D0340346

LANGENSCHEIDT'S NEW STANDARD SPANISH DICTIONARY

Spanish-English English-Spanish

by

C. C. Smith
G. A. Davies
H. B. Hall

Revised and updated edition

LANGENSCHEIDT

NEW YORK · BERLIN · MUNICH · VIENNA · ZURICH

Printed in Norway by Norbok a.s

First Part

Spanish-English

Contents
Materias

Preface

Like every living language, Spanish is subject to constant change: new terms and new compounds come into being, antiquated words are replaced by new ones, regional and popular words and technical terms pass into ordinary speech.

This completely new, updated edition details the latest developments in the two languages. This dictionary is designed for wide use, and is suitable for college students, translators, businesspeople, tourists, anyone who requires a detailed Spanish-English Dictionary.

Thousands of new Spanish words have been incorporated, among them the following examples: *despenalización* (legalization), *elepé* (long-playing record), *microonda* (microwave), *rockero* (rock singer), *videodisco* (video disk). Similarly, new compound forms have been added to existing headwords, e.g. *laboratorio espacial* (Skylab), *residuos radiactivos* (radioactive waste), *televisión por cable* (cable television).

In addition to this, special consideration has been given to Latin American Spanish. Thus, the dictionary contains a wealth of expressions which are either unknown in Spain or which, in the meanings given here, are used only in Latin America, e.g. *batiboleo* (*Cuba, Mex.* noise; confusion), *checar* (*Mex.* check), *escuelante* (*Col., Ven., Mex.* schoolboy, schoolgirl) or phrases such as *comer maíz* (*S.Am.* accept bribes).

This dictionary also offers information on the conjugation of Spanish verbs. Each verb in the dictionary includes a reference to a corresponding verb in the grammar appendix, where it is fully conjugated. Other useful information includes lists of current Spanish abbreviations and proper names, a table of numerals, and a table of weights and measures both in Spanish and English.

Based on the long-established Standard Dictionary of the Spanish and English Languages edited by C. C. Smith, G. A. Davies and H. B. Hall, it was developed in its present form by Walter Glanze Word Books, in cooperation with Dr. Roger J. Steiner, of the University of Delaware, and Dr. Gerald J. Mac Donald, the Curator of the Hispanic Society of America. To all of them our warmest appreciation.

Prólogo

Al igual que todas las lenguas vivas, el español se encuentra constantemente sometido a cambios impuestos por la formación de nuevos términos y expresiones, la sustitución de arcaísmos por nuevas palabras y la incorporación del léxico regional, popular y técnico al lenguaje cotidiano.

La presente edición completamente refundida de este diccionario da cuenta de los últimos desarrollos producidos en ambas lenguas. El diccionario ha sido concebido como una obra de consulta para todo tipo de público y es adecuado para estudiantes, traductores, hombres de negocio y turistas, o para cualquier persona que necesite un detallado diccionario español-inglés.

En esta edición se han incluido miles de palabras españolas nuevas. Así, por ejemplo: *despenalización* (legalization), *elepé* (long-playing record), *microonda* (microwave), *rockero* (rock singer), *videodisco* (video disk), etc. También se han incorporado expresiones bajo voces ya existentes, como por ejemplo: *laboratorio espacial* (Skylab), *residuos radiactivos* (radioactive waste) o *televisión por cable* (cable television).

Asimismo se ha prestado especial atención al uso del castellano en Latinoamérica, por lo que el diccionario es rico en expresiones y giros que o son desconocidos en España o que, en el sentido aquí citado, sólo se emplean en Latinoamérica, como por ejemplo: *batiboleo* (*Cuba, Mex.* noise; confusion), *checar* (*Mex.* check), escuelante (*Col., Ven., Mex.* schoolboy, schoolgirl) o *comer maíz* (*S.Am.* accept bribes).

El diccionario también contiene información sobre la conjugación de los verbos españoles. En cada verbo, se remite a un verbo correspondiente cuya conjugación aparece íntegramente en el apéndice gramatical. Además, el índice de abreviaturas españolas corrientes, la lista de nombres propios, la tabla de números y el cuadro de pesos y medidas constituyen una fuente más de información útil.

Basado en el conocido Standard Dictionary of the Spanish and English Languages, editado por C.C. Smith, G.A. Davies y H.B. Hall, este diccionario ha sido desarrollado hasta su forma presente por Walter Glanze Word Books, en cooperación con el Dr. Roger J. Steiner, de la Universidad de Delaware, y el Dr. Gerald J. Mac Donald, "Curator of the Hispanic Society of America". A todos ellos nuestro más sincero agradecimiento.

Directions for the Use of the Dictionary

Advertencias para facilitar la consulta del diccionario

1. Arrangement. A strict alphabetical order has been maintained throughout. The following will therefore be found in alphabetical order: the irregular forms of verbs; the various forms of the pronouns and article, etc.; and compounds.

Proper names and abbreviations are collected in special lists at the end of the dictionary.

2. Vocabulary. In many cases, the rarer words formed with e.g. *-idad, -ción, -ador, -ante, -oso, in-, des-* are excluded, to avoid extending the dictionary beyond all reasonable limits. The reader having some slight acquaintance with the processes of word-formation in the two languages will be able to look up the root word and form derived words from it.

Abstract nouns are often dealt with very briefly when they are adjacent to a root word which has been fully dealt with. Thus the entry **elegancia** *f* elegance *etc.* means: see the adjective *elegante* and form other abstract nouns accordingly.

3. Separation of different senses. The various senses of each Spanish word are made clear:

a) by symbols and abbreviated categories (see list on pp. 10–12);

b) by explanatory additions in italics, which may be a synonym (e.g. *emparejar* [*aparear*] match), or a complement (e.g. *enloquecedor jaqueca* splitting), or the object of a transitive verb (e.g., *echar mirada* cast), or the subject of an intransitive or reflexive verb (e.g., *empalmar* [*trenes*] connect), or again some other indication which while

1. El orden alfabético queda rigurosamente establecido. Ocupan su lugar alfabético, por tanto: las formas irregulares de los verbos; las diferentes formas de los pronombres y del artículo, etcétera, y las palabras compuestas.

Los nombres propios y las abreviaturas van reunidos en listas especiales que se imprimen como apéndices.

2. Vocabulario. En muchos casos se excluyen las palabras derivadas menos corrientes, que se forman, p.ej., con *-idad, -ción, -ador, -ante, -oso, in-, des-*, a fin de no extender más de lo razonable los límites del diccionario. El lector que tenga algún conocimiento de cómo se forman las palabras derivadas en los dos idiomas podrá buscar la palabra radical y formar sobre ella las derivadas que quiera.

Los sustantivos abstractos están tratados a menudo en forma somera cuando la palabra radical se ha tratado en forma extensa. Por tanto, el artículo **elegancia** *f* elegance *etc.* quiere decir: véase el adjetivo *elegante* para formar luego los sustantivos abstractos correspondientes.

3. Separación de las diversas acepciones. Las diversas acepciones de cada palabra española se indican:

a) mediante signos y categorías abreviadas (véase la lista en las págs. 10–12);

b) mediante aclaraciones impresas en bastardilla, las cuales pueden ser un sinónimo (p.ej., *emparejar* [*aparear*] match), o complemento (p.ej., *enloquecedor jaqueca* splitting), u objeto de verbo transitivo (p.ej. *echar mirada* cast) o sujeto de verbo intransitivo o reflexivo (p.ej. *empalmar* [*trenes*] connect), u otra indicación no precisamente sinó-

not exactly synonymous will none the less help the user in his search through the article for the required word.

nima pero que todavía le podrá ayudar al lector en la elección de la palabra justa.

Sometimes, e.g. with many abstract nouns, these explanations are omitted, but can easily be supplied from the adjacent entry for the corresponding adjective or other root word.

Estas aclaraciones suelen omitirse en el caso de muchos sustantivos abstractos, etcétera, pero es fácil suplirlas refiriéndose al artículo del adjetivo o palabra radical correspondiente.

In the first (Spanish-English) part of the dictionary all these indications are in Spanish, and in the second (English-Spanish) part they are in English. This arrangement is in accordance with the best modern theory. The indications have been kept as simple as possible and users knowing little of the other language should not find them difficult to understand when translating from the foreign language into their own. The abbreviations, largely English but often bilingual, are of course the same in both parts.

En la primera parte (Español-Inglés) de este diccionario todas estas indicaciones van en español, y en la segunda parte (Inglés-Español) van en inglés. Esto está de acuerdo con la más autorizada teoría actual. Las indicaciones son las más sencillas posibles para que el lector que no domine muy bien el otro idioma pueda comprenderlas sin demasiada dificultad al traducir una palabra de la lengua extranjera a la suya propia. Las abreviaturas, en inglés en su mayoría pero bilingües muchas, son desde luego idénticas en ambas partes.

It must be emphasized that such indications and explanations are intended only as the most elementary guide to the user, and are in no way complete definitions or exclusive rules about usage. There are many cases in which, given the limited space available, it has not been possible to provide indications of any sort.

Hay que insistir en que estas indicaciones y aclaraciones se le ofrecen al lector como guías sumamente sencillas y elementales, nada más; no pretenden de ningún modo formular definiciones completas ni ofrecer reglas exclusivas para el uso. Y son muchos los casos donde, dentro de los límites del diccionario, no ha sido posible dar indicación alguna.

4. The different parts of speech are indicated by numbers within each entry; the grammatical indication *adj.*, *adv.*, etc., is omitted in all cases where the category is obvious.

4. Las diferentes partes de la oración están indicadas dentro de cada artículo mediante números; las indicaciones gramaticales *adj.*, *adv.*, etcétera están suprimidas cuando la categoría es obvia.

5. The gender of every Spanish noun headword is indicated. In the case of a noun referring to a person which has a form for each gender, both are given; where the final *o* or *e* changes to *a* for the feminine, we write *pasajero m, a f* passenger; where the *a* has to be added for the feminine, we write *escritor m, -a f* writer. In this second class, some endings carry an accent in the masculine which is not needed in the feminine, and this suppression is not indicated in the dictionary. The endings affected are: *-án, ín-*,

5. Se indica el género de cada sustantivo español que encabeza artículo. En el caso de los sustantivos de persona que tienen distintas formas para los dos géneros, se ponen las dos formas; cuando la *o* o la *e* final se cambia en *a* para formar el femenino, ponemos *pasajero m, a f* passenger; cuando hay que añadir una *a* para la forma femenina, ponemos *escritor m, -a f* writer. En ciertas desinencias de esta segunda clase, el acento que lleva el género masculino se suprime en el femenino, supresión que no está indi-

-*ón* and -*és*, so that *danés m*, -*a f* means *danés m, danesa f*.

6. Phonetic transcription. This is given only in rare cases in which the pronunciation of a Spanish word does not correspond perfectly to its spelling. For the rest it will be sufficient for the reader to consult pp. 13–15 to know from its written form how any Spanish word is pronounced and stressed.

7. Translation. In rare cases, accurate single-word translation is impossible or meaningless. Recognizing this obvious linguistic fact, we have in such cases either provided an explanation in italics, or have introduced the translation with the warning abbreviation *approx.* (= approximately).

8. Brackets enclosing part of a word. When certain letters stand within brackets, we indicate

a) two forms that may be used indifferently, e.g. *sond(e)ar*;

b) two forms that may for convenience be run together because the translation of both is the same, e.g. *abarquillar(se)*, since the English word "curl up" covers both the transitive and reflexive senses.

9. As appendices, the reader will find: a list of abbreviations, a list of proper names, a table of numerals, a table of the conjugation of Spanish regular and irregular verbs (to which the numbers and letters placed after verb headwords refer, e.g. *abalanzar* [1f], *vender* [2a]), and a table of weights and measures.

cada en el diccionario. Estas desinencias son: -*án*, -*ín*, -*ón*, -*és*, de manera que *danés m*, -*a f* quiere decir: *danés m, danesa f*.

6. La pronunciación figurada se da únicamente en aquellos casos excepcionales donde la pronunciación de una palabra española (generalmente un extranjerismo) no concuerda con su escritura. Para las demás, bastará con que el lector consulte las págs. 13–15 para saber cómo hay que pronunciar y acentuar cualquier palabra española.

7. La traducción. En muy contados casos, la traducción exacta o resulta imposible o carece de sentido práctico. Ante este innegable hecho lingüístico, ponemos en dichos casos o una explicación en bastardilla, o, como advertencia al lector, la abreviatura *approx.* (= aproximadamente).

8. El paréntesis que encierra parte de una palabra. Cuando ciertas letras están en paréntesis, indicamos

a) dos formas que se pueden usar sin distinción, p.ej. *sond(e)ar*;

b) dos formas que pueden ponerse juntas porque se traducen las dos por la misma palabra, p.ej. *abarquillar(se)*, puesto que la palabra inglesa 'curl up' traduce los dos sentidos transitivo y reflexivo.

9. Como apéndices, el diccionario tiene: una lista de abreviaturas, una lista de nombres propios, una tabla de numerales, una tabla de la conjugación de los verbos españoles regulares e irregulares (tabla a la cual se refieren los números y letras colocados tras cada verbo que encabeza artículo, p.ej. *abalanzar* [1f], *vender* [2a]), y una tabla de pesos y medidas.

Key to the Symbols and Abbreviations

Explicación de los signos y abreviaturas

1. Symbols – Signos

~ ~ is the mark of repetition or tilde (swung dash). Sometimes when several compound words have their first element in common, that element is replaced by the thick tilde: **radio...: ~captar, ~difusión.** The thin tilde (~) used within the entry indicates the repetition of the headword, e.g. **rato...** *un buen ~, ~s pl. perdidos, pasar el ~.*

When the initial letter of the headword changes from a capital to a small letter, or vice versa, the normal tilde mark is replaced by the sign ♀: **sede...** *Santa* ♀.

~ ~ es la tilde o raya que indica repetición. Alguna vez cuando varias palabras compuestas tienen el primer elemento en común sustituimos ese elemento por la raya gruesa: **radio...: ~captar, ~difusión.** La tilde delgada (~) empleada dentro del artículo indica la repetición de la palabra que encabeza el artículo, p.ej. **rato...** *un buen ~, ~s pl. perdidos, pasar el ~.*

El signo ♀ significa la repetición de la palabra que encabeza el artículo con inicial cambiada (mayúscula en minúscula o viceversa): **sede...** *Santa* ♀.

F familiar, colloquial, *familiar, coloquial*

† archaic, *arcaico*

✧ rare, little used, *raro, poco usado*

📖 scientific, learned, *científico, culto*

✿ botany, *botánica*

⊕ technology, handicrafts, *tecnología, artes mecánicas*

⚒ mining, *minería*

⚔ military, *milicia*

⚓ nautical, *náutica*

☤ commerce, *comercio*

🚂 railway, *ferrocarriles*

✈ aviation, *aviación*

📯 postal affairs, *correos*

♪ music, *música*

△ architecture, *arquitectura*

⚡ electrical engineering, *electrotecnia*

⚖ jurisprudence, *jurisprudencia*

A mathematics, *matemáticas*

⛏ farming, *agricultura*

⚗ chemistry, *química*

⚕ medicine, *medicina*

2. Abbreviations – Abreviaturas

a.	and, also; *y, también*	*inf.*	infinitive, *infinitivo*
abbr.	abbreviation, *abreviatura*	*int.*	interjection, *interjección*
acc.	accusative, *acusativo*	*invar.*	invariable, *invariable*
adj.	adjective, *adjetivo*	*iro.*	ironical, *irónico*
adv.	adverb, *adverbio*		
Am.	Americanism, *americanismo*	*lit.*	literary, *literario*
anat.	anatomy, *anatomía*		
approx.	approximately, *aproximadamente*	*m*	masculine, *masculino*
		metall.	metallurgy, *metalurgia*
Arg.	Argentine, *Argentina*	*meteor.*	meteorology, *meteorología*
ast.	astronomy, *astronomía*	*Mex.*	Mexico, *México*
attr.	attributive, *atributivo*	*m/f*	masculine and feminine, *masculino y femenino*
biol.	biology, *biología*	*min.*	mineralogy, *mineralogía*
b.s.	bad sense, *mal sentido, peyorativo*	*mot.*	motoring, *automovilismo*
		mount.	mountaineering, *alpinismo*
		m/pl.	masculine plural, *masculino al plural*
C.Am.	Central America, *América Central*	*mst*	mostly, *por la mayor parte*
cj.	conjunction, *conjunción*		
co.	comic(al), *cómico*	*opt.*	optics, *óptica*
Col.	Colombia, *Colombia*	*orn.*	ornithology, *ornitología*
comp.	comparative, *comparativo*	*o.s.*, o.s.	oneself, *uno mismo, sí mismo*
contp.	contemptuous, *despectivo*		
C.R.	Costa Rica, *Costa Rica*	*p.*, p.	person, *persona*
		paint.	painting, *pintura*
dat.	dative, *dativo*	*parl.*	parliamentary, *parlamentario*
		pharm.	pharmacy, *farmacia*
eccl.	ecclesiastical, *eclesiástico*	*phls.*	philosophy, *filosofía*
Ecuad.	Ecuador, *Ecuador*	*phot.*	photography, *fotografía*
e.g.	for example, *por ejemplo*	*phys.*	physics, *física*
esp.	especially, *especialmente*	*physiol.*	physiology, *fisiología*
etc.	et cetera, *etcétera*	*pl.*	plural, *plural*
euph.	euphemism, *eufemismo*	*poet.*	poetry, poetic, *poesía, poético*
		pol.	politics, *política*
f	feminine, *femenino*	*p.p.*	past participle, *participio del pasado*
fenc.	fencing, *esgrima*		
fig.	figurative, *figurativo, figurado*	*P.R.*	Puerto Rico, *Puerto Rico*
		pred.	predicative, *predicativo*
f/pl.	feminine plural, *femenino al plural*	*pret.*	preterit(e), *pretérito*
		pron.	pronoun, *pronombre*
freq.	frequently, *frecuentemente*	*prov.*	provincialism, *provincialismo*
gen.	generally, *generalmente*	*prp.*	preposition, *preposición*
geog.	geography, *geografía*		
geol.	geology, *geología*	*rhet.*	rhetoric, *retórica*
ger.	gerund, *gerundio*		
gr.	grammar, *gramática*	*S.Am.*	Spanish Americanism, *hispanoamericanismo*
Guat.	Guatemala, *Guatemala*		
		sew.	sewing, *costura*
hist.	history, *historia*	*sg.*	singular, *singular*
hunt.	hunting, *montería*	*sl.*	slang, *argot, germanía*
		s.o., s.o.	someone, *alguien*
ichth.	ichthyology, *ictiología*	*s.t.*, s.t.	something, *algo*
indic.	indicative, *indicativo*	*su.*	substantive, *sustantivo*

subj.	subjunctive, *subjuntivo*
sup.	superlative, *superlativo*
surv.	surveying, *topografía*
tel.	telegraphy, *telegrafía*
teleph.	telephony, *telefonía*
telev.	television, *televisión*
th.	thing, *cosa*
thea.	theater, *teatro*
typ.	typography, *tipografía*
univ.	university, *universidad*
Urug.	Uruguay, *Uruguay*
v.	vide (see), *véase*
v/aux.	auxiliary verb, *verbo auxiliar*
Ven.	Venezuela, *Venezuela*
vet.	veterinary, *veterinaria*
v/i.	intransitive verb, *verbo intransitivo*
v/r.	reflexive verb, *verbo reflexivo*
v/t.	transitive verb, *verbo transitivo*
W.I.	West Indies, *Antillas*
zo.	zoology, *zoología*

The Pronunciation of Spanish

Accentuation

1. If the word ends in a vowel, or in *n* or *s*, the penultimate syllable is stressed: *espada, biblioteca, hablan, telefonean, edificios.*
2. If the word ends in a consonant other than *n* or *s*, the last syllable is stressed: *dificultad, hablar, laurel, niñez.*
3. If the word is to be stressed in any way contrary to rules **1** and **2**, an acute accent is written over the stressed vowel: *rubí, máquina, crímenes, carácter, continúa, autobús.*
4. **Diphthongs and syllable division.** Of the 5 vowels, *a e o* are considered "strong", *i* and *u* "weak":
   a) A combination of weak + strong forms a diphthong, the stress falling on the stronger element: *reina, baile, cosmonauta, tiene, bueno.*
   b) A combination of weak + weak forms a diphthong, the stress falling on the second element: *viuda, ruido.*
   c) Two strong vowels together remain as two distinct syllables, the stress falling according to rules **1** and **2**: *ma/estro, atra/er.*
   d) Any word having a vowel combination not stressed according to these rules bears an accent: *traído, oído, baúl, río.*

Value of the letters

Since the pronunciation of Spanish is (in contrast with English) adequately represented by orthography, the Spanish headwords have not been provided with a transcription in the I.P.A. alphabet, except in a very few cases of recent loan-words whose spelling and pronunciation are not in accord. The sounds of Spanish are described below, each with its corresponding I.P.A. symbol.

The pronunciation described is that of educated Castilian, and does NOT refer to that of certain Spanish provinces or of Spanish America (although a few outstanding features of the latter's pronunciation are mentioned).

It should be further realized that is it impossible to explain adequately the sounds of one language in terms of another; what is said below is no more than a very approximate guide.

Vowels

Spanish vowels are clearly and sharply pronounced, and single vowels are free from the tendency to diphthongization which is noticeable in English. When they are in an unstressed position they are relaxed only very slightly, again in striking contrast to English. Stressed vowels are more open and short before *rr* (compare *parra* with *para, perro* with *pero*).

a [a] Not so short as in English *fat*, nor so long as in English *father*: *paz, pata.*

e [e] Like *e* in English *they* (but without the following sound of *y*): *grande, pelo.* A shorter sound when followed by a consonant in the same syllable, like *e* in English *get*: *España, renta.*

i	[i]	Like *i* in English *machine*, though somewhat shorter: *pila, rubí*.
o	[o]	Not so short as in English *hot*, nor so long as in English *November*: *solo, esposa*. A shorter sound when followed by a consonant in the same syllable, like *o* in English *hot*: *costra, bomba*.
u	[u]	Like *oo* in English *food*: *puro, luna*. Silent after *q* and in *gue, gui*, unless marked with a diaeresis (*antigüedad, argüir*).
y	[i]	when a vowel (in the conjunction *y* "and" and at the end of a word), is pronounced like *i*.

Diphthongs

ai	[aj]	like *i* in English *right*: *baile, vaina*.
ei	[ej]	like *ey* in English *they*: *reina, peine*.
oi	[oj]	like *oy* in English *boy*: *boina, oigo*.
au	[aw]	like *ou* in English *rout*: *causa, áureo*.
eu	[ew]	like the vowel sounds in English *may-you*, without the sound of the *y*: *deuda, reuma*.

Semiconsonants

i, y	[j]	like *y* in English *yes*: *yeso, tiene*; in some cases in *S.Am.* this *y* is pronounced like the *s* [ʒ] in English *measure*: *mayo, yo*.
u	[w]	like *w* in English *water*: *huevo, agua*.

Consonants

b, v		These two letters represent the same value in Spanish. There are two distinct pronunciations:
	[b]	**1.** At the start of the breath-group and after *m, n* the sound is plosive like English *b*: *batalla, venid*; *tromba, invierno*.
	[β]	**2.** In all other positions the sound is a bilabial fricative, unknown in English, in which the lips do not quite meet: *estaba, cueva, de Vigo*.
c	[k]	**1.** *c* before *a, o, u* or a consonant is like English *k*: *caló, cobre*.
	[θ]	**2.** *c* before *e, i* is like English *th* in *thin*: *cédula, cinco*. In *S.Am.* this is pronounced like English voiceless *s* in *chase* [s]. N.B. In words like *acción*, both types of *c*-sound are heard [kθ].
ch	[tʃ]	like English *ch* in *church*: *mucho, chocho*.
d		Three distinct pronunciations:
	[d]	**1.** At the start of the breath-group and after *l, n*, the sound is plosive like English *d*: *doy, aldea, conde*.
	[ð]	**2.** Between vowels and after consonants other than *l, n* the sound is relaxed and approaches English voiced *th* [ð] in *this*: *codo, guardar*; in parts of Spain it is further relaxed and even disappears, particularly in the *-ado* ending.
		3. In final position, this type **2** is further relaxed or altogether omitted: *usted, Madrid*.
f	[f]	like English *f*: *fuero, flor*.
g		Three distinct pronunciations:
	[x]	**1.** Before *e, i* is the same of the Spanish *j* (below): *coger, general*.

	[g]	**2.** At the start of the breath-group and after *n*, the sound is that of English *g* in get: *Granada, rango.*
	[γ]	**3.** In other positions the sound is as in **2** above, but with no more than a close approximation of the vocal organs: *agua, guerra.*
		N.B. In the group *gue, gui* the *u* is silent (*guerra, guindar*) unless marked with the diaeresis (*antigüedad, argüir*). In the group *gua* all letters are sounded.
h	[-]	always silent: *honor, buhardilla.*
j	[x̧]	A strong guttural sound not found in English, but like the *ch* in Scots *loch*, Welsh *bach*, German *Achtung*: *jota, ejercer.* Silent at the end of the word: *reloj.*
k	[k]	like English *k*: *kilogramo, kerosene.*
l	[l]	like English *l*: *león, pala.*
ll	[ʎ]	approximating to English *lli* in *million*: *millón, calle.* In *S.Am.* like the *s* [ʒ] in English *measure.*
m	[m]	like English *m*: *mano, como.*
n	[n]	like English *n*: *nono, pan*; except before *v*, when the group is pronounced like *mb*: *enviar, invadir.*
ñ	[ɲ]	approximating to English *ni* in *onion*: *paño, ñoño.*
p	[p]	like English *p*, but without the slight aspiration which follows it: *Pepe, copa.* Silent in *septiembre, séptimo.*
q	[k]	like English *k*; always in combination with *u*, which is silent: *que, quiosco.*
r	[r]	a single trill stronger than any *r* in English, but like Scots *r*: *caro, querer.* Somewhat relaxed in final position. Pronounced like *rr* at the start of a word and after *l, n, s*: *rata.*
rr	[rr]	strongly trilled: *carro, hierro.*
s	[s]	voiceless *s*, like *s* in English *chase*: *rosa, soso.* But before a voiced consonant (*b, d*, hard *g, l, m, n*) is a
	[z]	voiced *s*, like English *s* in *rose*: *desde, mismo, asno.* Before "impure *s*" in recent loan-words, an extra *e*-sound is inserted in pronunciation: *e-sprint, e-stand.*
t	[t]	like English *t*, but without the slight aspiration which follows it: *patata, tope.*
v	[-]	see *b*.
w	[-]	found in a few recent loan-words only; usually pronounced like an English *v* or like Spanish *b, v*: *wáter.*
x	[gs]	like English *gs* in *big sock*: *máximo, examen.* Before a consonant like English *s* in *chase*: *extraño, mixto.*
z	[θ]	like English *th* in *thin*: *zote, zumbar.* In *S.Am.* like English voiceless *s* in *chase.*

The Spanish Alphabet

a [a], b [be], c [θe], ch [tʃe], d [de], e [e], f ['efe], g [x̧e], h ['atʃe], i [i], j ['x̧ota], k [ka], l ['ele], ll ['eʎe], m ['eme], n ['ene], ñ ['eɲe], o [o], p [pe], q [ku], r ['ere], rr ['erre], s ['ese], t [te], u [u], v ['uβe], x ['ekis], y [i'γrjeγa], z ['θeta] *or* ['θeða].

The letters are of the feminine gender: "Madrid se escribe con una *m* mayúscula."

A

a a) *lugar*: *a la mesa* at the table; *al lado de* at the side of; *a la derecha* on the right; *a retaguardia* in the rear; *subir a un tren* get on a train; *caer al mar* fall into the sea; *distancia*: *a 2 km.* (de) 2 km. away (from); *dirección*: *fue a la estación* he went to the station; *ir a casa* go home; b) *tiempo*: *¿a qué hora?* (at) what time?; *a las 3* at 3 o'clock; *a la noche* at nightfall; *a 15 de mayo* on the fifteenth of May; *a los 30 años* at 30 years of age; *a los pocos días* within a few days; c) *manera etc.*: *a la española* in (the) Spanish fashion; *a escape* at full speed; *a mano* by hand, manually; *a pie* on foot; *a solicitud* on request; d) *modo, velocidad*: *poco a poco* little by little; *paso a paso* step by step; *a 50 km. por hora* at 50 km. an hour; e) *medio, instrumento*: *bordado a mano* hand-embroidered; *girar a mano* turn by hand; *a sangre y fuego* by fire and sword; *a puñetazos* with (his) fists; *a nado* (by) swimming; *a lápiz* in pencil; f) *precio*: *¿a qué precio?* at what price?; *a 20 pesetas el kilo* at (*or* for) 20 pesetas a kilo; g) *propósito*: *¿a qué?* why?, for what purpose?; h) *sabor, olor*: *saber a vinagre* taste of vinegar; i) *dativo*: (*le*) *doy el libro a Juan* I give the book to John; j) *objeto personal* (*no se traduce*): *vio a su padre* he saw his father; k) *construcción con verbo*: *voy a comer* I am going to eat; *decidirse a inf.* decide to *inf.*; l) *se lo compré a él* I bought it from him; m) *al entrar* on entering; n) *equivale a si*: *a no ser él mi padre* if he were not my father; *a saberlo yo* had I known; *a decir verdad* to tell the truth; o) *elíptico*: *a que no lo adivinas* I bet you won't guess.

abacería *f* grocer's (shop), grocery store; **abacero** *m* grocer, provision merchant; *esp.* ⚓ chandler.

ábaco *m* abacus.

abad *m* abbot.

abadejo *m ichth.* cod(fish); (*insecto*) Spanish fly.

abadesa *f* abbess; **abadía** *f* abbey; [(*oficio*) abbacy.]

abajadero *m* slope, incline.

abajeño *S.Am.* **1.** lowland; **2.** *m*, **a** *f* lowlander.

abajo (*situación*) down, below, underneath; (*movimiento*) down, downwards; downstairs *en casa*; *¡~ X!* down with X!; *aquí ~* down here; *del rey ~* from the king down; *desde ~* from (down) below; *hacia ~* down(wards); *más ~* lower down; *la parte de ~* the lower part; *río ~* downstream; *~ de prp.* below.

abalanzar [1f] weigh, balance; (*el caballo*) rear; (*lanzar*) hurl; **~se** spring (*a* at); rush (*a* into); pounce, hurl o.s. (*sobre* on).

abaldonar [1a] degrade, debase; affront.

abalear [1a] *S.Am.* shoot.

abalone *zo.* abalone.

abalorio *m* glass bead; bead work, beading; *no valer un ~* be not worth a dime.

abanar [1a] fan.

abanderado *m* standard bearer, ensign; **abanderar** [1a] ⚓ register; **abanderizar** [1f] organize into bands; **~se** join a band, band together.

abandonado abandoned; *lugar etc.* deserted; godforsaken; *aspecto etc.* forlorn; *edificio* derelict; (*desaliñado*) slovenly, careless; **abandonar** [1a] *v/t.* abandon, leave (behind); forsake; (*salir de*) leave; (*huir*) flee, leave; *fig.* drop, give up; (*no hacer caso*) ignore; *v/i.* *deportes*: withdraw, scratch; **~se** (*desánimo*) give in, lose heart; (*desaliño*) let o.s. go, get slovenly; *~ a* yield to, give o.s. over to; **abandono** *m* abandonment; dereliction *de edificio, deber*; desertion *de hogar*; (*desaliño*) slovenliness; *fig.* abandon *de vida*; recklessness; indulgence (*a* in); *deportes*: withdrawal, scratching; *por ~* by default.

abanicar(se) [1g] fan (o.s.); **abanico** *m* fan; fan-shaped object; (*ventana*) fanlight; ⚓ derrick; **abani-**

queo *m* fanning; gesticulation *con manos*.

abaratamiento *m* cheapening; **abaratar** [1a] *v/t.* cheapen, make cheaper; *precio* lower; *v/i.*, **~se** get cheap, get cheaper.

abarca *f* sandal; brogue.

abarcar [1g] embrace, include, take in, extend to; contain, comprise; *tiempo* span; *S.Am.* corner, monopolize.

abarquillar(**se**) [1a] curl up, roll up; (*esp. papel*) crinkle.

abarraganamiento *m* illicit cohabitation; **abarraganarse** [1a] live together (as man and wife).

abarrancadero *m fig.* pitfall, difficult situation; **abarrancar** [1g] (*lluvia*) open fissures in; **~se** fall into a pit; *fig.* get into difficulties.

abarrotar [1a] ⚓ stow, pack tightly; *fig.* overstock; **~se** *S.Am.* † become a glut on the market; **abarrote** *m* ⚓ stowing, packing; **~s** *pl. S.Am.* groceries; *tienda de* **~s** grocer's (shop); **abarrotero** *m S.Am.* grocer.

abastar [1a] supply; **abastecedor** *m*, **-a** *f* supplier, purveyor, victualler; **abastecer** [2d] supply, provide, provision (*de* with); **abastecimiento** *m* supply, provision; (*acto*) supplying, provisioning; catering; **abastero** *m S.Am.* cattle dealer; **abasto** *m* supply; provisioning; *dar* **~** *a* supply.

abatanado skilled, skilful; **abatanar** [1a] ⊕ full, mill.

abatí *m S.Am.* maize, corn.

abatible collapsible; folding; **abatido** (*ruin*) abject, despicable; *ánimo* downcast, dejected, depressed; prostrate (*por dolor etc.* with); † depreciated; **abatimiento** *m* Δ *etc.* knocking down, dismantling; *fig.* dejection, depression, low spirits; gloom; **abatir** [3a] *casa etc.* knock down, dismantle; *tienda* take down; *árbol* fell; ✈ shoot down; *bandera* strike, lower; *fig.* humble, humiliate; (*desanimar*) discourage, get *s.o.* down, depress; prostrate *de dolor*; **~se** (*ave*) swoop, pounce; *fig.* be disheartened, get depressed.

abdicación *f* abdication; **abdicar** [1g] abdicate (*en* in favor of), renounce.

abdomen *m* abdomen; **abdominal** abdominal.

abducción *f* ⚕ abduction.

abecé *m* ABC; rudiments; *no saber el* **~** be very ignorant; **abecedario** *m* alphabet; (*libro*) primer, spelling book.

abedul *m* (silver) birch; *vara de* **~** birch.

abeja *f* bee; **~** *machiega*, **~** *reina* queen bee; **~** *obrera* worker; **abejar** *m* apiary; **abejarrón** *m* bumblebee; **abejaruco** *m* bee eater; **abejón** *m* drone; **abejorro** *m* bumblebee; (*escarabajo*) cockchafer; **abejuno** bee(like).

abellacado mean, villainous.

aberenjenado violet-colored.

aberración *f* aberration (*a. ast., opt.*); **aberrante** aberrant; **aberrar** [1k] be mistaken.

abertura *f* (*agujero*) aperture, opening, gap; (*grieta*) slit, crack, cleft; *geog.* (*ensenada*) cove; (*valle*) wide valley, gap; *fig.* openness, frankness.

abeto *m* fir; **~** *blanco* silver fir; **~** *del Norte*, **~** *rojo* spruce.

abierto 1. *p.p. of abrir*; **2.** *adj.* open, opened; *campo, mente, rostro* open; *ciudad* open, unfortified; *p.* frank, forthcoming; *S.Am.* conceited.

abigarrado variegated, many-colored; *animal* piebald; *fig.* motley; (*inconexo*) disjointed; **abigarramiento** *m* variegation; motley coloring; **abigarrar** [1a] variegate; paint *etc.* in a variety of colors.

abigotado mustachioed.

ab intestato ⚖ intestate; *fig.* neglected.

abiótico abiotic, lacking living organisms.

abisinio *adj. a. su. m*, **a** *f* Abyssinian.

abismal abysmal; **abismar** [1a] *fig.* cast down, humble; (*dañar*) spoil, ruin; **~se** *S.Am.* be surprised; **~** *en* plunge into, sink into; *dolor etc.* give o.s. over to; *estar abismado en* be lost in; **abismo** *m* abyss (*a. fig.*); *estar en el borde del* **~** be on the brink of ruin.

abjurar [1a] abjure, forswear (*a.* **~** *de*).

ablactación *f* weaning.

ablandabrevas *m/f* good-for-nothing; **ablandar** [1a] *v/t.* soften; *vientre* loosen; *mot.* run in; *fig.* soothe, mollify; *v/i.* (*viento*) moderate; (*frío*) become less severe; **~se** soften, get soft; ⊕ melt; (*rigor etc.*) relent; moderate, become less severe; (*esp. p.*) mellow.

ablativo *m* ablative (case).
abnegación *f* self-denial, abnegation; **abnegado** self-denying; **abnegarse** [1h *a.* 1k] deny o.s., go without.
abobado stupid(-looking); *fig.* amazed; **abobamiento** *m* stupidity; **abobar** [1a] make stupid; **~se** get stupid.
abocado *vino* smooth; **abocamiento** *m* biting; approach; meeting; **abocar** [1g] *v/t.* seize with the mouth; ⚔ bring up; *vino* pour, decant; *v/i.* ⚓ enter a river (*or* channel); **~se** approach; *~ con* meet, have a interview with.
abocinado trumpet-shaped; **abocinar** [1a] flare; F fall on one's face.
abochornado flushed, overheated; *fig.* ashamed (*de* at); **abochornar** [1a] burn up, overheat; *fig.* shame, embarrass; **~se** feel overheated; ⚘ wilt; *~ de fig.* feel ashamed at.
abofellar [1a] swell; puff out.
abofetear [1a] slap in the face.
abogacía *f* legal profession; **abogado** *m* lawyer; *~ criminalista* criminal lawyer; *~ de secano* quack lawyer; *ejercer de ~* practice law; *recibirse de ~* be called to the bar; **abogar** [1h] advocate, plead; *~ por* hold a brief for (*a. fig.*); *fig.* advocate, champion.
abolengo *m* ancestry, lineage; (*herencia*) inheritance.
abolición *f* abolition; **abolicionista** *m/f* abolitionist; **abolir** [3a; *defective*] abolish; revoke.
abolorio *m* ancestry.
abolsado full of pockets, baggy; **abolsarse** [1a] be baggy, form pockets.
abolladura *f* dent; (*arte*) embossing; **abollar** [1a] dent; bruise; (*arte*) emboss, do repoussé work on; **~se** get dented *etc.*; **abollonar** [1a] *metal* emboss.
abombado convex; *S.Am.* (*aturdido*) stunned; (*borracho*) drunk; **abombar** [1a] make convex; F stun, confuse; **~se** *S.Am.* (*pudrirse*) decompose; be stunned; get drunk.
abominable abominable; **abominación** *f* abomination (*a. fig.*), execration; **abominar** [1a] abhor, detest (*a. ~ de*).
abonable payable; **abonado 1.** trustworthy; **2.** *m*, **a** *f* subscriber *a periódico etc.*; 🚂, *thea. etc.* season-ticket holder; **abonador** *m*, **-a** *f* ☤ guarantor.
abonanzar [1f] clear up (*a. fig.*); ⚓ abate, calm down.
abonar [1a] **1.** *v/t. p.* vouch for, guarantee; ☤ credit, pay; improve (*a.* ⛏); ⛏ manure, dress, fertilize; *v. cuenta*; **2.** *v/i.* clear (up); **3. ~se** subscribe (*a periódico etc.* to); become a member (*a sociedad* of); 🚂, *thea.* take out a season ticket; **abonaré** *m* promissory note; **abono** *m* ☤ *etc.* voucher, guarantee; subscription *a periódico*; 🚂 *thea.* season ticket; improvement *de tierras*; ⛏ (*sustancia*) manure, dressing, fertilizer; *~ (de temporada)* season ticket; *~ químico* (chemical) fertilizer; *~ verde* leaf mold.
abordable *p.*, *lugar* approachable; *lugar* easy of access; **abordaje** *m* ⚓ boarding; **abordar** [1a] *v/t.* ⚓ board; (*atracar*) dock; *p.* accost, *fig.* approach; *problema* tackle; *tarea etc.* undertake, get down to; *tema* broach, begin on; *v/i.* ⚓ (*chocar*) run foul; (*aportar*) put in (*en* at).
aborigen *adj. a. su. m* aboriginal.
aborrascarse [1g] get stormy.
aborrecer [2d] hate, detest; (*aburrir*) bore; *nido* abandon; **aborrecible** hateful, abhorrent; invidious; **aborrecido** (*aburrido*) boring; **aborrecimiento** *m* hatred, hate, abhorrence; (*aburrimiento*) boredom.
aborregado: *cielo ~* mackerel sky.
abortar [1a] abort; ⚕ have a miscarriage; *fig.* miscarry, fail; **abortista** *m/f* abortionist; **abortivo** abortive; **aborto** *m* abortion; ⚕ miscarriage; ⚖ (criminal) abortion; *fig.* monster; *~ despenalizado* legalized abortion; **abortón** *m* abortion (*animal*).
abota(r)garse [1h] become bloated, swell up.
abotonador *m* button hook; **abotonar** [1a] *v/t.* button (up); *v/i.* bud.
abovedado *m* △ vaulting; **abovedar** [1a] arch, vault.
abozalar [1a] muzzle.
abra *f* (*ensenada*) bay, cove; (*valle*) dale; *geol.* fissure; *Mex.* clearing.
abracadabra *f* hocuspocus.
abrasado burnt up; *fig.* ashamed; *~ en cólera* in a raging temper; **abrasador** burning, scorching; *fig.* with-

ering; **abrasar** [1a] burn (up); ⚘ *etc.* parch; (*frío*) scorch, nip; (*viento*) sear; *dinero* squander; *fig.* shame; **~se** burn; be parched; *fig.* burn (*de amores* with love), be on fire; *~ de sed* (*de calor*) be dying of thirst (of the heat).

abrasión *f* graze, abrasion; **abrasivo** *m* abrasive.

abrazadera *f* bracket, brace, clasp; paper clip; *typ.* bracket.

abrazar [1f] embrace (*a. fig.*); clasp, take in one's arms, hug; *fig.* take in, include; *doctrina* espouse; *negocio* take charge of; **~se** *a, con, de* embrace; clasp; **abrazo** *m* embrace, hug; *un ~ (afectuoso, cordial etc.)* (*en carta*) best wishes, kind regards; with love from *s.o.*

ábrego *m* southwest wind.

abrebotellas *m* bottle opener; **abrecartas** *m* letter opener; **abrelatas** *m* can opener; **abreostras** *m* oyster knife.

abrevadero *m* drinking trough; (*lugar*) watering place; **abrevar** [1a] *animal* water, give a drink to; *tierra* irrigate; *pieles* soak; **~se** (*animal*) quench its *etc.* thirst; *fig. ~ en sangre* wallow in blood.

abreviación *f* abbreviation; reduction; **abreviadamente** in an abridged form; **abreviar** [1b] *v/t. palabra etc.* abbreviate; *materia* abridge, reduce; *período* shorten, lessen; *suceso* hasten; *fecha* bring forward; *v/i.* be quick; be short; **abreviatura** *f* abbreviation.

abridor *m* opener; can opener; grafting knife.

abrigada *f*, **abrigadero** *m* shelter, wind break; **abrigado** sheltered, protected; *enramada etc.* cozy; **abrigaño** *m* shelter; ⚓ haven.

abrigar [1h] shelter, protect (*de viento etc.* from, against); (*vestido etc.*) keep warm, cover; (*ayudar*) aid, support; *esperanzas etc.* harbor, cherish, entertain; **~se** take shelter (*de aguacero etc.* from); ⚓ seek shelter (*de temporal* from); protect o.s.; wrap o.s. up *con ropa*; **abrigo** *m* shelter; *esp.* ⚓ haven; (*sobretodo*) (over)coat; *fig.* covering, protection *de ropa*; (*ayuda*) aid, support; *al ~ de* sheltered from; *viento* in the lee of; *peligro* safe from; *de mucho ~ ropa* warm, heavy; *~ antiaéreo* air-raid shelter; *~ de pieles* fur coat.

abril *m* April; *fig.* springtime (*de la vida* of life); *~es pl.* years (of one's youth); *de 20 ~es* of 20 summers; *estar hecho un ~* be dressed to kill; **abrileño** April *attr.*

abrillantar [1a] ⊕ cut into facets; (*pulir*) polish, brighten; *fig.* enhance.

abrir [3a; *p.p. abierto*] **1.** *v/t.* open (*a. fig.*); begin; *~ (con llave)* unlock; ⚕ cut open; *agujero* make; *zanja* dig; *pozo* sink; *lámina* engrave; *grifo etc.* turn on; *camino* clear, make; *senda* beat; *bosque* clear; *cuenta* open; *lista, procesión* head; *apetito* whet; **2.** *v/i.* ⚘ *etc.* open, unfold; begin; *v. ojo*; **3. ~se** (*puerta etc.*) open; (*flor etc.*) open out; (*extenderse*) spread (out); *~ a, ~ con* unbosom o.s. to, be frank with.

abrochador *m* button hook; **abrochadura** *f* buttoning; hooking; fastening; **abrochar** [1a] button; hook, fasten (up) *con corchete*; clasp *con hebilla etc.*

abrogación *f* abrogation; **abrogar** [1h] abrogate, repeal.

abrojo *m* caltrop (*a.* ⚔); thistle; thorn; **abrojos** ⚓ hidden rocks.

abroncar [1g] F (*avergonzar*) shame; ridicule; (*enfadar*) annoy.

abroquelarse [1a] *fig.*: *~ con, ~ de* shield o.s. with.

abrumador crushing, overwhelming; (*molesto*) wearisome; **abrumar** [1a] crush, oppress; swamp, weigh down (*de trabajo* with); **~se** get foggy.

abrupto steep, abrupt.

abrutado brutish.

absceso *m* abscess.

absentismo *m* absenteeism; absentee landlordism; **absentista** *m/f* absentee; absentee landlord.

ábside *m* apse; **absidial** apsidal.

absintio *m* absinth.

absolución *f* absolution; ⚖ acquittal; **absoluta** *f* authoritative assertion, dictum; ⚔ discharge; ⚔ *tomar la ~* leave the service; **absolutamente** absolutely; positively; just; *~ nada* nothing at all; **absolutismo** *m* absolutism; **absoluto** absolute (*a.* ♏, *pol.*); *fig.* utter, absolute; *genio* tyrannical; *fe* implicit; *phls. lo ~* the absolute; *en ~* nothing at all; *¡en ~!* certainly not!; *está* *prohibido en* ~ it is absolutely forbidden; *no sabe nada en* ~ he knows nothing at all; **absolutorio** ⚖ of acquittal.

absolvederas *f/pl*. F (*de un confesor*) tendency to absolve lightly; **absolver** [2h; *p.p. absuelto*] absolve; ⚖ acquit, clear (*de* of); release (*de empeño* from).

absorbente 1. absorbent; *fig*. absorbing; (*que exige tiempo*) demanding; **2.** *m*: ~ *higiénico* sanitary napkin; **absorber** [2a] absorb (*a. fig*.), suck up; imbibe, take in; ✝ *capital* use up; *fig*. engross; **~se** become absorbed (*en* in); **absorción** *f* absorption (*a. fig*.); *fig*. engrossment; **absorto** *fig*. absorbed, engrossed (*en* in); (*admirando*) entranced, amazed; intent (*en proyecto* on); F in the clouds; ~ *en meditación* buried in thought.

abstemio abstemious, temperate; (*por completo*) teetotal.

abstención *f* abstention; nonparticipation; **abstencionismo** *m* nonparticipation; abstentionism; **abstencionista** *m/f* nonparticipant; **abstenerse** [2l] abstain, refrain (*de inf*. from *ger*.); forbear (*de inf*. to *inf*.); **abstinencia** *f* abstinence; (*ayuno*) fast; *fig*. forbearance; **abstinente** abstemious.

abstracción *f* abstraction; omission; (*distracción*) absence of mind, engrossment; ~ *hecha de* leaving *s.t.* on one side; **abstracto** abstract; *en* ~ in the abstract; **abstraer** [2p] *v/t*. abstract; *v/i*. (*a*. **~se**): ~ *de* do without, leave aside; **~se** be abstracted, be absorbed; **abstraído** absentminded; withdrawn.

abstruso abstruse.

absuelto 1. *p.p. of absolver*; **2.** *adj*. acquitted; absolved.

absurdidad *f* absurdity; **absurdo 1.** absurd; preposterous; farcical; **2.** *m* absurdity; farce.

abubilla *f orn*. hoopoe.

abuchear [1a] F hoot at, howl down, *approx*. boo; **abucheo** *m* F hooting, *approx*. booing.

abuela *f* grandmother; *fig*. old woman; F *¡cuéntaselo a tu* ~*!* tell that to the Marines!; **abuelita** *f* F grandma, granny; **abuelito** *m* F grandpa, grandad; **abuelo** *m* grandfather; *fig*. (*antepasado*) ancestor; (*viejo*) old man; ~*s pl*. grandparents.

abulense *adj. a. su. m/f* (native) of Avila.

abulia *f* lack of will power; **abúlico** lacking in will power, weak-willed.

abultado bulky, massive, unwieldy; **abultar** [1a] *v/t*. make large, enlarge; *fig*. exaggerate; *v/i*. be bulky; *fig*. loom large.

abundamiento *m* abundance, plenty; *a mayor* ~ furthermore; **abundancia** *f* abundance, plenty; *en* ~ in plenty, in abundance; **abundante** abundant, plentiful; heavy, copious; generous; **abundar** [1a]: ~ *de*, ~ *en* abound in, teem with, be rich in; ~ *en la opinión de* wholeheartedly agree with; **abundoso** abundant.

abur *v. agur*.

aburguesado middle-class; bourgeois; **aburguesarse** [1a] become middle-class; become bourgeois.

aburilar [1a] engrave.

aburrido wearisome, tiresome, boring; ghastly F; *rutina* humdrum; (*que está* ~) bored; **aburrimiento** *m* boredom, weariness, tedium; **aburrir** [3a] bore, weary; annoy, tire; F *tiempo* spend, while away; *dinero* blue; **~se** be bored, get bored (*con, de, por* with).

abusar [1a] go too far, take an unfair advantage; ~ *de autoridad, hospitalidad* abuse; *dinero* misapply; *confianza* betray; *amistad* presume upon; *amigos* impose upon; **abusión** *f* abuse; superstition; **abusionero** superstitious; **abusivo** improper, corrupt; **abuso** *m* abuse; misuse, misapplication *etc*.; **abusón** F uppish.

abyecto *condición* abject; (*ruin*) craven, vile.

acá here, around here, over here; hither *lit*.; ~ *y a(cu)llá* here and there; *de* ~ *para allá* to and fro; *de ayer* ~ since yesterday; *más* ~ nearer, more this way; *muy* ~ right here; *¡ven* ~*!* come (over) here!

acabado 1. perfect, complete; *fig*. consummate, polished; *salud* ruined, wrecked; ~ *de llegar* just after arrival; **2.** *m* finish; **acabador** *m* ⊕ finisher; **acabamiento** *m* completion, finishing; (*fin*) end; (*muerte*) death.

acabalar [1a] complete.

acabar [1a] **1.** *v/t*. finish, conclude,

complete; put the finishing touches to; (*matar*) kill off; **2.** *v/i.* finish, come to an end; (*morir*) die; ~ *con* make an end of, put paid to; destroy; *recursos* use up; *letra* end with; ~ *de inf.* have just *p.p.*: *acabo de hacerlo* I have just done it; *acababa de hacerlo* I had just done it; ~ *en punta etc.* end in; ~ *mal* come to a bad (*or* sticky) end; ~ *por inf.*, ~ *ger.* end up by *ger.*, finish up by *ger.*; F *es cosa de nunca* ~ there's no end to it; **3.** ~**se** stop, come to an end (*a. fig.*); (*morir*) die; (*estar terminado*) be all over; (*existencias*) run out; (*suministro*) fail; *se me acabó el dinero* I ran out of money; F *¡(todo) se acabó!* it's all up!; F *se acabó para él* he's had it; F *el acabóse* the pay-off, the end.
acabildar [1a] organize into a group, get together.
acabóse *v. acabar.*
acacia *f* acacia; ~ *falsa* locust tree.
acachetear [1a] slap, box.
academia *f* academy; ~ *gastronómica* domestic science college; **académico 1.** academic (*a. fig.*); **2.** *m* academician, member of an academy.
acaecedero possible; **acaecer** [2d] happen, occur, befall; **acaecimiento** *m* happening, occurrence.
acalorado heated, hot; (*fatigado*) tired (out); *fig. discusión* heated; *partidario* passionate; **acaloramiento** *m* ardor, heat; passion, anger; **acalorar** [1a] (*ejercicio*) warm, make hot; (*fatigar*) tire; *fig. pasiones* inflame, incite; (*animar*) encourage, stir up; ~**se** (*tomar calor*) get too hot, become overheated; (*irritarse*) get angry (*por* about); (*discusión*) become heated.
acallar [1a] silence (*a. fig.*), hush, quiet (down); *fig.* assuage, pacify.
acamar [1a] beat down, lay.
acampanado bell-shaped.
acampar [1a] ⚔ (en)camp.
acampo *m* common pasture.
acanaladura *f* groove; △ fluting; **acanalar** [1a] groove; △ flute; *papel etc.* corrugate.
acanallado disreputable; vile; degraded; low.
acantilado 1. *costa* (*en escalones*) shelving; rocky; (*escarpado*) precipitous, steep; **2.** *m* cliff.
acanto *m* acanthus.
acantonar [1a] quarter (*en* on); ~**se** limit one's activities (*en* to).
acaparador *m* monopolizer, monopolist; profiteer; **acaparamiento** *m* monopolizing (*de* of), cornering the market (*de* in); hoarding *de víveres*; **acaparar** [1a] monopolize; corner, corner the market in; *víveres* hoard; hog F.
acápite *m S.Am.* paragraph; *punto* ~ full stop, new paragraph.
acaramelado *fig.* oversweet, overpolite.
acar(e)ar [1a] *ps.* bring face to face; *peligro etc.* face (up to).
acardenalarse [1a] get bruised, go black and blue.
acariciar [1b] caress; *animal* pat, fondle; *esperanza* cherish, harbor; *proyecto* have in mind.
ácaro *m zo.* mite.
acarrear [1a] transport, cart, haul; (*río*) bring (down), carry; *fig.* occasion, bring in its train (*or* wake); **acarreo** *m* haulage, cartage (*a. precio*); *geol. terrenos de* ~ drift.
acartonarse [1a] get like cardboard; *fig.* (*p.*) become wizened.
acaso 1. *adv.* perhaps, maybe; *por si* ~ (just) in case; **2.** *m* chance, accident; *al* ~ at random.
acastañado chestnut-colored.
acatamiento *m* respect, esteem; **acatar** [1a] respect, esteem; treat with deference; revere; *ley* accept, adhere to.
acatarrarse [1a] catch a cold; *S.Am.* F get high (from alcohol).
acato *m* respect, esteem; attention.
acaudalado wealthy, well-off; **acaudalar** [1a] accumulate, acquire.
acaudillar [1a] lead, command.
acceder [2a] accede, agree (*a* to).
accesible accessible; ~ *a* open to, accessible to; **accesión** *f* (*acto*) assent (*a* to); (*cosa*) accessory; (*entrada*) access, entry; ⚕ attack, onset; **accésit** *m* second prize, consolation prize; **acceso** *m* (*acto de entrar*) admittance; (*camino*) access, approach (*a.* ✈); ⚕ attack, fit; *fig.* fit *de generosidad etc.*; outburst, fit *de cólera*; *de fácil* ~ easy to approach; ~**s** *pl.* approaches; **accesoria** *f* annex, outbuilding; **accesorio 1.** accessory; dependent; (*secundario*) incidental; **2.** *m* ac-

cessory, attachment; ~s *pl.* ⊕ accessories; *thea.* properties; props.

accidentado ⚕ in a faint; (*turbado*) upset; *vida* stormy, troubled, eventful; *terreno* hilly, rough; *superficie* uneven; **accidental** accidental; unintentional; incidental, casual; **accidentarse** [1a] faint (after an accident); **accidente** *m* accident; misadventure, mishap; ⚕ faint(ing fit); *gr.* accidence; roughness, unevenness *de terreno*; *por* ~ by accident.

acción *f* action; ✝ share; ⚔ action, engagement; *thea.* action, plot; ~es *pl.* ✝ stock(s), shares; *thea.* ~ *aparte* by-play; ~ *de gracias* thanksgiving; ~ *liberada* stock dividend; ~ *preferente* preference share; ~ *primitiva* ordinary share; ⚖ *ejercitar una* ~ bring an action; **accionado** *m* ⊕ action; **accionar** [1a] *v/t.* ⊕ work, drive; *v/i.* gesticulate; **accionista** *m/f* shareholder, stockholder.

acebo *m* holly (tree).

acecinar [1a] salt, cure; ~**se** get very thin.

acechadura *f* ambush; **acechador** *m*, -**a** *f* spy, watcher; **acechar** [1a] spy on, lie (*or* be) in wait for; *hunt. etc.* stalk; **acecho** *m* ambush; spying; *al* ~, *en* ~ in wait, on the watch; *cazar al* ~ stalk; **acechón** F spying, prying; F *hacer la acechona* spy, pry.

acedar [1a] make sour; *fig.* sour, embitter; (*molestar*) vex; ~**se** turn sour; ⚘ turn yellow.

acedera *f* sorrel.

acedía *f* sourness (*a. fig.*); (*desabrimiento*) unpleasantness; asperity *de genio*; ⚕ heartburn; **acedo** sour (*a. fig.*), acid; disagreeable.

aceitar [1a] oil, lubricate; **aceite** *m* oil; (*a.* ~ *de oliva*) olive oil; (*perfume*) essence; ~ *alcanforado* camphorated oil; ~ *combustible* fuel oil; ~ *de hígado de bacalao* cod-liver oil; ~ *de linaza*, ~ *secante* linseed oil; ~ *mineral* coal oil; ~ *de ricino* castor oil; **aceitera** *f* oilcan; **aceitero 1.** oil *attr.*; **2.** *m* oil merchant; **aceitón** *m* thick dirty oil; **aceitoso** oily, greasy; **aceituna** *f* olive; **aceitunado** olive(-colored); **aceitunero** *m*, **a** *f* dealer in olives; **aceitunil** olive *attr.*; olive-colored; **aceituno 1.** *S.Am.* olive(-colored); **2.** *m* olive (tree).

aceleración *f* acceleration, speeding-up; **acelerada** *f* acceleration, speed-up; **aceleradamente** speedily, swiftly; **acelerador** *m* accelerator; throttle; **acelerar** [1a] accelerate; *paso* quicken; *fig.* speed up, expedite; ~ *la marcha* go faster, accelerate; ~**se** hasten, hurry.

acémila *f* beast of burden; mule; **acemilero** *m* muleteer.

acemite *m* bran and flour mixed; (*potaje*) porridge.

acendrado pure, refined (*a. fig.*); **acendrar** [1a] purify; ⊕, *estilo* refine.

acensuar [1d] tax.

acento *m* accent; stress; ~ *agudo* acute accent; ~ *ortográfico* written accent; **acentuar** [1e] accent, accentuate; stress.

aceña *f* water mill; **aceñero** *m* miller.

acepción *f* meaning, sense; preference.

acepilladora *f* ⊕ planer; **acepilladura** *f* (wood) shaving; **acepillar** [1a] brush; ⊕ plane, shave.

aceptable acceptable; palatable; **aceptación** *f* acceptance (*a.* ✝); approval, approbation; ~ *de personas* discrimination; partiality; **aceptar** [1a] accept, *trabajo* accept, take on, undertake; *hechos* face; ~ *a inf.* agree to *inf.*; **acepto:** ~ *a*, ~ *de* acceptable to, welcome to, welcomed by.

acequia *f* irrigation ditch (*or* channel).

acera *f* pavement, sidewalk; row *de casas*.

acerado ⊕ steel *attr.*; (*cortante*) biting, cutting (*a. fig.*); *fig. dicho etc.* caustic; **acerar** [1a] ⊕ turn into steel; put a steel tip *etc.* on; *fig.* make sharp, make biting.

acerbidad *f* acerbity; harshness; **acerbo** sour, sharp (*a. fig.*); *lenguaje etc.* harsh, scathing.

acerca: ~ *de* about, concerning, on.

acercamiento *m* bringing (*or* drawing) near; *pol.* rapprochement; approach; **acercar** [1g] bring near(er); ~**se** approach (*a acc.*), come near (*a* to); ~ *a* go up to; *fig.* verge on, approach.

acería *f* steelworks.

acerico *m* small cushion; *sew.* pincushion.

acero *m* steel (*a. fig.*); ~ *colado* cast

steel; ~ *en lingotes* ingot steel; ~ *inoxidable* stainless steel; ~ *al manganeso* manganese steel; F *tener buenos* ~*s* (*ser valiente*) have a lot of pluck; (*tener hambre*) be ravenous; **acerocromo** *m* chromium steel.
acérrimo staunch, out-and-out, fierce.
acerrojar [1a] bolt, lock.
acertado right, correct; (*prudente*) wise, sound; (*hábil*) skilful; *dicho* well-aimed; apt; *idea* bright, well-conceived; *en esto no anduvo muy* ~ it was rather unwise of him; he was far off the mark; **acertante** *m*/*f* winner; **acertar** [1k] *v*/*t*. *blanco etc.* hit; *solución* guess right, get right; do *s.t.* right; *v*/*i*. (*dar en el blanco*) hit the mark; (*tener razón*) be right, guess right; (*tener éxito*) succeed; ~ *a inf.* (*hacer por casualidad*) happen to *inf.*; (*lograr*) succeed in *ger.*, manage to *inf.*; ~ *con* happen (up)on, hit on; find.
acertijo *m* riddle, puzzle.
acervo *m* heap; store; hoard; ~ *común* undivided estate.
acetato *m* acetate; **acético** acetic.
acetileno *m* acetylene.
acetona *f* acetone; **acetoso** acetous, acid.
acetre *m* small bucket; *eccl.* holy-water container.
acezar [1f] pant, puff (and blow).
aciago ill-fated, of ill omen.
aciano *m* cornflower.
acíbar *m* aloes; *fig.* bitterness, affliction; **acibarar** [1a] make bitter (with aloes); *fig.* embitter; ~ *la vida a* make *s.o.'s* life a burden.
acicalado *arma* bright and clean; *p.* spruce, neat; *b.s.* dressed to kill, dressy F; **acicalar** [1a] polish, clean; *fig.* dress up, bedeck; ~**se** *fig.* spruce o.s. up, get dressed up.
acicate *m* spur; *fig.* spur, incentive.
acidez *f* acidity; **acidificar** [1g] acidify; **ácido 1.** *fruta etc.* sharp, sour, acid; **2.** *m* acid; ~ *carbólico* carbolic acid; ~ *clorhídrico* hydrochloric acid; ~ *nítrico* nitric acid; ~ *oxálico* oxalic acid; ~ *sulfúrico* sulphuric acid; **acidular** [1a] acidulate; **acídulo** acidulous.
acierto *m* (*tiro*) good shot, hit (*a. fig.*); *fig.* (*acción*) good choice, wise move; (*conjetura*) good guess; (*habilidad*) skill; aptness *de observación*; (*éxito*) success; (*tino*) discretion.
acitrón *m* candied citron.
aclamación *f* acclamation; *por* ~ by acclamation; **aclamar** [1a] acclaim; ~ *a uno por jefe* hail s.o. as leader.
aclaración *f* explanation; rinsing; clearing; brightening (up); **aclarar** [1a] *v*/*t*. *asunto* clarify, explain, cast light on; *ropa* rinse; *bosque* clear, thin (out); *salsa* thin; *v. voz*; *v*/*i*. (*tiempo*) brighten (up), clear (up); **aclaratorio** explanatory; illuminating.
aclimatación *f* acclimatization; **aclimatar** [1a] acclimatize; ~**se** get acclimatized.
acné *f* ⚕ acne.
acobardar [1a] cow, intimidate, unnerve; ~**se** flinch, shrink (back) (*ante* from, at), get frightened.
acobrado copper-colored.
acocear [1a] kick; *fig.* maltreat, trample on.
acochinar [1a] F bump off.
acodado elbowed, elbow *attr.*
acodalar [1a] shore up, prop up.
acodar [1a] *vid etc.* layer; ~**se** lean (*sobre* on).
acodiciarse [1b]: ~ *a* covet.
acodo *m* 🌱 layer.
acogedor *ambiente*, *p.* welcoming, hospitable; *cuarto* snug; **acoger** [2c] *visita etc.* welcome, receive; *fugitivo* harbor, give refuge to; *noticia* admit, accept; ~**se** take refuge (*a* in); ~ *a fig. pretexto* take refuge in; *promesa* avail o.s. of; **acogible** welcome; acceptable; **acogida** *f* welcome, reception; acceptance; meeting place *de aguas*; asylum.
acogollar [1a] *v*/*t*. cover up, protect; *v*/*i*. sprout.
acogotar [1a] kill (with a blow on the neck); *p.* knock down.
acohombrar [1a] earth up.
acojinar [1a] ⊕ cushion.
acolchar [1a] *sew.* quilt; pad.
acólito *m* acolyte (*a. fig.*), server; *fig.* minion.
acollador *m* ⚓ lanyard.
acollar [1m] 🌱 earth up; ⚓ caulk.
acomedido *S.Am.* obliging.
acometer [2a] attack, set upon, assail; *fig. tarea etc.* undertake, have a go at F; (*sueño etc.*) overcome, overtake; (*dudas*) assail; **acometida** *f* attack, assault; ⚡ connec-

tion; **acometimiento** *m* attack; **acometividad** *f* aggressiveness, fight; enterprise, energy *en dificultades*.

acomodable adaptable; **acomodación** *f* accommodation; **acomodadizo** accommodating, obliging; acquiescent; **acomodado** (*conveniente*) suitable; *precio* moderate; *p.* wealthy, well-to-do, well off F; **acomodador 1.** obliging; **2.** *m thea.* usher; **acomodadora** *f thea.* usherette; **acomodamiento** *m* convenience; (*arreglo*) transaction, agreement.

acomodar [1a] **1.** *v/t.* (*componer*) arrange; (*encontrar sitio para*) fit in, find room for, accommodate; *acción* suit, adapt (*a* to); *ejemplo* apply (*a* to); *instrumento* adapt (*a uso* for); adjust, put right; *criado etc.* place (*a. fig.*); *thea.* show to a seat; *visitantes* make comfortable; *enemigos* reconcile; **2.** *v/i.* suit, fit; be suitable; **3.** **~se** (*conformarse*) comply; adapt o.s.; ~ *a circunstancias* adapt o.s. to; *situación nueva* settle down to; ~ *a inf.* settle down to *inf.*; ~ *con* reconcile o.s. to; (*avenirse*) come to an agreement with; *dictamen* comply with; ~ *de* provide o.s. with; **acomodo** *m* arrangement; lodgings; job; *S.Am.* neatness.

acompañado *sitio* busy, frequented; *p.* assistant; **acompañamiento** *m* accompaniment (*a.* ♪); (*p.*) escort; (*ps.*) retinue; *thea.* extras; *sin* ~ unaccompanied; **acompañanta** *f* chaperon, escort; ♪ accompanist; **acompañante** *m* companion; escort; ♪ accompanist; **acompañar** [1a] accompany (*a.* ♪), go with; *mujer freq.* chaperon; enclose *en carta*; ~ *a la puerta freq.* see out; ~ *a una p. en* join a p. in; *le acompaño en sus sentimientos* I sympathize with you (in your loss); *seguir acompañando a* keep with, stay with; **~se** *con* ♪ accompany o.s. on.

acompasado rhythmic, regular, measured; *fig.* (*hablando*) slow (of speech); (*andando*) slow, steady; **acompasar** [1a] ♪ mark the rhythm of; & measure with a compass; ~ *la dicción* speak with a marked rhythm.

acomunarse [1a] join forces.

acondicionado ⊕ conditioned; *bien* ~ (*genio*) nice; (*estado*) well set up, in good condition; *mal* ~ (*genio*) bad-tempered; (*estado*) badly off, in bad condition; **acondicionador** *m*: ~ *de aire* air conditioner; **acondicionamiento** *m*: ~ *de aire* air conditioning; **acondicionar** [1a] arrange, prepare; ⊕ condition; fix up.

aconcharse [1a] lean (*a* against); ⚓ run aground.

acónito *m* aconite.

aconsejable advisable, politic; *poco* ~ inadvisable; **aconsejar** [1a] advise, counsel; *virtud etc.* preach; **~se** seek (*or* take) advice; ~ *con*, ~ *de* consult with; ~ *mejor* think better of it.

aconsonantar [1a] rhyme (*con* with).

acontecer [2d] happen, occur; **acontecimiento** *m* happening, event; new development.

acopiar [1b] gather together, collect; *miel* hive; **acopio** *m* (*acto*) gathering, collecting; store (*a. fig.*), collection; abundance.

acoplado *m S.Am.* trailer; **acoplador** *m radio*: coupler; **acoplamiento** *m* ⊕ coupling; joint; ⚡ hookup, connection; ~ *de manguito* sleeve coupling; ~ *universal* universal joint; **acoplar** [1a] ⊕ (*unir*) join, couple, fit together; (*encajar*) fit (into place); ⚡ connect, join up; *bueyes* yoke, hitch; *S.Am.* 🚂 couple (up); **~se** *zo.* mate, pair; F be reconciled.

acoquinar [1a] scare; **~se** F get the jitters, get scared.

acorazado 1. armor-plated, ironclad; F forbidding; **2.** *m* battleship; **acorazamiento** *m* armor; armor plating; **acorazar** [1f] armor-plate; **~se** *fig.* arm o.s., steel o.s. (*contra* against).

acorchado spongy, corklike.

acordada *f* ⚖ decree; **acordadamente** by common consent; unanimously; **acordado** agreed; *lo* ~ that which has been agreed upon; **acordar** [1m] **1.** *v/t.* decide, resolve (*que subj.* to *inf.* [*or* that *subj.*]; *inf.* to *inf.*); remind (*algo a alguien* s.o. of s.t.); ♪ tune; *colores* blend; *diversos pareceres* reconcile; **2.** *v/i.* agree; correspond; **3.** **~se** agree, come to an agreement (*con* with); ~ (*de*) remember; *si mal no me*

acuerdo if my memory serves me right; *se acordó hacer* it was agreed to do; **acorde 1.** agreed; in accord; ♪ in harmony, in tune, harmonious; *estar* ~ *con* be in agreement with; **2.** *m* harmony, chord.
acordeón *m* accordion.
acordonado corded, ribbed; **acordonar** [1a] tie up; *corsé* lace up; *lugar* cordon off; *moneda* mill.
acornar [1m], **acornear** [1a] butt; (*penetrando*) gore.
acorralado cornered, at bay; **acorralamiento** *m* corraling; *fig.* intimidation; **acorralar** [1a] *animales* pen, corral, round up; *p.* corner (*a. fig.*); *fig.* intimidate.
acorrer [2a] run (up), hasten (*a* to).
acortar [1a] shorten, cut down; *camino, paso, vela* shorten; *cuento* cut short; *S.Am. fig.* tone down; **~se** *fig.* be slow, be timid.
acosar [1a] pursue, hound (*a. fig.*); *fig.* harass, badger, bait; **acoso** *m* pursuit; *fig.* harrying, baiting.
acostar [1m] lay (down); *niño etc.* put to bed; ⚓ bring alongside (*a acc.*); **~se** lie down; go to bed; *S.Am.* (*mujer*) be confined; *estar acostado* be lying down; be in bed.
acostumbrado usual, customary, habitual; *estar* ~ *a* be accustomed to, be used to; **acostumbrar** [1a] *v/t.* accustom, get *s.o.* used (*a* to); inure (*a apuros etc.* to); *v/i.*: ~ (*a*) *inf.* be in the habit of *ger.*, be accustomed to *inf.*; **~se** accustom o.s., get accustomed (*a* to).
acotación *f* (*mojón*) boundary mark; *surv.* elevation mark; (*apunte*) marginal note; *thea.* stage direction; **acotamiento** *m* boundary mark; annotation; stage direction; *S.Am.* shoulder (of road); **acotar** [1a] *terreno* survey, mark out; *árbol* lop, top; *página* annotate; *oferta* accept; F (*escoger*) choose; F (*atestiguar*) vouch for.
acotillo *m* sledge (hammer).
acoyundar [1a] yoke.
acre *olor* acrid, pungent; *sabor* tart, sharp; *genio* disagreeable, sour.
acrecencia *f* increase, growth; ⚖ accretion; **acrecentar** [1k] increase; *p.* promote, advance; **acrecer** [2d] increase.
acreditación *f* accrediting; clearance *por policía*; **acreditado** accredited; reputable; reputed (*de* to be); **acreditar** [1a] *embajador etc.* accredit (*cerca de* to); ✝ credit; (*afamar*) do credit to, add to the reputation of; (*garantizar*) vouch for, guarantee; **~se** get a reputation (*de* for); justify o.s.
acreedor 1. deserving (*a* of); **2.** *m*, **-a** *f* creditor; ~ *hipotecario* mortgagee; **acreencia** *f S.Am.* credit balance.
acribar [1a] sift, riddle; **acribillado** (*balas*) peppered, riddled; (*agujeros*) honeycombed; **acribillar** [1a] pepper, riddle (*a balas etc.* with); fill (*a puñaladas* with); *fig.* pester, harass.
acriminación *f* incrimination; **acriminador** incriminating; **acriminar** [1a] incriminate.
acrimonia *f* acridness, pungency; *fig.* acrimony; **acrimonioso** acrimonious.
acriollarse [1a] *S.Am.* go native.
acrisolar [1a] ⊕ purify, refine; *fig. verdad etc.* reveal, show, declare; clarify, bring out.
acristianar [1a] F Christianize; *niño* baptize.
acritud *f* = *acrimonia.*
acrobacia *f* acrobatics (*a.* ✈); ~ *aérea* aerobatics; **acróbata** *m/f* acrobat; **acrobático** acrobatic.
acrónimo *m* acronym.
acta *f* minutes, record *de reunión*; transactions *de sociedad*; certificate *de elección*; ~ *notarial* affidavit; *levantar* ~ take the minutes; *levantar* ~ *de* minute (*v/t.*); **~s** *pl.* life, acts *de santo*; minutes, record *de reunión.*
actitud *f* attitude (*a. fig.*), posture; outlook; *en* ~ *de inf.* getting ready to *inf.*; **activar** [1a] activate, energize; *trabajo* expedite, speed up; *fuego* brighten up; **actividad** *f* activity; promptness *en obrar*; bustle, movement *de muchedumbre etc.*; *en* ~ in operation, in action; *volcán* in eruption; *en plena* ~ in full swing; **activista** *m/f* activist; **activo 1.** active (*a. gr.*); *fig.* active, energetic; prompt; (*ocupado*) busy; *en* ~ on active service; **2.** *m* ✝ assets; ~ *de la quiebra* bankrupt's estate.
acto *m* act, action; ceremony, function; *thea.* act; 2*s pl. de los Apóstoles* Acts (of the Apostles); ~ *de fe* act of faith; *en el* ~ forthwith, immediately;

on the spot; ~ *continuo* straight afterwards, there and then.
actor *m* actor; *fig.* protagonist; **actora:** *parte* ~ prosecution; plaintiff; **actriz** *f* actress; *primera* ~ leading lady.
actuación *f* action; performance (*a. thea.*), behavior; ~ *en directo thea.* live performance; *S.Am.* role; **actual** present(-day); *cuestión* topical; **actualidad** *f* present (time); (*cuestión*) question of the moment, live issue; *en la* ~ at the present time, nowadays; *ser* (*or correr*) *de* ~ be current, be alive; *ser de gran* ~ be of immediate interest; be highly topical; ~*es pl.* current events; (*película*) newsreel; **actualmente** at present, at the moment, nowadays.
actuar [1e] *v/t.* actuate, set in motion, operate; work; *v/i.* act (*de* as); perform; ⊕ operate; ~ *sobre* act on.
actuario *m* ⚖ clerk; ✝ ~ (*de seguros*) actuary.
acuadrillar(se) [1a] band together.
acuarela *f* water color; **acuarelista** *m/f* water-colorist.
acuario *m* aquarium.
acuartelado *heráldica*: quartered; **acuartelar** [1a] quarter, billet; ~**se** withdraw to barracks.
acuático aquatic, water *attr.*; **acuátil** aquatic.
acucia *f* diligence; (*prisa*) haste; (*deseo*) keen desire; **acuciante** pressing; **acuciar** [1b] urge on, hasten, prod (on); (*desear*) desire keenly; **acucioso** diligent, keen; (*deseoso*) eager.
acuclillarse [1a] squat (down).
acuchillado knifelike; *fig.* experienced, wary; **acuchillar** [1a] stab (to death), knife; *sew.* slash; *madera* hack, gash; ~**se** fight with knives.
acudir [3a] come up *al ser llamado etc.*; come to the rescue *para socorrer*; come, turn up (*a cita* for, at), present o.s.; (*replicar*) respond, answer; ⛏ produce, yield; ~ *a* call on, turn to, have recourse to; *médico* go to see.
acueducto *m* aqueduct.
ácueo aqueous.
acuerdo *m* agreement, understanding; (*conformidad*) accord; harmony; (*recuerdo*) remembrance; *parl.* resolution; ~ *verbal* verbal (*or* gentleman's) agreement; *de* ~ in agreement; *¡de* ~*!* I agree!, agreed!; *de* ~ *con* in accordance with; *de común* ~ with one accord; *estar de* ~ *con* agree with, be in agreement with; *llegar a un* ~ come to an understanding (*con* with); *ponerse de* ~ come to an agreement, agree; *tomar un* ~ pass a resolution.
acuitar [1a] afflict, grieve; ~**se** be grieved (*por* by, at).
acular [1a] back (*a* against); F corner.
acullá over there, yonder.
acumulación *f* accumulation (*a. acto*); pile; hoard; **acumulador** *m* accumulator, storage battery; **acumular(se)** [1a] accumulate, gather, pile up; **acumulativo** accumulative.
acunar [1a] rock in a cradle.
acuñación *f* minting; **acuñar** [1a] *moneda* coin, mint; *medalla* strike; ⊕ (*meter cuñas*) wedge.
acuoso watery; *fruta* juicy.
acupuntura *f* ⚕ acupuncture.
acurrucarse [1g] squat; huddle up, curl up.
acusación *f* accusation; *esp.* ⚖ charge, indictment; *negar la* ~ plead not guilty; **acusado 1.** marked, pronounced; **2.** *m*, **-a** *f* accused, defendant; **acusador 1.** accusing, reproachful; **2.** *m*, **-a** *f* accuser; **acusar** [1a] accuse (*de* of); ⚖ accuse, indict (*de, por* of, on a charge of); *fig. culpable* point to, proclaim the guilt of; (*mostrar*) show, reveal; *cartas* show, declare; *recibo* acknowledge; ~**se** confess (*de su.* to; *de adj.* to being); **acusativo** *m* accusative (case); **acusatorio** accusatory; **acuse** *m* acknowledgment (*de recibo* of receipt); **acusete** *m/f S.Am.* informer; **acusón** F **1.** telltale; **2.** *m*, **-a** *f* telltale; gossip.
acústica *f* acoustics; **acústico 1.** acoustic; **2.** *m* hearing aid.
acutángulo *adj.* acute-angled.
achacar [1g]: ~ *a* attribute to, impute to, put *s.t.* down to; **achacoso** sickly, infirm; indisposed, ailing.
achaflanar [1a] chamfer, bevel.
achantarse [1a] F hide away; sing small.
achaparrado *árbol* dwarf, shrub-sized; *p.* stocky, thick-set, stumpy.
achaque *m* ⚕ sickliness, infirmity;

ailment; (*asunto*) matter, subject; pretext; defect, fault; F ⚕ period, monthlies; ~s *pl. mañaneros* morning sickness.
achatar [1a] flatten.
achicado childlike.
achicador *m* scoop, baler; **achicar** [1g] make smaller; *sew.* take in; (*humillar*) humble; intimidate, browbeat; ⚓ bale (out); *S.Am.* F kill; **~se** *fig.* eat humble pie, submit to humiliation.
achicoria *f* chicory.
achicharradero *m* hothouse, inferno; **achicharrar** [1a] *cocina*: fry crisp; (*demasiado*) overcook, burn; scorch, overheat; F plague; *S.Am.* squeeze; **~se** get burned, get scorched *etc.*
achín *m C.Am.* peddler; door-to-door salesman.
achinado *S.Am.* degraded; coarsened; (*color*) coppery; **achinar** [1a] F scare.
achiquitarse [1a] *S.Am.* lose heart; cower.
achispado lit-up, jolly; **achisparse** [1a] get tipsy.
achocar [1g] dash (*or* hurl) against a wall; stone *con piedra*; club *con palo*; F hoard.
achocharse [1a] F get doddery, begin to dodder, be in one's second childhood.
achubascarse [1g] (*cielo*) become threatening.
achuchar [1a] F crush, squeeze; (*azuzar*) urge on; **achuchón** *m* F squeeze; (*empujón*) push, jostle.
achula(pa)do ill-mannered, uncouth; spivvish *sl.*
achurar [1a] *S.Am.* wound; kill; gut, disembowel.
adagio *m* adage; ♪ adagio.
adalid *m* leader, champion.
adamado effeminate; F *mujer* flashy.
adamantino adamantine.
adamascado damask; **adamascar** [1g] damask.
adán *m* F slovenly character.
adaptabilidad *f* adaptability; **adaptable** adaptable; *p. freq.* versatile; **adaptación** *f* adaptation; **adaptador** *m* adapter; **adaptar** [1a] adapt; fit, make suitable (*para* for); **~se** adapt o.s. (*a* to).
adaraja *f* ⚠ toothing.
adarga *f* (oval) shield.
adarme: *por* ~s in driblets.
adecentar [1a] make decent, tidy up.
adecuado adequate; fit, suitable (*a, para* for); **adecuar** [1d] fit, adapt.
adefesio *m* F (*disparate*) absurdity, piece of nonsense; (*traje*) outlandish dress; (*p.*) odd guy.
adehala *f* (*propina*) gratuity, tip; bonus *sobre pago*.
adelantado 1. precocious, advanced; *reloj* fast; (*atrevido*) forward; ✝ *por* ~ in advance; **2.** *m* † governor, captain-general; **adelantamiento** *m* advancement, furtherance; progress, improvement; **adelantar** [1a] *v/t.* move forward, move on; *fecha, reloj* put forward; *pago* advance; (*pasar*) overtake, outstrip; *fig.* further, advance; *v/i.* make headway, get on; progress, improve; (*reloj*) be fast, gain; **~se** go forward, go ahead; (*reloj*) be fast, gain; ~ *a* get ahead of (*a.* ~ *de*); overtake (*a. mot.*); *fig.* steal a march on, beat *s.o.* to it; **adelante** ahead; forward(s), onward(s); ¡~! (*a interlocutor*) go ahead!, go on!, fire away!; (*a visita*) come in!; *más* ~ further on; later; (*de aquí or de hoy*) *en* ~ from now on, in the future; *por el camino* ~ from the opposite direction; **adelanto** *m* advance (*a.* ✝), progress, advancement.
adelfa *f* rosebay; oleander.
adelgazamiento *m* slimming; **adelgazar** [1f] *v/t.* make thin; (*régimen etc.*) help *s.o.* to slim; *vara* pare; *fig.* purify, refine; *entendimiento* sharpen; *v/i.* grow thin; (*de propósito*) slim, reduce; *fig.* split hairs; **~se** grow thin.
ademán *m* gesture, movement; flourish, motion *de mano*; *paint. etc.* attitude; ~es *pl.* manners; *en* ~ *de inf.* as if to *inf.*; *hacer* ~ *de inf.* make a move to *inf.*; *hacer* ~es gesture, make signs.
además 1. *adv.* besides, moreover, further(more); **2.** ~ *de prp.* besides, not to mention, aside from; ~ *de eso* moreover.
adentellar [1a] sink one's teeth into.
adentrar(se) [1a]: ~ *en* penetrate into, go into, get into, get inside;
adentro 1. = *dentro*; *v. tierra*; **2.** ~s *m/pl.* innermost being; *para sus* ~s to o.s.

adepto 1. *m* follower, supporter; **2.** adept; proficient.
aderezar [1f] prepare, get ready; *p. etc.* make beautiful, dress up; *fig.* embellish, adorn; *comida* season, garnish; *ensalada* dress; *bebidas* mix, blend; *tela* gum; **aderezo** *m* (*acto*) preparation; dressing; (*efecto*) adornment; *cocina*: seasoning, dressing; equipment; set *de joyas*; gumming *de tela*.
adeudado in debt; **adeudar** [1a] *v/t. dinero* owe; *impuestos* be liable for; *cuenta* debit, charge to; *v/i.* become related (by marriage); **~se** run into debt; **adeudo** *m* debt; customs duty *en aduana*; debit *en cuenta*.
adherencia *f* adherence; *fig.* connection; **adherente 1.**: *~ a* adhering to, sticking to; **2.** *m* follower, adherent; **adherir**(**se**) [3i] adhere, stick (*a* to); *~ a fig.* espouse, embrace; adhere to; **adhesión** *f* adhesion; *fig.* support, adherence; **adhesivo** *adj. a. su. m* adhesive.
adiamantado diamondlike.
adición *f* addition, adding-up; (*cuenta*) check; acceptance; **adicional** additional, extra; **adicionar** [1a] (*sumar*) add (up); add (*a* to).
adicto 1.: *~ a* devoted to; given to; **2.** *m* supporter; fan.
adiestramiento *m* training; breaking in; *caballo* breaking; **adiestrar** [1a] (*enseñar*) train, teach; (*guiar*) guide, lead; **~se** train o.s. (*a inf.* to *inf.*).
adinerado moneyed, well-off F.
adiós 1. *int.* good-bye!; **2.** *m* good-bye; farewell; **¡adiosito!** F bye-bye!
adiposo adipose, fat.
aditamento *m* addition.
aditivo *adj. a. su. m* additive.
adivinable guessable; **adivinación** *f* prophecy, divination; guessing; *~ de pensamientos* thought reading; **adivinanza** *f* riddle, conundrum; **adivinar** [1a] *porvenir etc.* prophesy, foretell; (*descubrir*) guess; *pensamientos* read; *enigma* solve; **adivino 1.** *m*, **a** *f* fortuneteller; **2.** *m zo.* praying mantis.
adjetivar [1a] *gr.* modify; make attributive; *fig.* apply epithets to; **adjetivo 1.** *m* adjective; **2.** adjectival; *~ gentilicio* adjective of nationality, gentilic.
adjudicación *f* award; **adjudicar** [1g] award, adjudge; knock down *en subasta* (*a* to, *en* for); **~se** *algo* appropriate.
adjuntar [1a] subjoin, append; enclose *en carta*; **adjunto 1.** joined on; *fig.* attached (*a* to); *p.* assistant; enclosed *en carta*; *remitir ~* enclose; *lo remitimos ~* we enclose it, we send it herewith; **2.** *m* addition, adjunct; (*p.*) assistant.
adjutor *m*, **-a** *f* assistant.
adminículo *m* accessory; **~s** *pl.* emergency kit.
administración *f* administration; management; running; *en ~* in trust; *obras en ~* books handled by us, books for which we are agents; **administrador** *m*, **-a** *f* administrator; (*jefe*) manager; (*síndico*) steward; (land) agent *de finca*; *~ de correos* postmaster; *es buena ~a* (*en casa*) she's a good manager; **administrar** [1a] administer; manage; run; *justicia* dispense, administer; **administrativo** administrative; managerial.
admirable admirable; **admiración** *f* admiration; wonder(ment); **admirador** *m*, **-a** *f* admirer; **admirar** [1a] (*respetar*) admire; look up to; (*sorprender*) cause surprise (to), astonish; *me admira su atrevimiento* I am amazed at your boldness; **~se** be surprised, be amazed, wonder (*de* at); **admirativo** admiring, full of admiration.
admisible admissible; *excusa etc.* legitimate; **admisión** *f* admission (*a* to); (*recepción*) acceptance; ⊕ intake, inlet; **admitir** [3a] admit (*a. fig.*; *a* to, *en* into); accept, recognize; *fig.* be susceptible of; *propina, explicación* accept; *dilación* permit, allow; *dudas* leave room for.
admonición *f* warning; **admonitorio** warning *attr.*
adobado *m* pickled meat; **adobar** [1a] dress, prepare; *carne* pickle; *piel* tan, dress; (*guisar*) cook, prepare; **adobe** *m* adobe; **adobera** *f S.Am.* brick-shaped cheese; mold for brick-shaped cheese; **adobo** *m* preparation, dressing; pickle.
adocenado commonplace, ordinary.

adoctrinar [1a] indoctrinate (*en* with).
adolecer [2d] fall ill (*de* with); ~ *de* suffer from (*a. fig.*).
adolescencia *f* adolescence; **adolescente** *adj. a. su. m/f* adolescent.
adonde 1. where; **2.** *¿adónde?* where (to)?
adopción *f* adoption; **adoptar** [1a] adopt (*a. fig.*); *fig.* embrace; *actitud* adopt, strike, take up; *parl.* pass, approve; **adoptivo** adoptive; *hijo* adopted.
adoquín *m* squared stone, sett; **adoquinado** *m* paving (of blocks); **adoquinar** [1a] pave (with setts).
adorable adorable; **adoración** *f* adoration; worship; **adorar** [1a] adore; worship.
adormecedor sleep-inducing; soporific; *a. fig.* lulling; **adormecer** [2d] send to sleep; *fig.* calm, lull; **~se** fall asleep, drowse (off); (*miembro*) get numb, go to sleep; *fig.* ~ *en* persist in; **adormecido** drowsy; numb; *fig.* inactive; **adormecimiento** *m* drowsiness; numbness; **adormidera** *f* opium poppy; **adormilarse** [1a], **adormitarse** [1a] doze.
adornar [1a] adorn, embellish (*de* with); *sew.* trim (*de* with); *cuarto* decorate; *comida* garnish; *p.* grace; *le adornan mil virtudes* he is blessed with every virtue; **adornista** *m/f* decorator; **adorno** *m* adornment; ornament; decoration; *sew.* trimming; motif *en diseño*; ~*s pl. fig.* trappings.
adosar [1a] lean (*a* against).
adquirir [3i] acquire; obtain; ✝ purchase; earn; *hábito* acquire, form; **adquirido** acquired; *mal* ~ *ganancias* ill-gotten; **adquisición** *f* acquisition; ✝ purchase; **adquisitivo** acquisitive; ✝ *poder* purchasing; **adquisividad** *f* acquisitiveness.
adrede on purpose, intentionally.
adrenalina *f* adrenalin.
adresógrafo *m* addressograph.
adscribir [3a; *p.p. adscrito*]: ~ *a* assign to; *adscrito a(l servicio de)* attached to.
aduana *f* customs; custom house; (*derechos de*) ~ customs duty; *exento de* ~, *libre de* ~ duty-free; *sujeto a* ~ dutiable; **aduanero 1.** customs *attr.*; **2.** *m* customs officer.
aducir [3o] adduce, bring forward; *prueba* furnish.
adueñarse [1a]: ~ *de* take possession of.
aduje *etc. v. aducir.*
adulación *f* flattery, adulation; **adulador** *m*, **-a** *f* flatterer; **adular** [1a] flatter, fawn on, make up to; **adulón** F **1.** cringing, fawning; **2.** *m*, **-a** *f* toady, creep.
adúltera *f* adulteress; **adulteración** *f* adulteration; **adulterar** [1a] *v/t.* adulterate; *v/i.* commit adultery; **adulterino** adulterous; *moneda* falsified, counterfeit; **adulterio** *m* adultery, misconduct; **adúltero 1.** adulterous; *fig.* corrupt; **2.** *m* adulterer.
adultez *f C.Am.* adulthood; **adulto** *adj. a. su. m*, **a** *f* adult, grownup.
adunar [1a] join, unite.
adustez *f* grimness, austerity; **adusto** *región etc.* scorching; *fig.* austere, grim; *estilo* severe.
aduzco *etc. v. aducir.*
advenedizo 1. foreign, (from) outside; *contp.* upstart, parvenu; **2.** *m*, **a** *f* foreigner, outsider; *contp.* upstart, parvenu; **advenimiento** *m* advent; accession *al trono*; **adventicio** adventitious.
adverbial adverbial; **adverbio** *m* adverb.
adversario *m*, **a** *f* adversary, opponent; **adversidad** *f* adversity; **adverso** *suerte* adverse, untoward; *lado* opposite.
advertencia *f* (*amonestación*) warning; caveat; (*recordatorio*) reminder; foreword *en libro*; **advertido** capable; (*despierto*) wide-awake; **advertir** [3i] *v/t.* notice, observe; (*enseñar*) point out, draw attention to; (*aconsejar*) advise (*que* that); (*amonestar*) warn (of); caution; *v/i.*: ~ *en* notice, observe; (*tener en cuenta*) take notice of.
Adviento *m* Advent.
advocación *f eccl.* name, dedication; *bajo la* ~ *de* in the name of.
adyacente adjacent (*a.* ⩚).
aechaduras *f/pl.* chaff; *v. ahechar.*
aeración *f* aeration; **aéreo** aerial, air *attr.*; *ferrocarril etc.* overhead; **aerodinámico** aerodynamic; *mot. etc.* streamlined; *v. túnel*; **aerodinamizar** [1f] streamline; **aeródromo** *m* aerodrome, airfield;

aerofoto *f* aerial photograph; **aerolito** *m* aerolite; **aeromodelismo** *m* aeromodelling; **aeromoza** *f S.Am.* air hostess, stewardess; **aeronáutica** *f* aeronautics; **aeronáutico** aeronautic(al); **aeronave** *f* airship; **aeropuerto** *m* airport; **aerosol** *m* ⚕ aerosol; **aerostática** *f* aerostatics; **aerostático** aerostatic(al); *v. globo*; **aeróstato** *m* aerostat, balloon; **aerotaxi** *m* air taxi; **aerotransportado** airborne; **aerovía** *f* airway.

afabilidad *f* affability, geniality, good nature; **afable** affable, genial, good-natured; *trato* easy, smooth.

afamado famed, noted (*por* for); **afamar** [1a] make famous.

afán *m* industry, exertion; anxiety; zeal, desire, urge (*de* for); **afanarse** [1a] exert o.s., strive, labor (*por inf.* to *inf.*); *C.Am.* work for pay; F drudge (*or* toil) away (*en* at); **afanoso** *trabajo* laborious, heavy; *tarea* troublesome, uphill; *p.* solicitous.

afasia *f* aphasia.

afeamiento *m* defacing; disfigurement; condemnation; **afear** [1a] deface, make ugly; *esp. cara* disfigure; *fig.* condemn, decry.

afección *f* affection (*a.* ⚕); (*alteración*) change, effect; ~ *cardíaca* heart complaint, heart trouble; ~**es** *pl. del alma* emotions; **afectación** *f* affectation, pose; pretence, affectation *de ignorancia etc.*; **afectado** affected, unnatural; *estilo* stilted, precious, affected; **afectar** [1a] (*dejarse sentir en*) affect, have an effect on; (*conmover*) affect, move; *S.Am.* hurt, injure; (*fingir*) affect, pretend; *celo etc.* put on a show of; desire; ⚖ tie up, encumber; *por lo que afecta a* regarding, as for; **afectísimo** *msl* affectionate; *suyo* ~ yours truly; **afectivo** affective; **afecto 1.** affectionate, fond; ⚖ subject to tax; tied; ~ *a* fond of; inclined to; ~ *de* afflicted with; **2.** *m* affection, fondness (*a* for); emotion, feeling; **afectuosidad** *f* fondness, affection; **afectuoso** affectionate.

afeitada *f*, **afeitado** *m* shave, shaving; **afeitar** [1a] *barba* shave; *cara* make up, paint; *cola* trim; *planta* prune; ~**se** (have a) shave; **afeite** *m* make-up; cosmetic; (*aderezo*) putting right, fixing.

afelpado plush(y), velvety.

afeminación *f* effeminacy; **afeminado 1.** effeminate, sissy *sl.*; **2.** *m* effeminate person, sissy *sl.*; (*maricón*) homosexual *sl.*

aferrado stubborn; *fig.* ~ *a*, ~ *en opinión etc.* wedded to; **aferrar** [1k] *v/t.* grapple, seize; ⚓ grapple; *vela, bandera* furl; *v/i.*, ~**se** grapple (with, together); ⚓ (*anclar*) anchor, moor; ⚓ (*asirse*) grapple; *fig.* ~ *a*, ~ *en* stick to.

afestonado festooned.

afianzamiento *m* guarantee, security; ⚖ bail; *fig.* backing; **afianzar** [1f] *muro* support, prop up; (*sujetar*) fasten; (*asir*) seize; *fig.* (*apoyar*) back, support; *p. etc.* guarantee, vouch for.

afición *f* fondness, liking (*a* for), taste (*a música etc.* for); (*pasatiempo*) hobby; (*ps.*) fans, public; *pinta de* ~ he paints as a hobby; *tomar* ~ *a* take (a liking) to; **aficionado 1.** (*no profesional*) amateur; ~ *a música etc.* fond of, with a taste for; *deportes etc.* keen on; *estar* ~ *a* like, be fond of; *ser muy* ~ *a* be very keen on; **2.** *m*, **a** *f* (*no profesional*) amateur; enthusiast; *deportes*: fan, follower (*a* of); *thea., cine*: fan; ~ *a la música etc.* music *etc.* lover, lover of music *etc.*; *tenis para* ~**s** amateur tennis; *es un simple* ~ he's just an amateur; **aficionar** [1a] make *s.o.* keen (*a algo* on); inspire affection in *s.o.* (*a alguien* for s.o.); ~**se** *a*, ~ *de* get fond of, take (a fancy) to; *deporte etc.* become a follower (*or* fan) of; ~ *a inf.* become fond of *ger.*

afiebrarse [1a] *S.Am.* get a fever.

afilada *f S.Am.* grinding; sharpening; **afiladera** *f* grindstone; **afilado** *filo* sharp, keen; *punto* tapering; **afilador** *m* (*p.*) knife grinder; ⊕ strop; **afiladura** *f* sharpening, whetting; **afilalápices** *m* pencil sharpener; **afilar** [1a] sharpen, make sharp, put an edge on; put a point on; *navaja* strop; ~**se** get sharp *etc.*; (*cara*) get peaked, grow thin; (*dedo*) taper.

afiliación *f* affiliation; **afiliado** affiliated (*a* to); ✝ subsidiary; **afiliarse** [1a]: ~ *a* affiliate (o.s.) to.

afiligranado ⊕ filigreed; *fig.* delicate, fine.

afilón *m* strop.

afín 1. (*colindante*) bordering; related, similar; *ideas* kindred, akin; **2.** *m/f* relation by marriage.

afinación *f* refining; ♪ tuning; **afinado** in tune; **afinador** *m* ♪ tuning key; (*p.*) tuner; **afinar** [1a] *v/t.* perfect; ⊕ purify, refine; *fig.* refine, polish; ♪ tune; *v/i.* sing (*or* play) in tune.

afinidad *f* affinity (*a.* ⚗); fellow feeling; kinship (*con* with); *por* ~ by marriage.

afino *m* ⊕ refinement.

afirmación *f* affirmation, assertion; **afirmar** [1a] (*reforzar*) strengthen, secure; (*estabilizar*) steady; (*declarar*) affirm, assert; state, lay (it) down (*que* that); **~se** steady o.s.; **afirmativa** *f* affirmative; **afirmativo** affirmative; positive.

aflicción *f* sorrow, affliction, trial; **aflictivo** distressing; *pena* corporal; **afligido 1.** distressed, heartbroken; stricken (*por* with); **2.**: *los ~s m/pl.* the bereaved; **afligir** [3c] afflict; (*pena etc.*) grieve, trouble, pain; *Mex.* beat; whip; **~se** grieve (*con, de, por* at).

aflojamiento *m* slackening, loosening (*a.* ⚕); *fig.* relief, relaxation; **aflojar** [1a] *v/t. cuerda, paso* slacken; *tornillo etc.* loosen (*a.* ⚕, *a. fig.*); *presión* release; *fig.* relax; *v/i. fig.* (*ablandarse*) relent; grow cool (*en devoción* in); get slack (*en estudios* in); **~se** slacken (off); work loose *etc.*; *fig.* (*calor,* ⚕) abate; (*devoción*) cool (off); (*interés*) flag.

afloramiento *m* outcrop; **aflorar** [1a] crop out, crop up, outcrop.

afluencia *f* (*flujo*) inflow, influx; (*gente etc.*) crowd, jam; *hora(s) de ~* rush hour; attendance *en reunión*; abundance; eloquence; **afluente 1.** flowing; eloquent; **2.** *m geog.* tributary, feeder; **afluir** [3g] flow (*a. fig.*; *a* into); **aflujo** *m* ⚕ afflux, congestion.

aforador *m* gauger; **aforar** [1a] ⊕ gauge; *fig.* appraise, value.

aforismo *m* aphorism; **aforístico** aphoristic.

aforo *m* gauging; *fig.* appraisal.

aforrar [1a] line, face; **~se** put on plenty of underclothes; F feed one's face, tuck it away.

afortunado fortunate, lucky; *tiempo* stormy.

afrancesado *adj. a. su. m,* **a** *f* Francophile; Frenchified; **afrancesarse** [1a] go French; become Gallicized.

afrecho *m* bran; *~ remojado* mash.

afrenta *f* affront; indignity, outrage; **afrentar** [1a] affront; dishonor; **~se** be ashamed (*de* of); **afrentoso** insulting, outrageous.

africano *adj. a. su. m,* **a** *f* African.

afrodisíaco *adj. a. su. m* aphrodisiac.

afrontamiento *m* confrontation; **afrontar** [1a] confront, bring face to face; *enemigo etc.* face (up to).

afuera 1. *adv.* outside; *¡~!* out of the way!; **2.** *~s f/pl.* outskirts; suburbs.

afufar [1a] F beat it, clear off.

agachada *f* F trick, dodge; **agachadiza** *f* snipe; F *hacer la ~* pretend not to have been seen; **agachar** [1a] F *cabeza* bow; *sombrero* slouch; **~se** crouch, double up; (*esconderse*) duck; (*retirarse*) go into hiding, make o.s. scarce, lie low.

agalla *f* ⚘ gall (nut); *~ (de roble)* oak apple; *ichth.* gill; F *tener (muchas) ~s* have guts.

ágape *m hist.* love feast; F banquet.

agarrada *f* F scrap, brawl; **agarradera** *f S.Am.* hold; grip; handle; *tener ~s* have connections; **agarradero** *m* handle, grip; ⊕ lug; F pull, influence; **agarrado** F stingy, tight(-fisted); **agarrafar** [1a] F grab hold of; **agarrar** [1a] *v/t.* grip, grasp, lay (*or* catch) hold of; grab *con fuerza*; F get, wangle; *v/i.* take hold (*de* of); *S.Am. ~ para* strike out for; **~se** grasp one another, grapple; *~ a* hold on to, seize; grip; *carretera* hold; *~ de* seize, fasten (up)on; F *se le agarró la fiebre* the fever took hold of him; **agarro** *m* grasp, hold; **agarrón** *m S.Am.* brawl; fight.

agarrotar [1a] *fardo* tie tight; *p.* squeeze tight; *reo* garrotte; (*camisa*) be tight for; **~se** ⚕ stiffen; ⊕ seize up.

agasajar [1a] treat kindly, make much of; (*con banquete etc.*) regale, entertain lavishly; give *s.o.* a royal welcome; **agasajo** *m* consideration, kindness; (*regalo*) royal welcome, lavish hospitality.

ágata *f* agate.

agave *f* agave, American aloe.

agavilladora *f* 🖋 binder; **agavillar**

[1a] bind (in sheaves); **~se** F gang up, band together.
agazapar [1a] F catch, grab (hold of); **~se** F (*esconderse*) hide; (*agacharse*) crouch down, duck.
agencia *f* agency (*a. fig.*); bureau; *S.Am.* pawnshop; ~ *de noticias* news agency; ~ *de transportes* carriers, removal business; ~ *de turismo*, ~ *de viajes* tourist office, travel agency; **agenciar** [1b] bring about, engineer; procure, obtain; *trato* negotiate; *b.s.* wangle; **~se** manage, get along; **agencioso** active, diligent.
agenda *f* notebook; (*diario*) engagement diary.
agente *m* agent; ~ (*de policía*) policeman; ~ *de cambio* bill broker; ~ *de negocios* broker; ~ *provocador* agent provocateur; ~ *marítimo* shipping agent; ~ *de publicidad* ✝ advertising agent; *thea. etc.* publicity agent; ~ *de transportes* carrier; ~ *de turismo* travel agent; courier; *S.Am.* ~ *viajero* commercial traveler, salesman.
agestado: *bien* ~ well-favored; *mal* ~ ill-favored.
agible workable, feasible.
agigantado gigantic; **agigantar** [1a] make *s.t.* (seem) huge.
ágil agile, nimble, quick; **agilidad** *f* agility *etc.*; **agilitar** [1a] enable, make it easy for; **~se** limber up.
agio *m* speculation; agio; **agiotaje** *m* speculation; (stock) jobbery, jobbing; **agiotista** *m* speculator; jobber.
agitación *f* waving; shaking *etc.*; ⚓ roughness; *fig.* ~ (*de ánimo*) agitation; (*movimiento*) bustle, stir, flurry; (*tumulto*) stir, ferment; **agitado** ⚓ rough, choppy; ✈ bumpy; *fig.* agitated, upset, excited; **agitador** *m* (*p.*) agitator, rabble rouser; ⊕ agitator, shaker.
agitanado gipsylike.
agitar [1a] *bandera etc.* wave; *brazo* shake, wave; *ala* flap; (*circularmente*) whirl; *líquido* shake up, stir; *fig.* stir up; (*inquietar*) worry, make anxious; **~se** shake, wave to and fro; (*bandera etc.*) flutter, flap; ⚓ get rough; *fig.* get excited, get worked up; get worried.
aglomeración *f* mass, agglomeration; ~ *de tráfico* traffic jam; **aglomerado** *m* agglomerate; coal briquet; **aglomerar**(**se**) [1a] form a mass, agglomerate; (*gente*) crowd together.
aglutinación *f* agglutination; **aglutinar**(**se**) [1a] agglutinate.
agnado *adj. a. su. m*, **a** *f* agnate.
agobiador, agobiante *carga* oppressive; *trabajo* overwhelming; *pobreza* grinding; **agobiar** [1b] weigh down, bow down (*de* with); oppress, burden (*a. fig.*); (*agotar*) exhaust, wear out; **~se** *con*, ~ *de* be weighed down with (*a. fig.*), bow beneath; **agobio** *m* burden; oppression; ⚕ nervous strain, anxiety.
agolpamiento *m* rush, crush, throng *de gente etc.*; bunch *de cosas*; crop *de penas*; flood *de lágrimas*; **agolparse** [1a] crowd together, throng; (*penas*) come on top of one another; (*lágrimas*) come in a flood.
agonía *f* agony; throes (*a. fig.*); (*ansia*) yearning; **agónico** *fig.* agonizing; **agonizante 1.** dying; **2.** *m/f* dying person; *eccl. monk who assists the dying*; **agonizar** [1f] *v/t.* F harass, pester; *v/i.* be in the throes of death.
agorar [1n] predict, prophesy; **agorero 1.** *p.* who prophesies; *ave* of ill omen; **2.** *m*, **a** *f* fortune teller, soothsayer.
agostar [1a] *plantas* parch, burn up; *tierra* plough (in summer); **~se** wither; *fig.* fade away; **agostizo** ↗ sickly, weak; **agosto** *m* August; *fig.* harvest; F *hacer su* ~ feather one's nest; make hay while the sun shines.
agotable exhaustible; **agotado** exhausted, worn out; *libro* out of print; *batería* run down; ✝ *estar* ~ be sold out; **agotamiento** *m* exhaustion (*a.* ⚕); depletion, draining; ~ *nervioso* strain; **agotar** [1a] exhaust (*a.* ⚕); *cisterna* drain, empty; *filón* work out; *provisión*, *recursos* drain, deplete, use up; *p.* tire, wear out; *paciencia* exhaust; **~se** be(come) exhausted; (*suministro etc.*) be used up, give out, run out; (*filón*) peter out; (*libro*) go out of print.
agraceño tart, sour.
agraciado graceful; *cara etc.* attractive, nice; blessed (*de* with); **agraciar** [1b] improve the looks of, make more attractive; *reo* pardon; (*favorecer*) reward (*con* with).
agradable pleasant, enjoyable, nice;

p. nice ([*para*] *con* to), agreeable; **agradar** [1a] please, be pleasing to.

agradecer [2d] *p.* thank; *favor* be grateful (*or* thankful) for; *agradezco tu carta* I am grateful for your letter; *se lo agradezco* I am grateful to you, I am much obliged; *agradecería que* I should be much obliged if; *¡se agradece!* much obliged; **agradecido** grateful (*a* to; *por* for); appreciative; *muy* ~ much obliged (*por* for); **agradecimiento** *m* gratitude.

agrado *m* affability; (*gusto*) taste, liking; *no es de mi* ~ it is not to my liking.

agrandar [1a] make bigger, enlarge; *dificultad* magnify.

agranujado *piel* pimply.

agrario agrarian; *reforma etc. freq.* land *attr.*

agravación *f*, **agravamiento** *m* aggravation, worsening; increase *de pena, impuesto*; ⚕ change for the worse; **agravante 1.** aggravating; **2.** *f* additional burden; unfortunate circumstance; **agravar** [1a] weigh down, make heavier; *pena, impuesto* increase; *dolor, situación* make worse; *pueblo* oppress; **~se** worsen, get worse.

agraviar [1b] wrong, offend; **~se** take offence, be offended (*de, por* at); **agravio** *m* offence, wrong; *a.* ⚖ grievance; **~s** *pl. de hecho* assault and battery; **agravioso** offensive, insulting.

agraz *m* sour grape; (*zumo*) sour grape juice; *fig.* bitterness, displeasure; *en* ~ prematurely; **agrazar** [1f] *v/t.* embitter; (*disgustar*) annoy; *v/i.* taste sour, have a sharp taste; **agrazón** *m* F annoyance, bother.

agredir [3a; *defective*] assault, attack, do violence to.

agregado *m* (*conjunto*) aggregate; (*p.*) attaché; ⊕ concrete block; *S.Am.* tenant; **agregar** [1h] (*añadir*) add (*a* to); (*juntar*) gather, collect; *p.* appoint, attach (*a* to); **~se** be joined (*a, con* to, with).

agremiar [1b] form into a union; **~se** form a union.

agresión *f* aggression; **agresivo** aggressive; *fig.* pushing, assertive, militant; **agresor** *m*, **-a** *f* aggressor, assailant.

agreste rural, country *attr.*; *fig.* rustic, countrified.

agrete sourish.

agriar [1b *or* 1c] (make) sour; *fig.* exasperate; **~se** turn (sour); *fig.* get exasperated, get irritated.

agrícola agricultural, farming *attr.*; **agricultor 1.** agricultural, farming *attr.*; **2.** *m*, **-a** *f* farmer, agriculturalist; **agricultura** *f* agriculture, farming.

agridulce bittersweet.

agriera *f Col., P.R.* heartburn.

agrietar [1a] crack (open), make cracks in; **~se** crack (open); get cracked; (*manos*) chap.

agrifolio *m* holly.

agrimensor *m* (land) surveyor; **agrimensura** *f* (land) surveying.

agringarse [1h] *S.Am.* act like a foreigner; pretend to be a gringo.

agrio 1. sour, acid, tart (*a. fig.*); *fig.* disagreeable; *camino* uneven, rough; *materia* fragile, breakable; *color* harsh, garish; **2.** *m* (sour) juice; ~*s pl.* citrus fruits.

agronomía *f* agronomy, agriculture; **agrónomo 1.** agricultural, farming *attr.*; *ingeniero* ~ = **2.** agricultural adviser, farming expert; **agropecuario** farming (and stock breeding) *attr.*

agrupación *f*, **agrupamiento** *m* association, group; (*acto*) grouping (together), coming together; **agrupar** [1a] group (together); (*apiñar*) bunch (*or* crowd) together; **~se** (*ps.*) crowd (around); (*cosas*) cluster, bunch together; *pol. etc.* rally, come together.

agrura *f* sourness (*a. fig.*).

agua *f* **1.** water; (*lluvia*) rain; ⚓ (*estela*) wake; (*abertura*) leak; △ slope of a roof; ~ *bendita* holy water; ~ *blanda* soft water; ~ *corriente* running water; ~ *de bebida* drinking water; ~ *de Colonia* eau de Cologne; ~ *dulce* fresh water; *de* ~ *dulce pez etc.* freshwater; ~ *de espliego* lavender water; ~ *llovediza*, ~ (*de*) *lluvia* rainwater; ~ (*de*) *manantial* spring water; ~ *potable* drinking water; ~ *abajo* downstream; ~ *arriba* upstream; *bailarle el* ~ *a* dance attendance on; *echar al* ~ launch; *echar el* ~ *a su molino* be on the make; *hacer* ~ leak, take in water; *se me hace la boca* ~ my mouth waters; *que hace* ~ *tela* moiré; *pescar en ~ turbia* fish in troubled waters; *retener el ~* hold water; *volverse ~ de cerrajas* (*proyecto etc.*) come to nothing; *¡hombre al ~!* man overboard!; **2.** *~s pl.* waters; ⚓ tide; ⚕ urine; sparkle *de joya*; *~ jurisdiccionales*, *~ territoriales* territorial waters; *~ mayores* excrement; *~ menores* urine; *~ minerales* mineral waters; *~ residuales* sewage; *hacer ~* make water, relieve o.s.; *nadar entre dos ~* sit on the fence.

aguacate *m* ♀ avocado; pear-shaped emerald.

aguacero *m* (heavy) shower; **aguacha** *f* stagnant water; **aguachirle** *f* slops, swill; *fig.* dish water; (*cosa*) trifle, mere nothing; **aguada** *f* ⚓ water supply; ⚒ flooding; *paint.* water color, wash; **aguado** watery, watered (down); *sopa* thin; *fig. fiesta etc.* spoiled, interrupted; **aguador** *m* water carrier, water seller; **aguaducho** *m* freshet; **aguafiestas** *m/f* wet blanket, killjoy; **aguafuerte** *f* etching; *grabar al agua fuerte* etch; **aguaje** *m* (*marea*) (spring) tide; current; (*provisión*) water supply; *C.Am.* cloudburst; reprimand; **aguamanil** *m* ewer, water jug; (*palangana*) wash stand; **aguamar** *m* jellyfish; **aguamarina** *f* aquamarine; **aguanieve** *f* sleet; **aguanoso** watery, wet; *terreno* waterlogged.

aguantada *f S.Am.* patience; forebearance; **aguantar** [1a] *v/t. techo* hold up; *aliento* hold; *dolor etc.* endure, withstand; *tempestad* weather; (*tolerar*) bear, stand, put up with; *v/i.* last, hold out; **~se** hold o.s. back, restrain o.s.

aguar [1i] water (down); *fig.* mar, spoil; *v. fiesta*.

aguardada *f* wait(ing); **aguardadero** *m hunt.* stand, hide; **aguardar** [1a] *v/t.* wait for, await; *v/i.* wait; *b.s.* lie in wait.

aguardentería *f* liquor store; **aguardiente** *m* brandy; *~ de caña* rum.

aguarrás *m* (oil of) turpentine.

aguatero *m S.Am.* water seller.

aguatocha *f* pump.

aguaturma *f* Jerusalem artichoke.

aguaza *f* sap.

aguazal *m* puddle.

agudeza *f* acuteness, sharpness (*a. fig.*); (*chiste*) witticism; (*lo ingenioso*) wit(tiness); **agudo** sharp, pointed; ⚕, 𝄞, *gr.* acute; *nota* high(-pitched); *sonido* piercing; *sabor etc.* pungent; *sentido* keen, acute; *pregunta* searching; *crítica* sharp, trenchant; (*gracioso*) lively, witty; *ingenio* ready, lively.

agüero *m* (*arte*) augury; (*pronóstico*) forecast; (*señal*) omen; *de buen ~* lucky, propitious; *de mal ~* ill-omened, of ill omen.

aguerrido hardened; inured; **aguerrir** [3a; *defective*] inure, harden.

aguijada *f* goad; **aguijar** [1a] *v/t.* goad (*a. fig.*); *fig.* urge on, incite; *v/i.* hurry along, make haste; **aguijón** *m* goad; *zo.* sting; ♀ prickle, sting; *fig.* spur, incitement; *dar coces contra el ~* kick against the pricks; **aguijonazo** *m* prick; *zo.*, ♀ sting; **aguijonear** [1a] = *aguijar*.

águila *f* eagle; *fig.* superior mind, genius; (*astuto*) wily bird; *~ pescadora* osprey.

aguileña *f* columbine.

aguileño *nariz* aquiline; *cara* sharp-featured.

aguilera *f* eyrie; **aguilón** *m* large eagle; jib *de grúa*; ⚠ gable (end); **aguilucho** *m* eaglet.

aguinaldo *m* Christmas (*or* New Year) gift; (*propina*) gratuity.

aguja *f sew.* needle; (*roma*) bodkin; hand *de reloj*; gnomon *de reloj de sol*; pointer *de esfera*; ⚠ spire, steeple; 🚂 (*a. ~s pl.*) points, switch rail; *~s pl. anat.* ribs; *~ capotera*, *~ de zurcir* darning needle; *~ de gancho* crochet hook; *~ hipodérmica* hypodermic needle; *~ magnética*, *~ de marear* compass (needle); *~ de (hacer) media* knitting needle; *buscar una ~ en un pajar* look for a needle in a haystack; **agujazo** *m* jab, prick; **agujereado** full of holes; *vasija* leaky; **agujerear** [1a] make holes in; pierce; **agujero** *m* hole; (*alfiletero*) needle case; ⊕ *~ de hombre* manhole; **agujetas** *f/pl.* ⚕ stitch; **agujón** *m* hatpin.

¡agur! F so long!; *iro. etc.* good-bye.

agusanado maggoty.

agustin(ian)o *adj. a. su. m*, **a** *f* Augustinian.

aguzar [1f] sharpen (*a. fig.*); *apetito* whet; *v. oreja, vista*.

¡ah! ah!; ha!; *¡~ de la casa!* hello inside!; *¡~ del barco!* ship ahoy!
ahechar [1a] sift; *trigo* winnow.
aherrojar [1a] fetter, put in irons; *fig.* subjugate, oppress.
aherrumbrarse [1a] get rusty; (*agua*) taste of iron.
ahí there, just there; *de ~ que* with the result that; *por ~* over there, that way; somewhere around; *fig.* more or less; *¡~ va!* there he goes!; (*sorpresa*) goodness me!; *estará por ~* he's knocking around somewhere.
ahijado *m*, **a** *f* godchild; *fig.* protegé(e); **ahijar** [1a] *v/t. p.* adopt; *animal* mother; *fig.* impute (*a* to); *v/i.* have children.
ahilar [1a] *v/t.* line up; *v/i.* go in single file; **~se** ⚕ faint with hunger; (*planta*) grow poorly; (*árbol*) grow tall; (*vino etc.*) go sour, go bad.
ahincadamente earnestly, hard; **ahincado** earnest, emphatic, energetic; **ahincar** [1g] press, urge; **~se** make haste, hurry up; **ahinco** *m* earnestness, intentness, energy; *con ~* earnestly, hard.
ahitar [1a] surfeit, cloy; **~se** stuff o.s. (*de* with) F; ⚕ have (*or* get) indigestion; **ahito 1.** surfeited, satiated; *fig.* fed up (*de* with); **2.** *m* ⚕ indigestion; *fig.* surfeit, satiety.
ahogadero *m* (*collar*) throatband; halter, headstall *de caballo*; *fig.* Black Hole of Calcutta; **ahogado** *cuarto* close, stifling; *fig.* spent up; **ahogar** [1h] drown *en agua*; suffocate, smother *por falta de aire* (*a. fig.*); *fuego* put out, extinguish; *proyecto de ley* kill; *planta* soak; *fig.* afflict, oppress; *morir ahogado* = **~se** drown; (*suicidarse*) drown o.s.; suffocate; **ahogo** *m* ⚕ shortness of breath, tightness of the chest; *fig.* affliction, sorrow; † stringency, embarrassment; *perecer por ~* drown; **ahoguío** *m* = *ahogo* ⚕.
ahondar [1a] *v/t.* deepen, make deeper; *fig.* penetrate, go into; *v/i.* *~ en* penetrate, go (deep) into; **~se** go (*or* sink) in more deeply; **ahonde** *m* deepening; digging.
ahora 1. *adv.* now; (*hace poco*) (just) now; (*dentro de poco*) in a little while; *desde ~* from now on, hence-forward; *hasta ~* up till now, as yet, hitherto; *por ~* for the present; *~ mismo* right now, this very minute; **2.** *cj.* now; *~ bien* now then; *~ pues* well then; *~ ... ~* whether ... or.
ahorcadura *f* hanging.
ahorcajarse [1a] sit astride; *~ en* straddle.
ahorcar [1g] hang; *v. hábito*; **~se** be hanged; (*suicidarse*) hang o.s.
ahorita *esp. S.Am.* F right away.
ahormar [1a] adjust (*a* to); *zapatos* break in, stretch; *fig.* make *s.o.* see sense.
ahorquillado forked; **ahorquillar** [1a] (*asegurar*) prop up, stay; *alambre etc.* shape like a fork; **~se** fork, become forked.
ahorrar [1a] *mst* save; *disgusto, peligro* avoid; *esclavo* free; *fig.* save (*de* from); **~se** spare o.s., save o.s.; *no ~(las) con nadie* be afraid of nobody; **ahorrativo** thrifty; *b.s.* stingy; **ahorro** *m* economy, saving; *~s pl.* savings.
ahoyar [1a] make holes in; perforate.
ahuchar [1a] hoard, put by; *Col., Ven., Mex.* bait; incite.
ahuecar [1g] *v/t.* hollow (out), make a hollow in; (*mullir*) loosen, soften; *voz* deepen, make solemn; *v/i.* F beat it; **~se** F put on airs.
ahulado 1. *C.Am., Mex.* waterproof(ed); impermeable; **2.** *m C.Am.* overshoe.
ahumado 1. *tocino etc.* smoked; *cristal etc.* smoky; **2.** *m* smoking, curing; **ahumar** [1a] *v/t. tocino etc.* smoke, cure; (*ahuyentar*) smoke out; *v/i.* (give out) smoke; **~se** (*comida*) taste burnt; (*cuarto*) be smoky, get smoked up; F get boozed.
ahusado tapering; **ahusarse** [1a] taper.
ahuyentar [1a] drive away, scare away; *fig.* banish, put out of mind; **~se** run away.
airado angry, furious; *vida* immoral, depraved; **airar** [1a] anger, irritate, **~se** get angry (*de, por* at).
aire *m* air (*a. fig.*: *aspecto, elegancia*); (*viento*) wind, draft; ♪ tune, air; *~ colado* draft; *~ comprimido* compressed air; *~ de familia* family resemblance; *~ líquido* liquid air; *~ viciado* stale air; *al ~ fig.* (up) in the air; *al ~ libre adj.* outdoor; *adv.* in the fresh (*or* open) air; outdoors; *de buen* (*mal*) *~* in a good (bad) temper;

cambiar de ~(*s*) have a change of air; *darse* ~*s* put on airs; *darse* ~*s de* boast of being; *tener* ~ *de* look like; *tomar el* ~ go for a stroll; *volar por los* ~*s* fly through the air.

airear [1a] air, ventilate; ~**se** take the air; ⚕ catch a chill.

airosidad *f* grace(fulness), elegance; **airoso** *lugar* airy; *tiempo* blowy; *cuarto* drafty; *fig*. graceful, elegant; airy, jaunty; (*con lucimiento*) successful; *quedar* ~, *salir* ~ come out with flying colors.

aislación *f* insulation; ~ *de sonido* soundproofing; **aislacionismo** *m* isolationism; **aislado** isolated; cut off; (*retirado*) lonely, out of the way; ⚡, ⊕ insulated; **aislador** ⚡ **1.** insulating; **2.** *m* insulator, nonconductor; **aislamiento** *m* isolation; ⚡ insulation; ⚡ insulating material; **aislante** *m* ⚡ insulator; **aislar** [1a] isolate (*a. fig.*), separate, cut off (*de* from); ⚡ insulate; ~**se** isolate o.s. (*de* from); live in isolation.

¡ajá! fine!, good!, all right!

ajamiento *m* (c)rumpling, crushing; *fig*. abuse.

ajamonarse [1a] F get plump, run to fat.

ajar [1a] (c)rumple, mess up; *esp. vestido* crush; batter; *p*. abuse; dress down; ~**se** get (c)rumpled *etc.*; ♀ fade.

ajardinar [1a] landscape.

ajedr(ec)ista *m/f* chess player; **ajedrez** *m* chess; (*fichas*) chess set, chess pieces, chessmen; **ajedrezado** checkered.

ajenjo *m* ♀ wormwood; (*bebida*) absinth.

ajeno (*de otro*) somebody else's, not one's own, other people's; (*de fuera*) outside; alien, foreign (*a manera de pensar etc.* to); (*impropio*) unsuitable; inappropriate (*a*, *de* to, for); different; ~ *a control etc.* outside, beyond; ~ *de preocupaciones etc.* without, free from; *los bienes* ~*s*, *lo* ~ other people's property; *estar* ~ *de sí* be detached.

ajete *m* young garlic; garlic sauce.

ajetreado *vida* tiring, busy; **ajetrearse** [1a] bustle about; (*afanarse*) slave (away); (*fatigarse*) tire o.s. out; **ajetreo** *m* (*trajín*) bustle, much coming and going; (*afanes*) drudgery.

ají *m* chili; red pepper; **ajiaceite** *m* sauce of garlic and olive oil; **ajilimoje** *m*, **ajilimójili** *m* F pepper and garlic sauce; ~*s pl.* F bits and pieces; buttons and bows; **ajo** *m* (clove of) garlic; F ✝ shady deal; F (*palabra*) swear word, dirty word; *harto de* ~*s* badly brought up, brought up in the gutter; F *tieso como un* ~ hoity-toity, high and mighty; F *soltar* ~*s y cebollas* swear like a trooper.

ajobar [1a] carry on one's back; **ajobo** *m* load; *fig*. burden, trouble.

ajorca *f* bracelet, bangle.

ajornalar [1a] hire by the day.

ajuar *m* household furnishings *de casa*; dowry *de novia*; trousseau.

ajuiciado sensible; **ajuiciar** [1b] bring to one's senses.

ajustable adjustable; **ajustado** right, fitting; *ropa* close-fitting, tight, clinging; **ajustador** *m* waistcoat; corselet; ⊕ finisher; fitter; **ajustar** [1a] **1.** *v/t*. ⊕ (*encajar etc.*) fit (*a* to, into); (*cerrar*, *ponerse etc.*) fasten; *mecanismo* adjust, regulate; (*corregir*) put right, set right; (*adaptar*, *cambiar*) adjust, adapt (*a* to); *agravio* pay off; *boda* arrange; *criado* hire, engage; *cuenta* settle; *página* make up; *precio* fix; **2.** *v/i*. fit; ~ *bien* be a good fit; **3.** ~**se** (*convenir*) fit, go; adapt o.s., get adjusted (*a* to); conform (*a* to); (*ponerse de acuerdo*) come to an agreement (*con* with); **ajustamiento** *m* ✝ settlement; **ajuste** *m* ⊕ *etc.* fitting; adjustment; *sew*. fit, fitting; engagement *de criado*; ✝ settlement; reconciliation; *typ*. making up; ⚖ retaining fee; *mal* ~ maladjustment.

ajusticiar [1b] execute.

al = *a* + *el*; ~ *llegar* on arriving.

ala *f* wing (*a.* ⚔, △, *pol. a. fig.*); ✈ wing, main plane; △ (*alero*) eaves; *anat*. auricle; blade *de hélice*; leaf *de mesa*; brim *de sombrero*; ~*s pl. fig*. courage; F *ahuecar el* ~ beat it; F *arrastrar el* ~ (*enamorado*) court; (*alicaído*) be depressed; *caérsele a uno las* ~*s* lose heart; *cortar las* ~*s a fig.* clip *s.o.'s* wings; F *tomar* ~*s* get frisky, get smart.

alabador approving, eulogistic; **alabamiento** *m* praise; **alabancioso** F boastful; **alabanza** *f* praise; eulogy; ~*s pl.* praises; *cantar las* ~*s de* sing the praises of; **alabar** [1a]

praise; ~se be pleased, be satisfied; (*jactarse*) boast (*de* of being).
alabarda *f* halberd; **alabardero** *m* halberdier; *thea.* hired applauder.
alabastro *m* alabaster (*a. fig.*); **alabastrino** alabaster *attr.*
alabear(**se**) [1a] warp; **alabeo** *m* warping; *tomar* ~ warp.
alacena *f* recess cupboard.
alacrán *m* scorpion.
alacridad *f* alacrity, readiness.
alada *f* fluttering; **alado** winged; *fig.* swift.
alagartado motley, variegated.
alambicado distilled; overrefined; *fig.* given sparingly (*or* grudgingly); *estilo etc.* subtle, precious; **alambicar** [1g] distill; *fig.* scrutinize; *estilo* make oversubtle; **alambique** *m* still; *por* ~ sparingly; *pasar por* ~ *fig.* go through *s.t.* with a tooth comb.
alambrada *f* barbed-wire entanglement; **alambrado** *m* (*valla*) wire fence; (*red*) wire mesh; ⚡ wiring; **alambre** *m* wire (*a.* ⚡); ~ *cargado* live wire; ~ *forrado* covered wire; ~ *de púas* barbed wire; **alambrar** [1a] wire; **alambrera** *f* wire mesh; wire cover *para carne etc.*; fire guard *para lumbre.*
alameda *f* ⚘ poplar grove; (*paseo*) walk; **álamo** *m* poplar; ~ *blanco* white poplar; ~ *de Italia* Lombardy poplar; ~ *negro* black poplar; ~ *temblón* aspen.
alamparse [1a]: ~ *por* have a craving for.
alano *m* mastiff.
alarde *m* ⚔ review; *fig.* display, parade; *hacer* ~ *de* make a show (*or* parade) of; **alardeado** vaunted; **alardear** [1a] boast, brag; **alardeo** *m* boasting, bragging.
alares *m/pl. sl.* trousers, pants.
alargadera *f* ⚗ adapter; ⊕ extension; **alargamiento** *m* elongation, extension *etc.*; **alargar** [1h] lengthen, prolong; extend; (*estirar*) stretch; (*pasar*) reach, hand; *mano* reach out; *cuello* crane; *cuerda* pay out; *paso* hasten; *cuento* spin out; *sueldo* increase; ~se (*días etc.*) draw out, lengthen; (*irse*) go away, withdraw; (*discurso etc.*) be long-winded, drag out; *se alargó en la conferencia* his lecture was long drawn out.
alarido *m* yell, shriek, howl; *dar* ~*s* yell *etc.*
alarife *m* architect; builder; *S.Am.* swindler.
alarma *f* alarm (*a. fig.*); ~ *aérea* air-raid warning; ~ *falsa* false alarm; *de* ~ warning *attr.*, alarm *attr.*; *dar la* ~ raise the alarm; **alarmante** alarming, startling; **alarmar** [1a] ⚔ call to arms, alert, sound the alarm among; *fig.* alarm; ~se be (*or* become) alarmed; **alarmista** *m/f* alarmist.
alazán *adj. a. su. m* sorrel.
alba *f* dawn; *eccl.* alb; (*al*) *romper el* ~ (at) dawn.
albacea *m* executor; *f* executrix.
albacora *f ichth.* albacore; swordfish.
albahaca *f* basil.
albanega *f* hair net.
albanés *adj. a. su. m*, -**a** *f* Albanian.
albañal *m* sewer, drain; ⛏ dunghill, compost heap.
albañil *m* bricklayer; mason, builder; **albañilería** *f* (*obra*) brickwork; masonry; (*arte*) bricklaying; building.
albarán *m* rent sign.
albarda *f* packsaddle; **albardilla** *f* cushion, pad; ⚠ cope, coping; (*tocino*) lard; (*batido*) batter.
albaricoque *m* apricot; **albaricoquero** *m* apricot (tree).
albayalde *m* white lead.
albedrío *m* (*a. libre* ~) free will; (*capricho*) whim, fancy; *al* ~ *de uno* at one's own pleasure, to suit o.s.
albéitar *m* veterinarian.
alberca *f* pond, cistern; *S.Am.* swimming pool.
albergar [1h] *v/t.* harbor, shelter; lodge, put up; *v/i.*, ~se (find) shelter; lodge; **albergue** *m* shelter, refuge (*a. mount.*); (*alojamiento*) lodging; *zo.* lair; ~ *de carretera* road house; ~ *para jóvenes* youth hostel; *dar* ~ *a* give *s.o.* lodging, take *s.o.* in.
albero 1. white; **2.** *m* pipeclay; (*paño*) tea towel; **albillo** white; **albina** *f* salt lake, salt marsh; **albino** *adj. a. su. m*, **a** *f* albino; **albis:** F *quedarse in* ~ not have a clue; **albo** *lit.* white.
albogue *m* rustic flute; (*gaita*) bagpipes; ~*s pl.* (*platillos*) cymbals.
albóndiga *f* meat ball; fish ball.
albor *m* whiteness; (*luz*) dawn (light); ~ *de la vida* childhood, youth;

~es *pl.* dawn; **alborada** *f* dawn; ⚔ reveille; *poet.*, ♪ aubade; **alborear** [1a] dawn.

albornoz *m* burnous(e) *de árabe*; bathing wrap, bath robe.

alborotadizo turbulent; *p.* restive, jumpy; **alborotado** hasty, rash; **alborotador 1.** riotous; boisterous; **2.** *m*, **-a** *f* agitator; rioter; mischief maker; **alborotar** [1a] *v/t.* disturb, agitate, stir up; *S.Am.* excite curiosity in; *v/i.* make a racket; **~se** (*p.*) get excited; (*turba*) riot; (*mar*) get rough; **alboroto** *m* (*vocerío etc.*) disturbance, racket, uproar; (*motín*) riot; (*pelea*) brawl; (*sobresalto*) scare, alarm.

alborozado merry, cheerful; **alborozar** [1f] cheer (up), gladden; **~se** be glad; **alborozo** *m* merriment, gaiety; jollification.

albricias *f/pl.* reward (for p. bringing good news); *¡~!* good news!; congratulations!; *en ~ de* as a token of.

álbum *m* album; *~ de recortes* scrapbook.

albumen *m* ♀ albumen; (*clara*) white of an egg; **albúmina** *f* ⚗ albumin; **albuminoso** albuminous.

albur *m ichth.* dace; *fig.* risk, chance.

albura *f* whiteness; white *de huevo*.

alcabala *f hist.* sales tax.

alcachofa *f* artichoke.

alcahueta *f* procuress, bawd; (*mensajera*) go-between; F gossip, tale bearer; **alcahuete** *m* procurer, pimp; go-between; *thea.* drop-curtain; **alcahuetear** [1a] procure; **alcahuetería** *f* procuring, pandering.

alcaide *m* † *castillo*: governor, castellan; *cárcel*: (*jefe*) governor; (*subordinado*) warder, jailer.

alcaldada *f* arbitrary action; abuse of power; **alcalde** *m* mayor; F *tener el padre ~* have influence; **alcaldear** [1a] F lord it, be bossy; **alcaldesa** *f* mayoress; **alcaldía** *f* mayoralty; (*casa*) mayor's residence (*or* office).

álcali *m* alkali; **alcalino** alkaline.

alcance *m* reach *de mano* (*a. fig.*); ⚔ range; *hunt.* pursuit; ✉ special delivery; (*periódico*) stop press; ✝ deficit; *fig.* scope *de programa etc.*; purview *de libro etc.*; range, grasp *de inteligencia*; (*talento*) capacity; significance, import; *al ~* within reach (*de* of; *a. fig.*); ⚔ within range; *al ~ del oído* within hearing, within earshot; *al ~ de la voz* within call; *de cortos ~s* dim(-witted); *fuera de su ~* out of one's reach; *fig.* over one's head; *andar* (*or ir*) *en los ~s a* spy on *s.o.*; *poner al ~ de* make *s.t.* accessible to; **alcancía** *f* money box; *S.Am. eccl.* collection box.

alcándara *f* clothes rack; *orn.* perch.

alcandora *f* beacon.

alcanfor *m* camphor; **alcanforar** [1a] camphorate.

alcantarilla *f* sewer; conduit; (*a. boca de ~*) drain; *S.Am.* cistern; **alcantarillado** *m* sewer system, drains; **alcantarillar** [1a] lay sewers in, provide sewers for.

alcanzadizo easily attainable (*or* reachable); **alcanzado** hard up, broke; **alcanzar** [1f] *v/t.* (*llegar*) reach; (*igualarse*) catch up with, overtake; *época* live through, live on into; (*coger*) grasp, catch (hold of); (*con sentidos*) perceive; *problema etc.* grasp, understand; *empleo* get, obtain; *v/i.* reach (*a, hasta* to *or acc.*); *~ a inf.* manage to *inf.*; *~ para todos* be enough, go round.

alcaparra *f* ♀ caper.

alcaparrosa *f* ⚗ vitriol.

alcaraván *m* stone curlew.

alcaravea *f* carraway.

alcatraz *m orn.* gannet; pelican.

alcaudón *m* shrike.

alcayata *f* meat hook; ⊕ tenter-hook.

alcazaba *f* citadel.

alcázar *m* fortress, citadel; royal palace; ⚓ quarter-deck.

alcazuz *m* liquorice.

alce *m zo.* elk; *naipes*: cut; *~ de América* moose.

alción *m orn.* kingfisher; (*mitológico*) halcyon.

alcista ✝ **1.** bull(ish); **2.** *m* bull.

alcoba *f* bedroom.

alcohol *m* alcohol; *~ desnaturalizado*, *~ metilado* methylated spirit; *lámpara de ~* spirit lamp; **alcohólico** *adj. a. su. m*, **a** *f* alcoholic; **alcoholismo** *m* alcoholism; **alcoholizado** *m*, **a** *f* alcoholic; **alcoholizar** [1f] alcoholize.

alcor *m* hill.

alcornoque *m* cork oak; *fig.* blockhead.

alcorza *f cocina*: icing, frosting; *fig.*

delicate little thing; **alcorzar** [1f] *cocina*: ice.
alcubilla *f* reservoir.
alcucero F having a sweet tooth; (*goloso*) greedy.
alcurnia *f* ancestry, lineage.
alcuza *f* olive-oil bottle; *S.Am.* cruet; water jug.
alcuzcuz *m approx.* couscous.
aldaba *f* (door) knocker; (*barra etc.*) bolt, crossbar; hitching ring *para caballo*; tener buenas ~s have pull, have influence; **aldabada** *f* knock (on the door); *fig.* fright; **aldabilla** *f* latch, catch; **aldabón** *m* = aldaba; (*asa*) handle.
aldea *f* village; **aldeano 1.** village *attr.*; *b.s.* uncouth, rustic; **2.** *m*, **a** *f* villager; **aldehuela** *f* hamlet; **alderorrio** *m* F rural backwater.
alderredor = alrededor.
aleación *f* alloy; **alear**[1] [1a] *metall.* alloy.
alear[2] [1a] *orn.* flap (its wings); (*p.*) move one's arms up and down; *fig.* ⚕ convalesce.
alebrarse [1a] lie flat; *fig.* cower.
aleccionador instructive, enlightening; **aleccionar** [1a] teach, give lessons to; instruct, coach.
alechugar [1h] fold, pleat.
aledaño 1. bordering; **2.** *m* boundary, limit.
alegación *f* allegation; **alegador** *S.Am.* quarrelsome; litigious; **alegar** [1h] plead (*a.* ⚖); allege; *autoridades etc.* quote, bring up; *dificultades* plead; *razones* put forward, adduce; **alegato** *m* ⚖ (*escrito*) bill; (*exposición*) pleading.
alegoría *f* allegory; **alegórico** allegoric(al); **alegorizar** [1f] allegorize.
alegrador 1. cheering; **2.** *m* spill; **alegrar** [1a] gladden, cheer (up); (*avivar*) brighten up, cheer up, enliven; *fuego* stir up, brighten up; *toro* excite; ⚓ *cabo* slacken; **~se** be glad, be happy, rejoice; cheer up (de *noticia* at); F (*achisparse*) get merry; ~ de, ~ con, ~ por be glad (because) of, rejoice at; ~ de *inf.* be happy (*or* glad) to *inf.*; **alegre** *p.*, *cara etc.* happy; *ánimo* joyful, glad; *carácter* cheerful, sunny; *música etc.* merry; *noticia* cheering, good; *color* bright, cheerful; (*osado*) reckless; F merry, tipsy; ~ (de corazón) light-hearted; **alegría** *f* happiness; joy(fulness), gladness; gaiety, merriment *etc.*; **alegrón 1.** F tipsy; high; **2.** *m* sudden joy; flare-up *de fuego*.
alejamiento *m* (*acto*) removal; (*lo remoto*) remoteness; distance; **alejar** [1a] move *s.t.* away (de from), remove; place at a distance; *peligro* remove; **~se** move away (de from); move to a distance; go away; (*peligro etc.*) recede.
alelar [1a] stupefy; make dull; **~se** (*viejo*) get feeble-minded; *fig.* gape stupidly.
aleluya 1. *f* (*grito*) hallelujah; *paint.* Easter print; F (*versos*) doggerel; F (*p. etc.*) bag of bones; **2.** *m* Easter time.
alemán 1. *adj. a. su. m*, **-a** *f* German; **2.** *m* (*idioma*) German.
alentada *f* deep breath; **alentado** (*animoso*) brave; (*altanero*) haughty; **alentador** encouraging; **alentar** [1k] encourage, inspire (a *inf.* to *inf.*); *resistencia* bolster up; *espíritu* buoy up; **~se** ⚕ get well.
alerce *m* larch.
alergia *f* allergy; **alérgico** allergic.
alero *m* ⚠ eaves; *mot.* fender; wing; **alerón** *m* aileron.
alerta 1.: ¡~! watch out!; estar (ojo) ~ be on the alert, stand by; **2.** *m* alert.
aleta *f* small wing; *ichth.* fin; flipper *de foca* (*a. sl.* = *mano*); *mot.* wing; ⊕, ✈ blade; ~s *sport* flippers; frogfeet.
aletargar [1h] benumb, drug; **~se** become lethargic.
aletazo *m orn.* flap of the wing, wingbeat; *ichth.* movement of the fin; **aletear** [1a] flap its wings, flutter; **aleteo** *m* fluttering, flapping; *fig.* palpitation.
aleudar [1a] leaven.
aleve = alevoso; **alevosía** *f* treachery, perfidy; **alevoso 1.** treacherous, perfidious; **2.** *m* traitor.
alfabético alphabetic(al); **alfabetizar** [1f] make literate, teach to read and write; **alfabeto** *m* alphabet.
alfalfa *f* lucerne, alfalfa.
alfanje *m* cutlass; *ichth.* swordfish.
alfaque *m* bar, shoal.
alfar *m* (*taller*) pottery; (*arcilla*) clay; **alfarería** *f* pottery; (*tienda*) pottery stall; **alfarero** *m* potter.
alfarjía *f* door frame; window frame; (*larguero*) batten.

alféizar *m* (*puerta*) splay(ing), embrasure; (*ventana*) (window)sill.

alfeñicarse [1g] F get awfully thin; (*remilgarse*) be prim and proper, be finicky; **alfeñique** *m* almond paste; F (*p.*) delicate sort, mollycoddle; (*remilgo*) squeamishness; affectation.

alférez *m* ⚔ second lieutenant, subaltern; ~ *de fragata* ensign; ~ *de navío* lieutenant j. g. (= junior grade).

alfil *m ajedrez*: bishop.

alfiler *m* pin; (*broche*) brooch, clip; ~*es pl. fig.* pin money; ~ *de corbata* tiepin; ~ *de seguridad* safety pin; F *de 25* ~*es* dressed to kill; F *pedir para* ~*es* ask for a tip; F *prendido con* ~*es* shaky, suspect; **alfilerar** [1a] pin (up); **alfilerazo** *m* pinprick (*a. fig.*); **alfiletero** *m* needle case.

alfolí *m* ✓ granary; salt warehouse.

alfombra *f* carpet (*a. fig.*); (*esp. pequeña*) rug; ~ *de baño* bath mat; **alfombrado** *m* carpeting; **alfombrar** [1a] carpet (*a. fig.*); **alfombrero** *m* carpet maker; **alfombrilla** *f* rug; *mot.* floormat; ⚕ German measles.

alforfón *m* buckwheat.

alforjas *f/pl.* saddle bags; (*comestibles*) provisions; *sacar los pies de las* ~ go off on a different tack.

alforza *f* pleat, tuck; *fig.* scar, slash.

alga *f* seaweed, alga 🕮.

algaida *f* (*bosquecito*) thicket; (*matorral*) bush, undergrowth; ⚓ dune.

algalia *f* civet.

algarabía *f* Arabic; *fig.* gibberish; F (*palabras atropelladas*) gabble; (*gritería*) din, hullabaloo.

algarada *f* outcry; *hacer una* ~ kick up a fuss.

algarrada *f hist.* catapult; *toros*: bull-baiting.

algarroba *f* carob (bean); **algarrobo** *m* carob tree, locust tree.

algazara *f* (Moorish) battle cry; *fig.* uproar, din.

álgebra *f* algebra; **algebraico** algebraic.

álgido ⚕ cold, chilly; F culminating, decisive.

algo 1. *pron.* something; ~ *es* ~ something is better than nothing; *eso ya es* ~ that is something; *¡por* ~ *será!* there must be some reason behind it!; *tomar* ~ have a drink; **2.** *adv.* rather, somewhat; *es* ~ *grande* it's on the big side, it's rather big.

algodón *m* cotton; ⚘ cotton plant; ⚕ swab; wadding *para orejas etc.*; ~ *en hojas* cotton batting; ~ *hidrófilo* cotton wool; ~ *pólvora* guncotton; *estar criado entre* ~*es* be born with a silver spoon in one's mouth; **algodonar** [1a] stuff (with cotton), wad; **algodonero 1.** cotton *attr.*; **2.** *m* (*p.*) cotton dealer; ⚘ cotton plant; **algodonosa** *f* cotton grass; **algodonoso** cottony.

alguacil *m* bailiff, constable.

alguien someone, somebody.

alguno 1. *adj.* (*algún delante de su. m singular*) some, any; (*tras su.*) (not ...) any; *algún libro que otro* some book or other; an occasional book; *no tengo dinero* ~ I don't have any money; *v. otro, tanto etc.*; **2.** *pron.* some; one; someone, somebody; ~*s pl.* some; ~ *de ellos* one of them; ~ *que otro* one or two, an occasional one; *¿ha venido* ~*?* has somebody (*or* anybody) come?; *tengo* ~*s* I have some, I have a few.

alhaja *f* jewel, gem; (*mueble*) fine piece; F (*p.*) treasure, gem; *buena* ~ *iro.* fine one, rogue; **alhajar** [1a] *casa* furnish, appoint (in good taste); **alhajera** *f S.Am.* jewelry box.

alharaca *f* fuss, ballyhoo, song and dance; *hacer* ~*s* make a fuss, create; **alharaquiento** demonstrative, emotional; strident.

alhelí *m* wallflower; gillyflower.

alheña *f* privet; (*tizón*) mildew.

alhóndiga *f* corn exchange.

alhucema *f* lavender.

aliado 1. allied; **2.** *m*, **a** *f* ally;

alianza *f* alliance (*a. fig.*); (*anillo*) wedding ring; *Biblia*: ♀ Covenant;

aliar [1c] ally; ~**se** become allied; form an alliance.

alias *adv. a. su. m* alias.

alicaído with drooping wings; *fig.* ⚕ weak, drooping; (*abatido*) downcast, down in the mouth.

alicantina *f* trick, ruse.

alicantino *adj. a. su. m*, **a** *f* (native) of Alicante.

alicates *m/pl.* pliers.

aliciente *m* incentive, inducement; *esp. b.s.* lure; mainspring (*a, de, para acción etc.* for).

alienación *f* alienation (*a.* ⚕); ⚕ mental derangement; **alienado 1.** distracted; insane, mentally ill; **2.**

m, **a** *f* mad person, lunatic; **alienar**(se) = *enajenar(se)*; **alienista** *m/f* psychiatrist, alienist.

aliento *m* (*un* ~) breath; (*acto*) breathing; *fig.* bravery, strength; *de un* ~ in one breath; *fig.* in one go; *sin* ~ out of breath; *cobrar* ~ take heart; *dar* ~ *a* encourage; *le huele mal el* ~ his breath smells; *tomar* ~ take breath.

aligación *f* bond, tie; *metall.* alloy.

aligeramiento *m* easing; alleviation; ~ *de impuestos* tax relief; **aligerar** [1a] *carga* lighten (*a. fig.*); (*abreviar*) shorten; *fig.* ease, relieve, alleviate; *paso* quicken; **~se** *de ropa* put on lighter clothing.

alijar [1a] *barco* unload; (*aligerar*) lighten; *contrabando* land; *madera* sandpaper; **alijo** *m* (*acto*) unloading; lightening; contraband; ~ *de armas* cache of arms.

alimaña *f* animal; *esp.* vermin.

alimentación *f* nourishment, feeding; (*comida*) food; ~ *forzada* ⚕ force feeding; ⊕ feed, supply; *fig.* nurture, fostering; ⊕ *dispositivo etc. de* ~ = **alimentador** *m* ⊕, ⚡ feed(er); **alimentante** *m/f* ⚖ person obliged to provide child support; **alimentar** [1a] feed, nourish (*a. fig.*); *fig. familia* maintain; (*criar*) bring up, nurture; *pasión etc.* foster, add fuel to; ⊕ feed; **~se** feed (*de, con* on); **alimenticio** *manjar* nourishing; nutritious, nutritive; *valor etc.* food *attr.*; *artículos* ~s foodstuffs; **alimentista** *m/f* pensioner; **alimento** *m* food (*a. fig.*); *fig.* incentive; encouragement; ⚖ ~s *pl.* alimony, allowance; **alimentoso** nourishing.

alindado foppish, dandified; **alindar**[1] [1a] make pretty, make nice; *p.* get up F.

alindar[2] [1a] *v/t. surv.* mark out; *v/i.* be adjacent, adjoin.

alineación *f* alignment (*a.* ⊕); line-up; *fuera de* ~ out of alignment; **alineado 1.** aligned; *no* ~ nonaligned; Third World *attr.*; **2.** *m* = *alineación*; **alinear** [1a] align, line (up); ⚔ form up; **~se** line up; ⚔ *etc.* fall in, form up.

aliñar [1a] *cocina*: dress, season; *S.Am. hueso* set; **aliño** *m* dressing, seasoning; (*acto*) preparation.

aliquebrado F drooping, crestfallen.

alisador *m* ⊕ (*p.*) polisher; (*instrumento*) smoothing blade;

alisar[1] [1a] smooth (down); polish; *esp.* ⊕ surface, finish; *pelo* smooth, sleek.

alisar[2] *m*, **aliseda** *f* alder grove.

alisios *m/pl.* (*a. vientos* ~) trade winds.

aliso *m* alder.

alistamiento *m* enlistment, recruitment; **alistar** [1a] (put on a) list; enroll *como miembro*; ⚔ enlist; ⚓ clear (for action); **~se** enroll; ⚔ enlist, join up; F sign up.

aliteración *f* alliteration; **aliterado** alliterative.

alivianar [1a] *S.Am.* lighten.

aliviar [1b] lighten (*a. fig.*); *fig.* relieve, give relief to, soothe; (*acelerar*) haste, speed up; *paso* quicken; ~ *de peso etc.* relieve s.o. of; **~se** get (*or* gain) relief; (*confesarse*) unburden one's heart (*de* of); **alivio** *m* relief (*a.* ⚕), alleviation; mitigation; (*mejora*) betterment; ~ *de luto* half-mourning.

aljaba *f* quiver.

aljama *f* Moorish (*or* Jewish) gathering; ⛪ mosque *de moros*, synagogue *de judíos*; **aljamía** *f Castilian written in Arabic characters.*

aljibe *m* (rainwater) cistern; ⚓ water tender; *mot.* oil tanker.

aljofaina *f* (wash)basin, (wash)bowl.

aljófar *m* pearl (*a. fig.*).

aljofifa *f* floor cloth; **aljofifar** [1a] wash, mop (up).

alma *f* soul; spirit; *fig.* (*p.*) (living) soul; (*aliento, fuente de inspiración*) heart and soul, lifeblood, moving spirit; crux, heart *de asunto*; ⚘ pith; ⊕, ⚡ core; ⚔ bore; F ~ *de caballo* twister; F ~ *de Caín* fiend; ~ *de Dios* good soul; ¡~ *mía!* my precious!; *con* (*toda*) *el* ~ heart and soul; *con toda mi* ~ with all my heart; *arrancársele a uno el* ~ be deeply shocked (*por* at, by); *caérsele a uno el* ~ *a los pies* be deeply moved; (*desanimarse*) be disheartened; *echarse el* ~ *a las espaldas* not be in the least concerned; *entregar* (*or rendir*) *el* ~ give up the ghost; *írsele a uno el* ~ *tras* be taken up with, fall for; F *me llegó al* ~ it came home to me; *tener el* ~ *en un hilo* have one's heart in one's mouth; *volver a uno*

el ~ al cuerpo calm down, recover one's peace of mind.
almacén *m* (*depósito*) warehouse, store (*a. fig.*); (*tienda*) shop; (*tienda grande*) department store; (*muebles*) depository; ⚔ magazine; *S.Am.* grocer's (shop); *~ de depósito* bonded warehouse; *en ~* in store; **almacenaje** *m* storage (charge); *~ frigorífico* cold storage; **almacenamiento** *m* storage; (*ordenador*) data storage, memory; **almacenar** [1a] put in store, store (up); (*esp. tienda*) stock up, lay in stock; *fig.* keep, collect; *b.s.* hoard; **almacenero** *m* storekeeper, warehouseman; *S.Am.* grocer; **almacenista** *m* warehouse (*or* shop) owner, warehouseman.
almadía *f* raft.
almadraba *f* tunny fishing; (*red*) tunny net(s).
almadreña *f* wooden shoe, clog.
almagrar [1a] raddle, ruddle; *fig.* defame; **almagre** *m* red ochre, ruddle.
almanaque *m* almanac; calendar; F *hacer ~s* muse.
almazara *f* oil mill.
almeja *f* shellfish, clam.
almena *f* merlon; *~s pl.* battlements; **almenado** battlemented, castellated.
almenara *f* beacon; (*araña*) chandelier.
almendra *f* ♀ almond; (*hueso*) kernel, stone; drop *de araña*; *~ garapiñada* praline; *~ tostada* burnt almond; F *de la media ~* kid-glove, finicky; **almendrada** *f* almond shake; **almendrado 1.** almond-shaped, pear-shaped; **2.** *m* macaroon; **almendral** *m* almond grove; **almendrera** *f*, **almendro** *m* almond (tree); **almendruco** *m* green almond.
almiar *m* haycock; hayrick.
almíbar *m* syrup; fruit juice; **almibarado** syrupy (*a. fig.*); *fig.* sugary, honeyed, oversweet; **almibarar** [1a] preserve (*or* serve) in syrup; *~ las palabras* use honeyed words.
almidón *m* starch; **almidonado** starched; F dapper, spruce; **almidonar** [1a] starch.
almilla *f* bodice; ⊕ tenon; (*carne*) breast of pork.
alminar *m* minaret.
almirantazgo *m* admiralty; **almirante** *m* admiral.
almirez *m* (metal) mortar.
almizcle *m* musk; **almizcleño** musky; **almizclero** *m* (*ciervo*) musk deer; (*roedor*) muskrat, musquash.
almo *poet.* nourishing; venerable.
almodrote *m* cheese and garlic sauce; F mixture; hodgepodge.
almohada *f* cushion *de silla*; pillow *de cama*; (*funda*) pillowcase; *~ neumática* air cushion; *consultar algo con la ~* sleep on s.t.; **almohadilla** *f* small cushion, small pillow; ⊕ pad; *~ (de entintar)* ink pad; ⚠ projection, relief; **almohadillado 1.** padded, stuffed; *piedra* dressed; **2.** *m* ashlar, dressed stone; **almohadón** *m* sofa cushion; hassock *para pies*.
almohaza *f* curry comb; **almohazar** [1f] *caballo* curry, groom, brush down; *pieles* dress.
almoneda *f* (*subasta*) auction; (*saldo*) clearance sale; **almoned(e)ar** [1a] (put up for) auction.
almorranas *f/pl.* piles; hemorrhoids.
almorzada *f* double handful; heavy breakfast; **almorzar** [1f *a.* 1m] *v/t.* have for lunch, lunch on; *v/i.* (have) lunch; (*desayuno*) (have) breakfast; *vengo almorzado* I've had lunch.
almuecín *m*, **almuédano** *m* muezzin.
almuerzo *m* lunch; formal luncheon; (*desayuno*) breakfast; (*de boda*) wedding breakfast; (*juego*) dinner service.
alnado *m*, **a** *f* stepchild.
alocado mad, wild.
alocución *f* allocution.
áloe *m* ♀ aloe; *pharm.* aloes.
alojamiento *m* lodging(s), F digs; ⚔ (*acto*) billeting; (*casa*) billet, quarters (*a.* ⚓); **alojar** [1a] lodge, put *s.o.* up; accommodate, house; ⚔ billet, quarter; *~se* lodge; ⚔ be billeted, be quartered; **alojo** *m S.Am.* accommodations; lodging.
alondra *f* (*a. ~ común*) lark.
alongar [1m] = *alargar*; *~se* remove, move away.
alpaca *f zo.* alpaca; alpaca wool; alpaca cloth; German silver.
alpargata *f* rope sandal; rubber and canvas sandal; **alpargatilla** *m/f* crafty sort.
alpende *m* lean-to; tool shed.

alpestre Alpine; *fig.* mountainous, wild; **alpinismo** *m* mountaineering; **alpinista** *m/f* mountaineer, climber; alpinist; **alpino** Alpine.
alpiste *m* ⚘ canary grass; (*semilla*) birdseed; F brandy; F *quedarse uno* ~ have one's trouble for nothing.
alquería *f* farmhouse.
alquiladizo 1. for rent; for hire; **2.** *m*, **a** *f* hireling; **alquilar** [1a] (*dueño*): *casa* rent (out), let; *coche etc.* hire out; (*inquilino etc.*): *casa, garaje, televisor* rent; *coche etc.* hire; *autocar* hire, charter; **~se** (*casa*) be let (*en precio* at, for); (*taxi etc.*) be out for hire, be on hire; (*anuncio*): *se alquila* (*casa*) to let; (*en general*) on hire; **alquiler** *m* (*acto*) letting; hire, hiring; renting; (*precio*) rent(al); rent *de casa*; ~ *de caballos* livery; *de* ~ for hire, on hire; *coche de* ~ rental car; *control de* ~*es* rent control; *exento de* ~*es* rent-free.
alquimia *f* alchemy; **alquímico** alchemic(al); **alquimista** *m* alchemist.
alquitara *f* still; **alquitarar** [1a] distil.
alquitrán *m* tar; ~ *de hulla*, ~ *mineral* coal tar; **alquitranado 1.** tarry; **2.** *m* (*firme*) tarmac; (*lienzo*) tarpaulin; **alquitranar** [1a] tar.
alrededor 1. *adv.* around; **2.** *prp.* ~ *de* around, about; *fig.* about, in the region of; **3.** ~*es m/pl.* outskirts, environs *de ciudad*; (*contornos*) surroundings, neighbourhood; setting *de local*.
alsaciano *adj. a. su. m*, **a** *f* Alsatian.
alta *f* ⚕ discharge (from hospital); *dar de* ~ discharge (from hospital); cure; ⚔ pass (as) fit; *darse de* ~ join, be admitted.
altanería *f meteor.* upper air; soaring *de ave*; *hunt.* falconry; *fig.* haughtiness; **altanero** *ave* high-flying, soaring; *fig.* haughty; high-handed.
altar *m* altar; ~ *mayor* high altar.
altavoz *m radio*: loudspeaker; ⚡ amplifier.
alterabilidad *f* changeability; **alterable** alterable; **alteración** *f* alteration; (*deterioro*) change for the worse, upset, disturbance; (*emoción*) agitation, strong feeling; (*altercado*) quarrel, dispute; ⚕ irregular pulse; **alterado** *fig.* agitated, upset, disturbed; *estómago* upset, disordered; **alterar** [1a] alter, change; ⚕ *etc.* change for the worse, upset; *b.s.* falsify; (*perturbar*) disturb, stir up; excite; **~se** *fig.* be disturbed, be upset (*por* by); (*leche*) go sour; (*voz*) falter.
altercado *m* argument, altercation; **altercar** [1g] quarrel, argue, bicker.
alternación *f* alternation, rotation; (*entre sí*) interchange; **alternador** *m* ⚡ alternator; **alternar** [1a] *v/t.* alternate (*con* with); interchange; vary; *v/i.* alternate; take turns; change about; ⊕ reciprocate; *sl.* pub crawl; ~ *con amigos* go around with; *sociedad* move in; ~ *de igual a igual* be on the same footing; **alternativa** *f* service by rotation; (*trabajo*) shift work; (*elección*) alternative, choice; *no tener* ~ have no alternative; ~*s pl. esp.* ups and downs, fluctuations; **alternativo, alterno** alternate; alternating (*a.* ⚡); (*a elegir*) alternative; *combustible* ~ alternate fuel; *energías alternas* alternate energy sources.
alteza *f* height; *fig.* sublimity; (*título*) highness.
altibajos *m/pl.* ups and downs, unevenness *de terreno*; *fig.* ups and downs, vicissitudes.
altillo *m* hillock; *S.Am.* attic.
altimático *cabina etc.* pressurized.
altímetro *m* altimeter.
altiplanicie *f* high plateau.
altísimo very high; *el* ♀ The Almighty.
altisonante high-flown, high-sounding.
altitud *f* height; *geog.*, ✈ altitude.
altivarse [1a] put on airs; **altivez** *f* haughtiness, arrogance; **altivo** haughty, arrogant.
alto[1] **1.** *adj. mst* high; *p., edificio, árbol* tall; *agua* deep; *mar* (*abierto*) high, deep, open; (*agitado*) rough, high; *voz* loud; *hora(s)* late, small; *clase, país, piso, río* upper; *fig.* elevated, high, sublime; (*el*) *más* ~ uppermost, highest, top; *de* ~ high (*adv.*); *de lo* ~ from above; *en (lo)* ~ up, high (up); *en lo* ~ *de* up, on top of; *por lo* ~ overhead; *tiene 2 metros de* ~ it is 2 meters high; **2.** *adv.* *lanzar* high (up); *gritar*

loudly; *v. pasar etc.*; **3.** *m geog.* height, hill; Δ upper floor, upper flat.

alto² *m* ⚔ *etc.* halt; *esp. fig.* stop, standstill; *¡~ ahí!* halt!, stop!; ⚓ avast!; *¡~ al fuego!* cease fire!; *hacer ~* halt (*a.* ⚔), stop.

altoparlante *m* loudspeaker.

altozano *m* hill(ock); hilly part *de ciudad*; *S.Am.* paved terrace.

altramuz *m* lupin(e).

altruismo *m* altruism; **altruista 1.** altruistic, unselfish; **2.** *m/f* altruist, unselfish person.

altura *f mst* height; height, tallness, stature *de p.*; depth *de agua*; height, altitude *de monte*; *geog.* latitude; ⚓ high seas; ♪ pitch; *fig.* loftiness, sublimity; *~s pl. geog. a. fig.* heights; *eccl.* heaven; *~ de caída* (*agua*) head; *~ de elevación* lift; *a la ~ de geog.* on the same latitude as; ⚓ *a la ~ de Vigo* off Vigo; *estar a la ~ de tarea etc.* be up to, measure up to; *estar a la ~ de las circunstancias* be up to the mark; *de ~* high; *pesca etc.* deepwater *attr.*; *en las ~s* on high; *tiene 2 metros de ~* it is 2 meters high; ✈ *tomar ~* climb.

alubia *f* string bean.

alucinación *f* hallucination, delusion; **alucinar** [1a] hallucinate, delude; *fig.* fascinate; **~se** be hallucinated, be deluded.

alud *m* avalanche.

aludir [3a]: *~ a* allude to, mention (in passing); *el aludido* the aforesaid; *darse por aludido* take the hint.

alumbrado 1. F lit-up, tight; **2.** *m* lighting (system); illumination; *~ fluorescente* fluorescent lighting; *~ de gas* gaslight; *~ público* street lighting; *red de ~* electricity grid; **3.** *m*, **a** *f hist.* illuminist; **alumbramiento** *m* ⚡ lighting, illumination; ⚕ childbirth; *tener un feliz ~* be safely delivered; **alumbrar** [1a] *v/t.* light (up), illuminate; *p.* light the way for; *ciego* give sight to; *agua* strike, find; *fig.* enlighten; *v/i.* ⚕ give birth; ⚡ *esto alumbra bien* this gives a good light; **~se** ⚡ light (up); F get tipsy.

alumbre *m* alum.

alúmina *f* alumina; **aluminio** *m* aluminum, *British* aluminium.

alumnado *m* student body; **alumno** *m*, **a** *f univ. etc.* student, pupil; ⚖ foster child, ward; *antiguo ~* alumnus, old boy *de colegio*; alumnus, old student *de universidad*; old pupil *de profesor*.

alunado lunatic, insane; *tocino* tainted.

alunizaje *m* moon landing; **alunizar** [1f] land on the moon.

alusión *f* allusion, mention, reference; *hacer ~ a* allude to, refer to; **alusivo** allusive.

aluvial alluvial; **aluvión** *m* alluvion (*a.* ⚖); (*depósito*) alluvium; *geol. de ~* alluvial; *~ de improperios* shower of insults.

álveo *m* bed (of a stream).

alveolar alveolar; **alvéolo** *m* alveolus, cell *de panal*; *anat.* socket.

alvino abdominal, bowel *attr.*

alza *f* ✝ rise, advance; ⚔ rear sight; ✝ *al ~* going up, buoyant; ✝ *jugar al ~* bull, speculate; **alzada** *f* height *de caballo*; ⚖ appeal;

alzado 1. elevated, raised; *S.Am.* insolent; brazen; rebellious; *precio* fixed, settled; **2.** *m* Δ front elevation; *typ.* gathering; **alzamiento** *m* (*acto*) lift(ing), raising; rise, advance *de precio*; (*quiebra*) fraudulent bankruptcy; (*postura*) higher bid; *pol.* (up)rising, revolt; **alzaprima** *f* (*palanca*) lever; (*cuño*) wedge; ♪ bridge;

alzar [1f] raise, lift (up), hoist; *mantel etc.* put away; (*llevarse*) take away; *cosecha* get in; *hostia* elevate; *pantalón* hitch up; *typ.* take up and arrange; *¡~!* up (you get)!; **~se** rise (up); *pol.* revolt, rise; ✝ go bankrupt (fraudulently); *~ con* make off with; *~ a mayores* get stuck up; **alzaválvulas** *m* ⊕ tappet; **alzo** *m C.Am.* theft.

allá (over) there; (*tiempo*) way back, long ago; F *¡~ tú!* that's your concern!, that's your problem; *más ~* further away (*or* over); farther on; *más ~ de* beyond, past; *límites* outside; *el más ~ fig.* the beyond; *por ~* thereabouts; ⚔ *¿quién va ~?* who goes there?; *¡~ voy!* I'm coming!

allanamiento *m* leveling, flattening; ⚖ submission (*a* to); *~ de morada* housebreaking; **allanar** [1a] *v/t.* (*hacer llano*) level (out), flatten; even; (*alisar*) smooth (down); *dificultad* smooth away, iron out; *país* subdue; *esp.* ⚖ permit entry into; *morada* break into; *v/i.* level out; **~se** level out, level off; (*caer*) tumble down; *~ a* accept, conform to.

allegadizo gathered at random; **allegado 1.** near, close; *p. related* (de to); *S.Am.* foster; **2.** *m*, **a** *f* (*pariente*) relation, relative; (*secuaz*) partisan, follower; **allegar** [1h] gather (together), collect; (*añadir*) add; **~se** go up (*a* to); (*llegar*) arrive, approach; ~ *a secta* become attached to; *dictamen* agree with.

allende beyond; ~ *de* besides; (*de*) ~ *los mares* (from) overseas.

allí there; ~ *dentro* in there; *de* ~ *a poco* shortly after(wards); *por* ~ (down) that way.

ama *f* mistress *de casa*; (*dueña*) owner, proprietress; foster mother *que cría*; (*de pensión etc.*) landlady; *S.Am.* ~ *de brazos* nursemaid; ~ *de casa* housekeeper, housewife; ~ *de cría*, ~ *de leche* wet nurse, foster mother; ~ *de llaves* housekeeper; matron *de colegio*.

amabilidad *f* kindness; amiability; *tener la* ~ *de inf.* be kind enough to *inf.*; **amable** kind; lovable; amiable, nice; *ser* ~ *con* be kind to; *qué* ~ *ha sido Vd. en inf.* how kind of you to *inf.*; **amachinarse** [1a] *S.Am.* cohabit; get intimate; **amado** *m*, **a** *f* love(r), sweetheart; **amador 1.** loving; **2.** *m*, **-a** *f* lover.

amadrigar [1h] welcome (with open arms); **~se** go into its hole, burrow; *fig.* go into retirement; withdraw into one's shell.

amaestrado *animal* trained, performing; *proyecto* well-contrived; **amaestramiento** *m* training *etc.*; **amaestrar** [1a] *animal* train; *caballo* break in; *p.* train, coach.

amagar [1h] *v/t.* threaten, show signs of, portend; *v/i.* threaten, be impending; *esp. fig.* be in the offing; ⚕ show the first signs; ⚔, *fenc.* feint; ~ *a inf.* threaten to *inf.*, show signs of *ger.*; **amago** *m* threat; (*indicio*) sign, symptom; ⚔, *fenc.* feint.

amainar [1a] *v/t. vela* take in, shorten; *furia* calm; *v/i.*, abate (*a. fig.*); (*viento etc.*) slacken, moderate; *amainó en su furia* his rage subsided; **~se** abate; slacken; lessen; **amaine** *m* abatement *etc.*

amaitinar [1a] spy on, pry into.

amalgama *f* amalgam; *fig.* concoction, medley; **amalgamación** *f* amalgamation; **amalgamar** [1a] amalgamate (*a. fig.*); *fig.* mix (up); combine; **~se** amalgamate (*a. fig.*).

amamantar [1a] suckle.

amancebado: *vivir* ~*s* = *amancebarse;* **amancebamiento** *m* cohabitation; common-law marriage; **amancebarse** [1a] live in sin.

amancillar [1a] stain, spot; *fig.* tarnish.

amanecer 1. [2d] dawn; appear (at dawn); (*p.*) wake up (*en* in), find o.s. at dawn; *fig.* begin to show; **2.** *m* dawn; *al* ~ at dawn; **amanecida** *f* dawn.

amanerado mannered, affected; **amaneramiento** *m* affectation; *lit.* mannerism (of style); **amanerarse** [1a] become affected (*or* mannered).

amanojar [1a] gather *s.t.* by the handful.

amansado tame; **amansador** *m*, **-a** *f* tamer; *S.Am.* horse breaker; **amansar** [1a] *animal* tame; *caballo* break in; *p.* subdue; *pasiones* soothe; **~se** (*pasión etc.*) moderate, abate.

amante 1. loving, fond; **2.** *m/f* lover; *f* mistress; ~*s pl.* lovers.

amanuense *m* amanuensis; scribe.

amañado (*hábil*) skilful, adroit; (*contrahecho*) fake(d), phon(e)y *sl.*; **amañar** [1a] do skilfully, do cleverly; fake; **~se** be handy, be expert; ~ *a inf.* settle down to *inf.*; ~ *con* get along with; **amaño** *m* skill, expertness; ~*s pl.* ⊕ tools; (*traza*) intrigue, guile; *tener* ~ *para* have an aptitude for.

amapola *f* poppy.

amar [1a] love.

amaraje *m* ✈ landing (on the sea); ditching.

amaranto *m* amaranth.

amarar [1a] land (on the sea); ditch *para evitar accidente*.

amargar [1h] *v/t.* make bitter; *fig.* embitter, spoil, upset; *v/i.* taste bitter; **~se** get bitter; *fig.* become (*or* grow) embittered; **amargo 1.** bitter (*a. fig.*); *fig.* embittered; **2.** *m* bitterness; ~*s pl.* bitters; **amargor** *m*, **amargura** *f* bitterness (*a. fig.*); *fig.* grief, affliction.

amaricado F effeminate; *es un* ~ he's a pansy.

amarillear [1a] show yellow; be yellowish; **amarillecer** [2d] (turn) yellow; **amarillento** yellowish; *tez etc.* sallow; **amarillez** *f* yellow(ness); sallowness; **amarillo** *adj. a. su. m* yellow.

amarra *f* mooring line, painter; ~s *pl.* moorings; *fig.* support, protection; *echar las* ~s moor; **amarradero** *m* (*poste*) bollard; (*cuerdas*) moorings; (*sitio*) berth; **amarraje** *m* mooring charges; **amarrar** [1a] *v/t. barco* moor; *cuerda* lash, belay; hitch, tie (up); *S.Am.* tie; *cartas* stack; *v/i.* F get down to it.

amartelado in love; lovesick; lovestruck; *andar ~ de* be in love with; **amartelamiento** *m* infatuation; **amartelar** [1a] *p.* woo, court; *corazón* win; ~**se** fall in love.

amartillar [1a] hammer; *pistola* cock.

amasada *f S.Am.* batch of dough; batch of mortar; **amasadera** *f* kneading trough; **amasador** *m* baker; **amasadora** *f* kneading machine; **amasadura** *f* (*acto*) kneading; (*masa*) batch; **amasamiento** *m* kneading; ⚕ massage; **amasar** [1a] *masa* knead; *harina, yeso* mix; *patatas* mash; *comida* prepare; ⚕ massage; F cook up; **amasijo** *m* kneading; mash *etc.*; F (*mezcla*) mixture; hodgepodge; (*complot*) plot.

amatista *f* amethyst.

amatorio love *attr.*; amatory, amorous.

amazacotado heavy, clumsy (*a. fig.*); *fig.* shapeless, jumbled; *obra freq.* stodgy.

amazona *f* amazon; (*jinete*) horsewoman; *contp.* horsy type.

ambages *m/pl.* beating about the bush, circumlocutions; *sin* ~ in plain language; **ambagioso** roundabout, involved.

ámbar *m* amber; ~ *gris* ambergris; **ambarino** amber *attr.*

ambición *f* ambition; **ambicionar** [1a] strive after, seek, be out for; hanker after; covet; **ambicioso 1.** ambitious; *b.s.* pretentious; **2.** *m*, **a** *f* ambitious person, careerist; ~ *de figurar* social climber.

ambidextro ambidextrous.

ambiente 1. ambient; *medio* ~ environment; situation; **2.** *m* atmosphere (*a. fig.*); *fig.* climate; (*que rodea*) milieu, environment, surroundings.

ambigú *m* buffet supper; cold supper; refreshment counter.

ambigüedad *f* ambiguity; **ambiguo** ambiguous; *género* common; (*incierto*) uncertain; (*evasivo*) noncommittal, equivocal; *cumplido* backhanded.

ámbito *m* ambit, compass; ⚠ confines.

ambos, ambas *adj. a. pron.* both; ~ *a dos* both.

ambrosia *f* ambrosia (*a. fig.*); **ambrosíaco** ambrosial.

ambulancia *f* ambulance; ⚔ field hospital; ~ *de correos* 🚂 mail car; **ambulante** (*que anda*) walking; (*que viaja*) roving, itinerant; *actor* strolling; *vendedor* traveling; **ambulatorio 1.** ambulatory; **2.** *m* ambulance.

amedrentar [1a] scare; intimidate; ~**se** be frightened, get scared.

amelonado F lovesick.

amén 1. *m* amen; F *decir ~ a todo* agree to anything; **2.** *prp.*: ~ *de* except (for); (*además de*) besides.

amenaza *f* threat, menace; **amenazador, amenazante** threatening, menacing; intimidating; **amenazar** [1f] *v/t.* threaten, menace; ~ *de muerte* threaten with death; *v/i.* threaten, loom, impend; ~ *con inf.* threaten to *inf.*

amenguar [1i] lessen, diminish; *fig.* defame, dishonor.

amenidad *f* pleasantness *etc.*; **amenizar** [1f] make pleasant, make nice; add charm to; *conversación* liven up; **ameno** pleasant, agreeable, nice; *trato, estilo etc.* pleasant; *lectura* light; *escritor* delightful.

amento *m* catkin.

americana *f* coat, jacket; **americanismo** *m* Americanism; *S.Am. pol.* Yankee imperialism; **americanizar** [1f] Americanize; **americano** *adj. a. su. m*, **a** *f* (*norte-*) American; (*sud-, central-*) Latin-American.

amerizar [1f] ✈ land (on the sea).

ametralladora *f* machine gun; ~ *antiaérea* antiaircraft gun; **ametrallar** [1a] machine-gun.

amiba *f*, **amibo** *m* ameba.

amiga *f* friend; (*novia*) girlfriend, sweetheart; *b.s.* mistress; *fig.* lover (de of); **amigable** friendly; *fig.* harmonious; **amigarse** [1h] get friendly; *b.s.* live in sin.

amígdala *f* tonsil; **amigdalitis** *f* tonsilitis.

amigo 1. friendly; ~ *de* given to, fond of; *ser muy* ~*s* be very good friends; **2.** *m* friend; (*novio*) boyfriend, sweetheart; *b.s.* lover; *fig.* lover (*de* of); ~ *de confianza* intimate; F *¡~ mío!* my friend!; old boy!; *hacerse* ~ *de* make friends with; *esp. b.s.* get in with; *ser* ~ *de fig.* be fond of; **amigote** *m* F old pal; **amiguita** *f* girlfriend.

amiláceo starchy.

amilanar [1a] intimidate, cow; ~**se** be cowed, be scared.

aminorar [1a] lessen; *gastos etc.* cut down; *paso* slacken.

amistad *f* friendship; ~*es pl.* (*ps.*) friends, acquaintances; *estrechar* ~ *con* get friendly with; F *hacer las* ~*es* make it up; *romper las* ~*es* fall out; **amistado** friendly (*con* with); **amistar** [1a] bring together, make friends; ~**se** become friends; (*después de riña*) make it up; ~ *con* make friends with; **amistoso** friendly; (*de vecino*) neighborly.

amnesia *f* loss of memory, amnesia; ~ *temporal* blackout.

amnistía *f* amnesty; **amnistiar** [1c] amnesty, grant an amnesty to.

amo *m* master *de casa etc.*; head of the family; (*dueño*) owner, proprietor; boss, overseer *en el trabajo*; ~ *de casa* householder.

amodorramiento *m* sleepiness, drowsiness; **amodorrarse** [1a] get sleepy, get drowsy; (*dormirse*) go to sleep; **amodorrido** drowsy, sleepy; numb.

amohinar [1a] vex, annoy; ~**se** get vexed, get annoyed; (*esp. niño*) sulk.

amojonar [1a] mark out.

amolador 1. F tedious; **2.** *m* (knife-) grinder; **amolar** [1m] grind, sharpen; F bore; pester; **amoladura** *f* grinding.

amoldar [1a] mold (*a. fig.*; *a modelo* on); adapt (*a circunstancias* to); ~**se** *fig.* adapt o.s., adjust o.s. (*a* to).

amonarse [1a] F get drunk.

amondongado flabby, gross.

amonedar [1a] coin, mint.

amonestación *f* warning; *esp.* ⚖ caution; *eccl.* (marriage) banns; *correr las* ~*es* publish the banns; **amonestador** warning *attr.*, cautionary; **amonestar** [1a] (*advertir*) warn; (*recordar*) remind; (*reprobar*) reprove, admonish; *eccl.* publish the banns of.

amoníaco 1. ammoniac(al); **2.** *m* ammonia.

amontonamiento *m* accumulation, piling up; **amontonar** [1a] heap (up), pile (up), accumulate; *nieve, nubes* bank (up); *esp. nieve* drift; *bienes* hoard, store (up); *fig. citas etc.* pile up; *alabanzas etc.* heap (*sobre* on); ~**se** pile (up), accumulate, collect; (*arena, nieve*) drift; (*nubes*) gather, pile up; (*gente*) crowd (together), huddle together; F get annoyed, go up in smoke.

amor *m* love (*a* for; *de* of); (*p.*) love; ~*es pl.* love affair, romance; ~ *cortés* courtly love; ~ *fracasado* disappointment in love; ~ *maternal* mother love; *¡~ mío!* (my) darling!; ~ *a la patria* love of one's country; ~ *propio* amour propre, self-respect; *al* ~ *del agua* with the current; *al* ~ *de la lumbre* by the fireside; *por* ~ for love; *por el* ~ *de* for the love of; *por el* ~ *de Dios* for God's sake; *hacer el* ~ *a* make love to; *picar a uno en el* ~ *propio* wound s.o.'s self-respect.

amoral amoral, unmoral; **amoralidad** *f* amorality.

amoratado purple; blue (*de frío* with cold).

amorcillo *m* flirtation, light-hearted affair.

amordazar [1f] *perro* muzzle (*a. fig.*); *p.* gag (*a. fig.*).

amorfo formless, shapeless, amorphous *esp.* 📖.

amorío *m* (*a.* ~*s pl.*) love affair, romance; ~ *secreto* intrigue; **amoroso** *p.* loving, affectionate; *b.s.* (*a. co.*) amorous; *carta, poesía etc.* of love, love *attr.*; *fig.* ⛏ workable; ⊕ malleable; *tiempo* mild, pleasant.

amorrar [1a] F bow one's head; *fig.* sulk.

amortajar [1a] shroud, lay out.

amortecer [2d] *ruido* muffle, deaden; ♪, *fuego* damp (down); ~**se** ⚕ faint, swoon; **amortecimiento** *m* muffling, deadening; ⚕ fainting.

amortiguación *f* deadening, muffling; absorbing, cushioning; **amortiguador 1.** deadening *etc.*; **2.** *m* damper; ⊕ shock absorber; 🚂 buffer; *mot. a.* bumper; ~ *de luz* dimmer; **amortiguar** [1i] **1.** *mst* =

amortecer; *choque* absorb; *golpe* cushion; *luz* dim; *color* tone down, kill.

amortizable ✝ redeemable; **amortización** *f* ⚖ amortization; ✝ redemption; *v. fondo*; **amortizar** [1f] ⚖ amortize; *préstamo* pay off, refund; *empleo* declare redundant; ~ *por desvalorización* write off.

amoscarse [1g], **amostazarse** [1f] F get peeved, get uptight.

amotinado mutinous; **amotinador** **1.** mutinous, riotous; **2.** *m* mutineer, rioter; **amotinamiento** *m* mutiny, rising, insurrection; **amotinar** [1a] incite to mutiny (*or* riot); **~se** mutiny, riot; rise up, rebel; *fig.* be upset, get upset.

amovible (re)movable, detachable; *empleado etc.* temporary.

amparador **1.** helping, protecting; **2.** *m*, **-a** *f* protector; **amparar** [1a] (*ayudar*) help; protect, shelter (*de* from); **~se** seek help; seek protection *etc.*; defend o.s. (*contra* against); ~ *a* have recourse to; ~ *con*, ~ *de* seek the protection of; **amparo** *m* help; protection; refuge, shelter; defense; favor.

amperímetro *m* ammeter; **amperio** *m* ampere.

ampliación *f* enlargement (*a. phot.*); (*ensanche*) extension; **ampliadora** *f phot.* enlarger; **ampliar** [1c] amplify; enlarge (*a. phot.*); (*ensanchar*) extend; *poderes* extend, widen; *declaración* amplify, elaborate; **amplificación** *f* amplification (*a. rhet., phys.*); ⚡ gain; **amplificador** *m radio*: amplifier; **amplificar** [1g] enlarge; amplify (*a. rhet., phys.*); **amplio** *espacio etc.* ample; *vestido* full, roomy; *falda* full; *cuarto* spacious, big; *poderes* ample, wide, generous; (*robusto*) assertive, full-blooded; *dibujo* bold; **amplitud** *f* ampleness; fullness; amplitude; *esp. fig.* breadth, extent.

ampo *m* dazzling white(ness); *como el* ~ *de la nieve* white as the driven snow.

ampolla *f* ⚕ blister; (*burbuja*) bubble; (*vasija*) flask; ⚕ (*vasija*) ampoule; **ampollarse** [1a] blister; **ampolleta** *f* (*vasija*) vial; (*reloj*) sandglass, hourglass; bulb *de termómetro*.

ampón *paquete* bulky; *p.* tubby.

ampulosidad *f* bombast, pomposity; **ampuloso** bombastic, pompous.

amputación *f* amputation; **amputar** [1a] amputate, cut off.

amuchachado boyish.

amueblado furnished; **amueblar** [1a] furnish; appoint.

amujerado effeminate.

amuleto *m* amulet, charm.

amuñecado doll-like.

amura *f* beam *de barco*; tack *de vela*; *cambiar de* ~ go about.

amurallar [1a] wall (in).

amurar [1a] ⚓ tack.

amusgar [1h] *orejas* throw back; *ojos* narrow.

anabaptista *m/f* anabaptist.

anacarado mother-of-pearl *attr.*

anacoreta *m/f* anchorite, anchoret.

anacrónico anachronistic; **anacronismo** *m* anachronism; (*objeto*) out-of-date object.

ánade *m* duck; ~ *real* mallard; **anadear** [1a] waddle; **anadón** *m* duckling.

anales *m/pl.* annals.

analfabetismo *m* illiteracy; **analfabeto** *adj. a. su. m*, **a** *f* illiterate.

analgesia *f* analgesia; **analgésico** *adj. a. su. m* analgesic.

análisis *mst m* analysis; ✝ ~ *de mercados* market research; **analista** *m* ☂ analyst; **analítico** analytic(al); **analizador** *m* analyst; **analizar** [1f] analyse; *gr.* parse.

analogía *f* analogy; **análogo** analogous, similar.

ananá(s) *m* pineapple.

anaquel *m* shelf; **anaquelería** *f* shelves, shelving.

anaranjado *adj. a. su. m* orange.

anarquía *f* anarchy; **anárquico** anarchic(al); **anarquismo** *m* anarchism; **anarquista** **1.** anarchic(al); *pol.* anarchist(ic); **2.** *m/f* anarchist.

anatema *mst m* anathema; **anatematizar** [1f] *eccl.* anathematize; (*maldecir*) curse; *fig.* reprimand.

anatomía *f* anatomy; ~ *macroscópica* gross anatomy; **anatómico** **1.** anatomical; **2.** *m* = **anatomista** *m/f* anatomist; **anatomizar** [1f] anatomize; *paint. músculos etc.* bring out, emphasize.

anca *f* haunch; rump, croup *de caballo*; F buttock; *~s pl.* rump; F *no sufre ~s* he can't take a joke.

anciana *f* old woman, old lady; **ancianidad** *f* old age; **anciano 1.** old, aged; **2.** *m* old man; *eccl.* elder.

ancla *f* anchor; ⚓ *~ de la esperanza* sheet anchor; *fig. ~ de salvación* sheet anchor; *echar (levar) ~s* drop (weigh) anchor; **ancladero** *m* anchorage; **anclar** [1a] (drop) anchor.

ancón *m* cove.

áncora *f* anchor (*a.* ⊕, *fig.*).

ancheta *f* ✝ (*géneros*) small amount; (*ganancia*) gain, profit; *Arg.* foolishness; ridiculous act.

ancho 1. wide, broad; *esp. fig.* ample, full; *ropa* loose(-fitting); *falda* full; *fig.* liberal, broad(-minded); *~ de conciencia* not overscrupulous; *~ de 3 metros, 3 metros de ~* 3 meters wide, 3 meters in width; F *ponerse a sus ~as* spread o.s., be at one's ease; *le viene muy ~ (chaqueta etc.)* it's on the big side for him; *fig.* I bet he's crying his eyes out; *le viene muy ~ el cargo* the job is too much for him; **2.** *m* width, breadth; 🚂 gauge.

anchoa *f* anchovy.

anchura *f* width, breadth, wideness; *esp. fig.* ampleness *etc.* (*v. ancho*); **anchuroso** *calle etc.* broad; *lugar* spacious.

andadas *f/pl. hunt.* tracks; *volver a las ~* backslide, return to one's old ways; **andaderas** *f/pl.* (child's) walker; go-cart; **andadero** *sitio* passable, easily traversed; **andado** worn, well-trodden; (*común*) ordinary; *ropa* worn, old; **andador 1.** fast-walking; (*carácter*) fond of walking, fond of gadding about; **2.** *m*, **-a** *f* (child's) walker; (*callejero*) gadabout; **3.** *~es pl.* leading strings; **andadura** *f* (*acto*) walking; (*paso*) gait, walk; pace *de caballo.*

andalucismo *m* Andalusianism; Andalusian trait(s); **andaluz** *adj. a. su. m*, **-a** *f* Andalusian; **andaluzada** *f* F tall story.

andamiada *f*, **andamiaje** *m* scaffold(ing), staging; **andamio** *m* scaffold(ing); (*tablado*) stage, stand; *~ óseo* skeleton.

andana *f* row, line; *llamarse ~* go back on one's word.

andanada *f* ⚓ broadside; (*tribuna*) covered grandstand; *fig.* scolding, telling-off F; *soltar la (or una) ~ a* haul *s.o.* over the coals.

andante 1. walking; *caballero* errant; **2.** *m* ♪ andante; **andanza** *f* incident; fortune, fate.

andar 1. [1q] *v/t. camino* walk; *distancia* go, cover; *v/i.* (*a pie*) walk, go; (*moverse*) move; (*comportarse*) behave; (*reloj, trabajo etc.*) go; ⊕ go, run, work; (*horas*) pass, elapse; *~ adj.* be, feel; *anda muy alegre* he's very cheerful; *seguir andando* go on walking, carry on walking; *ando escribiendo un libro* I'm in the course of writing a book; *vinimos andando* we came on foot, we walked; *¿cómo anda eso?* how are things going?: *¿cómo andas de dinero?* how are you off for money?; *¡anda!* (*ánimo*) come on!, go on!; (*sorpresa*) you don't mean to say!; *¡anda, anda!* don't be silly!; *¡andando!* that's all!; *~ a caballo etc.* ride, go on horseback; *puñetazos* go about it with; *~ a una* be at one, agree; *~ bien* (*reloj*) keep (good) time; *~ en pleitos* be engaged in, be involved in; **~se** (= *v/i.*, *but freq. indicates personal involvement*): *~ con circunloquios etc.* make use of, use; *~ en* indulge in; *se me anda la cabeza* my head is spinning; *¡todo se andará!* it will all work out!; (*promesa*) it shall be done!; **2.** *m* gait, pace; *a largo ~* in time, in due course; *estar a un ~* be on the same level.

andariego = *andador*; **andarín** *m* walker; *ser gran ~* be a great walker; **andas** *f/pl.* (*silla*) litter, sedan chair; portable platform *en procesión*; (*féretro*) bier; **andén** *m* 🚂 platform; (*acera*) footpath, sidewalk *S.Am.*; ⚓ quayside.

andinismo *m S.Am.* mountain climbing in the Andes; **andino** Andean.

andito *m* balcony.

andorga *f* F belly.

andorrear [1a] F gad about, bustle around; **andorrero** *m*, **a** *f* F gadabout.

andrajo *m* rag, tatter; (*p.*) scallywag, good-for-nothing; (*cosa*) trifle; *~s pl.* rags, tatters; **andrajoso** ragged, in tatters.

andrómina *f* F (*cuento*) fib, tale; (*engaño*) trick, fraud.

andurriales *m/pl.* out of the way place, wilds.

aneblar [1k] cover with mist (*or* cloud); *fig.* cast a cloud over, darken; **~se** cloud over, get misty; get dark.

anécdota *f* anecdote, story; **anecdótico** anecdotal; *contenido ~* story content, story value.

anegación *f* flooding *etc.*; **anegadizo** *terreno* subject to flooding; **anegar** [1h] (*ahogar*) drown (*en* in; *a. fig.*); (*inundar*) flood; *fig.* destroy, overwhelm; **~se** (*p.*) drown (*a. fig.*); (*campos*) be flooded; (*barco*) sink, founder; *~ en llanto* dissolve into tears.

anejo 1. attached; dependent; *~ a* attached to, joined on to; *edificio ~* = **2.** *m* ⚠ annex, outbuilding; *fig.* dependency; supplement *de revista.*

anemómetro *m* anemometer.

anémona *f*, **anemone** *f* anemone; *~ de mar* sea anemone.

anestesia *f* anesthesia; **anestesiar** [1b] anesthetize, give an anesthetic to; **anestésico** *adj. a. su. m* anesthetic.

anexar [1a] annex; *adjunto* attach, append; **anexión** *f* annexation; **anexionar** [1a] annex; **anexo 1.** *documento, edificio* attached; dependent (*a. eccl.*); *llevar algo ~* have s.t. attached; **2.** *m* annex; dependency (*a. eccl.*).

anfibio 1. amphibious; amphibian (*a.* ✈); **2.** *m* amphibian.

anfiteatro *m* amphitheater; *thea.* balcony, dress circle; *~ anatómico* dissecting room.

anfitrión *m lit. a. co.* host; **anfitriona** *f* hostess.

ánfora *f* amphora; *S.Am.* ballot box.

anfractuosidad *f* (*desigualdad*) roughness; (*vuelta*) bend, turning; *anat.* convolution, fold.

angarillas *f/pl.* handbarrow; (*cestas*) panniers; (*vinagrera*) cruet-stand.

ángel *m* angel; *~ custodio, ~ de la guarda* guardian angel; *tener ~* have charm; **angelical, angélico** angelic(əl); **angelón** *m*: F *~ de retablo* fat old thing; **angelote** *m* (*p.*) chubby child; **ángelus** *m* Angelus.

angina *f* angina, quinsy; *~ de pecho* angina pectoris; *tener ~s* have a sore throat.

anglicano *adj. a. su. m,* **a** *f* Anglican; **anglicismo** *m* Anglicism; **anglófilo** *adj. a. su. m,* **a** *f* Anglophile; **angloparlante** *adj. a. su. m/f* English-speaking; **anglosajón** *adj. a. su. m,* **-a** *f* Anglo-Saxon.

angostar(**se**) [1a] narrow; **angosto** narrow; **angostura** *f* narrowness; ⚓ strait, narrows; *geog.* narrow defile.

angra *f* cove, creek.

anguila *f* eel; *~ de mar* conger eel; ⚓ *~s pl.* slipway.

angular angular; *piedra* corner *attr.*; **ángulo** *m* angle (*a.* ⩘); (*esquina*) corner, turning; ⊕ knee, bend; *~ agudo* (*obtuso, recto*) acute (obtuse, right) angle; *phot.* de *~ ancho* wide-angle; *en ~* at an angle; **anguloso** angular; *camino etc.* full of corners.

angurria *f S.Am.* raging hunger; greed.

angustia *f* anguish, distress; ⚕ *~ vital* anxiety state; **angustiado** distressed, anguished; (*avaro etc.*) grasping, mean; **angustiar** [1b] grieve, distress; **~se** be distressed (*por* at); break one's heart; **angustioso** anguished, distressed; *voz* anxious; *situación* distressing, heart-breaking.

anhelante ⚕ (*a. respiración ~*) panting; *fig.* (*ansioso*) eager; (*nostálgico*) wistful, longing; **anhelar** [1a] *v/t.* be eager for; yearn for, pine for; *v/i.* ⚕ gasp, pant; *~ inf.* yearn to *inf.*; *~ por inf.* aspire to *inf.*; *~ por su.* hanker after *su.*; **anhelo** *m* eagerness; yearning, longing (*de, por* for); appetite (*de, por* for); **anheloso** ⚕ gasping, panting; *respiración* heavy, difficult; *fig.* eager.

anidar [1a] *v/t.* shelter, take in; *v/i. orn.* make its nest; *fig.* live, make one's home.

anieblar [1a] = *aneblar.*

anilina *f* aniline.

anillado ringed; *forma* ring-shaped; **anillar** [1a] make into a ring; (*sujetar*) (fasten with a) ring; **anillo** *m* ring (*a. ast.*); cigar band; *~ de boda* wedding ring; *fig. de ~* honorary; *venir como ~ al dedo* be just right; meet the case perfectly.

ánima *f* soul; soul in purgatory; *eccl. las ~s* sunset bell, Angelus.

animación *f* liveliness, life; vivacity

de carácter; sprightliness *de movimientos*; (*movimiento*) bustle, life, animation; **animado** lively; sprightly, vivacious; in high spirits; *fiesta* merry; (*concurrido*) well attended; busy; *zo.* animate.

animadversión *f* censure, animadversion; (*ojeriza*) ill-will.

animal 1. animal; *p.* stupid; **2.** *m* animal; *fig.* (*estúpido*) blockhead; F beast, brute; **animalada** *f* F stupidity; (*palabra*) silly thing (to say); **animálculo** *m* animalcule; **animalejo** *m* small creature; **animalidad** *f* animality; **animalucho** *m* F ugly brute.

animar [1a] *biol.* give life to, animate; *fig.* (*alegrar*) cheer up; (*estimular*) ginger up; *fuego, vista, cuarto* brighten up; *discusión* enliven, liven up; (*alentar*) encourage (*a inf.* to *inf.*); **~se** (*p.*) brighten up, cheer up; (*reunión, discusión*) get livelier, brighten up; (*cobrar ánimo*) take heart, feel encouraged; (*atreverse*) dare, make up one's mind (*a inf.* to *inf.*); *¡anímate!* buck up!; make up your mind!; **ánimo** *m* soul; spirit (*a. fig.*); (*valor*) courage, nerve; energy; attention, thought; *¡~!* cheer up!; *deportes*: go it!, come along!; *cobrar ~* pluck up courage, take heart; *dar ~(s) a, infundir ~ a* encourage; *dilatar el ~* gladden the heart; *estar con ~ de, tener ~s para* be in the mood for, feel like.

animosidad *f* (*valor*) courage, nerve; (*ojeriza*) animosity, ill will; **animoso** spirited, brave; ready (*para* for).

aniñado *cara etc.* childlike, of a child; *b.s.* childish, puerile; **aniñarse** [1a] act childishly.

aniquilación *f*, **aniquilamiento** *m* annihilation, obliteration; **aniquilar** [1a] annihilate, destroy; **~se** be wiped out; *fig.* ⚕ waste away; (*hacienda*) be frittered away; deteriorate, decline.

anís *m* ⚘ anise; (*grana*) aniseed; (*bebida*) *approx.* anisette; F *llegar a los ~es* turn up late; **anisete** *m* anisette.

aniversario *m* anniversary.

ano *m* anus.

anoche last night; *antes de ~* the night before last; **anochecedor** *m*, **-a** *f* late bird; **anochecer 1.** [2d] get dark; arrive at nightfall; **2.** *m* nightfall, dusk; *al ~* at nightfall; **anochecida** *f* nightfall, dusk.

anodino anodyne (*a. su.*); *fig.* harmless, inoffensive; *b.s.* insipid, dull.

ánodo *m* anode.

anomalía *f* anomaly; **anómalo** anomalous.

anonadación *f*, **anonadamiento** *m* annihilation *etc.*; **anonadar** [1a] annihilate, destroy; *fig.* overwhelm; **~se** be humiliated; (*desanimarse*) be discouraged.

anónimo 1. anonymous; nameless; ✝ *sociedad* limited; **2.** *m* (*en general*) anonymity; (*p.*) s.o. unknown; (*carta*) anonymous letter.

anorexia *f* ⚕ anorexia.

anormal abnormal; **anormalidad** *f* abnormality.

anotación *f* (*acto*) annotation; note; *S.Am.* score; **anotar** [1a] annotate; (*apuntar*) note (down), jot down; ✝ book; *S.Am.* score.

ánsar *m* goose; **ansarino** *m* gosling.

ansia *f* ⚕ anxiety, tension; (*angustia*) anguish; (*deseo*) longing, yearning (de for); *~s pl.* ⚕ nausea; **ansiar** [1b] *v/t.* long for, yearn for, covet; *~ inf.* long to *inf.*, crave to *inf.*; *v/i.*: *~ por* be head over heels in love with; **ansiedad** *f* anxiety (*a.* ⚕); solicitude; suspense; **ansioso** anxious (*a.* ⚕), worried; solicitous; *~ de, ~ por* eager for, greedy for, avid for.

antagónico antagonistic, opposed; **antagonismo** *m* antagonism; **antagonista** *m/f* antagonist.

antañazo a long time ago; **antaño** last year; *fig.* long ago.

antártico Antarctic.

ante[1] *m* elk; buffalo; (*piel*) buckskin, suède.

ante[2] *juez etc.* before, in the presence of; *enemigo, peligro etc.* in the face of, faced with; *asunto* with regard to.

anteanoche the night before last; **anteayer** the day before yesterday.

antebrazo *m* forearm.

antecámara *f* antechamber, anteroom; lobby.

antecedente 1. previous, preceding; **2.** *m* antecedent (*a.* ℞, *gr.*, *phls.*); *~s pl.* record, past history; *~s pl. penales* criminal record; *sin ~s* with a clean record; *estar en ~s* know all about it; *poner en* ~*s* put *s.o.* in the picture; **anteceder** [2a] precede, go before; **antecesor 1.** preceding; **2.** *m*, **-a** *f* predecessor; (*abuelo*) ancestor, forefather.

antedatar [1a] antedate.

antedicho aforesaid, aforementioned.

antediluviano antediluvian.

anteiglesia *f eccl.* porch.

antelación: *con* ~ = **antemano:** *de* ~ in advance, beforehand.

antena *f zo.* antenna, feeler; ⚡ aerial, antenna; F ⚡ ~ *de conejo* rabbit ears; ~ *de cuadro* loop aerial; ~ *direccional* directional aerial; ~ *interior* indoor aerial; ~ *interior incorporada* built-in antenna; *en* ~ on the air.

antenombre *m* title.

anteojera *f* spectacle case; ~*s pl.* blinkers; **anteojero** *m* optometrist; optician; **anteojo** *m* telescope, spyglass (*a.* ~ *de larga vista*); eye glass; ~*s pl.* spectacles, glasses; *mot. etc.* goggles; blinkers *de caballo*; ~ *binóculo* binoculars, field glasses; ~*s pl. de concha* hornrimmed spectacles; ~ *prismatico* prism binoculars; ~ *de teatro* opera glasses.

antepagar [1h] pay beforehand, prepay.

antepasado 1. before last; **2.** *m* forbear, forefather.

antepecho *m* balcony, ledge *de ventana*; parapet, guard rail *de puente etc.*; ⚔ breastwork, parapet.

antepenúltimo last but two, antepenultimate.

anteponer [2r] place *s.t.* in front; *fig.* prefer; ~**se** come in front, come in between; ~ *a fig.* overcome.

anteproyecto *m* preliminary sketch (*or* plan); *fig.* blueprint.

antepuerto *m* outer harbor.

antera *f* anther.

anterior (*orden*) preceding, previous; anterior (*a. gr.*); (*delantero*) front, fore; (*tiempo*) previous (*a* to), earlier (*a* than), former; **anterioridad** *f* precedence; priority; *con* ~ previously; *con* ~ *a* before, prior to.

antes 1. *adv.* before; formerly; (*en otro tiempo*) once, previously; (*con anticipación*) sooner, before now; ~ (*bien*) rather, on the contrary; ~ *que yo* (*tiempo*) before I did; (*preferencia*) rather (*or* sooner) than I; *cuanto* ~, *lo* ~ *posible* as soon as possible; *mucho* ~ long before; *poco* ~ just before; **2.** *prp.*: ~ *de* before; ~ *de inf.* before *ger.*; ~ *de terminada la función* before the show was over; **3.** *cj.*: ~ (*de*) *que* before.

antesala *f* antechamber; *hacer* ~ wait to be received; *fig.* cool one's heels.

anti... anti...; ~**ácido** *adj. a. su. m* antacid; ~**-adherente** nonstick; ~**aéreo** antiaircraft; *cañón* ~ antiaircraft gun; ~**biótico** *m* antibiotic; ~**ciclón** *m* anticyclone.

anticipación *f* anticipation, forestalling; ☤ advance; *con* ~ in advance; *llegar con bastante* ~ arrive in good time; *llegar con 5 minutos de* ~ arrive 5 minutes early; **anticipadamente** in advance; **anticipado** future, prospective; ☤ advance; **anticipar** [1a] *fecha etc.* advance, bring forward; ☤ advance; ~ *con placer* look forward to; ~ *las gracias* thank in advance; ~**se** take place (*or* happen) early; ~ *a acción* anticipate, forestall; *suceso* be ahead of; *p.* steal a march on; ~ *a inf. vb.* ahead of time; **anticipo** *m* foretaste; (*préstamo*) advance; (*pago*) advance payment; ⚖ retainer, retaining fee.

anti...: ~**clerical** anticlerical; ~**conceptivo** *m* contraceptive; ~**congelante** *m* (*a. solución* ~) antifreeze, defreezer; ~**corrosivo** anticorrosive; ~**constitucional** unconstitutional; ~**cristo** *m* Antichrist.

anticuado old-fashioned, out-of-date; *máquina etc.* antiquated; obsolete; **anticuarse** [1d] become old-fashioned; become antiquated; **anticuario** *m* 🕮 antiquarian; ☤ antique dealer; **anticuerpo** *m* antibody.

anti...: ~**derrapante** nonskid; ~**deslizante** nonslipping; *mot.* nonskid; ~**deslumbrante** antidazzle; ~**detonante** *mot.* antiknock.

antídoto *m* antidote (*a. fig.*; *de* against, for, to).

anti...: ~**económico** uneconomic(al); wasteful; ~**estético** inartistic; unsightly, offensive; ~**fascista** *adj. a. su. m/f* antifascist; ~**faz** *m* mask; veil; ~**friccional** antifriction *attr.*

antigualla *f* antique; F relic; (*cuento*) old story; (*p.*) has-been; ~*s* *pl. contp.* junk; **antiguamente** (*en lo antiguo*) in ancient times, of old; (*antes*) formerly, once; **antiguar** [1i] attain seniority; **~se** = *anticuarse*; **antigüedad** *f* antiquity; † seniority; **~es** *pl.* antiquities; **antiguo 1.** old; ancient; (*anterior*) former, late, one-time; *alumno etc.* old, former; † *más* ~ senior (*que* to); *socio más* ~ senior partner; *de* ~ from time immemorial; **2.**: *los* ~*s pl.* the ancients.

antihalo *m phot.* antihalo.

antihigiénico insanitary, unhygienic.

antílope *m* antelope.

antimonio *m* antimony.

antioxidante antirust.

antipara *f* screen.

antiparras *f/pl.* F glasses, specs.

antipatía *f* dislike (*hacia* for), aversion (*hacia* to, from); antipathy, unfriendliness (*entre* between); **antipático** disagreeable, unpleasant, not nice; *ambiente* uncongenial; *me es muy* ~ I don't like him at all; **antipatizar** [1f] *S.Am.* feel unfriendly; ~ *con* dislike.

antipatriótico unpatriotic.

antípoda 1. antipodal; *fig.* contrary, quite the opposite; **2.** *m* antipode; ~*s f/pl. geog.* antipodes.

antirreflejos *adj.* nonreflecting.

antirresbaladizo *mot.* nonskid.

antisemita *m/f* antisemite; **antisemítico** antisemitic; **antisemitismo** *m* antisemitism.

antiséptico *adj. a. su. m* antiseptic.

antisubmarino antisubmarine;

antiterrorista antiterrorist.

antítesis *f* antithesis; **antitético** antithetic(al).

antitóxico antitoxic; **antitoxina** *f biol.* antitoxin.

antojadizo capricious; given to sudden fancies; faddy; **antojado** eager, desirous; **antojarse** [1a] take a fancy to; ~ *que* imagine that, have the feeling that; *se me antoja visitar la ciudad* I have a mind to visit the city; *no se le antoja ir* he doesn't feel like going; **antojo** *m* caprice, whim, passing fancy; (*juicio*) hasty judgment; craving *de encinta*; ⚕ mole, birthmark; *a su* ~ as one pleases.

antología *f* anthology.

antónimo *m* antonym.

antorcha *f* torch; *fig.* lamp; ~ *a soplete* blowtorch.

antracita *f* anthracite.

ántrax *m* anthrax.

antro *m* cavern.

antropofagía *f* cannibalism; **antropófago 1.** man-eating, anthropophagous 📖; **2.** *m*, **a** *f* cannibal; **antropoide** anthropoid; **antropología** *f* anthropology; **antropólogo** *m* anthropologist.

antruejo *m* carnival.

antuviada *f*, **antuvión** *m* (sudden) blow (*or* bump); *de* ~ suddenly, unexpectedly.

anual annual; **anualidad** *f* † annuity; (*suceso*) annual occurrence; **anuario** *m* yearbook.

anubarrado cloudy, overcast.

anublar [1a] *cielo* cloud; (*oscurecer*) darken, dim (*a. fig.*); ⚘ dry up, wither; **~se** cloud over; darken; *fig.* fade away.

anudar [1a] knot, tie; join, unite (*a. fig.*); *narración* resume, take up again; *voz* strangle; **~se** get into knots *etc.*; ⚘ *etc.* remain stunted; ~*le a uno la lengua* get tongue-tied.

anulación *f* annulment *etc.*; **anular**[1] [1a] annul, cancel, nullify; *ley* revoke; set aside; *decisión* override, overrule; *p.* remove (from office), discharge; *gol* disallow; **~se** be deprived of authority, be removed; (*ser postergado*) be passed over; be humiliated.

anular[2] **1.** ring(-shaped); **2.** *m* ring finger.

anunciación *f* announcement; **anunciante** *m/f* † advertiser; **anunciar** [1b] announce; proclaim; *brindis* propose; (*pronosticar*) foretell; *b.s.* forebode, foreshadow; † advertise; **anuncio** *m* announcement; proposal; † (*esp. impreso*) advertisement; ad; (*cartel*) placard, poster; *thea. etc.* bill; notice *en tablón*; (*indicio*) sign, omen; ~ *luminoso* illuminated sign; ~*s pl. por palabras* classified advertisements, small ads.

anuo annual.

anverso *m* obverse.

anzuelo *m* (fish)hook; *fig.* lure, bait; *picar en* (*or tragar*) *el* ~ swallow the bait, be taken in.

añada *f* ✓ year, season; (*terreno*) piece of land.

añadido *m* false hair, switch; **añadi-**

dura *f* addition; ✝ extra measure; *de* ~ extra, into the bargain; *por* ~ besides, in addition, over (and above), to boot; **añadir** [3a] add (*a* to); (*aumentar*) increase; *fig.* add, lend (*a* to).

añagaza *f* decoy, lure (*a. fig.*); *fig.* bait, enticement.

añal 1. *suceso* yearly; ✓ *etc.* year-old; **2.** *m* year-old lamb *etc.*

añascar [1g] F get together bit by bit.

añejar [1a] age, make old; *b.s.* make stale; **~se** age; (*vino etc.*) improve with age; *b.s.* get stale, go musty; **añejo** old; *vino* mellow, mature; *b.s.* stale.

añicos *m/pl.* bits, pieces, shreds; *splinters* de madera; *hacer* ~ *papel etc.* tear up; *madera etc.* smash to smithereens.

añil *m* indigo (*a.* ⚘); bluing *para lavado.*

añinos *m/pl.* lamb's wool.

año *m* year; **~s** *pl.* (*cumpleaños*) birthday; ~ *bisiesto* leap year; ~ *de Cristo* Anno Domini (A.D.); ~ *de gracia* year of grace; ~ *económico* fiscal year; ~ *luz* light-year; ~ *de nuestra salud* year of our Lord; ♀ *Nuevo* New Year; *día de* ♀ *Nuevo* New Year's Day; *un* ~ *con otro* in an average year, on a yearly average; *de pocos* **~s** small, young; *entrado en* **~s** elderly, advanced in years; *¡mal* ~ *para él!* he's got a hard time coming!; *por los* **~s** *de 1600* about (the year) 1600; *¡por muchos* **~s**! here's luck!; F *estar de buen* ~ be in good shape, be fat; *v. tener.*

añojal *m* fallow (land).

añoranza *f* longing, nostalgia (*de* for), hankering (*de* after); sense of loss (*de pérdida* after); **añorar** [1a] long for, pine for, hanker after; *muerto etc.* grieve for, mourn.

añoso aged, full of years.

añublo *m* mildew, blight.

añudar [1a] = *anudar.*

añusgar [1h] choke; **~se** F get cross.

aojar [1a] put the evil eye (*or* hoodoo) on; **aojo** *m* evil eye, hoodoo.

aovado egg-shaped, oval; **aovar** [1a] lay eggs.

apabullar [1a] F squash, flatten (*a. fig.*).

apacentadero *m* pasture (land); **apacentar** [1k] pasture, graze; *fig. rebaño* minister to; *entendimiento* feed; *b.s.* feed, gratify, pander to; **~se** ✓ graze; *fig.* feed (*con, de* on).

apacibilidad *f* gentleness *etc.*; **apacible** gentle, mild, meek; *tiempo* mild, calm; *viento* gentle; (*ánimo*) even-tempered, peaceable.

apaciguamiento *m* appeasement *etc.*; **apaciguar** [1i] pacify, appease, mollify; (*aquietar*) calm down; **~se** calm down, quieten down.

apadrinar [1a] *empresa etc.* sponsor; *escritor* be a patron to; *eccl. niño* act as godfather to; *novio* be best man for; *fig.* support, approve.

apagado *volcán* extinct; *color* dull, lustreless; *voz* quiet; *sonido* muted, muffled; *p.* listless, spiritless; **apagafuego** *m*, **apagaincendios** *m* fire extinguisher; **apagar** [1h] *fuego* put out, extinguish; ⚡ *luz* turn off, turn out, switch off; *radio etc.* switch off; *color* tone down; *sonido* muffle; ♪ mute; *sed* quench, slake; *cal* slake; *afecto, dolor* kill, deaden; (*aplacar*) calm, soothe; **~se** go out; be extinguished; (*sonido etc.*) die away; (*p.*) calm down; **apagón** *m* ⚔ blackout; ⚡ power cut.

apalabrar [1a] agree to; *p.* engage; **~se** come to an agreement (*con* with).

apalabrear [1a] *S.Am.* make an appointment.

apaleamiento *m* beating *etc.*; **apalear** [1a] beat, thrash; *alfombra* beat; ✓ winnow; ~ *oro*, ~ *plata* be rolling in money; **apaleo** *m* ✓ winnowing.

apanalado honeycombed.

apandar [1a] F swipe, knock off; snitch.

apandillar [1a] form into a gang; **~se** band together, gang up.

apantanar [1a] flood, make swampy.

apañado *fig.* handy, skilful; (*apropiado*) suitable (*para* for); F *¡estás* ~*!* you've had it!; **apañar** [1a] (*coger*) pick up; (*asir*) take hold of; *b.s.* steal, swipe; (*ataviar*) dress up; F (*arropar*) wrap up; **~se** *para inf.* contrive to *inf.*; **~las** *por su cuenta* fend for o.s.; **apaño** *m* F (*remiendo*) mend, repair; (*habilidad*) knack, handiness; (*lío*) mess.

apañuscar [1g] F rumple, crumple; *S.Am.* jam together; (*robar*) steal, swipe.
aparador *m* sideboard, buffet; (*vitrina*) showcase; (*escaparate*) shop window; ⊕ workshop; **aparar** [1a] arrange; adorn; ⚘ weed, clean; *falda etc.* stretch out.
aparato *m* ⚗ *etc.* apparatus; (*dispositivo*) device, piece of equipment; ⊕ machine; ✈ airplane; *radio etc.*: set; *teleph.* instrument; *phot., gimnasia etc.*: apparatus, equipment; *fig.* ostentation, show; sign; symptom (*a.* ⚕); ⚕ (*vendaje*) bandage; (*apósito*) application; ~ *auditivo* hearing aid; ~ *eléctrico meteor.* display of lightning; ~*s pl. de mando* controls; ~ *de relojería* clockwork; ~ *fotográfico* camera; ~*s pl. sanitarios* bathroom fixtures; **aparatosidad** *f* ostentation *etc.*; **aparatoso** ostentatious, showy; pretentious; *caída, función etc.* spectacular.
aparcamiento *m* parking; ~ *subterráneo* underground garage; **aparcar** [1g] park (a vehicle).
aparcería *f* partnership; **aparcero** *m* partner; sharecropper; *S.Am.* companion.
aparear [1a] make even, level up; *animales* pair, mate; *fig.* pair (off), match.
aparecer [2d] appear; turn up, show up; loom (up) *en niebla etc.*; **aparecido** *m* appearance; ghost, specter.
aparejado fit, ready (*para* for); **aparejador** *m* foreman, overseer; Δ architect's assistant, builder; **aparejar** [1a] prepare, get ready; *meteor.* threaten; *caballo* harness; ⚓ fit out, rig out; *paint. etc.* prime, size; ~**se** prepare o.s., get ready (*para* for); **aparejo** *m* preparation; (*caballo*) harness; ⚓ rigging; ⊕ lifting gear, (block and) tackle; Δ bond; *paint.* priming, sizing; ~*s pl.* ⊕ tools, gear, equipment.
aparentar [1a] feign, affect; *edad* seem to be, look; ~ *inf.* make as if to *inf.*; **aparente** apparent, seeming; *manifestación* outward, visible; convenient, suitable; *esp. b.s.* plausible; **aparición** *f* appearance; (*espectro*) apparition; *de próxima* ~ *libro* forthcoming; **apariencia** *f* appearance, look(s); (*exterior*) outside; *esp. b.s.* semblance, (outward) show; probability; ~*s pl. thea.* décor; *salvar las* ~*s* keep up appearances, save one's face.
apartadero *m mot.* turnout; stopping place; rest area; 🚂 siding; **apartadijo** *m* (small) portion; = **apartadizo** *m* recess, alcove, nook; **apartado 1.** isolated, remote, secluded; *camino* devious; **2.** *m* (*a.* ~ *de correos*) post-office box; (*cuarto*) spare room; *typ.* paragraph; section *de documento*; **apartamento** *m esp. S.Am.* flat; **apartamiento** *m* (*acto*) withdrawal *etc.*; (*efecto*) isolation, remoteness; (*lugar*) secluded spot; **apartar** [1a] separate, take away (*de* from); isolate; ✉ *etc.* sort (out); (*quitar de en medio*) move away; *p.* (*a un lado*) take aside, draw aside; turn away, dissuade, sidetrack (*de propósito* from); (*a.* ~ *de sí*) put aside, put out of one's mind; ⚒ extract; ~**se** (*dos ps.*) separate (*a. casados*); (*alejarse*) move away; withdraw, retire (*de* from); (*mantenerse aparte*) keep away (*de* from), stand aside; ~ *de camino* leave, turn from; **aparte 1.** apart, aside (*de* from); **2.** *m thea.* aside; *typ.* (new) paragraph, indention.
apasionado passionate; (*fogoso*) fiery, impassioned, intense; (*aficionado*) passionately fond (*a, por* of); **apasionamiento** *m* passion, enthusiasm (*de, por* for); great fondness (*de, por* for); (*amorío*) infatuation; **apasionante** thrilling, exciting; **apasionar** [1a] stir deeply, make a strong appeal to; *enamorado* infatuate; afflict, torment; ~**se** get excited; ~ *de*, ~ *por* be mad about, enthuse over; (*enamorarse*) fall in love with.
apatía *f* apathy; ⚕ listlessness; **apático** apathetic; ⚕ listless.
apátrida stateless.
apatuscar [1g] F hurry, botch; **apatusco** *m* F frills, buttons and bows; Δ gingerbread.
apeadero *m* horse block; 🚂 wayside station; (*alojamiento*) (temporary) lodging, pied à terre; **apear** [1a] help *s.o.* down (*de* from); (*bajar*) take *s.t.* down; *árbol* fell; *caballo* hobble; *rueda* scotch (*a. fig.*); Δ prop up; *surv.* measure, survey; *problema* solve, work out; *dificultad* overcome; F make *s.o.* budge (*de opinión*

from); *tratamiento* drop; **~se** dismount, get down (*de caballo* from); ♪ *etc.* get off, get out; (*hospedarse*) stay, put up (*en* at); F back down.
apechugar [1h]: ~ *con* F put up with, swallow.
apedazar [1f] cut (*or* tear) into pieces; (*remendar*) mend, patch.
apedrear [1a] *v/t.* stone, pelt with stones; *v/i.* hail; **~se** be damaged by hail; **apedreo** *m* stoning; *meteor.* hail.
apegadamente devotedly; **apegado**: ~ *a* attached to, fond of; **apegarse** [1h] *a* become attached to, grow fond of; **apego** *m*: ~ *a* attachment to, fondness for.
apelación *f* appeal; *sin* ~ without appeal, final; *interponer* ~ give notice of appeal; **apelante** *m/f* appellant; **apelar** [1a] ⚖ appeal (*de* against); ~ *a fig.* appeal to; have recourse to; **apelativo** *m* *C.Am.* surname; family name.
apeldar [1a]: F ~*las* beat it.
apelmazado compressed, compact; *líquido* thick, lumpy; *escritura* clumsy; **apelmazar** [1f] compress; **~se** cake; get lumpy.
apelotonar [1a] make into a ball; **~se** (*gente*) crowd together.
apellidar [1a] name; (*calificar*) call; proclaim (*por rey* as); **~se** be called, have as a surname; **apellido** *m* surname; name; (*mote*) nickname; ~ *de soltera* maiden name.
apenar [1a] grieve, trouble; **~se** grieve, sorrow.
apenas scarcely, hardly (*a.* ~ *si*); (only) just; ~ ... *cuando* no sooner ... than.
apendectomía *f* appendectomy; **apéndice** *m* appendix (*a.* ⚕); appendage; *esp.* ⚖ schedule; **apendicitis** *f* appendicitis.
apercibimiento *m* preparation; provision; (*aviso*) warning, notice; ⚖ summons; **apercibir** [3a] prepare; provide; *ánimo* prepare (*para* for); (*avisar*) warn; ⚖ serve a summons on, summon; **~se** get (*o.s.*) ready, prepare (*o.s.*) (*para* for); ~ *de* provide o.s. with.
apercollar [1m] grab by the neck; (*acogotar*) fell (with a blow to the neck).
apergaminado parchmentlike; *p.* wizened.
aperitivo *m* appetizer; (*bebida*) aperitif.
apero *m* tools, equipment, gear; ⚒ implements, tackle (*a.* ~*s pl.*); *S.Am.* riding outfit.
aperreador F tiresome; **aperrear** [1a] set the dogs on; F (*molestar*) bother, plague; (*cansar*) tire out; **~se** F slave (away), overwork.
apersogar [1h] tether.
apersonado: *bien* ~ presentable; **apersonarse** [1a] ⚖ appear; appear in person; ✝ have a business interview.
apertura *f mst* opening; ⚖ reading (of a will).
apesadumbrado grieved, distressed; **apesadumbrar** [1a], **apesarar** [1a] grieve, distress, sadden; **~se** be grieved *etc.* (*con*, *de* at).
apesgar [1h] weigh down, overburden.
apestado *de* infested with; **apestar** [1a] *v/t.* ⚕ infect (with plague); *fig.* corrupt, vitiate; (*fastidiar*) annoy, bother; *v/i.* stink; **apestoso** (*que huele*) stinking; *olor* pestilential; F sickening, annoying.
apetecer [2d] *v/t.* crave (for), long for, hunger for; *v/i.*: *me apetece la leche* I'd like some milk, I could do with some milk; *me apetece ir* I feel like going; **apetecible** desirable; tempting; **apetencia** *f* hunger; *fig.* hunger, craving, desire (*de* for); **apetite** *m* appetizer; *fig.* incentive; **apetito** *m* appetite (*a. eccl.*); *esp. fig.* relish; *abrir el* ~ whet one's appetite; **apetitoso** appetizing; inviting, tasty; *p.* fond of delicate fare.
apiadar [1a] move to pity; *víctima* = **~se** *de* take pity on.
apicarado *niño* spoilt, naughty; **apicararse** [1a] go to the bad.
ápice *m* apex; *fig.* whit, iota; *estar en los* ~*s de* be well up in.
apicultor *m*, **-a** *f* beekeeper; **apicultura** *f* beekeeping, apiculture.
apilar(se) [1a] pile up, heap up.
apiñado jammed, packed, congested (*de* with); *barrio* overcrowded; **apiñadura** *f*, **apiñamiento** *m* congestion; squeeze, squash, jam; **apiñar** [1a] squeeze (together); bunch (*or* herd) together *en grupo*; overcrowd *en barrio*; **~se** (*gente*) crowd together;

(*esp. cosas*) be squashed (*or* jammed) together.
apio *m* celery.
apiolar [1a] F (*prender*) nab; (*matar*) do away with, bump off.
apiparse [1a] F guzzle.
apisonadora *f* road roller, steam-roller; **apisonar** [1a] roll; tamp, ram *con pisón*.
apitonar [1a] *v/t. huevo* crack, break through; *v/i.* sprout, begin to show; **~se** F have words, have a shouting match.
aplacar [1g] appease, placate; calm down.
aplanacalles *m/f S.Am.* idler; lazy person; **aplanamiento** *m* smoothing *etc.*; **aplanar** [1a] smooth, level, roll flat, make even; F knock out, bowl over; ~ *calles* F loaf; bum around; **~se** △ collapse; F lose heart.
aplastante overwhelming, crushing; **aplastar** [1a] squash, flatten (out); *fig.* leave *s.o.* speechless, flatten; *S.Am.* tire out.
aplaudir [3a] applaud, cheer; **aplauso** *m* applause; **~s** *pl.* applause, cheering, clapping; *fig.* acclaim.
aplazada *f S.Am.* = **aplazamiento** *m* postponement *etc.*; **aplazar** [1f] postpone, defer, put off; *sesión* hold over, adjourn; *cita* set a time *etc.* for; (*convocar*) summon, convene.
aplebeyar [1a] degrade, demean; **~se** lower o.s., demean o.s.
aplicabilidad *f* applicability; **aplicable** applicable; **aplicación** *f* application (*a.* ⚕); (*asiduidad*) industry, studiousness; **aplicar** [1g] *mst* apply (*a* to); *manos, color etc.* lay (*sobre* on); *hombres etc.* assign (*a, para* to); *delito* impute; *bienes* adjudge; *p.* enter, put in (*a profesión* for); **~se** *algo* claim for o.s.; ~ *a* apply to, be applicable to; *estudio etc.* apply o.s. to, give one's mind to.
aplomar [1a] △ plumb; make perpendicular; **~se** collapse, fall to the ground; **aplomo** *m fig.* seriousness, gravity; (*seguridad*) nonchalance, aplomb, self-possession; (*atrevimiento*) coolness.
apocado (*de poco ánimo*) spiritless; spineless; (*tímido*) diffident; (*vil*) common, mean.
apocalíptico apocalyptic; *estilo* obscure, enigmatic; F frightening.
apocamiento *m* spinelessness *etc.*; **apocar** [1g] make smaller, reduce; *fig.* limit; (*despreciar*) belittle, run down; humiliate; **~se** humble o.s.
apócrifo apocryphal.
apodar [1a] nickname, dub; label.
apoderado *m* agent, representative; ⚖ proxy; **apoderamiento** *m* authorization; ⚖ power of attorney; **apoderar** [1a] authorize, empower; ⚖ grant power of attorney to; **~se** *de* (*asir*) seize, take hold of; *fig.* get hold of, take possession of.
apodo *m* nickname; label.
apogeo *m ast.* apogee; *fig.* peak, summit, zenith.
apolilladura *f* moth hole; **apolillado** moth-eaten; **apolillarse** [1a] get moth-eaten.
apolítico apolitical; nonpolitical.
apologética *f* apologetics; **apología** *f* defense; encomium, eulogy; **apologista** *m/f* apologist.
apoltronado idling, lazy; **apoltronarse** [1a] get lazy; loaf around.
apoplejía *f* stroke, apoplexy; **apopléctico** apoplectic.
aporcar [1g] earth up.
aporrar [1a] F be unable to say a word; dry up; **~se** F become a bore (*or* nuisance).
aporreado *vida* poor, wretched; *Cuba, Mex.* chopped beef stew; *p.* rascally; **aporrear** [1a] beat, club; beat up; *mesa, teclas etc.* thump (on), pound (on); *fig.* bother, pester; **~se** slave away, be always at it; **aporreo** *m* beating(-up).
aportación *f* contribution; **~es** *pl. de la mujer* dowry; **aportar** [1a] *v/t.* bring; contribute; (*aducir*) bring forward; ⚖ bring as a dowry; *v/i.* reach port; F come out at an unexpected place; **aporte** *m S.Am.* contribution.
aportillar [1a] *muralla* breach; (*romper*) break down, break open; **~se** fall, collapse.
aposentar(**se**) [1a] lodge, put up; **aposento** *m* room; (*hospedaje*) lodging.
aposesionarse [1a]: ~ *de* take possession of.
aposición *f* apposition.
apósito *m* ⚕ (external) application; (*cataplasma*) poultice.
aposta(**damente**) purposely; **apostadero** *m* station, stand; ⚓ naval

station; **apostar**[1] [1a] ⚔ post, station.

apostar[2] [1m] *v/t. dinero* lay, wager, stake (a on); *v/i.* bet (a, por on; a que that); *v/i.*, **~se** compete (con with), be rivals; ~las a, ~las con compete with (en punto a for, in).

apostasía *f* apostasy; **apóstata** *m/f* apostate; **apostatar** [1a] *eccl.* apostatize (de from); *fig.* change sides.

apostema *f* abscess.

apostilla *f* note, comment; **apostillar** [1a] annotate; **~se** break out in pimples.

apóstol *m* apostle; **apostólicamente** F unostentatiously; **apostólico** apostolic.

apostrofar [1a] apostrophize; insult; (*reconvenir*) rebuke; **apóstrofe** *m or f* apostrophe; taunt, insult; rebuke, expostulation; **apóstrofo** *m gr.* apostrophe.

apostura *f* gracefulness; neatness.

apoteósico *éxito etc.* huge, tremendous; **apoteosis** *f* apotheosis (*a. fig.*).

apoyador *m* support, bracket, clamp; **apoyapié** *m* footrest; **apoyar** [1a] *v/t. codo etc.* lean, rest (en, sobre on); △ *etc.* support, hold up; *fig.* (*respaldar*) support, back; (*ayudar*) aid, stand by; *b.s.* abet; (*confirmar*) support, bear out; *v/i.*, **~se** en *base* rest on; *edificio* abut on; *bastón* lean on; *p.* rely on; *argumento* rest on; *datos* base o.s. on; **apoyo** *m* support (*a. fig.*); *fig.* backing, help; approval; favor.

apreciable appreciable, considerable; (*tasable*) measurable; *fig.* worthy, estimable; **apreciación** *f* appreciation, appraisal; † valuation; **apreciador** *m* appraiser; evaluator; **apreciar** [1b] value, assess (en at; *a. fig.*); *esp. fig.* estimate; *música etc.* appreciate; (*tener en mucho*) esteem, value (por for); ~ en mucho set great value on; **aprecio** *m* appreciation, appraisal; esteem; tener en gran ~ esteem; **apreciativo** of appraisal *etc.*

aprehender [2h] *criminal* apprehend; *bienes* seize; *fig.* perceive; **aprehensión** *f* capture; seizure; *fig.* perception.

apremiador, apremiante *mandato* urgent; *razón* pressing, compelling; **apremiar** [1b] (*obligar*) compel, force; (*instar*) urge on, press; (*dar prisa a*) hurry; (*oprimir*) oppress; el tiempo apremia time presses; **apremio** *m* compulsion *etc.*; ⚖ writ, judgment; summons; por ~ de tiempo because of pressure of time.

aprender [2a] learn (a *inf.* to *inf.*).

aprendiz *m*, **-a** *f* apprentice (de to); (*principiante*) learner; poner de ~ apprentice (con *p.* to); **aprendizaje** *m* apprenticeship; F pagar su ~ learn the hard way.

aprensar [1a] *uvas* crush, press; *fig.* oppress, crush; (*angustiar*) distress.

aprensión *f* apprehension, fear, worry; (*infundada*) strange notion; **aprensivo** apprehensive, worried; timid; ⚕ hypochondriac.

apresador *m*, **-a** *f* captor; **apresamiento** *m* capture *etc.*; **apresar** [1a] *p.* capture, take prisoner; ⚖ seize; (*asir*) seize, grasp.

aprestado ready; ~ para *inf.* calculated to *inf.*; **aprestar** [1a] prepare, make (*or* get) ready; *paint.* prime; *tela* size; **~se** prepare, get ready (para *inf.* to *inf.*); ~ para la lucha gird o.s. for the fray; **apresto** *m* (*acto*) preparation; (*equipo*) kit, outfit; *paint.* priming; size; sizing.

apresuración *f* haste(ning); **apresurado** hasty, hurried, quick; **apresuramiento** *m* haste(ning); **apresurar** [1a] hurry (up, along); hustle *sin ceremonia*; *paso etc.* speed up, accelerate; **~se** hasten, make haste (a, en, por *inf.* to *inf.*).

apretadamente hard, tight(ly); **apretadera** *f* strap, rope; ~s *pl.* F pressure; **apretado** *vestido etc.* tight; *lugar* (*pequeño*) cramped; (*lleno*) chock-a-block; dense, thick; *escritura* close, cramped; *lance etc.* tight, difficult, dangerous; F stingy, tight(-fisted); ~ de dinero short of money; **apretador** *m* ⊕ wedge; **apretar** [1k] **1.** *v/t. tuerca etc.* tighten; *lío etc.* squeeze; *contenido* pack in, pack tight; *p.* hug, squeeze (a to; entre *brazos* in); *mano* clasp, grip; (*saludo*) shake; *puño* clench; *dientes* set, grit; *botón* press; (*vestido*) be tight for, be small on; (*zapato*) pinch; *fig. disciplina* tighten up; afflict; (*angustiar*) distress (*a.* ⚕); (*acosar*) harass (*a.* ⚔), pester (*por* for); ⚔ *ataque* intensify; **2.** *v/i.* (*vestido*) be tight; (*zapato*) pinch; (*empeorar*) get worse; insist; ~ *a correr* break into a run; ~ *con enemigo* close with; *¡aprieta!* baloney!; nonsense!; **3.** **~se** (*estrecharse*) (get) narrow; (*ps.*) squeeze up, huddle together; *fig.* be distressed *etc.*

apretón *m* squeeze, pressure; (*abrazo*) hug; (*ahogo*) distress; F dash, run; ~ *de manos* handshake; *estar en un* ~ be in a quandary; **apretujar** [1a] F squeeze *etc.* hard; *p.* hug; sandwich *entre dos cosas*; **apretujón** *m* F (hard) squeeze; hug; crush, squash *de gente*; **apretura** *f* = *apretujón*; *fig.* distress; **aprieto** *m* crush, jam, squeeze; *fig.* (*apuro*) fix, quandary; (*aflicción*) distress; *estar en un* ~ be in a hole, be in trouble; *poner en un* ~ put in a fix.

aprisa quickly, hurriedly.

aprisco *m* sheepfold.

aprisionar (*encarcelar*) imprison; shackle, fetter (*a. fig.*).

aprobación *f* approval *etc.*; **aprobado** **1.** approved; worthy, excellent; **2.** *m univ. etc.* pass (mark); **aprobar** [1m] *v/t.* approve (*de* as); endorse; consent to; *examen, estudiante, parl.* pass; *v/i. univ.* pass; **aprobatorio** approving, of approval.

aproches *m/pl.* ⚔ approaches.

aprontamiento *m* quick service, quick dispatch; **aprontar** [1a] get ready quickly; *dinero* hand over without delay.

apropiación *f* adaptation *etc.*; **apropiado** appropriate (*a, para* to), suitable (*a, para* for); **apropiar** [1b] adapt, fit (*a* to); apply (*a caso, p.* to); (*dar*) give, bequeath; **~se** *algo* appropriate.

apropincuarse [1d] *co.* approach; (come) near.

aprovechable available; useful; **aprovechado** (*frugal*) thrifty; (*ingenioso*) resourceful; (*aplicado*) industrious; *tiempo* well-spent; **aprovechamiento** *m* use *etc.*; (*ventaja*) profit, advantage; (*adelanto*) improvement, progress; **aprovechar** [1a] *v/t.* (*explotar*) make (good) use of, use; *oferta etc.* take advantage of; *enseñanza etc.* profit by; *ocasión* seize, avail o.s. of; *posibilidades* make the most of; *v/i.* be of use; progress, improve (*en* in); ~ *a p.* be of use to, profit; ~ *poco* be of little avail; *¡que aproveche! hoping that those eating will enjoy their meal*; **~se** *de* = *v/t.*

aproximación *f* approach; (*efecto*) nearness, closeness; ⚓ *etc.* approximation; (*lotería*) consolation prize; **aproximado** approximate; near, rough; **aproximar** [1a] bring near(er), draw up (*a* to); **~se** come near(er), approach; ~ *a* near, approach; *fig.* approximate to; **aproximativo** approximate, near.

aptitud *f* (*idoneidad*) suitability (*para* for); (*capacidad*) aptitude, ability; **apto** suitable, fit (*para su.* for); ~ *a inf.*, ~ *para inf.* quick to *inf.*; ~ *para inf.* suitable for *ger.*

apuesta *f* bet, wager.

apuesto neat, spruce; *esp. iro.* dapper, natty.

apuntación *f* note; ♪ notation; **apuntado** pointed, sharp; ⚠ pointed, Gothic; **apuntador** *m thea.* prompter.

apuntalamiento *m* underpinning; **apuntalar** [1a] prop (up), shore (up), underpin; ⊕ strut.

apuntamiento *m* (*apunte*) note; ⚔ aiming; ⚖ judicial report; **apuntar** [1a] **1.** *v/t. fusil* aim (*a* at), train (*a* on); *blanco* aim at; (*señalar*) point out; (*tomar nota*) note (down), take a note of; *tantos* score; *partida* enter; *herramienta* sharpen; (*remendar*) patch; (*zurcir*) darn; *naipes*: stake, put up; *thea.* prompt; ~ *que* point out that; **2.** *v/i.* (*bozo etc.*) begin to show; (*día*) dawn; F ~ *y no dar* fail to keep one's word; **3.** **~se** turn sour; F get tight; **apunte** *m* note; jotting; (*partida*) entry; (*dibujo*) sketch; *thea.* (*p.*) prompt, prompter; (*libro*) promptbook; *naipes*: stake; *sacar* **~s** take notes.

apuñalar [1a] stab, knife; *v. mirada.*

apuñar [1a] seize (in one's fist); **apuñ(et)ear** [1a] punch, pummel.

apuradamente F precisely; **apurado** (*pobre*) needy, hard up; (*difícil*) hard, dangerous; exact; **apurar** [1a] *líquido, vaso* drain; *surtido* exhaust, finish, use up; (*llevar a cabo*) carry out, finish; ⊕ refine, purify; (*averiguar*) verify, check (on); (*molestar*) annoy; (*apremiar*) hurry, press; **~se** fret, worry, upset o.s. (*por* over); *S.Am.* hurry; *~ por inf.* strive to *inf.*; **apuro** *m* (*a. ~s pl.*) hardship, need, distress; (*aprieto*) difficulty, fix; F spot; *estar en el mayor ~, verse en ~s* be in trouble; be up against it; *pasar ~s* suffer hardship; *sacar de ~* get *s.o.* out of a jam.

aquejar [1a] (*molestar*) worry, harass; (*afligir*) distress; (*fatigar*) weary.

aquel, aquella *adj.* that; *aquellos, aquellas pl.* those.

aquél, aquélla *pron.* that (one); (*el anterior*) the former; *aquéllos, aquéllas pl.* those; (*los anteriores*) the former; **aquél** *m* F charm; (sex) appeal, it F.

aquello *pron.* that.

aquí here; *~ dentro* in here; *~ mismo* right here, on this very spot; *de ~* from here; (*tiempo*) from now; *de ~ a 8 días* in a week's time, within a week; *de ~ en adelante* from now on; *de ~ para allá* to and fro; *de ~ que* hence; *hasta ~* so far, as far as here; (*tiempo*) up till now; *por ~* this way; *por ~* (*cerca*) hereabouts, round here.

aquiescencia *f* acquiescence.

aquietar [1a] quieten (down), calm; pacify; *temores* allay.

aquilatar [1a] *metall.* assay; *fig.* weigh up, test, value.

aquilón *m* north wind.

ara *f* altar; (*piedra*) altar stone; *en ~s de* in honor of.

árabe 1. Arab(ic); △ Moresque; **2.** *m/f* Arab; **3.** *m* (*idioma*) Arabic; **arabesco 1.** Arab(ic); **2.** *m* △ arabesque; **arábigo 1.** Arab(ic); **2.** *m* Arabic; F *está en ~* it's Greek to me; *hablar en ~* talk double Dutch; **arabismo** *m* (*estudio*; *voz*; *rasgo*) Arabism; **arabista** *m/f* Arabist.

arable arable.

arácnido *m* arachnid.

arada *f* (day's) plowing; (*terreno*) plowed land; **arado** *m* plow; (*reja*) (plow)share; **arador** *m* plowman.

aragonés *adj. a. su. m*, **-a** *f* Aragonese; **aragonesismo** *m* Aragonese expression (*or* trait).

arambel *m* tatter, shred.

arana *f* trick, swindle; (*mentira*) lie.

arancel *m* tariff, duty; *~ protector* protective tariff; **arancelar** [1a] *C.Am.* pay; **arancelario** tariff *attr.*, customs *attr.*

arándano *m* bilberry, whortleberry; *~ agrio* cranberry.

arandela *f* ⊕ washer; candle stand *para vela*.

araña *f zo.* spider; (*a. ~ de luces*) chandelier; *fig.* resourceful person; *b.s.* sponger; **arañar** [1a] scratch; F scrape together; **arañazo** *m* scratch.

arar [1a] plow; till.

arbitrador *m*, **-a** *f* arbiter, arbitrator; **arbitraje** *m* arbitration; ✝ arbitrage (*de cambio* of exchange); **arbitram(i)ento** *m* arbitrament; **arbitrar** [1a] *deportes*: (*tenis*) umpire; (*fútbol, boxeo*) referee; ⚖ *etc.* arbitrate; *phls.* judge, determine freely; **~se** get along, manage; **arbitrariedad** *f* arbitrariness; (*acto*) outrage, arbitrary act; ⚖ illegal act; **arbitrario** arbitrary; **arbitrio** *m* (*albedrío*) free will; (*medio*) means, expedient; ⚖ adjudication; *~s pl.* ✝ excise taxes; **arbitrista** *m/f* armchair politician; bright-eyed idealist; **árbitro** *m* arbiter, moderator; *deportes*: umpire, referee.

árbol *m* ♀ tree; ⊕ axle, shaft; ⚓ mast; *~ frutal* fruit tree; *~ genealógico* family tree, pedigree; *~ de levas* camshaft; *~ motor* drive shaft; **arbolado 1.** *paisaje* wooded; *avenida* lined with trees; ⚓ having a mast; **2.** *m* woodland; **arboladura** *f* ⚓ masts and spars; **arbolar** [1a] *bandera* hoist; ⚓ mast; (*arrimar*) put up (*a* against); **~se** rear up, get up on its hind legs; **arboleda** *f* grove, plantation; **arboledo** *m* woodland; **arbóreo** *zo.* arboreal; *forma* treelike; **arborescente** arborescent; **arboricultura** *f* arboriculture.

arbotante *m* flying buttress.

arbusto *m* shrub.

arca *f* (*caja*) chest, coffer; ✓ hutch; (*depósito*) tank, reservoir; *~s pl.* safe, strong room; *~ de agua freq.* water tower; *~ de la alianza* Ark of the Covenant; *~ de Noé* Noah's Ark.

arcada *f* arch(es) *de puente*; △ series of arches, arcade; ⚕ retching.

arcadio *adj. a. su. m*, **a** *f* Arcadian.

arcaduz *m* pipe, conduit; (*cangilón*) bucket; *fig.* ways and means.

arcaico archaic; **arcaísmo** *m* archaism; **arcaizante** archaic; *p.*, *estilo* given to archaisms.

arcano 1. secret, enigmatic, recondite; **2.** *m* mystery, (great) secret.
arcángel *m* archangel.
arcar [1g] = *arquear* △, ⊕.
arce *m* maple (tree).
arcediano *m* archdeacon.
arcén *m* border, edge; △ curb.
arcilla *f* clay; ~ *de alfarería*, ~ *figulina* potter's clay, argil; **arcilloso** clay(ey); argillaceous 🕮.
arcipreste *m* archpriest.
arco *m* △, *anat.* arch; ⩘, ⚡ arc; ⚔ (long)bow; ♪ bow; hoop *de barril etc.*; ⚡ (*luz*) spotlight; ~ *de herradura* Moorish arch; ~ *iris* rainbow; ~ *ojival* pointed arch; ~ *triunfal* triumphal arch; ~ *voltaico* arc lamp.
arcón *m* bin, bunker.
archidiácono *m* archdeacon.
archiducado *m* archduchy; **archiduque** *m* archduke; **archiduquesa** *f* archduchess.
archimillonario *m* multimillionaire.
archipámpano *m* F *co. imaginary tycoon.*
archipiélago *m* archipelago; F labyrinth *de calles etc.*
archivador *m* (*p.*) filing clerk; (*mueble*) filing cabinet; **archivar** [1a] file (away); store away; deposit in the archives; F hide away; **archivero** *m*, **a** *f* filing clerk *en oficina*; 🕮 archivist, keeper; registrar; **archivo** *m* archives; registry; ♀ *Nacional* Record Office; ~*s pl.* ✝ *etc.* files; 🕮, *hist.* muniments, records.
ardentía *f* ⚕ heartburn; ⚓ phosphorescence.
arder [2a] burn (*a. fig.*); (*resplandecer*) glow, blaze; *fig.* (*espada etc.*) flash; ~ *de*, ~ *en amor etc.* burn with; ~ *en guerra* be ablaze with; ~ *sin llamas* smolder; ~**se** burn up, burn away; ⚘ be parched.
ardid *m* ruse, device, scheme; ~*es pl.* wiles.
ardido ✓ spoiled, burnt up; bold; *S.Am.* angry, irritated; **ardiente** burning (*a. fig.*); (*radiante*) glowing, blazing; *color* bright, glowing; *flor* bright red; *fiebre, deseo etc.* burning; *interés* keen, lively; *partidario* passionate, ardent.
ardilla *f* squirrel; F *andar como una* ~ be always on the go.
ardimiento *m* burning; *fig.* courage, dash.
ardite: F *no me importa un* ~ I don't care the least bit; F *no vale un* ~ it's not worth a dime.
ardor *m* heat, warmth; *fig.* (*celo*) ardor, eagerness; heat *de disputa etc.*; (*valor*) courage, dash; ~ *de estómago* heartburn; **ardoroso** burning, fiery; *fig.* enthusiastic; lively, vigorous.
arduo arduous, hard, tough, strenuous.
área *f* area (*a.* ⩘); (*medida*) are; ~ *de castigo* penalty area; ~ *de descansar* rest area; ~ *de meta* goal area; ~ *de servicio* service area.
arena *f* sand; grit; (*circo*) arena; ~*s pl.* ⚕ stones, gravel; ~ *movediza* quicksand; ~*s pl. de oro* fine gold; **arenal** *m* sandy ground, sands; (*cantero*) sandpit; ⚓ quicksand; **arenar** [1a] (sprinkle with) sand; ⊕ polish (*or* rub) with sand.
arenga *f* harangue (*a.* F); F scolding; **arengar** [1h] harangue; scold.
arenillas *f/pl.* ⚕ gravel.
arenisca *f* sandstone; grit; **arenisco** sandy; gravelly, gritty; **arenoso** sandy, sand *attr.*
arenque *m* herring; ~ *ahumado* kipper.
arepa *f S.Am.* cornbread; corn griddlecake.
arete *m* earring.
argadijo *m* ⊕ reel, bobbin; F busybody.
argado *m* prank, trick.
argalia *f* catheter.
argamandijo *m* F set (of tools *etc.*).
argamasa *f* △ mortar; plaster.
árgana *f* ⊕ crane.
argelino *adj. a. su. m*, **a** *f* Algerian.
argén *m* argent; **argentado** silvery; ⊕ silvered; **argentar** [1a] silver (*a.* ⊕, *fig.*); **argénteo** silver(y) (*a. fig.*); ⊕ silver-plated; **argentería** *f* silver (*or* gold) embroidery (*or* filigree); **argentino**[1] silvery.
argentino[2] *adj. a. su. m*, **a** *f* Argentinian.
argento *m poet.* silver; ~ *vivo* quicksilver.
argolla *f* (large) ring; knocker *de puerta*; *deportes*: croquet.
argonauta *m* Argonaut (*a. zo.*).
argot *m* slang; cant; argot.
argucia *f* sophistry, hairsplitting.
argüir [3g] *v/t.* argue; indicate, point to; impute (*a* to); accuse (*de*

of); *v/i.* argue (*contra* against, with); **argumentación** *f* argumentation; (line of) argument; **argumentador** argumentative; **argumentar** [1a] argue; **argumento** *m* argument; line of argument, reasoning; *thea. etc.* plot.

aria *f* aria.

aridecer [2d] *v/t.* make arid; *v/i.*, **~se** become arid (*or* dry); **aridez** *f* aridity, dryness (*a. fig.*); **árido** **1.** arid, dry (*a. fig.*); **2.** *~s m/pl.* dry goods (*esp.* ✓).

ariete *m* battering ram.

arillo *m* earring.

ario *adj. a. su. m,* **a** *f* Aryan, Indo-European.

arisco (*displicente*) fractious, cross; (*áspero*) surly; (*huraño*) shy, unsociable; *caballo* vicious.

arista *f* ♀ beard; *mount.* arête; ⚔ edge; ⚠ arris; ⚠ *~ de encuentro* groin.

aristocracia *f* aristocracy (*a. fig.*); **aristócrata** *m/f* aristocrat; **aristocrático** aristocratic.

aristón *m* ⚠ edge, corner.

aritmética *f* arithmetic; **aritmético** **1.** arithmetical; **2.** *m* arithmetician.

arlequín *m fig.* buffoon; **arlequinada** *f* (piece of) buffoonery; tomfoolery; **arlequinesco** *fig.* ridiculous, grotesque.

arma *f* arm, weapon; *~s pl.* arms (*a. heráldica*); *~ arrojadiza* missile; *~ atómica* atomic weapon; *~ blanca* steel (blade); *~s pl. cortas* small-arms; *~ de fuego* firearm, gun; *~ de infantería* infantry arm; *¡~s al hombro!* slope arms!, shoulder arms!; *alzarse en ~s* rise up in arms; *¡descansen ~s!* order arms!; *estar sobre las ~s* stand by; *pasar por las ~s* shoot; *tocar (al) ~* (sound the) call to arms; *tomar las ~s* take up arms.

armada *f* fleet; navy; *la* ♀ *Invencible* the Armada (*1588*).

armadijo *m* trap, snare.

armadillo *m* armadillo.

armado armed; equipped; ⊕ reinforced; *P.R., Mex.* stubborn; **armador** *m* shipowner; (*corsario*) privateer; **armadura** *f* ⚔ (suit of) armor; ⊕ *etc.* frame(work); ⚡ armature; *anat.* skeleton; ♪ key signature; **armamentismo** *m* military preparedness; **armamentista** **1.** arms *attr.*; militarist(ic); **2.** *m* arms dealer; *carrera ~* arms race; **armamento** *m* ⚔ (*acto*) arming; (*conjunto*) armament(s); ⚓ equipment, fitting-out.

armar [1a] *p. etc.* arm (*de, con* with; *a. fig.*); *arma* load; ⊕ *etc.* mount, assemble, put together; ⚠ set (*sobre cimientos* on; *a. fig.*); ⚓ equip, fit out; *hormigón* reinforce; *tienda* pitch, set up; *trampa* set; *fig.* prepare, arrange; *jaleo etc.* stir up, start; *caballero* dub, knight; *pleito* bring; F *~la* raise hell; start a row; **~se** arm o.s. (*de* with; *a. fig.*); *fig.* get ready; *S.Am.* put money in one's pocket.

armario *m* cupboard; (*ropa*) wardrobe; closet; *~ (para libros)* bookcase.

armatoste *m contp.* hulk; *esp.* ⊕ contraption; *mot.* crock, grid; F fat old thing.

armazón *f* frame(work); body; ✈ chassis; ⚠ *etc.* shell, skeleton; frame, carcass *de mueble.*

armella *f* eyebolt, screw eye.

armenio *adj. a. su. m,* **a** *f* Armenian.

armería *f* museum of arms; ⚔ armory; (*tienda*) gun shop; **armero** *m* gunsmith, armorer; (*estante*) gun rack.

armiño *m zo.* stoat; (*piel, heráldica*) ermine.

armisticio *m* armistice.

armón *m* ⚔ limber.

armonía *f* harmony (*a. fig.*); agreement; accord; *en ~* in harmony (*con* with); **armónica** *f* harmonica; *~ (de boca)* mouth organ, harmonica; **armónico** **1.** ♪ harmonic; *sonido* harmonious; **2.** *m* harmonic, overtone; **armonio** *m* harmonium; **armonioso** harmonious (*a. fig.*); *melodía* tuneful; **armonizar** [1f] *v/t.* harmonize, bring into harmony (*a. fig.*); *diferencias* reconcile; *v/i.* harmonize (*con* with); (*colores etc.*) go together; tone (*con* in with).

arnés *m* ⚔ armor; *~es pl.* harness; *fig.* gear, outfit.

árnica *f* arnica.

aro *m* hoop, ring; *~ de émbolo* piston ring; F *entrar por el ~* have no option.

aroma *m* aroma, fragrance; bouquet *de vino*; **aromático** aromatic; **aromatizar** [1f] give fragrance to; *líquido* spice, flavor (with herbs).

arpa *f* harp.

arpado toothed, jagged; *poet.* sweet-singing.

arpar [1a] scratch, claw (at); (*romper*) tear up, tear to pieces.
arpeo *m* grapnel, grappling iron.
arpía *f* harpy; *fig.* (*regañona*) termagant, shrew; (*flaca*) bag of bones.
arpillera *f* sacking, sackcloth.
arpista *m/f* harpist.
arpón *m* gaff, harpoon; **arpon**(**e**)**ar** [1a] harpoon.
arquear [1a] *v/t.* ▲ arch; ⊕ *lana* beat; ⚓ gauge; *v/i.* F retch; **~se** arch; (*superficie*) camber; **arqueo** *m* arching; ⚓ tonnage, burden; ✝ checking (of contents).
arqueología *f* archaeology; **arqueólogo** *m* archaeologist.
arquería *f* arcade; **arquero** *m* archer, bowman; ✝ cashier; *S.Am.* *sport* goalkeeper.
arquetipo *m* archetype.
arquimesa *f* desk, escritoire.
arquitecto *m* architect; ~ *de jardines* landscape gardener; **arquitectónico** architectural, architectonic; **arquitectura** *f* architecture.
arrabal *m* suburb; **~es** *pl.* outskirts, outlying area; **arrabalero 1.** suburban; F common, ill-bred; **2.** *m*, **a** *f* surburbanite; F common sort.
arracada *f* earring (with pendant).
arracimado clustered, clustering; **arracimarse** [1a] cluster (*or* bunch) together.
arraigado (firmly) rooted (*or* established); *fig.* ingrained; ✝ property-owning; **arraigar** [1h] *v/t.* establish, strengthen (*en fe etc.* in); *v/i.* ⚘ root, take root (*a. fig.*), strike root; *v/i.*, **~se** (*p.*) become a property owner, settle *en lugar*; *fig.* establish a hold; ~ *en p.* (*costumbre*) grow on; **arraigo** *m* hold (*a. fig.*); ✝ property, real estate; ⚘ *de fácil* ~ easily rooted.
arrancaclavos *m* nail claw; nail puller; **arrancada** *f* sudden start; quick acceleration; **arrancadero** *m* starting point; **arrancado** F on the rocks, broke; (*malo*) terrible; **arrancador** *m mot.* starter; **arrancamiento** *m* pulling out *etc.*; **arrancar** [1g] **1.** *v/t.* ⚘ *etc.* pull up, root out; (*arrebatar*) snatch away (*a*, *de* from); *página, botón etc.* tear off; *espada etc.* wrest, wrench (*a* from); *motor* start; *fig. victoria* snatch, wrest; *apoyo* win, get; *promesa etc.* force out (*a* of) *con fuerza*, wangle out (*a* of) *con astucia*; *p.* tear away (*de vicio* from); *suspiro* fetch, utter; **2.** *v/i. mot. etc.* start; pull away; (*salir*) start out; F get away (*de* from); *fig.* ~ *de* arise from, spring from (*a.* ▲).
arranchar [1a] *costa* skirt, sail close to; *velas* brace; *S.Am.* snatch away, snaffle; **~se** gather together; (*comer*) mess together.
arranque *m* (*sudden*) start, jerk; ▲, *anat.* starting point; *fig.* impulse; (*ira*) fit, outburst; (*ingenio*) sally; ~ (*automático*) (self-)starter.
arrapiezo *m* rag; F whippersnapper.
arras *f/pl.* deposit, pledge; *13 coins given by bridegroom to bride.*
arrasar [1a] *v/t.* raze, demolish; (*allanar*) level, flatten; *vasija* fill to the brim; *v/i. meteor.* clear (up); **~se** *en lágrimas* (*ojos*) fill with tears.
arrastradizo dangling, trailing; *fig.* maltreated; **arrastrado 1.** F poor, wretched; (*bribón*) rascally; **2.** *m* rascal; **arrastrar** [1a] *v/t.* drag (along), pull, haul; (*hacer bajar*) drag down (*a. fig.*); *falda etc.* trail; *palabras* drawl; *afecto* draw (*tras* to); *público* win over, carry; *v/i.*, **~se** (*reptar*) crawl, creep; (*p.*) drag o.s. along; (*colgar*) drag, trail, touch the ground; ⚘ trail; (*horas, obra*) drag; (*humillarse*) grovel, creep; **arrastre** *m* drag(ging) *etc.*; (*transporte*) haulage; *natación*: crawl; ~ *de espaldas* backstroke.
arrayán *m* myrtle.
¡arre! get up!; *sl.* giddap!
arreador *m* foreman; *S.Am.* whip; **arrear** [1a] *v/t.* urge on; (*enjaezar*) harness; *v/i.* F hurry along; F *¡arrea!* get a move on!; (*sorpresa*) get along with you!
arrebañaduras *f/pl.* scrapings, remains; **arrebañar** [1a] scrape together; (*comer*) eat up, clear up.
arrebatadizo excitable; hot-tempered, irascible; **arrebatado** *movimiento* sudden, violent; (*impetuoso*) rash, reckless; (*absorto*) rapt; *cara* flushed; **arrebatamiento** *m* snatching *etc.*; *fig.* fury; ecstasy; **arrebatar** [1a] (*quitar*) snatch (away) (*a* from); (*con fuerza*) wrench, wrest (*a* from); (*llevarse*) carry away (*or* off); *parte* rip off; *fig.* captivate; *público* move, stir;

♀ parch; ~**se** get carried away (*en* by); *cocina*: burn; **arrebatiña** *f* = *rebatiña*; **arrebato** *m* fury; ecstasy, rapture.

arrebol *m* red, glow *de cielo*; (*afeite*) rouge; **arrebolar** [1a] redden; ~**se** redden, flush; (*maquillarse*) rouge.

arrebozar [1f] = *rebozar*.

arrebujar [1a] jumble up; (*cubrir*) wrap up, cover; ~**se** wrap (*o.s.*) up (*con* with, in).

arreciar [1b] grow worse, get more severe; ~**se** ⚘ get stronger, pick up.

arrecife *m* causeway; ⚓ reef; ~ *de coral* coral reef.

arrechucho *m* F fit, outburst; ⚘ [(queer) turn.]

arredrar [1a] drive back; *fig.* scare, daunt; ~**se** draw back, move away (*de* from), shrink (*ante* at, before); *fig.* get scared; *sin* ~ nothing daunted.

arregazado *falda etc.* tucked up; *nariz* turned up; **arregazar** [1f] tuck up.

arreglado regulated, (well-)ordered; *fig.* moderate; *vida* of moderation, orderly; **arreglar** [1a] arrange, order, regulate; adjust (*a* to); (*componer*) put in order, put straight; ⊕ fix, repair; *aspecto, pelo, cuarto etc.* tidy up; *disputa* settle, make up; *cita, detalles* arrange, fix up; ~**se** come to terms (*a, con* with; *a.* ✝); F ~*las* get by; manage (*para inf.* to *inf.*); *todo se arreglará* it will be all right, things will work out; **arreglo** *m* arrangement *etc.*; settlement; F deal; (*regla*) rule, order; (*acuerdo*) agreement, ♪ setting; *con* ~ *a* in accordance with; *vivir con* ~ live quietly.

arregostarse [1a]: F ~ *a* take a fancy to; **arregosto** *m* F fancy, taste (*de* for).

arrellenarse [1a] lounge, sprawl; *fig.* be happy in one's work.

arremangado *nariz* turned up; **arremangar** [1h] turn up, roll up; *falda etc.* tuck up; ~**se** roll up one's sleeves *etc.*; *fig.* take a firm stand.

arremeter [2a] *v/t. caballo* spur on; *v/i.* rush forth, attack; *fig.* (*vista*) offend; ~ *a*, ~ *con*(*tra*) attack, rush at; *fenc.* lunge at; **arremetida** *f*, **arremetimiento** *m* attack; lunge *con arma*; (*impetu*) (on)rush; (*empujón*) push.

arremolinarse [1a] (*gente*) crowd around; (*agua*) swirl; (*polvo etc.*) whirl.

arrendable rentable; *casa* to let; **arrendador** *m*, **-a** *f* (*dueño*) lessor; (*inquilino*) tenant.

arrendajo *m* jay.

arrendamiento *m* (*acto*) letting *etc.*; (*precio*) rent(al); (*documento*) contract; *contrato de* ~ lease; *tomar en* ~ rent; **arrendar**[1] [1k] (*dueño*): *casa* let, lease; *máquina etc.* hire out; (*inquilino etc.*): *casa* rent, lease; *máquina etc.* hire.

arrendar[2] [1k] tie, tether.

arrendatario *m*, **a** *f* tenant, lessee; leaseholder; hirer; renter.

arreo *m* adornment; ~*s pl.* harness, trappings; (*equipo*) gear.

arrepentido 1. sorry, regretful (*de* for); (*a. eccl.*) repentant; **2.** *m*, **a** *f* penitent; **arrepentimiento** *m* repentance; regret; **arrepentirse** [3i] repent (*de* of); ~ *de* regret.

arrequives *m/pl.* F best clothes; finery, trimmings, buttons and bows; *fig.* circumstances.

arrestado bold, daring; **arrestar** [1a] arrest, take into custody; ~**se** *a* rush boldly into; **arresto** *m* arrest; (*reclusión*) imprisonment, ⚔ detention; *fig.* boldness, daring.

arriada *f* flood; **arriarse** [1c] flood, become flooded.

arriar [1c] *vela etc.* lower, haul down; *cable* slacken; F let go.

arriate *m* ⚘ bed, border; trellis *de madera*; (*camino*) road.

arriba a) *situación*: above; on top; upstairs *en casa*; (*movimiento*) up, upwards; upstairs *en casa*; b) *de la cintura* (*para*) ~ from the waist up; *de 5 libras para* ~ from 5 pounds upwards; *de* ~ *abajo* from top to bottom; from beginning to end; *por la calle* ~ up the street; *desde* ~ from (up) above; *hacia* ~ up(wards); *más* ~ higher up; further up; *río* ~ upstream; c) ~ *de prp.* above; further up than; d) *attr.*: *de* ~ upper; *la parte de* ~ the upper part; *los de* ~ those above; those on top; ⊕ *de* ~ overhead; *lo* ~ *escrito* what we have said above; e) *int.* ¡~! up you get!; ¡~ *España!* Spain for ever!

arribada *f* ⚓ arrival; ~ *forzosa* ⚓ emergency call (*or* stop); **arribar** [1a] ⚓ put into port; arrive; (*noticia*) come to hand; F ⚕, ♆ recover; ~ *a inf.* manage to *inf.*; **arribeño** *m*, **a** *f S.Am.* highlander; inlander; **arribista** *m/f* parvenu, upstart; **arribo** *m* arrival.

arriendo *m* = *arrendamiento.*

arriero *m* muleteer.

arriesgado risky, dangerous, hazardous; *p.* bold, daring; **arriesgar** [1h] *vida etc.* risk, endanger; *conjetura* hazard; *posibilidades* jeopardize; *dinero* stake; **~se** take a risk, expose o.s. to danger; ~ *a inf.* risk *ger.*; ~ *en empresa* venture upon; **arriesgo** *m S.Am.* risk; hazard.

arrimadero *m* support; **arrimadizo** *fig.* **1.** parasitic, sycophantic; **2.** *m*, **a** *f* toady, sycophant; **arrimado** *imitación* close; **arrimar** [1a] (*acercar*) move up, bring close (*a* to); *escala etc.* lean (*a* against); *carga* stow; *golpe etc.* give; (*quitar*) move out of the way; (*arrinconar*) put away; *p.* push aside; (*deshacerse de*) get rid of; (*abandonar*) lay aside; **~se** come close(r) *etc.*; (*unirse*) join together; ~ *a* come close to (*a. fig.*); lean on; (*afectuoso*) cuddle (*or* snuggle) up to; *fig.* seek the protection of; **arrimo** *m* support (*a. fig.*); (*afición*) attachment; **arrimón** *m* loafer; sponger; F *estar de* ~ hang (*or* loaf) around.

arrinconado *fig.* forgotten, neglected; isolated; **arrinconar** [1a] *fig.* lay aside, put away; (*deshacerse de*) get rid of; *p.* push aside; *asunto* shelve; *enemigo* corner; **~se** withdraw from the world.

arriscado *geog.* craggy; *fig.* bold, resolute; agile.

arriscar [1g] risk; **~se** take a risk; (*engreírse*) grow conceited.

arritmia *f* ⚕ arrhythmia; **arrítmico** arrhythmic.

arrivista = *arribista.*

arroba *f measure of weight = 11.502 kg.; variable liquid measure.*

arrobamiento *m* ecstasy, rapture; trance; **arrobar** [1a] entrance; **~se** go into ecstasies; (*espiritista*) go into a trance.

arrodillado kneeling, on one's knees; **arrodillarse** [1a] kneel (down), go down on one's knees.

arrogancia *f* arrogance; pride; **arrogante** arrogant; brave.

arrogarse [1h] *algo* arrogate to o.s.

arrojadizo: *v. arma*; easily thrown; for throwing; **arrojado** *fig.* daring, dashing; **arrojallamas** *m* flamethrower; **arrojar** [1a] throw; (*con fuerza*) fling, hurl; *deportes*: *pelota* bowl, pitch; *pesa* put; *pesca*: cast; *humo* emit, give out; *flores* put out; ⚒, ♆ yield, produce; *fig.* ~ *de sí* cast from one, fling aside; **~se** throw o.s. (*a* into, *por* out of); *fig.* rush, fling o.s., plunge (*a*, *en* into); **arrojo** *m* daring, dash; rashness.

arrollador *fig.* sweeping, overwhelming; devastating; **arrollar** [1a] (*enrollar*) roll (up); *esp.* ⊕, ⚡ coil, wind; (*agua etc.*) sweep away; *enemigo* throw back, rout; *mot.* knock down; *fig. p.* dumbfound, leave speechless.

arromar [1a] blunt, dull.

arropar [1a] wrap (up); tuck up *en cama*; **~se** wrap up; tuck o.s. up.

arrope *m* syrup.

arrostrar [1a] *v/t.* face (up to), brave; *v/i.*: ~ *a* show a liking for; ~ *con*, ~ *por* = *v/t.*; **~se** throw o.s. into battle.

arroyada *f* gully; (*crecida etc.*) flood; **arroyo** *m* stream, brook, watercourse; gutter *en calle*; F *poner en el* ~ put out of the house.

arroz *m* rice; ~ *con leche* rice pudding; F ~ *y gallo muerto* lots to eat; thrown-together meal.

arruga *f* wrinkle, line; crease, fold; **arrugado** wrinkled, lined; creased, crinkly; **arrugar** [1h] *cara* wrinkle, line; *ropa* crease, pucker; (*ajar*) crumple; *papel* crease; *entrecejo* knit, pucker up; **~se** get wrinkled *etc.*; ⚘ shrivel up.

arruinamiento *m* ruin(ation); **arruinar** [1a] ruin (*a.* ♆, *fig.*), destroy; demolish; *esperanzas* wreck, blight; **~se** △ fall into ruins, fall down; ♆ be ruined; *fig.* go to rack rand ruin

arrullar [1a] *v/t. niño* lull to sleep; F say sweet nothings to; *v/i.* coo; **~se** bill and coo (*a.* F); **arrullo** *m* cooing; ♪ lullaby.

arrumaje *m* ⚓ stowage; **arrumar** [1a] stow.

arrumbar[1] [1a] put aside, put on one side, forget; *p.* silence *en conversación.*

arrumbar[2] [1a] ⚓ take one's bearings; **~se** ⚕ get seasick.

arrurruz *m* arrowroot.
arsenal *m* ⚓ (naval) dockyard, shipyard; ⚔ arsenal; *fig.* storehouse, mine.
arsénico 1. arsenical; **2.** *m* arsenic.
arte *m a. f* art; (*maña*) trick, cunning; (*habilidad*) knack; (*hechura*) workmanship; ~ *griego* Greek art; ~ *mecánica* mechanical skill; ~ *de vivir* art of living; *no tener* ~ *ni parte en* have nothing to do with; ~*s mst f/pl. univ.* arts; *bellas* ~ fine arts; ~ *liberales* liberal arts; *malas* ~ trickery, guile; ~ *y oficios* arts and crafts; **artefacto** *m* ⊕ appliance, contrivance; *esp. arqueología*: artefact; F *mot.* old crock, jalopy.
artejo *m* knuckle, joint.
artería *f* cunning, artfulness.
arteria *f* artery (*a. fig.*); ⚡ feeder; **arterial** arterial; **arteriosclerosis** *f* arteriosclerosis.
artero cunning, artful.
artesa *f* (kneading) trough; ⚒ ~ *oscilante* cradle.
artesanía *f* handicraft, skill; (*arte, hechura*) craftsmanship; **artesano** *m* craftsman, artisan.
artesiano: *pozo* ~ Artesian well.
artesón *m* kitchen tub; ⚠ panel; molding *de techo*; coffer; **artesonado** *m* paneling; stuccoed (*or* plaster) ceiling; coffered ceiling; **artesonar** [1a] mold, stucco; panel.
ártico arctic.
articulación *f anat.*, ⊕ joint; *gr. etc.* articulation; ~ *esférica* ball joint; ~ *universal* universal joint; **articulado** *anat.*, ⊕ articulated, jointed; **articular** [1a] articulate; ⊕ join (together, up); ⚖ *etc.* article; **articulista** *m/f* article writer, contributor (to paper); **artículo** *m* article (*a. gr.*, ⚖, ✝); *anat.* articulation, joint; entry *en libro de consulta*; ~*s pl. de consumo* consumer goods; ~ *de fondo* leader, leading article, editorial; ~*s de gran consumo* mass-consumption articles; *eccl.* ~ *de la muerte* point of death; ~*s pl. de primera necesidad* basic commodities; ~ *suelto* oddment.
artífice *m/f* artist, craftsman; maker; *fig.* architect; **artificial** artificial; *b.s.* imitation *attr.*; **artificio** *m* (*arte*) art, skill; (*hechura*) workmanship, craftsmanship; ⊕ contrivance, appliance; *fig.* artifice; *b.s.* (piece of) double-dealing; **artificioso** artistic, fine, skillful; *fig.* cunning, artful; **artilugio** *m contp.* ⊕ contraption; gadget; (*treta*) gimmick; (*que no se nombra*) thingamajig.
artillado *m* = **artillería** *f* artillery; cannon (*pl.*); **artillero** *m* ⚔ artilleryman; ⚔, ✈, ⚓ gunner.
artimaña *f* trap; *fig.* cunning.
artista *m/f* artist; *thea. etc.* artiste; ~ *de cine* film actor (*f* actress); **artístico** artistic.
artrítico arthritic; **artritis** *f* arthritis.
arveja *f* vetch.
arzobispado *m* archbishopric; **arzobispal** archiepiscopal; **arzobispo** *m* archbishop.
arzón *m* saddle tree.
as *m* ace; one *en dado*; *fig.* ace, wizard.
asa[1] *f* handle; *fig.* handle, pretext; F *ser muy del* ~ be well in.
asa[2] *f* ⚘ juice.
asado 1. roast(ed); *bien* ~ well done; *poco* ~ underdone; **2.** *m* roast (meat); **asador** *m* spit, broach; (*máquina*) roasting jack; **asaduras** *f/pl.* entrails, offal; F *tiene* ~ he's as lazy as they come.
asaetear [1a] hit (with an arrow); *fig.* bother, pester.
asalariado 1. paid; wage-earning; **2.** *m*, **a** *f* wage earner.
asaltar [1a] *fortaleza etc.* storm, rush; *p.* fall on, attack; *fig.* (*duda*) assail; (*pensamiento*) cross one's mind; (*muerte etc.*) overtake; **asalto** *m* attack, assault; *fenc.*, *boxeo*: round; *por* ~ by storm.
asamblea *f* assembly; ⚔ *llamar a* ~ assemble, muster.
asar [1a] roast; *fig.* pester, plague (*con* with); ~**se** *fig.* (*a.* ~ *vivo*) be boiling hot, be nearly roasted.
asaz † *a. lit.* very, exceedingly; enough.
asbesto *m* asbestos.
ascendencia *f* ancestry, line; **ascendente** ascending; upward; *carrera, plumada, tren* up...; *marea* incoming; **ascender** [2g] *v/t.* promote, raise (*a* to); *v/i.* (*subir*) go up, ascend; (*en rango*) be promoted, move up; ✝ boom; ♃ ~ *a* amount to, add up to; **ascendiente 1.** = *ascendente*; **2.** *m/f* ancestor; **3.** *m* ascendancy, influence (*sobre* over).

ascensión *f* ascent; *eccl.* ascension; *fig.* = *ascenso*; *eccl.* *Día de la* ♀ Ascension Day; **ascensional** *ast.* ascendant, rising; *movimiento* upward; **ascensionista** *m/f* balloonist; **ascenso** *m* promotion, rise; grade; **ascensor** *m* elevator, lift; ⊕ elevator; **ascensorista** *m/f* elevator operator.

asceta *m/f* ascetic; **ascético** ascetic; **ascetismo** *m* asceticism.

asco *m* loathing, disgust, revulsion; (*cosa*) abomination, disgusting thing; *coger* ~ *a* get sick of; *dar* ~ *a* sicken, disgust; *me da* ~ *el queso* I loathe cheese; F *estar hecho un* ~ be filthy; *hacer* ~*s de* turn up one's nose at.

ascua *f* live coal, ember; *¡*~*s!* ouch!; F *arrimar el* ~ *a su sardina* know which side one's bread is buttered; make the most of one's opportunity; F *estar en* ~*s* be on tenterhooks; F *sacar el* ~ *con la mano del gato* get s.o. else to do the dirty work.

aseado clean, neat, tidy, trim; *p.* well-groomed; **asear** [1a] adorn, embellish; (*limpiar*) tidy up; **~se** tidy (o.s.) up; freshen (o.s.) up.

asechanza *f* trap, snare (*a. fig.*); **asechar** [1a] waylay, ambush; *fig.* set a trap for.

asediador *m* besieger; **asediar** [1b] besiege; *fig.* pester; (*amor*) chase, set one's cap at; **asedio** *m* siege; ✝ run (*de* on).

asegurable insurable; **asegurado** *m*, **a** *f* insured, insurant; **asegurador** *m* fastener; (*p.*) insurer, underwriter; **asegurar** [1a] (*fijar*) secure, fasten; *cimientos etc.* make firm; *fig.* guarantee, assure; affirm (*que* that); ✝ insure (*contra* against); *sitio* make secure (*contra ataque* against); *derechos etc.* safeguard; *se lo aseguro* I assure (*or* promise) you; *le aseguré de mi fidelidad* I assured him of my loyalty; **~se** make o.s. secure (*de peligro* from); ~ *de hechos* make sure of.

asemejar [1a] *v/t.* make alike; *fig.* liken (*a* to); **~se** be alike; ~ *a* be like, resemble.

asendereado *camino* beaten, well trodden; *vida* wretched, of drudgery; **asenderear** [1a] chase up hill and down dale.

asenso *m* assent; *dar* ~ *a* give credence to.

asentada *f* sitting; session; *de una* ~ at one sitting; **asentaderas** *f/pl.* F behind, bottom; **asentado** *fig.* established, settled; **asentador** *m* ⚠ stone mason; (*suavizador*) strop; **asentar** [1k] **1.** *v/t.* *p.* seat, sit *s.o.* down; *cosa* place, fix; *tienda* pitch; *cimientos* make firm; *ciudad* found; *tierra* level, tamp down; *golpe* fetch; *cuchillo* sharpen; *fig.* establish, consolidate; (*anotar*) enter, set down; *principio* lay down; ⚖ award; *impresión* fix in the mind; (*conjeturar*) suppose; **2.** *v/i.* be suitable, suit; **3.** **~se** seat o.s.; *fig.* establish o.s.; (⚠, *líquido*) settle.

asentir [3i] assent; ~ *a* consent to; *petición* grant; *arreglo* accept; *verdad* give in to.

asentista *m* (military) contractor; supplier.

aseo *m* tidiness; cleanliness; *persona* grooming; *cuarto de* ~, ~*s pl. euph.* restroom, toilet.

aséptico aseptic; free from infection.

asequible obtainable, available; *fin* attainable.

aserradero *m* sawmill; **aserrador** *m* sawyer; **aserradora** *f* power saw; **aserradura** *f* saw cut; ~*s pl.* sawdust; **aserrar** [1k] saw (up); **aserruchar** [1a] *S.Am.* saw.

aserto *m* assertion.

asesina *f* murderess; **asesinar** [1a] murder; *pol. etc.* assassinate; *fig.* plague (to death); **asesinato** *m* murder; *pol.* assassination; ~ *legal* judicial murder; **asesino 1.** murderous; **2.** *m* murderer, killer; *pol. etc.* assassin; *fig.* thug, cutthroat.

asesor *m*, **-a** *f* adviser; consultant; **asesorar** [1a] advise; act as a consultant to; **~se** seek (*or* take) advice (*con*, *de* from); consult; ~ *de situación* take stock of; **asesoría** *f* (task of) advising; (*honorarios*) adviser's fee.

asestar [1a] (*apuntar*) aim (*a* at); *arma* shoot, fire; *golpe* deal, strike; *fig.* try to hurt.

aseveración *f* assertion, contention; **aseveradamente** positively; **aseverar** [1a] assert, asseverate.

asexual asexual.

asfaltado *m* asphalting; asphalt (pavement *etc.*); **asfaltar** [1a] asphalt; **asfalto** *m* asphalt.

asfixia *f* asphyxia 🕮; suffocation, asphyxiation; **asfixiador, asfi-**

xiante asphyxiating, suffocating; *gas* poison *attr.*; **asfixiar** [1b] asphyxiate; suffocate; ⚔ gas; **~se** be asphyxiated, suffocate.
asgo *v. asir.*
así 1. *adv.* a) so, in this way, thus; thereby; F ~ ~ not too bad, middling; ~ *pues* and so, so then; *o* ~ or so; ~ *que* ~ anyway; F ~ *que asá* it makes no odds; ~ *es que* and so (it is that); ¡~ *sea!* so be it!; b) *comp. etc.*: ~ *como* (in the same way) as; as well as; ~ *A como B* both A and B; ~ *adj. que* so *adj.* that; ~ *de grande* so big, as big as that; **2.** *adj.*: *un hombre* ~ such a man, a man like that; ~ *es la vida* such is life; **3.** *cj.*: ~ *como*, ~ *que* as soon as.
asiático 1. Asian, Asiatic; **2.** *m*, **a** *f* Asian.
asidero *m* hold(er), handle; *fig.* handle, pretext.
asiduo 1. assiduous; frequent, regular, persistent; **2.** *m*, **a** *f* habitué, regular.
asiento *m* seat, place; site *de pueblo etc.*; ⚗ settling; (*fondo*) bottom; sediment; (*partida*) entry; ⚓ trim; seat(ing) *de válvula*; *fig.* stability; (*cordura*) wisdom, judgement; **~s** *pl.* buttocks; ~ *lanzable* ✈ ejection seat; *tome Vd.* ~ take a seat.
asignación *f* assignment *etc.*; † allowance, salary; **asignar** [1a] assign, apportion; *premio* award; *tarea* set; *causas* determine; **asignatorio** *m S.Am.* heir; inheritor; **asignatura** *f univ.* course, subject.
asilado *m*, **a** *f* inmate.
asilo *m eccl. a. pol.* asylum; *fig.* shelter, refuge; home *de viejos*; poorhouse, workhouse *de pobres*; ~ *de huérfanos* orphanage; ~ *para locos* lunatic asylum.
asimetría *f* asymmetry; **asimétrico** asymmetric(al).
asimilación *f* assimilation; **asimilar** [1a] assimilate; = *asemejar(se)*.
asimismo likewise, in like manner.
asir [3a; *present like salir*] *v/t.* seize, grasp (*con* with, *de* by); *pie etc.* catch, get caught (*en* in); *v. brazo*; *v/i.* ⚘ take root; **~se** *a*, ~ *de* take hold of, seize (*a. fig.*); ~ *con* grapple with.
asirio Assyrian.
asistencia *f* attendance (*a.* ⚕), presence (*a* at); (*ayuda*) help; (domestic) help; *S.Am.* boarding house; *Mex.* visitors' room; ⚕ nursing; **~s** *pl.* allowance, maintenance; ~ *médica* medical attendance; ~ *social* welfare (work); **asistenta** *f* assistant; (*criada*) cleaning woman; daily help; **asistente** *m* assistant; ⚔ orderly; **~s** *pl.* people present, those present; **asistir** [3a] *v/t.* help, aid; *rey etc.* attend, accompany; ⚕ attend; *v/i.* attend (*a acc.*), be present (*a* at); *escena freq.* be a witness of.
asma *f* asthma; **asmático** *adj. a. su. m*, **a** *f* asthmatic.
asna *f* (female) ass; **asnada** *f* silly thing; foolish act; **asnal** asinine (*a. fig.*); F beastly; **asnería** *f* silly thing; **asno** *m* donkey, ass (*a. fig.*); F fathead.
asociación *f* association; society; † partnership; **asociado 1.** associate(d); **2.** *m*, **a** *f* associate, partner; **asociar** [1b] associate (*a*, *con* with); *esfuerzos etc.* pool, put together; *categoría etc.* bracket (*con* with); *socio* take into partnership; **~se** associate; team up, join forces (*con* with); † become partners, enter into partnership.
asol(an)ar [1a] ⚘ dry up, parch.
asolar [1m] destroy, raze (to the ground), lay waste; **~se** (*líquido*) settle.
asoleada *f*, **asoleadura** *f S.Am.* sunstroke; **asolear** [1a] put (*or* keep) in the sun; **~se** sun o.s., bask; (*tostarse*) get sunburned.
asomada *f* brief appearance; surprise view; **asomar** [1a] *v/t.* show, put out, stick out (*a*, *por* at, through); (*falda etc.*) let *s.t.* show; *v/i.* begin to show, appear; loom up *en niebla etc.*; **~se** show, stick out; (*costa etc.*) loom up; ~ *a*, ~ *por* show o.s. at, lean (*or* hang) out of; F get merry.
asombradizo easily alarmed; **asombrador** = *asombroso*; **asombrar** [1a] shade, cast a shadow on; *color* darken; *fig.* (*asustar*) frighten; (*admirar*) amaze, astonish; **~se** be amazed (*de* at); be shocked; ~ *de inf.* be surprised to *inf.*; **asombro** *m* fear, fright; surprise, astonishment; F spook; **asombroso** amazing, astonishing.
asomo *m* appearance; sign, indication; hint, trace; *ni por* ~ by no means.
asonada *f* mob, rabble.

asonancia *f* assonance; *fig.* *no tener* ~ *con* bear no relation to; **asonantar** [1a] assonate (*con* with); **asonante 1.** assonant; **2.** *f* assonance; **asonar** [1m] assonate.

asordar [1a] deafen.

aspa *f* cross (X); ⩓ cross piece; sail *de molino*; ⊕ reel, winding frame; **aspado** F trussed up (*en* in); **aspar** [1a] ⊕ wind, reel; F vex, annoy; ~**se** writhe; F go all out (*por* for).

aspaventero 1. fussy; excitable, emotional; **2.** *m*, **a** *f* fussy *etc.* person; **aspaviento** *m* fuss.

aspecto *m* aspect; look(s), appearance *de p. etc.*; aspect, side *de problema*; *a(l) primer* ~ at first sight; *bajo ese* ~ from that point of view.

aspereza *f* roughness *etc.* (*v.* *áspero*).

asperges *m* F sprinkling; *quedarse* ~ come away empty-handed.

asperillo *m* sourness; bitterness.

asperjar [1a] sprinkle (*eccl.* with holy water).

áspero rough *al tacto*; *filo* jagged; *terreno* rough; *país* rugged; tart, sour, bitter *al gusto*; *voz* harsh, rasping; *clima* hard; *trato* surly, gruff; *genio* sour, surly; **asperón** *m* sandstone; ⊕ grindstone.

aspersión *f* sprinkling; ✓ spraying.

áspid *m* asp.

aspillera *f* loophole, embrasure.

aspiración *f* breath; inhalation; *phonet.* aspiration; ♪ short pause; ⊕ air intake; **aspirada** *f* aspirate; **aspirado** aspirate; **aspirador 1.** ⊕ suction *attr.*; **2.** *m* ~ *de polvo* = **aspiradora** *f* vacuum cleaner; **aspirante 1.** ⊕ suction *attr.*; **2.** *m/f* applicant, candidate (*a* for); **aspirar** [1a] *v/t.* breathe in, inhale; *phonet.* aspirate; ⊕ suck in; *v/i.* aspire (*a* to; *a inf.* to *inf.*).

aspirina *f* aspirin.

asquear [1a] *v/t.* loathe; *v/i.* feel loathing, feel disgust; **asqueroso** loathsome, disgusting, nasty; sickening; F lousy, awful; *p.* (*delicado*) squeamish.

asta *f* shaft *de lanza etc.*; (*lanza*) spear, lance; flagstaff *de bandera*; (*mango*) handle; *zo.* horn; *a media* ~ at half-mast.

ástaco *m* crayfish.

astado 1. horned; **2.** *m* bull.

aster *m* aster.

asterisco *m* asterisk.

astigmático astigmatic; **astigmatismo** *m* astigmatism.

astil *m* handle; shaft *de saeta*; beam *de balanza*.

astilla *f* splinter, chip; *hacer(se)* ~*s* = **astillar(se)** [1a] splinter, chip; ~**se** F be (full to) bursting; **astillero** *m* shipyard, dockyard.

astracán 1. F grotesque; **2.** *m* astrakhan.

astrágalo *m* ⩓, ⚔ astragal; ⩓ beading; *anat.* talus, astragalus.

astral of the stars, astral.

astreñir [3h *a.* 3i] = *astringir*; **astringente 1.** astringent, binding; **2.** *m* astringent, binding medicine; **astringir** [3c] *anat.* contract; ⚕ bind; *fig.* bind, compel.

astro *m* star (*a. cine*), heavenly body; F beauty; **astrología** *f* astrology; **astrológico** astrological; **astrólogo 1.** astrological; **2.** *m* astrologer; **astronauta** *m* astronaut; **astronave** *f* spaceship; ~ *tripulada* staffed spaceship; **astronavegación** *f* space travel; astronavigation; **astronomía** *f* astronomy; **astronómico** astronomical (*a. fig.*); **astrónomo** *m* astronomer.

astroso dirty, untidy, shabby; (*desgraciado*) unfortunate; (*vil*) contemptible.

astucia *f* astuteness *etc.*; (*una* ~) trick, piece of trickery.

asturiano *adj.a. su. m*, **a** *f* Asturian.

astuto astute, shrewd, smart; *b.s.* crafty, cunning.

asueto *m* (*a. día de* ~) day off, holiday; (*tarde*) afternoon off.

asumir [3a] assume, take on; *actitud* strike.

asunción *f* assumption; *eccl.* ♀ Assumption.

asunto *m* matter, thing; (*negocio*) business, affair; (*tema*) subject; ~ *concluido* that's an end of the matter; ~*s pl. exteriores* foreign affairs; *Ministerio de* ♀*s Exteriores* State Department.

asurar [1a] burn; ✝ parch; *fig.* worry.

asustadizo easily frightened; jumpy, panicky F; *caballo* skittish; **asustar** [1a] frighten, scare; startle, alarm; ~**se** be frightened *etc.* (*con, de, por* of, at).

atabal *m* kettledrum; **atabalear**

[1a] (*caballo*) stamp; drum *con dedos*; **atabalero** *m* kettledrummer.

atacable attackable; **atacado** irresolute; (*tacaño*) mean, stingy; **atacador 1.** *m*, **-a** *f* attacker; **2.** *m* ⚔ ramrod; **atacadura** *f* fastening, fastener; **atacar** [1g] (*embestir*) attack (*a.* ♫, ⚕, *fig.*); corner, press hard *en discusión*; (*atar*) fasten, button, do up; ⚒, *cañón* ram, tamp; *costal etc.* stuff, pack.

ataderas *f/pl.* F garters; **atadero** *m* (*cuerda*) rope, cord; (*parte*) place for tying; (*broche etc.*) fastening; (*anillo*) ring; F *eso no tiene* ~ you can't make head or tail of it; **atadijo** *m* F loose bundle; **atado 1.** *fig.* timid, shy, inhibited; **2.** *m* bundle; (*manojo*) bunch; **atadora** *f* ⚘ binder; **atadura** *f* (*acto*) fastening *etc.*; (*cuerda*) string, cord; ⚓ lashing; ⚘ tether; *fig.* bond, tie.

atafagar [1h] suffocate, overcome; *fig.* pester the life out of.

ataguía *f* coffer dam, caisson.

atajar [1a] *v/t.* stop, intercept; head off; *deportes*: tackle; ⚠ partition off; *escrito* cross off; *discusión* cut short; *discurso* interrupt; (*terminar*) call a halt to, put a stop to; *v/i.* take a short cut; *mot.* cut corners; **~se** be abashed; (*nervioso*) be all of a dither F; **atajo** *m* short cut (*a. fig.*); *deportes*: tackle; *echar por el* ~ *fig.* get out of it, get out quick.

atalaya 1. *f* watchtower; *fig.* height, vantage point; **2.** *m* lookout, sentinel; **atalayador** *m*, **-a** *f* lookout; *fig.* snooper, spy; **atalayar** [1a] watch (over), guard; *p.* spy on.

atañer [2f; *defective*]: ~ *a* concern; *en lo que atañe a* with regard to; *no me atañe* it's no concern of mine.

ataque *m* attack (*a, contra* on; ⚕ *de* of; *a. fig.*); ✈ *a.* raid; ~ *al corazón*, ~ *cardíaco* heart attack; ⚕ ~ *fulminante* stroke, seizure; ~ *por sorpresa* surprise attack.

atar [1a] tie (up), fasten; ⚘ tether; *fig.* paralyse, root to the spot; F ~ *corto a* keep a close watch on; F *no* ~ *ni desatar* talk nonsense; get nowhere; **~se** *fig.* get stuck (*en dificultades* in); ~ *a opinión* stick to.

atardecer 1. [2d] get dark, get late; **2.** *m* late afternoon, evening; *al* ~ at dusk.

atareado very busy; **atarear** [1a] give a job to, assign a task to; **~se** be very busy (*con, en* with); ~ *a inf.* be very busy *ger.*

atarjea *f* sewage pipe, culvert.

atarugar [1h] (*asegurar*) fasten, wedge, peg; *agujero* plug, stop; (*llenar*) stuff, fill (*de* with); F shut *s.o.* up; **~se** F swallow the wrong way, choke.

atascadero *m* mire, bog; *fig.* stumbling block; difficulties; **atascar** [1g] *agujero* plug, stop; *tubo* obstruct (*a. fig.*), clog (up); **~se** ⊕ *etc.* clog, get stopped up; get stuck, get bogged down (*en fango* in; *a. fig.*); (*coches*) get into a jam; (*motor*) stall; get stuck *en discurso*; **atasco** *m* obstruction; *mot. etc.* jam.

ataujía *f* ⊕ damascene (work), damask.

ataviar [1c] (*adornar*) deck, array; (*vestir*) dress up, get up (*con, de* in).

atávico atavistic.

atavío *m* (*a.* **~s** *pl.*) dress, finery; *sl.* glad rags.

atavismo *m* atavism.

ataxia *f* ataxy.

atediante boring, tiresome; **atediar** [1b] bore, tire.

ateísmo *m* atheism; **ateísta** atheistic(al).

atelaje *m* team; (*arreos*) harness.

atemorizar [1f] scare, frighten; **~se** get scared (*de, por* at).

atemperar [1a] moderate, temper; adjust, accommodate (*a* to).

atención *f* attention; (*cortesía*) *a.* civility; ¡~! attention!; (*aviso*) look out!; (*en paquete*) with care; **~es** *pl.* attentions; duties, responsibilities; *en* ~ *a* in view of; *llamar la* ~ attract *s.o.'s* attention; *llamar la* ~ *sobre* draw *s.o.'s* attention to; *prestar* ~ listen (*a* to); pay attention (*a* to); **atender** [2g] *v/t.* attend to, pay attention to; ⚕ look after; *consejo, voz* heed; ⊕ service; *v/i.*: ~ *a* = *v/t.*; *detalles etc.* take note of; *necesidad etc.* see about, see to; ~ *por* answer to the name of.

atenerse [2l]: ~ *a verdad* stand by, hold to; *regla* abide by, go by; *fuerzas etc.* rely on.

ateniense *adj. a. su. m/f* Athenian.

atentado 1. prudent, cautious; **2.** *m* illegal act, offense; assault (*contra* on), attempt (*a, contra vida* on); (*terrorista etc.*) outrage; **atentar**

[1a] *v/t. acto* do illegally; *crimen* attempt; *v/i.*: ~ *a*, ~ *contra* make an attempt on.

atento attentive (*a* to), observant (*a* of); mindful (*a pormenor* of); (*cortés*) polite, thoughtful, kind; ~ *a prp.* in view of; † *su* ~*a carta* your esteemed letter; *atentamente le saluda* yours faithfully.

atenuación *f* attenuation; ⚖ extenuation; **atenuante:** ⚖ *circunstancias* ~*s* extenuating circumstances; **atenuar** [1e] attenuate; *delito* extenuate; *importancia* minimize; ~**se** weaken.

ateo 1. atheistic(al); **2.** *m*, **a** *f* atheist.

aterciopelado velvety; velvetized; velvet *attr.*

aterido numb, stiff with cold; **aterirse** [3a; *defective*] get stiff with cold.

aterrada *f* ⚓ landfall.

aterrador frightening, terrifying.

aterraje *m* ✈ landing.

aterrar[1] [1k] *v/t.* demolish, destroy; cover with earth; *v/i.* ✈ land; ~**se** ⚓ stand inshore; *navegar aterrado* sail inshore.

aterrar[2] [1a] terrify, fill with terror; ~**se** be terrified (*de* at); panic.

aterrizaje *m* ✈ landing; ~ *forzoso* (*o forzado*) forced landing; ~ *a vientre* pancake landing; ~ *sin choque* soft landing; ~ *violento* crash landing; **aterrizar** [1f] ✈ land.

aterronarse [1a] get lumpy; (*tierra*) cake.

aterrorizar [1f] terrify; *pol. etc.* terrorize.

atesorar [1a] hoard (up); *virtudes* possess.

atestación *f* attestation; **atestado** *m* ⚖ affidavit, statement.

atestado[1] (*terco*) stubborn.

atestado[2] *p.p.* cram-full (*de* of), packed (*de* with); **atestar**[1] [1k] pack, stuff, cram (*de* with); *cuba* fill up; F stuff (*de comida* with).

atestar[2] [1a] attest, testify to.

atestiguación *f* deposition; attestation; **atestiguar** [1i] testify to, attest; bear witness to.

atezado tanned, swarthy; black; **atezar** [1f] blacken; ~**se** get tanned.

atiborrar [1a] stuff (*de* with); ~**se** stuff (*o.s.*) (*de* with), gorge (*de* on).

ático 1. Attic; **2.** *m* △ attic.

atierre *m* cave-in; *S.Am.* (land)fill.

atiesar [1a] stiffen; (*apretar*) tighten (up); ~**se** get stiff, stiffen (up) *etc.*; △ *etc.* bind.

atigrado 1. striped; *gato* tabby; **2.** *m* tabby (cat).

atildado neat, spruce, stylish; **atildar** [1a] *typ.* put a tilde over; *fig.* criticize, find fault with; (*asear*) clean (up), put right; ~**se** titivate, spruce *o.s.* up.

atinado (*discreto*) wise; *juicio* keen; *dicho* pertinent; **atinar** [1a] *v/t.* find, hit on; *v/i.* guess (right); be right, do the right thing; ~ *a blanco* hit; ~ *a*, ~ *con*, ~ *en solución etc.* hit on, guess (right); ~ *a inf.* manage to *inf.*

atiparse [1a] F stuff o.s., guzzle.

atiplado treble; **atiplarse** [1a] speak with a high (*or* squeaky) voice.

atirantar [1a] make taut; brace; ~**se** *Mex.* die, pass away.

atisbadero *m* peephole; **atisbador** *m*, **-a** *f* watcher, spy; **atisbar** [1a] spy on, watch; peep at *por agujero etc.*; **atisbo** *m* watching, spying; *fig.* slight sign, inkling, glimmerings.

atizador *m* poker; ⊕ feed(er); ~ *de la guerra* warmonger; **atizar** [1f] (*remover*) poke, stir; stoke *con combustible*; *vela* snuff; *fig.* rouse, stir up; F *puntapié* give; *¡atiza!* gosh!

atizonar [1a] ♀ blight, smut.

atlas *m* atlas.

atleta *m/f* athlete; *fig.* giant; *sl.* jock; **atlético** athletic; *deportes* ~*s* = **atletismo** *m* athletics.

atmósfera *f* atmosphere; *fig.* sphere (of influence); feeling *hacia una p.*; *radio*: *mala* ~ atmospherics; **atmosférico** atmospheric.

atocinado F fat, well-upholstered; well-padded; **atocinar** [1a] *puerco* cut up; *carne* cure; F do in, cut up; ~**se** F (*irritarse*) get huffish; (*enamorarse*) F get it bad.

atolón *m* atoll.

atolondrado thoughtless, reckless; **atolondramiento** *m* bewilderment; amazement; thoughtlessness; **atolondrar** [1a] stun, bewilder, amaze.

atolladero *m* mire, muddy spot; F

estar en un ~ be in a hole; **atollarse** [1a] stick in the mud; *fig.* get into a hole.
atómico atomic; *energía* ~*a* atomic power (*or* energy); **atomizador** *m* atomizer; (scent) spray; **átomo** *m* atom (*a. fig.*); *fig.* tiny particle, speck; spark *de vida*.
atonal atonal; **atonalidad** *f* atonality, serial music; **atonía** *f* atony; **atónico** atonic.
atónito thunderstruck (*con, de, por* by); aghast (*con, de, por* at).
átono atonic, unstressed.
atontado dim(-witted), muddle-headed; **atontar** [1a] bewilder, confuse.
atorar [1a] obstruct, stop up; ~**se** choke, swallow the wrong way.
atormentador *m*, **-a** *f* tormentor; **atormentar** [1a] torture (*a. fig.*); *fig.* torment; plague; (*aliciente*) tantalize.
atornillar [1a] (*poner*) screw on; (*apretar*) screw up; *dos cosas* screw together.
atortillar [1a] *S.Am.* squash, flatten.
atortolar [1a] F (*acobardar*) rattle; (*aturdir*) flabbergast.
atortujar [1a] squeeze flat.
atosigar [1h] poison; *fig.* harass, plague; put the pressure on.
atrabancado *Mex.* rash; thoughtless; **atrabancar** [1g] rush; ~**se** be in a fix; **atrabanco** *m* hurry.
atrabiliario *fig.* difficult, moody, morose; **atrabilis** *f fig.* difficult temperament, bad temper.
atracada *f S.Am.* quarrel; row; **atracadero** *m* berth, wharf; **atracador** *m* gangster, holdup man; **atracar** [1g] *v/t.* ⚓ bring alongside, tie up; *p.* hold up, waylay; F stuff; *v/i.* come alongside, tie up; ~ *al muelle* berth, dock; ~**se** F stuff (*o.s.*) (*de* with), overeat.
atracción *f* attraction; attractiveness, appeal *de p.*; (*diversión*) amusement; ~*es pl. thea.* entertainment; (*cabaret*) floor show; ~ *sexual* sex appeal.
atraco *m* holdup; **atracón** *m* F blowout; *darse un* ~ make a pig of o.s. (*de* over).
atractivo 1. attractive; *fuerza* of attraction; *fig.* charming, engaging, fetching F; **2.** *m* = *atracción*;

atraer [2p] attract; draw; *imaginación etc.* appeal to; *atención a.* engage; *dejarse* ~ *por* allow o.s. to be drawn to(wards).
atragantarse [1a] choke (*con* on), swallow the wrong way; F get all mixed up, lose the thread.
atramparse [1a] fall into a trap; (*tubo*) clog; (*pestillo*) stick, catch; F get stuck, get into a hole.
atrancar [1g] *v/t. puerta* bar; *tubo* clog, stop up; *v/i.* F take big steps; skip a lot *leyendo*; **atranco** *m* = *atascadero*.
atrapamoscas *f* Venus's-flytrap; **atrapar** [1a] F nab, catch; *empleo etc.* get, land (*o.s.*); (*engañar*) take in.
atrás *ir* back(wards); *estar* behind; (*tiempo*) previously; *de* ~ back *attr.*; *desde muy* ~ a long time (ago); *días* ~ days ago; *hacia* ~ back, backwards; *marcha* ~ *mot.* reverse (gear); **atrasado** slow (*a. reloj*), late, behind (time); overdue; *país* backward; (*pobre*) poor, needy; ~ (*en los pagos*) behind, in arrears; ~ *de noticias* behind the times; **atrasar** [1a] *v/t.* slow up, slow down, retard; *reloj* put back; *v/i.* (*reloj*) lose; *mi reloj atrasa* (*10 minutos*) my watch is (10 minutes) slow; ~**se** be behind; be slow, be late; ✝ be in arrears; **atraso** *m* slowness *de reloj*; (*demora*) time lag, delay; backwardness *de país*; ✝ ~*s pl.* arrears; ~*s pl.* backlog *de pedidos etc.*; *salir del* ~ make up leeway.
atravesada *f S.Am.* crossing; **atravesado** (*ojo*) squinting, cross-eyed; *animal* mongrel, cross-bred; *fig.* wicked; **atravesar** [1k] (*cruzar*) go over, go across, cross (over); *madero etc.* lay across (*en la calle* the street); pierce (*con, de bala* with); *periodo etc.* go through; *dinero* bet, stake; *S.Am.* ✝ monopolize, corner; F *le tengo atravesado* I can't stand him; ~**se** (*espina*) get stuck; *se me atraviesa* X I can't stand X; ~ *en conversación* butt into; *negocio ajeno* meddle in.
atrayente = *atractivo*.
atrenzo *m S.Am.* trouble, fix.
atreverse [2a] dare (*a inf.* to *inf.*); ~ *a empresa* (dare to) undertake; *competidor* compete with; ~ *con(tra)* be cheeky to; **atrevido** daring, bold; *b.s.* forward, impudent; **atrevimiento** *m* daring, boldness;

(spirit of) adventure; *b.s.* impudence.
atribución *f* attribution; functions, powers *de cargo*; **atribuible** attributable; **atribuir** [3g]: ~ *a* attribute to, put *s.t.* down to; *funciones* assign to; **~se** assume, claim for o.s.
atribular(se) [1a] grieve.
atributivo attributive (*a. gr.*); **atributo** *m* attribute.
atrición *f eccl.* attrition; ⚕ bruise.
atril *m eccl.* lectern; ♪ music stand; ♪ rostrum *de director*; book rest.
atrincherar [1a] entrench, fortify (with trenches); **~se** entrench, dig in.
atrio *m* inner courtyard, atrium (*a.* [*eccl.*, *anat.*]).
atrocidad *f* atrocity, outrage; F (*dicho*) stupid remark; F *¡qué ~!* how dreadful!
atrofia *f* atrophy; **atrofiar(se)** [1b] atrophy.
atronado reckless, thoughtless; **atronador** deafening; *aplausos* thunderous; **atronamiento** *m fig.* stunning; bewilderment; **atronar** [1m] deafen; *res* stun; *fig.* bewilder.
atropelladamente pell-mell, helter-skelter; **atropellado** hasty *en obrar*; brusque, abrupt *en hablar*; **atropellar** [1a] **1.** *v/t.* (*pisar*) trample underfoot; (*derribar*) knock down (*a. mot.*); (*empujar*) push past; hustle *por puerta*; *héroe* mob; *trabajo* hurry through; *obligación* disregard; *oposición* ride roughshod over; (*injuriar*) insult, outrage; **2.** *v/i.*: ~ *por* push one's way through; *fig.* disregard; **3. ~se** act *etc.* hastily; **atropello** *m mot.* accident; *fig.* outrage, excess; disregard (de for).
atroz atrocious, outrageous; F terrific, huge.
atuendo *m* pomp, show; (*vestido*) rig, attire.
atufar [1a] *fig.* anger, vex; **~se** (*comida*) go smelly; (*vino*) turn sour; *fig.* get vexed (*con*, *de* at, with).
atún *m* tunny; F nitwit.
aturar [1a] F close (up) tight.
aturdido thoughtless, reckless; **aturdimiento** *m fig.* bewilderment *etc.*; **aturdir** [3a] stun, daze *con golpe*; (*vino etc.*) fuddle, stupefy; *fig.* (*desconcertar*) bewilder, perplex; (*pasmar*) stun, dumbfound; (*confundir*) confuse, fluster; **~se** be stunned; get bewildered *etc.*
aturrullar [1a] F bewilder, perplex muddle.
atusar [1a] trim *con tijeras*; smooth *con mano*; comb *con peine*; **~se** dress swankily.
audacia *f* boldness, audacity; **audaz** bold, audacious.
audible audible; **audición** *f* hearing; ♪ (*prueba*) audition; ♪ concert; **audiencia** *f* audience (*con* with, of); hearing (*a.* ⚖); ⚖ (*tribunal*) high court; **audífono** *m* earphone; hearing aid; **audiofrecuencia** *f* audiofrequency; **audión** *m* audion; **audiovisual** audiovisual; **auditivo 1.** hearing *attr.*, auditory; **2.** *m teleph.* earpiece, receiver; **auditor** *m* (*a.* ~ *de guerra*) judge-advocate; **auditorio** *m* (*ps.*) audience; (*sala*) auditorium.
auge *m* peak, summit; heyday; (*aumento*) increase; ✝ boom; *estar en ~* thrive, be in its heyday; ✝ boom.
augurar [1a] (*cosa*) augur, portend; (*p.*) predict; **augurio** *m* augury, omen, portent; prediction; **~s** *pl. fig.* best wishes.
augusto august; stately.
aula *f* classroom; *univ.* lecture room; ~ *magna* assembly hall.
aulaga *f* furze, gorse.
aullar [1a] howl; **aullido** *m*, **aúllo** *m* howl.
aumentador *m* ⚡ booster; **aumentar** [1a] *v/t.* increase, add to, augment; enlarge (*a. phot.*); *opt.* magnify; *precio* increase, put up; ⚡, *producción etc.* boost, step up; *v/i.*, **~se** (be on the) increase; rise, go up; (*valor*) appreciate; **aumentativo** *gr.* augmentative; **aumento** *m* increase, rise; enlargement (*a. phot.*); *opt.* magnification; *Mex.*, *Guat.* postscript; addition; ✝ ~ (*en valor*) appreciation; *ir en ~* (be on the) increase.
aun even; ~ (*siendo esto*) *así* even so; ~ *cuando* although; *ni ~* not even.
aún still, yet; ~ *no ha venido* he still has not come, he has not come yet.
aunar [1a] join, unite; **~se** join up, combine.
aunque although, even though; ~ *más* however much.
¡aúpa! up (you get)!; *¡~ Madrid!*

up Madrid!; F de ~ posh, swanky; **aupar** [1a] F help up; *pantalón* hitch up; *fig.* boost, praise up.
aura *f* (gentle) breeze; *fig.* popularity, popular favour.
áureo *poet.* golden; **aureola** *f*, **auréola** *f opt. a. eccl.* aureole; *opt. a. fig.* halo.
aurícula *f* auricle; **auricular** **1.** auricular, of the ear, aural; **2.** *m anat.* little finger; *teleph.* receiver, earpiece; ~**es** *pl.* earphones, headphones; headset.
aurora *f* dawn (*a. fig.*); ~ *boreal*, ~ *polar* aurora borealis.
auscultar [1a] ⚕ sound, auscultate.
ausencia *f* absence; **ausentarse** [1a] go away, absent o.s.; stay away; **ausente** **1.** absent; missing (de from); away from home; **2.** *m/f* absentee; ⚖ missing person.
auspiciar [1b] *S.Am.* support, foster; **auspicio** *m fig.* protection, patronage; *bajo los* ~*s de* under the auspices of.
austeridad *f* austerity *etc.*; **austero** austere; *p.* stern, severe; *sabor* harsh.
austral southern.
australiano *adj. a. su. m*, **a** *f* Australian.
austríaco *adj. a. su. m*, **a** *f* [Austrian.]
austro *m* south wind.
autarquía *f* autarchy, self-sufficiency.
auténtica *f* certificate; authorized copy; **autenticar** [1a] authenticate; **autenticidad** *f* authenticity; **auténtico** authentic, genuine, real.
auto[1] *m* ⚖ edict, judicial decree; writ (*de ejecución* of execution); *thea. approx.* mystery play; ~*s pl.* ⚖ documents, proceedings; ~ *de fe* auto-da-fé; ~ *del nacimiento* nativity play; ~ *sacramental* eucharistic play; F *estar en* ~*s* be in the know; F *poner en* ~*s* put *s.o.* in the picture.
auto[2] *m mot.* car.
auto[3] ... self-..., auto...; ~**abastecimiento** *m* self-sufficiency; ~**adhesivo** self-adhesive; ~**biografía** *f* autobiography; ~**biográfico** autobiographic(al); ~**biógrafo** *m*, **a** *f* autobiographer; ~**bombo** *m* self-advertisement; *hacer* ~ shoot a line; ~**bote** *m* motorboat; ~**bús** *m* (omni)bus; ~**camión** *m* motor truck; ~**car** *m* (motor) coach; ~**casa** *f* trailer; mobile home.
autocracia *f* autocracy; **autócrata** *m/f* autocrat; **autocrático** autocratic.
autocrítica *f* self-examination, self-criticism.
autóctono autochthonous.
autodefensa *f* self-defense; **autodestrucción** *f* self-destruction.
autodeterminación *f* self-determination; **autodidacta** self-educated, self-taught; **autodominio** *m* self-control; **autódromo** *m* race-track; **auto-escuela** *f* driving school; **autoexpresión** *f* self-expression; **autógena** *f* welding.
auto...: ~**giro** *m* autogiro; ~**gobierno** *m* self-government; ~**grafía** *f* autography; ~**gráfico** autographic; **autógrafo** *adj. a. su. m* autograph; ~**limpiador**, ~**limpiante** self cleaning.
autómata *m* automaton (*a. fig.*), robot; *fig.* puppet; **automático** automatic; self-acting.
auto...: ~**matización** *f* automation; ~**motor** *m* Diesel train; ~**motriz** self-propelled; ~**móvil** **1.** self-propelled; **2.** *m* car, automobile; *ir en* ~ go by car; ~**movilismo** *m* motoring; ⊕ car industry; ~**movilista** **1.** (*a.* ~**movilístico**) motoring; car *attr.*, automobile *attr.*; **2.** *m/f* motorist.
autonomía *f* autonomy, home rule; ⚓, ✈ range; *de gran* ~ long-range; **autónomo** autonomous, independent.
autopiano *m S.Am.* player-piano.
autopista *f* motorway, motor road, turnpike.
autopropulsado self-propelled.
autopsia *f* postmortem, autopsy.
autor *m*, **-a** *f* author, writer; perpetrator *de crimen*; creator, originator *de idea*; **autora** *f* authoress; **autoridad** *f* authority; *fig.* show, pomp; ~*es pl.* authorities; **autoritario** authoritarian; peremptory, dogmatic; **autorización** *f* authorization, licence (*para inf.* to *inf.*); **autorizado** authorized; official; **autorizar** [1f] authorize (*a inf.* to *inf.*); license; give (*or* lend) authority to.
autorretrato *m* self-portrait.
autorzuelo *m* scribbler, hack.

autoservicio *m* self-service restaurant.
autostop *m* hitchhiking; *hacer* ~ hitchhike.
auxiliar 1. auxiliary (*a. gr.*); subsidiary; **2.** *m/f* assistant; **3.** [1b] help, assist; **auxilio** *m* help, assistance; relief; ~ *social* social work; welfare (service); *primeros* ~*s pl.* first aid.
avahar [1a] *v/t.* blow on; *v/i.*, ~**se** (give off) steam.
aval *m* endorsement.
avalancha *f* avalanche.
avalar [1a] ✝ endorse (*a. fig.*); *p.* answer for.
avalent(**on**)**ado** arrogant, boastful.
avalorar [1a] = *valorar*; *fig.* encourage; **avaluar** [1e] = *valorar*.
avance *m* advance (*a.* ⚔); ✝ (*anticipo*) advance (payment), credit; balance; ⚡ lead; ⊕ feed; **avanzada** *f* ⚔ outpost; (*tropa*) advance party; **avanzado** advanced (*de edad* in years); *fig.* advanced, avant-garde; *hora* late; **avanzar** [1f] *v/t.* advance (*a.* ✝), move on, move forward; *proposición* advance, put forward; *v/i.*, ~**se** advance (*a.* ⚔); move on, push on; (*noche etc.*) advance, draw on; **avanzo** *m* ✝ balance (sheet); (*presupuesto*) estimate.
avaricia *f* miserliness, avarice; greed(iness); **avaricioso, avariento** miserly, avaricious; **avaro 1.** miserly, mean; greedy; sparing, chary (*de alabanzas* of); *ser* ~ *de palabras* be a man of few words; **2.** *m*, **a** *f* miser.
avasallar [1a] subdue, enslave; ~**se** *fig.* submit, yield.
avatar *m* change, transformation.
ave *f* bird; ~ *can(t)ora* songbird; ~ *de corral* chicken, fowl; *pl. a.* poultry; ~ *de paso* bird of passage (*a. fig.*), migrant; ~ *de rapiña* bird of prey; ~ *zancuda* wader.
avecin(**d**)**arse** [1a] take up one's residence, settle.
avechucho *m* ugly bird; F ragamuffin, ne'er-do-well; bum.
avefría *f* lapwing.
avejentar(**se**) [1a] age (before one's time).
avejigar(**se**) [1h] blister.
avellana *f* hazelnut; **avellanado** *color* hazel, nut-brown; *piel etc.* shriveled, wizened; **avellanar 1.** *m* hazel wood; **2.** [1a] ⊕ countersink; ~**se** shrivel up; **avellanera** *f*, **avellano** *m* hazel.
avemaría *f* Ave Maria; Hail Mary; ¡℘! goodness gracious!; *al* ~ at dusk; F *en un* ~ in a twinkling; F *saber como el* ~ know inside out.
avena *f* oat(s); *de* ~ oaten; *copos de* ~ rolled oats.
avenado a bit mad.
avenamiento *m* drainage; **avenar** [1a] drain.
avenencia *f* agreement, bargain; ✝ deal.
avenida *f* avenue; flood, spate *de río*; (*afluencia*) gathering.
avenir [3s] reconcile; ~**se** come to an agreement, be reconciled (*con* with); ~ *a inf.* agree to *inf.*; ~ *con* be in agreement with, conform to; *p.* get along with; F *¡allá te las avengas!* that's your problem.
aventador *m* ↗ winnowing fork; fan, blower *para fuego*; **aventadora** *f* winnowing machine.
aventajado outstanding, superior; ~ *de estatura* very tall; **aventajar** [1a] (*exceder*) surpass, outstrip, beat; (*preferir*) put *s.t.* first; ~ *con mucho* outclass; ~ *en un punto* go one better than; ~**se** *a* surpass; get the advantage of; **aventón** *m S.Am. mot.* push; lift; (free) ride.
aventar [1k] ↗ winnow; fan, blow (on); (*viento*) blow away; F throw out; ~**se** fill, swell (up); F beat it.
aventura *f* (*lance*) adventure; *b.s.* escapade; (*casualidad*) chance, coincidence; (*riesgo*) risk, danger; **aventurado** risky, hazardous; **aventurar** [1a] venture; *vida* risk, hazard; *capital* stake; ~**se** venture, take a chance; ~ *a inf.* venture to *inf.*, risk *ger.*; **aventurera** *f* adventuress; **aventurero 1.** adventurous; **2.** *m* adventurer; ⚔ soldier of fortune; fortune hunter, social climber *en sociedad*.
avergonzado ashamed (*de, por* at); *expresión* shamefaced; **avergonzar** [1f *a.* 1m] (put to) shame; abash; embarrass; ~**se** be ashamed (*de, por* of, at, about; *de inf.* to *inf.*).
avería[1] *f orn.* aviary; (*bandada*) flock of birds.
avería[2] *f* damage; *mot. etc.* breakdown; fault *de construcción*; **averiado** damaged; *mot. quedar* ~ have a breakdown; **averiar** [1c] damage; ~**se** get damaged.

averiguable ascertainable; **averiguación** *f* ascertainment *etc.*; **averiguar** [1i] find out, ascertain; look up *en libro*; investigate, inquire into; *C.Am.*, *Mex.* get into a fight; **~se** *con* F tie *s.o.* down; (*entenderse*) get along with.
aversión *f* aversion (*hacia*, *por algo* to; *a alguien* for); disgust, distaste; *cobrar* ~ *a* take a strong dislike to.
avestruz *m* ostrich.
avetado veined, streaked, grained.
avetoro *m* bittern.
avezado accustomed; **avezar** [1f] accustom; **~se** get accustomed (*a* to).
aviación *f* aviation; (*cuerpo*) air force; **aviador** *m* aviator, airman, flyer; pilot.
aviar [1c] *v/t.* get ready, prepare; equip, provide (*de* with); F get *s.o.* ready; *S.Am.* lend; F *estar aviado* be in a mess; F *dejar aviado* leave *s.o.* in the lurch; *v/i.* F hurry up; *¡vamos aviando!* let's get a move on!
avícola *granja* chicken *attr.*, poultry *attr.*; **avicultor** *m* poultry farmer, poultry keeper; (*canarios etc.*) bird fancier; **avicultura** *f esp.* poultry keeping.
avidez *f* greed(iness), avidity; **ávido** greedy, avid (*de* for).
avieso distorted (*a. fig.*); *p.* perverse, wicked.
avilés *adj. a. su. m*, **-a** *f* (native) of Avila.
avillanado rustic, boorish.
avinagrado sour, jaundiced; embittered; **avinagrar(se)** [1a] (turn) sour.
avío *m* preparation, provision; *S.Am.* loan; *¡al ~!* get on with it!; *hacer su* ~ † make one's pile; *iro.* make a mess of it; *~s pl.* kit, tackle, gear; *iro.* paraphernalia.
avión *m* plane, airplane; aircraft; *orn.* martin; ~ *de caza* pursuit plane; ~ *de combate* fighter; ~ *de travesía* airliner; ~ *supersónico* supersonic aircraft; ~ *transporte* (air) transport; ~ *a chorro*, ~ *a reacción* jet plane; *en* ~ by air; ✉ *por* ~ (by) airmail; **avioneta** *f* light aircraft.
avisado prudent, wise; *mal* ~ rash; **avisador** *m*, **-a** *f* informant; *b.s.* informer; *thea. etc.* messenger; **avisar** [1a] inform, notify, let *s.o.* know; (*amonestar*) warn; ~ *con una semana de anticipación* give a week's notice; **aviso** *m* (*consejo*) advice; (*noticia*) piece of information, tip; (*advertencia*) warning; prudence, discretion; *con poco tiempo de* ~ at short notice; *hasta nuevo* ~ until further notice; *salvo* ~ *en contrario* unless otherwise informed; *según* (*su*) ~ as (you) ordered; *estar sobre* ~ be on the lookout.
avispa *f* wasp; F wily bird; **avispado** F wide awake, sharp; *S.Am.* startled; scared; **avispar** [1a] *caballo* spur on; F stir up, wake up; **~se** fret, be worried; **avispero** *m* wasps' nest (*a. fig.*); F mess; **avispón** *m* hornet.
avistar [1a] descry, sight; **~se** have an interview (*con* with).
avitaminosis *f* vitamin deficiency.
avituallar [1a] victual, provision.
avivar [1a] *fuego* stoke (up); *color*, *luz* make brighter; *fig.* enliven, revive; *interés* whip up; *efecto* enhance, heighten; *disputa* add fuel to; *combatientes* urge on; *v. ojo*; **~se** revive *etc.*
avizor 1.: *estar ojo* ~ be on the alert; **2.** *m* watcher; **~es** *pl. sl.* peepers; **avizorar** [1a] watch, spy on.
avutarda *f* great bustard.
axioma *m* axiom; **axiomático** axiomatic.
axiómetro *m* ⚓ telltale.
ay 1. *int. ¡~! dolor físico*: ouch!; *pena*: oh!, oh dear!; *rhet.* alas!; *admiración*: oh!; *¡~ de mí!* poor me!, it's very hard (on me)!; *¡~ del que ...!* woe betide the man who ...!; **2.** *m* sigh; groan, cry *de dolor*.
aya *f* governess.
ayear [1a] cry with pain; heave sighs.
ayer yesterday.
ayo *m* tutor.
ayuda 1. *f* help, aid, assistance; ⚕ enema; **2.** *m* page; ~ *de cámara* valet; **ayudador** *m*, **-a** *f*, **ayudante** *m/f* helper, assistant; *esp.* ⊕ mate; ⚔ adjutant; ~ *de laboratorio* laboratory assistant; **ayudantía** *f* assistantship; **ayudar** [1a] help, aid, assist (*a inf.* to *inf.*, in *ger.*); help out; (*servir*) be of use to, serve; ~ *a salir etc.* help *s.o.* out.
ayunar [1a] fast (*a* on); *fig.* go without; **ayunas:** *en* ~ without breakfast;

F *estar etc. en* ~ be (left) in the dark; (*no entender*) miss the point; **ayuno 1.** fasting; *fig.* without; F in the dark (de about); **2.** *m* fast(ing); *v. ayunas.*
ayuntamiento *m* town (*or* city) council; (*edificio*) town (*or* city) hall; ~ *sexual* sexual intercourse; *sl.* sex.
azabache *m min.* jet.
azacán *m*, **-a** *f* drudge.
azada *f* hoe; **azadón** *m* (large) hoe, mattock; **azadonar** [1a] hoe.
azafata *f* air hostess, stewardess.
azafrán *m* ⚘ crocus; *cocina*: saffron.
azahar *m* orange blossom.
azalea *f* azalea.
azar *m* (*el* ~) chance, fate; (*desgracia*) misfortune, piece of bad luck; *al* ~ at random; *v. juego*; **azararse** [1a] go wrong; (*p.*) get rattled; **azaroso** risky, hazardous, chancy; (*desgraciado*) unlucky; *vida* eventful.
ázimo unleavened.
azogado 1. *fig.* restless, fidgety; *temblar como un* ~ shake like a leaf; **azogar** [1h] *espejo* silver; **~se** F be restless, get agitated; **azogue** *m* mercury, quicksilver; F *ser un* ~ be always on the go; F *tener* ~ be fidgety.
azoico azoic.
azonzado *S.Am.* stupid; dumb.
azor *m* goshawk.
azoramiento *m* confusion; excitement; embarrassment; **azorar** [1a] disturb, upset; excite; embarrass; (*animar*) egg on; **~se** be disturbed *etc.*
azotacalles *m* loafer, lounger; gadabout; **azotado** variegated; **azotaina** *f* F spanking; **azotar** [1a] whip, flog; *niño* thrash, spank; (*mar, lluvia etc.*) lash; *calles* loaf around; **azotazo** *m* lash(ing); spank(ing) *en nalgas*; **azote** *m* whip, lash; (*golpe*) spank; *fig.* scourge; F **~s** *y galeras* the same old stuff.
azotea *f* flat roof, terrace (roof).
azteca *adj. a. su. m/f* Aztec.
azúcar *m a. f* sugar; ~ *blanco* castor sugar; ~ *cande* rock candy; ~ *de remolacha* beet sugar; ~ *moreno*, ~ *terciada* brown sugar; ~ *en terrón* lump sugar; **azucarado** sugary, sweet (*a. fig.*); **azucarar** [1a] sugar; (*bañar*) coat with sugar; F sugar (over); *p.* sweeten; **azucarera** *f* sugar bowl; sugar refinery; **azucarero 1.** sugar *attr.*; **2.** *m* sugar bowl.
azucena *f* (Madonna) lily; ~ *atigrada* tiger lily.
azud *m*, **azuda** *f* water wheel; (*presa*) dam.
azuela *f* adze.
azufrar [1a] sulfur(ize ⊕); **azufre** *m* sulfur, brimstone.
azul 1. blue; **2.** *m* blue; blueness; ~ *celeste* sky-blue; ~ *de cobalto* cobalt blue; ~ *eléctrico* electric blue; ~ *de mar*, ~ *marino* navy blue; ~ *de Prusia* Prussian blue; ~ *de ultramar* ultramarine; **azulado** blue; bluish; **azular** [1a] dye (*or* color) blue.
azulejar [1a] tile; **azulejo** *m* glazed tile.
azulina *f* cornflower; **azulino** bluish.
azumbrado F tipsy, drunk; **azumbre** *m liquid measure = 2.016 liters.*
azuzar [1f] *perro* set on; *fig.* irritate; (*estimular*) egg on.

B

baba *f* spittle, slobber; *biol.* mucus; slime *de caracol*; *caérsele a uno la* ~ (*alegre*) jump for joy; (*bobo*) get soft; *echar* ~ slobber; F say nasty things (*contra* about); **babador** *m* bib; **babaza** *f* slime, mucus; *zo.* slug; **babear** [1a] slobber, drivel; F be sloppy, drool (over women).
babel *m or f* babel, bedlam; confusion, mess.
babeo *m* slobbering, drooling; **babero** *m* bib.
babieca F **1.** simple-minded, stupid; **2.** *m/f* blockhead, dolt.
babilonia *f* babel, bedlam.
babilonio *adj. a. su. m,* **a** *f* Babylonian.
babilla *f vet.* stifle.
bable *m* Asturian dialect.
babor *m* port (side), larboard; *de* ~ port, larboard *attr.*
babosa *f zo.* slug; **babosada** *f C.Am., Mex.* stupidity; foolish act; **babosear** [1a] slobber over, drool over (*a.* F *fig.*); **baboseo** *m* slobbering; F calf love, infatuation; **baboso** slobbering *etc.*; F sloppy (over women); (*adulón*) fawning, snivelling; (*sucio*) dirty; (*bobo*) silly.
babucha *f* slipper, mule.
baca *f* top *de autobús*; luggage hold *para equipaje*; (*cubierta*) rainproof cover.
bacalao *m*, **bacallao** *m* cod(fish); F wet fish, drip; F *cortar el* ~ be the boss; give the keynote *en conversación.*
bacanal 1. bacchanal(ian), bacchantic; **2.** *f* orgy; ~**es** *pl.* bacchanalia; **bacante** *f* bacchanal, bacchante; *fig.* drunken and riotous woman.
bacía *f* (barber's) bowl; basin, vessel.
bacilar bacillary; **bacilo** *m* bacillus, germ; ~ *de Koch* T.B. germ.
bacín *m* large chamber pot; beggar's bowl; F wretch; **bacineta** *f* small chamber pot; beggar's bowl.
bacteria *f* bacterium, germ; **bacteriano, bactérico** bacterial; **bacteriología** *f* bacteriology; **bacteriológico** bacteriological; **bacteriólogo** *m* bacteriologist.
báculo *m* staff (*a. eccl.*); *fig.* staff, prop, support.
bache *m* rut, (pot)hole; ~ *de aire* air pocket.
bachiller 1. garrulous; **2.** *m*, **-a** *f pupil who has passed his graduation exam*; † *univ.* bachelor; *fig.* windbag; **bachillerato** *m* bachelor's degree; graduation examination; **bachillerear** [1a] F prattle (away); **bachillería** *f* F prattle; (piece of) nonsense.
badajo *m* (bell) clapper; F chatterbox.
badajocense, badajoceño *adj. a. su. m,* **a** *f* (native) of Badajoz.
badana *f* (dressed) sheepskin; F *zurrar la* ~ *a* tan *s.o.'s* hide; *fig.* haul s.o. over the coals.
badén *m* gully; gutter.
badil *m*, **badila** *f* fire shovel, *approx.* poker.
badulaque *m* F nitwit, simpleton; *S.Am.* boor, ill-bred fellow.
bagaje *m* ⚔ baggage; (*acémila*) beast of burden; *fig.* equipment.
bagatela *f* trinket, knickknack; *fig.* trifle; ~**s** *pl.* trivialities, things of no importance.
bagre *S.Am.* showy; gaudy; coarse.
¡bah! *desprecio*: bah!, pooh!; *incredulidad*: hum(ph)!, ho!
bahía *f* bay.
bahorrina F slop, filth; *fig.* riffraff.
bailable 1. that you can dance to; **2.** *m* ballet; dance number; **bailadero** *m* dance hall, dance floor; **bailador** *m*, **-a** *f* dancer; **bailar** [1a] *v/t.* dance; *peonza etc.* spin; *v/i.* dance (*a. fig.*); (*peonza*) spin (around); (*retozar*) jump (about); F ~ *al son que tocan* conform; adapt o.s. to circumstances; F *éste es otro que bien baila* here's another one (of the same kind); **bailarín** *m*, **-a** *f* (professional) dancer; ballet dancer; *f thea.* ballerina; dancing girl; **baile** *m* (*acto*) dance; dancing; (*reunión*) ball, dance; *thea.* ballet; ~ *de candil*

village dance, hop; ~ *de etiqueta* dress ball, formal dance; ~ *de máscaras* masked ball; ~ *de San Vito* St Vitus's dance; ~ *de trajes* fancy (dress) ball; **bailotear** [1a] dance about, hop around.

baivel *m* ⚠ bevel.

baja *f* ✝ drop, fall; ⚔ casualty; (*puesto*) vacancy; ✝ *etc. dar* ~, *ir de* (*or en*) ~ lose value; *dar de* ~ mark absent; drop *de lista*; *darse de* ~ drop out, retire; F *seguir en* ~ go from bad to worse.

bajá *m* pasha.

bajada *f* slope; (*acto*) going down, descent; **bajamar** *f* low tide; **bajar** [1a] **1.** *v/t. objeto* take down, get down; lower, let down; *brazo, ojos, precio, voz etc.* lower; *p.* help down, lead down; *cabeza* bow, bend; *gas, radio etc.* turn down; *escalera* go down, descend; *fig.* humiliate; **2.** *v/i.* go down, come down (*a* to); (✝, *agua*) fall; 🚂 *etc.* get off, get out; ~ *de* get off, get out of; **3.** **~se** bend down; *fig.* lower o.s., humble o.s.

bajel *m lit.* vessel, ship.

bajero lower, under...; **bajeza** *f* meanness *etc.*; lowliness *etc.*; (*acto*) vile deed, mean thing; *v. bajo*.

bajío *m* shoal, sandbank; shallows; *S.Am.* lowland.

bajista *adj. a. su. m* ✝ bear.

bajo 1. *mst* low; *terreno* low(-lying); (*inferior*) lower, under(most); *agua* shallow; (*a.* ~ *de cuerpo*) short; *cabeza* bent, lowered; *ojos* downcast; *sonido, voz* deep, low; (*débil*) low, faint; *color* dull; *fig.* mean, common; *calidad* low, poor; *condición* low(ly); *tarea* menial; ~ *de ley* base; *por lo* ~ secretly; **2.** *m* deep place, depth; ⚓ = *bajío*; ♪ bass; ⚠ ground floor; **3.** *adv.* down; *hablar* in a low voice; **4.** *prp.* under(neath); *reinado* in; *punto de vista* from; *palabra, pena* on.

bajón *m* decline (*a.* ⚕) drop; slump [*en moral*; ♪ bassoon.

bajorrelieve *m* bas-relief.

bajura *f* lowness, lack of height; shortness *de p.*

bala *f* ⚔ bullet; ✝ bale; ~ *de cañón* cannon ball; ~ *perdida* stray shot; ~ *trazadora* tracer bullet; F *como una* ~ like a shot; *ni a* ~ *S.Am.* under no circumstances; **balaceo** *m S.Am.* shooting; shootout.

balada *f lit.*, ♪ ballad.

baladí trivial, paltry; low-class; cheap; *material* trashy.

baladrar [1a] scream, screech; **baladrero** noisy, riotous; **baladro** *m* scream, screech.

baladrón 1. boastful; **2.** *m*, **-a** *f* braggart; **baladronada** *f* boast; boasting; (*acto*) (piece of) bravado; **baladronear** [1a] boast, brag; (*acto*) show brave.

balalaika *f* balalaika.

balance *m* to-and-fro motion; rocking, swinging; ⚓ roll(ing); *fig.* hesitation; ✝ balance (sheet); ✝ stock taking *de existencias*; ~ *de comercio* balance of trade; ~ *de pagos* balance of payments; **balancear** [1a] *v/t.* balance; *v/i.*, **~se** rock, swing; ⚓ roll; *fig.* hesitate, waver, be in two minds; **balanceo** *m* = *balance*; **balancín** *m* balance beam; ⊕ beam; ⊕ (*eje*) rocker (arm); yoke *para transportar*; ⚓ outrigger; seesaw *de niños*; balancing pole *de volatinero*.

balandra *f* sloop; **balandrista** *m* yachtsman; **balandro** *m* yacht; small sloop.

balanza *f* scales, weighing machine; balance (*a.* ✝, ⚗); *ast.* ♎ Scales; *fig.* judgement; ~ *romana* steelyard; *en la* ~ in the balance.

balar [1a] bleat.

balastar [1a] 🚂 ballast; **balasto** *m* ballast.

balaustrada *f* balustrade; banisters *de escalera*; **balaustre** *m* baluster; banister *de escalera*.

balazo *m* shot; ⚕ bullet wound.

balbucear [1a], **balbucir** [3f; *defective*] stammer, stutter; babble; (*niño*) lisp, make the first sounds; **balbuceo** *m* stammer *etc.*

balcón *m* balcony; (*barandilla*) railing; *fig.* vantage point; **balconero** *m* cat burglar.

baldaquín *m* canopy, tester.

baldar [1a] cripple; *naipes*: trump; *fig.* put out, inconvenience.

balde[1] *m esp.* ⚓ (canvas) pail, bucket; (zinc) bath.

balde[2]: *de* ~ free, for nothing; (*sobrante*) over; *en* ~ in vain, for nothing.

baldear [1a] wash (down), swill; (*achicar*) bale out.

baldío uncultivated; waste; *argumento etc.* empty, baseless; *p.* idle.

baldón *m* affront, insult; (*oprobio*)

stain; **baldonar** [1a] insult; stain, disgrace.
baldosa *f* (floor) tile; **baldosado** *m* tiled floor; **baldosar** [1a] tile.
balduque *m* (official) red tape.
balear[1] [1a] *S.Am.* shoot (at).
balear[2] *adj. a. su. m/f*, **baleárico** (native) of the Balearic Isles; **baleo** *m S.Am.* shooting.
balido *m* bleat(ing).
balín *m* small bullet; ~*es pl.* (buck) shot.
balística *f* ballistics.
balita *f* small bullet; *S.Am.* marble.
baliza *f* (lighted) buoy, marker.
balneario 1. thermal, medicinal; spa, health *attr.*; *estación ~a* = **2.** *m* health resort, spa.
balompié *m* football.
balón *m* (foot)ball; ✝ bale; ~ *volea* volleyball; **baloncesto** *m* basketball; **balonmano** *m* handball.
balota *f* ballot, **balotar** [1a] ballot.
balsa[1] *f* ⚘ balsa.
balsa[2] *f geog.* pond; F *ser una ~ de aceite* be like the tomb, be as quiet as a mouse.
balsa[3] *f* ⚓ raft; **balsadera** *f*, **balsadero** *m* ferry.
balsámico balsamic, balmy; *fig.* soothing, healing; **bálsamo** *m* balsam, balm (*a. fig.*).
balsear [1a] *río* cross by ferry; *ps. etc.* ferry across; **balsero** *m* ferryman.
baluarte *m* bulwark (*a. fig.*).
balumba *f* (great) bulk; big pile; F confusion; row; **balumbo** *m* bulky thing.
ballena *f* whale; (*lámina*) whalebone; stay *de corsé*; **ballenera** *f* whaler; **ballenero 1.** whaling *attr.*; **2.** (*p. a. barco*) whaler.
ballesta *f* crossbow; ⚙, *mot.* spring; **ballestero** *m* crossbowman.
ballet [bæ'le] *m* ballet.
bambalear [1a] = *bambolear*; *fig.* not be safe (*or* firm).
bambalinas *f/pl. thea.* flies.
bambarria *m/f* F dolt.
bambolear(se) swing, sway; (*mueble*) wobble; roll, reel *al andar*; **bamboleo** *m* sway(ing) *etc.*
bambolla *f* F show, ostentation; fuss; **bambollero** F showy, flashy.
bambú *m* bamboo.
banal banal; *p.* superficial, commonplace.
banana *f* banana (tree); *prov. a. S.Am.* banana; **bananal** *m* banana plantation; **bananero 1.** banana *attr.*; **2.** *m* = **banano** *m* banana (tree).
banasta *f* large basket, hamper; **banastro** *m* large round basket.
banca *f* (*asiento*) bench; (*frutería*) fruit stall; ✝ banking; *juegos*: bank; *hacer saltar la ~* break the bank; **bancada** *f* stone bench; ⊕ bench; ⚓ thwart; **bancal** *m* ✓ patch, plot; (*rellano*) terrace; **bancario** ✝ bank *attr.*, banking *attr.*; financial; **bancarrota** *f* (*esp.* fraudulent) bankruptcy; *fig.* failure; *hacer ~* go bankrupt; **banco** *m* (*asiento*) bench (*a.* ⊕), form *esp. en escuela*; ✝ bank; ⚓ bank, shoal; (*peces*) shoal; *min.* stratum, layer; *~ de ahorros* savings bank; *~ de arena* sandbank; *~ de crédito* credit bank; *~ de liquidación* clearing house; *~ de sangre* blood bank.
banda *f* (*faja*) sash, band; (*cinta*) ribbon; zone, strip; ♪, *radio*: band; side *de mar, barco*; *billar*: cushion; (*ps.*) band, gang; *orn.* flock; *~ de rodamiento* tread; *~ sonora* sound track; *de la ~ de acá* (on) this side; F *cerrarse a la ~* stand firm; **bandada** *f* flock (*a. fig.*), flight.
bandearse [1a] move to and fro; *fig.* get along, shift for o.s.
bandeja *f* tray; salver; *S.Am.* (meat *etc.*) dish.
bandera *f* flag, banner; ⚔ colors; *~ de parlamento* flag of truce, white flag; *~ de proa* jack; *a ~s desplegadas* in the open; *con ~s desplegadas* with flying colors (*a. fig.*); *dar a uno la ~* give pride of place to s.o.; **bandería** *f* faction; **banderilla** *f* banderilla; F *poner una ~ a* taunt; give *s.o.* what for; **banderín** *m* little flag; pennant; ⚔ recruiting office; ⚙ signal; **banderita** *f* small flag; *día de la ~* flagday; **banderola** *f* (signaling) flag; ⚔ pennant, pennon.
bandidaje *m* banditry; **bandido** *m* bandit; outlaw; desperado; F rascal; F *co.* ¡~! you little rat!, you so-and-so!; **banditismo** *m* banditry.
bando *m* edict, proclamation; faction, party; ~*s pl.* marriage banns.
bandolera *f* bandoleer; **bandolerismo** *m* brigandage, banditry; **bandolero** *m* brigand, bandit.
bandullo *m* F guts, belly.
bandurria *f* bandurria (*a kind of lute*).

banjo *m* banjo.
banquero *m* banker (*a. juegos*).
banqueta *f* stool.
banquetazo *m* F spread, feast; **banquete** *m* banquet; (*esp. en casa particular*) dinner party; **banquetear** [1a] banquet, feast.
banquillo *m* bench; footstool; ⚖ *approx.* dock.
banquisa *f* ice field; (*trozo*) ice floe.
bañador 1. *m*, **-a** *f* bather; **2.** *m* ⊕ tub, trough; (*traje*) bathing outfit; **bañar** [1a] bathe; bath *en bañera*; dip (*a.* ⊕); (*mar*) bathe, wash; *fig.* bathe (*con, de, en* in); (*luz etc.*) bathe, flood, fill, suffuse (*de* with); *estar bañado en agua de rosas* walk on air; **~se** bath *en bañera*; bathe *en mar etc.*; *ir a ~* go for a bath; **bañera** *f* bath(tub); **baño** *m* bath (*a.* ⊕, ⚕); (*bañera*) bath(tub); (*en general*) bathing; *paint.* coating, wash; *cocina*: coating; *~s pl.* ⚕ baths; spa; *~ de asiento* hip bath; *~ de ducha* shower; *~ turco* Turkish bath; F *dar un ~ a* teach a lesson to; *ir a ~s* take the waters.
bao *m* ⚓ beam.
baque *m* thud, bump, bang; bruise.
baquelita *f* bakelite.
baqueta *f* ramrod; *~s pl.* ♪ drumsticks; *a la ~* severely, harshly; tyrannically; *correr ~s* run the gauntlet; **baqueteado** inured, used to it; *ser un ~* know one's way about; **baquetear** [1a] *fig.* bother, put out; **baqueteo** *m* imposition, awful bind F.
bar *m* bar, *approx.* public house; snack bar.
barahunda *f* uproar; racket, din; hubbub.
baraja *f* pack (of cards); *fig.* confusion, mix-up; **barajadura** *f* shuffling, shuffle; **barajar** [1a] *v/t.* shuffle; *fig.* mix up, shuffle around; *v/i.* quarrel; **~se** get jumbled up, get mixed up.
baranda *f* rail(ing); *billar*: cushion; **barandal** *m*, **barandilla** *f* rail(ing), hand rail; banisters *de escalera*; balustrade.
barata *f Col., Mex.* junk shop; rummage sale; **baratear** [1a] sell cheaply; sell at a loss; **baratero** cheap; **baratía** *f S.Am.* cheapness; **baratija** *f* trinket, trifle; ✝ *freq.* novelty; *~s pl.* cheap goods, *b.s.* junk; **baratillo** *m* (*géneros*) second-hand goods; (*tienda*) second-hand shop, junk shop; (*puesto*) bargain counter; (*venta*) bargain sale; *de ~* gimcrack;
barato 1. cheap; *de ~* for nothing; *dar de ~* admit (for the sake of argument), grant; *echar* (*or meter*) *a ~* heckle, barrack; **2.** *m* bargain sale; F *cobrar el ~* (be a) bully; **baratura** *f* cheapness.
baraúnda *f* = *barahunda*.
barba 1. *f* chin; (*pelo*) beard (*a.* ⚘); whiskers; *orn.* wattle; *~ cerrada, ~ bien poblada* full beard; *~s pl. de chivo* goatee; *~ honrada* distinguished personage; *a ~ regalada* abundantly, fully; *en las ~s de* under the (very) nose of; *por ~* apiece, per head; *decir algo en sus propias ~s a* say s.t. to *s.o.* to his face; *hacer la ~* shave (o.s.); *hacer la ~ a* shave; *fig.* (*fastidiar*) pester; (*adular*) fawn on; **2.** *m thea.* old man's part; (*malo*) villain.
barbacoa *f S.Am.* barbecue.
barbado 1. bearded; **2.** *m* ⚘ seedling; *plantar de ~* transplant; **barbar** [1a] grow a beard; ⚘ strike root.
barbárico barbaric; **barbaridad** *f* barbarity (*a. fig.*); *fig.* atrocity, outrage; F huge amount; *~es pl. fig.* nonsense; terrible things, awful things; naughty things; F *una ~* (*como adv.*) terribly, awfully; *nos divertimos una ~* we had a tremendous time; *¡qué ~!* how awful!;
barbarie *f* barbarism, barbarousness; (*crueldad*) barbarity; **barbarismo** *m gr.* barbarism; *fig.* = *barbaridad*; F lack of polish;
bárbaro 1. *hist.* barbarian, barbarous; *fig.* barbarous, cruel; (*arrojado*) daring; (*inculto*) rough, unpolished; F smashing, tremendous; F *¡qué ~!* my (goodness)!; **barbarote** *m* F brute.
barbear [1a] be as tall (*or* high) as (*a. v/i. ~ con*).
barbechar [1a] leave fallow; (*arar*) plow for sowing; **barbechera** *f*, **barbecho** *m* fallow (land); *firmar como en un barbecho* sign a blank check.
barbería *f* barber's (shop); (*oficio*) hairdressing; **barbero 1.** *m* barber, hairdresser; **2.** *Mex. adj.* flattering; fawning.
barbi...: **~cano** gray-bearded, white-bearded; **~hecho** freshly

shaven; **~lampiño** smooth-faced, beardless; **~lindo** dapper, spruce; *b.s.* dandified.
barbilla *f* (tip of the) chin.
barbiponiente F beginning to grow a beard; *fig.* raw, novice.
barbo *m* barbel.
barbón *m* man with a beard; *zo.* billy goat; F graybeard.
barbot(e)ar [1a] mutter, mumble;
barboteo *m* mutter(ing) *etc.*
barbudo bearded; with a long beard.
barbulla *f* uproar, clamor, hullabaloo; **barbullar** [1a] babble away, talk noisily.
barca *f* (small) boat; ~ *de pesca*, ~ *pesquera* fishing boat; **barcada** *f* boat load; (*viaje*) boat trip, crossing; **barcaza** *f* lighter, barge; ~ *de desembarco* landing craft.
barcelonés *adj. a. su. m*, **-a** *f* (native) of Barcelona.
barcia *f* chaff.
barco *m* boat; (*grande*) ship, vessel; ~ *cisternas m* tanker; ~ *de guerra* warship; ~ *minero* collier; ~ *náufrago* shipwreck; ~ *de vela* sailing ship.
barda *f* thatch (on wall); **bardal** *m* thatched wall.
bardana *f* burdock.
bardar [1a] thatch.
bardo *m* bard.
baremo *m* (*escala*) scale; rate table.
bario *m* barium.
barítono *m* baritone.
barjuleta *f* knapsack; ⊕ tool bag.
barlovento *m* windward.
barman *m* bartender.
barniz *m* varnish; *cerámica*: glaze; ✈ dope; (*afeite*) make-up; *fig.* veneer; smattering *de conocimientos*; *dar de* ~ varnish; **barnizado** *m* varnishing; **barnizar** [1f] varnish; polish; glaze.
barométrico barometric(al); **barómetro** *m* barometer.
barón *m* baron; **baronesa** *f* baroness; **baronía** *f* barony.
barquero *m* boatman, waterman;
barquía *f* skiff, row(ing) boat.
barquilla *f* ✈ gondola, nacelle, car; ⚓ log.
barquillero *m* wafer seller; **barquillo** *m cocina*: *approx.* horn, cone, rolled wafer; (*helado*) cornet.
barquinazo *m* F tumble, hard fall; *mot.* jolt; (*vuelco*) spill, overturning.
barra *f* bar (*a.* ⚓, ⚖, *fig.*); ⊕ rod; ⚖ *a.* dock; stick, bar *de jabón etc.*; *heráldica*: bend; ~ *de cortina* curtain rod; ~ *de labios* lipstick; ~*s pl. paralelas* bars; *las* ~*s de Aragón* the pallets of Aragon; *llevar a la* ~ bring *s.o.* to justice; *no pararse en* ~*s* stick (*or* stop) at nothing.
barraca *f* hut, cabin; *esp.* Valencian thatched house; *S.Am.* storage shed.
barragana *f* concubine.
barranca *f*, **barranco** *m* gully, ravine; *fig.* obstacle.
barrar[1] [1a] daub, smear.
barrar[2] [1a], **barrear** [1a] barricade.
barredera *f* (street)sweeper; ~ *de alfombras* carpet sweeper; **barredura** *f* sweep(ing); ~*s pl.* sweepings; (*desperdicios*) refuse; **barreminas** *m* minesweeper.
barrena *f* auger; bit, drill *de berbiquí etc.*; (*esp.* ~ *de mano*) gimlet; ✈ spin; ⚒ ~ *de percusión* jumper; ✈ *entrar en* ~ go into a spin;
barrenar [1a] drill (through); ⚓ scuttle; F upset, make a mess of; ⚖ violate, infringe.
barrendero *m*, **a** *f* sweeper.
barrenillo *m zo.* borer; **barreno** *m* large drill, borer; (*agujero*) bore, bore hole; ⚒ blast hole; ⚓ *dar* ~ *a* scuttle.
barreño *m* washbowl; (dish)pan.
barrer [2a] *v/t.* sweep (out, clean *etc.*); (*a. fig.*) sweep away; clear (*de* of); ⚔, ⚓ rake; *v/i.* sweep; F ~ *hacia dentro* look after number one.
barrera *f* barrier (*a. fig.*), rail; ⚔ *etc.* barricade; ~ (*de fuego*) barrage; 🚂 level-crossing gate; *fig.* obstacle; refuge, help; ~ *de fuego móvil* creeping barrage; ~ *de portazgo* tollgate, turnpike; ~ *racial* color bar; ~ *del sonido* (*o* ~ *sónica*) sound barrier.
barriada *f* quarter, district.
barrial *m S.Am.* mudhole; muddy ground.
barrica *f* large barrel.
barricada *f* barricade.
barrido *m* = *barredura*; F *vale tanto para un* ~ *como para un fregado* he can turn his hand to anything.
barriga *f* belly (*a. de vasija*); △ bulge; **barrigón**, **barrigudo** potbellied.
barril *m* barrel; *de* ~ *cerveza etc.*

draught *attr.*; **barrilero** *m* cooper; **barrilete** *m* keg; ⊕ dog, clamp; chamber *de revólver*.
barrio *m* quarter, district; suburb; F *el otro* ~ the other world; ~*s pl. bajos* poor quarter, working-class district; *b.s.* slums, slum area.
barrisco: *a* ~ jumbled together; indiscriminately.
barritar [1a] (*elefante*) trumpet.
barrizal *m* muddy place, mire; **barro** *m* mud; *cerámica*: clay; (*búcaro*) earthenware pot; *anat.* pimple (on the face); ~*s pl.* earthenware; crockery; *de* ~ *búcaro etc.* earthen(ware); F *tener* ~ *a mano* be in the money.
barroco 1. baroque; *lit.* mannered, full of conceits; *b.s.* extravagant, in bad taste; **2.** *m* the Baroque (style *etc*); **barroquismo** *m* baroque style; extravagance.
barroso muddy; mud-colored; *cara* pimply.
barrote *m* (heavy) bar.
barruntar [1a] guess, conjecture; **barrunte** *m* sign, indication; **barrunto** *m* guess, conjecture; = *barrunte*.
bartola: *tumbarse a la* ~ be lazy, take it easy.
bartolina *f C.Am.* cell; dungeon; [jail.]
bártulos *m/pl.* things, belongings, bits and pieces; goods; ⊕ tools; kit; F *liar los* ~ pack up (one's traps); F *preparar los* ~ get ready, get set.
barullo *m* uproar, din.
barzón *m* saunter, stroll; *dar* ~*es* = **barzonear** [1a] stroll around, wander around.
basa *f* ⚠ base (of a column); *fig.* basis, foundation.
basáltico basaltic; **basalto** *m* basalt.
basar [1a] base; *fig.* base, found, ground (*sobre* on); ~**se** *en* be based on; base o.s. on, rely on.
basca *f* ⚕ (*mst* ~*s pl.*) queasiness, nausea; F fit of rage, tantrum; *dar* ~*s a* make *s.o.* sick, turn *s.o.*'*s* stomach; **bascosidad** *f* filth, dirt; **bascoso** ⚕ queasy; squeamish; *S.Am.* filthy.
báscula *f* scale, weighing machine; **basculante** *m* tip-up truck; **báscula-puente** *f* weighbridge; **bascular** [1a] tilt, tip up; (*oscilar*) rock to and fro; *pol. etc.* swing.
base *mst* base; ⊕ mount(ing); bed; *surv.* base (line); *fig.* basis, foundation; ~ *aérea* air base; ~ *avanzada* forward base; ~ *naval* naval base; *a* ~ *de* on the basis of; by means of;
básico ⚗ basic.
basílica *f esp. hist.* basilica; *eccl.* large church, privileged church.
basilisco *m* basilisk; F *estar hecho un* ~ be hopping mad.
basquear [1a] feel sick; *hacer* ~ *a* make *s.o.* sick, turn *s.o.*'*s* stomach.
basquetbol *m* basketball.
basquiña *f* skirt.
basta *f* tacking stitch.
bastante 1. *adj.* enough (*para* for; *para inf.* to *inf.*); **2.** *adv.* (*que basta*) enough; (*más o menos*): ~ *bueno* quite good, fairly good, rather good; **bastantemente** sufficiently, fully;
bastar [1a] be enough, be sufficient (*para inf.* to *inf.*); suffice, be (quite) enough; *¡basta!* that's enough!; right!, stop!; *¡basta ya!* that's quite enough (of that)!; *basta y sobra* that's more than enough; ~**se** *a sí mismo* be self-sufficient.
bastardear [1a] *v/t.* debase; adulterate; *v/i.* ⚘ *a. fig.* degenerate; fall away (*de* from); **bastardía** *f* bastardy; *fig.* wicked thing; **bastardilla:** (*letra*) ~ italic(s); *en* ~ in italics; *poner en* (*letra*) ~ italicize; **bastardo** *adj. a. su. m,* **a** *f* bastard; ⚠ *etc.* hybrid.
bastear [1a] *sew.* baste, tack.
bastedad *f* coarseness; roughness; *C.Am.* abundance; excess.
bastidor *m* frame (*a. sew.,* ⊕); frame, case *de ventana etc.*; (*con lienzo*) stretcher; *thea.* wing; *thea. a. fig. entre* ~*es* behind the scenes; (*de*) *entre* ~*es* off-stage; *dirigir entre* ~*es* work the oracle.
bastilla *f* hem; **bastillar** [1a] hem.
bastimentar [1a] supply, provision; **bastimento** *m* supply, provision; ⚓ vessel.
basto 1. coarse, rough; (*grosero*) rude, ill-mannered; **2.** *m* pack-saddle; *naipes*: ~*s pl.* clubs.
bastón *m* (walking) stick; ⚔ *etc.* baton; *heráldica*: pallet, pale; *fig.* control, command; ~ *de estoque* swordstick; ~ *de mando* baton; sign of authority; ~ *de montaña* walking stick; *empuñar el* ~ take charge; *meter el* ~ intervene; **bastonazo** *m* blow

with a stick; caning; **bastonear** [1a] beat (with a stick), cane; **bastonero** *m* master of ceremonies.
basura *f* rubbish, refuse; (*esp. papeles*) litter; (*polvo*) dust; ⚘ dung, manure; **basural** *m S.Am.* dump; trash pile; garbage heap; **basurero** *m* (*p.*) dustman; scavenger; (*sitio*) rubbish dump; ⚘ dungheap.
bata *f* dressing gown; housecoat; négligée; smock *de encinta*; ⚗ *etc.* laboratory coat.
batacazo *m* thud, bump.
bataclán *m S.Am.* burlesque show.
batahola *f* F hullabaloo, rumpus.
batalla *f* battle; *esp. fig.* fight, contest; *fig.* (inner) struggle, agitation (of mind); *mot.* wheel base; ~ *campal* pitched battle; *librar* (*trabar*) ~ do (join) battle; **batallador** *m* fighter; *fenc.* fencer; **batallar** [1a] battle, fight (*con* with, against, *por* over); *fig.* vacillate, waver; **batallón 1.** *cuestión etc.* vexed; **2.** *m* battalion.
batán *m* fulling mill; (*máquina*) fulling hammer; **batanar** [1a] full, beat; F = **batanear** [1a] F (*zurrar*) give *s.o.* a hiding; (*sacudir*) give *s.o.* a shaking; **batanero** *m* fuller.
bataola *f* = *batahola*.
batata *f* sweet potato, yam; *S.Am.* bashfulness.
batatazo *m* F stroke of luck, fluke.
batayola *f* ⚓ rail.
batea *f* (*bandeja*) tray; (*artesilla*) deep trough; ⚓ flat-bottomed boat; 🚂 truck, wagon, flatcar.
batel *m* small boat; skiff; **batelero** *m* boatman.
batería *f mst* battery; ⚡ bank *de luces*; *thea.* footlights; ~ *de cocina* kitchen utensils; **baterista** *m/f* ♪ drummer.
batiboleo *m Cuba, Mex.* noise; confusion.
batida *f* ⚔, *hunt.* drive; ⚔ reconnaissance; *fig.* search; **batidero** *m* continuous beating (*or* striking); rough ground; F coming and going; **batido 1.** *seda* shot, chatoyant; *camino* well-trodden, beaten; **2.** *m cocina*: batter; ~ (*de leche*) milkshake; **batidor** *m* ⊕, *hunt.* beater; ⚔ scout; (*peine*) comb; = *batidora*; **batiente** *m* (*marco*) jamb *de puerta*; frame, case *de ventana*; (*hoja*) leaf *de puerta*; ♪ damper; ⚓ open coast line; **batidora** *f* whisk; ⚡ (electric) mixer;
batintín *m* gong.
batir [3a] **1.** *v/t. metall., hunt.*, ⚔, *adversario, alas, huevos, marca* beat; *campo, terreno* comb, reconnoitre; *casa* knock down; *costa* beat (on); *crema* whip; *chocolate* mill; *manos* clap; *mantequilla* cream; *moneda* mint; *pelo* comb; *privilegio* do away with; *talones, vuelo* take to; *tiendas* strike; *toldo etc.* take down; (*sol*) beat down on; **2.** *v/i.* ⚘ beat (violently); **3.** ~**se** (have a) fight.
batiscafo *m* bathyscaphe.
batista *f* cambric, batiste.
bato *m* simpleton.
batracio *adj. a. su. m* batrachian.
batucar [1g] shake (up).
batueco *m* F stupid, silly.
batuque *m S.Am.* F to-do, rumpus.
baturrillo *m* hotchpotch.
baturro 1. uncouth; **2.** *m*, **a** *f* Aragonese peasant.
batuta *f* ♪ baton; F *llevar la* ~ be the boss, rule the roost.
baúl *m* (⚓ cabin) trunk; F corporation; ~ *mundo* large (*or* Saratoga) trunk; ~ *ropero* wardrobe trunk.
bauprés *m* bowsprit.
bausán *m* dummy, straw man; F simpleton.
bautismal baptismal; **bautismo** *m* baptism; F *romper el* ~ *a* break *s.o.*'s nut; **Bautista** *m*: *El* ~, *San Juan* ~ St. John the Baptist; **bautisterio** *m* baptistery; **bautizar** [1f] baptize (*a. fig.*); *fig.* name, give a name to; F *vino* water; F *p.* drench, soak; **bautizo** *m* baptism; christening.
bauxita *f* bauxite.
baya *f* berry.
bayeta *f* baize; (*trapo*) floor cloth.
bayo 1. biscuit(-colored); *caballo* bay *approx.*; **2.** *m approx.* bay (horse).
bayoneta *f* bayonet; **bayonetazo** *m* bayonet thrust, bayonet wound.
bayu(n)ca *f C.Am.* bar; tavern.
baza *f naipes*: trick; F *hacer* ~ get on; F *meter* ~ butt in, shove one's oar in; *meter* ~ *en* interfere in; F *no dejar meter* ~ *a* not let *a p.* get a word in edgeways.
bazar *m* bazaar.
bazo 1. yellowish-brown; **2.** *m anat.* spleen.
bazofia *f* leftovers; (pig)swill, hogwash (*a. fig.*); *fig.* vile thing, filth.
bazucar [1g], **bazuquear** [1a] stir,

shake; **bazuqueo** *m* stirring, shaking; ~ *gástrico* rumblings (in the stomach).
be[1]**:** *por* ~ down to the last detail; *tener algo las tres* ~*s* be really very nice.
be[2] *m* baa.
beata *f* lay sister; sister of charity; F devout woman; *b.s.* goody-goody; **beatería** *f* cant, sanctimoniousness; **beatificación** *f* beatification; **beatificar** [1g] beatify; **beatitud** *f* beatitude, blessedness; *Su* ♀ His Holiness; **beato 1.** happy, blessed; pious; *b.s.* hypocritical; sanctimonious, canting; **2.** *m approx.* lay brother; F devout man.
bebé *m* baby.
bebedero 1. drinkable, good to drink; **2.** *m* drinking trough; spout *de vasija*; **bebedizo 1.** drinkable; **2.** *m* ⚕ potion; † philtre, (love) potion; **bebedor 1.** hard-drinking, bibulous; **2.** *m*, **-a** *f* (hard) drinker, toper; **beber 1.** *m* drink(ing); **2.** *v/t.* drink (up); *esp. fig.* drink in, imbibe; ~ *con la lengua* lap up; ~ *de* drink out of; *v/i.* drink (*a. b.s.*); ~ *mucho*, ~ *a pote* drink a lot, be a heavy drinker; **beberrón** = *bebedor*; **bebezón** *m S.Am.* drinking spree; **bebible** drinkable, good to drink; **bebida** *f* drink (*a. alcohol*); beverage; ~ *alcohólica* liquor, alcoholic drink; *dado a la* ~ hard-drinking, given to drink; **bebido** tipsy, merry; **bebistrajo** *m* F filthy stuff (to drink).
beca *f* scholarship, grant (for study); insignia; **becario** *m*, **a** *f* scholar, scholarship holder.
becerrillo *m* calf skin; **becerro** *m* yearling calf; ⊕ calf skin; *eccl.* record (book).
becuadro *m* ♪ natural (sign).
bedel *m esp. univ. approx.* porter.
beduino 1. *adj. a. su. m*, **a** *f* Bedouin; **2.** *m fig.* barbarian.
befa *f* jeer; **befar** [1a] scoff at, jeer at.
befo 1. thick-lipped; (*zambo*) knock-kneed; **2.** *m* lip.
begonia *f* begonia.
beige [beis] *m* beige.
béisbol *m* baseball; **beisbolero** (*a.* **beisbolista**) *m* baseball player.
bejuco *m* liana.
beldad *f* beauty (*a. p.*).
belén *m eccl.* crib, nativity scene; *fig.* confusion, bedlam; (*lance*) risky venture.
beleño *m* henbane.
belfo = *befo*.
belga *adj. a. su. m/f*, **bélgico** Belgian.
belicista militaristic, war-minded; **bélico** warlike; *material etc.* war *attr.*; **belicoso** warlike; militant; **beligerancia** *f* belligerancy; militancy, warlike spirit; **beligerante** *adj. a. su. m/f* belligerent.
belitre *m* rogue, scoundrel.
belvedere *m* belvedere.
bellaco 1. wicked; astute, sly, cunning; **2.** *m*, **a** *f* scoundrel, rogue; miscreant; (*astuto*) knowing one.
belladona *f* deadly nightshade, belladonna (*a.* ⚕).
bellaquear [1a] cheat, be crooked; *S.Am.* (*caballo*) rear; *fig.* be stubborn; **bellaquería** *f* (*acto*) dirty trick; (*dicho*) mean (*or* nasty) thing to say; (*maldad*) wickedness.
belleza *f* beauty, loveliness; (*p.*) beauty, lovely thing; **bello** beautiful, lovely; *lo* ~ *ideal* beau ideal.
bellota *f* ♀ acorn; perfume box; F *anat.* Adam's apple.
bemol *m* ♪ flat; F *esto tiene muchos* ~*es* this is a tough one.
bencedrina *f* benzedrine.
benceno *m* benzene; **bencina** *f mot.* benz(ol)ine.
bendecir [*approx.* 3p] bless; consecrate; (*alabar*) praise, extol; ~ *la mesa* say grace; **bendición** *f* blessing, benediction; ~ (*de la mesa*) grace; ~*es pl. nupciales* wedding ceremony; *echar la* ~ give one's blessing (*a. fig.*); F *echar la* ~ *a* say good-bye to; have no more to do with; F *llovía que era una* ~ you should have seen how it rained; **bendito** saintly, blessed; *agua* holy; (*feliz*) happy; F simple (-minded); **benedícite** *m* grace; **benedictino** *adj. a. su. m* Benedictine (*a. licor*); F *ser obra de* ~ be a long job.
beneficencia *f* (*virtud*) doing good; charity; (*obra*) benefaction; (*fundación*) charity, charitable organization; **beneficiado** *m eccl.* incumbent, beneficiary; **beneficial:** *terreno* ~ glebe(land); **beneficiar** [1b] *v/t.* benefit, be of benefit to; ⚒ cultivate; ⚒ *mina* exploit, work;

material process, smelt; ✝ sell at a discount; *empleo* bribe one's way into; *S.Am.* (*ganado*) slaughter; *v/i.* be of benefit; **~se** de take advantage of; *S.Am.* shoot dead; **beneficiario** *m*, **a** *f* beneficiary; **beneficio** *m* benefit, good; (*donativo*) benefaction; *eccl.* living, benefice; ✝, ⚒, ✓ yield, profit; ⚒ processing, smelting; *thea.* benefit (performance); *a ~ de* for the benefit of; **beneficioso** beneficial, useful, profitable; **benéfico** good (*a, para* for); *obra etc.* charitable (*para con* towards).
benemérito worthy, meritorious; *un ~ de la patria* a national hero; *la* ℒ*a* the Civil Guard, the police.
beneplácito *m* approval, consent.
benevolencia *f* benevolence, kind(li)ness; **benévolo** benevolent, kind(ly); well-disposed (*con* to, towards).
benignidad *f* kind(li)ness *etc.*; **benigno** kind(ly); gracious, gentle; *clima* kindly, mild; ⚕ mild; *tumor* benign.
benito = *benedictino.*
benjamín *m* baby (of the family); favourite child.
beodez *f* drunkenness; **beodo** drunk(en).
bequista *m/f C.Am., Cuba* scholarship holder; grant winner.
berberecho *m zo.* cockle.
berberí, berberisco Berber.
berbiquí *m* (carpenter's) brace; *~ y barrena* brace and bit.
bereber *adj. a. su. m/f* Berber.
berenjena *f* aubergine, eggplant; **berenjenal** *m* aubergine bed; *fig* fine how-d'ye-do, fine pickle; *en buen ~ nos hemos metido* we've got ourselves into a fine mess.
bergante *m* scoundrel, rascal.
bergantín *m* brig.
berilo *m* beryl.
bermejo red(dish), russet; *esp. pelo* red(dish), auburn; *gato* ginger; **bermellón** *m* vermilion.
bernardina *f* F tall story.
berrear [1a] low, bellow; F fly off the handle; **berrenchín** *m* F rage, tantrum; **berrido** *m* lowing, bellow(ing); ♪ screech (*a. fig.*); **berrinche** *m* F rage, tantrum.
berro *m* watercress.
berza *f* cabbage; F *mezclar ~s con capachos* be all over the place, jumble things up; **berzal** *m* cabbage patch.
besamanos *m* royal audience, levee.
besar [1a] kiss; *fig.* graze, touch; ⚓ *a ~* chock-a-block; *~ la mano, ~ los pies fig.* pay one's respects (*a* to); **~se** kiss (each other); *fig.* bump heads together; **beso** *m* kiss; *echar un ~ a* blow a kiss to.
bestia 1. *f* beast; *~ de carga* beast of burden; *~ negra* bête noire, pet aversion; **2.** *m/f* dunce, ignoramus; (*rudo*) boor; F beast; F *¡~!* you idiot!; F *¡no seas ~!* don't be an idiot!; **bestial** beastly, bestial; *apetito* terrific; F stunning, swell; **bestialidad** *f* bestiality; *fig.* (piece of) stupidity.
besucar [1g] F pet, neck.
besugo *m* sea bream; *fig. de ~ ojos* bulging; (*tristes*) like a spaniel's; **besuguera** *f* ⚓ fishing boat; *cocina:* fish pan.
besuquearse [1a] F pet, neck; **besuqueo** *m* F petting, necking.
bético *lit.* Andalusian.
betún *m* ⚗ bitumen; (*zapatos*) shoe polish, blacking; F *darse ~* swank, show off.
bezo *m* thick lip; ⚕ proud flesh; **bezudo** thick-lipped.
bi... bi...
biberón *m* feeding bottle.
Biblia *f* Bible; *fig. saber la ~* know everything; **bíblico** biblical.
bibliografía *f* bibliography; **bibliográfico** bibliographic(al); **bibliógrafo** *m* bibliographer; **bibliomanía** *f* bibliomania; **bibliómano** *m* bibliomaniac.
biblioteca *f* library; (*estante*) bookcase; *~ circulante* lending (*or* circulating) library; *~ de consulta* reference library; **bibliotecario** *m*, **a** *f* librarian.
bicarbonato *m*: *~ sódico, ~ de sosa* bicarbonate of soda; household soda.
biceps *m* biceps.
bici *f* F (push)bike; **bicicleta** *f* (bi)cycle; *andar en ~, ir en ~* ride a bicycle, (bi)cycle.
bicoca *f* F trifle.
bicolor two-color; *mot.* two-tone.
bicha *f euph.* snake; *fig.* bogy; **bichería** *m S.Am.* vermin; **bicho** *m* small animal, largish insect *etc.*, *S.Am.* bug; *toros:* fighting bull; *Mex.* cat; (*p.*) odd bird; *~s pl.* vermin; *mal ~ fig.*

nasty piece of work; *S.Am. de puro ~* out of spite; F *todo ~ viviente* every living soul; *S.Am. tener ~* have a raging thirst.
bidé *m* bidet.
bidón *m* drum, can.
biela *f* connecting rod.
bielda *f approx.* pitchfork; **bieldar** [1a] winnow; **bieldo** *m* winnowing rake.
bien 1. *m* good; (*beneficio*) advantage, profit; (*bienestar*) welfare, wellbeing; property, possession; *mi ~* (*p.*) my dear(est); *~ público* common good; *sumo ~* highest good; *en ~ de* for the good of; *hacer ~* do good; be charitable; **2. ~es** *pl.* wealth, riches; property, possessions; *~ dotales* dowry; *~ heredables* hereditament; *~ inmuebles, ~ raíces* real estate, realty; landed property; *~ mostrencos* unclaimed (*or* ownerless) property; *~ muebles* personal property; (goods and) chattels; *~ relictos* estate, inheritance; *~ de la tierra* produce; *~ vinculados* entail; *decir mil ~ de* speak highly of; **3.** *adv.* well; (*correctamente*) right; (*de buena gana*) gladly, readily; easily; *~ ... ~* either ... or; *~ (así) como* just as, just like; *de ~ en ~* better and better; *más ~* rather; *o ~* or else; *~ que mal* one way or another, by hook or by crook; **4.** (*como int.*) *¡~!* all right!, okay!; *¡muy ~!* (*a orador etc.*) hear hear!; yes indeed!; *¡hizo muy ~!* and he was quite right too!; **5.** *cj. ~ que, si ~* although; *a ~ que* perhaps; *no ~* no sooner, as soon as.
bienal biennial (*a. planta ~*).
bien...: ~andante happy; prosperous; **~andanza** *f* happiness; prosperity; **~aventurado** happy, fortunate; *eccl.* blessed; F simple, naïve; **~aventuranza** *f* well-being, prosperity; *eccl.* (state of) blessedness; *las ~s pl.* the Beatitudes; **~estar** *m* well-being, welfare; **~hablado** nicely-spoken; **~hadado** lucky; **~hechor 1.** beneficent; **2.** *m* benefactor; **~hechora** *f* benefactress; **~intencionado** well-meaning.
bienio *m* (period of) two years.
bien...: ~oliente fragrant; **~querencia** *f* affection; (*buena voluntad*) good will; **~querer 1.** [2u] like, be fond of; **2.** *m* affection; good will.
bienquistar [1a] bring together, reconcile; **~se** become reconciled; **bienquisto** well thought-of, well-liked (*con, de, por* by).
bienvenida *f* welcome; greeting; (*llegada*) safe arrival; *dar la ~ a* welcome; **bienvenido** welcome; *¡~!* welcome!
bienvivir [3a] live in comfort; live decently.
bifásico ⚡ two-phase.
bifocal bifocal.
biftec *m* (beef)steak.
bifurcación *f* fork, junction *en camino*; branch; **bifurcado** forked; **bifurcarse** [1g] (*caminos etc.*) fork, branch; bifurcate; diverge.
bigamia *f* bigamy; second marriage *de viudo*; **bígamo 1.** bigamous; twice married; **2.** *m*, **a** *f* bigamist.
bigardear [1a] F loaf around; **bigardo** *m* loafer.
bigarro *m zo.* winkle.
bigornia *f* (double-headed) anvil.
bigote *m* (*a. ~s pl.*) mustache; whiskers *de gato etc.*; **bigotudo** with a big mustache.
bigudí *m* hair curler.
bikini *m* bikini (swimsuit).
bilateral bilateral (*a.* ✝), two-sided.
bilbaíno *adj. a. su. m*, **a** *f* (native) of Bilbao.
bilbilitano *adj. a. su. m*, **a** *f* (native) of Calatayud.
biliar bile *attr.*; gall *attr.*
bilingüe bilingual.
bilioso bilious (*a. fig.*); *fig.* peevish, difficult; **bilis** *f* bile (*a. fig.*); *descargar la ~* vent one's spleen; *exaltársele a uno la ~* get annoyed, get cross.
billar *m* billiards; (*mesa*) billiard table; *~ automático, ~ romano* pin table.
billete *m* ticket; ✝ (bank) note, bill; (*carta*) note, letter; *~ de abono* season ticket; *~ amoroso* love letter, billet-doux; *~ de banco* bank note, bill; *~ de ida y vuelta* return ticket; *~ kilométrico approx.* runabout ticket, mileage book; *medio ~* half fare; *~ sencillo* single ticket; **billetera** *f* wallet, bill-fold.
billón *m* (*Gran Bretaña*) billion; (*EE.UU.*) trillion; **billonésimo** billionth.
bimba *f* F top hat; *Mex.* drinking spree; drunkenness.

bimotor twin-engined.
binadera *f*, **binador** *m* hoe; **binar** [1a] hoe, dig over.
binario binary; ♪ *compás* two-four.
binocular binocular; **binóculo** *m* binoculars; *thea.* opera glasses; (*gafas*) pince-nez.
biofísica *f* biophysics.
biografía *f* biography, life; **biográfico** biographic(al); **biógrafo** *m*, **a** *f* biographer.
biología *f* biology; **biológico** biologic(al); **biólogo** *m* biologist.
biombo *m* (folding) screen.
biopsia *f* ⚕ biopsy.
bioquímica *f* biochemistry; **bioquímico 1.** biochemical; **2.** *m* biochemist.
bipartido bipartite.
bípedo *adj. a. su. m*, **a** *f* biped; F human.
biplano *m* biplane.
biplaza *m* ✈ two-seater.
birimbao *m* Jew's harp.
birlar [1a] knock down (*or* kill) with one shot; F *p.* swindle out of, do out of; *cosa* pinch; *le birlaron el empleo* he was done out of the job.
birlibirloque: *por arte de* ~ (as if) by magic.
birlocha *f* kite.
birlonga: *a la* ~ carelessly, sloppily.
birmano *adj. a. su. m*, **a** *f* Burmese.
birreactor *adj. a. su. m* ✈ twin jet.
birreta *f* biretta, cardinal's hat; **birrete** *m eccl.* biretta; *univ. approx.* cap, mortarboard F.
birria *f* F (*feo*) monstrosity, ugly old thing; (*inútil*) bungling piece of work; useless object.
bis 1. *adv.* twice; *thea.* ¡~! encore!; **2.** *m* encore.
bisabuela *f* great-grandmother; **bisabuelo** *m* great-grandfather; ~**s** *pl.* great-grandparents.
bisagra *f* hinge; F waggle *de caderas.*
bisar [1a] *thea. etc.* repeat.
bisbisar [1a] mutter, mumble; **bisbiseo** *m* mutter(ing), mumbling.
biscuter *m* minicar.
bisecar [1g] bisect; **bisección** *f* bisection.
bisel *m* bevel (edge); **biselado** bevel *attr.*; **biselar** [1a] bevel; *superficie* splay.
bisemanal twice-weekly.
bisiesto: *v. año* ~.
bisílabo two-syllable.
bismuto *m* bismuth.
bisnieto *m* great-grandson; ~*s pl.* great-grandchildren.
bisojo cross-eyed, squinting.
bisonte *m* bison.
bisoñada *f* naïve remark; **bisoño 1.** green, inexperienced; *soldado* raw; **2.** *m*, **a** *f* greenhorn; ⚔ recruit, rookie.
bisté *m*, **bistec** *m* (beef)steak.
bisturí *m* scalpel.
bisutería *f* imitation jewellery, paste.
bitácora *f* binnacle.
bitoque *m* faucet; spigot; bung; *C.Am.* sewer.
bituminoso bituminous.
bivio *m S.Am.* road junction.
bizantino 1. Byzantine; *fig.* decadent; *discusión* pointless; over-subtle, Jesuitical; **2.** *m*, **a** *f* Byzantine.
bizarría *f* gallantry; generosity; (*esplendor*) show; **bizarro** gallant, generous; (*gallardo*) dashing, smart.
bizcar [1g] *v/t.* wink; *v/i.* squint; **bizco** cross-eyed, squinting; *mirada* ~*a* squint; F *quedarse* ~ be dumbfounded.
bizcocho *m* sponge (cake); biscuit; (*loza*) biscuit (ware); ⚓ hardtack, ship's biscuit; ~ *borracho* tipsy cake.
bizma *f* poultice; **bizmar** [1a] poultice.
biznieto *etc. v. bisnieto.*
bizquear [1a] squint.
blanca *f* (*p.*) white (woman); ♪ minim; F *estar* (*or quedarse*) *sin* ~ be broke; **blanco 1.** white; *piel* white, light; *tez* fair; *página, verso* blank; F yellow, cowardly; **2.** *m* white(ness); (*p.*) white (man); ⚔ target (*a. fig.*); (*página etc.*) blank (space); interval; ~ *del ojo* white of the eye; ~ *de plomo* white lead; *en* ~ blank; *calentar al* ~ make white-hot; *dar en el* ~ hit the mark (*a. fig.*); *dejar en* ~ leave blank; *firmar en* ~ sign a blank check; *pasar la noche en* ~ not sleep a wink; *poner los ojos en* ~ roll one's eyes; *quedarse en* ~ fail to see the point; not understand a word; **blancor** *m* whiteness; **blancote** (sickly) white; F *p.* yellow; **blancura** *f* whiteness.
blandear[1] [1a] = *blandir.*
blandear[2] *v/t. fig.* convince, persuade; *v/i.*, ~**se** soften, yield, give in.

blandengue *m* F softie.
blandir [3a; *defective*] *v/t.* brandish, wave aloft; *v/i.* **~se** wave to and fro.
blando *mst* soft; *pasta etc.* smooth; *carne b.s.* flabby; *fig.* mild, gentle; mellow; *p. b.s.* soft, indulgent; sensual; F cowardly; *clima* mild; *palabras* bland; *ojos* tender; *~ de boca fig.* talkative, loose-tongued; **blanducho** F on the soft side, softish; *esp. carne* flabby, loose; **blandujo** F on the soft side; **blandura** *f* softness *etc.*; (*halago*) flattery, flattering words; (*requiebro*) sweet nothings.
blanqueadura *f* whitening; bleaching; whitewashing; **blanquear** [1a] *v/t. tela etc.* bleach, whiten; *pared* whitewash; ⊕ blanch; *v/i.* (*volverse*) turn white, whiten; (*mostrar*) show white; **blanqueador** *m*, **-a** *f* bleacher; **blanquecer** [2d] = *blanquear*; **blanquecino** whitish; **blanqueo** *m* bleaching *etc.*; **blanquillo** *pan etc.* white; **blanquimiento** *m* bleacher, bleaching solution.
blasfemador 1. blaspheming, blasphemous; **2.** *m*, **-a** *f* blasphemer; **blasfemar** [1a] blaspheme (*contra* against); *fig.* curse (and swear); *~ de* curse, revile; **blasfemia** *f eccl.* blasphemy; insult; (*palabrota*) oath, swearword; **blasfemo** = *blasfemador.*
blasón *m* (*en general*) heraldry; (*escudo*) coat of arms, escutcheon; (*señal, pieza*) armorial bearings, charge; *fig.* honour, glory; **blasonar** [1a] *v/t.* (em)blazon; *v/i.* boast (de of being), brag.
bledo: F *no se me da un ~* I don't care two hoots (de about).
blenda *f* blende.
blinda *f* = *blindaje*; **blindado** ⚔ armoured; ⊕ shielded; **blindaje** *m* ⚔, ⚓ armor (plating); ⊕ shield; **blindar** [1a] ⚔ armor; ⊕ shield.
bloc *m* (writing)pad; calendar pad.
blocao *m* blockhouse; pillbox.
blof *m* bluff; **blofear** [1a] bluff.
blonda *f* blond (lace); **blondo** blond; light; *esp. pelo* flaxen.
bloque *m* △, ⊕ block; *fig.* group; *pol.* bloc; *en ~* en bloc; *~ de cilindros* cylinder block; **bloquear** [1a] ⚔, ⚓ blockade; *mot.* brake, pull up; ✝ freeze, block; **bloqueo** *m* blockade; ✝ freeze, squeeze; ⚓ *burlar* (*or forzar*) *el ~* run the blockade.
blufar [1a] bluff; **bluff** *m* [bluf] bluff; *hacer un ~ a* bluff.
blusa *f* blouse; jumper *de lana*; overalls *de obrero.*
boa *f* boa.
boato *m* show(iness), ostentation; pomp, pageantry *de ceremonia etc.*
bobada *f* silly thing; *decir ~s* talk a lot of nonsense, talk rot; *¡no digas ~s!* get along with you!; **bobalías** *m/f* F dolt, ass; **bobalicón** F **1.** utterly stupid, quite silly; **2.** *m*, **-a** *f* nitwit, mutt; **bobático** F half-witted, doltish; **bobear** [1a] (*hablar*) talk (a lot of) twaddle; (*obrar*) act like a fool; fool around; **bober(í)a** *f* = *bobada.*
bóbilis: F *de ~ ~* (*gratis*) for nothing; (*sin trabajo*) without lifting a finger.
bobina *f* bobbin, spool (*a. phot.*), reel; ⚡ coil; **bobinado** *m* ⚡ winding; **bobinar** [1a] wind (on to a spool *etc.*).
bobo 1. (*corto*) stupid, simple; (*tonto*) silly; (*ingenuo*) naïve, green; *~ con* crazy about, mad about; **2.** *m*, **a** *f* fool, dolt, mutt; (*ingenuo*) greenhorn; *thea.* clown, funny man.
boca *f* mouth; muzzle *de fusil*; (cutting) edge *de escoplo etc.*; pincer *de crustáceo*; *fig.* mouth, entrance; (*sabor*) taste, flavor; *~ de agua* fireplug; *~ de escorpión fig.* evil tongue; *~ del estómago* pit of the stomach; *~ de mina* pithead; *~ de riego* hydrant; *a ~* by word of mouth; *a ~ de cañón* at close range; *a ~ de jarro beber* immoderately; ⚔ at close range; point-blank; *~ abajo* (*arriba*) face downward (upward); *andar etc. de ~ en ~* (*cuento*) go round, be common talk; F *¡cállate la ~!* shut up!, hold your tongue!; *meterse en la ~ del lobo* put one's head in the lion's mouth; *no decir esta ~ es mía* not open one's mouth; *quedarse con la ~ abierta fig.* be dumbfounded; *tapar la ~ a* shut *s.o.* up.
bocacalle *f* street entrance; intersection; *la primera ~* the first corner; **bocacha** *f* F big mouth; ⚔ blunderbuss; **bocadear** [1a] divide into pieces; **bocadillo** *m* snack; meat (*or* cheese *etc.*) roll, sandwich; **bocado** *m* mouthful; (*un poco de comida*)

morsel, bite; (*mordedura*) bite; (*parte del freno*) bit; (*freno*) bridle; **bocal** *m* pitcher; jar; **bocallave** *f* keyhole; **bocamanga** *f* cuff, wristband; **bocamina** *f* pithead, mine entrance; **bocanada** *f* mouthful *de vino etc.*; puff *de humo, viento*; F ~ *de gente* crush; **bocaza** *f* loudmouth; gossip; **bocera** *f* smear (on lips), moustache (*fig.*).

boceto *m* sketch, outline.

bocina *f* ♪ trumpet; horn (*a. mot., gramófono*); (*portavoz*) megaphone, speaking trumpet; ear trumpet *de sordo*; *mot. tocar la* ~ = **bocinar** [1a] *mot.* hoot, blow the horn, honk; speak through a megaphone; **bocinazo** *m mot.* hoot, honk, toot.

bocio *m* goiter.

bock *m* beer glass, tankard.

bocón 1. big-mouthed; F boastful; **2.** *m*, **-a** *f* F braggart.

bocoy *m* hogshead, large cask.

bocha *f* bowl; *juego de las* ~*s* bowls.

bochar [1a] *Mex., Ven.* turn down; reject; insult.

bochinche *m* uproar, din; *prov.* pub; *S.Am.* general stores.

bochorno *m* sultry weather, sultriness; stifling atmosphere; (*viento*) hot summer breeze; *fig.* turn F; flush *de cara*; embarrassment; *b.s.* dishonor, stigma; **bochornoso** *tiempo* sultry, thundery; *ambiente etc.* stifling; *fig.* embarrassing; *b.s.* shameful, degrading.

boda *f* wedding (*a.* ~*s pl.*), marriage; wedding reception; ~*s pl. de diamante* (*oro, plata*) diamond (golden, silver) wedding.

bodega *f* wine cellar; (*despensa*) pantry; (*depósito*) storeroom, granary; ⚓ warehouse; ⚓ hold *de barco*; *S.Am.* grocery store; **bodegón** *m* cheap restaurant; *b.s.* low dive; *paint.* still life.

bodijo *m* F quiet wedding; *b.s.* unequal match, misalliance.

bodoque *m* pellet; lump; F nitwit.

bodorrio *m* = *bodijo*.

bofe 1. *m* lung; ~*s pl.* lights *de animal*; F *echar los* ~*s* slog, slave; F *echar los* ~*s por* go all out for; **2.** *C.Am.* unpleasant; disgusting.

bofetada *f* slap in the face (*a. fig.*); *dar de* ~*s* hit, punch; **bofetón** *m* (hard) slap.

boga[1] *f* vogue (*por* for), popularity; *en* ~ in fashion, in vogue.

boga[2] ⚓ **1.** *f* rowing; **2.** *m/f* rower; **bogada** *f* stroke (of an oar); **bogador** *m*, **-a** *f* rower; **bogar** [1h] row; (*navegar*) sail; **bogavante** *m* ⚓ stroke; *zo.* lobster.

bogotano *adj. a. su. m*, **a** *f* (native) of Bogotá.

bohardilla *f* = *buhardilla*.

bohémico *geog.*, **bohemio** *adj. a. su. m*, **a** *f fig.*, **bohemo** *adj. a. su. m*, **a** *f geog.* Bohemian.

boicotear [1a] boycott; **boicoteo** *m* boycott(ing).

boina *f* beret.

boj *m* ⚘ box(wood).

bol *m* (punch) bowl; (*bolo*) ninepin.

bola *f* ball; ⚓ signal (with disks); *naipes*: slam; (*betún*) blacking, shoe polish; F fib; ~*s pl.* ⊕ ball bearings; *S.Am. hunt.* bolas; (*juego de [las]*) ~*s* American skittles; ~ *de naftalina* mothball; ~ *de nieve* snowball; F *¡dale* ~*!* come off it!; *v. pie*; *dejar que ruede la* ~ let things take their course; **bolada** *f* throw; *S.Am.* ✝ lucky break.

bolardo *m* bollard.

bolchev(iqu)ismo *m* Bolshevism; **bolchev(iqu)ista** *adj. a. su. m/f* Bolshevik, Bolshevist.

boleada *f S.Am.* hunt; **boleadoras** *f/pl. S.Am.* bolas; **bolear** [1a] *v/t.* F throw; *S.Am.* hunt; *Mex.* polish shoes; *v/i.* play for fun; F tell fibs; *S.Am.* play a dirty trick; ~**se** (*caballo*) rear; *fig.* stumble; *S.Am.* make a mistake; **bolera** *f* (*sitio*) bowling alley, skittle alley; (*juego*) skittles.

bolero *m* bolero; *Mex.* shoeshine (boy).

boleta *f* pass, ticket; ✝ authorization, permit; *S.Am.* ballot (paper), **boletería** *f S.Am.* 🚂 booking office; *thea.* box office; **boletín** *m* (*informe etc.*) bulletin; = *boleta*; ~ *de inscripción* registration form; ~ *meteorológico* weather forecast; ~ *naviero* shipping register; ~ *de noticias* news bulletin; ~ *oficial* (*del Estado*) official gazette; ~ *de pedido* application form; **boleto** *m S.Am.* ticket.

bolichada *f* F lucky break, stroke of luck; *de una* ~ at one stroke; **boliche** *m* (*bola*) jack; (*juego*) bowls; (*pista*) bowling green; ⊕ small furnace; *S.Am.* skittles.

bólido *m* meteorite.

bolígrafo *m* ball-point pen.

bolillo *m* bobbin (for making lace); *S.Am.* bread roll; ~*s pl.* toffee bars.

bolina *f* ⚓ bowline; F racket, row, uproar; ⚓ *de* ~ close-hauled.

bolita *f* pellet; (*canica*) marble.

boliviano *adj. a. su. m*, **a** *f* Bolivian.

bolo 1. *m* ninepin; *naipes*: slam; *pharm.* large pill; (*juego de*) ~*s pl.* ninepins, skittles; *echar a rodar los* ~*s fig.* create a disturbance; **2.** *C.Am.*, *Mex.* drunk.

bolonio *m*, **a** *f* F dunce, ignoramus.

bolsa *f* purse *para dinero*; (*saquillo*) bag, pouch; handbag *de mujer*; ⚔, *geol.* pocket; bag *en vestido, tela*; *S.Am.* sack; *anat.* cavity, sac; ✝ stock exchange, stock market; *fig.* fortune; ~ *de agua caliente* hot-water bottle; ~ *de aire* air pocket; ~ *de granos* corn exchange; ~ *de herramientas* tool bag, tool kit; *S.Am.* ~ *negra* black market; ~ *de trabajo* labor exchange, employment bureau; *hacer* ~ (*vestido*) bag; (*arrugarse*) pucker (up); *jugar a la* ~ play the market; **bolsero** *m S.Am.* sponger; *Mex.* pickpocket.

bolsillo *m* pocket (*a. fig.*); (*saquillo*) purse, money bag; *de* ~ pocket *attr.*, pocket-size; **bolsín** *m* ✝ bucket shop, curb market; **bolsista** *m* (stock) broker; *S.Am.* pickpocket; **bolso** *m* bag, purse; ~ *de mano*, ~ *de mujer* handbag, purse; *hacer* ~ (*vela*) belly.

bollería *f* pastry shop, bakery; **bollero** *m* baker, muffin man; **bollo** *m cocina*: muffin, bun, roll; dent *en metal*; *sew.* puff; ⚕ bump, lump; F to-do, mix-up; **bollón** *m* (ornamental) stud; (*pendiente*) button earring.

bomba *f* pump; glass, globe *de lámpara*; ✈ bomb; ⚔ shell; *S.Am.* (*burbuja*) bubble; (*chistera*) top hat; ¡~! attention please!; ~ *de aire* air pump; ~ *aspirante* suction pump; ~ *atómica* atom bomb; ~ *de engrase* grease gun; *mot.* ~ *de gasolina* fuel pump; ~ *de hidrógeno*, ~ *H* hydrogen bomb; ~ *estomacal* stomach pump; ~ *impulsora* force pump; ~ *incendiaria* incendiary bomb; ~ *de incendios* fire engine; ~ *de mano* grenade; ~ *de relojería*, ~ *de retardo* time bomb; ~ *neutrónica* neutron bomb; ~ *revientamanzanas* blockbuster; *a prueba de* ~*s* bombproof; *caer como una* ~ fall like a bombshell; *coche* ~ car bomb; *dar a la* ~ pump; F *estar a tres* ~*s* be very cross; *estar echando* ~*s* be boiling hot.

bombardear [1a] ⚔, *phys.* bombard (*a. fig.*; *de* with); ⚔ shell; ✈ bomb, raid; **bombardeo** *m* ⚔ bombardment (*a. phys.*), shelling; ✈ bombing; ~ *aéreo* (air) raid; **bombardero 1.** bombing; **2.** *m* bomber.

bombasí *m* fustian.

bombear [1a] ⚔ shell; *sew.* pad; *S.Am. agua* pump (out); *S.Am.* fire, dismiss; *S.Am.* spy on; *fig.* = *dar bombo a*; ~**se** ⚠ camber; (*madera etc.*) bulge; **bombeo** *m* camber; crown *de carretera*; bulging, warping.

bombero *m* fireman; pumper; (*cuerpo de*) ~*s pl.* fire department.

bombilla *f* ⚡ bulb; chimney *de lámpara*; ~ *de flash*, ~ *fusible* flash bulb.

bombo 1. F dumbfounded; **2.** *m* ♪ bass drum; ⚓ lighter; F excessive praise; *thea. etc.* write-up, *S.Am.* ballyhoo; F *dar* ~ *a* praise to the skies; *thea.* write up, ballyhoo; *S.Am. irse al* ~ fail, come to grief.

bombón *m* sweet, candy; chocolate; F (*p.*) good sort; (*mujer*) peach; (*cosa*) beauty.

bombona *f* carboy.

bombonera *f* candy box; F cozy little place.

bonachón good-natured, kindly; *b.s.* naïve, unsuspecting.

bonaerense *adj. a. su. m/f* (native) of Buenos Aires.

bonancible *meteor.* calm, fair; **bonanza** *f* ⚓ fair weather; *min.* bonanza; ✝ prosperity, bonanza; ✝ *estar en* ~ be booming; ⚓ *ir en* ~ have fair weather; *fig.* go well, prosper.

bonazo = *buenazo.*

bondad *f* goodness; kind(li)ness *etc.*; *tener la* ~ *de inf.* be so kind (*or* good) as to *inf.*; **bondadoso** kind(ly), kind-hearted, good(-natured).

bonete *m eccl.* hat, biretta; *univ. approx.* cap, mortarboard F; F *a tente* ~ doggedly; **bonetería** *f* hat shop; notions store.

bongo *m S.Am.* barge; canoe.

bonificación *f* improvement (*a.* ⚘); ✝ allowance, discount; **bonificar** [1g] improve (*a.* ⚘).

bonísimo *sup. of bueno.*
bonitamente stealthily, craftily; little by little; **bonito**[1] pretty, nice (*a. fig.*).
bonito[2] *m* tunny, bonito.
bono *m* voucher; ✝ bond.
boom *m* (*florecimiento*) boom (*a. lit.*).
boqueada: *dar la última* ~ breathe one's last; **boquear** [1a] *v/t.* pronounce, say; *v/i.* be at one's last gasp; *fig.* be in its last stages; **boquera** *f* ↙ sluice; ⚕ lip sore; ~*s pl.* F hunger; **boquerel** *m* nozzle; **boquerón** *m* wide opening; *ichth.* anchovy; **boquete** *m* gap, opening, hole; **boquiabierto** open-mouthed; *fig.* aghast; *estar* ~ gape; *mirar* ~ gape (at); **boquifresco** F outspoken; cheeky; **boquilla** *f* ♪ mouthpiece; ⊕ nozzle; burner *de gas*; stem *de pipa*; cigarette holder; **boquirroto** F talkative, garrulous; **boquirrubio** = *boquirroto*; (*candoroso*) simple, naïve; glib, indiscreet.
bórax *m* borax.
borboll(e)**ar** [1a] bubble, boil up; *fig.* splutter; **borbollón** *m* bubbling, boiling; *a* ~*es* impetuously, with a rush; **borbollonear** [1a] = *borboll*(*e*)*ar*.
borbónico Bourbon *attr.*
borbotar [1a] (*fuente*) bubble up, gush forth; bubble, boil *al hervir*; **borbotón** *m* = *borbollón*; *hablar a* ~*es* talk impetuously, splutter; *manar a* ~*es* gush forth.
borceguí *m* high shoe, laced boot, buskin; booty *de niño.*
borda *f* ⚓ gunwale; ⚓ (*vela*) mainsail; (*choza*) hut; ⚓ *de fuera de* ~ outboard *attr.*; *tirar por la* ~ throw overboard; **bordada** *f* ⚓ tack; *dar* ~*s* ⚓ tack; F keep on going to and fro.
bordado *m* embroidery, needlework; **bordadora** *f* needlewoman; **bordadura** *f* embroidery; **bordar** [1a] embroider (*a. fig.*).
borde *m* edge; side *de camino etc.*; brink *de abismo*; lip *de taza*; brim, rim *de vaso*; ledge *de ventana*; *sew.* selvage; ⚓ board; ~ *del camino* roadside, verge; ~ *del mar* seaside, seashore; *al* ~ *de* at the side (*or* edge) of; **bordear** [1a] *v/t.* skirt, go along the edge of; *v/i.* ⚓ tack; **bordillo** *m* curb.
bordo *m* ⚓ side; (*bordada*) tack; *a* ~ on board; *al* ~ alongside; *de alto* ~ large, seagoing; *fig.* of importance, influential.
bordón *m* pilgrim's staff; *fig.* guide, helping hand; ♪ bass string; *poet.* refrain; *fig.* = **bordoncillo** *m* pet phrase.
boreal north(ern).
Borgoña *m* (*a. vino de* ~) burgundy
borla *f* tassel; pompon *en sombrero*; tuft *de hebras*; bob *de pelo*; powder puff *para empolvarse*; *univ.* doctor's insignia.
borne *m* ⚡ terminal.
borneadizo easily warped; flexible; **bornear** [1a] *v/t.* twist, bend; △ put in place, align; *v/i.* ⚓ swing at anchor; ~**se** warp, bulge; **borneo** *m* twisting, bending; swaying *al bailar.*
boro *m* boron.
borona *f* corn, maize; millet; (*pan*) corn bread.
borra *f* (*lana*) thick wool, flock; stuffing *de almohada*; (*pelusa*) fluff; ⚘ down; sediment, lees; F (*palabras*) useless talk; F (*cosas*) trash; ~ *de algodón* cotton waste.
borrachear [1a] (go on the) booze; **borrachera** *f* (*estado*) drunkenness; (*a. juerga de* ~) spree, binge; *fig.* great excitement; *tomar una* ~ go on a spree; **borrachería** *f* foolish act; *Mex.* tavern; **borrachez** *f* drunkenness; *fig.* mental disturbance; **borrachín** *m* drunkard, sot, toper; **borracho 1.** drunk; (*de costumbre*) drunken, hard-drinking, fond of the bottle; *bizcocho* tipsy; *color* violet; *fig.* blind, wild (*de ira etc.* with); **2.** *m*, **a** *f* drunk(ard), sot.
borrador *m* rough copy, first draft; (*libro*) book for rough work; ✝ day book; (*goma*) rubber, eraser; duster *para pizarra*; **borradura** *f* erasure; **borrajear** [1a] scribble; (*distraído*) doodle; **borrar** [1a] erase, rub out *con borrador*; cross out *con rayas*; blot, smear *con tinta*; *fig.* erase, wipe away, wipe out; *imagen* blur, blot out.
borrasca *f* storm (*a. fig.*); *meteor. a.* depression, cyclone; (*riesgo*) hazard; (*contratiempo*) setback; **borrascoso** stormy (*a. fig.*); *viento* squally, gusty; *fig.* = **borrasquero** riotous, wild.
borrego *m*, **a** *f* (yearling) lamb; F simpleton; **borreguillo** *m* fleecy cloud; ~*s pl.* mackerel sky.

borrica *f* (female) donkey, ass; F ass (of a woman); **borricada** *f* piece of nonsense; **borrico** *m* donkey, ass (*a. fig.*); ⊕ sawhorse; **borricón** *m* F, **borricote** *m* F poor devil; **borriquete** *m* ⊕ sawhorse.
borrón *m* blot, smudge; (*borrador*) rough draft, sketch (*a. paint.*); *fig.* blemish; stain, stigma, slur *en reputación*; *lit.* estos ~es these humble jottings; **borronear** [1a] = *borrajear*; **borroso** *líquido* muddy, dirty; *imagen* blurred, indistinct; *paint.* woolly; *superficie* smudgy.
borujo *m* lump; pack; **borujón** *m* ⚕ lump, bump; (*lío*) bundle; **borujoso** lumpy.
boscaje *m* small wood, grove; *paint.* woodland scene; **boscoso** wooded; **bosque** *m* wood(s), woodland; (*grande*) forest; **bosquecillo** *m* copse, spinney.
bosquejar [1a] sketch, outline (*a. fig.*); ⊕ design; *proyecto* draft; **bosquejo** *m* sketch, outline (*a. fig.*); draft *de proyecto*.
bostezar [1f] yawn; **bostezo** *m* yawn.
bota *f* boot; (*odre*) leather wine bottle; ~s *pl. de campaña* top boots; ~s *pl. de goma* gum boots; ~s *pl. de montar* riding boots; *morir con las* ~s *puestas* die with one's boots on; F *ponerse las* ~s strike lucky, make one's pile.
botado cheeky; *S.Am.* *niño* abandoned; *S.Am.* ✝ dirt-cheap.
botador *m* ⚓ (punting) pole; ⊕ claw hammer; *S.Am.* spendthrift; **botadura** *f* launching; **botafuego** *m* hothead; **botalón** *m* boom, outrigger; ~ *de foque* jib boom.
botánica *f* botany; **botánico 1.** botanic(al); **2.** *m*, **a** *f* = **botanista** *m/f* botanist.
botar [1a] *v/t.* hurl, fling; *empleado* fire, dismiss; *pelota* pitch; *barco* launch; *timón* put over; *S.Am.* throw away; *fortuna* fritter away; *v/i. mot. etc.* bump, bounce; (*caballo*) buck; **~se** *S.Am.* throw o.s. (*a* into); **botaratada** *f* F wild thing; wild scheme; **botarate** *m* F wild fellow, madcap; *S.Am.* spendthrift.
botarga *f* motley, clown's outfit; (*p.*) clown.
botavara *f* ⚓ boom, sprit.
bote[1] *m* (*golpe*) thrust, blow; buck *de caballo*; bounce *de pelota etc.*; *Mex.* prison; jail; *dar* ~s bounce; *esp. mot.* bump, jolt; *estar de* ~ *en* ~ be packed, be crowded out.
bote[2] *m* (*vasija*) can, tin; pot, jar; *naipes*: jackpot; *mot.* F jalopy.
bote[3] *m* ⚓ boat; ~ *de paso* ferryboat; ~ *de remos* row(ing) boat; ~ *de salvamento*, ~ *salvavidas* lifeboat.
botella *f* bottle; ~ *de Leiden* Leyden jar.
botica *f* drug store; F *de todo como en* ~ everything under the sun; **boticario** *m* druggist.
botija *f* earthenware jug; *S.Am.* belly; F *estar hecho una* ~ be as fat as a sow; **botijo** *m* earthenware jar (with spout and handle); *v. tren.*
botillería *f* refreshment stall.
botín[1] *m* ⚔ booty, plunder, spoils.
botín[2] *m* (*polaina*) spat; = **botina** *f* bootee; high shoe.
botiquín *m* medicine chest; (*a.* ~ *de emergencia*) first-aid kit.
boto 1. dull, blunt; *fig.* dull, slow (-witted); **2.** *m* leather wine bottle.
botón *m sew.*, ⚡ button; ~ (*de camisa*) stud; ~ (*de puerta*) doorknob; *radio*: knob; tip *de florete*; ⚘ bud; F (*mujer*) peach; ⚘ ~ *de oro* buttercup; kingcup; **botonar** [1a] *S.Am.* button (up); **botones** *m* buttons, bellboy, bellhop.
bóveda *f* △ vault; dome; cavern; ~ *celeste* arch of heaven; **bovedilla:** F *subirse a las* ~s go up in smoke.
bovino bovine.
boxeador *m* boxer; **boxear** [1a] box; **boxeo** *m* boxing.
boya *f* ⚓ buoy; float *de red*.
boyada *f* drove of oxen.
boyante buoyant; *fig.* lucky; **boyar** [1a] float.
boyero *m* oxherd, drover; (*perro*) cattle dog.
bozal 1. (*novato*) raw, green; *potro* wild, untamed; F silly, stupid; *S.Am.* speaking broken Spanish; **2.** *m* muzzle; *S.Am.* halter.
bozo *m* (*vello*) down (on upper lip); (*boca*) mouth, lips; halter, headstall *de caballo*.
bracear [1a] swing one's arms; (*nadar*) swim, *esp.* crawl; *fig.* wrestle, struggle; **bracero** *m* (unskilled) laborer, worker; farmhand; *servir de* ~ be an escort; *de* ~ = **bracete:** *de* ~ arm in arm.
braco 1. pug-nosed; **2.** *m hunt.* setter.
bráctea *f* bract.

braga *f* ⊕ rope, sling; F diaper *de niño*; *~s pl.* breeches *de hombre*; knickers, panties *de mujer*; **bragado** *fig.* energetic; *b.s.* wicked; **bragadura** *f anat.* crotch; *sew.* gusset; **bragazas** *m* henpecked husband; **braguero** *m* ⚕ truss; **bragueta** *f* fly, flies; **braguillas** *m* F brat.
brama *f zo.* rut.
bramante *m* twine, fine string.
bramar [1a] roar, bellow (*a. fig.*); (*viento*) howl, roar; (*mar*) thunder, roar; **bramido** *m* roar, bellow *etc.*
branquia *f* gills.
brasa *f* (live) coal; *estar en ~s fig.* be on tenterhooks; *estar hecho una ~* be very flushed; **brasero** *m* brazier; *hist.* stake.
brasil *m* brazilwood; *Mex.* hearth.
brasileño *adj. a. su. m*, **a** *f* Brazilian.
bravata *f* threat; (piece of) bravado; *echar ~s = bravear*; **bravatear** [1a] *S.Am. = bravear*; **braveador 1.** blustering, bullying; **2.** *m* bully; **bravear** [1a] boast, talk big; bluster.
bravera *f* vent, chimney.
braveza *f* ferocity; *meteor. etc.* fury; (*valor*) bravery, courage; **bravío 1.** fierce, ferocious; (*indómito*) untamed, wild; *fig.* uncouth, coarse; **2.** fierceness; **bravo 1.** (*valiente*) brave; *b.s.* boastful, blustering; fine, excellent; (*guapo*) spruce, fine; sumptuous, magnificent; *animal* fierce; *mar* rough; *paisaje* rugged; *genio* bad-tempered, irritable; (*enojado*) very cross; *¡~!* bravo!; **2.** *m* thug; **bravucón** *m* F boaster, braggart; **bravura** *f* ferocity; (*valor*) bravery; *= bravata*.
braza *f approx.* fathom (*= 1.67 m*); (*cabo*) brace; **brazada** *f* (*remo, natación*) stroke; (*brazado*) armful; *~ de pecho* breaststroke; **brazado** *m* armful; **brazal** *m* armband; ✝ irrigation channel; **brazalete** *m* bracelet, wristlet; **brazo** *m* arm (*a.* ⊕, *fig.*); *zo.* foreleg; ⚘ limb, branch; (*soporte*) bracket; *fig.* energy, enterprise; (*valor*) courage; *~s pl. fig.* backers, protectors; (*obreros*) hands, workers; *~ derecho fig.* right-hand man; *~ de dirección* steering arm; *~ de lámpara* lamp bracket; *~ de lámpara de gas* gas bracket; *~ de mar* sound, arm of the sea; F *estar hecho un ~ de mar* be dressed (up) to kill; *a ~ partido* hand to hand; *con los ~s abiertos* with open arms (*a. fig.*); *asidos del ~* arm in arm; *cruzarse de ~s* fold one's arms; *estarse con los ~s cruzados fig.* (sit back and) do nothing; F *no dar su ~ a torcer* stand fast, not give in; *mover a ~* manhandle; F *tener ~* (*voz*) be husky;
brazuelo *m zo.* shoulder.
brea *f* tar, pitch; **brear** [1a] abuse, ill-treat; (*zumbar*) make fun of; *~ a golpes* beat up.
brebaje *m pharm.* potion, mixture; *b.s.* brew, nasty stuff (to drink).
brécol(es) *m(pl.)* broccoli.
brecha *f* ⚔ breach; ⚠ gap, opening; *abrir ~ en muro* breach; *abrir* (*or hacer*) *~ en fig.* make an impression on.
brega *f* (*lucha*) struggle; (*riña*) quarrel, row; (*chasco*) trick, joke; F *andar a la ~* slog away; *dar ~ a* play a trick on; **bregar** [1h] struggle, fight (*con* with, against; *a. fig.*); (*ajetrearse*) slog away.
breña *f*, **breñal** *m* scrub, rough ground; **breñoso** rough, scrubby.
brete *m* fetters, shackles; *fig.* tight spot, jam; *poner en un ~* get *s.o.* in a fix.
bretones *m/pl.* Brussels sprouts.
breva *f* ⚘ (early) fig; flat cigar; F chicken feed, cinch; *¡no caerá esa ~!* no such luck!
breve 1. short; brief (*esp. de duración*); *estilo* terse; *en ~* before long, shortly; **2.** *m* ♪ breve; *eccl.* (papal) brief; **brevedad** *f* shortness; brevity; conciseness *de estilo*; *con la mayor ~* as soon as possible; **breviario** *m* breviary; *fig.* compendium; (*lectura*) bedside companion.
brezal *m* moor(land), heath; **brezo** *m* heather.
briba: *andar* (*or vivir*) *a la ~* loaf around; **bribón 1.** idle, loafing; (*bellaco*) rascally; **2.** *m*, **-a** *f* loafer; rascal, scamp; **bribonada** *f* dirty trick; **bribonear** [1a] loaf around; **bribonería** *f* idle life; (*bellaquería*) roguery.
brida *f* bridle; ⊕ fishplate; ⊕ (*anillo*) collar; *a toda ~* at top speed; **bridón** *m* snaffle; ⚔ bridoon.
brigada 1. *f* ⚔ brigade; squad, gang *de obreros etc.*; *~ sanitaria* sanitation department; **2.** *m approx.* staff sergeant; **brigadier** *m* brigadier.

brigantino *adj. a. su. m,* **a** *f* (native) of Corunna.
brillante 1. brilliant (*a. fig., p.*), shining, bright; *joya, escena* glittering; *aspecto* cheerful; *conversación* scintillating; **2.** *m* brilliant; **brillantez** *f* brilliance *etc.*; **brillantina** *f* brillantine; metal polish; **brillar** [1a] shine (*a. fig., p.*); glitter, gleam, glisten; beam *con sonrisa*; glow, light up (*de emoción* with); ~ *por su ausencia* be conspicuous by one's absence; **brillo** *m* shine *etc.*; luster, sheen *esp. de superficie*; glow, radiance; *fig.* splendor, brilliance; *sacar ~ a* polish, shine.
brin *m* fine canvas, duck.
brincar [1g] *v/t. niño* dandle; F *pasaje* skip, miss out; *v/i.* skip, jump, leap about; F go off the deep end, blow one's top (*por* at); **brinco** *m* jump, leap, skip; *en un ~* in a trice.
brindar [1a] *v/t.* offer (*a* to; *a alguien con algo* s.t. to s.o.); *toro etc.* dedicate; invite (*a inf.* to *inf.*); *fig. sombra etc.* lend, offer; *v/i.* invite; *~ a, ~ por* drink (a toast) to, toast; *~se a inf.* offer to *inf.*; **brindis** *m* toast.
brío *m* (*freq. ~s pl.*) spirit, dash; liveliness; vigor; determination, resolution; (*garbo*) jauntiness; *cortar los ~s a* clip *s.o.'s* wings; **brioso** spirited, dashing; determined, resolute; jaunty.
briqueta *f* briquette.
brisa *f* breeze.
británico British; **britano 1.** *esp. hist.* British; **2.** *m,* **a** *f hist. a. poet.* Briton.
brizna *f* strand, thread, filament; fragment, piece.
broca *f sew.* reel, bobbin; ⊕ drill, bit; tack *de zapato*; *~ de avellanar* countersinking bit.
brocado 1. brocaded; **2.** *m* brocade.
brocal *m* curb *de pozo*; cigarette holder.
brocha *f* (large paint) brush; *~ de afeitar* shaving brush; *de ~ gorda fig.* slapdash, crude; **brochada** *f,* **brochazo** *m* brush stroke; (*pintura*) dab (of paint).
broche *m* clasp (*a. de libro*), fastener; (*joya etc.*) brooch; *~ de oro* punch line.
brochón *m* whitewash brush.
broma *f* (*chanza*) joke; prank; ~ (*estudiantil*) rag; (*algazara*) fun, merriment; *~ pesada* practical joke, hoax; *b.s.* poor sort of joke; *en ~* in fun; *lo decía en ~* I was only kidding; *estar de ~* be in a joking mood; *no estoy para ~s* I'm in no mood for jokes; *gastar una ~* play a joke (*a* on); **bromear** [1a] joke (*a. ~se*); rag; (*burlarse*) pull *s.o.'s* leg; **bromista 1.** fond of joking *etc.*; **2.** *m/f* (*salado*) joker, wag; (*chancero*) leg puller.
bromo *m* bromine; **bromuro** *m* bromide.
bronca *f* F (*riña*) row, scrap, wrangle; (*reprensión*) rap over the knuckles; (*broma*) poor sort of joke; *armar una ~* start a row; *echar una ~ a* rap *s.o.* over the knuckles.
bronce *m* bronze; *~ de cañón* gun metal; *~ dorado* ormolu; **bronceado 1.** bronze(-colored); *piel* tanned, sunburned; **2.** *m* ⊕ bronze finish; tan *de piel*; **bronceador** *m* suntan lotion; **broncear(se)** [1a] ⊕ bronze; *piel* tan, bronze, brown.
bronco *superficie* rough, unpolished; *metal* brittle; *voz* gruff, harsh; ♪ rasping, harsh; *trato* gruff; (*grosero*) uncouth, coarse; **bronquedad** *f* roughness *etc.*
bronquial bronchial.
bronquina *f* F scrap, quarrel.
bronquitis *f* bronchitis.
broquel *m* shield (*a. fig.*); **broquelarse** [1a] shield o.s.
broqueta *f* skewer.
brota *f* shoot, bud; **brotar** [1a] *v/t.* ⚘ sprout, put out; *fig.* pour out; *v/i.* ⚘ sprout, bud; (*agua etc.*) spring up, gush forth; (*río*) rise; ⚕ break out, show; *fig.* spring up; **brote** *m* ⚘ shoot, bud; ⚕ rash, pimples; ⚕ outbreak *de enfermedad*.
broza *f* ⚒ chaff *de trigo etc.*; (*hojas etc.*) dead leaves, dead wood; (*maleza*) brushwood; *fig.* rubbish, refuse; (*escrito*) trash.
bruces: *de ~* face downwards; *caer de ~* fall flat on one's face.
bruja *f* witch; F hag, harridan; *orn.* owl; **brujería** *f* sorcery, witchcraft, magic; **brujo** *m* sorcerer, magician, wizard.
brújula *f* ⚓ compass; *fig.* guide; *~ giroscópica* gyrocompass; F *perder la ~* lose one's touch; **brujulear** [1a]

cartas uncover; F (*adivinar*) guess; (*gestionar*) manage, contrive.
bruma *f* (*esp.* sea) mist, fog; **brumoso** misty, foggy.
bruñido *m* (*acto*) polish(ing); (*efecto*) shine, gloss; **bruñidor** *m*, **-a** *f* polisher, burnisher; **bruñir** [3h] polish, burnish; *C.Am.* annoy; **~se** F put on make-up.
brusco *ataque* sudden; *movimiento* brusque; *curva* sharp; *fig.* brusque, abrupt, offhand.
bruselas *f/pl.* (*unas* a pair of) tweezers.
brusquedad *f* suddenness *etc.*; *hablar con* ~ speak sharply.
brutal 1. brutal; (*brusco*) sudden, unexpected; F terrific; **2.** *m* brute; **brutalidad** *f* brutality, bestiality; (*acto*) piece of brutality, crime; stupidity; **bruto 1.** brute, brutish; bestial; (*malcriado*) uncouth, coarse; *material* rough, unpolished; *peso* gross; stupid; F terrific; *en* ~ (in the) rough; raw; *piedra* unpolished; **2.** *m* brute; F dolt.
bruza *f* brush *para caballo* (*a. typ.*); scrubbing brush *para fregar*.
bu *m* bogey (man); *hacer el* ~ *a* scare.
búa *f* pimple; **buba** *f*, **bubo** *m* tumor.
bucal oral, of the mouth.
bucanero *m* buccaneer.
búcaro *m* (fragrant) clay; (*vasija*) vase.
buccino *m* whelk.
buceador *m* diver; **bucear** [1a] dive; work as a diver; *fig.* delve, search below the surface; **buceo** *m* diving.
buces *v. bruces.*
bucle *m* curl, ringlet; *fig.* curve, bend, loop.
bucólica *f* pastoral poem, bucolic; F meal; **bucólico** pastoral, bucolic.
buchada *f* = *bocanada*; **buche** *m* *orn.* crop; *zo. a.* F maw; F belly; (*bocado*) mouthful; *sew.* pucker; *fig.* inside, bosom; *sew. hacer* ~ be baggy, pucker; F *llenar bien el* ~ tuck in; F *sacar el* ~ show off; F *sacar el* ~ *a* make *s.o.* talk.
budín *m* pudding.
budión *m* butterfly fish.
buen *v. bueno*; **buenamente** (*fácilmente*) easily, freely; (*de buena gana*) willingly, voluntarily; **buenaventura** *f* (good) luck; fortune; *decir la* ~ *a* tell *s.o.'s* fortune; **buenazo** kind(ly), good-natured.
bueno 1. *mst* good; *p.* good, kind, nice; *calentura* high; *constitución* sound, strong; *doctrina* sound; *sociedad* polite; *tiempo* good, fine, fair; *iro.* fine, pretty; F (*sencillo*) gullible, naïve; ~ *para inf.* suitable for *ger.*, good for *ger.*; *ser* ~ *para con* be kind to; ~ *de comer* (*sabroso*) good to eat; (*sano*) fit to eat; *el* ~ *de Pedro* good old Peter; *de* ~*as a primeras* (*de pronto*) suddenly, out of nowhere; (*en seguida*) straightaway; *por las* ~*as* gladly, willingly; *por las* ~*as o por las malas* by fair means or foul; *por las* ~*as y las malas* through thick and thin; *estar* ~ be well; F *está* ~*a* she's pretty hot; F *¡estaba buenísima!* she looked a real treat!; F *estar de* ~*as* be in a good mood; *¡ésa sí que es* ~*a!* that's a good one!; **2.** (*como int. etc.*): *¡*~*!* all right!, well then!; *duda*: come, come!, come off it!; *sorpresa*: you don't say!; *mandato*: *¡*~ (*está*)*!* that's enough!, that'll do!; *¿adónde* ~*?* where are you off to?; *¡cuánto* (*or tanto*) ~ *por aquí!* hullo (there)!, it's good to see you!; F *¡*~*as!* hullo!; **3.** *cj.*: ~ *que* although, even though.
buey *m* bullock, steer; ox *para labrar etc.*; F ~ *suelto* free man, free agent; (*soltero*) bachelor; *trabajar como un* ~ work like a Trojan.
búfalo *m* buffalo.
bufanda *f* scarf, muffler.
bufar [1a] snort (*a. fig.*; *de* with); (*gato*) spit.
bufete *m* desk; ⚖ lawyer's office; *S.Am.* snack.
bufido *m* snort (*a. fig.*; *de* of).
bufo 1. farcical, slapstick; *ópera* comic; **2.** *m* clown; **bufón 1.** funny, comical, clownish; **2.** *m*, **-a** *f* buffoon, clown; *hist.* jester; **bufonada** *f* (*acto*) buffoonery, clowning; (*dicho*) joke; (*sátira*) comic piece; **bufonearse** [1a] clown, play the fool; (*burlarse*) joke; **bufonesco** = *bufón 1.*
bugui-bugui *m* boogie-woogie.
bugle *m* bugle.
buhard(ill)a *f* dormer window; (*desván*) garret; *S.Am.* skylight.
buho *m* (*a.* ~ *real*) (eagle) owl; *fig.* unsociable person, hermit.
buhonero *m* peddler; hawker.
buitre *m* vulture.
buje *m* axle box; bushing.

bujería *f* trinket, gewgaw.
bujía *f* candle; (*candelero*) candlestick; ⚡ candle power; *mot.* spark-plug.
bula *f* (papal) bull; F *no poder con la* ~ have no strength left for anything; F *no me vale la* ~ *de Meco* I'm done for, I don't have a chance in hell.
bulbo *m* ⚘, ⚕ bulb; *S.Am. radio*: valve; **bulboso** ⚘ bulbous; bulb-shaped.
bulevar *m* boulevard, avenue.
búlgaro *adj. a. su. m*, **a** *f* Bulgarian.
bulimia *f* ⚕ bulimia.
bulón *m* bolt; spring pin.
bulto *m* (*volumen*) bulk(iness), volume, mass(iveness); (*que se distingue mal*) shape, form; ⚕ swelling, lump; (*fardo*) package, bundle, bale; bust; *S.Am.* briefcase; ~*s pl. de mano* hand luggage; *a* ~ in the mass, broadly; *de* (*mucho*) ~ heavy, massive; *fig.* important; *de poco* ~ small, which does not take up much room; F *buscar el* ~ *a* steal up behind; F *escurrir el* ~ dodge, get out of it.
bulla *f* (*ruido*) noise, uproar; (*movimiento*) bustle; fussing about; (*gente*) crowd; *meter* ~ kick up a row; **bullaje** *m* crush, crowd; **bullanguero 1.** riotous, rowdy; **2.** *m*, **a** *f* rioter, troublemaker; **bull**(**ar**)**anga** *f* disturbance, riot, unrest; **bullebulle** *m/f* busybody, mischiefmaker; (*inquieto*) fusspot; **bullicio** *m* (*ruido*) uproar; rowdiness; din, hum *de calle etc.*; (*movimiento*) bustle; (*alboroto*) uproar, confusion, disturbance; **bullicioso** *multitud*, *asamblea* noisy; *calle* bustling, busy; noisy; (*alborotador*) riotous, turbulent; *fiesta* boisterous, rowdy; (*inquieto*) restless; **bullir** [3h] *v/t.* move; *v/i.* (*hervir*) boil (*a. fig.*); (*con burbujas*) bubble (up); (*moverse*) move about, get around; bustle around; *fig.* teem, swarm (*de*, *en* with); ~**se** stir, budge.
buñuelo *m approx.* cruller; doughnut, fritter; F botched job, mess.
buque *m* ship, boat, vessel; (*casco*) hull; (*cabida*) capacity, tonnage; ~ *almirante* flagship; ~ *de carga* freighter; ~-*escuela* training ship; ~ *de guerra* warship; man-of-war †; ~ *mercante* merchantman; ~ *minador* minelayer; ~ *nodriza* mother ship; ~ *tanque* tanker; ~ (*de*) *vapor* steamer, steamship; ~ *de vela*, ~ *velero* sailing ship.
burbuja *f* bubble; *hacer* ~*s* = **burbujear** [1a] bubble, form bubbles.
burdégano *m* hinny.
burdel *m* brothel.
burdo coarse.
burgalés *adj. a. su. m*, **-a** *f* (native) of Burgos.
burgués 1. middle-class, bourgeois (*a. contp.*); (*de ciudad*) town *attr.*; **2.** *m*, **-a** *f* bourgeois, member of the middle class; townsman *de ciudad*; **burguesía** *f* middle class, bourgeoisie.
buril *m* burin, graver; **burilar** [1a] engrave.
burla *f* (*palabra*) gibe, taunt; (*chanza*) joke; (*chasco*) trick, hoax, practical joke; (*engaño*) trick, deception; (*esp.* ~*s pl.*) mockery, ridicule, joking, fun; ~ *burlando* unawares; (*con disimulo*) on the quiet; *de* ~*s* in fun; *gastar* ~*s con* make fun of; *hacer* ~ *de todo* make fun of everything; **burladero** *m* refuge, covert (in bullring); **burlador 1.** *m*, **-a** *f* wag, practical joker, leg puller F; **2.** *m* seducer.
burlar [1a] *v/t.* (*zumbar*) take in, hoax; (*engañar*) deceive; *enemigo etc.* outwit, outmaneuver; *ambición* frustrate; *bloqueo* run; *deseos etc.* disappoint; cheat *s.o.* of; *mujer* seduce; *v/i.*, ~**se** joke, banter; scoff; *yo no me burlo* I'm in dead earnest; I'm serious; F I'm not kidding; ~ *de* make fun of, poke fun at, scoff at; **burlería** *f* trick; (*cuento*) tall story, fairy tale; **burlesco** funny, comic; (*satírico*) mock, burlesque.
burlete *m* seal; weather strip(ping).
burlón 1. joking, bantering; *tono* mocking; *esp. risa* sardonic; **2.** *m*, **-a** *f* wag, joker, leg puller F; *b.s.* scoffer.
buró *m* bureau, (roll-top) desk; *Mex.* night table.
burocracia *f* public service, civil service; *esp. b.s.* bureaucracy; *contp.* officialdom; *fig.* red tape; **burócrata** *m/f* civil servant, administrative official; *contp.* bureaucrat, F pencil-pusher; **burocrático** bureaucratic; official.
burra *f* donkey, female ass; *fig.* stupid woman; (*sufrida*) drudge, slave; **burrada** *f fig.* silly thing, piece of stupidity; *decir* ~*s* talk non-

sense; **burro 1.** *m* donkey, ass; ⊕ sawhorse; *fig.* ass, dolt; ~ *de carga fig.* glutton for work; *b.s.* drudge, slave; F ~ *cargado de letras* pompous ass.

bursátil stock market *attr.*

burujo *m etc. v. borujo.*

busca *f* search, hunt (de for); *en* ~ *de* in search of; **buscada** *f* = *busca*; **buscador** *m*, **-a** *f* searcher; **buscapié** *m* hint; **buscapiés** *m* squib, cracker; **buscapleitos** *m S.Am.* troublemaker; F shyster; F ambulance chaser.

buscar [1g] **1.** *v/t.* look for, search for; seek (for, after); hunt for, have a look for; *enemigo* seek out; *cita* look up; *ganancia* be out for; *palabra* grope for; *camorra* ask for; *ir a* ~ (go and) fetch; **2.** *v/i.* look, search; **3.** **~se:** *se busca* (*aviso*) wanted; F *buscársela* manage to get along; (*camorra*) look for trouble, ask for it.

buscarruidos *m* troublemaker; **buscavidas** *m/f* snoop, busybody; (*trabajador*) hard worker, hustler; *b.s.* social climber, go-getter; **buscón** *m b.s.* petty thief, small-time crook; **buscona** *f* whore; *v. buscón.*

busilis *m* F (real) difficulty, snag; *dar en el* ~ put one's finger on the spot; *ahi está el* ~ there's the snag.

búsqueda *f* = *busca.*

busto *m* bust.

butaca *f* armchair, easy chair; *thea.* orchestra seat.

butano *m*: *gas* ~ butane (*or* cylinder) gas.

buz *m* kiss (of respect); F *hacer el* ~ bow and scrape.

buzo *m* diver.

buzón *m* ☏ letterbox; canal, conduit; *echar al* ~ mail.

C

¡ca! F get away with you!, not a bit of it!, oh no!

cabal 1. *adj.* exact, right; finished, complete, consummate; *esfuerzo etc.* all-out, thorough; *estar en sus ~es* be in one's right mind; **2.** *adv.* exactly; perfectly (right); **3.** *int.* quite right!

cábala *f fig.* cabal, intrigue; *~s pl.* guess, supposition.

cabalgada *f* troop of riders; ⚔ cavalry raid; **cabalgadura** *f* mount, horse; (*de carga*) beast of burden; **cabalgar** [1h] *v/t. yegua* cover; *v/i.* ride (on horseback); **cabalgata** *f* ride; (*desfile*) cavalcade.

cabalista *m fig.* schemer; **cabalístico** cab(b)alistic(al); *fig.* occult, mysterious.

caballa *f* mackerel.

caballada *f* drove of horses; *S.Am.* nonsense; stupid act; *S.Am.* dirty trick; **caballar** horse *attr.* (*a. rostro*), equine; **caballejo** *m* pony; *b.s.* nag; **caballerear** [1a] put on airs, pretend to be somebody; **caballeresco** *hist.* of chivalry, chivalric; *sentimientos* fine, noble; *carácter* gentlemanly; *trato* chivalrous; **caballerete** *m* F stuck-up young fellow, dude; **caballería** *f* mount, steed; horse, mule *etc.*; ⚔ cavalry; (*orden*) order of knighthood; *hist.* knighthood, chivalry; *~ andante* knight-errantry; F *andarse en ~s* overdo the compliments; **caballeriza** *f* stable (*a. fig., deportes*); stud *de cría*; *~ de alquiler* livery stable; **caballerizo** *m* groom, stable man.

caballero 1. riding, mounted (*en* on); *fig.* persistent, obstinate (*en* in); **2.** *m* gentleman; mister, sir *en trato directo*; *hist.* knight, noble, nobleman; knight *de Malta etc.*; *~ andante* knight-errant; *~ de industria* swindler, adventurer; *armar ~ a* knight; *ser cumplido ~, ser todo un ~* be a real gentleman; *es un mal ~* he's no gentleman; **caballerosidad** *f* gentlemanliness; chivalry; nobility; **caballeroso** gentlemanly; chivalrous; **caballerote** *m* F so-called gentleman.

caballete *m* ⚒, ⚠ ridge; ⊕ (saw)horse; (*madero*) trestle; cap *de chimenea*; *paint.* easel; bridge *de nariz.*

caballista *m* horseman; **caballito** *m* little horse, pony; *~ (de niños)* hobby-horse; *~ del diablo* dragonfly; *~ de mar* seahorse; *~s pl.* merry-go-round.

caballo *m* horse; *ajedrez*: knight; *naipes*: queen; ⊕ sawhorse; ⊕ *~ (de fuerza)* horsepower; *~ de balancín, ~ mecedor* rocking horse; *~ de batalla fig.* forte, speciality; *~ blanco* backer; F *~ de buena boca* accommodating fellow; *~ de carga* pack horse; *~ de carrera(s)* race horse; *~ de caza* hunter; *~ de guerra* war horse; *~ padre* stallion; *~ de tiro* cart horse; *a ~* on horseback; *a ~ de* astride, on; *a mata ~* at breakneck speed; ⚔ *de a ~* mounted; *ir (or montar) a ~* ride (on horseback); **caballón** *m* ⚒ ridge; **caballuno** horselike, horsy.

cabaña *f* cabin, hut; (*rebaño*) flock; *billar*: balk; *~ de madera* log cabin; **cabañero** *m* shepherd; **cabañuelas** *f/pl. Mex.* winter rain.

cabaret [kaβaˈre] *m* cabaret; night club.

cabás *m* satchel.

cabe *m*: F *~ de pala* windfall, lucky break; F *dar un ~ a* do harm to.

cabecear [1a] *v/t. sew.* bind; *deportes*: head; *v/i.* nod; (*negación*) shake one's head; ⚓ pitch; *mot.* lurch; (*carga*) slip; **cabeceo** *m* nod; shake of the head; ⚓ pitching; *mot.* lurch(ing); **cabecera** *f* head *de cama, mesa, puente etc.*; headboard *de cama*; end *de cuarto etc.*; (*almohada*) pillow, bolster; *geog.* administrative center, chief town; *typ.* headline; (*adorno*) head piece; heading *de documento*; *de ~ libro* bedside *attr.*; *médico* family *attr.*; *a la ~ de* at *s.o.*'s bedside.

cabecilla 1. *m/f* F hothead, wrong-headed sort; **2.** *m* ringleader.

cabellera *f* head of hair; (*peluca*) wig; scalp *de piel roja*; *ast.* tail; **cabello** *m* hair (*a.* ~*s pl.*); ~ *merino* thick curly hair; ⚘ ~*s pl. de Venus* maidenhair; *en* ~ with one's hair down; *en* ~*s* bare-headed; *pendiente de un* ~ hanging by a thread; F *asirse de un* ~ use any excuse; *traído por los* ~*s* irrelevant, quite off the point; *símil* far-fetched; **cabelludo** hairy; shaggy; ⚘ fibrous; *v. cuero*.

caber [2m] **1.** fit, go (*en caja* into); ~ *en espacio* be contained in; *cabe(n)* X there is room for X; *en esta caja no cabe* it won't go into this box, this box won't hold it; *¿cabemos todos?* is there room for us all?; *no cabe por esta puerta* it won't get through this door; **2.** *fig.* be possible; ~ *a* befall, happen to; (*suerte*) fall to (one's lot); *no cabe más* that's the limit; *no* ~ (*en sí*) *de alegría etc.* be bursting with; *no* ~ *en sí* be swollen-headed; *cabe preguntar si* one may ask if; *todo cabe en ese chico* that lad is capable of anything; *no cabe en él hacerlo* it is not in him to do it; *v. duda, suerte*.

cabestrillo *m* ⚕ sling; **cabestro** *m* halter; (*buey*) leading ox; F pimp; *llevar del* ~ *fig.* lead by the nose.

cabeza *f mst* head; top, summit *de monte*; top, head *de lista etc.*; *geog.* capital; *fig.* origin, beginning; (*p.*) head, chief; F ~ *de chorlito* nitwit; ~ *de dragón* snapdragon; ~ *de familia* head of the household; ~ *de guerra* warhead; ~ *de partido* county town; ~ *de playa* beachhead; ~ *de puente* bridgehead; ~ *de turco* scapegoat, whipping boy; *a la* ~ *de* at the head of; *de* ~ *estar* on end; *caer* head first, headlong; *por* ~ per head; F *tocado de la* ~ touched, round the bend; F *alzar la* ~ ✝ get on one's feet again; ⚕ be up and about; *calentarse la* ~ get fagged out; *escarmentar en* ~ *ajena* learn by another's mistakes; F *ir de* ~ be snowed under; *írsele a uno la* ~ be giddy; *meterse de* ~ *en* plunge into; *metérsele a uno en la* ~ get *s.t.* into one's head; *perder la* ~ lose one's head; F *romperse la* ~ rack one's brains; F *sentar la* ~ settle down; *subírsele a uno a la* ~ (*vino a. fig.*) go to one's head; *volver la* ~ look round.

cabezada *f* (*golpe*) butt *con cabeza*, blow on the head *en cabeza*; (*movimiento*) nod; ⚓ pitch(ing); *dar* ~*s* nod; *darse de* ~*s fig.* rack one's brains; **cabezal** *m* pillow; *mot.* headrest; (*imprenta*) heading; **cabezazo** *m* butt; *deportes*: header; **cabezo** *m* hillock, small hill; (*cumbre*) top; ⚓ reef; **cabezón 1.** = *cabezudo*; **2.** *m* hole for the head; collar band; *llevar de los* ~*es* force *s.o.* to go; **cabezota 1.** *f* big head; **2.** *m/f* F pig-headed sort; **cabezudo** big-headed; *fig.* pig-headed; *vino* heady; **cabezuela** *f* ⚘ head.

cabida *f* space, room; capacity (*a.* ⚓); extent *de terreno*; *tener* ~ *para* have room for, hold.

cabildear [1a] lobby; **cabildero** *m* lobbyist, intriguer; **cabildo** *m eccl.* chapter; *pol.* town council; (*junta*) chapter *etc.* meeting.

cabillo *m* end; ⚘ stalk, stem.

cabina *f* ✈, ⚓ *etc.* cabin; (*camión*) cab; ✈ *a.* cockpit; ~ *de teléfono*, ~ *telefónica* telephone booth.

cabio *m* joist, rafter; lintel *de puerta*.

cabizbajo *fig.* crestfallen, dejected.

cable *m* cable (*a.* ⚓, ⚡, *medida*), rope, hawser; ~ *de remolque* tow line, towrope; **cablegrafiar** [1c] cable; **cablegrama** *m* cable(gram).

cabo *m* end (*a. fig.*); *geog.* cape; (*mango*) handle; ⚓ cable, rope; ⊕ thread; end, bit *que queda*; stub, stump *de vela, lápiz etc.*; (*p.*) chief, head; ⚔ corporal; ~*s pl.* accessories *del vestido*; ~*s pl. fig.* odds and ends; ~ *suelto* loose end; *al* (*fin y al*) ~ in the end; *al* ~ *de* at the end of; *de* ~ *a rabo* from beginning to end; *atar* ~*s* put two and two together; *dar* ~ *a* finish off; *dar* ~ *de* put an end to; *llevar a* ~ carry *s.t.* out; *negocio* transact; *decisión* implement; *ponerse al* ~ *de* get the point of.

cabotaje *m* ⚓ coasting trade.

cabra *f* female goat, nanny goat F; *estar como una* ~ be crazy.

cabrahigo *m* wild fig.

cabrerizo 1. goat *attr.*; **2.** *m* = **cabrero** *m* goatherd.

cabrestante *m* capstan.

cabria *f* hoist, derrick.

cabrio *m* = *cabio*.

cabrío 1.: *macho* ~ male goat, billy goat; **2.** *m* flock of goats.
cabriola *f* caper; gambol; prance; *dar* ~*s* = **cabriolar** [1a] cut capers; (*cordero*) gambol; (*caballo*) prance; frisk about.
cabriolé *m* cab(riolet).
cabritilla *f* kid(skin); **cabrito** *m zo.* kid; *carne de* ~ kid; F *a* ~ astride; **cabrón** *m fig.* cuckold; complaisant husband; (*como injuria, a. co.*) bastard; rat; *S.Am.* pimp; **cabronada** *f* F (*mala pasada*) dirty trick; (*trabajo*) tough job, fag; **cabruno** goat *attr.*
cabuya *S.Am.*: *dar* ~ moor, tie up; F *ponerse en la* ~ cotton on.
caca *f* F excrement; filth; defect.
cacahuete *m* peanut, monkey nut; (*planta*) groundnut.
cacalote *m S.Am.* raven; *S.Am.* popcorn; *Cuba, Mex.* blunder; foolishness.
cacao *m* cocoa; *S.Am.* chocolate.
cacareado vaunted, much boasted of; **cacarear** [1a] *v/t.* boast about, make much of; *v/i.* (*gallina*) cackle; (*gallo*) crow; **cacareo** *m* cackling; crowing (*a. fig.*).
cacatúa *f* cockatoo.
cacería *f* (*partida*) shoot, hunt; (*pasatiempo*) shooting, hunting; (*muertos*) bag.
cacerola *f* (sauce)pan; casserole.
cacique *m S.Am.* chief, headman; *pol.* (local) boss; **caciquismo** *m pol.* (local) bossism; *approx.* machine politics.
caco *m* pickpocket; F coward.
cacofonía *f* cacophony.
cacto *m* cactus.
cacha *f* handle; *S.Am.* horn; F *hasta las* ~*s* up to the hilt.
cachar [1a] *plato* smash, break; *madera* cut with the grain; ⚒ plow up.
cacharro *m* earthenware pot, crock; *fig.* piece of junk; F *mot. etc.* jalopy, old crock; *C.Am., P.R.* jail; ~*s pl.* earthenware, (coarse) pottery.
cachaza *f* calm; *b.s.* slowness; (*bebida*) rum; **cachazudo 1.** calm, phlegmatic; slow; **2.** *m* slow sort.
cachear [1a] frisk (for weapons).
cachería *f S.Am.* F small business, sideline.
cachete *m* punch in the face; ⚕ swollen cheek; = **cachetero** *m* dagger; **cachetina** *f* fist fight.
cachicán 1. F sly, crafty; **2.** *m* ⚒ foreman, gaffer; F sly fellow.
cachigordo F squat, chunky.
cachiporra *f* billy; billy club *de policía*; blackjack *de criminal.*
cachivache *m* (*p.*) useless fellow; ~*s pl.* pots and pans; *contp.* junk.
cacho 1. bent, crooked; **2.** *m* crumb *de pan*; (*pedazo*) bit, slice; *ichth.* chub; F *estar fuera de* ~ be in safekeeping.
cachondeo *m* F farce, poor show; **cachondo** *zo.* in heat; *sl. mujer* hot, sexy.
cachorr(ill)o *m* pocket pistol; **cachorro** *m*, **a** *f* (*perro*) pup(py); (*león etc.*) cub.
cachupín *m*, **-a** *f* Spanish settler in America.
cada each; (*con número etc.*) every; ~ *2 semanas* every 2 weeks; ~ *cual*, ~ *uno* each one, everyone; *¿~ cuánto?* how often?
cadalso *m* scaffold; ⊕ platform.
cadáver *m* (dead) body, corpse; carcass *de animal*; **cadavérico** *fig.* cadaverous; ghastly, deathly pale.
cadena *f* chain; ~ *antirresbaladiza* skid chain; ~ *de televisión* channel; network; ~ *perpetua* life imprisonment; *phys. en* ~ chain *attr.*
cadencia *f* cadence, rhythm; ♪ (*trozo*) cadenza; **cadencioso** rhythmic(al).
cadeneta *f* chain stitch.
cadera *f* hip.
cadetada *f* F thoughtless action, irresponsible act; **cadete** *m* cadet.
caducar [1g] (*viejo*) dodder, be in one's dotage; get out of date *por antiguo*; ⚖, ✝ expire, lapse; **caducidad** *f* feebleness; lapse; expiration; **caduco** decrepit, feeble; ⚘ deciduous; *bienes* perishable, fleeting; ⚖ which has lapsed.
caedizo weak; frail; ready to fall;
caer [2o] *mst* fall (down *etc.*; *a.* ~**se**); (*viento, sol etc.*) go down; (*cortina*) hang; (*color*) fade; (*conversación*) flag; (*costumbre*) lapse; F *no caigo* I don't get it; F *ya caigo* I get it; ~ *a*, ~ *hacia* look towards, look out on to; ~ *bien a* (*vestido*) suit, look well on; ~ *de suyo* be obvious, go without saying; ~ *de tonto etc.* be very silly *etc.*; ~ *en capítulo* come in; *fecha fall on*; ~ *en que* realize that; ~ *por fecha* fall around; ~ *sobre* fall on; (*animal*)

pounce on; *dejar* ~ drop; *tono* lower; *dejarse* ~ let o.s. go (*or* fall); *fig.* be wily; *estar al* ~ be on the point of falling.

café *m* coffee; (*casa*) café; (*color de*) ~ coffee-colored; ~ *cantante approx.* night club; ~ *con leche* white coffee; ~ *solo* black coffee; **cafeína** *f* caffeine; **cafetal** *m* coffee plantation; **cafetalero** *m S.Am.* coffee planter; coffee dealer; **cafetear** [1a] drink coffee; **cafetera** *f* coffee pot; ~ (*eléctrica, filtradora*) percolator; *approx.* kettle *para hervir agua*; **cafetería** *f* cafeteria; milk bar; **cafetero** *m*, **a** *f* café proprietor; **cafetín** *m* little café; **cafeto** *m* coffee plant.

cáfila *f* F flock; string *de disparates.*

cafre 1. Kaffir; *fig.* cruel; (*zafio*) uncouth; **2.** *m/f* Kaffir.

cagada *f* shit; *fig.* shocking mistake; **cagado** F yellow, funky; **cagar** [1h] *v/t.* shit; *fig.* make a mess of; *v/i.* (have a) shit; **cagatinta**(**s**) *m* pencil pusher; **cagón** F *adj. a. su. m* (-**a** *f*) cowardly.

caída *f* fall (*a. fig.*); (*tropezando*) tumble; (*declive*) drop; *geol.* dip; fold *de cortina*; set, hang *de vestido*; *fig.* decline; collapse, downfall; *thea.* flop; *la* ~ the Fall; ~*s pl.* ⊕ shoddy; ~*s pl.* F witty remarks; ~ *de agua* waterfall; ~ *de cabeza* header; *a la* ~ *de la tarde* in the evening; *a la* ~ *del sol* at sunset; **caído 1.** fallen; *cabeza etc.* drooping; *cuello* turn-down; *fig.* crestfallen, dejected; ~ *de color* pale; **2.** ~*s m/pl.*; *los* ~ the fallen; ✝ income due; *monumento a los* ~ war memorial.

caigo *etc. v. caer.*

caimán *m* alligator, caiman.

caimiento *m* fall; ⚕ decline.

cairel *m* wig; (*fleco*) fringe; **cairelear** [1a] fringe.

cairino, cairota Cairene; from Cairo; *a. su. m/f.*

caja *f* box (*a.* ⊕, ⚡); case (*a. typ., de reloj, violín etc.*); chest; *mot.* body; *radio*: cabinet; (*ataúd*) coffin, casket; ⚔ drum; well *de escalera*; ⊕ housing, casing; ⚘ seed case, capsule; ✝ cash box; ~ *de ahorros* savings bank; ~ (*de caudales*) safe, strongbox; ✝ counter; cashier's office; ~ (*de fusil*) (gun)stock; ~ (*postal*) *de ahorros* (post office) savings bank; ~ *de cambio* (*de marchas*), ~ *de velocidades* gear box; ~ *de construcciones approx.* building society; ~ *de eje* axle box; ~ *de empalmes* junction box; ~ *de fuego* fire box; ~ *de fusibles* fuse box; ~ *de grasas* journal box; ~ *de herramientas* tool box; ~ *de menores* petty cash; ~ *de música* musical box; ~ *registradora* cash register; ~ *de registro* manhole; ~ *de resonancia* sounding board (*a. fig.*); ~ *de sebo* grease box, grease cup; ~ *sorpresa* jack-in-the-box; *despedir con* ~*s destempladas* send *s.o.* packing.

cajero *m*, **a** *f* ✝ cashier, (bank) teller; **cajeta** *f* small box; **cajetilla** *f* packet, pack; **cajista** *m* compositor, typesetter; **cajita** *f* small box; ~ *de cerillas* box of matches, matchbox; **cajón** *m* big box, case; drawer *de armario etc.*; space *entre estantes*; ✝ till; (*casilla*) stall; *S.Am.* coffin; ⊕ (*a.* ~ *hidráulico*, ~ *de suspensión*) caisson; ~ *de embalaje* packing case; F ~ *de sastre* odds and ends; (*p.*) muddle-headed fellow; *ser de* ~ be the usual thing, be a matter of course; **cajonería** *f* set of drawers.

cal *f* lime; ~ *apagada* slaked lime; ~ *viva* quicklime; F *de* ~ *y canto* strong, tough.

cala *f geog.* creek, cove, inlet; ⚓ fishing ground; hold *de barco*; ⚕ probe (*a. fig.*); ~ *de construcción* slipway.

calabacín *m* ⚘ marrow; F dolt; **calabaza** *f* pumpkin, gourd; F dolt; F *dar* ~*s a estudiante* fail; *novio* jilt; *recibir* ~*s* get jilted; F *salir* ~ be a flop; **calabazada** *f* butt (with the head); blow on the head; **calabazazo** *m* F bump on the head.

calabobos *m* drizzle.

calabozo *m* (*cuarto*) cell; (*cárcel*) prison; ⚔ F calaboose; jug; † dungeon.

calabrote *m* ⚓ hawser.

calada *f* soaking *etc.*; F *dar una* ~ *a* haul *s.o.* over the coals; **calado** *m* ⊕ fretwork; *sew.* drawn thread work; ⚓ draught.

calafate *m* caulker; **calafatear** [1a] caulk.

calamar *m* squid.

calambre *m* (*a.* ~*s pl.*) cramp.

calamidad *f* calamity; F (*p.*) dead loss; F *es una* ~ it's a great pity; F *¡vaya* ~*!* what bad luck!

calamina *f* calamine.
calamitoso calamitous.
cálamo *m poet.* pen; ♪ reed; *empuñar el* ~ take up the pen; *menear* ~ wield a pen.
calamocano F merry, tipsy.
calamoco *m* icicle.
calamorra *f* F nut, noddle.
calandrar [1a] calender; **calandria**[1] *f* ⊕ calender.
calandria[2] *f* calandra lark.
calaña *f* model, pattern; *fig.* nature, stamp, kind.
calañés *m Andalusian hat with turned-up brim.*
calar[1] **1.** lime *attr.*; **2.** *m* limestone quarry.
calar[2] [1a] **1.** *v/t.* (*líquido*) soak; pierce *con barrena*; ⊕ *metal* cut openwork in; *madera* cut fretwork in; *bayoneta, mastelero* fix; *puente, red* lower; *sombrero* pull down; *p., situación* size up; *p., intención* see through; *secreto* find out; **2.** *v/i.* (*líquido*) sink in; (*zapato*) leak, let in water; ⚓ draw; (*ave,* ✈) swoop (down); (*motor*) stop; **~se** get soaked (*hasta los huesos* to the skin), get drenched; (*ave*) swoop (down); *sombrero* pull down; *gafas* stick on, (*ya puestas*) push back.
calavera 1. *f* skull; **2.** *m* lively fellow; *b.s.* rake; *fig.* necio; *Mex. mot.* tail-light; **calaverada** *f* madcap escapade, foolhardy thing; **calaverear** [1a] carouse; *b.s.* lead a wild life.
calcañal *m*, **calcañar** *m* heel.
calcar [1g] trace; *fig.* ~ *en* base on, model on.
calcáreo lime *attr.*, calcareous 🕮.
calce *m* (*llanta*) tire; (*cuña*) wedge; (*hierro*) iron tip.
calceta *f* (knee-length) stocking; (*grillete*) fetter, shackle; *hacer* ~ knit; **calcetería** *f* hosiery; hosier's (shop); **calcetero** *m*, **a** *f* hosier; **calcetín** *m* sock.
calcificar(**se**) [1g] calcify; **calcina** *f* concrete; **calcinación** *f* calcination; **calcinar** [1a] calcine; burn, reduce to ashes; F bother; **calcio** *m* calcium.
calco *m* tracing; **calcomanía** *f* transfer.
calculable calculable; **calculador 1.** calculating; scheming; **2.** *m* (*máquina*) calculator; ~ *de mano* hand-held calculator; ~ *de bolsillo* pocket calculator; **calcular** [1a] calculate; add up, work out; *fig.* reckon (*que* that); **cálculo** *m* calculation; reckoning; estimate; ⚕ (gall)stone; ~ *de coste* costing; ~ *diferencial* differential calculus; ~ *mental* mental arithmetic; *según mis* ~*s* according to my reckoning; *obrar con mucho* ~ act cautiously.
caldas *f/pl.* hot springs.
caldeamiento *m* warming, heating; **caldear** [1a] heat (up), warm (up); *estar caldeado* be very hot; **~se** get overheated, get very hot.
caldera *f* boiler (*a.* ⊕); kettle; *S.Am.* coffee pot; F *las* ~*s de Pedro Botero* hell; **calderero** *m* boilermaker; ~ *remendón* tinker; **caldereta** *f* small boiler; *cocina*: fish stew; lamb stew; *eccl.* = **calderilla** *f eccl.* holy-water vessel; ✝ copper(s), small change; **caldero** *m* copper; ~ *de colada* ladle; **calderón** *m* large boiler; cauldron; *typ.* paragraph sign; ⚓ hold; **caldillo** *m* light broth; sauce for fricassee; *Mex.* meat bits in broth.
caldo *m* broth; consommé, clear soup; (*aderezo*) dressing, sauce; ~*s pl.* liquid derived from fruit *etc.*; ~ *concentrado de carne* beef broth; ~ *de cultivo* culture medium; F *hacer el* ~ *gordo a* play into *s.o.*'s hands.
cale *m* slap, smack.
calefacción *f* heating; *de* ~ heating *attr.*; ~ *central* central heating; ~ *por agua* (*aire*) *caliente* hot water (air) heat(ing); ~ *solar* solar heat(ing).
cal(**e**)**idoscopio** *m* kaleidoscope.
calendario *m* calendar; F *hacer* ~*s* muse.
caléndula *f* marigold.
calentador *m* heater; ~ (*de inmersión*) immersion heater; † ~ *de cama* warming pan; ~ *a gas* gas heater, geyser *de baño*; **calentamiento** *m* heating; **calentar** [1k] *v/t. horno etc.* heat (up); *comida, cuarto, piernas, silla etc.* warm (up); *negocio etc.* speed up, get moving; F warm, tan; ~ *al blanco* (*al rojo*) make white-hot (red-hot); *v/i.* be hot, be warm; **~se** heat (up), (get) warm, get hot; warm o.s. *a la lumbre*; *fig.* (*disputa*) get heated; (*exaltarse*) get excited; *zo.* be on heat; **calentura** *f* ⚕ temperature,

fever; *Col.* anger; **calenturiento** feverish.
calera *f* limestone quarry; (*horno*) = **calero** *m* lime kiln.
calesa *f* chaise, buggy.
calesera *f Andalusian jacket.*
calesín *m* gig, fly.
calesitas *f/pl. S.Am.* merry-go-round.
caleta *f* cove, inlet.
caletre *m* F acumen; judgment; gumption.
calibrador *m* gauge; calipers; **calibrar** [1a] gauge; calibrate; **calibre** *m* ⚔ calibre (*a. fig.*), bore; 🚂 gauge; = *calibrador*; ~ *estrangulado* choke bore.
calicó *m* calico.
calidad *f* quality; ✝ *a.* grade; (social) standing; character; term, stipulation *en contrato*; ~*es pl.* (moral) qualities; gifts; *a* ~ *de que* provided that; *de* ~ of quality, of importance; *en* ~ *de* in the capacity of; ~ *de vida* quality of life.
cálido hot; *color* warm.
calidoscopio *m* kaleidoscope.
calientacamas *m* ⚡ electric blanket; **calientapiés** *m* foot warmer; **calientaplatos** *m* hotplate; **caliente** hot; warm; *disputa* heated; *batalla* raging; (*fogoso*) fiery; *zo.* on heat; *en* ~ hot; *fig.* at once; *montar en* ~ shrink on.
califa *m* caliph; **califato** *m* caliphate.
calificación *f* qualification; assessment; label; mark *en examen*; **calificado** qualified; well-known, eminent; *prueba, rival* undisputed; *robo* proven, manifest; **calificar** [1g] qualify (*de* as; *a. gr.*); *p.* (*acreditar*) distinguish, give *s.o.* his fame; ennoble; *examen* mark; *escritos* correct; ~ *de* call, label; characterize as, describe as; ~**se** *S.Am.* register as a voter.
caliginoso *poet.* darkling, misty.
caligrafía *f* penmanship, calligraphy; **caligráfico** calligraphic.
calina *f* haze, mist.
calistenia *f* calisthenics.
cáliz *m eccl.* chalice, communion cup; *poet.* cup, goblet; ⚘ calyx.
caliza *f* limestone; **calizo** lime *attr.*; *terreno* limy.
calma *f* calm; calmness; ⚓ calm weather; (*lentitud*) slowness, laziness; lull (*en* in), cessation (*de* of); ~ *chicha* dead calm; *con* ~ calmly; *en* ~ calm; *fig.* in abeyance; ✝ steady; *perder la* ~ get ruffled; **calmante** soothing; sedative (*a. su. m*); **calmar** [1a] *v/t.* calm (down), quieten (down); *dolor* relieve; *nervios* soothe, steady; *v/i.* abate, fall; ~**se** calm down *etc.*; **calmoso** calm; F slow, lazy.
caló *m* gipsy slang; slang; *Madrid equivalent of Cockney.*
calofriarse [1c] feel chilly, get the shivers; **calofrío** *m* chill; **calofríos** *m/pl.* chill(y sensation), shivers.
calor *m* heat (*a.* ⊕, *phys.*, *fig. de batalla, disputa etc.*); (*esp. agradable*) warmth (*a. fig. de acogida etc.*); *fig.* enthusiasm, zeal; ~ *rojo* red heat; ¡*qué* ~! isn't it hot!; *entrar en* ~ get warm, begin to feel warm; warm up *con ejercicios*; *hace* (*mucho*) ~ it is (very) hot; *tener* ~ be hot, feel hot; **caloría** *f* caloric; **calórico** caloric; **calorífero 1.** heat-producing; **2.** *m* heating system; furnace, stove; heater; **calorífico** calorific; **calorifugar** [1h] *caldera* lag; **calorífugo** heat-resistant, nonconducting; (*incombustible*) fireproof.
calotear [1a] *S.Am.* cheat; gyp.
calta *f* (*a.* ~ *palustre*) marsh marigold.
calumnia *f* slander; (*esp. escrito*) libel (*de* on); **calumniador** *m*, **-a** *f* slanderer; libeler; **calumniar** [1b] slander; malign; libel; **calumnioso** slanderous; libelous.
caluroso warm, hot; *fig.* warm, enthusiastic.
calva *f* bald patch; ⚘ clearing.
Calvario *m* Calvary; (*estaciones del*) ~ Stations of the Cross; ♀ *fig.* cross; F string of debts, misfortunes.
calvatrueno *m* F bald pate; (*p.*) madcap; **calvero** *m* glade, clearing; **calvicie** *f* baldness; ~ *precoz* premature baldness.
calvinismo *m* Calvinism.
calvo 1. bald; hairless; *terreno* barren, bare; **2.** *m* bald man.
calza *f* wedge, scotch, chock; F stocking; ~*s pl.* hose, breeches; tights; *en* ~*s prietas fig.* in a fix.
calzada *f* highway, roadway; causeway; (carriage) drive *a casa*; **calzado 1.** *p.p.* ~ *de* shod with, wearing; **2.** *m* footwear; **calzador** *m* shoehorn; **calzar** [1f] **1.** *v/t. p. etc.*

put shoes on, provide with footwear; *zapatos etc.* put on; *número* wear, take; *bala* take; wedge, scotch, chock *con calce*; **2.** *v/i.*: *calza bien* he wears good shoes; F *calza poco* he's pretty dim; **3.** **~se** *zapatos etc.* put on; wear; *fig.* get; *p.* keep under one's thumb.

calzo *m* wedge, scotch; ⚓ chock, skid; **calzón** *m* (*a.* **~es** *pl.*) breeches; shorts; *S.Am.* trousers; **~es** *pl. blancos* (under)pants, drawers; F *ponerse etc. los* **~es** wear the trousers; **calzonazos** *m* F easy-going (*or* weak-willed) fellow; (*marido*) henpecked husband; **calzoncillos** *m/pl.* (under)pants.

callada: F *a las ~s, de ~* on the quiet; *dar la ~ por respuesta* say nothing; **callado** silent, quiet; reserved, secretive; **callandico** F, **callandito** F softly, stealthily; **callar** [1a] **1.** *v/t. secreto* keep; *trozo etc.* pass over (in silence), not mention; *cosa vergonzosa* keep quiet about, hush up; **2.** *v/i.*, **~se** keep quiet, be (*or* remain) silent; (*cesar*) stop talking (*or* ♪ playing, ⊕ working *etc.*), become quiet; (*mar, viento*) be hushed; *¡calla!, ¡cállate!* shut up!, hold your tongue!; *¡calla! fig.* you don't say!; *hacer ~* make *s.o.* stop talking *etc.*, shut *s.o.* up F.

calle *f* street; road; *deportes*: lane; *~ de dirección única* one-way street; *~ mayor* high street, main street; *azotar ~s* wander around; pass time walking; F *dejar en la ~* put *s.o.* out of a job; F *echar por la ~ de en medio* push on regardless; *hacer ~* clear the way; F *poner en la ~* kick out, chuck out; F *quedarse en la ~* not have a penny to one's name; **calleja** *f* = *callejuela*; **callejear** [1a] stroll around; *b.s.* hang about, loaf; **callejero** street *attr.*; (*p.*) fond of walking about town; **callejón** *m* alley(way), lane, passage; *~ sin salida* cul-de-sac; *fig.* blind alley; impasse; **callejuela** *f* narrow street, side street; alley(way); *fig.* way out (of it).

callista *m/f* corncutter; chiropodist; **callo** *m* corn *esp. en pie*; callus; *~s pl. cocina*: tripe; *criar etc. ~s* have no feelings, be a callous type; **callosidad** *f* callosity, hardness (on hands *etc.*); **calloso** callous; *manos* horny, hard.

cama *f* bed; 🌾 bedding, litter; *zo.* lair; floor *de carro*; *~ de matrimonio* double bed; *~-litera* double-decker bed; *~ turca* divan bed; ⚕ *caer en (la) ~* fall ill, take to one's bed; ⚕ *estar en ~, guardar ~* be confined to bed; *hacer (or poner) la ~ a* work harm for *s.o.* behind his back; *levantarse por los pies de la ~* get out of bed on the wrong side; **camada** *f zo.* litter, brood; (*capa*) layer; course *de ladrillos*; (*ps.*) gang.

camafeo *m* cameo.

camal *m* halter.

camaleón *m* chameleon.

camamila *f* camomile.

camándula *f* rosary; F *tener muchas ~s* be a sly one, be a bit of a rogue; **camandulear** [1a] be a hypocrite, be overdevout; **camandulería** *f* prudery, priggishness; **camandulero** F hypocritical.

cámara *f* room; chamber (*a.* ⊕, ⚓, ⚖, *parl.*); *parl. a.* house; ⚓ (*camarote*) cabin; ⚓ (*sala*) saloon; ⚔ *a.* breech; 🌾 granary; *anat.* cavity; *phot.* (*a. ~ fotográfica*) camera; *mot.* (*a. ~ de aire*) inner tube ⚕ *~s pl.* diarrhea; *~ cinematográfica* cinecamera; *♀ de Comercio* Chamber of Commerce; *mot. ~ de combustión* combustion chamber; *♀ de Diputados* Chamber of Deputies (Spain); *♀ de Representantes* House of Representatives (U.S.); *~ de gas* gas bag; *♀ de los Comunes* (*Lores*) House of Commons (Lords); *~ de niebla* cloud chamber; *~ de televisión, ~ televisora* television camera; *a ~ lenta* (in) slow motion; *de ~* royal.

camarada *m* comrade, companion; mate; **camaradería** *f* comradeship; team spirit *en deportes etc.*

camarera *f* waitress *en restaurante*; (chamber)maid *en hotel*; ⚓ stewardess; parlormaid *en casa*; lady's maid *de dama*; **camarero** *m* waiter; ⚓ steward; chamberlain *de rey*.

camarilla *f* clique, coterie; caucus *de partido*.

camarín *m eccl.* niche for an image; *thea.* dressing room; (*tocador*) boudoir; (*pieza retirada*) side room.

camaró(n) *m* shrimp; *C.Am.* tip.

camarote *m* ⚓ cabin, stateroom.

camastro *m* rickety old bed; **camastrón** F sly, not to be trusted.

cambalache *m* swap, exchange;

cambalach(e)ar [1a] swap, exchange.
cámbaro *m* crab.
cambiable changeable; exchangeable; **cambiante 1.** fickle, temperamental; **2.** *m* money changer; ~s *pl.* changing colors, iridescence.
cambiar [1b] **1.** *v/t.* change, exchange (*con, por* for); change, turn (*en* into); † *a.* trade (*por* for); (*de sitio*) shift, move; *saludos etc.* exchange; **2.** *v/i.*, **~se** change (*a.* ~ *de*); ~ *de sitio* shift, move; ~ *de sombrero etc. con* exchange hats *etc.* with; **cambiazo** *m* † F switch; *dar el* ~ switch the goods; **cambio** *m* change; (*trueque*) exchange; † (*tipo*) rate of exchange; (*vuelta*) change; turn *de marea*; change, shift, switch *de política etc.*; † *libre* ~ free trade; (*palanca de*) ~ *de marchas* gear lever, gearshift; ~ *de tiempo* change in the weather; 🚂 ~ *de vía* switch; *a* ~ *de*, *en* ~ *de* in exchange for; *en* ~ instead, in return; (*por otra parte*) on the other hand; **cambista** *m* money changer; *S.Am.* switchman.
camelar [1a] F *mujer* flirt with; cajole; tease.
camelia *f* camellia.
camelo *m* F flirtation; (*chasco*) joke, hoax; (*mentira*) cock-and-bull story; (*halago*) (piece of) blarney; *dar* ~ *a* make fun of; *me huele a* ~ it's fishy.
camello *m* camel (*a.* ⚓).
camellón *m* drinking trough; ⚒ ridge.
camerino *m thea.* dressing room.
camero 1. bed *attr.*; **2.** *m* maker (seller) of bedding; highway.
camerógrafo *m* cameraman.
camilla *f* ⚕ stretcher; sofa, couch; *table with heater underneath*; **camillero** *m* stretcher bearer.
caminante *m/f* wayfarer, traveler; walker; **caminar** [1a] *v/t. distancia* cover, travel, do; *v/i.* travel, journey; (*andar*) walk; (*rio, fig.*) move, go; F ~ *derecho* behave properly; **caminata** *f* F hike, ramble; jaunt, outing; **caminero** *v. peón.*
camino *m* road; way (*de* to; *a. fig.*); *esp. fig.* course, path; ~ *de* on the way to; ~ *de entrada* approach (road); ~ *de herradura* bridle path; ~ *real* high road (*a. fig.*); ~ *de Santiago* Milky Way; ~ *de sirga* towpath; ~ *trillado* well-trodden path; *fig.* beaten track; ~ *vecinal* country road, lane; *a medio* ~ halfway; *de* ~ *attr.* traveling; (*adv.*) in passing; *2 horas de* ~ 2 hours' journey; *en el* ~ on the way, en route; *abrir(se)* ~ make one's way (*por* through); *fig.* find a way; *allanar el* ~ smooth the way; *echar* ~ *adelante* strike out; *errar el* ~ lose the way; *llevar por mal* ~ lead astray; *partir el* ~ *con* meet *s.o.* halfway; *ponerse en* ~ set out, start; *traer a buen* ~ put *s.o.* on the right road.
camión *m mot.* truck; (*carro*) heavy wagon, dray; *S.Am.* bus; ~ *blindado* troop carrier; ~ *de la basura* garbage truck; ~ *grúa* tow truck; **camionaje** *m* haulage, cartage; **camionero** *m* truck driver; teamster; **camioneta** *f* van.
camisa *f* shirt; ~ (*de mujer*) chemise; ⊕ jacket (*a. de libro*), sleeve; ⚘ skin; mantle *de luz*; folder *de legajo*; ~ *de agua* water jacket; ~ *de fuerza* straitjacket; *en* (*mangas de*) ~ in one's shirt sleeves; *en* ~ *fig.* without a dowry; *dejar sin* ~ fleece; **camisería** *f* outfitter's; **camisero** *m*, **a** *f* shirtmaker; outfitter; **camiseta** *f* vest, undershirt; *deportes*: singlet; **camisón** *m* (*de noche*) night dress, nightgown.
camomila *f* camomile.
camorra *f* F row, set-to, scrap, quarrel; *armar* ~ kick up a row; **camorrista** F **1.** fond of scraps; **2.** *m* quarrelsome sort; hooligan.
campal *batalla* pitched.
campamento *m* camp; encampment; ~ *de trabajo* labor camp.
campana *f* bell; *eccl. fig.* parish (church); ~ *de bucear* diving bell; ~ *de cristal* bell glass; glass cover; *a* ~ *herida, a toque de* ~ to the ring of bells; F *oír* ~*s y no saber dónde* get hold of the wrong end of the stick; **campanada** *f* stroke (of the bell); (sound of) ringing; F commotion; **campanario** *m* belfry, church tower; **campanear** [1a] ring out; *campaneado fig.* much talked-of; **campanero** *m* ⊕ bell founder; ♪ (bell) ringer.
campanilla *f* handbell; ⚡ electric bell; (*burbuja*) bubble; (*adorno*) tassel; ⚘ bellflower; *anat.* uvula; ~ *azul* harebell; ~ *blanca* snowdrop; F *de muchas* ~*s* big, grand; **campanillazo** *m* loud ring; **campanillear**

[1a] tinkle, ring; **campanilleo** *m* tinkling, ringing.
campante outstanding; *b.s.* (*a. tan* ~) self-satisfied, smug.
campanudo bell-shaped; *falda* wide; *lenguaje* high-flown, bombastic; *orador* pompous.
campaña *f geog.* (flat) countryside, plain; ⚔, *pol.*, *fig.* campaign; ⚓ cruise, expedition, trip; ↗ season; ⚔ *de* ~ *freq.* field *attr.*; ⚔ *batir la* ~ reconnoitre; *hacer* ~ campaign (*en pro de* for).
campañol *m* vole.
campar [1a] ⚔ *etc.* camp; (*descollar*) stand out, excel; **campear** [1a] (*animales*) go to graze; (*trigo*) show green; ⚔ reconnoitre; *S.Am.* scour the countryside.
campechano hearty, good-hearted, open; generous.
campeón *m* champion; **campeonato** *m* championship.
campero (out) in the open; open-air *attr.*; ↗ sleeping in the open.
campesino 1. country *attr.*; *zo.* field *attr.*; *contp.* rustic; **2.** *m*, **a** *f* peasant (*a. contp.*); countryman (-woman); farmer; **campestre** country *attr.*; ⚘ wild.
camping *m* camping (ground).
campiña *f* countryside; open country.
campo *m* ↗ field (*a. fig.*, *phys.*, *heráldica*); (*depoblado*) country (side); *deportes*: field, ground, pitch; (golf) course; (*campamento*) camp; (*fondo*) background; ~ *de aterrizaje* landing ground; ~ *de aviación* airfield; ~ *de batalla* battlefield; ~ *de concentración* concentration camp; ~ *de deportes* playing field, recreation ground; ~ *de minas* minefield; ~ *petrolífero* oil-field; ~ *de pruebas* testing grounds; ~ *magnético* magnetic field; ~ *raso* open country; *a* ~ *raso* in the open; ~ *santo* cemetery, churchyard; ~ *de tiro* range; *a* ~ *traviesa* cross-country; *dejar el* ~ *libre* leave the field open (*para* for); *levantar el* ~ strike camp; *fig.* give up; *reconocer el* ~ reconnoiter; **camposanto** *m* cemetery, churchyard.
camuesa *f* pippin; **camueso** *m* pippin tree; F dolt.
camuflaje *m* camouflage; **camuflar** [1a] camouflage.
can *m zo.* dog; ⚔ trigger; ⚠ corbel.
cana *f* (*a.* ~*s pl.*) white hair, gray hair; F *echar una* ~ *al aire* let one's hair down; F *peinar* ~*s* be getting on.
canadiense *adj. a. su. m/f* Canadian.
canal *mst m geog.* ⚓ channel (*a. telev.*, *radio*), strait(s); navigation channel *de puerto*; (*artificial*) canal, waterway; ↗ (*a.* ~ *de riego*) irrigation channel; *geog.* narrow valley; *anat.* canal, tract; ⚠ gutter, spout; drain pipe; (*estría*) groove; ⊕ conduit; pipe *de agua, gas*; (*res*) dressed carcass; ~ *de navegación* ship canal; ~ *de la Mancha* English Channel; ~ *digestivo anat.* alimentary canal; *abrir en* ~ cut down the middle, slit open; **canaladura** *f* = *acanaladura*; **canalete** *m* paddle; **canalización** *f* canalization; ⊕ piping; ⚡ wiring; power source; main supply *de gas etc.*; *S.Am.* sewerage system; **canalizar** [1f] *río* canalize; *aguas* harness; *aguas de riego* channel; ⊕ pipe; **canalizo** *m* navigable channel; **canalón** *m* ⚠ spout; drain pipe; (*sombrero*) shovel hat.
canalla 1. *f* rabble, riffraff, mob; **2.** *m* swine, rotter; F rat; **canallada** *f* dirty trick; (*dicho*) nasty thing; **canallesco** mean, rotten; *diversión* low.
canana *f* cartridge belt.
canapé *m* sofa, settee.
canario 1. *adj. a. su. m*, **a** *f* (native) of the Canary Isles; **2.** *m orn.* canary; **3.** *int.* Holy Smoke!, Great Scott!
canasta *f* (round) basket; *naipes*: canasta; **canastilla** *f* small basket; layette *de niño*; **canastillo** *m* wicker tray; **canasto** *m* hamper; basket; *¡*~*s!* darn it!, confound it!
cancamurria *f* F blues; **cancamusa** *f* F trick; *armar una* ~ *a* throw sand in *s.o.*'s eyes.
cáncano *m* F louse; *andar como* ~ *loco* go round in circles.
cancel *m* wind-proof door; (*mueble*) folding screen; **cancela** *f* lattice gate.
cancelación *f* cancellation; **cancelar** [1a] cancel; *deuda* write off, wipe out; *fig.* dispel, do away with; banish (from one's mind).
cáncer *m* cancer; *ast.* 2 Cancer; **cancerado** cancerous; *fig.* corrupt; **cancerarse** [1a] (*úlcera*) become cancerous; (*p.*) have cancer; *fig.* become corrupt; **cancerología** *f*

study of cancer; cancer research; oncology; **canceroso** cancerous.

canciller *m* chancellor; **cancilleresco** *fig.* formal, ruled by protocol; **cancillería** *f* chancellery.

canción *f* song; *poet.* lyric, song; ~ *de cuna* lullaby, cradle song; ~ *infantil* nursery rhyme; F *volvemos a la misma* ~ here we go again; **cancionero** *m* ♪ song book; *poet.* anthology, collection of verse.

cancro *m* ⚘ canker; ⚕ cancer.

cancha *f* field, ground; *pelota*: court; *S.Am. caballos*: racecourse, race track; *gallos*: cockpit; ~ *de tenis* tennis court; (*espacio*) open space; *S.Am. estar en su* ~ be in one's element; **canchear** [1a] be out for a good time.

candado *m* padlock; clasp *de libro*; **candar** [1a] lock up, put away.

cande: *v. azúcar.*

candeal *pan* white.

candela *f* candle; *phys.* candlepower; (*candelero*) candlestick; F light *para cigarrillo*; F *arrimar* ~ *a* give *s.o.* a hiding; **candelaria** *f* Candlemas; **candelero** *m* candlestick; (*velón*) oil lamp; F *en* ~ high up; F *poner en* ~ give *s.o.* a high post; **candelilla** *f* bougie; ⚘ blossom, catkin; *S.Am.* glowworm; **candelizo** *m* F icicle.

candente *hierro* white-hot, red-hot; glowing, burning; *cuestión* burning.

candidato *m* candidate (*a* for); **candidatura** *f* candidature.

candidez *f* candor *etc.*; (*dicho*) silly remark; **cándido** *poet.* snow-white; *fig.* guileless, innocent; *b.s.* naïve; (*tonto*) stupid.

candil *m* oil lamp; F *arder en un* ~ (*vino*) be very strong; *fig.* be pretty strong stuff; **candilejas** *f/pl. thea.* footlights.

candonga *f* F (*lisonja*) blarney; (*engaño*) trick; (*chasco*) hoax, practical joke; teasing; F *dar* ~ *a* tease, kid; **candongo** F **1.** (*lisonjero*) smooth; (*astuto*) sly; (*holgazán*) lazy; **2.** *m*, **a** *f* cajoler, toady; sly sort; lazy blighter; **candonguear** [1a] F *v/t.* tease, kid; *v/i.* shirk, dodge work; **candonguero** = *candongo.*

candor *m poet.* pure whiteness; *fig.* innocence, guilelessness; **candoroso** innocent, guileless; *confesión etc.* frank, candid.

canela *f* cinnamon; F lovely thing; ¡~! good gracious!; ~ *de la China* cassia; **canelo 1.** cinnamon(-colored); **2.** *m* cinnamon (tree).

canelón *m* = *canalón*; (*carámbano*) icicle.

canesú *m sew.* yoke; (*vestido*) underbodice, camisole.

cangilón *m* pitcher; bucket, scoop *de noria etc.*

cangreja *f* ⚓ spanker.

cangrejo *m*: ~ (*de río*) crayfish; ~ (*de mar*) crab; ⚓ gaff.

canguelo *m* F funk.

canguro *m* kangaroo.

caníbal 1. cannibalistic, human-eating, man-eating; *fig.* savage; **2.** *m* cannibal; **canibalismo** *m* cannibalism.

canica *f* marble; (*juego*) marbles.

canicie *f* whiteness of the hair.

canícula *f* dog days; **canicular 1.**: *calores* ~*es* midsummer heat; **2.** ~*es m/pl.* dog days.

canijo F weak, sickly.

canilla *f anat.* shin(bone), arm bone; ⊕ bobbin, spool; spout, cock *de tonel*; rib *de tela*; *S.Am.* tap; *Mex.* force, power; *a* ~ by force.

canino 1. canine, dog *attr.*; *hambre* ravenous; **2.** *m* canine (tooth).

canje *m* exchange, interchange; **canjear** [1a] exchange, interchange.

cano white-haired; (*con algunas canas*) gray(-haired); *fig.* aged, venerable; *poet.* snow-white.

canoa *f* canoe; boat, launch; ~ *automóvil* motor launch.

canódromo *m* dog track.

canon *m eccl.*, ♪, *paint.* canon; ✝ tax; ⚒ rent; *typ. gran* ~ canon; ~*es pl.* ⚖ canon law; **canonical** canonical; *vida* easy; **canonicato** *m* canonry; F cushy job; **canónico** canonical; **canóniga** *f* F nap before lunch; F *coger una* ~ have one over the eight; **canónigo** *m* canon; **canonización** *f* canonization; **canonizar** [1f] canonize; *fig.* applaud, show approval of; **canonjía** *f* canonry: F cushy job.

canoro *ave* (sweet-)singing; *voz etc.* melodious.

canoso gray(-haired); *barba* grizzled.

canotaje *m* boating.

cansado tired, weary (*de* of); ⚕

exhausted; *vista* tired, strained; (*que cansa*) tedious, trying, tiresome; *pluma etc.* well-worn, past its best; **cansancio** *m* tiredness, weariness; *esp.* ⚕ fatigue; (*tedio*) boredom; F *estar muerto de* ~ be dog-tired; **cansar** [1a] **1.** *v/t.* tire, weary *esp. lit.*; ⚕ exhaust; *fig.* bother, bore (*con* with); *apetito* jade; *paciencia* wear out; *tierra* exhaust; *vista* tire, strain, try; **2.** *v/i.* tire; (*p.*) be trying, be tiresome; **3.** ~**se** tire, get tired (*con, de* of); tire o.s. out (*en inf. ger.*); **cansera** *f* F bother; **cansino** lazy; sluggish; tired.

cantábrico Cantabrian.

cantador *m*, **-a** *f* folk singer, singer of popular songs.

cantal *m* boulder; (*cantizal*) stony ground.

cantante 1. singing; *v. voz*; **2.** *m/f* (professional) singer; vocalist; **cantar** [1a] **1.** *v/t.* sing (*fig.* the praises of); chant; F ~*las claras* speak up; (*con descaro*) be cheeky; **2.** *v/i.* sing; *zo.* chirp; ⊕ squeak, grind; F squeal, blab; ~ *a dos voces* sing a duet; F ~ *de plano* tell all one knows; **3.** *m* song, poem; ~ *de gesta* epic; ♀ *de los* ♀*es* Song of Songs, Canticles; F *ése es otro* ~ that's another story.

cántara *f* large pitcher; *liquid measure* = *16.13 liters.*

cantárida *f*: (*polvo de*) ~ Spanish fly, *pharm.* cantharides.

cantarín 1. fond of singing; *tono* singsong; **2.** *m*, **-a** *f* singer.

cántaro *m* pitcher; (*cabida*) pitcherful; F *a* ~*s* in plenty; *llover* cats and dogs.

cante *m* singing; popular song; ~ *flamenco*, ~ *jondo Andalusian gipsy singing.*

cantera *f* (stone) quarry, pit; *fig.* talent, genius; **cantería** *f* (*arte, obra*) masonry, stonework; (*porción*) piece of masonry; **cantero** *m* (stone) mason; quarryman; (*extremo*) end; ~ *de pan* crust.

cántico *m eccl.* canticle; *fig.* song.

cantidad *f* quantity; amount, number; sum *de dinero*; (*una*) *gran* ~ *de* a great quantity of, lots of; *phys.* ~ *de movimiento* momentum; *en* ~ in quantity.

cantil *m* (*escalón*) coastal shelf; [(*acantilada*) cliff.]

cantilena *f* ballad, song; F *la misma* ~ the same old song.

cantimplora *f* water bottle, canteen; decanter *para vino*; ⊕ syphon.

cantina *f* 🚂 refreshment room, buffet; ⚔ *etc.* canteen; snack bar; bar(room); (*bodega*) wine cellar; (*fiambrera*) lunch box.

cantizal *m* stony ground.

canto[1] *m* (*acto, arte*) singing; (*pieza*) song; *eccl.* chant(ing); *poet.* lyric, song; canto *de épica*; ~ *del cisne* swan song; ~ *llano* plainsong; *al* ~ *del gallo* at cockcrow, at daybreak.

canto[2] *m* (*borde*) edge; rim; (*extremo*) end, point; (*esquina*) corner; back *de cuchillo*; crust *de pan*; (*piedra*) rock, boulder (*a.* ~ *rodado*); (*guijarro*) pebble; *de* ~ on edge, edgeways; on end; *faltar a uno el* ~ *de un duro* F have a narrow shave; *tener 2 cm. de* ~ 2 cm. thick.

cantón *m* corner; *pol.*, *heráldica*: canton; ⚔ cantonment; **cantonada**: *dar* ~ *a* shake *s.o.* off; **cantonear** [1a] loaf around; **cantonera** *f* corner band *de libro*; corner table; corner cupboard; **cantonero** *m* loafer, good-for-nothing.

cantor 1. (sweet-)singing; **2.** *m* **-a** *f* singer; *orn.* singing bird, songster.

cantorral *m* stony ground.

canturía *f* singing, vocal music; singing exercise; *b.s.* monotonous singing; **canturrear** [1a], **canturriar** [1b] hum, croon.

canuto *m* = *cañuto.*

caña *f* ♀ reed; (*tallo*) stem, cane; *anat.* shin(bone); arm bone; leg *de media, bota*; ⚒ gallery; (*vaso*) (long) glass; *S.Am.* rum; ~ *de azúcar*, ~ *melar* sugar cane; ~ *de pescar* fishing rod; ~ *del timón* tiller.

cañada *f geog.* gully; (*grande*) glen; (*a. real* ~) drover's road.

cañamazo *m* canvas; burlap; **cañameño** hempen; **cañamero** hemp *attr.*

cañamiel *f* sugar cane.

cáñamo *m* hemp; (*tela*) hempen cloth; *S.Am.* string; **cañamón** *m* hemp seed; ~*es pl.* bird seed.

cañaveral *m* reed field, reed bed; ⚘ sugar-cane plantation.

cañería *f* pipe, piece of piping; pipeline; (*desagüe*) drain; ♪ organ pipes; ~*s pl.* pipes, piping; ~ *maestra* water *etc.* main; **cañero** *m* plumber,

fitter; **cañete** *m* small pipe; **cañizo** *m* ↙ hurdle (for drying fruit *etc.*).
caño *m* tube, pipe (*a.* ♪); (*albañal*) drain, sewer; jet, spout *de fuente*; ⚓ channel; ⚒ gallery; (*bodega*) wine cellar; **cañón** *m* ⊕ tube, pipe (*a.* ♪); ⚔ gun, cannon; barrel *de fusil, pluma*; stem *de pipa*; shaft, stack *de chimenea*; *mount.* chimney; *S.Am.* canyon; ~ *antiaéreo* antiaircraft gun; *de dos* ~*es fusil* double-barreled; **cañonazo** *m* gunshot; F bolt from the blue; ~*s pl.* gunfire; *salva de 21* ~*s* 21-gun salute; **cañonear** [1a] shell; **cañoneo** *m* shelling, gunfire; **cañonera** *f* embrasure; **cañonero** *m* ⚓ gunboat.
cañoso reedy.
cañutería *f* gold or silver embroidery; **cañutero** *m* pincushion; **cañutillo** *m* glass tube; *sew.* gold (*or* silver) twist; **cañuto** *m* ⊕ tube, container; ⚘ internode; F telltale.
coaba *f* mahogany.
caolín *m* kaolin.
caos *m* chaos; **caótico** chaotic.
capa *f* (*vestido*) cloak; *eccl.* (*a.* ~ *pluvial*) cope; *toros*: cape; wrapper *de cigarro etc.*; layer *de atmósfera, piel etc.*; *geol.* stratum, bed; *cocina*: coating; *paint.* coat; covering *de nieve*; film, layer *de polvo*; pall *de humo*; *fig.* varnish; *b.s.* cloak, mask; *primera* ~ undercoat, ground; ~ *aguadera* raincoat; F ~ *rota* secret emissary; ~ *social* social level; *de 3* ~*s madera* 3-ply; *so* ~ *de* under the guise of; *abrirse de* ~ pluck up courage; F *andar de* ~ *caída* be in a bad way; *echar una* ~ *a* cover up for; *estar(se) etc. a la* ~ ⚓ lie to; *hacer de su* ~ *un sayo* do what one likes with one's own things.
capacidad *f* capacity (*a. phys.*, ⚕); size *de sala etc.*; *fig.* (cap)ability, capacity; intelligence; efficiency; ~ *para* aptitude for; ~ *adquisitiva*, ~ *de compra* purchasing power; ~ *competitiva* competitiveness; ~ *de carga* carrying capacity; ~ *útil* effective capacity; **capacitar** [1a]: ~ *para inf.* enable, empower *s.o.* to *inf.*; ~ *para su.* qualify *s.o.* for *su.*; ~**se** *para* qualify for, fit o.s. for.
capacha *f* frail, basket; **capacho** *m* wicker basket; ⚠ hod.
capar [1a] castrate; *fig.* cut down, curtail.
caparazón *m* caparison; *zo.* shell; nose-bag *para pienso.*
caparrón *m* bud.
caparrosa *f* vitriol; ~ *azul* copper sulphate, blue vitriol.
capataz *m* foreman; *esp.* ↙ overseer, bailiff.
capaz a) *p.* (cap)able, efficient, competent (*a.* ⚖; *de inf.* to *inf.*); ~ *de* capable of; ~ *para* qualified for; *ser* ~ *de inf.* be capable of *ger.*, be up to *ger.*; ¡*sería* ~! one could well believe it of him!; ⊕ ~ *de funcionar* operational; b) *cabida*: large, capacious; ~ *de*, ~ *para* that holds, with room for, with a capacity of.
capcioso wily, deceitful.
capear [1a] *v/t.* wave the cape at; F take *s.o.* in; ⚓ *temporal* ride out; *v/i.* ⚓ ride out the storm; lie to.
capellán *m* chaplain; (*en general*) priest; ~ *castrense* army chaplain; **capellanía** *f* chaplaincy.
capero *m* hat stand, hall stand.
caperuza *f* (pointed) hood; ⊕ cowl, cowling; cowl *de chimenea.*
capibara *f S.Am.* capybara.
capicúa *f* palindrome.
capigorra *m* F, **capigorrón** *m* F loafer, idler.
capilar 1. capillary (*a. anat., phys.*), hair *attr.*; *tubo etc.* ~ = **2.** *m* capillary; **capilaridad** *f* capillarity.
capilla *f eccl.* chapel; ♪ choir; (*capucho*) hood, cowl; *typ.* proof sheet; ~ *ardiente* funeral chapel; oratory *en casa*; ~ *de la Virgen* Chapel of Our Lady; ~ *mayor* choir, chancel; *typ. en* ~*s* in proof; F *estar en (la)* ~ *fig.* be on tenterhooks; **capillo** *m* bonnet *de niño*; hood *de halcón*; = *capullo.*
capirotazo *m* flip, flick.
capirote *m* hood; hennin *de mujer*; hood *de halcón*; flip, flick *con dedos*; **capirucho** *m* F hood.
capitación *f* poll tax, head tax, capitation.
capital 1. *mst* capital; *característica* main, principal; *enemigo, pecado* mortal; *importancia* supreme, paramount; *punto* essential, fundamental; *lo* ~ the main thing; **2.** *f pol.* capital *de país*; chief town, center *de región*; ~ *de provincia approx.* county town; **3.** *m* ⚕ capital; ~ *de explotación* working capital; ~ *de inversión* investment capital; ~ *social* share capital; **capitalismo** *m* capitalism; **capita-**

lista 1. capitalist(ic); 2. *m/f* capitalist; **capitalización** *f* capitalization; *interés* compounding; **capitalizar** [1f] capitalize; *interés* compound.
capitán *m* captain (*a.* ~ *de navío*); ~ *de fragata* commander; ~ *general* captain general; 5-star general; ~ *de puerto* harbor-master; **capitana** *f* flagship; **capitanear** [1a] captain, lead (*a. fig.*), command; **capitanía** *f* captaincy, captainship; (*grupo*) company; (*derechos*) harbor dues.
capitel *m* ⚠ capital.
capitolio *m* capitol; *fig.* imposing edifice; F *subir al* ~ get to the top.
capitoste *m* F boss; big shot.
capitulación *f* agreement; ⚔ capitulation; ~*es pl.* (*de boda*) marriage contract; **capitular**[1] *eccl.* chapter *attr.*; **capitular**[2] [1a] *v/t.* agree to; ⚖ charge (*de* with); *v/i.* come to terms (*con* with); ⚔ capitulate; **capítulo** *m* chapter (*a. eccl.*); item *de presupuesto*; heading; (*sala*) chapter house; *eccl.* reprimand; ~ *de culpas* charge; ~*s pl. matrimoniales* marriage contract; *llamar etc. a* ~ take *s.o.* to task.
capó *m mot.* hood.
capoc *m* kapok.
capón[1] *m* rap on the head.
capón[2] *m* (*p.*) eunuch; (*pollo*) capon; **caponera** *f* ✓ chicken coop; *fig.* open house; *sl.* clink.
capota *f mot.* hood, top; bonnet *de mujer*.
capotaje *m* somersault; ✈ loop; **capotar** [1a] ✈, *mot.* turn over; **capote** *m* cloak (with sleeves); *toros*: bullfighter's cloak (*a.* ~ *de brega*); F frown; *naipes*: slam; *meteor.* mass of dark clouds; *a* (*or para*) *mi* ~ to my way of thinking; *decir para su* ~ say to o.s.; **capotear** [1a] *fig.* get out of, duck, shirk; (*engañar*) bamboozle.
Capricornio *m* Capricorn.
capricho *m* whim, (passing) fancy, caprice (*a.* ♪); (*deseo*) keen desire, sudden urge (*por* for); *b.s.* craze, fad, pet notion; quirk (of the imagination); (*en general*) whimsicality; *por puro* ~ just to please oneself; *fue un* ~ *suyo* it was one of his mad ideas; *tiene sus* ~*s* he has his moods; **caprichoso, caprichudo** capricious; F quirky; *niño etc.* wayward; (*inconstante*) temperamental, moody; *idea, obra* fanciful, whimsical; (*con ideas raras*) full of one's own pet notions.
cápsula *f* cap *de botella*; ⚘, *anat.*, *pharm.* capsule; ⚘ boll *de algodón etc.*; case *de cartucho*; ~ *fulminante* detonating cap, percussion cap; **capsular** capsular; *en forma* ~ in capsule form.
captar [1a] *confianza etc.* win, get; *voluntad* gain control over; *aguas* dam, harness; (*entender*) catch, get the drift of; *radio*: pick up; **captura** *f* capture, seizure; **capturar** [1a] capture, seize, take.
capucha *f* hood; *eccl.* cowl; top *de pluma*; *gr.* circumflex accent; **capuchina** *f eccl.* Capuchin sister; ⚘ nasturtium; **capuchino** *m* Capuchin; **capucho** *m* cowl, hood; **capuchón** *m* lady's hooded cloak; *mot.* valve cap.
capullo *m zo.* cocoon; ⚘ bud; cup *de bellota*.
capuz *m* hood; *eccl.* cowl; (*capote*) cloak; (*chapuz*) dive.
caqui *m* khaki.
cara *f* face (*a. fig.*); side *de disco, sólido*; ⚠ façade, front; (*superficie*) surface, face; heads *de moneda*; *fig.* expression, look, appearance; ~ *de aleluya* cheerful face; ~ *o cruz* heads or tails; ~ *de cuchillo* hatchet face; ~ *de hereje* ugly face; (*triste*) hang-dog look; ~ *de juez* grim-looking face; *mala* ~ (*ademán*) pout, grimace, face F; ~ *de pascua* smiling face; ~ *de viernes* hang-dog look; ~ *de vinagre* sour expression, sourpuss; *sl.*; ~ *a* ~ face to face; ~ *adelante* (*atrás*) facing forwards (backwards); *a* ~ *descubierta* openly; *de* ~ opposite, facing; in the face; *dar* ~ *a* face up to; *dar la* ~ *por otro* answer for s.o. else; *echar* (*or jugar*) *a* ~ *o cruz* toss (up) (*acc.* for); *echar algo en* ~ *a* reproach *s.o.* for s.t.; bring up, allude to; *hacer* ~ *a* face (*a. fig.*); *enemigo* face up to, stand up to; F *lavar la* ~ *a* lick *s.o.'s* boots; *poner mala* ~ pout, make a face F; *tener* ~ *de inf.* look as if *condicional*; *tener buena* ~ ⚕ look well; look nice; *tener mala* ~ ⚕ look ill; look bad; *tener* ~ *de roñoso* look mean; *nos veremos las* ~*s* well, we shall see.
carabela *f* ⚓ caravel.
carabina *f* ⚔ carbine; F chaperon; *hacer etc. de* ~ go as chaperon; F *ser la* ~ *de Ambrosio* be quite useless; **carabinero** *m* carabineer.

caracol *m zo.* snail; (*concha*) snail shell, sea shell; (*pelo*) curl; *¡~es!* great Scott!; *de ~ escalera* spiral; *en ~* spiral, corkscrew *attr.*; *hacer ~es* (*p.*) zigzag; *b.s.* reel, stagger; (*caballo*) = **caracolear** [1a] *caballo* caracole.
carácter *m* character (*a. biol.*); *typ.* (*una letra*) character; (*cursivo etc.*) hand(writing); (*condición*) position; *de ~* (*firme etc.*) of character; *de ~ ...* ...-natured; *thea. de ~ heroico* cast in a heroic mold; *de medio ~* of an ill-defined nature; *caracteres pl.* (*de imprenta*) type (face); **característica** *f* characteristic; **característico** characteristic (*de* of); **caracterizado** distinguished, of note; **caracterizar** [1f] characterize; distinguish, set apart; (*enaltecer*) confer distinction on; *thea.* play with great effect; *~se thea.* make up, dress for the part.
caradura 1. *f* scoundrel; **2.** *adj.* brazen, shameless.
carajo *m* F prick; *¡~!* hell!
¡caramba! *sorpresa*: well, I'll be damned!, good gracious!; *enfado*: damn it!
carámbano *m* icicle.
carambola *f billar*: cannon; *fig.* trick, ruse; *por ~* by chance; in a roundabout way.
caramelo *m* sweet, toffee, caramel.
caramillo *m* ♪ recorder, pipe; *poet.* reed; (*montón*) untidy heap; (*chisme*) (piece of) gossip; *armar etc. un ~* start a gossipping campaign; **caramilloso** F fussy.
carantamaula *f* F (*cara*) ugly mug; **carantoña** *f* F (*cara*) ugly mug; (*mujer*) mutton dressed up as lamb; *~s pl.* petting, fondling; *hacer ~s a* make faces at; (*amor*) make sheep's eyes at; coax, wheedle.
carapacho *m* shell; *meterse en su ~* go into one's shell.
caraqueño *adj. a. su. m*, **a** *f* (native) of Caracas.
carátula *f* mask; *S.Am.* title page.
caravana *f* caravan; *fig.* group; *en ~* in a gang; **caravasar** *m* caravanserai.
¡caray! F confound it!
carbohidrato *m* carbohydrate.
carbólico carbolic.
carbón *m min.* coal (*a. ~ de piedra*); ⚡ carbon; *~ bituminoso* soft coal; *~ de leña, ~ vegetal* charcoal (*a. paint.*); *~ menudo* small coal, slack; (*papel*) *~* carbon (paper); *copia al ~* carbon copy; **carbonato** *m* carbonate; **carboncillo** *m paint.* charcoal; *mot.* carbon; **carbonear** [1a] make charcoal of; **carbonero 1.** coal *attr.*; charcoal *attr.*; **2.** *m* coal merchant; charcoal burner; **carbónico** carbonic; **carbonilla** *f* small coal; cinder; *mot.* carbon; **carbonización** *f* ⚗ carbonization; charring; **carbonizar** [1f] ⚗ carbonize; char; *leña* make charcoal of; *quedar carbonizado* ⚡ be electrocuted; (*edificio etc.*) be reduced to ashes; *~se* ⚗ carbonize; be charred; be reduced to ashes; **carbono** *m* carbon; **carbonoso** carbonaceous.
carbunclo *m min.*, **carbunco** *m* ⚕ carbuncle.
carburador *m* carburetor; **carburante** *m* fuel; **carburar** [1a] carburet; **carburo** *m* carbide.
carcaj *m* quiver; *S.Am.* rifle case.
carcajada *f* (loud) laugh, guffaw, peal of laughter; *reírse a ~s* roar with laughter; *soltar una* (*or la*) *~* burst out laughing.
carcamal *m* F old crock; **carcamán** ⚓ tub.
cárcel *f* prison, jail; ⊕ clamp; *poner en la ~* send to jail, put in prison; **carcelario** prison *attr.*; **carcelería** *f* imprisonment, detention; **carcelero 1.** prison *attr.*; **2.** *m* warder, jailer.
carcinógeno 1. *m* carcinogen; **2.** carcinogenic; cancer-causing; **carcinoma** *m* ⚕ carcinoma.
carcoma *f* woodworm; *fig.* anxiety, perpetual (cause for) worry; (*p.*) spendthrift; **carcomer** [2a] bore into, eat away; *fig.* undermine; *fortuna* eat away; *~se* get worm-eaten; *fig.* be eaten away; **carcomido** worm-eaten, wormy.
carda *f* (*acto*) carding; (*instrumento*) card, comb; teasel (*a.* ⚘); *fig.* rap over the knuckles; **cardar** [1a] card, comb; F *~ la lana a* haul *s.o.* over the coals.
cardenal *m* cardinal; ⚕ bruise; **cardenalato** *m* cardinalate.
cardencha *f* ⚘, ⊕ teasel.
cardenillo *m* verdigris; **cárdeno** purple, violet; lurid; *agua* opalescent.
cardíaco 1. cardiac, heart *attr.*; **2.** *m*, **a** *f* heart case.

cardinal cardinal.
cardo *m* thistle.
cardumen *m* shoal.
carear [1a] *v/t. ps.* bring face to face; *textos* compare, collate; *v/i.*: ~ *a* face towards; **~se** come face to face, meet; ~ *con* face (up to).
carecer [2d]: ~ *de* lack, be in need of, want (for).
carena *f* ⚓ careening; F ragging; *dar* ~ *a* = **carenar** [1a] careen.
carencia *f* lack (*de* of), need (*de* for); deficiency (*a.* ⚕); **carencial:** *mal* ~ deficiency disease.
careo *m* confrontation; collation; comparison.
carero F expensive, dear; high-priced.
carestía *f* scarcity, shortage; famine; ✝ high price(s); ~ *de la vida* high cost of living; *año de* ~ lean (*or* bad) year.
careta *f* mask; ⚒ *etc.* respirator; ~ *antigás* gas mask, respirator; *quitar la* ~ *a* unmask.
carey *m* tortoiseshell; *zo.* turtle.
carga *f* (*acto*) loading; charge *de cañón, caballería, horno,* ⚡; (*peso*) load (*a.* ⊕, ⚡); ⚓ cargo; *fig.* load, burden, onus; obligation(s), responsibilities; (*propiedad etc.*) encumbrance; (*cuidado*) worry, anxiety; tax (*sobre recursos* on); ⚡ ~ *máxima* peak load; ~ *personal* personal commitments; ⚒ ~ *de pólvora* blast; ⚓ ~ *de profundidad* depth charge; ~ *útil* payload; F *a* ~*s* galore, in plenty; *barco de* ~ cargo boat; ⊕ *con plena* ~ at full load; *de* ~ loading *attr.*; *bestia* pack *attr.*, of burden; *echar la* ~ *a* put the blame (*or* onus) on; F *echarse con la* ~ throw up the sponge; F *llevar la* ~ carry the can; *tomar* ~ load; *volver a la* ~ keep at it, return to the attack.
cargadero *m* loading point; ⚠ lintel;
cargado loaded; *esp. fig.* laden (*de* with); ⚡ charged, live; ~ (*con bala*) live; *dado* loaded; *té etc.* strong; *cielo* overcast; (*bochornoso*) sultry; F *mujer* in the family way; ~ *de años* very old; *v. espalda*; **cargador** *m* loader; ⚓ stevedore; ⚔ ramrod; filler *de pluma*; ~ (*de acumulador*) (battery) charger; **cargamento** *m* cargo, freight; (*acto*) loading; **cargante** F boring, tiresome; *niño* trying; *tarea* irksome.
cargar [1h] **1.** *v/t.* load (*de* with; *a, en* on); (*demasiado*) overload; weigh down on; *cañón* load; ⚡, *enemigo* charge; *horno* stoke; *sl. estudiante* plough; *impuestos* increase (*a* on); *velas* take in; *S.Am.* wear; *fig.* burden, load down (*con, de* with); encumber (*de deudas* with); *imaginación* fill (*de* with); *culpa* lay (*a* on); *responsabilidad* entrust (*a* to), *b.s.* saddle (*a* on); (*imputar*) charge (*de adj.* with being; *con su.* with); F annoy, bore; **2.** *v/i.* load (up), take on a load; ⚓ take on (a) cargo; *meteor.* turn, veer (*a, hacia* to); (*acento*) fall (*sobre* on); (*ps.*) crowd together; F overeat; drink too much; ~ *con peso* take, carry; *esp. fig.* shoulder; (*llevarse*) take *s.t.* away; ~ *sobre* (⚠, *responsabilidad*) rest on; (*importunar*) pester; **3. ~se** *peso etc.* take on o.s.; *meteor.* become overcast; F get bored, get annoyed; ~ *de* be full of, be loaded with; *fig.* get one's fill of; F ~*la* get into hot water; *¡algún día me lo cargaré!* I'll get him one day!; **cargareme** *m* (deposit) voucher.
cargazón *f* load; ⚓ cargo; ⚕ heaviness; *meteor.* mass of heavy cloud; ~ *de espaldas* stoop; **cargo** *m* load, weight; *fig.* obligation, duty; responsibility; (*custodia*) charge, care; (*empleo*) post; ✝ debit; ⚖ *etc.* charge; ~ *alto* high office; high official; VIP; *girar* (*or librar*) *a* ~ *de* draw on; *hacer* ~ *de* charge *s.o.* with; *hacerse* ~ *de* take charge of; see about; (*darse cuenta de*) realize; *ser en* ~ *a* be indebted to; *vestir el* ~ look the part;
carguero 1. *attr.* freight; of burden; **2.** *m* freighter; cargo boat; *S.Am.* beast of burden.
cariacontecido down in the mouth; aghast *de sobresalto*.
cariado rotten, carious 📖; **cariarse** [1b] decay, become decayed.
Caribe 1. Caribbean; **2.** *m/f* Carib; savage.
caricatura *f* caricature; *fig.* caricature (of a man); **caricaturista** *m/f* caricaturist; **caricaturizar** [1f] caricature.
caricia *f* caress; pat, stroke *a perro etc.*; *fig.* endearment.
caridad *f* charity, charitableness; *hacer la* ~ *a* give alms to.
caries *f* (dental) decay, caries.
carilla *f* mask; *typ.* page.

carinado *zo.*, ⚘ keeled.
cariño *m* affection, love; fondness, liking (*a* for); *Mex., C.Am.* gift; ~*s pl.* endearments, show of affection; *tener* ~ *a* be fond of; *tomar* ~ *a* take (a liking) to; **cariñoso** affectionate, fond, loving.
carioca 1. of Rio de Janeiro; **2.** *f* carioca (dance).
cariparejo F poker-faced; **carirredondo** F round-faced.
caritativo charitable (*con, para* towards).
cariz *m* look (of the sky); F look; F *esto va tomando mal* ~ this is getting to look bad.
carlinga *f* ✈ cockpit.
carlismo *m* Carlism; **carlista** *adj. a. su. m/f* Carlist.
carlota *f* charlotte.
carmen *m* ▲ *prov.* villa.
carmenar [1a] *pelo* untangle; *seda etc.* unravel; *lana* card; F pull *s.o.'s* hair; F (*desplumar*) fleece, swindle.
carmesí *adj. a. su. m* crimson; **carmín** *m* carmine; ⚘ dog rose; **carmíneo** carmine, crimson.
carnada *f* bait (*a. fig.*); **carnal** carnal, of the flesh; *pariente* full, blood-; *primo* first; **carnalidad** *f* lust, carnality; **carnaval** *m* carnival; (*época*) Shrovetide.
carne *f anat.*, ⚘, *eccl.* flesh; meat *de comer*; ~ *adobada* salt meat; ~ *congelada* frozen (*or* chilled) meat; ~ *de carnero* mutton; ~ *de cerdo* pork; ~ *de cordero* lamb; ~ *de gallina fig.* goose flesh; ~ *de membrillo* quince jelly; ~ *mollar* lean meat; ~ *picada* mince(d meat); ~ *de ternera* veal; ~ *de vaca* beef; ~ *de venado* venison; *de* ~ *y hueso* of flesh and blood; *de abundantes* (*or muchas*) ~*s* fat; *de pocas* ~*s* thin; *echar* ~*s Mex.* swear; curse; *en* ~ *viva* on the raw; *en* ~*s* with nothing on; F *cobrar* (*or criar, echar*) ~*s* put on weight; *perder* ~*s* lose weight; *no ser ni* ~ *ni pescado* be nondescript, be quite undistinguished.
carné = *carnet*.
carnear [1a] *S.Am.* slaughter; F take in.
carnero *m zo.* sheep; (*macho*) ram; (*carne*) mutton.
carnestolendas *f/pl.* Shrovetide; carnival.
carnet [kar'ne] *m* notebook; travel voucher *de turista*; ~ (*de identidad*) identity card; *mot.* ~ (*de conducir*) driving licence.
carnicería *f* butcher's (shop); *fig.* carnage, slaughter; *hacer una* ~ *de* massacre; **carnicero** *m* **1.** *zo.* carnivorous; F fond of meat; F *fig.* savage, inhuman; **2.** *m* (*p.*) butcher (*a. fig.*); *zo.* carnivore; **cárnico** meat *attr.*
carnívoro 1. carnivorous; **2.** *m* carnivore.
carnoso *anat.*, ⚘ fleshy; meaty; *p.* = **carnudo** beefy, fat.
caro † dear, expensive; *p.* dear, beloved.
caroca: F *hacer* ~*s* put it on, give o.s. airs.
carótida *f* carotid (artery).
carpa *f* carp; ~ *dorada* goldfish.
carpanta *f* F raging hunger.
carpeta *f* folder, file, portfolio; (*cartera*) briefcase; table cover *de mesa*; *S.Am.* bookkeeping department; **carpetazo:** *dar* ~ *a* shelve, put on one side.
carpetovetónico terribly Spanish, as Spanish as they come.
carpintería *f* (*arte*) carpentry, joinery; carpenter's shop; **carpintero** *m* carpenter; ~ (*de blanco*) joiner; ~ *de carretas* wheelwright; ~ *de ribera* ship's carpenter.
carraca *f* ⚓ *contp.* tub, hulk; ♪ rattle; **carraco** F **1.** feeble, decrepit; **2.** *m* old crock.
carrasca *f* kermes oak.
carraspear [1a] be hoarse, have a frog in one's throat; **carraspera** *f* hoarseness.
carrera *f* run (*a.* ♪, ⚓, *béisbol etc.*); (*certamen*) race; (*pista*) track; (*calle*) avenue; (*raya*) parting; run, ladder *en medias*; *ast.* course; (*hilera*) row, line; ▲ beam; ⊕ stroke *de émbolo*, lift *de válvula*; *fig.* course of human life; (*profesión*) career; *univ.* (degree) course, studies; ~*s pl.* racing, races; *de* ~(*s*) racing ..., race *attr.*; ~ *armamentista* (*a. de armamentos*) arms race; ~ *ascendente* upstroke; ~ *corta* dash, short run; ~ *de caballos* horse race; ~ *descendente* downstroke; ~ *del émbolo* piston stroke; ~ *de Maratón* Marathon (race); ~ *de obstáculos* obstacle race; ~ *de relevos* relay race; ~

de resistencia endurance race; ~ *de vallas* hurdle race, hurdles; *caballos*: steeplechase; *a* ~ (*abierta*) at full speed; *correr a* ~ *tendida* career, go full out; *dar* ~ *a* give *s.o.* his education; *dar libre* ~ *a* give free rein to; *no poder hacer* ~ *con* make no headway with; **carrerista 1.** horsy; **2.** *m/f* racing man (*or* woman); punter *que apuesta*.

carreta *f* cart; ~ *de mano* = *carretilla*; **carretada** *f* cart load; *a* ~*s* in loads, galore; **carretaje** *m* cartage, haulage; **carrete** *m* reel (*a. de caña*), spool (*a. phot.*), bobbin; ⚡ coil; ~ *de inducción* induction coil; **carretear** [1a] *v/t.* cart, haul; *carro* drive; *v/i.* ✈ taxi; ~**se** pull hard; **carretel** *m* reel, spool.

carretera *f* (main) road, highway; *por* ~ by road; **carretería** *f* wheelwright's; (*conjunto*) carts; **carretero** *m* carter; (*constructor*) wheelwright, cartwright; *jurar como un* ~ swear like a trooper; **carretilla** *f* truck; hand cart, barrow; ✓ wheelbarrow; go-cart *de niño*; F *de* ~ by heart; **carretón** *m* small cart; = *carretilla*.

carricoche *m* caravan, covered wagon; F old crock; **carricuba** *f* water cart.

carril *m* (*surco*) rut, track; ✓ furrow; (*camino*) cart track, lane; 🚂 rail.

carrillo *m* cheek, jowl; ⊕ pulley; F *comer a dos* ~*s* eat a lot; *fig.* get the best of both worlds.

carrizal *m* reed bed; **carrizo** *m* reed.

carro *m* cart, wagon; *S.Am.* car; † (*a.* ~ *de guerra*) chariot; ⚔ car; carriage *de máquina de escribir*; (*carga*) cart load; ~ *alegórico* float; ~ *blindado* armored car; ~ *de combate* tank; ~ *cuba* tank truck; ~ *fuerte* heavy trolley, platform carriage; ~ *fúnebre* hearse; ~ *de mudanza* removal van; ~ *de riego* water cart; ~*-patrulla S.Am.* patrol car; police car; police cruiser.

carrocería *f mot.* coachwork, body; **carrocero** *attr.* body; coach; *taller* ~ *mot.* body shop; **carromato** *m* covered wagon.

carroña *f* carrion; **carroño** foul, putrid.

carroza *f* (state) coach, carriage; float *en desfile*; ⚓ awning; **carruaje** *m* carriage; vehicle.

carrusel *m* merry-go-round; carrousel.

carta *f* letter; document; *naipes*: (playing) card; *hist.* charter; ⚓ (*a.* ~ *de marear*) chart; ~ *adjunta* covering letter; ~ *de amor* love letter; ~ *blanca* carte blanche, free hand; ~ *certificada* registered letter; ~ *de crédito* letter of credit; ~ *de figura* court card; ~ *geográfica* map; ~ *meteorológica* weather map; ~ *de naturaleza* naturalization papers; ~ *partida* ⚓ charter party; ~ *de pedido* order; *S.Am.* ~ *postal* postcard; ~ *de privilegio* charter; ~ *de recomendación* letter of introduction; ~ *de solicitud* (letter of) application; ~ *de venta* bill of sale; *a* ~ *cabal* thoroughly, in every way; *a* ~*s vistas* with one's cards on the table; *a la* ~ à la carte; *echar las* ~*s* tell one's fortune; *poner las* ~*s boca arriba* put one's cards on the table; *no saber a qué* ~ *quedarse* not know what to think; *tomar* ~*s en* take part in, intervene in; *¡*~ *canta!* there it is in black and white!

cartabón *m* set square *de dibujante*; ⚠ bevel; *surv.* quadrant.

cartapacio *m* (*cartera*) briefcase; *escuela*: satchel; (*cuaderno*) notebook.

cartearse [1a] correspond (*con* with).

cartel *m* poster, placard, bill; *escuela*: wall chart; † cartel; F *thea. tener* ~ be all the rage; **cartelera** *f* billboard; *thea. fig.* list of plays; *mantenerse en la* ~ run, be on; **cartelero** *m* bill sticker.

carteo *m* correspondence.

cárter *m* housing, case; ~ *del cigüeñal* crankcase.

cartera *f* wallet, pocketbook; portfolio (*a. pol.*), letter file; (*bolsa*) briefcase; *sew.* (pocket) flap; *pol. sin* ~ without portfolio; **carterista** *m* pickpocket; **cartero** *m* postman.

cartílago *m* cartilage 🕮, gristle; **cartilaginoso** cartilaginous 🕮, gristly.

cartilla *f* primer; ~ (*de ahorros*) deposit book; ~ (*de identidad*) identity card; ~ (*de racionamiento*) ration book; F *leer la* ~ *a* give *s.o.* a severe ticking-off; F *no saber la* ~ not know a blind thing.

cartografía *f* mapmaking, cartography; **cartógrafo** *m* mapmaker, cartographer.
cartomancia *f* fortune telling (*with cards*).
cartón *m* cardboard, pasteboard; *paint.* cartoon; board *de libro*; (*caja*) cardboard box, carton; ~ *piedra* papier mâché.
cartuchera *f* cartridge belt; **cartucho** *m* cartridge; roll *de monedas*; paper cone; ~ *sin bala*, ~ *en blanco* blank cartridge; *hasta quemar el último* ~ to the last ditch.
cartulina *f* fine cardboard.
casa *f* house; (*hogar*) home; (*piso*) flat, apartment; (*ps.*) household; (*a.* ~ *de comercio*) firm, business house; (*descendencia*) house, line; square *de tablero*; ~ *de banca* banking house; ~ *de campo* country house; ~ *de citas*, ~ *pública*, ~ *de putas* brothel; ~ *consistorial* town hall, civic center; ~ *de corrección* reformatory, remand home; ~ *de correos* post office; ~ *editorial* publishing house; ~ *embrujada*, ~ *de fantasmas* haunted house; ~ *de empeños* pawnshop; ~ *de fieras* zoo, menagerie; ~ *de guarda* lodge; ~ *de huéspedes* boarding house; ~ *de juego* casino; ~ *de locos*, ~ *de orates* asylum; ~ *de maternidad* maternity hospital; ~ *matriz* head office; ~ *de* (*la*) *moneda* mint; ~ *de pisos* apartment house; ~ *real* royal house (*or* family); ~ *religiosa* monastery; convent; ~ *solariega* ancestral home, family seat; ~ *de vecindad* apartment house; *a* ~ home(wards); *ir a* ~ *de Juan* go to John's; de ~ home, household *attr.*; *deporte*, *ropa* indoor; *animal* pet; *en* ~ (at) home; indoors; *en* ~ *de* ✉ care of; *estar en* ~ *de Juan* be at John's; *por la* ~ about the house; *abandonar la* ~ leave home, move out; *echar la* ~ *por la ventana* go to a lot of expense; *estar de* ~ be in one's everyday clothes; *hacer* ~ get rich; *llevar la* ~ keep house; *poner* ~ set up house; *aquí tiene Vd. su* ~ you're always very welcome; *voy para* ~ I'm off home.
casabe *m* cassava bread; cassava flour; manioc.
casaca *f* dress coat; *cambiar de* ~, *volver* ~ be a turncoat.
casación *f* cassation, annulment.
casada *f* married woman; **casadero** marriageable; **casado 1.** married; *mal* ~ unhappily married; *estar* ~ *con* be married to; **2.** *m* married man; **casal** *m* country house; pair of lovers.
casamata *f* casemate.
casamentero *m*, **a** *f* matchmaker; **casamiento** *m* marriage; wedding (ceremony); *prometer en* ~ betroth.
casar[1] *m* hamlet.
casar[2] [1a] *v/t.* (*sacerdote*) marry, join in marriage; *hija* marry (off), give in marriage (*con* to); *fig.* match; *v/i.*, **~se** marry (*con acc.*), get married (*con* to); *fig.* match.
casca *f* tan, bark (for tanning).
cascabel *m* (little) bell; *de* ~ *gordo* pretentious; *poner el* ~ *al gato* bell the cat; **cascabelear** [1a] *v/t.* beguile, take *s.o.* in; *v/i.* jingle; *fig.* behave frivolously; **cascabeleo** *m* jingle; **cascabelero** F featherbrained; **cascabillo** *m* (little) bell; ⚘ husk, chaff; ⚘ acorn cup.
cascada *f* waterfall, cascade.
cascado *p.* broken down, infirm; *cosa* broken (down); *voz* harsh, unmelodious.
cascajo *m* (piece of) grit, (piece of) gravel; *esp.* ⚠ rubble; F junk, rubbish; (*trasto*) old crock; F *estar hecho un* ~ be a wreck; **cascajoso** gritty, gravelly.
cascanueces *m* (*un* a pair of) nutcrackers.
cascar [1g] *v/t.* crack, split; *nueces* crack; *salud* break; F bash, slosh; F *deportes*: beat hollow, wipe the floor with; *v/i.* chatter (away); **~se** crack, split; (*salud*) crack up; (*voz*) break, crack.
cáscara *f* shell *de huevo*, *nuez*, *edificio*; rind, peel *de fruta*; husk *de grano*; *S.Am.* bark; *¡~s!* well I'm blowed!; F *ser de la* ~ *amarga* be wild; *pol.* have advanced ideas; **cascarón** *m* (broken) egg-shell; **cascarrabias** *m* F quick-tempered fellow.
casco *m anat.* skull; ⚔ *etc.* helmet; crown *de sombrero*; skin *de cebolla*; ⚓ hull; ⚓ (*viejo*) hulk; hoof *de caballo*; piece *de vasija*; (*tonel*) cask, barrel; ⊕ casing; ⚠ city area; *~s pl.* F nut; ~ *protector* crash helmet; ~ *urbano* city limits; *ligero* (*or alegre*) *de ~s* featherbrained, dim; F *romper los ~s a* break *s.o.'s* head; F *romperse los ~s* rack one's brains.

cascote *m* (piece of) rubble, (piece of) debris; *S.Am.* old fogey.
caseína *f* casein.
casería *f* country house; *S.Am.* ✝ clientèle; **caserío** *m* hamlet, settlement; (*casa*) country house; **casero 1.** domestic, household *attr.*; *pan etc.* home-made; *tela* homespun; *traje* (for use about the) house, indoor; *función* family *attr.*; *p.* home loving; **2.** *m*, **a** *f* (*dueño*) landlord; (*custodio*) caretaker; (*gerente*) building manager; (*inquilino*) tenant; (*que queda en casa*) stay-at-home, home-lover; *S.Am.* customer; **caserón** *m* big tumbledown house, barracks (of a place); **caseta** *f* stall, booth *de mercado*; *deportes*: pavilion; bathing hut *de playa*.
casete *m* cassette.
casi nearly, almost; ~ *nada* next to nothing; ~ *nunca* hardly ever; *2 años o* ~ 2 years or thereabouts; ~ ~ very nearly.
casilla *f* ⚠ hut, cabin; 🚂 cab; *thea.* box office; pigeonhole *de casillero*; compartment *de caja*; square *de papel*, *tablero*; *S.Am.* ✉ box number; F *sacar de sus* ~*s* shake *s.o.* up; (*irritar*) make *s.o.* go off the deep end; F *salir de sus* ~*s* fly off the handle; **casillero** *m* (set of) pigeonholes.
casimir *m* cashmere.
casinista *m* clubman; **casino** *m* club; casino *para jugar*.
casita *f* little house; cottage *de campo*.
caso *m* case (*a.* ⚖, *gr.*); (*suceso*) event, occurrence; (*ejemplo*) case, instance; ~ *fortuito* mischance; act of God; *en* ~ *de* in the event of; (*en*) ~ *que*, *en el* ~ *de que* in case *verb*, in the event of *ger.*; *en tal* ~ in such a case; *en todo* ~ in any case; *en último* ~ in the last resort; *según el* ~ as the case may be; *el* ~ *es que* the fact is that; *hablar al* ~ speak to the point; F *hacer* (*or venir*) *al* ~ be relevant; be suitable; *hacer* ~ *a* mind, notice; *¡no haga Vd.* ~*!* never mind!, take no notice!; F *hacer* ~ *de* take into account; *p.* take notice of; *sin hacer* ~ *de* regardless of; *hacer* ~ *omiso de* not mention, pass over; *pongamos por* ~ *que* let us suppose that; *servir para el* ~ serve one's purpose; *¡vamos al* ~*!* let's get to the point!; *verse en el* ~ *de inf.* find o.s. obliged to *inf.*
casorio *m* F hasty (*or* unwise) marriage.
caspa *f* dandruff, scurf.
¡cáspita! my goodness!; come off it!
casquete *m* ⚔ helmet; skullcap; ~ *polar* polar cap.
casquijo *m* gravel.
casquillo *m* tip, cap; ferrule *de bastón*; case *de cartucho*; *S.Am.* horseshoe.
casquivano F scatterbrained.
casta *f* caste; *biol.* breed, race; *fig.* quality; *venir de* ~ be natural to one.
castaña *f* chestnut; ~ (*de Indias*) horse chestnut, conker F; (*moño*) bun; **castañar** *m* chestnut grove; **castañero** *m*, **a** *f* chestnut seller; **castañeta** *f* snap; ♪ ~*s pl.* castanets; **castañetazo** *m* click *de castañuelas*; snap; crack; **castañetear** [1a] *v/t. dedos* snap; *v/i.* ♪ play the castanets; (*dedos*) snap, click; (*dientes*) chatter, rattle; (*huesos*) crack; **castaño 1.** chestnut (-colored); **2.** *m* chestnut (tree); ~ (*de Indias*) horse chestnut (tree); F *pasar de* ~ *oscuro* be too much; **castañuelas** *f/pl.* castanets; **castañuelo** chestnut.
castellanizar [1f] give a Spanish form to; **castellano** *adj. a. su. m*, **a** *f* Castilian.
casticidad *f* purity, correctness; **casticismo** *m* love of purity and correctness (*in language etc.*); **casticista** *m/f* purist; **castidad** *f* chastity, chasteness.
castigador *m* F seducer; **castigar** [1h] punish (*de*, *por* for); *deportes*: penalize; *esp. fig.* castigate, chastise; *cuerpo* mortify; *estilo* refine; **castigo** *m* punishment, penalty (*a. deportes*); *esp. fig.* castigation; refinement.
castillejo *m* ⚠ scaffolding; go-cart *de niño*; **castillete** *m min.* ⊕ derrick; tower; **castillo** *m* castle; ~ *en el aire* castle in Spain; ~ *de naipes* house of cards; ~ *de proa* forecastle.
castizo *biol.* purebred, pedigree; *fig.* pure, correct; authentic, genuine; F *es un tipo* ~ he's one of the best; **casto** chaste, pure.
castor *m* beaver; **castóreo** *m pharm.* castor.
castración *f* castration; **castrar** [1a] castrate; *animal a.* geld, doctor F; ⚘ cut back.
castrense army *attr.*, military.

castrista Castroist; of Castro; Castro *attr.*
casual fortuitous, chance *attr.*; (*no esencial*) incidental; *gr.* case *attr.*; **casualidad** *f* chance, accident; *por* ~ by chance; *da la* ~ *que* as it happens, it happens that; *entrar por* ~ drop in; *se encontraba allí por* ~ he happened to be there; *¡qué* ~ *encontrarle a Vd.!* fancy meeting you!
casuc(h)a *f* hovel, slum, shack.
casuista *m/f* casuist; **casuística** *f* casuistry.
casulla *f* chasuble.
cata *f* testing, sampling; *S.Am.* test bore; F *ir en* ~ *de* go in search of; **catacaldos** *m* F rolling stone; dilettante *en artes*, (*entrometido*) meddler.
cataclismo *m* cataclysm.
catacumba *f* catacomb.
catador *m* taster, sampler; (*aficionado*) connoisseur; **catadura** *f* tasting, sampling; F mug, puss.
catafoto *m* (rear) reflector.
catalán 1. *adj. a. su. m*, **-a** *f* Catalan, Catalonian; **2.** *m* (*idioma*) Catalan; **catalanismo** *m* (*voz*; *expresión*; *rasgo*; *movimiento*) Catalanism.
catalejo *m* (spy)glass, telescope.
catalizador *m* catalyst.
catalogar [1h] catalogue; **catálogo** *m* catalogue.
cataplasma *f* poultice; F bore; ~ *de mostaza* mustard plaster.
¡cataplum! bang!, crash!
catapulta *f* catapult.
catar [1a] (*probar*) taste, sample, try; *fig.* examine, have a look at; (*mirar*) look at; (*buscar*) look out for; *¡cata!, ¡cátale!* just look at him!; *¡cátate eso!* you just think!
catarata *f* waterfall; ⚕ cataract.
catarral catarrhal; **catarro** *m* cold; (*permanente*) catarrh; ~ *crónico del pecho* chest trouble.
catarsis *f* catharsis.
catástrofe *f* catastrophe; **catastrófico** catastrophic.
catavinos *m* wine sampler; F boozer.
catecismo *m* catechism.
catecúmeno *m*, **a** *f* catechumen; *fig.* convert.
cátedra *f univ.* chair, professorship; (*asignatura*) subject; (*aula*) lecture room, classroom; (*ps.*) class, group; ~ *del Espíritu Santo* pulpit; *explicar una* ~ hold a chair (*de* of); **catedral** *f* cathedral; **catedrático** *m univ.* professor, lecturer; ~ *de instituto* grammar school teacher.
categoría *f* category; class, group; standing, rank *en sociedad etc.*; *de* ~ important, of importance; *de segunda* ~ *freq.* second-rate; **categórico** categorical, positive; *mentira* downright; *orden* express.
catequizar [1f] catechize, instruct in Christian doctrine; F win *s.o.* over, talk *s.o.* round.
caterva *f* host, throng.
catódico cathode *attr.*; *tubo de rayos* ~*s* cathode ray tube; CRT; **cátodo** *m* cathode.
catolicismo *m* (Roman) Catholicism; **católico** *adj. a. su. m*, **a** *f* (Roman) Catholic; *adj. fig.* sure, beyond doubt; F *no estar muy* ~ be none too good; ⚕ be under the weather.
catorce fourteen; (*fecha*) fourteenth.
catre *m* cot *de niño*; ~ (*de tijera*) camp-bed, folding-bed; **catrecillo** *m* camp-stool, folding-seat.
caucásico *adj. a. su. m*, **a** *f* Caucasian; white.
cauce *m* riverbed; ⚒ irrigation channel.
caución *f* caution, wariness; ⚖ bail; (*palabra*) pledge, security; *admitir a* ~ admit to bail; **caucionar** [1a] ⚖ bail; *daño* prevent.
cauchero rubber *attr.*; **caucho** *m* rubber; (*impermeable*) raincoat; ~ *esponjoso* foam rubber.
caudal *m* volume, flow *de río*; fortune, property, wealth *de p.*; wealth, abundance, stock *de cosas*; **caudaloso** *río* large, carrying much water; *fig.* wealthy, rich.
caudillaje *m* leadership; political bossism; **caudillo** *m* leader, chief; *pol.* el ♀ chief of state.
causa *f* cause (*a. pol.*); reason; grounds *de queja*; ⚖ suit, case; ⚖ prosecution *de oficio*; *a* (*or por*) ~ *de* on account of, because of, owing to; *sin* ~ for no good reason; *hacer* ~ *común con* make common cause with; *instruir* ~ take legal proceedings; **causal 1.** causal; **2.** *f* reason, grounds; **causalidad** *f* causality; **causar** [1a] cause; *gastos, trabajo* entail; *enojo, protesta* provoke; **causativo** causative.

cáustico *adj. a. su. m* caustic (*a. fig.*).
cautela *f* caution, cautiousness, wariness; (*astucia*) cunning; **cautelar** [1a] guard against; **~se** be on one's guard (*de* against); **cauteloso** cautious, careful, wary; (*astuto*) cunning.
cauterio *m* cautery; *fig.* eradication; **cauterización** *f* cauterization; **cauterizar** [1f] cauterize; *fig.* eradicate; *p.* reproach.
cautivar [1a] take *s.o.* prisoner; *fig. espíritu* enthral; *auditorio* charm, captivate, win over; *corazón* steal; **cautiverio** *m*, **cautividad** *f* captivity; *esp. fig.* bondage; **cautivo** *adj. a. su. m*, **a** *f* captive.
cauto cautious, wary, careful.
cava *f* cultivation; **cavar** [1a] *v/t.* dig; *pozo* sink; *v/i.* dig; ⚒ go deep; *fig.* delve (*en* into); medidate deeply (*en* on).
caverna *f* cave, cavern; **cavernícola** *m/f* cave dweller; **cavernoso** cavernous; cave *attr.*; *montaña etc.* honeycombed with caves; *voz* hollow.
caviar *m* caviar(e).
cavidad *f* cavity, hollow.
cavilación *f* deep thought; = *cavilosidad*; **cavilar** [1a] ponder (deeply), brood over; be obsessed with; **cavilosidad** *f* (unfounded) suspicion; **caviloso** suspicious.
cayado *m* 🌱 crook; *eccl.* crosier.
cayo *m* cay; key; *♀s de la Florida* Florida Keys.
caz *m* mill-race.
caza **1.** *f* (*en general*) hunting; shooting *con escopeta*; (*una ~*) hunt; chase, pursuit; (*animales*) game; *~ furtiva* poaching; F *~ de grillos* wild-goose chase; *~ mayor* big game; *a ~ de* in search of; *andar a ~ de* go out for; *dar ~* give chase; *dar ~ a* go after, chase; hunt down; *fig.* search out; *ir a la ~, ir de ~* go hunting; go out shooting; F *levantar la ~* set the ball rolling; **2.** *m* ✈ fighter; *~-bombardero* fighter-bomber; *~ nocturno* night fighter; **cazadero** *m* hunting ground; **cazador** *m* hunter, huntsman; *~ (de alforja)* trapper; *~ furtivo* poacher; **cazadora** *f* huntress; hunting jacket; **cazanoticias** *m* newshawk; **cazaperros** *m* dogcatcher; **cazar** [1f] *animales* hunt; *total de muertos* bag; (*perseguir*) chase, go after, hunt down; F (*obtener*) get hold of, wangle; *p.* win over *halagando*, take in *engañando*; (*sorprender*) catch;
cazasubmarinos *m* subchaser, submarine chaser.
cazcalear [1a] F buzz about, fuss around.
cazo *m* ladle; *~ (de cola)* glue pot; **cazolero** = *cominero*; **cazoleta** *f* bowl *de pipa*; guard *de espada*; ⊕ housing; **cazonete** *m* toggle; **cazuela** *f* pan, casserole (*a. plato*); pan *de arma*; *thea.* gods.
cazurro sullen; rustic; coarse.
ce: *¡~!* hey!; pst!; F *~ por be* down to the last detail.
cebada *f* barley; *~ perlada* pearl barley; **cebadal** *m* barley field; **cebadera** *f* nose bag; ⊕ hopper; **cebadura** *f* 🌱 fattening; ⊕ stoking; ⚔ priming; **cebar** [1a] **1.** *v/t.* 🌱 feed, fatten (*con* on); *arma, lámpara, máquina* prime; *cohete* light; *horno* stoke; *fig.* feed (*con* with); *ira* inflame; *esperanza* nurse, cherish; **2.** *v/i.* grip, go in, catch; **3. ~se** *en víctima* vent one's fury on, batten on; (*peste*) rage among; *estudio* devote o.s. to.
cebellina *f zo.* sable.
cebo *m* 🌱 feed; lure, incentive; ⚔ charge, priming; primer; ⊕ oven load; *pesca*: bait (*a. fig.*).
cebolla *f* onion; bulb *de tulipán etc.*; *~ escalonia* shallot; **cebollana** *f* chive; **cebollino** *m* young onion, spring onion; (*simiente*) onion seed; (*cebollana*) chive.
cebón **1.** fat, fattened; **2.** *m* fattened animal.
cebra *f* zebra.
ceca: *andar de ~ en Meca* go from place to place.
cecear [1a] lisp; *pronounce* [s] *as* [θ]; *español* use Castilian pronunciation;
ceceo *m* lisp(ing); *pronunciation of* [s] *as* [θ]; **ceceoso** lisping, with a lisp.
cecina *f* dried meat.
cedazo *m* sieve.
ceder [2a] *v/t.* hand over, give up, yield; *cosa querida* part with; ⚖ grant; *propiedad* make over; *territorio* cede; *v/i.* give in, yield (*a* to); (*disminuir*) decline, go down; (*viento*, ⚒ *etc.*) abate; *~ de pretensión* give up; *~ en honra etc.* redound to.

cedizo high, tainted.
cedro *m* cedar.
cédula *f* document, (slip of) paper, certificate; ✝ warrant; ~ *en blanco* blank check; ~ *personal*, ~ *de vecindad* identity card; *dar* ~ *a* license.
cefálico cephalic.
céfiro *m* zephyr (*a. tela*).
cegajoso weepy.
cegar [1h *a.* 1k] *v/t.* (make) blind; (*tapar*) block up, stop up; *v/i.* go blind; *fig.* = **~se** become blinded (*de* by); **ceguedad** *f*, **ceguera** *f* blindness (*a. fig.*); blackout.
ceja *f anat.* eyebrow; ▲ *etc.* projection; ⊕ rim, flange; *geog.* brow, crown; *meteor.* cloud cap; *fruncir las* **~s** knit one's brow, frown; *quemarse las* **~s** burn the midnight oil; *tener a uno entre* ~ *y* ~ look with disfavor on s.o.
cejar [1a] (move) back; ⚓ go astern; *fig.* give way, back down; climb down *en discusión*; relax, weaken *en esfuerzo*; *no* ~ keep it up, hold out; *no* ~ *en trabajo etc.* keep at; *sin* ~ unflinchingly.
cejijunto with bushy eyebrows; *fig.* scowling, frowning.
celada *f* ambush, trap (*a. fig.*); **celador** *m* guard, watchman; ⊕ maintenance man; ⚡ lineman; *mot.* parking attendant.
celaje *m* ▲ skylight; *fig.* sign, token; **~s** *pl.* sunset clouds.
celar[1] [1a] *v/t.* keep a watchful eye on, keep a check on; monitor; see that *leyes etc.* are kept, see that *justicia* is done; *v/i.*: ~ *por* watch over, guard.
celar[2] [1a] (*encubrir*) conceal, hide.
celda *f* cell; ~ *de castigo* solitary confinement; **celdilla** *f zo.* cell; cavity, hollow; ▲ niche.
celebérrimo *sup. of célebre*; **celebración** *f* celebration *etc.*; **celebrante** *m eccl.* celebrant; **celebrar** [1a] *v/t. aniversario, suceso feliz* celebrate; *misa* say; *matrimonio* perform, celebrate; *reunión* hold; *fiesta* keep; (*alabar*) praise; (*aprobar*) applaud, welcome; *chiste* laugh at; *ventajas* preach; ~ *inf.* be glad to *inf.*; *lo celebro* I'm very glad; *v/i. eccl.* say mass; **~se** (*tener lugar*) take place, be held; **célebre** famous, noted, celebrated (*por* for); F funny, witty; F *¡fue* ~*!* it was priceless!; **celebridad** *f* celebrity; (*festejo*) celebration(s).
celeridad *f* speed, swiftness; *con* ~ quickly, speedily; promptly.
celeste celestial; *ast.* heavenly; *color* sky-blue; **celestial** heavenly (*a. fig.*), celestial; F silly.
celestina *f* bawd, procuress.
celibato *m* celibacy; F bachelor; **célibe 1.** single, unmarried; **2.** *m/f* unmarried person; celibate.
celo *m* zeal, fervor; conscientiousness; *b.s.* envy, distrust; *zo.* rut heat; *época de* ~ mating season; *caer etc. en* ~ be in heat, rut; **~s** *pl.* jealousy; *dar* **~s** give occasion for jealousy; *tener* **~s** be jealous (*de* of).
celofán *m* cellophane.
celosía *f* lattice, blind, shutter; *fig.* jealousy; **celoso** (*con celo*) zealous (*de* for), keen (*de* about, on); (*con celos*) jealous (*de of*); (*receloso*) suspicious; ⊕ very sensitive.
celta 1. Celtic; **2.** *m/f* Celt; **3.** *m* (*idioma*) Celtic; **celtibérico, celtíbero** *adj. a. su. m*, **a** *f* Celtiberian; **céltico** Celtic; **celtohispan(ic)o** Celto-Hispanic.
célula *f* cell; ~ *fotoeléctrica* photoelectric cell; ~ *voltaica* voltaic cell; **celular** cellular; **celuloide** *m* celluloid; **celulosa** *f* cellulose.
cementar [1a] ⊕ caseharden; cement.
cementerio *m* cemetery, graveyard.
cemento *m* cement (*a. anat.*); (*hormigón*) concrete.
cena *f* supper, evening meal; (*oficial, de homenaje etc.*) dinner; 2 *m* Cenacle (site of the Last Supper).
cenáculo *m lit.* group, coterie.
cenador *m* arbor; (*casita*) summer house.
cenegal *m* quagmire, morass; F sticky business; **cenagoso** muddy, boggy.
cenar [1a] *v/t.* have for supper; *v/i.* have one's supper *etc.*, dine; *venir etc. cenado* have had one's supper.
cenceño thin, skinny.
cencerrada *f noisy serenade given to widower who remarries*; **cencerrear** [1a] (*cencerro*) jangle; ♪ play terribly; ⊕ *etc.* rattle, clatter; **cencerreo** *m* jangle *etc.*; **cencerro** *m* cowbell; *a* **~s** *tapados* stealthily.

cendal *m* gauze.
cenefa *f* border (*a.* ⚠), trimming, edge.
cenicero *m* ashtray *para cigarro*; ash pan *de hogar*; trash can *para basuras*; **ceniciento** ashen, ash-colored; *la* ⁀*a* Cinderella.
cenit *m* zenith.
ceniza *f* ash(es); ~*s pl. fig.* ashes, mortal remains; **cenizo** *m* F wet blanket; **cenizoso** ashy; *fig.* ashen.
cenotafio *m* cenotaph.
censo *m* census *de población*; (*impuesto*) tax; ground rent *de propiedad*; (*hipoteca*) mortgage; ~ *electoral* electoral roll; F *ser un* ~ be a constant source of trouble; **censor** *m* censor; *fig.* critic; ~ *jurado de cuentas* certified public accountant; CPA; **censural** census *attr. etc.*; **censura** *f pol. etc.* censorship; (*crítica*) censure, stricture; criticism, judgment *de obra*; **censurable** reprehensible, blameworthy; **censurar** [1a] *pol. etc.* censor; (*criticar*) censure, condemn; find fault with; blame.
centaura *f* centaury.
centauro *m* centaur.
centavo *adj. a. su. m* hundredth; *S.Am.* cent.
centella *f* (*chispa*) spark (*a. fig.*); (*rayo*) flash of lightning; **centelleante** sparkling (*a. fig.*); flashing; **centell(e)ar** [1a] sparkle (*a. fig.*); flash; (*metal etc.*) gleam, glint; (*estrella*) twinkle; **centelleo** *m* sparkling, flashing *etc.*
centena *f* hundred; **centenar** *m* hundred; *a* ~*es* by the hundred, in hundreds; **centenario 1.** *adj. a. su. m* centenary; **2.** *m*, **a** *f* centenarian.
centeno *m* rye.
centésimo *adj. a. su. m* hundredth; **centígrado** centigrade; **centigramo** *m* centigram; **centímetro** *m* centimeter; **céntimo 1.** hundredth; **2.** *m* cent (*hundredth part of a peseta*).
centinela *m/f* sentry, guard, sentinel; *estar etc. de* ~ be on guard; *hacer* ~ *fig.* keep watch, be on the lookout.
centolla *f* (large) crab.
centón *m sew.* patchwork quilt; *lit.* cento.
central 1. central, middle; *esp. fig.* pivotal; **2.** *f* ✝ head office; ~ *de correos* main post office; ~ *depuradora* waterworks; ~ *eléctrica* power station; ~ *telefónica* telephone exchange; **centralista** *m/f* telephone operator; **centralita** *f teleph.* switchboard; **centralización** *f* centralization; **centralizar** [1f] centralize; **centrar** [1a] center; hit the center; ~**se** *en* concentrate on; stress; **céntrico** central, middle; *lugar* central, convenient; **centrifugadora** *f* centrifuge; centrifugal machine; spin-drier; **centrífugo** centrifugal; **centrípeto** centripetal; **centro** *m* center (*a.* ♘), middle; *fig.* center, hub *de actividad etc.*; (*objeto*) goal, purpose; ~ *de gravedad* center of gravity; ~ *de mesa* centerpiece; ~ *social* community center; *deportes*: *delantero* ~ center forward; *medio* ~ center half; *hallarse en su* ~ be in one's element; **centroamericano** Central American.
centuplicar [1g] centuple; **céntuplo 1.** hundredfold, centuple; **2.** *m* centuple.
centuria *f* century.
ceñido *vestido* tight, close-fitting; clinging; svelte, lithe; *fig.* sparing, frugal; ~ *y corto* straight to the point; **ceñir** [3h *a.* 3l] *espada* gird on; *cinturón etc.* put on; (*llevar*) wear; *frente etc.* bind, encircle (*con*, *de* with); wreathe (*con*, *de flores etc.* with); (*atar*) tie; *fig.* (*mar etc.*) girdle, surround; ⚔ besiege; *narración* cut down; ~**se** ✝ tighten one's belt; limit o.s., be brief *en palabras*; ~ *a tema* limit o.s. to, concentrate on; *se ciñó la corona* he became king.
ceño *m* frown, scowl; *meteor.* threatening look; *mirar con* ~ (*v/i.*) frown, scowl; (*v/t.*) frown at, give *s.o.* black looks; **ceñudo** frowning; *mirada etc.* black, grim.
cepa *f* stump *de árbol*; stock *de vid*; (*vid*) vine; ⚠ pier; *Mex.* pit, hole; *fig.* stock; *de buena* ~ *p.* of good stock; *cosa* of good quality.
cepillar [1a] brush; ⊕ plane; *S.Am.* flatter; *univ. sl.* plough; **cepillo** *m* brush; ⊕ plane; *eccl.* poorbox; ~ *de dientes* toothbrush; ~ *para las uñas* nail brush.
cepo *m* ⚘ branch; *hunt.* snare, trap; ⚔ *etc.* mantrap; stocks *de reo*; ⊕ reel; *eccl.* poorbox.

cequión *m* water race; *Ven.* stream, canal.
cera *f* (bees)wax; *Col., Ecuad., Mex.* candle; ~ (*de lustrar*) (wax) polish; ~s *pl.* honeycomb.
cerámica *f* (*arte*) ceramics; (*objetos*) pottery (*a.* ~s *pl.*); **cerámico** ceramic.
cerbatana *f* peashooter; ⚔ blowgun; ⚕ ear trumpet; *sl.* mouthpiece; spokesperson.
cerca[1] *f* fence; (*tapia*) wall; ~ (*viva*) hedge.
cerca[2] **1.** *adv.* near(by), close; *de* ~ near; ⚔ *etc.* at close range; *examinar* closely; *por aquí* ~ somewhere round here, nearby; **2.** *prp.* ~ *de* near, close to; in the neighborhood of; *número* about; (*embajador etc.*) to; ~ *de inf.* near *ger.*, on the point of *ger.*; **3.** *m*: *tiene buen* ~ it looks good close up; ~s *pl. paint.* objects in the foreground.
cercado *m* enclosure; garden, orchard; = *cerca*[1].
cercanía *f* nearness; ~s *pl.* outskirts *de ciudad*; neighborhood; *de* ~s 🚂 suburban; **cercano** near, close; *pueblo etc.* nearby, next; *muerte* approaching; ~ *a* near to; **cercar** [1g] fence in, enclose; wall *con tapia*, hedge *con seto*; (*rodear*) surround, ring (*de* with); ⚔ besiege; (*esp. enemigo, montañas*) hem in.
cercén: *a* ~ entirely; *cortar a* ~ nip in the bud; **cercenar** [1a] cut the edge off; clip, trim; *extremo* slice off; *moneda* clip; *gastos* cut down, curtail.
cerceta *f*: ~ (*común*) teal.
cerciorar [1a] inform, assure; **~se** *de* find out about, make sure of, ascertain.
cerco *m* ⚒ *etc.* enclosure; *S.Am.* hedge; hoop *de tonel*; rim *de rueda*; ⚠ frame; ⚔ siege; *meteor.* halo; ⚔ *poner* ~ *a* lay siege to.
cerda *f* bristle; horsehair; *hunt.* noose, snare; *zo.* sow; **cerdear** [1a] ♪ rasp, grate; F hold back, jib; **cerdo** *m* pig (*a. fig.*); (*carne de*) ~ pork; **cerdoso** *animal* shaggy, hairy; *barbilla etc.* bristly, stubbly.
cereal **1.** cereal, grain *attr.*; **2.** *m* cereal; ~es *pl.* grain, cereals.
cerebral cerebral, intellectual; brain *attr.*; F brainy; **cerebro** *m* brain (*a. fig.*).
ceremonia *f* ceremony; *eccl. a.* service; *falta de* ~ informality; *de* ~ *adv.* with all due ceremony; *attr.* formal; *por* ~ as a matter of form; *sin* ~ *adv.* informally, with no fuss; *attr.* informal; *hacer* ~s stand on ceremony; **ceremonial** *adj. a. su. m* ceremonial; **ceremonioso** ceremonious; *recepción* formal; *b.s.* stiff, overpolite.
céreo wax(en).
cereza *f* cherry; (*rojo*) ~ cherry (-red); **cerezo** *m* cherry (tree).
cerilla *f* match; (*vela*) wax taper; *anat.* earwax; **cerillo** *m* *S.Am.* match.
cernejas *f/pl.* fetlock.
cerner [2g] *v/t.* sift (*a. fig.*); *fig.* scan; *v/i.* ⚘ bud, blossom; *meteor.* drizzle; **~se** (*p.*) waddle; *orn.* hover, soar; *fig.* threaten; ~ *sobre* be poised over, hang over.
cernícalo *m* sparrow hawk, kestrel; F lout, dolt; rude ignoramus; F *coger un* ~ get boozed.
cernidillo *m* waddle; *meteor.* drizzle; **cernido** *m* sifting; (*harina*) sifted flour.
cero *m* (*nada*) nothing; ⚡ (*cifra*) nought; *phys. etc.* zero; *deportes*: nil; *tenis*: love; F ~ *a la izquierda* nonentity, back number; *empezar de* ~ start from the beginning.
ceroso (*de cera*) waxen; (*parecido a cera*) waxy; **cerote** *m* wax; F funk, jitters.
cerquita quite near, close by.
cerradero **1.** *caja* that can be locked; *aparato* locking, lock *attr.*; **2.** *m* strike (*of lock*); purse strings *de bolsa*; clasp; **cerrado** *asunto* obscure; *p.* (*callado*) quiet, secretive; F ~ (*de mollera*) dense; all-too-typical *de carácter*; with a broad accent *en habla*; *acento* broad, thick; *atmósfera* heavy; *barba* full; *cielo* overcast; *curva* sharp, tight; *noche* dark; *aquí huele a* ~ it's stuffy in here.
cerradura *f* (*acto*) closing, shutting; locking *con llave*; (*aparato*) lock; ~ *de combinación* combination lock; ~ *dormida* deadlock; **cerraja** *f* lock; **cerrajero** *m* locksmith.
cerrar [1k] **1.** *v/t.* close, shut; lock (up) *con llave*, bolt *con cerrojo*; *grifo etc.* turn off; *agujero* close (up), stop; *puño* clench, close; *carta* seal; ⚡ *circuito* make, close; *puerto* close; *trato* strike; *procesión* bring

up the rear of; *cuenta, discusión* close; *fábrica etc.* close down, shut down; **2.** *v/i.* close, shut; (*noche*) set in; ~ *con* close with, close in on; *dejar sin* ~ leave open; **3.** **~se** close *etc.*; ⚕ close up, heal; ⚔ close ranks; *meteor.* cloud over; ~ *en inf.* persist in *ger.*; **cerrazón** *f* threatening sky.

cerrero *animal* wild; *p.* uncouth, rough; **cerril** *terreno* rough; = *cerrero*; **cerro** *m* hill, height; *zo.* neck; *irse etc. por los* ~*s de Ubeda* get off the track; F talk a lot of rubbish.

cerrojo *m* bolt; *táctica de* ~ stonewalling; *echar el* ~ bolt the door.

certamen *m* competition, contest.

certero sure, certain; *tirador* good, crack; *golpe* well-aimed; (*sabedor*) well-informed; **certeza** *f* certainty; *tener la* ~ *de que* know for certain that, be quite sure that; **certidumbre** *f* certainty.

certificación *f* certification; ✉ registration; ⚖ affidavit; **certificado 1.** ✉ registered; **2.** *m* certificate; ✉ registered packet *etc.*; ~ *de aptitud* testimonial; ~ *médico* medical certificate; **certificar** [1g] certify; vouch for *s.o.*; ✉ register.

cerúleo sky-blue.

cerumen *m* earwax.

cervato *m* fawn.

cervecería *f* brewery; (*taberna*) public house, bar; **cervecero** *m* brewer; **cerveza** *f* beer.

cervical neck *attr.*, cervical 📖; **cerviz** *f* (nape of the) neck; *bajar* (*or doblar*) *la* ~ submit, bow down; *ser duro de* ~ be wild, be headstrong.

cesación *f* cessation; suspension, stoppage; **cesante 1.** out of a job; on half pay; **2.** *m civil servant who has been retired*; **cesantía** *f state of being a cesante*; (*paga*) retirement pension; **cesar** [1a] *v/t.* stop; *v/i.* stop, cease; (*empleado*) leave, quit; ~ *de inf.* stop *ger.*, leave off *ger.*; ~ *en el trabajo* give up one's work; *sin* ~ ceaselessly; **cese** *m* ✝ stoppage; stop-payment; ~ *de fuego*, ~ *de hostilidades* cease-fire.

cesión *f* ⚖ grant(ing), cession (*a. pol.*); **cesionario** *m*, **a** *f* grantee, assign; **cesionista** *m/f* grantor, assignor.

césped *m* grass, turf; lawn *esp. de casa*; green *para bolos*; (*tepe*) sod, turf.

cesta *f* basket; *pelota*: wicker racquet; **cestada** *f* basketful; **cestería** *f* wickerwork, basket work; (*tienda*) basket shop; **cestero** *m*, **a** *f* basket maker; **cesto** *m* (large) basket; hamper *esp. para comida*; ~ (*de la colada*) clothes basket; ~ (*para papeles*) waste-paper basket; F idiot; F *estar metido en un* ~ be a spoilt child.

cesura *f* caesura.

cetáceo *adj. a. su. m* cetacean.

cetrería *f* falconry; **cetrero** *m* falconer.

cetrino greenish-yellow; *rostro* sallow; *fig.* jaundiced.

cetro *m* sceptre; *fig.* power, dominion; *empuñar el* ~ ascend the throne.

cianotipia *f*, **cianotipo** *m* blueprint.

cianuro *m* cyanide; ~ *de potasio* cyanide of potassium.

ciar [1c] ⚓ go astern; (*bote*) back water; *fig.* go backwards; (*ceder*) back down, give in.

ciática *f* sciatica.

cibernética *f* ⚡ cybernetics.

cicatear [1a] F be stingy; **cicatería** *f* stinginess; **cicatero 1.** stingy, mean; **2.** *m*, **a** *f* mean sort, skinflint.

cicatriz *f* scar (*a. fig.*); **cicatrización** *f* healing; **cicatrizar**(**se**) [1f] heal (up); heal over, form a scar.

cicerone *m* guide, cicerone.

ciclamino *m* cyclamen.

cíclico cyclic(al); **ciclismo** *m* cycling; (*carreras*) cycle racing; **ciclista** *m/f* cyclist; **ciclo** *m* cycle; *escuela*: term; course, series *de clases*; **ciclón** *m* cyclone; **ciclotrón** *m* cyclotron.

cicuta *f* hemlock.

cidra *f* citron; **cidro** *m* citron (tree); (*género*) citrus.

ciega *f* blind woman; **ciego 1.** blind (*a. fig.*; de with); *caño etc.* blocked, stopped up; *a* ~*as* blindly (*a. fig.*); *fig.* thoughtlessly; *caminar a* ~*as* grope one's way; **2.** *m* blind man.

cielo *m* sky; *ast.* sky, heavens; *eccl.* heaven; climate; ~ (*raso*) ceiling; roof *de boca*; canopy *de cama*; ¡~*s*! heavens above!; good grief!; *a* ~

abierto in the open air (*a. a ~ raso*); ⚒ opencast; *a ~ descubierto* in the open; F *bajado del ~* marvelous; *cosa llovida del ~* godsend; F *juntársele a uno el ~ con la tierra* be in an awful mess; *tomar el ~ con las manos* ask for trouble, be overoptimistic; *venirse el ~ abajo* rain cats and dogs; *ver el ~ abierto* see a way out.
ciempiés *m* centipede.
cien *v. ciento*; *~ por ~ fig.* a hundred percent, wholehearted.
ciénaga *f* marsh, bog.
ciencia *f* science; (*saber en general*) knowledge, learning; *~-ficción* science fiction; *~s pl. ocultas* occult sciences; occultism; *~s pl. naturales* natural sciences; *hombre de ~* scientist; *saber a ~ cierta* know for certain, know for a fact.
cieno *m* mud, silt, ooze.
científico 1. scientific; **2.** *m* scientist.
ciento *adj. a. su m* (a) hundred, one hundred; *por ~* percent.
cierne: *en ~(s)* ⚘ in blossom, in flower; *fig. cosa* in its infancy; *p.* budding.
cierre *m* (*acto*) closing *etc.*; shutdown *de fábrica*; (*huelga*) lockout; (*mecanismo*) snap (lock); fastener *de vestido*; clasp *de libro*; catch *de puerta*; shutter *de tienda*; *mot.* choke; *~ de cremallera*, *~ relámpago* zipper; *~ metálico* (roll) shutter; **cierro** *m* = *cierre*; *S.Am.* envelope.
cierto (*seguro*) sure, certain; *promesa* definite; (*verdadero*) true; (*determinado*) a certain; *~s pl.* some, certain; *por ~* indeed, certainly; (*a propósito*) by the way; *¡sí, por ~!* yes of course!; es *~ que* it is true that; *no es ~* it is untrue; *estar en lo ~* be right; *saber de ~* know for certain.
cierva *f* hind; **ciervo** *m* deer; (*macho*) stag; *~ común* red deer.
cierzo *m* north wind.
cifra *f* ✠ number, numeral; quantity, amount; ✝ sum; (*escritura*) code, cipher; monogram; abbreviation; *en ~* in code; *fig.* mysteriously; (*en breve*) in a shortened form; **cifrado** in code; **cifrar** [1a] write in code; *fig.* summarize; *esperanza etc.* set, concentrate, place (*en* on).
cigarra *f* cicada.
cigarrera *f* cigar case; **cigarrería** *f* *S.Am.* tobacco store; **cigarrillo** *m* cigarette; **cigarro** *m* cigar (*a. ~ puro*); cigarette; *~ habano* Havana (cigar).
cigüeña *f orn.* stork; ⊕ crank, handle; **cigüeñal** *m* crankshaft.
cilampa *f C.Am.* drizzle.
ciliar ciliary.
cilindrada *f* cylinder capacity; **cilindrar** [1a] roll; **cilíndrico** cylindric(al); **cilindro** *m* cylinder (*a.* ⊕); *typ. etc.* roller; *~ de caminos* (road)roller.
cima *f* top *de árbol*; top, summit *de monte*; *fig.* summit, height; *dar ~ a* complete, carry *s.t.* out successfully.
cimarrón *S.Am. zo.*, ⚘ wild.
címbalo *m* cymbal.
cimbel *m* decoy (*a. fig.*).
cimbor(r)io *m* (base of a) dome.
cimbr(e)ar [1a] *vara* shake, swish; bend; F thrash; F *le cimbró de un bastonazo* he gave him one with his stick; *~se* sway, swing; (*doblarse*) bend; **cimbreño** pliant; *p.* willowy; **cimbreo** *m* sway(ing) *etc.*
cimentar [1k] ⚠ lay the foundations of; *fig.* found; (*afirmar*) cement, strengthen.
cimera *f* crest; **cimero** top, uppermost.
cimiento *m* foundation, groundwork; *fig.* basis, source; ⚠ *~s pl.* foundations.
cinabrio *m* cinnabar.
cinc *m* zinc; ✝ counter.
cincel *m* chisel; **cincelar** [1a] carve, chisel; engrave.
cinco five (*a. su.*); (*fecha*) fifth; *las ~* five o'clock; F *le dije cuántas son ~* I told him a thing or two; F *saber cuántas son ~* know what's what, know a thing or two; F *¡vengan esos ~!* shake!
cincuenta fifty.
cincha *f* girth; **cinchar** [1a] *silla* secure; ⊕ band, hoop; **cincho** *m* (*faja*) belt, sash; ⊕ band, hoop.
cine *m* cinema, movies; *~ mudo* silent film; **cineasta** *m/f* film producer; film actor (*f* actress); movie fan; **cinema** *m* cinema; **cinemateca** *f* film library; **cinematografía** *f* films; film making; **cinematografiar** [1c] film; **cinematográfico** movie *attr.*, film *attr.*; **cinematógrafo** *m* cinema(tograph); (*má-*

quina) film projector; motion-picture theater; movie house.
cinerario *urna* cinerary; = *ceniciento*.
cinética *f* kinetics; **cinético** kinetic.
cingalés *adj. a. su. m*, **-a** *f* Sinhalese.
cínico 1. cynical; *fig.* brazen, shameless; **2.** *m*, **a** *f* cynic; *fig.* humbug; **cinismo** *m* cynicism; *fig.* shamelessness, effrontery; humbug.
cinta *f sew. etc.* ribbon; band, strip; tape *de papel, magnetofón, a. deportes*; *cine*: film; (*rollo*) reel; kerb *de acera*; ⚠ fillet; ~ *adhesiva* adhesive tape; ~ *aisladora* insulating tape; ~ *de freno* brake lining; ~ *para máquina de escribir* typewriter ribbon; ~ *métrica* tape measure; **cintero** *m* girdle *de mujer*; (*maroma*) rope; **cinto** *m* ⚔ belt; girdle; *armas de* ~ side arms; **cintura** *f anat.* waist; waistline; (*faja*) girdle; *meter en* ~ keep *s.o.* under; make *s.o.* see reason; *tener poca* ~ have a slim waist; **cinturón** *m* belt; girdle; ~ *de seguridad* safety belt; ~ *retractil* retractable safety belt.
cipayo *m* sepoy.
cíper *m Mex.* zipper.
cipo *m* memorial stone; milestone *de camino*; road sign.
ciprés *m* cypress (tree).
circo *m* circus.
circuir [3g] circle, surround; **circuito** *m* circuit (*a.* ⚡); *deportes*: lap; circumference; ~ *en bucle* loop line; ~ *cerrado* closed circuit, loop; *corto* ~ short circuit; **circulación** *f* circulation (*a.* ⚕, ⚘); *mot.* (movement of) traffic; *fig.* propagation; ~ *rodada* wheeled traffic; ⚕ *poner en* ~ issue, put into circulation; **circulante** circulating; **circular 1.** *adj. a. su. f* circular; **2.** [1a] *v/t.* circulate; *v/i.* circulate (*a.* ⚕, ⚘, *fig.*); *mot.* move (freely); (*p.*) walk round, move about (*a.* ~ *por*); *¡circulen!* move along!; *hacer* ~ *ps.* move on, *coches* keep moving; **círculo** *m* circle (*a. fig.*); club; (*aro*) ring, band; (*extensión*) compass, extent; ♀ *Polar Artico* Arctic Circle; ~ *vicioso* vicious circle.
circun... circum...; **~cidar** [1a] circumcise; *fig.* curtail; moderate; **~cisión** *f* circumcision; **~dante** surrounding; **~dar** [1a] surround; **~ferencia** *f* circumference; **~flejo** *m* circumflex; **~locución** *f*, **~loquio** *m* roundabout expression, circumlocution; **~navegación** *f* circumnavigation; **~navegar** [1h] sail round, circumnavigate; **~scribir** [3a; *p.p. circunscrito*] circumscribe (*a. fig.*); *fig.* limit; **~se** *fig.* be limited, be confined (*a* to); **~scripción** *f* circumscription; *pol. etc.* (sub)division; **~specció́n** *f* cautiousness, circumspection; prudence; **~specto** circumspect, prudent, deliberate; *palabras* guarded; **~stancia** *f* circumstance; situation; *en las* ~*s* in (*or* under) the circumstances; **~stanciado** detailed, minute; **~stancial** circumstantial; *arreglo* makeshift, emergency *attr.*; **~stante 1.** surrounding; present; **2.** *m/f* onlooker, bystander; **~vecino** adjacent, surrounding; **~volar** ✈ circumnavigate; fly around.
cirio *m eccl.* (wax) candle.
cirro *m* cirrus.
ciruela *f* plum; ~ *claudia* greengage; ~ *damascena* damson; ~ *pasa* prune; **ciruelo** *m* plum (tree); F dolt.
cirugía *f* surgery; ~ *estética*, ~ *plástica* plastic surgery; **cirujano** *m* surgeon.
ciscar [1g] F dirty, soil; **~se** move the bowels; soil o.s.; **cisco** *m* slack; F row, shindy; F *armar un* ~, *meter* ~ start a row; F *estar hecho* ~ be done up.
cisma *m eccl.* schism; *pol. etc.* split; *fig.* disagreement; **cismático** *eccl.* schismatic(al); *fig.* troublemaking; dissident.
cisne *m* swan.
cisterna *f* (water)tank, cistern; toilet tank.
cistitis *f* cystitis.
cita *f* engagement, appointment, meeting; (*lugar*) rendezvous; (*con novia etc.*) date; *lit.* quotation; reference; *darse* ~ make a date (*con* with); **citación** *f lit.* quotation; ⚖ summons, citation; **citar** [1a] make an appointment (*or* date) with; ⚖ summon; *lit.* quote, cite; *toro* incite; *la cité para las 6* I arranged to meet her at 6.
cítara *f* zither; *hist.* lyre.
cítrico citric.
ciudad *f* city; town; **ciudadanía** *f*

citizenship; **ciudadano 1.** civic, city *attr.*; **2.** *m*, **a** *f* city dweller; *pol.* citizen; ~*s pl. freq.* townsfolk, townspeople; ~ *de honor* honorary citizen; **ciudadela** *f* citadel; *S.Am.* tenement; **cívico 1.** civic; *fig.* public-spirited, patriotic; domestic; **2.** *m S.Am.* policeman; **civil 1.** civil (*a. fig.*); ⚔ *guerra* civil; *población* civilian; **2.** *m* policeman; **civilidad** *f* civility; **civilización** *f* civilization; **civilizar** [1f] civilize; **~se** become civilized; **civismo** *m* public spirit; patriotism; community spirit; good citizenship; civic-mindedness.

cizalla *f* (*una* a pair of) (metal) shears; wire cutters; ~*s pl.* clippings.

cizaña *f* ⚘ darnel; *Biblia*: tares; *fig.* vice, harmful influence; *sembrar* ~ sow discord; **cizañero** *m*, **a** *f* troublemaker.

clamar [1a] *v/t.* cry out for; *v/i.* cry out (*contra* against, *por* for); **clamor** *m* (*grito*) cry; (*protesta*) outcry, clamor; (*ruido*) noise, clamor; (*toque*) knell; **clamorear** [1a] *v/t.* cry out for, clamor for; appeal for; *v/i.* (*campana*) toll; **clamoreo** *m* clamor; (*protesta*) outcry; **clamoroso** noisy; loud, shrieking; *éxito* resounding.

clandestinidad *f* secrecy; **clandestino** secret, clandestine; *pol. etc. a.* underground, undercover.

claque *m* claque; hired applauders.

clara *f* white of an egg; bald spot *en cabeza*; *meteor.* bright interval.

claraboya *f* skylight; transom.

clarear [1a] *v/t.* brighten; *color* make lighter; *v/i.* dawn; *meteor.* clear up; **~se** (*tela*) be transparent; F give the game away.

clarete *m* claret.

claridad *f* brightness *etc.*; clearness, clarity (*a. fig.*); ~*es pl.* plain speaking, blunt remarks; **claridoso** *C.Am., Mex.* frank; open; **clarificación** *f* clarification (*a. fig.*); illumination; **clarificar** [1g] illuminate, light up; clarify (*a. fig.*); *bosque* clear.

clarinada *f* F uncalled-for remark.

clarinete *m* clarinet.

clarión *m* chalk; **clarioncillo** *m* crayon.

clarividencia *f* far-sightedness; discernment; clairvoyance; **clarividente 1.** far-sighted; discerning; **2.** *m/f* clairvoyant(e).

claro 1. *adj. día, ojos etc.* bright; *agua, lenguaje, prueba, voz* clear; *cristal* clear, transparent; *cuarto, cerveza, color* light; *contorno* clear, distinct, bold; *líquido* thin; (*ralo*) thin, sparse; *fig.* illustrious; ~ *como la luz del día* plain as day; *más* ~ *que el sol* as clear as day (light); *¡~!* naturally!, of course!; *¡(pues)~!* I quite agree with you!; ~ *(que)* ...,~ *está* naturally ..., of course ...; *¡~ que sí!* of course it is!; *a las ~as* clearly; openly; *poner* (*or sacar*) *en* ~ explain, clarify; **2.** *adv.* clearly; *hablar* ~ *fig.* speak plainly; **3.** *m* opening, gap; space; ⛵ light, window; *paint.* highlight, light tone; clearing *en bosque*; egg white.

clase *f mst* class; (*género*) *a.* sort, kind; *univ. a.* lecture; (*sala*) classroom; *univ.* lecture room; ~ *alta* upper class(es); ~ *baja* lower class(es); ~ *media* middle class(es); ~ *obrera* working class; ~ *turista* tourist class; ⚔ ~*s pl.* (*de tropa*) noncommissioned officers; *de una misma* ~ of the same kind; *toda* ~ *de* every kind of, all manner of; *de toda* ~ of every kind, of all sorts; *dar* ~ give a lesson; *dar* ~*s* (*enseñar*) teach; (*aprender*) learn; F *fumarse la* ~ cut a class.

clásico 1. classical; *esp. fig.* classic; traditional; typical; *coche etc.* vintage; (*común*) ordinary; **2.** *m* classic; (*erudito*) classicist.

clasificación *f* classification; rating (*a.* ⚓); **clasificador** *m* filing cabinet; **clasificar** [1g] classify; grade, rate; sort (out).

claudia *f* greengage.

claudicar [1g] limp; F back down; give in; *fig.* act crookedly; (*ceder*) give way, abandon one's principles.

claustro *m* cloister (*a. fig.*); *univ. approx.* senate.

cláusula *f* clause; *gr.* sentence.

clausura *f* (*acto*) closing (ceremony), closure; *eccl.* monastic life; *eccl.* de ~ *convento* enclosed; **clausurar** [1a] close; suspend, adjourn.

clava *f* club; **clavado** *vestido* just right; *a las 5* ~*as* at 5 sharp; *estar* ~ (*reloj*) be stopped (*en* at); *quedar* ~ *fig.* be dumbfounded; **clavar** [1a] *clavo* knock in, drive in; *tablas* nail (together); (*asegurar*) fasten, pin, fix; *puñal* stick, thrust (*en* into); *joya* set; *cañón* spike; *vista* fix (*en*

on), rivet (*en* to); F diddle, sting.
clave 1. *f* ♪ clef; ⚠ keystone; *fig.* key (*de* to); ~ *de sol* treble clef; **2.** *adj.* key *attr.*
clavel *m* carnation; **clavellina** *f* pink.
clavero *m* ♀ clove (tree); (*p.*) keeper of the keys.
clavetear [1a] *puerta etc.* stud; *cordón etc.* put a tip on; *fig.* close, clinch, wind up.
clavícula *f* collarbone, clavicle.
clavija *f* pin, peg (*a.* ♪), dowel; ⚡ plug; ~ *hendida* cotter pin; F *apretar las* ~*s a* put the screws on.
clavillo *m* pin, rivet; ♀ clove.
clavo *m* nail; spike; stud; ♀ clove; ⚕ (*callo*) corn; (*dolor*) sharp pain; *fig.* anguish; ~ *de rosca* screw; F *dar en el* ~ hit the nail on the head; F *remachar el* ~ make matters worse; F *ser de* ~ *pasado* be as plain as a pike staff; (*fácil*) be a cinch.
claxon *m mot.* horn; *tocar el* ~ sound one's horn, hoot; honk.
clemencia *f* clemency, mercy; **clemente** merciful, forgiving; lenient.
cleptomanía *f* kleptomania; **cleptómano** *m*, **a** *f* kleptomaniac.
clerecía *f* priesthood; (*ps.*) clergy; **clerical** clerical; **clericalismo** *m* clericalism; **clericato** *m*, **clericatura** *f* priesthood; **clérigo** *m* (*esp. católico*) priest; (*esp. anglicano*) clergyman; **clero** *m* clergy.
cliché *m typ.* stencil; *lit.* cliché; = *clisé.*
cliente *m/f* ✝ customer, client (*a.* ⚖); ⚕ patient; **clientela** *f* customers, clients, clientèle; ⚕ practice, patients.
clima *m* climate; **climático** climatic; **climatización** *f* air conditioning.
clímax *m rhet.* climax.
clincha *f* clinch.
clínica *f* clinic, hospital; (*esp. privado*) nursing home; (*que enseña*) teaching hospital; (*enseñanza*) clinical training; ~ *de reposo* convalescent home; **clínico** clinical.
clip *m* paper clip; (*joya*) clip.
clisar [1a] stereotype; **clisé** *m typ.* cliché, plate; *phot.* plate.
clisos *m/pl. sl.* peepers.
cloaca *f* sewer (*a. fig.*).
cloquear [1a] cluck; harpoon.
cloral *m* chloral; **clorhídrico** hydrochloric; **cloro** *m* chlorine; **cloroformizar** [1f] chloroform; **cloroformo** *m* chloroform; **cloruro** *m* chloride; ~ *de cal* chloride of lime.
clóset *m S.Am.* (wall) closet.
club *m* club.
clueca broody (*f* hen).
coacción *f* coercion, duress; F pressure; **coactivo** coercive.
coadjutor *m* coadjutor; **coadyuvar** [1a] assist, contribute to.
coagulación *f* coagulation; **coagular(se)** [1a] coagulate.
coalición *f* coalition.
coartada *f* alibi; **coartar** [1a] limit, restrict.
coba *f* F (*embuste*) neat trick; (*halago*) soft soap; flattery; *dar* ~ *a* soap *s.o.* up, play up to *s.o.*
cobalto *m* cobalt.
cobarde 1. cowardly; faint-hearted; **2.** *m/f* coward; **cobardear** [1a] be a coward, show cowardice; **cobardía** *f* cowardice; faint-heartedness; **cobardón** *m* real coward.
cobaya *f*, **cobayo** *m* guinea pig.
cobertera *f* lid, cover; **cobertizo** *m* shed; outhouse; lean-to; (*refugio*) shelter; **cobertor** *m* bedspread; **cobertura** *f* cover(ing); bedspread *de cama.*
cobija *f* coping tile; *S.Am.* blanket; *S.Am.* ~*s pl.* bedclothes; **cobijar** [1a] cover (up), close; *fig.* take in, give shelter to; ~**se** take shelter; **cobijo** *m fig.* cover, shelter; lodging *en casa.*
cobista F *adj. a. su. m/f* flattering; fawning.
cobrable, cobradero *precio* chargeable; *suma* recoverable; **cobrador** *m* ✝ collector; conductor *de autobús*; (*perro*) retriever; **cobranza** *f* = *cobro*; **cobrar** [1a] **1.** *v/t.* (*recuperar*) recover; *precio* charge; *suma* collect; *cheque* cash; *sueldo* draw, get; *hunt.* retrieve; *cuerda* pull in; *fig. golpe* get; *cariño* take (*a* to); *crédito, fama, odio* get, acquire; *ánimo* summon up, muster; *fuerzas* gather; *carnes* put on; *S.Am.* press (for payment); ✝ *por* ~ outstanding; receivable; **2.** *v/i.* (*en empleo*) get one's pay; F *¡vas a* ~*!* you'll cop it!; **3.** ~**se** ⚕ recover;

(*volver en sí*) come to; ~ *de pérdida* make up for.

cobre *m* copper; ♪ brass (*a.* ~*s pl.*); *cocina*: copper pans; *batirse el* ~ go all out (*por inf.* to *inf.*); (*disputa*) get really worked up; **cobreño** copper *attr.*, coppery; **cobrizo** coppery.

cobro *m* recovery; collection *etc.*; ✝ *poner en* (*or al*) ~ make *s.t.* payable; (*cuenta*) send out a bill.

coca *f* F nut; (*golpe*) rap on the head; kink *en cuerda*; *Mex. de* ~ free; gratis.

cocaína *f* cocaine.

cocción *f* cooking *etc.*; ⊕ baking, firing.

cóccix *m* coccyx.

cocear [1a] kick (*a.* F).

cocer [2b *a.* 2h] *v/t.* cook; (*hervir*) boil; *pan* bake; ⊕ bake; *barros* fire; *v/i.* cook; boil; (*vino*) ferment; ~**se** ⚕ be in continual pain; F *no se le cuece el pan* he's like a cat on hot bricks; **cocido** *m* stew (*of meat, bacon a. vegetables*).

cociente *m* quotient; ~ *intelectual* intelligence quotient (I.Q.).

cocina *f* kitchen; (*arte,* ~ *francesa etc.*) cooking, cookery, cuisine; (*aparato*) stove, cooker; *de* ~ *utensilio etc.* kitchen *attr.*; *libro etc.* cookery *attr.*; ~ *económica* range, cooker; ~ *de* (*or a*) *gas* gas stove, gas cooker; ~ *de petróleo* oil stove; **cocinar** [1a] *v/t.* cook; *v/i.* do the cooking; F meddle; **cocinero** *m*, **a** *f* cook; **cocinilla** *f* spirit stove; chafing dish *para mesa*.

coco[1] *m* ♀ coconut; = *cocotero*.

coco[2] *m* bogey man; (*mueca*) face; *hacer* ~*s a* make faces at; (*amor*) make eyes at; *parecer un* ~ be an ugly devil.

cocodrilo *m* crocodile.

cócora *m/f* F bore.

cocotero *m* coconut palm.

cóctel *m* (*fiesta*) cocktail party; (*bebida*) cocktail; **coctelera** *f* cocktail shaker.

cochambre *m* F filth; filthy thing.

coche *m* car, automobile; † coach, carriage (*a.* 🚂); ~ *de alquiler*, ~ *de punto* taxi; ~ (*de tipo*) *medio* medium-size car; ~ *de reparto* delivery car; van; ~ *blindado* armored car; ~-*cama* sleeper, sleeping car; ~-*comedor* dining car; ~*s pl. de choque* dodgems; ~ *fúnebre* hearse; ~-*habitación* caravan; ~-*salón* saloon car; ~ *de turismo* touring car; *ir en* ~ go by car; drive, motor; **cochecillo** *m*: ~ *de inválidos* invalid carriage; **cochecito** *m* (*de niño*) baby carriage, stroller; **cochera** *f* garage; carport; ~ *de alquiler* livery stable; **cochero 1.**: *puerta* ~*a* carriage entrance; **2.** *m* coachman.

cochina *f* sow; *fig.* trollop; **cochinada** *f* F, **cochinería** *f* F filth(iness); (*acto*) dirty trick; (*palabra*) beastly thing; *hacer una* ~ play a dirty trick (*a* on); **cochinilla** *f zo.* woodlouse; (*colorante*) cochineal; *de* ~ *Cuba, Mex.* unimportant; **cochinillo** *m* suckling (pig); **cochino 1.** filthy, dirty (*a. fig.*); (*sin valor*) rotten, measly; **2.** *m* pig (*a. fig.*); **cochiquera** *f*, **cochitril** *m* pigsty (*a.* F).

cochura *f* = *cocción*; (*pan*) batch of dough.

codal *m* ♀ vine shoot; ⚠ strut, prop; frame *de sierra*.

codazo *m* jab, poke (with one's elbow); (*ligero*) nudge; **codear** [1a] elbow, jostle; *abrirse paso codeando* elbow one's way through; ~**se** *con* hobnob with, rub shoulders with.

códice *m* manuscript, codex.

codicia *f* greed(iness), lust (*de* for); keen desire (*de* for); **codiciable** covetable; **codiciar** [1b] covet.

codicilo *m* codicil.

codicioso greedy, covetous; F hard-working.

codificación *f* codification; **codificar** [1g] codify; **código** *m* ⚖, *tel.* code; ~ *de circulación* highway code; ~ *de leyes a.* statute book; ~ *penal* penal book.

codillo *m zo.* knee; ⊕ elbow (joint); ♀ stump; (*estribo*) stirrup; **codo** *m* elbow; *zo.* knee; ⊕ elbow (joint); *Mex., Guat.* miser; tightwad; *dar de(l)* ~ *a* nudge; *fig.* despise; F *empinar el* ~ knock them back; *hablar por los* ~*s* talk too much; F *mentir por los* ~*s* tell the most frightful lies.

codorniz *f* quail.

coeducación *f* coeducation.

coeficiente *adj. a. su. m* coefficient.

coercer [2b] coerce, constrain; **coerción** *f* coercion, constraint; **coercitivo** coercive.

coetáneo *adj. a. su. m*, **a** *f* contemporary.

coexistencia *f* coexistence; **coexistente** coexistent; **coexistir** [3a] coexist (*con* with).

cofa *f* ⚓ top; ~ *mayor* maintop.
cofia *f* cap *de criada etc.*; (*red*) hair net.
cofrade *m* member (of a brotherhood *etc.*); **cofradía** *f* brotherhood, fraternity; (*gremio*) guild.
cofre *m* chest; **cofrecito** *m* casket.
cogedero 1. ready to be picked; **2.** *m* handle; **cogedor** *m* picker; gatherer; dustpan; (*pala*) shovel.
coger [2c] *flores etc* pick, gather, collect; (*recoger*) take (up), gather (up); (*asir*) catch (hold of), take hold of, seize; ~ (*al vuelo*) snatch; *catarro, frío* catch; (*conseguir*) get (hold of); (*apresar*) trap; *dedos* catch (*en* in); (*toro*) toss, gore; (*alcanzar*) catch up with; (*noche*) overtake; (*sorprender*) catch; (*encontrar*) find; (*entender*) catch, gather, take in; (*contener*) take; *extensión* cover; **cogida** *f* ✓ picking, harvesting; *toros*: goring; **cogido 1.:** ~*s de la mano* hand in hand; **2.** *m* fold, gather.
cognado *adj. a. su. m*, **a** *f* cognate.
cognición *f* cognition.
cogollo *m* heart *de lechuga, col*; head *de col*.
cogotazo *m* blow on the back of the neck, rabbit punch; **cogote** *m* back of the neck, nape.
cogujón *m* point, corner.
cogulla *f* cowl.
cohabitación *f* cohabitation; **cohabitar** [1a] live together, cohabit (*a. b.s.*).
cohechar [1a] bribe; **cohecho** *m* bribe.
coheredero *m*, **a** *f* coheir(ess *f*).
coherencia *f* coherence; *phys.* cohesion; **coherente** coherent; **cohesión** *f* cohesion; **cohesivo** cohesive; **cohesor** *m radio*: coherer.
cohete *m* rocket; missile; ~ *de alcance medio* intermediate-range rocket; ~ *de señales* distress signal, flare.
cohibición *f* restraint; inhibition; **cohibido** restrained, restricted; (*carácter*) inhibited, full of inhibitions; self-conscious; **cohibir** [3a] restrain, check; inhibit.
cohombro *m* cucumber.
cohonestar [1a] gloss over, explain away, whitewash.
coima *f* rakeoff; bribe; *mujer* concubine.
coime *m* croupier.
coincidencia *f* coincidence; *en ~ con* in agreement with; **coincidente** coincident(al); **coincidir** [3a] coincide (*con* with).
coito *m* (sexual) intercourse, coitus 🕮.
cojear [1a] limp, be lame (*de* in); (*mueble*) wobble, rock; F slip up, be at fault (*de* in); *sabemos de qué pie cojea* we know his weaknesses; **cojera** *f* lameness; (*visible*) limp.
cojijoso peevish.
cojín *m* cushion; **cojinete** *m* small cushion, pad; ⊕ ~ (*a bolas*) (ball) bearing; ⊕ journal box; 🚂 chair.
cojo 1. lame, limping; crippled; *mueble* wobbly; *fig.* lame, shaky; **2.** *m*, **a** *f* lame person; cripple.
cok *m* coke.
col *f* cabbage; ~ (*rizada*) kale; ~ *de Bruselas* Brussels sprouts; ~ *de Saboya* savoy; *entre ~ y ~, lechuga* variety is the spice of life.
cola[1] *f zo.*, ✈, *ast.* tail (*a. de frac*); (*extremo*) (tail) end; bottom *de clase*; train *de vestido largo*; (*ps. etc.*) queue, line; ⊕ ~ *de milano* dovetail; *a la ~* at the back, behind; *de ~ posición* rear; *hacer ~* queue (up), line up; *tener ~* have serious consequences.
cola[2] *f* glue; ~ (*de retal*) size; ~ *de pescado* fish glue; (*gelatina*) isinglass.
colaboración *f* collaboration; *lit.* contribution (*a, en* to); **colaborador** *m*, **-a** *f* collaborator; *lit.* contributor; **colaborar** [1a] collaborate; ~ *a lit.* contribute to, write for.
colación *f* collation (*a. eccl.*); (*merienda*) snack; (*boda*) reception, wedding breakfast; *S.Am.* sweet; *sacar a ~* bring up, drag in; *traer a ~* adduce as proof; **colacionar** [1a] collate.
colada *f* wash(ing); (*lejía*) bleach; *geog.* defile; **coladera** *f*, **coladero** *m*, **colador** *m* (tea *etc.*) strainer; colander *para legumbres*; **colado** ⊕ *hierro* cast; *aire ~* draught; **coladura** *f* straining; F (piece of) nonsense; (*plancha*) blunder; ~*s pl.* dregs.
colapso *m* collapse, breakdown.
colar [1m] *v/t. líquido* strain; *ropa* bleach; pass, squeeze (*por* through);

F palm *s.t.* off, foist *s.t.* off (*a* on); *moneda* pass; *noticia* make *s.o.* believe; *v/i.* (*líquido*) filter, percolate; (*aire*) get in (*por* through); = **~se** slip through; (*p.*) slip in, sneak in; F (*mentir*) fib; (*equivocarse*) make a slip, put one's foot in it.

colcha *f* bedspread, counterpane; **colchón** *m* mattress.

cole *m* F = *colegio.*

colear [1a] wag its *etc.* tail; F *todavía colea* it's still not settled.

colección *f* collection; **coleccionador** *m* collector; **coleccionar** [1a] collect; **coleccionista** *m/f* collector; **colecta** *f* collection (for charity); *eccl.* collect; **colectar** [1a] collect; **colecticio** ⚔ untrained, raw; *tomo* omnibus; **colectividad** *f* (*conjunto*) sum total, whole; group; ~ (*social*) whole community; *pol.* collective ownership; **colectivismo** *m* collectivism; **colectivo** collective (*a. gr.*); *acción freq.* joint, group *attr.*; **colector** *m* collector (*a.* ⚡); (*canal*) sewer.

colega *m* colleague.

colegial 1. school *attr.*, college *attr.*; *eccl.* collegiate; **2.** *m* schoolboy; *Mex.* greenhorn; beginner; **colegiala** *f* schoolgirl; **colegiata** *f* collegiate church; **colegio** *m* (*mst independent*) grammar school, high school; primary school; *univ.*, *eccl.*, ⚕ *etc.* college.

colegir [3c *a.* 3l] gather, collect; conclude, gather (*de* from).

cólera 1. *f* anger; *physiol.* bile; *montar en* ~ get angry; **2.** ⚕ *m* cholera; **colérico** angry, irate; irascible.

colesterol *m* cholesterol.

coleta *f* pigtail; F postscript; *S.Am.* burlap; *cortarse la* ~ quit; **coletazo** *m* lash, blow with the tail; 🚗 *etc.* sway(ing).

coleto *m* leather jacket; F body; oneself; *decir para su* ~ say to o.s.; *echarse algo al* ~ eat (*or* drink) s.t. up.

colgadero *m* hook, hanger, peg; **colgadizo 1.** hanging; **2.** *m* lean-to, penthouse; **colgado** *fig.* uncertain, doubtful; F *dejar* ~ let *s.o.* down, disappoint; F *quedarse* ~ be disappointed; **colgadura**(**s**) *f*(*pl.*) hanggings, drapery; **colgajo** *m* rag, tatter; ⚘ bunch; **colgante 1.** hanging; drooping, floppy; *puente* suspension *attr.*; **2.** *m* (*joya*) drop, pendant; ⚠ festoon.

colgar [1h *a.* 1m] **1.** *v/t.* hang (*a.* ⚖; *de* from, *en* on); *ropa etc.* hang up; *pared* decorate with hangings, drape; *univ.* F plough; *culpa* pin (*a* on); *que me cuelguen si lo hago* I'll be hanged if I will; **2.** *v/i.* hang (*de* on, from); droop, dangle; *teleph.* hang up, ring off; *fig.* ~ *de* hang on.

colibrí *m* hummingbird.

cólico *m* colic.

colicuar [1d] melt, fuse.

coliflor *f* cauliflower.

coligado allied, in league; **coligarse** [1h] join together, make common cause.

colilla *f* stub; stump; cigarette (*or* cigar) butt.

colimbo *m* grebe.

colina *f* hill.

colindante adjoining, neighboring.

coliseo *m* coliseum; arena.

colisión *f* collision (*a. fig.*); *fig.* clash.

colitis *f* ⚕ colitis.

colmado 1. full (*de* of), overflowing (*de* with); **2.** *m* grocer's (shop); cheap restaurant; **colmar** [1a] fill (up), fill to overflowing; *esperanzas etc.* fulfill, more than satisfy; ~ *de fig.* shower with, overwhelm with; ~ *de favores* lavish favors upon.

colmena *f* (bee)hive; *fig.* hive; **colmenar** *m* apiary; **colmenero** *m* beekeeper.

colmillo *m anat.* eyetooth, canine; *zo.* fang; tusk *de elefante*; F *escupir por el* ~ brag, talk big.

colmo *m fig.* height *de locura etc.*; *fig.* limit; *a*(*l*) ~ in plenty; *con* ~ *llenar* to overflowing; *para* ~ *de desgracias* to make matters worse; ¡*es el* ~! that does it!, it's the last straw!

colocación *f* (*acto*) placing *etc.*; position; (*puesto*) job, situation; ✝ investment; **colocar** [1g] put, place (in position); arrange; ✝ invest; *tropas etc.* position, station; *p.* place (in a job), find a situation for; **~se** be placed (*a. deportes*) *etc.*; (*p.*) get a job.

colodión *m* collodion.

colodrillo *m* back of the neck.

colofón *m* colophon.

colofonia *f* rosin, colophony.

colombiano *adj. a. su. m,* **a** *f* Colombian.
colon *m anat., gr.* colon.
colonia *f* colony; (*barrio*) suburb; *sew.* silk ribbon; ~ *veraniega* holiday camp; **colonial** colonial; *productos* imported; **colonización** *f* colonization; settlement; **colonizador** *m* colonist; settler; pioneer; **colonizar** [1f] colonize; settle; **colono** *m pol.* colonist, settler; ✓ (tenant) farmer.
coloquial colloquial; **coloquio** *m* conversation, talk; 🕮 colloquium; *lit.* dialogue.
color *m* color; (*matiz*) hue; (*colorante*) dye; *fig.* color(ing); ~*es pl.* ⚔ colors; *de* ~ *p. etc.* colored; *zapatos* brown; *en* ~*es película* color *attr.*; ~ *local* local color; *v. rosa*; *so* ~ *de* under pretext of; *v. subido*; *mudar de* ~ change color, blanch; (*sonrojarse*) blush; *sacar los* ~*es a* make *s.o.* blush; *le salieron los* ~*es* she blushed; **coloración** *f* coloration, coloring; *zo. etc.* markings; **colorado** colored; (*rojo*) red; *chiste* blue, rude; *argumento* plausible; *ponerse* ~ blush; **coloradote** red-faced; **colorante** *m* coloring (matter); **colorar** [1a] color, dye (*de azul* blue); stain (*a.* ⊕); **colorear** [1a] *v/t. motivo* show in a favorable light; *acción etc.* gloss over; *v/i.* redden, show red; **colorete** *m* rouge; **colorido** *m* color(ing); **colorines** *m/pl.* bright colors; *¡qué* ~ *tiene!* (*niño*) what rosy cheeks he's got!; **colorir** [3a; *defective*] *v/t.* color; *fig.* gloss over; *v/i.* take on a color; **colorista** *m/f* colorist.
colosal colossal; **coloso** *m* colossus (*a. fig.*).
columbrar [1a] glimpse, spy, sight; *fig.* guess.
columna *f mst* column; ⚠ *a.* pillar (*a. fig.*); *quinta* ~ fifth column; ~ *de dirección mot.* steering column; ~ *vertebral* spinal column; **columnata** *f* colonnade; **columnista** *m* columnist.
columpiar [1b] swing; ~**se** swing (to and fro); seesaw; (*cuerpo etc.*) sway; waddle *al andar*; **columpio** *m* swing; (*tabla*) seesaw.
colusión *f* collusion.
colza *f* ⚘ rape, colza.
collado *m* hill; (*desfiladero*) pass.
collar *m* (*adorno*) necklace; collar *de perro* (*a.* ⊕); (*insignia*) chain (of office); ~ *de fuerza* stranglehold.
coma[1] *f gr.* comma; *sin faltar una* ~ down to the last detail.
coma[2] *m* ⚕ coma.
comadre *f* ⚕ midwife; F best friend, crony; (*chismosa*) gossip; **comadrear** [1a] F gossip; **comadreja** *f* weasel; **comadreo** *m* F, **comadrería** *f* F gossip(ing); **comadrero** *m,* **a** *f* gossip, busybody; **comadrón** *m* accoucheur; **comadrona** *f* midwife.
comandancia *f* command; (*grado*) rank of major; **comandante** *m* commandant, commander; (*grado*) major; **comandar** [1a] command; lead; **comandita** *f* silent partnership; **comanditario** *socio* silent; **comando** *m* command; ⚔ (*grupo*) commando; (*abrigo*) duffel coat; ~ *a distancia* remote control.
comarca *f* region, part (of the country); **comarcano** neighboring, bordering.
comba *f* bend; bow; *esp.* bulge, warp, sag; (*juego*) skipping; (*cuerda*) skipping rope; *saltar a la* ~ skip; **combadura** *f* bend(ing) *etc.*; camber *de carretera*; **combar** [1a] bend, curve; ~**se** bend, curve; (*madera*) bulge, warp, sag.
combate *m* fight, engagement, combat; *fig.* battle, struggle; ~ *singular* duel, single combat; *fuera de* ~ out of action; *boxeo*: knocked out; *poner fuera de* ~ *boxeo*: knock out; **combatiente** *m* combatant; **combatir** [3a] *v/t.* ⚔ attack; *costa* beat upon; *mente* assail, harass; *tendencia etc.* combat, fight against; *v/i.,* ~**se** fight, struggle (*con, contra* against); **combatividad** *f* fighting spirit, fight; *b.s.* aggressiveness; **combativo** fighting *attr.*; aggressive.
combés *m* ⚓ waist.
combinación *f* combination; (*arreglo*) arrangement, set-up; (*proyecto*) idea, scheme; (*prenda*) slip; 🚂 connexion; (*bebida*) cocktail; ~*es pl. fig.* plans, measures; **combinar** [1a] combine; *colores etc.* blend, mix; *plan* work out; ~**se** combine.
combo bent, warped, bowed.

combustible 1. combustible; **2.** *m* fuel, combustible; **combustión** *f* combustion.
comedero 1. eatable; **2.** *m* ↙ trough, manger; (*comedor*) dining room.
comedia *f* play, drama (*a. fig.*); (*festiva*) comedy; (*fingimiento*) farce, pretence; *hacer la* ~ make believe; *ir a la* ~ go to the play; **comediante** *m*, **a** *f* (*esp.* comic) actor (actress *f*).
comedido courteous, polite; moderate; **comedimiento** *m* courtesy *etc.*
comediógrafo *m* playwright, dramatic author.
comedirse [3l] be restrained (*en* in), restrain o.s.; be moderate.
comedón *m* blackhead.
comedor 1. = *comilón 1*; **2.** *m* dining room; (*muebles*) dining-room suite.
comején *m* termite, white ant.
comendador *m* commander (*of an order of knighthood*); **comendatorio** of recommendation.
comensal *m/f* dependant; (*compañero*) companion at table, fellow diner.
comentador *m* commentator; **comentar** [1a] comment on; expound; **comentario** *m* comments, remarks; *esp. lit.* commentary; ~*s pl.* gossip, tittle-tattle; **comentarista** *m* commentator; **comento** *m* comment; *lit.* commentary; *b.s.* lie, pretense.
comenzar [1f *a.* 1k] begin, start (*diciendo* by saying; *a inf.* to *inf.*; *con* with; *por su.* with *su.*; *por inf.* by *ger.*).
comer [2a] **1.** *v/t.* eat; ⊕ *etc.* eat away, corrode; (*consumir*) use up, eat up; *color* fade; *renta* enjoy; *ajedrez*: take; F ~ *vivo* have it in for; *me come la pierna* my leg is itching; *sin* ~*lo ni beberlo* without having a hand in it; **2.** *v/i.* eat; have a meal, *esp.* (have) lunch; *dar de* ~ *a* feed; *ser de buen* ~ eat anything; *tener qué* ~ *fig.* have enough to live on; *pero ¡~ y callar!* but I'd better shut up!; **3.** ~**se** *comida* eat up (*a. fig.*); *consonante* drop; *sílaba* slur over; *texto* skip; *fig.* ~ *unos a otros* be at loggerheads.
comerciable marketable; *fig.* sociable; **comercial** commercial, business *attr.*, trading *attr.*; *barrio freq.* shopping *attr.*; **comercializar** [1f] commercialize; **comerciante** *m/f* trader, dealer, merchant; ~ *al por mayor* wholesaler; ~ *al por menor* retailer; **comerciar** [1b] (*ps.*) have dealings; traffic; ~ *con mercancías*, ~ *en* deal in, handle; ~ *con p.*, *país* trade with, do business with; **comercio** *m* (*en general*) trade, business, commerce; (*negocio particular*) trade, traffic; (*conjunto de comerciantes*) business interest(s), (big) business; (*sociedad*) business, firm; (*tienda*) shop; *fig.* intercourse; ~ *exterior* foreign trade; ~ *sexual* sexual intercourse.
comestible 1. eatable; ⚘ *etc.* edible; **2.** *m* food(stuff); ~*s pl.* food(stuffs); (*comprados*) groceries; *tienda de* ~*s* grocer's (shop).
cometa[1] *m ast.* comet.
cometa[2] *f* kite.
cometer [2a] *crimen etc.* commit; *error* make; *negocio* entrust (*a* to); *gr.* use; **cometido** *m* assignment, commission.
comezón *f* itch (*a. fig.*; *de inf.* to *inf.*; *por* for), itching; tingle, tingling (sensation) *de calor etc.*; *sentir* ~ itch *etc.*
comible F eatable, palatable.
cómica *f* (*esp.* comic) actress; comedienne; **comicastro** *m* ham; **comicidad** *f* comicalness, humor; **cómico 1.** comic(al), funny; comedy *attr.*; *autor* dramatic; **2.** *m* (*esp.* comic) actor; comedian.
comida *f* (*alimento*) food; (*acto*) eating; (*a hora determinada*) meal; *esp.* lunch, dinner; (*manutención*) keep, board; **comidilla** *f* F hobby, first love; ~ *de la ciudad* talk of the town; **comido:** *estar* ~ have had lunch *etc.*; F ~ *por servido* it just doesn't pay.
comienzo *m* beginning, start; (*a.* ⚕) onset; birth, inception *de proyecto etc.*
comilón F **1.** fond of eating; *b.s.* greedy; **2.** *m*, **-a** *f* big eater; *b.s.* pig; **comilona** *f* F spread, blowout.
comillas *f/pl.* quotation marks, inverted commas.
comino *m* ⚘ cumin; cuminseed; *no vale un* ~ it's not worth two cents.
comisaría *f* police station; = **comisariato** *m* commissariat; **comisario** *m* commissary (*a.* ⚔); ~ *de policía* police superintendent; **comisión** *f*

commission (*a.* ✝); *parl. etc.* committee; ✝ (*junta*) board; (*encargo*) assignment, errand, commission; ~ *permanente* standing committee; ~ *planificadora* planning board; **comisionado** *m* commissioner; *parl. etc.* committee member; ✝ member of the board; **comisionar** [1a] commission; **comisionista** *m* commission agent; **comiso** *m* (*acto*) confiscation; (*cosas*) confiscated goods.

comisquear [1a] F keep on nibbling away (at).

comistrajo *m* F awful meal; *fig.* hodgepodge.

comisura *f* join; ~ *de los labios* corner of the mouth.

comité *m* committee.

comitiva *f* retinue, suite.

como a) *comp. su.*: like, the same as; *verb*: as; *algo así* ~ something like; ~ *si* as if; *v. así, tal etc.*; *la manera* ~ *sucedió* the way it happened; b) *en calidad de*: as; c) *cj. causa*: as, since; *condición*: if; ~ *no venga mañana* if he doesn't come tomorrow, unless he comes tomorrow; ~ *sea* as the case may be; ~ *no sea para inf.* unless it be to *inf.*; ~ *quiera* as you like; (*porque*) because; *así* ~, *tan luego* ~ as soon as; *libre* ~ *estaba* free as he was.

cómo a) *interrogative*: how?; (*por qué*) why?, how is it that ...?; *¿~ está Vd.?* how are you ?; *¿~ es?* what's he like?, what does he look like?; *¿~ es de grande?* how big is it?; *¿~ así?*, *¿~ eso?* how can that be?, how come?; (*enfado*) what do you mean?; *¿~ no?* why not?; *¿a ~ es el pan?* how much is the bread?; b) *int. ¿~?* (*pidiendo repetición*) eh?, what did you say?; (*sorpresa*) what?; (*enfado*) how dare you!; *¡~!* of course!; c) *su.*: *el porqué y el ~ de* the whys and wherefores of.

cómoda *f* chest of drawers; commode; **comodidad** *f* comfort, convenience; (self-)interest, advantage; *~es pl. de la vida* good things of life; **comodín 1.** *Col.*, *Mex.*, *P.R. adj.* cozy; **2.** *m naipes*: wild card; joker; *fig.* stand-by, useful gadget; **cómodo** comfortable; *cuarto etc. freq.* snug, cozy; convenient, handy; **comodón** F comfort-loving.

comodoro *m* commodore.

compacto compact; *typ. etc.* close.

compadecer [2d] (*a.* *~se de*) pity, be sorry for; sympathize with; *~se con* agree with; harmonize with.

compadre *m* godfather; F friend, pal; **compadrear** [1a] F be pals.

compaginar [1a] arrange; *typ.* make up; ~ *con* reconcile *s.t.* with, bring *s.t.* into line with; *~se* agree, tally (*con* with).

compañerismo *m* comradeship; *deportes etc.*: team spirit; **compañero** *m*, **a** *f* companion; partner; mate; ~ *de armas* comrade in arms; ~ *de clase* schoolmate; ~ *de cuarto* roommate; ~ *de juego* playmate; ~ *de rancho* messmate; ~ *de viaje* fellow traveler (*a. fig.*); **compañía** *f* company; society; ~ *inversionista* investment trust; ~ *de seguros* insurance company; ~ *matriz* parent company; ~ *tenedora* holding company; ♀ *de Jesús* Society of Jesus.

comparable comparable; **comparación** *f* comparison; *en* ~ *con* in comparison with, beside; **comparado** comparative; **comparar** [1a] compare (*con* with, to); liken (*con* to); **comparativo** *adj. a. su. m* comparative.

comparecencia *f* ⚖ appearance (in court); **comparecer** [2d] ⚖ appear (in court); **comparendo** *m* ⚖ summons; subpoena.

comparsa 1. *m/f* extra (*a. thea.*), super(numerary); **2.** *f* masquerade; *thea.* = **comparsería** *f* extras.

compartimiento *m* division, sharing; (*departamento*) *a.* ⚓ compartment; **compartir** [3a] divide up, share (out); *opinión* share; ~ *con* share with.

compás *m* ⚒ compasses; ⚓ compass; ♪ (*tiempo*) time, measure; (*ritmo*) beat, rhythm; (*división*) bar; *fig.* rule; *a* ~ in time; *llevar el* ~ beat (*or* keep) time; **compasado** measured, moderate; **compasar** [1a] = *acompasar*; *fig.* arrange, organize.

compasión *f* pity, compassion; *¡por ~!* for pity's sake!; **compasivo** compassionate; understanding, sympathetic.

compatibilidad *f* compatibility; **compatible** compatible, consistent (*con* with).

compatriota *m/f* compatriot, fellow countryman (countrywoman).

compeler [2a] compel (*a inf.* to *inf.*). **compendiar** [1b] abridge, summarize; **compendio** *m* abridgment, summary; (*libro*) compendium, digest; *en* ~ in brief; **compendioso** compendious, brief.

compenetración *f fig.* mutual understanding, natural sympathy; **compenetrarse** [1a] ⚗ *etc.* interpenetrate; *fig.* share each other's feelings; ~ *de algo* enter into (the spirit of); *p.* share the feelings of; absorb, take in.

compensación *f* compensation; ⚖ redress; *esp. fig.* recompense; ✝ clearing; *cámara de* ~ clearing house; **compensador** compensatory; **compensar** [1a] *pérdida* compensate for, make up (for); *error* redeem; *p.* compensate.

competencia *f* competition (*a.* ✝); rivalry; ⚖ competence; (*idoneidad*) suitability; (*incumbencia*) domain, field; *a* ~ vying with each other; *en* ~ *de* in competition with; *hacer* ~ *con* compete against (*or* with); *ser de la* ~ *de* be within *s.o.'s* province; **competente** *trabajo*, ⚖ competent; (*apropiado*) suitable, adequate; **competer** [2a]: ~ *a* be incumbent on; **competidor** 1. competing; 2. *m*, -**a** *f* competitor (*a.* ✝); rival (*a* for); **competir** [3l] compete (*a.* ✝, *deportes*; *con* with, against; *para* for); *fig.* ~ *con* rival, vie with; *poder* ~ be competitive.

compilación *f* compilation; **compilar** [1a] compile.

compinche *m* F pal, chum.

complacencia *f* pleasure, satisfaction; willingness *en obrar*; **complacer** [2x] please; *cliente* oblige; *tirano* humor; *deseo* gratify; ~**se** *en* take pleasure in *su.*, *ger.*; be pleased to *inf.*; **complacido** complacent; satisfied; **complaciente** genial, cheerful; obliging, helpful *en ayudar*.

complejidad *f* complexity; **complejo** *adj. a. su. m* complex; ~ *de inferioridad* inferiority complex.

complementar [1a] complement; complete, make up; F go well with; **complementario** complementary; **complemento** *m* complement (*a. gr.*, ⚔); *fig.* perfection, culmination; ~ *(in)directo* (in)direct object.

completar [1a] complete; make up; *pérdida* make good; *fig.* perfect; **completo** complete; 🚌 *etc.* full; *registro* thorough; *pensión* inclusive, all-in; *por* ~ completely, utterly.

complexión *f physiol.* constitution; make-up; complexion; **complexionado:** *bien* ~ strong, robust; *mal* ~ weak, frail; **complexional** *physiol.* constitutional; (*genio*) temperamental.

complicación *f* complication (*a.* ⚕); complexity, complex structure; **complicado** complex, complicated; *método freq.* elaborate; ~ *con* mixed up with; **complicar** [1g] complicate; ~**se** get complicated; (*embrollarse*) get tangled, get involved; **cómplice** *m/f* accomplice; **complicidad** *f* complicity, implication (*en* in).

complot [kom'plo] *m* plot, intrigue; conspiracy; scheme.

componedor *m typ.* composing stick; **componenda** *f* compromise; *b.s.* shady deal; **componente** 1. component; 2. *m* ⚗, ⊕ component; ingredient *de bebida etc.*; **componer** [2r] compose (*a. typ.*, ♪), constitute, make up; *typ. a.* set up (in type); *lit.* write; *salón* decorate; *p.* dress up; *comida etc.* prepare; *lo roto*, ⊕ repair, mend, overhaul; *diferencias*, *enemigos* reconcile; *disputa* settle; *mal asunto* patch up; F ⚕ settle; *ánimo* quieten, soothe; ~**se** (*mujer*) dress up; make up; ~*(las) con* come to terms with; ~ *de* be composed of, be made up of; F ~*las para inf.* manage to *inf.*, contrive to *inf.*

comportable bearable; **comportamentismo** *m* ⚕ behaviorism; **comportamiento** *m* behavior; ⊕ performance; **comportar** [1a] put up with, bear; *S.Am.* entail; cause; ~**se** behave, conduct o.s.; **comporte** *m* = *comportamiento*.

composición *f mst* composition; make-up; (*ajuste*) settlement; (*convenio*) agreement; **compositor** *m* composer; **compostura** *f* composition, make-up; (*reparo*) mending, repair(ing); (*aseo*) neatness; (*mesura*) sedateness; (*ajuste*) arrangement, settlement.

compostelano *adj. a. su. m* (**a** *f*) of, from Santiago de Compostela.

compota *f* compote, preserve; sauce *de manzanas etc.*
compra *f* purchase; buy; *~s pl.* shopping; *~ a plazos* installment purchase; *ir de ~s* shop, go shopping; **comprador** *m*, **-a** *f* shopper, customer *en tienda*; purchaser, buyer *de artículo*; **comprar** [1a] buy, purchase (*a* from); *fig.* buy off, bribe; *~ a plazos* buy on installment; **compraventa** *f* ⚕ contract of sale; (*tienda*) antique shop.
comprender [2a] *v/t.* (*abarcar*) comprise, include; (*entender*) understand; *no comprendido* not including; *todo comprendido* everything included, all in; *v/i.* understand, see; *¿comprendes?* see?; *¡ya comprendo!* I see; **comprensible** understandable, comprehensible (*para* to); **comprensión** *f* understanding; grasp; inclusion; **comprensivo** understanding; intelligent; (*que incluye*) comprehensive.
compresa *f* compress; *~ higiénica* sanitary napkin; **compresibilidad** *f* compressibility; **compresión** *f* compression; *de alta ~ attr.* high compression; *índice de ~* compression ratio; **compresor** *m* compressor; **comprimido 1.** *aire* compressed; **2.** *m pharm.* tablet; pill; **comprimir** [3a] compress (*a.* ⊕); squeeze, press down; *fig.* restrain, repress; *lágrimas* keep back.
comprobación *f* checking *etc.*; (*prueba*) proof; *en ~ de* in (*or* as) proof of; **comprobador** *m*: *~ de lámparas* tube tester; **comprobante 1.** of proof; **2.** *m* proof; ⚕ voucher, guarantee; **comprobar** [1m] check, verify; prove; ⊕ test, overhaul; *~ que* establish that.
comprometer [2a] (*poner en peligro*) jeopardize, endanger; *reputación* compromise; put *s.o.* in a compromising situation; *~ a* nail *s.o.* down to, hold *s.o.* to; *asunto* agree to entrust *s.t.* to; *~ a inf.*, *~ a que subj.* force *s.o.* to *inf.*; **~se** get involved (*en* in); ⚕ commit o.s.; *~ a inf.* engage to *inf.*, undertake to *inf.*; *se compromete a todo* he'll say yes to anything; **comprometido** embarrassing; ⚕ *etc. estar ~* be (already) engaged; **compromiso** *m* obligation, pledge, undertaking; (*cita*) engagement; compromising situation; (*aprieto*) tight corner, predicament; ⚕ *libre de ~*, *sin ~* without obligation; *por ~* out of a sense of duty; *poner en un ~* place *s.o.* in an embarrassing situation; *le puse en el ~ de inf.* I placed him in the position of having to *inf.*
compuerta *f* sluice, floodgate; hatch *en puerta*.
compuesto 1. *p.p. of componer*; *estar ~ de* be composed of, be made up of; **2.** *adj.* ⚗, ⚕, *gr.* compound; ⚘, ▲ *etc.* composite; *fig.* composed, calm; **3.** *m* compound (*a.* ⚗).
compulsar [1a] ⚖ check; make a copy of; **compulsión** *f* compulsion; **compulsivo** compulsory; compelling, compulsive.
compunción *f* compunction; (*tristeza*) sorrow; **compungido** remorseful, sorry; **compungirse** [3c] feel remorse (*por* at), feel sorry (*por* for).
computacional computational; *attr.* computing, computer; **computador** *m* (*a.* **-a** *f*) computer; *~ personal* personal computer; **computar** [1a] calculate, reckon; **cómputo** *m* calculation, computation; estimate.
comulgante *m/f* communicant; **comulgar** [1h] *v/t.* administer communion to; *v/i.* take communion.
común 1. common (*a* to; *a. b.s.*); *opinión a.* widespread, generally held; *de ~ con* in common with; *en ~* in common; *attr.* joint; *fuera de lo ~* out of the ordinary; *por lo ~* generally; *hacer en ~* do *s.t.* all together; *Mercado ~* Common Market (= *approx. Comunidad Económica Europea*); **2.** *m*: *el ~ de las gentes* most people, the common run (of people); **comuna** *f* commune; **comunal** communal.
comunicable communicable; F sociable; **comunicación** *f* communication; (*ponencia*) paper; (*parte*) message; **comunicado** *m* communiqué; **comunicar** [1g] *mst* communicate (*a.* ▲; *con* with); *noticia* give, convey, deliver (*a* to); (*legar*) bestow (*a* on); *periodismo*: report (*de* from); *~ que* report that, inform *s.o.* that; *teleph. estar comunicando* be engaged; **~se** (*ps.*) communicate; be in touch; ▲ (inter)communicate; **comunica-**

tivo communicative; *fig.* sociable; *risa etc.* infectious; **comunidad** *f* community; ~ *Económica Europea* (*CEE*) European Economic Community (EEC) (*approx.* Common Market); **comunión** *f* communion; **comunismo** *m* communism; **comunista 1.** communist(ic); **2.** *m/f* communist.

con with; (*a pesar de*) in spite of, despite; (*para* ~) to, towards; ~ *llegar tan tarde* arriving so late; ~ *que* whereupon; (*resumen*) and so, so (then); *v. todo, tal.*

conato *m* attempt, endeavor (*de inf.* to *inf.*); (*empeño*) effort; ⚖ ~ *de* attempted; *poner* ~ *en* put everything into.

concatenación *f* concatenation, linking; **concatenar** [1a] link together, concatenate.

concavidad *f* concavity; (*sitio*) hollow; **cóncavo 1.** concave; hollow; **2.** *m* hollow, cavity.

concebible conceivable, thinkable; **concebir** [3l] conceive.

conceder [2a] (*otorgar*) grant; concede; admit (*que* that); *premio* award.

concejal *m* (town) councilor; councilman; alderman; **concejo** *m* council; ~ *municipal* town council.

concentración *f* concentration (*a.* ⚗); **concentrar** [1a] concentrate (*a.* ⚗; ⚔ *en lugar* in; *en escena* on); *fig.* restrain, conceal; **~se** concentrate (*a.* ⚔), be concentrated; center (*en* on).

concepción *f* conception; (*facultad*) understanding; feast of the Immaculate Conception; *Inmaculada* ~ Immaculate Conception; **concepto** *m* concept (*a. phls.*), notion; opinion; *lit.* conceit; *bajo todos los* ~*s*, *por todos* ~*s* from every point of view; *en* ~ *de* by way of; *en mi* ~ in my view; *tener buen* ~ *de*, *tener en buen* ~ think well of; **conceptuar** [1e]: ~ *de*, ~ *por* deem *s.t.* to be, judge *s.t.* to be; ~ *como* regard *s.t.* as; **conceptuoso** witty; *estilo* mannered.

concerniente: ~ *a* concerning, relating to.

concertar [1k] *v/t.* (*arreglar*) arrange; *convenio etc.* conclude; *precio* fix (*en* at); *p.* reconcile (*con* with); harmonize; ♪ tune up; *v/i.* agree (*a. gr.*); harmonize; **~se** agree; be(come) reconciled.

concertina *f* concertina.

concesión *f* grant, award; ✝, *fig.* concession; **concesionario** *m* concessionaire; licensee; **concesivo** concessive (*a. gr.*).

conciencia *f* (*conocimiento*) knowledge, awareness; *phls.* consciousness; (*moral*) conscience; moral sense; *a* ~ conscientiously; *en* ~ with a clear conscience; **concienzudo** conscientious, thorough.

concierto *m* order, concert; ♪ harmony; (*pieza*) concerto; (*función*) concert; (*convenio*) agreement; *de* ~ in concert.

conciliación *f* conciliation; (*semejanza*) affinity, similarity; favor; **conciliador 1.** conciliatory; **2.** *m* conciliator; **conciliar** [1b] reconcile; *respeto etc.* win; ~ *el sueño* get to sleep; **~se** *algo* win, gain; **conciliatorio** conciliatory; propitiatory.

concilio *m eccl.* council.

concisión *f* conciseness, terseness; **conciso** concise, terse.

concitar [1a] stir up, incite.

conciudadano *m*, **a** *f* fellow citizen.

cónclave *m* conclave.

concluir [3g] *v/t.* end; conclude (*de* from; *a uno de* s.o. to be); convince; (*acallar*) silence; *v/i.* end (*gr. etc. con, en, por* in); *¡vamos a* ~ *de una vez!* let's get it over with!; ~ *de inf.* finish *ger.*; **conclusión** *f* conclusion; *en* ~ lastly, in conclusion; **concluyente** conclusive.

concomitancia *f* concomitance; **concomitante** concomitant.

concordancia *f* concordance (*a. eccl.*); *gr.*, ♪ concord; **concordante** concordant; **concordar** [1m] *v/t.* reconcile; *gr.* make *s.t.* agree; *v/i.* agree (*a. gr.*); ~ *con* agree with, tally with, fit in with; **concordato** *m* concordat; **concorde** in agreement; *poner* ~*s* bring about agreement between; **concordia** *f* concord, harmony; conformity, agreement; (*sortija*) ring.

concreción *f* concretion; ⚕ stone; **concretar** [1a] *fig.* make *s.t.* concrete; reduce to its essentials, boil down; *para* ~ to sum up; to be more specific; **~se** *a inf.* confine o.s. to *ger.*; **concretera** *f* concrete mixer; **concreto 1.** concrete; *aceite*

thick; *fig. punto etc.* definite, actual, specific; *en* ~ to sum up; exactly, specifically; *nada en* ~ nothing in particular; **2.** *m* concretion; *S.Am.* concrete.
concubina *f* concubine; **concubinato** *m* concubinage.
concupiscencia *f* lust, concupiscence; **concupiscente** lewd, lustful.
concurrencia *f* (*asistencia*) attendance, turnout; (*multitud*) crowd, gathering; † competition; concurrence *de circunstancias etc.*; **concurrente** present; concurrent; † competing; **concurrido** *lugar* crowded; *función* well-attended; **concurrir** [3a] (*reunirse*) gather, meet (*a* at, *en* in); *fig.* come together, conspire (*para inf.* to *inf.*); coincide (*con* with); † *etc.* compete; (*convenir*) agree; cooperate (*en* in); ~ *a concurso* compete in, take part in; *éxito* contribute to; ~ *con dinero* contribute; **concursante** *m/f* contestant, participant; **concurso** *m* (*reunión*) gathering; concurrence *de circunstancias*; (*ayuda*) help; competition (*a. a puesto*), contest; (*función*) show, exhibition; *deportes*: match, meeting; *tenis*: tournament; ~ *hípico* horse show; ~ *radiofónico* quiz show; *por* ~ by competition; *attr.* competitive.
concusión *f* ⚖ extortion; *sl.* shakedown; **concusionario** *m* extortioner.
concha *f zo.* shell; (*marisco*) shellfish; (*carey*) tortoiseshell; *thea.* prompter's box; ~ *de perla* mother-of-pearl; *meterse en su* ~ retire into one's shell; F *tener muchas* ~*s* be wide awake.
conchabarse [1a] hire (out); F gang up (*contra* on).
condado *m hist.* earldom; (*tierras, provincia*) county; **conde** *m* earl, count.
condecoración *f* ⚔ *etc.* decoration; insignia; **condecorar** [1a] decorate (*con* with).
condena *f* sentence; term; ~ *a perpetuidad* life sentence; *cumplir su* ~ serve one's sentence; **condenable** condemnable; **condenación** *f* condemnation; = *condena*; *eccl.* damnation; F *¡*~*!* damn!; **condenado 1.** F damned, ruddy; **2.** *m*, **a** *f* ⚖ criminal, convicted person; *eccl.* one of the damned; ~ *a muerte* condemned man; **condenador** condemnatory; **condenar** [1a] condemn (*a* to); *esp.* ⚖ convict, find guilty (*por ladrón* of stealing); ⚖ sentence (*a multa* to, *a presidio* to hard labor); *eccl.* damn; ▲ close up; ~**se** ⚖ confess (one's guilt); *eccl.* be damned.
condensable condensable; **condensación** *f* condensation; **condensador** *m* ⊕, ⚡ condenser; ~ *variable* variable condenser; **condensar** [1a] condense.
condesa *f* countess.
condescendencia *f* willingness (to help); acquiescence (*a* in); **condescender** [2g] acquiesce, say yes; ~ *a* consent to, say yes to; ~ *en inf.* agree to *inf.*
condestable *m hist.* constable; ⚓ deck petty officer; gunner.
condición *f* condition; ~ (*social*) status, position; character, nature; ~*es pl.* † *etc.* conditions, terms; circumstances; *humilde* ~ humble origin; ~*es pl. de vida* living conditions; *a* ~ (*de*) *que* on condition that; *de* ~ *attr.* noble; *de* ~ ... ...-natured; *estar en* ~*es de inf.* be in a condition (*or* fit state) to *inf.*; be in a position to; **condicionado, condicional** conditional (*a. gr.*).
condimentar [1a] season; flavor; (*con escpecias*) spice; **condimento** *m* seasoning; flavor(ing); dressing.
condiscípulo *m*, **a** *f* fellow student.
condolencia *f* condolence; **condolerse** [2h]: ~ *de* be sorry for; ~ *por* sympathize with.
condominio *m* ⚖ joint ownership; dual control; *pol.* condominium.
condonación *f* condonation, forgiveness; **condonar** [1a] *acto* condone; *deuda* forgive, forget.
cóndor *m orn.* condor; *Chile, Ecuad.* gold coin.
conducción *f* leading *etc.*; transport(ation); piping *de aguas*; *mot.* driving; *phys.* conduction; † agreement; ~ *a* (*la*) *derecha* right-hand drive; **conducente** conducive (*a* to); **conducir** [3o] **1.** *v/t.* lead, guide (*a* to); conduct; *negocio* conduct, manage; *mot.* drive; *mot.*, ⚓ steer; *carga* transport, convey; **2.** *v/i. mot. etc.* drive; ~ *a* lead to; *resultado etc.* make for; **3.** ~**se** be-

have, conduct o.s.; **conducta** *f* ⚚ *etc.* management, direction; conduct, behavior *de p.*; *mala* ~ misbehavior, misconduct; **conductibilidad** *f* conductibility; conductivity; **conductivo** *phys.* conductive; **conducto** *m* conduit (*a.* ⚡); tube; *esp. anat.* duct, canal; *fig.* agency; (*p.*) agent, intermediary; *por* ~ *de* through; **conductor 1.** leading, guiding; *phys.* conductive; **2.** *m phys.* conductor; ⚡ lead; **3.** *m*, **-a** *f* leader, guide; *mot. etc.* driver.

condueño *m*, **a** *f* part owner.

condumio *m* F food.

conectar [1a] ⚡, ⊕ connect (up); (*poner*) switch on; *boxeo*: *golpe* land; ~ *a tierra* ⚡ ground; ⚡ *estar conectado* be on; **conectivo** connective.

conejal *m*, **conejar** *m*, **conejera** *f* warren, burrow; F den, dive; **conejillo** *m*: ~ *de Indias* guinea pig; **conejo** *m* rabbit.

conexión *f* connexion (*a.* ⚡); relationship; **conexo** connected, related.

confabulación *f* plot, intrigue; ⚚ ring; **confabularse** [1a] plot, scheme.

confección *f* (*acto*) making; (*arte*) workmanship; *pharm.* confection, concoction; (*traje*) ready-made suit; **confeccionado** *ropa* ready-made, ready-to-wear; **confeccionar** [1a] make (up); **confeccionista** *m/f* ready-made clothier.

confederación *f* confederacy; confederation, league; **confederado** *adj. a. su. m* confederate; **confederarse** [1a] form a confederation, confederate.

conferencia *f* (*discurso*) lecture; *pol. etc.* meeting, conference; *teleph.* call; ~ *interurbana* long-distance call; ~ *de prensa* press conference; **conferenciante** *m/f* lecturer; **conferenciar** [1b] be in conference, confer; **conferencista** *m/f S.Am.* lecturer; **conferir** [3i] *v/t. dignidad* confer, bestow (*a* on); *premio* award (*a* to); *negocio* discuss; compare (*con* with); *v/i.* confer.

confesante *m* penitent; **confesar** [1k] *v/t.* confess (*a. eccl.*), own up to, admit; *v/i.*, **~se** confess (*con* to), make one's confession; **confesión** *f* confession; **confesional** confessional; **confes(i)onario** *m* confessional; (*garita a.*) confession box; **confesor** *m* confessor.

confiabilidad *f* reliability, trustworthiness; **confiable** reliable, trustworthy; **confiado** (*presumido*) vain, conceited; (*crédulo*) unsuspecting, gullible; ~ *en sí* (*mismo*) self-confident, self-reliant; **confianza** *f* confidence (*en* in); trust (*en* in), reliance (*en* on); familiarity (*con* with); ~ *en sí* (*mismo*) self-confidence; *b.s.* conceit; *con toda* ~ with complete confidence; *de* ~ *p.* reliable, trustworthy; *amigo* intimate; *puesto* responsible; *manera etc.* informal; *en* ~ trustingly; (*en secreto*) in confidence, confidentially; *tener* ~ *con* be on close terms with; **confiar** [1c] *v/t.*: ~ *a*, ~ *en* entrust *s.t.* to; *v/i.* (have) trust; ~ *en* trust, trust in (*or* to); rely on, count on; *éxito etc.* be confident about; ~ *en que* trust that; **confidencia** *f* confidence; *de mayor* ~ top secret; *hacer* ~*s a* confide in, reveal secrets to; **confidencial** confidential; **confidente** *m*, **a** *f* confidant(e *f*); informer; detective; spy.

configuración *f* shape, configuration; ~ *del terreno* lie of the land; **configurar** [1a] form, shape.

confín *m* limit, boundary; horizon; ~*es pl.* confines (*a. fig.*); **confinar** [1a] *v/t.* confine (*a*, *en* in); *v/i.*: ~ *con* border on; **~se** shut o.s. up.

confirmación *f* confirmation (*a. eccl.*); **confirmar** [1a] confirm (*a. eccl.*; *de*, *por* as); endorse, bear out; **confirmatorio** confirmative, confirmatory.

confiscación *f* confiscation; **confiscar** [1g] confiscate.

confitar [1a] preserve; *frutas* candy; *fig.* sweeten; **confite** *m* sweet; candy; confection; **confitería** *f* confectionery; (*tienda*) confectioner's; candy store; sweetshop; **confitero** *m*, **a** *f* confectioner; **confitura** *f* preserve; (*mermelada*) jam.

conflagración *f* conflagration; *fig.* flare-up.

conflictivo conflicting; anguished; troubled; **conflicto** *m* conflict (*a. fig.*); (*apuro*) difficulty, fix; ~ *laboral* labor dispute.

confluencia *f* confluence (*a.* ⚡);

confluente 1. confluent; **2.** *m* confluence; **confluir** [3g] meet, join; *fig.* come together.

conformación *f* structure, form; conformation; **conformar** [1a] *v/t.*: ~ *a*, ~ *con* adjust *s.t.* to, bring *s.t.* into line with; *v/i.* agree (*con* with); **~se** conform; ~ *con original* conform to; *regla* comply with, abide by; *política etc.* fall into line with, adjust o.s. to; *destino* resign o.s. to; **conforme 1.** *adj.* similar; in agreement, in line (*con* with); (*ps.*) agreed; **2.** *prp.*: ~ *a* in conformity with, in accordance with; *carácter etc.* in keeping with; **3.** *cj.* as; (*luego que*) as soon as; ~ ... *así* as ... so; **4.** *int.* ¡~! agreed!, right!, O.K.!; **conformidad** *f* similarity, conformity; agreement; proportion; resignation (*con* to); forbearance; *de* ~ *con* in accordance with; *en* ~ accordingly.

confort *m* comfort; **confortable** comfortable; *noticia etc.* comforting; **confortante** comforting; **confortar** [1a] invigorate, strengthen; *afligido* comfort.

confraternidad *f* confraternity; *fig.* good understanding, intimacy.

confrontación *f* confrontation; showdown; **confrontar** [1a] *v/t. ps.* bring face to face, confront (*con* with); *textos* compare; *v/i.* border (*con* on); **~se** *con* face, confront.

confucianismo *m* confucianism.

confundir [3a] (*mezclar*) mix, mingle (*con* with); *b.s.* mix up, jumble up; (*equivocar*) confuse (*con* with), mistake (*con* for), mix up; *enemigo* confound; floor *en debate*; *ánimo* perplex, bewilder; (*humillar*) make *s.o.* feel small; **confusamente** in (utter) confusion; *recordar* hazily; **confusión** *f* confusion; **confuso** *mst* confused; *cosas a.* mixed up, in disorder; *recuerdo a.* hazy.

confutación *f* confutation; **confutar** [1a] confute.

conga *f* conga (*popular dance of Cuba*); **congal** *m Mex.* brothel; whorehouse.

congelación *f* congealing; freezing (*a.* ✝); ⚕ frostbite; ~ *de salarios* wage freeze; **congelado** *carne* chilled, frozen; ⚕ frost-bitten; **congelador** *m* freezer; **congeladora** *f* deep-freeze; **congelar**(**se**) [1a] (*esp. sangre*) congeal; (*agua a. fig.*) freeze; ⚕ get frost-bitten.

congenial kindred; **congeniar** [1b] get on (*con* with).

congénito congenital.

congestión *f* congestion; **congestionar** [1a] produce congestion in, congest.

conglomeración *f* conglomeration; **conglomerado** *adj. a. su. m* conglomerate; **conglomerar**(**se**) [1a] conglomerate.

congoja *f* anguish, distress; **congojoso** distressing, heartbreaking.

congraciador ingratiating; **congraciarse** [1b] *con* get into *s.o.'s* good graces; *b.s.* ingratiate o.s. with, get in with.

congregación *f* gathering, assembly; *eccl.* congregation; **congregar** (**se**) [1h] gather, congregate; **congresista** *m/f* delegate, member (of a congress); **congreso** *m* congress.

congrio *m* conger (eel).

congruencia *f* suitability; congruence (*a.* ⩓), congruity; **congruente, congruo** suitable; congruent (*a.* ⩓), congruous.

cónico conical; ⩓ *sección* conic section; **conífera** *f* conifer; **conífero** coniferous.

conjetura *f* conjecture, surmise; *por* ~ by guesswork; **conjetural** conjectural; **conjeturar** [1a] guess (at) (*de*, *por* from); ~ *que* surmise that, infer that.

conjugación *f* conjugation (*a. biol.*); **conjugar** [1h] conjugate.

conjunción *f* conjunction; **conjuntiva** *f* conjunctiva; **conjuntivitis** *f* conjunctivitis; **conjuntivo** conjunctive; *tejido* connective; **conjunto 1.** united, joint; related *por afinidad*; **2.** *m* whole; group; team; (*vestido*, ♪) ensemble; *thea.* chorus; *de* ~ *attr.* overall; *en* ~ altogether, as a whole; *en su* ~ in its entirety.

conjura(**ción**) *f* conspiracy, plot; **conjurado** *m*, **a** *f* conspirator, plotter; **conjurar** [1a] *v/t.* (*suplicar*) entreat, beseech; swear *s.o.* in *con juramento*; *diablo* exorcize; *peligro* stave off, ward off; *v/i.*, **~se** plot, conspire (together); **conjuro** *m* conjuration, incantation; (*súplica*) entreaty.

conllevar [1a] *penas* help *s.o.* to bear; *p. etc.* put up with.
conmemoración *f* commemoration; **conmemorar** [1a] commemorate; **conmemorativo** commemorative; memorial *attr*.
conmensurable commensurable.
conmigo with me; with myself.
conminar [1a] threaten; **conminatorio** threatening.
conmiseración *f* pity, sympathy; (*acto*) commiseration.
conmoción *f* *geol.* shock (*a. fig.*); *fig.* commotion, disturbance; ~ *cerebral* concussion; **conmovedor** (*enternecedor*) moving, touching; poignant; (*que perturba*) disturbing; (*emocionante*) exciting, stirring; **conmover** [2h] shake, disturb; *fig.* move, touch; shock, disturb.
conmutador *m* ⚡ switch; commutator; *S.Am.* telephone exchange; **conmutar** [1a] exchange (*con*, *por* for); ⚖ *etc.* commute (*en* into).
connatural innate, inherent.
connivencia *f* connivance; (*complot*) conspiracy.
connotación *f* connotation; (*parentesco*) distant relationship; **connotar** [1a] connote.
cono *m* cone (*a.* ⚘); ~ *de proa cohetería* nose cone.
conocedor *m*, **-a** *f* connoisseur, (good) judge (*de* of); expert (*de* in); **conocer** [2d] *v/t.* know; be familiar with; distinguish, tell (*en*, *por* by); *peligro etc.* recognize; (*llegar a* ~) *p.* meet; *lugar etc.* (get to) know; (*entender*) understand, know about; *¿de qué le conoces?* how do know him?; *dar a* ~ introduce; *darse a* ~ make a name for o.s.; *v/i.* know; ~ *de*, ~ *en* know a lot about; **~se** know o.s.; (*dos ps.*) (*estado*) know each other; (*acto*) meet, get to know each other; *se conoce que* it is known that, it is established that; **conocible** knowable; **conocido 1.** *p. etc.* well-known; familiar; noted (*por* for); **2.** *m*, **a** *f* acquaintance; **conocimiento** *m* knowledge; understanding; ⚕ consciousness; (*p.*) acquaintance; ⚓ bill of lading; **~s** *pl.* knowledge (*de* of); information (*de* about); *obrar con* ~ *de causa* know what one is up to; *perder* (*recobrar*) ~ lose (regain) consciousness; *poner en* ~ *a* inform, let *s.o.* know; *tener* ~ *de* know about, have knowledge of; *venir en* ~ *de* learn of, hear about.
conque 1. (and) so, (so) then; **2.** *m* F condition (*para* of).
conquibus *m* F wherewithal.
conquista *f* conquest; **conquistador** *m*, **-a** *f* conqueror; *hist.* conquistador; **conquistar** [1a] conquer (*a* from); *fig.* win over, win round.
consabido well-known, well established; above-mentioned.
consagración *f* consecration; **consagrado** consecrated (*a* to); *expresión* time-honored; **consagrar** [1a] consecrate (*a* to); deify; *tiempo etc.* devote (*a* to); *palabra* sanction, authorize; **~se** *a* devote o.s. to.
consanguíneo related by blood, consanguineous; **consanguinidad** *f* blood relationship, consanguinity.
consciente conscious (*de* of).
conscrito *m* *S.Am.* recruit; conscript; draftee.
consecución *f* acquisition; *de difícil* ~ difficult to get hold of; **consecuencia** *f* consequence, outcome; consistency *de conducta*; *como* ~ in consequence; *de* ~ of consequence; *en* ~ accordingly; *en* ~ *de* as a consequence of; *traer a* ~ bring *s.t.* up; **consecuente** *phls.* consequent; *conducta etc.* consistent; **consecutivo** consecutive (*a. gr.*); **conseguir** [3d *a.* 3l] obtain, get, secure; ~ *inf.* succeed in *ger.*; *conseguí que se fuera* I managed to make him go.
conseja *f* (fairy) tale; **consejero** *m*, **a** *f* adviser; counselor; *pol.* councilor; **consejo** *m* (*dictamen*) advice, counsel; (*un* ~) piece of advice; hint; *pol. etc.* council; ⚖ tribunal, court; ✝ *etc.* board; ~ *de administración* board of directors; ~ *de guerra* (*sumarísimo*) (drumhead) court martial; ~ *de ministros* cabinet.
consenso *m* (unanimous) assent, consensus; **consentido** *niño* spoilt; *marido* complaisant; **consentidor** (*débil*) weak(-minded); *madre* indulgent; *marido* complaisant; **consentimiento** *m* consent; **consentir** [3i] *v/t.* consent to; permit, allow (*a.* ⚖; *que alguien subj.* s.o. to *inf.*); (*tolerar, admitir posibilidad*) admit; *niño* pamper, spoil; *v/i.* consent, say yes, agree (*en* to); (*ceder*) give

in; (*creer*) believe (*en que* that); ~ *con* be indulgent with; = **~se** ⊕ loosen, give; (*rajándose*) split, crack (up).

conserje *m* porter; caretaker, janitor; **conserjería** *f* porter's office.

conserva *f* (*en general*) preserved foods; (*fruta etc.*) preserve(s); (*mermelada*) jam; (*carne etc.*) pickle; **~s** *pl. alimenticias* canned goods; *en* ~ preserved; pickled; canned; **conservación** *f* preservation *etc.*; ⚠ *freq.* upkeep; **conservador 1.** preservative; *pol.* conservative; *ser* ~ *de salud etc.* preserve; **2.** *m*, **-a** *f pol.* conservative; **3.** *m* 📖 curator; **conservar** [1a] *p., salud, frutas,* ⚠ preserve; *esp.* 📖 conserve; can, tin *en lata*; *costumbres, hacienda etc.* keep up; *amigos, secreto* keep; (*guardar*) keep; **~se** last (out); ~ (*bien*) keep (well); ⚕ take good care of o.s.; ~ *con* (*or en*) *salud* keep well; **conservatismo** *m* conservatism; **conservativo** preservative, conservative; **conservatorio** *m* ♪ conservatory; *S.Am.* greenhouse; **conservero** *industria* canning *attr.*

considerable considerable, substantial, sizeable; **consideración** *f* consideration; respect, regard; *en* ~ *a* considering, in consideration of; *por* ~ *a* out of respect for; *sin* ~ *hablar* inconsiderately; *sin* ~ *a* irrespective of; *ser de* ~ be important, be of consequence; **considerado** (*amable*) considerate, thoughtful; respected; deliberate; **considerar** [1a] consider (*que* that; *como* as, to be, *or acc.*), regard (*como* as); show consideration for, respect.

consigna *f* order; slogan; ⚔, *pol.* watchword; 🚂 cloakroom; checkroom; **consignación** *f* consignment; deposit; **consignador** *m* consigner; **consignar** [1a] (*enviar*) consign; dispatch, remit (*a* to); deposit; *renta etc.* assign (*para* to); (*citar*) point out, record; **consignatario** *m* ✝ consignee; ✝ agent; ⚖ assign(ee).

consigo with him, with her, with you *etc.*

consiguiente consequent (*a* upon); *por* ~ consequently, so, therefore.

consistencia *f* consistency, consistence *etc.*; **consistente** consistent; solid, substantial; *razón etc.* sound, valid; **consistir** [3a]: ~ *en* consist of (*or* in); lie in; be due to.

consistorio *m eccl.* consistory; *pol.* town council.

consocio *m* fellow member; ✝ partner, associate.

consola *f* console table; ♪, ⚠ console.

consolación *f* consolation; **consolador 1.** consoling, comforting; **2.** *m*, **-a** *f* comforter; **consolar** [1m] console, comfort; **~se** find consolation (*con* in).

consolidación *f* consolidation; **consolidados** *m/pl.* consols; **consolidar** [1a] consolidate (*a.* ✝, *fig.*); *deuda* fund; *fig. a.* strengthen, cement.

consomé *m* broth; clear soup, consommé.

consonancia *f* consonance (*a. gr.*), harmony; *fig.* harmony, conformity; *en* ~ *con* in accordance with; **consonante 1.** *adj. a. su. f* consonant; **2.** *m* rhyming word, rhyme; **consonar** [1m] ♪ be in harmony (*a. fig.*); *lit.* rhyme.

consorcio *m* ✝ consortium; association; *fig.* harmony, good fellowship; **consorte** *m/f* consort; *fig.* partner, companion; ⚖ **~s** *pl.* partners in crime.

conspicuo eminent, prominent.

conspiración *f* conspiracy; **conspirador** *m*, **-a** *f* conspirator; **conspirar** [1a] conspire, plot (*contra* against); ~ *a inf.* conspire to *inf.*

constancia *f* constancy; steadiness *etc.*; proof, evidence; *dejar* ~ *de* place *s.t.* on record; *fig.* show evidence of; *trabajar con* ~ work steadily; **constante 1.** constant; steady; *amigo etc.* faithful, staunch; (*duradero*) lasting; **2.** *f* Ⱥ constant; **constar** [1a]: ~ *de* be clear from, be evident from; consist of; ~ *en* be on record in; ~ *por* be shown by; *hacer* ~ record; certify; reveal (*que* that); *consta que* it is a fact that; *me consta que* I have evidence that; *conste que* ⚖ *etc.* let it be on record that; F remember that, bear in mind that; *no consta* it is not listed; (*libro*) not available.

constatación *f* proof; establishment *de un hecho*; **constatar** [1a] show; state; establish; prove.

constelación *f* constellation; climate; **constelado** starry, full of stars; *fig.* bespangled (de with).

consternación *f* consternation, dismay; **consternar** [1a] (fill with) dismay.

constipado *m* ⚕ (head) cold; **constiparse** [1a] catch a cold; *estar constipado* have a cold.

constitución *f* constitution; **constitucional 1.** constitutional; **2.** *m* constitutionalist; **constituir** [3g] constitute; *colegio etc.* set up, establish; *principios etc.* erect (en into); ~ en *oficial etc.* make; *obligación* force *s.o.* into; **~se** en, ~ por set (o.s.) up as; **constitutivo** *adj. a. su. m* constituent; **constituyente** *pol.* constituent.

constreñir [3h *a.* 3l] force (*a inf.* to *inf.*); ⚕ constipate; **constricción** *f* constriction; **constrictor 1.** ⚕ costive, binding, **2.** *m anat.* constrictor.

construcción *f* building, construction (*a. gr.*); ~ *de buques* ship building; *en (vía de)* ~ under construction; **constructor 1.** building, construction *attr.*; **2.** *m* builder; ~ *de buques* ship builder; **construir** [3g] construct (*a.* ⚒), build; *edificio freq.* put up; *gr.* construe.

consuelda *f* comfrey.

consuelo *m* consolation, solace; joy, comfort.

consuetudinario habitual; ⚖ common.

cónsul *m* consul; **consulado** *m* (*cargo*) consulship; (*oficina*) consulate; **consular** consular.

consulta *f* consultation; (*parecer*) opinion; ⚕ (*horas de*) ~ office hours; *de* ~ *libro etc.* reference *attr.*; **consultación** *f* consultation; **consultar** [1a] consult; *referencia* look up; *asunto* discuss, take up (*a, con* with); (*aconsejar*) advise; **consultivo** consultative; **consultor** *m* consultant; **consultorio** *m* information bureau; ⚕ surgery, consulting room; problem (*or* advice) page *de periódico*.

consumación *f* consummation; end, extinction; **consumado** consummate, perfect; accomplished (*en* in); **consumar** [1a] carry out, accomplish; *matrimonio* consummate.

consumición *f* consumption *etc.*; food or drink taken in a café *etc.*; **consumido** F ⚕ skinny; fidgety, fretful; **consumidor** *m* ✝ consumer; (*cliente*) customer; **consumir** [3a] *mst* consume; F get on *s.o.'s* nerves, get *s.o.* down; wear *s.o.* out; **~se** burn out, be consumed *en fuego*; ⚕ waste away (*a. fig.*); *fig.* pine away, mope (*de* because of); **consumo** *m*, **consunción** *f* consumption.

consuno: *de* ~ together, with one accord.

contabilidad *f* accounting, bookkeeping; (*profesión*) accountancy; **contabilista** *m/f* accountant; bookkeeper; **contable** *m* accountant; bookkeeper.

contacto *m* contact; *poner(se) en* ~ *con* put (get) into touch with.

contado 1. *adj.* ~*s pl.* few; rare; *son* ~*s los que* there are few who; ~*as veces* seldom; **2.** *adv.*: *al* ~ cash down, (for) cash; *por de* ~ naturally; **contador** *m* counter *de café*; ✝ accountant, bookkeeper; ~ *de Geiger* Geiger counter; ~ *público titulado* (*or jurado*) certified public accountant (CPA); ⊕ meter; ~ *de gas* gas meter; **contaduría** *f* accountancy; bookkeeping; (*oficina*) accounts department; *thea.* box office.

contagiar [1b] infect (*con* with; *a. fig.*); **~se** become infected; ~ *de* ⚕ catch; *herejía* be tainted with; **contagio** *m* contagion (*a. fig.*); (*enfermedad*) infection; **contagioso** contagious, catching (*a. fig.*); *p.* infectious.

contaminación *f* contamination; (*baldón*) stain; ~ *ambiental* environmental pollution; **contaminar** [1a] contaminate (*a. fig.*); *agua* pollute; *vestido* soil; *texto* corrupt; *eccl.* profane; (*pervertir*) defile, stain; **~se** be contaminated (*con, de* by).

contante ready; *v. dinero*; **contar** [1m] *v/t.* ⚒ *etc.* count (*por dedos* on); (*considerar*) count (*entre* among, *por* as); *historia* tell; ~ *inf.* count on *ger.*, expect to *inf.*; *sin* ~ not counting, not to mention; except for; *cuenta 20 años* he's 20; *tiene los días contados* his days are numbered; *v/i.* count; ~ *con* rely on, count on; (*poseer, tener*) have; *no* ~ *con freq.* not bargain for.

contemplación *f* contemplation; ~es *pl.* indulgence; *sin* ~es without any explanation, without more ado; *no me vengas con* ~es don't come to me with excuses; **contemplar** [1a] gaze at, look at; *fig.*, *eccl.* contemplate; show consideration for; **contemplativo** contemplative.

contemporáneo *adj. a. su. m*, **a** *f* contemporary; **contemporizador** *m* time server; **contemporizar** [1f] temporize.

contención *f* ⚔ *etc.* containing, containment; (*contienda*) contention; rivalry; ⚖ suit; **contencioso** contentious; *p.* captious; **contender** [2g] contend; compete, be rivals (*en* in); ~ *con* fight with, *fig.* dispute with (*sobre* over); **contendiente** *m* contestant.

contenedor *m* container; **contener** [2l] contain (*a.* ⚔), hold; *multitud* keep in check; *rebeldes* keep down; *emoción* keep back, bottle up; *cólera* contain; *bostezo*, *risa* smother; ~**se** *fig.* hold o.s. in check, contain o.s.; **contenido 1.** *fig.* restrained; **2.** *m* contents; content.

contentadizo: *bien* (*mal*) ~ easy (hard) to please; **contentamiento** *m* contentment; **contentar** [1a] satisfy, content; ✝ endorse; ~**se** *con*, ~ *de* be contented with, be satisfied with; ~ *con inf.* content o.s. with *ger.*; **contento 1.** contented; (*alegre*) pleased; glad, happy; *estar* ~ *de* be glad about; (*satisfecho*) be pleased with; *quedar* ~ *de inf.* be content to *inf.*; *no caber de* ~ jump for joy; **2.** *m* joy, contentment; *a* ~ to one's satisfaction.

conteo *m* calculation; reckoning; count.

contérmino conterminous.

contero *m* ⚠ beading.

contertuli(an)o *m*, **a** *f* fellow member (of a *tertulia*).

contestable debatable; **contestación** *f* answer, reply; ⚖ ~ *a la demanda* plea; **contestar** [1a] answer (*a. v/i.* ~ *a*); ⚖ corroborate; **contesto** *m* reply; answer.

contexto *m lit.* context; (*enredo*) interweaving, web; **contextura** *f* contexture; make-up *de p.*

contienda *f* struggle, contest.

contigo with you; (†, *a. Dios*) with thee.

contigüidad *f* nearness, closeness; adjacency; **contiguo** adjacent (*a* to), adjoining.

continencia *f* continence; **continental** continental; **continente 1.** continent; **2.** *m geog.* continent; (*vasija*) container; *fig.* air, mien; (*porte*) bearing.

contingencia *f* contingency; **contingente 1.** contingent; **2.** *m* contingent (*a.* ⚔); contingency; ✝ *etc.* quota.

continuación *f* continuation; *a* ~ later (on); below *en texto*; *decir a* ~ go on to say; *a* ~ *de* after; **continuar** [1e] *v/t.* continue, go on with; *v/i.* continue, go on (*con* with; *ger.* ger.); ~ *con salud* keep in good health; ~ *en su puesto* stay at one's job, carry on with one's work; *continuará* (*cuento*) to be continued; ~(**se**) *con geog.*, ⚠ adjoin, connect with; **continuidad** *f* continuity; continuance; **continuo 1.** continuous; continual; ⊕ *cinta etc.* endless; *p.* persevering; *a la* ~*a*, (*de*) ~ continuously; **2.** *m* continuum.

contonearse [1a] swagger, strut; **contoneo** *m* swagger, strut.

contorno *m* form, shape; *paint. etc.* outline; ~*s pl.* environs; *en* ~ around.

contorsión *f* contortion; **contorsionista** *m/f* contortionist.

contra 1. *prp.* against (*a. en* ~ *de*); ⚠ opposite, facing; *ir en* ~ *de* run counter to, go against; **2.** *adv.* (*en*) ~ against; *opinar etc. en* ~ disagree; **3.** *m v. pro*; **4.** *f fenc.* counter; F bind, snag; *llevar la* ~ *a* oppose, contradict.

contra...: ~**almirante** *m* rear admiral; ~**atacar** [1g] counterattack; ~**ataque** *m* counterattack; ~**bajo** *m* double bass; ~**balancear** [1a] counterbalance; ~**balanza** *f* counterbalance; contrast; ~**bandista** *m/f* smuggler; ~**bando** *m* (*acto*) smuggling; (*géneros*) contraband; ~ *de armas* gun running; *de* ~ contraband *attr.*; *pasar de* ~ smuggle (in *or* out).

contracción *f* contraction.

contra(con)ceptivo *m* contraceptive.

contracorriente *f* crosscurrent; undercurrent.

contractable contractible; **contráctil** *m* contractile; **contractual** contractual.

contra...: **~cultura** *f* counterculture; **~decir** [3p] contradict; **~dicción** *f* contradiction; *fig.* incompatibility; *espíritu de* ~ contrariness; **~dictorio** contradictory.

contraer [2p] *mst* contract; *discurso* condense; *contrato etc.* enter into; *costumbre* acquire.

contra...: **~espionaje** *m* counterespionage; **~fuerte** *m* ⚠ buttress; *geog.* spur; **~golpe** *m* counterstroke; **~hacer** [2s] copy, imitate; *moneda* counterfeit; *documento* forge, fake; *p.* impersonate; **~hecho** counterfeit, fake(d); *anat.* hunchbacked; **~hechura** *f* counterfeit; counterfeiting *etc.*; **~jugada** *f* countermove.

contralto 1. *f* contralto; **2.** *m* countertenor.

contra...: **~luz:** *a* ~ against the light; **~maestre** *m* ⊕ foreman; ⚓ warrant officer; ⚓ boatswain; **~mandar** [1a] countermand; **~mandato** *m* countermand; **~marca** *f* countermark; **~marcar** [1g] countermark; **~marcha** *f* ⚔ countermarch; *mot. etc.* reverse; **~marchar** [1a] countermarch; **~orden** *f* counterorder; **~pelo:** *a* ~ *acariciar etc.* the wrong way; *fig.* against the grain; **~pesar** [1a] (counter)balance (*con* with); *fig.* offset, compensate for; **~peso** *m* counterbalance, counterweight; ✝ makeweight; **~poner** [2r] compare; (*oponer*) ~ *a* set *s.t.* up against; **~posición:** *en* ~ *a* in contrast to; **~prestación** *f* return favor; quid pro quo; **~producente** self-defeating; boomerang *attr.*; **~punto** *m* counterpoint.

contrariar [1c] go against, be opposed to; (*estorbar*) impede, thwart; (*molestar*) annoy; **contrariedad** *f* opposition; obstacle; (*disgusto*) bother, annoyance; **contrario 1.** contrary (*a* to); (*nocivo*) harmful (*a* to); (*enemigo*) hostile (*a* to); *lado* opposite; *suerte* adverse; *al* ~, *por lo* ~ on the contrary; *al* ~ *de* unlike; *en* ~ to the contrary; *lo* ~ the opposite, the reverse; *de lo* ~ otherwise; *todo lo* ~ quite the reverse; *llevar la* ~*a a* oppose, contradict; **2.** *m*, **a** *f* (*p.*) enemy, adversary; ⚖ *etc.* opponent; **3.** *m* contrary, reverse (*de* of); obstacle.

contra...: **♀rreforma** *f* Counterreformation; **~rrestar** [1a] counteract, offset; *pelota* return; **~rresto** *m* counteraction; **~sentido** *m* misinterpretation; contradiction; (*disparate*) piece of nonsense; **~seña** *f* countersign (*a.* ⚔); *thea.* ticket.

contrastar [1a] *v/t.* resist; ✝ *metal* assay, hallmark; *medidas* check; *radio*: monitor; *v/i.* contrast (*con* with); ~ *a*, ~ *con(tra)* face up to; **contraste** *m* contrast; ✝ assay; (*marca del*) ~ hallmark; *en* ~ *con* in contrast to; *por* ~ in contrast.

contrata *f* contract; *por* ~ by contract; **contratante** *m* ⚖ contracting party; ✝ contractor; **contratar** [1a] negotiate for, contract for; *p.* hire, engage; *jugador etc.* sign up.

contratiempo *m* setback, reverse.

contratista *m/f* (government) contractor; **contrato** *m* contract.

contra...: **~tuerca** *f* locknut; **~validación** *f documento* validation; **~validar** [1a] validate; confirm; **~vención** *f* contravention, infringement; **~veneno** *m* antidote (*de* to); **~venir** [3s]: ~ *a* contravene, infringe; **~ventana** *f* shutter.

contribución *f* contribution; (*carga*) tax; ~*es pl.* taxes, taxation; *exento de* ~*es* tax-free; **contribuir** [3g] contribute (*a*, *para* to, towards; *a inf.* to *ger.*); pay (in taxes); **contribuyente** *m* contributor; *esp.* taxpayer.

contrición *f* contrition.

contrincante *m* opponent; rival.

contristar [1a] sadden.

contrito contrite.

control *m* control; inspection, check(ing); ✝ (*cuenta*) audit; ~ *de la natalidad* (*or de los nacimientos*) birth control; ~ *remoto* remote control; *perder* ~ get out of control, lose control; **controlador** *m* controller; ~ *aéreo* air-traffic controller; **controlar** [1a] control; inspect, check; ✝ audit.

controversia *f* controversy; **controvertible** controversial; **controvertir** [3i] argue (*v/t.* over).

contumacia *f* obstinacy *etc.*; ⚖ contempt (of court); **contumaz** obstinate; wayward, perverse; ⚖ guilty of contempt, contumacious.
contumelia *f* contumely; **contumelioso** contumelious.
contundente *fig.* convincing, impressive; **contundir** [3a] bruise, contuse.
conturbar [1a] trouble, dismay.
contusión *f* bruising, contusion.
convalecencia *f* convalescence; **convalecer** [2d] get better, convalesce (de after); **convaleciente** *adj. a. su. m/f* convalescent.
convección *f* convection.
convencer [2b] convince (de of, de que that); **convencimiento** *m* (act of) convincing; conviction.
convención *f* convention; **convencional** conventional; **convencionalismo** *m* conventionalism.
convenible suitable; *p.* accomodating; *precio* fair; **conveniencia** *f* suitability *etc.*; (*conformidad*) agreement; conformity; ~s *pl.* ⚕ property; (*decoro*) decencies; **conveniente** (*apropiado*) suitable, fit(ting); proper, right; (*útil*) useful, profitable; juzgar ~ see fit (*inf.* to *inf.*); **convenio** *m* agreement; **convenir** [3s] agree (con with; en about, on; en *inf.* to *inf.*; en que that); ~ a suit, be suited to; be suitable for, befit; *impersonal*: ~ *inf.* be as well to *inf.*, be important to *inf.*; conviene beber agua it's a good thing to drink water; conviene a saber namely; ~**se** come to an agreement, agree.
conventículo *m* conventicle; **convento** *m* monastery; ~ (de monjas) convent, nunnery; **conventual** conventual.
convergencia *f* convergence; *fig.* common direction; concurrence; **converger** [2c], **convergir** [3c] converge (en on); *fig.* concur, be in accord (con with).
conversación *f* conversation, talk; **conversar** [1a] converse.
conversión *f* conversion; ⚔ wheel; **converso** *m*, **a** *f* convert; **convertible** convertible; **convertidor** *m* ⊕, ⚡ converter; **convertir** [3i] convert (*a.* ⊕, ⚡, ⚕; en into, *eccl.* a to); *ojos, armas, pensamientos* turn; ~**se** *eccl.* be(come) converted; ~ en turn into, become.
convexidad *f* convexity; **convexo** convex.
convicción *f* conviction; **convicto** convicted, found guilty.
convidada: F dar una ~, pagar la ~ stand a round; **convidado** *m*, **a** *f* guest; **convidar** [1a]: ~ a invite *s.o.* to; *bebida esp.* treat to, stand; *fig.* stir to, move to; ~ a uno con offer *s.t.* to s.o.; ~**se** volunteer.
convincente convincing.
convite *m* invitation; party, banquet.
convivencia *f* living together, life together; **convivir** [3a] live together; share the same life; ~ con *fig.* exist side by side with.
convocar [1g] summon; call.
convoy *m* ⚓ convoy; 🚂 train; F procession; **convoyar** [1a] escort.
convulsión *f* convulsion (*a. fig.*); **convulsionar** [1a] convulse; **convulsivo** convulsive; **convulso** convulsed (de with).
conyugal married, conjugal; **cónyug(u)e** *m/f* spouse, partner; ~s *pl.* married couple, husband and wife.
coñac *m* brandy.
¡**coño**! (*enojo*) damn it all!; (*sorpresa*) well I'll be damned!; (*injuria a p.*) idiot!
cooperación *f* cooperation; **cooperador** *m*, **-a** *f* cooperator; **cooperar** [1a] cooperate (a in); ~ en take part (together) in; **cooperario** *m* cooperator; **cooperativa** *f* cooperative; (mutual) association; **cooperativo** cooperative.
cooptar [1a] coopt.
coordenada *f* ⩘ coordinate; **coordinación** *f* coordination; **coordinar** [1a] coordinate.
copa *f mst* glass; *poet.* goblet; F *vino* drink; *deportes*: cup (*a. fig. de dolor*); crown *de sombrero*; ⚘ top; *naipes*: ~s *pl.* hearts; F llevar una ~ de más have one over the eight; tomar unas ~s have a drink or two.
copar [1a] ⚔ surround; *naipes*: sweep the board (*a. fig.*).
copear [1a] F have a drink.
copete *m anat.* tuft (of hair); forelock *de caballo*; *orn.*, *geog.* crest; de alto ~ aristocratic; important; tener mucho ~ be stuck-up; **copetín** *m S.Am.* cocktail; **copetudo** tufted; *fig.* stuck-up.

copia *f* copy; abundance; ~ *al carbón* carbon copy; ~ *en limpio* fair copy; **copiadora** *f* copy(ing) machine; duplicator; **copiante** *m/f* copyist; **copiar** [1b] copy (*a. fig.*); *dictado* take down; **copioso** copious, plentiful; **copista** *m/f* copyist.

copita *f* (small) glass.

copla *f* verse; couplet; ♪ popular song, folk song; ~*s pl.* verse(s), poetry; ~*s pl. de ciego* doggerel.

copo *m* ⊕ tuft; ~ *de nieve* snowflake.

copudo bushy, thick.

coque *m* coke.

coqueluche *f* whooping cough.

coqueta 1. flirtatious, flighty, coquettish; 2. *f* flirt, coquette; **coquetear** [1a] flirt (*con* with); **coqueteo** *m*, **coquetería** *f* flirtation; flirtatiousness, coquetry; *fig.* affectation; **coquetón** 1. (*majo*) smart; *hombre* attractive (to women); *mujer* = *coqueta*, 2. *m* lady-killer; F wolf.

coquitos: *hacer* ~ make faces.

coraje *m* (*ira*) anger; (*ánimo*) (fighting) spirit; **corajina** *f* F (fit of) temper; **corajudo** F quick-tempered.

coral[1] ♪ 1. choral; 2. *m* chorale.

coral[2] *m zo.* coral; **coralina** *f* coralline; **coralino** coral *attr.*

Corán *m* Koran; **coránico** Koranic.

coraza *f hist.* cuirass; ⚓ armor plate; *zo.* shell.

corazón *m* heart (*a. fig.*); *naipes*: ~*es pl.* hearts; *duro de* ~ hard-hearted; *de* ~ *adv.* willingly; *de buen* ~ kind-hearted; *de todo* ~ from the heart; *con el* ~ *en la mano* frankly, sincerely; *llevar el* ~ *en la mano* wear one's heart on one's sleeve; *poner el* ~ *en* set one's heart on; *tener el* ~ *para inf.* have the heart to *inf.*; *no tener* ~ *para* not feel up to; *estar enfermo del* ~ have heart trouble; **corazonada** *f* rash impulse; presentiment, hunch F.

corbata *f* (neck)tie; ~ *de lazo* = **corbatín** *m* bowtie.

corbeta *f* corvette.

corcel *m* steed, charger.

corcova *f* hunchback, hump; **corcovado** 1. hunchbacked; 2. *m*, **a** *f* hunchback; **corcovar** [1a] bend (over); **corcovear** [1a] buck, plunge; **corcovo** *m* buck; *fig.* crookedness.

corchea *f* ♪ quaver.

corcheta *f sew.* eye; **corchete** *m* snap fastener, clasp; *sew.* hook and eye; *typ.* bracket; ⚖ † constable.

corcho *m* cork; cork mat *para mesa*; *pesca*: float; **corchoso** corky.

cordaje *m* rigging.

cordel *m* cord, line; *a* ~ in a straight line; **cordelero** *m* cord maker, rope maker; **cordería** *f* cordage.

corderillo *m*, **corderina** *f* lambskin; **cordero** *m*, **a** *f* lamb (*a. fig.*); (*piel de*) ~ lambskin.

cordial 1. cordial; heartfelt; *pharm.* tonic; 2. *m* cordial; **cordialidad** *f* warmth, cordiality; frankness.

cordillera *f* (mountain) range.

cordobán *m* cordovan (leather); **cordobana:** F *andar a la* ~ go about with nothing on; **cordobés** *adj. a. su. m*, **-a** *f* Cordovan.

cordón *m* cord (*a. anat.*); (shoe)lace *de zapato*; ⚡ flex; ⚓ strand *de cabo*; cordon *de policía etc.* (*a.* ⚔, △); *de 3* ~*es lana* 3-ply; ~ *sanitario* sanitary cordon; ~ *umbilical* umbilical cord; **cordoncillo** *m sew.* rib; milling, milled edge *de moneda.*

cordura *f* good sense, wisdom.

corear [1a] *fig.* answer in a chorus; say all together; **corifeo** *m* coryphaeus; *fig.* leader; **corista** 1. *m/f eccl.* chorister; 2. *f thea.* chorus girl.

cormorán *m*: ~ (*grande*) cormorant.

cornada *f* goring; **cornadura** *f*, **cornamenta** *f* horns; antlers *de ciervo.*

cornamusa *f* bagpipe; *hunt.* hunting horn.

córnea *f* cornea.

cornear [1a] gore, butt.

corneja *f* crow; ~ *negra* carrion crow.

córneo horny, corneous 🕮.

corneta 1. *f* bugle; ~ (*de llaves*) cornet; ~ (*de monte*) hunting horn; 2. *m* ⚔ bugler; ♪ cornet player.

cornezuelo *m* (*hongo*) ergot.

cornisa *f* cornice (*a. mount.*); **cornisamento** *m* entablature.

cornucopia *f* cornucopia; **cornudo** 1. horned; 2. *m* cuckold.

coro *m* ♪ (*pieza*), *thea.*, *fig.* chorus; *ps.*, *eccl.*, △ choir; *a* ~ in a chorus; *a* ~*s* in turn; *de* ~ by heart, by rote; *hacer* ~ *de* (*or a*) *palabras* echo.

corola *f* corolla; **corolario** *m* corollary.

corona *f* crown; *ast.* corona; *meteor.* halo; *eccl.* tonsure; ~ (*de flores*) chaplet; wreath; **coronación** *f* coronation; = **coronam(i)ento** *m* crowning, conclusion; △ crown, coping stone; **coronar** [1a] crown (*con, de* with; *por rey acc.*); **coronario** coronary.

coronel *m* colonel; △ top molding.

coronilla *f* crown, top of the head; F *bailar de* ~ slog away; F *estar hasta la* ~ be fed up.

corotos *m/pl.* belongings; utensils; implements.

corpa(n)chón *m* F, **corpazo** *m* F carcass.

corpiño *m* bodice.

corporación *f* corporation; association; **corporal** corporal, bodily; *higiene etc.* personal; **corporativo** corporate; **corpóreo** corporeal, bodily; **corpulencia** *f* stoutness *etc.*; **corpulento** stout; *esp. p.* well-built, burly; **Corpus** *m* Corpus Christi; **corpúsculo** *m* corpuscle.

corral *m* (farm)yard; ~ *de madera* lumber yard; F ~ *de vacas* slum; ~ *de vecindad* tenement; *hacer* ~*es* play truant; F play hookey; **corralillo** *m* playpen.

correa *f* (leather) strap; thong; *esp.* ⊕ belt; (*calidad*) leatheriness; ~ *sin fin* endless belt; ~ *de transmisión* driving-belt; ~ *transportadora* conveyor (belt); *besar la* ~ eat humble pie; F *tener* ~ be able to take it; **correaje** *m* belts, straps; ⊕ belting.

corrección *f* correction; (*castigo*) punishment; (*formalidad*) correctness; **correccional** *m* reformatory; **correctivo** *adj. a. su. m* corrective; **correcto** correct (*a. fig.*), right; *fig.* polite; *facciones etc.* regular; **corrector** *m typ.* proofreader.

corredera *f* slide; ⊕ slide valve; ⚓ log; *de* ~ *puerta etc.* sliding; **corredizo** sliding; *nudo* running, slip *attr.*; *grúa* traveling; **corredor** *m*, **-a** *f* runner; ✝ agent, broker; ~ *automovilista* road racer; ~ *de bolsa* (stock) broker; ~ *de casas* house agent; ~ *de fincas rurales* land agent; F ~ *de noticias* gossip; **correduría** *f* brokerage.

corregidor *m hist.* chief magistrate; **corregir** [3c *a.* 3l] correct; put right; (*castigar*) punish, reprimand; *fig.* temper.

correlación *f* correlation; **correlacionar** [1a] correlate; **correlativo** *adj. a. su. m* correlative.

correligionario *m*, **a** *f* coreligionist.

correlón *adj. S.Am.* fast; swift; *Col., Mex.* cowardly.

correntón F gadabout; (*bromista*) jolly, fond of a lark.

correo *m* ✉ post, mail (*a.* ~*s pl.*); (*p.*) courier; ✉ mailman, postman; ⚔ dispatch rider; (*tren*) ~ mail train; (*casa de*) ~*s pl.* post office; ~ *aéreo* airmail; ~ *diplomático* courier; ~ *urgente* special delivery; *a vuelta de* ~ by return (of mail); *por* ~ by mail; through the mails; *echar al* ~, *poner en el* ~ mail, post.

correoso leathery, tough.

correr [2a] **1.** *v/t. terreno* traverse, travel over; ⚔ overrun; *caballo* race; *toros* fight; (*acosar*) chase, pursue; *cortina* draw (back); *vela* (un)furl; *pestillo* throw; *llave* turn; *silla* pull up, draw up; *fig. p.* embarrass, cover with confusion; *aventura* have; *riesgo* run; *sl. clase* cut; F ~*la* have one's fling; (*juerga*) go on the spree; **2.** *v/i.* run (*a. líquido, plazo, fig.*); (*líquido a.*) flow; (*surtidor*) play; (*viento*) blow; (*tiempo*) pass, elapse; (*moneda*) pass; (*doctrina etc.*) circulate, be commonly held; (*rumor*) go round; *a todo* ~ at full speed; *a todo turbio* ~ however bad things may be; *que corre mes etc.* current; ✝ ~ *a*, ~ *por* sell at; ~ *con* be in charge of; *gastos* meet; (*entender*) understand; **3.** ~**se** (*deslizarse*) slide (*por* along); (*derretirse*) melt; (*vela*) gutter; *fig.* get embarrassed; (*excederse*) go too far; **correría** *f* ⚔ raid, foray; excursion.

correspondencia *f* correspondence (*a.* ✉); communication(s), contact *entre lugares etc.*; 🚂 connexion; return *de afecto*; gratitude; **corresponder** [2a] correspond (*con* to), tally (*con* with); △ communicate; 🚂 connect (*con* with); ~ *a* correspond to; *afecto, favor* return, reciprocate, repay (*con* with); (*deber*) fall to; (*asunto*) concern; ~**se** correspond (*a.* ✉; *con* with); (*en afecto etc.*) agree; have regard for one another; **correspondiente** **1.** *a.* ⚗ corresponding; respective; **2.** *m* correspondent; **corresponsal** *m* (newspaper) correspondent.

corretaje *m* brokerage; **corretear** [1a] gad about; (*jugando*) run around; **corretero** *m*, **a** *f* gadabout; **correve(i)dile** *m* F gossip.

corrida *f* run, dash; ~ *de toros* bullfight; *de* ~ fast; **corrido** *fig.* sheepish, abashed; (*experimentado*) wise, knowing; *S.Am.* continuous; uninterrupted; ~ *de vergüenza* covered with shame; *de* ~ fluently.

corriente 1. *agua etc.* running; *estilo* flowing, fluid; *mes etc.* present; *cuenta* current; *moneda* accepted, normal; common, ordinary, everyday; *procedimiento* normal, standard; (*sabido*) well-known; *noticia* topical; F ~ *y moliente* regular; **2.** *m* current month; *el 10 del* ~ the 10th of this month; *estar al* ~ *de* be informed about; be well up with; *mantenerse al* ~ *de* keep in touch with; *tener al* ~ *de* keep *s.o.* informed about; **3.** *f* current (*a. fig.*, ⚡; *alterna* alternating, *continua* direct), stream; ~ *de aire* draught; ~ *submarina* undercurrent; *con* ~ *alambre* live; *dejarse llevar de la* ~ *fig.* follow the crowd.

corrillo *m* knot of people, huddle; *fig.* clique, coterie.

corrimiento *m* ⚕ discharge; ~ (*de tierras*) landslide; *fig.* embarrassment, sheepishness.

corro *m* ring, circle (of people); open space; *hacer* ~ make room.

corroboración *f* corroboration *etc.*; **corroborar** [1a] strengthen; *fig.* corroborate; **corroborativo** corroborative.

corroer [2za] corrode (*a. fig.*); *geol.* erode.

corromper [2a] *v/t.* corrupt (*a. fig.*); *madera* rot; *comida, placeres* spoil; *juez* bribe; *mujer* seduce; F annoy, put out; *v/i.* smell bad.

corrosión *f* corrosion; *geol.* erosion; **corrosivo** *adj. a. su. m* corrosive.

corrupción *f* corruption; corruptness; ⚚, ⚖ *a.* graft; rotting *etc.*; **corruptela** *f* corruption; abuse; bad habit; **corruptible** corruptible; *comida etc.* perishable; **corruptivo** corruptive; **corrupto** corrupt; **corruptor 1.** corrupting; **2.** *m*, **-a** *f* corrupter.

corsario *m* privateer; corsair.

corsé *m* corset.

corso *adj. a. su. m*, **a** *f* Corsican.

corta *f* felling, clearing.

corta...: **~bolsas** *m* pickpocket; **~césped** lawn mower; **~circuitos** *m* circuit breaker.

cortada *f S.Am.* gash; cut; **cortado** *leche* sour; *estilo* abrupt; ~ *a pico* precipitous; **cortador 1.** cutting; **2.** *m*, **-a** *f* cutter (*a.* ⊕); **cortadura** *f* cut; (*acto*) cutting (*a. de periódico*); *geog.* pass; **cortalápices** *m* pencil sharpener; **cortante 1.** cutting; *frío* bitter; *viento* biting; **2.** *m* cleaver, chopper.

corta...: **~papeles** *m* paper knife; **~pisa** *f sew.* trimming; *fig.* (*gracia*) charm, wit; conditions; difficulty; **~plumas** *m* penknife.

cortar [1a] **1.** *v/t.* cut (*a.* ⚗, *naipes*); (*recortar, suprimir*) cut out; (*amputar*) cut off; *carne* carve; *árbol etc.* cut down; *enemigo, provisión, región* cut off; *conversación* cut into, interrupt; (*acortar*) cut short; *agua, gas,* ⚡ cut off, turn off; ~ *de vestir sew.* cut out; *fig.* backbite; **2.** *v/i.* cut (*a. naipes*); (*frío etc.*) be biting; **3.** **~se** (*manos*) get chapped; (*leche*) turn (sour); (*p.*) get embarrassed, get tongue-tied; **cortaúñas** *m* nail clipper.

corte[1] *m* cut; (*acto*) cutting; (*filo*) edge; (*tela*) piece, length; ⚠, ⚗ (cross) section; ⚡ failure, cut; ⊕ job; ⚒ stint; *S.Am.* harvest; (*sastrería*) tailoring; cut, style *de traje*; (*marca*) make; ~ *de corriente* power cut.

corte[2] *f* court (*a. S.Am.* ⚖); (*patio*) court(yard); (*corral*) yard; (*ciudad*) capital (city); *la* ~ *freq.* Madrid; **~s** *pl. Spanish parliament*; **~s** *pl. constituyentes* constituent assembly; *hacer la* ~ *a* pay court to.

cortedad *f* shortness *etc.*; *fig.* bashfulness; backwardness *etc.*

cortejar [1a] attend; *mujer, poderoso* court; **cortejo** *m* courting; (*séquito*) entourage; (*agasajo*) treat; (*p.*) beau; (*desfile*) procession; ~ *fúnebre* funeral procession.

cortés polite, courteous; *amor* courtly; **cortesana** *f* courtesan; **cortesanía** *f* politeness, good manners; **cortesano 1.** of the court; = *cortés*; **2.** *m* courtier; **cortesía** *f* politeness; courtesy; title; *de* ~ *entrada* complimentary.

corteza *f* bark *de árbol*; peel, skin, rind *de fruta*; crust *de pan*; *fig.* outside; (*grosería*) coarseness.

cortijo *m* farm(house).

cortina *f* curtain; ~ *de hierro fig.* iron curtain; ~ *de humo* smoke screen.

corto short; brief; slight; (*escaso*) scant(y), deficient; (*defectuoso*) defective; *fig.* (*tímido*) bashful, shy; tongue-tied; (*lerdo*) backward, stupid; *quedarse* ~ not know what to say; **~circuito** *m* short circuit; *poner(se) en* ~ short-circuit; **~metraje** *m cine*: short.

coruñés *adj. a. su. m*, **-a** *f* (native) of Corunna.

corvadura *f* curve (*a.* △), bend; curvature; **corvo** curved, arched.

corvejón *m* hock *de caballo*; spur *de gallo*.

corzo *m*, **a** *f* roe (deer).

cosa *f* thing; (*algo*) something; (*no* ... ~) nothing; ~ *de* about, a matter of; *es* ~ *de 2 horas* it takes about 2 hours; *¡~s pl. de Juan!* one of John's tricks!; that's typical of John!; *¡~s pl. de España!* *contp.* what can you expect in Spain?; *otra* ~ something else; *poca* ~ nothing much; ~ *de* a matter of; ~ *de nunca acabar* bore; tiresome thing; ~ *rara* strange thing; *¡~ (más) rara!* how strange!; the funny thing is ...!; *a* ~ *hecha* as good as done; *como si tal* ~ as if nothing had happened; *es poca* ~, *no es gran* ~ it isn't up to much; *tal como están las* ~*s* as things stand; *ni* ~ *que valga* nor anything of the sort; *las* ~*s van mejor* things are going better.

cosaco *adj. a. su. m*, **a** *f* Cossack.

coscoja *f* kermes oak.

coscorrón *m* bump on the head.

cosecha *f* crop, harvest (*a. fig.*); (*acto*) harvesting; (*época*) harvest time; *de* ~ *propia* ❦ home-grown; *de su propia* ~ *fig.* out of one's own head, of one's own invention; *la* ~ *de 1949* (*vino*) the 1949 vintage; **cosechadora** *f* ⊕ (combine) harvester; **cosechar** [1a] harvest, gather (in); *esp. fig.* reap; **cosechero** *m*, **a** *f* harvester, reaper.

coseno *m* cosine.

coser [2a] sew (up, on); stitch (up; *a.* ⚕); *fig.* join closely (*con* to); *v. puñalada*; *ser cosa de* ~ *y cantar* be smooth sailing, be a cinch; **~se** *con* become attached to; **cosido** *m* sewing.

cosmético *adj. a. su. m* cosmetic.

cósmico cosmic; **cosmografía** *f* cosmography; **cosmógrafo** *m* cosmographer; **cosmonauta** *m* cosmonaut; **cosmonave** *f* spaceship; **cosmonavegación** *f* space travel; **cosmopolita** *adj. a. su. m/f* cosmopolitan; **cosmos** *m* cosmos; universe.

cosquillar [1a] tickle; **cosquillas** *f/pl.* tickling (sensation); F *buscarle a uno las* ~ stir s.o. up; *hacer* ~ *a* tickle; *fig.* tickle *s.o.'s* curiosity; *tener* ~ be ticklish; *tener malas* ~ be touchy; **cosquillear** [1a] tickle; **cosquilleo** *m* tickling (sensation); **cosquilloso** ticklish; *fig.* touchy.

costa[1] *f* † cost, price; ~*s pl.* ⚖ costs; † *a* ~ at cost; *a* ~ *de* at the expense of; *a toda* ~ at any price.

costa[2] *f* ⚓ coast; coastline, (sea) shore; **costado** *m anat.*, ⚓ side; ⚔ flank; *de cuatro* ~*s* downright; *por los cuatro* ~*s* on both sides of the family; **costal** *m* sack, bag; F ~ *de huesos* bag of bones; **costaneras** *f/pl.* △ rafters; **costanero** steep; ⚓ coastal.

costar [1m] cost (*a. fig.*); *fig.* cost dear(ly); *cuesta caro* it costs a lot; *cueste lo que cueste* cost what it may.

costarricense *adj. a. su. m/f*, **costarriqueño** *adj. a. su. m*, **a** *f* Costa Rican.

coste *m* cost, price; *a* ~ *y costas* at cost; without profit; **costear**[1] [1a] pay for, defray the cost of; (*poder* ~) afford.

costear[2] [1a] ⚓ (sail along the) coast.

costera *f* side *de paquete*; *geog.* slope; ⚓ coast; *pesca*: fishing season; **costero** coastal; coasting.

costilla *f* rib; ~*s pl.* F back; F *mi* ~ my better half; *medir las* ~ *a* tan; **costilludo** strapping.

costo *m* cost; ~ *de la vida* cost of living; **costoso** costly, expensive.

costra *f* crust; ⚕ scab; **costroso** crusty, incrusted; ⚕ scabby.

costumbre *f* custom, habit; ~*s pl.*

customs, ways; (*moralidad*) morals; *de* ~ usual(ly); *como de* ~ as usual; *tener por* ~ *inf.* be in the habit of *ger.*

costura *f* sewing, needlework, dressmaking; (*unión*) seam; *alta* ~ fashion designing; *de* ~ *francesa medias* fully-fashioned; *sentar las* ~*s a fig.* tan; **costur(e)ar** [1a] *C.Am.*, *Mex.* sew; **costurera** *f* dressmaker, seamstress.

cota *f*: ~ *de malla* coat of mail.

cotejar [1a] compare, collate; **cotejo** *m* comparison, collation.

cotí *m* ticking.

cotidiano daily, everyday.

cotiledón *m* cotyledon.

cotización *f* quotation, price *en bolsa*; quota; dues *de asociación*; **cotizar** [1f] quote (*en* at); *cuota* fix.

coto *m* ⚘ enclosed pasture; preserve *de caza*; (*mojón*) boundary post; ~ *cerrado fig.* closed shop; *poner* ~ *a* put a stop to.

cotorra *f* parrot; (*urraca*) magpie; **cotorrear** [1a] chatter (away); gossip; F gab; **cotorreo** *m* chatter, gabble; **cotorrera** *f* F chatterbox.

coturno *m* buskin; *de alto* ~ lofty, elevated.

coy *m* ⚓ hammock.

coyuntura *f anat.* joint; *fig.* juncture, occasion; opportunity.

coz *f* kick (*a.* ⚔); (*culata*) butt; F insult; *dar coces, dar de coces a* kick; *v. aguijón*; *tirar coces* lash out (*a. fig.*).

crac *m* † crash; ¡~! snap!, crack!

crampón *m* crampon.

cráneo *m* skull, cranium 📖.

crápula *f* drunkenness; *fig.* dissipation; **crapuloso** drunken; *fig.* dissipated.

crasitud *f* fatness; **craso** *p.* fat; *liquido* thick, greasy; *fig.* gross, crass.

cráter *m* crater.

creación *f* creation; **creador** **1.** creative; **2.** *m*, **-a** *f* creator; originator; **crear** [1a] create, make; *idea etc.* originate; found, establish.

crecer [2d] *mst* grow (*a. fig.*; *en* in); increase; (*luna*) wax; (*precio, río*) rise; (*días*) get longer; *dejar* ~ *barba* grow; ~**se** assume greater authority (*or* importance); **creces** *f/pl.* growth; increase; F *con* ~ with a vengeance; *devolver etc.* with interest; **crecida** *f* spate, flood; **crecido** large; ⚘, *p. etc.* (full-)grown; *río* in flood; **creciente** **1.** growing, increasing; *ast. cuarto* ~ crescent (moon); **2.** *m* crescent; **3.** *f* ⚓ ~ (*del mar*) high tide; *ast.* crescent moon; **crecimiento** *m* growth, increase; † rise in value; ~ *cero* zero growth.

credenciales *f/pl.* credentials; **credibilidad** *f* credibility; believability; **crediticio** † credit *attr.*; **crédito** *m mst* credit; authority, standing; (*creencia*) belief; *a* ~ on credit; *abrir* ~ *a* give credit to; *dar* ~ *a fig.* believe (in).

credo *m* creed; credo; F *en menos que se canta un* ~ in a jiffy; **credulidad** *f* credulity, gullibility; **crédulo** credulous, gullible; **creederas:** F *tiene buenas* ~ he'll swallow anything; **creencia** *f* belief; **creer** [2e] believe (*en* in; *que* that); think (*que* that); *creo que sí* (*no*) I (don't) think so; *lo creo* I think so; *¡ya lo creo!* you bet (your life)!, rather!; I should say so!; ~**se** believe o.s. (to be); **creíble** believable, credible; **creído** credulous; *S.Am.* gullible.

crema *f* (*nata*) cream (*a fig.*); (*natillas*) custard, cream; (*salsa*) sweet sauce; (*cosmético*) cold cream; ~ *dental* (*or dentífrica*) toothpaste.

cremación *f* cremation.

cremallera *f* ⊕ rack; *mot. dirección de* ~ rack and pinion steering; (*cierre de*) ~ zipper.

crémor *m*: ~ (*tártaro*) cream of tartar; **cremoso** creamy.

crencha *f pelo* part, parting.

creosota *f* creosote.

crepitar [1a] (*leña etc.*) crackle; (*tocino*) sizzle; crepitate (*a.* ⚕).

crepuscular twilight; *luz* ~ = **crepúsculo** *m* twilight, dusk.

cresa *f* maggot.

crespo curly; *estilo* involved; *p.* cross; **crespón** *m* crape.

cresta *f* crest.

creta *f* chalk; **cretáceo** cretaceous.

cretinez *f* utter stupidity; **cretino** *m* cretin (*a. fig.*).

cretona *f* cretonne.

cretoso chalky.

creyente *m/f* believer.

creyón *m* crayon.

cría *f* keeping, breeding *etc.*; (*pequeño*) young child *or* animal; (*conjunto*) litter, young, brood; de ~ *attr.* breeding; ~ *de ganado* cattle breeding, stock raising; **criada** *f* maid, servant; ~ *por horas* charwoman; ~ *para todo* general housemaid; **criadero** *m* ⊕ nursery; *zo.* breeding ground; ⚒ vein; **criado** **1.**: *bien* ~ well-bred, well brought up; *mal* ~ ill-bred; **2.** *m* servant; **criador** *m* breeder; **crianza** *f* raising, rearing; *physiol.* lactation; *fig.* breeding; *sin* ~ ill-bred; **criar** [1c] *ganado etc.* keep, breed, raise; (*educar*) bring up; (*cebar*) fatten; ~ (*a los pechos*) breast-feed, nurse; (*tierra*) produce, grow; *fig.* foster, nurture; *necesidad etc.* create; **~se** ⚘ *etc.* grow; **criatura** *f* creature (*a. fig.*); (*nene*) infant, baby.

criba *f* sieve, screen; **cribar** [1a] sift, sieve, screen.

cric *m* ⊕ jack; ~ *de cremallera* ratchet jack.

crimen *m* crime; **criminal** *adj. a. su. m/f* criminal; **criminalidad** *f* criminality; **criminología** *f* criminology.

crin *f* mane (*a.* ~*es pl.*); horsehair.

crío *m* F kid, child.

criollo *adj. a. su. m,* **a** *f* Creole.

cripta *f* crypt.

crisálida *f* chrysalis.

crisis *f* crisis; ~ *energética* energy crisis; ~ *nerviosa* nervous breakdown; *llegar a la* ~ come to a head.

crisma *f eccl.* chrism; *sl.* nut, bean; *sl. romper la* ~ *a* brain.

crisol *m* crucible; *fig.* melting pot.

crispar [1a] make; *s.t.* twitch; **~se** twitch.

cristal *m* glass, crystal (*a. phys., poet.*); (*hoja*) pane (of glass); (*espejo*) mirror; *de* ~ glass *attr.*; ~*es pl. emplomados* leaded lights; ⚓ ~ *de patente* bull's-eye; ~ *de roca* rock crystal; ~ *tallado* cut glass; **cristalería** *f* (*arte*) glasswork; (*fábrica*) glassworks; (*objetos*) glassware; **cristalino** *phys.* crystalline; *agua* limpid; **cristalización** *f* crystallization; **cristalizar**(**se**) [1f] crystallize.

cristianar [1a] F christen, baptize; **cristiandad** *f* Christendom; **cristianismo** *m* Christianity; **cristianizar** [1f] Christianize; **cristiano** **1.** *adj. a. su. m,* **a** *f* Christian; **2.** *m* F (*p.*) (living) soul; person; (*idioma*) Spanish; **cristo** *m* crucifix.

criterio *m* criterion; yardstick; (*juicio*) judgment; *formar un* ~ *sobre* arrive at an assessment of.

crítica *f* criticism; (*reseña*) review, notice; *b.s.* gossip; **criticador** **1.** critical; **2.** *m,* **-a** *f* critic; **criticar** [1g] criticize; **crítico** **1.** critical; **2.** *m* critic; **criticón** **1.** faultfinding, (over)critical; **2.** *m,* **-a** *f* faultfinder, critic; **critiquizar** [1f] F be over-critical of, be down on.

croar [1a] croak.

croata *adj. a. su. m/f* Croat(ian).

croché *m* crochet (work); *hacer* ~ crochet.

cromado **1.** chromium-plated, chrome; **2.** *m* chromium plating; **cromo** *m* chromium; *paint.* transfer; F color reproduction, picture; **cromolitografía** *f* chromolithograph.

crónica *f* chronicle; account; (*periódico*) newspaper; (*artículo*) report; feature story; ~ *literaria* literary page; **crónico** chronic; *vicio* ingrained; **cronista** *m/f* chronicler; (*periodista*) reporter, feature writer; **cronología** *f* chronology; **cronológico** chronological; **cronometrador** *m* timekeeper; **cronometraje** *m* ⊕ timing; **cronometrar** [1a] time; F clock; **cronómetro** *m* chronometer; *deportes etc.*: stop watch.

croqueta *f* croquette, rissole *approx.*

croquis *m* sketch.

crótalo *m* rattlesnake.

cruce *m* cross(ing); 🚸 *etc.* intersection; ~ *de caminos* crossroads; *teleph. hay un* ~ *en las líneas* the wires are crossed; **crucero** *m* ⚓ (*barco*) cruiser; ⚓ (*viaje*) cruise; ⛪ transept; (*encrucijada*) crossroads, crossing (*a.* 🚂); *misil* ~ ⚔ cruise missile; **cruceta** *f* crosspiece; **crucificar** [1g] crucify; *fig.* mortify; **crucifijo** *m* crucifix; **crucifixión** *f* crucifixion; **cruciforme** cruciform; **crucigrama** *m* crossword.

crudeza *f* rawness *etc.*; *con* ~ *hablar* harshly, roughly; **crudo** *comida, seda, tiempo etc.* raw; (*áspero*) rough; *agua, verdad* hard; *legumbres etc.* green, uncooked; *fruta*

unripe; *pan* doughy; *fig. expresión, manera* crude.
cruel cruel; **crueldad** *f* cruelty.
cruento *lit.* gory, bloody.
crujía *f* △ corridor; △ bay *entre muros*; ⚕ ward; *pasar etc. una* ~ have a tough time.
crujido *m* rustle *etc.*; **crujir** [3a] (*hojas, papel, seda*) rustle; swish *por el aire*; (*madera*) creak; (*hueso*) crack; (*tierra*) crunch; (*dientes*) gnash, grind.
crup *m* ⚕ croup.
crustáceo *m* crustacean.
cruz *f* cross (*a. fig.*); tails *de moneda*; crown *de ancla*; *zo.* withers; ~ *de Malta* Maltese cross; ♀ *Roja* Red Cross; *¡~ y raya!* that's enough!; *en* ~ crosswise; (*brazos*) crossed; *firmar con una* ~ make one's mark; *hacer la* ~ *a* have done with; *hacerse cruces* cross o.s.; *fig.* show one's surprise; *quedar en* ~ be in an agonizing situation; **cruza** *f S.Am.* intersection; crossbreeding; **cruzada** *f* crusade; **cruzado 1.** crossed; *chaqueta* double-breasted; *zo.* crossbred, hybrid; **2.** *m hist.* crusader; *~s pl. paint.* shading; **cruzar** [1f] *mst* cross; *palabras* have, exchange; **~se** pass each other.
cuaco *m S.Am.* horse.
cuaderna *f* ⚓ timber; ⚓ frame; **cuaderno** *m* notebook; (*folleto*) folder; ~ *de bitácora*, ~ *de trabajo* logbook.
cuadra *f* ⚒ stable; ⚕ ward; (*sala*) hall; ⚔ hut; *S.Am.* △ block; **cuadrada** *f* breve; **cuadrado 1.** square (*a.* ∡); *tela* checkered; *p.* square-shouldered; *niño* handsome; *b.s.* stupid; **2.** *m* square; (*regla*) ruler; ⊕ die; *sew.* gusset; *typ.* quadrat; **cuadragésimo** fortieth; **cuadrante** *m* ∡, ⚓ quadrant; *radio etc.*: dial; *reloj* face; **cuadrar** [1a] *v/t.* square (*a.* ∡); (*agradar*) please; (*convenir*) suit; *v/i.*: *~ con* square with, tally with; **~se** ⚔ stand to attention; F get very solemn; (*resistir*) refuse to budge; **cuadratura** *f* quadrature; **cuadricular** squared; **cuadrilátero** *adj. a. su. m* quadrilateral; *boxeo*: ring; **cuadrilongo** *adj. a. su. m* oblong.
cuadrilla *f* party, gang; *esp.* ⚔ squad; group; *toros*: matador's team; **cuadrillero** *m* chief, leader; ⊕ foreman.
cuadrito *m*: *cortar en ~s pl. cocina*: dice.
cuadro *m* square (*a.* ∡); (*tabla*) table, chart; ⚡ *etc.* panel; *paint.* picture (*a. televisión*), painting; (*marco, bastidor*) frame; pane *de vidrio*; ⚒ bed; ⚔ (*p.*) staff, cadre; *thea.* scene; *lit.* (vivid) picture; ~ *alpino* rock garden; *teleph.* ~ *de conexión manual*, ⚡ ~ *de distribución* switchboard; ~ *de mando mot.* dashboard; instrument panel; ~ *vivo* tableau; *a ~s tela* check; *2 metros en* ~ 2 meters square; **cuadrúpedo** *adj. a. su. m* quadruped; four-legged; **cuádruple** quadruple; **cuadruplicar**(**se**) [1g] quadrupl(icat)e; **cuádruplo** *m* quadruple.
cuajada *f* curd; (*requesón*) cream cheese; **cuajado** *fig.* dumbfounded; F asleep; ~ *de* full of; **cuajaleche** *m* ⚘ bedstraw; **cuajar** [1a] *v/t. leche* curdle; *sangre etc.* coagulate, congeal; F be to *s.o.'s* liking; *Mex.* tell a lie; *v/i.* F (*proyecto*) take shape; (*tener éxito*) come off; **~se** curdle *etc.*; set; *fig.* sleep soundly; F ~ *de* fill with; **cuajarón** *m* clot; **cuajo** *m* rennet; *de* ~ by the roots.
cual 1. *adj.* (such) as, of the kind (that); **2.** *pron. el etc.* ~ which; (*p.*) who; *lo* ~ (a fact) which; *con lo* ~ at which, whereupon; *por lo* ~ (and) so, and because of this; whereby; **3.** *prp.* ~ *su.* like; ~ *verb* (just) as; ~ ... *tal su.*: like ... like; *verb*: just as ... so; *a* ~ *más* vying with each other; *gritar a* ~ *más* see who can shout the loudest; **4.** *cj.*: ~ *si* as if; *v. tal.*
cuál which (one)?; *~(es)* ... *~(es)* some ... some; *si* ..., *¿~ debe ser el hijo?* if ..., what must the son be like?
cualidad *f* quality, characteristic; *phls. etc.* property; **cualitativo** qualitative.
cualquier(**a**), *pl.* **cualesquier**(**a**) **1.** *adj.* any (... you like); ~ *que* whichever, whatever; **2.** *pron.* anyone; ~ *que* (*cosa*) whichever; (*p.*) whoever; *un* ~ a nobody.
cuan: *tan* ... ~ as ... as.
cuán how.
cuando 1. *cj.* when; (*aunque*) (even) if, although; (*puesto que*) since; ~

más at most; ~ *menos* at least; ~ *quiera* whenever; *de* ~ *en* ~ from time to time; **2.** *prp.* at the time of.

cuándo when?; ~ ... ~ sometimes ... sometimes; *¿de* ~ *acá?* how come?

cuantía *f* quantity; importance; *de mayor* ~ first-rate; *de poca* ~ of small account, not much of a ...; **cuantioso** large, substantial; numerous; **cuantitativo** quantitative.

cuanto 1. *adj.* all that, as much as, whatever; ~*s pl.* all that; *unos* ~*s* a few, some; ~*s más ... tantos más* the more ... the more; *creía* ~*as historias escuchaba* he believed all the stories he heard; **2.** *pron.* all that (which), as much as; ~*s pl.* all those that, as many as; *v. tanto*; ~*(s) más, mejor* the more the merrier; **3.** *adv. a. cj.*: *en* ~ inasmuch as; *tiempo*: as soon as, directly; *(en)* ~ *a* as for, with regard to; ~ *más* at least; ~ *más adv.* the more *adv.*; ~ *más que* all the more because; *por* ~ ... *por tanto* inasmuch as ... therefore; ~ *más ... menos* the more ... the less.

cuánto how much?; ~*s pl.* how many?; ~ *(tiempo)* how long?; *¿a* ~*s estamos?* what is the date?; *¡*~ *me alegro!* I'm so glad!

cuarenta forty; **cuarentena** *f* (about) forty; ⚕ quarantine.

cuaresma *f* Lent; **cuaresmal** Lenten.

cuarta *f* ⅍ quarter, fourth; ⚓ point; span *de mano*; **cuartazos** *m* F fat old thing; **cuartear** [1a] quarter; *(descuartizar)* cut up; *brújula* box; ~**se** crack, split.

cuartel *m* ⚔ barracks; *heráldica*: quarter; ⛏ bed; ~*es pl.* ⚔ quarters; ~ *general* headquarters; *no dar* ~ give no quarter; **cuartelazo** *m* *S.Am.* military take-over; putsch; **cuarteto** *m* ♪ quartet; *poet.* quatrain; **cuartilla** *f (hoja)* sheet; *anat.* pastern; **cuartillo:** F *andar a tres* ~*s* be on the rocks.

cuarto 1. fourth; **2.** *m* ⅍, *ast.* quarter; ⚠ room; joint *de carne*; ~*s pl.* F dough, brass; ~ *de baño* bathroom; ~ *creciente (menguante)* first (last) quarter; ~ *de hora* quarter of an hour; *las 2 y* ~ a quarter past 2; *las 2 menos* ~ a quarter to 2; ~ *oscuro* dark room; ~ *trasero* hindquarters; *cocina*: rump; F *de tres al* ~ worthless; *en* ~ *typ.* quarto; F *por cuatro* ~*s* for a song; F *sin un* ~ stone-broke; F *tener* ~*s* be rolling in it; F *no tener un* ~ not have a cent.

cuarzo *m* quartz.

cuaternario quaternary; **cuatrillizos** *m/pl.*, ~**as** *f/pl.* quadruplets; **cuatrimotor** four-engine(d).

cuatro four *(a. su.)*; *(fecha)* fourth; *las* ~ four o'clock; *Mex.* deceit; swindle; F *más de* ~ quite a few; **cuatrocientos** four hundred.

cuba *f* cask, barrel; *(abierta)* vat; F boozer.

cubano *adj. a. su. m*, **a** *f* Cuban.

cubertería *f* silver(ware); tableware; cutlery.

cubeta *f* keg; *(cubo)* pail; *phot.* tray.

cubicar [1g] ⅍ cube; *phys.* determine the volume of; **cúbico** cubic, cubical; *raíz* cube *attr.*; **cubículo** *m* cubicle.

cubierta *f* cover(ing); ⊕ casing; ⚓ deck; *(sobre)* envelope; cover, jacket *de libro*; *mot.* tire(casing); ~ *de cama* coverlet; **cubierto 1.** *p.p. of cubrir*; **2.** *m* ⚠ roof; place *en mesa*; *(juego)* knife fork and spoon; *(comida)* meal; ~*s pl.* cutlery; ~ *de 30 pesetas* 30 peseta menu; *precio de* ~ cover charge; *ponerse a* ~ take cover, shelter (*de* from).

cubil *m* den, lair.

cubilete *m cocina*: copper pan; *(juego)* dice box.

cubismo *m* cubism; **cubista** *m* cubist.

cúbito *m* ulna.

cubo *m* bucket, pail; tub; ⊕ drum; hub *de rueda*; ⅍ cube; ~ *de basuras* trash pail; garbage can.

cubrecama *m* coverlet.

cubrir [3a; *p.p. cubierto*] *mst* cover (up, over; *con, de* with); ⚠ roof; *deuda* repay; *fuego* bank up; *vacante* fill; *me cubre (agua)* I'm out of my depth; ~**se** *(con sombrero)* put on one's hat.

cuca *f sl.* tart, whore.

cucaña *f* F cinch; **cucañero** *m*, **a** *f* F fly one; *(gorrón)* hanger-on; *(ambicioso)* social climber.

cucaracha *f* roach, cockroach.

cuclillas: *sentarse en* ~ squat, sit on one's heels.

cuclillo *m* cuckoo; F cuckold.
cuco 1. (*bonito*) pretty, cute; *situación*: fine; (*taimado*) crafty; **2.** *m orn.* cuckoo; F gambler; *hacer ~ a* poke fun at.
cucurucho *m* (paper) cone, cornet; (*sombrero*) horn, hennin.
cuchara *f* spoon; scoop (*a.* ⚓); ⊕ ladle; **cucharada** *f* spoonful; *meter su ~* butt in *en conversación*; meddle *en asunto*; **cucharear** [1a] spoon out, ladle out; ↗ pitch; **cucharetear** [1a] F *fig.* meddle; **cucharilla** *f*, **cucharita** *f* small spoon, teaspoon; **cucharón** *m* ladle.
cuchichear [1a] whisper; **cuchicheo** *m* whispering.
cuchilla *f* (large) knife; chopper *de carnicero*; runner *de patín*; blade *de arma*; *geog.* ridge; **cuchillada** *f* (*golpe*) slash; (*herida*) gash; *~s pl. sew.* slash, slit; *fig.* fight; **cuchillería** *f* cutlery; ✝ cutler's (shop); **cuchillero** *m* cutler; **cuchillo** *m* knife; ⚠ upright; *pasar a ~* put to the sword.
cuchipanda *f* F feed, beano.
cuchitril *m* den, hole; ⚠ hovel.
cuchufleta *f* F joke, crack.
cuelga *f* ⚘ bunch; F birthday present; **~capas** *m* coat hanger; (*mueble*) hall stand.
cuello *m* neck; collar *de camisa*; F *levantar el ~* get on one's feet again.
cuenca *f* wooden bowl; *anat.* (eye) socket; *geog.* bowl; basin, catchment area *de río*; *~ hullera*, *~ minera* coalfield; **cuenco** *m* saucer, shallow basin; *fig.* hollow.
cuenta *f* ℞ calculation, count(ing), reckoning; ✝ account, bill; *~* (*de banco*) bank account; (*registro*) check, tally; (*exposición, narración*) account; bead *de rosario*; *boxeo*: count; *~ atrás* countdown; *~ corriente* current account; *~ de diversos* sundries; *~ de gastos* expense account; *~ indistinta*, *~ en participación* joint account; *a ~* on account; *de ~ attr.* important; *de ~ y riesgo de* at *s.o.'s* own risk; *en resumidas ~s* in short, in a nutshell; *por su propia ~* on one's own account, for o.s.; *abonar en ~ a* credit to (*s.o.'s* account); *ajustar ~s* settle up (*con* with); *ajustar ~s viejas fig.* pay off old scores; F *le ajusté las ~s* I told him where to get off; F *caer en la ~* catch on (*de* to); *cargar en ~ a* charge to (*s.o.'s* account); *correr por ~ de* be *s.o.'s* business; F *esto corre por mi ~* this one's on me; *dar ~ de* (*narrar*) give an account of; (*explicar*) account for; F finish off; *dar buena ~ de sí* give a good account of o.s.; *darse ~* (*de*) realize; *sin darse ~* without noticing; *pedir ~s a* bring to account; *perder la ~* lose count; *tener en ~* bear in mind, take into account; F *no tener ~ inf.* be no point in *ger.*; *¡vamos a ~s!* let's get down to business!
cuentacorrentista *m/f* depositor.
cuentakilómetros *m* odometer; speedometer.
cuentista *m/f* storyteller (*a. b.s.*); *lit.* short-story writer; (*chismoso*) gossip.
cuento *m* story, tale (*a. b.s.*); *lit.* (short) story; F trouble; *~ de hadas* fairy tale; *~ de viejas* old wives' tale; *sin ~* countless; *dejarse de ~s* come to the point; *es el ~ de nunca acabar* it's an endless business; F *¡es puro ~!* rubbish!; *traer a ~* bring up, *b.s.* drag in; *venir a ~* be apt.
cuerda *f* rope; (*delgado*) string (*a.* ♪), cord (*a. anat.*); ℞, *anat., poet.* chord; *anat.* tendon; spring *de reloj*; ♩ (*tenor etc.*) voice; *~ de arco* bowstring; *~ floja* tightrope; *~ de plomada* plumb line; *~ salvavidas* lifeline; *~ de tripa* (♪ cat)gut; *~s pl. vocales* vocal cords; F *bajo ~* on the side; *aflojar* (*apretar*) *la ~ fig.* ease (tighten) up; *dar ~ a reloj* wind (up); *estar en su ~* be in one's element.
cuerdo sensible; sane.
cuerna *f* drinking horn; ♪ horn; antler *de ciervo*; **cuerno** *m mst* horn; antler *de ciervo*; *~ de la abundancia* horn of plenty; *poner en los ~s* place in danger; *poner los ~s a* cuckold; *saber a ~ quemado fig.* leave a nasty taste; F *¡vaya al ~!* go to hell!
cuero *m* leather; *zo.* skin, hide; pelt *de conejo, zorro*; (*odre*) wine skin; *~ cabelludo* scalp; *en ~s* stark naked; F *estar hecho un ~* be as drunk as a lord.
cuerpo *m mst* body (*a.* ℞, *ast.*); (*talle*) build, figure; (*grueso*) bulk; ⚗ substance; *sew.* bodice; (*libro*) volume; ⚠ wing, part; ⚔, *baile, diplomática*: corps; (*personal*) force, brigade; corporation; *carreras*: length; *~ de baile*

corps de ballet; ~ *de bomberos* fire department; ~ *del delito* corpus delicti; ~ *de sanidad* medical corps; ~ *a* ~ hand to hand; *a* ~, *en* ~ without a coat; *a* ~ *de rey* like a prince; *de* (*mucho*) ~ *vino* full-bodied; *de* ~ *entero* full-length; *fig.* thoroughgoing; *de medio* ~ half-length; *en* ~ *y alma* fully; *dar* ~ *a* thicken; *dar con el* ~ *en tierra* fall down; *estar de* ~ *presente* be laid out, (*rey etc.*) lie in state; *hacer del* ~ relieve o.s.; *hurtar el* ~ swerve, dodge; *tomar* ~ grow, get bigger.
cuervo *m* raven.
cuesco *m* ⚘ stone.
cuesta *f* slope; hill *en carretera*; ~ *abajo* downhill; ~ *arriba* uphill; *a* ~*s* on one's back; *echar etc. a* ~*s* take on one's shoulders; *hacérsele a uno* ~ *arriba inf.* go against the grain to *inf.*, find it hard to *inf.*; *ir* ~ *abajo fig.* go downhill.
cuestación *f* (charity) collection.
cuestión *f* matter, question, issue; *b.s.* quarrel, dispute; ⚘ problem; ~ *batallona* vexed question; ~ *candente*, ~ *palpitante* burning question; *en* ~ in question, at issue; **cuestionable** questionable; **cuestionar** [1a] question, argue about; place in doubt; **cuestionario** *m* questionnaire; question paper *en examen*.
cueva *f* cave; cellar *de casa*.
cuévano *m* pannier.
cuidado *m* (*esmero*) care; (*aprensión*) worry, concern; (*negocio*) concern, affair; *¡~!* look out!, mind!; (*en paquete*) with care; *¡~ con ...!* careful with ...!; beware of ...!; *¡~ con inf.!* be careful to *inf.*, see you *inf.*; *¡~ conmigo!* you watch your step!; *al* ~ *de* care of; *enfermar de* ~ fall seriously ill; *estar con* ~ be anxious; ⚕ *estar de* ~ be gravely ill; *¡no hay ~!*, *¡pierda Vd. ~!* don't worry!; *poner* ~ *en inf.* take great care in *ger.*; *tener* ~ take care; be careful (*con* of), watch out (*con* for); *tener* ~ *de* mind; *v. tener*, *traer*; **cuidadora** *f Mex.* nursemaid; **cuidadoso** careful; mindful (*de* of); solicitous (*de* for); concerned, anxious (*de*, *por resultado etc.* about).
cuidar [1a] *v/t.* take care of, look after (*a.* ⚕); see to; *v/i.*: ~ *de* look after; *obligación* attend to; ~ *de que* see (to it) that; ~**se** ⚕ look after o.s.; *b.s.* look after number one; ~ *de* worry about; ~ *de inf.* be careful to *inf.*
cuita *f* worry, affliction; **cuitado** worried; timid.
cuja *f* bedstead.
culata *f zo.* haunch; butt *de fusil*; breech *de cañón*; head *de cilindro*; **culatazo** *m* kick, recoil.
culebra *f* snake; ~ *de cascabel* rattlesnake; **culebrear** [1a] wriggle (along).
culí *m* coolie.
culibajo F dumpy.
culinario culinary.
culminación *f* culmination; **culminante** highest, top(most); *fig.* outstanding; **culminar** [1a] culminate, reach its highest point.
culo *m* seat; bottom; anus; F behind.
culpa *f* fault, blame; *esp.* ⚖ guilt; *echar la* ~ *a* blame (*de* for); *tener la* ~ be to blame (*de* for); *Vd. tiene la* ~ it's your fault; **culpabilidad** *f* guilt; **culpable 1.** *p.* to blame, at fault; *esp.* ⚖ guilty; *acto* to be condemned, ⚖ culpable; *confesarse* ~ plead guilty; **2.** *m/f* culprit; *esp.* ⚖ offender, guilty party; **culpado 1.** guilty; **2.** *m*, **a** *f* culprit; ⚖ accused; **culpar** [1a] blame; condemn; ~ *de* accuse *s.o.* of being.
cultivable cultivable; **cultivadora** *f* ⊕ cultivator; **cultivador** *m*, **-a** *f* farmer, cultivator; grower; **cultivar** [1a] cultivate (*a. fig.*); *tierras a.* work, till; *plantas a.* grow; *memoria etc.* develop; **cultivo** *m* cultivation; (*plantas*) crop; *biol.* culture; **culto 1.** cultured, refined; *gr.* learned; **2.** *m* worship; cult (*a* of); *rendir* ~ *a* worship; *fig.* pay homage to; **cultura** *f* culture; education; *de* (*gran*) ~ cultured; **cultural** cultural.
cumbre *f* summit, top; *fig.* summit, height; *conferencia en la* ~ summit meeting.
cumpa *m S.Am.* pal, buddy; comrade; *sl.* gumbah.
cumpleaños *m* birthday; **cumplido 1.** full, complete; *p.* courteous; **2.** *m* courtesy; ~*s pl.* compliments; *de* ~ formal; *por* ~ as a compliment; out of politeness; *¡sin ~s!* make yourself at home!; *venir de* ~ come out of a sense of duty.
cumplimentar [1a] congratulate;

(*visitar*) pay one's respects to; ⚖ carry out; **cumplimentero** effusive; **cumplimiento** *m* (*acto*) fulfillment *etc.*; (*cumplido*) compliment; courtesy; *de* ~ courtesy *attr.*; *por* ~ as a matter of courtesy; *hacer* ~*s* pay compliments.

cumplir [3a] *v/t. amenaza, deber, promesa* carry out, fulfil; *deseo* realize; *acto* perform; *años* reach; *condena* serve; *hoy cumplo 6 años* I'm 6 (years old) today; *¡que los cumplas muy felices!* many happy returns of the day!; *v/i.* (*plazo etc.*) expire; ⚔ finish one's service; *no le cumple a él inf.* it is not his place to *inf.*; ~ *con* = *v/t.*; *p.* do one's duty by; ~ *por* act on behalf of; *por* ~ as a mere formality; ~**se** be fulfilled *etc.*; (*plazo*) expire.

cumulativo cumulative; **cúmulo** *m* heap; *fig.* lot; *meteor.* cumulus.

cuna *f* cradle (*a.* ⚓, *fig.*); (*asilo*) home; *fig.* family; birth.

cundir [3a] spread (*a. fig.*); (*arroz*) swell; *fig.* multiply; *b.s.* be rampant, be rife.

cuneiforme cuneiform.

cuneta *f* ditch, gutter.

cuña *f* wedge; chock *de rueda*.

cuñada *f* sister-in-law; **cuñado** *m* brother-in-law.

cuñete *m* keg.

cuño *m* (die) stamp; *fig.* stamp.

cuota *f* quota; share; tuition; fare; ~ (*de socio*) membership fee; ~ *de enseñanza* school fees.

cupe *etc. v. caber.*

cupo *m* quota; share.

cupón *m* coupon; ~*es pl. en rama* ✝ stripped coupons.

cúpula *f* dome, cupola.

cuquería *f* craftiness.

cura[1] *m*: ~ (*párroco*) parish priest; (*en general*) priest.

cura[2] *f* (*acto*) healing; cure; (*método*) cure, treatment; ~ *de reposo* rest cure; ~ *de urgencia* emergency treatment, first aid; *tener* ~ be curable; F *no tiene* ~ it's quite hopeless; **curable** curable; **curación** *f* = *cura*[2]; ~ *primera* first aid; **curandero** *m* quack; **curar** [1a] *v/t. enfermedad, p., carne* cure (de of); *llaga* heal (*a. fig.*); (*tratar*) treat; *piel* tan; *madera* season; *mal etc.* remedy, put right; *v/i.*: ~ de look after; *palabras etc.* take notice of; ~**se** recover (*de* from), get better; **curativo** healing; curative.

curda: F *estar* (*con la*) ~ be tight.

cureña *f* gun carriage; F *a* ~ *rasa* out in the open.

curiosear [1a] *v/t.* (*mirar*) glance at, look over; (*husmear*) nose out; *tiendas etc.* have a look round; *v/i.* poke about, nose around; *b.s.* snoop; **curiosidad** *f* curiosity; *b.s.* inquisitiveness; (*objeto*) curio; (*aseo*) cleanness; **curioso 1.** curious; *b.s.* inquisitive; (*aseado*) neat, clean; (*esmerado*) careful; F odd; ~ *de* eager for; ~ *por inf.* eager to *inf.*; **2.** *m*, **a** *f* bystander, onlooker; *b.s.* busybody; *S.Am.* quack doctor; *los* ~*s de la literatura* those interested in literature.

curro *prov.* smart; *b.s.* showy; **currutaco** F **1.** swell, showy; **2.** *m* dude, sport.

cursado experienced, skilled; **cursante** *m/f S.Am.* student; **cursar** [1a] *v/t. lugar* frequent; *asignatura* take; *solicitud* facilitate, dispatch; *v/i.*: *el mes que cursa* the present month.

cursear [1a] *S.Am.* have diarrhea.

cursi 1. (*de mal gusto*) in bad taste, cheap, vulgar; pretentious, posh, genteel; affected; (*llamativo*) loud, flashy; (*desaseado*) shabby-genteel, dowdy; **2.** *m/f* = *cursilón*; **cursilería** *f* vulgarity; pretentiousness *etc.*; **cursilón** *m*, **-a** *f* F posh sort, one of the genteel sort; flashy type.

cursivo cursive.

curso *m* course; *univ.* (*ps., año*) year; *moneda de* ~ *legal* legal tender; *dar* ~ *a solicitud* deal with; **cursor** *m* ⊕ slide.

curtido 1. *piel* leathery; *tez* tanned, weather-beaten; *estar* ~ *en* be skilled in; be accustomed to; **2.** *m* tanning; ~*s pl.* tanned hides; **curtidor** *m* tanner; **curtiduría** *f* tannery; **curtir** [3a] tan (*a. fig.*); (*acostumbrar*) inure, harden.

curva *f* curve; *mot. etc. a.* bend; ~ *de nivel* contour line; **curvatura** *f* curvature; **curvo** curved.

cúspide *f geog.* peak; ⩓ apex.

custodia *f* care, safe keeping; ⚖ *etc.* custody; (*p.*) guard; *eccl.* monstrance; ~ *preventiva* protective custody; **custodiar** [1b] keep; (*vigilar*) guard, watch over; **custodio** *m* guard(ian), keeper; caretaker *de casa*.

cususa *f S.Am.* rum.

cutáneo cutaneous.

cúter *m* cutter.

cutí *m* ticking.

cutícula *f* cuticle.

cutis *m* skin, complexion.

cuyo whose; *en ~ caso* in which case.

¡cuz, cuz! here boy! (*dog*).

Ch

chabacanería *f* (piece of) vulgarity, bad taste; (*objeto*) shoddy piece of work; (*dicho*) platitude; (*dicho grosero*) coarse thing; **chabacano** vulgar, in bad taste; shoddy; crude, coarse.
chabola *f* shack.
chacal *m* jackal.
chacarero *m S.Am.* farm laborer.
chacolotear [1a] clatter.
chacota *f* fun and games, high jinks; *echar a* ~, *hacer* ~ *de* make fun of; **chacotear** [1a] have fun; **chacotero** fond of a laugh.
chacra *f S.Am.* small farm.
chacuaco 1. crude, repugnant; **2.** *m C.Am.* cigar butt.
chacha *f* F (nurse)maid.
cháchara *f* F small talk, chatter; ~*s pl.* junk; **chacharear** [1a] F chatter, jaw; **chacharero** *m*, **a** *f* F chatterbox.
chacho *m* F boy, lad.
chafallar [1a] F botch, make a mess of; **chafallo** *m* F botched job.
chafar [1a] (*aplastar*) flatten; (*arrugar*) crumple; F bring *s.o.* up short.
chafarote *m* cutlass; F sword.
chafarrinón *m* stain, spot; *echar un* ~ *a* throw dirt at (*a. fig.*).
chaflán *m* bevel, chamfer; **chaflanar** [1a] bevel, chamfer.
chagrén *m* shagreen.
chaira *f* steel *de carnicero*; shoemaker's knife.
chal *m* shawl.
chalado F dotty, round the bend; *estar* ~ *por* be crazy about.
chalán *m* (*esp.* horse) dealer.
chalana *f* wherry, scow.
chalanear [1a] *v/t. p.* beat down, haggle with; *negocio* handle cleverly; *v/i.* bargain shrewdly.
chalar [1a] F drive *s.o.* round the bend; ~**se** go crazy; ~ *por* be crazy about.
chaleco *m* vest; ~ *salvavidas* life jacket; *al* ~ *Mex.* by force; for nothing; **chalecón** *m Mex.* crook.
chalet [tʃaˈle] *m* (*rural*) villa, cottage; (*suizo*) chalet; house *en ciudad*; *golf*: clubhouse.
chalina *f* cravat.
chalote *m* shallot.
chalupa 1. *f* (open) boat, launch; *S.Am.* corncake; **2.** *m sl.* madman; **3.** *adj. sl.* crazy.
chamaco *m*, **a** *f C.Am., Mex., Col.* boy; girl; youngster.
chamarasca *f* brushwood (fire).
chamarra *f* sheepskin jacket.
chamba *f* F fluke.
chambelán *m* chamberlain.
chambón F awkward, clumsy; (*con suerte*) lucky; **chambonada** *f* F clumsiness; (*chiripa*) fluke.
chambra *f* housecoat.
chamizo *m* F den, joint.
champaña *m* champagne.
champiñón *m* mushroom.
champú *m* shampoo.
champurrar [1a] *bebidas* mix.
chamullar [1a] *sl.* speak, talk.
chamuscar [1g] scorch, singe; **chamusquina** *f* F row; dispute; *huele a* ~ it smells fishy.
chance *m S.Am.* chance; **chancear(se)** [1a] crack jokes; fool around (*con* with), play about; **chancero 1.** fond of joking *etc.*; **2.** *m* one for a lark.
chancillería *f* chancery.
chancla *f* old shoe; = **chancleta 1.** *f* slipper; **2.** *m/f* F good-for-nothing; **chanclo** *m* clog; galosh, overshoe *de goma*.
chancro *m* ⚕ chancre.
chanchi *sl.* **1.** *adv. sentar etc.* marvelously; *me fue* ~ I had a fine time; **2.** *adj.*: *¡estás* ~*!* I think you're wonderful!
chancho *S.Am.* **1.** dirty; **2.** *m* pig.
chanchullero *m* F crook, twister; **chanchullo** *m* F dirty business, fiddle, wangle; *andar en* ~*s* be on the fiddle.

chanflón misshapen; (*basto*) coarse, crude.
changarro *m S.Am.* small shop.
chantaje *m* blackmail; **chantajista** *m* blackmailer, racketeer.
chantre *m* cantor; precentor.
chanza *f* (*dicho*) joke; (*hecho*) piece of tomfoolery; ~*s pl.* banter; tomfoolery; *de* ~ in fun.
chao *m* chow (*de perro*).
chapa *f* plate, sheet *de metal*; metal top *de botella*; check *de guardarropa etc.*; board, panel *de madera*; (*enchapado*) veneer; (*afeite*) rouge; flush *en mejillas*; *fig.* good sense; **chapado:** ~ *a la antigua* old-fashioned.
chapalear [1a] splash (about); (*ola*) lap; = *chacolotear*.
chapar [1a] plate, cover *con metal*; veneer *con madera*; F *respuesta* come out with.
chaparra *f* kermes oak.
chaparrada *f*, **chaparrón** *m* downpour, cloudburst.
chapear [1a] = *chapar*.
chapeta *f* flush (on the cheeks).
chapín *m* clog; sandal; (dance) slipper.
chapitel *m* capital; spire *de torre*.
chapotear [1a] *v/t.* sponge (down), wet; *v/i.* splash *para salpicar*; paddle *con pies*; dabble *con manos*.
chapucear [1a] botch, bungle; **chapucería** *f* botched job, shoddy piece of work; **chapucero 1.** *objeto* badly made; *trabajo* clumsy, amateurish; *p.* bungling, slapdash; **2.** *m* bungler, bungling amateur.
chapurr(e)ar [1a] *bebidas* mix; *idioma* speak badly.
chapuz *m* ducking; dive; (*obra mala*) botched job; (*insignificante*) odd job; *dar* ~ duck, dive; **chapuzar** [1f] *v/t.* duck, dip; *v/i.*, **~se** duck, dive.
chaqué *m* morning coat; **chaqueta** *f* jacket.
chaquete *m* backgammon.
chaquetón *m* reefer, shooting jacket.
charada *f* charade.
charanga *f* brass band; **charanguero** = *chapucero*.
charca *f* pond, pool; **charco** *m* puddle; pool *de tinta etc.*; F *pasar el* ~ cross the water.
charla *f* talk (*a. radio etc.*), chat; *b.s.* chatter; (*chismes*) gossip; ~ *de chimenea* fireside chat; **charlador** talkative, gossipy; **charladuría** *f* small talk, gossip; **charlar** [1a] chat, talk; *b.s.* chatter; **charlatán 1.** talkative; **2.** *m*, **-a** *f* chatterbox, gossip; (*embaidor*) trickster; ⚕ quack; **charlatanismo** *m* charlatanism; loquacity; ⚕ quackery.
charnela *f* hinge.
charol *m* varnish; (*cuero*) patent leather; F *darse* ~ swank; **charolar** [1a] varnish, japan.
charrada *f* (piece of) bad breeding, coarse thing; F example of bad taste; flashy ornament; **charrán** *m* rascal; **charranada** *f* dirty trick.
charretera *f* epaulette.
charro 1. *p.* coarse, ill-bred; *cosa* flashy, tawdry; *vestido* loud; **2.** *m*, **a** *f fig.* coarse person; flashy person.
chascar [1a] *v/t. lengua* click; (*ronzar*) crunch; (*engullir*) swallow; *v/i.* crack; **chascarrillo** *m* funny story; **chasco** *m* trick, joke; (*decepción*) disappointment; *dar* ~ *a* pull *s.o.'s* leg; *dar un* ~ *a* play a trick on; *llevarse un* ~ be disappointed.
chasis *m* chassis.
chasquear[1] [1a] *p.* play a trick on; (*zumba*) pull *s.o.'s* leg; (*decepcionar*) disappoint; *promesa* break.
chasquear[2] [1a] *v/t. látigo* crack; *lengua* click; *dedos* snap; *v/i.* (*madera*) crack; **chasquido** *m* crack; click; snap.
chatarra *f* scrap iron, junk.
chateo *m* (*ir de* go on a) pub crawl.
chato 1. *p.* snub-nosed; pug-nosed; *nariz* snub; *cosa* low, flat; *S.Am.* common; *S.Am.* *¡~a mía!* darling!; **2.** *m* small (wine) glass.
chatunga *f sl.* smart piece.
¡chau! *S.Am.* hi there!; (*despedida*) so long!
chauvinismo *m* chauvinism; **chauvinista 1.** chauvinistic; **2.** *m/f* chauvinist.
chaval *m* F lad, boy, kid; **chavala** *f* F girl, kid.
chaveta *f* cotter(pin); F *perder la* ~ go off one's rocker; F *perder la* ~ *por* be crazy about.
¡che! *S.Am.* hey!; say!
checar [1a] *Mex.* check.
checo 1. *adj. a. su. m*, **a** *f* Czech; **2.** *m*

(*idioma*) Czech; **checoslovaco** *adj. a. su. m*, **a** *f* Czechoslovak(ian).
chelín *m* shilling.
cheque *m* check; cheque; ~ *de viajeros* traveler's check; **chequear** [1a] *C.Am., W.I.* examine; check; control; **chequeo** *m* control; checkup; **chequera** *f* checkbook.
chica *f* girl; (*chacha*) maid.
chicle *m* chewing gum.
chico 1. small, little; **2.** *m* boy; F (*hombre, camarada*) lad, fellow, chap; *los* ~*s* (*pequeños*) kids, children; ~ *de la calle* street urchin; *es buen* ~ he's a good lad.
chicolear [1a] F say nice things; flirt; **chicoleo** *m* F compliment; flirting; *decir* ~*s* say nice things; **chicolero** F flirtatious.
chicoria *f* chicory.
chicota *f* F fine girl; **chicote** *m* F fine lad; cigar (stub); **chicotear** [1a] *S.Am.* beat up; kill.
chicha[1] *f S.Am.* corn liquor; F *ni* ~ *ni limonada* not one thing or the other; (*sin interés*) dull.
chicha[2] F meat; *tener pocas* ~*s* be thin; *fig.* be weak.
chicharrero *m* oven, hothouse; F suffocating heat; **chicharro** *m* caranx, horse mackerel; **chicharrón** *m* fried crackling; *estar hecho un* ~ *cocina*: be burned to a cinder; (*p.*) be as red as a lobster.
chichear [1a] hiss.
chicho *m* hair curler.
chichón *m* ⚕ bump, swelling.
chifla *f* hiss(ing), whistle; **chiflado** F daft, barmy; **chifladura** *f* hissing, whistling; F daftness; (*acto*) daft thing; crazy idea; **chiflar** [1a] *thea.* hiss; *vino* knock back; ~**se** go wacky; go nuts; ~ *por, a. estar chiflado por* be crazy about.
chileno, chileño *adj. a. su. m*, **a** *f* Chilean.
chilla[1] *f hunt.* call.
chilla[2] *f*: (*tabla de*) ~ weatherboard, clapboard.
chillar [1a] (*gato etc.*) howl; (*ratón*) squeak; (*ave*) squawk, screech; (*p.*) (let out a) cry, yell; (*tocino*) sizzle; (*puerta*) creak; (*radio*) blare; (*frenos*) screech; (*colores*) jar; **chillido** *m* howl *etc.*; **chillón** *niño* noisy; *sonido, voz* shrill, strident; *color* gaudy, lurid.
chimenea *f* (*exterior*) chimney; ⚓ funnel; ⚒ shaft; (*hogar*) hearth; ~ (*francesa*) fireplace; (*marco de*) ~ chimney piece.
chimpancé *m* chimpanzee.
china[1] *f* china.
china[2] *f geol.* pebble.
china[3] *S.Am.* (*novia*) girlfriend; (*querida*) mistress; (*criada*) maid; (*niñera*) nursemaid.
chinarro *m* large pebble, stone.
chinchar [1a] F pester; *S.Am.* do in.
chinche *f* bug; F bore, tiresome person; *morir como* ~*s* die like flies; = **chincheta** *f* drawing pin.
chinchilla *f S.Am.* chinchilla.
chinchoso F tiresome.
chinela *f* slipper; (*chanclo*) clog.
chinesco Chinese; **chino**[1] **1.** *adj. a. su. m*, **a** *f* Chinese; **2.** *m* (*idioma*) Chinese; F double Dutch.
chino[2] *m*, **a** *f S.Am.* half-breed; mulatto; Indian.
chino[3] *m geol.* pebble.
chinorri *f sl.* dame, wench.
chipirón *m* squid.
chiquero *m* pigsty; pen *de toro.*
chiquilicuatro *m* F schemer.
chiquillada *f* childish prank; *contp.* childish thing (to do); **chiquillería** *f* F (*una* ~) crowd of youngsters; *la* ~ the kids; **chiquillo** *m*, **a** *f* kid, youngster; **chiquitín** F **1.** tiny; **2.** *m*, **-a** *f* tiny tot; **chiquito 1.** small, tiny; **2.** *m*, **a** *f* kid, youngster; F *andarse en* ~*as* beat about the bush, hum and ha.
chiribita *f* spark; ~*s pl.* F spots before the eyes; F *echar* ~*s* blow one's top; *le hacían* ~*s los ojos* his eyes lit up.
chiribitil *m* garret; (*escondrijo*) cubbyhole; F (*cuarto*) hole.
chirigota *f* F joke; (*p.*) laughing stock.
chirimbolos *m/pl.* F kitchen things.
chirimoya *f* custard apple.
chiripa *f billar*: lucky break; F fluke, stroke of luck; **chiripero** *m* lucky sort.
chirivía *f* parsnip.
chirle F tasteless, wishy-washy.
chirlo *m* gash; (*cicatriz*) long scar.
chirona *f sl.* jug; jail; slammer; clink.
chirriar [1b] (*grillo*) chirp; (*ave*) chirp, squawk; (*rueda*) creak,

squeak; (*frenos*) screech; (*tocino*) sizzle; (*p.*) sing (*or* play) out of tune; **chirrido** *m* chirp(ing) *etc.*

chirrión *m* tumbrel; squeaky cart; *S.Am.* whip.

¡chis! sh!; hush!

chisgarabís *m* F meddler, interfering sort.

chisme *m* (*murmuración*) (piece of) gossip, tale; (*trasto*) thing; ⊕ gadget; *~s pl.* gossip, tittle-tattle; (*trastos*) things, odds and ends; ⊕ tackle, paraphernalia; **chismear** [1a] gossip, tell tales; **chismería** *f*, **chismografía** *f* gossip, scandal; **chismoso 1.** gossipy; **2.** *m*, **a** *f* gossip, scandal-monger.

chispa 1. *f* spark (*a.* ⚡); *fig.* sparkle; (*gota*) drop; *caen ~s* it's drizzling; F *no dar ~* be utterly dull; *sl. estar con la ~, tener la ~* be tight; *ser una ~, tener (mucha) ~* be a lively sort; **2.** *adj. sl.*: *estar ~* be tight; **chispazo** *m* spark (*a. fig.*); (*cuento*) gossip, scandal; **chispeante** *fig.* sparkling; **chispear** [1a] spark; (*relucir*) sparkle (*a. fig.*); *meteor.* spot with rain; **chispero** spark(l)ing; **chispita** *f* F drop (of wine); **chisporrotear** [1a] (*leña*) crackle; (*aceite etc.*) splutter; (*tocino*) sizzle.

chistar [1a] speak; *no ~* not open one's mouth; *sin ~ (ni mistar)* without a word.

chiste *m* joke, funny story; (*suceso*) funny thing; *~ goma* shaggy dog story; *caer en el ~* get it; *no veo el ~* I don't see the joke.

chistera *f* (fish) basket; wicker racket; F top hat.

chistoso 1. funny, witty; **2.** *m*, **a** *f* wit.

chistu *m* (*Basque*) flute.

chita: *a la ~ callando* quietly; F on the quiet, on the sly.

chiticalla *m/f* F clam.

¡chito!, ¡chitón! sh!; shush!; quiet!

chivatazo *m sl.* tip-off; **chivatear** [1a] F split (*contra* on), squeal; **chivato** *m zo.* kid; F stool pigeon, stoolie, informer; *S.Am.* rascal; **chivo** *m* billy goat; *Col., Ecuad., Ven.* (fit of) rage.

chocante shocking; (*sorprendente*) startling, striking; *Mex.* intolerable; **chocar** [1a] *v/t.* shock; startle; ⚡ give a shock to; *vasos* clink; *mano* shake; *sl.* please; F *¡chócala!* shake (on it)!; *v/i.* ⚔ clash; *mot. etc.* collide; (*vasos*) clink; (*platos*) clatter; *~ con(tra)* knock into, run into; *mot. etc.* hit, collide with, crash into.

chocarrería *f* coarse joke; **chocarrero** coarse, dirty.

chocolate *m* chocolate; drinking chocolate; **chocolatera** *f* chocolate pot; F *mot.* crock; ⚓ hulk; **chocolatería** *f* chocolate factory; chocolate shop.

chocha perdiz *f* woodcock.

chochear [1a] dodder, be in one's dotage; (*enamorado*) be soft; **chochera** *f*, **chochez** *f* dotage; (*acto*) silly thing.

chochín *m* wren.

chocho doddering; *enamorado* silly, soft.

chófer *m* driver; (*empleado*) chauffeur.

cholo *adj. a. su. m*, **a** *f S.Am.* half-breed; half-civilized.

cholla *f* F nut.

chopa *f sl.* jacket.

chopo *m* ♀ black poplar; ⚔ F gun.

choque *m* shock (*a.* ⚡, ⚕); impact, jar, jolt; blast *de explosión*; *mot.*, 🚂 crash, smash, collision; (*ruido*) crash, clatter; clink *de vasos*; ⚔ *a. fig.* clash; *~ eléctrico* ⚕ shock therapy; *~ en cadena mot.* pile-up; mass collision.

choquezuela *f* kneecap.

chorizo *m* sausage, salami.

chorlito *m* plover; *v. cabeza.*

chorra *f sl.* luck.

chorrear [1a] *v/t.* ⚔ *sl.* dress down; *v/i.* spurt, gush (forth), spout (out); (*gotear*) drip; F trickle (away *etc.*); *~ de sudor* run with; **chorrera** *f* spout; channel; **chorretada** *f* spurt, squirt; **chorro** *m* jet (*a.* ⊕, ✈); spurt, spout; *fig.* stream; *C.Am.* faucet; tap; ✈ *a ~* jet *attr.*; *a ~s fig.* in plenty; *llover a ~s* pour; *salir a ~s* squirt out, gush forth.

chotacabras *m orn.* goatsucker, nighthawk.

chotis *m* schottische.

chova *f* chough.

choza *f* hut, shack.

christmas [ˈkrismas] *m* F Christmas card.

chubasco *m* squall, heavy shower; **chubascoso** squally, stormy; **chubasquero** *m* oilskins.

chuchería *f* knickknack; (*golosina*) tidbit, sweet.

chucho *m* F dog; ¡~! down!

chufa *f* earth almond, chufa.

chula *f* flashy sort; *S.Am.* girlfriend; **chulada** *f* vulgar thing; mean trick; (*gracioso*) funny thing; **chulear** [1a] F make fun of; *sl.* pinch, swipe; **chulería** *f* funny thing; (*aire*) flamboyant manner; **chulesco** = *chulo.*

chuleta *f* chop, cutlet; *univ. sl.* crib.

chulo 1. pert, saucy; *C.Am., Mex.* pretty; *b.s.* common, flashy; **2.** *m* *lower class madrileño*; *sl.* clever dude; (*alcahuete*) pimp.

chumacera *f* ball bearing; pillow block; journal bearing; ⚓ oarlock.

chumbera *f* prickly pear; **chumbo** *v. higo.*

chunga *f* F (*chiste*) joke; bit of fun; *estar de ~, tomar las cosas en ~* = **chungar(se)** [1a] F take things as a joke, joke, have a bit of fun.

chupada *f* suck; drag *de cigarro*; **chupado** F skinny; *falda* tight; ~ *de cara* lantern-jawed; **chupador** *m* teething ring; teat *de biberón*; **chupar** [1a] suck; ⚘ absorb, take in; *pipa* puff at; F *p.* milk; *caudal* eat away; F *a. S.Am.* smoke; *S.Am.* (*beber*) drink; *sl.* ¡*chúpate eso!* put that in your pipe and smoke it!; **~se** waste away; **chupatintas** *m contp.* pencil pusher; **chupete** *m* dummy; *S.Am.* lollipop; **chupón** *m* ⚘ sucker; drag *de cigarro*; (*p.*) swindler.

churre *f* thick grease; (*mugre*) filth.

churro *m* fritter.

churruscar(se) [1g] burn.

chus: *no decir ~ ni mus* not say a word.

chuscada *f* funny thing; **chusco** funny, droll.

chusma *f* rabble, riffraff.

chutar [1a] *deportes*: shoot; kick (*fútbol*).

chuzo *m* pike; *llover a ~s* rain cats and dogs.

D

dable possible, feasible, viable.
¡daca! hand it over!
dactilar *v. huella*; **dactilografía** *f* typing; **dactilógrafo** *m*, **a** *f* typist.
dadaísmo *m* Dadaism.
dádiva *f* gift, present; *fig.* sop; **dadivosidad** *f* generosity; **dadivoso** generous, open-handed, bounteous.
dado[1] *m* die; **~s** *pl.* dice.
dado[2] *p.p. of dar*; *dada su corta edad* in view of his youth; *~ a* given to; *~ que* given that; granted that; **dador** *m*, **-a** *f* giver, donor; bearer *de carta*.
dafodelo *m* daffodil.
daga *f* dagger.
dalia *f* dahlia.
daltoniano color-blind; **daltonismo** *m* color-blindness.
dama *f* lady; (*noble*) lady, gentlewoman; (*querida*) mistress; *juego de damas*: king; (*juego de*) **~s** *pl.* checkers; *primera ~ thea.* leading lady; *pol.* first lady; *~ de honor* lady-in-waiting; maid of honor *en boda*.
damajuana *f* demijohn.
damasco *m* damask; **damasquinado** ⊕ damask; **damasquinar** [1a] damask.
damero *m* checkerboard.
damisela *f* † damsel.
damnificar [1g] hurt, injure; *los damnificados* those affected, those who have suffered loss; the injured parties.
danés 1. *adj.* Danish; **2.** *m*, **-a** *f* Dane; **3.** *m* (*idioma*) Danish.
danza *f* dance; (*arte*) dancing; F (*negocio*) shady business; F (*jaleo*) row, rumpus; *~ de figuras* square dance; *~ guerrera* war dance; F *meterse en la ~* get caught up in a shady business; **danzante** *m*, **a** *f* dancer; F (*activo*) hustler, person who is always on the go; (*casquivano*) scatterbrain; **danzar** [1f] dance (*a. fig.*); F meddle, shove one's oar in; **danzarín** *m*, **-a** *f* dancer; F = *danzante* F; **danzón** *m* danzon (*Cuban dance*).
dañado wicked, bad; **dañar** [1a] hurt, harm, damage; (*echar a perder*) spoil; **~se** get damaged; spoil; ⚕ hurt o.s.; **dañino** harmful, destructive; **daño** *m* damage; hurt, harm, injury; ✝ loss; *S.Am.* witchcraft; ⚖ *~s pl. y perjuicios* damages; *por mi ~* to my cost; *hacer ~ a* = *dañar*; *estómago* upset; *hacerse ~* hurt o.s.; **dañoso** harmful, bad, injurious.
dar [1r] **1.** *v/t. mst* give; (*pasar*) pass, hand; *permiso etc.* grant, concede; *fig.* lend, give; *batalla* fight; *buenos días etc.* wish; *cartas* deal; *cosecha* produce, yield; *ejemplo* set; *golpe* give, strike, fetch; *grito* give, utter; *hora* strike; *paseo, paso* take; *tema para discusión* propose; *ir dando cuerda* pay out; *¡dale! boxeo etc.*: hit him!; *deportes*: get on with it!; *iro.* look at him!; what again?; are you still at it?; (*bastante*) that's enough!; **2.:** *lo mismo da* it makes no odds; *lo mismo me da* it's all the same to me; *¿qué más da?* what does it matter?; never mind!; **3.** *v/i. con prp.* (*para muchas frases, v. el correspondiente su. o verbo*): *~ a* (*ventana*) look on to, overlook; (*casa*) face (towards); *~ con p.* meet, run into; *idea, solución etc.* hit (up)on, strike; *dio con la cabeza contra un árbol* he hit his head against a tree; *~ con algo en el suelo* knock s.t. to the ground, drop s.t.; *no doy con el nombre* I can't think of the name; *~ consigo en* land in, end up in; *~ contra* hit, strike; *~ de v. espalda etc.*; *~ de sí* (*tela*) give, stretch; ↗ yield (well), produce (a lot); *~ en hábito, trampa* fall into; *cárcel* end up in; *chiste* see, catch on to; *~ en inf.* begin to *inf.*; persist in *ger.*; *~ por* consider (as); *le ha dado por inf.* he has taken to *ger.*; *~ sobre* overlook; **4. ~se** (*entregarse*) give o.s. up; (*producirse, existir*) occur, be found; *no se le da nada* he doesn't give a

damn; ~ *a* devote o.s. to; *b.s.* abandon o.s. to, indulge in; *v. conocer etc.*; ~ *cuenta de* realize; ~*las de* pose as, fancy o.s. as; ~ *por* consider o.s.
dardo *m* dart, shaft.
dares y tomares *m/pl.* F give and take, disputes, arguments, bickerings; *andar en ~ con* argue with.
dársena *f* ⚓ dock.
darviniano Darwinian, Darwinist; **darvinismo** *m* Darwinism.
data *f* date; ✝ item; **datar** [1a] date (de from).
dátil *m* ⚘ date; **datilera** *f* date (palm).
dativo *m* dative (case).
dato *m* fact, piece of information, datum; ~*s pl.* data, facts, information; ~*s pl. personales* personal details, facts about o.s.
de a) *posesión, pertenencia*: of; *tras sup.*: *el mejor del mundo* the best in the world; *los árboles del jardín* the trees in the garden; b) *materia*: *una moneda de plata* a silver coin, a coin of silver; *tras verbo*: *amueblado de nogal* furnished in walnut; *vestido de negro* dressed in black; *contenido*: *un vaso de vino* a glass of wine; *asunto*: *un libro de física* a physics book; *acerca de*: of, about, concerning; c) *partitivo*: *uno de ellos* one of them; ⅍ *de cada 7,6* 6 out of (every) 7; d) *comp.*: *más de 20* more than 20; e) *origen, procedencia*: from; *de A a B* from A to B; *de puerta en puerta* from door to door; f) *que va a*: *el camino de Madrid* the road to Madrid, the Madrid road; g) *tiempo*: *a las 6 de la mañana* at 6 in the morning; *de día* by day; *edad*: *un niño de 8 años* an 8-year-old boy, a boy of 8; *cuando*: *de niño* as a child; h) *causal*: *de miedo* for fear; *de puro cansado* out of sheer tiredness; i) *en cuanto a*: *mejor de salud* better in health; j) *aposición*: *la ciudad de Roma* the city of Rome; *frases*: F *el animal de Juan* that beast (of a) John; *el pobre de Juan* poor (old) John; k) *agente de pasivo*: *amado de todos* beloved of all *lit.*, loved by all; l) *condicional*: *de serle a Vd. posible* if you can; *de no ser así* if it were not so.
dé *v. dar.*
deambular [1a] stroll, saunter; wander (about).
deán *m eccl.* dean; **deanato** *m*, **deanazgo** *m* deanship.
debajo (*a. por* ~) underneath, below; ~ *de* under(neath), below; beneath.
debate *m* debate, discussion; **debatir**[1] [3a] *v/t.* debate, discuss.
debatir[2] [3a] *v/i.* struggle; flail about.
debe *m* debit (side).
deber 1. [2a] *v/t.* owe; *v/i.*: ~ *inf.* must *inf.*, have to *inf.*; *debería inf.*, *debiera inf.* ought to *inf.*, should *inf.*; *debíamos ir* we were to go, we were to have gone; ~ *de inf.* must *inf.*; *debe de haber ido* he must have gone; *no debe (de) ser muy difícil* it can't be very difficult; ~*se a* be owing to, be due to, be on account of; ~ *a que* be because, be due to the fact that; *puede ~ a que* it may be because; **2.** *m* duty, obligation; ✝ debt; ~*es pl. escuela*: homework; **debidamente** duly, properly, in due form; **debido** due, right, just; *como es* ~ as is only right, as is proper; ~ *a* owing to, due to, through; ~ *a ello* because of this; ~ *a que* because (of the fact that).
débil *mst* weak; feeble; *salud a.* poor; *esfuerzo a.* half-hearted; *luz* dim; *grito etc. a.* faint; **debilidad** *f* weakness *etc.*; *esp.* ⚕ debility; ~ *senil* senility; **debilitación** *f* weakening, enfeeblement, debilitation; **debilitar** [1a] weaken, debilitate (*esp.* ⚕); *resistencia etc.* impair, lower; ~**se** get weak(er).
debutante *m/f* debutant(e); beginner; **debutar** [1a] make one's début.
década *f* decade.
decadencia *f* decadence, decline; **decadente** decadent, effete; **decaer** [2o] decay, decline; flag; ~ *de ánimo* lose heart.
decaimiento *m* decay; weakness.
decano *m univ. etc.* dean; (*más antiguo*) doyen.
decantar[1] praise, laud.
decantar[2] [1a] *vino etc.* decant.
decapitar [1a] behead, decapitate.
decena *f* (about) ten; **decenal** decennial.
decencia *f* decency *etc.*

decenio *m* decade.
decente decent; seemly, proper; (*limpio*) clean; modest.
decepción *f* disappointment; (*engaño*) deception; **decepcionante** disappointing; **decepcionar** [1a] disappoint.
decidido determined, decided; **decidir** [3a] decide (*inf.* to *inf.*); *cuestión* settle, decide; **~se** decide, make up one's mind (*a inf.* to *inf.*).
decidor witty, lively.
décima *f* tenth; *eccl.* tithe; *poet. a 10-line stanza*; **decimación** *f* decimation; **decimal 1.** *adj. a. su. m* decimal; **2.** *f*: *~ periódica pura* recurring decimal; **décimo 1.** tenth; **2.** *m* tenth; (tenth part of a) lottery ticket; **decimoctavo** *etc. v. Apéndice.*
decir 1. [3p] say; tell; *verdad* speak, tell; *misa* say; (*texto*) say, read; (*llamar*) call; *~ bien* be right; *~ mal* be wrong; *~ para* (*or entre*) *sí* say to o.s.; *~ que sí* say yes; es *~* that is (to say); *por mejor ~* or rather; *por ~lo así* so to speak; *no hay más que ~* there is nothing more to be done about it; *no hay que ~ que* it goes without saying that; *no hay para qué ~* of course; *dar que ~ a la gente* make people talk; *me permito ~ que* I submit that, I venture to say that; *querer ~* mean (*con* by); *¡digo, digo!* just listen to this!; now wait a minute!; *como quien dice, como si dijéramos* so to speak, in a manner of speaking; *usted dirá* it's for you to say; (*echando vino etc.*) say when; *ello dirá* the event will show; *el qué dirán* what people (will) say; *¡diga(me)! teleph.* hello!; *diga lo que diga* whatever he says; F *¡no me diga(s)!* you don't say!; *no digamos* not exactly, not really; *mejor dicho* rather; *no es para dicho* it's not fit to be told; *lo dicho freq.* what has been said; *dicho y hecho* no sooner said than done; *he dicho* I have spoken; **~se:** *se dice* it is said, they say; (*cuento*) the story goes; *se me ha dicho que* I have been told that; **2.** *m* saying; *al ~ de* according to.
decisión *f* decision; (*ánimo*) determination; *forzar una ~* force the issue; **decisivo** decisive; *consideración* overriding; *voto* casting.
declamación *f* declamation; recitation; **declamador** *m* orator; *b.s.* ranter; **declamar** [1a] *v/t.* declaim; recite; *v/i.* hold forth, speak out (*contra* against); *b.s.* rant; **declamatorio** declamatory.
declarable declarable; **declaración** *f* declaration; pronouncement, statement; ⚖ evidence; *naipes*: bid; *~ de derechos* bill of rights; *~ de renta* tax return; *prestar ~* give evidence;
declarado professed, declared; **declarar** [1a] declare; pronounce, state; profess; ⚖ (*testigo*) testify, give evidence; (*juez*) find; *naipes*: bid; **~se** declare o.s.; ✱ *etc.* break out; *~ por* side with, come out on the side of.
declinación *f* decline, falling-off; *ast.*, ⚓ declination; *gr.* declension; **declinar** [1a] *v/t.* decline, refuse; ⚖ reject; *gr.* decline; inflect; *v/i.* decline, fall off; degenerate; (*terreno etc.*) slope (away); *gr.* decline.
declive *m* slope, incline, declivity; *~ económico* slump; *en ~* sloping; downhill.
decolorar [1a] discolor; **~se** get discolored.
decoración *f* decoration; *~ de interiores* interior decoration; *thea.* (*a. ~es pl.*) = **decorado** *m* decoration; décor; *thea.* scenery, set; **decorador** *m*, **-a** *f* decorator; **decorar**[1] [1a] decorate, adorn.
decorar[2] [1a] *lección* learn, memorize.
decorativo decorative, ornamental.
decoro *m* decorum, propriety; proprieties; honor; respect; modesty; **decoroso** decorous, proper, seemly; respectful; decent; modest.
decrecer [2d] decrease; (*aguas etc.*) go down; **decremento** *m* decrease.
decrépito decrepit; **decrepitud** *f* decrepitude.
decretar [1a] decree, ordain; *premio* award, adjudge; **decreto** *m* decree; *parl.* act; *~-ley m* decree, law.
dechado *m* model, paragon; pattern; *sew.* sampler.
dedada *f* thimbleful; pinch *de rapé etc.*; spot, dab *de mermelada etc.*; **dedal** *m* thimble; *fig.* thimbleful; **dedalera** *f* foxglove.

dedicación *f* dedication (*a* to); (*aplicación*) diligence; *eccl.* consecration; *fig.* devotion (*a* to); *en* (*or con*) *plena* ~ full-time; **dedicar** [1g] dedicate; *eccl. a.* consecrate; *libro* dedicate, *ejemplar* inscribe; *tiempo etc.* devote, give (*a* to), put in (*a* at); **~se** *a* devote o.s. to; *trabajo a.* be engaged in; *estudio a.* go in for, take up; *¿a qué se dedica Vd.?* what do you do?, what is your line of business?; **dedicatoria** *f* inscription, dedication; **dedicatorio** dedicatory.
dedil *m* fingerstall; finger guard.
dedillo: F *saber al* ~ have *s.t.* at one's fingertips, have *s.t.* (off) pat.
dedo *m* finger; ~ (*del pie*) toe; F spot, bit; ~ *anular* ring finger; ~ *auricular*, ~ *meñique* little finger; ~ *del corazón*, ~ *cordial* middle finger; ~ *índice* forefinger, index finger; ~ *pulgar* thumb; (*del pie*) big toe; *a dos ~s de* within an inch (*or* ace) of; on the verge of; *chuparse los ~s* eat with relish; smack one's lips (*a. fig.*); *no mamarse el* ~ be pretty smart; *meter el* ~ *en la boca a* try to get *s.o.* to talk; *poner el* ~ *en la llaga* put one's finger on the spot; *no tener dos ~s de frente* be an oaf.
deducción *f* deduction; derivation; ♪ diatonic scale; **deducible** deducible; inferable; **deducir** [3o] deduce (*de, por* from); infer; ⚖ deduct; **deductivo** deductive.
defección *f* defection, desertion; **defectible** fallible, imperfect; **defectivo** defective (*a. gr.*); **defecto** *m* defect, flaw; ⊕, ⚡ fault; (*esp. moral*) shortcoming, failure; lack, absence; ~ *de fonación* speech defect, impediment; **defectuoso** defective, faulty, unsound.
defender [2g] defend (*a.* ⚖; *contra* against, *de* from); protect (*contra, de frío etc.* against, from); *causa* champion, uphold; **~se** defend o.s.; F manage, get along, keep one's end up; **defendible** defensible; **defensa 1.** *f* defence (*a.* ⚖, *deportes*); shelter, protection; ⚓ *etc.* fender; ⚔ **~s** *pl.* defences, defence works; **2.** *m deportes*: back; **defensiva** *f* defensive; *estar a la* ~ be on the defensive; **defensivo** defensive; **defensor** *m*, **-a** *f* defender; protector; champion, upholder *de causa*; ⚖ counsel (for the defence; *a. abogado* ~).
deferencia *f* deference; **deferente** deferential; **deferir** [3i] *v/t.* ⚖ refer, delegate (*a* to); *v/i.*: ~ *a* defer to.
deficiencia *f* deficiency, defect; **deficiente** deficient, wanting (*en* in); defective; **déficit** *m* ✝ deficit; *fig.* shortage.
definible definable; **definición** *f* definition; **definido** definite (*a. gr.*); **definir** [3a] define; **definitiva:** *en* ~ definit(iv)ely; **definitivo** definitive.
deflación *f* deflation; **deflacionar** [1a] deflate; **deflacionista** deflationary.
deformación *f* deformation; distortion (*a. radio*); ⊕ strain; **deformar** [1a] deform; distort; ⊕ strain; **deforme** deformed, misshapen; abnormal; **deformidad** *f* deformity, malformation; abnormality; *fig.* moral shortcoming.
defraudar [1a] cheat, defraud; deceive; *esperanzas* cheat, disappoint, dash.
defuera (*a. por* ~) outwardly, on the outside.
defunción *f* death; passing; decease, demise.
degeneración *f* degeneration; (*moral*) degeneracy; **degenerado** *adj. a. su. m*, **a** *f* degenerate (type); **degenerar** [1a] degenerate (*en* into).
deglución *f* swallowing; **deglutir** [3a] swallow.
degollación *f* throat cutting; (*a.* ⚖) beheading, decapitation; **degolladero** *m anat.* neck, throat; (*matadero*) slaughterhouse; (*cadalso*) scaffold; **degollar** [1n] cut the throat of; behead, decapitate; *fig.* massacre; *comedia etc.* murder, make nonsense of.
degradación *f* degradation; ⚔ demotion, reduction in rank; **degradar** [1a] degrade, debase; ⚔ demote, reduce (in rank); **~se** demean o.s.
degüello *m* = *degollación*; shaft, slender part *de arma*; *entrar a* ~ *en* put *the inhabitants of* to the sword.

degustación *f* tasting.
dehesa *f* pasture, meadow; range.
deidad *f* deity; divinity; F beauty; **deificar** [1g] deify; apotheosize (*a. fig.*); **deísmo** *m* deism; **deísta 1.** deistic(al); **2.** *m/f* deist.
dejación *f* ⚖ abandonment, relinquishment; *S.Am.*, *Col.* slovenliness; **dejadez** *f* neglect, slovenliness *etc.*; **dejado** slovenly; (*flojo*) lazy, slack; (*abatido*) dejected.
dejar [1a] **1.** *v/t. mst* leave; *empresa, trabajo freq.* give up; *pasajero* drop, set down; ✝ *pérdida* show, leave; (*prestar*) lend; (*omitir*) forget, leave out; (*desamparar*) abandon, forsake; (*permitir*) let (*inf. inf.*), allow (*inf.* to *inf.*); ~ *atrás* leave behind, outstrip, outdistance; ~ *así las cosas* leave it at that; leave things as they are; ~ *para después* leave till later, put off; ~ *entrar* let in; ~ *salir* let out; ~ *por* leave *s.t.* as (being); *deja mucho que desear* it leaves much to be desired; *¡deja eso!* drop that!, stop that!; *v. caer etc.*; *como dejo dicho* as I have said; *dejado de la mano de Dios* beyond redemption; godforsaken; **2.** *v/i.*: ~ *de inf.* (*cesar*) stop *ger.*, leave off *ger.*; give up *ger.*; (*omitir*) fail to *inf.*, neglect to *inf.*; *no deja de extrañarme* I cannot but be surprised; *no poder* ~ *de inf.* not be able to help *ger.*; **3.** **~se** let o.s. go, get slovenly; ~ *decir que* let slip that; ~ *persuadir* allow o.s. to be persuaded; ~ *de bromas etc.* cut out, stop; *¡déjese de eso!* stop that!, cut it out! F.
dejo *m* (*gustillo*) aftertaste, tang; *fig.* touch, smack; reminder; (*habla*) (trace of) accent.
delación *f* denunciation, accusation; information.
delantal *m* apron.
delante in front (*a. por* ~); ahead; ~ *de* in front of; ahead of; **delantera** *f* front (part); *thea.* front row; (*ventaja*) lead, advantage; *coger* (*or tomar*) *la* ~ *a* get ahead of; get a start on; *llevar la* ~ lead; *tomar la* ~ take the lead; **delantero 1.** *fila, parte* front; *pata* fore; foremost *en progreso etc.*; *línea etc.* forward; *tracción* ~*a mot.* front (wheel) drive; **2.** *m* forward.
delatar [1a] denounce; inform against; (*traicionar*) betray (*a. fig.*); **delator** *m*, **-a** *f* accuser; informer; betrayer.
dele *m typ.* dele.
delectación *f* delight.
delegación *f* delegation; *parl.* ~ (*de poderes*) devolution; (*oficina*) local office; ~ *de hacienda local Treasury office*; (*comisaría*) police station; **delegado** *m*, **a** *f* delegate; ✝ agent; **delegar** [1h] delegate (*a* to).
deleitable enjoyable, delectable (*esp. co., lit.*); **deleitar** [1a] delight; **~se** *con*, ~ *de* (take) delight in; **deleite** *m* pleasure, delight, joy; **deleitoso** delightful, pleasing, pleasurable.
deletéreo deleterious.
deletrear [1a] spell out; *fig.* decipher, interpret.
deleznable (*que rompe*) fragile, brittle; (*resbaladizo*) slippery; *fig.* frail; ephemeral, insubstantial.
delfín *m* dauphin; *ichth.* dolphin.
delgadez *f* thinness *etc.*; **delgado** thin; *p. a.* slim, slender, slight; *fig.* delicate, light; (*agudo*) clever; **delgaducho** skinny; slight.
deliberación *f* deliberation; **deliberar** [1a] *v/t.* debate; ~ *inf.* decide to *inf.*; *v/i.* deliberate (*sobre* on), debate; **deliberativo** deliberative.
delicadeza *f* delicacy *etc.*; **delicado** delicate; dainty; *color* soft, delicate; *distinción* nice; *punto* tender, sensitive; sore; *situación* delicate, touchy; tricky; (*difícil de contentar*) hard to please, fastidious; (*ingenioso*) subtle; squeamish, overscrupulous.
delicia *f* delight(fulness); **delicioso** delicious; delightful.
delictivo punishable; criminal.
delimitación *f* delimitation; **delimitar** [1a] delimit, define.
delincuencia *f* delinquency, criminality; ~ *de menores* juvenile delinquency; **delincuente 1.** delinquent, criminal; **2.** *m/f* delinquent, criminal, offender; ~ *juvenil* juvenile delinquent; ~ *sin antecedente penal* first offender.
delineación *f* delineation; **delineante** *m* draftsman; **delinear** [1a] delineate, outline.
delinquir [3e] commit a crime, offend.
deliquio *m* swoon.
delirante delirious; light-headed;

delirar [1a] be delirious, rave; *fig.* talk nonsense; **delirio** *m* delirium; ravings, wanderings; *fig.* frenzy; (*disparates*) nonsense; *fig.* *con* ~ madly; F *¡el ~!* it was great!; **delirium** *m* **tremens** delirium tremens. [deed; ~ *de incendio* arson.]

delito *m* crime; offense; *fig.* mis-}

delta *m* (*geog.*) *a. f* delta.

delusorio delusive; **deludir** [3a] delude.

demacración *f* emaciation; **demacrado** emaciated; **demacrarse** [1a] waste away.

demagogia *f* demagogy; **demagógico** demagogic(al); **demagogo** *m* demagogue.

demanda *f* demand (*a.* ✝), request (*de* for); inquiry; petition; *thea.* call; ⚖ action, lawsuit; ~ *máxima* ⚡ peak load; *en ~ de* in search of; *entablar ~* take legal proceedings, bring an action; ✝ *tener ~* be in demand; **demandado** *m*, **a** *f* defendant; respondent *en divorcio*; **demandador** *m*, **-a** *f*, **demandante** *m/f* plaintiff, claimant; **demandar** [1a] demand; claim; ⚖ sue (*a una p.* a p.; *de, por* for).

demarcación *f* (*línea de* line of) demarcation; **demarcar** [1g] mark out, demarcate.

demás **1.** *adj.* other, rest of the; **2.** *pron.*: *lo ~* the rest; *los ~* the others, the rest (of them); *por lo ~* for the rest, otherwise; **3.** *adv.* = *además*; *por ~* in vain; moreover; *y ~* etcetera; *v. estar de más*;

demasía *f* (*superávit*) surplus; *fig.* excess, outrage; wicked thing; insolence; *en ~* too much, excessively; **demasiado** **1.** *adj.* too much; overmuch; *~s pl.* too many; **2.** *adv.* too; too much, excessively; ~ *bueno* too good (*para* for; *para inf.* to *inf.*).

demencia *f* madness, insanity; **dementado** *S.Am.* = **demente** **1.** mad, insane, demented; **2.** *m/f* lunatic.

demérito *m* demerit; unworthiness.

democracia *f* democracy; **demócrata** *m/f* democrat; **democrático** democratic; **democratizar** [1f] democratize.

demoler [2h] demolish (*a. fig.*), pull down; **demolición** *f* demolition.

demoníaco demoniac(al), demonic; **demonio** *m* demon; devil (*a. fig.*); *¡(qué) ~!* damn it!; what the devil!; *¿qué ~s?* what the hell?; *¿dónde ~s ...?* where the devil ...?; *ir como el ~* go hell for leather; *¡que se lo lleve el ~!* to hell with it!; **demontre** *m* F = *demonio*.

demora *f* delay; ⚓ bearing;

demorar [1a] *v/t.* delay, hold up (*or* back); *v/i.* stay on, linger on, delay.

demostrable demonstrable; **demostración** *f* demonstration; show *de cariño etc.*; gesture; **demostrar** [1m] show, demonstrate; prove; **demostrativo** *adj. a. su. m* demonstrative.

demudar [1a] change, alter; **~se** change color, change countenance; *sin ~* without a flicker of emotion.

denegación *f* refusal, rejection;

denegar [1h *a.* 1k] refuse, reject; ⚖ deny, reject, overrule.

dengoso affected, finicky; **dengue** *m* affectation, finickiness; prudery; *hacer ~s* be finicky; *no me vengas con ~s* I don't want to hear your silly complaints; **denguero** = *dengoso*. [insult.]

denigrar [1a] denigrate, revile;}

denodado bold, intrepid.

denominación *f* naming, designation; denomination; **denominador** *m* denominator; ~ *común* common denominator; **denominar** [1a] name, designate; denominate.

denostar [1m] insult, abuse.

denotar [1a] denote; reveal, indicate, show.

densidad *f* density (*a. phys.*); thickness *etc.*; **denso** *mst* dense; *humo, líquido a.* thick; solid; *libro* heavy, dry.

dentado *rueda* cogged, toothed; *filo* jagged; *sello* perforated; ⚘ dentate; **dentadura** *f* denture, set of teeth; *mala ~* bad teeth; ~ *postiza* false teeth, denture(s); **dental** *adj. a. su. f* dental; **dentar** [1k] *v/t.* furnish with teeth *etc.*; ⊕ *etc.* indent; *filo* make jagged; *sello* perforate; *sin ~ sello* imperforate; *v/i.* teethe; **dentellada** *f* bite, nip; (*señal*) tooth mark; *a ~s* with one's teeth; **dentellar** [1a] chatter; *el miedo le hizo ~* fear made his teeth chatter; **dentellear** [1a] bite, nibble (at); **dentera** *f* the shivers F; F envy, jealousy; *dar ~ a* set *s.o.'s* teeth on edge, give *s.o.* the shivers; *fig.* (*deseo*) make *s.o.'s* mouth water; **dentición** *f* teething; dentition; *estar con la ~* be teething; **dentífrico 1.** tooth *attr.*; **2.** *m* dentifrice; **dentista** *m* dentist; **dentistería** *f* dentistry.

dentro 1. inside; *sentir etc.* inwardly; (*en casa*) indoors; (*a. hacia ~, para ~*) in, inwards; *de ~, desde ~* from inside; *por ~* (on the) inside; **2.** *prp.*: *~ de estar* in, inside, within; *meter* into, inside.

dentudo toothy; large-toothed.

denudación *f* denudation; **denudar** [1a] denude; lay bare.

denuedo *m* boldness, daring.

denuesto *m* insult.

denuncia *f* denunciation (*a.* ⚖); ⚖ accusation; **denunciable** *ofensa* indictable; **denunciación** *f* = *denuncia*; **denunciador** *m*, **-a** *f*, **denunciante** *m/f* accuser; informer; **denunciar** [1b] (*publicar*) proclaim; (*pronosticar*) announce, foretell; (*comunicar*) give notice of; (*mostrar*) reveal; ⚖ denounce, accuse.

deparar [1a] provide, present (with), offer; ... *que deparó la suerte* which presented itself.

departamental departmental; **departamento** *m* department; compartment *de caja etc.* (*a.* 🚂); *Arg., Chile, Peru, Urug.* apartment; *~ de máquinas* engine room.

departir [3a] talk, chat.

depauperar [1a] impoverish; ⚕ weaken, deplete.

dependencia *f* dependence (*de* on); reliance (*de* on); dependency (*a. pol.*); ✝ branch office; ⚠ outbuilding, outhouse; (*negocio*) (piece of) business, affair; (*ps.*) sales staff, employees; *~s pl.* accessories; **depender** [2a] depend; follow (*de* from); **dependienta** *f* salesgirl, shop assistant, clerk; **dependiente 1.** dependent (*de* on); **2.** *m* employee; ✝ salesman, shop assistant, clerk.

depilatorio *adj. a. su. m* depilatory.

deplorable deplorable; lamentable, regrettable; **deplorar** [1a] deplore, regret.

deponente *adj.* (*gr.*) *a. su. m* (⚖) deponent.

deponer [2r] *v/t.* (*bajar*) lay down; (*apartar*) lay aside; (*quitar*) remove, take away, take down; *rey* depose, *ministro* remove from office; *v/i.* ⚖ give evidence; give a deposition; depose.

deportación *f* deportation; **deportado** *m*, **a** *f* deportee; **deportar** [1a] deport.

deporte *m* sport; game; **deportista 1.** sports *attr.*; sporting; **2.** *m* sportsman; **3.** *f* sportswoman; **deportividad** *f* sportsmanship; **deportivo** *club, periódico etc.* sports *attr.*; *actitud etc.* sporting, sportsmanlike.

deposición *f* deposition (*a.* ⚖), removal; ⚖ evidence.

depositador *m*, **-a** *f* ✝ depositor; **depositar** [1a] *mst* deposit; store, put away, lodge; entrust (*en* to); *~se* (*líquido*) settle; **depositaría** *f* depository; trust; **depositario 1.** deposit *attr.*; **2.** *m*, **a** *f* depositary, trustee; repository *de secreto etc.*; **depósito** *m* (*almacén*) store (house), warehouse, depot; ⚔ depot, dump; reservoir, tank *de líquido*; ✝, ⚗ deposit; *~ de agua* water tank, cistern; *~ de basura* (garbage) dump; *~ de cadáveres* mortuary; *~ de equipajes* cloakroom; *~ de gasolina* gasoline tank; *~ de maderas* lumber yard; ✝ *en ~* in bond.

depravación *f* depravity, depravation; **depravado** depraved; **depravar** [1a] deprave.

depreciación *f* depreciation; **depreciar(se)** [1b] depreciate.

depresión *f mst* depression (*a.* ⚕, ✝, *meteor.*); drop, fall *de mercurio*; dip *de horizonte, camino*; (*hueco*) depression, hollow; **depresivo, deprimente** depressing; **deprimido** ⚕ depressed; **deprimir** [3a] depress (*a.* ⚕, *fig.*); *nivel* lower, reduce; *fig.* humiliate; (*rebajar*) belittle, disparage.

depuración *f* purification; *pol.* purge; **depurador 1.** *m* purifier; **2.** cleansing; purifying; purging; *estación ~a* sewage-disposal plant; **depurar** [1a] purify, cleanse, purge (*a. pol.*).

derecha *f* right hand; (*lado*) right side; *pol.* right; *a la ~ estar* on the right, *torcer etc.* (to the) right; *a ~s* rightly; **derechamente** straight, directly; *fig.* properly, rightly; **derechazo** *m boxeo*: right; **derechista 1.** right-wing; **2.** *m/f* right-winger.

derecho 1. *adj. lado, mano* right; (*recto*) straight; (*vertical*) upright, erect, straight, standing; *C.A.* lucky; *más ~ que una vela* as straight as a die; **2.** *adv.* straight, direct; (*verticalmente*) straight, upright; **3.** *m* right (*a* to, *de inf.* to *inf.*); ⚖ (*ciencia*) law; (*en abstracto*) justice; right side *de papel*; *~s pl.* ✝ due(s); (*profesionales*) fee(s); (*impuestos*) tax(es); *~s pl. de aduana*, *~s pl. arancelarios* customs duty; *~s pl. de autor* royalties; *~ canónico* canon law; *~s pl. civiles* civil rights; *~ consuetudinario* common law; *~ divino* divine right; *~s pl. de entrada* import duties; *~ de gentes*, *~ internacional* international law; *~ de paso* right of way; *~ penal* criminal law; *~ preferente* preferential duty; *~s pl. de puerto* harbor dues; *con ~* rightly, justly; *con ~ a* with a right to; *conforme a ~* according to law; *por ~ propio* in his own right; *según ~* by right(s); F *¡no hay ~!* it's not fair!; *reservados todos los ~s* copyright; *tener ~ a* have a right to, be entitled to.

derechura *f* straightness; directness; *fig.* rightness; *en ~ hablar* plainly; *hacer* right away.

deriva *f* ⚓ drift; leeway *de rumbo*; *a la ~* adrift, drifting; *ir a la ~* drift; **derivación** *f* derivation (*a. gr.*); origin, source; ⚡ shunt; *hacer una ~ en alambre* tap; **derivado 1.** derivative (*a. gr.*); **2.** *m* derivative (*a. gr.*); ⚗ by-product; **derivar**[1] [1a] *v/t.* derive (*de* from); *v/i.*, **~se** derive, be derived.

derivar[2] [1a] ⚓ drift.

derivativo *adj. a. su. m* derivative.

dermatitis *f* dermatitis; **dermatología** *f* dermatology; **dermatólogo** *m* dermatologist.

derogación *f* repeal, abolition; *hacer ~ a* = **derogar** [1h] repeal, abolish.

derramadero *m* spillway; dumping ground, dump; **derramamiento** *m* spilling *etc.*; **derramar** [1a] pour out; spill; (*esparcir*) scatter, spread; *sangre* shed; *lágrimas* weep; *fig. noticia* spread; (*malgastar*) squander, waste; **~se** spill, overflow, run over; (*sangre*) flow, be shed; (*esparcirse*) scatter; spread; **derrame** *m* spilling *etc.*; (*salida*) overflow, outflow; (*pérdida*) leakage, waste; ⚕ discharge.

derrapar [1a] *mot.* skid; ⚓ yaw; **derrape** *m* skid; yaw.

derredor: *al ~ (de)*, *en ~ (de)* around, about.

derrelicto *m esp.* ⚓ derelict.

derrengado bent, crooked; (*cojo*) lame; **derrengar** [1h] bend, twist; *~ (a palos)* break *s.o.'s* back, cripple.

derretido melted; *metal* molten; *estar ~ por* be crazy about; **derretir** [3l] melt; *nieve a.* thaw; *fortuna* squander; **~se** melt; run; thaw; *~ por* be crazy about; F fret and fume.

derribar [1a] *casa* knock down, pull down; *puerta* batter down; *res* throw, fell; *adversario* knock down, lay out F; *hunt.*, ✈ shoot down, bring down; *gobierno etc.* overthrow; *fig.* humiliate; **~se** fall down, collapse; (*p.*) throw o.s. to the ground; **derribo** *m* knocking down *etc.*; *~s pl.* debris, rubble.

derrocadero *m* cliff, precipice; **derrocar** [1g] hurl down *desde lo alto*; *casa* knock down; *gobierno etc.* overthrow; oust, topple (*de* from); *fig.* humble; **~se** *por* throw o.s. over.

derrochador *adj. a. su. m* spendthrift; **derrochar** [1a] waste, squander; lavish; **derroche** *m* waste, squandering; lavish expenditure, extravagance.

derrota[1] *f* ⚓ course; (*camino*) road, path, way.

derrota[2] *f* defeat, rout; débâcle; **derrotar** [1a] defeat, rout; *ropa* tear; *salud etc.* ruin.

derrotero *m* ⚓ course; *fig.* course, plan of action.

derrotismo *m* defeatism; **derrotista** *m/f* defeatist.

derruir [3g] raze, demolish, tear down.

derrumbadero *m* cliff; *fig.* pitfall, hazard; **derrumbamiento** *m* headlong fall; collapse (*a. fig.*), caving in; **derrumbar** [1a] hurl down, throw down; **~se** (*p. etc.*) hurl o.s. (*por* over); fall headlong (*por* down); (*edificio a. fig.*) collapse; (*techo*) fall in, cave in; **derrumbe** *m* *C.Am.* collapse; cave-in.

desabillé *m* deshabille.

desabotonar [1a] *v/t.* unbutton; *v/i.* ⚘ blossom; **~se** come undone.

desabrido *sabor* tasteless, insipid (*a. fig.*); (*áspero*) harsh, rough; *debate* bitter; *p.* surly; *contestación* sharp.

desabrigado *fig.* unprotected, defenceless; **desabrigo** *m* bareness, exposure; *fig.* unprotectedness; destitution.

desabrimiento *m* insipidness *etc.*; (*sentimiento*) depression, uneasiness; *con* ~ *contestar* sharply; **desabrir** [3a] *fig.* embitter.

desabrochar [1a] undo, unfasten; *fig.* penetrate; **~se** F unbosom o.s. (*con* to).

desacatador disrespectful; **desacatar** [1a] be disrespectful to; **desacato** *m* disrespect; *esp.* ⚖ (act of) contempt.

desacertado mistake, wrong; (*imprudente*) unwise; *observación etc.* infelicitous; F off-the-track; **desacertar** [1k] be wrong; **desacierto** *m* mistake, miscalculation, miss; (*dicho etc.*) unfortunate remark.

desacomedido *S.Am.* rude, impolite.

desacomodado unemployed; badly off; **desacamodar** [1a] put out, inconvenience; *criado* discharge; **~se** lose one's post.

desaconsejado ill-advised.

desacoplar [1a] ⚡ disconnect; ⊕ uncouple.

desacorde discordant.

desacostumbrado unusual, odd; **desacostumbrar** [1a]: ~ *a uno de* break s.o. of the habit of, wean s.o. away from.

desacreditar [1a] discredit, bring into disrepute; (*denigrar*) run down.

desacuerdo *m* disagreement; error; discord; derangement; unconsciousness; (*olvido*) forgetfulness; *en* ~ *con* out of keeping with, at variance with.

desadvertido careless.

desafecto *m* disaffection; ill will, dislike.

desafiador **1.** defiant; challenging; **2.** *m*, **-a** *f* challenger; **desafiar** [1c] defy; challenge; dare; ~ *a inf.* challenge *s.o.* to *inf.*, dare *s.o.* to *inf.*

desaficionarse [1a]: ~ *de* come to dislike.

desafinado out of tune, off key; **desafinar** [1a] be (*or* go) out of tune; F speak out of turn.

desafío *m* challenge (*a. fig.*); defiance; ⚔ duel; rivalry; competition.

desaforado lawless, disorderly; (*grande*) huge; *grito etc.* mighty; *ser un* ~ be a violent sort; **desaforarse** [1m] act in an outrageous way; get worked up.

desafortunado unfortunate, unlucky.

desafuero *m* excess, outrage.

desagradable disagreeable, unpleasant; **desagradar** [1a] displease; dissatisfy; **desagradecido** ungrateful; **desagradecimiento** *m* ingratitude; **desagrado** *m* displeasure; dissatisfaction.

desagraviar [1b] *daño* make amends for; *p.* make amends to, indemnify; **~se** get one's own back; restore one's honor; **desagravio** *m* amends, compensation; *en* ~ *de* as amends for.

desagregación *f* disintegration; **desagregar**(**se**) [1h] disintegrate.

desaguadero *m* drain (*a. fig.*; *de* on); outlet; **desaguar** [1i] *v/t.* drain, empty; *fig.* squander; *v/i.*: ~ *en* drain into; **desagüe** *m* drainage, draining; (*caño etc.*) outlet, drain; *de* ~ *tubo etc.* waste *attr.*, outlet *attr.*

desaguisado **1.** illegal; **2.** *m* offence, outrage.

desahogado (*descarado*) impudent, brazen; (*despejado*) free; *vida* comfortable; **desahogar** [1h] *dolor etc.* ease; *p.* console; *pasión* vent; **~se** make things more comfortable; get out of trouble (*or* debt *etc.*); (*hablar*) relieve one's feelings, get s.t. off one's chest; (*confesarse*) unbosom o.s.; **desahogo** *m* (*alivio*) relief; (*medio para aliviarse*) outlet (*de* for); (*descaro*) impudence; (*libertad*) excessive freedom; comfort, comfortable circumstances; *vivir con* ~ be comfortably off.

desahuciado *caso* hopeless, bad; **desahuciar** [1b] eject, evict; oust; *enfermo* give up hope for; **desahucio** *m* ejection, eviction.

desairado unattractive, shabby;

quedar ~ be unsuccessful, come off badly; **desairar** [1a] slight, snub; **desaire** *m* slight, snub; (*falta de garbo*) lack of charm.
desalentar [1k] make breathless; *fig.* discourage; **~se** get discouraged; **desaliento** *m* discouragement; depression; (*debilidad*) weakness.
desaliñado slovenly, down-at-the-heels; (*temporalmente*) untidy, disheveled; (*descuidado*) slovenly, neglectful, careless; **desaliño** *m* slovenliness *etc.*
desalmado cruel, brutal; inhuman; **desalmarse** [1a]: ~ *por* long for, crave.
desalojar [1a] *v/t.* oust, eject, dislodge (*a.* ⚔); *v/i.* move out.
desalquilado vacant; **desalquilar** [1a] vacate; **~se** become vacant.
desamar [1a] dislike, detest.
desamarrar [1a] untie; ⚓ cast off.
desamor *m* coldness, indifference; dislike; **desamorado** cold-hearted.
desamparado helpless, abandoned; needy; deprived; **desamparar** [1a] desert, abandon, forsake; **desamparo** *m* (*acto*) desertion *etc.*; (*estado*) helplessness.
desamueblado unfurnished; stripped; **desamueblar** [1a] remove the furniture from, clear out; strip.
desandar [1q]: ~ *el camino*, ~ *lo andado* retrace one's steps, go back.
desangramiento: *morir de* ~ bleed to death; **desangrar** [1a] bleed; *lago* drain; *fig.* bleed white; **~se** lose a lot of blood; bleed to death.
desanidar [1a] *v/t.* oust, dislodge; *v/i.* (begin to) fly.
desanimado downhearted, low-spirited; lifeless; **desanimar** [1a] discourage, depress; **~se** get discouraged; **desánimo** *m* discouragement, despondency; lifelessness.
desanudar [1a] untie; disentangle.
desapacible *mst* unpleasant; *ruido* sharp, jangling; *tono* harsh; *debate* bitter; *sabor* sharp.
desaparecer [2d] *v/t.* hide, remove, take away; *v/i.* disappear; vanish; drop out of sight; (*efectos etc.*) wear off; **desaparecido** missing; **~s** missing persons; **desaparición** *f* disappearance.
desapasionado dispassionate.
desapego *m* coolness, indifference (*a* towards); dislike.
desapercibido (*desprevenido*) unprepared; (*inadvertido*) unnoticed.
desaplicación *f* slackness, laziness; **desaplicado** slack, lazy.
desapoderado (*precipitado*) headlong; wild; *gula etc.* excessive; *orgullo* overweening.
desaprensión *f* freedom from worry, nonchalance; unscrupulousness; **desaprensivo** unworried, nonchalant; *b.s.* unscrupulous.
desapretar [1k] loosen.
desaprobación *f* disapproval; **desaprobar** [1m] disapprove of, frown on; *petición* reject.
desapropiar [1b] divest, deprive (*de* of).
desaprovechado unproductive, below expectations; *estudiante etc.* slack; **desaprovechar** [1a] *v/t.* waste, fail to make the best use of; *v/i.* lose ground, slip back.
desarbolar [1a] dismast.
desarmamiento *m* disarmament; arms reduction; **desarmar** [1a] *v/t.* ⚔ disarm; ⊕ dismantle, take to pieces, take apart, strip (down); *fig.* *cólera etc.* calm, appease; *v/i.* disarm; **desarme** *m* = *desarmamiento*.
desarraigar [1h] root out, uproot, dig up; *fig.* eradicate; **desarraigo** *m* uprooting; *fig.* eradication.
desarrebujar [1g] *enredo* disentangle; (*descubrir*) uncover, unwrap; *fig.* explain, elucidate.
desarreglado out of order; (*desaliñado*) slovenly, untidy; *conducta etc.* disorderly; **desarreglar** [1a] disarrange, disturb; upset, mess up; **desarreglo** *m* disorder; confusion, chaos; *vivir en el mayor* ~ live in complete chaos.
desarrimado *m* lone wolf; F loner; **desarrimo** *m* lack of support; F stand-offishness.
desarrollar [1a] *lo arrollado* unroll, unwind, unfold; *ecuación* expand; *tesis* expound; *fig.* develop; evolve; **~se** *fig.* develop; unfold; evolve; **desarrollo** *m* development; evolution; growth; run *de juego etc.*; *ayuda al* ~ developmental aid.
desarroparse [1a] undress, uncover o.s.
desarrugar [1h] smooth (out).

desarticulado disjointed; **desarticular** [1a] separate, take apart; *huesos* put out.

desarzonar [1a] throw, unseat.

desaseado (*sucio*) dirty, slovenly; (*desaliñado*) untidy, unkempt, shabby; **desasear** [1a] dirty, soil; mess up; **desaseo** *m* dirtiness *etc.*

desasimiento *m* loosening *etc.*; *fig.* detachment, disinterest; **desasir** [3a; *present like salir*] loosen, let go; **~se** *de* let go of; *fig.* (*ceder*) give up; (*deshacerse de*) get rid of; *situación* extricate o.s. from.

desasosegado uneasy; restless; **desasosegar** [1h *a.* 1k] disturb, make uneasy; make restless; **desasosiego** *m* disquiet, uneasiness, anxiety; restlessness.

desastrado dirty, shabby; (*infeliz*) unlucky; **desastre** *m* disaster; **desastroso** disastrous.

desatado *fig.* wild, violent; **desatar** [1a] untie, undo, unfasten, loose(n); *fig.* solve, unravel; **~se** come undone *etc.*; *fig.* (*hablar*) get worked up; (*obrar*) go too far, forget o.s.; (*tempestad*) burst, break; (*calamidad*) fall (*sobre* on); **~** *de compromiso* get out of; **~** *en injurias etc.* burst into, (begin to) pour out.

desatascar [1g] *carro* pull out of the mud; *cañería* clear; *fig.* get *s.o.* out of a jam.

desatención *f* inattention; (*grosería*) discourtesy; (*desacato*) disrespect, disregard; F snub; **desatender** [2g] ignore, disregard, pay no attention to; *deber* neglect; (*ofender*) slight; F snub; **desatentado** thoughtless, inconsiderate; (*imprudente*) unwise; excessive, extreme; **desatento** inattentive; heedless, careless; (*grosero*) unmannerly, impolite.

desatinado foolish; mindless; nonsensical, silly; wild; **desatinar** [1a] *v/t.* perplex, bewilder; *v/i.* act foolishly; blunder (along); (*hablar*) talk nonsense; (*como loco*) rave; **desatino** *m* foolishness, folly; (*despropósito*; *esp.* **~s** *pl.*) nonsense, silly things.

desatornillar [1a] unscrew.

desatrancar [1g] *puerta* unbar; *pozo* clean out; *cañería* clear.

desatufarse [1a] go out for a breather; *fig.* calm down.

desautorizado unauthorized; unwarranted; discredited.

desavenencia *f* disagreement; friction, unpleasantness, rift; **desavenido** in disagreement, incompatible; **desavenir** [3s] cause a rift between, split; **~se** disagree (*con* with), fall out (*con* with).

desaventajado unfavorable.

desavisado unadvised; ill-advised; thoughtless, careless.

desayunar(se) [1a] (have) breakfast (*con* on); *estar desayunado* have had breakfast; **~** *de fig.* get the first news of; **desayuno** *m* breakfast.

desazón *f* (*soso*) tastelessness; poorness *de suelo*; *fig.* ⚕ trouble, discomfort; *fig.* annoyance; frustration; **desazonar** [1a] *comida* make tasteless; *fig.* upset, annoy; **~se** feel ill.

desbancar [1g] F *juego*: *v/t.* bust; *v/i.* go broke.

desbandada: *a la* **~** in disorder; **desbandarse** [1a] ⚔ *etc.* (*irse*) disband; (*huir*) flee in disorder; disperse in confusion.

desbarajustar [1a] throw into confusion; **desbarajuste** *m* confusion, disorder, chaos.

desbaratar [1a] *v/t.* ruin, spoil, mess up F; *proyecto*, *tentativa* thwart, foil; *teoría* debunk F; *fortuna* squander; ⚔ *etc.* throw into confusion; ⊕ take to pieces; *v/i.* talk nonsense; **~se** F blow up, go off the deep end.

desbarbar [1a] cut (back), trim (off); ✓ cut the roots of; F shave (*a.* **~se**).

desbarrancadero *m S.Am.* precipice.

desbarrar [1a] unbar; unlock; F talk a lot of rubbish.

desbastar [1a] ⊕ plane (down), smooth (out, down); F knock the corners off; **desbaste** *m* ⊕ planing *etc.*

desbocado *caballo* runaway; *p.* foul-mouthed; **desbocar** [1g]: **~** *en* (*río*) run into, flow into; (*calle*) open into; **~se** (*caballo*) bolt; (*p.*) let loose a stream of insults *etc.*, start to swear.

desbordante overflowing; uncontrolled; **desbordar(se)** [1a] overflow, run over; *fig.* lose one's self-control, fly off the handle; **~** *de alegría* be bursting with joy.

desbravador *m* horse breaker; **des-**

bravar [1a] *v/t.* break in, tame; *v/i.*, **~se** get less wild; diminish; (*licor*) lose its strength.
descabalgar [1h] dismount.
descabellado *p.* disheveled; *proyecto etc.* wild, crazy; bizarre; rash; mindless; **descabellar** [1a] *p. etc.* dishevel, rumple; *toro* kill with a thrust in the neck.
descabezado headless; *fig.* wild, crazy; rash; **descabezar** [1f] behead; *árbol* lop, poll; *planta* top; *fig. dificultad* begin to get over; *trabajo* be over the worst part of; *v. sueño*; **~se** rack one's brains.
descalabrado: *salir* ~ come out the loser (*de* in); **descalabrar** [1a] hit *etc.* in the head; (*en general*) hit, hurt; (*romper*) damage, smash; **descalabro** *m* blow, setback, misfortune; (*daño*) damage; ⚔ defeat.
descalcificar [1g] decalcify.
descalificación *f* disqualification; **descalificar** [1g] disqualify.
descalzar [1f] *zapato etc.* take off; *p.* take off *s.o.'s* shoes *etc.*; **~se** take off one's shoes *etc.*; (*caballo*) lose a shoe; **descalzo** bare-foot(ed), shoeless *etc.*; *eccl.* discalced; *estar* ~ *freq.* have one's shoes off; *ir* ~ go bare-footed.
descamarse [1a] scale (off).
descaminado *fig.* misguided, ill-advised; **descaminar** [1a] mislead, put on the wrong road; *fig.* lead astray; *S.Am.* hold up.
descamisado 1. ragged, wretched; **2.** *m* poor devil, wretch.
descampado: *al* ~ in the open air; *en* ~ in open country.
descansadero *m* stopping place, resting place; **descansado** rested, refreshed; *vida* free from care; (*que tranquiliza*) restful; **descansapié**(**s**) *m mot.* footrest; **descansar** [1a] *v/t.* (*ayudar*) help, give a hand to; (*apoyar*) rest, lean (*sobre* on); *¡descansen armas!* order arms!; *v/i.* (*no trabajar*) rest, take a rest, have a break (*de* from); (*dormir*) rest, sleep; (*enfermo*) rest, lie down; (*yacer*) lie; ✔ lie fallow; *no* ~ *freq.* not have a moment's rest; *¡que Vd. descanse!*, *¡descanse bien!* sleep well!; ~ *en* △, ⊕ rest upon, be supported by; *fig.* rely on; **descansillo** *m* △ landing; **descanso** *m* (*reposo*) rest; (*pausa*) rest, break; (*alivio*) relief; *deportes*: half-time, interval; *thea.* interval; △ landing; ⊕ support, rest; bracket; *sin* ~ *trabajar etc.* without a break.
descarado shameless, brazen; cheeky, saucy; blatant; F nervy;
descararse [1a] behave in an impudent way (*con* towards); ~ *a pedir* have the nerve to ask (for).
descarburar [1a] decarbonize.
descarga *f* unloading; off-loading; firing, discharge; ~ (*cerrada*) volley; ⚡ discharge; **descargadero** *m* unloading place; wharf; **descargador** *m* docker; **descargar** [1h] **1.** *v/t. barco, carro etc.* unload; off-load; *arma* fire, shoot, discharge; ⚡ discharge; *golpe* let fly (*en* at), strike (*en* on); *fig. p.* relieve, release (*de obligación* from); clear, acquit (*de culpa* of); free (*de deuda* of); *conciencia* ease; *ira etc.* vent (*en* on); **2.** *v/i.* ⚡ discharge; (*tempestad*) burst, break; ~ *en* (*río*) flow into; (*calle etc.*) open into; **3. ~se** resign; ⚖ clear o.s. (*de* of); ~ *de* get rid of, disburden o.s. of; ~ *en uno de algo* unload s.t. on to s.o.; **descargo** *m* unloading *de barco etc.*; ✝ receipt, voucher; ✝ discharge *de deuda*; ⚖ (*alegato*) evidence; ⚖ acquittal (*de acusación* of); release (*de obligación* from); **descargue** *m* unloading; off-loading.
descarnado lean, scrawny F; cadaverous; **descarnar** [1a] *hueso* remove the flesh from; *fig.* wear down, eat away; **~se** lose flesh.
descaro *m* shamelessness; impudence, cheek; blatancy.
descarriar [1c] misdirect, put on the wrong road; **~se** stray; *fig.* go astray.
descarrilamiento *m* derailment; **descarrilar** [1a] (*a.* **~se** *S.Am.*) be derailed, go off the rails; *fig.* wander from the point.
descartar [1a] discard, reject; **~se** *naipes*: discard; ~ *de* shirk; **descarte** *m naipes*: discard; *fig.* excuse.
descascar [1g] peel; shell; **~se** smash to pieces; F chatter; **descascarar** [1a] peel; shell; **~se** peel (off).
descendedero *m* ramp; **descendencia** *f* descent (*de* from), origin; (*hijos*) offspring; **descendente** descending, downward; *tren* down;

descender [2g] *v/t.* get down, take down; *escalera* go down; *v/i.* descend, come down, go down; (*fluir, pasar*) run, flow; ~ de descend from, be descended from; *fig.* derive from; **descendiente** *m/f* descendant; **descendimiento** *m* descent (*a. eccl.*); **descenso** *m* descent; (*disminución*) fall, decline, falling-off (de in); (*socavón*) subsidence; (*desnivel*) slope, drop.
descentrado off center; out of plumb; **descentralización** *f* decentralization; **descentralizar** [1f] decentralize.
descercar [1g] *ciudad* relieve; raise the siege of; **descerco** *m* relief.
descerrajado F raving mad; (*malo*) wicked; **descerrajar** [1a] break open; F *tiro* let off.
descifrable decipherable; **desciframiento** *m* deciphering, decoding; resolving; **descifrar** [1a] decipher, read; *mensaje en cifra* decode; *fig.* puzzle out, make out.
desclasificación *f* disqualification; **desclasificar** [1g] disqualify.
descocado F cheeky; brazen, insolent, forward; **descocarse** [1g] F be cheeky *etc.*; **descoco** *m* F cheek; brazenness.
descoger [2c] spread out, unfold.
descolar [1a] *vet.* tail; crop; cut the tail off.
descolgar [1h *a.* 1m] take down, get down, unhook; *auricular* lift; pick up; **~se** let o.s. down (de from; con by); come down; *fig.* turn up unexpectedly; ~ con *fig.* come out with.
descoloramiento *m* discoloration; **descolorar**(**se**) [1a] discolor; **descolorido** faded, discolored; *fig.* colorless.
descollante outstanding; **descollar** [1m] stand out.
descombrar [1a] clear, disencumber.
descomedido excessive; intemperate; (*grosero*) rude, disrespectful; **descomedimiento** *m* rudeness *etc.*; **descomedirse** [3l] be rude *etc.*
descompaginar [1a] mess up, disorganize.
descompasado out of all proportion; **descompasarse** [1a] be rude.
descomponer [2r] *orden* disturb, upset, disarrange; *facciones* distort; *fig.* shake up, put out; (*desmontar*) take apart; (*estropear*) tamper with, put out of order; *conjunto* split up; *ps.* create bad feeling between; *calma* ruffle, disturb; (*pudrir*) rot, decompose; ⚗ separate into its elements; **~se** (*pudrirse*) rot, decompose; (*irritarse*) lose one's temper; ~ con fall out with; **descomposición** *f* disturbance *etc.*; distortion; *opt.* dispersal; (*putrefacción*) decomposition (*a.* ⚗); *fig.* discomposure; **descompostura** *f* disorder, disorganization; (*desaseo*) untidiness; *fig.* discomposure; (*descaro*) brazenness; **descompuesto** out of order; *rostro* twisted; *fig.* (*descarado*) brazen; (*descortés*) rude; (*colérico*) angry.
descomunal huge, enormous; *sl.* humongous.
desconcertado disconcerted, taken aback; puzzled, bewildered; **desconcertador, desconcertante** disconcerting, upsetting, embarrassing; **desconcertar** [1k] ⊕ put out of order, damage; *anat.* dislocate; *proyecto* dislocate, throw out of gear; *orden* disturb; *p.* disconcert, put out; embarrass; (*problema*) baffle; puzzle, bewilder; **desconcierto** *m* disorder, confusion; ⊕ damage; *fig.* (*desavenencia*) disagreement; embarrassment; bewilderment.
desconcharse [1a] peel off, flake off.
desconectar [1a] ⚡, ⊕ disconnect.
desconfiado distrustful, suspicious; **desconfianza** *f* distrust; **desconfiar** [1c]: ~ de distrust, mistrust, suspect.
desconformar(**se**) [1a] disagree, dissent; **desconforme** in disagreement, dissident; **desconformidad** *f* disagreement (con with), dissent (de from).
descongelación *f* thaw; thawing out; **descongelador** *m* defroster; **descongelar** [1a] melt; defrost; † unfreeze, defreeze; **descongestión** *f* decongestion; freeing up; clearing; **descongestionar** [1a] decongest; free up.
desconocer [2d] not know; be ignorant of, be unfamiliar with; (*no reconocer*) not recognize; (*fingiendo*)

pretend not to know; ignore, disregard; (*rechazar*) disown, repudiate; **desconocido 1.** unknown (*de, para* to); strange, unfamiliar; (*cambiado*) much changed; (*ingrato*) ungrateful; **2.** *m*, **a** *f* stranger; **desconocimiento** *m* ignorance; repudiation; ingratitude.

desconsideración *f* inconsiderateness; **desconsiderado** inconsiderate.

desconsolado disconsolate; *rostro* woebegone; **desconsolador** distressing; **desconsolar** [1m] grieve, distress; **desconsuelo** *m* grief, distress.

descontable discountable.

descontaminación *f* decontamination; ~ *de radiactividad* radioactive decontamination; **descontaminar** [1a] decontaminate.

descontar [1m] take away; † discount (*a. fig.*), rebate; (*a. dar por descontado*) take for granted, assume.

descontentadizo hard to please; testy, peevish; restless, unsettled; **descontentar** [1a] displease; dissatisfy; **descontento 1.** dissatisfied (*de* with); discontented; disgruntled (*de* at); **2.** *m* dissatisfaction, displeasure; *esp. pol.* discontent.

descontinuación *f* discontinuation; **descontinuar** [1e] discontinue.

descontrolado *S.Am.* uncontrolled; unregulated; deregulated; **descontrolar** [1a] † deregulate; decontrol.

descorazonar [1a] *fig.* discourage; **~se** get discouraged.

descorchador *m* corkscrew; **descorchar** [1a] ⚘ *árbol* strip, bark; *botella* uncork, open.

descornar [1m] dehorn, poll.

descorrer [2a] *cortina* draw back.

descortés discourteous, rude; **descortesía** *f* discourtesy, rudeness.

descortezar [1f] *árbol* skin, bark; *pan* cut the crust off; F polish up a bit.

descoser [2a] unstitch; rip (apart); **~se** burst at the seams, come apart; F fart; **descosido 1.** big-mouthed; (*desastrado*) shabby, slovenly; **2.** *m sew.* open seam; tear; F *comer como un* ~ eat an awful lot.

descoyuntar [1a] put out of joint, dislocate; *fig.* bother, annoy.

descrédito *m* discredit; disrepute; **descreer** [2e] disbelieve (*a. eccl.*); **descreído 1.** unbelieving; godless; **2.** *m*, **a** *f* unbeliever; **descreimiento** *m* unbelief.

describir [3a; *p.p. descrito*] describe (*a.* ⚒); **descripción** *f* description; **descriptible** describable; **descriptivo** descriptive.

descrismar [1a] F bash *s.o.* on the head; **~se** F blow one's top.

descuajar [1a] dissolve; ⚘ uproot; *fig.* eradicate; F discourage.

descuajaringarse [1h] F be dog-tired; *S.Am.* fall to bits.

descuartizar [1f] carve up.

descubierto *situación* open, exposed; ⚔ *freq. a.* under fire; *p.* bareheaded; *cabeza* bare; † *a* ~ unbacked; *a(l)* ~ in the open; † *en* ~ overdrawn; *poner al* ~ lay *s.t.* bare; *quedar al* ~ be exposed; **descubridero** *m* look-out; **descubridor** *m* discoverer; ⚔ scout; **descubrimiento** *m* discovery; detection; **descubrir** [3a; *p.p. descubierto*] discover; detect, spot; bring to light, unearth, uncover; *petróleo etc.* strike; (*alcanzar a ver*) see; (*mostrar*) reveal; *estatua etc.* unveil; **~se** take off one's hat; (*saludo*) raise one's hat.

descuento *m* discount, rebate; *a* ~ below par; *al* ~ at a discount.

descuerar [1a] *S.Am.* skin; flay; F slander, libel.

descuidado careless; slack, negligent; forgetful; (*desaseado*) slovenly, unkempt; (*desprevenido*) off one's guard; **descuidar** [1a] *v/t.* neglect, disregard; *v/i.*, **~se** not worry, not bother (*de* about); *¡descuide Vd.!* don't worry!; **descuidero** *m* sneak thief; **descuido** *m* carelessness, slackness *etc.*; (*un* ~) oversight, mistake; *al* ~ nonchalantly; *por* ~ by an oversight.

deschavetar [1a] *S.Am.* get rattled; go mad; F flip one's lid.

desde *tiempo* since; *tiempo, lugar* from; ~ *hace 3 días* for 3 days; these last 3 days; ~ ... *hasta* from ... to; ~ *que* since.

desdén *m* disdain; scorn.

desdeñable contemptible; **desdeñador** = *desdeñoso*; **desdeñar** [1a] scorn, disdain, despise; turn up

one's nose at; ~**se** *de inf.* not deign to *inf.*; **desdeñoso** scornful, disdainful, contemptuous.
desdibujarse [1a] blur, fade (away).
desdicha *f* unhappiness; misery; wretchedness; (*una* ~) misfortune; **desdichado 1.** unhappy, unlucky; wretched; **2.** *m* poor devil, wretch.
desdinerarse [1a] F cough up.
desdoblar [1a] unfold, spread out; ⚗ break down (*en* into).
desdorar [1a] tarnish (*a. fig.*); **desdoro** *m* blot, stigma.
deseable desirable; **desear** [1a] want, desire, wish for; *desearía tiempo* I should like time; ~ *inf.* want to *inf.*, wish to *inf.*
desecación *f* desiccation; **desecar** [1g] dry up (*a. fig.*), desiccate.
desechar [1a] *desechos etc.* throw out; *lo inútil* jettison, scrap; *consejo, miedo etc.* cast aside; *proyecto, oferta* reject; *cargo* throw up; *talento etc.* underrate; blame; censure; *llave* turn; **desecho** *m* residue, waste; chaff *de grano*; *fig.* contempt, low opinion; ~ *de hierro* scrap iron; ~*s pl.* rubbish, debris, waste.
desembalar [1a] unpack.
desembanastar [1a] unpack; *secreto* blurt out, give away.
desembarazado (*despejado*) free, open; (*sin carga*) light; *fig.* free and easy; **desembarazar** [1f] *camino, sala* clear (*de* of); *fig.* ~ *de* rid *s.o.* of; ~**se** *de* get rid of, free o.s. of; **desembarazo** *m* freedom; lack of restraint.
desembarcadero *m* pier; wharf; landing place; **desembarcar** [1g] *v/t. ps.* land, put ashore; *mercancías* unload; *v/i.* land, disembark, go ashore; **desembarco** *m* debarkation; disembarkation; landing (*a. de escalera*) *etc.*
desembargar [1h] free.
desembarque *m* unloading, landing.
desembaular [1a] unpack, get out; F unburden o.s. of.
desembocadura *f* mouth; outlet, outfall; opening *de calle*; **desembocar** [1g]: ~ *en* (*río*) flow into; (*calle*) open into, meet; *fig.* end in.
desembolsar [1a] disburse; pay out; **desembolso** *m* outlay, expenditure; ~ *inicial* deposit.
desembragar [1h] disengage, disconnect; *mot.* declutch; **desembrague** *m* disengagement; *mot.* declutching.
desembriagar(**se**) [1h] sober up.
desembrollar [1a] F unravel.
desembuchar [1a] disgorge; F spill the beans; *¡desembucha!* out with it!
desemejante dissimilar; unlike (*a.* ~ *de*); **desemejanza** *f* dissimilarity; **desemejar** [1a] *v/t.* alter, change (for the worse); *v/i.* not look alike.
desempacar [1g] unpack.
desempacho *m* ease, confidence; unconcern.
desempaquetar [1a] unpack, unwrap.
desempatar [1a] break the tie between; **desempate** *m* (*a. partido de* ~) play-off.
desempeñar [1a] *prenda* redeem, take out of hock; *deudor* free from debt; *p.* get out of a jam; *deber* discharge; perform; *papel* play; **desempeño** *m* discharge *etc. de deber*; *thea.* performance, acting.
desempleado jobless; out of work, unemployed; **desempleo** *m* unemployment; joblessness; ~ *en masa* mass unemployment.
desempolvar [1a] dust.
desenamorar [1a] alienate; ~**se** grow apart; F get fed up (*de* with).
desencadenar [1a] unchain; *esp. fig.* unleash; ~**se** *fig.* break loose; (*tempestad, fig.*) burst.
desencajado *cara* contorted; *ojos* wild; **desencajar** [1a] dislocate; ⊕ disconnect; **desencajonar** [1a] take out, unpack.
desencallar [1a] refloat.
desencantar [1a] disenchant, disillusion; **desencanto** *m* disenchantment, disillusion(ment).
desenconar(**se**) [1a] *fig.* calm down; (*odio*) die down, abate.
desencorvar [1a] unbend, straighten.
desenchufar [1a] disconnect, unplug.
desenfadaderas *f/pl.* wits; resources; F *tener buenas* ~ be unflappable, be good at getting out of jams; **desenfadado** free, uninhibited; unconventional; **desenfadar**(**se**) [1a] calm down; **desenfado** *m* freedom, lack of inhibition.

desenfocado out of focus.
desenfrenado wild; (*vicioso*) unbridled, licentious; **desenfrenarse** [1a] lose all control; run riot, (go on the) rampage; indulge one's passions; (*tempestad*) burst, rage; **desenfreno** *m* wildness, lack of control; (*vicio*) licentiousness.
desenganchar [1a] unhook, unfasten; ⊕ disengage; *caballo* unhitch.
desengañar [1a] undeceive; disabuse (*de* of); **~se** see the light; become disillusioned; *¡desengáñese Vd.!* don't you believe it!; **desengaño** *m* disillusion(ment); (*chasco*) disappointment.
desenlace *m* outcome; *lit.* ending, dénouement; ~ *fatal* tragic ending; **desenlazar** [1f] undo, unlace; **~se** *lit.* end, turn out.
desenmarañar [1a] unravel, disentangle.
desenmascarar [1a] unmask, expose, show up.
desenojar [1a] appease, calm down.
desenredar [1a] free, disentangle (*a. fig.*); *fig.* resolve, straighten out; **~se** extricate o.s.; *fig.* get clear of trouble; ~ *de* get out of; **desenredo** *m* disentanglement; *lit.* dénouement.
desenrollar(**se**) [1a] unroll, unwind.
desensillar [1a] unsaddle.
desentenderse [2g]: ~ *de* wash one's hands of; affect ignorance of; *hacerse el desentendido* pretend not to have noticed.
desenterrar [1k] unearth, dig up (*a.* F); *muerto* disinter.
desentonar [1a] be out of tune (*con* with; *a. fig.*); **~se** *fig.* speak disrespectfully; **desentono** *m fig.* rudeness, rude tone of voice.
desentorpecer [2d] stretch; F polish *s.o.* up a bit.
desentramparse [1a] F get out of the red.
desentrañar [1a] disembowel; *fig.* puzzle out, get to the bottom of.
desentrenado out of practice.
desentumecer [2d] *miembro* stretch; *músculos* loosen up.
desenvainar [1a] *espada* unsheathe; ⚘ shell; F bring out, show.
desenvoltura *f* ease, assurance; *b.s.* boldness; brazenness; **desenvolver** [2h; *p.p. desenvuelto*] *paquete* unwrap; *rollo* unwind; *enredo* disentangle; (*desarrollar*) develop; **desenvolvimiento** *m* development; **desenvuelto** *fig.* free and easy, self-assured; *b.s.* bold; *mujer* brazen.
deseo *m* wish, desire (*de* for; *de inf.* to *inf.*); **deseoso** *de inf.* desirous of *ger.*, eager to *inf.*
desequilibrado unbalanced (*a. fig.*); (*desigual*) one-sided, lopsided; **desequilibrar** [1a] unbalance; throw off balance; **desequilibrio** *m* unbalance (*a.* ⚕).
deserción *f* desertion; **desertar** [1a] desert (*a.* ~ *de*); **desertor** *m* deserter.
deservicio *m* disservice.
desescarchador *m mot.* defroster.
desesperación *f* despair, desperation; F *ser una* ~ be unbearable; **desesperado** desperate; in despair; *condición* hopeless; **desesperanzar** [1f] deprive of hope; **desesperar** [1a] drive to despair; F drive to distraction; *v/i.*, **~se** despair (*de* of), lose hope; get desperate.
desestimar [1a] have a low opinion of; belittle, disparage; (*rechazar*) reject; discount.
desfachatado F brazen, barefaced; cheeky; **desfachatez** *f* F brazenness; impudence.
desfalcar [1g] embezzle; **desfalco** *m* embezzlement.
desfallecer [2d] *v/t.* weaken; *v/i.* get weak; faint away; (*voz*) fail; ~ *de ánimo* lose heart; **desfallecimiento** *m* weakness; faintness.
desfavorable unfavorable; **desfavorecer** [2d] disfavor.
desfiguración *f* disfiguration *etc.*; **desfigurado** altered; deformed; *phot.* blurred; **desfigurar** [1a] *rostro* disfigure; *cuadro etc.* deface; *voz* alter, disguise; *suceso etc.* distort, misrepresent.
desfiladero *m* defile, pass; **desfilar** [1a] parade; (*a.* ~ *ante*) march past, file past; **desfile** *m* procession; ⚔ parade, march past.
desflorar [1a] deflower; *asunto* treat superficially.
desfogar [1h] vent (*a. fig.*); **~se** *fig.* let o.s. go, blow off steam; **desfogue** *m* vent; *fig.* venting.

desfondar [1a] stave in (*a.* ⚓); ⚒ plough deeply.
desgaire *m* (*desaliño*) slovenliness; (*descuido*) nonchalance; *al* ~ in a slovenly way; scornfully; *mirar al* ~ sneer at.
desgajar [1a] tear off, break off; **~se** come off, break off; *fig.* tear o.s. away (*de* from); (*cielo*) get stormy.
desgalichado F clumsy, sloppy.
desgana *f* lack of appetite; *fig.* disinclination, reluctance; *a* ~ reluctantly; **desganado:** *sentirse* ~ have no appetite; **desganarse** [1a] lose one's appetite; *fig.* get fed up.
desgañitarse [1a] F bawl, scream o.s. hoarse.
desgarbado clumsy, ungainly; (*desaliñado*) slovenly.
desgarrador *fig.* heartbreaking, heartrending; **desgarrar** [1a] tear, rip up; *fig.* rend, shatter; **desgarro** *m* tear; *fig.* effrontery; boastfulness; **desgarrón** *m* big tear.
desgastado worn (out); used up; eroded; *llanta* treadless, bald; *tela* threadbare; **desgastar** [1a] wear away; *geol.* erode, weather; *cuerda etc.* chafe, fray; *metal* corrode; *fig.* spoil, ruin; **~se** wear away *etc.*; ⚕ get weak, wear o.s. out; **desgaste** *m* wear; erosion *etc.*; attrition (*a.* ⚔); (*pérdida*) waste, wastage.
desglosar [1a] remove, detach.
desgobernado uncontrollable, undisciplined; ungovernable; **desgobernar** [1k] misgovern, misrule; *asunto* mismanage, handle badly; *anat.* dislocate; **desgobierno** *m* misgovernment; mismanagement.
desgoznar [1a] unhinge, take off the hinges; **~se** *fig.* go off the rails; be thrown out of gear.
desgracia *f* (*mala suerte*) misfortune; (*suceso*) mishap, misfortune; (*pérdida de favor*) disgrace; (*aspereza*) unfriendliness; *por* ~ unfortunately; *caer en la* ~ fall into disgrace; **desgraciadamente** unfortunately; regrettably; **desgraciado 1.** unlucky, unfortunate; wretched; (*sin gracia*) graceless; (*desagradable*) unpleasant; **2.** *m*, **a** *f* wretch, unfortunate.
desgranar [1a] *trigo* thresh; *racimo* pick the grapes from; *guisantes* shell; **~se** ⚘ fall, seed; (*cuentas*) come unstrung.
desgreñado disheveled; **desgreñar** [1a] tousle, ruffle; muss.
desguarnecer [2d] ⊕ strip down; *plaza* abandon, dismantle; *caballo* unharness.
desguazar [1f] ⚓ break up; *madera* dress.
deshabitado unhabited; **deshabitar** [1a] move out of.
deshabituarse [1e] lose (*or* break) the habit.
deshacer [2s] *lo hecho* undo, unmake; spoil, destroy; (*dividir*) cut up; (*romper*) pull to pieces; ⊕ take apart; *maleta* unpack; *paquete* open; (*desgastar*) wear down; (*liquidar*) melt, dissolve; *agravio* right; *enemigo* rout; *tratado* violate; *miembro* (*a.* **~se**) hurt, bump (*contra* on); **~se** fall to pieces, come apart *al caer etc.*; (*liquidarse*) melt; (*afligirse*) grieve; get impatient *esperando*; ⚕ get weak; ~ *de* get rid of; *carga* throw off; ✈ dump, unload; part with *de mala gana*; ~ *en lágrimas* dissolve into; *cumplidos etc.* overdo, be lavish with; ~ *por inf.* struggle to *inf.*
desharrapado ragged, shabby.
deshebillar [1a] unbuckle.
deshebrar [1a] unthread.
deshecho 1. *p.p. of deshacer*; undone; *salud* broken; F *estoy* ~ I'm worn out; **2.** *adj. lluvia* violent; *suerte* tremendous.
deshelar [1k] thaw, melt, defrost (*a.* **~se**); ✈ de-ice.
desherbar [1k] weed.
desheredar [1a] disinherit.
desherrarse [1k] lose a shoe.
deshidratación *f* dehydration; **deshidratado** dehydrated.
deshielo *m* thaw; melting; defrosting.
deshilachar [1a] pull threads out of; **~se** fray; **deshilar** [1a] unravel.
deshilvanado *fig.* disconnected, disjointed; **deshilvanar** [1a] untack; unbaste.
deshinchar [1a] *neumático* let down; go flat; deflate; *cólera* give vent to; **~se** ⚕ go down; F get off one's high horse.
deshojado leafless; *flor* stripped of its petals; **deshojar** [1a] strip the leaves (*or* petals) off; **~se** lose its leaves *etc.*

deshollinador *m* (chimney) sweep; **deshollinar** [1a] sweep; F take a close look at.
deshonestidad *f* indecency *etc.*; **deshonesto** indecent, lewd, improper; **deshonor** *m* dishonor; insult (*de* to); **deshonorar** [1a] dishonor; be unworthy of; (*afear*) spoil, disfigure; (*despedir*) dismiss; **deshonra** *f* dishonor, disgrace, shame; shameful act; *tener algo a* ~ think s.t. shameful; **deshonrar** [1a] dishonor, disgrace; insult; *mujer* seduce; **deshonroso** dishonorable, ignominious.
deshora: *a* ~ at the wrong time; (*sin avisar*) unexpectedly; *hacer etc. a* ~ *freq.* mistime.
deshuesador *m* pitter; boner; **~a** *f fruta* pitter; pit-removing device; **deshuesar** [1a] *carne* bone; ⚘ stone.
desiderátum *m* desideratum.
desidia *f* laziness, idleness; **desidioso** lazy, idle.
desierto 1. *casa etc.* deserted; *isla* desert; *paisaje* bleak, desolate; *certamen*: void; **2.** *m* desert; wilderness.
designación *f* designation, appointment; **designar** [1a] designate, appoint; name; **designio** *m* design, plan.
desigual unequal; *superficie* uneven, rough, bumpy; *filo* ragged; *progreso etc.* erratic; *distribución* uneven, patchy; *contienda* unequal, one-sided; *tiempo* changeable; *fig.* arduous, tough; **desigualdad** *f* inequality; unevenness *etc.*
desilusión *f* disappointment; disillusion(ment); **desilusionar** [1a] disappoint, let down; disillusion; **~se** get disillusioned.
desinencia *f gr.* ending.
desinfección *f* disinfection; **desinfectante** *m* disinfectant; **desinfectar** [1a] disinfect.
desinflación *f* disinflation; deflation; **desinflacionar** [1a] ✝ deflate; **desinflar** [1a] deflate.
desinsectación *f insectos* extermination; fumigation; **desinsectar** [1a] exterminate insects (*de* from); fumigate.
desintegración *f*: ~ *nuclear* nuclear fission.
desinterés *m* disinterestedness; **desinteresado** disinterested; unselfish.
desintoxicación *f* sobering (up); detoxification; **desintoxicarse** [1g] sober up; get detoxified.
desistir [3a] desist; ~ *de* desist from; *derecho etc.* waive.
desjarretar [1a] hamstring; F ⚕ lay out.
deslavazado faded, colorless.
desleal disloyal; **deslealtad** *f* disloyalty.
desleído *ideas* woolly; **desleír** [3m] dissolve; dilute; *fig.* be long-winded about.
deslenguado foul-mouthed; scurrilous.
desliar [1c] untie, undo; **~se** come undone.
desligar [1h] untie, undo; *fig.* detach, separate; (*desenredar*) unravel; absolve, free (*de juramento* from).
deslindar [1a] mark out; *fig.* define.
desliz *m* slide; *mot.* skid; *esp. fig.* slip, lapse; **deslizadero** *m* slippery spot; **deslizadizo** slippery; **deslizamiento** *m* slide, sliding; skid; glide; ~ *de tierra* landslide; **deslizar** [1f] *v/t.* slide (*por* along), slip (*en* into, *por* through); *observación* slip in; *secreto* let slip; *v/i.*, **~se** (*resbalar*) slip (*en* up on); slide (*por* along); *mot.* skid; (*culebra etc.*) glide, slither; (*introducirse*) squeeze in; (*huir*) slip away; (*secreto*) slip out; (*equivocarse*) slip up, blunder; *b.s.* get into bad ways.
deslomar [1a] break the back of; **~se** F work one's guts out.
deslucido unadorned; dull, lifeless; undistinguished; *quedar etc.* ~ *fig.* be unsuccessful; **deslucimiento** *m* dullness *etc.*; **deslucir** [3f] tarnish, dull; *fig.* spoil, fail to give life to; **~se** *fig.* be unsuccessful.
deslumbrador dazzling (*a. fig.*), glaring; **deslumbramiento** *m* glare, dazzle; *fig.* confusion, bewilderment; **deslumbrante** dazzling; **deslumbrar** [1a] dazzle (*a. fig.*), blind; *fig.* confuse, bewilder.
deslustrado dull, lusterless (*a. fig.*); *vidrio* frosted, ground; **deslustrar** [1a] tarnish (*a. fig.*), dull; **deslustre** *m* dullness; tarnish; *fig.* stain, stigma.
desmadejar [1a] weaken; enervate.

desmallarse [1a] (*medias*) run.
desmán *m* excess; piece of bad behavior.
desmandado uncontrollable, out of hand; obstreperous; **desmandarse** [1a] behave badly, be insolent; get out of hand.
desmanotado awkward.
desmantelamiento *m* dilapidation; (*acto*) dismantling; **desmantelar** [1a] dismantle; *casa* abandon, forsake; **~se** get dilapidated.
desmaña *f* awkwardness *etc.*; **desmañado** awkward, clumsy; unpractical.
desmarcado *deportes*: unmarked.
desmayado ⚕ unconscious; ⚕ *fig.* weak, faint; languid; apathetic; *color* pale; **desmayar** [1a] *v/t.* dismay, distress; *v/i.* lose heart, get depressed; **~se** faint; **desmayo** *m* ⚕ faint(ing fit); ⚕ (*en general*) unconsciousness; *fig.* depression; *con ~ hablar* in a small voice, falteringly; *sin ~* unfaltering(ly); unflagging(ly).
desmedido excessive, disproportionate; *ambición etc.* boundless; **desmedirse** [3l] forget o.s., go too far.
desmedrar [1a] v/t. impair; *v/i.* decline, fall off; **desmedro** *m* decline, deterioration.
desmejorar [1a] spoil, impair; **~se** decline, deteriorate; ⚕ lose one's health; lose one's charms; *queda muy desmejorada* she's lost her looks; she's looking quite ill.
desmelenado disheveled.
desmembración *f* dismemberment; **desmembrar** [1k] dismember.
desmemoriado forgetful, absentminded; **desmemoriarse** [1b] get absentminded.
desmentida *f* denial; *dar una ~ a* give the lie to; **desmentir** [3i] *v/t.* give the lie to; *acusación* deny, refute; *carácter* belie; *rumor* scotch, scout; *teoría* explode; *v/i.*: *~ de* belie.
desmenuzable crumbly, crumbling, flaky; **desmenuzar** [1f] *pan* crumble; *carne* chop (up), grind, mince; *queso etc.* shred; *fig.* take a close look at.
desmerecer [2d] *v/t.* be unworthy of; *v/i.* deteriorate, lose value; *~ de* compare unfavorably with; not live up to; *no ~ de* be every bit as good as; **desmerecimiento** *m* unworthiness.
desmesura *f* excess; intemperance; immoderation; **desmesurado** disproportionate, inordinate; *ambición etc.* boundless; (*descarado*) impudent; **desmesurarse** [1a] forget o.s.
desmigajar [1a], **desmigar** [1h] crumble.
desmilitarización *f* demilitarization; **desmilitarizado** demilitarized; *zona ~a* demilitarized zone; **desmilitarizar** [1f] demilitarize.
desmirriado F ⚕ run down, under the weather; weedy *de natural.*
desmochar [1a] top; *árbol* lop, pollard; *texto etc.* cut.
desmontable detachable; **desmontaje** *m* ⊕ dismantling *etc.*; **desmontar** [1a] *v/t.* ⊕ dismantle, take to pieces, strip (down); ⚠ knock down; *escopeta* uncock; *vela* take in; *solar* level, clear; *árboles* fell; (*ayudar a bajar*) help *s.o.* down; *v/i.*, **~se** dismount, alight; **desmonte** *m* ⊕ *dismantling etc.*; levelling; 🚂 cutting.
desmoralización *f* demoralization; **desmoralizador** demoralizing; **desmoralizar** [1f] *ejército* demoralize; *costumbres etc.* corrupt.
desmoronadizo crumbling, crumbly; **desmoronado** dilapidated, tumbledown; **desmoronarse** [1a] *geol.* crumble; (*casa*) fall into disrepair, get dilapidated; (*caer*) collapse; *fig.* decline, decay.
desmovilización *f* demobilization; **desmovilizar** [1f] demobilize.
desmultiplicar [1g] ⊕ gear down.
desnacionalizado denationalized; *p.* stateless.
desnatar [1a] *leche* skim; *fig.* take the cream off; *leche sin ~* whole milk.
desnaturalizado unnatural; ⚗ denatured; **desnaturalizer** [1f] alter fundamentally; pervert, corrupt; ⚗ denature; *intenciones* misrepresent; **~se** (*p.*) give up one's nationality.
desnivel *m* unevenness; ⚠ cant, tilt; *fig.* inequality, difference, gap; **desnivelar** [1a] make uneven.
desnucar [1g] break the neck of; *res* fell; **~se** break one's neck.

desnudar [1a] strip (*a.* ⚘, *fig.*; de of); undress; *brazo etc.* bare; *espada* draw; **~se** undress, get undressed, strip; ~ de *hojas etc.* shed; *fig.* cast aside; **desnudez** *f* nakedness, nudity; bareness (*a. fig.*); **desnudismo** *m* nudism; **desnudista** *m/f* nudist; **desnudo 1.** naked, nude; bare; *fig.* (*sin adorno*) bare; (*pobre*) penniless; *verdad etc.* plain; ~ de devoid of, bereft of; **2.** *m* nude.

desnutrición *f* malnutrition, undernourishment; **desnutrido** ill-fed; undernourished.

desobedecer [2d] disobey; **desobediencia** *f* disobedience; **desobediente** disobedient.

desobstruir [3g] unblock, clear.

desocupación *f* leisure; *b.s.* idleness; (*paro*) unemployment; **desocupado** *cuarto* vacant, unoccupied; *tiempo* spare, leisure *attr.*; *p.* at leisure; *b.s.* idle; (*parado*) unemployed; (*libre*) free, not busy; **desocupar** [1a] *casa etc.* vacate; *cajón* empty.

desodorante *m* deodorant; **desodorizar** [1f] deodorize.

desoír [3q] ignore, disregard.

desojarse [1a] strain one's eyes.

desolación *f* desolation; *fig.* grief; **desolar** [1m] lay waste; **~se** grieve.

desolladero *m* slaughterhouse; F talking shop; **desollado** F brazen, barefaced; **desollador** *m fig.* extortioner, robber; **desolladura** *f* ⚕ graze, bruise; **desollar** [1m] skin, flay; F ~ *vivo* make *s.o.* pay through the nose; (*criticar*) flay.

desorbitado: *con los ojos* ~*s* wide-eyed, popeyed.

desorden *m mst* disorder; turmoil, confusion; (*objetos*) litter, mess; *fig.* loose living; **desordenado** disordered; *conducta etc.* disorderly; *objetos, cuarto* untidy; *niño etc.* wild, unruly; *país* lawless; **desordenar** [1a] throw into confusion, mess up, disarrange.

desorganización *f* disorganization, disruption; **desorganizar** [1f] disorganize, disrupt.

desorientación *f* disorientation; confusion; confusedness; going astray; **desorientar** [1a] make *s.o.* lose his way; *fig.* confuse; **~se** lose one's bearings.

desovar [1a] spawn; (*insecto*) lay eggs; **desove** *m* spawning; egg-laying; **desovillar** [1a] unwind; unravel (*a. fig.*).

despabiladeras *f/pl.* (*unas* a pair of) snuffers; **despabilado** wide awake (*a. fig.*); **despabilar** [1a] *vela* snuff; *lámpara* trim; *fig. p.* wake up, liven up; F (*robar*) swipe; (*matar*) do in; *fortuna* squander; *negocio* do quickly; **~se** wake up (*a. fig.*); *S.Am.* clear out; *¡despabílate!* get a move on!

despacio 1. slowly; gently; gradually; *S.Am.* (*voz*) soft; low; *¡~!* gently!, easy there!; **2.** *m S.Am.* delaying tactic; **despacioso** slow, phlegmatic; **despacito** = *despacio*.

despachaderas: F *tener buenas* ~ be practical, be on the ball; **despachante** *m S.Am.* clerk; ~ *de aduana S.Am.* customhouse broker; **despachar** [1a] *v/t.* (*concluir*) dispatch, settle; *negocio* do, transact; (*enviar*) dispatch, send, post; (*dar prisa a*) expedite; (*vender*) deal in; (*despedir*) send packing; F kill, dispatch; *v/i.* get it settled, come to a decision; (*darse prisa*) hurry; **despacho** *m* office *para negocios*; study *en casa*; (*tienda*) shop; (*mensaje*) dispatch; ~ (*de aduana*) clearance; ~ *de billetes* booking office; *tener buen* ~ be on top of one's job.

despachurrar [1a] F squash, crush, squelch; *comida* mash; *cuento* make a mess of; *p.* flatten, knock sideways.

despampanante F upsetting; disturbing; F stunning, tremendous; **despampanar** [1a] *v/t.* ⚘ prune; F knock *s.o.* sideways, bowl *s.o.* over; *v/i.* F talk freely; **~se** F get a nasty knock.

desparej(ad)o uneven; odd.

desparpajo *m* ease of manner; self-confidence, charm *en el trato*; *b.s.* glibness; savoir faire *en obrar*; *b.s.* (*descaro*) nerve, cheek.

desparramado wide, open; **desparramar** [1a] scatter, spread (*por* over); *fortuna* squander; **~se** F have a whale of a time.

despatarrada *f* F the split; **despatarrarse** [1a] F do a split; sprawl on the floor.

despavorido terrified.
despeado foot-sore; **despearse** [1a] get foot-sore.
despectivo contemptuous, scornful; derogatory; *gr.* pejorative.
despechar [1a] spite; (*irritar*) stir up, enrage; **despecho** *m* spite; despair; *a* ~ *de* in spite of; *orden etc.* in defiance of; *por* ~ out of spite.
despedazar [1f] tear apart, tear to pieces; *fig. honra* ruin; *corazón* break.
despedida *f* farewell, send-off; leave-taking; dismissal; *de* ~ farewell *attr.*, parting *attr.*; **despedir** [3l] *amigo* see off *en estación*, see out *en puerta*; *importuno* send away; *obrero* dismiss, discharge, sack; *olor* emit, give off; (*soltar*) get rid of; ~ *de sí fig.* put out of one's mind; **~se** say goodbye, take one's leave; ~ *de* say goodbye to, take leave of; see off *en estación etc.*
despegar [1h] *v/t.* unstick, detach; *sobre* open; *v/i.* ✈ take off; **~se** come unstuck; ~ *con* not go well with; **despego** *m* = *desapego*; despegue *m* ✈ take-off; ~ *vertical* vertical take-off.
despeinado dishevelled, unkempt; **despeinar** [1a] tousle, ruffle.
despejado clear, open; *cielo* cloudless; *fig. p.* bright, smart; **despejar** [1a] clear (*a. deportes*); *fig.* clear up, clarify; ⚒ find; **~se** *meteor.* clear up; *fig.* amuse o.s., relax; be free and easy *en el trato*; **despeje** *m deportes*: clearance; **despejo** *m* self-confidence, ease of manner; brightness.
despellejar [1a] skin (*a. sl.*).
despenalización *f* legalization; **despenalizar** [1f] legalize; condone.
despenar [1a] F bump off, do in.
despendedor extravagant.
despensa *f* pantry, larder; ⚓ *etc.* store room; (*comida*) stock of food; daily marketing; **despensero** *m* butler, steward.
despeñadamente hastily; boldly; **despeñadero** *m* cliff; *fig.* risk, danger; **despeñadizo** precipitous; **despeñar** [1a] hurl (*por* over, down); **~se** hurl o.s. down; fall headlong; *fig.* ~ *en* plunge into; **despeño** *m fig.* failure, collapse.
despepitarse [1a] bawl, shriek; ~ *por* be crazy about.
desperdiciar [1b] waste, fritter away; *oportunidad* throw away; **desperdicio** *m* waste, wasting; **~s** *pl.* rubbish, refuse; scraps; *biol.* waste products; F *no tener* ~ be just fine.
desperdigar [1h] scatter, separate.
desperezarse [1f] stretch (o.s.).
desperfecto *m* (*daño*) slight damage; (*falta*) flaw, imperfection.
despernado weary, footsore.
despertador *m* alarm clock; (*p.*) knocker-up; *fig.* warning; **despertamiento** *m* awakening; *eccl. etc.* revival; **despertar** [1k] *v/t.* wake (up); *fig. recuerdos* revive, recall; *esperanzas* raise; (*excitar*) arouse, stir up; *v/i.*, **~se** wake up, awaken.
despiadado merciless, remorseless.
despicar [1g] satisfy; **~se** get satisfaction, get even.
despido *m* discharge; firing; termination.
despierto awake; *fig.* alert, watchful; (*listo*) wide awake.
despilfarrado(r) extravagant, wasteful; (*andrajoso*) shabby; **despilfarrar** [1a] waste, squander; **despilfarro** *m* extravagance, waste, wastefulness; (*desaseo*) shabbiness, slovenliness.
despintar [1a] *v/t.* take the paint off; strip; *fig.* spoil, alter, distort; *v/i.*: ~ *de* be unworthy of; **~se** fade, lose its color; *no se me despinta* I always remember it (*or* him *etc.*).
despiojar [1a] delouse; F rescue *s.o.* from the gutter.
despique *m* revenge.
despistado F **1.** (all) at sea, off the beam; absent-minded; **2.** *m* absent-minded sort; **despistar** [1a] *hunt. a. fig.* throw *s.o.* off the scent; *fig.* mislead; **despiste** *m mot.* swerve; F absence of mind; confusion; (*desliz*) slip; *tener un terrible* ~ be hopelessly unpractical.
desplacer 1. [2x] displease; **2.** *m* displeasure.
desplantador *m* trowel; **desplantar** [1a] pull up, uproot; *fig.* move out of vertical.
desplazado *m*, **a** *f* outsider; misfit; (*refugiado*) displaced person; **desplazamiento** *m* ⚓ displacement; **desplazar** [1f] ⚓ displace; *fig.*

displace, take the place of; **~se** move, shift; (*p.*) go, travel.
desplegar [1h *a.* 1k] (*en general*) open (out), unfold; *alas etc.* spread; *velas* unfurl; ⚔ deploy; *energía etc.* display; *lo oculto* clarify, elucidate; **~se** open (out) *etc.*; **despliegue** *m fig.* display; ⚔ deployment.
desplomarse [1a] ⚠ lean, bulge; (*caer*) collapse, tumble (down); ✈ make a pancake landing; *fig.* (*p.*) crumple up; (*gobierno*) collapse; **desplome** *m* collapse *etc.*; ✈ pancake landing; *fig.* collapse, downfall.
desplumar [1a] pluck; *fig.* fleece.
despoblación *f* depopulation; ~ *del campo* drift from the land; **despoblado** *m* deserted spot, uninhabited place; **despoblar** [1m] depopulate; *fig.* lay waste.
despojar [1a]: ~ *de* strip of; *esp. fig.* divest of, denude of; ⚖ dispossess of; **~se** *de ropa* strip off, take off; *hojas etc.* shed; *fig.* divest o.s. of, give up; **despojo** *m* (*acto*) spoliation, despoilment; (*lo robado*) plunder, spoils; **~s** *pl.* leavings, scraps; offal *de animal*; (*restos mortales*) mortal remains; ⚠ rubble; *geol.* debris.
despolvorear [1a] dust.
desportilladura *f* chip; **desportillar**(se) [1a] chip.
desposado recently married; *los* **~s** the bridal couple; **desposar** [1a] marry; **~se** get engaged; (*casarse*) get married.
desposeer [2e] dispossess (*de* of), oust (*de* from); **~se** *de* give up; **desposeído:** *los* **~s** *m/pl. fig.* the have-nots; **desposeimiento** *m* dispossession.
desposorios *m/pl.* engagement.
despostar [1a] *S.Am. res* cut up; carve; butcher.
déspota *m* despot; **despótico** despotic; **despotismo** *m* despotism; ~ *ilustrado* enlightened despotism.
despotricar [1g] F rant, carry on.
despreciable *p.* despicable; (*de baja calidad*) trashy, worthless; miserable; (*muy pequeño*) negligible; **despreciar** [1b] scorn, despise, look down on; (*desairar*) slight, spurn; (*subestimar*) underrate; **~se** *de inf.* think it beneath one to *inf.*; **despreciativo** *tono etc.* contemptuous; *observación* disparaging, derogatory; **desprecio** *m* scorn, contempt.
desprender [2a] unfasten, detach; separate; *gas etc.* give off; **~se** ⊕ *etc.* work loose, fall off, fly off; ~ *de* give up; *fig.* follow from, be implied by; *se desprende que* we learn that; **desprendimiento** *m fig.* disinterestedness; generosity; ~ *de tierras* landslide.
despreocupación *f* unconcern *etc.*; **despreocupado** unconcerned, nonchalant, carefree; unconventional, free and easy; impartial.
desprestigiar [1b] disparage, run down; cheapen; **~se** lose caste, lose prestige; **desprestigio** *m* loss of prestige; unpopularity.
desprevención *f* unreadiness; lack of foresight; **desprevenido** unprepared; *coger* ~ catch *s.o.* unawares (*or* off guard).
desproporción *f* disproportion; **desproporcionado** disproportionate.
despropósito *m* (piece of) nonsense, silly thing.
desprovisto *de* devoid of.
después 1. *adv.* afterwards, later; (*en orden*) next; (*desde entonces*) since (then); (*luego*) next, then; *poco* ~ soon after; **2.** *prp.*: ~ *de* after; since; ~ *de inf.* after *ger.*; *el primero* ~ *de* the next to; ~ *de descubierta América* after the discovery of America; **3.** *cj.*: ~ (*de*) *que* after.
despuntado blunt; **despuntar** [1a] *v/t.* blunt; *v/i.* ⚘ sprout, begin to show; (*alba*) dawn, appear; (*p.*) sparkle; (*descollar*) stand out.
desquiciar [1b] *puerta* unhinge (*a. fig.*); *fig.* upset, turn upside down; (*turbar*) disturb; F lever *s.o.* out.
desquitarse [1a] get satisfaction; ☤ get one's money back; (*vengarse*) get even (*con* with), get one's own back (*con* on); **desquite** *m* revenge, retaliation; (*partido de*) ~ return match.
desrazonable unreasonable.
desrielar [1a] *S.Am.* derail.
destacado outstanding; **destacamento** *m* ⚔ detachment; **destacar** [1g] emphasize, give due promi-

nence to; *paint.* make *s.t.* stand out; ⚔ detach, detail; **~se** stand out (*a. paint. etc.*); *~ contra*, *~ en*, *~ sobre* stand out against; *cielo etc.* be silhouetted against.

destajar [1a] arrange for, contract for; *baraja* cut; **destajero** *m*, **destajista** *m* pieceworker; **destajo** *m* (*en general*) piecework, contract work; (*tarea*) job, stint; *a ~* by the job; *fig.* eagerly, keenly; *trabajar a ~* be on piecework; *trabajo a ~* piecework; F *hablar a ~* talk nineteen to the dozen.

destapar [1a] *botella* open, uncork; *caja* open, take the lid off; *fig.* reveal; **destaponar** [1a] uncork.

destartalado *casa* tumbledown; (*mal dispuesto*) rambling; *máquina etc.* rickety.

destazar [1f] cut up.

destejer [2a] undo, unravel; *fig.* upset.

destellar [1a] flash; sparkle; glint, gleam; **destello** *m* flash *etc.*

destemplado ♪ out of tune; *voz* harsh, unpleasant; **destemplanza** *f meteor.* inclemency, bleakness; ♪ indisposition; *fig.* lack of moderation; **destemplar** [1a] upset, disturb; ♪ untune; **~se** ♪ get out of tune; *fig.* get worked up; **destemple** *m* upset (*a.* ⚕), disturbance; dissonance.

desteñir [3l] fade, take the color out of.

desternillarse [1a]: *v. risa.*

desterrado *m*, **a** *f* exile; **desterrar** [1k] exile; banish (*a. fig.*).

destetar [1a] wean; **destete** *m* weaning.

destierro *m* exile.

destilación *f* distillation; **destilador** *m* ⚗ still; (*p.*) distiller; **destilar** [1a] *v/t.* distill; *sangre etc.* ooze, exude; *v/i.* fall (drop by drop); filter through; **destilatorio** *m* still; **destilería** *f* distillery.

destinación *f* destination; goal; **destinar** [1a] destine (*a*, *para* for, to); intend, mean (*a*, *para* for); *fondos etc.* earmark (*a* for); *empleado* appoint, assign (*a* to); ⚔ *etc.* post (*a* to); *estar destinado a inf.* be destined to *inf.*; *venir destinado a* (*carta*) be addressed to; **destinatario** *m*, **a** *f* addressee; **destino** *m* (*suerte*) destiny, fate; (*blanco*, 🚂 *etc.*) destination; (*puesto*) job, post; *con ~ a* bound for; *salir con ~ a* leave for.

destitución *f* destitution; depriving; dismissal; **destituir** [3g] dismiss, remove (*de* from).

destorcer [2b *a.* 2h] untwist; *vara etc.* straighten; **~se** ⚓ get off course.

destornillador *m* screwdriver; **destornillar** [1a] unscrew; **~se** *fig.* go out of one's mind.

destrabar [1a] loosen; *preso* unfetter.

destraillar [1a] unleash.

destral *m* hatchet.

destreza *f* skill, handiness, dexterity.

destripaterrones *m* F clodhopper; **destripar** [1a] gut, draw, paunch; disembowel; *fig.* mangle, crush; *cuento* spoil.

destronar [1a] dethrone; *fig.* overthrow.

destroncar [1g] ✿ chop off; *p.* maim; *fig.* ruin; *animal* wear out.

destrozar [1f] smash (*a.* ⚔), shatter; mangle; tear to pieces; *esp. fig.* ravage, ruin; **destrozo** *m* destruction; massacre *de ps.*; *esp.* *~s pl.* ravages, havoc; **destrozón** F hard on one's clothes.

destrucción *f* destruction; **destructible** destructible; **destructivo** destructive; **destructor 1.** destructive; **2.** *m* destroyer (*a.* ⚓); **destruir** [3g] destroy; ruin, wreck; *argumento* demolish; **~se** ₳ cancel out.

desuncir [3b] unyoke.

desunión *f* disconnection, separation; *fig.* disunity; **desunir** [3a] separate, sever; ⊕ disconnect, disengage; *fig.* cause a rift between.

desuñarse [1a] work one's fingers to the bone (*por inf.* to *inf.*).

desusado obsolete, out of date; *~ de* no longer in use by; **desusar** [1a] stop using; **~se** go out of use; **desuso** *m* disuse; *caer en ~* fall into disuse; *caído en ~* obsolete.

desvaído gaunt; *color* dull.

desvainar [1a] shell; pod.

desvalido *niño etc.* helpless; *p.* destitute; *pol.* underprivileged.

desvalijar [1a] rob, plunder.

desvalimiento *m* helplessness.

desvalorización *f* devaluation;

desvalorizar [1f] devalue; devaluate.
desván *m* loft, attic; garret.
desvanecer [2d] make *s.o.* disappear; *duda etc.* dispel; **~se** disappear, vanish; (*atenuarse*) melt away, dissolve; evaporate; *esp. fig.* fade away, fade out (*a. radio*); ⚕ faint; **desvanecimiento** *m* disappearance *etc.*; ⚕ fainting fit; dizzy spell; *fig.* vanity; *radio*: fading.
desvarar [1a] refloat.
desvariar [1c] rave, talk nonsense; ⚕ be delirious; **desvarío** *m* delirium; *fig.* whim, strange notion; *esp.* **~s** *pl.* ravings, ramblings.
desvelado sleepless, wakeful; vigilant; **desvelar** [1a] keep *s.o.* awake; **~se** stay awake, have a sleepless night; ~ *por su.* be much concerned about; ~ *por inf.* do everything possible to *inf.*; **desvelo** *m* watchfulness, vigilance; **~s** *pl.* care, concern.
desvencijado ramshackle, rickety; **desvencijarse** [1a] fall apart, break down.
desventaja *f* disadvantage; (*estorbo*) handicap, liability; **desventajado** disadvantaged; deprived; **desventajoso** disadvantageous.
desventura *f* misfortune; **desventurado 1.** unfortunate; miserable, wretched; **2.** *m*, **a** *f* wretch, unfortunate.
desvergonzado 1. shameless; impudent; unblushing; **2.** *m*, **a** *f* scoundrel, rascal; shameless person; **desvergonzarse** [1f *a.* 1m] behave in a shameless way, be impudent (*con* to); **desvergüenza** *f* shamelessness; impudence; *¡qué ~!* what a nerve!; what a shocking thing!; *tener la ~ de inf.* have the nerve to *inf.*
desvestir (*a.* **~se**) [3l] undress.
desviación *f* deflection, deviation (*a. de brújula*); *mot.* diversion; (*carretera*) bypass; *fig.* departure (*de* from); **desviado** (gone) astray; off the track; lost; **desviar** [1c] turn aside, deflect, divert (*a. fig.*, *mot.*; *de* from); 🚂 switch; *golpe* parry, ward off; *fig.* dissuade, sidetrack (*de propósito* from); ween away (*de mala compañía* from); **~se** deviate (*de curso etc.* from); turn aside, turn away; *mot. etc.* swerve; ⚓ sheer off; ⚓ go off course; wander (*de tema* from); **desvío** *m* deflection, deviation; *mot. etc.* swerve; (*camino*) detour; 🚂 siding; *fig.* coldness, dislike.
desvirtuar [1e] impair, spoil; detract from; **~se** spoil.
desvivirse [3a]: ~ *por su.* crave, be crazy about; ~ *por inf.* go out of one's way to *inf.*, be eager to *inf.*
detallado detailed; *conocimiento* intimate; **detallar** [1a] itemize, specify; *suceso etc.* tell in detail; **detalle** *m* detail; item; F token, (nice) gesture **~s** *pl. a.* particulars; *al ~* retail; *en ~* in detail; F *¡qué ~!* how sweet of you!; *vender al ~* retail; **detallista** *m/f* retailer.
detective *m* detective.
detector *m* ⚓, *radio*: detector.
detención *f* stoppage, hold-up; (*retraso*) delay; ⚖ detention; ~ *ilegal* unlawful detention; **detener** [2l] (*parar*) stop, hold up, check; (*guardar*) keep, hold (back), retain; *p.* (*retrasar*) keep, delay; (*abordar*) stop, accost; ⚖ detain; **~se** stop (*a inf.* to *inf.*); delay, linger; pause *antes de obrar*; **detenidamente** thoroughly; at (great) length; **detenido** *cuento* detailed; lengthy; *examen* thorough; *fig.* timid; (*escaso*) sparing, niggardly; **detenimiento** *m* delay; thoroughness; care; *con ~* thoroughly.
detergente *adj. a. su. m* detergent.
deteriorar [1a] spoil, damage, impair; **~se** deteriorate, spoil; **deterioro** *m* deterioration; damage; (*desgaste*) wear (and tear).
determinable determinable; **determinación** *f* determination; decision; **determinado** (*resuelto*) determined, purposeful; (*cierto*) certain, set; *un libro ~* a given book, some particular book; **determinante** *adj. a. su. m* determinant; **determinar** [1a] *mst* determine; *fecha, precio a.* fix; *contribución, daños a.* assess; *curso a.* shape; *pleito* decide; ~ *a uno a inf.* lead s.o. to *inf.*; ~ *inf.* = **~se a** *inf.* decide to *inf.*, determine to *inf.*
detestable detestable, odious; damnable; **detestación** *f* detestation, loathing; **detestar** [1a] detest, hate, loathe.
detonación *f* detonation; **detona-**

dor *m* detonator; **detonar** [1a] detonate, explode.

detracción *f* disparagement; **detractor 1.** slanderous; **2.** *m*, **-a** *f* slanderer, detractor.

detrás behind; *por* ~ behind; *atacar etc.* from behind, from the rear; ~ *de* behind; *por* ~ *de fig.* behind *s.o.'s* back.

detrimento *m* damage, detriment.

detrito *m* detritus, debris.

deuda *f* debt; (*en general*) indebtedness; (*pecado*) sin; ~*s pl.* (*pasivas*) liabilities; ~ *pública* national debt; *lleno de* ~*s* heavily in debt; *estar en* ~ owe (*por* for); *estar en* ~ *con* be indebted to; **deudo** *m* relative; **deudor 1.** *saldo* debit *attr.*; *le soy muy* ~ I am much indebted to you; **2.** *m*, **-a** *f* debtor.

devanadera *f sew.* reel, winding frame; **devanado** *m* ⚡ winding; **devanar** [1a] wind; *v.* seso.

devanear [1a] rave, talk nonsense; **devaneo** *m* ravings, nonsense; ⚕ delirium; (*amorío*) affair.

devastación *f* devastation; **devastar** [1a] devastate, lay waste.

devengar [1h] *sueldo* draw; *interés* earn, bear.

devenir 1. [3s] become; **2.** *m* evolution, process of development.

devoción *f* devotion (*a* to); devoutness, piety; *fig.* liking (*a* for); *estar a la* ~ *de* be completely under *s.o.'s* thumb; *tener gran* ~ *a* be greatly devoted to; *tener por* ~ *inf.* be in the habit of *ger.*; **devocionario** *m* prayerbook.

devolución *f* return; ✝ repayment, refund; **devolver** [2h; *p.p.* *devuelto*] return, give back, send back; ✝ repay, refund; *golpe* return; restore (*a estado primitivo* to); F throw up; ~**se** *S.Am.* return.

devorador devouring; **devorar** [1a] devour (*a. fig.*).

devoto 1. *eccl.* devout; devoted; *obra etc.* devotional; **2.** *m*, **a** *f eccl.* devout person; worshipper *en iglesia*; *fig.* devotee, votary; ~ *del volante* car enthusiast; *los* ~*s* the faithful.

deyección *f* (*a.* ~*es pl.*) ⚕ motion; *geol.* debris, lava.

di *etc. v. dar.*

día *m* day; daytime; daylight; *¡buenos* ~*s!* good morning!, good day!; *ocho* ~*s freq.* week; *quince* ~*s freq.* fortnight; ~ *de boda* wedding day; ~ *feriado*, ~ *festivo*, ~ *de fiesta* holiday; *eccl.* feast day; ~ *hábil* working day; ⚖ court day; ~*-hombre* man-day; ~ *laborable* working day, weekday; ~ *libre* free day; day off; ~ *malo*, ~ *nulo* off day; ♀ *de la Raza* Columbus Day (*12 October*); ~ *señalado* red-letter day; *todo el santo* ~ the whole day long; *al* ~ up to date; (*proporción*) a day; *a los pocos* ~*s* within a few days; *al otro* ~ on the following day; *el otro* ~ the other day; *otro* ~ some other day; another day; *algún* ~ some day, sometime; F *¡cualquier* ~*!* not on your life!; *de* ~ by day, in the daytime; *del* ~ fashionable, up to date; *el* ~ *de hoy* today; *v.* *hoy*; *el mejor* ~ some fine day; *el* ~ *menos pensado* when you least expect it; *en pleno* ~ in broad daylight; *en* ~*s de Dios* never; ~ *tras* ~ day after day, day in day out; *un* ~ *sí y otro no* on alternate days, every other day; ✝ *poner al* ~ write up; *ponerse al* ~ get up to date, catch up; *vivir al* ~ live from hand to mouth.

diabetes *f* diabetes; **diabético** *adj. a. su. m*, **a** *f* diabetic.

diabla *f* carding machine; F she-devil; F *a la* ~ any old how; **diablillo** *m* F imp, monkey; **diablo** *m* devil (*a. fig.*); *¡(qué)* ~*(s)!* the devil!, oh hell!; F *como el* ~ like the devil; *un ruido de todos los* ~*s* a hell of a noise; *pobre* ~ poor devil; F *ahí será el* ~ there'll be the devil to pay; F *tener el* ~ *en el cuerpo* (*niño*) be full of mischief; *¡vete al* ~*!* go to hell!; **diablura** *f* devilry; (*de niño*) mischief; ~*s pl.* monkey tricks; **diabólico** diabolic(al), devilish, fiendish.

diaconía *f* deaconry; **diaconisa** *f* deaconess; **diácono** *m* deacon.

diadema *f* diadem; tiara *de mujer.*

diáfano diaphanous, transparent; filmy; *agua* limpid.

diafragma *m* diaphragm; **diagnosis** *f* diagnosis; **diagnosticar** [1g] diagnose; **diagnóstico** *m* diagnosis; **diagonal** *adj. a. su. f* diagonal; **diagrama** *m* diagram.

dialéctica *f* dialectics; **dialéctico** dialectic(al); **dialecto** *m* dialect; **dialectología** *f* dialectology.

dialogar [1h] *v/t.* write in dialogue form; *v/i.* talk, converse; **diálogo** *m* dialogue.
diamante *m* diamond; *naipes*: ~*s pl.* diamonds; **diamantino** diamond-like, adamantine; **diamantista** *m* diamond cutter; ✝ diamond merchant.
diametral diametrical; **diámetro** *m* diameter.
diana *f* ⚔ reveille.
¡diantre! F oh hell!
diapasón *m* diapason; ~ (*normal*) tuning fork.
diapositiva *f* (lantern) slide; *phot.* transparency.
diario 1. daily; day-to-day; everyday; **2.** *m* (*periódico*) newspaper, daily; (*relación personal*) diary; ✝ daybook; (*gastos*) daily expenses; ~ *de a bordo*, ~ *de navegación* logbook; *a* ~ daily; **diarismo** *m S.Am.* journalism; **diarista** *m/f* diarist.
diarrea *f* diarrhea.
diarrucho *m S.Am.* F rag.
diatermia *f* diathermy.
diatónico diatonic.
diatriba *f* diatribe, tirade.
dibujante *m* ⊕ draftsman (*a. paint.*), designer; cartoonist *de periódico*; **dibujar** [1a] draw, sketch; ⊕ design; *fig.* draw, depict; ~**se** *contra* be outlined against; **dibujo** *m* (*en general*) drawing, sketching; (*un* ~) drawing, sketch; ⊕ design; cartoon *de periódico*; caricature; *fig.* description; *cine*: ~ *animado* cartoon; ~*s pl.* comics; comic strips; F funnies.
dicción *f* diction; (*palabra*) word; **diccionario** *m* dictionary; ~ *geográfico* gazetteer.
diciembre *m* December.
díceres *m/pl.* sayings; rumor(s).
dictado *m* dictation; title of honor; ~*s pl.* dictates; *escribir al* ~ take dictation, take down; **dictador** *m* dictator; **dictadura** *f* dictatorship; **dictáfono** *m* dictaphone; **dictamen** *m* opinion, dictum; judgment; *tomar* ~ *de* consult with; **dictaminar** [1a] *v/t. juicio* pass; *v/i.* pass judgment (*en* on); **dictar** [1a] dictate; inspire; *sentencia* pass, pronounce; *S.Am. clase* give, *conferencia* deliver; **dictatorial, dictatorio** dictatorial; **dicterio** *m* taunt, insult.
dicha *f* happiness; (*suerte*) (good) luck; *por* ~ by chance.
dicharachero *m* F witty person; *b.s.* coarse sort; **dicharacho** *m* dirty thing, coarse remark.
dicho 1. *p.p. of decir*; ~ *y hecho* no sooner said than done; *lo* ~, ~ I stand by what I said; **2.** *m* (*proverbio*) saying; tag; (*chiste*) bright remark; F insult; F ~ *gordo* rude thing.
dichoso (*feliz*) happy; (*con suerte*) lucky; (*que trae dicha*) blessed (*a.* F).
didáctico didactic.
dieciséis sixteen; *fecha* sixteenth (*v. Apéndice*).
diente *m* tooth (*a.* ⊕, *fig.*); cog *de rueda*; ~ *de ajo* clove of garlic; ~ *canino* canine (tooth); ~ *incisivo* incisor; ~ *de leche* milk tooth; ♀ ~ *de león* dandelion; ~*s pl. postizos* false teeth; *daba* ~ *con* ~ his teeth were chattering; he was trembling like a leaf; F *enseñar los* ~*s* show fight, turn nasty; F *estar a* ~ be ravenous; *hablar entre* ~*s* mumble; *hincar el* ~ *en* sink one's teeth into; *fig.* get one's knife into; *tener buen* ~ be a hearty eater.
Diesel: *motor* ~ diesel engine; **diesel-eléctrico** *adj.* diesel electric, **dieselización** *f* dieselization.
diestra *f* right hand; **diestro 1.** (*derecho*) right; (*hábil*) skilful (*en* in, at); handy, deft *con manos*; (*sagaz*) shrewd; *b.s.* sly; *a* ~ *y siniestro* wildly, all over the place; **2.** *m toros*: matador.
dieta *f* diet (*a. pol.*); ~*s pl.* subsistence allowance; *estar a* ~ (be on a) diet; *poner a* ~ put on a diet; **dietético 1.** dietary; **2.** *m* dietician.
diez ten (*a. su.*); (*fecha*) tenth; *las* ~ ten o'clock; **diezmar** [1a] decimate (*a. fig.*); **diezmo** *m* tithe.
difamación *f* slander, defamation; libel (*de* on); **difamador 1.** slanderous, libelous, defamatory; **2.** *m*, **-a** *f* defamer; scandalmonger; **difamar** [1a] slander, defame; libel *esp. por escrito*; malign; **difamatorio** = *difamador* 1.
diferencia *f* difference; *a* ~ *de* unlike; in contrast to; *con corta* ~ more or less; *partir la* ~ split the difference; *fig.* meet s.o. halfway; **diferencial 1.** differential; *impuesto*

discriminatory; **2.** *f* ⊕, *mot.* differential; **diferenciar** [1b] *v/t.* differentiate between; *v/i.* differ (*de* from), be in disagreement (*en* over); **~se** (*discordar*) differ (*de* from); (*ser diferente*) be distinguishable; differentiate (*a.* ⚘ *etc.*); *fig.* distinguish o.s.; **diferente** different (*de* from); unlike (*de acc.*); **~s** *pl.* (*varios*) several; **diferir** [3i] *v/t.* defer, put off, hold over; *v/i.* differ, be different (*de* from).

difícil difficult, hard (*de inf.* to *inf.*); *es ~ que* it is unlikely that, it is doubtful if; **difícilmente** with difficulty; *~ será verdad* this can hardly be true; **dificultad** *f* difficulty; trouble; objection; **dificultar** [1a] make *s.t.* difficult; hinder, obstruct; interfere with; *~ que* think it unlikely that; **dificultoso** awkward, troublesome; F ugly; F (*que estorba*) awkward, full of silly objections.

difteria *f* diphtheria.

difundir [3a] spread, diffuse, disseminate; *alegría etc.* radiate.

difunto dead, defunct; *el ~, la ~a* the deceased; *el ~ rey* the late king; *día de* ♀*s* All Souls' Day.

difusión *f* spread, diffusion, dissemination; (*prolijidad*) diffuseness; (*radio*) broadcasting; **difusivo** diffusive; **difuso** widespread; *luz* diffused; (*prolijo*) diffuse, discursive.

digerible digestible; **digerir** [3i] digest (*a. fig.*); (*tragar*) swallow; (*aguantar*) stomach; **digestibilidad** *f* digestibility; **digestible** digestible; **digestión** *f* digestion; **digestivo** digestive; **digesto** *m* ⚖ digest.

digitación *f* ♪ fingering; **digital** **1.** digital; *huella etc.* finger *attr.*; **2.** *f* ⚘ foxglove; **dígito** *m* digit.

dignación *f* condescension; **dignarse** [1a]: *~ inf.* condescend to *inf.*; deign to *inf.*; **dignatario** *m* dignitary; **dignidad** *f* (*gravedad*) dignity; (*cargo*) rank; (*respeto*) self-respect; (*p.*) worthy, dignitary; **dignificar** [1g] dignify; **digno** (*honrado*) worthy; (*grave*) dignified; (*apropiado*) fitting; *~ de* worthy of, deserving; fit for; *~ de mención* worth mentioning; *~ de verse* worth seeing; *ser ~ de a.* deserve.

digresión *f* digression.

dije[1] *etc. v. decir.*

dije[2] *m* trinket; medallion, locket; amulet; F (*p.*) treasure, gem.

dilación *f* delay; procrastination; *sin ~* without delay, forthwith.

dilapidación *f* waste; squandering; **dilapidar** [1a] squander.

dilatación *f* dilat(at)ion; *phys.* expansion; *fig.* calm; **dilatado** vast, extensive; numerous; (*prolijo*) long-winded; **dilatar** [1a] stretch, dilate, distend, expand (*a. phys.*); *fama etc.* spread; (*retrasar*) delay, put off; protract; **~se** stretch *etc.*; *fig.* be long-winded; *~ en, ~ sobre* dilate upon, linger over; **dilativo** dilatory; **dilatorias** *f/pl.* delaying tactics.

dilema *m* dilemma.

diletante *m/f* dilettante.

diligencia *f* diligence; † stagecoach; (*prisa*) speed; F errand, piece of business; **~s** *pl. previas* inquest; F *hacer una ~* run an errand; *poner ~ en inf.* be careful to *inf.*; **diligenciar** [1b] see about; **diligente** diligent, assiduous; (*pronto*) quick; *poco ~* slack.

dilucidación *f* explanation; enlightenment; **dilucidar** [1a] elucidate.

dilución *f* dilution; **diluir** [3g] dilute, water down (*a. fig.*).

diluvial *geol.* diluvial; **diluviar** [1b] pour (with rain); **diluvio** *m* deluge, flood (*a. fig.*).

dimanar [1a]: *~ de* arise from.

dimensión *f* dimension; **~es** *pl.* dimensions, size.

dimes y diretes: F *andar en ~ con* argue with.

diminutivo *adj. a. su. m* diminutive; **diminuto** tiny, minute; dwarf; miniature.

dimisión *f* resignation; **dimitir** [3a] resign (*de* from).

dinamarqués = *danés.*

dinámica *f* dynamics; *fig.* dynamic; **dinámico** dynamic (*a. fig.*).

dinamita *f* dynamite.

dínamo *f* dynamo.

dinastía *f* dynasty; **dinástico** dynastic.

dinerada *f*, **dineral** *m* mint of money; *valer un ~* cost (*or.* be worth) a fortune; **dinerillos** *m/pl.*: *tener ~* have a bit of money; **dinero** *m* money; currency, coinage *de un país*; *hombre de ~* man of means; *~*

contante cash; ~ *contante y sonante* hard cash, ready money; *andar mal de* ~ be badly off; *dar* ~ (*negocio*) make money, pay.

dintel *m* lintel; threshold.

diocesano *adj. a. su. m* diocesan; **diócesi(s)** *f* diocese.

Dios *m* God; ♀ god; ~ *delante* with God's help; ~ *mediante* God willing, D.V.; *¡~ mío!* good gracious!; I ask you!; *a* ~ *gracias* thank heaven; *a la buena de* ~ innocently; *a la de* ~ (*es Cristo*) rashly; *una de* ~ *es Cristo* a bust-up; *armar la de* ~ *es Cristo* raise hell; *¡por ~!* for goodness sake!, hang it (all)!; *como* ~ *manda* as is proper; *¡plegue a ~!* please God!; ~ *sabe* God knows; *¡válgame ~!* bless my soul!; *vaya con* ~ goodbye; F *iro.* and the best of luck; **diosa** *f* goddess.

diploma *m* diploma; **diplomacia** *f* diplomacy; **diplomado** qualified; **diplomática** *f* diplomatics; (*carrera*) diplomatic corps; **diplomático 1.** diplomatic; tactful; **2.** *m* diplomat(ist) (*a. fig.*).

dipsomanía *f* dipsomania; **dipsomaníaco** *m*, **a** *f* dipsomaniac.

diptongación *f* diphthongization; **diptongar** [1a] diphthongize; **diptongo** *m* diphthong.

diputación *f* deputation, delegation; ~ *provincial approx.* county council (offices); **diputado** *m*, **a** *f* delegate; ~ (*a Cortes*) deputy, member of Parliament; **diputar** [1a] delegate, depute.

dique *m* (*muro*) dike, seawall; (*malecón*) jetty, mole; dam *en río*; dock *de puerto*; ~ *de carena* graving dock; ~ *flotante* floating dock; ~ *seco* dry dock; *entrar en* ~, *hacer* ~ dock; *poner un* ~ *a fig.* check, restrain.

diré *etc. v. decir.*

dirección *f* (*línea de movimiento*) direction; way; (*tendencia*) trend, course; (*gobierno*) direction; ✝ *etc.* management; leading, leadership *de partido etc.*; ♪ conductorship; *mot. etc.* steering; *fig.* guidance; ✝ (*cargo*) directorship; (*junta*) (board of) directors; (*despacho*) manager's office; (*señas*) address; ~ *prohibida* no entry, no thoroughfare; *mot.* de ~ *columna etc.* steering *attr.*; (*calle de*) ~ *única* one-way (street); ⚡ *conmutador de 2* ~*es* 2-way switch; *en la* ~ *de* in the direction of; ~ *de tiro* ⚔ fire control; *servo*~ *mot.* power steering; **direccional** directional; **directivo** *junta etc.* managing, governing; *clase* managerial; administrative; **directo 1.** direct (*a. fig.*), straight; 🚂 through, nonstop; **2.** *m tenis etc.*: forehand; **director 1.** leading, guiding; = *directivo*; **2.** *m* director (*a.* ✝, *eccl.*); ✝ manager, executive; editor *de periódico*; ♪ ~ (*de orquesta*) conductor; headmaster *de escuela*; *univ.* master *de colegio*, warden *de residencia*; ~ *de escena* stage manager; producer; ~ *gerente* managing director; **directora** *f* headmistress (*a.* ~ *de colegio*); *univ.* warden; **directorio** *m* (*norma*) directive; (*junta*) directorate, ✝ board of directors; (*libro*) directory.

dirigencia *f* leadership; **dirigente** *m* leader; **dirigible 1.** *buque etc.* navigable; *misil* ~ guided missile; **2.** *m* dirigible; **dirigir** [3c] direct (*a, hacia* at, to, towards); *carta, palabra, protesta* address (*a* to); *libro* dedicate (*a* to); *mirada* turn, direct; ⚓, *mot. etc.* steer; *empresa* run, manage, operate; ♪ conduct; *p.* guide, advise (*en* in); *partido* lead, head; *periódico* edit; *manga* play (*a* on); *actores* produce; *fig. curso* shape; *esfuerzos* concentrate (*a* on), direct (*a* towards); ~**se** *a* go to, make one's way to; ⚓ *etc.* steer for, make for; *p.* address (o.s. to); apply to *solicitando*; ~ *hacia* head for.

discar [1g] *S.Am. teleph.* dial.

discernidor discerning, discriminating; **discernimiento** *m* discernment, discrimination; *edad de* ~ years of discretion; **discernir** [3i] discern; distinguish (*de* from); *premio* award.

disciplina *f mst* discipline; doctrine; *auto*~ self-control; self-discipline; **disciplinar** [1a] discipline; (*enseñar*) school, train; **disciplinario** disciplinary; ⚔ punishment *attr.*; **discipulado** *m* discipleship; **discípulo** *m*, **a** *f* disciple; pupil.

disco *m* disk; *deportes*: discus; 🚂 signal; *teleph.* ~ (*de marcar*) dial; ~ (*de gramófono*) (Gramophone) record; ~ *microsurco* long-playing record; ~ *vertebral* spinal disk; **discóbolo** *m* discus thrower.

díscolo uncontrollable; *niño* mischievous.

disconforme *etc. v. desconforme.*

discontinuo discontinuous (*a.* ⚔).

discordante discordant; **discordar** [1m] (*ps.*) disagree (de with), differ (de from); ♪ be out of tune; **discorde** discordant; (*ps.*) in disagreement; ♪ *sonido* discordant; *instrumento* out of tune; **discordia** *f* discord, disagreement.

discoteca *f* record library; discotheque.

discreción *f* discretion, tact; discrimination; wisdom, shrewdness; secrecy; wit; *a* ~ at one's discretion; ⚔ unconditionally; *cocina*: to taste; *comer etc.* ad-lib F; **discrecional** discretionary; optional; *parada* request *attr.*

discrepancia *f* discrepancy, disagreement; divergence; **discrepante** divergent; dissenting; **discrepar** [1a] differ (de from), disagree (de with).

discretear [1a] try to be clever, be frightfully witty; **discreto** discreet; tactful; unobtrusive; (*sagaz*) wise, shrewd; (*ingenioso*) witty; *phys. etc.* discrete.

discriminación *f*: ~ *racial* racial discrimination, **discriminar** [1a] *S.Am.* discriminate against.

disculpa *f* excuse, plea; apology; **disculpable** pardonable, excusable; **disculpar** [1a] excuse, pardon; exonerate (de from); **~se** apologize (con to, de for).

discurrir [3a] *v/t.* invent, think up; *v/i.* (*andar*) roam, wander; (*agua*) flow; (*tiempo*) pass; (*meditar*) reason; (*hablar*) discourse (sobre about, on); ~ en reflect on; **discursista 1.** *adj.* long-winded; F windy; **2.** *m/f* windbag; big talker; **discurso** *m* speech, address; (*en general, tratado*) discourse; course *del tiempo.*

discusión *f* discussion; argument; disagreement; **discutible** debatable, arguable; **discutidor** argumentative; **discutir** [3a] *v/t.* discuss, debate, talk over; argue about; contradict; *v/i.* argue (sobre about, over); ¡no discutas! don't argue!

disecar [1g] *anat.* dissect (*a. fig.*); stuff *para conservar*; **disección** *f* dissection.

diseminar [1a] scatter; *esp. fig.* disseminate, spread.

disensión *f* dissension.

disentería *f* dysentery.

disentimiento *m* dissent; **disentir** [3i] dissent (de from).

diseñador *m* designer; **diseñar** [1a] draw, sketch; ⊕ design; **diseño** *m* drawing, sketch; ⊕ *etc.* design.

disertación *f* dissertation, disquisition; **disertar** [1a]: ~ *acerca de* discuss, expound on.

disfavor *m* disfavor.

disforme badly proportioned; monstrous; (*feo*) ugly.

disfraz *m* disguise; mask *de cara*; fancy dress *para baile*; **disfrazado** de disguised as, in the guise of; *ir* ~ de masquerade as; **disfrazar** [1f] disguise (de as; *a. fig.*); *fig.* conceal, cloak; **~se** de disguise o.s. as.

disfrutar [1a] *v/t.* enjoy; *v/i.* F enjoy o.s.; ¡cómo disfruto! this is the life!; ~ con, ~ de enjoy; **disfrute** *m* enjoyment; use; benefit.

disfunción *f* ⚕ dysfunction.

disgregación *f* disintegration; **disgregar(se)** [1h] disintegrate.

disgustar [1a] displease, annoy; **~se** be annoyed, get angry (con, de about); (*enemistarse*) fall out (con with); (*aburrirse*) get bored (de with); **disgusto** *m* (*desazón*) displeasure, annoyance; (*pesadumbre*) grief, chagrin; (*molestia*) trouble, bother, difficulty; (*disputa*) quarrel, unpleasantness; *a* ~ against one's will.

disidencia *f* dissidence; *eccl.* dissent; **disidente 1.** dissident, dissentient; **2.** *m f* dissident, dissentient; *esp. eccl.* dissenter, nonconformist; **disidir** [3a] dissent.

disílabo 1. disyllabic; **2.** *m* disyllable.

disimulación *f* dissimulation, pretence; **disimulado** furtive, covert, underhand; **disimular** [1a] *v/t.* (*ocultar, fingir no sentir*) hide; cloak, disguise; (*perdonar*) excuse; *falta de otro* overlook, condone; *ofensa* pass off; *v/i.* dissemble, pretend; **disimulo** *m* dissimulation; indulgence; con ~ craftily.

disipación *f* dissipation (*a. fig.*); **disipado** dissipated, raffish; (*manirroto*) extravagant; **disipador** *m* spendthrift; **disipar** [1a] dissipate; *nubes, ilusiones* dispel; *fortuna* fritter away (*en* on); **~se** vanish; ⚗ evaporate.

dislate *m* silly thing, absurdity; nonsense.

dislocación *f* dislocation; *geol.* slip; **dislocar** [1g] dislocate.

disminución *f* diminution, decrease *etc.*; ~ *física* ⚕ handicap; disability; *sin* ~ unabated; **disminuir** [3g] *v/t. a. v/i.* diminish, decrease, lessen.

disociación *f* dissociation; **disociar** [1b] dissociate, separate.

disoluble dissoluble, dissolvable; **disolución** *f* dissolution; ⚗ solution; (*moral*) dissoluteness; **disoluto** dissolute, dissipated; **disolvente** *adj. a. su. m* dissolvent; **disolver(se)** [2h; *p.p. disuelto*] dissolve (*a. fig.*), melt.

disonancia *f* discord, dissonance; **disonante** discordant, dissonant; **disonar** [1m] ♪ be discordant, sound wrong; *fig.* lack harmony; be out of keeping (*con* with).

dispar different; unlike; unequal, disparate; **disparada** *f S.Am.* sudden flight; *a la* ~ like a shot; **disparado:** *ir* ~ go hell for leather; *salir* ~ be off like a shot; **disparador** *m* ⚔ trigger; escapement *de reloj*; *phot.*, ⊕ release; F *poner en el* ~ drive s.o. nuts; **disparar** [1a] *v/t.* ⚔ shoot, fire; let off; *piedra etc.* throw, let fly (*contra* at); *v/i.* ⚔ fire *etc.*; = *disparatar*; **~se** ⚔ go off; (*caballo*) bolt, run away; (*p. etc.*) rush off, dash away.

disparatado absurd, nonsensical, crazy; **disparatar** [1a] talk nonsense; **disparate** *m* silly thing, foolish remark (*or* idea *etc.*), absurdity; **~s** *pl.* nonsense, rubbish.

disparidad *f* disparity.

disparo *m* ⚔ shot, report; ⊕ trip, release; *fig.* = *disparate*.

dispendio *m* waste; extravagance; **dispendioso** expensive.

dispensa *f eccl. etc.* dispensation; exemption *de examen*; **dispensable** dispensable; **dispensación** *f* dispensation; **dispensador** *m* dispenser; **dispensar** [1a] (*distribuir*) dispense; (*eximir*) exempt, excuse (*de inf.* from *ger.*); *falta* excuse, pardon; *¡dispense Vd.!* excuse me!; *no puedo* **~me** *de inf.* I cannot help *ger.*; ~ *que subj.* excuse *s.o.* for *ger.*; **dispensario** *m* dispensary.

dispepsia *f* dyspepsia; **dispéptico** dyspeptic.

dispersar [1a] disperse, scatter (*a.* ⚔ **~se**); *manifestación etc.* break up; **dispersión** *f* dispersion (*a. phys.*), dispersal; **disperso** scattered; straggling; (*escaso*) sparse.

displicencia *f* indifference; bad temper, peevishness; **displicente** disagreeable, peevish, bad-tempered; fretful.

disponer [2r] *v/t.* (*arreglar*) arrange, dispose, lay out; line up *en fila*; (*preparar*) get ready (*para* for); (*determinar*) decide; ~ *que* order that, arrange that, provide that; *v/i.*: ~ *de* (*usar*) make use of, avail o.s. of; (*tener listo*) have *s.t.* available, have at one's disposal; **~se** *a inf.*, ~ *para inf.* get ready to *inf.*

disponibilidad *f* availability; **disponible** available; on hand, spare; **disposición** *f* (*arreglo*) arrangement, disposition; layout (*a.* △); (*temperamento*) disposition; aptitude (*para* for), turn (of mind); **~es** *pl.* preparations (*para* for), measures; ~ *de ánimo* attitude of mind; *última* ~ last will and testament; *a la* ~ *de* at the disposal of; *a la* ~ *de Vd.*, *a su* ~ at your service; *está a su* ~ you are welcome to it; *en* ~ *de inf.* in a position to *inf.*

dispositivo *m* device, appliance, gadget.

dispuesto 1. *p.p. of disponer*; *bien* ~ well-disposed (*hacia* towards); △ well designed; *mal* ~ ⚕ indisposed; *poco* ~ *a inf.* reluctant to *inf.*, loath to *inf.*; *estar* ~ *a inf.* be prepared to *inf.*, be disposed to *inf.*; **2.** *adj.* handsome; graceful; (*hábil*) clever.

disputa *f* dispute, argument; *en* ~ at issue; *sin* ~ beyond dispute; **disputable** debatable, disputable; **disputador 1.** disputatious; **2.** *m* disputant; **disputar** [1a] *v/t.* dispute, challenge; debate; *v/i.* debate (*de, sobre* on; *con* with); argue (*de, sobre* about); **~se** *algo* fight for.

distancia *f* distance (*a. fig.*); ~ *focal* focal distance; *a* ~ at a distance; *a gran* ~, *a larga* ~ *attr.* long-distance; *mantener a* ~ keep *s.o.* away,

hold *s.o.* off; *mantenerse a* ~ keep one's distance, stand aloof; **distanciar** [1b] *objetos* space out; *rival* outdistance; ~**se** (*dos ps.*) be estranged; ~ *de rival* get ahead of; **distante** distant; **distar** [1a]: *dista 10 km. de aquí* it is 10 km. (away) from here; *dista mucho* it is a long way away; *¿dista mucho?* is it far?; *dista de ser adj.* it is a long way from being *adj.*
distender [2g] distend; **distensión** *f* distension.
dístico *m* distich.
distinción *f* distinction (*a. honor*), difference; (*lo distinto*) distinctness; *fig.* elegance; *a* ~ *de* unlike; **distingo** *m* reservation; objection; subtle distinction; **distinguible** distinguishable; **distinguido** distinguished; *modales etc.* gentlemanly, ladylike; elegant; **distinguir** [3d] (*divisar*) distinguish, make out; (*separar*) distinguish (*de* from, *entre* between), tell (*de* from); (*caracterizar*) distinguish, mark; single *s.o.* out; *amigo* have a special regard for; honor, bestow an honor upon; ~**se** distinguish o.s.; stand out, be distinguished; **distintivo 1.** distinctive; *señal* distinguishing; **2.** *m* badge; *fig.* distinguishing mark, characteristic; **distinto** different, distinct (*de* from); clear, distinct; ~**s** *pl.* (*varios*) several.
distorsión *f radio*: distortion; **distorcionar** [1a] distort; twist; bend.
distracción *f* distraction; amusement; absence of mind; *por* ~ through sheer forgetfulness; **distraer** [2p] *v/t.* distract, divert, lead *s.o.* away (*de* from); (*entretener*) amuse; (*moralmente*) lead *s.o.* astray; *v/i.*: *el paseo distrae* walking is a relaxation; ~**se** amuse o.s.; **distraído** absentminded; vague, dreamy; *b.s.* inattentive, lackadaisical; *S.Am.* careless; slovenly.
distribución *f* distribution; (*arreglo*) arrangement; ⊕ timing gears; **distribuido:** ⚠ *bien* ~ well designed; **distribuidor** *m* distributor (*a. mot.*); ✝ dealer, supplier; ~ *automático* vending machine; **distribuidora** *f* ✝ distributor(s); **distribuir** [3g] distribute; hand out; give out, send out; ✉ deliver; ⚠ design, plan; **distributivo** distributive (*a. gr.*).
distrito *m* district, administrative area; ⚖ circuit; ~ *electoral* constituency *de diputado*, ward *de concejal*.
disturbio *m* disturbance; ~ *aerodinámico* wash.
disuadir [3a] dissuade (*de inf.* from *ger.*), deter, discourage; **disuasión** *f* disuasion *etc.*; **disuasivo** deterrent, dissuasive.
disyuntivo disjunctive (*a. gr.*).
diurético *adj. a. su. m* diuretic.
diurno day *attr.*, diurnal 📖.
diva *f* prima donna.
divagación *f* digression; ~**es** *pl.* wanderings, ramblings; **divagador** rambling; **divagar** [1h] ramble *en discurso*; wander *en mente*; (*salir del tema*) digress.
diván *m* divan; ~ *cama* day bed.
divergencia *f* divergence; **divergente** divergent; **divergir** [3c] diverge.
diversidad *f* diversity, variety; **diversificación** *f* diversification; **diversificar** [1g] diversify.
diversión *f* amusement, entertainment; pastime; ⚔ diversion; ~**es** *pl. de salón* indoor games; **diverso 1.** diverse; different (*de* from); ~**s** *pl.* several, various, sundry; **2.** *m/pl.* ✝ (*en lista*) miscellaneous.
divertido *libro etc.* entertaining, enjoyable; *fiesta* merry, gay; *chiste, p.* funny, amusing; *S.Am.* tight, tipsy; **divertimiento** *m* amusement, entertainment; **divertir** [3i] amuse, entertain; ~**se** have a good time, amuse o.s. (*en hacer* doing); ~ *con amor etc.* toy with.
dividendo *m* dividend; **dividir** [3a] divide (up; *en* into, *por* by); split (up), part company.
divieso *m* boil.
divinidad *f* divinity; godhead; (*dios pagano*) god(dess *f*); *fig.* beauty; **divinizar** [1f] deify; *fig.* exalt; **divino** divine (*a. fig.*).
divisa *f* emblem, badge; *heráldica*: motto, device; ~**s** *pl.* ✝ foreign exchange; *control de* ~**s** exchange control.
divisar [1a] make out; (e)spy.
divisible divisible; **división** *f* division (*a.* ⚔); *pol. etc.* split; *deportes*

class; category; **divisional** ⚔ divisional; **divisor** *m*: *máximo común* ~ highest common factor; **divisoria** *f geog.* divide; **divisorio** dividing; *línea ~a de las aguas* watershed.

divorciado *m*, **a** *f* divorcee; **divorciar** [1b] divorce (*a. fig.*); **~se** get divorced, get a divorce (de from); **divorcio** *m* divorce.

divulgación *f* disclosure *etc.*; **divulgar** [1h] *secreto* divulge, disclose, let out; (*publicar*) make known; spread, circulate; popularize; **~se** (*secreto*) leak out; (*rumor*) get about.

dobladillar [1a] hem; **dobladillo** *m* hem; cuff *de pantalón*; **doblado** double; (*cuerpo*) thickset; *terreno* rough; (*taimado*) sly; **dobladura** *f* fold, crease; **doblaje** *m cine*: dubbing; **doblar** [1a] *v/t.* double (*a. thea., bridge*); (*plegar*) fold (up), crease; *página etc.* turn down, *dobladillo etc.* turn up; (*torcer*) bend; ⚓ *cabo* round; *esquina* turn, round; *cine*: dub; *v/i.* (*torcer*) turn; ♪ toll; *thea.* stand in; **~se** double; (*plegarse*) fold (up); bend, buckle; (*ceder*) give in (*a* to), yield.

doble 1. double (*a.* ⚘, *sentido*); *fondo* false; *mando* dual; *paño extra* thick; *p.* two-faced, deceitful; **2.** *m* (*pliegue*) fold, crease; ♪ knell; ♪ tolling; *el* ~ twice the quantity; ✝ twice the amount; *pagar el ~ por* pay twice as much for; *ser el ~ de p.* be the double of; *tenis etc.*: *juego de ~s* doubles; *al ~* doubly; **3.** *m/f cine etc.*: double, stand-in.

doblegar [1h] (*plegar*) fold; (*torcer*) bend; *p.* persuade, sway; (*rendir*) force *s.o.* to give in; **~se** (*p.*) give in.

doblez 1. *m* fold, crease; **2.** *f* double-dealing, duplicity.

dócar *m* dog cart.

doce twelve (*a. su.*); (*fecha*) twelfth; *las* ~ twelve o'clock; **docena** *f* dozen; ~ *de fraile* baker's dozen; *a ~s* by the dozen.

docente educational; *centro, personal* teaching attr.; **dócil** docile; obedient; gentle; **docilidad** *f* docility; gentleness.

docto 1. learned; **2.** *m* scholar; **doctor** *m* doctor; **doctora** *f* F blue-stocking; ⚕ woman doctor; **doctorado** *m* doctorate; **doctoral** doctoral; **doctorarse** [1a] take one's doctorate.

doctrina *f* doctrine; teaching; (*saber*) learning; **doctrinal** doctrinal; **doctrinar** [1a] teach; **doctrinario** *adj. a. su. m* doctrinaire.

documentación *f* documentation; papers *de identidad*; **documental** *adj. a. su. m* documentary; documentary film; **documento** *m* document; record; certificate; ⚖ exhibit.

dogal *m* halter; noose *de verdugo*; *estar con el ~ al cuello* be in an awful jam.

dogma *m* dogma; **dogmático** dogmatic(al); **dogmatismo** *m* dogmatism; **dogmatizador** *m* dogmatist; **dogmatizar** [1f] dogmatize.

dogo *m* bulldog.

dólar *m* dollar.

dolencia *f* ailment, complaint; **doler** [2i] ⚕ hurt, pain; ache; *fig.* grieve, distress; *me duele el costado* my side hurts, I have a pain in my side; **~se** *de* be sorry for, grieve for; (*compadecer*) pity, sympathize with; *pecados* repent of; (*quejarse*) complain about; (*a voces*) moan, groan; **doliente 1.** ⚕ suffering, ill; sad, sorrowful; **2.** *m/f* sufferer; mourner *en entierro*.

dolomita *f* dolomite.

dolor *m* ⚕ pain, ache; pang; (*pesar*) grief, sorrow; regret; ~ *de cabeza* headache; ~ *de muelas* toothache; **dolorido** ⚕ sore, tender, aching; *p.* grief-stricken; *tono* plaintive, pained; **doloroso** painful, grievous.

doloso deceitful; fraudulent.

domable tamable; **domador** *m*, **-a** *f* trainer, tamer; ~ *de caballos* horse breaker; **domar** [1a] tame, train; *fig.* master, control; **domeñar** [1a] = *domar*.

domesticación *f* domestication; taming; **domesticado** tame; (*de casa*) pet; **domesticar** [1g] tame, domesticate; **domesticidad** *f* (*animal*) (state of being in) captivity; (*p.*) domesticity, homeliness; **doméstico 1.** *animal* tame, pet; *vida* home *attr.*, family *attr.*, domestic; *gastos* housekeeping *attr.*; *quehaceres* household *attr.*; **2.** *m*, **a** *f* domestic.

domiciliar [1b] domicile; house; **~se** take up (one's) residence; **domiciliario** house *attr.*, domiciliary; **domicilio** *m* home; 🕮, ⚖ domicile, dwelling, abode; ✝ ~ *social* head office; *deportes*: *a* ~ at home; *servicio a* ~ delivery service.
dominación *f* domination; dominance; rule, power; **dominador** controlling; *carácter* domineering; **dominante** dominant (*a.* ♪); *carácter* domineering, masterful; *amor* possessive; **dominar** [1a] dominate, subdue; *p. etc.* overpower; *pasión* control, master; *lengua* know well, have a command of; (*edificio etc.*) dominate, tower over, look down on; **~se** control o.s.
domingo *m* Sunday; ♀ *de Ramos* Palm Sunday; ♀ *de Resurrección* Easter Sunday; **dominguero** F, **dominical** Sunday *attr.*; **dominicano** Dominican; **domínico** *m* Dominican.
dominio *m* dominion, power, sway (*sobre* over); *esp. fig.* grip, hold (*de* on); command *de lengua*; (*superioridad*) ascendancy; (*tierras*) domain; *de* ~ *público noticia* generally known; ~ *sobre sí mismo* self-control.
dominó *m* (*ficha, vestido*) domino; (*juego de*) ~ dominoes.
don[1] *courtesy title, used before Christian names; on envelopes* *Señor Don* = Esquire; *in other cases not translated.*
don[2] *m* gift (*a. fig.*); ~ *de acierto* happy knack; ~ *de lenguas* gift for languages; ~ *de mando* leadership, ⚔ generalship; *tener* ~ *de gentes* have a way with people, be a good mixer, have charm; **donación** *f* donation; ⚖ gift; *escritura de* ~ deed of gift; **donador** *m*, **-a** *f* donor.
donaire *m* charm, wit *de habla*; grace, elegance; (*chiste*) witticism.
donante *m/f* donor; ~ *de sangre* blood donor; **donar** [1a] grant, donate; **donativo** *m* contribution, donation.
doncella *f* virgin; *esp. lit.* maid(en); (*criada*) (lady's) maid; **doncellez** *f* maidenhood; *anat.* maidenhead.
donde where; in which; *S.Am. casa, tienda, etc.* at; to; *en* ~ wherein; *por* ~ whereby; *¿dónde?* where? (*a. a* ~); *¿de dónde vienes?* where do you come from?; *¿por dónde?* (*lugar*) whereabouts?; (*dirección*) which way?; (*motivo*) why?; **dondequiera 1.** *adv.* anywhere; *por* ~ all over the place; **2.** *cj.* wherever.
donoso witty, funny; *iro.* fine.
donostiarra *adj. a. su. m/f* (native) of San Sebastián.
doña *courtesy title, used before Christian names; mst not translated.*
dorado 1. golden; gilded; ⊕ *etc.* gilt; **2.** *m* gilding; **dorador** *m* gilder; **doradura** *f* gilding; **dorar** [1a] gild (*a. fig.*); *cocina*: brown.
dormidera *f* ⚘ poppy; *tener buenas* ~*s* get off to sleep easily; **dormilón 1.** sleepy; **2.** *m*, **-a** *f* sleepyhead; **dormir** [3k] *v/t.* send to sleep; *resaca etc.* sleep off; *siesta* have; *v/i.* sleep; *quedarse dormido* drop off, go to sleep; *durmiendo se me pasó la hora* I overslept; **~se** go to sleep (*a. miembro*), fall asleep; **dormirela** *f* nap; **dormitar** [1a] doze, snooze; **dormitorio** *m* bedroom; dormitory *de colegio etc.*
dorsal back *attr.*, dorsal 🕮; **dorso** *m* back (*a. fig.*).
dos two (*a. su.*); (*fecha*) second; *las* ~ two o'clock; *los* ~ (*ambos*) both of them *etc.*; *tenis*: *a* ~ deuce; *de* ~ *en* ~ in twos, two by two; *en* ~ in two; *en un* ~ *por tres* in a second; *para entre los* ~ between you and me; **doscientos** two hundred.
dosel *m* canopy; **doselera** *f* valance.
dosis *f* dose; (*inyección*) shot; ~ *excesiva* overdose.
dotación *f* endowment; (*ps.*) staff; ⚓ complement, crew; **dotado** *de* ⊕ *etc.* equipped with, fitted with; (*p.*) endowed with; **dotar** [1a] *mujer* give a dowry to; *la dotó de X ptas* he gave her X ptas as a dowry; *fundación* endow (*de* with; *a. fig.*); *puesto* fix a salary for; ~ *de* ⚓ man with; (*taller etc.*) staff with; ⊕ equip with, fit with; **dote** *mst f* dowry, marriage portion; *fig.* gift, talent, endowment.
doy *v. dar.*
dozavo *adj. a. su. m* twelfth; *en* ~ [*typ.* in duodecimo.]
dracma *f* drachm, dram.
draga *f* dredge; (*barco*) dredger; **dragado** *m* (*a. obras de* ~) dredging;

dragaminas *m* minesweeper; **dragar** [1h] dredge; *minas* sweep.
dragón *m* dragon; ⚔ dragoon; **dragona** *f* ⚔ shoulder knot; **dragonear** [1a] *S.Am.* boast; flirt.
drama *m* drama (*a. fig.*); **dramática** *f* dramatic art, drama; **dramático 1.** dramatic; **2.** *m* dramatist; **dramatizar** [1f] dramatize; **dramaturgo** *m* dramatist; playwright.
drástico drastic.
drenaje *m* drainage (*a.* ⚕); **drenar** [1a] drain.
dríada *f* dryad.
driblar [1a] *deportes*: dribble.
dril *m* duck, drill; denim.
driza *f* halyard.
droga *f* drug (*a. b.s.*), medicine; substance; *fig.* (*trampa*) trick; (*molestia*) nuisance; **drogadicto** *m* drug addict (*a. adj.*); **droguería** *f* drug store; pharmacy.
dromedario *m* dromedary.
druida *m* druid.
dual *gr.* dual; **dualismo** *m* dualism.
ducado *m* duchy, dukedom; † ducat; **ducal** ducal.
dúctil soft, ductile; *fig.* easy to handle; **ductilidad** *f* softness, ductility.
ducha *f* shower (bath); ⚕ douche; **duchar** [1a] ⚕ douche; **~se** have a shower (bath).
ducho: **~** *en* skilled in, well versed in.
duda *f* doubt; misgiving; suspense; *fuera de toda* **~** past all doubt; *sin* **~** no doubt, doubtless; *no cabe* **~** (*de*) *que* there can be no doubt that; *poner en* **~** call in question; **dudar** [1a] *v/t.* doubt; *v/i.* doubt (*que, si* whether); **~** *de* doubt; mistrust; **~** *en inf.* hesitate to *inf.*; **dudoso** doubtful, dubious, uncertain; *punto* debatable; *resultado* indecisive.
duela *f* stave.
duelista *m* duelist; **duelo**[1] *m* ⚔ duel; *batirse en* **~** (fight a) duel.
duelo[2] *m* grief, sorrow; bereavement; mourning *por muerto*; (*ps.*) mourners; **~s** *pl.* hardships.
duende *m* imp, goblin; (*fantasma*) ghost; **duendecillo** *m* gremlin, jinx.
dueña *f* owner; proprietress; mistress *de casa etc.*; (*dama*) lady; † duenna; **dueño** *m* owner; proprietor; master; **~** *de sí mismo* self-possessed; *ser* **~** *de* own, be the owner of; *situación* be the master of; *ser muy* **~** *de inf.* be perfectly free to *inf.*; *ser* **~** *del baile* be the master of the situation.
duermevela *f* F nap, snooze.
dulcamara *f* nightshade.
dulce 1. *mst* sweet; *carácter, clima* mild, gentle; *agua* fresh; *metal* soft; **2.** *m* sweet, candy; **dulcera** *f* candy jar; **dulcería** *f* candy shop; **dulcificar** [1g] sweeten; *fig.* soften, make more gentle; **dulzarrón** F sickly-sweet, cloying; *fig.* sugary, sickening; **dulzoso** sweetish; **dulzura** *f* sweetness; gentleness *etc.*
dumping *m* † dumping; *hacer* **~** dump (goods).
duna *f* dune.
dúo *m* duet.
duodecimal duodecimal; **duodécimo** twelfth.
duplicación *f* duplication; **duplicado** *adj. a. su. m* duplicate; *por* **~** in duplicate; **duplicador** *m* duplicator; **duplicar** [1g] duplicate; repeat; ♠ double; **duplicidad** *f* deceitfulness, duplicity.
duque *m* duke; **duquesa** *f* duchess.
durabilidad *f* durability; **durable** durable, lasting; **duración** *f* duration; length of time; *de larga* **~** *disco* long-playing; **duradero** *tela* hard-wearing, serviceable; durable; (*que perdura*) lasting, permanent; **durante** during; **~** *todo el año* all the year round; *habló* **~** *una hora* he spoke for an hour; **durar** [1a] *cierto tiempo* last, go on for; (*permanecer*, **~** *en pie*) stand, survive; (*recuerdo etc.*) survive, endure; (*tela*) wear (well).
durazno *m* peach (tree).
dureza *f* hardness *etc.*
durmiente 1. sleeping; **2.** *m/f* sleeper; *la Bella* **~** Sleeping Beauty; **3.** *m* 🚂 sleeper, (cross)tie; girder.
duro 1. hard; *pan* stale; (*resistente*) tough; *fig. p. etc.* hard (*con* on), cruel (*con* to), callous; *estilo* harsh; **~** *de oído* hard of hearing; ♪ tone-deaf; F *ser* **~** *de pelar* (*or roer*) be a tough job; **2.** *m Spanish coin = 5 pesetas.*
dux *m* doge.

E

e and.
¡ea! come on!; here!, hey!
ebanista *m* cabinetmaker; **ebanistería** *f* cabinetmaking, woodwork.
ébano *m* ebony.
ebonita *f* ebonite.
ebrio intoxicated, drunk; blind *de ira*.
ebullición *f* boiling.
ebúrneo ivory.
ecléctico *adj. a. su. m* eclectic.
eclesiástico **1.** ecclesiastic(al); **2.** *m* clergyman, priest; ecclesiastic.
eclipsar [1a] eclipse (*a. fig.*); *fig.* outshine, overshadow; **eclipse** *m* eclipse (*a. fig.*); **eclíptica** *f* ecliptic.
eclisa *f* fishplate.
eco *m* echo; *hacer ~ fig.* correspond; *hacerse ~ de* echo; voice; *tener ~* catch on.
ecología *f* ecology; **ecológico** ecologic(al); **ecologista** *m/f*, **ecólogo** *m* ecologist.
economato *m* cooperative store; company store *para empleados*; commissary; guardianship.
economía *f* economy; (*un ahorro*) economy, saving; (*virtud*) thrift, thriftiness; *~ dirigida* planned economy; *~ política* economics; **económico** economic(al); (*que ahorra*) economical, thrifty; (*barato*) economical, inexpensive; **economista** *m/f* economist; **economizar** [1f] economize (*en* on); save *para la vejez etc.*; *b.s.* skimp, pinch.
ecuación *f* equation; **ecuador** *m* equator; **ecuánime** *carácter* equable, level-headed; *estado* calm, composed; **ecuanimidad** *f* equanimity, level-headedness; composure; **ecuatorial** equatorial.
ecuatoriano *adj. a. su. m*, **a** *f* Ecuador(i)an.
ecuestre equestrian.
ecuménico oecumenical.
eczema *f* eczema.
echada *f* throw, pitch, shy, cast; toss *de moneda*; *S.Am.* boast;
echadizo spying; *propaganda* secretly spread; *material* waste; **echado:** *estar ~* lie, be lying (down); *C.Am., Mex., P.R.* have an easy job (*or* life).
echar [1a] **1.** (*arrojar*) throw; cast, pitch, fling, toss; *desperdicios etc.* throw away; *p.* eject, turn out *de un sitio*; expel *de una sociedad*; dismiss *del trabajo*; *carta* post; *cimientos* lay; *culpa* lay, put (*a* on); *freno* put on, apply; *humo etc.* emit, give off; *impuesto* levy, impose; *líquido* pour (out); *llave* turn; *mirada* cast; *partida* play, have; *pelo etc.* begin to grow, sprout; *pestillo* slide; *pitillo* smoke, have; *raíz* strike; *retoño* put forth; *sangre* shed, lose; *suertes* cast, draw; *~ a inf.* begin to *inf.*; *~ abajo* demolish; *fig.* overthrow; *~ atrás* push back; *~ de menos* miss; *~la de* pose as, give o.s. the airs of, fancy o.s. as; *~ de sí* throw off; *piel* slough (off); *~ por dirección* take, turn to; *calle* go down; **2.** **~se** (*arrojarse*) throw o.s.; (*tenderse*) lie (down), stretch out; *~ a inf.* begin to *inf.*; *~las de* pose as, fancy o.s. as; *~ sobre* rush at, fall upon.
echazón *f* jettison; jetsam.
echona *f S.Am.* sickle.
edad *f* age; *de ~* elderly; *de corta ~* young; *de mediana ~*, *de ~ madura* middle-aged; *~ de hierro* Iron Age; *~ de oro* golden age; *♀ Media* Middle Ages; *mayor ~* majority; *mayor de ~* of age, adult, grown-up; *menor ~* minority; *menor de ~* under age, juvenile; *a una ~ avanzada* at an advanced age, late in life; *~ viril* manhood.
edecán *m* aide-de-camp.
edén *m* paradise, (garden of) Eden.
edición *f mst* edition; issue, publication; *♀es pl.* Pérez Pérez Publications; *~ príncipe* first edition; *ser la segunda ~ de* be the very image of.
edicto *m* edict, proclamation.

edificación *f* △ construction, building; *fig.* edification, uplift; **edificante** edifying, improving; **edificar** [1g] build; *fig.* edify, improve, uplift; **edificio** *m* building; *fig.* edifice, structure.

editar [1a] (*publicar*) publish; (*corregir etc.*) edit; **editor 1.** publishing *attr.*; **2.** *m* (*que publica*) publisher; (*que corrige etc.*) editor; **editorial 1.** publishing *attr.*; *política etc.* editorial; **2.** *m* leading article, editorial; **3.** *f* publishing house.

edredón *m* eiderdown.

educable teachable, educable; **educación** *f* education; training; (*crianza*) upbringing; (*modales*) manners, breeding; *mala* ~ *freq.* bad manners; *sin* ~ *freq.* bad-mannered; ¡*qué falta de* ~! what bad manners!; how coarse!; **educacional** educational; **educacionista** *m/f* education(al)ist; **educado** well-mannered; cultivated; *mal* ~ ill-mannered, unmannerly; **educando** *m*, **a** *f* pupil; **educar** [1g] educate; train; (*criar*) bring up; **educativo** educative.

edulcorante 1. *adj* sweetening; **2.** *m* sweetener; sweetening.

efectismo *m* straining after effect; **efectista** sensational; **efectivamente** sure enough; (*realmente*) in fact, really; (*contestación*) precisely; **efectivo 1.** effective; (*real*) actual, real; *hacer* ~ *check* cash, clear; **2.** *m* cash; specie; ~*s pl.* ⚔ effectives, establishment; *en* ~ in cash; **efecto** *m* effect; impression, impact; ~*s pl.* (*propiedad*) effects; (*capital etc.*) assets; (*enseres*) things; *esp.* ☤ goods, articles, merchandise; ~ *calorífico* heat value; ~*s pl. de consumo* consumer goods; ~*s pl. de escritorio* writing materials; ~*s pl. sonoros* sound effects; *al* ~ for the purpose; *en* ~ (*como contestación*) (yes) indeed; (*en realidad*) in fact; in effect; *hacer* ~ make an impression; *poner en* ~ give effect to; *surtir* ~ (*dar resultado*) work, take effect; (*dejarse sentir*) tell (*en* on); (*idea etc.*) get across.

efectuación *f* accomplishment; **efectuar** [1e] effect, effectuate; *parada etc.* make; (*causar*) bring about; *proyecto, reparación* carry out; *recuperación etc.* stage, make; ~**se** take place; be carried out.

efervescencia *f* effervescence (*a. fig.*); **efervescente** effervescent (*a. fig.*).

eficacia *f* efficacy; efficiency; **eficaz** effective, efficacious, effectual; (*que funciona bien*) efficient; (*que se deja sentir*) telling; **eficiencia** *f* efficiency; **eficiente** efficient.

efigie *f* effigy.

efímero ephemeral, short-lived.

efluvio *m* effluvium.

efusión *f* effusion (*a. fig.*), outpouring (*a. fig.*); *fig. b.s.* gush; ~ *de sangre* bloodshed; **efusivo** effusive; *gracias* warmest; *b.s.* gushing.

égida *f* aegis.

egipcio *adj. a. su. m*, **a** *f* Egyptian.

eglefino *m* haddock.

égloga *f* eclogue.

egocéntrico self-centered; **egoísmo** *m* egoism; selfishness; **egoísta 1.** egoistic(al); selfish; **2.** *m/f* egoist; **egolatría** *f* self-worship; self-glorification; **egotismo** *m* egotism; **egotista 1.** *adj.* egotistic(al); **2.** *m/f* egotist.

egregio eminent, distinguished.

¡**eh!** hey!; hi!; hoy!

eje *m* ⊕ axle *de ruedas*; (*árbol, husillo*) shaft, spindle; ⚙, *phys.*, *geog.*, *pol.* axis; *fig.* (*centro*) hinge, hub; (*esencia*) crux, core; central idea; ~ *de balancín* rocker (shaft); ~ *del cigüeñal* crankshaft; ~ *flotante* floating axle; ~ *tándem* dual axle; dual rear.

ejecución *f* execution (*a.* ⚖, ♪); fulfilment; enforcement *de ley*; ♪ performance, rendition; *poner en* ~ carry into effect; **ejecutante** *m/f* performer; **ejecutar** [1a] execute (*a.* ⚖, ♪); perform (*a.* ♪); *órdenes* fulfil; **ejecutivo 1.** executive; (*apremiante*) pressing, insistent; (*sin demora*) prompt; **2.** *m* executive; **ejecutor** *m*: ~ *testamentario* executor; **ejecutoria** *f* letters patent; (*genealogía*) pedigree.

¡**ejem!** ahem!

ejemplar 1. exemplary; **2.** *m* example; copy *de libro*; *zo. etc.* specimen; (*modelo*) model, example; **ejemplaridad** *f* exemplariness; **ejemplificar** [1g] exemplify; be illustrative of; **ejemplo** *m* example, instance; (*lección*) object lesson; *por* ~ for example, for instance; *sin* ~ unexampled; *dar* ~ set an example.

ejercer [2b] exercise; *influencia* exert, bring to bear; *poder* exercise, wield; *profesión* practice (de as), follow; **ejercicio** *m* exercise (*a.* ⚔); practice; tenure *de oficio*; ✝ fiscal year; ~ *de castigo escuela*: imposition; *hacer* ~*s* take exercise; **ejercitar** [1a] exercise; *profesión* practice; ⚔ *etc.* train, drill; ~**se** exercise; practice; train; **ejército** *m* army.

ejido *m* common.

el 1. *artículo*: the; **2.** *pron.*: ~ *de* that of; ~ *de Juan* John's; ~ *de Madrid* the Madrid one, the one from Madrid; *v. que*.

él (*p.*) he; (*cosa*) it; (*tras prp.*) him; it.

elaboración *f* elaboration *etc.*; **elaborar** [1a] elaborate; *producto* make, manufacture, prepare; *metal, madera etc.* work; *proyecto* work on, work up.

elasticidad *f* elasticity; give, spring(iness); *fig.* resilience; **elástico 1.** elastic; *superficie etc.* springy; *fig.* resilient; **2.** *m* elastic.

elección *f* choice, selection; *pol. etc.* election; **electivo** elective; **electo** elect; **elector** *m*, **-a** *f* elector; **electorado** *m* electorate; **electoral** electoral; *potencia etc.* voting *attr.*

electricidad *f* electricity; **electricista** *m* electrician; **eléctrico** electric(al); **electrificar** [1g], **electrizar** [1f] electrify (*a. fig.*); **electrocutar** [1a] electrocute; **electrodinámica** *f* electrodynamics; **electrodo** *m* electrode; **electrólisis** *f* electrolysis; **electromotor** *m* electric motor; **electrón** *m* electron; **electrónica** *f* electronics; **electrónico** electronic; electron *attr.*; **electrotecnia** *f* electrical engineering.

elefante *m*, **a** *f* elephant; **elefantino** elephantine.

elegancia *f* elegance *etc.*; **elegante** elegant; *movimiento etc.* graceful; (*distintivo*) stylish; (*majo*) smart; (*de moda, sociedad*) fashionable; (*de buen gusto*) tasteful; *frase etc.* polished, well-turned.

elegía *f* elegy; **elegíaco** elegiac.

elegibilidad *f* eligibility; **elegible** eligible; **elegido** elect; **elegir** [3c *a.* 3l] choose, select; *pol. etc.* elect.

elemental elementary; elemental; **elemento** *m mst* element (*a.* ⚡); ⚡ cell *de pila*; *fig.* ingredient; factor *de situación*; ~*s pl. fig.* (*medios*) means, resources; (*materia*) material, ingredients.

elenco *m* catalogue, list; *thea.* cast.

elepé 1. *disco* long-playing; LP; **2.** *m* long-playing record.

elevación *f* elevation; height, altitude; *fig.* exaltation; rise *de precios etc.*; **elevado** elevated; *edificio etc.* high; *fig. posición etc.* exalted, high, lofty; *estilo* grand; **elevador** *m* hoist; *S.Am.* elevator; ~ *de granos* (grain) elevator; **elevalunas** *m mot.* window lifts; ~ *eléctrico* electric window lifts; **elevar** [1a] raise (*a.* ⚗, *precios*), lift (up), elevate; exalt *a dignidad*; *producción* step up; ⚡ boost; ~**se** rise; (*edificio etc.*) soar, tower; *fig.* get conceited.

elidir [3a] elide.

eliminación *f* elimination, removal; *deportes*: ~ *progresiva* knockout; **eliminar** [1a] eliminate, remove; *necesidad etc.* obviate; **eliminatoria** *f deportes*: heat.

elipse *f* ellipse; **elipsis** *f* ellipsis; **elíptico** elliptic(al).

elisión *f* elision.

elitista *adj. a. su. m/f* elitist.

elixir *m* elixir.

elocución *f* elocution.

elocuencia *f* eloquence; **elocuente** eloquent.

elogiar [1b] praise, eulogize; **elogio** *m* praise, eulogy; tribute.

elucidar [1a] elucidate.

eludible avoidable; **eludir** [3a] elude, evade, escape; avoid.

ella (*p.*) she; (*cosa*) it; (*tras prp.*) her; it; **ellas** *pl.* they; (*tras prp.*) them.

ello it; ~ *es que* the fact is that; ~ *dirá* the event will show; F *¡a por* ~! here goes!

ellos *pl.* they; (*tras prp.*) them.

emanación *f* emanation (*a. phys.*); (*olor*) effluvium; **emanar** [1a]: ~ *de* emanate from, come from, originate in.

emancipación *f* emancipation; **emancipar** [1a] emancipate.

embadurnar [1a] (be)daub, smear.

embaidor *m* trickster, deceiver, cheat; **embaimiento** *m* imposture; **embaír** [3a; *defective*] trick; deceive; swindle; *sl.* con.

embajada *f* embassy; **embajador** *m* ambassador.

embalador *m*, **-a** *f* packer; **embalaje** *m* packing; **embalar** [1a] *v/t.* pack, bale, parcel up; *v/i.* F *deportes*: sprint; *mot.* step on it.

embaldosado *m* tiled floor; **embaldosar** [1a] tile.

embalsadero *m* boggy place.

embalsamar [1a] embalm.

embalsar [1a] dam (up); *este mes se han embalsado X metros cúbicos* reservoir stocks have gone up by X cubic meters this month; **embalse** *m* dam; reservoir; dammed-up water.

embanderar [1a] bedeck with flags.

embarazada pregnant; **embarazar** [1f] (*estorbar*) obstruct, hamper, hinder; (*empreñar*) make pregnant, get with child; **embarazo** *m* (*estorbo*) obstacle, hindrance; (*preñado*) pregnancy; **embarazoso** awkward, inconvenient; embarrassing.

embarcación *f* craft, boat, vessel; (*embarco*) embarkation; **embarcadero** *m* pier, landing stage, jetty; **embarcar** [1g] *ps.* embark, put on board; *cargamento* ship; *fig.* launch (*en empresa* on); **~se** embark, go on board; *fig.* get involved (*en* in); **embarco** *m* embarkation.

embargar [1h] *propiedad* seize, distrain upon, impound; (*estorbar*) impede; *sentidos* blunt, paralyse; **embargo** *m* ⚖ seizure, distraint; ⚕ indigestion; *sin ~* still, however, none the less.

embarque *m* shipment, loading (of cargo).

embarradura *f* smear.

embarrancarse [1g] run into a ditch, get stuck.

embarrar [1a] smear, bedaub (*de* with), begrime; splash with mud; *C.Am., Mex.* involve in a dirty deal.

embarullar [1a] make a mess of, muddle.

embate *m* ⚔ sudden attack; brunt *de ataque*; dashing, breaking *de olas*; **~s** *pl. de la fortuna* blows of fortune.

embaucador *m*, **-a** *f* trickster, swindler; humbug; impostor; *sl.* con man; **embaucamiento** *m* swindle; humbug; **embaucar** [1g] trick, fool, impose upon; F bamboozle; con.

embaular [1a] pack (into a trunk); F stuff o.s. with, tuck into.

embazar [1f] *v/t.* (*teñir*) dye brown; (*pasmar*) astound; (*estorbar*) hinder; *v/i.* be dumbfounded; **~se** have had enough.

embebecer [2d] entertain; **~se** be lost in wonder.

embeber [2a] *v/t.* absorb, soak up; *esp. fig.* imbibe; *vestido* take up, gather in; (*introducir*) insert; contain; *v/i.* shrink; **~se** (*absorto*) be absorbed; (*extático*) be enraptured; *~ de fig.* imbibe, be soaked in.

embelecar [1g] deceive, cheat; **embeleco** *m* fraud, deceit; F bore; **embelequería** *f W.I., Col., Mex.* fraud; swindle.

embelesado spellbound; **embelesador** ravishing, entrancing; **embelesar** [1a] enrapture, enthrall, fascinate; **embeleso** *m* rapture, bliss, delight.

embellecer [2d] embellish, beautify; **embellecimiento** *m* embellishment.

embestida *f* assault, onslaught; charge *de toro etc.*; **embestir** [3l] assault, assail; rush upon; (*toro*) charge; F pester (for a loan).

embetunar [1a] *zapatos* blacken; polish black; tar.

emblandecer [2d] soften; *fig.* mollify.

emblanquecer [2d] whiten, bleach.

emblema *m* emblem, device.

embobamiento *m* wonderment; **embobarse** [1a] gape, be amazed (*con, de, en* at); **embobecer** [2d] make silly.

embocadura *f* mouth *de río*; tip *de cigarrillo*; ♪ mouthpiece; bit *de freno*; *thea.* proscenium arch; **embocar** [1g] put into the mouth; F *comida* cram, scoff; *~ algo a uno* make s.o. believe s.t., put one over on s.o.

embolado *m thea.* minor role; F trick; **embolar** [1a] *toro* fit with wooden balls (on the horns); polish; **~se** *C.Am., Mex.* get drunk.

embolia *f* clot; embolism; ~ *cerebral* clot on the brain.

embolismar [1a] gossip about; **embolismo** *m* confusion, mess; F (*chismes*) gossip; F (*engaño*) hoax.

émbolo *m* piston; plunger.

embolsar [1a] pocket; *pago* collect.

emboque *m* F trick, hoax.

emboquillado *cigarrillo* tipped.

emborrachar [1a] intoxicate, get drunk; **~se** get drunk (*con*, *de* on).

emborrar [1a] (*llenar*) stuff; F = *embocar*.

emborronar [1a] *papel* scribble over, cover with scribble; *carta*, *renglones* scribble.

emboscada *f* ambush; **emboscarse** [1g] lie in ambush, hide.

embotado dull, blunt (*a. fig.*); **embotar** [1a] blunt, dull (*a. fig.*); *fig.* weaken, enervate.

embotellamiento *m* traffic jam *de coches*; bottleneck *en calle estrecha* (*a. fig.*); **embotellar** [1a] bottle; *fig.* bottle up.

embozado muffled up; **embozar** [1f] muffle (up); *fig.* cloak, disguise; **~se** muffle o.s. up; **embozo** *m* covering of the face, muffler, mask; (*cama*) turned-down bedclothes; *fig.* cunning, concealment; *sin* ~ frankly, openly.

embragar [1h] *engranaje* engage; *piezas* connect, couple; **embrague** *m* clutch; ~ *de disco* disk clutch.

embravecer [2d] *v/t.* enrage; *v/i.* ⚘ flourish; **~se** (*mar*) get rough.

embrear [1a] tar, cover with pitch.

embriagador intoxicant, intoxicating; *vino etc.* heady; **embriagar** [1h] make drunk, intoxicate; *fig.* enrapture; **~se** get drunk; **embriaguez** *f* drunkenness, intoxication; *fig.* rapture.

embrión *m* embryo; *en* ~ in embryo; **embrionario** embryonic.

embrocación *f* embrocation.

embrocar [1g] *hilos* wind (on a bobbin); *zapatos* tack; (*vaciar*) empty; (*volver boca abajo*) invert, turn upside down.

embrollar [1a] muddle, entangle, dislocate; *esp. ps.* embroil; **~se** get into a muddle; ~ *en* get involved in; **embrollo** *m* (*enredo*) tangle, muddle; (*situación difícil*) imbroglio; (*lío*) embroilment, entanglement; **embrollón** *m*, **-a** *f* troublemaker.

embromar [1a] tease, make fun of, rag; (*engañar*) hoodwink, kid F; **~se** *S.Am.* loiter; (*aburrirse*) get bored.

embrujar [1a] *p.* bewitch; *casa* haunt.

embrutecer [2d] brutalize, coarsen; **embrutecimiento** *m* brutalization; becoming brutal; coarsening.

embuchado *m* pork sausage; F blind; **embuchar** [1a] stuff (with mincemeat); F *comida* bolt.

embudar [1a] fit with a funnel; *fig.* trick; **embudo** *m* funnel; *fig.* trick.

emburujar [1a] jumble (up), pile (up).

embuste *m* (*mentira*) lie, story F; (*engaño*) trick, fraud; imposture, (piece of) chicanery; **~s** *pl.* trinkets; **embustería** *f* imposture, trick; **embustero 1.** deceitful; **2.** *m*, **a** *f* liar, storyteller F; cheat.

embutido *m cocina*: sausage; ⊕ inlay, marquetry; **embutir** [3a] stuff, cram; ⊕ inlay; F *comida* cram, scoff; F ~ *algo a uno* make s.o. swallow s.t.

emergencia *f* (*acto*) emergence; (*caso de urgencia*) emergency; ⚘ emergence; **emergente** resultant; **emerger** [2c] emerge; (*submarino*) surface.

emeritense *adj. a. su. m/f* (native) of Mérida.

emético *adj. a. su. m* emetic.

emigración *f* (e)migration; **emigrado** *m*, **a** *f* emigrant; *esp. pol.* emigré; **emigrante** *adj. a. su. m/f* emigrant; **emigrar** [1a] (e)migrate.

eminencia *f* (*colina etc.*, *título*, *fig.*) eminence; (*lo muy alto*) loftiness; *fig.* prominence; **eminente** (*muy alto*) lofty; *fig.* eminent; prominent, distinguished.

emisario *m* emissary; **emisión** *f* emission; issue; *radio*: (*acto*) broadcasting; (*una* ~) broadcast, program; **emisor** *m* transmitter; **emisora** *f* radio station; **emitir** [3a] emit, give off (*or* forth, out); *moneda*, *sellos* issue; *moneda falsa* utter; *empréstito* float, launch; *radio*: broadcast.

emoción *f* emotion; (*entusiasmo etc.*) excitement; (*estremecimiento*, *escalofrío*) thrill; tension *al esperar etc.*; **emocionado** deeply moved; **emo-**

cionante exciting, thrilling; moving; **emocional** emotional; **emocionar** [1a] (*entusiasmar*) excite, thrill; (*conmover*) move; **~se** get excited; be moved.

emolumentos *m/pl.* emoluments.

emotivo emotive; emotional.

empacar [1g] pack (up); **~se** be obstinate; (*cortarse*) get rattled F; *S.Am.* balk, shy.

empachado awkward; **empachar** [1a] upset, cause indigestion to; **~se** get embarrassed; become bashful; **empacho** *m* ⚕ indigestion; *fig.* embarrassment, bashfulness; **empachoso** indigestible; *fig.* embarrassing, shaming, shameful.

empadronamiento *m* census (taking), registration; **empadronar** [1a] take the census of, register.

empalagar [1h] (*empachar*) pall (*a* on; *a. fig.*), cloy (*a. fig.*); (*fastidiar*) bore, weary; **empalago** *m* cloying, disgust; *fig.* bore(dom); **empalagoso** sickly, rich, gooey F; *fig.* wearisome, trying.

empalar [1a] impale; **empalizada** *f* stockade.

empaliar [1b] decorate with bunting.

empalmar [1a] *v/t. cuerda* splice; *fig.* couple, join; *v/i.* (*líneas*) join, meet; (*trenes*) connect (*con* with); **empalme** *m* splice; ⊕ joint, connection; 🚂 junction *de líneas*; connection *de trenes*.

empanada *f* (meat) pie, patty; *fig.* fraud; shady business; **empanar** [1a] roll in bread crumbs, roll in pastry.

empantanar [1a] flood, swamp; *fig.* bog down; **~se** *fig.* get bogged down.

empañado *ventana* misty, steamy; **empañar** [1a] *niño* swaddle, wrap up; *ventana etc.* mist; *imagen* blur (*a. fig.*); *honor* tarnish; **~se** (*imagen etc.*) dim, blur; (*ventana etc.*) film over, get misty.

empapar [1a] soak, saturate, steep (*a. fig.*); (*lluvia etc.*) drench; **~se** *en* soak up; *fig.* steep o.s. in.

empapelado *m* papering, paperhanging; **empapelador** *m* paperhanger; **empapelar** [1a] *pared* paper; *caja* line with paper; *objeto* wrap in paper.

empaque *m* packing; *fig.* appearance, presence; solemnness; *S.Am.* brazenness; **empaquetador** *m*, **-a** *f* packer; **empaquetadura** *f* packing; ⊕ gasket; filling; **empaquetar** [1a] pack (up), parcel up, package.

emparedado *m* sandwich; **emparedar** [1a] immure, confine.

emparejar [1a] *v/t.* (*aparear*) match; (*allanar*) level; *v/i.* catch up (*con* with); **~se** match.

emparentado related by marriage (*con* to); **emparentar** [1k] become related by marriage; **~** *con familia* marry into.

emparrado *m* (trained) vine.

empastar [1a] paste; *libro* bind (in stiff covers); *diente* fill, stop; **empaste** *m* filling.

empatar [1a] *deportes*: draw, tie; *pol. etc.* tie; **empate** *m* draw, tie *en juego*; dead heat *en carrera*; *pol. etc.* tie; **empatía** *f* empathy.

empavesado *m* bunting; **empavesar** [1a] deck; *buque* dress.

empecatado incorrigible; (*desgraciado*) ill-fated.

empecinamiento *m* stubbornness; determination; covering with tar; **empecinar** [1a] tar; dip in pitch; **~se** *S.Am.* be stubborn; persist.

empedernido (*cruel*) heartless; (*sin compasión*) obdurate; *pol. etc.* diehard; inveterate *en un hábito*; *corazón* stony; **empedernir** [3a; *defective*] harden; **~se** harden one's heart.

empedrado **1.** *superficie* pitted; *cara* pockmarked; (*manchado*) dappled, flecked; **2.** *m* paving; stone work; **empedrar** [1k] pave.

empeine *m* groin; instep *de pie*; **~s** *pl.* ⚕ tetter.

empelotarse [1a] F get muddled; (*reñir*) get involved in a row; *S.Am.* undress; strip.

empella *f* vamp.

empellón *m* push, shove; *a* **~es** roughly; *dar* **~es** jostle.

empeñar [1a] pawn, pledge; *fig.* engage, compel; **~se** insist (*en* on), persist (*en* in); (*obligarse*) bind o.s.; **~** *en inf.* insist on *ger.*, be set on *ger.*; **~** *por* intercede for, mediate on behalf of; **empeño** *m* pledge; obligation; determination, insistence; (*esfuerzo*) endeavor; *con* **~** insistently; (*con ilu-*

sión) eagerly; **empeñoso** diligent; eager.

empeoramiento *m* deterioration, worsening; **empeorar** [1a] *v/t.* make worse, worsen; *v/i.*, **~se** get worse, worsen, deteriorate.

empequeñecer [2d] dwarf; (*despreciar*) belittle; (*quitar importancia a*) minimize.

emperador *m* emperor; **emperatriz** *f* empress.

emperejilarse [1a] F dress up, doll (o.s.) up.

empernar [1k] bolt.

empero but, yet, however.

emperrarse [1a] F (*obstinarse*) get stubborn; (*irritarse*) lose one's temper.

empezar [1f *a.* 1k] begin, start (*a inf.* to *inf.*; *por inf.* by *ger.*).

empinado *cuesta* steep; (*alto*) high; **empinar** [1a] *v/t. vaso etc.* raise; (*enderezar*) straighten; *v. codo*; *v/i.* F drink; **~se** (*p.*) stand on tiptoe; (*caballo*) rear; (*edificio*) tower; ✈ soar, zoom.

empingorotado F stuck-up; haughty; high and mighty.

empírico empiric(al); **empirismo** *m* empiricism.

emplastar [1a] plaster, poultice; *cara* make up; F *negocio* block; **emplasto** *m* plaster, poultice; *fig.* makeshift arrangement; F weakling.

emplazamiento *m* ⚖ summons; ⚔ emplacement; **emplazar** [1f] summon(s).

empleado *m*, **a** *f* employee; clerk *en oficina etc.*; **emplear** [1a] use; employ; *tiempo* occupy, spend; *~ mal* misuse; **empleo** *m* use; (*trabajo en general*) employment; (*puesto*) employment, job; *modo de ~* usage; instructions for use; *sin ~* unemployed; *pleno ~* full employment.

emplomar [1a] lead, cover (*or* weight *etc.*) with lead.

emplumar [1a] *v/t.* (tar and) feather; *v/i.* = **emplumecer** [2d] fledge, grow feathers.

empobrecer [2d] *v/t.* impoverish; *v/i.*, **~se** become poor; **empobrecimiento** *m* impoverishment.

empolvado powdery; *superficie etc.* dusty; **empolvar** [1a] *cara* powder; *superficie* cover with dust; **~se** (*p.*) powder o.s., powder one's face; (*superficie*) gather dust, get dusty.

empollar [1a] *v/t.* incubate; hatch; *v/i.* (*gallina*) sit, brood (*a. fig.*); (*insectos*) breed; F swot, cram; **empollón** *m*, **-a** *f* F swot.

emponzoñamiento *m* poisoning; **emponzoñar** [1a] poison (*a. fig.*); *fig.* corrupt.

emporcar [1g *a.* 1m] dirty, foul; begrime.

emporio *m* emporium; mart; cultural center; commercial center.

empotrar [1a] embed; ⊕ build in.

emprendedor enterprising; ambitious; energetic; **emprender** [2a] undertake, take on, tackle; (*empezar*) begin on, embark (up)on; F *~la con p.* (*para aclarar*) have it out with, tackle; (*reñir*) fall out with.

empreñar [1a] *p.* make pregnant, get with child; *animal etc.* impregnate; **~se** become pregnant.

empresa *f* enterprise, undertaking (*a.* ⚕); venture; ⚕ company, concern; *thea.* management; **empresario** *m thea.* manager; showman; impresario *de ópera etc.*; promoter *de boxeo etc.*

empréstito *m* (public) loan; *~ de guerra* war-loan.

empujadora-niveladora *f* bulldozer.

empujar [1a] push, shove; (*introducir*) push, thrust (*en* into); (*propulsar*) drive, propel; *botón* press; *fig. p.* sack, give the push to F; (*para obtener algo*) work behind the scenes for, intrigue for; **empujatierra** *f* bulldozer; earth mover; **empuje** *m* push, shove; (*presión*) pressure; *fig.* push, (pushfulness), energy, drive; ⊕ thrust; **empujón** *m* push, shove; dig, poke *con dedo etc.*; *a ~es* roughly; (*a intervalos*) by fits and starts.

empulgueras *f/pl.* thumbscrew.

empuñadura *f* hilt *de espada*; grip *de herramienta*; opening *de cuento*; **empuñar** [1a] grasp, grip, clutch.

emulación *f* emulation; **emulador** **1.** emulous (*de* of); **2.** *m*, **-a** *f* rival; **emular** [1a] emulate, rival; **émulo** **1.** emulous; **2.** *m* rival, competitor.

emulsión *f* emulsion.

en (*dentro*) in; (*hacia dentro*) into; (*sobre*) on, upon; (*en un lugar, ciudad etc.*) in, at; (*por un precio*) for, at; (*porcentaje*) by; *está ~ la caja* it's in the box; *meter ~ la caja* put in(to) the box; *está ~ la mesa* it's on the table; *~ Madrid* in Madrid; *pasan un mes ~ Lloret* they're spending a month at Lloret; *en un 20 por ciento* by 20 per cent; *le conocí ~ su andar* I recognized him by his walk; *~ viéndole* (*pasado*) the moment I saw him; (*presente, futuro*) the moment I see him; *~ que* in that; *¿~ qué lo notas?* how can you tell?

enaguas *f/pl.* petticoat, slip.

enaguazar [1f] flood.

enajenación *f* alienation; estrangement; (*distracción*) absentmindedness; *~ mental* derangement; **enajenar** [1a] *propiedad* alienate; *derechos* dispose of; *p.* drive mad; **~se** (*estar absorto*) be lost in wonder; (*amigos*) become estranged; *~ de algo* deprive o.s. of.

enaltecer [2d] exalt, extol.

enamoradizo susceptible (to women); **enamorado**: *estar ~ de* be in love with; **enamoramiento** *m* falling in love; **enamorar** [1a] inspire love in, win the love of; **~se** fall in love (*de* with); **enamoricarse** [1g] be just a bit in love (*de* with).

enangostar(se) [1a] narrow.

enano 1. dwarf; stunted; **2.** *m* dwarf; midget; *contp.* runt.

enarbolar [1a] raise, hang out, hoist; (*en la mano*) brandish; wave; **~se** (*caballo*) rear.

enarcar [1g] *barril* hoop; *cejas* arch, raise.

enardecer [2d] *fig.* fire, inflame; **~se** get excited; blaze (*de* with).

enarenar [1a] sand; **~se** ⚓ run aground.

encabezamiento *m* (*título, titular*) heading, headline, caption *de dibujo etc.*; preamble *de documento*; ✝ billhead; (*oficial*) register; census; tax list; *~ de factura* billhead; **encabezar** [1f] head, lead; *papel* put a heading to; *dibujo etc.* caption; (*empadronar*) take a census of; *vino* fortify.

encabritarse [1a] rear; prance.

encadenación *f*, **encadenamiento** *m* chaining; *fig.* connexion, concatenation; **encadenar** [1a] (en-) chain; (*trabar*) shackle; *fig.* connect, link.

encajadura *f* (*acto*) insertion, fitting; (*hueco*) socket; (*ranura*) groove; **encajar** [1a] **1.** *v/t.* (*introducir*) insert, fit (*into* en); (*unir*) join, fit together; ⊕ encase, house *en caja*; F *observación* intrude, get in; F *cuento* come out with, tell at the wrong time; F *golpe* land; F (*lanzar*) chuck (*a* at); F (*hacer escuchar*) make *s.o.* listen to; F *~ algo a uno* palm (*or* foist) s.t. off on s.o.; **2.** *v/i.* fit (properly); *fig.* be appropriate; *~ con* fit, match; (*cuadrar*) square with, be in line with; **3. ~se** F (*introducirse*) squeeze in; *fig.* intrude (*en* upon), gate-crash (*en acc.*); **encaje** *m* (*acto*) insertion, fitting; (*hueco*) socket; (*ranura*) groove; (*caja*) housing; *sew.* lace; (*taracea*) inlay, inlaid work, mosaic; *~ de aplicación* appliqué (work);

encajera *f* lace maker.

encajonado *m* cofferdam; **encajonar** [1a] pack *en caja etc.*; box (up); ⊕ *etc.* box in, (en)case; squeeze in, squeeze through *en sitio estrecho*.

encalabrinar [1a] ⚕ make *s.o.* dizzy; F get *s.o.* worked up; F *amante* hook, click with; **~se** F get an obsession, get the bit between one's teeth.

encaladura *f* whitewash(ing); ⚒ liming; **encalar** [1a] *pared* whitewash; ⚒ lime.

encalmado ⚓ becalmed; ✝ slack; **encalmarse** [1a] be becalmed.

encalvecer [2d] go bald.

encalladero *m* shoal, sandbank; **encalladura** *f* stranding; **encallar** [1a] run aground, run ashore; *fig.* fail; get stuck, get tied up *en negocio*.

encallecido hardened.

encamarse [1a] put oneself to bed; (*animal*) crouch, hide; (*trigo*) bend over.

encaminar [1a] guide, set on the right road (*a* to); *energías* direct (*a* towards); **~se** *a* set out for, take the road to, make for; *fig.* be directed at, be intended for.

encandecer [2d] make white-hot.

encandilado F high, erect; **encandilar** [1a] dazzle, bewilder; *lumbre* poke; *emoción* kindle; **~se** (*ojos*) glow, sparkle, glitter.

encanecer(se) [2d] (*pelo*) grey; (*p.*) grow old; (*mohoso*) go mouldy.

encanijado puny; **encanijarse** [1a] grow weak, begin to look ill.
encanillar [1a] (wind on a) spool.
encantado delighted, charmed, pleased; *casa* rambling; *lugar* romantic; (*distraído*) absent-minded; (*absorto*) in a trance; *¡~!* how do you do?, pleased to meet you; *yo, ~* it's all right with me; **encantador 1.** enchanting, charming, delightful, lovely; **2.** *m*, **-a** *f* magician; *fig.* charmer; **encantamiento** *m* enchantment; **encantar** [1a] bewitch; *fig.* enchant, charm, delight; fascinate; *nos encantó la ciudad* we were charmed with the city; **encante** *m* auction; public sale; **encanto** *m* charm, spell, enchantment, delight; *el niño es un ~* the child is a real treasure; *la casa es un ~* it's a marvelous house.
encañada *f* ravine; **encañado** *m* conduit; **encañar** [1a] *v/t. agua* pipe; *terreno* drain; *planta* stake; *v/i.* form stalks; **encañonar** [1a] *v/t.* pipe; *sl.* stick up, hold up; *v/i.* grow feathers.
encapotado *cielo* overcast; *Cuba p.* sad; depressed; glum; **encapotarse** [1a] put on a cloak; (*p.*) frown; (*cielo*) cloud over.
encapricharse [1a] persist in one's foolishness; *~ por* take a fancy to, get infatuated with.
encapuchado hooded.
encarado: *bien ~* having good features, good-looking; *mal ~* ill-favored, terribly plain.
encaramar [1a] raise, lift up; (*alabar*) extol; F elevate; *~se* perch; *~ a* climb, get to the top of.
encarar [1a] *v/t. arma* point, aim; *problema* face; *v/i., ~se con* face, confront.
encarcelación *f*, **encarcelamiento** *m* imprisonment; incarceration; jailing; **encarcelar** [1a] imprison, jail; F lock up, put behind bars.
encarecer [2d] *v/t.* ✝ put up the price of; *p.* recommend; (*alabar*) extol; exaggerate; *dificultad* stress; *v/i., ~se* get dearer; **encarecidamente** insistently; **encarecimiento** *m* ✝ rise in price; *fig.* exaggeration, overrating; *con ~* insistently.
encargado 1.: *~ de* in charge of; **2.** *m* agent, representative; person in charge; *univ. ~ de curso* lecturer in charge; *~ de negocios* chargé d'affaires; **encargamiento** *m* duty; obligation; charge; **encargar** [1h] (*encomendar*) entrust; charge (*un deber* with a duty), commission; recommend; (*pedir*) order; *~se de* (*tomar sobre sí*) take charge of, take over; (*cuidar de*) look after, see about; *~ de inf.* undertake to *inf.*, see about *ger.*; **encargo** *m* (*deber etc.*) charge, commission, assignment, job; (*pedido*) order; (*puesto*) office, post; *por ~ de* on the orders of; on behalf of.
encariñamiento *m* endearment; **encariñarse** [1a]: *~ con* grow fond of.
encarnación *f* incarnation; embodiment; **encarnado** (*color*) red; Caucasian-skin-colored; *tez* florid; (*que ha encarnado*) incarnate; **encarnar** [1a] *v/t.* embody, personify; *anzuelo* bait; *v/i.* become incarnate; (*herida*) heal (up); (*arma*) enter the flesh; **encarnecer** [2d] put on flesh; **encarnizado** *ojo* bloodshot; *batalla* bloody, bitter, fierce; **encarnizamiento** *m* bitterness; **encarnizar** [1f] *fig.* (*irritar*) enrage; make cruel; *~se* (*irritarse*) get angry; (*luchar*) fight fiercely; *~ en carne* gorge on; *víctima* treat cruelly.
encarpetar [1a] file away, pigeonhole.
encarrilar [1a] set on the right road, direct; *fig.* put on the right track, set right; *ir encarrilado fig.* be on the right track; *b.s.* be in a rut.
encartar [1a] *criminal* outlaw; (*empadronar*) enroll, register; sign up.
encasar [1a] *hueso* set.
encasillar [1a] pigeonhole; file, classify.
encasquetar [1a] *sombrero* pull on tight, jam on; *idea* put into *s.o.'s* mind; *~se* get an idea firmly fixed.
encastillado ⚠ castellated; *fig.* haughty; **encastillar** [1a] fortify; *~se* ⚔ take to the hills; *fig.* refuse to yield.
encauchado 1. rubberized; rubber-lined; **2.** *m S.Am.* rubber-lined poncho; **encauchar** [1a] rubberize.
encausar [1a] prosecute, put on trial.
encáustico encaustic; **encausto** *m* encaustic.

encauzar [1f] channel; *fig.* channel, guide.
encefálico encephalic.
encenagado mud-stained; *fig.* sunk in vice; **encenagarse** [1h] get muddy; *fig.* wallow in vice.
encendedor *m* lighter; cigarette lighter; (*p.*) lamplighter; **encender** [2g] light, set fire to, ignite; kindle (*a. fig.*); *cerilla* strike; *luz*, ⚡ turn on, switch on; *fig.* inflame; **~se** catch (fire), ignite; (*arder más*) flare up; *fig.* (*p.*) get excited; (*cara*) blush; **encendido 1.** *adj. luz* on, lighted; *alambre* live; (*color*) glowing (*de* with); *cara* red, inflamed; **2.** *m mot.* ignition, firing; ~ *transistorizado* solid-state ignition; **encendimiento** *m* burning, kindling; *fig.* (*ardor*) eagerness; intensity.
encerado 1. waxy, wax-colored; **2.** *m* oilcloth; ⚕ sticking plaster; *escuela:* blackboard; **enceradora** *f* polishing machine; **encerar** [1a] wax; *suelo* polish.
encerradero *m* fold, pen; enclosure; **encerrar** [1k] enclose, shut in, shut up; lock in, lock up *con llave*; (*rodear etc.*) confine, hem in; *fig.* contain, include; (*implicar*) involve, imply; **encerrona** *f* dilemma, tight spot; F trap, fix.
encespedar [1a] turf.
encestar [1a] put in a basket; F sink a basketball.
encía *f* gum.
encíclica *f* encyclical.
enciclopedia *f* encyclopedia; **enciclopédico** encyclopedic.
encierro *m* confinement, shutting-up; (*lugar*) enclosure; (*prisión*) prison; *toros*: corralling.
encima (*en el aire*) above, over, overhead; (*en la cumbre*) at the top; on top; (*sobre*) on; (*además*) besides, over and above; ~ *de* on, upon; on top of; *por* ~ over; *fig.* superficially; *por* ~ *de* over; *¿tienes cambio ~?* do you have any change on you?
encina *f* holm oak, ilex; **encinar** *m* wood of holm oaks.
encinta pregnant; *zo.* with young; *mujer* ~ expectant mother; *dejar* ~ make pregnant; impregnate.
encintado *m* curb(stone).
encizañar [1a] *fig.* sow discord (*v/t.* among).
enclaustrar [1a] cloister; *fig.* hide away.
enclavar [1a] nail; (*traspasar*) pierce; F cheat; **~se** interlock; **enclave** *m geog.* enclave; **enclavijar** [1a] peg, pin.
enclenque weak(ly), sickly.
enclocar [1g *a.* 1m], **encloquecer** [2d] go broody.
encobar [1a] brood, sit.
encocorar [1a] F vex; **~se** get upset.
encoger [2c] *v/t.* shrink; *p.* intimidate, fill with fear; *v/i.*, **~se** shrink, contract; (*p.*) (*acobardarse*) cringe; (*desanimarse*) get disheartened; ~ *de hombros* shrug (one's shoulders); **encogido** shrunken, contracted; *p.* bashful; **encogimiento** *m* shrinkage, contraction; *fig.* bashfulness; ~ *de hombros* shrug.
encojar [1a] cripple, lame; **~se** go lame; F pretend to be ill.
encolar [1a] glue; size *antes de pintar*; (*pegar*) stick (down, together).
encolerizar [1f] provoke, anger, incense; **~se** get angry, see red.
encomendar [1k] commend, entrust; **~se** *a* send greetings to.
encomiar [1b] extol, praise.
encomienda *f* (*encargo*) charge, commission; recommendation; protection; *hist. land or office held from military order* (*in America, from king*).
encomio *m* praise, tribute.
enconar [1a] ⚕ inflame; *p.* irritate, provoke; **~se** fester; *fig.* fester, rankle; **encono** *m* rancor, spite, spitefulness, bad blood; **enconoso** resentful, rancorous.
encontradizo: *hacerse el* ~ contrive an apparently chance meeting; **encontrado** opposed, contrary, conflicting; **encontrar** [1m] find; meet; *esp. fig.* encounter; **~se** be, be situated (*en* in); (*ps.*) meet; (*coches etc.*) collide; (*opiniones*) clash, conflict; ~ *adj. etc.* be, feel, find o.s.; ~ *con* meet (with), encounter; **encontrón** *m*, **encontronazo** *m* crash, collision.
encopetado (*linajudo*) of noble birth; (*que presume*) high and mighty, haughty; **encopetarse** [1a] give o.s. airs, get conceited.
encorar [1m] cover with leather.
encorchar [1a] cork; *abejas* hive.

encordar [1m] *raqueta, violín* string; (*atar*) lash with ropes; **encordelar** [1a] tie with string.
encornado: *bien* ~ with good horns; **encornadura** *f* horns.
encorralar [1a] corral, pen.
encorvada *f* stoop; slouch; F *hacer la* ~ malinger, pretend to be ill; **encorvadura** *f* bend(ing); curving, curvature; **encorvar** [1a] bend, curve; hook; inflect; **~se** bend (over, down), stoop; (*romperse*) buckle.
encrespado curly; **encrespador** *m* curling tongs; **encrespar** [1a] *pelo* curl; *plumas* ruffle; *agua* ripple; **~se** curl; ripple; (*mar*) get rough; (*p.*) get angry.
encrestado haughty.
encrucijada *f* crossroads, intersection; ambush.
encuadernación *f* binding; (*taller*) bindery; **encuadernador** *m* book binder; **encuadernar** [1a] bind; *sin* ~ unbound.
encuadrar [1a] frame; (*encajar*) fit in, insert.
encubierta *f* fraud; **encubierto** hidden, undercover; **encubridor** **1.** concealing; **2.** *m*, **-a** *f* ⚖ accessory (after the fact), abettor; **encubrimiento** *m* concealment; ⚖ abetment; **encubrir** [3a; *p.p. encubierto*] hide, conceal, cloak; ⚖ *crimen* conceal, abet; *sospechoso* harbour.
encuentro *m* meeting (*a. deportes*), encounter (*a.* ⚔, *deportes*); collision *de coches etc.*; clash *de opiniones*; *salir al* ~ *a, ir al* ~ *de* go to meet (*a. fig.*).
encuesta *f* poll; (*investigación*) inquiry, probe F; ~ *demoscópica* opinion poll.
encuitarse [1a] grieve.
encumbrado high, lofty, towering; **encumbramiento** *m* (*acto*) raising; (*altura*) height, loftiness; *fig.* exaltation; **encumbrar** [1a] raise (up); *p.* (*elevar*) exalt; (*ensalzar*) extol; **~se** (*edificio*) tower; soar (*a. fig.*); (*p.*) be proud.
encurtido *m* pickle; **encurtir** [3a] pickle.
enchapado *m* plating; veneer; **enchapar** [1a] plate *con metal*; veneer *con madera etc.*
encharcada *f* pool, puddle; **encharcado** stagnant; **encharcar** [1g] swamp, cover with puddles; **~se** fill (*or* get covered) with water.
enchicharse [1a] *S.Am.* get drunk; *C.Am.* get angry.
enchilada *f S.Am.* enchilada; corn cake with chili.
enchufable ⚡ plug-in; **enchufar** [1a] connect, fit together; (*como telescopio*) telescope; ⚡ plug in; ✝ merge; **enchufe** *m* ⊕ joint, connection; (*manguito*) sleeve; (*hueco*) socket; ⚡ plug, point, socket; F (*p. etc.*) connection, useful contact; (*sinecura*) cushy job; F *tener* ~ have pull, have influence, have connections; **enchufismo** *m* F wire pulling; connections; getting things done through contacts; **enchufista** *m* F wire puller, contact man.
ende: † *por* ~ therefore.
endeble ⚕ feeble, frail; *fig.* flimsy; **endeblez** *f* feebleness; *fig.* flimsiness.
endecasílabo **1.** hendecasyllabic; **2.** *m* hendecasyllable.
endecha *f* dirge; **endecharse** [1a] grieve, mourn.
endémico endemic; *fig.* rife.
endemoniado possessed of the devil; *fig.* devilish, fiendish; furious, wild; **endemoniar** [1b] F provoke, stir up.
endenante(**s**) *S.Am.* recently.
endentadura *f* serration; **endentar** [1k] ⊕ mesh, engage; **endentecer** [2d] teethe.
enderezado favorable, opportune; **enderezar** [1f] (*poner derecho*) straighten (out), unbend; (*poner vertical*) set up, right (*a.* ⚓); *fig.* direct; dedicate; (*gobernar*) manage; (*arreglar*) put in order; **~se** straighten (up), draw o.s. up; ✈ flatten out; ~ *a inf.* take steps to *inf.*
endeudamiento *m* indebtedness; **endeudarse** [1a] run into debt.
endiablado devilish, fiendish; *co.* impish, mischievous; *cara* ugly; *S.Am.* complicated.
endibia *f* endive.
endilgar [1h] F send, direct; ~ *algo a uno* (*encajar*) spring s.t. on s.o., unload s.t. on to s.o.
endiosamiento *m* pride, haughtiness, vanity; absorption; **endiosar** [1a] deify; **~se** give o.s. airs; (*absorto*) be absorbed.

endocrino ⚕ endocrine; *glándula* ductless.
endogamia *f* inbreeding; *engendrado por* ~ inbred.
endomingado in one's Sunday best, dressed up; **endomingarse** [1h] dress up (in one's Sunday best).
endosante *m/f* endorser; **endosar** [1a] endorse; **endosatario** *m* endorsee; **endoso** *m* endorsement.
endrina *f* sloe; **endrino** *m* sloe (bush), blackthorn.
endulzar [1f] sweeten (*a. fig.*); soften, mitigate.
endurecer [2d] harden, toughen (*a. fig.*); stiffen; *fig.* inure (*a* to); **~se** harden, set; *fig.* become cruel; **endurecido** hard; *fig.* hardy, inured *a fatigas etc.*; (*cruel*) callous, hard-boiled F; **endurecimiento** *m* (*acto*) hardening; (*estado*) hardness; *fig.* callousness.
enebro *m* juniper.
enema *f* enema.
enemiga *f* enmity; **enemigo 1.** enemy, hostile; *fig.* inimical (*de* to); **2.** *m*, **a** *f* enemy; **enemistad** *f* enmity; **enemistar** [1a] set at odds, make enemies of; **~se** fall out (*con* with), become enemies.
energético energy *attr.*; power *attr.*; **energía** *f* energy, ⊕, ⚡ *etc.* power, energy; *fig.* drive, go F; ~ *atómica* atomic energy; ~ *solar* solar energy; **enérgico** energetic; *tono etc.* emphatic; *p.* energetic, vital, active; *esfuerzo* strenuous; *campaña* high-pressure; *medida etc.* bold, drastic.
energúmeno *m*, **a** *f* crazy person; person possessed of the devil; *fig* demon, madman; *sl.* nut.
enero *m* January.
enervación *f* enervation; **enervador** enervating; **enervar** [1a] enervate.
enésimo n^{th}, umpteenth F.
enfadadizo irritable; **enfadar** [1a] annoy, anger, vex; **~se** get angry, be cross (*de* at, *con* with); **enfado** *m* annoyance, irritation; (*afán*) trouble, bother; **enfadoso** annoying, vexatious; (*fatigoso*) irksome.
enfangar [1h] cover with mud; **~se** *fig.* F get involved in dirty work; (*depravarse*) wallow in vice.
énfasis *m* emphasis; stress; **enfático** emphatic; positive.
enfermar [1a] *v/t.* make ill; *v/i.* fall ill, be taken ill; **enfermedad** *f* illness, sickness, disease; *fig.* malady; ~ *profesional* occupational disease; ~ *del sueño* sleeping-sickness; *una* ~ *que duró 3 meses* an illness which lasted 3 months; *una* ~ *muy peligrosa* a very dangerous disease; **enfermería** *f* sick bay *de colegio etc.*; (*hospital*) infirmary; **enfermera** *f* nurse; ~ *jefa* matron; **enfermero** *m* male nurse; ⚔ orderly; **enfermizo** sickly, infirm; unhealthy; *mente* morbid; **enfermo 1.** ill, sick; ~ *de amor* lovesick; *caer* ~, *ponerse* ~ fall (*or* take) ill; **2.** *m*, **a** *f* patient, invalid.
enfiestarse [1a] *S.Am.* have a good time; celebrate.
enfilada *f* enfilade; **enfilar** [1a] ⚔ enfilade; (*alinear*) line up; (*ensartar*) thread.
enflaquecer [2d] *v/t.* make thin; weaken; *v/i.*, **~se** get thin, lose weight; *fig.* weaken; **enflaquecimiento** *m* loss of weight; *fig.* weakening.
enflautado F pompous.
enfocar [1g] *phot. etc.* focus; *fig. problema* approach, consider, look at; size up; envisage; **enfoque** *m* *phot. etc.* focus(ing); (*aumento*) magnification; *fig.* grasp.
enfoscar [1g] fill with mortar; **~se** (*p.*) sulk; plunge (*en negocio* into); (*cielo*) cloud over.
enfrascar [1g] bottle; **~se** get entangled, get involved; bury o.s. (*en libro* in).
enfrenar [1a] *caballo* bridle; ⊕ brake; *fig.* restrain.
enfrentamiento *m* confrontation (*policía*; *masas*); **enfrentar** [1a] *v/t.* put face to face, confront; *v/i.* face; **~se** *con* face (up to).
enfrente (*en el lado opuesto*) opposite; (*delante*) in front; (*en pugna*) against, in opposition; ~ *de* opposite (to); *la casa de* ~ the house opposite.
enfriadera *f* coolingjar; **enfriadero** *m* cold storage; **enfriamiento** *m* cooling; ⚕ cold; **enfriar** [1c] cool (*a. fig.*), chill; **~se** cool (down *or* off); *fig.* grow cold, cool off.
enfundar [1a] sheathe, (put in its) case; (*llenar*) stuff.
enfurecer [2d] enrage, madden; **~se** (*p.*) get furious; (*mar*) get rough.
enfurruñarse [1a] F get angry; (*ponerse mohino*) sulk.

engaitar [1a] F wheedle, humbug, talk round.
engalanar [1a] adorn, (be)deck; **~se** dress up.
enganchar [1a] hook, hitch; (*colgar*) hang up; *caballo* harness; ⊕ couple; *fig.* inveigle, rope in; ⚔ persuade to join up; **~se** get hooked up, catch; ⚔ enlist; **enganche** *m* (*acto*) hooking (up); 🚂, ⊕ coupling; ⚔ recruiting, enlisting; (*dinero*) bounty.
engañabobos *m* (*p.*) trickster; (*trampa*) trick, trap; **engañadizo** gullible; **engañador 1.** deceptive; **2.** *m*, **-a** *f* cheat, impostor, deceiver; **engañar** [1a] deceive, fool F; (*timar*) cheat, trick; mislead *con consejos falsos*; beguile *con encantos*; delude *con promesas vanas*; *hambre* stay; *tiempo* kill, while away; *dejarse ~ por* be taken in by; **~se** (*equivocarse*) be mistaken; delude o.s. *con esperanzas etc.*; **engañifa** *f* F trick, swindle; **engaño** *m* deceit; (*timo etc.*) fraud, trick; (*apariencia falsa*) sham; (*decepción*) delusion; (*equivocación*) mistake, misunderstanding; *~s pl.* wiles; **engañoso** *p. etc.* deceitful; *apariencia etc.* deceptive; *consejo etc.* misleading.
engarabitarse [1a] F climb, shin up; (*aterirse*) get stiff with cold.
engarce *m* linking, connection; setting *de joya*; **engarzar** [1f] *cuentas* thread; *joya* mount, set; (*rizar*) curl; *fig.* link, connect.
engastar [1a] set, mount; **engaste** *m* setting, mount(ing).
engatado thievish; **engat(us)ar** [1a] F coax, cajole, inveigle (*para que* into *ger.*).
engendrar [1a] beget, breed (*a. fig.*); generate (*a.* Å); *fig.* engender; **engendro** *m biol.* foetus; *fig.* bungled affair, abortion; F *mal ~* bad lot.
englobar [1a] lump together.
engolfar [1a] ⚓ lose sight of land; **~se** *en fig.* plunge into; launch (out) into.
engolondrinarse [1a] F give o.s. airs; (*enamoricarse*) have a flirtation.
engolosinar [1a] tempt, entice; **~se** *con* grow fond of; grow accustomed to.
engolletarse [1a] give o.s. airs.
engomar [1a] gum, stick.
engordar [1a] *v/t.* fatten; *v/i.* get fat, fill out; F get rich; **engorde** *m* fattening.
engorrar [1a] *S.Am.* vex, bother; **engorro** *m* bother, nuisance; **engorroso** bothersome, vexatious, trying.
engranaje *m* gear(s), gearing, mesh; (*dientes*) gear teeth; **engranar** [1a] *v/t.* gear; put into gear; *~ con* gear into, engage (with); *v/i.* interlock; ⊕ engage (*con* in, with), mesh (*con* with); *estar engranado* be in mesh.
engrandecer [2d] enlarge, magnify (*a. fig.*); (*alabar*) extol; exalt; **engrandecimiento** *m* enlargement; *fig.* exaltation *etc.*
engrane *m* mesh(ing).
engrapador *m* (**-a** *f*) stapler; **engrapar** [1a] clamp; staple.
engrasador *m* greaser; *~ de compresión* grease gun; **engrasar** [1a] grease, oil, lubricate; **engrase** *m* greasing, lubrication.
engreído conceited, proud, stuck-up F; **engreimiento** *m* conceit, vanity; **engreír** [3l] make conceited; *S.Am.* spoil; **~se** get conceited; *~ con S.Am.* grow fond of.
engrosar [1m] *v/t.* (*aumentar*) increase, swell; (*ensanchar*) enlarge; (*espesar*) thicken; *v/i.* get fat; **~se** swell, expand.
engrudar [1a] paste; **engrudo** *m* paste.
enguijarrado *m* cobbles; **enguijarrar** [1a] cobble.
enguirnaldar [1a] garland; *fig.* wreathe.
engullir [3a *a.* 3h] gulp (down), bolt, gobble.
enhebrar [1a] thread.
enhestar [1k] (*poner derecho*) erect; (*elevar*) raise high, hoist up; **enhiesto** (*derecho*) erect; (*p.*) bolt upright; (*elevado*) lofty.
enhilar [1a] *aguja* thread; (*ordenar*) arrange, order.
enhorabuena *f* congratulations; *¡~!* (*aprobación*) well and good; (*felicitación*) congratulations!, best wishes!; *dar la ~ a* congratulate; **¡enhoramala!** good riddance!; *¡vete ~!* go to the devil!
enhuerar [1a] addle.
enigma *m* enigma; puzzle; **enigmático** enigmatic(al); puzzling.
enjabonar [1a] soap; lather; F (*dar jabón*) soap up; F (*injuriar*) abuse.

enjaezar [1f] harness.
enjalbegar [1h] whitewash; *cara* paint.
enjambrar [1a] *v/t.* hive; *v/i.* swarm; **enjambre** *m* swarm (*a. fig.*).
enjarciar [1b] rig.
enjaular [1a] cage; coop up, pen in; F jail.
enjertar [1a] = *injertar*.
enjoyar [1a] set with precious stones; *fig.* (be)jewel, embellish.
enjuagar [1h] *platos, boca etc.* rinse; *cubo etc.* swill (out); **enjuague** *m* (*acto*) rinse, rinsing; (*licor*) mouthwash; *fig.* intrigue, scheme.
enjugamanos *m S.Am.* towel; **enjugaparabrisas** *m mot.* windshield wiper; **enjugar** [1h] wipe; dry; *deuda* wipe out.
enjuiciamiento *m* judgment; ⚖ (*civil*) lawsuit, (*criminal*) trial; ~ *civil* civil suit; ~ *criminal* criminal prosecution; **enjuiciar** [1b] examine, judge; ⚖ (*procesar*) prosecute, try; sentence.
enjundia *f fig.* substance; (*vigor*) drive.
enjuto lean, spare; (*seco*) wizened; [*v. pie.*]
enlabiar [1b] take in, bamboozle F; **enlabio** *m* humbug, honeyed words.
enlace *m* link, connexion (*a.* 🚂), tie-up; ⚔ *etc.* liaison; ⚗ linkage; (*casamiento*) union.
enladrillado *m* brick paving; **enladrillar** [1a] pave with bricks.
enlatar [1a] can, tin; line with metal; *S.Am.* put a tin roof on.
enlazar [1f] *v/t.* connect, link, tie (together), knit (together); *S.Am.* lasso; *v/i.* 🚂 connect; **~se** (*unirse*) link (up), be linked; (*engranar*) interlock; (*familias*) become connected by marriage.
enlodar [1a], **enlodazar** [1f] muddy, cover with mud; *fig.* (*manchar*) stain; defame.
enloquecedor maddening; *jaqueca* splitting; **enloquecer** [2d] *v/t.* madden, drive mad; *v/i.* go mad; **enloquecimiento** *m* madness.
enlosar [1a] pave.
enlozado 1. *S.Am.* enameled; **2.** *m S.Am.* enamelware.
enlucido *m* plaster; **enlucidor** *m* plasterer; **enlucir** [3f] plaster; *metal* polish.
enlutado in mourning; **enlutar** [1a] dress in mourning; *fig.* darken; **~se** go into mourning.
enmaderado timbered; **enmaderamiento** *m* timbering; **enmaderar** [1a] timber.
enmarañar [1a] (en)tangle; *fig.* complicate, involve; confuse, make a mess of; **~se** get tangled *etc.*
enmascarar [1a] mask; *fig.* mask, disguise; **~se** *fig.* masquerade (*de* as).
enmendación *f* emendation *etc.*; **enmendar** [1k] emend, correct; *ley etc.* amend; reform *moralmente etc.*; *pérdida* repair, make good; **~se** reform, mend one's ways; **enmienda** *f* emendation; amendment; compensation.
enmohecer [2d] rust; ⚘ make moldy; **~se** rust; ⚘ get moldy; **enmohecido** rusty; ⚘ moldy, mildewed.
enmudecer [2d] *v/t.* silence; *v/i.*, **~se** (*callar*) be silent; remain silent (*debiendo hablar*); (*perder el habla*) become dumb.
enmugrecer [2d] (be)grime.
ennegrecer [2d] blacken, dye *etc.* black.
ennoblecer [2d] ennoble; *fig.* embellish, adorn, dignify.
enojadizo short-tempered, testy, peevish; **enojar** [1a] anger; annoy, vex; **~se** get angry, lose one's temper, get annoyed (*con, contra* with; *de* at); **enojo** *m* anger; annoyance, vexation; **enojoso** irritating, annoying.
enorgullecer [2d] fill with pride; **~se** swell with pride; ~ *de* be proud of, pride o.s. on.
enorme enormous, huge; *fig.* heinous; **enormidad** *f fig.* enormity, heinousness *de pecado etc.*; (*maldad*) wickedness; (*acto*) monstrous thing.
enotecnia *f* wine making; oenology.
enrabiar [1b] enrage.
enraizar [1f] take root.
enramada *f* arbor, bower.
enrarecer [2d] *v/t.* rarefy, thin; *v/i.*, **~se** (*gas etc.*) become rarefied, grow thin; (*escasear*) get scarce.
enredadera *f* (*en general*) creeper, climber; (*especie*) bindweed.
enredador *m*, **-a** *f* (*chismoso*) gossip, busybody; (*embustero*) mischief-maker; **enredar** [1a] (*coger con red*)

net; (*enmarañar*) (en)tangle; (*entretejer*) intertwine; (*mezclar*) mix up, make a mess of; *fig.* (*meter en empeño*) embroil, involve, implicate; sow discord between; **~se** get (en-)tangled; *fig.* get involved; **enredo** *m* tangle (*a. fig.*); *fig.* (*confusión*) entanglement, mess; mix-up F, maze *de detalles etc.*; (*lío*) embroilment; *thea. etc.* plot; **enredoso** tangled, tricky.

enrejado *m* lattice (work) *de ventana*; trellis *de jardín*; (*cerca*) railing(s); *sew.* openwork; **enrejar** [1a] *ventana* fix a grating to; (*cercar*) fence, put railings round.

enrevesado *v. revesado*.

enriquecer [2d] enrich, make rich; **~se** get rich, prosper; **enriquecimiento** *m* enrichment.

enriscado craggy; **enriscar** [1g] raise; **~se** hide among rocks.

enristrar [1a] string; *dificultad* straighten out.

enrizar(**se**) (1f) curl.

enrocar [1g] *ajedrez*: castle.

enrojecer [2d] *v/t.* redden; *metal* make red-hot; *v/i.*, **~se** blush, redden.

enrolarse [1a] *S.Am.* enlist, enrol.

enrollar [1a] roll (up), wind (up), coil.

enronquecer [2d] *v/t.* make hoarse; *v/i.* grow hoarse, get hoarse; **enronquecido** hoarse.

enroque *m ajedrez*: castling.

enroscadura *f* twist; kink; coil; **enroscar**(**se**) [1g] (*torcer*) twist, twine; (*rizar*) curl (up); *alambre etc.* coil, wind; *esp. fig.* wreathe.

ensacar [1g] sack, bag.

ensalada *f* salad; *fig.* (*confusión*) mix-up F; (*mezcla*) medley; *mot.* traffic jam; **ensaladera** *f* salad bowl; **ensaladilla** *f* (Russian *etc.*) salad.

ensalmador *m* bone setter, quack; **ensalmar** [1a] *hueso* set; cure by quack remedies; **ensalmo** *m* ⚕ quack treatment; (*fórmula*) charm, incantation; (*como*) *por* ~ as if by magic.

ensalzamiento *m* exaltation; **ensalzar** [1f] exalt; (*alabar*) extol.

ensamblador *m* joiner; **ensambladura** *f* joint; (*arte*) joinery; ~ *dentada* joggle; ~ *francesa* scarf; ~ *de inglete* mitre joint; **ensamblar** [1a] join; assemble.

ensanchador *m* ⊕ stretcher; **ensanchar** [1a] enlarge, widen, extend; (*estirar*) stretch; *sew.* let out; **~se** stretch, expand; **ensanche** *m* enlargement, widening; extension, expansion; stretch(ing); new development *de ciudad etc.*; *sew.* room to let out.

ensangrentado blood-stained, gory; **ensangrentar** [1k] stain with blood; **~se** *fig.* get angry; ~ *con*, ~ *contra* treat cruelly, treat vindictively.

ensañamiento *m* cruelty, barbarity; **ensañar** [1a] enrage; **~se** *en* vent one's anger on; delight in tormenting (*or* hurting).

ensartar [1a] *cuentas etc.* string; *aguja* thread; *fig.* reel off, trot out.

ensayar [1a] test, try (out); *metal* assay; *thea.*, ♪ rehearse; **~se** practice; ~ *a inf.* practice *ger.*; **ensaye** *m* (*metales*) assay; **ensayista** *m/f* essayist; **ensayo** *m* test, trial; assay *de metal*; (*entrenamiento*) practice; *lit.* essay; *thea.*, ♪ rehearsal; *rugby*: try; ~ *de choque mot.* crash test; ~ *general* dress rehearsal; *de* ~ tentative; *viaje etc.* trial *attr.*; *vuelo* test *attr.*; *hacer* ~*s* practice (*en* on).

enseguida at once; immediately.

enselvado wooded.

ensenada *f* inlet, cove, creek.

enseña *f* standard, ensign; **enseñado** trained, informed; *bien* ~ *perro* house-trained; **enseñanza** *f* teaching, instruction, education; schooling; tuition; *primera* ~, ~ *primaria* elementary education; *segunda* ~ secondary education; ~ *superior* higher education; **enseñar** [1a] (*instruir*) teach; train; (*mostrar*) show; (*indicar*) point out; **~se** *a* accustom o.s. to.

enseñorearse [1a]: ~ *de* take possession of, take over.

enseres *m/pl.* goods and chattels; (*accesorios*) gear, equipment.

ensiladora *f* silo; **ensilar** [1a] store in a silo.

ensillar [1a] saddle (up).

ensimismamiento *m* reverie, brown study; **ensimismarse** [1a] be absorbed, be in a brown study; *S.Am.* be conceited.

ensoberbecerse [2d] become proud; (*mar*) get rough.
ensombrear [1a] overshadow; **ensombrecer** [2d] darken; **~se** become gloomy.
ensordecedor deafening; **ensordecer** [2d] *v/t. p.* deafen; *ruido* muffle; *v/i.* go deaf; (*fingir*) pretend not to hear.
ensortijar [1a] curl; *nariz* ring.
ensuciamiento *m* soiling; *mst fig.* pollution; **ensuciar** [1b] soil, dirty, mess up, (be)foul; *fig.* defile, pollute; **~se** soil o.s. *en vestido*, wet one's bed *en cama*.
ensueño *m* dream, reverie; *de* ~ dreamlike.
entablado *m* (floor) boarding; **entabladura** *f* boarding, planking; **entablar** [1a] ⊕ board (up); ⚕ splint; ⚖ bring, institute; *tablero* set up; *conversación etc.* enter into, strike up; **~se** (*viento*) settle.
entablillar [1a] ⚕ splint.
entallador *m* sculptor; engraver; **entalladura** *f*, **entallamiento** *m* sculpture; carving; engraving; (*corte*) slot, groove; **entallar** [1a] *v/t.* (*esculpir*) carve; (*grabar*) engrave; (*hacer cortes en*) notch, slot; *v/i.* (*vestido*) fit; *traje que entalla bien* well tailored suit.
entallecer [2d] shoot, sprout.
entapizado ⚘ overgrown (*de* with); **entapizar** [1f] upholster; *pared* hang with tapestry; *silla etc.* cover with fabric.
entarascar(se) [1g] F dress up, doll up.
entarimado *m* (floor) boarding; (*mosaico*) inlaid floor; ~ (*de hojas quebradas*) parquet; **entarimar** [1a] board, plank.
entarugado *m* block flooring, block paving.
ente *m* entity, being; F guy, ass.
enteco weak(ly), sickly.
entelerido shivering with cold (*or* fright); *S.Am.* frail.
entendederas *f/pl.* capacity to understand; F brains; *sl.* smarts; F *tener malas* ~, *ser corto de* ~ be slow on the uptake; **entendedor** *m*, **-a** *f* understanding person; *al buen* ~ *pocas palabras* a word to the wise is enough.
entender [2g] *mst* understand; (*tener intención, querer decir*) intend, mean; (*creer*) believe; *no entiendo palabra* it's Greek to me; *a mi* ~ in my opinion; ~ *de* know about, be good at, be experienced as (*carpintería* a carpenter); *no* ~ *de a.* be no judge of; ~ *en* (*versado*) be familiar with, know all about; (*que trata*) deal with; *dar a* ~ give to understand, imply; purport; *hacer* ~ put across; *hacerse* ~ make o.s. understood, get across; *lograr* ~ manage to understand, get the hang of; **~se** have one's reasons; (*dos ps.*) understand one another, get along well together; *se entiende que* it is understood that; *eso se entiende* that is understood; ~ *con* know how to manage *en el trato*; (*acuerdo*) come to an agreement with; *eso no se entiende conmigo* that's not my concern; **entendido** (*sabio*) wise, knowing; (*enterado*) (well-) informed; *bien* ~ *que* on the understanding that; *no darse por* ~ pretend not to understand; **entendimiento** *m* understanding; (*inteligencia*) mind; (*juicio*) judgement.
entenebrecer [2d] darken; *asunto* fog; **~se** get dark.
enterado knowledgeable, (well-) informed; *S.Am.* conceited; *estar* ~ be informed (*de* about), be in the know; **enterar** [1a] inform; **~se** *de* learn, find out, hear of, get to know (about).
entereza *f* entirety; *fig.* integrity, strength of mind; fortitude; firmness; (*severidad*) strictness.
entérico enteric; **enteritis** *f* enteritis.
enterizo in one piece, one-piece.
enternecedor moving, pitiable; **enternecer** [2d] soften; *fig.* touch, move (to pity *etc.*); **~se** be touched, be moved; **enternecimiento** *m* compassion, tenderness.
entero 1. entire, whole; complete; *fig.* (*recto*) upright; firm; (*sano*) sound; robust; ⅍ integral, whole; *por* ~ wholly, completely; **2.** *m* ⅍ integer.
enterrador *m* gravedigger; **enterramiento** *m* burial, interment; **enterrar** [1k] bury (*a. fig.*), inter.
entibiar [1b] cool (*a. fig.*), take the chill off.
entibo *m* ⚒ prop.
entidad *f* entity; ✝ firm, concern;

pol. etc. body, organization; *de* ~ of moment, of consequence.

entierramuertos *m* gravedigger; **entierro** *m* burial, interment; (*funeral, procesión*) funeral; F treasure trove.

entintar [1a] ink (in); **entinte** *m* inking.

entoldado *m* awning; (*tienda grande*) marquee; **entoldar** [1a] put an awning over; (*adornar*) decorate (with hangings); **~se** (*cielo*) cloud over; (*p.*) give o.s. airs.

entomología *f* entomology.

entonación *f* intonation; *fig.* conceit; **entonado** haughty, starchy; ♪ in tune; **entonar** [1a] *v/t. canción etc.* intone; (*afinar*) sing in tune; *nota* pitch, give *para empezar*; *phot., paint.*, tone; ⚕ tone up; *alabanzas* sound; *v/i.* be in tune; **~se** give o.s. airs.

entonces then, at that time; (*siendo así*) and so; well then; *desde* ~ since then; ever since; *en aquel* ~ at that time.

entono *m* (*acto*) intoning; (*canto afinado*) being in tune; *fig.* haughtiness.

entontecer [2d] *v/t.* make silly; *v/i.*, **~se** get silly.

entornar [1a] half-close; *puerta* leave ajar; (*volcar*) upset; **entorno** *m* environment.

entorpecer [2d] dull, (be)numb, stupefy; *fig.* obstruct, set back, slow up; **entorpecimiento** *m* numbness, torpor; *fig.* obstruction, delay, slowdown.

entrada *f* (*en general*) entrance, way in; (*parte de edificio etc.*) porch, doorway, gateway, entrance hall; (*acto*) entry (*en* into); admission (*en academia etc.* to); (*derecho*) right of entry; beginning *de año etc.*; *thea. etc.* (*localidad*) ticket; (*total*) house; *deportes*: (*total*) gate; *béisbol etc.*: innings; influx *de turistas etc.*; *cocina*: entrée; ⊕ input, intake; ☤ entry *en libro mayor*; (*ingresos*) income, receipts; ~ *de favor*, ~ *de regalo* complimentary ticket, pass; ~ *llena* full house; *derechos de* ~ import duties; *dar* ~ *a* admit; give an opening to; *prohibida la* ~ keep out, no admittance.

entramado *m* △ truss.

entrambos *lit.* both.

entrampar [1a] trap, (en)snare; F (*enredar*) mess up; ☤ burden with debts; **~se** F get into a mess; ☤ get into debt.

entrante 1. *p.* incoming; *mes etc.* next; *ángulo* reentrant; **2.** *m* inlet.

entrañable (*querido*) intimate, dearly loved; (*afectuoso*) affectionate; **entrañar** [1a] (*introducir*) bury deep; (*contener*) contain, harbor; **~se** become very intimate; ~ *en* reach the heart of;

entrañas *f/pl.* entrails, bowels (*a. fig.*), inside(s) F; *fig.* (*lo más oculto*) innermost parts; (*centro, ánimo*) heart; disposition.

entrar [1a] **1.** *v/t.* (*hacer entrar*) bring in, show in; (*influir*) get at, influence; ⚔ attack; (*estudio etc.*) attract; *no me entran las matemáticas* I can't get the hang of maths; **2.** *v/i.* go in, come in, enter; (*año etc.*) begin; ~ *a inf.* begin to *inf.*; ~ *bien* (*convenir*) be fitting; (*venir al caso*) be to the point; ~ *en* enter, go into; *esp. fig.* enter into; (*encajar*) fit into; *sociedad* join, be admitted to; *profesión* adopt; *número* be one of, be counted among; (*río*) flow into.

entre between *dos*, among(st) *varios*; (*en medio de*) in the midst of; ~ *tú y yo* (between) the two of us; *de* ~ out of, from among; *decir* ~ *sí* say to o.s.

entre... inter...; **~abierto** half-open; **~acto** *m* interval; **~ayudarse** [1a] help one another; **~cano** grayish; **~cejo** *m* space between the eyebrows; *fig.* frown; *fruncir el* ~ frown; **~cierre** *m* interlock; **~coger** [2c] catch, intercept; *fig.* press; (*hacer callar*) silence; **~cortado** intermittent; **~cortar** [1a] partially cut; interrupt.

entrecruzar [1f] interlace; **~se** *biol.* interbreed.

entre...: ~cubiertas *f/pl.* betweendecks; **~chocarse** [1g] collide; **~dicho** *m* prohibition, ban; ⚖ injunction; **~fino** medium-quality.

entrega *f* (*acto*) delivery; surrender; instalment, part *de novela etc.*; 📯 post, delivery; ~ *contra paga* (*or reembolso*) cash on delivery; ~ *en fecha futura* forward delivery;

entregar [1h] (*dar, poner en manos*) deliver; hand (over), hand in;

(*ceder*) surrender; give up, part with; *sl.* *~la* kick the bucket; ✝ *a ~* to be supplied; **~se** surrender, give in; *~ a* devote o.s. to, indulge in; *b.s.* abandon o.s. to; *~ de* take possession of.

entre...: **~lazar(se)** [1f] entwine, interlace; **~listado** striped; **~medias** (in) between; in the meantime; **~més** *m thea.* interlude; *~es pl.* hors d'oeuvres; **~meter** [2a] insert; *v. entrometer*; **~mezclar** [1a] intermingle; intersperse.

entrenador *m deportes*: trainer (*a.* ✈), coach; **entrenamiento** *m* training; **entrenar** [1a] train, coach; **~se** train.

entre...: **~oír** [3q] half-hear; **~paño** *m* (door) panel; (*estante*) shelf; **~pierna(s)** *f* (*pl.*) crotch, crutch; **~puente** *m* between-decks; steerage; **~rrenglón** *m* space between the lines; interline; **~sacar** [1g] *pelo, árboles etc.* thin out; (*escoger*) pick out; (*examinar*) sift; **~semana** *f S.Am.* weekdays; workdays; **~sijo** *m* mesentery; *fig.* secret; difficulty, snag; *tener muchos ~s* be complicated; (*p.*) be very deep; **~suelo** *m* mezzanine, entresol; **~tanto 1.** *adv.* meanwhile, meantime; **2.** *m* meantime; **~tejer** [2a] entwine, interweave; (*trabar*) mat; *palabras etc.* put in, insert; **~tela** *f* interlining; *~s pl.* heartstrings; **~telar** [1a] interline.

entretener [2l] (*divertir*) entertain; (*ocupar*) keep (occupied); keep in suspense; engage *en conversación*; (*demorar*) hold up, delay; *tiempo* while away; ⊕ maintain; **entretenida:** *dar* (*con*) *la ~ a* hedge with, keep *s.o.* talking; **entretenido** entertaining, amusing; **entretenimiento** *m* entertainment, amusement; recreation; (*manutención*) upkeep; ⊕ maintenance; **~tiempo** *m* transition; meantime; spring; fall.

entre...: **~ver** [2v] glimpse; *fig.* guess, suspect; **~verado** *tocino* streaky; **~verar** [1a] intermingle; mix up; **~vero** *m* jumble, mix-up F; **~vía** *f* 🚂 gauge.

entrevista *f* interview, conference; **entrevistar** [1a] interview; **~se** *con* interview, have an interview with.

entristecer [2d] sadden, grieve; **~se** grow sad, grieve.

entrometerse [2a] meddle, interfere (*en* in, with), intrude; **entrometido 1.** meddlesome, interfering; **2.** *m*, **a** *f* busybody.

entroncar [1g] be related, be connected (*con* to, with), join; *S.Am.* 🚂 connect (*con* with).

entronizar [1f] enthrone; *fig.* exalt.

entronque *m* relationship, connexion; *S.Am.* 🚂 junction.

entruchada *f* F trap, trick; **entruchar** [1a] F decoy, lure.

entuerto *m* wrong, injustice.

entumecer [2d] (be)numb; **~se** (*miembro*) get numb, go to sleep; (*río*) swell; (*mar*) surge; **entumecido** stiff, numbed, cramped; **entumecimiento** *m* stiffness *etc.*

enturbiar [1b] *agua* muddy, disturb; *fig.* obscure, fog, confuse.

entusiasmar [1a] excite, fire, fill with enthusiasm; **~se** get excited (*por* about, over); *~ por* be enthusiastic about, be keen on, rave about; **entusiasmo** *m* enthusiasm (*por* for); keenness, zeal, zest; **entusiasta 1.** enthusiastic; keen (*de* on); zealous (*de* for); **2.** *m/f* enthusiast; fan F; **entusiástico** enthusiastic.

enumeración *f* enumeration; **enumerar** [1a] enumerate.

enunciación *f* enunciation; declaration; **enunciar** [1b] enunciate; declare; **enunciativo** enunciative; *gr.* declarative.

envainar [1a] sheathe; *sl.* *¡enváinala!* shut your trap!

envalentonamiento *m* boldness, daring; *b.s.* bravado; **envalentonar** [1a] embolden; *b.s.* fill with Dutch courage; **~se** take courage; put on a bold front.

envanecer [2d] make vain; **~se** grow vain; swell with pride (*con, de* at); **envanecimiento** *m* pride; vanity; conceit.

envaramiento *m* stiffness; **envararse** [1a] get stiff; get numb.

envasar [1a] *v/t.* pack(age), wrap; bottle; can, tin; *v/i. fig.* tipple; **envase** *m* (*acto*) packing *etc.*; (*recipiente en general*) container; (*papel*) wrapping; bottle; (*lata*) can, tin; *~ de hojalata* tin can; *sin ~* loose, unwrapped; *~s pl. a devolver* returnable empties.

envedijarse [1a] get tangled.
envejecer [2d] *v/t.* age, make old; *v/i.*, **~se** age, grow old, get old; **envejecido** aged, (looking) old.
envenenador *m*, **-a** *f* poisoner; **envenenamiento** *m* poisoning; **envenenar** [1a] poison (*a. fig.*); *relaciones etc.* embitter.
enverdecer [2d] turn green.
envergadura *f* ⚓ breadth; ✈ ~ (*de alas*) wingspan; (*extensión*) expanse, spread, span; *fig.* scope, compass, reach.
envés *m* back, wrong side *de tela*; flat *de espada*; F *anat.* back.
enviado *m* envoy; **enviar** [1c] send (*por* for).
enviciar [1b] corrupt; *fig.* vitiate; **~se** *con* (*or en*) become addicted to.
envidar [1a] bid.
envidia *f* envy, jealousy; *tener* ~ *a* envy; **envidiable** enviable; **envidiar** [1b] envy, begrudge (*algo a uno* a p. a th.); (*desear*) covet; **envidioso** envious, jealous; (*deseoso*) covetous.
envilecer [2d] debase, degrade; **~se** degrade o.s.; grovel; **envilecimiento** *m* degradation.
envío *m* (*acto*) sending, dispatch; ✝ consignment *de mercancías*, remittance *de dinero*; ⚓ shipment; *gastos de* ~ postage and handling.
envión *m* push, shove.
envite *m* stake, side bet; *fig.* (*ofrecimiento*) offer; (*empujón*) push, shove.
enviudar [1a] become a widow(er), be widowed.
envoltorio *m* bundle; **envoltura** *f* cover(ings), casing, wrapping; ⚘, ✈ *etc.* envelope; **~s** *pl.* swaddling clothes; **envolvedor** *m* cover, wrapping; **envolvente** *movimiento* encircling, enveloping; **envolver** [2h; *p.p. envuelto*] (*con papel etc.*) wrap (up), tie up, do up; (*con ropa*) wrap, swathe; (*contener, ceñir*) envelop, enfold; muffle *contra frío, ruido etc.*; ⚔ encircle, surround; *fig.* involve, imply; **~se** *fig.* become involved; **envolvimiento** *m* envelopment; ⚔ encirclement; *fig.* involvement.
enyesado *m* plastering; **enyesar** [1a] plaster.
enzarzar [1f] *fig.* involve, entangle; **~se** get involved, get tied up.
enzima *f* enzyme; **enzímico** enzymatic; **enzimología** *f* enzymology.
épica *f* epic; **épico** epic.
epicúreo *adj. a. su. m* epicurean.
epidemia *f* epidemic; **epidémico** epidemic.
epidermis *f* epidermis.
Epifanía *f* Epiphany.
epígrafe *m* inscription; (*lema*) motto, device; (*título*) title; (*titular*) headline.
epigrama *m* epigram; **epigramático** epigrammatic(al).
epilepsia *f* epilepsy; **epiléptico** *adj. a. su. m*, **a** *f* epileptic.
epilogar [1h] sum up; **epílogo** *m* epilogue.
episcopado *m* (*oficio*) bishopric; (*período*) episcopate; (*obispos*) bishops, episcopate, episcopacy; **episcopal** episcopal.
episodio *m* episode; incident; **episódico** episodic(al).
epístola *f* epistle; **epistolar** epistolary; **epistolario** *m* collected letters.
epitafio *m* epitaph.
epíteto *m* epithet.
epitomar [1a] condense, abridge, epitomize; **epítome** *m* compendium, epitome.
época *f* period, time, epoch; *de* ~ period *attr.*; *coche etc.* vintage; *hacer* ~ be a landmark, be epoch-making.
epopeya *f* epic (*a. fig.*).
equidad *f* equity (*a.* ⚖); fairness, impartiality.
equidistante equidistant.
equilátero equilateral.
equilibrado balanced; *p.* sensible; even-tempered; **equilibrar** [1a] (*poner en equilibrio*) balance, poise; (*igualar*) balance, adjust, redress; **equilibrio** *m* balance, equilibrium; *esp. fig.* poise; ~ *político* balance of power; **equilibrista** *m/f* tightrope walker, acrobat.
equino equine 🕮, horse *attr.*
equinoccio *m* equinox.
equipaje *m* luggage, piece of luggage; (*equipo*) equipment, kit; ⚓ crew; *hacer el* ~ pack (up); **equipar** [1a] equip, furnish, fit out, fit up (*con* with).
equiparar [1a] consider equal, equalize, put on a level (with); compare; **~se** *con* rank with.

equipo *m* equipment, outfit, kit; system; shift *de obreros*; (*grupo, deportes etc.*) team; (*acto*) fitting-out; ~ *de alta fidelidad* stereo system; hi-fi set.

equitación *f* (*acto*) riding; (*arte*) horsemanship; *escuela de* ~ riding school.

equitativo equitable, reasonable; [*trato* fair, square.]

equivalencia *f* equivalence; **equivalente** *adj. a. su. m* equivalent (*a* to); **equivaler** [2q]: ~ *a* be equivalent to; amount to; (*en nivel, grado*) rank as, rank with.

equivocación *f* mistake, error; (*descuido*) oversight; (*malentendido*) misunderstanding; F goof, slip; *por* ~ in error, by mistake; **equivocado** wrong, mistaken; *cariño etc.* misplaced; **equivocar** [1g] mistake (*A con B* A for B); **~se** be wrong, make a mistake; be mistaken (*con* for); ~ *de casa* go to the wrong house; **equívoco 1.** equivocal, ambiguous; **2.** *m* equivocation, ambiguity; (*palabra*) ambiguous word, word having two meanings; (*juego de palabras*) pun, word play.

era[1] *etc. v. ser.*

era[2] *f* era, age; ~ *atómica* atomic age.

era[3] *f* ✓ threshing floor; (*cuadro*) bed, plot.

erario *m* exchequer, treasury.

erección *f* erection; building, raising; *fig.* establishment.

eremita *m* hermit; recluse.

ergio *m* erg.

ergotismo *m* argumentativeness; ergotism.

erguido erect; *cuerpo etc.* straight; **erguir** [3n] (*levantar*) raise; (*poner derecho*) straighten; **~se** straighten up; *fig.* swell with pride.

erial 1. uncultivated; **2.** *m* common; (*yermo*) waste land.

erigir [3c] erect, build, raise; *fig.* establish; ~ *en* set *s.o.* up as; **~se** *en* set up as.

erisipela *f* erysipelas.

erizado bristly; bristling (*de* with); **erizarse** [1f] bristle; (*pelo*) stand on end; **erizo** *m zo.* hedgehog; ♀ bur; F surly fellow; ~ *de mar* sea urchin.

ermita *f* hermitage; **ermitaño** *m* hermit.

erogación *f* distribution (of wealth); *S.Am.* payment; gift.

erosión *f* erosion; wearing (out); reduction; **erosionar(se)** [1a] erode; **erosivo** erosive.

erótico erotic; *poesía etc.* love *attr.*; **erotismo** *m* eroticism; **erotomanía** *f* (pathological) eroticism; **erotómano** (pathologically) erotic.

errabundeo *m* wanderings; **errabundo** wandering.

erradicar [1g] eradicate.

erradizo wandering; **errado** (*equivocado*) mistaken; (*inexacto*) wide of the mark; (*imprudente*) unwise; **errante** (*no fijo*) wandering, roving, itinerant; (*perdido*) stray; *fig.* errant; **errar** [1l] *v/t. tiro, vocación* miss; (*no cumplir*) fail (in one's duty to); *v/i.* wander, rove, roam (about); = **~se** err, go astray; ~ *en vocación* miss; **errata** *f* misprint, erratum; **errático** erratic.

erre: F ~ *que* ~ obstinately.

erróneo wrong, mistaken, erroneous; **error** *m* error, mistake; fault; fallacy *en teoría etc.*; ~ *de imprenta* misprint; ~ *judicial* miscarriage of justice; ~ *de pluma* clerical error.

eructar [1a] belch; **eructación** *f*, **eructo** *m* belch, eructation 📖.

erudición *f* erudition, learning, scholarship; **erudito 1.** erudite, learned, scholarly; **2.** *m*, **a** *f* scholar.

erupción *f* eruption (*a.* ⚕); outbreak; ~ (*cutánea*) rash; *entrar en* ~ erupt; **eruptivo** eruptive.

esa *etc. v.* ese.

esbeltez *f* slenderness *etc.*; **esbelto** slim, slender, svelte.

esbirro *m* myrmidon, henchman; *sl.* mug; enforcer; (*alguacil*) constable, bailiff.

esbozar [1f] sketch, outline; **esbozo** *m* sketch, outline.

escabechar [1a] pickle, souse; F do in, carve up; F *univ.* plow; **escabeche** *m* pickle, souse; (*pescado*) pickled fish; *esp.* pickled tuna fish.

escabel *m* (foot)stool.

escabiosa *f* scabious.

escabrosidad *f* roughness, ruggedness *etc.*; **escabroso** *terreno* rough, rugged; (*desigual*) uneven; *fig.* (*áspero*) harsh; *asunto* difficult, thorny; *cuento* risky, scabrous.

escabullirse [3a] make o.s. scarce,

slip away, clear out; ~ *por* slip through.
escafandra *f* diving suit; ~ *espacial* space helmet.
escala *f* (*escalera*) ladder; (*graduación etc.*) scale (*a.* ℞, ♪); range *de velocidades etc.*; ⚓ port of call; (*parada*) intermediate stop; ~ *móvil* sliding scale; *según* ~ to scale; *sin* ~*s* nonstop; *en gran*(*de*) ~ on a large scale, in a big way; *hacer* ~ *en* put in at, call at; **escalada** *f* scaling, climbing; **escalafón** *m* establishment, list of officials, scale.
escalamera *f* ⚓ oarlock; rowlock.
escalar [1a] scale, climb; *casa* burgle, break into.
escaldado F wary, fly; *mujer* loose.
escaldadura *f* scald; **escaldar** [1a] scald; *metal* make red-hot.
escalera *f* stairs, staircase *en casa*; (flight of) steps *esp. al descubierto*; (*escala*) ladder; *mot.* tailboard; ~ *de caracol* spiral staircase; ~ *de incendios* fire escape; ~ *mecánica*, ~ *móvil*, ~ *rodante* escalator, moving staircase; ~ *de servicio* backstairs; ~ *de tijera* steps, stepladder.
escalfador *m* chafing dish; **escalfar** [1a] *huevo* poach.
escalinata *f* (flight of) steps.
escalo *m* burglary; break-in; digging (to enter or escape).
escalofriado chilly; **escalofrío** *m* chill (*a.* ⚕); (*estremecimiento*) shivering, shiver(s).
escalón *m* step, stair *de escalera*; rung *de escala*; *fig.* (*grado*) stage, grade; stepping stone, ladder *hacia un fin etc.*; ⚔ echelon; **escalonamiento** *m* gradation; graduation; **escalonar** [1a] spread out at intervals; step; *horas*, ⊕ stagger; ⚔ echelon.
escalpar [1a] scalp.
escalpelo *m* scalpel.
escama *f zo.* scale; *fig.* (*resentimiento*) grudge; (*recelo*) suspicion; **escamado** distrustful, wary; **escamar** [1a] scale; F make wary, make suspicious; ~**se** F get wary, get suspicious, be once bitten twice shy; **escamón** apprehensive, suspicious.
escamondar [1a] prune (*a. fig.*).
escamoso *pez* scaly; *sustancia* flaky.
escamoteador *m* conjurer; *fig.* swindler; **escamot**(**e**)**ar** [1a] whisk away, make *s.t.* vanish; *carta* palm; F steal, swipe; **escamoteo** *m* sleight of hand, conjuring; (*un* ~) conjuring trick.
escampar [1a] *v/t.* clear out; *v/i.* clear up, stop raining; *fig.* give up.
escampavía *f* revenue cutter.
escanciador *m* wine waiter; **escanciar** [1b] *vino* pour (out), serve; *vaso* drain.
escandalizar [1f] scandalize, shock; ~**se** be shocked; be offended; **escándalo** *m* scandal; (*alboroto, protesta etc.*) row, uproar; bad example; *armar un* ~ make a scene; **escandaloso** scandalous, shocking; *ofensa etc.* flagrant; *vida etc.* disorderly; *niño etc.* undisciplined, uncontrollable.
escandallo *m* ⚓ lead.
escandinavo *adj. a. su. m*, **a** *f* Scandinavian.
escandir [3a] scan; **escansión** *f* scansion.
escantillón *m* pattern, template, scantling.
escaño *m* bench, settle.
escapada *f* (*huida*) escape; (*travesura*) escapade; flying visit; ~ *en una tabla* narrow squeak; **escapar** [1a] escape (*a acc.*, *de* from); run away; ~ *de manos* elude; ~**se** escape; run away; get out; (*gas etc.*) leak (out); ~ *con* make off with; *se me escapa fig.* it eludes me; ~*le algo a uno fig.* (*decir etc.*) let s.t. slip; (*no ver*) escape one's notice.
escaparate *m* showcase, display cabinet; show window *de tienda*; *Cuba, Col., Ven.* clothes closet; **escaparatista** *m/f* window dresser.
escapatoria *f* (*huida*) escape, getaway; *fig.* loophole, excuse; escape *del trabajo etc.*
escape *m* escape, flight, get-away; ⊕ exhaust (*a. tubo de* ~, *gases de* ~); leak(age) *de gas, líquido*; ⊕ escapement; *a* ~ at full speed; ⊕ *de* ~ exhaust *attr.*; **escapismo** *m* escapism.
escapular scapular; **escapulario** *m* scapular(y).
escaque *m* square (*of* chessboard).
escara *f* ⚕ crust, slough.
escarabajear [1a] *v/t.* F bother, worry; *v/i.* wriggle, squirm; (*escribir*) scrawl, scribble; **escarabajo** *m* beetle; ⊕ flaw; F runt, dwarf; ~*s pl.* F scrawl.
escaramujo *m* dogrose, brier; (*fruta*) hip.

escaramuza *f* skirmish, brush; **escaramuzar** [1f] skirmish.

escarapela *f* rosette, cockade; F set-to.

escarbadientes *m* toothpick; **escarbador** *m* scraper; **escarbar** [1a] scratch; *lumbre* poke; *dientes* pick; *fig.* delve into.

escarcha *f* (hoar)frost; **escarchado** *fruta* crystallized; **escarchar** [1a] *v/t. pastel* ice; *v/i.* freeze.

escarcho *m* roach.

escarda *f* weeding hoe; (*labor*) weeding, hoeing; **escardar** [1a] weed (out) (*a. fig.*); **escardillo** *m* weeding hoe.

escariador *m* reamer; **escariar** [1b] ream.

escarificación *f* ⚒, ⚕ scarification; **escarificador** *m* scarifier; **escarificar** [1g] scarify.

escarlata *f* scarlet; scarlet cloth; **escarlatina** *f* scarlet fever.

escarmenar [1a] *lana* comb; *fig.* punish; F do out of *s.t.* bit by bit.

escarmentar [1k] *v/t.* punish severely, teach a lesson (to); *v/i.* learn one's lesson; **escarmiento** *m* punishment; warning, lesson; *para* ~ *de* as a lesson to; *servir de* ~ be a warning (*a* to).

escarnecer [2d] scoff at, ridicule; **escarnio** *m* jibe, jeer; derision.

escarola *f* endive.

escarolar [1a] curl; frill.

escarpa *f* scarp, escarpment, slope; **escarpado** steep, sheer; craggy; **escarpadura** *f* = *escarpa*; **escarpar** [1a] *terreno* (e)scarp; (*raspar*) rasp.

escarpia *f* spike, tenterhook.

escarpín *m* (*zapato*) pump; (*calcetín*) extra sock; ~*es pl.* ankle socks *de muchacha.*

escasamente barely; hardly.

escasear [1a] *v/t.* be sparing with, skimp; *v/i.* be scarce, get scarce, fall short; **escasez** *f* scarcity, shortage; (*tacañería*) stinginess; **escaso** scarce; scant(y); (*miserable*) meagre, skimpy; *cosecha, público* thin, sparse; *posibilidad, recursos* slim, slight; *dinero* tight; *provisión* short; *p.* (*tacaño*) stingy; (*económico*) sparing; ~ *de* short of; *6 metros* ~*s* barely 6 meters; *por una cabeza* ~*a* by a short head.

escatimar [1a] skimp, give grudgingly, stint, be sparing of; *esfuerzo* spare; **escatimoso** scrimpy, mean.

escena *f mst* scene; (*parte del teatro*) stage; ~ *muda* by-play; *poner en* ~ stage, perform; **escenario** *m* (*parte del teatro*) stage; scene, setting *de acción*; *cine*: continuity; **escénico** scenic; **escenógrafo** *m* scene painter.

escepticismo *m* scepticism; **escéptico 1.** sceptical; **2.** *m*, **a** *f* sceptic, doubter.

escindir [3a] split; **escisión** *f* scission; *fig.* split, division; ~ *nuclear* nuclear fission.

esclarecer [2d] *v/t.* (*aclarar*) explain, elucidate; illuminate; *fig.* ennoble; *v/i.* dawn; **esclarecido** illustrious.

esclavina *f* cape, tippet.

esclavitud *f* slavery, bondage; **esclavizar** [1f] enslave; **esclavo** *adj. a. su. m*, **a** *f* slave.

esclerosis *f* sclerosis.

esclusa *f* lock, sluice; floodgate.

escoba *f* broom; **escobada** *f* sweep; **escobar** [1a] sweep; **escobazo** *m* quick sweep; *echar a* ~*s* kick out; **escobilla** *f* whisk; brush (*a.* ⚡); ~ *de limpiaparabrisas* (windshield) wiper blade; **escobillón** *m* ⚕, ⊕ swab; **escobón** *m* long-handled broom; scrub brush *para fregar*; ⚕, ⊕ swab.

escocer [2b *a.* 2h] *v/t.* annoy; *v/i.* smart, sting; ~**se** chafe.

escocés 1. Scots, Scotch, Scottish; **2.** *m* Scot(sman); (*idioma*) Scots; **escocesa** *f* Scot(swoman).

escofina *f* rasp; **escofinar** [1a] rasp.

escoger [2c] choose, select, pick out; elect *en elección*; **escogido** select, choice; *obras* selected.

escolar 1. scholastic; school *attr.*; **2.** *m* pupil, schoolboy; **escolástica** *f*, **escolasticismo** *m* scholasticism; **escolástico 1.** scholastic; **2.** *m* schoolman.

escolta *f* escort; **escoltar** [1a] escort, guard, protect; ⚓ convoy, escort.

escollo *m* reef, rock; *fig.* pitfall, stumbling block.

escombrar [1a] clear out, clean out; **escombrera** *f* tip, dump; *metall.* slag heap; **escombro** *m ichth.* mackerel; ~*s pl.* debris, wreckage, rubble.

escondedero *m* hiding place; **esconder** [2a] hide, conceal (*de* from);

~se hide; lurk; **escondid(ill)as:** *a ~* by stealth, on the sly; *a ~ de* behind the back of; **escondite** *m* hiding place, cache; (*juego*) hide-and-seek; **escondrijo** *m* hiding place, hide-out; *fig.* nook.

escopeta *f* shotgun; *~ de dos cañones* double-barreled shotgun; *~ de viento* air-gun; **escopetazo** *m* (*tiro*) gun-shot; (*herida*) gunshot wound; *fig.* bad news, blow; *S.Am.* sarcasm; insult; **escopetear** [1a] shoot at (with a shotgun); **~se** *a* shower one another with; **escopeteo** *m* shooting; burst; lively exchange *de injurias etc.*; **escopetero** *m* gunsmith.

escoplear [1a] chisel; **escoplo** *m* chisel.

escora *f* ⚓ level line; (*inclinación*) list.

escorbuto *m* scurvy.

escoria *f metall.* slag, dross; scum (*a. fig.*); **escorial** *m* slag-heap, dump.

escorpión *m* scorpion.

escorzar [1f] foreshorten; **escorzo** *m* foreshortening.

escota *f* ⚓ sheet.

escotado décolleté, low(-necked); **escotadura** *f* low neck; *thea.* large trapdoor; **escotar** [1a] *v/t. sew.* cut to fit; *río etc.* draw water from; *v/i.* pay one's share; **escote** *m sew.* (low) neck, décolletage; share *de dinero*; *ir a ~, pagar a ~* pay one's share.

escotilla *f* hatch(way); **escotillón** *m* trapdoor.

escozor *m* smart, sting; *fig.* grief.

escriba *m* scribe; **escribanía** *f* (*escritorio*) writing desk; writing case; (*tintero*) inkstand; (*oficio*) clerkship; **escribano** *m* ⚖ clerk; † notary; *~ municipal* town clerk; **escribiente** *m* amanuensis; (*empleado*) clerk; **escribir** [3a; *p.p. escrito*] write; (*ortografiar*) spell; *¿cómo se escribe eso?* how is that spelled?; *el que esto escribe* the (present) writer; **escrito 1.** *p.p. of escribir*; **2.** *adj.* written; **3.** *m* writing, document; manuscript; ⚖ brief; *~s pl.* writings, works; *por ~* in writing, in black and white; *poner por ~* write down, commit to writing; **escritor** *m*, **-a** *f* writer; **escritorio** *m* writing desk, bureau; (*caja*) writing case; (*oficina*) office; **escritorzuelo** *m* hack, penny-a-liner; **escrituario** Scriptural; **escritura** *f* (*acto, arte*) writing; (*símbolos*) writing, script; (*propia de p.*) (hand)writing; ⚖ deed, document; indenture *de aprendiz*; *~ aérea* sky writing; *~ normal* longhand; *Sagrada ♀* Scripture; *~ de traspaso* conveyance; **escriturar** [1a] ⚖ execute by deed; *actor etc.* book.

escrófula *f* scrofula; **escrofuloso** scrofulous.

escroto *m* scrotum.

escrupulizar [1f] scruple; (*dudar*) hesitate; **escrúpulo** *m* (*inquietud*) scruple (*a. pharm.*); (*duda*) hesitation; = **escrupulosidad** *f* scrupulousness; **escrupuloso** scrupulous; (*minucioso etc.*) particular, precise.

escrutador 1. searching; **2.** *m parl.* teller; returning officer, scrutineer *en elecciones*; **escrutar** [1a] scrutinize; *votos* count; **escrutinio** *m* scrutiny, count *de votos*; (*votación*) ballot; (*examen*) scrutiny.

escuadra *f* ⚠ square; *~* (*de hierro*) bracket, angle iron; ⚔ squad; ⚓ fleet, squadron; *~ de delineante* set square; *~ falsa* bevel square; *a ~* square, at right angles; *fuera de ~* out of true; **escuadrar** [1a] square; **escuadrilla** *f* ✈ squadron, flight; ⚓ flotilla; **escuadrón** *m* ⚔ squadron.

escuálido pale, weak; (enjuto) skinny, scraggy.

escucha 1. *f* (*acto*) listening; *eccl.* chaperon; *estar a la ~* listen in; **2.** *m* ⚔ scout; *radio*: monitor; **escuchar** [1a] *v/t.* listen to; *consejos etc. a.* mind, heed, pay attention to; *v/i.* listen.

escudar [1a] shield (*a. fig.*); **~se** shelter, shield o.s.

escudero *m hist.* squire; page.

escudete *m sew.* gusset.

escudilla *f* bowl, basin.

escudo *m* shield (*a. fig.*); *~ de armas* coat of arms; *~ térmico* heat shield (of space capsule).

escudriñar [1a] scrutinize, scan, examine; inquire into, investigate.

escuela *f* school; *phls.* school (of thought); *~ de artes y oficios* trade school; *~ automovilista* driving school; ~ *elemental*, ~ *primaria* elementary school, primary school, grade school; ~ *de hogar* domestic science college; ~ *nocturna* night school; ~ *de párvulos* infant school, kindergarten; ~ *preparatoria* prep school; **escuelante** *m/f Col., Ven., Mex.* schoolboy; schoolgirl.

escueto plain, unadorned; bare, bald.

esculpir [3a] sculpture, carve; *inscripción* cut; **escultor** *m* sculptor; **escultura** *f* sculpture, carving; **escultural** sculptural; *figura* statuesque.

escupidera *f* spittoon; *S.Am.* chamber pot; **escupidura** *f* spit, spittle; phlegm; **escupir** [3a] spit (*a* at, *en* on); (*echar fuera*) spit out; *fig. llamas etc.* belch, spit, hurl forth; (*echar de sí*) throw off; cast aside.

escurreplatos *m* plate rack.

escurribanda *f* F loophole, way out; ⚕ looseness; ⚕ running *de úlcera*.

escurridero *m* draining board; **escurridizo** slippery; ⊕ aerodynamic; **escurrido** *S.Am.* abashed; **escurridor** *m* wringer *para ropa*; plate rack *para platos*; colander *para legumbres*; **escurriduras** *f/pl.* dregs, lees; **escurrir** [3a] *v/t. ropa* wring (out); *platos, líquido* drain; *v/i.* (*líquido etc.*) drip, trickle; (*superficie*) be slippery; ~**se** drain; slip, slide *en hielo etc.*; F (*p. etc.*) sneak off; (*deslizarse*) glide away; (*palabra*) slip out.

esdrújulo *adj. a. su. m* antepenultimate; accented on second before last syllable; having dactylic stress [- ⏑⏑].

ese[1] *f*: *hacer* ~*s* zigzag; (*borracho*) reel, stagger.

ese[2], **esa** *adj.* that; **esos, esas** *pl.* those.

ése, ésa *pron.* that (one); (*el anterior*) the former; *ésa* your town, the place where you are; **ésos, ésas** *pl.* those; (*los anteriores*) the former; *ni por ésas* on no account.

esencia *f* essence; core *de problema etc.*; **esencial** *adj. a. su. m* essential; *lo* ~ the main thing.

esfera *f* sphere; globe; face *de reloj*, dial *de instrumento*; *fig.* sphere, plane; field *de actividad*; ~ *de acción* scope; **esférico** spherical; **esferoide** *m* spheroid.

esfinge *f* sphinx (*a. fig.*).

esfínter *m* sphincter.

esforzado valiant; vigorous, energetic; **esforzar** [1f *a.* 1m] *v/t.* strengthen, invigorate; (*animar*) encourage; ~**se** strain, exert o.s.; ~ *en inf.*, ~ *por inf.* strive to *inf.*, struggle to *inf.*, endeavor to *inf.*;

esfuerzo *m* effort, endeavor, exertion; stress; stretch, effort *de imaginación*; (*ánimo*) courage, spirit; *sin* ~ effortlessly; *no escatimar* ~*s* spare no effort (*para inf.* to *inf.*).

esfumar [1a] *paint.* shade, tone down; ~**se** fade away; (*p.*) make o.s. scarce.

esgrima *f* (*deporte*) fencing; (*arte*) swordsmanship; **esgrimidor** *m* fencer; (*que maneja bien la espada*) swordsman; **esgrimir** [3a] *v/t.* wield (*a. fig.*); *v/i.* fence.

esguince *m* swerve, avoiding action; ⚕ sprain; *fig.* (*disgusto*) scowl; (*desdén*) scornful look.

eslabón *m* link *de cadena* (*a. fig.*); steel *para sacar fuego, afilar*; ⊕, ⚓ shackle; ~ *giratorio* swivel; **eslabonar** [1a] (inter)link; *fig.* link, knit together.

eslálom *m* slalom.

eslavo 1. *adj. a. su. m*, **a** *f* Slav; **2.** *m* (*idioma*) Slavic.

eslinga *f* ⚓ sling; **eslingar** [1h] sling.

eslogan *m* slogan.

eslora *f* ⚓ length.

eslovaco 1. Slovakian; **2.** *m*, **a** *f* Slovak.

esloveno 1. Slovenian; **2.** *m*, **a** *f* Slovene.

esmaltar [1a] enamel; *uñas* varnish, paint; *fig.* embellish, adorn with different colors; **esmalte** *m* enamel (*a. anat.*); (*obra*) smalt; ~ (*para uñas*) nail polish; *fig.* lustre.

esmerado painstaking, careful, neat.

esmeralda *f* emerald.

esmerarse [1a] take pains, take great care (*en* over); (*lucirse*) shine, do well.

esmerejón *m* merlin.

esmeril *m* emery; **esmerilar** [1a] polish with emery.

esmero *m* care(fulness), neatness; refinement, niceness; *poner* ~ *en* take care over.

esmirriado *v. desmirriado.*

esnob 1. *p.* snobbish; (*de buen tono*

etc.) posh; **2.** *m/f* snob; **esnobismo** *m* snobbery.

eso *pron.* that; ~ es that's right, that's it; *¡~ a él!* that's his problem!; *v.* *sí*[1]; *a ~ de las 5* (round) about 5 o'clock; *antes de ~* before then, by that time; *por ~* therefore, and so.

esófago *m* esophagus, gullet.

esotérico esoteric.

espabilado bright; intelligent; know the ropes; be informed; **espabilar** [1a] snuff; **~se** F: *¡espabílate!* get a move on!

espaciador *m* space bar (of typewriter); **espacial** spatial; *viaje etc.* space *attr.*; **espaciar** [1b] space (out) (*a. typ.*); *noticia* spread; **~se** (*dilatarse*) expatiate, spread o.s.; (*esparcirse*) relax, take one's ease; **espacio** *m* space (*a. typ.*); (*lugar*) space, room; ♪ interval; (*tardanza*) delay, slowness; *~ exterior* outer space; *~ muerto* clearance; *~ vital* living space, Lebensraum; **espacioso** spacious, roomy; capacious; *movimiento* slow, deliberate.

espada **1.** *f* sword; *entre la ~ y la pared* between the devil and the deep blue sea; *naipes*: *~s pl.* spades; **2.** *m* swordsman; *b.s.* bully, swashbuckler; *toros*: matador.

espadaña *f* bulrush.

espadín *m* dress sword, ceremonial sword; **espadón** *m* broadsword; ⚔ F brass hat.

espagueti *m* spaghetti.

espalda *f* back, shoulder(s) (*mst ~s pl.*); *a ~s (vueltas)* treacherously; *a ~s de uno* behind one's back; *~ con ~* back to back; *de ~s a* with one's back to; *cargado de ~s* round-shouldered; *caer de ~s, dar de ~s* fall on one's back; *echar a las ~s* forget about; *echar sobre las ~s* take on, take charge of; *volver la ~* (*apartarse*) turn away; (*huir*) turn tail; *volver las ~s a p.* cold-shoulder.

espaldar *m* back *de silla*; ⚘ espalier, trellis; **espaldarazo** *m* slap on the back; accolade; **espaldera** *f* espalier, trellis; **espaldilla** *f* shoulder-blade; **espaldón** *m* mortise.

espantable = *espantoso*; **espantada** *f* (*huida*) stampede; (*miedo*) cold feet; **espantadizo** shy, timid; **espantajo** *m* scarecrow (*a. fig.*); *fig.* sight, fright; (*coco*) bogy; **espantapájaros** *m* scarecrow.

espantar [1a] scare, frighten (away, off); (*horrorizar*) appal; **~se** get scared, get frightened; (*admirarse*) be amazed; **espanto** *m* fright, terror; (*asombro*) consternation; (*amenaza*) menace; *S.Am.* ghost; **espantosidad** *f* *S.Am.* fright; frightfulness; awfulness; **espantoso** frightful, dread(ful); appalling.

español **1.** Spanish; **2.** *m*, **-a** *f* Spaniard; **3.** *m* (*idioma*) Spanish; **españolada** *f* Spanish mannerism (*or* remark); **españolería** *f* Spanishness; hispanophilia (*a.* = *españolada*); **españolismo** *m* (*amor*) love of Spain, love of things Spanish; (*lo típico*) Spanishness; (*giro*) Spanish turn of phrase; **españolizar** [1f] make Spanish, hispanicize; **~se** adopt Spanish ways.

esparadrapo *m* sticking plaster.

esparaván *m* *orn.* sparrow hawk; *vet.* spavin.

esparcido scattered; *fig.* jolly, cheerful; **esparcimiento** *m* scattering, spreading; *fig.* (*descanso*) relaxation, recreation; (*alegría*) joviality; **esparcir** [3b] scatter, spread, sow; **~se** *fig.* relax.

espárrago *m* asparagus.

esparrancado (with legs) wide apart, set wide; **esparrancarse** [1g] F do a split.

esparto *m* esparto grass.

espasmo *m* spasm; jerk; **espasmódico** spasmodic(al); jerky, fitful.

espato *m* *geol.* spar.

espátula *f* spatula; *paint.* palette knife.

especia *f* spice; **especiado** spicy, spiced.

especial (e)special; *en ~* especially; **especialidad** *f* speciality; line F; **especialista** *m/f* specialist; **especializarse** [1f] specialize (*en* in, on *Am.*).

especie *f* *biol.* species; (*clase*) sort, kind; (*asunto*) matter; (*noticia*) news, rumor; pretext; *pagar en ~* pay in kind.

especificación *f* specification; **especificar** [1g] specify; itemize; **específico** **1.** specific; **2.** *m* (*natural*) specific; (*fabricado*) patent medicine; **espécimen** *m* specimen; **especioso** specious, plausible.

espectacular spectacular; **espectáculo** *m* spectacle; show, entertain-

ment; sight; **espectador** *m*, **-a** *f* spectator; onlooker, looker-on.
espectral *opt.* spectral; ghostly, unearthly; **espectro** *m opt.* spectrum; spectre, ghost.
especulación *f* speculation; **especulador** *m*, **-a** *f* speculator; **especular** [1a] *v/t.* contemplate, reflect on; *v/i.* speculate (*en* on; ✝ *sobre* in); **especulativo** speculative.
espejado glassy, bright; **espejear** [1a] shine, glint; **espejismo** *m* mirage (*a. opt.*), wishful thinking; **espejo** *m* mirror (*a. fig.*), (looking) glass; *fig.* model; ~ *retrovisor* driving mirror.
espeleología *f* spel(a)eology, pot-holing.
espelta *f* spelt.
espeluznante hair-raising; lurid.
espera *f* wait; waiting; ⚖ stay, respite; (*paciencia*) restraint; *en* ~ *de* waiting for; **esperanza** *f* hope; prospect; *dar* ~*s de* hold out a prospect of; *tener la* ~ *puesta en* set one's heart on; pin one's faith to; **esperanzador** encouraging, hopeful; **esperanzar** [1f] give hope to, buoy up (with hope); **esperar** [1a] **1.** *v/t.* (*tener esperanza de*) hope for; expect (*de* of); (*estar en espera de*) await, wait for; *niño* expect; *ir a* ~ go to meet; **2.** *v/i.* (*tener esperanza*) hope; (*estar en espera*) wait; (*permanecer*) stay; ~ *que indic.* hope that; ~ *que subj.* expect that; ~ (*a*) *que subj.* wait until; ~ *inf.* hope to *inf.*; ~ *en Dios* trust in God; ~ *desesperando* hope against hope.
esperma *f* sperm; ~ *de ballena* = **espermaceti** *m* spermaceti; **espermatozoo** *m* spermatozoon.
esperpento *m* F (*p.*) fright; monstrosity; freak; nonsense.
espesar [1a] thicken; *tela* weave tighter; ~**se** thicken, get thicker; coagulate, solidify; **espeso** thick, dense; *pasta etc.* stiff; (*sucio*) dirty; **espesor** *m* thickness, density; *tener 2 metros de* ~ be 2 meters thick; **espesura** *f* thickness; dirtiness; ⚘ thicket.
espetar [1a] *carne* skewer, spit; *p.* run through; (*en general*) impale, transfix; *orden* rap out; *sermón etc.* read; F ~ *algo a uno* spring s.t. on s.o.; ~**se** F get on one's high horse; F (*asegurarse*) steady o.s., settle o.s.;
espetón *m* skewer, spit; (*alfiler*) pin; (*golpe*) jab, poke.
espía *m/f* spy; tattletale; *sl.* cop.
espiantar [1a] *S.Am.* F hop it, scram.
espiar [1c] spy (*v/t.* on).
espichar [1a] *v/t.* prick; *v/i.* F peg out; **espiche** *m* spike, peg.
espiga *f* ⚘ ear *de trigo*, spike *de flores*; ⊕ spigot; (*clavo*) tenon, peg, pin; ⚔ fuse; clapper *de campana*; tang *de cuchillo*; ⚓ masthead; **espigadera** *f*, **espigador** *m*, **-a** *f* gleaner; **espigado** ⚘ ripe, ready to seed; *p.* tall, grown-up; **espigar** [1h] *v/t.* glean (*a. fig.*); ⊕ tenon; *v/i.* (*trigo*) form ears, come into ear; run to seed; (*p.*) ~**se** shoot up; **espigón** *m zo.* sting; (*púa*) spike; ⚘ ear; point *de herramienta etc.*; ⚓ breakwater; **espigueo** *m* gleaning.
espina *f* ⚘ thorn, spine, prickle; *ichth.* fish bone; ~ (*dorsal*) spine; *fig.* suspicion, doubt; *dar mala* ~ *a* worry; *estar en* ~*s* be on tenterhooks; *sacarse la* ~ get even.
espinaca(**s**) *f*(*pl.*) spinach.
espinal spinal; **espinapez** *m* ⊕ herring bone; **espinar 1.** [1a] *fig.* hurt *s.o.'s* feelings, sting; **2.** *m* thorn brake; *fig.* difficulty; **espinazo** *m* spine, backbone.
espineta *f* spinet.
espinilla *f anat.* shin(bone); ⚕ blackhead.
espino *m* hawthorn; **espinoso 1.** ⚘ thorny, prickly; *pez* spiny; *fig.* thorny, knotty; **2.** *m* stickleback.
espionaje *m* spying, espionage.
espira *f* ⩓ spiral; ⚡ turn (*a. de espiral*); *zo.* whorl.
espiráculo *m* spiracle; blowhole.
espiral 1. spiral, helical; corkscrew *attr.*; **2.** *m* hairspring; **3.** *f* spiral; wreath *de humo etc.*; ⊕ whorl.
espirar [1a] *v/t.* exhale, breathe out; *v/i.* breathe; *poet.* blow gently.
espiritado F like a wraith; **espiritismo** *m* spiritualism; **espiritista** *m/f* spiritualist; **espiritoso** *licor* spirituous; *p.* spirited; **espíritu** *m* spirit; mind; soul; ghost; ~ *Santo* Holy Ghost; ~ *de vino* spirits of wine; **espiritual** spiritual; unwordly; ghostly; **espiritualidad** *f* spirituality.

espita *f* spigot, tap, cock; F drunkard, soak; **espitar** [1a] tap, broach.
espleen *m v. spleen.*
esplendidez *f* splendor; magnificence *etc.*; **espléndido** splendid; magnificent, grand; (*liberal*) generous, lavish; **esplendor** *m* splendor; brilliance; glory; **esplendoroso** magnificent; brilliant.
esplénico splenetic.
espliego *m* lavender.
esplín *m v. spleen.*
espolada *f* prick with a spur; F ~ *de vino* drink of wine; **espolazo** *m* = *espolada*; **espolear** [1a] spur; *fig.* spur on; **espoleta** *f* ⚔ fuse; *anat.* wishbone; **espolón** *m zo., geog.* spur; ⚓ ram; ⚓ seawall, dike; cutwater *de puente*; ⚠ buttress; (*paseo*) promenade; F chilblain.
espolvorear [1a] dust (off).
espondeo *m* spondee (— —).
esponja *f* sponge; F sponger; **esponjar** [1a] make spongy; *lana etc.* make fluffy; ~**se** *fig.* swell with conceit; F ⚕ glow with health; look prosperous; **esponjosidad** *f* sponginess; **esponjoso** spongy; porous; (*empapado*) soggy.
esponsales *m/pl.* betrothal.
espontanearse [1a] (*falta*) own up; (*cosa intima*) unbosom o.s.; **espontaneidad** *f* spontaneity; **espontáneo** spontaneous; impromptu.
espora *f* spore.
esporádico sporadic.
esportillo *m* basket, pannier; **esportón** *m* large basket.
esposa *f* wife; ~*s pl.* handcuffs, manacles; *poner las* ~*s a* = **esposar** [1a] handcuff; **esposo** *m* husband; ~*s pl.* husband and wife, couple.
esprínter *m* sprinter.
espuela *f* spur (*a. fig.*); ~ *de caballero* larkspur; **espuelar** [1a] *S.Am.* spur; goad (on).
espuerta *f* basket, pannier.
espulgar [1h] delouse, rid of fleas; *fig.* scrutinize.
espuma *f* ⚓ *etc.* foam, spray, surf; froth *en cerveza etc.*; (*desechos*) scum; ~ (*de jabón*) lather; ~ *de caucho*, ~ *de látex* foam rubber; ~ *de mar* meerschaum; *echar* ~ foam; **espumadera** *f* (*paleta*) skimmer; spray nozzle *de atomizador*; **espumajear** [1a] froth at the mouth; **espumajoso** foamy, frothy; **espumar** [1a] *v/t.* skim; *v/i.* foam, froth; **espumarajo** *m* froth (at the mouth); **espumoso** foamy, frothy; *vino* sparkling.
espurio spurious; *p.* bastard.
esputar [1a] spit; **esputo** *m* spit, spittle; ⚕ sputum.
esqueje *m* slip, cutting.
esquela *f* note; ~ (*de defunción*) announcement of death.
esqueleto *m* skeleton (*a. fig.*).
esquema *m* diagram, plan, scheme; (*dibujo*) sketch; **esquemático** diagrammatic; schematic.
esquí *m* ski; (*deporte*) skiing; ~ *acuático* water skiing; **esquiador** *m*, **-a** *f* skier; **esquiar** [1c] ski.
esquife *m* skiff.
esquila[1] *f* (*campanilla*) handbell; (*cencerro*) cowbell.
esquila[2] *f* shearing; **esquilador** *m* shearer; **esquilar** [1a] shear, clip; **esquileo** *m* shearing.
esquilimoso F finicky.
esquilmar [1a] *cosecha* harvest; *suelo* exhaust, impoverish (*a. fig.*); **esquilmo** *m* harvest, yield.
esquimal *adj. a. su. m/f* Eskimo.
esquina *f* corner; **esquinado** having corners; *fig.* unsociable, prickly; **esquinazo** F: *dar* ~ *a* dodge, give [*a p.* the slip.
esquirla *f* splinter.
esquirol *m* blackleg, scab.
esquisto *m* schist.
esquite *m S.Am., Mex.* popcorn.
esquivar [1a] avoid, shun, elude, sidestep; ~ *inf.* avoid *ger.*, be chary of *ger.*; **esquivez** *f* aloofness *etc.*; **esquivo** aloof, shy; evasive *en contestar etc.*; (*desdeñoso*) scornful.
esquizofrenia *f* schizophrenia; **esquizofrénico** schizophrenic.
esta *etc. v.* este².
estabilidad *f* stability; **estabilización** *f* stabilization; **estabilizador** *m* stabilizer; **estabilizar** [1f] stabilize; steady; *precios* peg; **estable** stable; steady; firm; ⚜ regular.
establecer [2d] establish; set up, found; *gente etc.* settle; *afirmación etc.* substantiate; *residencia* take up; ~**se** establish o.s., settle *en casa, ciudad etc.*; ⚜ set up in business; **establecimiento** *m mst* establishment (*a. acto*); institution; settlement; ⚖ statute.

establo *m* cowshed; stable; stall.
estaca *f* stake, paling; (tent) peg *de tienda*; (*porra*) cudgel; ⚘ cutting; **estacada** *f* (*cerca*) fencing, fence; ⚔ palisade, stockade; F *dejar en la* ~ leave in the lurch; F *quedar en la* ~ succumb; (*fracasar*) fail disastrously; **estacar** [1g] *terreno* stake out (*or* off); *animal* tie to a stake; **~se** remain rooted to the spot.
estación *f* 🚂 *etc.* station (*a. fig.*), depot; season *del año*; ~ *balnearia* spa, health resort; ~ *carbonera* coaling station; ~ *depuradora* sewage farm; ~ *de empalme*, ~ *de enlace* junction; ~ *de gasolina* gas station; ~ *espacial* space station; ~ *meteorológica* weather station; ~ *muerta* off season; ~ *de servicio* service station; ~ *veraniega* summer resort; **estacional** seasonal; **estacionamiento** *m* *mot.* parking; **estacionar** [1a] station; *mot.* park; **~se** remain stationary; (*colocarse*) station o.s.; *mot.* park; **estacionario** stationary.
estada *f* stay.
estadía *f* ⚓ demurrage; *S.Am.* stay.
estadio *m* *deportes*: stadium; (*fase*) stage, phase.
estadista *m* *pol.* statesman; ⚗ statistician; **estadística** *f* statistics; (official) returns; **estadístico 1.** statistical; **2.** *m* statistician.
estado *m* state (*a. pol.*); condition; status; class, rank; list *de empleados etc.*; (*resumen*) summary; (*informe*) report, statement; ~ *de ánimo* state of mind; ~ *asistencial*, ~ *benefactor* welfare state; *en buen* ~ in good condition, in good order; ~ *civil* marital status; ~ *de cuenta(s)* statement of account; ~ *de guerra* state of war; *hombre de* ~ statesman; ~ *llano* third estate, commoners; ~ *mayor* staff; ~ *de sitio* state of siege; ~ *tapón* buffer state.
estadounidense United States *attr.*
estafa *f* swindle, trick; ⚓ racket F; *sl.* con job; **estafador** *m* swindler, trickster; racketeer F; *sl.* con man; **estafar** [1a] swindle; cheat; *sl.* con.
estafeta *f* post; (*oficina*) (sub) post office; (*p.*) courier; ~ *diplomática* diplomatic bag.
estalactita *f* stalactite; **estalagmita** *f* stalagmite.
estallar [1a] burst, explode, go off; (*como volcán*) erupt; (*látigo*) crack; *fig.* break out, flare up; *hacer* ~ set off, spark off; **estallido** *m* explosion, report; crash, crack; *fig.* outbreak.
estambre *m* worsted; ⚘ stamen.
estameña *f* serge; bunting.
estampa *f* *typ.* print, engraving; (*imprenta*) printing press; *fig.* stamp, aspect; *fig.* (*huella*) imprint; *dar a la* ~ print; **estampado 1.** *vestido* print(ed); **2.** *m* (cotton) print; **estampar** [1a] *typ.* print, engrave, stamp; *esp. fig.* imprint.
estampía: de ~ suddenly, unexpectedly.
estampida *f* *S.Am.* stampede; = **estampido** *m* report; boom, crash, bang.
estampilla *f* (rubber) stamp; *S.Am.* (postage) stamp; **estampillar** [1a] stamp.
estancado stagnant (*a. fig.*); *fig.* static; **estancamiento** *m* stagnancy, stagnation (*a. fig.*); *fig.* deadlock; **estancar** [1g] *aguas* stem, check; *negocio* suspend; *negociación* bring to a standstill, deadlock; *mercancía* monopolize (officially), *b.s.* corner; **~se** stagnate.
estancia *f* (*permanencia*) stay; (*morada*) dwelling, abode; (*cuarto*) living-room; *poet.* stanza; *S.Am.* farm, ranch; **estanciero** *m* *S.Am.* farmer, rancher.
estanco 1. watertight; **2.** *m* state monopoly; (*tienda*) tobacconist's (shop).
estándar *m* norm; standard; **estandar(d)ización** *f* standardization; **estandar(d)izar** [1f] standardize.
estandarte *m* standard, banner.
estanque *m* pond, pool, small lake; reservoir *para riego etc.*
estanquero *m* tobacconist.
estante *m* (*mueble*) rack, stand; bookcase; (*una tabla*) shelf; **estantería** *f* shelves, shelving.
estantigua *f* hobgoblin; phantom; apparition; F fright, sight.
estañar [1a] tin; (*soldar*) solder; **estaño** *m* tin.
estaquilla *f* peg, pin; **estaquillar** [1a] pin, peg (down).
estar [1p] be; (~ *en casa etc.*) be in; stand; (*asistir*) be present (*en* at); *estoy leyendo* I am reading; *¿cómo*

estás? how are you (keeping)?; *¿cómo estamos?* how do we stand?; *deportes*: what's the score?; *¿está Juan?* is John in?; ~ *a 10 ptas* cost 10 ptas, stand at 10 ptas; *estamos a 3 de mayo* today is the third of May; *¿a cuántos estamos?* what date is it?; *está bien* all right; (*basta*) that will do; ~ *bien a* suit; be fitting for; ~ *bien con* be on good terms with; ~ *con* ⚕ have; ~ *de rango* be acting as, be an acting ...; ~ *de más* be superfluous; (*p.*) be in the way; ~ *en asunto* be mixed up in; ~ *en que* understand that; ~ *en sí* be in one's right mind; ~ *fuera* (*de casa*) be out; (*de ciudad*) be away, be out of town; ~ *mal* ⚕ be ill; ~ *mal con* be on bad terms with; have a low opinion of; F *no está mal* it's not bad; ~ *para inf.* be about to *inf.*; ~ *para su.* be in the mood for; ~ *por inf.* (*dispuesto a*) be inclined to *inf.*; (*que queda por*) be still to be *p.p.*, remain to be *p.p.*; *está por ver* it remains to be seen; ~ *por su.* be in favor of; ~ *por p.* side with, support; **~se** stay (at home *etc.*); *¡estáte quieto!* keep still!

estarcido *m* stencil; **estarcir** [3b] stencil.

estatal state *attr.*

estática *f* statics; **estático** static.

estatificar [1g] nationalize.

estatua *f* statue; **estatuaria** *f* statuary; **estatuario** statuesque.

estatuir [3g] establish, enact; (*arreglar*) arrange; (*demostrar*) prove; **estatura** *f* stature, height; **estatutario** statutory; **estatuto** *m* statute; by-law *de municipio etc.*; (standing) order *de comité etc.*

estay *m* ⚓ stay.

este[1] **1.** *parte* east(ern); *dirección* easterly; *viento* east(erly); **2.** *m* east.

este[2], **esta** this; **estos, estas** *pl.* these.

éste, ésta this (one); (*último*) the latter; **éstos, éstas** *pl.* these; (*últimos*) the latter.

estela *f* ⚓ wake, wash; trail *de cohete etc.*; ⚠ stela; **estelar** stellar; *thea.* star *attr.*

estenografía *f* shorthand, stenography; **estenografiar** [1c] take down in shorthand; **estenógrafo** *m*, **a** *f* stenographer, shorthand writer; **estenotipia** *f* stenotypy; machine stenography.

estentóreo stentorian.

estepa *f* steppe.

estera *f* mat, matting; **~s** *pl.* caterpillar tread.

estercoladura *f* manuring; **estercolar** [1a] manure, dung; **estercolero** *m* dungheap, dunghill.

estereo...: ~fónico stereophonic; **~scopio** *m* stereoscope; **~tipar** [1a] stereotype (*a. fig.*); **~tipo** *m* stereotype.

estéril sterile, barren; **esterilidad** *f* sterility; **esterilización** *f* ⚕ sterilization; **esterilizar** [1f] sterilize.

esterilla *f* mat.

esterlina: *libra* ~ pound sterling.

esternón *m* breastbone, sternum 📖.

estero *m* matting; *geog.* estuary, inlet.

estertor *m* death rattle.

estética *f* aesthetics; **estético** aesthetic.

estetoscopio *m* stethoscope.

esteva *f* plow handle; **estevado** bowlegged, bandy-legged.

estiaje *m* low water.

estiba *f* ⚔ rammer; ⚓ stowage; **estibador** *m* stevedore, longshoreman; **estibar** [1a] pack tight; ⚓ stow, house.

estiércol *m* dung, manure.

estigma *m* stigma; mark; brand; **estigmatizar** [1f] stigmatize.

estilar [1a] *v/t.* draw up in due form; *v/i.*, **~se** be in fashion, be worn; ~ *inf.* be customary to *inf.*

estilete *m* stiletto.

estilista *m/f* stylist; **estilizado** stylized; **estilo** *m* style (*a.* ⚘); (*pluma*) stylus; (*modo, manera*) manner; *natación*: stroke; *algo por el* ~ something of the sort, that sort of thing; *y otros por el* ~ and such like.

estilográfica *f* fountain pen.

estima *f* esteem; ⚓ dead reckoning; **estimable** estimable, reputable; *cantidad* considerable; **estimación** *f* (*acto*) estimation; (*aprecio, tasa*) estimate, estimation; (*estima*) regard, esteem; **estimar** [1a] (*juzgar, medir*) estimate, reckon, gauge; (*respetar etc.*) esteem, value, respect; think a lot of; (*considerar*) think, reckon (*que* that).

estimulante 1. stimulating; **2.** *m* stimulant; **estimular** [1a] stimulate; encourage; excite; prompt;

discusión etc. promote; **estímulo** *m* stimulus, stimulation; encouragement; inducement.
estío *m* summer.
estipendio *m* stipend.
estipulación *f* stipulation; proviso, condition; **estipular** [1a] stipulate.
estirado *fig.* stiff, starchy; (*mojigato*) prim; (*tacaño*) tight-fisted.
estirajar [1a] F = **estirar** [1a] stretch, pull out; (*demasiado*) strain; *cuello* crane; *ropa* run the iron over; *poderes* extend unduly; *dinero, discurso* spin out; **~se** stretch; **estirón** *m* pull, tug; stretch; *dar un ~ fig.* shoot up.
estirpe *f* stock, race, lineage.
estival summery, summer *attr.*
esto *pron.* this; *con ~* herewith; *en ~* at this point; *en ~ de* in the matter of; *~ es* that is to say.
estocada *f* (sword) thrust, stab, lunge.
estofa *f* quilted material; *fig.* quality, class; **estofado** *m* stew, hot pot; **estofar** [1a] *cocina*: stew; *sew.* quilt.
estoicismo *m* stoicism; **estoico** **1.** stoic(al); **2.** *m* Stoic.
estola *f* stole.
estolidez *f* stupidity; **estólido** stupid.
estomacal *adj. a. su. m* stomachic; stomach *attr.* **estomagar** [1h] give indigestion to; F annoy; **estómago** *m* stomach; F *tener buen ~* (*no ofenderse*) be thick-skinned; *b.s.* have an elastic conscience, be none too scrupulous.
estopa *f* tow; ⚓ oakum; **estopilla** *f* cheesecloth.
estoque *m* rapier; ⚘ gladiolus; **estoquear** [1a] stab.
estorbar [1a] *v/t.* hinder, impede, obstruct; get in the way of; interfere with; *v/i.* be in the way; **estorbo** *m* hindrance, obstruction, obstacle; drag; curb.
estornino *m* starling.
estornudar [1a] sneeze; **estornudo** *m* sneeze.
estoy *etc. v. estar.*
estrabismo *m* squint.
estrada *f* road, highway.
estrado *m* dais, stage; ♪ bandstand; † drawing room; *~s pl.* law courts; *citar para ~s* subpoena.
estrafalario F outlandish, eccentric, screwball, zany; *vestido* slovenly, sloppy.
estragar [1h] corrupt, ruin; pervert; spoil; **estrago** *m* ruin, destruction; *~s pl.* havoc, ravages; *hacer ~s en(tre)* play havoc with, wreak havoc among.
estrambótico F odd, eccentric.
estrangul *m* ♪ mouthpiece.
estrangulación *f* strangulation; **estrangulador** *m* ⊕ throttle; choke; **estrangular** [1a] strangle; ⚕ strangulate; ⊕ throttle; ⊕ choke.
estraperlista *m* black marketeer; **estraperlo** *m* black market.
estrapontín *m* jump seat; folding seat.
estratagema *f* stratagem; **estratega** *m* strategist; **estrategia** *f* strategy; generalship; **estratégico** strategic.
estratificar(se) [1g] stratify; **estrato** *m* layer, stratum.
estratosfera *f* stratosphere; **estratosférico** stratospheric; *avión ~* stratocruiser.
estraza *f* rag.
estrechar [1a] narrow; *vestido* reduce, take in; (*apretar*) tighten (up); squeeze; *mano* grasp, shake; hug, enfold *en brazos*; *fig.* constrain, compel; **~se** narrow; tighten (up); *fig.* get very friendly (*con* with); stint o.s., economize; **estrechez** *f* narrowness; tightness; *fig.* closeness, intimacy *de amistad*; austerity, privation; *~ de miras* narrow-mindedness; insularity; *estreceheces pl. fig.* straits; **estrecho** **1.** narrow; tight; *cuarto* cramped; *fig. amistad, relación* close, intimate; strict, rigid; austere; (*tacaño*) mean; **2.** *m* strait(s), narrows.
estregadera *f* scrub brush; scraper *en la puerta*; **estregar** [1h *a.* 1k] rub, scrape; (*con agua etc.*) scrub, scour.
estrella *f* star (*a. fig., thea.*); *zo.* blaze; ⚔ pip, star *en uniforme*; *~ fija* fixed star; *~ fugaz* shooting star, falling star; *~ polar* polestar; *~ de rabo* comet; *nacer con ~* be born under a lucky star; F *ver las ~s* see stars; **estrelladera** *f* slice (*tool*); **estrelladero** *m* pan; **estrellado** *cielo* starry; *vestido* spangled; *huevo* fried; **estrellar** [1a] shatter, smash, dash; *huevo* fry; **~se** shatter,

dash (*contra* against); (*coche etc.*) smash (*contra* into); *esp.* ✈ crash (*contra* into); ~ *con* come up against; **estrellón** *m S.Am.* crash.
estremecer [2d] shake (*a. fig.*); **~se** (*edificio etc.*) shake; (*p.*) tremble (*ante* at, *de miedo* with); shudder (*de horror* with); shiver (*de frío* with); tingle, thrill (*de emoción* with); **estremecimiento** *m* shaking; trembling; shudder *etc.*
estrenar [1a] use (*or* wear *etc.*) for the first time; *thea.* perform for the first time; *película* give its première, release; **~se** make one's début; (*comedia*) open; **estreno** *m* first appearance *etc.*; début *esp. de p.*; *thea.* first night; *cine*: première, release.
estreñido constipated; **estreñimiento** *m* constipation; **estreñir** [3h *a.* 3l] constipate, bind.
estrépito *m* noise, racket, row, din; **estrepitoso** noisy, loud, deafening; *p.*, *fiesta etc.* rowdy.
estreptomicina *f* streptomycin.
estría *f* groove; ⚠ flute, fluting; **estriado** grooved, striate(d); ⚠ fluted; **estriar** [1c] groove, striate; ⚠ flute.
estribación *f geog.* spur; **~es** *pl.* foothills; **estribar** [1a]: ~ *en* be supported by; *fig.* rest (up)on, be based (up)on.
estribera *f* stirrup.
estribillo *m poet.* refrain; ♩ chorus; *fig.* pet word, pet phrase.
estribo *m* stirrup; ⊕ bracket, brace; *geog.* spur; ⚠ buttress, abutment; ⚠ pier; *mot.* running board, step; *fig.* basis, foundation; *perder los ~s* lose one's head; get hot under the collar *en conversación.*
estribor *m* starboard.
estricnina *f* strychnine.
estricto strict.
estridente strident, raucous; jangling; **estridor** *m* screech; stridence.
estro *m* inspiration.
estrofa *f* verse, stanza; strophe.
estropajo *m* scourer *para fregar*; dishcloth, swab; F dirt, rubbish; **estropajoso** F *carne* tough; *habla* indistinct; *p.* slovenly.
estropear [1a] *p.* hurt, maim; *mecanismo etc.* damage, tamper with; (*echar a perder*) spoil, ruin; *texto etc.* mangle; **~se** get damaged; spoil, go bad; **estropicio** *m* F (*destrozo*) breakage, smashing; *fig.* rumpus, fuss.
estructura *f* structure; frame; **estructural** structural; **estructurar** [1a] construct, organize.
estruendo *m* crash, din, clatter, thunder; *fig.* uproar, confusion; **estruendoso** noisy; *esp. p.* obstreperous.
estrujadura *f* squeeze, press(ing); **estrujar** [1a] squeeze, press, crush; F drain, bleed white; **estrujón** *m* squeeze, press(ing); F crush, jam.
estuario *m* estuary.
estucar [1g] stucco; **estuco** *m* stucco, plaster.
estuche *m* (*caja*) box, case; (*vaina*) sheath; ~ *de afeites* vanity case; F *ser un* ~ be quite an expert.
estudiante *m/f* student; **estudiantil** student *attr.*; **estudiantina** *f* student band; **estudiar** [1b] study; **estudio** *m mst* study (*a. paint.*, ♩; *cuarto particular*); *paint.*, *cine*, *radio*: studio; (*proyecto preliminar*) plan, design (*de* for); planning (*de* for); (*reconocimiento general*) survey; (*erudición*) learning; (*aplicación*) studiousness; **estudioso** studious; bookish.
estufa *f* stove; heater; ✓ hothouse; ~ *de gas* gas fire; ~ *de petróleo* oil stove; **estufilla** *f* small brazier; muff *para manos.*
estulticia *f* stupidity; **estulto** stupid.
estupefacción *f* stupefaction; **estupefaciente** *adj. a. su. m* narcotic; **estupefacto** stupefied, thunderstruck, speechless; *dejar* ~ leave speechless, stupefy.
estupendo stupendous; F marvelous, terrific, great; ¡~! wonderful!, that's fine!
estupidez *f* stupidity, foolishness; **estúpido** stupid, foolish.
estupor *m* stupor (*a. fig.*); *fig.* amazement.
estuprar [1a] rape; **estupro** *m* rape.
esturión *m* sturgeon.
estuve *etc. v. estar.*
etapa *f* stage, phase; *deportes*: lap, leg; ⚔ ration; ⚔ (*lugar*) stopping place.
etarra *m/f* member of ETA; Basque terrorist; **etarrista** *adj.* of ETA; ETA *attr.*

etcétera et cetera; and so on.
éter *m* ether; **etéreo** ethereal; **eterizar** [1f] etherize.
eternidad *f* eternity; **eternizar** [1f] etern(al)ize; perpetuate; *b.s.* prolong endlessly; **eterno** eternal.
ética *f* ethics; **ético**[1] ethical.
ético[2] ⚕ consumptive; *fig.* frail.
etimología *f* etymology; ~ *doble* doublet; ~ *popular* folk (*or* popular) etymology; **etimológico** etymological.
etíope *adj. a. su. m/f* Ethiopian.
etiqueta *f* (*ceremonial*) etiquette; punctilio, formality; (*rótulo*) label, ticket; *de* ~ *traje* formal; **etiquetero** ceremonious, punctilious; prim.
etnografía *f* ethnography; **etnología** *f* ethnology.
eucalipto *m* eucalyptus, gum tree.
Eucaristía *f* Eucharist.
eufemismo *m* euphemism; **eufemístico** euphemistic(al).
eufonía *f* euphony; **eufónico** euphonic, euphonious.
euforia *f* euphoria, exuberance; **eufórico** euphoric, exuberant.
eugenesia *f*, **eugenismo** *m* eugenics.
eunuco *m* eunuch.
¡eureka! eureka!
europeizar [1f] Europeanize, make a part of Europe; **europeo** *adj. a. su. m*, **a** *f* European.
éuscaro *adj. a. su. m* Basque; **euskera, eusquera** *m* Basque language.
eutanasia *f* euthanasia, mercy killing.
evacuación *f* evacuation; **evacuado** *m*, **a** *f* evacuee; **evacuar** [1d] evacuate; void; *vientre* have a movement of; *fig. encargo* fulfil; *negocio* transact.
evadido *m* fugitive; escaped prisoner; **evadir** [3a] evade; **~se** escape, break out.
evaluación *f* evaluation; **evaluar** [3c] evaluate.
evanescente evanescent.
evangélico evangelic(al); **Evangelio** *m* Gospel; **evangelizador** *m* evangelist; **Evangelista** *m* Evangelist; **evangelizar** [1f] evangelize.
evaporación *f* evaporation; **evaporar**(se) [1a], **evaporizar**(se) [1f] evaporate (*a. fig.*); vaporize.
evasión *f* escape; *fig.* evasion; ~ *fiscal* tax evasion; *literatura de* ~ escapist literature; **evasiva** *f* evasion; loophole, excuse; **evasivo** evasive, noncommittal; elusive.
evento *m* (unforeseen) event, eventuality, contingency; **eventual** *trabajo etc.* temporary, casual; (*interino*) acting; stopgap; (*sujeto a contingencia*) conditional; fortuitous.
evidencia *f* (*lo evidente*) obviousness; (*prueba etc.*) evidence; **evidenciar** [1b] show, prove, make evident; **evidente** obvious, evident.
evitable avoidable, preventable;
evitar [1a] *peligro etc.* avoid, escape; *molestia* save; (*precaver*) prevent; *tentación etc.* shun; ~ *inf.* avoid *ger.*, be chary of *ger.*
evocación *f* evocation; invocation; **evocador** evocative; reminiscent; **evocar** [1g] *recuerdo etc.* evoke, call up, conjure up; *espíritus etc.* invoke, call up.
evolución *f* evolution (*a. biol.*); ⚔ maneuver; change *de política etc.*; **evolucionar** [1a] evolve (*a. biol.*); ⚔ maneuver; (*política etc.*) change; **evolucionista** *adj. a. su. m/f* evolutionist; evolutionary; **evolutivo** evolutionary.
ex... ex-; former, late; ~ *ministro* ex-minister.
exacción *f* exaction, extortion; demand; levy.
exacerbar [1a] exacerbate, aggravate.
exactitud *f* exactness *etc.*; **exacto** exact, accurate, precise; right, correct; punctual; ¡~! quite right!, just so!
exageración *f* exaggeration; **exagerado** exaggerated; *relato etc. a.* highly-colored, overdone; *precio etc.* excessive, steep F; *p.* fulsome, demonstrative; theatrical; (*raro*) peculiar, odd; **exagerar** [1a] exaggerate; overdo, overstate; enlarge upon.
exaltación *f* exaltation; overexcitement; **exaltado 1.** exalted; *carácter* hot-headed, excitable; *estado temporal* overexcited, worked up; *pol.* extreme; **2.** *m pol.* extremist, hothead; **exaltar** [1a] exalt; (*celebrar*) extol; elevate *a dignidad*; (*inflamar*) excite, work up, fire; **~se** get excited, get worked up, work o.s. up.
examen *m* examination (*a. univ.*

etc.); inspection; interrogation; test; (*indagación*) inquiry (*de* into); **examinador** *m* examiner; **examinando** *m*, **a** *f* examinee; **examinar** [1a] examine; inspect, scan, go over, go through; (*poner a prueba*) test; *sospechoso* interrogate; investigate, inquire into, look into; **~se** take an examination (*de* in).
exangüe bloodless; *fig.* weak.
exánime lifeless; *fig.* in a faint.
exasperación *f* exasperation; **exasperar** [1a] exasperate, irritate; **~se** lose patience.
excarcelación *f* release; **excarcelar** [1a] release.
excavación *f* excavation; **excavador** *m* excavator (*p.*); **excavadora** *f* power shovel, excavator (*machine*); **excavar** [1a] excavate; (*ahuecar*) hollow (out).
excedente 1. excessive; (*sobrante*) excess, surplus; **2.** *m* excess, surplus; **exceder** [2a] exceed, surpass; outdo; transcend *en importancia etc.*; ~ *de* exceed; **~se** excel o.s.; *b.s.* overreach o.s., overdo it.
excelencia *f* excellence; ♀ Excellency; *por* ~ par excellence; **excelente** excellent.
excelso lofty, sublime.
excéntrica *f* ⊕ eccentric; **excentricidad** *f* eccentricity; **excéntrico 1.** eccentric; erratic; **2.** *m* eccentric.
excepción *f* exception; *a* ~ *de* with the exception of; *hacer una* ~ make an exception; **excepcional** exceptional; **excepto** except (for), excepting; **exceptuar** [1a] except, exclude; ⚖ *etc.* exempt.
excesivo excessive; over...; (*indebido*) unreasonable, undue; **exceso** *m* excess (*a. fig.*); extra; surfeit *esp. de comida*; ~ *de peso* excess luggage; *en* ~ *de* in excess of, over and above; *llevar al* ~ carry to excess, overdo.
excisión *f* excision.
excitabilidad *f* excitability; **excitable** excitable; temperamental; highly strung; **excitación** *f* excitation, excitement; ~ *loca* hysteria; **excitador** *m* ⚡ exciter, discharger; **excitante 1.** exciting; ⚕ stimulating; **2.** *m* stimulant; **excitar** [1a] excite (*a.* ⚡); *dudas, esperanzas* raise; *emoción* rouse, stir up; ⚡ energize.

exclamación *f* exclamation; **exclamar** [1a] exclaim; cry, shout; **exclamatorio** exclamatory.
excluir [3g] exclude; shut out; *posibilidad etc.* preclude, rule out; **exclusión** *f* exclusion; *con* ~ *de* to the exclusion of; **exclusiva** *f* sole right; **exclusive** exclusively; **exclusivista** exclusive; *grupo etc.* clannish; **exclusivo** exclusive; sole.
excombatiente *m* exserviceman.
excomulgar [1h] *eccl.* excommunicate; ban; **excomunión** *f eccl.* excommunication; ban.
excoriar [1b] skin, flay; **~se** graze o.s., skin o.s.
excrecencia *f* excrescence.
excreción *f* excretion; **excremental** excremental; **excremento** *m* excrement; **excretar** [1a] excrete.
exculpación *f* exoneration, exculpation; ⚖ acquittal; **exculpar** [1a] exonerate, exculpate; ⚖ acquit (*de* of).
excursión *f* excursion; (*mst breve*) outing, trip; ~ (*a pie*) hike F, ramble; ⚔ raid; **excursionismo** *m* hiking, rambling; sightseeing; **excursionista** *m*/*f* hiker F, rambler *por el campo*; tripper *esp. que va a la costa*; (*turista*) sightseer.
excusa *f* excuse; apology.
excusable excusable; **excusado 1.** unnecessary, superfluous; exempt (*de impuesto* from); reserved; ~ *es decir* needless to say; **2.** *m* toilet; lavatory; *sl.* john; **excusar** [1a] (*disculpar*) excuse; (*evitar*) avoid, prevent; (*prescindir de*) forget about, do without, not bother with; spare; **~se** apologize.
execrable execrable; **execración** *f* execration; **execrar** [1a] execrate.
exención *f* exemption; immunity; **exentar** [1a] exempt (*de* from); **exento** exempt (*de impuesto etc.* from); free (*de cuidados etc.* from); *lugar* clear, open.
exequias *f*/*pl.* funeral rites, obsequies.
éxeunt exeunt.
exhalación *f* exhalation; *astr.* shooting star; vapor; **exhalar** [1a] exhale; *vapor etc.* emit, give out; *suspiro* breathe, heave.
exhaustivo exhaustive; **exhausto** exhausted.
exhibición *f* exhibition, show; ~ *venta* sales exhibit; **exhibicionista**

m/f exhibitionist; **exhibir** [3a] exhibit, show.
exhortación *f* exhortation; **exhortar** [1a] exhort; **exhorto** *m* ⚖, *eccl.* charge.
exhumación *f* exhumation; **exhumar** [1a] exhume.
exigencia *f* demand, requirement; exigency; **exigente** exigent, exacting; particular; **exigir** [3c] *rentas etc.* exact (*a* from); (*pedir*) demand, require (*a* of), call for (*a* from); *exige mucho* he's very demanding.
exiguo meagre, scanty, exiguous.
exilado *m*, **a** *f* exile; **exilar** [1a], **exiliar** [1b] exile; **exilio** *m* exile.
eximio select; *p.* distinguished, eminent.
eximir [3a] exempt, free, excuse (*de* from).
existencia *f* existence; being; ✝ *en* ~ in stock; ~*s pl.* ✝ stock; **existencialismo** *m* existentialism; **existente** in existence, in being, existent; *esp. texto* extant; **existir** [3a] exist; be.
éxito *m* result, outcome; (*buen*) ~ success; *fig.*, *thea.*, ♪ hit; ~ *de librería* best seller; *tener (buen)* ~ be successful; *tener* ~ *en* be successful in, make a success of; **exitoso** successful.
éxodo *m* exodus.
exonerar [1a]: ~ *de deber etc.* relieve of, free from.
exorbitancia *f* exorbitance; **exorbitante** exorbitant.
exorcismo *m* exorcism; **exorcista** *m/f* exorcist; **exorcizar** [1f] exorcize.
exornar [1a] adorn, embellish.
exótico exotic.
expansible expandable; **expansión** *f* expansion; *fig.* (*desahogo*) expansiveness; (*solaz*) relaxation; **expansionar** [1a] expand; ~**se** *fig.* (*confesarse*) open one's heart; (*esparcirse*) relax; **expansivo** expansive (*a. fig.*); *fig.* affable, good-natured.
expatriación *f* expatriation; exile; **expatriado** *m*, **a** *f* expatriate; exile; **expatriarse** [1b] expatriate o.s., go into exile.
expectación *f* expectation; **expectante** expectant; **expectativa** *f* expectation; hope; prospect; ~ *de vida* expectation of life; *estar a la* ~ *de* look out for.
expectorar [1a] expectorate.
expedición *f* expedition (*a. fig.*); *fig.* speed; **expedicionario** expeditionary; **expedidor** *m* ⚓ shipper.
expediente *m* (*medio*) expedient, makeshift, device; ⚖ action, proceedings; (*papeles*) dossier, file.
expedir [3l] *mercancías* send, forward; *negocio* dispatch; *órdenes etc.* issue; **expeditar** [1a] *S.Am.* expedite; handle without delay; F speed, rush; **expeditivo** expeditious.
expeler [2a] expel, eject.
expendedor *m*, **-a** *f* dealer, retailer; tobacconist; *thea.* ticket agent; **expendeduría** *f* tobacco shop; cigar store; state retail store; **expender** [2a] (*gastar*) expend; (*vender*) sell, retail; be an agent for; *moneda falsa* pass.
expensas *f/pl.* expense(s); ⚖ costs; *a* ~ *de* at the expense of.
experiencia *f* experience; 📖 experiment; **experimentado** experienced; **experimental** experimental; **experimentar** [1a] *v/t.* experience, undergo, go through; *emoción* feel; ⊕ test; *v/i.* experiment (*con* with, *en* on); **experimento** *m* experiment.
experto 1. expert, skilled, experienced; **2.** *m* expert.
expiación *f* expiation; **expiar** [1c] expiate, atone for.
expiración *f* expiration; **expirar** [1a] expire.
explanación *f* leveling; *fig.* explanation, elucidation; **explanar** [1a] level; 🚂 grade; *fig.* explain, elucidate; unfold.
explayar [1a] extend, enlarge; ~**se** spread, open out; *fig.* spread o.s. *en discurso*; (*esparcirse*) relax; ~ *con* confide in, unbosom o.s. to.
explicable explicable, explainable; **explicación** *f* explanation; **explicar** [1g] (*declarar, aclarar, justificar*) explain; *doctrina etc.* expound; *curso* lecture on; *conferencia* give; ~**se** explain o.s.; *no me lo explico* I can't understand it; **explicatorio** explanatory.
explícito explicit.
exploración *f* exploration; **explorador** *m* explorer; pioneer; ⚔ *etc.* scout; (*niño*) ~ Boy Scout; **exploradora** *f* Girl Guide; **explorar**

[1a] explore; open up, pioneer; ⚔ *etc.* scout.

explosión *f* explosion (*a. fig.*); *fig.* outburst; *hacer* ~ explode; **explosivo** *adj. a. su. m* explosive.

explotación *f* exploitation; ⚒ working *etc.*; ~ *abusiva geol.* over-exploitation (of resources); **explotar** [1a] *v/t.* exploit (*a. b.s.*); ⚒ work; develop; operate; *recursos* tap; *v/i.* explode.

exponente 1. *m/f* exponent; *fig.* interpreter, apologist; **2.** *m* & index, exponent; **exponer** [2r] expose (*a. phot.*); *vida etc.* risk; *cuadro etc.* show, exhibit; *argumento, hechos* set forth, expound, state; *idea* unfold; ⚖ *acusación* bring; *niño* abandon; **~se** *a* expose o.s. to, lay o.s. open to.

exportable exportable; **exportación** *f* (*acto*) export(ation); (*mercancías*) export(s); **exportador** *m* exporter; shipper; **exportar** [1a] export.

exposición *f* (*acto*) exposing, exposure (*a. phot.*), exposition; *paint. etc.* exhibition, show; ✝ show, fair; statement *de hechos etc.*; petition *a autoridades*; ~ *universal* world's fair; **exposímetro** *m* exposure meter; **expósito** *m*, **a** *f* foundling (*a. niño* ~); **expositor** *m*, **-a** *f* exhibitor; exponent *de teoría*.

expresado above-mentioned; **expresar** [1a] express; voice; phrase, word, put; **~se** express o.s.; **expresión** *f* expression; **~es** *pl. fig.* greetings; **expresivo** expressive; affectionate; **expreso 1.** express, specific, clear; **2.** *m* 🚂 express (train); (*p.*) special messenger; *por* ~ by express delivery.

exprimelimones *m* lemon squeezer; **exprimidera** *f*, **exprimidor** *m* squeezer; **exprimir** [3a] squeeze out, express.

exprofeso on purpose.

expropiación *f* expropriation; **expropiar** [1b] expropriate.

expuesto 1. *p.p. of exponer*; **2.** *adj. lugar* exposed; (*peligroso*) dangerous; *artículo* on show, on view; ~ *a* exposed to, open to.

expugnar [1a] take by storm.

expulsar [1a] expel, eject, turn out; **expulsión** *f* expulsion, ejection; **expulsor** *m* ⊕ ejector.

expurgar [1h] expurgate; **expurgatorio** expurgatory.

exquisito exquisite; delicious; (*culto*) genteel, refined; *b.s.* affected.

extasiarse [1c] go into ecstasies, rhapsodize (*ante* over); **éxtasis** *m* ecstasy; rapture; trance *de espiritista etc.*; **extático** ecstatic, rapturous.

extemporáneo untimely; inopportune; unreasonable.

extender [2g] extend; stretch, expand; (*desenvolver, desplegar*) spread (out), open (out), lay out; *lo espeso, lo amontonado* spread; *cheque etc.* make out; *documento* draw up; write out; **~se** extend *etc.*; (*ocupar espacio*) extend, lie; (*ocupar tiempo*) extend, last (*de* from, *a* to, till); *fig.* range *entre dos puntos etc.*; *fig.* spread o.s. *en discurso*; ~ *a* (*propagarse, influir*) extend to; (*alcanzar, subir a*) reach, amount to, run into; **extendido** spread out, open; *miembro* outstretched; *fig.* prevalent, widespread.

extensible extending, extensible; **extensión** *f* (*acto, propagación*) extension; (*dimensión*) extent, size; (*lo espacioso*) spaciousness; expanse, stretch *de terreno etc.*; span, duration *de tiempo*; range *entre dos puntos etc.*; ♪ range, compass; *fig.* (*alcance*) scope, range, reach; **extensivo** extensive; **extenso** extensive; broad, spacious; *imperio* far-flung; *relato* full; (*general*) widespread; *por* ~ in full, at (great) length.

extenuación *f* emaciation; **extenuado** emaciated; **extenuar** [1e] emaciate; weaken.

exterior 1. exterior, external, outer; *manifestación etc.* outward; *comercio etc.* foreign; **2.** *m* exterior, outside; (*aspecto*) outward appearance; *deportes*: wing; *del* ~ *noticias, correo etc.* foreign, from abroad; **exterioridad** *f* externals; (*aspecto*) outward appeararance; **exteriorizar** [1f] reveal, express outwardly.

exterminar [1a] exterminate; **exterminio** *m* extermination.

externo 1. external; outward; **2.** *m*, **a** *f* day pupil.

extinción *f* extinction; **extingui-**

dor *m S.Am.* (*incendios*) fire extinguisher; **extinguir** [3d] extinguish; exterminate; **extinto** extinct; **extintor** *m* (fire) extinguisher.

extirpación *f* extirpation, eradication; **extirpar** [1a] extirpate, eradicate, stamp out.

extra 1. extra; *horas* ~ overtime; **2.** *m* extra *en cuenta*; **3.** *m/f cine*: extra; **4.** F: ~ *de* besides, in addition to.

extracción *f* extraction (*a.* ⚒); drawing *en lotería*.

extracorto *onda* ultrashort.

extractar [1a] *libro* abridge; **extracto** *m* ⚗ extract; *lit.* abstract; **extractor** *m* extractor; remover; ~ *de aire* ventilator; ~ *de humos* smoke evacuator.

extradición *f* extradition; **extradicionar** [1a] extradite.

extraer [2p] extract (*a.* A, ⚒), take out.

extra...: ~fino superfine; **~judicial** extrajudicial; **~limitarse** [1a] go too far, exceed one's authority; **~muros** *adv.* outside the city.

extranjerismo *m* foreign word (*or* expression *etc.*); **extranjero 1.** foreign; **2.** *m*, **a** *f* (*p.*) foreigner; **3.** *m* (*un país*) foreign country; (*en general*) foreign lands, foreign parts; *en el* ~ abroad; *ir al* ~ go abroad.

extrañamiento *m* estrangement; **extrañar** [1a] find strange, wonder at; *amigo* estrange; (*desterrar*) banish; *S.Am.* miss; *me extraña su conducta* I am surprised at your conduct; **~se** be amazed, be surprised (*de* at); (*amigos*) become estranged; (*rehusar*) refuse; **extrañeza** *f* strangeness, oddity, surprise, amazement; estrangement; **extraño** (*raro*) strange, odd; (*extranjero*) foreign; (*que no tiene que ver*) extraneous; ~ *a* unconnected with.

extraoficial unofficial; informal.

extraordinario 1. extraordinary; unusual; *edición*, *número* special; *precio etc.* extra, supplementary; **2.** *m* treat; (*plato*) extra dish.

extrasensorial extrasensory; **extraterrestre** extraterrestrial; otherworldly.

extravagancia *f* extravagance; eccentricity; (*capricho*) vagary; (*tonterías*) nonsense (*a.* ~*s pl.*); **extravagante** extravagant; eccentric; fancy *attr.*; (*tonto*) nonsensical.

extraviado stray, lost; **extraviar** [1c] *p.* lead astray; mislead, misdirect *en camino etc.*; *cosa* mislay, misplace; **~se** go astray (*a. fig.*), get lost, stray, wander; ⚕ miscarry; **extravío** *m* (*pérdida*) misplacement, loss; wandering; deviation (*from de*); *fig.* misconduct, evil ways.

extremado extreme; intense; excessive, overdone; **extremar** [1a] carry to extremes; overdo; **~se** do one's utmost; ~ *en inf.* go to great lengths to *inf.*

extremaunción *f* extreme unction; last rites (Roman Catholic).

extremeño *adj. a. su. m*, **a** *f* (native) of Extremadura.

extremidad *f* extremity; tip; edge; ~*es pl.* extremities *del cuerpo*; **extremismo** *m* extremism; **extremista** *m/f* extremist; **extremo 1.** extreme; (*sumo*) utmost; (*más remoto*) outermost; (*último*) last; **2.** *m* end; extreme; (*sumo grado*) highest degree; *fig.* great care; *con* ~ in the extreme; with a vengeance; *por* ~ extremely; *deportes*: ~ *derecho* outside right; *hacer* ~*s* gush; *pasar de un* ~ *a otro* go from one end to the other; *fig.* pass from one extreme to the other; **extremoso** effusive, gushing.

extrínseco extrinsic.

extroversión *f* extroversion; **extrovertido** *m*, **a** *f* extrovert.

exuberancia *f* exuberance; ⚘ luxuriance; **exuberante** exuberant; ⚘ luxuriant.

exudación *f* exudation; **exudar** [1a] exude, ooze.

exultación *f* exultation; **exultar** [1a] exult.

exvoto *m* votive offering.

eyector *m* ⊕ ejector.

F

fábrica *f* ⊕ factory, works, plant, mill; manufacture; ⚠ fabric; ⚠ masonry; (*edificio*) building, structure; ✝ (*marca*) make; ~ *experimental* pilot plant; ~ *de gas* gas works; ✝ *en* ~ *precio* ex-factory; **fabricación** *f* manufacture, making; make; *de* ~ *casera* homemade; *de* ~ *propia* our own make; ~ *en serie* mass production; **fabricante** *m* manufacturer, maker; **fabricar** [1g] ⊕ manufacture, make; ⚠ build; *fig.* fabricate, invent; (*juntar*) put together; ~ *en serie* mass-produce; **fabril** manufacturing.
fábula *f* fable; rumor; (*cuento*) tale; story, plot *de comedia etc.*; (*p.*) laughing stock; **fabuloso** fabulous; mythical.
facción *f pol. etc.* faction; feature *de cara*; ⚔ *estar de* ~ be on duty; **faccioso 1.** factious; rebellious; **2.** *m* rebel.
faceta *f* facet (*a. fig.*).
facial facial; *valor* face *attr.*
fácil easy, simple; (*pronto*) ready; *explicación b.s.* glib; facile; *p.* compliant; *mujer* loose; *es* ~ *que* it is likely that; **facilidad** *f* ease, facility; ~*es pl.* facilities; **facilitar** [1a] (*hacer fácil*) facilitate, help; (*proveer*) provide, supply; *me facilitó el libro* he let me have the book, he supplied me with the book.
facineroso *adj. a. su. m* criminal.
facsímil(e) *adj. a. su. m* facsimile; **facsimilar** [1a] facsimile; copy (mechanically).
factible feasible; workable.
facticio artificial, factitious.
factor *m* factor (*a.* ✝, ⚗); ✝ agent; 🚂 clerk; **factoría** *f* factory; ✝ agency, trading post.
factótum *m* factotum, jack-of-all-trades; *b.s.* busybody.
factura *f* invoice, bill; **facturar** [1a] ✝ invoice; 🚂 check.
facultad *f* (*potencia*) faculty (*a. univ.*); (*derecho etc.*) power (*de* of *su.*, to *inf.*); permission; **facultar** [1a] authorize; **facultativo 1.** optional; ⚕ medical; **2.** *m* doctor, practitioner.
facundia *f* eloquence, fluency; **facundo** eloquent, fluent.
facha *f* F look; (*p.*) sight, object; ⚓ *ponerse en* ~ bring to, lie to.
fachada *f* ⚠ façade (*a. fig.*), frontage; *typ.* frontispiece; F outward show.
fachenda *f* F bragging; boasting; **fachendear** [1a] F show off; brag; boast; **fachendón** F, **fachendoso** F swanky, snooty, conceited.
faena *f* (*tarea*) task, job; (*deber*) duty; ⚔ fatigue; F (*trabajo ingrato*) fag, sweat; F (*mala pasada*) dirty trick; *S.Am.* gang of workers; *S.Am.* overtime; extra job; *toros*: play with the cape; ~*s pl.* chores.
faisán *m* pheasant.
faja *f* strip, band *de tela etc.*; (*vestido*) sash (*a.* ⚔), belt; (*corsé*) girdle, corset; ✉ wrapper; *fig.* strip, belt, zone; **fajar** [1a] *v/t.* wrap, swathe; *v/i.* F ~ *con* go for, lay into; **fajín** *m* ⚔ sash; **fajina** *f* 🌾 shock, rick; (*leña*) faggots, kindling; ⚔ bugle call; **fajo** *m* sheaf *de papeles*; roll, wad *de billetes*.
falacia *f* deceit.
falange *f* phalanx; ♀ *Spanish Fascist party*.
falaz *p.* deceitful; *doctrina etc.* fallacious; *apariencia etc.* deceptive, misleading.
falda *f* skirt; (*regazo*) lap; *geog.* slope, hillside; *cosido a las* ~*s de* tied to the apron strings of; *mini*~ miniskirt.
faldellín *m* short skirt; underskirt; **faldero:** F *es muy* ~ he's a great one for the ladies; **faldillas** *f/pl.* tail *de traje*, coattails; **faldón** *m* skirt, tail *de traje*; flap; ⚠ gable.
falencia *f* deceit; mistake.
falena *f* moth.
falibilidad *f* fallibility; **falible** fallible.
fálico phallic; **falo** *m* phallus, penis.
falsario *m*, **a** *f* forger; (*mentiroso*)

liar; **falseador** *m*, **-a** *f* forger; **falsear** [1a] *v/t.* falsify, forge, fake; counterfeit; juggle with; *cerradura* pick; *v/i.* buckle, give way; ♪ be out of tune; **falsedad** *f* falsity, falseness *etc.* (*v. falso*); **falsete** *m* ⊕ bung; ♪ falsetto; **falsía** *f* falsity *etc.*; **falsificación** *f* falsification; forgery; fabrication; **falsificador** *m*, **-a** *f* forger; **falsificar** [1g] falsify; forge, fake, counterfeit; *elección* rig, fiddle; *razones* misrepresent; **falso** *mst* false; counterfeit, fake; *moneda* bad; (*simulado*) bogus, sham; (*insincero*) hollow, insincere; (*traidor*) treacherous; *testimonio* perjured, untrue; *opinión* unsound; *en* ~ without proper support; *jurar en* ~ perjure o.s.

falta *f* lack, want, need; absence; (*escasez*) shortage; (*defecto en el obrar*) failure, shortcoming; (*equivocación*) fault, mistake; (*desperfecto*) fault; ⊕ trouble; ⚖ default; *deportes*: foul; *tenis*: fault; ~ *de freq.* non...: ~ *de asistencia* non-attendance; *a* ~ *de prp.* failing; = *por* ~ *de* for want of, for lack of; *sin* ~ without fail; *hacer* ~ be necessary; *me hace* (*mucha*) ~ I need it (badly); *el hombre que hace* ~ the right man.

faltar [1a] (*estar ausente*) be missing, be lacking; be absent; (*necesitarse*) be needed; (*acabarse, fallar, dejar de ayudar a*) fail; default *en pago etc.*; *faltan 5* there are 5 missing, five short; *faltan 3 días para el examen* the exam is 3 days off; *falta poco para terminar* it's almost over; it's almost finished; *le falta dinero* he needs money, he lacks money; *¡no faltaba más!* it's the limit!, it's the last straw!; ~ *a cita* break, not turn up for; *clase* be absent from, cut, miss; *decencia* offend against; *deber* neglect; *palabra* go back on.

falto short, deficient; (*apocado*) poor, wretched; ~ *de* short of; *cualidades etc.* wanting in, lacking in, void of.

faltriquera *f* fob, (watch) pocket.

falúa *f* tender, launch.

falla *f* fault (*a. geol.*), failure; ~ *de encendido*, ~ *de tiro* misfire.

fallada *f naipes*: ruff.

fallar [1a] *v/t. naipes*: trump, ruff; ⚖ pronounce sentence on; *v/i.* (*tiro*) miss; (*escopeta etc.*) misfire, fail to go off; (*cuerda, soporte etc.*) give way, snap; (*frenos, memoria, cosecha etc.*) fail; (*proyecto*) fail, miscarry; ⚖ find, pass judgement; *el amigo me ha fallado* my friend has failed me (*or* let me down).

falleba *f* bolt.

fallecer [2d] pass away, die; **fallecido** late; **fallecimiento** *m* decease, demise.

fallido unsuccessful; ☤ (*a. su. m*) bankrupt; ⊕ (*a. su. m*) dud.

fallo *m* decision, ruling; ⚖ sentence, verdict; findings; ⊕ trouble; *deportes*: mistake, mix-up; *naipes*: void (*a* in); ~ *humano* human error.

fama *f* fame; reputation; rumor; glory; *mala* ~ *esp. de p.* notoriety; ☤ *etc.* bad reputation.

famélico starving, famished.

familia *f* family; household; *venir de* ~ run in the family; **familiar** **1.** (*conocido*; *sin ceremonia*) familiar; (*relativo a la familia*) family *attr.*; (*doméstico*) homely; *palabra* colloquial; *estilo etc.* informal; **2.** *m* (*conocido*) close acquaintance; (*pariente*) relation, relative; **familiaridad** *f* familiarity *etc.*; **familiarizar** [1f] familiarize, acquaint; **~se** become familiar; ~ *con* become conversant with, get to know.

famoso famous; F great.

fanal *m* lantern; (*torre*) lighthouse; (*campana*) bell glass.

fanático **1.** fanatical; bigoted; **2.** *m* fanatic; bigot; fiend F (*de* for); *S.Am.* fan; devotee; **fanatismo** *m* fanaticism; bigotry.

fandango *m* fandango.

fanega *f grain measure = 55.5 liters*; *ground area = 1.59 acres.*

fanfarrear [1a] = *fanfarronear*; **fanfarria** *f* bluster, bragging; ♪ fanfare; **fanfarrón** **1.** blustering, boastful; **2.** *m* blusterer, braggart; bully; **fanfarronada** *f* bluster, bluff, swagger; **fanfarronear** [1a] bluster, rant; swagger; **fanfarronería** *f* blustering, bragging.

fangal *m* bog, quagmire; **fango** *m* mud, mire, slush; **fangoso** muddy, slushy.

fantasía *f* fantasy; imagination; fancy; ♪ fantasia; *de ~ artículo* fancy; *joya* imitation; **fantasioso** F vain, stuck-up; **fantasma 1.** *m* ghost, phantom; F solemn and vain person; **2.** *f* bogey; **fantasmagoría** *f* phantasmagoria; **fantasmagórico** phantasmagoric; dreamlike; **fantasmal** phantom *attr.*; **fantástico** fantastic; weird; unreal(istic); fanciful, whimsical.

fantoche *m* puppet; nincompoop.

faquir *m* fakir.

faramalla *f* F claptrap; sham; trash.

farándula *f* † troupe of strolling players; F claptrap, pack of lies; **farandulero 1.** theater *attr.*; **2.** *m*, **a** *f* † strolling player; *b.s.* cheat, plausible rogue.

faraute *m* herald; F busybody.

fardel *m* knapsack; F ragbag; = **fardo** *m* bundle; bale, pack.

farfulla 1. *f* F splutter, jabber; **2.** *m*/*f* F gabbler, jabberer; **farfullar** [1a] F splutter, jabber, gabble; *trabajo* bungle.

farináceo starchy, farinaceous.

faringe *f* pharynx.

farisaico pharisaical, hypocritical; smug; **fariseo** *m* pharisee, hypocrite.

farmacéutico 1. pharmaceutical; **2.** *m* chemist, pharmacist, druggist; **farmacia** *f* (*ciencia*) pharmacy; (*tienda*) chemist's (shop); **farmacología** *f* pharmacology.

farero *m* lighthouse keeper; **faro** *m* beacon; ⚓ (*torre*) lighthouse; ⚓ lantern, light; *mot.* headlamp, headlight; *~ piloto*, *~ trasero* tail light, rear lamp; **farol** *m* lantern, lamp; street lamp; 🚗 headlight; F swank; **farola** *f* street lamp; **farolear** [1a] F swank; brag; **farolero** *m* lamppost; (*p.*) lamp lighter; F swank; **farolillo** *m* fairy light; ⚘ Canterbury bell.

fárrago *m* medley, hodgepodge.

farraquista *m* scatterbrain; muddlehead; **farrear** [1a] celebrate; F goof off.

farsa *f* farce; *fig.* humbug, masquerade; **farsante** *m* F humbug, fraud, fake.

fas: *por ~ o por nefas* by hook or by crook, rightly or wrongly.

fascículo *m* fascic(u)le.

fascinación *f* fascination; **fascinador** fascinating; **fascinar** [1a] fascinate; captivate; bewitch.

fascismo *m* Fascism; **fascista** *adj. a. su. m*/*f* fascist.

fase *f* (*a.* ⚡) phase; stage.

fastidiar [1b] annoy, bother, vex; bore; irk; *¡no me fastidies!* cut it out!; stop bothering me!; *¡no fastidies!* you don't mean it!, you're kidding!; **fastidio** *m* annoyance, bother, nuisance; boredom; *¡qué ~!* what a nuisance!; **fastidioso** annoying, vexing; tedious, tiresome; irksome.

fastos *m*/*pl.* annals.

fastuoso magnificent, pompous, lavish.

fatal fatal; fateful; irrevocable; F ghastly; **fatalidad** *f* fate; (*desgracia*) mischance, ill luck; fatality; **fatalismo** *m* fatalism; **fatalista 1.** fatalistic; **2.** *m*/*f* fatalist.

fatídico prophetic.

fatiga *f* fatigue (*a.* ⊕); weariness; (*trabajo*) toil; (*apuro*) hardship; **fatigante** tiresome; wearying; fatiguing; **fatigar** [1h] tire, weary; (*molestar*) annoy; **fatigoso** *trabajo etc.* tiring, exhausting; *p.* tired; (*penoso*) labored; F trying, tiresome.

fatuidad *f* inanity, fatuity; (*presunción*) conceit; **fatuo** inane, fatuous; conceited.

fauces *f*/*pl. anat.* gullet; *fig.* jaws.

fauna *f* fauna.

fauno *m* faun.

fausto *m* splendor, pomp, luxury.

fautor *m* accomplice; instigator.

favor *m* favor; (*servicio*) favor, good turn, kindness; protection; *a ~ de política* in favor of; *medio* with the help of; *p.* on behalf of; *noche etc.* under cover of; *por ~* please; *hacer el ~ de su.* oblige with *su.*; *¿me hace el ~ de inf.?* would you be so kind as to *inf.*?, please *inf.*; *haga el ~ de esperar* kindly wait; **favorable** favorable; auspicious; (*benévolo*) kind; **favorecer** [2d] favor; help; treat favorably; (*fortuna etc.*) smile on; (*traje, retrato*) flatter; **favoritismo** *m* favoritism; **favorito** *adj. a. su. m*, **a** *f* favorite (*a. deportes*).

faz *f lit.*, *fig.* face; aspect.

fe *f* faith (*en* in); belief; fidelity; certificate; *~ de bautismo* birth certificate; *~ de erratas* errata; *a ~ mía* on my honor; *de buena ~*

in good faith; *en ~ de* in witness of; *dar ~ de* testify to.
fealdad *f* ugliness.
febrero *m* February.
febrífugo *adj. a. su. m* febrifuge.
febril fevered, feverish (*a. fig.*); *fig.* hectic.
fécula *f* starch; **feculento** starchy.
fecundación *f* fertilization; *~ artificial* artificial insemination; **fecundar** [1a] fertilize; **fecundidad** *f* fertility; *esp. fig.* fruitfulness; **fecundizar** [1f] fertilize; **fecundo** fertile; prolific; *esp. fig.* fruitful.
fecha *f* date; *~ tope* closing date; *de larga ~* long-range, -dated; *hasta la ~* (up) to date; **fechar** [1a] date.
fechoría *f* misdeed.
federación *f* federation; **federal** federal; **federativo** federative.
feérico fairy.
fehaciente reliable; authentic.
felicidad *f* happiness; good luck; success; *~es pl.* congratulations; best wishes; **felicitación** *f* congratulation; **felicitar** [1a] congratulate.
feligrés *m*, **-a** *f* parishioner; **feligresía** *f* parish.
felino feline, catlike.
feliz *mst* happy; (*de buena suerte*) lucky; (*de buen éxito*) successful.
felonía *f* treachery; meanness.
felpa *f.* plush; F (*zurra*) hiding; F (*regaño*) talking-to; **felpar** [1a] cover with plush; *fig.* carpet; **felpudo 1.** plush(y); **2.** *m* doormat.
femenil feminine, womanly; **femenino 1.** feminine; ♀ female; *equipo ~* women's team; **2.** *m gr.* feminine.
fementido treacherous, false.
feminidad *f* femininity; **feminismo** *m* feminism; **feminista** *m/f* feminist.
fenecer [2d] *v/t.* finish, close; *v/i.* (*morir*) die; perish; (*acabar*) come to an end; **fenecimiento** *m* death; end, close.
fenicio *adj. a. su. m* Phoenician.
fénix *m* phoenix; *fig.* marvel.
fenomenal phenomenal; F tremendous, terrific; **fenómeno** *m* phenomenon; (*cosa anormal*) freak.
feo 1. ugly; unsightly; hideous; *olor etc.* nasty; *juego, tiempo* foul, dirty; **2.** *m* F insult; *hacer un ~ a* insult; **feote, feota** F shockingly ugly.
feraz fertile.
féretro *m* coffin, bier.
feria *f* (*mercado etc.*) fair, market; carnival; (*descanso*) holiday; ⚘ (agricultural) show; *C.Am., Mex.* tip, gratuity; change; *~ de muestras* trade fair; **feriado:** *día ~* holiday; **ferial** *m* market; **feriante** *m/f* stall holder; **feriar** [1b] *v/t.* buy, sell (in a market); *v/i.* take time off.
ferino savage; *v. tos.*
fermata *f* ♪ run.
fermentación *f* fermentation; **fermentar** [1a] ferment; **fermento** *m* ferment; leaven(ing).
ferocidad *f* fierceness *etc.*; **feroz** fierce, ferocious, savage, wild.
férreo iron; 🚂 rail...; **ferrería** *f* ironworks, foundry; **ferretería** *f* (*material*) ironmongery, hardware; (*tienda*) ironmonger's (shop), hardware shop; **ferretero** *m* ironmonger; **férrico** ferric; **ferrocarril** *m* railway, railroad; *~ elevado* overhead railway; **ferrohormigón** *m* ferroconcrete; **ferroso** ferrous; **ferroviario 1.** railway *attr.*; **2.** *m* railwayman.
ferry *m* ferry(boat).
fértil fertile, fruitful; rich (*en* in); **fertilidad** *f* fertility, fruitfulness; **fertilizante** *m* fertilizer; **fertilizar** [1f] fertilize; enrich.
férula *f* ferule, birch; *fig.* domination, rule.
férvido fervid, ardent; **ferviente** fervent; **fervor** *m* fervor, ardor; **fervoroso** fervent, ardent.
festejar [1a] entertain, fête, feast; (*galantear*) woo, court; *S.Am.* beat; **festejo** *m* entertainment, feast; courting; **festín** *m* feast, banquet; **festival** *m* festival; **festividad** *f* festivity, merrymaking; (*día*) holiday; (*agudeza*) wit; **festivo** (*alegre*) festive, gay; (*chistoso*) humorous, droll; (*agudo*) witty; jovial; *poema* burlesque, humorous; *día ~* holiday.
festón *m sew.* festoon, scallop; garland *de flores*; **festonear** [1a] *sew.* festoon, scallop; garland.
fetiche *m* fetish; mumbo jumbo F.
fetidez *f* rankness *etc.*; **fétido** rank, stinking, fetid.
feto *m* fetus.

feúcho F horribly ugly.

feudal feudal; **feudalidad** *f* feudality; **feudalismo** *m* feudalism; **feudatario** *adj. a. su. m* feudatory; **feudo** *m* fief; manor; ~ *franco* freehold.

fiable trustworthy.

fiado: *al* ~ on credit, on trust; **fiador** *m* (*p.*) *esp.* ⚖ surety, guarantor; *esp.* † sponsor; ⊕ catch, trigger; (*cierre etc.*) fastener; ⚔ safety catch; tumbler *de cerradura*; F bottom; *salir* ~ *por* go bail for, stand security for.

fiambre 1. cold; *noticia* stale; **2.** *m* (*carne etc.*) cold meat, cold food; F (*noticia*) (piece of) stale news; F (*chiste*) old joke, chestnut; F (*p.*) corpse, stiff; **fiambrera** *f* lunch basket, dinner pail; lunch box.

fianza *f* surety (*a. p.*), security; deposit; ~ *de aduana* bond; ~ *carcelera* bail; **fiar** [1c] *v/t.* entrust (*a* to); *p.* guarantee, stand security for, go bail for; † sell on credit; *v/i.* trust (*en* in); *de* ~ reliable; **~se** *de* trust in, rely (up)on.

fiasco *m* fiasco.

fíat *m* fiat.

fibra *f* fiber; grain *de madera*; *fig.* vigor, sinews; **~s** *pl. del corazón* heartstrings; **fibrina** *f* fibrin; **fibroso** fibrous.

ficción *f* fiction (*a.* ⚖), invention, fabrication; *ciencia* ~ science fiction; **ficticio** fictitious, imaginary.

ficha *f juegos*: counter, piece, marker; *póker*: chip; ~ (*del dominó*) domino; (*como moneda*) check, tally; (*papeleta etc.*) (index) card, record card; ⚡ plug; **fichar** [1a] *v/t.* file; *v/i.* sign on (*por* for); **fichero** *m* card index; (*mueble*) filing cabinet.

fidedigno trustworthy, reliable.

fideicomisario 1.: *banco* ~ trust company; **2.** *m* trustee; **fideicomiso** *m* trust.

fidelidad *f* fidelity, loyalty; (*exactitud*) accuracy; *de alta* ~ high-fidelity, hi-fi.

fideos *m/pl.* vermicelli.

fiduciario *adj. a. su. m* fiduciary.

fiebre *f* fever (*a. fig.*); ~ *aftosa* foot-and-mouth disease; ~ *amarilla* yellow fever; ~ *del heno* hay fever.

fiel 1. faithful, loyal; (*exacto*) accurate, true; **2.** *m* pointer, needle *de balanza.*

fieltro *m* felt; (*sombrero*) felt hat.

fiera *f* wild beast; (*p.*) fiend; (*mujer*) dragon; shrew; *casa* (*or colección*) *de* **~s** zoo, menagerie; **fiereza** *f* fierceness; cruelty; **fiero** fierce; cruel; (*horroroso*) frightful; (*feo*) ugly.

fierro *m S.Am.* branding iron; **~s** *pl. Ecuad., Mex.* tools.

fiesta *f* (*día*) holiday; *eccl.* feast, day *de santo etc.*; (*alegría, diversión*) festivity, celebration; party *esp. en casa particular*; fête, festival *en pueblo etc.*; *día de* ~ holiday; ~ *de guardar*, ~ *de precepto* holy day; ~ *nacional* national sport (*i.e. bullfighting*); *por fin de* ~ to round it all off; *aguar la* ~ be a killjoy, spoil the fun; F *estar de* ~ be in a good mood; F *no estar para* **~s** be in no mood for jokes; *hacer* **~s** *a* make a great fuss of; F *tengamos la* ~ *en paz* none of that, cut it out.

figura *f mst* figure; (*forma exterior, trazado*) shape; image; (*cara*) face; ~ *de nieve* snowman; *hacer* ~ cut a figure; **figurado** figurative; **figurante** *m*, **a** *f thea.* super (numerary), walker-on; *fig.* figurehead; **figurar** [1a] *v/t.* figure, shape; represent; *v/i.* figure (*como* as, *entre* among); **~se** suppose, imagine, figure; *¡figúrate!*, *¡figúrese!* just imagine!; (*ya*) *me lo figuraba* I thought as much; **figurativo** figurative.

figurín *m* fashion plate, model; **figurina** *f* figurine, statuette; **figurón** *m* F pompous ass; stuffed shirt.

fijación *f* (*acto*) fixing; (*psicológica*) fixation; **fijador** *m phot.* (*líquido*) fixer; (*cubeta*) fixing bath; hair lotion *para pelo*; **fijar** [1a] fix (*a. phot.*); secure, fasten; *sello etc.* stick (on), affix; *cartel* post; *fecha, hora, precio* fix, set; *pelo* set; *residencia* take up; *atención* focus, fix (*en* on); (*decidir*) settle (on), determine; *prohibido* ~ *carteles* stick no bills; **~se** settle, lodge; *¡fíjese!* just imagine!; ~ *en* (*notar*) notice; (*atender*) pay attention to; (*mirar fijamente*) stare at; seize upon; **fijativo** *adj. a. su. m* fixative; **fijeza** *f* firmness; fixity; *mirar con* ~ stare at; **fijo** fixed; firm, steady, secure; permanent; determined; *de* ~ certainly, without

doubt; F *ésa es la ~a* that's for sure; F *ésta es la ~a* this is it.
fil *m derecho* leapfrog.
fila *f* row (*a. thea.*), line, file; rank (*a.* ⚔); F dislike; *~ india* Indian file; *de dos ~s chaqueta* double-breasted; *en ~* in a row; ⚔ *en ~s* on active service; with the colors; ⚔ *romper ~s* fall out, dismiss.
filadelfiano Philadelphian.
filamento *m* filament.
filantropía *f* philanthropy; **filantrópico** philanthropic; **filántropo** *m* philanthropist.
filarmónica *f Mex.* accordeon; **filarmónico** philharmonic.
filatelia *f* philately, stamp collecting; **filatelista** *m/f* philatelist, stamp collector.
filete *m* ⚓, *cocina*: fillet; ⊕ worm; thread *de tornillo*; *sew.* narrow hem.
filfa *f* F fake, fraud, hoax.
filiación *f* filiation; connexion *de ideas*.
filial 1. filial; ✝ subsidiary; **2.** *f* ✝ subsidiary.
filibustero *m* pirate, freebooter.
filigrana *f* filigree; *typ.* watermark; F clever piece of play.
filípica *f* philippic.
filipino 1. Philippine; **2.** *m*, **a** *f* Philippine, Filipino.
filisteo *m* Philistine; *fig.* big man, giant.
film, filme *m* film; **filmación** *f* filming; **filmadora** *f* movie camera; **filmar** [1a] film, shoot; **fílmico** film *attr.*
filo *m* edge, cutting edge, blade; dividing line; *de dos ~s* double-edged; *por ~* exactly.
filo... philo...
filocomunista 1. fellow traveling, pro-Communist; **2.** *m/f* fellow traveler, pro-Communist.
filología *f* philology; **filológico** philological; **filólogo** *m* philologist.
filón *m* seam, vein, lode; F goldmine.
filosofal: *piedra ~* philosophers' stone; **filosofar** [1a] philosophize; **filosofía** *f* philosophy; **filosófico** philosophic(al); **filósofo** *m* philosopher.
filoxera *f* phylloxera.
filtración *f* filtration; (*accidental*) leakage; **filtrar** [1a] *v/t.* filter; strain; *v/i.*, **~se** filter through, percolate, seep; **filtro** *m* filter; † philtre.
filván *m* feather edge.
fin *m* (*término*) end, ending; (*objeto*) purpose, aim; *~ de semana* weekend; *a ~ de inf.* in order to *inf.*; *a ~ de que* so that; *a ~es de mayo* at (*or* about) the end of May; *al ~* finally, at the end; *en ~* (*como exclamación*) well (then), well now; *en ~, por ~* (*finalmente*) finally, at last; (*en suma*) in short; *al ~ y al cabo* in the end; *sin ~* endless(ly); ⊕ endless; *poner ~ a* stop, put a stop to.
finado 1. late; **2.** *m*, **a** *f* deceased.
final 1. final, last, ultimate; eventual; **2.** *m* end; ♪ finale; **3.** *f deportes*: final; **finalidad** *f* object, purpose; **finalista** *m/f* finalist; **finalizar** [1f] *v/t.* finish; finalize; *v/i.* end.
financiamiento *m S.Am.* financing, financial backing; **financiar** [1b] finance; **financiero 1.** financial; **2.** *m* financier; **finanzas** *f/pl.* finance.
finar [1a] die.
finca *f* property; (country) estate; country house; *S.Am.* ranch.
finchado F stuck-up.
finés *v. finlandés.*
fineza *f* fineness *de material etc.*; (*regalo*) little gift; *naipes*: finesse; *fig.* kindness, courtesy.
fingido false, mock; sham, fake; make-believe; **fingimiento** *m* simulation; pretense; **fingir** [3c] pretend; feign, fake; invent; make believe; *~ dormir, ~se dormido* pretend to be asleep; **~se** *su.* pretend to be *su.*
finiquitar [1a] *cuenta* close, balance up; **finiquito** *m* settlement.
finlandés 1. Finnish; **2.** *m*, **-a** *f* Finn; **3.** *m* (*idioma*) Finnish.
finito finite.
fino fine; *material etc.* delicate, thin; *producto* select, quality *attr.*; *gusto* discriminating; *inteligencia etc.* acute, shrewd; *ironía etc.* subtle; *oído* sharp; *p. etc.* polite, courteous, refined; *b.s.* cunning.
finta *f* feint; *boxeo*: *hacer ~s* spar.
finura *f* fineness *etc.*
firma *f* signature; (*acto*) signing; [✝ firm.]
firmamento *m* firmament.
firmante *adj. a. su. m/f* signatory;

el abajo ~ the undersigned; **firmar** [1a] sign.
firme 1. firm; steady, secure; *superficie etc.* hard, firm; *mercado* steady; *precio* set, stable; *p.* staunch, steadfast; ⚔ *¡~s!* attention!; ⚓ *en* ~ firm; **2.** *m* surface; **firmeza** *f* firmness *etc.*
fiscal 1. fiscal; **2.** *m* prosecutor, district attorney; **fiscalizar** [1f] inspect; oversee; *b.s.* pry into; ⚖ prosecute; **fisco** *m* exchequer.
fisga *f fig.* banter; *hacer* ~ *a* make fun of, tease; **fisgar** [1h] *v/t. pez* harpoon; *fig.* pry into; *v/i.* pry; (*burlarse*) mock, scoff; **fisgón 1.** F nosy, prying; **2.** *m*, **-a** *f* busybody; nosy person; **fisgonear** [1a] F = *fisgar*; **fisgoneo** *m* F nosiness.
física *f* physics; ~ *del estado sólido* solid-state physics; ~ *nuclear* nuclear physics; **físico 1.** physical; **2.** *m* physicist; ⚕ † physician; *anat.* physique; (*aspecto*) appearance.
físil fissile; fissionable.
fisiografía *f* physiography.
fisiología *f* physiology.
fisión *f* fission; ~ *nuclear* nuclear fission; **fisionable** fissionable.
fisonomía *f* physiognomy, features.
fístula *f* fistule.
fisura *f* fissure.
fláccido flaccid, flabby.
flaco 1. thin, lean, skinny; *fig.* weak; *memoria* bad, short; **2.** *m* weakness, weak point, foible; **flacura** *f* thinness *etc.*
flagelación *f* flagellation, whipping; **flagelar** [1a] flagellate, whip; *fig.* flay.
flagrante flagrant; *en* ~ red-handed.
flamante brilliant; *fig.* brand-new.
flameante flamboyant (*a.* ▲); **flamear** [1a] flame; (*bandera*) flutter.
flamenco[1] *m orn.* flamingo.
flamenco[2] **1.** Flemish; Andalusian gipsy *attr.*; F flashy, gaudy; **2.** *m*, **a** *f* Fleming; **3.** *m* (*idioma*) Flemish.
flámula *f* streamer.
flan *m* cream caramel, caramel custard.
flanco *m* flank; **flanquear** [1a] flank; ⚔ outflank.
flaquear [1a] weaken, flag; slacken; (*viga etc.*) give (way); **flaqueza** *f* leanness *etc.*; weakness, frailty; *fig.* failing, weakness *de la carne etc.*
flash *m* newsflash; *phot.* flash(light); ~*back* (*retrospección*) flashback.
flato *m* flatulence, wind; *S.Am.* gloominess; **flatulencia** *f* flatulence; **flatulento** flatulent.
flauta *f* flute; **flautín** *m* piccolo.
flebitis *f* phlebitis.
fleco *m* fringe *de pelo etc.*; (*adorno*) tassel; ~*s pl.* gossamer.
flecha *f* arrow; *alas en* ~ swept back wings; **flechar** [1a] wound *etc.* with an arrow, wing; *arco* stretch; F make a hit with; **flechazo** *m* arrow wound; F love at first sight; **flechero** *m* archer, bowman.
flema *f* phlegm (*a. fig.*); **flemático** phlegmatic, matter-of-fact; *sl. a. fig.* cool.
flemón *m* gumboil.
flequillo *m* fringe.
fletamento *m* charter(ing); **fletar** [1a] charter; freight; **flete** *m* freight; (*precio*) freightage.
flexibilidad *f* flexibility *etc.*; **flexible 1.** flexible; supple, pliable; *sombrero* soft; *p.* compliant, readily persuaded; **2.** *m* soft hat; ⚡ flex; **flexión** *f* flexion; *gr.* inflection; **flexional** *gr.* inflected; **flexor:** (*músculo*) ~ flexor.
flirt *m*, **flirtación** *f* flirting; **flirtear** [1a] flirt; **flirteo** *m* (*en general*) flirting; (*un* ~) flirtation.
flojear [1a] weaken; slacken; **flojedad** *f* looseness, slackness *etc.*; **flojel** *m* nap *de paño*; *orn.* down; **flojera** *f* F = *flojedad*; **flojo** (*no tirante*) loose, slack; (*no apretado*) loose; (*débil*) weak, feeble; limp; *viento* light; *vino etc.* weak; *precio* low, sagging; *mercado* slack, dull; *p.* lax, lazy, slack; *estudiante* weak.
flor *f* flower (*a. fig.*), blossom; bloom *en fruta*; grain *de cuero*; ~ *de la vida* prime of life; ~ *y nata fig.* cream; élite, the pick; *a* ~ *de* (on a) level with; *a* ~ *de agua* at water level; awash; *en* ~ in flower; *echar* ~*es a* pay compliments to, flirt with; **flora** *f* flora; **floración** *f* flowering; bloom; **floral** floral; **florar** [1a] flower; **florear** [1a] *v/t.* adorn with flowers; *v/i.* ♪ play a flourish; **florecer** [2d] ⚘ flower, bloom; *fig.* flourish, thrive; **floreciente** ⚘ in flower, blooming; *fig.* flourishing, thriving; **florecimiento** *m* flower-

ing; **floreo** *m fenc.*, ♪ flourish; *fig.* witty talk; **florero** *m* vase; **florescencia** *f* florescence; **floresta** *f* wood, grove; glade; beauty spot; *lit.* anthology.

florete *m* foil.

floricultura *f* flower growing.

florido *campo etc.* flowery; *estilo etc.* flowery, florid; *calidad* select; **florilegio** *m* anthology; **florista** *m/f* florist; **floristería** *f* florist's.

florín *m* florin.

florón *m* ⚠ finial; *typ.* tail piece.

flota *f* (*en general*) shipping; (*escuadra*) fleet; **flotación** *f* floating, flotation; **flotador** *m* float; **flotante** floating; *fig.* hanging loose; **flotar** [1a] float; ride; hang loose; stream *al viento*; **flote:** *a* ~ afloat; *poner a* ~, *sacar a* ~ (re)float, raise; *ponerse a* ~ *fig.* get out of a jam; **flotear** [1a]: ~ (*en el aire*) hover; **flotilla** *f* flotilla.

fluctuación *f* fluctuation; *fig.* uncertainty; **fluctuante** fluctuating; **fluctuar** [1e] fluctuate; (*p.*) waver, hesitate.

fluidez *f* fluidity; *fig.* fluency; **flúido 1.** fluid; *fig.* fluent, smooth; **2.** *m* fluid; ~ *eléctrico* electric current; **fluir** [3g] flow, run.

flujo *m* flow; flux; stream; ⚓ rising tide; ~ *de sangre* hemorrhage; ~ *de vientre* diarrhea.

fluorescencia *f* fluorescence; **fluorescente** fluorescent.

fluorización *f* fluoridation; **fluorizar** [1f] (*agua potable*) fluoridate.

fluvial river *attr.*

flux *m naipes*: flush.

fobia *f* phobia.

foca *f* seal.

focal focal; **foco** *m* focus (*a. fig.*); source *de calor, luz*; ⚡ floodlight; *fig.* center; hotbed *de vicios etc.*

fofo soft, spongy; insubstantial.

fogarada *f*, **fogata** *f* blaze, bonfire.

fogón *m* stove, kitchen range; 🚂 firebox; ⊕ vent; ⚓ galley; **fogonazo** *m* flash; **fogonero** *m* stoker, fireman.

fogosidad *f* fire, dash, verve; **fogoso** (high-)spirited, mettlesome, ardent; *caballo* fiery, frisky.

foliación *f* foliation; **foliar** [1b] foliate, number the pages of; **folio** *m* folio.

folklore *m* folklore; **folklórico** folk *attr.*, folklore *attr.*; **folklorista** *adj. a. su. m/f* folklorist(ic).

follaje *m* ⚘ foliage, leaves; *fig.* (*adorno*) excessive ornamentation; (*palabras*) verbiage.

folletín *m* newspaper serial; **folletista** *m* pamphleteer; **folleto** *m* pamphlet; folder, brochure, leaflet.

follón 1. (*perezoso*) lazy, slack; (*arrogante*) puffed-up, blustering; **2.** *m* ⚘ sucker; (*p.*) good-for-nothing F; F (*jaleo*) rumpus, row, shindy; F *hacer* ~ (*estudiantes*) have a rag, riot.

fomentación *f* ⚕ fomentation; **fomentar** [1a] encourage, promote, foment (*a.* ⚕), further, foster; *rebelión* stir up; **fomento** *m* encouragement *etc.*; ⚕ fomentation; *Ministerio de* ♀ *ministry responsible for public works, agriculture etc.*

fonda *f* inn; restaurant; 🚂 buffet.

fondeadero *m* anchorage; berth; **fondear** [1a] *v/t. fondo* sound; *barco* search; *fig.* examine; *v/i.* drop anchor.

fondero *m S.Am.* innkeeper.

fondillos *m/pl.* seat (of trousers).

fondista *m/f* innkeeper.

fondo *m* (*parte más baja*) bottom (*a.* ⚓); (*parte más lejana*) back, far end; (*profundidad*) depth; ⚓, *paint.*, *sew.* ground; *paint.*, *fig.* background; (*esencia*) substance, matter; disposition *de p.*; ⚘ fund; *fig.* fund, reservoir *de humor etc.*; ⚘ ~*s pl.* funds; finance; ~ *de amortización* sinking fund; *doble* ~, ~ *falso* false bottom; *bajos* ~*s pl. sociales* dregs of society; *a* ~ thoroughly; *al* ~ *de escena etc.* at the back of; *deportes*: *de* ~ long-distance, endurance *attr.*; *en el* ~ *fig.* at bottom, at heart; *dar* ~ anchor; *echar a* ~, *irse a* ~ sink.

fonema *m* phoneme; **fonética** *f* phonetics; **fonético** phonetic; **fonetista** *m/f* phonetician.

fonoabsorbente sound-absorbent; sound-deadening; **fonógrafo** *m* record player; phonograph; **fonología** *f* phonology.

fontanal *m*, **fontanar** *m* spring.

fontanería *f* plumbing; **fontanero** *m* plumber.

foque *m* jib.

forajido *m* outlaw, bandit, desperado.

forastero 1. alien, strange; **2.** *m*, **a** *f* stranger, outsider, visitor.
forcej(e)ar [1a] struggle, wrestle; flounder (about); **forcejudo** strong, powerful.
fórceps *m* forceps.
forense forensic.
forestal forest *attr.*; *v. repoblación etc.*
forja *f* forge; foundry; (*acto*) forging; **forjado** wrought; **forjar** [1a] forge, shape; *fig.* concoct.
forma *f* form, shape; (*modo*) way, means; formula; *typ.* format; ∼*s pl.* social forms, conventions; *de esta* ∼ in this manner; *de* ∼ *que* so that; *de todas* ∼*s* anyway, at any rate; *en debida* ∼ duly; *estar en* ∼ be in (good) form; *ver la* ∼ *de inf.* see one's way to *ger. or inf.*; **formación** *f* formation; education; training *para profesión*; **formal** (*relativo a la forma*) formal; *asunto* serious; official; *permiso etc.* formal, express; *promesa* definite; *manera* earnest; *p.* reliable, dependable; (*de edad*) adult, grown-up; **formalidad** *f* formality; form; seriousness *etc.*; *pura* ∼ matter of form; **formalismo** *m* conventionalism; (*administrativo etc.*) bureaucracy, red tape; **formalista** *m/f* formalist; **formalizar** [1f] formalize; formulate; regularize, put in order; ∼**se** take offense; grow serious; **formar** [1a] (*dar forma a*) form, shape; (*reunir, componer*) form, make up; *proyecto* make, lay; *tropas* parade; *alumno* train; ∼**se** form, shape; develop; ⚔ *etc.* form up, line up; **formativo** formative; **formato** *m* format.
fórmico: *ácido* ∼ formic acid.
formidable formidable, redoutable; tremendous (*a.* F).
formón *m* chisel.
fórmula *f* formula; (*receta*) formula, prescription; *por pura* ∼ just for form's sake; **formulación** *f* formulation; **formular** [1a] formulate; *queja* lodge; *pregunta* frame, pose; **formulario 1.** formulary; **2.** *m* formulary; form.
fornicación *f* fornication; **fornicar** [1g] fornicate; F have sex.
fornido strapping, hefty.
foro *m hist.* forum; ⚖ bar; *thea.* backstage.
forrado *m* lining; padding.
forraje *m* fodder, forage; (*acto*) foraging; F hodgepodge; **forrajear** [1a] forage.
forrar [1a] *mst* line; *ropa* line, pad; *libro etc.* cover; ⊕ face; ⊕ lag *para retener el calor*; **forro** *m* lining, padding; cover; ⊕ facing, sheathing; F *ni por el* ∼ not by a long shot.
fortalecer [2d] strengthen; ⚔ *etc.* fortify; *moral* stiffen; encourage *en una opinión etc.*; **fortalecimiento** *m* strengthening *etc.*; **fortaleza** *f* ⚔ fortress, stronghold; (*fuerza*) strength; fortitude, resolution; **fortificación** *f* fortification; **fortificar** [1g] fortify; *fig.* strengthen; **fortín** *m* pillbox, bunker; fort.
fortuito fortuitous; accidental, chance *attr.*
fortuna *f mst* fortune; luck; *por* ∼ luckily; ⚓ *correr* ∼ weather a storm; *probar* ∼ try one's luck, have a shot F.
forzado forced *etc.*; **forzar** [1f *a.* 1m] force, compel (*a inf.* to *inf.*); *puerta* break open; *cerradura* pick; *propiedad* enter by force; *mujer* ravish, rape; *sentido*, *ojos* strain; **forzoso** necessary; inescapable; *aterrizaje* forced; **forzudo** strong, tough.
fosa *f* grave; *anat.* fosse.
fosfato *m* phosphate; **fosforera** *f* matchbox; **fosforescencia** *f* phosphorescence; **fosforescente** phosphorescent; **fosfórico** phosphoric; **fósforo** *m* match; ⚗ phosphorus; **fosforoso** phosphorous.
fósil *adj. a. su. m* fossil (*a. fig.*); **fosilizado** fossilized.
foso *m* pit; ditch, trench; ⚔ fosse, moat; *thea.* pit; ∼ *de reconocimiento* inspection pit; *venirse al* ∼ flop.
fotinga *f S.Am.* F jalopy.
foto *f* (*a. m*) F photo; ∼**copia** *f* photocopy, print; ∼**copiadora** *f* photocopier; ∼**cromia** *f* color photography; ∼**eléctrico** photoelectric; ∼**génico** photogenic (*a.* F); ∼**grabado** *m* photogravure; ∼**grafía** *f* (*arte*) photography; (*foto*) photograph; ∼ *aérea* aerial photograph; ∼ *instantánea* snapshot; ∼**grafiar** [1c] photograph; ∼**gráfico** photographic; **fotógrafo** *m* photographer; **fotómetro** *m* exposure meter, photometer; **fotopila** *f* solar battery; **fotosíntesis** *f* photosynthesis; **fotostatar**

[1a] photostat; **fotóstato** *m* photostat; **fototelegrafía** *f* phototelegraphy; **fototipo** *m* phototype.
fox [fos] *m* foxtrot.
frac *m* dress coat, tail coat; F tails.
fracasar [1a] fail; fall through; **fracaso** *m* failure.
fracción *f* ⚹ *etc.* fraction; division; (*partido*) faction, splinter group; (*acto*) breaking; **fraccionamiento** *m* breaking up; **fraccionar** [1a] break up, divide; **fraccionario** fractional.
fractura *f* fracture, break; ~ *complicada* compound fracture; **fracturar** [1a] fracture, break.
fragancia *f* fragrance, perfume; **fragante** fragrant, sweet-smelling; *crimen* flagrant; *en* ~ in the act.
fragata *f* frigate; ~ *portaprojectiles teleguiados* guided missile frigate.
frágil fragile; brittle; *fig.* frail; **fragilidad** *f* fragility; brittleness; *fig.* frailty.
fragmentario fragmentary; *b.s.* scrappy; **fragmento** *m* fragment; scrap, piece, bit.
fragor *m* crash, clash; din; uproar.
fragosidad *f* roughness *etc.*; (*camino*) rough road; **fragoso** rough, uneven; *terreno* difficult; *selva* dense.
fragua *f* forge; **fraguar** [1i] *v/t.* ⊕ forge; *fig. mentira* concoct; *complot* hatch; *v/i.* ⊕ *cemento* set.
fraile *m* friar; monk; F priest; ~ *rezador entomology* praying mantis; **frailuno** *contp.* monkish.
frambuesa *f* raspberry; **frambueso** *m* raspberry (cane).
francachela *f* F spree, jamboree; (*comida*) spread.
francés 1. French; *despedirse a la* ~*a* take French leave; **2.** *m* (*p.*) Frenchman; (*idioma*) French; **francesa** *f* Frenchwoman.
franciscano *adj. a. su. m* Franciscan.
francmasón *m* (free)mason; **francmasonería** *f* (free)masonry.
franco 1. frank, open, forthright; (*pleno*) full; (*liberal*) generous; ⚕ free; *camino* open; ~ *a bordo* free on board; *v. porte*; **2.** *hist.* Frankish; ~*-español* Franco-Spanish; ~*canadiense adj. a. su. m/f* French-Canadian; **3.** *m* franc; *hist.* Frank.
francófilo *adj. a. su. m* (**a** *f*) Francophile; **francote** blunt, bluff.
francotirador *m* sniper.
franchute *m*, **a** *f* F Frenchy.
franela *f* flannel; *Mex.*, *Ven.*, *Col.*, *W.I.* undershirt.
frangollar [1a] F bungle, botch, rush; make a mess of.
franja *f* fringe, trimming; band (*a. fig.*).
franquear [1a] *contribuyente* exempt; *esclavo* free, liberate; *derecho* grant; allow; *camino* clear; *río etc.* cross; ✉ frank, stamp; ~**se** fall in with s.o.'s wishes; open one's heart (*a, con* to); **franqueo** *m* franking; postage; **franqueza** *f* frankness *etc.*; **franquicia** *f* exemption; ~ *postal* privilege of franking letters.
franquista *adj. a. su. m/f* pro-Franco; supporting (*or* devoted to) Francisco Franco.
frasco *m* flask, bottle.
frase *f* sentence; (*locución*) phrase; ~ *hecha* stock phrase, cliché; idiom; proverb; **fraseología** *f* phraseology.
fraternal brotherly, fraternal; **fraternidad** *f* brotherhood, fraternity; **fraternización** *f* fraternization; **fraternizar** [1f] fraternize; **fraterno** brotherly, fraternal.
fratricida 1. fratricidal; **2.** *m* fratricide (*p.*); **fratricidio** *m* fratricide (*act*).
fraude *m* fraud; false pretenses; dishonesty; ~ *fiscal* tax evasion; **fraudulencia** *f* fraudulence; **fraudulento** fraudulent; dishonest.
fray *m eccl.* brother.
frecuencia *f* frequency (*a.* ⚡); *alta* ~ high frequency; *con* ~ frequently; **frecuentador** *m*, **-a** *f* frequenter; **frecuentar** [1a] frequent; haunt; **frecuente** frequent; common; *costumbre etc.* prevalent, rife.
fregadero *m* (kitchen) sink; **fregado** *m* scrub(bing); washing-up *de platos*; F (*enredo*) mess; F (*jaleo*) row; **fregador** *m* (*pila*) sink; (*trapo*) dish cloth; (*estropajo*) scrubber, scourer; **fregar** [1h *a.* 1k] scrub, scour; *suelo* scrub, mop; *platos* wash; *S.Am.* annoy; **fregasuelos** *m* mop; **fregona** *f* kitchen maid; *contp.* skivvy.
freiduría *f* fried-fish shop; **freír** [3m; *p.p. frito*] fry.

fréjol *m* kidney bean.
frenar [1a] brake; *fig.* check, restrain; **frenazo** *m* sudden (*or* violent) braking; *fig.* putting a halt to.
frenesí *m* frenzy; **frenético** frantic, frenzied; wild.
freno *m* ⊕ brake; bit *de caballo*; *fig.* check, curb; ~ *de mano* hand brake; ~ *de disco* disk brake; ~ *de tambor* drum brake; *servo*~ power brake(s).
frenología *f* phrenology.
frente 1. *f* forehead, brow; (*cara*) face; **2.** *m todos sentidos*: front; *al* ~ in front; ✝ carried forward; *de* ~ *mover* forward; *marchar* abreast; *chocar* head on; *¡de* ~ *(mar)!* forward march!; *del* ~ brought forward; *en* ~ opposite, in front; *hacer* ~ *a* resist; *gastos* meet; ⚓ *tempestad* ride out; **3.** *prp.*: ~ *a* opposite (to); in front of; *fig.* as opposed to.
fresa *f* ⚘ (*mst* wild) strawberry; bit, drill *de dentista*; ⊕ milling cutter; **fresadora** *f* milling machine; **fresal** *m* strawberry bed; **fresar** [1a] mill.
fresca *f* fresh air, cool air; F piece of one's mind; *tomar la* ~ get some fresh air; **frescachón** glowing with health; bouncing; *mujer* buxom; **fresco 1.** *mst* fresh; (*algo frío*) cool; *agua* cold; *huevo* new-laid; F fresh, saucy, cheeky; F *quedarse tan* ~ not bat an eyelid, remain unmoved; **2.** *m* fresh air, cool air; ⚠ *etc.* fresco; *al* ~ in the open air, out of doors; *tomar el* ~ take the air, get some fresh air; **frescor** *m* freshness; coolness; **frescote** F blooming; buxom; **frescura** *f* freshness; coolness; F cheek, sauce, nerve.
fresno *m* ash (tree).
fresón *m* strawberry.
fresquera *f* meat closet; icebox.
freudiano *adj. a. su. m* (**a** *f*) Freudian; **freudismo** *m* Freudianism.
freza *f* spawn; (*acto, época*) spawning; **frezar** [1f] spawn.
friable friable.
frialdad *f* coldness; coolness, indifference.
fricasé *m* fricassee.
fricción *f* rubbing, rub; ⊕ friction (*a. fig.*); ⚕ massage; **friccionar** [1a] rub; ⚕ massage.
friega *f* rubbing; scrubbing; ⚕ massage; F bother, fuss; *S.Am.* thrashing; **friegaplatos** *m* dishwasher.
frigidez *f* frigidity; **frígido** frigid.
frigorífico 1. refrigerating; *camión* ~ refrigerator truck; **2.** *m* refrigerator; *S.Am.* cold-storage plant; ⚓ refrigerator ship.
frío 1. cold; *bala* spent; **2.** *m* cold; coldness; *hace (mucho)* ~ it is (very) cold; *tener* ~ be cold, feel cold; **friolento** chilly, shivery; **friolera** *f* trifle, mere nothing; **friolero** chilly, shivery.
frisar [1a] *v/t. tela* frizz, rub; *v/i.* get along; ~ *en* border on; *años* be getting on for.
frizo *m* frieze; wainscot, dado.
fritada *f* fry; **frito 1.** fried; F *tener* ~, F *traer* ~ defeat; worry to death; F *el inglés me trae* ~ English just gets me down; F *ese hombre me trae* ~ that chap is forever bothering me; **2.** *m* fry; ~*s pl. variados* mixed grill.
frivolidad *f* frivolity *etc.*; **frívolo** frivolous; *pretexto etc.* flimsy, trivial; *p.* shallow; *charla* idle.
fronda *f* frond; **frondosidad** *f* leafiness; luxuriance; **frondoso** leafy; luxuriant.
frontal *adj. a. su. m* frontal.
frontera *f* frontier, border; **fronterizo** frontier *attr.*, border *attr.*; *casa* opposite.
frontis *m* façade; **frontispicio** *m* frontispiece.
frontón *m* ⚠ pediment; gable; *deportes*: pelota court.
frotación *f*, **frotadura** *f* rub, rubbing; ⊕ friction; **frotar** [1a] rub; *cerilla* strike; *quitar frotando* rub off; **frote** *m* rub, rubbing.
fructífero productive; *fig.* fruitful; **fructificar** [1g] produce, yield a crop; *fig.* yield (a profit); **fructuoso** fruitful.
frugal frugal; thrifty; **frugalidad** *f* frugality; thrift(iness).
fruición *f* enjoyment, delight; perverse satisfaction.
frunce *m*, **fruncido** *m*, **fruncimiento** *m* pleat, gather(ing), pucker; **fruncir** [3b] pucker, wrinkle, ruffle; *sew.* pleat, gather, pucker; *labios* purse; *entrecejo* knit.
fruslería *f* trifle.
frustrar [1a] frustrate, thwart, balk; ~**se** fail, miscarry.
fruta *f* fruit; *fig.* result; ~ *de sartén* fritter; **frutal 1.**: *árbol* ~ = **2.** *m* fruit

tree; **frutar** [1a] fruit; **frutería** *f* fruit store; **frutero 1.:** *plato* ~ fruit dish; **2.** *m* fruit seller; **fruticultura** *f* fruit-growing; **frutilla** *f S.Am.* strawberry; **fruto** *m* fruit; *fig.* fruits, profit, results; *dar* ~ fruit.

fu: *ni* ~ *ni fa* neither one thing nor the other.

fucilazo *m* sheet lightning.

fuco *m.* wrack.

fucsia *f* fuchsia.

fuego *m* fire; light *para cigarrillo*; ⚓ beacon; ⚕ rash; ⚔ *¡~!* fire!; *~s pl. artificiales* fireworks; ~ *fatuo* will-o'-the-wisp; *abrir* ~ open fire; *echar* ~ *por los ojos* glare, look daggers; *hacer* ~ fire (*sobre* at, on); *jugar con* ~ play with fire; *pegar* ~ *a* set fire to; *poner a* ~ *y sangre* lay waste; *romper el* ~ open up.

fuelle *m* bellows (*a. phot.*); *mot.* folding hood; F gossip, talebearer.

fuente *f* fountain, spring; (*plato*) large dish, bowl; *fig.* source; ~ *termal* hot spring.

fuer: *a* ~ *de hombre honrado* as an honest man.

fuera 1. *adv.* outside; out; away; *deportes*: (*pelota*) *estar* in touch, out; *poner* into touch; (*equipo*) *jugar* away (from home); *¡~ (de aquí)!* off with you!; *por* ~ on the outside; *v. estar*; **2.** *prp.*: ~ *de* out of, outside (of); *fig.* in addition to, besides, beyond; ~ *de eso* apart from that; ~ *de mentir* short of lying; ~ *de servicio* out of service; inoperative; F down; ~ *de sí* beside o.s.

fuero *m* jurisdiction; (*código*) code (of laws); charter *de ciudad*; privilege *de grupo*.

fuerte 1. strong; sturdy; vigorous; *automóvil, motor etc.* powerful; *golpe* hard; *calor etc.* intense; *comida, gasto, lluvia* heavy; *ruido* loud; ~ *en* well up in; **2.** *adv.* strongly; *golpear* hard; *tocar* loud, loudly; *poner más* ~ *radio* turn up; **3.** *m* ⚔ fort, stongpoint; ♪, *fig.* forte.

fuerza *f* strength; force; power (*a.* ⚡); intensity; heaviness; effect *de argumento etc.*; *~s pl.* ⚔ forces; strength *de p.*; ~ *de gravedad* force of gravity; ~ *mayor* force majeure; act of God; ~ *motriz* motive power; *a la* ~ by force, willy-nilly; *a* ~ *de* by dint of; *a viva* ~ *entrada* forced; *por* ~ perforce; *por* ~ *mayor* under coercion; by main force; *hacer* ~ *de vela* crowd on sail; *tener ~s para* have the strength to *inf.* (for *su.*).

fuete *m S.Am.* (horse)whip.

fuga *f* flight, escape; leak *de gas etc.*; ♪ fugue; *poner en* ~ put to flight; *apelar a la* ~, *darse a la* ~, *ponerse en* ~ take to flight; ~ *de capitales* capital flight; **fugarse** [1h] flee, escape; ~ (*de la ley*) abscond; ~ *con* run away with; **fugaz** (*pasajero*) fleeting, short-lived; ephemeral; (*difícil de coger*) elusive; **fugitivo** *adj. a. su. m*, **a** *f* fugitive; = *fugaz*.

fui, fuimos *etc. v. ir, ser.*

fulana *f* F tart, whore; **fulano** *m*, **a** *f* (Mr *etc.*) So-and-so.

fulcro *m* fulcrum.

fulero F useless.

fulgente, fúlgido brilliant, bright; **fulgor** *m* brilliance, glow; **fulgurante** shining, bright; **fulgurar** [1a] shine, gleam; flash; **fulguroso** shining; flashing.

fulminación *f* fulmination; **fulminante** *polvo etc.* fulminating; ⚕ fulminant; F *éxito etc.* tremendous; **fulminar** [1a] *v/t.* fulminate; *amenazas etc.* thunder; ~ *con la mirada* look daggers at; *v/i.* fulminate, explode; **fulminato** *m* fulminate; ~ *mercúrico* ⚗ mercury fulminate.

fullería *f* cardsharping; trick; **fullero** *m* (card)sharper; F cheat, crook; dodger.

fumada *f* whiff (*or* puff) of smoke; **fumadero** *m* smoking room; ~ *de opio* opium den; **fumador** *m*, **-a** *f* smoker; **fumar** [1a] smoke; *prohibido* ~ no smoking; *~se* F *sueldo* squander; *clase* cut; **fumarada** *f* (*humo*) puff of smoke; pipeful *de tabaco.*

fumigación *f* fumigation; **fumigar** [1h] fumigate.

funámbulo *m*, **a** *f* tightrope walker.

función *f* function; duty; *thea.* show, entertainment; performance; ~ *taquillera* draw; *entrar en ~es* take up one's duties; **funcional** functional; **funcionamiento** *m* functioning; ⊕ *etc.* working, running; performance; behavior; ⊕ *en* ~ in order, in operation; *en pleno* ~ *sociedad etc.* going; **funcionar** [1a] function; work, run, go (*a.* ⊕); perform (*a.* ⊕); behave; *no funciona* (*como letrero*) out of order; *hacer* ~ operate; **funcionario** *m* official, functionary; civil servant.

funda *f* case, sheath; (*bolsa*) carryall; ~ *de almohada* pillow case.

fundación *f* foundation; **fundador** *m*, **-a** *f* founder; **fundamental** fundamental; basic; essential; **fundamentar** [1a] lay the foundations of; base (*en* on); **fundamento** *m* foundation; basis; (*trabajo preliminar*) groundwork; (*razón, motivo*) ground(s); reliability, trustworthiness *de p.*; ~*s pl. fig.* fundamentals; **fundar** [1a] found, set up, establish, institute; endow *con dinero*; *argumento etc.* base (*en* on); *bien fundado* well grounded.

fundente 1. melting; **2.** *m* ⚗ flux; ⚕ dissolvent; **fundible** fusible; **fundición** *f* (*acto*) fusion; ⊕ (*acto*) melting, smelting; (*fábrica*) foundry, forge; *typ.* fount; **fundido** melted; ↯ burned out; shorted; blown (out); *S.Am. p.* ruined; **fundidor** *m* smelter, founder; **fundir** [3a] fuse; ⊕ (*derretir*) melt (down), smelt; (*formar*) found, cast; ~**se** fuse (*a.* ↯), merge, blend; (*metal*) melt; ↯ blow, burn out.

fúnebre funereal; (*relativo a funeral*) funeral *attr.*; *fig.* mournful, lugubrious; **funeral 1.** funeral *attr.*; **2.** *m*, ~*es pl.* funeral; **funeraria** *f* undertaker's; *director de* ~ funeral director; **funerario, funéreo** funer(e)al.

funesto ill-fated, unfortunate; disastrous, fatal (*para* for).

fungoso fungous.

funicular *adj. a. su. m* funicular.

furgón *m* wagon, van; luggage van (*a.* ~ *de equipajes*); guard's van (*a.* ~ *de cola*); **furgoneta** *f* van; station wagon; light truck.

furia *f* fury; rage; *a toda* ~ like fury; *hecho una* ~ furiously angry; **furibundo, furioso** furious; violent; frantic; **furor** *m* rage; passion; frenzy; *hacer* ~ be all the rage (*or* go).

furriel *m* ⚔ *approx.* quartermaster.

furtivo furtive; stealthy; sly, shifty; *edición* pirated.

furúnculo *m* boil.

fuselaje *m* fuselage.

fusible 1. fusible; **2.** *m* fuse; *caja de* ~*s* fuse box.

fusil *m* rifle; gun; **fusilamiento** *m* shooting, execution; **fusilar** [1a] shoot, execute; **fusilazo** *m* rifle-shot; **fusilero** *m* rifleman, fusilier.

fusión *f* fusion (*a. fig.*); melting *de metal*; ⚚ merger; **fusionar(se)** [1a] fuse; ⚚ merge.

fusta *f* long whip; (*leña*) brushwood.

fustán *m* fustian.

fuste *m* wood; shaft *de arma etc.*; (*silla*) saddle tree; *de* ~ *fig.* of consequence, important.

fustigar [1h] whip, lash (*a. fig.*).

fútbol *m* football; **futbolista** *m* footballer.

futesa *f* trifle, mere nothing.

fútil trifling; **futilidad** *f* trifling nature, unimportance.

futura *f* ⚖ reversion; F fiancée; **futurismo** *m* futurism; **futuro 1.** future; **2.** *m* future (*a. gr.*); F fiancé; ~*s pl.* ⚚ futures; *en el* ~, *en lo* ~ in (the) future.

G

gabacho *m*, **a** *f* F Frenchy, froggy; Frenchified Spanish.
gabán *m* overcoat, topcoat.
gabardina *f* gaberdine; mackintosh, raincoat.
gabarra *f* lighter, barge.
gabarro *m* flaw; *vet.* pip; *fig.* error; (*estorbo*) snag.
gabinete *m* study, library; (*despacho*) office; consulting room; (*cuarto particular*) private (sitting) room; laboratory; museum; *pol.* cabinet; *de* ~ *p.* armchair *attr.*; ~ *de lectura* reading room.
gacela *f* gazelle.
gaceta *f* gazette, journal; *S.Am.* newspaper; **gacetero** *m* journalist; **gacetilla** *f* gossip column; news in brief; F gossip; **gacetillero** *m* gossip columnist; *contp.* penny-a-liner; **gacetista** *m/f* gossip.
gacilla *f C.Am.* safety pin.
gacha *f* thin paste; ~*s pl.* pap; *approx.* porridge.
gachí *f sl.* dame, girl.
gacho drooping, floppy; *borde etc.* turned down; *sombrero* slouch; *a* ~*as* on all fours.
gachón F nice, charming.
gaditano *adj. a. su. m*, **a** *f* (native) of Cadiz.
gafa *f* grapple; ~*s pl.* spectacles, glasses; **gafancia** *f* F constant bad luck; **gafar** [1a] hook, claw; F bring bad luck to, put the jinx on; **gafe:** F *ser* ~ have constant bad luck.
gaita *f* (*a.* ~ *gallega*) bagpipe; (*dulzaina*) flageolet; (*organillo*) hurdy-gurdy; *estar de* ~ be merry; **gaitero 1.** gaudy, flashy; (*alegre*) merry; **2.** *m* piper.
gaje *m* (*mst* ~*s pl.*) pay, emoluments; perquisites; ~*s pl. del oficio iro.* occupational risks.
gajo *m* (*rama*) (torn-off) branch; small cluster *de uvas*; segment *de fruta*; (*punta*) prong; *geog.* spur.
gala *f* full dress; elegance, gracefulness; *fig.* cream, flower, chief ornament; ~*s pl.* finery, trappings; *de* ~ state, (full-)dress, gala *attr.*; *hacer* ~ *de* parade, show off; glory in; *tener a* ~ *inf.* be proud to *inf.*
galafate *m* cunning thief.
galán *m* handsome fellow; ladies man; (*amante*) gallant, beau; *thea.* ~ *joven* juvenile lead; *primer* ~ leading man; **galano** smart, spruce; gaily dressed; *fig.* elegant; **galante** gallant, attentive (to women); *mujer* flirtatious; *b.s.* licentious; **galantear** [1a] court, woo; flirt with; **galanteo** *m* courting; flirtation; **galantería** *f* courtesy, compliment; gallantry; **galanura** *f* prettiness, charm, elegance.
galápago *m zo.* freshwater tortoise; *metall.* pig, ingot; (*silla*) light saddle.
galardón *m lit.* reward, prize; **galardonar** [1a] reward; *obra* give an award (*or* prize) to.
galaxia *f* galaxy.
galbana *f* laziness; shiftlessness.
galeón *m* galleon.
galeote *m* galley slave.
galera *f* ⚓, *typ.* galley; (*carro*) (covered) wagon; ⚕ hospital ward; **galerada** *f* galley (proof).
galería *f mst* gallery; (*pasillo*) passage; ~ *de tiro* shooting gallery.
galés 1. Welsh; **2.** *m* (*p.*) Welshman; (*idioma*) Welsh; **galesa** *f* Welshwoman.
galga *f* boulder.
galgo *m*, **a** *f* greyhound; F *¡échale un* ~*!* search me!
galicano Gallican; Gallic; **galicismo** *m* Gallicism; **gálico** *m* ⚕ syphilis.
galimatías *m* gibberish, double-talk; rigmarole.
galo 1. Gallic; **2.** *m*, **a** *f* Gaul.
galocha *f* clog, patten.
galón *m* braid; ⚔ stripe, chevron; **galonear** [1a] (trim with) braid.
galopada *f* gallop; **galopante** ⚕ galloping; **galopar** [1a] gallop; **galope** *m* gallop; *a* ~, *de* ~ at a gallop; in

great haste; *a ~ tendido* at full gallop; *medio ~* canter.

galopín *m* ragamuffin, urchin; (*brigón*) rogue; ⚓ cabin boy; F smart Alec.

galpón *m S.Am.* (large) shed.

galvánico galvanic; **galvanismo** *m* galvanism; **galvanizar** [1f] galvanize (*a. fig.*); electroplate; **galvanoplástico** galvanoplastic.

gallardear [1a] be graceful; bear o.s. well; **gallardete** *m* pennant, streamer; **gallardía** *f* gracefulness *etc.*; **gallardo** graceful, elegant; (*excelente*) fine; (*apuesto*) upstanding; (*bizarro*) dashing, gallant.

gallear [1a] bluster, throw one's weight about; (*descollar*) excel, stand out.

gallego *adj. a. su. m*, **a** *f* Galician.

gallera *f* cockpit.

galleta *f* biscuit; wafer; F slap; **galletero** *m* biscuit barrel.

gallina 1. *f* hen, fowl; *~ ciega* blindman's-buff; *~ de Guinea* guinea fowl; **2.** *m/f* F coward, funk; **gallinero** *m* henhouse, coop; *thea.* gods, gallery; (*voces*) babel; (*p.*) chicken farmer *que cría*; poulterer *que vende*; **gallipavo** *m* ♪ false note; **gallito** *m* cock o'-the walk; **gallo** *m* cock, rooster; ♪ false note, break in the voice; *Col.*, *C.R.*, *Mex.* strong man; *boxeo:* bantam weight; F boss; *~ de pelea* fighting cock; *alzar el ~* put on airs, brag; *tener mucho ~* F be cocky.

gama[1] *f zo.* doe.

gama[2] *f* (*letra*) gamma; ♪ scale; range, gamut *de colores etc.*; *~ de frecuencias* frequency range; *~ de ondas* wave range.

gamba *f* prawn; *sl.* 100 pesetas.

gamberrada *f* F piece of hooliganism; **gamberrear** [1a] F go around causing trouble, act like a hooligan; loaf; **gamberrismo** *m* F hooliganism; **gamberro** *m* F lout, hooligan.

gambito *m* gambit.

gamella *f* trough.

gamo *m* buck (of fallow deer).

gamuza *f zo.* chamois; (*cuero*) chamois leather, wash leather; (*trapo*) yellow duster.

gana *f* desire; appetite; inclination; *de buena ~* willingly, readily; *de mala ~* unwillingly, reluctantly, grudgingly; *dar etc. de mala ~* (be)grudge; *me da la (real) ~ de inf.* I feel like *ger.*, I want to *inf.*; *tener ~s de inf.* feel like *ger.*, care to *inf.*, have a mind to *inf.*

ganadería *f* livestock; (strain of) cattle; (*cría*) cattle raising, stock breeding; (*granja*) cattle ranch, stock farm; **ganadero** *m* stock breeder, rancher; cattle dealer; **ganado** *m* (*en general*) livestock; (*vacas*) cattle; (*rebaño*) herd, flock; *~ mayor* cattle horses and mules; *~ menor* sheep and goats; *~ porcino* pigs; *~ vacuno* cattle.

ganador 1. winning; **2.** *m*, **-a** *f* winner; **ganancia** *f* gain; ✝ profit; (*aumento*) increase; *~s pl.* winnings, earnings; *~s pl. y pérdidas* profit and loss; **ganancial** profit *attr.*; **ganancioso 1.** (*provechoso*) gainful, profitable, lucrative; (*ganador*) winning; **2.** *m*, **a** *f* gainer *en trato*; winner *en juego*.

ganapán *m* (*recadero*) messenger, porter; (*jornalero*) casual laborer; F boor.

ganar [1a] *v/t.* gain; ✝ earn; (*vencer*) win; (*obtener*) get; ⚔ conquer, take; (*llegar a*) reach; *tantos* score; *p.* (*atraer*) win over; (*vencer*) beat, outstrip (*en* at, in); *v/i.* thrive, improve.

ganchillo *m* crochet hook; crochet (work); **gancho** *m* hook; F (*p.*) tout; (*atractivo*) sex appeal, charm; *S.Am.* hairpin; **ganchoso, ganchudo** hooked.

gandul F **1.** idle, good-for-nothing, lazy; **2.** *m*, **-a** *f* loafer, good-for-nothing, slacker; **gandulear** [1a] F loaf, idle, slack; **gandulería** *f* F loafing, laziness.

ganga *f* bargain; gift F; cinch; snap.

gangoso nasal, with a twang.

gangrena *f* gangrene; **gangrenarse** [1a] become gangrenous; **gangrenoso** gangrenous.

gángster *m* gunman, gangster, mobster; **gangsterismo** *m* gangsterism; mobsterism.

ganguear [1a] speak with a (nasal) twang; **gangueo** *m* (nasal) twang.

ganoso anxious, keen (*de inf.* to *inf.*).

gansada *f* F (piece of) stupidity;

ganso 1. *m* gander; **2.** *m*, **a** *f* goose; *fig.* dolt, dope F; (*rústico*) bumpkin.

ganzúa *f* lock picker.

gañán *m* farmhand.

gañido *m* yelp, howl; **gañir** [3h] (*perro*) yelp, howl; (*ave*) croak; (*p.*) wheeze.

gañón *m* F, **gañote** *m* F throat, gullet.

garabatear [1a] hook; (*escribir*) scribble; F beat about the bush; **garabato** *m* hook, meat hook; pot-hook (*a. fig.*); (*letra*) scrawl; F sex appeal.
garaje *m* garage; **garajista** *m* garage man.
garambaina *f* tawdry finery; ~*s pl.* F grimaces; (*letra*) scrawl.
garante *m/f* guarantor; surety; **garantía** *f* guarantee; ⚖ warranty; (*prenda*) security; (*promesa*) undertaking; ~ *anticorrosión mot.* antirust warranty; **garantir** [3a; *defective*], **garantizar** [1f] guarantee, warrant, vouch for.
garañón *m* stud jackass.
garapiña *f* sugar icing; coagulated liquid; **garapiñar** [1a] ice (with sugar); (*helar*) freeze, clot; *fruta* candy; **garapiñera** *f* freezer.
garatusa: *hacer* ~*s a* coax, wheedle.
garbanzo *m* chickpea; ~ *negro fig.* black sheep.
garbeo *m* walk; promenade.
garbera *f* ⸸ shock.
garbillar [1a] ⸸ sift; ⚒ riddle, screen; **garbillo** *m* sieve, riddle.
garbo *m* jauntiness; graceful bearing; elegance; glamour, attractiveness; gallantry; generosity; **garboso** (*airoso*) jaunty; sprightly, graceful; elegant, spruce; *mujer* glamorous, attractive; generous.
garceta *f*: ~ *común* little egret.
garduña *f zo.* marten; **garduño** *m*, **a** *f* sneak thief.
garete: *al* ~ adrift.
garfa *f* claw; **garfada** *f* clawing.
garfio *m* hook; gaff; ⊕ grapple, grappling iron, claw; *mount.* climbing iron.
gargajear [1a] spit phlegm, hawk; **gargajo** *m* phlegm.
garganta *f* throat; gullet; *geog.* gorge, ravine; instep *de pie*; neck *de botella*; ♪ singing voice; **gargantear** [1a] warble, quaver; **gargantilla** *f* necklace.
gárgara *f* gargling; *hacer* ~*s* gargle; **gargarismo** *m* gargle; **gargarizar** [1f] gargle.
gárgol *m* groove.
gárgola *f* gargoyle.
garguero *m* gullet; (*traquea*) windpipe.
garita *f* cabin, hut; ⚔ sentry box; (*portería*) porter's lodge; (*atalaya*) lookout; F toilet; ~ *de señales* signal box.
garito *m* gambling den.
garlito *m* fish trap; *fig.* snare, trap; *caer en el* ~ fall into the trap; *coger en el* ~ catch in the act.
garlopa *f* jack plane.
garra *f* claw; talon; *fig.* hand; ~*s pl.* grip; *fig.* jaws; *caer en las* ~*s de* fall into the clutches of.
garrafa *f* carafe, decanter; large bottle.
garrafal enormous, terrific; *error etc.* monumental; awful.
garrapata *f zo.* tick; F disabled horse; **garrapatear** [1a] scribble, scrawl; **garrapato** *m* (*mst* ~*s pl.*) scribble, scrawl.
garrido neat, graceful; (*hermoso*) handsome, pretty.
garrocha *f* goad; *toros*: spear; *deportes*: vaulting pole.
garrón *m* spur, talon; (*pata*) paw.
garrote *m* cudgel, club; ⚕ tourniquet; garrote *para estrangular*; *dar* ~ *a* garrote; **garrotillo** *m* ⚕ croup.
garrucha *f* pulley.
garrulería *f* chatter; **garrulidad** *f* garrulity; **gárrulo** garrulous, chattering; *ave* chirping; *viento* noisy.
garúa *f S.Am.*, ⚓ drizzle; **garuar** [1e] drizzle.
garulla *f* loose grapes; F (*golfo*) urchin; (*turba*) mob, rabble.
garza *f* (*a.* ~ *real*) heron; (blue) crane; ~ *imperial* purple heron.
garzo blue(ish).
gas *m* gas; fumes; (*a.* ~ *del alumbrado*) coal gas; ~ *asfixiante* poison gas; ~*es pl. de escape* exhaust (fumes); ~ *hilarante* laughing gas; ~ *lacrimógeno* tear gas; ~ *de los pantanos* marsh gas; ~ *pobre* producer gas.
gasa *f* gauze; (*paño*) crape.
gaseiforme gaseous, gasiform; **gaseosa** *f* aerated water, mineral water; *esp.* soda (pop); soda water; fizz F; ~ *de limón* lemonade; **gaseoso** gaseous; aerated, gassy; *bebida* fizzy; **gasista** *m* gas fitter; **gas-oil** [ga'sojl] *m* diesel oil; **gasolina** *f* gasoline; **gasolinera** *f* gas station; motorboat; **gasómetro** *m* gasometer.
gastable expendable; **gastado** spent; (*usado*) worn-out; *vestido* shabby, threadbare; *fig.* outworn, hackneyed; **gastador 1.** extrava-

gant, wasteful; **2.** *m*, **-a** *f* spender, spendthrift; **3.** *m* ⚖ convict; ⚔ sapper; **gastar** [1a] *dinero* spend, expend, lay out (*en* on); (*perder*) waste; (*desgastar*) wear away, wear down, wear out; (*agotar*) use up; *ropa etc.* wear, sport; show habitually; possess; *bromas* crack; F *~las* behave, act; **~se** wear out; waste; (*agotarse*) run out; **gasto** *m* (*acto*) spending; (*lo gastado*) expenditure, expense; ☤ cost; (*desgaste*) wear; consumption; (rate of) flow *de gas etc.*; ☤ *~s pl.* expenditure, expenses; *~s pl. de acarreo* haulage; *~s pl. de explotación* operating costs; ☤ *~s pl. generales* overhead; ☤ *~s pl. menores* petty cash; *cubrir ~s* cover expenses; *meterse en ~s* (*con*) go to (the) expense (of); **gastoso** extravagant.

gástrico gastric; **gastritis** *f* gastritis; **gastroenterología** *f* gastroenterology; **gastronomía** *f* gastronomy; **gastronómico** gastronomic; **gastrónomo** *m*, **a** *f* gastronome(r), gastronomist.

gata *f* (she-)cat; F Madrid woman; *Mex.* (domestic) maid; *meteor.* hill cloud; *a ~s* on all fours; *andar a ~s* creep, crawl; **gatada** *f* sly trick; **gatear** [1a] *v/t.* claw, scratch; F pinch, swipe; *v/i.* (*subir*) clamber; (*ir a gatas*) creep, crawl.

gatillo *m* dental forceps; ⚔ trigger, hammer; *zo.* nape; F young thief.

gato *m* (tom)cat; ⊕, *mot.* jack; ⊕ grab; ☤ money bag; F sneak thief; F native of Madrid; *~ de algalia* civet cat; *~ montés* wildcat; *~ de tornillo* screw jack; *dar ~ por liebre* cheat, put one over *on s.o.*; *aquí hay ~ encerrado* there's more in this than meets the eye, I smell a rat; **gatuno** catlike, feline.

gatuperio *m* (*mezcla*) hodgepodge; (*trampa*) snare, fraud.

gaucho *S.Am.* **1.** *m* cowboy, herdsman, gaucho; **2.** gaucho *attr.*; *fig.* (*taimado*) sly; (*grosero*) coarse.

gaudeamus *m* F celebrating; merrymaking.

gaveta *f* drawer; ☤ till.

gavia *f* ✓ ditch; ⚓ topsail.

gavilán *m orn.* sparrow hawk.

gavilla *f* ✓ sheaf; (*ps.*) gang, band.

gaviota *f* (sea)gull.

gayo (*alegre*) merry; (*vistoso*) showy.

gayola *f* cage; F jail.

gaza *f* loop; ⚓ bend, bight.

gazafatón *m* F = *gazapatón*; **gazapa** *f* F fib, lie; **gazapatón** *m* F (*plancha*) bloomer; (*disparate*) piece of nonsense; **gazapera** *f* rabbit warren; F den of thieves; (*riña*) brawl; **gazapo** *m* young rabbit; (*p.*) sly fellow; (*plancha*) blunder.

gazmoñada *f*, **gazmoñería** *f* hypocrisy, cant; (*recato excesivo*) prudery; (*gravedad afectada*) demureness; **gazmoñ**(**er**)**o 1.** hypocritical, canting; strait-laced, prudish; demure; **2.** *m*, **a** *f* hypocrite; prude (*mst f*); prig.

gaznápiro *m*, **a** *f* simpleton, booby.

gaznate *m* (*garganta*) gullet; (*tráquea*) windpipe, throttle; F *remojar el ~* wet one's whistle.

gazpacho *m cold soup of oil, vinegar, garlic, onion, bread etc.*

gazuza *f* F hunger.

géiser *m geog.* geyser.

gelatina *f* gelatin(e), jelly; *~ explosiva* gelignite; **gelatinizar**(**se**) (1f) gelatinize; **gelatinoso** gelatinous.

gema *f* gem; ⚘ bud.

gemelo 1. twin; *buque* sister *attr.*; **2.** *m*, **a** *f* twin; *~s pl.* cufflinks; *opt.* field glasses, binoculars; *~s pl. de teatro* opera glasses.

gemido *m* groan; moan; wail; **gemir** [3l] groan; moan; wail; lament; (*viento, animales*) howl, whine.

Géminis *m ast., zodíaco* Gemini.

gen *m* gene.

genciana *f* gentian.

gendarme *m* gendarme; **gendarmería** *f* gendarmerie.

genealogía *f* genealogy; pedigree; **genealógico** genealogical.

generación *f* generation; (*hijos*) progeny; (*descendencia*) succession; **generador 1.** generating; **2.** *m* generator (*a.* ⚡, ⊕).

general 1. general; universal; (*corriente*) prevailing, rife; (*vasto*) wide; *en ~, por lo ~* generally, for the most part; *médico ~* general practitioner; **2.** *m* general; *~ de brigada* brigadier; *~ de división* major general; *capitán ~ de ejército* General of the Army; five-star general; **3.** *~es f/pl.* personal particulars; **generalato** *m* generalship; **generalidad** *f* generality; majority; vagueness; *~*

former Catalan government; **generalísimo** *m* generalissimo; **generalización** *f* generalization; **generalizar** [1f] generalize; make widely known, bring into general use; **~se** become general.
generar [1a] generate (*a.* ⚡); **generativo** generative.
genérico generic; **género** *m* 📖 genus; (*clase*) kind, nature; *lit.* genre; *gr.* gender; ✝ line; (*paño*) cloth, material; ~ *chico thea.* comic one-act pieces; ~ *humano* human race, mankind; *~s pl.* ✝ goods, merchandise, wares; *~s pl. de punto* knitwear.
generosidad *f* generosity; nobility; valor; **generoso** generous, liberal (*con, para* to, with); noble; magnanimous; valiant; *vino* rich, full-bodied.
genésico genetic; **génesis 1.** *f* genesis; **2.** *m* ♀ Genesis; **genética** *f* genetics; **genético** genetic.
genial inspired, of genius; (*propio del genio de uno*) in character; (*placentero*) pleasant, cheerful; **genialidad** *f* genius; temperament; eccentricity; (*una* ~) stroke of genius; **genio** *m* temper; disposition; character, nature; (*inteligencia superior*) genius; (*deidad*) spirit; *buen* ~ good nature; *mal* ~ (bad) temper; *de mal* ~ bad-tempered, ill-tempered, cross; *corto de* ~ slow-witted; *tener* ~ be temperamental.
genista *f* broom, genista.
genital genital; (*órganos*) *~es pl.* genitals; **genitivo 1.** reproductive, generative; **2.** *m* genitive (case); **genitourinario** genitourinary.
genocidio *m* genocide.
genovés *adj. a. su. m*, **-a** *f* Genoese.
gente *f* people; folk; followers; troops; nation; (*parientes*) relatives, folks F; F ~ *bien* upper-class people; well-off people; respectable people; ~ *de bien* honest folk, decent people; ~ *menuda* (*sin importancia*) small fry; (*niños*) children; (*humildes*) humble folk; *¡~ de paz!* friend!; ~ *de pelo* well-to-do folk; ~ *de medio pelo* people of limited means; ~ *principal* nobility, gentry; **gentecilla** *f* unimportant people; *contp.* riffraff; **gentil 1.** graceful, elegant; (*amable*) charming; F *iro.* remarkable, pretty; *eccl.* pagan, heathen; **2.** *m/f* gentile, heathen; **gentileza** *f* grace, charm, elegance; (*bizarría*) dash; (*ostentación*) show; politeness, courtesy; **gentilhombre** *m* † gentleman; **gentilicio** national; tribal; family *attr.*; **gentílico** heathen(ish), pagan; **gentío** *m* crowd, throng; mob; **gentualla** *f*, **gentuza** *f* rabble, mob; riffraff.
genuflexión *f* genuflection.
genuino genuine, real; pure; true.
geodesía *f* geodesy; **geofísica** *f* geophysics; **geografía** *f* geography; **geográfico** geographic(al); **geógrafo** *m* geographer; **geología** *f* geology; **geológico** geologic(al); **geólogo** *m* geologist; **geometría** *f* geometry; ~ *del espacio* solid geometry; **geométrico** geometric(al); **geopolítica** *f* geopolitics.
geranio *m* geranium.
gerencia *f* (*en general*) management; (*cargo*) managership; (*oficina*) manager's office; **gerente** *m* manager; executive.
geriatría *f* geriatrics; **geriátrico** geriatric.
germanesco slang; **germanía** *f* thieves' slang, cant.
germánico Germanic; **germano** German(ic).
germen *m biol.*, ⚘ germ; *fig.* germ, seed, source; **germicida 1.** germicidal; **2.** *m* germicide; **germinación** *f* germination; **germinal** germinal; **germinar** [1a] germinate; sprout.
gerundense *adj. a. su. m/f* (native) of Gerona.
gerundiano bombastic.
gerundio *m* gerund, present participle.
gesta *f* † heroic deed(s).
gestación *f* gestation.
gestear [1a] (*cara*) grimace; (*manos*) gesticulate; **gesticulación** *f* grimace; gesticulation; **gesticular** [1a] grimace; gesticulate.
gestión *f* negotiation; (*dirección*) management, conduct (of affairs); (*diligencia*; *esp. ~es pl.*) effort, measure, step; **gestionar** [1a] negotiate; manage; promote; (take steps to) procure.
gesto *m* (expression of one's) face; (*mueca*) grimace; gesture *con manos*; *estar de buen* (*mal*) ~ be in a good (bad) humor; *hacer ~s* make

(*or* pull) faces; gesture; *hacer un* ~ *de asco* look disgusted; *poner mal* ~ make a wry face.
gestor *m* manager; promoter; agent; **gestoría** *f* agency (for dealing with government departments).
giba *f* hump, hunch(back); F nuisance, bother; **gibar** [1a] F annoy, bother; **giboso** hunchbacked, humped.
giganta *f* giantess; ⚘ sunflower; **gigante 1.** giant, gigantic; **2.** *m* giant; **gigantesco** gigantic, giant, mammoth; **gigantón** *m*, **-a** *f* giant (carnival) figure.
gilda *f* F lollipop.
gilí *adj.* foolish; stupid.
gimnasia *f* gymnastics; physical training; ~ *respiratoria* deep breathing; **gimnasio** *m* gymnasium; **gimnasta** *m/f* gymnast; **gimnástico** gymnastic.
gimotear [1a] F whine; wail; (*lloriquear*) snivel, grizzle; **gimoteo** *m* F whining *etc.*
ginebra *f* gin; *fig.* bedlam, confusion.
ginecología *f* gynecology; **ginecológico** gynecological; **ginecólogo** *m* gynecologist.
gira *f* trip, outing; picnic *con comida*; *deportes etc.*: tour.
girado *m*, **a** *f* ⚕ drawee; **girador** *m*, **-a** *f* ⚕ drawer.
girald(**ill**)**a** *f* weathercock.
girar [1a] *v/t.* ⊕ *etc.* turn, twist, rotate; ⚕ *letra* draw, issue; *v/i.* rotate, turn (round), go round, revolve; (*esp. rápidamente*) gyrate, whirl, spin; (*de un lado a otro*) swivel, swing; (*sobre gozne*) hinge; (*sobre pivote*) pivot; spin; ⚕ do business; ⚕ ~ *a cargo de*, ~ *contra* draw on; ⚕ ~ *en descubierto* overdraw; ~ *hacia la izquierda* turn (to the) left.
girasol *m* sunflower.
giratorio gyratory; *puerta etc.* revolving; *puente etc.* swivel(ing), swing *attr.*; **giro** *m* turn (*a. fig.*); revolution, rotation, gyration; spin; *fig.* trend, course; *gr.* turn of phrase, expression; (line of) business; ⚕ draft; ⚕ ~ *en descubierto* overdraft; ~ *postal approx.* money order, postal order; *tomar otro* ~ change one's mind; **girocompás** *m* gyrocompass; **giroscópico** gyroscopic; **giroscopio** *m* gyroscope.
gitanada *f* gipsy trick; *fig.* fawning, wheedling; **gitanear** [1a] wheedle, cajole; **gitanería** *f* (*gitanos*) band of gipsies; (*dicho*) gipsy saying; (*mimos*) wheedling, cajolery; **gitanesco** gipsyish; gipsylike; gipsy *attr.*; **gitano 1.** gipsy *attr.*; (*taimado*) sly; (*zalamero*) smooth-tongued; (*insinuante*) engaging; **2.** *m*, **a** *f* gipsy.
glaciación *f* glaciation; freezing; **glacial** glacial; *viento etc.* icy, freezing; *fig.* cold, stony, indifferent; **glaciar** *m* glacier.
glacis *m* glacis.
gladiador *m* gladiator.
gladio *m*, **gladíolo** *m* gladiolus.
glándula *f* gland; **glandular** glandular; **glanduloso** glandulous.
glasear [1a] *papel etc.* glaze.
glauco light green, sea-green.
gleba *f* clod.
glicerina *f* glycerine; *nitro*~ nitroglycerine.
global global; total, overall; *cantidad* lump *attr.*; *investigación etc.* comprehensive, full; **globo** *m* globe, sphere; ~ (*aerostático*) balloon; ~ *cautivo* captive balloon; ~ *del ojo* eyeball; *en* ~ all in all, as a whole; ⚕ in bulk; **globosidad** *f* globosity; **globoso, globular** globular, spherical; **glóbulo** *m* globule; corpuscle *de sangre*.
gloria *f* glory; *una vieja* ~ a has-been; *saber a* ~ taste wonderful, be delicious; *estar en la* ~, *estar en sus* ~*s* be in one's element; **gloriarse** [1c] glory, rejoice (*en* in); boast (*de* of); **glorieta** *f* summerhouse, bower *de jardín*; circus, street intersection; **glorificación** *f* glorification; **glorificar** [1g] glorify; ~**se** glory (*de*, *en* in); **glorioso** glorious; *santo* blessed, in glory; *b.s.* proud, boastful; *la Gloriosa eccl.* the Virgin; F *the 1868 revolution.*
glosa *f* gloss; **glosar** [1a] gloss; *fig.* put an unfavorable construction on, criticize; **glosario** *m* glossary.
glosopeda *f* foot-and-mouth disease.
glotis *f* glottis.
glotón 1. gluttonous; **2.** *m*, **-a** *f* glutton, gourmand; **glotonear** [1a] gormandize; **glotonería** *f* gluttony.
glucosa *f* glucose, grape sugar.
gluglú *m* (*agua*) gurgle; (glug-)glug;

(*pavo*) gobble; *hacer* ~ gurgle; gobble; **gluglutear** [1a] (*pavo*) gobble.
glutinoso glutinous.
gnómico gnomic.
gnomo *m* gnome.
gnóstico *adj. a. su. m*, **a** *f* gnostic.
gobernable governable; ⚓ navigable; **gobernación** *f* governing, government; *Ministerio de la* ♀ *approx.* Ministry of the Interior; **gobernador 1.** governing; **2.** *m* governor; **gobernalle** *m* rudder, helm; **gobernante 1.** ruling; **2.** *m/f* ruler; **3.** *m* F (self-appointed) boss; **gobernar** [1k] *v/t.* govern, rule; (*manejar*) manage, handle; guide, direct; ⚓ steer, sail; ~ *mal* misgovern; *v/i.* govern; ⚓ handle, steer; **gobierno** *m* government; (*puesto*) governorship; control; management; guidance; ⚓ helm, steering; ~ *de la casa* housekeeping; *para tu* ~ for your guidance.
gobio *m* gudgeon.
goce *m* enjoyment; possession.
godo 1. Gothic; **2.** *m*, **a** *f* Goth; *S.Am. contp.* Spaniard; *S.Am. pol.* conservative, reactionary.
gol *m* goal (*score*).
gola *f* throat, gullet; ⚔ gorget; ⚠ ogee.
goleta *f* schooner.
golf *m* golf.
golfear [1a] loaf; live a street urchin's life; **golfería** *f* (*ps.*) street urchins; (*vida*) loafing, life in the gutter; (*mala pasada*) dirty trick; **golfillo** *m* street urchin, guttersnipe; **golfo**[1] *m* ragamuffin; little scoundrel; F loafer, tramp.
golfo[2] *m geog.* gulf, bay; open sea.
golilla *f* ruff.
golondrina *f* swallow; *empresa* ~ fly-by-night outfit; ~ *de mar* tern; **golondrino** *m* tramp; ⚔ deserter; **golondro** *m* F whim, fancy; *campar de* ~ sponge, live by one's wits.
golosina *f* tidbit (*a. fig.*), delicacy, sweet; (*cosa inútil*) bauble; (*antojo*) fancy; (*gusto por dulces*) sweet tooth; (*gula*) greed; **goloso** sweet-toothed; (*glotón*) greedy.
golpe *m* blow, knock (*a. fig.*); (*palmada*) smack; (*latido*) beat; (*choque*) shock, clash; surprise; *deportes*: stroke, hit, shot *con palo, raqueta etc.*; punch, blow *en boxeo*; kick, shot *en fútbol etc.*; (*multitud*) crowd, mass; (*pestillo*) spring lock; (*cartera*) pocket flap; ~ *bien dado* hit; ~ *de agua* heavy fall of rain; ~ *de estado* coup d'état; ~ *de fortuna* stroke of luck; ~ *franco* free-kick; ~ *de gente* crowd; ~ *de gracia* coup de grâce; ~ *de mano* ⚔ surprise attack; ~ *de mar* heavy sea, surge; ~ *maestro* masterstroke; ~ *de vista* glance; *de* ~ suddenly; abruptly; *de un* ~ at one stroke, outright; *abrir de* ~ fling open; *abrirse de* ~ fly open; *cerrar de* ~ slam; F *dar* ~ be a sensation, be a big hit; *dar* ~*s en* thump, pound (at); **golpear** [1a] *v/t.* strike, knock, hit; thump, bang *con ruido*; (*repetidamente*) beat; punch *con puño*; (*zurrar*) thrash; *v/i.* throb; ⊕ knock; **golpecito** *m* tap, rap; **golpeo** *m* knocking *etc.*; ⊕ knock; **golpete** *m* door catch; window catch; **golpeteo** *m* knocking; rattling; hammering; drumming.
gollería *f* (*golosina*) tidbit; extra, special treat.
gollete *m* throat; (*cuello*) neck (*a.* [*de botella*).
goma *f* gum; (*caucho*) rubber; (*liga*) rubber (*or* elastic) band; *S.Am.* F hangover; ~ *arábiga* gum arabic; ~ *de borrar* rubber, eraser; ~ (*elástica*) India rubber; **gomita** *f* elastic band; **gomoso 1.** gummy, sticky; **2.** *m* F dandy; dude.
góndola *f* gondola.
gong(o) *m* gong.
gorda *f* F: *hist. la* ♀ *the 1868 revolution*; *se armó la* ~ there was a great hullabaloo; *ahora nos va a tocar la* ~ now we're for it.
gordal fat, thick, big.
gordi(n)flón F pudgy, fat, chubby.
gordo 1. fat; *p. a.* stout, plump; (*craso*) greasy, oily; (*grande*) big; *premio* first, big; (*basto*) coarse, gross; *agua* hard; *traje de hombre* portly; *algo* ~ something really big; *hablar* ~ talk big; **2.** *m* fat, suet; F first prize; F *fig. sacarse el* ~ bring home the bacon; **gordura** *f* corpulence, stoutness; (*grasa*) grease, fat.
gorgojo *m* weevil, grub; *fig.* dwarf.
gorgoritear [1a] F trill, warble; **gorgorito** *m* F trill, quaver.
gorgotear [1a] gurgle; **gorgoteo** *m* gurgle.

gorguera *f* ruff; ⚔ gorget.
gorigori *m* F dirge, wailing racket.
gorila *m* gorilla; F tough, thug; strong-arm man.
gorja *f* gorge, throat; F *estar de* ~ be very cheerful.
gorjear [1a] warble, chirp, twitter; **~se** (*niño*) gurgle, crow; **gorjeo** *m* warble *etc.*
gorra 1. *f* (peaked) cap; bonnet; ~ *de visera* peaked cap; **2.** *m* (*a.* **gorrero** *m*) freeloader; sponger; F *colarse de* ~ gate-crash; F *ir etc.* de ~ scrounge, sponge; **gorrear** [1a] F sponge; freeload.
gorrinería *f* dirt; *fig.* dirty trick; **gorrino** *m*, **a** *f* small pig; hog (*a. fig.*).
gorrión *m* sparrow.
gorrista *m/f* F sponger.
gorro *m* cap; bonnet; ~ *de baño* bathing cap; ~ *de dormir* nightcap.
gorrón[1] *m* pebble; ⊕ pivot, journal.
gorrón[2] *m* F cadger, sponger; **gorronear** [1a] F scrounge, cadge, sponge.
gota *f* drop; bead, blob; ⚕ gout; ~ *a* ~ drop by drop; *caer a* ~ drip; *parecerse como dos* ~*s de agua* be as like as two peas in a pod; **goteado** speckled; **gotear** [1a] drip; dribble; trickle (*a. fig.*); (*vela*) gutter; ~**(se)** leak; **goteo** *m* drip(ping) *etc.*; **gotera** *f* leak; drip(ping); (*cenefa*) valence; ⚕ ailment; *lleno de* ~*s p.* full of aches and pains; **goteras** *f/pl. Col.* environs, outskirts.
gótico Gothic; *fig.* noble.
gotita *f* droplet.
gotoso gouty.
gozar [1f] *v/t.* enjoy; possess, have; *v/i.* enjoy o.s.; ~ de = *v/t.*; **~se** rejoice; ~ *en inf.* take pleasure in *ger.*
gozne *m* hinge.
gozo *m* joy, gladness; pleasure, delight, enjoyment; *un* ~ *para la retina* a joy to see, a sight for sore eyes; F *¡mi* ~ *en el pozo!* I'm sunk; *no caber de* ~ be beside o.s. with joy; **gozoso** glad, joyful (*con, de* about, over).
grabación *f* recording; ~ *en, de, sobre cinta* tape recording; **grabado** *m* engraving, print; (*esp. en libro*) illustration, picture; ~ *al agua fuerte* etching; ~ *al agua tinta* aquatint; ~ *en cobre* copperplate; ~ *en madera* woodcut; **grabador** *m* engraver; **grabadora** *f* recorder; ~ *de cinta* tape recorder; **grabador-reproductor** *m* cassette player; **grabadura** *f* engraving; **grabar** [1a] engrave; record *en disco etc.*; tape-record *en, sobre cinta*; *fig.* engrave, imprint; ~ *algo en el ánimo* impress s.t. on one's mind.
gracejo *m* wit, humor; repartee (*en contestar*).
gracia 1. *f* grace (*a. eccl.*); favor, pardon; gracefulness, attractiveness; (*agudeza*) wit; (*chiste*) joke; (*esencia de chiste*) point; F name; *¿cuál es su* ~*?* what's your name?; *¡qué* ~*!* what a nerve!, the very idea!; *de* ~ free, for nothing; *en* ~ *a* on account of, for the sake of; *sin* ~ graceless; *caer en* ~ *a* find favor with, make a hit with F; *dar en la* ~ *de decir* harp on; *hacerle a uno* ~ strike s.o. as funny; *tener* ~ be funny, be surprising; **2.** ~*s pl.* thanks; *¡*~*s!* thank you!; *muchas* ~*s* many thanks, thanks very much; ~*s a* thanks to; *¡*~*s a Dios!* thank goodness!; *¡y* ~*s! iro.* and be thankful!; *dar las* ~*s a* thank; **graciable** gracious; affable; (*fácil de conceder*) easily granted; **grácil** slender; small; delicate; **gracioso 1.** (*elegante*) graceful; (*afable*) gracious; attractive; (*agudo*) witty; (*divertido*) funny, amusing; (*gratuito*) free; *lo* ~ *del caso es que* the funny thing about it is that; **2.** *m thea.* fool, funny man.
grada *f* step *de escalera*; *thea. etc.* tier, row (of seats; grandstand, bleachers; ⚓ slipway, slips; ✓ harrow; ~ *de discos* disk harrow; **gradación** *f* gradation; *rhet.* climax; *gr.* comparison; **gradar** [1a] harrow; **gradas** *f/pl.* stone steps; (*Chile, Peru*) atrium; ~ *al aire libre* bleachers; **gradería** *f* flight of steps; *thea. etc.* rows of seats, tiers.
grado *m* (*peldaño*) step; *univ.*, ⅄, *phys. a. fig.* degree; (*nivel*) level; (*rango*) grade, rank; *escuela*: class, year; ~*s pl. eccl.* minor orders; ~ *de elaboración* stage of production; *de* (*buen*) ~ willingly; *de* ~ *en* ~ by degress; *de* ~ *o por fuerza* willy-nilly; *de mal* ~, (*a*) *mal mi etc.* ~ unwillingly; *en sumo* ~ to a great extent.
graduable adjustable; **graduación** *f* gradation; graduation; grading; ⚔ rank; alcoholic strength; **graduado** *m*, **a** *f* graduate; **gradual** gradual;

graduando *m*, **a** *f* (*persona próxima a graduarse en la universidad*) graduate; **graduar** [1e] (*clasificar*) grade; *termómetro etc.* graduate; (*medir*) gauge, measure; ⊕ calibrate; *vista* test; *univ.* confer a degree (⚔ rank) on; **~se** graduate, take one's degree (*en* in); ⚔ take a commission; *~ de* receive the degree of.
grafía *f* graph.
gráfica *f* graph; **gráfico 1.** graphic (*a. fig.*); pictorial, illustrated; **2.** *m* ⚗ graph; chart; diagram; (*horario*) timetable; *~ de temperatura* temperature chart.
grafito *m* graphite, blacklead.
grafología *f* graphology.
gragea *f* colored candy; sugar-coated pill.
grajear [1a] caw; (*niño*) gurgle; **grajilla** *f* jackdaw; **grajo** *m* rook.
grama *f* grass.
gramática *f* grammar; F *~ parda* native wit; **gramatical** grammatical; **gramático 1.** grammatical; **2.** *m* grammarian.
gramo *m* gram, *British* gramme.
gramófono *m*, **gramola** *f* Gramophone, phonograph.
gran *v. grande.*
grana[1] *f* ⚘ seeding; (*época*) seeding-time; (*semilla*) small seed; *dar en ~* go (*or* run) to seed.
grana[2] *f zo.* cochineal; kermes; (*color*) scarlet; (*paño*) scarlet cloth; *de ~* scarlet.
granada *f* ⚘ pomegranate; ⚔ grenade *de mano*, shell *de cañón*; *~ de mano* hand grenade; *~ de metralla* shrapnel; *~ extintora* fire extinguisher; *~ fallida* dud; *a prueba de ~* shell-proof; **granadero** *m* grenadier.
granadilla *f* passionflower.
granadina *f* grenadine.
granadino *adj. a. su. m*, **a** *f* (native) of Granada.
granado[1] *m* ⚘ pomegranate tree.
granado[2] notable, distinguished; select; mature; (*alto*) tall; *lo más ~* the pick.
granar [1a] run to seed.
granate *m* garnet.
granazón *f* seeding.
grande 1. big, large; (*a. fig.*) great; (*grandioso*) grand; *número, velocidad* high; (*alto*) tall; *en ~* as a whole; on a large scale, in a big way; F *estar en ~* be going strong; F *pasarlo en ~* have a whale of a time; F *vivir en ~* live in style; **2.** *m ~* (*de España*) grandee; *los ~s* the great; **grandemente** greatly; extremely; **grandeza** *f* bigness; greatness; (*grandiosidad*) grandeur; (*tamaño*) size; (*nobleza*) nobility; **grandilocuencia** *f* grandiloquence; **grandílocuo** grandiloquent; **grandiosidad** *f* grandeur, magnificence; **grandioso** magnificent, grand; (*esp. b.s.*) grandiose; **grandor** *m* size; **grandote** F whacking big; **grandullón** overgrown, oversize.
graneado granulated; **granear** [1a] *semilla* sow; *cuero* grain; (*puntear*) stipple; **granel:** *a ~* (*sin orden*) at random; (*en montón*) in a heap; ⚓ in bulk, loose; *dar* in abundance, lavishly; **granero** *m* granary (*a. fig.*); **granilla** *f* grain (in cloth).
granítico granite *attr.*; **granito** *m* granite; ⚕ pimple.
granizada *f* hailstorm; hail (*a. fig.*); = **granizado** *m* iced drink; **granizar** [1f] hail; *fig.* shower; **granizo** *m* hail.
granja *f* farm; farmhouse; (*quinta*) country house; (*vaquería*) dairy; *~ avícola* poultry farm.
granjear [1a] gain, earn; win; **~se** *algo* win (for o.s.).
granjería *f* farming; farm earnings; profit; **granjero** *m* farmer.
grano *m* grain (*a. pharm.*); (*semilla*) seed; (*baya*) berry; bean *de café*; (*partícula*) speck; ⚕ pimple, spot; ⚘ *~s pl.* grain, cereals; *con un ~ de sal* with a pinch of salt; *ir al ~* come to the point, get down to brass tacks; **granoso** granular.
granuja *m* ragamuffin, urchin; rogue, scoundrel; *f* loose grape; grape seed.
granujiento, granujoso pimply.
granujo *m* F pimple.
granulación *f* granulation; **granular** granular; **granular(se)** [1a] granulate; **gránulo** *m* granule.
grapa *f* clip; paper fastener; staple *de dos puntas*; ⚠ cramp.
grasa *f* fat; (*unto*) grease; (*sebo*) suet; (*aceite*) oil; (*mugre*) filth; ⚒ *~s pl.* slag; *~ de ballena* blubber; **grasiento** greasy, oily; filthy; **graso 1.** fatty; greasy; **2.** *m* fattiness; greasiness.

grata *f* ✝ favor; wire brush; **gratificación** *f* (*premio*) reward; (*propina*) tip, gratuity; bounty; indulgence; **gratificar** [1g] tip; reward; (*dar gusto*) gratify; *deseo* indulge; *se gratificará* (*anuncios*) a reward is offered; **gratis** free (of charge), for nothing, gratis; **gratitud** *f* gratitude; **grato** pleasing, pleasant; welcome, gratifying; (*agradecido*) grateful; *nos es ~ informarle* we are pleased to inform you; **gratuito** free; *observación etc.* gratuitous, uncalled-for; *acusación* unfounded; **gratulatorio** congratulatory.

grava *f* gravel; crushed stone; metal *de camino.*

gravamen *m* obligation; burden; (*carga*) encumbrance; *impuestos*: assessment; **gravar** [1a] encumber, burden; *impuestos*: assess; **gravativo** burdensome.

grave (*de peso*) heavy; *fig.* grave, serious; important, momentous; *enfermedad* grave; *herida, pérdida* grievous, severe; *p.* sedate, dignified; ♪ low, deep; *gr. palabra* paroxitone; *acento* grave; *estar ~* be critically ill; **gravedad** *f* gravity (*a. phys.*) *etc.*; *herido de ~* severely injured (*or* wounded); *~ nula* weightlessness, zero gravity.

grávido pregnant (*a. fig.*).

gravitación *f* gravitation; **gravitacional** gravitational; **gravitar** [1a] *phys. etc.* gravitate; *~ sobre* (*descansar*) rest on; (*pesar*) weigh down on; *fig.* be a burden to; **gravitatorio** gravitational; **gravoso** onerous; oppressive, burdensome; ✝ costly; (*molesto*) tiresome; *ser ~ a* weigh on.

graznar [1a] squawk; (*grajo*) caw, croak; (*ganso*) cackle; (*pato*) quack; **graznido** *m* squawk *etc.*

greco 1. Greek; 2. *m*, **a** *f* Greek.

greda *f geol.* clay; (*de batán*) fuller's earth; **gredoso** clayey.

gregario gregarious; herd *attr.*; (*servil*) slavish.

gremial 1. guild *attr.*; trade(s) union *attr.*; 2. *m* guild member; trade unionist; **gremio** *m* guild, corporation; association; (*obrero*) trade(s) union.

greña *f* (*mst pl.*) shock (*or* mat, mop) of hair; *fig.* entanglement, tangle; *andar a la ~* squabble; **greñudo** dishevelled.

gres *m geol.* potter's clay; (*loza*) earthenware, stoneware.

gresca *f* (*jaleo*) uproar, hubbub; (*riña*) row, brawl.

grey *f eccl.* flock, congregation.

grial *m* Grail.

griego **1.** Greek; **2.** *m*, **a** *f* Greek; F cheat; **3.** *m* (*idioma*) Greek; *fig.* gibberish, double Dutch.

grieta *f* fissure, crack; crevice; chink; chap *en piel*; **grietado** **1.** crackled; **2.** *m* crackleware; **grietarse** [1a] = *agrietarse.*

grifo **1.** kinky, tangled; ✝ script; *Mex.* drunk; **2.** *m* faucet, spigot; *lit.* griffin; *S.Am.* gas station; *Mex.* marijuana; (*servido*) *al ~* on tap, (on) draft.

grilla *f* female cricket; ⚡ grid; *S.Am.* fight, quarrel; *S.Am.* annoyance, bother; F *ésa es ~* (*y no canta*) that's a cock-and-bull story.

grillete *m* fetter, shackle.

grillo *m zo.* cricket; ⚘ shoot, sprout; *~s pl.* fetters, irons; *fig.* shackles.

grima *f* annoyance; horror; *me da ~* it gets on my nerves; (*escalofrío*) it gives me the shivers.

grímpola *f* pennant.

gringo *m*, **a** *f contp.* foreigner (*mst N. American*); F *hablar en ~* talk nonsense.

gripe *f* influenza, 'flu.

gris **1.** gray; *día* dull, gloomy; **2.** *m* gray; F *hace ~* there's a nasty cold wind; **grisáceo** grayish.

grisú *m* ⚒ firedamp.

grita *f* uproar, outcry; *dar ~ a* hoot, boo; **gritar** [1a] shout, yell, cry out; (*desaprobar*) hoot; (*bramar*) bellow; **gritería** *f*, **griterío** *m* shouting, uproar; **grito** *m* shout, yell; cry; hoot; bellow; scream; call; *a ~ herido, a ~ pelado, a voz en ~* at the top of one's voice; F *poner el ~ en el cielo* kick up a great fuss; **gritón** screaming, shouting.

groenlandés **1.** Greenland *attr.*; **2.** *m*, **-a** *f* Greenlander.

grosella *f* (red) currant; *~ espinosa, ~ silvestre* gooseberry; **grosellero** *m* currant bush; *~ silvestre* gooseberry bush.

grosería *f* coarseness *etc.*; (*dicho*)

rude thing; **grosero** (*basto*) coarse, rough; discourteous, rude; indelicate, gross; vulgar; (*zafio*) loutish; **grosor** *m* thickness; **grosura** *f* fat; (*régimen*) meat diet.
grotesco grotesque, bizarre, absurd.
grúa *f* ⊕ crane; derrick; ~ *de auxilio* wrecking crane; ~ *de caballete* gantry crane; ~ *puente* overhead crane.
gruesa *f* gross.
grueso 1. thick; (*corpulento*) fat; *p.* stout, thick-set; (*abultado*) large, bulky; (*basto*) coarse; (*poco agudo*) dull; *artillería, mar* heavy; **2.** *m* (*grosor*) thickness; (*bulto*) bulk; (*parte principal*) major portion; ⚔ main body; *el ~ del pelotón carreras*: the ruck; *en ~* in bulk.
grulla *f orn.* (*a. ~ común*) crane.
grumete *m* cabin boy.
grumo *m* clot *de sangre*; dollop; cluster *de uvas*; ~ *de leche* curd; **grumoso** clotted, lumpy.
gruñido *m* grunt; growl; snarl; **gruñir** [3h] (*esp. cerdo*) grunt; (*perro, oso*) growl, snarl; *fig.* grumble; (*puerta etc.*) creak; **gruñón** F grumpy.
grupa *f* croup, rump, horse's hindquarters; **grupada** *f* squall; **grupal** group; **grupera** *f* pillion.
grupo *m* group (*a. pol.*); cluster, bunch F; clump *de árboles*; ⊕ unit, set; ~ *electrógeno* generating set, power plant; ~ *de presión* pressure group.
grupúsculo *m* splinter group.
gruta *f* cavern, grotto.
guaca *f S.Am.* Indian tomb; buried treasure; **guacamayo** *m* macaw.
guaco *m S.Am. zo.* curassow (*kind of turkey*).
guachapear [1a] *v/t.* paddle in, splash; *fig.* botch, bungle; *v/i.* rattle, clatter.
guacho *S.Am.* motherless, orphaned; *zapato etc.* odd.
guadal *m S.Am.* bog; dune.
guadamecí *m* embossed leather.
guadaña *f* scythe; **guadañadora** *f* mowing machine; **guadañar** [1a] scythe, mow; **guadañero** *m* mower.
guagua *f* trifle; *S.Am.* bus; (*rorro*) baby; *de ~* free, for nothing.
gualdo yellow, golden.
gualdrapa *f* trappings; F tatter.
guano *m* guano.
guantada *f*, **guantazo** *m* slap; **guante** *m* glove; ~*s pl. fig.* tip, commission; ~ *con puño* gauntlet glove; ~*s pl. de cabritilla* kid gloves; *como un ~ ajustarse* like a glove; *convenir* down to the ground; *arrojar* (*recoger*) *el ~* throw down (take up) the gauntlet; F *echar el ~ a* lay hands on, seize; *echar un ~* make a collection (*a beneficio de* for); **guantelete** *m* gauntlet; **guantero** *m*, **a** *f* glover.
guapear [1a] F swagger; cut a dash; bluster; **guapetón** F very good-looking; (*bizarro*) dashing; (*ostentoso*) flashy; **guapeza** *f* prettiness; dash *etc.*; **guapo 1.** *mujer* pretty; *hombre* handsome; good-looking; (*aseado*) smart; (*ostentoso*) flashy; (*valiente*) dashing, bold; **2.** *m* F lover, gallant; (*matón*) bully; (*fanfarrón*) braggart; (*elegante*) swell.
guarda 1. *m* guard; keeper, custodian; ~ *de coto* gamekeeper; ~ *de la aduana* customhouse officer; ~ *forestal* forest ranger; **2.** *f* guard(ing); (safe) keeping, custody; observance *de ley*; flyleaf, end paper *de libro*; ward *de cerradura*; guard *de espada* (*a.* ⊕).
guarda...: ~barro(s) *m* mudguard; **~bosque** *m* ranger, forester; gamekeeper; **~brisa** *m mot.* windshield; **~cabo** *m* ⚓ thimble; **~cenizas** *m* ash pan; **~costas** *m* coastguard.
guardador watchful; (*tacaño*) stingy.
guarda...: ~espaldas *m* henchman, bodyguard; **~fango** *m* mudguard; **~frenos** *m* brake(s)man; **~fuego** *m* fire guard; fender; **~lmacén** *m/f* storekeeper; **~lodos** *m* mudguard; **~mano** *m* guard (*of sword*); **~meta** *m* goalkeeper; **~muebles** *m* furniture repository; **~pelo** *m* locket; **~polvo** *m* dust cover, dust sheet; (*vestido*) dust coat; overall(s).
guardar [1a] (*retener*) keep; (*proteger*) guard (*de* against, from); preserve, save (*de* from); (*poner aparte*) put away, lay by; (*vigilar*) watch; *ganado* tend; *fiesta, mandamiento* observe; *¡guarda!* look out!; **~se** *de* avoid; look out for; ~ *de inf.* keep from *ger.*, avoid *ger.*, guard against *ger.*; F *~la a* have it in for.

guardarropa 1. *m* checkroom; (*mueble*) wardrobe; **2.** *m/f* checkroom attendant; **guardarropía** *f thea.* wardrobe; (*accesorios*) properties, props F; *de ~* make-believe, fake.
guardavía *m* 🚂 linesman.
guardia 1. *f* (⚔ *servicio, regimiento, esgrima*) guard; police; custody, care; defense, protection; ⚓ watch; *~ civil* rural policeman; *~ marina* midshipman; *~ urbano* policeman; *~s pl. montadas* horse guards; *~ municipal* town police; *~ real* household troops; *en ~* on guard; *estar de ~* be on guard, be on duty; keep watch; *montar la ~* mount guard; *relevar la ~* change guard; **2.** *m* ⚔ guard(sman); policeman; *~s pl. de asalto* shock troops; *~ civil* civil guard; *~ marina* midshipman.
guardián *m*, **-a** *f* keeper, custodian; warden; (*vigilante*) watchman.
guardilla *f* attic, garret.
guardoso careful; *b.s.* niggardly.
guarecer [2d] shelter, protect, take in; preserve; **~se** shelter, take refuge (de from).
guarida *f zo.* lair, den; (*refugio*) shelter, cover; hideout, haunt *de p.*
guarismo *m* figure, numeral.
guarnecer [2d] (*adornar*) garnish, embellish (de with); equip, provide (de with); ⚔ man, garrison; *sew.* trim; *frenos* line; *pared* plaster; *joya* set; **guarnecido** *m* plaster; **guarnición** *f* equipment, provision; fitting; ⚔ garrison; ⊕ packing; *sew.* trimming, binding; lining *de frenos*; setting *de joya*; guard *de espada*; *~es pl.* harness *de caballo*; fittings, fixtures; *~es pl. del alumbrado* light fixtures; **guarnicionar** [1a] garrison; **guarnicionero** *m* harness maker.
guarra *f* sow; **guarro 1.** *m* pig; **2.** filthy.
guasa *f* F (*sosería*) dullness; (*burla*) joke; badinage, kidding; **de ~** jokingly.
guasearse [1a] F joke, kid, rag; **guaso** *S.Am.* coarse, uncouth; **guasón** *m*, **-a** *f* F joker, tease; (*lerdo*) dolt.
guatemalteco *adj. a. su. m*, **a** *f* Guatemalan.
guateque *m* F do, party, celebration.
guau 1. bow-wow!; **2.** *m* bark.
guayaba *f* guava (jelly).
guayacán *m* lignum vitae.
gubernamental 1. governmental; loyalist; **2.** *m/f* loyalist; **gubernativo** governmental.
gubia *f* gouge.
guedeja *f* long hair, lock; mane *de león.*
guerra *f* war; warfare; conflict, struggle, fight; *~ atómica* atomic warfare; *~ bacteriológica*, *~ bacteriana* germ warfare; *~ fría* cold war; *~ de guerrillas* guerrilla warfare; *~ mundial* world war; *~ de nervios* war of nerves; *~ nuclear* nuclear war; *~ relámpago* blitzkrieg; *~ a tiros* shooting war, hot war; *de ~* military, war *attr.*; *Ministerio de ≗* War Department; *en ~ con* at war with; *dar ~ a* (*molestar*) be a nuisance to, annoy; (*bromear*) rag; *hacer la ~* make war (*a* on); **guerrear** [1a] wage war, fight; *fig.* resist, put up a fight; **guerrero 1.** fighting; war *attr.*; warlike, martial; **2.** *m* warrior, soldier, fighter; **guerrilla** *f* guerrilla band, band of partisans; **guerrillero** *m* guerrilla, partisan, irregular.
guía 1. *m/f* (*p.*) guide; leader; adviser; **2.** *m* ⚔ marker; **3.** *f* (⊕, *fig.*, *libro*) guide; (*acto*) guidance; guide book, handbook; guide post; handlebars *de bicicleta*; (*caballo*) leader; *~s pl.* reins; *cine*: *~ sonora* sound track; *~ telefónica*, *~ de teléfonos* telephone directory; *~ del viajero* guide book; *~ vocacional* vocational guidance;
guiar [1c] guide; lead; manage; *planta* train; ⚓ *etc.* steer; *mot.* drive; ✈ pilot; **~se** *por* go by, be guided (*or* ruled) by.
guija *f* pebble; cobble *de calle*; **guijarral** *m* stony place; shingle *de playa*; **guijarro** *m* pebble; boulder; cobblestone; **guijarroso** *playa* pebbly, shingly; *terreno* boulder-strewn; **guijo** *m* (*grava*) gravel; granite chips *para carretera*; shingle *de playa.*
guillame *m* rabbet plane.
guillotina *f* guillotine (*a.* ⊕); **guillotinar** [1a] guillotine.
guinda *f* morello cherry.
guindaleza *f* hawser.
guindar [1a] hang on high; F pinch, swipe, snaffle.
guindilla *m* F cop, policeman.

guindola *f* lifebuoy.
guiñada *f* wink; blink; ⚓ yaw.
guiñapo *m* rag, tatter; (*p.*) ragamuffin.
guiñar [1a] wink; blink; ⚓ yaw; **guiño** *m* wink; *hacer* ~*s a* wink at, make eyes at.
guión *m* (*p. etc.*) leader; *typ.* hyphen, dash; (*escrito*) explanatory text, handout F; *cine*: script, scenario; *eccl.* processional cross (*or* banner); royal standard; ~ *de codornices* corncrake; **guionista** *m/f* script writer.
guirigay *m* gibberish, jargon; (*ruido*) hubbub.
guirnalda *f* garland, chaplet; wreath *esp. de entierro*.
guisa: *a* ~ de as, like, in the manner of; *de tal* ~ in such a way.
guisado *m* stew; **guisante** *m* pea; ~ *de olor* sweet pea; **guisar** [1a] (*cocinar*) cook; (*hervir*) stew; *fig.* prepare, arrange; **guiso** *m* cooked dish; seasoning; **guisote** *m* F *contp.* hash.
guita *f* twine; *sl.* dough, lolly.
guitarra *f* guitar; **guitarrista** *m/f* guitarist.
gula *f* gluttony; **gulusmear** [1a] (*comer*) nibble titbits; (*oler*) sniff the cooking.
gurrumino F **1.** uxorious; **2.** *m* henpecked husband.
gusanillo *m*: F *andarle a uno el* ~ be peckish; F *matar el* ~ take a nip first thing in the morning; **gusano** *m* worm; maggot, grub; caterpillar *de mariposa etc.*; *fig.* meek creature; ~ *de luz* glowworm; ~ *de seda* silkworm; ~ *de tierra* earthworm; **gusanoso** worm-eaten, maggoty.
gustación *f* tasting, trying; **gustar** [1a] *v/t.* taste, try, sample; *v/i.* please, be pleasing; *la comedia no gustó* the play was not much liked, the play was a flop; *me gustan los plátanos* I like bananas; *¿te gustaría ir a Madrid?* would you like to go to Madrid?; *¿te gustó la comedia?* did you enjoy the play?; *si Vd. gusta* if you don't mind; *¿Vd. gusta?* would you care for some?; *como Vd. guste* as you wish; ~ *de inf.* be fond of *ger.*, have a taste for *ger.*, enjoy *ger.*; **gustazo** *m* great (*or* fiendish) pleasure; **gustillo** *m* suggestion, touch, tang.
gusto *m* taste; (*sabor*) flavor; (*placer*) pleasure; (*afición*) liking (*por* for); (*capricho*) fancy, whim; *¡tanto* ~*!* how do you do?; *a* ~ at will; (*a sus anchas*) at ease, in comfort; *encontrarse a* ~ be happy, like it (here *etc.*); *al* ~ to taste; *a* ~ *de* to the liking of; *con mucho* ~ gladly, with pleasure; *de buen* (*mal*) ~ in good (bad) taste; *dar* ~ *a* please; *ser del* ~ *de* be to the liking of; *tanto* ~ glad to meet you; *tener* ~ *en inf.* be glad to *inf.*; *tengo mucho* ~ *en conocerle* I'm very glad to meet you; *tomar* ~ *a* take a liking to; **gustoso** (*sabroso*) tasty, savory; (*agradable*) pleasant; *lo haré* ~ I'll do it with pleasure.
gutapercha *f* gutta-percha.
gutural guttural, throaty.

H

ha *v. haber.*
¡ha! ah!
haba *f* (broad) bean; lima bean; *en todas partes cuecen ~s* it's the same the whole world over; *son ~s contadas* it's a certainty.
habano *m* Havana (cigar).
hábeas corpus *m* habeas corpus.
haber 1. [2k] *v/t.* catch, lay hands on; † have; *bien haya* blessed be; *que Dios haya* God rest his *etc.* soul; *habidos y por haber* present and future; *v/aux.* have; *~ de inf.* have to *inf*; must *inf.*; be (due) to *inf.*; *¿qué he de hacer?* what am I to do?, what must I do?; *ha de ser tonto* he must be a fool; *ha de cantar esta noche* he is to sing tonight; *verbo impersonal*: hay: (*sg.*) there is, (*pl.*) there are; *hay sol* it is sunny; *¿cuánto hay de aquí a Madrid?* how far is it to Madrid?; *¡no hay de qué!* you're welcome!, don't mention it!; *¿qué hay?* what's the matter?; *¿hay plátanos?* (*en tienda*) do you have any bananas?; *años ha* years ago; *habrá ocho días* about a week ago; *~ que inf.* be necessary to *inf.*; *hay que comer para vivir* one must eat to live; *no hay que decírselo* there's no need to tell him; he mustn't be told; **~se:** *tener que habérselas con* have to deal with, be up against; **2.** *m* property, goods (*mst ~es pl.*); income; ☤ assets, credit (side).
habichuela *f* kidney bean; *~ verde* string bean.
hábil clever, skillful; proficient, expert, good (*en* at); capable; *b.s.* cunning; fit (*para* for); ⚖ competent; **habilidad** *f* cleverness, skill *etc.*; **habilidoso** clever; **habilitación** *f* qualification; financing; equipment; **habilitado** *m* paymaster; **habilitar** [1a] enable, capacitate; entitle, qualify; empower; equip, fit out; ☤ *p.* finance.
habitable (in)habitable; **habitación** *f* (*cuarto*) room; (*morada*) dwelling, habitation; residence; (*alojamiento*) lodging(s); *biol.* habitat; *~ doble* double room; *~ individual* single room; *~ lacustre* lake dwelling; **habitante** *m* inhabitant; occupant *de casa*; **habitar** [1a] *v/t.* inhabit, live in, dwell in; *casa* occupy; *v/i.* live, dwell; **habitat** *m* habitat.
hábito *m todos sentidos*: habit; F *ahorcar* (*or colgar*) *los ~s* leave the priesthood; *tomar el ~* enter religion; take holy orders.
habituado *m*, **a** *f* habitué; **habitual** habitual, customary; *mst b.s.* inveterate; *criminal* hardened; regular; **habituar** [1e] habituate, accustom (*a* to); **~se** *a* become accustomed to, get used to.
habla *f* (*facultad*) speech; (*idioma*) language; (*regional*) dialect, speech; talk, speech *de clase, profesión etc.*; *al ~* in communication, in conversation; speaking; *teleph.* speaking, on the line; ⚓ within hail; *de ~ española* Spanish-speaking; *dejar sin ~* dumbfound; *negar* (*or quitar*) *el ~ a* not be on speaking terms with; *perder el ~* be speechless; **hablado:** *bien ~* well-spoken; *mal ~* coarse, rude; (*indecente*) foul-mouthed; **hablador 1.** talkative; **2.** *m*, **-a** *f* talker, chatterbox; (*y chismoso*) gossip; **habladuría** *f* rumor; bragging; malicious remark; (*chismes*) idle chatter, (piece of) gossip; **hablanchín** F, **hablantín** F talkative, chatty; **hablante 1.** speaking; **2.** *m/f* speaker.
hablar [1a] speak, talk (*con* to); *habla bien el español, pero habla tonterías* he speaks Spanish well, but he talks nonsense; *que hable él* let him have his say; *¡ni ~!* no fear!, not likely!, the very idea!; *~ alto* speak up; *~ claro* talk straight from the shoulder; *~lo todo* talk too much; *~ por (sólo) ~* talk for the sake of talking; *estar hablando* (*retrato*) be a speaking likeness; **~se:** *se habla español* Spanish (is) spoken here; *se habla de inf.* there is talk of

ger.; *no nos hablamos* we are not on speaking terms.

hablilla *f* rumor; idle gossip, tittle-tattle.

hacedero practicable, feasible; **hacedor** *m*, **-a** *f* maker; ♀ Maker.

hacendado **1.** landed, property owning; **2.** *m*, **a** *f* landowner, man *etc.* of property; *S.Am.* rancher; **hacendero** industrious, thrifty; **hacendista** *m* economist, financial expert; **hacendoso** diligent, hard-working; bustling, busy.

hacer [2s] **1.** *v/t.* a) make; create; ⊕ manufacture; ⚠ build, construct; compose, fashion, form; b) do; perform; practice; put into practice, execute; cause; compel, oblige; effect; (*proveer*) provide (*con*, *de* with); accustom (*a* to); suppose *a. p.* to be; c) Ꜭ amount to, make; *apuesta* lay; ✝ *balance* strike; *cama* make; *comedia* perform, do; *comida* prepare, cook, get; *corbata* tie; *dinero* earn, make; *discurso* make, deliver; *guerra* wage; *humo* give off, produce; *maleta* pack; *objeción* raise; *papel* play, act, take; *pregunta* put, pose; *prodigios* work; *sombra* cast; *visita* pay; d) ~ *adj.* turn *adj.*, render *adj.*, send (*esp. p.* F) *adj.*; e) ~ *inf.* have (*or* make) *a p. inf.*; have (*or* get) *s.t. p.p.*; *hágale entrar* show him in, have him come in; *me hago cortar el pelo* I have (*or* get) my hair cut; ~ *que subj.* see to it that; f) ~ *bien* do good; ~ *bien* (*mal*) *en inf.* be right (wrong) to *inf.*; ~ *bueno acusación* make good; F *la ha hecho buena* he's made a hash of it; *te hacíamos en Madrid* we thought (*or* supposed) you were in Madrid; *nos hizo con dinero* he provided us with money; *¿qué (le) hemos de ~?* what's to be done (about it)?; *tener que* ~ have s.t. to do; **2.** *v/i.* be important, matter, signify; (*convenir*) be suitable, be fitting; ~ *a todo* (*p.*) be good for anything; *la llave hace a las dos puertas* the key fits (*or* does for) both doors; ~ *que hacemos* pretend to be busy; *¿hace?* will it do?, is it a go? F; *no le hace* never mind, it doesn't matter; ~ *como que*, ~ *como si* act as if; ~ *de* act as; ~ *para inf.*, ~ *por inf.* make to *inf.*; try to *inf.*; *dar que* ~ give trouble; make work; **3.** *verbo impersonal*: a) *meteor.* be; *v. calor, tiempo etc.*; b) *hace 2 horas que llegó* he arrived 2 hours ago, it is 2 hours since he arrived; *está aquí desde hace 2 horas* he has been here for 2 hours; *v. tiempo*; **4.** **~se** (*transformarse*) become, grow, get (*or* come) to be, turn (into); (*crecer*) grow; (*fingirse*) pretend to be; *cortesías* exchange; ~ *soldado* become a soldier, turn soldier; ~ *viejo* grow old, get old; ~ *a* become accustomed to; ~ *atrás* fall back; ~ *con*, ~ *de* appropriate, get hold of; *se me hace imposible creerlo* I find it impossible to believe it; *¡eso no se hace!* that isn't done, that's not on! F.

hacia toward(s); (*cerca de*) about, near; ~ *abajo* down(wards); ~ *adelante* forward(s); ~ *arriba* up(wards); ~ *atrás* back(wards); ~ *las 3* at about 3 o'clock; ~ *dentro* inward; ~ *fuera* outward.

hacienda *f* (landed) property; (*finca*) (country) estate; fortune; *S.Am.* ranch; (*ganado*) livestock; **~s** *pl.* household chores; ~ *pública* federal income; (*Ministerio de*) ♀ Treasury.

hacina *f esp.* ⛏ stack, rick; (*montón*) pile, heap; **hacinamiento** *m* stacking *etc.*; **hacinar** [1a] stack; pile (up), heap (up); accumulate.

hacha[1] **1.** *f* axe, chopper; (*ligera*) hatchet; ⚔ (*a.* ~ *de armas*) battle-axe; **2.:** F *ser un* ~ be a wizard, be brilliant.

hacha[2] *f* torch; large candle.

hachazo *m* axe blow, axe stroke, hack.

hache *f letter H*; *llámele Vd.* ~ call it what you will, it's all the same.

hachear [1a] *v/t.* hew; *v/i.* wield an axe; **hachero** *m* woodcutter, lumberjack; ⚔ sapper.

hachich *m*, **hachís** *m* hashish.

hacho *m* beacon; **hachón** *m* (large) torch.

hada *f* fairy; ~ *madrina* fairy godmother; *de* **~s** fairy *attr.*; **hadado:** *bien* ~ lucky; *mal* ~ ill-fated; **hado** *m* fate, destiny.

haga, **hago** *v. hacer.*

¡hala! hi (there)!, hoy!; ⚓ *etc.* heave!

halagar [1h] show affection to, make up to F; (*acariciar*) caress; cajole, blandish *para persuadir*;

(*adular*) flatter; (*agradar*) gratify; **halago** *m* caress; cajolery; blandishment(s); flattery; gratification, delight; **halagüeño** flattering; pleasing, attractive, alluring; *perspectiva* hopeful.
halar [1a] ⚓ *v/t.* haul (at, on), pull; *v/i.* pull ahead.
halcón *m* falcon; *pol.* hawk; ~ *común* peregrine; **halconería** *f* falconry, hawking; **halconero** *m* falconer.
halda *f* skirt; *poner* ~*s en cinta* F roll up one's sleeves.
halibut *m* halibut.
halito *m* vapor; *from the mouth* breath; *poet.* gentle breeze.
halo *m* halo.
halterio *m* dumbbell; **halterofilia** *f* weightlifting; **halterofilista** *m/f* weightlifter.
hall [xol] *m* hall; *thea.* foyer.
hallar [1a] *mst* find; discover; locate; come across *sin buscar*; (*averiguar*) find out; ~**se** find o.s.; be; *se halla en Burgos* he is in Burgos; *se hallaba muy enfermo* he was very ill; ~ *con obstáculo* encounter; ~ *en todo* have a hand in everything; **hallazgo** *m* (*acto*) finding; discovery; (*cosa hallada*) find; (*recompensa*) reward (to finder); *100 ptas de* ~ 100 ptas reward.
hamaca *f* hammock; **hamaquear** [1a] *S.Am.* rock.
hambre *f* hunger (*a. fig.*; *de* for); famine; starvation; *fig.* longing (*de* for); ~ *canina* ravenous hunger; *entretener el* ~ stave off hunger; *matar el* ~ satisfy one's hunger; (*hacer*) *morir de* ~ starve (to death); *padecer* ~ starve; *pasar* ~ go hungry; *tener* ~ be hungry; *esp. fig.* hunger (*de* after, for); **hambrear** [1a] *v/t.* starve; *v/i.* starve, go hungry; **hambriento** hungry, famished, starving; *fig.* starved (*de* of), longing (*de* for).
hamburguesa *f* hamburger.
hamo *m* fish hook.
hampa *f* rogue's life, vagrancy; underworld, low life; (*a. gente del* ~) riffraff; **hampón** *m* tough, rowdy, thug.
hámster *m* hamster.
han *v. haber.*
handicap *m* handicap; **handicapar** [1a] *deportes*: handicap.
hangar *m* hangar.
haragán 1. idle, good-for-nothing; **2.** *m*, **-a** *f* idler, loafer, good-for-nothing; **haraganear** [1a] idle; lounge, loaf (about), hang about; **haraganería** *f* idleness *etc.*
harapiento, **haraposo** in rags, ragged, tattered; **harapo** *m* rag, tatter; *hecho un* ~ in rags.
harén *m* harem.
harina *f* flour, meal; (*polvo*) powder; ~ *de avena* oatmeal; ~ *de huesos* bone meal; ~ *lacteada* malted milk; ~ *de maíz* cornflour, corn meal; *es* ~ *de otro costal* that's (quite) another story, that's a horse of a different color; **harinero 1.** flour *attr.*; **2.** *m* (*p.*) flour merchant; flour bin; **harinoso** floury, mealy.
harnero *m* sieve.
harpillera *f* sacking, sackcloth.
hartar [1a] satiate, stuff, surfeit, glut (*con* with); *fig.* (*aburrir*) weary, bore; (*agobiar*) overwhelm (*de* with); ~ *de palos a* shower blows on; ~**se** gorge (*con* on), eat one's fill (*con* of); *fig.* weary (*de* of); get fed up (*de* with) F; **hartazgo** *m* glut, fill, bellyful; *darse un* ~ *de* eat one's fill of; *fig.* overdo; **harto 1.** *adj.* full (*de* of), glutted (*de* with); *fig.* tired (*de* of), fed up (*de* with); **2.** *adv.* quite, very; enough; **hartura** *f* surfeit, glut; abundance; *fig.* full satisfaction (of a desire); *con* ~ in abundance.
has *v. haber.*
hasta 1. *prp. espacio*: as far as, up to, down to; *tiempo*: till, until; as late as, up to; pending; *cantidad*: as much as, as many as; *v. ahora, vista etc.*; **2.** *adv.* even; quite; **3.** *cj.* even, also; ~ *que* until.
hastial[1] *m* ⚠ gable end.
hastial[2] *m* hulking lout.
hastiar [1c] (*cansar*) weary; (*repugnar*) disgust; (*disgustar*) annoy; (*aburrir*) bore; **hastío** *m* weariness; disgust; annoyance; boredom.
hatajo *m* F lot; **hato** *m* 🖍 herd; flock *de ovejas*; group *de ps.*; *b.s.* gang; *S.Am.* cattle ranch; *fig.* lot; (*víveres*) provisions; (*ropa*) clothes; personal effects; F *liar el* ~ pack up; F *menear el* ~ *a* beat up; *revolver el* ~ stir up trouble.
hay *v. haber.*

haya *f* beech (tree); **hayuco** *m* beechnut, beechmast.
haz[1] *m* ⸗ sheaf *de mieses etc.*, truss *de paja*; bundle *de leña etc.*; bunch; *haces pl. hist.* fasces; ~ *de luz* beam of light.
haz[2] *f mst fig. or lit.* face; (*superficie*) surface; right side *de tela*; ~ *de la tierra* face of the earth; *de dos haces fig.* two-faced.
haz[3] *v. hacer.*
hazaña *f* feat, exploit, (heroic) deed; achievement; **hazañería** *f* fuss; **hazañoso** heroic, valiant, dauntless.
hazmerreír *m* butt, laughing-stock, joke (*p.*).
he[1] *v. haber.*
he[2]: *mst lit.* ~ *aquí* here is, here are; lo (and behold)!; *¡heme* (*or héteme*) *aquí!* here I am!; *¡helos allí!* there they are!
hebdomadario *adj. a. su. m* weekly.
hebilla *f* buckle, clasp.
hebra *f* (length of) thread; strand; fibre; grain *de madera*; ⚒ vein; *fig.* thread (of the conversation); ~*s pl. poet.* hair; *pegar la* ~ strike up a conversation.
hebraico Hebraic; **hebreo 1.** *adj. a. su. m*, **a** *f* Hebrew; **2.** (*idioma*) Hebrew.
hebroso fibrous; *carne* stringy.
hecatombe *f* hecatomb.
hectárea *f* hectare.
héctico ⚕ consumptive.
hectolitro *m* hectolitre.
hechicera *f* sorceress, witch; enchantress; **hechicería** *f* sorcery, witchcraft; spell, enchantment (*a. fig.*); *fig.* charm, fascination; **hechicero 1.** magic; bewitching, enchanting (*a. fig.*); *fig.* charming; **2.** *m* wizard, sorcerer; witch doctor *de salvajes*; **hechizar** [1f] bewitch (*a. fig.*), cast a spell on; *b.s.* bedevil; *fig.* charm, enchant, delight; **hechizo 1.** artificial, false; (*amovible*) detachable; ⊕ manufactured; **2.** *m* magic; charm, spell (*a. fig.*); *fig.* glamour; ~*s pl.* (woman's) charms.
hecho 1. *p.p. of hacer*; *¡~!* all right!, O.K., it's a deal!; *a lo ~, pecho* what's done can't be undone; *bien* ~ well-made; *p.* well proportioned; *¡bien ~!* well done!, quite right!; *de* ~ in fact; *en ~ de verdad* as a matter of fact; *estar en el ~ de* catch on to; *estar ~ un ...* be like a ...; *estar ~ a* be accustomed to, be hardened to; **2.** *adj.* complete, mature; (*acabado*) finished; *sew.* ready-made, ready-to-wear; *frase* stock; ~ *y derecho* complete, proper, full-fledged; **3.** *m* deed, act, action; fact; (*elemento*) factor; (*asunto*) matter; (*suceso*) event; *los* ~*s de los Apóstoles* the Acts of the Apostles; *el ~ es que* the fact is that; *a* ~ continuously; all together; indiscriminately; *de* ~ in fact, as a matter of fact; *volvamos al* ~ let's get back to the matter in hand.
hechura *f* make, making; creation; creature (*a. fig.*); form, shape; build *de p.*; cut *de traje*; (*artesanía*) workmanship; *de* ~ *sastre* tailor-made; *somos* ~ *de Dios* we are God's handiwork.
heder [2g] stink, reek (*a* of); *fig.* annoy, be intolerable; **hediondez** *f* stench; stinking thing; **hediondo** stinking, foul-smelling; filthy (*a. fig.*); intolerable.
hedonismo *m* hedonism.
hedor *m* stench, stink, reek.
hegemonía *f* hegemony.
helada *f* frost; freeze(-up); ~ *blanca* hoarfrost; **heladera** *f* refrigerator; **heladería** *f* ice-cream parlor; **helado 1.** frozen (*a. fig.*); freezing, icy; (*preso*) ice-bound; *fig.* chilly, disdainful; **2.** *m* ice cream; water ice; cold drink; **helar** [1k] freeze; ice; chill (*a. fig.*); (*pasmar*) astonish; (*desalentar*) dishearten; ~**se** freeze; be frozen; (*avión, riel etc.*) ice (up); (*coagularse*) set.
helecho *m* fern, bracken.
helénico Hellenic, Greek; **heleno** *m*, **a** *f* Hellene, Greek.
hélice *f* spiral; ⚘, ⚡, *anat.* helix; ⚓ screw, propeller; ✈ propeller, airscrew; **helicoidal** spiral, helicoid(al).
helicóptero *m* helicopter.
helio *m* helium; **heliograbado** *m* heliogravure; **heliógrafo** *m* heliograph; **heliotropo** *m* heliotrope.
hembra *f zo.*, ⚘, ⊕ female; *zo.* she-...; *orn.* hen; *sew.* eye; ⊕ nut; F woman; *un pez* ~ a female fish; *una real* ~ a fine figure of a woman; **hembrilla** *f* ⊕ nut.

hemiciclo *m* semicircle; semicircular theater; *parl.* floor; **hemisferio** *m* hemisphere; **hemistiquio** *m* hemistich.

hemofilia *f* hemophilia; **hemorragia** *f* hemorrhage; **hemorroides** *f/pl.* hemorrhoids.

henal *m* hayloft; **henar** *m* meadow, hayfield.

henchir [3h] fill (up), stuff, cram; **~se** (*p.*) stuff o.s.

hendedura *f* cleft, split; (*incisión*) slit; (*grieta*) crack; *mst geol.* rift, fissure; **hender** [2g] cleave (*a. fig.*); split; crack; slit *con cuchillo*; *fig.* make a way through; **hendidura** *f* = *hendedura*.

henil *m* hayloft; **heno** *m* hay.

heñir [3h *a.* 3l] knead; *hay mucho que ~* F there's still a lot of work to do.

hepático hepatic.

heptágono *m* heptagon.

heráldica *f* heraldry; **heráldico** heraldic; **heraldo** *m* herald (*a. fig.*).

herbáceo herbaceous; **herbaje** *m* herbage, grass, pasture; **herbaj(e)ar** *v/t.* put to pasture, graze; *v/i.* graze, browse; **herbario** **1.** herbal; **2.** *m* herbarium; (*p.*) herbalist; **herbazal** *m* grassland; **herbívoro** herbivorous; **herbolario** **1.** crazy; **2.** *m* herbalist; **herborizar** [1f] gather herbs; (*como estudio*) botanize; **herboso** grassy.

hercúleo Herculean.

heredable (in)heritable; **heredad** *f* (country) estate, farm; domain; landed property; **heredar** [1a] inherit (*de* from), be heir to; *p.* name as one's heir; **heredera** *f* heiress; **heredero** *m* heir (*de* to), inheritor (*de* of); owner of an estate; *~ forzoso* heir apparent, heir at law; *~ único* universal heir; **hereditario** hereditary.

hereje *m/f* heretic; **herejía** *f* heresy (*a. fig.*).

herencia *f* inheritance; estate; legacy; *esp. fig.* heritage; *biol.* heredity.

herético heretic(al).

herida *f* wound, injury; (*ofensa*) insult, outrage; *fig.* affliction; **herido** **1.** injured; ⚔ wounded; **2.** *m* injured (⚔ wounded) man; *los ~s pl.* the wounded; **herir** [3i] hurt, injure; *esp.* ⚔ wound (*a. fig.*); (*golpear*) strike, hit; (*sol*) beat down on; ♪ pluck, strike; *fig.* touch, move; *fig.* offend.

hermafrodita *adj. a. su. m* hermaphrodite.

hermana *f* sister (*a. eccl.*); (*cosa*) twin; *~ de leche* foster sister; *~ política* sister-in-law; *media ~* half sister; **hermanar** [1a] match; (*unir*) join; harmonize; **hermanastro** *m* stepbrother; **hermandad** *f* brotherhood (*a. fig.*), sisterhood; *fig.* close relationship; **hermano** **1.** *m* brother (*a. fig., eccl.*); (*costa*) twin; *~s pl.* brother(s) and sister(s); *~ carnal* blood brother; *~ de leche* foster brother; *~ político* brother-in-law; *medio ~* half brother; **2.** *adj.* similar, matching; sister *attr.* (*fig.*).

hermético hermetic, airtight; watertight; *fig.* impenetrable.

hermosear [1a] beautify, make beautiful; adorn; **hermoso** beautiful; *esp. hombre* handsome; lovely; fine, splendid; **hermosura** *f* beauty; loveliness; (*p.*) belle, beauty.

hernia *f* rupture, hernia.

héroe *m* hero; **heroicidad** *f* (act of) heroism; **heroico** heroic; **heroicocómico** mock-heroic; **heroína**[1] *f* heroine.

heroína[2] *f pharm.* heroin; **heroinómano** *m* heroin addict.

heroísmo *m* heroism.

herpes *m/pl. or f/pl.* ⚕ shingles, herpes.

herrador *m* farrier; **herradura** *f* horseshoe; *curva en ~ mot.* hairpin bend; **herraje** *m* ironwork, metal fittings; **herramental** *m* tool bag, tool kit; **herramienta** *f* tool, implement; appliance; set of tools; F (bull's) horns; F (*dientes*) teeth; *~ de filo* edge tool; *~ mecánica* power tool; **herrar** [1k] *caballo* shoe; *ganado* brand; ⊕ bind (*or* trim) with iron; **herrería** *f* smithy, blacksmith's (shop), forge; (*fábrica*) ironworks; (*oficio*) blacksmith's trade; *fig.* uproar.

herrerillo *m* tit.

herrero *m* (black)smith; *~ de grueso* ironworker; *~ de obra* steelworker.

herrete *m* tag, metal tip; *S.Am.* branding iron.

herrumbre *f* rust; *fig.* taste of iron; *a prueba de ~* rustproof, rust-resistant; **herrumbroso** rusty.
hervidero *m* boiling, bubbling, seething (*a. fig.*); (*fuente*) bubbling spring; *fig.* swarm, throng; **hervidor** *m approx.* kettle; boiling pan; cooker; **hervir** [3i] boil, seethe (*a. fig.*); (*mar*) surge; *~ de, ~ en* swarm with, teem with; **hervor** *m* boiling, seething; *fig.* fire (of youth), restlessness; *alzar el ~* come to the boil.
heterodino *adj. a. su. m* heterodyne.
heterodoxo unorthodox, heterodox.
heterogéneo heterogeneous.
hético = *héctico.*
hexágono *m* hexagon.
hez *f*: *mst pl.* heces sediment, lees; dregs (*a. fig.*); excrement; *fig.* scum.
hiato *m gr.*, ⚕ hiatus.
hibernación *f* hibernation; **hibernal** wintry, winter *attr.*; **hibernar** [1a] hibernate.
híbrido hybrid.
hice *v. hacer.*
hidalga *f* noblewoman; **hidalgo** **1.** noble, illustrious; (*propio de ~*) gentlemanly; generous; **2.** *m* nobleman; **hidalguía** *f* nobility (*esp.* of conduct).
hidra *f* hydra.
hidratar(**se**) [1a] hydrate; **hidrato** *m* hydrate.
hidráulica *f* hydraulics; **hidráulico** hydraulic, water *attr.*; *fuerza ~a* water power.
hidro(**avión**) *m* seaplane; hydroplane; **hidrocarburo** *m* hydrocarbon; **hidrodinámica** *f* hydrodynamics; **hidroeléctrico** hydroelectric; **hidrófilo** absorbent, F bibulous; **hidrofobia** *f* hydrophobia; rabies; **hidrófobo** hydrophobic; **hidrófugo** damp-proof, water-repellent; **hidrógeno** *m* hydrogen; **hidrom**(**i**)**el** *m* mead; **hidropesía** *f* dropsy; **hidrópico** dropsical; **hidroplano** *m* seaplane; **hidrostática** *f* hydrostatics; **hidrostático** hydrostatic; **hidróxido** *m* hydroxide.
hiedra *f* ivy.
hiel *f* bile, gall (*a. fig.*); *fig.* bitterness, sorrow; *~es pl.* troubles; *echar la ~* overwork.
hielo *m* ice; frost; freezing; *fig.* coldness, indifference; *~ a la deriva, ~ movedizo, ~ flotante* drift ice; *~ seco* dry ice; *romper el ~ fig.* break the ice.
hiena *f* hyena.
hierba *f* grass; *esp.* ⚕ herb; small plant; *~s pl.* pasture; *~ cana* groundsel; *~ mora* nightshade; *~ rastrera* cotton grass; *mala ~* weed; *fig.* bad influence; **~buena** *f* mint.
hierro *m* iron; head *de lanza etc.*; (*de marcar*) brand; *~s pl.* irons; *~ acanalado, ~ ondulado* corrugated iron; *~ colado, ~ fundido* cast iron; *~ forjado* wrought iron; *~ en lingotes* pig iron; *~ viejo* scrap iron; *a ~ candente, batir de repente* strike while the iron's hot; *machacar en ~ frío* beat one's head against a wall, flog a dead horse.
higa *f* scorn, contempt.
hígado *m* liver; *~s pl.* F guts, pluck; F *echar los ~s* wear o.s. out.
higiene *f* hygiene; **higiénico** hygienic; sanitary; healthy.
higo *m* ⚘ (green) fig; *vet.* thrush; *~ chumbo, ~ de tuna* prickly pear; *de ~s a brevas* once in a blue moon; *no se me da un ~* I don't care a rap (*de* about).
higrómetro *m* hygrometer.
higuera *f* fig tree.
hija *f* daughter, child (*a. fig.*); *~ política* daughter-in-law; **hijastro** *m* stepson; **hijito** *m* F sonny; **hijo** *m* son, child (*a. fig.*); F (*vocativo*) son(ny), my boy; *~s pl.* children, son(s) and daughter(s); (*prole*) offspring, descendants; *cada ~ de vecino* F every man Jack, every mother's son; *~ de leche* foster child; *~ de su padre* F chip off the old block; *~ de sus propias obras* self-made man; *~ político* son-in-law; *Juan Lanas ~* Juan Lanas Junior; **hijuela** *f* little girl; ⊕ accessory; ⚖ portion, inheritance; **hijuelo** *m* little boy; ⚘ shoot; *~s pl. zo.* young.
hila *f* row, line; *a la ~* in single file; *~s pl.* ⚕ lint.
hilacha *f*, **hilacho** *m* raveled thread; fraying; *~ de vidrio* spun glass.
hilada *f* row, line; ⚠ course.
hilado *m* (*acto*) spinning; (*hilo*) yarn, thread; **hilandería** *f* (*arte*) spinning; (*fábrica*) (spinning) mill; **hilandero** *m*, **a** *f* spinner; **hilar**

[1a] spin; *fig.* reason, infer; ~ *delgado* draw it fine.
hilarante hilarious; *gas* laughing; **hilaridad** *f* hilarity, mirth.
hilaza *f* yarn, (coarse) thread; *descubrir la* ~ show o.s. in one's true colors.
hilera *f* row, rank (*a.* ⚔); line, string; *sew.* fine thread; ⚒ drill.
hilo *m* thread (*a. fig.*); yarn; (*tejido*) linen; (*alambre*) (thin) wire; trickle *de líquido*; string *de perlas etc.*; *fig.* train *del pensamiento*; course *de la vida*; *a* ~ uninterruptedly; *al* ~ *sew.* on the straight; *colgado de un* ~ hanging by a thread; *coger el* ~ pick (*or* take) up the thread; ~ *bramante* twine; ~ *de masa* ⚡ ground; ~ *dental* dental floss; *irse tras el* ~ *de la gente* follow the crowd; *manejar los* ~*s* pull strings; *perder el* ~ *de* lose the thread of.
hilván *m sew.* tacking, basting; **hilvanar** [1a] *sew.* tack, baste; *fig.* throw together, knock up.
himen *m* hymen, maidenhead; **himeneo** *m* Hymen.
himnario *m* hymnal, hymnbook; **himno** *m* hymn; ~ *nacional* national anthem.
hincapié: *hacer* ~ make a stand; *hacer* ~ *en* dwell on, insist on, emphasize.
hincar [1g] thrust (in); *clavo etc.* drive (in), sink; *pie* set (firmly); *v. diente, rodilla.*
hincha F **1.** *f* grudge, bad blood, ill-will; (*p.*, *cosa*) pet aversion; **2.** *m/f deportes*: supporter, fan, rooter; **hinchado** *lenguaje etc.* high-flown, pompous, stilted; *p.* vain, puffed-up; **hinchar** [1a] swell; distend; inflate, pump up, blow up *con aire*; *fig.* exaggerate; ~**se** swell (up), get distended; *fig.* be(come) puffed up (*or* vain); **hinchazón** *f* swelling; bump, lump; *fig.* vanity, conceit *de p.*; pomposity *de lenguaje*.
hindú *adj. a. su. m*, **-a** *f* Hindu.
hiniesta *f* ⚘ broom.
hinojo[1] *m* ⚘ fennel.
hinojo[2] *m* knee; *de* ~*s* on bended knee.
hipar [1a] **1.** hiccup, hiccough; (*perro*) pant; *fig.* be worn out; long, yearn (*por* for *su.*, to *inf.*); **2.** [xi'par] whimper.
hipérbola *f* ⅍ hyperbola; **hipérbole** *f rhet.* hyperbole; **hiperbólico** hyperbolic(al); exaggerated; **hipercrítico** hypercritical, carping, censorious; **hipertrofia** *f* hypertrophy.
hípico equine 🕮, horse *attr.*
hipnosis *f* hypnosis; **hipnótico** hypnotic; **hipnotismo** *m* hypnotism; **hipnotista** *m/f* hypnotist; **hipnotizar** [1f] hypnotize, mesmerize.
hipo *m* hiccup(s), hiccough(s); (*deseo*) longing; (*odio*) grudge, enmity; *tener* ~ *contra* have it in for; *tener* ~ *por* long for.
hipocampo *m* seahorse.
hipocondría *f* hypochondria; **hipocondríaco** **1.** hypochondriacal; **2.** *m*, **a** *f* hypochondriac.
hipocresía *f* hypocrisy; **hipócrita** **1.** hypocritical; **2.** *m/f* hypocrite.
hipodérmico hypodermic.
hipódromo *m* race track.
hipopótamo *m* hippopotamus.
hipoteca *f* mortgage; **hipotecar** [1g] mortgage; **hipotecario** mortgage *attr.*
hipotenusa *f* hypotenuse.
hipótesis *f* hypothesis, supposition; **hipotético** hypothetical.
hiriente offensive; wounding, cutting.
hirsuto hairy, hirsute, bristly; *fig. p.* brusque, rough.
hirviendo boiling; **hirviente** boiling, seething.
hisopear [1a] *eccl.* sprinkle (with holy water); **hisopo** *m eccl.* sprinkler; ⚘ hyssop.
hispalense *adj. a. su. m/f* Sevillian.
hispánico Hispanic; **hispanidad** *f* Spanishness; *pol.* (solidarity of the) Spanish world; **hispanismo** *m gr.* Hispanicism; 🕮 Hispanism; **hispanista** *m/f* Hispanist; **hispano** Spanish, Hispanic; **hispanoamericano** *adj. a. su. m*, **a** *f* Spanish-American, Latin-American; **hispanófilo** *adj. a. su. m*, **a** *f* Hispanophile.
histérico hysteric(al); *paroxismo* ~ hysterics; **histerismo** *m* hysteria.
histología *f* histology.
historia *f* history; (*narración, cuento*) story; (*esp. inventada*) tale; ~*s pl.* (*chismes*) gossip; ~*s de alcoba* bedtime stories; ~ *natural* history; ♀ *Sacra*, ♀

Sagrada biblical history; Scripture *en la escuela*; ~ *universal* world history; *dejarse de* ~*s* come to the point; *mujer que tiene* ~ woman with a past; **historiador** *m*, **-a** *f* historian; **historial 1.** historical; **2.** *m* (*historia, antecedentes*) record; (*ficha*) dossier; ⚕ (case) history; **historiar** [1b] tell the (hi)story of; chronicle; (*representar*) depict; **histórico** historical; (*notable*) historic; **historieta** *f* (short) story, tale, anecdote; ~ *gráfica* comic strip; **historiógrafo** *m* historiographer.

histrión *m* actor, player; buffoon; *b.s.* playactor; **histriónico** histrionic; **histrionismo** *m* histrionics; (*arte*) acting; (*ps.*) actors.

hita *f* ⊕ sprig, brad; (*mojón*) = **hito** *m* boundary post, milestone; ⚔ target; *fig.* aim, goal; ~ *kilométrico* kilometer stone; *a* ~ fixedly; *dar en el* ~ hit the nail on the head; *mirar de* ~ *en* ~ stare at, look *s.o.* up and down.

hocicar [1g] (*puerco*) root; (*con cariño*) nuzzle; (*p.*) fall on one's face; *fig.* run into trouble; **hocico** *m* snout, muzzle *de animal*; F snout, mug *sl. de p.*; *dar de* ~*s* fall on one's face; *dar de* ~*s contra* bump into; *estar de* ~ be in a bad temper; *meter el* ~ meddle; *poner* ~ pull a face.

hockey ['oki] *m* hockey; ~ *sobre patines*, ~ *sobre hielo* ice hockey.

hogaño *mst* † this year; these days.

hogar *m* hearth, fireplace; ⊕ furnace; 🚂 firebox; *fig.* home, house; family life; **hogareño** home *attr.*, family *attr.*; fireside *attr.*; *p.* home-loving, stay-at-home.

hogaza *f* large loaf.

hoguera *f* bonfire; (*llamas*) blaze.

hoja *f* ⚘ leaf (*a. de libro, puerta*); ⚘ petal; sheet *de metal, papel*; blade *de espada etc.*; pane *de vidrio*; (*documento*) form; ~ *clínica* clinical chart; ~ *de afeitar* razor blade; ~ *de embalaje* packing slip; ~ *de encuadernador libros* end paper; ~ *de estaño* tinfoil; ~ *de estudios* transcript; ~ *de guarda* flyleaf; ~ *de lata* tin(plate); ~ *de paga* pay roll; ~ *plegadiza* (table) flap; ~ *de ruta* waybill; ~ *de servicios* record of service; ~ *de tocino* flitch, side of bacon; ~ *volante* leaflet, handbill; *doblar la* ~ *fig.* change the subject; *volver la* ~ *fig.* turn over a new leaf; change the subject.

hojalata *f* tin (plate); **hojalatero** *m* tinsmith.

hojaldre *m* puff pastry.

hojarasca *f* dead (*or* fallen) leaves; *fig.* trifles, trash, rubbish; (*palabras*) useless words.

hojear [1a] turn the pages of, skim (*or* glance) through; **hojoso** leafy; **hojuela** *f* little leaf; (*escama*) flake; *metall.* foil; *cocina*: pancake.

¡hola! *saludo*: hello!, hey!; *extrañeza, reprensión*: hello!, hey!

holandés 1. Dutch; **2.** *m* Dutchman; **3.** *m* (*idioma*) Dutch; **holandesa** *f* Dutch woman; *a la* ~ *libro* quarter-bound.

holgado (*ocioso*) leisured, idle, unoccupied; *vestido etc.* loose, roomy, baggy; comfortable, cosy; (*casi rico*) comfortably off, well-to-do; **holganza** *f* (*ocio*) ease, leisure; (*descanso*) rest; (*placer*) enjoyment; **holgar** [1h *a.* 1m] (*descansar*) rest, take one's ease; (*estar ocioso*) be idle, be out of work; (*cosa*) be unused; be unnecessary; (*alegrarse*) be pleased (*con, de* with, about); *huelga decir* needless to say; ~**se** be glad (*con, de* about, at, of; *de que* that); enjoy o.s.

holgazán 1. idle, lazy; **2.** *m*, **-a** *f* idler, slacker, loafer; bum F; ne'er-do-well; **holgazanear** [1a] laze, loaf, slack; **holgazanería** *f* laziness *etc.*

holgorio *m* = *jolgorio*.

holgura *f* enjoyment, merrymaking; ease, comfort; looseness, roominess *de vestido*; ⊕ play.

holocausto *m* holocaust; burnt offering; *fig.* sacrifice.

hollar [1m] tread (on); trample underfoot (*a. fig.*); *fig.* humiliate.

hollejo *m* ⚘ skin, peel.

hollín *m* soot; **holliniento** sooty.

hombrachón *m* hulking fellow; **hombrada** *f* manly act; piece of bravado; **hombradía** *f* manliness; courage.

hombre 1. *m* man; (*género humano*) man, mankind; F husband; *¡~ al agua!*, *¡~ a la mar!* man overboard!; ~ *de armas* man-at-arms; ~ *de bien* honest man, man of honor; ~ *de buenas prendas* man of parts; ~ *de la*

calle man in the street; ~ *de ciencia* man of science; ~ *de dinero* man of means; ~ *de estado* statesman; ~ *hecho* grown man; ~ *de letras* man of letters; ~ *medio* average man; ~ *de mundo* man of the world; *v. muy*; ~ *de negocios* businessman; *pobre* ~ poor devil; slow-witted fellow; ~ *de pro(vecho)* honest man; man of worth; **2.** *int.* ¡~! *sorpresa*: good heavens!, my God!; *confirmación*: you bet!; *condoliéndose*: dear dear; yes I know; ¡*pero* ~! *protesta*: but my dear fellow!; heavens man!
hombre-anuncio *m* sandwich man.
hombrear[1] [1a] play the man; (*a.* ~**se**) ~ *con* try to keep up with.
hombrear[2] [1a] shoulder; put one's shoulder to.
hombrecillo *m* little man; ⚘ hop.
hombrera *f* shoulder strap; ⚔ epaulette.
hombre-rana *m* frogman.
hombría *f* manliness; ~ *de bien* honesty, uprightness.
hombro *m* shoulder; ~ *a* ~ shoulder to shoulder; ⚔ *sobre el* ~ ¡*armas!* slope arms!; *arrimar el* ~ put one's shoulder to the wheel, lend a hand; *echar al* ~ shoulder, take upon o.s.; *encogerse de* ~*s* shrug (one's shoulders); *mirar por encima del* ~ look down on, despise; *salir en* ~*s* be carried off on the shoulders of the crowd.
hombruno mannish, masculine.
homenaje *m* homage (*a. fig.*); allegiance; *fig.* tribute, testimonial; (*don*) gift; *en* ~ *a* in honor of; *rendir* ~ *a* do (*or* pay, render) homage to, swear allegiance to.
homeópata *m* homeopath(ist); **homeopatía** *f* homeopathy; **homeopático** homeopathic.
homicida 1. murderous, homicidal; **2.** *m* murderer; **3.** *f* murderess; **homicidio** *m* murder, homicide; manslaughter.
homilía *f* homily.
homogeneidad *f* homogeneity; **homogéneo** homogeneous; **homología** *f* homology; **homólogo 1.** *adj.* homologous; **2.** *m* colleague; **homónimo** *m* homonym; (*p.*) namesake; **homosexual** *adj. a. su. m/f* homosexual, gay.
honda *f* sling, catapult.
hondear [1a] ⚓ sound; (*descargar*) unload.
hondo 1. deep; low; *fig.* profound; *sentimiento* deep, heartfelt; **2.** *m* depth(s); bottom; **hondón** *m* bottom *de vaso, valle*; eye *de aguja*; *geog.* = **hondonada** *f* (*depresión*) hollow; (*tierra baja*) lowland; (*barranco*) gully, ravine; **hondura** *f* depth; profundity; *meterse en* ~*s* get out of one's depth, get into deep waters.
honestidad *f* decency, decorum *etc.*; **honesto** decent, decorous; modest; chaste; fair, just; honorable; honest.
hongo *m* (*en general*) fungus; (*comestible*) mushroom; (*venenoso*) toadstool; (*sombrero*) bowler (hat), derby.
honor *m* honor; virtue *esp. de mujer*; (*reputación*) good name; ~*es pl.* honors, honorary status; ~ *profesional* professional etiquette; *de* ~ *dama etc.* in waiting, of honor; *en* ~ *a la verdad* as a matter of fact, to tell the truth; *en* ~ *de* in honor of; *hacer* ~ *a firma* honor; *hacer los* ~*es de la casa* do the honors; *hacer los debidos* ~*es a comida* do justice to; *tener el* ~ *de inf.* have the honor to *inf.*, be proud to *inf.*
honorable honorable, worthy; **honorario 1.** honorary; honorific; **2.** *m* honorarium; *mst* ~*s pl.* fees, charges.
honra *f* self-esteem; dignity; (*reputación*) good name; honor; chastity; ~*s pl.* (*fúnebres*) last honors, obsequies; ¡*a mucha* ~! delighted!; *tener a mucha* ~ *inf.* be proud to *inf.*; *tener algo a mucha* ~ be proud of s.t.; **honradez** *f* honesty, honorableness, integrity; **honrado** honest, honorable; upright; **honrar** [1a] honor (*a.* ✝); respect, esteem, revere; do honor to; ~**se** be honored (*con* by, with; *de inf.* to *inf.*); **honrilla:** *por la negra* ~ for the sake of appearances, out of a sense of shame; **honroso** honorable; respectable, reputable.
hopa *f* cassock.
hora *f* hour; time (of day); *altas* ~*s pl.* small hours; ~ *de aglomeración* rush hours; ~ *de cierre* closing time; ~ *de comer* mealtime; time to eat; ~ *de verano* daylight-saving time; ~ *de irse* time to go; ~ *legal*, ~ *oficial* standard time; ~ *punta* peak hour; rush hour; ~*s pl. de consulta* office hours; ~*s de*

ocio leisure hours; *~s extraordinarias* overtime; *~-hombre* person-hour; man-hour; *~s pl. de oficina* business hours; *~s pl. punta* peak hours; *~ de recreo* playtime; *última ~ (periódico)* stop press; *a última ~* at the last moment; *a buena ~* opportunely; *a la ~* punctually; *en buen(a) ~* fortunately; safely; *en mala ~* unluckily; *fuera de ~s* out of hours; *por ~s* by the hour; *dar ~* fix a time; *dar la ~* strike (the hour); *ya es ~ de que* it is high time that; *¡ya era ~!* about time too!; *¿qué ~ es?* what is the time?, what time is it?; *poner en ~ reloj* set; *trabajar por ~s* work part-time; *no ver la ~ de* be hardly able to wait for.

horadar [1a] drill, bore (through); perforate, pierce.

horario 1. hourly; hour *attr.*; time *attr.*; **2.** *m* hour hand *de reloj*; 🚂 *etc.* timetable, schedule.

horca *f* gallows, gibbet; ⚘ (pitch-)fork; (*cebollas*) string; **horcadura** *f* fork (of a tree); **horcajadas:** *a ~* astride; **horcajadura** *f anat.* crotch; **horcajo** *m* ⚘ yoke; *geog.* fork (of a river).

horchata *f* orgeat; **horchatería** *f* resfreshment stall; *approx.* ice-cream parlor.

horda *f* horde; (*pandilla*) gang.

horero *m* hour hand.

horizontal horizontal; flat, level; **horizonte** *m* horizon (*a. fig.*); (*línea del ~*) skyline.

horma *f* ⊕ form, mold; (*a. ~ del calzado*) last, boot tree; (*muro*) dry stone wall; *hallar la ~ de su zapato* meet one's match.

hormiga *f* ant.

hormigón *m* concrete; *~ armado* reinforced concrete; *~ pretensado* prestressed concrete; **hormigonera** *f* ⊕ concrete mixer.

hormiguear [1a] ⚕ itch; (*abundar*) swarm, teem; **hormigueo** *m* ⚕ itch(ing), tingling, creeps F; *fig.* uneasiness; swarming; **hormiguero** *m* anthill (*a. fig.*); *fig.* swarm (of people).

hormillón *m* hat block.

hormón *m*, **hormona** *f* hormone.

hornacina *f* (vaulted) niche.

hornada *f* batch (of bread), baking; *fig.* crop, batch; **hornero** *m*, **a** *f* baker; **hornillo** *m* ⊕ small furnace; stove *de cocina*; bowl *de pipa*; ⚔ mine; *~ eléctrico* hot plate; *~ de gas* gas ring; **horno** *m* ⊕ furnace; *cerámica*: kiln; *cocina*: oven; *alto ~* blast furnace; *~ de cal* lime kiln; *~ crematorio* crematorium; *~ de fundición* smelting furnace; *~ de ladrillos* brick kiln.

horóscopo *m* horoscope; *sacar un ~* cast a horoscope.

horqueta *f todos sentidos*: fork; *S.Am.* (*ángulo agudo en un río*) bend; **horquilla** *f* ⚘ pitchfork; hairpin *para pelo*; fork *de bicicleta*; ⊕ yoke.

horrendo horrible, dire, frightful.

hórreo *m prov.* (*esp.* raised) granary.

horrible horrible, ghastly, dreadful (*a.* F); F unspeakable, nasty; **horripilante** hair-raising, horrifying, weird, creepy F; **horripilar** [1a] make *s.o.'s* hair stand on end, give *s.o.* the creeps F; **horror** *m* (*sentimiento*) horror, dread; abhorrence; (*calidad*) horror; repulsiveness; enormity; (*acto*) atrocity; *¡qué ~!* how horrible!; F goodness!, well did you ever!; *tener ~ a* have a horror of; *tener en ~* abhor, detest; **horrorizar** [1f] horrify; terrify; **~se** be horrified; **horroroso** horrifying; horrible, frightful, grim (*a.* F); F ghastly, dreadful.

horrura *f* filth, dirt, rubbish.

hortaliza *f* vegetable; **hortelano** *m*, **a** *f* (market) gardener.

hortensia *f* hydrangea.

hortera *f* wooden bowl; F *Madrid*: shop assistant, grocer's boy.

hortícola horticultural; **horticultor** *m*, **-a** *f* horticulturist, gardener; (*m*) nurseryman; **horticultura** *f* horticulture; gardening.

hosco dark, gloomy; *p.* surly, sullen, grim.

hospedaje *m* (cost of) lodging; **hospedar** [1a] put up, lodge, receive as a guest; **~se** put up, lodge, stop, stay (*en* at); **hospedera** *f* hostess; innkeeper's wife; **hospedero** *m* host; innkeeper; **hospicio** *m* poorhouse; hospice; (*niños*) orphanage; **hospital** *m* hospital, infirmary; *esp. eccl.* hospice; *~ de aislamiento*, *~ de contagiosos* isolation hospital; *~ de la sangre* poor relations; *~ de primera sangre* ⚔ field hospital; *estar hecho un ~* (*p.*) be full of aches and pains;

hospitalario hospitable; **hospitalidad** *f* hospitality; **hospitalizar** [1f] send to hospital.

hosquedad *f* gloom; sullenness *etc.*

hostelería *f* restaurant and hotel business; **hostelero** *m* innkeeper; **hostería** *f* inn.

hostia *f eccl.* Host; wafer; sacrificial victim.

hostigar [1h] lash, whip; *fig.* harass, plague.

hostil hostile; **hostilidad** *f* hostility; hostile act; *romper las ~es* start hostilities; **hostilizar** [1f] ⚔ harass, attack; (*enemistar*) antagonize.

hotel *m* hotel; (*casa*) detached house, mansion, villa; **hotelero 1.** hotel *attr.*; **2.** *m*, **a** *f* hotelkeeper.

hoy today; *~ en día*, *~ día* nowadays; *~ por ~* at the present; (*de*) *~ en 8 días* this day a week, a week today; *de ~ a mañana* any time now, when you least expect it; *de ~ en adelante* from now on, henceforward; *por ~* for the present.

hoya *f* pit, hole; (*tumba*) grave; *geog.* vale; *S.Am.* river basin; ✓ seed bed; **hoyada** *f* depression, hollow; **hoyanca** *f* potter's field; **hoyo** *m* hole (*a. golf*), cavity; (*tumba*) grave; ⚕ pock mark; **hoyoso** full of holes; **hoyuelo** *m* dimple.

hoz *f* ✓ sickle; *geog.* defile, ravine, gorge; *de ~ y de coz* headlong, recklessly.

hozar [1f] (*puerco*) root.

hube *v. haber.*

hucha *f* bin; (*arca*) chest; money box *para dinero*; *fig.* savings; *buena ~ fig.* nest egg.

hueco 1. hollow; (*vacío*) empty; blank; (*mullido*) soft; *tierra etc.* spongy; *fig. p.* conceited; *estilo* pompous; *voz* resounding, booming; **2.** *m* hole, hollow, cavity; (*intervalo*) gap, opening; (*vacío*) void, empty space; (*puesto*) vacancy; ⚠ recess, window; *~ de la axila* armpit; *~ de escalera* stairwell; **~-grabado** *m* photogravure.

huelga *f* (*laboral*) strike; (*descanso*) rest; (*ocio*) leisure, *b.s.* idleness; ⊕ play; *~ de brazos caídos* sit-down strike; *~ de hambre* hunger strike; *~ patronal* lockout; *~ por solidaridad* sympathetic strike; *en ~* on strike; *~ sentada* sit-down strike; *declararse* (*or ponerse*) *en ~* (go on) strike, walk out; **huelgo** *m* breath; space; ⊕ play; **huelguista** *m/f* striker.

huella *f* (*impresión de pie*) footprint; (*acto*) tread(ing); (foot)step; (*pista*) track; (*señal*) trace, mark, imprint, sign; tread *de escalón, neumático*; *~ dactilar*, *~ digital* fingerprint; *~ de sonido* sound track; *seguir las ~s de* follow in the footsteps of; **huello:** *camino de buen* (*mal*) *~* good (bad) road for walking.

huérfano 1. orphan(ed); *fig.* unprotected, uncared-for; *~ de madre* motherless; **2.** *m*, **a** *f* orphan.

huero *huevo* rotten; *fig.* empty; sterile; dud F.

huerta *f* (large) market garden; *~* (*de árboles frutales*) orchard; *esp. Valencia a. Murcia* irrigated region; **huerto** *m* (kitchen) garden, market garden; orchard *de árboles frutales.*

huesa *f* grave.

hueso *m anat.* bone; ⚘ stone; core; *fig.* hard work; *~ de la alegría* funny bone; *~ de la suerte* wishbone; *~ duro de roer* a hard nut to crack; *calarse hasta los ~s* get soaked to the skin; F *la sin ~* the tongue; *no dejar ~ sano a* pull to pieces, walk all over; *estar en los ~s* be nothing but skin and bone; *soltar la sin ~* F talk too much; F pour forth insults; **huesoso** bony, bone *attr.*

huésped *m* (*invitado*) guest; boarder, lodger *que paga*; (*que invita*) host; (*amo de la casa*) landlord; **huéspeda** *f* guest *etc.*; hostess; landlady.

huesudo bony; *p.* raw-boned.

hueva *f ichth.* (hard) roe; *~s pl.* spawn; **huevera** *f* eggcup; **huevo** *m* egg; *~ a la plancha*, *~ al plato*, *~ estrellado*, *~ frito* fried egg; *~ del té* tea ball; *~ de zurcir* darning egg *or* gourd; *~ en cáscara*, *~ pasado por agua* soft-boiled egg; *~ duro* hard-boiled egg; *~ escalfado* poached egg; *~s pl. revueltos* scrambled eggs.

hugonote *m*, **a** *f* Huguenot.

huida *f* flight, escape; shy(ing) *de caballo*; **huidizo** shy; elusive; (*pasajero*) fleeting; **huir** [3g] *v/t.* run away from, escape (from), flee; (*apartarse*) avoid, shun; *v/i.* run away, flee (de from) (*a.* **~se**); (*tiempo*) fly.

hule *m* oilcloth, oilskin; (*caucho*)

rubber; F *toros*: goring; F *habrá* ~ there's going to be trouble.

hulla *f* (soft) coal; **hullera** *f* colliery; ~ *azul* tide power; wind power; ~ *blanca* white power, water power; **hullero** coal *attr*.

humanar [1a] humanize; ~**se** become more human; *eccl.* become man; ~ *a inf. S.Am.* condescend to *inf.*; **humanidad** *f* humanity (*a. fig.*); humankind, mankind; F corpulence; ~*es pl.* humanities; **humanismo** *m* humanism; **humanista** *m/f* humanist; **humanitario** humanitarian; **humanización** *f* humanization; **humanizar** [1f] humanize; ~**se** become (more) human; **humano 1.** human; (*compasivo*) humane; *ciencias* ~*as* humane learning; **2.** *m* human (being).

humareda *f* cloud of smoke; **humazo** *m* dense (cloud of) smoke; F *dar* ~ *a* smoke out; **humeante** smoking, smoky, fuming; **humear** [1a] *v/t. S.Am.* fumigate; *v/i.* smoke; fume; steam; reek; *fig.* be not yet dead; (*altivecerse*) give o.s. airs.

humectar [1a]📖 = *humedecer*; **humedad** *f* humidity, damp(ness), moisture, wet(ness); *a prueba de* ~ damp-proof; **humedecer** [2d] damp, moisten, wet; ~**se** get damp *etc.*; **húmedo** damp, humid, moist, wet.

humera *f* F drunkenness.

humero *m* chimney, flue.

húmero *m* humerus.

humidificador *m* air humidifier.

humildad *f* (*virtud*) humility; (*condición*) humbleness, lowliness; (*acto*) submission; **humilde** humble; *carácter* humble, meek; *condición* low(ly), low-born; *voz* small; **humillación** *f* humiliation, mortification; **humillante** humiliating, humbling; degrading; **humillar** [1a] humiliate, humble; *cabeza* bow, bend; ~**se** humble o.s.; *b.s.* grovel.

humo *m* smoke; fumes; ~*s pl.* (*casas*) homes; *fig.* airs, conceit; *a* ~ *de pajas* thoughtlessly; F *bajar los* ~*s a* take *s.o.* down a peg; *echar* ~, *hacer* ~ smoke; *hacerse* ~, *irse todo en* ~ go up in smoke, vanish without trace; *tener muchos* ~*s* have a swelled head; F *vender* ~*s* brag, talk big; F peddle influence.

humor *m* humor (*a. anat.*); temper, mood; (*genio*) disposition; *buen* ~ good humor, high spirits; *estar de buen* (*mal*) ~ be in a good (bad) mood (*or* temper); *seguir el* ~ *a* humor; **humorada** *f* joke, witticism; **humorado:** *bien* ~ good-humored; *mal* ~ bad-tempered; **humorismo** *m* humor, humorousness; **humorista** *m/f* humorist; **humorístico** humorous, funny, comic.

humoso smoky.

humus *m* humus.

hundido sunken; *ojos* hollow; **hundimiento** *m* sinking *etc.*; **hundir** [3a] sink; submerge, engulf; plunge (*en* into); *fig.* destroy, ruin; *p.* confound *con razones*; ~**se** ⚓ *etc.* sink; plunge; ⚠ *etc.* collapse, cave in, tumble (down); (*tierra*) subside; *fig.* be destroyed, be ruined; disappear.

húngaro 1. *adj. a. su. m,* **a** *f* Hungarian; **2.** *m* (*idioma*) Hungarian.

huracán *m* hurricane.

huraño shy, diffident; unsociable; *animal* wild, shy.

hurgar [1h] poke; stir (up) (*a. fig.*), *lumbre* poke, rake; *fig.* incite, excite; *peor es hurgallo* (i. e., ~*lo*) better keep hands off; ~**se** pick one's nose; **hurgón** *m* poker, fire rake; **hurgonazo** *m* poke; jab; **hurgonear** [1a] *lumbre* poke; thrust at; jab.

hurón *m zo.* ferret; (*p.*) (*entrometido*) busybody, snooper; (*huraño*) shy unsociable person; **huronear** [1a] *fig.* ferret out, pry into; **huronera** *f fig.* den, lair.

hurtadillas: *a* ~ stealthily, on the sly.

hurtar [1a] steal, thieve; ✝ give short measure; (*mar*) encroach on, erode; *lit.* plagiarize; ~**se** keep out of the way, make off; **hurto** *m* (*acto*) theft, robbery; (*cosa*) thing stolen; ~ *doméstico* burglary, housebreaking; *a* ~ on the sly, by stealth.

húsar *m* hussar.

husillo *m* ⊕ (*eje*) spindle, shaft; *tornillo*) clamp screw; (*desagüe*) drain.

husma: *andar a la* ~ go prying around (*de* after); **husmear** [1a] *v/t.* scent, get wind of (*a. fig.*); F smell out, nose out, pry into; *v/i.* (*carne*) smell high; **husmeo** *m* scenting; sniff; F prying; **husmo** *m* high smell, gaminess; *estar al* ~ watch one's chance.

huso *m* spindle (*a.* ⊕); bobbin; drum *de torno*; ~ *horario* time zone.

¡huy! ow!, ouch!; (*sorpresa*) whew!

huyo *etc. v. huir.*

I

iba *etc. v. ir.*
ibérico Iberian; **ibero, íbero** *adj. a. su. m,* **a** *f* Iberian; **iberoamericano** Latin-American.
iceberg *m* iceberg.
icono *m* icon; **iconoclasta 1.** iconoclastic; **2.** *m/f* iconoclast.
ictericia *f* jaundice.
ictiología *f* ichthyology.
icurriña *f* Basque national flag.
ida *f* going; departure; *fig.* rash act; hastiness; (*rastro*) trail; (*viaje de*) ~ outward journey; ~*s pl. y venidas* comings and goings; ~ *y vuelta* round trip.
idea *f* idea; notion, opinion; (*ingenio*) inventiveness, talent; ~ *fija* obsession, bee in one's bonnet F; ~ *luminosa* bright idea; F *ni* ~ I haven't a clue; *hacerse etc. una* ~ *de* get an idea of; *mudar de* ~ change one's mind; *no tengo la menor* ~ I haven't the faintest idea; **ideación** *f* conception, thinking-out; **ideal 1.** ideal; notional, imaginary; **2.** *m* ideal; **idealismo** *m* idealism; **idealista 1.** idealistic; **2.** *m/f* idealist; **idealizar** [1f] idealize; **idear** [1a] think up; plan, design; invent; **ideario** *m* body of ideas; ideology.
ídem ditto, idem.
idéntico identical, (very) same; **identidad** *f* identity; sameness; **identificación** *f* identification; ~ *errónea* mistaken identify; **identificar** [1g] identify; recognize; pick out; ~**se** identify o.s., be identical (*con* with).
ideología *f* ideology; **ideológico** ideological.
idílico idyllic; **idilio** *m* idyll.
idioma *m* language; speech, idiom *de grupo*; **idiomático** idiomatic.
idiosincrasia *f* idiosyncrasy.
idiota 1. idiotic, stupid; *p.* simple; **2.** *m/f* idiot; **idiotez** *f* idiocy; **idiotismo** *m gr.* idiom(atic expression).
ido 1. wild, scatterbrained; *S.Am.* drunk; **2. los** ~**s** the dead.
idólatra 1. idolatrous; **2.** *m* idolater; **3.** *f* idolatress; **idolatrar** [1a] *ídolo* worship, adore; *fig.* idolize; **idolatría** *f* idolatry; **ídolo** *m* idol (*a. fig.*).
idoneidad *f* suitability; aptitude, ability; **idóneo** suitable; apt, fit, fitting.
iglesia *f* church; *cumplir con la* ~ fulfill one's religious obligations; *llevar a la* ~ lead to the altar.
iglú *m* igloo.
ignaro ignorant.
ígneo igneous; **ignición** *f* ignition.
ignominia *f* ignominy, shame(fulness), disgrace; **ignominioso** ignominious, shameful, disgraceful.
ignorancia *f* ignorance; **ignorante 1.** ignorant, uninformed; **2.** *m/f* ignoramus; **ignorar** [1a] not know, be ignorant (*or* unaware) of, be unacquainted with; *no* ~ be well aware of, know very well; **ignoto** unknown.
igual 1. equal (*a* to); (the) same; indifferent; (*parecido*) alike, similar; uniform, constant, (*liso*) smooth, level, even; *clima* equable; *temperamento* even; ~ *que* like, the same as; (*me*) *es* ~ it's all the same (to me); *ir* ~*es* be level, be even; **2.** *m/f* equal; match (*de* for); *al* ~, *por* ~ equally; *al* ~ *de* like, after the fashion of; *al* ~ *que* as; while, whereas; *en* ~ *de* instead of; *sin* ~ matchless; *no tener* ~ be unrivaled, have no equal; **igualación** *f* equalization *etc.*; **igualar** [1a] *v/t.* equalize; (*comparar*) match; **A** equate; (*allanar*) level (up, down), smooth (off), even (out; *a. fig.*); adjust; † agree upon; *v/i.*, ~**se:** ~ *a*, ~ *con* equal, be the equal of; **igualdad** *f* equality; sameness; evenness, smoothness; ~ *de ánimo* equanimity; **igualmente** equally; likewise; F the same to you; ~ *que* the same as.
ijada *f* flank; loin; ⚕ pain in the side, stitch; **ijar** *m* flank.
ilacación *f* inference; connexion; sequence; **ilativo** inferential.
ilegal illegal, unlawful; **ilegalidad** *f* illegality.

ilegible illegible, unreadable.
ilegítimo illegitimate; *acto* unlawful; *cosa* false, spurious.
ilerdense *adj. a. su. m/f* (native) of Lérida.
ileso unharmed, unhurt; untouched.
iletrado uncultured, illiterate.
iliberal illiberal.
ilícito illicit.
ilimitado unlimited, limitless.
ilógico illogical.
ilote *m* ear of corn.
iluminación *f* illumination, lighting; *fig.* enlightenment; **iluminado 1.** illuminated; **2.** *m* visionary; **iluminar** [1a] illuminate; light (up); *fig.* enlighten.
ilusión *f* illusion; delusion; (*esperanza*) (unfounded) hope, (day-) dream; (*entusiasmo*) excitement, eagerness; (*sentimiento de placer*) thrill; *¡qué ~!* how thrilling!; *forjarse ~es, hacerse ~es* build up high hopes, indulge in wishful thinking; *este proyecto me hace mucha ~* I am getting very excited about this scheme; *el viaje me hacía tanta ~* I was looking forward so much to the trip; **ilusionado** hopeful; excited, eager; *el viaje me trae muy ~* I am looking forward tremendously to the trip; **ilusionarse** [1a] indulge in wishful thinking; **ilusionismo** *m* wishful thinking; **iluso 1.** (easily) deluded, deceived; **2.** *m*, **a** *f* visionary, dreamer; **ilusorio** illusory, deceptive; unreal; empty.
ilustración *f* illustration; picture; *fig.* enlightenment, learning; **ilustrado** illustrated; *fig.* enlightened; **ilustrador 1.** illustrative; *fig.* enlightening; **2.** *m*, **-a** *f* illustrator; **ilustrar** [1a] illustrate; *fig.* enlighten, instruct; (*aclarar*) explain; (*hacer ilustre*) make *s.o.* famous; **ilustre** illustrious, famous; **ilustrísimo** most illustrious; *Vuestra* ~*a* Your Grace.
imagen *f mst* image; (mental) picture; (*semejanza*) likeness; *~es pl. rhet.* imagery; *a su ~* in his own image; *ser la viva ~ de* be the living image of; **imaginación** *f* imagination; (*fantasía*) fancy; **imaginar** [1a] imagine, visualize; (*inventar*) think up; **~se** suppose (*que* that); imagine, picture (to o.s.), fancy; *me imagino freq.* I can imagine; *¡imagínate!* just imagine!; **imaginario** imaginary, fanciful; **imaginativa** *f* imaginativeness, imagination; common sense, understanding; **imaginativo** imaginative; **imaginería** *f* statuary; fancy-colored embroidery; *rhet.* imagery.
imán *m* magnet; *~ de herradura* horseshoe magnet; *~ inductor* ⚡ field magnet; **iman(t)ación** *f* magnetization; **iman(t)ar** [1a] magnetize.
imbatible unbeatable; **imbatido** unbeaten.
imbécil 1. *p.* imbecile, feeble-minded; *cosa* silly; **2.** *m/f* imbecile, idiot; **imbecilidad** *f* imbecility *etc.*
imberbe beardless.
imbornal *m* drain hole.
imborrable ineffaceable.
imbuir [3g] imbue, infuse (*de, en* with).
imitación *f* imitation; *a ~ de* after, in imitation of; *de ~* imitation *attr.*, fake; **imitador 1.** imitative; **2.** *m*, **-a** *f* imitator; follower; **imitar** [1a] imitate; mimic, *b.s.* ape; *cosa b.s.* counterfeit.
impaciencia *f* impatience; **impacientar** [1a] exasperate, make *s.o.* lose patience; **~se** get impatient, fret (*por* at); **impaciente** impatient (*con, de, por* at); fretful.
impacto *m* impact; ⚔ hit; *~ directo* direct hit.
impar 1. odd, uneven (*a.* ⚕); (*que no tiene igual*) unmatched; **2.** *m* odd number.
imparcial impartial; (*que no entra en ningún partido*) nonpartisan; **imparcialidad** *f* impartiality.
impás *m* finesse.
impasible impassive, unmoved.
impávido dauntless, unflinching, intrepid.
impecable impeccable, faultless.
impedido disabled, crippled; *~ para* unfit for; **impedimento** *m* impediment (*a.* ⚖), obstacle, hindrance (*a* to); disability; **impedir** [3l] stop, prevent (*inf. or que subj.* [from] *ger.*); deter; (*frustrar*) thwart; (*estorbar*) hamper; **impeditivo** preventive.
impeler [2a] propel, drive; *fig.* impel, drive (*a inf.* to *inf.*).

impenetrable impenetrable (*a. fig.*); impervious; *fig.* unfathomable.
impenitencia *f* impenitence; **impenitente** impenitent, unrepentant.
impensado unexpected, unforeseen; (*fortuito*) random.
imperante ruling (*a.* ☤), prevailing; **imperar** [1a] rule, reign, *fig.* be in force, prevail; **imperativo 1.** commanding; **2.** *m* imperative (mood).
imperceptible imperceptible.
imperdible *m* safety pin.
imperdonable unpardonable, unforgivable.
imperecedero undying, imperishable; eternal.
imperfección *f* imperfection, flaw, fault; **imperfecto** imperfect (*a. gr.*); faulty; (*sin acabar*) unfinished.
imperial 1. imperial; **2.** *f* top, upper deck; **imperialismo** *m* imperialism; **imperialista 1.** imperialistic; **2.** *m*/*f* imperialist.
impericia *f* unskilfulness; *a prueba de ~* foolproof.
imperio *m* empire; (*autoridad*) rule, sway; *fig.* pride; **imperioso** imperious, lordly; (*urgente*) peremptory; (*necesario*) imperative.
imperito inexpert, unskilled; (*torpe*) clumsy.
impermeabilizar [1f] waterproof; **impermeable 1.** waterproof; impervious, impermeable; **2.** *m* raincoat, mackintosh.
impersonal impersonal.
impertérrito unafraid, unshaken.
impertinencia *f* irrelevance; impertinence *etc.*; **impertinente 1.** irrelevant; uncalled-for; (*insolente*) impertinent; (*susceptible*) touchy; (*nimio*) fussy; **2.** ~**s** *m*/*pl.* lorgnette.
imperturbable imperturbable, unruffled; **imperturbado** unperturbed.
ímpetu *m* impetus, impulse; momentum; (*movimiento*) (on)rush; (*prisa*) haste; violence; **impetuosidad** *f* impetuosity; impetus; **impetuoso** *p.* impetuous; headstrong; *acto* hasty; violent; *torrente* rushing.
impiedad *f* impiety *etc.*; heartlessness, pitilessness; **impío** impious, ungodly; wicked; heartless, pitiless.
implacable implacable, relentless; *competencia* cutthroat.
implantar [1a] implant, introduce.
implicación *f* contradiction (in terms).
implicar [1g] involve; *p. mst b.s.* implicate; *inferencia* imply; **implícito** implicit, implied.
implorar [1a] implore, beg.
impolítico imprudent; tactless; (*descortés*) impolite.
imponderable imponderable; (*indecible*) unutterable.
imponente 1. imposing, impressive; stately, grand; F terrific, tremendous; **2.** *m*/*f* ☤ depositor, investor; **imponer** [2r] *mst* impose (*a* on; *a. typ., eccl.*); *obediencia etc.* exact (*a* from), enforce (*a* upon); *tarea* set; *carga etc.* lay, thrust (*a* upon); instruct (*en* in); impute falsely (*a* to); (*impresionar*) impress; ☤ invest, deposit; ~**se** get one's way, assert o.s.; prevail (*a* over); (*costumbre*) grow up; ~ *de* acquaint o.s. with; **imponible** taxable.
impopular unpopular; **impopularidad** *f* unpopularity.
importación *f* import(s); (*acto*) importation; *de ~* imported; **importador** *m*, **-a** *f* importer; **importancia** *f* importance; significance; weight; magnitude; *sin ~* unimportant, minor; *dar mucha ~ a* make much of; *no dar ~ a* make light of; *darse ~* give o.s. airs; **importante** important; significant; weighty; (*grande*) considerable, sizeable; *lo* (*más*) ~ the main thing, **importar**[1] [1a] *v*/*t.* amount to, be worth; (*llevar consigo*) involve, imply; *v*/*i.* matter (*a* to), be of consequence; ~ *a* concern; *¡no importa!* it doesn't matter!, never mind!; *no importa (el) precio* cost no object; *¿te importa prestármelo?* do you mind lending it to me?; *¿qué importa?* what does it matter?, what of it?; **importar**[2] [1a] ☤ import (*a, en* into); **importe** *m* amount, value, cost.
importunar [1a] importune, pester, molest; **importunidad** *f* importunity, pestering; (*incomodidad*) annoyance; **importuno** importunate; inopportune; (*molesto*) troublesome, annoying.

imposibilidad *f* impossibility; inability; **imposibilitado** unable (*para inf.* to *inf.*); ⚕ disabled; (*pobre*) without means; **imposibilitar** [1a] make *s.t.* impossible, preclude; *p.* render unfit (*para* for), incapacitate; *me imposibilitó el salir* it prevented me going out; **imposible 1.** impossible; **2.** *m* the impossible; *hacer los ~s para inf.* do everything possible to *inf.*

imposición *f* imposition *etc.*; (*impuesto*) tax; *typ.* make-up; ✝ deposit; *~ de manos* laying-on of hands.

impostor *m*, **-a** *f* impostor, fraud; **impostura** *f* imposture, fraud, sham; (*imputación*) aspersion, slur.

impotable undrinkable.

impotencia *f* impotence (*a.* ⚕) *etc.*; **impotente** impotent (*a.* ⚕), powerless, helpless.

impracticabilidad *f* impracticability; **impracticable** impracticable, unworkable; *camino* impassable.

imprecación *f* imprecation, curse; **imprecar** [1g] imprecate, curse.

imprecisión *f* lack of precision, vagueness.

impredictible unpredictable.

impregnar [1a] impregnate, saturate; *fig.* pervade.

impremeditado unpremeditated.

imprenta *f* (*arte*) printing; (*oficina*) press, printing house; (*letra*) print; (*lo impreso*) printed matter; **imprentar** *la ropa S.Am.* press, iron; *S.Am.* mark.

imprescindible essential, indispensable.

impresión *f typ.* printing; (*letra, phot.*) print; (*tirada*) edition, impression; (*marca*) imprint; *fig.* impression; *~ dactilar*, *~ digital* fingerprint; **impresionable** impressionable, sensitive, susceptible; **impresionante** impressive, striking; moving; **impresionar** [1a] impress, strike; move; *disco etc.* record; **impresionista 1.** impressionist(ic); **2.** *m/f* impressionist; **impreso 1.** printed; **2.** *m* printed paper (*or* book); *~s pl.* printed matter; **impresor** *m* printer.

imprevisible unforeseeable; **imprevisión** *f* lack of foresight; thoughtlessness; **imprevisor** thoughtless; happy-go-lucky F; **imprevisto 1.** unforeseen, unexpected; **2.** *~s m/pl.* incidentals, unforeseen expenses.

imprimar [1a] *paint.* prime.

imprimir [3a; *p.p. impreso*] *typ.* print; (*estampar*) stamp; *fig.* stamp, imprint (*en* on).

improbabilidad *f* improbability, unlikelihood; **improbable** improbable, unlikely.

ímprobo dishonest; *tarea* arduous, thankless.

improcedencia *f* wrongness; inadmissibility; **improcedente** not right; ⚖ unfounded, inadmissible.

improductivo unproductive.

impronunciable unpronounceable.

improperio *m* insult, taunt.

impropicio inauspicious.

impropiedad *f* infelicity (of language); **impropio** improper (*a.* ℞); (*no apto*) inappropriate, unsuitable (*de, para* to, for); (*ajeno*) foreign (*de* to); *estilo* infelicitous.

impróvido improvident.

improvisación *f* improvisation; *b.s.* makeshift; *esp.* ♪ extemporization, impromptu; **improvisado** improvised; *b.s.* makeshift; ♪ *etc.* extempore, impromptu; **improvisar** [1a] improvise; extemporize (*a.* ♪); **improviso** unexpected, unforeseen; *al ~, de ~* unexpectedly; *hablar etc.* extempore; ♪ impromptu; **improvisto** = *improviso.*

imprudencia *f* imprudence *etc.*; *~ temeraria* criminal negligence; **imprudente** unwise, imprudent; rash, reckless; *palabras* indiscreet.

impudencia *f* impudence *etc.*; **impudente** impudent, brazen, shameless; **impudicia** *f* immodesty *etc.*; **impúdico** immodest, lewd, lecherous.

impuesto 1. *p.p. of imponer*; **2.** *m* tax, duty, levy (*sobre* on); *~s pl.* taxation; *sujeto a ~* taxable; *~ sobre la renta* income tax; *~ sobre el valor añadido* value-added tax.

impugnar [1a] oppose, contest; *teoría etc.* refute.

impulsar [1a] = *impeler*; **impulsión** *f* impulsion; ⊕ drive, propulsion; *fig.* impulse; *~ por reacción* jet propulsion; **impulsivo**

fig. impulsive; **impulso** *m* impulse (*a. fig.*), drive, thrust; impetus; *fig.* urge; *a* ~*s del miedo* driven by fear.
impune unpunished; **impunemente** with impunity; **impunidad** *f* impunity.
impuntual unpunctual; **impuntualidad** *f* unpunctuality.
impureza *f* impurity; **impurificar** [1g] adulterate; *fig.* defile; **impuro** impure.
imputación *f* imputation; **imputar** [1a] impute, attribute (*a* to).
inabordable unapproachable.
inacabable endless, interminable; **inacabado** unfinished.
inaccesible inaccessible.
inacción *f* inaction; drift.
inacentuado unaccented.
inaceptable unacceptable.
inactividad *f* inactivity *etc.*; **inactivo** inactive; (*perezoso*) idle, sluggish; ✝ dull.
inadaptación *f* maladjustment; **inadaptado** *m*, **a** *f* (*p.*) misfit.
inadecuado inadequate; unsuitable, inappropriate.
inadmisible inadmissible.
inadvertencia *f* inadvertence; (*error*) oversight, slip; **inadvertido** *p.* unobservant, inattentive; *error* inadvertent; *cosa* unnoticed; *pasar* ~ escape notice.
inagotable inexhaustible.
inaguantable intolerable.
inajenable, inalienable inalienable; not transferable.
inalámbrico wireless.
inalterable unalterable, unchanging; *color* fast; **inalterado** unchanged.
inamisto unfriendly.
inamovible irremovable, fixed; undetachable; (*incorporado*) built-in.
inanición *f* inanition, starvation; **inanidad** *f* inanity.
inanimado inanimate; **inánime** spiritless, lifeless.
inapeable incomprehensible; *p.* stubborn.
inapelable ⚖ unappealable; *fig.* inevitable.
inapercibido unperceived.
inapetencia *f* lack of appetite.
inaplicable inapplicable.
inapreciable invaluable, inestimable.
inapto unsuited (*para* for, to).
inarmónico unharmonious, unmusical.
inarrugable crease-resisting.
inarticulado inarticulate.
inasequible unattainable, out of reach; unobtainable.
inastillable nonshatterable, shatterproof.
inatacable unassailable.
inaudible inaudible; **inaudito** unheard-of, unprecedented; *fig.* outrageous.
inauguración *f* inauguration *etc.*; **inaugural** inaugural, opening; *viaje* maiden; **inaugurar** [1a] inaugurate; *exposición etc.* open; *estatua* unveil.
inca *m/f* Inca; **incaico** Inca.
incalculable incalculable; *riqueza* untold.
incalificable indescribable; (*infame, atroz*) unspeakable.
incambiable unchangeable.
incandescencia *f* incandescence, white heat, glow; **incandescente** incandescent, white-hot.
incansable tireless, unflagging.
incapacidad *f* incapacity; incompetence; inability (*para inf.* to *inf.*), unfitness (*para* for); **incapacitado** incapacitated; unfitted (*para* for); **incapacitar** [1a] incapacitate, render unfit (*para* for); disqualify (*para* for); **incapaz** incapable (*de* of); unfit; unable (*de inf.* to *inf.*); (*necio*) stupid; ⚖ incompetent.
incasable unmarriageable; (*que no quiere casarse*) opposed to marriage; *por su fealdad* unable to find a husband.
incautarse [1a]: ~ *de* ⚖ seize, attach.
incauto unwary, incautious.
incendajas *f/pl.* kindling.
incendiar [1b] set on fire, set alight; ~**se** catch fire; **incendiario** **1.** incendiary; *palabras* inflammatory; **2.** *m*, **a** *f* incendiary; **incendio** *m* fire.
incensar [1k] *eccl.* (in)cense; *fig.* flatter; **incensario** *m* censer.
incentivo *m* incentive.
incertidumbre *f* uncertainty.
incesante incessant.
incesto *m* incest; **incestuoso** incestuous.
incidencia *f* incidence (*a.* ⚕);

incident; *por* ~ by chance; **incidental** incidental; **incidente 1.** incidental; **2.** *m* incident.

incidir [3a] *v/t. esp.* ⚕ make an incision in; *v/i.* ~ *en culpa* fall into guilt; ~ *en*, ~ *sobre* strike, impinge on.

incienso *m* incense (*a. fig.*); (*olíbano*) frankincense.

incierto uncertain; (*falso*) untrue; inconstant.

incineración *f* incineration; ~ *de cadáveres* cremation; **incinerador** *m* incinerator; **incinerar** [1a] incinerate; *cadáver* cremate.

incipiente incipient.

incisión *f* incision; (*mordacidad en el lenguaje*) incisiveness, sarcasm; **incisivo 1.** sharp, cutting; *fig.* incisive; **2.** *m* incisor.

inciso *m gr.* clause; comma.

incitante provoking, inviting; **incitar** [1a] incite, prompt, spur on (*a* to).

incivil uncivil, rude; **incivilidad** *f* incivility; **incivilizado** uncivilized.

inclasificable unclassifiable, nondescript.

inclemencia *f* harshness; *a la* ~ exposed to wind and weather; **inclemente** harsh, severe.

inclinación *f* inclination (*a. fig.*); (*declive*) slope, incline; (*oblicuidad*) slant, tilt; stoop *de cuerpo*; nod *de cabeza*; (*reverencia*) bow; *fig.* leaning; **inclinado** sloping, leaning, slanting; *plano* inclined; **inclinar** [1a] *v/t.* incline (*a. fig.*; *a inf.* to *inf.*); slope, slant, tilt; *cabeza* (*bajar*) bend, nod *asintiendo*, bow *haciendo reverencia*; *p.* induce, persuade (*a inf.* to *inf.*); *v/i.*: ~ *a p.* resemble; ~**se** lean; slope; bend; *fig.* be inclined, tend (*a* to); ~ *a p.* resemble.

ínclito illustrious, renowned.

incluir [3g] include; contain, incorporate; (*comprender*) comprise; (*insertar*) enclose; *todo incluido* all found, inclusive terms; **inclusión** *f* inclusion; **inclusive 1.** *adv.* (*a.* **inclusivamente**) inclusive(ly); **2.** *prp.* including; **inclusivo** inclusive; **incluso 1.** *adj.* enclosed; **2.** *prp.* including; **3.** *adv.* inclusively; (*hasta, aun*) even.

incoar [1a] initiate; **incoativo** *gr.* inchoative, inceptive.

incobrable irrecoverable; *deuda* bad.

incógnita *f* unknown quantity; **incógnito 1.** unknown; **2.** *m* incognito; *de* ~ *adv.* incognito.

incoherencia *f* incoherence; **incoherente** incoherent, disconnected.

íncola *m* inhabitant.

incoloro colorless (*a. fig.*).

incólume safe, unharmed.

incombustible incombustible, fireproof.

incomible uneatable, inedible.

incomodar [1a] inconvenience, trouble, put out; ~**se** get annoyed; **incomodidad** *f* inconvenience; discomfort; annoyance; **incómodo 1.** inconvenient; uncomfortable; (*molesto*) tiresome, annoying; **2.** *m* = *incomodidad*.

incomparable incomparable.

incomparecimiento: *pleito perdido por* ~ undefended suit.

incompasivo pitiless, unsympathetic.

incompatible incompatible; *acontecimientos, citas, horas de clase etc.* conflicting.

incompetencia *f* incompetence; **incompetente** incompetent, unqualified.

incompleto incomplete, unfinished.

incomprensible incomprehensible.

incomunicación *f* isolation; ⚖ solitary confinement; **incomunicado** cut off; ⚖ in solitary confinement; incommunicado; **incomunicar** [1g] isolate, cut off; ⚖ put *s.o.* into solitary confinement.

inconcebible inconceivable, unthinkable.

inconciliable irreconcilable.

inconcluso incomplete, unfinished; **inconcluyente** inconclusive.

incondicional unconditional; *fe* implicit; *apoyo* wholehearted; *aserto* unqualified; *amigo, partidario etc.* staunch, stalwart.

inconexo unconnected; *fig.* incongruous; (*incoherente*) disjointed, disconnected; (*inaplicable*) irrelevant.

inconfeso unconfessed.

inconfundible unmistakable.

incongruencia *f* incongruity; **incongruente**, **incongruo** incongruous.

inconmensurable immeasurable, vast; (*desproporcionado*) incommensurate.

inconmovible unshakable.
inconquistable unconquerable; *fig.* unyielding.
inconsciencia *f* unconsciousness; unawareness; thoughtlessness, recklessness; **inconsciente** unconscious, unaware (*de* of); oblivious (*de* of, to); unwitting; (*irreflexivo*) thoughtless, reckless; *lo* ~ the unconscious.
inconsecuencia *f* inconsequence, inconsistency; **inconsecuente** inconsequent(ial), inconsistent.
inconsiderado thoughtless, inconsiderate; (*precipitado*) hasty.
inconsistencia *f* inconsistency *etc.*; **inconsistente** inconsistent; uneven; (*poco firme*) unstable; *argumento etc.* weak; *tela etc.* thin, flimsy; *terreno* loose.
inconsolable inconsolable.
inconstancia *f* inconstancy *etc.*; **inconstante** inconstant, changeable; (*poco firme*) unsteady; *p.* fickle.
inconstitucional unconstitutional.
inconsútil seamless.
incontable countless.
incontestable unanswerable; undeniable; **incontestado** unchallenged, unquestioned.
incontinencia *f* incontinence (*a.* ⚕); **incontinente 1.** incontinent (*a.* ⚕); **2.** *adv.* instantly, at once.
incontrastable *dificultad* insuperable; *argumento* unanswerable; *p.* unshakable.
incontrovertible incontrovertible.
inconveniencia *f* unsuitability; inconvenience; (*dicho*) tactless remark; silly thing; **inconveniente 1.** unsuitable; inconvenient; impolite; **2.** *m* obstacle, difficulty; (*desventaja*) drawback; objection; *poner un* ~ raise an objection; *no tengo* ~ (*en ello*) I have no objection, I don't mind.
incordiar [1b] F bother, annoy; **incordio** *m* F bore, nuisance.
incorporación *f* incorporation, association; embodiment; **incorporado** ⊕ built-in; **incorporar** [1a] incorporate (*a, con, en* in[to], with), embody (*a, con, en* in); mix (*con* with); make *p.* sit up; **~se** sit up; ~ *a buque etc.* join; **incorpóreo** incorporeal, bodiless.
incorrección *f* incorrectness *etc.*; **incorrecto** wrong, incorrect; *conducta* discourteous, improper; *facciones* irregular; **incorregible** incorrigible.
incorruptible incorruptible; **incorrupto** *cuerpo* uncorrupted; *fig.* pure, chaste.
incredibilidad *f* incredibility; **incredulidad** *f* incredulity, unbelief; **incrédulo 1.** incredulous, sceptical; **2.** *m*, **a** *f* unbeliever, sceptic; **increíble** incredible, unbelievable.
incremento *m* increase, addition; *tomar* ~ grow, increase.
increpar [1a] rebuke, reprimand.
incriminar [1a] accuse; incriminate; *falta* magnify.
incruento bloodless.
incrustación *f* incrustation; (*taracea*) inlay; **incrustar** [1a] incrust; inlay.
incubación *f* incubation (*a.* ⚕); **incubadora** *f* incubator; **incubar** [1a] incubate; hatch (*a. fig.*).
íncubo *m* incubus.
incuestionable unquestionable.
inculcar [1g] instil, inculcate (*en* in).
inculpable blameless; **inculpación** *f* accusation; **inculpar** [1a] accuse (*de* of); blame (*de* for).
inculto uncultivated (*a. fig.*); *fig.* uncultured, uncouth; **incultura** *f fig.* lack of culture.
incumbencia *f* obligation; *no es de mi* ~ it is not my in province, it has nothing to do with me; **incumbir** [3a]: ~ *a* be incumbent upon (*inf.* to *inf.*); *le incumbe inf.* it is his business (*or* job) to *inf.*
incumplido unfulfilled; **incumplimiento** *m* nonfulfillment; default.
incunables *m/pl.* incunabula.
incurable incurable; *fig.* irremediable.
incuria *f* negligence, carelessness; **incurioso** negligent, careless.
incurrir [3a]: ~ *en error* fall into; *deuda, ira etc.* incur; **incursión** *f* incursion, raid.
indagación *f* investigation, inquiry; **indagar** [1h] investigate, inquire into; (*descubrir*) ascertain.
indebidamente *adv.* unduly; **indebido** undue; *b.s.* improper.

indecencia *f* indecency *etc.*; **indecente** indecent, improper; obscene; F wretched, miserable.
indecible indescribable; *b.s.* unspeakable.
indecisión *f* indecision, hesitation; **indeciso** undecided; hesitant; vague; *resultado* indecisive.
indeclinable unavoidable; *gr.* indeclinable.
indecoroso unseemly, indecorous.
indefectible unfailing, infallible.
indefendible indefensible; **indefenso** defenseless.
indefinible indefinable; **indefinido** indefinite; vague; (*sin definir*) undefined.
indeleble indelible.
indemne undamaged; *p.* unhurt; **indemnidad** *f* (*seguridad contra un daño*) indemnity; **indemnización** *f* (*acto*) indemnification; (*pago*) indemnity; ~ *por despido* severance pay; ~*es pl.* reparations; **indemnizar** [1f] indemnify, compensate (*de* for).
independencia *f* independence; self-sufficiency; **independiente 1.** independent (*de* of); *cosa a.* self-contained; *p. a.* self-sufficient; **2.** *m/f* independent; **independizarse** [1f] become independent.
indescifrable undecipherable.
indescriptible indescribable.
indeseable undesirable.
indeshilachable nonfraying.
indesmallable runproof.
indestructible indestructible.
indeterminado indeterminate; inconclusive; *p.* irresolute.
indiana *f* printed calico.
indiano 1. Spanish American; **2.** *m Spaniard returning rich from America, approx.* nabob.
indicación *f* indication, sign; (*sugerencia*) hint; (*dato*) piece of information; reading *de termómetro etc.*; ~*es pl.* instructions, directions; *por* ~ *de* at the suggestion of; **indicado** right, suitable (*para* for); obvious; (*probable*) likely; *él es el más* ~ *para hacerlo* he is the best man to do it; *muy* ~ just the thing; just the person; **indicador** *m* indicator (*a.* ⊕, ⚘); gauge *de gasolina etc.*; (*aguja*) pointer; ~ *de velocidades* speedometer; **indicar** [1g] indicate; suggest; (*señalar*) point out, point to; ⊕ register, record; (*termómetro etc.*) read; **indicativo** *adj. a. su. m* indicative; **índice** *m mst* index; (*aguja*) pointer, needle; hand *de reloj*; catalogue *de biblioteca*; ~ *de compresión* compression ratio; ~ *de materias* table of contents; ~ *en el corte* thumb index; ~ *expurgatorio* Index; **indiciario** *prueba* circumstantial; **indicio** *m* indication, sign; (*prueba*) piece of evidence, clue (*de* to); (*huella*) trace; ⚖ ~*s pl. vehementes* circumstantial evidence.
indiferencia *f* indifference *etc.*; **indiferente** indifferent (*a* to); apathetic, unconcerned (*a* about); (*que no importa*) immaterial; *me es* ~ it makes no difference to me.
indígena 1. indigenous (*de* to), native; **2.** *m/f* native.
indigencia *f* indigence, poverty; **indigente 1.** indigent, destitute; **2.** *m/f* pauper.
indigestarse [1a] (*p.*) have indigestion; (*comida*) be indigestible; *fig.* be disliked, be unbearable; **indigestible** indigestible; **indigestión** *f* indigestion; **indigesto** undigested; (*incomible*) indigestible; *fig.* muddled.
indignación *f* indignation; **indignado** indignant (*con, contra p.* with; *de, por* at, about); **indignante** outrageous, infuriating; **indignar** [1a] anger, make *s.o.* indignant; ~**se** get indignant; **indignidad** *f* unworthiness; (*una* ~) unworthy act; (*afrenta*) indignity; **indigno** unworthy (*de* of); (*vil*) low.
indio *adj. a. su. m*, **a** *f* Indian.
indirecta *f* hint; insinuation; ~ *del padre Cobos* broad hint; *soltar una* ~ drop a hint; **indirecto** indirect; roundabout; oblique.
indisciplina *f* indiscipline, lack of discipline; **indisciplinado** undisciplined; lax.
indiscreción *f* indiscretion; **indiscreto** indiscreet, tactless.
indisculpable inexcusable.
indiscutible indisputable, unquestionable.
indisoluble indissoluble.
indispensable indispensable, essential.
indisponer [2r] *proyecto* spoil, upset; ⚕ upset, make unfit; ~ *con*

set *s.o.* against; **~se** ⚕ fall ill; ~ *con p.* fall out with; **indisponible** unavailable; **indisposición** *f* indisposition; **indispuesto** indisposed.
indisputable indisputable.
indistinción *f* indistinctness; indiscrimination; identity; **indistinguible** indistinguishable; **indistintamente** indiscriminately, without distinction; **indistinto** indistinct; vague; *luz etc.* faint, dim; *elección etc.* indiscriminate.
individual 1. individual; peculiar; *habitación* single; **2. ~es** *m/pl. tenis*: singles; **individualidad** *f* individuality; **individualista 1.** individualistic; **2.** *m/f* individualist; **individualizar** [1f], **individuar** [1e] individualize; **individuo** *adj. a. su. m*, **a** *f* individual (*a.* F); member *de sociedad*; **indivisible** indivisible; **indiviso** undivided.
indócil unmanageable, disobedient.
indocto unlearned, ignorant.
indocumentado 1. *adj.* unidentified; unqualified; without identification; **2.** *m*, **a** *f* nobody (*person of no account*).
indoeuropeo *adj. a. su. m* Indo-European.
índole *f* nature; character, disposition *de p.*; class, kind *de cosa*.
indolencia *f* indolence *etc.*; **indolente** indolent, lazy; apathetic; = **indoloro** painless.
indomable indomitable; *animal* untamable; unmanageable; **indomado** untamed; **indómito** indomitable; *animal* untamed; *b.s.* unruly.
indostanés *adj. a. su. m*, **-a** *f* Hindustani; **indostánico 1.** Hindustani; **2.** *m* (*a.* **indostaní** *m*) Hindustani.
indubitable indubitable.
inducción *f* inducement, persuasion; *phls.*, ⚡ induction; **inducido** *m* ⚡ armature; **inducir** [3o] induce (*a.* ⚡), persuade (*a inf.* to *inf.*); *phls.* infer; ~ *en error* lead *s.o.* into; **inductivo** inductive.
indudable undoubted; **indudablemente** undoubtedly, doubtless.
indulgencia *f* indulgence (*a. eccl.*); **indulgente** indulgent.
indultar [1a] ⚖ pardon, reprieve; exempt; **indulto** *m* ⚖ pardon, reprieve; exemption.
indumentaria *f*, **indumento** *m* clothing, dress.
industria *f* industry; (*destreza*) ingenuity, skill; (*oficio*) trade; ~ *pesada* heavy industry; *de* ~ on purpose; **industrial 1.** industrial; **2.** *m* industrialist, manufacturer; **industrialismo** *m* industrialism; **industrializar** [1f] industrialize; **industriarse** [1b] manage, find a way, get things fixed; **industrioso** industrious; (*hábil*) skilful, resourceful.
inédito unpublished; new, novel, unknown.
ineducado uneducated; *b.s.* ill-bred.
inefable ineffable, indescribable.
ineficacia *f* inefficacy *etc.*; **ineficaz** ineffective, ineffectual; inefficient; **ineficiencia** *f* inefficiency; **ineficiente** inefficient.
inelástico inelastic.
inelegancia *f* inelegance; **inelegante** inelegant.
inelegible inelegible.
ineluctable, ineludible inescapable.
inenarrable inexpressible.
inencogible unshrinkable, non-shrink.
inepcia *f* stupidity; = **ineptitud** *f* ineptitude, incompetence; **inepto** inept, incompetent; stupid.
inequidad *f* inequity.
inequívoco unequivocal, unmistakable.
inercia *f* inertia *etc.*
inerme unarmed, unprotected.
inerte inert (*a. phys.*); inactive; *fig.* passive; sluggish.
inescrutable inscrutable.
inesperado unexpected, unforeseen; unhoped-for.
inestabilidad *f* instability; **inestable** unstable, unsteady.
inestimable inestimable, invaluable.
inevitable inevitable, unavoidable.
inexacto inaccurate, inexact; *hecho* incorrect, untrue.
inexcusable inexcusable, unpardonable; unavoidable; essential, indispensable.
inexhausto *parte etc.* unused; unspent; (*inagotable*) inexhaustible.
inexistencia *f* nonexistence; **inexistente** nonexistent; defunct.

inexorable inexorable.
inexperiencia *f* inexperience *etc.*; **inexperto** inexperienced, raw; inexpert, unskilled.
inexplicable inexplicable; **inexplicado** unexplained; ⚓ uncharted.
inexplorado unexplored.
inexpresable inexpressible; **inexpresivo** inexpressive; wooden, dull.
inexpugnable impregnable; *fig.* firm, unshakable.
inextinguible inextinguishable, unquenchable.
inextricable inextricable.
infalibilidad *f* infallibility; **infalible** infallible.
infamar [1a] dishonor, discredit; (*defamar*) slander; **infamatorio** defamatory; **infame 1.** infamous, odious; vile; **2.** *m/f* villain; **infamia** *f* infamy.
infancia *f* infancy (*a. fig.*), childhood; (*ps.*) children; **infanta** *f* infant; *hist.* princess; **infante** *m* infant; *hist.* prince; ⚔ infantryman; **infantería** *f* infantry; ~ *de marina* marines, Marine Corps; **infanticida** *m/f* infanticide (*p.*); **infanticidio** *m* infanticide (*act*); **infantil** (*de niños*) infant, children's; (*inocente*) childlike; *b.s.* infantile, childish.
infatigable tireless.
infausto unlucky, unfortunate.
infección *f* infection (*a. fig.*); **infeccioso** infectious; **infectar** [1a] = *inficionar*; **infecto** foul; *fig.* corrupt, tainted.
infecundo infertile, sterile.
infelicidad *f* unhappiness; misfortune; **infeliz 1.** unhappy, wretched; unfortunate; **2.** *m* poor devil; good-natured simpleton.
inferencia *f* inference.
inferior 1. lower (*a* than); *calidad, rango* inferior (*a* to); ~ *a número* under, below, less than; **2.** *m* subordinate, inferior; *contp.* underling; **inferioridad** *f* inferiority; lower position.
inferir [3i] infer, deduce (*de, por* from); (*conducir a*) lead to, bring on; *herida* inflict.
infernáculo *m* hopscotch.
infernal infernal (*a.* F), hellish; F *un ruido* ~ a hell of a noise.
infértil infertile.
infestación *f* infestation; **infestar** [1a] overrun, infest; ⚕ infect.
inficionar [1a] infect, contaminate (*a. fig.*); *fig.* corrupt.
infidelidad *f* unfaithfulness *etc.*; **infidencia** *f* disloyalty, faithlessness; (*acto*) disloyal act; **infidente** faithless, disloyal; **infiel 1.** unfaithful, disloyal (*a, con, para* to); *relato* inaccurate; **2.** *m/f* unbeliever, infidel.
infiernillo *m* spirit lamp; chafing dish; **infierno** *m* hell; *fig.* inferno, hell; *en el quinto* ~ far, far away.
infiltración *f* infiltration; **infiltrar** [1a] infiltrate; *fig.* inculcate; **~se** filter (*en* in, through); percolate; *esp. fig.* infiltrate.
ínfimo lowest.
infinidad *f* infinity; *fig.* enormous number; **infinitesimal** infinitesimal (*a.* 𝔸); **infinitivo** *m* infinitive (mood); **infinito 1.** infinite; *fig.* boundless, limitless; enormous; **2.** *m* infinite; 𝔸 infinity; **3.** *adv.* infinitely; greatly, very much.
inflación *f* inflation (*a.* ☤); swelling; *fig.* conceit; **inflacionista** inflationary; **inflado** *m* inflation *of a tire.*
inflamable inflammable; **inflamación** *f* ignition, combustion; *fig.*, ⚕ inflammation; **inflamar** [1a] set on fire; *fig.* inflame (*a.* ⚕), excite; **~se** catch fire, flame up; *fig.* become inflamed (*a.* ⚕; *de, en* with), get excited.
inflar [1a] inflate (*a. fig.*), blow up; **~se** swell.
inflexible inflexible, unyielding; **inflexión** *f* inflexion.
infligir [3c] inflict (*a* on).
influencia *f* influence (*sobre* on); **influenciar** [1b] influence; **influir** [3g] have influence, carry weight (*con* with); ~ *en*, ~ *sobre* influence, affect; have a hand in; **influjo** *m* influence (*sobre* on); **influyente** influential.
información *f* (*una* a piece of) information; ⚔ intelligence; (*noticias*) news; ⚖ judicial inquiry; investigation; (*informe*) report; testimonial *sobre p.*; ⚖ *abrir una* ~ institute proceedings; **~es** *pl.* testimonial; **informador** *m*, **-a** *f* informant; **informal** irregular, incorrect; unconventional; *p.* unreliable,

off-hand, unbusinesslike; **informalidad** *f* irregularity; unreliability *etc.*; **informar** [1a] *v/t.* inform (*de* of, *sobre* about); (*dar forma a*) shape; *v/i.* report (*acerca de* on); ⚖ plead; ⚖ inform (*contra* against); **~se** inquire (*de* into), find out (*de* about), acquaint o.s. (*de* with); **informática** *f* data processing; computer science; **informativo** informative; news *attr.*; *junta etc.* consultative.

informe[1] shapeless.

informe[2] *m* report, statement; (piece of) information; ⚖ plea; *~s pl.* information; data; references; *~s confidenciales* inside information; *pedir ~s* make inquiries (*a* of; *sobre* about); *tomar ~s* gather information.

infortunado unfortunate, unlucky; **infortunio** *m* misfortune; mishap.

infracción *f* infringement; breach *de contrato*.

infraconsumo *m* underconsumption.

infracto unperturbable.

infra(e)scrito 1. undersigned; undermentioned; **2.** *m*, **a** *f* undersigned.

infraestructura *f* substructure; *fig.* underlying structure.

in fraganti red-handed.

infranqueable impassable; *fig.* insurmountable.

infrarrojo infrared.

infrecuente infrequent.

infringir [3c] infringe, contravene.

infructuoso fruitless.

ínfulas *f/pl. fig.* conceit; *darse ~* put on airs; *tener (muchas) ~ de* fancy o.s. as.

infundado unfounded, groundless.

infundio *m* F fairy tale, fib.

infundir [3a] infuse (*a, en* into); *fig.* instil (*a, en* into); *~ miedo a* fill *s.o.* with fear; **infusión** *f* infusion.

ingeniar [1b] devise, contrive, think up; **~se** manage, contrive (*a, para inf.* to *inf.*); make shift (*con* with); **ingeniería** *f* engineering; **ingeniero** *m* engineer (*a.* ⚓ ⚔); *v. agrónomo*; *~ de caminos, canales y puertos* civil engineer; *~ forestal*, *~ de montes* forestry expert; *~ de minas* mining engineer; *~ naval* shipbuilder, naval architect; **ingenio** *m* ingenuity, inventiveness; talent; wit; (*p.*) clever person; ⊕ apparatus; *~ nuclear* nuclear device; *S.Am.* *~ (de azúcar)* sugar refinery; **ingeniosidad** *f* ingenuity *etc.*; (*una ~*) clever idea; **ingenioso** ingenious, clever; resourceful; witty.

ingénito innate.

ingente huge, enormous.

ingenuidad *f* ingenuousness *etc.*; **ingenuo** ingenuous, naïve; candid.

ingerir [3i] swallow.

ingle *f* groin.

inglés 1. English, British; **2.** *m* (*p.*) Englishman, Briton; (*idioma*) English; F creditor; *el ~ medio* Middle English; *los ~es* the English, the British; **inglesa** *f* Englishwoman; *montar a la ~* ride sidesaddle; **inglesismo** *m* Anglicism.

ingobernable uncontrollable.

ingramatical ungrammatical.

ingratitud *f* ingratitude; **ingrato 1.** ungrateful; *tarea* thankless; disagreeable; (*desabrido*) harsh; **2.** *m/f* ingrate.

ingravidez *f* lightness, tenuousness; (*gravedad nula*) weightlessness; **ingrávido** weightless; light.

ingrediente *m* ingredient.

ingresar [1a] *v/t. dinero* deposit, put in; *v/i.* enter; † come in; *~ en sociedad* join, become a member of; **ingreso** *m* entry (*en* into); admission (*en sociedad* to); *~s pl.* income *de p.*; † receipts, profits; † revenue *del gobierno*.

íngrimo *S.Am.* all alone.

inhábil clumsy, unskillful; incompetent; (*inadecuado*) unfit, unqualified; **inhabilidad** *f* clumsiness *etc.*; **inhabilitación** *f* disqualification; disablement; *v. nota*; **inhabilitar** [1a] disqualify (*para* from), render *s.o.* unfit (*para* for).

inhabitable uninhabitable; **inhabitado** uninhabited.

inhalador *m* ⚕ inhaler; **inhalante** *m* inhalant; **inhalar** [1a] inhale.

inherente inherent (*a* in).

inhibición *f* inhibition; **inhibir** [3a] inhibit; **~se** keep out (*de* of), stay away (*de* from).

inhospitalario inhospitable; *fig.* uninviting, bleak; **inhospitalidad** *f* inhospitality; **inhóspito** inhospitable.

inhumación *f* burial.
inhumanidad *f* inhumanity; **inhumano** inhuman; *S.Am.* filthy.
inhumar [1a] bury, inter.
iniciación *f* initiation; beginning; **iniciado** *adj. a. su. m*, **a** *f* initiate; **iniciador** *m* pioneer; **inicial** *adj. a. su. f* initial; **iniciar** [1b] initiate (*en* into); (*comenzar*) begin; originate, pioneer, set on foot; **iniciativa** *f* initiative; resource, enterprise; lead(ership); ~ *privada* private enterprise; *tomar la* ~ take the initiative (*de* in).
inicuo wicked, iniquitous.
inigualado unequaled.
inimaginable unimaginable.
inimitable unimitable.
ininteligente unintelligent; **ininteligible** unintelligible.
ininterrumpido uninterrupted; sustained, steady.
iniquidad *f* iniquity, wickedness; injustice.
injerencia *f* interference, meddling; **injerir** [3i] insert, introduce; ✓ graft; (*tragar*) swallow; ~**se** interfere, meddle (*en* in); **injertar** [1a] ⚕, ✓ graft (*en* on, in); **injerto** *m* graft; (*acto*) grafting; ⚕ transplant.
injuria *f* insult, offense; outrage, injustice; (*daño*) injury, harm; ~*s pl. freq.* abuse; **injuriar** [1b] insult; revile; outrage, wrong; (*dañar*) injure, harm; **injurioso** insulting; outrageous; harmful.
injusticia *f* injustice *etc.*; **injustificable** unjustifiable; **injusto** unjust, unfair; wrong(ful).
inmaculado immaculate.
inmanejable unmanageable.
inmanente immanent.
inmarcesible, inmarchitable imperishable, undying.
inmaterial immaterial.
inmaturo unripe; *fig.* immature.
inmediaciones *f/pl.* neighborhood, environs; **inmediatamente** immediately, at once; **inmediato** immediate; (*contiguo*) adjoining, next; ~ *a* next to, close to.
inmejorable unsurpassable; perfect; *precio* unbeatable.
inmemorable, inmemorial immemorial.
inmensidad *f* immensity *etc.*; **inmenso** immense, huge, vast; **inmensurable** immeasurable.
inmerecido undeserved.
inmersión *f* immersion.
inmigración *f* immigration; **inmigrado** *m*, **a** *f*, **inmigrante** *adj. a. su. m/f* immigrant; **inmigrar** [1b] immigrate.
inminente imminent.
inmiscuirse [*inf. only*] meddle (*en* in).
inmoble immovable; motionless; *fig.* unmoved.
inmoderado immoderate; excessive.
inmodestia *f* immodesty; **inmodesto** immodest.
inmolar [1a] immolate.
inmoral immoral; **inmoralidad** *f* immorality.
inmortal *adj. a. su. m/f* immortal; **inmortalidad** *f* immortality; **inmortalizar** [1f] immortalize.
inmotivado groundless, unmotivated.
inmovible, inmóvil immovable, immobile; (*temporalmente*) motionless, still; *fig.* steadfast; **inmovilidad** *f* immobility *etc.*; **inmovilizar** [1f] immobilize; bring to a standstill; ✝ *capital* lock up; **inmueble** *m* property; ~*s pl.* (*a. bienes* ~*s*) real estate.
inmundicia *f* filth, dirt; (*basura*) rubbish; **inmundo** filthy, dirty, foul.
inmune exempt (*de* from); ⚕ immune (*contra* to); **inmunidad** *f* exemption; immunity; **inmunizar** [1f] immunize.
inmutable immutable, changeless; **inmutarse** [1a] change countenance, lose one's self-possession; *se inmutó* his face fell; *sin* ~ without batting an eye.
innato innate, inborn.
innatural unnatural.
innavegable unnavigable; *barco* unseaworthy.
innecesario unnecessary.
innegable undeniable.
innoble ignoble, base.
innocuo innocuous, harmless.
innovación *f* innovation; novelty; **innovador** *m*, **-a** *f* innovator; **innovar** [1a] introduce.
innumerable innumerable, countless.
inobediente disobedient.

inobservado unobserved; **inobservancia** *f* neglect.
inocencia *f* innocence; **inocentada** *f* naïve remark *etc.*; (*plancha*) blunder; (*broma*) practical joke; *S.Am.* April Fools' joke; **inocente** innocent (*de* of); (*tonto*) simple; **inocentón** *m*, **-a** *f* F simpleton.
inoculación *f* inoculation; **inocular** [1a] inoculate; *fig.* corrupt, contaminate.
inocuo innocuous, harmless.
inodoro 1. odorless; **2.** *m* lavatory.
inofensivo inoffensive, harmless.
inoficioso *S.Am.* useless.
inolvidable unforgettable.
inoperante inoperative.
inopinadamente unexpectedly; **inopinado** unexpected.
inoportuno inopportune, untimely; inconvenient; inexpedient.
inorgánico inorganic.
inoxidable rustless, stainless.
inquebrantable unbreakable; *fig.* unshakable.
inquietador, inquietante disturbing, disquieting; **inquietar** [1a] disturb, upset, worry; (*acosar*) stir up; **~se** worry, fret (*de, por* about); **inquieto** restless, unsettled; anxious, worried, uneasy (*por* about); **inquietud** *f* restlessness; anxiety, worry, disquiet.
inquilinato *m* tenancy; (*pago*) rent; (*impuesto de*) ~ rates; **inquilino** *m*, **a** *f* tenant; renter.
inquina *f* dislike, ill will; *tener* ~ *a* have one's knife into.
inquirir [3i] inquire into, investigate; **inquisición** *f* inquiry; ≈ Inquisition; **inquisidor** *m* inquisitor.
insaciable insatiable.
insalubre unhealthy, insalubrious; insanitary.
insanable incurable; **insania** *f* insanity; **insano** insane, mad.
insatisfactorio unsatisfactory; **insatisfecho** unsatisfied.
inscribir [3a; *p.p. inscrito*] inscribe (*a. fig.*, ✝, ⚖); (*apuntar*) list; enroll, enter *en padrón etc.*; register, record; **~se** enroll, register; **inscripción** *f* inscription; lettering; (*acto*) enrollment *etc.*
insecticida *adj. a. su. m* insecticide; **insectívoro** insectivorous; **insecto** *m* insect.
inseguridad *f* insecurity; **inseguro** unsafe, insecure; (*movedizo*) unsteady; (*dudoso*) uncertain.
inseminación *f* insemination.
insensatez *f* folly; **insensato** senseless, foolish; **insensibilidad** *f* insensitivity; ⚕ unconsciousness; **insensible** insensitive (*a* to); ⚕ unconscious; *miembro* numb; *fig.* unfeeling, callous.
inseparable inseparable.
inserción *f* insertion; **insertar** [1a] insert.
inservible useless, unusable.
insidia *f* snare; **insidioso** insidious.
insigne illustrious, distinguished; remarkable; **insignia** *f* badge, device; (*honorífica*) decoration; (*bandera*) flag; **~s** *pl.* insignia.
insignificancia *f* insignificance; (*cosa*) trifle; **insignificante** insignificant; petty, trivial.
insinuación *f* insinuation; **insinuante** insinuating, ingratiating; **insinuar** [1e] insinuate, imply, hint at; *observación* slip in; **~se** *en* worm one's way into, creep into; ~ *con* ingratiate o.s. with.
insipidez *f* insipidness *etc.*; **insípido** insipid, tasteless; *fig.* dull, flat.
insistencia *f* insistence; **insistente** insistent; persistent; **insistir** [3a] insist (*en, sobre* on; *en inf.* on *ger.*; *en que* that); ~ *en a.* stress, emphasize; *idea etc.* press.
insobornable incorruptible.
insociable unsociable.
insolación *f* exposure (to the sun); ⚕ sunstroke; *horas de* ~ hours of sunshine; **insolar** [1a] expose to the sun; **~se** ⚕ get sunstroke.
insolencia *f* insolence; **insolentarse** [1a] be(come) insolent; **insolente** insolent; (*orgulloso*) haughty; contemptuous; (*no avergonzado*) unblushing; *sonido* grating.
insólito unusual, unwonted.
insoluble insoluble.
insolvencia *f* insolvency, bankruptcy; **insolvente** insolvent, bankrupt.
insomne sleepless; **insomnio** *m* sleeplessness, insomnia.
insondable bottomless; *fig.* unfathomable, inscrutable.
insonorización *f* soundproofing;

insonorizado soundproof; **insonorizar** [1f] *v/t.* soundproof; **insonoro** noiseless, soundless.
insoportable unbearable.
insospechado unsuspected.
insostenible untenable.
inspección *f* inspection; check; survey; supervision; ~ *técnica de vehículos (I.T.V.)* automobile inspection, car inspection; **inspeccionar** [1a] inspect; (*comprobar*) check; (*velar*) supervise; survey; **inspector** *m* inspector; superintendent, supervisor.
inspiración *f* inspiration; **inspirar** [1a] breathe in; *fig.* inspire; ~**se** *en* be inspired by, find inspiration in.
instable = *inestable.*
instalación *f* (*acto, cosas*) installation; (*cosas*) fittings, equipment; ⊕ plant; **instalar** [1a] install, set up; *agua etc.* lay on; ~**se** settle, establish o.s.
instancia *f* request; (*escrito*) petition, application; (*hoja*) application form; *a* ~ *de* at the request of; *con* ~ *pedir* insistently.
instantánea *f phot.* snap(shot); **instantáneo** instantaneous.
instante *m* instant, moment; (*a*) *cada* ~ every moment, all the time; *al* ~ instantly; *en un* ~ in a flash; *por* ~*s* uninterruptedly; any time; **instantemente** insistently, urgently; **instar** [1a] urge, press (*a inf.*, *a que*, *para que* to *inf.*).
instaurar [1a] establish; restore.
instigación *f* instigation; *a* ~ *de* at the instigation of; **instigador** *m*, **-a** *f* instigator; **instigar** [1h] instigate; *p.* induce (*a inf.* to *inf.*), abet.
instilar [1a] instill.
instintivo instinctive; **instinto** *m* instinct; impulse, urge.
institución *f* institution, establishment; ~*es de un Estado* constitution; *de una ciencia, arte etc.* principles; **instituir** [3g] institute, establish, set up; **instituto** *m* institute, institution; *eccl.* rule; ~ *de segunda enseñanza*, ~ *de enseñanza media* high school; **institutriz** *f* governess.
instrucción *f* instruction; (*enseñanza*) education, teaching; ⚔ drill; (*conocimientos*) knowledge, learning; ⚖ proceedings; ~*es pl.* instructions, orders, directions; ~ *pública* (state) education; **instructivo** instructive; *película etc.* educational; **instructor** *m* instructor, teacher; **instructora** *f* instructress; **instruido** (well-)educated; **instruir** [3g] instruct (*de, en, sobre* in, about); educate; ⚔ drill; ⚖ draw up; ~**se** learn (*de, en, sobre* about).
instrumental 1. instrumental; **2.** *m* instruments; **instrumentar** [1a] score; **instrumentista** *m/f* instrumentalist; **instrumento** *m* instrument (*a. fig.*); (*herramienta, p.*) tool; (*apero*) implement; ⚖ deed, legal document; ~ *de cuerda* ♪ stringed instrument; ~ *de viento* ♪ wind instrument.
insubordinación *f* insubordination; unruliness; **insubordinado** insubordinate; unruly, rebellious; **insubordinar** [1a] rouse to rebellion; ~**se** rebel, be(come) insubordinate.
insuficiencia *f* insufficiency *etc.*; **insuficiente** insufficient, inadequate; *p.* incompetent.
insufrible unbearable.
insular insular.
insulina *f* insulin.
insulso tasteless, insipid; *fig.* dull, flat.
insultante insulting; **insultar** [1a] insult; **insulto** *m* insult.
insumergible unsinkable.
insumiso rebellious.
insuperable insuperable; *calidad* unsurpassable; **insuperado** unsurpassed.
insurgente *adj. a. su. m/f* insurgent.
insurrección *f* revolt, insurrection; **insurreccionar** [1a] rouse to rebellion; ~**se** rise in revolt; **insurrecto** *adj. a. su. m*, **a** *f* rebel.
insustituible irreplaceable.
intacto untouched; (*entero*) intact, whole; (*sin daño*) undamaged.
intachable irreproachable.
intangible intangible, impalpable.
integración *f* integration; **integral** *adj. a. su. f* ℞ integral; **integrante** integral; **integrar** [1a] integrate (*a.* ℞); (*componer*) make up, form; ✝ repay; **integridad** *f* wholeness,

completeness; *fig.* integrity; **íntegro** whole, complete; integral; *fig.* upright.

intelectiva *f* intellect, understanding; **intelecto** *m* intellect; brain(s); **intelectual** *adj. a. su. m/f* intellectual; **intelectualidad** *f* intellectuality; (*ps.*) intelligentsia.

inteligencia *f* intelligence; mind, wits; (*comprensión*) understanding; (*trato secreto*) collusion; **inteligente** intelligent, clever; (*instruido*) skilled, trained (*en* in); **inteligible** intelligible.

intemperancia *f* intemperance; **intemperie** *f* inclemency (of the weather); *a la* ~ in the open; **intempestivo** untimely, ill-timed.

intención *f* intention; *segunda* ~ underhandedness; *con* ~ deliberately; *con la* ~ *de inf.* intending to *inf.*; *con segunda* ~ meaningfully; *b.s.* nastily; *de* ~ on purpose; *llamar la* ~ catch the eye; *tener la* ~ *de inf.* intend to *inf.*, mean to *inf.*; **intencionado:** *bien* ~ well-meaning; *mal* ~ ill-disposed; **intencional** intentional.

intendencia *f* administration, management; ⚔ (*Cuerpo de*) ≈ *approx.* Service Corps; **intendente** *m* manager.

intensar(se) [1a] intensify; **intensidad** *f* intensity *etc.*; ⊕, ⚡ *etc.* strength; **intensificación** *f* intensification; **intensificar** [1g] intensify; **intensivo** intensive; **intenso** *mst* intense; *impresión* vivid; *emoción* strong, powerful.

intentar [1a] attempt, try (*inf.* to *inf.*); (*tener intención*) intend, mean (*inf.* to *inf.*; *con* by); **intento** *m* intention; (*cosa intentada*) attempt; *de* ~ on purpose; **intentona** *f* wild attempt; *pol.* putsch.

inter... inter...; **~acción** *f* interaction, interplay; **~calar** [1a] intercalate, insert; **~cambiable** interchangeable; **~cambiar** [1b] exchange; interchange; **~cambio** *m* exchange; interchange; **~ceder** [2a] intercede, plead (*con* with, *por* for); **~ceptación** *f* interception; stoppage, hold-up; **~ceptar** [1a] intercept, cut off; (*detener*) hold up; **~cesión** *f* intercession; **~conectar** [1a] interconnect; **~confesional** interdenominational; **~continental** intercontinental; **~decir** [3p] forbid; **~dependiente** interdependent; **~dicción** *f* prohibition; **~dicto** *m* interdict.

interés *m* interest (*a.* ☤); (*egoísmo*) self-interest; **~es** *pl.* interests, affairs; ~ *compuesto* compound interest; **~es** *pl. creados* vested interests; ~ *predominante* controlling interest; ~ *simple* simple interest; *en* ~ *de* in the interest of; *por* (*el*) ~ for money; *dar* (*or poner*) *a* ~ put out at interest; *poner* ~ *en* take an interest in; *sentir* ~ *por* be interested in; **interesado 1.** interested (*en* in); *b.s.* selfish; mercenary; having an ulterior motive; (*parcial*) biassed; **2.** *m*, **a** *f* person concerned, interested party; (*el que firma*) applicant; **interesante** interesting; **interesar** [1a] *v/t.* (*atraer*) interest (*en* in), be of interest to; appeal to; (*afectar*) concern, affect (*a.* ⚖), involve; *v/i.* be of interest; be important; **~se** be interested, take an interest (*en*, *por* in).

inter...: **~escolar** interscholastic, intercollegiate; **~estelar** interstellar; **~ferencia** *f* interference; *radio*: jamming; **~ferir** [3i] interfere with; *radio*: jam; **~foliar** [1b] interleave.

ínterin 1. *m* interim; *en el* ~ in the interim, in the meantime; **~es** *pl.* temporary incumbency; **2.** *adv.* meanwhile; **3.** *cj.* while, until; **interino 1.** provisional, temporary; *p.* acting; **2.** *m*, **a** *f* stand-in; ⚖, *eccl.* locum (tenens).

interior 1. interior, inner, inside; *fig.* inward, inner; *pol.* domestic, internal; *geog.* inland; **2.** *m* interior, inside; *fig.* mind, soul; **~es** *pl.* insides; *deportes*: ~ *derecho* inside right; *para mí* ~ to myself; *Ministerio del* ≈ Department of the Interior; *British* Home Office; **interiormente** inwardly.

inter...: **~jección** *f* interjection; **~lineal** interlinear; **~locutor** *m*, **-a** *f* speaker; *mi* ~ the person I was talking to; **~ludio** *m* interlude; **~mediario 1.** *m*, **a** *f* intermediary; mediator; **2.** *m* ☤ middleman; **~medio 1.** intermediate, halfway; intervening; **2.** *m* interval; (*a. thea.*) intermission; *por* ~ *de* through, by means of; **~mezzo** *m* intermezzo.

interminable unending, endless, interminable.

inter...: ~mitente intermittent (*a.* ⚕); **~nacional 1.** international; **2.** ♀*f pol.* International; **~nacionalismo** *m* internationalism; **~nacionalizar** [1f] internationalize.

internado 1. *m*, **a** *f* (*p.*) internee; **2.** *m* boarding school; (*estado*) boarding; (*ps.*) boarders; **internamiento** *m* internment; **internar** [1a] *v/t. pol.* intern; *v/i.*, **~se** *en país* penetrate into; *estudio* go deeply into; **interno 1.** internal; inside; **2.** *m*, **a** *f* boarder.

inter...: ~pelar [1a] implore; *parl.* ask *s.o.* for explanations; (*dirigirse a*) address, speak to; **~planetario** interplanetary; **~polación** *f* interpolation; **~polar** [1a] interpolate; interrupt momentarily; **~poner** [2r] interpose, insert, place between; **~se** intervene; **~pretación** *f* interpretation *etc.*; **~pretar** [1a] *mst* interpret; (*traducir a.*) translate; ♪ render, perform; *thea. papel* play, take; ~ *mal sentido* misinterpret; **intérprete** *m/f* interpreter; translator; ♪, *thea. etc.* exponent, performer.

inter...: ~regno *m* interregnum; **~rogación** *f* interrogation; (*pregunta*) question; *v. punto*; **~rogar** [1h] question, interrogate; ⚖ examine; **~rogativo** *gr. adj. a. su. m* interrogative; **~rogatorio** *m* questioning; (*hoja*) questionnaire; **~rumpir** [3a] interrupt; cut short, cut off; ⚡ switch off; *tráfico etc.* hold up; **~rupción** *f* interruption; stoppage; **~ruptor** *m* ⚡ switch; ~ *automático* ⚡ circuit breaker; ~ *del encendido mot.* ignition switch; ~ *de resorte* ⚡ snap switch; **~secarse** [1g] intersect; **~sección** *f* intersection; **~sticio** *m* interstice; interval, gap; (*grieta*) crack; ⊕ clearance; **~urbano** *teleph.* long-distance *attr.*; **~valo** *m tiempo*: interval (*a.* ♪), break; *espacio*: gap; *a* ~*s* at intervals; intermittently, off and on; **~vención** *f* intervention; participation; supervision; ✝ audit(ing); ⚕ operation; ~ *de los precios* price control; **~venir** [3s] *v/t.* supervise; ✝ audit; ⚕ operate on; *teleph.* tap; *v/i.* intervene (*en* in); (*tomar parte*) take part (*en* in); be involved (*en* in); **~ventor** *m* inspector, superintendent; ✝ auditor; **~viú** *f* interview; **~viuvar** [1a] interview, have an interview with.

intestado intestate.

intestinal intestinal; **intestino 1.** internal; **2.** *m* intestine, gut; ~ *ciego* caecum; ~ *delgado* small intestine; ~ *grueso* large intestine.

intimación *f* notification *etc.*; **intimar** [1a] notify, announce, intimate; order, require; *v/i.*, **~se** become intimate (*con* with).

intimidación *f* intimidation.

intimidad *f* intimacy, familiarity; privacy; *en la* ~ in private life.

intimidar [1a] intimidate, overawe; bully; **~se** be intimidated, get apprehensive.

íntimo intimate; (*interior*) innermost; private.

intitular [1a] entitle, call.

intocable *adj. a. su. m/f* untouchable.

intolerable intolerable, unbearable; **intolerancia** *f* intolerance *etc.*; **intolerante** intolerant (*con, para* of); bigoted, narrow-minded (*en* about).

intonso *libro* uncut.

intoxicar [1g] poison.

intraducible untranslatable.

intragable unpalatable (*a. fig.*).

intramuros within the city.

intranquilizar [1f] worry; **intranquilo** restless; uneasy, worried.

intranscribible unprintable.

intransferible untransferable.

intransigente intransigent; uncompromising; *esp. pol.* die-hard.

intransitable impassable; **intransitivo** intransitive.

intratable intractable; *p.* unsociable, difficult; *cosa* awkward.

intravenoso intravenous.

intrépido intrepid, undaunted; *b.s.* rash.

intriga *f* intrigue, plot (*a. lit.*), scheme; **intrigante** *m/f* intriguer, schemer; **intrigar** [1h] *v/t.* intrigue, puzzle; interest; *v/i.* intrigue, plot.

intrincado dense, impenetrable; *fig.* intricate; **intrincar** [1g] complicate.

intríngulis *m* F ulterior motive; (*dificultad*) (hidden) snag; (*misterio*) puzzle.

intrínseco intrinsic.
introducción *f* introduction; insertion; **introducir** [3o] introduce; *objeto* put in, insert; *p. a.* bring in, show in; (*ocasionar*) bring on; **~se** get in, slip in; (*entrometerse*) meddle.
intro...: ~misión *f* insertion; *b.s.* interference; **~specciόn** *f* introspection; **~spectivo** introspective; **~vertido** *adj. a. su. m,* **a** *f* introvert.
intrusión *f* intrusion; ⚖ trespass; **intruso 1.** intrusive; **2.** *m,* **a** *f* intruder, interloper; gate crasher *en reunión etc.*; ⚖ trespasser.
intuición *f* intuition; **intuir** [3g] know by intuition; **intuitivo** intuitive.
inundación *f* flood; **inundar** [1a] flood, inundate, swamp (*de, en* with; *a. fig.*).
inusitado unusual, unwonted; (*anticuado*) obsolete.
inútil useless; es *~ inf.* it is no use *ger.*, it's no good *ger.* F; **inutilidad** *f* uselessness; **inutilizar** [1f] make *s.t.* useless; disable, put out of action; (*estropear*) spoil; ✉ cancel.
invadir [3a] invade (*a. fig.*), overrun; *fig.* encroach upon.
invalidar [1a] invalidate, nullify; **invalidez** *f* nullity *etc.*; **inválido 1.** ⚖ invalid, null (and void); *p.* disabled; **2.** *m,* ⚕ **a** *f* invalid; **3.** *m* ⚔ pensioner, disabled soldier *etc.*
invariable invariable.
invasión *f* invasion (*a.* ⚕, *fig.*); encroachment (*de* on); *fig.* inroad (*de* into); **invasor 1.** invading; **2.** *m,* **-a** *f* invader.
invectiva *f* (*una* a piece of) invective; (*discurso*) tirade; **invectivar** [1a] inveigh against.
invencible invincible; *obstáculo* insuperable.
invención *f* invention; discovery; *poet.* fiction.
invendible unsalable.
inventar [1a] invent; devise; create; (*fingir*) make up; **inventariar** [1a] inventory, make an inventory of; **inventario** *m* inventory; ✝ *a.* stocktaking; **inventiva** *f* ingenuity *etc.*; **inventivo** inventive; ingenious, resourceful; **invento** *m* invention; **inventor** *m,* **-a** *f* inventor.
invernáculo *m,* **invernadero** *m* greenhouse, conservatory *de casa*; **invernal** wintry, winter *attr.*; **invernar** [1k] winter; *zo.* hibernate; **invernizo** wintry, winter *attr.*
inverosímil unlikely, improbable, implausible; **inverosimilitud** *f* unlikelihood *etc.*
inversión *f* inversion; reversal; ✝ investment; **inversionista** *m/f* investor; **inverso** inverse; reverse, contrary; *a la ~a* the other way round, on the contrary; *fig.* vice-versa; **inversor** *m* investor.
invertebrado *adj. a. su. m* invertebrate.
invertir [3i] invert, turn upside down; reverse (*a.* ⊕); ✝ invest; *tiempo* spend, put in.
investidura *f* investiture.
investigación *f* investigation, inquiry; 🕮 research (*de* into); **investigador** *m,* **a** *f* investigator, 🕮 research worker; **investigar** [1h] investigate, look into; 🕮 do research into.
investir [3l]: *~ con, ~ de* invest *s.o.* with, confer upon *s.o.*
inveterado *p.* inveterate; *hábito* deep-seated.
invicto unconquered.
invidente 1. blind; **2.** *m/f* blind person.
invierno *m* winter; *S.Am.* rainy season.
inviolable inviolable; **inviolado** inviolate.
invisibilidad *f* invisibility; **invisible** invisible; *en un ~* in an instant.
invitación *f* invitation; **invitado** *m,* **a** *f* guest; **invitar** [1a] invite (*a inf.* to *inf.*); call on (*a inf.* to *inf.*); attract, entice.
invocar [1g] invoke, call on.
involuntario involuntary; *ofensa etc.* unintentional.
invulnerable invulnerable.
inyección *f* injection; **inyectado:** *~ (en sangre)* bloodshot; **inyectar** [1a] inject (*en* into); **inyector** *m* injector; nozzle.
ion *m* ion; **iónico** ionic; **ionizar** [1f] ionize.
ir [3t] **1.** go; move; (*viajar*) travel; (*a pie*) walk; (*en coche*) drive; (*a caballo etc.*) ride; ⚕ be, get along, do; be at stake *en apuesta* (*a. fig.*); *va mucho de uno a otro* there is a great

difference between them; *de 5 a 3 van 2* 3 from 5 leaves 2; *con éste van 50* that makes 50; *eso no va para ti* that wasn't meant for you; *¿cuánto va?* what do you bet?; *van 5 duros a que no lo dices* I bet you 5 duros you don't say it; **2.** *modismos*: *¡voy!* (I'm) coming!; *a eso voy* I'm coming to that; *¡vamos!* let's go!, come on!; *fig.* well, after all; *¡vaya! sorpresa*: well!, there!, I say!; *aviso*: now now!; *¡vaya ...!* what a ...!; *¡vaya, vaya!* well I declare!; *¡qué va!* F nonsense!, not a bit of it!; *¿quién va?* who goes there?; **3.** *dativo*: *¿cómo te va (el libro)?* how are you getting on (with the book)?; *¿qué te va en ello?* what does it matter to you?; *vestido*: *te va muy bien* it suits you; **4.** *con prp.*: *~ a inf.* (*futuro próximo*) be going to *inf.*, be about to *inf.*; *voy a hacerlo en seguida* I am going to do it at once; *fui a verle* I went to see (F and saw) him; *~ de guía* act (*or* go) as guide; *v. para*; *~ por* (go to, go and F) fetch, go for; *carrera* go in for; *va por médico* he's going to be a doctor; *¡vaya por X!* here's toX!; *~ tras fig.* chase after; **5.** *v/aux. mst* be; *~ ger.* be *ger.*; *van corriendo* they are running; *iba oscureciendo* it was getting dark; (*ya*) *voy comprendiendo* I'm beginning to understand; *~ p.p.* be *p.p.*; *iba cansado* he was tired; *va vendido todo el género* all the goods are (already) sold; **6. ~se** go (away), leave, depart; (*morir*) die; (*líquido*) leak, ooze out; (*desbordar*) run over; (*gastarse*) wear out; (*envejecer*) grow old; (*resbalar*) slip, lose one's balance; (*pared etc.*) give way; *¡vete!* be off with you!, go away!; *¡vámonos!* let's go!

ira *f* anger, rage; *lit.* wrath; fury *de los elementos*; **iracundia** *f* irascibility; ire; **iracundo** irascible; irate.

irakí, iraquí *adj. a. su. m/f* Iraqi.

irascible irascible.

iridescencia *f* iridescence; **iridescente** iridescent; **iris** *m* rainbow; *opt.* iris; **irisado** iridescent.

irlandés 1. Irish; **2.** *m* (*p.*) Irishman; (*idioma*) Irish; *los ~es* the Irish; **irlandesa** *f* Irishwoman.

ironía *f* irony; **irónico** ironic(al).

irracional 1. irrational (*a.* ⩓); unreasoning; **2.** *m* brute.

irradiar [1b] (ir)radiate; (*difundir*) broadcast.

irrazonable unreasonable.

irreal unreal; **irrealidad** *f* unreality; **irrealizable** unrealizable, unattainable.

irrebatible irrefutable, unassailable.

irreconciliable irreconcilable; inconsistent, incompatible.

irreconocible unrecognizable.

irrecuperable irrecoverable.

irrecusable unimpeachable.

irredimible irredeemable.

irreducible irreducible.

irreemplazable irreplaceable.

irreflexivo thoughtless, unthinking; *p.* impetuous.

irrefutable irrefutable.

irregular irregular (*a. b.s.*); abnormal; **irregularidad** *f* irregularity.

irreligioso irreligious, ungodly.

irremediable irremediable.

irreparable irreparable.

irreprochable irreproachable.

irresistible irresistible.

irresoluble unsolvable; **irresoluto** irresolute, hesistant; (*sin resolver*) unresolved.

irrespetuoso disrespectful.

irresponsable irresponsible.

irreverente irreverent, disrespectful.

irrevocable irrevocable.

irrigar [1h] irrigate (*a.* ⚕).

irrisión *f* derision, ridicule; (*objeto*) laughingstock; **irrisorio** derisory, ridiculous.

irritable irritable; **irritación** *f* irritation; **irritador, irritante 1.** irritating; **2.** *m* irritant; **irritar** [1a] irritate (*a.* ⚕), anger, exasperate; *deseos* stir up; **~se** get angry (*de* at), be exasperated (*de* with).

irrompible unbreakable.

irrumpir [3a]: *~ en* burst into, rush into; *país* invade; **irrupción** *f* irruption; invasion.

isabelino *España*: Isabelline; *Inglaterra*: Elizabethan.

isla *f* island; ⚠ block; *~ de peatones*, *~ de seguridad* safety zone *for pedestrians*.

Islam *m* Islam; *el* ♀ Islam; **islámico** Islamic.

islandés 1. Icelandic; **2.** *m*, **-a** *f*

Icelander; **3.** *m* (*idioma*) Icelandic.
isleño 1. island *attr.*; **2.** *m*, **a** *f* islander; **isleta** *f* islet; **islote** *m* small (rocky) island.
iso... iso...; **isobara** *f* isobar; **isósceles** isosceles; **isoterma** *f* isotherm; **isótopo** *m* isotope.
israelí *adj. a. su. m/f* Israeli; **israelita** *adj. a. su. m/f* Israelite.
istmo *m* isthmus; neck.
italiano 1. *adj. a. su. m*, **a** *f* Italian; **2.** *m* (*idioma*) Italian.
ítem 1. *m* item; **2.** *adv.* item; also, moreover.
itinerario *m* itinerary, route.
izar [1f] ⚓ hoist; *bandera* run up.
izquierda *f* left hand; (*lado*) left side; *pol.* left; *a la ~ estar* on the left; *torcer etc.* (to the) left; **izquierdista 1.** left-wing; **2.** *m/f* left-winger, leftist; **izquierdo** left(-hand); (*zurdo*) left-handed; (*torcido*) crooked, twisted; ***levantarse del ~*** **get out of bed on the wrong side.**

J

¡ja! ha!

jabalí *m* wild boar; **jabalina** *f* ⚔, *deportes*: javelin.

jábega *f* seine, sweep net; (*barco*) fishing smack.

jabón *m* soap; (*un* ~) piece of soap; ~ *de olor*, ~ *de tocador* toilet soap; ~ *en polvo* soap powder, washing powder; *dar* ~ *a* soap; F soft-soap; F *dar un* ~ *a* tell *s.o.* off; **jabonado** *m* soaping; (*ropa*) wash; **jabonaduras** *f/pl.* lather, (soap) suds; **jabonar** [1a] soap; *ropa* wash; *barba* lather; F tell *s.o.* off; **jaboncillo** *m* toilet soap; ~ *de sastre* French chalk; **jabonera** *f* soap dish; **jabonoso** soapy.

jaca *f* pony.

jacal *m S.Am.* hut, shack.

jácara *f lit.* comic ballad (of low life); ♪ *a merry dance*; *estar de* ~ be very merry; *tener mucha* ~ have a fund of stories; **jacarandoso** lively.

jacaré *m S.Am.* alligator.

jacarero *m* jolly fellow, wag.

jácena *f* ⚠ girder.

jacinto *m* ⚘, *min.* hyacinth.

jaco *m* nag, hack.

jacobino *adj. a. su. m*, **a** *f* Jacobin.

jactancia *f* boasting; (*cualidad*) boastfulness; **jactancioso** boastful; **jactarse** [1a] boast (*de* about, of; *de inf.* of *ger.*).

jade *m min.* jade.

jadeante panting, gasping; **jadear** [1a] pant, puff (and blow), gasp (for breath); **jadeo** *m* pant(ing) *etc.*

jaez *m* (piece of) harness; *fig.* kind, sort; *jaeces pl.* trappings.

jaguar *m* jaguar.

jalar [1a] F pull, haul; ⚓ heave; **~se** *S.Am.* F get drunk; (*irse*) clear out.

jalbegar [1h] whitewash; F paint; **jalbegue** *m* whitewash(ing); F paint.

jalde, jaldo bright yellow.

jalea *f* jelly; *hacerse una* ~ F be madly in love.

jalear [1a] *perros* urge on; *bailadores* encourage (by shouting and clapping); **jaleo** *m* F (*jarana*) spree, binge; (*ruido*) row, racket; (*lío*) row, fuss; *armar un* ~ kick up a row; *estar de* ~ make merry.

jalón *m surv.* stake, pole; jerk, jolt, yank; *fig.* stage; **jalonar** [1a] stake out, mark out; *fig.* mark.

jamás never; (not) ever; *v. nunca, siempre.*

jamba *f* jamb.

jamelgo *m* F sorry nag, jade.

jamón *m* ham; ~ *en dulce* boiled ham; F *y un* ~ *con chorreras* and jam on it; **jamona** *f* F buxom (middle-aged) woman.

jangada *f* stupid remark; F dirty trick; ⚓ raft.

japonés 1. *adj. a. su. m*, **-a** *f* Japanese; **2.** *m* (*idioma*) Japanese.

jaque *m ajedrez*: check; F bully; ~ *mate* checkmate; *¡~ de aquí!* get out of here!; *dar* ~ *a* check; *dar* ~ *mate* (*a*) (check)mate; *estar muy* ~ F be full of pep; *tener en* ~ *fig.* hold a threat over; **jaquear** [1a] check; *fig.* harass.

jaqueca *f* headache; *dar* ~ *a* bore.

jaquetón *m* F bully.

jarabe *m* syrup; sweet drink; ~ *de pico* mere words, lip service; F *dar* ~ *a* butter *s.o.* up.

jarana *f* F spree, binge; (*pendencia*) rumpus; *andar de* ~ = **jaranear** [1a] F roister, carouse; lark about; **jaranero** roistering, merry.

jarcia *f* ⚓ rigging (*freq.* ~*s pl.*); (fishing) tackle; *fig.* heap.

jardín *m* (flower) garden; ~ *central baseball* center field; ~ *de la infancia* kindergarten, nursery school; ~ *derecho baseball*: right field; ~ *izquierdo baseball*: left field; ~ *zoológico* zoo; **jardinería** *f* gardening; **jardinero** *m*, **a** *f* gardener; *baseball*: fielder, outfielder.

jarope *m* syrup; F nasty drink.

jarra *f* pitcher, jar; *de* ~*s*, *en* ~*s* (with) arms akimbo.

jarrete *m* back of the knee; hock [*de animal.*]

jarro *m* jug, pitcher; F *echar un* ~ *de agua a* pour cold water on; **jarrón** *m* vase; ⚠ urn.

jaspe *m* jasper; **jaspear** [1a] marble, speckle.

jato *m*, **a** *f* calf.

jauja *f* promised land, earthly paradise; *¡esto es ~!* this is the life!; *¿estamos aquí o en ~?* where do you think you are?

jaula *f* cage (*a.* ⚒); crate *de embalaje*; *mot.* lock-up garage; cell *para loco*.

jauría *f* pack (of hounds).

jayán *m* hulking great brute.

jazmín *m* jazmine.

jazz [dʒaz] *m* jazz.

jeep [dʒip] *m* jeep.

jefa *f* (woman) head; manageress; **jefatura** *f* leadership; (*oficina*) headquarters; *~ de policía* police headquarters; **jefe** *m* chief, head, boss F; leader; (*gerente*) manager; ⚔ field officer; *~ de cocina* chef; *~ de coro* choirmaster; *~ de estación* stationmaster; *~ de estado mayor* chief of staff; *~ del estado* chief of state; *~ de redacción* editor in chief; *~ de ruta* guide; *~ de taller* foreman; *~ de tren* conductor; *~ de tribu* chieftain; *en ~* in chief.

jején *m S.Am.* gnat.

jengibre *m* ginger.

jeque *m* sheik(h).

jerarca *m* important person; F big shot; **jerarquía** *f* hierarchy; *fig.* (high) rank; *de ~* high-ranking; **jerárquico** hierarchic(al).

jerez *m* sherry; **jerezano** *adj. a. su. m*, **a** *f* (native) of Jerez.

jerga *f* jargon; slang *de ladrones etc.*; (*incomprensible*) gibberish.

jergón *m* palliasse; F ill-fitting garment; (*p.*) lumpish fellow; **jerigonza** *f* = *jerga*; F silly thing.

jeringa *f* syringe; *~ de engrase* grease gun; **jeringar** [1h] syringe; inject; squirt; F plague; **~se** F get bored, get annoyed; **jeringazo** *m* injection; squirt; syringing.

jeringuilla *f* mock-orange.

jeroglífico 1. hieroglyphic; **2.** *m* hieroglyph(ic); *fig.* puzzle.

jersé *m*, **jersey** *m* jersey, sweater, pullover; jumper *de mujer*; cardigan *con mangas*.

jesuita *adj. a. su. m* Jesuit; **jesuítico** Jesuitic(al).

jeta *f zo.* snout; F face, mug; F *fig.* nerve; F *poner ~* pout.

jíbaro *adj. a. su. m*, **a** *f S.Am.* peasant, rustic.

jibia *f* cuttlefish.

jícara *f* small cup; *S.Am.* gourd.

jifero 1. F filthy; **2.** *m* slaughterer, butcher; (*cuchillo*) knife.

jilguero *m* goldfinch; linnet.

jindama *f sl.* funk.

jinete *m* horseman, rider; ⚔ cavalryman; **jinetear** [1a] *v/t. S.Am.* break in; *v/i.* ride around.

jingoísmo *m* jingoism; **jingoísta 1.** jingoistic; **2.** *m/f* jingo.

jipijapa *m* straw hat.

jira *f* strip *de tela*; excursion, outing; (*merienda*) picnic; (*viaje*) tour; *en ~ deportes etc.*: on tour; *ir de ~* picnic; go on an outing.

jirafa *f* giraffe.

jirón *m* rag, shred; *fig.* bit.

jiu-jitsu *m* jujitsu.

jockey ['xoki] *m* jockey.

jocoserio seriocomic; **jocosidad** *f* humor; (*chiste*) joke; **jocoso** jocular, comic, humorous.

joder *vulgar v/i.* copulate; **jodienda** *f* dirty joke.

jofaina *f* washbasin.

jolgorio *m* F fun, merriment; (*un ~*) binge; lark.

jónico ▵ Ionic.

¡jopo! get out!, be off!

jornada *f* (day's) journey, stage; (*horas*) working day; ⚔ expedition; *fig.* lifetime; *thea.* † act; *~ ordinaria* full time; ⚔ *a largas ~s* by forced marches; *al fin de la ~* in the end; **jornal** *m* (day's) wage; (*trabajo*) day's work; *a ~* by the day; *~ mínimo* minimum wage; **jornalero** *m* (day) laborer.

joroba *f* hump, hunched back; *fig.* nuisance; **jorobado 1.** hunchbacked; **2.** *m*, **a** *f* hunchback; **jorobar** [1a] F annoy, pester, give *s.o.* the hump.

jota[1] *f letter J*; *fig.* jot, iota; F *no entiendo ni ~* I don't understand a word of it; *no saber ~* have no idea.

jota[2] *f Spanish dance.*

joven 1. young; youthful *en aspecto etc.*; **2.** *m* young man, youth; *los ~es* youth; young people; **3.** *f* young woman, girl; **jovencito** *m*, **a** *f*, **jovenzuelo** *m*, **a** *f* youngster.

jovial jolly, jovial, cheerful; **jovialidad** *f* joviality *etc.*

joya *f* jewel; *fig.* (*p.*) gem; *~s pl.* trousseau *de novia*; **joyería** *f* jewelry; (*tienda*) jeweler's (shop); **joyero** *m* jeweler; (*caja*) jewel case.

jubilación *f* retirement; (*renta*) pension; **jubilado** retired; **jubilar** [1a] *v/t. p.* pension off, retire; *cosa* discard, get rid of; *v/i.* rejoice; **~se** retire; F play hooky; **jubileo** *m* jubilee; F comings and goings; **júbilo** *m* jubilation, joy, rejoicing; **jubiloso** jubilant.

jubón *m* jerkin, close-fitting jacket; bodice *de mujer*.

judaísmo *m* Judaism; **judería** *f* ghetto; **judía** *f* Jewess; ⚘ kidney bean; *~ blanca* haricot (bean); *~ de España* scarlet runner; **judiada** *f* F cruel thing; ⚕ extortion.

judicatura *f* judicature; (*empleo*) judgeship; **judicial** judicial.

judío 1. Jewish; *fig.* usurious; **2.** *m* Jew (*a. fig.*).

juego[1] *etc. v. jugar.*

juego[2] *m* (*acto*) play(ing); (*diversión*) game (*a. fig.*), sport; gambling *con apuestas*; *naipes*: hand; (*conjunto de cosas*) set; suite *de muebles*; kit, outfit *de herramientas*; pack *de naipes*; ⊕ movement, play; play *de agua, luz etc.*; *~s pl. atléticos* (athletic) sports; *~ de azar* game of chance; *~ de bolas* ballbearing; *~ de bolos* ninepins; *~ de café* coffee set; *~ de campanas* chimes; *~ de damas* checkers; *~ de la pulga* tiddlywinks; *~ del corro* ring-around-a-rosy; *~ del salto* leapfrog; *~ limpio* (*sucio*) fair (foul) play; *~s pl. malabares* juggling; *~ de manos* sleight of hand; *~ de mesa* dinner service; *~ de naipes* card game; *~ de niños* (*cosa muy fácil*) child's play; *2s pl. Olímpicos* Olympic Games; *~ de palabras* pun, play on words; *~ de piernas* footwork; *~ de prendas* forfeits; *~ de salón* parlor game; *~ de suerte* game of chance; *~ de tejo* shuffleboard; *~ de vocablos*, *~ de voces* play on words, pun; *a ~ con* matching; *en ~* ⊕ in gear; *fig.* at stake; at hand; *fuera de ~* (*p.*) offside; (*pelota*) out; *por ~* in fun, for fun; *conocer el ~ a* know what *s.o.* is up to; *entrar en ~* take a hand; have a say; *hacer ~* (*con*) match, go (with); *poner en ~* set in motion; coordinate.

juerga *f* F (*ir de* go on a) binge, spree; **juerguista** *m* F reveler.

jueves *m* Thursday; *2 Santo* Maundy Thursday; *no es cosa del otro ~* it's nothing to write home about.

juez *m* judge (*a. fig.*); *~ árbitro* arbitrator, referee; *~ de línea* linesman; *~* (*municipal*) magistrate; *~ de paz approx.* Justice of the Peace.

jugada *f* play; (*una ~*) move; (*golpe*) stroke, shot; (*echada*) throw; (*mala*) *~* bad turn, dirty trick; **jugador** *m*, **-a** *f* player; *b.s.* gambler; *~ de manos* conjurer; **jugar** [1h *a.* 1o] *v/t. mst* play; (*arriesgar*) gamble, stake; *arma* handle; *v/i.* play (*a* at, *con* with); *b.s.* gamble; *~ con fig.* trifle with; (*hacer juego*) go with, match; *~ limpio* play the game; *de ~* toy *attr.*; **~se**: *~ el todo por el todo* stake one's all; **jugarreta** *f* F bad move; (*mala pasada*) dirty trick.

juglar *m* † minstrel; juggler, tumbler.

jugo *m* juice; gravy *de carne*; ⚘ sap (*a. fig.*); *fig.* essence; substance; **jugoso** juicy; *fig.* pithy, substantial.

juguete *m* toy; *esp. fig.* plaything; **juguetear** [1a] play, romp; **juguetería** *f* toyshop; **juguetón** playful.

juicio *m* judgment; (*seso*) sense; opinion; (*sana razón*) sanity, reason; ⚖ verdict (*a. fig.*); ⚖ (*proceso*) trial; *~ final* Last Judgment; *a mi ~* in my opinion; *asentar el ~* come to one's senses; *estar en su* (*cabal*) *~* be in one's right mind; *pedir en ~* sue; *perder el ~* go out of one's mind; **juicioso** judicious; wise, sensible.

julio *m* July.

jumento *m*, **a** *f* donkey (*a. fig.*).

juncia *f* sedge.

junco[1] *m* ⚘ rush, reed.

junco[2] *m* ⚓ junk.

jungla *f* jungle.

junio *m* June.

junquera *f* rush, bulrush; **junquillo** *m* jonquil; (*junco*) reed.

junta *f* (*reunión*) meeting, assembly; session; (*ps.*) board (*a.* ⚕), council, committee; (*juntura*) junction; ⊕ joint; ⊕ washer, gasket; *~ de comercio* board of trade; *~ directiva* board of management; *~ de sanidad* board of health; *~ militar* military junta; *~ universal* universal joint; *celebrar ~* sit; **juntamente** together (*con* with); at the same time; **juntar** [1a] join, put together; (*acopiar*) collect, gather (together); *esp. ps.* get together; *dinero* raise; **~se** join; (*ps.*) meet, gather (together); associate (*con* with); **junto 1.** *adj.* joined, together; *~s pl.* together; **2.** *adv.* together; *~ a* next to, near; *~ con* together with; (*de*) *por ~* all together; ✝ wholesale; *todo ~* all at once.

juntura *f* junction, join(ing); joint (*a. anat.*); ⊕ seam; ⊕ coupling.

jura *f* oath; **jurado** *m* jury; (*p.*) juryman, juror; **juramentar** [1a] swear *s.o.* in; **~se** take an oath; **juramento** *m* oath; *b.s.* oath, swear word; *bajo ~* on oath; *prestar ~* take an (*or* the) oath (*sobre* on); *tomar ~ a* swear *s.o.* in; **jurar** [1a] swear (*inf.* to *inf.*; *a. b.s.*); *v. falso*; *~selas a* have it in for; **jurídico** juridical, legal; **jurisdicción** *f* jurisdiction; district; **jurisdiccional** *v. agua*; **jurisprudencia** *f* jurisprudence, law; **jurista** *m/f* jurist, lawyer.

justa *f* joust, tournament; *fig.* contest.

justamente justly, fairly; (*exactamente*) just, precisely.

justar [1a] joust, tilt.

justicia *f* justice; fairness; right, rightness; (*ps.*) police; *en ~* by rights; *hacer ~ a* do justice to; **justiciable** actionable; **justiciero** (strictly) just; **justificable** justifiable; **justificación** *f* justification; **justificar** [1g] justify (*a. typ.*); (*probar*) substantiate; *sospechoso* clear (*de* of), vindicate; **justipreciar** [1b] evaluate; **justiprecio** *m* evaluation, appraisal; **justo 1.** *adj.* just, right, fair; (*virtuoso*) righteous; (*legítimo*) rightful; *cantidad etc.* exact; (*ajustado*) tight; **2.** *adv.* just; right; (*ajustadamente*) tightly; *¡~!* that's it!; *vivir muy ~* be hard up.

juvenil young; youthful; *obra* early; **juventud** *f* youth, early life; (*ps.*) young people.

juzgado *m* court, tribunal; **juzgar** [1h] judge (*a. fig.*); ⚖ pass sentence upon; *fig.* consider, deem; *~ de* pass judgment upon; *a ~ por* judging by (*or* from).

K

karate *m deportes*: karate.
kermes(**s**)**e** [ker'mes] *f* charitable fair, bazaar.
kerosén *m*, **kerosene** *m* kerosene, coal oil.
kilo *m* kilo; **~ciclo** *m* kilocycle; **~gramo** *m* kilogram; **~metraje** *m approx*. mileage; **kilómetro** *m* kilometer; **kilovatio** *m* kilowatt; **~s-hora** *m/pl*. kilowatt-hours.
kiosco *m v. quiosco*.
knock-out [kaw] *m* knockout (blow).

L

la 1. *artículo*: the; 2. *pron.* (*p.*) her; (*cosa*) it; (*Vd.*) you; 3. *pron. relativo*: ~ *de* that of; ~ *de Juan* John's; ~ *de Pérez* Mrs Pérez; *v. que*.
laberíntico labyrinthine; *casa* rambling; **laberinto** *m* labyrinth, maze (*a. fig.*); *fig.* tangle.
labia *f* F glibness, fluency; *tener mucha* ~ have the gift of the gab; **labial** *adj. a. su. f* labial; **labio** *m* lip (*a. fig.*, ⚕); (*reborde*) edge, rim; *fig.* tongue; ~ *leporino* harelip; *leer en los* ~*s* lip-read; *no morderse los* ~*s* be outspoken; ~**lectura** *f* lip reading; **labioso** fluent, smooth.
labor *f* labor, work; (*una* ~) piece of work; job; *esp.* ⚒ farm work, plowing; *sew.* (*una* a piece of) embroidery, sewing; ~ (*de aguja*) needlework; ~*es esp.* ⚒ workings; **laborable** workable; *v. día*; **laboral** labor *attr.*; **laboratorio** *m* laboratory; ~ *espacial* Skylab; ~ *de idiomas* language laboratory; **laborear** [1a] work (*a.* ⚒); ⚒ till; **laborioso** *p.* hard-working, painstaking; *trabajo* hard, laborious; **laborterapia** work therapy; **labradío** arable; **labrado** 1. worked; ⊕ wrought; *tela* patterned, embroidered; 2. *m* cultivated field; **labrador** *m* (*dueño*) farmer; (*empleado*) farm laborer; plowman *que ara*; (*campesino*) peasant; **labradora** *f* peasant (woman); **labrantío** arable; **labranza** *f* farming; (*hacienda*) farm; **labrar** [1a] work, fashion; ⚒ farm, till; *madera etc.* carve; (*toscamente*) hew; *fig.* bring about; **labriego** *m*, **a** *f* farm hand; peasant.
laburno *m* laburnum.
laca *f* shellac (*a. goma* ~); (*barniz*) lacquer; hair spray; ~ *negra* japan; ~ (*para uñas*) nail polish.
lacayo *m* footman, lackey.
lacear [1a] beribbon; (*atar*) tie with bows; (*coger*) snare.
lacerar [1a] lacerate, tear; *fig.* damage.
laceria *f* want, poverty; distress.
lacio ⚘ withered; (*flojo*) limp, languid; *pelo* lank.
lacónico laconic, terse; **laconismo** *m* terseness.
lacra *f* ⚕ mark; *fig.* defect, scar; **lacrar**[1] [1a] ⚕ strike; *fig.* damage.
lacrar[2] [1a] seal (with wax); **lacre** *m* sealing wax.
lacrimógeno *v. gas*; **lacrimoso** tearful, lachrymose.
lactancia *f* lactation, nursing; **lactar** [1a] *v/t.* nurse; *v/i.* feed on milk; **lácteo** milky; **láctico** lactic; **lactosa** *f* lactose.
lacustre lake *attr.*
ladear [1a] *v/t.* tilt, tip; *colina etc.* skirt; ✈ bank; *v/i.* lean, tilt; (*desviarse*) turn off; ~**se** lean, incline (*a. fig.*; *a* to, towards); *fig.* be even (*con* with); F ~ *con* break with; **ladera** *f* slope, hillside; **ladero** side *attr.*
ladino shrewd, smart, wily.
lado *m* side (*a. fig.*); ⚔ flank; ~ *débil* weak spot; ~ *a* ~ side by side; *al* ~ near, at hand; *al* ~ *de* by the side of, beside; (*casa*) next door to; *al otro* ~ *de* over, on the other side of; *de* ~ *adv.* sideways, edgeways; *de al* ~ *casa* next (door); *de un* ~ *a otro* to and fro; *por el* ~ *de* in the (general) direction of; *por todos* ~*s* on all sides; all round; *dejar a un* ~ pass over; *echar a un* ~ cast aside; finish; *hacer* ~ make room (*a* for); *hacerse a un* ~ stand aside, move over; *fig.* withdraw; *mirar de* (*medio*) ~ look askance at; steal a look at; *ponerse al* ~ *de* side with; *tener buenos* ~*s* have good connections.
ladrar [1a] bark; **ladrido** *m* bark(ing); *fig.* scandal(mongering).
ladrillado *m* brick floor; **ladrillo** *m* brick; (*azulejo*) tile; cake *de chocolate*; ~ *refractario* fire brick.
ladrón 1. thieving; 2. *m*, **-a** *f* thief; **ladronera** *f* den of thieves; (*acto*) robbery.
lagar *m* (wine *etc.*) press.
lagarta *f* lizard; F bitch; **lagartija** *f*

small lizard; **lagarto** *m* lizard; F sly rogue; ~ *de Indias* alligator.
lago *m* lake.
lagotería *f* F wheedling.
lágrima *f* tear; *fig.* drop; ~*s pl. de cocodrilo* crocodile tears; *deshacerse en* ~*s* burst (*or* dissolve) into tears; *llorar a* ~ *viva* sob one's heart out; **lagrimoso** tearful; *ojos* watery; (*triste*) sad.
laguna *f* pool; *esp.* ⚓ lagoon; *fig.* gap, lacuna 📖.
laicado *m* laity; **laical** lay; **laico 1.** lay; **2.** *m* layman.
lama *f* mud, slime, ooze.
lameculos *m* F bootlicker, toady.
lamentable regrettable (*que* that), lamentable; pitiful; (*quejoso*) plaintive; **lamentación** *f* lamentation; **lamentar** [1a] be sorry, regret (*que* that); *pérdida* lament; *muerto* mourn; ~**se** wail, moan (*de, por* over); complain (*de, por* at); **lamento** *m* lament; moan, wail; **lamentoso** = *lamentable*.
lamer [2a] lick; (*agua etc.*) lap; **lametada** *f* lick; lap; **lamido** (*flaco*) thin; pale; (*limpio*) scrubbed; (*relamido*) dandified.
lámina *f* sheet *de vidrio, metal etc.*; *metall., phot., typ.* plate; engraving; cut, picture, illustration; 📖 lamina; ~*s pl. de cobre etc.* sheet copper *etc.*; **laminado** *metal* sheet *attr.*; 📖 laminate(d); **laminador** *m* rolling mill; **laminar** [1a] *metal* roll; 📖 laminate.
lamiscar [1g] F lick greedily.
lámpara *f* lamp, light; (*bombilla*) bulb; *radio*: valve, tube; ~ *colgante* hanging lamp; ~ *de arco* arc lamp; ~ *de pie* standard lamp; ~ *de soldar* blowtorch; F *atizar la* ~ fill up the glasses; **lamparilla** *f* small lamp; (*vela*) nightlight; ⚘ aspen; **lamparón** *m* ⚕ scrofula.
lampazo *m* ⚘ burdock; ⚓ swab.
lampiño hairless; *p.* clean-shaven.
lamprea *f* lamprey.
lana 1. *f* wool; fleece; (*tela*) woolen cloth; **2.** *m S.Am.* man in the street; swindler; **lanar** wool *attr.*; *ganado* ~ sheep.
lance *m* (*acto*) throw, cast *de red*; (*jugada*) stroke, move; (*cantidad pescada*) catch; (*suceso*) occurrence, incident, event; (*trance*) critical moment; (*riña*) row; ~ *de honor* duel; *de* ~ second-hand; (*barato*) cheap.
lancero *m* lancer; ~*s pl.* (*baile*) lancers; **lanceta** *f* lancet; ⚕ *abrir con* ~ lance; **lancinante** piercing.
lancha *f* launch; (*bote*) (small) boat; lighter *para carga*; ~ *automóvil*, ~ *motora* motor launch; ~ *de desembarco* landing craft; ~ *rápida* speedboat, motor launch; ~ *salvavidas*, ~ *de socorro* lifeboat; **lanchón** *m* lighter, barge.
lanería *f* woollen goods; (*tienda*) wool shop; **lanero** wool *attr.*, woollen.
langosta *f* lobster; (*insecto*) locust (*a. fig.*); **langostín** *m*, **langostino** *m* prawn.
languidecer [2d] languish, pine (away); **languidez** *f* languor, lassitude; **lánguido** languid; (*débil*) weak; (*sin energía*) drooping, listless.
lanilla *f* nap; (*tela*) thin flannel; **lanoso, lanudo** woolly, fleecy.
lanza *f* spear, lance; pole *de coche*; nozzle *de manga*; ~ *en ristre* ready for action; *medir* ~*s* cross swords; **lanzabombas** *m* bomb release; trench mortar; **lanzacohetes** *m* rocket launcher; **lanzadera** *f* shuttle; **lanzaespumas** *m* foam extinguisher; **lanzallamas** *m* flamethrower; **lanzamiento** *m* throw(ing) *etc.*; launch(ing) *de barco*; ✈ drop (by parachute), jump; ~ *de pesos* putting the weight; **lanzaminas** *m* minelayer; **lanzar** [1f] throw, fling, cast, pitch; hurl *con violencia*; drop *en paracaídas*; ⚕ vomit; *barco*, † launch; *hojas etc.* put forth; ⚖ dispossess; *grito* give; *desafío* throw down; ~**se** throw o.s. (*a, en* into); rush (*sobre* at, on), dash; ✈ jump; *fig.* launch out (*a* into); ~ *sobre* fly at, fall upon; **lanzatorpedos** *m* torpedo tube.
laña *f* clamp; rivet; **lañar** [1a] clamp (together); *loza* rivet.
lapa *f* limpet.
lapicero *m* mechanical pencil; pencil holder; ~ *fuente* fountain pen.
lápida *f* memorial tablet, stone; ~ *mortuoria* headstone; ~ *sepulcral* gravestone; **lapidar** [1a] stone (to death); **lapidario** *adj. a. su. m* lapidary.

lápiz *m* pencil, lead pencil; *min.* black lead, graphite; ~ *estíptico* styptic pencil; ~ *labial* lipstick; *a* ~ in pencil.
lapón *m*, **-a** *f* Laplander.
lapso *m* lapse; **lapsus** *m*: ~ *calami* slip of the pen; ~ *linguae* slip of the tongue.
laquear [1a] lacquer; *uñas* polish.
lares *m/pl. fig.* home.
lard(e)ar [1a] lard, baste; **lardo** *m* lard.
largamente *contar* at length, fully; *vivir* comfortably; generously; (*largo rato*) long, for a long time; **largar** [1h] let loose, let go; *cable* let out; *velas, bandera* unfurl; F give; **~se** F beat it, hop it; **largo** **1.** long; *fig.* generous; abundant; F *p.* sharp; ⚓ loose, slack; ¡~ (*de aquí*)! clear off!; **~s** *años* long years, many years; *tardar* **~a** *media hora* take a good half hour; *le costó 100 ptas* **~as** it cost him all of 100 ptas; *tendido cuan* ~ *es etc.* full-length; *a la* **~a** in the long run; *a lo* ~ *de* along, alongside; (*tiempo*) throughout; *de* ~ in a long dress; *pasar de* ~ pass by (without stopping); *ponerse de* ~ put on grown-up clothes; *tirar de* ~ spend lavishly; **2.** *m* length; *tener 4 metros de* ~ be 4 meters long; **largometraje** *m* feature film; **largor** *m* length; **largucho** = *larguirucho*; **larguero** *m* ⚠ jamb; *deportes*: cross bar; bolster *de cama*; **largueza** *f fig.* generosity; **larguirucho** lanky; **largura** *f* length.
laringe *f* larynx; **laringitis** *f* laryngitis.
larva *f* larva 📖, grub.
las *v.* *los*.
lasca *f S.Am.* advantage, benefit.
lascivia *f* lasciviousness; lust; **lascivo** lascivious, lewd; (*juguetón*) playful.
laser *m* laser.
lasitud *f* lassitude, weariness; **laso** weary; (*flojo*) limp, languid.
lástima *f* pity; (*cosa*) pitiful object; (*quejido*) complaint; ¡*qué* ~! what a pity (*or* shame)!; *dar etc.* ~ be pitiful, cause pity; *es una* ~ it's a shame; *es* ~ *que* it is a pity that; *estar hecho una* ~ be a sorry sight; **lastimar** [1a] hurt, injure; offend; (*compadecer*) pity, sympathize with; **~se** hurt o.s. (*con, contra* on); ~ *de* complain about; (*compadecer*) feel sorry for; **lastimero** injurious; = **lastimoso** piteous, pitiful.
lastre *m* ballast; *fig.* steadiness, good sense.
lata *f* tin plate; (*envase*) tin can; (*tabla*) lath; F nuisance, bind; *en* ~ canned; F *dar la* ~ be a nuisance, annoy.
latente latent.
lateral lateral, side *attr.*
latero *m S.Am.* plumber; tinsmith.
latido *m* yelp, bark; beat(ing) *etc.*
latifundio *m* large estate.
latigazo *m* (*golpe*) lash (*a. fig.*); (*chasquido*) crack (of a whip); *fig.* harsh reproof; F strong nightcap; **látigo** *m* whip.
latín *m* Latin; **~es** *pl.* Latin tags; **latinajo** *m* F dog-Latin; **~s** *pl.* Latin tags; **latinismo** *m* Latinism; **latino** *adj. a. su. m*, **a** *f* Latin; **latinoamericano** *adj. a. su. m*, **a** *f* Latin-American.
latir [3a] (*perro*) yelp, bark; (*corazón etc.*) beat, throb.
latitud *f* latitude (*a. fig.*); (*anchura*) breadth; (*extensión*) area, extent; **lato** broad, wide.
latón *m* brass.
latoso F boring, annoying, tiresome.
latrocinio *m* robbery, theft.
laucha *f S.Am.* mouse.
laúd *m* ♪ lute.
laudable laudable, praiseworthy; **laudatorio** laudatory.
laurear [1a] crown with laurel; *fig.* reward, decorate; **laurel** *m* laurel; *fig.* laurels; reward.
lava *f* lava.
lavable washable; **lavabo** *m* washbasin; (*mesa*) washstand; (*cuarto*) lavatory; **lavacaras** *m/f* F fawner, flatterer, bootlicker; **lavadero** *m* laundry; (*tabla de lavar*) washboard; washing place *de río*; **lavado** *m* wash(ing), laundry; ~ *cerebral*, ~ *de cerebro* brainwashing; ~ *de cabeza* shampoo; ~ *a seco* dry cleaning; **lavadora** *f* washing machine; ~ *de platos* dishwasher; ~ *químico* dry cleaning; **lavadura** *f* washing; (*agua*) dirty water; **lavamanos** *m* washbasin.
lavanda *f* lavender.
lavandera *f* laundress, washerwoman; *orn.* wagtail; **lavandería** *f S.Am.* laundry; **lavaparabrisas** *m*

mot. windshield washer; **lavaplatos** *m/f p.* dishwasher; ⊕ dishwasher; **lavar** [1a] wash; *fig.* wipe out; **~se** (have a) wash; ~ *las manos* wash one's hands (*a. fig.*); **lavativa** *f* enema; F annoyance, bother; **lavavajillas** *m* ⊕ dishwasher; **lavazas** *f/pl.* dishwater, slops; **lavoteo** *m* F cat lick, quick wash.

laxante *adj. a. su. m* laxative; **laxar** [1a] ease, slacken; *vientre* loosen; **laxativo** laxative; **laxitud** *f* laxity, looseness; **laxo** lax, loose; *moral* lax.

laya *f* spade; *fig.* kind, sort.

lazada *f* bow, knot; **lazar** [1f] lasso, rope; **lazo** *m* bow, knot, loop; lasso, lariat *para caballos etc.*; snare, trap *para caza menor*; *fig.* link, bond; (*trampa*) trap; hairpin bend *en carretera*; ~ *corredizo* slip knot, noose; *caer en el* ~ fall into the trap; *tender un* ~ *a* set a trap for.

le *acc.* him; (*Vd.*) you; *dat.* (to) him, (to) her, (to) it; (*a Vd.*) (to) you.

leal loyal, faithful; true; **lealtad** *f* loyalty.

lebrato *m* leveret.

lebrel *m* greyhound.

lección *f* lesson (*a. eccl., fig.*); *univ.* lecture; reading *de ms. etc.*; *fig.* warning, example; ~ *práctica* object lesson; **lectivo** school *attr.*; **lector** *m*, **-a** *f* reader; foreign-language teacher; *univ.* lecturer; meter reader; ~ *mental* mind reader; **lectura** *f* reading; *de mucha* ~ widely read.

lecha *f* milt, (soft) roe; **lechada** *f* paste; (*cal*) whitewash; pulp *para papel*; **lechal 1.** sucking; **2.** *m* milky juice; **leche** *f* milk; ~ *desnatada* skimmed milk; ~ *de magnesia* milk of magnesia; ~ *de manteca* buttermilk; ~ *en polvo* powdered milk; **lechecillas** *f/pl.* sweetbreads; **lechera** *f* dairymaid; (*vasija*) milk can; **lechería** *f* dairy, creamery; **lechero 1.** milk *attr.*, dairy *attr.*; **2.** *m* dairyman; (*repartidor*) milkman; **lechigada** *f* litter, brood; *fig.* gang.

lecho *m mst* bed; (*fondo*) bottom; *geol.* layer; ~ *de plumas* feather bed; ~ *de roca* bedrock.

lechón *m*, **-a** *f* suckling pig; **lechoncillo** *m* sucking pig; **lechoso** milky.

lechuga *f* lettuce; *sew.* frill, flounce; **lechuguino** *m* young lettuce; F toff, masher.

lechuza *f* owl; ~ *común* barn owl.

leer [2e] read; interpret; † lecture (*en, sobre* on); ~ *entre líneas* read between the lines.

lega *f* lay sister.

legación *f* legation; **legado** *m* legate; ⚖ legacy, bequest.

legajo *m* file, bundle (of documents).

legal legal, lawful; *p.* trustworthy, truthful; **legalidad** *f* legality *etc.*; **legalizar** [1f] legalize; *documento* authenticate.

légamo *m* slime, mud; (*arcilla*) clay; **legamoso** slimy; clayey.

legañoso bleary.

legar [1h] ⚖ bequeath (*a. fig.*), leave; **legatario** *m*, **a** *f* legatee.

legendario legendary.

legibilidad *f* legibility; **legible** legible, readable.

legión *f* legion (*a. fig.*); ♀ *extranjera* Foreign Legion; **legionario** *adj. a. su. m* legionary.

legislación *f* legislation; **legislador** *m*, **-a** *f* legislator; **legislar** [1a] legislate; **legislativo** legislative.

legista *m* jurist.

legitimar [1a] legitimize; legalize; **~se** prove one's identity; **legitimidad** *f* legitimacy *etc.*; **legitimista** *adj. a. su. m/f* loyalist; **legítimo** legitimate, rightful; just; real, genuine.

lego 1. lay; *fig.* ignorant, uninformed; **2.** *m* layman; *eccl.* lay brother; *los* **~s** the laity.

legua *f* league; *a la* ~ far away.

legumbre *f* vegetable; **leguminoso** leguminous.

leíble legible; **leída** *f* reading; **leído** *p.* well-read.

lejanía *f* distance, remoteness; **lejano** distant, remote, far(-off).

lejía *f* bleach *para blanquear*; lye; F dressing-down.

lejos 1. far (off, away); ~ *de* far from (*a. fig.*; *de inf.* from *ger.*); *a lo* ~ in the distance; *de* ~, *desde* ~ from afar, from a distance; *está muy* ~ it is a long way away (*or* off); *ir* ~ go far; **2.** *m* distant view; (*vislumbre*) glimpse; *paint.* background; *tener buen* ~ look well at a distance.

lelo silly, stupid.

lema *m* (*mote*) motto, device; theme; *pol. etc.* slogan.

lencería *f* draper's (shop); (*géneros*) linen, drapery; lingerie *para mujer*.
lengua *f* tongue (*a. fig.*); (*idioma*) language; ♪ clapper; *mala* ~ gossip, evil tongue; ~ *de tierra* point, neck (of land); ~ *madre* parent language; ~ *materna* mother tongue; *de* ~ *en* ~ from mouth to mouth; *andar en* ~*s* be the talk of the town; *buscar la* ~ *a* pick a quarrel with; *írsele a uno la* ~ talk too much; *morderse la* ~ hold one's tongue; *tirar de la* ~ *a* make *s.o.* talk; *trabársele a uno la* ~ stammer; **lenguado** *m ichth.* sole; **lenguaje** *m* (*en general*) language, (faculty of) speech; (*modo de hablar*) idiom, parlance, (mode of) speech; *lit. etc.* style, diction; **lenguaraz** *b.s.* foul-mouthed; **lenguaz** garrulous; **lengüeta** *f* tab; ♪, ⊕ tongue (*a. de zapato*); pointer *de balanza*; *anat.* epiglottis; barb *de saeta etc.*; **lengüetada** *f* lick.
lenidad *f* lenience, lenity; **lenitivo** *adj. a. su. m* lenitive.
lente *mst m* lens, eyeglass *de miope*; ~*s pl.* glasses; ~ *de aumento* magnifying glass; ~ *de contacto* contact lens; **lentillas** *f/pl.* contact lenses.
lenteja *f* lentil.
lentejuela *f* spangle, sequin.
lentitud *f* slowness; **lento** slow.
leña *f* firewood, sticks; F beating; *echar* ~ *al fuego* add fuel to the flames; *hartar de* ~ thrash; *llevar* ~ *al monte* carry coals to Newcastle; **leñador** *m* woodcutter; **leño** *m* log; (*madera*) timber, wood; *fig.* blockhead; **leñoso** woody.
Léo *m ast.* Leo.
león *m* lion (*a. ast. a. fig.*); *S.Am.* puma; ~ *marino* sea lion; **leona** *f* lioness; **leonado** tawny; **leonera** *f* lion's cage, lion's den; F gambling den; F (*trastera*) lumber room.
leonés *adj. a. su. m*, **-a** *f* Leonese.
leopardo *m* leopard.
leotardos *m/pl.* leotards.
lepra *f* leprosy; **leproso 1.** leprous; **2.** *m*, **a** *f* leper.
lerdo dull, slow; clumsy *al moverse*.
les *acc.* them; (*Vds.*) you; *dat.* (to) them; (*a Vds.*) (to) you.
lesa majestad *f* lese-majesty.
lesión *f* wound; injury (*a. fig.*); **lesionado** *jugador* unfit; hurt; **lesionar** [1a] injure, hurt; ~**se** get hurt.
letal soporific; 🕮 deadly, lethal.
letanía *f* litany; *fig.* long list, rigmarole.
letárgico lethargic; **letargo** *m* lethargy (*a. fig.*).
letón *adj. a. su. m*, **-a** *f* Latvian.
letra *f mst* letter; (*modo de escribir*) (hand)writing; ♪ words, lyric; ✝ *a.* bill, draft; ~*s pl.* letters, learning; ~*s pl. univ.* Arts; *bellas* ~*s pl.* literature; *primeras* ~*s pl.* elementary education, *approx.* three Rs; ✝ ~ *abierta* letter of credit, open credit; ✝ ~ *de cambio* bill (of exchange), draft; ~ *cursiva* script; ~ *de imprenta typ.* type; ~ *de mano* handwriting; ~ *gótica* black letter; ~*s pl. humanas* humanities; ~*s pl. de molde* print, printed letters; ~ *muerta* dead letter; ~ *negrilla typ.* boldface; ~ *redonda*, ~ *redondilla typ.* roman; ~*s pl. sagradas* scripture; ✝ ~ *a la vista* sight draft; ✝ *a* ~ *vista* on sight; *a(l pie de) la* ~ *v. pie*; F *poner unas* (*or cuatro*) ~*s a* drop a line to.
letrado 1. learned; *b.s.* pedantic; **2.** *m* lawyer.
letrero *m* sign, notice; (*cartel*) placard; (*marbete*) label; (*palabras*) words; ~ *luminoso* illuminated sign.
letrina *f* lavatory; *fig.* filthy place.
leucemia *f* leukemia.
leudar [1a] leaven; ~**se** (*pan etc.*) rise.
leva *f* ⚓ weighing anchor; ⚔ levy; ⊕ cam; *mar de* ~ swell.
levadizo *v. puente*.
levadura *f* yeast, leaven.
levantamiento *m* raising *etc.*; (*sublevación*) (up)rising, revolt; ~ *del cadáver* inquest; ~ *del censo* census taking; ~ *de pesos* weight lifting; ~ *de planos* surveying; **levantar** [1a] raise, lift (up); ⚠ erect, build; (*recoger*) pick up; (*poner derecho*) straighten; *cerco, prohibición, tropa, voz* raise; *casa* (re)move; *caza* flush; *mesa* clear; *plano* draw (up); *sesión* adjourn; *testimonio* bear; *tienda* strike; *fig.* (*excitar*) rouse, stir up; (*animar*) hearten, uplift; ~**se** rise; get up *de cama*; (*ponerse de pie*) stand up; (*ponerse derecho*) straighten up; (*sublevarse*) rise, rebel; (*sobresalir*) stand out; ~ *con* make off with.
levante *m* east; east wind; *v. Nombres Propios*; **levantino** *adj. a. su. m*, **a** *f* Levantine.
levantisco restless, turbulent.

levar [1a]: ~ *anclas* weigh anchor; **~se** set sail.
leve light; *fig.* slight, trivial; **levedad** *f* lightness; *fig.* levity.
levita[1] *f* frock coat.
levita[2] *m* Levite.
léxico 1. lexical; **2.** *m* lexicon, dictionary; vocabulary; **lexicografía** *f* lexicography; **lexicógrafo** *m* lexicographer.
ley *f* law; *parl.* act, measure; (*regla*) rule; *fig.* loyalty, devotion; (*calidad*) (legal standard of) fineness; ~ *de la selva* law of the jungle; ~ *del menor esfuerzo* line of least resistance; ~ *de Lynch* lynch law; ~ *marcial* martial law; *a* ~ *de* on the word of; *de buena* ~ sterling, reliable; *de mala* ~ base, disreputable; *dar la* ~ set the tone; *tener* ~ *a* be devoted to.
leyenda *f* legend (*a. typ.*); inscription.
lezna *f* awl.
liar [1c] tie (up), bind; *paquete* do up, wrap up; *cigarrillo* roll; *fig.* embroil; F **~las** beat it; (*morir*) kick the bucket; **~se** *fig.* get involved (*con* with); F ~ *a inf.* start to *inf.*
libación *f* libation; **~es** *pl.* potations.
libanés *adj. a. su. m*, **-a** *f* Lebanese.
libar [1a] suck, sip; (*probar*) taste.
libelo *m* lampoon, libel (*contra* on); ⚖ petition.
libélula *f* dragonfly.
liberación *f* liberation, release; **liberado** ✝ paid up; **liberal 1.** liberal; generous; **2.** *m/f* liberal; **liberalidad** *f* liberality; **liberalismo** *m* liberalism.
libertad *f* liberty, freedom; (*excesiva*) license; familiarity *en el trato*; ~ *de cátedra* academic freedom; ~ *de comercio* free trade; ~ *de cultos* freedom of worship; ~ *de empresa* free enterprise; ~ *de enseñanza* academic freedom; ~ *de imprenta* freedom of the press; ~ *de los mares* freedom of the seas; ~ *de palabra* freedom of speech; ~ *de reunión* freedom of assembly; ~ *vigilada* probation; *plena* ~ free hand; *en* ~ at liberty, free; *poner en* ~ set free; **libertador** *m*, **-a** *f* liberator; **libertar** [1a] set free, release, liberate (*de* from); (*eximir*) exempt; (*preservar*) save (*de* from);
libertinaje *m* profligacy, licentiousness; **libertino 1.** profligate, rakish; (*incrédulo*) freethinking; **2.** *m* libertine, rake; freethinker.
libidinoso lustful, libidinous.
libio *adj. a. su. m*, **a** *f* Libyan.
libra *f* pound; ~ *esterlina* pound sterling; *ast.* ♎ Libra.
libraco *m* worthless book.
librado *m*, **a** *f* ✝ drawee; **librador** *m*, **-a** *f* ✝ drawer; **libramiento** *m* delivery, rescue; = **libranza** *f* ✝ draft, bill of exchange; *S.Am.* ~ *postal* money order; **librar** [1a] save, free, deliver (*de* from); ⚖ exempt (*de* from); *confianza* place; *sentencia* pass; *batalla* join; (*expedir*) issue; ✝ draw; **~se:** ~ *de* get out of, escape; (*deshacerse de*) get rid of; F *de buena nos hemos librado* that was a close shave; **libre** *mst* free (*de* from); (*atrevido*) free, outspoken; *b.s.* loose; *aire* open.
librea *f* livery.
librepensador *m*, **-a** *f* freethinker; **librepensamiento** *m* freethinking.
librería *f* (*tienda*) bookshop; ✝ bookselling, book trade; (*biblioteca*) library; (*armario*) bookcase; ~ *de viejo* second-hand bookshop; **librero** *m* bookseller; bookshelf; **libresco** bookish; **libreta** *f* notebook; ✝ account book; ~ *de banco* passbook, bank book; **libreto** *m* libretto; **libro** *m* book; ~ *de actas* minute book; ~ *de apuntes* notebook; ~ *de caja* cash book; ~ *de cheques* checkbook; ~ *de chistes* joke book; ~ *de cocina* cook book; ~ *de cuentas* account book; ~ *diario* journal; ~ *de lance* second-hand book; ~ *de lectura* reader; ~ *mayor* ledger; ~ *de mayor venta* best seller; ~ *de oro* guest book; ~ *parroquial* parish register; ~ *de pedidos* order book; ~ *de recuerdos* scrapbook; ~ *talonario* checkbook; ~ *de teléfonos* telephone book; ~ *de texto* textbook; ~ *de vuelo(s)* logbook; *ahorcar los* ~*s* give up studying; ~ *en rústica* paperbound book; *hacer* ~ *nuevo* turn over a new leaf; **librote** *m* F tome.
licencia *f mst* license; permission; ⚔ *etc.* leave; *univ.* degree; ⚔ ~ *absoluta* discharge; ~ *de armas* gun license; ~ *de caza* hunting license; *de* ~ on leave; **licenciado** *m*, **a** *f* licentiate,

approx. bachelor; *S.Am.* lawyer; **licenciar** [1b] license, give a permit to; ⚔ discharge; **~se** *univ.* graduate; **licenciatura** *f* degree; (*acto*) graduation; (*estudios*) degree course; **licencioso** licentious.

liceo *m* lyceum.

licitar [1a] bid for; *S.Am.* sell by auction; **lícito** lawful, legal; just; permissible.

licor *m* liquor, spirits; (*dulce*) liqueur; (*en general*) liquid; **~es** *pl. espiritosos* hard liquor; **licuar** [1d] liquefy; *metal* liquate; **licuefacción** *f* liquefaction.

lid *f* fight, contest; *en buena ~* in a fair fight.

líder *m* leader; leading; **liderar** *v/i.* lead; **liderato** *m* leadership; *deportes*: lead.

lidia *f toros*: bullfight(ing); *de ~ toro* fighting; **lidiador** *m*, **-a** *f* fighter; *toros*: bullfighter; **lidiar** [1b] *v/t.* fight; *v/i.* fight (*con, contra* against, *por* for); *fig.* contend, struggle (*con* with).

liebre *f* hare; *fig.* coward; *levantar la ~* blow the gaff.

liendre *f* nit.

lienzo *m* (*un* a piece of) linen; (*pañuelo*) handkerchief; *paint.* canvas; △ wall.

liga *f* suspender, garter; (*faja*) band; *pol.*, *deportes*: league; *metall.* alloy; (*mezcla*) mixture; ⚘ mistletoe; *orn.* bird lime; **ligado** *m* ♩ slur, tie; *typ.* ligature; **ligatura** *f* tie, bond; ♩, ⚕ ligature; **ligamento** *m* ligament; **ligar** [1h] tie, bind (*a. fig.*); *metall.* alloy; (*unir*) join; ⚕ ligature; **~se** band together; **ligazón** *f* bond, union.

ligeramente lightly; *conocer etc.* slightly; **ligereza** *f* lightness *etc.*; (*dicho etc.*) indiscretion; **ligero** light; rapid, swift, agile; *té* weak; (*superficial*) slight; *carácter etc.* fickle; (*poco serio*) flippant; *v. casco*; *~ de ropa* scantily clad; *a la ~a* perfunctorily, quickly; without fuss; *de ~* rashly, thoughtlessly; *juzgar a la ~a* jump to conclusions.

lignito *m* lignite.

ligustro *m* privet.

lija *f ichth.* dogfish; ⊕ (*a. papel de ~*) sandpaper; **lijar** [1a] sandpaper.

lila 1. *f* ⚘ lilac; **2.** *m* F boob, ninny; **lilailas** *f/pl.* F cunning, tricks.

lima[1] *f* ⚘ lime; *jugo de ~* lime juice.

lima[2] *f* ⊕ file; *fig.* polish, finish; *~ para las uñas* nail file; **limadura** *f* filing; *~s pl.* filings; **limar** [1a] file; *fig.* polish; (*suavizar*) smooth (over); (*cercenar*) cut down.

limazo *m* sliminess.

limbo *m* limbo; F *estar en el ~* be bewildered, be distracted.

limeño *adj. a. su. m*, **a** *f* (native) of Lima.

limero *m* ⚘ lime (tree).

limitación *f* limitation; **limitado** limited (*a.* ☤); *p.* slow-witted; **limitar** [1a] *v/t.* limit (*a inf.* to *ger.*); restrict; cut down; *v/i.*: *~ con* border on, be bounded by; **límite** *m* limit; *geog.* boundary, border; (*fin*) end; **limítrofe** bordering.

limo *m* slime, mud.

limón *m* lemon; **limonada** *f* lemonade; *~ (natural)* lemon squash; **limonado** lemon(-colored); **limonero** *m* ⚘ lemon (tree).

limosna *f* alms, charity; **limosnero 1.** charitable; **2.** *m* beggar.

limoso slimy, muddy.

limpia 1. *f* cleaning; **2.** *m* F bootblack; **~barros** *m* scraper; **~botas** *m* bootblack; **~chimeneas** *m* chimney sweep; **~dientes** *m* toothpick; **limpiadura** *f* cleaning; *~s pl.* scourings, dirt; **limpiaparabrisas** *m* windshield wiper; **limpiar** [1b] clean; cleanse (*a. fig.*); wipe *con trapo*; ⚘ prune; *zapatos* polish, shine; F clean out *en el juego*; *sl.* swipe; *~ en seco* dry-clean; **límpido** limpid; **limpieza** *f* (*acto*) cleaning *etc.*; (*calidad*) cleanness, (*a. hábito*) cleanliness; (*moral*) purity; (*destreza*) skill; fair play *en juego*; integrity, honesty; *~ de la casa* house cleaning; *~ de sangre* purity of blood; *~ en seco* dry cleaning; *hacer la ~* clean; **limpio** clean (*a. fig.*); pure; (*ordenado*) neat, tidy; *juego* fair (*a. adv.*); ☤ clear, net; *~ de* free from; *en ~ copia* fair; *poner en ~* make a fair copy of; F *estar ~* not know a thing; F *quedar(se) ~* be cleaned out (of money); *sacar en ~* understand, deduce; *no he podido sacar nada en ~ de ello* I couldn't make anything of it; **limpión** *m* wipe, (quick) clean; (*p.*) cleaner.

limusina *f* limousine.

linaje *m* lineage, parentage, family; *fig.* class, sort; ~*s pl.* (local) nobility; ~ *humano* mankind; **linajudo** high-born, blue-blooded F.
linaza *f* linseed.
lince *m* lynx; *fig.* sharp-eyed (*or* shrewd) person.
linchar [1a] lynch.
lindante adjoining, bordering; **lindar** [1a] adjoin (*con acc.*), border (*con* on); **linde** *m a. f* boundary; **lindero 1.** adjoining; **2.** *m* edge, border.
lindeza *f* prettiness *etc.*; (*dicho*) witticism; ~*s pl. iro.* insults; **lindo 1.** pretty, lovely, fine (*a. iro.*); excellent, superb; F *de lo* ~ a lot, a good deal; wonderfully; **2.** *m* fop, conceited person.
línea *f* line; figure *de p.*; (*contorno*) lines; (*linaje*) line; (*vía*) route; (*clase*) kind; ⚔ ~*s pl.* lines; ~ *aérea* overhead cable; ✈ airline; ~ *de base surv.* base line; ~ *delantera* forward line; ~ *derivada teleph.* extension; ~ *férrea* railway; ~ *de flotación* waterline; ~ *de (flotación con) carga* load line; ~ *internacional de cambio de fecha* international date line; ~ *lateral deportes*: touch line, sideline; ~ *de mira* line of sight; ~ *de montaje* assembly line; ~ *de puntos* dotted line; ~ *de saque* base line; ~ *de tiro* line of fire; ⚔ *de* ~ regular; *en* ~ in a row, in (a) line; *en su* ~ of its kind; *en toda la* ~ all along the line; *leer entre* ~*s* read between the lines; F *poner unas* ~*s a* drop a line to; **lineal** linear; *dibujo* line *attr.*; **linear** [1a] line, draw lines on; (*bosquejar*) sketch, outline.
linfa *f* lymph; **linfático** lymphatic.
lingote *m* ingot; *typ.* slug.
lingüística *f* linguistics; **lingüístico** linguistic.
linimento *m* liniment.
lino *m* ⚘ flax; (*tejido*) linen.
linóleo *m* linoleum.
linotipia *f* linotype.
linterna *f* lantern (*a.* ⚠), lamp; ⚡ spotlight; ~ *eléctrica* torch, flashlight; ~ *mágica* magic lantern.
lío *m* bundle, parcel, package; ✓ truss; F (*confusión*) mess, mix-up; F (*apuro*) jam; F (*jaleo*) row, rumpus; F (*amorío*) affair; F *armar un* ~ cause trouble; make a fuss, kick up a row; F *hacerse un* ~, F *meterse en un* ~ get into a jam.
liofilización *f* freeze-drying; **liofilizar** [1f] *v/t.* freeze-dry.
liquen *m* lichen.
liquidación *f* liquefaction; ✝ liquidation (*a. fig.*), winding-up; ✝ settlement *de cuenta*; (*venta*) (clearance) sale; **liquidador** *m*, **-a** *f* liquidator; **liquidar** [1a] liquefy; ✝, *pol.*, *fig.* liquidate; ✝ *negocio* wind up; ✝ *cuenta* settle; ✝ *deuda* clear, settle; ✝ *existencias* sell off; **líquido 1.** liquid (*a. gr.*); ✝ net; **2.** *m* liquid, fluid; ✝ net profit; ~ *imponible* net taxable income.
lira *f* lyre (*a. fig.*); **lírica** *f* lyrical poetry; **lírico** lyric(al); imaginary, utopian; *thea.* musical.
lirio *m* iris; lily; ~ *de agua* calla lily; ~ *de los valles* lily of the valley.
lirismo *m* lyricism; *b.s.* effusiveness; sentimentality; pipe dream.
lirón *m* dormouse; *dormir como un* ~ sleep like a log (*or* top).
lirondo: *v. mondo.*
lisiado 1. injured; (*tullido*) lame, crippled; **2.** *m*, **a** *f* cripple; **3.** *m*: ~ *de guerra* disabled veteran; **lisiar** [1b] injure (permanently); cripple, maim.
liso smooth, even; *pelo* straight; *fig.* plain; ~ *y llano* simple; *400 metros* ~*s* 400 meters flat.
lisonja *f* flattery; **lisonjear** [1a] flatter; (*agradar*) please, delight; **lisonjero 1.** flattering; pleasing; **2.** *m*, **a** *f* flatterer.
lista *f* list; catalogue; ⚔ roll (call); (*tira*) strip; slip *de papel*; stripe *de color*; ~ *de correos* general delivery; ~ *electoral* electoral roll; ~ (*de platos*) menu; ~ *de precios* price list; ~ (*de tandas etc.*) roster, rota; *pasar* ~ call the roll; **listado** striped.
listo ready (*para* for); (*avisado*) clever, smart, sharp; *v. pasarse.*
listón *m* ribbon; ⚠ lath.
lisura *f* smoothness *etc.*; *fig.* naiveté.
litera *f* litter; ⚓, 🚂 berth.
literal literal; **literario** literary; **literata** *f* literary lady; *contp.* bluestocking; **literato** *m* man of letters; **literatura** *f* literature.
litigación *f* litigation; **litigante** *adj. a. su. m/f* litigant; **litigar** [1h] go to law; *fig.* dispute, argue; **litigio** *m* lawsuit, litigation; *fig.* dispute; **litigioso** litigious.

litisexpensas *f/pl.* ⚖ costs.
litografía *f* lithography; (*estampa*) lithograph; **litografiar** [1b] lithograph.
litoral *adj. a. su. m* seaboard, littoral.
litro *m* liter.
lituano *adj. a. su. m*, **a** *f* Lithuanian.
liturgia *f* liturgy; **litúrgico** liturgical.
liviandad *f* fickleness *etc.*; **liviano** **1.** *fig.* fickle; frivolous; (*lascivo*) wanton; **2.** ~*s m/pl.* lights, lungs.
lívido livid, (black and) blue.
living ['liβin] *m* living room.
liza *f hist.* lists.
lo **1.** the, that which is *etc.*; ~ *bueno* the good, the good thing, goodness; ~ ... *que* how; *no sabe* ~ *grande que es* he doesn't know how big it is; ~ *mío* what is mine; ~ *ocurrido* what has happened; *no* ~ *hay* there isn't any; *a veces no se traduce*: ~ *sé* I know; *v. que*; **2.** *pron.* (*p.*) him; (*cosa*) it.
loa *f* praise; † *thea.* prologue; short play; **loable** praiseworthy, commendable; **loar** [1a] praise.
lobanillo *m* growth, tumor.
lobato *m*, **lobezno** *m* wolf cub; **lobo** *m* wolf; ~ *de mar* sea dog, old salt; ~ *marino* seal; ~ *solitario fig.* lone wolf; *gritar ¡el* ~*!* cry wolf; F *pillar un* ~ get drunk.
lóbrego murky, gloomy; **lobreguez** *f* murk, gloom(iness).
lóbulo *m* lobe.
local **1.** local; **2.** *m* premises, rooms; (*sitio*) site, scene, place; **localidad** *f* locality; *thea. etc.* seat, ticket; **localizar** [1f] locate, place; (*limitar*) localize.
loción *f* lotion; (*acto*) wash; ~ *capilar*, ~ *para el cabello* hair restorer; ~ *facial* shaving lotion.
loco **1.** mad; (*disparatado*) wild; ⊕ loose; *más* ~ *que una cabra* mad as a hatter; ~ *de atar* raving mad; ~ *por* mad about (*or* on); *volver* ~ drive *s.o.* mad; *volverse* ~ go mad; *es para volverse* ~ it's maddening; *estar para volverse* ~ be at one's wit's end; **2.** *m*, **a** *f* madman *etc.*, lunatic.
locomoción *f* locomotion; **locomotora** *f* locomotive, (railway) engine; ~ *de maniobras* shifting engine; **locomóvil** *m* traction engine.
locro *m S.Am.* stew.
locuacidad *f* loquacity *etc.*; **locuaz** loquacious, talkative, voluble; **locución** *f* expression, (turn of) phrase; diction.
locuelo *m*, **a** *f* madcap; **locura** *f* madness, lunacy; (*acto*) crazy thing; ~*s pl.* folly.
locutor *m*, **-a** *f radio*: announcer, commentator; **locutorio** *m eccl.* parlor; *teleph.* phone booth.
locha *f* loach.
lodazal *m* muddy place, quagmire; **lodo** *m* mud, mire; **lodoso** muddy.
logaritmo *m* logarithm.
lógica *f* logic; **lógico** **1.** logical; es ~ (*que*) it is natural (that), it stands to reason (that); **2.** *m* logician; **logística** *f* logistics; **logístico** logistic.
lograr [1a] get, obtain; attain, achieve; ~ *inf.* succeed in *ger.*, manage to *inf.*; ~ *que una p. haga* get s.o. to do; **logrero** *m* moneylender, usurer; *S.Am.* sponger; **logro** *m* achievement *etc.*; ✝ profit; *b.s.* usury; *a* ~ at (a high rate of) interest, at usurious rates.
logroñés *adj. a. su. m*, **-a** *f* (native) of Logrono.
loma *f* hillock, low ridge.
lombriz *f* (earth)worm; ~ *de tierra* earthworm; ~ *solitaria* tapeworm.
lomo *m anat.* back, (*carne*) loin; ✓ balk, ridge; shoulder *de colina*; spine *de libro*; ~*s pl.* ribs.
lona *f* canvas, sail cloth.
lonche *m S.Am.* lunch.
lonchería *f S.Am.* snack bar.
londinense **1.** London *attr.*; **2.** *m/f* Londoner.
longaniza *f* long pork sausage.
longevidad *f* longevity; **longevo** aged.
longitud *f* length; *geog.* longitude; ~ *de onda* wavelength; **longitudinal** longitudinal; **longitudinalmente** lengthwise.
lonja[1] *f* slice; rasher *de tocino etc.*
lonja[2] *f* ✝ exchange, market; (*tienda*) grocer's (shop).
lontananza *f paint.* background; *en* ~ far away, in the distance *or* background.
loor *m* praise.
loquear [1a] play the fool; *fig.* make merry.
loro *m* parrot.

los, las 1. *artículo*: the; **2.** *pron.* them; **3.** *pron. relativo*: ~ *de* those of; ~ *de Juan* John's; ~ *de casa* those at home; *v. que.*
losa *f* stone slab, flagstone; ~ (*sepulcral*) tombstone; (*trampa*) trap.
losange *m* diamond (shape); ⚔, *heráldica*: lozenge.
lote *m* portion, share; ✝ lot; **lotería** *f* lottery; *caerle a uno la* ~ win a prize in the lottery; F strike lucky; **lotero** *m*, **a** *f* lottery-ticket seller.
loto *m* lotus.
loza *f* crockery; ~ *fina* china(ware).
lozanear [1a] ⚘ flourish; (*p.*) be full of life; **lozanía** *f* luxuriance; vigour, liveliness; (*orgullo*) pride; **lozano** ⚘ lush, luxuriant, rank; *p.*, *animal* vigorous, lusty; (*orgulloso*) proud.
lubricidad *f fig.* lubricity; **lúbrico** slippery; *fig.* lewd.
lubri(fi)cación *f* lubrication; **lubri(fi)cador 1.** lubricating; **2.** *m* lubricator; **lubri(fi)cante** *adj. a. su. m* lubricant; **lubri(fi)car** [1g] lubricate, oil.
lucera *f* skylight.
lucerna *f* chandelier.
lucero *m* bright star, *esp.* Venus; ~ *del alba* morning star.
lucidez *f* lucidity; **lúcido** lucid, clear.
lucido splendid, brilliant; elegant; gallant, generous; successful; *quedar(se)* ~ *iro.* make a mess of things.
luciente bright, shining.
luciérnaga *f* glowworm.
lucimiento *m* brilliance; show; dash; (*éxito*) success.
lucio[1] *m ichth.* pike.
lucio[2] bright, shining.
lución *m* slowworm.
lucir [3f] *v/t.* show off, display, sport; *v/i.* shine (*a. fig.*); (*joyas etc.*) glitter, sparkle; cut a dash *con vestido etc.*; **~se** dress up; *fig.* shine; *iro.* make a fool of o.s.
lucrativo lucrative, profitable; **lucro** *m* profit.
luctuoso mournful, sad.
lucubración *f* lucubration.
lucha *f* fight, struggle (*por* for); conflict; *fig.* dispute; *deportes*: ~ (*libre*) wrestling; ~ *de clases* class struggle; ~ *de la cuerda* tug of war; **luchador** *m*, **-a** *f* fighter; wrestler; **luchar** [1a] fight, struggle (*por* for; *por inf.* to *inf.*); *deportes*: wrestle (*con* with; *a. fig.*).
ludibrio *m* derision, mockery.
luego immediately; (*después*) then, next; (*dentro de poco*) presently, later (on); ~ *que* as soon as; *¿y ~?* what next?; *desde* ~ of course, naturally; *hasta* ~ see you later.
lugar *m* place, spot; position; (*espacio*) room; (*pueblo*) village; *fig.* reason (*para* for), cause; opportunity; ~ *común* platitude, commonplace; (*retrete*) toilet, water closet; ~ *de cita* tryst; ~*es pl. estrechos* close quarters; ~ *religioso* place of burial; *en ~ de* instead of; *en primer ~* in the first place, firstly; for one thing; *en su ~* in his place; *fuera de ~* out of place; *dar ~ a* give rise to; *dejar ~ a* permit of; *hacer ~ para* make way (*or* room) for; *ponerse en su ~ fig.* stand on one's dignity; *tener ~* take place; **lugareño 1.** village *attr.*; **2.** *m*, **a** *f* villager; **lugarteniente** *m* deputy.
luge *f* (*trineo*) luge.
lugre *m* lugger.
lúgubre mournful, dismal.
lujo *m* luxury; *fig.* profusion, abundance; *de* ~ de luxe, luxury *attr.*; **lujoso** luxurious; ostentatious, showy; profuse, lavish; **lujuria** *f* lust, lechery; **lujuriar** [1b] lust; **lujurioso** lustful, lewd.
lumbago *m* lumbago.
lumbre *f* fire; (*luz, para cigarrillo*, △) light; brilliance, splendor; △ skylight; ~*s pl.* tinderbox; **lumbrera** *f* luminary (*a. fig.*); △ skylight; ⊕ vent; **luminarias** *f/pl.* illuminations; **luminoso** luminous, bright; *idea* brilliant, bright.
luna *f* moon; (*cristal*) plate glass; (*espejo*) mirror; (*lente*) lens; ~ *llena* full moon; *media* ~ half-moon; ~ *de miel* honeymoon; ~ *nueva* new moon; *a la ~ de Valencia* disappointed, in the lurch; **lunar 1.** lunar; **2.** *m* spot, mole; (*defecto*) flaw, blemish; ~ *postizo* beauty spot; **lunático** lunatic.
lunes *m* Monday.
luneta *f* lens; *thea.* stall; ~ *trasera mot.* rear window.
lunfardo *m S.Am.* thieves' slang.
lupa *f* magnifying glass.
lupanar *m* brothel.
lúpulo *m* ⚘ hop; hops.

lusitano *adj. a. su. m*, **a** *f* Portuguese.
lustrabotas *m* shoeshine boy.
lustrar [1a] shine, polish; **lustre** *m* polish, shine, gloss; *esp. fig.* luster; ~ *para metales* metal polish; *dar* ~ *a* polish; **lustroso** glossy, bright.
luterano *adj. a. su. m*, **a** *f* Lutheran.
luto *m* mourning; sorrow, grief; *medio* ~ half-mourning; ~ *riguroso* deep mourning; *estar de* ~ be in mourning (*por* for).
luz *f* light (*a.* ⚓, *fig.*); *luces pl. fig.* enlightenment; intelligence; ~ *de balizaje* ⚓ marker light; ~ *de costado*, ~ *de situación* side light; *luces de carretera* bright lights, brights; *luces de cruce* dimmers; ~ *de magnesio phot.* flash bulb; ~ *de matrícula* license-plate light; ~ *de parada* stop light; *luces de estacionamiento* parking lights; *luces de tráfico* traffic lights; ~ *trasera* tail light; *a la* ~ *de* in the light of; *a todas luces* anyway; everywhere; *entre dos luces* at twilight; F mellow; *dar a* ~ give birth (*v/t.* to); *fig.* publish; *mot. poner a media* ~ dim; *sacar a* ~ bring to light; *salir a* ~ come to light; (*libro*) appear.

Ll

llaga *f* ulcer, sore (*a. fig.*); (*herida*) wound; affliction; **llagar** [1h] wound, injure.

llama[1] *f* flame, blaze; *fig.* passion.

llama[2] *f zo.* llama.

llamada *f* call (*a.* ⚔, *teleph.*); ring (*or* knock) at the door; (*ademán*) signal, gesture; *typ.* reference (mark); **llamado** so-called; **llamamiento** *m* call; **llamar** [1a] *v/t.* call (*a. fig. a. teleph.*); (*convocar*) call, summon; (*invocar*) call upon (*a inf.* to *inf.*); beckon *con ademán*; (*atraer*) draw, attract; *v/i.* call; knock, ring *a puerta*; **~se** be called; *¿cómo te llamas?* what is your name?; *¡eso sí que se llama hablar!* now you're talking!, that's more like it!

llamarada *f* flare-up, sudden blaze; flush *de cara*; *fig.* outburst, flash.

llamativo gaudy, flashy, showy.

llamear [1a] blaze, flare.

llana *f* ⚠ trowel; = **llanada** *f* plain, level ground; **llanero** *m*, **a** *f* plain dweller; **llaneza** *f* plainness, simplicity; modesty; (*familiarity*) informality; **llano 1.** level, smooth, even; (*sin adorno*) plain, simple; (*claro*) clear, plain; (*sin dificultad*) straightforward; *gr.* paroxytone; *a la ~a* simply; *de ~* openly, clearly; **2.** *m* plain, level ground.

llanta *f* rim (of wheel); (*neumático*) tyre; *~ de oruga* track.

llantén *m* plantain.

llanto *m* weeping, crying; *fig.* lamentation.

llanura *f* flatness *etc.*; (*terreno*) plain.

llave *f* key (*a. fig.*); (gas *etc.*); tap; ⚡ switch; ⊕ spanner; ⊕ key; ♪ stop; ⚔, *lucha*: lock; *~ de caja*, *~ de cubo* socket wrench; *~ de caño*, *~ para tubos* pipe wrench; *~ de cierre* stopcock; *mot.* *~ de contacto* ignition key; *~ de estufa* damper; *~ inglesa* (monkey) wrench; *~ maestra* skeleton key, master key; *~ de mandíbulas dentadas* alligator wrench; *~ de paso* stopcock; passkey; *debajo de ~* under lock and key; *echar la ~* (*a*) lock up; **llavero** *m* key ring; (*p.*) turnkey; **llavín** *m* latch key.

llegada *f* arrival, coming; **llegar** [1h] *v/t.* bring up, draw up; *v/i.* arrive (*a* at), come; (*alcanzar*) reach; (*suceder*) happen; (*bastar*) be enough; *~ a* reach; (*importar*) amount to; (*igualar*) be equal to; *~ a inf.* reach the point of *ger.*; (*lograr*) manage to *inf.*; *~ a saber* find out; *~ a ser* become; *hacer ~ el dinero* make both ends meet; **~se** approach, come near.

llenar [1a] fill, stuff (de with); *espacio, tiempo* occupy, take up; *hoja* fill out (in, up); (*cumplir*) fulfill; (*satisfacer*) satisfy; (*colmar*) overwhelm (de with); *~ de insultos* heap insults upon; **~se** fill up; F stuff o.s.; *fig.* get cross; *~ de polvo* get covered in dust; **lleno 1.** full (de of), filled (de with); de *~* fully, entirely; **2.** *m* fill, plenty; *fig.* perfection; *thea.* full house; *ast.* full moon.

llevadero bearable; **llevar** [1a] carry (*a.* ⚕); *p.*, *cosa* take (*a* to); *p.* lead (*a* to); *casa, cuentas* keep; *armas, frutos, nombre* bear; *ropa* wear; *tiempo* spend; *precio* charge; *dirección* follow, keep to; *vida* lead; *premio* carry off; (*cercenar*) take off; (*aguantar*) bear, stand; (*dirigir*) manage; *~ p.p.* have (already) *p.p.*; *llevo escritas 3 cartas* I have written 3 letters; *~ mucho tiempo ger.* have been *ger.* a long time; *¿cuánto tiempo llevas aquí?* how long have you been here?; *te llevo 3 años* I am 3 years older than you; *~ adelante* push ahead with; *~ consigo*, *~ encima* carry, have with one; F *~la hecha* have got it all worked out; *~las de perder* be in a bad way; *~ lo mejor* (*peor*) get the best (worst) of it; *~ puesto* wear, have on; *no ~las* *todas consigo* have the wind up; **~se** *algo* take away, carry off; ~ *bien con* get on with.

llorar [1a] *v/t.* weep for, cry over; lament; *muerte* mourn; *v/i.* cry, weep; **lloriquear** [1a] snivel, whimper; **lloriqueo** *m* whimper, whimpering; **llorón 1.** sniveling, whining; **2.** *m*, **-a** *f* crybaby; **lloroso** tearful; sad.

llovedizo *techo* leaky; *v. agua*; **llover** [2h] rain (*a. fig.*); *como llovido* unexpectedly; *llueva o no* rain or shine; *como quien oye* ~ quite unmoved; *v. cielo*; **llovizna** *f* drizzle; **lloviznar** [1a] drizzle; **lluvia** *f* rain; (*cantidad*) rainfall; (*agua*) rainwater; *fig.* shower; mass; hail *de balas*; ~ *radiactiva* (radioactive) fallout; **lluvioso** rainy, wet.

M

macabro macabre.
macadán *m* macadam; **macadamizar** [1f] macadamize.
macana *f S.Am.* club; F (*disparate*) silly thing; F (*cuento*) fib, tale; F *¡qué ~!* what a bind!; **macanear** [1a] *S.Am.* F fib, lay it on; **macanudo** F smashing, super; (*disparatado*) silly.
macarrón[1] *m* ⚓ bulwark.
macarrón[2] *m*: *~* (*de almendra*) macaroon; *~es pl.* macaroni; **macarrónico** macaronic; *latín ~* dog-Latin.
macear [1a] hammer, pound.
macerar(se) [1a] macerate.
macero *m* mace bearer.
maceta *f* ⚘ flower pot.
macicez *f* massiveness.
macilento wan, haggard; (*flaco*) emaciated.
macillo *m* ♪ hammer.
macis *f* mace (*spice*).
macizo 1. massive; (*bien construido*) stout; *neumático, oro etc.* solid (*a. fig.*); **2.** *m geog.* mass(if); ⛏ bed.
macro... macro...
mácula *f* stain, blemish; *~ solar* sun spot.
machaca *m/f* (*p.*) pest, bore; **machacar** [1g] *v/t.* pound, crush, mash; F *precio* slash; *v/i.* go on, keep on; nag; *~ en* harp on; *¡no machaques!* don't go on so!, stop harping on it!; **machacón 1.** tiresome; **2.** *m*, **-a** *f* pest, bore.
machado *m* hatchet.
machamartillo: F *a ~* tightly; *creer etc.* implicitly; *cumplir* to the letter.
machaqueo *m* pounding *etc.*; *fig.* nagging.
machete *m* machete.
machihembrar [1a] ⊕ dovetail.
machismo *m* machismo.
macho 1. *biol.*, ⊕ male; *fig.* strong, tough; **2.** *m* male; mule; *v. cabrío*; ⚡ pin; ⊕ pin, peg; (*martillo*) sledge (hammer); *sew.* hook; F dolt; **machón** *m* buttress; **machote** *m sl.* he-man, tough guy.
machucar [1g] bruise.
machucho elderly; wise beyond one's years, prudent; sedate.
madeja *f* skein, hank *de lana*; mass *de pelo*; F *~ de nervios* bundle of nerves.
madera *f* wood; (*trozo*) piece of wood; *~* (*de construcción*) timber; *~ contrachapeada* plywood; *~ de deriva* driftwood; *de ~* wood(en);
maderaje *m*, **maderamen** *m* woodwork, timbering; **madero** *m* beam; F blockhead.
madrastra *f* stepmother; **madre** *f* mother (*a. attr., eccl., fig.*); *anat.* womb; bed *de río*; (*residuo*) sediment, dregs; *fig.* cradle *de civilización etc.*; *juegos*: *la ~* home; *~ adoptiva* foster mother; *~ de leche* wet nurse; *~ patria* mother country; old country; *~ política* mother-in-law; *sacar de ~* annoy, upset; *sin ~* motherless; *salirse de ~* overflow; **~selva** *f* honeysuckle.
madrigal *m* madrigal.
madriguera *f* den (*a. fig.*); burrow *en tierra*.
madrileño *adj. a. su. m*, **a** *f* (native) of Madrid.
madrina *f* godmother; *fig.* patron, patroness; *~ de boda approx.* bridesmaid.
madroño *m* strawberry tree.
madrugada *f* early morning; (*alba*) daybreak; *de ~* early; *las 3 de la ~* three o'clock in the morning; **madrugador 1.** that gets up early; **2.** *m*, **-a** *f* early riser, early bird; **madrugar** [1h] get up early; *fig.* get ahead; *deportes*: jump the gun.
madurar [1a] *v/t.* ripen; *fig.* mature; *p.* toughen (up), season; *proyecto etc.* think out; *v/i.* ripen; *fig.* mature; **madurez** *f* ripeness; *fig.* maturity; **maduro** ripe; *fig.* mature; *de edad ya ~a* middle-aged.
maestra *f* teacher (*a. fig.*); *~* (*de escuela*) schoolteacher;
maestranza *f* ⚓ dockyard; arsenal,

armory; **maestre** *m hist.* (grand) master; **maestría** *f* mastery; masterliness; *con* ~ in a masterly fashion; **maestro 1.** masterly; main, principal; *llave, obra etc.* master *attr.*; **2.** *m* master (*a. fig.*); ~ (*de escuela*) schoolteacher; ♪ maestro; ~ *de capilla* choirmaster; ~ *de ceremonias* master of ceremonies; ~ *de equitación* riding master; ~ *de obras* (*dueño*) (master)builder; foreman.

mafia *f* (*a. fig.*) Mafia.

magenta *f* magenta.

magia *f* magic; **mágico 1.** magic, magical; **2.** *m* magician.

magín *m* F fancy, imagination; mind.

magisterio *m* (*arte*) teaching; teaching profession; (*ps.*) teachers; **magistrado** *m* magistrate; **magistral** magisterial; *fig.* masterly; authoritative; **magistratura** *f* magistracy.

magnanimidad *f* magnanimity *etc.*; **magnánimo** magnanimous, generous; **magnate** *m* magnate, tycoon F; *hist.* baron.

magnesia *f* magnesia; **magnesio** *m* ⚗ magnesium; *phot.* flashlight.

magnético magnetic; **magnetismo** *m* magnetism; **magnetizar** [1f] magnetize; **magneto** *f* magneto; **magnetofón** *m* tape recorder; **magnetofónico** tape *attr.*, recording *attr.*; **magnetoscopia** *f* video recorder.

magnificencia *f* magnificence, splendor; **magnificar** [1g] *opt.* magnify; **magnífico** splendid, wonderful, superb, magnificent; *¡~!* splendid!; **magnitud** *f* magnitude (*a. ast.*); **magno** *lit.* great.

magnolia *f* magnolia.

mago *m* magician; *los tres Reyes Magos* the Three Wise Men.

magra *f* lean part; (*lonja*) slice, rasher; *¡~s!* rubbish!, not on your life!; **magro** (*flaco*) skinny; *carne* lean; (*escaso*) meager.

magulladura *f* bruise; **magullar** [1a] ⚕ bruise; batter, bash, mangle.

mahometano *adj. a. su. m*, **a** *f* Muslim, Mohammedan.

maitines *m/pl.* matins.

maíz *m* corn; *comer* ~ *S.Am.* accept bribes; **maizal** *m* cornfield.

majada *f* sheepfold; (*estiércol*) dung; **majadería** *f* silliness; (*dicho etc.*) silly thing; ~*s pl.* nonsense; **majadero 1.** silly; **2.** *m* idiot.

majar [1a] pound, grind, mash; ⚕ bruise; *fig.* bother.

majestad *f* majesty; stateliness; *Su* ~ His (*or* Her) Majesty; (*Vuestra*) ~ Your Majesty; **majestuoso** majestic, stately, imposing.

majo 1. lovely, nice, cute; (*elegante*) smart, natty; **2.** *m* toff, masher; flashy sort; (*valentón*) bully, lout.

majuelo *m* newly-planted vine.

mal 1. *adj.* = *malo*; **2.** *adv.* badly; (*difícilmente*) hardly; (*equivocadamente*) wrong(ly); *compuestos*: ~ *educado* ill-mannered, unmannerly; *v. parecido etc.*; *pero digo* ~ but I am wrong (to say ...); no, that's not right; ~ *que bien* willy-nilly; (*bien o mal*) any old how; *de* ~ *en peor* from bad to worse; *¡menos* ~*!* that's a relief!; *menos* ~ *que* it is just as well that; **3.** *m* evil, wrong; (*calamidad*) evil; (*daño*) harm, hurt, damage; (*desgracia*) misfortune; ⚕ disease; illness; ~ *caduco* epilepsy; ~ *de mar* seasickness; ~ *de ojo* evil eye; ~ *de rayos* radiation sickness; ~ *de la tierra* homesickness; ~ *de vuelo* airsickness; *caer en el* ~ fall into evil ways; *echar a* ~ scorn; *hacer* ~ (*a*) harm, hurt; *¡~ haya ...!* a curse on (*quien* him who); *llevar* (*or tomar*) *a* ~ resent, be offended at; *parar en* ~ come to a bad end.

mala *f* mail bag.

malabarista *m/f* juggler.

malacate *m* ⊕ winch, whim.

malaconsejado ill-advised.

malagueño *adj. a. su. m*, **a** *f* (native) of Málaga.

malandante unfortunate.

malandrín *m*, **-a** *f* scoundrel.

malaquita *f* malachite.

malaria *f* malaria.

malavenido in disagreement.

malaventura *f* misfortune; **malaventurado** unfortunate.

malayo 1. Malay(an); **2.** *m*, **a** *f* Malay; **3.** *m* (*idioma*) Malay.

malbaratar [1a] ⚚ sell off cheap; *fig.* squander.

malcasado unfaithful.

malcontento 1. discontented; **2.** *m*, **a** *f* malcontent.

malcriado ill-bred, coarse.

M N O

maldad *f* evil, wickedness; (*acto*) wicked thing.

maldecir [*approx.* 3p] *v/t.* curse; (*difamar*) = *v/i.*: ~ de run down, disparage; **maldiciente 1.** that speaks ill of everything, forever criticizing; slanderous; (*malhablado*) foul-mouthed; **2.** *m* grumbler, malcontent; slanderer; **maldición** *f* curse; ¡~! curse it!, damn!; **maldita** *f* F tongue; *soltar la* ~ talk too freely; (*encolerizarse*) blow up; **maldito** damned (*a. eccl.*); (*malo*) wicked; ~ *lo que me importa* I don't give a damn; *no saber ~a la cosa de* know a damn about; ¡~ *sea!* damn it!

maleable malleable (*a. fig.*).

maleante 1. wicked; **2.** *m/f* crook, hoodlum; vagrant; **malear** [1a] damage, spoil; *tierra* sour; *fig.* corrupt; **~se** spoil *etc.*, be ruined.

malecón *m* levee, dike, mole, jetty.

maledicencia *f* slander, scandal.

maleficio *m* curse, spell; **maléfico** evil, harmful.

malejo F pretty bad.

malentendido *m* misunderstanding.

malestar *m* ⚕ discomfort; *fig.* uneasiness, malaise; *pol.* unrest, discontent.

maleta 1. *f* (suit)case; *mot.* trunk; *hacer la(s) ~(s)* pack; **2.** *m* F bungler; *thea.* ham; **maletín** *m* valise, satchel.

malevolencia *f* malevolence, spite, ill will; **malévolo** malevolent, spiteful.

maleza *f* (*malas hierbas*) weeds; (*arbustos*) scrub; undergrowth, underbrush *en bosque*; (*soto*) thicket.

malformación *f* malformation.

malgastador spendthrift, thriftless; **malgastar** [1a] *hacienda* squander; *tiempo* waste; *salud* ruin.

malhablado foul-mouthed.

malhadado ill-starred, ill-fated.

malhecho *m* misdeed; **malhechor** *m*, **-a** *f* evildoer, malefactor.

malhumorado cross, bad-tempered, peevish.

malicia *f* (*maldad*) wickedness; (*astucia*) slyness; mischief *de niño etc.*; (*mala intención*) malice, maliciousness; **malicioso** wicked; sly; mischievous; malicious.

malignidad *f* malignancy *etc.*; **maligno** malignant (*a.* ⚕), malicious; *influjo etc.* evil, pernicious.

malintencionado unkind, ill-disposed.

malísimo dreadful, appalling.

malmandado F disobedient; obstinate.

malo 1. *mst* bad; *niño* naughty, mischievous; (*equivocado*) wrong; ⚕ ill; ~ *de inf.* hard to *inf.*; *lo* ~ *es que* the trouble is that; *andar a ~as con* be on bad terms with; *estar de ~as* be out of luck; *ponerse a ~as con* fall foul of; *venir de ~as* have evil intentions; **2.** *m thea.* villain.

malogrado abortive, ill-fated; *p.* late lamented; **malograr** [1a] spoil; *oportunidad* waste; **~se** fail, miscarry, come to grief; (*morir*) come to an untimely end; **malogro** *m* failure; (*muerte*) untimely end; waste *de tiempo etc.*

maloliente stinking, smelly.

malparado: *salir* ~ come off badly (*de* in); **malparar** [1a] damage, harm; ill-treat.

malparir [3a] have a miscarriage; **malparto** *m* miscarriage.

malpensado evil-minded; ¡*no seas* ~! don't be nasty!

malquerencia *f* dislike; **malquistar** [1a] cause a rift between, alienate; **~se** become estranged; **malquisto** disliked; *dos ps.* estranged.

malsano unhealthy; *mente* morbid; ⚕ sickly.

malsonante nasty, rude.

malsufrido impatient.

malta *f* malt.

maltés *adj. a. su. m*, **-a** *f* Maltese.

maltratamiento *m* maltreatment *etc.*; **maltratar** [1a] ill-treat, maltreat; knock about; abuse *de palabra*; **maltrato** *m* maltreatment etc.; **maltrecho** battered, damaged.

malucho F ⚕ poorly.

malva *f* ⚘ mallow; ~ *loca*, ~ *rósea* hollyhock; (*de*) *color de* ~ mauve; *ser como una* ~ be very meek and mild.

malvado 1. wicked, villainous; **2.** *m* villain.

malvarrosa *f* hollyhock; **malvavisco** *m* ⚘ marsh mallow.

malvender [2a] sell off cheap.
malversación *f* embezzlement; graft; **malversador** *m* embezzler; **malversar** [1a] embezzle, misappropriate.
malla *f* mesh; network; ⚔ (chain) mail.
mallo *m* mallet.
mallorquín *adj. a. su. m*, **-a** *f* Majorcan.
mamá *f*, **mamaíta** *f* F mommy, mom, mamma.
mamar [1a] suck; *fig.* learn as a child, acquire in infancy; (*a.* **~se**) F *destino* wangle, land; *recursos* milk; *fondos* pocket; *susto* have; *dar de ~ a* feed; **~se** F get tight; *~ a uno* get the best of s.o.
mamarracho *m* (*p.*) sight, object; (*obra*) unholy mess, botch; *paint.* daub.
mameluco *m* F chump.
mamífero 1. mammalian; **2.** *m* mammal.
mamola: *dar la ~ a* chuck *s.o.* under the chin.
mamón *m* ⚘ sucker; *zo.* suckling; *Mex.* baby bottle.
mamotreto *m* notebook; F whopping big book.
mampara *f* screen; **mamparo** *m* ⚓ bulkhead.
mamporro *m* bump *al caer*; punch, clout.
mampostería *f* △ masonry; **mampuesto** *m* (rough) stone; parapet; *de ~* spare, emergency *attr.*
mamut *m* mammoth.
maná *m* manna.
manada *f* ✓ flock, herd; pack *de lobos*; F crowd, mob; **manadero** *m* shepherd, herdsman.
manantial 1. flowing, running; **2.** *m* spring; *fig.* source; **manar** [1a] *v/t.* run with, flow with; *v/i.* flow, pour out; well up; *fig.* abound.
manceba *f* whore; (*concubina*) mistress; **mancebía** *f* brothel; wild oats; **mancebo** *m* youth.
mancilla *f* stain, spot; blemish, dishonor; **mancillar** [1a] stain, sully.
manco one-handed, one-armed; (*en general*) crippled, lame; *fig.* defective.
mancomún: *de ~* (con)jointly; **mancomunar** [1a] *recursos* pool; *intereses* combine; **~se** merge, combine; *~ en* associate in;
mancomunidad *f* pool; association; *pol.* commonwealth.
mancha *f zo. etc.* spot, mark; spot, fleck *en diseño*; (*suciedad*) spot, stain; smear; blot, smudge *de tinta*; *fig.* stain *en reputación*; (*defecto*) blemish; (*terreno*) patch; *~ solar* sunspot; **manchado** spotty, smudgy *etc.*; *esp. animal* dappled, spotted; *esp. ave* pied; **manchar** [1a] spot, mark; (*ensuciar*) soil, stain; smudge; *fig.* stain, tarnish; *reputación de otro* smear, tarnish.
manchego *adj. a. su. m*, **a** *f* (native) of La Mancha.
manda *f* bequest; **mandadero** *m*, **a** *f* messenger; (*m*) errand boy; **mandado** *m* order; commission, errand; *ir a los ~s* run errands; **mandamiento** *m* order; *eccl.* commandment; ⚖ writ, warrant; **mandar** [1a] **1.** *v/t.* order (*inf.* to *inf.*), (*gobernar*) rule (over); (*acaudillar*) lead, command; (*enviar*) send; (*legar*) bequeath; *~ (para acá y para allá)* order about; *~ a distancia* operate by remote control; *~ hacer algo* get (*or* have) s.t. done; *~ hacer un traje* have a suit made, order a suit; *~ salir* order *s.o.* out; **2.** *v/i.* be in command (*or* control); *b.s.* boss (people about); *~ por* send for; *aquí mando yo* I am the master here, I'm the boss; **3. ~se** △ communicate (*con* with); ⚕ get around (by o.s.).
mandarín *m* mandarin; **mandarina** *f* tangerine.
mandatorio *adj. a. su. m* mandatory; **mandato** *m* order; *pol. etc.* mandate; term *de presidente*; ⚖ writ, warrant (*de prisión* of arrest).
mandíbula *f* jaw (*a.* ⊕), mandible 🕮; jawbone.
mandil *m* (leather) apron; **mandilón** *m* apron; F coward.
mando *m* command, rule, control; leadership; ⊕ drive; ⊕ *~s pl.* controls; ⊕ *de ~* control *attr.*; *alto ~* high command; *~ a distancia* remote control; *~ a punta de dedo* fingertip control; *~ por botón* push-botton control; ⚔ *al ~ de* (*jefe*) in command of; (*subordinado*) under the command of; *tener el ~* be in control.
mandolina *f* mandolin(e).
mandón bossy, domineering.
mandrágora *f* mandrake.

mandria 1. worthless; **2.** *m/f* useless sort.

mandril[1] *m zo.* mandrill.

mandril[2] *m* ⊕ mandrel.

manear [1a] hobble.

manecilla *f* ⊕ pointer, hand; (*broche*) clasp.

manejable manageable; *herramienta etc.* handy; **manejar** [1a] manage, handle (*a. fig.*); *máquina a.* work, run, operate; *S.Am. coche* drive; **~se** ⚕ get around; *¿cómo te manejas para hacer eso?* how do you set about doing that?; **manejo** *m* management, handling *etc.*; *b.s.* intrigue; stratagem; *llevar todo el ~ de* be in sole charge of.

manera *f* way, manner; **~s** *pl.* manners *de p.*; *a la ~ de* in (*or* after) the manner of; *de esta ~* (in) this way, like this; *de otra ~* otherwise; *de ninguna ~* by no means; *¡de ninguna ~!* certainly not!; *de ~ que* so that; *¿de ~ que ...?* so ...?; *de todas ~s* at any rate; *en gran ~* in (a) great measure; *sobre ~* exceedingly; *no hay ~ de inf.* there's no way of *ger.*; *no había ~ de disuadirle* there was no dissuading him.

manga *f* sleeve; *~ (de riego)* hose, hose pipe; ✈ wind sock; ⚓ beam; *~ (de agua)* cloudburst, ⚓ water spout; *bridge*: game; *~ de viento* whirlwind; F *de ~* in league; *de ~ ancha* indulgent; *b.s.* not over-scrupulous; *en ~s de camisa* in one's shirt sleeves; *sin ~s* sleeveless; F *andar etc. ~ por hombro* be in a mess; *sl. pegar las ~s* kick the bucket.

manganeso *m* manganese.

mangante F **1.** brazen; **2.** *m* scrounger; **mangar** [1h] *sl.* swipe.

mango[1] *m* ♀ mango.

mango[2] *m* handle; **mangonear** [1a]: F *~ en* meddle in; *estudio etc.* dabble in; **mangoneón** *m* F busybody.

mangosta *f* mongoose.

manguera *f* hose pipe; ⚓ water spout; corral; (*tubo de ventilación*) funnel.

manguito *m* muff; ⊕ sleeve; *~ incandescente* gas mantle.

manía *f* mania; *fig.* mania, rage, craze (de for); (*capricho*) whim; (*rareza*) fad, peculiarity; *~ persecutoria* persecution mania; *dar en la ~ de inf.* take to *ger.*; *tener ~ a* dislike, have it in for; *tiene la ~ de inf.* he's got the habit of *ger.*;

maníaco 1. maniac(al); **2.** *m*, **a** *f* maniac.

maniatar [1a] tie *s.o.'s* hands.

maniático 1. maniacal; *fig.* mad, crazy; (*testarudo*) stubborn; (*raro*) eccentric, odd; **2.** *m*, **a** *f* maniac; *fig.* eccentric, odd type; **manicomio** *m* (lunatic) asylum, mental hospital.

manicura *f* manicure; **manicuro** *m*, **a** *f* (*p.*) manicurist.

manida *f* lair, den.

manido high, gamy.

manifestación *f* manifestation; show; declaration; *pol.* demonstration; **manifestante** *m/f* demonstrator; **manifestar** [1k] show; (*por palabra*) declare, express, state; **~se** show, be manifest; *pol.* demonstrate; *~ en* be evident in; **manifiesto 1.** clear, evident; *verdad* manifest; *error etc.* glaring; obvious; *poner de ~* make clear; *quedar ~* be plain; **2.** *m* ⚓ manifest; *pol.* manifesto.

manija *f* (*mango*) handle; (*abrazadera*) clamp, collar; 🚂 coupling.

manilargo *fig.* open-handed.

manilla *f* bracelet; (*grillete*) handcuff, manacle; hand *de reloj*; *~s pl. de hierro* handcuffs; **manillar** *m* handlebar.

maniobra *f* handling; maneuver (*a. fig.*); *fig.* move; *b.s.* stratagem, intrigue; *~s pl.* ⚔ maneuvers; 🚂 shunting; **maniobrable** maneuverable; **maniobrar** [1a] maneuver (*a. fig.*); 🚂 shunt.

maniota *f* hobble.

manipulación *f* manipulation; **manipulador 1.** *m*, **-a** *f* manipulator; **2.** *m* ⚡, *tel.* key, tapper; **manipular** [1a] manipulate; *fig.* handle, manage.

maniquí 1. *m* (tailor's) dummy, manikin; *fig.* puppet; *ir hecho un ~* be a fashion plate; **2.** *f* mannequin, model.

manirroto lavish, extravagant.

manivela *f* crank; *~ (de arranque)* starting handle.

manjar *m* dish; *~ exquisito* tidbit, delicacy.

mano *f* hand; *zo.* foot; coat *de pintura*; *naipes*: *ser ~* lead; *yo soy ~* it's my lead; ~ *de almirez* pestle; ~ *derecha* right-hand man; ~*s pl. limpias* extras, perquisites; F clean hands; ~*s pl. muertas* mortmain; ~ *de obra* labor; manpower; ~ *de papel* quire; ~*s puercas* F graft; *¡~s quietas!* hands off!; *última* ~ finishing touch; *a* ~ by hand; *escribir* in longhand; *a (la)* ~ at hand, on hand, handy; *a* ~ *airada* violently; *a* ~ *salva* without risk; *a* ~*s de dirigir* care of; *¡arriba las* ~*s!* hands up!; *bajo* ~ in secret, behind the scenes, underhandedly; *con las* ~*s en la masa* red-handed, in the act; *de la* ~ *llevar* by the hand; *de las* ~*s* hand in hand; *de primera* ~ at first hand; *de segunda* ~ second-hand; *de* ~*s a boca* suddenly, unexpectedly; *de* ~*s de* at the hands of; *recibir* from; *entre* ~*s* in hand, on hand; *¡fuera las* ~*s!* hands off!; *asidos de la* ~ hand-in-hand; *cargar la* ~ insist, press hard; *¡dame esa* ~*!* put it here!; *darse las* ~*s* join hands; (*estrechar*) shake hands; *dejar de la* ~ abandon; *no dejar de la* ~ *libro* not be able to put down; *echar una* ~ lend a hand; *naipes etc.*: play a game (de of); *echar* ~ *a* lay hands on; *echar* ~ *de* make use of, resort to; *escribir a la* ~ take dictation; *estrechar la* ~ *a* shake *s.o.'s* hand; *ganar por la* ~ *a* steal a march on; *hacerse la* ~ get one's hand in; *hecho a* ~ hand-made; *probar la* ~ try one's hand; *tener* ~ *con* have a way with, have influence on, have a pull with; *tener buena* ~ *para* be a good hand at; *untar la* ~ *a* grease *s.o.'s* palm; *venir a las* ~*s* come to blows; *vivir de la* ~ *a la boca* live from hand to mouth.

manojo *m* handful, bunch; tuft *de hierba etc.*

manómetro *m* gauge; ~ *de aceite* oil gauge.

manopla *f* (face) flannel; † gauntlet.

manoseado *fig.* hackneyed; **manosear** [1a] handle, finger; (*ajar*) rumple; *b.s.* paw, fiddle with, muck about with.

manotada *f*, **manotazo** *m* slap, smack; **manotear** [1a] *v/t.* slap, smack; *v/i.* gesticulate, use one's hands; **manoteo** *m* gesticulation.

mansalva: *a* ~ without risk; *a* ~ *de* safe from.

mansedumbre *f* mildness *etc.*; **manso** mild, gentle; *animal* tame.

manta *f* blanket; ~ *de coche* lap robe; ~ (*de viaje*) rug; F hiding; F *liarse la* ~ *a la cabeza* go the whole hog; press on regardless; F *tirar de la* ~ let the cat out of the bag; **mantear** [1a] toss in a blanket.

manteca *f* fat; *esp.* ~ (*de cerdo*) lard; ~ (*de vaca*) butter; **mantecado** *m approx.* ice cream; **mantecoso** buttery; lardy.

mantel *m* tablecloth; **mantelería** *f* table linen; **mantelillo** *m* table runner.

mantener [2l] keep *en equilibrio etc.*; ⚠ *etc.* hold up, support; (*alimentar*) sustain; ⊕ maintain, service; *opinión* maintain; *costumbre*, *relaciones etc.* keep up; ~**se** sustain o.s., subsist (*de* on); *fig.* stand firm; ~ (*en vigor*) stand; ~ *en un puesto* keep a job; **mantenimiento** *m* sustenance; maintenance *etc.*

mantequera *f* churn; butter dish *de mesa*; **mantequería** *f* dairy, creamery; **mantequilla** *f* butter.

mantilla *f* mantilla; ~*s pl.* baby clothes; *estar en* ~*s* (*p.*) be very innocent; (*proyecto*) be in its infancy.

mantillo *m* humus, mold.

manto *m* cloak (*a. fig.*); *eccl.*, ⚖ robe, gown; *zo.* mantle; ~ (*de chimenea*) mantel; **mantón** *m* shawl.

manuable handy; **manual 1.** manual, hand *attr.*; (*manuable*) handy; **2.** *m* manual, handbook; **manubrio** *m* handle, crank; winch.

manufactura *f* manufacture; (*edificio*) factory; **manufacturar** [1a] manufacture; **manufacturero 1.** manufacturing; **2.** *m* manufacturer.

manuscrito 1. handwritten, manuscript; **2.** *m* manuscript.

manutención *f* maintenance (*a.* ⊕).

manzana *f* apple; ⚠ block; ~ *de la discordia* apple of discord, bone of contention; ~ *silvestre* crab, crab apple; **manzanilla** *f* ⚘ camomile; (*infusión*) camomile tea; (*vino*) manzanilla (*a very dry sherry*); **manzano** *m* apple (tree).

maña *f* (*en general*) skill, ingenuity; *b.s.* guile, craft; (*una* ~) trick, knack; *b.s.* evil habit; *darse* ~ *para inf.* contrive to *inf.*

mañana 1. *f* morning; *de* ~, *por la* ~ in

the morning; *muy de* ~ early in the morning; *tomar la* ~ get up early; F have a shot of liquor before breakfast; **2.** *m*: *el* ~ the morrow, the future; **3.** *adv*. tomorrow; ~ *por la* ~ tomorrow morning; ¡*hasta* ~! see you tomorrow!; *pasado* ~ the day after tomorrow; **mañanear** [1a] *v/i*. be in the habit of getting up early; **mañanero** morning *attr*.; early-rising; **mañanica** *f* early morning, break of day.

mañoso skilful, clever; *b.s.* wily, sharp.

mapa *m* map.

mapache *m* rac(c)oon.

maque *m* lacquer; **maquear** [1a] lacquer.

maqueta *f* model.

maquillador *m thea*. make-up man; **maquillaje** *m* make-up; **maquillar(se)** [1a] make up.

máquina *f* machine (*a. fig.*); 🚂 engine, locomotive; ~ (*fotográfica*) camera; F bicycle; *mot*. F car; Δ palace, building; *fig*. scheme (of things), machinery; (*proyecto*) scheme; ~ *de afeitar* (safety) razor; ⚡ electric razor; ~ *de coser* sewing machine; ~ *de escribir* typewriter; ~ *herramienta* machine tool; ~ *infernal* infernal machine; ~ *de sumar* adding machine; ~ *sacaperras* slot machine; ~ *de vapor* steam engine; *a toda* ~ at full speed; *acabar* (*or coser etc.*) *a* ~ machine; *escribir a* ~ type; *hecho a* ~ machine-made; *typ*. typed; **maquinación** *f* machination, plot; **maquinador** *m*, **-a** *f* schemer; **maquinal** mechanical (*a. fig.*); **maquinar** [1a] plot; **maquinaria** *f* machinery; plant; **maquinista** *m* ⊕ operator, machinist; ⚓ *etc*. engineer; 🚂 engineer.

mar *m a. f* sea; ~ *alta* rough sea; ~ *ancha* high seas; ~ *bonanza* calm sea; ~ *de fondo* (ground) swell; ~ *llena* high tide; ~ *de nubes* cloud bank; ~ *de reconocimiento* ⚓ landmark, seamark; F *la* ~ *adv*. a lot; F *la* ~ *de* lots of, no end of; F *la* ~ *de tonto* no end of a fool; *al* ~ *caer etc.* overboard; *a* ~*es* copiously; *llorar a* ~*es* cry one's eyes out; *de alta* ~ seagoing; *en alta* ~ on the high seas; *por* ~ by sea; *hacerse a la* ~ put to sea.

maraña *f* ⚘ thicket; (*enredo*) tangle; *fig*. puzzle, jungle; (*embuste*) trick; **marañero 1.** scheming; **2.** *m* schemer.

marasmo *m* ⚕ wasting, consumption; *fig*. paralysis, stagnation.

maravilla *f* marvel, wonder; ⚘ marigold; *a* ~, *a las mil* ~*s* wonderfully, extremely well; **maravillar** [1a] surprise, amaze; ~**se** be amazed (*de* at); wonder, marvel (*de* at); **maravilloso** marvelous, wonderful.

marbete *m* label; tag, docket; *sew*. edge, border.

marca *f* mark(ing); stamp; (*fabricación*) make, brand; ⚓ landmark; ♪ beat; *naipes*: bid; *deportes*: record; *hist*. march(es); ~ *de agua* watermark; ~ *de fábrica*, ~ *registrada* (registered) trademark; ~ *de taquilla* box-office record; *de* ~ outstanding; *de* ~ *mayor* most outstanding; **marcación** *f* ⚓ bearing; **marcado** marked, pronounced; *acento* strong, broad; **marcador** *m* marker (*a. billar*); *deportes*: (*p.*) scorer; (*tanteador*) scoreboard; **marcapasos** *m* ⚕ pacemaker; **marcar** [1g] **1.** *v/t*. (*poner señal a*) mark; stamp, brand; *terreno etc.* mark out; (*señalar*) point out; (*reloj etc.*) show; (*termómetro etc.*) read, say; (*aplicar*) designate; ♪ *compás* keep, beat; *paso* mark; *deportes*: score; *teleph*. dial; **2.** *v/i*. *deportes*: score; *teleph*. dial; **3.** ~**se** ⚓ take one's bearings.

marcial martial; *porte* military.

marco *m paint*., Δ *etc*. frame; *fig*. setting; † mark; standard *de pesos etc.*; ~ *de chimenea* chimney piece; *poner* ~ *a paint*. frame.

marcha *f* ⚔, ♪ *a. fig*. march; ⊕ running, functioning; ⊕ (~ *atrás etc.*) gear; *fig*. progress; (*tendencia*) trend, course; (*velocidad*) speed; ⊕ *primera* ~ low gear; ~ *atrás* reverse (gear); *dar* ~ *atrás a*, *poner en* ~ *atrás coche etc.* reverse; ~ *forzada* forced march; ~ *nupcial* wedding march; *a toda* ~ (at) full blast; *en* ~ in motion, going; ⚓ *etc*. under way; ¡*en* ~! ⚔ forward march!; let's go!; *fig*. here goes!; (*a otro*) get going!; *sobre la* ~ immediately; *cerrar la* ~ bring up the rear; *poner en* ~ start; *fig*. set going, set in motion; *ponerse en* ~ start.

marchar [1a] (*caminar*) go; ⚔ march; ⊕ go, run, work; *fig.* go, come along; **~se** go (away), leave.
marchitar(se) [1a] wilt, wither, shrivel (up); **marchito** withered; faded (*a. fig.*).
marea *f* tide; (*viento*) sea breeze; ~ *alta* high tide, high water; ~ *baja* low tide; ~ *creciente*, ~ *entrante* flood tide; ~ *menguante* ebb tide; ~ *muerta* neap tide; ~ *viva* spring tide; **mareado** ⚕ sick; ⚓ seasick; *fig.* giddy, light-headed; F tipsy; **mareaje** *m* navigation; **marear** [1a] sail, navigate; *fig.* make *s.o.* cross; **~se** feel sick, feel dizzy; ⚓ feel (*or* be) seasick; **marejada** *f* swell, surge; *fig.* undercurrent; **mareo** *m* sick feeling, travel sickness; dizziness; ⚓ seasickness; **mareta** *f* surge (*a. fig.*).
marfil *m* ivory.
marga *f* marl.
margarina *f* margarine.
margarita *f* ⚘ daisy; *zo.* pearl; ~ (*impresora*) ⊕ *ordenador* daisy wheel.
margen 1. *mst m* border, edge; *typ.*, ✝ *etc.* margin; ~ *de error* margin of error; ~ *de seguridad* margin of safety; *al* ~ in the margin; *dar* ~ *para* give occasion for; F *dejar al* ~ leave out in the cold; **2.** *f* bank *de río etc.*; **marginal** marginal.
marica 1. *f orn.* magpie; **2.** *m* F milksop, sissy; **maricón** *m* F queer, pansy.
maridaje *m fig.* marriage; **marido** *m* husband.
mariguana *f* marijuana.
marimacho *m* F mannish woman.
marina *f* (*arte*) seamanship; (*buques*) shipping; ~ (*de guerra*) navy; *paint.* seascape; ~ *mercante* merchant navy; **marinería** *f* seamanship; (*ps.*) crew; **marinero 1.** seaworthy; **2.** *m* seaman, sailor; ~ *de primera* able seaman; **marino 1.** sea *attr.*; marine 📖; **2.** *m* seaman, sailor.
marioneta *f* marionette; *régimen* ~ puppet regime.
mariposa *f* butterfly; ~ (*nocturna*) moth; (*luz*) nightlight; **mariposear** [1a] flutter about; *fig.* act capriciously; (*amor*) flirt.
mariquita 1. *f* ladybird; **2.** *m* F milksop, sissy.
marisabidilla *f* F bluestocking.
mariscal *m* blacksmith; ~ *de campo* field marshal; † major general.
marisco *m* shellfish; **~s** *pl.* seafood.
marisma *f* marsh, swamp.
marital marital.
marítimo maritime; marine, sea *attr.*; *ciudad etc.* seaside *attr.*; *agente etc.* shipping *attr.*
marjal *m* moor; (*húmedo*) marsh, fen.
marmita *f* pot, kettle, boiler; *geol.* ~ *de gigante* pothole.
mármol *m* marble; **marmóreo** marble (*a. fig.*).
maroma *f* rope.
marmota *f* marmot; worsted cap; sleepyhead; ~ *de Alemania* hamster; ~ *de América* ground hog.
marqués *m* marquis; **marquesa** *f* marchioness.
marquesina *f* marquee; awning, canopy; Δ porch; Δ cantilever roof.
marquetería *f* marquetry.
marramizar [1f] caterwaul.
marrana *f* sow; F slut; **marrano 1.** dirty; **2.** *m* pig; F dirty pig; *hist.* Jew.
marrar [1a] miss; *fig.* go astray.
marras: F *de* ~ (that) you all know about; old, long-standing.
marrón 1. chestnut; maroon; **2.** *m* chestnut.
marroquí 1. *adj. a. su. m/f* Moroccan; **2.** *m* (*cuero*) Moroccan (leather); **marrueco** *adj. a. su. m*, **a** *f* Moroccan.
marrullería *f* smoothness, glibness; plausible excuses *etc.*; **marrullero 1.** smooth, glib, plausible; **2.** *m* smooth *etc.* sort.
marsopa *f* porpoise; **marsupial** *adj. a. su. m* marsupial.
marta *f* marten; (*piel*) sable.
martes *m* Tuesday; ~ *de carnaval*, ~ *de carnestolendas* Shrove Tuesday, Mardi Gras.
martillar [1a] hammer; **martillear** [1a] ⊕ knock; **martillo** *m* hammer; gavel *de presidente*; (*subastas*) auction room; ~ *picador* pneumatic drill.
martín *m* **pescador** kingfisher.
martinete *m* Δ pile driver; ⊕ drop hammer; ♪ hammer.
mártir *m/f* martyr; **martirio** *m* martyrdom; *fig.* torture; **martirizar** [1f] martyr(ize); *fig.* torment, torture.
marxismo *m* Marxism; **marxista** *adj. a. m/f* Marxist, Marxian.

marzo *m* March.
más 1. *comp.* more; *sup.* most; (*y*) plus, and; (*más tiempo*) longer; (*más rápidamente*) faster; *un libro de lo ~ interesante* a most interesting book; *~ quiero inf.* I would rather *inf.*; *~ bien* rather; *~ de*, *~ de lo que*, *~ que* more than; (*poco*) *~ o menos* more or less; *a ~* in addition (*de* to), besides (*de acc.*); *a lo ~* at (the) most; *como el que ~* as well as anyone, as well as the next man; *cuando ~* at (the) most, at the outside; *de ~* (*adicional*) extra; (*superfluo*) too much, too many; *v. estar*; *el que ~ y el que menos* every single one; *hasta no ~* to the limit; *los ~* most (people); *nada ~* nothing else; that's all; *ni ~ ni menos* just; *no ~* no more; *haber llegado etc.* just; *no ... ~* no longer, not any more; *no ~ que* only; just; *por ~ que* however much (*or* hard) *etc.*; *por ~ que yo quisiera* much as I should like; *¿qué ~?* what else?; what next?; *sin ~* (*ni ~*) without more ado; thereupon, at that; *es ~* furthermore; *hace no ~ de* no longer ago than, only ... ago; **2.** *m* ⩲ plus (sign); *tiene sus ~ y sus menos* it has its good and bad points.
mas *lit.* but.
masa[1] *f* (*pasta*) dough.
masa[2] *f* mass (*a. phys.*, *fig.*); *fig.* bulk, volume; *las ~s pl.* the masses; *~ coral* choir; *en ~* en masse; altogether.
masacrar [1a] massacre.
masaje *m* massage; *dar ~ a* massage; **masajista 1.** *m* masseur; **2.** *f* masseuse.
mascar [1g] chew; F mumble.
máscara *f* mask (*a. fig.*); *~ antigás* gas mask; *~s pl.* = **mascarada** *f* masque(rade); **mascarilla** *f* mask; (*vaciado*) death mask; **mascarón** *m*: *~ de proa* figurehead.
mascota *f* mascot.
masculinidad *f* masculinity, manliness; **masculino 1.** *biol.* male; *gr.* masculine; *fig.* masculine, manly; **2.** *m gr.* masculine.
mascullar [1a] F mumble, mutter.
masilla *f* putty.
masón *m* (free)mason; **masonería** *f* (free)masonry; **masónico** masonic.
masoquismo *m* masochism.
mastelero *m* topmast.
masticación *f* mastication; **masticar** [1g] masticate, chew; **masticatorio** masticatory, chewing.
mástil *m* pole, post; ⚓ mast; △ upright; ♪ neck; *~ de tienda* tent pole.
mastín *m* mastiff; *~ danés* Great Dane.
mastodóntico *fig.* elephantine.
mastoides *adj. a. su. f* mastoid.
mastuerzo *m* cress; F dolt.
mata *f* ⚘ shrub; (*pie de planta*) clump, root; (*hoja*) blade, sprig; mop, crop, head *de pelo*; *~s pl.* ⚘ scrub; *saltar de la ~* come out of hiding.
matachín *m* F bully.
matadero *m* slaughterhouse; F drudgery; **matador 1.** killing; **2.** *m*, **-a** *f* killer; *toros*: matador; *~ de mujeres* lady-killer; **matadura** *f vet.* sore, gall; **matafuego** *m* fire extinguisher; **mátalas callando** *m* F sly sort; **matanza** *f* slaughter; *esp.* ⚒ pig killing; *fig.* massacre; **matar** [1a] kill (*a. fig.*); *fuego* put out; *hambre* stay; *polvo* lay; *color* tone down; *así me maten* for the life of me; **~se** kill o.s.; get killed *en accidente*; *fig.* wear o.s. out; *~ con* quarrel with; *~ por inf.* struggle to *inf.*; **matarife** *m* butcher; *~ de caballos* knacker; **matasanos** *m* quack (doctor).
matasellar [1a] cancel, postmark; **matasello(s)** *m* postmark.
matasiete *m* bully, braggart.
mate[1] dull, matt.
mate[2] *m* (check)mate; *dar ~ a* (check)mate.
mate[3] *m S.Am.* ⚘ maté.
matemáticas *f/pl.* mathematics; **matemático 1.** mathematical; **2.** *m* mathematician.
materia *f* matter (*a. phys.*, ⚗); (*componentes*) material, stuff; (*asunto*) subject (matter); *escuela*: subject; *~ colorante* dyestuff; *~ fijo* 🚂 permanent way; *~ de guerra* matériel; *~ prima* raw material; *en ~ de* in the matter of, as regards; **material 1.** material; **2.** *m* material; ⊕ equipment, plant; *typ.* copy; *~ móvil*, *~ rodante* rolling stock; **materialismo** *m* materialism; **materialista 1.** materialistic; **2.** *m/f* materialist; **materializar(se)** [1f] materialize; **materialmente** *freq.* literally.

maternal motherly; maternal; **maternidad** *f* motherhood, maternity; (*a. casa de* ~) maternity hospital; **materno** maternal; *lengua etc.* mother *attr.*; *abuelo* ~ grandfather on the mother's side.
matinal morning *attr.*
matiz *m* shade (*a. fig.*); hue, tint; **matizar** [1f] (*casar*) blend, match; (*colorar*) tinge, tint (*de* with); *matizado de fig.* adorned with.
matón *m* bully, rough, lout.
matorral *m* thicket; brushwood, scrub.
matraca *f* rattle; F terrible bore, nuisance; *dar* ~ *a* give *s.o.* a hell of a time; (*mofarse*) jeer at; **matraquear** [1a] rattle; *fig.* jeer at.
matraz *m* ⚗ flask.
matrero 1. cunning; *S.Am.* suspicious; **2.** *m S.Am.* bandit.
matriarca *f* matriarch; **matricida** *m/f* matricide (*p.*); **matricidio** *m* matricide (*act*).
matrícula *f* list, register (*a.* ⚓), roll; *univ. etc.* (*acto*) matriculation, registration; (*permiso*) license; *mot.* registration number; **matriculación** *f* registration *etc.*; **matricular(se)** [1a] register, enroll.
matrimonial matrimonial; *vida* married; **matrimonio** *m* (*en general*) marriage, matrimony; (*acto*) marriage; (*ps.*) (married) couple; ~ *civil* civil marriage; ~ *consensual* common-law marriage; ~ *de conveniencia* marriage of convenience; *de* ~ *cama etc.* double; *contraer* ~ (*con*) marry.
matritense *adj. a. su. m/f* (native) of Madrid.
matriz *f anat.* womb; stub *de talonario*; ⊕ mold, die; ⊕ (*tuerca*) nut; *typ.*, ⚖ matrix.
matrona *f* matron.
matutino morning *attr.*
maula 1. *f* piece of junk; junk, trash; white elephant; *b.s.* dirty trick; **2.** *m/f* cheat, tricky sort; (*pesado*) bore; **maulero** *m*, **a** *f* cheat.
maullar [1a] mew, miaow; **maullido** *m* mew, miaow.
mausoleo *m* mausoleum.
maxilar 1. maxillary; **2.** *m* jaw, jaw-bone.
máxima *f* maxim; **máxime** especially; **máximo 1.** maximum; top; *grado etc.* highest; *esfuerzo etc.* greatest (possible); **2.** *m* = **máximum** *m* maximum.
maya *f* ⚘ daisy; (*p.*) May Queen.
mayal *m* ⚒ flail.
mayo *m* May; (*árbol*) maypole.
mayonesa *f* mayonnaise.
mayor 1. *adj. altar, misa* high; *parte, calle etc.* main, major (*a.* ♪); *p.* grown-up, of age; (*de edad avanzada*) elderly; **2.** *adj. comp.* bigger, larger, greater (*que* than); *edad*: older (*que* than), elder; senior (*que* to); *v. edad*; *hacerse* ~ *de edad* come of age; *ser* ~ *de edad* be of age; **3.** *adj. sup.* biggest; eldest *etc.*; **4.**: *al por* ~ wholesale; **5.** *m* chief, head; ⚔ major; ~*es pl.* ancestors; *fig.* elders; ~ *general* staff officer.
mayoral *m* ⊕ foreman, overseer; ⚒ head shepherd; † coachman.
mayorazgo *m* primogeniture; (*finca*) entailed estate; (*p.*) eldest son.
mayordomo *m* steward, butler.
mayoría *f* majority; larger part; *la* ~ *de* most; *en su* ~ in the main; **mayorista** *m* wholesaler; **mayormente** chiefly, mainly.
mayúscula *f* capital letter; **mayúsculo** *letra* capital; F pretty big, tremendous.
maza *f* mace; *deportes*: bat; ♪ drumstick; ~ *de gimnasia* Indian club.
mazacote *m* ⚠ concrete; ⚗ soda; F dry doughy food; F (*p.*) bore.
mazapán *m* marzipan.
mazmorra *f* dungeon.
mazo *m* mallet; (*manojo*) bunch; [(*p.*) bore.]
mazorca *f* ⚘ spike, clump; ear, cob *de maíz*; *sew* spindle; *comer maíz de la* ~, *comer maíz en la* ~ eat corn on the cob.
me (*acc.*) me; (*dat.*) (to) me; (*reflexivo*) (to) myself.
meadero *m* F bog, jakes; **meados** *m/pl.* F piss.
meaja *f* crumb; ~ *de huevo* tread.
meandro *m* meander.
mear [1a] F *v/t.* piss on; *v/i.* piss.
mecánica *f* mechanics; (*aparato*) mechanism, works; ~*s pl.* F household chores; **mecánico 1.** mechanical; machine *attr.*; *oficio* manual; ~ *dentista m/f* dental technician; **2.** *m* mechanic; engineer; machinist;
mecanismo *m* mechanism; works;

action, movement *de pieza*; *esp. fig.* machinery, structure; **mecanizar** [1f] mechanize; **mecanografía** *f* typing; ~ *al tacto* touch-typing; **mecanografiado** *adj. a. su. m* typescript; **mecanografiar** [1c] type; **mecanógrafo** *m*, **a** *f* typist.
mecedora *f* rocking chair.
mecenas *m* patron; **mecenazgo** *m* patronage.
mecer(se) [2b] *cuna etc.* rock; *rama etc.* sway; (*columpiar*) swing; (*agitar*) shake, stir up.
mecha *f* wick; ⚔ *etc.* fuse; = *mechón*; ~ *tardía* time fuse; **mechar** [1a] lard; **mechera** *f* F shoplifter; **mechero** *m* burner *de lámpara*; (*cada fuego*) jet; cigarette lighter; shoplifter; ~ *encendedor* pilot light; ~ *de gas* gas burner, gas jet; **mechón** *m* lock (of hair).
medalla *f* medal; = **medallón** *m* medallion; locket *con pelo etc.*; *typ.* inset.
médano *m*, **medaño** *m* sand dune; sandbank.
media *f* stocking; 𝔄 mean; *hacer* ~ knit; **mediación** *f* mediation; (*medio*) instrumentality; **mediado** half-full; *a* ~*s de* in the middle of; **mediador** *m*, **-a** *f* mediator; **medial** medial; **medianería** *f* party wall; **medianero 1.** *pared etc.* dividing; **2.** *m* mediator; (*mensajero*) go-between; **medianía** *f* (*punto medio*) half-way (point); (*promedio*) average; (*calidad*) mediocrity; ✝ modest means (*or* circumstances); **mediano** *punto* middle; ⚘ *etc.* median; *calidad* middling, medium, average; *b.s.* mediocre, indifferent; **medianoche** *f* midnight; **mediante** *prp.* by means of, through; **mediar** [1b] be in the middle; *fig.* mediate, intervene; *mediaba el mes de julio* it was half-way through July; *entre A y B median 50 km.* it is 50 km. from A to B.
médica *f* woman doctor; **medicamento** *m* medicine, drug; **medicastro** *m* quack; **medicina** *f* medicine; **medicinal** medicinal; **medicinar** [1a] treat, prescribe for.
medición *f* measuring, measurement; *surv.* survey(ing).
médico 1. medical; **2.** *m* doctor; medical practitioner; ~ *de cabecera* family doctor; ~ *dentista* dental surgeon; ~ *residente* house physician.
medida *f* 𝔄 measure(ment); (*acto*) measuring; (*regla, vasija*) measure; fitting, size *de zapato etc.*; *fig.* measure, step; *fig.* moderation; *a* ~ *de* in proportion to, according to; *a* ~ *que* as; *hecho a* ~ made to measure; *tomar* ~*s fig.* take steps (*para inf.* to *inf.*); **medidor** *m S.Am.* meter.
medieval medieval; **medievalista** *m/f* medievalist; **medievo** *m* Middle Ages.
medio 1. *adj. punto* mid(way), middle; 𝔄 mean; (*corriente*) average; (*mitad de*) half (a); ~ *pan* half a loaf; *a* ~ *tarde* in the middle of the afternoon; *las 2 y* ~*a* half-past 2; *a* ~*as hacer etc.* by halves; *dueño etc.* half; *dormido a* ~*as* half asleep; *ir a* ~*as* go halves (*con* with); **2.** *adv.* half; ~ *dormido* half asleep; *a* ~ *hacer* half done; **3.** *m* (*punto*) middle; (*mitad*) half; (*ambiente*) milieu, environment; medium *de comunicación etc.*; (*método*) means, way; (*medida*) measure; *deportes*: halfback; ~ *centro* center half; ~*s pl.* ✝ means; ~ *ambiente* environment; ~*s de comunicación* mass media; ~ *de cultivo* culture medium; *justo* ~ happy medium, golden mean; *de en* ~ middle; *de por* ~, *en* ~ in between; *en* ~ *de* in the middle (*or* midst) of; *por* ~ *de* by means of, through; *v. quitar*; *no regatear* ~ *para inf.* spare no effort to *inf.*
mediocre middling, average; *b.s.* mediocre; **mediocridad** *f* mediocrity; ✝ modest circumstances.
mediodía *m* midday, noon; *geog.* south.
medir [3l] measure (*a, por metros etc.* in; *a. fig.*); gauge; *surv.* survey; ~ (*con la vista*) size *s.o.* up; *poet.* scan; *mide 1,80 m.* (*p.*) he's 1.80 m. tall; ~**se** act with moderation.
meditabundo pensive, thoughtful; **meditación** *f* meditation *etc.*; **meditar** [1a] *v/t.* ponder, meditate (on); *proyecto* think out, plan; *v/i.* ponder, meditate; muse.
mediterráneo Mediterranean.
médium *m* medium (*p.*).
medra *f* increase; improvement; ✝ prosperity; **medrar** [1a] (*crecer*) grow; (*mejorar*) improve; ✝ *etc.* thrive, prosper, do well; *¡medrados*

estamos! now we're in a mess!, a fine thing you've done!
medroso fearful, timid; (*horroroso*) dreadful.
médula *f*, **medula** *f anat.* marrow; ⚘ pith; *fig.* essence; ~ *espinal* spinal cord.
medusa *f* jellyfish.
megaciclo *m* megacycle.
megáfono *m* megaphone.
megalomanía *f* megalomania.
megatón *m* megaton.
mejicano *adj. a. su. m*, **a** *f* Mexican.
mejido *huevo* beaten.
mejilla *f* cheek.
mejillón *m* mussel.
mejor 1. *adj. comp.* better; *sup.* best; *postor* highest; *lo* ~ the best thing (*or* part *etc.*); *a lo* ~ probably, maybe, with any luck; (*inesperadamente*) suddenly; **2.** *adv. comp.* better; *sup.* best; ~ *quisiera inf.* I would rather *inf.*; ~ *que* rather than; ~ *que* ~ all the better; **mejora** *f* improvement; ~*s pl.* ⚠ alterations; repairs; **mejoramiento** *m* improvement.
mejorana *f* marjoram.
mejorar [1a] *v/t.* improve; enhance; *postura* raise; *v/i.*, ~**se** improve (*a. meteor.*); ⚕ recover, get better; ⚕ *etc.* prosper; **mejoría** *f* improvement, recovery.
mejunje *m* F brew, mixture stuff.
melado *m* treacle, syrup.
melancolía *f* gloom(iness), melancholy; ⚕ melancholia; **melancólico** gloomy, sad, melancholy; (*pensativo*) dreamy, wistful.
melaza *f* (*a.* ~*s pl.*) molasses; treacle.
melena *f* long hair, loose hair; *esp.* pony tail; *zo.* mane; *estar en* ~ have one's hair down; **melenudo** long-haired; with flowing hair; *b.s.* bushy.
melifluo *fig.* mellifluous, sweet.
melindre *m fig.* daintiness; affectation; ~*s pl.* dainty ways; *b.s.* affectation; squeamishness; (*moral*) prudery; *gastar* ~*s* = **melindrear** [1a] F be affected, be finicky; **melindroso** affected; squeamish; finicky; (*moralmente*) prudish.
melocotón *m* peach; **melocotonero** *m* peach (tree).
melodía *f* melody, tune; (*calidad*) melodiousness; **melodioso** melodious, tuneful.
melodrama *m* melodrama; **melodramático** melodramatic.
melón *m* melon; F nut; (*p.*) idiot; ~ *de agua* watermelon; **melonada** *f* F silly thing.
meloso honeyed, sweet; *fig.* gentle, sweet.
mella *f* notch, nick, dent; (*hueco*) gap; *hacer* ~ (*reprensión etc.*) sink in, strike home; (*causar efecto*) *hacer* ~ *a* have an effect on; (*dañar*) *hacer* ~ *en* do damage to, harm; **mellado** *filo* jagged, ragged; gap-toothed; **mellar** [1a] notch, nick, dent; *fig.* damage.
mellizo *adj. a. su. m*, **a** *f* twin.
membrana *f* membrane; *orn. a.* web.
membrete *m* note, memo; (*inscripción*) letterhead, heading.
membrillo *m* ⚘ quince; (*carne de*) ~ quince jelly.
membrudo burly, brawny.
memez *f* silly thing; **memo** silly, stupid.
memorable memorable; **memorándum** *m* memorandum; (*librito*) notebook; **memoria** *f* memory; (*relación*) report, statement; (*nota*) memorandum; (*solicitud*) petition; (*ponencia*) paper; ~*s pl.* memoirs *de p.*; transactions *de sociedad*; (*saludo*) regards; ~ *anual* annual report; *digno de* ~ memorable; *flaco de* ~ forgetful; *de* ~ *aprender* by heart; *hablar* from memory; *en* ~ *de* in memory of; *hacer* ~ *de* bring up, recall; **memorial** *m* petition; ⚖ brief; **memorialista** *m* amanuensis.
mena *f* ore.
menaje *m* family, household; (*muebles*) furnishings.
mención *f* mention; **mencionar** [1a] mention, refer to, name; *sin* ~ let alone.
mendacidad *f* mendacity; **mendaz** mendacious, lying.
mendicante *adj. a. su. m/f* mendicant; **mendicidad** *f* begging; (*condición*) beggarliness; **mendigar** [1h] beg; **mendigo** *m*, **a** *f* beggar.
mendrugo *m* (hard) crust (of bread).
menear [1a] move; *cabeza etc.* shake, toss; *cola* wag; *caderas* swing, waggle; *cálamo* wield; *negocio* handle; F *peor es meneallo* leave well alone; ~**se** F bestir o.s., get a move

on; ¡~! get going!; **meneo** *m* shaking *etc.*; F hiding.
menester 1.: *ser* ~ be necessary; **2.** ~*es m/pl.* duties, jobs; F gear, tackle; F *hacer sus* ~*es euph.* do one's business; **menesteroso** needy.
menestral *m* workman, artisan.
mengano *m*, **a** *f* (Mr. *etc.*) So-and-so.
mengua *f* decrease, dwindling; decline; poverty; *en* ~ *de* to the discredit of; **menguado** (*cobarde*) cowardly, spineless; (*tonto*) silly; (*tacaño*) mean; **menguante 1.** dwindling *etc.*; **2.** *f* ⚓ ebb tide; waning *de luna*; *fig.* decline; **menguar** [1i] decrease, dwindle; (*marea etc.*) go down; (*luna*) wane; *fig.* decline, decay.
mengue *m* F devil.
meningitis *f* meningitis.
menor 1. *adj. órdenes*, ♪ *etc.* minor; **2.** *adj. comp.* smaller, lesser; *edad*: younger (*que* than), junior (*que* to); *v. edad*; **3.** *adj. sup.* smallest, least; youngest *etc.*; **4.:** *al por* ~ retail; *por* ~ in detail; **5.** *m/f* minor, young person; *apto para* ~*s cine*: U(niversal).
menos 1. *prp.* except; ⅄ less, minus; *5* ~ *3 son 2* 3 from 5 leaves 2; *las 2* ~ *cuarto* a quarter to 2; **2.** *adv. comp.* less; *sup.* least; ~ *de*, ~ *de lo que*, ~ *que* less than; *lo de* ~ the least of it; *5 de* ~ 5 short; *una libra de* ~ a pound less; *al* ~, (*a*) *lo* ~, *por lo* ~ at least; **3.** *cj.*: *a* ~ *que* unless; **4.** *adj. signo* minus; **5.** *m* minus (sign).
menos...: ~**cabar** [1a] lessen, reduce; (*dañar*) damage, impair; (*deslucir*) discredit; ~**cabo** *m* lessening; damage, loss; *en* ~ *de* to the detriment of; ~**preciar** [1b] (*desdeñar*) scorn, despise; (*insultar*) slight; (*subestimar*) underrate; ~**preciativo** scornful; slighting; ~**precio** *m* scorn, contempt.
mensaje *m* message; **mensajería** *f* public conveyance; ~*s pl.* transportation company; shipping line; **mensajero** *m*, **a** *f* messenger; *m* harbinger.
menstruación *f*, **menstruo** *m* } [menstruation.
mensual monthly; *100 ptas* ~*es* 100 ptas a month; **mensualidad** *f* monthly payment (*or* salary *etc.*); **mensualmente** monthly.
ménsula *f* bracket, corbel.
mensurable measurable; **mensuración** *f* mensuration.
menta *f* ♀ mint.
mental mental; *trabajo etc.* intellectual; **mentalidad** *f* mentality; **mentar** [1k] mention, name; **mente** *f* mind.
mentecato 1. silly, stupid; **2.** *m*, **a** *f* idiot.
mentidero *m* F talking shop; **mentir** [3i] lie, tell a lie (*or* lies); **mentira** *f* lie; (*en general*) lying, deceitfulness; *lit. etc.* fiction, invention; ¡*parece* ~! you don't say so!; well (I never)!; *parece* ~ *que* it seems impossible that; *aunque parece* ~ however unlikely it seems; **mentirijillas:** *de* ~ as a joke; *jugar* for fun; **mentirilla** *f* fib, white lie; **mentiroso 1.** lying, deceitful, false; **2.** *m*, **a** *f* liar; **mentís** *m* denial; *dar un* ~ *a* deny, give the lie to.
mentol *m* menthol.
mentón *m* chin.
mentor *m* mentor.
menú *m* menu.
menudear [1a] *v/t.* repeat frequently; tell in detail; *v/i.* be frequent, happen frequently; go into detail *contando*; F rain, come thick and fast; **menudencia** *f* trifle; ~*s pl.* trifles; little things, odds and ends; (*despojos*) offal; **menudeo:** ✝ *al* ~ retail; **menudillos** *m/pl.* giblets; **menudo 1.** small, tiny; slight, trifling; meticulous, exact; *a* ~ often; *por* ~ in detail; **2.** *m* small change; ~*s pl.* entrails.
meñique *m* little finger.
meollo *m anat.* marrow; *fig.* (*esencia*) gist; (*sustancia*) solid stuff, meat; (*seso*) brains.
mequetrefe *m* whippersnapper; (*entrometido*) busybody.
meramente merely, solely.
mercachifle *m* hawker, huckster; **mercadear** [1a] trade; **mercader** *m* merchant; **mercadería** *f* commodity; ~*s pl.* merchandise; **mercado** *m* market; ~ *negro* black market; **mercancía 1.** *f* commodity; ~*s pl.* goods, merchandise; **2.** ~*s m* 🚂 freight train; **mercante** ⚓ **1.** merchant *attr.*; **2.** *m* merchant ship; **mercantil** mercantile, commercial, trading *attr.*; *b.s.* mercenary; **mercar** [1g] buy.

merced *f*: *mst* † favor; benefit; reward; *vuestra* ~ your honor, your worship; *a* ~ voluntarily; ~ *a* thanks to; *estar a la* ~ *de* be at the mercy of.
mercenario 1. mercenary; **2.** *m* ⚔ mercenary; *fig.* hack, hireling.
mercería *f* haberdashery; (*tienda*) dry-goods store; *S.Am.* hardware store.
mercerizar [1f] mercerize.
mercero *m* haberdasher.
mercurial mercurial; **mercurio** *m* mercury.
merecedor deserving (*de* of); **merecer** [2d] *v/t.* deserve; be worth(y of); *alabanza etc.* earn (*a.* **~se**); (*necesitar*) need; *v/i.* be worthy; ~ *mucho* be very deserving; **merecido 1.**: *bien* ~ *lo tiene* it serves him right; **2.** *m* deserts; *llevar su* ~ get one's (just) deserts; **merecimiento** *m* deserts; merit, worthiness.
merendar [1k] *v/t.* have *s.t.* for lunch; (*acechar*) peep at; (*a.* **~se**) F wangle; *fortuna* squander; *v/i.* have lunch; picnic *en el campo.*
merengue *m* meringue.
meridiana *f* couch; chaise longue; **meridiano** *adj. a. su. m* meridian; *a la* ~*a* at noon; **meridional 1.** southern; **2.** *m/f* southerner.
merienda *f* lunch; (*bocadillo*) snack; packed meal *para viaje*; picnic *en el campo*; F hunchback; F *juntar* ~*s* join forces.
mérito *m* merit; worth, value; *hacer* ~ *de* mention; *hacer* ~*s* strive to be deserving; **meritorio** meritorious, worthy.
merluza *f* hake; *sl. estar* (*con la*) ~ F be stoned, be drunk.
merma *f* decrease; wastage, loss; **mermar** [1a] *v/t.* reduce, deplete; *ración etc.* cut down on; *v/i.* decrease, dwindle; (*líquido*) go down; *fig.* waste away.
mermelada *f* jam.
mero 1. *adj.* mere; pure, simple; *S.Am.* selfsame, very; **2.** *adv. S.Am.* soon, in a moment.
merodeador *m* marauder; **merodear** [1a] maraud.
mes *m* month.
mesa *f* table; desk *de trabajo*; counter *de oficina*; ⚠ landing; *geog.* tableland, plateau; (*junta*) presiding committee, board; ~ *de extensión* extension table; ~ *de juego* gambling table; ~ *de noche* bedside table; ~ *de operaciones* operating table; ~ *perezosa* drop table; ~ *redonda* table d'hôte; *hist. a. pol.* round table; ~ *de trucos* pool table; *alzar* (*or levantar*) *la* ~ clear away; *poner la* ~ lay the table.
mesana *f* mizzen.
mesarse [1a]: ~ *el pelo* tear one's hair.
mescolanza *f* = *mezcolanza.*
meseta *f* tableland, plateau; ⚠ landing; **mesilla** *f* occasional table; ~ *de chimenea* mantelpiece; **mesita** *f* stand, small table; ~ *portateléfono* telephone table.
mesmerismo *m* mesmerism.
mesón[1] *m phys.* meson.
mesón[2] *m* † inn; **mesonero** *m*, **a** *f* innkeeper.
mestizar [1f] crossbreed; **mestizo** *adj. a. su. m*, **a** *f* half-caste, half-breed; *zo.* crossbred, mongrel.
mesura *f* gravity *etc.*; **mesurado** grave; moderate, restrained; sensible; calm; **mesurarse** [1a] restrain o.s.
meta 1. *f* goal (*a. fig.*); winning post *en carrera*; **2.** *m* goalkeeper.
metabólico metabolic; **metabolismo** *m* metabolism.
metafísica *f* metaphysics.
metáfora *f* metaphor; **metafórico** metaphoric(al).
metal *m* metal; ♪ brass; timbre *de voz*; *fig.* quality; *el vil* ~ filthy lucre; ~ *blanco* nickel silver; **metálico 1.** metallic; metal *attr.*; **2.** *m* specie, coin; *en* ~ in cash; **metalífero** metalliferous; **metalistería** *f* metalwork; **metalurgia** *f* metallurgy; **metalúrgico** metallurgic(al).
metamorfosear [1a] metamorphose, transform; **metamorfosis** *f* metamorphosis, transformation.
metano *m* methane.
metedura *f* smuggling.
meteórico meteoric; **meteorito** *m* meteor; **meteoro, metéoro** *m fig.* meteor; atmospheric phenomenon; **meteorología** *f* meteorology; **meteorológico** meteorological, weather *attr.*; **meteorologista** *m/f* meteorologist.
meter [2a] put, insert, introduce (*en* in, into); (*apretando*) squeeze in; smuggle (in) *de contrabando*; *fig.* make, cause; *v. miedo etc.*; ~ *a una p. en* let a p. in for; *¿quién le mete en esto?* who told you to interfere?;

~se *fig.* meddle, interfere (*mucho* a lot); (*hacerse*) *monja* become; *soldado* turn; ~ *a su.* become; (*con ambición*) set o.s. up as; ~ *a inf.* take it upon o.s. to *inf.*; ~ *con* meddle with; *p.* pick a quarrel with; ~ *en* go into, get into; *fig.* interfere in; *dificultades* get into; *negocio* get involved in; *¡no te metas en lo que no te importa!* mind your own business!; *no ~ donde no le llaman* mind one's own business; ~ *en sí mismo* go into one's shell.
meticuloso meticulous, scrupulous.
metido 1.: ~ *en sí* introspective; *estar muy ~ con* be well in with; *estar muy ~ en* be deeply involved in; **2.** *m* shove, punch.
metilo *m* methyl.
metimiento *m* insertion; *fig.* influence.
metódico methodic(al); **método** *m* method; **metodología** *f* methodology.
metraje *m*: (*cinta de*) *largo* ~ full-length film; *cine*: *de corto* ~ short.
metralla *f* shrapnel.
métrica *f* metrics; **métrico** metric, metrical; **metro**[1] *m* ⚒, *poet.* meter; (*de cinta*) tape measure; (*plegable*) rule; (*recto*) ruler.
metro[2] *m* 🚇 subway.
metrónomo *m* metronome.
metrópoli *f* metropolis; *pol.* mother country; **metropolitano 1.** *adj. a. su. m eccl.* metropolitan; **2.** *m* 🚇 subway.
mexicano *adj. a. su. m,* **a** *f S.Am.* Mexican.
mezcla *f* mixture; *esp. fig.* blend; medley; ⚠ mortar; *sin ~ bebida* neat; **mezclador** *m* mixer; **mezclar** [1a] mix (up); blend; (*unir*) merge; *cartas* shuffle; **~se** mix, mingle (*con* with); *b.s.* get mixed (*en* up in); (*entrometerse*) meddle (*en* in); **mezcolanza** *f* hodgepodge, jumble.
mezquindad *f* meanness *etc.*; **mezquino** (*pobre*) poor, wretched; (*avaro*) mean; (*pequeño*) wretchedly small; (*insignificante*) petty, paltry.
mezquita *f* mosque.
mi, mis *pl.* my.
mí me.
miaja *f* crumb, bit.
miasma *m* miasma.
miau *m* mew, miaow.
mica *f min.* mica.
mico *m,* **a** *f* monkey; F *dar* (*or hacer*) ~ miss a date (*a* with).
micro... micro...
microbio *m* microbe.
microcosmo *m* microcosm.
microfilm *m* microfilm; **~s, ~es** *pl.* microfilms; **microfilmar** *v/t.* microfilm.
micrófono *m* microphone; *teleph.* mouthpiece.
microfundio *m* smallholding.
micrómetro *m* micrometer.
microonda *f* microwave.
microprocesador *m* microprocessor.
microscópico microscopic; **microscopio** *m* microscope.
microsurco 1. *adj. invar.* microgroove; **2.** *m* microgroove.
microteléfono *m* handset, French telephone.
micho *m,* **a** *f* F puss(y).
miedo *m* fear (*a* of); *por ~ de que* for fear that; *dar* (*or meter*) ~ *a* frighten; *tener* ~ be afraid (*a* of); **miedoso** scared, fearful; *carácter* timid.
miel *f* honey.
miembro *m anat.* limb; *anat., gr., p. etc.* member.
mientes: *parar ~ en* reflect on.
mientras while, as long as; ~ (*que*) whereas; ~ *más ... más* the more ... the more; ~ *tanto* meanwhile.
miércoles *m* Wednesday; ~ *de ceniza* Ash Wednesday.
mierda *f* F shit.
mies *f* corn, wheat, grain; **~es** *pl.* cornfields.
miga *f* bit; crumb *de pan*; *fig.* substance; F *hacer buenas* **~s** get on well, hit it off (*con* with); **migaja** *f* bit; crumb *de pan* (*a. fig.*); **~s** *pl.* leavings; **migar** [1h] crumble.
migración *f* migration.
migraña *f* migraine.
migratorio migratory.
mijo *m* millet.
mil a thousand; *dos* ~ two thousand; **~es** *pl.* thousands.
milagro *m* miracle; *fig. a.* wonder; *por* ~ by a miracle; *vivir de* ~ have a hard time of it; **milagroso** miraculous.
milano *m orn.* kite.
mildeu *m* mildew.

milenario 1. millennial; **2.** *m* = **milenio** *m* millennium.
milenrama *f* yarrow.
milésimo *adj. a. su. m* thousandth.
milicia *f* (*ps.*) militia; soldiery; (*profesión*) soldiering; (*período*) military service (*a.* **mili** *f* F); (*ciencia*) art of war; **miliciano** *m* militiaman.
miligramo *m* milligram; **mililitro** *m* milliliter; **milímetro** *m* millimeter.
militante militant; **militar 1.** military; (*guerrero*) warlike; *arte* of war; **2.** *m* soldier; serviceman; **3.** [1a] serve (in the army), soldier; *fig.* militate (*contra* against); **militarismo** *m* militarism; **militarizar** [1f] militarize.
milla *f* mile; ~ *marina* nautical mile.
millar *m* thousand; *a* ~*es* in thousands, by the thousand; **millarada** *f* (about a) thousand; **millón** *m* million; *3* ~*es de hombres* 3 million men; **millonario** *m*, **a** *f* millionaire; **millonésimo** *adj. a. su. m* millionth.
mimar [1a] (*acariciar*) pet, fondle; *fig.* pamper, spoil; *poderoso* humour.
mimbre *mst m* ⚘ osier; (*materia*) wicker; *de* ~(*s*) wicker(work) *attr.*; **mimbrear(se)** [1a] sway; **mimbrera** *f* osier willow.
mimeógrafo *m* mimeograph.
mimetismo *m* mimicry; **mímica** *f* gesticulation; sign language; (*remedo*) mimicry; (*una* ~) mime; **mímico** mimic; imitative; **mimo 1.** *m thea. etc.* mime; *hacer* ~ *de* mime; **2.** *m* pampering, indulgence; *hacer* ~*s a* make a fuss of; **mimoso** spoiled.
mina *f* mine (*a.* ⚔, ⚓, *fig.*); lead, refill *de lápiz*; *fig.* storehouse; ~ *de carbón* coal mine; **minador** *m* ⚔ sapper; ⚒ mining engineer; (*buque*) ~ minelayer; **minar** [1a] mine (*a.* ⚔, ⚓); (*cavar lentamente*) undermine, wear away; *fig.* undermine, sap.
mineral 1. mineral; **2.** *m* ⛏ mineral; ⚒ ore; ~ *de hierro* iron ore; **mineralizar** [1f] mineralize; **mineralogía** *f* mineralogy; **mineralogista** *m/f* mineralogist; **minería** *f* mining; **minero 1.** mining; **2.** *m* miner.
miniatura 1. *f* miniature; *en* ~ in miniature; **2.** *adj.* miniature; *perro etc.* toy.
mínimo 1. smallest, least; minimum; minimal; tiny; *sin la más* ~*a dificultad* without the slightest difficulty; *ni en lo más* ~ not in the slightest; **2.** *m* minimum; *meteor.* ~ *de presión* trough; **mínimum** *m* minimum.
minino *m*, **a** *f* F puss(y).
minio *m* red lead.
miniordenador *m* microcomputer.
ministerial ministerial; **ministerio** *m* ministry; **ministro** *m* minister; ~ *de asuntos exteriores* foreign minister; *primer* ~ prime minister.
minorar [1a] reduce, lessen; **minoría** *f*, **minoridad** *f* minority; **minorista** *m* retailer.
minucia *f* minuteness; ~*s pl.* details, minutiae; **minuciosidad** *f* thoroughness *etc.*; **minucioso** thorough, meticulous; minute.
minué *m*, **minuete** *m* minuet.
minúscula *f* small letter; **minúsculo** small (*a. typ.*), tiny.
minuta *f* (*borrador*) first draft; (*apunte*) minute, memorandum; list; (*comida*) menu; **minutar** [1a] draft; minute; **minutero** *m* minute hand; **minutisa** *f* sweet william; **minuto** *m* minute.
mío, mía 1. *pron.* mine; **2.** *adj.* (*tras su.*) of mine.
miope short-sighted; **miopía** *f* short-sightedness, miopia 🕮.
mira *f* ⚔ (*a.* ~*s pl.*) sights; *fig.* object, aim; *de amplias* ~*s* broad in outlook; *de* ~*s estrechas* narrow, narrow-minded; insular, parochial; *con* ~*s a inf.* with a view to *ger.*; *estar a la* ~ be on the lookout (*de* for); *poner la* ~ *en*, *tener* ~*s sobre* have designs on; **mirada** *f* look; glance; gaze; expression *de cara*; ~ *fija* stare; *apuñalar con la* ~ look daggers at; *echar una* ~ *a* glance at; (*vigilar*) keep an eye on; **miradero** *m* cynosure (of all eyes); (*asunto*) chief concern; (*lugar*) lookout, vantage point; **mirado** circumspect; *bien* ~ well thought of; **mirador** *m* △ bay window, balcony; (*lugar*) vantage point; **miramiento** *m* considerateness; caution; ~*s pl.* fuss; *sin* ~*s* unceremoniously; *tratar sin* ~*s freq.* ride roughshod over.
mirar [1a] **1.** *v/t.* look at; watch;

fig. look on, consider (*como* as); (*reflexionar sobre*) think carefully about; (*tener cuidado con*) watch, be careful about; ~ *fijamente* stare at; ~ *bien* like; ~ *mal* dislike; **2.** *v/i.* look; *¡mira!* look! (*protesta*) look here!; (*aviso*) look out!; ~ *a fig.* aim at, have in mind; *provecho* look to; ▲ *etc.* face, open on to; ~ *alrededor* look around; ~ *por ventana* look out of; *fig.* look after; ~ *de través* squint; **3. ~se** look at o.s.; (*recíproco*) look at each other; ~ *en ello* watch one's step.
mirasol *m* sunflower.
miríada *f* myriad.
miriápodo *m* millipede.
mirilla *f* peephole; *phot.* finder, viewfinder.
mirlo *m* blackbird; ~ *blanco* extraordinary thing; impossible dream.
mirón 1. inquisitive; **2.** *m*, **-a** *f* onlooker, kibitzer; *b.s.* busybody; *estar de* ~ look on.
mirra *f* myrrh.
mirto *m* myrtle.
misa *f* mass; ~ *del gallo* Midnight Mass; ~ *mayor* High Mass; ~ *rezada* Low Mass; **misal** *m* missal.
misantropía *f* misanthropy; **misantrópico** misanthropic(al); **misántropo** *m* misanthrope.
miscelánea *f* miscellany; **misceláneo** miscellaneous.
miserable 1. (*desdichado*) wretched; (*tacaño*) mean; *sueldo etc.* miserable, pitifully small; *conducta* contemptible; *lugar* squalid, sordid; **2.** *m/f* wretch; (*vil*) cad; **miseria** *f* misery, wretchedness; poverty; meanness; F (*una* ~) pittance; *vivir en la* ~ live in poverty; **misericordia** *f* pity; (*perdón*) forgiveness; mercy; **misericordioso** compassionate; merciful; **mísero** wretched.
misil *m* (guided) missile.
misión *f* mission; **misionero** *adj. a. su. m*, **a** *f* missionary; **misiva** *f* missive.
mismísimo selfsame, very same; **mismo** same (*que* as); *enfático*: *en ese* ~ *momento* at that very moment; *el* ~ *obispo* the same bishop; *el obispo* ~ the bishop himself; *yo* ~ I myself; *yo* ~ *lo vi* I saw it myself; *es la* ~*a bondad* he is kindness itself; *lo* ~ the same thing; *él hizo lo* ~ he did the same, he did likewise; *por lo* ~ for the same reason; *lo* ~ *que prp.* just like; *eso* ~ *digo yo* that's just what I say; *aquí* ~ right here; *v. ahora etc.*
misoginia *f* misogyny; **misógino** *m* misogynist.
misterio *m* mystery; secrecy; *thea.* mystery play; **misterioso** mysterious; mystifying, puzzling; **mística** *f*, **misticismo** *m* mysticism; **místico 1.** mystic(al); **2.** *m*, **a** *f* mystic; **mistificación** *f* hoax; hocus-pocus; **mistificar** [1g] hoax; mystify.
mitad *f* half; (*medio*) middle; *mi cara* ~ my better half; ~ *y* ~ half and half; *a* ~ *de camino etc.* half-way there; *a* ~ *de precio* half-price; *en la* ~ *de* in the middle of; *por la* ~ *partir* in halves, down the middle.
mítico mythical.
mitigación *f* mitigation *etc.*; **mitigar** [1h] *efecto* mitigate; *dolor* relieve; *cólera* appease, mollify; *severidad* temper.
mitin *m esp. pol.* meeting.
mito *m* myth; **mitología** *f* mythology; **mitológico** mythological.
mitón *m* mitten.
mitra *f* mitre.
mixomatosis *f* myxomatosis.
mixto 1. mixed; **2.** *m* match; 🚂 passenger and goods train; **mixtura** *f* mixture; **mixturar** [1a] mix.
mnemotécnica *f* mnemonics.
moaré *m* moiré.
mobiliario *m* suite; **moblaje** *m* (suite of) furniture.
mocear [1a] play around; **mocedad** *f* youth; *pasar las* ~*es* sow one's wild oats; **mocetón** *m* strapping youth; **mocetona** *f* big girl.
moción *f* motion (*a. parl.*), movement.
mocito 1. very young; **2.** *m*, **a** *f* youngster.
moco *m* mucus; snot; *metall.* slag; *llorar a* ~ *tendido* cry like a baby; **mocoso 1.** snotty; F ill-bred; **2.** *m* F brat.
mochila *f* rucksack, knapsack; ⚔ pack.
mocho 1. *zo.* hornless, polled; ⚘ pollard(ed); *torre* flat-topped; (*sin punta*) blunt; F shorn; **2.** *m* butt.
mochuelo *m*: ~ (*común*) little owl.

moda *f* fashion; style; *a la* ~, *de* ~ in fashion, fashionable; *alta* ~ haute couture; *fuera de* ~, *pasado de* ~ out of fashion, outdated; *muy de* ~ very much in the fashion.

modal 1. modal; **2.** ~*es m/pl.* manners.

modelado *m* modeling; **modelar** [1a] model (*sobre* on); (*dar forma a*) fashion, shape; **modelo 1.** *adj.* model; **2.** *m* model (*a. fig.*); pattern; form, blank; equal, peer; style; **3.** *f* model, mannequin.

moderación *f* moderation; **moderado** moderate (*a. pol.*); **moderar** [1a] moderate; *velocidad etc.* reduce; (*refrenar*) restrain; ~**se** (*p.*) control o.s., restrain o.s.

modernidad *f* modernity; **modernismo** *m* modernism; **modernizar** [1f] modernize; **moderno** modern; present-day; up-to-date.

modestia *f* modesty; **modesto** modest.

módico reasonable, moderate.

modificación *f* modification; **modificar** [1g] modify.

modismo *m* idiom.

modista *f* dressmaker; ~ (*de sombreros*) milliner; **modisto** *m* fashion designer.

modo *m* way, manner, mode (*a.* ♪); method, form *de gobierno etc.*; *gr.* mood; *fig.* moderation; ~*s pl.* manners; ~ *de empleo* (*en envase*) instructions for use; ~ *de ser* nature, disposition; *a mi* ~ *de ver* to my way of thinking; *a su* ~ in his own way; *al* ~ *inglés* in the English style; *uno a* ~ *de* a sort (*or* kind) of; *de ese* ~ at that rate; *de este* ~ (in) this way, like this; *de otro* ~ otherwise; *de un* ~ *u otro* somehow or other; *de ningún* ~ by no means; ¡*de ningún* ~! certainly not!; *de* ~ *que* so that; ¿*de* ~ *que* ...? so ...?; *de todos* ~*s* at any rate; *en cierto* ~ in some degree; in a way; *sobre* ~ extremely; *ver el* ~ *de inf.* see one's way to *ger. or inf.*

modorra *f* drowsiness, heaviness; *vet.* gid; **modorro** drowsy; *fig.* dull, stupid.

modoso quiet, nicely behaved.

modulación *f* modulation; *radio*: ~ *de frecuencia* frequency modulation; **modular** [1a] modulate.

mofa *f* mockery, derision; (*una* ~) taunt, gibe; *hacer* ~ *de* = *mofarse de*; **mofador** mocking *etc.*; **mofar** [1a] jeer, sneer; ~**se** *de* make fun of; mock, scoff at, sneer at.

mofeta *f* ⚒ firedamp; *zo.* skunk.

mofletudo fat-cheeked, chubby.

mogol *adj. a. su. m*, **-a** *f* Mongol, Mongolian; *el gran* ♀ the Great Mogul.

mogollón *m* F sponger, hanger-on; *comer de* ~ F scrounge a meal, sponge.

mohín *m* face, grimace; **mohina** *f* (*disgusto*) annoyance; (*murria*) sulkiness, sulks; (*resentimiento*) grudge; *fácil a las* ~*s* easily depressed; **mohino** (*triste*) gloomy, depressed; (*murrio*) sulky; (*malhumorado*) peevish.

moho *m* rust; ⚘ mold, mildew; **mohoso** rusty; ⚘ moldy, musty; *chiste* stale.

mojada *f* wetting, soaking; stab; **mojado** wet; soaked; damp, moist; **mojar** [1a] *v/t.* wet; (*ligeramente*) moisten; (*completamente*) drench, soak; *pluma* dip (*en* into); (*apuñalar*) stab; *v/i.*: ~ *en* F get mixed up in; ~**se** get drenched *etc.*

mojicón *m* sponge cake; (*bollo*) bun; F punch.

mojiganga *f* † masquerade, mummery; F pretentious thing.

mojigatería *f* hypocrisy; prudery *etc.*; **mojigato 1.** hypocritical; (*beato*) sanctimonious; (*puritano*) prudish; **2.** *m*, **a** *f* hypocrite; prude.

mojón *m* landmark, boundary stone; (*de camino*) milestone.

mola *f* ⚕ mole.

molar *m* molar.

molde *m* mold; cast *de yeso etc.*; *sew. etc.* pattern; *esp. fig.* model; *letra de* ~ printed; *venir de* ~ be just right; **moldear** [1a] mold; (*vaciar etc.*) cast; **moldura** *f* △ molding.

mole *f* mass; bulk; △ pile.

molécula *f* molecule; **molecular** molecular.

moledor *fig.* **1.** boring; **2.** *m* bore; **moler** [2h] grind, mill; pound; *fig.* (*fastidiar*) annoy; (*cansar*) weary; ~ *a palos* beat *s.o.* up; F *estoy molido* I'm done up.

molestar [1a] (*fastidiar*) annoy, bother; (*incomodar*) bother, put

out; (*perturbar*) upset; (*doler*) hurt, bother; *¿le molesta el ruido?* do you mind the noise?; *¿le molesta a Vd. que fume?* will it bother you if I smoke?; **~se** bother (*con* about, *en inf.* to *inf.*); put o.s. out; (*perder la calma*) be annoyed, get cross; **molestia** *f* annoyance; bother, nuisance; ⚕ *etc.* discomfort; *tomarse la ~ de inf.* take the trouble to *inf.*; **molesto** annoying, trying; *p. etc.* tiresome; *olor etc.* nasty; *trabajo* irksome; (*sentirse*) bothered; (*inquieto*) ill at ease; (*incómodo*) uncomfortable.
molicie *f* softness (*a. fig.*); *fig.* luxurious living; effeminacy.
molienda *f* grinding, milling; F weariness; (*una ~*) nuisance; **molinero** *m* miller; **molinete** *m* (toy) windmill, pinwheel; **molinillo** *m* mill, grinder *para café etc.*; mincer *para carne*; **molino** *m* mill; grinder; *~ harinero* gristmill, flour mill; *~ de sangre* animal-driven mill; *~ de viento* windmill; *luchar con los ~s de viento* tilt at windmills.
molusco *m* mollusk.
mollar soft, mushy; *carne* lean; *tierra* easily worked; **molleja** *f* gizzard; *criar ~* F get lazy; *~s pl.* sweetbread; **mollejón** *m*, **-a** *f* F (big) softy; **mollera** *f anat.* crown of the head; *freq.* noddle; F brains; *duro de ~* dense; (*porfiado*) pigheaded; F *tener buena ~* have brains.
momentáneo momentary; **momento** *m* moment; *phys.* momentum; *al ~* at once; *de ~ adv.* at (*or* for) the moment; *de poco ~* unimportant; *de un ~ a otro* at any moment.
momería *f* mummery, clowning.
momia *f* mummy; **momificar**(**se**) [1g] mummify.
momio 1. lean; *de ~* free; **2.** *m* bargain.
momo *m* funny face.
mona *f zo.* monkey; F (*p.*) ape; (*borracho*) drunk; (*borrachera*) drunk, hangover; F *coger* (*or pillar*) *una ~* get boozed; F *dormir la ~* sleep it off; F *hecho una ~* quite put out; F *pintar la ~* act important.
monacal monastic; **monacillo** *m* = *monaguillo*.
monada *f* (*bobada*) monkeyshine; (*gesto*) face, grimace; (*estupidez*) silliness; (*objeto*) lovely thing, beauty; (*p.*) pretty girl; (*lo bonito*) loveliness *etc.*; *~s pl.* flattery.
monag(**uill**)**o** *m* acolyte, server.
monarca *m* monarch; **monarquía** *f* monarchy; **monárquico 1.** monarchic(al); *pol.* royalist, monarchist; **2.** *m* royalist, monarchist; **monarquismo** *m* monarchism.
monasterio *m* monastery; **monástico** monastic.
monda *f* ⚘ pruning, lopping; (*piel*) peel(ings), skin; *sl. es la ~* it's the limit; (*p.*) *co.* he's a terror; **mondadientes** *m* toothpick; **mondaduras** *f/pl.* peel(ings), skin; **mondar** [1a] (*limpiar*) cleanse; *fruta* peel; *árbol* prune, lop; *dientes* pick; F *p.* cut *s.o.'s* hair; *fig.* fleece; **mondo** clean; pure; *el asunto ~ es esto* the plain fact of the matter is; *~ y lirondo* plain, pure and simple.
mondongo *m* guts.
moneda *f* currency, coinage; (*una ~*) coin; *~ dura* hard currency; *~ suelta* change; F *pagar en la misma ~* pay *s.o.* back; **monedero** *m*: *~ falso* counterfeiter.
monería *f* (*mueca*) funny face; (*mímica*) mimicry; (*broma*) playful trick; pretty ways *de niño*; (*bagatela*) trifle.
monetario monetary, financial.
monigote *m* rag doll; *paint.* botched painting; (*p.*) F sap, boob.
monises *m/pl.* F dough, brass.
monitorear *v/t. un programa* monitor.
monja *f* nun; **monje** *m* monk; **monjil** nun's, monk's, monkish.
mono[1] *m zo.* monkey; (*p.*) clown; *paint.* botched painting; *drogas* withdrawal symptom; *estar de ~s* be at daggers drawn.
mono[2] *m* overalls, coveralls; rompers *de niño*.
mono[3] F pretty, nice.
mono... mono...; **~cromo** *adj. a. su. m* monochrome; **monóculo** *m* monocle.
mono...: ~gamia *f* monogamy; **~grafía** *f* monograph; **~grama** *m* monogram; **~lito** *m* monolith; **monólogo** *m* monologue.
mono...: ~manía *f* monomania; **~motor** ✈ single-engine(d); **~plano** *m* monoplane; **~plaza** *m* ✈ single-seater; **~polio** *m* monopoly;

~polista *m/f* monopolist; **~polizar** [1f] monopolize; **~silábico** = **~sílabo 1.** monosyllabic; **2.** *m* monosyllable; **~teísmo** *m* monotheism; **~tonía** *f* monotony; sameness, dreariness; **monótono** monotonous; *rutina etc.* humdrum, dreary.

monserga *f* gibberish; drivel.

monstruo *m* monster (*a. fig.*); *biol.* freak; **monstruosidad** *f* monstrosity; freak; **monstruoso** monstrous, monster *attr.*; *biol.* freakish; *fig.* monstrous, hideous.

monta *f* ✠ total; *de poca ~* of small account; *cosa de poca ~* mere trifle.

montacargas *m* (service) lift, hoist.

montado mounted; ⊕ built-in; *artillería* horse *attr.*; **montador** *m* (*p.*) fitter; **montadura** *f* mounting; (*engaste*) setting; **montaje** *m* ⊕ assembly; △ erection; **montante** *m* ⊕ upright, stanchion; △ transom; ⚔ broadsword; ✝ total, amount.

montaña *f* mountain; *~ rusa* switchback, scenic railway; **montañero** *m*, **-a** *f* mountaineer; **montañés 1.** mountain *attr.*; **2.** *m*, **-a** *f* highlander; *native of Santander region*; **montañismo** *m* mountaineering; **montañoso** mountainous; mountain *attr.*

montaplatos *m* dumbwaiter.

montar [1a] **1.** *v/t. caballo etc.* (*subir*) mount, (*ir*) ride; ⊕ assemble, put together, mount; △ erect; *joya* set; *escopeta* cock; *negocio* start, set up; ✠ amount to (*a. fig.*); **2.** *v/i.* mount (*a, en acc.*), get up (*a, en* on); ✠ *~ a* amount to; *~ a caballo* ride; *~ en cólera* get angry; *tanto monta* it makes no odds.

montaraz 1. *zo.* mountain *attr.*; *fig.* wild; **2.** *m* keeper.

monte *m* mountain, hill; (*bosque*) woodland; (*despoblado*) wilds, wild country; *~ alto* forest; *~ bajo* scrub; *~ de piedad* pawnshop; *~ pío* pension fund for widows and orphans; mutual-benefit society; *~ tallar* tree farm; **montecillo** *m* hump, hummock; **montepío** *m* charitable organization; mutual-fund society.

montera *f* cloth cap.

montería *f* hunting; **montero** *m* huntsman, hunter.

montés *gato etc.* wild.

montículo *m* hillock, mound.

montón *m* heap, pile; drift *de nieve*; F stack; F *un ~ de gente* masses of people; F *un ~ de cosas* heaps of things; *~es pl.* F tons, loads; *a ~* together; *a ~es* in plenty, galore; *del ~* perfectly ordinary.

montuoso hilly.

montura *f* (*caballo*) mount; (*silla*) saddle; (*arreos*) harness; ⊕ mounting; *sin ~* bareback.

monumental monumental; **monumento** *m* monument (*a. fig.*); (*mausoleo*) memorial; *~s pl. freq.* sights *de interés turístico*.

monzón *m or f* monsoon.

moña: *sl. estar con la ~* be sozzled.

moño *m* bun, chignon; *orn.* crest; F *ponerse ~s* put it on.

moquero *m* handkerchief.

moqueta *f* moquette.

moquete *m* punch (on the nose).

moquillo *m vet.* distemper; *orn.* pip.

mora[1] *f* mulberry; blackberry *de zarza*.

mora[2]**:** *ponerse en ~* default.

morada *f* dwelling, home; (*estancia*) stay; *última ~* (last) resting place.

morado purple, dark violet.

morador *m*, **-a** *f* inhabitant.

moral[1] *m* ⚘ mulberry (tree).

moral[2] **1.** moral; **2.** *f* (*ciencia*) ethics; (*moralidad*) morals; morale *de ejército etc.*; **moraleja** *f* moral; **moralidad** *f* morality, morals, ethics; (*moraleja*) moral; **moralista** *m/f*, **moralizador** *m*, **-a** *f* moralist; **moralizar** [1f] moralize.

morar [1a] live, dwell, reside; (*permanecer*) stay.

moratoria *f* moratorium.

mórbido ⚕ morbid; **morbosidad** *f* morbidity, morbidness; **morboso** diseased, morbid.

morcilla *f* black pudding; *thea.* gag, unscripted bit.

mordacidad *f* pungency *etc.*; **mordaz** *fig.* biting, scathing, pungent; **mordaza** *f* gag; ⊕ clamp, jaw; **mordedura** *f* bite; **morder** [2h] bite; ⊕ wear down; ⊕ eat away; *fig.* gossip about, run down; **mordiscar** [1g] nibble; *p.* nip; (*caballo etc.*) champ; **mordisco** *m* nibble; nip; (*bocado*) bite.

morena[1] *f geol.* moraine.

morena[2] *f* dark girl, brunette;

moreno (dark) brown; *p.* dark; (*con exceso*) swarthy; (*de pelo* ~) dark-haired.

morera *f* mulberry (tree).

morfina *f* morphia, morphine; **morfinómano** *m* drug addict.

morfología *f* morphology.

moribundo 1. dying; *esp. fig.* moribund; **2.** *m* dying man.

morigerado well-behaved, law-abiding.

morillo *m* firedog.

morir [3k; *p.p. muerto*] *v/t.*: *fue muerto* he was killed; *v/i.* die (*a. fig.*); (*fuego etc.*) die down; 🚗 *etc.* (*línea*) end; (*calle*) come out (*en* in); *¡muera X!* down with X!; ~ *ahogado* drown; ~ *de frío* freeze to death; ~ *de hambre* starve (to death; *a. fig.*); ~ *helado* freeze to death; ~ *quemado* burn to death; ~ *de risa* die laughing; ~ *vestido* F die a violent death; **~se** die; (*miembro*) go to sleep; ~ *por* be dying for; ~ *por inf.* be dying to *inf.*

morisco 1. Moorish; **2.** *m*, **a** *f Moorish convert to Christianity*; **moro 1.** Moorish; **2.** *m*, **a** *f* Moor; *hay ~s en la costa* you'd better watch out.

morisqueta *f* dirty trick.

morosidad *f* slowness; **moroso 1.** slow, dilatory; ☤ slow to pay up; **2.** *m* ☤ defaulter.

morra *f* top of one's head; *andar a la* ~ come to blows; **morrada** *f* butt *de carnero*; bang on the head.

morral *m* haversack, knapsack; *hunt.* game bag; nose bag *de caballo*; F lout.

morriña *f* F blues; (*nostalgia*) homesickness.

morro *m zo.* snout; ✈ nose; *geog.* headland; *anat.* thick lip; *andar de* ~ be at odds; **morrocotudo** F (*pistonudo*) super, great; (*fuerte*) strong; *negocio* sticky; important.

morrongo *m* F cat.

morsa *f* walrus.

mortaja *f* shroud; **mortal** *adj. a. su. m/f* mortal; *herida etc.* fatal; **mortalidad** *f* mortality; toll, loss of life *en accidente*; (*estadística*) death rate; **mortandad** *f* mortality; death rate; ⚔ *etc.* slaughter, carnage; **mortecino** dying, failing; *luz* dim, fading; *color* dull; *hacer la ~a* play dead.

mortero *m* mortar (*a.* ⚔).

mortífero deadly, lethal; **mortificación** *f* mortification; humiliation; **mortificar** [1g] mortify; humiliate; (*despechar*) spite; (*doler*) hurt, kill; **mortuorio**: *esp. casa ~a* house of the deceased.

morueco *m zo.* ram.

mosaico[1] *eccl.* Mosaic.

mosaico[2] *m* mosaic.

mosca *f* fly; F ☤ dough; F (*p.*) nuisance, bore; *~s pl.* sparks; ~ *de la carne* meat fly; ~ *doméstica* house fly; ~ *de las frutas* fruit fly; ~ *muerta* hypocrite; ~ *del vinagre* fruit fly; *~s pl. volantes* spots before the eyes; F *aflojar* (*or soltar*) *la* ~ fork out; F *estar con* ~ be fed up to the teeth; F *papar ~s* gape, gawk; **moscarda** *f* blowfly, bluebottle; **moscardón** *m* = *moscarda*; (*avispón*) hornet; F nuisance, pest.

moscatel *adj. a. su. m* muscatel; F (*p.*) pest, nuisance.

moscón *m* F nuisance.

mosqueado spotted; brindled; **mosqueador** *m* fly whisk; **mosquearse** [1a] *fig.* take offense.

mosquete *m* musket; **mosquetero** *m* musketeer; *thea.* † groundling.

mosquita *f* **muerta** hypocrite; **mosquitero** *m* mosquito net; **mosquito** *m* mosquito; gnat.

mostacho *m* moustache.

mostachón *m* macaroon.

mostaza *f* mustard.

mosto *m* must, unfermented grape juice.

mostrador *m* counter; bar *de taberna*; ⊕ dial; **mostrar** [1m] show.

mostrenco ownerless, unclaimed; *título etc.* in abeyance; F *p.* homeless, *animal* stray; *obra* crude; *p.* (*zafio*) dense.

mota *f* burl *de paño*; (*hilacho*) thread; (*punto*) speck; *fig.* fault.

mote *m* nickname; (*lema*) motto.

motear [1a] speckle; dapple.

motejar [1a] nickname; ~ *de* brand *s.o.* as.

motín *m* revolt, rising; riot.

motivación *f* motivation; **motivar** [1a] cause, give rise to, motivate; justify; **motivo 1.** motive; *~s pl.* grounds, reasons; *S.Am.* finickiness, prudery; *de su ~ propio* on his own accord; **2.** *m* motive, reason (*de* for); ♪, *paint.* motif; ~ *conductor* ♪ leitmotif; *con ~ de* on the occasion of;

(*debido a*) owing to; *con este* ~ for this reason, because of this.

moto *f* F motorbike; **~carro** *m* three-wheeler; **~cicleta** *f* motorcycle; **~ciclista** *m/f* motorcyclist; ~ *de escolta* outrider; **~nave** *f* motor vessel.

motor 1. ⊕ motive; *anat.* motor; **2.** *m* motor, engine; ~ *de arranque* starter; ~ *de combustión interna*, ~ *de explosión* internal combustion engine; ~ *a chorro* jet engine; ~ *de fuera de borda* outboard motor; ~ *de reacción* jet engine; **motora** *f*, **motorbote** *m* motorboat; **motorismo** *m* motorcycling; *mot.* motoring; **motorista** *m/f* motorcyclist; *mot.* motorist; **motorizar** [1f] motorize; **motriz** *v. fuerza.*

movedizo loose, unsteady; *arenas* shifting; *fig. p. etc.* fickle; *situación etc.* troubled, unsettled; **mover** [2h] move; shift; ⊕ drive; *cabeza* shake *negando*, nod *asintiendo*; *cola* wag; *fig.* (*promover*) stir up; move (*a compasión* to); ~ *a inf.* prompt *s.o.* to *inf.*, lead *s.o.* to *inf.*; **~se** move, stir; **movible** movable; mobile; *fig.* changeable; **móvil 1.** = *movible*; **2.** *m* motive (*de* for); **movilidad** *f* mobility; **movilización** *f* mobilization; **movilizar** [1f] mobilize; **movimiento** *m* movement; *phys. etc.* motion; shake, nod *de cabeza*; ♩ tempo; (*animación*) activity, bustle *en calle etc.*; *thea. etc.* action; *mot. etc.* traffic; (*conmoción*) stir; ~ *máximo* peak traffic.

moza *f* girl; *contp.* wench; (*criada*) servant; *buena* ~, *real* ~ good-looking girl; ~ *de taberna* barmaid; **mozalbete** *m* lad.

mozárabe 1. Mozarabic; **2.** *m/f* Mozarab; **3.** *m* (*idioma*) Mozarabic.

mozo 1. young; (*soltero*) single; **2.** *m* lad, (*criado*) servant; 🚂 porter; *buen* ~ handsome fellow; (*fuerte*) well-built fellow; ~ *de caballos* groom; ~ *de cámara* cabin boy; ~ *de estación* station porter; ~ *de hotel* bellhop, bellboy; ~ *de restaurante* waiter; **mozuela** *f* girl; *contp.* wench; **mozuelo** *m* lad.

mucílago *m* mucilage; **mucosa** *f* mucous membrane; **mucosidad** *f* mucus; **mucoso** mucous.

muchacha *f* girl; (*criada*) maid; **muchachada** *f* boyish prank; **muchacho** *m* boy, lad.

muchedumbre *f* crowd; mass, throng, host; *contp.* mob, herd.

mucho 1. *adj.* a lot of; much, great; ~*s pl.* many, lots of; many a; (*como pron.*) ~*s pl. creen que* a lot of people think that; *somos* ~*s* there are a lot of us; **2.** *adv.* a lot, a great deal, much; *estimar etc.* highly, greatly; *trabajar* hard; *v. sentir*; (~ *tiempo*) long, a long time; (*muchas veces*) often; *¿estás cansado?* — *¡*~*!* are you tired? — very!; *con* ~ by far, far and away; *ni con* ~ not nearly, nothing like; *ni* ~ *menos* far from it; *v. por*; *no es* ~ *que* it is no wonder that; *no es para* ~ it isn't up to much.

muda *f* change of clothing; *zo.* molt; (*época*) molting season; *está de* ~ (*muchacho*) his voice is breaking; **mudable** changeable; shifting; *carácter etc.* fickle; **mudanza** *f* (*cambio*) change; removal, move *de domicilio*; ~*s pl. fig.* fickleness; (*humor*) moodiness; **mudar** [1a] *v/t.* change; *piel* slough (off), shed; *v/i.*, **~se** change (*de ropa*, *parecer etc. acc.*); (*trasladarse*) move; (*voz*) break; *zo.* molt.

mudez *f* dumbness; **mudo** dumb (*a. fig.*, *de* with); mute (*a. gr.*); speechless; *gr.*, *película* silent; *thea. papel* walk-on.

mueblaje *m* = *moblaje*; **mueble 1.** movable; **2.** *m* piece of furniture; ~*s pl.* furniture; fittings *de tienda etc.*

mueca *f* face, grimace.

muela *f* millstone *de molino*; grindstone *para afilar*; *anat.* molar, *freq.* tooth; ~ *cordal* wisdom tooth; ~ *de esmeril* emery wheel; ~ *del juicio* wisdom tooth; ~ *de molino* millstone.

muellaje *m* wharfage; **muelle**[1] *m* ⚓ wharf, quay; 🚂 unloading bay.

muelle[2] **1.** soft; *vida* luxurious; **2.** *m* ⊕ spring.

muérdago *m* mistletoe.

muerte *f* death; (*asesinato*) murder; *a* ~ *guerra* to the knife; *luchar* to the death; *de* ~ implacably; F *de mala* ~ lousy; **muerto 1.** dead; lifeless; *color* dull; F *más* ~ *que mi abuela* as dead as a doornail; *más* ~ *que una piedra* stone-dead; *dar por* ~ give *s.o.* up for dead; F *no tener*

donde caerse ~ be on the rocks; **2.** *m*, **a** *f* dead man *etc.*; (*cadáver*) corpse; *los* ~*s pl.* the dead; *tocar a* ~ (*campana*) toll; **3.** *m naipes*: dummy.
muesca *f* notch, groove, slot.
muestra *f* ✝ *etc.* sample; sign, signboard *de tienda etc.*; (*indicio*) sign, token; model; face *de reloj*; *dar* ~*s* de show signs of; **muestrario** *m* collection of samples; *sew.* pattern book.
mugido *m* moo; bellow; **mugir** [3c] (*vaca*) moo; (*toro*) bellow.
mugre *f* dirt; grease, grime; **mugriento** dirty; greasy, grimy.
mugrón *m* layer *de vid*; sucker.
muguete *m* lily of the valley.
mujer *f* woman; (*esposa*) wife; ~ *de faena* charwoman; **mujeriego 1.** fond of the women; *a* ~*as* sidesaddle; **2.** *m* F wolf; **mujeril** womanly.
mújol *m* (gray) mullet.
mula *f* mule.
muladar *m* dunghill; trash heap.
mulato *adj. a. su. m*, **a** *f* mulatto.
mulero *m* muleteer.
muleta *f* crutch; *fig.* prop; **muletilla** *f fig.* tag, pet phrase.
mulo *m* mule.
multa *f* fine; penalty; **multar** [1a] fine (*en 20 ptas* 20 ptas); *deportes*: penalize.
multi...: ~**color** multicolored; ~**copista** *m* duplicator; ~**forme** manifold, multifarious; ~**látero** multilateral; ~**millonario** *m*, **a** *f* multimillionaire; **multinacional** multinational; ~*es pl.* multinational corporations; **múltiple** manifold, multifarious; ⅍ multiple; *cuestión* many-sided; ~*s pl. freq.* many; ~ *de admisión* intake manifold; ~ *de escape* exhaust manifold; ~ *de uso* multipurpose.
multiplicación *f* multiplication; **multiplicar**(**se**) [1g] ⅍ multiply; increase; ⊕ gear up; **multiplicidad** *f* multiplicity; **múltiplo** *adj. a. su. m* multiple; **multitud** *f* multitude; crowd *de gente etc.*; *la* ~ *contp.* the masses; F ~ de lots of, heaps of.
mullir [3a] pound, knead; soften; *cama* shake up; ↗ *tierra* hoe, loosen; *plantas* hoe round.
mundanal, mundano worldly; of the world; (*de la buena sociedad*) society *attr.*; fashionable; social; **mundanería** *f* worldliness; **mundial** world-wide; *guerra, record etc.* world *attr.*; **mundo** *m* world (*a. fig., eccl.*); (*ps.*) people; (*esfera*) globe; *todo el* ~ everybody; *echar al* ~ bring into the world; *tener* (*mucho*) ~ be sophisticated, be experienced; *ver* (*mucho*) ~ see life, knock about F; **mundología** *f* F worldly wisdom; **mundonuevo** *m* peep show.
munición *f* (*a.* ~*es pl.*) stores, supplies; ⚔ ammunition, munitions; *de* ~ service *attr.*
municipal 1. municipal, town *attr.*; **2.** *m* policeman; **municipio** *m* municipality, township; (*ayuntamiento*) town council.
munificencia *f* munificence; **munífico** munificent.
muñeca *f anat.* wrist; doll; dummy *de modista*; **muñeco** *m* figure, guy; dummy *de sastre*; (*muñeca*) doll; *fig.* puppet; F (*niño*) little angel; (*afeminado*) gay; ~ *de nieve* snowman; **muñequera** *f* wrist watch.
muñón *m anat.* stump; ⊕ trunnion; journal, gudgeon.
mural mural; *mapa etc.* wall *attr.*; **muralla** *f* (city) wall, rampart; **murar** [1a] wall.
murciélago *m zo.* bat.
murmullo *m* murmur; ripple *etc.*; **murmuración** *f* gossip, slander; **murmurador** *m*, **-a** *f* gossip; grumbler; **murmurar** [1a] murmur; mutter *entre dientes*; whisper *al oído*; (*multitud etc.*) hum; (*aguas*) ripple; (*hojas etc.*) rustle; *fig.* (*quejarse*) grumble; mutter; (*chismear*) gossip (de about); ~ *de esp.* criticize.
muro *m* wall; ~ *del sonido* sound barrier.
murria *f* F blues; *tener* ~ be down in the dumps; **murrio** sulky; sullen.
mus *m a card game.*
musa *f* Muse.
musaraña *f zo.* shrew; (*animalejo*) bug, creepy-crawly; *mirar a las* ~*s* moon (about).
muscular muscular; **musculatura** *f* muscles; **músculo** *m* muscle; **musculoso** muscular.
muselina *f* muslin.
museo *m* museum; gallery; ~ *de arte etc.* art gallery.

musgaño *m* shrew.
musgo *m* moss; **musgoso** mossy.
música *f* music; (*ps.*) band; ~ *celestial* bunk, drivel; ~ *de fondo* background music; **musical = músico 1.** musical; **2.** *m*, **a** *f* musician, player.
musitar [1a] mumble, whisper.
muslo *m* thigh.
mustio *p*. depressed, gloomy; hypocritical, sanctimonious; ⚘ withered.
musulmán *adj. a. su. m*, **-a** *f* Moslem.
mutabilidad *f* changeability; **mutación** *f* change, mutation (*a. biol., gr.*); *thea.* change of scene.
mutilación *f* mutilation; **mutilado** *m*, **a** *f* cripple, disabled person; **mutilar** [1a] mutilate (*a. fig.*); (*lisiar*) cripple, maim; *texto* mutilate; *cuento* garble.
mutis *m thea.* exit; *hacer ~ thea.* exit; *fig.* not say a word; **mutismo** *m* dumbness; *fig.* silence.
mutualidad *f* mutuality; (*ayuda*) reciprocal aid; ✝ mutual-benefit association; **mutuo** mutual (*a.* ✝), reciprocal; joint.
muy very; greatly, highly; most; *es ~ de él* that's just like him; *es ~ de lamentar* it is much to be regretted; *el ~ tonto etc.* the big fool *etc.*; *es ~ hombre* he's a real man; *es ~ mujer* she's very feminine.

N

naba *f* ♣ rape.
nabab *m* nabob.
nabo *m* turnip; ~ *sueco* swede.
nácar *m* mother-of-pearl; **nacarado, nacarino** mother-of-pearl *attr.*; pearly.
nacer [2d] be born (*a. fig.*); ♣ come up, sprout; (*río*) rise; *fig.* spring, arise (de from); **nacido:** ~ *a*, ~ *para* born to (be); *bien* ~ of noble birth; *mal* ~ low-born; **naciente** nascent; recent; *sol* rising; **nacimiento** *m* birth (*a. fig.*); (*principio*) origin, start, beginning; source *de río*; (*manantial*) spring; (*belén*) nativity (scene); de ~ *ciego etc.* from birth.
nación *f* nation; de ~ by birth; **nacional** *adj. a. su. m/f* national; *producto freq.* home *attr.*; **nacionalidad** *f* nationality; **nacionalismo** *m* nationalism; **nacionalista** *adj. a. su. m/f* nationalist; **nacionalizar** [1f] nationalize; naturalize.
nada 1. *f* nothingness; *la* ~ the void; **2.** *pron.* nothing; ¡~, ~! not a bit of it!; ¡~ *de eso!* nothing of the kind!, far from it!; ~ *más* nothing else; (*solamente*) only; ¡*de* ~! not at all!, don't mention it!; *por* ~ *llorar etc.* for no reason at all; *por* ~ *del mundo* not for love nor money; *por menos de* ~ for two pins; ¡*pues* ~! not to worry!; *no ha sido* ~ it's nothing; **3.** *adv.*: ~ *fácil* not at all easy, far from easy.
nadaderas *f/pl.* waterwings; **nadador** *m*, **-a** *f* swimmer; **nadar** [1a] swim; (*corcho etc.*) float; ~ *en fig.* be rolling in, wallow in.
nadería *f* trifle.
nadie nobody, no-one; *no* ... ~ not ... anybody; *un* (*don*) ~ a nobody.
nadir *m* nadir.
nado: *pasar a* ~ swim (across).
nafta *f* naphtha; **naftaleno** *m*, **naftalina** *f* naphthalene.
naipe *m* (playing) card; *fig.* deck of cards; ~ *de figura* face card; *tener buen* ~ be lucky; ~*s pl.* cards.
nalgas *f/pl.* buttocks.
nana *f* F granny; ♪ lullaby.
napolitano *adj. a. su. m*, **a** *f* Neapolitan.
naranja *f* orange; F *media* ~ better half; **naranjada** *f* orangeade, orange squash; **naranjado** orange; **naranjal** *m* orange grove; **naranjo** *m* orange (tree).
narciso *m* narcissus; daffodil; *fig.* dandy.
narcosis *f* narcosis; **narcótico 1.** narcotic; **2.** *m* narcotic; sleeping pill; drug, dope; **narcotismo** *m* narcotism; **narcotizar** [1f] drug, dope, narcotize 📖; **narcotraficante** *m* drug dealer.
nardo *m* (spike)nard.
narigada *f S.Am.* snuff; **narigón, narigudo** big-nosed; **nariz 1.** *f* nose (*a. fig.*); (*cada orificio*) nostril; bouquet *de vino*; ~ *de pico de loro* hooknose; **2.** *narices pl. zo.* nostrils; F nose; ¡~! rubbish!; *cerrar la puerta en las* ~ *de* shut the door in *s.o.'s* face; *dar de* ~ land on one's nose; *hinchársele a uno las* ~ get annoyed; *sonarse las* ~ blow one's nose; *tabicarse las* ~ hold one's nose; *tener agarrado por las* ~ lead by the nose.
narración *f* narration; account, narrative; **narrador** *m*, **-a** *f* narrator; **narrar** [1a] tell, narrate; **narrativa** *f* narrative; **narrativo** narrative.
narval *m* narwhal.
nasa *f* ⚓ fish trap; (*cesta*) basket; bin *para pan etc.*
nasal *adj. a. su. f* nasal; **nasalidad** *f* nasality; **nasalizar** [1f] nasalize.
nata *f* cream (*a. fig.*); whipped cream; skim, scum; skin *en natillas etc.*; *v. flor.*
natación *f* swimming; ~ *de costado* sidestroke.
natal natal; *suelo etc.* native; **natalicio** *adj. a. su. m* birthday; **natalidad** *f* birth rate; *control de* ~ birth control.
natillas *f/pl.* custard.
natividad *f* nativity; **nativo** native

(*a.* ⚒); home *attr.*; natural, innate; **nato** born.

natural 1. *mst* natural (*a.* ♪); native; **2.** *m/f* native (de of), inhabitant; **3.** *m* nature, dispositition; *buen* ~ good nature; *al* ~ *descripción* true to life; (*sin arte*) rough; *bebida etc.* just as it comes; *vivir* according to nature; *del* ~ from nature, from life; **naturaleza** *f* nature; ~ *muerta* still life; *v. carta*; **naturalidad** *f* naturalness; *con la mayor* ~ as if nothing had happened; *hablar* in an ordinary tone; **naturalismo** *m* naturalism; **naturalista 1.** naturalistic; **2.** *m/f* naturalist; **naturalización** *f* naturalization; **naturalizar** [1f] naturalize; **naturismo** *m* nudism.

naufragar [1h] be (ship)wrecked, sink; *fig.* fail; **naufragio** *m* (ship)-wreck; *fig.* ruin; **náufrago 1.** shipwrecked; **2.** *m* shipwrecked sailor *etc.*, castaway.

náusea(**s**) *f* (*pl.*) nausea, sick feeling; *fig.* disgust; *dar* ~*s a* sicken; **nauseabundo** nauseating, sickening.

náutica *f* navigation, seamanship; **náutico** nautical.

navaja *f* (clasp) knife, jackknife; (*cortaplumas*) penknife; ~ (*de afeitar*) razor; **navajada** *f*, **navajazo** *m* slash.

naval naval.

navarro *adj. a. su. m*, **a** *f* Navarrese.

nave *f* ship; ⚠ nave; ~ *espacial* spaceship; ~ *central*, ~ *principal* nave; ~ *lateral* aisle; **navegable** navigable; **navegación** *f* navigation; (*viaje*) voyage; (*buques*) shipping; **navegador** *m*, **navegante** *m* navigator; **navegar** [1h] (*ir*) sail; (*dirigir*) navigate.

Navidad *f* Christmas (time); *por* ~*es* at Christmas (time); *¡Felices Navidades!* Merry Christmas!; **navidal** *m* Christmas card.

naviero 1. shipping *attr.*; **2.** *m* shipowner; **navío** *m* ship; ~ *de guerra* warship; ~ *de línea* ship of the line.

nazareno *adj. a. su. m*, **a** *f* Nazarene.

nazi *adj. a. su. m/f* Nazi; **nazismo** *m* Nazism.

neblina *f* mist; **nebulosa** *f* nebula; **nebulosidad** *f* mistiness *etc.*; **nebuloso** *ast.* nebular, nebulous; *cielo* cloudy; *atmósfera* misty; (*tétrico*) gloomy; *idea etc.* nebulous, vague; obscure.

necedad *f* silliness; (*acto, dicho*) silly thing, nonsense.

necesario necessary; **neceser** *m* hold-all; dressing case *de tocador*; ~ *de belleza* vanity case; ~ *de costura* workbox; **necesidad** *f* necessity; need (de for, of); (*hambre*) hunger; *euph.* business; *de* ~, *por* ~ of necessity; *de primera* ~ absolutely essential; *en caso de* ~ in case of need; **necesitado** needy, necessitous; *los* ~*s* the needy; **necesitar** [1a] *v/t.* want, need; *acción etc.* necessitate; ~ *inf.* must *inf.*, need to *inf.*; *v/i.*: ~ de need; ~**se**: *necesítase* (*anuncios*) wanted.

necio silly, stupid.

necrófago *m* ghoul; **necrología** *f* obituary (notice); **necromancía** *f* necromancy.

néctar *m* nectar.

nefando unspeakable; **nefario** nefarious.

nefasto unlucky, inauspicious.

negación *f* negation; denial; *gr.* negative; **negar** [1h *a.* 1k] *verdad etc.* deny; *permiso etc.* refuse (*a acc.*), withhold (*a* from); *responsabilidad* disclaim; (*vedar*) deny; ~ *que* deny that; ~**se** *a inf.* refuse to *inf.*; **negativa** *f* negative (*a. phot.*); denial, refusal; **negativo 1.** negative; ⚕ minus; **2.** *m phot.* negative.

negligencia *f* negligence *etc.*; **negligente** negligent; neglectful (de of), slack, careless.

negociable negotiable; **negociación** *f* negotiation; clearance *de cheque*; **negociador** *m*, **-a** *f* negotiator; **negociante** *m* businessman; merchant, dealer; **negociar** [1b] *v/t.* negotiate; *v/i.* negotiate; ~ *en* deal in, trade in; **negocio** *m* (*asunto*) affair, (piece of) business; ⚕ (*un* ~) deal, transaction; ⚕ (*en general*) trade, business; (*puesto*) job; ~*s pl.* business; *buen* ~ (good) bargain; *de* ~*s adj.* business *attr.*; *adv.* on business.

negra *f* black woman; **negrero** *m* slave trader; slave driver (*a. fig.*); **negrita** *f typ.* boldface; *en* ~*s* in bold type; **negrito** *m* (*muñeca*) golliwog; **negro 1.** black (*a. fig.*); dark; (*sombrío*) gloomy; F (*enfadado*) peeved; F broke; *suerte* awful, atrocious; ~ *como boca de lobo* pitch dark; F *pasar las* ~*as* have a rough time; **2.** *m* (*p.*) black,

black person; ~ *de humo* lampblack; **negroide** Negroid; **negrura** *f* blackness; **negruzco** blackish.
nene *m*, **a** *f* F baby.
nenúfar *m* water lily.
neo *m* neon.
neófito *m*, **a** *f* neophyte.
neolatino *lengua* Romance.
neologismo *m* neologism.
neón *m* neon.
neoyorquino *m*, **a** *f* New Yorker.
neozelandés *m*, **-a** *f* New Zealander.
nepotismo *m* nepotism.
nervadura *f* △ rib; **nervio** *m* nerve (*a. fig.*); ⚘ rib; *fig.* sinews; vigor; stamina, toughness; crux, key *de cuestión*; *sin* ~ weak, spineless; *crispar los* ~*s a* get on *s.o.'s* nerves; *poner los* ~*s en punta a* jar on, grate on; *tener* ~ possess character; *tener los* ~*s en punta* be all keyed up; **nerviosidad** *f*, **nerviosismo** *m* nervousness; (*temporal*) nerves F; **nervioso** *centro, célula* nerve *attr.*; *crisis, sistema* nervous; *p.* (*con miedo*) nervous, nervy F; highly strung; excitable; (*fuerte*) vigorous; *estilo* energetic; *poner* ~ *a alguien* get on s.o.'s nerves; *ponerse* ~ get excited, get worked up; **nervudo** wiry, sinewy.
nesga *f sew.* flare, gore; **nesgar** [1h] flare, gore.
neto pure, clean; neat, clear; ✝ net.
neumático 1. pneumatic; **2.** *m* tyre.
neuralgia *f* neuralgia; **neurastenia** *f* nervous exhaustion; neurasthenia 🕮; excitability; **neurasténico** highly strung, excitable; neurasthenic 🕮; **neuritis** *f* neuritis; **neurología** *f* neurology; **neurólogo** *m* neurologist; **neurona** *f* nerve cell; **neurosis** *f* neurosis; ~ *de guerra* shell shock; **neurótico** *adj. a. su. m*, **a** *f* neurotic.
neutral *adj. a. su. m/f* neutral; **neutralidad** *f* neutrality; **neutralizar** [1f] neutralize; *fig. a.* counteract; **neutro** *mst* neutral; *género* neuter; *verbo* intransitive.
neutrón *m* neutron.
nevada *f* snowstorm; (*cantidad*) snowfall; **nevado** snow-covered; *fig.* snowy; **nevar** [1k] *v/t.* whiten; *v/i.* snow; **nevasca** *f* snowstorm; **nevera** *f* refrigerator, icebox (*a. fig.*); **nevisca** *f* light snowfall, flurry of snow; (*aguanieve*) sleet; **neviscar** [1g] snow lightly; sleet; **nevoso** snowy; *temporal* snow *attr.*
nexo *m* link, connexion.
ni nor, neither; ~ ... ~ neither ... nor; *¡~ una palabra!* not a single word!; ~ *que* even though; ~ ... *siquiera* not even.
niara *f* ✓ stack.
nicotina *f* nicotine.
nicho *m* niche, recess.
nidada *f* (*huevos*) sitting, clutch; (*pollos*) brood; **nidal** *m* nest *de gallina*; (*huevo*) nest egg; F hangout; **nido** *m* nest (*a. fig.*).
niebla *f* fog; mist; ~ *artificial* smoke screen; *hay* ~ it is foggy.
nieta *f* granddaughter; **nieto** *m* grandson; *fig.* descendant; ~*s pl.* grandchildren.
nieve *f* snow; *Mex.* ice cream.
nigromancía *f* necromancy, black magic.
nihilismo *m* nihilism; **nihilista** *m/f* nihilist.
nilón *m* nylon.
nimbo *m* halo; *meteor.* nimbus.
nimiedad *f* insignificant detail; *con* ~ with a lot of details; **nimio** *detalle etc.* tiny, insignificant; *p.* small-minded; (*delicado*) fussy; *lit.* excessive (*en* in).
ninfa *f* nymph.
ningún, ninguno 1. *adj.* no; **2.** *pron.* none; (*p.*) nobody, no one; ~ *de ellos* none of them; ~ *de los dos* neither (of them).
niña *f* (little) girl; *anat.* pupil; ~*s pl. de los ojos de fig.* apple of *s.o.'s* eye; *desde* ~ from childhood; ~ *expósita* foundling; **niñada** *f* childish thing; **niñear** [1a] act childishly; **niñera** *f* nursemaid, nanny F; **niñería** *f* childish thing; *fig.* silly thing; **niñez** *f* childhood; **niño 1.** young; *b.s.* childish; **2.** *m* (little) boy; (*en general*) child; (*no nacido aún, recién nacido*) baby, infant; ~*s pl.* children; ~ *bonito*, ~ *gótico* playboy; ~ *explorador* boy scout; ~ *expósito* foundling; ~*-probeta* test-tube baby; *desde* ~ from childhood; *¡no seas* ~*!* don't be so childish!
níquel *m* nickel; chromium-plating; **niquelar** [1a] nickel(-plate); chromium-plate.
níspero *m*, **níspola** *f* medlar.
nitidez *f* spotlessness *etc.*; **nítido** bright, clean, spotless; *phot.* sharp.

nitrato *m* nitrate; **nítrico** nitric; **nitro** *m* nitre; **nitrogenado** nitrogenous; **nitrógeno** *m* nitrogen; **nitroso** nitrous.

nivel *m* level; ~ *de aire*, ~ *de burbuja* spirit level; ~ *sonoro* noise level; ~ *de vida* standard of living; *a* ~ level (*a.* 🚂); true; *al* ~ *de* (on a) level with; *ocasión* equal to, up to; **nivelación** *f* leveling; **nivelado** level; ⊕ *a.* flush; **niveladora** *f* ⊕ bulldozer; **nivelar** [1a] level; 🚂 *etc.* grade; *fig.* level up, even up.

níveo *fig.* snowy.

no *mst* not; (*usado solo*) no; *¿~? = ¿~ es verdad?*; *compuestos*: ~ *agresión* nonaggression; ~ *sea que* lest; ~ ... *sino* only; not ... but; *¡que ~!* I tell you it isn't!; no I won't!

nobiliario noble; **noble** *adj. a. su. m* noble; **nobleza** *f* nobility, aristocracy.

noción *f* notion, idea, *~es pl.* elements; smattering; **nocional** notional.

nocivo harmful, injurious.

nocturno night *attr.*; *zo. etc.* nocturnal; **noche** *f* night; nighttime; (*más bien tarde*) evening; (*oscuridad*) darkness; *¡buenas ~s!* good evening!; (*al despedirse o acostarse*) good night!; *esta* ~ tonight; *de* (*la*) ~ *función etc.* late-night *attr.*; ~ *toledana* sleepless night; *de* ~, *por la* ~ at night, by night; *de la* ~ *a la mañana* overnight; *hacerse de* ~ get dark; *quedarse a buenas ~s* be left in the dark; **nochebuena** *f* Christmas Eve; **nochero** sleepwalker; **noche vieja** New Year's Eve; watch night.

nodo *m* node.

nodriza *f* wet nurse.

nodular nodular; **nódulo** *m* nodule.

nogal *m*, **noguera** *f* walnut (tree).

nómada 1. nomadic; **2.** *m/f* nomad.

nombradía *f* fame, renown; **nombrado** *fig.* renowned; **nombramiento** *m* naming, designation; nomination; appointment; ⚔ commission; **nombrar** [1a] name; designate; (*proponer*) nominate; (*elegir etc.*) appoint; ⚔ commission; mention; **nombre** *m* name (*a. fig.*); *gr.* noun; ~ *comercial* firm name; ~ *de lugar* place name; ~ (*de pila*) Christian name, first name; ~ *de soltera* maiden name; *mal* ~ nickname; *por mal* ~ nicknamed; ~ *propio* proper name (*or* noun); *de* ~ by name; *en* ~ *de* in the name of, on behalf of; *sin* ~ nameless; *poner* ~ *a* call; **nomenclatura** *f* nomenclature.

nomeolvides *f* forget-me-not.

nómina *f* list; ✝ payroll; **nominación** *f* nomination; **nominal** nominal; titular; *valor* face *attr.*; *gr.* noun *attr.*; **nominativo** *m* nominative (case).

non odd; *andar de ~es* have nothing to do; *estar de* ~ be odd (man out); *fig.* be useless.

nonada *f* trifle, mere nothing.

nonagenario *adj. a. su. m*, **a** *f* nonagenarian; **nonagésimo** ninetieth.

nonato unborn.

nono ninth.

noqueada *f* knockout (blow); **noquear** [1a] knock out.

nordeste = *noreste.*

nórdico Nordic.

noreste 1. *parte* northeast(ern); *dirección* northeasterly; *viento* northeast(erly); **2.** *m* northeast.

noria *f* water wheel, chain pump.

norma *f* standard, rule, norm; method; ⊕, ⚓ square; *phys. etc.* ~ *de comprobación* control; **normal** normal (*a.* ⚛); natural; regular; *ancho etc.* standard; **normalizar** [1f] normalize, standardize; *~se* return to normal, settle down.

normando *adj. a. su. m*, **a** *f* Norman.

noroeste 1. *parte* northwest(ern); *dirección* northwesterly; *viento* northwest(erly); **2.** *m* northwest.

norte 1. *parte* north(ern); *dirección* northerly; *viento* north(erly); **2.** *m* north; *fig.* guide; lodestar; north wind; **norteamericano** *adj. a. su. m*, **a** *f* American; **norteño 1.** northern; **2.** *m*, **a** *f* northerner.

noruego 1. *adj. a. su. m*, **a** *f* Norwegian; **2.** *m* (*idioma*) Norwegian.

nos (*acc.*) us; (*dat.*) (to) us; (*reflexivo*) (to) ourselves; (*recíproco*) (to) each other; **nosotros, nosotras** *pl.* we; (*tras prp.*) us.

nostalgia *f* nostalgia, homesickness; **nostálgico** nostalgic, homesick.

nota *f* note (*a.* ♪); *escuela*: report; mark, class *en examen*; ~ *de adorno* grace note; ~ *de inhabilitación* endorsement; **notabilidad** *f* notability; (*p.*) notable; **notable 1.** notable, noteworthy (*por* for, on account of); remarkable; **2.** *m* worthy, notable; **notación** *f* notation; **notar** [1a] note, notice; (*apuntar*) note down; *escrito* annotate; *fig.* criticize; *hacer* ~ indicate, point out.

notarial notarial; **notario** *m* notary (public).

noticia *f* piece of news; (news) item *en periódico*; (*noción*) knowledge, idea (*de* of); ~*s pl.* news; **noticiar** [1b] notify; **noticiario** *m radio*: news (bulletin); *cine*: newsreel; **noticioso** *fuente* well-informed; **notificación** *f* notification; **notificar** [1g] notify; **notorio** well-known; *b.s.* notorious; obvious; blatant, flagrant.

novato 1. raw, green; **2.** *m* beginner, tiro.

novecientos nine hundred.

novedad *f* (*calidad*) newness, novelty, strangeness; (*cambio*) change, new development; (*cosa nueva*) novelty; (*noticia*) news; ~*es pl.* novelties; (*modas*) latest fashions; *sin* ~ as usual; ✈ the same as before; *llegar* safely, without incident; ⚔ all quiet; **novel 1.** new, inexperienced; **2.** *m* beginner; **novela** *f* novel; ~ *por entregas* serial; ~ *policíaca* detective story, whodunit *sl.*; **novelero** *p.* highly imaginative, romantic; **novelesco** *género* fictional; *suceso* romantic, fantastic; **novelista** *m/f* novelist; **novelón** *m* three-decker novel; **novelucha** *f* F yellowback, shocker.

noveno ninth; **noventa** ninety; **noventón** *adj. a. su. m*, **-a** *f* F nonagenarian.

novia *f* girlfriend, sweetheart; (*prometida*) fiancée; (*casada*) bride; **noviazgo** *m* engagement.

noviciado *m eccl.* novitiate; apprenticeship; **novicio** *m*, **a** *f* novice (*a. eccl.*); beginner; apprentice.

noviembre *m* November.

novilunio *m* new moon.

novilla *f* heifer; **novillada** *f* bullfight with young bulls; **novillero** *m toros*: novice bullfighter; F truant; **novillo** *m* young bull; steer, bullock; F cuckold; F *hacer* ~*s* play truant.

novio *m* boyfriend, sweetheart; (*prometido*) fiancé; (*casado*) bridegroom; *los* ~*s* (*casados*) the bridal couple.

novísimo newest, latest.

nubarrón *m* storm cloud; **nube** *f* cloud (*a. fig.*); ✈ film; *por las* ~*s* sky-high; *poner en* (*or por*) *las* ~*s* praise to the skies.

núbil nubile, marriageable.

nublado 1. cloudy; **2.** *m* storm cloud; *fig.* threat; (*copia*) swarm, abundance; **nubloso** cloudy; *fig.* gloomy.

nuca *f* nape.

nuclear nuclear; **núcleo** *m* nucleus; ⚡ core (*a. fig.*); ⚘ kernel; ~ *rural* village settlement.

nudillo *m* knuckle; **nudo** *m* knot (*a.* ⚓, ⚘, *fig.*); node; center *de comunicaciones*; (*enredo*) tangle; lump *en garganta*; *fig.* bond, tie; *thea.* plot; **nudoso** *madera etc.* knotty; *tronco* gnarled; *palo* knobbly.

nuera *f* daughter-in-law.

nuestro 1. *adj.* our; (*tras su.*) of ours; **2.** *pron.* ours; *los* ~*s* (*ps.*) our men, our side.

nueva *f* piece of news; ~*s pl.* news; *me cogió de* ~*s* it was news to me; **nuevamente** again; recently.

nueve nine (*a. su.*); (*fecha*) ninth; *las* ~ nine o'clock.

nuevo new; (*original*) novel; (*adicional*) further; *más* ~ (*p.*) junior; *de* ~ (all over) again; *¿qué hay de* ~*?* what's the news?

nuez *f* nut; (*de nogal*) walnut; ~ *de Adán*, ~ *de la garganta* Adam's apple; ~ *moscada* nutmeg.

nulidad *f* ⚖ nullity; incompetence *de empleado*; (*p.*) nonentity; **nulo** ⚖ (null and) void; invalid; *p. etc.* useless; *partido* drawn.

numen *m* talent, inventiveness; *de propio* ~ out of one's own head.

numeración *f* numeration; **numeral** numeral; **numerar** [1a] number; **numerario** *m* hard cash; **numérico** numerical; **número** *m* number (*a. de revista etc.*); *thea.* turn, number; item, number *en programa*; ~ *atrasado* back number; ~ *de serie* series number; *teleph.* ~ *equivocado* wrong number; ~ *extraordinario* special edition; *cargar al* ~ *llamado*, *cobrar al* ~ *llamado* call collect, reverse the charges; *de* ~ *miembro* full; *mirar por el* ~ *uno* look out for number one; *sin* ~ numberless; **numeroso** numerous.

numismática *f* numismatics; **numismático 1.** numismatic; **2.** *m* numismatist.
nunca never; ever; ~ *(ja)más* never again, nevermore; *casi* ~ hardly ever.
nuncio *m eccl.* nuncio, Papal envoy.
nupcial wedding *attr.*; **nupcias** *f/pl.* wedding; *casarse en segundas* ~ get married (for) a second time.
nutria *f* otter.
nutrición *f* nutrition, nourishment; **nutrido** *fig.* large, considerable; abundant; ⚔ *fuego* heavy; **nutrimento** *m* nutriment, nourishment; **nutrir** [3a] feed, nourish; *(fortalecer)* strengthen; *fig.* support, foment; **nutritivo** nourishing, nutritious; *valor* nutritional.
nylón *m* nylon.

Ñ

ñame *m* yam; F dunce.
ñapa *f S.Am.* tip; *S.Am. de* ~ to boot.
ñaque *m* junk; pile of junk.
ñiquiñaque *m* F trash, rubbish.
ñoño 1. whining; spineless; feeble-minded; **2.** *m*, **a** *f* drip.
ñudoso = *nudoso.*

O

o or; ~ ... ~ either ... or.
oasis *m* oasis.
obcecación *f* blind obstinacy; **obcecar** [1g] blind.
obedecer [2d] obey; ~ *a* (*ceder*) yield to; ~ *a*(*l hecho de que*) be due to, arise from; **obediencia** *f* obedience; **obediente** obedient.
obelisco *m* obelisk.
obenques *m/pl.* ⚓ shrouds.
obertura *f* overture.
obesidad *f* obesity; **obeso** obese.
óbice *m* obstacle.
obispado *m* bishopric; **obispo** *m* bishop.
óbito *m* decease.
objeción *f* objection; **objetante** *m/f* objector; **objetar** [1a] object; *objeciones* raise; *argumento* put forward; **objetividad** *f* objectivity; **objetivo** *adj. a. su. m* objective; **objeto** *m* object (*a. gr.*); (*fin a.*) end, purpose; (*asunto*) subject matter; ~ *volante no identificado* (*ovni*) unidentified flying object (UFO).
oblación *f*, **oblata** *f* oblation; **oblato** *eccl.* oblate.
oblea *f* wafer.
oblicuidad *f* obliquity; **oblicuo** oblique; *mirada* sidelong.
obligación *f* obligation; duty (*a, con, para* to); liability, responsibility; ✝ bond; ~ *de banco* bank note; ~*s pl.* ✝ bonds, securities; **obligar** [1h] force, compel, oblige (*a inf.* to *inf.*); ~**se** bind o.s. (*a* to); **obligatorio** obligatory, binding (*a* on), compulsory (*a* for).
oblongo oblong.
oboe *m* oboe.
óbolo *m* mite (*contribution*).
obra *f* work; piece of work; handiwork; ~*s pl. lit. etc.* works; ⚠ repairs, alterations; ~ *de* about, a matter of; ~*s pl. de caridad* good works; ~ *de consulta* reference book; ~ *de hierro* ironwork; ~ *maestra* masterpiece; ~*s pl. públicas* public works; ~ *de romanos* herculean task, tremendous undertaking; *¡manos a la* ~*!* let's get on with it!; ⚠ *estar en* ~*s* be closed for repairs; *poner por* ~ carry out, implement; put into practice; **obraje** *m* manufacture, processing; **obrar** [1a] *v/t.* build, make; *madera etc.* work; (*medicina*) work on, have an effect on; *v/i.* act, behave, proceed; *su carta obra en mi poder* your letter is to hand; **obrero** **1.** *clase etc.* working; labor *attr.*; *movimiento* working class; **2.** *m*, **a** *f* worker (*a. pol.*); **3.** *m* workman; man, hand.
obscenidad *f* obscenity; **obsceno** [obscene.
obscu... *v. oscu...*
obsequiar [1b] *amigo etc.* lavish attentions on; ~ (*con*) present *s.o.* with; give; ~ *a alguien con un banquete* hold a dinner for s.o.; **obsequio** *m* attention, courtesy; (*regalo*) present, gift; presentation *en jubilación etc.*; *en* ~ *de* in honor of; **obsequioso** attentive, obliging, helpful; *b.s.* obsequious.
observación *f* observation; (*dicho a.*) remark, comment; observance *de ley*; **observador** **1.** observant; **2.** *m*, **-a** *f* observer; **observancia** *f* observance; **observar** [1a] (*ver*) observe; watch; notice, spot F; *ley* observe, keep; *regla* adhere to; **observatorio** *m* observatory.
obsesión *f* obsession; **obsesionante** haunting; **obsesionar** [1a] obsess.
obstaculizar [1f] hold up, hinder; **obstáculo** *m* obstacle; hindrance; handicap.
obstante: *no* ~ **1.** *adv.* however, nevertheless; **2.** *prp.* in spite of; **obstar** [1a]: ~ *a* hinder, prevent.
obstetricia *f* obstetrics; **obstétrico** *m* obstetrician.
obstinación *f* obstinacy *etc.*; **obstinado** obstinate, stubborn; **obstinarse** [1a]: ~ *en inf.* persist in *ger.*
obstrucción *f* obstruction (*a. parl.*); **obstruccionista** *m/f* obstructionist; **obstructivo** obstructive; **obstruir** [3g] obstruct, block; hinder, interfere with.

obtención *f* obtaining; **obtener** [2l] get, obtain, secure.
obturador *m phot.* shutter; ⊕, *mot.* choke; **obturar** [1a] plug, stop up, seal off; *diente* fill.
obtuso blunt; &, *fig.* obtuse.
obús *m* howitzer; (*granada*) shell.
obviar [1c] *v/t.* obviate, remove; *v/i.* stand in the way; **obvio** obvious.
oca *f* goose.
ocasión *f* occasion, time; opportunity, chance (*de inf.* to *inf.*); *de* ~ second-hand; **ocasional** accidental; **ocasionar** [1a] cause, produce, occasion.
ocaso *m ast.* sunset; setting *de astro*; *geog.* west; *fig.* decline.
occidental western; **occidente** *m* west.
oceánico oceanic; **océano** *m* ocean.
ocio *m* leisure; *b.s.* idleness; *ratos de* ~ spare time; **ociosidad** *f* idleness; **ocioso** *p. etc.* idle, lazy; *obra* useless.
ocre *m* ochre.
octagonal octagonal; **octágono** *m* octagon; **octanaje:** *de alto* ~ high octane *attr.*; **octano** *m* octane; **octava** *f* octave; **octavilla** *f* pamphlet; **octavo** *adj. a. su. m* eighth; *typ. en* ~ octavo; **octogenario** *adj. a. su. m,* **a** *f* octogenarian; **octogésimo** eightieth; **octosílabo 1.** octosyllabic; **2.** *m* octosyllable; **octubre** *m* October.
ocular 1. ocular; *v. testigo*; **2.** *m* eyepiece; **oculista** *m/f* oculist.
ocultar [1a] hide (*a, de* from); screen, mask; **ocultismo** *m* occultism; **oculto** hidden, concealed; *fig.* secret; *ciencia* occult; *pensamiento* inner; *motivo* ulterior.
ocupación *f* occupation (*a.* ⚔); **ocupante** *m/f* occupant; **ocupar** [1a] *mst* occupy (*a.* ⚔); *puesto a.* fill, hold; *espacio, tiempo a.* take up; (*llenar*) fill (up); *atmósfera* pervade; *p.* keep *s.o.* busy; give employment to; (*molestar*) bother; **~se** *de* take care of, look after; pay attention to; ~ *en* be occupied in (*or* with), busy o.s. with; engage in; *estar ocupado* (*habitación, silla*) be taken, be occupied; (*p.*) be busy (*en* with), be engaged (*en* in); *teleph.* be engaged.
ocurrencia *f* occurrence; incident; (*chiste*) witty remark; (bright) idea; **ocurrente** witty; **ocurrir** [3a] happen, occur; **~se:** *se le ocurrió inf.* it occurred to him to *inf.*; he took it into his head to *inf.*
ochenta eighty; **ochentón** *adj. a. su. m,* **-a** *f* F octogenarian; **ocho** eight (*a. su.*); (*fecha*) eighth; *las* ~ eight o'clock; **ochocientos** eight hundred.
oda *f* ode.
odiar [1b] hate; **odio** *m* hatred; ill will; *~-amor* love-hate; ~ *de sangre* feud; *tener* ~ *a* hate; **odioso** odious, hateful; nasty.
odontología *f* odontology 🕮, dentistry.
odorífero sweet-smelling, odoriferous.
odre *m* wineskin; heavy drinker.
oeste 1. *parte* west(ern); *dirección* westerly; *viento* west(erly); **2.** *m* west.
ofender [2a] offend; wrong; *reputación etc.* injure; *vista etc.* hurt; (*injuriar*) insult; **~se** take offense (*de, por* at); take exception (*por* to); **ofensa** *f* offence; insult; **ofensiva** *f* offensive; *tomar la* ~ take the offensive; **ofensivo** offensive (*a.* ⚔); disgusting; (*grosero*) rude; **ofensor** *m,* **-a** *f* offender.
oferta *f* offer (*a.* ☿); proposal, proposition; ☿ tender, bid; ~ *y demanda* supply and demand; ☿ *en* ~ on offer; **ofertorio** *m* offertory.
office ['ofis] *m* pantry.
offset [of'set] *m typ.* offset.
oficial 1. official; **2.** *m* official, officer (*a.* ⚔); (*obrero*) skilled worker; journeyman; clerk *en oficina*; ~ *del día* orderly officer; ~ *de enlace* liaison officer; ~ *mayor* chief clerk; ~ *médico* medical officer; ⚓ *primer* ~ mate; **oficiala** *f* (*obrera*) skilled woman worker; clerk *en oficina*; **oficialidad** *f* officers; **oficiar** [1b] officiate (*de* as); **oficina** *f* office; ⚔ orderly room; *pharm.* laboratory; ⊕ workshop; ~ *de informacion*(*es*) information bureau; **oficinal** officinal; **oficinesco** office *attr.*; clerical; white-collar; **oficinista** *m/f* office worker, clerk; white-collar worker; **oficio** *m* (*profesión*) occupation; ⊕ craft, trade; (*papel*) function; (*cargo*) office; *eccl.* ~ (*divino*) (divine) service; *buenos* **~s** *pl.* good offices; *Santo* ♀ Inquisition, Holy Office; *de* ~ by trade, by pro-

fession; *miembro* ex officio; (*adv.*) officially; **oficioso** diligent; helpful; *b.s.* officious; (*no oficial*) informal, unofficial.
ofrecer [2d] *mst* offer; present; *bienvenida* extend; *gracias* give, offer; *respetos* pay; **~se** offer o.s.; volunteer; *~ a inf.* offer to *inf.*; **ofrecimiento** *m* offer(ing); **ofrenda** *f eccl.* offering; **ofrendar** [1a] give, contribute.
oftalmía *f* ophthalmia; **oftálmico** ophthalmic; **oftalmólogo** *m* ophthalmologist.
ofuscar [1g] dazzle; *fig.* mystify, confuse; *fama* dim.
ogro *m* ogre.
¡oh! o!, oh!
ohmio *m* ohm.
oída *f* hearing; *de ~s* by hearsay; **oído** *m* hearing; *anat.*, ♪ ear; ♪ *de ~* by ear; *aguzar los ~s* prick up one's ears; *dar ~s* listen (*a* to); *decir al ~ a* whisper to; *prestar ~ a* give ear to; *ser todo ~s* be all ears; **oidor** *m* † judge; **oigo** *v.* *oír*; **oír** [3q] hear; (*atender*) listen (to); *misa* attend, go to; *~ decir que* hear that; *~ hablar de* hear about, hear of; *¡oye!*, *¡oiga!* listen!; (*llamando*) hi!, hey!; (*sorpresa*) I say!; (*rechazando*) the very idea!; *¡oiga! teleph.* hullo!
ojal *m* buttonhole, eyelet.
¡ojalá! **1.** *int.* if only it would! *etc.*; no such luck!; **2.** *cj.* *~* (*que*) if only ...!; ... I hope that; *¡~ pudiera!* I wish I could!
ojazo: *echar los ~s a* ogle, make eyes at; **ojeada** *f* glance; *echar una ~ a* glance at; **ojear** [1a] eye, stare at; *hunt.* beat; **ojeras** *f/pl.* rings under the eyes; **ojeriza** *f* spite, ill will; *tener ~ a* have a grudge against; **ojeroso** seedy; **ojete** *m sew.* eyelet; **ojinegro** black-eyed.
ojiva *f* ogive; **ojival** ogival.
ojo *m* eye (*a. fig.*); span *de puente*; *~* (*de la cerradura*) keyhole; *¡~!* look out!; (*mucho*) *~ con* be very careful about, beware of; *¡~, mancha!* wet paint!, fresh paint!; *a los ~s de* in the eyes of; *a ~s cerrados* on trust; *a ~s vistas* publicly; *con buenos ~s* favorably; *en un abrir y cerrar de ~s* in the twinkling of an eye; *avivar el ~* be on the qui vive; F *costar un ~ de la cara* cost a small fortune; *echar el ~ a* have one's eye on; *guiñar el ~* wink (*a* at); turn a blind eye (*a* on); *hacer del ~* wink; *no pegar los ~s* not get a wink of sleep; *tener ~* go very carefully, keep one's wits about one; **ojuelos** *m/pl.* (bright) eyes.
ola *f* wave; *~ de calor* heat wave; *~ de frío* cold wave; *~ de marea* tidal wave; *batir las ~s* ply the seas.
¡olé! bravo!
oleada *f* ⚓ big wave; (*movimiento*) surge, swell; *fig.* wave *de huelgas etc.*
oleaginoso oily, oleaginous 🕮.
oleaje *m* surge, swell, surf.
óleo *m paint.*, *eccl.* oil; (*cuadro*) oil-painting; *al ~ pintura* oil *attr.*, *pintar* in oils; **oleoducto** *m* pipeline; **oleografía** *f* oleograph.
oler [2i] smell (*a* of, like); **olfatear** [1a] sniff, smell, scent (out; *a. fig.*); *fig.* nose out; **olfativo** olfactory; **olfato** *m* (sense of) smell; scent; **olfatorio** olfactory.
oligarquía *f* oligarchy.
olimpíada *f* Olympiad; **olímpico** Olympian; *v. juego.*
oliscar [1g] *v/t.* smell, sniff; *fig.* look into; *v/i.* smell (bad).
oliva *f* olive; **olivar** *m* olive grove; **olivo** *m* olive (tree); *tomar el ~ taurino*: duck behind the barrier; F beat it.
olmo *m* elm (tree).
olor *m* smell; odor; scent; *mal ~* stink, bad smell; **oloroso** sweet-scented, fragrant.
olvidadizo forgetful, absent-minded; **olvidado** forgetful; *~ de* forgetful of, oblivious of (*or* to); **olvidar** [1a] forget; leave behind; omit; **~se** (*propasarse*) forget o.s.; *~ de* = *v/t.*; *~ de inf.* forget to *inf.*; neglect to *inf.*; *se me olvidó* I forgot; **olvido** *m* (*estado*) forgetfulness; oblivion; omission, slip.
olla *f* pot, pan; (*guisado*) stew; pool *de río*; *mount.* chimney; *~ podrida* stew; *fig.* hodgepodge; *~ de presión* pressure cooker.
ombligo *m* navel; middle, center; F *encogérsele a uno el ~* have cold feet.
ominoso ominous; (*terrible*) awful, dreadful.
omisión *f* omission; failure (*de inf.* to *inf.*); (*dejadez*) neglect; **omitir** [3a] leave out, miss out, omit.
omni...: **~potencia** *f* omnipotence;

~**potente** omnipotent; ~**presencia** *f* omnipresence; ~**presente** omnipresent; ~**sciencia** *f* omniscience; ~**sciente,** ~**scio** omniscient; **omnívoro** omnivorous.
omóplato *m* shoulder blade.
once eleven (*a. su.*); (*fecha*) eleventh; *las* ~ eleven o'clock; **onceno** eleventh.
onda *f* wave (*a. phys., radio*); ~ *corta* shortwave; *de* ~ *corta* shortwave *attr.*; ~ *larga* long wave; ~ *luminosa* light wave; *radio*: ~ *portadora* carrier; ~ *sonora* sound wave; **ondeante** *superficie* undulating; *bandera* waving; **ondear** [1a] *v/t. pelo* wave; *sew.* pink; *v/i.* (*agua*) ripple; (*movimiento*) undulate; (*bandera etc.*) flutter, wave; (*pelo*) stream *al viento*, flow; ~**se** wave; swing; **ondímetro** *m* wavemeter; **ondulación** *f* undulation; wave (*a. pelo*), ripple; ~ *permanente* permanent wave; **ondulado** wavy; *camino* uneven; *terreno* rolling, undulating; *hierro, papel* corrugated; **ondulante** = *ondeante*; **ondular** [1a] = *ondear*; **ondulatorio** undulatory.
oneroso onerous, burdensome.
ónice *m* onyx.
onomástico **1.** name *attr.*, of names; **2.** *m* (*a. fiesta* ~*a*) saint's day; *approx.* birthday.
onomatopeya *f* onomatopoeia.
onubense *adj. a. su. m/f* (native) of Huelva.
onza *f* ounce (*a. zo.*).
opacidad *f* opacity; **opaco** opaque.
opalescente opalescent; **ópalo** *m* opal.
opción *f* option (*a* on); ~ *cero* zero option; *en* ~ as an option; **opcional** optional.
ópera *f* opera; ~ *semiseria* light opera; ~ *seria* grand opera.
operación *f* operation; **operador** *m*, **-a** *f cine etc.*: operator; ⚕ surgeon; **operar** [1a] *v/t.* ⚕ operate on (*de* for); *v/i.* operate; ~**se** ⚕ have an operation (*de* for); **operario** *m*, **a** *f* operative; workman; ~ *de máquina* machinist; **operativo** operative.
opereta *f* operetta, light opera.
opiata *f*, **opiato** *adj. a. su. m* opiate.
opinar [1a] think; ~ *que* be of the opinion that, judge that; **opinión** *f* opinion; ~ *pública* public opinion.
opio *m* opium.
oponer [2r] *dique etc.* set up (*a* against); *objeción etc.* raise (*a* to); *resistencia* offer; *dos pareceres* contrast; ~ *a adversario* pit against; ~ *A a B* play off A against B; ~**se** *a* oppose, be opposed to; defy; resist; *cátedra etc.* put in for.
oportunidad *f* opportunity (*de inf.* of *ger.*, to *inf.*), chance; (*lo oportuno*) opportuneness, expediency; **oportunismo** *m* opportunism; **oportunista** *m/f* opportunist; **oportuno** timely, opportune; expedient; apposite.
oposición *f* opposition; (*a.* ~*es pl.*) examination, competition (*a* for); **opositor** *m*, **-a** *f* competitor, candidate (*a* for).
opresión *f* oppression; oppressiveness; **opresivo** oppressive; **opresor** *m*, **-a** *f* oppressor; **oprimir** [3a] oppress; squeeze, press *con presión*; (*vestido*) be too tight for.
oprobio *m* shame, opprobrium; **oprobioso** shameful, opprobrious.
optar [1a] choose, decide (*entre* between; *por inf.* to *inf.*).
óptica *f* optics; **óptico** **1.** optic(al); **2.** *m* optician.
optimismo *m* optimism; **optimista** **1.** optimistic, hopeful; **2.** *m/f* optimist.
óptimo very good; optimum.
opuesto ♀, *lado* opposite; *opinión etc.* contrary, opposing.
opugnar [1a] attack.
opulencia *f* opulence, affluence; *vivir en la* ~ live in luxury; **opulento** opulent, rich; luxurious.
opúsculo *m* booklet, short work, tract.
oquedad *f* hollow; *fig.* hollowness.
ora: ~ ... ~ now ... now, now ... then.
oración *f* oration, speech; *eccl.* prayer; *gr.* sentence; **oráculo** *m* oracle; **orador** *m*, **-a** *f* orator; speaker; **oral** oral; **orar** [1a] speak, make a speech; *eccl.* pray (*a* to, *por* for).
orate *m/f* lunatic (*a.* F).
oratoria *f* oratory; **oratorio** **1.** oratorical; **2.** *m* ♪ oratorio; *eccl.* oratory.
orbe *m* orb; (*mundo*) world; **órbita** *f*

orbit (*a. fig.*); *entrar en* ~ go into orbit; **orbital** orbital.

orca *f* grampus.

órdago: F *de* ~ swell, neat.

ordalías *f/pl. hist.* (trial by) ordeal.

orden[1] *m* order; ~ *de colocación* word order; ~ *del día* agenda; ~ *público* law and order; *del* ~ *de* of the order of; *en* ~, *por (su)* ~ in order; *fuera de* ~ out of order (*a. parl.*); out of turn; *llamar al* ~ call to order; *poner en* ~ put into order; tidy up.

orden[2] *f mst* order; ⚖ *a.* writ, warrant; ~ *de allanamiento* search warrant; ⚔ ~ *del día* order of the day; ☤ ~ *de pago* money order; ☤ *a la* ~ to order; *hasta nueva* ~ till further orders; *por* ~ *de* on the orders of, by order of; *estar a las* ~*es de* be at *s.o.'s* service.

ordenación *f* order; arrangement; *eccl.* ordination; **ordenada** *f* ordinate; **ordenado** orderly, tidy; methodical; **ordenador** *m* ⊕ computer; ~ *de viaje* on-board computer; **ordenancista** *m* disciplinarian, martinet; **ordenanza 1.** *f* ordinance; decree; **2.** *m* ⚔ orderly, batman; **ordenar** [1a] (*arreglar*) arrange, order; marshal; (*poner en orden*) put into order; (*mandar*) order (*inf.* to *inf.*); *eccl.* ordain; ~**se** take (holy) orders.

ordeñadora *f* ⊕ milking machine; **ordeñar** [1a] milk; **ordeño** *m* milking.

ordinal *adj. a. su. m* ordinal.

ordinariez *f* commonness, coarseness; **ordinario** ordinary; usual; (*sin distinción*) ordinary, mediocre; (*vulgar*) common, coarse; *de* ~ usually.

orear [1a] air; ~**se** take a breather.

orégano *m* marjoram.

oreja *f* ear; (*lengüeta*) tab; (*asa*) lug, handle; *aguzar las* ~*s* prick up one's ears; **orejera** *f* ear flap; **orejeta** *f* ⊕ lug; **orejudo** big-eared, with big ears.

orfanato *m* orphanage; **orfandad** *f* orphanage; orphanhood.

orfebre *m* goldsmith, silversmith; **orfebrería** *f* gold *etc.* work.

orfelinato *m S.Am.* orphanage.

orfeón *m* glee club, choral society.

orgánico organic; **organillero** *m* organ grinder; **organillo** *m* barrel organ, hurdy-gurdy; **organismo** *m biol. etc.* organism; *pol.* organization; **organista** *m/f* organist; **organización** *f* organization; ♀ *de las Naciones Unidas* (*ONU*) United Nations (UN); **organizador** *m*, **-a** *f* organizer; **organizar** [1f] organize; **órgano** *m* organ; (*medio*) means, medium.

orgía *f* orgy.

orgullo *m* pride; (*arrogancia*) haughtiness, arrogance; **orgulloso** proud; haughty.

orientación *f* orientation; positioning; prospect *hacia sur etc.*; training; ⚓ trim; ~ *sur* southerly aspect, facing south; **oriental 1.** oriental; eastern; **2.** *m/f* oriental; **orientar** [1a] orientate; position; (*dirigir*) guide; train *para profesión*; ⚓ trim; *está orientado hacia el oeste* it faces (*or* looks, points) west; ~**se** *fig.* take one's bearings; **oriente** *m* east; ♀ Orient (*v. Apéndice*).

orificio *m* orifice; vent.

origen *m* origin; source; *dar* ~ *a* give rise to; **original 1.** original; novel; (*singular*) odd, eccentric; **2.** *m* original (*a. p.*); (*p.*) character; *typ.* copy; **originalidad** *f* originality; eccentricity; **originar(se)** [1a] originate; start, cause; **originario:** ~ *de* native to.

orilla *f* edge (*a. sew.*); bank *de río*; side *de lago*; shore *de mar*; rim *de taza*; *sew.* border, hem; ~ *del mar* seashore; ~*s pl. S.Am.* outskirts (of the city); *a* ~*s de* on the banks of; **orillar** [1a] *sew.* edge, trim (*de* with); *lago etc.* skirt; *asunto* touch briefly on; **orillo** *m* selvage, list.

orín *m* rust; *tomarse de* ~ get rusty.

orina *f* urine; **orinal** *m* chamber pot; **orinar** [1a] urinate; **orines** *m/pl.* urine.

oriundo: ~ *de* native to; *ser* ~ *de* come from, be a native of.

orla *f* border, edging, fringe; **orlar** [1a] border, edge (*de* with).

ornamental ornamental; **ornamentar** [1a] adorn; **ornamento** *m* ornament; adornment; ~*s pl. eccl.* ornaments; *fig.* moral qualities; **ornar** [1a] adorn, decorate; **ornato** *m* adornment, decoration.

ornitología *f* ornithology; **orni-**

tológico ornithological; **ornitólogo** *m* ornithologist.
oro *m* gold; *naipes*: *~s pl.* diamonds; *~ en barras* bullion; *~ batido* gold leaf; *~ laminado* rolled gold; *~ molido* ormulu; F *como un ~* spick and span; *de ~* gold(en).
oropel *m* tinsel (*a. fig.*); *de ~* tawdry; flashy; *gastar mucho ~* put on a bold front.
oropéndola *f* (golden) oriole.
orquesta *f* orchestra; **orquestal** orchestral; **orquestar** [1a] orchestrate.
orquídea *f* orchid, orchis.
ortiga *f* (stinging) nettle.
orto...: **~doncia** orthodontics; *aparato de ~* orthodontic appliance, braces; **~doxia** *f* orthodoxy; **~doxo** orthodox; sound; **~grafía** *f* spelling, orthography 🕮; **~gráfico** orthographic(al); **~pedia** *f* orthopedics; **~pédico** orthopedic; **~pedista** *m/f* orthopedist.
oruga *f zo.* caterpillar; ⚘ rocket.
orujo *m* bagasse of grapes *or* olives (*skins and stones after pressing*).
orza *f* ⚓ luff(ing); **orzar** [1f] luff.
orzuelo *m* ⚕ sty.
os (*acc.*) you; (*dat.*) (to) you; (*reflexivo*) (to) yourselves; (*recíproco*) (to) each other.
osadía *f* daring; **osado** daring, bold.
osamenta *f* bones; skeleton.
osar [1a] dare (*inf.* to *inf.*).
osario *m* ossuary, charnel house.
oscilación *f* oscillation, swing *etc*; **oscilador** *m* oscillator; **oscilar** [1a] oscillate, swing, sway; (*luz*) blink; *fig.* waver; **oscilatorio** oscillatory.
ósculo *m lit.* kiss.
oscurantismo *m* obscurantism; **oscurecer** [2d] *v/t.* obscure, darken; *fig.* confuse, fog; *fama* tarnish; *v/i.* get dark, grow dark; **oscuridad** *f* darkness; gloom, gloominess; *esp. fig.* obscurity; **oscuro** dark; gloomy; *esp. fig.* obscure; (*borroso*) indistinct; *a ~as* in the dark (*a. fig.*).
óseo bony, osseous 🕮; **osificación** *f* ossification; **osificar(se)** [1g] ossify.
oso *m* bear; *~ blanco* polar bear; *~ gris* grizzly bear; F *hacer el ~* play the fool.
ostentación *f* ostentation; pomp, display; *hacer ~ de* show off, parade; **ostentar** [1a] show; *b.s.* show off, flaunt, display; **ostentativo**, **ostentoso** ostentatious.
osteología *f* osteology.
ostra *f* oyster; *fig.* (*p.*) fixture.
ostracismo *m* ostracism.
ostral *m* oyster bed.
otario *S.Am.* silly.
otear [1a] spy on, watch from above; *fig.* examine, look into.
otero *m* hill, knoll.
otomana *f* ottoman; **otomano** *adj. a. su. m*, **a** *f* Ottoman.
otoñada *f* fall (season), autumn time; **otoñal** autumnal, fall *attr.*; **otoño** *m* fall, autumn.
otorgamiento *m* consent; (*acto*) granting; ⚖ execution; **otorgar** [1h] grant, give (*a* to); confer (*a* on); ⚖ execute.
otramente otherwise; in a different way; **otro 1.** *adj.* other; another; *thea.* *¡~a!* encore!; *~ que* other than; *no ~ que* no less a person *etc.* than; F *¡ésa es ~a!* here we go again!; *los tiempos son ~s* times have changed; *ser muy ~* be quite changed; **2.** *pron.* another one; *el ~* the other (one); *los ~s* the others, the rest; *algún ~* somebody else; *~ me dijo que* somebody else told me that; *como dijo el ~* as someone said; *v.* *alguno, tanto, uno etc.*
ovación *f* ovation; **ovacionar** [1a] applaud, cheer.
oval(ado) oval; **óvalo** *m* oval.
ovario *m biol.* ovary.
oveja *f* sheep, ewe; *cargar con la ~ muerta* be left holding the baby; **ovejuno** sheep *attr.*
ovetense *adj. a. su. m/f* (native) of Oviedo.
oviforme egg-shaped, oviform 🕮.
ovillar [1a] wind; **~se** curl up into a ball; **ovillo** *m* ball of wool *etc.*; *fig.* tangle; *hacerse un ~* curl up; cower *con miedo*; get tied up in knots *hablando*.
ovíparo oviparous; **ovoide** *adj. a. su. m* ovoid.
óvulo *m* ovum.
oxálico oxalic.
oxear [1a] shoo.
oxiacetilénico oxyacetylene *attr.*

oxidado rusty; ⚗ oxidized; **oxidar** [1a] ⚗ oxidize; rust; **~se** go rusty, get rusty (*a. fig.*); **óxido** *m* oxide; **oxigenar** [1a] oxygenate; **oxígeno** *m* oxygen.

¡oxte! shoo!; hop it!; *sin decir ~ ni moxte* without a word.

oye, oyendo *etc. v.* *oír*; **oyente** *m/f* listener, hearer.

ozono *m* ozone.

P

pabellón *m* (*edificio*) pavilion; summerhouse, hut *en jardín etc.*; block *de hospital etc.*; (*tienda*) bell tent; (*colgadura*) canopy, hangings; (*bandera*) flag; ⚔ stack; ♪ bell; *anat.* outer ear; ~ *de caza* shooting box.

pábilo *m*, **pabilo** *m* wick; (*quemado*) snuff.

pábulo *m fig.* encouragement, fuel; food *para pensamiento*; *dar* ~ *a* encourage, add fuel to.

paca *f* bale.

pacato peaceable; timid.

pacer [2d] *v/t. hierba* eat; *ganado* graze; *v/i.* graze.

paciencia *f* patience; forbearance; *¡~ y barajar!* keep trying!, don't give up!; *perder la* ~ lose one's temper; **paciente** *adj. a. su. m/f* patient; **pacienzudo** patient; long-suffering.

pacificación *f* pacification; peace (of mind), calm; **pacificador** *m*, **-a** *f* peacemaker; **pacificar** [1g] pacify; **~se** calm down; **pacífico** pacific, peaceable; peace-loving; **pacifismo** *m* pacifism; **pacifista** *adj. a. su. m/f* pacifist.

pacotilla *f fig.* trash; *de* ~ shoddy, catchpenny; F *hacer su* ~ make a modest profit, be doing nicely; F *hacer la* ~ *a* brown-nose, toady.

pactar [1a] stipulate, agree to, contract for; covenant; **pacto** *m* pact, covenant, agreement.

pachón **1.** *S.Am.* woolly; shaggy; **2.** *m* F dull type; (*perro*) pointer.

pachorra *f* F slowness, laziness; **pachorrudo** F slow, sluggish.

pachucho ⚘ overripe; F droopy, off-color, poorly.

padecer [2d] suffer (*de* from); endure; *error etc.* labor under, be a victim of; **padecimiento** *m* suffering.

padrastro *m* stepfather; *fig.* obstacle; *anat.* hangnail; **padrazo** *m* F indulgent father; **padre** *m* father (*a. eccl.*); *zo.* sire; (*tras nombre*) senior, the elder; *~s pl.* parents, father and mother; ancestors; ~ *espiritual* confessor; ~ *de familia* father of a family, man with family responsibilities; ≈ *Nuestro* Lord's Prayer; ≈ *Santo* Holy Father, Pope; F *de ~ y muy señor mío* terrific, a ... and a half; **padrino** *m eccl.* godfather, best man *en boda*; second *en duelo*; sponsor, patron *de empresa*.

padrón *m* (*nómina*) poll, census; register *de miembros etc.*; ⊕ *etc.* pattern; ⚠ commemorative column; *fig.* stain; F indulgent father.

paella *f Valencian rice dish with meat, shellfish etc.*

¡paf! bang!, plop!

paga *f* payment; (*sueldo*) pay, wages; fee; F *mala* ~ bad payer; **pagadero** payable, due; **pagado:** *~ de sí mismo* self-satisfied, smug; *estamos ~s* we are quits; **pagador** *m*, **-a** *f* payer; ⚔ (*oficial*) ~ paymaster.

paganismo *m* paganism; **pagano** *adj. a. su. m*, **a** *f* pagan, heathen.

pagar [1h] pay; repay; pay of[f] *compra* pay for; *favor, visita* retur[n] *fig.* atone for; *¡me las pagar[ás]* I'll pay you out for this!; *a* ~ postage due; *a* ~, *por* ~ *cuent[a]* unpaid; **~se** *de* be pleased with, take a liking to; ~ *de sí mismo* be conceited, be smug; **pagaré** *m* promissory note, IOU.

página *f* page; **paginación** *f* pagination; **paginar** [1a] paginate.

pago[1] **1.** *m* payment; repayment; *fig.* return, reward; ~ *anticipado* advance payment; ~ *al contado* cash (payment); ~ *a cuenta* payment on account; ~ *en especie* payment in kind; ~ *a plazos* deferred payment; ~ *contra recepción* cash on delivery; *en* ~ *de* in payment for; **2.** F paid, quits.

pago[2] *m* district; estate.

pagoda *f* pagoda.

pagote *m* F scapegoat.

paila *f* large pan.

país *m* country; land, region; *del* ~ *vino etc.* local; **paisaje** *m* landscape; countryside; scene(ry); **paisajista** *m/f* landscape painter; **paisanaje** *m* civil population; **paisano 1.** of the same country; **2.** *m*, **a** *f* fellow countryman; ⚔ civilian; *S.Am.* peasant; *de* ~ *soldado* in mufti, in civvies F; *policía* in plain clothes.

paja *f* straw; *fig.* trash; *lit.* padding; *de* ~ straw *attr.*; F *hombre de* ~ stooge; **pajar** *m* straw loft; rick.

pájara *f zo.* (hen) bird; (*cometa*) paper kite; F sharp one; ~ *pinta* forfeits; **pajarear** [1a] *fig.* loaf, loiter; *S.Am.* (*caballo*) shy; **pajarera** *f* aviary; **pajarero 1.** F *p.* merry, bright; *vestido* gaudy; **2.** *m* bird fancier; (*cazador*) bird catcher; **pajarilla** *f* paper kite; F *alegrárselas a uno las* ~*s* laugh o.s. silly; **pajarita** *f* paper kite, paper bird; **pajarito** *m* fledgling; **pájaro** *m* bird; F chap; F (*astuto*) clever fellow; F ~ *de cuenta* bigwig; ~ *carpintero* woodpecker; ~ *mosca* hummingbird; **pajarota** *f* F hoax; **pajarraco** *m* F slyboots.

paje *m* page; ⚓ cabin boy.

pajera *f* straw loft; **pajita** *f* (drinking) straw; **pajizo** straw *attr.*; straw-colored; **pajuela** *f* spill.

pala *f* shovel, spade; scoop; blade *de remo, hélice etc.*; *deportes*: bat, racquet; upper(s) *de zapato*; F wiliness.

palabra *f* word; (*facultad*) (power of) speech; F ¡~! honestly!, no kidding!; ~ *de casamiento* engagement (to marry); ~ *de honor* word of honor; ~*s pl. mayores* angry words; *a media* ~ at the least hint; ⚔ *bajo* ~ on parole; *de* ~ by word of mouth; *en una* ~ in a word; *por* ~ word for word, verbatim; *coger a uno la* ~ take a p. at his word; *pedir la* ~ ask to be allowed to speak; *tener la* ~ have (*or* hold) the floor; **palabrería** *f* F wordiness; verbiage; palaver; **palabrero 1.** windy, wordy; **2.** *m*, **a** *f* windbag; **palabrota** *f* rude word, swearword.

palaciano, palaciego 1. palace *attr.*, court *attr.*; **2.** *m* courtier; **palacio** *m* palace; ~ *de justicia* courthouse; ~ *municipal* city hall.

palada *f* shovelful; stroke *de remo.*

paladar *m* palate (*a. fig.*), roof of the mouth; *fig.* taste; **paladear** [1a] taste (with pleasure), relish.

paladín *m hist.* paladin; champion.

paladino open, public, clear.

palafrén *m* palfrey.

palanca *f* lever; crowbar; ~ *de freno* brake lever; ~ *de mando* control column; F *mover* ~*s* pull strings.

palangana *f* washbasin; **palanganero** *m* washstand.

palanqueta *f* small lever; jemmy *de ladrón.*

palatino *anat.* palatal; *pol.* palatine, palace *attr.*

palco *m* box; ~ *de proscenio* stage box; ~ *escénico* stage.

palenque *m* (*defensa*) palisade; (*público*) arena, ring.

paleografía *f* pal(a)eography.

paleontología *f* pal(a)eontology.

palestino *adj. a. su. m*, **a** *f* Palestinian.

palestra *f* arena; *fig.* lists; *salir a* ~ *fig.* take the floor (*or* field).

paleta *f* small shovel, scoop; (*badil*) fire shovel; ⚠ trowel; *paint.* palette; blade, vane, bucket *de rueda etc.*; **paletilla** *f* shoulder blade.

paleto *m zo.* fallow deer; F yokel, country bumpkin.

paliar [1b] palliate, alleviate; *fig.* conceal, gloss over; **paliativo 1.** palliative; *fig.* concealing; **2.** *m* palliative.

palidecer [2d] (turn) pale; **palidez** *f* paleness, pallor *etc.*; **pálido** pale, pallid; wan; sickly.

palillo *m* toothpick; ♪ drumstick; ~*s pl.* castanets; chopsticks; F trifles.

palinodia *f*: *cantar la* ~ recant.

palio *m* cloak; canopy; *eccl.* pall, pallium.

palique *m* F chat; small talk, chitchat; *estar de* ~ have a chat.

paliza *f* beating, thrashing; drubbing (*a. fig.*).

palizada *f* fenced enclosure; (*defensa*) stockade.

palma *f* ⚘, *anat. a. fig.* palm; *llevarse la* ~ carry off the palm, triumph; **palmada** *f* slap, pat *en el hombro etc.*; clapping, applause; *dar* ~*s* clap, applaud; **palmadita** *f* pat, tap.

palmar[1] *m* ⚘ palm grove.

palmar[2], **palmario** obvious, self-evident; patent.

palmatoria *f* candlestick; cane *para castigar.*

palmeado webbed.
palmear [1a] clap.
palmera *f* palm (tree).
palmeta *f* cane; (*acto*) caning; *ganar la ~ fig.* get in first; **palmetazo** *m* caning; *fig.* slap in the face.
palmípedo webfooted.
palmo *m* span; *avanzar ~ a ~* go forward inch by inch; *conocer a ~s* (*or ~ a ~*) know every inch of; *crecer a ~s* shoot up.
palmotear [1a] clap; **palmoteo** *m* applause.
palo *m* stick; pole; (*material*) wood; handle *de escoba etc.*; (golf *etc.*) club; ⚓ mast; ⚓ spar; (*golpe*) blow with a stick; *naipes*: suit; *~ dulce* liquorice root; *~ mayor* mainmast; *~ santo* lignum vitae; *dar ~s de ciego* lash out wildly; *dar de ~s* beat; *servir del ~* follow suit.
paloma *f* dove, pigeon; *fig.* meek and mild person; *fig. a. pol.* dove; *~s pl.* ⚓ whitecaps; *~ mensajera* carrier pigeon; *~ torcaz* woodpigeon; **palomar** *m* dovecot(e); **palomino** *m* young pigeon; **palomitas** *f/pl.* popcorn; **palomo** *m* (cock) pigeon.
palotada: F *no dar ~* not do a stroke.
palote *m* ♪ drumstick; downstroke *de pluma*, pothook; **palotear** [1a] F wrangle; **paloteo** *m* F wrangle.
palpable palpable; **palpar** [1a] touch, feel; (*a tientas*) grope along, feel one's way; *sl.* frisk.
palpitación *f* palpitation *etc.*; **palpitante** palpitating, throbbing; *cuestión* burning; **palpitar** [1a] palpitate, throb; flutter *de emoción*; (*estremecerse*) quiver.
palúdico marshy; ⚕ marsh *attr.*, malarial; **paludismo** *m* malaria.
palurdo 1. rustic; coarse; **2.** *m* rustic, yokel; *b.s.* lout.
palustre marshy.
pamema *f* F trifle; *~s pl.* (*cuentas*) humbug, nonsense; (*halagos*) wheedling; *¡déjate de ~s!* stop all that nonsense!
pampas *f/pl. S.Am.* pampas, prairie.
pámpana: F *zurrar la ~ a* tan.
pámpano *m* vine tendril; vine leaf.
pamplina *f* ⚘ chickweed; F silly remark, nonsense.
pan¹ *m* (*en general*) bread; loaf; ⚘ wheat; ⊕ gold leaf, silver leaf; cake *de jabón*; *~ de azúcar* sugar loaf; F *~ comido* chicken feed; *~ de cuco* stonecrop; *de ~ llevar tierra* arable; *con su ~ se lo coma* that's his problem, let him get on with it; *ganarse el ~* earn a living; *llamar al ~ ~ y al vino vino* call a spade a spade; F *venderse como ~ bendito* go like hot cakes.
pan² ... pan ... (*all*).
pana¹ *f* velveteen, corduroy.
pana² *f mot.* breakdown.
panacea *f* panacea, cure-all.
panadería *f* bakery, bakehouse; baker's (shop); **panadero** *m*, **a** *f* baker.
panadizo *m* ⚕ whitlow; F sickly sort.
panal *m* honeycomb.
panameño *adj. a. su. m*, **a** *f* Panamanian.
panamericano Pan-American.
pancarta *f* placard.
páncreas *m* pancreas.
pandear(se) [1a] bulge, warp, sag.
pandemonio *m* pandemonium.
pandeo *m* bulge, bulging.
pandereta *f* tambourine; **pandero** *m* tambourine; F idiot.
pandilla *f* set; *b.s.* gang, clique; ☦ ring; **pandillero** *m S.Am.* gangster.
pandorga *f* kite; F fat woman.
panecillo *m* roll.
panegírico *m* panegyric.
panel *m* panel; plywood.
panfleto *m* lampoon; pamphlet.
paniaguado *m* protégé; henchman.
pánico *adj. a. su. m* panic.
panizo *m* millet; maize.
panorama *m* panorama; vista; *paint.*, *phot.* view; **panoramicar** [1g] *cine*: pan; **panorámico** panoramic; *punto ~* viewpoint, vantage point.
pantalón *m*, *~es pl.* trousers, pants; (*de mujer*, *exterior*) slacks; (*interior*) knickers; *~es pl. cortos* shorts.
pantalla *f* screen (*a. cine*); (lamp)shade; *~ acústica* loudspeaker; *llevar a la ~* film; *pequeña ~* TV screen.
pantanal *m* marshland; **pantano** *m* marsh, bog, swamp; (*artificial*) reservoir; *fig.* obstacle; **pantanoso** marshy, swampy.
panteísmo *m* pantheism; **panteísta** pantheistic; **panteón** *m* pantheon.
pantera *f* panther.

pantomima *f* pantomime, dumb show.
pantoque *m* bilge; *agua de* ~ bilge water.
pantorrilla *f* calf (of the leg); **pantorrilludo** fat in the leg.
pantufla *f*, **pantuflo** *m* slipper.
panza *f* paunch, belly; **panzada** *f* F bellyful; *darse una* ~ have a blowout; **panzón** F, **panzudo** F paunchy, pot-bellied.
pañal *m* diaper *de niño*; tail *de camisa*; ~*es pl.* swaddling clothes; *fig.* early stages, infancy.
pañero *m* draper, clothier.
pañete *m* light cloth; ~*s pl.* shorts, trunks.
pañito *m*: ~ *de adorno* doily.
paño *m* cloth; stuff; (*medida*) breadth of cloth; duster, rag *para limpiar*; mist, cloudiness *en espejo etc.*; *sew.* panel; ~ *de cocina* dishcloth; ~ *higiénico* sanitary napkin; ~ *de lágrimas* stand-by; ~ *de manos* towel; ~ *de mesa* tablecloth; ~ *mortuorio* pall; ~*s pl. calientes fig.* half-measures; ~*s pl. menores* F underclothes, undies; *al* ~ *thea.* off-stage; *conocer el* ~ know one's business.
pañol *m* ⚓ store room; ~ (*del agua*) water store; ~ (*del carbón*) bunker.
pañoleta *f* fichu; **pañolón** *m* shawl; **pañuelo** *m* handkerchief; (head)scarf; ~ *de hierbas* bandanna.
papa[1] *m* pope.
papa[2] *f esp. S.Am.* potato; F fake, hoax; F food, grub; *S.Am.* snap, cinch; *ni* ~ *S.Am.* nothing; ~*s pl.* pap, mushy food.
papá *m* F dad(dy), papa.
papada *f* double chin (*a.* **papadilla** *f*); dewlap *de animal*.
papado *m* papacy.
papagayo *m* parrot; (*p.*) chatterbox.
papaíto *m* F = *papá*.
papal[1] papal.
papal[2] *m S.Am.* potato field.
papalina *f* cap with ear flaps; bonnet; F binge.
papamoscas *m orn.* flycatcher; F (*a.* **papanatas** *m* F) simpleton, sucker.
papar [1a] swallow, gulp; F eat; F *fig.* pass over hurriedly.
paparrucha *f* F hoax; worthless book *etc.*
papel *m* paper; piece of paper; *thea.* part, role (*a. fig.*); ~*es pl.* (identification) papers; ~ *de calcar* tracing paper; ~ *carbón* carbon paper; ~ *de cebolla* onionskin; ~ *cuadriculado* squared paper; ~ *de embalar*, ~ *de envolver* brown paper, wrapping paper; ~ *de empapelar* wallpaper; ~ *del Estado* government bonds; ~ *de estaño* tinfoil; ~ *de estraza* strong wrapping paper; ~ *de excusado* toilet paper; ~ *de filtro* filter paper; ~ *de fumar* cigarette paper; ~ *higiénico* toilet paper, toilet roll; ~ *de lija* sandpaper; ~ *marquilla* demy; ~ *mojado fig.* scrap of paper; triviality; ~ *moneda* paper money; ~ *ondulado* corrugated paper; ~ *de paja de arroz* rice paper; ~ *pintado* wallpaper; ~ *de plata* silver paper; ~ *secante* blotting paper, blotter; ~ *de seda* tissue paper; ~ *sellado* stamped paper; ~ *transparente* tracing paper; ~ *viejo*, ~*es pl. usados* waste paper; *desempeñar un* ~, *hacer un* ~ play a part (*a. fig.*); *hacer* ~ cut a figure.
papelear [1a] rummage through papers; F make a splash; **papeleo** *m* red tape; **papelería** *f* stationery; (*tienda*) stationer's (shop); (*lío*) sheaf of papers; **papelerío** *m* paperwork; **papelero** *m* stationer; paper manufacturer; **papeleta** *f* slip, card; *pol.* voting paper; *escuela*: report; (*empeño*) pawn ticket; **papelillo** *m* cigarette; **papelón** *m* waste paper; (*cartón*) pasteboard; F impostor; **papelote** *m*, **papelucho** *m* worthless bit of paper.
papera *f* mumps; goiter.
papilla *f* pap; *fig.* guile, deceit.
papiro *m* papyrus.
papirotazo *m*, **papirote** *m* flick.
papismo *m* papistry, popery; **papista 1.** popish; **2.** *m/f* papist.
papo *m* dewlap; crop *de ave*; **papujado** F swollen, puffed up.
paquebote *m* packet(boat).
paquete *m* parcel (*a.* 📯), packet, pack(age); ⚓ packet(boat); F toff; ~*s pl. postales* parcel post; ⚔ F *meter un* ~ *a* put on a charge, punish.
par 1. ⅍ even; equal; **2.** *m* pair, couple; (*noble*) peer; ~ *de torsión* torque; ~*es o nones* odds or evens; *a* ~*es* in pairs; *al* ~ equally; together; *de* ~ *en* ~ wide open; *sin* ~ unparalleled; peerless; *no tener* ~ have no parallel; **3.** *f* par; *a la* ~

equally; at the same time; ✝ at par; *a la ~ que* at the same time as; *golf*: *5 bajo ~* 5 under par; *estar sobre la ~* be at a premium.

para a) *destino, uso, fin*: for, intended for; *un hotel ~ turistas* a hotel (intended) for tourists, a tourist hotel; *una taza ~ el té* a teacup; *lo traje ~ ti* I brought it for you; *nació ~ poeta* he was born to be a poet; *salir ~ Madrid* leave for Madrid; *decir ~ sí* say to o.s.; b) *tiempo*: *~ mañana* for tomorrow; by tomorrow; *quede ~ mañana* let it wait till tomorrow; *va ~ 9 años* (*p.*) he's nearly 9; (*suceso pasado*) it's nearly 9 years ago, it's getting on for 9 years; c) *relación*: (*a. ~ con*) to, towards; *era amable ~ (con) todos* he was kind to everyone; *no hay hombre grande ~ su ayuda de cámara* no man is a hero to (*or* in the eyes of) his valet; d) *contraste*: *~ niño, lo hace muy bien* he does it very well for a child; e) *~ inf.* (*fin*): (in order) to *inf.*; *ahorrar ~ comprar algo* save (in order) to buy s.t.; f) *~ inf.* (*resultado*): *lo encontró ~ volver a perderlo* he found it only to lose it again; g) *~ inf.* (*con bastante, demasiado*): *tengo bastante ~ vivir* I have enough to live on; *es demasiado bueno ~ hacer eso* he is too good to do a thing like that; h) *~ que* in order that, so that; i) *¿~ qué?* why?, for what purpose?; *¿~ qué sirve?* what's it for?; what's the use of ...?

parabién *m* congratulations; *dar el ~ a* congratulate.

parábola *f lit.* parable; ⚹ parabola; **parabólico** parabolic.

para...: **~brisas** *m* windscreen, windshield; **~caídas** *m* parachute; *lanzar en ~* parachute; *lanzarse en ~* parachute, bale out *en emergencia*; **~caidista** *m* parachutist; ⚔ paratrooper; **~choques** *m mot.* bumper; ⊕ shock absorber; 🚂 buffer.

parada *f* stop; (*acto*) stopping; (*lugar*) stop; shutdown, standstill *de industria*; relay *de caballos*; dam *para agua*; stake, bet *en juego*; ⚔ parade; *fenc.* parry; *~ discrecional* request stop; *~ de taxi* taxi stand; *~ en seco* sudden stop; *formar en ~* parade.

paradero *m* whereabouts; stop; *S.Am.* 🚂 halt.

paradigma *m* paradigm.

paradisíaco heavenly.

parado slow, inactive; motionless; *salida* standing; *p.* unemployed; *S.Am.* standing up; *S.Am.* proud.

paradoja *f* paradox; **paradójico** paradoxical.

parador *m* † inn; (*moderno*) tourist hotel; (*p.*) heavy gambler.

parafina *f* paraffin wax.

parafrasear [1a] paraphrase; **paráfrasis** *f* paraphrase.

paraguas *m* umbrella.

paraguay(an)o *adj. a. su. m*, **a** *f* Paraguayan.

paragüero *m* umbrella stand.

paraíso *m* paradise, heaven; *thea.* gods, gallery.

paraje *m* place, spot; state, condition, situation.

paralela *f* parallel line; **~s** *pl.* parallel bars; **paralelismo** *m* parallelism; **paralelo** *adj. a. su. m* parallel (*a. geog.*); ⚡ *en ~* in parallel; **paralelogramo** *m* parallelogram.

parálisis *f* paralysis; **paralítico** *adj. a. su. m*, **a** *f* paralytic; **paralizar** [1f] paralyze (*a. fig.*); **~se** become paralyzed (*a. fig.*); *fig.* come to a standstill; stagnate.

paramento *m* ornament; hangings; trappings *de caballo*; face *de piedra*; **~s** *pl. eccl.* vestments.

parámetro *m* parameter, established boundaries.

páramo *m* bleak plateau, moor (-land).

parangón *m* comparison; **parangonable** comparable; **parangonar** [1a] compare.

paranoia *f* paranoia.

paraninfo *m univ.* central hall.

parapetarse [1a] protect o.s., take shelter; **parapeto** *m* parapet, breastwork.

parar [1a] **1.** *v/t.* stop; *progreso* check; *atención* fix (en on); *dinero* stake; *fenc.* parry; *golpe, amenaza* ward off; **2.** *v/i.* stop; stay, put up (*en hotel* at); (*terminar*) end up; *~ en* result in; 🚂 run to; *sin ~* without stopping, without a pause; *ir a ~ a* finish up at, end up at; **3. ~se** stop; *mot. etc.* stop, pull up, draw up; (*trabajo etc.*) stop, come to a standstill; *S.Am.* stand up; *~ en* pay attention to.

pararrayos *m* lightning rod.

parasitario, parasítico parasitic, parasitical; **parásito 1.** parasitic (*de* on); **2.** parasite (*a. fig.*); *radio*: ~s *pl.* atmospherics, statics.
parasol *m* parasol.
paratifoidea *f* paratyphoid.
parcela *f* plot, small-holding; **parcelar** [1a] parcel out.
parcial partial, part ...; *p. etc.* partial, prejudiced, partisan; **parcialidad** *f* partiality, prejudice.
parco sparing (*en alabanzas etc.* of); frugal (*en comer* in); temperate.
parcómetro *m* parking meter.
parchar [1a] *S.Am.* mend, patch; **parche** *m* ⚕ sticking plaster; *mot.* patch; ♪ drum(head).
pardal *m* sparrow; F sly fellow.
¡pardiez! by Jove!
pardillo *m* brown cloth; (*p.*) yokel, rustic; *orn.* (*a.* ~ *común*) linnet; *gente del* ~ country folk.
pardo 1. brown; dun; dark-skinned; *esp. S.Am.* dark gray; *cielo* cloudy, overcast; **2.** *m S.Am.* mulatto; **pardusco** grayish.
parear [1a] match; pair (*a. biol.*); **~se** pair off.
parecer [2d] **1.** seem, look; (*presentarse*) appear, turn up; (*dejarse ver*) show; ~ *inf.* seem to *inf.*; *a lo que parece, según parece* apparently, evidently; ~ *bien* look well, look all right *por el aspecto*; seem right *por lo justo etc.*; *parece que va a llover* it looks as though (*or* it seems that) it's going to rain; *me parece que sí* I think so; *¿qué te parece?* what do you think (of it)?; *si te parece* if you wish; just as you like; **2. ~se** look alike; ~ *a* resemble, look like; *padre etc.* take after; **3.** *m* opinion, view; looks *de cara*; *a mi* ~ in my opinion; *al* ~ apparently, evidently; *mudar de* ~ change one's opinion.
parecido 1. similar; ~ *a* like; *bien* ~ good-looking; personable; *mal* ~ plain; **2.** *m* resemblance, similarity (*a* to).
pared *f* wall; ~es *pl.* house; *dejar pegado a la* ~ nonplus; ~ *medianera* party wall; ~ *por medio* next door; **paredaño** adjoining, next-door; **paredón** *m* thick wall.
pareja *f* pair, couple; (dancing) partner; pair of Civil Guards; ~s *pl.* pair *de naipes*; *correr* ~s be on a par, keep pace, go together (*con* with); **parejero** *m S.Am.* race horse; **parejo** equal; *juntura etc.* even, smooth, flush; *por* ~ on a par; *ir* ~s go neck and neck.
parentela *f* relationship; (*ps.*) relations; **parentesco** *m* relationship, kinship.
paréntesis *m* parenthesis; (*signo*) bracket; *entre* ~ *fig. adj.* parenthetic(al); *adv.* by the way, incidentally.
paria *m/f* pariah.
parián *m S.Am.* market.
paridad *f* parity; comparison.
pariente *m*, **a** *f* relation, relative; F *la* ~*a* the wife, the missus.
parietal parietal.
parihuela *f* stretcher.
parir [3a] *v/t.* give birth to, bear; *v/i.* give birth, be delivered; (*vaca*) calve (*y hay palabras parecidas para otros animales*).
parisién *adj.*, **parisiense** *adj. a. su. m/f* Parisian.
parla *f* chatter, gossip; **parlador** talkative; *ojos etc.* expressive.
parlamentar [1a] talk, converse; (*enemigos*) parley; **parlamentario 1.** parliamentary; **2.** *m* parliamentarian; member of parliament;
parlamento *m parl.* parliament; parley *entre enemigos*; *thea.*, ⚖ speech.
parlanchín *m*, **-a** *f* F chatterbox;
parlante talking; loudspeaker;
parlar [1a] chatter, talk (too much);
parlatorio *m* chat, talk; **parlero** *p.* garrulous; (*chismoso*) gossiping; *pájaro* talking, song *attr.*; *ojo* expressive; **parleta** *f* F small talk, idle talk;
parlotear [1a] prattle, run on; **parloteo** *m* prattle.
parné *m sl.* tin, dough.
paro[1] *m orn.* tit.
paro[2] *m* stoppage, standstill; ~ (*forzoso*) unemployment.
parodia *f* parody, travesty (*a. fig.*), take-off F; **parodiar** [1b] parody, travesty, take off F; **parodista** *m/f* parodist.
parola *f* F chitchat, idle talk; (*soltura*) fluency.
parón *m* stop, delay.
paroxismo *m* paroxysm; ~ *de risa* convulsions of laughter.
parpadear [1a] blink, wink; (*luz*) flicker, twinkle; **parpadeo** *m*

blink(ing); flicker *etc.*; **párpado** *m* eyelid.

parque *m* park (*a.* ⚔, *mot.*); *S.Am.* ⚔ ammunition; ~ *de bomberos* fire station; ~ *zoológico* zoo.

parquear [1a] *v/t.* park.

parquedad *f* sparingness *etc.*

parquet [par'ke] *m* parquet.

parquímetro *m* parking meter.

parra *f* vine (*trained, climbing*); *hoja de* ~ *fig.* fig leaf.

párrafo *m* paragraph; F ~ *aparte* to change the subject; F *echar un* ~ have a chat.

parral *m* vine arbor.

parranda F: *andar* (*or ir*) *de* ~ go on a spree.

parricida *m/f* parricide (*p.*); **parricidio** *m* parricide (*act*).

parrilla *f* grating, gridiron; *cocina*: grill; (*restaurante*) grill room.

párroco *m* parish priest; **parroquia** *f* parish; parish church; † clientèle, custom(ers); **parroquial** parochial, parish *attr.*; **parroquiano** *m*, **a** *f* † patron, client, customer.

parsimonia *f* parsimony; moderation; (*lentitud*) slowness; *con* ~ *freq.* slowly, deliberately, unhurriedly; **parsimonioso** parsimonious; sparing *de palabras etc.*; (*lento*) slow, deliberate, unhurried.

parte[1] *m teleph. etc.* message; ⚔ dispatch, communiqué; (*informe*) report; ~ *meteorológico* weather forecast; *dar* ~ *a* inform.

parte[2] *f* part (*a.* ♪, *thea.*); share *en repartimiento*; ⚖ party; side; ~*s pl. fig.* parts, talents; ~*s pl.* (*pudendas etc.*) private parts; ~ *actora* prosecution; plaintiff; ~*s pl. contratantes* contracting parties; ~ *del león* lion's share; *la mayor* ~ the majority, most; ~ *de la oración* part of speech; *tercera* ~ (*p.*) third party; ~*s pl. vitales* vitals, vital parts; *de algún tiempo a esta* ~ for some time past; *de* ~ *a* ~ through and through; *de una* ~ *a otra* back and forth; *de* ~ *de* on behalf of, from; *en* ~ in part; *en buena* ~ in good part; *en gran* ~ to a great extent; *en* (*or a*) *alguna* ~ somewhere; *en* (*or a*) *otra* ~ somewhere else; *en ninguna* ~ nowhere; *en todas* ~*s* everywhere; *por* ~*s* systematically; one thing at a time, bit by bit; *por la mayor* ~ for the most part; *por mi* ~ as for me, for my (own) part; *por otra* ~ on the other hand; *por todas* ~*s* everywhere, on all sides; *por una* ~ on the one hand; *echar a mala* ~ look upon with disapproval; *palabra* use incorrectly; *ir a la* ~ go shares; *llevar la peor* ~ get the worst of it; *ponerse de* ~ *de* side with; *tener* ~ *en* share in; *tomar* ~ *en* take part in.

partear [1a] *mujer* deliver.

partenueces *m* nutcrackers.

partera *f* midwife.

partición *f* partition, division; sharing-out.

participación *f* participation; share *en repartimiento*; *deportes*: entry; *fig.* notification; ~ *en los beneficios* profit sharing; **participante** *m/f* participant; *deportes*: entrant, entry; **participar** [1a] *v/t.* inform, notify (of); *v/i.* participate; *deportes*: enter (*en* for); ~ *de* share in, partake of; ~ *en* participate in, (have a) share in; **partícipe** *m/f* participant; **participio** *m* participle; ~ *de pasado* past participle; ~ *de presente* present participle.

partícula *f* particle.

particular 1. particular; (e)special; private; ~ *a* peculiar to; **2.** *m* (*p.*) private individual; (*asunto*) particular, point; *nada de* ~ nothing special; *en* ~ (*en especial*) in particular; in private; **particularidad** *f* particularity, peculiarity; friendship, intimacy; **particularizar** [1f] particularize, specify; ~**se** be distinguished, stand out.

partida *f* (*salida*) departure; certificate *de bautismo etc.*; entry *en registro*; † entry, item *en lista*; † consignment *de mercancías*; *naipes etc.*: game; party *de personas*; ~ *de campo* picnic; *mala* ~, ~ *serrana* dirty trick; † ~ *doble* double entry; † ~ *simple*, ~ *sencilla* single entry.

partidario 1. partisan; **2.** *m*, **a** *f* partisan; supporter (de of); follower (de of); **partidismo** *m* partisan spirit; party politics (*b.s.*); **partidista** *adj. a. su. m/f* partisan.

partido 1. divided, split; **2.** *m pol.* party; *deportes etc.*: game, match; (*ps.*) side; *geog.* district, administrative area; *fig.* advantage, profit; (*apoyo*) support; (*acuerdo*) agreement; *de ~ soltero* eligible; *sacar ~ de* profit by (*or* from), put to use; *tomar ~* take sides, take a stand; **partija** *f* partition, division.

partir [3a] *v/t.* (*rajar etc.*) split, break; *nueces etc.* crack; (*repartir*) divide up, share (out); ✝ divide; *v/i.* set off, set out, depart, start (*de* from); *a ~ de* beginning from; since; *a ~ de hoy* from today.

partisano *m* partisan.

partitivo partitive.

partitura *f* score.

parto *m* (child)birth, delivery; labor; *fig.* product; *~ del ingenio* brainchild; *estar de ~* be in labor.

parva *f* ⚒ unthreshed corn; heap, pile.

parvulario *m* nursery school; kindergarten; **párvulo 1.** very small, tiny; *fig.* simple, innocent; **2.** *m*, **a** *f* child, infant.

pasa *f* raisin; *~ de Corinto* currant; *~ de Esmirna* sultana.

pasable passable.

pasada *f* (*acto*) passage, passing; enough to live on; *sew.* tacking stitch; F *mala ~* dirty trick; *de ~* in passing; **pasadera** *f* stepping-stone; ⚓ gangway; **pasadero** passable, tolerable; **pasadizo** *m* passage, corridor; gangway; **pasado 1.** past; *semana etc.* last; (*anticuado*) out-of-date; *comida* stale, bad; *comida guisada* overdone; **2.** *m* past (*a. gr.*); *~s pl.* ancestors; **pasador** *m* bolt, fastener *de ventana etc.*; pin *para pelo, corbata etc.*; *cocina*: colander; (*p.*) smuggler; *~es pl.* cuff links.

pasaje *m* (*acto, lugar,* ♪, *lit.*) passage; ⚓ (*travesía*) crossing, voyage; ⚓ (*precio*) passage money, fare; arcade *de tiendas*; **pasajero 1.** *calle etc.* busy; *fig.* transient, passing, fleeting; **2.** *m*, **a** *f* passenger; hotel guest.

pasamano *m* rail.

pasamontanas *m* winter cap, cap with ear flaps.

pasante *m* assistant (teacher *etc.*).

pasapasa *m* sleight of hand.

pasaporte *m* passport.

pasar [1a] **1.** *v/t.* pass; *río etc.* cross, go over; (*aventajar*) surpass, excel; *apuros* suffer, endure; *armadura etc.* pierce; *contrabando* smuggle in; *detalle* overlook; *enfermedad* give; *factura* send; *falta* overlook; *fruta* dry; *lista* call; *mano* pass, run (*por* over); *mercancías* take across, move, transfer; *moneda etc.* pass off; *noticia etc.* pass on, give; *propiedad* transfer; *tiempo* spend; *vehículo* pass, overtake; *~lo bien* enjoy o.s., have a good time; *~lo mal* have a bad time (of it); *~ por alto detalle etc.* leave out, overlook; *p.* ignore; **2.** *v/i.* pass; go; (*tiempo*) pass, elapse, wear on; (*suceso*) happen; (*efectos*) pass off, wear off; (*desaparecer*) pass away; (*cosa vieja*) last (out); get by, manage *con dificultad*; *naipes*: *paso* I pass, no bid; *¡pase Vd.!* come in!; after you!; *¿qué pasa?* what's going on?, what's up?; *¿qué le pasa a X?* what's the matter with X?; *hacer ~ p.* show in; *~ a inf.* go on to *inf.*; *~ a ser* become; *~ adelante* proceed; *~ de* exceed; *~ de los 60 años* be more than 60; *de ahí no paso* that is as far as I (can) go; there I stick; *~ de inf.* go beyond *ger.*; *~ por ciudad* pass through; *casa* call at; *~ por encima* (*de*) pass over; *~ por sabio* have a reputation for learning; *hacerse ~ por* pass o.s. off as, pose as; *~ sin* do without; **3.** *~se* (*comida*) go bad; *~ al enemigo* go over to the enemy; *~ de listo* be too clever (by half); *~ sin* do without, get by without.

pasarela *f* footbridge; ⚓ *etc.* gangway, gangplank.

pasatiempo *m* pastime, pursuit, hobby.

Pascua *f*, **pascua** *f*: *~ de los hebreos* Passover; *~ florida*, *~ de Resurrección* Easter; *~ de Navidad* Christmas; *~s pl.* Christmas holiday, Christmas time (*strictly, Christmas Day to Twelfth Night*; *¡Felices ~s!* Merry Christmas!; *de ~s a Ramos* once in a blue moon; *estar como unas ~s* be as happy as a sandboy; **pascual** paschal.

pase *m* pass.

paseante *m/f* stroller, walker; F *~ en corte* loafer; **pasear** [1a] *v/t.* *niño etc.* walk, take for a walk; parade (*por las calles* through the streets), show off; *v/i.*, *~se* stroll, walk, go for a walk; *~ en bicicleta* go for a cycle ride, go cycling; *~ a caballo* ride; *~ en coche* go for a drive, go for a run; **paseo** *m* stroll, walk; outing; (*calle*) parade, avenue; ~

(*marítimo*) promenade, esplanade; ~ *en bicicleta*, ~ *a caballo* ride; ~ *en coche* drive, run; *dar un* ~ go for a walk, take a walk (*or* stroll); *sl. llevar a* ~ take *s.o.* for a ride; *llevar de* ~ *niño* take out, take for a walk; F *mandar a* ~ send *s.o.* packing.

pasillo *m* passage, corridor; ⚓ *etc.* gangway; *thea.* short piece, sketch.

pasión *f* passion; *b.s.* bias, prejudice; **pasional** *p. etc.* passionate; *crimen* passionel; **pasionaria** *f* passion flower.

pasito *adv.* gently, softly.

pasividad *f* passiveness, passivity; **pasivo 1.** passive; *clases* ~*as* pensioners; **2.** *m* ✝ liabilities; debit side *de cuenta*.

pasmar [1a] amaze, astound, astonish; stun, dumbfound; ~**se** be amazed (*de* at) *etc.*; **pasmarota**(**da**) *f* F exaggerated show of surprise; **pasmo** *m* amazement, astonishment; awe; *fig.* wonder, marvel; ⚕ lockjaw; **pasmoso** amazing *etc.*, breath-taking; awesome; wonderful, marvelous.

paso[1] *fruta* dried.

paso[2] **1.** *m* step, pace; (*sonido*) footfall, footstep; (*huella*) footprint; (*modo de andar*) walk, gait; (*velocidad*) pace, rate; step, stair *de escalera*; *geog.* pass; ⚠ *etc.* passage, way (through); ⊕, ⚡ pitch; *sew.* stitch; *thea.* short piece, sketch; *fig.* (*acto*) passing; (*cambio*) passage, transition; progress, advance; incident, event; (*a. mal* ~) difficulty, jam F; *prohibido el* ~ no entry, no thoroughfare; ~ *de andadura* amble; ~ (*en*) *falso* slip, false move; ~ *de ganado* cattle crossing; ~ *de ganso* goose step; ~ *inferior* underpass; ~ *a nivel* grade crossing; ~ *subterráneo* subway; ~ *a* ~ step by step; *a buen* ~ quickly, hurriedly; *a cada* ~ at every step, at every turn; *a ese* ~ at that rate; *a dos* ~*s* near (*de* to); ⚔ *a* ~ *ligero* at the double; *al* ~ in passing; *al* ~ *que* while, whereas; *de* ~ in passing; by the way, incidentally; *abrir* ~ make (a) way (*para* for); *abrirse* ~ force one's way (*por* through); *aflojar el* ~ slacken one's pace, slow down; *apretar el* ~ step (it) out, hurry along; *ceder el* ~ make way; *mot.* give way; *ceder el* ~ *a fig.* give place to; *estar de* ~ be passing through; *llevar el* ~ keep in step, ⚔ mark time; *llevar al* ~ *caballo* walk; *salir al* ~ *a* waylay; confront; *salir del* ~ get out of a difficulty (*or* jam F); *seguir los* ~*s a* tail, shadow; *visitar de* ~ drop in (*or* by, over); *volver sobre sus* ~*s* retrace one's steps; **2.** *adv.* ¡~! not so fast!, easy there!; *hablar muy* ~ talk very softly.

paspartú *m* passe-partout.

pasquín *m* skit (*contra* on), lampoon.

pasta *f* paste; dough *para pan* (*a. sl.*); pastry *para hojaldre*; pulp *de madera*; (*cartón*) cardboard; (*encuadernación*) full leather; filling *de diente*; ~*s pl.* pastry, pastries; (*fideos*) noodles, spaghetti; ~ *de dientes*, ~ *dentífrica* toothpaste; *de buena* ~ kindly; *media* ~ half-binding; ~ *seca* cookie.

pastar [1a] graze.

pastel *m* (*dulce*) cake; pie *de carne etc.*; *paint.* pastel; F plot, undercover agreement; ~*es pl.* pastry, confectionery; **pastelear** [1a] F stall, spin it out to gain time; **pastelería** *f* (*arte*) confectionery, pastry; (*conjunto*) pastries; (*tienda*) confectioner's, cake shop; **pastelero** *m*, **a** *f* pastry cook; confectioner; **pastelillo** *m* small cake; pat *de mantequilla*.

pasteurizar [1f] pasteurize.

pastilla *f* tablet, pastille; cake *de jabón etc.*; bar *de chocolate*.

pastinaca *f* parsnip.

pasto *m* grazing; (*campo*) pasture; (*comida*) feed, grazing; *fig.* nourishment; fuel *para fuego etc.*; *a* ~ abundantly; *a todo* ~ freely, in great quantity; *de* ~ ordinary, everyday; *vino de* ~ ordinary wine; **pastor** *m* shepherd; herdsman, goatherd *etc.*; *eccl.* clergyman, pastor, protestant minister; **pastora** *f* shepherdess; **pastoral** *adj. a. su. f* pastoral; **pastorear** [1a] pasture; *eccl.* guide, lead; **pastorela** *f* pastoral, pastourelle; **pastoril** pastoral.

pastoso doughy; pasty; *voz* rich, mellow.

pastura *f* pasture; (*comida*) feed, fodder.

pata *f zo.* foot, paw, leg; leg *de mesa etc.*; *orn.* (female) duck; ~ *de cabra* crowbar; ~ *de gallo* crow's feet; F bloomer; F piece of nonsense; ~ *hendida* cloven hoof; ~ *de palo* peg

leg, wooden leg; *~s arriba* on one's back, upside down; *a cuatro ~s* on all fours; *a la ~ la llana* plainly, simply; *enseñar la ~, sacar la ~* give o.s. away; F *estirar la ~* peg out; F *meter la ~* put one's foot in it; butt in; *ser ~(s)* be even, tie; F *tener mala ~* be unlucky.
patada *f* stamp; (*puntapié*) kick; (*paso*) (foot)step; *a ~s* on all sides; **patalear** [1a] stamp; kick out, kick about; **pataleo** *m* stamping; kicking.
patán *m* F rustic, yokel; *b.s.* lout.
patarata *f* (piece of) nonsense, absurdity; gush, affectation; *~s pl.* tomfoolery.
patata *f* potato; *~s pl. fritas* chips; *~s pl. inglesas* crisps; **patatal** *m*, **patatar** *m* potato patch.
patatús *m* F dizzy turn.
pateadura *f*, **pateamiento** *m* stamping; kicking; *thea.* noisy protest, the bird F; **patear** [1a] F *v/t.* kick, boot; trample on; *v/i.* stamp (one's foot); *thea.* give the bird to a play; *fig.* bustle about.
patentado patent; proprietary; **patentar** [1a] patent; **patente 1.** patent (*a.* ✝), obvious, (self-) evident; **2.** *f* patent (*a. ~ de invención*); warrant; *de ~* patent; *S.Am.* first-class; *~ de privilegio* letters patent; *~ de sanidad* bill of health; **patentizar** [1f] make evident, reveal.
pateo *m* F stamping; *thea.* the bird.
paternal fatherly, paternal; **paternidad** *f* fatherhood; paternity *de niño etc.*; *~ literaria* authorship; **paterno** paternal; *abuelo ~* grandfather on the father's side.
patético pathetic, moving, poignant; **patetismo** *m* pathos, poignancy.
patiabierto F bowlegged.
patibulario horrifying, harrowing.
patíbulo *m* gallows, gibbet.
patidifuso F nonplussed, shattered.
patiestevado bandy-legged.
patillas *f/pl.* whiskers, sideburns.
patín *m* skate; runner *de trineo*; ✈ skid; ✈ *~ de cola* tail skid; *~ de ruedas* roller skate; **patinada** *f S.Am. mot.* skidding; **patinadero** *m* skating rink; **patinador** *m*, **-a** *f* skater; **patinaje** *m* skating; **patinar** [1a] skate; (*resbalar*) skid, slip; **patinazo** *m* skid; **patinet(te)** *f* scooter.
patio *m* court, (court)yard, patio; *thea.* pit; *~ de recreo* playground.
patita: F *poner de ~s en la calle* chuck out.
patito *m* duckling.
patizambo knock-kneed.
pato *m* duck; *~ (macho)* drake; F *estar hecho un ~* be slow, be awkward; F *pagar el ~* foot the bill, carry the can.
patochada *f* F blunder.
patología *f* pathology; **patológico** pathological; **patólogo** *m* pathologist.
patoso F **1.** boring; (*sabihondo*) smart; **2.** *m* bore.
patraña *f* story, fib; fake, hoax, swindle.
patria *f* mother country, native land; *~ chica* home town *etc.*; *fig.* home.
patriarca *m* patriarch; **patriarcal** patriarchal.
patricio *adj. a. su. m*, **a** *f* patrician.
patrimonial hereditary; **patrimonio** *m* inheritance; *fig.* heritage.
patrio native, home *attr.*; *potestad etc.* paternal; **patriota** *m/f* patriot; **patriotería** *f* jingoism, chauvinism; **patriotero** *adj. a. su. m*, **a** *f* jingo, chauvinist; **patriótico** patriotic; **patriotismo** *m* patriotism.
patrocinador *m*, **-a** *f* sponsor, patron; **patrocinar** [1a] sponsor; back; patronize; **patrocinio** *m* sponsorship; backing; patronage; **patrón** *m* landlord *de pensión*; (*jefe*) master, boss; ⚓ skipper; *eccl.* patron (saint); = *patrono*; *sew.* pattern; ⚘ stock; standard *para medidas etc.*; *~ oro* gold standard; *~ picado* stencil; *los ~es* the management; **patrona** *f* landlady *de pensión*; employer, owner; *eccl.* patron (saint); (*patrocinadora*) patron, patroness; **patronal** employer's; *eccl.* of a patron saint; **patronato** *m* (*acto*) patronage; ✝ employers' association; board of trustees *de obra benéfica etc.*; board *de turismo etc.*; **patrono** *m* employer, owner; *eccl.* patron (saint); (*patrocinador*) patron; sponsor; protector.
patrulla *f* patrol; **patrullar** [1a] patrol (*por acc.*); police.
patulea *f* F rabble, mob.
patullar [1a] trample, stamp about; F bustle about; F (*conversar*) chat.

paulatinamente gradually, bit by bit.
paulina *f* F telling-off, dressing-down; F (*carta*) poison-pen letter.
pauperismo *m* pauperism; **paupérrimo** very poor, terribly poor.
pausa *f* pause; break, respite; ♪ rest; *con* ~ slowly; **pausado** slow, deliberate; **pausar** [1a] *v/t.* slow down; interrupt; *v/i.* go slow; pause.
pauta *f* ruler *para rayar*; standard, norm; model, example; outline, plan, key; **pautar** [1a] *papel* rule; *fig.* give directions for.
pava *f* turkey hen; F plain woman; *S.Am.* pot, kettle; *S.Am. fig.* banter; F *pelar la* ~ do one's courting at a window grille.
pavesa *f* spark, cinder; *estar hecho una* ~ be a shadow of one's former self; F *ser una* ~ be very meek and mild.
pavimentar [1a] pave; **pavimento** *m* pavement, paving; flooring *de casa etc.*
pavisoso F, **pavitonto** F nice but a bit simple.
pavo *m* turkey; *sl.* 5 pesetas; ~ *real* peacock; F *comer* ~ be a wallflower; *sl. ponerse hecho un* ~, *tener mucho* ~ blush like a lobster; F *¡no seas* ~*!* don't be an idiot!
pavón *m* peacock; *metall.* bluing, bronzing; **pavonar** [1a] *metall.* blue, bronze; **pavonearse** [1a] swagger, strut, swank F.
pavor *m* terror, dread; **pavoroso** terrifying, frightful.
payasada *f* clowning, clownish stunt; ~*s pl.* tomfoolery; *thea. etc.* slapstick; **payaso** *m* clown.
payuelas *f/pl.* chickenpox.
paz *f* peace; peacefulness; rest; *en* ~ at peace; at rest; *dejar en* ~ leave alone, leave in peace; *descansar en* ~ rest in peace; *estar en* ~ be even (*con* with), be quits; *hacer las paces* make peace; make it up; *mantener la* ~ keep the peace.
pazguato simple, stupid.
pe: *de* ~ *a pa* from beginning to end.
peaje *m* toll; *barrera de* ~ toll bar, tollgate; *puente de* ~ toll bridge.
peana *f* stand, pedestal, base.
peatón *m* pedestrian, walker; ✉ country postman.
pebete *m* joss stick; ⚔ fuse; F thing that stinks; *S.Am.* F kid.
peca *f* freckle.
pecado *m* sin; **pecador 1.** sinning, sinful; **2.** *m*, **-a** *f* sinner; **pecaminoso** sinful; **pecar** [1g] sin; go astray; ~ *de confiado* be too trusting; ~ *por exceso de* err on the side of.
pececillos *m/pl.* fry.
pecera *f* fishbowl.
pecios *m/pl.* flotsam, wreckage.
pécora *f*: F *buena* ~, *mala* ~ nasty piece of work, cunning bitch; (*puta*) whore.
pecoso freckled.
pectoral 1. pectoral; **2.** *m eccl.* pectoral (cross).
pecuario cattle *attr.*
peculado *m* peculation.
peculiar peculiar; typical, characteristic; **peculiaridad** *f* peculiarity.
peculio *m* small savings; modest sum.
pecunia *f* F brass, cash; **pecuniario** pecuniary, money *attr.*
pechar [1a] pay (as a tax).
pechera *f* shirt front; bosom *de vestido*; (*armadura*) chest protector; F bosom; ~ (*postiza*) dicky.
pechero *m* commoner, plebeian.
pecho[1] *m anat.* chest; breast (*a. fig.*); (*esp. de mujer*) breast, bosom, bust; ~*s pl.* breasts, bust; *fig.* courage, spirit; *geog.* slope, gradient; *¡*~ *al agua!* courage!; *a* ~ *descubierto* unprotected; openly, frankly (*a. a* ~ *abierto*); *abrir su* ~, *descubrir su* ~ unbosom o.s.; *de dos* ~*s* double-breasted; *de un solo* ~ single-breasted; *dar el* ~ feed, nurse; *en* ~*s de camisa S.Am.* in shirt sleeves; *tomar a* ~(*s*) take to heart; *S.Am. tomarse a* ~*s* take seriously, make an issue of.
pecho[2] *m* tax, tribute.
pechuga *f* breast *de pollo etc.*; F breast, bosom *de mujer*; F *geog.* slope, hill.
pedagogía *f* pedagogy; **pedagógico** pedagogic(al); **pedagogo** *m* pedagogue (*a. b.s.*); teacher.
pedal *m* pedal; ~ *de acelerador* accelerator (pedal); ~ *de embrague* clutch (pedal); ~ *de freno* foot brake, brake (pedal); **pedalear** [1a] pedal.
pedante 1. pedantic; **2.** *m* pedant; **pedantería** *f* pedantry; **pedantesco** pedantic.

pedazo *m* piece, bit; scrap; ~ *del alma etc.* darling, apple of one's eye; F ¡~ *de animal!*, ¡~ *de bruto!* you idiot!; you beast!; *a* ~*s* in pieces; *hacer* ~*s* break to (*or* in) pieces, pull to pieces; shatter, smash; *hacerse* ~*s* fall to pieces, come apart, break up; *hecho* ~*s fig.* worn out.

pedernal *m* flint; flintiness.

pedestal *m* pedestal, stand, base.

pedestre *viaje* on foot; pedestrian (*a. fig.*).

pedíatra *m/f* pediatrician; **pediatría** *f* pediatrics.

pedicuro *m* chiropodist.

pedido *m* request; ☤ order; ~ *de repetición* repeat order; *a* ~ on request.

pedigüeño insistent, importunate; *niño* demanding.

pedimento *m* petition; ⚖ claim, bill.

pedir [3l] **1.** *v/t.* ask for; request, require; demand, need; beg; *paz* sue for; *comida etc.*; ☤ order; *me pidió dinero* he asked me for money; *no me pidas que lo haga* don't ask me to do it; ~ *prestado* borrow (*a* from); **2.** *v/i.* ask; ~ (*por Dios*) beg; *a* ~ *de boca* just right, just as one would wish.

pedrada *f* (*golpe*) hit with a stone; (*echada*) throw of a stone; *fig.* snide remark, dig; *matar a* ~*s* stone to death; **pedrea** *f* stone throwing; *meteor.* hailstorm; small prizes *en lotería*; **pedregal** *m* stony place; **pedregoso** stony, rocky; **pedrera** *f* stone quarry; **pedrería** *f* precious stones, jewels; **pedrisco** *m* shower of stones; heap of loose stones; *meteor.* hailstorm; **pedrusco** *m* rough stone, lump of stone; *meteor.* hailstorm, hailstones.

pega *f* (*acto*) sticking *etc.*; pitch, varnish *de vasija*; F (*chasco*) trick, practical joke; F (*zurra*) beating-up; F (*dificultad*) snag; F *de* ~ fake, sham; *pregunta de* ~ catch (*or* trick) question; *poner* ~*s* raise objections, make difficulties; **pegadizo** sticky; ⚕ infectious; ♪ catchy; *p.* parasitic; (*postizo*) sham, imitation; **pegado** *m* patch, sticking plaster; **pegajoso** sticky, adhesive; ⚕ infectious, catching; ♪ catchy; F (*suave*) soft, gentle; *vicio etc.* tempting; *p.* tiresome; (*sobón*) sloppy, oily, cloying.

pegar [1h] **1.** *v/t.* stick, glue, gum; unite, join; *botón etc.* sew on; *cartel etc.* post, stick; *p.* strike, slap, smack; *enfermedad* give; *sl. estar pegado* not have a clue; *estar pegado a fig.* be fond of; stick to, be inseparable from; **2.** *v/i.* stick *etc.*; (*fuego*) catch; (*colores*) match, go together; ⚘ take root; (*remedio etc.*) take; F *eso no pega ni con cola* that's miles off the point; F ~ *con p.* run into; **3.** ~**se** stick *etc.*; ⚕ be catching; *cocina*: catch; *fig.* intrude; ~ *a p.* stick to, attach o.s. to; *sl.* ~*la a marido* deceive, cuckold; *se la pega su mujer* his wife's deceiving him.

pegote *m* sticking plaster; F sticky mess; (*p.*) hanger-on, sponger; **pegotear** [1a] F sponge, cadge.

peina *f* ornamental comb, back comb; **peinada** *f* combing; *darse una* ~ comb one's hair, have a brush up; **peinado 1.** *p.* overdressed; *estilo* overdone, overnice; **2.** *m* coiffure, hairdo; hair style; **peinador** *m* hairdresser; (*vestido*) peignoir, dressing gown; dressing table; **peinadora** *f* hairdresser; **peinadura** *f* combing; ~*s pl.* combings; **peinar** [1a] *pelo* comb, do; style; *pelo, pieles, caballo* dress; *fig.* search, comb; ~**se** comb one's hair; **peine** *m* comb; F *buen* ~ sly one; *a sobre* ~ lightly; **peineta** *f* = *peina*.

peje *m* fish; F sly fellow.

pejiguera *f* F bother, nuisance.

pela *f sl.* one peseta.

pelado *cabeza etc.* shorn, hairless; *paisaje etc.* bare, treeless, bleak; *manzana etc.* peeled; *S.Am.* broke, penniless; *S.Am.* (*desvergonzado*) shameless; **peladura** *f* peeling *etc.*; ~*s pl.* peelings.

pelafustán *m*, **-a** *f* F good-for-nothing, layabout; **pelagallos** *m* F tramp, vagrant; **pelagatos** *m* F wretch, poor devil.

pelaje *m* coat, fur; *fig.* appearance, quality.

pelambre *m* hair; (*falta*) bare patch; **pelambrera** *f* thick hair, thick fur.

pelar [1a] cut the hair off, shear; *pollo* pluck; *fruta* peel, skin; F fleece, clean out *en el juego*; F rob;

S.Am. (*azotar*) beat; *S.Am.* (*desacreditar*) blacken, slander; **~se** (*p.*) lose one's hair; (*capa*) peel off; F *~las por* crave.

peldaño *m* step, stair; rung *de escala.*

pelea *f* fight, tussle; quarrel; struggle; scuffle, scrimmage; *~ de gallos* cockfight; *de ~ gallo* fighting; **peleador** combative, quarrelsome; **pelear** [1a] fight; scuffle; struggle; *fig.* vie; **~se** fight; scuffle; come to blows; (*desavenirse*) fall out (*con* with).

pelechar [1a] molt, shed one's hair; get new hair; F take a turn for the better.

pelele *m* rompers *de niño*; (*figura*) stuffed figure, dummy; F village idiot.

peleona *f* F row, set-to.

pelete *m* F poor fish, nobody; *en ~* without a stitch on; **peletero** *m* furrier; skinner.

peliagudo furry; long-haired; F *p.* crafty, clever; F *cosa* ticklish.

pelicano gray-haired.

pelícano *m* pelican.

pelicorto short-haired.

película *f* film; motion picture; *~ en colores* color film; *~ de dibujos* animated cartoon; *~ muda* silent film; *~ del Oeste* western; *~ sonora* sound film; *~ de terror* horror film, horror movie.

peligrar [1a] be in danger; **peligro** *m* danger; risk; *con ~ de vida etc.* at the risk of; *en ~* in danger; at stake; *fuera de ~* out of danger; *correr ~* be in danger; run a risk; *poner en ~* endanger; **peligroso** dangerous; risky; *herida, situación etc.* ugly, nasty.

pelillo *m* slight annoyance; F *echar ~s a la mar* make it up, bury the hatchet; *pararse en ~s* be easily upset, make a fuss about nothing at all.

pelinegro black-haired; **pelirrojo** red-haired, red-headed; **pelirrubio** fair-haired.

pelma(**zo**) *m* F bore; (*que tarda*) lump, sluggard.

pelo *m* hair; coat, fur *de animal*; down *de ave, fruta*; nap, pile *de tela, alfombra*; *~* (*de la barba*) whisker; F *a*(*l*) *~* just right; *~ arriba, contra ~* the wrong way; *con ~s y señales* with chapter and verse; *hombre de ~ en pecho* brave man; real man; *en ~* bare-back; F naked; F *a medios ~s* tight, half-seas-over; *de medio ~* trifling; (*postizo*) sham, fake; *cortar un ~ en el aire* be pretty smart; *cortarse el ~* have one's hair cut; F *echar ~s a la mar* make it up, bury the hatchet; *escaparse por un ~* have a narrow escape; *poner los ~s de punta* make one's hair stand on end; *tener el ~ de la dehesa* betray one's humble origins; *no tener ~s en la lengua* be outspoken, not mince words; (*hablar mucho*) talk nineteen to the dozen; *no tener ~ de tonto* be no fool; F *tomar el ~ a* pull one's leg; *venir al ~ a* suit down to the ground.

pelón hairless, bald; F stupid; F (*sin dinero*) broke; **pelona** *f* baldness; F death; **peloso** hairy.

pelota *f* ball; (*juego vasco*) pelota; *S.Am.* ferryboat; *~ base* baseball; *en ~* naked; **pelotari** *m* pelota player; **pelotear** [1a] *v/t. cuenta* audit; *v/i. tenis etc.*: knock up; *fútbol*: kick a ball about; F bicker, fall out; **peloteo** *m tenis*: knock-up *antes de comenzar*; rally *en el juego*; **pelotera** *f* F, **pelotero** *m* F row, quarrel, argument.

pelotilla: F *hacer la ~ a* suck up to, toady to; **pelotillero** *m* F toady, yes-man, stooge.

pelotón *m* ⚔ squad, party; small mat, tuft *de pelo*; crowd *de gente*; *~ de ejecución* firing squad.

peltre *m* pewter, spelter.

peluca *f* wig; F wigging, dressing-down.

peluco *m sl.* watch.

peludo 1. hairy, shaggy; *esp. animal* furry; *barba etc.* bushy; **2.** *m* thick mat.

peluquearse [1a] *S.Am.* get a haircut; **peluquería** *f* hairdresser's, barbershop; **peluquero** *m* hairdresser, barber; wigmaker.

pelusa *f* ⚘ down; fluff *de tela*; F envy.

pelvis *f* pelvis.

pella *f* ball, pellet; roll, round mass; ⚘ head; raw lard *de cerdo*; F sum of money; F *hacer ~* play truant.

pelleja *f* skin, hide; **pellejería** *f* skins, hides; (*fábrica*) tannery; *~s pl. S.Am.* upsets, troubles; **pellejo**

m skin, hide, pelt *de animal*; ⚘ peel; (*odre*) wineskin; F drunk, toper; *sl.* (*mujer*) whore; *no quisiera estar en su* ~ I wouldn't like to be in his shoes; F *salvar el* ~ save one's bacon.
pellizcar [1g] pinch, nip; *comida etc.* take a small bit of; **pellizco** *m* pinch, nip; small bit.
pena *f* (*aflicción*) sorrow, distress, grief; ⚕ pain(s); (*trabajo*) trouble; hardship; ⚖ punishment, penalty; ☤ forfeit, penalty; ~*s pl. S.Am.* ghosts; ~ *capital* capital punishment; ~ *de muerte* death penalty; *alma en* ~ soul in torment; *a duras* ~*s* with great difficulty; *¡qué* ~*!* what a shame!; *so* ~ *de* under pain of; *da* ~ *verle así* it grieves me to see him like that; *es una* ~ it's a shame, it's a pity; *merecer la* ~, *valer la* ~ be worthwhile (*ir*, *de ir* to go, going), be worth the trouble; *no vale la* ~ *inf.* (*a.*) there is no point in *ger.*; *que vale la* ~ *de leerse* (*visitarse*) worth reading (visiting); *morir de* ~ die of a broken heart; **penable** punishable.
penacho *m orn.* tuft, crest; plume *de casco*; plume, wreath *de humo*; *fig.* pride, arrogance; panache.
penado 1. grieved; laborious, difficult; **2.** *m* convict.
penal 1. penal; **2.** *m* prison; **penalidad** *f* trouble, hardship; ⚖ penalty; **penalista** *m* penologist, expert in criminal law; **penálty** *m* penalty.
penar [1a] *v/t.* penalize, punish; *v/i.* suffer; (*alma*) be in torment; ~ *por* pine for, long for; ~**se** grieve, mourn.
penca *f* ⚘ fleshy leaf; *hacerse de* ~*s* have to be coaxed into doing s.t.
pendencia *f* quarrel, fight, brawl; *armar* ~ brawl; **pendenciero 1.** quarrelsome, cantankerous; given to fighting; **2.** *m* brawler; tough F.
pender [2a] hang; dangle; droop; depend; ⚖ *etc.* be pending; **pendiente 1.** hanging; *asunto etc.* pending, unsettled; *fig.* dependent (*de* on); *estar* ~ *de los labios de* hang on *s.o.'s* lips; **2.** *m* earring; **3.** *f geog.* slope, incline; pitch *de techo*.
pendil *m* (woman's) mantle; F *tomar el* ~, *tomar* ~*es* pack up, clear out; sneak away.
péndola *f* pendulum *de reloj*; clock; *fig.* pen, quill; **pendolista** *m* penman, calligrapher.
pendón *m* banner, standard; pennon; F tall shabby person; *sl.* whore.
péndulo *m* pendulum; clock.
pene *m* penis.
peneque F pickled.
penetración *f* penetration (*a. fig.*); *fig.* insight, acuteness; **penetrador** penetrating, keen; **penetrante** penetrating; penetrative; *frío* biting; *mirada* searching; *mente* penetrating, keen, acute; *vista*, *viento* sharp; *sonido* piercing; **penetrar** [1a] *v/t.* penetrate, pierce; permeate; *misterio etc.* fathom, grasp; *intención* see through; *v/i.* penetrate (*en*, *entre*, *por acc.*); sink in, soak in; ~**se** *de* become imbued with.
penicilina *f* penicillin.
península *f* peninsula; **peninsular** peninsular.
penique *m* penny.
penitencia *f* penitence; (*acto*) penance; *hacer* ~ *fig.* take potluck; **penitenciado** *m S.Am.* convict; **penitencial** penitential; **penitenciar** [1b] impose a penance on; **penitenciaría** *f* prison, penitentiary (*a. eccl.*); **penitenciario** *m eccl.* confessor; ⚖ prison, penitentiary; **penitente** *adj. a. su. m/f* penitent.
penol *m* yard arm.
penoso arduous, laborious; painful, distressing.
pensado: *mal* ~ evil-minded, nasty-minded; *de* ~ on purpose; **pensador** *m* thinker; **pensamiento** *m* (*facultad*, *una idea*) thought; (*ideas de p.*) thinking; ⚘ pansy; *ni por* ~ not on any account; **pensante** thinking; **pensar** [1k] **1.** *v/t. pensamiento etc.* think; *problema* think over, give thought to; *número* think of; ~ *inf.* intend to *inf.*, propose to *inf.*, plan to *inf.*; ~ *de* think of, have an opinion of; *dar que* ~ *a* give food for thought to, give pause to; *¡ni* ~*lo!* not a bit of it!; **2.** *v/i.* think; ~ *en* think of, think about, reflect on; *sin* ~ unexpectedly; **pensativo** thoughtful, pensive.
penseque *m* F oversight, mistake.
pensión *f* (*renta etc.*) pension; annuity; allowance; (*casa*) boarding house, guest house, lodging house; lodgings *para estudiantes etc.*; (*que*

se paga) board and lodging; *fig.* burden; ~ *completa* full board (and lodging); ~ *vitalicia* annuity; **pensionado 1.** *m*, **a** *f* (*p.*) pensioner; **2.** *m* boarding school; **pensionar** [1a] pension; **pensionista** *m/f* pensioner; (*huésped*) paying guest, lodger; (*alumno*) boarder.

pentagonal pentagonal; **pentágono** *m* pentagon.

pentagrama *m* ♪ stave, staff.

Pentecostés *f* (*hebrea*) Pentecost; (*cristiana*) Whit(sun), Whitsuntide.

penúltimo last but one, next to last, penultimate.

penumbra *f* penumbra; half-light, semidarkness, shadow.

penuria *f* shortage, dearth.

peña *f* rock; cliff, crag; (*ps.*) group, circle; *b.s.* coterie, clique; ~ *deportiva* supporters' club; **peñascal** *m* rocky place; **peñasco** *m* rock; crag; pinnacle of rock; **peñascoso** rocky, craggy; **peñón** *m* (mass of) rock, crag; *el* ♀ The Rock (of Gibraltar).

peños *m/pl. sl.* teeth.

peón *m* (*peatón*) pedestrian; ⚔ infantryman, foot soldier; ⚠ *etc.* laborer; construction worker; *S.Am.* farmhand, peon; (*peonza*) top; *ajedrez*: pawn; ⊕ spindle, axle; ~ *caminero* member of a road gang, laborer; ~ *de albañil*, ~ *de mano* hod carrier; **peonada** *f* day's stint.

peonía *f* peony.

peonza *f* spinning top, whipping top; F busy little person.

peor *adj. a. adv. comp.* worse; *sup.* worst; *cada vez* ~, ~ *que* ~ worse and worse; *de mal en* ~ from bad to worse; *v. tanto*; **peoría** *f* worsening, deterioration.

pepinillos *m/pl.* (*en vinagre*) gherkins; **pepino** *m* cucumber.

pepita *f* ♀, *vet.* pip; *metall.* nugget; F *no tener* ~ *en la lengua* be outspoken, not mince words; (*hablar mucho*) talk nineteen to the dozen.

pepitoria *f fig.* hodgepodge, medley.

péptico peptic.

pequeñez *f* smallness, small size; shortness *de p.*; infancy *de niño*; *contp.* small-mindedness; *pequeñeces pl.* trifles; **pequeño** little, small; *estatura* short; *fig.* modest, humble; *los* ~*s* the children.

pera[1] *adj. sl.*: *muy* ~ posh, classy.

pera[2] *f* pear; (*barba*) goatee; ♀ switch; bulb *de claxon etc.*; F *partir* ~*s con* be on easy terms with; F *poner a uno las* ~*s a cuarto* put the screws on; tell a few home truths to; **peral** *m* pear (tree).

perca *f ichth.* perch.

percance *m* mishap, mischance; hitch *en proyecto etc.*; ☤ perquisite.

percatarse [1a]: ~ *de* take notice of; guard against.

percebe *m* barnacle; F idiot.

percepción *f* perception; appreciation, notion; ☤ collection, receipt; **perceptible** perceptible, noticeable, detectable; **percibir** [3a] *sueldo etc.* receive, get; *impuestos* collect; *impresión etc.* perceive, see, notice, detect; *peligro etc.* scent, sense.

percusión *f* percussion; **percusor** *m*, **percutor** *m* striker, hammer; **percutir** [3a] strike, tap.

percha *f* rack, coat stand; coat hanger; **perchero** *m* hall stand.

perdedor *m* loser; *buen* ~ good loser, good sport.

perder [2g] lose; *tiempo* waste; *tren etc.* miss; *univ. curso* fail; ⚖ *etc.* forfeit; (*echar a* ~) ruin, spoil; ~ *por 2 a 3* lose (by) 2—3; *echar a* ~ *comida etc.* spoil, ruin, *oportunidad* waste, lose; *echarse a* ~ spoil, be ruined; ~**se** (*en camino etc.*) lose o.s., get lost, stray; (*material, comida*) be spoiled; (*líquido, provisión*) go (*or* run) to waste; ~ (*de vista*) pass out of sight; ~ *por* be mad about.

perdición *f* perdition (*a. eccl.*), undoing, ruin.

pérdida *f* loss; waste *de tiempo*; ⚖ *etc.* forfeiture; wastage *de liquido etc.*; *fig.* ruination; ☤ *con* ~ at a loss, at a sacrifice; **perdidizo**: *hacer* ~ hide; lose on purpose; *hacerse el* ~ make o.s. scarce; **perdido 1.** *bala* stray; *momentos* idle, spare; F dirty; F *bebedor etc.* inveterate, hardened; ~ *por* mad about; *dar por* ~ give up for lost; **2.** *m* rake.

perdigar [1h] *carne* half-cook, brown; **perdigón** *m orn.* young partridge; ⚔ pellet; ~ *zorrero* buckshot; ~*es pl.* (small)shot, pellets.

perdiz *f* partridge.

perdón *m* forgiveness, pardon (*a.* ⚖): ¡~! sorry!; *con* ~ if I may, by your leave; *hablando con* ~ if I may say so; *pedir* ~ *a* ask *s.o.'s* forgiveness; **perdonable** pardonable, excusable; **perdonador** forgiving; **perdonar** [1a] pardon (*a.* ⚖), forgive, excuse (*algo a alguien* a p. a th.); *vida* spare; (*exceptuar*) exempt; *¡perdone!* pardon me!, I'm so sorry!; *no* ~ *ocasión* miss no opportunity; *no* ~ *medio de inf.* use all possible means to *inf.*; **perdonavidas** *m* F bully, tough.

perdulario 1. careless, sloppy; (*moralmente*) vicious; **2.** *m* rake.

perdurable (ever)lasting; abiding; **perdurar** [1a] last, endure, survive; stand.

perecedero perishable; *vida etc.* transitory; *p.* mortal; **perecer** [2d] perish; suffer; ~ *ahogado* drown; **~se** *por* pine for, crave, be dying for; *mujer* be mad about; ~ *por inf.* crave to *inf.*, be dying to *inf.*; ~ *de risa* die of laughing.

peregrinación *f* long tour, travels; *eccl.* pilgrimage; **peregrinar** [1a] travel extensively (abroad); *eccl.* go on a pilgrimage; **peregrino 1.** *p.* wandering; *ave* migratory; *fig.* strange; *belleza etc.* rare, exotic; **2.** *m*, **a** *f* pilgrim.

perejil *m* parsley; ~*es pl.* F buttons and bows, trimmings; F titles, handles.

perendengue *m* trinket, cheap ornament.

perenne everlasting, undying, perennial (*a.* ⚘); *de hoja* ~ evergreen.

perentorio peremptory, authoritative; urgent.

pereza *f* idleness, laziness, sloth (*a. eccl.*); **perezoso 1.** idle, lazy, slothful; slack; *movimiento* sluggish, slow; **2.** *m zo.* sloth.

perfección *f* perfection; completion; *a la* ~ to perfection; **perfeccionamiento** *m* perfection; improvement; **perfeccionar** [1a] perfect; improve; *proceso etc.* complete; **perfectamente** perfectly; *¡~!* precisely!, just so!; **perfectibilidad** *f* perfectibility; **perfectible** perfectible; **perfecto 1.** perfect; *proceso etc.* complete; **2.** *m gr.* perfect (tense).

perfidia *f* perfidy, treachery; **pérfido** perfidious, treacherous, disloyal.

perfil *m* profile; *phot. etc.* side view; ⚠, *geol.* (cross) section; outline *de edificio etc.*; ~*es pl.* finishing touches; ~ *aerodinámico* streamlining; **perfilado** *cara* elongated, long; *nariz* well-formed; *avión etc.* streamlined; **perfilar** [1a] outline; *avión etc.* streamline; **~se** show one's profile, give a side view; (*edificio etc.*) show in outline; F dress up.

perforadora *f* pneumatic drill; **perforar** [1a] perforate; pierce, puncture *accidentalmente*; *agujero* drill, bore; *pozo* sink; *tarjeta etc.* punch.

performance [perˈformans] *m deportes*: performance.

perfumar [1a] scent, perfume; **perfume** *m* scent, perfume; **perfumería** *f* perfume shop; perfumery; **perfumista** *m/f* perfumer.

pergamino *m* parchment.

pergeñar [1a] (*disponer*) arrange, fix up; (*bosquejar*) do roughly, do in rough; **pergeño** *m* rough draft.

pericia *f* skill, skillfulness; expertness, expertise; proficiency; **pericial** *testigo* expert.

perico *m orn.* parakeet; F chamber pot; F *es* ~ *entre ellas* he's a ladies' man.

periferia *f* periphery; outskirts *de* [*ciudad.*]

perifollo *m* ⚘ chervil; ~*s pl.* buttons and bows, frippery.

perífrasis *f* periphrasis; **perifrástico** periphrastic.

perilla *f* pear-shaped ornament; (*barba*) goatee; ~ (*de la oreja*) lobe of the ear; F *venir de* ~(*s*) come just right, be to the point.

perillán *m* F rogue, crafty sort.

perímetro *m* perimeter.

perinola *f* teetotum.

periódico 1. periodic(al); ⚕ recurrent; **2.** *m* (*diario, dominical*) newspaper; (*revista etc.*) periodical; **periodicucho** *m* F rag; **periodismo** *m* journalism; **periodista** *m/f* journalist; *m a.* pressman, newspaperman; **periodístico** journalistic, newspaper *attr.*

período *m* period; compound sentence; *phys.* cycle; ~ *lectivo* term *en la escuela.*

peripecia *f lit.* vicissitude; ~*s pl.* unforeseen changes, ups and downs.

peripuesto F dressy, overdressed.
periquete: F *en un ~* in a tick.
periquito *m* parakeet.
periscopio *m* periscope.
peristilo *m* peristyle.
peritaje *m* expert work; (*pago*) expert's fee; **perito 1.** skilled, skilful; experienced; qualified; expert, proficient (*en* at, in); **2.** *m* expert; technician; *~ electricista etc.* qualified electrician *etc.*
peritonitis *f* peritonitis.
perjudicar [1g] damage, harm, impair; *posibilidades etc.* prejudice; **perjudicial** harmful, injurious *a salud etc.*; prejudicial, detrimental (*a, para intereses etc.* to); **perjuicio** *m* (*daño*) damage, harm; ⚕ financial loss; (*injusticia*) wrong; prejudice; *en ~ de* to the detriment of; *sin ~ de* without prejudice to.
perjurar [1a] commit perjury; **~se** perjure o.s.; **perjurio** *m* perjury; **perjuro 1.** perjured; **2.** *m* perjurer.
perla *f* pearl (*a. fig.*; de of, among); *fig.* gem; F *me está* (*or viene*) *de ~s* it suits me a treat.
perlático paralytic, palsied; **perlesía** *f* paralysis, palsy.
permanecer [2d] stay, remain; **permanencia** *f* (*estado*) permanence; (*período*) stay; **permanente 1.** permanent; constant; *comisión, ejército* standing; **2.** *f* F perm; *hacerse una ~* have one's hair permed.
permanganato *m* permanganate.
permeable permeable, pervious (*a* to).
permisible allowable, permissible; **permisivo** permissive; **permiso** *m* permission; ⚔ *etc.* leave; (*documento*) permit, license; *~ de conducir* driving license; *~ de convalecencia* sick leave; *~ de entrada* entry permit; *~ de salida* exit permit; *con ~* if I may; (*levantándose de mesa etc.*) excuse me; *con ~ de Vd.* if you don't mind, by your leave; *estar de ~* be on leave; **permitir** [3a] allow, permit; permit of; enable; *no se permite fumar aquí* you can't smoke here, no smoking here; *si lo permite el tiempo* weather permitting.
permuta *f* barter, exchange; **permutación** *f esp.* ⅋ permutation; interchange; ⚕ barter, exchange;
permutar [1a] *esp.* ⅋ permute; ⚕ barter, exchange.
pernear [1a] kick one's legs; F hustle, get cracking; **pernera** *f* trouser leg; **perneta:** *en ~s* barelegged.
pernicioso pernicious, evil.
pernil *m* upper leg, haunch *de animal*; trouser leg.
pernio *m* hinge.
perno *m* bolt; *~ con anillo* ringbolt; *~ roscado* screw bolt.
pernoctar [1a] spend the night.
pero 1. *cj.* but; yet; **2.** *m* objection; snag; defect; *¡no hay ~ que valga!* there are no buts about it!; *poner ~(s) a* find fault with, raise objections to.
perogrullada *f* platitude, truism.
perol *m* (bowl-shaped) pan.
peroné *m* fibula, splint(er) bone.
peroración *f* peroration; conclusion of a speech; **perorar** [1a] perorate, make a speech; summarize; F orate; **perorata** *f* long-winded speech.
peróxido *m* peroxide.
perpendicular 1. perpendicular; at right angles; **2.** *f* perpendicular.
perpetración *f* perpetration; **perpetrador** *m*, **-a** *f* perpetrator; **perpetrar** [1a] perpetrate.
perpetuación *f* perpetuation; **perpetuar** [1e] perpetuate; **perpetuidad** *f* perpetuity; **perpetuo** perpetual; everlasting; ceaseless; *exilio etc.* (for) life.
perplejidad *f* perplexity; bewilderment; dilemma; hesitation; **perplejo** perplexed; *dejar ~* perplex, puzzle.
perra *f* bitch; tantrum; drunkenness; F *~ chica* 5-céntimo coin; F *~ gorda* 10-céntimo coin; F *~s pl.* small change; *sl. cogerse una ~ de* get an obsession about (*or* with), get a thing about; **perrada** *f* pack of dogs; F dirty trick; **perrera** *f* kennel; *fig.* badly paid job; drudgery; F tantrum; **perrería** *f* pack of dogs; (*ps.*) gang of thieves; (*palabra*) harsh word; F dirty trick; **perrillo** *m* puppy; (*raza pequeña*) miniature dog; ⚔ trigger; **perrito** *m*, **a** *f* puppy.
perro 1. *m* dog; *~ de aguas* spaniel; *~ caliente sl.* hot dog; *~ cobrador* retriever; *~ danés* Great Dane; *~ dogo* bulldog; *~ esquimal* husky; *~ faldero*

lap dog; ~ *guardián* watchdog; ~ *del hortelano* dog in the manger; ~ *de lanas* poodle; ~ *lebrel* whippet; ~ *lobo* alsatian; ~ *marino* dogfish; ~ *de muestra* pointer; setter; ~ *pastor* sheep dog; ~ *de presa* bulldog; ~ *raposero* foxhound; ~ *rastrero* tracker dog; ~ *de Terranova* Newfoundland dog; ~ *viejo fig.* old hand, wise old owl; *tiempo de* ~*s* dirty weather; *a otro* ~ *con ese hueso* tell that to the Marines; *dar* ~ *a uno* keep s.o. waiting; *darse a* ~*s* get wild; **2.** wretched, cruel, wicked.

perruna *f* dog biscuit; **perruno** ⚕ canine, dog *attr.*; *devoción etc.* doglike.

persa *adj. a. su. m/f* Persian.

persecución *f* persecution; (*caza*) pursuit, chase; **persecutorio:** *v. manía*; **perseguidor** *m*, **-a** *f* persecutor; pursuer; **perseguir** [3d *a.* 3l] persecute; (*dar caza a*) pursue, chase; (*acosar*) harass, beset; pick on; *objetivo* aim at, pursue.

perseverancia *f* perseverance; constancy; **perseverante** persevering; **perseverar** [1a] persevere; persist (*en* in).

persiana *f* (Venetian) blind; slatted shutter; window shade.

persignarse [1a] cross o.s.

persistencia *f* persistence; **persistente** persistent; **persistir** [3a] persist (*en* in; *en inf.* in *ger.*); persevere; continue.

persona *f* person; ~*s pl. freq.* people; *buena* ~ good sort, decent fellow; ~ *desplazada* displaced person; *tercera* ~ third party; *en* ~ in person, in the flesh; *en la* ~ *de* in the person of; *por* ~ per person; per capita; **personaje** *m* personage; *thea. etc.* character; F *ser un* ~ be somebody; **personal 1.** personal; **2.** *m* personnel, staff; (*total*) establishment; *esp.* ⚔ force; ⚓ complement; **personalidad** *f* personality; **personalismo** *m* selfishness, egoism; taking things in a personal way; **personalizar** [1f] personalize; embody; *virtud* personify; ~**se** become personal; **personarse** [1a] appear in person; **personificación** *f* personification; embodiment; **personificar** [1g] personify; embody; pick out for individual mention *en discurso etc.*

perspectiva *f* (*en* in) perspective: outlook, prospect *para el futuro*; appearance; (*vista*) view, scene.

perspicacia *f* perspicacity, discernment, perception; **perspicaz** perspicacious, discerning, perceptive; **perspicuo** clear, intelligible.

persuadir [3a] persuade; *dejarse* ~ be prevailed upon (*a inf.* to *inf.*); ~**se** be persuaded, become convinced; **persuasión** *f* persuasion; **persuasiva** *f* persuasion, persuasiveness; **persuasivo** persuasive.

pertenecer [2d] belong (*a* to); *fig.* ~ *a* concern, appertain to; **perteneciente:** ~ *a* appertaining to; **pertenencia** *f* ⚖ ownership; (*cosa*) property, possession; appurtenance, accessory.

pértica *f* = *2.571 m.*; *approx.* rod.

pértiga *f* pole.

pertinacia *f* pertinacity, obstinacy; ⚕ persistence; **pertinaz** pertinacious, obstinate; ⚕ persistent.

pertinencia *f* relevance, pertinence; **pertinente** relevant, pertinent, appropriate.

pertrechar [1a] ⚔ supply with ammunition and stores *etc.*; equip; *fig.* arrange, prepare; **pertrechos** *m/pl.* ⚔ supplies and stores *etc.*; ⚔ munitions; implements, equipment; ~ *de guerra* ordnance.

perturbación *f* (*mental*) perturbation; *pol.*, *meteor.*, ⚕ disturbance; ⚕ upset; ~ *del orden público* breach of the peace; **perturbador 1.** perturbing, disturbing; **2.** *m* disturber; *pol.* disorderly element; **perturbar** [1a] (*mentalmente*) perturb; *calma* ruffle; *orden*, ⚕ disturb; ⚕ *etc.* upset.

peruano *adj. a. su. m*, **a** *f* Peruvian.

perversidad *f* perversity, depravity; (*acto*) wrongdoing; **perversión** *f* perversion (*a.* ⚕), depravation; **perverso** perverse, depraved; *consejo etc.* evil; **pervertido** *m*, **a** *f* pervert; **pervertimiento** *m* perversion, corruption; **pervertir** [3i] pervert, corrupt; *texto etc.* distort; ~**se** become perverted.

pervinca *f* periwinkle.

pesa *f* weight; *deportes*: shot; dumbbell *para ejercicios*; **pesacartas** *m* letter scales.

pesadez *f* heaviness, weight; slowness; tiresomeness; harshness; *phys.* gravity.

pesadilla *f* nightmare; (*p. etc.*) pet aversion.

pesado heavy, weighty; *movimiento* slow, sluggish; ponderous; *sueño* deep; *libro etc.* boring, tedious; stodgy; *p.* boring, tiresome; **pesadumbre** *f* sorrow, grief; **pesaje** *m* weighing; *deportes*: weigh-in.

pésame: *dar el* ~ express one's condolences, send one's sympathy (*por* for, on).

pesantez *f* weight; gravity.

pesar [1a] **1.** *v/t.* weigh (*a. fig.*); *v/i.* weigh; be heavy; (*tiempo*) drag; (*opinión etc.*) count for a lot; *mal que le pese* whether he likes it or not; *me pesa mucho* I am very sorry about it, it grieves me greatly; *pese a* in spite of; *pese a quien pese* regardless of the consequences; **2.** *m* regret, sorrow; *a* ~ *de* in spite of, despite; *a mi* ~ to my regret; **pesaroso** regretful, sorrowful, sorry.

pesca *f* fishing; (*cantidad pescada*) catch; ~ *submarina* underwater fishing; ~ *de altura* deep-sea fishing; ~ *de bajura* off-shore fishing; F *andar a la* ~ *de* fish for; **pescada** *f* hake; **pescadería** *f* fish market; (*tienda*) fish shop; **pescadero** *m*, **a** *f* fishmonger; **pescadilla** *f* whiting; **pescado** *m* fish; **pescador** *m* fisherman; ~ *de caña* angler.

pescante *m mot.* driver's seat; ⊕ jib; ⚓ davit.

pescar [1g] *v/t.* (*coger*) catch; (*tratar de coger*) fish for; (*sacar del fondo*) dredge up (*a. fig.*); F *puesto* manage to get, land; F *p.* catch unawares, catch (in a lie *etc.*); F *no saber qué se pesca* not have a clue; *v/i.* fish.

pescozudo thick-necked; **pescuezo** *m* neck; scruff of the neck; *fig.* haughtiness.

pesebre *m* manger, crib; stall.

peseta *f* peseta; F *cambiar la* ~ be sick.

pesimismo *m* pessimism; **pesimista 1.** pessimistic; **2.** *m/f* pessimist.

pésimo vile, abominable, wretched.

peso *m* weight; (*que se sostiene*) burden, load; *esp. phys.* gravity; (*balanza*) balance, scales; *S.Am.* peso; *fig.* weight(iness); ~ *atómico* atomic weight; ~ *bruto* gross weight; ~ *específico* specific gravity; ~ *fuerte* heavyweight; ~ *gallo* bantamweight; ~ *ligero* lightweight; ~ *medio* middleweight; ~ *medio fuerte* cruiserweight; ~ *mosca* flyweight; ~ *de muelle* spring balance; ~ *muerto* dead weight; ~ *neto* net weight; ~ *pesado* heavyweight; ~ *pluma* featherweight; *de* ~ *fig.* weighty; *en* ~ *echar etc.* bodily; *coger* in the air; *eso cae de su* ~ it goes without saying.

pespunt(e)ar [1a] backstitch; **pespunte** *m* backstitch(ing).

pesquera *f* weir *en río*; = **pesquería** *f* fishery, fishing grounds; **pesquero** fishing *attr.*

pesquisa *f* inquiry, investigation; search; **pesquisar** [1a] inquire into, investigate; **pesquisidor** *m* investigator; (*juez*) examining magistrate.

pestaña *f* eyelash; ⊕ flange; rim *de llanta*; F *no pegar* ~ not get a wink of sleep; **pestañear** [1a] blink, wink; *sin* ~ without batting an eye; **pestañeo** *m* blink(ing), wink(ing).

peste *f* ⚕ plague, epidemic; (*olor*) stink, stench; *fig.* evil, menace; ~ *aviar* fowl pest; ~ *bubónica* bubonic plague; *echar* ~*s* swear (*contra* at); **pestífero** pestiferous; *olor* foul, noxious; **pestilencia** *f* pestilence, plague; **pestilencial** pestilential; **pestilente** pestilent.

pestillo *m* bolt, latch, catch.

petaca *f* cigarette case; tobacco pouch.

pétalo *m* petal.

petardear [1a] *v/t. fig.* cheat, swindle; *v/i. mot.* backfire; **petardista** *m/f* cheat, swindler; blackleg *en huelga*; **petardo** *m* ⚔ petard; (*fuegos artificiales*) firecracker; *fig.* swindle, fraud.

petate *m* roll of bedding; F luggage; F (*p.*) trickster; (*despreciable*) poor fish; F *liar el* ~ pack up (and clear out); (*morir*) peg out.

peteretes *m/pl.* sweets.

petición *f* request; petition *a autoridad etc.*; ⚖ suit, plea; ~ *de mano* formal betrothal; *a* ~ by request; *a* ~ *de* at the request to; *cometer* ~ *de principio* beg the question; **peticionario** *m*, **a** *f* petitioner.

petimetre *m* fop, beau.

petirrojo *m* robin.
peto *m* ⚔ breastplate; bodice *de mujer*.
pétreo stony; **petrificación** *f* petrification; **petrificar**(**se**) [1g] petrify (*a. fig.*).
petróleo *m min.* oil, petroleum; (*como combustible*) oil; ~ *combustible* fuel oil; ~ *crudo* crude oil; **petrolero** **1.** oil, petroleum *attr.*; **2.** *m* (*p.*) oil dealer; ⚓ (*a. buque* ~) tanker; **petrología** *f* petrology.
petulancia *f* pertness, insolence; **petulante** pert, insolent.
peyorativo pejorative; depreciatory.
pez[1] *m* fish; ~ *de plata entomol.* silverfish; ~ *sierra* sawfish; F ~ *gordo* big pot, big shot; F *estar* ~ (*en ello*) not have a clue; *estar como el* ~ *en el agua* F snug as a bug in a rug.
pez[2] *f* pitch, tar.
pezón *m* teat, nipple; ⚘ stalk.
pezuña *f* hoof.
piada *f* cheeping; F catch phrase.
piadoso pious, devout; (*benigno*) merciful, kind (*para con* to).
piafar [1a] paw the ground, stamp.
pianista *m/f* pianist; **piano** *m* piano; ~ *de cola* grand piano; ~ *de media cola* baby grand; ~ *vertical* upright piano.
piar [1c] cheep; F ~ *por* cry for.
piara *f* herd; drove.
pibe *m S.Am.* kid, child.
pica *f* pike; *poner una* ~ *en Flandes* bring off something difficult.
picada *f* sting; bite; peck; **picadero** *m* riding school; **picadillo** *m* minced meat; **picado** **1.** *material* perforated; *tabaco* cut; *mar* choppy; **2.** *m* ✈ dive; ~ *con motor* ✈ power dive; **picador** *m* horse trainer; *toros*: picador; ⚒ face worker; **picadura** *f* sting, bite; prick(ing); cut tobacco.
picajón, picajoso F touchy.
picante **1.** *sabor* hot, peppery; *fig.* piquant, racy, spicy; *observación* sharp, pungent; **2.** *m fig.* piquancy, spiciness; pungency.
picapedrero *m* stone cutter, quarryman.
picapleitos *m* F litigious person.
picaporte *m* door handle; latch; (*llave*) latch key.
picar [1g] **1.** *v/t.* prick, pierce, puncture; *billete* punch, clip; *papel* perforate; *superficie* pit, pock; *caballo* prick, spur on; *toro* stick; (*insecto*) sting, bite; (*culebra, pez*) bite; (*ave*) peck; *comida* nibble, pick at; *lengua* burn; *carne* mince, chop up; *paint.* stipple; *sew.* pink; *fig.* annoy, bother; pique; **2.** *v/i.* ⚕ smart; itch; (*sol*) burn, scorch; ✈ dive; *mot.* ~ (*por autoencendido*) pink; ~ *muy alto* be overambitious; ~ *en* be something of a; *estudio etc.* dabble in; **3.** ~**se** (*ropa*) get moth-eaten; (*vino*) turn sour; (*fruta*) go off; (*mar*) get choppy; (*p.*) take offense, bridle (*por* at); *sl. drogas*: get a fix, shoot up; ~ *de* boast of being.
picardear [1a] play about, play up, be mischievous; ~**se** go to the bad;
picardía *f b.s.* crookedness; (*una* ~) dirty trick; naughtiness *de niño*; (*palabra*) rude thing, naughty word; **picaresco** roguish; *lit.* picaresque; **pícaro** **1.** *b.s.* crooked; sly, crafty; *mst co.* rascally; *niño* naughty; *S.Am.* funny; **2.** *m lit.* picaro; *b.s.* rascal, rogue; (*niño*) rascal, scamp; **picaruelo** roguish.
picatoste *m* fried bread.
picaza *f* magpie.
picazo *m* jab, poke; **picazón** *f* ⚕ smarting, itch(ing); sting; F annoyance.
pícea *f* spruce.
pick-up [pi'ku(p)] *m* pick-up.
pico *m orn.* beak, bill; (*ave*) woodpecker; spout *de vasija etc.*; *geog.* peak, summit; (*punta*) sharp point, corner; (*herramienta*) pick(axe); F talkativeness; *20 y* ~ 20-odd; *a las 4 y* ~ just after 4; F *callar el* ~ keep one's trap shut; *irse del* ~ talk too much; *ser un* ~ *de oro, tener mucho* (*or buen*) ~ have the gift of the gab.
picor *m* smarting, itch(ing).
picoso pockmarked.
picota *f* pillory; *geog.* peak; △ point.
picotada *f*, **picotazo** *m* peck; **picotear** [1a] *v/t.* peck; *v/i.* F chatter; talk hot air, gas; ~**se** F squabble; **picotero** F **1.** chattering, talkative; **2.** *m*, **a** *f* chatterer, gas-bag.
pictórico pictorial; *dotes etc.* artistic.
picha *f sl.* penis.
pichel *m* tankard.

pichón *m* young pigeon; *S.Am.* young bird; F kid; ~ *de barro* clay pigeon; **pichona** *f* F darling.

pie *m* foot (*a.* ♪, *poet.*); foot, base *de columna etc.*; stand, support; trunk *de árbol*; stem *de vaso, planta*; sediment *de líquido*; foot *de cama, página*; *thea.* cue; catchword; *fig.* foothold *al trepar*; (*estado*) footing; ~ *de atleta* athlete's foot; ~ *de imprenta* imprint; ~ *marino* sea-legs; ~ *plano* flatfoot; *a* ~ on foot; *a cuatro* ~*s* on all fours; *a* ~ *enjuto* dry-shod; *fig.* without risk; *a* ~ *juntillo, a* ~ *juntillas fig. creer* firmly, absolutely; *al* ~ close, handy; ✝ *al* ~ *de fábrica* cost price, f.o.b. factory; *al* ~ *de la letra entender, citar* literally; *copiar* word for word, exactly; *de* ~ standing; up; *de a* ~ *soldado* foot *attr.*; *de* ~*s a cabeza* from head to foot; *en* ~ standing; up; *en* ~ *de guerra* on a war footing; *en un mismo* ~ *de igualdad* on an equal footing (*con* with); *dar* ~ *a* give cause for; *no dar* ~ *con bola* be continually wide of the mark; *estar de* (*or en*) ~ stand, be standing; *ir a* ~ walk, go on foot; *írsele a uno los* ~*s* slip, stumble; *irse por* ~*s* make off; *morir al* ~ *del cañón* die in harness; *nacer de* ~(*s*) be born with a silver spoon in one's mouth; *poner el* ~ tread; *ponerse de* (*or en*) ~ rise, stand up, get up; *volver* ~(*s*) *atrás* retrace one's steps.

piedad *f* piety, devoutness; (*lástima*) pity; (*filial*) piety; ¡*por* ~! for pity's sake!; *tener* ~ *de* take pity on.

piedra *f* stone; rock; *meteor.* hail, hailstone; flint *de mechero*; ~ *de afilar* hone; ~ *de amolar* grindstone; ~ *angular* cornerstone (*a. fig.*); ~ *arenisca* sandstone; ~ *caliza* limestone; ~ *de escándalo* source of scandal; bone of contention; ~ *fundamental* foundation stone; ~ *de molino* millstone; ~ *pómez* pumice (stone); ~ *preciosa* precious stone; *primera* ~ foundation stone; ~ *de toque* touchstone; *a tiro de* ~ within a stone's throw; *no dejar* ~ *sobre* ~ raze to the ground.

piel *f* skin; (*de animal*) skin, hide, pelt; (*con pelo*) fur; ♣ peel, rind, skin; ~ *de ante* buckskin, buff; ~ *de cerdo* pigskin; ~ *de foca* sealskin; ~ *de Rusia* Russia leather; ~ *roja m/f* redskin; ~ *de ternera* calf, calf leather.

piélago *m lit.* ocean, deep.

pienso[1] *m* ⚒ feed, fodder; ~*s pl.* feeding-stuffs.

pienso[2]: ¡*ni por* ~! the very idea!

pierna *f* leg; downstroke *con pluma*; *en* ~*s* bare-legged; *dormir a* ~ *suelta* (*or tendida*) sleep soundly.

pieza *f mst* piece; (*cuarto*) room; *hunt.* game, catch, example; *esp.* ⊕ part; *buena* ~, *linda* ~ crafty fellow; ~ *de convicción* convincing argument; ~ *fundida* cast(ing); ~ *de recambio*, ~ *de repuesto* spare part; ~ *de respeto* guest room; *de una* ~ in one piece.

pífano *m* fife.

pifia *f* F blunder, bloomer.

pigmento *m* pigment.

pigmeo *adj. a. su. m* pigmy.

pijama *m* pyjamas.

pijotero F *co.* **1.** wretched, beastly; **2.** *m* beast, rogue.

pila *f* (*montón*) pile, heap, stack; (*fregadero*) sink; (*abrevadero*) trough; *eccl.* font; ⚠ pier of bridge *etc.*; ⚡ battery; ~ *atómica* atomic pile; *sacar de* ~ *a* act as godparent to.

pilar *m* ⚠ pillar, pier; (*mojón*) milestone; basin, bowl *de fuente*.

píldora *f* pill; *dorar la* ~ sugar (*or* gild) the pill.

pileta *f* basin, bowl; sink.

pilón *m* (*abrevadero*) drinking trough; basin *de fuente*; (*mortero*) mortar; (*azúcar*) loaf sugar; ⚡ pylon; *S.Am.* tip, gratuity.

pilongo thin, lean.

pilot(e)ar [1a] steer; *coche* drive; *avión* pilot; **pilote** *m* ⚠ pile; **piloto 1.** *m* pilot; ~ *de puerto* harbor pilot; ~ *de prueba* test pilot; **2.** *luz* rear, tail *attr.*

piltrafa *f* skinny meat; ~*s pl.* offal, scraps.

pillada *f* dirty trick; **pillaje** *m* plunder, pillage; **pillar** [1a] plunder, pillage; (*perro*) worry; F catch, seize.

pillastre *m* F scoundrel, rogue; **pillería** *f* dirty trick; (*ps.*) gang of scoundrels; **pillín** *m* F *co.* scamp, rascal; **pillo** F **1.** blackguardly; rotten; *niño* mischievous; (*astuto*) sly, crafty; **2.** *m* rascal, rogue; rotter, cad; (*niño*) = **pilluelo** *m* F scamp, rascal; (*golfo*) urchin.

pimentero *m* pepperbox; ♣ pepper

plant; **pimentón** *m* cayenne pepper, red pepper; paprika; **pimienta** *f* black pepper; allspice, pimento; **pimiento** *m planta* pepper, black pepper; ♀ pepper plant.
pimpollo *m* sucker, shoot *de planta*; (*árbol*) sapling; rosebud; F handsome child.
pinabete *m* fir (tree).
pináculo *m* pinnacle.
pinar *m* pinewood, pine grove.
pinaza *f* pinnace.
pincel *m* paint brush; *fig.* painter; **pincelada** *f* (brush) stroke; *última* ~ *fig.* finishing touch.
pinchar [1a] pierce, prick, puncture (*a. mot.*); *fig.* F prod; *tener un neumático pinchado* have a puncture; *no* ~ *ni cortar* cut no ice; **~se** *sl. drogas*: get a fix, shoot up; **pinchazo** *m* prick, puncture (*a. mot.*); F prod.
pincho *m* prickle, spike.
pindonga *f* F gadabout.
pingajo *m* F tag; rag, shred.
pinganitos: F *estar en* ~ be high up, be well in.
pingo *m* F rag, shred; (*p.*) ragamuffin; *S.Am.* horse; *~s pl.* clothes.
pingüe fat, greasy; *fig. ganancia* rich, fat; *negocio* lucrative.
pingüino *m* penguin.
pinitos *m/pl.*: *hacer* ~ toddle, take one's first steps; **pino**[1]**:** *en* ~ upright, standing; *v. pinitos.*
pino[2] *m* pine (tree); ~ *albar* Scotch pine; ~ *negro* Swiss mountain pine; ~ *rodeno* cluster pine; ~ *de tea* pitch pine; **pinocha** *f* pine needle; **pinsapo** *m* Spanish fir.
pinta 1. *f* spot, mark; (*punto*) dot, spot; *fig.* F look(s), appearance, face; F (*lluvia*) drop of rain; F (*trago*) drop to drink; *naipes*: *¿a qué* ~? what's trumps?; **2.** *m* F *co. es un* ~ he's a fly one, he's a wily bird.
pintado spotted, mottled; *fig.* identical; F *como el más* ~ with the best; F *me sienta que ni* ~, *viene que ni* ~ it suits me a treat.
pintar [1a] *v/t.* paint (*de rojo* red; *a. fig.*); *esp. fig.* depict, picture; describe; F *~la* put it on; F *no pinta nada* he cuts no ice, he doesn't count; *v/i.* paint; ♀ begin to ripen; F show, turn out; ~ *como querer* indulge in wishful thinking; **~se** put on make-up; *¡ojo, se pinta!* wet paint!; **pintarraj**(**e**)**ar** [1a] F daub; **pintarrajo** *m* F daub.
pintiparado identical (*a* to); just the thing, just right (*para* for); **pintiparar** [1a] F compare.
pintor *m*, **-a** *f* painter; ~ *de brocha gorda* house painter; *b.s.* dauber; **pintoresco** picturesque; **pintura** *f* painting; (*color*) paint; *fig.* description; ~ *a la aguada* water color; ~ *al óleo* oil painting.
pinturero F **1.** conceited, swanky; **2.** *m*, **a** *f* show-off, swank.
pinza *f* (clothes) peg; *zo.* claw; **pinzas** *f/pl.* (*unas* a pair of) ⊕ pincers; (*pequeñas*) tweezers; forceps.
pinzón *m* (*a.* ~ *vulgar*) chaffinch; ~ *real* bullfinch.
piña *f* ♀ pine cone; (*comestible*) pineapple; (*ps.*) clique, cluster; **piñón** *m* ♀ pine kernel; *orn.*, ⊕ pinion; **piñonate** *m* candied pine kernel; **piñonear** [1a] click; **piñoneo** *m* click.
pío[1] *caballo* piebald.
pío[2] pious, devout; (*benigno*) merciful, kind.
pío[3] *m orn.* cheep; F itch, intense longing; *no decir ni* ~ not breathe a word.
piojería *f* verminous place; F wretchedness; **piojo** *m* louse; F ~ *resucitado* jumped-up fellow; parvenu; **piojoso** verminous, lousy; *fig.* mean.
pipa *f* pipe; ♪ reed; cask *de vino*; ♀ pip; *sl.* handgun.
pipiar [1c] chirp.
pipirigallo *m* sainfoin.
pipiripao *m* F slap-up do, spread.
pipote *m* keg, small cask.
pique *m* pique, resentment; *naipes*: spades; *a* ~ *de* in danger of; on the point of; *echar a* ~ sink; *fig.* wreck, ruin; *irse a* ~ sink, founder; *tener un* ~ *con* have a grudge against.
piqueta *f* pick(axe).
piquete *m* prick, jab; small hole *en ropa*; ⚔ picket.
pira *f* pyre.
piragua *f* canoe; shell; **piragüista** *m* canoeist; oarsman.
piramidal pyramidal; **pirámide** *f* pyramid.
pirarse [1a] F beat it (*a.* *~las*); [*clase* cut.

pirata *m* pirate; *fig.* hard-hearted villain; ~ *aéreo* hijacker; **piratear** [1a] buccaneer; *fig.* rob; **piratería** *f* piracy; ~ *aérea* hijacking; **pirático** piratical.
pirenaico Pyrenean.
pirita *f* pyrites.
piro... pyro...
piropear [1a] F say flirtatious things to; **piropo** *m* flirtatious remark, amorous compliment; *min.* garnet, carbuncle; *echar* ~*s a* = *piropear.*
pirotecnia *f* pyrotechnics; **pirotécnico** firework *attr.*, pyrotechnic(al).
pirrarse [1a] F: ~ *por* rave about, be crazy about.
pirueta *f* pirouette; **piruetear** [1a] pirouette.
pis *m sl.* piss; *hacer* ~ piss, pee.
pisa *f* tread(ing) *etc.*; **pisada** *f* (*ruido*) footstep, footfall, tread; (*huella*) footprint; **pisapapeles** *m* paperweight; **pisar** [1a] **1.** *v/t.* (*por descuido*) step on; (*apretando*) tread down; (*destruyendo*) trample (on, underfoot), flatten; (*estar una cosa sobre otra*) lie on, cover; ♪ *cuerda* pluck, *tecla* strike; *fig.* walk all over, abuse; **2.** *v/i.* tread, step; **pisaverde** *m* F toff, swell.
piscina *f* swimming pool; fishpond.
Piscis *m ast.* Pisces.
piscolabis *m* F snack, bite.
piso *m* (*acto*) tread(ing); sole *de zapato*; (*suelo*) flooring; (*habitaciones*) apartment, *British* flat; (*segundo etc.*) floor, story; ~ *alto* top floor; ~ *bajo* ground floor; ~ *principal* first floor; *casa de dos* ~*s* two-story house; **pisón** *m* ram, rammer; **pisotear** [1a] tread down; trample (on, underfoot); stamp on; **pisotón** *m* stamp on the foot.
pista *f* track, trail (*a. fig.*); *atletismo etc.*: race track; ~ *de aterrizaje* runway; ~ *de baile* dance floor; ~ *de ceniza* dirt track; ~ *de esquí* ski run; ~ *de patinaje*, ~ *de patinar* skating rink; ~ *de tenis* tennis court; *estar sobre la* ~ be on the scent; *seguir la* ~ *a* trail, be on the track of.
pistilo *m* pistil.
pisto *m* vegetable hash; ⚕ broth; *a* ~*s* little by little; sparingly; *darse* ~ give o.s. airs.
pistola *f* pistol; ~ *ametralladora* tommy gun, submachine gun; ~ *de arzón* horse pistol; ~ *engrasadora* grease gun; **pistolera** *f* holster; **pistolero** *m* gunman, gangster; **pistoletazo** *m* pistol shot; **pistolete** *m* pocket pistol.
pistón *m* ⊕ piston; ♪ key, piston; F *de* ~ = **pistonudo** F terrific, smashing.
pitada *f* whistle; hiss(ing) *de desaprobación*; F *dar una* ~ come out with an inappropriate remark.
pitanza *f* dole; F grub.
pitar [1a] blow a whistle; *mot.* sound the horn; *S.Am.* smoke; **pitido** *m* whistle, whistling.
pitillera *f* cigarette case; **pitillo** *m* cigarette; *echar un* ~ have a smoke.
pito *m* ♪ whistle; *mot.* horn; cigarette; *S.Am.* pipe; *no se me da un* ~ I don't care tuppence (*de* about, for); *no tocar* ~ *en* have nothing to do with; *no vale un* ~ it's not worth tuppence.
pitón[1] *m zo.* python.
pitón[2] *m* horn *de toro etc.*; spout, nozzle *de porrón*; ⚘ sprig, young shoot.
pitorrearse [1a]: F ~ *de* scoff at.
pitorro *m* spout, nozzle.
pituitario pituitary; *glándula* ~*a* pituitary.
pivote *m* pivot.
píxide *f* pyx.
pizarra *f min.* slate; *escuela*: blackboard; **pizarrín** *m* slate pencil; **pizarrón** *m S.Am.* blackboard; *deportes*: scoreboard; **pizarroso** slaty; full of slate.
pizca *f cocina*: pinch; crumb *de pan etc.*; *fig.* trace, speck; *ni* ~ not a bit, not a scrap.
pizcar [1g] F pinch, nip; **pizco** *m* F pinch, nip.
pizpereta *f* F, **pizpireta** *f* F smart little piece.
placa *f* plate (*a. phot.*); plaque *con inscripción etc.*; (*condecoración*) badge; ~ *esmerilada* focussing screen; ~ *giratoria* turntable; ~ *de matrícula* license plate.
pláceme *m* congratulations; *dar el* ~ *a* congratulate; **placentero** pleasant, agreeable; **placer**[1] **1.** *v/t.* [2x] please; **2.** *m* pleasure; enjoyment; delight; *a* ~ at one's pleasure.
placer[2] *m min.* placer; ⚓ sandbank.
placero *m*, **a** *f* stall holder, market trader; *fig.* loafer, gossip.

placidez *f* placidity; **plácido** placid.
plaga *f* ⚕ *etc.* plague; ↙ (*zo.*) pest, (⚘) blight; *fig.* scourge, calamity; blight; hardship; abundance, glut; **plagar** [1h] infest, plague (*de* with); sow (*de minas* with); *plagado de* full of, infested with; **~se** *de* become infested with.
plagiar [1b] plagiarize; *S.Am.* kidnap; **plagiario** *m*, **a** *f* plagiarist; **plagio** *m* plagiarism; *S.Am.* kidnapping.
plan *m* (*disposición, intento*) plan, scheme; △, *surv.* plan; (*nivel*) level; (*altitud*) height; F set-up, arrangement; F (*actitud*) attitude; *~ de estudios* curriculum; *~ quinquenal* five-year plan; F *en ~ de* as, on a basis of; *en ~ de viaje* making preparations for a trip; *en ~ de turismo* as a tourist; *en ~ económico* on the cheap; *en ese ~* in that way; *como sigas en ese ~* if you go on like that; *estar en ~ de divertirse* be out for a good time; *estar en un ~ imposible* be on an impossible basis; *sl. tener un ~ con casada* be having an affair with.
plana *f typ.* page; *escuela*: copywriting; ⚔, ⚓ *~ mayor* staff; *a ~ y renglón* line for line; *fig.* just right; *enmendar la ~ a* find fault with; correct mistakes of.
plancha *f* plate, sheet *de metal*; slab *de madera etc.*; iron *para planchar*; (*acto*) ironing; ⚓ gangway; F bloomer; *a la ~* grilled, *huevo* fried; *~ de blindaje* armor plate; ⊕ *~ de garnitura* bolster; *hacer la ~* float; F *hacer* (*or tirarse*) *una ~* make a bloomer, drop a brick; **planchado** *m* ironing; **planchar** [1a] iron; *traje* press; **planchear** [1a] plate; **plancheta** *f surv.* plane table; F *echárselas de ~* show off.
planeador *m* glider; **planear** [1a] *v/t.* plan; *v/i.* glide; soar; **planeo** *m* glide, gliding.
planeta *m* planet; **planetario 1.** planetary; **2.** *m* planetarium.
planicie *f* level ground, flat surface.
planificación *f* planning; **planificador** planning *attr.*; **planificar** [1g] plan, organize.
planilla *f S.Am.* payroll; (*billete*) ticket (*a. pol.*).
plano 1. flat, level; smooth; plane (*esp.* ✈); *de ~* clearly, plainly; *confesar* openly; *caer de ~* fall flat; *rechazar de ~* turn down (flat); **2.** *m* ✈ plane; plan *de edificio etc.*; map, street plan *de ciudad*; flat *de espada*; *~ de cola* tailplane; *~ focal* focal plane; *~ inclinado* inclined plane; *primer ~* foreground; *levantar el ~ de* survey, make a map of.
planta *f* ⚘, ⊕ plant; plantation; *anat.* sole, foot; △ (*piso*) floor, story; △ (ground) plan; (*proyecto*) plan, scheme; establishment *de personal*; *~ baja* ground floor, first floor; *~ piloto* pilot plant; *~ del sortilegio* ⚘ witch hazel; *de ~* from the foundations; *echar ~s* swagger, brag; F *tener buena ~* make a fine appearance; **plantación** *f* plantation; (*acto*) planting; **plantador** *m* (*p.*) planter; (*instrumento*) dibber.
plantar [1a] *planta, golpe* plant; *poste etc.* fix, set up; *fig.* set up; F (*a. dejar plantado*) *novio* jilt, walk out on; (*dejar en apuro*) leave high and dry; (*en cita*) stand *s.o.* up; F *~ en la calle* pitch into the street; *obrero* sack; **~se** plant o.s.; (*caballo*) refuse, balk; F (*llegar*) get (*en* to), be (*en* at).
plantear [1a) establish, set up, get under way; *problema* pose; *dificultad, cuestión* raise.
plantel *m* ⚘ nursery; (*gente*) body, group, establishment; (*educacional*) training establishment.
plantilla *f* inner sole *de zapato*; sole *de media*; ⊕ template, pattern; establishment *de personal*; *ser de ~* be on the establishment.
plantío *m* plot, bed; (*acto*) planting.
plantista *m* boaster, braggart.
plantón *m* ⚘ seedling, cutting; ⚔ guard, sentry; F *dar ~ a* stand *s.o.* up; F *estar de ~* be stuck, have to wait around.
plañidero mournful, plaintive; **plañir** [3h] mourn, grieve over.
plasma *m* plasma.
plasmar [1a] mold, shape; create.
plasta *f* soft mass; flattened mass; F badly-made thing, bungled job.
plasticidad *f* plasticity; *fig.* expressiveness, descriptiveness; **plasticina** *f* plasticine; **plástico 1.** plastic; *fig.* expressive, descriptive; **2.** *m* plastic.
plata *f* silver; *S.Am.* money; *~ de ley*

sterling silver; *como una* ~ like a new pin; F *en* ~ briefly; frankly.

plataforma *f* platform (*a. fig.*); stage; 🚂 turntable.

plátano *m* plane (tree); (*fruta*) banana.

platea *f thea.* pit.

plateado 1. silver *attr.*; silvery; ⊕ silver-plated; **2.** *m* silver plating; **platear** [1a] silver; silver-plate; **platería** *f* (*arte*) craft of the silversmith; (*tienda*) silversmith's; jeweler's; **platero** *m* silversmith; jeweler.

plática *f* talk, chat; *eccl.* sermon; **platicar** [1g] talk, chat, converse.

platija *f* plaice.

platillo *m* saucer; ♪ ~*s pl.* cymbals; ~ *de balanza* scale; ~ *volante* flying saucer; *pasar el* ~ pass the hat round.

platina *f* (microscope) slide.

platino *m* platinum; *mot.* ~*s pl.* contact points.

plato *m* plate, dish; (*primero etc.*) course; (*español, favorito etc.*) dish; (*porción*) plateful; ~ *fuerte* main course; ~ *giratorio*, ~ *de tocadiscos* turntable; F *nada entre dos* ~*s* much ado about nothing; *fregar* (*or lavar*) *los* ~*s* wash up; F *ser* ~ *de segunda mesa* feel neglected, be left out in the cold; be second-best.

plausible acceptable, admissible; (*loable*) praiseworthy, commendable.

playa *f* (sea)shore; beach; seaside (resort) *para veranear etc.*; *Santander tiene magníficas* ~*s* Santander has wonderful beaches; *pasar el día en la* ~ spend the day on the beach; *este año vamos a una* ~ this year we're going to the seaside; **playeras** *f/pl.* sandals, sand shoes; tennis shoes; **playero** beach *attr.*

plaza *f* square *en ciudad*; (*mercado*) market place; ⚔ (*a.* ~ *fuerte*) fortified town, stronghold; ✝ town, city, place; ✝ money market; (*sitio*) room, space; place, seat *en vehículo*; (*puesto*) post, job; (*vacante*) vacancy; ~ *de armas* parade ground; ~ *de gallos* cockpit; ~ *mayor* main square; ~ *de toros* bullring; *mot. etc. de dos* ~*s* two-seater; ✝ *en esa* ~ there, in your town; *sentar* ~ enlist (*de* as).

plazo *m* time, period; term; time limit; expiration date; *esp.* ✝ date; (*pago*) installment; *dentro de un* ~ *de 2 meses* within a period of 2 months; *a* ~*s* on credit, on easy terms; by installments; *a corto* ~ short-dated; *a largo* ~ long-dated; *compra a* ~*s* installment-plan purchase; *comprar a* ~*s* buy on the installment plan; *en* ~*s* in installments.

plazoleta *f*, **plazuela** *f* small square.

pleamar *f* high tide.

plebe *f* common people, the masses; *contp.* plebs; **plebeyo 1.** plebeian; **2.** *m*, **a** *f* plebeian, commoner.

plebiscito *m* plebiscite.

plegable pliable, pliant; *silla etc.* folding, collapsible; **plegadera** *f* paper knife; **plegadizo** = *plegable*; **plegado** *m*, **plegadura** *f* fold; pleat; (*acto*) folding; pleating; **plegar** [1h *a.* 1k] fold, bend, crease; *sew.* pleat; **~se** fold (up), bend, crease; *fig.* bow, submit.

plegaria *f* prayer.

pleitear [1a] plead, conduct a lawsuit; go to law (*con, contra* with; *sobre* over); **pleitista 1.** litigious; **2.** *m/f* litigious person; **pleito** *m* lawsuit, case; *fig.* dispute, controversy; ~*s pl.* litigation; *andar a* ~*s* be engaged in lawsuits; *estar a* ~ *con* be at odds with; *poner* ~ sue (*a acc.*), bring an action (*a* against).

plenario plenary, full.

plenilunio *m* full moon.

plenipotenciario *adj. a. su. m* plenipotentiary.

plenitud *f* plenitude, fullness; abundance; **pleno 1.** *mst fig.* full, complete; *sesión* plenary, full; *en* ~ *día* in broad daylight; *en* ~ *verano* at the height of summer; *en* ~*a vista* in full view; **2.** *m* plenum.

pleonasmo *m* pleonasm.

plétora *f* plethora; abundance, flood; **pletórico** plethoric; ~ *de* full of, brimming with.

pleuresía *f* pleurisy.

plexo *m*: ~ *solar* solar plexus.

pliego *m* (*hoja*) sheet; folder; (*carta*) sealed letter; ~ *cerrado* sealed orders; ~ *de condiciones* details, specifications *para oferta etc.*; tender; ~ *suelto* broadsheet; **pliegue** *m* fold (*a. geol.*); *sew. etc.* pleat, crease, tuck.

plinto *m* plinth.

plisado *m* pleating; **plisar** [1a] pleat.

plomada *f* ⚠ plumb, plummet; ⚓ sinker *de red*; ⚓ (sounding) lead *para sondar*; **plomar** [1a] seal with lead; **plomería** *f* ⚠ lead roofing; ⊕ plumbing; **plomero** *m* plumber; **plomizo** leaden (*a. fig.*); lead-colored; **plomo** *m* ⚗ lead; (*peso*) lead (weight); sinker *de red*; ⚠ plumbline; ⚔ bullet; ⚡ fuse; *a* ~ plumb, true, vertical(ly); *fig.* just right; *andar con pies de* ~ proceed very gingerly; *caer a* ~ fall flat.

plugo, pluguiere *etc. v. placer*[1].

pluma *f orn.* feather; (*de escribir*) pen (*a. fig.*); (*adorno*) plume; *fig.* penmanship; ~ *esferográfica* ball-point pen; ~ *estilográfica*, ~ *fuente* fountain pen; *dejar correr la* ~ let one's pen run on; *escribir al correr de la* ~, *escribir a vuela* ~ write quickly, write freely; *hacer a* ~ *y a pelo* waste nothing; **plumada** *f* stroke of a pen; **plumado** feathered; *pollo* fledged; **plumafuente** *f S.Am.* fountain pen; **plumaje** *m* plumage, feathers; plume, crest *de casco*; **plumazo** *m* feather mattress, feather pillow; (*plumada*) stroke of a pen (*a. fig.*).

plúmbeo leaden; heavy as lead.

plumero *m* (feather) duster; plume *de casco*; **plumón** *m* down; (*colchón*) featherbed; **plumoso** downy.

plural *adj. a. su. m* plural; **pluralidad** *f* plurality; majority *de votos etc.*; **pluriempleo** *m trabajo* moonlighting.

plus *m* extra pay, bonus.

pluscuamperfecto *m* pluperfect.

plusmarca *f deportes*: record; **plusmarquista** *m/f deportes*: record breaker.

plusvalía *f* enhanced value, appreciation.

plutocracia *f* plutocracy; **plutócrata** *m/f* plutocrat.

plutonio *m* plutonium.

pluvial rain *attr.*; **pluviómetro** *m* rain-gauge, pluviometer; **pluvioso** rainy.

población *f* population; (*ciudad etc.*) city, town, village; **poblacho** *m* down-at-heel town, decayed village; **poblachón** *m* F dump; **poblado** *m* town, village; inhabited place; built-up area; **poblador** *m*, **-a** *f* settler, founder.

poblar [1m] *tierra* settle, colonize, people; stock (*de peces* with); plant (*de árboles* with); *poblado de* peopled with, populated with (*or* by); *fig.* full of; **~se** ⚘ come into leaf.

pobo *m* white poplar.

pobre 1. poor (*de* in); *¡~ de mí!* poor (old) me!; **2.** *m/f* poor person; pauper; beggar *que mendiga*; *los ~s pl.* the poor; *un* ~ a poor man; *fig.* poor wretch; **pobrete 1.** poor, wretched; **2.** *m*, **a** *f* poor thing; well-meaning but ineffective person; **pobretería** *f* poverty; (*ps.*) poor people; **pobretón 1.** very poor; **2.** *m* poor man; **pobreza** *f* poverty; want, penury; slender resources.

pocilga *f* piggery, (pig)sty (*a. fig.*).

pócima *f*, **poción** *f pharm.* dose, draught; *vet.* drench; *fig.* brew, concoction.

poco 1. *adj.* little, slight, scanty; ~ *dinero* little money; *queda* ~ *vino* there isn't much wine left; *su inteligencia es ~a* his intelligence is slight; *la ganancia es ~a* the profit is small; *~s pl.* few; *~s libros* few books, not many books; *~s son los que ...* there are few who ...; *unos ~s* some few, a few; **2.** *m*: *un* ~ a little; *un* ~ *de dinero* a little money, some money; *un* ~ (*como adv.*): *le conozco un* ~ I know him slightly, I know him a little; *un* ~ *mejor* a little better; **3.** *adv.* little, not much; only slightly; *sabe* ~ he knows little; *cuesta* ~ it doesn't cost much; *a veces se traduce por el prefijo* un-: ~ *amable* unkind, ~ *amistoso* unfriendly; *a* ~ shortly (after); *a* ~ *de haber salido* shortly after he had gone out; ~ *a* ~ little by little, gradually; *¡~ a ~!* gently!, easy there!; *dentro de* ~ shortly, soon; *en* ~ *estuvo que se cayese* he almost fell, he very nearly fell; ~ *más o menos* more or less; *por* ~ almost, nearly; *hace* ~ a short time since; *tener en* ~ think little of, have no use for; *vida* hold cheap.

pocho discolored; *fruta* overripe; *S.Am.* chubby, squat.

pochola *f* F nice girl; *¡~!* darling!

poda *f* pruning (season); **podadera** *f* pruning shears, secateurs; pruning knife, bill hook; **podar** [1a] prune; lop.

podenco *m* hound, hunting dog.
poder 1. [2t] be able, can; *puede venir* he is able to come, he can come; *no puede venir* he is unable to come, he cannot come, he can't come; (*absoluto*) *los que pueden* those who can, those that are able (to); *puede que subj.* it may be that, it is possible that, perhaps; *puede ser* (it) may be (so); *puede ser que* it may be that; *¿se puede?* may I?; *no ~ con p. etc.* not be able to stand; *carga etc.* not be able to manage; *no ~ más* be exhausted; have had enough; *a más no ~* to the utmost; as hard as possible; *hasta más no ~* to the utmost; *comer etc.* to one's heart's content; *b.s.* excessively; *no ~ menos de inf.* not be able to help *ger.*, have no alternative but to *inf.*; *no puedo menos de creer* I can't help thinking; *~ mucho* have power, have influence; **2.** *m* power; authority; ⚖ power of attorney, proxy; ⊕ power, capacity, strength; ⊕ value; *~ adquisitivo* purchasing power; *~ legislativo* legislative power; (*plenos*) *~es pl.* full power, authority; *a ~ de* by dint of; *en ~ de* in the possession of, in the hands of; *por ~(es)* by proxy.
poderhabiente *m/f* attorney, proxy.
poderío *m* power; authority, jurisdiction; (*bienes*) wealth, substance.
poderoso powerful; *remedio etc.* potent, efficacious; (*rico*) rich, wealthy.
podómetro *m* pedometer.
podre *f* pus; **podredumbre** *f* rot, rottenness, decay, corruption; ⚕ pus; *fig.* gnawing doubt, uneasiness; **podrido** rotten, bad, putrid; **podrir** = *pudrir*.
poema *m* (*esp.* long) poem; **poesía** *f* poetry; (*una ~*) (*esp.* short *or* lyrical) poem; **poeta** *m* poet; **poetastro** *m* poetaster; **poética** *f* poetics; **poético** poetic(al); **poetisa** *f* poetess; **poetizar** [1f] *v/t.* poeticize; idealize; *v/i.* write poetry.
pogrom(o) *m* pogrom.
póker *m* poker.
polaco 1. Polish; **2.** *m*, **a** *f* Pole; **3.** *m* (*idioma*) Polish.
polaina *f* gaiter, legging.
polar polar; **polaridad** *f* polarity; **polarización** *f* polarization; **polarizar** [1f] polarize.
polca *f* polka.
polea *f* pulley; tackle block.
polémica *f* polemics; controversy; **polémico** polemical.
polen *m* pollen.
poli *m* F cop, police officer.
policía 1. *m* policeman; *~ femenino* policewoman; **2.** *f* police (force); *fig.* administration, order, (good) government; (*cortesía*) politeness; *~ militar* military police; *~ secreta* secret police; *~ urbana* street cleaning; **policíaco:** *v. novela.*
polifacético many-sided, versatile.
polifónico polyphonic.
poligamia *f* poligamy; **polígamo 1.** polygamous; **2.** *m*, **a** *f* polygamist.
poligloto *m*, **a** *f* polyglot.
poligonal polygonal; **polígono** *m* polygon.
polígrafo *m* writer on a wide variety of subjects.
polilla *f* (clothes) moth; bookworm.
polio(mielitis) *f* polio(myelitis).
pólipo *m* polyp.
polisílabo 1. polysyllabic; **2.** *m* polysyllable.
polisón *m* bustle.
politeísmo *m* polytheism.
politene *m*, **politeno** *m* polythene.
política *f* politics; (*e.g. ~ de Carlos V, ~ exterior*) policy; (*cortesía*) politeness, good manners; *~ del buen vecino* Good Neighbor Policy; *~ de café* parlor politics; **político 1.** political; polite, courteous; *padre etc. ~* father-*etc.* in-law; *familia ~a* relatives by marriage, in-laws F; **politicón** ceremonious, obsequious; **politiquear** [1a] F talk politics; **politiqueo** *m b.s.* party politics; political gossip; **politiquero** *m b.s.* politician.
póliza *f* certificate, voucher; (*giro*) draft, order; (*timbre*) tax stamp; *~ dotal* endowment policy; *~ de seguro(s)* insurance policy.
polizón *m* ⚓, ✈ stowaway; vagrant, tramp; *viajar de ~* stow away.
polizonte *m* F copper, cop.
polo *m geog.*, ⚡ pole; ⚡ (*borne*) terminal; (*juego*) polo; *~ acuático*, *~ de agua* water polo; *~ de atracción popular* drawing card.
poltrón idle, lazy; **poltrona** *f* reclining chair, easy chair.

polvareda *f* dust cloud; F *levantar una ~* cause a rumpus; **polvera** *f* powder compact, vanity case; **polvo** *m* dust; powder; pinch *de rapé etc.*; *~s pl.* face powder; *~(s) de arroz* rice powder; *~s pl. de blanqueo* bleaching powder; *~(s) de hornear*, *~(s) de levadura* baking powder; *lleno de ~* dusty, covered with dust; *en ~* powdered; F *hacer ~ cosa* ruin; *p.* shatter; flatten, crush *en discusión*; F *estoy hecho ~* I'm worn out; *hacer morder el ~* make *s.o.* bite the dust; *matar el ~* lay the dust; *ponerse ~s* powder one's face; *quitar el ~ (a)* dust; F *sacudir el ~ a* thrash; beat up.

pólvora *f* gunpowder; *fig.* life, liveliness; (*mal genio*) bad temper; *descubrir la ~* set the Thames on fire; F *gastar la ~ en salvas* fuss around uselessly; *propagarse como la ~* spread like wildfire; **polvorear** [1a] powder, dust, sprinkle; **polvoriento** dusty; powdery; **polvorilla** *m/f* F live wire; **polvorín** *m* powder magazine; **polvoroso** dusty; F *poner pies en ~* beat in.

polla *f orn.* pullet; *naipes*: pool, stake; F chick, girl; **pollada** *f* hatch, brood; **pollastro** *m* F sly fellow.

pollera *f* hen coop; **pollero** *m* chicken farmer; (*que vende*) poulterer.

pollino *m*, **a** *f* donkey; F ass.

pollita *f* pullet; **pollito** *m* chick; F *está Vd. hecho un ~* you're looking quite a youngster; **pollo** *m* chicken; chick *de ave no domesticada*; F young man, youth; **polluelo** *m* chick.

pomada *f* pomade.

pomar *m* apple orchard.

pomelo *m* grapefruit.

pómez: *v. piedra.*

pomo *m* (*frasco*) perfume bottle; pommel *de espada*; ⚘ fruit having pips; *~ de puerta* doorknob.

pompa *f* pomp; show, display, pageantry; procession; ⚓ pump; *~ de jabón* soap bubble; *director de ~s fúnebres* undertaker; **pomposidad** *f* pomposity; **pomposo** pompous; majestic, magnificent; *estilo* pompous, high-flown.

pómulo *m* cheekbone.

ponche *m* punch.

poncho *m S.Am.* poncho, blanket, cape.

ponderación *f fig.* deliberation, consideration; exaggeration; high praise; **ponderar** [1a] *fig.* weigh up; ponder (over); exaggerate; (*alabar*) praise highly; *estadística*: weight.

ponedero *m* nest(ing box); **ponedora** *f* laying; *buena ~* good layer.

ponencia *f* (learned) paper; report.

poner [2r] **1.** put; place; set; arrange; *cuidado* take, exercise (*en* in); *dinero* (*inversión*) put, invest; (*juego*) bet, stake; *escaparate* dress; *huevo* lay; *impuesto* impose; *luz, radio etc.* switch on, turn on, put on; *mesa* lay, set; *miedo* cause; *objeción* raise; *obra dramática* perform, put on; *película* show; *problema* set; *ropa* put on; *telegrama* send; *tiempo* take; *tienda* set up; *~ adj.* make, turn; *~ que* suppose that; *~ a alguien a inf.* set s.o. to *inf.*; *~ a alguien de* treat s.o. as; set s.o. up as; *~ aparte* set aside; F *eso pone mucho* that's asking a lot; *teleph. póngame con el Sr X* put me through to Mr X; **2. ~se** put o.s.; place o.s.; (*sol*) set; *~ adj.* turn; get, become; *~ a inf.* begin to *inf.*, set about *ger.*, proceed to *inf.*; *~ bien con* get in with, get on the good side of; *~ (a) mal con* get the wrong side of.

poney *m* pony.

ponga, pongo *etc. v. poner.*

poniente *m* west; west wind.

pontazgo *m* toll.

pontificado *m* pontificate, papacy; **pontifical** pontifical, papal; **pontificar** [1g] pontificate; **pontífice** *m* pope, pontiff; *Sumo ~* His Holiness the Pope; **pontificio** pontifical, papal.

pontón *m* pontoon; bridge of planks; pontoon bridge; ⚓ hulk.

ponzoña *f* poison; **ponzoñoso** poisonous; *fig.* noxious, harmful.

popa *f* stern, poop; *a ~* abaft, astern; *de ~ a proa* fore and aft; from stem to stern; *v. viento.*

popar [1a] scorn, jeer at.

popelín *m*, **popelina** *f* poplin.

populachería *f* cheap popularity, playing to the gallery; **populachero** common, vulgar, cheap; **populacho** *m* mob, plebs; lower orders; **popular** popular; *palabra* colloquial; **popularidad** *f* popularity;

popularismo *m* colloquialism; **popularizar** [1f] popularize; **~se** become popular; **populoso** populous.

poquedad *f* scantiness, paucity; fewness; timidity *de carácter*; (*cosa*) trifle; **poquísimo** very little; *~s pl.* very few; **poquito:** *un ~* a little bit (*su.* de of).

por 1. *prp.* a) *agente tras verbo pasivo*: by; *instrumento*: *comunicar ~ señas* talk by (means of) signs; *~ ferrocarril* by rail; *lo hizo ~ sí mismo* he did it by himself; b) *lugar*: *~ la ciudad* (*pasar*) through the town; (*pasearse*) round the town; *~ Medina* by way of Medina, via Medina (*a.* 🚂); *~ el túnel* through the tunnel; *~ la calle* along the street; *~ todo el país* over the whole country; *errar ~ los campos* wander in the fields; c) *tiempo*: *~ la noche* in the night, during the night; *~ Navidades* at (*or* about) Christmas time; *~ estas fechas* about this time; d) *motivo etc.*: *~ temor* out of fear, from fear; *cerrado ~ muerte del dueño* closed owing to (*or* on account of, because of) owner's death; *~ mí* for me, for my sake; for myself, for my part; *~ la patria* for (the sake of) the country; *~ adj.* as being, as, because it is *etc.*; *lo dejó ~ imposible* he gave it up as impossible; e) *en nombre de*: *hablo ~ todos* I speak for (*or* in the name of, on behalf of) everybody; *intercedió ~ mí* he interceded for me (*or* on my behalf); f) *objetivo*: *mi admiración ~ ti* my admiration for you; g) *en busca de*: *vendrá ~ nosotros* he will come for us; h) *quedar etc.*: *quedan cartas ~ escribir* there are still some letters to be written; i) *cambio*: *lo compró ~ 150 pesetas* he bought it for 150 pesetas; *te doy éste ~ aquél* I'll give you this one in exchange for (*or* in place of) that one; j) *manera*: *~ docenas* in dozens, by the dozen; *~ escrito* in writing; *~ persona* per person; *120 kms. ~ hora* 120 kms. an hour; *recibir ~ esposa* take as one's wife; k) Ꜳ times; *3 ~ 5* 3 times 5; **2.** *cj. etc.*: *~ inf.* (*para*) in order to *inf.*; (*causa*) because; *~ haber venido tarde* through having come late, because he came late; *~ que subj.* in order that; *~ difícil que sea* however hard it is; *~ mucho* (*or más*) *que se esforzara* however hard (*or* much) he struggled; *¿~ qué?* why?; *yo sé ~ qué* I know why.

porcachón F, **porcallón** F filthy, dirty.

porcelana *f* porcelain; (*loza corriente*) china.

porcentaje *m* percentage; *esp.* ⊕ rate.

porcino porcine; *ganado ~* pigs.

porción *f* portion; part, share; *una ~ de cosas etc.* a number of things *etc.*

pordiosear [1a] beg; **pordiosero** *m*, **a** *f* beggar.

porfía *f* persistence, obstinacy, stubbornness; *a ~* in competition; in emulation; insistently; **porfiado** persistent, obstinate, stubborn; **porfiar** [1c] persist (*en* in), insist; argue obstinately; *~ por inf.* struggle obstinately to *inf.*

pórfido *m* porphyry.

pormenor *m* detail, particular; **pormenorizar** [1f] detail, set out in detail.

pornografía *f* pornography; **pornográfico** pornographic.

poro *m* pore; **porosidad** *f* porosity, porousness; **poroso** porous.

porque because; *~ subj.* in order that.

porqué *m* reason (*de* for), why; F quantity, amount; F (*dinero*) wherewithall.

porquería *f* F (*en general*) dirt, filth; nastiness; (*acto*) indecency, indecent act; (*mala pasada*) dirty trick; *la obra es una ~* the thing's a lot of old rubbish, it's a wretched piece of work; *vender por una ~* sell for next to nothing; **porqueriza** *f* pigsty; **porquerizo** *m*, **porquero** *m* pigman.

porra *f* stick, cudgel; truncheon *de policía*; (*herramienta*) large hammer; F bore, nuisance; *¡~s!* dash (it)!; (*a otra p.*) get away!, rubbish!; F *mandar a la ~* chuck out, send packing; F *¡vete a la ~!* go to hell!; **porrada** *f* thwack, thump; F stupidity; F (*montón*) pile, heap; **porrazo** *m* thwack, thump; bump *de caída*; **porrear** [1a] grind away, go on and on.

porreta *f* green leaf *de cebolla etc.*; F *en ~* stark naked; **porretada** *f* pile, heap; **porrillo:** F *a ~* in abundance,

by the ton; **porro** F dull, stupid; **porrón 1.** slow, stupid; sluggish; **2.** *m glass wine jar with long spout.*
porta(a)viones *m* aircraft carrier.
portada *f* ⚠ front, façade; (*puerta*) porch, doorway; cover *de revista*; *typ.* frontispiece, title page; **portado:** *bien* ~ well-dressed; well-behaved; **portador** *m*, **-a** *f* carrier, bearer; ✝ bearer, payee; ~ *de gérmenes* germ carrier.
porta...: **~equipajes** *m mot.* trunk; **~estandarte** *m* standard-bearer; **~fusil** *m* sling; **~hachón** *m* torch-bearer.
portal *m* vestibule, hall; (*puerta*) porch, doorway; street door *que da a calle*; gate(way) *de ciudad*.
portalámpara *m* socket, lamp holder.
portaligas *m* suspender belt.
portalón *m* ⚠ gate(way); ⚓ gangway.
porta...: **~manteo** *m* traveling bag; **~monedas** *m* pocketbook; purse; **~objeto** *m opt.* slide; stage; **~papeles** *m* brief case; **~placas** *m* plate holder; **~plumas** *m* penholder.
portarse [1a] behave; conduct o.s.; *se portó muy bien conmigo* he treated me very well.
portátil portable.
portavoz *m* megaphone; (*p.*) spokesman; *contp.* mouthpiece.
portazgo *m* toll.
portazo *m* bang, slam; *dar un* ~ slam the door.
porte *m* ✝ carriage; porterage; ✉ postage; *fig.* behavior, conduct, demeanor, bearing; disposition, character; *franco de* ~ ✝ freight free of charge; ✉ postage free; ~ *pagado* ✝ freight prepaid; ✉ postage prepaid; **portear**[1] [1a] ✝ carry, convey.
portear[2] [1a] slam, bang.
portento *m* marvel, prodigy; **portentoso** marvelous, extraordinary.
porteño *adj. a. su. m*, **a** *f* (native) of Buenos Aires.
porteo *m* carrying, portage.
portería *f* porter's lodge; *deportes*: goal; **portero** *m* porter, janitor, doorkeeper; *deportes*: goalkeeper; ~ *electrónico* automatic door opener.
portezuela *f* door; *sew.* pocket flap.
pórtico *m* portico, porch; arcade *de plaza etc.*

portilla *f* porthole; **portillo** *m* gap, opening, breach; (*puerta*) wicket; *geog.* narrow pass.
portón *m* large door, main door.
portorriqueño *v. puertorriqueño.*
portuario port *attr.*, harbor *attr.*; *trabajador* ~ docker.
portugués 1. *adj. a. su. m*, **-a** *f* Portuguese; **2.** *m* (*idioma*) Portuguese.
porvenir *m* future; *en el* ~, *en lo* ~ in the future.
pos: *en* ~ *de* after, in pursuit of; *ir en* ~ *de* chase, pursue.
posada *f* (*mesón*) inn; lodging house; (*casa*) house, dwelling; (*alojamiento*) lodging.
posaderas *f/pl.* buttocks.
posadero *m*, **a** *f* innkeeper.
posar [1a] *v/t. carga* lay down; *v/i.*, **~se** (*ave*) alight, settle, perch, rest; (*modelo*) sit, pose; (*polvo, líquido*) settle; lodge *en posada.*
posdata *f* postscript.
pose *f* pose; *phot.* time exposure.
poseedor *m*, **-a** *f* owner, possessor; holder *de marca, oficio*; **poseer** [2e] have; own, possess; *tema, lengua* know perfectly, have a complete mastery of; *ventaja* (*cosa*) have, hold; (*p.*) enjoy; **poseído** possessed; *fig.* crazed; **posesión** *f* possession; tenure *de oficio*; complete mastery *de tema, lengua*; *tomar* ~ take over; *tomar* ~ *de* = **posesionarse** [1a]: ~ *de* take possession of, take over; *oficio* take up; **posesivo** *adj. a. su. m* possessive; **poseso 1.** possessed; **2.** *m*, **a** *f* person possessed.
posfechar [1a] postdate.
posibilidad *f* possibility; chance; **posibilitar** [1a] make possible, facilitate; **posible 1.** possible; feasible; *en lo* ~ as far as possible; *v. pronto*; *a serme* ~ if I possibly can; *hacer lo* ~ do all in one's power, do as much as possible (*para, por inf.* to *inf.*); **2. ~s** *m/pl.* means, assets.
posición *f* position; situation; (*rango*) standing.
positiva *f phot.* positive, print; **positivismo** *m* positivism; **positivo 1.** positive (*a., phot.*); ⚡ positive, plus; *idea etc.* constructive; **2.** *m gr.* positive; *phot.* positive, print.

posma *m* F bore.
poso *m* sediment, deposit, dregs.
posponer [2r] subordinate.
posta 1. *f* relay *de caballos*; (*casa*) post-house; (*etapa*, *distancia*) stage; stake *en juego*; *hunt.* slug; F *a* ~ on purpose; *por la* ~ posthaste; **2.** *m* courier.
postal 1. postal; **2.** *f* (*a. tarjeta* ~) post card; ~ *ilustrada* picture post card.
poste *m* post, pole; (*persona muy alta y delgada*) beanpole; stake *de cerca etc.*; (*a.* ~ *telegráfico*) telegraph pole; ~ *de alumbrado*, ~ *de farol* lamppost; ~ *indicador* road sign, signpost; ~ *de llegada* winning post; ~ *de salida* starting post; F *dar* ~ *a* keep *s.o.* waiting; *oler el* ~ scent danger, smell a rat.
postema *m* ⚕ abscess, tumor; *fig.* bore, dull sort.
postergar [1h] delay, postpone; *p.* pass over.
posteridad *f* posterity; **posterior** *lugar*: rear, back; posterior; *tiempo*: later, subsequent; *ser* ~ *a* be later than; **posterioridad:** *con* ~ subsequently; *con* ~ *a* subsequent to, later than.
pos(t)guerra *f* postwar period; *de* (*la*) ~ postwar; *en la* ~ in the postwar period, after the war.
postigo *m* wicket, postern, small door; shutter *de ventana*.
postillón *m* postilion.
postín *m* F side, swank; (*boato*) show, luxury; *de* ~ posh, swanky; luxurious; *darse* ~ swank; **postinero** F posh, swanky.
postizas *f/pl.* castanets; **postizo 1.** *dentadura etc.* false, artificial; *cuello* detachable; *b.s.* sham, phon(e)y; dummy; **2.** *m* false hair.
postmeridiano postmeridian; afternoon *attr.*
postor *m* bidder; *mejor* ~ highest bidder.
postración *f* prostration; ~ *nerviosa* nervous exhaustion; **postrado** prostrate (*a. fig.*); **postrar** [1a] prostrate; *esp.* ⚕ weaken, exhaust; (*derribar*) overthrow; **~se** (*acto*) prostrate o.s.; (*estado*) be prostrate.
postre 1. *m* (*a.* ~*s pl.*) dessert, sweet; **2.:** *a la* ~ at last, in the end.
postremo, postrero last; rear, hindermost; **postrimerías** *f/pl.* dying moments; closing stages; *eccl.* four last things.
postulación *f* postulation; **postulado** *m* postulate, assumption, working hypothesis; **postulante** *m/f* petitioner; candidate; **postular** [1a] postulate; (*pedir*) seek, claim, demand.
póstumo posthumous.
postura *f* posture, pose, stance *del cuerpo*; *fig.* position, attitude; *pol. etc.* agreement; bet, stake *en el juego*; bid *en subasta*; *orn.* (*cantidad*) eggs; (*acto*) egg laying; ~ *del sol* sunset.
potable drinkable; *v. agua*.
potaje *m cocina*: mixed vegetables, stew; dried vegetables; mixed drink; *fig.* medley, mixture.
potasa *f* potash.
potasio *m* potassium.
pote *m* pot, jar; (*tiesto*) flower pot; (*guiso*) stew; *a* ~ in abundance.
potencia *f* power (*a.* ♘, *pol.*); potency; ⊕ (horse)power, capacity; *pol. las* ~*s* the Powers; ~ *electoral* voting power; ~ *mundial* world power; ⊕ ~ *real* effective power; **potencial 1.** potential; **2.** *m* potential; capacity; *gr.* conditional; **potencialidad** *f* potentiality.
potentado *m* potentate; *fig.* baron, tycoon.
potente powerful; potent; F big, strong.
potestad *f* power; authority, jurisdiction; (*p.*) potentate; ~ *marital* husband's authority.
potingue *m* F concoction, brew.
potosí *m*: *costar un* ~ cost the earth; *valer un* ~ be worth a fortune.
potra *f zo.* filly; ⚕ rupture, hernia; F *tener* ~ be lucky; **potro** *m zo.* colt; rack *de tormento*; ~ *de madera* vaulting horse.
poyo *m* stone bench.
pozanco *m* pool, puddle.
pozo *m* well; ⚒ shaft; pool *de río*; *S.Am.* pool, puddle; ~ *artesiano* Artesian well; ~ *negro* cesspool; ~ *de petróleo* oil well; ~ *de ventilación* upcast, ventilation shaft; *ser un* ~ *de ciencia* be immensely learned.
práctica *f* practice; method; *en la* ~ in practice; *la* ~ *hace maestro* practice makes perfect; *hacer* ~*s de piano etc.* practice; **practicable** practicable; workable, feasible; *thea. puerta* that opens; **practicante 1.** practicing; **2.** *m/f* practitioner; ⚕ male nurse, medical assistant,

orderly; **practicar** [1g] practice; exercise; (*poner por obra*) perform, carry out; *deporte* go in for; *agujero* cut, make; **~se:** ~ *en la enseñanza* do school practice; **práctico 1.** practical; handy; *proyecto* workable; *p.* practical, down-to-earth; **2.** *m* practitioner; ⚓ pilot.

prader(í)a *f* meadow(land); prairie *en el Canadá etc.*; **prado** *m* meadow, field, pasture.

pragmático pragmatic.

preámbulo *m* preamble; *b.s.* beating about the bush; *no andarse en* ~*s* F come to the point.

prebenda *f eccl.* prebend; F sinecure, soft job; **prebendado** *m* prebendary.

preboste *m* provost.

precalentar [1k] preheat.

precario precarious, uncertain.

precaución *f* precaution; (*cualidad*) foresight, forethought; wariness; *tomar* ~*es* take precautions.

precaver [2a] guard against, forestall; **~se** be on one's guard (*de* against), be forewarned, beware (*de* of); **precavido** cautious.

precedencia *f* priority, precedence; superiority; **precedente 1.** preceding, foregoing, former; **2.** *m* precedent; *sin* ~ unprecedented; **preceder** [2a] precede, go before; have priority over; *que precede freq.* preceding, foregoing.

preceptista *m/f* theorist; **precepto** *m* precept; order, injunction; rule; **preceptor** *m* teacher; tutor; **preceptorado** *m* tutorship; **preceptoral** tutorial.

preces *f/pl.* prayers, supplications.

preciar [1b] estimate, appraise; **~se** boast; ~ *de algo* pride o.s. on, boast of; ~ *de* (*ser*) boast of being; ~ *de inf.* boast of *ger.*

precintar [1a] (pre)seal, prepackage; **precinto** *m* seal.

precio *m* (*que se paga*) price; cost; (*valor*) value, worth; ✝ *a.* charge, figure, rate; *fig.* worth *de p. etc.*; *control de* ~*s* price control; *lista de* ~*s* price list; ~ *de cierre* closing price; ~ *de compra* purchase price; ~ *al contado* cash price; ~ *irrisorio* bargain price; ~ *tope* ceiling price; ~ *de venta* sale price; *a* ~ *de quemazón* F at a giveaway price; *al* ~ *de fig.* at the cost of; *poner a* ~ offer a reward for; *no tener* ~ *fig.* be priceless; **preciosidad** *f* preciousness; (*cosa*) beautiful thing; **preciosismo** *m* preciosity; **precioso** precious; valuable; *fig.* lovely, beautiful; charming, pretty.

precipicio *m* precipice; cliff.

precipitación *f meteor.* precipitation, rainfall; (*prisa*) haste; rashness; ~ *acuosa* rainfall; ~ *radiactiva* (radioactive) fallout; **precipitado 1.** *prisa* breakneck, headlong; *acción, modo* hasty; (*imprudente*) rash; **2.** *m* ⚗ precipitate.

precipitar [1a] hurl, cast down *desde lo alto*; (*acelerar*) hasten, speed up; precipitate (*a.* ⚗); **~se** rush, dash, dart; ~ *sobre* rush at; swoop on; pounce on.

precisamente precisely; ~ *por eso* for that very reason; *vengo* ~ *de allí* it so happens I come from there; **precisar** [1a] *v/t.* (*necesitar*) need, require; fix, determine exactly; *detalles* state precisely; *v/i.* be necessary; ~ *de* need; **precisión** *f* precision, preciseness, accuracy; need, necessity; ~*es* data; ⊕ *de* ~ precision *attr.*; **preciso** necessary, essential; (*exacto*) precise, exact, accurate; *estilo* concise; *es* ~ *que vayas* you must go, it is essential that you should go; *tener las cualidades* ~*as* have the requisite qualities; *tener el tiempo* ~ have just enough time (*para inf.* to *inf.*).

precitado above-mentioned.

preclaro illustrious, famous.

precocidad *f* precociousness *etc.*

preconcebido preconceived; *idea* ~*a* = **preconcepción** *f* preconception.

preconizar [1f] foresee; *se preconiza que* it is foreseen that, it is thought that.

precoz precocious, forward; *calvicie etc.* premature; ⚘ *etc.* early.

precursor *m*, **-a** *f* forerunner, precursor.

predecesor *m*, **-a** *f* predecessor.

predecir [3p] foretell, predict.

predestinación *f* predestination; **predestinar** [1a] predestine.

predeterminar [1a] predetermine.

prédica *f eccl.* sermon; harangue; **predicación** *f* preaching; sermon; **predicado** *m* predicate; **predicador** *m* preacher; **predicar** [1g] preach (*a. fig.*).

predicción *f* prediction, forecast; ~ *del tiempo* weather forecasting.

predilección *f* predilection; **predilecto** favorite.

predio *m* property, estate; ~ *rústico* country estate; ~ *urbano* town property.

predisponer [2r] predispose; prejudice (*contra* against); **predisposición** *f* predisposition, inclination; *b.s.* bias, prejudice.

predominante predominant; prevailing, prevalent; ⚕ *interés* controlling; uppermost *en la mente*; **predominar** [1a] predominate, prevail (*v/t.* over); **predominio** *m* predominance; prevalence; superiority (*sobre* over).

preeminencia *f* preeminence; superiority; **preeminente** preeminent; superior.

preempción *f* preemption.

preenfriar [1c] precool.

pre-estreno *m* preview.

preexistencia *f* preexistence; **preexistente** preexistent; **preexistir** [3a] preexist, exist before.

prefabricado prefabricated; **prefabricar** [1g] prefabricate.

prefacio *m* preface, foreword.

prefecto *m* prefect.

preferencia *f* preference; priority; *de* ~ preferably; *de* ~ *plaza* reserved; **preferente** preferential; preferable; ⚕ *acción* preference *attr.*; **preferentemente** preferably; **preferible** preferable; **preferir** [3i] prefer (*A a B* A to B; *hacer* to do, doing).

prefigurar [1a] foreshadow.

prefijar [1a] fix beforehand, prearrange; *gr.* prefix; **prefijo** *m* prefix.

pregón *m* proclamation, announcement; ⚕ street cry; **pregonar** [1a] proclaim, announce; *secreto* disclose; *méritos etc.* praise publicly; *mercancías* cry, hawk; **pregonero** *m* town crier.

preguerra *f* prewar period; *de* (*la*) ~ prewar; *en la* ~ in the prewar period, before the war.

pregunta *f* question; F *andar* (*or estar*) *a la cuarta* ~ be broke; *hacer una* ~ ask a question; **preguntar** [1a] *v/t.* ask (*algo a alguien* a p. a th., a th. of a p.); *v/i.* ask, inquire; ~ *por p. etc.* ask for, ask after; *salud de p. etc.* ask after; ~**se** wonder (*si* if, whether); **preguntón** inquisitive.

prehistórico prehistoric.

preignición *f* preignition.

prejuicio *m* prejudice; bias; (*acto*) prejudgment; *tener* ~ be biased; **prejuzgar** [1h] prejudge.

prelado *m* prelate.

preliminar **1.** preliminary; preparatory; **2.** *m* preliminary.

preludiar [1b] prelude (*a.* ♪); introduce; **preludio** *m* prelude (*a.* ♪).

premarital premarital.

prematuro premature; untimely.

premeditación *f* premeditation; *con* ~ with premeditation, deliberately; **premeditado** premeditated; deliberate, willful; *insulto* studied; **premeditar** [1a] premeditate.

premiado **1.** *adj.* prize *attr.*; **2.** *m*, **a** *f* prize winner; **premiar** [1b] reward, recompense; give an award (*or* prize) to *en certamen*; **premio** *m* reward, recompense; prize *en certamen*; ⚕ premium; ~ *de enganche* ⚔ bounty; ~ *gordo* first prize, big prize; *a* ~ at a premium.

premioso *vestido* tight; (*molesto*) troublesome, burdensome; *orden* strict; *p.* tongue-tied, slow of speech.

premisa *f* premise.

premonición *f* premonition; **premonitorio** premonitory.

premura *f* pressure; (*prisa*) haste, urgency.

prenatal prenatal, antenatal.

prenda *f* (*empeño*) pledge, security; (*alhaja*) jewel; ~ (*de vestir*) garment, article of clothing; *fig.* token, sign, favor; (*p.*) loved one, darling; ~**s** *pl.* qualities, talents, gifts; (*juego*) forfeits; ~**s** *interiores* underwear; ~ *perdida* forfeit; *en* ~ *de* as a pledge of; (*dejar*) *en* ~ (leave) in pawn; **prendar** [1a] pledge, pawn; *fig.* captivate, win over; ~**se** *de* take a fancy to; *p.* fall in love with.

prendedero *m*, **prendedor** *m* brooch, clasp, pin.

prender [2a; *p.p. a. preso*] *v/t.* seize, grasp; *p.* capture, catch; ⚖ arrest; pin, attach *con alfiler etc.*; *v/i.* ⚘ take root; (*fuego*) catch; (*vacunación etc.*) take; ~**se** (*mujer*) dress up.

prendería *f* second-hand shop; pawnbroker's; **prendero** *m* second-hand dealer; pawnbroker.

prendimiento *m* capture, seizure.
prenombrado above-mentioned, foregoing.
prensa *f* press; ⊕ gland, stuffing box; *de* ~ press *attr.*; ~ *de copiar* printing frame; ~ *rotativa* rotary press; ~ *taladradora* drill press; *dar a la* ~ publish; *entrar en* ~ go to press; *estar en* ~ be in press; *meter en* ~ F put the squeeze on; *tener mala* ~ have a bad press; **prensado** *m* sheen, shine; **prensaestopas** *m* ⊕ (packing) gland; **prensar** [1a] press; **prensil** prehensile.
preñada pregnant; **preñado 1.** *muro* bulging, sagging; ~ *de* full of; **2.** *m* = **preñez** *f* pregnancy.
preocupación *f* worry, concern, preoccupation; prejudice; **preocupado** worried, concerned, preoccupied; **preocupar** [1a] (*inquietar*) worry, preoccupy, exercise; (*predisponer*) prejudice; **~se** worry, care (*de, por* about); *¡no se preocupe!* don't bother!, don't trouble yourself!; don't worry about it!
preparación *f* preparation; (*instrucción*) training; ~ *militar etc.* military *etc.* preparedness; **preparador** *m deportes*: trainer; **preparar** [1a] prepare; ⊕ prepare, process; (*aprestar*) get ready; (*instruir*) train; **~se** prepare (o.s.); get ready; **preparativo 1.** preparatory; preliminary; **2.** *~s m/pl.* preparations; preliminaries; **preparatorio** preparatory.
preponderancia *f* preponderance; superiority; **preponderante** preponderant; superior; **preponderar** [1a] preponderate; prevail.
preposición *f* preposition; **preposicional** prepositional.
prepucio *m* foreskin, prepuce.
prerrogativa *f* prerogative, privilege.
presa *f* (*acto*) capture, seizure; (*cosa apresada*) prize (*esp.* ⚓), spoils, booty; (*animal que se caza*) prey, quarry; (*animal cazado*) capture, catch; weir, dam, barrage *de río*; (*conducto*) ditch, conduit; *~s pl.* fangs; *hacer* ~ seize; *ser* ~ *de* be a prey to.
presagiar [1b] betoken, forebode, presage; **presagio** *m* omen, portent.
presbicia *f* far-sightedness; **présbita, présbite** far-sighted.
presbiteriano 1. *adj.* Presbyterian; **2.** *m*, **a** *f* Presbyterian; **presbiterio** *m* presbitery, chancel; **presbítero** *m* priest.
presciencia *f* foreknowledge, prescience; **presciente** prescient.
prescindible dispensable, expendable; **prescindir** [3a]: ~ *de* do without dispense with; disregard.
prescribir [3a; *p.p. prescrito*] prescribe; **prescripción** *f* prescription; **prescrito** prescribed.
presea *f* jewel.
presencia *f* presence; ~ *de ánimo* presence of mind; **presencial** *v. testigo*; **presenciar** [1b] be present at, witness, watch.
presentable presentable; **presentación** *f* presentation; introduction; **presentador** *m*, **presentadora** *f televisión*: moderator; **presentar** [1a] *mst* present; *p. a otra* introduce; *p.* propose, nominate (*a puesto* for); (*mostrar*) display, show; *thea.* perform; *demanda* put in, present; *dimisión* tender; *película* show; *proyecto etc.* put forward; *pruebas* submit, present; *¡presenten armas!* present arms!; **~se** present o.s.; (*acudir*) turn up; report (*en* at); run *como candidato*; ~ *a puesto* put in for; ~ *para examen* sit, enter for.
presente 1. present; *¡~!* present!; *los ~s* those present; *la* ~ this letter; *con perdón de los ~s, mejorando lo* ~ present company excepted; *al* ~ at present; *hacer* ~ state, declare; *tener* ~ remember, bear in mind; **2.** *m* present; *gr.* present (tense).
presentimiento *m* premonition, presentiment; foreboding; **presentir** [3i] have a presentiment of; ~ *que* have a presentiment that.
preservación *f* preservation, protection; **preservar** [1a] preserve, protect (*contra* from, against).
presidencia *f pol. etc.* presidency; chairmanship; **presidencial** presidential; **presidente** *m*, **a** *f pol. etc.* president; chairman *de comité, reunión*; *parl.* speaker.
presidiario *m* convict; **presidio** *m* (*cárcel*) prison; (*condena*) hard labor; ⚔ (*ps.*) garrison; (*lugar*) fortress.

presidir [3a] preside (*acc.* at, over); take the chair (*acc.* at).
presilla *f* fastener, clip; press stud.
presión *f* pressure (*a.* ⊕, *meteor.*); press, squeeze *con mano etc.*; ⊕ de ~ pressure *attr.*; ~ *atmosférica* atmospheric (*or* air) pressure; ~ *de inflado* tire pressure; ~ *sanguínea* blood pressure; *a* ~ on draught; **presionar** [1a] press.
preso **1.** *p.p. of prender*; **2.** *m*, **a** *f* prisoner, convict; ~ *preventivo* pretrial prisoner.
prestación *f* lending, loan; **prestado:** *dar* ~ lend, loan; *pedir* ~, *tomar* ~ borrow; **prestador** *m*, **-a** *f* lender; **prestamista** *m* money lender; pawnbroker; **préstamo** *m* (*acto*) lending, borrowing; (*dinero*) loan; **prestar** [1a] *v/t.* lend, loan; *atención* pay; *ayuda* give; *juramento* take, swear; *v/i.* give, stretch; **~se** (*p.*) lend o.s., (*cosa*) lend itself (*a* to); **prestatario** *m* borrower.
presteza *f* quickness, speed, agility.
prestidigitación *f* prestidigitation, sleight of hand; **prestidigitador** *m* conjurer, juggler.
prestigio *m* prestige; face; (*fascinación*) spell; (*engaño*) trick; **prestigioso** famous, of some standing; (*fascinador*) captivating; (*engañoso*) illusory.
presto **1.** *adj.* (*vivo*) quick, prompt; agile, nimble; (*dispuesto*) ready; **2.** *adv.* quickly; at once, right away.
presumible presumable, to be presumed; **presumido** conceited; **presumir** [3a] *v/t.* presume; guess, surmise; *v/i.* be conceited, presume; give o.s. airs; ~ *de* fancy o.s. as *su.*, boast of being *adj.*; ~ *de listo* think o.s. very clever; *según cabe* ~ presumably; **presunción** *f* presumption; conceit; **presunto** supposed, presumed; *heredero* presumptive; **presuntuoso** conceited, vain; presumptuous; pretentious.
presuponer [2r] presuppose; **presuposición** *f* presupposition; **presupuestar** [1a] budget for; **presupuestario** budget *attr.*, budgetary; **presupuesto** *m* ⚚ budget; estimate *para un proyecto etc.*
presura *f* speed; promptness; (*porfía*) persistence; **presuroso** quick, speedy; prompt; hasty (*a. b.s.*).
pretencioso pretentious.
pretender [2a] claim; *mujer* court; *puesto* seek, try for; *honores etc.* aspire to; *objeto* aim at, try to achieve; ~ *que indic.* claim that, allege that; ~ *que subj.* expect that, suggest that, intend that; ~ *inf.* (*intentar*) seek to *inf.*, attempt to *inf.*, try to *inf.*; ~ *decir* mean (*con* by); ~ *poder inf.* claim to be able to *inf.*, purport to *inf.*; ~ *ser su.* profess to be, claim to be; **pretendido** supposed, pretended; alleged; **pretendiente** **1.** *m* suitor *de mujer*; **2.** *m*, **a** *f* claimant; applicant (*a puesto* for); pretender (*a trono* to).
pretensado prestressed.
pretensión *f* claim; aim, object; (*pretencioso*) pretension; pretense *para engañar*; *tener* **~es** *de* have pretensions to.
pretérito **1.** past; **2.** *m* preterit(e), past historic.
preternatural preternatural.
pretextar [1a] plead, use as an excuse; **pretexto** *m* pretext; pretense; plea, excuse; *so* ~ *de* under pretext of.
pretil *m* parapet *de puente*; hand rail, railing.
pretina *f* girdle, belt.
prevalecer [2d] prevail (*sobre* over, against); ⚘ take root.
prevalerse [2q]: ~ *de* avail o.s. of.
prevención *f* (*cualidad*) forethought, foresight; (*prejuicio*) prejudice; (*estado*) preparedness; (*acto*) prevention *etc.*; safety measure, precaution; (*aviso*) warning; (*comisaría*) police station; *a* ~, *de* ~ spare, emergency *attr.*; **prevenido** prepared, ready; *fig.* cautious, forewarned; **prevenir** [3s] prepare, make ready; (*impedir*) prevent; (*prever*) foresee, anticipate; provide for; (*advertir*) (fore)warn (*contra* against); (*predisponer*) prejudice (*contra* against); **~se** make ready, get ready; ~ *contra* prepare for; take precautions against; **preventivo** preventive (*a.* ⚕); precautionary.
prever [2v] foresee, forecast; envisage, visualize.
previo **1.** *adj.* previous, prior; *examen* preliminary; **2.** *prp.* after, following.

previsible foreseeable; **previsión** *f* foresight; far-sightedness; thoughtfulness; (*pronóstico*) forecast; ~ *social* social security; ~ *del tiempo* weather forecasting; **previsor** far-sighted; thoughtful.

prez *f* honor, glory.

prieto blackish, dark; *p.* mean; *S.Am.* dark, brunette.

prima *f* ⚕ bonus, bounty; premium *de seguros*; subsidy *de exportación etc.*

primacía *f* primacy; **primada** *f* F hoax, trick; piece of stupidity; **primado** *m* primate; **primal** *adj. a. su. m*, **-a** *f* yearling; **primar** [1a]: ~ *sobre* take precedence over; **primario** primary; **primato** *m* primate.

primavera *f* spring(time); ⚘ primrose; **primaveral** spring *attr.*; springlike.

primera *f* (*a.* ~ *clase*) first class; ~ *de cambio* first of exchange; F *de* ~ first-rate, first-class; F *estar de* ~ ~ feel fine; *viajar en* ~ travel first; **primeramente** first(ly), in the first place; chiefly; **primerizo** *m*, **a** *f* novice, beginner; **primero 1.** first; primary; foremost; *años etc.* early; (*anterior*) former; *necesidad* basic, prime; urgent; *materia* raw; *a* ~*s de* at the beginning of; *ser el* ~ *en inf.* be the first to *inf.*; **2.** *adv.* first; (*preferentemente*) rather, sooner.

primicias *f/pl.* first fruits.

primitivo primitive; original; *obra etc.* early; *color* prime.

primo 1. ℞ prime; *materia* raw; **2.** *m*, **a** *f* cousin; ~ *carnal*, ~ *hermano* first cousin; **3.** *m* F fool, sucker.

primogénito first-born; **primogenitura** *f* primogeniture; birthright.

primor *m* beauty, elegance, exquisiteness; (*habilidad*) skill; *es un* ~ it's a charming thing, it's a lovely piece of work.

primordial original; *hecho etc.* basic.

primoroso exquisite, fine, elegant; (*hábil*) skilful, neat.

princesa *f* princess; **principado** *m* principality.

principal 1. principal; chief, main; foremost; *piso* first; (*noble*) illustrious; **2.** *m* principal (*a.* ⚕, ⚖); head, chief.

príncipe *m* prince; ~*s pl.* prince and princess; ~ *consorte* prince consort; *v. edición*; ~ *de Gales* Prince of Wales; ~ *heredero* crown prince; **principesco** princely.

principiante 1. learner, who is beginning; **2.** *m*, **a** *f* beginner, learner, novice; **principiar** [1b] start, begin (*a inf.* to *inf. or ger.*; *con* with); **principio** *m* beginning, start; origin, source; *phls.*, *ciencias etc.*: principle; ⚗ *etc.* element, constituent; *cocina*: entrée; ~*s pl.* essentials, rudiments *de tema*; ~ *de admiración* inverted exclamation point; ~ *de interrogación* inverted question mark; *a* ~*s del mes* at the beginning of the month; *a* ~*s del siglo pasado* early last century; *al* ~ at first; in the beginning; *desde el* ~ from the first; *en* ~ in principle; *en un* ~ at first, at the beginning; *por* ~ on principle.

principote *m* F swank, swell; parvenu.

pringar [1h] *v/t. cocina*: dip in fat; *asado* baste; (*ensuciar*) stain with fat; *S.Am.* splash; F (*herir*) wound; F (*calumniar*) blacken, run down; *v/i. sl.* (*perder*) come a cropper, take a beating; ⚔ *sl.* sweat one's guts out; F ~ *en* dabble in, have a hand in; **~se** F make money on the side, clean up a packet; **pringón 1.** F greasy; **2.** *m* grease stain; **pringoso** greasy; **pringue** *m* grease, fat, dripping; grease stain.

prior *m* prior; **priora** *f*, **prioresa** *f* prioress; **priorato** *m* priory.

prioridad *f* priority; seniority; *de máxima* ~ of the highest priority.

prisa *f* hurry, haste; speed; urgency; *a* ~, *de* ~ quickly, hurriedly; *a toda* ~ as quickly as possible; *correr* ~ be urgent; *¿corre* ~ *este trabajo?* is this work urgent?; *¿te corre* ~*?* are you in a hurry?; *darse* ~ hurry; *¡date* ~*!* hurry up!, come along!; *despachar de* ~ *trabajo* hurry along, rush; *estar de* ~, *tener* ~ be in a hurry.

prisión *f* (*acto*) capture, arrest; (*cárcel*) prison; (*período*) imprisonment; ~*es pl.* shackles; **prisionero** *m* prisoner; *hacer* ~ take prisoner.

prisma *m* prism; **prismático**

1. prismatic; **2.** ~*s m/pl.* prism binoculars.
prístino pristine, original.
privación *f* (*acto*) deprivation; (*falta*) privation, want; **privado 1.** private; personal; **2.** *m* favorite; *en* ~ in private; **privanza** *f* favor; **privar** [1a] *v/t.* deprive (*de* of), dispossess (*de* of); starve (*de* of); (*destituir*) demote, remove (*de* from); (*vedar*) forbid; *v/i.* be in favor *en corte*; F be in vogue, be the thing; **~se** *de* deprive o.s. of, give up, forgo; **privativo** exclusive; particular; ~ *de* peculiar to, restricted to.
privilegio *m* privilege (*de inf.* of *ger.*); ⚖ sole right; *lit.* copyright; ~ *de invención* patent.
pro *m a. f* profit, advantage; *¡buena ~!* good appetite!; *de* ~ of note, of worth; *hombre de* ~ worthy man; *el* ~ *y el contra, los ~s y los contras* the pros and cons; *buena* ~ *le haga* and much good may it do him; *en* ~ *de* pro, for; on behalf of.
proa *f* bow(s), prow; *de* ~ bow *attr.*, fore.
probabilidad *f* probability, likelihood; chance, prospect; *según toda* ~ in all probability; *no tener* ~ *de ganar* be unlikely to win, have small chance of winning; **probable** probable, likely.
probanza *f* proof, evidence; inquiry.
probar [1m] **1.** *v/t.* prove; establish; (*ensayar*) try, try out, test; *vestido* try on; *comida etc.* taste, sample, try; *no pruebo nunca el vino* I never touch wine; **2.** *v/i.*: ~ *a inf.* try to *inf.*; *no me prueba bien el vino* wine doesn't agree with me; *¿probaremos?* shall we try?
probatorio probative, evidential; *documentos ~s de* documents in proof of.
probeta *f* ⚗ test tube; graduated cylinder; ⊕ test specimen; ~ *niño* test-tube baby.
probidad *f* integrity, rectitude.
problema *m* problem; puzzle; **problemático** problematic, doubtful.
probo upright, honest.
probóscide *f* proboscis.
procacidad *f* insolence *etc.*; **procaz** insolent, impudent; shameless.
procedencia *f* source, origin; ⚓ port of origin; ⚖ propriety; **procedente** fitting, reasonable; ⚖ proper, lawful; ~ *de* coming from, originating in; **proceder 1.** [2a] proceed (*a elección* to; *a inf.* to *inf.*; ⚖ *contra* against); (*portarse*) behave, act; (*convenir*) be proper; *si el caso procede* if the case warrants it; ~ *de* proceed from, flow from, spring from; originate in; **2.** *m* course, procedure; behaviour; **procedimiento** *m* procedure; proceeding; process; ⚖ proceedings.
proceloso stormy, tempestuous.
prócer *m* important person, chief, leader.
procesado *m*, **a** *f* accused; **procesal** procedural; ⚖ *costas etc.* legal; **procesar** [1a] ⚖ try, put on trial; prosecute; sue; *datos* process, data-process.
procesión *f* procession; F *la* ~ *va por dentro* still waters run deep.
proceso *m* process (*a. anat.*, ⚗); ⚖ trial; prosecution; proceedings, lawsuit; ~ *verbal S.Am.* minutes.
proclama *f* proclamation; ~*s pl.* banns; **proclamación** *f* proclamation; acclamation; **proclamar** [1a] proclaim; acclaim.
procreación *f* procreation; **procreador** procreative; **procrear** [1a] procreate; breed.
procuración *f* ⚖ letter (*or* power, warrant) of attorney; proxy; **procurador** *m* ⚖ attorney, *approx.* solicitor; *pol.* (*a.* ~ *a Cortes*) member of parliament; deputy, representative; **procurar** [1a] get; seek; cause, produce; ~ *inf.* try to *inf.*, strive to *inf.*, endeavor to *inf.*
prodigalidad *f* extravagance; plenty, abundance; **prodigar** [1h] *b.s.* waste, squander; *alabanzas etc.* lavish.
prodigio *m* prodigy; wonder, marvel; *niño* ~ child prodigy; **prodigioso** prodigious; marvelous.
pródigo 1. *b.s.* extravagant, wasteful; prodigal (*de* of), lavish (*de* with); *hijo* ~ prodigal son; **2.** *m*, **a** *f* spendthrift, prodigal.
producción *f* production; yield; produce; ~ *en masa*, ~ *en serie* mass production; **producir** [3o] *mst* produce; cause, generate; ~ *en serie* mass produce; *me produce la impresión de*

que it gives me the impression that; **~se** take place, come about, arise; come into being; *se produjo un cambio* a change came about; *se produjo una explosión* there was an explosion.

productividad *f* productivity; **productivo** productive; ✝ ~ *de interés* interest bearing; **producto** *m* product (*a.* ⚗, ⚘, ⊕); production; ✝ proceeds, yield; ~*s pl.* products, produce (*esp.* ⚘); ~ *alimenticio* foodstuff; **productor 1.** productive; producing; **2.** *m*, **-a** *f* producer; **produje, produzco** *etc. v. producir.*

proemio *m* preface, introduction.

proeza *f* exploit, heroic deed.

profanación *f* desecration; **profanar** [1a] desecrate, profane; **profano 1.** profane; indecent, immodest; **2.** *m* layman.

profecía *f* prophecy.

proferir [3i] utter; *indirecta* throw out; *injuria* hurl, let fly (*contra* at); *suspiro* fetch.

profesar [1a] *v/t.* profess; show, declare; *profesión* practice; *v/i. eccl.* take vows; **profesión** *f* profession, calling; declaration *de fe etc.*; *de* ~ professional; *hacer* ~ *de* pride o.s. on; **profesional** *adj. a. su. m/f* professional; **profesionalismo** *m* professionalism; **profesor** *m*, **-a** *f* teacher *en general*; (school)master, (school)mistress *de instituto*; *univ.* (*que tiene cátedra*) professor; (*subordinado*) lecturer; ~ *adjunto*, ~ *auxiliar approx.* assistant lecturer; ~ *agregado* visiting lecturer; **profesorado** *m* teaching profession; (*ps.*) teaching staff; (*puesto*) professorship.

profeta *m* prophet; **profético** prophetic(al); **profetizar** [1f] prophesy.

profiláctico *adj. a. su. m* prophylactic.

prófugo *m* fugitive; ⚔ deserter.

profundidad *f* depth; *esp. fig.* profundity; ⚗ height; *tener una* ~ *de 3 metros* be 3 meters deep; *poca* ~ shallowness; **profundizar** [1f] *hoyo* deepen, make deeper; (*a. v/i.* ~ *en*) *estudio* extend, make a careful study of; *misterio* fathom; **profundo** deep; *mst fig.* profound; *conocedor etc.* very knowledgeable; *tener 3 metros de* ~ be 3 meters deep.

profusión *f* profusion; extravagance; **profuso** profuse.

progenie *f* progeny; offspring *de p.*; *fig.* brood; **progenitor** *m* ancestor; **progenitura** *f* offspring.

programa *m* program; plan; schedule; ~ *de estudios* curriculum, syllabus; ~ *para ordenador* program(me); F software; **programación** *f* program(m)ing.

progresar [1a] progress, advance; **progresión** *f* progression (*a.* ⚗); **progresista** *adj. a. su. m/f pol.*, **progresivo** progressive; **progreso** *m* progress, advance; ~*s pl.* progress; *hacer* ~*s* make progress.

prohibición *f* prohibition (*de* of), ban (*de* on); embargo (*de* on); **prohibir** [3a] prohibit, forbid (*algo a alguien* a p. a th.); ban; stop; ~ *inf.* forbid *s.o.* to *inf.*; *v. dirección etc.*; *se prohibe fumar, prohibido fumar* no smoking; *queda terminantemente prohibido inf.* it is strictly forbidden to *inf.*; **prohibitivo** prohibitive.

prohijar [1a] adopt.

prohombre *m* leader, top man, man of authority.

prójima *f* F woman who is no better than she ought to be; **prójimo** *m* neighbor, fellow man, fellow being.

prole *f* offspring, progeny; *b.s.* brood, spawn.

proletariado *m* proletariat(e); **proletario** *adj. a. su. m*, **a** *f* proletarian.

proliferación *f* proliferation; **proliferar** [1a] proliferate; **prolífico** prolific (*en* of).

prolijidad *f* prolixity *etc.*; **prolijo** prolix, tedious, long-winded.

prologar [1h] preface; *libro prologado por X* book with a preface by X (*or* introduced by X); **prólogo** *m* prologue; preface, introduction *de libro etc.*

prolongación *f* prolongation; extension; **prolongar** [1h] prolong; extend; ⚗ *línea* produce.

promediar [1b] *v/t.* divide into two halves; *v/i.* (*interponerse*) mediate; *antes de* ~ *el mes* before the month is half-way through; **promedio** *m* average; middle *de una distancia.*

promesa *f* promise; **prometedor**

promising; *perspectiva* hopeful, rosy; **prometer** [2a] *v/t.* promise; pledge; *v/i.* have (*or* show) promise; *es un chico que promete* he's a promising lad; **~se** *algo* expect, promise o.s.; (*novios*) get engaged; *estar prometido* be engaged; **prometida** *f* fiancée; **prometido** *m* promise; (*p.*) fiancé.
prominencia *f* protuberance; *esp. fig.* prominence; **prominente** prominent; protuberant.
promiscuidad *f* mixture, jumble, confusion *de objetos*; promiscuity *de vida*; **promiscuo** *objetos* all mixed up, in disorder; ambiguous; *vida* promiscuous.
promisión *v. tierra.*
promoción *f* (*ascenso*) promotion; (*fomento*) promotion, advancement, furtherance; ⚔ *la ~ de 1987* the 1987 class.
promontorio *m* promontory, headland.
promotor *m*, **promovedor** *m* promoter; pioneer; instigator; **promover** [2h] (*ascender*) promote; (*fomentar*) promote, forward, further; *proyecto etc.* pioneer, set on foot; *rebelión* stir up, instigate.
promulgación *f* promulgation; **promulgar** [1h] promulgate; *fig.* proclaim, announce publicly.
pronombre *m* pronoun; **pronominal** pronominal.
pronosticación *f* prediction, prognostication; **pronosticar** [1g] forecast, predict, foretell, prognosticate; **pronóstico** *m* forecast, prediction; ⚕ prognosis; (*señal*) omen, prognostic; *~ del tiempo* weather forecast; ⚕ *de ~ leve* slight, not serious; *de ~ reservado* of uncertain gravity (*or* extent).
prontitud *f* promptness, speed; quickness, keenness *de ingenio*; **pronto 1.** *adj.* prompt, quick, speedy; *contestación* prompt, swift, ⚘ early; *curación* speedy; (*listo*) ready (*para inf.* to *inf.*); **2.** *adv.* quickly, promptly; soon; at once; early; *un poco ~* a bit early, on the early side; *lo más ~ posible* as soon as possible; *tan ~ como* as soon as; *de ~* suddenly; *¡hasta ~!* see you soon!; *por de ~, por lo ~* meanwhile, for the present; **3.** *m* sudden movement, jerk; F strong impulse (*or* urge).
prontuario *m* handbook, compendium.
prónuba *f* bridesmaid.
pronunciación *f* pronunciation; **pronunciado** *S.Am.* obvious, clear; emphasized; **pronunciamiento** *m* ⚔ revolt, insurrection; **pronunciar** [1b] pronounce; utter; *discurso* make, deliver; ⚖ *sentencia* pass, pronounce; **~se** declare (o.s.) (*en favor de* in favor of); ⚔ revolt, rebel.
propagación *f biol. etc.* propagation; *fig.* spreading, dissemination; **propaganda** *f* propaganda; ⚘ advertising; **propagandista** *m/f* propagandist; **propagar** [1h] *biol. etc.* propagate; *fig. ideas etc.* spread, disseminate.
propalar [1a] divulge, disclose.
propasarse [1a] go to extremes, go too far; forget o.s.
propender [2a] incline, tend (*a* to); **propensión** *f* inclination (*a* for), propensity (*a* to), tendency (*a* to, towards); bent (*a* for); proneness (*a* to); **propenso:** *~ a* inclined to; prone to, subject to; *~ a inf.* apt to *inf.*
propiamente properly; *la arquitectura ~ dicha* architecture proper.
propiciación *f* propitiation; **propiciar** [1b] propitiate; **propiciatorio** propitiatory; **propicio** propitious, auspicious; *p.* kind, helpful.
propiedad *f* (*bienes, finca*) property; (*atributo*) property (*a.* ⚗), attribute; (*dominio*) ownership; (*lo propio*) appositeness; *paint. etc.* likeness, resemblance; *~ literaria* copyright, rights; *en ~* properly; *es ~* copyright; **propietaria** *f* proprietress; **propietario 1.** proprietary; **2.** *m* proprietor; owner; (*terrateniente*) landowner, landlord.
propina *f* tip, gratuity; F *de ~* into the bargain; **propinar** [1a] *bebida* treat to; *golpe* deal; *paliza* give; **~se** *algo* treat o.s. to.
propincuidad *f* propinquity; **propincuo** near.
propio (*conveniente*) proper, suitable, fitting (*para* for); (*que per-*

tenece a uno) own, one's own; characteristic (*de* of), peculiar (*de* to), special; (*mismo*) same; natural, genuine; *el ~ obispo* the bishop himself; *sus ~as palabras* his very words; *lo hizo con su ~a mano* he did it with his own hand; *la casa es la suya ~a* the house is his very own; *la ciudad tiene un carácter ~* the city has a character of its own; F *haré lo ~ que tú* I'll do the same as you.

proponente *m* proposer; **proponer** [2r] propose; *teoría etc.* propound, put forward; **~se** *inf.* propose to *inf.*, plan to *inf.*

proporción *f* proportion; ratio; rate; *en ~ con* in proportion to; *no guardar ~* be out of proportion (*con* to, with); **proporcionado** proportionate; *bien ~* well-proportioned, shapely; **proporcional** proportional; **proporcionar** [1a] provide, supply, give; adjust, adapt.

proposición *f* proposition; proposal.

propósito *m* purpose, aim, intention; *buenos ~s pl.* good resolutions; *a ~* (*adj.*) appropriate, fitting (*para* for); *observación* apt, apposite; *a ~* (*adv.*) by the way, incidentally; *a ~ de* about; *de ~* on purpose, purposely, deliberately; *fuera de ~* off the point, out of place, irrelevant(ly); *sin ~ fijo* purposeless(ly).

propuesta *f* proposition, proposal.

propulsión *f* propulsion; *~ a cohete, ~ cohética* rocket propulsion; *~ a chorro, ~ por reacción* jet propulsion; **propulsor** *m* propellent.

prorrata *f* share, quota; *a ~* pro rata, proportionately; **prorratear** [1a] apportion, share out; average; **prorrateo** *m* apportionment, sharing.

prórroga *f* prorogation; ✝ extension; ⚖ stay, respite; *deportes*: extra time; **prorrogación** *f* prorogation; **prorrogar** [1h] (*suspender*) prorogue, adjourn; (*suprimir*) abolish; (*aplazar*) postpone; *plazo* extend; ⚖ stay, respite.

prorrumpir [3a] burst forth, break forth; *~ en gritos, lágrimas* burst into.

prosa *f* prose; F idle chatter; **prosador** *m*, **-a** *f* prose writer; F chatterbox, great talker; **prosaico** prosaic, prose *attr.*; *fig.* prosaic, prosy, ordinary; **prosaísmo** *m fig.* ordinariness.

prosapia *f* ancestry, lineage.

proscribir [3a; *p.p. proscrito*] (*prohibir*) prohibit, ban; *partido etc.* proscribe; (*desterrar*) banish; *criminal* outlaw; **proscripción** *f* ban (*de* on), prohibition (*de* of); proscription; banishment; **proscrito 1.** *p.p. of proscribir*; **2.** *adj.* banned; banished; outlawed; **3.** *m* exile; outlaw.

prosecución *f* prosecution, continuation; pursuit; **proseguir** [3d *a.* 3l] *v/t.* continue, proceed with, carry on; *demanda* push; *estudio, investigación* pursue; *v/i.* continue, go on.

proselitismo *m* proselytism; **prosélito** *m*, **a** *f* proselyte.

prosista *m/f* prose writer.

prosodia *f gr.* rules for pronunciation and accentuation; *poet.* prosody.

prosopopeya *f* F pomposity, solemnity.

prospección *f* exploration; ⚒ prospecting (*de* for); **prospecto** *m* prospectus; **prospector** *m* prospector.

prosperar [1a] prosper, thrive, flourish; **prosperidad** *f* prosperity; success, good fortune; (*período*) good times; **próspero** prosperous, thriving, flourishing; successful; *fortuna etc.* favorable.

prosternarse [1a] prostrate o.s.

prostíbulo *m* brothel.

prostitución *f* prostitution; **prostituir** [3g] prostitute (*a. fig.*); **prostituta** *f* prostitute.

protagonista *m/f* protagonist; main character, (*m*) hero, (*f*) heroine.

protección *f* protection; *~ aduanera* protective tariff; *~ a la infancia* child welfare; **proteccionista** *adj. a. su. m/f* protectionist; *impuesto* protective; **protector 1.** protective; *tono* patronizing; **2.** *m*, **-a** *f* protector; guardian; **protectorado** *m* protectorate; **proteger** [2c] protect (*de, contra* from, against); shield, shelter; defend; (*alentar*) support, encourage; **protegido** *m*, **a** *f* protegé(e).

proteína *f* protein.
protervo wicked, perverse.
protesta *f* protest; protestation *de amistad etc.*; **protestación** *f* protestation; ~ *de fe* profession of faith; **protestante** *adj. a. su. m/f* Protestant; **protestantismo** *m* Protestantism; **protestar** [1a] protest (*a.* ✝, ⚖; *contra, de* against; *de que* that); remonstrate; *fe* profess; ~ *de inocencia etc.* protest; **protesto** *m* ✝, ⚖ protest.
protocolo *m* protocol; etiquette *de sociedad.*
protón *m* proton.
protoplasma *m* protoplasm.
prototipo *m* prototype.
protuberancia *f* protuberance; **protuberante** protuberant.
provecto: *de edad ~a* elderly, advanced in years.
provecho *m* advantage, benefit, profit (*a.* ✝); *~s* perquisites; *negocio de ~* profitable business; *persona de ~* useful person, decent sort; *¡buen ~! hoping that those eating will enjoy their meal* good appetite!; good luck!; *¡buen ~ le haga!* and much good may it do him!; *de ~* useful; *sacar ~ de* benefit by (*or* from), profit by (*or* from); **provechoso** advantageous, beneficial, profitable (*a.* ✝).
proveedor *m*, **-a** *f* supplier, purveyor; caterer; ~ *casero* roundsman; **proveer** [2a; *p.p. provisto, a. proveído*] provide, supply (*de* with); *negocio* transact; ⚖ decree; *vacante* fill; ~ *a* cater for.
provenir [3s]: ~ *de* come from, arise from, stem from.
provenzal *adj. a. su. m* Provençal.
proverbial proverbial; **proverbio** *m* proverb.
providencia *f* forethought, foresight, providence; (*Divina*) ♀ Providence; **providencial** providential; **providente, próvido** provident.
provincia *f* province; *de ~(s) freq.* provincial, country *attr.*; **provincial** *adj. a. su. m*, **-a** *f* (*eccl.*) provincial; **provincialismo** *m* provincialism; **provinciano 1.** provincial, country *attr.*; **2.** *m*, **a** *f* provincial, country dweller.
provisión *f* provision; supply, store; *~es pl.* provisions *etc.*;
provisional provisional, temporary.
provocación *f* provocation; (*insulto*) affront; **provocador** provocative; **provocar** [1g] *v/t.* provoke; incite, tempt, move; (*fomentar*) promote, forward; *cambio, reacción etc.* provoke, bring about, induce; ~ *a cólera* rouse to fury; ~ *a lástima* move to pity; *el mar provoca a bañarse* the sea invites (*or* tempts) one to bathe; *v/i.* F be sick; **provocativo** provocative, provoking.
próximamente approximately; (*pronto*) shortly; **proximidad** *f* proximity, nearness; **próximo** near, next, neighboring; *pariente* close; *el mes ~* next month; *el mes ~ pasado* last month; *en fecha ~a* at an early date; *estar ~ a inf.* be on the point of *ger.*
proyección *f* projection; **proyectar** [1a] *película etc.* project, show; *sombra* cast; *casa, máquina etc.* plan, design; *viaje etc.* plan; ~ *inf.* plan to *inf.*; *estar proyectado para inf.* be designed to *inf.*; **proyectil** *m* projectile, missile; *esp.* ⚔ shell; ~ *buscador del blanco* homing missile; ~ *dirigido*, ~ *teleguiado* guided missile; **proyectista** *m/f* designer, planner; **proyecto** *m* project, scheme, plan; (*presupuesto*) detailed estimate; ~ *de ley* bill; *¿qué ~s tienes para las vacaciones?* what are your plans for the holiday?; **proyector** *m cine*: projector; ⚡, ⚔ searchlight.
prudencia *f* prudence, wisdom; sound judgement; **prudente** prudent, wise, sensible; judicious.
prueba *f* proof (*a.* ✗, *typ.*); (*indicio*) proof, sign, token; ⚖ proof, evidence (*a. fig.*); (*ensayo*) test, trial, try-out; *phot.* proof, print; *esp.* ⚗ experiment; taste, sample *de comida etc.*; fitting *de vestido*; *deportes*: event; *~s pl. typ.* proofs, proof sheets; *~s pl.* ⊕, *deportes etc.*: trials; ~ *de alcohol* alcohol-level test (for drunken driving); ~ *documental* documentary evidence; ~ *eliminatoria* heat; ~ *de fuego fig.* acid test; ~ *indiciaria* circumstantial evidence; *phot.* ~ *positiva* positive print; *de ~ freq.* test *attr.*, testing; *phot. copia de ~* test print; *a ~* on trial, on approval;

a ~ *de* proof against; *a* ~ *de agua* waterproof; *a* ~ *de bala* bulletproof; *a* ~ *de escaladores* burglarproof; *a* ~ *de incendio* fireproof; *a toda* ~ foolproof; *en* ~ *de* in proof of; *poner a* ~, *someter a* ~ (put to the) test, try out.

prurito *m* ⚕ itch; *fig.* itch, urge (*de inf.* to *inf.*).

prusiano *adj. a. su. m*, **a** *f* Prussian.

psicoanálisis *m* psychoanalysis; **psicoanalista** *m/f* psychoanalyst; **psicología** *f* psychology; **psicológico** psychological; **psicólogo** *m* psychologist; **psicoterapia** *f* psychotherapy; ~ *de grupo* group therapy; **psicosis** *f* psychosis; **psique** *f* psyche; **psiquiatra** *m* psychiatrist; **psiquiatría** *f* psychiatry; **psíquico** psychic(al).

ptomaína *f* ptomaine.

púa *f zo.*, ⚘ prickle, spike, spine; quill *de erizo*; ⚘ graft *para injertar*; tooth *de peine*; prong *de horquilla etc.*; barb *de anzuelo etc.*

pubertad *f* puberty.

publicación *f* publication; **publicar** [1g] publish; (*dar publicidad a*) publicize; *secreto* disclose, divulge; **publicidad** *f* publicity; ☤ advertising; **publicista** *m/f* publicist; **público 1.** public; state *attr.*; *hacer* ~ publish, disclose; **2.** *m* public; *thea. etc.* audience; *deportes etc.*: spectators; crowd; *un* ~ *numeroso* a large attendance; *en* ~ publicly, in public.

puchera *f* F pot; stew; **pucherazo** *m* F rigging of an election, fiddling with votes; **puchero** *m* pot; (*guisado*) stew; F daily bread; F (*gesto*) pout, face; F *hacer* ~*s* pout, screw up one's face; F *volcar el* ~ rig an election, fiddle the voting.

puches *m/pl.* porridge, gruel.

pucho *m* remnant; (*cigarro*) stump; tiny amount, trifle.

pude *etc. v. poder.*

pudendo: *partes* ~*as* private parts.

pudibundo modest, shy; chaste; **pudicicia** *f* modesty; chastity; **púdico** modest, shy; chaste.

pudiendo *v. poder.*

pudiente well-to-do; powerful.

pudor *m* modesty, shyness; virtue, chastity; (*vergüenza*) shame; *atentado al* ~ indecent offence; **pudoroso** modest, shy; chaste.

pudrición *f*, **pudrimiento** *m* rot, rottenness; putrescence; *pudrición seca* dry rot; **pudrir** [3a] rot; ~**se** rot, decay, putrefy; *fig.* rot, languish *en cárcel*; die (*de aburrimiento etc.* of).

pueblada *f S.Am.* revolt; **pueblero 1.** *S.Am.* village *attr.*; **2.** *m S.Am.* villager; **pueblo** *m* (*nación*) people, nation; (*plebe*) lower orders, common people; (*poblado*) town, village.

puedo *etc. v. poder.*

puente *m* bridge (*a.* ♪); ⚓ deck; ⚓ ~ (*de mando*) bridge; ~ *aéreo* air lift; ~ *colgante* suspension bridge; ~ *de engrase* grease lift; ~ *giratorio* swing bridge; ~ *levadizo* drawbridge; ~ *de pontones* pontoon bridge; *hacer* ~ take the intervening day off.

puerca *f* sow; F slut; **puerco 1.** *m* pig, hog; F pig; ~ *espín*, ~ *espino* porcupine; **2.** dirty, filthy.

puericia *f* boyhood; **pueril** childish; *contp.* puerile, childish; **puerilidad** *f* puerility, childishness.

puerro *m* leek; *sl.* joint; *sl.* hashish cigarette.

puerta *f* door; doorway; gate *de jardín, ciudad etc.*; gateway (*a. fig.*); ~ *accesoria* side door; ~ *excusada*, ~ *falsa* private door, side door; ~ *giratoria* swing door, revolving door; ~ *principal* front door; ~ *de servicio* tradesman's entrance; ~ *trasera* back door; ~ *ventana* french window; ~ *vidriera* glass door; *a* ~ *cerrada* behind closed doors; *a las* ~*s de la muerte* at death's door; *de* ~ *en* ~ from door to door; *tomar la* ~ leave, get out.

puerto *m* ⚓ port, harbor; (*ciudad*) port; *esp. fig.* haven; *geog.* pass; ~ *de escala* port of call; ~ *franco* free port; *entrar a* ~ put in.

puertorriqueño *adj. a. su. m*, **a** *f* (native) of Puerto Rico.

pues (*ya que*) since, for, because; (*continuativo*) then; well; well then; (*afirmación*) yes, certainly; ~ ... (*vacilando*) well ...; *ahora* ~ now, now then; ~ *bien* well then, very well; ~ *sí* well yes, yes certainly.

puesta *f* stake, bet *en el juego*; *orn.* egg-laying; ~ *del sol* sunset; ~ *en marcha* starting.

puesto 1. *p.p.* of *poner*; *ir bien* ~ be

well dressed; *con el sombrero* ~ with his hat on; **2.** *m* place, position, situation; (*empleo*) post, position; ⚔ post; booth, stall *de mercado*; (*quiosco*) stand; pitch *de vendedor ambulante*; ~ *de escucha* listening post; ~ *de policía* police post, police station; ~ *de socorro* first-aid post; **3.:** ~ *que* since, as.

¡puf! ugh!

púgil *m* boxer; **pugilato** *m* boxing.

pugna *f fig.* battle, struggle; *estar en* ~ *con* conflict with; **pugnacidad** *f* pugnacity; **pugnar** [1a] struggle, fight, strive (*por inf.* to *inf.*); **pugnaz** pugnacious.

puja *f* bid; F *sacar de la* ~ *a* get ahead of; get *s.o.* out of a jam.

pujante strong, vigorous; *p.* strapping; **pujanza** *f* strength, vigor; **pujar** [1a] *v/t. precio* raise, push up; *v/i.* bid up *en subasta*; *naipes*: bid; (*pugnar*) struggle, strain; (*no lograr hablar*) be at a loss for words, be tongue-tied; falter *hablando*; (*casi llorar*) be on the verge of tears.

pujo *m fig.* strong impulse, strong desire; F try, shot.

pulcritud *f* neatness *etc.*; **pulcro** neat, tidy, smart; exquisite, delicate.

pulga *f* flea; *aguantar* ~ stand for no nonsense; *de malas* ~*s* peppery; *hacer de una* ~ *un camello, hacer de una* ~ *un elefante* make a mountain out of a molehill; *tener malas* ~*s* be bad-tempered, be short-tempered.

pulgada *f* inch.

pulgar *m* thumb; **pulgarada** *f* pinch *de rapé etc.*; flip, flick *con el pulgar*; (*medida*) inch.

pulido (*pulcro*) neat, tidy; *trabajo etc.* polished; **pulidor** *m*, **-a** *f* polisher; **pulimentar** [1a] polish; (*alisar*) smooth; **pulimento** *m* polish; **pulir** [3a] polish; *fig.* polish up, touch up; F (*robar*) pinch; F (*vender*) flog; ~**se** *fig.* acquire polish; dress up.

pulmón *m* lung; **pulmonar** pulmonary, lung *attr.*; **pulmonía** *f* pneumonia.

pulpa *f* pulp; soft part *de carne, fruta*; ~ *de madera* wood pulp; **pulpejo** *m* fleshy part, soft part.

pulpería *f S.Am.* general store.

púlpito *m* pulpit.

pulpo *m* octopus.

pulposo pulpy; fleshy.

pulquérrimo *sup. of pulcro.*

pulsación *f* pulsation; throb(bing), beat(ing); F touch; tap *en máquina de escribir*; **pulsador** *m* push button; **pulsar** [1a] *v/t.* ♪ *instrumento* play; *tecla etc.* touch, strike, play; *botón* press, push; ⚕ feel the pulse of; *fig.* sound out, explore; *v/i.* pulsate, throb, beat.

pulsera *f* wristlet, bracelet.

pulso *m anat.* pulse; (*muñeca*) wrist; *fig.* steady hand, firmness of touch; (*cuidado*) care, caution; *a* ~ by sheer strength; by sheer hard work; *fig.* the hard way; *a* ~ *sudando* by the sweat of one's brow; *hecho a* ~ *dibujo* freehand; *tomar el* ~ *a* feel the pulse of; *tomar a* ~ lift clean off the ground; *S.Am.* F drink in one go.

pulular [1a] swarm, abound.

pulverización *f* pulverization; spray(ing) *de líquido*; **pulverizador** *m* spray(er); **pulverizar** [1f] pulverize; powder; *líquido* spray; **pulverulento** powdered, powdery.

pulla *f* taunt, cutting remark; dig; rude word, indecent remark.

¡pum! bang!; pop!

punción *f* ⚕ puncture.

punching ['puntʃin] *m* punch ball.

pundonor *m* point of honor; honor; face (*fig.*); **pundonoroso** honorable; punctilious, scrupulous.

pungir [3c] prick; sting.

punible punishable; **punición** *f* punishment; **punitivo** punitive.

punta *f* point (*a. geog.*); end, tip; end, butt *de cigarro*; ⊕ nail; toe *de zapato etc.*; horn *de toro*; sourness *de vino*; (*pizca*) touch, trace, tinge; ~ *del pie* toe; ~ *de lanza* spearhead (*a. fig.*); *de* ~ on end, endways; *estar de* ~ be at odds (*con* with); *hacer* ~ be first, go first; *poner(se) de* ~ (*pelo*) stand on end; *ponerse de* ~ *con* fall out with; *sacar* ~ *a* sharpen, point; *tener* ~ *de loco* have a streak of madness.

puntada *f* stitch (*a. S.Am.* ⚕).

puntal *m* ▲ prop, shore; stanchion; ⊕ strut; *fig.* prop, support; *S.Am.* snack.

puntapié *m* kick.

punteado *m* ♪ twang(ing), plucking;

puntear [1a] ♪ pluck, twang; *sew.* stitch; *dibujo etc.* dot, mark with dots; stipple; fleck.
puntera *f* toe (cap); F kick.
puntería *f* aim(ing); (*destreza*) marksmanship; *enmendar la* ~ correct one's aim; *hacer la* ~ *de* aim, sight; *tener mala* ~ be a bad shot.
puntiagudo sharp(-pointed).
puntilla *f* ⊕ tack, brad; *sew.* narrow lace edging; point *de pluma*; *de* ~*s* on tiptoe.
puntillo *m* punctilio; **puntilloso** punctilious.
punto *m* point (*a. fig.*; *sitio, momento, detalle, rasgo, estado, etc.*); (*sitio*) spot, place; dot *señalado en papel etc.*; *gr.* full stop; pip *de carta*; dot, speckle, fleck *de tela*; *sew.* stitch; (*malla*) mesh; *fig.* point of honor; *dos* ~*s gr.* colon; ~ *y coma* semicolon; ¡~ *en boca!* mum's the word!; ~ *por* ~ point by point; ~ *de admiración* exclamation mark; ~ *de apoyo* fulcrum; ~ *capital* crucial point, crux; ~*s pl. cardinales* cardinal points; ~ *de congelación* freezing point; ~*s pl. de consulta* terms of reference; ~ *de contacto* point of contact; ~ *de ebullición* boiling point; ~ *de fuga* vanishing point; ~ *de fusión* melting point; ~ *de honor* point of honor; ~ *de inflamación* flash point; ~ *de interrogación* question mark; ~ *de media* plain knitting; ~ *muerto* ⊕ dead center; *mot.* neutral (*a.* ~ *neutral*); *fig.* stalemate, deadlock; ~ *neutro mot.* neutral; ~ *de partida* starting point; ~*s pl. suspensivos three dots indicating hesitation etc.* (...); ~ *de vista* point of view; *a* ~ ready; *a* ~ *fijo* for sure; *al* ~ at once, instantly; *de todo* ~ completely; *en* ~ (*hora*) on the dot, sharp; *en* ~ *a* with regard to; *cocina*: *en su* ~ done to a turn; *hasta cierto* ~ up to a point; *hasta el* ~ *de inf.* to the extent of *ger.*; *hasta tal* ~ *que* to such an extent that; *por* ~*s* one thing at a time; *boxeo*: on points; *bajar de* ~ decline; *estar a* ~ *de inf.* be on the point of *ger.*; *hacer* ~ knit; *poner a* ~ *motor* tune up; *poner en su* ~ bring to perfection; *subir de* ~ grow; *b.s.* get worse.
puntuación *f gr.* punctuation; marking *de exámenes*; mark, class *en examen*; *deportes*: score; **puntual** prompt; *cálculo etc.* exact; *p. etc.* reliable, conscientious; **puntualidad** *f* punctuality *etc.*; **puntualizar** [1f] fix in the mind; *suceso* give an exact account of; (*acabar*) finish off; **puntuar** [1e] *v/t. gr.* punctuate; *examen* mark; *v/i. deportes*: score; *eso no puntúa* that doesn't count.
puntura *f* puncture, prick.
punzada *f* puncture, prick; ⚕ stitch *de costado*; ⚕ shooting pain, spasm, twinge; *fig.* pang; **punzante** *dolor* shooting, stabbing; *observación* biting, caustic; **punzar** [1f] *v/t.* puncture, pierce, prick; punch; *v/i.* (*dolor*) shoot, stab, sting; **punzón** *m* punch; graver, burin.
puñada *f* punch, clout.
puñado *m* handful (*a. fig.*).
puñal *m* dagger; **puñalada** *f* stab; *fig.* grievous blow; F *coser a* ~*s* cut up, carve up.
puñetazo *m* punch; *dar un* ~ *a* punch; *dar de* ~*s* punch, pommel.
puño *m anat.* fist; (*contenido*) fistful, handful; (*mango*) handle, haft, hilt; cuff *de camisa*; *de propio* ~ in one's own handwriting; *de* ~ *y letra de X* in X's own handwriting; *como un* ~ tangible, absolutely real; *por sus* ~*s* by oneself, on one's own; *meter en un* ~ intimidate, cow; domineer.
pupa *f* ⚕ pimple, blister.
pupila *f anat.* pupil; (*p.*) ward; **pupilo** *m* ward; boarder.
pupitre *m* desk.
puré *m* purée, soup; ~ *de patatas* mashed potatoes.
pureza *f* purity.
purga *f* purge (*a. pol.*), purgative; ⊕ *válvula de* ~ vent; **purgación** *f* purging; **purgante** *m* laxative; **purgar** [1h] purge (*a. pol.*); purify, refine; ⊕ vent, drain; *fig. pecado etc.* purge, expiate; ~**se** ⚕ take a purge; *fig.* purge o.s.; **purgativo** purgative; **purgatorio** *m* purgatory.
purificación *f* purification; **purificar** [1g] purify; cleanse; ⊕ refine.
Purísima: *la* ~ the Virgin.
purista *m/f* purist.
puritanismo *m* puritanism; **puritano 1.** puritanical; puritan; **2.** *m*, **a** *f* puritan.
puro 1. pure; (*sin mezcla*) pure, un-

adulterated, unalloyed; *verdad* plain, simple, unvarnished; *cielo* clear; *de ~ aburrimiento* out of sheer boredom; *de ~ bobo* out of sheer stupidity; **2.** *m* cigar.

púrpura *f* purple; purple cloth; **purpurar** [1a] purple; dye purple; **purpúreo, purpurino** purple.

purulento purulent.

pus *m* pus, matter.

puse *etc. v. poner.*

pusilánime faint-hearted, pusillanimous; **pusilanimidad** *f* faint-heartedness, pusillanimity.

pústula *f* pustule, sore, pimple.

puta *f* whore, prostitute.

putativo supposed, putative.

putrefacción *f* rot(tenness), putrefaction, decay; *~ fungoide* dry rot; **putrefacto** rotten, putrid; **putrescente** rotting, putrescent; **pútrido** putrid, rotten.

Q

que 1. *pron. relativo*: (*p.*) (*sujeto*) who, (*acc.*) whom; (*cosa*) which; (*p., cosa*) that; *en muchos casos se puede suprimir*; *el hombre ~ vi* the man (whom) I saw; *el ~* (*p.*) he who, whoever; who, the one who; (*cosa*) which, the one which; *la ~* she who *etc.*; *los ~*, *las ~* those who *etc.*; *lo ~* what, that which; (*esp. tras coma*) which, something which, a fact which; *lo ~ quiero* what I want; *todo lo ~ vi* all (that) I saw; *lo ~ es eso* as for that; *no tengo nada ~ hacer* I have nothing to do; **2.** *cj.* a) that; *en muchos casos se puede suprimir*: *yo sé ~ es verdad* I know (that) it is true; *dice ~ sí* he says yes; *¡~ sí, hombre!* I tell you it is!; *v.* *sí*[1]; b) (*pues*) for, because; *a menudo no se traduce*: *¡cuidado!, ~ viene un coche* look out! there's a car coming; c) *con subjuntivo*: *quiero ~ lo hagas* I want you to do it; *¡~ lo pases bien!* have a good time!; *¡~ entre!* let him come in!, send him in!; d) *comparaciones*: than; *más ~ yo* more than I; e) *el ~ subj.* the fact that, that; f) *~ ... ~* whether ... or; *yo ~ tú* if I were you; F *¡a ~ no!* I bet it isn't!, I bet you can't!; no, I tell you!

qué 1. *pron. interrogativo*: *¿~?* what?; *¿~ hiciste entonces?* what did you do then?; **2.** *¡~ perro más feo!* what an ugly dog!; *¡~ bonito!* how pretty!; *¡~ asco!* how disgusting!; *¿de ~ tamaño es?* how big is it?, what size is it?; *¿~ edad tiene?* how old is he?; *¡~ de ...!* how many ...!; **3.** *¿a ~?* why?; *¿a mí ~?* what's that got to do with me?; *¿de ~ le conoce?* how do you know him?; F *¿y ~?* so what?; what then?; *sin ~ ni para ~* without rhyme or reason.

quebrada *f* gorge, ravine; gap.

quebradero *m*: F *~ de cabeza* headache, worry; **quebradizo** fragile, delicate, brittle; *hojaldre* short; *salud, virtud* frail; **quebrado 1.** *terreno* rough, broken; ⚕ ruptured; ✝ bankrupt; **2.** *m* A fraction; **quebradura** *f* fissure, slit; ⚕ rupture; **quebraja** *f* fissure, slit; **quebrantadura** *f*, **quebrantamiento** *m* breaking, breakage *etc.*; ⚕ exhaustion, fatigue; **quebrantahuesos** *m* bearded vulture; **quebrantar** [1a] break (*a. fig.*); crack; shatter; *caja* break open; *cárcel* break out of; *color* tone down; *S.Am. potro* break in; *resistencia, salud* break, shatter; *p.* annoy; **quebranto** *m* (*acto*) breaking *etc.*; ⚕ weakness, poor health; *fig.* (*pérdida*) severe loss; (*pena*) great sorrow.

quebrar [1k] *v/t.* break, smash; *color* tone down; *v/i.* break; ✝ go bankrupt, fail; (*disminuir*) slacken, weaken; *~ con* break with; **~se** break, get broken; ⚕ be ruptured.

queche *m* smack, ketch.

queda *f* curfew.

quedar [1a] **1.** (*permanecer en un lugar etc.*) stay, remain; (*sobrar*) be left (over), remain; *~ adj., p.p.* be, remain, stay; keep; *quedé 3 días* I stayed 3 days; *quedan 3* there are 3 left; *me quedan 3* I have 3 left; *no quedan más que ruinas* there are only ruins left, there is nothing but ruins; *la cosa quedó así* there the matter rested; *~ inmóvil* keep still; *~ sentado* remain seated, stay sitting down; *quedó aterrado* he was terrified; *~ a deber* still owe; *~ bien* do o.s. justice, acquit o.s. well; *~ en inf.* agree to *inf.*; *~ en que* agree that; *¿en qué quedamos?* well, what do we say?; *~ por inf.* remain to be *p.p.*, be still to be *p.p.*; *el trabajo queda por hacer* the work is still to be done; *~ por encima de* come off better than, have the laugh of; *~ sin hacer* be left undone; **2. ~se** stay, remain; stay on, stay behind, linger (on); put up (*en hotel* at); *~ ciego* go blind; *~ con* (*retener*) keep, hold on to, retain; *~ en casa* stay in(doors); *no se quedó* *en menos* he was not to be outdone; *se me quedan chicos los zapatos* I have outgrown my shoes; ~ *sin gasolina etc.* run out of.

quedo 1. *adj.* quiet, still; **2.** *adv.* softly.

quehacer *m* job, task, duty; ~*es pl. domésticos* household jobs, chores; housekeeping.

queja *f* (*dolor*) moan, groan; whine; (*resentimiento*) complaint, grumble, grouse; ⚖ *etc.* protest, complaint; *tener* ~ *de* have a complaint to make about; **quejarse** [1a] (*dolor*) moan, groan; whine; complain (*de* about, of), grumble (*de* about, at); protest (*de* about, at); **quejido** *m* moan, groan; **quejoso** complaining, querulous; **quejumbroso** whining, plaintive; cantankerous.

quema *f* fire, burning; **quemador** *m* burner; ~ *de gas* gas burner; **quemadura** *f* burn; scald *de líquido etc.*; (*insolación*) sunburn; blowout *de fusible*; **quemar** [1a] **1.** *v/t.* burn; (*pegar fuego a*) kindle, set on fire; (*líquido*) scald; *boca* burn; *plantas* (*sol*) burn, scorch; (*helada*) burn, frost; *fusible* blow, burn out; F *precio* slash, cut; F *p.* annoy, upset; *v. tierra*; **2.** *v/i. fig.* be burning hot; **3.** ~**se** burn; scorch; feel burning hot; F (*buscando*) be warm; *¡qué te quemas!* you're getting warm!

quemarropa: *a* ~ point-blank.

quemazón *f* burn, burning; *fig.* intense heat; F (*comezón*) itch; F (*palabra*) cutting remark; F (*resentimiento*) pique, annoyance; *S.Am.* F ✝ bargain sale, cut-price sale.

quepo *etc. v. caber.*

querella *f* dispute, controversy; ⚖ *etc.* complaint, charge; **querellante** *m/f* ⚖ plaintiff, complainant; **querellarse** [1a] complain; ⚖ file a complaint, bring an action.

querencia *f zo.* (*guarida*) lair, haunt; *zo.* homing instinct; *fig.* den, haunt, favorite spot; *buscar la* ~ home.

querer 1. [2u] (*amar*) love; (*tener afición a*) like; (*desear*) want, wish; *quiero hacerlo* I want to do it; *quiero que lo hagas* I want you to do it; *te quiero mucho* I love you very much; *en la oficina le quieren mucho* he is well liked in the office; *quisiera saber* I should like to know; *como Vd. quiera* as you please, just as you wish; *como quiera* anyhow, anyway; *como quiera que* whereas; since, inasmuch as; *quiera o no quiera* willy-nilly; *v. decir*; *quiere llover* it is trying to rain; *sin* ~ inadvertently, unintentionally, by mistake; *lo hizo sin* ~ he didn't mean to do it; **2.** *m* love, affection.

querida *f b.s.* mistress; *¡sí,* ~*!* yes dear, yes darling; **querido 1.** dear, beloved, darling; **2.** *m b.s.* lover; *¡sí,* ~*!* yes dear, yes darling; *el* ~ *de las musas* the darling of the muses.

querosena *m* kerosene.

quesera *f* (*p.*) dairymaid; cheese maker; (*plato*) cheese dish; **quesería** *f* dairy *en granja*; cheese factory; **quesero** *m* dairyman; cheese maker; **queso** *m* cheese; ~ *crema* cream cheese; ~ *helado* brick ice cream; F *me lo dio con* ~ he put one over on me; ~ *para extender* cheese spread.

¡quiá! surely not!

quicio *m* hinge; *fig. fuera de* ~ out of joint; *sacar de* ~ exasperate.

quid [kið] *m* gist, core, nub.

quídam ['kiðan] *m* F (*fulano*) somebody or other; *contp.* nobody.

quiebra *f* (*grieta*) crack, fissure; (*pérdida*) loss, damage; ✝ bankruptcy *de p.*, failure *de sociedad*, slump, crash *de economía entera*.

quiebro *m* ♪ trill; *toros*: dodge, avoiding action; F *dar el* ~ *a p.* dodge.

quien (*sujeto*) who, (*acc.*) whom; (*en comienzo de frase*) he *etc.* who, whoever; *el hombre a* ~ *lo di* the man to whom I gave it, the man I gave it to; ~ ... ~ some ... others; *hay* ~ *dice* there are some who say.

quién (*sujeto*) who, (*acc.*) whom; *¿a* ~ *lo diste?* to whom did you give it?, who did you give it to?; *¿de* ~ *es este libro?* whose is this book?

quienquiera whoever.

quieto (*inmóvil*) still; (*silencioso*) quiet; calm, peaceful; *¡estáte* ~*!* keep still!; **quietud** *f* stillness *etc.*

quijotada *f* quixotic act; **quijote** *m* quixotic person, hopelessly unrealistic person; **quijotería** *f*, **quijotismo** *m* quixotism, hopeless lack of realism; **quijotesco** quixotic, hopelessly unrealistic.

quilatar [1a] = *aquilatar*; **quilate** *m* carat.
quilo[1] *m physiol.* chyle; F *sudar el* ~ slave, work like a slave.
quilo[2] *m* kilogram.
quilombo *m S.Am.* cottage, hut; *b.s.* brothel.
quilla *f* ⚓, *orn.*, ⚘ keel; *colocar la* ~ *de* lay down; *dar de* ~ keel over.
quimera *f* fantastic idea, fancy, chimera; *fig.* quarrel, dispute; **quimérico** fantastic, fanciful, chimerical; **quimerista** *m/f* quarrelsome sort, rowdy, brawler.
química *f* chemistry; **químico** **1.** chemical; **2.** *m* chemist.
quina *f* Peruvian bark, quinine.
quincalla *f* hardware, ironmongery; **quincallería** *f* hardware shop, ironmonger's (shop); **quincallero** *m* ironmonger.
quince fifteen (*a. su.*); (*fecha*) fifteenth; ~ *días freq.* two weeks, fortnight; F *dar* ~ *y raya a* wipe the floor with; **quincena** *f* two weeks, fortnight; **quincenal** every two weeks, fortnightly; **quinceno** fifteenth.
quincuagésimo fiftieth; **quingentésimo** five hundredth.
quinielas *f/pl.* football pool(s).
quinientos five hundred.
quinina *f* quinine.
quinqué *m* oil lamp; F *tener mucho* ~ be wide awake, know what's going on.
quinquenal quinquennial; *plan* ~ five year plan; **quinquenio** *m* quinquennium, five year period.
quinta *f* (*casa*) villa, country house; ♪ fifth; ⚔ draft; ⚕ coughing fit; *ir a* ~*s* be drafted; *redimirse de las* ~*s* be exempted from the draft.
quintaesencia *f* quintessence.
quintal *m Castilla*: = *46 kg.*; ~ *métrico* = *100 kg.*
quintar [1a] ⚔ conscript, draft.
quintería *f* farmhouse; **quintero** *m* farmer; farm laborer.
quinteto *m* quintet.
quintilla *f 5-line stanza.*
quinto **1.** fifth; **2.** *m* 𝔄 fifth; ⚔ conscript, recruit, draftee.
quintuplicar [1g] quintuple; **quíntuplo** quintuple, fivefold.
quiosco *m* stand, newsstand, kiosk *de calle*; summerhouse, pavilion *de jardín*; ~ (*de música*) bandstand; ~ (*de periódicos*) newsstand; ~ *de necesidad* public lavatory.
quiquiriquí *m* cock-a-doodle-doo.
quirófano *m* operating room.
quiromancia *f* palmistry, chiromancy.
quiropedia *f* chiropody, pedicure.
quirúrgico surgical.
quise *etc. v. querer.*
quisicosa *f* F puzzle(r).
quisquilla *f* trifle, triviality; (*a.* ~*s pl.*) quibbling, hair-splitting; *dejarse de* ~*s* stop fussing, stop quibbling; *pararse en* ~*s* bicker, quibble; **quisquilloso** touchy, cantankerous; fastidious, pernickety, choosy; captious, hair-splitting.
quiste *m* cyst.
quisto: *bien* ~ well-liked; well received; *mal* ~ disliked; unwelcome.
quita...: ~**esmalte** *m* nail-polish remover; ~**manchas** *m* (*p.*) dry cleaner; (*material*) cleaner, stain remover; ~**motas** *m/f* F bootlicker, toady; ~**nieves** *m*: (*máquina*) ~ snow plow; ~**pelillos** *m/f* F bootlicker, toady; ~**pesares** *m* F consolation, comfort; ~**piedras** *m* cowcatcher.
quitapón: *de* ~ detachable.
quitar [1a] **1.** take away, remove (*a* from); *ropa* take off; *pieza* take out, take off, remove; *golpe* avert; *fenc.* parry; *mesa* clear; (*robar*) steal; *abuso, dificultad etc.* do away with, remove; 𝔄 subtract, take away; *le quitaron el reloj* someone stole his watch; *no quita nada de su valor* it does not detract from its value at all; *me quitaron ese privilegio* they deprived me of that privilege; ~ *que subj.* prevent *ger.*; ~ *frotando etc.* rub *etc.* off; F *¡quita (allá)!* get away with you!; *de quita y pon* detachable; ~ *de en medio* remove, get rid of; ~ *de encima* shake off, get rid of; **2.** ~**se** *ropa* take off; (*mancha*) come out; (*p.*) withdraw (*de* from); ~ *de algo*, ~ *algo de encima* get rid of s.t., dispose of s.t.; ~ *de en medio* get out of the way; *¡quítate de ahí!* come out of that!, come away from that!
quitasol *m* sunshade, parasol.
quite *m* hindrance; *fenc.* parry; (*regate*) dodge, dodging; *estar al* ~ be forewarned.
quizá(s) perhaps, maybe; I dare say.

R

rábano *m* radish; ~ *picante*, ~ *rusticano* horseradish; F *tomar el* ~ *por las hojas* bark up the wrong tree, be on the wrong track.
rabear [1a] wag its tail.
rabí *m* rabbi.
rabia *f* ⚕ rabies; *fig.* rage, fury; *me da* ~ it maddens me; *tener* ~ *a* have a grudge against; **rabiar** [1b] *fig.* rage, rave; (*dolor*) be in great pain; *pica que rabia* it stings like the devil; F *esto está que rabia* (*bebida*) it's got a kick to it; ~ *por* be dying for; ~ *por inf.* be dying to *inf.*
rabieta *f* F paddy, tantrum.
rabillo *m* ⚘ stalk; (*con el*) ~ *del ojo* (out of the) corner of one's eye.
rabino *m* rabbi.
rabión *m* rapids.
rabioso ⚕ mad, rabid; *fig.* furious; *partidario* rabid; *dolor* raging, violent; *sabor* hot.
rabo *m* tail; = *rabillo*.
rabona: *hacer* ~ play hooky.
racanear [1a] F slack, swing the lead; **rácano** *m* F slacker; *hacer el* ~ = *racanear*.
racial racial, race *attr.*
racimo *m* cluster, bunch.
raciocinar [1a] reason; **raciocinio** *m* reason; (*acto*) reasoning; argument.
ración *f* ration; portion, helping *de plato*; *eccl.* prebend; ~ *de hambre* starvation wages; **racional** rational (*a.* Ⱥ); reasonable; **racionalismo** *m* rationalism; **racionalista** *m/f* rationalist; **racionamiento** *m* rationing; **racionar** [1a] ration; **racionero** *m eccl.* prebendary.
racismo *m* racialism.
racha *f meteor.* squall, gust; (*suerte*) stroke of luck; string, series *de sucesos*; *a* ~*s* fits and starts.
rada *f* ⚓ roads(tead).
radar *m* radar.
radiación *f* radiation; *radio*: broadcasting; **radiactividad** *f* radioactivity; **radiactivo** radioactive;
radiado radio *attr.*, broadcast *attr.*; **radiador** *m* radiator; **radial** radial; *S.Am.* radio *attr.*; **radiante** radiant (*a. fig.*); **radiar** [1b] *radio*: broadcast; *phys.* radiate.
radical 1. radical; **2.** *m pol.* radical; Ⱥ, *gr.* root; **radicalismo** *m* radicalism; **radicar** [1g] ⚘ *a. fig.* take root; be, be located *en lugar*; (*dificultad etc.*) lie (en in).
radio[1] *m* Ⱥ, *anat.* radius; spoke *de rueda*; ⚗ radium; ⚓, ✈ ~ *de acción* range; *en un* ~ *de* within a radius of.
radio[2] *f* radio; broadcasting; (*aparato*) radio (set); wireless telegram; ~**aficionado** *m*, **a** *f* ham (radio operator); ~**captar** [1a] monitor; ~**difundir** *v/t. a. v/i.* broadcast; ~**difusión** *f* broadcasting; ~**escucha** *m/f* listener; ~**emisora** *f* broadcasting station; ~**experimentador** *m* radio fan, ham; ~**fonía** *f* radio(phony); ~**fónico** radio *attr.*; ~**fonógrafo** *m S.Am.* radiogram; ~**frecuencia** *f* radio frequency; ~**goniómetro** *m* direction finder; ~**grafiar** [1c] ⚕ X-ray; ⚡ radio; ~**gráfico** X-ray *attr.*; ~**grama** *m* radiogram; ~**gramola** *f* radiogram; ~**logía** *f* radiology; ~**perturbación** *f* jamming; ~**rreceptor** *m* radio set (*or* receiver); ~ *de contrastación* monitor; ~**scopia** *f* radioscopy; ~**telefonía** *f* radio(telephony); ~**teléfono** *m* radiophone, radio telephone; ~**telegrafía** *f* radiotelegraphy, radio; ~**telegrafista** *m* radio operator; ~**telescopio** *m* radiotelescope; ~**terapia** *f* radiotherapy; **radioyente** *m/f* listener.
raedera *f* scraper; **raedura** *f* scraping; ⚕ abrasion; ~*s pl.* filings, scrapings; **raer** [2z] scrape; (*quitar*) scrape off; (*alisar*) smooth; chafe; ⚕ abrade; ~**se** chafe; (*tela*) fray.
ráfaga *f* squall, gust *de viento*; burst *de balas*; flurry *de nieve*; flash *de luz*.
raído *tela* frayed, threadbare; *aspecto* shabby; *fig.* shameless.

raigón *m* ⚘ large root; root, stump *[de diente.]*
rail *m* rail.
raíz *f* root; *fig.* foundation; origin; ~ *cuadrada* square root; ~ *cúbica* cube root; *a* ~ *de* soon after; as a result of; *de* ~ root and branch; *cortar de* ~ nip in the bud; *echar raíces* take root.
rajá *m* raja(h).
raja *f* crack, split, slit; gash; (*astilla*) sliver, splinter; slice *de melón etc.*; F *sacar* ~ look after number one; ⚕ get a rake-off; **rajadura** *f* = *raja*; **rajar** [1a] *v/t.* split, crack, slit; *melón etc.* slice; *v/i.* F shoot a line; (*hablar*) chatter; ~**se** split *etc.*; *sl.* back down, give up.
rajatabla: F *a* ~ down to the last detail, to the letter; at all costs, regardless; *S.Am.* on the dot.
ralea *f* breed, kind, sort.
ralo *pelo* sparse; *tela* loosely-woven; *phys.* rare.
rallador *m* grater; **rallar** [1a] grate; F grate on, annoy; **rallo** *m cocina*: grater; ⊕ large file, rasp.
rallye [ˈrali] *m mot.* rally; ~**-paper** *m* paper chase.
rama *f* branch (*a. fig.*); *en* ~ *algodón* raw; *libro* unbound; *andarse por las* ~*s* beat about the bush; get bogged down in details; **ramaje** *m* branches; **ramal** *m* strand *de cuerda*; (*ronzal*) halter; *fig.* offshoot; 🚂 branch line; **ramalazo** *m* (*golpe*) lash; (*señal*) weal, bruise; (*dolor*) stab of pain; (*pesar*) grief, blow.
ramera *f* whore.
ramificación *f* ramification; **ramificarse** [1g] ramify, branch (out).
ramillete *m* bouquet, posy; corsage *en vestido*; cluster; *fig.* collection.
ramita *f* twig, sprig; spray *de flores*.
ramo *m* branch, bough; bunch, bouquet *de flores*; ⚕ touch; *fig.* branch; department *de tienda etc.*; ⚕ line; **ramojo** *m* brushwood.
rampa *f* ramp; ~ *de lanzamiento* launching pad.
ramplón *zapato* heavy, rough; *fig.* vulgar, common; **ramplonería** *f* vulgarity, coarseness.
rana *f* frog; ~ *toro* bullfrog.
rancidez *f*, **ranciedad** *f* rancidness *etc.*; **rancio** rancid, rank, stale, musty; *fig. abolengo* ancient; *costumbre* time-honored; *vino* old.
ranchear [1a] *S.Am.* *v/t.* sack; *v/i.* build a camp, make a settlement; **ranchería** *f* settlement; **ranchero** *m* (mess) cook; *S.Am.* rancher; **rancho** *m* ⚔, ⚓ mess; camp, settlement; *S.Am.* hut; (*finca*) ranch; ⚔ F *asentar el* ~ prepare a meal; *fig.* get things organized, settle in; *hacer* ~ make room; ⚔ *hacer el* ~ have a meal; *hacer* ~ *aparte* F be a lone wolf, go one's own way.
rango *m* rank; status; class.
ranúnculo *m* buttercup.
ranura *f* groove, slot.
rapacidad *f* rapacity, greed.
rapapolvo *m* F ticking-off; *echar un* ~ *a* tick off.
rapar [1a] shave, crop; F pinch.
rapaz[1] rapacious, greedy; thieving; *zo.* predatory.
rapaz[2] *m* lad, youngster, young man; *contp.* kid; **rapaza** *f* lass, young woman, youngster.
rape *m* quick haircut (*or* shave); *fig.* ticking-off; *al* ~ cut close.
rapé *m* snuff.
rapidez *f* speed(iness), rapidity *etc.*; **rápido 1.** rapid, speedy, quick, swift; **2.** *m* express (train); ~*s pl.* rapids.
rapiña *f* robbery (with violence); *de* ~ predatory; *v. ave*; **rapiñar** [1a] F steal, make off with.
raposa *f* vixen, fox (*a. fig.*); **raposo** *m* (dog-)fox.
rapsodia *f* rhapsody.
raptar [1a] abduct, kidnap; **rapto** *m* abduction, kidnap(p)ing; *fig.* sudden impulse; *fig.* ecstasy; **raptor** *m* kidnap(p)er.
raque *m* beachcombing; *andar al* ~ go beachcombing; **raquear** [1a] beachcomb; **raquero** *m* beachcomber; pirate.
raqueta *f* racquet; ~ *de nieve* snowshoe; ~ *y volante* battledore and shuttlecock.
raquítico ⚕ rickety; *fig.* stunted; (*débil*) weak, feeble; **raquitis** *f*, **raquitismo** *m* rickets.
rareza *f* rarity, rareness, scarcity; *fig.* oddity, eccentricity; **raridad** *f* rarity; **rarificar** [1g] rarefy; **raro** rare, scarce, uncommon; *fig.* strange, odd; notable; *es* ~ *que* it is odd that; *¡qué hombre más* ~*!* what an odd man!; *¡cosa más* ~*a!* very strange!

ras *m* level(ness); ~ *con* ~ level; flush; *a* ~ close, even, flush; *a* ~ *de* on a level with; flush with; *a* ~ *de tierra* (almost) at ground level; **rasar** [1a] skim, graze; **~se** (*cielo*) clear.

rascacielos *m* skyscraper; **rascadera** *f* scraper; **rascador** *m* rasp, scraper; hairpin *para pelo*; **rascar** [1g] scrape (*a.* ♪ *co.*); scratch; rasp; **~se** *S.Am.* get drunk; **rascatripas** *m/f* F third-rate violinist; **rascón** sharp, sour.

rasete *m* satinet(te).

rasgado *ojos* large; *boca* wide; **rasgadura** *f* tear, rip; **rasgar** [1h] tear, rip, slash; *un papel* tear up; **rasgo** *m* stroke, flourish *de pluma*; *fig.* feature, characteristic; (*acto*) feat, deed; noble gesture; **~s** *pl.* features *de cara*; ~ *de ingenio* flash of wit; stroke of genius; *a grandes* ~*s* in outline; **rasgón** *m* tear, rent; **rasguear** [1a] ♪ strum; **rasguñar** [1a] scratch, scrape; *paint.* outline; **rasguño** *m* scratch; *paint.* outline.

raso **1.** level, flat, clear; *paisaje* bare; open; *asiento* backless; *cielo* cloudless; *soldado etc.* ordinary; *v. soldado*; **2.** *m sew.* satin; *al* ~ in the open air; in open country.

raspa *f ichth.* fishbone; ⚘ beard *de espiga*, stalk *de uvas*; **raspador** *m* scraper, rasp(er); **raspadura** *f* scrape *etc.*; erasure; **~s** *pl.* filings, scrapings; **raspante** *vino* sharp; **raspar** [1a] *v/t.* scrape, rasp, file *con raspador*; *piel etc.* graze; scale; *palabra* erase; F pinch; *S.Am.* F tick off; *v/i.* (*vino*) be sharp; **raspear** [1a] (*pluma*) scratch.

rastra *f* (*señal*) track, trail; (*carro*) sledge; ⚒ harrow; ⚓ drag, trawl; dredge; string *de cebollas etc.*; *a* ~(s) by dragging; *fig.* unwillingly; *llevar a* ~ drag; *pescar a la* ~ trawl; **rastreador** *m* tracker; ⚓ (*barco*) ~ trawler; **rastrear** [1a] *v/t.* (*seguir*) track, trail; (*encontrar*) track down, trace; (*llevar*) drag; ⚓ dredge, drag; *minas* sweep; *v/i.* ⚒ rake, harrow; ⚓ trawl; ✈ *etc.* skim the ground, fly low; **rastrero** *fig.* despicable; **rastrillar** [1a] rake; *lino etc.* dress; **rastrillo** *m* rake; ⚔ portcullis; ~ *delantero* cowcatcher; **rastro** *m* ⚒ rake, harrow; track, trail *de animal, de cosa arrastrada*; *fig.* trace, sign; path *de huracán*; ~ *de condensación* ✈ contrail; *sin dejar* ~ without leaving a trace behind; **rastrojera** *f* stubble field; **rastrojo** *m* stubble.

rasurador *m* (electric) razor; **rasurar** [1a] *cara* shave; ⊕ scrape.

rata **1.** *f* rat; **2.** *m* F sneak thief.

rataplán *m* drum beat, rub-a-dub.

ratear [1a] share out; (*robar*) pilfer, lift; filch; **ratería** *f* petty larceny, pilfering; **ratero** **1.** light-fingered; **2.** *m* pickpocket, small-time thief.

ratificación *f* ratification; **ratificar** [1g] ratify.

raticida *m* rat poison.

rato *m* (short) time, while, spell; *un* ~ (*como adv.*) awhile; *un buen* ~ a good while; *largo* ~ a long while; **~s** *pl. perdidos*, ~*s libres* spare time, leisure; *al poco* ~ shortly after; *a* ~*s* from time to time; F *pasar el* ~ while away the time; *pasar un buen* ~ have a good time; *pasar un mal* ~ have a bad time of it.

ratón *m*, **-a** *f* mouse; ~ *de biblioteca* bookworm; **ratonar** [1a] gnaw, nibble; **ratonera** *f* mouse trap; (*agujero*) mouse hole.

raudal *m* torrent; *fig.* plenty, abundance; *entrar etc. a* ~*es* flood in *etc.*; **raudo** swift, rushing; impetuous.

raya *f* stripe, streak *en tela etc.*; scratch, mark *en piedra etc.*; dash *con pluma* (*a. tel.*); line *que subraya etc.*; *deportes*: line, mark; parting *de pelo*; crease *de pantalón*; boundary, limit; *ichth.* ray, skate; *a* ~ (with)in bounds; *a* ~*s tela* striped; *hacerse la* ~ part one's hair; *mantener a* ~ keep off, keep at bay, keep in check; *pasar de (la)* ~ *fig.* go too far, overstep the mark; *poner a* ~ check, hold back; *tener a* ~ keep within bounds.

rayado **1.** striped *etc.*; **2.** *m* stripes; ruling *de papel*; ⊕ rifling.

rayano adjacent; borderline; ~ *en* bordering on.

rayar [1a] *v/t.* stripe, line, streak; *piedra etc.* scratch, score; *papel* rule, draw lines across; *fusil* rifle; (*tachar*) cross out; (*subrayar*) underline; *v/i.*: ~ *con* border on, be next to; *fig.* be equal to, match; ~ *en* border on (*a. fig.*), verge on; *al* ~ *el alba* at first light.

rayo[1] *etc. v. raer.*

rayo² *m* (*luz*) ray, beam, shaft; (*relámpago*) flash of lightning; thunderbolt *que daña*; spoke *de rueda*; ~s *pl. catódicos* cathode rays; ~s *pl. cósmicos* cosmic rays; ~s *pl. gama* gamma rays; ~ *mortífero* death ray; ~ *de sol* sunbeam; ~s *pl.* X X-rays; *caer como un* ~ fall like a bombshell; come down out of nowhere; *echar* ~s F blow up, hit the ceiling; *entrar* (*salir*) *como un* ~ dash in (out); *pasar como un* ~ flash past.

rayón *m* rayon.

raza¹ *f* race (*a. biol.*); breed, stock, strain; ~ *humana* human race, humankind, mankind; *de* ~ *caballo* thoroughbred; *perro etc.* pedigree.

raza² *f* crack, slit; ray of light.

razón *f* reason; right, justice; ratio; *S.Am.* message; ~ *de más* all the more reason; ~ *de ser* raison d'être; ✝ ~ *social* trade name; *a* ~ *de* at the rate of; *con* ~ *o sin ella* rightly or wrongly; *en* ~ *de* with regard to; *dar* ~ *de* give an account of, report on; *dar* ~ *de sí* give an account of o.s.; *meter en* ~, *poner en* ~ make *s.o.* see sense; *meterse en* ~ listen to reason, see sense; *perder la* ~ go mad; *puesto en* ~ reasonable; *tener* ~ be right; *no tener* ~ be wrong; **razonable** reasonable; rational; *aviso, posibilidad etc.* fair; **razonado** reasoned; **razonamiento** *m* reasoning; argument; **razonar** [1a] *v/t.* reason; argue; *problema* reason out; *v/i.* reason; (*discurrir*) talk.

re¹ ... re ..

re² ... *prefijo de intensificación*: very ...; *rebueno* very good.

reabrir(se) [3a; *p.p. reabierto*] reopen.

reacción *f* reaction (*ante* to); response (*a* to); ~ *en cadena* chain reaction; ✈ *a* ~ jet(-propelled); **reaccionar** [1a] react (*a, ante* to; *contra* against; *sobre* on); respond (*a* to); **reaccionario** *adj. a. su. m,* **a** *f* reactionary.

reacio obstinate, stubborn.

reacondicionar [1a] recondition.

reactivo *m* reagent; **reactor** *m phys.* reactor; ✈ jet engine; ~*-generador m* breeder reactor.

reafirmar [1a] reaffirm; reassert.

reajustar [1a] readjust; **reajuste** *m* readjustment.

real¹ real; genuine.

real² **1.** (*del rey*) royal; *aspecto etc.* kingly; *fig.* royal, splendid, generous; *moza etc.* fine; **2.** *m* fairground; ✝ *coin of 25 cents.*

realce *m* ⊕ raised work, embossing; *paint.* high light; *fig.* luster, splendor; *fig.* enhancement.

realeza *f* royalty.

realidad *f* reality; truth, sincerity; *en* ~ in fact, actually; *un sueño hecho* ~ a dream come true; **realismo** *m* realism; **realista** **1.** realistic; **2.** *m/f* realist; **realizable** realizable (*a.* ✝); *objetivo etc.* attainable; **realización** *f* realization (*a.* ✝); fulfillment, achievement; ✝ (*venta*) sale, selling-up; **realizar** [1f] realize (*a.* ✝); *objetivo* fulfill, achieve; *promesa etc.* carry out; ✝ (*vender*) sell out, sell up; ~**se** (*sueño etc.*) come true, materialize; **realmente** really, actually; *comer etc.* royally.

realquilar [1a] sublet, sublease; [relet.

realzar [1f] ⊕ emboss, raise; *fig.* enhance, heighten, add to; *paint.* highlight.

reanimar [1a] revive (*a. fig.*); *fig.* encourage; ~**se** revive, rally.

reanudación *f* renewal, resumption; **reanudar** [1a] renew; *viaje etc.* resume.

reaparecer [2d] reappear; **reaparición** *f* reappearance; recurrence, return.

reapertura *f* reopening.

reaprovisionar [1a] replenish, restock.

rearmar(se) [1a] rearm; **rearme** *m* rearmament.

reasegurar [1a] reinsure; **reaseguro** *m* reinsurance.

reasumir [1a] resume, reassume.

reata *f* string of horses *etc.*; (*cuerda*) lasso, rope; *de* ~ in single file; *fig.* submissively.

rebaja *f* lowering, reduction (*a.* ✝); **rebajamiento** *m* = *rebaja*; ~ *de sí mismo* self-abasement; **rebajar** [1a] reduce (*a.* ✝), lower, cut down; *paint.* tone down; *fig. p.* humble, deflate; *valor* detract from; (*desacreditar*) decry, disparage; ~**se** humble o.s.; ~ *a inf.* descend to *inf.*, stoop to *inf.*

rebajo *m* ⊕ rabbet; recess.

rebalsa *f* pool, puddle; **rebalsar** [1a] dam (up); ~**se** form a pool; become dammed up.

rebanada *f* slice; **rebanar** [1a] slice.
rebaño *m* flock (*a. fig.*), herd.
rebasar [1a] exceed, go beyond, overrun (*a.* ~ *de*).
rebatible easily refuted; *asiento* tip-up.
rebatiña: F *andar a la* ~ scramble, fight (*de* for).
rebatir [3a] *ataque* repel, ward off; *cantidad* reduce; *descuento* deduct; *argumento* rebut, refute.
rebato *m* alarm; ⚔ call to arms; ⚔ surprise attack; *llamar a* ~ sound the alarm.
rebeca *f* cardigan.
rebeco *m* chamois, ibex.
rebelarse [1a] rebel, revolt; resist; **rebelde 1.** rebellious, mutinous; *niño etc.* unruly; stubborn; *ser* ~ *a fig.* be in revolt against, resist; **2.** *m/f* rebel; ⚖ defaulter; **rebeldía** *f* rebelliousness, defiance, disobedience; ⚖ default; ⚖ contempt of court; *en* ~ by default; *caer en* ~ default; be in contempt; **rebelión** *f* revolt, rebellion; **rebelón** restive.
reblandecer [2d] soften.
rebolludo thick-set, chunky F.
reborde *m* ⊕ flange, rim; ledge.
rebosadero *m* overflow; **rebosante** overflowing (*a. fig.*; *de* with), brimful (*a. fig.*; *de* of); **rebosar** [1a] run over, overflow (*a. fig.*; *de, en* with); ~ *en dinero* have pots of money; ~ *de salud* be bursting with health.
rebotar [1a] *v/t. clavo etc.* clinch; *ataque* repel; F annoy, upset; *v/i.* bounce; rebound; (*bala*) ricochet; ~ *de soslayo* glance off; **rebote** *m* bounce; rebound; *de* ~ on the rebound.
rebozar [1f] muffle up; *cocina*: roll in flour (*or* batter *etc.*); ~**se** muffle up; **rebozo** *m* muffler; *S.Am.* shawl; *fig.* disguise; *de* ~ secretly; *sin* ~ openly, frankly; (*adj.*) above-board.
rebufar [1a] recoil; **rebufo** *m* recoil.
rebullicio *m* hubbub, uproar; **rebullir** [3a] stir; show signs of life.
rebusca *f* search; ↗ gleaning; *fig.* leavings, remains; **rebuscado** recherché; studied, elaborate; **rebuscar** [1g] search carefully for, hunt out; ↗ glean.
rebuznar [1a] bray; **rebuzno** *m* bray(ing).
recabar [1a] manage to get.
recadero *m* messenger; errand boy; **recado** *m* message; errand; (*regalo*) gift; (*compras*) daily shopping; (*seguridad*) safety, precaution; *v. recaudo*; ~ *de escribir* writing case; writing materials; *dejar* ~ leave a message; *enviar a un* ~ send on an errand; *mandar* ~ send word.
recaer [2o] fall back, relapse (*en* into); ⚕ suffer a relapse; ~ *en heredero* pass to; ~ *sobre* devolve upon; **recaída** *f* ⚕ relapse (*a. fig.*; *en* into).
recalar [1a] saturate.
recalcar [1g] (*apretar*) squeeze, press; cram, stuff (*de* with); *fig.* stress; make great play with.
recalcitrante recalcitrant; **recalcitrar** [1a] retreat, back down; resist, be stubborn.
recalentar [1k] overheat; *comida etc.* warm up.
recalmón *m* lull.
recamado *m* embroidery; **recamar** [1a] embroider.
recámara *f* dressing room; *S.Am.* bedroom; ⚔ breech (*a.* ⊕), chamber; F *tener mucha* ~ be on the careful side.
recambio *m* ⊕ spare; refill; ⚚ re-exchange; *de* ~ spare.
recapacitar [1a] think over.
recapitulación *f* recapitulation, summing-up; **recapitular** [1a] recapitulate, sum up.
recargado overloaded; *fig.* over-elaborate; **recargar** [1h] reload; (*demasiado*) overload; recharge; (*demasiado*) overcharge; *fig.* increase; **recargo** *m* new burden; extra load; ⚚ extra charge, surcharge; increase *de impuestos etc.*
recatado cautious, circumspect; *mujer* shy, demure; **recatar** [1a] hide; ~**se** be cautious; refrain from taking a stand; **recato** *m* caution; shyness, demureness; modesty.
recaudación *f* collection; recovery; (*oficina*) tax office; **recaudador** *m*: ~ *de contribuciones* tax collector; **recaudar** [1a] *impuestos* collect; *deudas* recover; *fig.* watch over, guard; **recaudo** *m* collection; *fig.* care, protection; *a buen* ~ in safe keeping.

recelar [1a] suspect, fear, distrust (*a.* ~ *de*, **~se**); ~ *que* suspect that; **~se** *inf.* be afraid of *ger.*; **recelo** *m* suspicion, fear; mistrust, misgiving; **receloso** suspicious, distrustful, apprehensive.
recensión *f* recension.
recepción *f* reception (*a. radio*); receipt; admission *a academia etc.*; (*cuarto*) drawing room; reception (desk) *en hotel*; **receptáculo** *m* receptacle (*a.* ⚘); holder; **receptador** *m* F fence, holder of stolen goods; **receptivo** receptive; **receptor** *m* receiver.
receso *m S.Am. parl.* recess.
receta *f cocina*: recipe; ⚕ prescription; **recetar** [1a] ⚕ prescribe.
recial *m* rapids.
recibidero receivable; **recibidor** *m*, **-a** *f* receiver, recipient; receptionist *en hotel*; **recibimiento** *m* (*cuarto*) hall; (*grande*) reception-room; (*acto*) reception; **recibir** [3a] receive; (*acoger*) welcome, receive, greet; (*salir al encuentro de*) (go and) meet; *título* take, receive; *ir a* ~ (go to) meet; *reciben mucho en casa* they entertain a good deal; *reciben los jueves* they receive visitors on Thursdays; **~se** *de* qualify as; **recibo** *m* = *recibimiento*, *recepción*; ☤ receipt; (*cuenta*) bill; *acusar* ~ acknowledge receipt (*de* of); *estar de* ~ be at home (to callers); *ser de* ~ be acceptable.
reciclable recyclable; **reciclado** *m*, **reciclaje** *m* recycling.
recién *adv.* newly; just; lately; ~ **casado** newly wed; ~ **llegado 1.** newly arrived; **2.** *m*, **a** *f* newcomer *en lugar*; latecomer *en reunión etc.*; ~ **nacido** newborn; ~ **puesto** *huevo* new-laid; **reciente** recent; *pan etc.* new, fresh.
recinto *m* enclosure, compound; precincts; area; place.
recio 1. *adj.* (*fuerte*) strong, robust; (*grueso*) thick, bulky; (*duro*) hard; (*áspero*) harsh, rough; *voz* loud; *tiempo* severe; **2.** *adv. hablar* loudly.
recipiente *m* (*p.*) recipient (*a. phys.*, ⚗); (*vaso*) vessel, container.
recíproca *f* & reciprocal; **reciprocar** [1g] reciprocate; **reciprocidad** *f* reciprocity; *usar de* ~ reciprocate; **recíproco** reciprocal.
recitación *f* recitation; **recitado** *m* recitation; ♪ recitative; **recital** *m* recital; **recitar** [1a] recite; **recitativo** *adj. a. su. m* recitative.
reclamación *f* claim, demand; objection; protest, complaint; **reclamar** [1a] *v/t.* claim, lay claim to; press for, demand; *socorro etc.* beg; ⚖ reclaim; *v/i.* protest (*contra* against).
reclamo *m orn.* (*ave*) decoy; (*grito*) call; *typ.* catchword; *fig.* lure, inducement; (*anuncio*) advertisement; slogan; blurb *de libro*; *S.Am.* complaint.
reclinar(**se**) [1a] recline, lean back.
recluir [3g] shut away; ⚖ intern, imprison; **reclusión** *f* seclusion; ⚖ imprisonment; ~ *perpetua* life imprisonment; **recluso 1.** ⚖ imprisoned; **2.** *m*, **a** *f* ⚖ prisoner, inmate; recluse.
recluta 1. *m* recruit; **2.** *f* = **reclutamiento** *m* recruitment; **reclutar** [1a] recruit; *S.Am. ganado* round up.
recobrar [1a] recover, get back; retrieve; *fugitivo* recapture; *tiempo* make up (for); **~se** ⚕ recover; (*volver en sí*) come to; *fig.* collect o.s.; **recobro** *m* recovery *etc.*
recocer [2b *a.* 2h] cook again; (*demasiado*) overcook; *metall.* anneal; **~se** suffer inwardly.
recodo *m* turn, bend *de camino etc.*; loop; ⊕ offset.
recogedor *m* (*p.*) picker, harvester; gleaner; (*herramienta*) rake; scraper; **recoger** [2c] (*levantar*) pick up; *deportes*: *pelota freq.* field, stop; (*juntar*) collect, gather together; *cosecha* get in, harvest; *frutos* pick; *noticia* pick up, come across; (*acoger*) take in; (*ir por*) get, fetch; *p.* come for; (*encoger*) contract, draw in; (*acortar*) shorten; *alas* fold; **~se** withdraw; (*acostarse*) go to bed, retire; (*ir a casa*) go home; (*refugiarse*) take shelter; **recogida** *f* withdrawal, retirement; ✓ harvest; ✉ post, collection; ~ *de basuras* garbage collection; **recogimiento** *m* (*acto*) gathering; ✓ harvesting; *eccl.* withdrawal, retreat; (*estado*) seclusion; *eccl.* quiet time, retreat.
recolección *f* ✓ harvest, picking; collection *de rentas*; gathering *de*

información etc.; (*resumen*) compilation; *eccl.* retreat; **recolectar** [1a] ✓ = *recoger*.

recomendable recommendable; (*aconsejable*) advisable; **recomendación** *f* recommendation; (*escrito*) reference, testimonial; **recomendar** [1k] recommend; ~ *inf.* urge to *inf.*; ~ *que* request that, ask that.

recomenzar [1f *a.* 1k] begin again.

recompensa *f* recompense; reward; compensation (*de pérdida* for); *en* ~ in return (*de* for); **recompensar** [1a] recompense (*acc.* for); compensate (*acc.* for); *trabajo etc.* reward.

recomponer [2r] ⊕ mend, repair; *typ.* reset.

reconcentrar [1a] concentrate, bring together; *sentimiento* hide; ~**se** become absorbed in thought; collect one's wits.

reconciliación *f* reconciliation **reconciliar** [1b] reconcile.

reconcomio *m* F suspicion.

recóndito recondite.

reconfortar [1a] comfort; cheer, encourage; ~**se** *con* fortify o.s. with.

reconocer [2d] recognize; know; *culpa, verdad etc. a.* admit, acknowledge; *hechos a.* face; inspect, examine (*a.* ⚕); *terreno* survey; ⚔ reconnoitre; spy out; *reconozco que no es normal* I realize it's not usual; *hay que* ~ *que* one must admit that; *ya se reconoce que* it is already acknowledged that; **reconocible** recognizable; **reconocido** grateful; **reconocimiento** *m* recognition; admission, acknowledgment; inspection, examination (*a.* ⚕); survey; ⚔ reconnaissance; ⚖ recognizance; (*agradecimiento*) gratitude; ~ *médico* inquest.

reconquista *f* reconquest; **reconquistar** [1a] reconquer.

reconsiderar [1a] reconsider.

reconstituir [3g] reconstitute, reform; reconstruct; **reconstituyente** *m* tonic, restorative.

reconstrucción *f* reconstruction *etc.*; **reconstruir** [3g] reconstruct; rebuild; *gobierno* reshuffle.

recontar [1m] recount, retell.

reconvención *f* expostulation, remonstrance; ⚖ (counter)charge; **reconvenir** [3s] reprimand; accuse; ⚖ countercharge; (*a.* ~ *a*) expostulate with, remonstrate with.

reconvertir [3i] reconvert.

recopilación *f* summary; compilation; ⚖ code; **recopilar** [1a] compile, collect; *leyes* codify.

record [ˈrekor] *adj. a. su. m* record.

recordable memorable; **recordación** *f* remembrance; *de feliz* ~ of happy memory; **recordar** [1m] *v/t.* remember, recall, recollect; remind (*algo a alguien* a p. of a th.); (*hacer pensar en*) call up, bring to mind; *si mal no* ~ F if I remember correctly; *v/i.*, ~**se** awaken; **recordativo** reminiscent; *carta* ~*a* follow-up letter, reminder; **recordatorio** *m* reminder; memento.

recorrer [2a] *país etc.* cross, travel, tour; go through; *plaza etc.* cross; *terreno* (*buscando*) range, scour; *distancia* travel (*a.* ⊕), cover; (*repasar, registrar*) look over, go over, survey; ⊕ repair, overhaul; ~ *de pie* travel on foot, walk; **recorrido** *m* run, journey; (*ruta*) path, route; ✈ flight; distance traveled; run; round *de proveedor casero etc.*; stroke *de émbolo*; ~ *de aterrizaje* landing run.

recortadito F very particular; **recortar** [1a] *lo sobrante* cut away, cut back, trim; *figura, periódico* cut out; *pelo* trim; *paint.* outline; ~**se** be outlined, stand out; **recorte** *m* cutting; trim; ~*s pl.* trimmings, clippings; *álbum de* ~*s* scrap book.

recostado reclining, recumbent; lying down; **recostar** [1m] lean; ~**se** lie back, lie down.

recoveco *m* turn, bend *de calle etc.*; ~*s pl.* ins and outs; innermost recesses; *fig.* subterfuges.

recreación *f* recreation; *escuela*: break, playtime; **recrear** [1a] recreate; amuse, entertain; ~**se** amuse o.s., take recreation.

recrecer [2d] *v/t.* increase; *v/i.* increase; (*ocurrir*) happen again; ~**se** recover one's good spirits.

recreo *m* recreation, relaxation; amusement; *escuela*: break.

recriminación *f* recrimination; **recriminar** [1a] recriminate; ~**se** exchange recriminations.

recrudecer [2d] recrudesce, break out again.

recta *f* straight line; *carreras*: the straight; ~ *de llegada* home straight; **rectangular** = **rectángulo 1.** rectangular, oblong; *triángulo etc.* right-angled; **2.** *m* rectangle, oblong.
rectificación *f* rectification; **rectificador** *m* rectifier; **rectificar** [1g] *mst* rectify (*a. fig.*); *trazado etc.* straighten; *cálculo* set right; *cilindro* rebore.
rectilíneo rectilinear.
rectitud *f* straightness; accuracy; *fig.* rectitude, uprightness; **recto 1.** straight; *ángulo* right; *gr.* literal, proper; *fig.* upright, honest; *juicio* sound; **2.** *m* rectum.
rector 1. governing, managing; **2.** *m* rector; *univ. approx.* vice chancellor; **3.** *m*, **-a** *f* principal, head *de comunidad*.
recua *f* mule train; F string, drove.
recubrir [3a; *p.p. recubierto*] recover; cover; ⊕ coat, surface.
recuento *m* recount; inventory; *hacer el* ~ *de* make a survey of.
recuerdo *m* memory, recollection; (*objeto*) souvenir, memento; ~**s** *pl.* (*saludo*) regards.
recuero *m* muleteer.
reculada *f* recoil; *fig.* retreat; **recular** [1a] recoil; *fig.* retreat, fall back; F back down; **reculones:** F *andar a* ~ go backwards.
recuperable recoverable, retrievable; recyclable; **recuperación** *f* recovery; **recuperar** [1a] recover, retrieve, recuperate; reclaim; **~se** ⚕ recover, recuperate.
recurrente recurrent; **recurrir** [3a]: ~ *a algo* have recourse to, resort to, fall back on; *p.* turn to; **recurso** *m* recourse, resort; expedient; refuge; ⚖ appeal; ~**s** *pl.* resources; means.
recusar [1a] ⚖ reject; challenge.
rechazamiento *m* rejection *etc.*; **rechazar** [1f] *ataque* repel, beat off; *oferta* reject, refuse, turn down; *tentación* resist; ⚖, *proyecto de ley* reject; **rechazo** *m* rebound *de pelota*; recoil *de cañón*; *fig.* repulse; *de* ~ on the rebound; *fig.* as a result.
rechifla *f* (*silbo*) whistle; hiss; *esp. thea.* catcall; (*silbos*) whistling *etc.*; *fig.* derision; **rechiflar** [1a] whistle (*v/t.* at), hiss, catcall.
rechinamiento *m* creak(ing) *etc.*; **rechinar** [1a] (*madera etc.*) creak; (*ludir dos cosas*) grate, grind; (*maquinaria*) clank; (*motor*) whirr, hum; (*sonido agudo*) squeak; *fig.* do *s.t.* with an ill grace; *hacer* ~ *dientes* gnash, grind; **rechino** *m* creak(ing) *etc.*
rechoncho F thick-set, stocky; squat; plump, tubby.
rechupete: F *de* ~ *comida* scrumptious; jolly good.
red *f* net (*a. fig.*); (*mallas*) mesh(es) (*a. fig.*); 🚂 *etc.* network, system; baggage netting; *agua*, ⚡ mains; *fig.* trap, snare; ~ *de alambre* wire netting; ~ *barredera* trawl; dragnet; *a* ~ *barredera* with a clean sweep; *caer en la* ~ *fig.* fall into the trap.
redacción *f* (*acto*) writing, redaction; editing; wording; (*oficina*) newspaper office; (*ps.*) editorial staff; **redactar** [1a] write; draft, word; *periódico* edit; **redactor** *m*, **-a** *f* (*jefe*) editor; (*subordinado*) sub-editor.
redada *f* (*acto*) cast; (*cantidad*) catch, haul (*a. fig.*); sweep *por policía*.
redaños *m/pl.* F pluck, guts.
redarguir [3g] turn an argument against its proposer; ⚖ impugn.
redecilla *f* small net; hair net *para pelo*.
rededor: *al* ~ *v. alrededor*.
redención *f* redemption (*a.* ✝); **redentor 1.** redeeming; redemptive; **2.** *m*, **-a** *f* redeemer; ♀ Redeemer.
redicho F affected, refined.
redil *m* sheepfold, pen.
redimible redeemable; **redimir** [3a] redeem; *cautivo* ransom.
rédito *m* interest, yield, return; **redituar** [1e] yield, produce.
redoblado stocky, thick-set; *paso* double-quick; **redoblante** *m* drum; **redoblar** [1a] *v/t.* redouble; (*replegar*) bend back, bend over; *clavo* clinch; *v/i.* ♪ play a roll on the drum; **redoble** *m* ♪ drum roll; roll, rumble *de trueno*.
redoma *f* flask, phial.
redomado sly, artful; (*completo*) out-and-out, utter.
redonda: *a la* ~ round (about); *de la* ~ in the neighborhood, of the area; **redondear** [1a] round off; round; **~se** get to be well off; get clear of

debts; **redondel** *m* bullring, arena; **redondez** *f* roundness; *en toda la ~ de la tierra* in the whole wide world; **redondilla** *f* quatrain; **redondo** round (*a. fig.*); *fig.* (*sin rodeos*) square, straightforward; *en ~* around; *2 metros en ~* 2 meters round; *caer ~* fall senseless.

red(r)opelo *m* F row; *al ~* the wrong way; against the grain; *traer al ~* ride roughshod over.

redro F (*detrás*) behind; (*atrás*) backwards.

redrojo *m* (*p.*) puny child, runt.

reducción *f* reduction, cut; (*copia*) miniature version; ⚕ setting; **reducible** reducible; **reducido** reduced; limited; *número etc. freq.* small; *precio* low; *espacio* limited, confined, narrow; **reducir** [3f] reduce (*a. fig.*; *a, hasta* to); diminish, lessen, cut; *fortaleza* reduce; *país* subdue; ⚕ *hueso* set; **~se** lessen *etc.*; *fig.* economize.

reducto *m* ⚔ redoubt.

reduje *m etc. v. reducir.*

redundante redundant, superfluous; **redundar** [1a]: *~ en* redound to.

reedificar [1g] rebuild.

reeditar [1a] republish, reprint; reedit.

reeducación *f* reeducation.

reelegible reeligible; **reelegir** [3c *a.* 3l] reelect.

reembolsable repayable; ☿ *no ~* irredeemable; **reembolsar** [1a] *p.* reimburse, repay; *dinero* pay back, refund; **~se** reimburse o.s.; *dinero* recover; **reembolso** *m* reimbursement; repayment, refund; *envío etc. contra ~* cash on delivery.

reemplazar [1f] replace (*con* with, by), change (*con* for); **reemplazo** *m* (*acto, p.*) replacement; ⚔ reserve; ⚔ *de ~* reserve.

reencuentro *m* collision; clash *de tropas.*

reenganchar [1a] *v/t. a.* **~se** reenlist.

reentrada *f* reentry.

reenviar [1c] forward; (*devolver*) send back.

reestreno *m thea.* revival.

reexpedir [3l] *carta* forward.

refacción *f* refreshment; *S.Am.* repair(s); F extra, bonus.

refectorio *m* refectory.

referencia *f* reference (*a.* ☿, *recomendación sobre p.*); account, report; **referente:** *~ a* relating to; **referéndum** *m* referendum; **referir** [3i] recount, report; *cuento* tell; *~ que* say that; *~ a* (*dirigir*) refer to; **~se** *a* refer to; apply to; *por lo que se refiere a* as regards, as for.

refilón: *mirar de ~* take a quick look at.

refinación *f* refining; **refinado** refined; **refinadura** *f* refining; **refinamiento** *m fig.* refinement; nicety; neatness; **refinar** [1a] refine; *estilo etc.* polish; **refinería** *f* refinery; **refino** refined, extra fine.

reflector *m* reflector; ✈ *etc.* searchlight; *mot. ~ posterior* rear reflector; **reflejar** [1a] reflect; mirror; reveal; **~se** be reflected; **reflejo 1.** *luz* reflected; *acto* reflex; *verbo* reflexive; **2.** *m* reflection; gleam, glint; *physiol.* reflex (action); *~ patelar, ~ rotuliano* knee jerk; **reflexión** *f* reflection, thought; **reflexionar** [1a] *v/t.* reflect on, think about; *v/i.* reflect (*en, sobre* on), muse; think, pause *antes de obrar*; **reflexivo** thoughtful, reflective; *gr.* reflexive.

refluir [3g] flow back; **reflujo** *m* ebb (tide); *fig.* retreat.

refocilación *f* (huge) enjoyment, (great) pleasure; (*alegría*) cheerfulness; **refocilar** [1a] give (great) pleasure to; (*alegrar*) cheer up; **~se** *con* enjoy (hugely), have a fine time with; **refocilo** *m* = *refocilación.*

reforma *f* reform; reformation; (*mejora*) improvement; ≗ Reformation; **~s** *pl.* ⚠ alterations, repairs; *~ agraria* land reform; **reformación** *f* reform(ation); **reformado** reformed; **reformador** *m* **-a** *f* reformer; **reformar** [1a] reform; (*mejorar*) improve; revise, reorganize; *abusos* put right, correct; ⊕ mend, repair; ⚠ alter, repair; **~se** reform; (*contenerse*) restrain o.s.; **reformatorio** *m* reformatory; **reformista** *m/f* reformer.

reforzador *m* ⚡ booster; *phot.* intensifier; **reforzar** [1f *a.* 1m] reinforce (*a.* ⚔), strengthen; boost (*a.* ⚡); *fig.* buttress, bolster up; (*animar*) encourage.

refracción *f* refraction; **refractar** [1a] refract; **refractario** fireproof; *fig.* refractory, recalcitrant; *ser* ~ *a* resist.
refrán *m* proverb, saying; *como dice el* ~ as the saying goes.
refregar [1h *a.* 1k] rub; F dress down, tick off; **refregón** *m* rub(bing).
refrenar [1a] *caballo* rein back, rein in; *fig.* curb, restrain.
refrendar [1a] endorse, countersign; authenticate.
refrescar [1g] *v/t.* refresh; cool; *acción* renew; *memoria* refresh, jog; *v/i.*, **~se** (*tiempo*) cool down, get cooler; (*salir*) take the air; (*beber*) take a drink; ⚓ (*viento*) blow up; **refresco** *m* cool drink, soft drink; **~s** *pl.* refreshments.
refriega *f* scuffle, affray.
refrigeración *f* refrigeration; cooling *de motor*; ~ *por agua* watercooling; **refrigerador** *m* refrigerator; ice bucket; **refrigerante** refrigerating, cooling; ⚗ refrigerant (*a. su. m*); **refrigerar** [1a] refrigerate; cool; refresh; **refrigerio** *m* refreshment; cooling drink; *fig.* relief.
refuerzo *m* strengthening; brace; **~s** *pl.* reinforcements.
refugiado *m*, **a** *f* refugee; **refugiarse** [1b] take refuge; shelter; go into hiding; *se refugió en Francia* he fled to France; **refugio** *m* refuge, shelter (*a. fig.*); *eccl.* sanctuary; *fig.* haven; ~ *antiaéreo* air-raid shelter; ~ *antiatómico* fallout shelter; ⚔ ~ *subterráneo* dugout.
refulgente brilliant, refulgent.
refundición *f* revision, recasting; (*obra*) adaptation; **refundir** [3a] ⊕ recast; *fig.* revise; *texto* remodel, adapt, rewrite.
refunfuñar [1a] grunt, growl; (*murmurar*) grumble; **refunfuño** *m* grunt, growl; grumble.
refutación *f* refutation; **refutar** [1a] refute.
regadera *f* watering can; (*reguera*) irrigation ditch; sprinkler *para calle etc.*; **regadío 1.** irrigable; *tierra* **~a**, *tierra de* ~ = **2.** irrigated land; **regadura** *f* watering, irrigation; sprinkling.
regala *f* gunwale.
regalado dainty, delicate; *vida etc.* of luxury, comfortable, pleasant; **regalar** [1a] *regalo* give; (*dar gratis*) make a present of, give away; (*acariciar*) caress, fondle; (*halagar*) make a fuss of; (*convidar*) treat (*con* to), regale (*con* on, with); *dar medio regalado* sell for a song; *no lo quisiera ni* ~ I wouldn't want it at any price; **~se** regale o.s. (*con* on, with); indulge o.s.
regalía *f fig.* perquisite, privilege; bonus; **~s** *pl.* royal prerogatives.
regaliz *m*, **regaliza** *f* liquorice.
regalo *m* gift, present; (*comida*) treat, delicacy; *fig.* pleasure; comfort, luxury; **~s** *de fiesta* favors; *de* ~ *entrada* complimentary; **regalón** F *p.* pampered, spoiled; *vida* soft, comfortable.
regañadientes: *a* ~ reluctantly.
regañar [1a] *v/t.* F scold; nag (at); *v/i.* (*perro*) snarl, growl; (*p.*) grouse; (*dos ps.*) quarrel; **regaño** *m* snarl, growl; (*gesto*) scowl; *fig.* grouse; F scolding; **regañón** *p.* grumbling, irritable; *mujer* **~a** shrew, virago.
regar [1h *a.* 1k] *planta* water; *tierra* water, irrigate; *calle* hose; *geog.* (*río*) water; spray *con insecticida etc.*; (*esparcir*) sprinkle, scatter.
regata[1] *f* 🌱 irrigation ditch.
regata[2] *f* ⚓ (*carrera*) race; (*conjunto de carreras*) regatta.
regate *m* swerve, dodge (*a.* F); **regatear**[1] [1a] *v/t.* haggle over; bargain away; (*por menor*) sell retail; *v/i.* haggle, bargain; F bicker; F (*hurtar el cuerpo*) swerve, duck, dodge.
regatear[2] [1a] ⚓ race.
regateo *m* haggling *etc.*; **regatón**[1] **1.** haggling; F niggling, argumentative; **2.** *m* retailer.
regatón[2] *m* ferrule *de bastón*.
regazo *m* lap (*a. fig.*).
regencia *f* regency.
regeneración *f* regeneration; **regenerar** [1a] regenerate; ⊕ reclaim.
regentar [1a] manage, direct; preside over; *cátedra* occupy, hold; *b.s.* domineer, boss F; **regente 1.** *príncipe* regent; *director etc.* managing; *fig.* ruling; **2.** *m/f* (*real*) regent; manager *de fábrica, finca*; *typ.* foreman.
regicida *m/f* regicide (*p.*); **regicidio** *m* regicide (*act*).

régimen *m pol.* régime; ⚕ diet; (*reglas*) rules, regulations; system, regimen; *gr.* government; ~ *alimenticio* diet; ~ *de hambre* starvation diet; ~ *de justicia* rule of law; ~ *lácteo* milk diet; **regimiento** *m* administration *etc.*; ⚔ regiment.
regio royal, regal; *apariencia* regal, kingly; *fig.* royal.
región *f* region; part, area; *anat.* tract, region; **regional** regional; local; **regionalismo** *m* regionalism.
regir [3c *a.* 3l] *v/t. país etc.* rule, govern (*a. gr.*); *sociedad etc.* manage, control; (*conducir*) guide, steer; *v/i.* (*ley, precio*) be in force; (*condición*) prevail; ⚓ obey the helm; *el mes que rige* the present month; **~se** *por* be ruled by, go by.
registrador *m* recorder, registrar; inspector; register; **registrar** [1a] *hecho* register, record; *partida etc.* enter; file *en archivo*; *voz etc.* record; (*examinar*) survey, inspect, look through; *equipaje* examine; *p.*, *sitio* search; **registro** *m* (*acto*) registration; (*libro, archivo*) register, record; (*archivos*) registry, record office; (*partida*) entry; recording *en disco etc.*; ♪ (*extensión, altura*) register; ♪ stop *de órgano*; ♪ pedal *de piano*; regulator *de reloj*; bookmark(er) *para libro*; damper *de estufa*; (*abertura*) manhole; *typ.* register; survey, inspection; examination; search; ~ *domiciliario* search of a house; ~ *parroquial* parish register.
regla *f* rule (*a.* ⅍, *deportes, eccl.*); regulation; (*base*) law, principle; ruler *para trazar líneas*; order, discipline; **~s** *pl.* ⚕ period; ~ *de cálculo* slide rule; ~ *T* T-square; ~ *de tres* rule of three; *en* ~ in order; *por* ~ *general* as a rule; on the average; *hacerse una* ~ *de inf.* make it a rule to *inf.*; *salir de* ~ go too far; *ser de* ~ be the rule; **reglaje** *m* ⊕ overhaul; adjustment.
reglamentación *f* regulation; **reglamentar** [1a] regulate, provide regulations for; **reglamentario** regulation *attr.*, set; statutory; **reglamento** *m* regulation, rule; (*código*) rules and regulations; standing order *de asamblea*; by-law *de sociedad, municipio*; ~ *del tráfico* rule of the road.
reglar [1a] *línea* rule; *fig.* regulate; **~se** *por* conform to, be guided by.
regleta *f typ.* space; **regletear** [1a] *typ.* space out.
regocijado merry; exultant; *carácter* jolly, cheerful; **regocijar** [1a] gladden, cheer (up); **~se** rejoice (*de, por* at); make merry; exult (*por* at, in); **regocijo** *m* joy, rejoicing; elation; gaiety, merriment; **~s** *pl.* festivities.
regodearse [1a] F crack jokes; ~ *con*, ~ *en* delight in; **regodeo** *m* F delight; amusement.
regoldar [1m] belch.
regordete F chubby, dumpy.
regosto *m* craving (*de* for).
regresar [1a] go back, come back, return; **regresión** *f* regression; retreat; **regresivo** re(tro)gressive; **regreso** *m* return; *estar de* ~ be back.
regüeldo *m* belch(ing).
reguera *f* irrigation ditch; ⚓ moorings; **reguero** *m* ✓ irrigation ditch; trickle *de sangre etc.*; (*señal*) streak, track; ~ *de pólvora* train of gunpowder; *ser un* ~ *de pólvora* spread like wildfire.
regulable adjustable; **regulación** *f* regulation; adjustment; control; **regulador** *m* ⊕ regulator, throttle, governor; control; *radio*: (control) knob; *radio*: ~ *de volumen* volume control; **regular 1.** regular (*a.* ⚔, *eccl.*); (*mediano*) fair, middling, medium; F *salud, progreso etc.* fair, so-so; (*conveniente*) suitable; normal, usual; *por lo* ~ as a rule; **2.** *m eccl.* regular; **3.** [1a] regulate; *esp.* ⊕ adjust; *precios etc.* control; *reloj* put right; *despertador* set; *negocios etc.* put in order; **regularidad** *f* regularity; **regularizar** [1f] regularize; standardize.
regurgitar [1a] regurgitate.
rehabilitación *f* rehabilitation; **rehabilitar** [1a] rehabilitate; reinstate *en oficio*; *casa* restore, renovate; ⊕ overhaul.
rehacer [2s] redo, do again; *objeto* remake; (*reparar*) mend, repair; **~se** ⚕ recover; ⚔ rally; **rehecho** *p.* thick-set.
rehén *m* hostage.
rehilar [1a] quiver, reel; (*flecha*) whizz; **rehilete** *m* dart; (*volante*)

shuttlecock; *fig.* dig, cutting remark.

rehuir [3g] (*apartar*) remove; (*evitar*) avoid, decline.

rehusar [1a] refuse (*inf.* to *inf.*), decline, turn down.

reidero F laughable; **reidor** laughing, merry.

reimpresión *f* reprint; **reimprimir** [3a] reprint.

reina *f* queen (*a. ajedrez, abeja*); ~ *madre* queen mother; **reinado** *m* reign; **reinante** reigning; prevailing; **reinar** [1a] reign; rule; (*condiciones*) prevail.

reincidir [3a] relapse (*en* into); backslide.

reincorporarse [1a]: ~ *a* rejoin.

reino *m* kingdom.

reinstalar [1a] reinstall; *p.* reinstate.

reintegración *f* ⚕ refund, reimbursement; restitution *etc.*; **reintegrar** [1a] ⚕ refund, pay back; restore; ~**se** *a* return to; ~ *de* recover, recoup; **reintegro** *m* restoration, restitution.

reinvertir [3i] reinvest; plough back.

reír(se) [3m] laugh (*de* at, over); F (*vestido*) tear; ~ *con alguien* laugh at s.o.'s jokes; ~ *de* (*burlarse*) laugh at, make fun of; *cosa de* ~ joke.

reja *f* grating, grid(iron); grille, bar(s) *de ventana*; ~ (*del arado*) plowshare; **rejado** *m* grille, grating; **rejilla** *f* grating; lattice; screen; wickerwork *de silla etc.*; 🚂 luggage rack; *radio*: grid, grille; small stove; **rejo** *m* spike, sharp point; *zo.* sting; *fig.* vigor; **rejón** *m* pointed iron bar; *toros*: lance.

rejuvenecer [2d] *v/t.* rejuvenate; *v/i.*, ~**se** be rejuvenated.

relación *f* (*conexión*) relation(ship) (*con* to, with); (*narración*) account, statement, report; tale, recital *de dificultades etc.*; (*informe oficial*) record, return; list; 𝔄 ratio; proportion; ~*es pl.* relation(ship); (*amorosas*) courting, courtship; betrothal, engagement; *llevan 2 años de ~es* they've been courting 2 years; *buenas ~es pl.* good relations; *~es pl. comerciales* business connections, trade relations; ⚕ *~es pl. personales* personnel management; *~es pl. públicas* public relations; *no guardar ~ con* be out of proportion to, bear no relation to; *mantener ~es con* keep in touch with; **relacionado** related; ~ *con* that has to do with; bound up with; **relacionar** [1a] relate (*con* to); connect (*con* with); ~**se** be related; ~ *con* relate to; *p.* get to know.

relai(s) [reˈle] *m* ⚡ relay.

relajación *f* relaxation *etc.*; laxity *de moralidad*; ⚕ hernia; **relajado** *vida* dissolute; **relajar** [1a] relax, slacken, loosen; *moralidad* weaken; (*distraer*) relax, amuse; ~**se** relax; ⚕ be ruptured; (*moralidad*) become lax.

relamerse [2a] lick one's lips; *labios* smack, lick; *fig.* gloat (*de* over); (*afeitarse*) paint one's face; **relamido** prim and proper; affected; (*pulcro*) overdressed.

relámpago 1. *m* lightning, flash (*a. fig.*); flash of wit; ~*s pl.* lightning; ~ *fotogénico* flash bulb; *pasar como un* ~ go by like lightning; **2.** *attr.* lightning; **relampagueante** lightning; flashing; **relampaguear** [1a] lighten; flash (*a. fig.*); **relampagueo** *m* lightning; flashing.

relanzar [1f] repel, repulse.

relatar [1a] relate, report; *anécdota* tell.

relatividad *f* relativity; **relativo** **1.** relative (*a. gr.*; *a* to); comparative; ~ *a* regarding, relating to; **2.** *m gr.* relative.

relato *m* story, tale; (*informe*) report; **relator** *m* narrator, teller; ⚖ court reporter.

relé *m* ⚡ relay; ~ *de televisión* television relay system.

releer [2e] reread.

relegación *f* relegation; exile; **relegar** [1h] relegate; (*desterrar*) exile; ~ *al olvido* banish from memory.

relevación *f* relief (*a.* ⚔); replacement *etc.*; **relevante** outstanding; **relevar** [1a] *v/t.* ⊕ emboss, carve in relief; relieve (*de cargo etc.* of; *a.* ⚔); absolve, exonerate (*de culpa* from); *empleado* replace; *v/i.* stand out; **relevo** *m* relief (*a.* ⚔); *deportes*: ~*s pl.* relay (race).

relicario *m* shrine; (*caja*) reliquary.

relieve *m* relief; *fig.* prominence; ~*s pl.* leftovers; *bajo* ~ bas-relief;

de ~ *fig.* of importance; *en* ~ in relief, raised; *estampar en* ~ emboss; *poner de* ~ set off (*contra* against); *fig.* emphasize, point out.
religión *f* religion; religious sense, piety; *entrar en* ~ take vows; **religiosa** *f* nun; **religioso 1.** religious (*a. fig.*); **2.** *m* monk.
relimpio F spick and span.
relinchar [1a] neigh, whinny; **relincho** *m* neigh(ing), whinny.
reliquia *f* relic; ~*s pl.* ⚕ after-effects; *fig.* relics, traces *del pasado etc.*; remains; ~ *de familia* heirloom.
reloj [rei'lou] *m* (*grande*) clock; (*portátil*) watch; ⊕ clock, meter; ~ *de arena* sandglass, hourglass; ~ *automático* timer; ~ *de bolsillo* pocket watch; ~ *de caja* grandfather clock; ~ *de carillón* chime clock; ~ *de cuarzo* quartz watch; ~ *de cuclillo* cuckoo clock; ~ *despertador* alarm clock; ~ *de estacionamiento* parking meter; ~ *de ocho días cuerda* eight-day clock; ~ *de pulsera* wrist watch; ~ *registrador* time clock; ~ *registrador de tarjetas* punch clock; ~ *de sol* sundial; *como un* ~ like clockwork; *contra el* ~ against the clock; F *estar como un* ~ feel on top of the world; **relojera** *f* watch case; watch pocket; **relojería** *f* (*arte*) watchmaking; (*tienda*) watchmaker's shop; (*aparato de*) ~ clockwork; *v. bomba*; **relojero** *m* watchmaker.
reluciente shining, brilliant; glittering, gleaming; sparkling; **relucir** [3f] shine (*a. fig.*); glitter, gleam; sparkle; *sacar a* ~ bring out, show off.
relumbrar [1a] shine; sparkle; glare; **relumbrón** *m* flash; glare; *de* ~ flashy, showy, tawdry; *vestirse de* ~ dress flashily.
rellano *m* ▲ landing.
rellenado *m* replenishment *etc.*; **rellenir** [1a] refill, replenish; (*henchir*) stuff, cram; pad; *pollo* stuff; ~**se** F stuff o.s.; **relleno 1.** full, packed; *cocina*: stuffed; **2.** *m* filling, stuffing; padding (*a. fig.*), wadding; *cocina*: stuffing.
remachar [1a] ⊕ *clavo* clinch; *metales* rivet; *fig.* drive home; **remache** *m* rivet; (*acto*) riveting *etc.*
remada *f* stroke; **remador** *m* oarsman.
remanente 1. *phys.* remanent; ✝ *etc.* surplus.
remansarse [1a] form a pool; eddy; become stagnant; **remanso** *m* pool; eddy; backwater.
remar [1a] row; *fig.* toil.
rematado hopeless, out-and-out; *loco* raving; *tonto* utter; **rematante** *m* highest bidder; **rematar** [1a] *v/t. p.*, *trabajo* finish off; ▲ *etc.* top, crown; *subasta*: knock down (*a* to, *en* for); *v/i.* end (▲ *en* in); *deportes*: shoot, score; ~*se* be ruined; **remate** *m* (*fin*) end; (*toque*) finishing touch; ▲ *etc.* top, crest; (*postura*) highest bid; (*adjudicación*) sale; *bridge*: bidding, auction; **de** ~ utterly, completely, hopelessly; *tonto etc.* utter; *por* ~ finally; *poner* ~ *a* cap, top.
remedar [1a] imitate, copy; (*para burlarse*) ape, mimic.
remediable that can be remedied; **remediar** [1b] *perjuicio etc.* remedy; *daño etc.* repair; save, help *en peligro*; (*evitar*) prevent (*que* from *ger.*); **remedio** *m* remedy; help; ⚖ recourse; *sin* ~ inevitable, having nothing to stop it; F *ni para un* ~ not for love nor money; *no hay* ~ *para él* it's all up with him; *no hay más* ~ there's no help for it; *no hay más* ~ *que inf.* the only thing is to *inf.*; *no tener* ~ be unavoidable; (*p. etc.*) be past redemption; *no tengo más* ~ *que inf.* I have no alternative but to *inf.*
remedo *m* imitation; *b.s.* poor imitation, travesty.
remendar [1k] mend, repair, patch; *fig.* correct; **remendón** *m* cobbler.
remero *m* oarsman.
remesa *f* remittance; shipment, consignment; **remesar** [1a] *dinero* remit, send; *mercancías* send, ship, consign.
remiendo *m* (*acto*) mending *etc.*; (*tela etc.*) mend, patch; spot *en piel*; *fig.* correction; *a* ~*s* piecemeal.
remilgado (*gazmoño*) prudish, prim; (*afectado*) affected, overnice; (*delicado*) finicky, fussy; squeamish; **remilgarse** [1h] be fussy *etc.*; **remilgo** *m* prudery; affectation; (*mueca*) simper, smirk.
reminiscencia *f* reminiscence; ♪ *a. fig.* echo.
remirado overcautious, excessively scrupulous; pernickety; **remirar** [1a] look at again; ~**se** take great pains (*en* over).

remisión *f* (*envío*) sending; forgiveness *de pecado etc.*; **remiso** slack, remiss; *movimiento* sluggish; **remisor** *m S.Am.* ✝ sender; **remitente 1.** ⚕ remittent; **2.** *m/f* sender; **remitir** [3a] *v/t.* send, remit; *pena etc.* forgive, pardon; *lector* refer (*a* to); *sesión* adjourn; *v/i.* slacken, let up; *remite* (*en sobre*) sender; **~se** *a* refer to.

remo *m* oar; (*deporte*) rowing; *fig. anat.* arm, leg; *fig.* toil; *a ~ y vela fig.* speedily; *aguantar los ~s* lie (*or* rest) on one's oars; *andar al ~* be hard at it; *pasar a(l) ~* row across.

remoción *f* removal.

remodelación *f* remodeling.

remojar [1a] soak, steep; dip; F celebrate with a drink; *~ la palabra* F wet one's whistle; **remojo** *m* soaking *etc.*; *dejar etc. en ~* soak, steep; *poner en ~* put off to a more suitable time; **remojón** *m* soaking *etc.*

remolacha *f* beet(root); *~ azucarera* sugar beet; *azúcar de ~* beet sugar; *raíz de ~* beetroot.

remolcador *m* ⚓ tug; **remolcar** [1g] (take in) tow; tug; *avión remolcado* sailplane.

remoler [2h] grind up small.

remolin(e)ar(se) [1a] (*agua*) swirl, eddy; whirl, spin *en aire*; (*gente etc.*) swirl, mill around, crowd together; **remolino** *m* (*agua*) swirl, eddy; whirlpool; (*aire*) whirl, whirlwind; (*polvo*) whirl, cloud; (*pelo*) tuft; (*gente*) throng, crush.

remolón 1. slack, lazy; **2.** *m*, **-a** *f* shirker, slacker; *hacerse el ~* = **remolonear** [1a] F shirk, slack; skulk; (*no moverse*) refuse to budge.

remolque *m* towing; (*cable*) tow rope; (*cosa remolcada*) tow, ship *etc.* on tow; *mot.* trailer; caravan *para turismo*; *a ~* in tow; *dar ~ a* take in tow; *llevar al ~* tow.

remonta *f* ⚔ remount; cavalry horses; mending, repair; **remontar** [1a] ⚔ remount; *zapatos etc.* mend, repair; *río* go up; *fig.* raise; **~se** rise, tower; ✈ soar (*a. fig.*); *fig.* get excited; *~ a* go (*or* date) back to.

remoquete *m* punch; *fig.* cutting remark; F (*nombre*) nickname; F (*amoroso*) flirting, spooning; F *dar ~ a* bother.

rémora *f fig.* hindrance; loss of time.

remorder [2h] *fig. p.* cause remorse to; *conciencia* nag, prick; *mente* prey upon; **~se** show remorse; **remordimiento** *m* remorse, regret; pang of conscience.

remoto remote (*a. fig.*); unlikely; *estar ~* be rusty.

remover [2h] *p.*, *cosa* remove, move; (*agitar*) stir, shake up; *tierra* turn over, dig up; *sentimientos* disturb, upset; **removimiento** *m* removal.

remozarse [1f] look much younger.

rempujar [1a] F push, shove, jostle; **rempujón** *m* F push, shove.

remuneración *f* remuneration; *~ por rendimiento* wage for piece work; **remunerador** remunerative; rewarding; **remunerar** [1a] remunerate; reward.

renacer [2d] be reborn; ⚘ appear again; ⚕ recover; *fig.* revive; *hacer ~* revive; **renacimiento** *m* rebirth; revival; ♀ Renaissance.

renacuajo *m* tadpole; F shrimp, runt.

renal kidney *attr.*, renal 📖.

rencilla *f* (*disputa*) quarrel; (*odio de sangre*) feud; (*rencor*) bad blood, ill will; *me tiene ~* he's got it in for me; **rencilloso** quarrelsome.

rencor *m* ill feeling, spite(fulness), rancor; *guardar ~* have a grudge, bear malice (*a* against); **rencoroso** spiteful; vicious, malicious.

rendición *f* surrender; ✝ yield, profits; **rendido** obsequious, submissive; *admirador* humble; *~* (*de cansancio*) worn-out.

rendija *f* crack, crevice, chink; aperture; *fig.* rift, split.

rendimiento *m* ⊕ (*producto*) output; ⊕ efficiency, performance; ✝ yield; *fig.* obsequiousness; (*cansancio*) exhaustion; **rendir** [3l] **1.** *v/t.* (*conquistar*) *país* conquer, subdue; defeat; *fortaleza* take; (*entregar*) surrender; (*sujetar*) overcome; (*devolver*) return, give back; ✝ *producto* produce; *ganancia etc.* yield; *interés, fruto* bear; *gracias* give, render; *homenaje* pay, do; ⚔ *guardia* hand over; (*cansar*) tire, wear out; F throw up; *le rindió el sueño* sleep overcame him; **2.** *v/i.*: *~ bien* yield well; *este negocio no rinde* this business does not pay;

3. ~se ⚔ surrender; yield, give up; (*cansarse*) wear o.s. out; ~ *a evidencia* bow to.
renegado 1. renegade; F gruff, bad-tempered; **2.** *m*, **a** *f* renegade, turncoat; F nasty piece of work; **renegar** [1h *a*. 1k] *v/t*. deny vigorously; detest; *v/i*. turn renegade, *eccl*. apostatize; blaspheme; F curse; ~ **de** forsake, disown; detest.
renglón *m* line; *leer entre ~es* read between the lines; F *poner unos ~es a* drop a line to.
renguear [1a] *S.Am*. limp.
reniego *m* curse, oath.
reno *m* reindeer.
renombrado renowned; **renombre** *m* renown, fame; (*apellido*) surname.
renovable renewable; **renovación** *f* renewal; renovation; *paint*. redecoration; *etc*.; **renovar** [1m] renew; renovate; *cuarto* redecorate; *aviso etc*. repeat; *moda* reintroduce; *país, organización* transform, reorganize.
renquear [1a] limp.
renta *f* (*ingresos*) income; interest, return; (*acciones*) stock; ~ *nacional* gross national product; *~s pl. públicas* revenue; ~ *vitalicia* annuity; **rentar** [1a] yield, produce; **rentero** *m* tenant farmer; **rentista** *m/f* (*accionista*) stockholder; bondholder; financier; rentier, person of independent means; financial expert; **rentístico** financial.
renuencia *f* reluctance; **renuente** reluctant, unwilling.
renuevo *m* ⚘ shoot, sprout; (*acto*) renewal.
renuncia *f* renunciation, surrender; resignation *etc*.; **renunciar** [1b] *v/t*. (*a*. *v/i*. ~ *a*) *derecho etc*. renounce (*en* in favor of), surrender, relinquish; *demanda* drop, waive; *proyecto*, *hábito* give up; *puesto* resign; *trono* abdicate; *v/i*. *naipes*: revoke; **renuncio** *m* revoke; F lie, fib; F *coger en un* ~ catch out, show up.
reñidero *m*: ~ (*de gallos*) cockpit.
reñido *p*. on bad terms, at odds (*con* with); *batalla* bitter; *en lo más* ~ *de* in the thick of; **reñir** [3h *a*. 3l] *v/t*. scold, tell off; *v/i*. (*disputar*) quarrel; (*pelear*) fight, come to blows; (*enemistarse*) fall out (*con* with).
reo 1. *adj*. guilty, criminal; **2.** *m*, **a** *f* offender, criminal, culprit; ⚖ defendant, accused.
reojo: *mirar de* ~ look askance (at); F look scornfully at.
reorganización *f* reorganization; **reorganizar** [1f] reorganize.
reorientar [1a] reorientate, readjust.
reóstato *m* rheostat.
repanchigarse, repantigarse [1h] loll (about), lounge, sprawl.
reparación *f* ⊕ repair(ing), mending; *fig*. reparation, redress; *~es pl*. repairs.
reparador 1. faultfinding; *alimento* fortifying; **2.** *m*, **-a** *f* ⊕ repairer; (*criticón*) faultfinder, critical observer.
reparar [1a] *v/t*. ⊕ repair, mend; (*satisfacer*) make good, make amends for; *fortunas* retrieve; *fuerzas* restore; *error* correct; *golpe* parry; = *v/i*.: ~ *en* notice; pay attention to; **~se** check o.s., restrain o.s.
reparo *m* ⊕ *etc*. repairs; ⚠ restoration; ⚕ restorative; criticism; doubt, objection; protection; *fenc*. parry; *poner ~s a* raise objections to; find fault with; **reparón** F **1.** critical, faultfinding; **2.** *m*, **-a** *f* faultfinder.
repartición *f* distribution; division, sharing-out; **repartidor** *m* distributor; **repartimiento** *m* distribution; **repartir** [3a] distribute, divide, share (out); parcel out; *tareas etc*. allot; *territorio* partition; *octavillas, vasos etc*. give out, hand round; ✉ deliver; *naipes*: deal; *castigos* mete out; *thea*. *papeles* cast; **reparto** *m* = *repartición*; ✉ delivery; *thea*. cast; deal *de naipes*; ~ *de acciones gratis* stock dividend; stock split.
repasar [1a] *lugar* pass by again; *calle* go along again; *fig*. reexamine, review; *texto, lección* read (*or* go) over; *ropa* mend; *mecanismo etc*. check, overhaul; **repasata** *f* F ticking-off; **repaso** *m* review, revision *etc*.; *sew*. mending; ⊕ checkup, overhaul; F ticking-off; ~ *general* general overhaul; *curso de* ~ refresher course; *ropa de* ~ mending.

repatriado 1. repatriated; **2.** *m*, **a** *f* repatriate; **repatriar** [1b] repatriate; send home; **~se** return home.
repecho *m* sharp gradient, steep slope; *a ~* uphill.
repelente repulsive; repellent; **repeler** [2a] repel, repulse; *idea etc.* reject.
repensar [1k] reconsider, rethink.
repente *m* start, sudden movement; *fig.* sudden impulse; *~ (de ira)* fit of anger; *de ~* suddenly, all at once; **repentino** sudden; swift; *vuelta* sharp; **repentizar** [1f] ♪ sight-read, improvise; **repentón** *m* F violent start.
repercusión *f* repercussion (*a. fig.*), reverberation; **repercutir(se)** [3a] (*cuerpo*) rebound; (*sonido*) reverberate, reecho; *fig. ~ en* have repercussions on.
repertorio *m thea. etc.* repertoire; index, repertory.
repetición *f* repetition; recurrence; *thea.* encore; **repetir** [3l] *v/t.* repeat; do *etc.* again; *sonido* echo; *lo grabado* play back; *lección etc.* recite, rehearse; *v/i.* repeat; **~se** (*p.*) repeat o.s.; (*pintor etc.*) copy o.s.; (*suceso*) recur.
repicar [1g] *campana* ring, peal; *carne* chop up small; **~se** boast.
repintar [1a] repaint; **~se** use too much make-up.
repipi F (*redicho*) posh, la-di-da; arty; (*resabido*) know-it-all; *niña ~* little madam.
repique *m* peal(ing), chime; F tiff, squabble; **repiquete** *m* merry (*or* lively) peal; ⚔ clash; **repiquetear** [1a] *campana* ring merrily; **~se** F squabble, wrangle; **repiqueteo** *m* merry pealing; rapping, tapping; clatter *de máquina*.
repisa *f* ledge, shelf; bracket; *~ de chimenea* mantelpiece; *~ de ventana* window sill.
replantar [1a] replant.
replegable folding; ✈ retractable; **replegar** [1h *a.* 1k] fold over; refold; ✈ retract; **~se** ⚔ fall back (*sobre* on).
repleto replete, crammed; obese.
réplica *f* answer, argument; retort, rejoinder; **replicar** [1g] retort, rejoin; *b.s.* argue, answer back; **replicón** F argumentative, saucy.
repliegue *m* fold, crease; convolution; ⚔ retirement.
repoblación *f* repopulation; restocking; *~ forestal* (re)afforestation;
repoblar [1m] *país* repopulate; *estanque* restock; ⚘ (re)afforest.
repollo *m* cabbage; *~ morado S.Am.* red cabbage; **repolludo** round-headed; *fig.* tubby.
reponer [2r] replace, put back; restore; *thea.* revive; (*contestar*) reply; *repuso* he replied; **~se** ⚕ *etc.* recover, pick up; *~ de* recover from, get over.
reportaje *m* report, article; **reportar** [1a] fetch, carry; *fig.* restrain; **~se** control o.s.; **reporte** *m* report, news item; **repórter** *m*, **reportero** *m* reporter.
reposacabezas *m* head rest; **reposado** quiet, restful; solemn; **reposar** [1a] rest, repose; sleep; (*yacer*) lie; **~se** (*líquido*) settle.
reposición *f* replacement; *thea.* revival; ⚕ *etc.* recovery.
repositorio *m* repository.
reposo *m* rest (*a.* ⚕), repose.
repostería *f* (*tienda*) confectioner's (shop); pantry *en casa*; (*arte*) pastry making, confectionery; **repostero** *m*, **a** *f* pastry cook, confectioner.
reprender [2a] reprimand, take to task (*algo a alguien* s.o. for s.t.); **reprensible** reprehensible; **reprensión** *f* reprimand, rebuke.
represa *f* (*acto*) recapture; (*parada*) check, stoppage; dam, weir *en río*; *~ de molino* mill pond.
represalia *f* reprisal; *tomar ~s* take reprisals, retaliate.
represar [1a] (*tomar*) recapture; (*parar*) halt, check; *agua* dam (*a. fig.*); stem (*a. fig.*).
representación *f* representation; *thea.* production; performance; acting; *de ~ hombre* of importance; *en ~ de* representing; *hacer ~es a* make representations to; **representante** *m/f* representative (*a.* ✝); *thea.* performer; **representar** [1a] *mst* represent; stand for; act for; (*informar*) state, declare; (*ser la imagen de*) show, express; *edad* look; *thea.* perform, play; act; **~se** *algo* imagine, picture (to o.s.); envisage; **representativo** representative.
represión *f* repression; suppression; **represivo** repressive.

reprimenda *f* reprimand.

reprimir [3a] repress, curb; *levantamiento* suppress.

reprobar [1m] condemn, reprove; *univ. etc.* fail; **réprobo** *adj. a. su. m,* **a** *f* reprobate; *eccl.* damned.

reprochar [1a] reproach (*algo a alguien* s.o. with *or* for a th.); censure, condemn; **reproche** *m* reproach, reproof (*a* for); reflection (*a* on).

reproducción *f* reproduction; **reproducir(se)** [3o] reproduce.

reptil *m* reptile.

república *f* republic; **republicanismo** *m* republicanism; **republicano** *adj. a. su. m,* **a** *f* republican.

repudiación *f* repudiation; **repudiar** [1b] repudiate; *herencia etc.* renounce; disavow, disown; **repudio** *m* repudiation *etc.*

repudrirse [3a] F eat one's heart out, pine away.

repuesto *m* store, stock, supply; (*sustituto*) replacement; ⊕ refill; ⊕ (*pieza*) spare (part), extra; ⊕ *de* ~ spare, extra.

repugnancia *f* aversion (*hacia, por* from, to), loathing (*hacia, por* for); disgust; (*desgana*) reluctance; opposition; **repugnante** disgusting, revolting; **repugnar** [1a] disgust, revolt; (*estar en pugna con*) conflict with; contradict; do reluctantly; *me repugna hacerlo* I hate doing it.

repulgado affected; **repulgar** [1h] hem; **repulgo** *m* hem; *cocina*: fancy edging; F ~ *de empanada* trifle.

repulir [3a] repolish; refurbish; **~se** dress (up) to the nines; spruce o.s. up.

repulsa *f* rejection, refusal; rebuff; ⚔ check; **repulsar** [1a] reject, refuse; ⚔ repulse, check; **repulsión** *f* = *repulsa*; (*antipatía*) repulsion (*a. phys.*); **repulsivo** repulsive.

repuntar [1a] (*marea*) turn; **~se** (*vino*) turn; F fall out (*con* with); **repunte** *m* turn (of the tide).

reputación *f* reputation, name; standing; **reputar** [1a] repute, esteem; *bien reputado* highly reputed.

requebrar [1k] say nice things to, try to flirt with; *fig.* flatter; ~ *de amores a* court.

requemado *piel* tanned; parched; overdone; **requemar** [1a] ⚘ *etc.* parch, scorch; *comida* overdo, burn; *lengua* burn, sting; *sangre etc.* inflame; **~se** (*piel*) get tanned; ⚘ get parched, dry up; *fig.* smolder (*de* with).

requerir [3i] (*necesitar*) require (*a* of), need; (*llamar*) summon; (*enviar por*) send for; intimate, notify; investigate; ~ *de amores a* court.

requesón *m* curd; cream cheese.

requiebro *m* flirtatious remark.

réquiem *m* requiem.

requilorios *m/pl.* F time-wasting formalities; (*adornos*) frills, buttons and bows; (*accesorios*) bits and pieces.

requisar [1a] requisition; **requisición** *f* ⚔ requisition; **requisito** *m* requisite; requirement; ~ *previo* prerequisite; *llenar los* ~*s* fulfil the requirements.

res *f* beast, animal; (*esp. como número*) head of cattle; *S.Am.* steak.

resabiado knowing, that has learned his lesson; (*taimado*) crafty; **resabiarse** [1b] acquire a bad habit; get fed up; **resabido** would-be expert, pretentious; **resabio** *m* nasty taste; *fig.* bad habit; *tener* ~*s de* smack of.

resaca *f* ⚓ undertow, undercurrent; F hangover.

resalado witty, lively, vivacious.

resaltar [1a] jut (out); *fig.* stand out; *hacer* ~ throw into relief, set off (*contra* against); **resalte** *m,* **resalto** *m* projection.

resarcimiento *m* indemnification, repayment; **resarcir** [3b] indemnify (*de* for), repay; **~se** *de* make up for, retrieve.

resbaladero *m* slippery place, slide; **resbaladizo** slippery; **resbalar** [1a] slip (up); slide; skid; *fig.* slip up; **resbalón** *m* slip (*a. fig.*); slide; skid; **resbaloso** *S.Am.* slippery.

rescatar [1a] *p.* ransom; *cosa empeñada etc.* redeem; (*salvar*) rescue; *terrenos* reclaim; retail; *tiempo* make up for; **rescate** *m* ransom; redemption; rescue; ~ *de terrenos* land reclamation.

rescindir [3a] rescind.
rescoldo *m* embers; smoldering; *fig.* scruple, lingering doubt; *arder en* ~ smolder.
rescontrar [1m] ✝ offset, balance.
resecar [1g] dry thoroughly; (*dañar*) parch, scorch; **reseco** very dry; parched.
reseda *f* mignonette.
resentido resentful, sullen; *es un* ~ he's got a chip on his shoulder; *estar* ~ *de* feel the effect of; **resentimiento** *m* resentment; **resentirse** [3i]: ~ *de*, ~ *por* resent; be offended at; *defecto* suffer from; *consecuencias* feel the effects of.
reseña *f lit.*, ⚔ review; *paint.* sketch; **reseñador** *m* reviewer, critic; **reseñar** [1a] review; sketch.
reserva *f* reserve (*a.* ✝, ⚔); (*acto etc.*) reservation; discretion, reticence; privacy; ~ *de caza* game preserve; ~ *de Indios* Indian reservation; ~ *mental* mental reservation; *absoluta* ~, *con la mayor* ~ in the strictest confidence; *a* ~ *de* with the intention of; *de* ~ in reserve; *sin* ~ unreservedly; **reservación** *f* reservation; **reservado 1.** *p.* reserved, reticent; discreet; *lugar* private; *asiento* reserved; **2.** *m* 🚃 reserved compartment; ~ *de señoras* ladies-only compartment; **reservar** [1a] reserve; set aside, keep; (*encubrir*) conceal; ~**se** save o.s. (*para* for); (*desconfiar*) beware (*de* of); **reservista** *m* reservist.
resfriado *m* cold; chill; **resfriar** [1c] *v/t.* cool (*a. fig.*), chill; *v/i.* turn cold; ~**se** ⚕ catch cold; *fig.* cool off.
resguardar [1a] protect, shield (*de* from); ~**se** shelter; safeguard o.s.; **resguardo** *m* protection; safeguard; shelter; guard; (*documento*) certificate; (*papeleta*) slip, check.
residencia *f* residence; *univ.* hall of residence, hostel; ~ *de ancianos* home for the aged, nursing home; **residencial** residential; **residente** *adj. a. su. m/f* resident; **residir** [3a] reside; live; *fig.* lie; *fig.* ~ *en* consist in, reside in; rest with; **residual** residual, residuary; **residuo** *m* residue; ⚗ remainder; ⚗, ⚗ residuum; ~*s pl.* refuse, remains; ~*s radiactivos* radioactive waste.
resignación *f* resignation; **resignado** resigned; **resignar** [1a] resign; renounce; *mando etc.* hand over (*en* to); ~**se** resign o.s. (*a* to).
resina *f* resin; **resinoso** resinous.
resistencia *f* resistance (*a.* ⚔, *phys.*, ⚡); strength; endurance, stamina, staying power; opposition; (*acto*) stand; ✈ ~ *al avance* drag; ~ *pasiva* passive resistance;
resistente resistant; tough; *tela etc.* hard-wearing; ⚘ hardy; ~ *al rayado* scratch-resistant; **resistir** [3a] *v/t.* stand, bear; *tentación* resist; *v/i.* resist; (*durar*) last; *esp.* ⚔ hold out; fight back; ~ *a* resist, withstand; make a stand against; stand up to; (*soportar*) stand, bear; ~**se** resist, struggle; ~ *a inf.* refuse to *inf.*, find it hard to *inf.*; **resistor** *m* resistor.
resma *f* ream.
resobado hackneyed, trite.
resol *m* glare of the sun; **resolana** *f*, **resolano** *m* sun trap.
resolución *f* resolution (*a. parl.*); (*acto*) solving; decision; *fig.* resolution, resolve; boldness; *en* ~ in short, to sum up; *tomar una* ~ take a decision; **resoluto** = *resuelto*; **resolver** [2h; *p.p. resuelto*] *problema* solve, do; think out, puzzle out; *cuestión* settle; *cuerpo, materia* resolve (*en* into); *conjunto* analyse, divide (up); ⚗ *etc.* dissolve (away); *acción* decide on; ~**se** resolve itself, work out; ~ *a inf.* resolve to *inf.*
resollar [1m] puff (and blow); snort; wheeze; F *no* ~ give no sign of life.
resonancia *f* resonance; echo; *tener* ~ *fig.* cause a stir, have repercussions; **resonante** resonant; resounding, ringing, echoing; **resonar** [1m] resound, ring, echo (*de* with).
resoplar [1a] puff, blow, snort; **resoplido** *m* puff, snort.
resopón *m* nightcap.
resorte *m* ⊕ spring; elasticity, springiness; *fig.* means, expedient; ~ *espiral* coil spring; F *tocar* ~*s* pull wires.
respailar *v/i.*: *ir respailando* F scurry along.
respaldar [1a] endorse; *fig.* support, back; ~**se** lean back; sprawl; **respaldo** *m* back *de silla, hoja*; endorsement *en papel*; *fig.* support, backing.

respectar [1a] concern; *por lo que respecta a* ... as far as ... is concerned; **respectivo** respective; **respecto** *m* respect, relation; *(con)* ~ *a*, *(con)* ~ *de* with regard to; in relation to; *a ese* ~ on that score; *al* ~ in the matter; *bajo ese* ~ in that respect; **respetabilidad** *f* respectability; **respetable** respectable; worthy; **respetar** [1a] respect; **respeto** *m* respect, regard, consideration; *de* ~ spare, extra; *por* ~ *a* out of consideration for; ~*s pl.* respects; *campar por sus* ~*s* strike out on one's own; *b.s.* be self-centered; be bone idle; *estar de* ~ be all dressed up.

réspice *m* F curt reply; *(reprensión)* ticking-off.

respingado *nariz* snub; **respingar** [1h] shy, start; *fig.* kick; **respingo** *m* shy, start; *fig.* gesture of disgust; **respingón** *nariz* snub; *caballo* difficult, *S.Am.* surly.

respiración *f* breathing; **respiradero** *m* ⊕ vent, air valve; *fig.* respite, breathing space; **respirar** [1a] breathe; *gas etc.* breathe in; breathe again *después de mal momento*; *(descansar)* get one's breath; *sin* ~ without a break; **respiratorio** respiratory; breathing *attr.*; **respiro** *m* breathing; *(descanso)* breathing space; lull, respite; *(prórroga)* grace; reprieve.

resplandecer [2d] shine (*a. fig.*); glitter, glow, blaze; **resplandeciente** shining *etc.*; **resplandor** *m* brilliance, radiance; glitter, glow, blaze.

responder [2a] *v/t.* answer; *injuria etc.* answer with; *v/i.* answer, reply; *esp. fig.* respond; *(ser respondón)* answer back; ~ *de*, ~ *por* answer for, be responsible for; **respondón** F cheeky, saucy, pert.

responsabilidad *f* responsibility *etc.*; *de* ~ *limitada* limited liability *attr.*; *bajo mi* ~ on my responsibility; **responsable** responsible (*de* for); liable (*de* for); *la p.* ~ the person in charge.

responsorio *m eccl.* response.

respuesta *f* answer, reply; response.

resquebra(ja)dura *f* crack, split; **resquebrajar(se)** [1a] crack, split; **resquebrar** [1k] begin to crack.

resquemar [1a] *lengua* burn, sting; ⚘ parch; *comida* burn; **resquemo(r)** *m* burn, sting; burnt taste *de comida*; *fig.* sorrow; resentment.

resquicio *m* chink, crack; *fig.* chance, opening.

resta *f* Ꭿ subtraction; *(residuo)* remainder.

restablecer [2d] reestablish; restore; revive; **~se** recover.

restallar [1a] crack; *(crujir)* crackle.

restante 1. remaining; *los* ~*s* the rest; **2.** *m* rest, remainder.

restañar [1a] stanch.

restar [1a] *v/i.* Ꭿ subtract, take away; deduct; *pelota* return; *autoridad, valor etc.* reduce; *v/i.* remain, be left.

restauración *f* restoration; **restaurán** [resto'ran] *m*, **restaurante** *m* restaurant; café; ~ *automático* automat; **restaurar** [1a] restore; repair; recover.

restitución *f* return, restitution; **restituir** [3g] restore, return.

resto *m* rest; remainder (*a.* Ꭿ); *deportes*: *(p.)* receiver; *(acto)* return; ~*s pl.* remains; *cocina*: leftovers; ⚓ *etc.* wreckage; ~*s de serie* remnants; ~*s pl. mortales* mortal remains; *a* ~ *abierto* F without limit; *echar el* ~ stake all one's money; F go the whole hog; do one's utmost (*por inf.* to *inf.*).

restorán *m S.Am.* restaurant.

restregar [1h *a.* 1k] scrub, rub (hard).

restricción *f* restriction; limitation; restraint; ~ *mental* mental reservation; **restrictivo** restrictive; **restringir** [3c] restrict.

resucitar [1a] *v/t.* resuscitate; *fig.* resurrect, revive; *v/i.* resuscitate return to life; revive.

resuelto 1. *p.p. of resolver*; **2.** resolute, determined; steadfast; prompt; *estar* ~ *a inf.* be determined to *inf.*

resuello *m* *(respiración)* breathing; *(un* ~*)* breath; *(ruidoso, penoso)* puff; snort; wheeze; *corto de* ~ short-winded.

resulta: *de* ~*s de* as a result of; **resultado** *m* result, outcome; issue; sequel; effect; *dar* ~ produce results; **resultar** [1a] be, prove (to be), turn out (to be); ~ *de* result from, stem from; be evident from;

~ *(ser) verdadero* prove (to be) true; *esto resulta difícil* this is awkward; *resulta que* it emerges that, it appears that; *resulta de todo esto que* it follows from all this that; *ahora resulta que no puedo* now it turns out that I can't; *con todo lo que después resultó* with all that ensued; *no me resultó muy bien aquello* it didn't work out very well for me; F *esto no me resulta* I can't get along with this.

resumen *m* summary, résumé; *en* ~ to sum up, in short; **resumir** [3a] sum up, summarize; **~se** be included.

resurgimiento *m* resurgence; revival; **resurgir** [3c] revive, reappear; be resurrected; **resurrección** *f* resurrection.

retablo *m* reredos, altar piece.

retaguardia *f* rearguard; *a* ~ in the rear.

retahila *f* row, line, string; *fig.* volley, string.

retajar [1a] cut round.

retal *m* remnant, oddment.

retama *f* Spanish broom; ~ *de escoba* furze.

retar [1a] challenge; F tick off.

retardar [1a] slow down, slow up, retard; *reloj* put back; **retardo** *m* slowing-up; delay; time lag; **retardriz** *acción* delaying.

retazo *m* remnant; *fig.* bit, fragment; ~*s pl.* odds and ends; snippets; *labor de* ~*s* patchwork.

rete... very ...; **retebién** very well, jolly well.

retemblar [1k] shudder, shake (*de* at, with).

retén *m* reserve (*a.* ⚔), store; ⊕ stop, catch, lock.

retención *f* retention (*a.* ⚕); ☤ deduction; **retener** [2l] retain, keep (back), hold (back); *(deducir)* withhold, deduct; ⚖ detain; **retenida** *f* guy (rope); **retentivo** retentive (*a.* ⚕).

reticencia *f* irony, sarcasm; *(una* ~*)* half-truth; **reticente** ironical, sarcastic; misleading, full of half-truths.

retícula *f phot.* screen; *opt.* reticule; **retículo** *m* reticle; network.

retina *f* retina.

retintín *m* tinkle, tinkling; jingle; ring(ing); F nastily sarcastic tone; **retiñir** [3h] tinkle; jingle; ring.

retirada *f* ⚔ withdrawal (*a.* ☤), retreat (*a. toque*); recall *de embajador*; *(sitio)* retreat, place of refuge; *batirse en* ~ retreat; **retirado** *oficial* retired; *lugar* secluded, remote; **retirar** [1a] withdraw (*a.* ⚔, ☤; *de* from); take away, remove (*a* from); ⊕ *pieza* take out, take off; *tapa* take off; *mano, cubierta* draw back; *embajador* recall; **~se** ⚔ retreat, withdraw; retire *a su cuarto*; *(apartarse de la gente)* retire, go into seclusion; shrink back (*ante peligro etc.* at, from); *(jubilarse)* retire; *deportes*: drop out, retire; scratch *antes de salida*; **retiro** *m* ⚔, ☤ withdrawal; *(sueldo)* pension, retirement pay; *(jubilación)* retirement; *eccl.* retreat; *(recogimiento)* seclusion; *(lugar)* retreat; *vivir en el* ~ live in retirement (*or* seclusion).

reto *m* challenge; *(amenaza)* threat; *S.Am.* insult.

retocar [1g] retouch, touch up (*a. phot.*).

retoñar [1a] ⚘ sprout; *fig.* reappear, recur; **retoño** *m* ⚘ shoot.

retoque *m* retouching, touching-up; *(última mano)* finishing touch; ⚕ touch.

retorcer [2b *a.* 2h] twist; *manos* wring; *argumento* turn; *sentido* twist; **~se** twist, twine; writhe, squirm *de dolor*.

retórica *f* rhetoric; ~*s pl.* quibbles; **retórico 1.** rhetorical; **2.** *m* rhetorician.

retornar [1a] *v/t.* return, give back; turn back; *v/i.* return; **retorno** *m* return; *(pago)* reward, payment; *(cambio)* barter; ~ *terrestre* ⚡ ground.

retorsión *f* twisting; writhing.

retorta *f* ⚗ retort.

retortero: F *andar al* ~ bustle around, fuss about; F *traer al* ~ lead *s.o.* a dance, push *s.o.* around.

retortijón *m*: ~ *de tripas* gripe.

retozar [1f] frolic, frisk, gambol, romp; **retozo** *m* frolic *etc.*; ~ *de la risa* giggle, titter; **retozón** frisky, playful.

retractar [1a] retract, withdraw; **~se** recant, retract; **retráctil** retractable.

retraer [2p] bring back, bring again; *fig.* dissuade, discourage; **~se** retire, retreat; take refuge; retract; ~ *de* withdraw from, give up; shun; **retraído** retiring, shy; unsociable; *b.s.* backward; **retraimiento** *m* (*acto*) withdrawal *etc.*; (*lugar*) retreat, refuge; (*lo retirado*) seclusion.

retransmisión *f radio*: repeat (broadcast); **retransmitir** [3a] repeat; relay.

retrasar [1a] *v/t.* delay, defer, put off; *evolución etc.* retard, slow down; *reloj* put back; *retrasado* (mentally) retarded; *v/i.* (*reloj*) be slow; = **~se** (*p.*, 🚂 *etc.*) be late, be behind time; lag behind *en estudios etc.*; **retraso** *m* delay; time lag; slowness, lateness; *con* ~ late; behindhand; *con 20 minutos de* ~ 20 minutes late; *tener* ~ be late.

retratar [1a] portray (*a. fig.*); *fig.* describe; **retratista** *m/f* portrait painter; **retrato** *m* portrait; *fig.* description; *fig.* (*imagen fiel*) likeness; *ser el vivo* ~ *de* be the very image of.

retrechería *f* F dodge; **retrechero** F clever, crafty; (*atractivo*) lovely, nice.

retreparse [1a] lean back, lounge.

retreta *f* ⚔ (*toque de*) ~ tattoo; retreat; *S.Am.* outdoor band concert.

retrete *m* lavatory, toilet.

retribución *f* (*recompensa*) reward, payment; (*pago*) pay; compensation (*a.* ⊕); **retribuido** *puesto* salaried; *trabajo* paid; **retribuir** [3g] reward, repay; pay.

retro... retro...; **~activo** retroactive; retrospective; **~carga**: *de* ~ breech-loading; *arma de* ~ breech-loader; **~ceder** [2a] draw back, stand back; go back, turn back *en viaje etc.*; back down, flinch (*ante peligro* from); (*agua etc.*) fall; ⚔ retreat, fall back; ⚔ (*arma*) recoil; *hacer* ~ force back; **~ceso** *m* backward movement, falling back; ⚔ withdrawal; ⚔ recoil *de arma*; ☤ recession, slump; ⚕ renewed attack, flare-up; ⊕ rewind; **retrocohete** *m* retrorocket; **retrodisparo** *m* retro-firing; **retrógrado** retrograde; *esp. pol.* reactionary; **retrogresión** *f* retrogression.

retronar [1m] rumble.

retro...: **~propulsión** *f* ✈ jet propulsion; **~spección** *f* retrospect, retrospection; **~spectivo** retrospective; *cine*: *escena* **~***a* flashback; **~visor** *m*: (*espejo*) ~ rear-view mirror.

retruécano *m* play on words.

retumbante booming, resounding; *fig.* bombastic; **retumbar** [1a] boom, rumble, reverberate; **retumbo** *m* boom *etc.*

reuma *m* rheumatism; **reumático** rheumatic; **reumatismo** *m* rheumatism.

reunión *f* meeting, gathering; reunion; *pol.* meeting, rally; (*fiesta*) party; **reunir** [3a] *cosas separadas* join (together), (re)unite; *cosas dispersas* gather (together), assemble, get together; *colección* make; *datos etc.* collect; *fondos* raise; *cualidades* combine; **~se** (*juntarse*) meet, get together, gather; (*unirse*) unite; (*concurrir*) conspire; ~ *con* (re)join; meet up with.

revalidar [1a] confirm, ratify.

revalor(iz)ación *f* revaluation; **revalorar** [1a], **revalorizar** [1f] revalue; reassess.

revancha *f* revenge; *deportes*: return match; *tomar su* ~ get one's own back.

revelación *f* revelation; disclosure; **revelado** *m phot.* developing; **revelador 1.** revealing, telltale; **2.** *m phot.* developer; **revelar** [1a] *mst* reveal; disclose, betray, give away; *phot.* develop.

revendedor *m*, **-a** *f* retailer; *b.s.* speculator; **revender** [2a] resell, retail; *b.s.* speculate in; *entradas* tout.

revenirse [3s] (*encogerse*) shrink; (*vino*) turn sour; (*secarse*) dry out; (*ceder*) give way.

reventa *f* resale.

reventadero *m* rough ground; F tough job, grind; **reventar** [1k] **1.** *v/t.* burst; crush, smash; *fig.* ruin; F (*cansar*) bore to tears; F (*molestar*) rile; F (*hacer trabajar*) overwork, work to death; **2.** *v/i.* burst; explode, pop; (*brotar*) burst forth; (*olas*) break; *fig.* explode (*de ira etc.* with); F die; ~ *de risa* split one's sides; ~ *por inf.* be bursting to *inf.*; **3. ~se** burst *etc.*; **reventón** *m* burst; explosion; *mot.* blowout; *fig.* steep hill, tough climb; (*apuro*) jam; *darse un* ~ sweat, slog (*para inf.* to *inf.*).

rever [2v] review, revive; ⚖ *fallo* review; *pleito* retry.
reverberar [1a] (*ruido*) reverberate; (*luz*) play (*en* on), be reflected (*en* from); **reverbero** *m* reverberation; (*espejo*) reflector; (*farol*) street lamp.
reverdecer [2d] grow green again; *fig.* acquire new vigor.
reverencia *f* reverence; (*saludo*) bow *de hombre*, curtsy *de mujer*; ≈ Your *etc.* Reverence; **reverencial** reverential; **reverenciar** [1b] revere, venerate; **reverendo** respected, reverend; *eccl.* reverend; F solemn; **reverente** reverent.
reversible *mst* reversible; ⚖ reversionary; **reversión** *f* reversion; **reverso** *m* back, other side; reverse *de moneda*; el ~ de la medalla *fig.* the other side of the picture; (*p.*) the exact opposite; **reverter** [2g] revert.
revés *m* (*cara*) back, other side, underside; (*golpe*) slap; *tenis*: backhand; *fig.* reverse, setback; al ~ *tela etc.* inside out, upside down; (*adv.*) on the contrary; al ~ de lo que esperaba contrary to what I expected; todo le salió al ~ it all turned out wrong for him; volver al ~ turn inside out, turn upside down; **revesado** complicated; *fig.* unmanageable.
revestimiento *m* facing, coating; lining; ⚔ revetment; **revestir** [3l] *ropa* put on, wear; *superficie* clothe (de in); *esp.* ⊕ face, coat; line; sheathe; *fig. suelo etc.* carpet (de with); *cuento* adorn (de with); *p.* invest (con, de with); *importancia* have; **~se** be carried away; (*engreírse*) be haughty; ~ con, ~ de *autoridad etc.* be invested with.
reviejo very old.
revisada *f S.Am.* examination, revision; **revisar** [1a] revise; reexamine; review (*a.* ⚖); check; *esp.* ⊕ overhault; **revisión** *f* revision; review (*a.* ⚖); check; *esp.* ⊕ overhaul; **revisor** *m*, **-a** *f* reviser; 🚂 ticket collector, conductor.
revista *f* review (*a.* ⚓, ⚔), inspection; revision; *thea.* revue; *lit.* review, magazine; ⚖ retrial; pasar ~ a = **revistar** [1a] ⚓, ⚔ inspect, review; **revistero** *m* reviewer, critic; contributor.
revivificar [1g] revitalize; **revivir** [3a] revive, be revived; live again.
revocación *f* revocation, repeal; reversal; **revocar** [1g] *orden etc.* revoke, repeal; *decisión* reverse; dissuade (de from); *casa* plaster; whitewash; **revocatoria** *f S.Am.* recall; cancellation, repeal; **revoco** *m* = revocación; ⚠ = revoque.
revolcar [1g *a.* 1m] *p. etc.* knock down, knock over, send flying; F *adversario* floor; **~se** roll, flounder about; (*esp. animal*) wallow (*a. fig.*, en in); (*empeñarse*) dig one's heels in.
revolear [1a] fly around; **revolotear** [1a] flutter, flit; wheel; hover.
revoltijo *m*, **revoltillo** *m* jumble, mess, litter; *fig.* mess.
revoltoso **1.** rebellious, unruly; *niño* naughty; **2.** *m* rebel; *pol.* troublemaker, agitator.
revolución *f mst* revolution (*a.* ⊕); turn; **revolucionar** [1a] revolutionize; **revolucionario** *adj. a. su. m*, **a** *f* revolutionary.
revólver *m* revolver.
revolver [2h; *p.p.* revuelto] (*agitar, sacudir*) shake; *líquido* stir (up); *tierra* turn up, turn over; *objeto* turn round, turn over (*or* upside down); *papeles etc.* look through, rummage among; *lo ordenado* mix up, upset, disarrange; *estómago* turn; *asunto* turn over *en mente*; *ánimos* upset, sow discord among; *p.* get into trouble (con with); (*envolver*) wrap up; **~se** turn (right) round, turn over *etc.*; toss and turn *en cama*; *ast.* revolve; (*tiempo*) change, turn stormy.
revoque *m* (*acto*) plastering; whitewashing; (*materia*) plaster; whitewash.
revuelco *m* fall, tumble.
revuelo *m* disturbance; rumpus; de ~ incidentally, in passing.
revuelta *f* (*motín*) revolt; disturbance; turn, bend *de camino*; change *de parecer etc.*; (*disputa*) quarrel, row; **revuelto** **1.** *p.p. of revolver*; *agua* troubled; *v. huevo*; **2.** *adj.* in disorder, higgledy-piggledy; (*travieso*) naughty; *asunto* complicated.
rey *m* king (*a. naipes, ajedrez*); **~es** *pl.* king and queen; ~ de zarza wren; día (*or* noche) de ≈es Twelfth Night; los

℞es *Católicos* Ferdinand and Isabella; *los* ℞es *Magos* the Magi, the Three Wise Men (*equivalent to Santa Claus as bringers of presents*); *ni ~ ni roque* F nobody.
reyerta *f* quarrel; fight, brawl.
rezagado *m* late-comer; loiterer; ⚔ straggler; **rezagar** [1h] outdistance, leave behind; (*aplazar*) postpone; **~se** fall (*or* get left) behind; lag (behind); straggle.
rezar [1f] *v/t.* say; *v/i.* pray, say one's prayers; (*texto*) read, say, run; F grumble; F *~ con* have to do with; **rezo** *m* (*acto*) praying; (*una oración*) prayer; (*oraciones*) prayers; devotions; office, daily service.
rezongar [1h] grumble, mutter; growl; **rezongo** *m* grumble; growl; **rezongón** grumbling, cantankerous.
rezumar [1a] *v/t.* ooze, exude; *v/i.* ooze (out), seep, leak out (*a. fig.*).
ría[1] *etc. v. reír.*
ría[2] *f* estuary, mouth of a river; *approx.* sea loch, fiord.
riachuelo *m* brook, stream.
riada *f* flood.
ribera *f* shore, beach; bank *de río*; **ribereño** riverside *attr.*; *esp.* ⚖ riparian.
ribete *m sew. etc.* edging, border; *fig.* addition; *fig.* trimmings, embellishments *de cuento*; *~s pl. fig.* streak, touch; *tener sus ~s de* have some pretentions to, have some appearance of being *etc.*
ricacho *m*, **ricachón** *m* F nouveau riche.
rico 1. rich, wealthy; (*fértil, suntuoso*) rich (*en* in); *comida* tasty, delicious; *dulces etc.* rich; *fruto* luscious; F cute; F lovely; F *sí, rica* yes darling; **2.** *m*, **a** *f* rich person, wealthy man *etc.*; *nuevo ~* nouveau riche.
rictus *m* (involuntary) twisting of the lips; sneer; grin.
ridiculez *f* absurdity; **ridiculizar** [1f] ridicule, deride; guy; **ridículo** ridiculous, absurd, ludicrous; (*delicado*) touchy; *poner en ~* ridicule, make a fool of; *ponerse en ~* make a fool (*or* exhibition) of o.s.
riego *m* watering; irrigation; *fig.* sprinkling; *~ por aspersión* spray.
riel *m* 🚂 rail; *metall.* ingot.
rielar [1a] *poet.* shimmer; twinkle.
rienda *f* rein; *a ~ suelta* at top speed; *fig.* without the least restraint; *dar ~ suelta a* give free rein to; give *s.o.* his head; *deseos* indulge; *soltar las ~s* take off the brakes; kick over the traces.
riente laughing, merry; *paisaje* smiling, bright.
riesgo *m* risk; danger; *correr ~ de inf.* run the risk of *ger*; **riesgoso** *S.Am.* risky.
rifa *f* raffle; (*riña*) quarrel, fight; **rifar** [1a] *v/t.* raffle; *v/i.* quarrel, fight.
rifle *m* rifle; *~ de repetición* repeater; **riflero** *m* rifleman.
rigidez *f* rigidity *etc.*; *~ cadavérica* rigor mortis; **rígido** rigid; stiff; *fig.* strict, stern (*con, para* towards), unbending; *b.s.* wooden; hidebound; **rigor** *m* rigor, severity (*a. meteor. etc.*); harshness, strictness; stringency; *en ~* strictly speaking; *ser de ~* be de rigueur, be the order of the day; **rigorismo** *m* strictness; austerity; **rigorista** *m/f* strict observer, stickler; **rigurosidad** *f* rigor, severity; **riguroso** rigorous; *crítico, pena, tiempo etc.* severe, harsh; strict; stringent.
rija *f* quarrel, fight; **rijo** *m* lust(fulness); **rijoso** quarrelsome; (*sensual*) lustful.
rima *f* rhyme; *~s pl.* poems, poetry; *octava ~* ottava rima; *tercia ~* terza rima; **rimador** *m*, **-a** *f* rhymester; **rimar** [1a] rhyme (*con* with).
rimbombancia *f* resonance, echo; *fig.* bombast; showiness, flashiness; **rimbombante** resounding, echoing; *fig.* bombastic; (*vistoso*) showy, flashy.
rimero *m* stack, heap.
rincón *m* (inside) corner; *fig.* corner, nook, retreat; patch *de terreno etc.*; **rinconada** *f* corner.
ringl(er)a *f* row, line; swath *de hierba segada.*
ringorrango *m* F flourish *de pluma*; *fig.* trimmings, frills.
rinoceronte *m* rhinoceros.
riña *f* quarrel; (*con golpes*) fight, scuffle, fracas; *~ de gallos* cockfight.
riñón *m anat.* kidney; *fig.* heart,

core; F *tener el ~ bien cubierto* be well-heeled.
río *m* river; *~ abajo* downstream; *~ arriba* upstream; *~ de oro fig.* gold mine; *a ~ revuelto* in disorder; *pescar en ~ revuelto* fish in troubled waters.
rió *etc. v. reír.*
riolada *f* F flood, stream.
rioplatense *adj. a. su. m/f* (native) of the River Plate region.
riosta *f* brace, strut.
ripio *m* residue, refuse; (*cascote*) debris, rubble; *fig. poet.* word used to fill up the line; (*palabrería*) verbiage, padding; *no perder ~* not miss a trick.
riqueza *f* wealth, riches; (*fertilidad, sabor, de estilo*) richness; *~s pl. del subsuelo* mineral resources; *vivir en la ~* live in luxury.
risa *f* (*una ~*) laugh; (*en general*) laughter, laughing; *hubo ~s* there was laughter; *el libro es una verdadera ~* the book's a laugh from start to finish; *cosa de ~* joke, laughing matter; *¡qué ~!* what a joke!, how funny!; *desternillarse de ~* split one's sides; *morirse de ~* die of laughing; *tomar a ~* laugh *s.t.* off.
risco *m* cliff, bluff, crag; **riscoso** craggy.
risible ludicrous, laughable.
risotada *f* guffaw, horselaugh.
ristra *f* string of onions, string of garlic; F string, row, file.
ristre: (*lanza*) *en ~* at the ready, all set.
risueño smiling; *disposición* cheerful, sunny; *paisaje* smiling; *perspectiva* bright.
rítmico rhythmic(al); **ritmo** *m* rhythm.
ito *m* rite; ceremony; **ritual** *adj. a. su. m* ritual.
rival 1. rival, competing; **2.** *m/f* rival, competitor; **rivalidad** *f* rivalry; enmity; **rivalizar** [1f] compete, vie; *~ con* rival.
rizado *pelo* curly; *superficie* crinkly; crisp; **rizador** *m* curling iron, hair curler; **rizar** [1f] *pelo* curl; crisp; *superficie* crinkle; *agua* ripple, ruffle; *~ el rizo* ✈ loop the loop; *~se* curl *etc.*; **rizo 1.** curly; **2.** *m* curl, ringlet; ripple *de agua*; *~s pl.* ⚓ reefs; ✈ *hacer* (*or rizar*) *el ~* loop the loop; **rizoso** curly.
roano roan.
robar [1a] *poseedor* rob (*algo a alguien* s.o. of s.t.); *posesión* steal (*a* from); (*secuestrar*) abduct, kidnap; *caja* break into, rifle; *casa* break into, burgle; *cartas* draw, take.
roblar [1a] rivet, clinch.
roble *m* oak (tree); **robledal** *m*, **robledo** *m* oak wood.
roblón *m* rivet.
robo *m* robbery; theft, thieving; *~ en la vía pública* highway robbery; *~ con escalamiento* burglary; *~ relámpago* smash-and-grab raid.
robot *m* robot; **robotización** *f* robotization, use of robots.
robustecer [2d] strengthen; *~se* grow stronger; **robustez** *f* robustness *etc.*; **robusto** robust; strong, sturdy; tough; hardy.
roca *f* rock.
roce *f* rub(bing); *esp.* ⊕ friction; graze *en piel*; *fig.* close contact, familiarity; *tener ~ con* be in close contact with.
rociada *f* dash, splash; shower, sprinkling; (*aspersión*) spray; *fig.* shower *de piedras*, hail *de balas*; F *echar una ~ a* dress down; **rociador** *m* spray, sprinkler; **rociar** [1c] *v/t.* sprinkle, spray (*de* with); spatter *de lodo etc.*; *fig.* scatter, shower; *v/i.*: *rocía esta mañana* there is a dew this morning.
rocín *m* hack, nag; F lout; **rocinante** *m* poor old horse.
rocío *m* dew; (*llovizna*) drizzle; *fig.* sprinkling.
rockero *m* F rock singer.
rococó *adj. a. su. m* rococo.
rocoso rocky.
roda *f* ⚓ stem.
rodaballo *m* turbot; *~ (menor)* brill.
rodada *f* rut, (wheel) track; *S.Am.* fall.
rodado *circulación* wheeled, on wheels; *piedra* rounded; *v. canto*; *caballo* dappled; *estilo* rounded, fluent; **rodaja** *f* (*rueda*) small wheel, castor; disk, round; slice *de pan etc.*; **rodaje** *m* ⊕ (set of) wheels; *cine*: shooting, filming; *mot. en ~* running-in; **rodamiento** *m* bearing; tread *de un neumático*; *~s pl.* running gear; **rodante** rolling; **rodapié** *m* skirting board; **rodar** [1m] *v/t. vehículo* wheel; *cosa redonda* roll; *mot.* run in;

película shoot, film; *v/i.* roll (*por* along, down *etc.*); go, run, travel *sobre ruedas*; rotate, revolve *en eje*; *fig.* wander about, roam; abound; ~ *por alguien* be at s.o.'s beck and call; *echarlo todo a* ~ spoil everything.

rodear [1a] *v/t.* surround (*de* by, with); ring, encircle, shut in; *S.Am. ganado* round up; *v/i.* go round; (*camino*) make a detour; *fig.* beat about the bush; **~se** turn, toss, twist; **rodeo** *m* detour *de camino*; roundabout way, long way round; *fig.* dodge; pretext; circumlocution; ⚘ cattle pen; *S.Am.* ⚘ roundup, rodeo; *sin* ~*s* outright; *andarse con* ~*s*, *ir por* ~*s* beat about the bush; *dejarse de* ~*s* come to the point.

rodera *f* rut, cart track.

rodete *m* coil, bun *de pelo*; pad *para peso*; ward *de cerradura*; ⊕ articulator.

rodilla *f* knee; (*trapo*) floor cloth; *de* ~*s* kneeling; *caer de* ~*s* fall on one's knees; *estar* (*or hincarse, ponerse*) *de* ~*s* kneel (down); *hincar la* ~ kneel down; *fig.* bow, humble o.s. (*ante* to); **rodillazo** *m* push with the knee; *dar un* ~ *a* knee.

rodillo *m* roller; *cocina*: rolling pin; ink-roller *para entintar*; ~ *pintor* paint roller; ~ *de vapor* steamroller.

rodrigón *m* ⚘ stake, prop.

roedor 1. gnawing (*a. fig.*); **2.** *m* rodent; **roer** [2z] gnaw; nibble; *hueso* pick; *metal* corrode, eat into; (*pesar, duda*) gnaw.

rogación *f* petition; *eccl.* rogation; ~*s pl. eccl.* rogations; **rogar** [1h *a.* 1m] *v/t. p.* beg; plead with; *cosa* beg for, ask for, plead for; ~ *que* beg *inf.*; ask that; *v/i.* beg, plead (*por* for); (*orar*) pray; *hacerse* (*de*) ~ have to be coaxed; *no se hizo de* ~ he didn't have to be asked twice.

rojear [1a] redden, turn red; **rojete** *m* rouge; **rojez** *f* redness; **rojillo** *pol.* pink; **rojizo** reddish; ruddy; **rojo 1.** red (*a. pol.*); ruddy; **2.** *m* red (*a. pol.*); ~ *cereza* cherry-red; ~ *de labios* lipstick; *calentar al* ~ make red-hot.

rol *m* list, catalog(ue), roll; ⚓ muster.

rollizo *p.* plump; stocky, sturdy; *niño* chubby; *mujer* plump, buxom; *objeto* cylindrical.

rollo *m* roll; *cocina*: rolling pin; F awful bore.

romadizo *m* head cold.

romana *f* steelyard.

romance 1. *lengua* romance; **2.** *m* romance (language); Spanish (language); *lit.* ballad; **romancero** *m* collection of ballads; **románico** *lengua* romance; ⚠ Romanesque, *en Inglaterra* Norman; **romano** *adj. a. su. m*, **a** *f* Roman (*a. typ.*); *v. obra*; **romanticismo** *m* romanticism; **romántico** *adj. a. su. m* romantic.

romaza *f* dock, sorrel.

rombo *m* rhomb(us).

romería *f eccl.* pilgrimage; gathering at a shrine; *fig.* trip, excursion; F festivities, fair, open-air dance *etc.*; **romero**[1] *m*, **a** *f* pilgrim.

romero[2] *m* ⚘ rosemary.

romo blunt; *p.* snub-nosed.

rompecabezas *m* (*problema*) puzzle, teaser; (*acertijo*) riddle; (*dibujo*) jig-saw puzzle; **rompedero** fragile, breakable; **rompedora-cargadora** *f* ⚒ power loader; **rompehielos** *m* ice breaker; **rompehuelgas** *m* strike breaker; **rompeolas** *m* breakwater; **romper** [2a; *p.p. roto*] **1.** *v/t. plato etc.* break, smash, shatter; *cuerda etc.* break, snap; *presa, cerca etc.* break through, breach; *papel, tela* tear (up), rip (up); *ropa* tear; wear out; *tierra* break up; *aguas* cleave; *niebla, nubes* break through; *ayuno* break; *hostilidades* open up, start; *relaciones* break off; **2.** *v/i.* (*día, olas*) break; ⚘ burst (open); (*guerra etc.*) break out; (*ps.*) fall out (*con* with); ~ *a inf.* suddenly start to *inf.*; F *de rompe y rasga* determined; **rompiente** *m* (*ola*) breaker; (*escollo*) reef; ~*s pl.* breakers, surf; **rompimiento** *m* (*acto*) breaking *etc.*; (*abertura*) opening, breach, crack; *fig.* outbreak *de guerra*; break (*con p.* with); breaking-off *de relaciones*.

ron *m* rum; ~ *de laurel*, ~ *de malagueta* bay rum.

ronca *f* F nasty threat; (*reprimenda*) ticking-off; *echar* ~*s* bully.

roncar [1g] snore; (*mar etc.*) roar; F threaten, bully.

roncear [1a] kill time; work *etc.* unwillingly; F cajole; **roncería** *f* time wasting; unwillingness; F ca-

jolery; **roncero** (*tardo*) slow; F grumpy; (*que halaga*) smooth, smarmy.
ronco *p.* hoarse; throaty, husky; *sonido* harsh, raucous.
roncha *f* bruise, weal; swelling *de picadura.*
ronda *f* night patrol, (night) watch; beat *de policía*; (*ps.*) watch, patrol; (*con canto*) serenaders; round *de bebidas etc.*; ~ *negociadora* round of negotiations; **rondar** [1a] *v/t.* patrol, go the rounds of; *fig.* haunt, hang about; F pester; ~ *la calle a una joven* hang about the street where a girl lives; *luz* (*mariposa*) fly round; *v/i.* (*policía*) be on patrol, go the rounds; prowl (round), hang about; roam the streets at night; ♪ go serenading.
rondón: *entrar de* ~ rush in.
ronquear [1a] talk hoarsely; **ronquedad** *f*, **ronquera** *f* hoarseness *etc.*; **ronquido** *m* snoring; (*un* ~) snore; *fig.* roar.
ronronear [1a] purr; **ronroneo** *m* purr(ing).
ronzal *m* halter.
ronzar [1f] crunch, munch.
roña *f vet.* scab *de oveja*, mange *de perro*; ⚘ rust; (*mugre*) filth, grime; = **roñería** *f* meanness; **roñoso** scabby, mangy; filthy; F mean, stingy.
ropa *f* clothing, clothes, dress; ~ *blanca* linen; ~ *blanca* (*de mujer*) lingerie; ~ *de cama* bedclothes, bedding; ~ *dominguera* Sunday best; ~ *hecha* ready-made clothes; ~ *interior* underwear, underclothes; ~ *lavada*, ~ *por lavar*, ~ *sucia* laundry, washing; *a quema* ~ point-blank; *tentarse la* ~ think long and hard; **ropaje** *m* (*ropa*) clothing, (*vestido*) gown, robe; (*paños*) drapery; *fig.* garb; **ropavejero** *m* old-clothes dealer; **ropería** *f* clothing trade; (*tienda*) clothier's; **ropero** *m* clothier; (*mueble*) wardrobe.
roque *m* rook, castle (*chess*).
roquedal *m* rocky place.
rorro *m* F baby, kid.
rosa *f* rose; red spot, birthmark *en cuerpo*; *caminito de* ~*s* primrose path; ~ *de los vientos*, ~ *náutica* compass; *color (de)* ~ rose, pink; *verlo todo color de* ~ see everything through rose-colored spectacles; **rosado** pink, rosy; **rosal** *m* rose tree, rose bush; ~ *silvestre* dog rose; ~ *trepador* rambler rose; **rosaleda** *f* rose garden, rose bed.
rosario *m* rosary, beads, chaplet; *rezar el* ~ tell one's beads.
rosbif *m* roast beef.
rosca *f* coil, spiral; ⊕ screw, thread *de tornillo*; *cocina*: ring-shaped roll *etc.*; ⚓ *en* ~ light; F *hacer la* ~ *a* suck up to; *pasarse de* ~ have a crossed thread; F bite off more than one can chew; F *tirarse una* ~ plough.
róseo roseate, rosy.
roseta *f* ⚘ small rose; rose *de regadera*; red patch *en mejilla*; (*adorno*) rosette; ~*s pl.* popcorn; **rosetón** *m* ⚠ rosette; ⚠ rose (window).
rosicler *m* red of dawn, rosy tint.
rostro *m anat.* countenance, face; ⚓ beak; *hist.*, *zo. etc.* rostrum; *dar en* ~ *a alguien con algo* throw s.t. in s.o.'s face; *hacer* ~ *a* face (up to).
rotación *f* rotation; revolution; turnover *de mano de obra*; ~ *de cultivos* rotation of crops; **rotativo** rotary; revolving; **rotatorio** rotary, rotatory.
rotisería *f S.Am.* fast-food restaurant.
roto 1. *p.p. of romper*; **2.** broken; torn; (*andrajoso*) ragged; *fig.* debauched.
rotunda *f* rotunda.
rotor *m* rotor.
rotoso *S.Am.* ragged.
rótula *f* kneecap; ⊕ ball-and-socket joint.
rotulación *f* (*acto*) labeling; lettering; (*profesión*) sign painting; **rotulador** *m* felt pen; **rotular** [1a] label, ticket; letter; mark, inscribe; (*titular*) head, entitle; **rotulata** *f* label, ticket, tag; **rotulista** *m* sign painter; **rótulo** *m* label, ticket, tag; inscription, lettering; (shop) sign *de tienda*; title, heading; (*cartel*) poster.
rotundamente roundly, flatly; **rotundo** *negativa etc.* round, flat; *lenguaje etc.* sonorous.
rotura *f* (*acto*) breaking *etc.*; (*abertura*) opening, breach, break; tear, hole *en tela etc.*; **roturación** *f* ✓ reclamation; **roturar** [1a] ✓ break up.
roya *f* ⚘ rust, blight.

rozadura *f* rub(bing); chafing; *esp.* ⚕ abrasion, graze, sore spot; **rozagante** striking; *b.s.* showy; *fig.* proud; **rozamiento** *m* friction (*a.* ⊕), rubbing; **rozar** [1f] *v/t. a. v/i. tierra* clear; *hierba* crop, graze; nibble; (*ludir*) rub (against, on), chafe, scrape; ⚕ *piel* chafe, graze; (*tocar ligeramente*) shave, graze; *superficie* skim; **~se** *fig.* hobnob, rub shoulders (*con* with).

roznar [1a] *v/t.* crunch, gnaw; *v/i.* bray.

ruano roan.

rubéola *f* German measles.

rubí *m* ruby; jewel *de reloj.*

rubia *f* (*p.*) blonde; *mot.* shooting brake; ⚘ madder; *sl.* one peseta; ~ *de bote*, ~ *oxigenada* peroxide blonde; ~ *platino* platinum blonde; **rubicundo** reddish; ruddy; rubicund; **rubio** fair, fair-haired, blond(e); *tabaco* Virginian.

rublo *m* rouble.

rubor *m* bright red; blush, flush *en cara*; *fig.* bashfulness; **ruborizarse** [1f] blush (*de* at, with), flush, redden; **ruboroso** blushing, red; *fig.* bashful.

rúbrica *f* rubric (*a. eccl.*), heading; (*señal*) red mark; flourish *tras firma*; *ser de* ~ be in line with custom; **rubricar** [1g] sign with a flourish; (*y sellar*) sign and seal.

rucio 1. *caballo* (silver-)gray; *p.* gray-haired; **2.** *m* gray.

ruda *f* rue.

rudeza *f* coarseness *etc.*

rudimental, rudimentario rudimentary; **rudimento** *m* rudiment; **~s** *pl.* rudiments.

rudo (*tosco*) coarse, rough, crude; (*áspero*) rough; *golpe* hard; (*penoso*) hard, tough; (*grosero*) rude, ill-mannered; (*bobo*) simple.

rueca *f* distaff.

rueda *f* wheel; roller, castor *de mueble etc.*; ring, circle *de ps. etc.*; (*suplicio*) rack; (*rebanada*) round; ~ *de andar* treadmill; ~ *de cadena* sprocket wheel; ~ *dentada* gear wheel; cog (wheel); ~ *de escape* escapement wheel; ~ *de fuego* pinwheel; ~ *libre* free wheel; ~ *de molino* millstone; ~ *motriz* drive wheel; ~ *de paletas* paddle wheel; ~ *de presos criminales* line-up; ~ *de prensa* press conference; ~ *de recambio* spare wheel; ~ *de trinquete* ratchet wheel; *en* ~ in a ring; F *hacer la* ~ *a* suck up to; F *ir sobre* **~s** go with a swing; **ruedecilla** *f* roller, castor; **ruedero** *m* wheelwright; **ruedo** *m* (*giro*) turn, rotation; edge, circumference; (*estera*) mat; *toros*: bullring, arena.

ruego *m* request; entreaty.

rufián *m* pimp, pander; (*brutal*) lout, hooligan.

rufo red-haired, sandy; (*rizado*) curly; (*fuerte*) tough.

rugby *m* rugby.

rugido *m* roar *etc.*; **rugir** [3c] (*león*) roar; (*toro etc.*) bellow; (*tempestad*) roar, howl; (*tripas*) rumble.

rugoso wrinkled, creased.

ruibarbo *m* rhubarb.

ruido *m* noise; sound; (*muy ruidoso*) din, row; noisiness; *fig.* repercussions; (*protestas*) outcry, stir; *mucho* ~ *y pocas nueces* much ado about nothing; *hacer* ~ *fig.*, *meter* ~ make a stir, be a sensation; F *quitarse de* **~s** keep out of trouble; **ruidoso** noisy, loud; *suceso* sensational; *oposición* vocal, noisy.

ruin (*vil*) mean, despicable; (*pequeño*) small; (*mezquino*) petty; (*avaro*) mean; *trato* shabby, heartless; *animal* vicious.

ruina *f mst* ruin; downfall, collapse, wreck; **~s** *pl.* ruins; *estar hecho una* ~ be a wreck.

ruindad *f* meanness *etc.*

ruinoso ruinous, tumbledown, ramshackle; *empresa* disastrous; (*sin valor*) worthless.

ruiseñor *m* nightingale.

ruleta *f* roulette; **ruletero** *m Mex.* taxi driver.

rulo *m* roll; roller; rolling pin.

rumano 1. *adj. a. su. m*, **a** *f* Rumanian; **2.** *m* (*idioma*) Rumanian.

rumbo *m esp.* ⚓ course, direction, bearing; F show(iness), pomp; *S.Am.* noisy celebrating; ~ *nuevo fig.* departure; *con* ~ *a* bound for, headed for; in the direction of; *hacer* ~ *a* set a course for, head for; *por aquellos* **~s** in those parts; F *de mucho* ~ = **rumbón** F, **rumboso** F very fine, big, splendid; (*generoso*) free with one's money *etc.*

rumia(**ción**) *f* rumination; **rumiante** *adj. a. su. m* ruminant; **ru-**

miar [1b] *v/t.* chew; F chew over, brood on (*or* over); *v/i.* chew the cud; F ruminate, brood.
rumor *m* murmur, mutter, buzz *de voces*; (*voz*) rumor; **rumorear** [1a]: *se rumorea que* it is rumored that; **rumoroso** noisy, loud; *arroyo etc.* murmuring.
runa *f* rune; **rúnico** runic.
runrún *m* F purr(ing) *de gato*; (*ruido*) murmuring, buzz; (*voz*) buzz.
ruptura *f fig.* rupture; breaking *de contrato*; breaking-off *de relaciones*.
rural rural; country *attr*.
ruso 1. *adj. a. su. m*, **a** *f* Russian; **2.** *m* (*idioma*) Russian.
rusticidad *f* rusticity *etc.*; **rústico 1.** rustic, country *attr.*; *b.s.* coarse, uncouth; *en ~a* paperback *attr.*, paperbacked; **2.** *m* rustic, yokel.
ruta *f* route; (*señal de carretera*) main road, through road; *~ aérea* air lane.
rutilante *poet.* shining.
rutina *f* routine; round; *por ~* as a matter of course; **rutinario** routine; everyday; humdrum; *p.* unimaginative; **rutinero 1.** = *rutinario*; **2.** *m* man who just sticks to routine.

S

sábado *m* Saturday; (*judío*) Sabbath.
sábana *f* sheet; *eccl.* altar cloth; *sl.* 1000 pesetas.
sabana *f* savanna(h).
sabandija *f* bug, creepy-crawly F; ~s *pl.* vermin.
sabañón *m* chilblain.
sabelotodo *m* F know-it-all.
saber [2n] **1.** *v/t.* know; (*estar enterado de*) know about, be aware of; *en pretérito freq.* learn, get to know, find out; ~ *inf.* know how to *inf.*, can *inf.*; *hacer* ~ inform; ~ *de* know about, know of; *p. ausente* hear from; *a* ~ namely; *sin* ~*lo yo* without my knowledge; *vete a* ~ your guess is as good as mine; *¡qué sé yo!* how do I know?, how should I know?; *¡qué sé yo qué más!* and what not; *el Sr no sé cuántos* Mr what's his name; *un no sé qué* a certain something; *un no sé qué de elegante* a certain elegance; *demasiado sé que* I know only too well that; *que yo sepa* as far as I know; F *¿sabe(n)?* you know (what I mean)?; *¿quién sabe?* who can tell?; *sepa Vd.* I would have you know; **2.** *v/i.:* ~ *a* taste of, taste like; *esp. fig.* smack of; **3.** *m* knowledge, learning; *según mi leal* ~ *y entender* to the best of my knowledge.
sabidillo *m*, **a** *f* know-it-all; **sabido** well-informed, knowledgeable; *de* ~ for sure; **sabiduría** *f* wisdom; knowledge, learning; **sabiendas:** *a* ~ knowingly; *a* ~ *de que* knowing full well that; **sabihondo** *adj. a. su. m*, **a** *f* know-it-all, smart aleck; **sabio 1.** wise, learned; knowing; *animal* trained; **2.** *m*, **a** *f* learned man *etc.*; wise person; 📖 scholar, savant; *hist.* sage.
sablazo F: *dar un* ~ *a* F hit for a loan; *vivir de* ~*s* live by sponging.
sable *m* saber, cutlass.
sablista *m* F sponger, cadger.
sabor *m* taste, flavor; *con* ~ *a miel* honey-flavored; **saborear** [1a] flavor; (*percibir el sabor de*) savor, relish, taste; ~**se** smack one's lips; **saborete** *m* F slight flavor.
sabotaje *m* sabotage; **saboteador** *m* saboteur; **sabotear** [1a] sabotage.
sabroso tasty, delicious; F salty.
sabueso *m* bloodhound (*a. fig.*).
saburra *f* coat, fur.
saca[1] *f* big sack.
saca[2] *f* (*acto*) taking out; ☤ export, exporting; *estar de* ~ be on sale; F be of an age to marry.
saca...: ~**bocados** *m* ⊕ punch; ~**botas** *m* boot jack; ~**corchos** *m* corkscrew; ~**cuartos** *m* F, ~**dineros** *m* F cheap trinket; (*maña*) cheat; ~**manchas** *m/f* dry cleaner; ~**muelas** *m* F dentist; ~**puntas** *m* pencil sharpener.
sacar [1g] (*extraer*) take out, get out, pull out, draw out; extract (*a.* ⚒); withdraw; (*quitar*) remove; (*exceptuar*) exclude, remove; (*obtener*) get; *arma* draw; *billete, entrada* buy, book; *copia* make; *cuentas* make up; *dinero* draw (out) *de banco*; *foto* take; *lengua, mano etc.* put out, stick out; *mancha* get out, get off; *notas* make; *pelota* (*fútbol*) throw in, (*tenis*) serve; *premio* win; *producto nuevo* bring out; *provecho* derive (de from); *publicación* bring out; *puesto* get; *secreto* draw out; *título* (*univ.*) ge[t]; take; *verdad* get at; *saca bu*[...] *retrato* he takes well; F *¿qué sac*[...] *con eso?* what are you driving at[?]; *¿de dónde has sacado esa idea?* where did you get that idea?; ~ *de sí* drive *s.o.* crazy.
sacarina *f* saccharin.
sacerdocio *m* priesthood; ministry; **sacerdotal** priestly; **sacerdote** *m* priest; **sacerdotisa** *f* priestess.
saciar [1b] satiate, surfeit (de on, with); *hambre, deseos etc.* appease; **saciedad** *f* satiation, surfeit.
saco[1] *m* bag, sack; ⚔ kitbag; *sl.* 1000 pesetas; *S.Am.* jacket; ~ *de dormir*

sleeping bag; ~ *de noche* overnight bag; ~ *de viaje* traveling bag.

saco[2] *m* ⚔ sack; *entrar a* ~ sack, loot.

sacramental sacramental; *fig.* time-honored; **sacramento** *m* sacrament; **sacrificar** [1g] sacrifice; slaughter *en matadero*; *perro etc.* put to sleep; **sacrificio** *m* sacrifice; slaughter(ing); ~ *del altar* Sacrifice of the Mass; **sacrilegio** *m* sacrilege; **sacrílego** sacrilegious; **sacristán** *m* verger, sacrist(an); sexton; ~ *de amén* yes man; **sacristía** *f* vestry, sacristy; **sacro** sacred, holy; **sacrosanto** most holy; sacrosanct.

sacudida *f* shake; jerk; jolt, bump *esp. de vehículo*; shock *de terremoto etc.*; blast *de explosión*; jerk, toss *de cabeza*; *pol. etc.* upheaval; **sacudidura** *f*, **sacudimiento** *m* shaking *etc.*; **sacudir** [3a] (*agitar*) shake; *brazo, pasajeros etc.* jerk, jar, jolt; *cabeza etc.* jerk, toss; (*hacer oscilar*) rock; beat *para quitar polvo*; (*mover de arriba abajo, alas etc.*) flap; (*arrojar*) toss; (*quitar de encima*) shake off; (*debatirse*) thrash about.

sádico sadistic; **sadismo** *m* sadism.

saeta *f* ⚔ arrow, dart; hand *de reloj*; magnetic needle; ♪ *sacred song esp. during Holy Week.*

saetín *m* mill race; ⊕ tack.

saga *f* saga.

sagacidad *f* shrewdness *etc.*; **sagaz** shrewd, clever, sagacious.

Sagitario *m ast.* Sagittarius.

sagrado 1. sacred, holy; **2.** *m* sanctuary; *acogerse a* ~ seek sanctuary; **sagrario** *m* sanctuary, shrine.

sagú *m* sago.

sahumar [1a] perfume; smoke, fumigate.

saín *m* fat, grease; fish oil *para alumbrar*; **sainete** *m* = *saín*; sauce, seasoning; *fig.* (*bocado*) tidbit; (*sabor*) spice, relish; *thea.* one-act comedy.

sajar [1a] ⚕ cut, lance.

sajón *adj. a. su. m*, **-a** *f* Saxon.

sal[1] *f* salt; *fig.* (*donaire*) charm; (*viveza*) liveliness; (*agudeza*) wit, wittiness; ~ *amoníaca* sal ammoniac; ~*es pl.* (*aromáticas*) smelling salts; ~ *de fruta* fruit salts; ~ *gema* rock salt; ~ *de la Higuera* Epsom salts; ~ *de sosa* washing soda; ~ *de la tierra* salt of the earth; ~ *volátil* sal volatile.

sal[2] *v. salir.*

sala *f* (*a.* ~ *de estar*) drawing room, sitting room, lounge; (*pública*) hall; *thea.* house, auditorium; ⚕ ward; ⚖ court; ~ *de calderas* boiler room; ~ *del cine* movie theater; ~ *de lo civil* civil court; ~ *de conferencias* lecture room; ~ *de enfermos* infirmary; ~ *de espectáculos* concert room, hall; ~ *de espera* waiting room; ~ *de estar* living room, sitting room; ~ *de fiestas* night club; ~ *de justicia* law court; ~ *de lectura* reading room; ~ *de máquinas* engine room; ~ *de muestras* show room; ~ *de operaciones* operating room; ~ *de recibo* parlor; ~ *de subastas* sale room; *en* ~ *deporte* indoor.

salacidad *f* salaciousness.

saladar *m* salt marsh; **salado** salt(y); *fig.* (*encantador*) charming, cute; (*vivo*) lively; *lenguaje etc.* racy; (*agudo*) witty; *S.Am.* † expensive; (*desgraciado*) unlucky.

salamandra *f* salamander.

salamanquesa *f* lizard.

salami *m* salame.

salar [1a] salt, cure; (*sazonar*) add salt to.

salario *m* wage(s).

salaz salacious, prurient.

salceda *f*, **salcedo** *m* willow plantation.

salcochar [1a] boil (in salt water).

salchicha *f* (pork) sausage; **salchichería** *f* pork butcher's; **salchichón** *m* (salami) sausage.

saldar [1a] *cuenta* settle; *cuentas* balance; *existencias* sell off; *libros* remainder; **saldo** *m* (*acto*) settlement; (*cantidad*) balance; (*venta*) (clearance) sale; (*géneros*) remnant(s); ~ *acreedor* credit balance; ~ *deudor* debit balance.

saledizo *m* projection.

salero *m* salt cellar; (*almacén*) salt store; F wit; charm; (*gancho*) sex appeal; **saleroso** F = *salado*.

salida *f* (*puerta etc.*) way out, exit; ⊕ *etc.* outlet, vent; *geog.* outlet (*al mar* to the sea); (*acto*) going out *etc.*; emergence; 🚂, ✈ departure; rising *de sol*; *deportes*: start; leak *de gas, líquido*; ⚔ sally, sortie; ⊕ output; † (*inversión*) outlay; (*venta*) sale; (*mercado*) outlet, opening; (*resultado*) issue, outcome, result; ⚠ projection; (*escapatoria*) loophole, way out; F crack, joke; ~ *de baño* bathrobe; ~ *de emergencia* emergency exit; ~ *fácil* ready market; ~ *lanzada* flying start, running start; ~ *del sol* sunrise; ~ *de teatro* evening wrap; ~ *de teatros* after-theater party; ~ *de tono* remark out of place; *dar* ~ *a cólera etc.* vent; ✝ place, find an outlet for; ✝ *tener* ~ sell well; F *tener buenas* ~*s* be full of wisecracks.

salido projecting, bulging; *hembra* on heat; **salidizo** *m* projection; **saliente 1.** ⚠ *etc.* projecting; *rasgo* prominent; *sol* rising; *miembro etc.* retiring, outgoing; **2.** *m* projection.

salina *f* salt mine; ~*s pl.* saltworks; **salinidad** *f* salinity, salt(i)ness; **salino** saline, salty.

salir [3r] (*pasar fuera*) come out, go out; appear; emerge (*de* from), issue; arise; (*sol*) rise; *thea.* (*a.* ~ *a escena*) come on, go on; (*partir*) leave, depart (*a.* 🚂, ✈; *para* for); ⚓ sail; ⚘ come up (*a. puesto*); (*escapar*) get out (*de* of), escape (*de* from); (*mancha*) come off; (*sobresalir*) project, jut out, stick out *etc.*; *deportes*: start; *ajedrez*: have first move; *naipes*: lead; (*lotería*) win a prize (*a.* ~ *premiado*); (*resultar*) prove, turn out (to be); *le salió un diente* he cut a tooth; ~ *corriendo etc.* run *etc.* out; ~ *ganando deportes*: win; *fig.* be the gainer; ✝ be in pocket; ~ *perdiendo deportes*: lose; *fig.* be the loser; ✝ be out of pocket; ~ *elegido* be elected; ~ *bien* (*p.*) succeed, make good; pass *en examen*; (*suceso*) go off well; ~ *mal* (*p.*) fail, do badly; (*proyecto etc.*) miscarry; ~ *a calle* open into; *padre* take after; ✝ come to, work out at; ~ *caro* come expensive; ~ *con carta* lead; *novio* go out with; *observación* come out with; *pretensión* succeed in; ~ *de enfermedad* get over; ~ *por fig.* stand security for; ~**se** (*líquido, vasija*) leak; (*desbordarse*) overflow; boil over; ~ *de tema* wander from.

salitre *m* saltpeter.

saliva *f* spit, spittle, saliva; (*no*) *gastar* ~ (not) waste one's breath (*en* on); *tragar* ~ swallow one's feelings; **salivar** [1a] salivate.

salmantino *adj. a. su. m*, **a** *f* Salamancan.

salmo *m* psalm; **salmodia** *f* psalmody; F singsong, drone, monotonous singing; **salmodiar** [1b] drone, sing monotonously.

salmón *m* salmon; **salmonete** *m* (red) mullet.

salmuera *f* pickle, brine.

salobre salt(y).

saloma *f* ♪ (sea) shanty.

salón *m* lounge, drawing room; (*público*) hall; *paint.* salon; *esp.* ⚓ saloon; common room *de colegio*; ~ *de actos* auditorium; ~ *del automóvil* automobile show; ~ *de baile* ballroom, dance hall; ~ *de belleza* beauty parlor; ~ *de demostraciones* showroom; ~ *de pintura* art exhibition; ~ *de refrescos* ice-cream parlor; ~ *de sesiones* assembly hall; ~ *social* lounge; *juego de* ~ parlor game.

salpicadero *m mot.* dashboard; **salpicadura** *f* splash(ing) *etc.*; **salpicar** [1g] splash, spatter (*de* with); sprinkle (*de* with); *fig.* bespatter; pepper; *tela etc.* dot, fleck; *discurso* interlard (*de* with); **salpicón** *m* (*carne*) salmagundi; = *salpicadura*.

salpimentar [1a] season; *fig.* sweeten.

salpresar [1a] salt.

salpullido *m* ⚕ rash; swelling *de picadura*.

salsa *f* sauce; gravy *para carne asada*; dressing *para ensalada*; *fig.* appetizer; ~ *de ají* chile sauce; ~ *inglesa* Worcestershire sauce; ~ *de tomate* tomato sauce; catsup, ketchup; **salsera** *f* sauce boat; gravy boat.

saltabanco *m* quack, mountebank; (*malabarista*) juggler; **saltadura** *f* chip; **saltamontes** *m* grasshopper.

saltar [1a] **1.** *v/t.* leap (over), jump (over); vault; skip *en lectura*; **2.** *v/i.* leap, jump, spring (*a* on, *por* over); vault; dive, plunge (*a agua* into); hop, skip *a la comba etc.*; (*rebotar*) bounce, fly up; (*tapón*) pop out; (*botón*) come off; ⊕ (*pieza*) fly off; (*líquido*) spurt up, shoot up; (*vaso*) break, crack; burst; explode; *biol.* ~ *atrás* revert; ~ *sobre* pounce on; *hacer* ~ (*volar*) blow up; *trampa* spring; *caballo* (make) jump; **saltarín** *m*, **-a** *f* dancer; F restless sort.

salteador *m*: ~ *de caminos* highwayman, robber; **salteamiento** *m* holdup; **saltear** [1a] hold up; *fig.* overcome suddenly.

salterio *m* psalter; ♪ psaltery.

saltimbanqui *m* = *saltabanco.*

salto *m* leap, jump, spring, bound; vault; hop, skip; dive, plunge; pounce *sobre presa*; (*sima*) chasm; passage skipped, part missed *en lectura*; ~ *de agua* waterfall; ⊕ chute; ~ *de altura* high jump; ~ *de ángel* swan dive; ~ *de cabeza* header; ~ *de cama* négligée; dressing gown; ~ *de carpa* jackknife (dive); ~ *a ciegas* leap in the dark; ~ *de esquí* ski jump; ~ *con garrocha*, ~ *con pértiga* pole vault; ~ *de longitud* long jump; ~ *mortal* somersault; ~ *ornamental* fancy dive; ~ *de palanca* high dive; *triple* ~ hop step and jump; ~ *de trampolín* (springboard) dive; ~ *de viento* ⚓ sudden shift in the wind; *a* ~*s* by leaps and bounds; (*a empujones*) by fits and starts; *de un* ~ in one bound; *bajar etc. de un* ~ jump down *etc.*; *en un* ~ *fig.* in a jiffy; **saltón 1.** *ojos* bulging; *dientes* protruding; **2.** *m* grasshopper.

salubre healthy, salubrious; **salubridad** *f* healthiness; *S.Am.* (public) health; **salud** *f* ⚕ health; *fig.* welfare, wellbeing; *eccl.* salvation; ¡(*a su*) ~! good health!; *beber a la* ~ *de* drink (to) the health of; *estar bien* (*mal*) *de* ~ be in good (bad) health; **saludable** healthy; *fig.* salutary; **saludar** [1a] greet; say hullo to F; hail; *esp.* ⚔ salute; *fig.* hail, welcome; **saludo** *m* greeting; *esp.* ⚔ salute; ~*s* (*en carta*) best wishes; *un* ~ *afectuoso* kind regards; **salutación** *f* greeting.

salva *f* ⚔ salute, salvo; (*bienvenida*) greeting; volley, salvo *de aplausos.*

salvabarros *m* mudguard.

salvación *f eccl. etc.* salvation; rescue, delivery (*de* from).

salvado *m* bran.

salvador *m*, **-a** *f* rescuer, deliverer; ♀ Saviour.

salvadoreño *adj. a. su. m*, **a** *f* Salvadoran.

salvaguardar [1a] safeguard; **salvaguardia** *f* safe conduct; *fig.* safeguard.

salvajada *f* barbarity, savage deed *etc.*; **salvaje 1.** *mst* wild; (*feroz*) savage; **2.** *m/f* savage; **salvajería** *f* savagery; (*acto*) barbarity; **salvajino** wild; savage; *carne* gamy; **salvajismo** *m* savagery.

salvamanteles *m* table mat.

salvamento *m* rescue; salvage; *fig.* salvation; (*lugar*) place of safety; *de* ~ life-saving; *v. bote etc.*;

salvar [1a] save (*a. eccl.*), rescue (*de* from); *barco etc.* salvage; *arroyo etc.* jump over, clear; *rápidos* shoot; *distancia* cover; *obstáculo* negotiate, clear; *dificultad* get round; resolve; ~**se** save o.s., escape (*de* from); *eccl.* save one's soul; *salvando prp.* excepting; *sálvese el que pueda* every man for himself; **salvavidas** *m*: (*cinturón*) ~ lifebelt; *v. bote etc.*; **salvedad** *f* reservation, proviso.

salvia *f* ⚘ sage.

salvilla *f* salver.

salvo 1. *adj.* safe; saved; **2.** *adv.*, *prp.* except (for), save, barring; ~ *error u omisión* (*s.e.u.o.*) barring error or omission; *a* ~ safely; out of danger; *a* ~ *de* safe from; *en* ~ out of danger; ~ *que* except that; unless; *dejar a* ~ make an exception of; *poner a* ~ put in a safe place; *ponerse a* ~ escape, reach safety; **salvoconducto** *m* safe conduct; **salvohonor** *m* F backside.

samaritano *adj. a. su. m*, **a** *f* Samaritan; *buen* ~ good Samaritan.

sambenito *m fig.* dishonor, disgrace; F *quedó con su* ~ *toda la vida* he was disgraced for life.

san saint (*mst escrito* St.); F ¡*voto a* ~*es*! in heaven's name!

sanable curable; **sanalotodo** *m fig.* panacea, cure-all; **sanar** [1a] *v/t.* cure (*de* of), heal; *v/i.* (*p.*) recover; (*herida*) heal; **sanativo** healing; **sanatorio** *m* sanatorium; nursing home.

sanción *f* sanction; penalty; **sancionar** [1a] sanction.

sancochar [1a] parboil.

sandalia *f* sandal.

sándalo *m* sandal(wood).

sandez *f* foolishness; *sandeces pl.* nonsense.

sandía *f* watermelon.

sandío foolish, silly.

sandunga *f* F charm; wit; **sandunguero** F charming; witty.

saneamiento *m* ⚖ surety; indemnification; drainage; sanitation *de* *casa*; **sanear** [1a] ⚖ guarantee; indemnify; *terreno* drain.

sangradera *f* ⚕ lancet; **sangradura** *f* ⚕ bleeding, blood-letting; outlet, draining; **sangrar** [1a] *v/t.* ⚕ bleed; *fig.* ⚒ *etc.* drain; *árbol, horno* tap; *typ.* indent; *v/i.* bleed; F *estar sangrando* be still fresh; be perfectly clear; **sangre** *f* blood; ~ *azul* blue blood; ~ *fría* sangfroid, coolness; *a* ~ *fría* in cold blood; *a* ~ *y fuego* by fire and sword; without mercy; *mala* ~ bad blood; *pura* ~ *m/f* thoroughbred; *de pura* ~ thoroughbred; ~ *vital* life blood; *echar* ~ bleed; *se me heló la* ~ my blood ran cold; **sangría** *f* bleeding; tapping *etc.*; (*bebida*) sangria; **sangriento** bloody; gory; *arma etc.* bloodstained; *p.* bloodthirsty; *injuria* deadly; **sangrigordo** *S.Am.* unpleasant; **sangriligero** *S.Am.* nice; **sangripesado** *S.Am.* unpleasant; **sanguijuela** *f* leech (*a. fig.*); **sanguinario** bloodthirsty, bloody; **sanguíneo** *vaso etc.* blood *attr.*; *fig.* blood-red; **sanguinolento** bloody, bloodstained; *fig.* blood-red.

sanidad *f* sanitation; (*lo sano*) health(iness); ~ *pública* public health; *inspector de* ~ sanitary inspector; **sanitario** sanitary; *instalación* ~*a* sanitation; **sano** *p.* healthy, fit; *comida etc.* wholesome; *fruta, doctrina etc.* sound; F whole, undamaged; ~ *y salvo* safe and sound; *cortar por lo* ~ take desperate measures; cut one's losses.

sánscrito *adj. a. su. m* Sanskrit.

santa *f* saint.

santabárbara *f* (powder) magazine.

santiamén: F *en un* ~ in a trice.

santidad *f* holiness, sanctity; saintliness; *su* ♀ His Holiness; **santificar** [1g] sanctify; hallow, consecrate.

santiguar [1i] make the sign of the cross over; F slap; ~**se** cross o.s.

santo 1. holy; *esp. p.* saintly; *mártir* blessed (*a.* F); **2.** *m* saint; saint's day; ~ *y seña* password; *fig.* watchword; F *¿a* ~ *de qué?* what on earth for?; *desnudar a un* ~ *para vestir a otro* rob Peter to pay Paul; F *no es* ~ *de mi devoción* I'm not very keen on him; F *quedar para vestir* ~*s* be on the shelf; **santuario** *m* sanctuary; **santurrón 1.** sanctimonious; hypocritical; **2.** *m*, **-a** *f* sanctimonious person; hypocrite.

saña *f* anger, fury (*a. fig.*); cruelty; **sañoso, sañudo** furious.

sapo *m* toad; F *echar* ~*s y culebras* swear black and blue.

saque *m tenis etc.*: service, serve; (*línea*) base line, service line; (*p.*) server; *fútbol*: throw-in; ~ *inicial* kickoff; ~ *de esquina* corner kick; ~ *de portería* goal kick; *tener buen* ~ F be a heavy drinker and eater.

saqueador *m* looter; **saquear** [1a] loot, sack, plunder; *fig.* rifle, ransack; **saqueo** *m* looting *etc.*

sarampión *m* measles.

sarao *m* soirée, evening party.

sarcasmo *m* sarcasm; **sarcástico** sarcastic.

sarcófago *m* sarcophagus.

sardina *f* sardine; ~ *arenque* pilchard; *como* ~*s en banasta, como* ~*s en lata* F (packed in) like sardines; **sardinero** sardine *attr.*

sardo *adj. a. su. m*, **a** *f* Sardinian.

sargentear [1a] *v/t.* ⚔ command; F boss about; *v/i.* F be bossy; **sargento** *m* sergeant; **sargentona** *f* F big blowzy woman.

sargo *m* bream.

sarmentoso twining; **sarmiento** *m* vine shoot.

sarna *f* itch, scabies; *vet.* mange; **sarnoso** that has the itch; itchy; *vet.* mangy.

sarraceno *adj. a. su. m*, **a** *f* Saracen.

sarracina *f* free fight.

sarro *m* incrustation; fur *de vasija, lengua*; tartar *de dientes*; **sarroso** incrusted; furry; covered with tartar.

sarta *f*, **sartal** *m* string (*a. fig.*); line, series.

sartén *mst f* frying pan.

sastre *m* tailor; ~ *de teatro* costumier; *hecho por* ~ tailor-made; **sastrería** *f* tailoring; (*tienda*) tailor's.

satánico satanic, devilish.

satélite 1. satellite; ~ *de comunicaciones* communications satellite; **2.** *m* satellite (*a. pol.*); (*p.*) minion, henchman.

satén *m* sateen; **satinado** glossy.

sátira *f* satire; **satírico** satiric(al); **satirizar** [1f] satirize.

sátiro *m* satyr (*a. fig.*).
satisfacción *f* satisfaction; ~ *de sí mismo* self-satisfaction, smugness; *a* ~ to one's satisfaction; **satisfacer** [2s] *mst* satisfy; *deuda* pay; *necesidad, petición* meet; (*dar placer a*) gratify, please; **~se** satisfy o.s., be satisfied; (*vengarse*) take revenge; **satisfactorio** satisfactory; **satisfecho** satisfied; pleased ~ (*de sí mismo*) self-satisfied, smug.
saturar [1a] saturate; permeate.
saturnino saturnine.
sauce *m* willow; ~ *llorón* weeping willow; **saucedal** *m* willow plantation.
saúco *m* ⚘ elder.
saurio *m* saurian.
savia *f* sap.
saxofón *m* saxophone.
saya *f* skirt; dress; **sayo** *m* smock, tunic; long loose gown.
sayón *m* executioner; F ugly customer.
sazo *m sl.* hankie.
sazón *f* ripeness, maturity; (*ocasión*) season, time; *a la* ~ then, at that time; *en* ~ ⚘ ripe; *actuar* opportunely; **sazonado** ⚘ *etc.* mellow; *plato* tasty; *frase* witty; **sazonar** [1a] *v/t.* season, flavor; *fig.* bring to maturity; *v/i.* ripen.
se 1. *pron. reflexivo*: a) *sg.* himself, herself, itself; (*con Vd.*) yourself; *pl.* themselves; (*con Vds.*) yourselves; b) *recíproco*: each other, one another; c) *con inf.*: oneself, *e.g. hay que protegerse* one must protect oneself; d) *impersonal*: *freq. se traduce por la voz pasiva, por* one, *por* people: *se dice que* it is said that, people say that; *no se sabe por qué* it is not known why; *se habla español* Spanish (is) spoken here; **2.** *pron. personal que corresponde a* le, les: *se lo di* I gave it to him; *se lo buscaré* I'll look for it for you.
sé *v. saber, ser.*
sebo *m* grease, fat; tallow *para velas*; suet *para cocina*; **seboso** greasy, fatty; tallowy; suety.
seca *f* drought; (*época*) dry season; (*arena*) sandbank; **secador** *m*: ~ *para el pelo* hair dryer; **secadora** *f* wringer; **secano** *m* (*a. tierras de* ~) dry land, unirrigated land; region having little rain; ⚓ sandbank; *fig.* very dry thing; **secante 1.** drying; *S.Am.* annoying; *papel* ~ = **2.** *m* blotting paper; **secar** [1g] dry (up); *superficie* wipe dry; *frente* wipe, mop; blot *con papel secante*; *líquido derramado* mop up; *fig.* annoy, vex; bore; **~se** (*río etc.*) dry up, run dry; (*p.*) dry o.s.; ⚘ dry up, wilt; (*animal*) get thin; **secarropa** *f* clothes dryer; ~ *de travesaños* clotheshorse.
sección *f* section; ⚠ (*corte*) cross section; *fig.* section (*a.* ⚔), division, department *de organización*; ~ *vertical* vertical section; **seccional** sectional; **seccionar** [1a] divide up.
secesión *f* secession.
seco *mst* dry; *legumbres etc.* dried; *planta* dried-up; (*flaco*) lean; (*áspero*) sharp, harsh; *golpe etc.* sharp; (*riguroso*) strict; *respuesta* curt; *estilo* plain, bare; *a* **~as** simply, just; *en* ~ high and dry (*a. fig.*); *río* dry; *fig.* abruptly; *parar*(*se*) *en* ~ stop dead.
secoya *f* sequoia.
secreción *f* secretion; **secretar** [1a] secrete.
secretaría *f* secretariat(e); (*oficio*) secretaryship; (*oficina*) secretary's office; **secretario** *m*, **a** *f* secretary; **secretear** [1a] F talk confidentially; **secreto 1.** secret; (*no visible*) hidden; **2.** *m* secret; (*lo* ~) secrecy; (*escondrijo*) secret drawer, hiding place; ~ *de correspondencia* sanctity of the mails; ~ *de estado* state secret; ~ *a voces* open secret; *en* ~ in secret; in private; ⚖ in camera; *estar en el* ~ be in the secret; *hacer* ~ *de* be secretive about.
secta *f* sect; denomination; **sectario 1.** sectarian; denominational; **2.** *m*, **a** *f* follower, devotee; sectarian.
sector *m mst* sector; section *de opinión*; ~ *de distribución* house current, power line.
secuaz *m* follower, partisan; *b.s.* underling.
secuestrador *m*, **-a** *f* kidnap(p)er; **secuestrar** [1a] kidnap; *bienes* seize; **secuestro** *m* kidnap(p)ing; ⚖ seizure.
secular secular; (*viejo*) age-old, ancient; **secularización** *f* secularization; **secularizar** [1f] secularize.
secundar [1a] second, help; **secundario** *mst* secondary; minor, side..., by...; **secundinas** *f/pl.* after birth.

sed *f* thirst (*de* for; *a. fig.*); *apagar la* ~ quench one's thirst; *tener* ~ be thirsty; *fig. tener* ~ *de* thirst for.
seda *f* silk; (*cerda*) bristle; *de* ~ silk(en); *como una* ~ (*adj.*) smooth (as silk); (*adv.*) smoothly; **sedal** *m* fishing line.
sedante 1. sedative; *fig.* soothing; **2.** *m* = **sedativo** *adj. a. su. m* sedative.
sede *f eccl.* see; seat *de gobierno*; headquarters *de sociedad etc.*; ~ *social* head office; *Santa* ~ Holy See.
sedentario sedentary.
sedeño silken; silky; **sedería** *f* silks, silk goods; (*comercio*) silk trade; (*tienda*) silk shop; **sedero** silk *attr.*
sedic(i)ente self-styled, so-called.
sedición *f* sedition; **sedicioso 1.** seditious; **2.** *m*, **a** *f* rebel.
sediento thirsty (*a.* ⚘); *fig.* eager (*de* for).
sedimentar [1a] deposit (sediment); **~se** settle; **sedimentario** sedimentary; **sedimento** *m* sediment.
sedoso silky.
seducción *f* (*acto*) seduction *etc.*; (*aliciente*) lure, charm; **seducir** [3o] seduce; entice, lure, lead astray; (*cautivar*) charm, beguile; (*sobornar*) bribe; **seductivo** seductive; *fig.* charming, captivating; **seductor 1.** = *seductivo*; **2.** *m* seducer.
sefardí 1. Sephardic; **2.** *m/f* Sephardi; **~es** *pl.* Sephardim.
segador *m* harvester, reaper; **segadora** *f* reaper; mower, mowing machine; ~*-atadora f* binder; ~*-trilladora f* combine (harvester); ~ *de césped* lawn mower; **segar** [1h *a.* 1k] *trigo etc.* reap, cut; *heno*, *hierba* mow; *fig.* cut off; mow down.
seglar 1. secular, lay; **2.** *m* layman.
segmento *m* segment; ~ *de émbolo* piston ring.
segregación *f* segregation; **segregacionista** *adj. a. su. m/f* segregationist; **segregar** [1h] segregate; *physiol.* secrete.
seguida: *de* ~ uninterruptedly, straight off; *en* ~ at once, right away; **seguido** continued, successive; *camino etc.* straight; **~s** *pl.* in a row, in succession; *3 días* **~s** 3 days running; *todo* ~ *adv.* straight ahead; **seguimiento** *m* chase, pursuit; continuation; **seguir** [3d *a.* 3l] **1.** *v/t.* follow; (*cazar*) chase, pursue; (*acosar*) hound; *pasos* dog; *consejo* follow, take; *curso* pursue; continue; **2.** *v/i.* follow; come after, come next; go on, continue; (*caminar etc.*) proceed; *como sigue* as follows; *¿cómo sigue?* ⚕ how is he?; *¡siga!* go on!; *siga a la derecha* keep to the right; ~ *ger.* keep (on) *ger.*, go on *ger.*; ~ *leyendo etc.* read on *etc.*; ~ *en su sitio* still be in the same place; ⚽ *hacer* ~ forward; ~ *adelante* go on, carry (straight) on; *mot.* drive on (*hasta* as far as); ~ *bueno* (*tiempo*) hold, stay fine; ~ *con* go on with; ~ *en error* continue in; **3. ~se** follow, ensue; (*sucederse*) follow one another; *síguese que* it follows that.
según 1. *prp.* according to; in accordance with; ~ *lo que dice* from what he says; ~ *este modelo* on this model; **2.** *adv.* depending on circumstances; ~ (*y como*), ~ (*y conforme*) it (all) depends; **3.** *cj.* as; ~ *esté el tiempo* depending on the weather.
segunda *f* ♪ second; ~ (*intención*) second (*or* veiled) meaning; hidden purpose; **segundante** *m boxeo*: second; **segundero** *m* second-hand; **segundo 1.** second; **2.** *m* second; ⚓ mate; *sin* ~ unrivaled; **segundón** *m* second (*or* younger) son.
seguridad *f* safety, safeness; security; reliability; (*certeza*) certainty; ⚖ security, surety; ~ *colectiva* collective security; ~ *contra incendios* fire precautions; *de* ~ *cinturón etc.* safety *attr.*; *para mayor* ~ to be on the safe side; *tener la* ~ *de que* be sure that; **seguro 1.** (*sin peligro*) safe, sure; secure; (*confiable*) reliable, dependable; (*cierto*) certain, sure; (*firme*) stable, steady; *¿está Vd.* ~*?* are you sure?; *estar* ~ *de que* be sure that; **2.** *m* safety; certainty; confidence; ✝ insurance; (*lugar*) safe place; tumbler *de cerradura*; ⚔ safety catch; ⊕ pawl, catch; ~ *de desempleo*, ~ *de desocupación* unemployment insurance; ~ *de enfermedad* health insurance; ~ *de incendios* fire insurance; ~ *social* social insurance (*or* security); ~ *de vida* life insurance; (*póliza de*) ~ *sobre la vida* life insurance (policy); *a*

buen ~, *de* ~ surely, truly; *sobre* ~ without risk; *saber a buen* ~ know for certain.

seis six (*a. su.*); (*fecha*) sixth; *las* ~ six o'clock; **seiscientos** six hundred.

seísmo *m* earthquake.

selección *f* selection (*a. biol.*); ♪ ~*es pl.* selections; **seleccionador** *m* selector; **seleccionar** [1a] pick, choose; **selectivo** selective (*a. radio*); **selecto** *calidad* select, choice; *obras etc.* selected; *club* select, exclusive.

seltz [selθ, sel]: *agua* (*de*) ~ soda water, seltzer (water).

selva *f* forest, wood(s); (*esp. tropical*) jungle; **selvático** ⚘ wild; *escena etc.* sylvan; *fig.* rustic; **selvoso** wooded.

selladura *f* seal(ing); **sellar** [1a] seal; stamp *con timbre etc.*; **sello** *m* seal; signet; ✉ stamp; ✝ brand, seal; *fig.* (*huella*) impression, mark; hallmark *de calidad*; ⚕ capsule, pill; ~ *fiscal* revenue stamp.

semáforo *m* semaphore; 🚂 signal; *mot.* traffic light.

semana *f* week; ~ *inglesa* five-and-a-half day week; ♀ *Santa* Holy Week; *entre* ~ during the week; **semanal, semanario** *adj. a. su. m* weekly.

semántica *f* semantics.

semblante *m lit.* visage; *fig.* appearance, look; *componer el* ~ recover one's composure; *mudar de* ~ change color; **semblanza** *f* biographical sketch.

sembradera *f*, **sembradora** *f* drill; **sembrado** *m* sown field; **sembrador** *m*, **-a** *f* sower; **sembradura** *f* sowing; **sembrar** [1k] sow; *fig.* sprinkle, scatter, strew (*de* with); *discordia* sow; *noticia* spread.

semejante 1. similar (*a.* ⅍); ~*s pl.* alike, similar; ~ *a* like; *no hice cosa* ~ I never did such a thing; **2.** *m* fellow man, fellow creature; *no tiene* ~ it has no equal; **semejanza** *f* similarity, resemblance; *a* ~ *de* like, as; **semejar**(**se**) [1a] be alike, be similar, resemble each other.

semen *m* semen; **semental 1.** *caballo* stud, breeding; **2.** *m* sire; **sementera** *f* (*acto*) sowing; (*campo*) sown land; (*época*) seed time, sowing time.

semestral half-yearly; **semestre** *m* period of six months.

semi... semi...; half...; ~**breve** *f* semibreve; ~**círculo** *m* semicircle; ~**conductor** *m* ⚡ semiconductor; ~**corchea** *f* semiquaver; ~**final** *f* semifinal.

semilla *f* seed; **semillero** *m* seed bed; nursery; *fig.* hotbed; ~ *de césped* grass seed; **seminal** seminal.

seminario *m* seminary; *univ.* seminar; ⚘ seed bed; nursery; **seminarista** *m* seminarist.

semioficial semiofficial.

semita 1. Semitic; **2.** *m*/*f* Semite; **semítico** Semitic.

semitono *m* semitone.

semivocal *f* semivowel.

sémola *f* semolina.

sempiterna *f* evergreen; **sempiterno** everlasting.

senado *m* senate; **senador** *m* senator; **senatorial, senatorio** senatorial.

sencillez *f* simplicity *etc.*; **sencillo 1.** simple, straightforward, easy; *billete*, ⚘ single; *p. etc.* unsophisticated, natural; *b.s.* simple; *vestido, estilo etc.* simple, plain; **2.** *m S.Am.* loose change.

senda *f*, **sendero** *m* (foot)path, track, lane (*a. mot.*).

sendos one ... each; *les dio* ~ *golpes* he struck each of them; *llevaban* ~ *fusiles* they each carried a rifle.

senectud *f* old age; **senil** senile; **senilidad** *f* senility.

seno[1] *m* (*pecho*) breast; (*pechos*) bosom, bust; (*útero*) womb; (*frontal*) sinus; *fig.* bosom; lap; (*hueco*) hollow; *geog.* small bay; ⚓ trough *de ola*; *esconder algo en el* ~ hide s.t. in one's bosom; *en el* ~ *de la familia* in the bosom of the family.

seno[2] *m* ⅍ sine.

sensación *f* sensation (*a. fig.*); sense, feeling; feel; thrill; *hacer* ~ cause a sensation; **sensacional** sensational; **sensacionalismo** *m* sensationalism.

sensatez *f* good sense, sensibleness; **sensato** sensible.

sensibilidad *f* sensitivity (*a* to); **sensibilizado** *phot.* sensitive; sensitized; **sensible** (*que siente*) sensible; *aparato etc.* sensitive; (*que se conmueve*) sensitive, responsive (*a* to); (*apreciable*) perceptible, noticeable; (*lamentable*) regrettable; *pér-*

dida considerable; ⚕ tender, sore; *phot.* sensitive; ~ *de mejora* capable of improvement; ~ *del honor que se me hace* fully aware of the honor being done me; **sensiblería** *f* sentimentality, mush; squeamishness; **sensiblero** sentimental, mushy; squeamish; **sensitiva** *f* mimosa; **sensitivo** *órgano etc.* sense *attr.*; sensitive; *ser* sentient; **sensorio** sensory; **sensual** sensual, sensuous; **sensualidad** *f* sensuality; **sensualismo** *m* sensualism; **sensualista** *m/f* sensualist.

sentada *f* sitting; *de una* ~ at one sitting; **sentadero** *m* seat; **sentado** sitting, seated; (*establecido*) settled; permanent; *carácter* sedate; sensible; *dar por* ~ take for granted, assume; *dejar* ~ leave a clear impression of; *dejar* ~ *que* lay (it) down that; *estar* (*or quedar*) ~ sit, be sitting (down), be seated; **sentar** [1k] **1.** *v/t. p.* seat, sit; (*asentar*) set up, establish; † put down (*en la cuenta de* to); **2.** *v/t. a. v/i.* (*vestido*) fit *por tamaño*, suit *por estilo*; ~ *bien fig.* go down well; ~ *bien a* (*comida*) agree with; ~ *mal fig.* go down badly, produce a bad impression; ~ *mal a* (*comida*) disagree with; **3.** **~se** sit (down); settle (o.s.).

sentencia *f* ⚖ sentence; (*máxima*) dictum, saying; **sentenciar** [1b] *v/t.* ⚖ sentence (*a* to); *v/i.* pronounce, give one's opinion; **sentencioso** sententious; dogmatic; *dicho* pithy; oracular.

sentidamente regretfully; **sentido** **1.** (*hondo*) heartfelt, keen; (*que se ofende*) sensitive; (*convincente*) moving, feeling; **2.** *m* (*facultad*) sense; (*significado*) sense, meaning; (*juicio*) sense, good sense; (*aprecio*) feeling (*de música* for); way, direction; ~ *común* common sense; *doble* ~ double meaning; *en cierto* ~ in a sense; *sin* ~ meaningless; ⚕ senseless, unconscious; *cobrar* ~ begin to mean s.t.; F *costar un* ~ cost the earth; *perder el* ~ lose consciousness; *tener* ~ make sense.

sentimental sentimental; *mirada* soulful; *aventura, vida etc.* love *attr.*; **sentimentalismo** *m* sentimentality; **sentimiento** *m* feeling; sentiment; (*pesar*) grief, regret; consciousness; *v. acompañar.*

sentina *f* ⚓ bilge; *fig.* sink, sewer.

sentir **1.** [3i] *v/t.* feel; sense, perceive; (*oír*) hear; (*tener pesar*) regret, be sorry for; *lo siento* (*mucho*) I am (very *or* so) sorry; *siento tener que hacerlo* I am sorry to have to do it; *dejarse* ~ let itself be felt; *v/i.* judge, think; *sin* ~ inadvertently; *dar que* ~ give cause for regret; **~se** feel, *e.g.* ~ *enfermo* feel ill, ~ *obligado a* feel obliged to; (*quejarse*) complain, be offended, be resentful; (*quebrarse*) crack; ~ *de* ⚕ have a pain in; *palabra etc.* take offence at; **2.** *m* feeling; opinion; *a mi* ~ in my opinion.

seña *f* sign, token; mark *en cara etc.*; ⚔ password; **~s** *pl.* address; description; **~s** *pl. personales* personal description; *por las* **~s** F to all appearances; *por más* **~s** to clinch the matter; *dar* **~s** *de* show signs of; *hablar por* **~s** talk by signs; *hacer* **~s** *a*, *llamar con* **~s** make signs to, beckon (to).

señal *f* sign, mark; (*indicio*) sign, token, indication; mark(ing) *de identidad*; brand *de animal*; sign, signal *con mano*; *radio mot.*, 🚂 *etc.* signal; (*mojón*) landmark; bookmark *en libro*; ⚕ scar, mark; (*huella*) trace; † deposit; (*prenda*) pledge, token; ~ *de carretera* road sign; ~ *digital* fingerprint; ~ *horaria* time signal; **~es** *pl. luminosas*, **~es** *pl. de tráfico* traffic signals; ~ *para marcar* dial tone; ~ *de ocupado* busy signal; ~ *de peligro* danger signal; ~ *de trama* 🚂 block signal; ~ *de video* video signal; † *en* ~ as a deposit; *en* ~ *de* as a token of; *sin la menor* ~ *de* without a trace of; **señaladamente** especially; **señalado** notable, distinguished; **señalar** [1a] point out, point to, indicate *con dedo*; (*mostrar*) show; (*comunicar*) signal; mark, stamp; *animal* brand; denote; *fecha etc.* fix, set; *p. etc.* appoint, name; ⚕ leave a scar (on); **~se** *fig.* make one's mark; **señalizar** [1f] signpost.

señor *m* gentleman, man; (*dueño*) master, owner; (*noble, feudal, dueño fig.*) lord; *delante de apellido*: Mister (*escrito* Mr.); *en trato directo*: sir; (*a noble*) my lord; *¡sí* ~*!* yes indeed!; *pues sí* ~ well that's how it is; *El* ♀ The Lord; *muy* ~ *mío* Dear Sir; *hacer el* ~

lord it; ~es *pl.* gentlemen; ✝ Messrs.; *los ~es Smith* the Smiths.

señora *f* lady; (*dueña*) mistress, owner; (*noble*) lady; (*esposa*) wife; *delante de apellido*: Mrs. ['misiz]; *en trato directo*: madam; (*a noble*) my lady; *la ~ de Smith* Mrs. Smith; *Nuestra* ♀ Our Lady *para católicos*, the Virgin (Mary) *para protestantes*.

señorear [1a] rule; lord it over; *pasiones* master; **~se** control o.s.; *~ de* seize.

señoría *f* rule, sway; lordship; ladyship; *tratamiento*: *su etc.* ♀ (Your, His) Lordship, (Your, Her) Ladyship; my lord, my lady; **señori(a)l** *fig.* lordly, commanding; **señorío** *m hist.* manor; domain; *fig.* dominion, sway, rule (*sobre* over); (*dignidad*) lordliness.

señorita *f* young lady; *delante de apellido*: Miss; *en trato directo freq. no se traduce*; **señorito** *m* young gentleman; (young) master; (*de mucho mundo*) man about town; *contp.* playboy; **señorón** *m* F big shot.

señuelo *m* decoy; *fig.* bait, lure.

sépalo *m* sepal.

separable separable; ⊕ detachable; **separación** *f* separation (*a.* ⚖); dismissal (*de puesto* from); ⊕ removal; *eccl.* disestablishment; *~ del matrimonio* legal separation; **separado** separate; *esp.* ⊕ detached; *por ~* separately; ✉ under separate cover; *vive ~ de su mujer* he is separated from his wife, he doesn't live with his wife; **separador** *m* separator; **separar** [1a] separate (*de* from); sever; divide; (*clasificar*) sort; *mueble etc.* move away (*de* from); ⊕ *pieza* remove, detach; (*despedir*) dismiss; **~se** separate (*de* from); part company (*de* with); (*piezas*) come apart; retire, withdraw; (*estado etc.*) secede; **separata** *f* offprint; **separatismo** *m* separatism; **separatista** *m/f* separatist.

sepia *f zo.* cuttlefish; *paint.* sepia.

sepsis *f* sepsis.

septentrión *m* north; **septentrional** north(ern).

séptico septic.

se(p)tiembre *m* September.

séptimo *adj. a. su. m* seventh; **septuagenario** *adj. a. su. m*, **a** *f* septuagenarian; **septuagésimo** seventieth.

sepulcral sepulchral (*a. fig.*); *fig.* gloomy, dismal; **sepulcro** *m* tomb, grave; (*Biblia*) sepulcher; **sepultar** [1a] bury; *fig.* entomb; *fig.* (*esconder*) bury, hide away; **sepultura** *f* (*acto*) burial; (*tumba*) grave; *dar ~ a* bury; *estar con un pie en la ~* have one foot in the grave; **sepulturero** *m* gravedigger, sexton.

sequedad *f* dryness *etc.*; **sequía** *f* drought; (*temporada*) dry season.

séquito *m* retinue, entourage; party.

ser 1. [2w] be; a) *identidad*: *soy yo* it's me, it is I *lit.*; *teleph.* *¡soy Pérez!* Pérez speaking, this is Pérez; b) *origen*: *yo soy de Madrid* I am from Madrid; c) *materia*: *la moneda es de oro* it is a gold coin; d) *hora*: *es la una* it is one o'clock; *son las 2* it is 2 o'clock; *serán las 9* it will be about 9; *serían las 9* it would be (*or* have been) about 9; e) *posesión*: *el coche es de mi padre* the car belongs to my father; f) *destino*: *¿qué ha sido de él?* what has become of him?; F *¿qué es de tu vida?* what's the news?; g) *pasivo*: *ha sido asesinado* he has been murdered; h) *frases*: *~ para poco* be of next to no use; *de no ~ así* were it not so; *a no ~ por* but for; were it not for; *a no ~ que* unless; *¡cómo ha de ~!* what else do you expect?; *es de esperar que* it is to be hoped that; *es de creer que* it may be assumed that; *es que* the fact is that; *soy con Vd.* I'll be with you in a moment; *siendo así que* so that; *o sea* that is to say, or rather; *sea ... sea* whether ... or whether; *sea lo que sea* (*or fuere*) be that as it may; *no sea que* lest; *érase que se era* once upon a time (there was); *era de ver* you ought to have seen it, it was worth seeing; *presidente que fue* ex-president; former(ly) president; **2.** *m* being; (*vida*) life; essence; *~ humano* human being.

sera *f* pannier, basket.

seráfico seraphic, angelic; F poor; **serafín** *m* seraph.

serenar [1a] calm; quieten, pacify; *líquido* clarify; **~se** grow calm; *meteor.* clear up; (*p.*) calm down; (*líquido*) clear.

serenata *f* serenade.

serenidad *f* serenity *etc.*; **sereno**[1] serene, calm; *tiempo* settled, fine; *cielo* cloudless; *temperamento* even; F (*no borracho*) sober.

sereno[2] *m* (night) watchman; (*rocío*) dew; *al* ~ in the open (air).

serial *m* serial; *radio*: soap opera; *radio*: serial; ~ *lacrimógeno* soap opera; ~ *radiado* serial; **serie** *f* series (*a.* Å, ⚡, *biol.*); sequence; set; *de* ~ stock; *coche de* ~ stock car; ⚡ *arrollado en* ~ series-wound; *v. fabricar*; *en* ~ mass; *fuera de* ~ out of order, not in the proper order; (*extraordinario*) special, custom-built; outsize.

seriedad *f* seriousness *etc.*; **serio** *mst* serious; grave; solemn; sober, staid; (*confiable*) reliable, trustworthy; (*justo*) fair, fair-minded; (*genuino*) true, real; *en* ~ seriously; *poco* ~ *freq.* frivolous; (*no confiable*) unreliable; *etc.*

sermón *m* sermon (*a. iro.*); **sermonear** [1a] F *v/t.* lecture; *v/i.* sermonize; **sermoneo** *m* F lecture.

serón *m* pannier, large basket.

serpa *f* ⚘ runner.

serpentear [1a] *zo.* wriggle, snake; (*camino*) wind; (*río*) wind, meander; **serpenteo** *m* wriggling *etc.*; **serpentín** *m* coil; **serpentina** *f min.* serpentine; (*papel*) streamer; **serpentino** snaky, sinuous; winding; **serpiente** *f* snake; (*mitológica, fig.*) serpent; ~ *de cascabel* rattlesnake; ~ *de mar* sea serpent.

serpollo *m* sucker, shoot.

serraduras *f/pl.* sawdust.

serrallo *m* harem, seraglio.

serranía *f* mountainous area, hill country; **serrano 1.** highland *attr.*, mountain *attr.*; *fig.* rough, rustic; *jugada* dirty; **2.** *m* highlander.

serrar [1k] saw; **serrín** *m* sawdust; **serruchar** [1a] *S.Am.* saw; **serrucho** *m* handsaw.

servible serviceable; **servicial** helpful, obliging; dutiful; **servicio** *m* service (*a.* ⚔, *eccl., hotel, tenis*); service, set *de vajilla*; *hotel*: service (charge); *S.Am.* lavatory; ~*s pl.* sanitation *de casa*; ~ *activo* active service; ~ *de café* coffee set; ~ *doméstico* (domestic) service; domestic help; (*ps.*) servants; ~ *de grúa mot.* towing service; ~ *militar* military service; ~ *postventa* customer service; ~ *social* social service, welfare work; *al* ~ *de* in the service of; ⚔ *etc. de* ~ on duty; ⚔ *en condiciones de* ~ operational; *franco de* ~ off duty; *hacer un flaco* ~ *a* play a dirty trick on; *libre* ~ self-service; ⚔ *prestar* ~ serve, see service.

servidor *m*, **-a** *f* servant; *un* ~ my humble self; ~ *de Vd.* at your service; *su seguro* ~ yours faithfully; **servidumbre** *f* servitude; *fig.* self-control; (*obligación*) compulsion; (*ps.*) servants, staff; ~ *de la gleba* serfdom; ~ *de paso* right of way; **servil** servile; (*rastrero*) groveling, abject; *imitación* slavish; *oficio* menial; **servilismo** *m* servility *etc.*

servilleta *f* serviette, napkin.

servio 1. Serbian; **2.** *m*, **a** *f* Serb; **3.** *m* (*idioma*) Serbo-Croat.

servir [3l] **1.** *v/t. mst* serve; *ps. a la mesa* wait on; *cargo* carry out, fulfill; *cañón* man; *máquina* tend; (*hacer un servicio a*) do a favor to, oblige; *ser servido de inf.* be pleased to *inf.*; **2.** *v/i.* serve (*a.* ⚔, *tenis*; *de* as, for); (*ser servible*) be useful, be of use; serve, wait *a la mesa*; (*ser criado*) be in service; ⚔ *está sirviendo* he is doing his military service; ~ *en lugar de* do duty for; *para* ~ *a Vd.* at your service; ~ *para* be good for, be used for; *no sirve para nada* (*p.*) he's no earthly use; *¿para qué sirve?* what is the good of it?; (eso) *no sirve* that's no good, that won't do; **3.** ~**se** help o.s. *a la mesa*; ~ *inf.* be good enough to *inf.*; deign to *inf.*; *sírvase inf.* please *inf.*; ~ *de* make use of; put to use.

sésamo *m* ⚘, *fig.* sesame; *¡~ ábrete!* open sesame!

sesear [1a] *pronounce* c (*before* e, i) *and* z [θ] *as* [s].

sesenta sixty; **sesentón** *adj. a. su. m*, **-a** *f* F sexagenarian.

seseo *m pronunciation of* c (*before* e, i) *and* z [θ] *as* [s].

sesera *f* brain pan; F brain (box).

sesgado slanting, oblique; *gorra etc.* awry; **sesgar** [1h] slant, slope; (*cortar*) cut on the slant; *sew.* cut (on the) bias; ⊕ bevel; (*torcer*) twist to one side; **sesgo** *m* slant, slope; *esp. sew.* bias; (*torcimiento*) warp, twist; *fig.* (mental) twist, turn; *fig.* compromise; *al* ~ slanting; awry; *cortar etc.* on the bias.

sesión *f* session, sitting; meeting;

cine: ~ *continua* continuous showing; ~ *de espiritismo* séance; *levantar la* ~ adjourn.
seso *m* brain; *fig.* sense, brains; ~*s pl.* brains (*a. cocina*); *devanarse los* ~*s* rack one's brains; *v. tapa*; *perder el* ~ go mad.
sestear [1a] take a siesta (*or* nap).
sesudo sensible, wise; (*inteligente*) brainy.
set *m tenis*: set.
seta *f* mushroom, toadstool; bristle.
setecientos seven hundred; **setenta** seventy; **setentón** *adj. a. su. m*, **-a** *f* F septuagenarian.
setiembre *m* September.
seto *m* fence; ~ (*vivo*) hedge.
seudo... pseudo...; **seudónimo** 1. pseudonymous; 2. *m* pseudonym.
severidad *f* severity *etc.*; **severo** *mst* severe; stringent, exacting; hard, harsh; stern; *ser* ~ *con* (*or para*) be hard on.
sevillano *adj. a. su. m*, **a** *f* Sevillian.
sexagenario *adj. a. su. m*, **a** *f* sexagenarian; **sexagésimo** sixtieth.
sexo *m* sex; *el bello* ~ the fair sex; *el* ~ *débil* the gentle sex.
sextante *m* sextant.
sexteto *m* sextet, sestet.
sexto *adj. a. su. m* sixth.
sexual sexual; sex *attr.*; **sexualidad** *f* sexuality.
sí[1] **1.** *adv.* yes; indeed; ~ *tal* yes indeed, surely; *enfático etc.*: *él* ~ *fue* he did go, he certainly went; *él no lo sabe pero yo* ~ he doesn't know (it) but I do; *ellos* ~ *vendrán* they are sure to come, they at least will come; F *porque* ~ because that's the way it is; because I say so; *lo hizo porque* ~ *b.s.* he did it out of pure cussedness; *por* ~ *o por no* in any case; *¡eso* ~ *que no!* not on any account!; *un día* ~ *y otro no* on alternate days, every other day; **2.** *m* yes; consent; *dar el* ~ say yes.
sí[2] *pron. sg.* himself, herself, itself; (*con Vd.*) yourself; *pl.* themselves; (*con Vds.*) yourselves; *recíproco*: each other; ~ *mismo* himself *etc.*; (*con inf.*) oneself; *de* ~ in itself; spontaneously; *de por* ~ separately, individually; per se; in itself *etc.*; *fuera de* ~ beside o.s.; *por* ~ (*solo*) by oneself *etc.*; *v. dar etc.*
si *cj.* if; whether; ~ *no* if not; otherwise; *¿*~ ...*?* what if ...?, suppose ...?; *¡*~ *fuera verdad!* if only it were true!; *¿*~ *vendrá?* I wonder if he'll come?; *por* ~ *acaso* (just) in case.
siamés *adj. a. su. m*, **-a** *f* Siamese.
siberiano *adj. a. su. m*, **a** *f* Siberian.
sibilante *adj. a. su. f* sibilant.
sicalipsis *f* eroticism, suggestiveness; **sicalíptico** erotic, suggestive.
siciliano *adj. a. su. m*, **a** *f* Sicilian.
sico... *v. psico...*
sicofanta, sicofante *m* informer, spy; slanderer.
sicomoro *m* sycamore.
sideral, sidéreo sidereal; astral; *casco etc.* space *attr.*
siderurgia *f* iron and steel industry; **siderúrgico** iron and steel *attr.*; *la* ~*a* iron and steel works.
sidra *f* cider.
siega *f* reaping, mowing; (*época*) harvest.
siembra *f* (*acto*) sowing; (*campo*) sown field; (*época*) sowing time; *patata de* ~ seed potato.
siempre always; all the time; ever; *como* ~ as usual; *de* ~ usual, inevitable; *lo de* ~ the same old thing; (*de una vez*) *para* ~ once and for all, for good; *para* ~ for ever; *para* (*or por*) ~ *jamás* for ever and ever; ~ *que indic.* whenever, as often as; *subj.* provided that.
sien *f anat.* temple.
sierpe *f* snake, serpent.
sierra *f* ⊕ saw; *geog.* mountain range; ~ *de arco* (*para metales*), ~ *de armero* hacksaw; ~ *cabrilla* whipsaw; ~ *de calados* fretsaw; ~ *circular* circular saw, buzz saw; ~ *continua*, ~ *sin fin* band saw; ~ *de espigar* tenon saw; ~ *de vaivén* jigsaw.
siervo *m*, **a** *f* slave; ~ (*de la gleba*) serf, servant.
sieso *m* anus.
siesta *f* siesta, (afternoon) nap; (*calor*) hottest part of the day; *dormir* (*or echar*) *la* ~ take a nap.
siete seven (*a. su.*); (*fecha*) seventh; *las* ~ seven o'clock; F *hablar más que* ~ talk nineteen to the dozen.
sífilis *f* syphilis; **sifilítico** syphilitic.
sifón *m* siphon; ⊕ trap; *con* ~ *bebida* and soda.
sigilo *m* secrecy, discretion; ~ *sacramental* secrecy of the confessional; **sigiloso** discreet, secret; reserved.
sigla *f* symbol, abbreviation.
siglo *m* century; (*mucho tiempo*) age;

(*época*) age, time(s); *eccl.* world; ♀ *de las Luces* Age of Enlightenment; ♀ *de Oro* Golden Age; *eccl. en el* ~ in the world; *por los* ~*s de los* ~*s* world without end.

signar [1a] mark, sign; make the sign of the cross over; ~**se** cross o.s.; **signatura** *f typ.*, ♪ signature; (catalog) number *de biblioteca*.

significación *f* significance; **significado 1.** *S.Am.* well-known; important; **2.** *m* meaning *de palabra*; intention; (*importancia*) significance; **significante** significant; **significar** [1g] *v/t.* (*hacer saber*) make known, signify; (*querer decir*) mean (*para* to), signify; *v/i.* be important; **significativo** significant; *mirada etc.* meaning, expressive.

signo *m mst* sign; ♒ *a.* symbol; mark *en lugar de firma*; ~ *externo* status symbol; ~ *de admiración* exclamation mark; ~ *de interrogación* question mark.

sigo *etc. v. seguir.*

siguiente next, following.

sílaba *f* syllable; **silabeo** *m* syllabification; **silábico** syllabic.

silba *f* hiss(ing), catcall; **silbar** [1a] *v/t. melodía* whistle; *silbato* blow; *comedia etc.* hiss (*en Inglaterra*: boo); *v/i.* ♪ *etc.* whistle; (*bala etc.*) whine; (*flecha etc.*) whizz, swish; *thea. etc.* hiss (*en Inglaterra*: boo, catcall); **silbato** *m* whistle; **silbido** *m*, **silbo** *m* whistle; whistling; hiss, hissing; whine *etc.*; *silbido de oídos* ringing in the ears.

silenciador *m* silencer; **silenciar** [1b] *hecho* keep silent about; *p.* silence; **silencio** *m* silence; quiet; hush; ♪ rest; ¡~! quiet!; *en* ~ in silence (*a. fig.*); *guardar* ~ keep quiet; *entregar al* ~ forget about; *pasar en* ~ omit all reference to; **silencioso 1.** silent, quiet; soundless; *esp.* ⊕ noiseless; **2.** *m* ⊕ muffler, silencer.

silicato *m* silicate; **sílice** *f* silica.

silo *m* ⚘ silo; *fig.* cave(rn).

silogismo *m* syllogism.

silueta *f* silhouette; outline *de edificio*; skyline *de ciudad*; (*talle de p.*) figure.

silvestre *esp.* ⚘ wild; uncultivated; *fig.* rustic; **silvicultura** *f* forestry.

silla *f* (*en general*) seat; (*mueble*) chair; ~ (*de montar*) saddle; ~ *eléctrica* electric chair; ~ *de manos* sedan chair; ~ *plegadiza*, ~ *de tijera* camp stool, folding chair; ~ *de ruedas* wheelchair; ~*s apilables* chairs that can be stacked or nested.

sillería *f* (set of) chairs; seating; *eccl.* stall, choir stalls; ⚠ masonry; **silleta** *f* small chair; (*orinal*) bedpan; **sillico** *m* chamber pot; commode; **sillín** *m* saddle; **sillón** *m* armchair, easy chair; ~ (*de montar*) sidesaddle; ~ *de orejas* wing chair; ~ *de ruedas* Bath chair.

sima *f* abyss, pit; chasm.

simbiosis *f* symbiosis.

simbólico symbolic(al); token *attr.*; **simbolismo** *m* symbolism; **simbolizar** [1f] symbolize; be a token of; typify, represent; **símbolo** *m* symbol; *eccl.* creed.

simetría *f* symmetry; *fig.* harmony; **simétrico** symmetrical; *fig.* harmonious.

simiente *f* seed; sperm.

simiesco apish, simian.

símil 1. similar; **2.** *m* simile; comparison; **similar** similar; **similigrabado** *m typ.* half-tone; **similitud** *f* similarity, resemblance.

similor *m* pinchbeck; *de* ~ *fig.* fake, sham.

simonía *f* simony.

simpar unequaled, unmatched.

simpatía *f* (*afecto*) liking (*hacia, por* for), friendliness (*hacia, por* towards); congeniality *de ambiente*; (*correspondencia*) sympathy; fellow feeling; (*lo atractivo*) charm; (*no*) *tener* ~ *a* (dis)like; *tomar* ~ *a* take a liking for; **simpático** *p.* nice, likeable; pleasant; *ambiente* congenial, agreeable; 🕮, *phys. etc.* sympathetic; **simpatizante** *m/f* sympathizer (*de* with); **simpatizar** [1f] get on well together; ~ *con p.* get on well with; *carácter etc.* harmonize with, be congenial to.

simple 1. *mst* simple; (*no doble*) single; (*incauto*) gullible, simple; (*corriente*) ordinary; *por* ~ *descuido* through sheer carelessness; **2.** *m* simpleton; ⚘~*s pl.* simples; **simpleza** *f* silliness; (*acto etc.*) silly thing; (*pequeñez*) mere trifle; *decir* ~*s* talk nonsense; **simplificar** [1g] sim-

plify; **simplón** F **1.** gullible, simple; **2.** *m*, **-a** *f* simple soul.
simulación *f* simulation; make-believe; *b.s.* pretense; **simulacro** *m* image, idol; (*fantasma*) vision; (*apariencia*) semblance, pretense; ~ *de combate* sham fight; **simulado** fake; ✝ pro forma; **simular** [1a] simulate; feign, sham.
simultáneo simultaneous.
sin without; with no; ...less; un...; apart from, not counting; ~ *embargo* nevertheless, however; ~ *gasolina* out of petrol; ~ *sombrero* without a hat, hatless; ~ *inf.* without *ger.*; ~ *hablar* without speaking; ~ *almidonar* unstarched; ~ *lavar* unwashed; *cuenta* ~ *pagar* bill to be paid, unpaid bill; ~ *que subj.* without ... *ger.*
sinagoga *f* synagogue.
sinapismo *m* ⚕ mustard plaster; F nuisance, bore.
sincerar [1a] vindicate, justify; **~se:** ~ *a*, ~ *con* open one's heart to; **sinceridad** *f* sincerity; **sincero** sincere; genuine, heartfelt.
síncopa *f* ♪ syncopation; *gr.* syncope; **sincopar** [1a] syncopate; *fig.* abridge; **síncope** *m* ⚕ fainting fit.
sincrónico synchronous; synchronized; **sincronismo** *m* synchronism; coincidence *de fechas etc.*; **sincronizar** [1f] synchronize.
sindical trade(s) union *attr.*; syndical; **sindicalismo** *m* trade(s) unionism; syndicalism; **sindicalista** *m/f* trade(s) unionist; syndicalist; **sindicar** [1g] *obreros* form into a trade union; syndicate; *propiedad* put in trust; **sindicato** *m* syndicate; (*laboral*) trade(s) union, labor union; **síndico** *m* trustee; ⚖, ✝ *approx.* (official) receiver.
sindíos 1. godless; **2.** *m/f* atheist.
síndrome *m* syndrome; ~ *de imunidad deficiente adquirida* (*SIDA*) acquired immune-deficiency syndrome (AIDS).
sinecura *f* sinecure.
sinfín *m* = *sinnúmero*.
sinfonía *f* symphony; **sinfónico** symphonic.
singladura *f* ⚓ (day's) run.
singular 1. *mst* singular (*a. gr*); (*destacado*) outstanding; *combate* single; (*raro*) peculiar, odd; **2.** *m gr.* singular; **singularidad** *f* singularity; peculiarity *etc.*; **singularizar** [1f] single out; **~se** stand out, distinguish o.s.; be conspicuous.
siniestrado 1. hurt by an accident; **2.** *m*, **a** *f* victim.
siniestro 1. left; *fig.* sinister; (*funesto*) disastrous; **2.** *m* accident, catastrophe, disaster.
sinnúmero: *un* ~ *de* a great many, a great amount of.
sino[1] *m* fate, destiny.
sino[2] **...** (*chino*) sino...
sino[3] but; except; ~ *que* but.
sínodo *m* synod.
sinónimo 1. synonymous; **2.** *m* synonym.
sinopsis *f* synopsis.
sinrazón *f* wrong, injustice.
sinsabor *m* trouble, unpleasantness; (*pesar*) sorrow.
sinsostenismo *m* F bra-less fashion.
sintáctico syntactic(al); **sintaxis** *f* syntax.
síntesis *f* synthesis; **sintético** synthetic(al); **sintetizar** [1f] synthesize.
síntoma *m* symptom; sign; ~ *de abstinencia* withdrawal symptom; **sintomático** symptomatic.
sintonía *f radio*: tuning; ♪ signature tune; **sintonización** *f* tuning; **sintonizar** [1f] *radio*: tune; *programa* tune in to; ⚡ syntonize.
sinuosidad *f* sinuosity; **sinuoso** winding, sinuous; wavy.
sinusitis *f* sinusitis.
sinvergüenza *m* F scoundrel.
siqu... *v.* *psiqu...*
siquiera 1. *adv.* at least; *dame un beso* ~ give me a kiss at least; *ni* ~ not even, not so much as; *ni me besó* ~ he didn't even kiss me; *tan* ~ even; **2.** *cj.* even if, even though.
sirena *f* (*p.*) mermaid; (*clásica*) siren; ♪ siren, hooter; ~ *de la playa* bathing beauty; ~ *de niebla* foghorn.
sirga *f* towrope; **sirgar** [1h] tow.
sirio *adj. a. su. m*, **a** *f* Syrian.
sirvienta *f* servant, maid; **sirviente** *m* servant; waiter.
sisa *f* petty theft; *sew.* dart; **sisar** [1a] pilfer; *sew.* put darts in, take in.
sisear [1a] hiss; **siseo** *m* hiss.
sísmico seismic; **sismógrafo** *m* seismograph.
sisón 1. thieving, light-fingered; **2.** *m*, **-a** *f* petty thief.

sistema *m mst* system; method; framework; *el* ~ the establishment (established order); **sistemático** systematic; **sistematizar** [1f] systematize; organize.
sitiador *m* besieger; **sitiar** [1b] besiege; *fig.* surround, hem in; **sitio** *m* (*lugar determinado*) place, spot; site, location; (*espacio*) room; ⚔ siege; *en estado de* ~ in a state of siege; under martial law; *¿hay* ~*?* is there (any) room?; *hay* ~ *de sobra* there's plenty of room; *levantar el* ~ raise the siege; *poner* ~ *a* lay siege to; *quedarse en el* ~ die on the spot; **sito** situated, located (*en* in); **situación** *f* situation; position; location, locality; (*social*) position, standing; *S. Am. precios de* ~ bargain prices; **situado** situated, placed; **situar** [1e] place, put, set; *esp. edificio* site, locate; ⚔ *etc.* post, station; ✝ lay aside; place; ~**se** take place.
slogan [cz'logan] *m* slogan.
smoking [ez'mokin] *m* dinner jacket.
snob [ez'nob] *etc. v. esnob etc.*
so[1] *prp.* under.
¡so![2] whoa!
soba *f* kneading *de masa*; slap, dab *con mano*; F hiding; F *dar* ~ *a* tan.
sobaco *m* armpit; armhole *de vestido*.
sobado rumpled, messed up; *libro* well-thumbed, dog-eared; *S. Am.* F terrific; **sobajar** [1a] crush, rumple, mess up; *fig.* humiliate.
sobaquera *f* armhole; **sobaquina** *f* underarm odor.
sobar [1a] *masa etc.* knead; squeeze; F (*zurrar*) tan; F (*manosear*) paw, finger, feel; (*novios, a.* ~**se**) pet, cuddle.
soberanía *f* sovereignty; **soberano** *adj. a. su. m,* **a** *f* sovereign.
soberbia *f* pride *etc.*; **soberbio** (*orgulloso*) proud, haughty; arrogant; grand; (*colérico*) angry.
sobón F (*que manosea*) too free with his *etc.* hands; *fig.* too familiar by half, fresh; (*enamorado*) mushy, spoony; (*taimado*) work-shy.
sobornable bribable, venal; **sobornado** twisted, out of shape; **sobornar** [1a] bribe; buy off; **soborno** *m* bribe; (*en general*) bribery, graft.
sobra *f* excess, surplus; ~*s pl.* leavings, leftovers; scraps; *de* ~ (*adj.*) (to) spare, surplus, extra; (*adv.*) more than enough; (*saber*) only too well; F *estar de* ~ (*p.*) be one (*etc.*) too many; be left out; *b.s.* be in the way; **sobradamente** too; (only) too well; **sobradillo** *m* penthouse; **sobrado 1.** excessive, more than enough; *p.* wealthy; *estar* ~ *de* be well provided for; **2.** *m* attic, garret.
sobrancero unemployed.
sobrante 1. spare, extra, surplus; **2.** *m* surplus (*a.* ✝); ✝ balance in hand; margin; **sobrar** [1a] *v/t.* exceed, surpass; *v/i.* be left over, be to spare; remain; be more than enough; *nos sobra tiempo* we have heaps (*or* lots, plenty) of time; *me parece que aquí sobro* it seems I'm not needed here.
sobre[1] *m* envelope; letter cover; (*señas*) address.
sobre[2] on, upon; on top of; (*encima de*) over, above; (*acerca de*) about; *1* ~ *4* 1 in 4; ~ *las 5* about 5 o'clock; ~ *inf.* on top of (being), in addition to (being).
sobre[3]**...** super...; over...; ~**abundante** superabundant; ~**abundar** [1a] superabound (*en* in, with); ~**alimentado** ⊕ supercharged; ~**alimentador** *m* ⊕ supercharger; ~**alimentar** [1a] ⊕ supercharge; *p.* overfeed; ~**calentar** [1k] overheat; ~**cama** *m* bedspread; ~**carga** *f* extra load; (*soga*) rope; ✝, 📮 surcharge; ~**cargar** [1h] *carro* overload; ⚡ *etc.* overcharge; *p. etc.* weigh down; ✝, 📮 surcharge; ~**cargo** *m* ⚓ supercargo; ~**cejo** *m,* ~**ceño** *m* frown.
sobrecoger [2c] startle, (take by) surprise; ~**se** be startled, start (*a* at, *de* with); (*achicarse*) be overawed, be abashed.
sobre...: ~**cubierta** *f* outer cover; jacket *de libro*; ~**dicho** above (mentioned); ~**dorar** [1a] gild; *fig.* gloss over; ~**dosis** *f* overdose.
sobre(e)ntender [2g] understand; deduce, infer; ~**se** be implied *etc.*
sobre...: ~**(e)xcitado** overexcited; ~**(e)xcitar** [1a] overexcite; ~**(e)xponer** [2r] *phot.* overexpose; ~**faz** *f* surface, outside; ~**giro** *m* overdraft; ~**haz** *f* = ~*faz*; (*cubierta*) cover; ~**herido** slightly wounded; ~**humano** superhuman; ~**llevar** [1a] (help to) carry; *fig. carga de otro* ease;

molestias bear, endure; *faltas de otro* be tolerant towards; **~manera** exceedingly; **~marcha** *f mot.* overdrive; **~mesa** *f* (*tapete*) table cover; (*postre*) dessert; (*tiempo*) sitting on after a meal; *de ~ charla etc.* after-dinner; *reloj etc.* table *attr.*; **~nadar** [1a] float; **~natural** supernatural; unearthly, weird; *ciencia* occult; **~nombre** *m* nickname; by-name; title.

sobrentender *etc. v. sobre(e)ntender etc.*

sobre...: ~paga *f* rise, bonus; **~parto** *m* ⚕ confinement; *morir de ~* die in childbirth; **~pasar** [1a] surpass; *límite* exceed; *marca* beat; ✈ *pista* overshoot; **~peine 1.** slightly, briefly; **2.** *m* hair trimming; **~pelliz** *f* surplice; **~peso** *m* overweight; **~población** *f* overcrowding.

sobreponer [2r] put on top, put *one thing* on *another*, superimpose; **~se** *fig.* pull o.s. together; win through *en adversidad*; make the best of a bad job; *~ a dificultad* overcome; *susto* get over; *rival etc.* triumph over.

sobre...: ~precio *m* surcharge; **~producción** *f* overproduction; **~puesto 1.** added, superimposed; **2.** *m* addition; **~pujar** [1a] outdo; outbid.

sobrero extra, spare.

sobre...: ~saliente 1. outstanding, brilliant; *univ.* first class; **2.** *m/f* substitute; *thea.* understudy; **3.** *m univ.* first class, distinction; **~salir** [3r] ⚠ *etc.* project, jut out; stick out (*or* up), protrude; *fig.* stand out, excel (*en* at).

sobresaltar [1a] fall upon, rush at; (*asustar etc.*) startle; shock; **~se** start, be startled (*con*, *de* at); **sobresalto** *m* fright, scare; shock; *de ~* suddenly.

sobre...: ~sanar [1a] ⚕ heal superficially; *defecto* hide, gloss over; **~scrito** *m* superscription; address *en carta*; **~seer** [2e] desist; default *en obligación*; **~seimiento** *m* giving up; default; ⚖ stay of proceedings; **~sello** *m* double seal; **~stante** *m* overseer; foreman; **~stimar** [1a] overvalue; overestimate; **~sueldo** *m* extra pay, bonus; **~tasa** *f* surcharge; **~todo** *m* overcoat; **~venir** [3s] supervene, ensue; happen (unexpectedly); **~viviente 1.** surviving; **2.** *m/f* survivor; **~vivir** [3a] survive; *~ a* survive; outlive, outlast; **~volar** [1m] fly over.

sobriedad *f* sobriety *etc.*

sobrina *f* niece; **sobrino** *m* nephew.

sobrio sober, moderate; temperate; *fig.* sober, restrained.

socaire *m* lee; *al ~* to leeward; F *ponerse al ~* shirk.

socaliñar [1a] get by a swindle; **socaliñero 1.** swindling; **2.** *m* swindler.

socapa *f* F subterfuge; *a ~* surreptitiously.

socarrón sly, crafty, artful; (*guasón*) mocking, with sly humor; malicious; **socarronería** *f* slyness; sly humor *etc.*

socava(**ción**) *f* undermining; **socavar** [1a] undermine, dig under; *fig.* sap, undermine; **socavón** *m* ⚒ mine gallery, tunnel; hole *en calle*; ⚠ sudden collapse.

sociable *p.* sociable; *animal etc.* social, gregarious; **social** social; ✝ company *attr.*; **socialismo** *m* socialism; **socialista** *adj. a. su. m/f* socialist; **socializar** [1f] socialize, nationalize.

sociedad *f* society; association; ✝ company, firm; ✝ *etc.* partnership *de dos ps.*; *alta ~*, *buena ~* (high) society; *~ anónima* stock company, corporation; *Pérez y García* ♀ *Anónima* Pérez y García Incorporated (Limited); *~ de control* holding company; ♀ *de las Naciones* League of Nations; *~ secreta* secret society; *~ de socorro mutuo* friendly (*or* provident) society.

socio *m*, **a** *f* member *de club etc.*; fellow *de sociedad científica etc.*; ✝ partner; ✝ associate; F fellow; *~ comanditario*, *~ pasivo* sleeping partner; *~ de honor*, *~ honorario* honorary member; *~ de número* full member; **sociología** *f* sociology; **sociológico** sociological; **sociólogo** *m* sociologist.

socorrer [2a] help; *necesidades*, *ciudad* relieve; **socorrido** *p. etc.* helpful, cooperative; *cosa útil* handy; (*bien provisto*) well-stocked; (*trillado*) hackneyed; **socorrismo** *m* first aid; **socorro** *m* help, aid; relief (*a.* ⚔); *¡~!* help!; *~s pl. mutuos* mutual aid; *trabajos de* ~ relief work.

soda *f* ⚗ soda; (*bebida*) soda (water).

sodio *m* sodium.

soez dirty, obscene; crude.

sofá *m* sofa, settee; **~-cama** *f* day bed.

sofisma *m* sophism; **sofista 1.** sophistic(al); **2.** *m* sophist; **sofistería** *f* (piece of) sophistry; **sofisticación** *f* ⊕ sophistication; **sofisticado** *p. etc.* (*a.* ⊕) sophisticated; **sofístico** sophistic, sophistical; false, fallacious.

sofocación *f* suffocation; *fig.* vexation; annoying rebuff; **sofocante** stifling, suffocating; **sofocar** [1g] choke, stifle, suffocate; *incendio* smother, put out; *fig.* make *s.o.* blush; (*irritar*) make *s.o.* angry; F bother; **~se** choke *etc.*; (*corriendo etc.*) get out of breath; *fig.* flush, get embarrassed; (*encolerizarse*) get worked up, get hot under the collar; **sofoco** *m* embarrassment; F *pasar un* ~ have an embarrassing time; **sofocón** *m* F stunning blow.

sofrenada *f* sudden check; F ticking-off; **sofrenar** [1a] rein back suddenly; *fig.* restrain; F bawl out.

soga *f* rope; halter; *con la* ~ *al cuello* up to one's neck in it; F *dar* ~ *a* make fun of; *echar la* ~ *tras el caldero* throw in one's hand, chuck it all up; F *hacer* ~ lag behind.

soja *f* soya; *semilla de* ~ soya bean.

sojuzgar [1h] subjugate, subdue.

sol *m* sun; sunshine, sunlight; F *como un* ~ bright as a new pin; *de* ~ *día* sunny; **de** ~ *a* ~ from sunrise to sunset; *no dejar a* ~ *ni a sombra* drive *s.o.* from pillar to post, give *s.o.* no respite; *hacer* ~ be sunny; *tomar el* ~ sun o.s., bask.

solado *m* tiling, tiled floor.

solamente only; solely.

solana *f* sunny spot; (*cuarto*) sun lounge; **solanera** *f* ⚕ sunburn; (*lugar*) sunny spot.

solano *m* east wind.

solapa *f* lapel; flap *de sobre*; *fig.* excuse; **solapadamente** in an underhand way, by crooked means; **solapado** sly, sneaky; **solapar** [1a] *fig.* *v/t.* overlap; (*ocultar*) cover up, keep dark; *v/i.* overlap; **~se** get hidden underneath; **solapo** *m sew.* lapel; overlap; F chuck under the chin; F *a* ~ by underhand methods.

solar[1] *m* ⚠ lot, site, piece of ground; (*casa*) ancestral home, family seat; *S.Am.* backyard.

solar[2] solar, sun *attr.*

solar[3] [1m] *calzado* sole; *suelo* floor, tile.

solariego *casa* ancestral; *familia* ancient and noble; *hist.* manorial; *hist.* *tierras* ~*as* demesne.

solario *m* sun porch.

solaz *m* relaxation, recreation; (*consuelo*) solace; **solazar** [1f] give relaxation to, amuse; (*consolar*) solace, comfort; **~se** enjoy o.s., amuse o.s., relax.

solazo *m* F scorching sun(shine).

soldada *f* pay, wages.

soldadesca *f* (brutal and licentious) soldiery; **soldadesco** soldierly; *a la* ~*a* like a soldier; **soldado** *m* soldier; ~ *de infantería* infantryman; ~ *de juguete* toy soldier; ~ *de marina* marine; ~ *de a pie* foot soldier; ~ *de plomo* tin soldier; ~ *de primera* private first class; ~ *raso* buck private.

soldador *m* soldering iron; (*p.*) welder; **soldadura** *f* (*metal*) solder; (*acto*) soldering, welding; (*juntura*) soldered joint, welded seam; ~ *autógena* welding; **soldar** [1a] ⊕ solder, weld; *fig.* join; *disputa* patch up; correct; **~se** (*huesos*) knit.

soleado sunny; sunned; **solear** [1a] (put in the) sun.

solecismo *m* solecism.

soledad *f* solitude; loneliness; (*lugar*) lonely place.

solemne solemn; dignified; grave, weighty; F *error* terrible; **solemnidad** *f* solemnity *etc.*; (*acto*) solemn ceremony; formalities; F *pobre de* ~ miserably poor; F *rico de* ~ stinking with money; **solemnizar** [1f] solemnize; celebrate.

soler [2h; *defective*]: ~ *inf.* be in the habit of *ger.*; *suele venir a las 5* he generally (*or* usually) comes at 5; *solía hacerlo* I used to do it; *como se suele* as is customary.

soleta: F *tomar* ~ beat it.

solevantar [1a] raise up, heave up; *fig.* rouse, stir up.

solfa *f* ♪ solfa; musical notation; *fig.* music; F tanning; F *poner en* ~ make a mockery of; **solfear** [1a] ♪ solfa; F tan; **solfeo** *m* ♪ solfa; F tanning.

solicitador *m*, **-a** *f*, **solicitante** *m/f* applicant; petitioner; **solicitar** [1a] request, solicit (*algo* a th.; *algo a alguien* a th. of a p.); *puesto etc.* apply for, put in for; *votos* canvass; *atención*, *phys.* attract; *ser solicitado fig.* be sought after, be in demand; **solícito** diligent, careful; solicitous (*por* about, for); **solicitud** *f* care, concern; (*acto, petición*) request; application (*de puesto* for); *a* ~ on request, on demand; † *dinero* on call.

solidaridad *f* solidarity; **solidario** jointly liable; *esp.* ⚖ jointly; *compromiso etc.* mutually binding; ~ *de* integral with; **solidez** *f* solidity *etc.*; **solidificar**(**se**) [1g] solidify; harden; **sólido 1.** solid (*a.* A, *fig.*); stable, firm; (*robusto*) strong, stout; hard; *aspecto* solid, massive; (*duradero*) solid, lasting; *argumento* sound; *color* fast; **2.** *m* solid.

soliloquiar [1b] soliloquize, talk to o.s.; **soliloquio** *m* soliloquy, monologue.

solista *m/f* soloist.

solitaria *f* tapeworm; **solitario 1.** solitary; desolate, lonely, bleak; *en* ~ solo; **2.** *m*, **a** *f* (*p.*) recluse, hermit; **3.** *m* solitaire.

soliviantar [1a] rouse, stir up; win over *con promesas etc.*; **soliviar** [1b] lift up; **~se** half rise, get up on one elbow *etc.*

solo 1. (*único*) only, sole; (*sin compañía*) alone, by o.s.; single; (*solitario*) lonely; ♩ solo; *sentirse muy* ~ feel very lonely (*or* isolated); *ni un* ~ *punto* not one single point; *a solas* by o.s., alone; **2.** *m* ♩, *naipes*: solo.

sólo only, solely; merely; just; *tan* ~ only.

solom(**ill**)**o** *m* sirloin.

solsticio *m* solstice.

soltar [1m] (*desatar*) untie, unfasten; (*aflojar*) loose(n), slacken; (*desenmarañar*) free; (*dejar caer*) drop, let go of; *mano etc.* release; (*poner en libertad*) release, let go, (set) free; *animal etc.* let out, let (*or* set, turn) loose; *amarras* cast off; *carcajada* let out; *dificultad* solve; F *dinero* cough up; ⊕ *embrague* disengage, *freno* release; *exclamación* let out; *golpe* let fly; *injurias* utter, let fly (a string of); *presa* let go of; **~se** (*pieza*) (*aflojarse*) work loose; (*desprenderse*) come off, come undone; (*escapar*) get free; (*perfeccionarse*) become expert; *b.s.* let o.s. go; ~ *a inf.* begin to *inf.*

soltera *f* unmarried woman; *b.s.* spinster; **soltero 1.** single, unmarried; **2.** *m* bachelor, unmarried man; **solterón** *m* old (*or* confirmed) bachelor; **solterona** *f* older unmarried woman; *contp.* spinster, old maid.

soltura *f* (*acto*) release *etc.*; ⊕ looseness *de pieza*; agility, freedom of movement; *fig.* (*desvergüenza*) shamelessness, liberty *de lengua*; (*inmoralidad*) licentiousness; ease, fluency *en hablar*; *hablar idioma con* ~ speak fluently; ⚕ ~ *de vientre* looseness of the bowels.

soluble soluble; **solución** *f mst* solution; answer (*de problema* to); resolving *de duda*; *thea.* dénouement; ~ *de continuidad* interruption, break in continuity; **solucionar** [1a] (re)solve.

solvencia *f* † solvency; settlement *de cuenta*; *de* ~ discerning; *de toda* ~ *moral* of excellent character, completely trustworthy; **solventar** [1a] † settle, pay; *dificultad* resolve; **solvente** *adj.* (†) *a. su. m* (⚖) solvent; (*juicioso*) discerning; credible, believable.

sollamar [1a] scorch, singe.

sollo *m* sturgeon.

sollozar [1f] sob; **sollozo** *m* sob.

somanta *f* F tanning.

sombra *f* (*que proyecta un objeto*) shadow; (*para resguardarse del sol*; *luz y* ~) shade; (*oscuridad*) darkness, shadow(s); (*fantasma*) ghost, shade; *fig.* shadow *de duda etc.*; protection, favour; (*atracción*) charm, wit; *paint.* (*tierra de*) ~ umber; *a la* ~ in the shade; F in clink; *ni por* ~ by no means; *dar* ~ *a* shade; *hacer* ~ *a fig.* put *s.t.* in the shade; F *tener buena* ~ be lucky, bring good luck; be likeable; *tener mala* ~ bring bad luck; be not much liked; *no tener* ~ *de* not be a bit like; **sombraje** *m*, **sombrajo** *m* shelter from the sun; *hacer* **~s** get in the light; **sombreado** *m* shading; **sombrear** [1a] shade; *fig.* overshadow.

sombrerera *f* milliner; (*caja*) hatbox; **sombrerería** *f* millinery,

hats; (*tienda*) hat shop; **sombrerero** *m* hatter; **sombrerete** *m* little hat; ⊕ bonnet; cowl *de chimenea*; cap *de seta, cubo*; **sombrero** *m* hat; headgear; ~ *de candil*, ~ *de tres picos* three-cornered hat, cocked hat; ~ *de copa* top hat; ~ *flexible* soft hat, trilby; ~ *gacho* slouch hat; ~ *hongo* derby; ~ *de paja* straw hat; ~ *de pelo S.Am.* high hat.
sombrilla *f* parasol, sunshade.
sombrío shady; *fig.* sombre, dismal; *p.* gloomy, morose.
somero superficial, shallow.
someter [2a] *informe etc.* submit, present; (*conquistar*) conquer; ~ *a prueba etc.* subject to, put to; **~se** yield, submit.
somier *m* spring mattress.
somnambulismo *m* sleep-walking; **somnámbulo** *m*, **a** *f* sleep-walker; **somnífero** sleep-inducing; **somnolencia** *f* sleepiness, drowsiness; **somnolento** = *soñoliento*.
somorgujar [1a] duck, submerge; **~se** dive, plunge; **somorgujo** *m* grebe.
son *m* (pleasant) sound; *fig.* news, rumor; *¿a qué ~?, ¿a ~ de qué?* why?; *a ~ de* to the sound of; *en ~ de* like, as, in the manner of; *en ~ de broma* as a joke; *por este ~* in this way; *sin ~* for no reason at all; **sonado** talked-of, famous; sensational.
sonaja *f* little bell; **sonajear** [1a] jingle; **sonajero** *m* rattle.
sonámbulo 1. moonstruck; **2.** *m* sleepwalker.
sonar [1m] **1.** *v/t.* sound; *campana* ring; ♪ play; *sirena, narices* blow; **2.** *v/i.* sound; (*campana*) ring; ♪ play; (*reloj*) strike; *gr.* be pronounced; F (*tripas*) rumble; F *fig.* sound familiar, ring a bell; *no me suena* it doesn't ring a bell with me; *su nombre suena mucho* he is much talked about; *no quiero que suene mi nombre* I don't want my name mentioned; F *así como suena* just as I'm telling you; ~ *a* sound like; ~ *a hueco* sound hollow; **3. ~se** (*a.* ~ *las narices*) blow one's nose; *se suena que* it is rumored that.
sonata *f* sonata.
sonda *f* (*acto, medida*) sounding; (*instrumento*) ⚓ lead; ⊕ bore; ⚕ probe; ~ *acústica* echo sounder; **sondaje** *m* ⚓ sounding; ⊕ boring; *fig. de ~* exploratory; *organismo de ~* public-opinion poll; **sond(e)ar** [1a] ⚓ sound, take soundings of; ⚕ probe, sound; ⊕ drill, bore into; *fig. terreno* explore; *p., intenciones* sound out; *misterio* plumb; **sondeo** *m* sounding *etc.*; *fig.* (*encuesta*) poll, inquiry; *pol. etc.* feeler, overture.
soneto *m* sonnet.
sonido *m* sound (*a. gr., phys.*); noise; ~ *silencioso* ultrasound.
sonorizar(se) [1f] *gr.* voice; **sonoro** sonorous; loud, resounding; *voz a.* rich; *gr.* voiced; *banda, efectos etc.* sound *attr.*
sonreír(se) [3m] smile (*de* at); **sonriente** smiling; **sonrisa** *f* smile.
sonrojarse [1a] blush, flush (*de* at); **sonrojo** *m* blush(ing); *fig.* naughty word, dubious remark.
sonrosado rosy, pink.
sonsacar [1g] remove *s.t.* surreptitiously (*or* craftily); *p.* entice away; *fig. p.* pump, draw out; *secreto* worm out (*a* of).
sonsonete *m* (*golpecitos*) tapping; din, jangling, rumbling; *fig.* sing-song, chant; (*frase con rima*) jingle; (*desprecio*) mocking undertone.
soñación: F *ni por ~* not on your life; **soñador 1.** dreamy; **2.** *m*, **-a** *f* dreamer; **soñar** [1m] dream (*con* about, of; *con inf.* of *ger.*); ~ *despierto* day-dream; F *ni ~lo* not on your life; F *me va que ni soñado* it suits me a treat; **soñera** *f* drowsiness; **soñolencia** *f* = *somnolencia*; **soñoliento** sleepy, drowsy, somnolent; (*que adormece*) soporific.
sopa *f* soup; sop *en leche*; F *hecho una ~* soaked to the skin; F *comer la ~ boba* scrounge a meal; F *quitar la ~ a*, F *quitarse la ~* sober up.
sopapear [1a] F shake violently; bash, punch; **sopapo** *m* F punch; F slap; F tap.
sopesar [1a] lift, try the weight of.
sopetón *m* punch; *de ~* unexpectedly; *entrar de ~* pop in, drop in.
soplado F affected, overnice; (*engreído*) stuck-up; *sl.* tight, lit up.
soplamocos *m* F punch on the nose.

soplar [1a] **1.** *v/t.* (*apartar*) blow away; blow up, inflate; *fig.* inspire; (*apuntar*) prompt, help *s.o.* along with; (*robar*) pinch; F (*zampar*) hog, guzzle; *sl.* split on; **2.** *v/i.* blow (*a. viento*); puff; *sl.* split (*contra* on), blab; **soplete** *m* blowlamp, torch; ~ *oxiacetilénico* oxyacetylene burner; **soplido** *m* = **soplo** *m* blow(ing), puff *de boca*; puff, gust *de viento*; *esp.* ⊕ blast; *fig.* instant; F (*aviso*) tip; F (*delación*) tales; = **soplón** *m*, **-a** *f* F (*niño*) telltale; informer *de policía*.

soponcio *m* F dizzy spell.

sopor *m* ⚕ drowsiness; *fig.* lethargy; **soporífero 1.** soporific; **2.** *m* nightcap; ⚕ sleeping draft.

soportable bearable.

soportal *m* porch; ~**es** *pl.* arcade *con tiendas*; colonnade.

soportar [1a] (*apoyar*) carry, hold up; (*aguantar*) endure, bear, stand; **soporte** *m* support; mount(ing); base, stand; holder, bracket.

soprano *f* soprano.

sor *f eccl.* sister.

sorber [2a] sip; (*chupar*) suck (in); ~ (*por las narices*) sniff; *medicamento* inhale; absorb, soak up; (*tragar*) swallow (up); **sorbete** *m* sherbet; (*bebida*) iced fruit drink; **sorbetón** *m* F gulp, mouthful; **sorbo** *m* sip; gulp, swallow; sniff.

sordera *f*, **sordez** *f* deafness.

sordidez *f* nastiness *etc.*; **sórdido** nasty, dirty; *fig.* mean.

sordina *f* ♪ mute, muffler; damper *de piano*; *a la* ~ on the quiet.

sordo 1. *p.* deaf (*a. fig.*; *a* to); (*silencioso*) quiet, noiseless; *sonido* muffled, dull; *gr.* voiceless; ~ *como una tapia* deaf as a post; *a la* ~*a*, *a* ~*as* noiselessly; **2.** *m*, **a** *f* deaf person; *hacerse el* ~ pretend not to hear; turn a deaf ear (*a* to); **sordomudo 1.** deaf and dumb; **2.** *m*, **a** *f* deaf-mute.

sorna *f* slyness; sluggishness, slowness; *con* ~ slyly, sarcastically.

soroche *m S.Am.* mountain sickness.

sorprendente surprising; amazing; startling; **sorprender** [2a] (*maravillar*) surprise; amaze; (*sobresaltar*) startle; (*coger desprevenido*) (take by) surprise, catch; *conversación* overhear; *secreto* discover; ~**se** be surprised (*de* at); **sorpresa** *f* surprise; ¡*qué* ~!, ¡*vaya* ~! what a surprise!; *coger de* ~ take by surprise; ⚔ *coger por* ~ surprise; **sorpresivo** surprising.

sortear [1a] *v/t.* (*rifar*) raffle; *deportes etc.*: toss up for; (*evitar*) dodge; *v/i.* toss up; draw lots; (*esquivarse*) dodge.

sortija *f* ring; curl, ringlet *de pelo*; ~ *de sello* signet ring.

sortilegio *m* spell, charm; (*brujería*) sorcery; (*adivinación*) fortunetelling.

sosa *f* soda.

sosegado quiet, calm, peaceful; gentle; restful; **sosegar** [1h *a.* 1k] *v/t.* calm (down); quieten; *ánimo* reassure; *dudas* allay; *v/i.* rest; ~**se** calm down.

sosería *f* tastelessness *etc.*

sosiego *m* quiet(ness), calm, peace, peacefulness.

soslayar [1a] put *s.t.* sideways, place *s.t.* obliquely; *dificultad* get round; *pregunta* dodge; **soslayo:** *al* ~, *de* ~ obliquely, at a slant, sideways; *mirada* sidelong; *mirar de* ~ look at *s.o.* out of the corner of one's eye; *fig.* look askance at.

soso tasteless, insipid; (*sin azúcar*) unsweetened; *fig.* dull, colorless; flat.

sospecha *f* suspicion; **sospechar** [1a] *v/t.* suspect; *v/i.*: ~ *de* suspect, have one's suspicions about; **sospechoso 1.** suspicious; (*no confiable*) suspect; **2.** *m*, **a** *f* suspect.

sostén *m* ⚠ *etc.* support, prop; stay; stand; bra(ssière) *de mujer*; *fig.* support, prop; mainstay, pillar; **sostener** [2l] ⚠, ⊕ support, hold up; *lo inestable* prop up; *peso* bear; *carga* carry; *fig.* sustain (*a.* ♪); (*entretener*) maintain; (*tolerar*) bear; *p. etc.* sustain *con comida*; maintain *con dinero*; *opinión* uphold; *proposición* maintain; *presión* keep up, sustain; *resistencia* bolster up; ~ *que* hold that; ~**se** support o.s. *etc.*; (*perdurar*) last (out); ~ (*en pie*) stand up; **sostenido** *adj. a. su. m* ♪ sharp; **sostenimiento** *m* support; maintenance *etc.*

sota *f* jack, knave.

sotabanco *m* attic, garret.

sotana *f* cassock; F hiding.

sótano *m* basement; (*almacén*) cellar.

sotavento *m* lee(ward).
sotechado *m* shed.
soterrar [1k] bury; *fig.* hide away.
soto *m* thicket; copse; grove.
soviet *m* soviet; **soviético** soviet *attr.*
soya *f S.Am.* soy bean.
spleen [es'plin] *m* boredom, depression.
sprint [es'print] *m* sprint; **sprintar** [esprin'tar] [1a] sprint.
stand [es'tand] *m* stand.
stándard [es'tandar] *adj. a. su. m* standard.
store [es'tor] *m* sun blind.
su, sus (*un poseedor*) his, hers, its, one's; (*de Vd.*) your; (*varios poseedores*) their; (*de Vds.*) your.
suave (*blando*) soft; (*liso*) smooth; (*dulce, agradable*) sweet; *aire* soft, mild; *carácter* gentle; docile; *modales, movimiento, tacto, viento* gentle; *música, olor* sweet; *pasta* smooth; *ruido* soft; *sabor* smooth, mild; **suavidad** *f* softness *etc.*; **suavizador** *m* razor strop; **suavizar** [1f] soften; (*alisar*) smooth (out, down); *navaja* strop; *fig. dureza* ease, soften; temper; relax; *color* tone down; *p.* mollify, soften; *carácter* mellow.
sub... *mst* sub...; under...
subalimentado undernourished, underfed.
subalterno 1. subordinate; auxiliary; minor, inferior; **2.** *m* subordinate.
subarrendar [1k] sublet, sublease; **subarrendatario** *m*, **a** *f* subtenant.
subasta *f* auction sale, (sale by) auction; *poner en* (*or sacar a*) *pública* ~ sell by auction; **subastador** *m* auctioneer; **subastar** [1a] auction (off).
subcampeón *m* runner-up.
subcomisión *f* subcommittee.
subconsciencia *f* subconscious.
subconsciente subconscious.
subcontrato *m* subcontract.
subcutáneo subcutaneous.
subdesarrollado underdeveloped.
súbdito *adj. a. su. m*, **a** *f pol.* subject.
subdividir(se) [3a] subdivide; **subdivisión** *f* subdivision.
subestación *f* substation.
subestimación *f* underestimation; understatement; **subestimar** [1a] *capacidad, contrario* underestimate, underrate; *propiedad* undervalue; *proposición* understate.
subida *f* (*acto*) climb(ing) *etc.*; (*cuesta*) slope, hill; (*aumento*) rise, increase; promotion; **subido** *color* bright; *olor* strong; *precio* high, stiff; *calidad* superior; ~ *de color cara* florid, rosy; flushed *de vergüenza*; *cuento* dirty, rude.
subinquilino *m*, **a** *f* subtenant.
subir [3a] **1.** *v/t.* (*levantar*) raise, lift up; (*llevar*) take up; get up; *escalera* climb, go up; *montaña* climb; *p.* promote; *precio, sueldo* raise, put up; ✝ *artículo* put up the price of; ♪ raise the pitch of; **2.** *v/i.* go up, come up; move up; climb; (*aumentarse*) rise, increase; (*precio, río, temperatura*) rise; (*fiebre*) get worse; (*ser ascendido*) rise, move up; ~ *a* (*precio*) come to; ~ *a*, ~ *en vehículo* get into, get on; *caballo* mount; *árbol* climb; **3.** **~se** rise, go up; ~ *a*, ~ *en* get into *etc.*
súbito sudden; *de* ~ suddenly.
subjetivo subjective.
subjuntivo *m* subjunctive (mood).
sublevación *f* (up)rising; **sublevar** [1a] stir up a revolt among; **~se** rise, revolt.
sublimación *f* sublimation; **sublimado** *m* sublimate; **sublimar** [1a] exalt; *deseos etc.*, ⚗ sublimate; **sublime** sublime; high, lofty; noble, grand; *lo* ~ the sublime; **subliminal** subliminal.
submarinismo *m* scuba diving; skin diving; **submarinista** *m/f* scuba diver; **submarino 1.** underwater; **2.** *m* submarine.
subnormal retarded (mentally).
suboficial *m* noncommissioned officer.
subordinado *adj. a. su. m*, **a** *f* subordinate; **subordinar** [1a] subordinate.
subproducto *m* by-product.
subrayar [1a] underline (*a. fig.*); *lo subrayado es mío* my italics.
subrepticio surreptitious.
subsanar [1a] *falta* overlook; *error* put right; *pérdida* make up; *daño* repair.
subscr... *v. suscr...*
subsecretario *m* undersecretary.
subsidiarias *f/pl.* feeder industries; **subsidiario** *m* subsidiary.

subsidio *m* subsidy, grant; aid; (*de seguro social*) benefit; ~ *familiar* family allowance; ~ *de natalidad* maternity benefit; ~ *de paro* unemployment insurance; ~ *de vejez* old age pension.
subsiguiente subsequent.
subsistir [3a] (*vivir*) subsist, live; (*existir aún*) endure, last (out); (*ley etc.*) be still in force; (*edificio*) still stand.
subst... *v. sust...*
subsuelo *m* subsoil.
subteniente *m* second lieutenant.
subterfugio *m* subterfuge; way out, dodge.
subterráneo 1. underground, subterranean; **2.** *m* cavern; cellar; *S.Am.* underground.
subtítulo *m* subtitle, subhead(ing); caption.
suburbano suburban; **suburbio** *m* suburb; *b.s.* shantytown, outlying slum.
subvención *f* subsidy, grant; **subvencionar** [1a] subsidize, aid; **subvenir** [3s]: ~ *a gastos* meet, defray; *necesidades* provide for.
subversión *f* subversion; (*acto*) overthrow; **subversivo** subversive; **subverter** [3i] subvert; *orden* disturb; undermine.
subyacente underlying.
subyugar [1h] subdue, subjugate; overpower; *ánimos etc.* (come to) dominate.
succión *f* suction; **succionar** [1a] suck; apply suction to.
suceder [2a] (*ocurrir*) happen; (*seguir*) succeed, follow; (*heredar*) inherit; ~ *a p.* succeed; *puesto, trono* succeed to; *bienes* inherit; **~se** follow one another; **sucesión** *f* sucession (*a* to), sequence; (*hijos*) issue, offspring; **sucesivamente** successively; *y así* ~ and so on; **sucesivo** successive; consecutive; *en lo* ~ in the future; (*desde entonces*) thereafter; **suceso** *m* event, happening; incident; (*resultado*) outcome; **sucesor** *m*, **-a** *f* successor; (*heredero*) heir.
suciedad *f* dirt(iness) *etc.*; (*palabra*) dirty word, obscene remark.
sucinto succinct, concise.
sucio dirty, filthy; grimy, grubby, soiled; *fig.* dirty, obscene; *juego* foul; *color* blurred.
suculencia *f* succulence; **suculento** succulent; luscious, juicy; *plato* tasty.
sucumbir [3a] succumb (*a* to).
sucursal *f* branch (office); subsidiary.
sud *m* south; **sudamericano** *adj. a. su. m*, **a** *f* South American.
sudar [1a] sweat (*a.* F); **sudario** *m* shroud.
sudeste 1. *parte* southeast(ern); *dirección* southeasterly; *viento* southeast(erly); **2.** *m* southeast; **sudoeste** *v. suroeste.*
sudor *m* sweat (*a. fig.*); *con el* ~ *de su frente* by the sweat of one's brow; **sudoriento, sudo(ro)so** sweaty, sweating.
suecia *f* suede.
sueco 1. Swedish; **2.** *m*, **a** *f* Swede; F *hacerse el* ~ act dumb; **3.** *m* (*idioma*) Swedish.
suegra *f* mother-in-law; **suegro** *m* father-in-law.
suela *f* sole; sole leather; (*poner*) *media* ~ halfsole; F *de siete* ~*s* downright; *no llegarle a uno a la* ~ *del zapato* not be able to hold a candle to s.o.
sueldo *m* salary, pay; *a* ~ on a salary; *b.s.* (gangster) on a contract, hired (to kill).
suelo *m* (*tierra*) ground, soil, land; (*superficie de la tierra*) ground; (*piso*) floor; (*material de piso*) flooring; bottom *de vasija*; hoof *de caballo*; ~ *natal* native land; *caer al* ~ fall to the ground; *echarse por los* ~*s* grovel; F *estar por los* ~*s* be dirt-cheap.
suelto 1. (*no atado*) loose, free; (*libre*) free, at large; (*sin trabas*) unhampered; (*separado*) detached, unattached; (*no en serie*) odd, separate; *ejemplar, número* single; *fig.* (*ligero*) light, quick; (*hábil*) expert; (*libre, atrevido*) free, daring; *estilo* easy, fluent; *verso* blank; ~ *de lengua* (*parlanchín*) talkative; (*respondón*) cheeky; (*soplón*) blabbing; (*obsceno*) foul-mouthed; ~ *de vientre* loose; **2.** *m* ✝ small change; news item *en periódico*; *typ.* paragraph.
sueño *m* sleep; (*fantasía*) dream (*a. fig.*); *en(tre)* ~*s* in a dream; ~*s dorados* daydreams; ~ *hecho realidad* dream come true; *conciliar el* ~ (*p.*) get to

sleep; (*droga*) make *s.o.* sleep; *descabezar el* ~, *echar un* ~ have a nap; *tener* ~ be sleepy; *tener el* ~ *ligero* be a light sleeper.

suero *m* ⚕ serum; whey *de leche*.

suerte *f* (good) luck; fortune, chance; (*hado*) fate, destiny, lot; condition, state; (*género*) kind; *toros*: stage; (*de capa*) play with the cape; ~*s pl.* juggling; *buena* ~ (good) luck; *mala* ~ bad luck, hard luck; *de mala* ~ unlucky; *de* ~ *que* so that; (*en principio de frase*) (and) so; *por* ~ luckily; by chance; *caber en* ~ *a* fall to; *no me cupo tal* ~ no such luck; *echar* ~*s* draw lots; *la* ~ *está echada* the die is cast; *estar de* ~ be in luck; *probar* ~ try one's luck, have a go; *quiso la* ~ *que* as luck would have it; *tener* (*buena*) ~ be lucky; *¡que tengas* (*mucha*) ~*!* I wish you luck!; *trae mala* ~ *inf.* it's unlucky to *inf.*; *unirse a la* ~ *de* throw in one's lot with.

sueste *m* sou'wester.

suéter *m* jumper, sweater.

suficiencia *f* adequacy, fitness; (*aire de*) ~ self-importance; smugness, self-satisfaction; *darse aires de* ~ get on one's high horse; *una* ~ *de* enough; **suficiente** enough, sufficient; (*apto*) adequate, fit; *b.s.* smug, self-satisfied, superior.

sufijo *m* suffix.

sufragar [1h] *v/t.* aid, support; ✝ defray (the costs of); *v/i. S.Am.* vote; **sufragio** *m* (*derecho de votar*) suffrage, franchise; (*voto*) vote; ballot; (*ayuda*) aid; ~ *universal* universal suffrage.

sufrido 1. patient, long-suffering; *color, tela etc.* hard-wearing; *marido* complaisant; **2.** *m* F complaisant husband; **sufrimiento** *m* patience; tolerance; (*padecimiento*) suffering, misery; **sufrir** [3a] *v/t.* (*padecer*) suffer; *pérdida* suffer, sustain; (*experimentar*) undergo, experience; (*soportar*) bear, put up with; (*permitir*) suffer, permit; *v/i.* suffer.

sugerencia *f* suggestion; **sugerente** full of suggestions; **sugerir** [3i] suggest; hint; *pensamiento etc.* prompt; **sugestión** *f* suggestion; hint; prompting; stimulus; (*psychological*) autosuggestion, self-hypnotism; **sugestionar** [1a] hypnotize; *fig.* influence, dominate the will of; **sugestivo** attractive; (*que hace pensar*) stimulating, thought-provoking.

suicida 1. suicidal; **2.** *m/f* suicide (*p.*); **suicidarse** [1a] commit suicide; **suicidio** *m* suicide (*act*).

suizo[1] *adj. a. su. m,* **a** *f* Swiss.

suizo[2] *m* sugared bun.

sujeción *f* subjection; (*acto de fijar*) fastening *etc.*; **sujetador** *m* fastener; bra; clip *de pluma*; ~ *de libros* book end; **sujetapapeles** *m* paper clip; **sujetar** [1a] (*fijar etc.*) fasten, hold in place; (*agarrar*) lay hold of, seize; (*dominar*) subdue; keep down, keep under; ~**se** *a* subject o.s. to, submit to; **sujeto 1.**: ~ *a* subject to, liable to; **2.** *m gr.* subject; F fellow, character; F *mal* ~ bad lot.

sulfato *m* sulfate.

sulfurar [1a] ⚗ sulfurate; *fig.* annoy, rile; ~**se** blow up, see red; **sulfúreo** sulfur(e)ous; **sulfúrico** sulfuric; **sulfuro** *m* sulfide.

sultán *m* sultan; **sultana** *f* sultana.

suma *f* (*agregado*) sum, total; (*dinero*) sum; (*acto*) adding-up; (*resumen*) summary; substance, essence; ~ *y sigue* carried forward; ~ *global* lump sum; *en* ~ in short; **sumadora** *f* adding machine; **sumamente** extremely, highly; **sumar** [1a] add up, total; (*compendiar*) summarize; sum up; *suma y sigue* add and carry; ~**se** *a* join, become attached to; **sumario** *adj. a. su. m* summary (*a.* ⚖).

sumergir [3c] submerge; sink; dip, plunge, immerse; *fig.* plunge (*en* into); ~**se** submerge; sink *etc.*; **sumersión** *f* submersion, submergence; immersion; *fig.* absorption (*en* in).

sumidero *m* drain, sewer; overflow; sink; *esp.* ⊕ sump.

suminstrador *m,* **-a** *f* supplier; **suministrar** [1a] supply; **suministro** *m* supply; ~*s pl.* supplies; ~ *de combustible* fuel supply.

sumir [3a] sink; plunge, immerse; *fig.* plunge (*en* into); ~**se** sink.

sumisión *f* submission; (*cualidad*) submissiveness; **sumiso** submissive, obedient; unresisting; (*sin quejar*) uncomplaining.

sumo great, extreme; *sacerdote* high; *pontífice* supreme; *con* ~*a*

dificultad with the greatest difficulty; *a lo* ~ at (the) most.
suntuario sumptuary; **suntuoso** *mst* sumptuous; lavish, rich.
supeditar [1a] oppress, crush; (*avasallar*) subdue; *fig.* subordinate (*a* to).
super... super...; over...
superable surmountable; *obra* that can be done.
superabundante superabundant.
superar [1a] surpass *en cantidad*; excel *en calidad*; *dificultad* overcome, surmount; *expectativa* exceed; *límites* transcend; *marca* break, beat.
superávit *m* surplus.
supercarburante *m* high-test fuel.
superconsumo *m* overconsumption.
superchería *f* fraud, trick(ery); **superchero** fraudulent; bogus.
super...: ~directa *f mot.* overdrive; **~empleo** *m* overemployment; **~entender** [2g] supervise; **~estructura** *f* superstructure; **~ferolítico** F finicky.
superficial *medida* surface *attr.*; *fig. mst* superficial (*a.* ⚕); facile; perfunctory; *p. etc.* shallow; **superficie** *f* surface; area; outside; face; ~ *inferior* underside; *mot.* ~ *de rodadura* tread; ~ *de sustentación* ✈ airfoil.
superfino superfine.
superfluo superfluous.
super...: ~heterodino *m* superhet(erodyne); **~hombre** *m* superman; **~intendencia** *f* supervision; **~intendente** *m* superintendent, supervisor; overseer; ~ *de patio* 🚂 yardmaster.
superior 1. upper, higher; *fig.* superior, better; high, higher; first-rate; *clase social etc.* upper; *p.* chief, head...; master ...; ~ *a cifra* more than, larger than; *calidad* better than; *nivel etc.* above, higher than; **2.** *m* superior; *mis* ~*es* my superiors *en categoría*; *fig.* my betters; **superiora** *f* mother superior; **superioridad** *f* superiority.
superlativo *adj. a. su. m* superlative.
super...: ~mercado *m* supermarket; **~numerario** *adj. a. su. m*, **a** *f* supernumerary; **~poblado** *barrio etc.* overcrowded, congested; *región* overpopulated; **~poner** [2r] superimpose; **~producción** *f* overproduction; **~sónico** supersonic.
superstición *f* superstition; **supersticioso** superstitious.
supervisar [1a] supervise.
supervivencia *f* survival; **superviviente** *m/f* survivor.
suplantar [1a] supplant.
suplefaltas *m/f* F scapegoat.
suplemental supplemental; **suplementario** *mst* supplementary; *precio etc.* extra; *empleo* ~, *negocio* ~ sideline; *tren* ~ relief train, extra train; **suplemento** *m* supplement; 🚂 excess fare; ~ *dominical diario* Sunday supplement.
suplente 1. substitute, deputy, reserve; *maestro* supply *attr.*; **2.** *m/f* substitute, deputy; *thea. etc.* understudy; *deportes*: reserve.
supletorio supplementary.
súplica *f* supplication; ⚖ petition; ~*s pl.* pleading(s); **suplicante 1.** *tono etc.* imploring; **2.** *m/f* ⚖ *etc.* petitioner; applicant; **suplicar** [1g] *p.* plead with, implore; beg; *ayuda etc.* plead for, beg (for); ⚖ appeal, petition (*de* against).
suplicio *m* (*castigo*) punishment; (*tormento*) torture; (*dolor*) torment; *fig.* ordeal, anguish.
suplir [3a] *necesidad, omisión* supply; *falta* make good, make up for; supplement; *p. etc.* (*mst* ~ *a*) replace, take the place of; substitute for.
suponer [2r] *v/t.* suppose, assume; entail, imply *como consecuencia*; *supongo que sí* I suppose so; *Vd. puede* ~ *lo que pasó* you can guess what happened; *v/i.* be important; **suposición** *f* supposition, surmise; *fig.* authority; distinction; (*mentira*) imposture.
supremacía *f* supremacy; **supremo** supreme.
supresión *f* suppression *etc.*; **supresor** *m radio*: suppressor; **suprimir** [3a] *rebelión, crítica etc.* suppress; *costumbre, derecho* abolish; *dificultad, desechos* remove, eliminate; *restricciones* lift; *pasaje* delete, cut out.
supuesto 1. *p.p. of suponer*; **2.** *adj.* supposed, ostensible; (*sedicente*) self-styled; *nombre* assumed; ~ *que* since, inasmuch as; granted that; **3.** *m* assumption, hypothesis; *por* ~ of course; *dar por* ~ take *s.t.* for granted.

supurar [1a] discharge, run, suppurate 🕮.
sur 1. *parte* south(ern); *dirección* southerly; *viento* south(erly); **2.** *m* south.
surcar [1g] *tierra etc.* furrow, plow (through *etc.*); (*hacer rayas*) score, groove; *agua* cleave; **surco** *m* ⸙ *etc.* furrow; (*raya*) groove, line; groove *de disco*; (*arruga*) wrinkle; track *en agua*; F *echarse en el* ~ lie down on the job.
surgir [3c] arise, emerge, appear; (*líquido*) spout, spurt (up); spring up; loom up; (*dificultad etc.*) arise, crop up; (*p.*) appear unexpectedly; ⚓ anchor.
suroeste 1. *parte* southwest(ern); *dirección* southwesterly; *viento* southwest(erly); **2.** *m* southwest.
surrealismo *m* surrealism; **surrealista** *m/f* surrealist.
surtido 1. mixed, assorted; **2.** *m* (*gama*) range, selection, assortment; (*provisión*) stock, supply; *de* ~ stock; **surtidor** *m* fountain; (*chorro*) jet; ~ *de gasolina* gas(oline) pump; **surtir** [3a] *v/t.* supply, stock; *esp. fig.* provide; *efecto* have, produce; *bien surtido* well stocked (*de* with); *v/i.* spout, spurt; ⚓ anchor; **~se** *de* provide o.s. with.
susceptible susceptible; sensitive, touchy; impressionable; ~ *de mejora etc.* capable of, open to; *daño* liable to.
suscitar [1a] *rebelión etc.* stir up; provoke; *cuestión, duda etc.* raise.
suscribir [3a; *p.p. suscrito*] subscribe (*a* to); *opinión* subscribe to; (*firmar*) sign; **~se** subscribe (*a* to, for); **suscripción** *f* subscription; **suscriptor** *m*, **-a** *f* subscriber.
susodicho above(-mentioned).
suspender [2a] hang (up), suspend; *fig. mst* suspend; *candidato* fail; (*admirar*) astonish; **suspensión** *f* hanging (up), suspension (*a. mot.*); *fig. mst* suspension; ⚖ stay; ~ *de armas*, ~ *de hostilidades* cease-fire; **suspensivo:** *v. punto*; **suspenso 1.** suspended, hanging; *candidato* failed; *fig.* amazed; bewildered; **2.** *m univ. etc.* fail(ure); *en* ~ *negocio* in suspense, pending; ⚖ in abeyance; *quedar en* ~ stand over.
suspicacia *f* suspicion, mistrust; **suspicaz** suspicious, distrustful.
suspirado longed-for; **suspirar** [1a] sigh (*por* for); **suspiro** *m* sigh; *exhalar el último* ~ breathe one's last.
sustancia *f* substance; essence; *en* ~ in substance; **sustancial** substantial; important, vital; **sustancioso** substantial; *comida* nourishing; **sustantivo 1.** substantive; *gr.* substantival; **2.** *m* noun, substantive.
sustentación *f* lift; = **sustentamiento** *m* maintenance; sustenance; **sustentar** [1a] sustain; maintain; support; (*alimentar*) feed, nourish; *tesis* defend; **~se** sustain o.s.; subsist (*con* on); **sustento** *m* sustenance, food; maintenance; *fig.* (*vida que se gana*) livelihood; (*esencia vital*) lifeblood.
sustitución *f* substitution; replacement; **sustituir** [3g] *v/t.* substitute (*A por B* B for A), replace (*A por B* A by B, A with B); *v/i.* substitute; deputize; ~ *a* replace; deputize for; **sustituto** *m*, **a** *f* substitute; deputy; replacement.
susto *m* fright, scare; *¡ay qué ~!* what a fright you gave me!; *darse un* ~ have a fright.
sustracción *f* 𝔄 subtraction; deduction; **sustraer** [2p] 𝔄 subtract; deduct; (*robar*) steal; **~se** *a* withdraw from, contract out of; avoid.
sustrato *m* substratum.
susurrar [1a] whisper; *fig.* (*arroyo*) murmur; (*hojas*) rustle; (*viento*) whisper; *susurran que, se susurra que* it is whispered that; **~se** *fig.* be whispered about; **susurro** *m fig.* whisper; murmur; rustle.
sutil *tela etc.* thin, fine; tenuous; (*perspicaz*) keen, observant; *distinción etc.* subtle; **sutileza** *f* thinness *etc.*; subtlety; finesse; **sutilizar** [1f] *v/t.* thin down, fine down; *fig.* polish, perfect; refine (up)on; *b.s.* split hairs about; *v/i.* quibble.
sutura *f* suture; **suturar** [1a] suture.
suyo, suya 1. *pron. a. adj.* (*tras verbo ser*) (*un poseedor*) his, hers,

its, one's; (*de Vd.*) your; (*varios poseedores*) theirs; (*de Vds.*) yours; **2.** *adj.* (*tras su.*) of his *etc.*; de ~ naturally; intrinsically; per se; on its own; eso es *muy* ~ that's just like him; *salirse con la* ~*a* have one's way; carry one's point *en debate.*

svástica *f* swastika.

T

¡ta! careful!; easy there!
taba *f* anklebone; (*juego*) knuckle bones; F *menear las ~s* bustle about; F *tomar la ~* start speaking; show who is boss.
tabacal *m* tobacco field; **Tabacalera** *f Spanish state tobacco monopoly*; **tabacalero 1.** tobacco *attr.*; **2.** *m* tobacconist; **tabaco** *m* tobacco; (*puro*) cigar; (*cigarrillos*) cigarettes; ⚘ tobacco plant; *~ en polvo* snuff; *~ en rama* leaf tobacco; *~ rubio* Virginian tobacco; **tabacoso** *dedos* tobacco-stained.
tabalada *f* F punch; knock, bump *de caída*; **tabalear** [1a] *v/t.* shake, rock; *v/i.* drum (with one's fingers).
tábano *m* horsefly.
tabaquera *f* (*caja*) snuffbox; bowl *de pipa*; *S.Am.* pouch; **tabaquería** *f* tobacconist's (shop); **tabaquero** *m* tobacconist.
taberna *f* pub(lic house), bar.
tabernáculo *m* tabernacle.
tabernario *fig.* rude, dirty; **tabernero** *m* publican, landlord; (*empleado*) barman.
tabicar [1g] wall up, partition off; *fig.* cover up; **tabique** *m* partition (wall), thin wall.
tabla *f* (*madera*) plank, board; (*piedra*) slab; *paint.* panel; *anat.* flat (*or* wide) part; ✓ bed, patch; *sew.* broad pleat; ✝ meat stall; & *etc.* table; (*lista*) table, list; chart; index *de libro*; *~s pl. thea.* boards, stage; *fig.* theater; *~s pl. ajedrez etc.*: draw; *~ de dibujo* drawing board; *~ de lavar* washboard; *~ de materias* table of contents; *~ de multiplicar* multiplication table; *~ de planchar* ironing board; *~ de salvación* last resort; lifesaver; *escapar en una ~* have a narrow escape; *hacer ~ rasa de* make a clean sweep of; *quedar ~s fig.* be deadlocked; **tablado** *m* plank floor, platform, stand; *thea. etc.* stage; (*cadalso*) scaffold; **tablaje** *m*, **tablazón** *f* planks, planking, boards; **tablear** [1a] cut into boards; ✓ divide into beds; *sew.* pleat; **tablero** *m* boards, planks; *ajedrez etc.*: board; (*encerado*) blackboard; counter *de tienda*; ⚡ switchboard; *~ (de instrumentos)* instrument panel, *mot.* dashboard; ✓ beds, plots; (*juego*) gambling den; *~ de ajedrez* chessboard; *~ de dibujo* drawing board; *poner al ~* risk; **tableta** *f* small board; (*taco*) tablet; bar *de chocolate*; **tabletear** [1a] rattle; **tablilla** *f* small board; ⚕ splint; **tablón** *m* plank, beam; *~ de anuncios* notice board.
tabú *m* taboo.
tabuco *m* slum, wretched little place.
tabular [1a] tabulate.
taburete *m* stool, footstool.
tacañería *f* meanness; **tacaño** mean, stingy, close-fisted.
tácito tacit; *observación etc.* unspoken; *ley* unwritten; **taciturno** taciturn; (*triste*) moody, sulky, glum.
taco *m* plug, bung, stopper; (*empaquetadura*) wad(ding); *billar*: cue; ⚔ rammer; (*juguete*) popgun; *S.Am.* heel; *~ (de papel)* writing pad; F (*bocadillo*) snack; F swig, mouthful *de vino*; F (*palabra*) oath, curse; *S.Am.* heel; *S.Am.* muddle, mess; F *soltar un ~* swear.
tacón *m* heel; **taconear** [1a] click one's heels *al saludar etc.*; stamp with one's heels.
táctica *f* tactics; *fig.* move; way (of doing things); gambit; **táctico 1.** tactical; **2.** *m* tactician.
táctil tactile; **tacto** *m* (*sentido*) (sense of) touch; touch *de mecanógrafa etc.*; (*acto*) touch(ing), feel; *fig.* tact; *ser áspero etc. al ~* feel rough *etc.*
tacha[1] *f* ⊕ large tack, stud.
tacha[2] *f* flaw, blemish, defect; *sin ~* flawless; *poner ~ a* find fault with; **tachar** [1a] cross out; *fig.* fault, criticize, attack; *~ de* accuse of being.
tachines *m/pl. sl.* feet.
tachón[1] *m* stroke, crossing-out.
tachón[2] *m* ⊕ stud, boss; *sew.* trim-

ming; **tachonar** [1a] ⊕ stud (*a. fig.*).
tachoso defective, faulty.
tachuela *f* (tin)tack.
tafetán *m* taffeta; ~*es pl. fig.* flags; F buttons and bows; ~ *adhesivo*, ~ *inglés* court plaster.
tafilete *m* morocco leather.
tahona *f* bakery, bakehouse.
tahur *m* gambler; *b.s.* card sharper, cheat.
taifa *f* F gang of thieves; *hist.* band, faction.
taimado sly, crafty.
taja *f* cut; division; **tajada** *f* slice, cut *de carne etc.*; *S.Am.* cut, slash; F (*ronquera*) hoarseness; F (*borrachera*) drunk; F ✝ rake-off; F *sacar* ~ look after number one; get something out of it; ✝ get a rake-off; **tajadera** *f* chopper; ⊕ cold chisel; **tajadero** *m* chopping block; **tajado** *peña* sheer; **tajamar** *m* stem, cutwater; *S.Am.* dike, dam; **tajante** cutting, sharp; *fig.* incisive, sharp; **tajar** [1a] *carne etc.* slice, cut; chop; hew; **tajo** *m* (*corte*) cut; slash *con espada*; (*filo*) cutting edge; *geog.* sheer cliff; (*tajadero*) chopping block; block *de verdugo*; (*tarea*) job; *tirar* ~*s* slash (*a* at).
tal 1. *adj.* such (a); (*con su. abstracto*) such; ~*es pl.* such; *el* ~ *Pérez* this Pérez, that fellow Pérez; *un* ~ *Pérez* a man °called Pérez, one Pérez; **2.** *pron.* (*p.*) such a one, someone; (*cosa*) such a thing, something; F *en la calle de* ~ in such-and-such a street; *el* ~ this man *etc.* (we're talking about); such a person; ~ *como* such as; *como* ~ as such; ~ *cual libro* an odd book, one or two books; ~ *o cual* such-and-such; ~ *para cual* two of a kind; *sí* ~ yes indeed; *y* ~ and such; ~ *hay que* there are those who; *no hay* ~ nothing of the sort; *no hay* ~ *como inf.* there's nothing like *ger.*; **3.** *adv.* so, in such a way; ~ *como* just as; ~ *cual* (*adv.*) just as it is; *era* ~ *cual deseaba* it was just what he wanted; (*como adj.*) middling, so-so; *¿qué* ~? how goes it?, how's things?; *¿qué* ~ *el libro?* what do you think of the book?; *¿qué* ~ *te gustó?* how did you like it?; **4.** *cj.*: *con* ~ *que* provided (that).
talabartería *f* saddlery; **talabartero** *m* saddler.
taladradora *f* drill; ~ *de fuerza* power drill; **taladrar** [1a] bore, drill, punch, pierce; *que taladra los oídos* earsplitting; **taladro** *m* drill; gimlet; bore(r); auger; (*agujero*) drill hole.
tálamo *m* marriage bed.
talante *m* (*semblante*) look; (*ánimo*) frame of mind; (*deseo*) will, pleasure; (*modo de hacer*) method, way; *de buen* (*mal*) ~ *estar* in a good (bad) mood; *hacer* with a good (bad) grace.
talar [1a] *árbol* fell, cut down; ⚠ *etc.* pull down; *fig.* devastate.
talco *m* tinsel; talc; ~ *en polvo* talcum powder.
talcualillo F so-so, middling (*a.* ⚕).
talega *f* bag, sack; diaper *de niño*; ~*s pl.* money, wealth; **talego** *m* long sack, poke; F (*p.*) ragbag; F *tener* ~ have money tucked away.
talento *m* talent (*a. hist.*); gift; (*inteligencia*) brains, ability; ~*s pl.* talents; accomplishments; **talentoso** talented, gifted.
talismán *m* talisman.
talmente in such a way, so.
talón *m anat.* heel; stub, counterfoil *de cheque etc.*; 🚂 receipt for luggage; **talonar** [1a] heel; **talonario** *m* (*a. libro* ~) book of tickets; receipt book; check book; **talonear** [1a] hurry along.
talud *m* slope, bank; *geol.* talus.
talla *f* (*escultura*) carving; (*grabado*) engraving; height, stature *de p.*; size *de traje etc.*; rod, scale *para medir*; ⚖ reward; *diamante* cut, polish; *obra de* ~ carving; *poner a* ~ offer a reward for; *tener poca* ~ be on the short side;
tallado 1. carved *etc.*; *bien* ~ shapely, well-formed; *diamante* cut, polished; **2.** *m* carving *etc.*; **tallar** [1a] *v/t.* carve; shape, work; (*grabar*) engrave; *diamante* cut; *p.* measure; *fig.* value, appraise; *v/i. S.Am.* chat.
tallarín *m* noodle.
talle *m* (*cintura*) waist; (*cuerpo*) figure *esp. de mujer*; build, physique *esp. de hombre*; *fig.* outline; look, appearance.
taller *m* ⊕ workshop, shop; (*grande*) mill, factory; workroom *de sastre*; studio *de pintor*; ~*es pl. gráficos* printing works; ~ *agremiado* closed shop; ~ *franco* open shop; ~ *de máquinas* machine shop; ~ *de montaje* as-

sembly shop; ~ *penitenciario* workhouse; ~ *de reparaciones* repair shop.

tallo *m* ⚘ stem, stalk; blade *de hierba*; (*renuevo*) shoot.

talluda: F *es una ~ ya* she's no chicken; **talludo** ⚘ tall; *p.* lanky.

tamañito: *dejar ~* crush, make *s.o.* feel small; **tamaño 1.** (*grande*) so big, such a big; huge; (*pequeño*) so small *etc.*; *abrir ~ ojos* open one's eyes wide; *~ como* as big as; **2.** *m* size; capacity, volume; *de ~ extra(ordinario)* outsize; *de ~ natural* full-size, life-size; *¿de qué ~ es?* how big is it?

tamarindo *m* tamarind; **tamarisco** *m*, **tamariz** *m* tamarisk.

tambalear(se) [1a] (*p.*) stagger, reel, totter; (*cosa*) wobble; (*vehículo*) lurch, sway; *ir tambaleándose* lurch along *etc.*

también also, as well, too; beside(s); *¡~!* that as well?, not that too!; *yo ~* so am I, me too.

tambo *m S.Am.* inn.

tambor *m* ♪, ⊕ drum; *sew.*, ⚠ tambour; *anat.* eardrum; (*p.*) drummer; *a ~ batiente* drums beating; in triumph; *~ mayor* drum major; **tambora** *f* bass drum; **tamboril** *m* small drum; **tamborilada** *f* F, **tamborilazo** *m* F bump on one's bottom; (*espaldarazo*) slap on the shoulder; **tamborilear** [1a] drum *con dedos*; (*lluvia*) patter; **tamborileo** *m* drumming; patter; **tamborilero** *m* drummer.

tamiz *m* sieve; **tamizar** [1f] sift, sieve.

tamo *m* fluff; (*polvo*) dust (*a.* ✓).

tampoco neither, not ... either; nor; *ni éste ni aquél ~* neither this one nor that one; *yo ~ lo sé, yo no lo sé ~* I don't know either; *ni yo ~* nor I either.

tampón *m* plug (*a.* ✱), *~ (de entintar)* ink pad.

tan so; *~ bueno* so good; *coche ~ grande* such a big car; *~ ... como* as ... as; *~ es así que* so much so that; *un ~* such a.

tanda *f* shift, gang, relay *de ps.*; shift, turn, spell *en el trabajo*; turn *de riego etc.*; (*tarea*) job; (*capa*) layer, coat; (*partida*) game; (*lote*) batch; *S.Am. thea.* show; *S.Am.* bad habit.

tándem *m* tandem; ⚡ *en ~* tandem.

tanganillas: *en ~* unsteadily; **tanganillo** *m* prop, wedge.

tangencial tangential; **tangente** *f* tangent.

tangible tangible.

tango *m* tango.

tanque *m* tank (*a.* ⚔); **tanquero** *m S.Am.* ⚓ tanker.

tantán *m* tomtom; **tantarantán** *m* drumbeat, rub-a-dub; F punch.

tanteador *m* scoreboard; (*p.*) scorer; **tantear** [1a] *v/t.* (*examinar*) weigh up; (*ensayar*) feel, test; (*comparar*) measure, weigh; *intenciones*, *p.* sound out; *deportes*: keep the score of; *v/i. deportes*: score, keep (the) score; (*ir a tientas*) grope; *¡tantee Vd.!* *S.Am.* just imagine!, fancy that!; **tanteo** *m* weighing-up; calculation; trial, test(ing); trial and error; *deportes*: score; *al ~* by guesswork.

tanto 1. *adj.* so much; *~s pl.* so many; *~ como* as much as; *~s como* as many as; *20 y ~s* 20-odd; *a ~s de mayo* on such-and-such a day in May; *a las ~as* in the small hours; **2.** *adv.* so much; as much; *trabajar etc.* so hard; *permanecer etc.* so long; *él come ~ como yo* he eats as much as I do; *~ A como B* both A and B; *~ más* the more, all the more ... as; *~ más cuanto que* all the more (...) because; *~ mejor* all the better; *~ peor* so much the worse; *no es para ~* there's no need to make such a fuss; it's not as bad as all that; *~ que* so much so that; *en(tre) ~* meanwhile; F *¡ni ~ así!* not in the least little bit; *por (lo) ~* so, therefore; **3.** *cj.*: *con ~ que* provided (that); **4.** *m* ✝ *etc.* so much, a certain amount; (*ficha*) counter, chip; *deportes*: point, goal; *apuntar los ~s* keep score; *~ por ciento* percentage, rate; ✝ *al ~* at the same price; *algún ~*, *un ~* rather; *otro ~* as much again, the same thing again; *estar al ~ de* be in touch with, know about; *poner al ~ de* give *s.o.* the news about, put *s.o.* in the picture about.

tañer [2f] ♪ play; *campana* ring; **tañido** *m* sound *de instrumento*; ringing *de campana*; twang *de guitarra*; tinkle *al caer etc.*

tapa *f* lid; (*tapón*) top, cap; cover *de libro*; (*plato*) *approx.* dish of hors d'oeuvres, snack (taken with a drink); *~ de los sesos* brain box, brain pan, skull; *levantarse la ~ de los sesos* blow one's brains out.

tapabalazo *m S.Am.* fly *of trousers*.
tapa(a)gujeros *m* F jerry builder; *fig.* stopgap.
tapaboca *f*, **tapabocas** *m* slap; (*bufanda*) muffler.
tapacubos *m* hubcap.
tapadera *f* lid, cover, cap; **tapadero** *m* stopper; **tapadillo:** *de ~* secretly; **tapado** *m S.Am.* (woman's) coat.
tapagujeros *m* F bungling mason; F substitute, replacement.
tapar [1a] *vasija* put the lid on; *botella* put the cap on, stopper; *cara* cover up; muffle up; (*cegar etc.*) stop (up), block (up); *visión* obstruct, hide; *fig.* conceal; *defecto* cover up; *fugitivo* hide; *delincuente* cover up for; **~se** wrap (o.s.) up.
taparrabo *m* loincloth *de indio etc.*; swimming trunks.
taperujarse [1a] F cover up one's face.
tapete *m* rug; (table) runner; *~ verde* card table, gambling table; *estar sobre el ~* be under discussion.
tapia *f* (garden) wall; mud wall; **tapiar** [1b] wall in; *fig.* stop up.
tapicería *f* (*colgada*) tapestry, tapestries, hangings; upholstery *de mueble*; (*arte*) tapestry making; upholstery.
tapioca *f* tapioca.
tapiz *m* tapestry; carpet; **tapizar** [1f] *pared* hang with tapestries; *mueble* upholster; *suelo* carpet (*a. fig.*, *con*, *de* with).
tapón *m* stopper, cap *de botella*; (*corcho*) cork; ⊕ plug, bung; wad; ⚕ tampon; *~ de algodón* ⚕ swab; *~ de cubo mot.* hubcap; *~ de desagüe* drain plug; *~ de tráfico* traffic jam; **taponar** [1a] stopper, cork; *conducto* plug, stop up; ⚕ tampon; **taponazo** *m* pop.
tapujarse [1a] F muffle o.s. up; **tapujo** *m* muffler; F subterfuge; F *sin ~s* straight, no messing.
taquigrafía *f* shorthand, stenography; **taquígrafo** *m*, **a** *f* shorthand writer, stenographer.
taquilla *f* 🚂 booking office; *thea.* box office; (*carpeta*) file; **taquillero 1.** *éxito etc.* box office *attr.*; **2.** *m*, **a** *f* clerk.
taquimeca(nógrafa) *f* shorthand typist.
taquímetro *m* speedometer; *surv.* tachymeter.
tara *f* ✝ tare; (*palito*) tally stick.
tarabilla 1. *f* F chatter; **2.** *m/f* F (*hablador*) chatterbox; (*casquivano*) useless sort, dreamer; *soltar la ~* F talk a blue streak.
taracea *f* inlay, marquetry; **taracear** [1a] inlay.
tarado defective, damaged.
tarambana *adj. a. su. m/f* F harum-scarum; crackpot.
tarántula *f* tarantula.
tarar [1a] tare.
tararear [1a] hum.
tarasca *f hist.* (processional) dragon; F old bag; **tarascada** *f* bite; F tart reply, rude answer; **tarascar** [1g] bite, snap at.
tardanza *f* slowness; (*retraso*) delay; **tardar** [1a] take a long time, be long; delay; (*sin partir etc.*) linger (on); (*llegar tarde*) come late, be late; *~ en inf.* be slow to *inf.*, be long in *ger.*; be late in *ger.*; *~ mucho en inf.* take a long time to *inf.*; *~ dos horas en inf.* take two hours to *inf.*; *¿cuánto tardaremos en llegar?* how long shall we take to get there?; *a más ~* at the latest.
tarde 1. *adv.* late; (*demasiado*) too late; *de ~ en ~* from time to time; *~ o temprano* sooner or later; *más ~* later (on); *se hace ~* it is getting late; **2.** *f* (*de 12 a 5 o 6*) afternoon; (*de 5 o 6 al anochecer*) evening; *¡buenas ~s!* good afternoon, good evening; *de la ~ a la mañana* overnight; *fig.* in no time at all; **tardecer** [2d] get dark; **tardecita** *f* dusk.
tardío (*lento*) slow; (*que llega o madura tarde*) late; (*atrasado*) belated, overdue; **tardo** slow, sluggish; **tardón** F slow; (*lerdo*) dim.
tarea *f* job, task; duty, duties; (*cuidado*) worry; *~ de ocasión* chore; *~ suelta* odd job.
tarifa *f* tariff; rate, charge; price list *en café etc.*; (*pasaje*) fare; *~ recargada* extra fare; *~ turística* tourist class; **tarifar** [1a] price.
tarima *f* platform; (*soporte*) stand; (*asiento*) stool, bench; (*cama*) bunk.
tarja *f* tally; F swipe, slash; **tarjar** [1a] keep a tally of.
tarjeta *f* card; *~ de crédito* credit card; *~ de felicitación*, *~ de buen deseo*

greeting card; ~ *de identidad* identity card; ~ *navideña* Christmas card; ~ *perforada* punch card; ~ *postal* post card; ~ *de visita* visiting card.
tarraconense *adj. a. su. m/f* (native) of Tarragona.
tarro *m* pot, jar.
tarta *f* tart, cake.
tártago: F *darse un* ~ slog, sweat.
tartajear [1a] stammer; **tartajoso** stammering, tongue-tied; **tartalear** [1a] F stagger, reel; (*hablando*) get stuck for words; **tartamudear** [1a] stutter, stammer; **tartamudeo** *m* stutter(ing); **tartamudez** *f* stutter, speech defect; **tartamudo 1.** stuttering; **2.** *m*, **a** *f* stutterer.
tartán *m* Scotch plaid; tartan.
tártaro *m* ⚗ tartar; (*p.*) Tartar.
tarugo *m* wooden peg; (*tapón*) plug, stopper; ⚠ wooden paving block.
tarumba: F *volver* ~ daze, fog.
tasa *f* (fixed, official) price; rate; *fig.* estimate; (*acto*) valuation *etc.*; (*medida, norma*) measure, standard; *sin* ~ boundless, unstinted; **tasable** ratable; **tasación** *f* valuation; fixing *de precios*; *fig.* appraisal; **tasadamente** in moderation, sparingly; **tasador** *m* valuer; **tasar** [1a] *artículo* fix a price for, price (*en* at); *trabajo etc.* assess, rate (*en* at); *fig.* appraise; regulate; put a limit on, restrict.
tasca *f* F bar, pub; eating house; *b.s.* low dive.
tata *f* F maid; (*niñera*) nanny.
tatarabuelo *m* great-great-grandfather.
tatas: F *andar a* ~ (*niño*) toddle; (*a gatas*) get down on all fours.
¡tate! 1. *admiración*: goodness!, well well!; (*ya caigo*) oh I see; *cuidado*: look out!; **2.** *m sl.* drug addict, smoker of hashish.
tatuaje *m* tattoo; (*acto*) tattooing; **tatuar** [1d] tattoo.
taumaturgo *m* miracle worker.
taurino bullfighting *attr.*; *zo.* bull *attr.*; **Tauro** *m ast.* Taurus; **taurófilo** *m*, **a** *f* bullfight fan; **tauromaquia** *f* (art of) bullfighting; **tauromáquico** bullfighting *attr.*
tautología *f* tautology.
taxativo limiting, restricting.
taxi *m* taxi(cab).
taxidermista *m/f* taxidermist.
taxímetro *m* taximeter, clock F;
taxista *m* taxi driver.
taz: *S.Am.* ~ *con* ~ side by side; equal, even.
taza *f* cup; basin *de fuente*.
tazarse [1f] fray.
tazón *m* large cup, bowl; *prov.* wash-basin.
te (*acc.*) you; (*dat.*) (to) you; (*reflexivo*) (to) yourself; (†, *a Dios*) thee, (to) thee, (to) thyself.
té *m* tea.
tea *f* torch.
teatral of the theater, theatrical; *fig.* dramatic; *esp. b.s.* histrionic, stagey; **teatralidad** *f* drama, sense of theater; showmanship; **teatro** *m* theater (*a.* ⚔); scene *de acontecimiento*; (*profesión*) the theater, the stage; (*obras*) dramatic works; ~ *de estreno* first-run house; ~ *de la ópera* opera house; ~ *de repertorio* stock company; *dar* ~ *a* ballyhoo.
tebeo *m* children's comic.
teca *f* teak.
tecla *f* key; ~ *de cambio* shift key; ~ *de escape* margin release; ~ *de espacios* space bar; ~ *de retroceso* backspacer; F *dar en la* ~ get the hang of a thing; fall into a habit; **teclado** *m* keyboard; manual *de órgano*; **teclear** [1a] *v/t.* F *asunto* approach from various angles; *v/i.* strum, thrum; F drum *con dedos*; **tecleo** *m* fingering *etc.*; touch, fingerwork.
técnica *f* technique; **tecnicidad** *f* technicality; **tecnicismo** *m* technicality, technical term; **técnico 1.** technical; **2.** *m* technician; expert, specialist; **tecnicolor** *m* technicolor; **tecnología** *f* technology; **tecnológico** technological; **tecnólogo** *m* technologist.
tecomate *m S.Am.* gourd.
techado *m* roof; *bajo* ~ indoors, under cover; **techar** [1a] roof (in, over); **techo** *m*, **techumbre** *f* roof; ceiling *de habitación* (*a.* ✈).
tedio *m* boredom; tedium.
teja *f* tile, roofing tile; shovel hat; yew tree; linden tree; ~ *de madera* shingle; *a toca* ~ on the nail, in hard cash; *de* ~*s abajo* in the natural way of things; *de* ~*s arriba* with God's help; up aloft; supernatural; as far as the supernatural is concerned; **tejadillo** *m* top, cover; **tejado** *m* (tiled)

roof; *fig.* housetop; **tejar** [1a] tile.
tejedor *m*, **-a** *f* weaver; **tejedura** *f* weaving; (*textura*) weave, texture; **tejeduría** *f* weaving; (*fábrica*) textile mill; **tejer** [2a] weave (*a. fig.*); *S.Am.* knit; *fig.* scheme; ~ *y destejer* blow hot and cold; **tejido** *m* fabric, material; tissue (*a. anat.*); web; (*textura*) weave, texture; **~s** *pl.* textiles.
tejo *m* ♣ yew; (*aro*) quoit.
tejoleta *f* bit of tile, sherd; brickbat.
tejón *m* badger.
tela *f* cloth, fabric, material; web *de araña etc.*; (*nata*) skin, film; skin *de fruta*; *sl.* dough; *fig.* subject, matter; ~ *de araña* spider's web; **~s** *pl. del corazón* heartstrings; ~ *cruzada* twill; ~ *metálica* wire fencing, chicken wire; ~ *de punto* stockinet; *hay ~ que cortar* (*or para rato*) it's an awkward business, it's a long job; *poner en ~ de juicio* (call in) question; test, look closely at.
telar *m* loom; *thea.* gridiron.
telaraña *f* spider's web, cobweb.
tele...: **~comando** *m*, **~control** *m* remote control; **~diario** *m* daytime television news; **~fonear** [1a] telephone; **~fonema** *m* telephone message; **~fónico** telephonic; telephone *attr.*; **~fonista** *m/f* (telephone) operator, telephonist; **teléfono** *m* telephone; ~ *automático* dial telephone; ~ *público* pay station; *llamar al* (*or por*) ~ telephone, ring (up).
tele...: **~fotografía** *f* telephoto; **~grafía** *f* telegraphy; **~grafiar** [1c] telegraph; **~gráfico** telegraphic; telegraph *attr.*; **~grafista** *m/f* telegraphist; **telégrafo** *m* telegraph; **~s** *m* F telegram boy; **telegrama** *m* telegram; **teleimpresor** *m* teleprinter; **teleloca** *f* television; **telémetro** *m* range finder.
tele...: **~patía** *f* telepathy; **~pático** telepathic; **~scopar(se)** [1a] telescope; **~scópico** telescopic; **~scopio** *m* telescope; **~spectador** *m*, **-a** *f* (tele)viewer; **~squí** *m* ski lift; **~tipo** *m* teletype; **~visar** [1a] televise; **~visión** *f* television; ~ *por cable* cable television; ~ *en circuito cerrado* closed-circuit television; ~ *en colores* color television; *aparato de* ~ = **~visor** *m* television set.
telón *m* curtain; *pol.* ~ *de acero* iron curtain; ~ *de boca* front curtain; drop (curtain); ~ *de fondo*, ~ *de foro* backcloth, backdrop; ~ *de seguridad* safety curtain.
tema[1] *m* theme (*a.* ♪); subject (*a. paint.*), topic; motif; *gr.* stem.
tema[2] *f* fixed idea, mania; *a* ~ in emulation; *tener* ~ be stubborn; *tener* ~ *a* have a grudge against.
temblar [1k] tremble (*ante* at, *de* at, with); shake, quiver, shiver; (*tambalearse*) totter, sway; ~ *de frío* shiver with cold; ~ *por su vida* fear for one's life; **temblequear** [1a] F be all of a quiver; **temblón** 1. trembling; *álamo* ~ = 2. *m* aspen; **temblor** *m* tremble, trembling *etc.*; tremor; shiver(ing) *esp. de frío*; ~ *de tierra* earthquake; **tembloroso** trembling.
temer [2a] *v/t.* be afraid of, fear; dread; *v/i.* be afraid; ~ *por* fear for; ~ *inf.*; fear to *inf.*; ~ *que* fear that; be afraid that; *no temas* don't be afraid.
temerario *p.*, *acto* rash, reckless; *juicio* hasty; unfounded; **temeridad** *f* rashness *etc.*, temerity.
temeroso timid; = **temible** dreadful, frightful; *adversario etc.* redoubtable; **temor** *m* fear, dread; (*recelo*) misgiving; *sin ~ a* fearless of.
témpano *m*: ~ (*de hielo*) ice floe; (*grande*) iceberg.
temperamento *m* temperament, nature; *fig.* compromise; **temperancia** *f* temperance; **temperante** *S.Am.* 1. teetotal; 2. *m/f* teetotaler; **temperar** [1a] *v/t.* temper, moderate; *pasión etc.* calm; *v/i. S.Am.* go on holiday; **temperatura** *f* temperature; **temperie** *f* (state of the) weather.
tempestad *f* storm (*a. fig.*); ~ *de arena* sandstorm; ~ *de risas* gales of laughter; ~ *en un vaso de agua* tempest in a teapot; **tempestuoso** stormy (*a. fig.*), rough.
templado moderate, restrained; *agua* tepid; *clima* mild, temperate; ♪ in tune; **templanza** *f* temperance; mildness; **templar** [1a] temper, moderate; (*suavizar*) soften; *temperatura* cool; *solución* dilute; *metal* temper; *colores* blend; ♪ tune (up); **~se** (*p.*) control o.s.; (*tiempo*) moderate; **temple** *m* temper(ing)

de metal; ♪ tuning; *meteor.* (state of the) weather; temperature; *fig.* disposition; spirit, mettle; *pintar al ~, pintura al ~* distemper.

templete *m* bandstand.

templo *m* temple; (*cristiano*) church, chapel.

temporada *f* time, period; spell (*a. meteor.*); (*social, deportiva etc.*) season; *~ alta* midseason; *de ~* temporarily; vacationing; *en plena ~* at the height of the season; **temporal** **1.** *eccl. etc.* temporal; (*provisional*) temporary; **2.** *m* storm; **temporáneo** temporary; **témporas** *f/pl.* ember days; **temporero** temporary; **temporizar** [1f] temporize; **tempranal** ⚘ *etc.*, **tempranero, temprano** early.

tenacidad *f* toughness *etc.*

tenacillas *f/pl.* tongs *para azúcar etc.*; curling tongs *para pelo*; ⚕ *etc.* tweezers, forceps; (*despabiladeras*) snuffers.

tenaz tough, resistant; (*pegajoso*) that sticks fast; *creencia, resistencia* stubborn; *p.* tenacious, persevering.

tenazas *f/pl.* ⊕ (*unas* a pair of) pliers, pincers; tongs *para carbón*.

tenazón: *a ~, de ~* without taking aim; offhand.

tenca *f* tench.

tendajo *m* small shop.

tendal *m* awning.

tendalera *f* F mess, litter.

tendejón *m* small shop.

tendencia *f* tendency, trend; inclination; tenor *de observación etc.*; ✝ trend, run *de mercado*; *con ~ a* tending to(wards).

tendencioso tendentious.

ténder *m* 🚂 tender.

tender [2g] **1.** *v/t.* stretch; spread (out), lay out; *paint.*, ⚠ put on; *arco* draw; *cable, vía* lay; *ferrocarril, puente* build; *mano* stretch out; *ropa* hang out; *trampa* set (*a* for); **2.** *v/i.*: *~ a su.* tend to, tend towards, incline to; *~ a inf.* tend to *inf.*; **3.** *~se* lie down, stretch (o.s.) out; (*caballo*) run at a full gallop; *naipes*: lay down; F let things go to pot.

tendero 1. *m*, **a** *f* shopkeeper, storekeeper; grocer; **2.** *m* tentmaker.

tendido 1. lying (down), flat; **2.** *m* laying *de cable etc.*; (*ropa*) washing; (*yeso*) coat of plaster; *toros*: front row.

tendón *m* tendon, sinew.

tendré *etc. v. tener.*

tenducho *m* poky little shop.

tenebroso dark; gloomy, dismal; *asunto* sinister, dark; *negocio* shady; *estilo* obscure.

tenedor *m* fork; (*p.*) holder, bearer; *~ de acciones* stockholder; *~ de bonos* bondholder; *~ de libros* bookkeeper; *~ de obligaciones* bondholder; **teneduría** *f*: *~ de libros* bookkeeping.

tenencia *f* tenure *de oficio etc.*; possession *de propiedad*.

tener [2l] have; have got; (*tener en la mano, asir etc.*) hold; (*retener*) keep; (*contener*) hold, contain; *¿qué tienes?* what's the matter with you?; *~ 9 años* be 9 (years old); *¿cuántos años tienes?* how old are you?; *~ 3 metros de ancho* be 3 meters wide; *eso me tiene sin cuidado* I'm not bothered (about that); *~ puesto el sombrero* have (got) one's hat on; F *no ~las todas consigo* have the wind up; *¡ten!, ¡tenga!* here you are!; (*al lanzar*) catch!; *~ a bien inf.* think it proper to *inf.*; *~ a menos inf.* think it beneath o.s. to *inf.*; *~ en más* think all the more of; *~ en menos* think the less of; *~ en mucho* value, esteem; *v. poco*; *~ para sí que* think that; *~ por* consider as; *le tengo por listo* I think him pretty clever; *~ que inf.* have to *inf.*, must *inf.*; *~ trabajo que hacer* have work to do; *~se* hold (fast); stand firm; catch o.s. *al caer*; (*detenerse*) stop; *¡tente!* hold it!, wait a moment!; *~ a* stick to; *~ con* stand up to; *~ en pie* stand up; *~ por* think o.s.

tenería *f* tannery.

tengo *etc. v. tener.*

tenia *f* tapeworm.

teniente *m* lieutenant; *~ coronel* lieutenant colonel; *~ general* lieutenant general; *~ de navío* ⚓ lieutenant.

tenis *m* tennis; *~ de mesa* table tennis; **tenista** *m/f* tennis player.

tenor[1] *m* ♪ tenor.

tenor[2] *m* state; (*sentido*) tenor, purport; *a este ~* like this; *a ~ de* on the lines of.

tenorio *m* lady-killer.

tensar [1a] tauten; tense; **tensión** *f*

tension; stress, strain; rigidity; *alta* ~ high tension; *de alta* ~ high-tension; ~ *arterial*, ~ *sanguínea* blood pressure; ⚕ ~ *excesiva*, ~ *nerviosa* (over)strain; ~ *superficial* surface tension; **tenso** tense, taut; **tensor** *m* ⊕ guy; *anat.* tensor.

tentación *f* temptation.

tentáculo *m* tentacle, feeler.

tentador 1. tempting; **2.** *m* tempter; **tentadora** *f* temptress; **tentar** [1k] (*palpar*) touch, feel; ⚕ probe; *camino* feel; (*intentar*) try, attempt; (*emprender*) undertake; (*seducir*) tempt; lure, entice; **tentativa** *f* try, attempt; effort; ~ *de asesinato* attempted murder; **tentativo** tentative.

tentempié *m* F snack, bite.

tenue (*delgado*) thin, slender; *hilo* fine; *esp. fig.* tenuous, slight; *aire*, *olor* thin; *línea*, *ruido* faint; *asunto* trifling; **tenuidad** *f* thinness *etc.*

teñir [3h *a.* 3l] *mst* dye (*de negro* black); color; stain, tinge.

teocracia *f* theocracy.

teodolito *m* theodolite.

teología *f* theology; *no meterse en* ~*s* keep out of deep water; **teólogo** *m* theologian.

teorema *m* theorem; **teoría** *f* theory; ~ *atómica* atomic theory; ~ *cuántica*, ~ *de los cuanta* quantum theory; **teórico 1.** theoretic(al); **2.** *m* = **teorizante** *m* theorist; **teorizar** [1f] theorize.

tepe *m* turf, sod.

tequila *f S.Am.* brandy.

terapeuta *m/f* therap(eut)ist; **terapéutica** *f* therapeutics; = **terapia** *f* therapy; ~ *laboral* occupational therapy.

tercera *f* ♪ third; **tercería** *f* mediation; *b.s.* procuring; **tercermundista** Third World; **tercermundo** *m* Third World; **tercero 1.** *adj. a. su. m* ⩓ third; **2.** *m*, **a** *f* go-between; (*árbitro*) mediator; ⚖ third person (*or* party); *b.s.* procurer, pimp; **terceto** *m* ♪ trio; *poet.* tercet; ~*s pl.* terza rima; **terciado** *azúcar* brown; **terciar** [1b] *v/t.* slope, slant; ⩓ divide into three; *v/i.* fill in, stand in; ~ *en* take part in, join in; (*como árbitro*) mediate in; **tercio** *m* third; ⚔ *hist.* regiment; *hacer buen* ~ *a* do (*s.o.*) a good turn.

terciopelo *m* velvet.

terco obstinate, stubborn.

terebrante *dolor* piercing.

tergiversación *f* distortion *etc.*; **tergiversar** [1a] *v/t.* distort, misrepresent; *v/i.* prevaricate; be undecided, blow hot and cold.

terliz *m* tick(ing).

termal thermal; **termas** *f/pl.* hot springs, hot baths; **térmico** thermic.

terminación *f* ending (*a. gr.*), conclusion; **terminacho** *m*, **terminajo** *m* F (*grosero*) rude word, coarse expression; (*feo, bárbaro*) ugly word; (*mal usado*) malapropism, howler; **terminal** *adj. a. su. m* (⚡), *f* (*puerto*) terminal; **terminante** final, definitive; (*claro*) conclusive; *negativa* flat; *prohibición* strict; **terminar** [1a] end, finish; ~ *de inf.* stop *ger.*; finish *ger.*; ~ *en* end in (*a. fig.*); ~ *por inf.* end (up) by *ger.*; ~**se** come to an end, draw to a close, stop; ~ *hacia* lead to; **término** *m* end, finish; (*mojón*) boundary, limit; 🚂 *etc.* terminus; (*plazo*) period, time; outlying part *de ciudad*; (*palabra*, *phls.*, ⩓) term; (*arbitrio*) compromise solution; *medio* ~ subterfuge, evasion; *primer* ~ foreground; *segundo* ~ middle distance; *último* ~ background; *en último* ~ *fig.* in the last analysis; ~ *medio* compromise, middle way; (*promedio*) average; *de* ~ *medio* average; *por* ~ *medio* on the average; ~ *municipal* township; *en* ~*s de* in terms of; *en otros* ~*s* in other words; *poner* ~ *a* put an end to; **terminología** *f* terminology.

termita *m* termite.

termodinámica *f* thermodynamics; **termómetro** *m* thermometer; **termonuclear** thermonuclear; **termopila** *f* thermopile; **termos** *m* vacuum (*or* thermos) flask; hot-water heater; ~ *de acumulación* ⚡ off-peak heater; **termóstato** *m* thermostat.

terne 1. big, tough; *b.s.* bullying; **2.** *m* bully.

ternera *f* (heifer) calf; (*carne*) veal; **ternero** *m* (bull) calf.

terneza *f* tenderness; ~*s pl.* sweet nothings, nice things.

ternilla *f* gristle; **ternilloso** gristly.

terno *m* set of three, trio; (*traje*) three-piece suit; F swearword.
ternura *f* tenderness; (*palabra*) endearment.
terquedad *f* obstinacy.
terrado *m* = *terraza*.
terraja *f* ⊕ die stock.
terranova *m* Newfoundland (dog).
terraplén *m* 🚂 *etc.* embankment; ✐ terrace; mound; ⚔ rampart, earthwork; **terraplenar** [1a] terrace; *hoyo* fill in; (*levantar*) bank up.
terrateniente *m/f* landowner.
terraza *f* terrace; (*tejado*) flat roof; balcony *de piso*; ✐ flower bed, border.
terrazgo *m* field, plot; (*pago*) rent.
terremoto *m* earthquake.
terrenal = **terreno 1.** earthly, wordly; **2.** *m geol. etc.* (*superficie*) terrain; (*naturaleza del suelo*) soil, land; (*extensión*) piece of ground, grounds; ✐ plot, patch, field; *deportes*: pitch, ground; *fig.* field, sphere; ~ *echadizo* refuse dump; ~ *de pasto* run, pasture; *sobre el* ~ *fig.* on the spot; *ceder* ~ give ground; *ganar* ~ gain ground; *preparar el* ~ *fig.* pave the way (*a* for).
térreo earthen; (*parecido a tierra*) earthy; **terrero 1.** earthly; earthen; *fig.* humble; **2.** *m* pile, heap; **terrestre** terrestrial, land *attr.*; *vía etc.* overland.
terrible terrible, dreadful; **terrífico** terrifying.
territorial territorial; **territorio** *m* territory.
terrón *m* clod; lump (*a. azúcar*); ✐ patch.
terror *m* terror, dread; **terrorífico** terrifying; **terrorismo** *m* terrorism; **terrorista** *m* terrorist.
terroso earthy; (*sucio*) dirty.
terruño *m* clod, lump; (*espacio*) piece of ground; *fig.* native soil.
terso (*liso*) smooth; (*y brillante*) glossy; (*brillante*) shining, bright; *estilo* smooth, flowing; **tersura** *f* smoothness *etc.*
tertulia *f* (*reunión*) social gathering, get-together F; (*grupo*) party, group, circle; set *de café etc.*; *estar de* ~, *hacer* ~ get together (and talk); **tertuliano** *m*, **a** *f* member of a social gathering *etc.*; regular member; partygoer.
terylene *m* terylene.
tesar [1k] tense; ⚓ tauten.
tesis *f* thesis.
teso tense, taut.
tesón *m* insistence; tenacity, firmness *en resistir*; **tesonero** *S.Am.* obstinate, stubborn, tenacious.
tesorería *f* treasury; (*oficio*) treasurership; **tesorero** *m*, **a** *f* treasurer; **tesoro** *m* treasure; hoard; (*edificio, ministerio*) treasury; (*diccionario*) thesaurus; ≈ *público* Exchequer, Treasury.
test *m* test.
testa *f* head; (*frente, cara*) front; F brains; ~ *coronada* crowned head.
testador *m* testator; **testadora** *f* testatrix.
testaferro *m* man of straw; figurehead; 🃏 dummy.
testamentario 1. testamentary; **2.** *m* executor; **3. a** *f* executrix; **testamento** *m* will, testament; *Antiguo, Viejo* (*Nuevo*) ≈ Old (New) Testament; **testar** [1a] make a will.
testarada *f* butt with the head; F pig-headedness; **testarudez** *f* stubbornness; **testarudo** stubborn, pigheaded F; **testera** *f* front, face; forehead *de animal*.
testículo *m* testicle.
testificar [1g] give evidence, testify; *fig.* attest; **testigo** *m/f* witness; ~ *de cargo* witness for the prosecution; ~ *de descargo* witness for the defense; ~ *ocular*, ~ *presencial*, ~ *de vista* eyewitness; **testimoniar** [1b] testify to, bear witness to; **testimonio** *m* testimony, evidence; *dar* ~ give evidence; *dar* ~ *de* testify to, give evidence of.
teta *f* breast; (*pezón*) teat.
tétano *m* tetanus.
tetera *f* teapot; tea urn; teakettle.
tetilla *f* nipple; teat *de biberón*.
tétrico gloomy; sullen, sad; *luz* dim, dismal.
teutónico Teutonic.
textil 1. textile; **2.** ~*es m/pl.* textiles.
texto *m* text; *fuera de* ~ full-page; **textual** textual.
textura *f* texture (*a. fig.*).
tez *f* complexion, skin.
ti you; (†, *a Dios*) thee.
tía *f* aunt; ~ *abuela* grandaunt; F (*grosera*) coarse woman; (*vieja*) old bag; (*puta*) whore; (*chica*) dame, bird; ~ *abuela* great-aunt; F *¡no hay tu*

~! nothing doing!; F ¡*cuéntaselo a tu* ~! tell that to the Marines!
tiberio *m* F set-to.
tibia *f* tibia.
tibieza *f* lukewarmness *etc.*; **tibio** lukewarm, tepid, cool (*a. fig.*).
tiburón *m* shark.
tic *m* tic.
tictac *m* tick(tock); *hacer* ~ (*reloj*) tick; (*corazón*) go pit-a-pat.
tiempo *m* time; *meteor.* weather; *gr.* tense; ♪ (*parte*) movement; ♪ (*compás*) time, tempo; *deportes*: half; *los buenos* ~*s* the good old days; *en mis buenos* ~*s* in my prime; ~ *libre* spare time, leisure; *deportes*: *primer* ~ first half; *a* ~ in (good) time, early; *a un* ~, *al mismo* ~ at the same time; *a su debido* ~ in due course; *al poco* ~ very soon; *con* ~ in (good) time, early; *con el* ~ eventually, in time; *de 4* ~*s motor* 4-stroke; *el* ♀ Father Time; *en* ~ *de Maricastaña, en* ~ *del rey que rabió* long ago, in the year dot; *fuera de* ~ at the wrong time; *más* ~ *quedar etc.* longer; ¿*cuánto* ~ *más?* how much longer?; *mucho* ~ a long time; *de mucho* ~ of long standing; *en otro* ~ formerly; *andando el* ~ in due course, in time; *darse buen* ~ have a good time; *hacer* ~ while away the time; *hace buen* ~ it is fine, the weather is good; *hace mucho* ~ a long time ago; *desde hace mucho* ~ for a long time; *hace mucho* ~ *que no le veo* it's a long time since I saw him; *matar el* ~ kill time; *perder el* ~ waste time.
tienda *f* shop, store; ~ (*de campaña*) tent; (*toldo*) awning; ~ *de campaña* army tent; camping tent; ~ *de modas* ladies' dress shop; ~ *de objetos de regalo* gift shop; ~ *de raya Mex.* company store; *poner* ~ set up shop.
tienta *f* ⚕ probe; *fig.* cleverness; *a* ~*s* gropingly; *andar a* ~*s* grope, feel one's way (*a. fig.*); **tiento** *m* (*tacto*) touch, feel(ing); stick *de ciego*; *zo.* feeler; *fig.* (*seguridad*) steady hand; (*cuidado*) wariness; ♪ flourish; F (*golpe*) punch; (*trago*) swig; *S.Am.* snack; *a* ~ by touch; *fig.* uncertainly; *con* ~ cautiously; *ir con* ~ watch one's step, go carefully; F *dar un* ~ *a* take a swig from.
tierno *mst* tender; (*blando*) soft; *pan* new.
tierra *f ast.* earth; *geog.* world, earth; (*no mar*) land; (*finca. terreno*) land; (*materia del suelo*) ground, earth, soil; (*patria*) native land, one's (own) country; region; ⚡ earth; *de batán* fuller's earth; ~ *firme* mainland; dry land; ~ *de nadie* no man's land; ~ *de pan llevar* corn land; ~ *prometida*, ~ *de promisión* promised land; ~ *quemada* scorched earth; ♀ *Santa* Holy Land; ~ *adentro* inland; up-country; *por* ~ by land, overland; *caer a* ~ fall down; *dar en* ~ *con, echar por* ~ knock down; *fig.* upset; *echar a* ~ raze to the ground; *echar* ~ *a fig.* hush up; *poner en* ~ ground; ✈ land; ⚓ *tomar* ~ land.
tieso 1. *adj.* stiff, rigid (*a. fig.*); (*tirante*) taut; *fig.* brave; grave; (*terco*) stubborn; (*engreído*) stuck-up; *tenérselas* ~*as con* stand up to; **2.** *adv.* strongly, hard.
tiesto *m* flower pot; (*fragmento*) piece of pottery, sherd.
tiesura *f* stiffness.
tifo 1. *adj.* full, satiated; **2.** *m* typhus; ~ *de América* yellow fever; ~ *de Oriente* bubonic plague.
tifoidea: *fiebre* ~ typhoid.
tifón *m* typhoon; (*tromba*) water spout.
tifus *m* typhus; *thea. sl.* free seats, complimentaries; ~ *exantemático* spotted fever; *thea. sl. entrar de* ~ get in free.
tigre *m* tiger; *S.Am.* jaguar; **tigresa** *f* tigress.
tijera *f* (*p.*) gossip; *tener una* ~ have a sharp tongue; **tijeras** *f/pl.* (*unas* a pair of) scissors; (*grandes, de jardín*) shears, clippers; *de* ~(*s*) folding; **tijeretada** *f*, **tijeretazo** *m* snip, cut; **tijereta** *f* ⚘ vine tendril; *zo.* earwig; **tijeretear** [1a] snip, cut, snick.
tildar [1a] *letra* put a tilde over; (*tachar*) cross out; *fig.* brand, stigmatize (*de* as); **tilde** *mst f typ.* tilde (~); *fig.* jot.
tilín *m* tinkle, ting-a-ling; F *hacer* ~ be well liked; F *tener* ~ be nice, have a way with people.
tilo *m* lime (tree).
timador *m* swindler, confidence trickster; **timar** [1a] steal; *p.* swindle; ~**se** F make eyes at each other; ~ *con* make eyes at.

timbal *m* ♪ (kettle)drum; *cocina*: meat pie.
timbrar [1a] stamp; ✉ postmark; **timbre** *m* ✉ stamp; (*impuesto del* ~) tax stamp, stamp duty; (*campanilla*) bell; ~*s* glockenspiel; timbre *de voz etc.*; ~ *nasal* twang.
timidez *f* timidity *etc.*; **tímido** timid, shy, nervous; bashful, coy.
timo *m* F swindle, confidence trick; (*broma*) gag; *dar un* ~ *a* cheat; (*burlar*) play a joke on.
timón *m* ⚓, ✈ rudder; *esp. fig.* helm; ✓ beam; ~ *de dirección* rudder; ~ *de profundidad* elevator; **timonel** *m*, **timonero** *m* steersman, helmsman; cox(swain) *de trainera etc.*
timorato god-fearing.
tímpano *m* △, *anat.* tympanum, eardrum; ♪ (kettle)drum.
tina *f* vat, tub; (*baño*) bathtub; large jar; ~ *de lavar* washtub; **tinaja** *f* vat, (large earthen) jar.
tinctura *f* tincture (*a. fig.*).
tinerfeño *adj. a. su. m*, **a** *f* (native) of Tenerife.
tinglado *m* platform; (*cobertizo*) shed; *fig.* trick; *conocer el* ~ see through it.
tinieblas *f/pl.* darkness (*a. fig.*), dark, shadows.
tino *m* (*habilidad*) skill, knack; feel, (sure) touch; (*juicio*) good judgment; *a* ~ gropingly; *a buen* ~ by guesswork; *sin* ~ immoderately; (*sin propósito*) foolishly, aimlessly; *coger el* ~ get the hang of it; *perder el* ~ get all mixed up; *sacar de* ~ *a* bewilder.
tinta *f* ink; dye *para teñir*; (*matiz*) tint, shade, hue; ~ *de copiar* copying ink; ~ *china* Indian ink; ~ *de imprenta* printer's ink; ~ *de marcar* marking ink; ~ *simpática* invisible ink; *media* ~ half-tone, tint; F *medias* ~*s pl.* half-baked ideas; *de buena* ~ on good authority; F *sudar* ~ slog; **tinte** *m* (*acto*) dyeing; (*materia*) dye(stuff); (*color*) tint, hue, tinge; ⊕ stain; (*tintorería*) dry cleaner's; *fig.* disguise; **tinterillo** *m* F pen pusher; **tintero** *m* inkstand; inkwell; F *dejar en el* ~, F *quedar* (*or quedársele a uno*) *en el* ~ forget clean about.
tintín *m* clink, chink *de vasos etc.*; jingle *de cadena etc.*; tinkle, ting-a-ling *de timbre*; **tintinear** [1a] clink *etc.*
tinto dyed; *vino* red; **tintorería** *f* dry cleaner's *que limpia*; dyer's *que tiñe*; (*arte*) dyeing; (*fábrica*) dyeworks; **tintura** *f* dye; rouge *de cara*; ⊕ stain; *pharm.* tincture; *fig.* smattering.
tiña *f* ⚕ ringworm; F meanness; **tiñoso** scabby, mangy; F mean.
tío *m* uncle; F (*viejo*) old fellow; F (*sujeto*) fellow, chap; ~*s pl.* uncle and aunt; ~ *abuelo* great-uncle; *el* ~ *Lucas* old Lucas; F *¡qué* ~*!* the old so-and-so!, what a fellow (he is)!; **tiovivo** *m* roundabout, merry-go-round.
típico typical; *fig.* picturesque; quaint, cute, of interest to (*or* popular with) tourists; *p. fig.* original; **tipismo** *m* quaintness *etc.*
tiple 1. *m* treble, boy soprano; **2.** *f* soprano.
tipo *m mst* type; (*clase a.*) sort, kind; (*físico*) shape, figure, build; F fellow, chap; ~*s pl. typ.* type; ~ *bancario* bank rate; ~ *de cambio* rate of exchange; ~ *de ensayo*, ~ *de prueba* eye-test chart; ~ *de impuesto* tax rate; ~ *de interés* rate of interest; ~ *de letra* typeface; ~ *menudo* small print; ~ (*de*) *oro* gold standard; *tiene buen* ~ (*m*) he is well-built; (*f*) she has a good figure; **tipografía** *f* printing; typography; **tipográfico** printing *attr.*; typographical.
típula *f* daddy-longlegs, cranefly.
tiquete *m S.Am.* ticket.
tiquismiquis F **1.** *m* fussy sort; **2.** *m/pl.* silly scruples; (*cortesías*) bowing and scraping; (*molestias*) pinpricks.
tira *f* (long *or* narrow) strip; slip *de papel*; ~ *cómica* comic strip; ~ *proyectable* film strip.
tirada *f* (*acto*) throw; distance, stretch; *typ.* printing, edition; ~ *aparte* offprint; *de una* ~ at one stroke, at a stretch; **tirado** ✝ dirt cheap; ⚓ rakish; *letra* cursive; **tirador** *m* handle, knob *de puerta etc.*; bell rope; ⚡ cord; ⚔ (*p.*) shot, marksman; ~ *apostado*, ~ *certero*, ~ *emboscado* sniper.
tiralevitas *m* F climber, creep.
tiralíneas *m* drawing pen; ⚒ compasses.
tiranía *f* tyranny; **tiránico** tyrannical; *amor* possessive; *encanto*

irresistible; **tiranizar** [1f] *v/t.* tyrannize; *v/i.* be a tyrant, domineer; **tirano 1.** tyrannical; domineering; **2.** *m*, **a** *f* tyrant.

tirante 1. taut, tight; *relaciones etc.* tense, strained; ✝ tight; **2.** *m* ⚠ tie, brace; ⊕ strut; trace *de guarnición*; shoulder strap *de vestido*; ~s *pl.* braces, suspenders; **tirantez** *f* tautness *etc.*; *fig.* tension; ✝ stringency.

tirar [1a] **1.** *v/t.* throw; cast, toss, sling; *desperdicios* throw away; (*disipar*) waste; *alambre* draw out; (*arrastrar*) haul; *línea* draw; ⚔ shoot, fire; *typ.* print, run off; *beso* blow; ~*le de* fancy o.s. as, as, pose as; **2.** *v/i.* (*chimenea*) draw; ⚔ fire (*a* at, on), shoot (*a* at); (*atraer*) appeal; (have a) pull; (*durar*) last; ~ *a su.* tend towards; ~ *a color* approach, have a touch of; ~ *a inf.* aim to *inf.*; ~ *a la derecha* turn to the right, keep right; ~ *a viejo* be elderly; ~ de (*arrastrar*) pull, haul; *cuerda etc.* pull on, tug; (*imán*) attract; *espada* draw; *v. largo*; ~ *por calle* turn down, go off along; *a todo* ~ at the most; F *ir tirando* get along, manage; **3.** ~**se** throw o.s., jump (*por ventana* out of; *risco* over); (*abalanzarse*) rush (*a* at), spring (*a* at, on); (*echarse*) lie down.

tirilla *f* neckband; ~ *de bota* bootstrap; ~ *de camisa* collarband.

tirillas *m* F nobody; (*pequeño*) runt; (*como int.*) little man, buster.

tiritaña *f* F trifle.

tiritar [1a] shiver (*de* with); **tiritón** *m* shiver.

tiro *m* throw; ⚔ shot (*a. deportes, p.*); (*alcance*) range; ⚔ (*sitio*) rifle range; shooting gallery *de feria*; team *de caballos*; trace *de guarnición*; (*cuerda*) rope; *sew.* length; flight *de escalera*; (*broma*) practical joke; ~ *con arco* archery; ~ *al blanco* target practice; ~ *de fusil* gunshot; *a* ~ within range; *a* ~ *de fusil* within gunshot; *a* ~ *de piedra* within a stone's throw; *ni a* ~*s* not for love nor money; *de* ~ *caballo* draft; *de* ~*s largos* all dressed up; *errar el* ~ miss; *hacer* ~ *a* aim at, have designs on; *matar a* ~*s* shoot; F *salir el* ~ *por la culata* backfire.

tiroideo thyroid; **tiroides** *m* (*a. glándula* ~) thyroid (gland).

tirón *m* pull, tug; jerk; hitch; (*estirón*) stretch; *de un* ~ in one go, straight off; *mover etc. a* ~*es* tug, jerk.

tirotear [1a] blaze away at; ~**se** exchange shots repeatedly; **tiroteo** *m* firing, shooting.

tirria *f* dislike; *tener* ~ *a* have a grudge against.

tísico 1. tubercular; **2.** *m*, **a** *f* tuberculous person, tubercular patient, tubercular; **tisis** *f* tuberculosis.

tisú *m* tissue.

titán *m* titan; **titánico** titanic.

títere *m* marionette, puppet; (*teatro de*) ~*s pl.* puppets, puppet show; **titiritero** *m*, **a** *f* puppeteer; acrobat; (*malabarista*) juggler.

titubeante halting, stammering; **titubear** [1a] (*tambalear*) reel, stagger, totter; (*vacilar*) hesitate; stammer, falter *al hablar*; **titubeo** *m* hesitation *etc.*

titular 1. titular, official; **2.** *m typ.* headline; **3.** *m/f* holder; **4.** [1a] (en)title, call; **titulillo** *m* running title, page heading; F *andar en* ~*s* watch out for every little thing; **título** *m mst* title; headline *de periódico*; (*certificado*) diploma, qualification; *univ.* degree; ✝ bond; ~*s* credentials; ~ (*de nobleza*) title; ~ *de propiedad* title deed; *a* ~ *de* by way of; as a, in the capacity of; *¿a* ~ *de qué?* by what right?

tiza *f* whitening; chalk *para escribir*.

tizna *f* black, grime; *paint.* crayon; **tiznar** [1a] blacken; smudge; (*manchar*) spot, stain; *fig.* stain, tarnish; brand; **tizne** *mst m* (*hollín*) soot; (*suciedad*) smut, grime; **tiznón** *m* smut, spot of soot, smudge; **tizón** *m* half-burned piece of wood; ⚘ smut; *fig.* stain; **tizonear** [1a] poke.

tizos *m/pl. sl.* fingers.

toalla *f* towel; ~ *de rodillo* roller towel; **toallero** *m* towel rack.

tobera *f* nozzle.

tobillera *f* ankle sock; F teenager; **tobillo** *m* ankle.

tobogán *m* toboggan.

toca *f* headdress.

tocadiscos *m* record player; jukebox *de café*; ~ *automático* record changer.

tocado headdress; (*pelo*) coiffure, hairdo.

tocador[1] *m*, **-a** *f* ♪ player.

tocador[2] *m* (*mueble*) dressing table; (*cuarto*) boudoir, dressing room; (*estuche*) toilet case; *de* ~ *freq.* toilet *attr.*
tocante: ~ *a* with regard to.
tocar[1] [1g] **1.** *v/t.* (*palpar, estar en contacto con*) touch; (*palpar*) feel; (*manosear*) touch, handle; (*chocar*) collide with, hit; ⚓ go aground on; ♪ play; *trompeta* blow; *tambor* beat; *disco* play; *timbre* ring; *tema* touch on; **2.** *v/i.*: ~ *a puerta* knock at; *pariente* be related to; (*caber en suerte*) fall to one's lot (*or share*); *le tocó el premio* he got the prize; (*importar a*) concern, affect; *le toca de cerca* it closely concerns him; (*deber*) *le toca a Vd. decidir* it is for you (*or* up to you) to decide; (*turno*) *me toca a mí* it's my turn (*inf.* to *inf.*), it's my go; *¿a quién le toca (jugar)?* whose turn is it?; **3.** *v/i.*: ~ *en* ⚓ touch at, call at; (*estar junto*) be next to; *b.s.* impinge upon; interfere with; **4.** ~**se:** F ~*selas* beat it.
tocar[2] [1g] *pelo* do; arrange, set; ~**se** cover one's head.
tocayo *m*, **a** *f* namesake.
tocino *m* bacon; salt pork.
tocón *m* ⚘, *anat.* stump.
todavía still, yet; ~ *no* not yet; ~ *en 1900* as late as 1900.
todo 1. all; whole, entire; every; *velocidad etc.* full; ~ *el dinero* all the money, the whole of the money; *por* ~*a Europa* all over Europe, throughout Europe; ~*s los días* every day; ~ *el que* everyone who; *lo comió* ~ he ate it all; *lo sabe* ~ he knows everything; (*nada menos que*) ~ *un hombre* every inch (*or* bit) a man; ~ *cuanto* all that which; ~*s cuantos* all those who; **2.** *adv.*: *ante* ~ first of all; primarily; *a pesar de* ~, *así y* ~ even so, in spite of everything; all the same; *con* ~ still; however; *del* ~ wholly, completely; *no del* ~ not quite; *después de* ~ after all; *sobre* ~ above all, especially, most of all; F *y* ~ and so on, and what not; **3.** *m* all, everything; (*el* ~) whole; F *ser el* ~ run the show; be the mainstay; ~*s pl.* everybody; every one of them; ~*s y cada uno* all and sundry.
todopoderoso almighty.
toga *f hist.* toga; *univ. etc.* gown; ⚖ gown, robe.
tojo *m* gorse, furze.
toldilla *f* ⚓ roundhouse; **toldo** *m* sunshade, awning; (*pabellón*) marquee; cloth, tarpaulin *de carro*; *S.Am.* hut; *fig.* pride.
tole *m* hubbub, uproar; (*protesta*) outcry; *levantar el* ~ kick up a fuss; F *tomar el* ~ get out quick.
toledano *adj. a. su. m*, **a** *f* Toledan; *noche* sleepless.
tolerable tolerable; **tolerancia** *f* tolerance (*a.* ⊕), toleration; **tolerante** tolerant; broad-minded; **tolerar** [1a] tolerate; endure, put up with.
tolondro 1. scatter-brained; **2.** *m* bump, lump.
toma *f* taking; ⚔ capture; ⚕ dose; (*entrada*) inlet, intake; (*salida*) tap, outlet; ⚡ (*a.* ~ *de corriente*) (*enlace*) lead; (*enchufe*) plug, point; ~ *de declaración* taking of evidence; ~ *de hábito* taking of vows; ~ *de posesión* taking-over; (*presidente etc.*) inauguration; ~ *de tierra* ⚡ ground wire; ✈ landing; **tomacorriente** *m*, **tomada** *f S.Am.* ⚡ plug; ⚡ tap, outlet; ⚡ current collector; **tomado** F tight; ~ (*de orín*) rusty; **tomadura** *f* = *toma*.
tomar [1a] **1.** *v/t. mst* take; *ánimo, fuerzas* get, gain; *aspecto* take on; *bebida, comida, lecciones* have; *costumbre* get into, acquire; *frío* get, catch; ~ *por* take *s.o.* for; ~ *sobre sí* take upon o.s.; ~*la con* pick a quarrel with; **2.** *v/i.*: ~ *por la derecha* turn to the right; ~ *por una calle* turn down a street; *toma y daca* give and take; *¡toma!* fancy that!; well there you are!; of course!; **3.** ~**se:** ~ (*de orín*) go rusty.
tomate *m* tomato.
tomavistas *m phot.* motion-picture camera; cameraman.
tomillo *m* thyme; ~ *salsero* savory.
tomo *m* volume; (*lo grueso*) bulk; *fig.* importance; *de* ~ *y lomo* bulky; F big, important.
ton: *sin* ~ *ni son* without rhyme or reason.
tonada *f* tune, song; **tonadilla** *f* little tune; merry tune; *thea.* interlude; **tonalidad** *f* ♪ tonality; ♪ key; shade *de color*; *radio*: *control de* ~ tone control.
tonel *m* barrel, cask; **tonelada** *f* ton;

tonelaje *m* tonnage; **tonelero** *m* cooper; **tonelete** *m* cask, keg; (*falda*) short skirt; kilt *de hombre*.
tongo *m* F *deportes*: fixing, nobbling; *aquí hay* ~ it's been fixed.
tónica *f* ♪ tonic; (*nota*) ~ keynote; **tónico 1.** ⚕, ♪, *acento* tonic; *sílaba* accented; **2.** *m* ⚕ tonic (*a. fig.*); **tonificar** [1g] tone up, fortify; **tonillo** *m* singsong, monotonous note; **tono** *m mst* tone; ♪ (*calidad etc.*) tone; ♪ (*altura*) pitch; ♪ (*de fa etc.*) key; ♪ (*pieza*) slide; (*matiz*) shade; *teleph.* ~ *de marcar* dialing tone; ~ *mayor* (*menor*) major (minor) key; ♪ *a* ~ in key; *a* ~ *con* in tune with; *de buen* ~ fashionable; elegant; genteel; *de mal* ~ vulgar; *bajar el* ~ lower one's voice; *dar el* ~ *fig.* set the tone; *darse* ~ put on airs; *subir(se) de* ~ put it on; live in style.
tonsila *f* tonsil; **tonsilitis** *f* tonsilitis.
tonsura *f eccl.* tonsure; **tonsurar** [1a] *eccl.* tonsure; 🌾 shear, clip.
tontada *f* rubbish, nonsense; **tontaina** *m/f* F dimwit; **tontear** [1a] talk nonsense; fool; **tontería** *f* (*lo tonto*) silliness; (*acto*) silly thing; (*palabra*; *a.* ~*s pl.*) nonsense, rubbish; *¡déjate de* ~*s!* come off it!; **tonto 1.** silly, foolish; **2.** *m*, **a** *f* fool, idiot; (*payaso*) funny man, clown; *a* ~*as y a locas* all over the place, haphazardly; *hacer el* ~ play the fool; F *hacerse el* ~ act dumb; **tontuna** *f* = *tontería*.
topacio *m* topaz.
topar [1a] *v/t.* (*chocar*) bump (against, into), knock (against, into); (*encontrar*, *a. v/i.* ~ *con*) run into, bump into; *v/i. zo.* butt (each other); (*juego*) take a bet; (*tropezar*) stumble; (*dificultad*) lie; (*salir bien*) succeed, manage it; **tope** *m* (*cabo*) butt, end; ⚓ masthead; 🚂 buffer; *mot.* bumper; ⊕ stop, check; (*choque*) collision; bump, knock; *fig.* snag; (*riña*) quarrel; (*reyerta*) scuffle; *v. fecha etc.*; ~ *de puerta* doorstop; *al* ~ end to end; *hasta el* ~ to the brim; *estar hasta los* ~*s* ⚓ be loaded to the gunwales; *fig.* be fed up; *ahí está el* ~ that's the snag.
topera *f* molehill.
topetada *f*, **topetazo** *m* butt, bump; **topetar** [1a] butt, bump; *fig.* bump into; **topetón** *m* bump.
tópico 1. local; **2.** *m* commonplace, cliché, catch phrase; *S.Am.* topic.
topo *m* mole; F great lump.
topografía *f* 🕮 topography; *surv.* surveying; **topográfico** topograph-ic(al); **topógrafo** *m* 🕮 topographer; *surv.* surveyor; **toponimia** *f* study of place names; *la* ~ *de Aragón* the place names of Aragon; **topónimo** *m* place name.
toque *m* (*acto*) touch (*a. paint.*); (*ensayo*) test, trial; peal(ing) *de campana*; ring *de timbre*; beat *de tambor*; hoot *de sirena*; ⚔ (bugle) call; *S.Am.* turn; ~ *de diana* reveille; ~ *de difuntos* knell; ~ *de queda* curfew; ~ *de retreta* ⚔ tattoo; ~ *de tambor* drumbeat; *dar un* ~ *a* test; *p.* sound out.
toquilla *f* headscarf; shawl.
torada *f* herd of bulls.
tórax *m* thorax.
torbellino *m* (*viento*) whirlwind; (*agua*) whirlpool; *fig.* whirl.
torcedor *m* ⊕ spindle; **torcedura** *f* twist(ing); ⚕ sprain, strain; (*vino*) weak wine; **torcer** [2b *a.* 2h] **1.** *v/t.* twist; (*encorvar*) bend, curve; (*alabear*) warp; *manos, cuello* wring; *cara* screw up; *músculo* strain; *tobillo* sprain, twist; *esquina* turn; *fig. sentido* twist; *justicia* pervert; **2.** *v/i.* turn (*a* to); (*pelota*) swerve, spin; **3.** ~**se** twist; bend; (*alabearse*) warp; (*cambiar de lugar*) slew (round); (*extraviarse*) go astray; (*vino etc.*) turn sour; **torcida** *f* wick, lampwick; curl-paper; **torcido 1.** twisted; bent; *camino etc.* full of turns, twisty; *fig.* crooked; *S.Am.* unlucky; **2.** *m* curl *de pelo*; twist *de seda etc.*; **torcimiento** *m* twisting *etc.*
tordo 1. dappled; **2.** *m* thrush.
torear [1a] *v/t. toro* fight, play; *fig.* deceive; (*burlarse*) tease, draw on; *v/i.* fight (bulls); (*como profesión*) be a bullfighter; **toreo** *m* (art of) bullfighting; **torería** *f* (class of) bullfighters; F prank; **torero** *m* bullfighter; **torete** *m* young bull; F bouncing child; **toril** *m* bullpen.
tormenta *f* storm; *fig.* misfortune; (*confusión*) turmoil, upheaval; **tormento** *m* torment; anguish, agony; torture (*a. fig.*); **tormentoso** stormy, wild.
torna *f* return; *volver las* ~*s* turn the

tables (*a* on); *se han vuelto las* ~*s* now the boot's on the other foot; **tornada** *f* return; **tornadizo 1.** changeable; renegade; **2.** *m*, **a** *f* turncoat, renegade.

tornado *m* tornado.

tornar [1a] *v/t.* give back; (*volver*) turn, make; *v/i.* go back, return; ~ *a escribir* write again; **~se** turn, become; **tornasol** *m* ⚘ sunflower; ⚗ litmus; sheen *de tela*; **tornasolado** iridescent, sheeny; *seda* shot; **tornavía** *f* turntable; **tornavoz** *f* sounding board; *eccl.* canopy; *hacer* ~ cup one's hands to one's mouth.

tornear [1a] turn (on a lathe).

torneo *m* tournament, competition; *hist.* tourney, joust.

tornero *m* turner, lathe operator.

tornillo *m* (*rosca*) screw; (*torno*) small lathe; ⚔ F desertion; ~ *de banco* vice, clamp; ~ *sin fin* worm (gear); ~ *mariposa*, ~ *de orejas* thumbscrew; ~ *para metales* machine screw; ~ *de presión* setscrew; *apretar los* ~*s a* put the screws on; *le falta un* ~, *tiene flojos los* ~*s* he has a screw loose.

torniquete *m* turnstile; ⚕ tourniquet.

torniscón *m* F slap (*or* smack) in the face; (*con dedos*) pinch.

torno *m* ⊕ lathe; ⊕, ⚓ winch, drum; (*freno*) brake; bend *de río*; (*vuelta*) turn; ~ *de alfarero* potter's wheel; ~ *de asador* spit; ~ *de banco* vice, clamp; ~ *de hilar* spinning wheel; ~ *revolvedor* turret lathe; ~ *de tornero* turning lathe; *en* ~ around, round about; *en* ~ *suyo* about him; *en* ~ *a* around, about; *labrar a* ~ turn on the lathe.

toro *m* bull; ~*s pl.* bullfight; (*arte*) bullfighting; ~ *de lidia* fighting bull; *echar* (*or soltar*) *el* ~ *a* pull no punches with; *irse a la cabeza del* ~ take the bull by the horns; *ver los* ~*s desde la barrera* sit on the fence.

toronja *f* grapefruit; **toronjil** *m* ⚘ balm.

torpe *movimiento* ungainly, heavy; *mente* slow; (*desmañado*) clumsy, awkward; (*tosco*) crude; indecent, lewd; dishonorable.

torpedear [1a] torpedo (*a. fig.*); **torpedero** *m* torpedo boat; **torpedo** *m* torpedo (*a. ichth.*).

torpeza *f* slowness *etc.*

torrar [1a] toast.

torre *f* ▲ tower; ⚔, ⚓, ✈ turret; *radio*: mast; *ajedrez*: rook; ~ *de conducción eléctrica* pylon; ~ *del homenaje* keep; ~ *de lanzamiento* launching tower; ~ *maestra* donjon, keep; ⚓ ~ *de mando* conning tower; ~ *de marfil fig.* ivory tower; ~ *de perforación* oil derrick; ~ *de refrigeración* cooling tower; ~ *reloj* clock tower; ⚓ ~ *de vigía* crow's nest.

torrencial torrential; **torrente** *m* mountain stream, torrent; *fig.* torrent, rush, flood *de palabras etc.*; (*ímpetu*) (on)rush; **torrentera** *f* gully.

torreón *m* ▲ turret; fortified tower.

torrero *m* lighthouse keeper.

torreta *f* ⚓, ✈ turret; conning tower *de submarino*.

torrezno *m* rasher, piece of bacon.

tórrido torrid.

torsión *f* ⊕ torsion; twist; *esp.* ✈ warping; **torsional** torsional.

torso *m* torso; *paint.* head and shoulders; *escultura*: bust.

torta *f cocina*: cake, tart; *fig.* cake; *typ.* fount; F slap; F *costar la* ~ *un pan* come out dearer than expected; F *ser* ~*s y pan pintado* be child's play; **tortazo** *m* F slap.

tortícolis *m* crick in the neck, stiff neck.

tortilla *f* omelet(te); ~ *a la española* potato omelet; ~ *a la francesa* plain omelet; ~ *de tomate* Spanish omelet; F *hacer* ~ *a p.* beat up; *cosa* smash; *asunto* make a mess of; F *se volvió la* ~ it came out all wrong; his *etc.* luck turned.

tortita *f* pancake.

tórtola *f* turtledove; **tórtolo** *m* turtledove; F lovebird.

tortuga *f* tortoise; ~ (*marina*) turtle.

tortuoso winding, tortuous; *fig.* devious.

tortura *f* torture (*a. fig.*); **torturar** [1a] torture.

torvo *aspecto* grim; *mirada* fierce.

tos *f* cough(ing); ~ *ferina* whooping cough.

tosco course, rough, crude; *p. etc.* uncouth.

toser [2a] cough; F *a mí nadie me tose*

I'll not stand for that; no one's going to push me around.

tósigo *m* poison; sorrow.

tosquedad *f* coarseness *etc* (*v. tosco*).

tostada *f* (piece of) toast; F *dar* (*or pegar*) *una* ~ *a* have *s.o.* on; **tostado 1.** *pan* toasted; *color* dark brown; ~ (*por el sol*) sunburnt, tanned; **2.** *m* tan; **tostador** *m* toaster; roaster; **tostadora** *f* ⚡ toaster; **tostar** [1m] *pan* toast; *café* roast; *fig.* (*calentar*) toast; *p.* tan; **~se** (*al sol*) tan, get brown; **tostón** *m* toasted chickpea; roast sucking pig; (*pan*) buttered toast; F (*p.*) bore; F (*obra*) dreadful piece of work; lemon F.

total 1. *adj.* total; whole; *esp.* ⚕ gross; *ruina etc.* utter; **2.** *adv.* all in all; and so; anyway, when all is said and done; ~ *que* the upshot of it was that; to cut a long story short; **3.** *m* total; whole; sum; *en* ~ in all; **totalidad** *f* whole; totality; *en su* ~ as a whole; **totalitario** totalitarian; **totalitarismo** *m* totalitarianism; **totalizador** *m* totalizator; **totalizar** [1f] add up.

tóxico 1. toxic, poisonous; **2.** *m* poison; **toxicomanía** *f* drug addiction; **toxicómano 1.** addicted to drugs; **2.** *m*, **a** *f* drug addict; **toxina** *f* toxin.

tozudo obstinate.

traba *f* link, bond *que une*; lock *que cierra, sujeta*; ✓ hobble; *fig.* hindrance, obstacle; **~s** *pl. fig.* trammels; *echar* (*or poner*) **~s** *a* shackle; **trabacuenta** *f* mistake; *andar con* **~s** be engaged in endless controversies; **trabado** *fig.* strong, tough.

trabajado worn out; *estilo etc.* strained; **trabajador 1.** hard-working, industrious; **2.** *m* worker; laborer; **trabajar** [1a] *v/t. madera etc.* work; work on; *p.* work, drive; *p.* (*con maña*) get to work on; *caballo* train; *mente* trouble; *v/i.* work (*de* as; *en* at); (*torcerse*) warp; ~ *mucho* work hard; ~ *con fig.* (get to) work on; ~ *por inf.* strive to *inf.*; *hacer* ~ *dinero* make work; *agua, recursos* harness; **trabajo** *m* (*en general, a. phys.*) work; (*un* ~) piece of work; (*tarea, colocación*) job; (*fermentación*) working(s); (*los obreros*) labor, the workers; *fig.* trouble, difficulty; **~s** *pl. fig.* hardships; ~ *en el propio campo* fieldwork; ~ *a destajo* piecework; **~s** *pl. forzados* hard labor; ~ *de menores* child labor; ~ *de oficina* clerical work; ~ *de taller* shopwork; *me cuesta* ~ *inf.* I find it hard to *inf.*; *estar sin* ~ be out of a job; *tomarse el* ~ *de inf.* take the trouble to *inf.*; **trabajoso** hard, laborious; deficient; ⚕ sickly.

trabalenguas *m* tongue twister; **trabar** [1a] join, link; (*aherrojar*) shackle, fetter (*a. fig.*); (*sujetar*) lock, fasten; (*asir*) seize; *caballo* hobble; *sierra* set; *amistad* strike up; *batalla* join; *conversación* start; **~se** (*cuerdas*) get tangled; ⊕ lock, jam; **trabazón** *f* link; consistency; *fig.* bond, connexion.

trabucar [1g] turn upside down; *fig.* confuse; *palabras etc.* mix up; **~se** get all mixed up; **trabuco** *m hist.* catapult; blunderbuss; (*juguete*) popgun.

tracción *f* traction; haulage; ~ *a las 4 ruedas* 4-wheel drive; ~ *delantera* front drive; ~ *trasera* rear drive.

tracería *f* tracery.

tractor *m* tractor; ~ *de oruga* caterpillar tractor.

tradición *f* tradition; **tradicional** traditional; *costumbre freq.* time-honored; *ley* unwritten; *canción etc.* folk *attr.*

traducción *f* translation; rendering; ~ *automática* machine translation; **traducir** [3f] translate; render; express; **traductor** *m*, **-a** *f* translator.

traer [2p] bring, get, fetch; (*atraer*) attract, draw; *ropa* wear; (*llevar consigo*) have, carry; (*causar*) bring (about); (*acarrear*) involve, bring in its train; *autoridades* adduce; *me trae sin cuidado* it doesn't bother me; *me trae loco* it's driving me mad; *le trae muy preocupado* he's very worried about it; **~se:** ~ *bien* (*mal*) be well (badly) dressed; (*comportarse*) behave properly (badly); **~las** be up to something; *problema que se las trae* difficult problem.

tráfago *m* ⚕ traffic, trade; (*faena*) drudgery, routine job; **trafagón** F hustling, lively; F slick, tricky; **traficante** *m* trader; **traficar** [1g] trade, deal (*en* in); buy and sell; F come and go; **tráfico** *m mot. etc.* traffic; ✝ trade, business, traffic.

tragaderas *f/pl.* throat; F *tener buenas* ~ be gullible; be very easy-going; **tragadero** *m* throat, gullet; **trágala** *m/f* F, **tragaldabas** *m/f* F greedy sort; **tragaleguas** *m/f* F quick walker; great one for walking; **tragaluz** *m* skylight; **tragantada** *f* F swig, mouthful; **tragar** [1h] **1.** *mst* swallow; (*y terminar*) drink up, swallow down; (*engullir*) gulp (down); (*con dificultad*) get down; **2.** *fig.* (*a.* ~**se**) *barco etc.* swallow up, engulf; *material* use up, take; *cosa desagradable, increíble* swallow; *p.* stick, stand; *tenerse tragado algo* have got used to the idea (of s.t. happening); **3.** *v/i. sl.* sleep around.

tragedia *f* tragedy; **trágico 1.** tragic(al); **2.** *m* tragedian.

trago *m* drink, draught; swallow, gulp; F *mal* ~ bad time; nasty blow; *a* ~*s* little by little; *de un* ~ at one go; *echar un* ~ have a swig; F *pasar un* ~ *amargo* have a rough time of it; **tragón** F greedy.

traición *f* treachery; treason (*a.* ⚖); (*una* ~) betrayal, act of treason; *alta* ~ high treason; **traicionar** [1a] betray, be a traitor to; **traicionero** treacherous.

traída *f*: ~ *de aguas* water supply; **traído** worn, threadbare; ~ *y llevado* knocked about; *fig.* well-worn.

traidor 1. *p.* treacherous; *acto* treasonable; **2.** *m* traitor; betrayer; *thea.* villain; **traidora** *f* traitress.

traílla *f* lead, leash; (*látigo*) lash; (*perros*) team of dogs; ⚒ harrow.

trainera *f* (small) boat, fishing boat.

traje[1] *etc. v. traer.*

traje[2] *m* (*en general*) dress; costume (*a. de mujer*); suit *de hombre*; *fig.* garb, guise; ~ *de baño* swimsuit; swimming trunks; ~ *de calle* lounge suit; *en* ~ *de calle policía* in plain clothes; ~ *de campaña* battledress; ~ *de ceremonia*, ~ *de etiqueta* full dress; dress suit, evening dress; ~ *de cuartel* undress; ~ *hecho* ready-made suit; ~ *de luces* bullfighter's costume; ~ *de malla* tights; ~ *de montar* riding habit; ~ *de novia* wedding dress; ~ *de paisano* civilian clothes (*v. a. paisano*); **trajear** [1a] clothe, dress; *co.* get up, rig out; ~**se** dress up *etc.*

trajín *m* haulage, transport; F coming and going; (*bullicio*) bustle; **trajinante** *m* carrier, haulage contractor; **trajinar** [1a] *v/t.* carry, convey; *v/i.* be on the go; hustle, bustle.

tralla *f* whipcord; (*látigo*) lash.

trama *f* weft, woof; *fig.* plot, scheme; *thea. etc.* plot; **tramar** [1a] weave; *fig.* plot, contrive; *complot* hatch; *¿qué estarán tramando?* I wonder what they're up to?

tramitación *f* transaction; steps, procedure; ~ *automática de datos* data processing; **tramitar** [1a] transact, negotiate; **trámite** *m* (*paso*) movement, transit; (*en negocio*) step, move; ~*s pl.* procedure; ~*s pl. de costumbre* usual channels; ~*s pl. oficiales* official channels.

tramo *m* flight *de escalera*; length, section *de camino etc.*; stretch; span *de puente*; (*terreno*) plot.

tramoya *f* piece of stage machinery; F *armar una* ~ kick up a fuss; **tramoyista** *m* scene shifter; *fig.* swindler; humbug.

trampa *f hunt.* trap, snare, trapdoor *en suelo*; 🚂 fender; *fig.* snare, catch, pitfall; (*ardid*) trick, ruse; (*criminal*) fraud; fiddle F, wangle F; ✝ bad debt; ~ *explosiva* booby trap; *armar* ~ *a* set a trap for; *caer en la* ~ fall for it; *hacer* ~*s* cheat; (*con manos*) juggle; *hay* ~ there's a catch somewhere; **trampantojo** *m* F sleight of hand, trick; **trampear** [1a] *v/t.* cheat, swindle; *v/i.* get money by false pretenses; *ir trampeando* get by; **trampería** *f* monkey business; **trampista** *m* = *tramposo* 2.

trampolín *m* springboard (*a. fig.*).

tramposo 1. tricky, crooked; **2.** *m* twister, crook.

tranca *f* beam, pole; (cross)bar *de puerta*; *S.Am.* F binge; *a* ~*s y barrancas* through fire and water; **trancada** *f* stride; **trancar** [1g] *v/t. puerta* bar; *v/i.* F stride along; **trancazo** *m* swipe, bang; ⚕ F flu.

trance *m* moment, juncture; (*mal paso, apuro*) critical juncture; ~ *mortal* dying moments; *a todo* ~ at all costs; *en* ~ *de* in the act of; *muerte* at the point of.

tranco *m* big step, stride; *a* ~*s* pell-mell; *en dos* ~*s* in a couple of ticks.

tranquilidad *f* stillness *etc.*; *con toda* ~ with one's mind at ease; **tranquilizador** *noticia* reassuring; *música etc.* soothing; **tranquilizante** *m* ⚕ tranquilizer; **tranquilizar** [1f] still, calm; *ánimo* reassure, relieve; *¡tranquilícese!* calm yourself!; don't worry!; **tranquilo** still, calm, tranquil; (*sin ruido*) quiet; *mar* calm; *ánimo* calm, untroubled.

tranquilla *f* latch; trap, red herring *en conversación*.

trans... trans...; *v. a. tras...*; ~**acción** *f* compromise, settlement; ✝ transaction; (*volumen de*) ~*es pl.* turnover; ~**atlántico 1.** transatlantic; **2.** *m* liner; ~**bordador** *m* ferry; (*puente*) transporter bridge; ~**bordar** [1a] *v/t.* 🚂 *etc.* transfer; ⚓ tranship; ferry *en río*; *v/i.* 🚂 change; **bordo** *m* transfer; change; ⚓ transhipment; 🚂 *hacer* ~ change (*en* at); ~**cribir** [3a; *p.p. transcrito*] transcribe; ~**cripción** *f* transcription; ~**currir** [3a] go by, elapse; ~**curso** *m*: *en el* ~ *de* in the course of; ~**eúnte 1.** transitory, transient; **2.** *m/f* passer-by; (*que vive fuera*) nonresident; ~**ferencia** *f* transfer (*a.* ⚖); transference; ~**ferible** transferable; ~**ferir** [3i] transfer; ~**figurar** [1a] transfigure; ~**formable** *mot.* convertible; ~**formación** *f* transformation, change; ~**formador** *m* ⚡ transformer; ~**formar** [1a] transform; change; ~**formismo** *m biol.* transmutation; ~**formista** *m thea.* quick-change actor.

tránsfuga *m* ⚔ deserter; *pol.* turncoat.

trans...: ~**fundir** [3a] transfuse; (*comunicar*) tell, spread; ~**fusión** *f* transfusion; ~ *de sangre* blood transfusion; ~**gredir** [3a] transgress; ~**gresor** *m*, **-a** *f* transgressor.

transición *f* transition; **transicional** transitional.

transido: ~ *de dolor* racked with pain; ~ *de hambre* overcome with hunger.

transigente accommodating, compromising; **transigir** [3c] compromise (*con* with); be tolerant (*con* towards).

transistorio *m* ⚡ transistor.

transitable passable; **transitar** [1a] travel, go from place to place; **transitivo** transitive; **tránsito** *m* (*acto*) transit, passage; (*parada*) stop(ping place); traffic; transfer *a puesto*; *calle de mucho* ~ busy street; *horas de máximo* ~ rush hours; *de* ~, *en* ~ in transit; *hacer* ~ make a stop; *el* ~ *de este camino es difícil* this road is hard going; **transitorio** transitory.

trans...: ~**lúcido** translucent; ~**marino** overseas; ~**migrar** [1a] (trans)migrate; ~**misión** *f* transmission (*a.* ⊕, ⚡); *radio a.* broadcast; ~ *en circuito* hook-up; ⚔ (*cuerpo de*) ~*es pl.* signals; ~**misor 1.:** *estación* ~*a* transmitting station; **2.** *m* transmitter; ~**mitir** [3a] *mst* transmit (*a. radio*); *posesión* pass on, hand down; ~**mutación** *f* transmutation; ~**mutar** [1a] transmute; ~**parencia** *f* transparency; ~**parentarse** [1a] (*vidrio etc.*) be transparent; (*objeto visto*) show through; (*intención*) be clear; ~**parente 1.** transparent (*a. fig.*); limpid; filmy; *aire etc.* clear; **2.** *m* curtain, blind; ~**piración** *f anat.* perspiration; ⚘ transpiration; ~**pirar** [1a] *anat.* perspire; ⚘ transpire; (*rezumarse*) seep through; *fig.* transpire, become known; ~**pirenaico** (*situado*) on the other side of the Pyrenees; *tráfico* through the Pyrenees.

transponer [2r] move, change the places of, transpose; *esquina* disappear round; ~**se** hide behind s.t.; (*sol*) set; (*dormirse*) get sleepy.

transportable transportable; **transportación** *f* transportation; **transportador** *m* ⚒ protractor; **transportar** [1a] transport; haul, carry; ⚓ *a.* ship; *diseño etc.* transfer; ♪ transpose; ~**se** *fig.* get carried away; **transporte** *m* transport (*a. buque*); (*a.* ~*s pl.*) transportation; *fig.* transport, ecstasy; ~*s pl.* (*negocio*) haulage business; (*mudanzas*) removals; ~ *colectivo* public transportation; *Ministerio de* ~*s* Ministry of Transport.

transposición *f* transposition (*a.* ♪); move, change of places.

transubstanciación *f* transubstantiation.
transvasar [1a] decant.
transversal, transverso transverse; oblique; *calle etc.* cross.
tranvía *m* streetcar; (*sistema*) streetcar system.
trapacear [1a] be on the fiddle; **trapacería** *f* racket, fiddle; **trapacero** swindling; **trapacista** *m* racketeer; cheat, swindler.
trápala 1. *f* uproar, shindy; clatter *de caballo*; F swindle; **2.** *m* F talkativeness; **3.** *m/f* chatterbox; (*embustero*) cheat, swindler; **trapalear** [1a] F chatter, jabber; (*mentir*) fib; (*trapacear*) be on the fiddle; **trapalón** F lying; swindling.
trapatiesta *f* F roughhouse, shindy.
trapaza *f* = *trapacería*.
trapecio *m* trapeze; ⅍ trapezium.
trapería *f* rags, old clothes; (*tienda*) junk shop; **trapero** *m* ragman.
trapichear [1a] F plot.
trapillo: F *estar de* ~ be dressed up to the nines; **trapío:** *tener buen* ~ have real class; have a fine presence.
trapisonda *f* F (*jaleo*) row, shindy; (*enredo*) monkey business, dirty work; (*mentira*) fib; **trapisondear** [1a] F scheme, plot; **trapisondista** *m* F scheme, intriguer.
trapito *m* rag; ~*s pl. de cristianar* Sunday best; **trapo** *m* rag; duster; ⚓ canvas, sails; F ~*s pl.* clothes, dresses; *v. trapito*; *a todo* ~ in full sail; F *poner como un* ~ haul *s.o.* over the coals; (*difamar*) tear *s.o.* to pieces; *soltar el* ~ burst out laughing; (*llorar*) burst into tears.
traque *m* crack, bang; (*pólvora*) fuse.
tráquea *f* windpipe, trachea 🕮 (*a. zo.*).
tranque(te)ar [1a] *v/t.* (*agitar*) shake; rattle *con ruido*; F muck about with; *v/i.* crackle, bang *como cohete*; (*máquina, vehículo etc.*) rattle; jolt, joggle; **traque(te)o** *m* crack(le); rattle *etc.*; **traquido** *m* crack, bang.
tras 1. *prp. lugar*: behind, after; *tiempo*: after; **2.** *cj.*: ~ *de inf.* besides *ger.*, in addition to *ger.*; **3.** *m* F bottom; **4.** *int.* ¡~, ~! bang, bang!
tras... trans...; *v. a. trans...*; **~alcoba** *f* dressing room; **~cendencia** *f* importance; result; implications; *esp. phls.* transcendence; *de* ~ important, significant; ~**cendental** far-reaching; momentous, of great significance; *esp. phls.* transcendent(al); **~cender** [2g] (*oler*) smell strongly (*a* of); (*divulgarse*) become known, leak out; (*extenderse*) spread, have a wide effect; ~ *a fig.* suggest, evoke; **~cocina** *f* scullery; **~colar** [1m] strain; *fig.* get *s.t.* across; **~conejarse** [1a] get lost; **~corral** *m* back yard; F bottom.
trasegar [1h *a.* 1k] *v/t.* decant; pour into another bottle; *botellas* rack; *fig.* upset, turn upside down; *puestos* reshuffle; *v/i.* F booze.
trasera *f* back, rear; **trasero 1.** back, rear, hind; **2.** *m* hind quarters, rump *de animal*; bottom *de p.*; F ~*s pl.* ancestors.
trasfondo *m* background; (*honduras*) uttermost depths; undertone *de crítica etc.*
trasgo *m* goblin; imp (*a. niño*); bogy.
trashojar [1a] *v/t.* leaf through.
trashumación *f* migration, move to new pastures; **trashumante** *tribu, p.* nomadic; *ganado* migrating, on the move to new pastures; **trashumar** [1a] make the move to new pastures.
trasijado skinny.
traslación *f* transfer, move, removal (*a* to); copy(ing); **trasladar** [1a] transfer, move (*a* to); *función* postpone; *documento* copy; (*traducir*) translate; **~se** move; ~ *a puesto etc.* transfer to, move to; *otro sitio* move to, go on to, proceed to; **traslado** *m* transfer, move; copy.
tras...: ~lapar(se) [1a] overlap; **~lapo** *m* overlap; **~laticio** *sentido* figurative; **~lucirse** [3f] (*cuerpo*) be translucent; (*hecho*) be plain to see; (*noticia*) leak out; **~luz** *m* diffused light; reflected light; *al* ~ against the light; **~nochada** *f* last night; (*vela*) sleepless night; (*vigilia*) watch; ⚔ night attack; **~nochado** *comida, cuento* stale; *p.* hollow-eyed, run down; **~nochador** *m* (*p.*) night owl; **~nochar** [1a] *v/t. pro-*

blema sleep on; *v/i.* (*sin dormir*) have a sleepless night; (*pernoctar*) spend the night; (*estar fuera*) stay out all night, have a night on the tiles F; **~oír** [3q] mishear; **~ojado** haggard, hollow-eyed; **~país** *m* hinterland, interior; **~palar** [1a] shovel; **~papelar** [1a] mislay.

traspasar [1a] (*trasladar*) move; (*cruzar*) cross (over); *negocio* make over, transfer; *jugador* transfer; *esp.* ⚖ convey; *cuerpo* pierce, run through, transfix; *ley* violate; (*dolor*) rack, torture; **~se** go too far; **traspaso** *m* move; transfer; *esp.* ⚖ conveyance; (*dolor*) anguish, pain.

traspatio *m S.Am.* backyard.

traspié *m* stumble, slip; (*zancadilla*) trip; *dar un ~* stumble.

traspintarse [1a] F turn out all wrong.

trasplantar [1a] transplant; **~se** *fig.* emigrate, uproot o.s.

tras...: ~pontín *m* F bottom; **~portín** *m* pillion seat; F bottom; **~puesta** *f* transposition, changing over; removal; *geog.* fold, rise; (*escondite*) hiding place; (*patio*) backyard; (*huida*) escape; **~punte** *m thea.* call boy; **~quiladura** *f* shearing; **~quilar** [1a] *oveja* shear, clip; *pelo de p.* make a mess of; *fig.* cut down.

trastada *f* dirty trick; (*broma*) practical joke; **trastazo** *m* whack, thump; **traste** *m* ♪ fret; *S.Am.* F backside; F *dar al ~ con* chuck away; *fig.* mess up, spoil; **trastear** [1a] *v/t.* ♪ play (well); *toro* play; F *p.* manage, get round; *v/i.* move things around; *fig.* make bright conversation; **trastera** *f* lumber room; **trastería** *f* lumber, junk; (*tienda*) junk shop; F = *trastada*.

trastienda *f* back room (of a shop); F *tener mucha ~* be pretty smart.

trasto *m* (*mueble*) piece of furniture; (*utensilio*) crock; (*cosa inútil*) piece of junk; *thea.* furniture and properties; F (*p. inútil*) dead loss, failure; washout F; (*p. molesta*) nuisance; (*p. rara*) queer type; *~s pl.* tools, tackle; *~s pl. de matar* weapons; *~s pl. de pescar* fishing tackle; *~s pl. viejos* junk; F *coger* (*or liar*) *los ~s* pack up and go.

trastornar [1a] (*volcar*) turn upside down; overturn, upset; *orden de objetos* mix up; *fig.* (*inquietar*) trouble; *sentidos* daze, make dizzy; *nervios* shatter; *orden político etc.* disturb; **trastorno** *m* (*acto*) overturning *etc.*; *fig. pol. etc.* upheaval; disorder, trouble; ⚕ upset, disorder; *~ mental* mental disorder, breakdown.

trastrocar [1g *a.* 1m] reverse, invert, change round; **trastrueco** *m*, **trastrueque** *m* reversal *etc.*

trasunto *m* copy; *fig.* (*a. ~ fiel*) faithful copy, exact image.

trasvolar [1m] fly over.

trata *f* slave trade; *~ de blancas* white slavery.

tratable tractable, manageable; *p.* sociable, easy to get on with.

tratado *m lit.* treatise, tract; *pol.* treaty; ✝ *etc.* agreement.

tratamiento *m* treatment (*a.* ⚕, ⊕); ⊕ processing; treatment, handling *de p.*, *problema*; title, style (of address); *apear el ~* drop *s.o.'s* title; *dar ~ a* give *s.o.* his full title.

tratante *m* dealer, trader (*en* in).

tratar [1a] **1.** *v/t. mst* treat (*a.* ⊕; ⚗ *con, por* with; *de loco etc.* as); ⊕ *a.* process; (*manejar*) handle, deal with; *~ de p.* (*con título, de tú*) address as; **2.** *v/i.*: *~ con* have dealings with; *~* (*acerca*) *de*, *~ sobre* deal with, treat of; *tema* discuss, be about; *~ de inf.* try to *inf.*; *~ en* deal in, trade in; **3. ~se** *bien* live well, do o.s. well; *se trata de inf.* it is a question of *ger.*; *se trata de su.* it is about *su.*; *¿de qué se trata?* what's it about?; what's wrong?

trato *m* treatment; (*entre ps.*) intercourse, dealings; relationship; manner; title, style (of address); ✝ deal, bargain; *~ colectivo* collective bargaining; *~ comercial* business deal; *~ doble* double-dealing; *~ sexual* sexual intercourse; *de fácil ~* easy to get on with; *cerrar un ~* strike a bargain, do a deal; *hacer un buen ~* drive a good bargain; *¡~ hecho!* it's a deal!; *tener buen ~* be easy to get on with.

través *m* bend, turn; (*torcimiento*) bias; ▲ cross beam; ⚔ traverse; *fig.* upset; *a(l) ~ de* through; across; over; *de ~* sideways; crooked; **travesaño** *m* ▲, ⊕ transom, crossbar (*a. deportes*); bolster *de cama*; **travesear** [1a] play up, be mischievous; *fig.* talk wittily; **travesero 1.** sideways; cross *attr.*; **2.** *m* bolster; **travesía** *f* (*calle*) cross street; main road *dentro de pueblo*; ⚓ crossing, voyage; *S.Am.* plain; **travesura** *f* prank, lark, (piece of) mischief; clever trick; (*ingenio*) wit, sparkle; **traviesa** *f* 🚂 sleeper; ⚠ cross beam; ⚓ crossing, voyage; **travieso** = *travesero 1*; *fig. muchacho* naughty, mischievous; (*inquieto*) restless; (*sagaz*) clever.

trayecto *m* (*espacio*) distance, way; (*viaje*) journey *de p.*, run *de vehículo*; flight *de bala etc.*; **trayectoria** *f* trajectory, path.

traza *f* ⚠ *etc.* plan, design; (*medio*) device, scheme; (*aspecto*) looks; *por las* ~*s* by all the signs; F *darse* ~ get along, manage; *discurrir* ~*s para* contrive schemes for; *llevar buena* ~ look all right; *tener* ~*s de inf.* look like *ger.*; **trazado 1.:** *bien* ~ good-looking; *mal* ~ unattractive; **2.** *m* (*dibujo*) outline, sketch; (*plano*) plan, layout; (*línea*) route; **trazador 1.** *phys.*, ⚔ tracer *attr.*; **2.** *m* (*p.*) planner, designer; *phys. etc.* tracer; **trazar** [1f] sketch, outline; design, plan, lay out; *límites* mark out; *línea* draw, trace; *curso etc.* plot; *medios* contrive, devise; **trazo** *m* sketch, outline; line, stroke.

trebejo *m* old-fashioned thing; *ajedrez*: chessman; ~*s pl. de cocina* kitchen utensils.

trébol *m* clover, trefoil (*a.* ⚠); *naipes*: ~*es pl.* clubs.

trece thirteen; (*fecha*) thirteenth; F *estarse etc. en sus* ~ stand firm, stick to one's guns.

trecho *m* stretch, way; (*tiempo*) while; *un buen* ~ a good way; *a* ~*s* intermittently; *de* ~ *en* ~ at intervals; *muy de* ~ *en* ~ only once in a while.

tregua *f* ⚔ truce; *fig.* respite, lull, let-up; *no dar* ~ give no respite.

treinta thirty; (*fecha*) thirtieth; **treintena** *f* (about) thirty.

trematodo *m* fluke.

tremebundo terrible; **tremendo** (*horrendo*) dreadful, frightful; (*digno de respeto*) imposing; (*muy grande*) tremendous; F terrific, tremendous.

trementina *f* turpentine.

tremolar [1a] *v/t.* hoist; (*agitar*) wave; *fig.* make a show of; *v/i.* flutter, wave; **tremolina** *f* rustle; F bustle, great doings; (*jaleo*) row; **trémulo** quivering, tremulous; *luz* flickering; *voz* timid, small.

tren *m* 🚂 train; ⚔ convoy; ⊕ set *de engranajes etc.*; outfit, equipment *de viaje*; (*ps.*) retinue; (*boato*) pomp; ~ *ascendente* up train; ~ *de aterrizaje* landing gear; ~ *botijo*, ~ *de recreo* excursion train; ~ *correo* mail train; slow train; ~ *descendente* down train; ~ *expreso* express train; ~ *de laminación* rolling mill; ~ *de mercancías* freight train; ~ *ómnibus* local train, local, accommodation train; ~ *de viajeros* passenger train; *en* ~ by train.

trena *f sl.* clink.

trencilla *f*, **trencillo** *m* braid; **trenza** *f* plait, pigtail, pony tail; braid; twist *de hebras*; plait *de esparto etc.*; *en* ~ with one's hair down; **trenzado** *m* plaits; **trenzar** [1f] *pelo* plait, braid; *hebras etc.* twist, intertwine, weave.

trepa 1. *f* climb(ing); (*voltereta*) somersault; *hunt.* hide; ⊕ drilling, boring; *sew.* trimming; grain *en madera*; F slyness; F (*castigo*) hiding; **2.** *m* F social climber; **trepado** *m* 📯 perforation; **trepador 1.** climbing, rambling; **2.** *m* (*a.* **trepadora** *f*) climber, rambler; **trepar** [1a] *v/t.* climb; ⊕ drill, bore; *sew.* trim; *v/i.* (*a.* ~ *a*) climb (up); clamber up; scale; ⚘ climb (*por* up).

trepe: F *echar un* ~ *a* tick off.

trepidar [1a] shake, vibrate.

tres three (*a. su.*); (*fecha*) third; *las* ~ three o'clock; **trescientos** three hundred.

tresnal *m* shock, stack.

treta *f fenc.* feint; *fig.* trick, stratagem; wheeze F; gimmick *publicitaria etc.*; *S.Am.* bad habit.

trezavo 1. thirteenth; **2.** *m*, **a** *f* thirteenth.

triangular triangular, three-cornered; **triángulo** *m* triangle (*a.* ♪)

tribal tribal; **tribu** *f* tribe (*a. zo.*), **tribual** tribal.

tribulación *f* tribulation.

tribuna *f* rostrum *de orador*; *hist.* tribune; platform *en mitin*; gallery (*a. eccl.*); *deportes*: (grand)stand; ~

del acusado dock; ~ *del jurado* jury box; ~ *de órgano* ♪ organ loft; ~ *de la prensa* press box; **tribunal** *m* ⚖ court; (*ps.*) court, bench; tribunal *de investigación etc.*; *univ.* board of examiners; *fig.* tribunal; forum *de opinión etc.*; ~ *marítimo* prize court; ~ *de menores* juvenile court; ♀ *Supremo* High Court, Supreme Court; *en pleno* ~ in open court.

tributar [1a] *todos sentidos*: pay; **tributario** *adj. a. su. m* tributary; **tributo** *m* tribute (*a. fig.*); (*impuesto*) tax.

tricentenario *m* tercentenary.

triciclo *m* tricycle.

tricolor *m* tricolor.

tricornio *m* three-cornered hat.

tridente *m* trident.

tridimensional three-dimensional.

trienal triennial; **trienio** *m* period of three years.

trifásico ⚡ three-phase, triphase.

trifulca *f* F row, roughhouse.

trigal *m* wheat field.

trigésimo thirtieth.

trigo *m* wheat; *sl.* dough; ~ *candeal* bread wheat; ~ *sarraceno* buckwheat; *de* ~ *entero* wholemeal; *meterse en* ~*s ajenos* meddle in s.o. else's affairs (*or* subject *etc.*).

trigonometría *f* trigonometry.

trigueño *pelo* corn-colored; *tez* olive; *p.* olive-skinned.

triguero 1. wheat *attr.*; **2.** *m* corn sieve.

trilingüe trilingual.

trilla *f* threshing; **trillado** *camino* beaten, well-trodden; *fig.* trite, hack(neyed); **trillador** *m* thresher; **trilladora** *f* threshing machine; **trilladura** *f* threshing; **trillar** [1a] thresh; *fig.* frequent.

trillizos *m/pl.* triplets.

trillo *m* threshing machine.

trillón *m* trillion (*Gran Bretaña*).

trimestral *revista etc.* quarterly; *univ.* terminal, termly; **trimestre** *m* quarter, period of three months; *univ.* term; ✝ quarterly payment (*or* rent *etc.*).

trinado *m* ♪ trill; *orn.* warble; **trinar** [1a] trill; *orn.* sing, warble; F fume, blow one's top; F *está que trina* he's hopping mad.

trinca *f* group (*or* set) of three; threesome; F gang.

trincar[1] [1g] break up; tear up.

trincar[2] [1g] (*atar*) tie up; ⚓ lash.

trincar[3] [1g] F have a drink.

trinchar [1a] carve, slice; F do in;

trinchera *f* ⚔ *etc.* trench; entrenchment; 🚂 cutting; (*abrigo*) trench coat.

trineo *m* sled(ge), sleigh; ~ *balancín* bobsleigh.

Trinidad *f* Trinity.

trinitaria *f* ✿ heartsease; pansy *de jardín*.

trino *m* = *trinado*.

trinquete *m* ⚓ (*palo de*) ~ foremast; (*vela*) foresail; ⊕ pawl, trip; ratchet.

trinquis *m* F drink, swig.

trío *m* trio.

tripa *f* intestine, gut; (*panza*) belly; ~*s pl. anat.* insides, guts; *cocina*: tripe; *hacer de* ~*s corazón* pluck up courage; put on a bold front; F *tener malas* ~*s* be cruel.

tripartito tripartite.

triple 1. triple; threefold; **2.** *m* triple; *es el* ~ *de lo que era* it is three times (*or* treble) what is was; **triplicado** (*por* in) triplicate; **triplicar**(**se**) [1g] treble, triple; do three times.

trípode *mst m* tripod.

tripón *m* F pot-bellied.

tríptico *m* triptych; (*hoja*) form in three parts.

tripulación *f* crew; **tripulante** *m* crew member, man; **tripular** [1a] man.

trique *m* crack, swish; *a cada* ~ at every turn.

triquiñuela *f* F trick, funny business; *tío* ~*s* artful old cuss.

tris *m* (*ruido*) crack, tinkle; F trice; *en un* ~ within an inch; *estuvo en un* ~ *que lo hiciera* he very nearly did it.

trisca *f* crushing noise; (*retozo*) romp; (*jaleo*) rumpus, row; **triscar** [1g] *v/t.* (*mezclar*) mix, mingle; (*enredar*) mix up; *sierra* set; *v/i.* stamp one's feet; (*retozar*) romp, frisk about.

trisílabo 1. trisyllabic; **2.** *m* trisyllable.

trismo *m* lockjaw.

triste *mst* sad; *aspecto* sad-looking, gloomy; *carácter* melancholy; (*afligido*) sorrowful; (*sombrío*) gloomy, dismal; *paisaje etc.* desolate, dreary;

(*despreciable*) wretched, miserable; es ~ *no poder ir* it's a pity we can't go.
tritón *m zo.* newt.
triturar [1a] triturate; grind (up), pound, pulverize.
triunfador 1. triumphant; **2.** *m* victor, winner; **triunfal** triumphal; **triunfante** triumphant; (*jubiloso*) jubilant, exultant; **triunfar** [1a] triumph (de over); exult (de, *sobre* over); *naipes*: trump; **triunfo** *m* triumph (*a. fig.*); *fig.* success; *naipes*: trump; *sin* ~ no trumps; *palo de(l)* ~ trump(s suit).
trivial trivial; (*trillado*) trite; (*grosero*) vulgar; **trivialidad** *f* triviality; triteness; *decir* ~*es* talk in platitudes.
triza *f* shred, bit; ~*s pl. fig.* ribbons; *hacer* ~*s* shred, tear up; smash to bits.
trocar [1g *a.* 1m] ✝ *etc.* exchange, barter; change (*con, por* for); *posiciones etc.* change over; *palabras* exchange; (*equivocar*) mix up, twist; ~**se** change.
trocha *f* by-path, narrow path; *S.Am.* 🚂 gauge.
trochemoche: *a* ~ helter-skelter, pellmell; all over the place.
trofeo *m* trophy; *fig.* victory, success.
troglodita *m* caveman, troglodyte; *fig.* brute; (*comilón*) glutton.
troj(e) *f* barn, granary.
trola *f* F fib.
trole *m* trolley; **trolebús** *m* trolley bus.
trolero *m* F fibber.
tromba *f* whirlwind; column *de polvo etc.*; ~ (*marina*) waterspout; ~ *terrestre* tornado.
trombón *m* trombone.
trombosis *f* thrombosis.
trompa *f* ♪ horn; (*trompo*) humming top; trunk *de elefante*; proboscis *de insecto etc.*; *sl.* hooter, conk; *anat.* tube, duct; *sl. cogerse una* ~ get boozed; **trompada** *f* F, **trompazo** *m* F bump, bang; (*golpe*) punch.
trompeta 1. *f* trumpet; **2.** *m* = *trompetero*; **trompetazo** *m* trumpet blast; blast, blare; **trompetear** [1a] (play the) trumpet; **trompetero** *m* ♪ trumpet player; ⚔ trumpeter; **trompetilla** *f*: ~ (*acústica*) ear trumpet.
trompicar [1g] *v/t.* trip up; F fiddle the promotion of; *v/i.* stumble; **trompicón** *m* stumble, trip.
trompis *m* F punch, swipe.
trompo *m* top; F clumsy dancer; **trompón** *m S.Am.* bump, bang; F clumsy individual.
tronada *f* thunderstorm; **tronado** F broke; **tronar** [1m] thunder; (*cañón etc.*) thunder, rumble; F fail, be ruined; F ~ *con* fall out with; ~ *contra* denounce, fulminate against; storm at; F *por lo que pueda* ~ just in case.
troncal: *línea* ~ trunk line; **tronco** *m* ⚘ (*de árbol*), *anat.* trunk; stem, stalk *de flor*; (*leño*) log; team *de caballos*; 🚂 trunk line; (*familia*) stock; F *estar hecho un* ~ be sleeping like a log.
tronchar [1a] chop off, lop off; (*romper*) smash.
tronera 1. *f* ⚔ loophole, embrasure; ⚓ narrow window; *billar*: pocket; **2.** *m/f* crazy sort.
tronido *m* thunderclap; ~*s pl.* thunder.
trono *m* throne.
tronzar [1f] smash, shatter; *sew.* pleat.
tropa *f* (*gente*) troop, flock, body; ⚔ (*soldados*) troop; (*no oficiales*) men, rank and file; *S.Am.* herd; *en* ~ straggling; ~*s pl.* troops; ~*s de asalto* shock troops, storm troops; **tropel** *m* (*movimiento*) rush, bustle; (*prisa*) rush, hurry; (*confusión*) jumble, mess; (*muchedumbre*) throng; *de* ~, *en* ~ in utter chaos; in a mad rush; **tropelía** *f* = *tropel*; *fig.* outrage; **tropero** *m S.Am.* cowboy.
tropezar [1f *a.* 1k] trip, stumble (*con, en* on, over); (*reñir*) fall out (*con* with); *fig.* ~ *con*, ~ *en dificultad* run into, run up against; (*encontrar*) stumble upon; *p.* run into; **tropezón** *m* stumble, trip; *a* ~*es* by fits and starts; *hablar etc.* falteringly; *dar un* ~ stumble.
tropical tropic(al); **trópico** *m* tropic; ~*s pl.* tropics.
tropiezo *m* stumble, trip; *fig.* snag obstacle; (*falta*) slip; (*riña*) squabble.
tropo *m* trope, figure of speech.
troquel *m* ⊕ die.
troqueo *m* trochee (- ‿).
trotamundos *m* globe-trotter; **tro-**

tar [1a] trot; F be on the go, hustle; **trote** *m* trot; ~ *cochinero*, ~ *de perro* jog trot; *al* ~ at a trot; *fig.* quickly, right away; *para todo* ~ for everyday wear; F *andar en malos* ~*s* have a rough time; F *tomar el* ~ dash off.

trovador *m* troubadour.

troyano *adj. a. su. m*, **a** *f* Trojan.

trozo *m* bit, piece; ♪, *lit. etc.* passage; *a* ~*s* piecemeal, in bits.

trucaje *m* trick photography; **truco** *m* F trick, wheeze, dodge; ~ *de naipes* card trick; ~ *de propaganda* gimmick.

trucha *f* trout; ⊕ derrick, crane.

trueco *m* = *trueque*.

trueno *m* thunder; (*un* ~) clap of thunder; bang, report; F crazy sort; F ~ *gordo* big row.

trueque *m* exchange; barter; *a* ~ *de* in exchange for.

trufa *f* truffle; F fib, story; **trufar** [1a] *v/t.* stuff with truffles; *v/i.* F fib.

truhán *m* rogue, crook; (*gracioso*) clown, funny man; **truhanesco** crooked; funny.

truísmo *m* truism.

truncar [1g] truncate; cut short, curtail; *escrito etc.* slash.

trust *m* trust, cartel.

tú you; (†, *a Dios*) thou; *tratar etc. de* ~ = *tutear*.

tu, tus *pl.* your; (†, *a Dios*) thy.

tubérculo *m* ⚘ tuber; *anat., zo.,* ⚕ tubercle; **tuberculosis** *f* tuberculosis; **tuberculoso** tuberculous, tubercular.

tubería *f* tubing; piping, pipes; **tubo** *m* tube (*a. anat., televisión*); pipe; ~ *acústico* speaking tube; ~ *de aspiración* breathing tube; ~ *capilar* capillary; ~ *de chimenea* chimney pot; ~ *de desagüe* waste pipe; drain pipe; ~ *digestivo* alimentary canal; ~ *de ensayo* test tube; ~ *de escape* exhaust (pipe); ~ *de humo* flue; ~ *de imagen televisión*: picture tube; ~ *de lámpara* lamp glass; ~ *de paso* bypass; ~ *de rayos catódicos* cathode ray tube; ~ *sonoro* chime; ~ *de vacío* vacuum tube; **tubular** tubular.

tudesco *adj. a. su. m*, **a** *f* German.

tuerca *f* nut; ~ *mariposa* wing nut.

tuerto 1. (*torcido*) twisted, crooked; (*de ojo*) one-eyed, blind in one eye; F *a* ~*as* upside down, back to front; *a* ~*as o a derechas* rightly or wrongly; by hook or by crook; (*sin pensar*) hastily; **2.** *m*, **a** *f* one-eyed person; **3.** *m* wrong.

tuétano *m anat.* marrow; ⚘ pith; *hasta los* ~*s* through and through; *enamorado hasta los* ~*s* head over heels in love.

tufarada *f* bad smell; **tufo** *m* vapour, gas; (*olor*) bad smell, stink; F ⚕ bad breath; F ~*s pl.* swank.

tugurio *m* ⚒ shepherd's hut; (*cuarto*) poky little room; (*casucha*) slum, hovel.

tul *m* tulle, net.

tulipán *m* tulip.

tullido 1. crippled; paralytic; **2.** *m*, **a** *f* cripple; **tullir** [3h] cripple, maim; paralyse; *fig.* abuse.

tumba[1] *f* grave, tomb.

tumba[2] *f* (*voltereta*) somersault; *S.Am.* felling of trees; **tumbacuartillos** *m* F old soak; **tumbar** [1a] *v/t.* knock down, knock over; F (*vino*) lay *s.o.* out; *v/i.* fall down; ⚓ capsize; *estar tumbado* lie, be lying down; ~**se** lie down; stretch out, sprawl; **tumbo** *m* fall, tumble; (*vaivén*) shake, lurch; *fig.* critical moment; *dar un* ~ tumble; (*a. dar* ~*s*) lurch; **tumbón** F bone-idle; **tumbona** *f* easy chair.

tumefacción *f* swelling; **túmido** swollen; **tumor** *m* tumor, growth.

túmulo *m* tumulus, barrow; *geog.* mound.

tumulto *m* turmoil, tumult; *pol. etc.* riot; **tumultuario, tumultuoso** tumultuous; riotous.

tuna *f* ♪ *student music group.*

tunante 1. crooked; **2.** *m* rogue, crook; *esp. co.* scamp, villain.

tunda *f* shearing; F hiding; **tundir** [3a] *paño* shear; *hierba* mow, cut; F tan.

túnel *m* tunnel; ~ *aerodinámico*, ~ *del viento* wind tunnel; ~ *de lavado* automatic car wash.

tungsteno *m* tungsten.

túnica *f hist., anat. etc.* tunic; (*vestido largo*) robe, gown.

tuno = *tunante*.

tuntún: F *al* (*buen*) ~ thoughtlessly, trusting to luck.

tupé *m* toupee; F nerve, cheek.

tupido thick, dense (*a.* F); *paño* close-woven; **tupir** [3a] pack tight, press down; ~**se** F stuff o.s.

turba[1] *f geol.* peat, turf.
turba[2] *f* crowd; swarm; (*chusma*) mob.
turbación *f* confusion; disturbance; (*de p.*) embarrassment; distress; trepidation; **turbador** disturbing.
turbamulta *f* mob, rabble.
turbante *m* turban.
turbar [1a] *orden etc.* disturb, upset; *agua* stir up; *fig.* darken; *p., ánimo* disturb, upset, worry; (*desconcertar*) embarrass; **~se** get embarrassed, feel awkward; get all mixed up, get confused; (*inquietarse*) begin to worry, get upset.
turbina *f* turbine.
turbio *agua* muddy, turbid; *líquido* thick, cloudy; *aguas fig.* dark, troubled; *época, vida* unsettled; *negocio* shady; *medio* dubious; *estilo* confused, obscure.
turbión *m* heavy shower, squall; *fig.* shower; swarm; hail *de balas*.
turbocompresor *m* turbocompressor; **turbohélice** *adj. a. su. m* turboprop; **turbopropulsor** *m motor*: turboprop; **turborreactor** *adj. a. su. m* turbo jet.
turbulencia *f* turbulence *etc.*; **turbulento** turbulent; *niño* noisy, unruly; *espíritu etc.* restless; *época* troubled; *ejército etc.* mutinous, disorderly.
turca *f* F binge, boozing; *coger una ~* get boozed.
turco 1. Turkish; **2.** *m*, **a** *f* Turk; **3.** *m* (*idioma*) Turkish.
turgente, túrgido swollen, turgid.
turismo *m* tourism, tourist trade; touring; sightseeing; (*coche de*) ~ tourer; **turista** *m/f* tourist; sightseer; visitor, holiday maker; **turístico** tourist *attr.*
turnar [1a] take turns; **turno** *m* (*vez*) turn; (*tanda*) spell, shift; turn, go *en juegos*; *por ~* in rotation, in turn; *por ~s* by turns; *esperar su ~* take one's turn; *es su ~, le toca el ~* it's his turn; *estar de ~* be on duty.
turolense *adj. a. su. m/f* (native) of Teruel.
turón *m* polecat.
turquesa *f min.* turquoise; ⊕ mold.
turquí deep blue.
turrón *m sweet made of almond, honey etc. in a hard block, approx.* nougat; F plum, easy job.
turulato F dazed, stunned.
¡tus! good dog!; F *sin decir ~ ni mus* without a word.
tusar [1a] *S.Am.* cut, shear.
tute *m a card game, approx.* bezique.
tutear [1a] *address as tú*; be on familiar terms with.
tutela *f* ⚖ guardianship; *fig.* protection, tutelage; *bajo ~* in ward.
tuteo *m addressing a p. as tú.*
tutiplén: F *comer a ~* eat hugely.
tutor *m* guardian, tutor; **tutora** *f* guardian; **tutoría** *f* guardianship, tutelage.
tuve *etc. v. tener.*
tuyo, tuya 1. *pron.* yours; (†, *a Dios*) thine; **2.** *adj.* (*tras su.*) of yours.

U

u or (*before words beginning with o or ho*).
ubicación *f* location, position, situation; **ubicar** [1g] *v/t. S.Am.* place, put; *v/i.*, **~se** be, lie, stand, be located; **ubicuidad** *f* ubiquity; **ubicuo** ubiquitous.
ubre *f* udder; (*cada pezón*) teat; **ubrera** *f* ⚕ thrush.
ucranio *adj. a. su. m*, **a** *f* Ukranian.
¡uf! *cansancio*: phew!; *repugnancia*: ugh!
ufanarse [1a] boast; ~ de pride o.s. on, boast of; **ufanía** *f* pride; *b.s.* vanity, conceit; **ufano** proud; exultant; (*alegre*) cheerful; satisfied (de with); easy, smooth *en obrar*; *b.s.* vain, conceited.
ujier *m* usher, attendant.
úlcera *f* ulcer; (*esp. externo*) sore; **ulceración** *f* ulceration; **ulcerar** [1a] ulcerate; make a sore on; **~se** ulcerate, fester; **ulceroso** ulcerous; full of sores.
ulterior *lugar*: farther, further; *tiempo*: later, subsequent.
ultimación *f* conclusion; **últimamente** lastly, finally; (*recientemente*) lately, of late; **ultimar** [1a] end, finish; *trato etc.* conclude; **ultimátum** *m pol.* ultimatum; **último** (*en ~ lugar*) last; latter *de dos*; (*más reciente*) latest; (*más remoto*) furthest; (*extremo*) utmost; *piso* top; *calidad* finest, superior; ~ *suplicio* capital punishment; este ~ the latter; *a ~s de mes* in the latter part of; *en estos ~s años* in the last few years; *por ~* last(ly), finally; F *estar en las ~as* be down and out, be on one's last legs; *llegar el ~* be last; *ser el ~ en inf.* be the last to *inf.*; F *ser la ~a* be all the rage.
ultra... ultra...
ultrajador, ultrajante outrageous; insulting, offensive; **ultrajar** [1a] outrage; insult, revile; **ultraje** *m* outrage; insult; **ultrajoso** outrageous.
ultramar: *de ~, en ~* overseas; **ultramarino** **1.** overseas; **2.** *~s m/pl.* groceries; (*tienda de*) ~ grocer's, delicatessen.
ultramoderno ultramodern.
ultramontano *adj. a. su. m* ultramontane.
ultranza: *a ~* to the death; *fig.* regardless, at all costs.
ultratumba: *de ~ vida* beyond the grave; *voz* from beyond the grave.
ultravioleta ultraviolet.
ulular [1a] howl, shriek; (*buho*) hoot; **ululato** *m* howl, shriek; hoot.
umbela *f* umbel.
umbilical umbilical.
umbral *m* threshold (*a. ~es pl. fig.*).
umbrío, umbroso shady; shadowy.
un, una **1.** *artículo*: a, (*delante de vocal y h muda*) an; **2.** *adj. numeral*: one; *¡a la una, a las dos, a las tres!* (*subasta*) going, going, gone!; (*carreras*) ready, steady, go!
unánime unanimous; **unanimidad** *f* unanimity; *por ~* unanimously.
unción *f eccl. a. fig.* unction; ⚕ ointment.
uncir [3b] yoke.
undécimo eleventh.
undulación *f etc. v. ondulación etc.*
ungir [3c] anoint (*a. eccl.*), apply ointment to; **ungüento** *m* ointment, salve.
unguiculado ungual; **ungulado** *adj. a. su. m* hoofed (animal), ungulate 🕮.
uni... uni...; one-..., single-...
únicamente only; solely.
unicameral single-chamber.
único only; sole, single, solitary; (*singular, extraordinario*) unique; *distribuidor etc.* sole, exclusive; *hijo ~* only child; *su ~ cuidado* his one care; *este ejemplar es ~* this specimen is unique.
unicolor one-color; *esp.* ⚘ self.
unicornio *m* unicorn.
unidad *f* unity; oneness; ⚔, ⚗, ⊕ *etc.* unit; **unido** united; (*liso*) smooth; *mantener(se) ~(s)* keep together; remain united; **unificación** *f* unification; **unificar** [1g] unite, unify.
unifamiliar *casa* one-family.

uniformar [1a] make uniform; *p.* put into uniform; **uniforme 1.** *mst* uniform; *velocidad etc. a.* steady, unvarying, regular; *superficie a.* level, even, true; **2.** *m* uniform; **uniformidad** *f* uniformity *etc.*

Unigénito: *el* ~ the only Begotten Son.

unilateral one-sided, unilateral.

unión *f* union (*a.* ⚕); (*unidad*) unity; (*casamiento*) union, marriage; ⊕ union, joint; (*punto de*) ~ junction.

unir [3a] *cosas* join; *mst fig.* unite; *sociedades, intereses* merge; *familias, novios* unite (by marriage); **~se** join (together) unite; *esp.* ⚕ merge; ~ *a* join.

unísono unisonous; *voces etc.* in harmony; *al* ~ in unison, with one voice.

unitario 1. unitary; *eccl.* Unitarian; **2.** *m*, **a** *f* Unitarian.

universal universal; world-wide; **universalidad** *f* universality; generality; **universidad** *f* university; **universitario 1.** university *attr.*; academic; **2.** *m/f* university student; **3.** *m*, **a** *f* university professor; **universo** *m* universe.

uno 1. *adj.* one; identical, one and the same; *Dios es* ~ God is one; *la verdad es una* truth is one and indivisible; *~s pl.* some, a few; *unos 20 km* some 20 km, about 20 km; **2.** *pron.* one; ~ *que vino a verme* someone who came to see me; ~ *no sabe* one does not know; ~ *necesita amigos* a man needs friends; ~ *a* ~ one by one; ~(s) *a otro*(s) one another, each other; ~ *que otro* an occasional, the odd; ~ *y otro* both; *cada* ~ each one, everyone; *en* ~ at one; *una de dos* either one (thing) or the other; *a una* all together; *la una* one o'clock; **3.** *m* one.

untadura *f* (*acto*) smearing *etc.*; ⚕ ointment; ⊕ grease; (*mancha*) smear, dab; **untar** [1a] smear, dab (*de* with); (*engrasar*) grease, oil; *pan, mantequilla* spread; *fig.* bribe, grease the palm of; **unto** *m* grease; fat *de animal*; **untuoso** greasy, sticky; *mst fig.* unctuous; **untura** *f* = *untadura.*

uña *f anat.* nail; (*garra*) claw; hoof *de caballo*; sting *de alacrán*; ⚓ fluke, bill; ⊕ pallet; ⊕ claw; ⚘ ~ *de caballo* coltsfoot; *a* ~ *de caballo* at full gallop; *largo de ~s* light-fingered; *comerse las ~s* bite one's nails; F *ser* ~ *y carne* be thick (as thieves), be hand in glove; **uña**(**ra**)**da** *f* nail mark; (*arañazo*) scratch; **uñero** *m* ingrowing nail; ⚕ whitlow.

¡upa! up, up!

uranio *m* uranium.

urbanidad *f* refinement, urbanity; **urbanismo** *m* city planning; **urbanista** *m/f* city planner; **urbanística** *f* city planning; **urbanístico** city planning; **urbanización** *f* urbanization; development; **urbanizado** built-up; **urbanizar** [1f] *terreno* urbanize, develop, build on; *p.* civilize; **urbano** urban, city *attr.*; *fig.* polite, refined, urbane; **urbe** *f* large city, metropolis; *La* ♀ *esp.* Madrid.

urdimbre *f* warp; **urdir** [3a] warp; *fig.* contrive, plot, conspire to bring about, scheme.

urente burning, stinging.

urgencia *f* urgency; pressure; haste; emergency; pressing need; *de* ~ *medida, salida* emergency *attr.*; *botiquín etc.* first-aid *attr.*; *en caso de* ~ in case of necessity; *pedir con* ~ press for; **urgente** (*que corre prisa*) urgent; (*apremiante*) pressing; *demanda etc.* imperative, insistent; *pedido* rush *attr.*; *carta* express; **urgir** [3c] be urgent, press; ~ *inf.* it is absolutely necessary to *inf.*

úrico uric; **urinario 1.** urinary; **2.** *m* urinal.

urna *f* urn; glass case; ~ *electoral* ballot box; *~s pl. electorales fig.* voting place; *acudir a las ~s* vote, go to the polls.

urraca *f* magpie.

urticaria *f* nettle rash, hives.

uruguayo *adj. a. su. m*, **a** *f* Uruguayan.

usado used; (*gastado*) worn; *p.* skilled, experienced.

usagre *m* ⚕ impetigo; *vet.* mange.

usanza *f* custom; *a* ~ *de* according to the custom of.

usar [1a] *v/t., a. v/i.* ~ *de* use, make use of; *sin* ~ unused; *sello etc.* mint; ~ *inf.* be accustomed to *inf.*; **~se** be used, be in use; (*estilarse*) be in fashion; (*gastarse*) wear out.

usina *f S.Am.* factory.

uso *m* (*empleo*) use; (*usufructo*) use, enjoyment; (*deterioro*) wear (and tear); (*costumbre*) usage, custom; (*moda*) fashion, style; *al* ~ in keeping with custom; *al* ~ *de hacer etc.* for the use of; *vestir etc.* in the style of; *en* ~ in use; *hacer* ~ *de* make use of; *hacer* ~ *de la palabra* speak.
usted, ustedes *pl.* you.
usual usual, customary; **usuario** *m*, **a** *f* user; **usufructo** *m* usufruct, use; ~ (*vitalicio*) life interest (*de* in); **usufructuario** *m*, **a** *f* usufructuary.
usura *f* usury, interest; (*ganancia excesiva*) profiteering; **usurario** usurious; **usurear** [1a] lend money at high rates of interest; *fig.* profiteer; **usurero** *m* usurer; *fig.* profiteer, loan shark.
usurpación *f* usurpation; *fig.* encroachment (*de* upon), inroad (*de* into); **usurpador** *m* usurper; **usurpar** [1a] usurp (*a. fig.*); *fig.* encroach upon, make inroads into.
utensilio *m* tool, implement; utensil *esp. de cocina.*
uterino uterine; *hermanos* born of the same mother; **útero** *m* womb, uterus.
útil 1. useful; helpful, handy; usable, serviceable; **2.** *m* usefulness; ~*es pl.* (set of) tools, implements, equipment; **utilidad** *f* use(fulness), utility; (*provecho*) profit, benefit, good; **utilitario** utilitarian; *ropa etc.* utility *attr.*; **utilizable** usable; fit for use, ready to use; ⊕ *desechos* reclaimable; **utilización** *f* use, utilization; ⊕ reclamation; **utilizar** [1f] use, make use of, utilize; ⊕ *desechos* reclaim; *recursos naturales, potencia* harness; **utillaje** *m* = *útiles.*
utopía *f* Utopia; **utópico, utopista** *m*/*f* Utopian.
uva *f* grape; ~ *crespa*, ~ *espín*, ~ *espina* gooseberry; ~ *pasa* raisin; ~ *de Corinto* currant; *estar hecho una* ~ be dead drunk.
úvula *f* uvula; **uvular** uvular.

V

va *etc. v. ir.*
vaca *f* cow; (*carne*) beef; (*cuero*) cowhide; ~ *lechera* milker; ~ *marina* sea cow; ~ *de San Antón* ladybird; F *pasar las* ~*s gordas* have a whale of a time.
vacación *f* vacation (*a.* ~*es pl.*); (*puesto*) vacancy; ~*es pl. retribuidas* vacation with pay; *de* ~*es* on vacation; *marcharse de* ~*es* go off on vacation; **vacacionista** *m/f* vacationist.
vacada *f* herd of cows.
vacante 1. vacant, unoccupied; **2.** *f* vacancy; **vacar** [1g] be vacant, remain unfilled; ~ *a*, ~ *en* engage in, attend to.
vaciadero *m* sink, drain; **vaciado 1.** ⊕ hollow ground; **2.** *m* cast, molding; plaster cast *de yeso*; **vaciador** *m* scoop; (*p.*) cutler.
vaciar [1c] *v/t. vasija, bolsillo etc.* empty; *vaso etc.* drain; *contenido* empty out; *líquido* pour away, run off; cast, mold *en molde*; (*ahuecar*) hollow out; (*afilar*) grind, sharpen; *v/i.* (*río*) flow, empty (*en* into); ~**se** F tell all one knows, spill the beans.
vaciedad *f* = *vacuidad*; *fig.* piece of nonsense; ~*es pl.* nonsense.
vacilación *f* hesitancy, hesitation, vacillation; **vacilante** *luz* flickering; *movimiento* unsteady; *habla* halting; *fig.* hesitant, vacillating; **vacilar** [1a] (*luz*) flicker; (*mueble etc.*) be unsteady, shake; (*habla*) falter; *fig.* hesitate, waver, vacillate; hang back *al avanzar*; (*memoria*) fail; ~ *en su.* hesitate about; *inf.* hesitate to *inf.*
vacío 1. empty; *puesto etc.* vacant, unoccupied; *papel* blank; *charla* idle; (*inútil*) vain, useless; (*presuntuoso*) vain, proud; **2.** *m phys.* vacuum; (*el espacio, la nada*) void; (*lo vacío*) emptiness; (*un espacio*) empty space, gap; (*hueco*) hollow; (*ijada*) side, ribs; (*puesto*) vacancy; *caer en el* ~ fall flat; *hacer el* ~ *a* send *s.o.* to Coventry; *llenar un bien sentido* ~ fill a long-felt want; ⊕ *marchar en* ~ idle, tick over; (*fuera de control*) race.
vacuidad *f* emptiness; vacancy; *mst fig.* vacuity.
vacuna *f* vaccine; **vacunación** *f* vaccination; **vacunar** [1a] vaccinate; **vacuno** bovine; *ganado* ~ cattle.
vade *m* satchel.
vadeable fordable; *fig.* not insuperable; **vadear** [1a] *v/t. río* ford; *agua* wade through; *fig. dificultad* get around, overcome; *p.* sound out; *v/i.* wade.
vademécum *m* vademecum; (*bolsa*) satchel.
vado *m* ford; *fig.* way out, expedient; *no hallar* ~ see no way out; *tentar el* ~ look into matters, study the ground.
vagabundear [1a] wander, roam; (*holgazanear*) loaf, idle; **vagabundo 1.** vagabond; wandering, vagrant; **2.** *m*, **a** *f* wanderer, rover; *b.s.* tramp, bum; vagabond, vagrant; **vagancia** *f* vagrancy; idleness; **vagante** vagrant; **vagar 1.** [1h] wander, rove, roam; prowl *esp. de noche*; (*cazcalear*) saunter; *b.s.* loiter; (*vivir ocioso*) be idle, be at leisure; *b.s.* loaf; **2.** *m* leisure; *andar de* ~ be at leisure.
vagido *m* wail, cry.
vago 1. vague, indeterminate; *perfil etc.* ill-defined, indistinct; *ideas* vague, woolly; *control etc.* loose, lax; (*holgazán*) lazy; (*errante*) roving, wandering; *en* ~ in vain; (*sin firmeza*) unsteadily; *golpe etc.* in the air; **2.** *m* (*holgazán*) lazy sort; (*no confiable*) unreliable sort; (*confuso*) woolly-minded sort.
vagón *m* car, railroad car; ~ *ca*[...] sleeping car; ~ *carbonero* coal car; ~ *de carga* freight car; ~ *cerrado* bo[x] car; ~ *cisterna* tank car; ~ *de col*[a] caboose; ~ *frigorífico* refrigerator car; ~ *de mercancías* freight car; ~ *de plataforma* flatcar; ~ *salón* parlor car; ~ *tolva* hopper-bottom car; ~ *volquet*

V W X

dump car; **vagoneta** *f* ⚒ *etc.* tip car; *S.Am.* delivery van.
vaguear [1a] = *vagar*; **vaguedad** *f* vagueness; indistinctness; (*dicho*) vague remark.
vaharada *f* puff; whiff, reek;
vah(e)ar [1a] steam, send out vapor, give out fumes; (*oler*) whiff, reek;
vahido *m* fainting spell, dizzy spell;
vaho *m* vapor, steam, fumes; (*olor*) reek, whiff; (*aliento*) breath.
vaina *f* sheath, scabbard; (⊕, *estuche*) case; ⚘ pod, husk, shell; **vainica** *f* *sew.* hemstitch; **vainilla** *f* vanilla.
vaivén *m* oscillation, rocking; swing, sway; movement to and fro; (*ir y venir*) coming and going, constant movement; *fig.* unsteadiness; *pol. etc.* swing, seesaw; ~*es pl.* ups and downs.
vajilla *f* (*en general*) crockery; (*una* ~) set of dishes, service; ~ *de oro* gold plate; ~ *de plata* silver plate; ~ *de porcelana* chinaware; *lavar la* ~ wash the dishes.
valdré *etc. v. valer.*
vale *m* promissory note, IOU; (*cédula*) voucher, warrant; **valedero** valid, binding; ~ *para 3 meses* valid for 3 months; *ser* ~ (*afirmación etc.*) hold good; **valedor** *m*, **-a** *f* protector.
valencia *f* ⚗ valency.
valenciano *adj. a. su. m*, **a** *f* Valencian.
valentía *f* courage, bravery; (*acto*) brave deed; *b.s.* boastfulness;
valentón **1.** boastful; arrogant; **2.** *m* braggart; **valentonada** *f* brag, bragging, boast(ing).
valer [2q] **1.** *v/t.* (*tener el valor de*) be worth, be valued at; cost; (*sumar*) amount to; be equal to, be equivalent to; *castigo etc.* earn; (*ayudar, servir*) avail, be of help to, protect; *¿cuánto vale?* how much is it?; *¡válgame Dios!* goodness!, bless my soul!; *no* ~ *nada* be worthless; *v. pena*; **2.** *v/i.* (*ser valioso*) be valuable; (*ser valedero*) be valid; (*p. etc.*) have one's merits; count *en juegos etc.*; *es un hombre que vale* he is a man of some quality; *¿vale?* is that all right?, will that do?; *eso no vale* that won't do, that's no good; (*juegos etc.*) that doesn't count; *más vale así* it's just as well, it's better this way; *más vale que yo vaya* I had better go; *más vale tarde que nunca* better late than never; ~ *para* be useful for; ~ *por* be worth be as good as; *hacer* ~ *derechos* assert; **3.** ~**se**: *no poder* ~ be helpless; ~ *de* make use of, avail o.s.; *derecho* exercise; ~ *por sí mismo* help o.s.; **4.** *m* value, worth.
valeriana *f* valerian.
valeroso brave; effective, powerful.
valetudinario *adj. a. su. m*, **a** *f* valetudinarian.
valía *f* value, worth; influence.
validar [1a] ratify, validate; **validez** *f* validity; **válido** valid; (*sano*) strong, fit; **valido** *m pol.* favorite.
valiente brave, gallant; (*excelente*) fine, first-rate; *iro.* fine.
valija *f* case; ✉ (*saco*) mail bag; (*correo*) mail, *British* post; ~ *diplomática* diplomatic bag.
valimiento *m* influence (*cerca de* with); favor, protection.
valioso valuable; useful, worthwhile; (*rico*) wealthy; (*poderoso*) powerful.
valor *m* value (*a.* ♪, ♈), worth; price; value, denomination *de moneda etc.*; importance; (*sentido*) meaning; (*ánimo*) courage; (*atrevimiento*) nerve, audacity; ✝ ~*es pl.* securities, bonds, stock; ~ *alimenticio* nutritional value; ~*es pl. en cartera* investments; ~*es pl. habidos* holdings; ~ *nominal* face value, nominal value; ~ *sentimental* sentimental value; *objetos de* ~ valuables; *sin* ~ worthless.
valoración *f* ✝ valuation; *fig.* assessment; ⚗ titration; **valorar** [1a] value; price; *esp. fig.* assess, rate, appraise; ⚗ titrate; **valorizar** [1f] valorize; = *valorar*.
vals *m* waltz; **valsar** [1a] waltz.
valuar [1e] *etc.* = *valorar etc.*
valva *f* ⚘, *zo.* valve.
válvula *f* valve; ~ *de admisión* intake valve; ~ *de escape* exhaust valve; ~ *de escape libre* cutout; ~ *de purga* vent; ~ *de seguridad* safety valve.
valla *f* fence; (*defensa*) barricade, stockade; ~ (*de construcción*) hoarding; *fig.* obstacle; *deportes*: hurdle; ~ *paranieves* snow fence; *v. carrera*;
valladar *m*, **vallado** *m* = *valla*;
vallar [1a] fence in, enclose.
valle *m* valley; roadside advertising sign; ~ *de lágrimas* vale of tears.

vallisoletano *adj. a. su. m,* **a** *f* (native) of Valladolid.
vamos *v. ir.*
vampiresa *f* vamp; **vampiro** *m* vampire; *fig.* vampire, bloodsucker.
vanadio *m* vanadium.
vanagloria *f* vainglory; **vanagloriarse** [1b]: ~ *de* boast of; **vanaglorioso** vainglorious, boastful.
vandálico Vandal(ic); **vandalismo** *m* vandalism; **vándalo** *m,* **a** *f* Vandal; *fig.* vandal.
vanguardia *f* van(guard) (*a. fig.*).
vanidad *f* vanity; uselessness *etc.*; **vanidoso** vain, conceited, smug; **vano** useless, vain, idle; (*ilusorio*) vain; (*frívolo*) inane, idle, frivolous; *en* ~ in vain.
vapor *m* steam (*a.* ⊕), vapor; (*natural*) vapor, mist; (*con olor*) fumes; ⚕ faintness, giddiness; ⚓ steamer, steamship; ⚕ ~*es pl.* vapors, hysteria; ~ *de agua* water vapor; ~ *correo* mailboat; ~ *de ruedas* paddle steamer; ~ *volandero* tramp (steamer); *al* ~ by steam; at full speed; *de* ~ steam *attr.*; *cocer al* ~ steam; *echar* ~ steam; **vaporizador** *m* vaporizer; spray *de perfume etc.*; **vaporizar** [1f] vaporize; *perfume etc.* spray; **vaporoso** steamy, misty, vaporous; *fig.* light, airy.
vapulear [1a] thrash, flog; beat up; **vapuleo** *m* thrashing *etc.*
vaquería *f* dairy; (*vacada*) herd of cows; **vaqueriza** *f* cow shed; **vaquer(iz)o** *m* herdsman, cowboy; **vaqueta** *f* cowhide; **vaquill(on)a** *f S.Am.* heifer.
vara *f* stick, rod (*a.* ⊕), bar; wand *de mando*; shaft *de coche*; (*medida*) *approx.* yard (*2.8 feet*); ~ *de adivinar* divining rod; ~ *alta* authority, power; ~ *de oro* goldenrod; ~ *de pescar* fishing rod; **varada** *f* launching; (*encalladura*) stranding; **varadero** *m* shipyard; **varal** *m* long pole, long stick; F lamppost; **varapalo** *m* long pole; (*golpe*) blow with a stick; F trouble; setback, disappointment.
varar [1a] *v/t.* (*botar*) launch; beach *en playa etc.*; *v/i.*, ~**se** run aground, be stranded; *fig.* get bogged down.
varazo *m* blow with a stick; **varear** [1a] *p.* beat, strike; beat *como castigo*; *fruta* knock down; *toro* stir up; *paño* sell by the yard.
varec *m* seaweed.
variabilidad *f* variability; **variable** 1. variable (*a.* ⅍), changeable, up-and-down; 2. *f* ⅍ variable; **variación** *f* variation (*a.* ♪); **variado** varied; mixed; *superficie etc.* variegated, checkered; **variante** *adj. a. su. f* variant; **variar** [1c] *v/t.* vary, change; alter, modify; *v/i.* vary; change; range (*de* from; *a* to); ~ *de opinión* change.
várice: ~**s** *f/pl.* varicose veins.
varicela *f* chickenpox.
variedad *f* variety (*a. biol.*); *teatro de* ~*es* variety show, vaudeville.
varilla *f* (thin) stick; ⊕ rod, bar, link; spoke *de rueda*; rib *de paraguas etc.*; curtain rod; stay *de corsé*; ~ *de nivel* dipstick; ~ (*de virtudes, mágica*) wand; F *anat.* jawbone; ~ *de zahorí* divining rod; **varillaje** *m* rods, linkage; ribs, ribbing.
vario various, varied; *colorido* variegated, motley; *actividades* multifarious; (*inconstante*) changeable; ~*s pl.* several, some, a number of.
varioloso pockmarked.
varita *f*: ~ *mágica* wand.
varón *m* (*hombre*) man; (*macho*) male; (*de edad viril*) adult male; (*respetable*) worthy man, great man; *hijo* ~ male child, boy; *santo* ~ nice old fellow; **varonil** manly, virile; *biol.* male, masculine.
vasallaje *m hist.* vassalage; *fig.* subjection; **vasallo** *m* vassal.
vasco(ngado) 1. *adj. a. su. m,* **a** *f* Basque; 2. *m* (*idioma*; *a.* **vascuence** *m*) Basque.
vascular vascular.
vase = *se va*; *v. ir.*
vaselina *f* Vaseline; petroleum jelly.
vasija *f* vessel; container.
vaso *m* glass, tumbler; (*en general*) vessel; *hist.* vase; (*cantidad*) glassful; *anat.*, ⚘ vessel, duct; hoof *de caballo*; ~ *capilar* capillary; ~ *de engrase* ⊕ grease cup; ~ *graduado* measuring glass, measuring cup; ~ *de noche* chamber pot; ~ *sanguíneo* blood vessel.
vástago *m* ⊕ rod, stem; ⚘ shoot, bud; *fig.* scion, offspring; ~ *de válvula* valve stem; ~ *de émbolo* piston rod.
vastedad *f* vastness; **vasto** vast, immense.
vate *m* poet, bard; **vaticinar** [1

prophesy, predict; **vaticinio** *m* prophecy, prediction.
vatiaje *m* wattage; **vatímetro** *m* wattmeter; **vatio** *m* watt; **vatio-hora** *m* watt-hour.
vaya *v. ir.*
vecinal *camino* local; **vecindad** *f* neighborhood, vicinity; (*ps.*) neighborhood, neighbors; **vecindario** *m* neighborhood; community; (*cifra etc.*) population, inhabitants; **vecino 1.** neighboring, adjoining; *casa etc.* next; (*cercano*) near, close; *fig.* close, similar (*a* to); **2.** *m*, **a** *f* (*de al lado*) neighbor; (*habitante*) resident, inhabitant, citizen.
veda *f* (*acto*) prohibition; (*tiempo*) close season; **vedado** *m* preserve; *cazar etc. en* ~ poach; **vedar** [1a] forbid, prohibit; (*impedir*) stop, prevent; *proyecto etc.* veto.
vedette [be'ðet] *f* star.
vedija *f* tuft of wool (*or* hair); (*greña*) mat, matted hair.
vega *f* fertile plain; water meadow(s); *S.Am.* tobacco plantation.
vegetación *f* vegetation; (*desarrollo*) growth; *~es adenoideas* adenoids; **vegetal 1.** plant *attr.*, vegetable; **2.** *m* plant, vegetable; **vegetar** [1a] grow; *esp. fig.* vegetate; **vegetariano** *adj. a. su. m*, **a** *f* vegetarian; **vegetativo** vegetative.
veguero 1. country *attr.*, lowland *attr.*; **2.** *m* farmer; *S.Am.* tobacco planter; (*puro*) cigar.
vehemencia *f* vehemence *etc.*; **vehemente** vehement, passionate; *partidario etc.* fervent, red-hot; *deseo* eager, fervent.
vehículo *m* vehicle (*a. fig.*); *~ espacial* space vehicle.
veinte twenty; (*fecha*) twentieth; **veintena** *f* a score, (about) twenty; **veintiuna** *f* pontoon (*game*).
vejación *f* vexation; **vejamen** *m* vexation; (*reprensión*) sharp rebuke; (*pulla*) taunt.
vejancón *m* F, **vejarrón** *m* F old boy, geezer.
vejar [1a] vex, annoy; **vejatorio** vexatious, annoying.
vejestorio *m*, **vejete** *m* old boy, little old man.
vejez *f* old age; *fig.* old story.
vejiga *f anat.* bladder (*a. de pelota*); (*ampolla*) blister; *~ de la bilis*, *~ de la hiel* gall bladder; *~ natatoria* air bladder.
vela[1] *f* ⚓ sail; (*toldo*) awning; *~ de cruz* square sail; *~ mayor* mainsail; F *entre dos ~s* half-seas-over; *darse* (*or hacerse*) *a la ~* (set) sail, get under way.
vela[2] *f* wakefulness, being awake; (*trabajo*) night work; (*romería*) pilgrimage; (*velación*) vigil; candle; *~ romana* (*fuegos artificiales*) Roman candle; *pasar la noche en ~* have a sleepless night; **velada** *f* evening party, soirée; party, social *para divertirse*; = *vela*; *~ musical* musical evening; **velador** *m* candlestick; (*p.*) watchman, caretaker.
velamen *m* sails.
velar[1] [1a] veil (*a. fig.*); *phot.* fog veil; *fig.* shroud; *~se phot.* fog.
velar[2] [1a] *v/t.* keep watch over, watch; *enfermo* sit up with; *v/i.* (*no dormir*) stay awake; stay up, sit up at night; *eccl. etc.* keep vigil; (*trabajar*) work late; *~ por* watch over, look after; *~ por que* see to it that.
veleidad *f* fickleness; (*capricho*) whim; (*intento*) half-hearted attempt (*de* at); **veleidoso** fickle, inconstant; capricious, flighty.
velero 1. swift; **2.** *m* ⚓ sailing ship; ✈ glider.
veleta *f* weathervane, weathercock; float *de pescar*; F person who chops and changes; *~ de manga* ✈ air sleeve, air sock.
velo *m* veil; *fig.* veil, shroud, film; pretext; *phot.* fog, veil(ing); *~ del paladar* soft palate; *tomar el ~* take the veil.
velocidad *f* speed, pace, rate; velocity; (*ligereza*) swiftness; ⊕, *mot.* speed; (*engranaje*) gear; *de alta ~* high speed; *~ de crucero* cruising speed; *~ económica* cruising speed; *límite de ~*, *~ máxima permitida* speed limit; *primera ~* low gear, bottom gear; *segunda ~* second gear; *a toda ~* at full speed; **velocímetro** *m* speedometer; **velódromo** *m* cycle track.
velón *m* oil lamp.
veloz fast, speedy; (*ligero*) swift, quick.
vello *m* down, hair; ⚘ bloom; **vellocino** *m* fleece; *~ de oro* Golden Fleece; **vellosidad** *f* hairiness *etc.*; **vellón** *m* (*lana*) fleece; (*piel*) sheep-

skin; *metall.* copper alloy; **velloso** hairy; downy; fluffy; **velludo** shaggy.

vena *f anat.* vein; (*filón*) vein, seam; grain *de piedra, madera*; streak *de locura etc.*; *poet.* inspiration; *estar de* ~ be in (good) form; *estar en* ~ be in the vein, be in the mood (*para* for).

venablo *m* dart, javelin; F *echar* ~*s* blow one's top.

venado *m* deer, stag; (*carne*) venison.

venal[1] *anat.* venous.

venal[2] that can be bought; for sale; *p.* venal, mercenary; *no* ~*es libros* not to be sold; **venalidad** *f* venality.

venatorio hunting *attr.*

vencedor 1. *equipo etc.* winning; *general, país* conquering, victorious; **2.** *m*, **-a** *f* winner; victor, conqueror.

vencejo *m orn.* swift; (*lazo*) band, string.

vencer [2b] *v/t. enemigo* defeat, beat, conquer; *deportes*: beat; *rival* surpass, outdo; *pasión etc.* master; *dificultad* get over, surmount; *v/i.* win; ✝ (*plazo*) expire; (*obligaciones*) mature, fall due; ~**se** control o.s.; **vencida:** *a la tercera va la* ~ (*para animar*) third time lucky; (*aviso*) you won't get away with it next time; *ir de* ~ be all in, be on one's last legs; **vencido** *equipo etc.* losing; ✝ mature; due, payable; *darse por* ~ give in, give up; **vencimiento** *m* ✝ expiration; maturity.

venda *f* bandage; **vendaje** *m* dressing, bandaging; ~ *enyesado* plaster cast; ~ *provisional* first-aid bandage; **vendar** [1a] *herida* bandage, dress; *ojos etc.* cover; (*atar*) bind; *fig.* blind.

vendaval *m* gale, strong wind.

vendedor *m* seller, vendor; salesman *de tienda etc.*; ~ *ambulante* peddler, hawker; **vendedora** *f* seller; salesgirl, saleswoman *en tienda etc.*; **vender** [2a] sell; market; *fig.* sell, betray, give away; ~**se** sell (*bien etc.*); be sold; ~ *a*, ~ *por* sell at, sell for, fetch; *se vende* (*anuncios*) for sale; **vendible** saleable, marketable.

vendimia *f* grape harvest; vintage *esp. de 1960 etc.*; *fig.* big profit, killing; **vendimiador** *m*, **-a** *f* vintager; **vendimiar** [1b] pick, gather; *fig.* profit by, take a profit from.

vendré *etc. v. venir.*

veneciano *adj. a. su. m*, **a** *f* Venetian.

veneno *m* poison, venom; **venenoso** poisonous, venomous.

venera *f zo.* scallop; (*cáscara*) scallop shell.

venerable venerable; **veneración** *f* veneration, worship; **venerar** [1a] venerate, revere, worship.

venéreo venereal.

venero *m* spring; *min.* lode; *fig.* source, origin.

venezolano *adj. a. su. m*, **a** *f* Venezuelan.

vengador 1. avenging; **2.** *m*, **-a** *f* avenger; **venganza** *f* vengeance, revenge; retaliation; **vengar** [1h] avenge; ~**se** take revenge (*de* for, *en* on); retaliate (*en* on, against); **vengativo** vindictive; *medida etc.* retaliatory.

vengo *etc. v. venir.*

venia *f* pardon, forgiveness; (*permiso*) leave, consent; (*saludo*) nod; **venial** venial.

venida *f* (*llegada*) arrival, coming; (*regreso*) return; *fig.* impetuosity, rashness; **venidero** coming, forthcoming, future; *los* ~*s* future generations, posterity.

venir [3s] come (*a* to; *de* from); *el mes que viene* next month; *eso vengo diciendo* that's what I've been saying all along; *vengo cansado* I'm tired; *¿a qué viene ...?* what's the point of ...?; *¡venga!* come along!; *¡venga un beso!* let's have a kiss!; *¡venga el libro ese!* let's have a look at that book!; *venga lo que viniere* come what may; (*estar a*) *ver* ~ sit on the fence, wait and see; ~ *a su.* agree to, consent to; ~ *a inf.* come to *inf.*; (*terminar*) end by *ger.*, end up *ger.*; (*suceder*) happen to *inf.*; (*acertar*) manage to *inf.*; ~ *a ser* (*sumar*) amount to, work out at; (*resultar*) turn out to be; ~ *a menos* come down in the world; ~ *bien* ⚘ *etc.* do well, grow well; (*objeto*) come in handy; ~ *bien a* (*vestido*) fit, suit; *te viene muy estrecho* it's too tight for you; ~ *en inf.* resolve to *inf.*, agree to *inf.*; ~ *por* come for; ~**se** ferment; ~ *abajo*, ~ *a tierra* collapse, tumble down.

venoso *sangre* venous; *hoja etc.* veined.

venta *f* sale; selling, marketing; (*me-*

són) inn; ~ *al contado* cash sale; ~ *de liquidación* clearance sale; ~ *a plazos* installment plan; ~ *por balance* clearance sale; ~ *pública* (public) auction; *precio de* ~ selling price; *de* ~ on sale, on the market; *en* ~ for sale; *poner a la* ~ put on sale, market.

ventada *f* gust of wind.

ventaja *f* advantage; asset; start *en carrera*; *tenis*: vantage; odds *en juego*; (*sobresueldo*) bonus; (*ganancia*) gain, profit; *llevar la* ~ *a* be ahead of, have the upper hand over; **ventajoso** advantageous; ✝ profitable.

ventana *f* window; ~ *batiente* casement; ~ *de guillotina* sash window; ~ *de la nariz* nostril; ~ *salediza* bay window; **ventanaje** *m* windows; **ventanal** *m* large window; sash window; **ventanear** [1a] F be always at the window; **ventanilla** *f* small window; ticket window; window *de coche etc.*; *anat.* nostril; **ventanillo** *m* small window; peephole *en puerta*.

ventarrón *m* gale, high wind.

ventear [1a] *v/t.* (*perro etc.*) sniff, scent; *ropa* air, put out to dry; *fig.* smell out; *v/i.* snoop, come sniffing around; *impersonal*: blow; **~se** (*henderse*) split; (*arruinarse*) spoil (out in the air); **venteo** *m* sniff(ing); *fig.* snooping.

ventero *m*, **a** *f* innkeeper.

ventilación *f* ventilation (*a. fig.*); *fig.* airing, discussion; **ventilado** drafty, breezy; **ventilador** *m* ventilator, (electric) fan; ~ *aspirador* exhaust fan; **ventilar** [1a] ventilate (*a. fig.*); *fig.* air, discuss.

ventisca *f* blizzard, snowstorm; **ventiscar** [1g] blow a blizzard; **ventisquero** *m* blizzard; glacier; (*montón*) snowdrift.

ventolera *f* gust of wind; (*molinete*) (toy) windmill; F smugness, conceit; whim, wild idea.

ventosa *f* ⚕ cupping glass; *zo.* sucker; (*abertura*) vent, air hole; **ventosear** [1a] break wind; **ventosidad** *f* wind, flatulence; **ventoso** windy.

ventral ventral.

ventregada *f* brood, litter.

ventrículo *m* ventricle.

ventrílocuo *m*, **a** *f* ventriloquist; **ventriloquia** *f* ventriloquism.

ventura *f* luck, (good) fortune; (*dicha*) happiness; *a la* (*buena*) ~ at random; hit or miss; *por* ~ by chance; (*quizá*) perhaps; (*afortunadamente*) luckily; **venturoso** lucky, fortunate, happy.

ver [2v] **1.** *mst* see; (*mirar*) look at; (*examinar*) look into; ⚖ hear, try; *le vi llegar* I saw him arrive; *lo vi hacer* I saw it done; *lo veo* I see; *según voy viendo* as I am now beginning to see; *véase* see, vide; *¡a* ~*!* let's see, let's have a look; *a mi modo de* ~ in my opinion; ~ *y creer* seeing is believing; *dejarse* ~ (*p.*) show one's face, show up; (*efecto*) become apparent; *dejarse* ~ *en* tell on; *no dejarse* ~ keep away; *echar de* ~ notice; *estar por* ~ remain to be seen; *hacer* ~ *que* make *s.o.* see that; make the point that *en discusión*; *no poder* ~ not be able to stand; *ser de* ~ be worth seeing; *no tener nada que* ~ *con* have nothing to do with; *vamos a* ~ let me see; **2. ~se** be seen; (*reflexivo*) see o.s.; (*recíproco*) see each other; (*encontrarse*) (*una p.*) find o.s., be; (*dos ps.*) meet; *ya se ve* naturally; *ya se ve que* it is obvious that; ~ *con* see, have a talk with; **3.** *m* sight, vision; (*aspecto*) looks, appearance; opinion; *a mi* ~ in my opinion; *tener buen* ~ look all right.

vera *f* edge, verge; *a la* ~ *de* near, beside.

veracidad *f* truthfulness, veracity.

veranda *f* veranda(h).

veraneante *m/f* vacationist; **veranear** [1a] spend the summer vacation; spend the vacation; **veraneo** *m* summer vacation; *lugar de* ~, *punto de* ~ summer resort; **veraniego** summer *attr.*; summery; *fig.* slight, trivial; **veranillo** *m*: ~ *de San Martín* Indian summer; **verano** *m* summer.

veras *f/pl.* truth, reality; (*seriedad*) earnestness; serious matters, hard facts; *de* ~ really; (*en serio*) in earnest; *¿de* ~*?* really?, indeed?; *va de* ~ it's the real thing.

veraz truthful, veracious.

verbal verbal; oral.

verbena *f* fair; (*velada*) evening party; *eccl.* night festival; *hist.* wake; ⚘ verbena.

verbigracia for example.

verbo *m gr.* verb; *el* ~ the Word; **verborrea** *f* F, **verbosidad** *f* wordiness, verbosity; **verboso** wordy, verbose.

verdad *f* truth; *la ~ lisa y llana* the plain truth; *la pura ~* es the fact of the matter is; *a la ~* really, in truth; *de ~* real, proper; *en ~* really, truly; *es ~* it is true (*que* that); *¿no es ~?*, *¿~?* isn't it?, don't you? *etc.*; isn't that so?; *decir cuatro verdades a* tell *s.o.* a few home truths, give *s.o.* a piece of one's mind; **verdaderamente** really, truly, indeed; **verdadero** *historia etc.* true, truthful; *p.* truthful; (*real, cierto*) true, real, veritable.

verde 1. green; *fruta* green, unripe; *madera* unseasoned; (*fresco*) fresh; (*lozano*) young, vigorous, lusty; *cuento etc.* dirty, low, smutty; *¡están ~s!* sour grapes!; F *poner ~* abuse; run down; dress down; **2.** *m* green; ⚘ greenery, foliage; *darse un ~* take a bit of time off; **verdear** [1a], **verdecer** [2d] (*estar*) look green; (*hacerse*) turn green, grow green; **verdegay** *m adj. a. su. m* light green; **verdemar** *m* sea-green; **verdete** *m* verdigris; **verdín** *m* ⚘ scum *en estanque*, moss *en árbol*; (*verdete*) verdigris; **verdinegro** dark green; **verdor** *m* greenness; *esp.* ⚘ verdure; *fig.* youthful vigor; **verdoso** greenish.

verdugo *m* executioner, hangman; *fig.* (*p.*) tormentor; (*cosa*) torment; ⚘ shoot, sucker; (*azote*) lash; = **verdugón** *m* weal, welt.

verdulera *f fig.* vulgar woman; **verdulería** *f* greengrocery; (*tienda*) greengrocer's (shop); **verdulero** *m*, **a** *f* greengrocer.

verdura *f* greenness; *esp.* ⚘ greenery, verdure; *~s pl.* greens(tuff), vegetables.

vereda *f* path, lane; *S.Am.* pavement.

veredicto *m* verdict.

verga *f* ⚓ yard(arm), spar; *anat.* penis; **vergajo** *m* whip.

vergonzante shamefaced; **vergonzoso** (*tímido*) bashful, shy; (*pudoroso*) modest; (*que causa vergüenza*) shameful, disgraceful; *anat. partes* private; **vergüenza** *f* shame; bashfulness, shyness; modesty; honor; (*oprobio*) shame; *~s pl.* genitals, privates, private parts; *¡qué ~!* shame (on you)!, what a disgrace!; *me da ~ inf.* it upsets me to have to *inf.*, I find it embarrassing to *inf.*; *tener ~* be ashamed (*de inf.* to *inf.*).

vericueto *m* rough track.

verídico true, truthful; **verificable** verifiable; **verificación** *f* checking, check-up, verification; proving; realization *de suceso etc.*; **verificar** [1g] (*comprobar*) check (up on), verify; *hechos* establish, substantiate; *testamento* prove; *contador etc.* inspect; (*efectuar*) carry out; **~se** (*tener lugar*) take place; (*ser verdad*) prove true, come true.

verismo *m* realism, truthfulness.

verja *f* (*reja*) grating, grill; (*puerta*) (iron) gate; (*valla*) railing(s).

vermicida *m* vermicide; **vermicular** vermicular; **vermiforme** vermiform; **vermífugo** *m* vermifuge.

verminoso verminous.

vermut *m* [berˈmu] vermouth.

vernáculo vernacular; *lengua ~a* vernacular.

vernal spring *attr.*, vernal.

vernier *m* vernier.

verónica *f* ⚘ veronica, speedwell; *a pass in bullfighting.*

verosímil likely, probable; *relato* credible; **verosimilitud** *f* likeliness, probability; *lit. etc.* verisimilitude; credibility.

verraco *m* boar; **verraquear** [1a] F grunt; (*niño*) howl with rage; **verraquera** *f* violent crying.

verruga *f* wart (*a.* ⚘); *fig.* defect; (*p.*) bore, nuisance; **verrugoso** warty.

versado: *~ en* versed in, conversant with.

versal *adj. a. su. f typ.* capital; **versalitas** *f/pl. typ.* small capitals.

versar [1a] turn, go round; *~ sobre fig. materia* deal with, discuss; *tema* turn on.

versátil *miembro etc.* mobile, easily turned; (*inconstante*) changeable, fickle; (*talentoso*) versatile; *arma* multipurpose; **versatilidad** *f* changeableness *etc.*

versículo *m* verse; **versificación** *f* versification; **versificar** [1g] *v/t.* versify; *v/i.* write verses.

versión *f* version; draft; translation.
verso *m* (*en general*) verse; (*un* ~) line; ~ *suelto* blank verse.
vértebra *f* vertebra; **vertebrado** *adj. a. su. m* vertebrate; **vertebral** vertebral.
vertedero *m* rubbish dump, tip; = **vertedor** *m* (*canal*) overflow, drain; spillway *de río*; ⚓ scoop (*a. de tendero*), bailer; **verter** [2g] *v/t. líquido, sal etc.* pour (out); (*por accidente*) spill; *luz, lágrimas* shed; *desechos* dump, tip; *vasija* empty, tip up; (*traducir*) translate (*a* into); *v/i.* flow, run.
vertical vertical (*a.* ✈), upright; **vértice** *m* apex, vertex; *anat.* crown of the head.
verticilo *m* whorl.
vertiente *mst f* slope.
vertiginoso giddy, dizzy, vertiginous; **vértigo** *m* giddiness, dizziness, vertigo.
vesícula *f* vesicle; (*ampolla*) blister; ~ *biliar* gall bladder.
vespertino evening *attr.*
vestal *adj. a. su. f* vestal.
vestíbulo *m* vestibule; hall, lobby; *thea.* foyer.
vestido *m* (*en general*) dress, clothing; dress, frock *de mujer*; (*conjunto*) costume, suit; ~ *de ceremonia* dress suit; ~ *de etiqueta*, ~ *de serio* evening clothes; ~ *de noche*, ~ *de etiqueta* evening gown; ~ *de gala* ⚔ full dress; ~ *de tarde-noche* cocktail dress; **vestidor** *m* dressing room; **vestidura** *f* clothing; ~s *pl. eccl.* vestments.
vestigial vestigial; **vestigio** *m* vestige, trace, sign; relic; ~s *pl.* (*restos*) remains.
vestimenta *f* raiment, clothing.
vestir [3l] **1.** *v/t. p. etc.* dress, clothe (*de* in); (*cubrir*) dress, cover, drape (*de* in, with); (*adornar*) dress up; embellish, trim; *vestido* (*ponerse*) put on, (*llevar*) wear; (*sastre*) make clothes for; *vestido de* dressed in, clad in; (*como disfraz etc.*) dressed as; **2.** *v/i.* dress (*bien* well); ~ *de* dress in, wear; **3.** ~**se** (*p.*) dress, get dressed; (*cubrirse*) get covered (*de* with); *importancia* assume.
vestuario *m* (*vestidos*) clothes, wardrobe; *thea.* (*trajes*) wardrobe; (*cuarto*) dressing room; ⚔ uniform; *deportes*: changing room, pavilion; (*guardarropa*) checkroom.
veta *f* seam, vein; grain *en madera etc.*; *fig.* talents, inclinations.
vetar [1a] veto.
veteado 1. veined; *madera etc.* grained; **2.** *m* graining.
veterano *adj. a. su. m* veteran.
veterinaria *f* veterinary science; **veterinario** *m* vet(erinary surgeon).
veto *m* veto; *poner* ~ *a* veto.
vetustez *f* great age, antiquity; **vetusto** very old, ancient; hoary.
vez *f* **1.** time, occasion; (*caso*) instance; (*turno*) turn; *a la* ~ at a time, at the same time; *a su* ~ in his turn; *alguna* ~ sometimes; *¿le ves alguna* ~? do you ever see him?; (*alg*)*una* (*que otra*) ~ occasionally; *cada* ~ every time; *cada* ~ *más* increasingly, more and more; *le veo cada* ~ *más delgado* he seems to get thinner and thinner; *de una* ~ in one go, at once, outright; *de una* ~ (*para siempre*) once and for all, for good; *de* ~ *en cuando* now and again, from time to time; *en* ~ *de* instead of; *otra* ~ again; *rara* ~ seldom; *tal* ~ perhaps; *una* ~ (*que*) once; **2. veces** *pl.* times *etc.*; *dos* ~ twice; *dos* ~ *tanto* twice as much; *a* ~ at times; *algunas* ~ sometimes; *¿cuántas* ~? how many times?, how often?; *las más* ~ in most cases, most times; *muchas* ~ often; *pocas* ~ seldom; *repetidas* ~ repeatedly, time after time; *hacer las* ~ *de* act as, take the place of.
veza *f* vetch.
vía 1. *f* road; route, way; 🚃 (*rieles*) track, line; (*ancho*) gauge; (*número de andén*) platform; *anat.* passage, tract; *fig.* way, means; (*oficial etc*). channel; ✉ ~ *aérea* airmail; ~ *de agua* leak; waterway; ~ *ancha* broad gauge; ~ *doble* double track; *de* ~ *estrecha* narrow-gauge; ~ *férrea* railway; ~ *fluvial* waterway; ~s *de hecho* ⚖ assault and battery; ♀ *Láctea* Milky Way; ~ *muerta* siding; ~ *normal* standard gauge; ~ *pública* thoroughfare; *en* ~ *de* in process of; *por* ~ *de* via, by way of; *por* ~ *bucal* orally; *por* ~ *marítima* by sea; *por* ~ *terrestre* overland; **2.** *prp.* via.
viable viable; *proyecto* feasible.

viaducto *m* viaduct.
viajante 1. traveling; **2.** *m/f* traveler; **3.** *m* ✝ commercial traveler, salesman; **viajar** [1a] travel (*a.* ✝); go; ~ *en coche etc.* ride; ~ *por* travel (through); tour *de vacaciones*; **viaje** *m* journey; ⚓ voyage; (*breve, de excursión*) trip; (*jira, de vacaciones*) tour; (*en general*) travel (*mst* ~*s pl.*); ~ *en coche etc. a.* ride; ~ *de ensayo* trial run, trial trip; ~ *de ida y vuelta* return journey; ~ *de novios* honeymoon; ~ *de pruebas* ⚓ shakedown cruise; ~ *de recreo* pleasure trip; *¡buen* ~*!* have a good trip!, bon voyage!; *estar de* ~ be away (on one's travels); be on tour; **viajero** *m*, **a** *f* traveler; 🚗 *etc.* passenger.
vianda *f* (*a.* ~*s pl.*) food.
viandante *m/f* traveler.
viático *m* travel allowance; food for a journey; *eccl.* viaticum.
víbora *f* viper (*a. fig.*).
vibración *f* vibration; throb(bing); *phonet.* roll, trill; **vibrante** vibrating; *phonet.* rolled, trilled; *fig.* vibrant (de with); **vibrar** [1a] *v/t.* vibrate; *phonet.* roll, trill; *v/i.* vibrate; throb, pulsate; **vibratorio** vibratory.
vicario *m eccl.* curate; (*suplente*) deputy; ~ *general* vicar general.
vice... vice; ~**almirante** *m* vice admiral; ~**canciller** *m* vice chancellor; ~**cónsul** *m* vice consul; ~**gerente** *m* assistant manager; ~**presidencia** *f* vice presidency; vice chairmanship; ~**presidente** *m pol. etc.* vice president; vice chairman *de comité*.
viceversa vice versa.
viciado *aire* foul, thick, stale; *texto* corrupt; **viciar** [1b] *aire* make foul; *comida etc.* taint, spoil; *texto* corrupt, falsify; *costumbres* corrupt, pervert; *contrato*, ⚖ nullify; (*quitar valor a*) vitiate, spoil; ~**se** *fig.* get depraved; **vicio** *m mst* vice; defect; *gr. etc.* mistake; *de* ~, *por* ~ (*de mimo*) from being spoiled; (*por costumbre*) out of sheer habit; **vicioso 1.** *mst* vicious (*a. phls.*); *gusto etc.* depraved; ⊕ defective, faulty; *niño* spoiled; ⚘ rank, luxuriant; **2.** *m*, **a** *f* addict, fiend.
vicisitudes *f/pl.* vicissitudes.
víctima *f* victim; (*p. o animal sacrificado*) sacrifice; prey *de ave etc.*; ~ *propiciatoria* scapegoat; *ser* ~ *de fig.* be a prey to.
victoria *f* victory; **victorioso** victorious.
vid *f* vine.
vida *f mst* life; (*duración*) life(time); (*modo de vivir*) way of life, living; (*modo de sustentarse*) livelihood; *de* ~ *airada* loose-living; ~ *de perros* dog's life; *¡*~ *mía!* my love!, darling!; *¡por* ~ *mía!* upon my soul!; *de por* ~ for life; *de toda la* ~ lifelong; *en la* ~, *en mi* ~ never in my life; *en* ~ in his *etc.* lifetime; *darse buena* ~ live in style, do o.s. proud; *dar mala* ~ *a* ill-treat; *estar con* ~ be alive; *ganarse la* ~ earn a living; *hacer* ~ *b.s.* live together.
vidente *m/f* seer; clairvoyant.
videocassette *m* video cassette; **videodisco** *m* video disk; **videograbación** *f* video-tape recording; **video-juego** *m* video game; **videotocadiscos** *m* video record player.
vidriado 1. glazed; **2.** *m* glaze, glazing; (*loza*) glazed earthenware; **vidriar** [1b] glaze, glass; **vidriera** *f eccl.* stained-glass window; *S.Am.* shopwindow; (*puerta*) ~ glass door; **vidriería** *f* glass works; (*vasos*) glassware; **vidriero** *m* glazier; **vidrio** *m* glass; ~ *cilindrado* plate glass; ~ *de color* stained glass; ~ *deslustrado* frosted glass, ground glass; ~ *tallado* cut glass; F *pagar los* ~*s rotos* carry the can; **vidrioso** glassy; *mirada* glazed, glassy; (*resbaladizo*) like glass; (*quebradizo*) brittle; delicate; *p.* touchy, sensitive.
vieja *f* old woman; **viejo 1.** old; (*anticuado*) old(-fashioned); *noticia* stale; **2.** *m* old man; ~ *verde* gay old dog; *b.s.* old goat, dirty old man.
vienés *adj. a. su. m*, **-a** *f* Viennese.
viento *m* wind (*a.* ♪, *fig.*, Γ); air; *hunt.* scent; (*cuerda*) guy (rope); *fig.* vanity; ~*s pl. alisios* trade winds; ✈ ~ *ascendente* up-current; ✈ ~ *de cola* tail wind; ~ *contrario* headwind; ~ *de la hélice* slipstream; ~ *en popa* tail wind; *ir* ~ *en popa fig.* get along splendidly; F *beber etc. los* ~*s por* be crazy about; *hacer* ~ be windy.
vientre *m* belly (*a. fig.*); (*útero*) womb; (*intestino*) bowels; ⚕ ~ *flojo* looseness of the bowels.
viernes *m* Friday; ♀ *Santo* Good Friday.

viga *f* ⚠ beam, rafter; girder *de metal*; (*madero*) balk, timber.
vigencia *f* operation, validity; *en* ~ = **vigente** in force, valid.
vigésimo twentieth.
vigía **1.** *f* watchtower; ⚓ reef; **2.** *m* lookout, watch.
vigilancia *f* vigilance, watchfulness; *bajo* ~ *médica* under the care of a physician; **vigilante** **1.** vigilant, watchful; **2.** *m* watchman, caretaker; warder *de cárcel*; shopwalker *en tienda*; ~ *de noche*, ~ *nocturno* night watchman; **vigilar** [1a] watch (over), keep an eye on (*a.* ~ *por*); *trabajo etc.* supervise, superintend; *máquina* tend; *frontera* guard, police; **vigilia** *f eccl. etc.* vigil; (*día de*) ~ fast day; (*desvelo*) watchfulness; (*víspera*) eve; (*trabajo*) study, night work, lucubrations; *comer de* ~ abstain from meat; *pasar la noche de* ~ spend a night without sleep.
vigor *m mst* vigor; validity; (*resistencia*) stamina, hardiness; (*ímpetu*) drive; *en* ~ in force, operative; *entrar en* ~ come into force; *poner en* ~ put into effect, enforce; **vigorizar** [1f] invigorate; (*animar*) encourage; **vigoroso** *mst* vigorous; strong, forceful; *esfuerzo a.* strenuous; *proyecto etc. a.* bold; *niño etc. a.* sturdy.
viguería *f* beams, rafters; (*metal*) steel frame; **vigueta** *f* joist, small beam.
vigués *adj. a. su. m*, **-a** *f* (native) of Vigo.
vil villainous, blackguardly; low, base; *hecho* vile, foul; *tratamiento* shabby; **vileza** *f* vileness *etc.*; (*acto*) base deed.
vilipendiar [1b] vilify; (*despreciar*) despise, scorn; **vilipendio** *m* vilification; contempt, scorn; **vilipendioso** contemptible.
vilo: *en* ~ in the air; *fig.* all in the air, undecided.
villa *f* (*romana, quinta, de veraneo*) villa; (*población*) small town; (*municipio*) borough; *La* ♀ *esp.* Madrid; **villalata** *f* shack, tin hut; **villanaje** *m* peasantry, villagers.
villancico *m* carol.
villanesco peasant *attr.*; *fig.* rustic; **villanía** *f* baseness, villainy; (*acto etc.*) foul thing; (*nacimiento*) humble birth; **villano** **1.** rustic; *fig.* coarse; **2.** *m*, **a** *f hist.* villein; low-born person; peasant (*a. fig.*).
villorrio *m* one-horse town, dump.
vinagre *m* vinegar; **vinagrera** *f* vinegar bottle; *S.Am.* heartburn; ~*s pl.* cruet stand; **vinagroso** vinegary; *fig.* bad-tempered.
vinatería *f* wine shop; wine trade; **vinatero** **1.** wine *attr.*; **2.** *m* wine merchant, vintner.
vinaza *f* nasty wine; **vinazo** *m* strong wine.
vinculación *f* linking *etc.*; ⚖ entail; **vincular** [1a] (*ligar*) link, bind; *esperanzas* base, found (*en* on); perpetuate; ⚖ entail; **vínculo** *m* link, bond, tie; ⚖ entail.
vindicación *f* vindication; **vindicar** [1g] vindicate; **vindicativo** vindictive.
vine *etc. v. venir.*
vínico wine *attr.*; **vinícola** wine (growing) *attr.*; **vinicultor** *m* wine grower; **vinicultura** *f* wine growing, production of wine; **vinillo** *m* weak wine; **vino** *m* wine; ~ *añejo* mellow wine; ~ *blanco* white wine; ~ *espumoso* sparkling wine; ~ *generoso* strong wine, full-bodied wine; ~ *de Jerez* sherry; ~ *de mesa*, ~ *de pasto* table wine; ~ *de Oporto* port (wine); ~ *de postre* dessert wine; ~ *seco* dry wine; ~ *tinto* red wine; *dormir el* ~ sleep off a hangover; **vinoso** like wine, vinous; *p.* too fond of wine.
viña *f* vineyard; **viñador** *m* vine grower; wine grower; **viñedo** *m* vineyard.
viñeta *f* vignette.
viola *f* ♪, ⚘ viola; **violáceo** violet.
violación *f mst* violation; ~ (*de la ley*) offence, infringement; outrage (*de* on); rape; **violador** *m*, **-a** *f* violator *etc.*; **violar** [1a] *mst* violate; *ley a.* break, offend against; (*ultrajar*) outrage; *lugar sagrado a.* desecrate; *mujer* rape.
violencia *f* violence (*a. fig.*); *fig.* fury; embarrassment; embarrassing situation; ⚖ assault, violence; *hacer* ~ *a* = **violentar** [1a] *casa* break into; ⚖ assault; *fig.* do violence to, outrage; *sentido* distort, force; ~**se** force o.s.; **violento** *mst* violent; *fig. a.* wild; *postura* awkward, unnatural; *situación etc.* awkward, embarrassing; *sentido*

distorted; *mostrarse* ~ turn violent, offer violence; *sentirse* ~ feel awkward, feel embarrassed.

violeta *f* violet.

violín *m* violin; (*p.*) = **violinista** *m/f* violinist; **violón** *m* double-bass; F *tocar el* ~ have a silly sort of job; **violencelista** *m/f* cellist; **violoncelo** *m* cello.

vira *f* dart; welt *de zapato.*

virada *f* tack(ing); **viraje** *m* ⚓ tack, turn; bend *de camino*; swerve, turn *de coche*; *pol.* swing *de votos*, volte-face *de política*; *phot.* toning; ~ *en horquilla* hairpin bend; **virar** [1a] *v/t.* put about; *phot.* tone; *v/i.*, ~**se** ⚓ go about, tack; veer (round) (*a. fig.*); *mot.*, ✈ turn, swerve; *pol.* (*votos*) swing; (*política*) veer round, change round.

viral virus *attr.*

virgen *adj. a. su. f* virgin; **virginal** maidenly, virginal; **virginidad** *f* virginity; **virgo** *m* virginity; *ast.* ♍ Virgo.

viril virile; *esp. carácter* manly; *v. edad*; **virilidad** *f* virility; manliness; (*edad*) manhood.

virola *f* collar; ⊕ ferrule.

virolento pockmarked.

virote *m* arrow; F (*joven*) man about town; (*p. grave*) solemn sort.

virreinal viceregal; **virreinato** *m* viceroyalty; **virrey** *m* viceroy.

virtual virtual; *fuerza* potential; *imagen etc.* apparent.

virtud *f* virtue; efficacy; *en* ~ *de* in (*or* by) virtue of, by reason of; **virtuosismo** *m* virtuosity; **virtuoso 1.** virtuous; **2.** *m* virtuoso.

viruela *f* smallpox, variola; ~*s pl.* pockmarks.

virulencia *f* virulence; **virulento** virulent.

virus *m* virus; *enfermedad por* ~ virus disease.

viruta *f* ⊕ shaving; **virutilla** *f* thin shaving; ~*s pl. de acero* steel wool.

vis *f* **cómica:** *tener* ~ be witty, sparkle.

visado *m* visa; ~ *de permanencia* residence permit; ~ *de tránsito* transit visa.

visaje *m* face, grimace; *hacer* ~*s* grimace, smirk.

visar *m pasaporte* visa; *documento* endorse, pass.

vísceras *f/pl.* viscera.

viscosidad *f* 📖 viscosity; stickiness *etc.*; **viscoso** 📖 viscous; sticky, slimy; *líquido a.* thick.

visera *f* ⚔ visor; peak *de gorra*; eye shade *contra el sol.*

visibilidad *f* visibility; **visible** visible; (*manifiesto*) evident, in evidence; *¿está* ~ *el duque?* is the duke free?, will the duke see a visitor?

visión *f* sight, vision (*a. eccl.*); (*imaginación vana*) fantasy; *fig.* (*p.*) sight, scarecrow; ~ *de conjunto* (complete) picture; ~ *negra* blackout *del aviador*; F *ver* ~*es* be seeing things; **visionario** *adj. a. su. m*, **a** *f* visionary.

visita *f* visit; call; (*p.*) visitor, caller; *hacer* (*pagar*) *una* ~ pay (return) a visit; **visitación** *f eccl.* visitation; **visitador** *m*, **-a** *f* frequent visitor; (*oficial*) inspector; **visitante 1.** visiting; **2.** *m/f* visitor; **visitar** [1a] visit; call on, (go and) see; (*en viaje oficial*) inspect; **visiteo** *m* frequent visiting; **visitero 1.** forever visiting; **2.** *m*, **a** *f* constant visitor.

vislumbrar [1a] glimpse, catch a glimpse of; *fig.* get some idea of, conjecture; **vislumbre** *f* glimpse; (*reflejo*) gleam, glimmer; *fig.* (*esp.* ~*s pl.*) inkling, general idea.

viso *m* sheen, gloss *de tela*; gleam, glint *de metal*; ~*s pl. fig.* appearance; *a dos* ~*s* having a double purpose; *de* ~ of some importance; *hacer* ~*s* shimmer.

visón *m* (*a. piel de* ~) mink.

visor *m phot.* viewfinder; ✈ bomb sight.

visorio visual.

víspera *f* eve, day before; ~*s pl.* vespers, evensong; *la* ~ *de*, *en* ~*s de* on the eve of; *en* ~*s de inf.* on the point of *ger.*

vista *f* (*facultad, sentido*) sight, vision, eyesight; (*que se dirige a un punto*) eyes, glance, gaze; (*cosa vista*) sight; (*panorama*) view, scene, vista; (*apariencia*) appearance, looks; (*perspectiva*) outlook, prospect; intention; ✝ sight; ⚖ trial *de p.*, hearing *de pleito*; ~*s pl.* view, outlook; *corto de* ~ short-sighted; *doble* ~ second sight;

cine: ~ *fija* still; ~ *de pájaro* bird's-eye view; ✝ *a la* ~ at sight, on sight; *a la* ~ *de* (with)in sight of; *a* ~ *de* in sight of; (*ante*) in the presence of; *a primera* ~ at first sight, on the face of it; *a simple* ~ with the naked eye; *con* ~*s al mar* overlooking the sea; *con* ~*s al norte* with northerly aspect; *de* ~ (*conocer etc.*) by sight; *en plena* ~ in full view; *¡hasta la* ~*!* cheerio!, so long!; *aguzar la* ~ look more closely; *clavar la* ~ *en* stare at; clap eyes on; *hacer la* ~ *gorda a* turn a blind eye to, wink at; *medir con la* ~ size up; *perder de* ~ lose sight of; *no perder de* ~ keep in view; *salta a la* ~ it hits you in the eye; *torcer la* ~ squint.

vistazo *m* look, glance, glimpse; *de un* ~ at a glance; *dar un* ~ have a look (*a* at); *fig.* pop in; *echar un* ~ *a* take a look at, glance at.

vistillas *f/pl.* viewpoint, high place.

visto 1. *p.p. of ver*; ~ *bueno* passed, approved, O.K.; *bien* ~ approved of, thought right; *mal* ~ thought wrong; ~ *que* seeing that; *por lo* ~ evidently; by the look of things; ~ *todo esto* in view of all this; *no* ~, *nunca* ~ unheard-of; *está* ~ *que* it is clear that; **2.:** ~ *bueno m* approval, authorization.

vistoso showy, attractive, gay; *b.s.* loud, gaudy.

visual 1. visual; **2.** *f* line of sight.

vital vital; *espacio* living; **vitalicio 1.** life *attr.*; **2.** *m* life annuity; life-insurance policy; **vitalidad** *f* vitality; **vitalizar** [1f] vitalize; **vitamina** *f* vitamin; **vitamínico** vitamin *attr.*

vitela *f* vellum.

vitícola vine growing, vine *attr.*; **viticultor** *m* vine grower; **viticultura** *f* vine growing, viticulture.

vitola *f S.Am.* looks, appearance.

¡vítor! hurrah!; **vitorear** [1a] cheer, acclaim.

vítreo glassy, vitreous 🕮; **vitrificar(se)** [1g] vitrify; **vitrina** *f* glass case, showcase; display cabinet (*a.* ~ *de exposición*); *S.Am.* shop window.

vitriolo *m* vitriol.

vitualla(s) *f(pl.)* provisions, victuals.

vituperar [1a] condemn, inveigh against, vituperate; **vituperioso** vituperative; **vituperio** *m* condemnation, vituperation; insult, affront.

viuda *f* widow; **viudedad** *f* widow's pension; **viudez** *f* widowhood; **viudo 1.** widowed; **2.** *m* widower.

¡viva! *v. vivir.*

vivacidad *f* vivacity, liveliness *etc.*

vivaque *m* bivouac; **vivaquear** [1a] bivouac.

vivar *m* (*conejos*) warren; (*peces*) fish pond.

vivaracho *p. etc.* jaunty, frisky, lively; *ojos* lively, intelligent.

vivaz (*de larga vida*) long-lived; ⚘ perennial; (*que dura*) enduring, lasting; active, vigorous; (*lleno de vida*) lively; (*agudo*) sharp, quick-witted.

víveres *m/pl.* provisions, supplies, stores.

vivero *m* fish pond; ⚘ nursery.

viveza *f* liveliness *etc.* (*v. vivo*).

vividero habitable; **vividor** *m* F sharp one.

vivienda *f* housing, accommodation; (*morada*) dwelling; *escasez de* ~*s* housing shortage; *problema de la* ~ housing problem.

viviente living; *los* ~*s* the living.

vivificador, vivificante life-giving; reviving; **vivificar** [1g] revitalize, enliven, bring to life.

vivíparo viviparous.

vivir 1. [1a] live (*de* by, off, on; *en* at, in); *¡viva!* hurrah!; *¡viva X!* long live X!, hurrah for X!; *¿quién vive?* who goes there?; *dar el quién vive a* challenge; ~ *para ver* live and learn; *tener con qué* ~ have enough to live on; **2.** *m* life; living; (*modo de* ~) way of life; *de mal* ~ loose-living; ⚖ criminal, outside the law.

vivisección *f* vivisection.

vivo 1. (*no muerto*) alive, living; live; *lengua* modern, living; (*lleno de vida*) lively, bright; *dolor* sharp, acute; *emoción* keen, deep, intense; *inteligencia* sharp; *imaginación* lively; *ingenio* ready; *paso* quick, smart; *escena, recuerdo, colorido etc.* vivid; *color* rich, bright; *carne* raw; *los* ~*s* the living; *al* ~ to the life; *herir en lo* ~ cut to the quick; strike home; **2.** *m sew.* edging, border.

vizcaíno *adj. a. su. m*, **a** *f* Biscayan.
vizconde *m* viscount; **vizcondesa** *f* viscountess.
vocablo *m* word; *jugar del* ~ (make a) pun; **vocabulario** *m* vocabulary.
vocación *f* calling, vocation; **vocacional** vocational.
vocal 1. vocal; **2.** *m* voting member; **3.** *f* vowel; **vocálico** vocalic, vowel *attr.*; **vocalizar** [1f] *v/t.* vocalize; voice; *v/i.* ♪ hum; **~se** vocalize; **vocativo** *m* vocative (case).
voceador 1. vociferous, loud-mouthed; **2.** *m* town crier; **vocear** [1a] *v/t.* (*publicar*) shout, announce loudly; acclaim loudly; (*llamar*) shout to; F make a fuss about *s.t.* in public; *v/i.* shout, bawl; **vocejón** *m* rough voice; **vocería** *f*, **vocerío** *m* shouting, uproar, hullabaloo F; **vocero** *m* spokesman; **vociferar** [1a] vociferate, scream; **vocinglería** *f* shouting, shrieking, uproar; **vocinglero** vociferous, loud-mouthed; (*parlanchín*) chattering; *fig.* blatant.
vodú *v. vudú.*
voladero flying, that can fly; **voladizo** ⚠ projecting; **volador 1.** flying; *fig.* swift; **2.** *m* rocket; *ichth.* flying fish; **voladura** *f* blowing-up, demolition *etc.*; **volandas**: *en* ~, *a las* ~ in the air, through the air; *fig.* on wings.
volandera *f* ⊕ washer; grindstone *de molino*; F fib; **volandero** fledged, ready to fly; *p.* restless; **volante 1.** flying; *fig.* unsettled; **2.** *m mot.* steering wheel; ⊕ flywheel; balance *de reloj*; (*juego*) badminton; shuttlecock *con que se juega*; *sew.* ruffle, frill, flounce; (*papel*) note; *un buen* ~ a good driver; **volantón** *m* fledgling.
volar [1m] *v/t.* explode; *edificio etc.* blow up, demolish; *mina* explode, spring; blast *en cantera*; *v/i.* fly (*a. fig.*); flutter; hurtle; (*irse volando*) fly away, disappear; (*ir rápidamente*) fly, run fast, go fast; (*noticia*) spread quickly; (*tiempo*) fly; ~ *sin motor* ✈ glide.
volatería *f* (*aves*) birds, fowls; (*caza*) falconry; fowling *con señuelo*.
volátil ⚗ volatile (*a. fig.*); (*mudable*) changeable; **volatilidad** *f* volatility; **volatilizar(se)** [1f] volatilize, vaporize.
volatín *m*, **volatinero** *m*, **a** *f* tightrope walker, acrobat.
volcán *m* volcano; **volcánico** volcanic.
volcar [1g *a.* 1m] *v/t.* overturn, tip over; upset, knock over *por accidente*; *coche etc.* overturn, turn over; ⚓ capsize; *contenido* empty out, dump; *fig.* (*turbar*) make *s.o.* dizzy; (*hacer cambiar*) make *s.o.* change his mind; tease, irritate; *v/i.*, **~se** overturn *etc.*; F ~ *por inf.* do one's utmost to *inf.*
volear [1a] volley; **voleo** *m* volley; F *de un* ~ at one blow.
volframio *m* wolfram.
volición *f* volition.
volquete *m* tipcart.
voltaico voltaic; **voltaje** *m* voltage.
volteador *m*, **-a** *f* acrobat; **voltear** [1a] *v/t.* (*girar*) swing, whirl; (*poner al revés*) turn round; (*volcar*) upset, overturn; transform; *S.Am.* turn; *v/i.* roll over, somersault; **voltereta** *f* somersault, roll; tumble; ~ *sobre las manos* hand spring.
voltímetro *m* voltmeter; **voltio** *m* volt.
volubilidad *f fig.* fickleness; instability; **voluble** (*que gira*) revolving; ⚘ winding; *fig.* fickle, changeable; unstable.
volumen *m mst* volume; (*bulto*) bulk(iness); *radio*: ~ *sonoro* volume (of sound); **voluminoso** voluminous; bulky, big.
voluntad *f mst* will; (*energía*) will power; (*cariño*) affection, fondness; *buena* ~ goodwill; *mala* ~ ill will, malice; *su santa* ~ his own sweet will; *última* ~ last wish; ⚖ last will and testament; *a* ~ *obrar etc.* at will; (*cantidad*) ad-lib F; *por* ~ *propia* of one's own free will; *ganarse la* ~ *de* win over; **voluntariedad** *f* waywardness, willfulness; **voluntario 1.** voluntary; ⚔ volunteer *attr.*; **2.** *m* volunteer; **voluntarioso** wayward, headstrong, willful.
voluptuosidad *f* voluptuousness; **voluptuoso 1.** voluptuous; *b.s.* sensual; **2.** *m*, **a** *f* voluptuary.
voluta *f* ⚠ scroll, volute; spiral, column *de humo etc.*
volver [2h; *p.p. vuelto*] **1.** *v/t.* turn; turn round; *página etc.* turn (over); (*invertir*) turn upside down; *ojos etc.* turn, cast; *arma etc.* turn (*a* on),

direct, aim (*a* at); *puerta* close, pull to; (*devolver*) send back; *favor, visita* return, repay; (*reponer*) put back, replace (*a* in); (*restablecer*) restore (*a* to); ~ *adj.* turn, make, render; *v. loco*; **2.** *v/i.* return, come back, go back, get back; (*torcer*) turn, bend; ~ *a hábito, tema etc.* revert to, return to; ~ *a hacer* do again; ~ *atrás* turn back; ~ *en sí* come to, regain consciousness; ~ *por* stand up for; ~ *sobre sí* recover one's calm; **3.** **~se** turn (round); (*regresar*) = *v/i.*; (*vino*) turn (sour); (*opinión*) change one's mind; ~ *adj.* turn, become, go, get; ~ *atrás fig.* look back; (*cejar*) back out; ~ *contra* turn on; *v. loco.*

vomitado F sickly, seedy; **vomitar** [1a] vomit, bring up, throw up; *fig. llamas etc.* belch forth, spew; *ganancias* disgorge; *injurias* hurl; **vomitivo** *m* emetic; **vómito** *m* vomit; (*acto*) being sick, vomiting; ~*s del embarazo* morning sickness; **vomitona** *f* F bad sick turn.

voracidad *f* voracity, voraciousness.

vorágine *f* whirlpool, maelstrom.

voraz voracious, greedy, ravenous.

vórtice *m* whirlpool, vortex.

vos † ye; *S.Am.* you; **vosear** [1a] *S.Am.* address as *vos* (*i.e., treat familiarly*).

vosotros, vosotras *pl.* you.

votación *f* vote, voting; *esp. parl.* division; ~ *por manos levantadas* show of hands; *someter a* ~ put to the vote, take a vote on; **votante** **1.** voting; **2.** *m/f* voter; **votar** [1a] *v/t. ley* pass; *candidato* vote for; *v/i.* vote (*por* for); vow *a Dios etc.*; (*renegar*) curse, swear; **votivo** votive; **voto** *m pol. etc.* vote; (*p.*) voter; vow *a Dios etc.*; (*reniego*) curse, swearword; ~*s pl. fig.* (good) wishes; ~ *de calidad* casting vote; ~ *de confianza* vote of confidence; ~ *informativo* straw vote; *echar* ~*s* curse, swear; *hacer* ~ *de inf.* swear to *inf.*, (make a) vow to *inf.*; *hacer* ~*s para que* earnestly hope that.

voy *etc. v. ir.*

voz *f* voice (*a. gr.*); (*vocablo*) word; (*voto*) vote, support; (*grito*) shout; noise *de trueno etc.*; rumor, report; *voces pl.* (*gritos*) shouting; ~ *común* hearsay, rumor; *a una* ~ with one voice; *a media* ~ in a low voice; *v. grito*; *de viva* ~ viva voce; by word of mouth; *en* ~ in (good) voice; *en* ~ *alta* aloud, out loud; *en* ~ *baja* in an undertone; *aclarar la* ~ clear one's throat; *corre la* ~ *de que* there's a rumor going round that; *dar voces* shout, call out; *dar la* ~ *de alarma* sound; *dar cuatro voces* make a great fuss; F *llevar la* ~ *cantante* be the boss; *estar pidiendo a voces que* be crying out to *inf.*; *tener* ~ *y voto* have a say; *no tener* ~ *en capítulo* have no say *in a thing.*

vozarrón *m* F loud harsh voice.

vudú *m* voodoo; **vuduísmo** *m* voodoo religion; **vuduísta** *adj. a. su. m/f* voodoo.

vuelco *m* upset, spill, overturning; *dar un* ~ overturn; (*corazón*) jump.

vuelo *m* ✈ flight; fullness *de vestido*; (*adorno*) lace, frill; △ projecting part; *de mucho* ~ *falda* full; ~ *a ciegas* blind flying; ~ *de enlace* connecting flight; ~ *de ensayo* test flight; ~ *sin motor*, ~ *a vela* gliding; ~ *en picado* dive; *al* ~ on the wing, in flight; *fig.* at once; *alzar el* ~ take flight; F dash off; *tocar a* ~ peal; *tomar* ~ grow, develop.

vuelta *f* turn, revolution; *deportes*: lap, circuit *en carrera*; round *de torneo*; (*jira*) tour; (*paseo*) stroll; (*recodo*) turn, bend, curve; (*regreso*) return; (*devolución*) return, giving back; (*dinero*) change; (*revés*) back, other side; (*repetición*) repeat; *sew.* cuff; F hiding; ⚓ ~ *de cabo* hitch; ~ *de campana* somersault; ~ *del mundo* trip around the world; *a la* ~ (*de regreso*) on one's return; (*página*) on the next page, overleaf; *a la* ~ *de esquina* round; *años etc.* after, at the end of; *v. correo*; *dar* ~ *a llave* turn; *coche etc.* reverse, turn round; *dar la* ~ *a* go round; *dar una* ~ take a stroll; *dar una* ~ *de campana* turn completely over; *dar media* ~ face about; ⚔ about turn; *dar* ~*s* turn, go round, revolve; (*camino*) twist and turn; (*cabeza*) (be in a) whirl; *dar* ~*s a manivela etc.* wind, turn; *botón* turn; twirl *en dedos*; *no hay que darle* ~*s* it's no use going on (with it); *estar de* ~ be back, be home; F be in the know; F be mighty clever; *poner de* ~ *y media* heap insults upon; *no tiene* ~ *de hoja* there's no denying it.

vuelto 1. *p.p. of volver*; **2.** *m S.Am.* change.
vuestro 1. *adj.* your; (*tras su.*) of yours; **2.** *pron.* yours.
vulcanita *f* vulcanite; **vulcanizar** [1f] vulcanize.
vulgar *lengua* vulgar; *opinión etc.* common, general; *término* ordinary, accepted; (*corriente*) ordinary, everyday; banal; trivial, trite; **vulgaridad** *f* commonness *etc.*; (*cosa vulgar*) triviality; *~es pl. freq.* small talk; platitudes; **vulgarismo** *m* popular form; *b.s.* slang (word), vulgarism; **vulgarizar** [1f] popularize, vulgarize; *texto etc.* translate into the vernacular; **Vulgata** *f* Vulgate; **vulgo** *m* common people, lower orders, common herd.
vulnerable vulnerable; **vulnerar** [1a] damage.
vulpeja *f* fox; (*hembra*) vixen; **vulpino** vulpine.

W, X

wáter [ˈbater] *m* lavatory, toilet, water closet.

wélter [ˈbelter] *m boxeo*: welterweight.

whisk(e)y [ˈwiski] *m* whisk(e)y.

wolfram [ˈbolfram] *m* wolfram.

xilófono [s-] *m* xylophone.

xilografía [s-] *f* xylography, wood engraving.

xilógrafo [s-] *m* xylographer, wood engraver.

Y

y and; *las 2 y media* half-past two.
ya (*en momento pasado*) already, before now; (*ahora*) now; (*más adelante*) in due course, sometime; (*en seguida*) at once; *¡~!* now I remember, of course!; *~, ~* yes, yes; *~ ..., ~ ...* (*ora*) now ..., now ...; (*si*) whether ..., or ...; *~ en 1977* as long ago as 1977, as early as 1977; *~ no* no longer, not any more; *~ que* as, since; now (that).
yacaré *m* crocodile.
yacente *estatua* recumbent; **yacer** [2y] †, *lit.* lie; *aquí yace* here lies; **yacija** *f* bed; (*tumba*) grave, tomb; *ser de mala ~* sleep badly; (*inquieto*) be restless; (*carácter*) be a bad lot; **yacimiento** *m* bed, deposit; *~ de petróleo* oil field.
yámbico iambic; **yambo** *m* iambus.
yanqui *adj. a. su. m/f* Yankee.
yate *m* yacht.
yedra *f* ivy.
yegua *f* mare; **yeguada** *f* stud.
yelmo *m* helmet.
yema *f* yolk *de huevo*; ⚘ (leaf) bud, eye; (*lo mejor*) best part; *fig.* snag; *~ del dedo* fingertip; *~ mejida* eggnog; *dar en la ~* put one's finger on the spot.
yendo *v. ir.*
yerba *f v. hierba.*
yermar [1a] lay waste; **yermo 1.** waste, uninhabited; **2.** *m* waste (land), wilderness.
yerno *m* son-in-law.
yerro *m* error, mistake; *~ de cuenta* miscalculation; *~ de imprenta* printer's error.
yerto stiff, rigid.
yesca *f* tinder (*a. fig.*); fuel *de pasión etc.*; *~s pl.* tinderbox.
yesería *f* plastering, plasterwork; **yesero** *m* plasterer; **yeso** *m geol.* gypsum; ⚠ *etc.* plaster; (*vaciado*) plaster cast; *~ mate* plaster of Paris.
yip *m S.Am.* jeep.
yo I; *el ~* the self, the ego.
yódico iodic; **yodo** *m* iodine; **yoduro** *m* iodide.
yola *f* gig, yawl; *deportes*: sailing boat, shell.
yonquí *m sl. drogas*: junkie (*drug addict*).
yugo *m* yoke (*a. fig.*).
yugo(e)slavo *adj. a. su. m*, **a** *f* Jugoslav.
yugular jugular.
yungas *f/pl. S.Am.* valleys.
yungla *f* jungle.
yunque *m* anvil; *fig.* tireless worker, devil for work.
yunta *f* yoke, team *de bueyes*; (*pareja*) couple, pair.
yute *m* jute.
yuxtaponer [2r] juxtapose; **yuxtaposición** *f* juxtaposition.

Z

zabordar [1a] run aground.
zabullir *etc. v. zambullir etc.*
zafado *S.Am.* (*vivo*) wide awake; (*descarado*) brazen.
zafar [1a] loosen, untie; **~se** keep out of the way, hide o.s. away; ~ *de p. etc.* shake off, dodge, ditch F; *compromiso* wriggle out of.
zafarrancho *m* ⚓ clearing for action; F row, set-to; ~ *de combate* (call to) action stations.
zafio coarse, loutish.
zafiro *m* sapphire.
zafo: *salirse* ~ come out (*de* of) unharmed.
zaga *f* rear; *a la* ~, *en* ~ behind, in the rear; *no ir en* ~ *a* be every bit as good as; *no ir en* ~ *a nadie* be second to none.
zagal *m* lad, youth; ✎ shepherd boy; **zagala** *f* lass, girl; ✎ shepherdess.
zagalón *m* big lad; **zagalona** *f* big girl.
zagual *m* puddle.
zaguán *m* vestibule, hall(way).
zaguero rear, back; bottom *en liga*; *p.* slow.
zahareño wild, unsociable.
zaherir [3i] attack, criticize (sarcastically); reproach, upbraid; ~ *con* throw *s.t.* in *s.o.'s* face.
zahorí *m* seer, clairvoyant; (*que busca agua*) water diviner.
zahurda *f* pigsty.
zaino *animal* chestnut; *p.* treacherous, false.
zalamería *f* flattery, cajolery *etc.*; **zalamero 1.** flattering, cajoling; unctuous, suave, oily; **2.** *m*, **a** *f* flatterer; servile person.
zalea *f* sheepskin.
zalema *f* salaam, bowing and scraping.
zamarra *f* sheepskin (jacket); **zamarrear** [1a] shake, worry; *fig.* shake up, knock about; **zamarro** *m* sheepskin; F yokel; **~s** *pl. S.Am.* riding breeches.
zambo 1. knock-kneed; **2.** *m*, **a** *f* Indian-black (*mixed Indian and black*).
zambomba *f sort of rustic drum*; F ¡~! phew!; **zambombo** *m* coarse fellow, yokel.
zambra *f* F uproar, row.
zambucar [1g] F jumble up, mix up.
zambullida *f* dive, plunge; duck, ducking; **zambullir** [3h] duck, plunge; **~se** dive, plunge; duck; *fig.* hide, cover o.s. up.
zampabollos *m/f* F (*comilón*) greedy pig, glutton; (*grosero*) coarse sort; **zampar** [1a] whip smartly, shoot (*en* into); F (*comer*) wolf, demolish, put away; **~se** whip, vanish (*en* into); **zampatortas** *m/f* F = *zampabollos*; **zampón** F greedy.
zampoña *f* shepherd's pipes.
zampuzar [1f] duck *en agua*; *fig.* = *zampar*.
zanahoria *f* carrot.
zanca *f* shank; **~s** *pl.* F long shanks; **zancada** *f* stride; F *en dos* **~s** in a couple of ticks; **zancadilla** *f* trip *con pie*; (*aparato*) booby trap; (*engaño*) trick; *echar la* ~ *a* trip (up); **zancajear** [1a] rush around; **zancarrón** *m* F leg bone; big bone; (*p.*) old bag of bones; **zanco** *m* stilt; *en* **~s** *fig.* well up, in a good position; **zancudo** long-legged; *orn.* wading; *ave* **~a** wader.
zangamanga *f* F funny business, piece of dirty work; **zanganada** *f* F sauce, saucy remark.
zanganear [1a] F loaf, (be a) spiv; **zángano** *m* drone; F drone, idler, slacker.
zangarrear [1a] strum on a guitar.
zangarri(an)a *f* F ⚕ small upset; headache; *fig.* blues.
zangolotear [1a] F *v/t.* keep playing with, fidget with; *v/i.* (be on the) fidget; **~se** (*ventana*) rattle.
zangón *m* big lazy guy.
zanguanga: F *hacer la* ~ swing the lead; **zanguango** F lazy; silly.
zanja *f* ditch, trench; *S.Am.* irri-

gation ditch; *abrir las* ~*s* lay the foundations; **zanjar** [1a] trench, ditch; *dificultad* get round.

zanquilargo F leggy; **zanquivano** spindly.

zapa[1] *f* (*lija*) shagreen, sharkskin.

zapa[2] *f* ⚔ (*pala*) spade; (*trinchera*) trench, sap; **zapador** *m* sapper, pioneer.

zapallo *m S.Am.* gourd, pumpkin.

zapapico *m* pick(axe); **zapar** [1a] sap, undermine.

zaparrazo *m* F claw, scratch.

zapata *f* shoe *de freno etc.*; **zapatazo** *m* bump, bang; **zapateado** *m* tap dance; **zapatear** [1a] *v/t.* kick, prod with one's foot; tap with one's foot; F give *s.o.* a rough time; *v/i.* tap-dance; **zapatería** *f* shoe shop; (*arte*) shoemaking; **zapatero** *m* shoemaker; ~ *remendón*, ~ *de viejo* cobbler; **zapatilla** *f* slipper *para casa*; pump *para bailar*; ⊕ washer; **zapato** *m* shoe; *como tres en un* ~ like sardines; *saber dónde aprieta el* ~ know which side one's bread is buttered; know where s.o.'s weakness lies.

¡zape! shoo!; **zapear** [1a] shoo, scare away.

zaque *m* wineskin; F boozer; F *estar hecho un* ~ be sozzled.

zaquizamí *m* poky little place, hole.

zar *m* tsar, czar.

zarabanda *f* sarabande; *fig.* row.

zaragata *f* F row, set-to; **zaragatero** *m* F rowdy, hooligan.

zaragozano *adj. a. su. m,* **a** *f* (native) of Saragossa.

zaranda *f* sieve; **zarandajas** *f/pl.* F trifles, odds and ends; **zarandear** [1a] sift, sieve; shake up; ~**se** be on the go, never be still; **zarandillo** *m* F active person, lively sort; F *traer como un* ~ keep *s.o.* on the go; **zarandón** *m sl.* booze-up.

zarapito *m* curlew.

zarcillo *m* ⚘ tendril; (*joya*) earring.

zarco light blue.

zarigüeya *f* opossum.

zarpa *f* claw, paw; F *echar la* ~ grab hold (*a* of); **zarpada** *f* clawing, blow with the paw; **zarpar** [1a] weigh anchor, set sail; **zarpazo** *m* = *zarpada*; *fig.* thud, bump.

zarrapastrón F, **zarrapastroso** ragged, slovenly, shabby.

zarza *f* bramble, blackberry; **zarzal** *m* (clump of) brambles; **zarzamora** *f* blackberry.

zarzo *m* (*tejido*) wattle; hurdle *de cerca etc.*

zarzuela *f* operetta, light opera, musical comedy.

¡zas! bang!, slap!

zascandil *m* F busybody.

zepelín *m* zeppelin.

zigzag *m* zigzag; *en* ~ *relámpago* forked; **zigzaguear** [1a] zigzag.

zinc *m* zinc.

zipizape *m* F set-to, rumpus.

zócalo *m* socle, base of a pedestal; *Mex.* public square, center square.

zoclo *m* clog, wooden shoe; galosh, overshoe *de goma*.

zodiacal zodiacal; **zodíaco** *m* zodiac.

zona *f* zone; belt, area; ~ *a batir* target area; ~ *edificada* built-up area; ~ *de pruebas* testing ground; ~ *siniestrada* disaster area; ~ *tórrida* torrid zone; **zonal** zonal.

zoo... zoo...; **zoología** *f* zoology; **zoológico** zoological; **zoólogo** *m* zoologist.

zopenco F **1.** stupid, silly; **2.** *m* nitwit, dunce, blockhead.

zoquete *m* (*madera*) block, piece; (*pan*) bit of bread; F (*tonto*) chump, duffer; (*grosero*) oaf, lout.

zorra *f* (*en general*) fox; (*hembra*) vixen; F whore; **zorrera** *f* foxhole; F worry, anxiety; **zorrería** *f* foxiness, craftiness; **zorrero** foxy, crafty; **zorro 1.** *m* (dog) fox; F old fox, crafty sort; F *hacerse el* ~ act dumb; **2.** foxy, crafty, slippery.

zorzal *m* thrush; F sly fellow; *S.Am.* F mutt.

zozobra *f* ⚓ sinking, capsizing; *fig.* worry, anxiety; unrest; **zozobrar** [1a] ⚓ sink, capsize, overturn; *fig.* (*peligrar*) be in danger; (*afligirse*) worry, fret.

zueco *m* clog, wooden shoe.

zulú *m* Zulu.

zumba *f fig.* banter, chaff, teasing; *hacer* ~ *a* rag, tease; **zumbador** *m* ⚡ buzzer; **zumbar** [1a] *v/t.* F rag, chaff; *univ. sl.* plow; *golpe* let *s.o.* have; *S.Am.* throw, chuck; *v/i.* (*abeja*) buzz, hum, drone; (*oídos*) sing, ring; (*máquina*) whirr, drone, hum; (*zumbador*) buzz; ~**se** de rag, chaff; **zumbido** *m* buzz(ing) *etc.*; F

punch, hit; **zumbón 1.** *p.* waggish, funny; *tono etc.* bantering; **2.** *m*, **-a** *f* wag, funny man *etc.*; banterer, tease.
zumo *m* juice; (*como bebida*) fruit juice and soda; *fig.* advantage, profit; ~ *de cepas*, ~ *de parras* F fruit of the vine; ~ *de limón* lemonade and soda; ~ *de uva* grape juice; **zumoso** juicy.
zuncho *m* band, hoop, ring.
zupia *f* muddy wine; *fig.* trash.
zurcido *m* darn, mend; **zurcidura** *f* (*acto*) darning, mending; = *zurcido*; **zurcir** [3b] darn, mend, sew up; *fig.* put together; *mentira* concoct, think up.
zurdo left-handed.
zurra *f* dressing, tanning; F (*paliza*) tanning, spanking; (*trabajo*) grind, drudgery; (*riña*) set-to; **zurrador** *m* tanner.
zurrapa *f* dregs; F trash, muck; **zurraposo** thick, muddy.
zurrar [1a] dress, tan; F tan, wallop, spank; **~se** dirty o.s.
zurriaga *f* whip; **zurriagar** [1h] whip; **zurriagazo** *m* lash; *fig.* bad knock, stroke of bad luck; **zurriago** *m* whip.
zurriar [1b] hum, buzz.
zurribanda *f* F = *zurra* F.
zurriburri *m* F mess, mix-up.
zurrón *m* pouch, bag.
zutano *m*, **a** *f* (Mr. *etc.*) So-and-so.

Appendices
Apéndices

Spanish Abbreviations

Abreviaturas españolas

Each entry contains an expansion of the Spanish abbreviation, and wherever possible the equivalent English abbreviation with its expansion in parentheses.

A

a *área.*
A: bomba A *bomba atómica* A-bomb (atomic bomb).
(a) *alias* alias.
ab.[1] *abril* Apr. (April).
a.c. *año corriente* current year, present year.
A. (de) C. *año de Cristo* A.D. (Anno Domini).
a/c *al cuidado* c/o (care of).
acr. *acreedor* creditor.
adj. *adjunto* Enc. (enclosure, enclosed).
adm(ón). *administración* admin. (administration).
a/f. *a favor* in favor.
afmo. *afectísimo*: *suyo* ~ yours truly.
ag. *agosto* Aug. (August)
a. (de) J.C. *antes de Jesucristo* B.C. (before Christ).
AI *Amnistía Internacional* AI (Amnesty International).
Al.º *Alonso personal name.*
amp. *amperios* amp. (ampères).
Ant.º *Antonio personal name.*
ap. *thea. aparte* aside.
apdo. *apartado (de correos)* P.O.B. (Post Office Box).
art., art.º *artículo* art. (article).
arz. *arzobispo* abp. (archbishop).
A.T. *Antiguo Testamento* O.T. (Old Testament).
atmo. *atentísimo*: *suyo* ~ yours truly.
atta. *atenta.*
atte. *atentamente.*
a/v. *a vista* at sight.
Av., Av.ᵈᵃ *Avenida*, Av., Ave. (Avenue).

B

B. *eccl. beato* blessed.
B.A. *Buenos Aires capital of Argentina.*
Bº *banco* bk. (bank).
Bón. *batallón* Battn, Bn. (battalion).

C

c. *capítulo* ch. (chapter).
C. *compañía* Co. (company).
c^3 *centímetro cúbico* c.c. (cubic centimeter).
c.ª *compañía* Co. (company).
c.a. *corriente alterna* A.C. (alternating current).
C.A.E. *cóbrese al entregar* C.O.D. (cash on delivery).
cap. *capítulo* ch. (chapter).
Cap.ⁿ *Capitán* Capt. (Captain).
cap.º *capítulo* ch. (chapter).
c.c. *centímetro cúbico* c.c. (cubic centimeter).
c.c. *corriente continua* D.C. (direct current).
c/c *cuenta corriente* C/A (current account).
C.D. *Club Deportivo* S.C. (Sports Club).
c/d *con descuento* with discount.
C. de J. *Compañía de Jesús* S.J. (Society of Jesus).
CECA *Comunidad Europea de Carbón y del Acero* ECSC (European Coal and Steel Community).
CEE *Comunidad Económica Europea* E(E)C (European [Economic] Community).
C.F. *Club de Fútbol* F.C. (Football Club).
cg. *centigramo* centigram.

Cía *compañía* Co. (company).
c.i.f. *costo, seguro y flete* c.i.f. (cost, insurance, freight).
cl. *centilitro* centiliter.
cm. *centímetro* cm. (centimeter).
cm^2 *centímetro cuadrado* sq. cm. (square centimeter).
cm^3 *centímetro cúbico* c.c. (cubic centimeter).
Cnel *Coronel* Col. (Colonel).
COI *Comité Olímpico Internacional* IOC (International Olympic Committee).
col., col.[a] *columna* col. (column).
comp. *compárese* cf. (confer).
comp.[a] *compañía* Co. (company).
corrte. *corriente, de los corrientes* inst. (instant).
C.P. *contestación pagada* R.P. (reply paid).
cs. *céntimos; centavos* cents.
c.s.f. *costo, seguro, flete* c.i.f. (cost, insurance, freight).
cta, c.[ta] *cuenta* A/C (account).
cte *corriente, de los corrientes* inst. (instant).
cts. *céntimos; centavos* cents.
c/u *cada uno* ea. (each).
c.v. *caballo(s) de vapor* HP (horsepower).

Ch

ch. *cheque* chq. (cheque).

D

D. *debe* debit side.
D. *Don* Esq. (Esquire) (*Sr. D., en el sobre delante del nombre de pila*; Esq., *en el sobre después del apellido*).
Da. *Doña title of courtesy to ladies: no equivalent.*
dcho., dcha. *derecho, derecha* right.
d. (de) J.C. *después de Jesucristo* A.D. (Anno Domini).
D.F. *México: Distrito Federal* Federal District.
dg. *decigramo* decigram.
Dg. *decagramo* decagram.
D.G.T. *Dirección General del Turismo state tourist organization.*
dho. *dicho* aforesaid.
dic.[e] *diciembre* Dec. (December).
dl. *decilitro* deciliter.
Dl. *decalitro* decaliter.
dm. *decímetro* decimeter.
Dn *Don* (*v. D.*).
d.[na] *docena* doz. (dozen).
do. *descuento* dis., dist (discount).
doc. *docena* doz. (dozen).
dom.[o] *domingo* Sun. (Sunday).
d/p. *días plazo* day's time.
Dr. *Doctor* Dr (doctor).
dro., dra. *derecho, derecha* right.
d.[to] *descuento* dis., dist (discount).
dup.[do] *duplicado* duplicate.
d/v. *días vista* d.s., d/s. (days after sight).

E

E *este* E. (East[ern]).
ed. *edición* ed. (edition).
EE.UU. *Estados Unidos* U.S., U.S.A. (United States [of America]).
E.M. *Estado Mayor* staff.
Encia. *Eminencia* Eminence.
en.[o] *enero* Jan. (January).
E.P.D. *en paz descanse* R.I.P. (requiescat in pace).
ES *Ejército de Salvación* S.A. (Salvation Army).
esq. *esquina* corner.
etc. *etcétera* etc. (et caetera, etcetera).
EU *Estados Unidos* US (United States).
Exc. *Excelencia* Excellency.
Exmo. *Excelentísimo courtesy title.*

F

f. *femenino* f., fem. (feminine).
fa *factura* bill, account.
f.a.b. *franco a bordo* f.o.b. (free on board).
f.c. *ferrocarril* Rly. (railway).
feb.[o] *febrero* Feb. (February).
Fern.[do] *Fernando personal name.*
fha. *fecha* d. (date).
FMI *Fondo Monetario Internacional* I.M.F. (International Monetary Fund).
f.[o]**, fol.** *folio* fo., fol. (folio).
Fr. *Fray* Fr. (Friar).
Fran.[co] *Francisco personal name.*

G

g. *gramo(s)* gr(s). (gram[s], *British* gramme[s]).
G *giro* draft, money-order.
gde. *guarde: que Dios guarde* whom God protect.

Genl *General* Gen. (General).
G.º *Gonzalo personal name.*
gob.ⁿᵒ *gobierno* Govt. (Government).
Gral, gral. *General* Gen. (General).
grs. *gramos* grs. (grams).

H

h. *habitantes* pop. (population).
h. *hacia* c. (circa).
H. *haber* Cr. (credit).
H: bomba H *bomba de hidrógeno* H-bomb (hydrogen bomb).
hect. *hectárea* hectare.
Hg. *hectogramo* hectogram.
Hl. *hectolitro* hectoliter.
Hnos. *Hermanos* Bros. (Brothers).
H.P. (*inglés* – horse-power) *caballos, caballaje* H.P. (horse-power).

I

ib., ibid. *ibídem* ibid. (ibidem).
igl.ª *iglesia* church.
Il. *ilustre courtesy title.*
Ilmo. *ilustrísimo courtesy title.*
Imp. *Imprenta* printers, printing works.
I.N.I. *Instituto Nacional de Industria state industrial council.*
IVA *Impuesto sobre el valor agregado* (*o añadido*) VAT (value-added tax).
izdo., izda. *izquierdo, izquierda* left.

J

J.C. *Jesucristo* Jesus Christ.
JJ.OO. *Juegos Olímpicos* Olympic Games.
juev. *jueves* Thurs. (Thursday).

K

k/c *kilociclos* k/c. (kilocycles).
Kg. *kilogramo* kg. (kilogram).
Kl. *kilolitro* kiloliter.
Km. *kilómetro* km. (kilometer).
Km./h. *kilómetros por hora* kilometers per hour.
kv. *kilovatio* kw. (kilowatt).

L

l. ⚖ *ley* law.
l. *libro* bk. (book).
l. *litro* l. (liter).
lbs. *libras* lbs. (pounds).
lib. *libra* lb. (pound).
lib., lib.º *libro* bk. (book).
Lic. en Fil. y Let. *Licenciado en Filosofía y Letras* B.A. (Bachelor of Arts).
lun. *lunes* Mon. (Monday).

M

m. *minuto* m. (minute).
m. *metro* m. (meter).
m. *masculino* m., masc. (masculine).
m. *muerto, murió* d. (died).
m² *metro cuadrado* sq. m. (square meter).
m³ *metro cúbico* cu. m. (cubic meter).
M. *Madrid capital of Spain.*
Ma. *María personal name.*
mart. *martes* Tues. (Tuesday).
M.C. *Mercado Común* C.M. (Common Market).
Md. *Madrid capital of Spain.*
M.F. *modulación de frecuencia* F.M. (frequency modulation).
mg *miligramo* mg. (milligram).
miérc. *miércoles* Weds. (Wednesday).
mm *milímetro* mm. (millimeter).
Mons. *Monseñor* Mgr. (Monsignor).
MS *manuscrito* MS (manuscript).
MMS *manuscritos* MSS (manuscripts).

N

n. *nacido, nació* b. (born).
N *norte* N. (North[ern]).
nal. *nacional* national.
Na. Sra. *Nuestra Señora* Our Lady, The Virgin.
N.B. *nótese bien* N.B. (nota bene).
NE *noreste* N.E. (North East[ern]).
NNE *nornordeste* NNE (north-northeast).
NNO *nornordoeste* NNW (north-northwest).
NN.UU. *Naciones Unidas* U.N. (United Nations).
n.º *número* No. (number).
NO *noroeste* N.W. (North West[ern]).
nov.ᵉ *noviembre* Nov. (November).
nro., nra. *nuestro, nuestra* our.
N.S. *Nuestro Señor* Our Lord.
N.T. *Nuevo Testamento* N.T. (New Testament).

ntro., ntra. *nuestro, nuestra* our.
N.U. *Naciones Unidas* U.N. (United Nations).
Núm. *número* No. (number).

O

O *oeste* W. (West[ern]).
O.A.A *Organización de Agricultura y Alimentación* F.A.O. (Food and Agriculture Organization).
O.A.C.I. *Organización de Aviación Civil Internacional* I.C.A.O. (International Civil Aviation Organization).
ob., obpo. *obispo* Bp. (bishop).
obr. cit. *obra citada* op. cit. (opere citato).
OCDE *Organización de Cooperación y Desarrollo Económico* O.E.C.D. (Organization for Economic Cooperation and Development).
oct.[e] *octubre* Oct. (October).
OEA *Organización de los Estados Americanos* O.A.S. (Organization of American States).
OIT *Organización Internacional de Trabajo* ILO (International Labor Organization).
OLP *Organización para la Liberación de Palestina* P.L.O. (Palestine Liberation Organization).
OMS *Organización Mundial de la Salud* W.H.O. (World Health Organization).
ONU *Organización de las Naciones Unidas* UNO (United Nations Organization).
O.P. *Orden de Predicadores* O.S.D. (Order of St. Dominic).
O.P. *Obras Públicas* P.W.D. (Public Works Department).
OPEP *Organización de Países Exportadores de Petróleo* OPEC (Organization of Petroleum-Exporting Countries).
O.S.B. *Orden de San Benito* O.S.B. (Order of St. Benedict).
OTAN *Organización del Tratado del Atlántico Norte* NATO (North Atlantic Treaty Organization).
OTASE *Organización del Tratado del Sudeste Asiático* (*or del Asia Sudeste*) SEATO (South East Asia Treaty Organization).
OVNI *u* **ovni** *objeto volante no identificado* UFO (unidentified flying object).

P

p. *punto, puntada* st. (stitch).
P. *papa* pope.
P. *padre* Fr. (Father).
P% *por cien(to)* %, p. c. (per cent).
pág. *página* p. (page).
págs. *páginas* pp. (pages).
p.c. *por cien(to)* %, p.c. (per cent).
PC *Partido Comunista* C.P. (Communist Party).
P.D. *posdata* P.S. (postscript).
PDC *Partido Demócrata Cristiano* Christian Democratic Union.
pdo. *pasado* ult. (ultimo).
Pe. *Padre* Fr. (Father).
PED *Procesamiento Electrónico de Datos* E.D.P. (electronic data processing).
p. ej. *por ejemplo* e.g. (exempli gratia, for example).
pmo. *próximo* prox. (proximo).
PNB *producto nacional bruto* G.N.P. (gross national product).
P.[o] *Pedro personal name.*
P.[o] *Paseo* Avenue.
p.[o] **n.**[o] *peso neto* nt. wt. (net weight).
p.o. *por orden* per pro(c)., p.p. (per procurationem, by proxy).
p.p. *por poder* per pro(c)., p.p. (per procurationem, by proxy).
P.P. *porte pagado* C.P. (carriage paid).
p.pdo. (*el mes*) *próximo pasado* ult. (ultimo).
pral. *principal* first.
pr. fr. *próximo futuro* prox. (proximo).
Prof. *Profesor* Prof. (Professor).
prov. *provincia* province.
PS *Partido Socialista* Socialist Party.
ps. *pesos* pesos.
P.S. *postscriptum* (*posdata*) P.S. (postscript).
ptas. *pesetas* pesetas.
P.V.P. *precio de venta al público* retail price.
pzs *piezas* pcs. (pieces).

Q

q.D.g. *que Dios guarde* whom God protect (*used after mention of king*).
q.e.p.d. *que en paz descanse* R.I.P. (requiescat in pace).
q.e.s.m. *que estrecha su mano courtesy formula.*
quil. *quilates* carats.
qts. *quilates* carats.

R

R. *Real* Royal.
R. *Reverendo* Rev. (Reverend).
R.A.C.E. *Real Automóvil Club de España equivalent to British* A.A. *and* R.A.C.
Rdo *Reverendo* Rev. (Reverend).
RENFE *Red Nacional de Ferrocarriles Españoles Spanish railway company.*
RFA *República Federal de Alemania* FRG Federal Republic of Germany.
R.M. *Reverenda Madre* Reverend Mother.
R.O. *real orden* royal decree.
R.P. *Reverendo Padre* Reverend Father.
rúst. *en rústica* paper-backed.

S

s/ *su* yr. (your).
S. *San(to), Santa* St. (Saint).
S *sur* S. (South[ern]).
s.a. *sin año* s.a. (sine anno).
S.A. *Su Alteza* H.H. (His [*or* Her] Highness).
S.A. ✝ *Sociedad Anónima* Inc. (Incorporated); Ltd. (Limited).
sáb. *sábado* Sat. (Saturday).
SE *sudeste* S.E. (South East[ern]).
sept.[e] *septiembre* Sept. (September).
s.e.u.o. *salvo error u omisión* E. & O.E. (errors and omissions excepted).
s.f. *sin fecha* n.d. (no date).
sgte. *siguiente* f. (following).
SIDA *síndrome de inmunidad deficiente adquirida* AIDS (acquired immune-deficiency syndrome).
sigs. (*y*) *siguientes* et seq. (et sequentia), ff. (following).
S.I.M. *Servicio de Información Militar* M.I. (Military Intelligence).
s.l.ni f. *sin lugar ni fecha* n.p. or d. (no place or date).
s/n. *sin número* not numbered.
S.M. *Su Majestad* H.M. (His [*or* Her] Majesty).
SO *suroeste* S.W. (South West[ern]).
Sr. *Señor* Mr (Mister).
Sra. *Señora* Mrs (Mistress).
S.R.C. *se ruega contestación* R.S.V.P. (répondez s'il vous plaît).
Sres. *Señores* Messrs (Messieurs).
Srio. *Secretario* Sec. (Secretary).
S.R.M. *Su Real Majestad* H.M. (His [*or* Her] Majesty).
Srta. *Señorita* Miss.
SS *Seguridad Social British* N.I. (National Insurance); *Am.* (Social Security).
SS. *Su Santidad* His Holiness.
SS *Santos* SS (Saints).
SSE *sudsudeste* SSE (south-south-east).
SSO *sudsudoeste* SSW (south-south-west).
s.s.s. *su seguro servidor* yours truly.

T

t. *tomo*(s) vol(s). (volume[s]).
Tel. *teléfono* Tel. (Telephone).
Tente. *Teniente* Lieut. (Lieutenant).
Tlf. *teléfono* Tel. (Telephone).
T.R.B. *toneladas registradas brutas* G.R.T. (gross register tonnage).
Tte *Teniente* Lieut. (Lieutenant).
TV *televisión* T.V. (television).

U

Ud. *usted* you.
Uds. *ustedes* you.
U.E.P. *Unión Europea de Pagos* E.P.U. (European Payments Union).
U.P.U. *Unión Postal Universal* U.P.U. (Universal Postal Union).
URSS *Unión de las Repúblicas Socialistas Soviéticas* U.S.S.R. (Union of Soviet Socialist Republics).

V

v. *voltio* v. (volt).
v. *véase* see.
V. *usted* you.
Vd. *usted* you.
Vda de *viuda de* widow of.
Vds. *ustedes* you.
verso *versículo* v. (verse).
v.g., v.gr. *verbigracia* viz. (videlicet).
vid. *vide* see.
vier. *viernes* Fri. (Friday).
V.M. *Vuestra Majestad* Your Majesty.
V.º B.º *visto bueno* O.K. (all correct?).
v(t)ro., v(t)ra. *vuestro, vuestra* yr. (your).

W

w. *watio* w. (watt).

X

Xpo. *Cristo* Christ.

Spanish Proper Names

Nombres propios españoles

A

Abisinia *f* Abyssinia.
Abrahán Abraham.
Adán Adam.
Adén Aden.
Adolfo Adolf, Adolphus.
Adriano Hadrian.
Adriático *m* Adriatic.
Afganistán *m* Afghanistan.
Africa *f* Africa; ~ *del Norte* North Africa.
Agustín Augustine.
Aladino Aladdin.
Albania *f* Albania.
Alberto Albert.
Albión *f* Albion.
Alejandría Alexandria.
Alejandro Alexander; ~ *Magno* Alexander the Great.
Alemania *f* Germany.
Alfredo Alfred.
Alicia Alice.
Alpes *m/pl.* Alps.
Alsacia *f* Alsace.
Alto Volta *m* Upper Volta.
Amalia Amelia.
Amazonas *m* Amazon.
Amberes Antwerp.
América *f* America; ~ *Central* Central America; ~ *del Norte* North America; ~ *del Sur* South America; ~ *Latina* Latin America.
Ana Ann(e).
Anacreonte Anacreon.
Andalucía *f* Andalusia.
Andes *m/pl.* Andes.
Andrés Andrew.
Angola *f* Angola.
Aníbal Hannibal.
Antártida *f* Antarctic.
Antillas *f/pl.* West Indies, Antilles; *Grandes* ~ Greater Antilles; *Pequeñas* ~ Lesser Antilles.
Antioquía Antioch.
Antonio Anthony.
Apeninos *m/pl.* Apennines.
Aquiles Achilles.
Arabia *f* Arabia; ~ *Saudita o Saudí* Saudi-Arabia.
Aragón *m* Aragon.
Arcadia *f* Arcady.
Ardenas *m/pl.* Ardennes.
Argel Algiers.
Argelia *f* Algeria.
Argentina *f* the Argentine.
Aristófanes Aristophanes.
Aristóteles Aristotle.
Arlequín Harlequin.
Armenia *f* Armenia.
Arquímedes Archimedes.
Arturo Arthur.
Artús: *el* **Rey** ~ King Arthur.
Asia *f* Asia; ~ *Menor* Asia Minor.
Asiria *f* Assyria.
Asunción *Capital of Paraguay.*
Atenas Athens.
Atila Attila.
Atlántico *m* Atlantic.
Augusto Augustus.
Australia *f* Australia.
Austria *f* Austria.
Auvernia *f* Auvergne.
Aviñón Avignon.
Azores *m/pl.* Azores.

B

Babia: *estar en* ~ go woolgathering, have one's mind somewhere else.
Babilonia *f* Babylon.
Baco Bacchus.
Bahamas *f/pl.* Bahamas.
Balcanes *m/pl.* Balkans.
Baleares *f/pl.* Balearic Isles.
Báltico *m* Baltic.
Bangla Desh *m* Bangladesh.
Barba Azul Bluebeard.
Bartolomé Bartholomew.
Basilea Bâle, Basle.
Baviera *f* Bavaria.
Beatriz Beatrice.

Belcebú Beelzebub.
Belén Bethlehem; *estar en ~* daydream, go woolgathering.
Bélgica *f* Belgium.
Belgrado Belgrade.
Belice *m* Belize.
Benedicto Benedict.
Bengala *f* Bengal.
Benito Benedict.
Benjamín Benjamin.
Berlín Berlin.
Berna Berne.
Bernardo Bernard.
Birmania *f* Burma.
Bizancio Byzantium.
Blancanieves Snow-white.
Bocacio Boccaccio.
Bogotá *Capital of Columbia.*
Bolivia *f* Bolivia.
Borbón Bourbon.
Borgoña *f* Burgundy.
Bósforo *m* Bosphorus.
Brasil *m* Brazil.
Bretaña *f* Brittany.
Brígida Bridget.
Briján: *saber más que ~* be very bright.
Brujas Bruges.
Bruselas Brussels.
Bruto Brutus.
Buda Buddha.
Buenos Aires *Capital of Argentina.*
Bulgaria *f* Bulgaria.
Burdeos Bordeaux.
Burundi *m* Burundi.

C

Cabo *m* **de Buena Esperanza** Cape of Good Hope.
Cabo *m* **de Hornos** Cape Horn.
Cabo *m* **Cañaveral** Cape Canaveral.
Cabo: (Ciudad *f* **de) El ~** Cape Town.
Cachemira *f* Kashmir.
Cádiz Cadiz.
Caín Cain; F *pasar las de ~* have a terrible time.
Cairo: El ~ Cairo.
Camboya *f* Cambodia.
Camerún *m* Cameroons.
Canadá *m* Canada.
Canal *m* **de la Mancha** English Channel.
Canal *m* **de Panamá** Panama Canal.
Canal *m* **de Suez** Suez Canal.
Canarias *f/pl.* Canaries.
Cantórbery Canterbury.
Caperucita Roja Red Riding-Hood.
Caracas *Capital of Venezuela.*
Caribe *m* Caribbean (Sea).
Carlitos Charlie.
Carlomagno Charlemagne.
Carlos Charles.
Carlota Charlotte.
Cárpatos *m/pl.* Carpathians.
Cartago Carthage.
Casa Blanca: *la ~* the White House.
Casandra Cassandra.
Castilla *f* Castile.
Catalina Catherine, Catharine; Katherine; Kathleen.
Cataluña *f* Catalonia.
Catón Cato.
Catulo Catullus.
Cáucaso *m* Caucasus.
Cecilia Cecily.
Ceilán *m* Ceylon.
Cenicienta: (La) ~ Cinderella.
Cerdeña *f* Sardinia.
César Caesar.
Cicerón Cicero.
Cíclope *m* Cyclops.
Clemente Clement.
Colombia *f* Colombia.
Colón Columbus.
Colonia Cologne.
Concha, Conchita *pet names for Concepción.*
Congo *m* the Congo.
Constantinopla Constantinople.
Constanza Constance.
Copenhague Copenhagen.
Córcega *f* Corsica.
Córdoba Cordova.
Corea *f* Korea; *~ del Norte* North Korea; *~ del Sur* South Korea.
Corinto Corinth.
Cornualles *m* Cornwall.
Coruña: La ~ Corunna.
Costa *f* **de Marfil** Ivory Coast.
Costa Rica *f* Costa Rica.
Creta *f* Crete.
Creso Croesus.
Cristo Christ.
Cristóbal Christopher.
Cuba *f* Cuba.
Cupido Cupid.

Ch

Chad *m* Chad.
Champaña *f* Champagne.

Checoslovaquia *f* Czechoslavakia.
Chile *m* Chile, Chili.
China *f* China; ~ *Nacionalista* Taiwan.
Chipre *f* Cyprus.

D

Dafne Daphne.
Dahomey *o* **Dahomé** *m* Dahomey.
Dalmacia *f* Dalmatia.
Damasco Damascus.
Dámocles Damocles.
Danubio *m* Danube.
Dardanelos *m/pl.* Dardanelles.
Darío Darius.
David David.
Delfos Delphi.
Demóstenes Demosthenes.
Diego James.
Dinamarca *f* Denmark.
Domiciano Domitian.
Don Quijote Don Quixote.
Dorotea Dorothy.
Dublín Dublin.
Dunquerque Dunkirk.
Durero Dürer.
Durmiente: *la* **Bella** ~ Sleeping Beauty.

E

Ecuador *m* Ecuador.
Edén *m* Eden.
Edimburgo Edinburgh.
Edipo Oedipus.
Eduardo Edward.
Egeo (Mar) *m* Aegean Sea.
Egipto *m* Egypt.
Elena Helen.
Elíseo *m* Elysium.
Emilia Emily.
Emilio Emil(e).
Eneas Aeneas.
Enrique Henry, Harry.
Erasmo Erasmus.
Ernesto Ernest.
Escandinavia *f* Scandinavia.
Escipión Scipio.
Escocia *f* Scotland.
Esmirna Smyrna.
Esopo Aesop.
España *f* Spain.
Esparta Sparta.
Esquilo Aeschylus.
Estados *m/pl.* **Unidos (de América)** United States (of America).
Esteban Stephen.
Estocolmo Stockholm.
Estonia *f* Estonia.
Estrasburgo Strasbourg.
Estuardo Stuart.
Etiopía *f* Ethiopia.
Euclides Euclid.
Eugenio Eugene.
Eurípedes Euripedes.
Europa *f* Europe.
Eva Eve.

F

Federico Frederick.
Felipe Philip.
Fernando Ferdinand.
Filadelfia Philadelphia.
Filipinas *f/pl.* Philippines.
Finlandia *f* Finland.
Flandes *m* Flanders.
Florencia Florence.
Frankfort-del-Meno Frankfurt on Main.
Francia *f* France.
Francisca Frances.
Francisco Francis.

G

Gabón *m* Gaboon.
Galeno Galen.
Gales *m* Wales.
Galilea *f* Galilee.
Gante Ghent.
Garona *m* Garonne.
Gascuña *f* Gascony.
Génova Genoa.
Geofredo Geoffrey.
Gertrudis Gertrude.
Getsemaní Gethsemane.
Ghana *f* Ghana.
Gibraltar *m* Gibraltar; *Estrecho de* ~ Straits of Gibraltar; *Peñón de* ~ Rock of Gibraltar.
Gil Giles.
Ginebra Geneva; (*p.*) Guinevere.
Godofredo Godfrey.
Golfo *m* **Pérsico** Persian Gulf.
Golfo *m* **de Vizcaya** Bay of Biscay.
Goliat Goliath.
Gran Bretaña *f* Great Britain.
Granada Granada; Grenada.
Gran Cañón *m* Grand Canyon.
Grecia *f* Greece.
Gregorio Gregory.
Groenlandia *f* Greenland.

Guadalupe *f* Guadeloupe.
Gualterio Walter.
Guatemala *f* Guatemala.
Guayana *f* **(Francesa)** (French) Guiana.
Guido Guy.
Guillermo William; ~ *el Conquistador* William the Conqueror.
Guinea *f* Guinea; ~ *Ecuatorial* Equatorial Guinea.
Gustavo Gustave.
Guyana *f* Guyana.

H

Habana: La ~ Havana.
Habsburgo Hapsburg.
Haití *m* Haiti.
Hamburgo Hamburg.
Hawai *m* Hawaii.
Haya: La ~ The Hague.
Hébridas *f/pl.* Hebrides.
Helena Helen.
Hércules Hercules.
Herodes Herod.
Himalaya *m* the Himalayas.
Hipócrates Hippocrates.
Hispanoamérica *f* Spanish America.
Holanda *f* Holland.
Homero Homer.
Honduras *f* Honduras.
Horacio Horace.
Hugo Hugh, Hugo.
Hungría *f* Hungary.

I

Iberia *f* Iberia.
Ignacio Ignatius.
India: *la* ~ India.
Indias *f/pl.* Indies; ~ *Occidentales* West Indies.
Indonesia *f* Indonesia.
Indostán *m* Hindustan.
Inés Agnes.
Inglaterra *f* England.
Irak *m* Irak, Iraq.
Irán *m* Iran.
Irlanda *f* Ireland; ~ *del Norte* Northern Ireland.
Isabel Isabel, Elizabeth.
Isabelita Bess(ie), Bessy, Betty.
Iseo Isolde.
Islandia *f* Iceland.
Islas *f/pl.*: ~ *Bahamas* Bahamas; ~ *Baleares* Balearic Isles; ~ *Bermudas* Bermuda; ~ *Británicas* British Isles; ~ *de Cabo Verde* Cape Verde Islands; ~ *Canarias* Canary Isles; ~ *Hawai* Hawaii; ~ *Normandas* Channel Isles; ~ *de Sotavento* Leeward Isles.
Isolda Isolde.
Israel *m* Israel.
Italia *f* Italy.

J

Jacob Jacob.
Jacobo (*reyes de Escocia e Inglaterra*) James.
Jaime James.
Jamaica *f* Jamaica.
Japón *m* Japan.
Jehová Jehovah.
Jenofonte Xenophon.
Jeremías Jeremy.
Jericó Jericho.
Jerónimo Jerome.
Jerusalén Jerusalem.
Jesús Jesus; ¡~! good heavens!; (*estornudo*) bless you!; *en un decir* ~ in a trice; *Jesucristo* Jesus Christ.
Joaquín *m* Joachim.
Job Job.
Jordán *m* Jordan (*river*).
Jordania *f* Jordan (*country*).
Jorge George.
José Joseph.
Josefina Josephine.
Josué Joshua.
Juan John; *un buen* ~, ~ *Lanas* simple soul.
Juana Jane; Joan; ~ *de Arco* Joan of Arc.
Juanito Jack; Johnny.
Judá *f* Judah.
Judas Judas.
Judea *f* Judaea.
Julieta Juliet.
Julio Julius.
Júpiter Jupiter; Jove.

K

Kenia *f* Kenya.
Kuwait *m* Kuwait.

L

Lacio *m* Latium.
Lanzarote Lancelot.
Laos *m* Laos.
La Paz *Capital of Bolivia.*
Laponia *f* Lapland.

Lausana Lausanne.
Lázaro Lazarus.
Leandro Leander.
Leida, Leide(n) Leyden.
Leningrado Leningrad.
Leonor Eleanor.
Lepe: *saber más que ~* be pretty smart.
Letonia *f* Latvia.
Levante *m* Levant; *South-east part (or coasts) of Spain.*
Líbano *m* Lebanon.
Liberia *f* Liberia.
Libia *f* Libya.
Lieja Liège.
Lima *Capital of Peru.*
Liorna Leghorn.
Lisboa Lisbon.
Lituania *f* Lithuania.
Livio Livy.
Loira *m* Loire.
Lola, Lolita *pet names for Dolores.*
Lombardía *f* Lombardy.
Londres London.
Lorena *f* Lorraine.
Lorenzo Laurence.
Lovaina Louvain.
Lucano Lucan.
Lucas Luke.
Lucerna Lucerne.
Lucrecia Lucretia.
Lucrecio Lucretius.
Luis Louis.
Lutero Luther.
Luxemburgo *m* Luxembourg.
Lyón Lyons.

M

Madera *f* Madeira.
Magallanes *m* Magellan; *Estrecho de ~* Magellan Straits.
Magdalena *f* Magdalen.
Maguncia Mainz.
Mahoma Mahomet.
Málaga Malaga.
Malawi *m* Malawi.
Malaysia *f* Malaysia.
Malí *m* Mali.
Mallorca *f* Majorca.
Malvinas *f/pl.* Falkland Isles.
Managua *Capital of Nicaragua.*
Manolo *pet name for Manuel.*
Manuel Emmanuel.
Mar *m*: *~ Adriático* Adriatic Sea; *~ Báltico* Baltic Sea; *~ Caribe* Caribbean (Sea); *~ Caspio* Caspian Sea; *~ de las Indias* Indian Ocean; *~ Mediterráneo* Mediterranean Sea; *~ Muerto* Dead Sea; *~ Negro* Black Sea; *~ del Norte* North Sea; *~ Rojo* Red Sea.
Marcial Martial.
Marcos Mark.
Margarita Margaret.
María Mary; *~ Antonieta* Marie Antoinette.
Maricastaña: *en tiempo de ~* long ago, in the year dot.
Marruecos *m* Morocco.
Marsella Marseilles.
Marsellesa *f* Marseillaise.
Marte Mars.
Martín Martin.
Martinica *f* Martinique.
Mateo Matthew.
Matilde Mat(h)ilda.
Mauricio Mauritius; (*p.*) Maurice.
Mauritania *f* Mauretania.
Meca: La ~ Mecca.
Mediterráneo *m* Mediterranean.
Méjico *m* Mexico.
Menorca *f* Minorca.
Mercurio Mercury.
Mesías Messiah.
México *m* Mexico.
Midas Midas.
Miguel Michael; *~ Angel* Michelangelo.
Milán Milan.
Misisipí *m* Mississippi.
Misurí *m* Missouri.
Moisés Moses.
Montevideo *Capital of Uruguay.*
Moscú Moscow.
Mosela *m* Moselle.
Montañas *f/pl.* **Rocosas** Rocky Mountains.
Montes *m/pl.* **Apalaches** Appalachian Mountains.
Mozambique *f* Mozambique.

N

Napoleón Napoleon.
Nápoles Naples.
Narbona Narbonne.
Navarra *f* Navarre.
Nazaret Nazareth.
Nepal *m* Nepal.
Neptuno Neptune.
Nerón Nero.
Niágara Niagara.
Nicaragua *f* Nicaragua.
Nicolás Nicholas.

Níger *m* Niger.
Nigeria *f* Nigeria.
Nilo *m* Nile.
Niza Nice.
Noé Noah.
Normandía *f* Normandy.
Noruega *f* Norway.
Nueva Escocia *f* Nova Scotia.
Nueva Gales *f* **del Sur** New South Wales.
Nueva Guinea *f* New Guinea.
Nueva York New York.
Nueva Zelanda *f* New Zealand.

O

Océano *m*: ~ *Atlántico* Atlantic Ocean; ~ *glacial Antártico* Southern Ocean; ~ *glacial Artico* Arctic Ocean; ~ *Indico* Indian Ocean; ~ *Pacífico* Pacific Ocean.
Octavio Octavian.
Olimpo Olympus.
Oliverio Oliver.
Orcadas *f/pl.* Orkney Islands.
Orfeo Orpheus.
Oriente *m* East; *Extremo* ~ Far East; ~ *Medio* Middle East; *Próximo* ~ Near East.
Ostende Ostend.
Ovidio Ovid.

P

Pablo Paul.
Pacífico *m* Pacific.
Paca *pet name for Francisca.*
Paco *pet name for Francisco* Frank.
País *m* **Vasco** Basque Country.
Países *m/pl.* **Bajos** Netherlands.
Pakistán *m* Pakistan.
Palestina *f* Palestine.
Panamá *m* Panama.
Paquita *pet name for Francisca* Frances.
Paquito *pet name for Francisco* Frank.
Paraguay *m* Paraguay.
París Paris.
Parnaso Parnassus.
Patillas F the devil, Old Nick; *ser un* ~ be a poor fish, be a nobody.
Patricio Patrick.
Pedro Peter.
Pegaso Pegasus.
Pekín Pekin(g).
Península *f* **Ibérica** Iberian Peninsula.
Pensilvania *f* Pennsylvania.
Pepa *pet name for Josefa.*
Pepe *pet name for José* Joe.
Pepita *pet name for Josefa.*
Perico *pet name for Pedro* Pete; ~ *el de los Palotes* somebody, so-and-so, any Tom Dick or Harry.
Pero Grullo: *frase de* ~ = *perogrullada.*
Perpiñán Perpignan.
Perú *m* Peru.
Petrarca Petrarch.
Piamonte *m* Piedmont.
Picardía *f* Picardy.
Pilatos Pilate.
Píndaro Pindar.
Pío Pius.
Pirineos *m/pl.* Pyrenees.
Pitágoras Pythagoras.
Platón Plato.
Plinio Pliny.
Plutarco Plutarch.
Plutón Pluto.
Polichinela Punch.
Polinesia *f* Polynesia.
Polonia *f* Poland.
Pompeya Pompeii.
Poncio Pilato(s) Pontius Pilate.
Portugal *m* Portugal.
Praga Prague.
Provenza *f* Provence.
Prusia *f* Prussia.
Psique Psyche.
Puerto Rico *m* Puerto Rico.
Pulgarcito Tom Thumb.

Q

Quito *Capital of Ecuador.*

R

Rafael Raphael.
Raimundo, Ramón Raymond.
Raquel Rachel.
Rebeca Rebecca.
Reginaldo, Reinaldos Reginald.
Reino *m* **Unido** United Kingdom.
Renania *f* Rhineland.
República *f* **Centroafricana** Central African Republic.
República *f* **Dominicana** Dominican Republic.
República *f* **Malgache** Republic of Madagascar.
República *f* **Popular de China** People's Republic of China.

República *f* **Sudafricana** Republic of South Africa.
Ricardo Richard.
Rin *m* Rhine.
Roberto Robert.
Ródano *m* Rhône.
Rodas *f* Rhodes.
Rodesia *f* Rhodesia.
Rodrigo Roderick.
Roldán, Rolando Roland.
Roma Rome.
Rosa Rose.
Rosellón *m* Roussillon.
Ruán Rouen.
Ruanda *f* Ruanda.
Rumania *f* Rumania.
Rusia *f* Russia.

S

Saboya *f* Savoy.
Sáhara *m* Sahara.
Sajonia *f* Saxony.
Salomón Salomon.
Salvador: El ~ El Salvador.
Samuel Samuel.
San José *Capital of Costa Rica.*
San Salvador *Capital of El Salvador.*
Sansón Samson.
Santiago Saint James; *Capital of Chile.*
Santo Domingo *Capital of the Dominican Republic.*
Sarre *m* Saar.
Satanás Satan.
Saturno Saturn.
Saúl Saul.
Sena *m* Seine.
Senegal *m* Senegal.
Servia *f* Serbia.
Sevilla Seville.
Siberia *f* Siberia.
Sibila Sibyl.
Sicilia *f* Sicily.
Sierra Leona *f* Sierra Leone.
Simbad Sin(d)bad.
Singapur Singapore.
Sión *m* Zion.
Siracusa Syracuse.
Siria *f* Syria.
Sócrates Socrates.
Sofía Sofia; (*p.*) Sophia.
Sófocles Sophocles.
Somalia *f* Somaliland.
Sri Lanka *m* Sri Lanka.
Sudán *m* S(o)udan.
Suecia *f* Sweden.
Suiza *f* Switzerland.
Surinam *m* Surinam.

T

Tácito Tacitus.
Tailandia *f* Thailand.
Tajo *m* Tagus.
Támesis *m* Thames.
Tangañica *f* Tanganyika.
Tánger Tangier.
Tanzania *f* Tanzania.
Tegucigalpa *Capital of Honduras.*
Tejas *m* Texas.
Terencio Terence.
Teresa Theresa.
Terranova *f* Newfoundland.
Tesalia *f* Thessaly.
Tíber *m* Tiber.
Tibet *m* Tibet.
Ticiano Titian.
Tierra *f* **Santa** Holy Land.
Timoteo Timothy.
Togo *m* Togo.
Toledo Toledo.
Tolomeo Ptolemy.
Tolón Toulon.
Tolosa (de Francia) Toulouse.
Tomás Thomas.
Trento Trent.
Trinidad *f* **y Tobago** *m* Trinidad and Tobago.
Trípoli Tripoli.
Tristán Tristram.
Troya Troy; *¡arda ~!* press on regardless!; *¡aquí fue ~!* now there's nothing but ruins; that's where the trouble began; that was a battle royal.
Túnez Tunis; Tunisia.
Tunicia *f* Tunisia.
Turquía *f* Turkey.

U

Ucrania *f* Ukraine.
Uganda *m* Uganda.
Unión *f* **de Emiratos Arabes** United Arab Emirates.
Unión *f* **de India** Union of India.
Unión *f* **de Repúblicas Socialistas Soviéticas (U.R.S.S.)** Union of Soviet Socialist Republics (U.S.S.R.).
Unión *f* **Soviética** Soviet Union.

Uruguay *m* Uruguay.
Utopia *f* Utopia.

V

Varsovia Warsaw.
Vascongadas *f/pl.* Basque Provinces.
Vaticano *m* Vatikan.
Velázquez Velasquez.
Venecia Venice.
Venezuela *f* Venezuela.
Venus Venus.
Versalles Versailles.
Vesubio *m* Vesuvius.
Vicente Vincent.
Viena Vienna.
Vietnam *o* **Viet Nam** *m* Viet Nam.
Villadiego: F *tomar las de* ~ beat it.
Virgilio Virgil.
Vizcaya *f* Biscay.
Vosgos *m/pl.* Vosges.
Vulcano Vulcan.

Y

Yemen *m* Yemen.
Yugo(e)slavia *f* Jugoslavia.

Z

Zaire *m* Zaïre.
Zambia *f* Zambia.
Zaragoza Saragossa.
Zimbabue *m* Zimbabwe.

Numerals – Numerales

Cardinal Numbers – Números cardinales

0 cero *nought*
1 uno, una *one*
2 dos *two*
3 tres *three*
4 cuatro *four*
5 cinco *five*
6 seis *six*
7 siete *seven*
8 ocho *eight*
9 nueve *nine*
10 diez *ten*
11 once *eleven*
12 doce *twelve*
13 trece *thirteen*
14 catorce *fourteen*
15 quince *fifteen*
16 dieciséis *sixteen*
17 diecisiete *seventeen*
18 dieciocho *eighteen*
19 diecinueve *nineteen*
20 veinte *twenty*
21 veintiuno *twenty-one*
22 veintidós *twenty-two*
30 treinta *thirty*
31 treinta y uno *thirty-one*
40 cuarenta *forty*
50 cincuenta *fifty*
60 sesenta *sixty*
70 setenta *seventy*
80 ochenta *eighty*
90 noventa *ninety*
100 cien(to) *a (one) hundred*
101 ciento uno *a hundred and one*
110 ciento diez *a hundred and ten*
200 doscientos, -as *two hundred*
300 trescientos, -as *three hundred*
400 cuatrocientos, -as *four hundred*
500 quinientos, -as *five hundred*
600 seiscientos, -as *six hundred*
700 setecientos, -as *seven hundred*
800 ochocientos, -as *eight hundred*
900 novecientos, -as *nine hundred*
1000 mil *a thousand*
1959 mil novecientos cincuenta y nueve *nineteen hundred and fifty-nine*
2000 dos mil *two thousand*
1.000.000 un millón (de) *a (one) million*
2.000.000 dos millones (de) *two million*

Ordinal Numbers – Números ordinales

(The ordinal numbers in Spanish agree with the noun in number and gender, *primero -a -os -as etc.*)

1 primero *first*
2 segundo *second*
3 tercero *third*
4 cuarto *fourth*
5 quinto *fifth*
6 sexto *sixth*
7 séptimo *seventh*
8 octavo *eighth*
9 noveno, nono *ninth*
10 décimo *tenth*
11 undécimo *eleventh*
12 duodécimo *twelfth*
13 decimotercero, decimotercio *thirteenth*
14 decimocuarto *fourteenth*
15 decimoquinto *fifteenth*
16 decimosexto *sixteenth*
17 decimoséptimo *seventeenth*
18 decimoctavo *eighteenth*
19 decimonoveno, decimonono *nineteenth*
20 vigésimo *twentieth*
21 vigésimo prim(er)o *twenty-first*
22 vigésimo segundo *twenty-second*

30 trigésimo *thirtieth*
31 trigésimo prim(er)o *thirty-first*
40 cuadragésimo *fortieth*
50 quincuagésimo *fiftieth*
60 sexagésimo *sixtieth*
70 septuagésimo *seventieth*
80 octogésimo *eightieth*
90 nonagésimo *ninetieth*
100 centésimo *hundredth*
101 centésimo primero *hundred and first*
110 centésimo décimo *hundred and tenth*
200 ducentésimo *two hundredth*
300 tricentésimo *three hundredth*
400 cuadringentésimo *four hundredth*
500 quingentésimo *five hundredth*
600 sexcentésimo *six hundredth*
700 septingentésimo *seven hundredth*
800 octingentésimo *eight hundredth*
900 noningentésimo *nine hundredth*
1000 milésimo *thousandth*
2000 dos milésimo *two thousandth*
1.000.000 millonésimo *millionth*
2.000.000 dos millonésimo *two millionth*

En inglés, los números ordinales suelen abreviarse **1st., 2nd., 3rd., 4th., 5th.,** etc.; in Spanish, the ordinal numbers may be written **1°, 2°** etc.

Fractions and other Numerals – Números quebrados y otros

$\frac{1}{2}$ medio, media *one (a) half*; **$1\frac{1}{2}$** uno y medio *one and a half*; **$2\frac{1}{2}$** dos y medio *two and a half*; **$\frac{1}{2}$** hora *half an hour*; **$1\frac{1}{2}$** kilómetros *a kilometer and a half*

$\frac{1}{3}$ un tercio, la tercera parte *one (a) third*; **$\frac{2}{3}$** dos tercios, las dos terceras partes *two thirds*

$\frac{1}{4}$ un cuarto, la cuarta parte *one (a) quarter*; **$\frac{3}{4}$** tres cuartos, las tres cuartas partes *three quarters*; **$\frac{1}{4}$** hora *a quarter of an hour*; **$1\frac{1}{4}$** horas *an hour and a quarter*

$\frac{1}{5}$ un quinto *one (a) fifth*; **$3\frac{4}{5}$** tres y cuatro quintos *three and four fifths*

$\frac{1}{11}$ un onzavo *one (an) eleventh*; **$\frac{5}{12}$** cinco dozavos *five twelfths*; **$\frac{75}{100}$** setenta y cinco centésimos *seventy-five hundredths*

$\frac{1}{1000}$ un milésimo *one (a) thousandth*

simple *single*
doble, duplo *double*
triple *treble, triple, threefold*
cuádruplo *fourfold*
quíntuplo *fivefold etc.*

una vez *once*
dos veces *twice*
tres veces *three times etc.*
siete veces más grande *seven times as big*; doce veces más *twelve times more*

en primer lugar *firstly*
en segundo lugar *secondly etc.*

7 + 8 = 15 siete y (*or* más) ocho son quince *seven and eight are fifteen*

10 − 3 = 7 diez menos tres resta siete, de tres a diez van siete *three from ten leaves seven*

2 × 3 = 6 dos por tres son seis *two times three are six*

20 ÷ 4 = 5 veinte dividido por cuatro es cinco *twenty divided by four is five*

Notes on the Spanish Verb

The simple tenses and parts of the three conjugations and of irregular verbs are set out in the following pages, but certain general points may be summarized here:

1. **Compound tenses** etc. are formed with the auxiliary *haber* and the past participle:

perfect:	he mandado (*subj.*: haya mandado)
pluperfect:	había mandado (*subj.*: hubiera mandado, hubiese mandado)
future perfect:	habré mandado
perfect infinitive:	haber mandado
perfect gerund:	habiendo mandado

2. The **imperfect** is regular for all verbs except *ser* (*era* etc.), *ver* (*veía* etc.) and *ir* (*iba* etc.).

3. The **conditional** is formed like the future on the infinitive: *mandar/ía*. If the future is irregular, so will be the conditional: *salir — saldré, saldría*; *decir — diré, diría*.

4. The **imperfect subjunctives** I and II are formed from the 3rd person plural of the preterite, using as a stem what remains after removing the final *-ron* syllable, and adding *-ra* or *-se*:

   mandar: manda/ron — mandara, mandase
   querer: quisie/ron — quisiera, quisiese
   traer: traje/ron — trajera, trajese
   conducir: conduje/ron — condujera, condujese.

5. **Imperative.** The "true" imperative is limited to the familiar forms or true second persons (*tú, vosotros*) used affirmatively: *habla, mándamelo, hacedlo*. The imperative affirmative with *Vd., Vds.* is formed with the subjunctive: *mándemelo Vd., háganlo Vds.* The imperative negative for all persons is formed with the subjunctive: *no lo hagas* (*tú*), *no vayan Vds.*

6. **Continuous tenses** are formed with *estar* and the gerund: *estoy trabajando, estábamos discutiendo*. Other auxiliary verbs may be used according to sense: *vamos avanzando, según voy viendo, vengo diciendo eso.*

7. The **passive** is formed with tenses of *ser* and the past participle: *es recibido, será vencido, fue construido*. In passive uses the past participle agree in number and gender with the subject: *las casas fueron derribadas.*

First Conjugation

[1a] **mandar**

Infinitive: mandar **Gerund:** mandando **Past Participle:** mandado

Indicative

Present	*Imperfect*	*Preterite*
mando	mandaba	mandé
mandas	mandabas	mandaste
manda	mandaba	mandó
mandamos	mandábamos	mandamos
mandáis	mandabais	mandasteis
mandan	mandaban	mandaron

Future	*Conditional*
mandaré	mandaría
mandarás	mandarías
mandará	mandaría
mandaremos	mandaríamos
mandaréis	mandaríais
mandarán	mandarían

Subjunctive

Present	*Imperfect I*	*Imperfect II*
mande	mandara	mandase
mandes	mandaras	mandases
mande	mandara	mandase
mandemos	mandáramos	mandásemos
mandéis	mandarais	mandaseis
manden	mandaran	mandasen

Imperative

Affirmative	*Negative*
manda (tú)	no mandes (tú)
mande Vd.	no mande Vd.
mandad (vosotros)	no mandéis (vosotros)
manden Vds.	no manden Vds.

Infinitive	Present Indicative	Present Subjunctive	Preterite
[1b] **cambiar.** The *i* of the stem is not stressed and the verb is regular	cambio cambias cambia cambiamos cambiáis cambian	cambie cambies cambie cambiemos cambiéis cambien	cambié cambiaste cambió cambiamos cambiasteis cambiaron
[1c] **variar.** In forms stressed on the stem, the *i* is accented	varío varías varía variamos variáis varían	varíe varíes varíe variemos variéis varíen	varié variaste varió variamos variasteis variaron

	Infinitive	Present Indicative	Present Subjunctive	Preterite
[1d]	**evacuar.** The *u* of the stem is not stressed and the verb is regular	evacuo evacuas evacua evacuamos evacuáis evacuan	evacue evacues evacue evacuemos evacuéis evacuen	evacué evacuaste evacuó evacuamos evacuasteis evacuaron
[1e]	**acentuar.** In forms stressed on the stem, the *u* is accented	acent**ú**o acent**ú**as acent**ú**a acentuamos acentuáis acent**ú**an	acent**ú**e acent**ú**es acent**ú**e acentuemos acentuéis acent**ú**en	acentué acentuaste acentuó acentuamos acentuasteis acentuaron
[1f]	**cruzar.** The stem consonant *z* is written *c* before *e*	cruzo cruzas cruza cruzamos cruzáis cruzan	cru**c**e cru**c**es cru**c**e cru**c**emos cru**c**éis cru**c**en	cru**c**é cruzaste cruzó cruzamos cruzasteis cruzaron
[1g]	**tocar.** The stem consonant *c* is written *qu* before *e*	toco tocas toca tocamos tocáis tocan	to**qu**e to**qu**es to**qu**e to**qu**emos to**qu**éis to**qu**en	to**qu**é tocaste tocó tocamos tocasteis tocaron
[1h]	**pagar.** The stem consonant *g* is written *gu* (*u* silent) before *e*	pago pagas paga pagamos pagáis pagan	pa**gu**e pa**gu**es pa**gu**e pa**gu**emos pa**gu**éis pa**gu**en	pa**gu**é pagaste pagó pagamos pagasteis pagaron
[1i]	**fraguar.** The *u* of the stem is written *ü* (so that it should be pronounced) before *e*	fraguo fraguas fragua fraguamos fraguáis fraguan	frag**ü**e frag**ü**es frag**ü**e frag**ü**emos frag**ü**éis frag**ü**en	frag**ü**é fraguaste fraguó fraguamos fraguasteis fraguaron
[1k]	**pensar.** The stem vowel *e* becomes *ie* when stressed	p**ie**nso p**ie**nsas p**ie**nsa pensamos pensáis p**ie**nsan	p**ie**nse p**ie**nses p**ie**nse pensemos penséis p**ie**nsen	pensé pensaste pensó pensamos pensasteis pensaron
[1l]	**errar.** As [1k], but the diphthong is written *ye* at the start of the word	**ye**rro **ye**rras **ye**rra erramos erráis **ye**rran	**ye**rre **ye**rres **ye**rre erremos erréis **ye**rren	erré erraste erró erramos errasteis erraron

Infinitive	Present Indicative	Present Subjunctive	Preterite
[1m] **contar.** The stem vowel *o* becomes *ue* when stressed	c**ue**nto c**ue**ntas c**ue**nta contamos contáis c**ue**ntan	c**ue**nte c**ue**ntes c**ue**nte contemos contéis c**ue**nten	conté contaste contó contamos contasteis contaron
[1n] **agorar.** The stem vowel *o* becomes *üe* when stressed	ag**üe**ro ag**üe**ras ag**üe**ra agoramos agoráis ag**üe**ran	ag**üe**re ag**üe**res ag**üe**re agoremos agoréis ag**üe**ren	agoré agoraste agoró agoramos agorasteis agoraron
[1o] **jugar.** The stem vowel *u* becomes *ue* when stressed; the stem consonant *g* is written *gu* (*u* silent) before *e*; *conjugar*, *enjugar* are regular	j**ue**go j**ue**gas j**ue**ga jugamos jugáis j**ue**gan	j**ue**g**u**e j**ue**g**u**es j**ue**g**u**e jug**u**emos jug**u**éis j**ue**g**u**en	jug**u**é jugaste jugó jugamos jugasteis jugaron
[1p] **estar.** Irregular. Imperative: *está* (*tú*)	estoy estás está estamos estáis están	esté estés esté estemos estéis estén	estuve estuviste estuvo estuvimos estuvisteis estuvieron
[1q] **andar.** Irregular.	ando andas anda andamos andáis andan	ande andes ande andemos andéis anden	anduve anduviste anduvo anduvimos anduvisteis anduvieron
[1r] **dar.** Irregular.	doy das da damos dais dan	dé des dé demos deis den	di diste dio dimos disteis dieron

Second Conjugation

[2a] **vender**

Infinitive: vender **Gerund:** vendiendo **Past Participle:** vendido

Indicative

Present	*Imperfect*	*Preterite*
vendo	vendía	vendí
vendes	vendías	vendiste
vende	vendía	vendió
vendemos	vendíamos	vendimos
vendéis	vendíais	vendisteis
venden	vendían	vendieron

Future	*Conditional*
venderé	vendería
venderás	venderías
venderá	vendería
venderemos	venderíamos
venderéis	venderíais
venderán	venderían

Subjunctive

Present	*Imperfect I*	*Imperfect II*
venda	vendiera	vendiese
vendas	vendieras	vendieses
venda	vendiera	vendiese
vendamos	vendiéramos	vendiésemos
vendáis	vendierais	vendieseis
vendan	vendieran	vendiesen

Imperative

Affirmative	*Negative*
vende (tú)	no vendas (tú)
venda Vd.	no venda Vd.
vended (vosotros)	no vendáis (vosotros)
vendan Vds.	no vendan Vds.

Infinitive	Present Indicative	Present Subjunctive	Preterite
[2b] **vencer.** The stem consonant *c* is written *z* before *a* and *o*	ven**z**o vences vence vencemos vencéis vencen	ven**z**a ven**z**as ven**z**a ven**z**amos ven**z**áis ven**z**an	vencí venciste venció vencimos vencisteis vencieron
[2c] **coger.** The stem consonant *g* is written *j* before *a* and *o*	co**j**o coges coge cogemos cogéis cogen	co**j**a co**j**as co**j**a co**j**amos co**j**áis co**j**an	cogí cogiste cogió cogimos cogisteis cogieron

Infinitive	Present Indicative	Present Subjunctive	Preterite
[2d] **merecer.** The stem consonant *c* becomes *zc* before *a* and *o*	mere**zco**	mere**zca**	mereci
	mereces	mere**zca**s	mereciste
	merece	mere**zca**	mereció
	merecemos	mere**zca**mos	merecimos
	merecéis	mere**zcá**is	merecisteis
	merecen	mere**zca**n	merecieron
[2e] **creer.** Unstressed *i* between vowels is written *y*. Past participle: *creído* Gerund: *creyendo*	creo	crea	creí
	crees	creas	creíste
	cree	crea	cre**yó**
	creemos	creamos	creímos
	creéis	creáis	creísteis
	creen	crean	cre**y**eron
[2f] **tañer.** Unstressed *i* after *ñ* and *ll* is omitted. Gerund: *tañendo*	taño	taña	tañí
	tañes	tañas	tañiste
	tañe	taña	ta**ñó**
	tañemos	tañamos	tañimos
	tañéis	tañáis	tañisteis
	tañen	tañan	ta**ñe**ron
[2g] **perder.** The stem vowel *e* becomes *ie* when stressed	p**ie**rdo	p**ie**rda	perdí
	p**ie**rdes	p**ie**rdas	perdiste
	p**ie**rde	p**ie**rda	perdió
	perdemos	perdamos	perdimos
	perdéis	perdáis	perdisteis
	p**ie**rden	p**ie**rdan	perdieron
[2h] **mover.** The stem vowel *o* becomes *ue* when stressed. Verbs in *-olver* form their past participle in *-uelto*	m**ue**vo	m**ue**va	moví
	m**ue**ves	m**ue**vas	moviste
	m**ue**ve	m**ue**va	movió
	movemos	movamos	movimos
	movéis	mováis	movisteis
	m**ue**ven	m**ue**van	movieron
[2i] **oler.** As [2h], but the diphthong is written *hue* at the start of the word	**hue**lo	**hue**la	olí
	hueles	**hue**las	oliste
	huele	**hue**la	olió
	olemos	olamos	olimos
	oléis	oláis	olisteis
	huelen	**hue**lan	olieron
[2k] **haber.** Irregular throughout. Future: *habré*	he	haya	hube
	has	hayas	hubiste
	ha	haya	hubo
	hemos	hayamos	hubimos
	habéis	hayáis	hubisteis
	han	hayan	hubieron
[2l] **tener.** Irregular throughout. Future: *tendré* Imperative: *ten* (*tú*)	tengo	tenga	tuve
	tienes	tengas	tuviste
	tiene	tenga	tuvo
	tenemos	tengamos	tuvimos
	tenéis	tengáis	tuvisteis
	tienen	tengan	tuvieron

Infinitive	Present Indicative	Present Subjunctive	Preterite
[2m] **caber.** Irregular throughout. Future: *cabré*	quepo cabes cabe cabemos cabéis caben	quepa quepas quepa quepamos quepáis quepan	cupe cupiste cupo cupimos cupisteis cupieron
[2n] **saber.** Irregular throughout. Future: *sabré*	sé sabes sabe sabemos sabéis saben	sepa sepas sepa sepamos sepáis sepan	supe supiste supo supimos supisteis supieron
[2o] **caer.** Irregular. Unstressed *i* between vowels is written *y*, as [2e] Past participle: *caído* Gerund: *cayendo*	caigo caes cae caemos caéis caen	caiga caigas caiga caigamos caigáis caigan	caí caíste cayó caímos caísteis cayeron
[2p] **traer.** Irregular throughout. Past participle: *traído* Gerund: *trayendo*	traigo traes trae traemos traéis traen	traiga traigas traiga traigamos traigáis traigan	traje trajiste trajo trajimos trajisteis trajeron
[2q] **valer.** Irregular. Future: *valdré*	valgo vales vale valemos valéis valen	valga valgas valga valgamos valgáis valgan	valí valiste valió valimos valisteis valieron
[2r] **poner.** Irregular throughout. Future: *pondré* Past participle: *puesto* Imperative: *pon* (*tú*)	pongo pones pone ponemos ponéis ponen	ponga pongas ponga pongamos pongáis pongan	puse pusiste puso pusimos pusisteis pusieron
[2s] **hacer.** Irregular throughout. Future: *haré* Past participle: *hecho* Imperative: *haz* (*tú*)	hago haces hace hacemos hacéis hacen	haga hagas haga hagamos hagáis hagan	hice hiciste hizo hicimos hicisteis hicieron
[2t] **poder.** Irregular throughout. In present tenses like [2h]. Future: *podré* Gerund: *pudiendo*	puedo puedes puede podemos podéis pueden	pueda puedas pueda podamos podáis puedan	pude pudiste pudo pudimos pudisteis pudieron

	Infinitive	Present Indicative	Present Subjunctive	Preterite
[2u]	**querer.** Irregular. In present tenses like [2g]. Future: *querré*	quiero quieres quiere queremos queréis quieren	quiera quieras quiera queramos queráis quieran	quise quisiste quiso quisimos quisisteis quisieron
[2v]	**ver.** Irregular. Past participle: *visto* Gerund: *viendo* Imperfect: *veía etc.* Imperative: *ve (tú)*, *ved (vosotros)*	veo ves ve vemos veis ven	vea veas vea veamos veáis vean	vi viste vio vimos visteis vieron
[2w]	**ser.** Irregular throughout. Past participle: *sido* Gerund: *siendo* Future: *seré* Imperfect: *era, eras etc.* Imperative: *sé (tú)*, *sed (vosotros)*	soy eres es somos sois son	sea seas sea seamos seáis sean	fui fuiste fue fuimos fuisteis fueron

[2x] **placer.** Used only in 3rd person sg. Irregular forms: Present subj. *plega*, *plegue* or *plazca*; Preterite *plugo* or *plació*; Imperfect subj. I *pluguiera* or *placiera*, Imperfect subj. II *pluguiese* or *placiese*.

[2y] **yacer.** (Mostly †). Irregular forms: Present indic. *yazco*, *yazgo* or *yago*; Present subj. *yazca*, *yazga*, *yaga* etc. Imperative *yace* (*tú*) or *yaz* (*tú*).

[2z] **raer.** Alternative forms in present tenses: Present indic. *raigo* or *rayo* etc.; Present subj. *raiga* or *raya* etc.

[2za] **roer.** Alternative forms in present tenses: Present indic. *roigo* or *royo*; Present subj. *roiga* or *roya*.

Third Conjugation

[3a] **recibir**

Infinitive: recibir **Gerund:** recibiendo **Past Participle:** recibido

Indicative

Present	*Imperfect*	*Preterite*
recibo	recibía	recibí
recibes	recibías	recibiste
recibe	recibía	recibió
recibimos	recibíamos	recibimos
recibís	recibíais	recibisteis
reciben	recibían	recibieron

Future	*Conditional*
recibiré	recibiría
recibirás	recibirías
recibirá	recibiría
recibiremos	recibiríamos
recibiréis	recibiríais
recibirán	recibirían

Subjunctive

Present	*Imperfect I*	*Imperfect II*
reciba	recibiera	recibiese
recibas	recibieras	recibieses
reciba	recibiera	recibiese
recibamos	recibiéramos	recibiésemos
recibáis	recibierais	recibieseis
reciban	recibieran	recibiesen

Imperative

Affirmative	*Negative*
recibe (tú)	no recibas (tú)
reciba Vd.	no reciba Vd.
recibid (vosotros)	no recibáis (vosotros)
reciban Vds.	no reciban Vds.

Infinitive	Present Indicative	Present Subjunctive	Preterite
[3b] **esparcir.** The stem consonant *c* is written *z* before *a* and *o*	espar**z**o esparces esparce esparcimos esparcís esparcen	espar**z**a espar**z**as espar**z**a espar**z**amos espar**z**áis espar**z**an	esparcí esparciste esparció esparcimos esparcisteis esparcieron
[3c] **dirigir.** The stem consonant *g* is written *j* before *a* and *o*	diri**j**o diriges dirige dirigimos dirigís dirigen	diri**j**a diri**j**as diri**j**a diri**j**amos diri**j**áis diri**j**an	dirigí dirigiste dirigió dirigimos dirigisteis dirigieron

	Infinitive	Present Indicative	Present Subjunctive	Preterite
[3d]	**distinguir.** The *u* after the stem consonant *g* is omitted before *a* and *o*	distin**g**o distingues distingue distinguimos distinguís distinguen	distin**g**a distin**g**as distin**g**a distin**g**amos distin**g**áis distin**g**an	distinguí distinguiste distinguió distinguimos distinguisteis distinguieron
[3e]	**delinquir.** The stem consonant *qu* is writen *c* before *a* and *o*	delin**c**o delinques delinque delinquimos delinquís delinquen	delin**c**a delin**c**as delin**c**a delin**c**amos delin**c**áis delin**c**an	delinquí delinquiste delinquió delinquimos delinquisteis delinquieron
[3f]	**lucir.** The stem consonant *c* becomes *zc* before *a* and *o*	lu**zc**o luces luce lucimos lucís lucen	lu**zc**a lu**zc**as lu**zc**a lu**zc**amos lu**zc**áis lu**zc**an	lucí luciste lució lucimos lucisteis lucieron
[3g]	**concluir.** The *i* of *-ió* and *-ie-* changes to *y*; a *y* is inserted before endings not beginning with *i*. Gerund: *concluyendo*	conclu**y**o conclu**y**es conclu**y**e concluimos concluís conclu**y**en	conclu**y**a conclu**y**as conclu**y**a conclu**y**amos conclu**y**áis conclu**y**an	concluí concluiste conclu**y**ó concluimos concluisteis conclu**y**eron
[3h]	**gruñir.** Unstressed *i* after *ñ*, *ll* and *ch* is omitted. Gerund: *gruñendo*	gruño gruñes gruñe gruñimos gruñís gruñen	gruña gruñas gruña gruñamos gruñáis gruñan	gruñí gruñiste gru**ñó** gruñimos gruñisteis gru**ñe**ron
[3i]	**sentir.** The stem vowel *e* becomes *ie* when stressed; unstressed *e* becomes *i* in 3rd persons of Preterite, 1st and 2nd persons pl. of Present Subjunctive. In *adquirir etc.* the stem vowel *i* becomes *ie* when stressed Gerund: *sintiendo*	s**ie**nto s**ie**ntes s**ie**nte sentimos sentís s**ie**nten	s**ie**nta s**ie**ntas s**ie**nta s**i**ntamos s**i**ntáis s**ie**ntan	sentí sentiste s**i**ntió sentimos sentisteis s**i**ntieron
[3k]	**dormir.** The stem vowel *o* becomes *ue* when stressed; unstressed *o* becomes *u* in 3rd persons of Preterite, 1st and 2nd persons pl. of Present Subjunctive. Gerund: *durmiendo*	d**ue**rmo d**ue**rmes d**ue**rme dormimos dormís d**ue**rmen	d**ue**rma d**ue**rmas d**ue**rma d**u**rmamos d**u**rmáis d**ue**rman	dormí dormiste d**u**rmió dormimos dormisteis d**u**rmieron

	Infinitive	Present Indicative	Present Subjunctive	Preterite
[3l]	**medir.** The stem	m**i**do	m**i**da	medí
	vowel *e* becomes *i*	m**i**des	m**i**das	mediste
	when stressed, and	m**i**de	m**i**da	m**i**dió
	also when unstressed	medimos	m**i**damos	medimos
	in 3rd persons of	medís	m**i**dáis	medisteis
	Preterite, 1st and 2nd	m**i**den	m**i**dan	m**i**dieron
	persons pl. of Present			
	Subjunctive.			
	Gerund: *midiendo*			
[3m]	**reír.** Irregular.	río	ría	reí
	Past participle: *reído*	ríes	rias	reíste
	Gerund: *riendo*	ríe	ría	rió
		reimos	riamos	reímos
		reis	riáis	reísteis
		ríen	rían	rieron
[3n]	**erguir.** Irregular.	irgo	irga	erguí
	Gerund: *irguiendo*	irgues	irgas	erguiste
	Imperative: *irgue* (*tú*)	irgue	irga	irguió
	or *yergue* (*tú*)	erguimos	irgamos	erguimos
		erguís	irgáis	erguisteis
		irguen	irgan	irguieron
		or	*or*	
		yergo	yerga	
		yergues	yergas	
		yergue	yerga	
		erguimos	yergamos	
		erguís	yergáis	
		yerguen	yergan	
[3o]	**conducir.** The stem	condu**zc**o	condu**zc**a	conduje
	consonant *c* becomes	conduces	condu**zc**as	condujiste
	zc before *a* and *o*, as	conduce	condu**zc**a	condujo
	[3f]. Irregular preter-	conducimos	condu**zc**amos	condujimos
	ite in *-uje*	conducís	condu**zc**áis	condujisteis
		conducen	condu**zc**an	condujeron
[3p]	**decir.** Irregular	digo	diga	dije
	throughout.	dices	digas	dijiste
	Future: *diré*	dice	diga	dijo
	Past participle: *dicho*	decimos	digamos	dijimos
	Gerund: *diciendo*	decís	digáis	dijisteis
	Imperative: *di* (*tú*)	dicen	digan	dijeron
[3q]	**oír.** Irregular.	oigo	oiga	oí
	Unstressed *i* between	oyes	oigas	oíste
	vowels becomes *y*.	oye	oiga	oyó
	Past participle: *oído*	oímos	oigamos	oímos
	Gerund: *oyendo*	oís	oigáis	oísteis
		oyen	oigan	oyeron

	Infinitive	Present Indicative	Present Subjunctive	Preterite
[3r]	**salir.** Irregular. Future: *saldré* Imperative: *sal* (*tú*)	salgo sales sale salimos salís salen	salga salgas salga salgamos salgáis salgan	salí saliste salió salimos salisteis salieron
[3s]	**venir.** Irregular throughout. Future: *vendré* Gerund: *viniendo* Imperative: *ven* (*tú*)	vengo vienes viene venimos venís vienen	venga vengas venga vengamos vengáis vengan	vine viniste vino vinimos vinisteis vinieron
[3t]	**ir.** Irregular throughout. Imperfect: *iba*, *ibas etc.* Gerund: *yendo* Imperative: *ve* (*tú*), *id* (*vosotros*)	voy vas va vamos vais van	vaya vayas vaya vayamos vayáis vayan	fui fuiste fue fuimos fuisteis fueron

Weights and Measures

Pesos y medidas

Metric system – Sistema métrico

(The various ancient measures still in use are listed and defined in the main part of the dictionary)

Multiples and fractions formed with the following prefixes are not listed separately:

deca- **10** times; *hecto-* **100** times; *kilo-* **1000** times;
deci- one tenth; *centi-* one hundredth; *milli-* one thousandth

1. Linear measures
Medidas de longitud

1 centímetro (centimeter)
= **10** milímetros (millimeters)
= **0.3937** inches

1 metro (meter)
= **100** centímetros (centimeters)
= **39.37** inches *or* **1.094** yards

1 kilómetro (kilometer)
= **1000** metros (meters)
= **0.6214** mile (almost exactly five-eighths of a mile)

2. Square measures
Medidas cuadradas

1 centímetro cuadrado (square centimeter)
= **0.155** square inch

1 metro cuadrado (square meter)
= **10.764** square feet

1 kilómetro cuadrado (square kilometer)
= **247.1** acres *or* **0.3861** square mile

1 área (are)
= **100** metros cuadrados (square meters)
= **119.6** square yards

1 hectárea (hectare)
= **100** áreas (ares)
= **2.471** acres

3. Cubic measures
Medidas de cubicación

1 centímetro cúbico (cubic centimeter)
= **0.061** cubic inch

1 metro cúbico (cubic meter)
= **35.31** cubic feet *or* **1.308** cubic yards

4. Measure of capacity
Medida de capacidad

1 litro (liter)
= **1000** centímetros cúbicos (cubic centimeters)
= **1.76** pints *or* **0.22** gallon

5. Weights – Pesos

1 gramo (gram, *British* gramme)
= **0.0352** ounce

1 kilo(gramo) (kilogram, *British* kilogramme)
= **2.2045** pounds

1 quintal métrico
= **100** kilogramos (kilograms)
= **220.45** pounds

1 tonelada
= **1000** kilogramos (kilograms)
= **0.9842** ton

Second Part

English-Spanish

Contents

Materias

Preface

Like every living language, English is subject to constant change. New terms and new compounds come into being, antiquated words are replaced by new ones; regional and popular words and technical terms pass into ordinary speech.

This completely new, updated edition details the latest developments in the two languages. This dictionary is designed for wide use, and is suitable for college students, translators, businesspeople, tourists, anyone who requires a detailed English-Spanish Dictionary.

Thousands of new English words have been incorporated. Among them, the following examples: *AIDS* (SIDA), *heliport* (helipuerto), *microwave* (microonda), *minicomputer* (miniordenador), *nuke* (*sl.* arma atómica; atacar con arma atómica). Similarly, new compound forms have been added to existing headwords, e.g. *acid rain* (lluvia ácida), *cable television* (televisión por cable), *video-tape recording* (videograbación).

Notable features of the dictionary are: a phonetic transcription, in the alphabet of the International Phonetic Association, is given for every English headword; the stress of every word is indicated; syllabification dots show where each word should be divided at the end of written line; in many cases, the "social class" of a word is indicated, and an attempt is made to render the word by another of equivalent class. The gender of every Spanish noun is given. Within each entry, the reader is offered many defining words to help his choice of an exact translation, and is given help with grammatical constructions.

Other useful information includes lists of current English abbreviations and proper names, a table of numerals, and a table of weights and measures both in English and Spanish.

Based on the long-established Standard Dictionary of the English and Spanish Languages edited by C. C. Smith, G. A. Davies and H. B. Hall, this dictionary was developed in its present form by Walter Glanze Word Books, in cooperation with Dr. Roger J. Steiner, of the University of Delaware, and Dr. Gerald J. Mac Donald, the Curator of the Hispanic Society of America. To all them our warmest appreciation.

Prólogo

Al igual que todas las lenguas vivas, el inglés se encuentra constantemente sometido a cambios impuestos por la formación de nuevos términos y expresiones, la sustitución de arcaísmos por nuevas palabras y la incorporación del léxico regional, popular y técnico al lenguaje cotidiano.

La presente edición completamente refundida de este diccionario da cuenta de los últimos desarrollos producidos en ambas lenguas. El diccionario ha sido concebido como una obra de consulta para todo tipo de público y es adecuado para estudiantes, traductores, hombres de negocios y turistas, o para cualquier persona que necesite un detallado diccionario inglés-español.

En esta edición se han incluido miles de palabras inglesas nuevas. Así por ejemplo: *AIDS* (SIDA), *heliport* (helipuerto), *microwave* (microonda), *minicomputer* (miniordenador), *nuke* (*sl.* arma atómica; atacar con arma atómica), etc. También se han incorporado expresiones bajo voces ya existentes, como por ejemplo: *acid rain* (lluvia ácida), *cable television* (televisión por cable), *video-tape recording* (videograbación).

Quien nos consulte apreciará las características siguientes: una pronunciación figurada, según el alfabeto de la Asociación Fonética Internacional, acompaña cada voz-guía inglesa; en todos los casos, se indica la acentuación de la palabra; hemos señalado la separación silábica por medio de puntos que indican dónde se debe dividir una palabra al final de un renglón escrito; en muchos casos, se ha señalado la «clase social» de una palabra, y se ha intentado traducirla con el equivalente castellano. Se precisa el género de cada sustantivo español. Dentro de cada artículo, el lector encontrará muchas palabras definidoras que le ayudarán a elegir la traducción exacta, y se le ayuda además con las construcciones gramaticales.

El índice de abreviaturas inglesas corrientes, la lista de nombres propios, la tabla de numerales y el cuadro de pesos y medidas constituyen una fuente más de información útil.

Basado en el conocido Standard Dictionary of the Spanish and English Languages, editado por C. C. Smith, G. A. Davies y H. B. Hall, este diccionario ha sido desarrollado hasta su forma presente por Walter Glanze Word Books, en cooperación con el Dr. Roger J. Steiner, de la Universidad de Delaware, y el Dr. Gerald J. Mac Donald, «Curator of the Hispanic Society of America». A todos

Prólogo

[illegible] que [illegible] en [illegible] se encuentra [illegible] términos [illegible] por [illegible] palabras y [illegible] del [illegible] español [illegible] lengua [illegible].

[illegible] de [illegible] productos [illegible] diccionario [illegible] de [illegible] para todo tipo de [illegible] nombres [illegible] detallado [illegible] inglés [illegible].

En este volumen [illegible] con [illegible] en [illegible] que [illegible].

[illegible] la [illegible] Nacional [illegible] en inglés [illegible] la [illegible] de [illegible] clase social [illegible]. Dentro de cada [illegible] de las que [illegible] con [illegible].

[illegible] del [illegible] de [illegible] y [illegible] de información [illegible].

[illegible] Spanish and [illegible] English Language [illegible] por [illegible] Dr. [illegible] de [illegible] y el Dr. Gerald [illegible] Donald [illegible] the [illegible]

Directions for the Use of the Dictionary

Advertencias para facilitar la consulta del diccionario

1. Arrangement. A strict alphabetical order has been maintained throughout. The following forms will therefore be found in alphabetical order: the irregular forms of verbs, nouns, comparatives and superlatives; the inflected forms of the pronouns; and compounds.

Proper names and abbreviations are collected in special lists at the end of the dictionary.

2. Vocabulary. In many cases, the rarer words formed with *-ing, -er, -ness, -ist, un-, in-, etc.*, are excluded, to avoid extending the size of the dictionary beyond all reasonable limits. The reader having some slight acquaintance with the processes of word-formation in the two languages will be able to look up the root word and form derived words from it.

Abstract nouns are often dealt with very briefly when they are adjacent to a root word which has been fully dealt with. Thus the entry *fineness* fineza *f* etc. means: see the adjective *fine* and form other abstract nouns accordingly.

3. Separation of different senses. The various senses of each English word are made clear:

a) by symbols and abbreviated categories (see list on pp. 538–539);

b) by explanatory additions in italics, which may be a synonym (e.g. *face* [*grimace*] mueca *f*), or a complement (e.g. *face* faz *f of the earth*), or the object of a transitive verb (e.g. *face danger* arrostrar), or the subject of an intransitive verb (e.g. *fall* [*wind*] amainar).

1. El orden alfabético queda rigurosamente establecido. Ocupan su lugar alfabético, por tanto: las formas irregulares de los verbos y sustantivos, del comparativo y del superlativo; las diferentes formas de los pronombres; y las palabras compuestas.

Los nombres propios y las abreviaturas van reunidos en listas especiales que se imprimen como apéndices.

2. Vocabulario. En muchos casos se excluyen las palabras derivadas menos corrientes, que se forman, p.ej., con *-ing, -er, -ness, -ist, un-, in-*, a fin de no extender más de lo razonable los límites del diccionario. El lector que tenga algún conocimiento de cómo se forman las palabras derivadas en los dos idiomas podrá buscar la palabra radical y formar sobre ella las derivadas que quiera.

Los sustantivos abstractos estan tratados a menudo en forma somera cuando la palabra radical que les corresponde se ha tratado en forma extensa. Por tanto, el artículo *fineness* fineza *f* etc. quiere decir: véase el adjetivo *fine* para formar luego los sustantivos abstractos correspondientes.

3. Separación de las diversas acepciones. Las diversas acepciones de cada palabra inglesa se indican:

a) mediante signos y categorías abreviadas (véase la lista en las págs. 538–539);

b) mediante aclaraciones impresas en bastardilla, las cuales pueden ser un sinónimo (p.ej., *face* [*grimace*] mueca *f*), o complemento (p.ej., *face* faz *f of the earth*), u objeto de verbo transitivo (p.ej., *face danger* arrostrar), o sujeto de verbo intransitivo (p.ej., *fall* [*wind*] amainar).

Sometimes, e.g. with many abstract nouns, these explanations are omitted, but can easily be supplied from the adjacent entry for the corresponding verb or root word.

4. The different parts of speech are indicated by numbers within each entry; the grammatical indication *adj.*, *su.*, etc., is omitted in all cases where the category is obvious.

5. The gender of every Spanish noun is indicated. Often in translating an English noun, two Spanish versions must be given, one for each gender: where the final *o* or *e* changes to *a* for the feminine, we write *passenger* pasajero (a *f*) *m*; where the *a* has to be added for the feminine, we write *teacher* profesor (-a *f*) *m*. In this second class, some endings carry an accent in the masculine which is not needed in the feminine, and this suppression is not indicated in the dictionary. The endings affected are: *-án, -ín, -ón* and *-és*, so that *idler* haragán (-a *f*) *m* means: haragán *m*, haragana *f*.

6. Syllabification dots. The centered dots within the English word show how it should be divided in writing, e.g. **ab·dom·i·nal.** If the syllabification dot coincides with the stress mark, the former is left out. The word may therefore also be divided at the point where the stress mark stands alone, e.g. **ab·ne'ga·tion.**

7. Phonetic transcription. The pronunciation of each headword and of many others is given in the alphabet of the International Phonetic Association (explanation on pp. 540–542). This is omitted only in the case of forms derived with one of the common suffixes (*-er, -ness*, etc.) and of compounds whose component parts are given independently elsewhere in the dictionary. In both cases, however, the stress of the word is always given.

Estas aclaraciones suelen omitirse en el caso de muchos sustantivos abstractos, etc., pero es fácil suplirlas refiriéndose al artículo del verbo o palabra radical correspondiente.

4. Las diferentes partes de la oración están indicadas dentro de cada artículo mediante números; las indicaciones gramaticales *adj.*, *su.*, etc., están suprimidas siempre cuando la categoría es obvia.

5. Se indica el género de cada sustantivo español. A veces, al traducir una palabra inglesa, hay que dar dos palabras españolas, una para cada género: cuando la *o* o la *e* final se cambia en *a* para formar el femenino, ponemos *passenger* pasajero (a *f*) *m*; cuando hay que añadir una *a* para la forma femenina, ponemos *teacher* profesor (-a *f*) *m*. En ciertas desinencias de esta segunda clase, el acento que lleva el género masculino se suprime en el femenino, supresión que no está indicada en el diccionario. Estas desinencias son: *-án, -ín, -ón, -és*, de manera que *idler* haragán (-a *f*) *m* quiere decir: haragán *m*, haragana *f*.

6. Puntos de silabeo. Los puntos centrales dentro de la palabra inglesa indican cómo se puede dividir la palabra escrita, p.ej., **ab·dom·i·nal.** Si el punto coincide con el acento, aquél queda suprimido. La palabra puede por tanto dividirse allí donde está el acento solo, p.ej., **ab·ne'ga·tion.**

7. La pronunciación figurada de cada palabra impresa en caracteres gruesos se da según el alfabeto de la Asociación Fonética Internacional (véase la explicación en las págs. 540–542). Esta pronunciación se omite en el caso de las palabras derivadas mediante uno de los sufijos corrientes (*-er, -ness*, etc.), y en el caso de las palabras compuestas cuyos elementos constan independientemente en otra parte del diccionario. En ambos casos, no obstante, se indica siempre dónde cae el acento.

8. Translation. In rare cases, accurate single-word translation is impossible or meaningless. Recognizing this obvious linguistic fact, we have in such cases either provided an explanation in italics in place of a translation, or have introduced the translation with the warning abbreviation *approx.* (= approximately).

When certain letters stand within brackets in a Spanish word, we indicate two forms that may be used indifferently or which are more or less synonymous, e.g. *village* puebl(ecit)o *m* means pueblo *m* and pueblecito *m*.

9. As appendices to the dictionary, the reader will find: a list of abbreviations, a list of proper names, a table of numerals, some notes on the conjugation of the English verb, with a list of the parts of irregular verbs, and a table of weights and measures.

8. La traducción. En muy contados casos, la traducción exacta o resulta imposible o carece de sentido práctico. Ante este innegable hecho lingüístico, ponemos en dichos casos o una explicación en bastardilla, o, como advertencia al lector, la abreviatura *approx.* (= aproximadamente).

Cuando en una voz española ciertas letras están entre paréntesis, se trata de dos formas que se pueden usar indiferentemente o que son más o menos sinónimas, p.ej. *village* puebl(ecit)o *m* quiere decir pueblo *m* y pueblecito *m*.

9. Como apéndices, el diccionario tiene: una lista de abreviaturas, una lista de nombres propios, una lista de numerales, unas notas sobre la conjugación del verbo inglés, con una lista de las partes de los verbos irregulares, y una tabla de pesos y medidas.

Key to the Symbols and Abbreviations

Explicación de los signos y abreviaturas

1. Symbols – Signos

~ ♀ ~ ♀ is the mark of repetition or tilde (swung dash). To save space, compound catchwords are frequently given with the aid of the tilde. The thick tilde (~) stands for the catchword at the beginning of the entry. The thin tilde (~) stands for: a) the preceding catchword, which itself may have been formed with the aid of a thick tilde; b) in the phonetic transcription, the entire pronunciation of the preceding catchword, or a part of it which remains unchanged. If the preceding catchword is given without phonetic transcription, the tilde refers to the last preceding phonetic transcription or indicates only a shifting stress.

~ ♀ ~ ♀ es la tilde o raya que indica repetición. Para reservar todo el espacio disponible a las voces-guia, las palabras compuestas se imprimen a menudo en forma abreviada mediante la tilde. La tilde gruesa (~) representa la voz-guía que encabeza el párrafo. La tilde delgada (~) representa: a) la voz-guía precedente, que puede ella misma estar formada mediante una tilde gruesa; b) en la pronunciación figurada, toda la pronunciación de la voz-guía precedente, o bien parte de ella que permanece intacta. Si la voz-guía se imprime sin pronunciación figurada, la tilde se refiere a la última pronunciación figurada, o bien indica solamente un cambio de acento.

When the initial letter changes from a capital to a small letter, or vice versa, the normal tilde mark is replaced by the sign ≈ or ≈ respectively.

Examples:
far ... ~-fetched
fore ... ~·gone: ~ *conclusion*
fair¹ [fer] **... fair²** [~]
favor ['feivər] **... favorable** ['~vərəbl]
foreign ... ≈ *Office*

□ after an adjective or participle, means that from it an adverb may be formed regularly by adding *-ly*, or from adjectives ending in *-ic* by adding *-ally*, or by changing *-le* into *-ly* or *-y* into *-ily*; examples:

rich □ = *richly*
frantic □ = *frantically*
acceptable □ = *acceptably*
happy □ = *happily*

El signo ≈ ≈ significa la repetición de la voz-guía con inicial cambiada (mayúscula en minúscula o vice-versa).

Ejemplos:
far ... ~-fetched
fore ... ~·gone: ~ *conclusion*
fair¹ [fer] **... fair²** [~]
favor ['feivər] **... favorable** ['~vərəbl]
foreign ... ≈ *Office*

□ después de un adjetivo o participio significa que de él se puede formar regularmente el adverbio añadiendo *-ly*, o añadiendo *-ally* a los adjetivos que terminan en *-ic*, o cambiando *-le* en *-ly* e *-y* en *-ily*; ejemplos:

rich □ = *richly*
frantic □ = *frantically*
acceptable □ = *acceptably*
happy □ = *happily*

F familiar, colloquial, *familiar, coloquial.*
† archaic, *arcaico.*
✧ rare, little used, *raro, poco usado.*
📖 scientific, learned, *científico, culto.*
❀ botany, *botánica.*
⊕ technology, handicrafts, *tecnología, artes mecánicas.*
⚒ mining, *minería.*
⚔ military, *milicia.*
⚓ nautical, *náutico.*
☤ commerce, *comercio.*
🚂 railway, *ferrocarriles.*
✈ aviation, *aviación.*
📯 postal affairs, *correos.*
♪ music, *música.*
⚠ architecture, *arquitectura.*
⚡ electrical engineering, *electrotecnia.*
⚖ jurisprudence, *jurisprudencia.*
Ꭿ mathematics, *matemáticas.*
⚘ farming, *agricultura.*
⚗ chemistry, *química.*
⚕ medicine, *medicina.*

2. Abbreviations – Abreviaturas

a. and, also, *y, también.*
abbr. abbreviation, *abreviatura.*
acc. accusative, *acusativo.*
adj. adjective, *adjetivo.*
adv. adverb, *adverbio.*
Am. Americanism, *americanismo.*
anat. anatomy, *anatomía.*
approx. approximately, *aproximadamente.*
Arg. Argentine, *Argentina.*
ast. astronomy, *astronomía.*
attr. attributive, *atributivo.*
biol. biology, *biología.*
Bol. Bolivia, *Bolivia.*
b.s. bad sense, *mal sentido, peyorativo.*
cj. conjunction, *conjunción.*

co. comic(al), *cómico*.
Col. Colombia, *Colombia*.
comp. comparative, *comparativo*.
contp. contemptuous, *despectivo*.

dat. dative, *dativo*.

eccl. ecclesiastical, *eclesiástico*.
e.g. for example, *por ejemplo*.
esp. especially, *especialmente*.
etc. et cetera, *etcétera*.
euph. euphemism, *eufemismo*.

f feminine, *femenino*.
fenc. fencing, *esgrima*.
fig. figurative, *figurativo, figurado*.
f/pl. feminine plural, *femenino al plural*.
freq. frequently, *frecuentemente*.

gen. generally, *generalmente*.
geog. geography, *geografía*.
geol. geology, *geología*.
ger. gerund, *gerundio*.
gr. grammar, *gramática*.

hist. history, *historia*.
hunt. hunting, *montería*.

ichth. ichthyology, *ictiología*.
indic. indicative, *indicativo*.
inf. infinitive, *infinitivo*.
int. interjection, *interjección*.
Ir. Irish, *irlandés*.
iro. ironical, *irónico*.
irr. irregular, *irregular*.

lit. literary, *literario*.

m masculine, *masculino*.
metall. metallurgy, *metalurgia*.
meteor. meteorology, *meteorología*.
m/f masculine and feminine, *masculino y femenino*.
min. mineralogy, *mineralogía*.
mot. motoring, *automovilismo*.
mount. mountaineering, *alpinismo*.
m/pl. masculine plural, *masculino al plural*.
mst mostly, *por la mayor parte*.

opt. optics, *óptica*.
orn. ornithology, *ornitología*.
o.s. oneself, *uno mismo, sí mismo*.

p. person, *persona*.

paint. painting, *pintura*.
parl. parliamentary, *parlamentario*.
pharm. pharmacy, *farmacia*.
phls. philosophy, *filosofía*.
phot. photography, *fotografía*.
phys. physics, *física*.
physiol. physiology, *fisiología*.
pl. plural, *plural*.
poet. poetry, poetic, *poesía, poético*.
pol. politics, *política*.
p.p. past participle, *participio del pasado*.
pred. predicative, *predicativo*.
pret. preterit(e), *pretérito*.
pron. pronoun, *pronombre*.
prov. provincialism, *provincialismo*.
prp. preposition, *preposición*.

rhet. rhetoric, *retórica*.

S.Am. Spanish Americanism, *hispanoamericanismo*.
Scot. Scottish, *escocés*.
sew. sewing, *costura*.
sg. singular, *singular*.
sl. slang, *argot, germanía*.
s.o. someone, *alguien*.
s.t. something, *algo*.
su. substantive, *sustantivo*.
subj. subjunctive, *subjuntivo*.
sup. superlative, *superlativo*.
surv. surveying, *topografía, agrimensura*.

tel. telegraphy, *telegrafía*.
teleph. telephony, *telefonía*.
telev. television, *televisión*.
th. thing, *cosa*.
thea. theater, *teatro*.
typ. typography, *tipografía*.

univ. university, *universidad*.

v. vide (see), *véase*.
v/aux. auxiliary verb, *verbo auxiliar*.
vet. veterinary, *veterinaria*.
v/i. intransitive verb, *verbo intransitivo*.
v/r. reflexive verb, *verbo reflexivo*.
v/t. transitive verb, *verbo transitivo*.

zo. zoology, *zoología*.

Signos de la Asociación Fonética Internacional aplicados al inglés

A. Vocales y Diptongos

[ɑː] sonido largo parecido al de *a* en *raro*: *far* [fɑːr], *father* ['fɑːðər].

[ʌ] *a* abierta, breve y oscura, que se pronuncia en la parte anterior de la boca sin redondear los labios: *butter* ['bʌtər], *come* [kʌm], *color* ['kʌlər], *blood* [blʌd], *flourish* ['flʌriʃ], *twopence* ['tʌpəns].

[æ] sonido breve, bastante abierto y distinto, algo parecido al de *a* en *parra*: *fat* [fæt], *ran* [ræn].

[ai] sonido parecido al de *ai* en *estáis, baile*: *I* [ai], *lie* [lai], *dry* [drai].

[au] sonido parecido al de *au* en *causa, sauce*: *house* [haus], *now* [nau].

[ei] *e* medio abierta, pero más cerrada que la *e* de *hablé*; suena como si la siguiese una [i] débil, sobre todo en sílaba acentuada: *date* [deit], *play* [plei], *obey* [ə'bei].

[e] sonido breve, medio abierto, parecido al de *e* en *perro*: *bed* [bed], *less* [les].

[ə] 'vocal neutra', siempre átona; parecida a la *e* del artículo francés *le* y a la *a* final del catalán *casa*: *about* [ə'baut], *butter* ['bʌtər], *connect* [kə'nekt].

[iː] sonido largo, parecido al de *i* en *misa, vino*: *scene* [siːn], *sea* [siː], *feet* [fiːt], *ceiling* ['siːliŋ].

[i] sonido breve, abierto, parecido al de *i* en *filfa, esbirro,* pero más abierto: *big* [big], *city* ['siti].

[ou] *o* larga, más bien cerrada, sin redondear los labios ni levantar la lengua; suena como si la siguiese una [u] débil: *note* [nout], *boat* [bout], *below* [bi'lou].

[ɔː] vocal larga, bastante cerrada, entre *a* y *o*; le es algo parecida la *o* de *por*: *fall* [fɔːl], *nought* [nɔːt], *or* [ɔːr], *before* [bi'fɔːr].

[ɔ] sonido breve y abierto, parecido al de la *o* en *porra, corro,* pero más cerrado: *god* [gɔd], *not* [nɔt], *wash* [wɔʃ], *hobby* ['hɔbi].

[ɔi] diptongo cuyo primer elemento es una *o* abierta, seguido de una *i* abierta pero débil; parecido al sonido de *oy* en *doy*: *voice* [vɔis], *boy* [bɔi], *annoy* [ə'nɔi].

[əː] forma larga de la 'vocal neutra' [ə], en sílaba acentuada; algo parecida al sonido de *eu* en la palabra francesa *leur*: *word* [wəːrd], *girl* [gəːrl], *learn* [ləːrn], *murmur* ['məːrmər].

[uː] sonido largo, parecido al de *u* en *cuna, duda*: *fool* [fuːl], *shoe* [ʃuː], *you* [juː], *rule* [ruːl], *canoe* [kə'nuː].

[u] *u* pura pero muy rápida, más cerrada que la *u* de *burra*: *put* [put], *look* [luk], *careful* ['kerful].

B. Consonantes

[b] como la *b* de *cambiar*: *bay* [bei], *brave* [breiv].

[d] como la *d* de *andar*: *did* [did], *ladder* ['lædər].

[f] como la *f* de *filo*: *face* [feis], *baffle* ['bæfl].

[g] como la *g* de *golpe*: *go* [gou], *haggle* ['hægl].

[h] se pronuncia con aspiración fuerte, sin la aspereza gutural de la *j* en *Gijón*: *who* [hu:], *behead* [bi'hed].

[j] como la *y* de *cuyo*: *you* [ju:], *million* ['miljən].

[k] como la *c* de *casa*: *cat* [kæt], *kill* [kil].

[l] como la *l* de *loco*: *love* [lʌv], *goal* [goul].

[m] como la *m* de *madre*: *mouth* [mauθ], *come* [kʌm].

[n] como la *n* de *nada*: *not* [nɔt], *banner* ['bænər].

[p] como la *p* de *padre*: *pot* [pɔt], *top* [tɔp].

[r] un sonido muy débil que no tiene nada de la vibración fuerte que caracteriza la *r* española; se articula elevando la punta de la lengua hacia el paladar duro: *rose* [rouz], *pride* [praid], *there* [ðer], *there is* [ðer'iz].

[s] como la *s* de *casa*: *sit* [sit], *scent* [sent].

[t] como la *t* de *pata*: *take* [teik], *patter* ['pætər].

[v] inexistente en español; a diferencia de *b*, *v* en español, se pronuncia juntando el labio inferior con los dientes superiores: *vein* [vein], *velvet* ['velvit].

[w] como la *u* de *huevo*: *water* ['wɔ:tər], *will* [wil].

[z] como la *s* de *mismo*: *zeal* [zi:l], *hers* [hə:rz].

[ʒ] inexistente en español; como la *j* de la palabra francesa *jour*: *measure* ['meʒər], *rouge* [ru:ʒ]. Aparece a menudo en el grupo [dʒ], que se pronuncia como el grupo *dj* de la palabra francesa *adjacent*: *edge* [edʒ], *gem* [dʒem].

[ʃ] inexistente en español; como *ch* en la palabra francesa *chose*: *shake* [ʃeik], *washing* ['wɔʃiŋ]. Aparece a menudo en el grupo [tʃ], que se pronuncia como la *ch* en *mucho*: *match* [mætʃ], *natural* ['nætʃərəl].

[θ] como la *z* de *zapato*: *thin* [θin], *path* [pæθ].

[ð] forma sonorizada del anterior, algo como la *d* de *todo*: *there* [ðer], *breathe* [bri:ð].

[ŋ] como la *n* de *banco*: *singer* ['siŋər], *tinker* ['tiŋkər].

[x] sonido que en rigor no pertenece al inglés, pero que se encuentra en palabras escocesas, alemanas, etc. que se usan en inglés: como la *j* de *jamás*: *loch* [lɔx].

Nota: Importa que el lector se dé cuenta de la casi imposibilidad de explicar de modo satisfactorio los sonidos de una lengua en términos de otra. Lo que aquí se dice es a modo de aproximación y de ayuda general, sin que pretenda tener ningún rigor científico. Importa además reconocer que los sonidos que se explican aquí pueden variar mucho en cuanto se emplean juntamente con otros sonidos o en frases enteras.

La tilde [˜], que aparece en la pronunciación figurada de ciertas palabras de origen francés, indica la nasalización de la vocal.

Los dos puntos [:] indican que la vocal anterior se pronuncia larga.

C. Acentuación

La acentuación de la palabra inglesa se indica colocando el acento ['] al principio de la sílaba acentuada, p.ej. *onion* ['ʌnjən]. Muchas palabras largas o compuestas tienen dos sílabas acentuadas (una quizá más ligeramente que la otra), lo cual se indica poniendo dos acentos: *falsification* ['fɔːlsifi'keiʃn], *upstairs* ['ʌp'sterz]. Uno de los acentos que lleva la palabra compuesta puede sin embargo suprimirse cuando la palabra tiene que someterse al ritmo de una frase entera, o cuando se emplea en función distinta (p.ej. como adjetivo o adverbio): *the upstairs rooms* [ði 'ʌpsterz 'ruːmz], *on going upstairs* [ɔn 'gouiŋ ʌp'sterz].

Véanse también las *Advertencias*, núm. 7, y la *Explicación de los Signos*.

D. Sufijos sin pronunciación figurada

Para ahorrar espacio, las palabras derivadas mediante uno de los sufijos corrientes suelen escribirse en el diccionario sin pronunciación figurada propia. Su pronunciación puede comprobarse consultando el lector la pronunciación figurada de la voz-guía que encabeza el párrafo, añadiendo después la pronunciación del sufijo según esta lista:

-ability [-əbiliti]
-able [-əbl]
-age [-idʒ]
-al [-(ə)l]
-ally [-(ə)li]
-an [-(ə)n]
-ance [-(ə)ns]
-ancy [-ənsi]
-ant [-ənt]
-ar [-ər]
-ary [-əri]
-ation [-eiʃn]
-cious [-ʃəs]
-cy [-si]
-dom [-dəm]
-ed [-d; -t; -id]*
-edness [-dnis; -tnis; -idnis]
-ee [-iː]
-en [-n]
-ence [-(ə)ns]
-ent [-(ə)nt]
-er [-ər]
-ery [-əri]
-ess [-is]
-fication [-fikeiʃn]
-ial [-(ə)l]
-ian [-(jə)n]
-ible [-əbl]
-ic(s) [-ik(s)]
-ical [-ikl]
-ily [-ili]
-iness [-inis]
-ing [-iŋ]
-ish [-iʃ]
-ism [-izm]
-ist [-ist]
-istic [-istik]
-ite [-ait]
-ity [-iti]
-ive [-iv]
-ization [-aizeiʃn]
-ize [-aiz]
-izing [-aiziŋ]
-less [-lis]
-ly [-li]
-ment(s) [-mənt(s)]
-ness [-nis]
-oid [-ɔid]
-oidic [-ɔidik]
-or [-ər]
-ous [-əs]
-ry [-ri]
-ship [-ʃip]
-(s)sion [-ʃn]
-sive [-siv]
-ties [-tiz]
-tion [-ʃn]
-tious [-ʃəs]
-trous [-trəs]
-try [-tri]
-y [-i]

* [-d] tras vocales y consonantes sonoras; [-t] tras consonantes sordas; [-id] tras *d* y *t* finales.

El alfabeto inglés

a [ei], b [biː], c [siː], d [diː], e [iː], f [ef], g [dʒiː], h [eitʃ], i [ai], j [dʒei], k [kei], l [el], m [em], n [en], o [ou], p [piː], q [kjuː], r [ɑːr], s [es], t [tiː], u [juː], v [viː], w ['dʌbljuː], x [eks], y [wai], z [ziː] (*British* [zed]).

Normas de ortografía en el inglés británico

Existen ciertas diferencias entre el inglés escrito en Gran Bretaña (British English, BE) y el inglés escrito en Estados Unidos (American English, AE). Son las principales:

1. **El guión** con que se escriben en BE muchas palabras compuestas se suprime a menudo en AE, p.ej. heeltap, soapbox, shinbone.
2. La **u** que se escribe en BE en las palabras que terminan en **-our** (p.ej. col*our*, hum*our*) se suprime en AE: col*or*, hum*or*.
3. Muchas palabras que en BE terminan en **-re** (p.ej. cent*re*, met*re*, theat*re*) se escriben en AE **-er,** p.ej. cent*er*, met*er*, theat*er* (pero no massacre).
4. En muchos casos, las palabras que en BE tienen **ll** en posición media se escriben en AE con una **l,** p.ej. counci*l*or, trave*l*ed. Sin embargo, hay palabras que en BE se escriben con una **l** que en AE se escriben con **ll,** p.ej. enro*ll*(s), ski*ll*ful, insta*ll*ment.
5. En ciertos casos, las palabras que en BE terminan en **-ence** (p.ej. def*ence*, off*ence*) se escriben en AE con **-ense:** def*ense*, off*ense*.
6. Ciertas vocales finales, que no tienen valor en la pronunciación, se escriben en BE (p.ej. catalog*ue*, dialog*ue*, prolog*ue*, programm*e*) pero no en AE: catalog, dialog, prolog, program.
7. Se ha extendido más en AE que en BE la costumbre de escribir **e** en lugar de **ae** y **oe,** p.ej. an(a)*e*mia, an(a)*e*sthesia, (o)*e*sophagus.
8. Algunas consonantes que en BE suelen escribirse dobles (p.ej. wa*gg*on) se escriben en AE sencillas, p.ej. wa*g*on, kidna*p*ed, worshi*p*ed.
9. En AE se suprime a veces la **u** del grupo **ou** que tiene BE, p.ej. m*o*(*u*)ld, sm*o*(*u*)lder, y se escribe en AE pl*o*w en lugar del BE pl*ou*gh.
10. En AE suele suprimirse la **e** muda en las palabras como abridg(*e*)ment, acknowledg(*e*)ment.
11. Hay otras palabras que se escriben de distinto modo en BE y AE, p.ej. BE cosy = AE *cozy*, BE moustache = AE *mustache*, BE sceptical = AE *skeptical*, BE grey = AE *gray*.

La pronunciación del inglés británico

Entre la pronunciación del inglés en Gran Bretaña (British English, BE) y la del inglés en Estados Unidos (American English, AE) existen múltiples diferencias que es imposible tratar aquí en forma adecuada. Señalamos únicamente las diferencias más notables:

1. **Intonación.** El AE se habla en un tono más monótono que el BE.
2. **Ritmo.** Las palabras que tienen dos sílabas o más después del acento principal [''] llevan en AE un acento secundario que no tienen en BE, p.ej. *dictionary* [AE ''dikʃə'neri = BE 'dikʃənri].
3. La **r** escrita en posición final después de una vocal o entre vocal y consonante es normalmente muda en BE, pero se pronuncia claramente en AE, p.ej. *car* [AE kɑːr = BE kɑː], *care* [AE ker = BE keə], *border* [AE 'bɔːrdər = BE 'bɔːdə].
4. Una de las peculiaridades más notables del AE es la **nasalización** de las vocales antes y después de las consonantes nasales [m, n, ŋ].
5. La **a** [BE ɑː] se pronuncia en AE como [æ] en palabras del tipo *pass* [AE pæs = BE pɑːs], *answer* [AE 'ænsər = BE 'ɑːnsə], *dance* [AE dæns = BE dɑːns], *laugh* [AE læf = BE lɑːf].
6. La sílaba final **-ile** (BE generalmente [-ail]) se pronuncia a menudo en AE como [-əl] o bien [-il], p.ej. *missile* [AE 'mis(ə)l, 'misil = BE 'misail].

A

a [ei; ə] *article*: un, una; *10 miles an hour* 10 millas por hora; *2 shillings a pound* 2 chelines la libra.
A 1 ['ei 'wʌn] F de primera calidad; F *feel* ~ estar como un reloj.
a·back [ə'bæk] F atrás, hacia atrás; ⚓ en facha; F *taken* ~ desconcertado.
ab·a·cus ['æbəkəs], *pl.* **ab·a·ci** ['~sai] ábaco *m* (*a.* △).
a·baft [ə'bæft] **1.** *adv.* a popa; **2.** *prp.* detrás de.
a·ban·don [ə'bændən] abandonar, desamparar; renunciar a, dejar; ~ *o.s. to* abandonarse a, entregarse a; **a'ban·doned** *adj.* abandonado, desamparado; **a'ban·don·ment** abandono *m*, desamparo *m*.
a·base [ə'beis] humillar, degradar; envilecer; **a'base·ment** humillación *f*, degradación *f*.
a·bash [ə'bæʃ] confundir, avergonzar; ~*ed* corrido, confundido; **a'bash·ment** confusión *f*, vergüenza *f*.
a·bate [ə'beit] *v/t.* disminuir, reducir; ⚖ suprimir, abolir; *price* rebajar; *enthusiasm etc.* moderar; *pride* abatir; *v/i.* menguar, disminuir; moderarse; (*price*) bajar; (*wind*) amainar; **a'bate·ment** disminución *f*; supresión *f*, abolición *f*; rebaja *f of price*; amaine *m*.
ab·a·tis [ə'bætis] estacada *f*.
ab·at·toir ['æbətwɑːr] matadero *m*.
ab·ba·cy ['æbəsi] abadía *f*; **'ab·bess** abadesa *f*; **ab·bey** ['æbi] abadía *f*, convento *m*; **ab·bot** ['æbət] abad *m*.
ab·bre·vi·ate [ə'briːvieit] abreviar; ⚗ simplificar; **ab·bre·vi'a·tion** abreviatura *f*.
ABC ['ei 'biː 'siː] abecé *m*, abecedario *m*; rudimentos *m/pl.*
ab·di·cate ['æbdikeit] *v/t.* abdicar, renunciar; *he* ~*s his principles* abdica de sus principios; *v/i.* abdicar (*in favor of* en favor de); **ab·di'ca·tion** abdicación *f*, renuncia *f*.
ab·do·men ['æbdəmen; ⚕ æb'doumen] abdomen *m*, vientre *m*;
ab·dom·i·nal [æb'dɔminl] abdominal.
ab·duct [æb'dʌkt] raptar; **ab'duction** rapto *m*; ⚖, ⚕ abducción *f*.
a·bed [ə'bed] en cama.
ab·er·ra·tion [æbə'reiʃn] aberración *f* (*a. ast. a. opt.*).
a·bet [ə'bet] incitar, instigar; ⚖ (*mst aid and* ~) encubrir, ser cómplice; **a'bet·ment** incitación *f*, instigación *f*; ⚖ encubrimiento *m*, complicidad *f*; **a'bet·tor** instigador *m*; ⚖ cómplice *m/f*, encubridor *m*, fautor *m*.
a·bey·ance [ə'beiəns] suspensión *f*; ⚖ *in* ~ en suspenso, en desuso.
ab·hor [əb'hɔːr] aborrecer, abominar; **ab·hor·rence** [əb'hɔrns] aborrecimiento *m*, abominación *f*; *hold in* ~ detestar; **ab'hor·rent** ☐ repugnante, detestable (*to* a).
a·bide [ə'baid] [*irr.*] *v/i. lit.* morar; ~ *by* atenerse a; conformarse con, cumplir con; *v/t.* aguardar; conformarse con; *I cannot* ~ *him* no le puedo ver; **a'bid·ing** ☐ permanente, perdurable.
a·bil·i·ty [ə'biliti] habilidad *f*, capacidad *f*, talento *m*; aptitud *f*; *to the best of one's* ~ lo mejor que pueda (*or* sepa) uno; **a'bil·i·ties** *pl.* dotes *f/pl.* intelectuales.
ab·ject ['æbdʒekt] ☐ abyecto, vil, ruin; ~ *poverty* la mayor miseria; **ab'jec·tion, 'ab·ject·ness** abyección *f*, bajeza *f*.
ab·jure [əb'dʒur] renunciar (a), abjurar.
ab·la·tive ['æblətiv] ablativo *m* (*a.* ~ *case*).
a·blaze [ə'bleiz] ardiendo; *fig.* ardiente, ansioso.
a·ble ['eibl] ☐ hábil, capaz; *be* ~ poder; (*know how to*) saber; ~ *to pay* solvente; ~**-bod·ied** ['~'bɔdid] sano, robusto; ⚓ ~ *seaman* marinero *m* de primera.
ab·lu·tion [ə'bluːʃn] ablución *f*.
ab·ne·gate ['æbnigeit] abnegar, renunciar, rehusar; **ab·ne'ga·tion** abnegación *f*, renuncia *f*.

ab·nor·mal [æb'nɔ:rml] □ anormal; deforme; **ab·nor'mal·i·ty** anormalidad *f*; deformidad *f*.
a·board [ə'bɔ:rd] ⚓ a bordo; *all* ~! ¡señores viajeros, al tren! (*etc.*).
a·bode [ə'boud] **1.** *pret. a. p.p. of abide*; **2.** morada *f*, domicilio *m*; *take up one's* ~ avecindarse, domiciliarse.
a·bol·ish [ə'bɔliʃ] abolir, anular, suprimir; **a'bol·ish·ment, ab·o·li·tion** [æbo'liʃn] abolición *f*, anulación *f*, supresión *f*; **ab·o'li·tion·ist** abolicionista *m/f*.
A-bomb ['eibɔm] = *atomic bomb* bomba *f* atómica.
a·bom·i·na·ble [ə'bɔminəbl] □ abominable, detestable; *taste etc.* pésimo; **a'bom·i·nate** [~neit] abominar; **a·bom·i'na·tion** abominación *f*; asco *m*.
ab·o·rig·i·nal [æbə'ridʒənl] **1.** □ aborigen, indígena; **2.** (*pl. mst* **ab·o'rig·i·nes** [~ini:z]) aborigen *m*.
a·bort [ə'bɔ:rt] abortar (*a. fig.*); **a'bor·tion** aborto *m*; engendro *m*; *fig.* malogro *m*, fracaso *m*; **a'bor·tion·ist** abortista *m/f*; **a'bor·tive** □ abortivo; ineficaz, sin resultado.
a·bound [ə'baund] abundar (*with, in* en).
a·bout [ə'baut] **1.** *prp.* (*nearly*) casi; *place* junto a; (*relating to*) de, acerca de; ~ *6 o'clock* a eso de las 6; ~ *6 days* unos 6 días; ~ *the end* casi al final; ~ *the fire* junto al fuego; ~ *the house* por la casa; *he looked* ~ *him* miró a su alrededor; *he took her* ~ *the waist* la cogió por la cintura; *I have no money* ~ *me* no llevo dinero encima; *speak* ~ *the matter* hablar del asunto; *ask questions* ~ *s.t.* hacer preguntas acerca de algo; *what is it* ~? ¿de qué se trata?; *v. how, what*; **2.** *adv.*: *be* ~ estar levantado; estar por aquí; *be* ~ *to do* estar para (*or* a punto de) hacer.
a·bove [ə'bʌv] **1.** *prp.* encima de, superior a; ~ *300* más de 300; ~ *all* sobre todo; *not to be* ~ *doing s.t.* ser capaz de hacer algo; *fig. get* ~ *o.s.* engreírse; *fig. it is* ~ *me* no lo entiendo; **2.** *adv.* (por) encima; arriba; *v. over*; **3.** *adj.* susodicho; **a'bove·'board** sin rebozo; legítimo; **a'bove-'men·tioned** sobredicho, antedicho, susodicho.
ab·ra·ca·dab·ra [æbrəkə'dæbrə] abracadabra *f*.
ab·rade [ə'breid] raer, raspar.
ab·ra·sion [ə'breiʒn] raedura *f*, rozadura *f*, raspadura *f*; abrasión *f*; **ab'ra·sive** ⊕ abrasivo *m*.
a·breast [ə'brest] de frente, de fondo; *fig.* ~ *of or with* al corriente de; al día de.
a·bridge [ə'bridʒ] abreviar; compendiar; privar; **a'bridg·ment** abreviación *f*; compendio *m*; privación *f of rights*.
a·broad [ə'brɔ:d] fuera; en el extranjero; *go* ~ ir al extranjero; *there is a rumor* ~ *that* corre el rumor de que; *it has got* ~ se ha divulgado.
ab·ro·gate ['æbrougeit] revocar, abrogar; **ab·ro'ga·tion** abrogación *f*.
ab·rupt [ə'brʌpt] □ brusco, rudo; *event* precipitado; *terrain* escarpado; *style* cortado; **ab'rupt·ness** brusquedad *f*, rudeza *f*; precipitación *f*.
ab·scess ['æbsis] absceso *m*.
ab·scond [əb'skɔnd] huir de la justicia; F zafarse.
ab·sence ['æbsns] ausencia *f*; falta *f*; ~ *of mind* distracción *f*, despiste *m* (F).
ab·sent 1. ['æbsnt] □ ausente; *be* ~ faltar; *fig.* = *absent-minded*; **2.** [æb'sent]: ~ *o.s.* ausentarse (*from* de); **ab·sen·tee** [æbsn'ti:] absentista *m/f*; **ab·sen'tee·ism** absentismo *m*; **'ab·sent-'mind·ed** □ distraído.
ab·sinth ['æbsinθ] ajenjo *m*.
ab·so·lute ['æbsəlu:t] □ absoluto (*a. gr.*); total; *denial* categórico, rotundo; *liar* redomado; *nonsense* puro; ~*ly* absolutamente *etc.*; ~*ly!* ¡perfectamente!; **'ab·so·lute·ness** lo absoluto; **ab·so'lu·tion** absolución *f*; **'ab·so·lut·ism** absolutismo *m*.
ab·solve [əb'zɔlv] absolver (*from* de).
ab·sorb [əb'sɔ:rb] absorber (*a. fig.*); *shock etc.* amortiguar; ~*ed in* absorto en; **ab'sorb·ent** absorbente, hidrófilo; **ab·sorp·tion** [əb'sɔ:rpʃn] absorción *f* (*a. fig.*).
ab·stain [əb'stein] abstenerse (*from* de); *freq.* abstenerse de las bebidas alcohólicas; **ab'stain·er** *approx.* abstemio *m* (*freq. total* ~); **ab·ste·mi·ous** [əb'sti:miəs] □ sobrio, abstemio; **ab·sten·tion** [æb'stenʃn] abstención *f* (*parl.* de votar); **ab·sti·nence** ['æbstinəns] abstinencia *f*

(*from* de); **ˈab·sti·nent** □ abstinente, abstemio.
ab·stract **1.** [ˈæbstrækt] □ abstracto (*a. gr.*); recóndito; *in the* ~ en abstracto; **2.** [~] resumen *m*, extracto *m*; **3.** [æbˈstrækt] abstraer (*mentally*); *euph.* hurtar; ⚗ extraer; *book* compendiar; **abˈstract·ed** □ *fig.* distraído; **ab·strac·tion** [æbˈstrækʃn] abstracción *f*; *euph.* hurto *m*; ⚗ extracto *m*; recogimiento *m* (del espíritu).
ab·struse [æbˈstruːs] □ abstruso; **abˈstruse·ness** lo abstruso; tenebrosidad *f*.
ab·surd [əbˈsəːrd] □ absurdo, irrazonable; ridículo; necio; **abˈsurd·i·ty** disparate *m*, absurdo *m*; tontería *f*, locura *f*.
a·bun·dance [əˈbʌndəns] abundancia *f*, copia *f*, caudal *m*; plenitud *f of heart etc.*; riqueza *f*; **aˈbun·dant** □ abundante, copioso; *water* caudaloso; ~ *in* abundante en, rebosante de; **aˈbun·dant·ly** copiosamente; ~ *clear* plenamente claro.
a·buse **1.** [əˈbjuːs] abuso *m*; (*insults*) denuestos *m/pl.*, improperios *m/pl.*; injurias *f/pl.*; **2.** [~z] abusar de; denostar; maltratar; **aˈbu·sive** □ abusivo; insultante; *be* ~ soltar injurias.
a·but [əˈbʌt] *v/t. a. v/i.*: ~ *with*, ~ *on* confinar con, lindar con; *v/i.*: ~ *on*, ~ *against* apoyarse en (*penthouse etc.*); **aˈbut·ment** contrafuerte *m*, estribo *m*; **aˈbut·ter** propietario *m* colindante.
a·bysm [əˈbizm] *poet.* = *abyss*; **aˈbys·mal** □ abismal; *fig.* profundo; **a·byss** [əˈbis] abismo *m*, sima *f*.
Ab·ys·sin·i·an [æbiˈsinjən] abisinio *adj. a. su. m* (a *f*).
a·ca·cia [əˈkeiʃə] acacia *f*.
ac·a·dem·ic [ækəˈdemik] □ académico; universitario; *argument etc.* bizantino, estéril; ~ *costume* toga *f*, traje *m* de catedrático; ~ *dress* vestidura *f* universitaria (*a. academicals pl.*); ~ *freedom* libertad *f* de cátedra, libertad de enseñanza; ~ *subjects pl.* materias *f/pl.* no profesionales; ~ *year* año *m* escolar; **ac·aˈdem·i·cal** □ universitario.
a·cad·e·mi·cian [əkædəˈmiʃn] académico *m*; **a·cad·e·my** [əˈkædəmi] academia *f*.
a·can·thus [əˈkænθəs] acanto *m* (*a.* ⩓).
ac·cede [ækˈsiːd]: ~ *to* consentir en, acceder a; *post* entrar en; *party* afiliarse a; *throne* subir a.
ac·cel·er·ate [ækˈseləreit] acelerar; apresurar; **ac·cel·erˈa·tion** aceleración *f*; **acˈcel·er·a·tor** *mot.* acelerador *m*.
ac·cent **1.** [ˈæksnt] acento *m*; **2.** [ækˈsent] acentuar; recalcar (*a. fig.*).
ac·cen·tu·ate [ækˈsentjueit] = *accent* 2; **ac·cen·tuˈa·tion** acentuación *f*.
ac·cept [əkˈsept] aceptar (*a.* ~ *of*, *a.* ✝); *p.* admitir; **ac·cept·aˈbili·ty** = *acceptableness*; **ac·cept·a·ble** [əkˈseptəbl] □ aceptable; grato; **acˈcept·a·ble·ness** aceptación *f*; aprobación *f*; **acˈcept·ance** aceptación *f* (*a.* ✝); acogida *f*; (*ideas*) acogida *f*, asenso *m*; **ac·cep·ta·tion** [æksepˈteiʃn] acepción *f* (de una palabra); **acˈcept·ed** □ acepto; **acˈcept·er**, **acˈcept·or** aceptador *m*; ✝ aceptante *m*.
ac·cess [ˈækses] acceso *m*, entrada *f* (*to* a); ⚕ acceso *m*, ataque *m*; *easy of* ~ abordable, tratable; accesible; **acˈces·sa·ry** = *accessory* 2; **ac·ces·si·bil·i·ty** [~iˈbiliti] accesibilidad *f*; **acˈces·si·ble** [~əbl] □ accesible (*to* a); asequible; **acˈces·sion** acceso *m*, entrada *f*; accesión *f* (*treaty etc.*); entrada *f* en posesión *of estate etc.*; subida *f to the throne*; (*property*) aumento *m*; ⚖ accesión *f*.
ac·ces·so·ry [ækˈsesəri] **1.** □ accesorio; **2.** accesorio *m*; ⚖ cómplice *m/f*; **acˈces·so·ries** [~riz] *pl.* accesorios *m/pl.*
ac·ci·dence [ˈæksidəns] *gr.* accidentes *m/pl.*
ac·ci·dent [ˈæksidənt] accidente *m*; ~ *insurance* seguro *m* contra accidentes; *by* ~ por casualidad; **ac·ci·den·tal** [æksiˈdentl] **1.** □ accidental, fortuito; ~ *death* muerte *f* accidental; **2.** ♪ accidente *m*.
ac·claim [əˈkleim] **1.** aclamar, ovacionar; **2.** aclamación *f*.
ac·cla·ma·tion [ækləˈmeiʃn] aclamación *f* (*freq.* ~*s pl.*); *by* ~ por aclamación.
ac·cli·mate [əˈklaimit] aclimatar.
ac·cli·ma·ti·za·tion [əklaimətai-

ˈzeiʃn] aclimatación *f*; **acˈcli·ma·tize** aclimatar.
ac·cliv·i·ty [əˈkliviti] subida *f*.
ac·com·mo·date [əˈkɔmədeit] (*adapt*) acomodar, adaptar (*to* a); ajustar; *differences* reconciliar, acomodar; proveer (*with* de); (*house*) alojar; **acˈcom·mo·dat·ing** □ acomodadizo; **ac·com·moˈda·tion** acomodación *f*, adaptación *f*; acuerdo *m*, convenio *m*; transigencia *f*; alojamiento *m*; ~*s* facilidades *f/pl.*, comodidades *f/pl.*; (*in a train*) localidad *f*; (*in a hotel*) alojamiento *m*; ⚕ ~ *bill* pagaré *m* de favor; *seating* ~ plazas *f/pl.*, asientos *m/pl.*; ~ *train* tren *m* ómnibus.
ac·com·pa·ni·ment [əˈkʌmpənimənt] acompañamiento *m* (*a.* ♪); accesorio *m*; **acˈcom·pa·nist** acompañante (a *f*) *m*; **acˈcom·pa·ny** acompañar (*by*, *with* de).
ac·com·plice [əˈkɔmplis] cómplice *m/f*, fautor *m*.
ac·com·plish [əˈkɔmpliʃ] acabar, completar; efectuar; *prophesy etc.* cumplir; **acˈcom·plished** consumado, logrado; *fact* realizado; *p.* hábil; **acˈcom·plish·ment** (*end*) conclusión *f*; logro *m*, éxito *m*; ~*s pl.* talentos *m/pl.*, habilidades *f/pl.*
ac·cord [əˈkɔːrd] **1.** acuerdo *m*, convenio *m*; armonía *f*; *of one's own* ~ espontáneamente, de su propio acuerdo; *with one* ~ de común acuerdo; **2.** *v/i.* concordar (*with* con); *v/t.* conceder; **acˈcord·ance** conformidad *f*; *in* ~ *with* conforme a, de acuerdo con; **acˈcord·ant:** ~ *to*, ~ *with* conforme a; **acˈcord·ing:** ~ *to* según; conforme a; ~ *as* según; **acˈcord·ing·ly** en conformidad: *and* ~ así pues, y por lo tanto.
ac·cor·di·on [əˈkɔːrdiən] acordeón *m*.
ac·cost [əˈkɔst] abordar.
ac·couche·ment [əˈkuːʃmənt] alumbramiento *m*, parto *m*; **ac·coucheur** [ækuːˈʃəːr], *f* **ac·couˈcheuse** [~z] comadrón (-a *f*) *m*.
ac·count [əˈkaunt] **1.** narración *f*, relato *m*; cuenta *f* (*a.* ⚕), cálculo *m*; estimación *f*, importancia *f*; *blocked* ~ cuenta *f* bloqueada; *current* ~ cuenta *f* corriente; *payment on* ~ pago *m* a cuenta; *by all* ~*s* por lo que dicen; *of no* ~ de poca importancia; *on his* ~ por él; *on his own* ~ por su propia cuenta; *on no* ~ de ninguna manera; *on* ~ *of* a causa de, por; *bring to* ~ pedir cuentas a; *give* (*or render*) *an* ~ *of* dar cuenta de; *buy on* ~ comprar a plazos; *give a good* ~ *of o.s.* dar buena cuenta de sí; *settle an* ~ liquidar una cuenta; *take into* ~, *take* ~ *of* tener en cuenta; *turn to* ~ aprovechar, sacar provecho de; **2.** *v/i.*: ~ *for* dar cuenta de, explicar; justificar; *I cannot* ~ *for it* no me lo explico; *v/t.* considerar, tener por; **ac·count·aˈbil·i·ty** responsabilidad *f*; **acˈcount·a·ble** □ responsable; **acˈcount·an·cy** contabilidad *f*; **acˈcount·ant** contador *m*, contabilista *m/f*; contable *m*; **acˈcount book** libro *m* de cuentas; **acˈcount·ing** contabilidad *f*.
ac·cou·tered [əˈkuːtərd] equipado; **ac·cou·ter·ments** [əˈkuːtərmənts] *pl.* arreos *m/pl.*; equipo *m*.
ac·cred·it [əˈkredit] acreditar (*a. diplomatic*); ~ *s.o. to a p.* acreditar a alguien cerca de una p.; ~ *s.t. to a p.* atribuir algo a una p.
ac·cre·tion [æˈkriːʃn] aumento *m*; ⚖ acrecencia *f*, accesión *f*.
ac·crue [əˈkruː] aumentarse.
ac·cu·mu·late [əˈkjuːmjuleit] acumular(se), amontonar(se); **ac·cu·muˈla·tion** acumulación *f*, aumento *m*; montón *m*; **ac·cu·mu·la·tive** [əˈkjuːmjulətiv] □ acumulativo; **acˈcu·mu·la·tor** ⚡ acumulador *m*.
ac·cu·ra·cy [ˈækjurəsi] exactitud *f*, precisión *f*; **ac·cu·rate** [ˈ~rit] □ exacto, preciso; correcto.
ac·curs·ed [əˈkəːrsid], **ac·curst** [əˈkəːrst] maldito; *lit.* ~ *be* ¡maldito sea!, ¡mal haya!
ac·cu·sa·tion [ækjuːˈzeiʃn] acusación *f*; ⚖ denuncia *f*, delación *f*; **ac·cu·sa·tive** [əˈkjuːzətiv] acusativo *m* (*a.* ~ *case*); **ac·cu·sa·to·ry** [əˈkjuːzətəri] acusatorio; **ac·cuse** [əˈkjuːz] acusar (*of* de); denunciar, delatar; *the* ~*d* ⚖ el acusado; **acˈcus·er** acusador *m*.
ac·cus·tom [əˈkʌstəm] acostumbrar, avezar (*to* a); **acˈcus·tomed** acostumbrado; usual.
ace [eis] as *m* (*dice*, *cards*, *a. tennis*; *a. sl. fig.*); F ~ *in the hole* triunfo *m* en reserva; *within an* ~ *of* a dos dedos de.
a·cer·bi·ty [əˈsəːrbiti] aspereza *f*.
ac·e·tate [ˈæsitit] acetato *m*; **a·ce·tic**

[əˈsiːtik] acético; ~ *acid* ácido *m* acético; **a·cet·i·fy** [əˈsetifai] *v/t.* acetificar; *v/i.* acetificarse; **ac·e·tone** [ˈæsitoun] acetona *f*; **ac·e·tous** [ˈ~təs] acetoso; agrio; **a·cet·y·lene** [əˈsetiliːn] acetileno *m*; ~ *torch* soplete *m* oxiacetilénico.

ache [eik] **1.** doler; **2.** dolor *m*; *full of ~s and pains* lleno de goteras.

a·chieve [əˈtʃiːv] lograr, conseguir; acabar; **aˈchieve·ment** realización *f*, logro *m*; hazaña *f*, proeza *f*.

A·chil·les heel [əˈkiliːzˈhiːl] talón *m* de Aquiles.

ach·ing [ˈeikiŋ] **1.** □ dolorido; **2.** dolor *m*.

ach·ro·mat·ic [ækrouˈmætik] □ acromático.

ac·id [ˈæsid] **1.** □ ácido, agrio; ~ *rain* lluvia *f* ácida; ~ *test* prueba *f* decisiva; *v. test*; **2.** ácido *m*; **a·cid·i·fy** [əˈsidifai] acidificar; **aˈcid·i·ty** acidez *f*; acedía *f of stomach*; **ac·i·do·sis** [æsiˈdousis] acidosis *f*; **ˈac·id·proof** a prueba de ácidos; **a·cid·u·late** [əˈsidjuleit] acidular; **a·cid·u·lous** [əˈsidjuləs] acídulo.

ac·knowl·edge [əkˈnɔlidʒ] reconocer; *crime etc.* confesar; *favor etc.* agradecer; ✝ ~ *receipt* acusar recibo; **acˈknowl·edg·ment** reconocimiento *m*; confesión *f*; agradecimiento *m*; ✝ acuse *m* de recibo.

ac·me [ˈækmi] *lit. fig.* cima *f*, apogeo *m*, colmo *m*; ~ *of perfection* suma perfección *f*.

ac·ne [ˈækni] acné *m*.

ac·o·lyte [ˈækəlait] acólito *m*.

ac·o·nite [ˈækənait] acónito *m*.

a·corn [ˈeikɔːrn] bellota *f*.

a·cous·tic, a·cous·ti·cal [əˈkuːstik(l)] □ acústico; **aˈcous·tics** acústica *f*; *pl. of a room* condiciones *f/pl.* acústicas de un local, acústica *f*.

ac·quaint [əˈkweint] enterar, avisar (*with*, *of* de); *be ~ed* conocerse; *be ~ed with* conocer; saber, estar al corriente de; *become ~ed with* (llegar a) conocer; ponerse al tanto de; **acˈquaint·ance** conocimiento *m* (*with* de); (*p.*) conocimiento *m*, conocido *m*.

ac·qui·esce [ækwiˈes] asentir (*in* a), conformarse (*in* con); **ac·quiˈes·cence** consentimiento *m*, aquiescencia *f* (*to* en); **ac·quiˈes·cent** □ condescendiente; acomodadizo.

ac·quire [əˈkwaiər] adquirir, obtener; *language* aprender; ~ *a taste for* tomar gusto a; **acˈquired** [~d] adquirido; ~ *immune-deficiency syndrome* (*AIDS*) síndrome *m* de inmunidad deficiente adquirida (SIDA); ~ *taste* gusto *m* adquirido; **acˈquire·ment** adquisición *f*; *~s pl.* conocimientos *m/pl*.

ac·qui·si·tion [ækwiˈziʃn] adquisición *f*; ganancia *f*; **ac·quis·i·tive** [æˈkwizitiv] □ adquisitivo; codicioso; **acˈquis·i·tive·ness** codicia *f*.

ac·quit [əˈkwit] absolver (*a.* ⚖), exculpar (*of* de); ~ *o.s. of duty etc.* desempeñar, cumplir; ~ *o.s. well* (*ill*) hacerlo bien (mal); **acˈquit·tal** ⚖ absolución *f*; descargo *m of debt*; desempeño *m*; **acˈquit·tance** ⚖ quita *f*; descargo *m of debt*.

a·cre [ˈeikər] acre *m* (= *40,47 áreas*); *God's* ~ camposanto *m*; **acre·age** [ˈeikəridʒ] superficie *f* en acres; extensión *f* (de tierras).

ac·rid [ˈækrid] acre; *fig.* áspero, desapacible.

ac·ri·mo·ni·ous [ækriˈmounjəs] □ áspero, desabrido; **ac·ri·mo·ny** [ˈækriməni] acrimonia *f*, aspereza *f*.

ac·ro·bat [ˈækrəbæt] acróbata *m/f*; **ac·roˈbat·ic** □ acrobático; **ac·roˈbat·ics** acrobacia *f*; ✈ vuelo *m* acrobático.

ac·ro·nym [ˈækrənim] acrónimo *m*.

a·cross [əˈkrɔs] **1.** *adv.* a través, de través; de una parte a otra, de un lado a otro; del otro lado; en cruz, transversalmente; **2.** *prp.* a(l) través de; del otro lado de; *~-the-board* comprensivo, general.

act [ækt] **1.** *v/i.* actuar, obrar; funcionar, marchar; comportarse, conducirse; *thea.* trabajar; ~ *as* actuar de, hacer de; ~ (*up*)*on* obrar con arreglo a; influir en; ⚕ atacar; ~ *for* representar; F ~ *up* travesear; *v/t. thea.* representar; desempeñar (un papel); **2.** acto *m*, acción *f*, obra *f*; *parl.* decreto *m*, ley *f*; *thea.* acto *m*, jornada *f*; F *in the* ~ con las manos en la masa; *2s pl. of the Apostles* Hechos *m/pl.* de los Apóstoles; **ˈact·a·ble** representable; **ˈact·ing 1.** *thea.* representación *f*; (*action, operation, performance*) actuación *f*, desempeño *m*; **2.** interino, suplente; ✝ ~ *partner* socio *m* interino.

ac·tion [ˈækʃn] acción *f* (*a.* ⚔, *thea.*), acto *m*, hecho *m*; ⊕ mecanismo *m*;

funcionamiento *m*, marcha *f*; (*horse*) marcha *f*; gesto *m*; ⚖ acción *f*, demanda *f*; *put into* ~ poner en marcha; *put out of* ~ inutilizar; parar; *take* ~ tomar medidas; ˈ**ac·tion·a·ble** justiciable.

ac·tive [ˈæktiv] □ activo (*a. gr. a.* ☤); enérgico; vigoroso; *be on the* ~ *list* estar en activo; **acˈtiv·i·ty** actividad *f*; energía *f*; vigor *m*; *in full* ~ en plena actividad; *pl. esp.* ☤ negocios *m/pl.*; esfera *f* de actividad.

ac·tor [ˈæktər] actor *m*, cómico *m*; **ac·tress** [ˈæktris] actriz *f*.

ac·tu·al [ˈæktjuəl] □ verdadero, real, efectivo; actual; **ac·tu·al·i·ty** [æktjuˈæliti] realidad *f*; actualidad *f*; **ac·tu·al·ize** [ˈæktjuəlaiz] actualizar; realizar; **ac·tu·al·ly** [ˈæktjuəli] en realidad.

ac·tu·ar·y [ˈæktjuəri] actuario *m* de seguros.

ac·tu·ate [ˈæktjueit] actuar; impeler; **ac·tuˈa·tion** actuación *f*.

a·cu·men [əˈkju:men] perspicacia *f*; juicio *m* crítico.

ac·u·punc·ture [ˈækjupʌŋktʃər] acupuntura *f*.

a·cute [əˈkju:t] □ *all senses*: agudo; **aˈcute·ness** agudeza *f*.

ad [æd] F = *advertisement*; *classified* ~*s pl.* anuncios *m/pl.* por palabras.

ad·age [ˈædidʒ] adagio *m*; refrán *m*.

ad·a·mant [ˈædəmənt] *fig.* firme, intransigente; insensible (*to* a); **ad·a·man·tine** [~ˈmæntain] adamantino; *fig.* = *adamant*.

Ad·am's ap·ple [ˈædəmzˈæpl] nuez *f*.

a·dapt [əˈdæpt] adaptar, acomodar, ajustar; *text* refundir; **a·dapt·aˈbil·i·ty** adaptabilidad *f*; capacidad *f* para acomodarse; **aˈdapt·a·ble** adaptable; **ad·apˈta·tion** adaptación *f* (*to* a); refundición *f*; **aˈdap·ter** *radio*: adaptador *m*.

add [æd] *v/t.* añadir, agregar (*to* a); Ⱥ sumar; ~*ed line* ♪ línea *f* suplementaria; *v/i.* ~ *to* aumentar; realzar; ~*ing machine* sumadora *f*, máquina *f* de sumar; ~ *up to* subir a; *fig.* venir a ser, equivaler a.

ad·den·dum [əˈdendəm], *pl.* **adˈden·da** [~ə] adición *f*, apéndice *m*.

ad·der [ˈædər] víbora *f*.

ad·dict 1. [əˈdikt]: ~ *o.s.* entregarse (*to* a), enviciarse (*to* en, con); 2. [ˈædikt] adicto (a *f*) *m*; (*drugs*) toxicómano (a *f*) *m*; **adˈdict·ed:** ~ *to* aficionado a, adicto a; entregado a; **adˈdic·tion** (*drugs*) toxicomanía *f*.

ad·di·tion [əˈdiʃn] añadidura *f*; adición *f*; Ⱥ suma *f*; *in* ~ además, a más; *in* ~ *to* además de; **adˈdi·tion·al** □ adicional; **ad·di·tive** [ˈæditiv] aditivo *m*.

ad·dle [ˈædl] **1.** huero; *fig.* huero, atontado; confuso; **2.** enhuerar (*v/t. a. v/i.*).

ad·dress [əˈdres] **1.** *p.* dirigir la palabra a; *letter*, *protest etc.* dirigir (*to* a); ☤ consignar; ~ *o.s. to p.* dirigirse a; *th.* aplicarse a; ~*ing machine* máquina *f* para dirigir sobres; **2.** (*house*) dirección *f*, señas *f/pl.*; sobrescrito *m*; ☤ consignación *f*; (*speech*) discurso *m*; (*skill*) destreza *f*; (*behavior*) maneras *f/pl.*, modales *m/pl.*; *give an* ~ pronunciar un discurso; *pay one's* ~*es to a lady* hacer la corte a una señorita; **ad·dress·ee** [ædreˈsi:] destinatario *m*; **adˈdress·o·graph** máquina *f* de direcciones, adresógrafo *m*.

ad·duce [əˈdju:s] aducir, alegar.

ad·e·noids [ˈædənɔidz] *pl.* vegetaciones *f/pl.* adenoides.

ad·ept [əˈdept] **1.** diestro, experto (*at*, *in* en); **2.** perito *m*; *be an* ~ *at* ser maestro en (*or* de).

ad·e·qua·cy [ˈædikwəsi] suficiencia *f*; adecuación *f*; **ad·e·quate** [ˈ~kwit] □ suficiente; apropiado, adecuado.

ad·here [ədˈhir]: ~ *to* adherir a, pegarse a; *fig.* adherirse a, allegarse a; *promise* cumplir; *rule* observar; **adˈher·ence**: ~ *to* adherencia *f* a, adhesión *f* a; (*rule*) observancia *f* de; **adˈher·ent 1**. adhesivo; **2.** partidario (a *f*) *m*.

ad·he·sion [ədˈhi:ʒn] *mst* = *adherence*; ⚕ adherencia *f*.

ad·he·sive [ədˈhi:siv] □ adhesivo; ~ *plaster* esparadrapo *m*; ~ *tape* cinta *f* adhesiva, tafetán *m* adhesivo.

a·dieu [əˈdju:] **1.** ¡adiós!; **2.** adiós *m*; *bid* ~ *to* despedirse de.

ad·i·pose [ˈaedipous] adiposo.

ad·it [ˈædit] entrada *f*, acceso *m*; ⚒ bocamina *f*.

ad·ja·cen·cy [əˈdʒeisənsi] adyacencia *f*, contigüidad *f*; **adˈja·cent** □ adyacente, contiguo, inmediato (*to* a).

ad·jec·ti·val [ædʒekˈtaivl] □ adjetival, adjetivo; **ad·jec·tive** [ˈædʒiktiv] adjetivo *m*.

ad·join [ə'dʒɔin] lindar con; **ad'join·ing** colindante, lindero.
ad·journ [ə'dʒə:rn] *v/t.* prorrogar, diferir; *session* clausurar, suspender; *v/i.*: ~ *to* trasladarse a; **ad'journ·ment** aplazamiento *m*; clausura *f*.
ad·judge [ə'dʒʌdʒ] decretar; condenar (*to* a); sentenciar, juzgar; *prize* adjudicar; ~ *s.o. guilty* declarar culpable a alguien; **ad'judg·ment** adjudicación *f*, sentencia *f*.
ad·ju·di·cate [ə'dʒu:dikeit] juzgar; declarar, pronunciar; **ad·ju·di'ca·tion** adjudicación *f*; juicio *m*, sentencia *f*.
ad·junct ['ædʒʌŋkt] auxiliar *m*, adjunto *m*; accesorio *m*.
ad·ju·ra·tion [ædʒu'reiʃn] conjuro *m*, imprecación *f*; juramento *m*; **ad·jure** [ə'dʒu:r] conjurar, imprecar; juramentar.
ad·just [ə'dʒʌst] ajustar; arreglar; *quarrel* conciliar; *apparatus etc.* ajustar, regular; ~ *o.s. to* adaptarse a; **ad'just·a·ble** □ ajustable, graduable, regulable; **ad'just·ment** ajuste *m*, regulación *f*; acuerdo *m*, convenio *m*; arreglo *m*.
ad·ju·tan·cy ['ædʒutənsi] ayudantía *f*; **'ad·ju·tant** ayudante *m*.
ad-lib [æd'lib] F **1.** a voluntad; a discreción; **2.** improvisar.
ad·min·is·ter [əd'ministər] *mst* administrar; *shock etc.* proporcionar; ~ *an oath* tomar juramento; **ad·min·is'tra·tion** administración *f*; gobierno *m*; dirección *f*; **ad'min·is·tra·tive** [~trətiv] administrativo; **ad'min·is·tra·tor** [~treitər] administrador *m*; **ad'min·is·tra·trix** [~triks] administradora *f*.
ad·mi·ra·ble ['ædmərəbl] □ admirable; excelente.
ad·mi·ral ['ædmərəl] almirante *m*; **'ad·mi·ral·ty** almirantazgo *m*; ♀ Ministerio *m* de Marina; *First Lord of the* ~ (*British*) Ministro *m* de Marina.
ad·mi·ra·tion [ædmi'reiʃn] admiración *f*.
ad·mire [əd'maiər] admirar; **ad'mi·rer** admirador (-a *f*) *m*.
ad·mis·si·bil·i·ty [ədmisə'biliti] admisibilidad *f*; **ad'mis·si·ble** □ admisible; **ad'mis·sion** admisión *f*, entrada *f* (*to* a); confesión *f* (*of* de); ~ *free* entrada *f* libre (*or* gratis).
ad·mit [əd'mit] *v/t.* admitir; aceptar; confesar, reconocer; *be* ~*ted to academy etc.* ingresar en; *v/i.*: ~ *of* admitir, dar lugar a; ~ *to* confesarse culpable de; **ad'mit·tance** entrada *f*, admisión *f*; ⚡ admitancia *f*; *no* ~ es prohibida la entrada; **ad'mit·ted·ly** indudablemente; de acuerdo que ..., es verdad que ...
ad·mix·ture [əd'mikstʃər] mezcla *f*, adición *f*.
ad·mon·ish [əd'mɔniʃ] amonestar; reprender; aconsejar (*to inf.*); **ad·mo·ni·tion** [ædmə'niʃn] amonestación *f*; reprensión *f*; consejo *m*; advertencia *f*; **ad·mon·i·to·ry** [əd'mɔnitəri] □ amonestador.
a·do [ə'du:] ruido *m*; aspaviento *m*; dificultad *f*; *without more* ~ sin más ni más; *much* ~ *about nothing* mucho ruido y pocas nueces.
a·do·be [ə'doubi] adobe *m*.
ad·o·les·cence [ædou'lesns] adolescencia *f*; **ad·o'les·cent** adolescente *adj. a. su. m/f.*
a·dopt [ə'dɔpt] adoptar; ~*ed son* hijo *m* adoptivo; **a'dop·tion** adopción *f*; *country of* ~ patria *f* adoptiva; **a'dop·tive** adoptivo; **a'dop·tive·ly** por adopción.
a·dor·a·ble [ə'dɔ:rəbl] □ adorable; **ad·o·ra·tion** [ædɔ:'reiʃn] adoración *f*; **a·dore** [ə'dɔ:r] adorar; **a'dor·er** adorador (-a *f*) *m*.
a·dorn [ə'dɔ:rn] adornar, engalanar, embellecer; **a'dorn·ment** adorno *m*.
ad·re·nal [əd'ri:nl] suprarrenal; ~ *gland* glándula *f* suprarrenal; **ad·ren·al·in** [əd'renəlin] adrenalina *f*.
a·drift [ə'drift] ⚓ al garete, a la deriva (*a. fig.*); *turn* ~ abandonar a su suerte.
a·droit [ə'drɔit] □ diestro, hábil; mañoso; **a'droit·ness** destreza *f*, habilidad *f*; maña *f*.
ad·u·late ['ædjuleit] adular, lisonjear; **ad·u'la·tion** adulación *f*, lisonja *f*; **'ad·u·la·tor** adulador (-a *f*) *m*, lisonjero (a *f*) *m*; **'ad·u·la·to·ry** lisonjero.
a·dult ['ædʌlt] adulto *adj. a. su. m* (a *f*); ~ *education* enseñanza *f* de adultos.
a·dul·ter·ant [ə'dʌltərənt] adulterante *adj. a. su. m*; **a'dul·ter·ate** **1.** [~reit] adulterar, falsificar; **2.** [~rit] adulterado, falsificado; **a·dul·ter·a·tion** [ədʌltə'reiʃn] adulteración *f*, falsificación *f*; impureza *f*;

a'**dul·ter·a·tor** adulterador (-a *f*) *m*; a'**dul·ter·er** adúltero *m*; a'**dul·ter·ess** adúltera *f*; a'**dul·ter·ous** □ adúltero; a'**dul·ter·y** adulterio *m*.
ad·um·brate ['ædʌmbreit] bosquejar; presagiar; **ad·um'bra·tion** bosquejo *m*; presagio *m*.
ad·vance [əd'væns] **1.** *v/i.* avanzar, adelantar(se); ascender *in rank*; (*price*) subir; *v/t.* avanzar, adelantar; *fig. cause etc.* fomentar, promover; *idea etc.* proponer; **2.** ⚔ *etc.* avance *m*; *fig.* progreso *m*, adelanto *m*; (*money*) anticipo *m*; *~s pl.* requerimiento *m* amoroso; *in ~* por adelantado, de antemano; *be in ~ of* adelantarse a; *thank in ~* anticipar las gracias; **3.** *adj.* adelantado, anticipado; *~ guard* avanzada *f*; **ad'vanced** *adj. gen. a. pol.* avanzado; adelantado; *study* superior, alto; *~ in years* entrado en años; **ad'vance·ment** progreso *m*; adelantamiento *m*; fomento *m*; ascenso *m*.
ad·van·tage [əd'væntidʒ] ventaja *f* (*a. tennis*); beneficio *m*, provecho *m*; *take ~ of* aprovechar(se de), sacar ventaja de; *b.s.* embaucar, valerse de, abusar de; *have the ~ of s.o.* llevar ventaja a alguien; *show to ~* lucir; **ad·van·ta·geous** [ædvən'teidʒəs] □ ventajoso, provechoso.
ad·vent ['ædvənt] advenimiento *m*; *eccl.* ♀ Adviento *m*; **ad·ven·ti·tious** [ædven'tiʃəs] □ adventicio.
ad·ven·ture [əd'ventʃər] **1.** aventura *f*; lance *m*; **2.** aventurar(se); arriesgarse; **ad'ven·tu·rer** aventurero *m*; **ad'ven·tur·ess** aventurera *f*; **ad'ven·tur·ous** □ aventurero, arrojado, emprendedor.
ad·verb ['ædvəːrb] adverbio *m*; **ad·ver·bi·al** [əd'vəːrbiəl] □ adverbial.
ad·ver·sar·y ['ædvərsəri] adversario (a *f*) *m*, contrario (a *f*) *m*; **ad·verse** ['~vəːrs] □ adverso, contrario; hostil; desfavorable; *~ balance* saldo *m* negativo; **ad·ver·si·ty** [əd'vəːrsiti] adversidad *f*; infortunio *m*.
ad·vert [əd'vəːrt]: *~ to* referirse a, hacer referencia a.
ad·ver·tise ['ædvərtaiz] *v/t.* anunciar; publicar; *~ one's weakness* patentizar debilidad; *v/i.* poner un anuncio; *~ for* buscar por medio de anuncios; **ad·ver·tise·ment** [əd'vəːrtismənt] anuncio *m*; **ad·ver·tis·er** ['ædvərtaizər] anunciante *m/f*; '**ad·ver·tis·ing 1.** publicidad *f*, propaganda *f*, anuncios *m/pl.*; **2.** publicitario, de anuncios; *~ agency* agencia *f* de publicidad, empresa *f* anunciadora.
ad·vice [əd'vais] consejo *m*; aviso *m*, informe *m*, noticia *f*; *a piece of ~* un consejo; *take medical ~* consultar al médico.
ad·vis·a·bil·i·ty [ədvaizə'biliti] conveniencia *f*; **ad·vis·a·ble** [əd'vaizəbl] □ aconsejable, prudente, conveniente; **ad'vise** *v/t.* aconsejar (*to inf.*); avisar, informar (*a.* ✝); *v/i.*: *~ on* ser asesor en; **ad'vised** □ deliberado; *well ~* prudente; *you would be well ~ to inf.* sería aconsejable que Vd. *subj.*; **ad'vis·ed·ly** [~idli] deliberadamente, adrede; **ad'vis·er, ad'vis·or** consejero *m*, asesor *m*; **ad'vi·so·ry** [~əri] consultivo.
ad·vo·ca·cy ['ædvəkəsi] ⚖ abogacía *f*; defensa *f*; intercesión *f*; **ad·vo·cate 1.** ['~kit] ⚖ abogado *m*; defensor *m*; **2.** ['~keit] abogar por; propugnar, defender; proponer.
adze [ædz] azuela *f*.
ae·gis ['iːdʒis] égida *f*.
Ae·o·li·an [iː'ouliən] eolio.
ae·on ['iːən] eternidad *f*; *phls.* eón *m*.
a·er·ate ['ereit] *v/t.* airear; **a·er·at·ed:** *~ water* (agua *f*) gaseosa *f*; **a·er'a·tion** aeración *f*.
a·e·ri·al ['eriəl] **1.** □ aéreo; *~ camera* aparato *m* de fotografía aérea; *~ photograph* aerofoto *f*; *~ railway* funicular *m* aéreo; **2.** antena *f*; *~ mast* torre *f* de antena.
aer·i·al·ist ['eriːəlist] volatinero *m*.
a·er·ie ['eri] *v. eyrie.*
a·er·o... ['erou] aero...; **a·er·o·bat·ics** [~'bætiks] *pl.* acrobacia *f* aérea; **a·er·o·drome** ['erədroum] aeródromo *m*, campo *m* de aviación; **a·er·o·dy·nam·ic** [~dai'næmik] aerodinámico; **a·er·o·gram** ['~græm] aerograma *m*, radiograma *m*; **a·er·o·lite** ['~lait] aerolito *m*; **a·er·o·naut** ['~nɔːt] aeronauta *m/f*; **a·er·o'nau·tic, a·er·o'nau·ti·cal** □ aeronáutico; **a·er·o'nau·tics** *sg. a. pl.* aeronáutica *f*; '**a·er·o·plane** avión *m*, aeroplano *m*; '**aer·o·sol** aerosol *m*; '**aer·o·space** aeroespacial; **a·er·o·stat** ['~stæt] aerostato *m*; **a·er·o'stat·ic** aerostático.
aes·thet... *v. esthet...*

a·far [ə'fɑːr] (*mst* ~ *off*) lejos, en (la) lontananza; *from* ~ (des)de lejos.

af·fa·bil·i·ty [æfə'biliti] afabilidad *f*.

af·fa·ble ['æfəbl] □ afable.

af·fair [ə'fer] asunto *m*, negocio *m*; F cosa *f*; amorío *m*; ~ *of honor* lance *m* de honor; ~*s* negocios *m/pl.*; ~*s of state* asuntos *m/pl.* de estado.

af·fect [ə'fekt] *assume or pretend* afectar; aficionarse a; *influence* conmover, enternecer, impresionar; tener que ver con; influir en; *he* ~*s the free thinker* se las echa de librepensador; **af·fec·ta·tion** [æfek'teiʃn] afectación *f*; amaneramiento *m*; cursilería *f*; melindre *m*, dengue *m*; **af·fect·ed** [ə'fektid] □ afectado; conmovido; amanerado; cursi; melindroso; **af'fect·ing 1.** □ conmovedor, tierno, patético; **2.** *prp.* relativo a; **af'fec·tion** afecto *m*, cariño *m*, amor *m*; *esp.* ⚕ afección *f*; **af'fec·tion·ate** [~kʃnit] □ cariñoso, afectuoso; **af'fec·tive** afectivo.

af·fi·ance [ə'faiəns] **1.** palabra *f* de casamiento; **2.** dar palabra de casamiento.

af·fi·da·vit [æfi'deivit] declaración *f* jurada.

af·fil·i·ate [ə'filieit] *v/t.* (a)filiar; ⚖ determinar la paternidad de; *v/i.* afiliarse (*with, to* a); ~*d company* sociedad *f* filial, compañía *f* subsidiaria; **af·fil·i'a·tion** afiliación *f*.

af·fin·i·ty [ə'finiti] afinidad *f*; atracción *f*.

af·firm [ə'fəːrm] afirmar, aseverar, declarar; **af·fir·ma·tion** [æfəːr'meiʃn] afirmación *f*, aseveración *f*, declaración *f*; **af·firm·a·tive** [ə'fəːrmətiv] **1.** □ afirmativo; **2.**: *answer in the* ~ dar una respuesta afirmativa.

af·fix 1. ['æfiks] *gr.* afijo *m*; añadidura *f*; **2.** [ə'fiks] fijar; pegar, unir; añadir.

af·flict [ə'flikt] afligir, acongojar; *be* ~*ed with* sufrir de; **af'flic·tion** aflicción *f*, congoja *f*; miseria *f*.

af·flu·ence ['æfluəns] afluencia *f*; opulencia *f*; **'af·flu·ent 1.** □ opulento, acaudalado; **2.** afluente *m*.

af·flux ['æflʌks] aflujo *m*.

af·ford [ə'fɔːrd] dar, proporcionar, proveer; (*pay for*) costear; *be able to* ~ (*to*) poder darse el lujo de, poder permitirse; *I can* ~ *it* tengo con que comprarlo, puedo permitírmelo.

af·fray [ə'frei] refriega *f*, reyerta *f*.

af·for·est [æ'fɔrist] poblar de árboles, repoblar; **af·for·est'a·tion** repoblación *f* (forestal).

af·fran·chise [æ'fræntʃaiz] franquear, manumitir.

af·front [ə'frʌnt] **1.** afrentar, injuriar, ultrajar; (*verbally*) denostar; arrostrar; **2.** afrenta *f*, injuria *f*, ultraje *m*; denuesto *m*; *put an* ~ *upon, offer an* ~ *to* afrentar *etc.*

a·field [ə'fiːld] en el campo, al campo; afuera; *far* ~ muy lejos.

a·fire [ə'faiər] ardiendo; *be* ~ arder.

a·flame [ə'fleim] en llamas.

a·float [ə'flout] a flote; en el mar; a nado; inundado; † en circulación; *keep* ~ mantener(se) a flote; *set* ~ poner a flote; *esp.* † sacar a flote.

a·foot [ə'fut] a pie; en pie; en marcha; *set* ~ poner en marcha; *what is* ~? qué se está tramando?

a·fore [ə'fɔːr] ⚓ *v. before*; **'~·men·tioned, '~·named, '~·said** antedicho, susodicho, precitado; **'~·thought** premeditado; *malice* ~ premeditación *f*.

a·foul [ə'faul] enredado; en colisión; *run* ~ *of* enredarse con.

a·fraid [ə'freid] temeroso, miedoso; *be* ~ tener miedo (*of* de, a), temer; *be* ~ *to* tener miedo de *inf*, temer *inf*; *be* ~ *for* temer por; F *I'm* ~ *I have to go now* siento tener que irme ahora; F *I'm* ~ *he won't come* me temo que no venga.

a·fresh [ə'freʃ] de nuevo, otra vez.

Af·ri·can ['æfrikən] africano *adj. a. su. m* (a *f*); **Af·ri·kaans** [~'kɑːns] africaans *m*; **Af·ri·kan·der** ['~kændər] africander *m*.

aft [æft] a popa; en popa.

aft·er ['æftər] **1.** *adv.* (*time*) después; (*place*) detrás; **2.** *prp.* (*time*) después de; (*place*) detrás de; ~ *all* después de todo, con todo, al fin y al cabo; *day* ~ *day* día tras día; *time* ~ *time* repetidas veces; *I'll go* ~ *him* voy detrás de él; ~ *Velázquez* según Velázquez; ≗ *you!* ¡Pase Vd.!; *soon* ~ *having seen him* poco después de haberle visto; ~ *hours* fuera de horas; **3.** *cj.* después (de) que; **4.** *adj.* posterior; ⚓ de popa; **'~·birth** secundinas *f/pl.*; **'~·crop** segunda cosecha *f*; **'~·din·ner** de sobremesa; **'~'din·ner 'speak·er** orador *m* de sobremesa; **'~'din·ner 'speech** discurso *m* de sobremesa; **'~·ef·fect** efecto *m* resultante, consecuencia *f*; ˈ**~·glow** celajes *m/pl.*; ˈ**~·life** vida *f* futura; resto *m* de la vida; ˈ**~·math** consecuencias *f/pl.*; repercusiones *f/pl.*; ˈ**~·noon** tarde *f*; *good ~!* ¡buenas tardes!; ˈ**~·pains** *pl.* dolores *m/pl.* de sobreparto; ˈ**~**ˈ**shave** ˈ**lo·tion** loción *f* para después del afeitado; ˈ**~·taste** dejo *m*, resabio *m*; ˈ**~·thought** ocurrencia *f* tardía; ˈ**~·treat·ment** tratamiento *m* postoperatorio; **~·wards** [ˈ~wərdz] después, más tarde.

a·gain [əˈgen] otra vez, de nuevo, nuevamente; *~ and ~, time and ~* repetidas veces; *as much (many) ~* otro (os, as) tanto (os, as); *now and ~* de vez en cuando, una que otra vez; *never ~* nunca más; *come ~* volver a venir; *do it ~* volver a hacerlo.

a·gainst [əˈgenst] contra; cerca de, al lado de; *(as) ~* en contraste con; *~ his coming* para su venida; *over ~* enfrente de; *be ~* oponerse a; *he was ~ it* estaba en contra.

a·gape [əˈgeip] boquiabierto.

ag·ate [ˈægət] ágata *f*.

a·ga·ve [əˈgeivi] agave *f*, pita *f*.

age [eidʒ] **1.** edad *f*; época *f*, siglo *m*; *(old) ~* vejez *f*, senectud *f*; *~ bracket, ~ group* grupo *m* de personas de la misma edad; *at the ~ of* a la edad de; *in the ~ of Queen Anne* en la época de (*or* en tiempos de) la reina Ana; *of ~* mayor de edad; *come of ~* llegar a mayor edad; *over ~* demasiado viejo; *under ~* menor de edad; *what is your ~?* ¿qué edad tiene Vd.?, ¿cuántos años tiene Vd.?; F *wait for ~s* esperar una eternidad; **2.** envejecer(se); **ag·ed** [ˈ~id] viejo, anciano; **aged** [eidʒd]: *~ 20* de 20 años; ˈ**age·less** que no tiene edad, inmemorial; eternamente joven; ˈ**age lim·it** edad *f* mínima *or* máxima; edad *f* de jubilación.

a·gen·cy [ˈeidʒənsi] agencia *f*; acción *f*; medio *m*, mediación *f*, instrumentalidad *f*.

a·gen·da [əˈdʒendə] orden *m* del día.

a·gent [ˈeidʒənt] agente *m*; apoderado *m*; representante *m*; 🚂 jefe *m* de estación.

a·gent-pro·voc·a·teur [æʒɑ̃prɔvɔkətəːr] agente *m* provocador.

age·worn [ˈeidʒwɔːrn] caduco.

ag·glom·er·ate [əˈglɔməreit] aglomerar(se); **ag·glom·er**ˈ**a·tion** aglomeración *f*.

ag·glu·ti·nate 1. [əˈgluːtineit] aglutinar(se); **2.** [~nit] aglutinado; **ag·glu·ti·na·tion** [~ˈneiʃn] aglutinación *f*; **ag·glu·ti·na·tive** [əˈgluːtinətiv] aglutinante.

ag·gran·dize [əˈgrændaiz] engrandecer, agrandar; **ag**ˈ**gran·dize·ment** engrandecimiento *m*, agrandamiento *m*.

ag·gra·vate [ˈægrəveit] agravar, exacerbar; F irritar, exasperar; **ag·gra**ˈ**va·tion** agravación *f*, exacerbación *f*; circunstancia *f* agravante; F exasperación *f*.

ag·gre·gate 1. [ˈægrigeit] *v/t.* agregar, unir; *v/i.* ascender a, sumar; **2.** [ˈ~git] □ agregado, unido, global; *~ value* valor *m* total (*or* global); **3.** [~] agregado *m*, total *m*, conjunto *m*; *in the ~* en conjunto, en total; **ag·gre·ga·tion** [~ˈgeiʃn] agregación *f*.

ag·gres·sion [əˈgreʃn] agresión *f*; **ag**ˈ**gres·sive** [əˈgresiv] □ agresivo; *fig.* emprendedor; *~ war* guerra *f* agresiva; **ag**ˈ**gres·sive·ness** acometividad *f*; **ag**ˈ**gres·sor** agresor (-a *f*) *m*.

ag·grieved [əˈgriːvd] ofendido, desairado; agraviado.

a·ghast [əˈgæst] espantado, horrorizado; pasmado (*at* de).

ag·ile [ˈædjəl] □ ágil.

a·gil·i·ty [əˈdʒiliti] agilidad *f*.

a·ging [ˈeidʒiŋ] envejecimiento *m*.

ag·i·o [ˈædʒou] agio *m*; **ag·i·o·tage** [ˈædʒətidʒ] agio *m*, agiotaje *m*.

ag·i·tate [ˈædʒiteit] *v/t.* agitar; perturbar, alborotar; *plans etc.* discutir (acaloradamente); *v/i.*: *~ for* hacer propaganda por; **ag·i**ˈ**ta·tion** agitación *f*; perturbación *f*; discusión *f*; *insidious ~* agitación *f* clandestina; ˈ**ag·i·ta·tor** agitador (-a *f*) *m*, instigador (-a *f*) *m*, alborotador (-a *f*) *m*.

a·glow [əˈglou] encendido, fulgurante.

ag·nate [ˈægneit] agnado *adj. a. su.* [*m* (a *f*).]

a·go [əˈgou]: *(it is) a year ~* hace un año; *long ~* hace mucho tiempo, tiempo ha.

a·gog [əˈgɔg] ansioso, anhelante, ávido (*for* de); *set ~* excitar.

ag·o·nize [ˈægənaiz] *v/t.* atormentar; *v/i.* retorcerse de dolor, sufrir intensamente; ˈ**ag·o·niz·ing** □ desgarrador, angustioso.

ag·o·ny ['ægəni] angustia *f*, congoja *f*; (~ *of death, mortal* ~) agonía *f*; F ~ *column sección de anuncios relativos a asuntos particulares (parientes desaparecidos, etc.).*
a·grar·i·an [ə'greriən] agrario *adj. a. su. m* (a *f*); **a'grar·i·an·ism** agrarismo *m*.
a·gree [ə'gri:] *v/i.* concordar (*esp. gr.*), estar de acuerdo (*with* con, *that* en que); ponerse de acuerdo; ~ *on*, ~ *to* convenir en, quedar en, acordar; *it does not* ~ *with me* no me sienta (bien); *v/t. be* ~*d* estar de acuerdo (*on* en, *that* en que); ~*d* convenido, aprobado; ~*d!* ¡Conforme!; **a'gree·a·ble** □ agradable, ameno; *p.* simpático; conforme (*to* con), dispuesto (*to* a); **a'gree·a·ble·ness** agrado *m*; amenidad *f*; **a'gree·ment** acuerdo *m*; convenio *m*; concordancia *f*; conformidad *f*; ~ *to differ* desacuerdo *m* amistoso; *come to an* ~ ponerse de acuerdo, concertarse.
ag·ri·cul·tur·al [ægri'kʌltʃərəl] agrícola; ~ *adviser* agrónomo *m*; **ag·ri·cul·ture** ['~tʃər] agricultura *f*; **ag·ri'cul·tur·(al·)ist** [~tʃər(əl)ist] agricultor (-a *f*) *m*.
a·ground [ə'graund] varado, encallado; *run* ~ varar, encallar.
a·gue ['eigju:] fiebre *f* intermitente; escalofrío *m*; **'a·gu·ish** palúdico; escalofriado.
ah [ɑ:] ¡ah!
a·ha [ɑ:'hɑ:] ¡ajá!
a·head [ə'hed] delante, al frente; ⚓ por la proa; adelante; *straight* ~ todo seguido; *be* ~ *of one's time* anticiparse a su época; *get* ~ *of a p.* adelantarse a una p.; *go* ~ ir adelante, continuar, avanzar; *go* ~*!* ¡adelante!; *send* ~ enviar por delante.
a·hoy [ə'hɔi] ¡ha!; *ship* ~! ¡Ah del barco!
aid [eid] **1.** ayudar, auxiliar, socorrer; ~ *and abet* auxiliar e incitar, ser cómplice de; **2.** ayuda *f*, auxilio *m*, socorro *m*; *by* (*with*) *the* ~ *of* con la ayuda de; al amparo de; *in* ~ *of* a beneficio de.
aide-de-camp ['eiddə'kɑ̃:ŋ] edecán *m*.
ai·grette ['eigret] airón *m*.
ai·guil·lette [eigwi:'let] cordones *m/pl*.
ail [eil] *v/i.* estar enfermo; sufrir; *v/t.* afligir; inquietar; *what* ~*s him?* ¿qué tiene?
ail·e·ron ['eilərɔn] alerón *m*.
ail·ing ['eiliŋ] enfermizo, achacoso; enfermo; **'ail·ment** achaque *m*, dolencia *f*, enfermedad *f*.
aim [eim] **1.** *v/i.* apuntar (*at* a); *fig.* ~ *at* aspirar a, ambicionar; ~ *to* aspirar a, intentar; *fig.* ~ *high* picar muy alto; *v/t. gun, remark etc.* apuntar (*at* a); *blow etc.* asestar (*at* a); **2.** puntería *f*; *fig.* mira *f*, meta *f*, blanco *m*, designio *m*; *take* ~ apuntar; **'aim·less** □ sin objeto; desatinado; ~*ly* a la buena ventura, a la deriva.
ain't [eint] F = *is not, are not etc.*; *has not, have not.*
air[1] [er] **1.** aire *m*; *by* ~ por avión; *in the* ~ *fig.* en el aire, indefinido; en proyecto; *in the open* ~ al aire libre, al raso; *castles in the* ~ castillos *m/pl.* en el aire; *war in the* ~ guerra *f* aérea; *on the* ~ en antena, en la radio; *be on the* ~ hablar por radio; emitir; *clear the* ~ airear la atmósfera; *put on the* ~ llevar a las antenas; *take the* ~ tomar el fresco; *walk on* ~ estar bañado en agua de rosas; **2.** airear, orear, ventilar (*a. fig.*).
air[2] [~] aire *m*, aspecto *m*; ademán *m*; porte *m*; *give o.s.* ~*s* darse tono, envanecerse; *put on* ~*s* darse aires; *with an* ~ con aplomo; con garbo; ~*s and graces* refinamiento *m* afectado.
air[3] [~] ♪ aire *m*, tonada *f*.
air...: **'~ base** base *f* aérea; **'~ bladder** vejiga *f* natatoria; **'~·borne** ✈ en el aire, despegado; ⚔ aerotransportado; *germs etc.* transmitido por el aire; **'~ brake** freno *m* neumático; **'~ cham·ber** cámara *f* de aire; **'~-con'di·tion** climatizar; **'~-con'di·tioned** con aire acondicionado, refrigerado; **'~ con'di·tion·er** acondicionador *m* de aire; **'~ con'di·tion·ing** acondicionamiento *m* del aire, clima *m* artificial; **'~-cooled** enfriado por aire; **'~·craft** avión *m*; ~ *carrier* portaaviones *m*; **'~ cush·ion** cojín *m* de aire, almohada *f* neumática; **'~·drop 1.** lanzamiento *m*; **2.** *v/t.* lanzar; **'~ ex·haust·er** aspirador *m*; **'~·field** campo *m* de aviación; **'~·foil** superficie *f* de sustentación; **'~ force** aviación *f*, fuerzas *f/pl.* aéreas; **'~ gun** escopeta *f* de

aire comprimido; ~ **host·ess** azafata *f*, aeromoza *f S.Am.*
air·i·ness [ˈerinis] buena ventilación *f*; airosidad *f*; *fig.* ligereza *f*; alegría *f*.
air·ing [ˈeriŋ] ventilación *f*; oreo *m*; paseo *m* (para tomar el aire); *take an* ~ orearse, dar una vuelta.
air...: ˈ~ **jack·et** chaqueta *f* salvavidas; ⊕ camisa *f* de aire; ˈ~**·less** sin aire; sin viento; ˈ~**·lift** puente *m* aéreo; ˈ~**·line** línea *f* aérea; línea *f* recta; ˈ~**·lin·er** avión *m* de pasajeros, transaéreo *m*; ˈ~ **mail** correo *m* aéreo; ~ *letter* carta *f* aérea; ~ *stamp* sello *m* aéreo; ˈ~**·man** aviador *m*; ˈ~ **meˈchan·ic** mecánico *m* de aviación; ˈ~ **pas·sen·ger** pasajero *m* de avión; ˈ~ **pho·to(·graph)** aerofoto *f*; ˈ~ **pi·lot** piloto *m*; ˈ~**·plane** avión *m*; ~ *carrier* portaaviones *m*; ~ *pilot* piloto *m*; ˈ~ **pock·et** bache *m* aéreo; ˈ~**·port** aeropuerto *m*; ˈ~ **pres·sure** presión *f* atmosférica; ˈ~ **pump** bomba *f* de aire; ˈ~ **raid** ataque *m* aéreo; ~ *shelter* refugio *m* antiaéreo; ~ *warning* alarma *f* aérea; ˈ~**·screw** hélice *f* de avión; ˈ~**·ship** aeronave *f*; ˈ~**·sick** mareado (en el aire); ˈ~**·sick·ness** mal *m* de vuelo; ˈ~ **speed** velocidad *f* relativa al aire; ~ *indicator* velocímetro *m* aéreo; ˈ~**·strip** pista *f* de aterrizaje; ˈ~**·tight** hermético; ˈ~**·waves** *pl.* ondas *f/pl.* de radio; ˈ~**·way** aerovía *f*, vía *f* aérea; ~ *lighting* balizaje *m*; ˈ~**·wom·an** aviadora *f*; ˈ~**·wor·thy** en condiciones de vuelo.
air·y [ˈeri] □ airoso; *esp. room* bien ventilado, ancho; *fig.* etéreo, ligero; (*rude*) impertinente; *airily* con desenvoltura; muy a la ligera.
aisle [ail] nave *f* lateral; *thea. etc.* pasillo *m*.
aitch [eitʃ] *nombre de la h inglesa.*
aitch·bone [ˈeitʃboun] rabad(ill)a *f*.
a·jar [əˈdʒɑːr] entreabierto, entornado; *fig.* en desacuerdo.
a·kim·bo [əˈkimbou]: *with arms* ~ en jarras.
a·kin [əˈkin] consanguíneo (*to* de), emparentado (*to* con); *fig.* análogo, semejante (*to* a).
al·a·bas·ter [ˈæləbæstər] **1.** alabastro *m*; **2.** alabastrino.
a·lack [əˈlæk] † *a.* ~*-a-day!* ¡ay!, ¡guay!
a·lac·ri·ty [əˈlækriti] alacridad *f*.
a·larm [əˈlɑːrm] **1.** alarma *f*; sobresalto *m*; ~ *and despondency* confusionismo *m* y desconcierto; *give the* ~, *raise an* ~, *sound the* ~ dar la alarma, tocar a rebato; **2.** alarmar, inquietar, asustar; **aˈlarm bell** (campana *f* de) rebato *m*, timbre *m* de alarma; **aˈlarm clock** (reloj *m*) despertador *m*; **aˈlarm cord** 🚃 freno *m* de alarma; **aˈlarm·ist 1.** alarmista *m/f*; **2.** alarmante.
a·lar·um [əˈlerəm] *mst* † *for alarm.*
a·las [əˈlæs] ¡ay!, ¡ay de mí!
alb [ælb] *eccl.* alba *f*.
Al·ba·ni·an [ælˈbeinjən] albanés *adj. a. su. m* (-a *f*).
al·ba·tross [ˈælbətrɔs] albatros *m*.
al·be·it [ɔːlˈbiːit] aunque, bien que.
al·bi·no [ælˈbainou] albino (a *f*) *m*.
al·bum [ˈælbəm] álbum *m*.
al·bu·men, al·bu·min [ˈælbjumin] ⚗ albúmina *f*; ⚘ albumen *m*; **alˈbu·mi·nous** albuminoso.
al·chem·ic, al·chem·i·cal [ælˈkemik(l)] □ alquímico; **al·che·mist** [ˈælkimist] alquimista *m*; **ˈal·che·my** alquimia *f*.
al·co·hol [ˈælkəhɔl] alcohol *m*; ~*-level test* prueba *f* de alcohol; **al·coˈhol·ic** alcohólico *adj. a. su. m* (a *f*), alcoholizado *adj. a. su. m* (a *f*); **ˈal·co·hol·ism** alcoholismo *m*; **ˈal·co·hol·ize** [ˈ~laiz] alcoholizar.
al·cove [ˈælkouv] nicho *m*, hueco *m*; gabinete *m of library*; cenador *m in garden*; trasalcoba *f in a bedroom.*
al·der [ˈɔːldər] aliso *m*.
al·der·man [ˈɔːldərmən] regidor *m*, concejal *m* (de cierta antigüedad); **al·der·man·ic** [~ˈmænik] de (un) concejal, edilicio; **al·der·man·ship** [ˈ~mənʃip] regidoría *f*, concejalía *f*.
ale [eil] ale *f* (*cerveza inglesa, obscura, espesa y amarga*).
a·lee [əˈliː] a sotavento.
a·lem·bic [əˈlembik] alambique *m*.
a·lert [əˈləːrt] **1.** □ vigilante; vivo, listo; **2.** alerta *m*; *be on the* ~ estar alerta, estar sobre aviso; **aˈlert·ness** vigilancia *f*; presteza *f*.
al·fal·fa [ælˈfælfə] alfalfa *f*.
al·ga [ˈælgə], *pl.* **al·gae** [ˈældʒiː] alga *f*; algas *f/pl.*
al·ge·bra [ˈældʒibrə] álgebra *f*; **al·ge·bra·ic** [~ˈbreiik] □ algebraico, algébrico.
a·li·as [ˈeiliæs] alias *adv. a. su. m.*
al·i·bi [ˈælibai] coartada *f*; F excusa *f*, pretexto *m*.

al·ien [ˈeiliən] **1.** ajeno, extraño (*to* a); extranjero; **2.** extranjero (a *f*) *m*; **ˈal·ien·a·ble** enajenable, alienable; **al·ien·ate** [ˈ~eit] enajenar, alienar; *be ~d from* enajenarse de; **al·ien·a·tion** enajenación *f*; alienación *f*; *~ of mind* enajenación *f* mental; **ˈal·ien·ist** alienista *m*/*f*.

a·light[1] [əˈlait] ardiendo, encendido, iluminado.

a·light[2] [~] bajar, apearse; ✈ aterrizar; *~ on* posarse sobre; *~ on one's feet* caer de pie.

a·lign [əˈlain] alinear; *~ o.s. with* alinearse con; ponerse al lado de; **aˈlign·ment** alineación *f*.

a·like [əˈlaik] **1.** *adj.* semejante, parecido; *look ~* parecerse; **2.** *adv.* igualmente, del mismo modo.

al·i·ment [ˈælimənt] alimento *m*; **al·i·men·ta·ry** [~ˈmentəri] alimenticio; *~ canal* tubo *m* digestivo, canal *m* alimenticio; **al·i·menˈta·tion** alimentación *f*.

al·i·mo·ny [ˈælimouni] alimentos *m*/*pl.*

a·line(·ment) [əˈlain(mənt)] = *align(-ment)*.

al·i·quot [ˈælikwɔt] (parte *f*) alícuota.

a·live [əˈlaiv] vivo, viviente, con vida; *fig.* vivaz, activo; sensible (*to* a), despierto (*to* para); *keep ~* mantener(se) en vigor; F *look ~* menearse; F *man ~!* ¡hombre!; *be ~ to* hacerse cargo de; apreciar; *~ with* rebosante de, hormigueante en.

al·ka·li [ˈælkəlai] álcali *m*; **al·ka·line** [ˈ~lain] alcalino.

all [ɔ:l] **1.** *adj.* todo; *~ day (long)* (durante) todo el día; *~ kind(s) of books* toda clase de libros, libros de toda clase; *for ~ that* con todo, no obstante, así y todo; **2.** todo *m*; todos *m*/*pl.*, todas *f*/*pl.*; *after ~* sin embargo; *my ~* todo lo que tengo; *~ of* todo el, todos los; *~ of them* (ellos) todos; *~ that* todo lo que, todos los que; *at ~* de cualquier manera; en lo más mínimo; siquiera un poco; *not at ~* de ninguna manera; no hay de qué; *for ~ (that) I care* igual me da; *for ~ I know* que yo sepa; quizá; **3.** *adv.* enteramente, del todo; *v. once*; *~ the better* tanto mejor; *~ but* casi, por poco; menos; *v. right, there.*

all-A·mer·i·can [ɔ:ləˈmerikən] que representa los EE.UU.; exclusivamente estadunidense.

all-around [ˈɔ:ləˈraund] cabal; † global; *player* competente en todos los aspectos del juego.

al·lay [əˈlei] apaciguar, aquietar; *pain* aliviar, mitigar.

al·le·ga·tion [æleˈgeiʃn] aseveración *f*, alegación *f*, alegato *m*; **al·lege** [əˈledʒ] declarar, sostener; (*as proof, excuse, etc.*) alegar; **alˈleged** alegado; (*mst falsely*) supuesto, pretendido.

al·le·giance [əˈli:dʒns] fidelidad *f*, lealtad *f*; (*a. oath of ~*) homenaje *m*; *swear ~ to* rendir homenaje a.

al·le·gor·ic, al·le·gor·i·cal [æleˈgɔrik(l)] □ alegórico; **al·le·go·rize** [ˈæligəraiz] alegorizar; **ˈal·le·go·ry** alegoría *f*.

al·le·lu·ia [æliˈlu:jə] aleluya *f*.

al·ler·gy [ˈælərdʒi] alergia *f*.

al·le·vi·ate [əˈli:vieit] aliviar; **al·le·viˈa·tion** alivio *m*.

al·ley [ˈæli] callejuela *f*, callejón *m*; paseo *m in park*; **ˈal·ley·way** callejuela *f*, callejón *m*; pasadizo *m*.

All Fools' Day [ˈɔ:lˈfu:lzdei] = *April Fools' Day*.

al·li·ance [əˈlaiəns] alianza *f*; *form an ~* formar una alianza.

al·li·ga·tor [ˈæligaitər] caimán *m*; *~ pear* aguacate *m*; *~ wrench* llave *f* de mandíbulas dentadas.

al·lit·er·ate [əˈlitəreit] usar aliteración; formar aliteración; **al·lit·erˈa·tion** aliteración *f*; **alˈlit·er·a·tive** □ aliterado.

all-met·al [ˈɔ:lˈmetl] enteramente metálico.

al·lo·cate [ˈæləkeit] asignar, señalar; repartir; **al·loˈca·tion** asignación *f*; reparto *m*.

al·lo·cu·tion [ælouˈkju:ʃn] alocución *f*.

al·lo·di·al [əˈloudiəl] □ alodial.

al·lot [əˈlɔt] asignar, adjudicar; repartir; **alˈlot·ment** asignación *f*; reparto *m*; lote *m*, porción *f*; parcela *f* (de tierra).

all-out [ˈɔ:lˈaut] **1.** *adj. supporter etc.* acérrimo; *effort etc.* total, máximo; **2.** *adv.* con todas las fuerzas; a máxima velocidad.

al·low [əˈlau] (*permit*) permitir, dejar (*to inf.*); (*grant*) conceder, dar; (*admit*) confesar; *discount* descontar; *he is ~ed to be* se reconoce que es; *~ for* tomar en consideración, tener en cuenta; *it ~s of no excuse* no admite disculpa; **alˈlow·a·ble**

□ permisible, admisible; **al'low·ance** (*grant*) concesión *f*; ración *f*, pensión *f*; (*discount*) descuento *m*, rebaja *f*; ⊕ tolerancia *f*; *make* ~ *for p.* disculpar; *th.* tener en cuenta.
al·loy [ə'lɔi] **1.** aleación *f*, liga *f*; *fig.* mezcla *f*; **2.** alear, ligar; *fig.* mezclar, adulterar.
all-pur·pose ['ɔːl'pəːrpəs] para todo uso, universal.
All Saints' Day ['ɔːl'seintsdei] Día *m* de Todos los Santos (*1 noviembre*).
All Souls' Day ['ɔːl'soulzdei] Día *m* de Difuntos (*2 noviembre*).
all·spice ['ɔːlspais] pimienta *f* inglesa.
all-star ['ɔːl'staːr] *sport, film, etc.*: compuesto de primeras figuras; ~ *game* juego *m* de estrellas.
al·lude [ə'luːd]: ~ *to* aludir a, hacer referencia a, mencionar.
al·lure [ə'ljuːr] atraer, fascinar; **al'lure·ment** atractivo *m*, aliciente *m*; fascinación *f*; **al'lur·ing** □ atractivo, tentador.
al·lu·sion [ə'luːʒn] alusión *f*, referencia *f* (*to* a); **al'lu·sive** □ alusivo, referente (*to* a).
al·lu·vi·al [ə'luːviəl] □ aluvial; **al'lu·vi·on** [~ən], **al'lu·vium** [~əm] aluvión *m*.
all·weath·er ['ɔːl'weðər] para todo tiempo.
al·ly[1] **1.** [ə'lai] aliarse, unirse; *fig.* emparentarse (*to, with* con); *allied fig.* conexo, parecido; *allied to fig.* relacionado con; **2.** ['ælai] aliado *m*, confederado *m*; *The Allies* Los Aliados *m/pl.*
al·ly[2] ['æli] bolita *f*, canica *f*.
al·ma·nac ['ɔːlmənæk] almanaque *m*.
al·might·i·ness [ɔːl'maitinis] omnipotencia *f*; **al'might·y 1.** □ todopoderoso; F imponente, grandísimo; **2.** ♀ Todopoderoso *m*.
al·mond ['ɑːmənd] almendra *f*; (*a.* ~ *tree*) almendro *m*; ~ *brittle* crocante *m*.
al·mon·er ['ælmənər] limosnero *m*.
al·most ['ɔːlmoust] casi.
alms [ɑːmz] *sg. a. pl.* limosna *f*; '~**·house** hospicio *m*, asilo *m*, casa *f* de beneficencia.
al·oe ['ælou] áloe *m*, acíbar *m*.
a·loft [ə'lɔft] hacia arriba, en alto; ⚓ en la arboladura.
a·lone [ə'loun] **1.** *adj.* solo; *let* ~ sin mencionar; y mucho menos; *leave* ~ no molestar; no mezclarse en; **2.** *adv.* solamente, sólo.
a·long [ə'lɔŋ] **1.** *adv.* a lo largo; adelante; *all* ~ desde el principio; ~ *with* junto con; **2.** *prp.* a lo largo de; por; al lado de; **a'long'side 1.** *adv.* ⚓ al costado, costado con costado; *bring* ~ costar; **2.** *prp. fig.* junto a, al lado de.
a·loof [ə'luːf] reservado, huraño; *keep* ~ apartarse, alejarse (*from* de); *stand* ~ mantenerse apartado, mantenerse a distancia; **a'loof·ness** reserva *f*.
a·loud [ə'laud] alto, en voz alta.
alp [ælp] *lit.* cumbre *f*; ♀*s pl.* Alpes *m/pl.*; **al·pen·stock** ['ælpinstɔk] alpenstock *m*.
al·pha·bet ['ælfəbit] alfabeto *m*; **al·pha·bet·ic, al·pha·bet·i·cal** [~'betik(l)] □ alfabético.
Al·pine ['ælpain] alpino, alpestre; ⚕ ~ *sun* sol *m* de montaña; '**al·pin·ist** alpinista *m/f*.
al·read·y [ɔːl'redi] ya; previamente, antes.
Al·sa·tian [æl'seiʃn] alsaciano *adj. a. su. m* (a *f*); ~ *dog* perro *m* lobo.
al·so ['ɔːlsou] también, además; *racing*: ~ *ran* (caballo *m*) que no logró colocarse; F fracasado *m*.
al·tar ['ɔːltər] altar *m*; ara *f* (*lit.*); *high* ~ altar *m* mayor; ~ *boy* acólito *m*, monaguillo *m*; ~ *cloth* sabanilla *f*, palia *f*; ~*piece* retablo *m*; ~ *rail* comulgatorio *m*.
al·ter ['ɔːltər] cambiar(se), alterar, modificar; *animal* castrar; '**al·ter·a·ble** mudable; **al·ter'a·tion** alteración *f*, cambio *m* (*of, to* de); ⚠ ~*s pl.* reformas *f/pl.*
al·ter·cate ['ɔːltəːrkeit] altercar; **al·ter'ca·tion** altercado *m*.
al·ter·nate 1. ['ɔːltəːrneit] alternar; *alternating current* corriente *f* alterna, corriente alternativa; **2.** [ɔːl'təːrnit] □ alterno, alternativo; *on* ~ *days* cada dos días, un día sí y otro no; **3.** suplente *m*, sustituto *m*; **al·ter·na·tion** [~'neiʃn] alternación *f*; **al'ter·na·tive** [~nətiv] **1.** □ alternativo; **2.** alternativa *f*; *I have no* ~ no puedo hacer otra cosa; no tengo elección; **al·ter·na·tor** ['~neitər] ⚡ alternador *m*.
al·though [ɔːl'ðou] aunque; si bien.
al·tim·e·ter [æl'timitər] altímetro *m*; **al·tim·e·try** [æl'timitri] altimetría *f*.

al·ti·tude ['æltitju:d] altitud *f*; altura *f*, elevación *f*; *high* ~ *flight* vuelo *m* de altura.
al·to ['æltou] contralto *f*.
al·to·geth·er [ɔ:ltə'geðər] enteramente, del todo; en conjunto, en total.
al·tru·ism ['æltruizm] altruismo *m*; **'al·tru·ist** altruista *m/f*; **al·tru'is·tic** □ altruista, desinteresado.
al·um ['æləm] alumbre *m*; **a·lu·mi·na** [ə'lju:minə] alúmina *f*; **al·u·mi·num** [ə'luminəm] aluminio *m*; **a'lu·mi·nous** [ə'lju:minəs] aluminoso.
a·lum·nus [ə'lʌmnəs] *m*, *pl*. **a·lum·ni** ['~nai]; **a·lum·na** ['~nə] *f*, *pl*. **a·lum·nae** ['~ni:] *mst* graduado (a *f*) *m*.
al·ve·o·lar [əl'vi:ələr] alveolar.
al·ways ['ɔ:lwəz] siempre; *as* ~ como (de) siempre.
am [æm; *in phrases freq.* əm] soy, estoy (*v. be*).
a·mal·gam [ə'mælgəm] amalgama *f*; **a'mal·gam·ate** [~meit] amalgamar(se); **a·mal·gam'a·tion** amalgamación *f*, unión *f* (*a*. ✝).
a·man·u·en·sis [əmænju'ensis], *pl*. **a·manu'en·ses** [~si:z] secretario *m*, amanuense *m*.
am·a·ranth ['æmərænθ] amaranto *m*.
a·mass [ə'mæs] acumular, amontonar.
am·a·teur ['æmətʃər] aficionado (a *f*) *m*; *b.s.* chapucero *m*, principiante *m/f*; ~ *performance* función *f* de aficionados; **am·a·teur·ish** [~'tʃuriʃ] superficial, inexperto, chapucero.
am·a·tive ['æmətiv], **am·a·to·ry** ['~tɔ:ri] amatorio, erótico.
a·maze [ə'meiz] asombrar, pasmar; **a'mazed** □ asombrado, pasmado (*at* de); *be* ~ *at* asombrarse de; **a'maze·ment** asombro *m*, aturdimiento *m*; pasmo *m*; **a'maz·ing** □ asombroso, pasmoso.
Am·a·zon ['æməzn] amazona *f*; *fig*. F marimacho *m*; **Am·a·zo·ni·an** [~'zounjən] amazónico.
am·bas·sa·dor [æm'bæsədər] embajador *m*; **am·bas·sa·do·ri·al** [~'dɔ:riəl] embajatorio; **am'bas·sa·dress** [~dris] embajadora *f*.
am·ber ['æmbər] **1.** ámbar *m*; **2.** ambarino, de ámbar; **am·ber·gris** ['~gri:s] ámbar *m* gris.
am·bi·dex·trous ['æmbi'dekstrəs] □ ambidextro.
am·bi·ent ['æmbiənt] ⚘ ambiente.
am·bi·gu·i·ty [æmbi'gjuiti] ambigüedad *f*, doble sentido *m*; **am'big·u·ous** □ ambiguo; equívoco, dudoso.
am·bi·tion [æm'biʃn] ambición *f* (*to*, *for* por), anhelo *m* (*to*, *for* de); **am'bi·tious** □ ambicioso; *idea*, *plan* grandioso; *be* ~ *of* (*or for*) ambicionar.
am·ble ['æmbl] **1.** (*horse etc.*) paso *m* de andadura; **2.** amblar; *fig*. andar despacio; **'am·bler** amblador *m*.
am·bro·si·a [æm'brouziə] ambrosía *f*; **am'bro·si·al** □ ambrosíaco; *fig*. celestial, delicioso.
am·bu·lance ['æmbjuləns] (coche *m*) ambulancia *f*; ~ *box* botiquín *m*; F ~ *chaser* abogado *m* especializado en pleitos sobre accidentes; ~ *man* ambulanciero *m*; ~ *station* puesto *m* de socorro; **'am·bu·lant** ambulante.
am·bu·la·to·ry ['æmbjulətɔ:ri] **1.** ambulatorio, móvil; **2.** paseo *m*; ⚠ galería *f*, deambulatorio *m*.
am·bus·cade [æmbəs'keid], **am·bush** ['æmbuʃ] **1.** emboscada *f*; *lay* (*make*) *an* ~ tender una celada (*for* a); *lie in* ~ estar en acecho (*or* en celada); **2.** acechar; tomar (*or* coger) por sorpresa.
a·me·ba [ə'mi:bə] amiba *f*.
a·mel·io·rate [ə'mi:liəreit] mejorar(se); **a·mel·io'ra·tion** mejora *f*, mejoramiento *m*.
a·men ['ɑ:'men] **1.** ¡amén!; **2.** amén *m*.
a·me·na·ble [ə'mi:nəbl] sumiso, dócil; ⚖ responsable; ~ *to argument* persuasible.
a·mend [ə'mend] enmendar (*a*. ⚖ *a. parl*.); rectificar, reformar; **a'mend·ment** enmienda *f*; enmienda *f* (de la Constitución de EE.UU.); **a'mends** [~dz] reparación *f*, recompensa *f*; *make* ~ *for* compensar, igualar; expiar.
a·men·i·ty [ə'meniti] amenidad *f*; *amenities pl*. atractivos *m/pl*., conveniencias *f/pl*.; comodidad *f*.
a·merce [ə'mə:rs] multar; **a'merce·ment** multa *f*.
A·mer·i·can [ə'merikən] **1.** americano; ~ *cloth* hule *m*; ~ *leather* cuero *m* artificial; ~ *Legion organización de veteranos de las guerras*; **2.** americano

(a *f*) *m*; **a'mer·i·can·ism** americanismo *m*; **a'mer·i·can·ize** americanizar(se).

Am·er·in·di·an, Am·er·ind [æmə'rindjən, 'æmərind] amerindio *m*.

am·e·thyst ['æmiθist] amatista *f*.

a·mi·a·bil·i·ty [eimjə'biliti] afabilidad *f*, amabilidad *f*; **'a·mi·a·ble** □ afable, amable; bonachón; simpático.

am·i·ca·ble ['æmikəbl] □ amigable, amistoso.

a·mid(st) [ə'mid(st)] entre, en medio de.

a·mid·ships [ə'midʃips] en medio del navío.

a·miss [ə'mis] mal, fuera de propósito; impropio; *take* ~ llevar a mal; *it would not be* ~ *(for him)* no (le) estaría de más; *what is* ~ *with it?* ¿qué le pasa?

am·i·ty ['æmiti] concordia *f*, amistad *f*.

am·me·ter ['æmitər] amperímetro *m*, anmetro *m*.

am·mo·ni·a [ə'mounjə] amoníaco *m*; *liquid* ~ amoníaco *m* líquido; **am'mo·ni·ac** [~æk], **am·mo·ni·a·cal** [æmou'naiəkl] amoníaco; *v. sal*.

am·mu·ni·tion [æmju'niʃn] **1.** municiones *f/pl.*; *fig.* pertrechos *m/pl.*; **2.** *attr.* de municiones.

am·nes·ty ['æmnesti] **1.** amnistía *f*, indulto *m*; **2.** indultar.

a·moe·ba [ə'mi:bə] = *ameba*.

a·mong(st) [ə'mʌŋ(st)] entre, en medio de; *from* ~ de entre.

a·mor·al [æ'mɔrəl] □ amoral.

am·o·rous ['æmərəs] □ amoroso; enamoradizo; *b.s.* mujeriego; **'am·o·rous·ness** enamoramiento *m*.

a·mor·phous [ə'mɔ:rfəs] *min.* amorfo (*a. fig.*); *fig.* heterogéneo, abigarrado.

am·or·ti·za·tion [əmɔ:rti'zeiʃn] amortización *f*; **am'or·tize** [~taiz] amortizar.

a·mount [ə'maunt] **1.**: ~ *to* valer, hacer, ascender a; *fig.* equivaler a, significar; **2.** cantidad *f*, suma *f*, importe *m*; *to the* ~ *of* hasta la cantidad de.

a·mour [ə'mu:r] *mst iro.* amorío *m*; ~ *propre* amor *m* propio.

am·pere ['æmper] amperio *m*; ~-*hour* amperio-hora *m*.

am·phib·i·an [æm'fibiən] **1.** anfibio *m*; **2.** = **am'phib·i·ous** □ anfibio.

am·phi·the·a·ter ['æmfiθiətər] anfiteatro *m*.

am·ple ['æmpl] amplio; abundante; liberal; bastante; **'am·ple·ness** amplitud *f*; abundancia *f*; suficiencia *f*.

am·pli·fi·ca·tion [æmplifi'keiʃn] amplificación *f* (*a. rhet. a. phys.*);

am·pli·fi·er ['~faiər] *radio*: amplificador *m*; **'am·pli·fy** amplificar, ampliar; dilatar, extender; *radio*: ~*ing valve* lámpara *f* amplificadora;

am·pli·tude ['~tju:d] amplitud *f*; extensión *f*; *phys.* amplitud *f* (de oscilación); ~ *modulation* modulación *f* de amplitud.

am·poule ['æmpu:l] ampolla *f*.

am·pu·tate ['æmpjuteit] amputar; **am·pu'ta·tion** amputación *f*.

a·muck [ə'mʌk]: *run* ~ enloquecer, desbocarse (*a. fig.*), desmandarse.

am·u·let ['æmjulit] amuleto *m*.

a·muse [ə'mju:z] divertir, entretener; distraer, solazar; **a'muse·ment** diversión *f*, entretenimiento *m*; pasatiempo *m*, recreo *m*; (*in a park or circus*) atracción *f*; ~ *park* parque *m* de atracciones; *for* ~ para divertirse; **a·mus·ing** □ divertido, entretenido; gracioso.

an [æn, ən] *article antes de sonido vocal*: un, una.

an·a·bap·tist [ænə'bæptist] anabaptista *m/f*.

a·nach·ro·nism [ə'nækrənizm] anacronismo *m*.

a·nae·mi... = *anemi...*

an·aes·the... = *anesthe...*

an·al·ge·si·a [ænəl'dʒi:ziə] analgesia *f*.

an·a·log·ic, an·a·log·i·cal [ænə'lɔdʒik(l)] □, **a·nal·o·gous** [ə'næləgəs] análogo; afín; **a'nal·o·gy** analogía *f*; afinidad *f*; *on the* ~ *of* por analogía con.

an·a·lyse ['ænəlaiz] analizar; **a·nal·y·sis** [ə'næləsis], *pl.* **a'nal·y·ses** [~i:z] análisis *mst m*; **ana·lyst** ['ænəlist] analizador *m*; *public* ~ jefe *m* del laboratorio municipal; **an·a·lyt·ic, an·a·lyt·i·cal** [ænə'litik(l)] □ analítico.

an·ar·chic, an·ar·chi·cal [æ'nɑ:rkik(l)] □ anárquico; **an·arch·ism** ['ænərkizm] anarquismo *m*; **'an·arch·ist** anarquista *m/f*; **'an·arch·y** anarquía *f*; desorden *m*.

a·nath·e·ma [ə'næθimə] anatema *m a. f*; **a'nath·e·ma·tize** anatematizar.

an·a·tom·i·cal [ænə'tɔmikl] □ anatómico; **a·nat·o·mist** [ə'nætəmist] anatomista *m/f*; **a'nat·o·mize** [~aiz] anatomizar; *fig.* analizar minuciosamente; **a'nat·o·my** anatomía *f* (*a. fig.*).
an·ces·tor ['ænsistər] antepasado *m*, progenitor *m*; **an·ces·tral** [~'sestrəl] ancestral, hereditario; **an·ces·tress** ['ænsistris] antepasada *f*; **'an·ces·try** ascendencia *f*, linaje *m*, abolengo *m*.
an·chor ['æŋkər] **1.** ⚓ *a. fig.* ancla *f*; *at* ~ al ancla, anclado; *cast* (*or drop*) ~ echar anclas; *weigh* ~ zarpar; **2.** *v/t.* anclar; sujetar; *v/i.* anclar, fondear; **'an·chor·age** ancladero *m*, fondeadero *m*.
an·cho·ret ['æŋkɔret], **an·cho·rite** ['~rait] anacoreta *m/f*.
an·cho·vy [æn'tʃouvi] anchoa *f*.
an·cient ['einʃənt] **1.** □ antiguo; vetusto; **2.** *the* ~*s pl.* los antiguos *m/pl.*
an·cil·lar·y ['ænsileri] auxiliar; subordinado (*to* a).
and [ænd, ənd, F ən] y; (*before* i-, hi-) e; *thousands* ~ *thousands* miles y miles, millares; *try* ~ *inf.* tratar de *inf.*; *try* ~ *take it* cógelo si puedes; *after verbs of motion*: a (*e.g.*, *go* ~ *see him* ir a verle).
An·dal·u·si·an [ændəl'u:ziən] andaluz *adj. a. su. m* (-a *f*).
and·i·ron ['ændaiərn] morillo *m*.
an·ec·do·tal [ænek'doutl], **an·ec·dot·i·cal** ['~dɔtikl] □ anecdótico; **an·ec·dote** ['ænikdout] anécdota *f*.
an·e·lec·tric [æni'lektrik] aneléctrico.
a·ne·mi·a [ə'ni:miə] anemia *f*; } **a'ne·mic** anémico.
an·e·mom·e·ter [æni'mɔmitər] anemómetro *m*.
a·nem·one [ə'nemənì] ⚘ anemone *f*; *zo.* anémona *f* (de mar).
an·er·oid ['ænərɔid] aneroide; ~ *barometer* barómetro *m* aneroide.
an·es·the·si·a [ænis'θi:ʒə] anestesia *f*; **an·es·thet·ic** [ænis'θetik] □ anestésico *adj. a. su. m*; **an·es·thet·ize** [ə'nesθətaiz] anestesiar.
a·new [ə'nju:] de nuevo, otra vez.
an·gel ['eindʒl] ángel *m*; **an·gel·ic, an·gel·i·cal** [æn'dʒelik(l)] □ angélico.
an·ger ['æŋgər] **1.** cólera *f*, ira *f*, saña *f*; **2.** enojar, encolerizar, provocar.
an·gi·na [æn'dʒainə] angina *f*; ~ *pectoris* angina *f* de pecho.
an·gle ['æŋgl] **1.** ángulo *m*; *fig.* punto *m* de vista; ~ *iron* ángulo *m* de hierro, hierro *m* angular; **2.** pescar con caña (*for acc.*); ~ *for* F ir a la caza de; **'an·gler** pescador (-a *f*) *m* con caña.
An·gles ['æŋglz] *pl.* anglos *m/pl.*
An·gli·can ['æŋglikən] anglicano *adj. a. su. m* (a *f*); *a.* inglés.
An·gli·cism ['æŋglisizm] anglicismo *m*.
an·gling ['æŋgliŋ] pesca *f* con caña.
An·glo-Sax·on ['æŋglou'sæksn] anglosajón *adj. a. su. m* (-a *f*).
an·gry ['æŋgri] □ colérico; enojado, enfadado; ⚕ inflamado; *become* ~ *at* enojarse de; *get* ~ encolerizarse, montar en cólera (*with p.* con *or* contra); *it makes me* ~ me enoja mucho.
an·guish ['æŋgwiʃ] angustia *f*, congoja *f*.
an·gu·lar ['æŋgjulər] □ angular; *fig.* torpe; ~ *point* vértice *m*; **an·gu·lar·i·ty** [~'læriti] calidad *f* de lo angular; *fig.* torpeza *f*.
an·hy·drous [æn'haidrəs] anhidro.
an·i·line ['ænilain] anilina *f*; ~ *dyes* colores *m/pl.* de anilina.
an·i·mad·ver·sion [ænimæd'və:rʒn] censura *f*, animadversión *f*; **an·i·mad·vert** [~'və:rt] censurar, reprochar ([*up*]*on acc.*); observar.
an·i·mal ['æniməl] **1.** animal *m*; bestia *f*; **2.** animal; ~ *spirits pl.* vitalidad *f*, ardor *m*, vivacidad *f*; **an·i·mal·cule** [~'mælkju:l] animálculo *m*; **an·i·mal·ism** ['~məlizm] sensualidad *f*; **an·i'mal·i·ty** animalidad *f*.
an·i·mate **1.** ['ænimeit] animar, alentar; **2.** ['~mit] vivo; **'an·i·mat·ed** □ *fig.* vivo, vivaz, animado; ~ *cartoon* película *f* de dibujos, dibujo *m* animado; **an·i·ma·tion** [æni'meiʃn] vivacidad *f*, animación *f*; (*of a cartoon*) animación *f*.
an·i·mos·i·ty [æni'mɔsiti], **an·i·mus** ['æniməs] animosidad *f*, rencor *m*, ojeriza *f*.
an·ise ['ænis] anís *m*; **an·i·seed** ['~si:d] **1.** anís *m*; **2.** *attr.* de anís.
an·kle ['æŋkl] tobillo *m*; ~ *bone* hueso *m* del tobillo; ~ *sock* escarpín *m*; ~ *support* tobillera *f*.
an·klet ['æŋklit] ajorca *f* para el pie.
an·nals ['ænlz] *pl.* anales *m/pl.*; *fig. a. lit.* fastos *m/pl.*
an·neal [ə'ni:l] recocer; templar (*a. fig.*).

an·nex 1. [ə'neks] añadir, adjuntar (*to* a); *esp. territory* anexar, apoderarse de; 2. ['æneks] apéndice *m*, aditamento *m*; edificio *m* anexo, pabellón *m*; **an·nex'a·tion** anexión *f*.
an·ni·hi·late [ə'naiəleit] aniquilar; **an·ni·hi'la·tion** aniquilamiento *m*.
an·ni·ver·sa·ry [æni'və:rsəri] aniversario *m*.
an·no·tate ['ænouteit] anotar; comentar, glosar; **an·no'ta·tion** anotación *f*; comentario *m* (*on, to* sobre).
an·nounce [ə'nauns] anunciar, proclamar; **an'nounce·ment** anuncio *m*, aviso *m*, proclama *f*; **an'nounc·er** *radio*: locutor (-a *f*) *m*.
an·noy [ə'nɔi] molestar, fastidiar, jorobar (F); **an'noy·ance** molestia *f*, fastidio *m*; enojo *m*; **an'noyed** enfadado, irritado, enojado; **an'noy·ing** □ molesto, fastidioso; *p.* importuno.
an·nu·al ['ænjuəl] 1. □ anual; ⚘ ~ *ring* cerco *m*; 2. anuario *m*, publicación *f* anual; ⚘ planta *f* anual, anual *m*.
an·nu·i·tant [ə'njuitənt] rentista *m/f*, censualista *m/f*; **an'nu·i·ty** [~iti] renta *f* vitalicia (*a.* ~ *bond*), pensión *f* vitalicia.
an·nul [ə'nʌl] anular, cancelar; *laws* abrogar.
an·nu·lar ['ænjulə] □ anular.
an·nul·ment [ə'nʌlmənt] anulación *f*, cancelación *f*; abrogación *f*.
An·nun·ci·a·tion [ənʌnsi'eiʃn] *eccl.* Anunciación *f*.
an·ode ['ænoud] 1. ánodo *m*; 2. *attr.* de ánodo; ~ *potential* potencial *m* anódico.
an·o·dyne ['ænoudain] anodino *adj. a. su. m.*
a·noint [ə'nɔint] *mst eccl.* untar, ungir; consagrar.
a·nom·a·lous [ə'nɔmələs] □ anómalo; **a'nom·a·ly** anomalía *f*.
a·non [ə'nɔn] 1. † luego, dentro de poco; *poet. ever and* ~ de vez en cuando; 2. *abbr.* = *anonymous*.
an·o·nym·i·ty [ænə'nimiti] anónimo *m*; **a·non·y·mous** [ə'nɔniməs] □ anónimo.
an·oth·er [ə'nʌðər] otro; *just such* ~ otro tal.
an·swer ['ænsər] 1. *v/t. p., question* contestar a, responder a, replicar a; ~ *a letter* contestar (a) una carta; ~ *the bell or the door* acudir a la puerta; *v/i.* responder, contestar, replicar; (*suffice*) servir, convenir; F ~ *back* ser respondón; ~ *for* responder de; ~ *to description* corresponder a; ~ *to the name of* atender por; 2. respuesta *f*, contestación *f* (*to* a); ⅍ solución *f*; ⚖ réplica *f*; '**an·swer·a·ble** □ responsable (*for* de).
ant [ænt] hormiga *f*.
an·tag·o·nism [æn'tægənizm] antagonismo *m*, rivalidad *f* (*between* entre); hostilidad *f* (*to* a); **an'tag·o·nist** antagonista *m/f*, adversario *m*; **an·tag·o'nis·tic** □ antagónico; contrario, opuesto (*to* a).
an·tag·o·nize [æn'tægənaiz] enemistarse con, contrariar.
ant·arc·tic [ænt'ɑ:rktik] antártico; *the* ♀ las Tierras *f/pl.* Antárticas; ♀ *Circle* Círculo *m* Polar Antártico.
an·te ['ænti] *poker etc.*: 1. tanto *m*, apuesta *f*; 2. F (*mst* ~ *up*) *v/t. a. v/i.* poner un tanto, apostar; *v/i. fig.* contribuir.
an·te·ced·ence [ænti'si:dəns] precedencia *f*; *ast.* retrogradación *f*; **an·te'ced·ent** 1. □ precedente, antecedente (*to* a); 2. antecedente *m* (*a. gr.*); *his* ~*s pl.* sus antecedentes *m/pl.*
an·te·cham·ber ['æntitʃeimbə] antecámara *f*.
an·te·date ['ænti'deit] antedatar; [preceder.]
an·te·di·lu·vi·an ['æntidi'lu:viən] antediluviano.
an·te·lope ['æntiloup] antílope *m*.
an·ten·na [æn'tenə], *pl.* **an'ten·nas** [~əs], **an'ten·nae** [~ni:] *all senses*: antena *f*.
an·te·ri·or [æn'ti:riər] anterior (*to* a).
an·te·room ['æntirum] antecámara *f*.
an·them ['ænθəm] motete *m*; *national* ~ himno *m* nacional.
an·ther ['ænθər] antera *f*.
ant·hill ['ænthil] hormiguero *m*.
an·thol·o·gy [æn'θɔlədʒi] antología *f*.
an·thra·cite ['ænθrəsait] antracita *f*.
an·thrax ['ænθræks] ántrax *m*.
an·thro·poid ['ænθrəpɔid] antropoide; **an·thro·pol·o·gist** [~'pɔlədʒist] antropólogo *m*; **an·thro'pol·o·gy** antropología *f*; **an·thro·poph·a·gy** [ænθrou'pɔfədʒi] antropofagia *f*.

an·ti... ['ænti-] *in compounds* anti...
an·ti·air·craft ['ænti'erkræft]: ~ *defense* defensa *f* antiaérea; ~ *gun* cañón *m* antiaéreo.
an·ti·bi·ot·ic ['æntibai'ɔtik] antibiótico *adj. a. su. m.*
an·ti·bod·y ['ænti'bɔdi] (*pl.* ~*bodies*) anticuerpo *m.*
an·tics ['æntiks] *pl.* bufonadas *f/pl.*, payasadas *f/pl.*; travesuras *f/pl.*, cabriolas *f/pl.*, gracias *f/pl.*
An·ti·christ ['æntikraist] Anticristo *m.*
an·tic·i·pate [æn'tisipeit] (*forestall*) anticipar, prevenir; (*foresee*) prever; (*expect*) esperar; (*look forward to*) prometerse; (*get ahead of*) anticiparse a; **an·tic·i'pa·tion** anticipación *f*, prevención *f*; previsión *f*; expectación *f*; esperanza *f*; *in* ~ de antemano; *in* ~ *of* esperando; **an'tic·i·pa·to·ry** [~pətɔ:ri] que anticipa.
an·ti·cler·i·cal ['ænti'klerikl] anticlerical.
an·ti·cli·max ['ænti'klaimæks] *rhet.* anticlímax *m*; *fig.* decepción *f.*
an·ti·cor·ro·sive ['æntikə'rousiv] anticorrosivo.
an·ti·cy·clone ['ænti'saikloun] anticiclón *m.*
an·ti·daz·zle ['ænti'dæzl] *mot.* antideslumbrante.
an·ti·dote ['æntidout] antídoto *m* (*against, for, to* contra).
an·ti·fas·cist ['ænti'fæʃist] antifascista *adj. a. su. m/f.*
an·ti·freeze ['ænti'fri:z] *mot.* (solución *f*) anticongelante.
an·ti·fric·tion ['ænti'frikʃn] ⊕ antifriccional.
an·ti·glare ['ænti'gler] antideslumbrante.
an·ti·ha·lo ['ænti'heilou] *phot.* antihalo *m.*
an·ti·knock ['ænti'nɔk] *mot.* antidetonante.
an·ti·mis·sile ['ænti'misl] antiproyectil.
an·ti·mo·ny ['æntiməni] antimonio *m.*
an·ti·pas·to ['ænti'pɑ:stou] aperitivo *m*, entremés *m.*
an·tip·a·thy [æn'tipəθi] antipatía *f* (*between* entre); repugnancia *f* (*to* hacia).
an·tip·o·dal [æn'tipədl] □ antípoda; **an'tip·o·des** [~di:z] *pl.* antípodas *m/pl.*; **an·ti·pode** ['~poud] *fig. sg.* antípoda *m.*
An·ti·py·rin(e) [ænti'pairin] antipirina *f.*
an·ti·quar·i·an [ænti'kweriən] anticuario *adj. a. su. m*; **an·ti·quar·y** ['~kwəri] anticuario *m*, aficionado *m* de antigüedades; **an·ti·quat·ed** ['~kweitid] anticuado.
an·tique [æn'ti:k] **1.** antiguo, viejo; **2.** antigüedad *f*, antigualla *f*; ~ *dealer* anticuario *m*; ~ *shop*, ~ *store* tienda *f* de antigüedades; **an·tiq·ui·ty** [~'tikwiti] antigüedad *f*; vetustez *f.*
an·ti·rust ['ænti'rʌst] antioxidante.
an·ti-Sem·ite [ænti'si:mait] antisemita *m/f*; **an·ti-Sem·i·tic** [~sə'mitik] antisemítico; **an·ti-Sem·i·tism** [~'semitizm] antisemitismo *m.*
an·ti·sep·tic [ænti'septik] antiséptico *adj. a. su. m.*
an·ti·skid ['ænti'skid] *mot.* antideslizante, antiderrapante.
an·tith·e·sis [æn'tiθisis], *pl.* **an·tith·e·ses** ['~si:z] antítesis *f*; **an·ti·thet·ic, an·ti·thet·i·cal** [~'θetik(l)] □ antitético.
an·ti·tox·in ['ænti'tɑ:ksən] antitoxina *f.*
an·ti·trust ['ænti'trʌst] anticartel.
an·ti·war ['ænti'wɔ:r] antibélico.
ant·ler ['æntlər] cuerna *f*; ~*s pl.* cornamenta *f*, cuernas *f/pl.*
an·to·nym ['æntənim] antónimo *m.*
a·nus ['einəs] ano *m.*
an·vil ['ænvil] yunque *m* (*a. fig.*).
anx·i·e·ty [æŋ'zaiəti] cuidado *m*; inquietud *f*, ansiedad *f* (*about* sobre); (*yearning*) ansia *f*, anhelo *m* (*for, to* de), ⚕ ansiedad *f.*
anx·ious ['æŋkʃəs] □ inquieto, preocupado, ansioso; (*desirous*) deseoso (*for, to* de); *be* ~ *about* inquietarse por.
an·y ['eni] **1.** *pron.* alguno; cualquiera; (*negative sense*) ninguno; **2.** *adj.* algún; cualquier; (*negative sense*) ningún; *are there* ~ *nails?* ¿hay clavos?; ~ *book you like* cualquier libro; ~ *place* dondequiera; ~ *time* cuando quiera; alguna vez; **3.** *adv. mst not translated*: ~ *more* más; '**~·bod·y**, '**~·one** alguien, alguno; *not* ~ nadie; '**~·how** en todo caso, de todos modos; con todo; de cualquier modo; '**~·thing** algo, cualquier cosa; ~ *else?* ¿algo más?; ~ *else* cualquier otra cosa; ~ *but* (*that*) todo menos (eso); *not* ~ nada; '**~·way** = *anyhow*;

'~**where** en todas partes, en cualquier parte, dondequiera.

a·pace [ə'peis] aprisa.

a·part [ə'pɑːrt] aparte, separadamente; aislado, separado; ~ *from* aparte de; *joking* ~ en serio; *fall* ~ caerse a pedazos; desunirse; ir al desastre; *live* ~ vivir separados; vivir aislado; *stand* ~ mantenerse apartado; *take* ~ descomponer, desarmar, desmontar; *tell* ~ distinguir; **a·part·heid** [ə'pɑːrtait, ə'pɑːrtheit] separación *f* racial (*Unión Sudafricana*); **a'part·ment** apartamento *m*, piso *m*; ~ *hotel* hotel *m* de familias; ~ *house* casa *f* de pisos; ~*s pl.* alojamiento *m*, casa *f*.

ap·a·thet·ic [æpə'θetik] □ apático; indiferente; '**ap·a·thy** apatía *f*; indiferencia *f* (*to* a).

ape [eip] **1.** mono *m* (*esp.* los antropomorfos); *fig.* mono (a *f*) *m* de imitación; remedador (-a *f*) *m*; **2.** imitar, remedar.

a·pe·ri·ent [ə'piːriənt] laxante *adj. a. su. m*; **a·pe·ri·tif** [ə'peritiv] aperitivo *m*.

ap·er·ture ['æpərtʃər] abertura *f*; rendija *f*.

a·pex ['eipeks], *pl. freq.* **ap·i·ces** ['eipisiːz] ápice *m*; *fig.* cumbre *f*.

aph·o·rism ['æfərizm] aforismo *m*, apotegma *m*; **aph·o'ris·tic** □ aforístico.

aph·ro·dis·i·ac [æfrou'diziæk] afrodisíaco *adj. a. su. m*.

a·pi·ar·y ['eipiəri] colmenar *m*; **a·pi·cul·ture** ['~kʌltʃər] apicultura *f*.

a·piece [ə'piːs] cada uno; por persona.

ap·ish ['eipiʃ] simiesco; *fig.* necio, tonto.

A·poc·ry·pha [ə'pɔkrifə] *pl.* libros *m/pl.* apócrifos de la Biblia; **a'poc·ry·phal** apócrifo.

ap·o·gee ['æpoudʒiː] apogeo *m*.

a·pol·o·get·ic [əpɔlə'dʒetik] **1.** □ lleno de disculpas; **2.** *mst* ~*s pl. eccl.* apologética *f*; **a'pol·o·gist** apologista *m/f*; **a'pol·o·gize** [~dʒaiz] disculparse (*for* de; *to* con); pedir perdón; **a'pol·o·gy** disculpa *f*, excusa *f*; *lit.* apología *f*, defensa *f*; *an* ~ *for a house* una birria de casa; *make an* ~ disculparse.

ap·o·plec·tic, ap·o·plec·ti·cal [æpə'plektik(l)] □ apoplético; '**ap·o·plex·y** apoplejía *f*.

a·pos·ta·sy [ə'pɔstəsi] apostasía *f*; **a'po·state** [~stit] apóstata *m/f*; **a'pos·ta·tize** [~stətaiz] apostatar (*from* de).

a·pos·tle [ə'pɔsl] apóstol *m*; **ap·os·tol·ic, ap·os·tol·i·cal** [æpə'stɔlik(l)] □ apostólico.

a·pos·tro·phe [ə'pɔstrəfi] *gr.* apóstrofo *m*; *rhet.* apóstrofe *m or f*; **a'pos·tro·phize** apostrofar.

a·poth·e·car·y [ə'pɔθikeri] † boticario (a *f*) *m*.

a·poth·e·o·sis [əpɔθi'ousis] apoteosis *f* (*a. fig.*).

ap·pal [ə'pɔːl] espantar; infundir pasmo (*or* horror); **ap'pall·ing** □ espantoso; *taste etc.* pésimo.

ap·pa·ra·tus [æpə'reitəs] aparato *m*.

ap·par·el [ə'pærəl] *lit.* **1.** ataviar, vestir (*esp. p.p.*); **2.** atavío *m*, vestido *m*; (*a. wearing* ~) ropa *f*.

ap·par·ent [ə'pærənt] □ aparente; claro, manifiesto; *v. heir*; ~*ly* según parece, por lo visto; aparentemente;

ap·pa·ri·tion [æpə'riʃn] aparición *f*; fantasma *m*.

ap·peal [ə'piːl] **1.** ⚖ apelar (*to* a; *against* de); suplicar (*to a p. for a th.* a una p. por algo); ser atrayente; ~ *to* llamar la atención de *s.o.*; atraer, interesar *acc.*; recurrir a; *v. country*; **2.** ⚖ apelación *f*, recurso *m* de casación; súplica *f*, instancia *f*; llamamiento *m* (*to* a); atractivo *m*; **ap'peal·ing** □ suplicante; atrayente.

ap·pear [ə'pir] parecer; aparecer (*mst suddenly*); *esp.* ⚖ comparecer; **ap'pear·ance** apariencia *f*, aspecto *m*; (*act*) aparición *f*; ⚖ comparecencia *f*; ~*s pl.* apariencias *f/pl.*; *keep up* (*or save*) ~*s* salvar las apariencias; *thea. make an* ~ salir; *put in an* ~ hacer acto de presencia; *to all* ~*s* aparentemente.

ap·pease [ə'piːz] apaciguar; *p.* desenojar; *hunger etc.* satisfacer, saciar; *passion* mitigar, aquietar; **ap'pease·ment** pacificación *f*.

ap·pel·lant [ə'pelənt] apelante *adj. a. su. m/f*; **ap·pel·late** [ə'pelit] apelante; ♀ *Court* Tribunal *m* de Apelación; ~ *judge* juez *m* de alzadas; **ap·pel·la·tion** [æpe'leiʃn] nombre *m*, título *m*.

ap·pel·lee [æpe'liː] apelado (a *f*) *m*.

ap·pend [ə'pend] añadir; adjuntar; colgar; **ap'pend·age** añadidura *f*;

accesorio *m*, apéndice *m*; **ap·pen·dec·to·my** [~ˈdektəmi] apendectomía *f*; **ap·pen·di·ci·tis** [~ˈsaitis] apendicitis *f*; **apˈpen·dix** [~diks], *pl. a.* **apˈpen·di·ces** [~disiːz] apéndice *m* (*a.* ⚕).

ap·per·tain [æpərˈtein]: ~ *to* pertenecer a; atañer a; relacionarse con; incumbir a.

ap·pe·tite [ˈæpitait] apetito *m*, apetencia *f* (*a. fig.*); *fig.* deseo *m*, anhelo *m* (*for* de); *eccl.* apetito *m* concupiscible.

ap·pe·tiz·er [ˈæpitaizər] apetite *m* (*a. fig.*); aperitivo *m*; **ˈap·pe·tiz·ing** □ apetitoso.

ap·plaud [əˈplɔːd] *v/t.* aplaudir (*a. fig.*); *fig.* celebrar; *v/i.* aplaudir, dar palmadas.

ap·plause [əˈplɔːz] aplauso *m* (*a. fig.*); *fig.* aprobación *f*, elogio *m*.

ap·ple [ˈæpl] manzana *f*; (*a.* ~ *tree*) manzano *m*; *Adam's* ~ nuez *f* de la garganta; ~ *of discord* manzana *f* de la discordia; ~ *of one's eye* niñas *f/pl.* de los ojos; ~ *polisher* F quitamotas *m/f*; ˈ~ **cart:** F *upset a p.'s* ~ dar al traste con los planes de una p.; ˈ**~·jack** aguardiente *m* de manzana; ˈ~ ˈ**pie** pastel *m* (*or* empanada *f*) de manzanas; F *in* ~ *order* en perfecto orden; ˈ**~·sauce** compota *f* de manzanas; *sl.* coba *f*, jabón *m*, música *f* celestial.

ap·pli·ance [əˈplaiəns] instrumento *m*, herramienta *f*; dispositivo *m*.

ap·pli·ca·bil·i·ty [æplikəˈbiliti] aplicabilidad *f*; ˈ**ap·pli·ca·ble** aplicable (*to* a); ˈ**ap·pli·cant** suplicante *m/f*, aspirante *m/f*, pretendiente (a *f*) *m* (*for a post* a un puesto); **ap·pliˈca·tion** aplicación *f* (*to* a; *a.* = *industry*); solicitud *f* (*for* por), petición *f* (*for* de, por); *make an* ~ solicitar; dirigirse (*to* a).

ap·pli·qué [əˈpliːkei] (*a.* ~ *work*) encaje *m* de aplicación.

ap·ply [əˈplai] *v/t.* aplicar (*to* a); ~ *o.s. to* aplicarse a; *v/i.* ser aplicable; interesar; *cross out what does not* ~ táchese lo que no interese; ~ *to* referirse a; acudir a, dirigirse a; ~ *for* solicitar, pedir *acc.*; *applied mathematics* matemáticas *f/pl.* aplicadas.

ap·point [əˈpɔint] *date etc.* señalar, designar; *p.* nombrar; *house* amueblar; proveer; *well* ~*ed* bien amueblado; bien provisto (de muebles *etc.*); **apˈpoint·ment** señalamiento *m*, designación *f*; nombramiento *m to post*; (*post*) oficio *m*; cita *f with p.*; *make an* ~ citar(se); *by* ~ (*with royal arms etc.*) proveedores de; (*for a conference*) cita *f* previa; ~*s pl.* equipo *m*, instalación *f*, accesorios *m/pl.*, adornos *m/pl.*

ap·por·tion [əˈpɔːrʃn] prorratear; **apˈpor·tion·ment** prorrateo *m*.

ap·po·site [ˈæpəzit] □ apropiado (*to* a); a propósito, oportuno; ˈ**ap·po·site·ness** propiedad *f*; acierto *m*; oportunidad *f*.

ap·po·si·tion [æpəˈziʃn] juxtaposición *f*; *gr.* aposición *f*; (*seal*) impresión *f*.

ap·prais·al [əˈpreizl] tasación *f*, valoración *f*; *fig.* aprecio *m*; **apˈpraise** [~eiz] tasar, valorar; *fig.* apreciar; **apˈpraise·ment** = *appraisal*; **apˈprais·er** tasador *m*.

ap·pre·ci·a·ble [əˈpriːʃəbl] □ apreciable, estimable; sensible, perceptible; **apˈpre·ci·ate** [~ʃieit] *v/t.* apreciar, estimar; percibir; *v/i.* aumentarse en valor; **ap·pre·ciˈa·tion** aprecio *m*, estimación *f*; percepción *f*; (*value*) aumento *m* en valor, plusvalía *f*; **apˈpre·ci·a·tive** □, **apˈpre·ci·a·to·ry** apreciativo; apreciador; agradecido; *be* ~ *of* agradecer *acc.*

ap·pre·hend [æpriˈhend] aprehender, prender; *fig.* percibir, entender; temer, sospechar; **ap·preˈhen·sion** aprehensión *f*, prendimiento *m*; percepción *f*, comprensión *f*; temor *m*, recelo *m*, aprensión *f*; **ap·preˈhen·sive** □ aprensivo, miedoso (*of* de; *that* de que); tímido; perspicaz, comprensivo; *grow* ~ intimidarse.

ap·pren·tice [əˈprentis] **1.** aprendiz (-a *f*) *m*; *fig.* novicio (a *f*) *m*; **2.** poner de aprendiz; *be* ~*d to* estar de aprendiz con; **apˈpren·tice·ship** aprendizaje *m*, noviciado *m*.

ap·prise [əˈpraiz] informar, avisar (*of* de).

ap·pro [ˈæprou] ✝ F: *on* ~ a prueba.

ap·proach [əˈproutʃ] **1.** *v/i.* acercarse, aproximarse (*a. fig.*; *freq. to* a); *v/t.* acercarse a, aproximarse a (*a. fig.*); *p.* abordar; *firm etc.* dirigirse a; **2.** acercamiento *m*; aproximación *f* (*to* a); acceso *m* (*a. fig.*); método *m*, camino *m*; camino *m* de entrada; ~es *pl.* ⚔ aproches *m/pl.*; accesos *m/pl.*; **ap'proach·able** abordable, accesible; **ap'proach·ing** próximo, cercano; que se acerca.

ap·pro·ba·tion [æprə'beiʃn] aprobación *f*; consentimiento *m*.

ap·pro·pri·ate **1.** [ə'prouprieit] apropiar(se); *funds etc.* destinar (*for* a); **2.** [~priit] □ apropiado (*to* a), a propósito; apto, pertinente; **ap·pro·pri'a·tion** apropiación *f*; consignación *f*.

ap·prov·al [ə'pru:vəl] aprobación *f*; consentimiento *m*; visto *m* bueno; *on* ~ a prueba; **ap'prove** aprobar, sancionar, confirmar; ~ *of* aprobar, dar por bueno; **ap'proved** probado, acreditado; ~ *school* correccional *m*.

ap·prox·i·mate **1.** [ə'prɔksimeit] aproximar(se) (*to* a); **2.** [~mit] □ aproximado, aproximativo; cercano, inmediato (*to* a); **ap·prox·i·ma·tion** [~'meiʃn] aproximación *f*; **ap'prox·i·ma·tive** [~ksimətiv] □ aproximativo.

ap·pur·te·nance [ə'pə:rtinəns] (*freq.* ~*s pl.*) dependencia *f*; pertinencia *f*.

a·pri·cot ['eiprikɔt] albaricoque *m*; ~ *tree* albaricoquero *m*.

A·pril ['eiprəl] abril *m*; '~ '**Fools' Day** día *m* de engañabobos, primer día de abril, en que se coge por inocente a la gente.

a·pron ['eiprən] delantal *m*; mandil *m of shoemaker, freemason etc.*; *thea.* visera *f*; '~ **string:** *tied to the* ~*s of* cosido a las faldas de.

ap·ro·pos [æprə'pou] **1.** *adj.* oportuno; **2.** *adv.* a propósito; **3.** *prp.* ~ *of* a propósito de; acerca de.

apse [æps] ábside *m*.

apt [æpt] □ apto; *remark etc.* a propósito; propenso (*to* a); listo (*at* en); **ap·ti·tude** ['~titju:d] aptitud *f*; '**apt·ness** acierto *m of remark etc.*

aq·ua for·tis ['ækwə 'fɔ:rtis] aguafuerte *f*.

aq·ua·lung ['ækwəlʌŋ] aparato *m* de aire comprimido (que suministra aire al buzo).

aq·ua·ma·rine [ækwəmə'ri:n] aguamarina *f*; color *m* verde mar.

aq·ua·plane ['ækwəplein] **1.** acuaplano *m*; **2.** correr en acuaplano.

aq·ua·relle [ækwə'rel] acuarela *f*; **aq·ua'rel·list** acuarelista *m/f*.

a·quar·i·um [ə'kweriəm] acuario *m*.

a·quat·ic [ə'kwætik] **1.** acuático, acuátil; ~*s pl.*, ~ *sports pl.* deportes *m/pl.* acuáticos; **2.** animal *m* acuático; planta *f* acuática.

aq·ua·tint ['ækwətint] acuatinta *f*.

aq·ue·duct ['ækwidʌkt] acueducto *m*; **a·que·ous** ['eikwiəs] □ ácueo; acuoso.

aq·ui·line ['ækwilain] aguileño; ~ *nose* nariz *f* aguileña.

Ar·ab ['ærəb] árabe *adj. a. su. m/f*; *zo.* caballo *m* árabe; ~ *quarter* morería *f*; F *street* ♀ golfillo *m*; chico *m* de la calle; **ar·a·besque** [~'besk] arabesco (*a. su. m*); *fig.* fantástico; **A·ra·bi·an** [ə'reibjən] árabe *adj. a. su. m/f*; *The* ~ *Nights* las Mil y una noches; **Ar·a·bic** ['ærəbik] **1.** árabe, arábigo; *gum* ♀ goma *f* arábiga; **2.** árabe *m*, arábigo *m* (*idioma*).

ar·able ['ærəbl] **1.** arable; **2.** (*or* ~ *land*) tierra *f* de labrantío.

a·rach·nid [ə'ræknid] arácnido *m*.

A·ra·gon·ese ['ærəgəni:z] aragonés *adj. a. su. m* (-a *f*).

ar·bi·ter ['ɑ:rbitər] árbitro (a *f*) *m*; arbitrador (-a *f*) *m*; **ar·bi·trage** [ɑ:rbi'trɑ:ʒ] ✝ arbitraje *m*; **ar'bit·ra·ment** *lit.* arbitramento *m*; '**ar·bi·trar·i·ness** arbitrariedad *f*; capricho *m*; '**ar·bi·trar·y** □ arbitrario; **ar·bi·trate** ['~treit] arbitrar; **ar·bi'tra·tion** arbitraje *m*; ⚖ arbitramento *m*; tercería *f*; *court of* ~ tribunal *m* de arbitraje; '**ar·bi·tra·tor** arbitrador *m*; ⚖ juez *m* árbitro.

ar·bor ['ɑ:rbər] ⊕ eje *m*, árbol *m*; emparrado *m*, glorieta *f*, cenador *m*; ♀ *Day* fiesta *f* del árbol; ~ *vitae* ♀ árbol *m* de la vida; **ar·bo·re·al** [ɑ:r'bɔ:riəl], **ar'bo·re·ous** arbóreo; **ar·bo·res·cent** [ɑ:rbə'resnt] □ arborescente; **ar·bo·re·tum** [ɑ:rbə'ri:təm] jardín *m* botánico de árboles; **ar·bo·ri·cul·ture** ['ɑrbərikʌltʃər] arboricultura *f*.

arc [ɑ:rk] *all senses*: arco *m*; **ar·cade** [ɑ:r'keid] arcada *f*; (*with shops*) pasaje *m*, soportales *m/pl.*, galería *f*.

Ar·ca·dian [ɑ:r'keidjən] arcadio *adj. a. su. m* (a *f*).

ar·ca·num [ɑ:r'keinəm], *pl.* **ar·ca·na** [ɑ:r'keinə] arcano *m*.

arch[1] [ɑ:rtʃ] **1.** △ *a. anat.* arco *m*; bóveda *f*; ~ *of heaven* bóveda *f* celeste; **2.** △ abovedar; arquear.

arch² [~] □ zumbón; chancero; travieso; astuto; *woman* coqueta.
arch³ [~] principal; consumado.
ar·chae·ol·o·gist [ɑːrkiˈɔlədʒist] arqueólogo *m*; **ar·chaeˈol·o·gy** arqueología *f*.
ar·cha·ic [ɑːrˈkeiik] □ arcaico; **ˈar·cha·ism** arcaísmo *m*.
arch·an·gel [ˈɑːrkeindʒl] arcángel *m*.
arch·bish·op [ˈɑːrtʃˈbiʃəp] arzobispo *m*; **archˈbish·op·ric** [~rik] arzobispado *m*.
arch·dea·con [ˈɑːrtʃˈdiːkən] arcediano *m*.
arch·duch·ess [ˈɑːrtʃˈdʌtʃis] archiduquesa *f*; **ˈarchˈduch·y** archiducado *m*.
arch·duke [ˈɑːrtʃˈdjuːk] archiduque *m*.
arch·en·e·my [ˈɑːrtʃˈenimi] archienemigo *m*.
arch·er [ˈɑːrtʃər] arquero *m*; **ˈarch·er·y** tiro *m* con arco.
ar·che·type [ˈɑːrkitaip] arquetipo *m*.
arch·fiend [ˈɑːrtʃˈfiːnd] Satanás *m*, el enemigo.
ar·chi·e·pis·co·pal [ɑːrkiiˈpiskəpl] arzobispal.
ar·chi·pel·a·go [ɑːrkiˈpeligou] archipiélago *m*.
ar·chi·tect [ˈɑːrkitekt] arquitecto *m*; *fig*. artífice *m/f*; **ar·chi·tec·ton·ic** [~ˈtɔnik] □ arquitectónico; **ar·chi·tec·ture** [ˈ~tʃər] arquitectura *f*.
ar·chives [ˈɑːrkaivz] *pl*. archivo *m*; **ˈar·chiv·ist** archivero (a *f*) *m*.
arch·ness [ˈɑːrtʃnis] socarronería *f*, salero *m*; astucia *f*; (*woman's*) coquetería *f*.
arch·way [ˈɑːrtʃwei] arcada *f*.
arc lamp [ˈɑːrk læmp] lámpara *f* de arco.
arc·tic [ˈɑːrktik] **1.** ártico; frígido; *the* ♀ las Tierras *f/pl*. Árticas; ♀ *Circle* Círculo *m* Polar Ártico; ♀ *Ocean* Océano *m* Boreal; **2.** zona *f* ártica; chanclo *m*.
arc weld·ing [ˈɑːrk ˈweldiŋ] soldadura *f* de arco.
ar·den·cy [ˈɑːrdənsi] ardor *m*, celo *m*; vehemencia *f*; **ˈar·dent** □ *mst fig*. ardiente, caluroso; fogoso; fervoroso, entusiasmado; ~ *spirits pl*. licores *m/pl*. espiritosos.
ar·dor [ˈɑːrdər] ardor *m*; *fig*. fervor *m*, celo *m*; ahinco *m*.
ar·du·ous [ˈɑːrdjuəs] □ arduo, penoso; riguroso; enérgico; (*steep*) escarpado.
are [ɑːr] somos; estamos *etc*. (*v*. *be*).
a·re·a [ˈeriə] área *f*, extensión *f*; *geog*. región *f*, comarca *f*; ⚠ *approx*. corral *m*, traspatio *m*; *danger* ~ zona *f* de peligro; *goal* ~ área *f* de meta; *prohibited* ~ zona *f* prohibida.
a·re·na [əˈriːnə] arena *f*, redondel *m*; *esp. bullfighting*: ruedo *m*; *fig*. lid *f*.
aren't [ɑːrnt] = *are not*.
a·rête [æˈreit] *mount*. arista *f*.
ar·gent [ˈɑːrdʒənt] argén *m*.
Ar·gen·tine [ˈɑːrdʒəntain] argentino *adj. a. su. m* (a *f*); *the* ~ la Argentina.
ar·gil [ˈɑːrdʒil] arcilla *f* figulina; **ar·gil·la·ceous** [~ˈleiʃəs] arcilloso.
Ar·go·naut [ˈɑːrgənɔːt] argonauta *m* (*a. zo.*).
ar·gu·a·ble [ˈɑːrgjuəbl] discutible; **ar·gue** [ˈ~gjuː] *v/t*. argüir; sostener; ~ *into* persuadir a; ~ *out of* disuadir de; *v/i*. disputar, argumentar.
ar·gu·ment [ˈɑːrgjumənt] argumento *m*; discusión *f*; disputa *f*, **ar·gu·menˈta·tion** raciocinación *f*, argumentación *f*; **ar·gu·men·ta·tive** [~ˈmentətiv] □ argumentador.
a·ri·a [ˈɑːriə] aria *f*.
ar·id [ˈærid] árido, seco (*a. fig.*); **aˈrid·i·ty** aridez *f*.
a·right [əˈrait] correctamente; acertadamente; a derechas; *set* ~ rectificar.
a·rise [əˈraiz] [*irr.*] *lit*. levantarse, alzarse; *fig*. surgir, aparecer; ~ *from* provenir de; **aˈris·en** *p.p. of arise*.
ar·is·toc·ra·cy [ærisˈtɔkrəsi] aristocracia *f* (*a. fig.*); **a·ris·to·crat** [ˈ~təkræt] aristócrata *m/f*; **a·ris·toˈcrat·ic**, **a·ris·toˈcrat·i·cal** □ aristocrático.
a·rith·me·tic [əˈriθmətik] aritmética *f*; **ar·ith·met·i·cal** [~ˈmetikəl] □ aritmético; **a·rith·me·ti·cian** [~məˈtiʃn] aritmético *m*.
ark [ɑːrk] arca *f*; ♀ *of the Covenant* arca *f* de la alianza; *Noah's* ♀ arca *f* de Noé.
arm¹ [ɑːrm] brazo *m* (*a. of sea, chair*); ♀ rama *f*, gajo *m*; ~ *in* ~ de bracete, de bracero, asidos del brazo; *infant in* ~*s* niño (a *f*) *m* de teta; *fig. with open* ~*s* con los brazos abiertos; *within* ~*'s reach* al alcance del brazo; *keep a p. at* ~*'s length* mantener a una p. a distancia; *take a p. in one's* ~*s* abrazar a una p.
arm² [~] **1.** ⚔ arma *f* (*mst in pl.*); *heraldry*: ~*s pl*. escudo *m*, blasón *m*; *infantry* ~ arma *f* de infantería; ~*s race*

carrera *f* de armamentos; *under* ~*s* sobre las armas; *fig. be* (*all*) *up in* ~*s* poner el grito en el cielo; *rise up in* ~*s* alzarse en armas; *take up* ~*s* tomar las armas; **2.** ⚔ armar(se); ⊕ armar.
ar·ma·da [ɑːrˈmɑːdə] armada *f*; *the* (*Invincible*) ♀ la (Armada) Invencible (*1588*).
ar·ma·ment [ˈɑːrməmənt] armamento *m*; **ar·ma·ture** [ˈ~tjur] armadura *f* (*a.* ⚡, *zo.*, ♀); (*dynamo*) inducido *m*; ~ *winder* bobinador *m*.
arm·chair [ˈɑːrmtʃer] **1.** (*theoretical*) de gabinete; **2.** silla *f* de brazos; butaca *f*; sillón *m*; ~ *politician etc.* político *m etc.* de café.
...-armed [ɑːrmd] de brazos...
Ar·me·ni·an [ɑːrˈmiːnjən] armenio *adj. a. su. m* (a *f*).
arm·ful [ˈɑːrmful] brazado *m*.
ar·mi·stice [ˈɑːrmistis] armisticio *m*.
arm·let [ˈɑːrmlit] brazal *m*.
ar·mo·ri·al [ɑːrˈmɔːriəl] heráldico.
ar·mor [ˈɑːrmər] **1.** ⚔ armadura *f* (*a. suit of* ~; *a. zo. a. fig.*); blindaje *m*; escafandro *m*; ~ *plate* plancha *f* de blindaje; ~*-plate* acorazar, blindar; **2.** blindar; ~*ed car* carro *m* (*or* coche *m*) blindado; ˈ**~-clad**, ˈ**~-plat·ed** blindado, acorazado; ˈ**ar·mor·er** armero *m*; ˈ**ar·mor·y** armería *f*; arsenal *m*.
arm·pit [ˈɑːrmpit] sobaco *m*, hueco *m* de la axila; ˈ**arm rest** apoyo *m* para el brazo, apoyabrazos *m*.
ar·my [ˈɑːrmi] ejército *m* (*a. fig.*); ~ *command*, ~ *staff* estado *m* mayor; ˈ**~ corps** cuerpo *m* de ejército; ˈ**~ˈlist** lista *f* de oficiales del ejército.
ar·ni·ca [ˈɑːrnikə] árnica *f*.
a·ro·ma [əˈroumə] aroma *m*, fragancia *f*; **ar·o·mat·ic** [ærouˈmætik] □ aromático, fragante.
a·rose [əˈrouz] *pret. of arise*.
a·round [əˈraund] **1.** *adv.* alrededor; a la redonda; por todos lados; F *be* ~ andar por allí; **2.** *prp.* alrededor de, en torno de; *number* cerca de.
a·rouse [əˈrauz] despertar (*a. fig.*); *fig.* mover, excitar.
ar·peg·gio [ɑːrˈpedʒou] arpegio *m*.
ar·rack [ˈærək] aguardiente *m* de palma.
ar·raign [əˈrein] ⚖ procesar; denunciar; reprender; **arˈraign·ment** ⚖ auto *m* de procesamiento; denuncia *f*; reprensión *f*.
ar·range [əˈreindʒ] *v/t.* arreglar, componer, ordenar; *time* fijar, citar; *dispute, agreement etc.* ajustar, componer; ♪ adaptar, refundir; *v/i.* hacer un arreglo (*with* con); convenir (*to* en); ~ *for* prevenir, disponer; **arˈrange·ment** arreglo *m*, ordenación *f*; concierto *m*, convenio *m*; ajuste *m*; orden *m*, disposición *f*; ♪ adaptación *f*, refundición *f*; *come to an* ~ llegar a un acomodo, entenderse (*with* con); *make one's own* ~*s* obrar por su propia cuenta.
ar·rant [ˈærənt] □ notorio, redomado, de siete suelas.
ar·ray [əˈrei] **1.** ⚔ orden *m* de batalla; *fig.* aparato *m*, pompa *f*; *poet.* gala *f*, atavío *m*; **2.** ⚔ formar las tropas; ataviar, componer.
ar·rear [əˈrir]: *mst* ~*s pl.* atrasos *m/pl.*; *in* ~*s* atrasado en pagos; **arˈrear·age** tardanza *f*.
ar·rest [əˈrest] **1.** arresto *m*, detención *f*; secuestro *m of goods*; parada *f*; prórroga *f of judgment*; *under* ~ bajo arresto; **2.** arrestar, detener; parar; prorrogar; *attention* llamar; **arˈrest·ing** impresionante.
ar·riv·al [əˈraivl] llegada *f*; persona *f or* cosa *f* que ha llegado; F *new* ~ recién nacido (a *f*) *m*; *fig.* advenimiento *m*; 🚂 ~ *platform* andén *m* de vacío; **arˈrive** llegar, arribar (*at* a).
ar·ro·gance [ˈærəgəns] arrogancia *f*, soberbia *f*; ˈ**ar·ro·gant** □ arrogante, soberbio; **ar·ro·gate** [ˈærougeit] *to o.s.* arrogarse; *qualities etc.* atribuirse, apropiarse.
ar·row [ˈærou] flecha *f*, saeta *f*; ˈ**~·head** punta *f* de flecha; **~·root** [ˈærəruːt] arrurruz *m*.
arse [ɑːrs] culo *m*.
ar·se·nal [ˈɑːrsinl] arsenal *m*.
ar·se·nic [ˈɑːrsnik] arsénico *m*; **arˈsen·i·cal** arsénico.
ar·son [ˈɑːrsn] delito *m* de incendiar.
art[1] [ɑːrt] arte *mst m in sg.*, *f in pl.*; habilidad *f*, destreza *f*; *black* ~*s pl.* magia *f* negra; *fine* ~*s pl.* bellas artes *f/pl.*; *liberal* ~*s pl.* artes *f/pl.* liberales; ~*s and crafts pl.* artes *f/pl.* y oficios; *Bachelor of* ♀*s* (*abbr. B.A.*) Licenciado (a *f*) *m* en Filosofía y Letras; *Master of* ♀*s* (*abbr. M.A.*) Maestro (a *f*) *m* en Artes; *Faculty of* ♀*s* Facultad *f* de Filosofía y Letras.
art[2] [~] † eres; estás (*v. be*).
ar·te·fact [ˈɑːrtifækt] artefacto *m*.
ar·te·ri·al [ɑːrˈtiriəl] arterial; ~ *road*

carretera *f* principal, autopista *f*; **ar·te·ri·o·scle·ro·sis** [ɑːrtiriouskli'rousis] arteriosclerosis *f*; **ar·ter·y** ['ɑːrtəri] arteria *f* (*a. fig.*).

Ar·te·sian well [ɑːrtiːzən 'wel] pozo *m* artesiano.

art·ful ['ɑːrtful] ☐ astuto, mañoso; diestro, ingenioso.

ar·thrit·ic [ɑːr'θritik] artrítico; **ar·thri·tis** [ɑːr'θraitis] artritis *f*.

ar·ti·choke ['ɑːrtitʃouk] alcachofa *f*; *Jerusalem* ~ *approx*. girasol *m*.

ar·ti·cle ['ɑːrtikl] **1.** artículo *m*; ~*s of apprenticeship* contrato *m* de aprendizaje; ~*s of association* escritura *f* (*or* reglamento *m*) para una sociedad anónima; *an* ~ *of clothing* una prenda de vestir; **2.** *law, text* articular; acusar; *apprentice etc.* pactar, comprometer por escrito; ~*d to* agregado a, unido a.

ar·tic·u·late 1. [ɑːr'tikjuleit] *speech* articular; *joints* enlazar; **2.** [~lit] ☐ (*a.* **ar'tic·u·lat·ed** [~leitid]) articulado; distinto; capaz de hablar; **ar·tic·u'la·tion** articulación *f*.

ar·ti·fice ['ɑːrtifis] artificio *m*; destreza *f*, maña *f*; **ar'tif·i·cer** artífice *m/f*; **ar·ti·fi·cial** [~'fiʃəl] ☐ artificial; postizo; afectado; ⚖ ~ *person* persona *f* jurídica; **ar·ti·fi·ci'al·i·ty** calidad *f* de lo artificial *etc.*

ar·til·ler·y [ɑːr'tiləri] artillería *f*; **ar'til·ler·y·man** artillero *m*.

ar·ti·san [ɑːrti'zæn] artesano (a *f*) *m*.

art·ist ['ɑːrtist] artista *m/f*; **ar·tiste** [ɑːr'tiːst] artista *m/f* de teatro *etc.*; **ar·tis·tic, ar·tis·ti·cal** [~'tistik(l)] ☐ artístico; artificioso.

art·less ['ɑːrtlis] ☐ natural, sencillo; ingenuo; *b.s.* desmañado; **'art·less·ness** naturalidad *f*, sencillez *f*; candidez *f*.

art·y ['ɑːrti] F ostentosamente artístico; *p.* cursi, repipi.

Ar·y·an ['eriən] ario *adj. a. su. m* (a *f*).

as [æz, əz] *adv. a. cj.* como; porque, ya que; a medida que; tal como; (*temporal*) cuando; (*result*) que, de manera que; ~ ... ~ tan ... como; *it is* ~ *good* ~ *lost* puede darse por perdido; *v. far*; ~ *for*, ~ *to* en cuanto a; ~ *from date* a partir de; ~ *if*, ~ *though* como si *subj.*; ~ *if to inf.* como para *inf.*; ~ *it seems* por lo visto, según parece; ~ *it were* por decirlo así; ~ *per* según; *v. such*; ~ *well* también; ~ *well* ~ así como; tan bien como; ~ *yet* hasta ahora.

as·bes·tos [æz'bestɔs] asbesto *m*.

as·cend [ə'send] *v/i.* subir (*a.* ♪); elevarse, encaramarse; (*time*) remontarse; *v/t. river* subir; *mountain, throne* subir a; **as'cend·an·cy** ascendiente *m*, dominio *m* (*over* sobre); **as'cend·ant 1.** ascendente; predominante; **2.** = *ascendancy*; *ast.* ascendiente *m*; *be in the* ~ estar predominante; estar en su cenit; **as'cend·en·cy, as'cend·ent** = *ascendancy, ascendant*.

as·cen·sion [ə'senʃn] *all senses*: ascensión *f*; ♀ *Day* Día *m* de la Ascensión.

as·cent [ə'sent] ascenso *m*; subida *f of mountain etc.*; (*slope*) cuesta *f*, pendiente *f*; tramo *m of stairs*.

as·cer·tain [æsər'tein] averiguar; **as·cer'tain·a·ble** ☐ averiguable; **as·cer'tain·ment** averiguación *f*.

as·cet·ic [ə'setik] **1.** ☐ ascético; **2.** asceta *m/f*; **as'cet·i·cism** [~tisizm] ascetismo *m*.

as·cor·bic [ə'skɔrbik] ascórbico; ~ *acid* ácido *m* ascórbico.

as·crib·a·ble [əs'kraibəbl] atribuible; **as'cribe** atribuir; imputar, achacar; **as·crip·tion** [əs'kripʃn] atribución *f*.

a·sep·tic [ei'septik] aséptico.

a·sex·u·al [ei'seksjuəl] asexual.

ash[1] [æʃ] ♆ fresno *m*.

ash[2] [~] (*freq. pl.* **ash·es** ['æʃiz]) ceniza *f*; ~*es pl.* cenizas *f/pl. of dead*; ♀ *Wednesday* Miércoles *m* de Ceniza.

a·shamed [ə'ʃeimd] ☐ avergonzado; *be* (*or feel*) ~ avergonzarse, sonrojarse (*at, of* de; *for* por); *be* ~ *of o.s.* tener vergüenza de sí.

ash·can ['æʃkæn] cubo *m* de la basura.

ash·en[1] ['æʃn] ♆ de fresno.

ash·en[2] [~] ceniciento; *face* pálido.

ash·lar ['æʃlər] sillar *m*.

a·shore [ə'ʃɔːr] a tierra; en tierra; *come* ~, *go* ~ desembarcar; *run* ~, *be driven* ~ encallar, varar.

ash...: '~ **pan** guardacenizas *m*; **'**~ **tray** cenicero *m*.

ash·y ['æʃi] cenizoso.

A·sian ['eiʒn], **A·si·at·ic** [eiʒi'ætik] asiático *adj. a. su. m* (a *f*).

a·side [ə'said] **1.** aparte, a un lado; ~ *from* además de; *step* ~ hacerse a un lado; **2.** *thea.* aparte *m*.

as·i·nine ['æsinain] asnal; *fig.* estúpido.

ask [æsk] *v/t.* preguntar (*a th.* algo; *a p. a th.* algo a una p.); pedir, rogar (*of, from* a); *~ in* invitar a entrar; *~ a p. for a th.* pedir algo a una p.; *~ that* pedir que; invitar (*to* a); *~ (a p.) a question* hacer una pregunta (a una p.); *v/i. ~ about, ~ after, ~ for* preguntar por; *~ for* pedir, reclamar; *sl. he ~ed for it* se la buscó; *for the ~ing* sin más que pedirlo, con solo pedir; F *that's ~ing a lot* eso pone mucho.

a·skance [ə'skæns], **a·skant** [ə'skænt] al soslayo, al sesgo; *look* con recelo.

a·skew [ə'skjuː] al soslayo, ladeado.

a·slant [ə'slænt] **1.** *adv.* oblicuamente; **2.** *prp.* a través de.

a·sleep [ə'sliːp] dormido, durmiendo; *fall ~* dormirse.

asp[1] [æsp] *zo.* áspid *m.*

asp[2] [~] ⚘ *v. aspen.*

as·par·a·gus [əs'pærəgəs] espárrago *m.*

as·pect ['æspekt] aspecto *m*; apariencia *f*; *with southern ~* con vistas al sur.

as·pen ['æspən] **1.** álamo *m* temblón; **2.** *wood* de álamo temblón; temblador.

as·per·gill, as·per·gil·lum ['æspərdʒil, ~'dʒiləm] hisopo *m.*

as·per·i·ty [æs'periti] aspereza *f.*

as·per·sion [əs'pəːrʒən] difamación *f*, calumnia *f.*

as·phalt ['æsfɔːlt] **1.** asfalto *m*; **2.** asfaltar.

as·pho·del ['æsfədel] asfódel *m.*

as·phyx·i·a [æs'fiksiə] asfixia *f*; **as'phyx·i·ate** asfixiar; **as·phyx·i'a·tion** asfixia *f.*

as·pic ['æspik] *manjar a base de gelatina, que contiene huevos, carne, etc.*

as·pir·ant [əs'pairənt] aspirante *m/f* (*after, for, to* a); **as·pi·rate 1.** ['æspərit] aspirado; **2.** [~] aspirada *f*; **3.** ['~reit] aspirar; **as·pi'ra·tion** ⚕ aspiración *f*; *fig.* anhelo *m* (*after, for* por); **as'pire** [əs'paiər] aspirar (*after, to* a), anhelar (*after, to acc.*); **as·pi·rin** ['æspərin] aspirina *f*; **as'pir·ing** [əs'pairiŋ] □ ambicioso.

ass [æs] asno *m*, burro *m*; *fig.* burro *m*, mentecato *m*; F culo *m*; *make an ~ of o.s.* ponerse en ridículo.

as·sail [ə'seil] acometer, arremeter contra; *fig.* asaltar; *fig.* inundar (*with* de); *task* acometer, emprender; **as'sail·ant, as'sail·ler** asaltador (-a *f*) *m*, agresor (-a *f*) *m*; atracador *m.*

as·sas·sin [ə'sæsin] asesino (a *f*) *m*; **as'sas·si·nate** [~neit] asesinar (*esp. por motivos políticos*); **as·sas·si'na·tion** asesinato *m.*

as·sault [ə'sɔːlt] **1.** asalto *m* (*a. fig.*; [*up*]*on* sobre); ⚔ carga *f*, ataque *m*; ⚖ violencia *f*; atraco *m*; *~ and battery* vías *f/pl.* de hecho, violencias *f/pl.*; **2.** asaltar; ⚔ cargar, atacar; ⚖ violentar; atracar.

as·say [ə'sei] **1.** ensaye *m*; **2.** *metals* ensayar; intentar, tratar (de); **as'say·er** ensayador *m.*

as·sem·blage [ə'semblidʒ] asamblea *f*, reunión *f*; ⊕ montaje *m*; **as'sem·ble** convocar; juntar(se), reunir(se); *troops* formar; ⊕ montar; **as'sem·bly** reunión *f*; asamblea *f* (*a.* ⚔), junta *f*; senado *m*; ⊕ montaje *m*, armadura *f*; *~ hall* aula *f* magna, paraninfo *m*; salón *m* de sesiones; *~ line* línea *f* de montaje, cadena *f* de montaje; *Am. pol. ~ man* asambleísta *m en la asamblea legislativa*; *~ plant* fábrica *f* de montaje; *~ room* sala *f* de reunión, sala *f* de fiestas; ⊕ taller *m* de montaje.

as·sent [ə'sent] **1.** asenso *m*, consentimiento *m*; aprobación *f*; **2.** consentir (*to* en), asentir (*to* a); *~ to* aprobar *acc.*

as·sert [ə'səːrt] afirmar, declarar; hacer valer; *~ o.s.* imponerse, hacer valer sus derechos; **as'ser·tion** afirmación *f*, declaración *f*; **as'ser·tive** □ asertivo; *character* agresivo, presumido.

as·sess [ə'ses] gravar (con impuestos); *damage, tax etc.* fijar, determinar; valorar; apreciar; **as'sess·a·ble** □ ✝ gravable; **as'sess·ment** gravamen *m*; valoración *f*; aprecio *m*; **as'ses·sor** tasador *m*; asesor *m.*

as·set ['æset] posesión *f*; *fig.* valor *m*; F ventaja *f*; **'as·sets** *pl.* ✝ activo *m*; *fig.* valores *m/pl.* positivos.

as·sev·er·ate [ə'sevəreit] aseverar, afirmar; **as·sev·er'a·tion** aseveración *f.*

as·si·du·i·ty [æsi'djuiti] asiduidad *f*, diligencia *f*; **as'sid·u·ous** □ asiduo, diligente, concienzudo.

as·sign [ə'sain] **1.** asignar, señalar; *goods* consignar, traspasar; achacar (*to* a *cause etc.*); **2.** ⚖ cesionario *m*, consignatorio *m*; **as'sign·a·ble** □

asignable; transferible; **as•sig•na-tion** [æsigˈneiʃn] asignación *f*; ✝ consignación *f*, traspaso *m*; cita *f with p.*; **as•sign•ee** [æsiˈniː] = *assign* 2; (*bankruptcy*) síndico *m*; apoderado *m*; **as•sign•ment** [əˈsainmənt] asignación *f*; consignación *f*; (*task*) comisión *f*, encargo *m*; **as•sign•or** [æsaiˈnɔːr] ⚖ cesionista *m*/*f*.

as•sim•i•late [əˈsimileit] asimilar(se) (*a. physiol. a. gr.*), asemejar(se) (*to, with* a); **as•sim•iˈla•tion** asimilación *f*.

as•sist [əˈsist] ayudar, auxiliar; ~ *at* asistir a; ~ *in* tomar parte en; ~ *in ger.* ayudar a *inf.*; **asˈsist•ance** ayuda *f*, socorro *m*, auxilio *m*; **asˈsist•ant 1.** auxiliar, ayudador; sub-; **2.** ayudante *m*, adjutor *m*.

as•size [əˈsaiz] tasa *f*; ~*s pl.* sesión *f* de un tribunal de justicia.

as•so•ci•a•ble [əˈsouʃiəbl] relacionable (*with* con); **asˈso•ci•ate 1.** [~ʃieit] asociar(se), juntar(se) (*with* a, con); ~ *in* mancomunarse en; **2.** [~ʃiit] asociado, coligado; con-; **3.** [~ʃiit] asociado *m*, socio *m* (*a.* ✝), consocio *m*; miembro *m* correspondiente (de una academia;) compañero *m*, camarada *m*/*f*; **as-so•ci•a•tion** [~siˈeiʃn] asociación *f*; agrupación *f*, sociedad *f*; (*a mutual* ~) cooperativa *f*; ~ *football* fútbol *m*.

as•so•nance [ˈæsənəns] asonancia *f*.

as•sort [əˈsɔːrt] *v*/*t.* clasificar, compaginar; ✝ proveer de un surtido; *v*/*i.* convenir, concordar (*with* con); ~ *well* (*ill*) (no) hacer juego (*with* con); **asˈsort•ment** clasificación *f*; ✝ surtido *m*.

as•suage [əˈsweidʒ] apaciguar, mitigar; *appetite, passion etc.* saciar; **asˈsuage•ment** mitigación *f*, alivio *m*.

as•sume [əˈsjuːm] *aspect* tomar; *authority etc.* apropiarse, agregarse; *burden* asumir; dar por sentado, suponer (*that* que); *assuming that* dado que; **asˈsum•ing** □ presuntuoso, presumido; **as•sump•tion** [əˈsʌmpʃn] asunción *f*; suposición *f*; presunción *f*; *eccl.* ♀ Asunción *f*; *on the* ~ *that* suponiendo que; **asˈsump•tive** □ supuesto; arrogante.

as•sur•ance [əˈʃuːrəns] aseguramiento *m*; declaración *f*; garantía *f*; ✝ seguro *m*; confianza *f* en sí mismo; *b.s.* descoco *m*; **asˈsure** asegurar (*a p. of a th.* a una p. de algo; *a.* ✝); declarar, afirmar; garantizar; **asˈsured 1.** (*adv.* **asˈsur•ed•ly** [~ridli]) confiado; *b.s.* presumido; ~*ly* seguramente, de seguro, sin duda, ciertamente; **2.** asegurado (a *f*) *m*; **asˈsur•er** [~rər] asegurado (a *f*) *m*; *a.* = **asˈsur•or** [~rər] asegurador *m*.

As•syr•i•an [əˈsiriən] asirio.

as•ter [ˈæstər] aster *m*; (*China aster*) reina *f* Margarita.

as•ter•isk [ˈæstərisk] asterisco *m*.

a•stern [əˈstəːrn] a popa; *go* ~ ciar.

asth•ma [ˈæzmə] asma *f*; **asth•mat-ic** [~ˈmætik] **1.** *a.* **asthˈmat•i•cal** □ asmático; **2.** asmático (a *f*) *m*.

as•tig•mat•ic [æstigˈmætik] □ astigmático; **aˈstig•ma•tism** [~mətizm] astigmatismo *m*.

a•stir [əsˈtəːr] en movimiento; levantado (de la cama).

as•ton•ish [əsˈtɔniʃ] asombrar, sorprender; pasmar; *be* ~*ed* asombrarse, maravillarse (*at* de, con); **asˈton-ish•ing** □ asombroso, sorprendente; **asˈton•ish•ment** asombro *m*, sorpresa *f*; pasmo *m*.

as•tound [əsˈtaund] pasmar; aturdir.

as•tra•khan [ˈæstrəkæn] astracán *m*.

as•tral [ˈæstrəl] astral, sidéreo.

a•stray [əˈstrei] extraviado, descarriado, despistado; *go* ~ extraviarse, descarriarse (*a. fig.*); *lead* ~ llevar por mal camino, extraviar.

a•stride [əˈstraid] **1.** *adv.* (*ride* montar) a horcajadas; **2.** *prp.* a caballo sobre, a horcajadas sobre.

as•trin•gent [əsˈtrindʒent] □ ⚕ astringente; *fig. style* adusto, austero.

as•trol•o•ger [əsˈtrɔlədʒər] astrólogo *m*; **as•tro•log•i•cal** [æstrəˈlɔdʒikl] □ astrológico, astrólogo; **as•trol•o-gy** [əsˈtrɔlədʒi] astrología *f*; **as-tron•o•mer** [əsˈtrɔnəmər] astrónomo *m*; **as•tro•nom•i•cal** [æstrəˈnɔmikl] □ astronómico; *fig.* tremendo; **as•tron•o•my** [əsˈtrɔnəmi] astronomía *f*.

as•tro•naut [ˈæstrənɔt] astronauta *m*/*f*; **as•troˈnau•tics** *sg.* astronáutica *f*; **as•troˈphys•ics** *sg.* astrofísica *f*.

as•tute [əsˈtjuːt] □ sagaz, perspicaz; astuto; **asˈtute•ness** perspicacia *f*; astucia *f*.

a•sun•der [əˈsʌndər] separadamente; en dos, a pedazos; *lit. tear* ~ hacer pedazos.

a·sy·lum [ə'sailəm] asilo *m*; amparo *m*.

at [æt, *unstressed* ət] en; a; hacia; por; ~ *Mérida* en Mérida; ~ *school* en la escuela; ~ *midday* a mediodía; ~ *Christmas* en (*or* por) Navidades; ~ *a low price* a un precio bajo; ~ *Mary's* en casa de María; ~ *that time* en aquella época; ~ *the door* a la puerta; ~ *table* a la mesa; ~ *peace* en paz; ~ *one blow* de un golpe; *be* ~ *s.t.* estar ocupado con algo.

at·a·vism ['ætəvizm] atavismo *m*.

a·tax·y [ə'tæksi] ataxia *f*.

ate [eit] *pret. of eat* 1.

a·the·ism ['eiθiizm] ateísmo *m*; **'a·the·ist** ateo (a *f*) *m*; **a·the'is·tic, a·the'is·ti·cal** □ ateísta, ateo.

ath·lete ['æθli:t] atleta *m/f*; ⚕ ~*'s foot* pie *m* de atleta; **ath·let·ic** [æθ'letik], **ath'let·i·cal** □ atlético; ~ *sports pl.* ejercicios *m/pl.* atléticos; **ath'let·ics** *pl.*, **ath'let·i·cism** [~tisizəm] atletismo *m*.

a·thwart [ə'θwɔ:rt] **1.** *prp.* a(l) través de; **2.** *adv.* de través, transversalmente.

a·tilt [ə'tilt] inclinado.

at·las ['ætləs] atlas *m*.

at·mos·phere ['ætməsfir] atmósfera *f*; *fig.* ambiente *m*; **at·mos·pher·ic, at·mos·pher·i·cal** [~'ferik(l)] □ atmosférico; **at·mos'pher·ics** *pl.* *radio*: mala atmósfera *f*, parásitos *m/pl*.

at·oll ['ætɔl] atolón *m*.

at·om ['ætəm] átomo *m* (*a. fig.*); ~ *smasher* rompeátomos *m*; **a·tom·ic** [ə'tɔmik] atómico; ~ *age* era *f* atómica; ~ *bomb* bomba *f* atómica; ~ *energy* energía *f* atómica; ~ *fission* fisión *f* nuclear; ~ *nucleus* núcleo *m* atómico; ~ *pile* pila *f* atómica; ~ *research* investigaciones *f/pl.* atómicas; ~ *weight* peso *m* atómico; **a'tom·ic-'pow·ered** impulsado por energía atómica; **at·om·ism** ['ætəmizm] atomismo *m*; **at·om'is·tic** □ atomístico; **'at·om·ize** reducir a átomos, atomizar; *liquid* pulverizar; **'at·om·izer** pulverizador *m*, vaporizador *m*.

a·ton·al [ei'tounəl] atonal; **a·ton'al·i·ty** atonalidad *f*.

a·tone [ə'toun] *v/t.* † conciliar; *v/i.*: ~ *for* expiar *acc.*; **a'tone·ment** expiación *f*; *Day of* ♀ Día *m* de la Expiación.

a·ton·ic [æ'tɔnik] □ átono, atónico; **at·o·ny** ['ætəni] atonía *f*.

a·tro·cious [ə'trouʃəs] □ atroz; F malísimo, infame; **a·troc·i·ty** [ə'trɔsiti] atrocidad *f* (*a.* F).

at·ro·phy ['ætrəfi] **1.** atrofia *f*; **2.** atrofiar(se).

at·tach [ə'tætʃ] *v/t.* atar, pegar, prender (*to* a); ☤ adjuntar; *importance, value etc.* dar, conceder (*to* a); ⚖ *p.* arrestar; *th.* incautarse; ~ *o.s. to* agregarse a; pegarse a; ~ *value to* conceder valor a, estimar; *fig. be* ~*ed to p. etc.* tener cariño a, aficionarse a; *be officially associated with* depender de; *v/i.* ~ *to* corresponder a; **at'tach·a·ble** separable; *p.* casadero; ⚖ incautable; **at·ta·ché** [atə'ʃei] agregado *m*; ~ *case* cartera *f* (grande, para documentos); **at'tached** *male etc.* comprometido; agregado (*to* a); ☤ adjunto (*to* a); **at'tach·ment** atadura *f*; ⊕ accesorio *m*; (*affection*) cariño *m* (*to* por, a), apego *m* (*to* a); (*loyalty*) adhesión *f*, lealtad *f*; ⚖ arresto *m*; incautación *f*, embargo *m*.

at·tack [ə'tæk] **1.** acometer, embestir (*a. fig.*); atacar (*a.* ⚕ *a.* ⚔); **2.** ataque *m* (*on* contra, a, sobre; *a. fig.*); ⚕ ataque *m*, acceso *m*; **at'tack·a·ble** atacable; **at'tack·er** agresor (-a *f*) *m*.

at·tain [ə'tein] *v/t.* alcanzar, lograr, conseguir; *v/i.*: ~ *to* llegar a; **at'tain·a·ble** realizable; accesible; **at'tain·der** ⚖ muerte *f* civil; **at'tain·ment** logro *m*, obtención *f*; ~*s pl.* talentos *m/pl.*, conocimientos *m/pl.*, dotes *f/pl.*, prendas *f/pl*.

at·tar ['ætər] esencia *f* de rosas.

at·tem·per [ə'tempər] atemperar (*a. fig.*); modificar; calmar; acomodar (*to* a).

at·tempt [ə'tempt] **1.** ensayar, intentar (*to inf.*), tentar (*to* de); *the life of a person* atentar a, atentar contra; **2.** tentativa *f*, conato *m* (*to* de); atentado *m* (*on life* a, contra).

at·tend [ə'tend] *v/t.* acompañar; cortejar, servir; † aguardar; *course etc.* asistir a; ⚕ atender a, asistir; *well attended* (muy) concurrido; *v/i.* prestar atención (*to* a); asistir (*at* a); ~ *on* servir; *sick* atender a, asistir; ~ *to work etc.* atender a; **at'tend·ance** (*presence*) presencia *f* (*at* en), asistencia *f* (*at* a); (*gathering*) concurrencia *f*; ⚕ asistencia *f*; obsequio *m* (*on* de); *be in*

~ asistir; *dance ~ on* estar pendiente de los menores detalles de; **at'tend-ant 1.** concomitante ([*up*]*on* a); asistente (*at* a); **2.** criado (a *f*) *m*, sirviente (a *f*) *m*; mozo (a *f*) *m*; ordenanza *m*; *thea. etc.* acomodador (-a *f*) *m*.
at·ten·tion [ə'tenʃn] atención *f* (*a. fig.*); *~!* ¡atención!; ⚔ *~!* ¡firmes!; *call ~ to* llamar la atención sobre; *give* (*or pay*) *~* prestar atención (*to* a); **at'ten·tive** □ atento (*to* a).
at·ten·u·ate [ə'tenjueit] atenuar (*a. fig.*); *attenuating circumstances pl.* circunstancias *f*/*pl.* atenuantes; **at'ten·u·at·ed** enflaquecido; **at·ten·u'a·tion** atenuación *f*.
at·test [ə'test] atestiguar; dar fe (*to* de); juramentar; **at·tes·ta·tion** [ætes'teiʃn] atestiguación *f*; atestación *f*; ⚖ autenticación *f*.
At·tic ['ætik] **1.** ático; **2.** ♀ desván *m*, sotabanco *m*; guardilla *f*.
at·tire [ə'taiər] *lit.* **1.** ataviar, adornar, componer; **2.** atavío *m*; adorno *m*.
at·ti·tude ['ætitju:d] actitud *f* (*a. fig.*; *to* a); ademán *m*; ✈ posición *f*; *strike an ~* tomar una postura; *~ of mind* actitud *f*, disposición *f* de ánimo; **at·ti'tu·di·nize** pavonearse; tomar posturas afectadas.
at·tor·ney [ə'tə:rni] abogado *m*; † apoderado (a *f*) *m*; † ⚖ procurador *m*; ⚖ *circuit* (*district*) *~* fiscal *m*; *letter* (*or warrant*) *of ~* poder *m*, procuración *f*; *power of ~* poder *m*; ♀ *General* fiscal *m* de la corona; procurador *m* general; *by ~* por poder.
at·tract [ə'trækt] atraer; *attention* llamar; **at'trac·tion** [~kʃən] atracción *f*; aliciente *m*; atractivo *m* of *p.esp.*; *thea.* programa *m*; **at'trac·tive** [~tiv] □ *mst fig.* atractivo, atrayente; agradable; **at'trac·tive·ness** atractivo *m*, hechizo *m*.
at·trib·ut·a·ble [ə'tribjutəbl] atribuible; **at·tri·bute 1.** [ə'tribju:t] atribuir, achacar; **2.** ['ætribju:t] atributo *m*; **at·tri'bu·tion** atribución *f*; **at·trib·u·tive** [ə'tribjutiv] □ atributivo.
at·tri·tion [ə'triʃn] roce *m*, desgaste *m*; *eccl.* atrición *f*; *war of ~* guerra *f* de agotamiento.
at·tune [ə'tju:n] ♪ afinar; *fig. ~ to* armonizar con.
au·burn ['ɔ:bərn] castaño rojizo.
auc·tion ['ɔ:kʃn] **1.** almoneda *f*, subasta *f*; *~ house* martillo *m*; *sell at ~*, *put up for ~* subastar, poner en pública subasta; *sale by ~* subasta *f*; **2.** subastar (*freq. ~ off*); **auc·tion·eer** [~'nir] **1.** subastador *m*; **2.** rematar, subastar.
au·da·cious [ɔ:'deiʃəs] □ audaz, osado; *b.s.* descarado, fresco; **au·dac·i·ty** [ɔ:'dæsiti] audacia *f*, osadía *f*; *b.s.* descaro *m*.
au·di·bil·i·ty [ɔ:di'biliti] capacidad *f* de ser oído; **au·di·ble** ['ɔ:dəbl] □ audible; **'au·di·ble·ness** = *audibility*.
au·di·ence ['ɔ:diəns] auditorio *m*, público *m*, audiencia *f* (*with*, *of* con).
au·di·o·fre·quen·cy ['ɔ:diou'fri:kwənsi] *radio*: audiofrecuencia *f*; **au·di·o·me·ter** [ɔ:di'ɔmitər] audiómetro *m*.
au·dit ['ɔ:dit] **1.** intervención *f*; **2.** intervenir; **au'di·tion** audición *f*; **'au·di·tor** interventor *m*; censor *m* de cuentas; **au·di·to·ri·um** [~'tɔ:riəm] sala *f*, anfiteatro *m*; **au·di·to·ry** ['~tɔ:ri] auditivo.
au·ger ['ɔ:gər] barrena *f*.
aught [ɔ:t] algo; (*with negation*) nada; *for ~ I care* igual me da; *for ~ I know* que yo sepa.
aug·ment [ɔ:g'ment] aumentar(se), engrosar(se); **aug·men'ta·tion** aumento *m*, acrecentamiento *m*; **aug'ment·a·tive** [~tətiv] □ aumentativo (*a. gr.*).
au·gur ['ɔ:gər] **1.** augur *m*; **2.** agorar, pronosticar; prometer (*well* bien, *ill* mal); *~ well* ser de buen agüero; **au·gu·ry** ['ɔ:gjuri] augurio *m*.
Au·gust 1. ['ɔ:gəst] agosto *m*; **2.** ♀ [ɔ:'gʌst] □ augusto; **Au·gus·tan** [ɔ:'gʌstən] augustal; clásico.
auk [ɔ:k] alca *f*.
aunt [ænt, ɑ:nt] tía *f*; **aunt·ie, aunt·y** ['~ti] F tía *f*.
au·ra ['ɔ:rə] ambiente *m*; emanación *f*.
au·ral ['ɔ:rəl] auricular.
au·re·ole ['ɔ:rioul] *eccl.*, *ast.*, aureola *f*.
au·ri·cle ['ɔ:rikl] aurícula *f*; **au·ric·u·la** [ɔ:'rikjulə] ⚘ oreja *f* de oso; **au·ric·u·lar** □ auricular; *~ witness* testigo *m* auricular.
au·rif·er·ous [ɔ:'rifərəs] aurífero.
au·rochs ['ɔ:rɔks] uro *m*.
au·ro·ra [ɔ:'rɔ:rə] aurora *f*; *~ borealis* aurora *f* polar (*or* boreal); **au'ro·ral** matutino; *color* rosáceo.

aus·cul·ta·tion [ɔːskəlˈteiʃn] auscultación *f*.
aus·pice [ˈɔːspis] auspicio *m*; protección *f*; *under the* ~*s of* bajo los auspicios de; **aus·pi·cious** [~ˈpiʃəs] □ propicio, favorable; de buen augurio.
aus·tere [ɔːsˈtir] □ austero, severo; *style etc.* adusto; *taste* acerbo; **aus·ter·i·ty** [~ˈteriti] austeridad *f*, severidad *f*; adustez *f*.
aus·tral [ˈɔːstrəl] austral.
Aus·tra·lian [ɔːsˈtreiljən] australiano *adj. a. su. m* (a *f*).
Aus·tri·an [ˈɔːstriən] austríaco *adj. a. su. m* (a *f*).
au·tarch·y [ˈɔːtɑːrki] autarquía *f*.
au·then·tic [ɔːˈθentik] □ auténtico; **auˈthen·ti·cate** [~keit] autenticar; refrendar; **au·then·tiˈca·tion** autenticación *f*; refrendación *f*; **au·thenˈtic·i·ty** autenticidad *f*.
au·thor [ˈɔːθər] autor (-a *f*) *m*; **au·thor·ess** [ˈɔːθəris] *esp. lit.* autora *f*; **au·thor·i·tar·i·an** [ɔːθɔriˈteriən] autoritario; **auˈthor·i·ta·tive** [~teitiv] □ autorizado; perentorio; autoritario; **auˈthor·i·ty** autoridad *f*; *the authorities* las autoridades; *on good* ~ de buenta tinta; *under the* ~ *of* bajo la autoridad de; *in* ~ *over* al mando de; **au·thor·i·za·tion** [ɔːθəraiˈzeiʃn] autorización *f*; **ˈau·thor·ize** autorizar; **ˈau·thor·ship** calidad *f or* profesión *f* de autor; paternidad *f* literaria *of work*.
au·tis·tic [ɔːˈtistik] autístico.
au·to [ˈɔːtou] automóvil *m*, coche *m*.
au·to... [ˈɔːto] auto...
au·to·bi·og·ra·pher [ɔːtoubaiˈɔgrəfər] autobiógrafo (a *f*) *m*; **ˈau·to·bi·o·graph·ic, ˈau·to·bi·o·graph·i·cal** [~ˈgræfik(l)] □ autobiográfico; **au·to·biˈog·ra·phy** [~grəfi] autobiografía *f*.
au·to·bus [ˈɔːtoubəs] autobús *m*.
au·to·cade [ˈɔːtoukeid] caravana *f* de automóviles.
au·toch·thon [ɔːˈtɔkθən] autóctono (a *f*) *m*; **auˈtoch·tho·nous** autóctono.
au·toc·ra·cy [ɔːˈtɔkrəsi] autocracia *f*; **au·to·crat** [ˈɔːtəkræt] autócrata *m/f*; **au·toˈcrat·ic, au·toˈcrat·i·cal** □ autocrático; autoritario.
au·to·gi·ro [ˈɔːtouˈdʒairou] autogiro *m*.
au·to·graph [ˈɔːtəgræf] **1.** autógrafo *adj. a. su. m*; ~ *seeker* cazaautógrafos *m*; **2.** firmar; dedicar; **au·to·graph·ic** [~ˈgræfik] autográfico; **au·tog·ra·phy** [ɔːˈtɔgrəfi] ⊕ autografía *f*.
au·to·mat [ˈɔːtəmæt] restaurante *m* automático; **au·to·mat·ic** [ɔːtəˈmætik] **1.** □ automático; ~ *clutch* servoembrague *m*; **2.** pistola *f* automática; **au·tomˈa·tion** automatización *f*, automación *f*; **au·tom·a·ton** [ɔːˈtɔmətən], *pl.* *mst* **auˈtom·a·ta** [~tə] autómata *m* (*a. fig.*).
au·to·mo·bile [ˈɔːtəmoubiːl] automóvil *m*, coche *m*; ~ *show* salón *m* del automóvil.
au·ton·o·mous [ɔːˈtɔnəməs] □ autónomo; **auˈton·o·my** autonomía *f*.
au·top·sy [ˈɔːtəpsi] autopsia *f*.
au·to·type [ˈɔːtotaip] **1.** autotipo *m*, facsímil *m*; **2.** producir por la autotipia.
au·tumn [ˈɔːtəm] otoño *m*; **au·tum·nal** [ɔːˈtʌmnəl] □ otoñal.
aux·il·ia·ry [ɔːgˈziliəri] **1.** auxiliar (*a. gr.*); subalterno; **2. auxˈil·ia·ries** [~iz] *pl.* tropas *f/pl.* auxiliares.
a·vail [əˈveil] **1.** beneficiar, valer; ~ *o.s. of* valerse de, aprovechar; **2.**: *of no* ~ inútil; *of what* ~ *is it?* ¿de qué sirve? (*to inf.*); **a·vail·aˈbil·i·ty** disponibilidad *f*; calidad *f* de asequible (*or* accesible); **aˈvail·a·ble** □ disponible, asequible; *p.* accesible, tratable; *ticket* válido; *make* ~ disponer.
av·a·lanche [ˈævəlæntʃ] alud *m*; *fig.* torrente *m*.
a·vant-garde [ˈɑːvɑːnˈgɑːrd] **1.** vanguardista; **2.** vanguardismo *m*.
av·a·rice [ˈævəris] avaricia *f*, mezquindad *f*; **av·aˈri·cious** □ avaro, avariento.
a·venge [əˈvendʒ] vengar, vindicar; ~ *o.s.* (*or be* ~*d*) vengarse ([*up*]*on* en); *avenging angel* ángel *m* vengador; **aˈveng·er** vengador (-a *f*) *m*.
av·e·nue [ˈævinjuː] avenida *f*; autopista *f*; *fig.* camino *m*, acceso *m*.
a·ver [əˈvəːr] afirmar, declarar.
av·er·age [ˈævəridʒ] **1.** promedio *m*, término *m* medio; ⚓ avería *f* (*general* gruesa, *particular* particular); *on* (*an or the*) ~ por regla general; **2.** medio, de término medio; *a.b.s.* mediano, ordinario; **3.** *v/t.* calcular el término medio de; prorratear; *v/i.* (*work etc.*) resultar por término medio, ser por regla general.

a·ver·ment [əˈvəːrmənt] declaración *f*; ⚖ comprobación *f*.
a·verse [əˈvəːrs]: ~ *from, to* opuesto a, adverso a; con antipatía hacia; *I am ~ to th.* siento repugnancia por; *I am ~ to ger.* tengo pocas ganas de *inf.*, me repugna *inf.*; **aˈverse·ness, aˈver·sion** [~ʒn] aversión *f* (*for, from, to* hacia), repugnancia *f* (*for, from, to* por); *v. pet.*
a·vert [əˈvəːrt] apartar; *blow etc.* impedir, quitar.
a·vi·ar·y [ˈeiviəri] avería *f*, pajarera *f*.
a·vi·a·tion [eiviˈeiʃn] aviación *f*; ~ *medicine* aeromedicina *f*; **ˈa·vi·a·tor** aviador (-a *f*) *m*.
av·id [ˈævid] □ ávido, ansioso (*of, for* de); **a·vid·i·ty** [əˈviditi] avidez *f*, ansia *f*.
av·o·ca·do [ɑːvəˈkɑːdou] aguacate *m*.
av·o·ca·tion [ævouˈkeiʃn] vocación *f*; ocupación *f* accesoria; † distracción *f*.
a·vo·cet [ˈævouset] avoceta *f*.
a·void [əˈvɔid] evitar (*doing* hacer); salvarse de; *duty etc.* eludir; ⚖ anular; **aˈvoid·a·ble** evitable; eludible; **aˈvoid·ance** evitación *f*; ⚖ anulación *f*; plaza *f* vacante.
av·oir·du·pois [ævərdəˈpɔiz] *sistema de pesos británico y estadounidense*; F gordura *f*.
a·vouch [əˈvautʃ] afirmar; garantizar; confesar.
a·vow [əˈvau] reconocer, confesar; **aˈvow·al** reconocimiento *m*, confesión *f*; **aˈvow·ed·ly** [~idli] sin rebozo, abiertamente.
av·unc·u·lar [əˈvʌŋkjuːlər] de un tío; como un tío.
a·wait [əˈweit] *lit. a. fig.* aguardar, esperar.
a·wake [əˈweik] **1.** despierto; *fig.* despabilado, listo; *keep ~* (*coffee etc.*) desvelar; *wide ~* completamente despierto (*a. fig.*); *fig.* astuto; **2.** [*irr.*] *v/t.* (*mst* **aˈwak·en**) despertar; ~ *a p. to a th.* ponerle a uno al corriente de algo; *v/i.* despertar(se) (*a. fig.*); ~ *to* darse cuenta de.
a·ward [əˈwɔːrd] **1.** adjudicación *f*; ⚖ sentencia *f*, fallo *m*; ⚔ *etc.* condecoración *f*; (*prize*) premio *m* (*chief* gordo); **2.** adjudicar; decretar; *prize etc.* conferir, conceder.
a·ware [əˈwer] consciente (*of* de); *be ~ of* estar enterado de; *become ~ of* enterarse de; darse cuenta de; **aˈware·ness** conciencia *f*, conocimiento *m*.
a·wash [əˈwɔʃ] a flor de agua; en el agua.
a·way [əˈwei] ausente; lejos;; en otro lugar; (*with verbs, e.g. work ~*) con ahinco, sin cesar; *be ~* estar fuera; ~ *with you!* ¡quita allá!; ¡lárgate!; F ~ *back* hace mucho tiempo; ~ *team* equipo *m* de fuera; *play ~* jugar fuera.
awe [ɔː] **1.** temor *m* reverencial, pasmo *m*; *stand in ~ of* reverenciar; **awe·some** [ˈ~səm] □ pasmoso; aterrador; **ˈ~-struck** pasmado.
aw·ful [ˈɔːful] □ tremendo, pasmoso; impresionante; F malísimo, muy feo; *~ly adv.* F excesivamente; terriblemente; **ˈaw·ful·ness** † veneración *f*; horror *m*; F enormidad *f*.
a·while [əˈwail] un rato; algún tiempo.
awk·ward [ˈɔːkwərd] □ *p. etc.* desmañado, torpe, lerdo; *situation* embarazoso; violento; *problem* peliagudo, difícil, delicado; ~ *squad* ⚔ pelotón *m* de los torpes; **ˈawk·ward·ness** desmaña *f*, torpeza *f*; delicadeza *f*.
awl [ɔːl] lezna *f*, subilla *f*.
awn [ɔːn] arista *f*.
awn·ing [ˈɔːniŋ] toldo *m*; (*cart*) entalamadura *f*; (*window*) marquesina *f*; ⚓ toldilla *f*.
a·woke [əˈwouk] *pret. a. p.p. of awake 2.*
a·wry [əˈrai] de través, al sesgo; *fig.* equivocadamente; *go ~, turn ~* salir mal, fracasar.
axe [æks] **1.** hacha *f*; *fig.* (*costs etc.*) reducción *f*, cercenamiento *m*; *have an ~ to grind* actuar de una manera interesada; **2.** *fig.* reducir, cercenar.
ax·i·om [ˈæksiəm] axioma *m*; **ax·i·oˈmat·ic** □ axiomático.
ax·is [ˈæksis], *pl.* **ax·es** [ˈ~siːz] eje *m* (*a.* ✈ *a.* ⚘); *physiol.* axis *m*.
ax·le [ˈæksl] eje *m*, árbol *m*; ~ *box* caja *f* de eje; **ˈ~ tree** eje *m* (de un carro).
ay(**e**) [ai] **1.** *parl. a.* ⚓ sí; *for ever and ~* siempre jamás; **2.** sí *m*; *parl. the ~s have it* han ganado los que votaron por la moción; **ay**(**e**) [e] siempre; *for ~* por siempre.
a·za·lea [əˈzeiljə] azalea *f*.
az·i·muth [ˈæziməθ] acimut *m*; **az·i·muth·al** [~ˈmjuːθl] □ acimutal.
a·zo·ic [əˈzouik] azoico.
az·ure [ˈæʒər] azul *adj. a. su. m.*

B

baa [bɑː] **1.** balar; **2.** balido *m.*
bab·ble [ˈbæbl] **1.** barbullar, barbotear; *fig.* charlar, parlar; hablar indiscretamente; (*stream*) murmurar; **2.** barboteo *m*; parloteo *m*; murmullo *m*; ˈ**bab·bler** charlatán (-a *f*) *m*; ˈ**bab·bling** *adj. talk* descosido.
babe [beib] niño *m*, a *f*; *sl.* chica *f.*
Ba·bel [ˈbeibl] Babel *m or f*; ♀ *fig.* babel *m or f.*
ba·boon [bəˈbuːn] mandril *m.*
ba·by [ˈbeibi] niño (a *f*) *m*; nene (a *f*) *m*, rorro (a *f*) *m*; F *b.s.* aniñado (a *f*) *m*; ~ *of the family* benjamín *m*; *be left holding the* ~ cargar con la oveja muerta; ~ **car·riage** cochecillo *m* para niños; ~ **grand** piano *m* de media cola; ˈ**~·hood** [~hud] infancia *f*; ˈ**ba·by·ish** infantil.
Bab·y·lo·ni·an [bæbiˈlounjən] babilonio *adj. a. su. m* (a *f*).
baby...: ˈ**~·sit** F vigilar (*a los niños dormidos en ausencia de sus padres*); ˈ**~-sit·ter** niñero (a *f*) *m* tomado (*f*: a) por horas, cuidaniños *m/f S.Am.*; ˈ~ **talk** habla *f* infantil.
bac·cha·nal [ˈbækənl] **1.** = *bacchante*; **2.** bacanal; ˈ**bac·cha·nals** *pl. or* **bac·cha·na·li·a** [~ˈneiljə] *pl.* bacanales *f/pl.*; **bac·chaˈna·li·an** bacanal; desenfrenado.
bac·chan·te [bəˈkænti] bacante *f*; **bacˈchan·tic** bacanal.
bac·cy [ˈbæki] F tabaco *m.*
bach·e·lor [ˈbætʃələr] soltero *m*; *old* ~ solterón *m*; *univ.* bachiller *m* (†), licenciado (a *f*) *m*; ~ *flat* piso *m* para soltero; ~ *girl* soltera *f* (que tiene sus propios recursos); ˈ**~·hood** [~hud] soltería *f.*
bac·il·la·ry [bəˈsiləri] bacilar; **baˈcil·lus** [~ləs], *pl.* **baˈcil·li** [~lai] bacilo *m.*
back [bæk] **1.** espalda *f*, dorso *m*; (*mountain*) lomo *m*; respaldo *m of chair*; dorso *m of check, hand etc.*; final *m of book*; *sport*: defensa *m*; (*at the*) ~ *of* tras, detrás de; *stage etc.* al fondo de; *behind one's* ~ a espaldas de uno (*a. fig.*); *on one's* ~ postrado, en cama; (*carrying s. t.*) a cuestas; *with one's* ~ *to the wall* entre la espada y la pared; F *get* (*or put*) *a p.'s* ~ *up* enojar a una p.; *turn one's* ~ *on* volver la espalda a; **2.** *adj.* trasero, posterior, de atrás; ~ *issue* número *m* atrasado; ~ *pay* sueldo *m* retrasado; **3.** *adv.* (hacia) atrás; otra vez; de vuelta; ~ *and forth* de una parte a otra; ~ *in period* allá por; *some months* ~ hace unos meses; **4.** *v/t.* apoyar (*a.* ~ *up*); *pol.* respaldar; *car* dar marcha atrás a; *horse* montar; (*bet*) apostar a; ✝ endosar; ~ *up* mover hacia atrás; ⚓ ~ *water* ciar; *v/i.* retroceder, moverse hacia atrás; (*esp. horse*) cejar; F ~ *down* ceder; rajarse; F ~ *out* echarse atrás, desdecirse; ˈ**~·ache** dolor *m* de espalda; ~ **al·ley** callejón *m* de atrás; ˈ**~-ˈben·cher** *diputado que no ocupa un escaño en la fila delantera*; ˈ**~·bite** [*irr.* (*bite*)] cortar de vestir, murmurar; ˈ**~·bone** espinazo *m*; *fig.* firmeza *f*; *fig. to the* ~ hasta la médula; ˈ**~·break·ing** deslomador; ˈ**~·chat** *sl.* réplica *f*; maldicencia *f*; ˈ**~·cloth** telón *m* de fondo; ˈ~ ˈ**door** puerta *f* trasera; ˈ**back·er** sostenedor (-a *f*) *m*; ✝ suscriptor (-a *f*) *m*, inversionista *m/f.*
back...: ˈ**~·fire 1.** *mot.* petardeo *m*, falsa explosión *f*; **2.** *mot.* petardear; *fig.* salir el tiro por la culata; ˈ**~ˈgam·mon** chaquete *m*; ˈ**~·ground** fondo *m*, último término *m*; *fig.* antecedentes *m/pl.*; educación *f*; ~ *music* música *f* de fondo; ˈ**~·ˈhand 1.** *tennis etc.*: revés *m*; **2.** = ˈ**~ˈhand·ed** dado con la vuelta de la mano; *fig.* falto de sinceridad, irónico; ˈ~ ˈ**hand·er** *tennis etc.*: revés *m*; ˈ**back·ing** apoyo *m*; *esp.* ✝ reserva *f.*
back...: ˈ**~·lash** ⊕ contragolpe *m*; *fig.* reacción *f* violenta; ˈ**~·log** atrasos *m/pl.* (de pedidos pendientes); ˈ~ ˈ**num·ber** número *m* atrasado; *fig.* cero *m* a la izquierda; ˈ~ **pay** sueldo *m* retrasado; ˈ**~-ˈped·al** dar marcha atrás con los pedales, contrapedalear; ˈ**~ˈseat** asiento *m* de atrás; F *take*

a ~ ceder su puesto, perder influencia; '~'**side** trasero *m*; nalgas *f/pl.*; '~·**slap·per** tipo *m* guasón, campechano *m*; '~·**slap·ping** espaldarazos *m/pl.*; *mutual* ~ bombo *m* mutuo; '~'**slide** [*irr.* (*slide*)] volver a las andadas, reincidir; '~'**slid·er** reincidente *m/f*; '~'**slid·ing** reincidencia *f*; '~·**stage** detrás del telón; entre bastidores; '~'**stairs 1.** escalera *f* de servicio; **2.** F por enchufe; por intriga; clandestino; '~·**stitch 1.** pespunte *m*; **2.** pespuntar; '~·**stop** reja *f* (*or* red *f*) para detener la pelota; '~-**stroke** arrastre *m* de espaldas; ~ **talk** F contestación *f* insolente; ~ **to back** dándose las espaldas; F sucesivamente; '~·**track** F volver pies atrás, retirarse.

back·ward ['bækwərd] **1.** *adj.* vuelto hacia atrás; *country, pupil* atrasado; *p.* (*shy*) retraído, corto; **2.** *adv.* (*a.* '**back·wards**) (hacia) atrás; al revés; ~*s and forwards* de acá para allá; '**back·ward·ness** atraso *m*; cortedad *f*.

back...: '~·**wa·ter** brazo *m* de río estancado; remanso *m*; *fig.* lugar *m* (*or* condición *f*) atrasado(a); '~-**woods** *pl.* región *f* apartada (*compare* Las Batuecas *in Spain*); '~-'**woods·man** patán *m*, hombre *m* de los *backwoods*; '~'**yard** patio *m* trasero, corral *m* trasero.

ba·con ['beikən] tocino *m*; F *save one's* ~ salvar el pellejo; *sl. bring home the* ~ sacarse el gordo.

bac·te·ri·al [bæk'tiriəl] □ bacteriano, bactérico; **bac·te·ri·o·log·i·cal** [bæktiəriə'lɔdʒikəl] □ bacteriológico; **bac·te·ri·ol·o·gist** [~'ɔlədʒist] bacteriólogo *m*; **bac'te·ri·um** [~iəm], *pl.* **bac'te·ri·a** [~iə] bacteria *f*.

bad [bæ:d] □ malo; infeliz, desgraciado; (*rotten etc.*) dañado, podrido; (*harmful*) nocivo, dañoso; ⚕ indispuesto, enfermo; *coin* falso; *debt* incobrable; F *not* ~ bastante bueno (*or* bien); F *not too* ~ así así; *things are not so* ~ las cosas van bastante bien; ~ *blood* mala sangre *f*; ~ *breath* mal aliento *m*; F *be in* ~ *with* tener enojada a una persona (*over* a causa de); *go* ~ (*food*) pasarse; *go to the* ~ caer en el mal; *look* ~ tener mala cara; F *he's a* ~ *one* [*freq.* ən] es un mal sujeto; *v.* *worse*; ~*ly adv.* mal; con urgencia; gravemente; ~*ly off* malparado; muy enfermo; *want* ~*ly* desear mucho; perderse por.

bade [beid] *pret. of bid.*

badge [bædʒ] insignia *f*, divisa *f*.

badg·er ['bædʒər] **1.** tejón *m*; **2.** molestar; fastidiar, acosar.

bad·i·nage [bædi'nɑ:ʒ] chanza *f*; guasa *f*.

bad·min·ton ['bædmintən] volante *m*.

bad·ness ['bædnis] maldad *f*; podredumbre *f*.

bad-tem·pered ['bæ:d'tempərd] de mal genio.

baf·fle ['bæfl] **1.** ⊕ (*a.* '~ *plate*) deflector *m*; *radio*: pantalla *f* acústica; **2.** frustrar, impedir; chasquear; desconcertar; *it* ~*s description* se escapa a la descripción; **baf·fling** ['bæfliŋ] perplejo; desconcertador.

bag 1. [bæ:g] maleta *f*; bolsa *f* (*a. zo.*, ⚕); (*hand*) bolso *m*; (*big*) saco *m*; (*shoulder*) zurrón *m*, mochila *f*; *hunt.* cacería *f* (de animales muertos de una vez); *diplomatic* ~ valija *f* diplomática; F ~*s pl.* pantalón *m*; F *it's in the* ~ es cosa segura; *pack* ~ *and baggage* tomar el tole; **2.** [bæg] *v/t.* ensacar; *sl.* coger, asegurarse; *hunt.* cazar; *v/i.* (*garment etc.*) hacer bolsa.

bag·a·telle [bægə'tel] bagatela *f*.

bag·gage ['bægidʒ] equipaje *m*; ⚔ bagaje *m*; *contp.* mujercilla *f*; fulana *f*; ~ *car* 🚃 furgón *m* de equipajes, vagón *m* de equipajes; ~ *check* contraseña *f* de equipajes, talón *m* de equipajes; ~ *rack* red *f* de equipajes; ~ *room* sala *f* de equipajes.

bag·gy ['bægi] holgado, que hace bolsa.

bag...: '~·**pipe** gaita *f*; '~·**snatch·er** ladrón *m* de bolsos, ratero (a *f*) *m*.

bail[1] [beil] ⚖ **1.** caución *f*, fianza *f*; ⚖ *admit to* ~ admitir a caución; *be* (*or go, stand*) ~ *for* salir fiador por; **2.** caucionar; ~ *out* poner en libertad bajo fianza.

bail[2] [~] ⚓ achicar.

bail[3] [~] *cricket*: travesaño *m* del rastrillo.

bail[4] [~] asa *f of kettle etc.*

bail·ee [bei'li:] ⚖ depositario *m*.

bail·iff ['beilif] ⚖ alguacil *m*, corchete *m*; mayordomo *m on estate*.

bail·ment ['beilmənt] ⚖ afianzamiento *m*; (*goods*) depósito *m*.

bail·or ['beilər] ⚖ depositador (-a *f*) *m*.

bairn [bern] *Scot.* niño (a *f*) *m.*
bait [beit] **1.** cebo *m*, carnada *f*; *fig.* aliciente *m*; (*deceitful*) señuelo *m*, añagaza *f*; *swallow the* ~ tragar el anzuelo; **2.** *trap etc.* poner cebo en; *dogs* azuzar; *horses on journey* dar pienso a; *fig.* acosar, atormentar.
bait·ing ['beitiŋ] acoso *m.*
baize [beiz] bayeta *f*; *green* ~ tapete *m* verde.
bake [beik] **1.** cocer al horno; *bricks etc.* cocer; endurecer; **2.** banquete *m* al aire libre; '**~·house** panadería *f*, tahona *f*.
ba·ke·lite ['beikəlait] baquelita *f.*
bak·er ['beikər] panadero *m*; **bak·er·y** panadería *f*; '**bak·ing** hornada *f*; cocción *f*; F *it's* ~ (*hot*) hace un calor sofocante; '**bak·ing pow·der** levadura *f* en polvo, polvos *m/pl.* de levadura, polvo *m* de hornear; '**bak·ing so·da** bicarbonato *m* de sosa.
bak·sheesh ['bækʃi:ʃ] propina *f.*
bal·a·lai·ka [bælə'laikə] balalaika *f.*
bal·ance ['bæləns] **1.** (*scales*) balanza *f*; equilibrio *m* (*a. fig.*); ✝ balance *m*; ✝ saldo *m of account etc.*; (*watch*) volante *m*; F resto *m*; ~ *in hand* ✝ alcance *m*; sobrante *m*; ~ *of payments* balance *m* de pagos; ~ *of power* equilibrio *m* político; ~ *of trade* balance *m* de comercio; *fig. in the* ~ en la balanza; *v. strike*; **2.** *v/t.* equilibrar; contrapesar (*with* con); ✝ saldar, finiquitar; *v/i.* equilibrarse, balancearse; menearse; ✝ ~ *up* finiquitar; '**~ sheet** ✝ balance *m*, avanzo *m.*
bal·co·ny ['bælkəni] balcón *m*, mirador *m*; *thea.* anfiteatro *m.*
bald [bɔ:ld] □ calvo; *countryside* pelado; *fig.* sin adornos, franco; escueto, desnudo.
bal·da·chin ['bɔ:ldəkin] baldaquín *m.*
bal·der·dash ['bɔ:ldədæʃ] galimatías *m*; disparate *m.*
bald...: '**~·head,** '**~·pate** calvo *m*; '**~'head·ed** calvo; F *go* ~ *into* meterse de ligero en; '**bald·ness** calvicie *f*; *fig.* desnudez *f.*
bal·dric ['bɔ:ldrik] tahalí *m.*
bale[1] [beil] ✝ **1.** fardo *m*, bala *f*; **2.** embalar.
bale[2] [~] ⚓ achicar; ✈ ~ *out* lanzarse en paracaídas.
bale·ful ['beilful] □ funesto; (*look*) triste.
balk [bɔ:k] **1.** ⚘ lomo *m* (entre surcos); *fig.* obstáculo *m*, estorbo *m*; (*timber*) viga *f*; (*billiards*) cabaña *f*; **2.** *v/t.* frustrar, impedir; perder, evitar; *v/i.* (*horse*) plantarse (*a. fig.*; *at* al ver), repropriarse.
Bal·kan ['bɔ:lkən] balcánico.
ball[1] [bɔ:l] **1.** bola *f*; globo *m*, esfera *f*; (*tennis etc.*) pelota *f*; (*football*) balón *m*; (*cannon*) bala *f*; (*wool*) ovillo *m*; *baseball*: tiro *m* falso; F *keep the* ~ *rolling* mantener en marcha (*esp.* la conversación); F *play* ~ cooperar (*with* con); **2.** convertir en bolas; *sl.* ~ *up* echarlo todo a rodar.
ball[2] [~] baile *m*; *dress* ~ baile *m* de etiqueta.
bal·lad ['bæləd] romance *m*; ♪ balada *f.*
ball-and-sock·et ['bɔ:lən'sɔkit]: ~ *joint* articulación *f* esférica.
bal·last ['bæləst] **1.** ⚓ lastre *m* (*a. fig.*); 🚂 balasto *m*; **2.** ⚓ lastrar; 🚂 balastar.
ball...: '**~ 'bear·ing** cojinete *m* a bolas; '**~ boy** mozo *m* que recoge las pelotas; '**~ car·tridge** cápsula *f* con bala; '**~ game** juego *m* de pelota; F béisbol *m.*
bal·let ['bælei] ballet *m*, baile *m.*
bal·lis·tics [bə'listiks] *mst sg.* balística *f.*
bal·loon [bə'lu:n] **1.** ⚗ *a.* ✈ globo *m*; *mot.* ~ *tire* llanta *f* balón; **2.** subir en un globo; ~ (*out*) hincharse como un globo; **bal'loon fab·ric** tela *f* de globo; **bal'loon·ist** ascensionista *m/f.*
bal·lot ['bælət] **1.** balota *f*, papeleta *f* (para votar); sufragio *m*; votación *f*; **2.** balotar, votar; ~ *for* determinar por balota; '**~ box** urna *f* electoral.
ball-point pen ['bɔ:lpɔint'pen] bolígrafo *m*, polígrafo *m*, pluma *f* esferográfica; *Arg.* birome *f*; *Bol.* punto *m* bola; *Col.* esfero *m.*
ball·room ['bɔ:lru:m] salón *m* de baile.
bal·ly·hoo [bæli'hu:] **1.** F alharaca *f*; bombo *m*; propaganda *f* sensacional; **2.** F dar bombo a.
balm [bɑ:m] bálsamo *m* (*a. fig.*).
balm·y ['bɑ:mi] □ balsámico, fragante; *sl.* chiflado.
ba·lo·ney [bə'louni] *sl.* sandez *f*, tontería *f.*
bal·sam ['bɔ:lsəm] bálsamo *m*; **bal·sam·ic** [~'sæmik] □ balsámico.
bal·us·ter ['bæləstər] balaustre *m.*

bal·us·trade [bæləs'treid] balaustrada *f*, barandilla *f*.
bam·boo [bæm'bu:] bambú *m*.
bam·boo·zle [bæm'bu:zl] F embaucar, capotear.
ban [bæn] **1.** bando *m*, edicto *m*; bando *m* de destierro; excomunión *f*; prohibición *f* (*on* de); **2.** prohibir; proscribir; excomulgar; ~ *a p. from a th.* prohibir a una p. (el uso de) algo.
ba·nan·a [bə'nænə] plátano *m*; banana *f S.Am.*; ~ *oil* esencia *f* de pera; *radio*: ~ *plug* clavija *f* con hembrilla.
band [bænd] **1.** banda *f* (*a. radio*), faja *f*; (*edge of garment*) cenefa *f*; (*hat-*) cintillo *m*; (*group*) cuadrilla *f*, gavilla *f*; ♪ banda *f*, música *f*; **2.** orlar; rayar *with stripes*; (*group*) apandillar(se), acuadrillarse; ~ *together* asociarse.
band·age ['bændidʒ] **1.** vendaje *m*, venda *f*; *first aid* ~ vendaje *m* provisional; **2.** vendar.
ban·dan·na [bæn'dænə] pañuelo *m* de hierbas.
band·box ['bændbɔks] caja *f* de cartón; *as if he came out of a* ~ aseadísimo, acicalado.
ban·dit ['bændit] bandido *m*; '**ban·dit·ry** bandolerismo *m*, bandidaje *m*.
band-mas·ter ['bændmæstər] director *m* de banda, músico *m* mayor.
ban·do·leer [bændə'lir] bandolera *f*.
bands·man ['bændzmən] músico *m* de banda; '**band·stand** quiosco *m* de música; '**band·wag·on** F *pol. a. fig.* partido *m* político que triunfa; *get* (*climb*) *on the* ~ adherirse al partido que gana.
ban·dy ['bændi] **1.** hockey *m* (sobre hielo) (*a.* '~ **ball**); **2.** *ball* pelotear, pasar de uno a otro; *words etc.* cambiar, trocar; *a. fig.* ~ *about* divulgar, esparcir; '~**-leg·ged** estevado.
bane [bein] azote *m*; ruina *f*; *it's the* ~ *of my life!* ¡causará mi perdición!; **bane·ful** ['beinful] ☐ funesto; nocivo.
bang [bæŋ] **1.** ¡pum!; **2.** F precisamente (~ *across etc.*); *sl.* ~ *on* acertado; **3.** detonación *f*; estallido *m*; golpe *m on head etc.*; contusión *f*; (*hair*) flequillo *m*; **4.** golpear, cerrar *etc.* con estrépito; cortar en flequillo; *sl. price* rebajar.
ban·gle ['bæŋgl] ajorca *f*.
bang-up ['bæŋ'ʌp] *sl.* de primera.
ban·ish ['bæniʃ] desterrar (*a. fig.*); '**ban·ish·ment** destierro *m*.
ban·is·ter ['bænistər] balaustre *m*; **ban·is·ters** ['~z] *pl.* barandilla *f*.
ban·jo ['bændʒou] banjo *m*.
bank [bæŋk] **1.** ribera *f*, orilla *f*, margen *f*; banda *f*, montón *m of clouds*; banco *m of sand*; (*hill*) loma *f*; batería *f of lamps*; hilera *f of oars*; ⚕ banco *m*; (*in games*) banca *f*; (*piggy-*) ~ hucha *f*, alcancía *f*; ~ *of deposit* banco *m* de depósito; ~ *of issue* banco *m* de emisión; **2.** *v/t. fire* cubrir (*a.* ~ *up*); *water* represar, estancar; *pile* amontonar (*a.* ~ *up*); ⚕ depositar; ✈ ladear; *v/i.* dedicarse a negocios de banca; depositar dinero (*with* en); ✈ ladearse; F ~ *on* contar con; '**bank·a·ble** recibidero (en un banco); '**bank ac·count** cuenta *f* de banco; '**bank bill** obligación *f* de banco; = *banknote*; '**bank book** libreta *f* (de depósitos); '**bank·er** banquero *m* (*a. in games*); '**bank hol·i·day** día *m* feriado en que están cerrados los bancos; '**bank·ing 1.** rampas *f/pl.*, terraplén *m*; ⚕ banca *f*; ✈ ladearse *m*; **2.** ⚕ bancario; '**bank·ing house** casa *f* de banca; '**bank·note** billete *m* de banco; '**bank rate** tipo *m* de interés (*or* descuento) bancario; '**bank roll** lío *m* de papel moneda; **bank·rupt** ['~rʌpt] **1.** quebrado *m*, fallido *m*; ~*'s estate* activo *m* de la quiebra; **2.** quebrado, insolvente; *fig.* ~ *in* (*or* ~ *of*) falto de; *go* ~ hacer bancarrota, quebrar; **3.** hacer quebrar, arruinar; **bank·rupt·cy** ['~rəptsi] bancarrota *f*, quiebra *f*; *declaration of* ~ declaración *f* de quiebra.
ban·ner ['bænər] **1.** bandera *f*, estandarte *m*; ~ *cry* grito *m* de combate; ~ *headlines pl.* titulares *m/pl.* sensacionales; **2.** *adj.* primero en dignidad.
banns [bænz] *pl.* amonestaciones *f/pl.* (de matrimonio); *call the* ~ amonestar, correr las amonestaciones.
ban·quet ['bæŋkwit] **1.** banquete *m*; **2.** banquetear (*v/i. a. v/t.*); ~*ing hall* comedor *m* de gala.
ban·shee [bæn'ʃi:] *Scot., Ir.* hada *f* que anuncia una muerte.
ban·tam ['bæntəm] gallinilla *f* (de) Bantam; *fig.* persona *f* de pequeña

talla y amiga de pelear; ˈ~**·weight** peso *m* gallo.
ban·ter [ˈbæntər] **1.** zumba *f*, chanza *f*; **2.** chancear(se con); burlar(se de); ˈ**ban·ter·er** zumbón (-a *f*) *m*.
bap·tism [ˈbæptizm] bautismo *m* (*a. fig.*); (*act*) bautizo *m*; **bap·tis·mal** [bæpˈtizməl] bautismal.
bap·tist [ˈbæptist] bautista *m*; (*sect*) baptista *m/f*; ˈ**bap·tis·ter·y** bautisterio *m*; **bap·tize** [~ˈtaiz] bautizar (*a. fig.*).
bar [bɑːr] **1.** barra *f* (*a.* ⚖ *a. heraldry*); vara *f*, varilla *f*; (*securing*) tranca *f*; (*window*) reja *f*; (*tavern*) bar *m*; (*counter*) mostrador *m*; (*river*) barra *f*; ♪ compás *m*; *fig.* impedimento *m* (*to* para); *fig.* tribunal *m of public opinion etc.*; *parallel* ~*s pl.* (barras) paralelas *f/pl.*; ~ *magnet* barra *f* imantada; ⚖ *be called to the* ~ recibirse de abogado; *behind* ~*s* entre rejas; ⚖ *prisoner at the* ~ acusado *m*; ⚖ *stand at the* ~ comparecer ante el tribunal (*a. fig.*); **2.** *door* atrancar; barrear; impedir, obstruir; prohibir; (*a.* ~ *out*) excluir; ~ *none* sin excepción.
barb [bɑːrb] lengüeta *f of arrow etc.*; *zo.* púa *f*; **barbed** armado de lengüetas (*or* púas); *fig.* incisivo, mordaz; ~ *wire* ⚔ alambre *m* de púas (de espino *for fences*).
bar·bar·i·an [bɑːrˈberiən] bárbaro *adj. a. su. m* (a *f*) (*a. fig.*); **bar·bar·ic** [~ˈbærik] □ barbárico; de ruda magnificencia; **bar·ba·rism** [ˈ~bərizm] barbarismo *m of language etc.*; barbarie *f*; **bar·bar·i·ty** [~ˈbæriti] barbaridad *f*; **bar·ba·rize** [ˈ~bəraiz] barbarizar; ˈ**bar·ba·rous** □ bárbaro.
bar·be·cue [ˈbɑːrbikjuː] barbacoa *f S.Am.*; *fiesta al aire libre en la que se come carne asada.*
bar·bel [ˈbɑːrbl] barbo *m*.
bar·ber [ˈbɑːrbər] barbero *m*, peluquero *m*; ~ *shop* peluquería *f*, barbería *f*.
bard [bɑːrd] bardo *m*.
bare [ber] **1.** □ desnudo; *head* descubierto; *landscape* pelado, raso; *clothes etc.* raído; *style* escueto; *room* con pocos muebles; desprovisto (*of* de); mero; *v. lay*; **2.** desnudar, descubrir; ˈ~**·back** montado en pelo; *adv.* en pelo, sin montura; ˈ**bare·faced** □ descarado, fresco; ˈ**bare·fac·ed·ness** descaro *m*, desfachatez *f*; ˈ**bareˈfoot·ed** descalzo; ˈ**bareˈhead·ed** descubierto; ˈ**bareˈlegged** en pernetas; ˈ**bare·ly** apenas, solamente; ˈ**bare·ness** desnudez *f* (*a. fig.*); desabrigo *m*.
bar·gain [ˈbɑːrgin] **1.** pacto *m*, convenio *m*; (*cheap th.*) ganga *f*; negocio *m* ventajoso (para el comprador); ~ *counter* baratillo *m*; ~ *price* precio *m* irrisorio; F *it's a* ~! ¡hecho!; *into the* ~ de añadidura; por más señas; *make* (*or strike*) *a* ~ cerrar un trato; *make the best of a bad* ~ poner a mal tiempo buena cara; **2.** negociar; F (*haggle*) regatear (*freq. away*); ~ *away* vender regalado; ~ *for* (*freq. with negative*) contar con.
barge [bɑːrdʒ] **1.** gabarra *f*, barcaza *f*; (*esp. ceremonial*) falúa *f*; **2.** F (*a.* ~ *about*) moverse pesadamente, dar tumbos; F ~ *in* entrar sin pedir permiso; irrumpir; F ~ *into* entrometerse en, inmiscuirse en; **barˈgee, ˈbarge·man** gabarrero *m*.
bar·i·tone [ˈbæritoun] barítono *m*.
bar·i·um [ˈberiəm] bario *m*.
bark[1] [bɑːrk] **1.** corteza *f*; ⊕ casca *f for tanning*; **2.** descortezar; *skin* raer.
bark[2] [~] **1.** ladrar (*a. fig.*: *at* a); ~ *up the wrong tree* tomar el rábano por las hojas; **2.** ladrido *m*; *sl.* tos *f*.
bark[3] [~] ⚓ *a. poet.* barca *f*.
bar·keep·er [ˈbɑːrkiːpər] tabernero *m*.
bar·ley [ˈbɑːrli] cebada *f*.
barm [bɑːrm] levadura *f* (de cerveza).
bar·maid [ˈbɑːrmeid] moza *f* de taberna.
bar·man [ˈbɑːrmən] *v. bartender*.
barm·y [ˈbɑːrmi] espumoso; *sl.* chiflado.
barn [bɑːrn] granero *m*, troje *f*; *esp.* establo *m*, cuadra *f*; ~ *owl* lechuza *f*, oliva *f*.
bar·na·cle [ˈbɑːrnəkl] *on boats* cirrópodo *m*; *orn.* bernicla *f*; *zo.* percebe *m*.
barn·storm [ˈbɑːrnstɔːrm] *Am. pol. ir por el campo pronunciando discursos políticos.*
barn·yard [ˈbɑːrnjɑːrd] corral *m*; ~ *fowl pl.* aves *f/pl.* de corral.
ba·rom·e·ter [bəˈrɔmitər] barómetro *m*; **bar·o·met·ric, bar·o·met·ri·cal** [bærəˈmetrik(l)] □ barométrico.

bar·on [ˈbærən] barón *m*; *fig*. potentado *m*; ~ *of beef* solomillo *m* doble (de carne de vaca); ˈ**bar·on·age** nobleza *f*; ˈ**bar·on·ess** baronesa *f*; **bar·on·et** [ˈ~it] baronet *m*; **bar·on·et·cy** [ˈ~si] título *m* de baronet; **ba·ro·ni·al** [bəˈrouniəl] baronial; **bar·o·ny** [ˈbærəni] baronía *f*.
ba·roque [bəˈrɔk] barroco *adj*. *a*. *su*. [*m*.]
barque [bɑːrk] barca *f*.
bar·rack [ˈbærək] **1.** (*mst* ~*s pl*.) cuartel *m*; F *approx*. caserón *m*; **2.** F mofarse de; ˈ~ **square,** ˈ~ **yard** plaza *f* de armas.
bar·rage [ˈbærɑːʒ] (*water*) presa *f*; ⚔ barrera *f* de fuego; ~ *balloon* globo *m* de barrera; *creeping* ~ barrera *f* de fuego móvil.
bar·rel [ˈbærl] **1.** tonel *m*, cuba *f*; (*gun*, *pen*) cañón *m*; (*capstan*, *watch*) cilindro *m*; ⊕ tambor *m*; **2.** embarrilar, entonelar; ˈ**bar·rel or·gan** ♪ organillo *m*.
bar·ren [ˈbærən] □ estéril; árido; *fig*. infructuoso; ˈ**bar·ren·ness** esterilidad *f*; aridez *f*.
bar·ri·cade [ˈbærikeid] **1.** barricada *f*; **2.** barrear, cerrar con barricadas.
bar·ri·er [ˈbæriər] barrera *f* (*a*. *fig*.); ✝ fielato *m*; ~ *reef* barrera *f* de arrecifes.
bar·ring [ˈbɑːriŋ] F excepto, salvo.
bar·ris·ter [ˈbæristər] (*a*. ~-*at-law*) *British*: *abogado que tiene derecho a alegar en los tribunales superiores*.
bar·row[1] [ˈbærou] carretilla *f*; carreta *f*.
bar·row[2] [~] *hist*. túmulo *m*.
bar·tend·er [ˈbɑːrtendər] tabernero *m*, barman *m*.
bar·ter [ˈbɑːrtər] **1.** permutación *f*, trueque *m* (de bienes); **2.** trocar, permutar (*for* por, con); *b.s*. (*mst* ~ *away*) derrochar, malvender.
ba·salt [ˈbəsɔːlt] basalto *m*; **ba·sal·tic** [bəˈsɔːltik] basáltico.
base[1] [beis] □ bajo, humilde; vil, ruin; infame; *metals* bajo de ley.
base[2] [~] **1.** base *f*; ⚠ basa *f*; **2.** basar, fundar ([*up*]*on* en; *a*. *fig*.); ✈ aterrizar; ~ *o.s. on* apoyarse en; *be* ~*d* [*up*]*on* estribar en, basarse en.
base...: ˈ~**·ball** béisbol *m*; ˈ~**·less** infundado; ˈ~**·line** *surv*. línea *f* de base; *tennis*: línea *f* de saque; ˈ**base·ment** sótano *m*.
base·ness [ˈbeisnis] bajeza *f*, vileza *f* *etc*. (*v*. *base*[1]).
bash·ful [ˈbæʃful] □ tímido, encogido; vergonzoso.
bas·ic [ˈbeisik] **1.** □ fundamental; 🜍 básico; 𝟐 *English* (= *British*, *American*, *Scientific*, *International*, *Commercial English*) inglés *m* básico; ~ *commodities pl*. artículos *m*/*pl*. de primera necesidad; ~ *slag* escoria *f* básica; **2.** ~*s pl*. asuntos *m*/*pl*. básicos.
ba·sil·i·ca [bəˈzilikə] basílica *f*.
bas·i·lisk [ˈbæzilisk] basilisco *m*.
ba·sin [ˈbeisn] (*small*) escudilla *f*, cuenca *f*; (*wash*) jofaina *f*; (*river*) cuenca *f*; (*port*) dársena *f*; (*fountain*) taza *f*.
ba·sis [ˈbeisis], *pl*. **ba·ses** [ˈ~iːz] base *f*, fundamento *m*; *on the* ~ *of* a base de.
bask [bæsk] asolcarse, tomar el sol.
bas·ket [ˈbæskit] cesta *f*; (*big*) cesto *m*; (*with two handles*) canasta *f*; ˈ~**·ball** baloncesto *m*, basquetbol *m*; ~ **din·ner,** ~ **sup·per** *approx*. comida *f* campestre; ˈ**bas·ket·ful** cestada *f*; ˈ**bas·ket·work** cestería *f*.
Basque [bæsk] **1.** vasco *adj*. *a*. *su*. *m* (*a f*); **2.** (*language*) vascuence *m*.
bas-re·lief [beisriˈliːf] bajorrelieve *m*.
bass[1] [beis] ♪ bajo *m*.
bass[2] [bæs] corteza *f* de tilo; ~ *wood* tilo *m* americano.
bas·si·net [bæsiˈnet] cuna *f* hecha de mimbres.
bas·so [ˈbæsou]: ~ *profundo* bajo *m* profundo.
bas·soon [bəˈsuːn] bajón *m*.
bas·tard [ˈbæstərd] □ bastardo *adj*. *a*. *su*. *m* (*a f*); ˈ**bas·tar·dy** bastardía *f*.
baste[1] [beist] *sew*. hilvanar.
baste[2] [~] *joint* pringar; F dar de palos.
bas·tion [ˈbæstiən] baluarte *m* (*a*. [*fig*.).]
bat[1] [bæt] *zo*. murciélago *m*; *blind as a* ~ más ciego que un topo.
bat[2] [~] **1.** *sport*: maza *f*; *off one's own* ~ sin ayuda; de suyo; F *right off the* ~ de repente, sin deliberación; **2.** golpear (con un palo *etc*.); F *come* (*or go*) *to* ~ *for* ayudar.
bat[3] [~] guiñar; *without* ~*ting an eye* sin emoción, sin pestañear, sin inmutarse.
batch [bætʃ] *cooking*: hornada *f*; colección *f*, grupo *m*; (*set*) tanda *f*; lío *m* *of papers*.
bate [beit] disminuir; *price* rebajar; *with* ~*d breath* con aliento suspenso.

Bath[1] [bæθ]: ~ *brick* piedra *f* para limpiar cuchillos; ~ *chair* silla *f* de ruedas.
bath[2] [bæθ] (*pl.* **baths** [bæðz]) baño *m*; piscina *f for swimming*; *fig. blood* ~ carnicería *f*; *take a* ~ tomar un baño.
bathe [beið] bañar(se); **ˈ~r** [~ər] bañista *m*/*f*.
bath·ing [ˈbeiθiŋ] **1.** baño *m*; **2.** *attr.* de baño; ~ *beach* playa *f* de baños; ~ *beauty* sirena *f* de la playa; ~ *cap* gorro *m* de baño; ~ *resort* estación *f* balnearia; ~ *suit* traje *m* de baño, bañador *m*; ~ *trunks pl.* taparrabo *m*; **3.** *go* ~ ir a bañarse.
ba·thos [ˈbeiθɔs] paso *m* de lo sublime a lo ridículo (*or* trivial).
bath...: **ˈ~·house** casa *f* de baños; caseta *f* de baños; **ˈ~·robe** albornoz *m*, bata *f* de baño; bata *f*, peinador *m*; **ˈ~·room** baño *m*, cuarto *m* de baño; ~ *fixtures pl.* aparatos *m*/*pl.* sanitarios; **ˈ~ salts** *pl.* sales *f*/*pl.* de baño; **ˈ~ tow·el** toalla *f* de baño; **ˈ~·tub** bañera *f*, bañadera *f*, baño *m*.
ba·tiste [bæˈtiːst] batista *f*.
bat·man [ˈbætmən] ordenanza *m*.
ba·ton [bæˈtɑːn] ⚔ bastón *m*; ♪ batuta *f*.
ba·tra·chi·an [bəˈtreikjən] batracio *adj. a. su. m*.
bat·tal·ion [bəˈtæljən] batallón *m*.
bat·ten [ˈbætn] **1.** alfarjía *f*, lata *f*, listón *m*; **2.** listonar; asegurar con listones (⚓ *a.* ~ *down*); *esp. fig.* ~ *on* cebarse en.
bat·ter [ˈbætər] **1.** pasta *f*, batido *m*; *sport*: bateador *m*; **2.** apalear; magullar; ⚔ cañonear; *fig.* criticar severamente; ~ *down*, ~ *in door etc.* derribar; **ˈbat·tered** [~tərd] apaleado; *fig.* ajado; **ˈbat·ter·ing** paliza *f*; castigo *m*; ~ *ram* ariete *m*; **ˈbat·ter·y** ⚔, ⚡, *baseball*: batería *f*; ⚡ pila *f*, acumulador *m*; ⚖ violencia *f* (*esp. assault and* ~); **ˈbat·ter·y charg·er** cargador *m* de acumulador.
bat·tle [ˈbætl] **1.** batalla *f*; combate *m*; ~ *royal* pelotera *f*; *do* ~ librar batalla; **2.** batallar (*against* contra; *with* con); luchar (*for* por); **ˈ~-axe** hacha *f* de combate; *fig. old* ~ mujer *f* severa.
bat·tle·dore [ˈbætldɔːr] raqueta *f* (*en el juego de volante*); ~ *and shuttlecock* raqueta *f* y volante.
bat·tle...: **ˈ~ dress** traje *m* de campaña; **ˈ~·field** campo *m* de batalla; **ˈ~·front** frente *m* de combate; **ˈ~·ground** campo *m* de batalla; **ˈ~·ments** [ˈbætlmənts] *pl.* almenas *f*/*pl.*; **ˈ~·ship** acorazado *m*.
bat·tue [bæˈtuː] *hunt.* batida *f*.
bau·ble [ˈbɔːbl] chuchería *f*.
baulk [bɔːk] *v. balk*.
baux·ite [ˈbɔːksait] bauxita *f*.
Ba·var·i·an [bəˈveriən] bávaro *adj. a. su. m* (a *f*).
baw·bee [bɔːˈbiː] *Scot.* = *halfpenny*.
bawd [bɔːd] alcahueta *f*; **ˈbawd·y** □ obsceno, impúdico.
bawl [bɔːl] *v*/*i.* vocear, desgañitarse (*freq.* ~ *out*); ~ *at s.o.* reñir a una p. en voz alta; *v*/*t.* F ~ *out* reñir, regañar.
bay[1] [bei] *horse* (caballo *m*) bayo *approx.*
bay[2] [~] ⚓ bahía *f*, abra *f*; (*large*) golfo *m*; ~ *salt* sal *f* morena.
bay[3] [~] ⚠ crujía *f*; ⛪ nave *f*.
bay[4] [~] ⚘ laurel *m*; ~ *rum* ron *m* de laurel, ron de malagueta.
bay[5] [~] **1.** ladrar, aullar; **2.** ladrido *m*, aullido *m*; *at* ~ acosado, acorralado; *keep at* ~ mantener a raya.
bay·o·net [ˈbeiənit] **1.** bayoneta *f*; **2.** herir (*or* matar) con la bayoneta.
bay win·dow [ˈbei ˈwindou] ventana *f* salediza, mirador *m*; *sl.* barriga *f*.
ba·zaar [bəˈzɑːr] bazar *m*.
ba·zoo·ka [bəˈzuːkə] bazuca *f*.
be [biː; bi] [*irr.*]: a) ser; estar; encontrarse; haber; existir; *he is a doctor* es médico; (*location*) *he is in Madrid* está en Madrid; (*temporary state*) *he is ill* está (*or* se encuentra) enfermo; *there is, there are* hay; *so be it* (*or be it so*) así sea; *be that as it may* sea como fuere; b) *auxiliary verb with present participle*: *I am working* trabajo, estoy trabajando; *he is coming tomorrow* viene mañana; c) *auxiliary verb with inf.*: *I am to go to Spain* he de ir a España; d) *auxiliary verb with p.p.*: ser, estar, quedar; *passive* (*action*): *he was followed by the police* fue seguido por la policía; *passive* (*state*): *the door is closed* la puerta está (*or* queda) cerrada; e) *idioms*: *mother to* ~ futura madre *f*; *my wife to* ~ mi futura (esposa); f) *for phrases with prp.*, *v. the prp.*
beach [biːtʃ] **1.** playa *f*; ~ *robe* albornoz *m*; ~ *shoe* playera *f*; ~ *umbrella* sombrilla *f* de playa; ~ *wagon* rubia *f*,

coche *m* rural; **2.** *v/t.* ⚓ varar; **'~-comb** raquear; *go ~ing* andar al raque; **'~·comb·er** raquero *m*; **'~-head** ⚔ cabeza *f* de playa.

bea·con ['bi:kn] **1.** almenara *f*, alcandora *f*; faro *m*; (*hill*) hacho *m*; *fig.* amonestación *f*, guía *f*; **2.** iluminar, guiar.

bead [bi:d] **1.** cuenta *f*, abalorio *m*; gota *f*; (*gun*) mira *f* globular; *~s pl.* sarta *f* de cuentas; rosario *m*; *tell one's ~s* rezar el rosario; **2.** *v/t.* adornar con abalorios; *v/i.* burbujear; **'bead·ing** abalorio *m*; △ astrágalo *m*, contero *m*.

bea·dle ['bi:dl] bedel *m*; *eccl.* pertiguero *m*.

bead·y ['bi:di] adornado con abalorios; burbujeante; *esp. eyes* que tienen apariencia de gotas.

beak [bi:k] pico *m*; nariz *f* (corva *esp.*); ⚓ rostro *m*; *sl.* magistrado *m*; **'beaked** picudo.

beak·er ['bi:kər] taza *f* grande; ⚗ probeta *f* con pico.

beam [bi:m] **1.** △ viga *f*; ⚓ bao *m*; ⚓ (*width*) manga *f*; (*plow*) timón *m*; ⚡ *etc. a. fig.* rayo *m*; (*balance*) astil *m*; ⊕ balancín *m*; *on her ~ ends* ⚓ a punto de volcar; F *fig. on one's ~ ends* sin blanca; F *on the ~* siguiendo el buen camino; **2.** brillar; *fig.* sonreír alegremente.

bean [bi:n] ⚘ haba *f*; judía *f*; *sl.* cabeza *f*; F *full of ~s* rebosando de vitalidad; **~ pole** ['~'poul] rodrigón *m* para frijoles; F (*tall, skinny person*) poste *m* de telégrafo.

bear[1] [ber] **1.** oso *m*; *fig.* hombre *m* ceñudo; ✝ bajista *m/f*; ✝ *~ market* mercado *m* bajista; **2.** ✝ jugar a la baja; ✝ hacer bajar el valor.

bear[2] [~] [*irr.*] *v/t.* llevar; (*endure*) soportar, aguantar; *arms, date, inscription, name* llevar; *interest* devengar; *love etc.* sentir, tener; *weight* cargar, sostener; *child* parir; *inspection etc.* tolerar, sufrir; *fruit etc.* rendir, producir; *costs etc.* pagar, costear; *~ away* llevarse; ganarse; *~ down* postrar; *~ o.s.* comportarse; *~ out* confirmar, apoyar; *v/i.* dirigirse (a); ⚓ *the ship ~s north* el barco lleva dirección norte; ⚓ *~ down upon* correr sobre; caer sobre; *~ (up)on* atañer a; F *~ up* cobrar ánimo; *~ with* tener paciencia con; *bring to ~ pressure etc.* ejercer ([*up*] *on* sobre); **'~·a·ble** □ llevadero.

beard [bird] **1.** barba *f*; ⚘ arista *f*; **2.** hacer cara a; retar; **'beard·ed** barbudo; ⚘ aristado; **'beard·less** imberbe, lampiño.

bear·er ['berər] portador (-a *f*) *m* (*a.* ✝); ⚘ árbol *m* fructífero; poseedor (-a *f*) *m of office*.

bear·ing ['beriŋ] aguante *m*; sustentamiento *m*; *p.'s* porte *m*, modales *m/pl.*; *heraldry*: blasón *m*; aspecto *m of th.*; relación *f* (*on* con); ⚓ marcación *f*; ⊕ cojinete *m*, apoyo *m*; *take one's ~s* ⚓ marcarse; *fig.* orientarse; *lose one's ~s* desorientarse.

bear·ish ['beriʃ] ✝ bajista; **'bear-skin** piel *f* de oso; (*military cap*) morrión *m*.

beast [bi:st] bestia *f*; *fig.* hombre *m* brutal; *fig.* persona *f* molesta; F *th.* cosa *f* mala (*or* molesta); *~ of burden* bestia *f* de carga; F *a ~ of a th.* molesto, pesado; **'beast·li·ness** bestialidad *f*; **'beast·ly** bestial; F molesto, desagradable.

beat [bi:t] **1.** [*irr.*] *v/t.* batir, golpear, pegar; (*defeat*) vencer; *record* batir, superar; F sobrepasar, aventajar; F *p.* confundir; *path* abrir; *hunt.* ojear; *drum* tocar; *carpet* apalear; ♪ *time* llevar; *v. retreat*; *sl. ~ it!* ¡lárgate!; F *to ~ the band* hasta más no poder; F *~ one's way* hacer un viaje sin pagar; *~ down* abatir; ✝ *price* rebajar; *~ off* rechazar; *~ up egg* batir; *sl. p.* aporrear; *v/i.* batir; (*heart*) latir; ⚓ *~ about* barloventear; F *~ about the bush* andarse por las ramas, ir por rodeos; **2.** golpe *m*; (*heart*) latido *m*; (*rhythm*) marca *f*; ♪ compás *m*; (*police*) ronda *f*; *off (outside) my ~* fuera de mi competencia; **3.** F deslumbrado, perplejo; engañado; *dead ~ sl.* rendido; **'beat·en** *p.p. of beat* 1; *track* trillado; *~ path* camino *m* trillado; **'beat·er** *hunt.* ojeador *m*.

be·at·i·fi·ca·tion [bi:ætifi'keiʃn] beatificación *f*; **be'at·i·fy** beatificar; **be'at·i·tude** [~tju:d] beatitud *f*; *the* ♀*s pl.* las Bienaventuranzas.

beau [bou] galán *m*; *b.s.* petimetre *m*; *~ ideal* lo bello ideal.

beau·ti·cian [bju:'tiʃən] embellecedora *f*, esteta *m/f*, esteticista *m/f*.

beau·ti·ful ['bju:təful] □ hermoso, bello; *~ly* F maravillosamente, muy bien.

beau·ti·fy ['bju:tifai] embellecer.

beau·ty ['bju:ti] belleza *f*, hermosura

f; (*woman*) beldad *f*; F *it's a* ~ es bárbaro; *sleeping* 2 la Bella Durmiente (del bosque); ~ *contest* concurso *m* de belleza; ~ *parlor* salón *m* de belleza; ~ *queen* reina *f* de la belleza; ~ *spot* (*face*) lunar *m* postizo; (*place*) sitio *m* pintoresco.

bea·ver [ˈbiːvər] *zo.* castor *m*; (*helmet*) babera *f*; (*hat*) sombrero *m* de copa.

be·bop [ˈbiːbɔp] *variación sobre el jazz tradicional.*

be·calm [biˈkɑːm] sosegar; ⚓ *be* ~*ed* encalmarse.

be·came [biˈkeim] *pret. of become.*

be·cause [biˈkɔːz] porque; ~ *of* a causa de.

beck [bek] seña *f*; *at the* ~ *and call of* a disposición de.

beck·on [ˈbekn] hacer seña (*to* a); llamar con señas; *fig.* atraer.

be·come [biˈkʌm] [*irr.* (*come*)] *v/i.* ser, hacerse (*of* de); *what will* ~ *of me?* ¿ qué será de mí?; *v/t. mst with su.* hacerse; *mst with adj.* ponerse; llegar a ser; convertirse en; (*action*) convenir a; (*clothes esp.*) sentar a, favorecer; **beˈcom·ing** □ decoroso; *clothes* que sienta bien.

bed [bed] **1.** cama *f*; (*a. animals*) lecho *m*; (*river*) cauce *m*; 🌱 macizo *m*, arriate *m*; ⊕ base *f*, apoyo *m*; *geol.* capa *f*, yacimiento *m*; ~ *and board* comida *f* y casa; ~ *jacket* mañanica *f*; *be brought to* ~ *of* parir; F *get up on the wrong side of the* ~ levantarse por los pies de la cama; *go to* ~ acostarse; *make the* ~ hacer la cama; *stay in* ~ guardar cama; *take to* (*one's*) ~ encamarse; **2.** acostar; ⊕ engastar, embutir; 🌱 ~ (*out*) plantar en un macizo.

be·daub [biˈdɔːb] embadurnar.

be·dazzle [biˈdæzl] deslumbrar.

bed·bug [ˈbedbʌg] chinche *f*.

bed·clothes [ˈbedklouðz] *pl.* ropa *f* de cama.

bed·ding [ˈbediŋ] ropa *f* de cama; colchón *m*; (*animals*) lecho *m*.

be·deck [biˈdek] acicalar, engalanar.

be·dev·il [biˈdevl] endiablar (*a. fig.*); hechizar; **beˈdev·il·ment** hechizo *m*; confusión *f*.

be·dew [biˈdjuː] *poet.* rociar.

bed·fel·low [ˈbedfelou] compañero *m* de cama.

be·dim [biˈdim] oscurecer.

bed·lam [ˈbedləm] manicomio *m*; *fig.* belén *m*.

bed·lin·en [ˈbedlinin] ropa *f* de cama; las sábanas.

Bed·ou·in [ˈbeduin] beduino *adj. a. su. m* (a *f*).

bed·pan [ˈbedpæn] silleta *f*.

bed·post [ˈbedpoust] pilar *m* de cama.

be·dragg·le [biˈdrægl] ensuciar; *clothes etc.* manchar.

bed...: ˈ~**·rid**(**·den**) postrado en cama; ˈ~**·ˈrock** *geol.* lecho *m* de roca; *fig.* fundamento *m*; ˈ~**·room** dormitorio *m*, alcoba *f*; ˈ~**·side:** *at the* ~ *of* a la cabecera de; *good* ~ *manner* mano *f* izquierda, diplomacia *f*; ~ *table* mesa *f* de noche; ˈ~**·ˈsit·ting-room** (F ˈ~-ˈ**sit·ter**) salón *m* con cama; ˈ~**·sore** úlcera *f* de decúbito; ˈ~**·spread** colcha *f*, sobrecama *m*; ˈ~**·stead** cuja *f*; ˈ~**·straw** cuajaleche *m*, amor *m* de hortelano; ˈ~**·tick** cutí *m*; ˈ~**·time** hora *f* de acostarse; ˈ~ **warm·er** calientacamas *m*.

bee [biː] abeja *f*; *fig.* reunión *f*; F *have a* ~ *in one's bonnet* tener una idea fija.

beech [biːtʃ] haya *f*; ˈ~**·nut** hayuco *m*.

beef [biːf] **1.** carne *f* de vaca; F fuerza *f* muscular; **2.** F quejarse; ˈ~**·eat·er** alabardero *m* de la Torre de Londres; ~**·steak** [ˈbiːfˈsteik] biftec *m*, bistec *m*; ˈ~ ˈ**tea** caldo *m* concentrado de carne; ˈ**beef·y** fornido; carnoso.

bee...: ˈ~**·hive** colmena *f*; ˈ~**·keep·er** colmenero *m*; ˈ~**·keep·ing** apicultura *f*; ˈ~ˈ**line** línea *f* recta *gen. in make a* ~ *for* ir en línea recta hacia.

been [biːn, bin] *p.p. of be.*

beer [bir] cerveza *f*; *dark* ~ cerveza *f* parda, cerveza negra; *light* ~ cerveza *f* clara; *small* ~ cerveza floja; F bagatela *f*; ˈ**beer·y** F de cerveza; alcohólico.

bees·wax [ˈbiːzwæks] cera *f* (de abejas).

beet [biːt] remolacha *f*; *v. sugar* ~.

bee·tle[1] [biːtl] ⊕ **1.** pisón *m*; **2.** apisonar.

beet·le[2] [~] *zo.* escarabajo *m*.

bee·tle[3] [~] **1.** (sobre)saliente; ceñudo; ~*-browed* cejijunto; (*sullen*) ceñudo; **2.** sobresalir.

beet·root [ˈbiːtruːt] raíz *f* de remolacha.

beet sug·ar [ˈbiːt ʃugər] azúcar *m* de remolacha.

be·fall [biˈfɔːl] [*irr.* (*fall*)] *v/t.* acontecer a, acaecer a; *v/i.* acontecer; **beˈfall·en** *p.p. of befall.*

be·fit [biˈfit] cuadrar a, convenir a; **be·fit·ting** □ propio, conveniente.
be·fog [biˈfɔg] aneblar; *fig.* ofuscar.
be·fore [biˈfɔːr] **1.** *adv.* (*place*) (a)delante; *go* ~ ir adelante; ~ *and behind* por delante y por detrás; (*time*) antes; anteriormente; **2.** *cj.* antes (de) que; **3.** *prp.* (*place*) delante de; *judge etc.* ante; (*time*) antes de; *be* (*or go*) ~ *a p.* ir delante de una p., ir primero; **beˈfore·hand** de antemano; *be* ~ *with* anticipar.
be·foul [biˈfaul] ensuciar, emporcar.
be·friend [biˈfrend] ofrecer amistad a; patrocinar.
beg [beg] *v/t.* suplicar, rogar (*of* a); (*as beggar*) mendigar; *v. pardon, question*; *v/i.* mendigar, pordiosear; rogar (*for a th. acc.*; *of a p.* a); *fig. go* ~*ging* ofrecerse algo sin presentarse aceptador ninguno; ✝ *I* ~ *to inform you...* tengo el gusto de informarle...
be·gan [biˈgæn] *pret. of begin.*
be·get [biˈget] [*irr.* (get)] engendrar (*a. fig.*); **beˈget·ter** engendrador *m.*
beg·gar [ˈbegər] **1.** mendigo (a *f*) *m*, pordiosero (a *f*) *m*; F *contp.* tio *m*; **2.** empobrecer; *fig.* excederse de; *it* ~*s description* supera a toda descripción; **ˈbeg·gar·ly** indigente; mezquino; **ˈbeg·gar·y** mendicidad *f*; miseria *f*; *reduce to* ~ reducir a la miseria.
be·gin [biˈgin] [*irr.*] comenzar, empezar (*to* a); iniciar; ~ *by* comenzar por; ~ *on s.t.* emprender algo; ~ *with* comenzar con, principiar con; *to* ~ *with* para empezar; en primer lugar; ~*ning from date* a partir de; **beˈgin·ner** principiante *m/f*; **beˈgin·ning** comienzo *m*, principio *m*; *from* ~ *to end* del principio al fin, de cabo a rabo (F).
be·gone [biˈgɔn] † ¡fuera!; ¡aléjate!
be·go·ni·a [biˈgounjə] begonia *f.*
be·got [biˈgɔt] *pret. a. p.p. of* beget; **be·got·ten** [biˈgɔtn] *p.p. of* beget; *the only* ♀ *Son* El Unigénito.
be·grime [biˈgraim] embadurnar, embarrar; tiznar *with soot etc.*
be·grudge [biˈgrʌdʒ] dar de mala gana; (*envy*) envidiar.
be·guile [biˈgail] engañar, seducir; *fig.* entretener; ~ *into* inducir (por engaño) en *acc.*, a *inf.*
be·gun [biˈgʌn] *p.p. of begin.*
be·half [biˈhæf]: *on* ~ *of* a favor de, en nombre de; por.
be·have [biˈheiv] (com)portarse; ⊕ *etc.* funcionar, actuar; ~ *o.s.* portarse bien; **beˈhav·ior** [~jər] conducta *f*, comportamiento *m*; ⊕ *etc.* funcionamiento *m*; **beˈhav·ior·ism** behaviorismo *m.*
be·head [biˈhed] descabezar; decapitar.
be·held [biˈheld] *pret. a. p.p. of* [*behold.*]
be·hest [biˈhest] orden *f.*
be·hind [biˈhaind] **1.** *adv.* (por) detrás; (hacia) atrás; *be* ~ (*late*) retrasarse; F *be a bit* ~ estar un poco atrasadillo; **2.** *prp.* detrás de; **beˈhind·hand** con retraso, retrasado.
be·hold [biˈhould] [*irr.* (*hold*)] *lit.* **1.** contemplar; advertir, columbrar; **2.** ¡he aquí!; ¡mira(d)!; **beˈhold·en** obligado; **beˈhold·er** observador (-a *f*) *m.*
be·hove [biˈhouv]: *it* ~*s a p. to inf.* incumbe a una p. *inf.*
beige [beiʒ] **1.** beige *m*; **2.** color de beige, amarillento.
be·ing [ˈbiːiŋ] ser *m*; existencia *f*; *in* ~ existente; *come into* ~ producirse; nacer.
be·jew·eled [biˈdʒuːəld] enjoyado.
be·la·bor [biˈleibər] apalear; *fig.* zurrar.
be·la·ted [biˈleitid] □ demorado, tardío.
be·lay [biˈlei] **1.** [*irr.*] ⚓ amarrar a una cabilla *or* hierro; **2.** *mount.* atadura *f.*
belch [beltʃ] **1.** eructar, regoldar; *fig.* echar, arrojar; **2.** eructación *f*, regüeldo *m.*
bel·dam [ˈbeldəm] *fig.* bruja *f.*
be·lea·guer [biˈliːgər] sitiar.
bel·fry [ˈbelfri] campanario *m.*
Bel·gian [ˈbeldʒən] belga *adj. a. su. m/f.*
be·lie [biˈlai] desmentir.
be·lief [biˈliːf] creencia *f*, crédito *m*; fe *f* (*in* en; *that* de que); (*opinion*) parecer *m*; *past all* ~ increíble; *to the best of my* ~ según mi leal saber y entender.
be·liev·a·ble [biˈliːvəbl] creíble.
be·lieve [biˈliːv] creer (*in* en); ~ *in story etc.* dar crédito a; F (*not*) ~ *in e.g. drink* (no) aprobar; *don't you* ~ *it!* ¡no lo crea(s)!; **beˈliev·er** creyente *m/f*; F partidario (a *f*) *m* (*in* de).

be·lit·tle [biˈlitl] *fig.* deprimir, despreciar.
bell [bel] campana *f*; (*hand*) campanilla *f* (*a.* ♀); (*electric*) timbre *m*; (*animal's*) cencerro *m*; cascabel *m*; ♪ pabellón *m of trumpet etc.*; *fig. that rings a* ~ eso me suena.
bell·boy [ˈbelbɔi] botones *m*.
belle [bel] beldad *f*, guapetona *f*.
belles-let·tres [ˈbelˈletr] bellas letras *f/pl*.
bell...: ˈ**~·flow·er** campanilla *f*; ˈ**~ found·er** ⊕ campanero *m*; ˈ**~ glass** campana *f* de cristal; ˈ**~·hop** *sl.* botones *m*.
bel·li·cose [ˈbelikous] belicoso; **bel·li·cos·i·ty** [~ˈkɔsiti] belicosidad *f*.
bel·lied [ˈbelid] panzudo; convexo, combado.
bel·lig·er·ent [biˈlidʒərənt] □ beligerante *adj. a. su. m/f*; **bel·lig·er·en·cy** beligerancia *f*.
bel·low [ˈbelou] **1.** bramar; (*p.*) gritar, dar voces; **2.** bramido *m*.
bel·lows [ˈbelouz] *pl.* (*a pair of* un) fuelle *m* (*a. phot.*); (*forge*) barquín *m*.
bell...: ˈ**~ ring·er** campanero *m*; ˈ**~ rope** cuerda *f* de campana; ˈ**~-shaped** acampanado.
bel·ly [ˈbeli] **1.** vientre *f*; barriga *f* (*a. of vessel*); *~ache sl.* dolor *m* de barriga; *v/i. sl.* quejarse; *~ button* F ombligo *m*; *~ dance* F danza *f* del vientre; *~-land* ✈ aterrizar de panza; **2.** combarse; (*sail*) hacer bolso; ˈ**bel·ly·ful** [~ful] *sl.* panzada *f*; F *have had a ~* estar harto ya (*of* de).
be·long [biˈlɔŋ] pertenecer (*to* a); corresponder (*to* a); **beˈlong·ings** [~iŋz] *pl.* efectos *m/pl.*, bártulos *m/pl.*; F cosas *f/pl*.
be·lov·ed [biˈlʌvid] querido *adj. a. su. m* (a *f*).
be·low [biˈlou] **1.** *adv.* abajo, debajo; *here ~* en este mundo; **2.** *prp.* debajo de; *fig.* inferior a.
belt [belt] **1.** cinturón *m* (*a.* ⚔), cinto *m*; (*corset*) faja *f*; ⊕ correa *f*, cinta *f*; *fig.* zona *f*; *fig. below the ~* sucio, suciamente; *fig. tighten one's ~* ceñirse; **2.** *sl.* golpear con correa.
bel·ve·dere [ˈbelvidir] belvedere *m* (en forma de torre).
be·moan [biˈmoun] lamentar.
be·muse [biˈmju:z] aturdir.
bench [ben(t)ʃ] banco *m* (*a.* ⊕); ⚖ tribunal *m*; ⚖ judicatura *f*; *be on the ~* ser juez (*or* magistrado); *v. treasury*; ˈ**bench·er** *approx.* decano *m* de los colegios de abogados.
bend [bend] **1.** curva *f*; recodo *m*, curva *f in road*; ⚓ gaza *f*; F *the ~s pl.* enfermedad *f* de los cajones de aire comprimido; F *go round the ~* volverse loco; **2.** [*irr.*] combar(se), encorvar(se); *body etc.* inclinar(se); *efforts etc.* dirigir (*to* a); *sail* envergar.
beneath [biˈni:θ] = *below*; *fig. ~ me* indigno de mí; *she married ~ her* se casó con hombre de clase inferior.
Ben·e·dic·tine [beniˈdiktain] benedictino *adj. a. su. m* (*a. liqueur* [~ti:n]).
ben·e·dic·tion [beniˈdikʃn] bendición *f*.
ben·e·fac·tion [beniˈfækʃn] beneficencia *f*; (*gift*) beneficio *m*; ˈ**ben·e·fac·tor** bienhechor *m*; ˈ**ben·e·fac·tress** bienhechora *f*.
ben·e·fice [ˈbenifis] beneficio *m*; **be·nef·i·cence** [biˈnefisns] beneficencia *f*; **beˈnef·i·cent** □ benéfico.
ben·e·fi·cial [beniˈfiʃl] □ beneficioso; ⚖ que goza el usufructo de una propiedad; **ben·eˈfi·ci·ar·y** beneficiario (a *f*) *m*; *eccl.* beneficiado *m*.
ben·e·fit [ˈbenifit] **1.** beneficio *m* (*a. thea.*); (*insurance*) lucro *m*; *~ performance* beneficio *m*; *for the ~ of* a beneficio de; **2.** beneficiar, aprovechar; sacar provecho (*by*, *from* de).
be·nev·o·lence [biˈnevələns] benevolencia *f*; **beˈnev·o·lent** □ benévolo; *society* caritativo.
Ben·gal [beŋˈgɔ:l] bengalí; **Benˈgal·i** [~li] bengalí *adj. a. su. m/f*.
be·night·ed [biˈnaitid] sorprendido por la noche; *fig.* ignorante.
be·nign [biˈnain] □ benigno (*a.* ⚕); **be·nig·nant** [biˈnignənt] □ saludable; benigno; **beˈnig·ni·ty** benignidad *f*.
bent [bent] **1.** *pret. a. p.p. of bend*²; *~ on* resuelto a, empeñado en; **2.** inclinación *f*, propensión *f* (*for* a).
be·numb [biˈnʌm] entorpecer, entumecer.
ben·zene [ˈbenzi:n] benceno *m*.
ben·zine [ˈbenzi:n] bencina *f*.
be·queath [biˈkwi:ð] legar (*a. fig.*).
be·quest [biˈkwest] legado *m* (*a. th.*), manda *f*.
be·reave [biˈri:v] [*irr.*] despojar; *esp.*

the ~*d* los afligidos; **be'reave·ment** *mst* aflicción *f*, duelo *m*.

be·reft [bi'reft] *pret. a. p.p. of bereave*; *be* ~ *of* ser (*a.* estar) privado de.

be·ret [bə'rei] boina *f*.

berke·li·um ['bə:rkiliəm] berkelio *m*.

ber·ry ['beri] baya *f*.

ber·serk [bər'sə:rk] **1.** frenético; **2.** frenéticamente.

berth [bə:rθ] **1.** ⚓ fondeadero *m*, amarradero *m for ship*; ⚓ F (*cabin*) camarote *m*; ⚓, 🚃 (*bunk*) litera *f*; F *fig.* puesto *m*; *give a wide* ~ *to* esquivar, evitar; **2.** anclar, atracar.

ber·yl ['beril] berilo *m*.

be·seech [bi'si:tʃ] suplicar (*for acc.*); **be'seech·ing** □ suplicante.

be·set [bi'set] [*irr.* (set)] acosar (*a. fig.*), perseguir; *road* obstruir; ~*ting sin* pecado *m* dominante.

be·side [bi'said] **1.** *adv. v.* ~*s*; **2.** *prp.* cerca de, junto a; en comparación con; ~ *o.s.* fuera de sí (*with* con); **be'sides** [~dz] **1.** *adv.* además, también; **2.** *prp.* además de; excepto.

be·siege [bi'si:dʒ] asediar (*a. fig.*), sitiar; **be'sieg·er** asediador *m*, sitiador *m*.

be·smear [bi'smir] embarrar, embadurnar.

be·smirch [bi'smə:rtʃ] ensuciar, manchar (*a. fig.*).

be·som ['bi:zm] escoba *f*.

be·sot·ted [bi'sɔtid] embrutecido.

be·sought [bi'sɔ:t] *pret. a. p.p. of beseech*.

be·spat·ter [bi'spætər] salpicar; *fig.* llenar (*with* de).

be·speak [bi'spi:k] [*irr.* (*speak*)] encargar; apalabrar; indicar; *poet.* hablar con.

be·spec·ta·cled [bi'spektəkld] con gafas.

be·spoke [be'spouk] *pret. a. p.p. of bespeak*; ~ *tailor* sastre *m* que confecciona a medida; ~ *work* trabajo *m* hecho a la medida; **be'spo·ken** *p.p. of bespeak*.

be·sprin·kle [bi'spriŋkl] salpicar (*a. fig.*), rociar.

best [best] **1.** *adj. sup.* mejor; óptimo; ~ *girl* novia *f*; ~ *man* padrino *m* de boda; *v. seller*; **2.** *adv. sup.* mejor; *at* ~ a lo más; *I had* ~ *go* más vale que yo vaya; **3.** *su.* lo mejor; *v. Sunday*; *do one's* ~ hacer como mejor pueda uno; *for the* ~ con la mejor intención; *be for the* ~ conducir al bien; F *get the* ~ *of it* vencer; *make the* ~ *of* salir lo mejor posible de; *make the* ~ *of a bad job* sobreponerse.

bes·tial ['bestjəl] □ bestial, brutal; **bes·ti·al·i·ty** [besti'æliti] bestialidad *f*, brutalidad *f*.

be·stir [bi'stə:r]: ~ *o.s.* menearse [(*fig.*).]

be·stow [bi'stou] conferir, otorgar ([*up*]*on* a); **be'stow·al** otorgamiento *m*, donación *f*.

be·strew [bi'stru:] [*irr.*] esparcir; desparramar.

be·strid·den [bi'stridn] *p.p. of bestride*.

be·stride [bi'straid] [*irr.*] montar a horcajadas; cruzar de un tranco.

be·strode [bi'stroud] *pret. of bestride*.

bet [bet] **1.** apuesta *f*; (*sum*) postura *f*; **2.** apostar (*on* a); F *you* ~ (*your life*)! ¡ya lo creo!, *I* ~ *you a shilling that* te apuesto un chelín a que; *I* ~ *you can* a que puedes.

be·take [bi'teik] [*irr.* (*take*)]: ~ *o.s. to* darse a, aplicarse a; ir a, acudir a.

be·think [bi'θiŋk] [*irr.* (*think*)]: ~ *o.s. of* recapacitar *acc.*; considerar, recordar *acc.*; ~ *o.s. to inf.* ocurrírsele a uno *inf.*

be·thought *pret. a. p.p. of bethink*.

be·tide [bi'taid]: *woe* ~ *the man who ...!* ¡ay del que ...!

be·times [bi'taimz] temprano; en sazón.

be·to·ken [bi'toukn] presagiar; anunciar, indicar.

be·took [bi'tuk] *pret. of betake*.

be·tray [bi'trei] traicionar; delatar (*a. fig.*); *fig.* revelar, dejar ver; **be'tray·al** traición *f*; *fig.* revelación *f*; ~ *of trust* abuso *m* de confianza; **be'tray·er** traicionero (a *f*) *m*, traidor (-a *f*) *m*.

be·troth [bi'trouð] prometer en matrimonio; *be* (*or become*) ~*ed* desposarse; **be'troth·al** desposorio *m*.

bet·ter[1] ['betər] **1.** *adj. comp.* mejor; *he is* ~ está mejor; *get* ~ mejorarse; *v. half*; **2.** *adv. comp.* mejor; ~ *off* más acomodado; *so much the* ~ tanto mejor; *I had* ~ *go* más vale que yo vaya; *think* ~ *of it* mudar de parecer; **3.** *su.* superior *m*; *my* ~*s pl.* mis superiores; *get the* ~ *of* llevar la ventaja a; **4.** *v/t.* mejorar; ~ *o.s.* mejorar su posición; *v/i.* progresar, mejorar(se).

bet·ter² [~] apostador (-a *f*) *m*.
bet·ter·ment mejoramiento *m*.
bet·ting [ˈbetiŋ] apostar *m*; juego *m*.
be·tween [biˈtwi:n] (*poet. or prov. a.* **be·twixt** [biˈtwikst]) **1.** *adv.* (*freq. in* ~) en medio, entremedias; *betwixt and* ~ entre lo uno y lo otro, ni fu ni fa (F); **2.** *prp.* entre; ~ *ourselves* entre nosotros; **beˈtween-decks** entrecubiertas *f/pl.*, entrepuentes *m/pl.*; **beˈtween decks** entrecubiertas.
bev·el [ˈbevl] **1.** biselado; **2.** ⊕ (*instrument*) cartabón *m*, escuadra *f* falsa; ⚓ baivel *m*; ⊕ bisel *m* (*a.* ~ edge); **3.** *v/t.* ⊕ biselar; *v/i.* inclinarse; ˈ~ **wheel** rueda *f* cónica.
bev·er·age [ˈbevəridʒ] bebida *f*.
bev·y [ˈbevi] (*birds*) bandada *f*; (*ladies*) grupo *m*.
be·wail [biˈweil] lamentar.
be·ware [biˈwer] precaverse (*of* de); ~! ¡atención!
be·wil·der [biˈwildər] aturdir, aturrullar; desconcertar; **beˈwil·der·ment** aturdimiento *m*; perplejidad *f*.
be·witch [biˈwitʃ] hechizar (*a. fig.*), embrujar; **beˈwitch·ment** hechizo *m* (*a. fig.*); encanto *m*.
be·yond [biˈjɔnd] **1.** *adv.* más allá (*a. fig.*), más lejos; F *it's* ~! ¡es el colmo!; **2.** *prp.* más allá de; además de; fuera de; superior a; ~ *the seas* allende los mares; *get* ~ *a p.* hacérsele imposible a una p.; *it is* ~ *me* está fuera de mi alcance; **3.** más allá *m*.
bi... [bai] bi...
bi·an·nu·al [baiˈænjuəl] semestral.
bi·as [ˈbaiəs] **1.** sesgo *m*, diagonal *f*; *fig.* pasión *f*, predisposición *f*, prejuicio *m*; *cut on the* ~ cortar al sesgo; **2.** sesgar; *fig.* influir en, torcer; *be* ~*sed* tener prejuicio, ser partidista.
bib [bib] babador *m*, babero *m*.
Bi·ble [ˈbaibl] Biblia *f*; **bib·li·cal** [ˈbiblikəl] □ bíblico.
bib·li·og·ra·pher [bibliˈɔgrəfər] bibliógrafo *m*; **bib·li·o·graph·ic, bib·li·o·graph·i·cal** [~ouˈgræfik(l)] □ bibliográfico; **bib·li·og·ra·phy** [~ˈɔgrəfi] bibliografía *f*; **bib·li·o·ma·ni·a** [~ouˈmeinjə] bibliomanía *f*; **bib·li·oˈma·ni·ac** [~niæk] bibliómano *m*; **bib·li·o·phile** [ˈ~oufail] bibliófilo *m*.
bib·u·lous [ˈbibjuləs] □ *p.* bebedor, borrachín; hidrófilo.
bi·cam·er·al [baiˈkæmərəl] bicameral.
bi·car·bon·ate of so·da [baiˈkɑ:rbənitəvˈsoudə] bicarbonato *m* sódico.
bi·ceps [ˈbaiseps] bíceps *m*.
bick·er [ˈbikər] (*quarrel*) altercar, pararse en quisquillas; (*stream*) murmurar; ˈ**bick·er·ing** riña *f*.
bi·cy·cle [ˈbaisikl] **1.** bicicleta *f*; **2.** andar en bicicleta; ˈ**bi·cy·clist** ciclista *m/f*.
bid [bid] **1.** [*irr.*] *lit.* mandar; ordenar; *cards*: pujar, marcar; licitar *at auction*; *adieu etc.* decir, dar; ~ *fair to inf.* prometer *inf.*, dar indicios de *inf.*; ~ *up* pujar; **2.** (*auction etc.*) oferta *f*, postura *f*; (*cards*) marca *f*; tentativa *f* (*to* de, para); *cards*: *no* ~ paso; ˈ**bid·den** *p.p. of bid*; ˈ**bid·der** licitador *m*, postor *m*; *highest* ~ mejor postor *m*; ˈ**bid·ding** orden *f*; (*auction*) licitación *f*, postura *f*; *cards*: (*open the* abrir la, *close the* cerrar la) declaración *f*.
bide [baid] † aguardar; ~ *one's time* esperar la hora propicia.
bi·en·ni·al [baiˈenjəl] ⚘ (planta *f*) bienal, bianual *m*.
bier [bir] féretro *m*, andas *f/pl.*
biff [bif] *sl.* bofetada *f*.
bi·fo·cal [ˈbaifoukl] **1.** bifocal; **2.** ~*s pl.* anteojos *m/pl.* bifocales.
bi·fur·cate [ˈbaifə:rkeit] **1.** bifurcarse; **2.** bifurcado; **bi·furˈca·tion** bifurcación *f*.
big [big] grande (*a. fig.*); abultado, voluminoso; (*mst* ~ *with child*) encinta; F engreído; *fig.* importante; ~ *shot sl.* pájaro *m* de cuenta, señorón *m*; ~ *toe* dedo *m* gordo o grande *del pie*; *sl. talk* ~ echar bravatas.
big·a·mist [ˈbigəmist] bígamo (a *f*) *m*; **big·a·mous** [~məs] □ bígamo; ˈ**big·a·my** bigamia *f*.
bight [bait] gaza *f*; (*bay*) caleta *f*.
big·ness [ˈbignis] grandeza *f*; (gran) tamaño *m*.
big·ot [ˈbigət] fanático (a *f*) *m*, intolerante *m/f*; ˈ**big·ot·ed** fanático, intolerante; ˈ**big·ot·ry** fanatismo *m*, intolerancia *f*.
big·wig [ˈbigwig] F pájaro *m* de cuenta, espadón *m*.
bike [baik] F bici *f*.
bi·lat·er·al [ˈbaiˈlætərl] □ bilateral.
bil·ber·ry [ˈbilbəri] arándano *m*.
bile [bail] bilis *f*; *fig.* displicencia *f*.

bilge [bildʒ] ⚓ pantoque *m*; ⚓ (*a.* ~ *water*) agua *f* de pantoque; (*barrel*) barriga *f*; *sl.* disparates *m/pl.*
bi·lin·gual [bai'liŋgwəl] bilingüe.
bil·ious ['biljəs] □ bilioso (*a. fig.*).
bilk [bilk] estafar, defraudar.
bill[1] [bil] **1.** *zo.* pico *m*; uña *f of anchor*; ✓ podadera *f* (*a.* ~ *hook*); *geog.* promontorio *m*; **2.** *esp. fig.* ~ *and coo* acariciarse, besuquearse.
bill[2] [~] **1.** ✝ cuenta *f*, factura *f*; *parl.* proyecto *m* de ley; ✝ billete *m*; ✝ letra *f* de cambio (*a.* ~ *of exchange*); (*notice*) cartel *m*; anuncio *m*; *thea.* programa *m*; ⚖ alegato *m*; pedimento *m*; ~ *of fare* minuta *f*; ⚓ ~ *of health* patente *m* de sanidad; ~ *of lading* conocimiento *m* de embarque; ~ *of rights* declaración *f* de derechos; ley *f* fundamental; ⚖ ~ *of sale* escritura *f* de venta; **2.** *thea. etc.* anunciar.
bill·board ['bil'bɔːrd] cartelera *f*, tablón *m* de anuncios.
bil·let ['bilit] **1.** ⚔ (lugar *m* de) alojamiento *m*; **2.** leño *m*; *metall.* lingote *m*; **3.** ⚔ alojar (*on* en casa de).
bil·let-doux [bilei'duː] carta *f* amorosa.
bill·fold ['bilfould] billetera *f*.
bill·hook ['bilhuk] podadera *f*.
bil·liard ['biljərd] de billar; '~ **cue** taco *m*; '**bil·liards** *pl.* billar *m*.
bil·lion ['biljən] *American* mil millones; *British* billón *m*.
bil·low ['bilou] **1.** oleada *f*; *poet.* ~*s pl.* piélago *m*; **2.** ondular, ondear; '**bil·low·y** ondoso.
bill-post·er ['bilpoustər] cartelero *m*.
bil·ly ['bili] (*a.* '~ **can**) lata *f* para calentar agua al aire libre; cachiporra *f*; '~ **goat** macho *m* cabrío.
bin [bin] hucha *f*, arcón *m*; (*bread*) nasa *f*.
bi·na·ry ['bainəri] binario.
bind [baind] **1.** [*irr.*] *v/t.* liar, atar (*to* a); ceñir (*with* con, de); *wound* vendar; *book* encuadernar; *cloth* ribetear; *corn* agavillar; ⚕ estreñir; *fig.* obligar; ⚖ ~ *over* obligar legalmente (*to* a); ~ *a p. apprentice* poner en aprendizaje a una p.; *v/i.* atiesarse, aglutinarse, adherirse; **2.** *sl.* lata *f*; '**bind·er** atador (-a *f*) *m*; ⚕ faja *f*; (*book*) encuadernador *m*; ✓ atadora *f*, agavilladora *f*; '**bind·ing** **1.** obligatorio; *food* que estriñe; **2.** ligadura *f*; (*book*) encuadernación *f*; *sew.* ribete *m*; '**bind·weed** enredadera *f*.
binge [bindʒ] *sl.* borrachera *f*; *go on a* ~ ir de juerga.
bin·na·cle ['binəkl] bitácora *f*.
bin·oc·u·lar [bai'nɔkjulər] binocular; **bin·oc·u·lars** [bi'nɔkjulərz] *pl.* gemelos *m/pl.*
bi·no·mi·al [bai'noumiəl] binomio.
bi·o·chem·i·cal ['baiou'kemikl] bioquímico; '**bi·o'chem·ist** bioquímico *m*; '**bi·o'chem·is·try** bioquímica *f*.
bi·o·de·grad·a·ble [baiədi'greidəbl] biodegradable.
bi·og·ra·pher [bai'ɔgrəfər] biógrafo (a *f*) *m*; **bi·o·graph·ic, bi·o·graph·i·cal** [~ou'græfik(l)] □ biográfico; **bi·og·ra·phy** [~'ɔgrəfi] biografía *f*.
bi·o·log·ic, bi·o·log·i·cal [baiə'lɔdʒik(l)] □ biológico; **bi·ol·o·gist** [~'ɔlədʒist] biólogo *m*; **bi'ol·o·gy** biología *f*.
bi·o·phys·i·cal [baiə'fizikl] biofísico; **bi·o·phys·ics** [baiə'fiziks] biofísica *f*.
bi·par·ti·san [bai'pɑːrtizn] de dos partidos políticos.
bi·par·tite [bai'pɑːrtait] bipartido.
bi·ped ['baiped] 📖 bípedo *adj. a. su. m.*
bi·plane ['baiplein] biplano *m*.
birch [bɔːrtʃ] **1.** ⚘ abedul *m*; vara *f* de abedul, férula *f*; **2.** varear.
bird [bəːrd] ave *f*, pájaro *m*; *sl.* sujeto *m*, tío *m*; F *be a night* ~ correrla; ~ *cage* jaula *f*; ~ *call* reclamo *m*; ~*s of a feather* gente *f* de una calaña; ~ *in the hand* pájaro *m* en mano; ~ *of passage* ave *f* de paso (*a. fig.*); ~ *of prey* ave *f* de rapiña; ~ *shot* perdigones *m/pl.*; *kill two* ~*s with one stone* matar dos pájaros de una pedrada; '~ **fan·ci·er** pajarero *m*; '~ **lime** liga *f*; '~ **seed** alpiste *m*; '**bird's-eye view** vista *f* de pájaro; '**bird's nest** **1.** nido *m* de pájaro; **2.** buscar nidos.
birth [bəːrθ] nacimiento *m* (*a. fig.*); ⚕ parto *m*; linaje *m*; *fig.* origen *m*, comienzo *m*; *by* ~ de nacimiento; *give* ~ *to* parir, dar a luz; ~ *certificate* partida *f* de nacimiento; ~ *control* control *m* de natalidad, limitación *f* de la natalidad; '~**·day** cumpleaños *m*; ~ *cake* pastel *m* de cumpleaños; ~ *present* regalo *m* de cumpleaños; '~**·mark** antojo *m*, nevo *m* materno; '~ **place** lugar *m* de nacimiento; '~ **rate** natalidad *f*; '~**·right** derechos

m/pl. de nacimiento; primogenitura *f.*

bis·cuit [ˈbiskit] **1.** galleta *f*; bizcocho *m* (*a. pottery*); **2.** bayo, pardusco.

bi·sect [baiˈsekt] bisecar; **biˈsec·tion** bisección *f.*

bish·op [ˈbiʃəp] obispo *m*; (*chess*) alfil *m*; ˈ**bish·op·ric** obispado *m.*

bis·muth [ˈbizməθ] bismuto *m.*

bi·son [baisn] bisonte *m.*

bis·sex·tile [biˈsekstail] bisiesto *adj. a. su. m.*

bit [bit] **1.** trozo *m*, porción *f*; (*horse's*) freno *m*; ⊕ barrena *f*; ~ *by* ~ poco a poco; *a good* ~ bastante, una buena cantidad; F (*p.*) *a* ~ *of a* hasta cierto punto; *not a* (*or one*) ~ ni pizca; *do one's* ~ hacer su contribución; *take the* ~ *in one's teeth* rebelarse; **2.** *pret. of bite* 2.

bitch [bitʃ] **1.** perra *f*; zorra *f*, loba *f*; (*woman*) zorra *f*, mujer *f* de mal genio; **2.** *sl.* chapucear.

bite [bait] **1.** mordedura *f*, dentellada *f*; bocado *m to eat*; (*snack*) refrigerio *m*; picadura *f of insect etc.*; *fig.* mordacidad *f*; *take a* ~ F comer algo; **2.** morder; (*fish, insect*) picar; ⊕ asir; (*acid*) corroer; (*sword*) herir; *sl. what's biting you?* ¿qué mosca te ha picado?; ~ *at* querer morder; ˈ**bit·er** mordedor (-a *f*) *m*; *the* ~ *bit* el cazado cazador; ˈ**bit·ing** □ penetrante; *fig.* mordaz.

bit·ten [ˈbitn] *p.p. of bite* 2; *be* ~ *fig.* ser engañado; F ~ *with* contagiado de.

bit·ter [ˈbitər] **1.** □ amargo (*a. fig.*); *fight etc.* encarnizado; *cold* cortante, penetrante; **2.** cerveza *f* clara.

bit·tern [ˈbitə:rn] avetoro *m* común.

bit·ter·ness [ˈbitərnis] amargura *f*, amargor *m*; encarnizamiento *m of fight etc.*

bit·ters [ˈbitərz] *pl.* bitter *m.*

bit·ter·sweet [ˈbitə:rswi:t] agridulce.

bitts [bits] bitas *f/pl.*

bi·tu·men [biˈtju:mən] betún *m*; **bi·tu·mi·nous** [~ˈtju:minəs] bituminoso.

biv·ouac [ˈbivuæk] **1.** vivaque *m* (al raso); **2.** vivaquear.

biz [biz] F *v. business.*

bi·zarre [biˈzɑ:r] raro, grotesco.

blab [blæb] F **1.** (*a.* **blab·ber**) chismoso (a *f*) *m*; **2.** chismear; parlar; divulgar; soplar (*sl.*).

black [blæk] **1.** □ negro (*a. fig.*); *fig.* aciago; *look* ceñudo; *look* ~ *at* mirar con ceño; ~ *and blue* amoratado, acardenalado; ♀ *Death* peste *f* negra; *in* ~ *and white* en blanco y negro; por escrito; *v. eye, market*; **2.** ennegrecer; *shoes* limpiar; **3.** negro (a *f*) *m* (*a. race*); color negro *m*; (*mourning*) luto *m.*

black...: ~·**a·moor** [ˈ~əmur] negro (a *f*) *m*; ˈ~·**ball** dar bola negra a; ˈ~**ber·ry** zarzamora *f*; ˈ~·**bird** mirlo *m*; ˈ~·**board** pizarra *f*; ~ *eraser* cepillo *m*; ˈ~·**box** *in airplanes* registrador *m* de vuelo; ˈ~-**coat·ed** en chaqueta negra; ~ *worker* oficinista *m/f*; ˈ**black·en** *v/t.* ennegrecer; *fig.* denigrar; *v/i.* ennegrecerse (*a. fig.*).

black...: ˈ~·**guard** [ˈblægɑ:rd] **1.** pícaro *m*, bribón *m*, canalla *m*; **2.** (*mst* ˈ~·**guard·ly**) pillo, vil; **3.** injuriar, vilipendiar; ~·**head** [ˈblækhed] ⚕ comedón *m*; ˈ~ ˈ**hole** *ast.* agujero *m* negro; ˈ**black·ing** betún *m*; ˈ**black·ish** negruzco.

black...: ˈ~·**jack** **1.** cantimplora *f* (de cuero); cachiporra *f* (con puño flexible); 2. aporrear; ˈ~ˈ**lead** **1.** ⚒ grafito *m*; lápiz *m*; **2.** ennegrecer con plombagina; ˈ~·**leg** esquirol *m in strike*; tramposo *m*; ˈ~ˈ**let·ter** *typ.* letra *f* gótica; ˈ~·**list** **1.** poner en la lista negra; **2.** lista *f* negra; ˈ~·**mail** **1.** chantaje *m*; **2.** amenazar con chantaje; ˈ~·**mail·er** chantajista *m/f*; ˈ**black·ness** negrura *f.*

black...: ˈ~·**out** **1.** apagón *m*; ⚕ amnesia *f* (*or* ceguera *f*) temporal; ✈ visión *f* negra *of an aviator*; **2.** *v/t.* apagar; *v/i.* padecer un ataque de amnesia (*or* ceguera) temporal; ˈ~ ˈ**sheep** *fig.* oveja *f* negra, garbanzo *m* negro; ˈ~·**smith** herrero *m*; ˈ~·**thorn** endrino *m*; ˈ~ ˈ**tie** corbata *f* de smoking, smoking *m.*

blad·der [ˈblædər] vejiga *f.*

blade [bleid] hoja *f of knife etc.*; (*cutting edge*) filo *m*; paleta *f of propeller*; hoja *f of grass*; pala *f of oar, axe, hoe*; (*p.*) buen mozo *m*; ⚡ cuchilla *f.*

blam·a·ble [ˈbleiməbl] □ culpable; ˈ**blam·a·ble·ness** culpabilidad *f.*

blame [bleim] **1.** culpa *f*; *bear the* ~ cargar con la culpa; *put* (*or lay*) *the* ~ *on* echar la culpa a (*for* de); **2.** culpar; *be to* ~ *for* tener la culpa de.

blame·ful [ˈbleimful] censurable; ˈ**blame·less** □ inculpable, intachable; ˈ**blame·less·ness** inculpabilidad *f*; ˈ**blame·wor·thi·ness** culpabilidad *f*; ˈ**blame·wor·thy** censurable.
blanch [blæntʃ] *cooking*: blanquear; blanquecer; (*p.*) palidecer.
blanc·mange [bləˈmɔnʒ] *approx.* crema *f* (de vainilla *etc.*).
bland [blænd] □ suave, blando; ˈ**blan·dish** engatusar, halagar; ˈ**blan·dish·ment** (*mst* ~*s pl.*) halago *m*, lisonja *f*.
blank [blæŋk] **1.** □ *paper etc.* en blanco; vacío; *fig.* desconcertado; *look* sin expresión; *verse* blanco, suelto; ~ *cartridge* cartucho *m* sin bala; ~ *check* firma *f* en blanco; *fig.* carta *f* blanca; *fire* ~ usar municiones de fogueo; **2.** (*space etc.*) blanco *m*; (*coin*) cospel *m*; *fig.* falta *f* de sensaciones *etc.*; billete *m* de lotería no premiado; *fig. draw* (*a*) ~ no encontrar nada.
blan·ket [ˈblæŋkit] **1.** manta *f*; cobija *f S.Am.*; *fig.* manto *m*; *fig. wet* ~ aguafiestas *m/f*; **2.** cubrir con manta; ⚓ quitar el viento a; *fig.* suprimir; (*p.*) mantear; **3.** comprensivo, general.
blank·ness [ˈblæŋknis] vacío *m*; falta *f* de expresión.
blare [bler] **1.** (*trumpet*) sonar; sonar muy fuerte; ~ (*out*) vociferar; **2.** trompetazo *m*; estrépito *m*.
blar·ney [ˈblɑːrni] **1.** zalamerías *f/pl.*, coba *f*; **2.** halagar, dar coba.
bla·sé [blɑːˈzei] hastiado; empalagado.
blas·pheme [blæsˈfiːm] blasfemar (*against* contra); **blasˈphem·er** blasfemador (-a *f*) *m*; **blas·phe·mous** [ˈblæsfiməs] □ blasfemo; ˈ**blas·phe·my** blasfemia *f*.
blast [blæst] **1.** ráfaga *f*; soplo *m of bellows*; trompetazo *m from trumpet*; carga *f* de pólvora; (*explosion*) sacudida *f*; presión *f*; ⚘ tizón *m*, añublo *m*; *in full* ~ en plena marcha; **2.** volar, barrenar; ⚘ añublar, marchitar; *fig.* arruinar; ~ (*it*)! ¡maldito sea!; ˈ~ **fur·nace** ⊕ alto horno *m*; ˈ**blast·ing 1.** de volar; **2.** voladura *f*; ˈ**blast-off** lanzamiento *m* de cohete.
bla·tan·cy [ˈbleitənsi] vocinglería *f*; descaro *m*; ˈ**bla·tant** □ vocinglero; descarado.
blath·er [ˈblæðər] **1.** charla *f*; disparates *m/pl.*; **2.** charlatanear.
blaze [bleiz] **1.** llamarada *f*; hoguera *f*; F incendio *m*; *fig.* ardor *m*; *fig.* resplandor *m*; señal *f* (*hecha en los árboles para que sirva de guía*); (*on horse, cow*) estrella *f*; *go to* ~*s!* ¡en tu padre!; **2.** *v/i.* arder, encenderse en llamas; *fig.* enardecerse; F ~ *away* ⚔ seguir tirando; trabajar con ahinco; *v/t. trail* abrir; publicar, proclamar (*mst* ~ *abroad*); ˈ**blaz·er** chaqueta *f* ligera.
bla·zon [ˈbleizn] **1.** blasón *m* (*a. fig.*); **2.** blasonar; proclamar; ˈ**bla·zon·ry** blasón *m*; boato *m*.
bleach [bliːtʃ] **1.** blanquear(se); **2.** ⚗ lejía *f*; ˈ**bleach·er** blanqueador (-a *f*) *m*; lejía *f*, blanquimiento *m*; ~*s pl.* gradas *f/pl.* al aire libre; ˈ**bleach·ing** blanqueo *m*; ˈ**bleach·ing pow·der** polvos *m/pl.* de blanqueo; cloruro *m* de cal.
bleak [bliːk] □ desierto, solitario; (*bare*) pelado; *weather* frío, crudo; *fig. prospect* nada prometedor; *welcome* inhospitalario; ˈ**bleak·ness** lo desierto; frío *m etc.*
blear [blir] **1.** (*a.* **blear·y** □) legañoso; turbio, indistinto; **2.** enturbiar.
bleat [bliːt] **1.** balido *m*; **2.** balar.
bleb [bleb] ampolla *f*.
bled [bled] *pret. a. p.p. of bleed.*
bleed [bliːd] [*irr.*] **1.** *v/i.* sangrar; ~ *to death* morir de desangramiento; **2.** *v/t.* sangrar, desangrar; ~ (*white*) desangrar; ˈ**bleed·ing 1.** ⚕ sangría *f*; **2.** *sl.* maldito.
blem·ish [ˈblemiʃ] **1.** mancha *f*, tacha *f* (*a. fig.*); **2.** manchar, tachar (*a. fig.*).
blench [blentʃ] cejar, recular.
blend [blend] **1.** mezclar(se), combinar(se); (*colors*) casar; **2.** mezcla *f*, combinación *f*.
blende [blend] blenda *f*.
bless [bles] bendecir; favorecer (*with* con); F ~ *me!*, ~ *my soul!* ¡válgame Dios!; **blessed** [blest] □ *p.p. of bless*; *well I'm* ~! ¡caramba!; *a.* **bless·ed** [ˈblesid] bendito, bienaventurado; agraciado (*with* con); F santo; ˈ**bless·ed·ness** bienaventuranza *f*, santidad *f*; ˈ**bless·ing** bendición *f* (*a. fig.*); beneficio *m*.
blest [blest] *poet. v. blessed.*
bleth·er [ˈbleðər] = *blather.*
blew [bluː] *pret. of blow*[2] *a. blow*[3].
blight [blait] **1.** ⚘ añublo *m*; ⚘ tizón

m, roya *f*; *fig.* plaga *f*, infortunio *m*; **2.** ⚘ atizonar; arruinar; ˈ**blight·er** *sl.* tío *m*; bribón *m*.
blind [blaind] **1.** □ ciego (*a.* ⚠ *a. fig.*; *with* de, *to* a); oculto; ~ *in one eye* tuerto; *fig.* ~ *alley* callejón *m* sin salida; ~ *date* cita *f* a ciegas; ~ *landing* aterrizaje *m* a ciegas; ~*ly fig.* a ciegas; **2.** venda *f*; (*window*) celosía *f*, persiana *f*; *fig.* pretexto *m*; *sl.* pantalla *f*; **3.** cegar; deslumbrar.
blind...: ˈ**~·fold 1.** con los ojos vendados; *fig.* sin reflexión; **2.** vendar los ojos a; ˈ**~·man's-buff** gallina *f* ciega; ˈ**blind·ness** ceguedad *f*; ˈ**blind-worm** lución *m*.
blink [bliŋk] **1.** parpadeo *m*; (*gleam*) destello *m*; *sl. on the* ~ incapacitado, desconcertado; **2.** *v/t.* guiñar, cerrar momentáneamente; no hacer caso de; *v/i.* parpadear; (*light*) oscilar; ˈ**blink·ers** *pl.* anteojera *f* (de caballo); ˈ**blink·ing** F maldito.
blip [blip] bache *m*.
bliss [blis] bienaventuranza *f*; arrobamiento *m*; ˈ**bliss·ful** □ bienaventurado; deleitoso; ˈ**bliss·ful·ness** embeleso *m*, éxtasis *m*.
blis·ter [ˈblistər] **1.** ampolla *f*, vejiga *f*; **2.** ampollar(se); ~*ing fig.* arrollador; *heat* abrasador.
blithe [blaið] □, **~·some** [ˈ~səm] □ *mst poet.* alegre, jovial.
blith·er·ing [ˈbliðəriŋ] *sl.* charlatán; *fig.* consumado.
blitz [blits] **1.** guerra *f* relámpago; *esp.* bombardeo *m* aéreo (alemán); **2.** ✈ bombardear; ˈ**~·krieg** [ˈ~kri:g] guerra *f* relámpago.
bliz·zard [ˈblizərd] ventisca *f*.
bloat [blout] hinchar(se), abotagarse; ~*ed* abotagado; *fig.* hinchado (*with* de); ˈ**bloat·er** arenque *m* ahumado.
blob [blɔb] gota *f*; burbuja *f*.
bloc [blɔk] bloque *m*; *en* ~ en bloque.
block [blɔk] **1.** *stone, a. pol. a. mot.* bloque *m*; zoquete *m of wood*; (*butcher's, executioner's*) tajo *m*; (*pulley*) polea *f*, aparejo *m*; ⚠ manzana *f*, cuadra *f S.Am.*; 🚂 bloqueo *m*; *fig.* obstáculo *m*; *fig.* grupo *m*; F ~*buster* bomba *f* revientamanzanas, bomba rompedora; ~ *letter* mayúscula *f*; ~ *and tackle* aparejo *m* de poleas; **2.** obstruir, cerrar; ✝ bloquear; ~ *in*, ~ *out* esbozar; ~ *up* tapar, cegar.
block·ade [blɔˈkeid] **1.** bloqueo *m*; *v. run*; **2.** bloquear; ˈ**~ run·ner** forzador *m* de bloqueo.
block...: ˈ**~·head** zoquete *m*, zopenco (a *f*) *m*; ˈ**~·house** blocao *m*; ˈ**~ system** sistema *m* de bloqueo.
bloke [blouk] F tío *m*, sujeto *m*.
blond [blɔnd] **1.** rubio; blondo; **2.** = **blonde** F rubia *f*; (*a.* ~ *lace*) blonda *f*.
blood [blʌd] sangre *f*; linaje *m*, parentesco *m*; *b. s.* ira *f*, cólera *f*; (*p.*) currutaco *m*, galán *m*; *in cold* ~ a sangre fría; ~ *bank* banco *m* de sangre; ~*curdling* horripilante; ~ *relation* pariente *m/f* consanguíneo; ~ *royal* estirpe *f* regia; ~ *stream* corriente *f* sanguínea; ~ *test* análisis *m* de sangre; ~ *transfusion* transfusión *f* de sangre; *his* ~ *ran cold* se le heló la sangre; *v. bad*; ˈ**~-guilt·y** culpable de homicidio; ˈ**~ heat** calor *m* de la sangre; ˈ**~·horse** caballo *m* de pura raza; ˈ**~·hound** sabueso *m* (*a. fig.*); ˈ**blood·less** □ exangüe; pálido; *fig.* pacífico, incruento.
blood...: ˈ**~·let·ting** sangría *f*; ˈ**~ poi·son·ing** envenenamiento *m* de la sangre; ˈ**~ pres·sure** tensión *f* arterial; (*high*) hipertensión *f*; ˈ**~·shed** efusión *f* de sangre; matanza *f*; ˈ**~-shot** *eye* inyectado (de sangre); ˈ**~·thirst·y** □ sanguinario; ˈ**~ ves·sel** vaso *m* sanguíneo; ˈ**blood·y** □ sangriento; *sl.* puñetero; *sl. as adv.* muy.
bloom[1] [blu:m] **1.** flor *f*; florecimiento *m*, floración *f*; vello *m on fruit*; *fig.* lozanía *f*; **2.** florecer; *fig.* lozanear.
bloom[2] [~] *metall.* changote *m*.
bloom·er [ˈblu:mər] F gazapatón *m*; F ~*s pl.* bragas *f/pl.*
bloom·ing [ˈblu:miŋ] □ floreciente (*a. fig.*); F condenado.
blos·som [ˈblɔsəm] **1.** flor *f*; flores *f/pl.*; *in* ~ en flor; **2.** florecer; *fig.* ~ *into* convertirse en.
blot [blɔt] **1.** borrón *m* (*a. fig.*); **2.** manchar; borrar; (*mst* ~ *out*) *light, view* oscurecer; *writing* borrar, tachar; *fig.* destruir; secar *with blotting paper*.
blotch [blɔtʃ] mancha *f*; erupción *f on skin*.
blot·ter [ˈblɔtər] papel *m* secante; borrador *m*.
blot·ting pa·per [ˈblɔtiŋpeipər] papel *m* secante.
blot·to [ˈblɔtou] *sl.* borracho.

blouse [blauz] blusa *f*.
blow[1] [blou] golpe *m*; bofetada *f* *with hand*; choque *m*; *at one* ~ de un golpe; *come to* ~*s* venir a las manos; *that was a* ~*!* ¡fue un golpe duro!
blow[2] [~] [*irr.*] *poet.* florecer.
blow[3] [~] [*irr.*] **1.** *v/i.* soplar (*a. whale*); (*puff*) jadear, resoplar; (*hooter etc.*) sonar; *sl.* irse; *sl.* ~ *in* entrar de sopetón; ~ *on s. t.* enfriar soplando; ~ *open* abrirse (por el viento); ~ *over* pasar; ser olvidado; ~ *up* estallar; *sl.* reventar (de ira); *v/t.* soplar; ♪ sonar, tocar; *fuse* quemar; *nose* sonar; (*fly*) depositar larvas en; *sl. money* despilfarrar; F ~*me!*, *I'm* ~*ed!* ¡no me digas!; ¡ahí va!; ~ *a kiss* echar un beso; ~ *out* apagar; ~ *up* volar, hacer saltar; *balloon etc.* inflar; **2.** soplo *m*, soplido *m*; F *go for a* ~ dar una vuelta; '**blow·er** soplador (-a *f*) *m*; ⊕ aventador *m*; *sl.* teléfono *m*.
blow...: '~**·fly** moscarda *f*; '~ **hole** *zo.* espiráculo *m*; respiradero *m*; '~**-off** ⊕ escape *m*; '~**·out** *mot.* pinchazo *m*, reventón *m*; ⚡ quemadura *f*, quemazón *f*; *sl.* banquetazo *m*, tertulia *f* concurrida, festín *m*; '~ **pipe** ⊕ soplete *m*; cerbatana *f of native*; '~**-torch** antorcha *f* a soplete, lámpara *f* de soldar; '**blow·y** ventoso.
blowz·y ['blauzi] desaliñado; *face* coloradote.
blub·ber ['blʌbər] **1.** grasa *f* de ballena; (*weeping*) llanto *m*; **2.** lloriquear; llorar hasta hincharse los carrillos; **3.** (*lips*) befo *m*.
bludg·eon ['blʌdʒn] **1.** cachiporra *f*; **2.** aporrear; *fig.* obligar a porrazos (*into ger.* a *inf.*).
blue [blu:] **1.** azul; *bruise etc.* lívido, amoratado; F abatido, melancólico; *talk a* ~ *streak* F soltar la tarabilla; **2.** azul *m*; ⚗ añil *m*; *pol.* conservador (-a *f*) *m*; **3.** azular; *washing* dar azulete a, añilar; F *money* despilfarrar.
blue...: '~**·ber·ry** ⚘ mirtilo *m*; '~-'**blood·ed** linajudo; '~ **book** *libro de informes oficiales*; *registro de empleados del gobierno*; '~**·bottle** moscarda *f*; ⚘ aciano *m* mayor; '~'**chip** valor *m* de primera fila; '~ '**dev·ils** *pl.* F melancolía *f*; '~**·jack·et** marinero *m* (de buque de guerra); '~**·jay** *zo.* cianocita *f*; ~ **laws** *pl.* leyes *f/pl.* rigoristas severas; '~'**moon** cosa *f* muy raro; *once in a* ~ cada muerte de obispo, de Pascuas a Ramos; '**blue·ness** azul *m*; '~-'**pen·cil** marcar o corregir con lápiz azul; '**blue·print** cianotipo *m*, ferroprusiato *m*; *fig.* programa *m*, bosquejo *m*, anteproyecto *m*; **blues** *pl.* morriña *f*, murrias *f/pl.*; ♪ *música de jazz melancólica*; '**blue·stock·ing** literata *f*; marisabidilla *f*.
bluff [blʌf] **1.** ☐ escarpado; *p.* brusco, francote; **2.** risco *m*, promontorio *m* escarpado; amenaza *f* que no se puede realizar, bluf *m*; fanfarronada *f*; *call s.o.'s* ~ cogerle la palabra a uno; **3.** engañar, embaucar.
blu·ish ['blu:iʃ] azulado, azulino.
blun·der ['blʌndər] **1.** patochada *f*, coladura *f*, patinazo *m*; **2.** hacer una patochada *etc.*; desatinar (*a.* ~ *along*); F ~ *out* descolgarse con; '**blun·der·er** desatinado (a *f*) *m*.
blunt [blʌnt] **1.** ☐ embotado (*a. fig.*), despuntado, *fig.* obtuso, torpe; *manner* francote; **2.** embotar, despuntar; '**blunt·ness** embotamiento *m*; *fig.* brusquedad *f*, franqueza *f*.
blur [blə:r] **1.** borrón *m*; contorno *m* borroso; **2.** manchar; borrar; empañar (*a. fig.*); ~*red esp. phot.* desfigurado, desdibujado.
blurb [blə:rb] *sl.* anuncio *m* efusivo (*esp. de editor*).
blurt [blə:rt] (*a.* ~ *out*) descolgarse con.
blush [blʌʃ] **1.** rubor *m*, sonrojo *m*; color *m* de rosa; *at first* ~ a primera vista; **2.** sonrojarse, ruborizarse (*at* de); ponerse colorado; ~ *to inf.* avergonzarse de *inf.*; '**blush·ing** ruboroso.
blus·ter ['blʌstər] **1.** borrasca *f* ruidosa; *fig.* jactancia *f*, fanfarronada *f*; **2.** *v/i.* (*wind etc.*) bramar; fanfarronear; *v/t.* ~ *forth*, ~ *out* decir ruidosamente; ~ *it out* defenderse echando bravatas; '**blus·ter·er** fanfarrón *m*; hombre *m* colérico.
bo·a ['bouə] boa *f* (*a. fur*).
boar [bɔ:r] verraco *m*; *wild* ~ jabalí *m*.
board [bɔ:rd] **1.** tabla *f*, tablero *m*; (*notice*) tablón *m*; cartón *m for binding*; ⚓ bordo *m*; ✝ *etc.* junta *f*, consejo *m* de administración; *thea. the* ~*s pl.* las tablas; ~ *of health* junta *f* de sanidad; (*full*) ~ *and lodging* pensión *f* completa, comida *f* y casa; ~ *of trade* junta *f* de comercio; ~ *of trustees* consejo *m* de administra-

ción; ~*walk* paseo *m* entablado a la orilla del mar; ⚓ *on* ~ a bordo; *go by the* ~ ser abandonado; *tread the* ~*s* ser actor (*or* actriz); **2.** *v/t.* entablar (*a.* ~ *up*); ⚓ abordar; ⚓ embarcarse en; 🚃 *etc.* subir a; *p.* dar pensión completa a; *v/i.* (*a.* ~ *with*) hospedarse (con); ˈ**board·er** huésped (-a *f*) *m*, cliente *m/f* habitual *or* fijo; *school*: interno (a *f*) *m*.
board·ing [ˈbɔːrdiŋ] entablado *m*; ⚓ abordaje *m*; ˈ~ **house** pensión *f*, casa *f* de huéspedes; ˈ~ **school** internado *m*.
board room [ˈbɔːrdruːm] sala *f* de juntas.
boast [boust] **1.** jactancia *f*; baladronada *f*; *make* ~ *of* hacer gala de; **2.** jactarse (*about, of* de); ~ *about*, ~ *of* hacer alarde de; *fig. th.* enorgullecerse de, cacarear; ˈ**boast·er** fanfarrón (-a *f*) *m*, plantista *m*; ˈ**boast·ful** □ jactancioso.
boat [bout] **1.** barca *f*, bote *m*; (*large*) barco *m*; ~ *hook* bichero *m*; ~*house* casilla *f* para botes; *be in the same* ~ correr los mismos peligros; *burn one's* ~*s pl.* quemar las naves; **2.** ir en bote; ˈ**boating** canotaje *m*; ˈ**boat race** regata *f*; ˈ**boat·swain** [ˈbousn] contramaestre *m*.
bob [bɔb] **1.** (*jerk*) sacudida *f*, meneo *m*; (*hair*) borla *f*; pelo *m* cortado corto; *sl.* chelín *m*; (*plumbline*) plomo *m*; **2.** *v/t.* menear, sacudir; *hair* cortar corto; *v/i.* menearse; (*a.* ~ *up and down*) fluctuar.
bob·bin [ˈbɔbin] carrete *m* (*a.* ⚡), bobina *f* (*a.* ⚡); *sew.* canilla *f*.
bob·ble [ˈbɔbl] F coladura *f*.
bob·by [ˈbɔbi] *sl.* polizonte *m*; ˈ~ **pin** horquillita *f* para el pelo; ˈ~**·socks** *pl.* escarpines *m/pl.*; ˈ~**·soxer** *sl.* chica *f* tobillera.
bob·sled [ˈbɔbsled], **bob·sleigh** [ˈbɔbslei] trineo *m* de balancín, bobsleigh *m*.
bob·tail [ˈbɔbteil] rabo *m* mocho; animal *m* rabón; cola *f* corta; cola cortada; *v. ragtag*.
bob·white [ˈbɔbˈwait] *zo.* colín *m* de Virginia.
bock beer [ˈbɔkbir] cerveza *f* de marzo.
bode [boud]: ~ *well* (*ill*) ser buena (mala) señal.
bod·ice [ˈbɔdis] corpiño *m*, almilla *f*; (*dress*) cuerpo *m*.
bod·i·less [ˈbɔdilis] incorpóreo.
bod·i·ly [ˈbɔdili] **1.** *adj.* corpóreo, corporal; **2.** *adv.* corporalmente; en conjunto; *lift etc.* en peso.
bod·kin [ˈbɔdkin] aguja *f* de jareta; (*hair*) espadilla *f*.
bod·y [ˈbɔdi] **1.** cuerpo *m*; persona *f*; (*dead*) cadáver *m*; ⊕ armazón *f*; *mot.* carrocería *f*, caja *f*; *in a* ~ en bloque, todos juntos; ⚔ *main* ~ grueso *m*; **2.** ~ *forth* dar cuerpo (*or* forma) a; encarnar; ˈ~**·guard** guardia *m* de corps; guardaespaldas *m*.
Boer [bɔːr] bóer *adj. a. su. m/f*.
bog [bɔg] **1.** pantano *m*, ciénaga *f*; **2.**: *get* ~*ged down* enfangarse; *fig.* empantanarse, atrancarse.
bog·gle [ˈbɔgl] sobresaltarse; cejar (*a. fig.*); ~ *at* vacilar (*or* titubear) ante.
bog·gy [ˈbɔgi] pantanoso.
bo·gie [ˈbougi] 🚃 bogie *m*; *a.*=*bogy*.
bo·gus [ˈbougəs] falso, superchero.
bo·gy [ˈbougi] duende *m*, trasgo *m*; *the* ~ *man* el coco; *fig.* espantajo *m*.
Bo·he·mi·an [bouˈhiːmjən] bohemo *adj. a. su. m* (a *f*); *fig.* bohemio *adj. a. su. m* (a *f*).
boil[1] [bɔil] ⚕ divieso *m*, furúnculo *m*.
boil[2] [~] **1.** hervir (*a. fig.*); *cooking*: cocer, salcochar; ~ *down* reducir por cocción; ~ *over* (*liquid*) irse; **2.**: *come to the* ~ comenzar a hervir; ˈ**boil·er** caldera *f* (*a.* ⊕); ~ *room* sala *f* de calderas; ~ *suit* mono *m*; ˈ**boil·ing** hervor *m*; cocción *f*; ~ *point* punto *m* de ebullición.
bois·ter·ous [ˈbɔistərəs] □ *wind etc.* borrascoso, proceloso; *p.* alborotador, bullicioso; *voices* vocinglero; ˈ**bois·ter·ous·ness** tumulto *m*, bullicio *m*; vocinglería *f of voices*.
bold [bould] □ atrevido, osado; *b.s.* desenvuelto, descocado; (*steep*) escarpado; *fig.* claro, vigoroso; *typ.* negrita, negrilla *f*; ~*face typ.* negrita *f*, negrilla *f*; *make* (*so*) ~ (*as*) *to* atreverse a; ˈ**bold·ness** osadía *f*; *b.s.* desenvoltura *f*, descoco *m*; *fig.* claridad *f*, vigor *m*.
bole [boul] tronco *m*.
boll [boul] cápsula *f*.
bol·lard [ˈbɔlərd] bolardo *m*.
bo·lo·ney [bəˈlouni] = *baloney*.
Bol·she·vism [ˈbɔlʃəvizm] bolchevismo *m*; ˈ**Bol·she·vist** bolchevista *adj. a. su. m/f*.
bolster [ˈboulstər] **1.** (*pillow*) travese-

ro *m*; **2.** (*mst* ~ *up*) sostener, reforzar; *fig.* alentar.
bolt [boult] **1.** (*door*) cerrojo *m*, pestillo *m*; ⚔ saeta *f*; (*thunder-*) rayo *m*; ⊕ perno *m*; salida *f* (*or* fuga *f*) repentina (*for* para alcanzar); ~ *upright* erguido; *fig.* ~ *from the blue* acontecimiento *m* inesperado, *b.s.* rayo *m*; **2.** *v/t. door* acerrojar; ⊕ sujetar con perno, empernar; F *food* engullir; *v/i.* fugarse, escaparse (*esp. horse*); ~ *out* salir de golpe; *Am. pol.* disidir; ˈ**bolt·er** tamiz *m*; *Am. pol.* disidente *m*.
bolt·hole [ˈboulthoul] *fig.* refugio *m*; escapatoria *f*.
bomb [bɔm] **1.** bomba *f*; (*hand*) granada *f*; ~ *crater* ⚔ embudo *m* de bomba; ~ *release* lanzabombas *m*; ~*shell* bomba *f*; ~*sight* mira *f* de bombardeo, visor *m*; *v. atomic, incendiary etc.*; *fig. fall like a* ~(*shell*) caer como una bomba; **2.** bombardear; ~*ed out* desalojado (por causa de bombardeo).
bom·bard [bɔmˈbɑːrd] bombardear; *fig.* llenar (*with* de); **bomˈbard·ment** bombardeo *m*.
bom·bast [ˈbɔmbæst] ampulosidad *f*, rimbombancia *f*; **bomˈbas·tic, bomˈbas·ti·cal** □ ampuloso, rimbombante.
bomb·er [ˈbɔmər] bombardero *m*.
bomb·proof [ˈbɔmpruːf] a prueba de bombas.
bo·na fi·de [ˈbɔnəˈfaidə] de buena fe.
bo·nan·za [bouˈnænzə] F **1.** *fig.* filón *m*; **2.** lucrativo.
bon·bon [ˈbɔnbɔn] bombón *m*, confite *m*.
bond [bɔnd] **1.** lazo *m*, vínculo *m* (*a. fig.*); ☤ obligación *f*; ☤ bono *m*; ☤ fianza *f* (de aduana); △ aparejo *m*; ☤ *in* ~ en depósito; **2.** ☤ obligar por fianza; ☤ depositar mercancías en la Aduana; ~*ed warehouse* depósito *m* comercial, almacén *m* de depósito; ˈ**bond·age** esclavitud *f* (*a. fig.*), cautiverio *m*; ˈ~**·hold·er** ☤ tenedor *m* de bonos; ˈ**bond**(**s**)**·man** siervo *m*; ˈ**bond**(**s**)**·wom·an** sierva *f*.
bone [boun] **1.** hueso *m*; (*fish-*) espina *f*; ~*s pl. a.* esqueleto *m*; huesos *m/pl. of the dead*; ~ *of contention* manzana *f* de la discordia; ~*head* F mentecato *m*, zapenco *m*; *feel in one's* ~*s* saber a buen seguro, estar totalmente seguro de; F *have a* ~ *to pick with* tener que habérselas con; F *make no* ~*s about* no andarse con rodeos en; **2.** *meat, fish* deshuesar; F (*a.* ~ *up*) quemarse las cejas, empollar; ˈ**bone meal** harina *f* de huesos; ˈ**bon·er** *sl.* patochada *f*; ˈ**bone set·ter** ensalmador *m*.
bon·fire [ˈbɔnfaiər] hoguera *f*.
bon·net [ˈbɔnit] **1.** (*woman's*) gorra *f*, papalina *f*; (*child's*) capillo *m*; gorra *f* escocesa: *mot.* capó *m*; ⊕ sombrerete *m*; ⚓ boneta *f*; **2.** cubrir (la cabeza).
bon·ny [ˈbɔni] *esp. Scot.* bonito, lindo; robusto.
bo·nus [ˈbounəs] adehala *f*; ☤ prima *f*.
bon·y [ˈbouni] huesudo; ✶ *etc.* huesoso.
boo [buː] **1.** *speaker etc.* silbar; **2.**: *not to say* ~ no decir chus ni mus.
boob [buːb] bobo *m*.
boo·by [ˈbuːbi] bobo *m*, mentecato *m*; *orn.* bubía *f*; ~ *prize* premio *m* de consolación; ˈ~ **trap** trampa *f* explosiva; zancadilla *f*.
boog·ie-woog·ie [ˈbugiˈwugi] bugui-bugui *m*.
boo·hoo [buˈhuː] lloriquear.
book [buk] **1.** libro *m*; libreta *f for notes etc.*; libro *m* talonario *of cheques, tickets*; *bring s. o. to* ~ pedirle cuentas a una p.; ☤ *close the* ~*s* cerrar el borrador; *be in a p.'s good* (*bad*) ~*s* estar bien (mal) con una p.; **2.** ☤ asentar, anotar; *artist* escriturar; *room* reservar; *ticket* sacar; F (*police*) reseñar; ~ *through to* sacar un billete hasta; ˈ~**·bind·er** encuadernador *m*; ˈ~**·case** armario *m* para libros, estante *m*; ˈ~ **end** sujetador *m* de libros; ˈ**book·ie** F = *bookmaker*; ˈ**book·ing** reservación *f of passage*; escritura *f of an actor*; ˈ**book·ing clerk** taquillero (a *f*) *m*; ˈ**book·ing of·fice** taquilla *f*; despacho *m* de billetes; ˈ**book·ish** □ *learning* libresco; *p.* estudioso; *b.s.* enteradillo; ˈ**book·keep·er** tenedor *m* de libros; ˈ**book·keep·ing** teneduría *f* de libros; ˈ**book·let** folleto *m*, opúsculo *m*.
book...: ˈ~**·mak·er** corredor *m* profesional de apuestas; ˈ~**·mark** señal *f* de libros; ˈ~ **plate** ex libris *m*; ˈ~ **rest** atril *m*; ˈ~ **reˈview** reseña *f*; ˈ~**·sell·er** librero *m*; ˈ~**·shelf** estante *m* para libros; ˈ~**·stand** mostrador *m* para libros; (*rack*) atril *m*; *selling books* puesto *m* de venta para libros;

ˈ~·**store** librería *f*; ˈ~·**worm** polilla *f*; *fig.* ratón *m* de biblioteca.

boom[1] [bu:m] ⚓ (*jib*) botalón *m*; botavara *f*.

boom[2] [~] ✝ **1.** auge *m*, prosperidad *f* repentina; **2.** ascender (los negocios), estar en bonanza.

boom[3] [~] **1.** estampido *m*; **2.** hacer estampido; estallar; (*voice*) resonar, retumbar.

boom·er·ang [ˈbu:məræŋ] bumerang *m*; *fig.* lo contraproducente.

boon[1] [bu:n] merced *f*, gracia *f*; (*gift*) dádiva *f*; favor *m*.

boon[2] [~] generoso, liberal; ~ *companion* amigo *m* íntimo, camarada *m*.

boor [buə] patán *m* (*a. fig.*); tosco *m*, palurdo *m*.

boor·ish [ˈbuəriʃ] □ patán, tosco, palurdo.

boost [ˈbu:st] **1.** empujar; ⚡ elevar; *fig.* promover, fomentar; ayudar; **2.**: *give a* ~ *to* dar bombo a; ˈ**boost·er** reforzador *m*; (*enthusiastic backer*) bombista *m/f*; ⚡ elevador *m* de tensión; *radio*: repetidor *m*; ~ *rocket* ⊕ cohete *m* lanzador; ~ *shot* ⚕ inyección *f* secundaria; ~ *station* ⊕ repetidor *m*.

boot[1] [bu:t] † **1.**: *to* ~ también; **2.** aprovechar.

boot[2] [~] **1.** bota *f*; *mot.* maleta *f*; F *the* ~ *is on the other foot* los papeles están trastrocados; *die with one's* ~*s on* morir al pie del cañón; **2.** patear; *sl.* ~ *out* poner en la calle; ˈ~·**black** limpiabotas *m*; ˈ**boot·ed** calzado con botas; **boot·ee** [bu:ˈti:] (*woman's*) botina *f*, borceguí *m*; (*child's*) bota *f* de lana, borceguí *m*.

booth [bu:ð] caseta *f*; (*market*) puesto *m*; *teleph.* cabina *f*.

boot...: ˈ~·**lace** cordón *m*; ˈ~·**leg·ger** contrabandista *m* en licores.

boots [bu:ts] *sg.* limpiabotas *m*, botones *m*.

boot-tree [ˈbu:ttri:] horma *f*.

boo·ty [ˈbu:ti] botín *m*, presa *f*.

booze [bu:z] F **1.** emborracharse; borrachear; **2.** bebida *f* (alcohólica); borrachera *f*; ˈ**booz·y** F borracho.

bop [bɔp] *especie de jazz*.

bo·rax [ˈbɔ:ræks] bórax *m*.

bor·der [ˈbɔ:rdər] **1.** borde *m*, margen *m*, orilla *f*; (*frontier*) frontera *f*; ⚘ arriate *m*; *sew.* orla *f*, orilla *f*; (*embroidered etc.*) cenefa *f*; **2.**: ~ *on* rayar en, frisar en; ~ *upon* lindar con, confinar con; **3.** fronterizo; ˈ~·**land** región *f* (*or* zona *f*) fronteriza; ˈ~·**line** *case etc.* dudoso, incierto.

bore[1] [bɔ:r] **1.** ⊕ taladro *m*, barreno *m*; ⚔ calibre *m*, alma *f*; *geol.* sonda *f*; *fig.* (*p.*) pelmazo *m*, pesado (a *f*) *m*, machaca *m/f*; (*th.*) molestia *f*, lata *f*; **2.** ⊕ taladrar, perforar; *fig.* aburrir; fastidiar, dar la lata a; *be* ~*d to death* aburrirse como una almeja.

bore[2] [~] *ola grande causada en los estuarios por la marea*.

bore[3] [~] *pret. of bear*[2].

bo·re·al [ˈbɔ:riəl] boreal, septentrional.

bore·dom [ˈbɔ:rdəm] aburrimiento *m*, fastidio *m*.

bor·er [ˈbɔ:rər] ⊕ barrena *f*, taladro *m*; *zo.* barrenillo *m*, *cualquier insecto que roe*.

bo·ric ac·id [ˈbɔ:rikˈæsid] ácido *m* bórico; **bo·ron** [ˈ~rɔn] boro *m*.

bor·ing [ˈbɔ:riŋ] □ aburrido, pesado.

born [bɔ:rn] **1.** *p.p. of bear*[2]; *be* ~ nacer; *I was* ~ nací; **2.** *adj. actor* nato; *liar* innato; *in all my* ~ *days* en mi vida.

borne [bɔ:rn] *p.p. of bear*[2] llevar *etc.*

bor·ough [ˈbʌrou] villa *f*; (*municipal*) ~ municipio *m*, municipalidad *f*; distrito *m* electoral de municipio.

bor·row [ˈbɔrou] pedir prestado (*of*, *from* a); *idea etc.* apropiarse; ˈ**bor·row·er** prestatario (a *f*) *m*, comodatorio *m*; el (la) que pide (*or* toma) prestado; ˈ**bor·row·ing** acto *m* de pedir (*or* tomar) prestado; empréstito *m*; (*word*) préstamo *m*.

bos·cage [ˈbɔskidʒ] espesura *f*, matorral *m*.

bosh [bɔʃ] F palabrería *f*, necedades *f/pl.*, música *f* celestial.

bos·om [ˈbuzəm] seno *m* (*a. fig.*), pecho *m*; (*garment*) pechera *f*; superficie *f of lake*; ~ *friend* amigo (a *f*) *m* íntimo (a).

boss[1] [bɔs] ⊕ clavo *m*, tachón *m*; protuberancia *f*; ⚠ crucería *f*.

boss[2] [~] F **1.** jefe (a *f*) *m*, patrón (-a *f*) *m*; *esp. Am. pol.* cacique *m*; **2.** regentar, dirigir; mandar, dominar.

boss·y [ˈbɔsi] □ F mandón; tiránico.

bo·tan·ic, bo·tan·i·cal [bəˈtænik(l)] □ botánico; **bot·a·nist** [ˈbɔtənist] botanista *m/f*, botánico *m/f*; **bot·a·nize** [ˈ~naiz] herborizar; ˈ**bot·a·ny** botánica *f*.

botch [bɔtʃ] **1.** chapucería *f*, chafallo *m*; **2.** chapucear, chafallar; ˈ**botcher** chapucero (a *f*) *m*.
both [bouθ] ambos, los dos; ~ ... *and* tanto ... como; ~ *of them* ambos, los dos.
both·er [ˈbɔðər] F **1.** molestia *f*, lata *f*; pejiguera *f*; **2.** molestar; ~ *to* tomarse la molestia de; ~ (*it*)! ¡porras!; *he's always* ~*ing me* me está majando continuamente; **both·erˈa·tion** F ¡porras!
bot·tle [ˈbɔtl] **1.** botella *f*; frasco *m*; (*water*) cantimplora *f*; (*baby's*) biberón *m*; (*scent*) pomo *m*; ~ *opener* abrebotellas *m*; F *hit the* ~ emborracharse; **2.** embotellar (*a.* ~ *up*; *esp. fig.*); ~ *up emotion* contener; ˈ~**neck** cuello *m* (de una botella); *fig.* embotellamiento *m*.
bot·tom [ˈbɔtəm] **1.** fondo *m* (*a. fig.*); lecho *m*, cauce *m of river*; asiento *m of chair, bottle*; ⚓ (*ship's*) quilla *f*, casco *m*; F trasero *m*; *fig.* base *f*, fundamento *m*; *at the* ~ en el fondo; en el otro extremo; *fig. at* ~ en el fondo; *get to the* ~ *of a matter* profundizar (*or* fondear) un asunto; topar con la explicación de una cosa; *fig. be at the* ~ *of* ser causa (*or* motivo) de; **2.** ínfimo, más bajo; último; ~ *dollar* último dólar *m*; **3.** poner fondo (*or* asiento) a; ˈ**bot·tom·less** sin fondo; insondable; ˈ**bot·tom·ry** préstamo *m* sobre casco y quilla.
bough [bau] rama *f*.
bought [bɔːt] *pret. a. p.p. of buy*.
bou·gie [ˈbuːʒiː] candelilla *f*.
boul·der [ˈbouldər] canto *m* rodado.
bounce [bauns] **1.** (re)bote *m*; F fanfarronería *f*; **2.** (re)botar; F fanfarronear; ~ *in* (*out*) entrar (salir) sin ceremonia; ~ *a p. out of a th.* disuadir a una p. de algo a fuerza de amenazas; ˈ**boun·cer** F embuste *m*, filfa *f*; *sl.*: *el que echa a los alborotadores de un café etc.*; ˈ**bounc·ing** fuerte, recio; frescachón.
bound[1] [baund] **1.** *pret. a. p.p. of bind*; **2.** *adj.* atado; *fig.* obligado; *fig.* ~ *to* seguro de *inf.*; ~ *up with* estrechamente relacionado con.
bound[2] [~]: ~ *for* con rumbo a, con destino a.
bound[3] [~] **1.** límite *m*, linde *m a. f*; *in* ~*s* a raya; *out of* ~*s* fuera de los límites; *fig. fix* (*the*) ~*s* fijar los jalones; **2.** limitar, deslindar.
bound[4] [~] **1.** salto *m*, brinco *m*; *v. leap*; **2.** saltar, brincar.
bound·ary [ˈbaundəri] límite *m*, linde *m a. f*; lindero *m*; ~ *stone* hito *m*, mojón *m*.
bound·less [ˈbaundlis] □ ilimitado.
boun·te·ous [ˈbauntiəs] □, **boun·ti·ful** [ˈ~tiful] □ liberal, generoso; dadivoso.
boun·ty [ˈbaunti] munificencia *f*; ⚔ *etc.* gratificación *f*, enganche *m*; (*esp. royal*) merced *f*, gracia *f*; ✝ prima *f*, subvención *f*.
bou·quet [buˈkei] ⚘ ramillete *m*, ramo *m*; (*wine*) aroma *m*, nariz *f*.
bour·geois[1] [ˈburʒwɑː] burgués *adj. a. su. m* (-a *f*).
bour·geois[2] [bəːrˈdʒɔis] *typ.* tipo *m* de 9 puntos.
bour·geoi·sie [burʒwɑːˈziː] burguesía *f*.
bout [baut] turno *m*; ⚕ ataque *m*; ⚔ encuentro *m*; *fenc.* asalto *m*.
bo·vine [ˈbouvain] bovino; *fig.* lerdo.
bow[1] [bau] **1.** reverencia *f*, inclinación *f*; *make one's* ~ presentarse, debutar; **2.** *v/i.* hacer una reverencia *f* (*to* a); *fig.* ~ *to* someterse a; ~ *beneath* agobiarse con (*or* de; *a. fig.*); *v/t.* inclinar; *fig.* agobiar, oprimir (*mst* ~ *down*).
bow[2] [~] ⚓ proa *f*.
bow[3] [bou] **1.** arco *m* (*a.* ♪); (*tie, knot*) lazo *m*; **2.** ♪ hacer pasos del arco.
bowd·ler·ize [ˈbaudləraiz] expurgar.
bow·el [ˈbauəl] intestino *m*; ~*s pl.* entrañas *f/pl.* (*a. fig.*); ~ *movement* evacuación *f* del vientre; *have a* ~ *movement* evacuar el vientre.
bow·er [ˈbauər] cenador *m*, glorieta *f*; *poet.* entramada *f*; *poet.* morada *f*; ⚓ (*a.* ~ *anchor*) ancla *f* de proa.
bow·ie·knife [ˈbouiˈnaif] cuchillo *m* de monte.
bowl[1] [boul] (*large*) (al)jofaina *f*, palangana *f*; (*small*) escudilla *f*, tazón *m*; *fig.* copa *f of wine*; hornillo *m of pipe*; pala *f of spoon*; *geog.* cuenca *f*.
bowl[2] [~] **1.** bola *f*, bocha *f*; ~*s sg. a. pl.* juego *m* de las bochas; **2.** *v/t.* rodar; *sport*: arrojar; *fig.* ~ *over* desconcertar; *v/i.* rodar; *sport*: jugar a las bochas; arrojar la pelota; ~ *along* rodar, ir de prisa.
bow·leg·ged [ˈbouˈlegid] estevado, con las piernas en arco.

bowl·er [ˈboulər] *el que arroja la pelota*; (*hat*) hongo *m*.
bow·line [ˈboulin] ⚓ bolina *f*.
bowl·ing [ˈbouliŋ] juego *m* de bolos, boliche *m*; ~ *alley* bolera *f*, boliche *m*; ~ *green* bolera *f* encespada.
bow...: **ˈ~·man** arquero *m*, flechero *m*; **ˈ~·shot** tiro *m* de flecha; **ˈ~·sprit** bauprés *m*; **ˈ~·string** cuerda *f* de arco; **ˈ~ ˈtie** (corbata *f* de) lazo *m*; **ˈ~ ˈwin·dow** ventana *f* salediza.
bow-wow [ˈbauˈwau] ¡guau!
box[1] [bɔks] **1.** ⚘ boj *m*; caja *f* (*a.* ⚡); (*large*) cajón *m*; cofre *m*, arca *f*; (*jewel-*) estuche *m*; ⊕ caja *f*, cojinete *m*; (*coach*) pescante *m*; *thea.* palco *m*; ~ *pleat* pliegue *m* de tabla; ~ *seat* asiento *m* de palco; **2.** encajonar (*a. fig.*; *esp.* ~ *up*); *compass* cuartear.
box[2] [~] **1.** boxear; ~ *a. p.'s ear* dar un cachete a una p.; **2.**: ~ *on the ear* cachete *m*, puñetazo *m*; **ˈ~ ˈcalf** boxcalf *m*, piel *f* de becerro; **ˈbox·er** boxeador *m*; *zo.* boxer *m*.
box·ing [ˈbɔksiŋ] boxeo *m*; ˈ**2**-*Day* = *fiesta de San Esteban* (*26 diciembre*); ~ *gloves pl.* guantes *m/pl.* de boxeo; ~ *match* partido *m* de boxeo; ~ *ring* cuadrilátero *m* de boxeo.
box...: **ˈ~ num·ber** apartado *m*; **ˈ~ of·fice** **1.** taquilla *f*; **2.** *adj.* seguro de éxito popular; ~ *hit* éxito *m* de taquilla; ~ *record* marca *f* de taquilla; *be good* ~ ser taquillero; **ˈ~ room** trastero *m*; **ˈ~·wood** boj *m*.
boy [bɔi] **1.** niño *m*; muchacho *m*, chico *m*; (*son*) hijo *m*; (*servant*) criado *m*, botones *m*; **2.** *adj.* joven; *v. scout*.
boy·cott [ˈbɔikɔt] **1.** boicotear; **2.** boicoteo *m*.
boy·hood [ˈbɔihud] muchachez *f*, puericia *f*; juventud *f*; **boy·ish** [ˈbɔiiʃ] □ amuchachado; juvenil.
bra [brɑ] F = *brassière*.
brace [breis] **1.** ⊕ abrazadera *f*; refuerzo *m*, laña *f*; ⚠ tirante *m*, riostra *f*; (*carriage*) sopanda *f*; *typ.* corchete *m*; ⚓ braza *f*; (*pair*) par *m*; ~*s pl.* tirantes *m/pl.*; ~ *and bit* berbiquí *m* y barrena; **2.** asegurar, reforzar; ⚓ bracear; *fig.*, *esp.* ~ *o.s.* vigorizar(se); prepararse.
brace·let [ˈbreislit] pulsera *f*, brazalete *m*.
brac·ing [ˈbreisiŋ] que da vigor (*or* tono); tónico.
brack·en [ˈbrækn] helecho *m*.
brack·et [ˈbrækit] **1.** ⚠ ménsula *f*, repisa *f*; (*gas*) mechero *m*; (*light*) brazo *m*; *typ.* corchete *m*; **2.** poner entre corchetes; *fig.* asociar, agrupar.
brack·ish [ˈbrækiʃ] salobre.
bract [brækt] bráctea *f*.
brag [bræg] **1.** fanfarronada *f*; **2.** fanfarronear; ~ *of*, ~ *about* jactarse de.
brag·gart [ˈbrægərt] fanfarrón *m*, matasiete *m*.
Brah·man [ˈbrɑːmən], *mst* **Brah·min** [ˈ~min] **1.** bracmán (-a *f*) *m*; **2.** bracmánico.
braid [breid] **1.** (*hair*) trenza *f*; trencilla *f*; ⚔ galón *m*; **2.** trenzar; galonear.
braille [breil] alfabeto *m* de los ciegos.
brain [brein] **1.** cerebro *m*, sesos *m/pl.*; *fig.* (*mst* ~*s pl.*) intelecto *m*, cabeza *f*; *have s.t. on the* ~ ser obsesionado por algo, no poder quitar algo de la cabeza; F *pick a p.'s* ~*s* sacarle a uno el jugo; *rack one's* ~*s* devanarse los sesos; **2.** *sl.* romper la crisma a.
brain...: **ˈ~child** parto *m* del ingenio; **ˈ~ drain** éxodo *m* de técnicos; **ˈ~ ˈfe·ver** meningitis *f* cerebroespinal; **ˈ~·less** □ tonto, insensato; **ˈ~ pan** cráneo *m*, tapa *f* de los sesos; **ˈ~-storm** frenesí *m*; **ˈ~ trust** consultorio *m* intelectual, grupo *m* de peritos; **ˈ~·wash·ing** lavado *m* cerebral, lavado de cerebro; **ˈ~ wave** onda *f* encefálica; F idea *f* luminosa; **ˈ~ work** trabajo *m* intelectual; **ˈbrain·y** □: *be* ~ ser sesudo, ser una hacha.
braise [breiz] guisar; estofar.
brake[1] [breik] ⚘ helecho *m*; soto *m*.
brake[2] [~] **1.** ⊕ freno *m* (*a. fig.*); (*flax*) agramadera *f*; *mot.* rubia *f*; ~ *lining* forro *m* del freno, guarnición *f* del freno; ~ *pedal* pedal *m* de freno; ~ *shoe* zapata *f*; **2.** ⊕ frenar; *flax* agramar; **ˈbrake(s)·man** 🚂 guardafrenos *m*.
bram·ble [ˈbræmbl] zarza *f*; **ˈbram·bly** zarzoso.
bran [bræn] salvado *m*.
branch [bræntʃ] **1.** ⚘ rama *f*; *fig.* ramo *m*, dependencia *f*; sección *f*; brazo *m of river*; † sucursal *f*; **2.** (*a.* ~ *out*) ramificarse; ⚘ echar ramas; extenderse; (*a.* ~ *off*) bifurcarse; separarse (*from* de); **ˈbranch·ing** ⚡ derivación *f*; **ˈbranch line** ramal *m*;

línea *f* local; ˈ**branch** ˈ**of·fice** sucursal *f*; ˈ**branch·y** ramoso.

brand [brænd] **1.** tizón *m*; ⚒ *etc.* hierro *m* de marcar; *esp. poet.* tea *f*; *poet.* espada *f*; ✝ marca *f*, sello *m*; **2.** marcar (con hierro candente); *fig.* tiznar (*acc.* de); ~*ing iron* hierro *m* de marcar.

bran·dish [ˈbrændiʃ] blandir.

brand-new [ˈbrændˈnjuː] enteramente nuevo, flamante.

bran·dy [ˈbrændi] coñac *m*; ˈ~ **ball** bombón *m* relleno de coñac.

brash [bræʃ] insolente, respondón; descarado; inculto; tosco.

brass [bræs] latón *m*; F pasta *f*; plancha *f* conmemorativa (de latón); *fig.* descaro *m*; ♪ *the* ~ el cobre; ~ *band* charanga *f*, banda *f*; ⚔ F ~ *hat* espadón *m*; F ~ *knuckles* boxeador *m*; *sl.* ~ *tacks pl.* lo esencial; *get down to* ~ *tacks* ir al grano; ˈ~ **found·er** latonero *m*.

brassière [brəˈzir] sostén *m*.

bras·sy [ˈbræːsi] de latón; *sound* áspero; *fig.* descarado; presuntuoso, presumido.

brat [bræt] F mocoso *m*, braguillas [*m*.]

bra·va·do [brəˈvɑːdou] bravata *f*, baladronada *f*.

brave [breiv] **1.** □ valiente, animoso; *lit.* magnífico, vistoso; **2.** desafiar, arrostrar; ˈ**brav·er·y** valor *m*, valentía *f*.

bra·vo [ˈbrɑːˈvou] (*pl.* ~[e]s) **1.** asesino *m* pagado; **2.** ¡bravo!

brawl [brɔːl] **1.** pendencia *f*; alboroto *m*; *poet.* murmullo *m*; **2.** alborotar, armar pendencia; ˈ**braw·ler** pendenciero (a *f*) *m*.

brawn [brɔːn] músculo *m*; *fig.* fuerza *f* muscular; (*meat*) carne *f* en gelatina; ˈ**brawn·i·ness** fortaleza *f*; ˈ**brawn·y** fuerte, vigoroso.

bray[1] [brei] **1.** rebuzno *m*; (*trumpet*) sonido *m* bronco; tintirintín *m*; (*laugh*) carcajada *f*; **2.** rebuznar; (*trumpet*) sonar con estrépito; (*laugh*) soltar una carcajada.

bray[2] [~] triturar.

braze [breiz] soldar.

bra·zen [ˈbreizn] □ de latón; *fig.* descarado; ˈ**bra·zen·ness** descaro *m*, desfachatez *f*.

bra·zier [ˈbreiʒər] brasero *m*; (*p.*) latonero *m*.

Bra·zil·ian [brəˈziliən] brasileño *adj. a. su. m* (a *f*).

Bra·zil-nut [brəˈzilˈnʌt] castaña *f* de Pará.

breach [briːtʃ] **1.** rompimiento *m* (*a. fig.*), rotura *f*; violación *f*, infracción *f of rule*; ⚔ brecha *f*; ~ *of contract* infracción *f* de contrato; ~ *of faith* falta *f* de fidelidad, infidencia *f*; ~ *of the peace* perturbación *f* del orden público; ~ *of promise* incumplimiento *m* de la palabra de matrimonio; ~ *of trust* abuso *m* de confianza; **2.** romper; ⚔ abrir brecha en.

bread [bred] pan *m* (*a. fig.*); ~ *basket* panera *f*, cesto *m* para el pan; *fig.* granero *m*; ~*board* tablero *m* para cortar el pan; ~*box* caja *f* para pan; ~ *and butter* pan *m* con mantequilla; pan de cada día; ~ *crumbs* pan *m* rallado; ~*ed* empanado; ~*fruit* fruto *m* del pan; ~ *knife* cuchillo *m* para cortar el pan; ~ *line* cola *f* del pan; ~ *winner* sostén *m* de la familia; *earn one's* ~ *and butter* ganarse el pan; *know which side one's* ~ *is buttered* saber a qué carta quedarse; ˈ~ **crumb** migaja *f* (de pan).

breadth [bredθ] anchura *f*; ⚓ (*beam*) manga *f*; *fig.* amplitud *f*; tolerancia *f*.

bread·win·ner [ˈbredwinər] el (la) que se gana la vida; productor (-a *f*) *m*.

break [breik] **1.** ruptura *f*; abertura *f*, grieta *f*; pausa *f*, intervalo *m*; interrupción *f*; (*rest*) descanso *m*; (*holiday*) asueto *m*; (*voice*) gallo *m*; (*carriage*) break *m*; partida *f at billiards*; ✝ (*price*) baja *f*; ~ *of day* alba *f*, amanecer *m*; *without a* ~ sin parar; F *give a p. a* ~ abrirle a uno la puerta; **2.** [*irr.*] *v/t.* romper, quebrantar (*a. fig.*); ⚡ interrumpir; *bank* quebrar; *horse* domar, amansar; *impact* amortiguar, suavizar; *news* comunicar; *p.* arruinar; *record* batir, superar; ⚒ abrir (*freq. fig.*: ~ *new ground* emprender algo nuevo); ~ *down* derribar; destruir; ~ *in* forzar, romper; ~ *in pieces* hacer pedazos; ~ *up* desmenuzar; *camp* levantar; *estate* parcelar; *organization* disolver; *ship* desguazar; *v/i.* romperse, quebrantarse; (*bank*) hacer bancarrota; (*boil*) reventar; (*day*) apuntar; (*health*) desfallecerse; (*voice*) mudar; ~ *away* desprenderse; separarse; ~ *down* perder la salud, decaer; prorrumpir en lágrimas; *mot.*,

⊕ tener averías; ~ *into a run* echar a correr; ~ *out* (*war*) estallar; ⚕ declararse; ~ *up* hacerse pedazos; disolverse; (*meeting*) levantarse; (*school*) cerrarse; *v. a. broken*; ˈ**break·a·ble** quebradizo, frágil; ˈ**break·age** rotura *f*; ⚓ indemnización *f* (por cosas quebradas); ˈ**break·a·way** *sport*: escapada *f*; ˈ**break·down** ⚕ colapso *m*; ⚕ (*nervous*) crisis *f* nerviosa; interrupción *f*, cesión *f*; *mot.* avería *f*; ˈ**break·er** ⚓ cachón *m*.

break...: ~**·fast** [ˈbrekfəst] **1.** desayuno *m*; **2.** desayunar(se); ~**·neck** [ˈbreiknek] precipitado; arriesgado; *at* ~ *speed* a mata caballo; ˈ~**·through** ⚔ ruptura *f*; *fig.* descubrimiento *m* sensacional; ˈ~ˈ**up** desmoronamiento *m*; desintegración *f*; disolución *f*; *school*: clausura *f*; ˈ~**·wa·ter** rompeolas *m*.

bream [bri:m] brema *f*; *sea* ~ besugo *m*.

breast [brest] **1.** pecho *m* (*a. fig.*); seno *m*; *fig.* corazón *m*; pechuga *f of bird*; *make a clean* ~ *of* confesar con franqueza; **2.** arrostrar, hacer cara a.

breast...: ˈ~**·bone** esternón *m*; ˈ~**·pin** alfiler *m* de pecho; ˈ~**·plate** peto *m*; ˈ~**·stroke** brazada *f* de pecho; ˈ~**·work** ⚔ parapeto *m*.

breath [breθ] aliento *m*, respiración *f*; (*animals*) hálito *m* (*a. poet.* = *breeze*); (*pause*) respiro *m*, pausa *f*; *out of* ~ sin aliento; *short of* ~ corto de resuello; *under one's* ~ en voz baja; *waste one's* ~ *on* gastar saliva en; **breathe** [bri:ð] *v/i.* respirar (*a. fig.*); (*heavily*) resollar; aspirar (*a.* ~ *in*); *v/t.* inspirar, respirar; exhalar; *fig.* sugerir; *v. last, word*; ˈ**breath·er** respiro *m*.

breath·ing [ˈbri:ðiŋ] respiración *f*; ˈ~ **space,** ˈ~ **time** descanso *m*, respiro *m*.

breath·less [ˈbreθlis] □ falto de aliento; ˈ**breath·less·ness** falta *f* de aliento.

breath·tak·ing [ˈbreθteikiŋ] □ *speed* vertiginoso; pasmoso.

bred [bred] *pret. a. p.p. of breed* 2.

breech [bri:tʃ] ⊕ recámara *f*; **breech·es** [ˈ~iz] *pl.* calzones *m/pl.*; F *wear the* ~ llevar los calzones; ˈ**breech·load·er** arma *f* de retrocarga.

breed [bri:d] **1.** casta *f*, progenie *f*; raza *f*; mestizo (a *f*) *m esp. White-Indian*; **2.** [*irr.*] *v/t.* criar, engendrar; *fig.* ocasionar, producir; educar; *v/i.* reproducirse; ˈ**breed·er** criador (-a *f*) *m*; ~ *reactor* reactor-generador *m*; ˈ**breed·ing** cría *f*; crianza *f* (*a. fig.*).

breeze[1] [bri:z] **1.** brisa *f*; F bronca *f*; **2.** F: ~ *in* entrar sin preocupación.

breeze[2] [~] *zo.* tábano *m*.

breez·y [ˈbri:zi] □ ventilado; (*windy*) ventoso; *p.* animado, jovial.

breth·ren [ˈbreðrin] hermanos *m/pl.*

breve [bri:v] cuadrada *f*, breve *m*.

bre·vet [ˈbrevit] graduación *f* honoraria.

bre·vi·ar·y [ˈbri:viəri] breviario *m*.

brev·i·ty [ˈbreviti] brevedad *f*.

brew [bru:] **1.** *v/t.* hacer, preparar; *fig.* urdir; *v/i.* prepararse; (*storm*) amenazar; **2.** poción *f*, brebaje *m*; mezcla *f*; ˈ**brew·er** cervecero *m*; ~*s yeast* levadura *f* de cerveza; ˈ**brew·er·y** fábrica *f* de cerveza.

bri·ar [ˈbraiər] = *brier*[1] *a. brier*[2].

brib·a·ble [ˈbraibəbl] sobornable; **bribe** [braib] **1.** soborno *m*, cohecho *m*; **2.** sobornar, cohechar; ˈ**brib·er** sobornador (-a *f*) *m*, cohechador (-a *f*) *m*; ˈ**brib·er·y** soborno *m*, cohecho *m*.

brick [brik] **1.** ladrillo *m*; F *a regular* ~ un buen sujeto; *sl. drop a* ~ hacer una plancha; **2.** (*mst* ~ *up*) cerrar (con ladrillos); ˈ~**·bat** trozo *m* de ladrillo; ˈ~ **kiln** horno *m* de ladrillos; ˈ~**·lay·er** ladrillador *m*; ˈ~**·works** tejar *m*, ladrillar *m*.

brid·al [ˈbraidl] **1.** □ nupcial; **2.** *mst poet.* boda *f*; ~ *wreath* corona *f* nupcial.

bride [braid] novia *f*, desposada *f*; ˈ~**·groom** novio *m*, desposado *m*; ˈ**brides·maid** madrina *f* de boda, prónuba *f*.

bridge[1] [bridʒ] **1.** puente *m* (*a.* ♪); (*nose*) caballete *m*; (*billiards*) violín *m*; **2.** tender un puente sobre; *fig.* ~ *the gap* llenar el vacío.

bridge[2] [~] *cards*: bridge *m*.

bridge·head [ˈbridʒhed] cabeza *f* de puente.

bri·dle [ˈbraidl] **1.** brida *f*, freno *m*; **2.** *v/t.* enfrenar; *fig.* refrenar, reprimir; *v/i.* levantar la cabeza; *fig.* picarse (*at* por); *fig.* erguirse; ˈ~ **path** camino *m* de herradura.

bri·doon [briˈdu:n] bridón *m*.

brief [bri:f] **1.** □ breve, conciso; (*fleeting*) fugaz, pasajero; **2.** epítome *m*, resumen *m*; (*papal*) breve *m*; ⚖ escrito *m*, memorial *m*; *hold a* ~ *for* abogar por (*a. fig.*); ˈ~ **case** cartera *f*; ˈ**brief·ing** órdenes *f/pl.*; informe *m* *of the press*; reunión *f* en que se dan las órdenes; ˈ**brief·ness** brevedad *f*.

bri·er[1] [ˈbraiər] ⚘ escaramujo *m*; zarza *f*.

bri·er[2] [~] pipa *f* (*esp.* aquélla hecha de madera de brezo; *a.* ~ *pipe*).

brig [brig] bergantín *m*.

bri·gade [briˈgeid] brigada *f*; **brig·a·dier** [brigəˈdir] brigadier *m*.

brig·and [ˈbrigənd] bandido *m*, bandolero *m*; ˈ**brig·and·age** bandolerismo *m*; latrocinio *m*.

bright [brait] **1.** □ claro, luminoso, brillante; *surface* lustroso, pulido; *color* subido; *fig.* (*cheerful*) vivo, alegre; (*clever*) listo, talentoso; **2.** ~*s mot.* luces *f/pl.* de carretera; ˈ**bright·en** *v/t.* pulir, abrillantar; *fig.* mejorar, avivar, animar; *v/i.* (*freq.* ~ *up*) avivarse, animarse; mejorar; ˈ**bright·ness** claridad *f*, brillantez *f*; resplandor *m*; lustre *m*; lo subido *of color*; *fig.* viveza *f*; talento *m*, viveza *f* de ingenio.

brill [bril] rodaballo *m*.

bril·liance [ˈbriljəns], **bril·lian·cy** [ˈbriljənsi] brillantez *f*, brillo *m*; ˈ**bril·liant 1.** □ brillante, refulgente; *fig.* excelente, sobresaliente; (*showy*) vistoso; **2.** brillante *m*.

brim [brim] **1.** borde *m*, orilla *f*; ala *f* *of hat*; **2.** (*a.* ~ *over*) rebosar (*with* de; *a. fig.*); ˈ~ˈ**ful**, ˈ~-ˈ**full** lleno hasta el borde; rebosante (*with* de); ˈ~·**less** *hat* sin ala.

brim·stone [ˈbrimstoun] azufre *m*.

brin·dle(**d**) [ˈbrindl(d)] manchado, mosqueado.

brine [brain] salmuera *f*; *poet.* piélago *m*.

bring [briŋ] [*irr.*] llevar; traer; conducir; ⚖ *charge* exponer; ⚖ *suit* entablar, armar; ~ *about* ocasionar, originar; ~ *along* llevar consigo; ~ *away* llevarse; ~ *back* devolver; *p.*, *th.* volver con; ~ *down price* rebajar; ✈ derribar; *thea.* ~ *down the house* hacer que se venga abajo el teatro; ~ *forth* dar a luz, parir; *fig.* producir; ~ *forward* presentar; *date* adelantar; ✝ llevar a otra cuenta; ~ *s.t. home to s.o.* hacer que alguien se dé cuenta de algo; ~ *in* presentar; *fashion etc.* introducir; *income etc.* producir, rendir; *p.* hacer entrar; *verdict* dar; ~ *off* ⚖ exculpar; *success* conseguir; ~ *on* causar, inducir; ~ *out th.* sacar, hacer salir; *book* sacar a luz, publicar; *p.* hacer más afable, ayudar a adquirir confianza; ~ *round* (*win over*) ganar, convertir; ⚕ hacer volver en sí; ~ *a p. to do s.t.* inducir a alguien a hacer algo; ~ *o.s. to inf.* resignarse a *inf.*, cobrar suficiente ánimo para *inf.*; ⚓ ~ *to* ponerse en facha; ~ *together* reunir; *enemies* reconciliar; ~ *under* sojuzgar, someter; ~ *up p.* criar, educar; *subject* sacar a colación; (*stop*) parar; F vomitar, arrojar; ˈ~·**ing** ˈ**up** educación *f*, crianza *f*.

brink [briŋk] borde *m*, orilla *f*; *fig.* *on the* ~ *of* a punto de.

brin·y [ˈbraini] salado, salobre.

bri·quette [briˈket] briqueta *f*.

brisk [brisk] **1.** □ enérgico, vigoroso; despejado; animado, activo; *gait etc.* gallardo, airoso; **2.** (*mst* ~ *up*) avivar, animar.

bris·ket [ˈbriskit] pecho *m* de un animal, *esp. carne cortada del pecho para asar*.

brisk·ness [ˈbrisknis] energía *f*; despejo *m*; *etc.*

bris·tle [ˈbrisl] **1.** cerda *f*; **2.** erizarse; *fig.* (*freq.* ~ *up*) montar en cólera; *fig.* estar erizado (*with* de); ˈ**bris·tled**, ˈ**bris·tly** cerdoso; erizado.

Bri·tan·nic [briˈtænik] británico.

Brit·ish [ˈbritiʃ] británico; inglés; *the* ~ *pl.* los ingleses; ˈ**Brit·ish·er** F natural *m/f* de Gran Bretaña.

Brit·on [ˈbritən] britano (a *f*) *m*; inglés (-a *f*) *m*.

brit·tle [ˈbritl] quebradizo, frágil; ˈ**brit·tle·ness** fragilidad *f*, friabilidad *f*.

broach [broutʃ] **1.** asador *m*; (*spire*) aguja *f*; ⊕ broca *f*; **2.** *cask* espitar; *fig.* mencionar por primera vez; (*start using*) decentar.

broad [brɔːd] □ ancho, amplio; extenso, vasto; *outline etc.* claro, explícito; (*coarse*) grosero; *story* verde; *mind*, *view* liberal, tolerante; *accent* marcado, cerrado; ~ *inoutlook* de amplias miras e ideas; ~*ly* en general; ˈ~·**axe** ⊕ hacha *f* de carpintero; ˈ~·**cast 1.** ↙ sembrado al vuelo; *fig.* diseminado, divulgado; **2.** [*irr.* (*cast*)] *v/t.* ↙ sembrar al vuelo; *fig.* diseminar, divulgar, difundir; *radio*:

emitir, radiar; *v/i.* hablar *etc.* por la radio; *~ing* radiodifusión *f*; *~ing station* emisora *f*, radioemisora *f*; **3.** *radio*: emisión *f*, programa *m*; ˈ**~·cloth** paño *m* fino; ˈ**broad·en** ensanchar(se); *fig.* ampliar(se); ˈ**broad-ˈmind·ed** liberal, tolerante; de miras amplias; ˈ**broad·ness** anchura *f*; *esp. fig.* amplitud *f*; liberalismo *m*, tolerancia *f*.

broad...: ˈ**~·sheet** hoja *f* suelta impresa; ˈ**~·side** ⚓ costado *m*, andanada *f*; *a.* = *broadsheet*; ˈ**~·sword** espadón *m*.

bro·cade [brəˈkeid] brocado *m*; **broˈcad·ed** espolinado.

broc·co·li [ˈbrɔkəli] brécol *m*.

bro·chure [brouˈʃur] folleto *m*.

brock [brɔk] tejón *m*.

brogue [broug] (*shoe*) abarca *f*; acento *m* irlandés.

broil [brɔil] **1.** pendencia *f*, camorra *f*; **2.** asar sobre ascuas (*or* a la parrilla); tostar (al sol); *~ing* tórrido; ˈ**broil·er** pollo *m* para asar.

broke [brouk] *pret. of break*; *sl.* sin blanca.

bro·ken [broukən] *p.p. of break*; *adj. ground* accidentado, desigual; *health* estropeado, deshecho; *language* chapurreado; *voice* cascado; (*despairing*) desesperado; ˈ**~-ˈdown** abatido; descompuesto; destartalado; ˈ**~-ˈheart·ed** traspasado de dolor; ˈ**bro·ken·ly** con la voz cascada; acongojado; ˈ**bro·ken-ˈwind·ed** *vet.* corto de resuello.

bro·ker [ˈbroukər] ⚚ corredor *m*; ⚚ agente *m* de negocios; prendero *m*; ˈ**bro·ker·age**, ˈ**bro·king** corretaje *m*.

bro·mide [ˈbroumaid] bromuro *m*; F perogrullada *f*; **bro·mine** [ˈ~mi:n] bromo *m*.

bron·chi·al [ˈbrɔŋkiəl] bronquial; **bron·chi·tis** [brɔŋˈkaitis] bronquitis *f*.

bron·co [ˈbrɔŋkou] potro *m* cerril; ˈ**~bust·er** *sl.* domador *m* de caballos, picador *m*.

bronze [brɔnz] **1.** bronce *m* (*a. fig.*); **2.** *attr.* de bronce; **3.** *v/t.* broncear; F (*beat*) zurrar; *v/i.* (*tan*) broncearse.

brooch [broutʃ] broche *m*.

brood [bru:d] **1.** camada *f*, cría *f*; *fig.* progenie *f*; *~ mare* yegua *f* de cría; **2.** empollar; *fig. ~ on, ~ over* rumiar *acc.*; meditar *acc.* melancólicamente; ˈ**brood·y** clueca; *fig.* melancólico.

brook¹ [bruk] arroyo *m*.

brook² [~] *lit.* (*mst negative*) sufrir, aguantar.

brook·let [ˈbruklit] arroyuelo *m*.

broom [bru:m] escoba *f*; ⚘ hiniesta *f*, retama *f*; **~·corn** [ˈbrumˈkɔ:rn] sorgo *m*; **~·stick** [ˈbrumstik] palo *m* de escoba.

broth [brɔθ] caldo *m*.

broth·el [ˈbrɔθl] burdel *m*, lupanar *m*.

broth·er [ˈbrʌðər] hermano *m* (*a. fig.*); **~·hood** [ˈ~hud] fraternidad *f*; (*a. guild*) hermandad *f*; ˈ**~-in-law** cuñado *m*; ˈ**broth·er·ly** fraternal.

brougham [ˈbru:əm] brougham *m*.

brought [brɔ:t] *pret. a. p.p. of bring*.

brow [brau] ceja *f*; (*forehead*) frente *f*; cumbre *f of hill*; *knit one's ~* fruncir las cejas; ˈ**~·beat** [*irr.* (*beat*)] intimidar (con palabras); (*dominate*) imponerse a.

brown [braun] **1.** pardo, castaño, moreno; *bread* moreno; *paper* de embalar, de estraza; *shoes* de color; *~ study* absorción *f*, pensamiento *m* profundo, ensimismamiento *m*; *~ sugar* azúcar *f* terciada; **2.** color *m* pardo *etc.*; **3.** (*skin etc.*) broncear(se); poner(se) moreno; *cooking*: dorar(se); *sl. be ~ed off* estar harto (*with* de); ˈ**brown·ie** duende *m* moreno; *miembro joven de las Niñas Exploradores*; ˈ**brown·ish** que tira a moreno; ˈ**brown·stone** *piedra arenisca de color pardo rojizo*.

browse [brauz] **1.** pimpollos *m/pl.*; **2.** herbajar; ramonear, rozar (*on acc.*); *fig.* leer por gusto.

bru·in [ˈbru:in] oso *m*.

bruise [bru:z] **1.** contusión *f*, cardenal *m*, magulladura *f*; **2.** magullar; (*batter*) majar, machacar; ˈ**bruis·er** *sl.* boxeador *m*.

bru·nette [bru:ˈnet] morena, trigueña *adj. a. su. f.*

brunt [brʌnt] ⚔ embate *m*, acometida *f*; *fig. bear the ~ of* aguantar lo más recio de.

brush [brʌʃ] **1.** cepillo *m*; (*large*) escoba *f*; *paint.* pincel *m*, brocha *f*; (*fox*) rabo *m*; ⚡ escobilla *f*; ⚔ escaramuza *f*; = *~wood, backwoods*; *~ stroke* pincelada *f*; *give a p. a ~* cepillar a una *p.*; *have a ~ with a p.* desavenirse con una p.; **2.** *v/t.* (a)cepillar; rozar *in passing*; ~ *aside* echar a un lado; ~ *away*, ~ *off* quitar con cepillo (*or* con la mano); ~ *down* (a)cepillar, limpiar, almohazar; ~ *up* acicalar; *fig.* repasar, refrescar; *v/i.*: ~ *against* rozar; ~ *by*, ~ *past* pasar rozando (*or* muy cerca); **'~·wood** matorral *m*, breñal *m*.

brusque [brusk] □ brusco, rudo.

Brus·sels ['brʌslz]: ~ *sprouts pl.* col *f* de Bruselas.

bru·tal ['bru:tl] □ brutal; feroz; **bru·tal·i·ty** [bru'tæliti] brutalidad *f*; ferocidad *f*; **bru·tal·ize** ['bru:təlaiz] embrutecer; **brute** [bru:t] **1.** brutal; (*stupid etc.*) bruto; **2.** bruto *m*, bestia *f* (*a. fig.*); monstruo *m*; **'brut·ish** □ = *brute* 1; **'brut·ish·ness** brutalidad *f*.

bub·ble ['bʌbl] **1.** burbuja *f*, ampolla *f*; *fig.* bagatela *f*; (*fraud*) engañifa *f*; ~ *and squeak carne fría frita con legumbres*; **2.** burbujear, borbotar; ~ *over fig.* rebosar (*with* de).

buc·ca·neer [bʌkə'nir] **1.** bucanero *m*; **2.** piratear.

buck [bʌk] **1.** *zo.* gamo *m*; (*goat*) macho *m* cabrío; (*rabbit*) conejo *m* macho; (*p.*) petimetre *m*; *sl.* dólar *m*; ~ *private* ⚔ soldado *m* raso; F *pass the* ~ echar la carga a otro; **2.** *v/i.* corcovear; F ~ *up* animarse, cobrar ánimo; F ~ *up!* ¡apúrate!; *v/t.* F hacer frente a; F embestir, arrojarse sobre; F ~ *up* animar.

buck·et ['bʌkit] cubo *m*, balde *m*; ⊕ paleta *f*; ~ *seat mot.* baquet *m*; F *a drop in the* ~ una nonada; *sl. kick the* ~ estirar la pata; **'~·ful** contenido *m* de un cubo; F *rain* ~*s* llover a chuzos.

buck·le ['bʌkl] **1.** hebilla *f*; **2.** *v/t.* hebillar; *v/i.* doblarse, encorvarse; ~ *down to* (*prp.*) dedicarse con empeño a; ~ *to* (*adv.*) emprender algo con ahinco; **'buck·ler** escudo *m*, rodela *f*.

buck·ram ['bʌkrəm] bucarán *m*.

buck...: **'~·shot** balines *m/pl.*; perdigón *m* zorrero; **'~·skin** cuero *m* de ante; **'~·wheat** alforfón *m*.

bud [bʌd] **1.** pimpollo *m*, brote *m*; *in* ~ en brote; *fig. nip in the* ~ cortar de raíz; **2.** *v/t.* ✓ injertar de escudete; *v/i.* brotar, echar pimpollos; ~*ding lawyer etc.* abogado *m etc.* en ciernes.

bud·dy ['bʌdi] F camarada *m*, compinche *m*.

budge [bʌdʒ] mover(se); *he did not dare to* ~ no osaba bullirse.

budg·et ['bʌdʒit] **1.** presupuesto *m*; *attr.* presupuestario; **2.** *v/i.*: ~ *for* presupuestar; **'budg·et·ar·y** presupuestario.

buff [bʌf] **1.** piel *f* de ante; *in* (*one's*) ~ en cueros; **2.** color de ante.

buf·fa·lo ['bʌfəlou], *pl.* **buf·fa·loes** ['~z] **1.** búfalo *m*; **2.** *v/t. sl.* intimidar.

buff·er ['bʌfər] 🚂 tope *m*; amortiguador *m*; F mastuerzo *m*; ~ *state* estado *m* tapón.

buf·fet[1] ['bʌfit] **1.** bofetada *f*; golpe *m*; **2.** abofetear; golpear; ~*ing* golpear *m* (*e.g. of sea*).

buf·fet[2] [bə'fei] 🚂 fonda *f*, cantina *f*; (*sideboard*) aparador *m*; ~ *car* coche *m* bar; ~ *lunch* servicio *m* de bufet; ~ *supper* ambigú *m*, bufet *m*.

buf·foon [bʌ'fu:n] bufón *m*; **buf'foon·er·y** bufonada *f*.

bug [bʌg] chinche *f*; bicho *m*, insecto *m*; *sl.* microbio *m*; *sl.* estorbo *m*, traba *f*; F *big* ~ señorón *m*; **~·a·boo** ['~əbu:], **'bug·bear** espantajo *m* (*a. fig.*); coco *m*; **'bug·gy** **1.** lleno de chinches; **2.** calesa *f*.

bu·gle[1] ['bju:gl] ♪ corneta *f*.

bu·gle[2] [~] abalorio *m*.

bu·gler ['bju:glər] corneta *m*.

buhl [bu:l] taracea *f*.

build [bild] **1.** [*irr.*] construir, fabricar; *fig.* edificar (*on* sobre); fundar, establecer, componer; ⊕ ~ *in* empotrar; ~ *up* componer *from parts*; armar; ✲ fortalecer; *fig.* crear; **2.** estructura *f*; *anat.* talle *m*; **'build·er** arquitecto *m*; constructor *m*; maestro *m* de obras; **'build·ing** edificio *m*; construcción *f*; *attr.* de construcción; relativo a edificios; ~ *contractor* contratista *m*; ~ *and loan association* sociedad *f* de crédito para la construcción; ~ *lot* solar *m*; ~ *site* terreno *m* para construir; ~ *trades pl.* oficios *m/pl.* de edificación; **'build-'up** composición *f*, acumulación *f*; *fig.* propaganda *f* previa.

built [bilt] *pret. a. p.p. of build* 1; **'built-'in** ⚠ empotrado; ⊕ incorporado, montado; ⚡ interior; **'built-'up** urbanizado.

bulb [bʌlb] ⚘ bulbo *m*; ⚡ bombilla *f*; ampolleta *f of thermometer*; **'bulbous** bulboso.

Bul·gar·i·an [bʌlˈgeriən] búlgaro *adj. a. su. m* (a *f*).

bulge [bʌldʒ] **1.** bombeo *m*, comba *f*, pandeo *m*; **2.** bombearse, combarse, pandearse; *bulging eyes* ojos *m/pl.* saltones.

bulk [bʌlk] bulto *m*, volumen *m*; grueso *m*; *fig.* la mayor parte; ⚓ carga *f*; *in* ~ a granel; ~ *goods pl.* mercancías *f/pl.* sueltas; ˈ**~·head** ⚓ mamparo *m*; ˈ**bulk·i·ness** volumen *m*, bulto *m*; ˈ**bulk·y** abultado, voluminoso.

bull[1] [bul] **1.** *zo.* toro *m*; ✝ *sl.* alcista *m*; *sl.* detective *m*, policía *m*; *take the ~ by the horns* irse a la cabeza del toro; *attr.* macho; **2.** ✝ *sl.* jugar al alza; *sl.* chapucear.

bull[2] [~] *eccl.* bula *f*.

bull[3] [~] disparate *m*.

bull·dog [ˈbuldɔg] dogo *m*; *univ.* F bedel *m*.

bull·doze [ˈbuldouz] F intimidar; *opposition* arrollar; ˈ**bull·doz·er** empujadora *f* niveladora, motoniveladora *f*.

bul·let [ˈbulit] bala *f* (de fusil); *~proof* a prueba de balas, blindado.

bul·le·tin [ˈbulitin] boletín *m*; anuncio *m*; *v. news* ~; *~board* tablón *m* de anuncios, tablilla *f*.

bull...: ˈ**~·fight** corrida *f* de toros; ˈ**~·finch** camachuelo *m*; ˈ**~·frog** rana *f* toro; ˈ**~·head·ed** obstinado, terco.

bul·lion [ˈbuljən] oro *m* (*or* plata *f*) en barras (*or* lingotes); (*fringe*) entorchado *m*.

bull·ock [ˈbulək] buey *m*.

bull·pen [ˈbulˈpen] toril *m*; F prevención *f* de policía.

bull's-eye [ˈbulzai] centro *m* del blanco; ⚓ cristal *m* de patente, portilla *f*; *tipo de dulce*; ~ *pane* vidrio *m* abombado.

bul·ly[1] [ˈbuli] **1.** matón *m*, valentón *m*; **2.** F de primera; *a. int.* ¡bravo!; **3.** intimidar; tiranizar; ~ *s.o. into* forzar a uno con amenazas a que *subj.*

bul·ly[2] [~] carne *f* de vaca conservada en latas (*a.* ~ *beef*).

bul·rush [ˈbulrʌʃ] junco *m*; espadaña *f*.

bul·wark [ˈbulwərk] baluarte *m* (*a. fig.*); ⚓ macarrón *m*.

bum[1] [bʌm] F culo *m*.

bum[2] [~] F **1.** (*p.*) holgazán *m*, vagabundo *m*; (*spree*) jarana *f*, juerga *f*; **2.** holgazanear, vagabundear (*a. go on the* ~); *sl.* beber a pote; *sl.* mendigar; **3.** *sl.* inferior, chapucero; *feel* ~ sentirse muy malo.

bum·ble·bee [ˈbʌmblbiː] abejorro *m*.

bum·boat [ˈbʌmbout] bote *m* vivandero.

bump [bʌmp] **1.** topetón *m*; batacazo *m in falling*; sacudida *f*; (*lump etc.*) chichón *m*, hinchazón *f*; protuberancia *f*; comba *f on surface*; **2.** chocar contra, topetar (*a.~against*); ~ *along* botar, dar sacudidas; F ~ *into p.* topar; *sl.* ~ *off* asesinar, despenar; **bump·er** [ˈbʌmpər] tope *m*; ⚔ *a. mot.* parachoques *m*; copa *f* llena; *attr.* muy grande, abundante.

bump·kin [ˈbʌmpkin] patán *m*.

bump·tious [ˈbʌmpʃəs] □ F engreído, presuntuoso.

bump·y [ˈbʌmpi] abollado; *land* desigual; *air* agitado; *road* lleno de baches.

bun [bʌn] bollo *m*; (*hair*) moño *m*.

bunch [bʌntʃ] **1.** manojo *m*, atado *m*; ramo *m of flowers*; racimo *m of grapes*; F grupo *m*; F montón *m*; **2.** agrupar, juntar; ˈ**bunch·y** racimoso.

bun·combe [bʌŋkəm] *v. bunk.*

bun·dle [ˈbʌndl] **1.** lío *m*, bulto *m*; legajo *m of papers*; haz *f of sticks*; **2.** *v/t.* arropar, envolver (*mst* ~ *up*); F ~ *off* despachar sin ceremonia; *v/i.* escaparse, irse.

bung [bʌŋ] **1.** bitoque *m*; **2.** tapar (con bitoque); cerrar; F *~ed up mst* hinchado; cerrado.

bun·ga·low [ˈbʌŋgəlou] bungalow *m*, casa *f* de campo.

bung·hole [ˈbʌŋhoul] piquera *f*.

bun·gle [ˈbʌŋgl] **1.** chapucería *f*; **2.** chapucear; ˈ**bun·gler** chapucero (a *f*) *m*; ˈ**bun·gling** **1.** □ chapucero; **2.** chapucería *f*.

bun·ion [ˈbʌnjən] hinchazón *f* en el pie, juanete *m*.

bunk[1] [bʌŋk] *sl.* palabrería *f*, música *f* celestial; *do a* ~ huir, volver la cara.

bunk[2] [~] camastro *m*, tarima *f* para dormir; F cama *f*.

bunk·er [ˈbʌŋkər] **1.** (*coal-*) carbonera *f*; ⚓ pañol *m* del carbón; *golf*: hoya *f* de arena, arenal *m*; **2.** ⚓ proveer de carbón; F *get ~ed* empantanarse.

bun·kum [ˈbʌŋkəm] *v. bunk.*

bun·ny [ˈbʌni] conejito *m*.

bun·ting[1] [ˈbʌntiŋ] *orn.* escribano *m*; *corn* ~ triguero *m*.

bun·ting[2] [~] ⊕ estameña *f*; ⚓ *etc.* banderas *f/pl.*, empavesado *m*.

buoy [bɔi] **1.** boya *f*; **2.** aboyar; ~ *up* mantener a flote; *fig.* alentar.

buoy·an·cy [ˈbɔiənsi] fluctuación *f*, facultad *f* de flotar; ✈ fuerza *f* ascensional; ˈ**buoy·ant** □ boyante; *fig.* alegre, animado; † al alza.

bur [bəːr] ♀ erizo *m*; *fig.* persona *f* muy pegadiza.

Bur·ber·ry [ˈbəːrbəri] gabardina *f*.

bur·den[1] [ˈbəːrdn] **1.** carga *f* (*a. fig.*), gravamen *m*; ⚓ arqueo *m*; ⚓ peso *m* de la carga; **2.** cargar (*a. fig.*; *with* de); ˈ**bur·den·some** oneroso, gravoso.

bur·den[2] [~] ♪ estribillo *m*; *fig.* tema *m* principal.

bur·dock [ˈbəːrdɔk] bardana *f*.

bu·reau [ˈbjurou], *pl. a.* **bu·reaux** [~z] escritorio *m*; oficina *f*, agencia *f*; ramo *m*, departamento *m*; **bu·reauc·ra·cy** [~ˈrɔkrəsi] burocracia *f*; **bu·reau·crat** [ˈbjuroukræt] burócrata *m/f*; **bu·reauˈcrat·ic** □ burocrático.

bur·geon [ˈbəːrdʒən] *lit.* **1.** retoño *m*; **2.** retoñar.

bur·gess [ˈbəːrdʒis] vecino (a *f*) *m* de una villa; burgués *m*, ciudadano *m*; alcalde *m* de un pueblo o villa; *hist.* diputado *m*.

burgh [ˈbʌrə] *Scot.* villa *f*.

bur·glar [ˈbəːrglər] escalador *m*; ~ *alarm* alarma *f* de ladrones; ~*proof* a prueba de escaladores; **bur·glar·ize** [ˈbəːrgləraiz] allanar, escalar; **bur·gla·ry** [ˈ~ri] allanamiento *m* de morada, robo *m* con escalamiento.

bur·gun·dy [ˈbəːrgəndi] vino *m* de Borgoña.

bur·i·al [ˈberiəl] entierro *m*; ˈ~ **ground** cementerio *m*.

bu·rin [ˈbjurin] buril *m*.

burl [bəːrl] mota *f* en el paño.

bur·lap [ˈbəːrləp] harpillera *f*.

bur·lesque [bəːrˈlesk] **1.** burlesco, festivo; ~ *show* espectáculo *m* de bailes y cantos groseros, music-hall *m*; **2.** parodia *f*; **3.** parodiar.

bur·ly [ˈbəːrli] membrudo, fornido.

Bur·mese [bəːrˈmiːz] birmano *adj. a. su. m* (a *f*).

burn [bəːrn] **1.** quemadura *f*; *Scot.* arroyo *m*; **2.** [*irr.*] *v/t.* quemar; (*sun*) abrasar; ⊕ *fuel* funcionar con; *house etc.* (*a.* ~ *down*) incendiar; ⚡ ~ *out* fundir, quemar; ~ *up* consumir (*a. fig.*; *with* con, en); *v/i.* quemar(se); arder; incendiarse (*a.* ~ *down*); ~ *out* apagarse; ⚡ fundirse, quemarse; ~ *up* consumirse; arder mejor; *fig.* ~ *with* arder en (*or* de); *the light is* ~*ing* la luz está encendida; ˈ**burn·er** mechero *m*; (*gas etc.*) quemador *m*, fuego *m*; ˈ**burn·ing** □ ardiente (*a. fig.*); ~ *question* cuestión *f* palpitante.

bur·nish [ˈbəːrniʃ] bruñir; ˈ**bur·nish·er** bruñidor *m*.

burnt [bəːrnt] *pret. a. p.p. of burn* 2; ~ *almond* almendra *f* dulce tostada; ~ *offering* holocausto *m*.

burr [bəːr] **1.** sonido *m* fuerte de la erre; **2.** pronunciar la erre con sonido fuerte.

bur·row [ˈbʌrou] **1.** madriguera *f*; (*rabbit's*) conejera *f*; **2.** socavar; (*a.* ~ *through*) horadar.

bur·sa·ry [ˈbəːrsəri] beca *f*; tesorería *f* de un colegio.

burst [bəːrst] **1.** reventón *m*; estallido *m*; (*leak*) fuga *f*; ⚔ ráfaga *f of fire*; *fig.* arranque *m*, ímpetu *m*; **2.** [*irr.*] *v/i.* reventar(se); estallar (*a. fig.*); ~ *into room* irrumpir en; *tears* prorrumpir en, deshacerse en; *threats etc.* desatarse en; ~ *out laughing* echarse a reír; ~ *with laughing* reventar de risa; *v/t.* reventar; romper.

bur·then [ˈbəːrðn] ⚓ arqueo *m*.

bur·y [ˈberi] enterrar, sepultar; *fig.* ocultar; ~*ing ground* cementerio *m*; *be buried in thought* estar absorto en meditación.

bus [bʌs] F autobús *m*; ~*boy* ayudante *m* de camarero; ~ *driver* conductor *m* de autobús; ~ *stop* parada *f* de autobús; *sl. miss the* ~ perder la ocasión.

bus·by [ˈbʌzbi] gorra *f* de húsar.

bush [buʃ] arbusto *m*; matorral *m*; ⊕ forro *m* de metal; **bush·el** [ˈbuʃl] *medida de áridos* (= *35,24 litros*; *British* = *36,36 litros*); ˈ**bush·rang·er** *Australia*: bandido *m*; **bush·y** [ˈbuʃi] *p.* peludo; *ground* matoso.

busi·ness [ˈbiznis] negocio *m*, comercio *m*; (*firm*) empresa *f*; negocios *m/pl.*; (*calling*) empleo *m*, ocupación *f*; (*matter*) asunto *m*, cuestión *f*; *big* ~ comercio *m* en gran escala; *on* ~ de negocios; ~ *connections pl.* relaciones *f/pl.* comerciales; ~ *deal* trato *m* comercial; ~ *district* barrio *m* comercial; ~ *hours pl.* horas *f/pl.* de oficina; ~ *house* casa *f* de comercio; ~ *quarter* barrio *m* comercial; ~ *suit* traje *m* de calle; ~ *trip* viaje *m* de negocios; *do* ~ *with* comerciar con; *have no* ~ *to inf.* no tener derecho a *inf.*; *make it one's* ~ *to inf.* proponerse *inf.*; F *mean* ~ actuar (*or* hablar) en serio; *mind one's own* ~ no meterse donde no le llaman; *send a p. about his* ~ mandarle a uno a paseo; **ˈ~·like** metódico, eficaz; negocioso; **ˈ~·man** hombre *m* de negocios.

bus·kin [ˈbʌskin] borceguí *m*; *thea.* coturno *m*.

bus·man [ˈbʌsmən] conductor *m* de autobús; *~'s holiday día de fiesta que pasa uno haciendo lo mismo que los otros días.*

bust[1] [bʌst] busto *m*; pecho *m* de mujer.

bust[2] [~] F **1.** reventón *m*; ✝ fracaso *m*; *go* ~ quebrar; **2.** romper(se), estropear(se).

bus·tard [ˈbʌstərd] avutarda *f*.

bus·tle [ˈbʌsl] **1.** bullicio *m*, animación *f*; (*esp. crowd*) bulla *f*; (*dress*) polisón *m*; **2.** *v/i.* menearse, apresurarse; (*a.* ~ *about*) bullir; *v/t.* impeler (a trabajar *etc.*); **ˈbus·tler** bullebulle *m/f*; **ˈbus·tling** □ hacendoso; *crowd* bullicioso.

bust-up [ˈbʌstˈʌp] F ✝ quiebra *f*; (*quarrel*) riña *f*; (*row*) una *f* de Dios es Cristo.

bus·y [ˈbizi] **1.** □ ocupado (*at, with* en); activo; *b.s.* entrometido; bullicioso; *place* muy concurrido, de mucha actividad; ~ *signal teleph.* señal *f* de ocupado; *keep* ~ (*v/t.*) ocupar, (*v/i.*) estar ocupado; **2.** (*mst* ~ *o.s.*) ocupar(se) (*about, at, in, with* en, de, con); **ˈ~·body** buscavidas *m/f*, entrometido (a *f*) *m*.

but [bʌt] **1.** *cj.* pero, mas (*lit.*); (*after negative*) sino; sino que; que no *subj.* (*e.g., not so busy* ~ *he can come* no tan ocupado que no pueda venir); *he never walks* ~ *he falls* nunca anda sin caer; **2.** *prp.* excepto; solamente; *I cannot* ~ *inf.* no puedo menos de *inf.*; *v. last*; ~ *for* a no ser por; **3.** *adv.* solamente; *v. all*; *nothing* ~ nada más que; ~ *little* muy poco; **4.** *su.* pero *m*, objeción *f*.

butch·er [ˈbutʃər] **1.** carnicero *m* (*a. fig.*); asesino *m*; ~ *knife* cuchilla *f* de carnicero; ~ *shop* carnicería *f*; **2.** *cattle* matar; dar muerte a; **ˈbutch·er·y** carnicería *f* (*a. fig.*); (*place*) matadero *m*.

but·ler [ˈbʌtlər] despensero *m*; mayordomo *m*.

butt[1] [bʌt] **1.** cabo *m*, extremo *m*; mocho *m*; culata *f of gun*; colilla *f of cigarette*; ⊕ cabeza *f* de biela; (*target*) blanco *m*; *fig.* hazmerreír *m*; cabezada *f with head*; *~s pl.* sitio *m* para tirar al blanco; **2.** dar cabezadas (*v/t.* contra); F ~ *in* interrumpir; *b.s.* entrometerse.

butt[2] [~] tonel *m*.

butte [bjuːt] cerro *m*, monte *m* [aislado.]

but·ter [ˈbʌtər] **1.** mantequilla *f*; ~ *dish* mantequillera *f*; *~scotch* bombón *m* escocés, bombón hecho con azúcar terciado y mantequilla; F ~ *would not melt in his mouth* es un mátalas callando, es una mosquita muerta; **2.** untar con mantequilla; F (*a.* ~ *up*) lisonjear; **ˈ~·cup** ranúnculo *m*; **ˈ~-fin·gered** desmañado en coger (la pelota *etc.*); **ˈ~·fly** mariposa *f* (*a. fig.*); **ˈ~·milk** leche *f* de manteca; **ˈbut·ter·y** despensa *f*.

but·tock [ˈbʌtək] nalga *f* (*mst pl.*).

but·ton [ˈbʌtn] **1.** botón *m* (*a.* ⚘); **2.** abotonar (*a.* ~ *up*); **ˈ~·hole 1.** ojal *m*; **2.** *sew.* abrir ojales en; *fig.* obligar a escuchar; **ˈ~·hook** abotonador *m*.

but·tress [ˈbʌtris] **1.** contrafuerte *m* (*a. geog.*); *fig.* sostén *m*, apoyo *m*; *flying* ~ arbotante *m*; **2.** apoyar, reforzar (*a. fig.*).

bux·om [ˈbʌksəm] rolliza; frescachona.

buy [bai] [*irr.*] *v/t.* comprar (*from* a); *fig.* (*a.* ~ *off*) comprar, sobornar; ~ *out partner* comprar la parte de; ~ *up* ✝ acaparar; *v/i. mst* ~ *and sell* traficar, comerciar; **ˈbuy·er** comprador (-a *f*) *m*; **ˈbuy·ing** compra *f*.

buzz [bʌz] **1.** zumbido *m*; ~ *bomb* bomba *f* volante; ~ *saw* sierra *f* circular; **2.** *v/i.* zumbar; ~ *about* cazcalear; *sl.* ~ *off* largarse; *teleph.* colgar; *v/t.* llamar por teléfono.

buz·zard [ˈbʌzərd] ratonero *m* común, águila *f* ratonera.

buzz·er [ˈbʌzər] ⚡ zumbador *m*.

by [bai] **1.** *prp.* por; *norm* según, de acuerdo con; (*in respect of*) de; (*time*) ~ *day* de día; ~ *3 o'clock* para las 3; ~ *now* ya, ahora; ~ *then* para entonces; antes de eso; *day* ~ *day* día por día; (*place*) ~ *me* cerca de mí, a mi lado; *north* ~ *east* norte por este; *side* ~ *side* lado a lado; (*manner*) ~ *easy stages* en cortas etapas; ~ *leaps and bounds* a pasos agigantados; ~ *lamplight* a la luz de una lámpara; ~ *land* por tierra; ~ *the dozen fig.* a docenas; ~ *twos* en pares; ♀ (*multiplication*) por; ~ *far*, ~ *half* con mucho; ~ *o.s.* solo; ~ *the* ~ a propósito; ~ *the way* de paso; a propósito; **2.** *adv.* cerca; a un lado; aparte; ~ *and* ~ luego, pronto; ~ *and large* de un modo general; *close* ~ cerca; **3.** *adj.* secundario, incidente.

bye-bye [ˈbaiˈbai] F ¡adiosito!; (*lulling children*) ¡ro ro!

by...: ˈ**~-e·lec·tion** elección *f* complementaria; ˈ**~·gone 1.** pasado; **2.** ~*s pl.*: *let* ~ *be* ~ olvidemos lo pasado; ˈ**~-law** estatuto *m*, reglamento *m*; ˈ**~-name** apodo *m*; ˈ**~·pass 1.** desviación *f*; ⊕ tubo *m* de paso; **2.** desviar; evitar (*a. fig.*); ˈ**~-path** trocha *f*; ˈ**~·play** *thea.* acción *f* aparte; escena *f* muda; ˈ**~-prod·uct** subproducto *m*; ⚗ derivado *m*; ˈ**~·road** camino *m* apartado; ˈ**~·stand·er** espectador (-a *f*) *m*, circunstante *m*/*f*; ˈ**~-street** callejuela *f*; ˈ**~·way** camino *m* apartado; camino *m* vecinal; ˈ**~·word** objeto *m* de burla (*or* oprobio); refrán *m*; *be a* ~ *for* ser notorio por.

By·zan·tine [biˈzæntain] bizantino *adj. a. su. m* (a *f*).

C

cab [kæb] taxi *m*; † cabriolé *m*; 🚂 casilla *f*; casilla *f*, cabina *f* (*of a truck*); ~ *stand* punto *m* de coches, punto de taxis.
ca·bal [kəˈbæl] cábala *f*.
cab·a·ret [kæbəˈrei] cabaret *m*.
cab·bage [ˈkæbidʒ] col *f*; repollo *m*.
cab·ba·lis·tic, cab·ba·lis·ti·cal [kæbəˈlistik(l)] □ cabalístico.
cab·by [ˈkæbi] F taxista *m*.
cab·in [ˈkæbin] cabaña *f*; ⚓ camarote *m*; *lorry*, ✈ cabina *f*; ˈ~ **boy** mozo *m* de cámara; grumete *m*.
cab·i·net [ˈkæbinit] vitrina *f*; armario *m*; (*radio*) caja *f*; *pol*. gabinete *m*, consejo *m* de ministros; *medicine* ~ botiquín *m*; ˈ~**mak·er** ebanista *m*.
ca·ble [ˈkeibl] **1.** ⚓, *tel*. cable *m* (*a*. F); *tel*. cablegrama *m*; ~ *address* dirección *f* cablegráfica; ~ *car* tranvía *m* de tracción por cable; ~ *television* televisión *f* por cable; **2.** cablegráfico; **3.** cablegrafiar; ˈ~**gram** cablegrama *m*; ˈ~ **stitch** punto *m* en cruz.
cab·man [ˈkæbmən] taxista *m*; † cochero *m*.
ca·boo·dle [kəˈbu:dl] *sl*.: *the whole* ~ lo todo.
ca·boose [kəˈbu:s] cocina *f* en la cubierta de un buque.
cab·ri·o·let [kæbriouˈlei] cabriolé *m*.
cab-stand [ˈkæbstænd] parada *f* de taxis.
ca·ca·o [kəˈkɑ:ou] cacao *m*.
cache [kæʃ] escondite *m*; ~ *of arms* alijo *m* de armas.
ca·chet [ˈkæʃei] sello *m*; *fig*. marca *f* de distinción.
cack·le [ˈkækl] **1.** cacareo *m*; risa *f* aguda; *sl*. cháchara *f*; **2.** cacarear; *sl*. chacharear; ˈ**cack·ler** cacareador (-a *f*) *m*; *fig*. parlanchín (-a *f*) *m*.
ca·coph·o·ny [kæˈkɔfəni] cacofonía *f*.
cac·tus [ˈkæktəs] cacto *m*.
cad [kæd] F sinvergüenza *m*, pillo *m*.
ca·dav·er·ous [kəˈdævərəs] □ cadavérico.
cad·die [ˈkædi] *golf*: *muchacho que lleva los instrumentos de juego*.
cad·dish [ˈkædiʃ] mal educado; de un malcriado.
cad·dy [ˈkædi] cajita *f* para té.
ca·dence [ˈkeidəns] cadencia *f*; compás *m*.
ca·det [kəˈdet] cadete *m*; hijo *m* menor.
cadge [kædʒ] *v/t*. obtener mendigando; *v/i*. gorronear, vivir de gorra; ˈ**cadg·er** gorrón (-a *f*) *m*.
ca·du·cous [kəˈdju:kəs] caduco.
cae·cum [ˈsi:kəm] intestino *m* ciego.
cae·sar·i·an [si:ˈzeriən] cesario (*a*. ⚕); cesariano.
cae·su·ra [siˈzju:rə] cesura *f*.
ca·fé [kəˈfei] café *m*; restaurante *m*.
caf·e·te·ri·a [kæfiˈtiriə] cafetería *f*.
caf·fe·ine [ˈkæfii:n] cafeína *f*.
cage [keidʒ] **1.** jaula *f* (*a*. ⚒); **2.** enjaular.
cage·y [ˈkeidʒi] □ F astuto, taimado; cauteloso, reservado.
cairn [kern] montón *m* de piedras (como señal o mojón).
cais·son [ˈkeisn] ⚔ cajón *m*; ⊕ cajón *m* hidráulico; ⚓ cajón *m* de suspensión.
ca·jole [kəˈdʒoul] halagar, camelar; ~ *s.o. into s.t.* conseguir por medio de halagos que una p. haga algo; **caˈjol·er** lisonjero (a *f*) *m*, zalamero (a *f*) *m*; **caˈjol·er·y** engatusamiento *m*, zalamería *f*.
cake [keik] **1.** pastelillo *m*, bollo *m*; bizcocho *m*; (*soap*) pastilla *f*; *sl*. *take the* ~ ganar el premio; ser el colmo; **2.** apelmazarse; endurecerse.
cal·a·bash [ˈkæləbæʃ] calabaza *f*.
cal·a·boose [ˈkæləbu:s] *sl*. calabozo *m*.
cal·a·mine [ˈkæləmain] calamina *f*.
ca·lam·i·tous [kəˈlæmitəs] □ calamitoso; **caˈlam·i·ty** calamidad *f*.
ca·lash [kəˈlæʃ] calesa *f*.
cal·car·e·ous [kælˈkeriəs] calcáreo.
cal·ci·fi·ca·tion [kælsifiˈkeiʃn] calcificación *f*; **cal·ci·fy** [ˈ~fai] calcificar(se); **cal·ci·na·tion** [kælsiˈneiʃn] calcinación *f*; **cal·cine** [ˈkælsain]

calcinar(se); ˈ**cal·cite** calcita *f*; **cal·ci·um** [ˈ~siəm] calcio *m*.

cal·cu·la·ble [ˈkælkjuləbl] calculable; **cal·cu·late** [ˈ~leit] *v/t*. calcular; ~*d to inf*. aprestado para *inf*.; *v/i*. calcular, conjeturar; ~ *on* contar con; *calculating machine* máquina *f* de calcular; sumadora *f*; *electronic calculating machine* calculadora *f* electrónica, computadora *f* electrónica; **cal·cu**ˈ**la·tion** cálculo *m*, calculación *f*; **cal·cu**ˈ**la·tor** *p*. calculador *m* (-a *f*), computador *m* (-a *f*); ⊕ calculadora *f*, computadora *f*; *v*. *computer*.

cal·en·dar [ˈkælindər] **1.** calendario *m*; lista *f*; ~ *month* mes *m* del año; **2.** poner en la lista.

cal·en·der [~] ⊕ **1.** calandria *f*; **2.** calandrar.

calf [kæf], *pl*. **calves** [kævz] ternero *m*; *fig*. F bobo *m*; (*or* ˈ~ **leath·er**) piel *f* de becerro; *anat*. pantorrilla *f*; *zo*. (*seal etc*.) cría *f*; *in* ~, *with* ~ preñada; F ~ *love* amartelamiento *m*; *kill the fatted* ~ celebrar una fiesta de bienvenida; ˈ~**·skin** piel *f* de becerro.

cal·i·ber [ˈkælibər] calibre *m*; *fig*. capacidad *f*, aptitud *f*; **cal·i·brate** [ˈkælibreit] calibrar.

cal·i·co [ˈkælikou] calicó *m*.

Cal·i·for·nian [kæliˈfɔːrnjən] californio *adj*. *a*. *su*. *m* (*a f*).

cal·i·pers [ˈkælipərz] *pl*. compás *m* de calibres, calibrador *m*.

ca·liph [ˈkælif] califa *m*; **cal·iph·ate** [ˈ~eit] califato *m*.

cal·is·then·ic [kælisˈθenik] **1.** calisténico; **2.** ~*s pl*. calistenia *f*.

calk [kɔːk] **1.** poner ramplones; **2.** ramplón *m* (*a*. **calk·in** [ˈkælkin]).

call [kɔːl] **1.** llamada *f*; grito *m*; visita *f* (*pay* hacer); ⚖ citación *f*; ⚔ toque *m*, llamada *f*; (*bird's*, *birdcatcher's*) reclamo *m*; *hunt*. chilla *f*; ☤ demanda *f*; *fig*. (~ *to*) obligación *f* (a, de), necesidad *f* (de); *thea*. llamamiento *m*; demanda *f* (*for* por); ~*boy thea*. traspunte *m*; (*in a hotel*) botones *m*; ~*er* visitante *m*/*f*; llamador (-a *f*) *m*; ~ *girl* prostituta *f*, mujer *f* de lujo, chica *f* de cita; ☤ ~ *money* dinero *m* a la vista; ~ *number teleph*. número *m* de teléfono; (*of a book*) número de clasificación; ~ *to the colors* ⚔ llamada *f* a filas; *radio*: ~ *sign* indicativo *m*; *port of* ~ puerto *m* de escala; *on* ~ disponible; ☤ a solicitud; *within* ~ al alcance de la voz; **2.** *v/t*. llamar; *meeting* convocar; invitar; calificar de; considerar, juzgar; *roll* pasar; llamar por teléfono; *cards*: (*bid*) marcar; *poker*: exigir la exposición de una mano; *attention* llamar (*to* sobre, a); *v*. *name*, *question*; *be* ~*ed* llamarse; *v*. *bar*; ~ *back* hacer volver; *teleph*. volver a llamar; ~ *down* pedir al cielo; F regañar; ~ *forth* sacar; *protest* originar, motivar; ~ *in p*. hacer entrar; *police* llamar; pedir la ayuda de; *thing issued* retirar; ~ *off* cancelar, abandonar; ~ *together* convocar; ~ *up memory* evocar; *teleph*. llamar; ⚔ llamar (al servicio militar); *v/i*. llamar (*a*. *teleph*.), dar voces; venir; hacer una visita; ~ *at house etc*. pasar por; ⚓ *port* hacer escala en; ~ *for* ir (*or* venir) por; exigir; pedir; ~ *on* acudir a (*for* en busca de); visitar; invitar (*to* a); ~ *out* dar voces; *sound the* ~ *to arms* ⚔ batir (*or* tocar) a llamada.

cal·la lil·y [ˈkæləˈliliː] lirio *m* de agua, calla *f*.

cal·li·graph·ic [kæliˈgræfik] □ caligráfico; **cal·lig·ra·phy** [kəˈligrəfi] caligrafía *f*.

call·ing [ˈkɔːliŋ] vocación *f*, profesión *f*; acción *f* de llamar *etc*.; ~ *card* tarjeta *f* de visita.

cal·los·i·ty [kæˈlɔsiti] callosidad *f*; ˈ**cal·lous** □ calloso; *fig*. duro, insensible.

cal·low [ˈkælou] inexperto, sin plumas.

calm [kɑːm] **1.** □ *weather* calmoso, bonancible; *p*. *etc*. tranquilo, sosegado; **2.** calma *f*; tranquilidad *f*, sosiego *m*; *v*. *dead*; **3.** (*a*. ~ *down*) calmar(se); tranquilizar(se), sosegar(se); ~ *down!* ¡tente quieto!; ˈ**calm·ness** calma *f*; tranquilidad *f*.

ca·lor·ic [kəˈlɔrik] calórico; *conductor of* ~ conductor *m* del calor; **cal·o·rie** [ˈkæləri] caloría *f*; **cal·o·rif·ic** [kæləˈrifik] calorífico.

ca·lum·ni·ate [kəˈlʌmnieit] calumniar; **ca·lum·ni**ˈ**a·tion** calumnia *f*; **ca**ˈ**lum·ni·a·tor** calumniador (-a *f*) *m*; **ca**ˈ**lum·ni·ous** □ calumnioso, difamador; **cal·um·ny** [ˈkæləmni] calumnia *f*.

Cal·va·ry [ˈkælvəri] Calvario *m*; ♀ calvario *m*.

calve [kæv] parir (*la vaca*); **calves** [kævz] *v*. *calf*.

Cal·vin·ism [ˈkælvinizm] calvinismo *m*.
ca·lyx [ˈkeiliks], *pl.* **cal·y·ces** [ˈ~lisiːz] ⚘ cáliz *m*.
cam [kæm] leva *f*.
cam·ber [ˈkæmbər] ⊕ **1.** combadura *f*; **2.** combarse, arquearse.
cam·bric [ˈkeimbrik] batista *f*.
came [keim] *pret. of come.*
cam·el [ˈkæml] *zo. a.* ⚓ camello *m*.
ca·mel·li·a [kəˈmiːlje] camelia *f*.
cam·e·o [ˈkæmiou] camafeo *m*.
cam·er·a [ˈkæmərə] máquina *f* (fotográfica); cámara *f* (de televisión); *~man* camarógrafo *m*, tomavistas *m*; *in ~* en secreto.
cam·o·mile [ˈkæməmail] camomila *f*; *~ tea* manzanilla *f*.
cam·ou·flage [ˈkæmuflɑːʒ] **1.** camuflaje *m*; **2.** camuflar.
camp [kæmp] **1.** campamento *m*; *~ bed* catre *m* de tijera; *~ chair*, *~ stool* silla *f* plegadiza, silla *f* de tijera, catrecillo *m*; *~ fire* hoguera *f* de campamento; **2.** acampar; F alojarse temporalmente; *~ing* camping *m*; *~ ground*, *~ing site* camping *m*.
cam·paign [kæmˈpein] **1.** campaña *f*; *election ~* campaña *f* electoral; **2.** hacer campaña (*for* a favor de); **camˈpaign·er** veterano *m* (*a. fig.*, *esp. old ~*); *fig.* paladín *m*.
cam·phor [ˈkæmfər] alcanfor *m*; **cam·phor·at·ed** [ˈ~reitid] alcanforado.
cam·pus [ˈkæmpəs] terrenos *m/pl.*, recinto *m* (de la Universidad).
cam·shaft [ˈkæmʃæft] árbol *m* de levas.
can[1] [kæn] [*irr.*] puedo; sé; *etc.*
can[2] [~] **1.** lata *f*, bote *m*; vaso *m* (de lata); *~ opener* abrelatas *m*; **2.** enlatar, conservar; *sl.* poner en la calle; *sl. carry the ~* pagar el pato; *~ning industry* industria *f* conservera.
Ca·na·di·an [kəˈneidjən] canadiense *adj. a. su. m/f.*
ca·nal [kəˈnæl] canal *m* (*a.* ⚕); **ca·nal·i·za·tion** [kænəlaiˈzeiʃn] canalización *f*; **ˈca·nal·ize** canalizar.
ca·nard [kæˈnɑːrd] noticia *f* falsa.
ca·nar·y [kəˈneri] canario *m*.
ca·nas·ta [kəˈnæstə] *cards*: canasta *f*.
can·cel [ˈkænsl] *v/t.* cancelar (*a. fig.*); *stamp* matar; *v/i.* ⅍ *~ out* destruirse; **can·cel·la·tion** [kænseˈleiʃn] cancelación *f*, supresión *f*.
can·cer [ˈkænsər] ⚕ cáncer *m*; ♋ *ast.* Cáncer *m*; *~ research* cancerología *f*; **ˈcan·cer·ous** canceroso.
can·de·la·brum [kændəˈlɑːbrəm] (*pl. ~bra* [~brə] *or ~brums* [~brəmz]) candelabro *m*.
can·did [ˈkændid] □ franco; *~ camera* cámara *f* indiscreta; *~ly* francamente.
can·di·date [ˈkændidit] candidato *m* (*for* para); opositor (-a *f*) *m*; **can·di·da·ture** [ˈ~ʃər] candidatura *f*.
can·died [ˈkændid] azucarado.
can·dle [ˈkændl] candela *f*, bujía *f*; vela *f*; *eccl.* cirio *m*; *~ power* bujía *f*; **Can·dle·mas** [ˈ~məs] candelaria *f*; **can·dle·stick** candelero *m*; (*low*) palmatoria *f*.
can·dor [ˈkændər] candor *m*; franqueza *f*.
can·dy [ˈkændi] **1.** azúcar *m* cande; bombón *m*, dulce *m*; *~ box* bombonera *f*, confitera *f*; *~ store* confitería *f*, dulcería *f*; **2.** *v/t.* azucarar; *v/i.* cristalizarse.
cane [kein] **1.** ⚘ caña *f*; ⚘ caña *f* de azúcar; (*stick*) bastón *m*; *school*: palmeta *f*; *~ chair* silla *f* de mimbre; *~ seat* asiento *m* de rejilla; *~ sugar* azúcar *m* de caña; **2.** *school*: castigar con palmeta.
ca·nine [ˈkeinain] **1.** canino; **2.** canino *m*, colmillo *m* (*a. ~ tooth*).
can·is·ter [ˈkænistər] bote *m*, lata *f*.
can·ker [ˈkæŋkər] **1.** ⚕ úlcera *f* en la boca; ⚘ cancro *m*; *fig.* corrupción *f*, peste *f*; **2.** ulcerarse; corromperse; **ˈcan·kered** *fig.* emponzoñado, corrompido; **ˈcan·ker·ous** ulceroso.
canned [kænd] envasado; en lata; *~ goods pl.* conservas *f/pl.* alimenticias; *sl. ~ music* música *f* en discos.
can·ner·y [ˈkænəri] fábrica *f* de conservas alimenticias, conservera *f*.
can·ni·bal [ˈkænibl] **1.** caníbal *m*; **2.** antropófago.
can·non [ˈkænən] **1.** ⚔ cañón *m*; artillería *f*; *billiards*: carambola *f*; *~ball* bala *f* de cañón; *~ fodder* carne *f* de cañón; **2.** hacer carambola; rebotar (*against*, *off* contra); **can·non·ade** [~ˈneid] cañoneo *m*.
can·not [ˈkænɔt] no puedo; no sé; *etc.*
can·ny [ˈkæni] □ *Scot.* astuto; frugal, económico.
ca·noe [kəˈnuː] **1.** canoa *f*; **2.** pasear en canoa.
can·on [ˈkænən] canon *m*; (*p.*) canó-

nigo *m*; *typ.* gran canon *m*; ~ *law* derecho *m* canónico; ˈ**can·on·ess** canonesa *f*; **canˈon·i·cal** canónico; **can·on·i·za·tion** [~naiˈzeiʃn] canonización *f*; ˈ**can·on·ize** canonizar; ˈ**can·on·ry** canonjía *f*.

can·o·py [ˈkænəpi] **1.** dosel *m*; ⚠ baldaquín *m*; cielo *m of bed*; **2.** endoselar.

cant[1] [kænt] **1.** inclinación *f*, sesgo *m*; vaivén *m*; (*crystal etc.*) bisel *m*, chaflán *m*; **2.** inclinar, sesgar; ladear (se); ~ *over* volcar.

cant[2] [~] **1.** lenguaje *m* insincero, gazmoñería *f*; (*jargon*) jerga *f*, germanía *f*; **2.** hablar insinceramente; hablar en jerga.

can't [kænt] = *cannot*.

can·ta·loupe [ˈkæntəloup] cantalupo *m*, melón *m*.

can·tan·ker·ous [kənˈtæŋkərəs] □ F arisco, intratable; quejumbroso; quisquilloso.

can·teen [kænˈti:n] cantina *f*; (*bottle*) cantimplora *f*; juego *m of cutlery*; ⚔ centro *m* de recreo.

can·ter [ˈkæntər] **1.** medio galope *m*; **2.** andar a medio galope.

can·thar·i·des [kænˈθæridi:z] *pl.* polvo *m* de cantárida.

can·ti·cle [ˈkæntikl] cántico *m*; ⌒*s pl.* Cantar *m* de los Cantares.

can·ti·le·ver [ˈkæntili:vər] viga *f* voladiza.

can·to [ˈkæntou] canto *m*.

can·ton 1. [ˈkæntən] cantón *m* (*a. heraldry*); **2.** [kənˈtu:n] ⚔ acantonar; ˈ**can·ton·ment** acantonamiento *m*.

can·vas [ˈkænvəs] canamazo *m*, lona *f*; *paint.* lienzo *m*; *under* ~ ⚔ en tiendas; ⚓ con las velas izadas.

can·vass [~] **1.** solicitación *f* (*esp.* de votos); sondeo *m*; escrutinio *m*, pesquisa *f*; **2.** *v/t.* escudriñar; *votes* solicitar; *opinion* sondear; *v/i.* solicitar; ˈ**can·vass·er** solicitador (-a *f*) *m*.

caou·tchouc [ˈkautʃuk] caucho *m*.

cap [kæp] **1.** gorra *f*; (*with peak*) gorra *f* de visera; (*cover*) tapa *f*, tapón *m*; caballete *m of chimney*; ⊕ casquete *m*; ⚓ tamborete *m*; cápsula *f of gun, bottle*; ~ *and bells* gorro *m* con campanillas; ~ *and gown* toga *f* y bonete; ~ *in hand* con el sombrero en la mano; *the* ~ *fits* viene de perilla; *polar* ~ casquete *m* polar; *put on one's thinking* ~ meditarlo bien; F *set one's* ~ *at a p.* proponerse conquistar a una p. como novio; **2.** *head* cubrir con gorra; *hill* coronar; *vessel* poner tapa a; *work* poner remate a; *to* ~ *it all* para colmo de desgracias.

ca·pa·bil·i·ty [keipəˈbiliti] capacidad *f*, habilidad *f*; ˈ**ca·pa·ble** □ capaz (*of* de), hábil.

ca·pa·cious [kəˈpeiʃəs] □ espacioso, capaz; *dress* holgado; **ca·pac·i·tate** [~ˈpæsiteit] habilitar, autorizar; **caˈpac·i·ty 1.** capacidad *f*; *mot.* cilindrada *f*; *in my* ~ *as* en mi calidad de; **2.** *attr.* máximo; *thea.* lleno.

cap-à-pie [kæpəˈpi:] de pies a cabeza.

ca·par·i·son [kəˈpærisn] *lit.* **1.** caparazón *m*; equipo *m*; **2.** engualdrapar; *fig.* vestir soberbiamente.

cape[1] [keip] *geog.* cabo *m*, promontorio *m*.

cape[2] [~] capa *f*, esclavina *f*.

ca·per[1] [ˈkeipər] ⚘ alcaparra *f*.

ca·per[2] [~] **1.** cabriola *f*; *fig.* travesura *f*; F lío *m*, embrollo *m*; *cut* ~*s* = **2.** cabriolar.

ca·pi·as [ˈkeipiæs]: *writ of* ~ orden [*f* de arresto.]

cap·il·lar·i·ty [kæpiˈlæriti] capilaridad *f*; **cap·il·lar·y** [kəˈpileri] **1.** capilar; **2.** tubo *m* (*or* vaso *m*) capilar.

cap·i·tal [ˈkæpitl] **1.** □ capital; ⚖ de capital; F excelente, magnífico; **2.** ⚖ capital *m*; (*town*) capital *f*; ⚠ capitel *m*; *typ.* (*or* ~ *letter*) mayúscula *f*; ~ *letter* letra *f* mayúscula; ~ *punishment* último suplicio *m*; *fig. make* ~ *out of* aprovechar; ˈ**cap·i·tal·ism** capitalismo *m*; ˈ**cap·i·tal·ist** capitalista *m*/*f*; **cap·i·talˈis·tic** capitalista; **cap·i·tal·i·za·tion** [kəpitəlaiˈzeiʃn] capitalización *f*; **capˈi·tal·ize** capitalizar; *typ.* escribir (*or* imprimir) con mayúscula; ~ *on* aprovecharse de.

cap·i·ta·tion [kæpiˈteiʃn] capitación *f*.

ca·pit·u·late [kəˈpitjuleit] capitular; **ca·pit·uˈla·tion** capitulación *f*.

ca·pon [ˈkeipən] capón *m*.

ca·price [kəˈpri:s] capricho *m*; **ca·pri·cious** [kəˈpriʃəs] □ caprichoso, caprichudo; **caˈpri·cious·ness** veleidad *f*, inconstancia *f*.

Cap·ri·corn [ˈkæprikɔ:rn] Capricornio *m*.

cap·ri·ole [ˈkæprioul] corveta *f*.

cap·size [kæpˈsaiz] *v/i.* volcar, zozobrar; *v/t.* tumbar, volcar.

cap·stan [ˈkæpstən] cabrestante *m*.
cap·su·lar [ˈkæpsjulər] capsular; **cap·sule** [ˈkæpsjuːl] ⚘ *a*. ⚕ cápsula *f*.
cap·tain [ˈkæptin] capitán *m* (*a. sport*); *~ of industry* gran industrial *m*; **cap·tain·cy, cap·tain·ship** [ˈkæptinsi, ˈ~inʃip] capitanía *f*.
cap·tion [ˈkæpʃn] **1.** encabezamiento *m*; pie *m*; *film*: subtítulo *m*; **2.** intitular.
cap·tious [ˈkæpʃəs] □ criticón, reparador; quisquilloso; falso.
cap·ti·vate [ˈkæptiveit] *fig*. cautivar, fascinar; **cap·tiˈva·tion** fascinación *f*; ˈ**cap·tive** cautivo *adj. a. su. m* (a *f*); *~ balloon* globo *m* cautivo; **cap·tiv·i·ty** [~ˈtiviti] cautiverio *m*.
cap·tor [ˈkæptər] apresador (-a *f*) *m*; **cap·ture** [ˈ~tʃər] **1.** apresamiento *m*; captura *f*; toma *f of city etc.*; (*p*.) prisionero (a *f*) *m*; presa *f*; **2.** apresar, capturar; *city etc.* tomar; *fig*. captar.
Cap·u·chin [ˈkæpjutʃin] capuchino *m*.
car [kɑːr] coche *m*, carro *m S.Am.*; (*tram-*) tranvía *m*; 🚃 vagón *m*, coche *m*; *~barn* cochera *f* de tranvías; *~boy* bombona *f*, garrafón *m*; *~ caller* avisacoches *m*; *~fare* pasaje *m* de tranvía o autobús; *~load* furgonada *f*, vagonada *f*; *~port* cochera *f*; *~-rental service* alquiler *m* de coches; *~ washer* lavacoches *m*.
car·a·bi·neer [kærəbiˈnir] carabinero *m*.
car·a·cole [ˈkærəkoul] **1.** caracol *m* (*horse*); **2.** caracolear.
ca·rafe [kəˈræf] garrafa *f*.
car·a·mel [ˈkærəmel] caramelo *m*.
car·at [ˈkærət] quilate *m*.
car·a·van [kærəˈvæn] caravana *f*; carricoche *m*; *mot*. remolque *m*; **car·aˈvan·se·rai** [~serai] caravasar *m*.
car·a·way [ˈkærəwei] alcaravea *f*.
car·bide [ˈkɑːrbaid] carburo *m*.
car·bine [ˈkɑːrbain] carabina *f*.
car·bo·hy·drate [ˈkɑːrbouˈhaidreit] ⚗ hidrato *m* de carbono; ⚕ carbohidrato *m*, fécula *f*.
car·bol·ic ac·id [kɑːrˈbɔlikˈæsid] ácido *m* carbólico.
car·bon [ˈkɑːrbən] carbono *m*; ⚡ carbón *m*; (*a. ~ paper*) papel *m* carbón; *~ copy* copia *f* al carbón; *~ dioxide* dióxido *m* de carbono; *~ monoxide* óxido *m* de carbono, monóxido *m* de carbono; **car·bo·na·ceous** [~ˈneiʃəs] carbonoso; **car·bon·ate** [ˈ~bənit] carbonato *m*; **car·bon·ic** [~ˈbɔnik] carbónico; *~ acid* ácido *m* carbónico; **car·bon·i·za·tion** [~bənaiˈzeiʃn] carbonización *f*; ˈ**car·bon·ize** carbonizar(se).
car·boy [ˈkɑːrbɔi] bombona *f*.
car·bun·cle [ˈkɑːrbʌŋkl] *min*. carbunclo *m*; ⚕ carbunco *m*; F grano *m*.
car·bu·ret [ˈkɑːrbjuret] carburar; ˈ**car·bu·ret·tor** carburador *m*.
car·case, *mst* **car·cass** [ˈkɑːrkəs] cadáver *m* (de un animal); res *f* muerta; (*frame*) armazón *f*.
car·cin·o·gen [kɑːrˈsinədʒən] carcinógeno *m*; **car·ci·no·ma** [ˈkɑːrsiˈnoumə] carcinoma *m*, cáncer *m*.
card¹ [kɑːrd] ⊕ **1.** carda *f*; **2.** *wool* cardar.
card² [~] (*playing*) carta *f*; ☏ *etc*. tarjeta *f*, postal *f*; (*index*) ficha *f*; F (tipo *m*) salado *m*; *~ catalogue* catálogo *m* de fichas, fichero *m*; *~ game* juego *m* de naipes; *~ index* fichero *m*, tarjetero *m*; *~ party* tertulia *f* de baraja; *~ trick* truco *m* de naipes; *game of ~s* partida *f* de cartas; *like a house of ~s* como un castillo de naipes; F *on the ~s* probable; *have a ~ up one's sleeve* tener ayuda en reserva; *put one's ~s on the table* poner las cartas boca arriba; *speak by the ~* hablar con conocimiento de causa.
card·board [ˈkɑːrdbɔːrd] cartón *m*; *~ box* caja *f* de cartón.
car·di·ac [ˈkɑːrdiæk] cardíaco.
car·di·gan [ˈkɑːrdigən] rebeca *f*, jersey *m*.
car·di·nal [ˈkɑːrdinl] **1.** □ cardinal; **2.** cardenal *m* (*a. orn*.); **car·di·nal·ate** [ˈ~eit] cardenalato *m*.
card...: ˈ**~ in·dex** fichero *m*; ˈ**~sharp** fullero *m*, tahur *m*.
care [ker] **1.** cuidado *m*, solicitud *f*; esmero *m*, atención *f*; cargo *m*, custodia *f*; *~ of* (*abbr. c/o*) ... a manos de; en casa de; *take ~* tener cuidado; *take ~ of* cuidar de; F atender a; *with ~!* ¡atención!; ¡cuidado!; **2.** tener cuidado; *~ about* preocuparse de (*or* por); *~ for* cuidar; (*love*) querer, amar; desear; *I don't ~ for that* no me gusta eso; *~ to* tener ganas de; *would you ~ to say?* ¿quiere Vd. decirme?; F *I don't ~* (*twopence etc.*)! ¡no se me da un bledo! (*for* de); *well ~d for* bien cuidado.

ca•reen [kəˈriːn] ⚓ carenar; volcar, inclinar.
ca•reer [kəˈrir] **1.** carrera *f*; ~ *diplomat* diplomático *m* de carrera; **2.** correr a carrera tendida; **ca•reer•ist** [kəˈririst] ambicioso (a *f*) *m*.
care•free [ˈkerfriː] despreocupado.
care•ful [ˈkerful] □ cuidadoso; esmerado; cauteloso; *appearance* acicalado; *be* ~ *to inf.* poner diligencia en *inf.*; *be* ~ *to say that* decir muy particularmente que; **ˈcare•ful•ness** cuidado *m*; esmero *m*; cautela *f*.
care•less [ˈkerlis] □ descuidado; desatento, desaplicado; alegre, sin cuidado; **ˈcare•less•ness** descuido *m*; negligencia *f*; indiferencia *f*; desaliño *m of appearance*.
ca•ress [kəˈres] **1.** caricia *f*; **2.** acariciar (*a. fig.*).
care•tak•er [ˈkerteikər] custodio *m*, conserje *m*; guardesa *f*.
care•worn [ˈkerwɔːrn] agobiado de inquietudes.
car•fare [ˈkɑːrfer] pasaje *m*.
car•go [ˈkɑːrgou] carga *f*, cargamento *m*; *mixed* (*or general*) ~ carga *f* mixta.
car•i•ca•ture [ˈkærikətʃər] **1.** caricatura *f*; (*newspaper*) dibujo *m*; **2.** caricaturizar; **car•i•ca•tur•ist** [ˈkærikətʃərist] caricaturista *m*/*f*, dibujante *m*/*f*.
car•i•es [ˈkeriiːz] caries *f*; **ˈcar•i•ous** cariado.
car•il•lon [ˈkærilɔn, kəˈriljən] carillón *m*.
car•mine [ˈkɑːrmain] **1.** carmín *m*; **2.** carmíneo.
car•nage [ˈkɑːrnidʒ] carnicería *f*, mortandad *f*; **ˈcar•nal** □ carnal; **car•nal•i•ty** [~ˈnæliti] carnalidad *f*; **car•na•tion** [~ˈneiʃn] **1.** clavel *m*; **2.** encarnado.
car•ni•val [ˈkɑːrnivl] carnaval *m*; fiesta *f*, feria *f*.
car•ni•vore [ˈkɑːrnivɔːr] carnívoro *m*; **car•niv•o•rous** [~ˈnivərəs] carnívoro.
car•ol [ˈkærl] **1.** villancico *m*; **2.** cantar villancicos.
car•om [ˈkærəm] **1.** carambola *f*; **2.** *v*/*i*. carambolear.
ca•rot•id [kəˈrɔtid] (*a.* ~ *artery*) carótida *f*.
ca•rouse [kəˈrauz] **1.** *a.* **caˈrous•al** jarana *f*, parranda *f*; **2.** jaranear, andar de parranda.
carp[1] [kɑːrp] *ichth.* carpa *f*.
carp[2] [~] criticar, censurar; ~ *at* quejarse de.
car park [ˈkɑːrpɑːrk] aparcamiento *m*.
car•pen•tar [ˈkɑːrpintər] **1.** carpintero *m*; **2.** carpintear; **ˈcar•pen•try** carpintería *f*.
car•pet [ˈkɑːrpit] **1.** alfombra *f*, tapete *m*; F *be on the* ~ estar sobre el tapete; F ser reprobado; **2.** alfombrar; *fig.* cubrir, revestir; F reprobar; **ˈ~•bag•ger** aventurero *m* político; **ˈcar•pet•ing** alfombrado *m*.
car•pet...: **ˈ~ ˈknight** soldado *m* de gabinete; **ˈ~ slip•pers** *pl.* zapatillas *f*/*pl.*; **ˈ~ sweep•er** barredera *f* de alfombras; (*machine*) aspirador *m* (de polvo).
car•riage [ˈkæridʒ] carruaje *m*; 🚃 vagón *m*; ⚔ cureña *f*; ✝ porte *m*; ⊕ carro *m*; (*bearing*) andares *m*/*pl.*, modo *m* de andar; ~ *free* franco de porte; ~ *paid* porte pagado.
car•riage...: **ˈ~-and-ˈpair** coche *m* de dos caballos; **ˈ~ door** portezuela *f*; **ˈ~ drive** calzada *f*; **ˈ~ road, ˈ~ way** carretera *f*; calzada *f*.
car•ri•er [ˈkæriər] porteador *m*; trajinante *m*; empresa *f* de transportes; ⚓ porta(a)viones *m*; ⚕ portador (-a *f*) *m*; *radio*: (*wave*) onda *f* portadora; **ˈ~ pi•geon** paloma *f* mensajera.
car•ri•on [ˈkæriən] carroña *f*; inmundicia *f*; ~ *crow* corneja *f* negra.
car•rot [ˈkærət] zanahoria *f*; **ˈcar•rot•y** F pelirrojo.
car•ry [ˈkæri] **1.** *v*/*t*. llevar, traer; transportar; llevar encima *on p.*; *goods* acarrear; *burden* sostener; *prize, election* ganar, lograr; ⚔ *fortress* conquistar, tomar; *proposition* hacer aceptar; ✝ *stock* tener en existencia; (*extend*) extender, llevar más lejos; ⚡ llevar; *fig.* comprender, implicar; *v. day, effect, weight*; ~ *o.s.* andar (con garbo *etc.*); ~ *along* llevar consigo; ~ *away* llevarse; *fig.* encantar, arrebatar; ~ *everything before one* arrollarlo todo; ✝ ~ *forward* pasar; ~ *off* llevarse; (*kill*) matar; ~ *s.t. off well* salir airoso; ~ *on* continuar; *esp.* ✝ dirigir; promover; ~ *out* (*or through*) *plan* realizar, llevar a cabo; *repairs* hacer; ~ *over* guardar para más tarde; ✝ pasar; ~ *through p.* sostener hasta el fin; *v*/*i*. (*reach*) alcanzar; ~ *on* continuar; F (*complain*) quejarse sin motivo;

(*misbehave*) travesar; insistir, machacar (*about* en); ~ *on!* ¡adelante!; ¡siga!; F ~ *on with* tener un amorío con; ~*ing capacity* capacidad *f* de carga; **2.** ⚔ alcance *m*.

cart [kaːrt] **1.** carro *m*, carreta *f*; ~ *horse* caballo *m* de tiro; *hand* ~ carretilla *f*, carretón *m*; *fig. put the* ~ *before the horse* trastrocar las cosas; *sl. in the* ~ en un atolladero; **2.** carretear; F llevar (*esp.* con dificultad); ˈ**cart·age** carretaje *m*; ✝ acarreo *m*.

carte blanche [ˈkaːrtblaːnʃ] carta *f* blanca.

car·tel [ˈkaːrtel] ✝ *a.* ⚔ cartel *m*.

cart·er [ˈkaːrtər] carretero *m*, trajinante *m*.

car·ti·lage [ˈkaːrtilidʒ] cartílago *m*; **car·ti·lag·i·nous** [~ˈlædʒinəs] cartilaginoso.

cart load [ˈkaːrtloud] carretada *f* (*a. fig.*).

car·tog·ra·pher [kaːrˈtɔgrəfər] cartógrafo *m*; **carˈtog·ra·phy** cartografía *f*.

car·ton [ˈkaːrtən] caja *f* de cartón, envase *m*.

car·toon [kaːrˈtuːn] **1.** *paint.* cartón *m*; caricatura *f*, dibujo *m*; *film*: dibujo *m* animado; **2.** caricaturizar.

car·touche [kaːrˈtuːʃ] △ cartela *f*.

car·tridge [ˈkaːrtridʒ] cartucho *m*; ~ *belt* canana *f*.

cart wheel [ˈkaːrtwiːl] rueda *f* de carro; *fig.* salto *m* mortal de lado; *sl.* dólar *m*.

cart·wright [ˈkaːrtrait] carretero *m*.

carve [kaːrv] *meat* trinchar; *stone etc.* esculpir, tallar (*in* en); *fig.* ~ *one's way through* hacerse un camino por; ˈ**carv·er** trinchador (-a *f*) *m*; tallista *m*/*f*; escultor (-a *f*) *m*; ~*s pl.* cuchillo *m* y trinchante.

carv·ing [ˈkaːrviŋ] acción *f* de trinchar; △ *etc.* escultura *f*; obra *f* de talla.

cas·cade [kæsˈkeid] cascada *f*.

case[1] [keis] **1.** caja *f* (*a. typ.*); estuche *m*; funda *f*; (*window etc.*) marco *m*, bastidor *m*; (*cartridge- etc.*) cápsula *f*; (*glass*) vitrina *f*; *typ. lower* ~ caja *f* baja; *upper* ~ caja *f* alta; **2.** encajonar; enfundar.

case[2] [~] caso *m* (*a.* ⚕ *a. gr.*); ⚖ causa *f*, pleito *m*; F persona *f* divertida; argumento *m* convincente; *a* ~ *for* una razón por; *have a strong* ~ tener un argumento fuerte; *as the* ~ *may be* según el caso; *in* ~ en caso que; por si acaso; *in* ~ *of* en caso de; *in any* ~ en todo caso; *in such a* ~ en tal caso.

case-hard·en [ˈkeishaːrdn] ⊕ cementar; *fig.* ~*ed* insensible.

ca·se·in [ˈkeisiiːn] caseína *f*.

case knife [ˈkeisnaif] cuchillo *m* con vaina.

case·mate [ˈkeismeit] casamata *f*.

case·ment [ˈkeismənt] ventana *f* a bisagra, ventana batiente; bastidor *m*, marco *m* (de una ventana); *poet.* ventana *f*.

cash [kæʃ] **1.** dinero *m* contante; pago *m* al contado; ~ *down, for* ~ al contado; *in* ~ en metálico; *be out of* ~ estar sin blanca; ~ *payment* pago *m* al contado; ~ *purchase* compra *f* al contado; ~ *and carry* pago *m* al contado con transporte al cargo del comprador; ~ *on delivery* pagar contra recepción; ~ *on hand* efectivo *m* en caja; ~ *register* caja *f* registradora; **2.** *check* cobrar, hacer efectivo; F ~ *in on* sacar provecho de; ˈ~ **book** libro *m* de caja; ˈ~**box** caja *f*; **cash·ier** [kæˈʃir] **1.** cajero (a *f*) *m*; **2.** destituir; degradar.

cash·ew [ˈkæʃuː] anacardo *m*, marañón *m*; ~ *nut* anacardo *m*, nuez *f* de marañón.

cash·mere [kæʃˈmir] casimir *m*.

cas·ing [ˈkeisiŋ] cubierta *f*, envoltura *f*; cerco *m of window*; ⊕ tubería *f* de revestimiento.

ca·si·no [kəˈsiːnou] casino *m*.

cask [kæsk] tonel *m*, barril *m*.

cas·ket [ˈkaskit] cajita *f*, cofrecito *m*; ataúd *m*.

cas·sa·tion [kæˈseiʃn] casación *f*.

cas·se·role [ˈkæsəroul] cacerola *f*.

cas·sette [kaˈset] casete *m*.

cas·si·a [ˈkæsiə] casia *f*; canela *f* de la China.

cas·sock [ˈkæsək] sotana *f*.

cas·so·war·y [ˈkæsəweri] casuario *m*.

cast [kæst] **1.** echada *f*; lance *m of net*; molde *m*, forma *f*; *fig.* apariencia *f*, estampa *f*; *thea.* reparto *m*, personal *m*; ⊕ pieza *f* fundida; ✝ balance *m*; (*eye*) mirada *f* bizca; (*colour*) tinte *m*; **2.** [*irr.*] *v/t.* echar, lanzar; desechar; *eyes* volver; *shadow* proyectar; ⊕ fundir; *thea. parts* repartir; *lots* echar; *sum* (*a.* ~ *up*) calcular, sumar;

~ *iron* hierro *m* colado; ~ *steel* acero *m* colado; ~ (*a th.*) *in a p.'s teeth* echar a uno en la cara; ~ *away* desechar, abandonar; ⚓ *be* ~ *away* ser un náufrago; ~ *down* derribar; *fig.* desanimar; *eyes* bajar; ~ *forth* despedir; ~ *a horoscope* sacar un horóscopo; ~ *loose* soltar; ~ *off* abandonar; ~ *on* (*knitting*) empezar con; ~ *out* arrojar; despedir; *v/i.* (*fishing*) lanzar, arrojar; ⊕ fundir; ~ *about for* buscar; ⚓ ~ *off* desamarrar.
cas·ta·net [kæstə'net] castañuela *f.*
cast·a·way ['kæstəwei] ⚓ náufrago (a *f*) *m*; réprobo (a *f*) *m.*
caste [kæst] casta *f*; *lose* ~ desprestigiarse.
cas·tel·lan ['kæstələn] castellano *m*, alcaide *m*; **cas·tel·lat·ed** ['kæsteleitid] almenado; encastillado.
cas·ter ['kæstər] = *castor*[2].
cas·ti·gate ['kæstigeit] castigar; **cas·ti'ga·tion** castigo *m.*
cast·ing ['kæstiŋ] **1.** *vote* decisivo; **2.** ⊕ pieza *f* fundida.
cast-i·ron ['kæst'aiərn] hecho de hierro fundido; *fig.* fuerte, duro.
cas·tle ['kæsl] **1.** castillo *m*; *chess*: torre *f*, roque *m*; ~ *in Spain* castillo *m* en el aire; **2.** *chess*: enrocar.
cast·off ['kæstɔːf] abandonado, desechado; *clothing* de desecho.
cas·tor[1] ['kæstər] *pharm.* castóreo *m*; *sl.* sombrero *m*; ~ *oil* aceite *m* de ricino.
cas·tor[2] [~] ruedecilla *f* de mueble; vinagrera *f*; ~*s pl.* angarillas *f/pl.*; ~ *sugar* azúcar *m* extrafino.
cas·trate ['kæstreit] castrar; **cas'tra·tion** castración *f.*
cas·u·al ['kæʒuəl] **1.** □ casual; descuidado, indiferente; ~ *laborer* obrero *m* casual; **2.** *persona que recibe caridad de vez en cuando*; **'cas·u·al·ty** accidente *m*; ⚔ baja *f*; víctima *f.*
cas·u·ist ['kæʒuist] casuista *m/f*; *b.s.* sofista *m/f*; **'cas·u·ist·ry** casuística *f*; razonamiento *m* falaz.
cat [kæt] gato *m*; azote *m* con nueve ramales; ~ *burglar* balconero *m*; ~*fish* bagre *m*; ~*nap* sueñecito *m*; ~*nip* hierba *f* gatera, nébeda *f*; ~*-o'-nine-tails* azote *m* con nueve ramales; ~*tail* anea *f*, espadaña *f*; amento *m*; ~*ty* felino, gatuno; (*spiteful*) malicioso; (*gossipy*) chismoso; ~*walk* pasadero *m*, pasarela *f*; *bell the* ~ ponerle cascabel al gato; F *let the* ~ *out of the bag* revelar el secreto, cantar.
cat·a·clysm ['kætəklizm] cataclismo *m.*
cat·a·comb ['kætəkoum] catacumba *f.*
cat·a·log, cat·a·logue ['kætəlɔg] **1.** catálogo *m*; fichero *m*; **2.** catalogar.
cat·a·lyst ['kætəlist] catalizador *m.*
cat·a·pult ['kætəpʌlt] catapulta *f*; honda *f.*
cat·a·ract ['kætərækt] catarata *f* (*a.* ⚕).
ca·tarrh [kə'tɑːr] catarro *m*; **ca·tarrh·al** [kə'tɑːrəl] catarral.
ca·tas·tro·phe [kə'tæstrəfi] catástrofe *f*; **cat·a·stroph·ic** [kætə'strɔfik] □ catastrófico.
cat·call ['kætkɔːl] **1.** rechifla *f*, silba *f*; **2.** rechiflar, silbar.
catch [kætʃ] **1.** cogida *f*; presa *f*, botín *m*; pesca *f of fish*; (*lock*) pestillo *m*, aldabilla *f*; ♪ canon *m* de carácter cómico; (*deceit*) trampa *f*; **2.** [*irr.*] *v/t.* coger, atrapar; agarrar, asir; *fig.* comprender; llegar a oír; *fig.* sorprender; *breath* suspender; F ~ *it* merecerse un regaño; ~ *in the act* coger con las manos en la masa; *v. cold, fire, hold etc.*; F ~ *out p.* cazar, sorprender; coger en una falta; ~ *up p.* alcanzar; *th.* asir; **3.** *v/i.* enredarse, engancharse; ⊕ engranar; (*fire*) encenderse; ⚕ *be* ~*ing* ser contagioso; ~ *at* tratar de asir (*or* coger); ~ *on* prender en; F coger el tino; caer en la cuenta; ~ *on to* F estar en el hecho de (*comprender*); ~ *up fig.* ponerse al día; ~ *up with* alcanzar, emparejar con; **'~·all** armario *m etc.* destinado a contener toda clase de objeto; **'catch·er** *sport*: receptor *m*, parador *m*; **'catch·ing** ⚕ contagioso; atrayente; ♪ pegajoso; **'catch·ment ba·sin** cuenca *f.*
catch...: **'~·pen·ny** ✝ de pacotilla; **'~ phrase** tópico *m*; **'~·pole** alguacil *m*, corchete *m*; **'~ ques·tion** pega *f*; **'~·word** *typ.* reclamo *m*; *thea.* pie *m*; **'catch·y** F pegajoso.
cat·e·chism ['kætikizm] catecismo *m*; (*method*) catequismo *m*; **cat·e·chize** ['~kaiz] catequizar; **cat·e·chu·men** [~'kjuːmən] catecúmeno (a *f*) *m.*
cat·e·gor·i·cal [kæti'gɔːrikl] □ categórico; **cat·e·go·ry** ['~gɔːri] categoría *f.*

cat·e·nar·y [kəˈtiːnəri] ⚭ catenaria *f*.
ca·ter [ˈkeitər]: ~ *for* abastecer, proveer; *fig.* proveer a; ˈ**ca·ter·er** abastecedor *m*; proveedor *m*; ˈ**ca·ter·ing** abastecimiento *m*.
ca·ter·pil·lar [ˈkætərpilər] oruga *f*.
cat·er·waul [ˈkætərwɔːl] marramizar; chillar.
cat·gut [ˈkætgʌt] cuerda *f* de tripa.
ca·thar·sis [kəˈθɑːrsis] catarsis *f*.
ca·the·dral [kəˈθiːdrl] catedral *f*.
Cath·er·ine wheel [ˈkæθərin ˈwiːl] ⚠ rosetón *m*; (*firework*) rueda *f* de fuegos artificiales.
cath·e·ter [ˈkæθitər] catéter *m*.
cath·ode [ˈkæθoud] cátodo *m*; ~ *ray tube* tubo *m* de rayos catódicos.
cath·o·lic [ˈkæθəlik] **1.** □ *eccl.* católico; liberal, de amplias miras; **2.** católico (a *f*) *m*; **caˈthol·i·cism** catolicismo *m*.
cat·kin [ˈkætkin] amento *m*.
cat's-paw [ˈkætspɔː] *fig.* instrumento *m*.
cat·sup [ˈketʃəp, ˈkætsəp] salsa *f* de tomate condimentada.
cat·ti·ness [ˈkætinis] malicia *f*.
cat·tle [ˈkætl] ganado *m* (vacuno); ~ *crossing* paso *m* de ganado; ~*man* ganadero *m*; ~ *raising* ganadería *f*; ~ *ranch* hacienda *f* de ganado; ˈ~ **breed·ing** cría *f* de ganado; ˈ~ **rus·tler** ladrón *m* de ganado; ˈ~ **show** exposición *f* de ganado.
Cau·ca·sian [kɔːˈkeiʒən] caucasiano, caucásico *adj. a. su. m* (a *f*).
cau·cus [ˈkɔːkəs] camarilla *f* política.
cau·dal [ˈkɔːdl] *zo.* caudal.
cau·dle [ˈkɔːdl] bebida *f* caliente.
caught [kɔːt] *pret. a. p.p. of catch* 2 *a.* 3.
caul·dron [ˈkɔːldrən] calderón *m*.
cau·li·flow·er [ˈkɔliflauər] coliflor *f*.
caulk [kɔːk] calafatear; ˈ**caulk·er** calafate *m*.
caus·al [ˈkɔːzl] □ causal; **cau·sal·i·ty** [~ˈzæliti] causalidad *f*; ˈ**caus·a·tive** causativo; **cause 1.** causa *f* (*a.* ⚖); *make common ~ with* hacer causa común con; **2.** causar; ˈ**cause·less** □ sin causa.
cause·way [ˈkɔːzwei] calzada *f*; (*sea*) arrecife *m*.
caus·tic [ˈkɔːstik] **1.** cáustico *m*; **2.** □ cáustico (*a. fig.*).
cau·ter·i·za·tion [kɔːtəraiˈzeiʃn] cauterización *f*; ˈ**cau·ter·ize** cauterizar; ˈ**cau·ter·y** cauterio *m*.
cau·tion [ˈkɔːʃn] **1.** cautela *f*; (*warning*) amonestación *f*; F persona *f* extraordinaria; ~ *money* caución *f*; **2.** advertir, amonestar (*against* contra); ˈ**cau·tion·ar·y** amonestador.
cau·tious [ˈkɔːʃəs] □ cauteloso, precavido; ˈ**cau·tious·ness** cautela *f*, circunspección *f*.
cav·al·cade [kævlˈkeid] cabalgata *f*.
cav·a·lier [kævəˈlir] **1.** caballero *m*; galán *m*; **2.** altivo, desdeñoso.
cav·al·ry [ˈkævlri] caballería *f*.
cave [keiv] **1.** cueva *f*; ~-*in* atierre *m*, hundimiento *m*, derrumbe *m*, socavón *m*; **2.** ~ *in*: *v/i.* hundirse, derrumbarse; *v/t.* F quebrar.
ca·ve·at [ˈkeiviæt] advertencia *f*; ⚖ advertencia *f* de suspensión.
cave·man [ˈkeivmən] troglodita *m*; hombre *m* de las cavernas.
cav·ern [ˈkævərn] caverna *f*, antro *m*; ˈ**cav·ern·ous** cavernoso.
cav·i·ar(e) [ˈkæviɑːr] caviar *m*.
cav·il [ˈkævil] **1.** crítica *f*, reparo *m*; **2.** sutilizar, critiquizar; ~ *at, about* poner peros a; ˈ**cav·il·er** criticón (-a *f*) *m*.
cav·i·ty [ˈkæviti] cavidad *f*.
ca·vort [kəˈvɔːrt] cabriolar.
caw [kɔː] **1.** graznar; **2.** graznido *m*.
cay·enne [keiˈen] (*a.* [ˈkeien] *pepper*) pimentón *m*.
cay·man [ˈkeimən] caimán *m*.
cay·use [ˈkaiˈjuːs] F jaca *f* india.
cease [siːs] *v/i.* cesar (*from* de); ~ *from* dejar de; *v/t.* suspender, cesar; ˈ~-ˈ**fire** cese *m* de hostilidades; ˈ**cease·less** □ incesante.
ce·dar [ˈsiːdər] cedro *m*.
cede [siːd] ceder.
ceil·ing [ˈsiːliŋ] techo *m*, cielo *m* raso; ✈ techo *m*; *fig.* punto *m* más alto; ~ *price* precio *m* tope.
cel·an·dine [ˈseləndain] celidonia *f*.
cel·e·brant [ˈselibrənt] *eccl.* celebrante *m*; ˈ**cel·e·brate** celebrar (*a. eccl.*); ˈ**cel·e·brat·ed** célebre, famoso (*for* por); **cel·eˈbra·tion** celebración *f*; (*party*) reunión *f*; *in ~ of* en conmemoración de; ˈ**cel·e·bra·tor** parrandista *m/f*.
ce·leb·ri·ty [siˈlebriti] celebridad *f* (*a. p.*).
ce·ler·i·ty [siˈleriti] celeridad *f*.
cel·er·y [ˈseləri] apio *m*.
ce·les·tial [siˈlestjəl] celestial (*a. fig.*).

cel·i·ba·cy ['selibəsi] celibato *m*; **cel-i·bate** ['~bit] célibe *adj. a. su. m/f.*
cell [sel] (*prison*) celda *f*; *biol.* célula *f*; *pol.* célula *f* (de comunistas); ⚡ elemento *m*; (*bees*) celdilla *f*.
cel·lar ['selər] **1.** sótano *m*; (*wine*) bodega *f*; **2.** embodegar; '**cel·lar-age** ['~idʒ] almacenaje *m* en una bodega.
cel·list ['tʃelist] violoncelista *m/f*; **cel·lo** ['tʃelou] violoncelo *m*.
cel·lo·phane ['seləfein] (papel *m*) celofán *m*.
cel·lu·lar ['seljulər] celular; **cel·lule** ['~ju:l] célula *f*; **cel·lu·loid** ['~julɔid] celuloide *m*; **cel·lu·lose** ['~lous] celulosa *f*.
Celt [selt, kelt] celta *m/f*; '**Celt·ic** céltico.
ce·ment [si'ment] **1.** cemento *m*; **2.** cementar; *fig.* consolidar; **ce·ment-a·tion** [si:men'teiʃn] cementación *f*.
cem·e·ter·y ['semitəri] cementerio *m*.
cen·o·taph ['senətæf] cenotafio *m*.
cense [sens] incensar; '**cen·ser** incensario *m*.
cen·sor ['sensər] **1.** censor *m*; **2.** censurar; **cen·so·ri·ous** [sen'sɔ:riəs] □ hipercrítico, criticón; **cen·sor·ship** ['~sərʃip] censura *f*.
cen·sur·a·ble ['senʃərəbl] □ censurable; **cen·sure** ['senʃər] **1.** censura *f*; **2.** censurar.
cen·sus ['sensəs] censo *m*; *take the* ~ levantar el censo.
cent [sent] centavo *m* (*Am.* = $^1/_{100}$ *dólar*); *per* ~ por ciento.
cen·taur ['sentɔ:r] centauro *m*.
cen·tau·ry ['sentɔ:ri] centaura *f*.
cen·te·nar·i·an [senti'neriən] centenario *adj. a. su. m* (a *f*); **cen·te-nar·y** [sen'ti:nəri] centenario *m*.
cen·ten·ni·al [sen'tenjəl] centenario *adj. a. su. m*.
cen·ter ['sentər] **1.** centrista, central; **2.** centro *m*; ~ *field baseball* jardín *m* central; ~ *forward* delantero *m* centro; ~ *half* medio centro *m*; ~*piece* centro *m* de mesa; ~ *punch* ⊕ punzón *m* de marcar, granete *m*; **3.** centrar; concentrarse (*on, about* en).
cen·tes·i·mal [sen'tesiml] □ centesimal.
cen·ti... ['senti]: '**~·grade** centígrado; '**~·gram** centígramo *m*; '**~·me-ter** centímetro *m*; '**~·pede** ['~pi:d] ciempiés *m*.
cen·tral ['sentrəl] □ central; ~ *heating* calefacción *f* central; **cen-tral·i·za·tion** [~lai'zeiʃn] centralización *f*; '**cen·tral·ize** centralizar.
cen·tric, cen·tri·cal ['sentrik(l)] □ céntrico; **cen·trif·u·gal** [sen'trif-jugl] □ centrífugo; **cen'trip·e·tal** [~pitl] □ centrípeto.
cen·tu·ple ['sentjupl] **1.** céntuplo; **2.** centuplicar.
cen·tu·ry ['sentʃuri] siglo *m*.
ce·ram·ic [si'ræmik] cerámico; **ce-'ram·ics** *pl.* cerámica *f*.
ce·re·al ['siriəl] cereal *adj. a. su. m*.
cer·e·bral ['seribrəl] cerebral.
cer·e·mo·ni·al [seri'mounjəl] □ ceremonial *adj. a. su. m*; **cer·e'mo-ni·ous** □ ceremonioso; **cer·e·mo-ny** ['seriməni] ceremonia *f*; *Master of Ceremonies* maestro *m* de ceremonias; *stand on* ~ hacer ceremonias.
cer·tain ['sə:rtn] □ cierto; *know for* ~ saber a buen seguro; *make* ~ asegurarse (de), cerciorarse (de); ~*ly* ciertamente; sin falta; '**cer·tain·ty** certeza *f*.
cer·tif·i·cate 1. [sər'tifikit] certificado *m*, título *m*; ~ *of baptism* (*death, marriage*) partida *f* de bautismo (defunción, casamiento); **2.** [sər'tifikeit] certificar; ~*d* con título; '**cer·ti·fi-ca·tion** certificación *f*; '**cer·ti·fied 'pub·lic ac'count·ant** censor *m* jurado de cuentas; **cer·ti·fy** ['~fai] certificar; garantizar; **cer·ti·tude** ['~tju:d] certeza *f*.
cer·vi·cal ['sə:rvikl] cervical; **cer-vix** ['~viks] (*pl.* **-vi·ces** ['~visi:z]) cervix *f*.
ces·sa·tion [se'seiʃn] cesación *f*; ~ *of hostilities* suspensión *f* de hostilidades.
ces·sion ['seʃn] cesión *f*.
cess·pool ['sespu:l] pozo *m* negro.
ce·ta·cean [si'teiʃjən] cetáceo *adj. a. su. m*.
chafe [tʃeif] **1.** *v/t.* rozar, raer; calentar (frotando); *fig.* irritar, enfadar; **2.** *v/i.* desgastarse (*against* contra); *fig.* irritarse, enfadarse; *chafing dish* escalfador *m*.
chaff [tʃæf] **1.** barcia *f*, aechaduras *f/pl.*; *b.s.* broza *f*, desecho *m*; (*banter*) zumba *f*, chanza *f*; **2.** *p.* zumbarse de, dar chasco a.
chaf·fer ['tʃæfər] regatear.
chaf·finch ['tʃæfintʃ] pinzón *m* vulgar.

cha·grin ['ʃægrin] **1.** desazón *f*, disgusto *m*; **2.** desazonar, apesadumbrar.
chain [tʃein] **1.** cadena *f*; *phys.* ~ *reaction* reacción *f* en cadena; ~ *store* tienda *f* de una cadena; **2.** encadenar; '~ **gang** cadena *f* de presidiarios, collera *f*, cuerda *f* de presos; '~**smo·ker** fumador (-a *f*) *m* de un pitillo tras otro.
chair [tʃer] **1.** silla *f*; cátedra *f* (*a. professorial* ~); presidencia *f of meeting*; presidente *m*; *take the* ~ presidir; **2.** *p. in authority* asentar; llevar en una silla; *meeting* presidir; '~·**man,** '~·**per·son,** '~·**wom·an** presidente *m*; '~·**man·ship** presidencia *f*.
chaise [ʃeiz] calesa *f*, landó *m*; ~-*longue* meridiana *f*.
chal·ice ['tʃælis] *eccl.* cáliz *m*.
chalk [tʃɔ:k] **1.** *geol.* creta *f*; tiza *f for drawing*; *French* ~ jaboncillo *m* de sastre; esteatita *f*; F *by a long* ~ de mucho; **2.** marcar con tiza; *fig.* apuntar (*mst* ~ *up*); '**chalk·y** cretoso.
chal·lenge ['tʃælindʒ] **1.** desafío *m* (*a. fig.*), reto *m*; ⚔ quién vive *m*; ⚖ recusación *f*; **2.** desafiar (*a. fig.*), retar; ⚔ dar el quién vive a; ⚖ recusar; disputar; dudar; '**chal·leng·er** desafiador (-a *f*) *m*; retador (-a *f*) *m*.
cha·lyb·e·ate [kə'libiit] ferruginoso.
cham·ber ['tʃeimbər] cámara *f*; recámara *f of gun*; *lit.* aposento *m*; ~ *music* música *f* de cámara; ~ *of commerce* cámara *f* de comercio; ~*s pl.* despacho *m* de un abogado (*or* juez); **cham·ber·lain** ['~lin] chambelán *m*, gentilhombre *m* de cámara; '**cham·ber·maid** camarera *f*, criada *f* (de un hotel); '**cham·ber·pot** orinal *m*.
cha·me·le·on [kə'mi:ljən] camaleón *m*.
cham·fer ['tʃæmfər] **1.** chaflán *m*; **2.** chaflanar.
cham·ois ['ʃæmwɑ:] *zo. a.* ⊕ gamuza *f*.
champ[1] [tʃæmp] morder; mordiscar.
champ[2] [~] F campeón *m*.
cham·pagne [ʃæm'pein] champaña *m*.
cham·pi·on ['tʃæmpjən] **1.** campeón *m* (*a. fig.*); paladín *m* (*of a cause etc.*); **2.** defender; abogar por; '**cham·pi·on·ship** campeonato *m*.
chance [tʃæns] **1.** ocasión *f*, oportunidad *f*; posibilidad *f*, probabilidad *f*; suerte *f*; riesgo *m*; *by* ~ por casualidad; *look out for the main* ~ estar a la caza de su propio provecho; *stand a* ~ tener una probabilidad (*of* de); *take a* (*or one's*) ~ aventurarse; *take no* ~*s* obrar con cautela; **2.** casual; fortuito; **3.** *v/i.* acontecer, suceder; ~ *upon* tropezar con; *v/t.* F arriesgar.
chan·cel ['tʃænsəl] coro *m* y presbiterio *m*; '**chan·cel·ler·y** cancillería *f*; '**chan·cel·lor** canciller *m*; '**chan·cel·lor·ship** cancillería *f*.
chan·cer·y ['tʃænsəri] ⚖ chancillería *f*; cancillería *f*.
chanc·y ['tʃænsi] F arriesgado.
chan·de·lier [ʃændi'lir] araña *f* (de luces).
chan·dler ['tʃændlər] (*p.*) velero *m*; abacero *m*.
change [tʃeindʒ] **1.** cambio *m*; transformación *f*; muda *f of clothing*; (*a. small* ~) moneda *f* suelta; (*money returned*) vuelta *f*; ~ *of heart* cambio *m* de sentimiento; ~*of life* menopausia *f*; *thea.* ~ *of scene* mutación *f*; *for a* ~ por cambiar; **2.** *v/t.* cambiar; transformar; (*replace*) reemplazar; *clothes*, *opinion* cambiar de; *color* demudarse; ~ *places* trocarse (*with* con); ~ *the subject* volver la hoja; *v/i.* cambiar, mudar; 🚂 transbordar, hacer transbordo; **change·a'bil·i·ty** alterabilidad *f*; mutabilidad *f*; '**change·a·ble** □ cambiable; inconstante, inestable; '**change·less** inmutable; '**change·ling** niño (a *f*) *m* cambiado por otro; '**change-'o·ver** cambio *m*; '**chang·ing-room** vestuario *m*.
chan·nel ['tʃænl] **1.** canal *m* (*a. radio*); brazo *m of river*; (*irrigation*) cacera *f*; *fig.* vía *f*; *through the official* ~*s* pasando por los trámites oficiales; *the* (*English*) ♀ el Canal de la Mancha; **2.** acanalar; *fig.* encauzar.
chant [tʃænt] **1.** canto *m* llano; (*talking*) sonsonete *m*; **2.** cantar (el canto llano); *fig.* (*mst.* ~ *away*) discantar, cantar la misma cantilena; '**chan·try** capilla *f* (dotada para decir misas).
cha·os ['keiɔs] caos *m*; **cha'ot·ic** □ caótico.
chap[1] [tʃæp] **1.** grieta *f*, hendedura *f*; **2.** agrietar(se).
chap[2] [~] mandíbula *f*, quijada *f*.

chap[3] [~] F tipo *m*, pájaro *m*; '**~book** librete *m* (de cuentos *etc.*).
chap·el ['tʃæpl] capilla *f*; templo *m* (de algunas sectas protestantes); *typ.* personal *m* de una imprenta.
chap·er·on ['ʃæpəroun] **1.** acompañanta *f* de señorita, carabina *f*; **2.** acompañar (a una señorita), ir de carabina.
chap·lain ['tʃæplin] capellán *m*; '**chap·lain·cy** capellanía *f*.
chap·let ['tʃæplit] guirnalda *f*, corona *f* de flores; *eccl.* rosario *m*.
chap·pie ['tʃæpi] *sl.* tipo *m*.
chap·ter ['tʃæptər] capítulo *m*; *eccl. mst* cabildo *m*; ~ *and verse* con todos sus pelos y señales.
char[1] [tʃɑːr] *ichth.* umbra *f*.
char[2] [~] carbonizar; chamuscar.
char·ac·ter ['kæriktər] carácter *m*; *thea.* personaje *m*; F tipo *m*, sujeto *m*; *in* ~ conforme al tipo; **char·ac·ter'is·tic 1.** □ característico; propio (*of* de); **2.** característica *f*; distintivo *m*; **char·ac·ter·i·za·tion** [~rai'zeiʃn] caracterización *f*; representación *f*; **char·ac·ter·ize** caracterizar.
cha·rade [ʃə'reid] charada *f*.
char·coal ['tʃɑːrkoul] carbón *m* vegetal; carboncillo *m for drawing*; '**~·burn·er** carbonero *m*.
charge [tʃɑːrdʒ] **1.** carga *f of gun* (*a.* ⚡); *fig.* cargo *m*; ⚔ carga *f*; *eccl.*, ⚖ exhortación *f*, exhorto *m*; ⚖ acusación *f*; (*price*) precio *m*; *heraldry*: blasón *m*; ~*s pl.* coste *m*; honorarios *m/pl.*; *in* ~ *of p.* a cargo de; *th.* encargado de; *free of* ~ gratis; *give a p. in* ~ entregar a la policía; *take* ~ *of* hacerse cargo de; **2.** *v/t.* cargar (*a.* ⚔, ⚡); *price* cobrar; ordenar, mandar (*to inf.*); *p.* cargar (*with* con, de); ~ *s.t. to* (*the account of*) cargarle algo a uno en cuenta; *v/i.* cobrar (*freq.* mucho); '**charge·a·ble** □ cobradero; ⚖ acusable (*with* de); '**charge account** cuenta *f* corriente, cuenta *f* abierta.
char·gé d'af·faires ['ʃɑːrʒei dæ'fer] encargado *m* de negocios.
charg·er ['tʃɑːrdʒər] *poet.* caballo *m* de guerra, corcel *m*; ⚡ cargador *m*.
char·i·ot ['tʃæriət] carro *m* romano, carro *m* de guerra; **char·i·ot·eer** [~'tir] (*classical*) auriga *m*.
cha·ris·ma [kə'rizmə] carisma *f*; **cha·ris·mat·ic** [~'mætik] □ carismático.
char·i·ta·ble ['tʃæritəbl] □ caritativo; benéfico; ~ *society* institución *f* benéfica.
char·i·ty ['tʃæriti] caridad *f*; *out of* ~ por caridad; '~ **per'form·ance** función *f* benéfica.
char·la·tan ['tʃɑːrlətən] charlatán *m*, curandero *m*; '**char·la·tan·ism** charlatanismo *m*.
char·lotte ['ʃɑːrlət] *cooking*: carlota *f*.
charm [tʃɑːrm] **1.** hechizo *m*, encanto *m*; amuleto *m*; *fig.* encanto *m*; ~*s pl.* hechizos *m/pl. of woman*; **2.** hechizar, encantar (*a. fig.*); ~ *away* hacer desaparecer como por magia; llevarse misteriosamente; '**charm·er** encantador *m*; *fig.* hombre *m* de mucho encanto; '**charm·ing** □ encantador.
char·nel-house ['tʃɑːrnlhaus] osario *m*.
chart [tʃɑːrt] **1.** ⚓ carta *f* de marear; tabla *f*, cuadro *m*; **2.** poner en una carta de marear; ~ *a course* trazar un derrotero.
char·ter ['tʃɑːrtər] **1.** carta *f*; carta *f* de privilegio, encartación *f*; **2.** estatuir; *ship* fletar; *bus etc.* alquilar; '~ **mem·ber** socio *m* fundador; '~ **par·ty** carta *f* partida.
char·wom·an ['tʃɑːrwumən] criada *f* por horas, asistenta *f*.
char·y ['tʃæri] □ avaro (*of* de); cuidadoso, cauteloso; *be* ~ *of ger.* esquivar, evitar *inf*.
chase[1] [tʃeis] **1.** caza *f*; persecución *f*; *give* ~ dar caza; *wild goose* ~ pretensión *f* disparatada; **2.** perseguir; ~ *after* ir en pos de; *fig.* ir tras; ~ *away* ahuyentar.
chase[2] [~] grabar; *jewel* engastar.
chase[3] [~] *typ.* rama *f*.
chas·er ['tʃeisər] ✈ avión *m* de caza; ⚓ cazasubmarinos *m*.
chasm ['kæzm] grieta *f*; sima *f*; *fig.* abismo *m*.
chas·sis ['ʃæsi] chasis *m*, armazón *f*.
chaste [tʃeist] □ casto; *fig.* castizo, sin adorno.
chas·ten ['tʃeisn] castigar; *style* acendrar, apurar (*mst p.p.*); templar; ~*ed p.* escarmentado.
chas·tise [tʃæs'taiz] *lit.* castigar; **chas·tise·ment** ['~tizmənt] castigo *m*.
chas·ti·ty ['tʃæstiti] castidad *f*; sencillez *f of style*.

chas·u·ble [ˈtʃæzjubl] casulla *f*.
chat [tʃæt] **1.** charla *f*, palique *m*; **2.** charlar.
chat·tels [ˈtʃætlz] *pl*. (*mst goods and* ~) bienes *m*/*pl*. muebles.
chat·ter [ˈtʃætər] **1.** (*p*.) chacharrear; (*birds*) chirriar; (*teeth*) castañetear; **2.** cháchara *f*; chirrido *m*; castañeteo *m*; ˈ**~·box** F parlanchín (-a *f*) *m*, tarabilla *f*.
chat·ty [ˈtʃæti] □ hablantín; *letter* lleno de noticias.
chauf·feur [ˈʃoufər] chófer *m*.
chau·vin·ism [ˈʃouvinizm] chauvinismo *m*; ˈ**chau·vin·ist** chauvinista *m*/*f*; **chau·vin**ˈ**is·tic** □ chauvinista.
chaw [tʃɔː] F mascar; *sl*. ~ *up* hacer polvo.
cheap [tʃiːp] □ barato; (*selling cheap*) baratero; *fig*. de mal gusto, chabacano; F *feel* ~ sentirse avergonzado; *hold* ~ despreciar; F *on the* ~ barato; ˈ**cheap·en** abaratar; *fig*. desprestigiar; ~ *o.s.* aplebeyarse; ˈ**cheap-skate** *sl*. tacaño (a *f*) *m*.
cheat [ˈtʃiːt] **1.** trampa *f*, fraude *m*; (*p*.) tramposo (a *f*) *m*, petardista *m*/*f*; **2.** trampear, petardear; defraudar; estafar ([*out*] *of acc*.); ˈ**cheat·ing** trampa *f*, engaño *m*.
check [tʃek] **1.** parada *f* (súbita); rechazo *m*, repulsa *f* (*a*. ⚔); impedimento *m* (*on* para), estorbo *m* (*on* a); control *m*, inspección *f* (*on* de); (*luggage*) talón *m*; billete *m* de reclamo; ficha *f in games*; ⊕ tope *m*; (*square*) cuadro *m*; (*cloth*) paño *m* a cuadros; *chess*: (*in* en) jaque *m*; cheque *m*; cuenta *f*; F *hand in one's* ~*s* estirar la pata; *hold in* ~ contener, refrenar; **2.** parar; rechazar, repulsar; impedir, estorbar; controlar, inspeccionar; *document* compulsar; *facts* comprobar; *baggage* facturar; *chess*: dar jaque a; ~ *in* inscribir el nombre (en el registro de un hotel); ~ *up* comprobar, verificar (*on acc*.); ˈ**check·book** talonario *m* de cheques; ˈ**check·ered** cuadrado; *fig*. variado; ˈ**check·ers** *pl*. juego *m* de damas; ˈ**check girl** moza *f* de guardarropa; ˈ**check·ing** control *m*, verificación *f*; ˈ**check·ing ac·count** cuenta *f* corriente; ˈ**check** ˈ**mate 1.** mate *m*; **2.** dar mate a; ˈ**check·out** (*from a hotel*) salida *f*; (*time*) hora *f* de salida; (*in a self-service retail store*) revisión *f* de pago; ˈ**check·out** ˈ**coun·ter** mostrador *m* de revisión; ˈ**check·point** punto *m* de inspección; ˈ**check·room** guardarropa *f*; ˈ**check·up** verificación *f*; ⚕ reconocimiento *m* general.
cheek [tʃiːk] mejilla *f*, carrillo *m*; F descaro *m*, frescura *f*; ⊕ quijada *f*; *v*. *jowl*; ˈ**~·bone** pómulo *m*; ˈ**cheek·y** F descarado.
cheep [tʃiːp] piar.
cheer [tʃir] **1.** humor *m* (*esp*. *of good* ~ de buen ánimo); comida *f* (*esp*. *make good* ~ banquetear); aplauso *m*; *three* ~*s* ¡viva! (*for acc*.); **2.** *v*/*t*. alegrar, consolar (*a*. ~ *up*); aplaudir; animar con aplausos (*a*. ~ *on*); *v*/*i*. alegrarse, animarse (*a*. ~ *up*); ~ *up!* ¡ánimo!; ˈ**cheer·ful** □ alegre; ˈ**cheer·ful·ness**, ˈ**cheer-i·ness** alegría *f*; complacencia *f*; **cheer·i·o** [ˈ~riˈou] F ¡adiós!; ¡hasta la vista!; ˈ**cheer·less** □ triste, melancólico; ˈ**cheer·y** □ animado; jovial; *atmosphere etc*. acogedor.
cheese [tʃiːz] queso *m*; *cream* ~ requesón *m*; ˈ**~·cloth** estopilla *f*; ˈ**~ par·ing 1.** *fig*., *mst* ~*s pl*. bagatelas *f*/*pl*., frioleras *f*/*pl*.; **2.** tacaño, roñoso.
chees·y [ˈtʃiːzi] caseoso; *sl*. tosco, sin valor.
chee·tah [ˈtʃiːtə] leopardo *m* indio.
chef [ʃef] jefe *m* de cocina.
chei·ro·man·cy [ˈkairəmænsi] quiromancia *f*.
chem·i·cal [ˈkemikl] **1.** □ químico; **2.** sustancia *f* química.
che·mise [ʃiˈmiːz] camisa *f* de mujer.
chem·ist [ˈkemist] ⚗ químico (a *f*) *m*; (*pharmaceutical* ~) boticario *m*, farmacéutico *m*; ~*'s* (*shop*) farmacia *f*; ˈ**chem·is·try** química *f*.
che·mo·ther·a·py [kiːmouˈθerəpi] quimoterapia *f*.
cheque [tʃek] = *check*.
cher·ish [ˈtʃeriʃ] estimar, apreciar; *hopes etc*. acariciar, abrigar.
che·root [ʃəˈruːt] *tipo de puro*.
cher·ry [ˈtʃeri] **1.** cereza *f*; (*a*. ~ *tree*) cerezo *m*; *fig*. *sl*. virginidad *f*; **2.** *attr*. rojo cereza (*a*. ˈ**~-red**).
cher·ub [ˈtʃerəb] querubín *m*; **che-ru·bic** [~ˈruːbik] querúbico.
cher·vil [ˈtʃəːrvil] perifollo *m*.
chess [tʃes] ajedrez *m*; ˈ**~·board** tablero *m* (de ajedrez); ˈ**~·man**, ˈ**~·piece** trebejo *m*, pieza *f*; ˈ**~·play-er** ajedrecista *m*/*f*.

chest [tʃest] arca *f*, cofre *m*; *anat.* pecho *m*; (*money*) caja *f*; ~ *of drawers* cómoda *f*; ~ *trouble* catarro *m* crónico del pecho; *get a th. off one's* ~ desahogarse; ˈ**chest·y** *sl.* engreído.

chest·nut [ˈtʃesnʌt] **1.** castaña *f*; (*a.* ~ *tree*) castaño *m*; F chiste *m* ya conocido; **2.** castaño, marrón.

chev·a·lier [ʃevəˈlir] caballero *m*.

chev·i·ot [ˈtʃeviət] cheviot *m*.

chev·ron [ˈʃevrən] ⚔ galón *m*; *heraldry*: cheurón *m*.

chev·y [ˈtʃevi] **1.** caza *f*; **2.** cazar; F acosar; F ~ *s.o. into ger.* empujar a una p. a *inf*.

chew [tʃuː] **1.** mascar, masticar; ~ *the cud* rumiar (*a. fig.*; *a.* ~ *s.t. over*); *sl.* ~ *the rag* dar la lengua; **2.** mascadura *f*; ˈ**chew·ing gum** chicle *m*.

chi·cane [ʃiˈkein] **1.** embuste *m*; **2.** embustar; **chi**ˈ**can·er·y** embuste *m*, trapaza *f*.

chick [ˈtʃik] pollito *m*; F crío (a *f*) *m*; **chick·en** [ˈtʃikin] pollo *m*, gallina *f*; F *she is no* ~ ya no es una pollita.

chick·en...: ˈ~ **coop** pollera *f*; ˈ~ **farm·er** avicultor *m*; ˈ~**·feed** *sl.* pan *m* comido; *sl.* breva *f*; ˈ~**·heart·ed** cobarde, gallina; ˈ~**·pox** varicela *f*; ˈ**chick·pea** garbanzo *m*.

chic·o·ry [ˈtʃikəri] chicoria *f*.

chide [tʃaid] [*irr.*] *lit.* reprobar.

chief [tʃiːf] **1.** □ principal; primero; ~ *clerk* oficial *m* mayor; ~ *executive* jefe *m* del gobierno; **2.** jefe *m*; ... *in* ~ ... en jefe; ~ *of staff* jefe *m* de estado mayor; ˈ**chief·ly** principalmente, mayormente; **chief·tain** [ˈ~tən] jefe *m*, cacique *m*.

chil·blain [ˈtʃilblein] sabañón *m*.

child [tʃaild] niño (a *f*) *m*; hijo (a *f*) *m*; *attr.* muy joven; ~*'s play fig.* cosa *f* de coser y cantar; *from a* ~ desde niño; *with* ~ encinta; ˈ~**·bed** parturición *f*; ˈ~**·birth** parto *m*; ˈ**child·hood** niñez *f*, infancia *f*; ˈ**child·ish** □ pueril; *b.s.* aniñado; ˈ**child·ish·ness** puerilidad *f*; niñería *f*; ˈ**child la·bor** trabajo *m* de menores; ˈ**child·less** sin hijos; ˈ**child·like** *fig.* propio de un niño; **chil·dren** [ˈtʃildrən] *pl. of child*; ˈ**child** ˈ**wel·fare** protección *f* a la infancia.

Chil·e·an [ˈtʃiliən] chileno *adj. a. su. m* (a *f*).

chi·li [ˈtʃili] ají *m*.

chill [tʃil] **1.** *lit.* frío; *manner* desapacible; **2.** frío *m*; escalofrío *m* (*a.* ⚕); *take the* ~ *off liquid* entibiar; *room* calentar ligeramente; **2.** *v/t.* enfriar (*a. metal*); *fig.* desalentar; ~*ed meat* carne *f* congelada; *v/i.* enfriarse; *esp.* ⚕ calofriarse; ˈ**chill·i·ness,** ˈ**chill·ness** frialdad *f* (*a. fig.*); ˈ**chill·y** frío (*a. fig.*); *p.* friolero; *feeling* escalofriado.

chime [tʃaim] **1.** campaneo *m*; (*peal*) repique *m*; carillón *m*; *fig.* conformidad *f*, acuerdo *m*; **2.** repicar, sonar; *fig.* estar en armonía; F ~ *in with* soltar, saltar.

chi·me·ra [kaiˈmiərə] quimera *f*; **chi·mer·i·cal** [~ˈmerik(l)] □ quimérico.

chim·ney [ˈtʃimni] chimenea *f* (*exterior*); tubo *m* de lámpara; *mount.* olla *f*, cañón *m*; ˈ~**·piece** marco *m* de chimenea; ˈ~ **pot** tubo *m* de chimenea; ˈ~ **sweep**(**·er**) limpiachimeneas *m*.

chim·pan·zee [tʃimpənˈziː] chimpancé *m*.

chin[1] [tʃin] barba *f*, barbilla *f*; *double* ~ papada *f*; F *keep one's* ~ *up* no desanimarse; F *take it on the* ~ mantenerse firme.

chin[2] [~] *sl.* parlotear.

chi·na [ˈtʃainə] porcelana *f*.

chine [tʃain] espinazo *m*; (*meat*) lomo *m*.

Chi·nese [ˈtʃaiˈniːz] **1.** chino *adj. a. su. m* (a *f*); **2.** (*language*) chino *m*.

chink[1] [tʃiŋk] grieta *f*, hendedura *f*; resquicio *m* (*a. fig.*).

chink[2] [~] **1.** sonido *m* metálico; tintineo *m*; **2.** sonar, tintinear.

chintz [tʃints] zaraza *f*.

chip [tʃip] **1.** astilla *f*, brizna *f*; lasca *f of stone*; (*defect*) saltadura *f*, desportilladura *f*; patata *f* frita; *poker*: ficha *f*; ~ *off the old block* de tal palo tal astilla, hijo *m* de su padre; F *have a* ~ *on one's shoulder* ser un resentido; **2.** desportillar(se), astillar(se); F ~ *in* interrumpir (una conversación) (*with* diciendo); **chip·munk** [ˈtʃipmʌŋk] ardilla *f* listada; ˈ**chip·py** *sl.* seco, poco interesante.

chi·rop·o·dist [kiˈrɔpədist] quiropodista *m*/*f*; **chi**ˈ**rop·o·dy** quiropodia *f*; **chi·ro·prac·tor** [ˈkairəpræktər] quiropráctico *m*.

chirp [tʃəːrp] **1.** gorjear, pipiar; (*cricket*) chirriar; F hablar alegremente; **2.** gorjeo *m*; chirrido *m*; ˈ**chirp·y** F alegre.

chis·el [ˈtʃizl] **1.** formón *m*, escoplo *m for wood*; cincel *m for stone*; **2.** escoplear; cincelar; *sl.* timar; ˈ**chis·el·er** F gorrón *m*.
chit[1] [tʃit] chiquillo (a *f*) *m*; ~ *of a girl* mujercilla *f*.
chit[2] [~] esquela *f*, nota *f*.
chit-chat [ˈtʃittʃæt] palique *m*; chismería *f*.
chiv·al·rous [ˈʃivlrəs] □ caballeroso; ˈ**chiv·al·ry** caballería *f*; (*spirit*) caballerosidad *f*.
chive [tʃaiv] cebollino *m*.
chiv·y [ˈtʃivi] F = *chevy*.
chlo·ral [ˈklɔːrl] cloral *m*; **chlo·ride** [ˈ~aid] cloruro *m*; ~ *of lime* cloruro *m* de cal; **chlo·rine** [ˈ~iːn] cloro *m*; **chlo·ro·form** [ˈ~əfɔːrm] **1.** cloroformo *m*; **2.** cloroformizar; **chlo·ro·phyll** [ˈ~əfil] clorofila *f*.
chock [tʃɔk] **1.** cuña *f*; combo *m of barrel*; ⚓ calzo *m*; **2.** acuñar; afianzar con combos (*or* calzos); ˈ**~-a-ˈblock** apretado; atestado (*with* de); ˈ**~-ˈfull** de bote en bote.
choc·o·late [ˈtʃɔkəlit] chocolate *m*.
choice [tʃɔis] **1.** elección *f*; preferencia *f*; ✝ *wide* ~ gran surtido *m*; *have no* ~ no tener alternativa; *make* (*or take*) *one's* ~ elegir, seleccionar; **2.** selecto, escogido.
choir [ˈkwaiər] coro *m*; ~*master* maestro *m* de capilla, jefe *m* de coro.
choke [tʃouk] **1.** *v/t.* estrangular; sofocar (*a. fig.*); tapar, atascar (*a.* ~ *up*); *fig.* ~ *back* retener; F ~ *off p.* parar; reprobar; *v/i.* sofocarse, ahogarse (*a. fig.*); atascarse, obstruirse; **2.** ⊕ cierre *m*, obturador *m*; *mot.* estrangulador *m*; *mot.* aire *m*; ~ *coil* bobina *f* de reacción; ˈ**~·bore** calibre *m* estrangulado; ˈ**~·damp** mofeta *f*; ˈ**chok·er** F cuello *m* alto.
chol·er·a [ˈkɔlərə] cólera *m*; ˈ**chol·er·ic** colérico, irascible.
cho·les·ter·ol [kəˈlestəroul, ~rɔl] colesterol *m*.
choose [tʃuːz] [*irr.*] escoger; elegir; seleccionar; ~ *between* optar entre; ~ *to inf.* optar por *inf.*; ˈ**choos·y** F melindroso, quisquilloso.
chop[1] [tʃɔp] **1.** golpe *m* cortante; tajada *f*; (*meat*) chuleta *f*; *sl.* ~*s pl.* boca *f*; labios *m/pl.*; ~*s and changes* altibajos *m/pl.*; cambios *m/pl.*; **2.** *v/t.* cortar, tajar; tronchar (*freq.* ~ *off*); desmenuzar (*freq.* ~ *up*); *meat* picar; *v/i.* cambiar súbitamente; (*wind*) virar; ~ *and change* variar; cambiar de parecer.
chop[2] [~] ✝ sello *m*; F *first* ~ de primera calidad.
chop·per [ˈtʃɔpər] (*p.*) tajador *m*; (*tool*) hacha *f*; (*butcher's*) cortante *m*, cuchilla *f*; *sl.* ✈ helicóptero *m*; ˈ**chop·ping block** tajo *m*; ˈ**chop·py** *sea* agitado, picado; ˈ**chop·stick** palillo *m* para comer (*de los chinos*).
cho·ral [ˈkɔːrl] □ coral; **cho·ral**(**e**) [kɔˈræl] coral *m*.
chord [kɔːrd] acorde *m*; (*string*, ♪, ⚕ *a. poet.*) cuerda *f*; *fig. strike the right* ~ juzgar bien el ambiente (de una reunión *esp.*).
chore [tʃɔːr] tarea *f* de ocasión; (*household*) ~*s pl.* quehaceres *m/pl.* domésticos.
cho·re·og·ra·phy [kɔriˈɔgrəfi] coreografía *f*.
chor·is·ter [ˈkɔristər] corista *m/f*.
cho·rus [ˈkɔːrəs] **1.** coro *m*; ~ *girl* corista *f*, conjuntista *f*; **2.** hablar (*or* cantar) en coro.
chose [tʃouz] *pret.*, ˈ**cho·sen** *p.p. of choose*.
chow [tʃau] chao *m*; *sl.* comida *f*; **~·der** [ˈ~dər] estofado *m* de almejas o pescado.
chrism [ˈkrizm] crisma *f*.
chris·ten [ˈkrisn] bautizar; **Chris·ten·dom** [ˈ~dəm] cristiandad *f*; ˈ**chris·ten·ing** bautismo *m*, bautizo *m*.
Chris·tian [ˈkristʃən] □ cristiano *adj. a. su. m* (a *f*); ~ *name* nombre *m* de pila; **Chris·ti·an·i·ty** [~tiˈæniti] cristianismo *m*; **Chris·tian·ize** [ˈ~tʃənaiz] cristianizar.
Christ·mas [ˈkrisməs] **1.** navideño; **2.** Navidad *f*, Navidades *f/pl.*, Pascua *f* de Navidad; ~ *card* aleluya *f* navideña, tarjeta *f* navideña, navidal *m*; ~ *carol* villancico *m*; ~ *Day* día *m* de Navidad; ~ *Eve* nochebuena *f*; ~ *gift* aguinaldo *m*, regalo *m* de Navidad; ~ *tree* árbol *m* de Navidad; *Merry* ~! ¡Felices Pascuas!, ¡Felices Navidades!
chro·mat·ic [krəˈmætik] □ cromático; **chroˈmat·ics** *pl. or. sg.* cromática *f*.
chrome [kroum] **1.** cromado; ~ *yellow* amarillo *m* de cromo; **2.** cromo *m*; (*plating*) cromado *m*; **3.** *v/t.* cromar; **chro·mi·um** [ˈ~jəm] cromo *m*; ˈ**chro·mi·um-plat·ed** croma-

do; **chro·mo'lith·o·graph** cromolitografía *f*.
chron·ic ['krɔnik] □ crónico; F terrible, muy serio; **'chron·i·cle 1.** crónica *f*; **2.** anotar; narrar; **'chron·i·cler** cronista *m*/*f*.
chron·o·log·i·cal [krɔnə'lɔdʒikl] □ cronológico; *~ly* en orden cronológico; **chro·nol·o·gy** [krə'nɔlədʒi] cronología *f*.
chro·nom·e·ter [krə'nɔmitər] cronómetro *m*.
chrys·a·lis ['krisəlis] crisálida *f*.
chrys·an·the·mum [kri'sænθəməm] crisántemo *m*.
chub [tʃʌb] cacho *m*; **'chub·by** rechoncho; *face* mofletudo.
chuck[1] [tʃʌk] **1.** (*hen*) cloqueo *m*; *my ~!* ¡amor mío!; **2.** cloquear.
chuck[2] [~] **1.** F arrojar; *~ out* echar; *~ it!* ¡basta ya!; *~ under the chin* dar la mamola a; **2.** mamola *f*.
chuck[3] [~] ⊕ manguito *m*.
chuck·le ['tʃʌkl] **1.** reír entre dientes, soltar una risa sofocada; **2.** risa *f* sofocada.
chum [tʃʌm] **1.** F compinche *m*, compañero *m*; *be great ~s* ser amigos íntimos; **2.** compartir un cuarto; F *~ up* entablar amistad.
chump [tʃʌmp] F zoquete *m*; (*meat*) lomo *m*; *sl.* melón *m*, calabaza *f*; *sl.* (*p.*) majadero *m*; *sl. off one's ~* chiflado.
chunk [tʃʌŋk] F pedazo *m* grueso; persona *f* rechoncha; **'chunk·y** F corto y grueso; rechoncho.
church [tʃə:rtʃ] **1.** iglesia *f*; *♀ of England* Iglesia *f* Anglicana; **2.**: *be ~ed* ser purificada *después de un parto*; **'~·go·er** devoto (a *f*) *m*; **'church mem·ber** feligrés *m*; **'church'ward·en** capiller *m*; **'church·y** F beato; **'church'yard** cementerio *m*, camposanto *m*.
churl [tʃə:rl] patán *m* (*a. fig.*), palurdo *m*; **churl·ish** □ palurdo, tosco; (*niggardly*) mezquino.
churn [tʃə:rn] **1.** mantequera *f*; **2.** batir en una mantequera; hacer (mantequilla); revolver, agitar (*a. ~ up*).
chute [ʃu:t] salto *m* de agua; canalón *m in house*; tolva *f in mill*; tobogán *m in swimming pool*.
chut·ney ['tʃʌtni] salsa *f* picante.
chyle [kail] quilo *m*.
chyme [kaim] quimo *m*.
ci·ca·da [si'keidə] cigarra *f*.
cic·a·trice ['sikətris] 🕮 cicatriz *f*;
cic·a·tri·za·tion [~trai'zeiʃn] cicatrización *f*; **'cic·a·trize** cicatrizar(se).
ci·ce·ro·ne [tʃitʃə'rouni] *lit.* cicerone *m*.
ci·der ['saidər] sidra *f*.
ci·gar [si'gɑ:r] (cigarro) puro *m*, cigarro *m*; *~ band* anillo *m* de cigarro; *~ case* cigarrera *f*, petaca *f*; *~ cutter* cortacigarros *m*; *~ holder* boquilla *f*; *~ store* estanco *m*, tabaquería *f*.
cig·a·ret, cig·a·rette [sigə'ret] cigarrillo *m*; pitillo *m*; **'~ case** petaca *f*, pitillera *f*; **'~ hold·er** boquilla *f*; **'~ light·er** mechero *m*; **'~ pa·per** papel *m* de fumar.
cil·i·ar·y ['siliəri] ciliar.
cinch [sintʃ] *sl.* breva *f*.
cinc·ture ['siŋktʃər] *lit.* cinturón *m*.
cin·der ['sindər] carbonilla *f*; *~s pl.* cenizas *f*/*pl*.
cin·e·cam·er·a ['sinikæmərə] cámara *f* cinematográfica.
cin·e·ma ['sinimə] cine *m*; **cin·e·mat·o·graph** [~'mætəgræf] **1.** cinematógrafo *m*; **2.** cinematografiar; **cin·e·mat·o·graph·ic** [~'græfik] □ cinematográfico.
cin·er·ar·y ['sinəreri] cinerario.
cin·na·bar ['sinəbɑ:r] cinabrio *m*.
cin·na·mon ['sinəmən] canela *f*.
ci·pher ['saifər] **1.** cifra *f*; cero *m*; (*p.*) cero *m* a la izquierda; *in ~* en cifra; **2.** cifrar; calcular.
cir·cle ['sə:rkl] **1.** círculo *m* (*a. fig.*); *thea.* anfiteatro *m*; **2.** circundar, cercar; (*go round*) dar vueltas (a); girar;
cir·clet ['~klit] venda *f*, faja *f* (para la cabeza).
cir·cuit ['sə:rkit] circuito *m* (*a.* ⚡); ⚖ *approx.* distrito *m*; *sport*: pista *f*; *v. short ~*; ⚡ *~ breaker* cortacircuitos *m*, interruptor *m* automático, disyuntor *m*; **cir·cu·i·tous** [sər'kjuitəs] □ tortuoso.
cir·cu·lar ['sə:rkjulər] **1.** □ circular; ✝ *~ note* carta *f* de crédito; *~ saw* sierra *f* circular; **2.** circular *f* (*a. ~ letter*).
cir·cu·late ['sə:rkjuleit] circular; **'cir·cu·lat·ing**: *~ library* biblioteca *f* circulante; *~ medium* moneda *f* corriente; **cir·cu'la·tion** circulación *f* (*a.* ✝).
cir·cum... ['sə:rkəm] circun...; **cir·cum·cise** ['~saiz] circuncidar; **cir-**

cum·ci·sion [~'siʒn] circuncisión *f*; **cir·cum·fer·ence** [sər'kʌmfərəns] circunferencia *f*; **cir·cum·flex** ['sə:rkəmfleks] circunflejo *m*; **cir·cum·ja·cent** [~'dʒeisnt] circunjacente; **cir·cum·lo·cu·tion** [~lə'kju:ʃn] circunlocución *f*; circunloquio *m*; **cir·cum·loc·u·to·ry** [~'lɔkjutəri] perifrástico; **cir·cum·nav·i·gate** [~'nævigeit] circunnavegar; **cir·cum·nav·i·ga·tion** circunnavegación *f*; **cir·cum·scribe** ['~skraib] circunscribir (*a. fig.*); **cir·cum·scrip·tion** [~'skripʃn] circunscripción *f*; **cir·cum·spect** □ ['~spekt] □ circunspecto; **cir·cum·spec·tion** [~'spekʃn] circunspección *f*; **cir·cum·stance** ['~stəns] circunstancia *f*; *be in easy ~s* estar acomodado; *in (or under) the ~s* en las circunstancias; *under no ~s* de ninguna manera; **cir·cum·stan·tial** [~'stænʃl] □ circunstancial; ⚖ *~ evidence* prueba *f* indiciaria, indicios *m/pl.* vehementes; **cir·cum·'stan·ti·ate** relatar con las circunstancias; **cir·cum·vent** [~'vent] embaucar; burlar.

cir·cus ['sə:rkəs] circo *m*; *British (traffic circle square or plaza)* plaza *f* redonda.

cir·rus ['sirəs], *pl.* **cir·ri** ['~ai] cirro *m*.

cis·co ['siskou] arenque *m* de lago.

cis·tern ['sistərn] arca *f*, depósito *m*; *(rainwater)* aljibe *m*; *hot-water ~* termo *m*.

cit·a·del ['sitədl] ciudadela *f*.

ci·ta·tion [sai'teiʃn] citación *f* (*a.* ⚖); ⚔ mención *f*; **cite** [sait] citar; ⚔ mencionar.

cit·i·zen ['sitizn] ciudadano (a *f*) *m*; ⚔ paisano *m*; *~s band (CB) radio*: banda *f* ciudadana; **cit·i·zen·ship** ['~ʃip] ciudadanía *f*.

cit·ric ac·id ['sitrik'æsid] ácido *m* cítrico; **cit·ron** ['sitrən] *(tree)* cidro *m*; *(fruit)* cidra *f*; **cit·rus** ['~rəs] **1.** auranciáceo; **2.** cidro *m* (*el género Citrus*); *~ fruit* agrios *m/pl.*, frutas *f/pl.* cítricas.

cit·y ['siti] **1.** ciudad *f*; *London*: *the ~ el centro comercial de Londres*; **2.** ciudadano; *~ clerk* archivero *m*; *~ council* ayuntamiento *m*; *~ editor* redactor *m* de periódico encargado de noticias locales; *~ fathers pl.* concejales *m/pl.*; *~ hall* casa *f* consistorial, palacio *m* municipal; *~ limits pl.* casco *m* urbano; *~ manager* administrador *m* municipal; *~ planner* urbanista *m/f*; *~ planning* urbanismo *m*; *~ room* redacción *f*.

civ·ic ['sivik] cívico; *~ center* casa *f* consistorial; conjunto *m* de edificios municipales; *~s sg.* estudio *m* de los deberes y derechos del ciudadano; *~-mindedness* civismo *m*.

civ·il ['sivl] □ civil; *~ defense* defensa *f* pasiva; *~ servant* funcionario (a *f*) *m* del Estado; *~ service* burocracia *f* oficial; **ci·vil·ian** [si'viljən] paisano (a *f*) *m*; *~ clothes pl.* traje *m* de paisano; **ci'vil·i·ty** civilidad *f*; **civ·i·li·za·tion** [~lai'zeiʃn] civilización *f*; **'civ·i·lize** civilizar.

clack [klæk] **1.** chasquido *m*; (*p.*) tarabilla *f*; *~ valve* chapaleta *f*; **2.** hacer chasquido; sonar; *(chatter)* charlar.

clad [klæd] *lit. pret. a. p.p. of clothe.*

claim [kleim] **1.** demanda *f* (*a.* ⚖); petición *f*; pretensión *f* (*to* a); ⚒ pertinencia *f*; *~ check* comprobante *m*; *lay ~ to* reclamar; **2.** demandar; reclamar; pretender (*to inf.*); afirmar; *attention* merecer; **'claim·a·ble** que se puede reclamar; **'claim·ant** demandante *m/f* (*a.* ⚖); pretendiente (a *f*) *m to throne.*

clair·voy·ance [kler'vɔiəns] clarividencia *f*; **clair'voy·ant(e)** visionario (a *f*) *m*; clarividente *m*.

clam [klæm] **1.** almeja *f*; F *(tight-lipped person)* chiticalla *m/f*; *~ chowder* estofado *m* de almejas; **2.** *v/i.* *~ up* F callarse la boca.

cla·mant ['kleimənt] *lit.* estrepitoso.

clam·ber ['klæmbər] gatear, trepar, subir gateando (*up* a).

clam·mi·ness ['klæminis] frío *m* húmedo; **'clam·my** □ frío y húmedo.

clam·or ['klæmər] **1.** clamor *m*, clamoreo *m*; **2.** clamorear, clamar (*for* por); **clam·or·ous** ['~əs] □ clamoroso.

clamp [klæmp] **1.** abrazadera *f*; *(screw)* tornillo *m* de banco; *(potato)* montón *m*; **2.** afianzar con abrazadera; *fig.* *~ down on* apretar los tornillos a; suprimir.

clan [klæn] clan *m* (*a. fig.*).

clan·des·tine [klæn'destin] □ clandestino.

clang [klæŋ] **1.** sonido *m* metálico

fuerte, clamoreo *m*; ~! ¡tolón!; **2.** (re)sonar; ˈ**clang·er** F: *drop a* ~ hacer una plancha; meter la pata; **clang·or** [ˈklæŋgər] estruendo *m*; **clang·or·ous** [ˈklæŋgərəs] estrepitoso.

clank [klæŋk] **1.** sonido *m* metálico seco, rechino *m*; **2.** rechinar.

clan·nish [ˈklæniʃ] exclusivista; unido.

clap [klæp] **1.** palmoteo *m*, aplauso *m*; (*thunder*) trueno *m*; golpe *m* seco; *sl.* gonorrea *f*; **2.** dar palmadas, aplaudir; dar un golpe a (*on* en); ~ *eyes on* clavar la vista en; F ~ *up* poner en la cárcel; = *place* 2, *put* 1; ˈ~**·board** chilla *f*; ˈ**clap·per** badajo *m*; ˈ**clap·trap 1.** faramalla *f*; farfolla *f*; **2.** faramallón.

claque [klæk] claque *f*, tifus *m*.

clar·et [ˈklærət] clarete *m*; *sl.* sangre *f*.

clar·i·fi·ca·tion [klærifiˈkeiʃn] aclaración *f*; **clar·i·fy** [ˈ~fai] clarificar, aclarar.

clar·i·net [klæriˈnet] clarinete *m*.

clar·i·ty [ˈklæriti] claridad *f*.

clash [klæʃ] **1.** choque *m*; fragor *m*; **2.** chocar (*a. fig.*; *with* con); (*colors*) desentonar (*with* con).

clasp [klæsp] **1.** broche *m*, corchete *m*; (*book*) broche *m*, manecilla *f*; (*shoe*) hebilla *f*; agarro *m of hand etc.*; (*handshake*) apretón *m*; **2.** abrochar; abrazar; agarrar; *hand* apretar; ˈ~ ˈ**knife** navaja *f*.

class [klæs] **1.** clase *f*; *good* ~ de buena calidad; F *that's* ~ (*for you*)! ¡su padre!; **2.** clasificar; ~ *with* comparar con; ˈ~-ˈ**con·scious** celoso de las distinciones sociales; ˈ~-ˈ**con·scious·ness** sentimiento *m* de clase.

clas·sic [ˈklæsik] clásico *adj. a. su. m*; *the* ~*s pl.* la obras clásicas (*esp.* griegas y latinas); las humanidades; ˈ**clas·si·cal** □ clásico.

clas·si·fi·ca·tion [klæsifiˈkeiʃn] clasificación *f*; **clas·si·fy** [ˈ~fai] clasificar.

class...: ˈ~**·room** aula *f*, clase *f*; ˈ~ ˈ**strug·gle** lucha *f* de clases; ˈ**class·y** F elegante, de primera, muy pera.

clat·ter [ˈklætər] **1.** martilleo *m*; repiqueteo *m*; estruendo *m*; trápala *f of hooves*; choque *m of plates*; rumor *m of conversation*; **2.** martillear; (*esp. metal*) guachapear; chocar; mover con estruendo confuso.

clause [klɔːz] cláusula *f* (*a. gr.*).

claus·tral [ˈklɔːstrəl] claustral.

clav·i·cle [ˈklævikl] clavícula *f*.

claw [klɔː] **1.** garra *f*; garfa *f esp. of bird of prey*; (*lobster's etc.*) pinza *f*; ⊕ garfio *m*, gancho *m*; **2.** arañar; agarrar; (*tear*) desgarrar.

clay [klei] arcilla *f*; ~ *pigeon* pichón *m* de barro; **clay·ey** [ˈkleii] arcilloso; ˈ**clay pit** barrera *f*.

clean [kliːn] **1.** *adj.* □ limpio (*a. fig.*); neto, distinto; *surface etc.* despejado, desembarazado; *limb etc.* bien formado; *fig.* diestro; ~ *bill of health* patente *f* limpia de sanidad; *sl. come* ~ cantar; **2.** *adv.* enteramente; **3.** limpiar; ~ *out* limpiar vaciando; *sl. be* ~*ed out* quedar limpio; ~ *up* arreglar; *sl.* sacar de ganancia; **4.** *su.* limpia *f*; ˈ**clean·ing** limpia *f*, limpiadura *f*; *attr.* de limpiar; ~ *fluid* quitamanchas *m*; ~ *woman* criada *f* que hace la limpieza, alquilona *f*; **clean·li·ness** [ˈklenlinis] limpieza *f*; esmero *m*; **clean·ly 1.** *adv.* [ˈkliːnli] limpiamente; en limpio; **2.** *adj.* [ˈklenli] esmerado; limpio; **clean·ness** [ˈkliːnnis] limpieza *f*; **cleanse** [klenz] *lit.* limpiar, purificar (*of* de); **clean·up** [ˈkliːnˈʌp] limpiadura *f*; *sl.* ganancia *f*.

clear [klir] **1.** □ claro; *sky* despejado; libre (*of* de); completo, total; ✝ sin deudas (*a. in the* ~); *as* ~ *as day* más claro que el sol; *get* ~ *of* deshacerse de, desembarazarse de; *place* salir de; **2.** *v/t.* aclarar, clarificar (*a.* ~ *up*); *table* despejar; (*a.* ~ *away*) levantar; *site* desmontar; quitar (*a.* ~ *away, off*); limpiar (*of* de); (*jump*) saltar por encima de; ⚖ absolver; probar la inocencia de; *ball* despejar; ✝ *check* hacer efectivo; ✝ *debt* liquidar (*a.* ~ *off*); ~ *a ship for action* alistar un buque para el combate; *v. throat*; *v/i.* abonanzar (*a.* ~ *up*); (*sky*) despejarse; F ~ *off* irse, escabullirse (*a.* ~ *out*); ˈ**clear·ance** espacio *m* libre; acreditación *f of personnel*; ✝ negociación *f*; ⚓, ✝ despacho *m*; ⊕ espacio *m* muerto; *sport*: despeje *m*; ~ *sale* venta *f* de liquidación; ˈ**clear-ˈcut** claro, bien definido; ˈ**clear·ing** claro *m in wood*; ✝ compensación *f*; ~ *house* cámara *f* de compensación; *v. clear* 1.

cleav·age [ˈkliːvidʒ] hendedura *f*; *fig.* división *f*; *sl.* escote *m*.

cleave[1] [kliːv] [*irr.*] hender (*a. fig.*).

cleave² [~] *fig.* adherirse (*to* a); ~ *together* ser inseparables.
cleav·er ['kliːvər] cuchilla *f* de carnicero.
clef [klef] clave *f*.
cleft [kleft] **1.** grieta *f*, hendedura *f*; ~ *palate* fisura *f* del paladar; **2.** *pret. a. p.p. of cleave*¹.
clem·en·cy ['klemənsi] clemencia *f* (*a. meteor.*); '**clem·ent** □ clemente.
clench [klentʃ] apretar, cerrar; = *clinch*.
cler·gy ['kləːrdʒi] clero *m*, clerecía *f*; '**~·man** clérigo *m*, sacerdote *m* (*esp. de la Iglesia Anglicana*); pastor *m*.
cler·i·cal ['klerikl] □ clerical; oficinista, *b.s.* oficinesco; ~ *error* error *m* de pluma; ~ *work* trabajo *m* de oficina.
clerk [kləːrk] oficinista *m*/*f*; dependiente (a *f*) *m*; ⚖ escribano *m*; *eccl.* clérigo *m*; *v. town*.
clev·er ['klevər] □ inteligente; hábil; listo; *b.s.* habilidoso; '**clev·er·ness** inteligencia *f*; habilidad *f*.
clew [kluː] ovillo *m*; *v. clue*.
cli·ché ['kliːʃei] cliché *m*, frase *f* hecha.
click [klik] **1.** golpecito *m* seco; piñoneo *m of gun*; chasquido *m of tongue*; taconeo *m of heels*; **2.** piñonear; chasquear; *sl.* enamorarse, hacerse novios.
cli·ent ['klaiənt] cliente *m*/*f*; **cli·en·tèle** [klaiən'tel] clientela *f*.
cliff [klif] risco *m*; (*sea*) acantilado *m*.
cli·mate ['klaimit] clima *m*; *fig.* ambiente *m*; **cli·mat·ic** [klai'mætik] □ climático.
cli·max ['klaimæks] *rhet.* clímax *m*; colmo *m*; cima *f* de intensidad, punto *m* álgido.
climb [klaim] [*irr.*] **1.** trepar, escalar; subir (a); F *fig.* ~ *down* cejar; desdecirse; **2.** subida *f*; '**climb·er** *mst* alpinista *m*/*f*; *fig.* buscavidas *m*, tiralevitas *m*; ⚘ enredadera *f*, trepadora *f*; '**climb·ing** *mst* alpinismo *m*; '**climb·ing i·ron** garfio *m*.
clinch [klintʃ] **1.** agarro *m*; ⊕ remache *m*; *boxing*: clincha *f*; **2.** agarrar; remachar; luchar cuerpo a cuerpo; *fig. argument* remachar; *v. clench*; '**clinch·er** ⊕ remachador *m*; *fig.* argumento *m* decisivo.
cling [kliŋ] [*irr.*] adherirse (*to* a), pegarse (*to* a) (*a. fig.*); ~ *to p.* abrazarse a, quedar abrazado a; '**cling·ing** suspendido; *p.* pegajoso; *dress* muy ajustado.
clin·ic ['klinik] **1.** clínica *f*; **2.** = '**clin·i·cal** □ clínico; ~ *thermometer* termómetro *m* clínico; **cli·ni·cian** [~'niʃn] clínico *m*.
clink [kliŋk] **1.** tintín *m*; choque *m of glasses*; *sl.* trena *f*; **2.** tintinear; chocar; '**clink·er** escoria *f* de hulla; ladrillo *m* muy duro.
clip¹ [klip] **1.** esquileo *m of wool*; F golpe *m*; **2.** trasquilar, esquilar; recortar; *coin* cercenar; *ticket* picar; *words* apocopar; F chapurrear; F (*hit*) golpear.
clip² [~] grapa *f*; (*paper*) sujetapapeles *m*; sujetador *m of pen*; (*brooch*) alfiler *m* de pecho, clip *m*.
clip·per ['klipər] (*a pair of* ~*s* una) cizalla *f*; ✂ tijeras *f*/*pl.* podadoras; ⚓, ✈ clíper *m*; '**clip·pings** *pl.* recortes *m*/*pl.*; trasquilones *m*/*pl. of wool*; retales *m*/*pl. of cloth*.
clique [kliːk] pandilla *f*; peña *f*.
cloak [klouk] **1.** capa *f* (*a. fig.*), capote *m*; ~ *and dagger* de capa y espada; **2.** encapotar; *fig.* encubrir, disimular; '**~·room** guardarropa *f*; *euph.* aseos *m*/*pl.*; 🚂 consigna *f*.
clock [klɔk] **1.** reloj *m*; *sport*: cronómetro *m*; ~*maker* relojero *m*; ~ *tower* torre *f* reloj; *against the* ~ contra el reloj; **2.**: ~ *in* fichar; '**~·wise** en la dirección de las agujas del reloj; '**~·work** aparato *m* de relojería; *like* ~ como un reloj.
clod [klɔd] tierra *f*, terrón *m*; (*p.*) palurdo *m* (*a.* '**~·hop·per**).
clog [klɔg] **1.** zueco *m*; *fig.* traba *f*; estorbo *m*; **2.** atascar(se) (*a. fig.*); (*hamper*) estorbar.
clois·ter ['klɔistər] **1.** claustro *m*; **2.** enclaustrar (*a. fig.*).
close 1. a) [klouz] fin *m*; conclusión *f*; *at the* ~ *of day* a la caída de la tarde; b) [klous] recinto *m*, cercado *m*; **2.** [klouz] *v*/*t.* cerrar (*a.* ⚡); *hole* tapar (*a.* ~ *up*); *treaty* concluir; ~*d car* coche *m* cerrado, conducción *f* interior; ~*d chapter* asunto *m* concluido; ~*d-circuit television* televisión *f* en circuito cerrado; ~*d season* veda *f*; ~*d shop* taller *m* agremiado; ~ *down* cerrar definitivamente; *closing* cerradura *f*, cierre *m*; *closing date* fecha *f* tope; *closing price* ✝ último precio *m*; *closing prices* ✝ precios *m*/*pl.* de

cierre; *v/i.* cerrar(se); terminar; ~ *in* acercarse rodeando; ~ *in on* rodear; ~ *up* ponerse más cerca; (*wound*) cicatrizarse; **3.** [klous] □ cercano, próximo; *friendship etc.* estrecho, íntimo; *weave etc.* compacto, tupido; *argument* minucioso; *atmosphere* sofocante, mal ventilado; *imitation* arrimado; *score* igual, casi empatado; *translation* fiel; F (*mean*) avaro, mezquino; ~ *by*, ~ *to* cerca de; ~ *call* F escape *m* por un pelo; ~ *quarters pl.* lugar *m* muy estrecho, lugares *m/pl.* estrechos; ~ *shave* afeitado *m* a ras; F escape *m* por un pelo; *v. quarter, season, shave*; ~*ly printed* de impresión compacta; **ˈ~ˈfist·ed** tacaño; **ˈ~ˈfit·ting** ajustado; **ˈ~ˈlipped** callado, reservado; **close·ly** [ˈklousli] de cerca; estrechamente; fielmente; atentamente; **ˈclose·ness** proximidad *f*; intimidad *f*; pesantez *f*, mala ventilación *f*; fidelidad *f to original*.

clos·et [ˈklɔzit] **1.** retrete *m*, gabinete *m*; (*cupboard*) armario *m*; *v. water...*; **2.**: *be* ~*ed with* estar encerrado con.

close-up [ˈklousʌp] vista *f* de cerca, fotografía *f* de cerca.

clo·sure [ˈklouʒər] **1.** cierre *m*; clausura *f*; fin *m*, término *m*; *parl. apply the* ~ terminar el debate; **2.** *debate* terminar.

clot [klɔt] **1.** grumo *m*; cuajarón *m of blood etc.*; *sl.* papanatas *m*; **2.** cuajarse, coagularse.

cloth [klɔθ], *pl.* **cloths** [klɔθs, klɔːðz] tela *f*, paño *m*; (*table*) mantel *m*; *fig.* clero *m*; *lay the* ~ poner la mesa; ~ *binding* encuadernación *f* en tela.

clothe [klouð] [*irr.*] vestir; *p.* trajear; *fig.* revestir; investir (*with* de).

clothes [klouðz] ropa *f*, vestidos *m/pl.*; **ˈ~·bas·ket** cesto *m* de la colada; **ˈ~·brush** cepillo *m* de ropa; **ˈ~ clos·et** ropero *m*; **ˈ~ dry·er** secadora *f* de ropa, secarropa *f*; **ˈ~ hang·er** colgador *m*, perchero *m*; **ˈ~·horse** enjugador *m*, secarropa *f* de travesaños; **ˈ~·line** cordel *m* para tender la ropa; **ˈ~·pin** pinza *f*; **ˈ~ press** guardarropa *f*, armario *m*; **ˈ~ tree** percha *f*.

cloth·ier [ˈklouðiər] fabricante *m* de ropa; (*dealer in cloth*) pañero *m*; (*p. who sells ready-made clothes*) ropero *m*.

cloth·ing [ˈklouðiŋ] ropa *f*, vestidos *m/pl.*; ropaje *m*; *attr.* textil.

cloud [klaud] **1.** nube *f* (*a. fig.*); *phys.* ~ *chamber* cámara *f* de niebla; *storm* ~ nubarrón *m*; *be under a* ~ estar desacreditado; estar mohino; *fig. in the* ~*s th.* quimérico, ilusorio; *p.* distraído, despistado; **2.** anublar (*a. fig.*); ~ (*over*) anublarse; **ˈ~·burst** chaparrón *m*; **ˈcloud·less** sin nubes, despejado; **ˈcloud·y** □ anublado, nuboso; *liquid* turbio; sombrío.

clout [klaut] **1.** F dar de bofetadas; **2.** F bofetada *f*; † trapo *m*.

clove¹ [klouv] clavo *m*; (*tree*) clavero *m*.

clove² [~] *pret. of cleave¹*; **ˈclo·ven** *p.p. of cleave¹*; *adj.*: ~ *hoof* pata *f* hendida.

clo·ver [ˈklouvər] trébol *m*; F *be in* ~ vivir holgadamente, darse buena vida; ~ *leaf* hoja *f* de trébol; *mot.* (*intersection*) cruce *m* en trébol.

clown [klaun] **1.** payaso *m in circus*; palurdo *m*; **2.** bufonearse; **ˈclown·ish** □ bufonesco.

cloy [klɔi] empalagar(se), hartar(se).

club [klʌb] **1.** porra *f*, cachiporra *f*; (*golf-*) palo *m*; (*society*) club *m*; casino *m*; *cards*: ~*s pl.* tréboles *m/pl.*, (*Spanish*) bastos *m/pl.*; **2.** *v/t.* aporrear; *v/i.*: ~ *together* unirse para el mismo fin; pagar cada uno su escote; **ˈ~·house** *golf*: chalet *m*; **ˈ~·man** casinista *m*.

cluck [klʌk] cloquear.

clue [kluː] indicio *m*; pista *f*.

clump [klʌmp] **1.** grupo *m* de árboles, arboleda *f*; masa *f* informe; **2.** andar pesadamente (*a.* ~ *along*).

clum·si·ness [ˈklʌmzinis] desmaña *f*, torpeza *f*; **ˈclum·sy** □ desmañado, torpe; (*badly done*) chapucero.

clung [klʌŋ] *pret. a. p.p. of cling*.

clus·ter [ˈklʌstər] **1.** grupo *m*; ⚘ racimo *m*; **2.** agruparse; ⚘ arracimarse; (*people*) apiñarse; ~ *around* reunirse en torno de.

clutch [klʌtʃ] **1.** agarro *m*; *mot.* (pedal *m* de) embrague *m*; nidada *f of eggs*; *in his* ~*es* en sus garras; **2.** agarrarse (*at* a); empuñar.

clut·ter [ˈklʌtər] **1.** desorden *m*, confusión *f*; (*with noise*) barahunda *f*; **2.** poner en confusión; *be* ~*ed up with* estar atestado de.

coach [koutʃ] **1.** coche *m*; diligencia *f*; 🚃 coche *m*, vagón *m*; *mot.* autocar *m*, pullman *m*; *sport*: entrenador *m*; **2.**

team etc. entrenar; *student* enseñar, preparar; '~ **build·er** carrocero *m*; '~ **house** cochera *f*; '~**·man** cochero *m*.
co·ad·ju·tor [kou'ædʒutər] coadjutor *m*.
co·ag·u·late [kou'ægjuleit] coagular; **co·ag·u'la·tion** coagulación *f*.
coal [koul] **1.** carbón *m*; hulla *f*; (*freq.* ~*s pl.*) ascua *f*, brasa *f*; ~ *bin* carbonera *f*; ~ *bunker* carbonera *f*; ~ *car* vagón *m* carbonero; ~ *dealer* carbonero *m*; ~ *industry* industria *f* hullera; ~ *mine* mina *f* de carbón; ~ *oil* aceite *m* mineral; ~*yard* carbonería *f*; *haul over the* ~*s* echar un rapapolvo a; *v.* *Newcastle*; **2.** ⚓ tomar carbón; ~*ing station* estación *f* carbonera.
co·a·lesce [kouə'les] unirse; combinarse; *pol. etc.* incorporarse; **co·a'les·cence** unión *f*; combinación *f*.
coal·field ['koulfi:ld] yacimiento *m* de carbón; cuenca *f* minera.
co·a·li·tion [kouə'liʃn] *pol.* coalición *f*; unión *f*, combinación *f*.
coal...: '~**·pit** mina *f* de carbón; '~'**scut·tle** cubo *m* para carbón; '~'**tar** alquitrán *m* mineral.
coarse [kɔ:rs] □ basto, tosco; *fig.* grosero, rudo; '**coarse·ness** tosquedad *f*; grosería *f*, *etc.*
coast [koust] **1.** costa *f*; litoral *m*; *the* ~ *is clear* no hay moros en la costa; **2.** costear; *mot.* ir en punto muerto; ~ *along* avanzar sin esfuerzo; '**coast·al** costanero; '**coast·er** ⚓ barco *m* costero; trineo *m*; ~ *brake* freno *m* de contrapedal; '**coast guard** guardacostas *m*; '**coast·ing** navegación *f* costera; ~ *trade* cabotaje *m*.
coat [kout] **1.** chaqueta *f*, americana *f*; (*overcoat*) abrigo *m*; (*layer*) capa *f*; mano *f of paint*; (*animal's*) pelo *m*; ~ *of arms* escudo *m* de armas; ~ *of mail* cota *f* de malla; *fig. turn one's* ~ cambiar de casaca; *cut the* ~ *according to the cloth* adaptarse a las circunstancias; **2.** cubrir, revestir (*with* con, de); dar una mano de pintura a; '~ **hang·er** colgador *m*; '**coat·ing** capa *f*, baño *m*; tela *f* para chaquetas *etc.*; '**coat stand** percha *f*.
coax [kouks] engatusar; conseguir por medio de halagos (*into ger.* que *subj.*); ~ *a p. out of doing s.t.* disuadir a una p. de hacer algo; '**coax·ing** □ lenguaje *m* almibarado; coba *f*; halagos *m/pl*.
cob [kɔb] jaca *f* fuerte; cisne *m* macho; (*loaf*) pan *m* redondo; (*maize*) mazorca *f*.
co·balt ['koubɔ:lt] cobalto *m*; ~ *blue* azul *m* de cobalto.
cob·bler ['kɔblər] zapatero *m*, remendón *m*; bebida *f* helada; pastel *m* de frutas; **cob·ble·stone** ['kɔbəlstoun] guijarro *m*.
cob·nut ['kɔbnʌt] avellana *f* grande.
cob·web ['kɔbweb] telaraña *f* (*a. fig.*).
co·caine [kə'kein] cocaína *f*.
coc·cyx ['kɔksiks] cóccix *m*.
coch·i·neal ['kɔtʃini:l] cochinilla *f*.
cock [kɔk] **1.** gallo *m*; macho *m* de ave; ⊕ grifo *m*, espita *f*; martillo *m of gun*; vuelta *f of hat*; ~ *of the walk* gallito *m* del lugar; **2.** *gun* amartillar; enderezar, volver hacia arriba; ladear *on side*; ~*ed hat* sombrero *m* de tres picos (*or* de candil); ~ *one's eye at s.o.* mirar con intención a una p.
cock·ade [kɔ'keid] escarapela *f*.
cock-and-bull sto·ry ['kɔkənd'bulstɔ:ri] cuento *m*, camelo *m*.
cock·a·too ['kɔkətu:] cacatúa *f*.
cock·a·trice ['kɔkətris] basilisco *m*.
cock·chaf·er ['kɔktʃeifər] abejorro *m*.
cock·crow ['kɔkkrou] canto *m* del gallo; aurora *f*; *at* ~ al amanecer.
cock·er ['kɔkər] cocker *m*.
cock...: ~**·eyed** ['kɔkaid] bizco; *sl.* ladeado; *sl. fig.* incomprensible, estúpido; '~**-fight**(**·ing**) pelea *f* de gallos.
cock·le[1] ['kɔkl] ⚘ cizaña *f*.
cock·le[2] [~] **1.** *zo.* berberecho *m*; *the* ~*s of the heart* lo más íntimo del corazón; **2.** arrugar(se) (*a.* ~ *up*).
cock·ney ['kɔkni] *habitante de Londres*; *dialecto de ciertos barrios de Londres*.
cock·pit ['kɔkpit] cancha *f*, reñidero *m* de gallos; ✈ cabina *f*, carlinga *f*; *fig.* sitio *m* de muchos combates.
cock·roach ['kɔkroutʃ] cucaracha *f*.
cocks·comb ['kɔkskoum] cresta *f* de gallo; '**cock·'sure** F demasiado seguro; presuntuoso; '**cock·tail** combinación *f*; ~ *party* cóctel *m*; '**cock·y** □ F engreído, hinchado.
co·co ['koukou] cocotero *m*.
co·coa ['koukou] cacao *m*; (*drink*) chocolate *m*.

co·co·nut ['koukənʌt] coco *m*; ~ *palm*, ~ *tree* cocotero *m*.
co·coon [kɔ'ku:n] capullo *m*.
cod [kɔd] bacalao *m*.
cod·dle ['kɔdl] mimar; *egg* cocer en agua caliente sin hervir.
code [koud] **1.** código *m* (⚖ *a. fig.*); cifra *f*; *tel.* alfabeto *m* Morse; *in* ~ en cifra; **2.** cifrar.
co·de·ine ['koudi:n] codeína *f*.
cod·fish ['kɔdfiʃ] bacalao *m*.
codg·er ['kɔdʒər] F (*freq. old* ~) tipo *m*, sujeto *m*.
cod·i·cil ['kɔdisil] codicilo *m*; **cod·i·fi'ca·tion** codificación *f*; **cod·i·fy** ['~fai] codificar.
cod·ling ['kɔdliŋ] ♀ manzana *f* de forma cónica.
cod-liv·er oil ['kɔdlivər'ɔil] aceite *m* de hígado de bacalao.
co-ed ['kou'ed] F **1.** coeducacional; **2.** alumna *f* de un colegio coeducacional.
co·ed·u·ca·tion [kouedju'keiʃn] coeducación *f*.
co·ef·fi·cient [koui'fiʃnt] coeficiente *adj. a. su. m*.
co·erce [kou'ə:rs] obligar, apremiar (*into ger.* a *inf.*); coercer; **co'er·ci·ble** coercible; **co'er·cion** [~ʃn] compulsión *f*; coerción *f*; *under* ~ por fuerza mayor; **co'er·cive** □ coercitivo.
co·e·val [kou'i:vəl] □ coetáneo; contemporáneo.
co·ex·ist ['kouig'zist] coexistir (*with* con); **'co·ex'ist·ence** coexistencia *f*, convivencia *f*; **'co·ex'ist·ent** coexistente.
cof·fee ['kɔfi] café *m*; *black* ~ café *m* solo; ~*bean* grano *m* de café; ~*cake* rosquilla *f* (que se come con el café); ~ *grinder*, ~ *mill* molinillo *m* de café; ~ *grounds pl.* poso *m* del café, heces *f/pl.* de café; ~ *plantation* cafetal *m*; ~ *pot* cafetera *f*; ~ *set* juego *m* de café; ~ *tree* cafeto *m*.
coff·er ['kɔfər] cofre *m*, arca *f*; △ artesón *m*; ~*s pl. fig.* fondos *m/pl.*; '~**·dam** ataguía *f*.
cof·fin ['kɔfin] **1.** ataúd *m*; **2.** *fig.* encerrar.
cog [kɔg] diente *m*; rueda *f* dentada.
co·gen·cy ['koudʒənsi] fuerza *f*; '**co·gent** □ convincente; lógico.
cogged [kɔgd] dentado; engranado.
cog·i·tate ['kɔdʒiteit] *v/i.* meditar, reflexionar; *v/t.* recapacitar; **cog·i'ta·tion** meditación *f*, reflexión *f*.
co·gnac ['kounjæk] coñac *m*.
cog·nate ['kɔgneit] cognado *adj. a. su. m* (a *f*); afín.
cog·ni·tion [kɔg'niʃn] cognición *f*.
cog·ni·za·ble ['kɔgnizəbl] cognoscible; ⚖ justiciable; '**cog·ni·zance** conocimiento *m*; ⚖ competencia *f*; *take* ~ *of* reparar en; '**cog·ni·zant** instruido, noticioso (*of* de).
cog·no·men [kɔg'noumen] apodo *m*; apellido *m*.
cog·wheel ['kɔgwi:l] rueda *f* dentada.
co·hab·it [kou'hæbit] cohabitar; **co·hab·i'ta·tion** cohabitación *f*, abarraganamiento *m*.
co·heir ['kou'er] coheredero *m*; **co·heir·ess** ['kou'eris] coheredera *f*.
co·here [kou'hir] adherirse, pegarse; (*ideas etc.*) enlazarse; **co'her·en·cy** coherencia *f*; **co'her·ent** □ coherente; **co·her·er** [kou'hirər] *radio*: cohesor *m*.
co·he·sion [kou'hi:ʒn] cohesión *f* (*a. fig.*); **co'he·sive** □ cohesivo.
coif·feur [kwɑ:'fə:r] peluquero *m*;
coif·fure [~'fjur] peinado *m*.
coign of van·tage [kɔinəv'væntidʒ] atalaya *f*; posición *f* ventajosa.
coil [kɔil] **1.** rollo *m*; ⚓ aduja *f of rope*; ⚡ carrete *m*; ⚗ serpentín *m*, † desorden *m*, barahunda *f*; ~ *spring* resorte *m* espiral; **2.** arrollar(se), enrollar(se); serpentear; ⚓ *rope* adujar.
coin [kɔin] **1.** moneda *f*; F *pay back in one's own* ~ pagar en la misma moneda; **2.** acuñar; *fig.* forjar; *word etc.* inventar, idear; '**coin·age** acuñación *f*; amonedación *f*; sistema *m* monetario; *fig.* invención *f*.
co·in·cide [kouin'said] coincidir (*with* con); **co·in·ci·dence** [kou'insidəns] coincidencia *f*; **co·in·ci'dent·al** □ coincidente; fortuito.
coin·er ['kɔinər] monedero *m* (*esp.* falso).
co·i·tus ['kouitəs] coito *m*.
coke [kouk] **1.** coque *m*; F Coca-Cola *f*; **2.** convertir en coque.
col·an·der ['kʌləndər] escurridor *m*.
cold [kould] **1.** □ frío (*a. fig.*); ~ *meat* carne *f* fiambre; *be* ~ (*p.*) tener frío; (*weather*) hacer frío; (*th.*) estar frío; *in* ~ *blood* a sangre fría; ~ *chisel* cortafrío *m*; ~ *comfort* poca consolación *f*; ~ *cream* colcrén *m*; ~ *cuts pl.*

fiambres *m/pl.*; ~ *feet pl.* F desánimo *m*, miedo *m*; F *have* ~ *feet* encogérsele a uno el ombligo; ~*hearted* duro, insensible; ~ *meat* carne *f* fiambre; *turn a* ~ *shoulder* F tratar con suma frialdad; ~ *snap* corto rato *m* de frío agudo; ~ *storage* conservación *f* en cámara frigorífica; ~ *war* guerra *f* fría; **2.** frío *m*; ⚕ resfriado *m*; *catch* ~ resfriarse, coger un resfriado; F *leave out in the* ~ dejar al margen; **'~-'blood·ed** *zo.* de sangre fría; *fig.* insensible; (*cruel*) desalmado; **'cold·ness** frialdad *f*; indiferencia *f*.

cole·slaw ['koul'slɔː] ensalada *f* de coles.

col·ic ['kɔlik] cólico *m*.

co·li·tis [kə'laitis] colitis *f*.

col·lab·o·rate [kə'læbəreit] colaborar; **col·lab·o'ra·tion** colaboración *f*; **col'lab·o·ra·tor** colaborador (-a *f*) *m*; ⚔ colaboracionista *m*.

col·lapse [kə'læps] **1.** ⚕ sufrir colapso; F desmayarse; △ *etc.* hundirse; *fig.* fracasar; **2.** ⚕ colapso *m*; hundimiento *m*; fracaso *m*; **col'laps·i·ble** plegable, abatible.

col·lar ['kɔlər] **1.** cuello *m*; (*animals a.* ⊕) collar *m*; F *slip the* ~ escaparse; **2.** prender por el cuello; *sl.* coger, prender; **'~·bone** clavícula *f*.

col·late [kɔ'leit] colacionar (*a. eccl.*); *text* cotejar.

col·lat·er·al [kɔ'lætərəl] □ colateral; ~ *security* garantía *f* subsidiaria.

col·la·tion [kɔ'leiʃn] colación *f* (*a. eccl.*); cotejo *m of text*.

col·league ['kɔliːg] colega *m*.

col·lect 1. ['kɔlekt] *eccl.* colecta *f*; **2.** [kə'lekt] *v/t.* acumular; reunir; *antiques etc.* coleccionar; *fares* cobrar; *taxes* colectar, recaudar; ~ *o.s.* recobrarse; ~ *one's wits* reconcentrarse; *v/i.* acumularse; reunirse; coleccionar; **col'lect 'call** *teleph.* llamada *f* por cobrar; **col'lect·ed** □ *fig.* sosegado; **col'lec·tion** colección *f*; montón *m*; recaudación *f of taxes*; ~ *agency* agencia *f* de cobros de cuentas; **col'lec·tive** □ colectivo (*a. gr.*); ~ *bargaining* trato *m* colectivo; ~ *farm* granja *f* colectiva; **col'lec·tive·ly** colectivamente; **col'lec·tiv·ism** colectivismo *m*; **col'lec·tor** coleccionador *m*; (*tax-*) recaudador *m*; ⚡ colector *m*.

col·leen ['kɔliːn, kɔ'liːn] *Ir.* muchacha *f*.

col·lege ['kɔlidʒ] colegio *m*; colegio *m* de universidad; **col·le·gi·an** [kə'liːdʒiən] colegial *m*; **col'le·gi·ate** [~dʒiit] colegial; colegiado.

col·lide [kə'laid] chocar (*with* con; *a. fig.*); *fig.* entrar en conflicto.

col·lie ['kɔli] perro *m* pastor, perro pastoril escocés.

col·lier ['kɔliər] minero *m* de carbón; ⚓ barco *m* minero; **col·lier·y** ['kɔljəri] mina *f* de carbón.

col·li·sion [kə'liʒn] colisión *f*, choque *m* (*a. fig.*).

col·lo·ca·tion [kɔlə'keiʃn] colocación *f*; disposición *f*.

col·lo·di·on [kə'loudiən] colodión *m*.

col·loid ['kɔlɔid] *adj. a. su.* coloide *m*.

col·lo·qui·al [kə'loukwiəl] □ popular, familiar; **col'lo·qui·al·ism** popularismo *m*.

col·lo·quy ['kɔləkwi] coloquio *m*.

col·lude [kə'luːd] coludir; **col·lu·sion** [kə'luːʒn] colusión *f*.

co·lon ['koulən] *typ.* dos puntos *m/pl.*; *anat.* colon *m*.

colo·nel ['kəːrnəl] coronel *m*; **'colo·nel·cy** coronelía *f*.

co·lo·ni·al [kə'lounjəl] **1.** colonial; **2.** colono *m*; **col·o·nist** ['kɔlənist] colonizador *m*; colono *m*; **col·o·ni·za·tion** [kɔlənai'zeiʃn] colonización *f*; **'col·o·nize** colonizar.

col·on·nade [kɔlə'neid] △ columnata *f*; soportales *m/pl.*

col·o·ny ['kɔləni] colonia *f*.

col·o·phon ['kɔləfən] colofón *m*.

col·o·pho·ny [kɔ'lɔfəni] colofonía *f*.

col·or ['kʌlər] **1.** color *m* (*a. fig.*); ⚔ ~*s pl.* bandera *f*; F *be off* ~ estar indispuesto; *change* ~ mudar de color, demudarse; ~ *film* película *f* en colores; ~ *photography* fotografía *f* en colores; ~ *salute* ⚔ saludo *m* con la bandera; ~ *sergeant* sargento *m* abanderado; ~ *screen phot.* pantalla *f* de color; ~ *television* televisión *f* en colores; *call to the* ~*s* llamar al servicio militar; *show one's* ~*s* dejar ver uno su verdadero carácter; *fig. with flying* ~*s* con lucimiento; **2.** *v/t.* colorear (*a. fig.*), colorar; *v/i.* sonrojarse (*a.* ~ *up*); **'~-blind** daltoniano; ciego para los colores (*a. fig.*); **'~-blind·ness** daltonismo *m*; **'colored** *p.* de color; (*specious*) coloreado (*a. fig.*); **col·or·ful** ['~ful] □ lleno de color; vivo, animado; **'col·or·ing** colorido *m*; colorante *m* (*a.* ~ *matter*);

(*complexion*) color *m*; ˈ**col·or·less** □ sin color, incoloro; *fig.* soso, insulso.
co·los·sal [kəˈlɔsl] □ colosal.
co·los·sus [kəˈlɔsəs] coloso *m*.
colt [koult] potro *m*; *fig.* mozuelo *m*; ˈ**colts·foot** ⚘ uña *f* de caballo.
col·um·bine [ˈkɔləmbain] aguileña *f*.
col·umn [ˈkɔləm] columna *f*; **co·lum·nar** [kəˈlʌmnər] de columna; **col·um·nist** [ˈkɔləmnist] periodista *m*, columnista *m*.
col·za [ˈkɔlzə] colza *f*.
co·ma [ˈkoumə] **1.** ⚕ coma *m*; **2.** ⚘ manojito *m* (de hebras sedosas); *ast.* cabellera *f*.
comb [koum] **1.** peine *m*; almohaza *f* *for horse*; (*cock's*) cresta *f*; ⊕ carda *f*; *v. curry* ~; *v. honey*-~; **2.** peinar; *wool* cardar; *fig.* registrar (*or* explorar) con minuciosidad.
com·bat [ˈkɔmbət] **1.** combate *m* (*a. fig.*); ~ *duty* servicio *m* de frente; **2.** combatir(se); ˈ**com·bat·ant** combatiente *m*; ˈ**com·bat·ive** □ peleador.
comb·er [ˈkoumər] ⊕ cardador *m*; ⚓ ola *f* encrestada.
com·bin·able [kəmˈbainəbl] combinable; **com·bi·na·tion** [kɔmbiˈneiʃn] combinación *f* (*a. garment*, *mst* ~*s pl.*); ~ *lock* cerradura *f* de combinación; **com·bine 1.** [kəmˈbain] combinar(se); **2.** [ˈkɔmbain] ✝ monopolio *m*; ⚒ (*a.* ~ *harvester*) cosechadora *f*.
comb·ings [ˈkoumiŋz] *pl.* peinaduras *f/pl.*
com·bus·ti·ble [kəmˈbʌstəbl] **1.** combustible; *fig.* ardiente; **2.** combustible *m*; **com·bus·tion** [kəmˈbʌstʃən] combustión *f*.
come [kʌm] [*irr.*] venir; ir; ~! ¡ven!, ¡venga!; *oh*, ~! ¡pero mire!; *how* ~? F ¿cómo eso?; *that's what* ~*s of hesitating* eso lo trae el vacilar; *coming!* ¡voy!; ~ *about* pasar; suceder (*that* que); realizarse; ~ *across p.* topar a; *th.* encontrar, dar con; ~ *along* venir, ir; ~ *along!* ¡vamos!; ~ *at* alcanzar; (*attack*) arrojarse sobre; ~ *away* retirarse, marcharse; salir de casa *etc.*; ~ *back* volver; ~ *before* anteponerse a; llegar antes; ~ *by* conseguir; ~ *down* bajar; *fig.* desplomarse; ~ *down on* caer sobre; F regañar; ~ *down with* ⚕ enfermar de; ~ *for* venir por; ~ *forward* presentarse, acudir; ~ *in* entrar; *fig.* ponerse en uso, ponerse de moda; empezar; llegar *in race*; ~ *in!* ¡adelante!; ~ *in useful* servir, ser útil; ~ *into estate* heredar; *v. own*; ~ *off* (*part*) soltarse; desprenderse; *fig.* (*event*) verificarse, celebrarse; (*succeed*) tener éxito, verse logrado; ~ *off it!* F ¡déjate de tonterías!; ~ *off well* salir airoso; ~ *on* (*grow*) crecer; (*improve*) mejorar, hacer progresos; (*prosper*) medrar; ~ *on!* ¡vamos!, ¡despabílate!; (*encouragement*) ¡ánimo!; ~ (*up*)*on* encontrarse con; descubrir; ~ *out* salir; salir a luz; (*as new*) estrenarse, debutar; (*news*) revelarse, traslucirse; (*workers*) declararse en huelga; ~ *out with* decir, revelar; ~ *over*: *what's* ~ *over you?* ¿qué te pasa?; ~ *over queer* F tener vahidos; ~ *round* ⚕ volver en sí; (*visit*) ir a ver; (*agree*) convenir, asentir; dejarse persuadir; ~ *to* a) *adv.* ⚕ volver en sí; ⚓ parar, fachear; b) *prp.* heredar; *sum* subir a; ~ *to mind* ocurrirse; ~ *up* subir; aparecer; acercarse (*to* a); mencionarse *in conversation*; *univ.* matricularse; ~ *up to* estar a la altura de; ~ *up with th.* proponer; ˈ~**·back** F rehabilitación *f*; respuesta *f* aguda; *stage a* ~ F rehabilitarse.
co·me·di·an [kəˈmiːdiən] cómico *m*, autor *m* de comedias; **co·me·di·enne** [~iˈen] cómica *f*.
come·down [ˈkʌmdaun] F desazón *f*, humillación *f*; desgracia *f*.
com·e·dy [ˈkɔmidi] comedia *f*; (*musical*) zarzuela *f*; (*behavior*) comicidad *f*.
come·li·ness [ˈkʌmlinis] gracia *f*, donaire *m*; ˈ**come·ly** gentil, apuesto.
come-on [ˈkʌmɔn] *sl.* añagaza *f*; desafío *m*; (*p.*) bobo *m*.
com·er [ˈkʌmər] F persona *f* que promete; *all* ~*s pl.* todos los contendientes.
co·mes·ti·bles [kəˈmestiblz] *pl.* comestibles *m/pl.*
com·et [ˈkɔmit] cometa *m*.
com·fort [ˈkʌmfərt] **1.** consuelo *m*, alivio *m*; (*physical*) confort *m*, comodidad *f*; bienestar *m*; ~ *loving* comodón; ~ *station* quiosco *m* de necesidad; **2.** consolar, aliviar; ⚖ ayudar; ˈ**com·fort·a·ble** □ cómodo, confortable; *living* desahogado, holgado; ˈ**com·fort·er** consolador (-a *f*) *m*; (*scarf*) bufanda *f* de lana; (*baby's*)

chupete *m*; colcha *f*, cobertor *m*; **ˈcom·fort·ing** □ consolador; **ˈcom·fort·less** □ desconsolado; desolado, triste; *room* sin comodidad.

com·frey [ˈkʌmfri] consuelda *f*.

com·fy [ˈkʌmfi] □ F = *comfortable*.

com·ic [ˈkɔmik] **1.** □ (*mst* **ˈcom·i·cal** □) cómico; divertido, entretenido; ~ *book* tebeo *m*; ~ *opera* ópera *f* cómica; ~ *strip* tira *f* cómica, historieta *f* gráfica; **2.** (*p.*) cómico *m*; revista *f* cómica (infantil), tebeo *m*; ~*s* F tiras *f/pl.* cómicas.

com·ing [ˈkʌmiŋ] **1.** que viene, venidero; **2.** venida *f*, llegada *f*; ~ *and going* trajín *m*, ajetreo *m*.

com·i·ty [ˈkɔmiti] cortesía *f*.

com·ma [ˈkɔmə] coma *f*.

com·mand [kəˈmænd] **1.** orden *f*, mandato *m*; mando *m*, dominio *m*; ⚔ comando *m*; ⚔, ⚓ comandancia *f*; dominio *m of language*; *be at the* ~ *of* estar a la disposición de; *be in* ~ estar al mando; **2.** mandar, ordenar (*to* a); *respect* merecer, imponer; ⚔, ⚓ comandar; **com·man·dant** [kɔmənˈdænt] comandante *m*; **com·man·deer** [~ˈdir] ⚔ *men* reclutar por fuerza; *stores etc.* expropiar; F apoderarse de; **com·mand·er** [kəˈmændər] ⚔ comandante *m*; ⚓ capitán *m* de fragata; comendador *m of Order*; **comˈmand·er in ˈchief** generalísimo *m*; **comˈmand·ing** comandante; *fig.* imponente, dominante; *appearance* señorial; **comˈmand·ment** mandamiento *m*.

com·mem·o·rate [kəˈmeməreit] conmemorar; **com·mem·oˈra·tion** conmemoración *f* (*in* ~ *of* en ... de); **comˈmem·o·ra·tive** □ conmemorativo.

com·mence [kəˈmens] comenzar, empezar (*ger. or to inf.* a *inf.*); **comˈmence·ment** comienzo *m*, principio *m*.

com·mend [kəˈmend] encomendar (*to* a); recomendar, alabar; **comˈmend·a·ble** □ loable, recomendable; **com·men·da·tion** [kɔmenˈdeiʃn] alabanza *f*, encomio *m*; recomendación *f*; **comˈmend·a·to·ry** [~ətəri] laudatorio; comendatorio.

com·men·su·ra·ble [kəˈmenʃərəbl] □ conmensurable; **comˈmen·su·rate** □ proporcionado; ~ *with* conforme a.

com·ment [ˈkɔment] **1.** comento *m*; comentario *m* (*on* sobre); observación *f* (*on* sobre); (*conversational*) dicho *m*; **2.** comentar (*on acc.*); observar (*that* que); **ˈcom·men·tar·y** comentario *m*; **ˈcom·men·ta·tor** comentador *m*, comentarista *m*; *radio*: locutor *m*.

com·merce [ˈkɔmə:rs] comercio *m*; *chamber of* ~ cámara *f* de comercio;

com·mer·cial [kəˈmə:rʃl] **1.** □ comercial; ~ *traveler* viajante *m*, agente *m* viajero *S.Am.*; **2.** *radio*: anuncio *m*, programa *m* publicitario; **comˈmer·cial·ism** mercantilismo *m*; **comˈmer·cial·ize** comercializar.

com·mis·er·ate [kəˈmizəreit] compadecer; ~ *with* condolerse de; **com·mis·er·a·tion** [~ˈreiʃn] conmiseración *f*.

com·mis·sar·i·at [kɔmiˈseriət] comisariato *m*, comisaría *f*; **com·mis·sar·y** [ˈ~səri] comisario *m* (*a.* ⚔).

com·mis·sion [kəˈmiʃn] **1.** comisión *f* (*a.* ✝); ⚔ nombramiento *m*; ⚖ perpetración *f of crime*; ✝ ~ *merchant* comisionista *m*; **2.** comisionar; ⚔ nombrar; *ship* poner en servicio activo; **com·mis·sion·aire** [~əˈner] portero *m*, conserje *m*; **comˈmis·sion·er** [~ər] comisionado *m*; miembro *m* de la junta municipal; ~ *for oaths* notario *m* público.

com·mit [kəˈmit] cometer; *business* confiar; *parl. bill* someter (a una comisión); (*v.s.*) comprometer(se); ⚖ *p.* encarcelar, internar; ~ *to memory* aprender de memoria; ~ *to writing* poner por escrito; **comˈmit·ment** obligación *f*; compromiso *m*; ⚖ auto *m* de prisión; *parl.* traslado *m* a una comisión; **comˈmit·tal** ⚖ auto *m* de prisión; entierro *m of body*; **comˈmit·tee** comité *m*, comisión *f*.

com·mode [kəˈmoud] cómoda *f*; (*a. night* ~) sillico *m*; **comˈmo·di·ous** □ cómodo, espacioso, holgado; **com·mod·i·ty** [kəˈmɔditi] mercancía *f*; cosa *f* útil.

com·mo·dore [ˈkɔmədɔ:r] comodoro *m*.

com·mon [ˈkɔmən] **1.** □ común; F ordinario; ~ *council* ayuntamiento *m*; ~ *carrier* empresa *f* de transportes públicos; ~ *law* derecho *m* consuetudinario; ~*-law marriage* matrimonio *m* consensual; ♀ *Market* Comunidad *f* Económica Europea (CEE); ~ *stock* acción *f* ordinaria; acciones *f/pl.* ordinarias; ~ *room* salón *m* (*de un colegio etc.*); ~ *sense* sentido *m* común; *attr.* ~*-sense* cuerdo, racional; ~ *weal* bien *m* público; *in* ~ en común; *fig. in* ~ *with* de común con; **2.** campo *m* común, ejido *m*; **com·mon·al·ty** ['~nlti] generalidad *f* de personas; **'com·mon·er** plebeyo *m*; *univ.* estudiante *m* que no tiene beca del colegio; *British parl.* miembro *m* de la Cámara de los Comunes; **'com·mon·ness** F ordinariez *f*; **'com·mon·place 1.** perogrullada *f*; lugar *m* común; **2.** común, trivial; **com·mons** ['~z] *pl.* estado *m* llano; (*food*) víveres *m/pl.*; (*room*) salón *m* de un colegio; *short* ~ ración *f* escasa; (*mst House of*) ♀ (Cámara *f* de) los Comunes; **'com·mon·wealth** nación *f*; república *f*; ♀ Mancomunidad *f*.

com·mo·tion [kə'mouʃn] conmoción *f*, tumulto *m*.

com·mu·nal [kəm'ju:nl, 'kɔmjunl] □ comunal; **com·mune 1.** [kə'mju:n] *eccl.* comulgar; comunicar (*with* con); **2.** ['kɔmju:n] *pol.* comuna *f*.

com·mu·ni·ca·bil·i·ty [kəmju:nikə'biliti] comunicabilidad *f*; **com'muni·ca·ble** □ comunicable; **com'mu·ni·cant** *eccl.* comulgante *m/f*; **com'mu·ni·cate** [~keit] comunicar (*with* con); *eccl.* comulgar; (*buildings*) mandarse (*with* con); **com·mu·ni'ca·tion** comunicación *f*; ~*s satellite* satélite *m* de comunicaciones; *be in* ~ *with* estar en contacto con; **com'mu·ni·ca·tive** □ comunicativo.

com·mun·ion [kəm'ju:njən] comunión *f*; ~ *rail* comulgatorio *m*.

com·mu·ni·qué [kəmju:ni'kei] comunicado *m*, parte *m*.

com·mu·nism ['kɔmju:nizm] comunismo *m*; **'com·mu·nist 1.** comunista *m/f*; **2.** = **com·mu'nis·tic** □ comunista.

com·mu·ni·ty [kəm'ju:niti] comunidad *f*; sociedad *f*; (*local*) vecindario *m*; ~ *center* centro *m* social; ~ *spirit* civismo *m*.

com·mut·a·ble [kəm'ju:təbl] conmutable; **com·mu·ta·tion** [kɔmju:'teiʃn] conmutación *f*; abono *m*; ~ *ticket* billete *m* de abono; **com·mu·ta·tive** [kə'mju:tətiv] conmutativo; **com·mu·ta·tor** ['kɔmju:teitər] ⚡ colector *m*; **com·mute** [kə'mju:t] *v/t.* conmutar (*for*, *to* por, *into* en); *v/i.* ser abonado al ferrocarril; viajar con billete de abono (*esp.* al trabajo); **com'mut·er** abonado *m* al ferrocarril.

com·pact 1. ['kɔmpækt] pacto *m*, convenio *m*; (*make-up*) estuche *m* de afeites; **2.** [kəm'pækt] compacto; conciso, breve; **3.** [~] condensar, hacer compacto; **com'pact·ness** densidad *f*; concisión *f*.

com·pan·ion [kəm'pænjən] compañero (a *f*) *m*; compañía *f*; ⚓ lumbrera *f*; ~ *in arms* compañero *m* de armas; **com'pan·ion·a·ble** □ sociable, simpático; **com'pan·ion·ship** compañerismo *m*.

com·pa·ny ['kʌmpəni] compañía *f* (*a.* ⚔ *a. thea.*); ✝ sociedad *f*, empresa *f*; F (*p.*) visita *f*; *bad* ~ amistades *f/pl.* sospechosas; F *good* ~ compañero *m* simpático (*or* entretenido); *keep s.o.* ~ acompañar a, estar con; ir juntos; *part* ~ separarse, tomar rumbos distintos; *fig.* desunirse.

com·pa·ra·ble ['kɔmpərəbl] □ comparable; **com·par·a·tive** [kəm'pærətiv] **1.** *gr.* comparativo *m*; **2.** □ comparado; *gr.* comparativo.

com·pare [kəm'per] **1.** *beyond* ~, *without* ~, *past* ~ sin comparación; **2.** *v/t.* comparar (*with*, *to* con); *as* ~*d with* comparado con; *v/i.* compararse (*with* con); **com·par·i·son** [~'pærisn] comparación *f*; *in* ~ *with* en comparación con.

com·part·ment [kəm'pɑ:rtmənt] compartimiento *m*; 🚂 departamento *m*.

com·pass ['kʌmpəs] **1.** ⚓ brújula *f*; ♪ extensión *f*, límites *m/pl.* (de la voz *etc.*); confín *m*, circuito *m*; *fig.* alcance *m*; (*a pair of* un) ~*es pl.* compás *m*; ~ *card* ⚓ rosa *f* náutica, rosa de los vientos; **2.** rodear, ceñir; (*contrive*) conseguir; *fig.* alcanzar, abarcar.

com·pas·sion [kəm'pæʃn] compasión *f*, piedad *f*; *have* ~ *on* tener piedad de; *move to* ~ mover a compasión; **com'pas·sion·ate** [~-

ʃənit] □ compasivo; *on* ~ *grounds* por compasión.

com·pat·i·bil·i·ty [kəmpætəˈbiliti] compatibilidad *f*; **comˈpat·i·ble** □ compatible.

com·pa·tri·ot [kəmˈpætriət] compatriota *m/f*.

com·pel [kəmˈpel] *p*. compeler (*to* a); *respect* imponer.

com·pen·di·ous [kəmˈpendiəs] □ compendioso.

com·pen·di·um [kəmˈpendiəm] compendio *m*.

com·pen·sate [ˈkɔmpenseit] *v/t*. compensar (*with* con); indemnizar (*for* de); *v/i*.: ~ *for* compensar; **com·penˈsa·tion** compensación *f*; indemnización *f*; ⊕ retribución *f*, recompensa *f*; **ˈcom·pen·sa·tive, ˈcom·pen·sa·to·ry** compensador, compensatorio.

com·pete [kəmˈpi:t] competir, hacer competencia (*for* para; *with* con).

com·pe·tence, com·pe·ten·cy [ˈkɔmpitəns(i)] competencia *f* (*a*. ⚖); capacidad *f*; aptitud *f*; **ˈcom·pe·tent** □ competente (*a*. ⚖); capaz, hábil.

com·pe·ti·tion [kɔmpiˈtiʃn] competencia *f*; concurso *m*; (*civil service etc*.) oposiciones *f/pl*.; *in* ~ *with* en competencia con; **com·pet·i·tive** [kəmˈpetitiv] □ competidor; *price* competitivo; *post* de (*or* por) concurso (*or* oposición); **comˈpet·i·tor** competidor (-a *f*) *m*; opositor (-a *f*) *m for post*.

com·pi·la·tion [kɔmpiˈleiʃn] compilación *f*; **com·pile** [kəmˈpail] compilar.

com·pla·cence, com·pla·cen·cy [kəmˈpleisns(i)] complacencia *f*; *b.s*. satisfacción *f* de sí mismo; **comˈpla·cent** □ satisfecho (con poca razón) (*about* de).

com·plain [kəmˈplein] quejarse (*about*, *of* de; *that* de que); ⚖ demandar; **comˈplain·ant** ⚖ demandante *m/f*; **comˈplaint** queja *f*; ⚖ querella *f*, demanda *f*; ⚕ enfermedad *f*, mal *m*; *lodge a* ~ hacer una reclamación.

com·plai·sance [kəmˈpleizns] complacencia *f*; deferencia *f*; **comˈplai·sant** □ complaciente, amable; *husband* consentido.

com·ple·ment [ˈkɔmplimənt] **1.** complemento *m* (*a*. *gr*., ♗); ⚓ personal *m*; **2.** complementar; **com·pleˈmen·tal, com·pleˈmen·ta·ry** complementario.

com·plete [kəmˈpli:t] **1.** □ completo, entero; consumado; **2.** completar, llevar a cabo; *form* llenar; **comˈple·tion** cumplimiento *m*, terminación *f*.

com·plex [ˈkɔmpleks] **1.** □ complejo; complicado; **2.** ⚕ complejo *m*; F idea *f* fija, prejuicio *m* irracional; **com·plex·ion** [kəmˈplekʃn] tez *f*, color *m* de la cara; aspecto *m*, carácter *m*; **comˈplex·i·ty** complejidad *f*.

com·pli·ance [kəmˈplaiəns] sumisión *f* (*with* a), condescendencia *f* (*with* a); *in* ~ *with* accediendo a; de acuerdo con; **comˈpli·ant** □ condescendiente; sumiso.

com·pli·cate [ˈkɔmplikeit] complicar; embrollar; **com·pliˈca·tion** complicación *f*.

com·plic·i·ty [kəmˈplisiti] complicidad *f*.

com·pli·ment **1.** [ˈkɔmplimənt] cumplimiento *m*, cumplido *m*; piropo *m to woman*; *send* ~*s* enviar saludos; **2.** [ˈ~ment] cumplimentar; felicitar (*on* sobre); **com·pliˈmen·ta·ry** lisonjero; *ticket etc*. de regalo, de cortesía; ~ *copy* ejemplar *m* de cortesía; ~ *ticket* billete *m* de regalo, pase *m* de cortesía.

com·ply [kəmˈplai] conformarse (*with* con); obedecer (*with* a); ~ *with* obrar de acuerdo con.

com·po·nent [kəmˈpounənt] componente *adj*. *a*. *su*. *m* (*a*. ~ *part*).

com·port [kəmˈpɔ:rt] convenir (*with* a); ~ *o.s*. comportarse.

com·pose [kəmˈpouz] componer (*a*. ♪ *a*. *typ*.); **comˈposed,** *adv*. **com·pos·ed·ly** [kəmˈpouzidli] *spirit* sosegado; compuesto (*of* de); *be* ~ *of* componerse de, estar compuesto de; **comˈpos·er** ♪ compositor *m*; autor *m*; **comˈpos·ing** composición *f*; *typ*. ~ *stick* componedor *m*; **com·pos·ite** [kəmˈpɔzit] **1.** compuesto; **2.** compuesto *m*; ⚘ ~*s pl*. compuestas *f/pl*.; **com·pos·i·tion** [kɔmpəˈziʃn] composición *f*; ✝ arreglo *m*, ajuste *m*; **com·pos·i·tor** [kəmˈpɔzitər] cajista *m*; **com·post** [ˈkɔmpɔst] 🌱 abono *m*; **com·po·sure** [kəmˈpouʒər] compostura *f*, serenidad *f*.

com·pote [ˈkɔmpout] compota *f*; conserva *f* (de fruta).

com·pound[1] **1.** ['kɔmpaund] compuesto; ~ *fracture* fractura *f* complicada; ~ *interest* interés *m* compuesto; **2.** [~] compuesto *m* (*a.* ⚗); *gr.* (*a.* ~ *word*) vocablo *m* compuesto; **3.** [kəm'paund] *v/t.* componer; *v/i.*: ~ *with* capitular con.

com·pound[2] ['kɔmpaund] comprender; encerrar, incluir.

com·pre·hen·si·ble [kɔmpri'hensəbl] □ comprensible; **com·pre'hen·sion** comprensión *f*; **com·pre'hen·sive** □ comprensivo; **com·pre'hen·sive·ness** extensión *f*, alcance *m*.

com·press 1. [kəm'pres] comprimir; **2.** ['kɔmpres] compresa *f*; **com·pres·si·bil·i·ty** [kəmpresi'biliti] compresibilidad *f*; **com·pres·sion** [~'preʃn] compresión *f*; ~ *ratio* índice *m* de compresión; **com'pres·sor** compresor *m*.

com·prise [kəm'praiz] comprender; constar de; *range* abarcar.

com·pro·mise ['kɔmprəmaiz] **1.** compromiso *m*, componenda *f*; **2.** *v/t.* *affair* arreglar; *p.* comprometer; *v/i.* comprometer(se); *b.s.* transigir.

com·pul·sion [kəm'pʌlʃn] compulsión *f*; **com'pul·so·ry** [~səri] □ obligatorio; compulsivo.

com·punc·tion [kəm'pʌŋkʃn] compunción *f*.

com·put·a·ble [kəm'pju:təbl] calculable; **com·pu·ta·tion** [kɔmpju:'teiʃn] cómputo *m*, cálculo *m*; **com·pute** [kəm'pju:t] computar, calcular; **com'put·er** ordenador *m*; *p.* computador *m* (-a *f*), calculador *m* (-a *f*); *v.* *calculator*; ~ *science* informática *f*.

com·rade ['kɔmreid] camarada *m*; ~ *in arms* compañero *m* de armas.

con[1] [kɔn] estudiar, repasar; aprender de memoria.

con[2] [~] *ship* gobernar.

con[3] [~] *abbr.* = *contra* contra; *pro and* ~ en pro y en contra; *the pros and* ~*s* el pro y el contra.

con[4] [~] *sl.* **1.** (*a.* ~ *man*) timador *m*; **2.** timar.

con·cat·e·nate [kɔn'kætineit] concatenar; **con·cat·e'na·tion** concatenación *f*.

con·cave ['kɔn'keiv] □ cóncavo; **con·cav·i·ty** [~'kæviti] concavidad *f*.

con·ceal [kən'si:l] ocultar (*from* a, de); ⚖ encubrir; **con'ceal·ment** disimulación *f* *of feelings etc.*; encubrimiento *m*; *place of* ~ escondrijo *m*.

con·cede [kən'si:d] conceder.

con·ceit [kən'si:t] presunción *f*, engreimiento *m*, ínfulas *f/pl.*; *lit.* concepto *m*; **con'ceit·ed** □ engreído, afectado; *style* conceptuoso; **con'ceit·ed·ness** engreimiento *m*.

con·ceiv·a·ble [kən'si:vəbl] □ concebible; **con'ceive** *v/i.* concebir; *v/t.* imaginar, formar concepto de; *child* concebir; *plan* idear.

con·cen·trate 1. ['kɔnsentreit] concentrar(se); ~ *on* concentrar la atención en; concentrarse (*on ger.* a *inf.*); *fig. hope etc.* cifrar (*on* en); **2.** ['~trit] *esp.* ⚗ sustancia *f* concentrada; **con·cen'tra·tion** concentración *f* (*a.* ⚗); ~ *camp* campo *m* de concentración; **con'cen·tric** □ concéntrico.

con·cep·tion [kən'sepʃn] concepción *f*; idea *f*, concepto *m*.

con·cern [kən'sə:rn] **1.** asunto *m*, negocio *m*; interés *m*, preocupación *f* (*for*, *with* por); inquietud *f* (*for* por); ✝ empresa *f*; F *esp. the whole* ~ el asunto entero; *of* ~ de importancia; *that's your* ~*!* ¡allá tú!; **2.** concernir, atañer; preocupar, inquietar; ~ *o.s. with* ocuparse de, interesarse por; *be* ~*ed in* estar interesado en; estar metido en; *be* ~*ed* estar preocupado (*with* por; *that* porque); *be* ~*ed to inf.* (me *etc.*) interesa *inf.*; *as far as he is* ~*ed* en cuanto le toca a él; *as* ~*s* respecto de; *to whom it may* ~ a quien pueda interesar, a quien corresponda; **con'cerned** □ interesado (*in* en); ocupado; inquietado (*at*, *about*, *for* por); *those* ~ los interesados; **con'cern·ing** *prp.* concerniente a; respecto de.

con·cert 1. ['kɔnsərt] concierto *m* (*a.* ♪); *in* ~ de concierto; ~*master* concertino *m*; **2.** [kən'sə:rt] concertar; **con·cer·ti·na** [kɔnsər'ti:nə] concertina *f*; **con·cer·to** [kən'tʃertou] concierto *m*.

con·ces·sion [kən'seʃn] concesión *f*; privilegio *m*; **con·ces·sion·aire** [kənseʃə'ner] concesionario *m*.

con·ces·sive [kən'sesiv] □ concesivo (*a. gr.*).

conch [kɔŋk] caracola *f*.

con·cil·i·ate [kən'silieit] conciliar;

(*win over*) ganar, granjear; **con·cil·i'a·tion** conciliación *f*; **con'cil·i·a·tor** conciliador *m*; **con'cil·i·a·to·ry** [~ətəri] conciliador, conciliatorio.

con·cise [kən'sais] □ conciso; **con'cise·ness** concisión *f* (*a.* **con'ci·sion**).

con·clave ['kɔnkleiv] cónclave *m*; asamblea *f*.

con·clude [kən'klu:d] concluir, terminar; sacar una consecuencia; *agreement* llegar a; *business* finalizar, dar por terminado; *to be ~d* continuará; **con'clud·ing** final.

con·clu·sion [kən'klu:ʒn] conclusión *f*; *in ~* en conclusión; *try ~s with* participar en una contienda con; **con'clu·sive** □ conclusivo; (*decisive*) decisivo.

con·coct [kən'kɔkt] mezclar, confeccionar; *fig.* tramar, urdir; **con'coc·tion** confección *f*; *fig.* maquinación *f*, trama *f*.

con·com·i·tance, con·com·i·tan·cy [kən'kɔmitəns(i)] concomitancia *f*; **con'com·i·tant** concomitante *adj. a. su. m.*

con·cord 1. ['kɔŋkɔ:rd] concordia *f*; *gr.*, ♪ concordancia *f*; **2.** [kən'kɔ:rd] concordar (*with* con); **con'cord·ance** concordancia *f* (*a. eccl.*); **con'cord·ant** □ concordante; **con'cor·dat** [~dæt] concordato *m*.

con·course ['kɔŋkɔ:rs] confluencia *f of rivers*; concurso *m*, reunión *f of people*; 🚂 gran salón *m*.

con·crete 1. ['kɔnkri:t] □ concreto; ⊕ de hormigón; **2.** [~] ⊕ hormigón *m*; *~ mixer* hormigonera *f*, concretera *f*; **3.** [kən'kri:t] cuajarse; solidificarse; **con·cre·tion** [kən'kri:ʃn] concreción *f*.

con·cu·bi·nage [kɔn'kju:binidʒ] concubinato *m*; **con·cu·bine** ['kɔŋkjubain] concubina *f*, barragana *f*.

con·cu·pis·cence [kən'kju:pisns] concupiscencia *f*; **con'cu·pis·cent** concupiscente.

con·cur [kən'kə:r] concurrir; convenir (*with* con; *in* en); **con·cur·rence** [~'kʌrəns] concurrencia *f*; unión *f*; (*agreement*) acuerdo *m*; (*assent*) asenso *m*; *in ~ with* de acuerdo con; **con'cur·rent** □ concurrente.

con·cus·sion [kən'kʌʃn] sacudimiento *m*; ⚕ conmoción *f* cerebral.

con·demn [kən'dem] condenar (*to* a); censurar; *~ed cell* celda *f* de los condenados a muerte; **con'dem·na·ble** condenable; **con·dem·na·tion** [kɔndem'neiʃn] condenación *f*; ⚖ condena *f*; censura *f*; **con·dem·na·to·ry** [kən'demnətəri] condenador.

con·den·sa·ble [kən'densəbl] condensable; **con·den·sa·tion** [kɔnden'seiʃn] condensación *f*; (*a.* 🕮) compendio *m of material*; **con·dense** [kən'dens] condensar; *material* abreviar; **con'dens·er** ⊕, ⚡ condensador *m*.

con·de·scend [kɔndi'send] condescender (*to* en); dignarse (*to inf.*); **con·de'scend·ing** □ condescendiente; que trata (*or* se comporta) con aire protector (*or* de superioridad); **con·de'scen·sion** [~ʃn] dignación *f*, condescendencia *f*.

con·di·ment ['kɔndimənt] condimento *m*.

con·di·tion [kən'diʃn] **1.** condición *f*; *~s pl.* condiciones *f/pl.*, circunstancias *f/pl.*; *on ~ that* a condición (de) que; **2.** condicionar, acondicionar; determinar; **con·di'tion·al** □ condicional (*a. gr.*); *~ upon* a condición de (que); **con'di·tion·al·ly** [~əli] con reservas; **con'di·tioned** (a)condicionado; determinado.

con·dole [kən'doul] condolerse (*with* de); **con'do·lence** pésame *m*, condolencia *f*; *express one's ~s* dar el pésame.

con·do·min·i·um [kɔndə'miniəm] condominio *m*.

con·do·na·tion [kɔndou'neiʃn] condonación *f*; **con·done** [kən'doun] condonar.

con·duce [kən'dju:s] conducir (*to* a); **con'du·cive** conducente, contribuyente (*to* a).

con·duct 1. ['kɔndəkt] conducta *f*; **2.** [kən'dʌkt] conducir; llevar; *orchestra* dirigir; ♪ (*v./i.*) llevar la batuta; *~ o.s.* comportarse; **con·duct·i·bil·i·ty** [kəndʌkti'biliti] conductibilidad *f*; **con'duct·i·ble** [~təbl] conductivo; **con'duct·ing** ♪ dirección *f*; dirigir *m*; **con'duc·tion** conducción *f*; **con'duc·tive** □ conductivo; conductor; **con·duc·tiv·i·ty** [kɔndʌk'tiviti] conductibilidad *f*; **con·duc·tor** [kən'dʌktər] conductor *m* (*a. phys.*); ♪ director *m*;

(*bus*) cobrador *m*; 🚂 revisor *m*; (*lightning*) pararrayos *m*; **con'duc·tress** cobradora *f*.

con·duit ['kɔndjuit] conducto *m*, canal *m*.

cone [koun] cono *m* (*a*. ⚘); (*ice-cream* ~) barquillo *m*.

co·ney ['kouni] conejo *m*.

con·fab ['kɔnfæb] F **1.** = **con·fab·u·late** [kən'fæbjuleit] confabular; **2.** = **con·fab·u'la·tion** confabulación *f*; plática *f*.

con·fec·tion [kən'fekʃn] confección *f*, hechura *f*; (*sweetmeat*) confite *m*; **con'fec·tion·er** confitero *m*; pastelero *m*; **con'fec·tion·er·y** confites *m/pl.*; pasteles *m/pl.*; (*shop*) confitería *f*; pastelería *f*.

con·fed·er·a·cy [kən'fedərəsi] confederación *f*; ⚖ complot *m*; **con'fed·er·ate 1.** [~rit] confederado; **2.** [~] confederado *m*; cómplice *m*; **3.** [~reit] confederarse; **con·fed·er'a·tion** confederación *f*.

con·fer [kən'fə:r] *v/t*. conferir (*on* a); *v/i*. conferir (*with* con; *about, upon* acerca de, sobre); **con·fer·ence** ['kɔnfərəns] conferencia *f*; (*assembly*) congreso *m*.

con·fess [kən'fes] confesar (*to p.* a); ~ *to th.* reconocer, admitir; ~ *to God* confesarse a Dios; **con'fess·ed·ly** [~idli] según se admite; francamente; **con·fes·sion** [~'feʃn] confesión *f* (*a. eccl.*); *eccl.* (*a.* ~ *of faith*) credo *m*, profesión *f* de fe; ~ *box* confesonario *m*; **con'fes·sion·al 1.** confesional; **2.** confesonario *m*; **con'fes·sor** (*priest*) confesor *m*; (*sinner*) confesante *m/f*, penitente *m/f*.

con·fi·dant [kɔnfi'dænt] confidente *m*; **con·fi'dante** [~] confidenta *f*.

con·fide [kən'faid] *v/i*.: ~ *in* confiar en, fiarse de; ~ *to* hacer confidencias a; *v/t. th.* confiar (*to* a, en); **con·fi·dence** ['kɔnfidəns] confianza *f* (*in* en); confidencia *f*, secreto *m*; *in* ~ en confianza; *gain* ~ adquirir confianza; ~ *man* timador *m*; **'con·fi·dent** □ seguro (*of* de; *that* de que); lleno de confianza; *b.s.* confiado; **con·fi'den·tial** □ confidencial; ~*ly* en confianza.

con·fig·u·ra·tion [kənfigju'reiʃn] configuración *f*.

con·fine 1. ['kɔnfain] *mst* ~*s pl.* confines *m/pl.* (*a. fig.*); **2.** [kən'fain] confinar (*s.o. to* en); encerrar; limitar; *be* ~*d to bed* tener que guardar cama; *be* ~*d* (*woman*) estar de parto; **con'fine·ment** confinamiento *m*; encierro *m*; encarcelamiento *m in prison*; ⚕ parto *m*, sobreparto *m*.

con·firm [kən'fə:rm] confirmar (*a. eccl.*); ratificar, revalidar; **con·fir·ma·tion** [kɔnfər'meiʃn] confirmación *f* (*a. eccl.*); **con·firm·a·tive** [kən'fə:rmətiv], **con'firm·a·to·ry** [~təri] confirmatorio; **con'firmed** confirmado (*a. eccl.*); (*by habit*) inveterado.

con·fis·cate ['kɔnfiskeit] confiscar; **con·fis'ca·tion** confiscación *f*; **con'fis·ca·to·ry** que confisca.

con·fla·gra·tion [kɔnflə'greiʃn] conflagración *f*.

con·flict 1. ['kɔnflikt] conflicto *m* (*a. fig.*); **2.** [kən'flikt]: ~ *with* estar en pugna con; **con'flict·ing** [~iŋ] *events, appointments, class hours, etc.* incompatible; *stories* contradictorio.

con·flu·ence ['kɔnfluəns] confluencia *f* (*a.* ⚕); **con·flu·ent** ['~fluənt] confluente *adj. a. su. m.*

con·form [kən'fɔ:rm] *v/t.* conformar (*to* con); *v/i.*: ~ *to* conformarse con, allanarse a; **con'form·a·ble** □ conforme (*to* con); **con·for·ma·tion** [kɔnfɔ:r'meiʃn] conformación *f*; **con·form·ist** [kən'fɔ:rmist] conformista *m/f*; *fig.* que se allana a todo; **con'form·i·ty** conformidad *f*; *in* ~ *with* conforme a.

con·found [kən'faund] confundir; vencer; F ~ *it!* ¡demonio!; **con'found·ed** □ F condenado.

con·fra·ter·ni·ty [kɔnfrə'tə:rniti] cofradía *f*; *fig.* confraternidad *f*.

con·front [kən'frʌnt] afrontar, carear; *s.o.* confrontar (*with* con); hacer cara a; *manuscripts* cotejar; *be* ~*ed with* encararse con; salírsele a uno; **con·fron·ta·tion** [kɔnfrʌn'teiʃn] confrontación *f*, afrontamiento *m*; cotejo *m*.

con·fuse [kən'fju:z] confundir (*s.t. with* con); ~ *the issue* oscurecer las cosas; **con'fused** confuso; perturbado, aturrullado; **con'fus·ed·ly** *adv.* confusamente; **con'fu·sion** confusión *f*; (*mental*) aturdimiento *m*; desorden *m*.

con·fut·a·ble [kən'fju:təbl] confutable; **con·fu·ta·tion** [kɔnfju:'teiʃn] confutación *f*; **con·fute** [kən'fju:t] confutar.

con·geal [kən'dʒiːl] congelar(se); (*blood*) coagular(se). **con·ge·la·tion** [kɔndʒi'leiʃn] congelación *f*. **con·gen·ial** [kən'dʒiːniəl] □ congenial; *atmosphere etc.* agradable; **con·ge·ni·al·i·ty** [~'æliti] simpatía *f*, afinidad *f*. **con·gen·i·tal** [kɔn'dʒenitl] □ congénito. **con·ge·ri·es** [kɔn'dʒiriːz] 🕮 congerie *f*. **con·ger** ['kɔŋgər] (*a.* ~ *eel*) congrio *m*. **con·gest** [kən'dʒest] congestionar(se) (*a.* ⚕); (*people*) apiñarse; ~*ed area* barrio *m* superpoblado; **con'ges·tion** congestión *f*; ~ *of traffic* aglomeración *f* del tráfico. **con·glom·er·ate 1.** [kɔn'glɔmərit] conglomerado *adj. a. su. m*; **2.** [~reit] conglomerar(se); **con·glom·er'a·tion** conglomeración *f*. **con·grat·u·late** [kən'grætjuleit] felicitar ([*up*]*on* por); **con·grat·u'la·tion** felicitación *f*, parabién *m*; ~*s*! ¡enhorabuena!; **con'grat·u·la·to·ry** congratulatorio. **con·gre·gate** ['kɔŋgrigeit] congregar(se); **con·gre'ga·tion** *eccl.* congregación *f*; auditorio *m*; los fieles (de una iglesia); **con·gre'ga·tion·al** congregacionalista. **con·gress** ['kɔŋgres] congreso *m*; ♀ Congreso *m* (*de Estados Unidos*); ~*man* congresista *m*; **con·gres·sion·al** [~'greʃnl] congresional. **con·gru·ence, con·gru·en·cy** ['kɔŋgruəns(i)] = *congruity*; ⅍ congruencia *f*; **'con·gru·ent** = *congruous*; ⅍ congruente; **con'gru·i·ty** congruencia *f*, conformidad *f*; **'con·gru·ous** □ congruo (*with* con); conforme (*with* a); ⅍ congruente (*to* respecto a). **con·ic, con·i·cal** ['kɔnik(l)] □ cónico; ⅍ ~ *section* sección *f* cónica. **co·ni·fer** ['kounifər] conífera *f*; **co'nif·er·ous** conífero. **con·jec·tur·al** [kən'dʒektʃərəl] □ conjetural; **con'jec·ture 1.** conjetura *f*; **2.** conjeturar (*from* de, por). **con·join** [kən'dʒɔin] juntar(se), unir(se); **con'joint** conjunto; **con'joint·ly** de mancomún. **con·ju·gal** ['kɔndʒugl] □ conjugal; **con·ju·gate** ['~geit] **1.** *v/t.* conjugar; *v/i. biol.* reproducirse; **2.** ['~git] ⚘ conjugado; **con·ju·ga·tion** ['~geiʃn] conjugación *f* (*a. biol.*). **con·junct** [kən'dʒʌŋkt] □ conjunto; **con'junc·tion** conjunción *f*; **con·junc·ti·va** [kɔndʒʌŋk'taivə] conjuntiva *f*; **con·junc·tive** [kən'dʒʌŋktiv] conjuntivo; ~ *mood* modo *m* conjuntivo; **con·junc·ti·vi·tis** [~'vaitis] conjuntivitis *f*; **con'junc·ture** [~tʃə] coyuntura *f*. **con·ju·ra·tion** [kɔndʒu'reiʃn] conjuro *m*; **con·jure 1.** [kən'dʒur] *v/t.* conjurar, pedir con instancia; **2.** ['kʌndʒər] *v/t.* conjurar, exorcizar (*a.* ~ *away*); ~ *up* hacer aparecer; *fig.* evocar; *v/i.* escamotear; practicar las artes mágicas; **'con·jur·er, 'con·jur·or** mágico *m*; escamoteador *m*, prestidigitador *m*; **'con·jur·ing trick** escamoteo *m*. **conk** [kɔŋk] F **1.** narigón *m*; **2.**: *mst* ~ *out* ⊕ parar, tener averías; ⚕ perder el conocimiento. **con·nect** [kə'nekt] conectar(se), conexionar(se); asociar(se), enlazar(se); 🚂 empalmar (*with* con); *teleph.* poner en comunicación (*with* con); **con'nect·ed** □ conexo; asociado; enlazado (*with* con); *well* ~ de buena familia; *be* ~ *with* estar asociado con; ⚚ ser un empleado de; **con'nect·ing** que une, que conecta; ~ *flight* vuelo *m* de enlace; ~ *rod* biela *f*. **con·nec·tion** [kə'nekʃn] conexión *f* (*a.* ⚡); *fig.* relación *f*; (*family* ~) parentesco *m*; unión *f*, enlace *m*; 🚂 correspondencia *f* (*with* con), empalme *m*; ⊕ acoplamiento *m*; *in* ~ *with* a propósito de; *in this* ~ con respecto a esto; **con·nec·tive** □ conectivo; *anat.* ~ *tissue* tejido *m* conjuntivo. **conn·ing tow·er** ['kɔniŋtauər] torreta *f*. **con·nip·tion** [kə'nipʃn] pataleta *f*, berrinche *m*. **con·niv·ance** [kə'naivəns] connivencia *f*; confabulación *f* (*at*, *in* para); **con'nive** hacer la vista gorda (*at* a); ~ *with* confabularse con. **con·nois·seur** [kɔni'səːr] conocedor (-a *f*) *m*; catador *m of wine*. **con·no·ta·tion** [kɔnou'teiʃn] connotación *f*; **con'note** connotar. **con·nu·bi·al** [kə'njuːbiəl] □ conjugal, connubial. **con·quer** ['kɔŋkər] conquistar (*a. fig.*), vencer; **'con·quer·or** conquistador (-a *f*) *m*; vencedor (-a *f*) *m*.

con·quest ['kɔŋkwest] conquista *f*.
con·san·guin·e·ous [kɔnsæŋ'gwiniəs] consanguíneo; **con·san'guin·i·ty** consanguinidad *f*.
con·science ['kɔnʃns] conciencia *f*; F *in all* ~ en realidad de verdad; ~ *money* dinero *m* que se paga para descargar la conciencia; '**con·science·less** desalmado; '**~-strick·en** contrito, arrepentido.
con·sci·en·tious [kɔnʃi'enʃəs] □ concienzudo; ~ *objector* pacifista *m* que se niega a tomar las armas; **con·sci'en·tious·ness** escrupulosidad *f*; industria *f*.
con·scious ['kɔnʃəs] □ consciente; intencional; *be* ~ hacerse cargo, tener conocimiento (*of* de; *that* de que); ⚕ tener conocimiento; '**con·scious·ness** conciencia *f*; ⚕ conocimiento *m*; *phls.* consciencia *f*; *lose* (*regain*) ~ perder (recobrar) el conocimiento.
con·script [kən'skript] reclutar; **con·script** ['kɔnskript] recluta *m*, quinto *m*; **con·scrip·tion** reclutamiento *m*; (llamada *f* al) servicio *m* militar obligatorio.
con·se·crate ['kɔnsikreit] consagrar (*a. fig.*); **con·se'cra·tion** consagración *f*.
con·sec·u·tive [kən'sekjutiv] consecutivo (*a. gr.*), sucesivo; **con'sec·u·tive·ly** sucesivamente.
con·sen·sus [kən'sensəs] consenso *m*.
con·sent [kən'sent] **1.** consentimiento *m* (*to* en); *by common* ~ según la opinión unánime; **2.** consentir (*to* en).
con·se·quence ['kɔnsikwəns] consecuencia *f*; *of* ~ de consecuencia; *in* ~ por consiguiente; *in* ~ *of* de resultas de; *take the* ~*s* aceptar las consecuencias; '**con·se·quent 1.** consiguiente; *phls.* consecuente; *be* ~ *on* ser consecuencia de; **2.** *gr.* consiguiente *m*; *phls.*, ⚖ consecuente *m*; **con·se·quen·tial** [~'kwenʃl] □ consiguiente; (*proud*) altivo; ~ *on* en consecuencia de; **con·se·quent·ly** ['~kwentli] por consiguiente.
con·ser·va·tion [kɔnsər'veiʃn] conservación *f*; **con·serv·a·tism** [kən'səːrvətizm] conservatismo *m*; **con'serv·a·tive** □ conservativo; *pol.* conservador (*a. su. m*); moderado, cauteloso; **con'ser·va·toire** [~twɑːr] conservatorio *m*; **con'ser·va·tor** conservador *m*; **con'serv·a·to·ry** [~tri] invernadero *m*; **con'serve 1.** conserva *f*, compota *f*; **2.** conservar.
con·sid·er [kən'sidər] considerar; **con'sid·er·a·ble** □ considerable; **con'sid·er·ate** [~rit] □ considerado; **con·sid·er·a·tion** [~'reiʃn] consideración *f*; ⚖ remuneración *f*; *in* ~ *of* en consideración a; *take into* ~ tomar en cuenta; *without due* ~ sin reflexión; **con'sid·er·ing 1.** *prp.* en consideración a; **2.** F *adv.* teniendo en cuenta las circunstancias.
con·sign [kən'sain] consignar (*a.* ⚖); confiar, entregar; **con·sig·na·tion** [kɔnsai'neiʃn] consignación *f*; **con·sign·ment** [kən'sainmənt] consignación *f* (*a.* ⚖); ⚖ envío *m*, remesa *f*; **con·sign·ee** [kɔnsai'niː] consignatorio *m*; **con·sign·er, con·sign·or** [kən'sainər] consignador *m*.
con·sist [kən'sist] consistir (*in*, *of* en); constar (*of* de); **con'sist·ence, con'sist·en·cy** consistencia *f*; consecuencia *f of actions*; **con'sist·ent** □ consistente; consonante (*with* con); *conduct* consecuente; ~*ly* sin excepción, continuamente; **con'sis·to·ry** consistorio *m*.
con·sol·a·ble [kən'souləbl] consolable; **con·so·la·tion** [kɔnsə'leiʃn] consolación *f*, consuelo *m*.
con·sole 1. [kən'soul] consolar; **2.** ['kɔnsoul] ▵ consola *f*.
con·sol·i·date [kən'sɔlideit] consolidar (*a.* ⚖); **con·sol·i'da·tion** consolidación *f*.
con·so·nance ['kɔnsənəns] consonancia *f*; '**con·so·nant 1.** □ consonante (*a.* ♪); ~ *with* compatible con, conforme a; **2.** *gr.* consonante *f*; ~ *shift* alteración *f* de consonantes.
con·sort 1. ['kɔnsɔːrt] consorte *m/f*; ⚓ buque *m* que acompaña a otro; *prince* ~ príncipe *m* consorte; **2.** [kən'sɔːrt]: ~ *with* asociarse con; (*agree*) concordar con.
con·spic·u·ous [kən'spikjuəs] □ visible, evidente; que llama la atención; *fig.* notable; *be* ~ *by one's absence* brillar por su ausencia.
con·spir·a·cy [kən'spirəsi] conspiración *f*, complot *m*; **con'spir·a·tor** [~tər] conspirador (-a *f*) *m*; **con·spire** [~'spaiər] *v/t.* urdir, maquinar; *v/i.* conspirar (*to* a).

con·sta·ble ['kʌnstəbl] policía *m* (*a. police* ~); *hist.* condestable *m*; **con·stab·u·lar·y** [kən'stæbjuləri] guardia *f* civil, policía *f*.
con·stan·cy ['kɔnstənsi] constancia *f*; fidelidad *f*; **'con·stant 1.** □ constante; incesante; (*persistent*) porfiado; **2.** ⚗ constante *f*.
con·stel·la·tion [kɔnstə'leiʃn] constelación *f* (*a. fig.*).
con·ster·na·tion [kɔnstər'neiʃn] consternación *f*.
con·sti·pate ['kɔnstipeit] estreñir; **con·sti'pa·tion** estreñimiento *m*.
con'stit·u·en·cy [kən'stitjuənsi] distrito *m* electoral; **con'stit·u·ent 1.** constitutivo; *pol.* constituyente; ~ *assembly* cortes *f*/*pl.* constituyentes; **2.** constitutivo *m*, componente *m*; ⚖ poderdante *m*; *pol.* elector *m*.
con·sti·tute ['kɔnstitju:t] constituir (*a p. judge* a una p. juez); **con·sti'tu·tion** constitución *f*; **con·sti'tu·tion·al 1.** □ constitucional; **2.** F paseo *m*; **con·sti'tu·tion·al·ist** constitucional *m*; **con'sti·tu·tive** □ constitutivo, constituidor.
con·strain [kən'strein] constreñir, obligar (*to* a); imponer; detener, encerrar *in prison*; ~*ed* (*embarrassed*) desconcertado; *smile* forzado; **con'straint** coacción *f*, constreñimiento *m*; encierro *m*; *fig.* desconcierto *m*.
con·strict [kən'strikt] apretar; (*shrink*) encoger; **con'stric·tion** constricción *f*; **con'stric·tor** *anat.* constrictor *m*.
con·struct [kən'strʌkt] construir (*a. gr.*); **con'struc·tion** construcción *f*; interpretación *f*, explicación *f*; *under* ~ en construcción; **con'struc·tive** constructivo; *denial etc.* implícito; **con'struc·tor** constructor *m*.
con·strue [kən'stru:] *gr.* construir; interpretar.
con·sue·tu·di·nar·y [kɔnswi'tju:dinəri] consuetudinario.
con·sul ['kɔnsl] cónsul *m*; **con·su·lar** ['kɔnsjulər] consular; **con·su·late** ['~lit] consulado *m*; **con·sul·ship** ['kɔnslʃip] consulado *m*.
con·sult [kən'sʌlt] consultar (*with* con); ~*ing attr.* consultor; ⚕ ~*ing room* consultorio *m*; **con'sult·ant** consultor *m*; ⚕ especialista *m*; **con·sul·ta·tion** [kɔnsəl'teiʃn] consulta *f* (*a.* ⚕), consultación *f*; **con'sult·a·tive** [kən'sʌltətiv] consultivo.
con·sum·a·ble [kən'sju:məbl] consumible; **con'sume** consumir (*a. fig.*); **con'sum·er** consumidor *m*; ~ *goods pl.* artículos *m*/*pl.* de consumo.
con·sum·mate 1. [kən'sʌmit] □ consumado, cabal; **2.** ['kɔnsʌmeit] consumar; **con·sum·ma·tion** [~'meiʃn] consumación *f*, perfección *f*.
con·sump·tion [kən'sʌmpʃn] consunción *f*; consumo *m of goods*; ⚕ tisis *f*; **con'sump·tive** □ consuntivo; ⚕ tísico *adj. a. su. m* (a *f*).
con·tact ['kɔntækt] **1.** contacto *m* (*a. fig.*, ⚡); ~ *breaker* ⚡ ruptor *m*; ~ *lenses* lentes *m*/*pl.* de contacto, lentes invisibles, lentillas *f*/*pl.*, microlentillas *f*/*pl.*; *get in* ~ *with* = **2.** [kən'tækt] F ponerse en contacto con.
con·ta·gion [kən'teidʒn] contagio *m* (*a. fig.*); **con'ta·gious** □ contagioso (*a. fig.*).
con·tain [kən'tein] contener (*a.* ⚔); *space* abarcar; ~ *o.s.* contenerse; *be* ~*ed in* caber en; ⚗ ser (exactamente) divisible por; **con'tain·er** continente *m*; ✝ *etc.* envase *m*, caja *f*; **con'tain·ment** ⚔ contención *f*.
con·tam·i·nate [kən'tæmineit] contaminar (*a. fig.*); *be* ~*ed by* contaminarse con (*or* de); **con·tam·i'na·tion** contaminación *f*; refundición *f*, fusión *f of text*.
con·tem·plate ['kɔntempleit] contemplar; proponerse (*doing* hacer); **con·tem'pla·tion** contemplación *f*; mira *f*, intención *f*; **'con·tem·pla·tive** □ contemplativo.
con·tem·po·ra·ne·ous [kəntempə'reinjəs] □ contemporáneo; **con'tem·po·rar·y** contemporáneo *adj. a. su. m* (a *f*); coetáneo *adj. a. su. m* (a *f*).
con·tempt [kən'tempt] desprecio *m*, desdén *m*; ⚖ ~ *of court* contumacia *f*, rebeldía *f*; *hold in* ~ despreciar; **con'tempt·i·ble** □ despreciable; **con'temp·tu·ous** [~juəs] □ despreciativo, despectivo; desdeñoso (*of* para, hacia).
con·tend [kən'tend] *v*/*i.* contender (*with ... over* con ... sobre); luchar (*for* por); (*argument*) sostener; *v*/*t.* afirmar, sostener.
con·tent [kən'tent] **1.** contento (*with*

de, con); *parl.* ~! ¡sí!; *not* ~! ¡no!; *be* ~ *to* quedar contento de; **2.** contentar; ~ *o.s.* contentarse (*with* con); **3.** contento *m*; *to one's heart's* ~ a gusto, hasta más no poder; **4.** ['kɔntent] contenido *m* (*freq.* ~*s pl.*); (*capacity*) cabida *f*; (*esp.* ⚗) componente *m*; **con'tent·ed** □ contento, satisfecho; **con'tent·ed·ness** contento *m*, satisfacción *f*.

con·ten·tion [kən'tenʃn] contienda *f*, disputa *f*; argumento *m*, aseveración *f* (*that* de que); **con'ten·tious** □ contencioso; (*quarrelsome*) pendenciero.

con·tent·ment [kən'tentmənt] contento *m*, satisfacción *f*.

con·ter·mi·nous [kɔn'təːrminəs] contérmino, limítrofe.

con·test 1. ['kɔntest] debate *m*, disputa *f*; (*fight*) contienda *f*, lid *f* (*a. fig.*); (*competition*) concurso *m*; **2.** [kən'test] disputar, impugnar; tomar parte en un concurso; *election* ser candidato en; **con'test·ant** contendiente *m/f*; contrincante *m*; rival *m/f*.

con·text ['kɔntekst] contexto *m* (*a. fig.*); **con·tex·tu·al** [kən'tekstjuəl] □ relativo al contexto; **con'tex·ture** [~tʃər] contextura *f*.

con·ti·gu·i·ty [kɔnti'gjuiti] contigüidad *f*; **con·tig·u·ous** □ [kən'tigjuəs] contiguo (*to* a).

con·ti·nence ['kɔntinəns] continencia *f*; **'con·ti·nent 1.** □ continente; **2.** continente *m*; *the* ♀ la Europa continental; **con·ti·nen·tal** [~'nentl] □ continental; ~ *climate* clima *m* continental.

con·tin·gen·cy [kən'tindʒənsi] contingencia *f*; **con'tin·gent 1.** □ contingente, eventual; dependiente (*on* de); **2.** contingente *m*.

con·tin·u·al [kən'tinjuəl] □ continuo, incesante; **con'tin·u·ance** continuación *f*; (*stay*) permanencia *f*; **con·tin·u'a·tion** continuación *f*; ✝ prórroga *f*; **con'tin·ue** *v/t.* continuar; mantener; ⚖ aplazar; *to be* ~*d* continuará; *v/i.* continuar(se); ~ *doing* continuar haciendo; **con·ti·nu·i·ty** [kɔnti'njuːiti] continuidad *f*; *film*: escenario *m*; **con·tin·u·ous** [kən'tinjuəs] □ continuo (*a.* ⚡); ~ *showing* sesión *f* continua; **con·tin·u·um** [kən'tinjuəm] continuo *m*.

con·tort [kən'tɔːrt] retorcer, deformar; **con'tor·tion** contorsión *f*; **con'tor·tion·ist** contorsionista *m/f*.

con·tour ['kɔntur] contorno *m*; ~ *line* curva *f* de nivel.

con·tra ['kɔntrə] (en) contra.

con·tra·band ['kɔntrəbænd] (*attr.* de) contrabando *m*.

con·tra·cep·tive [kɔntrə'septiv] anticonceptivo *m*, contraceptivo *m*.

con·tract 1. [kən'trækt] *v/t.* contraer; *friendship* entablar; *v/i.* contraerse; comprometerse por contrato (*to* a); ~ *for* contratar; ~*ing party* contratante *m*; **2.** ['kɔntrækt] contrato *m*; ✝ contrata *f*; *by* ~ por contrata; ~ *work* destajo *m*; **con·tract·ed** [kən'træktid] contraído; encogido; **con·tract·i'bil·i·ty** calidad *f* de contractable; **con'tract·i·ble** contractable; **con'trac·tile** [~tail] contráctil; **con'trac·tion** contracción *f*; **con'trac·tor** contratista *m/f*; contratante *m*; *anat.* esfínter *m*; **con'trac·tu·al** [~tjuel] contractual.

con·tra·dict [kɔntrə'dikt] contradecir; **con·tra'dic·tion** contradicción *f*; **con·tra'dic·to·ry** □ contradictorio; *p.* contradictor.

con·tra·dis·tinc·tion [kɔntrədis'tiŋkʃn] distinción *f* por oposición; *in* ~ *to* a diferencia de.

con·trail ['kɔntreil] ✈ rastro *m* de condensación, estela *f* de vapor.

con·trap·tion [kən'træpʃn] dispositivo *m*, artificio *m*; *contp.* armatoste *m*, artilugio *m*.

con·tra·ri·e·ty [kɔntrə'raiəti] contrariedad *f*; **con·tra·ri·ly** ['~trɔrili] con espíritu de contradicción; tercamente; **'con·tra·ri·ness** contrariedad *f*; (*obstinacy*) terquedad *f*; **con·tra·ri·wise** ['~waiz] en contrario; F tercamente; **'con·tra·ry 1.** contrario; F [kən'treri] obstinado, terco; que lleva la contra; *adv.* en contrario; ~ *to* contrario a; **2.** contrario *m*; *on the* ~ al contrario; *to the* ~ en contrario.

con·trast 1. ['kɔntræst] contraste *m*; *in* ~ por contraste; *in* ~ *to* en contraposición a; **2.** [kən'træst] *v/t.* poner en contraste; *v/i.* contrastar (*with* con).

con·tra·vene [kɔntrə'viːn] contravenir a; *statement* contradecir, resistir a; **con·tra·ven·tion** [~'venʃn] contravención *f*; ⚖ infracción *f*.

con·trib·ute [kən'tribjuːt] contribuir (*towards* a, para; *to ger.* a *inf.*); ~ *to paper* colaborar en; **con·tri·bu·tion** [kɔntri'bju:ʃn] contribución *f*; artículo *m*, escrito *m to paper*; **con·trib·u·tor** [kən'tribju:tər] contribuidor (-a *f*) *m*, contribuyente *m*; colaborador (-a *f*) *m to paper*; **con'trib·u·to·ry** contribuidor (*to* a).

con·trite [kən'trait] □ contrito; **con·tri·tion** [kən'triʃn] contrición *f*.

con·triv·ance [kən'traivəns] invención *f*; (*apparatus*) artificio *m*; plan *m*; **con'trive** *v/t.* inventar; urdir, tramar; *v/i.*: ~ *to* ingeniarse a, lograr; ~ *well* componérselas (*in* para).

con·trol [kən'troul] **1.** mando *m*, gobierno *m*; inspección *f*, intervención *f* (*esp.* ☤); control *m*; ⊕ regulador *m*; 🕮 norma *f* de comprobación; dirección *f*; *attr.* de mando, de control; ~*s pl. esp.* ✈ aparatos *m/pl.* de mando; *remote* ~ comando *m* a distancia, telecontrol *m*; ✈ ~ *column*, ~ *stick* mango *m* de escoba, palanca *f* de mando; ~ *knob radio*: botón *m*, regulador *m*; ✈ ~ *panel* tablero *m* de instrumentos; *be in* ~ tener el mando, mandar; *get out of* ~ perder control; *get under* ~ conseguir dominar; **2.** mandar, gobernar; controlar, comprobar; ⊕ regular; *price* controlar; ~ *o.s.* dominarse; **con'trol·ler** inspector *m*; ☤ interventor *m*; director *m*; ⊕ regulador *m*; **con'trol·ling** predominante, decisivo; ☤ ~ *interest* interés *m* predominante.

con·tro·ver·sial [kɔntrə'və:rʃl] □ controvertible; contencioso; '**con·tro·ver·sy** controversia *f*; '**con·tro·vert** controvertir.

con·tu·ma·cious [kɔntju'meiʃəs] □ contumaz (*a.* ⚖); **con·tu·ma·cy** ['kɔntjuməsi] contumacia *f*.

con·tu·me·li·ous [kɔntju'mi:liəs] □ contumelioso; **con·tu·me·ly** ['kɔntjumli] contumelia *f*.

con·tuse [kən'tju:z] contundir; **con'tu·sion** contusión *f*.

co·nun·drum [kə'nʌndrəm] acertijo *m*, adivinanza *f*.

con·va·lesce [kɔnvə'les] convalecer; **con·va'les·cence** convalecencia *f*; **con·va'les·cent** convaleciente *adj. a. su. m/f*; ~ *home* clínica *f* de reposo.

con·vec·tion [kən'vekʃn] convección *f*.

con·vene [kən'vi:n] *v/i.* juntarse, reunirse; *v/t. meeting* convocar.

con·ven·ience [kən'vi:njəns] conveniencia *f*; comodidad *f*; (*time*) oportunidad *f*; *at your earliest* ~ cuando le sea conveniente; *public* ~ aseos *m/pl.*; *marriage of* ~ matrimonio *m* de conveniencia; **con'ven·ient** □ conveniente; cómodo; *time* oportuno; apto; *spot* alcanzadizo, céntrico.

con·vent ['kɔnvənt] convento *m* (de religiosas); **con·ven·ti·cle** [kən'ventikl] conventículo *m*; **con'ven·tion** convención *f*; (*meeting*) asamblea *f*; **con'ven·tion·al** □ convencional; **con'ven·tion·al·ism** convencionalismo *m*; formalismo *m*; **con·ven·tion·al·i·ty** [~'næliti] formalismo *m*; apego *m* a las convenciones; **con'ven·tu·al** [~tjuəl] □ conventual.

con·verge [kən'və:rdʒ] convergir (*on* en); **con'ver·gence, con'ver·gen·cy** convergencia *f*; **con'ver·gent, con'verg·ing** convergente.

con·ver·sant [kən'və:rsənt] versado (*with* en); *become* ~ *with* familiarizarse con; **con·ver·sa·tion** [~'seiʃn] conversación *f*, plática *f*; **con·ver'sa·tion·al** □ de conversación; *p.* hablador, expansivo; **con·verse 1.** ['kɔnvə:rs] □ contrario, inverso; **2.** [~] plática *f*; 𝔄 inversa *f*; **3.** [kən'və:rs] conversar (*with* con); **con'ver·sion** conversión *f* (*to* a; *into* en); ☤ cambio *m*, conversión *f*; ☤, ⊕ reorganización *f*; ⚖ apropiación *f* ilícita.

con·vert 1. ['kɔnvə:rt] converso (a *f*) *m*, convertido (a *f*) *m*; **2.** [kən'və:rt] convertir (*to* a); ⚖ apropiarse ilícitamente (*to one's own use* para uso propio); **con'vert·er** ⊕, ⚡ convertidor *m*; **con·vert·i·bil·i·ty** [~ə'biliti] convertibilidad *f*; **con'vert·i·ble** □ convertible; *mot.* transformable; descapotable.

con·vex ['kɔn'veks] □ convexo; **con'vex·i·ty** convexidad *f*.

con·vey [kən'vei] transportar, llevar; *current* transmitir; *news* comunicar; dar a entender (*to* a); ⚖ traspasar; **con'vey·ance** transporte *m*; vehículo *m*; (*a.* ⚡) transmisión *f*; comunicación *f*; ⚖ (escritura *f* de) traspaso

m; *public* ~ vehículo *m* de transporte público; **con'vey·anc·er** escribano *m* que prepara escrituras de traspaso; **con'vey·or** (*or* ~ *belt*) correa *f* transportadora.
con·vict 1. ['kɔnvikt] presidiario *m*; **2.** [kən'vikt] condenar; declarar culpable (*of* de); **con·vic·tion** [kən'vikʃn] convencimiento *m*; ⚖ condena *f*; ~*s pl.* convicciones *f/pl.*, opiniones *f/pl.*
con·vince [kən'vins] convencer (*of* de); **con'vinc·ing** □ convincente.
con·viv·i·al [kən'viviəl] □ festivo, jovial; **con·viv·i·al·i·ty** [~vi'æliti] jovialidad *f*, sociabilidad *f*.
con·vo·ca·tion [kɔnvə'keiʃn] convocación *f*; (*meeting*) asamblea *f*.
con·voke [kən'vouk] convocar.
con·vo·lu·tion [kɔnvə'lu:ʃn] circunvolución *f* (*a.* ⚕), repliegue *m*.
con·vol·vu·lus [kən'vɔlvjuləs] convólvulo *m*.
con·voy ['kɔnvɔi] **1.** convoy *m*; **2.** convoyar.
con·vulse [kən'vʌls] agitar(se); *nerves* convulsionar; *be* ~*d with laughter* desternillarse de risa; **con'vul·sion** convulsión *f* (*a. fig.*); ~*s pl.* (*of laughter*) paroxismo *m* de risa; **con'vul·sive** □ *cough etc.* convulsivo; convulso.
coo [ku:] arrullar.
cook [kuk] **1.** cocinero (a *f*) *m*; **2.** cocinar; cocer, guisar; *meal* preparar; F *accounts* falsificar; *sl.* ~ *up* maquinar, tramar; **'cook·er** hervidor *m*; (*gas, etc.*) cocina *f*; ⚘ fruta *f* para cocer; **'cook·er·y** arte *m* de cocina; ~ *book* libro *m* de cocina; **'cook·ie** = *cooky*; **'cook·ing** cocina *f*; *attr.* de cocina(r); ~ *soda* bicarbonato *m* sódico; ~ *stove* cocina *f* económica; **'cook·y** pasta *f* seca, pastelito *m* dulce.
cool [ku:l] **1.** □ fresco; tibio (*a. fig.*); *fig.* indiferente, frío; sereno, tranquilo; *b.s.* descarado, audaz; F sin exageración; *a* ~ *thousand* mil libras contantes y sonantes; **2.** fresco *m*; **3.** refrescar(se); (*a.* ~ *down*) moderarse; ~ *down!* ¡cálmate!; ~ *off fig.* enfriarse; **'cool·er** refrigerador *m*; *sl.* trena *f*; **'cool-'head·ed** sereno, sosegado.
coo·lie ['ku:li] culí *m*.
cool·ing ['ku:liŋ] refrigeración *f*; *attr.* refrigerante; *drink* refrescante; ~ *tower* torre *f* de refrigeración; **'cool·ness** frescura *f*; tibieza *f* (*a. fig.*), *etc.*
coomb [ku:m] hondonada *f*.
coon [ku:n] F marrullero *m*; *zo.* mapache *m*.
coop [ku:p] **1.** gallinero *m*, caponera *f*; **2.**: ~ *up* encerrar, enjaular.
co-op [kou'ɔp] F = *cooperative* (*store*).
coop·er ['ku:pər] barrilero *m*, tonelero *m*; **'coop·er·age** tonelería *f*.
co·op·er·ate [kou'ɔpəreit] cooperar; **co·op·er'a·tion** cooperación *f*; **co'op·er·a·tive** [~pərətiv] **1.** cooperativo; *p.* socorrido; **2.** cooperativa *f*; ~ *store* tienda *f* cooperativa; **co'op·er·a·tor** [~reitər] cooperario *m*, cooperador (-a *f*) *m*.
co-opt [kou'ɔpt] *nombrar* (*a una p. a un comité*) *por votación extraordinaria.*
co·or·di·nate 1. [kou'ɔ:rdinit] □ coordenado; (*equal*) igual; *gr.* coordinante; **2.** [~] ⩓ coordenada *f*; **3.** [~neit] coordinar; **co·or·di'na·tion** coordinación *f*.
coot [ku:t] *zo.* focha *f* común; F bobo (a *f*) *m*; **coot·ie** ['~i] *sl.* piojo *m*.
cop [kɔp] *sl.* **1.** coger, prender; *you'll* ~ *it!* ¡las vas a pagar!; **2.** F polizonte *m*, esbirro *m*; *be a fair* ~ caerse con todo el equipo.
co·part·ner ['kou'pɑ:rtnər] consocio *m*; copartícipe *m/f*; **'co'part·ner·ship** coparticipación *f*; asociación *f*.
cope[1] [koup] **1.** *eccl.* capa *f* pluvial; ⚠ albardilla *f*; **2.** ⚠ poner albardilla a; abovedar.
cope[2] [~]: ~ *with* poder con, vencer.
cop·i·er ['kɔpiər] *p.* copiante *m/f*, copista *m/f*; *p.* imitador *m* (-a *f*); ⊕ copiador *m* (-a *f*).
co·pi·lot ['kou'pailət] copiloto *m*.
cop·ing ['koupiŋ] ⚠ albardilla *f*; ~ *stone* coronamiento *m*.
co·pi·ous ['koupjəs] □ copioso; **'co·pi·ous·ness** abundancia *f*, copia *f*.
cop·per[1] ['kɔpər] **1.** cobre *m*; (*utensil*) caldero *m*; (*money*) calderilla *f*; *zo.* ~*head* víbora *f* de cabeza de cobre; **2.** cubrir con cobre; **3.** de cobre, cobreño; (*color*) cobrizo; **'~·plate** plancha *f* de cobre; lámina *f*, estampa *f*; *attr.* bello, bien formado; **'~·smith** cobrero *m*; **'cop·per·y** cobreño; (*color*) cobrizo.
cop·per[2] [~] *sl.* polizonte *m*, esbirro *m*.

cop·pice [ˈkɔpis], **copse** [kɔps] soto *m.*
cop·u·late [ˈkɔpjuleit] tener ayuntamiento; **cop·uˈla·tion** ayuntamiento *m* carnal, coito *m*; **cop·u·la·tive** [ˈ~lətiv] copulativo.
cop·y [ˈkɔpi] **1.** copia *f*; ejemplar *m of book*; número *m of journal*; *typ.* material *m*, original *m*; *v. fair, rough*; **2.** copiar; imitar; (*counterfeit*) contrahacer; **ˈ~·book** cuaderno *m*; **ˈ~·cat** F imitador (-a *f*) *m*; **ˈ~·hold** posesión *f* por enfiteusis; **ˈcop·y·ing ink** tinta *f* de copiar; **ˈcop·y·ist** copista *m/f*; **ˈcop·y·right** derecho *m* de propiedad literaria, copyright *m*; **ˈcop·y-writ·er** escritor *m* de anuncios.
co·quet [kouˈket] coquetear; **co-quet·ry** [ˈ~kitri] coquetería *f*; **co-quette** [~ˈket] coqueta *f*; **coˈquet-tish** □ coquetón, coqueta.
cor·al [ˈkɔrəl] coral *m*; *attr.* coralino; **cor·al·line** [ˈ~lain] *zo.* coralina *f*.
cor·bel [ˈkɔːrbl] ménsula *f*, repisa *f*.
cord [kɔːrd] **1.** cuerda *f*; *anat.* cordón *m*; (*cloth*) pana *f*; **2.** acordonar; **ˈcord·age** ⚓ cordaje *m*; cordería *f*; **ˈcord·ed** acordonado.
cor·dial [ˈkɔːrdiəl] □ cordial *adj. a. su. m*; **cor·dial·i·ty** [~diˈæliti] cordialidad *f*.
cord·mak·er [ˈkɔːrdmeikər] cordelero *m.*
cor·don [ˈkɔːrdən] **1.** cordón *m*; *sanitary* ~ cordón *m* sanitario; **2.** ~ *off* aislar con un cordón.
cor·do·van [ˈkɔːrdəvən] cordobán *m.*
cor·du·roy [ˈkɔːrdərɔi] pana *f*; ~ *road* camino *m* de troncos.
core [kɔːr] **1.** corazón *m*, centro *m*; *fig.* quid *m*, esencia *f*; ⚕ foco *m*; alma *f of cable*; núcleo *m of electromagnet.*
co·re·li·gion·ist [ˈkouriˈlidʒənist] correligionario (a *f*) *m.*
co·re·spond·ent [ˈkourisˈpɔndənt] cómplice *m/f* del demandado en juicio de divorcio.
Co·rin·thi·an [kəˈrinθiən] corintio *adj. a. su. m* (a *f*).
cork [kɔːrk] **1.** corcho *m*; tapón *m* (de corcho); **2.** tapar con corcho (*a.* ~ *up*); **ˈcork·age** *sobrecarga que se cobra en un restaurante sobre una botella de vino*; **ˈcork·er** *sl.* argumento *m* irrefutable; (*lie*) camelo *m*; **ˈcork·ing** F excelente, bárbaro.
cork...: **ˈ~ jack·et** salvavidas *m* de corcho; **ˈ~·screw 1.** sacacorchos *m*; **2.** en caracol, en espiral; **3.** zigzaguear, moverse en espiral; **ˈ~-tipped** *cigarette* emboquillado; **ˈ~ tree** alcornoque *m*; **ˈcork·y** corchoso; F alegre, vivaracho.
cor·mo·rant [ˈkɔːrmərənt] cormorán *m* grande; *fig.* persona *f* rapaz.
corn[1] [kɔːrn] **1.** maíz *m*; *British* trigo *m*; *Scot.* avena *f*; (*kernel of corn, grain of wheat, etc.*) grano *m* (*de maíz, trigo*); (*liquor*) F aguardiente *m*; *sl.* trivialidad *f*, broma *f* gastada; ~ *bread* pan *m* de maíz; ~ *cake* tortilla *f* de maíz; ~ *on the cob* maíz *m* en la mazorca; **2.** acecinar; ~*ed beef* carne *f* de vaca conservada en lata.
corn[2] [~] ⚕ callo *m.*
corn...: **ˈ~·cob** mazorca *f* de maíz; ~ *pipe* pipa *f* de fumar hecha de una mazorca de maíz; **ˈ~·crib** granero *m* para maíz; **ˈ~ cure** ⚕ callicida *f*.
cor·ne·a [ˈkɔːrniə] córnea *f*.
cor·nel [ˈkɔːrnl] cornejo *m.*
cor·nel·ian [kɔːrˈniːljən] cornalina *f*.
cor·ne·ous [ˈkɔːrniəs] córneo.
cor·ner [ˈkɔːrnər] **1.** ángulo *m*; esquina *f* (*esp. street* ~); (*inside*) rincón *m* (*a. fig.*); *fig.* apuro *m*, aprieto *m*; *sport*: córner *m*; ✝ acaparamiento *m*; *fig. turn the* ~ ir saliendo del apuro, darse la vuelta a la tortilla; *out of the* ~ *of one's eye* con el rabillo del ojo; *cut* ~*s* atajar; ~ *flag* banderín *m*; ~ *room* habitación *f* de esquina; **2.** arrinconar (*a. fig.*); ✝ acaparar.
cor·ner...: **ˈ~ cup·board** rinconera *f*; **ˈ~·stone** piedra *f* angular (*a. fig.*); primera piedra *f of a new building*; **ˈ~·ways** diagonalmente.
cor·net [ˈkɔːrnit] ♪ corneta *f*; cucurucho *m of paper etc.*; (*ice cream*) barquillo *m.*
corn...: **ˈ~ ex·change** bolsa *f* de granos; **ˈ~·field** maizal *m*; *British* trigal *m*; *Scot.* avenal *m*; **ˈ~·flour** harina *f* de maíz; **ˈ~·flow·er** cabezuela *f*; **ˈ~·husk** perfolla *f*.
cor·nice [ˈkɔːrnis] cornisa *f* (*a. mount.*).
Cor·nish [ˈkɔːrniʃ] córnico *adj. a. su. m.*
corn...: **ˈ~ liq·uor** chicha *f*; **ˈ~·meal** harina *f* de maíz; **ˈ~ plas·ter** ⚕ emplasto *m* para los callos; **ˈ~ silk** cabellos *m/pl.*, barbas *f/pl.* del maíz; **ˈ~·stalk** tallo *m* de maíz; **ˈ~·starch** almidón *m* de maíz.
cor·nu·co·pi·a [kɔːrnjuˈkoupjə] cornucopia *f*.

corn·y [ˈkɔːrni] de trigo; de maíz; ⚕ calloso; *sl.* ♪ muy sentimental; *sl. joke etc.* pesado, gastado, trivial.
co·rol·la [kəˈrɔlə] corola *f*; **corˈol·la·ry** corolario *m*; consecuencia *f* natural.
co·ro·na [kəˈrounə], *pl.* **coˈro·nae** [~niː] corona *f*; ⚠ cornisa *f*, coronamiento *m*; **coˈro·nal** coronal, coronario; **ˈco·ro·na·ry** ⚕ coronario; ~ *thrombosis* trombosis *f* coronaria; **cor·o·na·tion** [kɔrəˈneiʃn] coronación *f*; **cor·o·ner** [ˈkɔrənər] juez *m* de primera instancia e instrucción; **cor·o·net** [ˈ~nit] corona *f* (de conde *or* marqués); diadema *f*.
cor·po·ral [ˈkɔːrpərəl] **1.** □ corporal; **2.** ⚔ cabo *m*; *eccl.* corporal *m*; **cor·po·rate** [ˈ~rit] □ corporativo; incorporado; **cor·po·ra·tion** [~ˈreiʃn] corporación *f*; F panza *f*, tripa *f*; ✝ sociedad *f* anónima; **cor·po·ra·tive** [ˈ~rətiv] corporativo; **cor·po·re·al** [~ˈpɔːriəl] □ corpóreo; ⚖ material, tangible.
corps [kɔːr], *pl.* **corps** [kɔːrz] cuerpo *m*; ~ *de ballet* cuerpo *m* de baile.
corpse [kɔːrps] cadáver *m*.
cor·pu·lence, cor·pu·len·cy [ˈkɔːrpjuləns(i)] corpulencia *f*; **ˈcor·pu·lent** corpulento.
cor·pus [ˈkɔːrpəs], *pl.* **cor·po·ra** [ˈ~pərə] cuerpo *m* (de leyes, escritos *etc.*); ♀ *Christi* Corpus *m*; ~ *delicti* cuerpo *m* de delito; **cor·pus·cle** [ˈkɔːrpʌsl] corpúsculo *m*; (*blood*) glóbulo *m*.
cor·ral [kɔˈræl] **1.** corral *m*; **2.** acorralar, encerrar.
cor·rect [kəˈrekt] **1.** □ exacto, justo; *behavior* correcto, cumplido; *be* ~ *freq.* tener razón, acertar; **2.** corregir; *exam* puntuar, calificar; **corˈrec·tion** corrección *f*; calificación *f of exam paper*; *I speak under* ~ puede que esté equivocado; **corˈrec·tive** correctivo *adj. a. su. m*; **corˈrect·ness** corrección *f*, urbanidad *f*; exactitud *f*, fidelidad *f*; **corˈrec·tor** corrector *m*.
cor·re·late [ˈkɔrileit] **1.** correlacionar; **2.** correlativo *m*; **cor·reˈla·tion** correlación *f*; **cor·rel·a·tive** [~ˈrelətiv] □ correlativo *adj. a. su. m.*
cor·re·spond [kɔrisˈpɔnd] corresponder (*to* a); corresponderse, cartearse (*with p.* con); **cor·reˈspond·ence** correspondencia *f*; (*collected letters*) epistolario *m*; **cor·reˈspond·ent 1.** □ correspondiente; **2.** correspondiente *m*; (*newspaper*) corresponsal *m*; el (la) que escribe cartas.
cor·ri·dor [ˈkɔridɔːr] pasillo *m*, corredor *m*.
cor·rob·o·rant [kəˈrɔbərənt] corroborante *adj. a. su. m*; **corˈrob·o·rate** [~reit] corroborar; **cor·rob·oˈra·tion** corroboración *f*; **corˈrob·o·ra·tive** [~rətiv] corroborativo.
cor·rode [kəˈroud] corroer (*a. fig.*); **corˈro·dent** corrosivo *adj. a. su. m*; **corˈro·sion** corrosión *f*; **corˈro·sive** □ corrosivo *adj. a. su. m.*
cor·ru·gate [ˈkɔrugeit] arrugar(se); ⊕ acanalar; ~*d iron* hierro *m* ondulado; ~*d paper* papel *m* ondulado.
cor·rupt [kəˈrʌpt] **1.** □ corrompido; *manners* estragado; *text* viciado, depravado; **2.** *v/t.* corromper; estragar; *v/i.* corromperse; (*rot*) podrirse; **corˈrupt·er** corruptor (-a *f*) *m*; **cor·rupt·i·bil·i·ty** [~əˈbiliti] corruptibilidad *f*; **corˈrupt·i·ble** □ corruptible; **corˈrup·tion** corrupción *f* (*a. fig.*); **corˈrup·tive** □ corruptivo.
cor·sage [kɔːrˈsɑːʒ] corpiño *m*, jubón *m*; ⚘ ramillete *m* para la cintura.
cor·sair [ˈkɔːrser] corsario *m*.
cors(e)·let [ˈkɔːrslit] sostén-faja *f*.
cor·set [ˈkɔːrsit] corsé *m*.
cor·ti·cal [ˈkɔːrtikl] cortical.
cor·us·cate [ˈkɔrəskeit] coruscar; **cor·usˈca·tion** brillo *m*, relampagueo *m*.
cor·vette [kɔːrˈvet] corbeta *f*.
cor·vine [ˈkɔːrvain] corvino.
cor·y·phae·us [kɔriˈfiːəs], *pl.* **cor·y·phae·i** [~ˈfiːai] corifeo *m*; **co·ry·phée** [~ˈfei] prima bailarina *f*.
cosh [kɔʃ] *sl.* **1.** cachiporra *f*; **2.** dar de golpes con una cachiporra.
co·sig·na·to·ry [ˈkouˈsignətəri] cosignatorio *adj. a. su. m* (a *f*).
co·sine [ˈkousain] coseno *m*.
co·si·ness [ˈkouzinis] comodidad *f*; calor *m* acogedor *of room etc.*
cos·met·ic [kɔzˈmetik] **1.** cosmético; **2.** cosmético *m*, afeite *m*.
cos·mic, cos·mi·cal [ˈkɔzmik(l)] □ cósmico; ~ *rays* rayos *m/pl.* cósmicos.
cos·mo·gra·pher [kɔzˈmɔgrəfər]

cosmógrafo *m*; **cos'mo·gra·phy** cosmografía *f*.
cos·mo·pol·i·tan [kɔzmə'pɔlitən] cosmopolita *adj. a. su. m/f*.
Cos·sack ['kɔsæk] cosaco *adj. a. su. m* (a *f*).
cos·set ['kɔsit] **1.** cordero *m* domesticado; **2.** mimar, acariciar.
cost [kɔst] **1.** precio *m*; coste *m*, costa *f*; ✝ *at* ~ a costa; *to my* ~ por mi daño; ~*-effective* económico; ~ *of living* costo *m* de la vida; ~*s pl.* ⚖ costas *f/pl.*; *at all* ~*s* a todo trance; **2.** [*irr.*] costar; ~ *what it may* cueste lo que cueste.
cos·ter ['kɔstər] = '~**·mon·ger** vendedor *m* ambulante (de frutas, pescado *etc.*).
cost·ing ['kɔstiŋ] cálculo *m* de coste.
cos·tive ['kɔstiv] □ estreñido.
cost·li·ness ['kɔstlinis] carestía *f*; (*luxury*) fausto *m*; '**cost·ly** costoso, suntuoso.
cost-price ['kɔstprais] (*adv.* al) precio *m* de coste.
cos·tume ['kɔstju:m] **1.** traje *m*; (*fancy dress*) disfraz *m*; ~ *ball* baile *m* de trajes; **2.** trajear; **cos'tum·i·er** [~miər] sastre *m* de teatro.
co·sy ['kouzi] = *cozy*.
cot [kɔt] catre *m*; camita *f* de niño, cuna *f*; ⚓ coy *m*.
co·te·rie ['koutəri] grupo *m*; camarilla *f*.
cot·tage ['kɔtidʒ] casita *f*; chalet *m*; (*laborer's etc.*) barraca *f*, choza *f*, cabaña *f*; ~ *cheese* requesón *m*, naterón *m*; '**cot·tag·er** habitante *m/f* de una choza; veraneante *m/f*.
cot·ter ['kɔtər] chaveta *f*; ~ *pin* clavija *f* hendida, chaveta *f*.
cot·ton ['kɔtn] **1.** algodón *m*; (*plant*) algodonero *m*; ~ *field* algodonal *m*; ~ *gin* ⊕ desmotadera *f* de algodón; ~ *picker* recogedor *m* de algodón; ⊕ máquina *f* para recolectar el algodón; ~*seed* semilla *f* de algodón; ~*seed oil* aceite *m* de algodón; ~ *waste* hilacha *f* de algodón, estopa *f* de algodón; ~*wood* ♀ chopo *m* del Canadá, chopo de Virginia; ~ *wool* algodón *m* (hidrófilo), ouata *f*; **2.** F convenir, congeniar; *sl.* ~ *on to* entender; F ~ *up* hacer buenas migas; '~ **grass** algodonosa *f*; '**cot·ton·y** algodonoso.
co·tyl·e·don [kɔti'li:dən] cotiledón *m*.
couch [kautʃ] **1.** sofá *m*, canapé *m*, meridiana *f*; *poet.* lecho *m*; **2.** acostar(se) (*now only p.p.*); *thoughts* expresar, formular; (*crouch*) agacharse; (*lie in wait*) emboscarse; '~ **grass** hierba *f* rastrera.
cough [kɔf] **1.** tos *f*; ~ *drop* pastilla *f* para la tos; ~ *syrup* jarabe *m* para la tos; **2.** toser; ~ *down speaker* hacer callar (tosiendo); ~ *up* expectorar; *sl.* descolgarse con; *sl.* sacar, producir; (*money*) desdinerarse.
could [kud] *pret. of can*.
couldn't ['kudnt] = *could not*.
cou·lee ['ku:li] cañada *f*, quebrada *f*.
coul·ter ['koultər] reja *f* (del arado).
coun·cil ['kaunsl] junta *f*, consejo *m*; *eccl.* concilio *m*; (*town*) concejo *m*, ayuntamiento *m*; **coun·cil·or** ['~ilər] concejal *m*; '**coun·cil·man** concejal *m*.
coun·sel ['kaunsəl] **1.** consejo *m*; deliberación *f*, consulta *f*; ⚖ abogado *m*; ~ *for the defense* defensor *m*; ~ *for the prosecution* fiscal *m*; *keep one's own* ~ guardar silencio; *take* ~ *with* consultar; **2.** aconsejar; **coun·sel·or** ['~lər] consejero (a *f*) *m*; abogado *m* (*a.* '~**-at-'law**).
count[1] [kaunt] **1.** cuenta *f*, cálculo *m*; suma *f*, total *m*; ⚖ cargo *m*; *boxing*: cuenta *f*; ~*down* cuenta *f* a cero, cuenta atrás; *lose* ~ perder la cuenta; **2.** *v/t.* contar; ~ *out* no incluir, no tener en cuenta; *boxing*: declarar vencido; *v/i.* contar; valer (*a.* ~ *for*); *that doesn't* ~ eso no vale; ~ *on* contar con; ~ *on one's fingers* contar por los dedos.
count[2] [~] conde *m*.
coun·te·nance ['kauntinəns] **1.** semblante *m*, figura *f*; *be out of* ~ estar desconcertado; *keep one's* ~ mantenerse tranquilo; abstenerse de reír; *lose* ~ perturbarse; *put out of* ~ desconcertar; **2.** dar aprobación a; (*encourage*) apoyar.
count·er[1] ['kauntər] (*shop etc.*) mostrador *m*, contador *m*; (*check*) ficha *f*, chapa *f*; (*horse's*) pecho *m*; ⚓ bovedilla *f*; *fenc.* contra *f*; *Geiger* ~ contador *m* Geiger; *sl. under the* ~ por la trastienda.
count·er[2] [~] **1.** en contra; ~ *to* contrario a, opuesto a; *run* ~ *to* oponerse a, ser contrario a; **2.** oponerse a; contradecir; contrarrestar; *blow* parar; ~ *with* contestar con.

coun·ter·act [kauntə'rækt] contrarrestar; neutralizar; **coun·ter'ac·tion** contrarresto *m*, neutralización *f*.
coun·ter·at·tack ['kauntərətæk] **1.** contraataque *m*; **2.** contraatacar.
coun·ter·at·trac·tion ['kauntərə'trækʃn] atracción *f* rival.
coun·ter·bal·ance **1.** ['kauntərbæləns] contrapeso *m*, contrabalanza *f*; **2.** [~'bæləns] contrapesar, contrabalancear.
coun·ter·blast ['kauntərblæst] *fig.* respuesta *f* vigorosa (*to* a); declaración *f* vigorosa.
coun·ter·charge ['kauntərtʃɑːrdʒ] recriminación *f*.
coun·ter·check ['kauntərtʃek] oposición *f*, estorbo *m*; ✝ segunda comprobación *f*.
coun·ter·clock·wise ['kauntər'klɔkwaiz] en sentido contrario al de las agujas del reloj.
coun·ter·cul·ture ['kauntər'kʌltʃər] contracultura *f*.
coun·ter·cur·rent ['kauntər'kʌrənt] contracorriente *f*.
coun·ter·es·pi·o·nage ['kauntər'espiənɑːʒ] contraespionaje *m*.
coun·ter·feit ['kauntərfit] **1.** falsificado, falseado, contrahecho; ~ *money* moneda *f* falsa; **2.** falsificación *f*, contrahechura *f*; *money* moneda *f* falsa; **3.** falsificar, falsear, contrahacer; '**coun·ter·feit·er** falsificador (-a *f*) *m*, falseador (-a *f*) *m*.
coun·ter·foil ['kauntərfɔil] talón *m*.
coun·ter·fort ['kauntərfɔːrt] contrafuerte *m*.
coun·ter·mand **1.** ['kauntər'mænd] contramandato *m*, contraorden *f*; **2.** [~'mænd] contramandar, revocar.
coun·ter·march ['kauntərmɑːrtʃ] **1.** contramarcha *f*; **2.** contramarchar.
coun·ter·mark ['kauntərmɑːrk] **1.** contramarca *f*; **2.** contramarcar.
coun·ter·move ['kauntərmuːv] contrajugada *f*.
coun·ter·or·der ['kauntərɔːrdər] contraorden *f*.
coun·ter·pane ['kauntərpein] colcha *f*, cobertor *m*.
coun·ter·part ['kauntərpɑːrt] copia *f*, imagen *f*; (*complement*) contraparte *f*, complemento *m*.
coun·ter·point ['kauntərpɔint] contrapunto *m*.
coun·ter·poise ['kauntərpɔiz] **1.** contrapeso *m*; **2.** contrapesar.
coun·ter·shaft ['kauntərʃæft] eje *m* intermedio.
coun·ter·sign ['kauntərsain] **1.** contraseña *f* (*a.* ⚔); ✝ *etc.* contramarca *f*; **2.** refrendar.
coun·ter·sink ['kauntərsiŋk] avellanar.
coun·ter·stroke ['kauntərstrouk] contragolpe *m*.
coun·ter·ten·or ['kauntər'tenər] contralto *m*.
coun·ter·weight ['kauntərweit] contrapeso *m*.
count·ess ['kauntis] condesa *f*.
count·ing house ['kauntiŋhaus] escritorio *m*, despacho *m*; oficina *f*.
count·less ['kauntlis] sin cuento.
coun·tri·fied ['kʌntrifaid] rústico, campesino; *contp.* palurdo.
coun·try ['kʌntri] **1.** país *m*; patria *f*; (*not town*) campo *m*; *parl. appeal* (*or go*) *to the* ~ celebrar elecciones generales; ⚔ *live off the* ~ vivir sobre el país; **2.** *attr.* de campo, rural; ~ *club* club *m* campestre; ~ *estate* finca *f*; ~ *folk* gente *f* del campo; ~ *house* quinta *f*, casa *f* de campo; ~ *life* vida *f* del campo; ~ *seat* finca *f*, casa *f* solariega; '~**·man** campesino *m*; *fellow* ~ compatriota *m*; '~**·side** campo *m*; (*open* ~) campiña *f*; '~**·wom·an** campesina *f*.
coun·ty ['kaunti] condado *m*; *attr.* aristocrático; ~ **seat** = ~ **town** cabeza *f* de partido.
coup [kuː] golpe *m*; ~ *d'état* golpe *m* de estado; ~ *de grâce* golpe *m* de gracia.
cou·ple ['kʌpl] **1.** par *m*; (*people*) pareja *f*; F dos más o menos; *married* ~ matrimonio *m*; **2.** juntar, unir; *animals* aparear; ⊕ acoplar, enganchar; F casar; '**cou·pler** *radio*: acoplador *m*; '**cou·plet** pareado *m*; par *m* de versos.
cou·pling ['kʌpliŋ] ⊕ acoplamiento *m*; 🚂 enganche *m*.
cou·pon ['kuːpɔn] cupón *m*; (*football*) boleto *m*.
cour·age ['kʌridʒ] valor *m*, valentía *f*; ~! ¡ánimo!; *pluck up* ~ hacer de tripas corazón; **cou·ra·geous** [kə'reidʒəs] □ valiente.
cour·i·er ['kuriər] estafeta *f*, correo *m* diplomático; agente *m* de turismo.
course [kɔːrs] **1.** curso *m*; ⚔ trayectoria *f*; *fig.* proceder *m*, camino *m*; ⚓ rumbo *m*; plato *m of meal*; transcurso *m*, paso *m of time*; hilada *f of bricks*;

corriente *f of water*; (*golf*) campo *m*; (*race*) pista *f*; *in due* ~ a su tiempo; andando el tiempo; *in the* ~ *of* durante; *of* ~ por supuesto, desde luego; *give* ~ *to* dar curso a; **2.** *v/t.* dar caza a, perseguir; *v/i.* correr (*freq.* ~ *along*).

court [kɔːrt] **1.** corte *f*; ⚖ tribunal *m*; *sport*: pista *f*; ⚠ patio *m*; (*house*) palacete *m*, mansión *f* suntuosa; *general* ~ asamblea *f* legislativa; *in open* ~ en pleno tribunal; *pay one's* ~ *to* hacer la corte a; **2.** cortejar, galantear; hacer la corte a; *favor etc.* solicitar, buscar; ˈ~ **card** carta *f* de figura; ˈ~ **day** día *m* hábil; **cour·teous** [ˈkəːrtiəs] □ cortés; **cour·tesan,** *a.* **cour·te·zan** [kɔːrtiˈzæn] cortesana *f*, hetera *f*; **cour·te·sy** [ˈkəːrtisi] cortesía *f*, gentileza *f*; **court·house** [ˈkɔːrtˈhaus] palacio *m* de justicia; **cour·ti·er** [ˈ~jər] cortesano *m*; ˈ**court·ly** urbano, elegante; *b.s.* obsequioso, halagüeño; ~ *love* amor *m* cortés.

court...: ˈ~-ˈ**mar·tial 1.** consejo *m* de guerra; **2.** someter a consejo de guerra; ˈ~ ˈ**plas·ter** esparadrapo *m*; ˈ~**·room** sala *f* de justicia, tribunal *m*; ˈ~**·ship** cortejo *m*; noviazgo *m*; ˈ~ˈ**yard** patio *m*, atrio *m*.

cous·in [ˈkʌzn] primo (a *f*) *m*; *first* ~, ~ *german* primo (a *f*) *m* carnal; *country* ~ pariente *m* pueblerino.

cove[1] [kouv] **1.** ⚓ cala *f*, ensenada *f*; escondrijo *m*; ⚠ bovedilla *f*; **2.** abovedar.

cove[2] [~] *sl.* tío *m*, tipo *m*.

cov·e·nant [ˈkʌvinənt] **1.** pacto *m*, convenio *m*; *Bible*: ♀ Alianza *f*; **2.** pactar, convenir.

cov·er [ˈkʌvər] **1.** (*lid*) tapa *f*, cubierta *f*; (*cutlery*) cubierto *m*; colcha *f on bed*; forro *m*, cubierta *f of book*; portada *f of magazine*; (*insurance*) cobertura *f*; *mot.* (*a. outer* ~) cubierta *f*; *fig. b.s.* disimulación *f*, pretexto *m*; ~ *charge* precio *m* del cubierto; ~ *girl* F muchacha *f* hermosa en la portada de una revista; ~*up* efugio *m*, subterfugio *m*; *break* ~ salir a campo raso; *take* ~ abrigarse (*from* de); esconderse; *under* ~ clandestinamente; *under* ~ *of* so pretexto de; *under separate* ~ por separado; **2.** cubrir (*a. fig.*); revestir; tapar *with lid etc.*; (*hide*) ocultar; *fig.* disimular; *fig.* incluir; *distance* recorrer; ⚔ apuntar a, dominar; *retreat* cubrir; (*stallion*) cubrir; ~ *in* llenar; ~ *over* cubrir, revestir (*with* de, con); ~ *up* tapar, correr el velo sobre; *fig.* ocultar; disimular; ~*ed bridge* puente *m* cubierto; ~*ed wagon* carromato *m*; ~*ed wire* alambre *m* forrado; ˈ**cov·er·ing** cubierta *f*, envoltura *f*; ~ *letter* carta *f* adjunta; **cov·er·let** [ˈ~lit] cubrecama *m*, colcha *f*.

cov·ert [ˈkʌvərt] **1.** □ cubierto, secreto, disimulado; **2.** *zo.* guarida *f*; abrigo *m*; ⚘ soto *m*.

cov·et [ˈkʌvit] codiciar; ˈ**cov·et·ous** □ codicioso (*of* de); avaro; ˈ**cov·et·ous·ness** codicia *f*; avaricia *f*.

cov·ey [ˈkʌvi] nidada *f* de perdices; *fig.* grupo *m*, peña *f*.

cow[1] [kau] vaca *f*; hembra *f* del elefante *etc.*

cow[2] [~] intimidar, acobardar.

cow·ard [ˈkauərd] □ cobarde *adj. a. su. m*; ˈ**cow·ard·ice,** ˈ**cow·ard·liness** cobardía *f*; ˈ**cow·ard·ly** cobarde.

cow·boy [ˈkaubɔi] vaquero *m*; gaucho *m S.Am.*; ˈ**cow·catch·er** 🚂 rastrillo *m* delantero, quitapiedras *m*.

cow·er [ˈkauər] agacharse (*esp.* por causa de miedo).

cow·herd [ˈkauhəːrd] pastor *m* de ganado; ˈ**cow·hide** cuero *m*; (*whip*) zurriago *m*.

cowl [kaul] capucha *f*; (*habit*) cogulla *f*; (*chimney*) sombrerete *m*.

cow...: ˈ~**·lick** mechón *m*, remolino *m* (*pelos que se levantan sobre la frente*); ˈ~**·pox** vacuna *f*; ˈ~**·punch·er** F vaquero *m*; ˈ~ **shed** establo *m*; ˈ~**·slip** primavera *f*.

cox [kɔks] F **1.** = *coxswain*; **2.** *v/i.* servir de timonel; *v/t.* gobernar.

cox·comb [ˈkɔkskoum] farolero *m*, mequetrefe *m*.

cox·swain [ˈkɔkswein, ˈkɔksn] timonel *m*.

coy [kɔi] □ reservado, tímido, recatado; ˈ**coy·ness** recato *m*, timidez *f*.

coz·en [ˈkʌzn] *lit.* defraudar, engañar.

co·zy [ˈkouzi] **1.** cómodo; **2.** cubretetera *f for teapot*.

crab[1] [kræb] cangrejo *m*, centolla *f*; *ast.* ♀ Cáncer *m*; ⊕ torno *m*; grúa *f*; *catch a* ~ faltar con el remo.

crab[2] [~] ⚘ (*freq.* ˈ~ **ap·ple**) manzana *f* silvestre; (*tree*) manzano *m* silvestre; F persona *f* desabrida, cascarrabias *m/f*; ~ *grass* garranchuelo *m*;

crab·bed ['~id] □ avinagrado, amargado; (*disagreeable*) desabrido, desapacible; *writing* indescifrable, mal formado.

crab louse ['kræblaus] ladilla *f*.

crack [kræk] **1.** grieta *f*, hendedura *f*; (*sound*) crujido *m*; chasquido *m* (*a. of whip*), estallido *m*; F instante *m*; *sl.* chiste *m*, cuchufleta *f*; *attr.* F de primera; F *shot* certero; *at* (*the*) ~ *of dawn* al romper el alba; **2.** *v/t.* agrietar, hender; hacer chasquear; *safe, bottle* abrir; *joke* decir, contar; *nut* cascar; *sl.* ~ *up* elogiar; *v/i.* agrietarse, henderse; chasquear; (*window*) rajarse; (*voice*) cascarse; F ~ *down on* castigar severamente; F ~ *up* fracasar; (✈ *etc.*) desbaratarse; ⚕ perder la salud; '~-**brained** chiflado, loco; '**cracked** agrietado; *window* rajado; F chiflado; '**crack·er** triquitraque *m*, petardo *m*; (*biscuit*) cracker *m*, blanco *m* de baja clase; '**crack·er·jack** F la monda, el non plus ultra; '**crack·jaw** trabalenguas *m*; '**crack·le 1.** crujir, crepitar; **2.** crujido *m*, crepitación *f*; '**crack·le·ware** grietado *m*; '**crack·ling** chicharrón *m*; = *crackle* 2; **crack·nel** ['~nl] *approx.* galleta *f* ligera; turrón *m*; '**crack-up** F fracaso *m*; ⚕ colapso *m*; ✈ aterrizaje *m* violento.

cra·dle ['kreidl] **1.** cuna *f* (*a.* ⚓ *a. fig.*); ⚒ artesa *f* oscilante; △ plataforma *f* colgante; ~ *song* canción *f* de cuna; **2.** poner en la cuna; *fig.* criar.

craft [kræft] oficio *m*, empleo *m*; (*skill*) destreza *f*; *b.s.* maña *f*, astucia *f*; ⚓ embarcación *f*, barco *m*; **craft·i·ness** astucia *f*, socarronería *f*; '**crafts·man** artesano *m*, artífice *m*; '**crafts·man·ship** artesanía *f*, artificio *m*; '**craft·y** □ astuto, socarrón.

crag [kræg] peñasco *m*, risco *m*, despeñadero *m*; '**crag·gy** peñascoso, escarpado, arriscado.

crake [kreik] polluela *f*.

cram [kræm] embutir, rellenar; *hen* cebar; F empollar; F ~ *o.s.* (*with food*) hartarse; '~-'**full** atestado, repleto (*of* de); '**cram·mer** F empollón (-a *f*) *m*.

cramp [kræmp] **1.** ⊕ grapa *f*; ⊕ abrazadera *f*; ⚕ calambre *m*; **2.** engrapar, lañar: ~ (*one's style*) cortarle las alas a uno; **cramped** estrecho, apretado; ⚕ entumecido; '**cramp iron** grapa *f*, laña *f*.

cram·pon ['kræmpən] garfio *m*, arpeo *m*; *mount.* crampón *m*.

cran·ber·ry ['krænbəri] arándano *m* agrio.

crane [krein] **1.** *orn.* grulla *f* (común); ⊕ grúa *f*; **2.** levantar (*or* mover) con grúa; *neck* estirar; **crane·fly** ['~flai] típula *f*; '**crane's-bill** geranio *m*, pico *m* de cigüeña.

cra·ni·um ['kreiniəm] cráneo *m*.

crank [kræŋk] **1.** ⊕ manivela *f*, manubrio *m*; F persona *f* rara, maniático *m*; extravagante *m*; concepto raro *m*; **2.** *mot.* hacer arrancar con la manivela (*a.* ~ *up*); '~**case** cárter *m* del cigüeñal; '**crank·i·ness** F chifladura *f*, desequilibrio *m*; '**crank·shaft** eje *m* del cigüeñal; '**crank·y** chiflado, extravagante.

cran·nied ['krænid] grietado, grietoso; '**cran·ny** grieta *f*, hendedura *f*.

crape [kreip] crespón *m*.

craps [kræps] juego *m* de los dados.

crap·u·lence ['kræpjuləns] crápula *f*; '**crap·u·lent** crapuloso.

crash [kræʃ] **1.** (*noise*) estrépito *m*, estallido *m*; *mot.*, 🚃 *etc.* accidente *m*, choque *m*, encontronazo *m*; *fig.* fracaso *m*; ⚚ quiebra *f*; ~ *dive* sumersión *f* instantánea *of submarine*; ~ *helmet* casco *m* protector; ~ *landing* aterrizaje *m* violento; ~ *program* programa *m* intensivo; **2.** romperse con estrépito; *mot.*, 🚃 tener un accidente; ✈ estrellarse; ⚚ quebrar; ~ *a party sl.* colarse, entrar de gorra; ~ *into* chocar con, estrellarse contra.

crass [kræs] tupido, espeso; *fig.* craso.

crate [kreit] caja *f*, cajón *m* (de embalaje); jaula *f* (de listones).

cra·ter ['kreitər] cráter *m*.

cra·vat [krə'væt] corbata *f*.

crave [kreiv] implorar, solicitar; ansiar, anhelar (*for, after acc.*).

cra·ven ['kreivn] cobarde *adj. a. su. m.*

crav·ing ['kreiviŋ] ansia *f*; regosto *m*, deseo *m* vehemente (*for* de).

craw·fish ['krɔːfiʃ] **1.** ástaco *m*; **2.** F desdecirse, rajarse.

crawl [krɔːl] **1.** arrastramiento *m*; (*on all fours*) gateamiento *m*; *swimming*: crol *m*, crawl *m*; corral *m* (para peces); **2.** arrastrarse; gatear, ir a gatas; F (*a.* ~ *along*) ir a paso de

tortuga; F *fig.* ~ *with* estar cuajado (*or* plagado) de; pulular de.
cray·fish ['kreifiʃ] ástaco *m*.
cray·on ['kreiən] **1.** creyón *m*, tizna *f*; **2.** dibujar con creyón.
craze [kreiz] **1.** manía *f* (*for* por), locura *f*; (*fashion*) moda *f*; *be the* ~ estar de moda; **2.** estriar; **crazed** enloquecido, alocado; '**cra·zi·ness** locura *f*; chifladura *f*; '**cra·zy** □ loco (*for, about* por); chiflado; *idea* disparatado; ⚠ en mosaico; ⚠ *building etc.* desvencijado; *drive* ~ volver loco; *quite* ~, *sl.* ~ *as a bedbug* loco rematado; ~ *quilt* centón *m*.
creak [kri:k] **1.** crujido *m*, chirrido *m*; rechinamiento *m*; **2.** crujir, chirriar; rechinar; '**creak·y** □ rechinador.
cream [kri:m] **1.** crema *f*; nata *f*; *fig.* flor *f* y nata (*of* de); *cold* ~ crema *f*; ~ *puff* bollo *m* de crema; ~ *separator* desnatadora *f*; ~ *of tartar* crémor *m* (tártaro); **2.** formar nata; *milk* desnatar; *butter* batir; *fig.* quitar lo mejor de; **3.** color de crema; '**cream·er·y** mantequería *f*; lechería *f*; '**cream·y** □ cremoso.
crease [kri:s] **1.** pliegue *m*, arruga *f*; (*fold*) doblez *m*; (*trousers*) raya *f*; ~ *resisting* inarrugable; **2.** arrugar(se), plegar(se).
cre·ate [kri'eit] crear; originar, ocasionar; *sl.* hacer alharacas; **cre'a·tion** creación *f*; **cre'a·tive** creador; fecundo; **cre'a·tor** creador *m*; **crea·ture** ['kri:tʃər] criatura *f*; (*p.*) hechura *f*; bicho *m*; ~ *comforts pl. las cosas que confortan el cuerpo.*
crèche [kreʃ] guardería *f* infantil.
cre·dence ['kri:dəns] fe *f*, creencia *f*; *give* ~ *to* dar fe a; **cre·den·tials** [kri'denʃlz] *pl.* credenciales *f/pl.*
cred·i·bil·i·ty [kredi'biliti] credibilidad *f*; **cred·i·ble** ['kredəbl] □ creíble.
cred·it ['kredit] **1.** crédito *m* (*a.* ✝); *on* ~ a crédito; *give* ~ *to* creer; ✝ abrir crédito a; *do a p.* ~ honrar; *take* ~ *for* atribuirse el crédito de; **2.** *attr.* ✝ crediticio; **3.** creer; ✝ acreditar; ~ *a p. with* atribuir a una p. el mérito de; '**cred·it·a·ble** □ estimable, honorable; '**cred·i·tor** acreedor (-a *f*) *m*.
cre·du·li·ty [kri'dju:liti] credulidad *f*; **cred·u·lous** □ crédulo.
creed [kri:d] credo *m*.
creek [kri:k] cala *f*, ensenada *f*; río *m*, riachuelo *m*.
creel [kri:l] cesta *f* (para pescado); jaula *f* de mimbre (para la langosta).
creep [kri:p] **1.** [*irr.*] arrastrarse; gatear; moverse despacio y con cautela; (*flesh*) sentir hormigueo; ~ *up on s.o.* acercarse a uno sin que se dé cuenta; **2.** arrastramiento *m*; *sl. be a* ~ reptar; ~*s pl.* hormigueo *m*; *give the* ~*s* horripilar; '**creep·er** (planta *f*) enredadera *f*; '**creep·y** hormigueante; horripilante.
cre·mate [kri'meit] incinerar; **cre'ma·tion** incineración *f* (de cadáveres); **crem·a·to·ri·um** [kremə'tɔ:riəm], **cre·ma·to·ry** ['~tɔ:ri] horno *m* crematorio.
cren·el·at·ed ['krenileitid] almenado.
Cre·ole ['kri:oul] criollo *adj. a. su. m* (a *f*).
cre·o·sote ['kriəsout] creosota *f*.
crep·i·tate ['krepiteit] crepitar; **crep·i'ta·tion** crepitación *f*.
crept [krept] *pret. a. p.p. of creep* 1.
cre·pus·cu·lar [kri'pʌskjulər] crepuscular.
cres·cent ['kresnt] **1.** creciente; **2.** cuarto *m* creciente (*or* menguante); *heraldry*: creciente *m*; (*street*) calle *f* en forma de cuarto creciente.
cress [kres] mastuerzo *m*.
cres·set ['kresit] tedero *m*.
crest [krest] cresta *f*; '**crest·ed** crestado; ~ *lark* cogujada *f*; '**crest·fall·en** alicaído, abatido.
cre·ta·ceous [kri'teiʃəs] cretáceo.
cre·tin ['kretin] cretino *m*.
cret·onne [kre'tɔn] cretona *f*.
cre·vasse [kri'væs] grieta *f* en un helero; brecha *f* en un dique.
crev·ice ['krevis] grieta *f*.
crew[1] [kru:] ⚓ tripulación *f*; equipo *m*; (*gang*) banda *f*, pandilla *f*.
crew[2] [~] *pret. of crow* 2.
crib [krib] **1.** pesebre *m*; cama *f* pequeña para niños; F *school*: chuleta *f*; F plagio *m*; hucha *f* para maíz; *sl. crack a* ~ robar una casa; **2.** F plagiar; F usar una chuleta; '**crib·bage** *juego de naipes.*
crick [krik] tortícolis *m* (*esp.* ~ *in the neck*); calambre *m*.
crick·et[1] ['krikit] *zo.* grillo *m*.
crick·et[2] [~] **1.** cricquet *m*; F juego *m* limpio; **2.** jugar al cricquet; '**crick·et·er** cricquetero *m*.
cri·er ['kraiər] pregonero *m*.

crime [kraim] crimen *m.*
crim·i·nal ['kriminl] criminal *adj. a. su. m/f*; ~ *code* código *m* penal; ~ *law* derecho *m* penal; ~ *negligence* imprudencia *f* temeraria; **crim·i·nal·i·ty** [~'næliti] criminalidad *f*; **crim·i·nol·o·gy** [~'nɔlədʒi] criminología *f.*
crimp[1] [krimp] ⚔, ⚓ reclutar por fuerza.
crimp[2] [~] **1.** rizar, encrespar; ~*ing iron* encrespador *m*; **2.** rizo *m*; *sl. put a* ~ *in* estorbar.
crim·son ['krimzn] **1.** carmesí *adj. a. su. m*; **2.** enrojecer(se).
cringe [krindʒ] **1.** agacharse, encogerse; *fig.* reptar; **2.** servilismo *m.*
crin·kle ['kriŋkl] **1.** arruga *f*; *sl.* parné *m*; **2.** arrugar(se); (*hair*) rizar (se); '**crink·ly** arrugado; rizado.
crin·o·line ['krinəli:n] crinolina *f.*
crip·ple ['kripl] **1.** lisiado (a *f*) *m*, mutilado *m* (a *f*), tullido (a *f*) *m*; **2.** lisiar, mutilar; *ship* desarbolar; *fig.* perjudicar, estropear.
cri·sis ['kraisis], *pl.* **cri·ses** ['~si:z] crisis *f.*
crisp [krisp] **1.** □ crespo, rizado; frágil pero duro; tostado; *style* cortado; *air* fresco, refrescante; *su.* ~*s pl.* patatas *f/pl.* inglesas; **2.** encrespar, rizar; tostar *in oven.*
criss·cross ['kriskrɔs] **1.** cruz *f*, líneas *f/pl.* cruzadas; **2.** *adv.* en cruz; **3.** trazar líneas cruzadas (sobre); entrecruzarse; F ~ (*my heart*)! ¡palabra de honor!
cri·te·ri·on [krai'tiriən], *pl.* **cri'te·ri·a** [~ə] criterio *m.*
crit·ic ['kritik] crítico *m*; *b.s.* criticón (-a *f*) *m*; '**crit·i·cal** □ crítico; (*hyper-*) criticón; *be* ~ *of* criticar; **crit·i·cism** ['~sizm], **cri·ti·que** [kri'ti:k] crítica *f*; **crit·i·cize** ['~saiz] criticar.
croak [krouk] **1.** (*crow*) graznar; (*frog*) croar; (*p.*) gruñir; *sl.* estirar la pata; **2.** graznido *m*; canto *m of frog*; '**croak·er** gruñidor *m.*
Cro·at ['krouət], **Cro·a·tian** [krou'eiʃn] croata *adj. a. su. m/f.*
cro·chet ['krouʃei] **1.** croché *m*; ~ *needle* aguja *f* de gancho; **2.** hacer croché; ~*ing* labor *f* de ganchillo.
crock [krɔk] vasija *f* de barro; F (*p.*) carcamal *m*; (*car*) cacharro *m*; '**crock·er·y** loza *f*; vajilla *f*, los platos.
croc·o·dile ['krɔkədail] cocodrilo *m*; ~ *tears* lágrimas *f/pl.* de cocodrilo.
cro·cus ['kroukəs] azafrán *m.*
croft·er ['krɔftər] arrendatario *m* de una finca pequeña.
crom·lech ['krɔmlek] crómlech *m.*
crone [kroun] vieja *f* arrugada.
cro·ny ['krouni] F compinche *m.*
crook [kruk] **1.** (*shepherd's*) cayado *m*; ⊕ gancho *m*; (*bend*) curva *f*; F criminal *m*, fullero *m*; *v. hook*; **2.** encorvar(se); **crook·ed** ['~kid] □ encorvado, curvo; *fig.* torcido, avieso; F *go* ~ torcerse.
croon [kru:n] canturrear; '**croon·er** vocalista *m/f* (sentimental).
crop [krɔp] **1.** cosecha *f* (*a. fig.*); *orn.* buche *m*; (*hair*) cabellera *f*, corte *m* de pelo; (*whip*) látigo *m* mocho; ~ *dusting* aerofumigación *f*, fumigación *f* aérea; **2.** *v/t.* cortar; desorejar; *top* desmochar; trasquilar (*a. fig.*); *grass* pacer; *v/i.* ~ *up geol.* aflorar; F manifestarse inesperadamente; salir; '**crop·per** ⚘ que da cosecha; *sl.* caída *f* severa; F *come a* ~ caer; fracasar.
cro·quet [krou'kei] juego *m* de croquet.
cro·sier ['krouʒər] báculo *m* del obispo.
cross [krɔs] **1.** cruz *f*; *biol.* cruzamiento *m*; (*burden*) cruz *f*; *on the* ~ diagonalmente; *make the sign of the* ♀ hacer la señal de la cruz; **2.** □ transversal; opuesto (*to* a); F malhumorado; F arisco, de mal genio; *get* ~ enfadarse, ponerse furioso; *at* ~ *purposes* sin comprenderse uno a otro; **3.** *v/t.* atravesar, cruzar; *p.* contrariar; *breed* cruzar; ~ *o.s.* santiguarse; ~ *out* tachar; ~ *one's mind* ocurrírsele a uno; *teleph. the wires are* ~*ed* hay un cruce en las líneas; *v/i.* cruzar (*a. letters*); ~ *over* atravesar de un lado a otro; '~**·bar** travesaño *m*; '~**·beam** viga *f* transversal; '~**-bench** *parl. escaños de los independientes*; ~**·bones** *pl.* huesos *m/pl.* cruzados (*símbolo de la muerte*); '~**·bow** ballesta *f*; '~**·breed 1.** híbrido; **2.** cruzar; '~'**coun·try** a campo traviesa; ~ *race* cross *m*; '~**·cur·rent** contracorriente *f*; '~**·cut saw** sierra *f* de trazar; '~**ex·am·i'na·tion** ⚖ repregunta *f*; interrogatorio *m* severo; ~**-ex·am·ine** ['krɔsig'zæmin] ⚖ repre-

guntar; interrogar rigurosamente; **ˈ~-eyed** bizco, bisojo, ojituerto; **ˈ~-grained** de contrafibra; *fig.* áspero, esquivo; *be* ~ ser de mala uva; **ˈcross·ing** ⚓ travesía *f*; (*roads*) cruce *m*; (*ford*) vado *m*; ~ *gate* barrera *f*, barrera de paso a nivel; ~ *point* punto *m* de cruce.

cross...: **ˈ~-ˈlegged** con las piernas cruzadas; en cuclillas; **ˈ~·ly** con enfado; resentido; **ˈ~·patch** F malhumorado (a *f*) *m*; **ˈ~·piece** travesaño *m*; **ˈ~ ˈref·er·ence** contrarreferencia *f*, remisión *f*; **ˈ~·road** camino *m* que cruza; (*a.* ~*s pl.*) cruce *m*, encrucijada *f*; **ˈ~ sec·tion** sección *f* transversal; *fig.* sección *f* representativa; **ˈ~ street** calle *f* traviesa, calle de travesía; **ˈ~·wise** al través; en cruz; **ˈ~·word** (*a.* ~ *puzzle*) crucigrama *m*.

crotch [krɔtʃ] bifurcación *f*; *anat.* horcajadura *f*; **crotch·et** [ˈ~it] ♪ negra *f*; capricho *m*; **ˈcrotch·et·y** F caprichoso; (*disagreeable*) desabrido.

crouch [krautʃ] agacharse, encogerse.

croup[1] [kru:p] (*horse's*) grupa *f*.

croup[2] [~] ⚕ crup *m*.

crou·pi·er [kru:ˈpjei, ˈkru:piər] coime *m*.

crow [krou] **1.** corneja *f*; *as the* ~ *flies* en derechura; F *eat* ~ cantar la palinodia; F *have a* ~ *to pick with* tener que habérselas con; **2.** [*irr.*] cantar (el gallo); *fig.* alardear, exultar; **ˈ~·bar** palanca *f*.

crowd [kraud] **1.** multitud *f*, muchedumbre *f*; gentío *m*; *contp.* vulgo *m*; *sport*: espectadores *m/pl.*; *follow the* ~ irse tras el hilo de la gente; *fig. pass in a* ~ no descollar; **2.** *v/t.* amontonar, atestar; *people* apiñar (*a.* ~ *together*); ~ *on sail* hacer fuerza de vela; ~*ed* atestado (*with* de); concurrido; *be* ~*ed out* (*place*) estar de bote en bote; (*p.*) ser excluido; *v/i.* agolparse, arremolinarse (*a.* ~ *together*, ~ *around*).

crow·foot [ˈkroufut] ranúnculo *m*.

crown [kraun] **1.** corona *f*; cruz *f of anchor*; copa *f of hat*; cima *f of hill*; ⚠ coronamiento *m*; ~ *prince* príncipe *m* heredero; ~ *princess* princesa *f* heredera; **2.** coronar; completar, terminar; (*reward*) premiar; *sl.* golpear en la cabeza; ~*d head* testa *f* coronada.

crow's-nest [ˈkrouznest] ⚓ torre *f* de vigía.

cru·cial [ˈkru:ʃiəl] □ decisivo, crítico; *shape* cruciforme; **cru·ci·ble** [ˈkru:sibl] crisol *m* (*a. fig.*); **cru·ci·fix** [ˈ~fiks] crucifijo *m*, cruz *f*; **cru·ci·fix·ion** [~ˈfikʃn] crucifixión *f*; **ˈcru·ci·form** cruciforme; **cru·ci·fy** [ˈ~fai] crucificar; *fig.* mortificar.

crude [kru:d] □ (*raw*) crudo; *fig.* tosco, grosero; *b.s. work* chapucero; ⚠ *etc.* sin labrar; **ˈcrude·ness, cru·di·ty** [ˈ~iti] tosquedad *f*; grosería *f*, rudeza *f*.

cru·el [ˈkruəl] □ cruel (*a. fig.*); **ˈcruel·ty** crueldad *f*.

cru·et [ˈkru:it] vinagrera *f*; **ˈ~ stand** angarillas *f/pl*.

cruise [kru:z] **1.** viaje *m* por mar, crucero *m*; excursión *f*; ~ *missile* misil crucero *m*; **2.** cruzar; *cruising radius* autonomía *f*; *cruising speed* velocidad *f* de crucero; *mot.* velocidad *f* económica; **ˈcruis·er** ⚓ crucero *m*; **ˈ~ weight** peso *m* medio fuerte.

crul·ler [ˈkrʌlər] buñuelo *m*.

crumb [krʌm] **1.** migaja *f* (*a. fig.*); miga *f of loaf*; **2.** desmigar; cubrir con migajas; **crum·ble** [ˈ~bl] *v/t.* desmigar; *v/i.* desmoronarse (*a. fig.*; *a.* ~ *away*); **ˈcrum·bling, ˈcrum·bly** desmenuzable, desmoronadizo; **crumb·y** [ˈkrʌmi] lleno de migajas.

crum·my [ˈkrʌmi] *sl.* sucio; *joke* gastado; *bar etc.* de baja categoría.

crum·pet [ˈkrʌmpit] bollo *m* blando tostado.

crum·ple [ˈkrʌmpl] arrugar(se), plegar(se); (*dress*) ajar(se); *fig.* (*a.* ~ *up*) ceder, desplomarse.

crunch [krʌntʃ] ronzar; (*ground*) crujir.

cru·sade [kru:ˈseid] **1.** cruzada *f* (*a. fig.*); **2.** participar en una cruzada; ~ *for* hacer campaña en pro de (*or* por); **cruˈsad·er** cruzado *m*.

crush [krʌʃ] **1.** aplastar; *grapes etc.* prensar, estrujar; *stones etc.* moler; *dress* ajar; *fig.* abrumar, anonadar; ~*ing fig.* aplastante; **2.** presión *f* violenta, aplastamiento *m*; (*crowd*) agolpamiento *m*, bullaje *m*; *sl. have a* ~ *on* perder la chaveta por; **ˈcrus·her** molino *m* (de piedra *esp.*).

crust [krʌst] **1.** corteza *f*; (⚕ *a. wine*) costra *f*; ⚕ escara *f*; (*old bread*) mendrugo *m*; **2.** encostrarse; **ˈcrust·y** □ costroso; *fig.* áspero, desabrido.

crutch [krʌtʃ] muleta *f* (*a. fig.*).
crux [krʌks] enigma *m*; lo esencial.
cry [krai] **1.** grito *m*; lloro *m*, lamento *m*; (*seller's*) pregón *m*; *be a far* ~ estar lejos, ser mucho camino; *have a* (*good*) ~ llorar (a mares); *in full* ~ acosando de cerca; **2.** gritar; llorar; *wares* pregonar; ~ *down* rebajar, desacreditar; ~ *for* clamar por; ~ *for joy* llorar de alegría; ~ *off* retirarse, rajarse; *s.t.* renunciar (a), romper; ~ *out* gritar, publicar en voz alta; ~ *out* (*against*) protestar (contra); ~ *up* encarecer; ˈ**~·ba·by** llorón (-a *f*) *m*; ˈ**cry·ing** *fig.* atroz, enorme.
crypt [kript] cripta *f*; ˈ**cryp·tic** □ oculto, misterioso.
crys·tal [ˈkristl] **1.** cristal *m*; ~ *ball* bola *f* de cristal; *as clear as* ~ tan claro como el agua; **2.** = **crys·tal·line** [ˈ~təlain] cristalino; **crys·tal·liˈza·tion** cristalización *f*; ˈ**crys·tal·lize** cristalizarse; ~*d fruit* fruta *f* escarchada.
cub [kʌb] cachorro *m*; *fig.* rapaz *m*.
cub·by-hole [ˈkʌbihoul] chiribitil *m*.
cube [kju:b] **1.** cubo *m*; ~ *root* raíz *f* cúbica; **2.** cubicar; ˈ**cu·bic,** ˈ**cu·bi·cal** □ cúbico.
cu·bi·cle [ˈkjubikl] cubículo *m*.
cu·bism [ˈkju:bizm] cubismo *m*; ˈ**cu·bist** cubista *m*.
cuck·old [ˈkʌkəld] **1.** cornudo *m*; **2.** encornudar, poner los cuernos a.
cuck·oo [ˈkuku:] **1.** cuc(lill)o *m*; **2.** *sl.* chiflado.
cu·cum·ber [ˈkju:kʌmbə] cohombro *m*, pepino *m*; *cool as a* ~ fresco como una lechuga; *fig.* sosegado.
cud [kʌd] bolo *m* alimenticio; *v.chew*.
cud·dle [ˈkʌdl] **1.** abrazo *m*, caricia *f*; **2.** acariciar, abrazar; ~ *up* arrimarse (*to* a).
cudg·el [ˈkʌdʒl] **1.** porra *f*; *take up the* ~*s for* ir a la defensa de; **2.** aporrear, apalear; ~ *one's brains* devanarse los sesos.
cue [kju:] *billiards*: taco *m*; *thea.* pie *m*, apunte *m*; (*hair*) coleta *f*; *take one's* ~ *from* seguir el ejemplo de.
cuff[1] [kʌf] **1.** bofetada *f*; **2.** abofetear, dar de bofetadas.
cuff[2] [~] (*shirt-, etc.*) puño *m*; (*hand-*) ~*s pl.* esposas *f/pl.*; ˈ**~ links** *pl.* gemelos *m/pl.*
cui·rass [kwiˈræs] coraza *f*.
cui·sine [kwiˈzi:n] cocina *f*.
cu·li·nar·y [ˈkʌlinəri] culinario.
cull [kʌl] *lit.* entresacar, espigar.
culm [kʌlm] cisco *m*.
cul·mi·nate [ˈkʌlmineit] culminar (*a. ast.*); ~ *in* terminar en; **cul·miˈna·tion** culminación *f*; *fig.* colmo *m*, apogeo *m*.
cul·pa·bil·i·ty [kʌlpəˈbiliti] culpabilidad *f*; **cul·pa·ble** □ culpable.
cul·prit [ˈkʌlprit] culpado (a *f*) *m*; reo *m*; ⸢ bribón *m*.
cult [kʌlt] culto *m*.
cul·ti·va·ble [ˈkʌltivəbl] cultivable.
cul·ti·vate [ˈkʌltiveit] cultivar (*a. fig.*); *fig.* ~*d* culto, refinado; **cul·tiˈva·tion** cultivo *m*; ˈ**cul·ti·va·tor** cultivador *m*; ⊕ cultivadora *f*.
cul·tur·al [ˈkʌltʃərəl] □ cultural.
cul·ture [ˈkʌltʃər] cultura *f*; cultivo (*a.* 🕮); ˈ**cul·tured** culto.
cul·vert [ˈkʌlvərt] alcantarilla *f*.
cum·ber [ˈkʌmbər] estorbar; molestar; **~·some** [ˈ~səm], **cum·brous** [ˈ~brəs] □ molesto, pesado.
cu·mu·la·tive [ˈkju:mjulətiv] □ cumulativo; **cu·mu·lus** [ˈ~ləs], *pl.* **cu·mu·li** [ˈ~lai] cúmulo *m*.
cu·ne·i·form [kju:ˈni:ifɔ:rm] cuneiforme.
cun·ning [ˈkʌniŋ] **1.** □ astuto, taimado; precioso, mono; **2.** astucia *f*; sagacidad *f*.
cup [kʌp] **1.** taza *f*; *eccl. a.* ⚘ cáliz *m*; (*fig. a. prize*) copa *f*; *in one's* ~*s* bebido; **2.** ahuecar; poner en forma de taza (*or* bocina); **~·board** [ˈkʌbərd] armario *m*, aparador *m*, alacena *f*; ~ *love* amor *m* interesado; ˈ**~-shaped** en forma de taza.
cu·pid·i·ty [kjuˈpiditi] codicia *f*.
cu·po·la [ˈkju:pələ] cúpula *f*.
cup·ping glass [ˈkʌpiŋglæs] ventosa *f*.
cu·pre·ous [ˈkju:priəs] cúprico; cobrizo.
cur [kə:r] perro *m* de mala raza; (*p.*) canalla *m.*
cur·a·bil·i·ty [kju:rəˈbiliti] curabilidad *f*; ˈ**cur·a·ble** curable.
cu·ra·cy [ˈkjurəsi] vicaría *f*; **cu·rate** [ˈ~rit] vicario *m*, cura *m*; **cu·ra·tor** [~ˈreitər] conservador *m*.
curb [kə:rb] **1.** barbada *f* (de la brida); (*pavement*) encintado *m*; (*well*) brocal *m*; *fig.* impedimento *m*, estorbo *m* (*on* para); **2.** proveer de barbada (*or* encintado); *fig.* refrenar, reprimir; ˈ**~** ˈ**mar·ket** ✝ bolsín *m*.
curd [kə:rd] cuajada *f*; **cur·dle** [ˈ~dl] cuajar(se); ~ *the blood* horripilar.

cure [kjuːr] **1.** cura *f*; *fig.* curato *m*; **2.** curar; **ˈ~-all** panacea *f*.
cur·few [ˈkəːrfjuː] queda *f*.
cu·ri·o [ˈkjuriou] curiosidad *f*; **cu·ri·ˈos·i·ty** [~ˈɔsiti] curiosidad *f*; **ˈcu·ri·ous** □ curioso.
curl [kəːrl] **1.** rizo *m*, bucle *m of hair*; espiral *f of smoke*; ondulación *f*; **2.** rizar(se), encrespar(se); ondular(se); *lips* fruncir; (*waves*) encresparse; ~ *up* arrollarse; (*p.*) acurrucarse; F abatirse.
curl·ing [ˈkəːrliŋ] *sport*: curling *m* (*juego sobre un campo de hielo*); **ˈ~ i·ron, ˈ~ tongs** *pl.* encrespador *m*; **ˈcurl·y** crespo, encrespado, rizado.
cur·mudg·eon [kəːrˈmʌdʒn] erizo *m*, mezquino *m*, cicatero *m*.
cur·rant [ˈkʌrənt] (*dried*) pasa *f* de Corinto; (*fresh*) grosella *f*; ~ (*bush*) grosellero *m*.
cur·ren·cy [ˈkʌrənsi] moneda *f* (en circulación); *fig.* uso *m* corriente; *fig.* extensión *f*, propagación *f*; **ˈcur·rent 1.** □ corriente; *be* ~ correr, ser de actualidad; ~ *events* actualidades *f/pl.*; ~*ly* actualmente; **2.** corriente *f* (*a.* ⚡).
cur·ric·u·lum [kəˈrikjuləm], *pl.* **curˈric·u·la** [~lə] programa *m* de estudios.
cur·ri·er [ˈkʌriər] curtidor *m*.
cur·ry[1] [ˈkʌri] **1.** cari *m*, curry *m*; **2.** preparar con cari; **ˈ~ pow·der** polvo *m* (de especias) para preparar el cari.
cur·ry[2] [~] *leather* curtir; *horse* almohazar; ~ *favor* buscar favores; **ˈ~·comb** almohaza *f*.
curse [kəːrs] **1.** maldición *f*; blasfemia *f*; (*oath*) palabrota *f*; **2.** *v/t.* maldecir; echar pestes de; *be* ~*d with* padecer de; tener que aguantar; *v/i.* blasfemar; (*a.* ~ *and swear*) soltar palabrotas.
cur·sive [ˈkəːrsiv] cursivo.
cur·so·ry [ˈkəːrsəri] □ precipitado, apresurado; *glance* rápido.
curt [kəːrt] □ brusco, áspero; conciso; **ˈcurt·ness** brusquedad *f*.
cur·tail [kəːrˈteil] cercenar (*a. fig.*), reducir; privar (*of* de); **curˈtail·ment** cercenamiento *m*, reducción *f*; privación *f*.
cur·tain [ˈkəːrtn] **1.** cortina *f* (*a.* ⚔); (*heavy*) cortinón *m*; *thea.* telón *m*; *pol. iron* ~ telón *m* de acero; **2.** proveer de cortina; separar con cortina (*a.* ~ *off*); **ˈ~ call** llamada *f* a la escena para recibir aplausos; **ˈ~ rais·er** pieza *f* preliminar; **ˈ~ ring** anilla *f*; **ˈ~ rod** barra *f* de cortina.
curt·sy [ˈkəːrtsi] **1.** reverencia *f*; *drop a* ~ = **2.** hacer una reverencia (*to* a).
cur·va·ture [ˈkəːrvətʃər] curvatura *f*.
curve [kəːrv] **1.** curva *f*; **2.** encorvar(se); voltear en curva *through air*.
cush·ion [ˈkuʃn] **1.** cojín *m*, almohadón *m*; *billiards*: baranda *f*; *fig.* ✝ colchón *m*; **2.** amortiguar; proteger con cojines; ⊕ acojinar.
cush·y [ˈkuʃi] *sl.* fácil, agradable; holgado.
cusp [kʌsp] cúspide *f*.
cuss [kʌs] F **1.** blasfemia *f*, ajo *m*; *sl.* tipo *m*, tío *m*; **2.** blasfemar, soltar un ajo; **ˈcuss·ed** [ˈkʌsid] maldito; **ˈcuss·ed·ness** terquedad *f* (*esp. pure* ~).
cus·tard [ˈkʌstərd] natillas *f/pl.*; flan *m*.
cus·to·di·an [kʌsˈtoudiən] custodio *m*; **cus·to·dy** [ˈkʌstədi] custodia *f*; *in* ~ en prisión; *take into* ~ arrestar.
cus·tom [ˈkʌstəm] costumbre *f*; ✝ clientela *f*, parroquia *f*; ~*s pl.* aduana *f*; derechos *m/pl.* de aduana; ~*-built* hecho por encargo, fuera de serie; ~*s clearance* despacho *m* de aduana; ~*s house* aduana *f*; ~*s officer* aduanero *m*; ~ *tailor* sastre *m* a la medida; ~ *work* trabajo *m* hecho a la medida; **cus·tom·ar·y** [ˈ~əri] □ acostumbrado, de costumbre; **ˈcus·tom·er** cliente *m*; F tío *m*; ~ *service* servicio *m* de postventa; **ˈcus·tom-made** hecho a la medida.
cut [kʌt] **1.** corte *m*; (*blow*) golpe *m* cortante, tajo *m*; tajada *f of meat*; (*deletion*) corte *m*; ✝ reducción *f*; ⚕ herida *f*, incisión *f*; corte *m*, hechura *f of dress*; (*proportion*) parte *f*; (*insult*) desaire *m*, zaherimiento *m*; ⚡ apagón *m*; *sl.* tajada *f*; ~*back* reducción *f*; discontinuación *f*, incumplimiento *m*; *cinema*: retorno *m* a una época anterior; *short* ~ atajo *m*; **2.** [*irr.*] *v/t.* cortar; *corn* segar; *esp. hole* practicar, hacer; *stone etc.* tallar; (*divide*) partir, dividir; ✝ *losses* abandonar; *class* fumarse; *p.* desairar, zaherir; fingir no ver; F *caper etc.* ejecutar, presentar; *tooth* salirle a uno (un diente); ~ *across* cortar al través; atravesar; *fig.* ir en contra de; ~ *away* separar (cortando); ~ *back* acortar, recortar; ~

down cortar, derribar; *costs* aminorar; *price* rebajar; ~ *off* cortar (*a.* ⚡); *leg* amputar; ~ *open* abrir (cortando); ~ *out* (re)cortar; *hole etc.* practicar, hacer; *stone* tallar, labrar; *fig.* suprimir; *be* ~ *out for* tener talento especial para; *have one's work* ~ *out* tener trabajo de sobra (*to inf.* para poder *inf.*); F ~ *it out!* ¡déjese de eso!; *v. short*; ~ *up* desmenuzar; *meat* picar; F *fig.* criticar severamente; F *be* ~ *up* acongojarse, afligirse (*about* por); *v/i.* cortar; ~ *in* interrumpir, interponerse; **3.** cortado; ⊕ labrado; ~ *glass* cristal *m* tallado; ~*away coat* chaqué *m*; ~ *and dried* preparado (*or* convenido) de antemano; monótono, poco interesante; ~ *glass* cristal *m* tallado; ~*water* espolón *m*, tajamar *m*; ~ *off* aislado, incomunicado.
cu·ta·ne·ous [kju'teiniəs] cutáneo.
cut·a·way ['kʌtəwei] (*a.* ~ *coat*) chaque *m*.
cute [kju:t] □ F mono; astuto.
cu·ti·cle ['kju:tikl] *anat.*, ⚘ cutícula *f*.
cut·lass ['kʌtləs] chafarote *m*.
cut·ler ['kʌtlər] cuchillero *m*; '**cut·ler·y** cuchillería *f*; cubertería *f*.
cut·let ['kʌtlit] chuleta *f*.
cut...: '~**-off** atajo *m*; '~'**out** diseño *m* para recortar; ⚡ portafusible *m*; ⊕ válvula *f* de escape libre; '~**·purse** carterista *m*; ratero *m*; '~**-rate** de precio reducido; '**cut·ter** cortador (-a *f*) *m*; ⊕ cortadora *f*; ⚓ cúter *m*; ⚓ escampavía *f*; '**cut·throat 1.** asesino *m*; **2.** sanguinario, cruel; *competition* intenso, implacable; '**cut·ting 1.** □ cortante; *fig.* mordaz; ~ edge filo *m*; **2.** corte *m*, cortadura *f*; (*paper*) recorte *m*; 🚂 *etc.* trinchera *f*, desmonte *m*; 🚂 zanja *f* ferroviaria.
cut·tle ['kʌtl] jibia *f* (*mst* '~**·fish**).
cy·a·nide ['saiənaid] cianuro *m*; ~ *of potassium* cianuro *m* de potasio.
cy·ber·net·ics [saibər'netiks] cibernética *f*.
cyc·la·men ['sikləmən] ciclamino *m*, pamporcino *m*.
cy·cle ['saikl] **1.** ciclo *m* (*a.* ♪ *etc.*); F bicicleta *f*; **2.** montar (*or* ir) en bicicleta; **cy·clic, cy·cli·cal** ['saiklik(l)] □ cíclico; '**cy·cling** ciclismo *m*; '**cy·clist** ciclista *m/f*.
cy·clo·pe·di·a, cy·clo·pae·di·a [saiklə'pi:diə] enciclopedia *f*.
cy·clone ['saikloun] ciclón *m*; borrasca *f*.
cy·clo·tron ['saiklətrɔn] ciclotrón *m*.
cyg·net ['signit] pollo *m* de cisne.
cyl·in·der ['silindər] cilindro *m*; ⊕ ~ *block* bloque *m* de cilindros; ~ *bore* alesaje *m*; *mot.* ~ *capacity* cilindrada *f*; ~ *head* (*of steam engine*) tapa *f* del cilindro; (*of gas engine*) culata *f* del cilindro; *hot-water* ~ termo *m*; **cy'lin·dric, cy'lin·dri·cal** □ cilíndrico.
cym·bal ['simbl] címbalo *m*.
cyn·ic ['sinik] **1.** (*a.* '**cyn·i·cal** □) cínico; **2.** cínico *m*; **cyn·i·cism** ['~sizm] cinismo *m*.
cy·no·sure ['sainəʃur] *fig.* (*esp.* ~ *of every eye*) miradero *m*.
cy·press ['saipris] ciprés *m*.
cyst [sist] quiste *m*; '**cyst·ic** *anat.* cístico; ⚕ quístico; **cys·ti·tis** [sis'taitis] cistitis *f*.
czar [zɑ:r] zar *m*; **czar·i·na** [zɑ:'rinə] zarina *f*.
Czech [tʃek] **1.** checo *adj. a. su. m* (a *f*); **2.** (*language*) checo *m*.
Czech·o·slo·vak ['tʃekou'slouvæk] checoslovaco *adj. a. su. m* (a *f*).

D

'd F = *had*; *would*.
dab [dæb] **1.** golpe *m* ligero; soba *f*; untadura *f of liquid*; brochazo *m of paint*; pizca *f*, porción *f* pequeña; *ichth.* lenguado *m*; *be a ~ hand at* ser perito en; **2.** golpear (*or* tocar) ligeramente; sobar; untar; *~ on paint* embadurnar de.
dab·ble ['dæbl] salpicar, mojar; *feet etc.* chapotear; *~ in* interesarse en, ser aficionado a; *b.s.* meterse en, mangonear en; ✝ especular en, jugar a; '**dab·bler** aficionado (a *f*) *m*.
dace [deis] albur *m*.
dad [dæd], **dad·dy** ['~i] F papá *m*, papaíto *m*.
dad·dy-long·legs ['dædi'lɔŋlegz] F típula *f*.
da·do ['deidou] friso *m* (de pared).
daf·fo·dil ['dæfədil] dafodelo *m*; narciso *m*.
dag·ger ['dægər] daga *f*, puñal *m*; *be at ~s drawn* ser enemigos; *look ~s at* apuñalar con la mirada.
da·go ['deigou] *sl. contp.* = *italiano*, *a. español, portugués*.
dahl·ia ['deiliə] dalia *f*.
dai·ly ['deili] diario *adj. a. su. m*; F asistenta *f*.
dain·ti·ness ['deintinis] delicadeza *f*, melindre *m*; primor *m*, esmero *m*; '**dain·ty 1.** □ delicado, regalado; de buen gusto, precioso; *b.s.* quisquilloso, esmerado; **2.** golosina *f*.
dair·y ['dɛəri] ✝ lechería *f*; (*farm*) quesería *f*, vaquería *f*; '**~·maid** lechera *f*; '**~·man** lechero *m*.
da·is ['deiis] estrado *m*.
dai·sy ['deizi] margarita *f*, maya *f*; *sl.* primor *m*.
dale [deil] valle *m*.
dal·li·ance ['dæliəns] frivolidad *f*; coquetería *f*; '**dal·ly** coquetear (*with* con); (*sport*) juguetear; (*delay*) tardar; (*idle*) holgar.
dam[1] [dæm] madre *f* (de un animal).
dam[2] [~] **1.** presa *f*; embalse *m*; **2.** represar (*a. fig.*); *~ up* cerrar, tapar.
dam·age ['dæmidʒ] **1.** daño *m*, perjuicio *m*; ⊕ *etc.* avería *f*; ⚖ *~s pl.* daños *m/pl.* y perjuicios; **2.** dañar, perjudicar; averiar; *mot. etc.* causar daño a; *mot. etc. be ~ed* sufrir daño; '**dam·age·a·ble** ⚖ susceptible de indemnización.
dam·a·scene ['dæməsi:n] ataujía *f*;
dam·ask ['dæməsk] **1.** damasco *m*; ⊕ ataujía *f*; damasquinado *m*; *attr.* de damasco; ⊕ de ataujía; **2.** *cloth* adamascar; ⊕ damasquinar.
dame [deim] dama *f*; *sl.* tía *f*.
damn [dæm] **1.** condenar (*a. eccl.*), censurar; maldecir; *~ it!* ¡maldito sea!, ¡demonio!; **2.** terno *m*, palabrota *f*; *sl. I don't give a ~* maldito lo que me importa; *sl. not worth a ~* de poca monta; '**dam·na·ble** □ detestable; **dam'na·tion** condenación *f*; *~!* ¡cáspita!; **damned** *eccl.* condenado; F maldito, condenado; *adv.* extremadamente; **damn·ing** ['dæmiŋ] damnificador.
damp [dæmp] **1.** húmedo; mojado; **2.** humedad *f*; *fig.* abatimiento *m*, desaliento *m*; **3.** (*a.* '**damp·en**) humedecer, mojar; (*dull*) amortiguar, amortecer; *fig.* desalentar; (*a. ~ down*) cubrir; '**damp·er** registro *m*; ♪ sordina *f*; tiro *m* (de chimenea), llave *f* de estufa; '**damp·ish** algo húmedo; '**damp-proof** a prueba de humedad.
dam·sel ['dæmzl] †, *lit.* damisela *f*.
dam·son ['dæmzn] ciruela *f* damascena.
dance [dæns] **1.** baile *m*, danza *f*; *formal ~* baile de etiqueta; **2.** bailar, danzar (*a. fig.*); '**~ band** orquesta *f* de jazz; '**~ floor** pista *f* de baile; '**~ hall** salón *m* de baile; '**danc·er** bailador (-a *f*) *m*; danzante (a *f*) *m*; (*professional*) bailarín (-a *f*) *m*.
danc·ing ['dænsiŋ] baile *m*; *attr.* de baile; '**~ girl** bailarina *f*, corista *f*; '**~ part·ner** pareja *f* de baile.
dan·de·li·on [dændi'laiən] diente *m* de león.
dan·der ['dændər] *sl.* cólera *f*, mal genio *m*; *get a p.'s ~ up* enojar a una p.

dan·dle [ˈdændl] *child* hacer saltar sobre las rodillas.
dan·druff [ˈdændrəf] caspa *f*.
dan·dy [ˈdændi] **1.** currutaco *m*; *sl.* cosa *f* excelente; **2.** *sl.* de primera; **ˈdan·dy·ism** dandismo *m*.
Dane [dein] danés (-a *f*) *m*; *Great* ∼ mastín *m* danés.
dan·ger [ˈdeindʒər] peligro *m*; *out of* ∼ fuera de peligro; **ˈ∼ list:** *be on the* ∼ estar de cuidado; **ˈ∼ mon·ey** prima *f* de riesgos; **ˈdan·ger·ous** □ peligroso; **ˈdan·ger sig·nal** señal *f* de peligro.
dan·gle [ˈdæŋgl] colgar(se) en el aire; bambolearse; ∼ *after* ir tras de.
Dan·ish [ˈdeiniʃ] danés *adj. a. su. m.*
dank [dæŋk] húmedo, liento.
dap·per [ˈdæpər] □ apuesto, gallardo.
dap·ple [ˈdæpl] motear, salpicar de manchas; **ˈdap·pled** moteado, salpicado de manchas; *horse* rodado; **ˈdap·ple-ˈgray** caballo *m* rucio rodado.
dare [der] *v/i.* osar (*to inf.*), atreverse (*to* a); *I* ∼ *say* quizá; concedo (*that* que); *v/t. s.o.* desafiar; *gaze* resistir; **ˈ∼·dev·il** temerario (a *f*) *m*; **ˈdar·ing** □ **1.** atrevido, osado; **2.** atrevimiento *m*, osadía *f*.
dark [dɑːrk] **1.** □ oscuro; *complexion* moreno, trigueño; enigmático, secreto; ignorante; (*evil*) malvado, alevoso; ∼ *Ages* edades *f/pl.* bárbaras; ∼ *horse fig.* ganador *m* inesperado; candidato *m* poco conocido; ∼ *meat* carne *f* del ave que no es la pechuga; ∼ *room* cuarto *m* oscuro; *get* ∼ hacerse de noche; *keep* ∼ mantener secreto, reservar; **2.** oscuridad *f*, tinieblas *f/pl.*; *in the* ∼ a oscuras (*a. fig.*); *keep s.o. in the* ∼ no revelar a una p. cierta noticia; **ˈdark·en** oscurecer(se); *fig.* entristecer; *fig.* confundir, turbar; *never* ∼ *a p.'s door* nunca ir a ver a una p.; **ˈdark·ish** algo oscuro; **ˈdark·ness** oscuridad *f*; *fig.* maldad *f*; *fig.* ignorancia *f*.
dar·ling [ˈdɑːrliŋ] **1.** querido (a *f*) *m*; *my* ∼! ¡amor mío!; **2.** querido, predilecto.
darn[1] [dɑːrn] F = *damn*.
darn[2] [∼] **1.** zurcido *m*, zurcidura *f*; **2.** zurcir.
darn·ing [ˈdɑːrniŋ] acción *f* de zurcir; zurcidura *f*; cosas *f/pl.* por zurcir; **ˈ∼ nee·dle** aguja *f* de zurcir.
dart [dɑːrt] **1.** ⚔ dardo *m*, venablo *m*; (*game*) rehilete *m*; movimiento *m* rápido; ∼*board* blanco *m*; **2.** lanzarse, precipitarse; moverse rápidamente.
Dar·win·ism [ˈdɑːrwinizm] Darvinismo *m*.
dash [dæʃ] **1.** choque *m*; rociada *f* *of water etc.*; pequeña cantidad *f*; raya *f with pen*; *typ.* guión *m*; *fig.* arrojo *m*, brío *m*; carrera *f* corta (*for* hasta *etc.*); *cut a* ∼ lucir; **2.** *v/t.* romper, estrellar (*against* contra); rociar, salpicar; despedazar (*mst* ∼ *to pieces*); *hope* frustrar; ∼ (*it*)! ¡porras!; ∼ *against* estampar contra: ∼ *off letter* escribir de prisa; *v/i.* estrellarse; (*waves*) romperse; correr; F ∼ *away*, ∼ *off* marcharse; F ∼ *in* (*out*) entrar (salir) como un rayo; F ∼ *up* acercarse (rápidamente); **ˈ∼·board** tablero *m* de instrumentos, panel *m*, salpicadero *m*, cuadro *m* de mando; **ˈdash·ing** □ brioso, arrojado; apuesto, guapo.
das·tard [ˈdæstərd] alevoso; **ˈdas·tard·ly** cobarde, alevoso, vil.
da·ta [ˈdeitə] *pl.* datos *m/pl.*; ∼ *bank* banco *m* de datos; ∼ *processing* tramitación *f* automática de datos, informática *f*; ∼ *storage* almacenamiento *m* de datos. [*f* (*a.* ∼ *palm*).]
date[1] [deit] ♣ dátil *m*; (*tree*) datilera
date[2] [∼] **1.** fecha *f*; F cita *f*; ✝ plazo *m*; F novio (a *f*) *m*; *what is the* ∼? ¿a cuántos estamos?; F *make a* ∼ citar (*with* a); *out of* ∼ anticuado; (*up*) *to* ∼ hasta la fecha; *up to* ∼ al día; moderno; **2.** fechar; F citar; ∼ *back to* remontarse a; ∼ *from* datar de; ∼*d* fechado; *fig.* anticuado; **ˈ∼·less** sin fecha; *fig.* inmemorial; **ˈ∼·line** línea *f* de cambio de fecha.
da·tive [ˈdeitiv] dativo *m* (*a.* ∼ *case*).
da·tum [ˈdeitəm] dato *m*.
daub [dɔːb] **1.** embadurnar; *paint.* pintorrear; **2.** embadurnamiento *m*; *paint.* pintarrajo *m*; **ˈdaub·(st)er** pintamonas *m*.
daugh·ter [ˈdɔːtər] hija *f*; ∼**-in-law** [ˈdɔːtərinlɔː] nuera *f*; **ˈdaugh·ter·ly** filial, como una hija.
daunt [dɔːnt] acobardar, desalentar; **ˈ∼·less** □ intrépido, impávido.
dav·en·port [ˈdævənpɔːrt] sofá *m* cama.
dav·it [ˈdævit] pescante *m*.
da·vy[1] [ˈdeivi] ⚒ (*mst* ∼ *lamp*) lámpara *f* de seguridad.

da·vy[2] [~]: *take one's ~* jurar, prestar juramento.
daw·dle ['dɔ:dl] F *v/i.* holgazanear; andar muy despacio; *v/t. ~ away* malgastar; '**daw·dler** F holgazán (-a *f*) *m*; *fig.* dormilón (-a *f*) *m*.
dawn [dɔ:n] **1.** amanecer *m*, alba *f*; *esp. fig.* aurora *f*; *from ~ to dusk* de sol a sol; *get up with the ~* madrugar; **2.** amanecer, apuntar el día; *fig. ~ on s.o.* caer uno en la cuenta.
day [dei] día *m*; *eccl.* fiesta *f*; *fig.* palma *f*, victoria *f*; *~ after ~, ~ in, ~ out* día tras día; *the ~ after* el día siguiente; *the ~ before* el día anterior; la víspera de *event etc.*; *by ~* de día; *by the ~* a jornal; *good ~!* ¡buenos días!; *to this ~* hasta el día de hoy; *call it a ~* dejar de trabajar *etc.*; *carry the ~* ganar la victoria; *v. off etc.*; '**~ bed** sofá *m* cama; '**~·book** diario *m*; '**~·break** amanecer *m*; '**~·dream 1.** ensueño *m*; **2.** soñar despierto; '**~'la·bor·er** jornalero *m*; '**~·light** luz *f* del día; *in broad ~* en pleno día; *fig. see ~* comprender; ver el final de un trabajo; *~-saving time* hora *f* de verano; '**~ 'nurse·ry** guardería *f* para niños; '**~ 'off** asueto *m*; '**~ star** *poet.* sol *m*; lucero *m* del alba; '**~·time 1.** diurno; **2.** día *m*; *~ television news* telediario *m*; '**~-to-'day** diario, cotidiano.
daze [deiz] **1.** aturdir, ofuscar; deslumbrar; **2.** aturdimiento *m*; *in a ~* aturdido.
daz·zle ['dæzl] **1.** deslumbrar (*a. fig.*), ofuscar; **2.** deslumbramiento *m*.
dea·con ['di:kn] diácono *m*; **dea·con·ess** ['di:kənis] diaconisa *f*; '**dea·con·ry** diaconía *f*.
dead [ded] **1.** muerto; difunto; insensible (*to* a); *leaf* marchito, seco; *hands etc.* entumecido; *color* apagado; *sound* sordo; ⚡ sin corriente; (*obsolete*) anticuado, obsoleto; *~ calm* calma *f* chicha; *~ center* punto *m* muerto; *v. heat*; *~ letter fig.* letra *f* muerta; *v. level*; *~ load* carga *f* fija; *v. loss*; *~ march* marcha *f* fúnebre; *~ stop* parada *f* en seco; *~ water* agua *f* tranquila; *~ weight* peso *m* muerto; *fig.* carga *f* onerosa; *~ wood* leña *f* seca; *fig.* material *m* inútil; **2.** *adv.* completamente, absolutamente; *~ drunk* borracho como un tronco; *~ set* empeñado (*on* en); *~ tired* hecho polvo, muerto de cansancio; **3.**: *the ~ pl.* los muertos; *fig.* lo más profundo; *in the ~ of night* en las altas horas; *in the ~ of winter* en lo más recio del invierno; '**~ 'beat** hecho polvo, agotado; '**~·beat** *sl.* gorrón (-a *f*) *m*; holgazán (-a *f*) *m*; '**~ bolt** cerrojo *m* dormido; '**~ 'calm** calma *f* chicha, calmazo *m*; '**~ 'center** punto *m* muerto; '**~ 'drunk** difunto de taberna; '**dead·en** amortiguar, amortecer; '**dead'end** callejón *m* sin salida (*a. fig.*); *~ kids* chicos *m/pl.* de las calles; '**~·latch** aldaba *f* dormida; '**dead·line** fecha *f* tope, línea *f* vedada; fin *m* del plazo; '**dead·lock 1.** *fig.* punto *m* muerto, desacuerdo *m* insuperable; (*lock*) cerradura *f* dormida; **2.** estancar; '**dead·ly 1.** mortal; fatal (*a. fig.*); *fig.* abrumador; **2.** *adv.* sumamente; '**dead·ness** inercia *f*; pérdida *f* de vida; falta *f* de vida.
dead...: '**~·net·tle** ortiga *f* muerta; '**~·pan** *sl.* (semblante *m*) sin expresión; '**~ 'reck·on·ing** ⚓ estima *f*; '**~ 'ring·er** segunda edición *f*; '**~·wood** leña *f* seca; *fig.* cosa *f* inútil, gente *f* inútil.
deaf [def] sordo (*to* a); *~ and dumb* sordomudo; *~ as a post* sordo como una tapia; '**deaf·en** ensordecer; (*noise*) asordar; *~ing* ensordecedor; '**deaf-'mute** sordomudo (a *f*) *m*; '**deaf·ness** sordera *f*.
deal[1] [di:l] tabla *f* de pino (*or* de abeto).
deal[2] [~] **1.** negocio *m*, negociación *f*; F ✝ trato *m*, transacción *f*; convenio *m*, acuerdo *m*; *cards*: reparto *m*, mano *f*; (*turn*) turno *m*; porción *f*; *a good ~* bastante; *a great ~* mucho; *it's a ~!* ¡trato hecho!; *give a square ~ to* tratar con justicia a; *make a great ~ of p.* estimar mucho a; *th.* dar importancia a; **2.** [*irr.*] *v/t. blow* asestar, dar; (*esp. ~ out*) repartir; *cards* dar; *v/i.* negociar, comerciar; (*in* en); *cards*: ser mano; *~ with p.* tratar a (*or* con); *subject* tratar de; '**deal·er** ✝ comerciante *m* (*in* en); *cards*: repartidor *m*, mano *f*; *sharp ~* taimado *m*; '**deal·ing** (*mst ~s pl.*) comercio *m*, trato *m*; relaciones *f/pl*.
dealt [delt] *pret. a. p.p. of deal*[2].
dean [di:n] *eccl.* deán *m*; *univ. etc.* decano *m*; '**dean·er·y** deanato *m*; (*residence*) decanato *m*.
dear [dir] **1.** □ *p. etc.* querido; *purchase* caro, costoso; *shop etc.* carero;

fig. pay ~*ly for* pagar caro *acc.*; **2.** querido (a *f*) *m*; persona *f* simpática; *my* ~*!* ¡querido (a) mío (a)!, ¡hombre!; **3.** F *oh* ~*!*, ~ *me!* ¡Dios mío!; ¡caramba!; ˈ**dear·ness** cariño *m*; ✝ carestía *f*; **dearth** [dəːrθ] carestía *f*, escasez *f*; **dear·y** [ˈdiri] F queridito (a *f*) *m*.

death [deθ] muerte *f*; fallecimiento *m*, defunción *f*; *be at* ~*'s door* estar a la muerte; *do (put) to* ~ dar la muerte a; ~ *certificate* fe *f* de óbito, partida *f* de defunción; ~ *house* capilla *f de los reos de muerte*; ~ *penalty* pena *f* de muerte; ~ *rattle* estertor *m* agónico; ~ *ray* rayo *m* mortífero; ~*watch* vela *f* de un difunto; guardia *f* de un reo de muerte; *tired to* ~ rendido, fatigado; *fig.* harto (*of* de); *to the* ~ a muerte; ˈ**~·bed** lecho *m* de muerte; ˈ**~·blow** golpe *m* mortal; ˈ**~·less** inmortal; ˈ**death·ly** mortal; *fig.* profundo; ˈ**death rate** mortalidad *f*; ˈ**death roll** número *m* de muertos; ˈ**death's-head** calavera *f*; ˈ**death war·rant** sentencia *f* de muerte.

dé·bâ·cle [deiˈbɑːkl] derrota *f*, caída *f*; fracaso *m*.

de·bar [diˈbɑːr] excluir (*from* de); prohibir.

de·bark [diˈbɑːrk] desembarcar; **de·bar·ka·tion** [dibɑːrˈkeiʃn] desembarco *m of passengers*; desembarque *m of freight*.

de·base [diˈbeis] degradar, envilecer; *coinage* adulterar; **deˈbase·ment** envilecimiento *m*.

de·bat·a·ble [diˈbeitəbl] □ discutible, contestable; dudoso; **deˈbate** **1.** debate *m*, discusión *f*; **2.** discutir, debatir (*with* con); disputar (*on* de, sobre; *with* con); (*think*) deliberar; **deˈbat·er** polemista *m/f*; controversista *m/f*; *parl. etc.* discutidor (-a *f*) *m*, orador (-a *f*) *m*.

de·bauch [diˈbɔːtʃ] **1.** libertinaje *m*; **2.** corromper; viciar; **deb·auˈchee** libertino (a *f*) *m*; **deˈbauch·er·y** libertinaje *m*.

de·ben·ture [diˈbentʃər] vale *m*; obligación *f*.

de·bil·i·tate [diˈbiliteit] debilitar; **deˈbil·i·ty** debilidad *f*.

deb·it [ˈdebit] **1.** debe *m* (*a.* ~ *side*); (*entry*) cargo *m*; **2.** cargar.

de·bouch [diˈbautʃ] desembocar.

de·bris [dəˈbriː, ˈdeibriː] escombros *m/pl.*, desechos *m/pl.*

debt [det] deuda *f*; *deeply in* ~ lleno de deudas; *be in* ~ tener deudas; *be 100 in* ~ deber 100 dólares (*to* a); *be in a p.'s* ~ *fig.* estar agradecido a una p.; *run into* ~ contraer deudas, endeudarse; ˈ**debt·or** deudor (-a *f*) *m*.

de·bunk [diːˈbʌŋk] F *p.* desenmascarar; desacreditar.

dé·but [diˈbjuː, ˈdeibuː] estreno *m*, debut *m*; *make one's* ~ *thea.* estrenarse, debutar; (*in society*) ponerse de largo, presentarse en la sociedad; **dé·bu·tante** [debjutɑ̃ːnt] muchacha *f* que se presenta en la sociedad.

dec·ade [ˈdekeid] década *f*; decenio *m*, década *of years*.

de·ca·dence [ˈdekədəns] decadencia *f*; ˈ**de·ca·dent** decadente.

de·camp [diˈkaemp] largarse, marcharse; ⚔ decampar, levantar el campo.

de·cant [diˈkaent] decantar; **deˈcant·er** garrafa *f*.

de·cap·i·tate [diˈkæpiteit] degollar; **de·cap·iˈta·tion** degollación *f*.

de·car·bon·ize [diˈkɑːrbənaiz] descarburar, quitar la carbonilla a.

de·cay [diˈkei] **1.** decadencia *f*, decaimiento *m*; caries *f of teeth*; podredumbre *f*; **2.** decaer; *esp.* ⚠ *a. fig.* desmoronarse; cariarse; pudrirse.

de·cease [diˈsiːs] *esp.* ⚖ **1.** fallecimiento *m*; **2.** fallecer; *the* ~*d* el (la) difunto (a).

de·ceit [diˈsiːt] engaño *m*; fraude *m*; **deˈceit·ful** □ engañoso; (*lying*) mentiroso; **deˈceit·ful·ness** duplicidad *f*, bellaquería *f*.

de·ceive [diˈsiːv] engañar; defraudar; *be* ~*d freq.* equivocarse; **deˈceiv·er** engañador (-a *f*) *m*, impostor (-a *f*) *m*.

de·cel·er·ate [diːˈseləreit] moderarse la marcha.

De·cem·ber [diˈsembər] diciembre *m*.

de·cen·cy [ˈdiːsnsi] decencia *f*; ˈ**de·cen·cies** *pl.*: *the* ~ las buenas costumbres *f/pl.*; (*comforts*) comodidades *f/pl.*

de·cen·ni·al [diˈsenjəl] decenal; **deˈcen·ni·um** [~jəm] decenio *m*.

de·cent [ˈdiːsnt] □ decente; F *he's a* ~ *sort* es (una) buena persona; F *he was* ~ *to me* estuvo amable conmigo.

de·cen·tral·i·za·tion [diːsentrəlai-

ˈzeiʃn] descentralización *f*; **deˈcen·tral·ize** descentralizar.
de·cep·tion [diˈsepʃn] engaño *m*, fraude *m*, decepción *f*; **deˈcep·tive** □ engañoso; ilusorio.
de·cide [diˈsaid] decidir (*to inf. or* -se a *inf.*; *in favor of* a favor de; [*up*]*on* por); *attitude* determinar; **deˈcid·ed** □ decidido, resuelto; indudable; *~ly* indudablemente.
de·cid·u·ous [diˈsidjuəs] ⚘ deciduo.
dec·i·mal [ˈdesiml] decimal *adj. a. su. m*; *~ point* punto *m* decimal, coma *f*; **dec·i·mate** [ˈ~meit] diezmar (*a. fig.*); **dec·iˈma·tion** decimación *f*.
de·ci·pher [diˈsaifər] descifrar (*a. fig.*); **deˈci·pher·a·ble** [~rəbl] descifrable; **deˈci·pher·ment** desciframiento *m*.
de·ci·sion [diˈsiʒn] decisión *f*; ⚖ resolución *f*, fallo *m*; (*resoluteness*) firmeza *f*; *make* (*or take*) *a ~* tomar una decisión; **de·ci·sive** [diˈsaisiv] □ decisivo; (*conclusive*) terminante.
deck [dek] **1.** ⚓ cubierta *f*; (*omnibus*) planta *f*; *cards*: baraja *f*; *~ hand* marinero *m* de cubierta; *~-land* apontizar; *~-landing* apontizaje *m*; *between ~s* ⚓ entre cubiertas; **2.** *lit.* ataviar, engalanar; *~ out* adornar, engalanar; **ˈ~ˈchair** hamaca *f*, tumbona *f*, silla *f* de cubierta; **...ˈdeck·er:** *e.g. two-~* de dos plantas.
de·claim [diˈkleim] declamar; *~ against* protestar contra.
dec·la·ma·tion [dekləˈmeiʃn] declamación *f*; **de·clam·a·to·ry** [diˈklæmətɔːri] declamatorio.
de·clar·a·ble [diˈklerəbl] declarable; **dec·la·ra·tion** [dekləˈreiʃn] declaración *f* (*a.* ⚖); **deˈclar·a·to·ry** [~təri] declaratorio; **de·clare** [diˈkler] declarar; afirmar; *~ o.s.* pronunciarse (*in favor of* en favor de); F *well, I ~!* ¡vaya, vaya!; *nothing to ~* nada de pago; **deˈclared** □ manifiesto.
de·clen·sion [diˈklenʃn] declinación *f* (*a. gr.*).
de·clin·a·ble [diˈklainəbl] declinable; **dec·li·na·tion** [dekliˈneiʃn] declinación *f* (*ast a.* ⚓); denegación *f*; **de·cline** [diˈklain] **1.** *v/t.* rehusar, no aceptar; *gr.* declinar; *v/i.* declinar (*a. fig.*); negarse (*to* a); **2.** declinación *f* (*a. fig.*); ⚕ *etc.* bajón *m*; ocaso *m of sun*; baja *f of prices*; F tisis *f*; *be on the ~* ir disminuyendo.
de·cliv·i·ty [diˈkliviti] declive *m*.
de·clutch [ˈdiːˈklʌtʃ] desembragar.
de·code [ˈdiːˈkoud] descifrar.
dé·colle·té(**e**) [deikəlˈtei] escotado.
de·com·pose [diːkəmˈpouz] descomponer(se); **de·com·po·si·tion** [diːkɔmpəˈziʃn] descomposición *f*.
de·con·tam·i·nate [diːkənˈtæmineit] descontaminar; **de·con·tam·iˈna·tion** descontaminación *f*; *~ squad* cuadrilla *f* de descontaminación.
de·con·trol [ˈdiːkənˈtroul] **1.** supresión *f* del control; **2.** suprimir el control (de).
dec·o·rate [ˈdekəreit] decorar, adornar; *room* empapelar, pintar; ⚔ condecorar; **dec·oˈra·tion** adorno *m*, ornato *m*; ⚔ condecoración *f*; ♀ *Day* (*30 mayo*) *día para decorar las tumbas de los soldados muertos en batalla* (*EE.UU.*); **dec·o·ra·tive** [ˈdekərətiv] □ decorativo; bonito; **dec·o·ra·tor** [ˈ~reitər] adornista *m/f*; (pintor *m*) decorador *m*.
dec·o·rous [ˈdekərəs] □ decoroso;
de·co·rum [diˈkɔːrəm] decoro *m*.
de·coy [diˈkɔi] **1.** señuelo *m* (*a. fig.*); (*a.* **deˈcoy duck**) reclamo *m*; trampa *f*; **2.** atraer con señuelo.
de·crease 1. [ˈdiːkriːs] disminución *f*; **2.** [diːˈkriːs] disminuir(se).
de·cree [diˈkriː] **1.** decreto *m*; **2.** decretar.
de·crep·it [diˈkrepit] decrépito; **deˈcrep·i·tude** [~tjuːd] decrepitud *f*.
de·cry [diˈkrai] desacreditar; rebajar.
dec·u·ple [ˈdekjupl] **1.** décuplo *adj. a. su. m*; **2.** decuplicar.
ded·i·cate [ˈdedikeit] dedicar; **ded·iˈca·tion** dedicación *f*; dedicatoria *f in book*; **ˈded·i·ca·to·ry** dedicatorio.
de·duce [diˈdjuːs] deducir; **deˈduc·i·ble** deducible.
de·duct [diˈdʌkt] restar; **deˈduc·tion** deducción *f*; ✝ descuento *m*; **deˈduc·tive** □ deductivo.
deed [diːd] **1.** hecho *m*, acto *m*, hazaña *f*; ⚖ escritura *f*, documento *m*; **2.** traspasar por escritura.
deem [diːm] juzgar, considerar; (*believe*) creer.
deep [diːp] **1.** □ hondo, profundo; ♪ grave, bajo; *color* oscuro; subido; *p.* insondable, astuto; *~ in debt* lleno de

deudas; ~ *in thought* absorto en la meditación; *fig.* ~ *in s.t.* muy metido en; F *go off the* ~ *end* montar en cólera; ~*-sea fishing* pesca *f* de gran altura; **2.** *poet.* piélago *m*; ˈ~ ˈ**breath·ing** gimnasia *f* respiratoria; ˈ~-ˈ**chest·ed** ancho de pecho; ˈ**deep·en** profundizar(se); *voice* ahuecar; *color* hacer(se) más oscuro (*or* subido); *sorrow* intensificar(se); ˈ**deep-**ˈ**root·ed** profundamente arraigado; ˈ**deep-**ˈ**seat·ed** con profundas raíces.

deer [dir] ciervo *m*; ˈ~ **stalk·er** cazador *m* de venado; ˈ~ **stalk·ing** caza *f* de venado.

de·face [diˈfeis] desfigurar, deformar; **deˈface·ment** desfiguración *f*, deformación *f*.

de·fal·cate [ˈdi:fælkeit] desfalcar; **de·falˈca·tion** desfalco *m*; ˈ**de·fal·ca·tor** defraudador (-a *f*) *m*.

def·a·ma·tion [defəˈmeiʃn] difamación *f*; **de·fam·a·to·ry** [diˈfæmətəri] difamatorio; **de·fame** [diˈfeim] difamar; mancillar; **deˈfam·er** difamador (-a *f*) *m*.

de·fault [diˈfɔ:lt] **1.** omisión *f*, descuido *m*; falta *f*, incumplimiento *m*; ⚖ rebeldía *f*; *in* ~ *of* por falta de; *make* ~ no comparecer; faltar; **2.** faltar; ⚖ caer en rebeldía; ponerse en mora; ⚕ demorar los pagos; **deˈfault·er** ⚖ rebelde *m*; ⚕ persona *f* que demora los pagos; ⚔ delincuente *m*.

de·feat [diˈfi:t] **1.** derrota *f*; **2.** vencer (*a. fig.*); derrotar; *fig. e.g. hopes* frustrar; **deˈfeat·ism** derrotismo *m*; **deˈfeat·ist** derrotista *m/f*.

de·fect [ˈdi:fekt, diˈfekt] defecto *m*; **deˈfec·tion** defección *f*, deserción *f*; **deˈfec·tive** □ defectuoso; defectivo (*a. gr.*); *child etc.* anormal; falto (*in* de).

de·fend [diˈfend] defender (*from* de); **deˈfen·dant** (*civil*) demandado (a *f*) *m*; (*criminal*) acusado (a *f*) *m*, reo *m*; **deˈfend·er** defensor *m*.

de·fense [diˈfens] defensa *f* (*a. sport*); **deˈfense·less** indefenso; **de·fen·si·ble** [diˈfensəbl] defendible; **deˈfen·sive 1.** □ defensivo; **2.** defensiva *f*; *be on the* ~ estar a la defensiva.

de·fer[1] [diˈfə:r] diferir, aplazar; ~*red payment* pago *m* a plazos; ~*red annuity* cuota *f* de pensión.

de·fer[2] [~] deferir (*to* a); **def·er·ence** [ˈdefərəns] deferencia *f*; *in* ~ *to*, *out of* ~ *to* obedeciendo a, teniendo respeto a; **def·er·en·tial** [~ˈrenʃl] □ deferente.

de·fer·ment [diˈfə:rmənt] aplazamiento *m*; prórroga *f* (*a.* ⚔).

de·fi·ance [diˈfaiəns] desafío *m*; oposición *f* terca; *bid* ~ *to* desafiar; *in* ~ *of* a despecho de, con infracción de; **deˈfi·ant** □ desafiador; provocativo.

de·fi·cien·cy [diˈfiʃənsi] deficiencia *f*, carencia *f*; ~ *disease* mal *m* carencial; **deˈfi·cient** insuficiente; incompleto; deficiente; *be* ~ *in* carecer de.

def·i·cit [ˈdefisit] déficit *m*.

de·fi·er [diˈfaiər] desafiador (-a *f*) *m*.

de·file[1] [diˈfail] **1.** desfiladero *m*; **2.** ⚔ desfilar.

de·file[2] [~] manchar, ensuciar (*a. fig.*); profanar, contaminar; **de·file·ment** profanación *f*, contaminación *f*.

de·fin·a·ble [diˈfainəbl] definible; **deˈfine** definir; delimitar, determinar; **def·i·nite** [ˈdefinit] □ definido (*a. gr.*); *statement etc.* categórico; distinto, preciso; *quite* ~ indudable; **def·iˈni·tion** definición *f*; claridad *f*; *by* ~ por definición; **deˈfin·i·tive** □ definitivo; categórico; ~*ly* en definitiva.

de·flate [di:ˈfleit] desinflar; ⚕ deflacionar; **deˈfla·tion** desinflación *f*; ⚕ deflación *f*; **deˈfla·tion·a·ry** deflacionista.

de·flect [diˈflekt] desviar (*a. fig.*; *from* de); **deˈflec·tion**, *mst* **de·flex·ion** [diˈflekʃən] desviación *f*.

de·flow·er [di:ˈflauər] desflorar; *fig.* despojar.

de·form [diˈfɔ:rm] deformar; ~*ed* deforme, mutilado; **de·forˈma·tion** deformación *f*; **deˈform·i·ty** deformidad *f*.

de·fraud [diˈfrɔ:d] defraudar (*of* de).

de·fray [diˈfrei] *costs* sufragar, costear.

de·freez·er [di:ˈfri:zər] anticongelante *m*.

de·frost·er [di:ˈfrɔstər] desescarchador *m*.

deft [deft] □ diestro (*at* en); *touch* ligero.

de·funct [diˈfʌŋkt] **1.** difunto; *fig.* muerto, inexistente; **2.** *the* ~ el (la) difunto (a).

de·fy [di'fai] desafiar (*a. fig.*); oponerse a.
de·gen·er·a·cy [di'dʒenərəsi] depravación *f*; **de'gen·er·ate 1.** [~rit] □ degenerado *adj. a. su. m* (a *f*); **2.** [~reit] degenerar (*into* en); **de·gen·er·a·tion** [~'reiʃn] degeneración *f*; **de'gen·er·a·tive** degenerativo.
deg·ra·da·tion [degrə'deiʃn] degradación *f*, envilecimiento *m*; **de·grade** [di'greid] degradar, envilecer; ~ *o.s. freq.* aplebeyarse.
de·gree [di'gri:] grado *m* (⚕ *etc.*); *univ.* título *m*, licenciatura *f*; † grada *f*; rango *m*, condición *f* social; *by* ~*s* poco a poco; *in no* ~ de ninguna manera; *in some* ~ hasta cierto punto; en cierto modo; *to the highest* ~ en sumo grado; *to a* ~ un tanto; *take a* ~ recibir un título; graduarse, licenciarse (*in* en).
de·hu·mid·i·fi·er [di:hju:'midifaiər] deshumedecedor *m*.
de·hy·drate [di:'haidreit] deshidratar; **de·hy·drat·ed** [di:'haidreitid] deshidratado; **de·hy'dra·tion** deshidratación *f*.
de-ice ['di:'ais] ✈ deshelar.
de·i·fi·ca·tion [di:ifi'keiʃn] deificación *f*; **de·i·fy** ['di:ifai] deificar.
deign [dein]: ~ *to* dignarse *inf*.
de·ism ['di:izm] deísmo *m*; **'de·ist** deísta *m/f*; **de'is·tic, de'is·ti·cal** □ deísta.
de·i·ty ['di:iti] deidad *f*; *the* ≈ Dios.
de·ject [di'dʒekt] abatir, desanimar; **de'ject·ed** □ abatido; **de'ject·ed·ness, de'jec·tion** abatimiento *m*.
de·lay [di'lei] **1.** tardanza *f*, retraso *m*; dilación *f*; **2.** *v/i.* tardar (*in* en); *v/t.* diferir, dilatar; ~*ed action attr.* de acción retardada.
de·le ['di:li:] *typ.* **1.** dele *m*; **2.** borrar, quitar.
de·lec·ta·ble [di'lektəbl] □ *co. or lit.* deleitable; **de·lec·ta·tion** [di:lek'teiʃn] delectación *f*.
del·e·ga·cy ['deligəsi] delegación *f*; **del·e·gate 1.** ['~geit] delegar (*to* a); *p.* diputar; **2.** ['~git] delegado (a *f*) *m*; diputado (a *f*) *m*; **del·e·ga·tion** [~'geiʃn] delegación *f* (*a. body*); diputación *f*.
de·lete [di:'li:t] tachar, suprimir, borrar; **del·e·te·ri·ous** [deli'tiəriəs] □ deletéreo; **de·le·tion** [di:'li:ʃn] supresión *f*.
delf(t) [delf(t)] porcelana *f* de Delft.
de·lib·er·ate 1. [di'libəreit] *v/t. s.t.* meditar; *v/i.* deliberar (*on* sobre); **2.** [~rit] □ premeditado, reflexionado; (*cautious*) cauto, circunspecto; *movement etc.* lento, espacioso; ~*ly freq.* de propósito, con premeditación; **de'lib·er·ate·ness** premeditación *f*; **de·lib·er·a·tion** [~'reiʃn] deliberación *f*; premeditación *f*; **de'lib·era·tive** [~reitiv] □ deliberativo.
del·i·ca·cy ['delikəsi] delicadeza *f*; (*titbit*) golosina *f*; **del·i·cate** ['~kit] □ delicado; *food* exquisito; *action* considerado; **del·i·ca·tes·sen** [delikə'tesn] tienda *f* que se especializa en manjares exquisitos, colmado *m*.
de·li·cious [di'liʃəs] □ delicioso, exquisito.
de·light [di'lait] **1.** deleite *m*, delicia *f*; *a* ~ *to the eye* un gozo para la retina; *take* ~ *in* deleitarse en *inf.*, con *su.*; **2.** deleitarse (*in* en, con); *be* ~*ed to* tener mucho gusto en; **de'light·ful** [~ful] □ delicioso, precioso; **de'light·ful·ness** encanto *m*, delicia *f*.
de·lim·it [di:'limit], **de'lim·i·tate** [~teit] delimitar; **de·lim·i'ta·tion** delimitación *f*.
de·lin·e·ate [di'linieit] delinear; bosquejar (*a. fig.*); **de·lin·e'a·tion** delineación *f*; bosquejo *m*; **de'lin·e·a·tor** delineador (-a *f*) *m*; ⊕ delineante *m*.
de·lin·quen·cy [di'liŋkwənsi] ⚖ delincuencia *f*; (*guilt*) culpa *f*; (*omission*) descuido *m*; **de'lin·quent** delincuente *adj. a. su. m/f*; culpable *adj. a. su. m/f*.
de·lir·i·ous [di'liriəs] □ delirante; **de'lir·i·ous·ness** delirio *m*; **de'lir·i·um** [~əm] delirio *m*; ~ *tremens* [~'tri:menz] delirium *m* tremens.
de·liv·er [di'livər] librar (*from* de); (*a.* ~ *up*, ~ *over*) entregar; ✉ distribuir, repartir; *speech* pronunciar; *blow* asestar; ⚕ *woman* partear; *message* comunicar; *ball* lanzar; *be* ~*ed of* parir *acc.*; **de'liv·er·ance** liberación *f*, rescate *m*; **de'liv·er·y** liberación *f*, salvación *f*; ✉ repartido *m*; ⚕ parto *m*, alumbramiento *m*; entrega *f of goods*, *writ*; modo *m* de expresarse; *attr.* de entrega; de reparto; ~*man* mozo *m* de reparto; ~ *room* ⚕ sala *f* de alumbramiento; ~ *service* servicio *m*

a domicilio; ~ *truck* sedán *m* de reparto.
dell [del] vallecito *m*.
de·louse [di:ˈlaus] despiojar, espulgar.
del·ta [ˈdeltə] delta *f*; *geog.* delta *m*.
de·lude [diˈlu:d] engañar, deludir (*into* para que); *easily* ~*d* iluso.
del·uge [ˈdelju:dʒ] **1.** diluvio *m*; **2.** inundar (*with* de).
de·lu·sion [diˈlu:ʒn] engaño *m*; ilusión *f*, alucinación *f*; **deˈlu·sive** [~siv] □, **deˈlu·so·ry** [~səri] delusorio, ilusorio; decepcionante.
de luxe [diˈlʌks] de lujo.
delve [delv] cavar (*into* en; *a. fig.*).
dem·a·gog·ic, dem·a·gog·i·cal [deməˈgɔgik(l)] □ demagógico; **dem·a·gogue** [ˈ~gɔg] demagogo *m*; **ˈdem·a·gog·y** demagogia *f*.
de·mand [diˈmænd] **1.** demanda *f* (*a.* ✝, ⚖); exigencia *f*; *on* ~ a solicitud; *be in* ~ tener demanda, *fig.* ser solicitado; ~ *note* apremio *m* de pago; **2.** demandar; exigir (*of* a), solicitar perentoriamente (*of* de); **deˈmand·ing** exigente.
de·mar·cate [ˈdi:mɑ:rkeit] demarcar; **de·marˈca·tion** (*line of* línea *f* de) demarcación *f*.
de·mean[1] [diˈmi:n] (*mst* ~ *o.s.*) degradar(se).
de·mean[2] [~]: ~ *o.s.* comportarse; **deˈmean·or** [~ər] porte *m*, conducta *f*.
de·ment·ed [diˈmentid] □ demente.
de·mer·it [di:ˈmerit] demérito *m*.
de·mesne [diˈmein] heredad *f*, hacienda *f*; tierras *f/pl.* solariegas (*freq.* ~ *land*).
dem·i... [ˈdemi] medio, semi...
dem·i·john [ˈdemidʒɔn] damajuana *f*.
de·mil·i·ta·ri·za·tion [di:militəraiˈzeiʃn] desmilitarización *f*; **deˈmil·i·ta·rize** desmilitarizar.
de·mise [diˈmaiz] **1.** ⚖ transferencia *f*; traspaso *m of title or estate*; fallecimiento *m of p.*; **2.** transferir, traspasar.
de·mob [di:ˈmɔb] F = *demobilize*; **de·mo·bi·li·za·tion** [ˈdi:moubilaiˈzeiʃn] desmovilización *f*; **deˈmo·bi·lize** desmovilizar.
de·moc·ra·cy [diˈmɔkrəsi] democracia *f*; **dem·o·crat** [ˈdeməkræt] demócrata *m/f*; **dem·oˈcrat·ic, dem·oˈcrat·i·cal** □ democrático;
de·moc·ra·tize [diˈmɔkrətaiz] democratizar.
de·mol·ish [diˈmɔliʃ] demoler, derribar; *argument etc.* destruir; F zamparse; **dem·o·li·tion** [deməˈliʃn] demolición *f*, derribo *m*.
de·mon [ˈdi:mən] demonio *m*; **de·mo·ni·ac** [diˈmouniæk] **1.** (*a.* **de·mo·ni·a·cal** [di:məˈnaiəkl] □) demoníaco; **2.** energúmeno (a *f*) *m*;
de·mon·ic [di:ˈmɔnik] demoníaco.
de·mon·stra·ble [ˈdemənstrəbl] □ demostrable; **dem·on·strate** [ˈ~streit] demostrar; *pol.* hacer una manifestación; **dem·onˈstra·tion** demostración *f*; *pol.* manifestación *f*; **de·mon·stra·tive** [diˈmɔnstrətiv] **1.** □ demostrativo (*a. gr.*); *p.* exagerado, exaltado; **2.** demostrativo *m*; **dem·on·stra·tor** [ˈdemənstreitər] demostrador (-a *f*) *m*; *univ.* ayudante *m*, mozo *m* de laboratorio; *pol.* manifestante *m*.
de·mor·al·i·za·tion [dimɔrəlaiˈzeiʃn] desmoralización *f*; **deˈmor·al·ize** desmoralizar; **deˈmor·al·iz·ing** desmoralizador.
de·mote [di:ˈmout] degradar; **deˈmo·tion** degradación *f*.
de·mur [diˈmə:r] **1.** reparo *m*, pega *f*; **2.** poner pegas, objetar.
de·mure [diˈmju·r] □ grave, solemne; (*modest*) recatado; *b.s.* gazmoño; **deˈmure·ness** gazmoñería *f*; recato *m*.
de·mur·rage [diˈmʌridʒ] estadía *f*; **deˈmur·rer** objeción *f*; ⚖ excepción *f*.
de·my [diˈmai] papel *m* marquilla.
den [den] (*animal's, robber's*) madriguera *f*; F (*room*) cuchitril *m*; F cuarto *m* de estudio; *opium* ~ fumadero *m* de opio.
de·na·tion·al·ize [di:ˈnæʃnəlaiz] desnacionalizar.
de·ni·a·ble [diˈnaiəbl] negable; **deˈni·al** negación *f*; (*refusal*) denegación *f*; (*a. self-*~) abnegación *f*; **deˈni·er** negador (-a *f*) *m*.
den·i·grate [ˈdenigreit] denigrar.
den·im [ˈdenim] (*freq.* ~*s pl.*) dril *m* de algodón.
den·i·zen [ˈdenizn] habitante *m/f*; extranjero (a *f*) *m* naturalizado (a).
de·nom·i·nate [diˈnɔmineit] denominar; **de·nom·iˈna·tion** denominación *f*; categoría *f*; *eccl.* secta *f*, confesión *f*; valor *m of coin etc.*;

de·nom·i'na·tion·al *mst eccl.* sectario; **de'nom·i·na·tive** [~nətiv] denominativo (*a. gr.*); **de'nom·i·na·tor** [~neitər] denominador *m*; *common* ~ denominador *m* común.

de·no·ta·tion [di:nou'teiʃn] denotación *f*; designación *f*; significación *f*; **de'note** denotar; señalar, designar; significar.

de·nounce [di'nauns] denunciar; censurar, reprender; **de'nounce·ment** denuncia *f*; censura *f*, reprensión *f*.

dense [dens] □ denso, compacto; *undergrowth etc.* tupido; F duro de mollera; **'dense·ness** *mst* estupidez *f*; **'den·si·ty** densidad *f* (*a. phys.*).

dent [dent] **1.** abolladura *f*; mella *f in edge*; **2.** abollar(se); mellar.

den·tal ['dentl] **1.** dental; odontológico; ~ *floss* hilo *m* dental; ~ *science* odontología *f*; **2.** 🕮 dental *f*; **den·tate** ['~teit] dentado; **den·ti·frice** ['~tifris] dentífrico *m*; **'den·tist** dentista *m*, odontólogo *m*; **'den·tist·ry** odontología *f*; **den·ture** ['~tʃər] dentadura *f* artificial; (*esp.* ~*s pl.*) dentadura *f* postiza.

den·u·da·tion [di:nju:'deiʃn] denudación *f*; despojo *m*; **de'nude** denudar; despojar (*of* de).

de·nun·ci·a·tion [dinʌnsi'eiʃn] denuncia *f* (*a.* ⚖), denunciación *f*; **de'nun·ci·a·tor** denunciador (-a *f*) *m*; ⚖ denunciante *m*/*f*.

de·ny [di'nai] negar; *request etc.* denegar; *report* desmentir; ~ *o.s.* abnegarse; ~ *o.s. th.* negarse, no permitirse.

de·o·dor·ize [di:'oudəraiz] desodorizar; **de'o·dor·ant** desodorante *m*.

de·part [di'pa:rt] *v*/*i*. partir, marcharse; (*train etc.*) salir, tener su salida; ~ *from truth etc.* apartarse de, desviarse de; *the* ~*ed* el (la) difunto (a); *v*/*t*.: ~ *this life* partir de esta vida; **de'part·ment** departamento *m*; sección *f*, ramo *m*; ministerio *m*; ~ *store* grandes almacenes *m*/*pl*.; **de·part'men·tal** □ departamental; **de'par·ture** [~tʃər] partida *f*, salida *f*; *fig.* desviación *f*; *attr.* 🚂 *etc.* de salida; *new* ~ un curso (*or* rumbo) nuevo.

de·pend [di'pend] ✎ pender, colgar; ~ (*up*)*on* depender de; *p. etc.* contar con, confiar en; F *it* ~*s* eso depende; **de'pend·a·ble** □ *p.* formal, confiable; seguro; **de'pend·ant** familiar *m*/*f* dependiente; **de'pend·ence** dependencia *f* (*on* de); confianza *f* (*on* en); apoyo *m* (*on* sobre); **de'pend·en·cy** *mst* posesión *f*, colonia *f*; **de'pend·ent 1.** □ dependiente (*on* de); pendiente (*on* de); *gr.* subordinado; **2.** *v. dependant*.

de·pict [di'pikt] representar, describir; *paint.* pintar, dibujar.

de·pil·a·to·ry [de'pilətəri] depilatorio *adj. a. su. m.*

de·plete [di'pli:t] agotar; *stock etc.* mermar; ⚕ depauperar; **de'ple·tion** agotamiento *m*; ⚕ depauperación *f*.

de·plor·a·ble [di'plɔ:rəbl] □ deplorable; **de·plore** [di'plɔ:r] deplorar.

de·ploy [di'plɔi] ⚔ desplegar; *fig.* organizar; **de'ploy·ment** despliegue *m*.

de·po·nent [di'pounənt] **1.** *gr.* deponente; **2.** ⚖ deponente *m*.

de·pop·u·late [di:'pɔpjuleit] despoblar; **'de·pop·u'la·tion** despoblación *f*.

de·port [di'pɔ:rt] deportar; ~ *o.s.* comportarse; **de·por'ta·tion** deportación *f*; **de·port·ee** [di:pɔ:r'ti:] deportado (a *f*) *m*; **de'port·ment** porte *m*, continente *m*; conducta *f*.

de·pose [di'pouz] deponer (*a.* ⚖).

de·pos·it [di'pɔzit] **1.** depósito *m* (*a.* ✝); *geol.* yacimiento *m*; ✝ señal *f*; (*house etc.*) desembolso *m* inicial; ⚗ poso *m*; ~ *account* cuenta *f* corriente; **2.** depositar (*with* en); ✝ dar para señal; ⚗ sedimentar; **de'pos·i·ta·ry** (*p.*) depositario (a *f*) *m*; **dep·o·si·tion** [depə'ziʃn] deposición *f* (*a.* ⚖); *eccl.*, *paint.* descendimiento *m* (de Cristo); **de·pos·i·tor** [di'pɔzitər] depositador (-a *f*) *m*; ✝ cuentacorrentista *m*/*f*, imponente *m*; **de'pos·i·to·ry** depositaría *f*, almacén *m*; *fig.* filón *m*.

de·pot ['depou] depósito *m*, almacén *m*; 🚂 estación *f*.

dep·ra·va·tion [deprə'veiʃn] depravación *f*, perversión *f*; **de·prave** [di'preiv] depravar; **de'praved** depravado; **de·prav·i·ty** [di'præviti] depravación *f*, estragamiento *m*.

dep·re·cate ['deprikeit] desaprobar, lamentar; **dep·re·ca·to·ry** ['~təri] de desaprobación.

de·pre·ci·ate [di'pri:ʃieit] depreciar(se); desestimar, despreciar; **de·pre·ci'a·tion** depreciación *f*; **de'pre·ci·a·to·ry** [\~təri] despectivo.
dep·re·da·tion [depri'deiʃn] depredación *f*; \~*s pl.* estragos *m/pl.*; **'dep·re·da·tor** depredador *m*.
de·press [di'pres] deprimir (*a. fig.*); (*dispirit*) desalentar, desanimar; *price* hacer bajar; \~*ed* alicaído, abatido; \~*ed area* zona *f* deprimida; **de'press·ing** □ deprimente; triste; **de·pres·sion** [di'preʃn] depresión *f* (*a.* ⚕, ⚓); ⚕ flojedad *f*; crisis *f* económica; *meteor.* depresión *f*, borrasca *f*; *geog.* hondonada *f*.
dep·ri·va·tion [depri'veiʃn] privación *f*; *a great* \~ una gran pérdida; **dep·ri·ve** [di'praiv] privar (*of* de).
depth [depθ] profundidad *f* (*a. fig.*); fondo *m of building*; \~ *charge* carga *f* de profundidad; *in the* \~ *of* en lo más recio de, en pleno ...; *be out of one's* \~ cubrirle a uno (el agua); *fig. get out of one's* \~ meterse en honduras; *the* \~ *s pl.* ⚓ el abismo, el piélago.
dep·u·ta·tion [depju'teiʃn] diputación *f*; **de·pute** [di'pju:t] diputar; **dep·u·tize** ['depjutaiz] diputar; \~ *for s.o.* sustituir a; **'dep·u·ty 1.** diputado *m* (*a. pol.*); sustituto *m*, suplente *m*; **2.** *attr.* teniente, suplente.
de·rail [di'reil] (hacer) descarrilar; **de'rail·ment** descarrilamiento *m*.
de·range [di'reindʒ] desarreglar, descomponer; *p.* volver loco; **de'range·ment** desarreglo *m*, descompostura *f*; ⚕ trastorno *m* mental.
de·rate [di:'reit] *property* reducir los impuestos sobre.
Der·by ['də:rbi] *sport*: derby *m*; **'der·by** (*hat*) hongo *m*; *sports*: carrera *f*.
der·e·lict ['derilikt] **1.** abandonado; negligente; **2.** *esp.* ⚓ derrelicto *m*; pelafustán (-a *f*) *m*; **der·e·lic·tion** [deri'likʃn] abandono *m*; desamparo *m*; \~ *of duty* negligencia *f* (de sus deberes).
de·ride [di'raid] ridiculizar, mofarse de; **de·ri·sion** [di'riʒn] mofa *f*, befa *f*; **de·ri·sive** [di'raisiv] □ mofador; **de'ri·so·ry** [\~səri] mofador; *quantity etc.* irrisorio, ridículo.
de·riv·a·ble [di'raivəbl] derivable; deducible; **der·i·va·tion** [deri'veiʃn] derivación *f*; **de·riv·a·tive** [di'rivətiv] **1.** □ derivativo, derivado (*a. gr.*); **2.** derivativo *m* (*a. gr.*, ⚕); **de·rive** [di'raiv] derivar(se) (*from* de); *profit* sacar (*from* de); *be* \~*d from* provenir de.
der·ma·tol·o·gist [də:rmə'tɔlədʒist] dermatológo *m*; **der·ma'tol·o·gy** dermatología *f*.
der·o·gate ['derəgeit] detraer (*from* de); *b.s.* desmerecerse; **der·o'ga·tion** menosprecio *m*; **de·rog·a·to·ry** [di'rɔgətɔ:ri] □ despreciativo, despectivo.
der·rick ['derik] grúa *f*; (*oil*) torre *f* de perforación, derrick *m*.
des·cant [dis'kænt] *fig.* discantar (*upon* sobre).
de·scend [di'send] descender, bajar (*from* de); \~ (*up*)*on* caer sobre; *fig.* \~ *to* rebajarse a; \~ (*or be* \~*ed*) *from* descender de; **de'scend·ant** descendiente *m/f*.
de·scent [di'sent] descendimiento *m* (*a. eccl.*); (*fall*) descenso *m* (*a. fig.*); (*origin*) descendencia *f* (*from* de); ⚖ herencia *f*; *geog.* declive *m*; *esp.* ⚓ invasión *f*.
de·scrib·a·ble [dis'kraibəbl] descriptible; **de'scribe** describir (*a.* ⚫); \~ *as* calificar de.
de·scrip·tion [dis'kripʃn] descripción *f*; clase *f*. género *m*; **de'scrip·tive** □ descriptivo; *style* pintoresco.
de·scry [dis'krai] divisar, columbrar.
des·e·crate ['desikreit] profanar; **des·e'cra·tion** profanación *f*.
des·ert¹ **1.** ['dezərt] a) desierto; inhabitado; b) desierto *m*, yermo *m*; **2.** [di'zə:rt] *v/t.* ⚔ desertar; abandonar, desamparar; *v/i.* ⚔, ⚖ desertar (*from* de; *to* a); ⚖ abandonar el domicilio conyugal.
de·sert² [di'zə:rt] (*a.* \~*s pl.*) merecimiento *m*, mérito *m*; *get one's (just)* \~*s* llevar su merecido.
de·sert·er [di'zə:rtər] desertor *m*; **de'ser·tion** deserción *f*, abandono *m*.
de·serve [di'zə:rv] merecer (*of* de, para con); *he got what he* \~*d* llevó su merecido; **de'serv·ed·ly** [\~vidli] merecidamente; **de'serv·ing** □ merecedor (*of* de); digno (*of* de).
des·ha·bille ['dezæbi:l] desabillé *m*.
des·ic·cate ['desikeit] desecar; **des·ic'ca·tion** desecación *f*.

de·sid·er·a·tum [di'sidə'reitəm] desiderátum *m*.

de·sign [di'zain] **1.** ⊕ *etc.* diseño *m*, traza *f*; (*pattern*) dibujo *m*; (*sketch*) bosquejo *m*; (*purpose*) designio *m*, intención *f*; *by* ~ intencionalmente; △ *modern* ~ estilo *m* moderno, moderno diseño *m*; F *have* ~*s on* tener sus proyectos sobre; **2.** diseñar, trazar; dibujar; (*purpose*) idear, proyectar; *be* ~*ed to* estar proyectado para; *well* (*badly*) ~*ed house* bien (mal) distribuido.

des·ig·nate 1. ['dezigneit] designar; nombrar; (*point to*) señalar; **2.** ['~nit] designado, nombrado; **des·ig'na·tion** nombramiento *m*; (*title etc.*) denominación *f*.

de·sign·ed·ly [di'zainidli] adrede; **de'sign·er** dibujante *m*; diseñador *m*; **de'sign·ing** intrigante.

de·sir·a·ble [di'zairəbl] □ deseable, apetecible; **de·sire** [di'zaiər] **1.** deseo *m* (*for*, *to* de); **2.** desear (*to inf.*, *a p. to* que una p. *subj.*); **de·sir·ous** [di'zairəs] □ deseoso (*of* de; *to inf.* de *inf.*; *that* de que *subj.*).

de·sist [di'zist] desistir (*from* de).

desk [desk] pupitre *m*; (*a. writing* ~) escritorio *m*; mesa *f*.

des·o·late 1. ['desəleit] asolar; *p.* entristecer; **2.** ['~lit] □ desierto, solitario; despoblado; (*in ruins*) arruinado; (*forlorn*) lúgubre, triste; **des·o'la·tion** soledad *f*; desolación *f*; (*act*) arrasamiento *m*.

de·spair [dis'per] **1.** desesperación *f*; **2.** desesperar (*of* de); **de·spair·ing** [dis'periŋ] □ desesperado.

des·patch = *dispatch*.

des·per·a·do [despə'rɑːdou] bandido *m*; forajido *m*.

des·per·ate ['despərit] □ desesperado; *situation etc.* grave; *fight* encarnizado; (*bold*) temerario; **des·per·a·tion** [despə'reiʃn] desesperación *f*; *in* ~ desesperado.

des·pi·ca·ble ['despikəbl] □ despreciable; vil, ruin.

de·spise [dis'paiz] despreciar; desdeñar. [de.]

de·spite [dis'pait] *prp.* a despecho

de·spoil [dis'pɔil] despojar (*of* de); **de'spoil·ment** despojo *m*.

de·spond [dis'pɔnd] desalentarse, desanimarse; desesperar (*of* de); **de'spond·en·cy** [~dənsi] desánimo *m*; desesperación *f*; **de'spond·ent** □ abatido, alicaído; *be* ~ andar de capa caída.

des·pot ['despɔt] déspota *m*; **des'pot·ic** □ despótico; **des·pot·ism** ['~pətizm] despotismo *m*.

des·sert [di'zəːrt] postre *m*; ~ *spoon* cuchara *f* de postre; *v. desert*[2].

des·ti·na·tion [desti'neiʃn] destino *m* (*a.* 🚂), paradero *m*; **des·tine** ['~tin] destinar (*to*, *for* a, para); *be* ~*d to* estar destinado a; **'des·ti·ny** destino *m*, hado *m*.

des·ti·tute ['destitjuːt] indigente; desprovisto (*of* de); **des·ti'tu·tion** indigencia *f*.

de·stroy [dis'trɔi] destruir (*a. fig.*); matar; (*annihilate*) aniquilar; **de'stroy·er** destructor *m* (*a.* ⚓).

de·struct·i·bil·i·ty [distrʌkti'biliti] destructibilidad *f*; **de'struct·i·ble** [~əbl] destructible; **de'struc·tion** destrucción *f* (*a. fig.*); ⚔ *etc.* estragos *m/pl.*; **de'struc·tive** □ destructivo (*a. fig.*); *child* revoltoso; nocivo (*of* a); **de'struc·tive·ness** espíritu *m* de destrucción; **de'struc·tor** incinerador *m* (de basuras).

des·ue·tude [di'sjuːitjuːd] desuso *m*.

des·ul·to·ri·ness ['desəltərinis] calidad *f* de inconexo (*or* deshilvanado); **'des·ul·to·ry** □ inconexo, deshilvanado; intermitente.

de·tach [di'tætʃ] separar, desprender; ⚔ destacar; **de'tach·a·ble** separable, desmontable; suelto; **de'tached** separado, desprendido; *fig.* imparcial, objetivo; ~ *house* hotel *m*; *become* ~ desprenderse, separarse; **de'tach·ment** separación *f*, desprendimiento *m*; *fig.* objetividad *f* (*of mind* de ánimo); ⚔ destacamento *m*.

de·tail 1. ['diːteil] detalle *m*, pormenor *m*; ⚔ destacamento *m*; *in* ~ en detalle; *go into* ~ menudear; **2.** [di'teil] detallar; ⚔ destacar; **'de·tailed** *account etc.* detallado, detenido.

de·tain [di'tein] detener (*a.* ⚖); (*delay*) retener; **de·tain·ee** [~'niː] detenido *m*; **de'tain·er** ⚖ detención *f*.

de·tect [di'tekt] descubrir, percibir; **de'tect·a·ble** perceptible; **de'tec·tion** descubrimiento *m*; **de'tec·tive** detective *m*; *attr.* policiaco, de detective; ~ *story* novela *f* policía-

ca (*or* policial); **deˈtec·tor** descubridor *m*; *radio a.* ⚓: detector *m*.
dé·tente [deiˈtɑ̃:nt] *pol.* détente *f*.
de·ten·tion [diˈtenʃn] detención *f*, arresto *m*; *unlawful* ~ detención *f* ilegal.
de·ter [diˈtəːr] disuadir (*from* de); impedir (*from* que *subj.*).
de·ter·gent [diˈtəːrdʒənt] detergente *adj. a. su. m*.
de·te·ri·o·rate [diˈtiriəreit] *v/t*. deteriorar; *v/i*. empeorarse; **de·te·ri·o·ˈra·tion** deterioro *m*, empeoramiento *m*.
de·ter·ment [diˈtəːrmənt] disuasión *f*.
de·ter·mi·na·ble [diˈtəːrminəbl] □ determinable; **deˈter·mi·nant** determinante *adj. a. su. m*; **deˈter·mi·nate** [~nit] □ determinado; definitivo, distinto; **de·ter·miˈna·tion** determinación *f*; (*resolve*) empeño *m*; **deˈter·mi·na·tive** [~neitiv] determinativo (*a. gr.*); **deˈter·mine** [~min] determinar (*to inf.*); determinarse (*to* a); ocasionar, dar motivo a; ~ *on* optar por; resolverse a; **deˈter·mined** □ resuelto; (*stubborn*) porfiado.
de·ter·rent [diˈterənt] **1.** disuasivo; **2.** lo que disuade; impedimento *m*; (*threat*) amenaza *f*.
de·test [diˈtest] detestar; **deˈtest·a·ble** □ detestable; **de·tes·ta·tion** [di:tesˈteiʃn] detestación *f*; persona *f* detestada; *hold in* ~ execrar.
de·throne [diˈθroun] destronar; **deˈthrone·ment** destronamiento *m*.
det·o·nate [ˈdetouneit] (hacer) detonar; **ˈdet·o·nat·ing cap** cápsula *f* fulminante; **det·oˈna·tion** detonación *f*; **det·o·na·tor** [ˈ~tər] detonador *m*, cápsula *f* fulminante.
de·tour [ˈdi:tur] desvío *m*, rodeo *m*.
de·tract [diˈtrækt]: ~ *from* quitar atractivo a; rebajar, quitar mérito a; **deˈtrac·tive** detractor; **deˈtrac·tor** calumniador (-a *f*) *m*.
de·train [di:ˈtrein] ⚔ (hacer) bajar del tren.
det·ri·ment [ˈdetrimənt] perjuicio *m*, detrimento *m*; *to the* ~ *of* en perjuicio de; **det·ri·men·tal** [detriˈmentl] □ perjudicial (*to* a, para).
de·tri·tus [diˈtraitəs] detrito *m*.
deuce [dju:s] **1.** *dice*: dos *m*; *tennis*: a dos; **2.** F diantre *m*, demonio *m*; *what the* ~ ...? ¿qué demonios ...?
de·val·u·a·tion [di:væljuˈeiʃn] desvalorización *f*; **deˈval·ue** desvalorizar.
dev·as·tate [ˈdevəsteit] devastar; **ˈdev·as·tat·ing** □ *fig.* arrollador; **dev·asˈta·tion** devastación *f*.
de·vel·op [diˈveləp] *v/t*. desarrollar (*a.* ♞), desenvolver; *phot.* revelar; *land* urbanizar; ⚒ *etc.* explotar; *v/i*. desarrollarse; F (*esp. be* ~*ing*) ir, progresar; **deˈvel·op·er** *phot.* revelador *m*; **deˈvel·op·ing** *phot.* revelado *m*; **deˈvel·op·ment** desarrollo *m*, desenvolvimiento *m*; *phot.* revelado *m*; (*a. urban* ~) urbanización *f*; ⚒ explotación *f*; *fig.* (*esp. new* ~) acontecimiento *m* nuevo, novedad *f*; ~ *area* zona *f* con tendencia a paro laboral severo.
de·vi·ate [ˈdi:vieit] desviar(se) (*from* de); **de·viˈa·tion** desviación *f* (*a. compass*).
de·vice [diˈvais] ⊕ dispositivo *m*, aparato *m*; *fig.* recurso *m*, ardid *m*; emblema *m*; (*motto*) lema *m*; *nuclear* ~ ingenio *m* nuclear; *leave to one's own* ~*s* dejar a uno que haga lo que le dé la gana.
dev·il [ˈdevl] **1.** diablo *m* (*a. fig.*); F arrojo *m*, ardor *m*; ⚖ abogado *m* principiante; *typ.* mozo *m* recadero; plato *m* picante; *the* ~! ¡diablos!; *poor* ~! ¡pobre diablo!; *between the* ~ *and the deep blue sea* entre la espada y la pared; F *like the* ~ como el diablo; F *talk of the* ~! ¡hablando (del ruin) de Roma, por la puerta asoma!; F *there'all be the* ~ *to pay* nos sentarán las costuras; F *raise the* ~ armarla; **2.** preparar con mucho picante; vejar; ⚖ ~ *for* trabajar de abogado para (un principal); **ˈdev·il·ish** □ diabólico; *adv.* F extremadamente; **ˈdev·il-may-ˈcare** F despreocupado; temerario; **ˈdev·il·ment** maldad *f*; (*mischief*) diablura *f*; **ˈdev·il·ry, ˈdev·il·try** diablura *f*.
de·vi·ous [ˈdi:viəs] □ apartado, aislado; *path* tortuoso.
de·vise [diˈvaiz] **1.** ⚖ legado *m*; **2.** idear, proyectar; hacer proyectos; ⚖ legar; **de·vis·er, de·vis·or** [diˈvaizər] autor *m*, inventor *m*; ⚖ testador *m*.
de·vi·tal·ize [di:ˈvaitəlaiz] debilitar.
de·void [diˈvɔid] desprovisto (*of* de).
dev·o·lu·tion [di:vəˈlu:ʃn] ⚖ traspaso *m*; *biol.* degeneración *f*; *parl.*

delegación *f* (de poderes); **de·volve** [di'vɔlv] *v/t.*: ~ *upon* transmitir a; transferir a; *v/i.*: ~ *upon*, ~ *to* incumbir a, corresponder a.

de·vote [di'vout] dedicar; ~ *o.s. to* dedicarse a; **de'vot·ed** □ devoto; dedicado (*to* a); (*letter*) *your* ~ *servant* suyo afmo.; **dev·o·tee** [devou'ti:] devoto (a *f*) *m*; **de·vo·tion** [di'vouʃn] devoción *f* (*to* a); (*studies etc.*) dedicación *f* (*to* a); ~*s pl.* oraciones *f/pl.*; rezo *m*; **de'vo·tion·al** □ piadoso, devoto.

de·vour [di'vauər] devorar (*a. fig.*); F *food* zamparse; ~*ed with* consumido de (*or* por); **de'vour·ing** devorador (*a. fig.*).

de·vout [di'vaut] □ devoto, piadoso; (*earnest*) cordial; **de'vout·ness** piedad *f*.

dew [dju:] **1.** rocío *m*; **2.** rociar; '~ **drop** gota *f* de rocío; '~**lap** papada *f*; '**dew pond** charca *f* formada por el rocío; '**dew·y** rociado; *eyes* húmedos; *fig.* ~ *eyed* ingenuo.

dex·ter·i·ty [deks'teriti] destreza *f*; **dex·ter·ous** ['~tərəs] □ diestro (*at, in* en).

di·a·be·tes [daiə'bi:ti:z] diabetes *f*; **di·a'be·tic** diabético *adj. a. su. m* (a *f*).

di·a·bol·ic, di·a·bol·i·cal [daiə'bɔlik(l)] □ diabólico.

di·a·dem ['daiədem] diadema *f*.

di·ag·nose ['daiəgnouz] diagnosticar; **di·ag'no·sis** [~sis], *pl.* **di·ag'no·ses** [~si:z] diagnosis *f*.

di·ag·o·nal [dai'ægənl] □ diagonal *adj. a. su. f* (⚒ *a. cloth*).

di·a·gram ['daiəgræm] diagrama *m*, esquema *m*; **di·a·gram·mat·ic** [daiəgrə'mætik] □ esquemático.

di·al ['daiəl] **1.** esfera *f*, cuadrante *m*; *teleph.* disco *m*; *radio*: dial *m*; **2.** *teleph.* marcar; ~*ing teleph.* marcaje *m*; **3.** ~ *telephone* teléfono *m* automático; ~ *tone teleph.* señal *f* para marcar.

di·a·lect ['daiəlekt] dialecto *m*; **di·a'lec·tic, di·a'lec·ti·cal** □ dialéctico; **di·a'lec·tics** dialéctica *f*.

di·a·log, di·a·logue ['daiəlɔg] diálogo *m*.

di·am·e·ter [dai'æmitər] diámetro *m*; **di·a·met·ri·cal** [daiə'metrikl] □ diametral; ~*ly opposed* diametralmente opuesto (*to* a).

di·a·mond ['daiəmənd] diamante *m*; (*shape*) losange *m*; *cards*: ~*s pl.* diamantes *m/pl.*, (*Spanish*) oros *m/pl.*; ~ *cut* ~ tal para cual; ~ *jubilee* sexagésimo aniversario *m*; ~ *wedding* bodas *f/pl.* de diamante; '~ '**cut·ter** diamantista *m*; '~**like** adiamantado.

di·a·pa·son [daiə'peizn] diapasón *m*; (*voice*) extensión *f*.

di·a·per ['daiəpər] pañal *m*.

di·aph·a·nous [dai'æfənəs] □ diáfano.

di·a·phragm ['daiəfræm] diafragma *m* (*a. teleph.*).

di·a·rist ['daiərist] diarista *m/f*.

di·ar·rhe·a [daiə'riə] diarrea *f*.

di·a·ry ['daiəri] diario *m*.

di·a·ther·my ['daiəθə:rmi] diatermia *f*.

di·a·ton·ic [daiə'tɔnic] diatónico.

di·a·tribe ['daiətraib] diatriba *f*.

dib·ble ['dibl] ⚘ **1.** plantador *m*; **2.** *plants* (*freq.* ~ *in*) plantar con plantador.

dibs [dibz] *sl.* parné *m*.

dice [dais] (*pl. of die*²) **1.** dados *m/pl.*; (*shape*) cubitos *m/pl.*, cuadritos *m/pl.*; *load the* ~ cargar los dados; **2.** jugar a los dados; *vegetables* cortar en cuadritos; '~ **box** cubilete *m*.

dick [dik] *sl.* detective *m*.

dick·ens ['dikinz] F diantre *m*; *the* ~ *of a* ... un tremendo ...

dick·er ['dikər] regatear.

dick·(e)y ['diki] F (*a.* ~*bird*) pájaro *m*; pechera *f* postiza *to wear*; *mot.* asiento *m* del conductor; asiento *m* trasero (descubierto).

dic·ta·phone ['diktəfoun] dictáfono *m*.

dic·tate 1. ['dikteit] mandato *m*; **2.** [dik'teit] dictar; mandar, disponer (*a. fig.*); **dic'ta·tion** dictado *m*; = *dictate*; *take* ~ escribir al dictado; **dic'ta·tor** dictador *m*; **dic·ta·to·ri·al** [diktə'tɔ:riəl] □ dictatorio; *manner etc.* dictatorial, mandón; **dic'ta·tor·ship** [dik'teitərʃip] dictadura *f*.

dic·tion ['dikʃn] dicción *f*, lenguaje *m*; **dic·tion·ar·y** ['dikʃəneri] diccionario *m*.

dict·um ['diktəm], *pl.* **dic·ta** ['~tə] aforismo *m*; ⚖ *etc.* dictamen *m*.

did [did] *pret. of do*.

di·dac·tic [dai'dæktik] □ didáctico.

did·dle ['didl] *sl.* estafar; engañar.

didn't ['didnt] = *did not*.

die[1] [dai] [*ger. dying*] morir (*of*,

from de); ~ *away* acabarse gradualmente; desaparecer; ~ *down* (*fire*) extinguirse, morir; sosegarse (*a. fig.*); ~ *off* morir, extinguirse; ~ *out* extinguirse, desaparecer; F ~ *hard* rendirse de mala gana; F *never say* ~! ¡ánimo!; *be dying to* morirse por; *be dying for* (*s.t.*) apetecer mucho, morir por (una cosa).

die[2] [~] [*pl. dice*] dado *m*; (*pl. dies* [daiz]) ⊕ troquel *m*; matriz *f*, molde *m*; *as straight as a* ~ más derecho que una vela; *the* ~ *is cast* la suerte está echada.

die...: ˈ~ ˈ**cast·ing** ⊕ pieza *f* fundida a troquel; ˈ**~-hard** intransigente (*a. su. m*); acérrimo, empedernido.

di·e·lec·tric [daiiˈlektrik] dieléctrico *adj. a. su. m.*

die·sel en·gine [ˈdi:zlˈendʒin] motor *m* diesel; ˈ**die·sel oil** gas-oil *m*.

die·stock [ˈdaistɔk] terraja *f*.

di·et [ˈdaiət] **1.** régimen *m*, dieta *f*; *pol. etc.* dieta *f*; **2.** *v/t.* poner a dieta; *v/i.* estar a dieta (*a. be on a* ~); ˈ**di·e·tar·y** dietético; **di·e·ti·cian** [daiəˈtiʃn] dietético *m*.

dif·fer [ˈdifər] diferenciar, discordar (*with, from* de); diferenciarse (*from* de); **dif·fer·ence** [ˈdifrəns] diferencia *f* (*a.* ♃); *it makes no* ~ lo mismo da; *split the* ~ partir la diferencia; ˈ**dif·fer·ent** □ diferente, distinto (*from* de); **dif·fer·ˈen·tial** [~ʃl] **1.** diferencial; ~ *calculus* cálculo *m* diferencial; **2.** diferencial *f* (♃ *a. mot.*); **dif·ferˈen·ti·ate** [~ʃieit] *v/t.* distinguir (*between* entre); *v/i.* diferenciarse (*a.* ⚘ *etc.*).

dif·fi·cult [ˈdifikəlt] □ difícil; ˈ**dif·fi·cul·ty** dificultad *f*; aprieto *m*; *difficulties pl.* ⚚ *etc.* aprietos *m/pl.*, apuros *m/pl.*; *make difficulties* poner reparos (*for s.o.* a).

dif·fi·dence [ˈdifidəns] cortedad *f*, timidez *f*; ˈ**dif·fi·dent** □ tímido, apocado.

dif·fuse 1. [diˈfju:z] difundir(se) (*a. fig.*); **2.** [~s] □ difuso (*a. fig.*); **difˈfused** [~zd] *light etc.* difuso; **difˈfu·sion** [~zən] difusión *f*; **difˈfu·sive** [~siv] □ difusivo; *speech* difuso.

dig [dig] **1.** [*irr.*] cavar, excavar; F empellar, empujar; ⚔ ~ *in* atrincherarse; F ~ *into* engolfarse en; ~ *up* desenterrar; **2.** empujón *m*; F *fig.* indirecta *f*, zumba *f*; F excavación *f*.

di·gest 1. [diˈdʒest] digerir (*a. fig.*); compendiar, resumir; **2.** [ˈdaidʒest] resumen *m*; ⚖ digesto *m*; **di·gest·i·bil·i·ty** [~əˈbiliti] digestibilidad *f*; **diˈgest·i·ble** digerible; **diˈges·tion** digestión *f*; **diˈges·tive** digestivo.

dig·ger [ˈdigər] cavador *m*; **dig·gings** [ˈ~iŋz] *pl.* F alojamiento *m*, pensión *f*; excavaciones *f/pl.*

dig·it [ˈdidʒit] ♃ dígito *m*; ˈ**dig·it·al** digital.

dig·ni·fied [ˈdignifaid] grave, solemne; **dig·ni·fy** [ˈ~fai] dignificar.

dig·ni·tar·y [ˈdignitəri] dignitario *m*; ˈ**dig·ni·ty** dignidad *f*; *beneath one's* ~ impropio; *stand* (*up*)*on one's* ~ indignarse, ponerse en su lugar.

di·gress [daiˈgres] hacer una digresión, apartarse del tema; **diˈgres·sion** [~ʃn] digresión *f*.

digs [digz] *pl.* F alojamiento *m*, pensión *f*.

dike [daik] **1.** dique *m* (*a. fig. a. geol.*); **2.** contener con un dique.

di·lap·i·date [diˈlæpideit] *furniture etc.* desmantelar(se); *house* desmoronar(se); **diˈlap·i·dat·ed** desmoronado; **di·lap·iˈda·tion** dilapidación *f of fortune*; desmoronamiento *m*; desmantelamiento *m*.

di·lat·a·bil·i·ty [daileitəˈbiliti] dilatabilidad *f*; **diˈlat·a·ble** dilatable; **dil·aˈta·tion** dilatación *f*; **diˈlate** dilatar(se) (*upon* sobre); **diˈla·tion** dilatación *f*; **dil·a·to·ri·ness** [ˈdilətərinis] tardanza *f*; ˈ**dil·a·to·ry** □ dilativo; tardón (F).

di·lem·ma [diˈlemə] dilema *m* (*a. phls.*), perplejidad *f*, apuro *m*; *be in a* ~ estar en un dilema.

dil·et·tan·te, *pl.* **dil·et·tan·ti** [diliˈtænti, *pl.* ~ˈtænti:] diletante *m/f*; aficionado (a *f*) *m*.

dil·i·gence [ˈdilidʒəns] diligencia *f*; ˈ**dil·i·gent** □ diligente, trabajador.

dil·ly·dal·ly [ˈdilidæli] F vacilar; (*loiter*) holgazanear, perder el tiempo.

di·lute [daiˈlu:t] **1.** diluir (*a. fig.*); **2.** diluido; **diˈlu·tion** dilución *f*.

di·lu·vi·al [daiˈlu:viəl] *geol.* diluvial; *hist.* diluviano.

dim [dim] **1.** □ *light* débil, mortecino; *fig.* confuso, indistinto; F atontado (*a.* **~-*witted***); F *take a* ~ *view of th.*

reprobar; **2.** amortiguar; *mot.* poner a media luz; *fig.* ofuscar, oscurecer; (*glass*) empañarse.

dime [daim] *moneda de diez centavos* (*de un dólar*); ~ *novel* novela *f* sensacional.

di·men·sion [di'menʃn] dimensión *f.*

di·min·ish [di'miniʃ] disminuir(se); **dim·i·nu·tion** [dimi'nju:ʃn] disminución *f*; **di'min·u·tive** [~jutiv] **1.** □ *gr.* diminutivo; (*small*) diminuto, menudo; **2.** *gr.* diminutivo *m.*

dim·ple ['dimpl] **1.** hoyuelo *m*; **2.** formar(se) hoyuelos; (*water*) rizar(se); '**dim·pled** que tiene hoyuelos.

din [din] **1.** estruendo *m* continuo; barahunda *f* (*e.g. of market*); **2.** atolondrar con reiteraciones.

dine [dain] *v/i.* cenar; ~ *out* cenar fuera; *v/t.* dar de cenar a; '**din·er** convidado *m*; comensal *m*; 🚃 cochecomedor *m.*

ding [diŋ] repicar; F repetir insistentemente; **~·dong** ['~'dɔŋ] repique *m*; tintín *m*; ~! ¡tolón!; *attr. battle* encarnizado.

din·gey, din·ghy ['diŋgi] bote *m*; ⚓ *rubber* ~ bote *m* salvavidas.

din·gle ['diŋgl] cañada *f* pequeña.

din·gy ['dindʒi] □ deslustrado, desmejorado; sórdido; *color* sombrío, tétrico.

din·ing... ['dainiŋ...]: '**~ car** cochecomedor *m*; '**~ hall** comedor *m*; '**~ room** comedor *m*; ~ *suite* juego *m* de comedor; ~ *table* mesa *f* de comer.

dink·ey ['diŋki] locomotora *f* de maniobras.

dink·y ['diŋki] F mono; pequeñito.

din·ner ['dinər] cena *f*; comida *f at midday*; banquete *m*; '**~ coat,** '**~ jack·et** smoking *m*; '**~ pail** fiambrera *f*; '**~ par·ty** banquete *m*; '**~ service** vajilla *f*; '**~ suit** smoking *m*; '**~ time** hora *f* de la cena o comida.

dint [dint] **1.** † golpe *m*; *by* ~ *of* a fuerza de; **2.** abollar.

di·o·ce·san [dai'ɔsisn] diocesano *adj. a. su. m*; **di·o·cese** ['daiəsis] diócesi(s) *f.*

di·op·tric [dai'ɔptrik] **1.** dióptrico; **2.** ~*s pl.* dióptrica *f.*

di·o·ra·ma [daiə'ræmə] diorama *m.*

dip [dip] **1.** *v/t.* bañar, sumergir (*a.* ⊕); *flag* bajar, saludar con; *pen* mojar; *cloth* teñir; meter, mojar (*into* en); *mot.* poner a media luz; ~*stick* varilla *f* de nivel; *v/i.* sumergirse; inclinarse hacia abajo, ladearse; (*disappear*) desaparecer, bajar; *geol.* buzar; F ~ *into* meterse en; *book* hojear; **2.** baño *m* (*a. liquid*), inmersión *f*; inclinación *f*, ladeo *m*; depresión *f in road, horizon*; F baño *m* de mar; (*candle*) vela *f* de sebo; *geol.* buzamiento *m.*

diph·the·ri·a [dif'θiriə] difteria *f.*

diph·thong ['difθɔŋ] diptongo *m.*

di·plo·ma [di'ploumə] diploma *m*; **di'plo·ma·cy** diplomacia *f*; **dip·lo·mat** ['dipləmæt] diplomático *m*; **dip·lo'mat·ic, dip·lo'mat·i·cal** □ diplomático; **dip·lo'mat·ics** *sg.* diplomática *f*; **di·plo·ma·tist** [di'ploumətist] diplomático *m* (*a. fig.*).

dip·per ['dipər] cazo *m*; *orn.* mirlo *m* acuático; *ast. the* ♀ el Carro; '**dip·py** *sl.* loco.

dip·so·ma·ni·a [dipsou'meiniə] dipsomanía *f*; **dip·so'ma·ni·ac** [~niæk] dipsomaníaco (a *f*) *m.*

dire ['daiər] horrendo, calamitoso; extremado.

di·rect [di'rekt] **1.** □ directo (*a. gr.*); sincero, abierto; ~ *current* corriente *f* continua; ⚔ ~ *hit* impacto *m* directo; ~ *speech* oración *f* directa; **2.** *adv.* derecho, en derechura; = ~*ly*; **3.** dirigir (*to, towards, at* a, hacia); mandar, ordenar (*to inf.*); **di'rec·tion** dirección *f*; (*order*) orden *f*, instrucción *f*; ~*s for use* modo *m* de empleo; *in the* ~ *of* en la dirección de; **di'rec·tion·al** *radio*: direccional; ~ *aerial* antena *f* orientable; **di'rec·tion find·er** radiogoniómetro *m*; **di'rec·tion find·ing** radiogoniometría *f*; **di'rec·tive** [~tiv] **1.** directivo; **2.** directorio *m*; **di'rect·ly 1.** *adv.* en el acto, en seguida; precisamente; **2.** *cj.* en cuanto; **di'rect·ness** derechura *f*; franqueza *f.*

di·rec·tor [di'rektər] director *m* (*a. film*); ⚕ *board of* ~*s* junta *f*, consejo *m* de administración; **di'rec·to·rate** [~rit] ⚕ dirección *f*; directorio *m*; **di'rec·tor·ship** cargo *m* de director; **di'rec·to·ry** directorio *m*; *teleph.* guía *f* telefónica.

dire·ful ['daiərful] □ calamitoso.

dirge [də:rdʒ] endecha *f.*

dir·i·gi·ble ['diridʒəbl] dirigible *adj. a. su. m.*

dirk [də:rk] puñal *m.*

dirt [də:rt] mugre *f*, suciedad *f*;

(*mud*) lodo *m*; (*filth, a. fig.*) porquería *f*; obscenidad *f*; F *fling* ~ *at* calumniar; ˈ~ˈ**cheap** F tirado; ˈ~ **road** camino *m* de tierra; ˈ~ **track** *sport*: pista *f* de ceniza; ˈ**dirt·y 1.** □ sucio (*a. fig.*); (*stained*) manchado; indecente, obsceno; ~ *linen* ropa *f* sucia; *air one's* ~ *linen in public* sacar los trapos sucios a relucir; ~ *trick sl.* perrada *f*, mala partida *f*; **2.** ensuciar; manchar.

dis·a·bil·i·ty [disəˈbiliti] inhabilidad *f*, impedimento *m*.

dis·a·ble [disˈeibl] inhabilitar, incapacitar (*for, from* para); **disˈa·bled** incapacitado; impedido; mutilado; ~ *veteran* lisiado *m* de guerra; **disˈa·ble·ment** inhabilitación *f*.

dis·a·buse [disəˈbjuːz] desengañar (*of* de).

dis·ac·cord [disəˈkɔːrd] **1.** desacuerdo *m*; **2.** discordar.

dis·ad·van·tage [disədˈvæntidʒ] desventaja *f*; *taken at a* ~ colocado en una situación violenta; **dis·ad·van·ta·geous** [disædvænˈteidʒəs] □ desventajoso.

dis·af·fect·ed [disəˈfektid] desafecto (*towards* hacia); **dis·afˈfec·tion** malquerencia *f*; *esp. pol.* descontento *m*.

dis·a·gree [disəˈgriː] desavenirse (*with* con); discrepar (*with* de); no estar de acuerdo (*on* sobre); (*quarrel*) altercar; ~ *with* (*food*) sentar mal a; **dis·aˈgree·a·ble** □ desagradable; *p.* displicente, de mal genio; desabrido (*to* con); **dis·aˈgree·ment** desacuerdo *m*; discrepancia *f*; disconformidad *f* (*with* con); (*quarrel*) altercado *m*.

dis·al·low [ˈdisəˈlau] desaprobar, rechazar; *goal* anular.

dis·ap·pear [disəˈpir] desaparecer; **dis·ap·pear·ance** [~ˈpirəns] desaparición *f*.

dis·ap·point [disəˈpɔint] decepcionar; desilusionar; *hopes* frustrar; **dis·apˈpoint·ing** □ decepcionante; **dis·apˈpoint·ment** decepción *f*, desilusión *f*; chasco *m*; ~ *in love* amor *m* fracasado.

dis·ap·pro·ba·tion [disæprouˈbeiʃn] desaprobación *f*.

dis·ap·prov·al [disəˈpruːvl] desaprobación *f*; **dis·apˈprove** desaprobar (*of th. acc.*); ~ *of p.* tener poca simpatía a.

dis·arm [disˈɑːrm] desarmar; **disˈar·ma·ment** desarme *m*, desarmamiento *m*.

dis·ar·range [ˈdisəˈreindʒ] desarreglar, descomponer; **dis·ar·range·ment** desarreglo *m*.

dis·ar·ray [disəˈrei] desorden *m*, descompostura *f*.

dis·as·ter [diˈzæstər] desastre *m*; ~ *area* zona *f* siniestrada; **disˈas·trous** □ desastroso, catastrófico.

dis·a·vow [ˈdisəˈvau] desconocer; repudiar, renunciar; **dis·aˈvow·al** desconocimiento *m*; repudio *m*, renuncia *f*.

dis·band [disˈbænd] *v/t. troops* licenciar; *organization* disolver; *v/i.* desbandarse; **disˈband·ment** licenciamiento *m*.

dis·bar [disˈbɑːr] ⚖ excluir del foro.

dis·be·lief [ˈdisbiˈliːf] incredulidad *f* (*a. eccl.*); **dis·be·lieve** [ˈdisbiˈliːv] descreer (*a. eccl.*); ˈ**dis·beˈliev·er** incrédulo (a *f*) *m*; *esp. eccl.* descreído (a *f*) *m*.

dis·bur·den [disˈbəːrdn] descargar; ~ *o.s. of* descargarse de.

dis·burse [disˈbəːrs] desembolsar; **disˈburse·ment** desembolso *m*.

disc [disk] = *disk*.

dis·card 1. [disˈkɑːrd] (*a. cards*) descartar, echar a un lado; **2.** [ˈdiskɑːrd] descarte *m*.

dis·cern [diˈsəːrn] discernir, percibir; **disˈcern·i·ble** [~əbl] □ perceptible; **disˈcern·ing** □ discernidor, perspicaz; **disˈcern·ment** discernimiento *m*, perspicacia *f*.

dis·charge [disˈtʃɑːrdʒ] **1.** *v/t.* descargar; *duty* desempeñar; *worker* despedir; *patient* dar de alta; *troops* licenciar; *abscess* sajar; *v/i.* (*river*, ⚡) descargar; ⚕ supurar; **2.** descarga *f*; descargo *m of debt*; desempeño *m*; despedida *f*, desacomodo *m*; ⚔ licenciamiento *m*; ⚕ supuración *f*; **disˈcharg·er** ⚡ excitador *m*.

dis·ci·ple [diˈsaipl] discípulo (a *f*) *m*; **disˈci·ple·ship** discipulado *m*.

dis·ci·plin·a·ble [ˈdisiplinəbl] disciplinable; castigable; **dis·ci·pli·nar·i·an** [~ˈneriən] ordenancista *m/f*; **dis·ciˈpli·na·ry** [~əri] disciplinario; **dis·ci·pline** [ˈ~plin] **1.** disciplina *f*; (*punishment*) castigo *m*; **2.** disciplinar; castigar.

dis·claim [disˈkleim] desconocer,

negar; ⚖ renunciar; **dis'claim·er** negación *f*; renuncia *f*.

dis·close [dis'klouz] revelar; divulgar, propalar; **dis'clo·sure** [~ʒər] revelación *f*; divulgación *f*.

dis·col·or·a·tion [diskʌlə'reiʃn] descoloramiento *m*; **dis'col·or** descolorar(se).

dis·com·fit [dis'kʌmfit] † derrotar; desconcertar; frustrar; **dis'com·fi·ture** [~tʃər] desconcierto *m*; frustración *f*.

dis·com·fort [dis'kʌmfərt] **1.** incomodidad *f*; **2.** inquietar.

dis·com·pose [diskəm'pouz] inquietar, desasosegar; (*ruffle*) descomponer; **dis·com'po·sure** [~ʒər] inquietud *f*; desconcierto *m*; descompostura *f*.

dis·con·cert [diskən'sə:rt] desconcertar; **dis·con'cert·ing** □ desconcertante.

dis·con·nect ['diskə'nekt] ⚡, ⊕ desconectar; desacoplar; **'dis·con'nect·ed** □ desconectado; *speech* inconexo; **'dis·con'nec·tion** desunión *f*; incoherencia *f*.

dis·con·so·late [dis'kɔnsəlit] □ desconsolado (*a. fig.*).

dis·con·tent ['diskən'tent] **1.** descontento *m*; **2.** descontentar; **'dis·con'tent·ed** □ descontento; **dis·con'tent·ment** descontento *m*.

dis·con·tin·u·ance ['diskən'tinjuəns] (*a.* **dis·con·tin·u'a·tion**) descontinuación *f*; **'dis·con'tin·ue** [~nju:] descontinuar; cesar de; *paper* anular el abono de; **'dis·con'tin·u·ous** □ discontinuo (*a.* 𝔄).

dis·cord ['diskɔ:rd], **dis'cord·ance** discordia *f*; ♪ disonancia *f*; *fig. sow* ~ sembrar cizaña; **dis'cord·ant** □ discorde (*a. fig.*); *fig.* disonante.

dis·co·theque [diskou'tek] discoteca *f*.

dis·count 1. ['diskaunt] descuento *m*, rebaja *f*; *at a* ~ al descuento; *fig. be at a* ~ no valorarse en su justo precio; **2.** [dis'kaunt] descontar (*a. fig.*); desestimar; *report* considerar exagerado; **dis'count·a·ble** descontable.

dis·coun·te·nance desaprobar; **dis'coun·te·nanced** desconcertado; (*abashed*) corrido.

dis·cour·age [dis'kʌridʒ] desalentar, desanimar; disuadir (*from* de); desaprobar; **dis'cour·age·ment** desaliento *m*; disuasión *f*; desaprobación *f*.

dis·course 1. ['diskɔ:rs] discurso *m*; *hold* ~ *with* platicar con; **2.** [dis'kɔ:rs] discurrir (*about, upon* sobre).

dis·cour·te·ous [dis'kə:rtiəs] □ descortés; **dis'cour·te·sy** [~tisi] descortesía *f*.

dis·cov·er [dis'kʌvər] descubrir; revelar; manifestar; **dis'cov·er·er** descubridor *m*; **dis'cov·er·y** descubrimiento *m*; revelación *f*; manifestación *f*.

dis·cred·it [dis'kredit] **1.** descrédito *m*; (*doubt*) duda *f*, desconfianza *f*; **2.** desacreditar; (*disbelieve*) descreer; **dis'cred·it·a·ble** □ ignominioso, deshonroso.

dis·creet [dis'kri:t] □ discreto.

dis·crep·an·cy [dis'krepənsi] discrepancia *f*.

dis·crete [dis'kri:t] □□ discreto; discontinuo.

dis·cre·tion [dis'kreʃn] discreción *f*; *at one's* ~ a discreción; *years* (*or age*) *of* ~ edad *f* de discernimiento; **dis'cre·tion·al** □, **dis'cre·tion·ar·y** discrecional.

dis·crim·i·nate [dis'krimineit] distinguir (*between* entre); ~ *against* hacer distinción en perjuicio de; **dis'crim·i·nat·ing** □ discernidor, perspicaz; de buen gusto, fino; ✝ *duty* diferencial; parcial; **dis'crim·i·na·tion** discernimiento *m*, discreción *f*; *b.s.* tratamiento *m* parcial (*against* de); *racial* ~ discriminación *f* racial; **dis'crim·i·na·tive** [~neitiv] □, **dis·crim·i'na·to·ry** □ discernidor; *b.s.* parcial.

dis·cur·sive [dis'kə:rsiv] □ divagador, difuso; *phls.* que raciocina.

dis·cus ['diskəs] *sport*: disco *m*.

dis·cuss [dis'kʌs] hablar de, tratar de; *theme etc.* versar sobre; (*argue*) discutir; **dis'cus·sion** discusión *f*; tratamiento *m*, exposición *f of theme*.

dis·dain [dis'dein] **1.** desdén *m*; **2.** desdeñar; **dis'dain·ful** [~ful] □ desdeñoso.

dis·ease [di'zi:z] enfermedad *f*; **dis'eased** enfermo; morboso; *fig.* depravado.

dis·em·bark ['disim'bɑ:rk] desembarcar; **dis·em·bar·ka·tion** [disembɑ:r'keiʃn] desembarco *m*.

dis·em·bar·rass ['disim'bærəs] desembarazar, despejar (*of* de); *fig.* librar de turbación.

dis·em·bod·y [disimˈbɔdi] *soul* separar del cuerpo; ⚔ licenciar.

dis·em·bow·el [disimˈbauəl] desentrañar.

dis·en·chant [ˈdisinˈtʃænt] desencantar (*a. fig.*).

dis·en·cum·ber [ˈdisinˈkʌmbər] descombrar; desembarazar (*of* de).

dis·en·gage [ˈdisinˈgeidʒ] ⊕ soltar, desenganchar; *p.*, ⚓ *etc.* desempeñar(se); ⚔ retirar(se); ˈ**dis·en·ˈgaged** *esp.* libre, desocupado; ˈ**dis·enˈgage·ment** *mot.* desembrague *m*; ⊕ desunión *f*; ⚓ *etc.* desempeño *m*; ⚔ retirada *f*; *pol.* neutralización *f*.

dis·en·tan·gle [ˈdisinˈtæŋgl] librar (*from* de); desenredar; *fig.* ~ *o.s. from* desenredarse de; ˈ**dis·enˈtan·gle·ment** desenredo *m*.

dis·es·tab·lish [ˈdisisˈtæbliʃ] *eccl.* separar del Estado; ˈ**dis·esˈtab·lish·ment** *eccl.* separación *f* del Estado.

dis·fa·vor [ˈdisˈfeivər] **1.** disfavor *m*; desaprobación *f*; *fall into* ~ caer en la desgracia; **2.** desfavorecer; *action* desaprobar.

dis·fig·ure [disˈfigər] desfigurar; **disˈfig·ure·ment** desfiguración *f*.

dis·fran·chise [ˈdisˈfræntʃaiz] privar de derechos de ciudadano; **dis·fran·chise·ment** [disˈfræntʃizmənt] privación *f* de derechos de ciudadano.

dis·gorge [disˈgɔːrdʒ] *v/t.* vomitar, arrojar; *fig. e.g. booty* devolver; *v/i.* (*river*) desembocar.

dis·grace [disˈgreis] **1.** desgracia *f*, disfavor *m*; ignominia *f*; escándalo *m*; *fall into* ~ caer en la desgracia; **2.** deshonrar, desacreditar; ~ *o.s.* deshonrarse, desacreditarse; **disˈgrace·ful** [~ful] □ ignominioso, vergonzoso; ~! ¡qué vergüenza!.

dis·grun·tled [disˈgrʌntld] descontento (*at* de); (*moody*) veleidoso.

dis·guise [disˈgaiz] **1.** disfrazar (*as* de; *a. fig.*); *voice* cambiar, disfrazar; **2.** disfraz *m*; *it's a blessing in* ~ no hay mal que por bien no venga.

dis·gust [disˈgʌst] **1.** repugnancia *f*, aversión *f* (*at* hacia); *fill with* ~ dar asco; **2.** repugnar, dar asco a; *be* ~*ed with* sentir repugnancia hacia; **disˈgust·ing** □ repugnante, asqueroso; ofensivo.

dish [diʃ] **1.** plato *m*, fuente *f*; *cooking*: plato *m*, manjar *m*; *wash the* ~*es* fregar los platos; **2.** servir en un plato; *sl.* vencer, burlar; F ~ *up* servir.

dis·ha·bille [disæˈbiːl] desabillé *m*.

dis·har·mo·ny [disˈhɑːrməni] disonancia *f*.

dish·cloth [ˈdiʃklɔθ] paño *m* de cocina, albero *m*; *approx.* estropajo *m*.

dis·heart·en [disˈhɑːrtn] desalentar; abatir.

di·shev·eled [diˈʃevld] *hair* despeinado, desgrenado; desaliñado.

dis·hon·est [disˈɔnist] □ fraudulento; no honrado; **dis·hon·est·y** [~ˈɔnisti] fraude *m*; falta *f* de honradez.

dis·hon·or [disˈɔnər] **1.** deshonra *f*, deshonor *m*; **2.** deshonrar, afrentar; *check etc.* negarse a aceptar (*or* pagar); **disˈhon·or·a·ble** □ deshonroso.

dish...: ˈ~**·pan** jofaina *f* para fregar los platos; ˈ~ **rack** escurreplatos *m*; ˈ~**·rag** albero *m*; ˈ~**·tow·el** paño *m* para secar platos; ˈ~**·wash·er** *p.* fregona *f*, friegaplatos *m*; ⊕ lavadora *f* de platos, lavaplatos *m*, lavavajillas *m*; ˈ~**·wa·ter** lavazas *f/pl*.

dis·il·lu·sion [disiˈluːʒn] **1.** desilusión *f*; **2.** desilusionar; **dis·ilˈlu·sion·ment** desilusión *f*.

dis·in·cli·na·tion [disinkliˈneiʃn] aversión *f*, antipatía *f* (*for*, *to* hacia); **dis·in·cline** [ˈ~ˈklain] *s.o.* hacer (a uno) poco dispuesto (*to* a); ˈ**dis·inˈclined** poco dispuesto (*to* a).

dis·in·fect [ˈdisinˈfekt] desinfectar; ˈ**dis·inˈfect·ant** desinfectante *m*; **dis·inˈfec·tion** desinfección *f*.

dis·in·fla·tion [ˈdisinˈfleiʃn] desinflación *f*.

dis·in·gen·u·ous [ˈdisinˈdʒenjuəs] □ doble, insincero.

dis·in·her·it [ˈdisinˈherit] desheredar; **dis·inˈher·it·ance** desheredación *f*.

dis·in·te·grate [disˈintigreit] desagregar(se), disgregar(se); **dis·in·teˈgra·tion** desagregación *f*, disgregación *f*.

dis·in·ter [ˈdisinˈtəːr] desenterrar.

dis·in·ter·est·ed [disˈintristid] □ desinteresado; **disˈin·ter·est·ed·ness** desinterés *m*.

dis·join [dis'dʒɔin] desunir; **dis'joint** [~t] dislocar; *fig.* desordenar; **dis'joint·ed** desarticulado; *speech* inconexo.
dis·junc·tion [dis'dʒʌŋkʃn] disyunción *f*; **dis'junc·tive** □ disyuntivo (*a. gr.*).
disk [disk] disco *m*; *mot.* ~ *clutch* embrague *m* de disco; ✓ ~ *harrow* grada *f* de discos; ~ *jockey* locutor *m* de un programa de discos, animador *m* de un programa de discos.
dis·like [dis'laik] **1.** *p.*: *I* ~ *him* le tengo aversión, me es antipático; *th.*: *I* ~ *that* eso no me gusta; *I* ~ *walking* no me gusta ir a pie; **2.** aversión *f*, antipatía *f* (*for, of* hacia, a); *take a* ~ *to* coger antipatía a; ~*d* malquisto; poco grato, impopular.
dis·lo·cate ['disləkeit] dislocar; *traffic* interceptar; *fig.* embrollar; **dis·lo'ca·tion** dislocación *f* (*a. geol.*); (*traffic*) interceptación *f*; *fig.* embrollo *m*.
dis·lodge [dis'lɔdʒ] desalojar (*a.* ⚔); quitar de su sitio, hacer caer.
dis·loy·al ['dis'lɔiəl] □ desleal; '**dis'loy·al·ty** deslealtad *f*.
dis·mal ['dizməl] □ *fig.* sombrío, tenebroso, tétrico; (*sad*) triste, lúgubre; F pésimo.
dis·man·tle [dis'mæntl] desmontar, desarmar; *house* desmantelar; ⚓ desaparejar; ⚔ desguarnecer; **dis'man·tling** desmonte *m*; desmantelamiento *m*.
dis·mast [dis'mæst] desarbolar.
dis·may [dis'mei] **1.** consternación *f*, conturbación *f*; (*discouragement*) desánimo *m*; **2.** consternar, turbar (*a. fill with* ~); desanimar.
dis·mem·ber [dis'membər] desmembrar; **dis'mem·ber·ment** desmembración *f*.
dis·miss [dis'mis] *v/t.* despedir, destituir; ⚔ licenciar; ⚖ rechazar; dar permiso a *p.* para irse; *possibility etc.* descartar, echar a un lado; ~ (*from one's mind*) poner en olvido; *be* ~*ed the service* ser separado del servicio; *v/i.* ⚔ romper filas; **dis'miss·al** despedida *f*, destitución *f*; ⚔ licenciamiento *m*; ⚖ rechazamiento *m*; permiso *m* para irse.
dis·mount [dis'maunt] desmontar (se).
dis·o·be·di·ence [disə'bi:djəns] desobediencia *f*; **dis·o'be·di·ent** □ desobediente; '**dis·o'bey** desobedecer.
dis·o·blige ['disə'blaidʒ] ser poco servicial a (*una p.*); '**dis·o'blig·ing** □ poco servicial.
dis·or·der [dis'ɔ:rdər] **1.** desorden *m*; ⚕ trastorno *m*; (*indisposition*) destemplanza *f*; tumulto *m*, motín *m*; *mental* ~ trastorno *m* mental; **2.** desordenar, desarreglar; **dis'or·dered** □ desordenado; *stomach* alterado; **dis'or·der·ly** desordenado; (*riotous*) alborotador; *conduct* escandaloso; ~ *conduct* conducta *f* contra el orden público; ~ *house euph.* burdel *m*.
dis·or·gan·i·za·tion [disɔ:rgənai'zeiʃn] desorganización *f*; falta *f* de organización; **dis'or·gan·ize** desorganizar.
dis·own [dis'oun] repudiar, desconocer; renegar de.
dis·par·age [dis'pæridʒ] desacreditar; (*with words*) menospreciar, hablar mal de; **dis'par·age·ment** descrédito *m*; menosprecio *m*, detracción *f*; **dis'par·ag·ing** □ despreciativo; ~*ly* en términos despreciativos, con desdén.
dis·pa·rate ['dispərit] □ dispar, distinto; **dis·par·i·ty** [dis'pæriti] disparidad *f*.
dis·pas·sion·ate [dis'pæʃnit] □ desapasionado, imparcial.
dis·patch [dis'pætʃ] **1.** despachar; *goods* consignar, enviar; (*death-blow*) rematar; *meal* despabilar; **2.** despacho *m*; consignación *f*; (*speed*) prontitud *f*; **dis'patch rid·er** correo *m*.
dis·pel [dis'pel] disipar, dispersar; *esp. fig.* desvanecer.
dis·pen·sa·ble [dis'pensəbl] dispensable; prescindible; **dis'pen·sa·ry** dispensario *m*; **dis·pen·sa·tion** [dispen'seiʃn] dispensación *f*; *eccl. etc.* dispensa *f*; designio *m* divino.
dis·pense [dis'pens] *v/t.* dispensar; ⚖ administrar; *pharm.* preparar; ~ *from* eximir de; *v/i.*: ~ *with* deshacerse de; prescindir de; *oath etc.* eximir de; **dis'pens·er** dispensador *m*; *pharm.* farmacéutico *m*.
dis·perse [dis'pə:rs] dispersar(se); **dis'per·sal, dis'per·sion** dispersión *f* (*a. of Jews*); *opt.* descomposición *f*; **dis'per·sive** □ dispersivo.

dis·pir·it [dis'pirit] desalentar; **dis'pir·it·ed** □ desalentado; abatido.
dis·place [dis'pleis] sacar de su sitio; destituir; (*replace*) suplir, reemplazar; *phys.* desplazar; ~*d person* (*abbr.* D. P.) desplazado (a *f*) *m*, persona *f* desplazada; **dis'place·ment** desplazamiento *m*; cambio *m* de situación, destitución *f*; remplazo *m* (*by* con).
dis·play [dis'plei] **1.** despliegue *m of quality*; exhibición *f*; pompa *f*, aparato *m*; ostentación *f* (*esp. b.s.*); ~ *cabinet* vitrina *f*; ~ *window* escaparate *m*; **2.** desplegar; exhibir; ostentar; *quality* revelar.
dis·please [dis'pli:z] desagradar, desplacer; (*annoy*) enojar, enfadar; **dis'pleased** □ disgustado (*at, with* de, con); enfadado, indignado; **dis'pleas·ing** □ desagradable, ingrato; **dis·pleas·ure** [~'pleʒər] desagrado *m*; disgusto *m* (*at* por, a causa de); enojo *m*, indignación *f*; *incur s.o.'s* ~ incurrir en el enojo de una p.
dis·port [dis'pɔ:rt]: ~ *o.s.* divertirse (*esp.* alborozadamente), juguetear.
dis·pos·a·ble [dis'pouzəbl] disponible; **dis'pos·al** disposición *f*; arreglo *m*, ajuste *m of a matter*; ✝ *etc.* consignación *f*, donación *f*; (*sale*) venta *f*; *at one's* ~ a su disposición; **dis'pose** *v/t.* disponer, arreglar; inducir, mover (to a); determinar, decidir; *v/i.* ~ *of* disponer de; (*rid*) deshacerse de, quitarse de; *rights* enajenar; *problem etc.* solucionar; *food* comer; *property* vender; **dis'posed** dispuesto (*to* a); *well* ~ bien dispuesto (*towards* hacia); **dis·po·si·tion** [~pə'siʃn] disposición *f*, orden *m*; (*character*) índole *f*, natural *m*; decreto *m*; ⚖ (*will*) legado *m*; propensión *f* (*to* a); plan *m*; ⚔ *make* ~*s* hacer preparativos.
dis·pos·sess [dispə'zes] desposeer, privar (*of* de); *tenant* desahuciar; **dis·pos·ses·sion** [~'zeʃn] desposeimiento *m*; desahucio *m*.
dis·pro·por·tion ['disprə'pɔ:rʃn] desproporción *f*; **dis·pro'por·tion·ate** [~it] □ desproporcionado; (*large*) desmesurado, indebido.
dis·prove ['dis'pru:v] confutar, refutar.
dis·pu·ta·ble [dis'pju:təbl] disputable; **dis'pu·tant** disputador *m*; **dis·pu·ta·tion** [~'teiʃn] disputa *f*; **dis·pu'ta·tious** □ disputador; **dis'pute 1.** disputa *f*, contienda *f*; *beyond* (*or without*) ~ sin disputa; *in* ~ disputado; **2.** *v/t.* disputar; *v/i.* disputar, discutir (*about, over* sobre).
dis·qual·i·fi·ca·tion [diskwɔlifi'keiʃn] inhabilitación *f*, impedimento *m*; *sport*: descalificación *f*; **dis'qual·i·fy** [~fai] inhabilitar, incapacitar (*for* para); *sport*: descalificar.
dis·qui·et [dis'kwaiət] **1.** inquietud *f*, desasosiego *m*; **2.** inquietar; **dis'qui·et·ing** inquietante; **dis·qui·e·tude** [~'kwaiitju:d] inquietud *f*.
dis·qui·si·tion [diskwi'ziʃn] disertación *f*, disquisición *f*.
dis·re·gard ['disri'gɑ:rd] **1.** indiferencia *f* (*for* a); (*neglect*) descuido *m*; *with complete* ~ *for* sin atender en lo más mínimo a; **2.** desatender, descuidar; (*ignore*) no hacer caso de.
dis·re·pair ['disri'per] mal estado *m*; *fall into* ~ desmoronarse (*esp. building*).
dis·rep·u·ta·ble [dis'repjutəbl] □ de mala fama, mal reputado; *house* de mal vivir; **dis·re·pute**['~ri'pju:t] mala fama *f*, descrédito *m*; *bring into* ~ desacreditar.
dis·re·spect ['disris'pekt] desacato *m*, falta *f* de respeto; **dis·re·spect·ful**['~'pektful] □ irrespetuoso, desacatador.
dis·robe ['dis'roub] desnudar(se) (*of* de; *a. fig.*).
dis·rupt [dis'rʌpt] romper; *fig.* desbaratar, desorganizar; **dis'rup·tion** rompimiento *m*; desordenamiento *m*, confusión *f*; desbaratamiento *m*, desorganización *f*.
dis·sat·is·fac·tion ['dissætis'fækʃn] descontento *m*; desagrado *m*; **'dis·sat·is'fac·to·ry** [~təri] □ poco satisfactorio; **'dis'sat·is·fy** [~fai] desagradar, descontentar.
dis·sect [di'sekt] disecar; *fig.* hacer la disección de; **dis·sec·tion** [di'sekʃn] disección *f*; análisis *m* minucioso.
dis·sem·ble [di'sembl] *v/t.* disimular, encubrir; *v/i.* disimular, ser hipócrita; **dis'sem·bler** disimulador (-a *f*) *m*.
dis·sem·i·nate [di'semineit] diseminar, difundir; **dis·sem·i'na·tion** difusión *f*.

dis·sen·sion [di'senʃn] disensión *f*, discordia *f*; *eccl.* disidencia *f*.
dis·sent [di'sent] **1.** disentir (*from* de); *eccl.* disidir; **2.** disentimiento *m*; *eccl.* disidencia *f*; **dis'sent·er** *mst eccl.* disidente *m*; **dis·sen·tient** [di'senʃiənt] **1.** disidente, disconforme; **2.** disidente *m*.
dis·ser·ta·tion [disər'teiʃn] disertación *f* (*on* sobre).
dis·serv·ice ['dis'sə:rvis] deservicio *m* (*to* a); *render a* ~ *to* perjudicar.
dis·sev·er [dis'sevər] partir, separar.
dis·si·dence ['disidəns] disidencia *f*; **'dis·si·dent** disidente *adj. a. su. m.*
dis·sim·i·lar ['di'similər] □ disimilar (*a. gr.*), desemejante (*to* de); **dis·sim·i·lar·i·ty** ['~'læriti] desemejanza *f*.
dis·sim·u·late [di'simjuleit] = *dissemble*; **dis·sim·u'la·tion** disimulación *f*.
dis·si·pate ['disipeit] *v/t.* disipar; *money* despilfarrar; *v/i.* disiparse; (*p.*) entregarse a los vicios; **'dis·si·pat·ed** disoluto; **dis·si'pa·tion** disipación *f* (*a. fig.*); libertinaje *m*.
dis·so·ci·ate [di'souʃieit] disociar; ~ *o.s. from* hacerse insolidario de; **dis·so·ci'a·tion** disociación *f*.
dis·sol·u·bil·i·ty [disɔlju'biliti] disolubilidad *f*; **dis·sol·u·ble** [di'sɔljubl] disoluble.
dis·so·lute ['disəlu:t] □ disoluto; **dis·so'lu·tion** disolución *f*.
dis·solv·a·ble [di'zɔlvəbl] disoluble; **dis'solve** *v/t.* disolver (*a. fig.*); *v/i.* disolverse; *fig.* desvanecerse; ~ *into tears* deshacerse en lágrimas; **dis'solv·ent** disolvente *adj. a. su. m.*
dis·so·nance ['disənəns] disonancia *f* (*a. fig.*); **'dis·so·nant** disonante (*a. fig.*).
dis·suade [di'sweid] disuadir (*from* de); **dis·sua·sion** [di'sweiʒən] disuasión *f*; **dis·sua·sive** [di'sweisiv] □ disuasivo.
dis·taff ['distæf] rueca *f*; *fig. on the* ~ *side* por parte de madre.
dis·tance ['distəns] **1.** distancia *f* (*a. fig.*); lejanía *f*, lontananza *f*; *fig.* reserva *f*, recato *m*; *paint.* término *m*; *at a* ~ a distancia; *in the* ~ a lo lejos, en lontananza; *from a* ~ de lejos; *fig. keep at a* ~ no tratar con familiaridad; *keep one's* ~ mantenerse a distancia; *striking* ~ alcance *m*; **2.** distanciar; *sport:* dejar atrás (*a. fig.*); **'dis·tant** □ distante; lejano; (*slight*) leve, ligero; *fig.* indiferente, frío; *relation* lejano; *be* ~ *with s.o.* tratar con frialdad.
dis·taste ['dis'teist] aversión *f*, repugnancia *f* (*for, towards* hacia, por); **dis'taste·ful** [~ful] □ desagradable, poco grato (*to* a); (*annoying*) enfadoso.
dis·tem·per[1] [dis'tempər] **1.** pintura *f* al temple; **2.** pintar al temple.
dis·tem·per[2] [~] *vet.* moquillo *m*; *pol.* desorden *m*, destemplanza *f*.
dis·tend [dis'tend] dilatar(se), distender(se), hinchar(se); **dis'ten·sion** distensión *f*, dilatación *f*.
dis·tich ['distik] dístico *m*.
dis·til(l) [dis'til] destilar (*a.* ⚗); **dis·til·late** ['~eit] ⚗ destilar; **dis·til·la·tion** [~'leiʃən] destilación *f*; **dis'till·er** destilador *m*; **dis'till·er·y** destilería *f*.
dis·tinct [dis'tiŋkt] □ distinto; claro, inequívoco; positivo; *as* ~ *from* a diferencia de; **dis'tinc·tion** distinción *f*; individualidad *f of style*; sobresaliente *m in exam*; *draw a* ~ *between* hacer una distinción entre; *have the* ~ *of ger.* haberse distinguido por *inf.*; **dis'tinc·tive** □ distintivo, característico; **dis'tinct·ness** claridad *f*.
dis·tin·guish [dis'tiŋgwiʃ] distinguir (*between* entre); ~ *o.s.* distinguirse; *be* ~*ed from* distinguirse de; **dis'tin·guish·a·ble** distinguible; **dis'tin·guished** distinguido; conocible (*by* por).
dis·tort [dis'tɔ:rt] torcer (*a. fig.*), deformar; **dis'tor·tion** torcimiento *m*, deformación *f*; *radio etc.*: distorsión *f*.
dis·tract [dis'trækt] distraer; (*confuse*) aturdir, confundir; (*madden*) volver loco; **dis'tract·ed** □ aturdido; enloquecido; **dis'tract·ing** □ que distrae (la atención); **dis'trac·tion** distracción *f*; diversión *f*; aturdimiento *m*, perplejidad *f*; locura *f*; *drive s.o. to* ~ volver loco.
dis·train [dis'trein]: ~ *upon* secuestrar, embargar; **dis'traint** secuestro *m*, embargo *m*.
dis·traught [dis'trɔ:t] demente; (*agitated*) muy turbado.
dis·tress [dis'tres] **1.** pena *f*, angus-

tia *f*; (*straits*) apuro *m*, miseria *f*; (*danger*) peligro *m*; = *distraint*; ⚕ agotamiento *m*; ~ *rocket* cohete *m* de señales; ~ *signal* señal *f* de peligro; **2.** apenar, afligir; agotar; **dis'tressed** *freq.* preocupado (*for* por); **dis'tress·ing** □ penoso, que da pena.

dis·trib·ute [dis'tribju:t] distribuir, repartir (*among* entre); **dis·tri'bu·tion** distribución *f*, repartimiento *m*; **dis'trib·u·tive** □ distributivo (*a. gr.*); **dis'trib·u·tor** distribuidor (-a *f*) *m*; ⊕, ⚡ distribuidor *m*; ✝ distribuidora *f* (*a. films*).

dis·trict ['distrikt] comarca *f*, región *f*; *pol.* distrito *m*; ⚖ jurisdicción *f*; ~ *attorney* fiscal *m*.

dis·trust [dis'trʌst] **1.** desconfianza *f*, recelo *m*; **2.** desconfiar de, recelar; **dis'trust·ful** [~ful] □ desconfiado; (*suspicious*) receloso.

dis·turb [dis'tə:rb] *p* molestar, estorbar; inquietar, perturbar; *order* alborotar; *balance of mind* trastornar; **dis'turb·ance** alboroto *m*, disturbio *m*; (*disquiet*) desasosiego *m*; trastorno *m of mind*.

dis·un·ion ['dis'ju:njən] desunión *f*; **dis·u·nite** ['disju'nait] desunir(se) (*a. fig.*).

dis·use ['dis'ju:s] desuso *m*; *fall into* ~ caer en desuso; **dis'used** [~zd] *mst building* abandonado.

di·syl·lab·ic ['daisi'læbik] □ disílabo; **di·syl·la·ble** [dai'siləbl] disílabo *m*.

ditch [ditʃ] **1.** zanja *f*; (*road*) cuneta *f*; ⚔ foso *m*; *to the last* ~ hasta quemar el último cartucho; **2.** *v/i.* abrir zanjas; *v/t. sl.* zafarse de; ✈ *sl.* ~ *a plane* amarar, tomar agua; **'ditch·er** cavador *m* de zanjas.

dith·er ['diðər] F **1.** estremecimiento *m*; nerviosismo *m*; *be all of a* ~, *be in a* ~ = **2.** estar muy nervioso, estar a(l) quite y pon; (*hesitate*) vacilar.

dit·to ['ditou] iden, ídem; ~ *mark* la sigla „ (*es decir*: id.).

dit·ty ['diti] cancioneta *f*.

di·ur·nal [dai'ə:rnl] □ diurno, diario.

di·va·ga·tion [daivə'geiʃn] divagación *f*.

di·van [di'væn] diván *m*; ~ *bed* cama *f* turca.

dive [daiv] **1.** sumergirse; *swimming*: zambullirse *into water*, bucear *under water*; ✈ picar; ~*-bomb* bombardear en picado; ~ *bombing* bombardeo *m* en picado; F ~ *into pocket* meter la mano en; *building* entrar de prisa en; *matter* engolfarse en; **2.** *swimming*: salto *m* de trampolín, zambullida *f*; ✈ picado *m*; F (*esp. low*) ~ tasca *f*; **'div·er** buzo *m*, zambullidor *m*, buceador *m*; (*person who works under water*) escafandrista *m*/*f*; *orn.* colimbo *m*, zambullidor *m*.

di·verge [dai'və:rdʒ] divergir; (*road*) bifurcarse; **di'ver·gence, di'ver·gen·cy** divergencia *f*; discrepancia *f*; **di'ver·gent** □ divergente; discrepante.

di·verse [dai'və:rs] □ diverso; variado; **di·ver·si·fi'ca·tion** diversificación *f*; **di'ver·si·fy** [~fai] diversificar; **di'ver·sion** [~ʃn] diversión *f* (*a.* ⚔); (*traffic-*) desviación *f*; **di'ver·si·ty** diversidad *f*.

di·vert [dai'və:rt] divertir; *traffic* desviar.

di·vest [dai'vest] desnudar; *fig.* despojar (*of* de); ~ *o.s. of fig.* renunciar a.

di·vide [di'vaid] **1.** *v/t.* partir, dividir (*freq.* ~ *up*; *into* en); ⅄ dividir (*by* por); *fig.* dividir, sembrar la discordia entre; ~ *out* repartir; *v/i.* dividirse (*into* en); **2.** *geog.* divisoria *f*; **div·i·dend** ['dividend] ✝, ⅄ dividendo *m*, **di·vid·ers** [di'vaidərz] *pl.* compás *m* de división, **di·vid·ing** [di'vaidiŋ] divisorio; ~ *line* línea *f* divisoria.

div·i·na·tion [divi'neiʃn] adivinación *f*; **di·vine** [di'vain] **1.** □ divino (*a. fig.*); *v. service*; **2.** sacerdote *m*; teólogo *m*; **3.** adivinar (*a. fig.*); **di'vin·er** adivinador *m*; (*water*) zahorí *m*.

div·ing ['daiviŋ] salto *m* de trampolín, el bucear *etc.*; **'~ bell** campana *f* de bucear; **'~ board** trampolín *m*; **'~ suit** escafandra *f*.

di·vin·ing rod [di'vainiŋrɔd] varilla *f* de zahorí; **di·vin·i·ty** [di'viniti] divinidad *f*; teología *f*; *the* ≈ Dios *m*.

di·vis·i·bil·i·ty [divizi'biliti] divisibilidad *f*; **di'vis·i·ble** [~zəbl] divisible; **di'vi·sion** [~ʒn] división *f* (*a.* ⅄, ⚔); sección *f*; *fig.* discordia *f*; división *f*; *parl.* votación *f*; **di'vi·sion·al** ⚔ divisional; **di'vi·sor** [~zər] divisor *m*.

di·vorce [di'vɔ:rs] **1.** disolución *f* del matrimonio; divorcio *m*; *fig.* separación *f*, divergencia *f*; *get a* ~ di-

vorciarse; **2.** divorciar; *fig.* separar; **di·vor'cee** [~sei] divorciado (a *f*) *m*.
di·vulge [dai'vʌldʒ] divulgar; revelar.
dix·ie ['diksi] ⚔ *sl.* olla *f* de campaña; ♀ *el Sur de Estados Unidos*.
diz·zi·ness ['dizinis] vértigo *m*; '**dizzy** **1.** □ vertiginoso; aturdido, confuso; *height* que produce vértigo; F alegre; *sl.* estupendo; *be* ~ tener vértigos; ⚕ tener vahidos; **2.** (*a.* *make* ~) causar vértigos, marear.
do [du:] [*irr.*] (*v. a. done*) **1.** *v/t.* hacer; obrar; ejecutar; terminar; *thea.* desempeñar, representar; *cooking*: asar, cocer; *distance* recorrer; *duty* cumplir con; *hair* peinar; *homage* rendir, tributar; *problem* resolver; *room* limpiar; *sl.* visitar de turista; *sl.* estafar, timar (*a.* ~ *down*); *v. best, death, time etc.*; F ~ *o.s. well!* regalarse; ~ (*over*) *again* repetir; *sl.* ~ *in* apalear; asesinar; F ~ *out* decorar; F ~ *out of* hacer perder; ~ *up laces etc.* liar, atar; *parcel* empaquetar; *room* renovar el papel *etc.* de; **2.** *v/i.* actuar, proceder; convenir, ser suficiente; estar, encontrarse; *that will* ~ basta ya; eso sirve; *that won't* ~ no sirve; no vale; *how do you* ~? encantado, mucho gusto; ¿cómo está Vd.?; ~ *badly* ir perdiendo, sufrir reveses; salir mal; ~ *well* tener éxito; salir bien *in exam*; ~ *away with* quitar, suprimir; ~ *for p.* ser cocinera (*or* asistenta) de; F acabar con; ~ *with* conformarse con; *I could* ~ *with* me apetece; necesito; *have nothing to* ~ *with* no tener nada que ver con; ~ *without* pasarse sin, prescindir de; **3.** *v/aux.* a) *question*: ~ *you know him?* ¿le conoce Vd.?; b) *negation with not*: *I* ~ *not know him* no le conozco; c) *emphasis*: *I* ~ *feel better* ciertamente me encuentro mejor; ~ *come and see me* le ruego que venga a verme; *I* ~ *tell the truth* yo sí que digo la verdad; d) *to avoid repetition of a verb*: ~ *you like London?—I* ~ ¿le gusta Londres?—Sí; *you write better than I* ~ Vd. escribe mejor que yo; *I take a bath every day—so* ~ *I* me baño todos los días—yo también; e) *inversion after adv.*: *seldom does she come here* (ella) rara vez viene por aquí; **4.** *su.* F (*swindle*) estafa *f*; (*party*) reunión *f*, guateque *m*; *make* ~ *with* conformarse con; hacer lo posible con.
doc [dɔk] F = *doctor*.
doc·ile ['dɔsl] dócil; **do·cil·i·ty** [dɔ'siliti] docilidad *f*.
dock[1] [dɔk] recortar; *tree* desmochar; *pay* reducir, rebajar.
dock[2] [~] ⚘ acedera *f*, romaza *f*.
dock[3] [~] **1.** ⚓ (*with gates*) dique *m*; dársena *f*; *esp.* muelle *m*; ⚖ barra *f*; ~*s pl.* puerto *m*; *dry* ~ dique *m* seco; *floating* ~ dique *m* flotante; ~*hand* portuario *m*; **2.** (hacer) entrar en dique; atracar al muelle; '**dock·er** trabajador *m* portuario, cargador *m*.
dock·et ['dɔkit] rótulo *m*, marbete *m*; etiqueta *f*; ⚖ orden *m* del día; *pay* ~ *approx.* sobre *m* de paga.
dock·yard ['dɔkjɑ:rd] arsenal *m*, astillero *m*.
doc·tor ['dɔktər] **1.** doctor *m* (*a.* ⚕); ⚕ médico *m*; **2.** F medicinar; reparar; F castrar; adulterar, falsificar; **doc·tor·ate** ['~rit] doctorado *m*.
doc·tri·naire [dɔktri'ner] doctrinario *adj. a. su. m*; **doc·tri·nal** ['dɔktrinl] □ doctrinal; **doc·trine** ['~trin] doctrina *f*.
doc·u·ment **1.** ['dɔkjumənt] documento *m*; **2.** ['~ment] documentar; **doc·u'men·tal, doc·u'men·ta·ry** □ documental; ~ (*film*) documental *m*; **doc·u·men'ta·tion** documentación *f*.
dod·der ['dɔdər] **1.** ⚘ cúscuta *f*; **2.** temblar; (*totter*) tambalear; '**dod·der·ing** chocho, temblón.
dodge [dɔdʒ] **1.** regate *m* (*a. fig.*); (*trick*) truco *m*; ⊕ ingenio *m*, artificio *m*; **2.** *v/t.* evadir (moviéndose bruscamente); (*elude*) dar esquinazo a; *v/i.* F *fig.* escurrir el bulto; ~ *around* andar a saltos; ~ *round the corner* volver la esquina; **dodg·ems** ['dɔdʒəms] coches *m/pl.* de choque; '**dodg·er** *fig.* remolón (-a *f*) *m*; fullero (a *f*) *m*; anuncio *m* de mano; pan *m* de maíz.
do·do ['doudou], *pl.* **-dos** *or* **-does** F inocente *m* de ideas anticuadas; *dead as a* ~ anticuado.
doe [dou] gama *f*; hembra *f* del conejo (*or* de la liebre).
do·er ['du:ər] hacedor *m*.
does [dʌz] hace *etc.* (*v. do*).
doe·skin ['douskin] piel *f* de ante.
dog [dɔg] **1.** perro *m*; *hunt.* sabueso *m*; (*male of fox*) zorro *m*; (*wolf*) lobo *m*; F

tío *m*; F *b.s.* tunante *m*; ⊕ grapa *f*; (*a. fire* ~) morillo *m*; F *go to the* ~*s* arruinarse; entregarse al vicio; F *put on the* ~ darse ínfulas; *gay* ~ calavera *m*; *every* ~ *has his day* todo llega en este mundo; ~*catcher* lacero *m*, cazaperros *m*; ~*house* perrera *f*; ~ *in the manger* el perro del hortelano; ~ *racing* carreras *f/pl.* de galgos; ~ *show* exposición *f* canina; ~*'s life* vida *f* miserable; ♀ *Star* Canícula *f*; ~ *tooth* colmillo *m*; ~*watch* ⚓ guardia *f* de cuartillo; ~*wood* ⚘ cornejo *m*; **2.** seguir de cerca, perseguir; **'~ cart** coche *m* de dos ruedas, dócar *m*; **'~ days** *pl.* canícula *f*.

doge [doudʒ] dux *m*.

dog·fight ['dɔgfait] *mst fig.* escaramuza *f*, refriega *f*; ✈ combate *m* aéreo.

dog·ged ['dɔgid] □ tenaz, terco; **'dog·ged·ness** tenacidad *f*.

dog·ger·el ['dɔgərəl] versos *m/pl.* ramplones.

dog·gy ['dɔgi] **1.** perrito *m*; **2.** canino; aparatoso, emperejilado; **'dog 'Lat·in** latín *m* macarrónico.

dog·ma ['dɔgmə] dogma *m*; **dog·mat·ic, dog·mat·i·cal** [dɔg'mætik(l)] □ dogmático (*a. fig.*); arrogante, autoritario; **dog'mat·ics** *pl. or sg.* dogmática *f*; **dog·ma·tism** ['~mətizm] dogmatismo *m*; **'dog·ma·tist** dogmatizador *m*; **dog·ma·tize** ['~taiz] dogmatizar.

dog...: **'~ rose** rosal *m* silvestre, escaramujo *m*; **'~('s)-eared** *book* sobado, muy usado; **'~-'tired** rendido, cansadísimo; **'~ track** canódromo *m*.

doi·ly ['dɔili] pañito *m* (de adorno).

do·ing ['du:iŋ] **1.** *present participle of do*; *nothing* ~*!* de ninguna manera; **2.:** *esp.* ~*s pl.* actos *m/pl.*, hechos *m/pl.*; conducta *f*; *sl.* ⊕ *etc.* chismes *m/pl.*; *great* ~*s* gran actividad *f*, tremolina *f*.

dol·drums ['dɔldrəmz] *pl.* ⚓ zona *f* de las calmas; *fig. be in the* ~ tener murria; (*th.*) languidecer.

dole [doul] **1.** limosna *f*; subsidio *m* de paro; F *be on the* ~ estar parado; **2.** repartir, distribuir (*mst* ~ *out*).

dole·ful ['doulful] □ triste, lúgubre; **'dole·ful·ness** tristeza *f*, melancolía *f*.

doll [dɔl] **1.** muñeca *f*; *sl.* mozuela *f*; **2.** F engalanarse, emperejilarse (*a.* ~ *up*).

dol·lar ['dɔlər] dólar *m*.

dol·lop ['dɔləp] F grumo *m*; porción *f*.

doll·y ['dɔli] F muñequita *f*.

dol·o·mite ['dɔləmait] dolomita *f*.

dol·o·rous ['dɔlərəs] † lastimoso, apenado; triste.

dol·phin ['dɔlfin] delfín *m*.

dolt [doult] bobalicón *m*, mastuerzo *m*; **'dolt·ish** □ bobalicón, atontado.

do·main [də'mein] dominio *m*; *fig.* campo *m*.

dome [doum] cimborrio *m*; cúpula *f*.

do·mes·tic [də'mestik] **1.** □ doméstico; casero; *pol. strife* intestino; ~ *science college* escuela *f* de hogar; academia *f* gastronómica; **2.** doméstico *m*; **do'mes·ti·cate** [~keit] domesticar; ~*d p.* hogareño; **do·mes·ti'ca·tion** domesticación *f*; **do·mes·tic·i·ty** [doumes'tisiti] domesticidad *f*.

dom·i·cile ['dɔmisail] **1.** *esp.* ⚖ domicilio *m*; **2.** domiciliar(se); **dom·i·cil·i·ar·y** [dɔmi'siljəri] domiciliario.

dom·i·nance ['dɔminəns] dominación *f*; **'dom·i·nant** dominante *adj. a. su. f* (♪); **dom·i·nate** ['~neit] dominar; **dom·i'na·tion** dominación *f*; **dom·i·neer** [dɔmi'nir] dominar, tiranizar (*over acc.*); **dom·i'neer·ing** □ dominante, dominador.

Do·min·i·can [də'minikən] **1.** dominicano; **2.** dominico *m*.

do·min·ion [də'minjən] dominio *m*; *the* ♀*s pl.* los dominios británicos.

dom·i·no ['dɔminou] (*carnival*) dominó *m*; ficha *f* del dominó; **dom·i·noes** ['~z] *pl.* (juego *m* de) dominó *m*.

don[1] [dɔn] *univ.* (*Oxford a. Cambridge*) preceptor *m*, catedrático *m*, *fellow* (*véase*) de un colegio.

don[2] [~] ponerse.

do·nate ['douneit] donar; **do'na·tion** donación *f*.

done [dʌn] **1.** *p.p. of do*; *freq.* ser hecho, estar hecho (*a. cooking*); *have* ~ haber terminado; *have* ~ *with th.* haber terminado con; *p. freq.* no tener nada que ver con; *ger.* haber terminado de *inf.*, haber dejado de *inf.*; *it's not* ~ *to inf.* no es elegante *inf.*; *well* ~*!* ¡bien!; **2.** *adj.* terminado; F (*a.* ~ *in*, ~ *up*) rendido, hecho cisco; F ~ *for* fuera de combate;

✠ desahuciado; **3.** *int.* ¡terminado!; ✝ ¡trato hecho!.
don·jon [ˈdɔndʒən] torre *f* del homenaje.
don·key [ˈdɔŋki] burro *m*; ~ *engine* pequeña máquina *f* de vapor.
do·nor [ˈdounər] donador *m*; donante *m/f*; *blood* ~ donante *m/f* de sangre.
don't [dount] **1.** = *do not*; **2.** F prohibición *f*.
doom [du:m] **1.** *mst b.s.* destino *m*, hado *m*; perdición *f*, muerte *f*; juicio *m* final; **2.** predestinar (a la muerte, a la perdición); condenar (a muerte); **dooms·day** [ˈdu:mzdei] día *m* del juicio final.
door [dɔ:r] puerta *f* (*a. fig.*); (*street-*) portal *m*; portezuela *f of vehicle*; ~*bell* campanilla *f* de puerta, timbre *m* de puerta; ~ *check* amortiguador *m*, cierre *m* de puerta; ~*frame* bastidor *m* de puerta, marco *m* de puerta; ~*head* dintel *m*; ~*jamb* jamba *f* de puerta; ~ *knob* botón *m* de puerta, pomo *m* de puerta; ~ *knocker* aldaba *f*; ~ *latch* pestillo *m*; ~*mat* felpudo *m* de puerta; ~ *scraper* limpiabarros *m*; ~*sill* umbral *m*; ~*step* escalón *m* delante de la puerta; escalera *f* exterior; ~*stop* tope *m* de puerta; *front* ~, *main* ~ puerta *f* principal; *side* ~ puerta *f* accesoria; *behind closed* ~*s* a puertas cerradas; *next* ~ en la casa de al lado; *next* ~ *to* al lado de; *fig.* que raya en; *out of* ~*s* al aire libre, afuera; *lay the blame at s.o.'s* ~ echarle a uno la culpa (*for* de); *show to the* ~ acompañar a la puerta; *show s.o. the* ~ enseñar la puerta a; ˈ~ **han·dle** tirador *m* (*or* resbalón *m*) de puerta; picaporte *m*; ˈ~**·man** portero *m*; (*one who helps people in and out of cars*) abrecoches *m*; ˈ~**·nail:** *dead as a* ~ más muerto que mi abuela; ˈ~**·post** jamba *f* (de una puerta); ˈ~**·way** portal *m*, puerta *f*; *stand in the* ~ estar a la puerta.
dope [doup] **1.** grasa *f* lubricante; barniz (*a.* ✈); *sl.* narcótico *m*; *sl.* informe *m*; *sl.* (*p.*) bobo *m*; ~ *friend sl.* toxicómano *m*; **2.** *sl.* dar (*or* poner) un narcótico a; *sl.* pronosticar; ~ *sheet sl.* hoja *f* confidencial sobre los caballos de carreras; ˈ**dope·y** *sl.* bobalicón.
dor·mant [ˈdɔ:rmənt] *mst fig.* durmiente, inactivo; latente.
dor·mer (**win·dow**) [ˈdɔ:rmər(ˈwindou)] buhardilla *f*.
dor·mi·to·ry [ˈdɔ:rmitɔ:ri] dormitorio *m*; ⚔ compañía *f*.
dor·mouse [ˈdɔ:rmaus] (*pl.* **dor·mice** [ˈdɔ:rmais]) lirón *m*.
dor·sal [ˈdɔ:rsl] □ dorsal.
dose [dous] **1.** dosis *f*; **2.** administrar una dosis a (*a.* ~ *a p. with*); *wine* adulterar.
dos·si·er [ˈdɔsiei] expediente *m*; (*police etc.*) ficha *f*.
dot [dɔt] **1.** punto *m*; ~*s and dashes tel.* puntos *m/pl.* y rayas; F *on the* ~ en punto; **2.** poner punto a; puntear, salpicar de puntos; *fig.* esparcir, desparramar (*a.* ~ *about*); *sl.* ~ *s.o. one* dar de bofetadas a; ~*ted line* línea *f* de puntos; ~*ted with* salpicado de.
dot·age [ˈdoutidʒ] chochez *f*; *be in one's* ~ chochear; **do·tard** [ˈ~ərd] viejo (a *f*) *m* chocho (a); **dote** [dout] chochear; ~ (*up*)*on* estar loco por (*or* con); ˈ**dot·ing** □ chocho (*a. fig.*); (*doltish*) lelo.
dot·ty [ˈdɔti] *sl.* chiflado.
dou·ble [ˈdʌbl] **1.** doble (*a.* ⚘); dos veces; doblado; *fig.* doble, falso; ~ *chin* papada *f*; ~ *date* cita *f* de dos parejas; ~*-decker bed* cama-litera *f*; ~*-header* tren *m* con dos locomotoras; *baseball*: dos partidos *m/pl.* jugados sucesivamente; ~*-jointed* de articulaciones dobles; ~ *meaning* doble sentido *m*; ~*talk* F galimatías *m*; F habla *f* ambigua para engañar; ~ *time* pago *m* doble por horas extraordinarias de trabajo; ⚔ paso *m* redoblado; ~ *track* doble vía *f*; **2.** doble *m* (*a. p.*); ~*s pl. tennis*: juego *m* de dobles; *at the* ~ a paso ligero; **3.** *v/t.* doblar (*a. bridge*); *p.* ser el doble de; ~*d up* doblado; agachado; *be* ~*d up with laughter* desternillarse de risa; *v/i.* doblarse; (*a.* ~ *up*) agacharse; ~*-park* aparcar en doble fila; F ~ *up* compartir dos la misma habitación; (*a.* ~ *back*) virar; ˈ~-ˈ**bar·reled** de dos cañones; *fig.* ambiguo; ˈ~ ˈ**bass** contrabajo *m*; ˈ~ ˈ**bed** cama *f* de matrimonio; ˈ~-ˈ**breast·ed** *jacket* cruzado, de dos filas, de dos pechos; ˈ~-ˈ**cross** *sl.* hacer una mala faena a; ˈ~-ˈ**deal·er** artero *m*; traidorzuelo *m*; ˈ~-ˈ**deal·ing** doblez *f*; ˈ~-ˈ**edged** de dos filos; ˈ~ ˈ**en·try** ✝ partida *f* doble; ˈ~ ˈ**fea·ture** de dos películas de largo metraje; ˈ**dou·ble-**

ˈ**quick** ⚔ a paso ligero (*or* redoblado); F lo más pronto posible.
dou·blet [ˈdʌblit] † jubón *m*; (*pair*) pareja *f*; etimología *f* doble.
doubt [daut] **1.** *v/i.* dudar (*whether* que *subj.*); tener dudas; *v/t.* dudar; *I ~ it* lo dudo; **2.** duda *f*; *beyond ~* sin duda; *in ~* dudoso; *no ~* sin duda; *without ~* indudablemente; *call in ~* poner en duda; ˈ**doubt·er** escéptico (a *f*) *m*; **doubt·ful** [ˈ~ful] □ dudoso (*a. character*); ˈ**doubt·less** *adv.* sin duda, indudablemente.
douche [du:ʃ] **1.** ducha *f*; ⚕ jeringa *f*, maqueta *f*; **2.** duchar(se).
dough [dou] masa *f*, pasta *f*; *sl.* pasta *f*, guita *f*; ˈ**~·boy** F soldado *m* de infantería; ˈ**~·nut** buñuelo *m*; ˈ**dough·y** pastoso; que sabe a pasta, crudo.
dour [ˈdur] severo, austero; (*obstinate*) terco.
douse [daus] mojar, calar *with water*; *v. dowse*.
dove [dʌv] paloma *f*; ˈ**~·cot**(**e**) palomar *m*; ˈ**~·tail** ⊕ **1.** cola *f* de milano; **2.** ensamblar a cola de milano; *fig.* corresponder, ajustarse.
dow·a·ger [ˈdauədʒər] viuda *f* de un titulado (*or* hidalgo); señora *f* anciana.
dow·dy [ˈdaudi] □ *n.*, *dress* poco elegante, poco atractivo; *dress* fuera de moda.
dow·el [ˈdauəl] clavija *f*.
dow·er [ˈdauər] viudedad *f*.
down[1] [daun] vello *m*; plumón *m of bird, mattress*.
down[2] [~] *geog.* (*esp.* *~s pl.*) *terreno ondulado y pelado sobre roca de creta*; = *dune*.
down[3] [~] **1.** *adv.* abajo; hacia abajo, para abajo; (*to ground*) en tierra; (*south*) hacia el sur; *~ below* allá abajo; *~ from* desde; *~ to* hasta; *be ~* (*price*) haber bajado; F estar abatido; (*battery etc.*) estar agotado; *sport*: quedarse atrás, perder; F *be ~ on p.* tener una inquina a; tratar severamente; *be ~ and out* estar arruinado, estar en las últimas; **2.** *prp.* abajo de; *~ river* río abajo; *~ the street* calle abajo; **3.** *int.* ¡abajo!; *~ with ...!* ¡muera ...!; **4.** *adj. train etc.* descendente; **5.** F echar a tierra; *food* tragar; *~ tools* declararse en huelga; **6.** *su. v. up 5*; **7.** *Down-Easter etc.* *habitante de la Nueva Inglaterra, esp. de Maine*; ˈ**~·cast** alicaído, abatido; ˈ**~·fall** caída *f*, ruina *f*; ˈ**~·grade:** F *be on the ~* ir cuesta abajo (*fig.*); ˈ**~-ˈheart·ed** abatido, desanimado; ˈ**~ˈhill 1.** *adj.* en declive; **2.** *adv.* cuesta abajo (*a. fig.*); ˈ**~·pour** chaparrón *m*; aguacero *m*; ˈ**~·right 1.** *lie etc.* categórico, absoluto; patente, evidente; *p.* franco, abierto; **2.** *adv.* absolutamente, completamente; ˈ**~ˈstairs 1.** abajo; en el piso de abajo; **2.** piso *m* inferior; ˈ**~ˈstream** aguas abajo, río abajo; ˈ**~·stroke** (*pen*) palote *m*, pierna *f*; ⊕ carrera *f* descendente; ˈ**~ˈtown** en el centro de la ciudad; ˈ**~·trod·den** pisoteado (*a. fig.*); oprimido; ˈ**~·ward 1.** descendente; **2.** (*a.* ˈ**~·wards**) hacia abajo.
down·y [ˈdauni] velloso; plumoso; *sl.* despabilado, taimado.
dow·ry [ˈdauri] dote *f*.
dowse [dauz] *light* apagar; ˈ**dows·er** zahorí *m*; ˈ**dows·ing rod** varilla *f* de zahorí.
do·yen [ˈdwaiən] decano *m*.
doze [douz] **1.** dormitar (*a. ~ away*); *~ off* quedarse medio dormido; **2.** sueño *m* ligero; *have a ~* echar una siestecita.
doz·en [ˈdʌzn] docena *f*; *baker's ~* docena *f* de fraile; *talk 19 to the ~* hablar más que 7.
drab [dræb] **1.** gris amarillento; *fig.* monótono; **2.** ramera *f*.
drachm [dræm], **drach·ma** [ˈdrækmə] dracma *f* (*a. pharm.*).
draft [dræft] **1.** (*of air*) corriente *f* de aire; (*pulling*; *current of air in a chimney*) tiro *m*; (*drink*) bebida *f*, trago *m*; ✝ giro *m*, letra *f* de cambio; ⚔ quinta *f*; (*sketch*) bosquejo *m*; (*first form of writing*) borrador *m*, versión *f of article etc.*; *attr. horse etc.* de tiro; ⚓ calado *m*; *beer* de barril, al grifo; *be exempted from the ~* redimirse de la quinta; *on ~* a presión; *~ age* edad *f* de quintas; *~ beer* cerveza *f* a presión; *~ board* ⚔ junta *f* de reclutamiento; *~ call* llamada *f* a quintas; *~ dodger* emboscado *m*; *~ee* conscripto *m*, quinto *m*; *~ horse* caballo *m* de tiro; *~ing room* sala *f* de dibujo; *~sman* dibujante *m*; (*man who draws up documents*) redactor *m*; (*professional*) delineante *m*; *~s* damas *f/pl.*, juego *m* de damas; *~ treaty* proyecto *m* de

convenio; ~y airoso, con corrientes de aire; **2.** dibujar; hacer un borrador de; *article* redactar; *plan* bosquejar; ⚔ quintar; ⚔ destacar; *be* ~*ed* ⚔ ir a quintas.

drag [dræg] **1.** rastra *f* (*a.* ⚓); ✓ grada *f*; narria *f for wood etc.*; ⚓ (*a.* ~ *net*) red *f* barredera; ✈ resistencia *f* al avance; *fig.* estorbo *m*, demora *f*; F cuesta *f* dura; *sl.* influencia *f*; **2.** *v/t.* arrastrar; ⚓ rastrear; = *dredge*[1] 2; ~ *along* arrastrar consigo (*or* tras sí); ~ *out* hacer demasiado largo (*or* lento); *v/i.* arrastrarse (*along the ground* por el suelo); ⚓ rastrear (*for* en busca de); ✝ decaer; (*time*) pesar.

drag·on [ˈdrægən] dragón *m*; F *fig.* fiera *f*; F (*duenna*) carabina *f*; ˈ~**·fly** libélula *f*, caballito *m* del diablo.

dra·goon [drəˈguːn] **1.** ⚔ dragón *m*; **2.** tiranizar; ~ *into ger.* obligar por intimidación a *inf.*

drain [drein] **1.** (*outlet*) desaguadero *m*; alcantarilla *f*, boca *f* de alcantarilla *in street*; *fig.* desaguadero *m* (*on* de); ~ *board* escurridero *m*; ~ *cock* llave *f* de purga; ~ *hole* imbornal *m*; ~ *pipe* tubo *m* de desagüe (*a. fig.*); ~ *plug* tapón *m* de desagüe, escurridero *m*; **2.** *v/t.* desaguar; ✓ avenar; ⚕ *wound* drenar; *glass* apurar; *lake* desangrar (*a.* ~ *off*); *vessel* escurrir; *v/i.* desaguar (*into* en); ˈ**drain·age** desagüe *m*, avenamiento *m*; (*system*) alcantarillado *m*; ~ *basin* cuenca *f* de un río; ✓ ~ *channel* zanja *f*.

drake [dreik] pato *m* macho.

dram [dræm] dracma *f*; cantidad *f* pequeña *of brandy etc.*

dra·ma [ˈdræmə, ˈdrɑːmə] drama *m* (*a. fig.*); **dra·mat·ic** [drəˈmætik] □ dramático (*a. fig.*); ~*s* representación *f* de aficionados; *pl.* obras *f/pl.* representadas por aficionados; **dram·a·tist** [ˈdræmətist] dramaturgo *m*; ˈ**dram·a·tize** dramatizar.

drank [dræŋk] *pret. of drink* 2.

drape [dreip] colgar, adornar con colgaduras; vestir (con telas de muchos pliegues; *in* de); ˈ**drap·er** pañero *m*, lencero *m*; ˈ**dra·per·y** colgaduras *f/pl.*, ropaje *m*; pañería *f* (*a.* ~ *shop*); (*haberdashery*) mercería *f*.

dras·tic [ˈdræstik] □ drástico.

draught [drɑːft, dræft] *mst British* = *draft*.

draw [drɔː] **1.** [*irr.*] *v/t.* arrastrar, tirar de (*a.* ~ *along*); (*take out*) sacar; (*lengthen*) alargar; atraer; *bow* tender; *breath* aspirar; *cheque* girar, librar; *curtain* correr; *drawing* dibujar; *fowl* destripar; *line* trazar, tirar; *lots* echar; *money, prize* sacar; *salary* cobrar; *sword, water* sacar; ⚓ *water* calar; ~ *aside p.* apartar; ~ *back* retirar; *curtain* descorrer; ~ *forth* hacer salir, producir; ~ *off* sacar, extraer; *liquid* trasegar; ~ *on p.* engatusar; *glove* ponerse; ~ *out* sacar; *p.* hacer hablar; *b.s.* sonsacar; ~ *up* redactar; *chair* acercar; ⚔ ordenar para el combate; ~ *o.s. up* enderezarse, ponerse en su lugar; ~ (*up*)*on* ✝ girar a cargo de; *fig.* inspirarse en; *v/i.* (*chimney*) tirar; *sport*: empatar; atraer; (*artist*) dibujar; moverse (*aside* a un lado *etc.*); ~ *back* retroceder, cejar (*a. fig.*); ~ *near* acercarse (*to* a); ~ *up* pararse (*sharp* en seco); ~ *to a close* estar para terminar; **2.** *sport*: empate *m*; *chess*: tablas *f/pl.*; *lottery*: sorteo *m*; F función *f* taquillera (*or* de mucho éxito); ˈ~**·back** inconveniente *m* (*to* en); ✝ (*excise*) reembolso *m*; ˈ~**·bridge** puente *m* levadizo; **drawˈee** ✝ librado *m*, girado *m*; ˈ**draw·er 1.** [ˈdrɔːə] dibujante *m*; ✝ girador *m*, librador *m*; **2.** [ˈdrɔː] cajón *m*; ~*s pl.* calzoncillos *m/pl.*; bragas *f/pl.* de mujer.

draw·ing [ˈdrɔːiŋ] dibujo *m*; ~ *instruments pl.* instrumentos *m/pl.* de dibujar; ˈ~ **acˈcount** cuenta *f* corriente; ˈ~ **board** tablero *m* de dibujo; ˈ~ **card** polo *m* de atracción popular; ˈ~**-pen** tiralíneas *m*; ˈ~ **pin** chincheta *f*; ˈ~ **room** salón *m*; recepción *f*; 🚂 departamento *m* reservado; *attr.* de buen gusto.

drawl [drɔːl] **1.** *v/t. words* arrastrar; *v/i.* hablar lentamente arrastrando las palabras; **2.** habla *f* lenta y pesada.

drawn [drɔːn] **1.** *p.p. of draw 1*; **2.** *adj. game* empatado; *face* ojeroso, cansado; ~ *butter* mantequilla *f* derretida; *sew.* ~ *work* calado *m*.

dray [drei] carro *m* (*esp.* para barriles de cerveza).

dread [dred] **1.** pavor *m*, temor *m*; *fill with* ~ infundir pavor a; **2.** temer; *I* ~ *to think of it* me horroriza pensar en ello; **3.** espantoso; **dread·ful** [ˈ~ful] **1.** □ terrible, espantoso; F desagradable; F malísimo; **2.**: *penny* ~ folletín

m horrendo; **dread·naught** [ˈ~nɔːt] ⚓ gran buque *m*, acorazado *m*.
dream [driːm] **1.** sueño *m* (*a. fig.*); (*a. day-*) ensueño *m*; **2.** [*irr.*] soñar (*of* con); ~ *away* (*e.g. the day*) pasar (el día) soñando; *~land* reino *m* del ensueño; *~like* de ensueño; ~ *world* tierra *f* de la fantasía; ˈ**dream·er** soñador (-a *f*) *m*; *fig.* fantaseador (-a *f*) *m*; **dreamt** [dremt] *pret. a. p.p. of dream* 2; ˈ**dream·y** □ *p.* distraído, muy en las nubes; entre sueños, nebuloso.
drear·i·ness [ˈdririnis] tristeza *f*; monotonía *f*; ˈ**drear·y** □ triste, melancólico; monótono.
dredge[1] [dredʒ] ⚓ **1.** draga *f*, rastra *f*; **2.** dragar; rastrear; ~ *up* pescar (*a. fig.*); ˈ**dredg·er**[1] ⚓ draga *f*; ˈ**dredg·ing** obras *f/pl.* de dragado.
dredge[2] [~] espolvorear; ˈ**dredg·er**[2] azucarero *m*, especiero *m*.
dregs [dregz] *pl* heces *f/pl.* (*a. fig.*).
drench [drentʃ] **1.** *vet.* poción *f*; (*shower*) chaparrón *m*; **2.** mojar, empapar; F *be ~ed* calarse, estar calado; ˈ**drench·er** F chaparrón *m*; ˈ**drench·ing** torrencial.
dress [dres] **1.** vestido *m*, ropa *f*; (*a. fig.*) atavío *m*; (*woman's*) vestido *m*; ~ *ball* baile *m* de etiqueta; *thea.* ~ *rehearsal* ensayo *m* general; *full* ~ traje *m* de etiqueta; *v. fancy*; **2.** *v/t.* vestir (*a. fig.*; *in black* de negro); (*a.* ~ *up*) ataviar, adornar (*in* con, de); *hair* peinar; *horse, skins* peinar, almohazar; *stone* labrar; *window* poner; *wound* curar, vendar; ✓ abonar; ⚔ alinear; ⊦ ~ *down* dar un rapapolvo a; *v/i.* (*a. get ~ed*) vestirse; ~ (*well*) vestir(se) (bien); ~ *up* acicalarse; vestirse de etiqueta; ˈ~ **ball** baile *m* de etiqueta; ˈ~ ˈ**cir·cle** *thea.* anfiteatro *m*; ˈ~ ˈ**coat** frac *m*; ˈ~ **deˈsign·er** modisto *m*; ˈ**dress·er** aparador *m* con estantes; cómoda *f* con espejo; ˈ~ **form** maniquí *m*; ˈ~ **goods** *pl.* géneros *m/pl.* para vestidos.
dress·ing [ˈdresiŋ] (*act*) el vestir(se); ⚕ vendaje *m*; (*food*) salsa *f*, condimento *m*; ✓ abono *m*; ˈ~ **case** neceser *m*; ˈ~-ˈ**down** F repasata *f*, regaño *m*; ˈ~ **gown** bata *f*; ˈ~ **room** vestidor *m*; *thea.* camarín *m*, camerino *m*; ˈ~ **sta·tion** puesto *m* de socorro; ˈ~ **ta·ble** tocador *m*.
dress...: ˈ**~·mak·er** costurera *f*, modista *f*; ˈ**~·mak·ing** costura *f*; ˈ~ **pa·rade** ⚔ parada *f*; ˈ~ **reˈhears·al** ensayo *m* general; ˈ~ ˈ**shirt** camisa *f* de pechera dura; ˈ~ **shop** casa *f* de modas; ˈ~ ˈ**suit** traje *m* de etiqueta; ˈ~ **tie** corbata *f* de smoking, corbata de frac; ˈ**dress·y** F acicalado; elegante.
drew [druː] *pret. of draw* 1.
drib·ble [ˈdribl] gotear, caer gota a gota; (*mouth*) babear; *football*: driblar.
drib·let [ˈdriblit] adarme *m*; *in ~s* por adarmes.
dried [draid] secado; *fruit* paso; *vegetables* seco; ~ *beef* cecina *f*; ~ *fig* higo *m* paso; ~ *peach* orejón *m*.
dri·er [ˈdraiər] enjugador *m*; (*for hair*) secador *m*; (*for clothes*) secadora *f*; (*rack for drying clothes*) tendedero *m* (de ropa).
drift [drift] **1.** (impulso *m* de una) corriente *f*; ⚓ deriva *f*; *fig.* sentido *m*, tendencia *f*; *fig.* giro *m*; *b.s.* (*esp. pol.*) inacción *f*; (*snow- etc.*) montón *m*; *geol.* terrenos *m/pl.* de acarreo; ⚒ galería *f* horizontal que sigue el filón; ~ *from the land* despoblación *f* del campo; **2.** *v/t.* impeler, llevar; amontonar; *v/i.* ir a la deriva (*a.* ~ *along*); *fig.* vivir sin rumbo; ˈ~ **ice** hielo *m* a la deriva, hielo flotante; ˈ**~·wood** madera *f* de deriva, madera flotante.
drill [dril] **1.** ⊕ taladro *m*; (*pneumatic*) ~ perforadora *f*, martillo *m* picador; ✓ hilera *f*; ✓ (*machine*) sembradora *f*; ⚔ instrucción *f*; *fig.* disciplina *f*; *sl.* rutina *f*; *~master* amaestrador *m*; ⚔ instructor *m*; ~ *press* prensa *f* taladradora; **2.** *v/t.* ⊕ taladrar; ✓ sembrar con sembradora; ⚔ enseñar instrucción a; *v/i.* perforar (*for oil* en busca de); ⚔ hacer instrucción; ˈ**drill·ing** perforación *f for oil etc.*
drink [driŋk] **1.** bebida *f*; beber *m* (en exceso); (*swig*) trinquis *m*, trago *m*; *have a* ~ tomar unas copas, tomar algo; *take a* ~ echar un trago; **2.** [*irr.*] beber (*a. fig.*); ~ *a p.'s health* brindar por alguien; ~ *down* beber de una vez; *esp. fig.* ~ *in* beber; ~ *out of* beber de; ~ *up* tragar, apurar; ˈ**drink·a·ble** bebible, potable; ˈ**drink·er** bebedor *m*.
drink·ing...: ˈ~ **bout**, ˈ~ **spree** juerga *f* de borrachera; bebezón *m S.Am.*; ˈ~ **cup** taza *f* para beber; ˈ~ **foun·tain** fuente *f*; ˈ~ **song** canción

f de taberna; **ˈ~ trough** abrevadero *m*; **ˈ~ wa·ter** agua *f* potable.
drip [drip] **1.** goteo *m*; ⚠ alero *m*; *sl.* bobalicón (-a *f*) *m*; tontaina *m*/*f*; **2.** gotear, caer gota a gota; ~ *coffee* café *m* de maquinilla; ~*-dry* de lava y pon; ~ *pan* colector *m* de aceite; F ~*ping wet* calado.
drip·ping [ˈdripiŋ] pringue *m*.
drive [draiv] **1.** *mot.* paseo *m* (en coche); calzada *f up to house*; *sport*: golpe *m* fuerte (*tennis*: a ras de la red); *fig.* vigor *m*, energía *f*; campaña *f* vigorosa (*to* para); ⊕ mecanismo *m* de transmisión; ✝ venta *f* de liquidación; *hunt.*, ⚔ batida *f*; ~ *shaft* árbol *m* de mando, eje *m* motor; ~*way* calzada *f*; camino *m* de entrada para coches; ~ *wheel* rueda *f* motriz; ~*-yourself service* alquiler *m* sin chófer; **2.** [*irr.*] *v*/*t.* impeler, empujar; mover, actuar (*a. fig.*); ⊕ impulsar; *mot. etc.* conducir, guiar; *p.* llevar en coche; *fig. p.* forzar (*to* a); *sport*: golpear con gran fuerza; *p. crazy etc.* volver; ~ *away* (*or off*) ahuyentar; ~ *back* obligar a retroceder; ~ *in* (*or home*) hincar, remachar; ~ *a good bargain* hacer un buen trato; *v*/*i.* conducir; ~ *at th. fig.* insinuar, querer decir; ~ *away* trabajar mucho; *mot.* ~ *on* seguir adelante; *the rain was driving down* llovía a chuzos.
drive-in [ˈdraivˈin]: ~ *movie theater* auto-teatro *m*; ~ *restaurant* restaurante *m* donde los clientes no necesitan dejar sus coches.
driv·el [ˈdrivl] **1.** babear; ~ *away fortune* malgastar; **2.** música *f* celestial, monserga *f*.
driv·en [ˈdrivn] *p.p. of drive* 2.
driv·er [ˈdraivər] conductor *m*; 🚂 maquinista *m*; ⊕ rueda *f* motriz; persona *f* despótica; ~ *license* permiso *m* (*or* carnet *m*) de conducir (*or* de chófer).
driv·ing [ˈdraiviŋ] **1.** conducción *f*; **2.** *adj. freq.* motriz; *rain* torrencial, recio; *attr.* ~ *instructor* instructor *m* de conducción; ~ *license* = *driver license*; ~ *mirror* retrovisor *m*; ~ *school* escuela *f* automovilista, auto-escuela *f*; **ˈ~ belt** correa *f* de transmisión.
driz·zle [ˈdrizl] **1.** llovizna *f*; cilampa *f S.Am.*; **2.** lloviznar.
droll [droul] (*adv. drolly*) gracioso, festivo; (*odd*) raro; **ˈdroll·er·y** chuscada *f*.
drom·e·dar·y [ˈdrʌmədəri] dromedario *m*.
drone [droun] **1.** *zo.* zángano *m* (*a. fig.*); (*noise*) zumbido *m*; **2.** zumbar; hablar monótonamente (*a.* ~ *on*).
drool [dru:l] **1.** babear; **2.** F bobería *f*.
droop [dru:p] *v*/*t.* inclinar, dejar caer; *v*/*i.* inclinarse; pender, colgar; *fig.* decaer; *fig.* (*lose heart*) desalentarse; **ˈdroop·ing** □ caído, inclinado; lánguido.
drop [drɔp] **1.** gota *f* (*a.* ⚕); (*fall*) baja *f*, caída *f* repentina; (*slope*) cuesta *f*, declive *m*, pendiente *f*; *mount.* precipicio *m*; lanzamiento *m by parachute*; *thea.* (*a.* ~ *curtain*) telón *m* de boca; ~ *by* ~ gota a gota; ~ *hammer* martinete *m*; ~*-leaf table* mesa *f* de hoja plegadiza; ~ *light* lámpara *f* colgante; ~*out* fracasado *m*, desertor *m* escolar; *become a* ~*out* ahorcar los libros; ~*per* cuentagotas *m*; ~ *shutter* obturador *m* de guillotina; ~ *table* mesa *f* perezosa; F *get* (*have*) *the* ~ *on* coger (llevar) la delantera a; F *take a* ~ beber; F *have taken a* ~ *too much* llevar una copa de más; **2.** *v*/*t.* dejar caer; inclinar; *hunt.* derribar; abandonar; omitir, suprimir; *claim* renunciar a; *consonant* comerse; *curtsy* hacer; *money* perder; *passenger*, *subject* dejar; *voice* bajar; ~ *that!* ¡deja eso!; *v. anchor*; ~ *a hint* soltar una indirecta; ~ *in the post* echar al buzón; *v*/*i.* caer; bajar (*a.* ~ *down*); (*crouch*) agacharse; *fig.* cesar, terminar; (*drip*) gotear; ~ *behind* quedarse atrás; ~ *dead* caer muerto; ~ *in* (*or by*, *over*) visitar de paso; ~ *off esp.* quedarse dormido; ~ *out* darse de baja, retirarse; ~ *out of sight* desaparecer; **ˈdrop·let** gotita *f*; **ˈdrop·ping** goteo *m*; ~*s pl.* excremento *m* (de los animales); **ˈdrop scene** telón *m* de boca.
drop·si·cal [ˈdrɔpsikl] □ hidrópico; **ˈdrop·sy** hidropesía *f*.
dross [drɔs] escoria *f* (*a. fig.*).
drought [draut], **drouth** [drauθ] sequía *f*; **ˈdrought·y** árido, seco.
drove [drouv] **1.** manada *f*, piara *f*; *fig.* muchedumbre *f*; **2.** *pret. of drive* 2; **ˈdro·ver** ganadero *m*; boyero *m*, pastor *m*.
drown [draun] *v*/*t.* anegar (*a. fig.*; *in* en); *sound* apagar; *v*/*i.* (*or be* ~*ed*) ahogarse; perecer ahogado, anegarse.

drowse [drauz] adormecer(se); ˈ**drow·si·ness** somnolencia *f*, modorra *f*; ˈ**drow·sy** □ soñoliento; *be* ~ tener sueño.

drub [drʌb] apalear; tundir; *fig.* vencer, derrotar; ˈ**drub·bing** paliza *f* (*a. fig.*); *fig.* derrota *f*.

drudge [drʌdʒ] **1.** esclavo *m* del trabajo (*or* de la cocina), azacán (-a *f*) *m*; **2.** azacanarse, afanarse; ˈ**drudg·er·y** perrera *f*, trabajo *m* penoso.

drug [drʌg] **1.** droga *f* (*a. b.s.*), medicamento *m*; (*esp. to sleep*) narcótico *m*; ✝ ~ *on the market* artículo *m* invendible; ~ *addict* toxicómano *m* (a *f*); ~ *addiction* toxicomanía *f*; ~ *dealer* narcotraficante *m*/*f*; ~ *habit* vicio *m* de los narcóticos; ~ *store* farmacia *f*, droguería *f*; ~ *traffic* contrabando *m* de narcóticos; **2.** administrar narcóticos a, narcotizar; aletargar; **drug·gist** [ˈdrʌgist] farmacéutico *m*, boticario *m*; ~'s (*shop*) farmacia *f*.

dru·id [ˈdru:id] druida *m*.

drum [drʌm] **1.** tambor *m* (*a.* ⊕); (*big*) timbal *m*; (*ear-*) tímpano *m*; (*oil etc.*) bidón *m*; **2.** *v*/*i.* ♪ tocar el tambor; tamborilear *with fingers*; *v*/*t.* ~ *into s.o.* meterle a uno en la cabeza; ⚔ ~ *out* expulsar; ˈ~ **beat** toque *m* de tambor; ˈ~ **corps** banda *f* de tambores; ˈ~**·fire** fuego *m* graneado, fuego nutrido; ˈ~**·head** piel *f* (*or* parche *m*) de tambor; ~ *court martial* consejo *m* de guerra sumarísimo (*or* al frente del enemigo); ˈ~ **ma·jor** tambor *m* mayor; ˈ**drum·mer** tambor *m*; ˈ**drum·stick** palillo *m*, maza *f*.

drunk [drʌŋk] **1.** *p.p. of drink* 2; **2.** borracho (*a. fig.*); *get* ~ emborracharse; **drunk·ard** [ˈ~ərd] borracho (a *f*) *m*; ˈ**drunk·en** borracho, dado a la bebida; ˈ**drunk·en·ness** embriaguez *f*.

dry [drai] **1.** □ seco; *climate etc.* árido; *fig.* aburrido, sin interés; *appearance* (*of p.*) enjuto; *humor approx.* raro, peculiar; F prohibicionista; F (*thirsty*) sediento; *bread freq.* sin mantequilla; ~ *battery* pila *f* seca; (*group of dry cells*) batería *f* seca; ~ *cell* pila *f* seca; ~ *dock* dique *m* seco; ~*er* = *drier*; ~*-eyed* ojienjuto; ~ *farming* cultivo *m* de secano; ~ *goods pl.* mercancías *f*/*pl.* generales (*tejidos, lencería, pañería, sedería*); ~ *ice* hielo *m* seco, carbohielo *m*; ~ *law* ley *f* seca; ~ *measure* medida *f* para áridos; ~ *season* estación *f* de la seca; ~ *wash* ropa *f* lavada y secada pero no planchada; **2.** secar(se) (*a.* ~ *up*); *sl.* ~ *up* callarse, dejar de hablar.

dry-clean [ˈdraiˈkli:n] limpiar en seco, lavar en seco; ˈ**dry clean·er** tintorero *m*; ~'s tintorería *f*; ˈ**dry clean·ing** limpieza *f* en seco, lavado *m* en seco.

dry·ness [ˈdrainis] sequedad *f*; (*climate*) aridez *f*.

dry...: ˈ~ ˈ**nurse** ama *f* seca, niñera *f*; ˈ~ ˈ**rot** ⚘ putrefacción *f* fungoide; *fig.* corrupción *f* interna; ˈ~-ˈ**shod** a pie enjuto.

du·al [ˈdju:əl] *gr.* dual; doble; ~ *control* doble mando *m*; ˈ**du·al·ism** dualismo *m*.

dub [dʌb] *film* doblar; *knight* armar caballero; apodar *with name*; ˈ**dub·bing** *film*: doblaje *m*.

du·bi·ous [ˈdju:biəs] □ dudoso; *be* ~ dudar, tener dudas (*of, about, over* sobre, de); ˈ**du·bi·ous·ness** duda *f*, incertidumbre *f*.

du·cal [ˈdju:kl] ducal.

duc·at [ˈdʌkət] ducado *m* (*dinero*).

duch·ess [ˈdʌtʃis] duquesa *f*.

duch·y [ˈdʌtʃi] ducado *m* (*título*).

duck[1] [dʌk] *orn.* pato *m*; ánade *m*.

duck[2] [~] **1.** zambullida *f in water*; agachada *f to escape*; **2.** chapuzar(se) *in water*; agachar(se) *to escape*; F ~ *out* esfumarse.

duck[3] [~] (*cloth*) dril *m*, brin *m*.

duck·ling [ˈdʌkliŋ] patito *m*, anadón *m*.

duck·y [ˈdʌki] mono, majo.

duct [dʌkt] conducto *m* (*a.* ⚕).

duc·tile [ˈdʌktil] □ dúctil (*a. fig.*); **duc·til·i·ty** [~ˈtiliti] ductilidad *f*.

dud [dʌd] **1.** ⚔ granada *f etc.* fallida; *fig.* fallo *m*; (*fake*) filfa *f*; **2.** fallido, huero; falso.

dude [du:d] petimetre *m*, cursi *m*; ~ *ranch* rancho *m* para turistas.

dudg·eon [ˈdʌdʒn]: *in high* ~ muy enojado.

due [dju:] **1.** *adj.* debido; ✝ pagadero; conveniente, oportuno; 🚂 *etc.* (que) debe llegar; ~ *to* por causa de; debido a; *be* ~ *to p.* deberse a; *th.* ser ocasionado por; *be* ~ *to inf.* deber *inf.*; (*time*) estar para *inf.*; *fall* ~ vencer; **2.** *adv.* ⚓ derecho, en derechura; precisamente; **3.** *su.* (*right*) derecho *m*; (*desert*) merecimiento *m*; (*debt*) deuda *f*; ~*s pl.* ✝ derechos *m/pl.*; *b.s.* get one's ~ llevar su merecido.

du·el [ˈdjuːəl] **1.** duelo *m*; **2.** batirse en duelo; ˈ**du·el·(l)ist** duelista *m.*

du·et(to) [djuˈet(ou)] dúo *m.*

duff·el [ˈdʌfl] paño *m* de lana basta; ~ *coat* comando *m.*

duff·er [ˈdʌfər] tonto *m*, zoquete *m.*

dug [dʌg] **1.** *pret. a. p.p. of dig*; **2.** *zo.* ubre *f*, pezón *m*; ˈ**~·out** ⚔ refugio *m* subterráneo; cobertizo *m* bajo.

duke [djuːk] duque *m*; ˈ**duke·dom** ducado *m.*

dull [dʌl] **1.** (*adv. dully*) lerdo, estúpido; insensible; (*tedious etc.*) insulso, aburrido; *color* apagado; *day* gris; *edge* embotado; *pain, sound* sordo; *surface* deslustrado, mate; ✝ inactivo, flojo; **2.** embotar (*a. fig.*); deslustrar; *enthusiasm* enfriar; *p.* entorpecer; ˈ**dull·ness** estupidez *f*; insensibilidad *f etc.* (*v. dull*).

du·ly [ˈdjuːli] *v. due*; debidamente; a su (debido) tiempo.

dumb [dʌm] □ mudo; F estúpido, lerdo; *deaf and* ~ sordomudo; *v. show*; *strike* ~ dejar sin habla, pasmar; ˈ**~·bell** pesa *f*, halterio *m*; *sl.* estúpido *m*; ˈ**~ˈfound** dejar sin habla, pasmar; ˈ**dumb·ness** mudez *f*; F estupidez *f*; ˈ**dumb ˈshow** pantomima *f*; ˈ**dumb ˈwait·er** estante *m* giratorio; montaplatos *m.*

dum·my [ˈdʌmi] **1.** (*tailor's*) maniquí *m*; ✝ envase *m* vacío; (*baby's*) chupete *m*; *bridge*: (*be* hacer de) muerto *m*; ✝ (*p.*) testaferro *m*; **2.** falso, postizo.

dump [dʌmp] **1.** descargar de golpe; (*rid*) deshacerse de; *rubbish* vaciar; ✝ *goods* inundar el mercado con, vender en grandes cantidades y a precios inferiores a los corrientes; F ~ *down* meter; **2.** basurero *m*, escorial *m*, vertedero *m*; (*garbage heap*) montón *m* de basuras, basural *m*; ⚔ depósito *m*; *sl. contp.* pueblucho *m*, poblachón *m*; F (*be* [*down*] *in the* tener) ~*s pl.* murria *f*; ˈ**dump·ing** ✝ dumping *m*; ˈ**dump·ing ground** basurero *m*; ˈ**dump·ling** *bola de masa hervida* (*or cocida*); ˈ**dump·y** regordete, culibajo.

dun[1] [dʌn] pardo, castaño oscuro.

dun[2] [~] **1.** acreedor *m* importuno; **2.** molestar, dar la lata a.

dunce [dʌns] zopenco (a *f*) *m*; ~ *cap* capirote *m* que se le pone al alumno torpe; **dun·der·head** [ˈdʌndərhed] zoquete *m.*

dune [djuːn] duna *f.*

dung [dʌŋ] **1.** estiércol *m*; **2.** estercolar.

dun·geon [ˈdʌndʒn] mazmorra *f*, calabozo *m.*

dung·hill [ˈdʌŋhil] estercolero *m.*

duo [ˈdjuːou] dúo *m.*

du·o·dec·i·mal [djuːouˈdesiml] duodecimal; **du·oˈdec·i·mo** [~mou] duodécimo, dozavo; *typ. in* ~ en dozavo.

dupe [djuːp] **1.** primo *m*, inocentón *m*; **2.** embaucar; (*swindle*) timar.

du·plex [ˈdjuːpleks] dúplice, doble; ~ *house* casa *f* para dos familias.

du·pli·cate **1.** [ˈduːplikit] a) (*in* por) duplicado; b) duplicado *m*; **2.** [ˈ~keit] duplicar; **du·pli·ca·tion** [~ˈkeiʃn] duplicación *f*; ˈ**du·pli·ca·tor** duplicador *m*, multicopista *m*; **du·plic·i·ty** [duːˈplisiti] duplicidad *f*, doblez *f.*

du·ra·bil·i·ty [djurəˈbiliti] durabilidad *f*, duración *f*; ˈ**du·ra·ble** □ durable, duradero; ~ *goods pl.* artículos *m/pl.* duraderos; **du·ra·tion** [~ˈreiʃn] duración *f.*

du·ress [djuˈres] (*under* por) coacción *f.*

du·ring [ˈdjuriŋ] durante.

durst [dəːrst] † *pret. of dare.*

dusk [dʌsk] crepúsculo *m*, anochecer *m*; *poet.* oscuridad *f*; ˈ**dusk·i·ness** oscuridad *f*; color *m* sombrío; ˈ**dusk·y** □ oscuro, sombrío; *complexion* moreno.

dust [dʌst] **1.** polvo *m*; (*refuse*) basura *f*; *fig.* cenizas *f/pl.*; *sl.* pasta *f*; *bite the* ~ morder el polvo; *raise a* ~ armarla; *throw* ~ *in one's eyes* engañar; **2.** quitar el polvo, despolvorear; *cooking*: espolvorear; ˈ**~·bin** *British* cubo *m* de la basura; ˈ**~ bowl** estepa *f*, cuenca *f* de polvo, terreno *m* estéril a causa de la erosión; ˈ**~ cart** camión *m* de la basura; ˈ**~·cloth** trapo *m* para quitar el polvo; ˈ**~ cloud** nube *f* de polvo, polvareda *f*; ˈ**~ cov·er** guardapolvo *m*; sobrecubierta *f of book*; ˈ**dust·er** plumero *m*; (*rag*) gamuza *f*, trapo *m*; (*blackboard*) borrador *m*; guardapolvo *m*; ˈ**dust·i·ness** calidad *f* de polvoroso (*or* empolvado); ˈ**dust·ing** *sl.*

paliza *f*; ˈ**dust** ˈ**jack•et** sobrecubierta *f*; ˈ**dust•pan** cogedor *m*; ˈ~ **rag** trapo *m* para quitar el polvo; ˈ~ **storm** tolvanera *f*; ˈ**dust**-ˈ**up** F riña *f*, pelea *f*; ˈ**dust•y** polvoriento, empolvado; *sl. not so* ~ bastante bien (*or* bueno).

Dutch [dʌtʃ] holandés *adj. a. su. m*; ~ *treat* F convite *m* a escote; *go* ~ F pagar a escote; *in* ~ en desgracia; F *double* ~ galimatías *m*, chino *m*; ˈ**Dutch•man** holandés *m*; ˈ**Dutch-wom•an** holandesa *f*.

du•ti•a•ble [ˈdjuːtiəbl] sujeto a derechos de aduana; **du•ti•ful** [ˈ~ful] □ obediente, respetuoso; (*obliging*) servicial.

du•ty [ˈdjuːti] deber *m*, obligación *f* (*to* a, para con); (*esp. duties pl.*) tarea *f*, faena *f*; ⚓ derechos *m/pl.* de aduana; *off* ~ libre; ⚔ franco de servicio; *on* ~ de servicio; de guardia; *in* ~ *bound* obligado (to a); *do* ~ *for* servir en lugar de; *take up one's duties* entrar en funciones; ˈ~-ˈ**free** ⚓ libre de derechos de aduana; ˈ~-**ser•geant** (*police*) sargento *m* de servicio.

dwarf [dwɔːrf] **1.** enano *m*; **2.** enano; diminuto; **3.** achicar; *fig.* empequeñecer; ˈ**dwarf•ish** □ enano, diminuto.

dwell [dwel] [*irr.*] morar, habitar; ~ (*up*)*on* explayarse en; hacer hincapié en; ˈ**dwell•ing** morada *f*, vivienda *f*; ˈ**dwell•ing house** casa *f*, domicilio *m*; **dwelt** [dwelt] *pret. a. p.p. of dwell*.

dwin•dle [ˈdwindl] disminuirse, menguar (*a.* ~ *away*); quedar reducido (*into* a); ˈ**dwin•dling** disminución *f*, mengua *f* (*a.* ~ *away*).

dye [dai] **1.** tinte *m*; matiz *m*, color *m*; *fig. of deepest* ~ de lo más vil; **2.** teñir (*s.t. black* de negro); ~*d in the wool* intransigente; *v. wool*; ˈ**dy•er** tintorero *m*; ˈ**dye•stuff** tinte *m*, materia *f* colorante; ˈ**dye works** tintorería *f*.

dy•ing [ˈdaiiŋ] **1.** moribundo; agonizante; *moments* final; **2.** *ger. of die*[1].

dy•nam•ic [daiˈnæmik] **1.** □ (*a.* **dyˈnam•i•cal** □) dinámico (*a. fig.*); **2.** *fig.* dinámica *f*; **dyˈnam•ics** *sg.* dinámica *f*; **dy•na•mite** [ˈdainəmait] **1.** dinamita *f*; **2.** volar con dinamita; **dy•na•mo** [ˈdainəmou] dínamo *f*.

dy•nas•tic [daiˈnæstik] □ dinástico; **dy•nas•ty** [ˈdainəsti] dinastía *f*.

dys•en•ter•y [ˈdisnteri] disentería *f*.

dys•pep•sia [disˈpepsiə] dispepsia *f*; **dysˈpep•tic** □ dispéptico; melancólico.

E

each [i:tʃ] **1.** *adj.* cada; todo; **2.** *pron.* cada uno; ~ *other* uno(s) a otro(s), el uno al otro; mutuamente; **3.** *adv.* por persona.

ea·ger [ˈi:gər] □ ansioso; anhelante; impaciente; vehemente; *be* ~ *for* anhelar; *be* ~ *to* tener vivo deseo de; **ˈea·ger·ness** ansia *f*; anhelo *m etc.*

ea·gle [ˈi:gl] águila *f*; *eye* (de) lince.

ear[1] [ir] ⚘ espiga *f*; ~ *of corn* ilote *m.*

ear[2] [~] oreja *f*; (*sense*) oído *m*; ♪ *by* ~ de oído; *be all* ~*s* ser todo oídos; *give* ~ *to* prestar oído a; *have a good* ~ tener buen oído; *turn a deaf* ~ hacerse el sordo; **~·ache** [ˈireik] dolor *m* de oídos; **ˈ~·drum** tímpano *m.*

earl [ə:rl] conde *m*; **earl·dom** [ˈ~dəm] condado *m.*

ear·ly [ˈə:rli] **1.** *adj.* temprano (*a.* ⚘); primero; primitivo; precoz; *reply* pronto; *at an* ~ *date* en fecha próxima; ~ *bird* madrugador (-a *f*) *m*; ~ *life* juventud *f*; **2.** *adv.* temprano; con tiempo; *arrive 5 minutes* ~ llegar con 5 minutos de anticipación; *book* ~ reservar con mucha anticipación; ~ *last century* a principios del siglo pasado; ~ *in the morning* muy de mañana.

ear·mark [ˈirmɑ:rk] *fig.* reservar, poner aparte (*for* para); destinar (*for* a).

ear·muff [ˈirmʌf] orejera *f.*

earn [ə:rn] ganar(se); adquirir, obtener; *praise etc.* merecer(se), granjearse; ✝ (*bonds*) *interest* devengar.

ear·nest[1] [ˈə:rnist] prenda *f*, señal *f*; (*a.* ˈ~ **mon·ey**) arras *f/pl.*

ear·nest[2] [~] □ serio; formal; *desire* ardiente; *in* (*good*) ~ (muy) de veras, en serio; **ˈear·nest·ness** seriedad *f*; formalidad *f.*

earn·ings [ˈə:rniŋz] *pl.* sueldo *m*; ingresos *m/pl.*; ganancias *f/pl.*

ear...: **ˈ~·phone** audífono *m*; **ˈ~·phones** *pl.* auriculares *m/pl.*; **ˈ~·piece** *teleph.* auricular *m*; **ˈ~·ring** (*long*) pendiente *m*; (*round*) arete *m*; **ˈ~·shot**: *within* ~ al alcance del oído; **ˈ~-split·ting** *shout* desaforado; *noise* que rompe el tímpano.

earth [ə:rθ] **1.** tierra *f* (*a.* ⚡); *zo.* madriguera *f*; F *cost the* ~ costar un potosí; *down-to-*~ práctico; *get back to* ~ volver a la realidad; *run to* ~ encontrar (tras larga búsqueda); **2.** ⚡ conectar a tierra; ⚒ ~ *up* acollar; **ˈearth·en** de tierra; *pot* de barro; **ˈearth·en·ware** loza *f* de barro; cacharros *m/pl.*; **ˈearth·ly** terrenal, mundano; F *he hasn't an* ~ no tiene posibilidad alguna; *be of no* ~ *use* no servir para nada en absoluto; **ˈearth·quake** terremoto *m*; **ˈearth·work** terraplén *m*; **ˈearth-worm** lombriz *f*; **ˈearth·y** terroso; *fig.* telúrico; (*coarse*) grosero.

ear...: **ˈ~ trum·pet** trompetilla *f* (acústica); **ˈ~·wax** cera *f* de los oídos; **ˈ~·wig** tijereta *f.*

ease [i:z] **1.** facilidad *f*; soltura *f*; comodidad *f of living etc.*; alivio *m from pain*; naturalidad *f of manner*; *at* ~ cómodo; a sus anchas; *ill at* ~ incómodo; ⚔ *stand at* ~*!* en su lugar ¡descanso!; *life of* ~ vida *f* desahogada; *take one's* ~ descansar; *with* ~ fácilmente, con facilidad; **2.** *v/t.* aliviar, mitigar; (*soften*) suavizar; *weight* aligerar; *pressure* aflojar; *mind* tranquilizar; *v/i.* (*wind*) amainar; (*rain*) moderarse; ~ *off*, ~ *up* suavizarse, aligerarse.

ea·sel [ˈi:zl] caballete *m.*

ease·ment [ˈi:zmənt] ⚖ servidumbre *f.*

eas·i·ness [ˈi:zinis] facilidad *f*; soltura *f.*

east [i:st] **1.** este *m*, oriente *m*; **2.** *adj.* del este, oriental; **3.** *adv.* al este, hacia el este.

East·er [ˈi:stər] pascua *f* florida (*or* de Resurrección); (*period*) semana *f* santa; *attr.* ... de pascua; ~ *Day*, ~ *Sunday* Domingo *m* de Resurrección; ~ egg huevo *m* duro decorado o huevo de imitación que se da como regalo en el día de Pascua de Resurrección.

east·er·ly [ˈi:stərli] *direction* hacia el este; *wind* del este; **east·ern** [ˈ~tərn] oriental; ˈ**east·ern·er** habitante *m/f* del este; **east·ern·most** [ˈistərn-moust] (el) más oriental; **east-ward**(s) [ˈi:stwərd(z)] hacia el este.

eas·y [ˈi:zi] **1.** □ fácil; *conditions* cómodo, holgado; *manner* natural, afable; *pace* lento, pausado; *virtue* laxo; *p.* de moralidad laxa; F *p.* fácil de engañar; *v. street, term*; ~ *mark* F víctima *f*, inocentón *m*; ~ *money* dinero *m* ganado sin pena; ✝ dinero abundante; ~ *payments* facilidades *f/pl.* de pago; ~ *to get on with* muy afable; ~ *to run* de fácil manejo; **2.** *adv.* F fácilmente; *take it* ~ descansar; *b.s.* haraganear; ir despacio; *take it* ~! ¡cálmese!; ˈ~ ˈ**chair** butaca *f*, sillón *m*; ˈ~**-going** acomodadizo; (*careless*) descuidado; (*lazy*) holgazán.

eat [i:t] **1.** [*irr.*] comer; *meal* tomar; consumir *with envy etc.*; *sl. what's* ~*ing you?* ¿qué mosca te ha picado?; ~ *away*, ~ *into* corroer; *fig.* carcomer; *fig.* mermar; ~ *up* comerse; devorar; **2.** *sl.* ~*s pl.* comida *f* (muy sabrosa); ˈ**eat·a·ble** comestible; **eat·a·bles** [ˈ~z] *pl.* comestibles *m/pl.*; ˈ**eat·en** *p.p. of eat* 1; ˈ**eat·er**: *be a big* ~ tener siempre buen apetito; ser comilón; ˈ**eat·ing** el comer; ˈ**eat·ing house** bodegón *m*.

eau de Co·logne [ˈoudəkəˈloun] (agua *f* de) Colonia *f*.

eaves [i:vz] *pl.* alero *m*; ˈ**eaves·drop** escuchar a las puertas; fisgonear; ˈ**eaves·drop·per** escuchador *m* escondido, fisgón *m*.

ebb [eb] **1.** menguante *m*, reflujo *m*; ~ *and flow* flujo *m* y reflujo; ~ *tide* marea *f* menguante; *at a low* ~ decaído; **2.** bajar; *fig.* decaer, disminuir.

eb·on·ite [ˈebənait] ebonita *f*; ˈ**eb·on·y** (*attr.* de) ébano *m*.

e·bul·li·ent [iˈbʌljənt] *fig.* exaltado, entusiasta; **eb·ul·li·tion** [ebəˈliʃn] *fig.* arranque *m*.

ec·cen·tric [ikˈsentrik] **1.** □ excéntrico; **2.** ⊕ excéntrica *f*; (*p.*) excéntrico *m*; **ec·cen·tric·i·ty** [eksen-ˈtrisiti] excentricidad *f* (*a. fig.*).

ec·cle·si·as·tic [ikli:ziˈæstik], *adj. mst* **ec·cle·siˈas·ti·cal** □ eclesiástico *adj. a. su. m.*

ech·e·lon [ˈeʃələn] **1.** escalón *m*; **2.** escalonar.

ech·o [ˈekou] **1.** eco *m*; **2.** *v/t.* repetir; *opinion* hacerse eco de; *v/i.* resonar; ~**sound·er** [ˈ~saundər] sonda *f* acústica.

é·clat [eiˈklɑ:] éxito *m* brillante; brillo *m*.

ec·lec·tic [ekˈlektik] □ ecléctico *adj. a. su. m*; **ecˈlec·ti·cism** [~tisizm] eclecticismo *m*.

e·clipse [iˈklips] **1.** eclipse *m* (*a. fig.*); **2.** eclipsar (*a. fig.*); **eˈclip·tic** eclíptica *f*.

ec·logue [ˈeklɔg] égloga *f*.

e·co·nom·ic [i:kəˈnɔmik], **e·co-ˈnom·i·cal** □ económico; frugal; *rent* justo; **e·coˈnom·ics** *pl.* economía *f* política; **e·con·o·mist** [iˈkɔn-əmist] economista *m/f*; **eˈcon·o·mize** [~maiz] economizar (*on* en); **eˈcon·o·my** economía *f*; frugalidad *f*.

ec·sta·sy [ˈekstəsi] éxtasis *m*; *go into ecstasies* extasiarse (*over* ante); **ec-stat·ic** [eksˈtætik] □ extático.

ec·u·men·i·cal [i:kju:ˈmenikl] □ ecuménico.

ec·ze·ma [ˈeksimə] eczema *m*.

ed·dy [ˈedi] **1.** remolino *m*; **2.** arremolinarse.

e·de·ma [i:ˈdi:mə] edema *m*.

edge [edʒ] **1.** (*cutting*) filo *m*, corte *m*; (*border*) margen *m*, borde *m*, orilla *f*; canto *m of table etc.*; (*end*) extremidad *f*; *on* ~ de canto; *fig.* nervioso; F *have the* ~ *on* llevar ventaja a; *put an* ~ *on* afilar; *set a p.'s teeth on* ~ dar dentera a una p.; **2.** *v/t.* afilar; orlar; *sew.* ribetear; *v/i.* ~ *along* avanzar de lado; ~ *in* abrirse paso (poco a poco); ~ *up to* acercarse con cautela a.

edge...: ˈ~ **tool** herramienta *f* de filo; ˈ~**·ways**, ˈ~**·wise** de canto, de lado; *not to let a p. get a word in* ~ no dejar meter baza a nadie.

edg·ing [ˈedʒiŋ] orla *f*, ribete *m*.

edg·y [ˈedʒi] F nervioso.

ed·i·ble [ˈedibl] comestible.

e·dict [ˈi:dikt] edicto *m*.

ed·i·fi·ca·tion [edifiˈkeiʃn] edificación *f*; **ed·i·fice** [ˈ~fis] edificio *m* (imponente); **ed·i·fy** [ˈ~fai] edificar; ˈ**ed·i·fy·ing** □ edificante.

ed·it [ˈedit] *script* preparar (*or* corregir) para la imprenta; *paper* dirigir, redactar; *book* editar; ~*ed by* (en) edición de; **e·di·tion** [iˈdiʃn] edición *f*; *typ.* tirada *f*; **ed·i·tor** [ˈeditər] director *m*, redactor *m of paper*; editor *m of book*; ~ *in chief* jefe *m* de redacción; **ed·i·to·ri·al** [~ˈtɔ:-

riəl] artículo *m* de fondo; ~ *staff* redacción *f*, cuerpo *m* de redacción; **ed·i·tor·ship** [ˈ~tərʃip] dirección *f*.
ed·u·cate [ˈedjukeit] educar; instruir; ~*d* culto; **ed·uˈca·tion** educación *f*; instrucción *f*; cultura *f*; *elementary* ~ primera enseñanza *f*; *secondary* ~ segunda enseñanza *f*; *Ministry of* ♀ Ministerio *m* de Educación (Nacional); **ed·uˈca·tion·al** □ educacional; docente; *film etc.* instructivo; ~ *institution* centro *m* docente; **ˈed·u·ca·tive** educativo; **ed·uˈca·tion(al)·ist** [~ʃn(əl)ist] educacionista *m/f*; **ˈed·u·ca·tor** educador (-a *f*) *m*.
e·duce [iˈdju:s] educir, sacar.
e·duc·tion [iˈdʌkʃn] educción *f*; ⊕ evacuación *f*; **eˈduc·tion pipe** tubo *m* de emisión.
eel [i:l] anguila; *be as slippery as an* ~ escurrirse como una anguila.
e'en [i:n] = *even*.
e'er [er] = *ever*.
ee·rie, ee·ry [ˈiri] □ misterioso; horripilante; inquietante.
ef·face [iˈfeis] borrar; ~ *o.s.* retirarse modestamente, lograr pasar inadvertido.
ef·fect [iˈfekt] **1.** efecto *m*; resultado *m*; impresión *f*; fuerza *f*; ~*s pl.* efectos *m/pl.*; *for* ~ sólo por impresionar; *in* ~ en efecto, en realidad; *law* vigente; *of no* ~ inútil; *to this* ~ con este propósito; *carry into* ~ poner en ejecución; *feel the* ~ *of* estar resentido de; *give* ~ *to* poner en efecto; *put into* ~ poner en vigor; *take* ~ (*law*) ponerse en vigor; (*remedy*) surtir efecto; **2.** efectuar, llevar a cabo; **efˈfec·tive 1.** □ eficaz; potente, impresionante; efectivo; ⚔, ⚓ útil para todos servicios; ⚖ *become* ~ entrar en vigor; ⊕ ~ *capacity* capacidad *f* útil; ⊕ ~ *power* potencia *f* real; **2.** ⚔ ~*s pl.* efectivos *m/pl.*; **efˈfec·tu·al** [~juəl] eficaz; **efˈfec·tu·ate** [~jueit] efectuar.
ef·fem·i·na·cy [iˈfeminəsi] afeminación *f*; **efˈfem·i·nate** [~nit] □ afeminado.
ef·fer·vesce [efərˈves] estar (*or* entrar) en efervescencia; bullir; **efferˈves·cence** efervescencia *f*; **efferˈves·cent** efervescente (*a. fig.*).
ef·fete [eˈfi:t] gastado; decadente.
ef·fi·ca·cious [efiˈkeiʃəs] □ eficaz; **ef·fi·ca·cy** [ˈ~kəsi] eficacia *f*.
ef·fi·cien·cy [eˈfiʃnsi] eficiencia *f*; eficacia *f*; capacidad *f*; ⊕ rendimiento *m*; **efˈfi·cient** [~ʃnt] □ eficiente; eficaz; capaz; ⊕ de buen rendimiento.
ef·fi·gy [ˈefidʒi] efigie *f*; *burn s.o. in* ~ quemar a uno en efigie.
ef·flo·resce [eflɔ:ˈres] ⚘ florecer; ⚗ eflorecerse; **ef·floˈres·cence** eflorescencia *f* (*a.* ⚗); **ef·floˈres·cent** eflorescente (*a.* ⚗).
ef·flu·ent [ˈefluənt] (corriente *f*) efluente; **ef·flu·vi·um,** *pl.* **efˈflu·vi·a** [eˈflu:viəm, ~viə] efluvio *m*, emanación *f*; tufo *m*.
ef·fort [ˈefərt] esfuerzo *m* (*to* por); F tentativa *f*; resultado *m*; *spare no* ~ *to* no regatear medio para; **ˈef·fort·less** □ fácil, nada penoso.
ef·fron·ter·y [eˈfrʌntəri] descaro *m*, impudencia *f*.
ef·fu·sion [iˈfju:ʒn] efusión *f*; **efˈfu·sive** [~siv] □ efusivo.
eft [eft] tritón *m*.
egg[1] [eg]: ~ *on* incitar (*to* a), impulsar (*to* a).
egg[2] [~] huevo *m*; *sl.* tío *m*; *sl. bad* ~ calavera *m*, sinvergüenza *m*; ~ *beater* batidor *m* de huevos; ~*cup* huevera *f*; ~ *flip* yema *f* mejida; ~*head* F intelectual *m/f*, erudito *m*; ~*nog* caldo *m* de la reina, yema *f* mejida; ~*plant* berenjena *f*; ~*shell* cascarón *m*, cáscara *f* de huevo.
eg·lan·tine [ˈegləntain] eglantina *f*.
e·go [ˈi:gou] el yo; **ˈe·go·ism** egoísmo *m*; **ˈe·go·ist** egoísta *m/f*; **e·goˈis·tic, e·goˈis·ti·cal** □ egoísta; **e·go·tism** [ˈegoutizm] egotismo *m*; **ˈe·go·tist** egotista *m/f*; **e·goˈtis·tic, e·goˈtis·ti·cal** □ egotista.
e·gre·gious [iˈgri:dʒəs] □ enorme, chocante.
e·gress [ˈi:gres] salida *f*.
E·gyp·tian [iˈdʒipʃn] egipcio *adj. a. su. m* (a *f*).
eh [ei] ¿cómo?; ¿qué?; ¿no?
ei·der [ˈaidər] (*a.* **ˈ~ duck**) eider *m*; **ˈ~·down** edredón *m*.
eight [eit] ocho (*a. su. m*); *sl. have one over the* ~ llevar una copa de más; ~*-day clock* reloj *m* de ocho días cuerda; **eight·een** [ˈeiˈti:n] dieciocho; **ˈeightˈeenth** [~θ] décimoctavo; **eighth** [~θ] octavo (*a. su. m*); **eight·i·eth** [ˈ~iiθ] octogésimo; **ˈeight·y** ochenta.

ei·ther [ˈiːðər] **1.** *adj.* cualquier ... de los dos; **2.** *pron.* uno u otro, cualquiera de los dos; **3.** *cj.* ~ ... *or* o ... o; **4.** *adv. not* ~ tampoco, no ... tampoco.

e·jac·u·late [iˈdʒækjuleit] exclamar, proferir (de repente); **e·jac·uˈla·tion** exclamación *f*.

e·ject [iˈdʒekt] expulsar, echar, arrojar; *tenant* desahuciar; **eˈjec·tion** expulsión *f*; desahucio *m from house*; **eˈjec·tor** ⊕ eyector *m*, expulsor *m*; ✈ ~ *seat* asiento *m* expulsor, asiento lanzable.

eke [iːk]: ~ *out* hacer llegar; suplir las deficiencias de (*with* con); *livelihood* ganar a duras penas.

el [el] F = *elevated* (*railroad*) ferrocarril *m* elevado.

e·lab·o·rate 1. [iˈlæbərit] □ complicado; primoroso; detallado; rebuscado; **2.** [~reit] *v/t.* elaborar; *v/i.* explicarse (~ *on* explicar) con muchos detalles; ~ *on* ampliar; **e·lab·o·ra·tion** [~ˈreiʃn] elaboración *f*; complicación *f etc.*

e·lapse [iˈlæps] pasar, transcurrir.

e·las·tic [iˈlæstik] □ elástico *adj. a. su. m*; ~ *band* gomita *f*; **e·las·tic·i·ty** [~ˈtisiti] elasticidad *f*.

e·late [iˈleit] regocijar, exaltar; *be* ~*d* alegrarse (*at, with* de); **eˈla·tion** regocijo *m*, viva alegría *f*, júbilo *m*.

el·bow [ˈelbou] **1.** codo *m* (*a.* ⊕); (*bend*) recodo *m*; *at one's* ~ a la mano; muy cerca; *out at* ~*s* raído; *bend the* ~ empinar el codo; **2.** empujar con el codo; ~ *one's way* (*through*) abrirse paso codeando; **ˈ~ grease** F codo *m*; esfuerzo *m*, aplicación *f*; muñeca *f*, jugo *m* de muñeca; **ˈ~ patch** codera *f*; **ˈ~ rest** ménsula *f*; **ˈ~·room** espacio *m* suficiente; libertad *f* de acción.

eld·er[1] [ˈeldər] **1.** mayor; ~ *statesman* veterano *m* de la política; **2.** mayor *m/f*; *eccl.* anciano *m*; ~*s pl.* jefes *m/pl.* (de tribu); *my* ~*s pl.* mis mayores.

el·der[2] [~] ⚘ saúco *m*.

eld·er·ly [ˈeldərli] mayor, de edad.

eld·est [ˈeldist] (el) mayor.

e·lect [iˈlekt] **1.** elegir, escoger; ~ *to* optar por *inf.*; decidir *inf.*; **2.** elegido; *eccl.* electo; *the* ~ los elegidos; *president* ~ presidente *m* electo; **eˈlec·tion** elección *f*; **e·lec·tionˈeer·ing** campaña *f* electoral; *b.s.* maniobras *f/pl.* electorales; **eˈlec·tive 1.** □ electivo; **2.** asignatura *f* electiva; **eˈlec·tor** elector (-a *f*) *m*; **eˈlec·tor·al** electoral; ~ *college* colegio *m* electoral; ~ *roll* lista *f* electoral; **eˈlec·tor·ate** [~rit] electorado *m*.

e·lec·tric [iˈlektrik] □ eléctrico; *fig.* cargado de emoción; muy tenso, candente; ~ *blanket* calienta-camas *m*; ~ *blue* azul (*m*) eléctrico; ~ *chair* silla *f* eléctrica; ~ *fan* ventilador *m* eléctrico; ~ *percolator* cafetera *f* eléctrica; ~ *shaver* electroafeitadora *f*; ~ *tape* cinta *f* aislante; **eˈlec·tri·cal** □ eléctrico; ~ *engineer* ingeniero *m* electricista; ~ *engineering* electrotecnia *f*; **e·lec·tri·cian** [~ˈtriʃn] electricista *m*; **e·lecˈtric·i·ty** [~siti] electricidad *f*; ~ *supply* suministro *m* eléctrico; **e·lec·tri·fiˈca·tion** electrificación *f*; **eˈlec·tri·fy** [~fai] electrificar; electrizar (*a. fig.*).

e·lec·tro... [iˈlektrou] electro...; **eˈlec·tro·cute** [~trəkjuːt] electrocutar; **e·lec·troˈcu·tion** electrocución *f*; **eˈlec·trode** [~troud] electrodo *m*; **eˈlec·tro·dyˈnam·ics** *sg.* electrodinámica *f*; **e·lec·trol·y·sis** [~ˈtrɔlisis] electrólisis *f*; **eˈlec·troˈmag·net** electroimán *m*; **eˈlec·troˈmet·al·lur·gy** electrometalurgia *f*; **eˈlec·troˈmo·tor** electromotor *m*.

e·lec·tron [iˈlektrɔn] electrón *m*; *attr.* = **e·lecˈtron·ic** □ electrónico; ~ *brain* cerebro *m* electrónico; **e·lecˈtron·ics** *sg.* electrónica *f*.

e·lec·tro·plate [iˈlektroupleit] **1.** galvanizar; **2.** artículo *m* galvanizado; **e·lec·tro·type** [iˈlektroutaip] electrotipo *m*.

e·lec·tu·ar·y [iˈlektjuəri] electuario *m*.

el·e·gance [ˈeligəns] elegancia *f*; **ˈel·e·gant** □ elegante.

el·e·gi·ac [eliˈdʒaiək] elegíaco.

el·e·gy [ˈelidʒi] elegía *f*.

el·e·ment [ˈelimənt] *all senses*: elemento *m*; ~*s pl.* elementos *m/pl.*, nociones *f/pl.*; *be in one's* ~ estar en su elemento; **el·eˈmen·tal** □ elemental; **el·eˈmen·ta·ry** □ elemental; ~ *school* escuela *f* primaria.

el·e·phant [ˈelifənt] elefante *m*; *white* ~ maula *f*; **el·e·phan·tine** [~ˈfæntain] elefantino; *fig.* mastodóntico.

el·e·vate [ˈeliveit] elevar; *p.* exaltar; ascender *in rank*; **ˈel·e·vat·ed** elevado (*a. fig.*); F (*a.* ~ *railroad*) ferrocarril *m* elevado; **el·eˈva·tion** *all* *senses*: elevación *f*; ˈ**el•e•va•tor** ascensor *m*; (*goods*) montacargas *m*; ✓ elevador *m* de granos; ✈ timón *m* de profundidad.

e•lev•en [iˈlevn] once (*a. su. m*); **eˈlev•enth** [~θ] undécimo, onceno; ~ *hour* último momento *m*.

elf [elf] duende *m*; (*dwarf*) enano *m*.

e•lic•it [iˈlisit] (son)sacar, lograr obtener.

e•lide [iˈlaid] elidir.

el•i•gi•bil•i•ty [elidʒəˈbiliti] elegibilidad *f*; ˈ**el•i•gi•ble** □ elegible; aceptable, adecuado; *bachelor* de partido.

e•lim•i•nate [iˈlimineit] eliminar; *solution etc.* descartar; suprimir; **e•lim•iˈnation** eliminación *f etc.*

e•li•sion [iˈliʒn] elisión *f*.

é•lite [eiˈliːt] élite *f*; lo selecto, flor *f* y nata.

e•lix•ir [iˈliksər] elixir *m*.

E•liz•a•be•than [ilizəˈbiːθn] isabelino.

elk [elk] alce *m*.

ell [el] † *approx.* ana *f* (= *45 pulgadas*).

el•lipse [iˈlips] elipse *f*; **elˈlip•sis** [~sis], *pl.* **elˈlip•ses** [~siːz] elipsis *f*; **elˈlip•tic, elˈlip•ti•cal** [~tik(l)] □ elíptico.

elm [elm] olmo *m*.

el•o•cu•tion [eləˈkjuːʃn] elocución *f*; (arte *m* de la) declamación *f*; **el•oˈcu•tion•ist** profesor (-a *f*) *m* de elocución.

e•lon•gate [ˈiːlɔŋgeit] alargar, extender; **e•lonˈga•tion** alargamiento *m*, extensión *f*; *ast.* elongación *f*.

e•lope [iˈloup] fugarse (con un amante); **eˈlope•ment** fuga *f* con un amante.

el•o•quence [ˈeləkwəns] elocuencia *f*; ˈ**el•o•quent** □ elocuente.

else [els] **1.** *adj.* otro; *all* ~ todo lo demás; *anyone* ~ (cualquier) otro; *nobody* ~ ningún otro; *nothing* ~ nada más; *how* ~? ¿de qué otra manera?; *what* ~? ¿qué más?; **2.** *adv.* (ade)más; F de otro modo; *or* ~ o bien, si no; ˈ**elseˈwhere** en (*or* a) otra parte.

e•lu•ci•date [iˈluːsideit] aclarar, dilucidar, elucidar; **e•lu•ciˈda•tion** aclaración *f*, elucidación *f*.

e•lude [iˈluːd] *blow etc.* eludir, esquivar, evitar; *grasp* escapar de; *it* ~*s me* se me escapa; **eˈlu•sive** [iˈluːsiv] □ fugaz; evasivo; *p.* difícil de encontrar; **eˈlu•sive•ness** lo fugaz *etc.*

elves [elvz] *pl. of elf*.

em [em] *typ.* eme *f*.

e•ma•ci•at•ed [iˈmeiʃieitid] demacrado, extenuado; **e•ma•ci•a•tion** [imeisiˈeiʃn] demacración *f*.

em•a•nate [ˈeməneit] emanar; **em•aˈna•tion** emanación *f* (*a. phys.*).

e•man•ci•pate [iˈmænsipeit] emancipar; **e•man•ciˈpa•tion** emancipación *f*; **eˈman•ci•pa•tor** emancipador *m*, libertador *m*.

e•mas•cu•late [iˈmæskjuleit] *fig.* mutilar, debilitar; estropear; ~*d style* empobrecido; **e•mas•cuˈla•tion** *fig.* mutilación *f*.

em•balm [imˈbɑːm] embalsamar; **emˈbalm•ment** embalsamamiento *m*.

em•bank•ment [imˈbæŋkmənt] terraplén *m*; dique *m*.

em•bar•go [emˈbɑːrgou] **1.** embargo *m*; prohibición *f* (*on* de), suspensión *f*; **2.** embargar.

em•bark [imˈbɑːrk] *v/t.* embarcar; *v/i.* embarcarse (*for* con rumbo a); ~ (*up*)*on* emprender; **em•bar•ka•tion** [embɑːrˈkeiʃn] embarco *m of people*; embarque *m of goods*.

em•bar•rass [imˈbærəs] desconcertar, turbar, azorar; molestar; poner en un aprieto; *be* ~*ed* azorarse, estar azorado; **emˈbar•rass•ing** □ embarazoso, desconcertador; vergonzoso; molesto; *moment, situation* violento; **emˈbar•rass•ment** desconcierto *m*, (per)turbación *f*, azoramiento *m*; apuro *m*; estorbo *m*.

em•bas•sy [ˈembəsi] embajada *f*.

em•bat•tled [imˈbætld] en orden de batalla; *city* sitiado; ⚠ almenado.

em•bed [imˈbed] empotrar, clavar, hincar (*in* en).

em•bel•lish [imˈbeliʃ] embellecer; adornar, guarnecer; **emˈbel•lish•ment** embellecimiento *m*; adorno *m*.

Em•ber days [ˈembərdeiz] *pl.* témporas *f/pl*.

em•bers [ˈembərz] *pl.* rescoldo *m*, ascua *f*.

em•bez•zle [imˈbezl] malversar, defalcar; **emˈbez•zle•ment** malversación *f*, desfalco *m*; **emˈbez•zler** malversador *m*.

em·bit·ter [imˈbitər] amargar; *relations* envenenar.
em·blem [ˈembləm] emblema *m*; **em·blem·at·ic, em·blem·at·i·cal** [embliˈmætik(l)] □ emblemático.
em·bod·i·ment [imˈbɔdimənt] encarnación *f*, personificación *f*; **emˈbod·y** encarnar, personificar; (*include*) incorporar.
em·bold·en [imˈbouldn] envalentonar.
em·bo·lism [ˈembəlizm] embolia *f*.
em·boss [imˈbɔs] realzar, labrar de realce; estampar en relieve.
em·brace [imˈbreis] **1.** abrazar(se); (*include*) abarcar; *offer* aceptar; **2.** abrazo *m*.
em·bra·sure [imˈbreiʒər] ⚠ alféizar *m*; ⚔ tronera *f*, cañonera *f*.
em·broˈca·tion [embrouˈkeiʃn] embrocación *f*.
em·broi·der [imˈbrɔidər] bordar, recamar; *fig*. adornar con detalles ficticios; **emˈbroi·der·y** bordado *m*.
em·broil [imˈbrɔil] embrollar, enredar; ~ *with* indisponer con; **emˈbroil·ment** embrollo *m*, enredo *m*.
em·bry·o [ˈembriou] **1.** embrión *m*; *in* ~ en embrión; **2.** = **em·bry·on·ic** [~ˈɔnik] □ embrionario.
e·mend [iːˈmend] enmendar; **e·menˈda·tion** enmienda *f*.
em·er·ald [ˈemərəld] **1.** esmeralda *f*; **2.** esmeraldino.
e·merge [iˈməːrdʒ] salir, surgir, emerger; aparecer; resultar (de una investigación) (*that* que); **eˈmer·gence** salida *f*, aparición *f*; **eˈmer·gen·cy** necesidad *f* urgente, aprieto *m*, situación *f* imprevista; ~ *brake* freno *m* de auxilio; ~ *exit* salida *f* de auxilio, salida *f* de urgencia; ~ *landing* aterrizaje *m* forzoso; ~ *landing field* aeródromo *m* de urgencia; ~ *measure* medida *f* de urgencia.
em·er·y [ˈeməri] esmeril *m*; ˈ~ **cloth** tela *f* de esmeril; ˈ~ **wheel** esmeriladora *f*, rueda *f* de esmeril, muela *f* de esmeril.
e·met·ic [iˈmetik] emético *adj. a. su. m*.
em·i·grant [ˈemigrənt] emigrante *adj. a. su. m/f*; **em·i·grate** [ˈ~greit] emigrar; **em·iˈgra·tion** emigración *f*.
em·i·nence [ˈeminəns] eminencia *f* (*a. title*); ˈ**em·i·nent** □ eminente.
em·is·sar·y [ˈemisəri] emisario *m*; **e·mis·sion** [iˈmiʃn] emisión *f*.
e·mit [iˈmit] emitir; *smoke etc*. arrojar, despedir; *cry* dar; *sound* producir.
e·mol·u·ment [iˈmɔljumənt] emolumento *m*.
e·mo·tion [iˈmouʃn] emoción *f*; **eˈmo·tion·al** □ emocional; *moment* de mucha emoción; *p*. exaltado; demasiado sensible; **eˈmo·tive** □ emotivo.
em·pan·el [imˈpænl] *jury* elegir, inscribir.
em·per·or [ˈempərər] emperador *m*.
em·pha·sis [ˈemfəsis], *pl*. **em·pha·ses** [ˈ~siːz] énfasis *m*; **em·pha·size** [ˈ~saiz] acentuar (*a. fig.*); *fig*. subrayar, recalcar; **em·phat·ic** [imˈfætik] □ enfático; enérgico; *be* ~ *that* insistir en que.
em·phy·se·ma [emfiˈsiːmə] enfisema *m*.
em·pire [ˈempaiər] imperio *m*.
em·pir·ic [emˈpirik] empírico *adj*. (*mst* **emˈpir·i·cal** □) *a. su. m*; **emˈpir·i·cism** empirismo *m*; **emˈpir·i·cist** empírico *m*.
em·place·ment [imˈpleismənt] sitio *m*, colocación *f*; ⚔ emplazamiento *m*.
em·ploy [imˈplɔi] **1.** emplear; servirse de; **2.** empleo *m*; servicio *m*; ocupación *f*; *in the* ~ *of* empleado por; **em·ploy·ee** [emplɔiˈiː] empleado (a *f*) *m*, dependiente (a *f*) *m*; **em·ploy·er** [imˈplɔiər] patrón *m*; **emˈploy·ment** empleo *m*; ocupación *f*, servicio *m*; *full* ~ pleno empleo *m*; *level of* ~ nivel *m* de trabajo; ~ *agency* agencia *f* de colocaciones.
em·po·ri·um [emˈpɔːriəm] emporio *m*.
em·pow·er [imˈpauər] autorizar (*to* a); habilitar (*to* para que); facultar (*to* para).
em·press [ˈempris] emperatriz *f*.
emp·ti·ness [ˈemptinis] vacío *m*; vaciedad *f*, vacuidad *f*; **emp·ty** [ˈempti] **1.** vacío; (*fruitless*) vano, inútil; *house, place* desocupado; *post* vacante; *vehicle* sin carga; F hambriento; **2.** *v/t*. vaciar; *contents* descargar, verter; *place* desocupar, dejar vacío; *v/i*. vaciarse; (*drain away*) desaguar; (*place*) ir quedando vacío (*or* desocupado); ~ *into* (*river*) desembocar en; **3.** botella *f*

etc. vacía; *empties pl.* envases *m/pl.*; '~-'**han·ded** con las manos vacías, manivacío.

e·mu ['i:mju:] emú *m.*

em·u·late ['emjuleit] emular; **em·u'la·tion** emulación *f*; '**em·u·lous** □ émulo; emulador (*of* de).

e·mul·sion [i'mʌlʃn] emulsión *f.*

en·a·ble [i'neibl] permitir (*to inf.*); habilitar (*to* para que); poner en condiciones (*to* para).

en·act [i'nækt] decretar; *law* dar, promulgar; *thea.* representar, realizar; **en'act·ment** ley *f*, estatuto *m*; promulgación *f of law.*

en·am·el [i'næml] **1.** esmalte *m*; **2.** esmaltar, pintar al esmalte; **~·ware** utensilios *m/pl.* de cocina de hierro esmaltado.

en·am·or [i'næmər] enamorar; *be ~ed of p.* estar enamorado de; *th.* tener gran afición a.

en·camp [in'kæmp] acampar(se); **en'camp·ment** campamento *m.*

en·case [in'keis] encaj(on)ar; encerrar.

en·cash·ment [in'kæʃmənt] cobro *m.*

en·chain [in'tʃein] encadenar.

en·chant [in'tʃænt] encantar (*a. fig.*); **en'chant·er** hechicero *m*; **en'chant·ing** □ encantador; **en'chant·ress** hechicera *f.*

en·cir·cle [in'sə:rkl] cercar; rodear, circunvalar; *waist* ceñir; ⚔, *pol.* envolver; **en'cir·cle·ment** ⚔, *pol.* envolvimiento *m.*

en·clave ['enkleiv] enclave *m.*

en·clit·ic [en'klitik] enclítico *adj. a. su. m.*

en·close [in'klouz] cercar, encerrar; (*include*) incluir; remitir adjunto, adjuntar *with letter*; **en'clo·sure** [~ʒər] (*place*) cercado *m*, recinto *m*; (*act*) encerramiento *m*; cosa *f etc.* inclusa *in letter.*

en·co·mi·ast [en'koumiæst] encomiasta *m/f*; **en'co·mi·um** [~miəm] encomio *m.*

en·com·pass [in'kʌmpəs] abarcar; (*surround*) rodear; (*bring about*) lograr.

en·core [ɑŋ'kɔ:r] **1.** ¡bis!; **2.** pedir la repetición de *a th.*, a *a p.*; **3.** repetición *f*, bis *m.*

en·coun·ter [in'kauntər] **1.** *all senses*: encuentro *m*; **2.** encontrar(se con), tropezar con.

en·cour·age [in'kʌridʒ] animar, alentar (*to* a); *industry* fomentar, reforzar; *growth* estimular; fortalacer *in a belief*; **en'cour·age·ment** estímulo *m*, incentivo *m*; aliento *m*; fomento *m*; *give ~ to* infundir ánimo(s) a; **en'cour·a·ging** □ alentador, esperanzador; favorable.

en·croach [in'kroutʃ] pasar los límites (*on* de); invadir (*on acc.*); *fig.* usurpar (*on acc.*); **en'croach·ment** invasión *f*; intrusión *f*; *fig.* usurpación *f.*

en·crust [in'krʌst] incrustar(se).

en·cum·ber [in'kʌmbər] estorbar; gravar, cargar *with debts etc.*; *place* llenar; **en'cum·brance** estorbo *m*; impedimento *m*; gravamen *m*, carga *f*; *without ~* sin familia.

en·cy·clo·pe·di·a, en·cy·clo·pae·di·a [ensaiklou'pi:diə] enciclopedia *f*; **en·cy·clo'pe·dic, en·cy·clo'pae·dic** enciclopédico.

end [end] **1.** fin *m*, final *m*; extremo *m*, cabo *m*; remate *m*; límite *m*; *sport*: lado *m*; desenlace *m of play*; (*object*) fin *m*, objeto *m*; *~ paper* hoja *f* de encuadernador; *at the ~ of* al cabo de; *century etc.* a fines de; *in the ~* al fin y al cabo; *on ~* de punta, de canto; *3 days on ~* 3 días seguidos; *for days on ~* durante una infinidad de días; *no ~ of* un sinfin de, la mar de; *to the ~ that* a fin de que; *to this ~* con este propósito; *be at an ~* estar terminado; *come to an ~* terminarse; *keep one's ~ up* no cejar, defenderse bien; *make an ~ of* acabar con; *make both ~s meet* hacer llegar el dinero; *put an ~ to* poner fin a; *stand on ~* poner(se) de punta; **2.** final; **3.** *v/t.* acabar, terminar; *v/i.* terminar (*in* en; *with* con; *by present participle*); acabar; (*route*) morir; *~ up* acabar; ir a parar (*at* en).

en·dan·ger [in'deindʒər] poner en peligro, comprometer.

en·dear [in'dir] hacer querer; *~ o.s. to* hacerse querer de; **en'dear·ing** □ atractivo, simpatiquísimo; **en'dear·ment** palabra *f* cariñosa, ternura *f*, caricia *f.*

en·deav·or [in'devər] **1.** esfuerzo *m*, empeño *m*; tentativa *f*; **2.** esforzarse (*to* por), procurar (*to inf.*).

en·dem·ic [en'demik] **1.** *a.* **en'dem·i·cal** □ endémico; **2.** endemia *f.*

end·ing ['endiŋ] fin *m*, conclusión *f*;

desenlace *m of book etc.*; *gr.* desinencia *f.*
en·dive [ˈendaiv] escarola *f*, endibia *f.*
end·less [ˈendlis] □ inacabable, interminable; ⊕ sin fin.
en·dorse [inˈdɔːrs] endosar; *fig.* aprobar, confirmar; *license* poner nota de inhabilitación en; **en·dor·see** [endɔːrˈsiː] endosatario *m*; **en·dorse·ment** [inˈdɔːrsmənt] endoso *m*; *fig.* aprobación *f*, confirmación *f*; nota *f* de inhabilitación *in license*; **enˈdors·er** endosante *m/f.*
en·dow [inˈdau] dotar (*a. fig.*) (*with* con, *fig.* de); fundar; **enˈdow·ment** dotación *f*; fundación *f*; *fig.* dote *f*, prenda *f.*
en·due [inˈdjuː] dotar (*with* de).
en·dur·a·ble [inˈdjurəbl] tolerable, soportable; **enˈdur·ance** resistencia *f*, paciencia *f*; aguante *m*; *past* ~ inaguantable; ~ *race* carrera *f* de resistencia; **en·dure** [inˈdjur] *v/t.* aguantar, soportar, tolerar; resistir; *v/i.* (per)durar; sufrir sin rendirse.
end·way(s) [ˈendwei(z)], **end·wise** [ˈ~waiz] de punta; de pie; de lado.
en·e·ma [ˈenimə] enema *f.*
en·e·my [ˈenimi] enemigo *adj. a. su. m* (a *f*) (*of* de); ~ *alien* extranjero *m* enemigo.
en·er·get·ic [enərˈdʒetik] □ enérgico; **ˈen·er·gize** activar; excitar (*a.* ⚡); **ˈen·er·gy** energía *f.*
en·er·vate [ˈenəːrveit] enervar; **ˈen·er·vat·ing** enervador, deprimente; **en·erˈva·tion** enervación *f.*
en·fee·ble [inˈfiːbl] debilitar; **enˈfee·ble·ment** debilitación *f.*
en·fi·lade [enfiˈleid] **1.** enfilar; **2.** enfilada *f.*
en·fold [inˈfould] envolver, abrazar; estrechar (entre los brazos).
en·force [inˈfɔːrs] *law* hacer cumplir, poner en vigor; *demand* insistir en; imponer (*upon* a); **enˈforce·ment** ejecución *f of law*; imposición *f.*
en·fran·chise [inˈfræntʃaiz] conceder el derecho de votar a; (*free*) emancipar; **enˈfran·chise·ment** [~tʃizmənt] concesión *f* del derecho de votar; emancipación *f.*
en·gage [inˈgeidʒ] *v/t.* (*contract*) apalabrar; *taxi etc.* alquilar; *servant* ajustar, tomar a su servicio; *attention* atraer, ocupar; *p.* entretener *in conversation*; ⊕ (*a.* ~ *with*) engranar con; ⊕ *coupling* acoplar; ⚔ *enemy* trabar batalla con; *be* ~*d* estar prometido (*to* para casarse con); *teleph.* estar comunicando; *be* ~*d in* estar ocupado en, dedicarse a; *get* ~*d* prometerse; *v/i.* (*promise*) comprometerse (*to* a); ⊕ engranar (*in, with* con); ~ *in* ocuparse en, dedicarse a; **enˈgage·ment** (*contract*) contrato *m*, ajuste *m*; (*appointment*) compromiso *m*, cita *f*; (*to marry*) palabra *f* de casamiento; (*period of* ~) noviazgo *m*; ⚔ combate *m*, acción *f.*
en·gag·ing [inˈgeidʒiŋ] □ simpático, atractivo, agraciado.
en·gen·der [inˈdʒendər] engendrar (*a.* †), dar lugar a, suscitar.
en·gine [ˈendʒin] motor *m*; 🚂 máquina *f*, locomotora *f*; ~ *house* cuartel *m* de bomberos; ~*man* maquinista *m/f*, conductor *m* de locomotora; **ˈen·gined** de ... motores; **ˈen·gine driv·er** maquinista *m.*
en·gi·neer [endʒiˈnir] **1.** ingeniero *m* (*a.* ⚔, ⚓); mecánico *m*; 🚂 maquinista *m*; **2.** F lograr, agenciar, gestionar; **en·giˈneer·ing** (*attr.* de) ingeniería *f.*
en·gine room [ˈendʒinrum] sala *f* de máquinas.
Eng·lish [ˈiŋgliʃ] inglés *adj. a. su. m*; *in billiards* efecto *m*; *the* ~ los ingleses; ~ *Channel* Canal *m* de la Mancha; ~ *daisy* margarita *f* de los prados; ♪ ~ *horn* corno *m* inglés, cuerno *m* inglés; ~*-speaking* de habla inglesa, anglo-parlante; **ˈEng·lish·man** inglés *m*; **ˈEng·lish·wom·an** inglesa *f.*
en·gorge [inˈgɔːrdʒ] atracar(se).
en·grain [inˈgrein] *v. ingrain.*
en·grave [inˈgreiv] grabar (*a. fig.*); burilar; **enˈgrav·er** grabador *m*; **enˈgrav·ing** grabado *m.*
en·gross [inˈgrous] absorber; ⚖ redactar en forma legal; poner en limpio; **enˈgross·ment** absorción *f*; copia *f* caligráfica.
en·gulf [inˈgʌlf] sumergir, hundir, tragar(se).
en·hance [inˈhæns] realzar; *price* aumentar; **enˈhance·ment** realce *m.*
e·nig·ma [iˈnigmə] enigma *m*; **e·nig·mat·ic, e·nig·mat·i·cal** [enigˈmætik(l)] □ enigmático.
en·join [inˈdʒɔin] mandar, ordenar (*to inf.*); imponer (*on* a); ⚖ prohibir (*from inf.*).

en·joy [inˈdʒɔi] *health, possessions* gozar de, disfrutar de; *advantages* poseer; *meal* comer con gusto; *he ~s swimming* le gusta nadar; *b.s. ~ ger.* gozarse en *inf.*; *~ o.s.* divertirse mucho, pasarlo bien; *did you ~ the play?* ¿le gustó la comedia?; **enˈjoy·a·ble** □ deleitable, agradable; divertido; **enˈjoy·ment** placer *m*; goce *m*; gusto *m*; disfrute *m of inheritance etc.*

en·lace [inˈleis] en(tre)lazar; ceñir.

en·large [inˈlɑːrdʒ] *v/t.* agrandar, ensanchar; aumentar; ampliar (*a. phot.*); *v/i.*: *~ upon* tratar con más extensión; exagerar; **enˈlarge·ment** ensanche *m*; extensión *f*; aumento *m*; ampliación *f* (*a. phot.*); **enˈlarg·er** *phot.* ampliadora *f*.

en·light·en [inˈlaitn] ilustrar, iluminar; instruir (*in* en); *can you ~ me?* ¿puede Vd. ayudarme? (*about* en el asunto de); **enˈlight·en·ment** ilustración *f*.

en·list [inˈlist] ⚔ alistar(se); *support* conseguir; ⚔ *~ed man* soldado *m* raso.

en·liv·en [inˈlaivn] vivificar, avivar, animar.

en·mesh [inˈmeʃ] coger en la red; ⊕ engranar.

en·mi·ty [ˈenmiti] enemistad *f*.

en·no·ble [iˈnoubl] ennoblecer.

e·nor·mi·ty [iˈnɔːrmiti] *fig.* enormidad *f*; **eˈnor·mous** □ enorme.

e·nough [iˈnʌf] bastante; suficiente; *be kind ~ to* tener la amabilidad de; *more than ~* más que suficiente (*to* para); *I've had ~ of him* estoy harto de él; *I had ~ to do to get home* me costó trabajo llegar a casa; *v. sure*; *that's ~!* ¡basta!

en·quire [inˈkwaiər] = *inquire*.

en·rage [inˈreidʒ] enfurecer, hacer rabiar.

en·rap·ture [inˈræptʃər] embelesar.

en·rich [inˈritʃ] enriquecer; *soil* fertilizar; **enˈrich·ment** enriquecimiento *m*; fertilización *f*.

en·rol(l) [inˈroul] alistar(se) (*a.* ⚔); inscribir(se), matricular(se); **enˈrol(l)·ment** alistamiento *m*; inscripción *f*.

en route [enˈruːt] en camino; *be ~ to* ir camino de, ir con rumbo a, dirigirse a.

en·sconce [inˈskɔns]: *~ o.s.* instalarse cómodamente, acomodarse.

en·semble [ɑ̃ːˈsɑ̃ːmbl] (*dress*) conjunto *m*; F traje *m*; ♪ agrupación *f*.

en·shrine [inˈʃrain] *fig.* encerrar.

en·sign [ˈensain] bandera *f*; alférez *m*.

en·slave [inˈsleiv] esclavizar; **enˈslave·ment** esclavitud *f*; (*act*) avasallamiento *m*.

en·snare [inˈsner] entrampar.

en·sue [inˈsuː] seguirse, resultar; sobrevenir.

en·sure [inˈʃur] asegurar.

en·tab·la·ture [enˈtæblətʃər] cornisamento *m*.

en·tail [inˈteil] **1.** vínculo *m*, vinculación *f*; **2.** ocasionar, causar; suponer; ⚖ vincular.

en·tan·gle [inˈtæŋgl] enmarañar, enredar; **enˈtan·gle·ment** embrollo *m*, enredo *m* (amoroso *etc.*); *barbed wire ~* alambrada *f*.

en·ter [ˈentər] *v/t.* entrar en; penetrar en; *society* ingresar en, matricularse en; *member* matricular; asentar, registrar *in records*; *protest* formular; ✝ *order* asentar, anotar; *child* inscribir como futuro alumno (*for* de); *~ a p.'s head* ocurrírsele a uno; *~ up* ✝ *ledger* hacer, llevar; *diary* poner al día; *v/i.* entrar; *thea.* entrar en escena; *sport*: participar (*for* en), presentarse (*for* a); *~ into* participar en; *agreement* firmar; *conversation* entablar; *plans* formar parte de; *relations* establecer; *~ into the spirit of* dejarse emocionar por; empaparse en; *~ (up)on career* emprender; *office* tomar posesión de; *term* empezar.

en·ter·ic [enˈterik] entérico; **en·ter·i·tis** [~təˈraitis] enteritis *f*.

en·ter·prise [ˈentərpraiz] empresa *f*; (*spirit*) iniciativa *f*; *private ~* iniciativa *f* privada; **ˈen·ter·pris·ing** □ emprendedor.

en·ter·tain [entərˈtein] (*amuse*) entretener, divertir; *guest* recibir; festejar, agasajar; *idea, hope* abrigar; considerar; *they ~ a great deal* reciben mucho en casa; **en·terˈtain·er** actor *m*, músico *m* (*etc.*); **en·terˈtain·ing** □ entretenido, divertido; **en·terˈtain·ment** entretenimiento *m*, diversión *f*; espectáculo *m*; función *f*; *~ tax* impuesto *m* sobre los espectáculos.

en·thral(l) [inˈθrɔːl] *fig.* encantar, embelesar; cautivar.

en·throne [in'θroun] entronizar; **en'throne·ment** entronización *f*.
en·thuse [in'θju:z] F: *~ over* entusiasmarse mucho por.
en·thu·si·asm [in'θju:ziæzm] entusiasmo *m* (*for* por); **en'thu·si·ast** [~æst] entusiasta *m*/*f*; **en·thu·si'as·tic** □ entusiasta; entusiástico; lleno de entusiasmo (*about*, *over* por).
en·tice [in'tais] tentar, atraer (con maña); seducir; **en'tice·ment** tentación *f*; seducción *f*.
en·tire [in'taiər] entero; completo; **en'tire·ly** enteramente; **en'tire·ty**: *in its ~* enteramente, completamente; en su totalidad.
en·ti·tle [in'taitl] *book* intitular; *~ to* dar derecho a (*acc.*, *inf.*); *be ~d to* tener derecho a.
en·ti·ty ['entiti] entidad *f*, ente *m*.
en·tomb [in'tu:m] sepultar.
en·to·mol·o·gy [entə'mɔlədʒi] entomología *f*.
en·tour·age [ɔntu'rɑ:ʒ] séquito *m*.
en·trails ['entreilz] *pl.* entrañas *f*/*pl*.
en·trance[1] ['entrəns] entrada *f*; ingreso *m*; *thea.* entrada *f* en escena; *~ examination* examen *m* de ingreso; *~ fee* cuota *f*.
en·trance[2] [in'træns] encantar, embelesar, hechizar; extasiar.
en·trant ['entrənt] principiante *m*/*f*; *sport*: participante *m*/*f*.
en·treat [in'tri:t] rogar, suplicar (insistentemente) (*to inf.*); **en'treat·y** ruego *m*, súplica *f* (insistente).
en·tree ['ɑ:ntrei] entrada *f*, ingreso *m*; *of meal*: entrada *f*, principio *m*.
en·trench [in'trentʃ] ⚔ atrincherar(se); *fig.* *~ o.s.* establecerse firmemente; **en'trench·ment** trinchera *f*, atrincheramiento *m*.
en·trust [in'trʌst] confiar (*to* a; *a p. with a th.* algo a alguien).
en·try ['entri] entrada *f*; ingreso *m*; (*street*) bocacalle *f*; ⚖ toma *f* de posesión (*on* de); *sport*: (*total*) participación *f*; (*p.*) participante *m*/*f*; artículo *m in dictionary*; apunte *m in diary*; ✝ partida *f*; *no ~* prohibido el paso; dirección prohibida; *~ permit* permiso *m* de entrada; *~ word* (*in a dictionary*) voz-guía *f*; *bookkeeping by double* (*single*) *~* contabilidad *f* por partida doble (simple).
en·twine [in'twain] entretejer; entrelazar.
e·nu·mer·ate [i'nu:məreit] enumerar; **e·nu·mer'a·tion** enumeración *f*.
e·nun·ci·ate [i'nʌnsieit] enunciar; pronunciar; **e·nun·ci'a·tion** enunciación *f*; pronunciación *f*.
en·vel·op [in'veləp] envolver (*in* en); ⚔ *~ing movement* movimiento *m* envolvente; **en·ve·lope** ['enviloup] sobre *m*; ✈ envoltura *f*; **en·vel·op·ment** [in'veləpmənt] envolvimiento *m*.
en·ven·om [in'venəm] envenenar (*a. fig.*).
en·vi·a·ble ['enviəbl] □ envidiable; **'en·vi·ous** □ envidioso; *be ~ of* tener envidia de.
en·vi·ron·ment [in'vairənmənt] medio *m* ambiente; *~al pollution* contaminación *f* ambiental; **en·vi·rons** [en'vairənz] *pl.* alrededores *m*/*pl.*, inmediaciones *f*/*pl*.
en·vis·age [in'vizidʒ] prever; concebir, representarse; contemplar.
en·voy ['envɔi] enviado *m*.
en·vy ['envi] **1.** envidia *f*; **2.** envidiar (*a p. a th.* algo a alguien); *p.* tener envidia a.
en·zyme ['enzaim] enzima *f*.
ep·au·let(**te**) ['epɔlət] charretera *f*.
e·pergne [i'pə:rn] centro *m* de mesa.
e·phem·er·al [i'fi:mərəl] efímero.
ep·ic ['epik] **1.** □ épico; **2.** épica *f*, epopeya *f*.
ep·i·cure ['epikjur] gastrónomo *m*; **ep·i·cu·re·an** [~'riən] epicúreo *adj. a. su. m* (*a. fig.*).
ep·i·dem·ic [epi'demik] **1.** □ epidémico; **2.** epidemia *f*.
ep·i·der·mis [epi'də:rmis] epidermis *f*.
ep·i·gram ['epigræm] epigrama *m*; **ep·i·gram·mat·ic, ep·i·gram·mat·i·cal** [~grə'mætik(l)] □ epigramático.
ep·i·lep·sy ['epilepsi] epilepsia *f*; **ep·i'lep·tic** epiléptico *adj. a. su. m* (a *f*).
ep·i·log, ep·i·logue ['epilɔg] epílogo *m*.
E·piph·a·ny [i'pifəni] Epifanía *f*.
e·pis·co·pa·cy [i'piskəpəsi] episcopado *m*; **e'pis·co·pal** episcopal; **e'pis·co·pate** [~pit] episcopado *m*.
ep·i·sode ['episoud] episodio *m*; **ep·i·sod·ic, ep·i·sod·i·cal** [~'sɔdik(l)] □ episódico.

e·pis·tle [iˈpisl] epístola *f*; **eˈpis·to·lar·y** [~təlari] epistolar.

ep·i·taph [ˈepitæf] epitafio *m*.

ep·i·thet [ˈepiθet] epíteto *m*.

e·pit·o·me [iˈpitəmi] epítome *m*, compendio *m*; *fig*. representación *f* en miniatura, resumen *m*; **eˈpit·o·mize** epitomar, compendiar; *fig*. representar en miniatura.

ep·och [ˈi:pɔk] época *f*; **ˈ~-mak·ing** que hace época.

Ep·som salts [ˈepsəmˈsɔ:lts] *pl*. sal *f* de la Higuera.

eq·ua·bil·i·ty [ekwəˈbiliti] uniformidad *f*; tranquilidad *f*, ecuanimidad *f*; **ˈeq·ua·ble** □ *climate etc*. igual, uniforme; *temperament* tranquilo, ecuánime.

e·qual [ˈi:kwl] **1.** □ igual (*to* a); *fig*. ~ *to task* con fuerzas para; *occasion* al nivel de; **2.** igual *m*/*f*; **3.** ser igual a; **e·qual·i·ty** [iˈkwɔliti] igualdad *f*; **e·qual·i·za·tion** [i:kwəlaiˈzeiʃn] igualación *f*; **ˈe·qual·ize** *v*/*t*. igualar; *v*/*i*. *sport*: lograr el empate.

e·qua·nim·i·ty [i:kwəˈnimiti] ecuanimidad *f*.

e·quate [iˈkweit] igualar, considerar equivalente (*to*, *with* a); **eˈqua·tion** ecuación *f*; **eˈqua·tor** ecuador *m*; **e·qua·to·ri·al** [ekwəˈtɔ:riəl] □ ecuatorial.

eq·uer·ry [ˈekweri] caballerizo *m* (del rey).

e·ques·tri·an [iˈkwestriən] **1.** ecuestre; **2.** jinete (a *f*) *m*.

e·qui·dis·tant [ˈi:kwiˈdistənt] □ equidistante.

e·qui·lat·er·al [ˈi:kwiˈlætərəl] □ equilátero.

e·quil·i·brist [i:ˈkwilibrist] equilibrista *m*/*f*; **e·quiˈlib·ri·um** [~əm] equilibrio *m*.

e·quine [ˈi:kwain] 🕮 equino; caballar, hípico.

e·qui·noc·tial [i:kwiˈnɔkʃl] equinoccial; **e·qui·nox** [ˈ~nɔks] equinoccio *m*.

e·quip [iˈkwip] equipar; ⊕ ~*ped with* dotado de; *be well* ~*ped to inf*. estar bien dotado para *inf*.; **e·quip·ment** [iˈkwipmənt] equipo *m*; material *m*; avíos *m*/*pl*.; equipaje *m*; pertrechos *m*/*pl*.; (*mental*) aptitud *f*.

e·qui·poise [ˈekwipɔiz] **1.** equilibrio *m*; contrapeso *m*; **2.** equilibrar; contrapesar.

eq·ui·ta·ble [ˈekwitəbl] □ equitativo; **ˈeq·ui·ty** equidad *f* (*a*. ⚖); ✝ *equities pl*. acciones *f*/*pl*. de dividendo no fijo.

e·quiv·a·lence [iˈkwivələns] equivalencia *f*; **eˈquiv·a·lent** equivalente *adj*. *a*. *su*. *m* (*to* a).

e·quiv·o·cal [iˈkwivəkl] □ equívoco, ambiguo; **eˈquiv·o·cate** [~keit] soslayar el problema, usar equívocos (para no contestar directamente); **e·quiv·oˈca·tion** equívoco *m*.

e·ra [ˈirə, ˈerə] era *f*, época *f*.

e·rad·i·cate [iˈrædikeit] desarraigar, extirpar; **e·rad·iˈca·tion** desarraigo *m*, extirpación *f*.

e·rase [iˈreis] borrar (*a*. *fig*.); **eˈras·er** goma *f* de borrar; **eˈra·sure** [~ʒər] borradura *f*.

ere [er] † **1.** *cj*. antes (de) que; **2.** *prp*. antes de; ~ *long* dentro de poco.

e·rect [iˈrekt] **1.** □ erguido, derecho; *hair etc*. erizado; **2.** erigir, construir, levantar; ⊕ montar; *principles* formular; constituir (*into* en); **eˈrec·tion** construcción *f*, estructura *f*; (*act*) erección *f*; ⊕ montaje *m*; **eˈrect·ness** lo erguido *etc*.; **eˈrec·tor** constructor *m*.

erg [ə:rg] ergio *m*.

er·got [ˈə:rgət] cornezuelo *m*.

er·mine [ˈə:rmin] armiño *m*.

e·rode [iˈroud] *soil* erosionar(se), causar erosión en; *metal etc*. corroer, desgastar(se).

e·ro·sion [iˈrouʒn] erosión *f*; desgaste *m*; **eˈro·sive** [~siv] erosivo.

e·rot·ic [iˈrɔtik] □ erótico; erotómano; (*obscene*) sicalíptico; **eˈrot·i·cism** [~sizm] erotomanía *f*; sicalipsis *f*.

err [ə:r] errar, equivocarse; (*sin*) pecar; ~ *on the side of* pecar por exceso de.

er·rand [ˈerənd] recado *m*, mandado *m*; *run* ~*s* ir a los mandados; **ˈ~ boy** mandadero *m*, recadero *m*.

er·rant [ˈerənt] errante; *knight* andante; (*erring*) equivocado.

er·rat·ic [iˈrætik] □ irregular, inconstante; *performance*, *record etc*. desigual; *behavior* excéntrico; *geol*., ⚕ errático; **er·ra·tum** [iˈreitəm], *pl*. **erˈra·ta** [~ə] errata *f*.

er·ro·ne·ous [iˈrounjəs] □ erróneo.

er·ror [ˈerər] error *m*, yerro *m*; equivocación *f*; *in* ~ por equivocación.

e·ruc·ta·tion [iːrʌkˈteiʃn] 🕮 eructo *m.*
er·u·dite [ˈerudait] □ erudito; **er·u·di·tion** [~ˈdiʃn] erudición *f.*
e·rupt [iˈrʌpt] (*volcano*) entrar en erupción; ⚕ hacer erupción; *fig.* irrumpir (*into* en); (*anger*) estallar; **eˈrup·tion** erupción *f* (*a.* ⚕); explosión *f of anger etc.*; **eˈrup·tive** eruptivo.
er·y·sip·e·las [eriˈsipiləs] erisipela *f.*
es·ca·la·tor [ˈeskəleitər] escalera *f* móvil (*or* rodante).
es·cal·lop [esˈkæləp] **1.** concha *f* de peregrino; *on edge of cloth* festón *m*; **2.** hornear a la crema y con migajas de pan; cocer (*ostras*) en su concha; *a piece of cloth* festonear; *~ed potatoes pl.* patatas *f/pl.* al gratén.
es·ca·pade [eskəˈpeid] travesura *f*, aventura *f*; **es·cape** [isˈkeip] **1.** *v/t.* evitar, eludir; *death* escapar a; *vigilance* burlar; (*forget*) olvidársele (a uno); (*meaning*) *p.* escaparse a; *~ notice* pasar inadvertido; *a cry ~d him* no pudo contener un grito; *v/i.* escapar(se); evadirse; (*gas etc.*) fugarse; *~ from p.* escaparse a; *prison* escaparse de; **2.** escape *m*, fuga *f*; fuga *f of gas etc.*; *fig.* escapatoria *f* (*from duties etc.*); *~ literature* literatura *f* de escape (*or* de evasión); *have a narrow ~* escaparse por un pelo; **es·cap·ee** [eskəˈpiː] evadido *m*; **esˈcape·ment** ⊕ escape *m*; *~ wheel* rueda *f* de escape; **esˈcap·ism** escapismo *m.*
es·carp [isˈkɑːrp] **1.** (*a.* **esˈcarp·ment**) escarpa *f*; **2.** escarpar.
es·cheat [isˈtʃiːt] **1.** reversión *f* de bienes mostrencos; **2.** *v/t.* confiscar; transferir (al estado *etc.*); *v/i.* revertir (al estado *etc.*).
es·chew [isˈtʃuː] evitar; renunciar a.
es·cort 1. [ˈeskɔːrt] ⚔ escolta *f*; acompañante *m/f*; **2.** [isˈkɔːrt] escoltar; acompañar.
es·cri·toire [eskriˈtwɑːr] escritorio *m.*
es·cutch·eon [isˈkʌtʃn] escudo *m* de armas; *fig.* honor *m.*
Es·ki·mo [ˈeskimou] esquimal *m/f.*
e·soph·a·gus [iːˈsɔfəgəs] esófago *m.*
e·so·ter·ic [esouˈterik] □ esotérico.
es·pal·ier [esˈpæljər] espaldar *m*, espalera *f.*
es·pe·cial [isˈpeʃl] □ especial; particular; **esˈpe·cial·ly** especialmente; sobre todo; máxime.
es·pi·o·nage [espiəˈnɑːʒ] espionaje *m.*
es·plan·ade [espləˈneid] paseo *m* (*mst* marítimo).
es·pous·al [isˈpauzl] *fig.* adhesión *f* (*of* a); **esˈpouse** [~z] casarse con; *fig.* adherirse a, abrazar.
es·py [isˈpai] divisar.
es·quire [isˈkwaiər] *on envelopes*: Sr. don; *v. squire*; ♀ (*abbr. Esq.*) título *m* de cortesía que se escribe después del apellido y que se usa en vez de *Mr.*
es·say 1. [eˈsei] intentar (*to inf.*); (*test*) ensayar; **2.** [ˈesei] ensayo *m*; **ˈes·say·ist** ensayista *m/f.*
es·sence [ˈesns] esencia *f*; **es·sen·tial** [iˈsenʃl] **1.** □ esencial; indispensable, imprescindible; *~ oil* aceite *m* esencial; **2.** esencial *m.*
es·tab·lish [isˈtæbliʃ] establecer; fundar; *facts* verificar; *~ that* comprobar que; *♀ed Church* iglesia *f* del Estado; **esˈtab·lish·ment** establecimiento *m*; fundación *f*; ⚔ efectivos *m/pl.*, fuerzas *f/pl.*; *the ♀ centro del poder efectivo en Inglaterra*; ⚓ *etc.* personal *m.*
es·tate [isˈteit] (*land etc.*) finca *f*, hacienda *f*, heredad *f*; ⚖ (*property*) bienes *m/pl.* (relictos); herencia *f*; *pol.* estado *m*; *~ agent* corredor *m* de fincas; *~ car* rubia *f*; *~ duty* impuesto *m* sobre los bienes relictos; *real ~* bienes *m/pl.* raíces; *third ~* estado *m* llano; F *fourth ~* la prensa.
es·teem [isˈtiːm] **1.** estima *f*; consideración *f*, aprecio *m*; **2.** estimar, apreciar; *I would ~ it a favor if* agradecería que.
es·ti·ma·ble [ˈestiməbl] estimable.
es·ti·mate 1. [ˈestimeit] estimar; apreciar; calcular (*that* que); computar, tasar (*at* en); hacer un presupuesto (*for* de); **2.** [ˈ~mit] estimación *f*; tasa *f*; cálculo *m*; presupuesto *m for work*; **es·tiˈma·tion** estimación *f*; *in my ~* según mis cálculos; en mi opinión.
Es·to·ni·an [esˈtounjən] **1.** estonio *adj. a. su. m* (a *f*); **2.** (*language*) estonio *m.*
es·trange [isˈtreindʒ] enajenar, apartar; *become ~d* malquistarse; **esˈtrange·ment** enajenamiento *m*, extrañamiento *m*; desavenencia *m.*
es·tu·ar·y [ˈestjuəri] estuario *m*, ría *f.*

et·cet·er·a [it'setrə] etcétera; *~s pl.* adiciones *f/pl.*, adornos *m/pl.*
etch [etʃ] grabar al agua fuerte; **'etch·ing** aguafuerte *f.*
e·ter·nal [i'tə:rnl] □ eterno; (*a. b.s.*) sempiterno; **e'ter·nal·ize** [~nəlaiz] eternizar; **e'ter·ni·ty** eternidad *f*; **e·ter·nize** [i:'tə:rnaiz] eternizar.
e·ther ['i:θər] éter *m*; **e·the·re·al** [i'θi:riəl] etéreo (*a. fig.*); **'e·ther·ize** eterizar.
eth·i·cal ['eθikl] □ ético; honrado; **'eth·ics** *mst sg.* ética *f*; moralidad *f.*
E·thi·o·pi·an [i:θi'oupiən] etíope *adj. a. su. m/f.*
eth·nog·ra·phy [eθ'nɔgrəfi] etnografía *f*; **eth'nol·o·gy** [~lədʒi] etnología *f.*
eth·yl ['eθil] etilo *m*; **eth·yl·ene** ['eθili:n] etileno *m.*
et·i·quette ['etiket] etiqueta *f*; honor *m* profesional.
E·ton crop ['i:tn'krɔp] corte *m* a lo garçón.
et·y·mo·log·i·cal [etimə'lɔdʒikl] □ etimológico; **et·y·mol·o·gy** [~'mɔlədʒi] etimología *f*; **ety·mon** ['etimɔn] étimo *m.*
eu·cha·rist ['ju:kərist] Eucaristía *f.*
eu·chre ['ju:kər] **1.** juego *m* de naipes; **2.** *v/t.* F ser más listo que.
eu·gen·ics [ju:'dʒeniks] *sg.* eugenismo *m*, eugenesia *f.*
eu·lo·gist ['ju:lədʒist] elogiador *m*; **eu·lo·gize** ['~dʒaiz] elogiar, encomiar; **eu·lo·gy** ['~dʒi] elogio *m*, encomio *m.*
eu·nuch ['ju:nək] eunuco *m.*
eu·phe·mism ['ju:fimizm] eufemismo *m*; **eu·phe'mis·tic, eu·phe'mis·ti·cal** □ eufemístico.
eu·phon·ic [ju:'fɔnik] □, **eu·phon·i·ous** ['~iəs] □ eufónico; **eu·pho·ny** ['ju:fəni] eufonía *f.*
eu·re·ka [ju'ri:kə] ¡eureka!
Eu·ro·pe·an [jurə'pi:ən] europeo *adj. a. su. m* (a *f*).
Eu·ro·vi·sion [jurə'viʒn] Eurovisión *f* (*sistema europeo de televisión*).
eu·tha·na·si·a [ju:θə'neizə] eutanasia *f.*
e·vac·u·ate [i'vækjueit] evacuar; desocupar; **e·vac·u'a·tion** evacuación *f*; **e·vac·u'ee** evacuado (a *f*) *m.*
e·vade [i'veid] evadir, eludir; *v. issue.*
e·val·u·ate [i'væljueit] evaluar; **e·val·u'a·tion** evaluación *f.*
ev·a·nesce [i:və'nes] desvanecerse; **ev·a'nes·cence** desvanecimiento *m*; **ev·a'nes·cent** □ evanescente.
e·van·gel·ic, e·van·gel·i·cal [i:væn'dʒelik(l)] □ evangélico; **e·van·ge·list** [i'vændʒilist] evangelizador *m*; *the* ♀ Evangelista *m*; **e'van·ge·lize** evangelizar.
e·vap·o·rate [i'væpəreit] evaporar(se) (*a. fig.*); *~d milk* leche *f* evaporada; **e·vap·o'ra·tion** evaporación *f.*
e·va·sion [i'veiʒn] evasiva *f*, evasión *f*; **e'va·sive** [~siv] □ evasivo; *be ~* contestar con evasivas.
eve [i:v] víspera *f*; *on the ~ of* la víspera de, en vísperas de.
e·ven[1] ['i:vn] **1.** *adj.* □ llano, liso; igual; *temperature etc.* constante, invariable; *treatment* imparcial; *temper* sereno, apacible; ⚘ par; *be ~* estar en paz (*with* con); *get ~* desquitarse (*with* con); *that makes us ~* (*game*) eso iguala el tanteo; **2.** *adv.* aun, hasta; incluso; tan siquiera; *~ as* precisamente cuando, en el mismo momento en que; *~ if*, *~ though* aunque, aun cuando; *~ so* aun así; *not ~* ni (...) siquiera; F *break ~* salir sin ganar ni perder; **3.** *v/t.* igualar, allanar; *~ out ps.* hacer iguales; *th.* repartir con justicia; *~ up score etc.* igualar, nivelar; *v/i.*: *~ up* pagar, ajustar cuentas (*with* con).
e·ven[2] [~] *poet.* anochecer *m.*
e·ven...: **'~-'hand·ed** imparcial; **'~-tem·pered** apacible, ecuánime.
eve·ning ['i:vniŋ] tarde *f*; anochecer *m*; noche *f*; *good ~!* ¡buenas tardes!; *musical ~* velada *f* musical; *attr. star etc.* vespertino; *paper* de la tarde; *~ clothes pl.* traje *m* de etiqueta; *~ dress* traje *m* de etiqueta; *~ gown* vestido *m* de noche *de mujer*; *~ primrose* hierba *f* del asno; *~ star* estrella *f* vespertina, lucero *m* de la tarde; *~ wrap* salida *f* de teatro.
e·ven·ness ['i:vənnis] igualdad *f*; lisura *f*; uniformidad *f*; imparcialidad *f*; serenidad *f.*
e·ven·song ['i:vənsɔŋ] vísperas *f/pl.*
e·vent [i'vent] suceso *m*, acontecimiento *m*; caso *m*; consecuencia *f*; *sport*: prueba *f*, carrera *f etc.*; *~s pl.* (*programme*) programa *m*; *at all ~s*, *in any ~* en todo caso; *in the*

~ *of* en caso de; e'**vent·ful** [~ful] □ *life* azaroso, accidentado; memorable; *match etc.* lleno de emoción, lleno de incidentes.

e·ven·tu·al [i'ventjuəl] □ final; consiguiente; eventual; ~*ly* finalmente, con el tiempo; al fin y al cabo; **e·ventu·al·i·ty** [~'æliti] eventualidad *f*.

ev·er ['evər] siempre; alguna vez; (*negative sense*) jamás, nunca; ~ *after*, ~ *since* desde entonces; (*cj.*) después (de) que; F ~ *so* (— *adj.*) muy; F ~ *so* (*much*) (*adv.*) muchísimo; F ~ *so many things* la mar de cosas; *as* ~ como siempre; (*in letter*) tu amigo, un abrazo; *as soon as* ~ *I can* lo más pronto que pueda; *for* ~ para siempre; *for* ~ *and* ~ por siempre jamás; *hardly* ~ casi nunca; *better than* ~ mejor que nunca; F *the best* ~ el mejor que se ha visto nunca; F *did you* ~? ¿se vió jamás tal cosa?, *did you* ~ *meet him?* ¿llegó Vd. a conocerle?; '**~·green** (planta *f*) de hoja perenne; **~'last·ing** □ sempiterno, perpetuo, perdurable; *b.s.* aburrido; '**~'more** eternamente; *for* ~ por siempre jamás.

ev·er·y ['evri] cada, todo; todos (los *etc.*); ~ *bit as good* de ningún modo inferior (*as* a); ~ *bit a man* todo un hombre; ~ *now and then* de vez en cuando; ~ *one* cada uno; ~ *one of them* todos ellos; ~ *other day* un día sí y otro no, cada dos días; ~ *ten years* cada diez años; *her* ~ *look* todas sus miradas; '**~·bod·y** todos, todo el mundo; '**~'day** diario; rutinario; acostumbrado, corriente; '**~·thing** todo; *he paid for* ~ lo pagó todo; *time is* ~ el tiempo lo es todo; '**~·where** en (por, a) todas partes; ~ *you go* (por) dondequiera que vayas.

e·vict [i'vikt] desahuciar; e'**vic·tion** desahucio *m*.

ev·i·dence ['evidəns] **1.** ⚖ prueba *f*, declaración *f*, testimonio *m*, deposición *f*; (*sign*) prueba *f*, indicio *m*; evidencia *f*; *in* ~ manifiesto, visible; *give* ~ deponer, prestar declaración, dar testimonio; **2.** evidenciar; *be* ~*d by* estar probado por; '**ev·i·dent** □ evidente, claro; manifiesto; *be* ~ *in* manifestarse en; *be* ~ *from* resultar de; deducirse de, quedar bien claro de; **ev·i·den·tial** [~'denʃl] □ indicador, probatorio.

e·vil ['i:vl] **1.** □ *p.* malo, malvado, perverso; *th.* pernicioso; *the* ~ *eye* aojo *m*, mal *m* de ojo; ~-*minded* mal pensado, malintencionado; *the* ♀ *One* el enemigo malo; **2.** mal *m*, maldad *f*; '**~'do·er** malhechor *m*; '**~'do·ing** malhecho *m*, maldad *f*.

e·vince [i'vins] dar señales de, mostrar; indicar.

e·vis·cer·ate [i'visəreit] destripar.

ev·o·ca·tion [evou'keiʃn] evocación *f*; **e·voc·a·tive** [i'vɔkətiv] □ evocador, sugestivo.

e·voke [i'vouk] evocar.

ev·o·lu·tion [i:və'lu:ʃn] evolución *f* (*a. biol. a.* ⚔); desarrollo *m*; ⅍ extracción *f* de raíces; **ev·o'lu·tion·ar·y** evolutivo.

e·volve [i'vɔlv] *v/t.* evolucionar, desarrollar; *heat etc.* desprender; *v/i.* evolucionar, desarrollarse.

ewe [ju:] oveja *f*.

ew·er ['ju:ər] aguamanil *m*.

ex [eks] **1.** *prp. dividend* sin participación en; *works* en; ~ *officio* de oficio; **2.** antiguo; ... que fue; ex...; ~-*minister* ex ministro *m*.

ex·ac·er·bate [eks'æsərbeit] exacerbar.

ex·act [ig'zækt] **1.** □ exacto; puntual; **2.** exigir (*from* a); *obedience etc.* imponer (*from* a); **ex'act·ing** exigente; *conditions* severo; **ex'ac·tion** exacción *f* (*a. b.s.*); **ex'act·i·tude** [~titju:d] exactitud *f*; **ex'act·ly** exactamente; (*time*) en punto; (*as answer*) exacto; *how many were there*, ~? ¿cuántos había, en concreto?; **ex'act·ness** exactitud *f*.

ex·ag·ger·ate [ig'zædʒəreit] exagerar; **ex·ag·ger'a·tion** exageración *f*.

ex·alt [ig'zɔ:lt] exaltar; elevar; ensalzar; **ex·al·ta·tion** exaltación *f*; elevación *f*; **ex·alt·ed** [ig'zɔ:ltid] exaltado, elevado.

ex·am [ig'zæm] F = **ex·am·i·na·tion** [igzæmi'neiʃn] examen *m*; ⚕ reconocimiento *m*; ⚖ interrogación *f*; investigación *f* (*into* de); registro *m of baggage*; *take an* ~ sufrir un examen, examinarse; **ex'am·ine** [~min] examinar; ⚖ interrogar; (*closely*) escudriñar; *baggage* registrar; ~ *into* indagar, investigar; **ex·am·i'nee** examinando (a *f*) *m*; **ex'am·in·er** examinador *m*; inspector *m*.

ex·am·ple [ig'zæmpl] ejemplo *m*; ejemplar *m*; ♧ problema *m*; *for* ~ por ejemplo; *make an* ~ *of* castigar de modo ejemplar; *set an* ~ dar ejemplo.

ex·as·per·ate [ig'sæspəreit] exasperar, irritar, sacar de quicio; **ex·as·per'a·tion** exasperación *f*.

ex·ca·vate ['ekskəveit] excavar; **ex·ca'va·tion** excavación *f*; **'ex·ca·va·tor** (*p*.) excavador *m*; ⊕ excavadora *f*.

ex·ceed [ik'si:d] exceder (de); *limit* rebasar; *speed limit* sobrepasar; *expectations* superar; ~ *o.s.* excederse; **ex'ceed·ing** extraordinario; † = **ex'ceed·ing·ly** sumamente, sobremanera.

ex·cel [ik'sel] *v/t.* aventajar, superar; *v/i.* sobresalir (*in* en); **ex·cel·lence** ['eksələns] excelencia *f*; **'Ex·cel·len·cy** Excelencia *f*; **'ex·cel·lent** □ excelente.

ex·cept [ik'sept] **1.** exceptuar, excluir; **2.** *cj.* † ~ (*that*) a menos que; **3.** *prp.* excepto, salvo, fuera de; ~ *for* excepto; dejando aparte, sin contar; **ex'cept·ing** *prp.* excepto, a excepción de; **ex'cep·tion** excepción *f*; *with the* ~ *of* a excepción de; *take* ~ ofenderse (*to* por); **ex'cep·tion·a·ble** recusable; **ex'cep·tion·al** □ excepcional.

ex·cerpt 1. [ek'sə:rpt] citar; sacar; **2.** ['eksə:rpt] cita *f*, extracto *m*; separata *f from journal*.

ex·cess [ik'ses] exceso *m* (*a. fig.*); *fig.* desmán *m*, desafuero *m*; ⚕ excedente *m*; *attr.* excedente, sobrante; *in* ~ *of* superior a; *carry to* ~ llevar al exceso; ~ *baggage* exceso *m* de equipaje; ~ *fare* suplemento *m*; ~*-profits tax* impuesto *m* sobre ganancias excesivas; ~ *weight* exceso *m* de peso; **ex'ces·sive** □ excesivo; sobrado.

ex·change [iks'tʃeindʒ] **1.** cambiar (*for* por); *prisoners, stamps etc.* canjear; *shots* cambiar; *courtesies* hacerse; **2.** cambio *m*; canje *m*; (*cultural etc.*) intercambio *m*; *teleph.* central *f* telefónica; ⚕ (*stock* ~) bolsa *f*; (*corn etc.*) lonja *f*; *in* ~ *for* a cambio de; *bill of* ~ letra *f* de cambio; ~ *control* control *m* de divisas; (*rate of*) ~ (tipo *m* de) cambio *m*; **ex'change·a·ble** cambiable, canjeable.

ex·cheq·uer [iks'tʃekər] erario *m*, hacienda *f*, tesoro *m* (público); *British Chancellor of the* ♀ Canciller *m* del Tesoro (= *Ministro de Hacienda*); ~ *bills* bonos *m/pl.* del Tesoro.

ex·cise[1] ['eksaiz] (recaudación *f* de) impuestos *m/pl.* interiores; ~ *tax* impuesto *m* sobre ciertas mercancías de comercio interior.

ex·cise[2] [ek'saiz] eliminar, quitar; cortar; **ex·ci·sion** [ek'siʒn] excisión *f*; corte *m*.

ex·cit·a·bil·i·ty [iksaitə'biliti] excitabilidad *f*; exaltación *f*; **ex'cit·a·ble** □ excitable; exaltado; nervioso; **ex·ci·ta·tion** [eksi'teiʃn] excitación *f*; **ex·cite** [ik'sait] emocionar; entusiasmar; (*stimulate*) excitar, estimular; (*rouse*) provocar; *get* ~*d* emocionarse; alborotarse; entusiasmarse (*about, over* por); **ex'cite·ment** emoción *f*; entusiasmo *m*; excitación *f*; **ex'cit·ing** □ emocionante; conmovedor; apasionante; excitante.

ex·claim [iks'kleim] *v/t.* decir con vehemencia; *v/i.* exclamar; ~ *against* acusar vivamente.

ex·cla·ma·tion [eksklə'meiʃn] exclamación *f*; ~ *mark* punto *m* de admiración; **ex·clam·a·to·ry** [~'klæmətəri] □ exclamatorio.

ex·clude [iks'klu:d] excluir; exceptuar.

ex·clu·sion [iks'klu:ʒn] exclusión *f*; *to the* ~ *of* con exclusión de; **ex'clu·sive** [~siv] □ exclusivo; privativo; *policy etc.* exclusivista; (*sole*) único; *club etc.* selecto; ~ *of* fuera de, sin contar.

ex·cog·i·tate [eks'kɔdʒiteit] excogitar.

ex·com·mu·ni·cate [ekskə'mju:nikeit] excomulgar; **ex·com·mu·ni'ca·tion** excomunión *f*.

ex·co·ri·ate [eks'kɔ:rieit] excoriar; *fig.* azotar.

ex·cre·ment ['ekskrimənt] excremento *m*; **ex·cre·men·tal** [~'mentl] excremental; **ex·cre·men·ti·tious** [~'tiʃəs] excrementicio.

ex·cres·cence [iks'kresns] excrecencia *f*; **ex'cres·cent** excrecente.

ex·crete [eks'kri:t] excretar; **ex'cre·tion** excreción *f*; **ex'cre·tive** excrementicio; **ex'cre·to·ry** excretorio.

ex·cru·ci·at·ing [iks'kru:ʃieitiŋ] □ agudísimo, atroz.

ex·cul·pate ['ekskʌlpeit] exculpar; **ex·cul'pa·tion** exculpación *f*.

ex·cur·sion [iks'kə:ʒn] excursión *f*; ~ *train* tren *m* botijo, tren *m* de recreo.
ex·cus·a·ble [iks'kju:zəbl] □ perdonable, disculpable; **ex'cuse 1.** [iks'kju:z] disculpar, perdonar (*a p. a th.* algo a alguien); excusar; dispensar (*from* de); ~ *me!* ¡dispense Vd.!; **2.** [iks'kju:s] excusa *f*; disculpa *f*; pretexto *m*.
ex·e·at ['eksiæt] permiso *m* (para estar ausente).
ex·e·cra·ble ['eksikrəbl] □ execrable; **ex·e·crate** ['~kreit] execrar; **ex·e'cra·tion** execración *f*; abominación *f*.
ex·e·cu·tant [ig'zekjutənt] ♪ ejecutante *m/f*; **ex·e·cute** ['eksikju:t] ejecutar (*a.* ♪); llevar a cabo, cumplir; ⚖ *man* ejecutar, ajusticiar; *document* otorgar; legalizar; **ex·e'cu·tion** ejecución *f* (*a.* ♪ *a.* ⚖); ⚖ otorgamiento *m*; legalización *f*; **ex·e'cu·tion·er** verdugo *m*; **ex·ec·u·tive** [ig'zekjutiv] **1.** □ ejecutivo; **2.** ✝ gerente *m*, director *m*; *pol.* poder *m* ejecutivo; autoridad *f* suprema; ejecutivo *m*; ♀ *Mansion* palacio *m* presidencial; **ex'ec·u·tor** [~tər] albacea *m*, ejecutor *m* testamentario.
ex·em·plar [ig'zemplər] modelo *m*, patrón *m*; **ex'em·pla·ri·ness** ejemplaridad *f*; **ex'em·pla·ry** ejemplar.
ex·em·pli·fi·ca·tion [igzemplifi'keiʃn] ejemplificación *f*; ⚖ copia *f* notarial; **ex'em·pli·fy** [~fai] ejemplificar; ⚖ hacer copia notarial de.
ex·empt [ig'zempt] **1.** exento (*from* de); **2.** exentar, eximir (*from* de); dispensar, exceptuar; **ex'emp·tion** exención *f*.
ex·e·quies ['eksikwiz] *pl.* funerales *m/pl.*
ex·er·cise ['eksərsaiz] **1.** *all senses*: ejercicio *m*; *take* ~ hacer ejercicios; **2.** *v/t. power, profession* ejercer; *care* poner (*in* en); *right* valerse de; (*train*) ejercitar (*in* en); *mind, p.* preocupar; *dog* llevar de paseo; *horse* entrenar; *v/i.* ejercitarse; hacer ejercicios.
ex·ert [ig'zə:rt] ejercer; ~ *o.s.* esforzarse; afanarse; trabajar *etc.* demasiado; **ex'er·tion** esfuerzo *m*; afán *m*; trabajo *m etc.* excesivo.
ex·e·unt ['eksiʌnt] éxeunt.
ex·fo·li·ate [eks'foulieit] exfoliar(se).
ex·ha·la·tion [ekshə'leiʃn] exhalación *f*; espiración *f of air*; **ex·hale** [~'heil] *air* espirar; exhalar.
ex·haust [ig'zɔ:st] **1.** agotar (*a. fig.*); *fig.* apurar; debilitar; (*tire*) cansar; *be* ~*ed* (*tired*) estar rendido; **2.** ⊕ (tubo *m* de) escape *m*; gases *m/pl.* de escape; *attr.* de escape; ~ *fan* ventilador *m* aspirador; ~ *manifold* múltiple *m* de escape; ~ *pipe* tubo *m* de escape; ~ *valve* válvula *f* de escape; **ex'haust·i·ble** agotable; **ex'haust·ing** □ duro, que agota; **ex'haus·tion** agotamiento *m* (*a. fig.*); *fig.* postración *f*; **ex'haus·tive** □ exhaustivo, comprensivo.
ex·hib·it [ig'zibit] **1.** *signs etc.* mostrar, manisfestar, exhibir; *exhibit* exponer; *film etc.* presentar; **2.** objeto *m* expuesto; pieza *f* de museo; ⚖ documento *m*; *on* ~ expuesto; **ex·hi·bi·tion** [eksi'biʃn] *paint. etc.* exposición *f*; exhibición *f*; demostración *f*; *univ.* beca *f*; *make an* ~ *of o.s.* ponerse en ridículo; *on* ~ expuesto; **ex·hi'bi·tion·er** becario *m*; **ex·hi'bi·tion·ist** exhibicionista *m/f*; **ex·hib·i·tor** [ig'zibitər] expositor *m*.
ex·hil·a·rate [ig'ziləreit] alegrar, regocijar; excitar; levantar el ánimo de; **ex'hil·a·rat·ing** □ que regocija *etc.*; tónico, vigorizante; **ex·hil·a'ra·tion** alegría *f*, regocijo *m*; excitación *f*.
ex·hort [ig'zɔ:rt] exhortar (*to* a); **ex·hor·ta·tion** [egzɔ:r'teiʃn] exhortación *f*; **ex'hor·ta·to·ry** [~tɔ:ri] exhortatorio.
ex·hu·ma·tion [ekshju:'meiʃn] exhumación *f*; **ex'hume** exhumar; desenterrar (*a. fig.*).
ex·i·gence, ex·i·gen·cy ['eksidʒəns(i)] exigencia *f*, necesidad *f* (urgente); caso *m* de urgencia; **'ex·i·gent** exigente; urgente.
ex·ile ['eksail] **1.** destierro *m*, exilio *m*; (*p.*) desterrado (a *f*) *m*, exilado (a *f*) *m*; **2.** desterrar, exil(i)ar.
ex·ist [ig'zist] existir; **ex'ist·ence** existencia *f*; vida *f*; *be in* ~ existir; *in* ~ = **ex'istent** existente; actual; **ex·ist'en·tial·ism** existencialismo *m*.
ex·it ['eksit] **1.** salida *f*; *thea.* mutis *m*; ~ *permit* permiso *m* de salida; **2.** *thea.* hacer mutis; ~ *Macbeth* váse Macbeth.
ex·o·dus ['eksədəs] éxodo *m*.
ex·on·er·ate [ig'zɔnəreit] exculpar,

disculpar (*from blame* de); exonerar (*from duty* de); **ex·on·er'a·tion** exculpación *f*; exoneración *f*.
ex·or·bi·tance [ig'zɔːrbitəns] exorbitancia *f*; **ex'or·bi·tant** □ exorbitante, excesivo.
ex·or·cism ['eksɔːrsizm] exorcismo *m*; **'ex·or·cist** exorcista *m/f*; **ex·or·cize** ['~saiz] exorcizar, conjurar.
ex·ot·ic [eg'zɔtik] **1.** □ exótico; **2.** ⚘ planta *f* exótica.
ex·pand [iks'pænd] *v/t.* extender; ensanchar; dilatar; *market etc.* expansionar; ⅍ *equation* desarrollar; *v/i.* extenderse; dilatarse; (*p.*) hacerse más expansivo; **ex·panse** [~'pæns] extensión *f*; envergadura *f* *of wings*; **ex'pan·si·ble** expansible; **ex'pan·sion** expansión *f*; dilatación *f*; ensanche *m of town etc.*; ⚕ desarrollo *m*; **ex'pan·sive** □ expansivo (*a. fig.*); **ex'pan·sive·ness** afabilidad *f*.
ex·pa·ti·ate [eks'peiʃieit] espaciarse; extenderse (*on* en alabanzas *etc.* de).
ex·pa·tri·ate [eks'pætrieit] **1.** desterrar; ~ *o.s.* expatriarse; **2.** expatriado (a *f*) *m*; **ex·pa·tri'a·tion** expatriación *f*.
ex·pect [iks'pekt] esperar (*of* de; *that* que *subj.*); contar con; prometerse; *baby* esperar; (*foresee*) prever; F suponer; F *be ~ing* estar encinta; F *I ~ he'll be there* supongo que estará allí; *just what I ~ed* ya me lo figuraba; **ex'pect·an·cy** (*state*) expectación *f*; expectativa *f* (*of* de); **ex'pect·ant** □ expectante; ~ *mother* mujer *f* encinta; **ex·pec'ta·tion** expectación *f*; expectativa *f*; *~s pl.* esperanza *f* de heredar *in will*; *beyond ~* mejor de lo que se esperaba; *in ~ of* esperando; *~ of life* expectativa *f* de vida, índice *m* vital.
ex·pec·to·rate [eks'pektəreit] expectorar; **ex·pec·to'ra·tion** expectoración *f*.
ex·pe·di·ence, ex·pe·di·en·cy [iks'piːdiəns(i)] conveniencia *f*; oportunidad *f*; **ex'pe·di·ent 1.** □ conveniente; oportuno; ventajoso; **2.** expediente *m*, recurso *m*; **ex·pe·dite** ['ekspidait] *progress* facilitar; *business* despachar; (*speed up*) acelerar; **ex·pe·di·tion** [~'diʃn] expedición *f*; **ex·pe'di·tion·ar·y** expedicionario; **ex·pe'di·tious** □ expeditivo, pronto.
ex·pel [iks'pel] expeler, despedir; arrojar; *p.* expulsar.
ex·pend [iks'pend] expender, gastar (*on* en; *in doing* haciendo); *time* pasar; *resources* consumir, agotar; **ex'pend·a·ble** prescindible; **ex'pend·i·ture** [~itʃə] gasto(s) *m*(*pl.*); desembolso *m*; **ex·pense** [~'pens] gasto *m*; costa *f*; expensas *f/pl.*; *at my ~* corriendo yo con los gastos; *at the ~ of fig.* a expensas de; *at great ~* gastándose muchísmo dinero; ~ *account* cuenta *f* de gastos; *go to ~* meterse en gastos; **ex'pen·sive** □ caro, costoso; *shop etc.* carero.
ex·pe·ri·ence [iks'piriəns] **1.** experiencia *f*; **2.** experimentar; *loss, fate* sufrir; *difficulty* tener; **ex'pe·ri·enced** experimentado; perito; versado (*in* en).
ex·per·i·ment 1. [iks'perimənt] experimento *m*; prueba *f*; **2.** [~ment] hacer experimentos, experimentar (*on* en, *with* con); **ex·per·i·men·tal** [eksperi'mentl] □ experimental.
ex·pert ['ekspəːrt] **1.** □ experto, perito (*at, in* en); hábil; ⚖ *witness* pericial; **2.** experto *m*, perito *m* (*at, in* en); **ex·pert·ise** [ekspəːr'tiːz], **'ex·pert·ness** pericia *f*; habilidad *f*.
ex·pi·ate ['ekspieit] expiar; **ex·pi'a·tion** expiación *f*; **ex·pi·a·to·ry** ['~tɔːri] expiatorio.
ex·pi·ra·tion [ekspi'reiʃn] vencimiento *m*, expiración *f of term*; espiración *f of air*; **ex'pire** [~'pair] *v/i.* (*die*) expirar; (*term*) vencer, expirar, cumplirse; (*ticket*) caducar; *v/t. air* expeler, espirar; **ex·pi·ry** [~'pairi] = *expiration*.
ex·plain [iks'plein] explicar; *mystery* aclarar; *plan* exponer; *conduct* explicar, justificar; ~ *o.s.* explicarse; hablar más claro; justificar su conducta; ~ *away* justificar hábilmente, dar razones convincentes de; *difficulty* salvar hábilmente; **ex'plain·a·ble** explicable.
ex·pla·na·tion [ekspləˈneiʃn] explicación *f*; aclaración *f*, *etc.*; **ex·plan·a·to·ry** [iks'plænətəri] explicativo.
ex·ple·tive [eks'pliːtiv] voz *f* expletiva, reniego *m*; (*oath*) palabrota *f*.
ex·pli·ca·ble ['eksplikəbl] explicable.
ex·plic·it [iks'plisit] □ explícito.
ex·plode [iks'ploud] *v/t.* volar, hacer saltar; *theory* refutar, desmentir;

v/i. estallar, hacer explosión; reventar *with anger etc.*
ex·ploit 1. [iks'plɔit] explotar; 2. ['eksplɔit] hazaña *f*, proeza *f*; **ex·ploi'ta·tion** explotación *f*.
ex·plo·ra·tion [eksplɔ:'reiʃn] exploración *f*; **ex'plor·a·to·ry** [~rətəri] preparatorio, de sondaje; **ex·plore** [iks'plɔ:r] explorar; *fig.* examinar, sondar; **ex'plor·er** explorador *m*.
ex·plo·sion [iks'plouʒn] explosión *f* (*a. fig.*); **ex'plo·sive** [~siv] □ explosivo *adj. a. su. m* (*a. fig.*).
ex·po·nent [eks'pounənt] exponente *m/f*; partidario (a *f*) *m*; intérprete *m/f*; ⚗ exponente *m*.
ex·port 1. [eks'pɔ:rt] exportar; 2. ['ekspɔ:rt] exportación *f* (*a.* ~*s pl.*); ~ *trade* comercio *m* de exportación; **ex'port·a·ble** exportable; **ex·por'ta·tion** exportación *f*; **ex'port·er** exportador *m*.
ex·pose [iks'pouz] exponer (*a. phot.*); *plot etc.* desenmascarar; ~ *o.s. to* exponerse a; *be* ~*d* quedar al descubierto; **ex'posed** *adj. position* expuesto, desabrigado, al descubierto; *flank* desguarnecido; **ex·po·si·tion** [ekspə'ziʃn] exposición *f*.
ex·pos·tu·late [iks'pɔstjuleit] protestar; ~ *with* reconvenir a; tratar de convencer a; **ex·pos·tu'la·tion** protesta *f*; reconvención *f*; esfuerzo *m* por convencer(le *etc.*).
ex·po·sure [iks'pouʒər] exposición *f* (*a. phot.*); desenmascaramiento *m of plot etc.*; *die from* ~ morir de frío; ~ *meter* fotómetro *m*, exposímetro *m*; ~ *time* tiempo *m* de exposición.
ex·pound [iks'paund] exponer, explicar; comentar.
ex·press [iks'pres] 1. □ expreso; explícito, categórico; *letter* urgente; ~ *company* compañía *f* de expreso, compañía de transportes rápidos; ~*man* empleado *m* del servicio de transportes rápidos; ~ *train* rápido *m*, tren *m* expreso; ~*way* carretera *f* de vía libre; 2. rápido *m* (*a.* ~ *train*), expreso *m*; *by* ~ 🚂 en gran velocidad; 3. *adv.* por carta (*etc.*) urgente; *for a special purpose* expresamente; por expreso; 4. expresar; *juice* exprimir; ~ *o.s.* expresarse; **ex'pres·sion** *all senses*: expresión *f*; **ex'pres·sive** □ expresivo; **ex'press·ly** expresamente, categóricamente; adrede.
ex·pro·pri·ate [eks'prouprieit] expropiar; **ex·pro·pri'a·tion** expropiación *f*.
ex·pul·sion [iks'pʌlʃn] expulsión *f*.
ex·punge [eks'pʌndʒ] borrar, tachar.
ex·pur·gate ['ekspə:rgeit] expurgar; **ex·pur'ga·tion** expurgación *f*; **ex'pur·ga·to·ry** [~gətɔ:ri] expurgatorio.
ex·qui·site ['ekskwizit] 1. □ exquisito, primoroso; *pain* agudísimo; 2. petimetre *m*.
ex-serv·ice·man ['eks'sə:rvismən] excombatiente *m*.
ex·tant [eks'tænt] existente.
ex·tem·po·rar·y [iks'tempərəri], **ex·tem·po·re** [eks'tempəri] 1. *adj.* improvisado; 2. *adv.* de improviso, sin preparación; *speak* ~ = **ex·tem·po·rize** [iks'tempəraiz] improvisar.
ex·tend [iks'tend] extender(se); *building etc.* ensanchar, ampliar; *hand* tender; *term etc.* prolongar (se); *thanks, welcome* dar, ofrecer; *athlete* exigir el máximo esfuerzo a; ~ *over*, ~ *to* (*include*) abarcar.
ex·ten·si·ble [iks'tensibl] extensible; **ex'ten·sion** extensión *f*; ⚠ *etc.* ensanche *m*, ampliación *f*; prolongación *f of term etc.*; ⚖ prórroga *f*; *teleph.* línea *f* derivada; ⚡ ~ *cord* cordón *m* de extensión; ~ *ladder* escalera *f* extensible; ~ *table* mesa *f* de extensión; **ex'ten·sive** □ extenso; vasto, dilatado; *use etc.* abundante, general; *travel* ~*ly* viajar por muchos países *etc.*
ex·tent [iks'tent] extensión *f*; alcance *m*; amplitud *f*; *to the* ~ *of* hasta el punto de; *to the full* ~ en toda su extensión; *to a certain* ~, *to some* ~ hasta cierto punto; *to a great* ~ en gran parte; *to such an* ~ *that* hasta tal punto que; *to that* ~ hasta ahí.
ex·ten·u·ate [eks'tenjueit] atenuar, disminuir, mitigar; *extenuating circumstances pl.* circunstancias *f/pl.* atenuantes; **ex·ten·u'a·tion** atenuación *f*, mitigación *f*.
ex·te·ri·or [eks'tiriər] exterior *adj. a. su. m.*
ex·ter·mi·nate [eks'tə:rmineit] exterminar; **ex·ter·mi'na·tion** exterminio *m*.
ex·ter·nal [eks'tə:rnl] 1. □ externo; exterior; ~ *trade* comercio *m* exte-

rior; **2.** ~s *pl.* exterioridad *f*, aspecto *m* exterior.
ex·tinct [iks'tiŋkt] *volcano etc.* extinto, apagado; *animal* extinto, extinguido; **ex'tinc·tion** extinción *f*.
ex·tin·guish [iks'tiŋgwiʃ] extinguir; apagar; *right etc.* suprimir; **ex'tin-guish·er** extintor *m*.
ex·tir·pate ['ekstə:rpeit] extirpar; **ex·tir'pa·tion** extirpación *f*.
ex·tol [iks'tɔl] ensalzar, celebrar.
ex·tort [iks'tɔ:rt] obtener (*or* sacar) por fuerza; **ex'tor·tion** *all senses*: exacción *f*; **ex'tor·tion·ate** [~ʃnit] □ exorbitante, excesivo; *p.*, *means* injusto; **ex'tor·tion·er** desollador *m*; concusionario *m*.
ex·tra ['ekstrə] **1.** *adj.* extra (...); de más, de sobra; *charge etc.* extraordinario, suplementario; *part* de repuesto; adicional; ~ *charge* suplemento *m*, recargo *m*; ~ *pay* sobresueldo *m*; *sport*: ~ *time* prórroga *f*; **2.** *adv.* especialmente, extraordinariamente; *with verbs*: más; de sobra; **3.** *su.* extra *m on bill*; exceso *m*; cosa *f* adicional; (pieza *f* de) repuesto *m*; *thea.* comparsa *m*/*f*; ~s *pl.* comparsería *f*.
ex·tract 1. ['ekstrækt] cita *f*, trozo *m*; *pharm.* extracto *m*; **2.** [iks'trækt] extraer (*a.* ⅍); sacar; **ex'trac·tion** extracción *f*.
ex·tra·dit·a·ble [ekstrə'daitəbl] sujeto a la extradición; **'ex·tra·dite** extradicionar, obtener la extradición de; **ex·tra·di·tion** [~'diʃn] extradición *f*.
extra...: **'~·ju'di·cial** extrajudicial; **'~'mu·ral** de extramuros; fuera del recinto de la escuela (*or* universidad *etc.*); *course* para externos.
ex·tra·ne·ous [eks'treinjəs] extraño; ajeno (*to* a).
ex·traor·di·nar·y [iks'trɔ:rdineri] □ extraordinario.
ex·trav·a·gance [iks'trævigəns] prodigalidad *f*, despilfarro *m*; gasto *m* (*or* lujo *m*) excesivo; extravagancia *f*; **ex'trav·a·gant** □ *p.* pródigo, despilfarrado(r); *price* exorbitante; *praise* excesivo; *living* muy lujoso; *ideas etc.* extravagante, estrafalario; **ex·trav·a·gan·za** [ekstrævə'gænzə] obra *f* extravagante y fantástica.
ex·treme [iks'tri:m] **1.** □ extremo; *case freq.* excepcional; ~*ly* extremadamente, sumamente; **2.** extremo *m*; extremidad *f*; *in the* ~ en sumo grado; *go to* ~*s* propasarse; pasar de lo razonable; tomar medidas extremas; **ex'trem·ist** extremista *m*/*f*; **ex·trem·i·ty** [~'tremiti] extremidad *f*; medida *f* extrema; rigor *m*; **ex'trem·i·ties** [~z] *pl.* extremidades *f*/*pl. of body*; medidas *f*/*pl.* extremas; *be driven to* ~ estar muy apurado.
ex·tri·cate ['ekstrikeit] librar, extraer, sacar (*from* de); **ex·tri'ca·tion** libramiento *m*, extricación *f*.
ex·trin·sic [eks'trinsik] □ extrínseco.
ex·tro·vert ['ekstrouvə:rt] extrovertido *m*.
ex·trude [eks'tru:d] empujar hacia fuera; sacar.
ex·u·ber·ance [ig'zju:bərəns] exuberancia *f*; euforia *f*; **ex'u·ber·ant** □ exuberante; eufórico.
ex·u·da·tion [eksju:'deiʃn] exudación *f*; **ex·ude** [ig'zju:d] *v*/*i.* exudar; rezumarse; *v*/*t.* dejar escapar, destilar, rezumar.
ex·ult [ig'zʌlt] exultar; regocijarse (*at*, *in* por; *to find* al encontrar); triunfar (*over* sobre); **ex'ult·ant** □ regocijado, ufano, triunfante; **ex·ul·ta·tion** [egzʌl'teiʃn] exultación *f*.
eye [ai] **1.** *mst* ojo *m*; *sew.* corcheta *f*; ⚘ yema *f*; ⚕ *black* ~ ojo *m* amoratado; ~ *of the morning* sol *m*; *in the* ~*s of* a los ojos de; *with an* ~ *to ger.* con la intención de *inf.*; pensando en *acc.*; *be all* ~*s* ser todo ojos; F *be up to one's* ~*s* tener trabajo hasta encima de la cabeza; *catch the* ~ llamar la atención; *catch s.o.'s* ~ atraer la atención de uno; *cry one's* ~*s out* llorar a mares; F *give the glad* ~ *to* echar los ojazos a; *have an* ~ *for* tener gusto por; saber apreciar *acc.*; *have an* ~ *to* vigilar; tener en cuenta; F *have one's* ~ *on* tener los ojos en; vigilar; (*desire*) echar el ojo a; F *it's all my* ~! ¡es puro cuento!; *keep an* ~ *on* vigilar; echar una mirada a; *make* ~*s at* hacer guiños a; *open s.o.'s* ~*s to* hacer que uno se dé cuenta de; (*not to*) *see* ~ *to* ~ (*with*) (no) estar completamente de acuerdo (con); *set* ~*s on a p.* ponerle los ojos encima a uno; *shut one's* ~*s to* hacer la vista gorda a; *not to shut one's* ~*s to* tener en cuenta; *turn a blind* ~ fingir no ver (*on acc.*), hacer la vista

gorda (*to* a); **2.** ojear; mirar (detenidamente *etc.*); **ˈ~·ball** globo *m* del ojo; **ˈ~·bolt** armella *f*, cáncamo *m*; **ˈ~·brow** ceja *f*; *raise one's ~s* arquear las cejas; **ˈ~ catch·er** cosa *f etc.* que llama la atención; **ˈ~·cup** ojera *f*, lavaojos *m*; **...eyed** [aid] de ... ojos, de ojos ...

eye...: ˈ~·glass anteojo *m*; lente *m*; monóculo *m*; ocular *m of optical instrument*; (*eyecup*) ojera *f*, lavaojos *m*; *~es* gafas *f/pl.*, anteojos *m/pl.*; **ˈ~·lash** pestaña *f*; **ˈeye·let** ojete *m*, ojal *m*; (*hole to look through*) mirilla *f*.

eye...: ˈ~·lid párpado *m*; **ˈ~·o·pen·er** revelación *f*, sorpresa *f* grande; acontecimiento *m* asombroso; **ˈ~·piece** *opt.* ocular *m*; **ˈ~·shade** visera *f*; **ˈ~ shadow** crema *f* para los párpados; **ˈ~ shot** alcance *m* de la vista; **ˈ~·sight** (alcance *m* de la) vista *f*; **ˈ~ socket** cuenca *f* del ojo; **ˈ~·sore** monstruosidad *f*, cosa *f* que ofende la vista; **ˈ~·strain** vista *f* fatigada; **ˈ~ test, ˈ~ chart** escala *f* tipográfica oftalmométrica, tipo *m* de ensayo, tipo de prueba; **ˈ~·tooth** colmillo *m*, diente *m* canino; *cut one's eyeteeth* F tener el colmillo retorcido; *give one's eyeteeth for* F dar los ojos de la cara por; **ˈ~·wash** colirio *m*; *sl.* tonterías *f/pl.*; protestación *f* insincera; alabanza *f* insincera, halago *m* para engañar; **ˈ~ˈwit·ness** testigo *m* presencial, testigo ocular.

ey·rie, ey·ry [ˈaiəri, ˈeri] aguilera *f*.

F

fa·ble [ˈfeibl] fábula *f*.

fab·ric [ˈfæbrik] tejido *m*, tela *f*; ⚠ fábrica *f*; **fab·ri·cate** [ˈ~keit] fabricar (*a. fig.*); *fig.* inventar, falsificar; **fab·riˈca·tion** fabricación *f*; *fig.* mentira *f*, falsificación *f*.

fab·u·lous [ˈfæbjuləs] □ fabuloso.

fa·çade [fəˈsɑːd] fachada *f*; *fig.* apariencia *f*, barniz *m*.

face [feis] **1.** cara *f*; semblante *m*, rostro *m*; superficie *f*; faz *f of the earth*; (*grimace*) mueca *f*; (*effrontery*) desfachatez *f*; (*prestige*) prestigio *m*, apariencias *f/pl.*; esfera *f of watch*; ⚒ cara *f* de trabajo; ~ *downwards* boca abajo; ~ *to* ~ cara a cara; *in* (*the*) ~ *of* ante; luchando contra; a pesar de; *on the* ~ *of it* a primera vista; *lose* ~ desprestigiarse; F *make* (*or pull*) ~*s* hacer carantoñas (*at* a), hacer muecas (*at* a); *save* (*one's*) ~ salvar las apariencias; *say s.t. to one's* ~ decir algo por (*or* en) la cara de uno; *set one's* ~ *against* mostrarse contrario a; F *show one's* ~ dejarse ver; ~ *value* ⚕ valor *m* nominal; *fig.* valor *m* aparente, significado *m* literal; **2.** *v/t. danger* arrostrar, hacer cara a; *p., enemy* encararse con; *problem* afrontar; *facts* reconocer, aceptar; (*building*) mirar hacia, estar enfrente de; ⊕ revestir; (a)forrar; ⊕ (*a.* ~ *off*) alisar; *be* ~*d with* presentársele a uno; ~ *it out* mantenerse firme; insistir descaradamente en ello; *v/i.*: ~ *about* dar media vuelta; ~ *on to* dar a, dar sobre; ~ *up to* dar cara a; ~ *up to it* reconocerlo; ˈ~ **card** figura *f*, naipe *m* de figura; ˈ~ **lift** cirugía *f* estética; ˈ~ **pow·der** polvos *m/pl.* de tocador; ˈ**fac·er** percance *m*; problema *m* desconcertante.

fac·et [ˈfæsit] faceta *f* (*a. fig.*); ˈ**fac·et·ed** labrado en facetas.

fa·ce·tious [fəˈsiːʃəs] □ gracioso, chistoso (*freq.* en momento inoportuno); guasón.

face worker [ˈfeiswəːrkər] ⚒ picador *m*.

fa·cial [ˈfeiʃl] **1.** □ facial; **2.** masaje *m* facial.

fac·ile [ˈfæsil] fácil, vivo; *b.s.* ligero, superficial; **fa·cil·i·tate** [fəˈsiliteit] facilitar; **fa·cil·iˈta·tion** facilitación *f*; **faˈcil·i·ty** facilidad *f*.

fac·ing [ˈfeisiŋ] ⊕ revestimiento *m*; *sew.*: ~*s pl.* vueltas *f/pl.*

fac·sim·i·le [fækˈsimili] facsímil *adj. a. su. m.*

fact [fækt] hecho *m*; realidad *f*; ~*s pl.* 🕮 datos *m/pl.*; *the* ~ *is that* ello es que; *the* ~ *of the matter* la pura verdad; *in* (*point of*) ~ en realidad; ˈ~ **find·ing** investigación *f*, indagación *f*.

fac·tion [ˈfækʃn] facción *f*; disensión *f*.

fac·tious [ˈfækʃəs] □ faccioso; ˈ**fac·tious·ness** disensión *f*, espíritu *m* de partido.

fac·ti·tious [fækˈtiʃəs] □ facticio.

fac·tor [ˈfæktər] factor *m* (⚗ *a. fig.*); *fig.* elemento *m*, hecho *m*; ⚕ agente *m*; ˈ**fac·to·ry** fábrica *f*, factoría *f*.

fac·to·tum [fækˈtoutəm] factótum *m*.

fac·tu·al [ˈfæktjuəl] □ objetivo; que consta de hechos (*or* datos).

fac·ul·ty [ˈfækəlti] *all senses*: facultad *f*.

fad [fæd] F manía *f*, capricho *m*; novedad *f*; ˈ**fad·dy** caprichoso; aficionado a novedades; descontentadizo.

fade [feid] desteñir(se), descolorar (se); (*flower*) marchitar(se); ~ *away*, ~ *out* desdibujarse; desvanecerse (*a. radio*); apagarse; ~ *in*, ~ *up* (hacer) aparecer gradualmente; *film*: ~ *to* fundir a; ˈ**fade·less** que no se descolora; ˈ**fad·ing** *radio*: desvanecimiento *m*

fae·ces [ˈfiːsiːz] *v.* feces.

fag [fæg] F **1.** faena *f*, trabajo *m* penoso; *school*: alumno *m* joven que trabaja para otro mayor; *sl.* pitillo *m*; *sl. contp.* (*homosexual*) maricón *m*; **2.** *v/i.* hacer faenas rudas; *v/t.* fatigar, cansar; *be* ~*ged out* estar rendido; ˈ~ ˈ**end** F cabo *m*, desperdicios *m/pl.*; *sl.* colilla *f*.

fag·ot, fag·got ['fægət] haz *m* (*or* gavilla *f*) de leña; astillas *f/pl.*; *sl. contp. homosexual* maricón *m.*

Fahr·en·heit ['færənhait]: ~ *thermometer* termómetro *m* de Fahrenheit.

fail [feil] **1.** *v/i.* fracasar; frustrarse, malograrse; no surtir efecto; (*supply*) acabarse; (*voice*) desfallecer; ser suspendido *in exam*; ⚕ quebrar, hacer bancarrota; ~ *to* dejar de; no lograr; *he ~ed to appear* no se presentó, ⚖ no compareció; *often not translated*: *I ~ to see how* no veo cómo; ~ *in duty etc.* faltar a; *v/t.* faltar a; *p.* faltar a sus obligaciones a; *pupil* suspender; *exam* salir mal en, no aprobar; (*strength etc.*) abandonar; *words ~ me* no encuentro palabras (para expresarme); **2.** F *univ.* suspenso *m*; *without ~* sin falta; '**fail·ing 1.** falta *f*, defecto *m*, flaqueza *f*; **2.** *prp.* a falta de; **fail·ure** ['feiljər] fracaso *m*; malogro *m*; falta *f*, omisión *f*; (*p.*) fracasado (a *f*) *m*; ⚡ corte *m*; suspenso *m in exam*; ⚕ quiebra *f*, bancarrota *f*; *the ~ to* el dejar de, la omisión de.

fain [fein] † **1.** *adj.* dispuesto; **2.** *adv.* de buena gana.

faint [feint] **1.** ☐ débil; *sound etc.* indistinto, casi imperceptible; *resemblance* ligero; *line etc.* tenue; *I haven't the ~est (idea)* no tengo la más remota idea; ⚕ *feel ~* tener vahidos; **2.** desmayarse, desfallecer (*with* de); **3.** desmayo *m*, desfallecimiento *m*; **~-heart·ed** ['~'hɑːtid] ☐ medroso, pusilánime; '**faint·ness** debilidad *f*; tenuidad *f*; ⚕ desfallecimiento *m.*

fair[1] [fer] **1.** ☐ (*beautiful*) hermoso, bello; *hair* rubio; *skin* blanco; (*just*) justo, equitativo; *hearing* imparcial; *name* honrado; *prospects* favorable; *sky* sereno, despejado; *weather* bueno; *chance*, *warning* razonable; (*middling*) regular, mediano; *it's not ~!* ¡no hay derecho!; *~ copy* copia *f* en limpio; *make a ~ copy of* poner en limpio; *~ game* caza *f* legal; *fig.* objeto *m* legítimo; *by ~ means* por medios rectos; *~ play* juego *m* limpio; *~ sex* bello sexo *m*; *~ to middling* bastante bueno, mediano; **2.** *adv.* directamente; exactamente; justamente; *play ~* jugar limpio; *speak a p. ~* hablar a una p. cortésmente.

fair[2] [~] feria *f*; (*fun*) parque *m* de atracciones; verbena *f*; '**~ ground** real *m*, campo *m* de una feria.

fair·ly ['ferli] *v. fair*[1]; bastante; medianamente; completamente; '**fair·ness** justicia *f*, imparcialidad *f*; blancura *f of skin*; *in all ~* para ser justo; '**fair-'spo·ken** bien hablado; '**fair·way** ⚓ canalizo *m*; '**fair-weath·er friend** amigo *m* en la prosperidad; amigo del buen viento.

fair·y ['feri] **1.** hada *f*; **2.** feérico, mágico; de hada(s); *~ godmother* hada *f* madrina; *~land* tierra *f* de las hadas; *~ light* farolillo *m*; *~ ring* corro *m* de brujas; *~ tale* 1. cuento *m* de hadas; *fig.* bella poesía *f*; 2. fantástico, de ensueño.

faith [feiθ] fe *f*; confianza *f* (*in* en); *in good ~* de buena fe; *break ~* faltar a la palabra (*with* dada a); *keep ~* cumplir su palabra (*with* dada a); **faith·ful** ['~ful] ☐ fiel, leal; puntual; *the ~ pl.* los fieles; *yours ~ly* atentamente le saluda; '**faith·ful·ness** fidelidad *f*, lealtad *f*; '**faith-heal·ing** curación *f* por fe; '**faith·less** ☐ infiel, desleal; falso; '**faith·less·ness** infidelidad *f*, deslealtad *f.*

fake [feik] F **1.** falsificación *f*, impostura *f*; filfa *f*; (*p.*) impostor *m*, farsante *m* (*a.* '**fak·er**); **2.** falso, fingido, falsificado; **3.** (*a. ~ up*) contrahacer, falsificar, fingir.

fal·con ['fɔːlkən] halcón *m*; '**fal·con·er** halconero *m*, cetrero *m*; '**fal·con·ry** halconería *f*, cetrería *f.*

fall [fɔːl] **1.** caída *f*; ⚕ baja *f*; otoño *m*; declive *m*, desnivel *m in ground*; (*water*) salto *m* de agua, cascada *f*, catarata *f* (*a. ~s pl.*); *the* ♀ la Caída; *ride for a ~* ir a acabar mal; **2.** [*irr.*] caer(se); disminuir; (*level, price*) bajar; ⚔ caer, rendirse; (*wind*) amainar; sucumbir (*to* ante); *his face fell* se inmutó; *the anniversary ~s on a Tuesday* el aniversario cae en martes; *~ asleep* dormirse; *~ away* enflaquecer; apostatar; *~ back* retroceder; ⚔ replegarse (*on* sobre); *~ back (up)on* recurrir a; *~ behind* quedarse atrás; *v. stool*; *~ down* caerse; F fracasar; *~ due* vencer; *~ flat* caer de bruces, caer de boca; (*suggestion*) caer en el vacío; *~ for p.* enamorarse de; *trick* dejarse engañar por; *~ in* (*roof*) desplomarse; ⚔ alinearse; *~ in love* enamorarse (*with* de); ~ *in with p.* encontrarse con; *idea* convenir en; ~ *into error etc.* incurrir en; *category* estar incluido en; *conversation* entablar; *habit* adquirir; *three parts etc.* dividirse en; ~ *off* desprenderse; caerse; (*quantity*) disminuir; (*quality*) empeorar; ~ *on* ⚔ *etc.* caer sobre, echarse sobre; ~ *out* reñir (*with* con), pelearse (*with* con), indisponerse (*with* con); resultar (*that* que); ⚔ romper filas; *v. short*; ~ *through* fracasar, quedar en nada; ~ *to* empezar a comer; (*duty*) competer a, corresponder a; ~ *to ger.* empezar a *inf.*

fal·la·cious [fəˈleiʃəs] □ erróneo, delusorio, ilusorio; *b.s.* sofístico.

fal·la·cy [ˈfæləsi] error *m*; sofisma *m*.

fall·en [ˈfɔːlən] *p.p. of fall* 2.

fall guy [ˈfɔːlˈgai] *sl.* pato *m*, cabeza *f* de turco.

fal·li·bil·i·ty [fæliˈbiliti] falibilidad *f*; **fal·li·ble** [ˈfæləbl] □ falible.

fall·ing [ˈfɔːliŋ]: ˈ~-ˈ**off** disminución *f*; empeoramiento *m*; ˈ~ ˈ**sick·ness** mal *m* caduco; ˈ~ **star** estrella *f* fugaz.

fall·out [ˈfɔːlaut] caída *f* radiactiva, lluvia *f* radiactiva, precipitación *f* radiactiva; ~ *shelter* refugio *m* antiatómico.

fal·low [ˈfælou] **1.** barbechado; *lie* ~ estar en barbecho; **2.** barbecho *m*; **3.** barbechar; ˈ~ **deer** gamo *m*.

false [fɔːls] □ falso; *p.* desleal, pérfido; *teeth etc.* postizo; *be* ~ *to*, *play* ~ traicionar; ~ *bottom* doble fondo *m*; ~ *imprisonment* detención *f* ilegal; **false·hood** [ˈ~hud] mentira *f*; falsedad *f*; ˈ**false·ness** falsedad *f*; perfidia *f*.

fal·set·to [fɔːlˈsetou] falsete *m*.

fal·si·fi·ca·tion [ˈfɔːlsifiˈkeiʃn] falsificación *f*; **fal·si·fy** [ˈ~fai] falsificar; **fal·si·ty** [ˈ~ti] falsedad *f*.

fal·ter [ˈfɔːltər] *v/i.* vacilar, titubear; (*voice*) desfallecer, empañarse; *v/t.* decir titubeando.

fame [feim] fama *f*; **famed** famoso (*for* por), afamado.

fa·mil·iar [fəˈmiljər] **1.** □ familiar (*to* a) (*a. b.s.*); conocido; íntimo; *be* ~ *with* estar familiarizado con, ser conocedor de; **2.** familiar *m* (*a. eccl.*; *a.* ~ *spirit*); **fa·mil·i·ar·i·ty** [~liˈæriti] familiaridad *f* (*a. b.s*); conocimiento *m*; intimidad *f*; **fa·mil·iar·i·za·tion** [~ljəraiˈzeiʃn] familiarización *f*; **faˈmil·iar·ize** familiarizar (*o.s. with* -se con).

fam·i·ly [ˈfæmili] **1.** familia *f*; **2.** familiar; casero; *business* de familia; *butcher etc.* doméstico; *in the* ~ *way* en estado de buena esperanza, encinta; ~ *allowance* subsidio *m* familiar; ~ *income* entradas *f/pl.* familiares; ~ *man* padre *m* de familia; hombre *m* casero; ~ *name* apellido *m*; ~ *tree* árbol *m* genealógico.

fam·ine [ˈfæmin] hambre *f*; carestía *f of goods.*

fam·ished [ˈfæmiʃt] famélico, hambriento.

fa·mous [ˈfeiməs] □ famoso, célebre (*for* por); F ~*ly* a las mil maravillas.

fan[1] [fæn] **1.** abanico *m*; ventilador *m*; ⚒ aventador *m*; (*machine*) aventadora *f*; **2.** abanicar; ventilar; ⚒ aventar; *fire* avivar, soplar; *fig.* excitar, atizar.

fan[2] [~] F aficionado (a *f*) *m*, entusiasta *m/f*; admirador (-a *f*) *m*.

fa·nat·ic, fa·nat·i·cal [fəˈnætik(l)] □ fanático *adj. a. su. m* (a *f*); **faˈnat·i·cism** fanatismo *m*.

fan·ci·er [ˈfænsiər] criador *m* aficionado.

fan·ci·ful [ˈfænsiful] □ caprichoso; fantástico; imaginario.

fan·cy [ˈfænsi] **1.** fantasía *f*; imaginación *f*; capricho *m*, antojo *m*; afición *f*, gusto *m*; quimera *f*, suposición *f* arbitraria; *take a* ~ *to* aficionarse a; *p.* prendarse de; *take* (*or tickle*) *one's* ~ atraer, cautivar; **2.** de fantasía; de lujo, de adorno; *ideas etc.* extravagante; *price* exorbitante; ~ *dress* disfraz *m*; ~ *dress ball* baile *m* de trajes; ~-*free* libre de amores; ~ *goods pl.* géneros *m/pl.* de fantasía; **3.** imaginar(se), figurarse; antojarse; aficionarse a, encapricharse por; ~ *meeting you!* ¡qué casualidad encontrarle a Vd.!; *just* ~! ¡imagínate!; ˈ~**work** *sew.* labores *f/pl.*

fan·fare [ˈfænfer] *approx.* toque *m* de trompeta, fanfarria *f*.

fan·light [ˈfænlait] abanico *m*.

fang [fæŋ] colmillo *m*; ⊕ diente *m*.

fan·mail [ˈfænmeil] F cartas *f/pl.* escritas por admiradores.

fan·ta·sia [fænˈteiziə] ♪ fantasía *f*; **fan·tas·tic** [~ˈtæstik] □ fantástico; **fan·ta·sy** [ˈ~təsi] fantasía *f*.

far [fɑːr] **1.** *adj.* lejano, distante; más lejano; **2.** *adv.* lejos, a lo lejos (*a.* ~ *away, off*); *how* ~ *is it* (*to*)? ~ ¿cuánto hay de aquí (a)?; ~ *and away* con mucho; ~ *and near,* ~ *and wide* por todas partes; ~ *better* mucho mejor; ~ *the best* con mucho el mejor; ~ *from ger.* lejos de *inf.*; ~ *from it!* ¡nada de eso!; ~ *be it from me to inf.* no permita Dios que *subj.*; *by* ~ con mucho; *as* ~ *as* hasta; *as* ~ *as I know* que yo sepa; *in so* ~ *as* en tanto que; *so* ~ hasta aquí; (*time*) hasta ahora; *go* ~ *to* contribuir mucho a; *go so* ~ *as to inf.* llegar a *inf.*; **~·a·way** [ˈfɑːrəwei] remoto; *look* preocupado, distraído.
farce [fɑːrs] farsa *f*; *fig.* tontería *f*, absurdo *m*; **far·ci·cal** [ˈ~ɪkl] □ ridículo, absurdo.
fare [fer] **1.** precio *m* (del billete); billete *m*; ⚓ pasaje *m*; (*p.*) pasajero (a *f*) *m*; (*food*) comida *f*; **2.** pasarlo, irle a uno (bien *etc.*); suceder; ˈ~ ˈ**well 1.** ¡adiós!; **2.** adiós *m*, despedida *f*; *bid* ~ despedirse (*to* de); **3.** ... de despedida.
far... [fɑːr]: ˈ~-ˈ**fetched** inverosímil, poco probable; forzado, traído por los cabellos; ˈ~-ˈ**flung** extenso.
far·i·na·ceous [færiˈneiʃəs] farináceo.
farm [fɑːrm] **1.** granja *f*; cortijo *m*; estancia *f S.Am.*; (*oyster etc.*) criadero *m*; = ~*house*; **2.** *v/t.* cultivar, labrar; ~ *out* arrendar, dar en arriendo; *v/i.* cultivar la tierra; ser agricultor; *he* ~*s in Kentucky* tiene tierras en Kentucky; ˈ**farm·er** granjero *m*, agricultor *m*; labrador *m*; estanciero *m S.Am.*; ˈ**farm·hand** labriego *m*; peón *m S.Am.*; ˈ**farm**ˈ**house** alquería *f*, cortijo *m*; ˈ**farm·ing 1.** agricultura *f*; labranza *f*, cultivo *m*; **2.** agrícola; *land* labrantío, de labor; **farm·stead** [ˈ~sted] alquería *f* (y sus dependencias); ˈ**farm**ˈ**yard** corral *m*.
far-off [ˈfɑːrˈɔːf] lejano, remoto.
far·ra·go [fəˈreigou] fárrago *m*.
far-reach·ing [ˈfarˈriːtʃiŋ] trascendental; de mucho alcance.
far·ri·er [ˈfæriər] herrador *m*; *vet.* albéitar *m*.
far·row [ˈfærou] **1.** lechigada *f*; **2.** parir (*la cerda*).
far·sight·ed [ˈfɑːrˈsaitid] □ clarividente; previsor; **far**ˈ**sight·ed·ness** clarividencia *f*; previsión *f*.
far·ther [ˈfɑːrðər], **far·thest** [ˈ~ðist] *comp. a. sup. of far*.
far·thing [ˈfɑːrðiŋ] cuarto *m* de penique; *fig.* ardite *m*.
fas·ci·nate [ˈfæsineit] fascinar, encantar; ˈ**fas·ci·nat·ing** □ fascinador, encantador; **fas·ci**ˈ**na·tion** fascinación *f*, encanto *m*.
fas·cism [ˈfæʃizm] fascismo *m*; ˈ**fas·cist** fascista *adj. a. su. m/f*.
fash·ion [ˈfæʃn] **1.** moda *f*; estilo *m*; uso *m*, manera *f*; buen tono *m*; *in* ~ de moda; *out of* ~ pasado de moda; *in the Spanish* ~ a la (manera) española; *set the* ~ imponer la moda (*for* de); **2.** formar; labrar; forjar; adaptar; modelar; ˈ**fash·ion·a·ble** □ de moda; de buen tono, elegante; *be* ~ estar de moda; ˈ**fash·ion de**ˈ**sign·er** modisto *m*; ˈ**fash·ion mod·el** modelo *m/f*; ˈ**fash·ion pa**ˈ**rade,** ˈ~ ˈ**show** desfile *m* de modelos; ˈ**fash·ion** ˈ**plate** figurín *m* de moda.
fast[1] [fæst] **1.** *adj.* rápido, veloz; ligero; (*firm*) fijo, firme; *color* sólido, inalterable; *friend* leal; *living* disoluto; F *woman* muy coqueta; fresca; ~-*food restaurant* rotisería *f*; *make* ~ sujetar, amarrar; F *pull a* ~ *one* jugar una mala pasada (*on* a); **2.** *adv.* rápidamente; de prisa; ~ *asleep* profundamente dormido; *be* ~ (*clock*) adelantar; *hold* ~ mantenerse firme.
fast[2] [~] **1.** ayuno *m*; **2.** ayunar; ˈ~**day** día *m* de ayuno.
fas·ten [ˈfæsn] *v/t.* asegurar, fijar; atar; sujetar, pegar; *door* cerrar; *dress* abrochar; ~ *on blame etc.* achacar a; *v/i.* ~ (*up*)*on* agarrarse de; *fig.* fijarse en; ˈ**fas·ten·er,** ˈ**fas·ten·ing** (*lock*) cerrojo *m*; cierre *m*; broche *m*, corchete *m on dress*; (*paper*) grapa *f*.
fas·tid·i·ous [fæsˈtidiəs] □ quisquilloso, delicado; exigente; descontentadizo.
fast·ness [ˈfæstnis] ⚔ plaza *f* fuerte; lo más intrincado *of mountain etc.*
fat [fæt] **1.** gordo, grueso; *land* fértil; *living, profits* pingüe; *meat* poco magro; F *iro. a* ~ *lot* muy poco; *get* ~ engordar; **2.** grasa *f*; *the* ~ *of the land* lo mejor y más rico de la tierra; *now the* ~ *is in the fire* aquí se va a armar la gorda.
fa·tal [ˈfeitl] □ fatal, funesto (*to* para); **fa·tal·ism** [ˈ~əlizm] fatalismo *m*; ˈ**fa·tal·ist** fatalista *m/f*; **fa-**

tal·i·ty [fəˈtæliti] fatalidad *f*; (*p.*) muerto *m*, muerte *f*.
fate [feit] hado *m*; suerte *f*, destino *m*; *the* ᴤs *pl.* las Parcas; **fat·ed** [ˈ~id] fatal; ~ *to* predestinado a; **fate·ful** [ˈ~ful] □ fatal, funesto, fatídico.
fat·head [ˈfæthed] F idiota *m*/*f*, tronco *m*, estúpido *m*.
fa·ther [ˈfɑːðər] **1.** padre *m*; ᴤ *Christmas* Papá Noel *m*; ᴤ *Time* el Tiempo *m*; **2.** engendrar; prohijar; servir de padre a; ~ *on* atribuir a, achacar a; **fa·ther·hood** [ˈ~hud] paternidad *f*; ˈ**fa·ther-in-law** suegro *m*; ˈ**fa·ther·land** patria *f*; ˈ**fa·ther·less** huérfano de padre; ˈ**fa·ther·ly** paternal.
fath·om [ˈfæðəm] **1.** braza *f*; **2.** ⚓ sond(e)ar (*a. fig.*); *fig.* penetrar; profundizar; entender; ˈ**fath·om·less** insondable (*a. fig.*).
fa·tigue [fəˈtiːg] **1.** fatiga *f* (*a.* ⊕), cansancio *m*; ⚔ faena *f*; ~ *clothes* ⚔ traje *m* de faena; ⚔ ~ *duty* faena *f*; **2.** fatigar, cansar; **faˈtigue par·ty** destacamento *m* de trabajo.
fat·ness [ˈfætnis] gordura *f*; fertilidad *f*; ˈ**fat·ten** engordar (*a. v/i.*); ˈ**fat·ty 1.** graso; ~ *degeneration* degeneración *f* grasosa; **2.** F gordi(n)flón *m*.
fa·tu·i·ty [fəˈtjuiti] fatuidad *f*, simpleza *f*; **fat·u·ous** [ˈfætjuəs] □ fatuo, simple.
fau·cet [ˈfɔːsit] grifo *m*, bitoque *m*.
faugh [fɔː] ¡bah!
fault [fɔːlt] **1.** falta *f* (*a. sport*); culpa *f*; imperfección *f in manufacture etc.*; ⊕, ⚡ avería *f*, desperfecto *m*, defecto *m*; *geol.* falla *f*; *at* ~ culpable; *to a* ~ excesivamente, sumamente; *it's your* ~ Vd. tiene la culpa; *find* ~ criticar, censurar (*with acc.*); **2.** tachar, encontrar defectos en; ˈ**~·find·er** criticón (-a *f*) *m*; ˈ**~·find·ing 1.** criticón, reparón; **2.** manía *f* de criticar; ˈ**fault·less** □ impecable, intachable; ˈ**fault·y** □ defectuoso, imperfecto.
faun [fɔːn] fauno *m*.
fau·na [ˈfɔːnə] fauna *f*.
fa·vor [ˈfeivər] **1.** favor *m*; (*approval*) aprobación *f*; (*support*) amparo *m*; privanza *f at court*; (*token*) prenda *f*; ✝ grata *f*, atenta *f*; ~*s pl.* favores *m*/*pl.* *of woman*; *at a party*: regalos *m*/*pl.* de fiesta, objetos *m*/*pl.* de cotillón; *in* ~ *of* a favor de; *be in* ~ *of p.* estar por; *th.* aprobar, ser partidario de; *ger.* estar por *inf.*, apoyar la idea de *inf.*; *be in* ~ tener mucha aceptación; *be in* ~ *with* tener el apoyo de; gozar de favor cerca de; *do a* ~ hacer un favor; *find* ~ *with s.o.* caerle en gracia a uno; **2.** favorecer; apoyar; **fa·vor·a·ble** [ˈ~vərəbl] □ favorable; **fa·vored** [ˈ~vərd] favorecido; *well* ~ bien parecido; **fa·vor·ite** [ˈ~vərit] **1.** favorito, predilecto; **2.** favorito (a *f*) *m* (*a. sport*); ˈ**fa·vor·it·ism** favoritismo *m*.
fawn[1] [fɔːn] *zo.* cervato *m*; color *m* de cervato.
fawn[2] [~] adular, lisonjear (*on acc.*); (*animal*) acariciar (*on acc.*); ˈ**fawn·ing** servil, lisonjero.
faze [feiz] F inquietar, molestar.
fe·al·ty [ˈfiːəlti] † homenaje *m*, fidelidad *f*.
fear [fir] **1.** miedo *m* (*of* a, de), temor *m*; aprensión *f*; *for* ~ *of* temiendo, por miedo de; *for* ~ *that* por miedo de que; *go in* ~ *of one's life* temer por su vida; F *no* ~! ¡ni hablar!; **2.** *v/t.* temer; *v/i.* tener miedo (*to inf.* de *inf.*); ~ *for* temer por; **fear·ful** [ˈ~ful] □ *p.* temeroso (*of* de), tímido, aprensivo; *th.* pavoroso, horrendo; ˈ**fear·less** □ intrépido, audaz; ~ *of* sin temor a; ˈ**fear·less·ness** intrepidez *f*.
fea·si·ble [ˈfiːzəbl] factible, posible; *make* ~ posibilitar.
feast [fiːst] **1.** banquete *m*, festín *m*; (*day*) fiesta *f*; **2.** *v/t.* festejar; agasajar; banquetear; ~ *one's eyes* recrear la vista (*on* mirando); *v/i.* banquetear; ~ *on* regalarse con.
feat [fiːt] hazaña *f*, proeza *f*.
feath·er [ˈfeðər] **1.** pluma *f*; ⊕ lengüeta *f*; ⊕ cuña *f*; *in fine etc.* ~ de buen humor; *show the white* ~ volver las espaldas, mostrarse cobarde; *that is a* ~ *in his cap* es un triunfo para él; **2.** emplumar; ~ *one's nest* ponerse las botas, hacer su agosto; ˈ**~·bed** plumón *m*, lecho *m* de plumas; ˈ**~-brained** cascabelero; ˈ**feath·ered** plumado; alado; ˈ**feath·er·edge** filván *m*; ˈ**feath·er stitch** punto *m* de espina; ˈ**feath·er·weight** peso *m* pluma; ˈ**feath·er·y** ligero como pluma.
fea·ture [ˈfiːtʃər] **1.** rasgo *m*; característica *f*; facción *f of face*; (*film*) atracción *f* principal, largometraje

m; artículo *m in paper*; ~*s pl.* facciones *f/pl.*; ~ *writer* articulista *m/f*; **2.** delinear; representar; *film* ofrecer; destacar; *actor* presentar; • **'feature·less** sin rasgos distintivos, monótono.
feb·ri·fuge ['febrifju:dʒ] febrífugo *adj. a. su. m.*
fe·brile ['fi:bril] febril.
Feb·ru·ar·y ['februəri] febrero *m.*
fe·ces ['fi:si:z] *pl.* excrementos *m/pl.*
feck·less ['feklis] □ irreflexivo, descuidado; débil.
fec·u·lent ['fekjulənt] feculento.
fe·cund ['fi:kʌnd] fecundo; **fe·cundate** ['fi:kʌndeit] fecundar; **fe·cun'da·tion** fecundación *f*; **fe·cun·di·ty** [fi'kʌnditi] fecundidad *f.*
fed [fed] *pret. a. p.p. of feed* 2; *be* ~ *up* estar harto (*with* de).
fed·er·al ['fedərəl] □ federal; ~ *income* hacienda *f* pública; **'fed·er·al·ism** federalismo *m*; **'fed·er·al·ist** federalista *m/f*; **'fed·er·al·ize** confederar(se); **fed·er·ate** ['~reit] confederar(se); **fed·er'a·tion** federación *f*; **fed·er·a·tive** ['~reitiv] federativo.
fee [fi:] derechos *m/pl.*; honorarios *m/pl.*; (*entrance*) cuota *f*; (*tip*) gratificación *f*; *school*: ~*s pl.* cuota *f* de enseñanza; ~ *simple* herencia *f* libre de condición.
fee·ble ['fi:bl] □ débil; flojo; irresoluto; '~-'**mind·ed** imbécil; '**fee·ble·ness** debilidad *f*; flojedad *f.*
feed [fi:d] **1.** comida *f*; ✓ pienso *m*, pasto *m*; F cuchipanda *f*, comilona *f*; ⊕ (tubo *m*, dispositivo *m* de) alimentación *f*; **2.** [*irr.*] *v/t.* dar de comer a; nutrir; alimentar (*a.* ⊕); *fire* cebar; ~ *up animals* cebar, engordar; *v. fed*; *v/i.* comer; alimentarse (*on* de); ✓ pacer; '~·**back** *radio*: realimentación *f*, regeneración *f*; *fig.* comentario *m* privado y confidencial, información *f* secreta, comentarios *m/pl.*; observaciones *f/pl.*, informaciones *f/pl.*; '**feed bag** cebadera *f*, morral *m*; '**feed·er** ⊕ alimentador *m*; *geog.* afluente *m*; (*baby's*) babero *m*; '**feed·er line** 🚂 ramal *m* tributario; '**feed·ing** alimentación *f*; ⊕ *attr.* de alimentación; '**feed·ing bot·tle** biberón *m*; '**feed·ing stuffs** ✓ piensos *m/pl.*
feel [fi:l] **1.** [*irr.*] *v/t.* sentir; experimentar, percibir; (*touch*) palpar, tocar; *pulse* tomar; reconocer; ~ *that* creer que, parecerle a uno que; *v/i.* sentirse; ~ *bad*, ~ *ill* sentirse mal; ~ *cold* (*p.*) tener frío; (*th.*) estar frío; ~ *for* condolerse de; ~ *like doing* tener ganas de hacer; ~ *rough etc.* ser áspero *etc.* al tacto; ~ *up to* creerse capaz de; *I don't* ~ *quite myself* no me encuentro muy bien de salud; **2.** tacto *m*; sensación *f*; '**feel·er** *zo.* antena *f*; *zo.* tentáculo *m*; *pol. etc.* sondeo *m*; tentativa *f*; '**feel·ing 1.** □ sensible; compasivo; ~*ly* con honda emoción; **2.** tacto *m*; sensación *f*; sentimiento *m*; sensibilidad *f*; (*opinion*) parecer *m*; (*foreboding*) presentimiento *m*; *with* ~ con emoción; (*angrily*) con pasión; *hurt one's* ~*s* herir los sentimientos de uno.
feet [fi:t] *pl. of foot* pies *m/pl.*
feign [fein] fingir; ~ *mad*(*ness*) fingirse loco; ~ *sleep* fingirse dormido; ~ *to do* fingir hacer; '**feigned** fingido.
feint [feint] **1.** artificio *m*, engaño *m*; (*fencing*) finta *f*; **2.** hacer una finta.
fe·lic·i·tate [fi'lisiteit] felicitar; **fe·lic·i'ta·tion** felicitación *f*; **fe'lic·i·tous** □ feliz, oportuno; **fe'lic·i·ty** felicidad *f*; ocurrencia *f* oportuna.
fe·line ['fi:lain] felino.
fell[1] [fel] **1.** *pret. of fall* 2; **2.** *tree* talar; derribar; *cattle* acogotar.
fell[2] [~] *poet.* cruel; feroz; destructivo.
fell[3] [~] *geog.* montaña *f*; (*moor*) páramo *m*, brezal *m.*
fel·low ['felou] compañero *m*; prójimo *m*; (*equal*) igual *m/f*; (*other half*) pareja *f*; *univ. approx.* miembro *m* de la junta de gobierno de un colegio; *univ.* becario *m*; socio *m*, miembro *m of society*; F tipo *m*, sujeto *m*, individuo *m*; *nice* ~ buen chico *m*; *poor* ~ (*!*) pobrecito *m*; *young* ~ chico *m*; *now listen, young* ~ oiga Vd., joven; *a* ~ *can't do this all day* uno no puede hacer esto todo el día; '~ '**be·ing** prójimo *m*; '~ '**cit·i·zen** conciudadano *m*; '~ '**coun·try·man** compatriota *m*; '~ '**crea·ture** prójimo *m*; '~ '**feel·ing** simpatía *f*, afinidad *f*; '~ '**mem·ber** consocio *m*; ~·**ship** ['~ʃip] compañerismo *m*; compañía *f*; hermandad *f*; *univ.* (*office*) dignidad *f* del *fellow*; *univ.* (*grant*) beca

f; ˈ~ ˈ**trav·el·er** compañero *m* de viaje (*a. fig.*); *pol.* filocomunista *m*/*f*.
fel·on [ˈfelən] criminal *m*, delincuente *m*/*f* de mayor cuantía; **fe·lo·ni·ous** [fiˈlounjəs] □ criminal; delincuente; **fel·o·ny** [ˈfeləni] crimen *m*, delito *m* de mayor cuantía.
felt[1] [felt] *pret. a. p.p. of feel* 1.
felt[2] [~] **1.** fieltro *m* (*a.* ~ *hat*); **2.** cubrir con fieltro.
fe·male [ˈfi:meil] hembra *adj. a. su. f* (*a.* ⊕); femenino.
fem·i·nine [ˈfeminin] femenino; *contp.* afeminado; **fem·iˈnin·i·ty** feminidad *f*; ˈ**fem·i·nism** feminismo *m*; ˈ**fem·i·nist** feminista *m*/*f*.
fen [fen] pantano *m*.
fence [fens] **1.** cerca *f*, valla *f*, cercado *m*; *sl.* receptor *m* de cosas robadas; *sit on the* ~ ver los toros desde la barrera; (estar a) ver venir; **2.** *v*/*t.* cercar; proteger, defender (*from* de); ~ *in* encerrar con cerca; ~ *off* separar con cerca; *v*/*i. fig.* defenderse con evasivas; *sport*: esgrimir; ˈ**fen·cer** esgrimidor (-a *f*) *m*; **fenc·ing** [ˈfensiŋ] esgrima *f*; *attr.* de esgrima; ~ *post* poste *m* de cerca.
fend [fend]: ~ *for o.s.* defenderse (a sí mismo), apañárselas por su cuenta; ~ *off* parar; desviar; ˈ**fend·er** guardafuego *m*; *mot.* parachoques *m*; guardafango *m*; 🚂 trompa *f*; ⚓ defensa *f*.
fen·nel [ˈfenl] hinojo *m*.
fen·ny [ˈfeni] pantanoso.
fer·ment 1. [ˈfə:rmənt] fermento *m*; fermentación *f*; *fig.* agitación *f*; **2.** [fərˈment] (hacer) fermentar; **fer·men·ta·tion** [fə:rmenˈteiʃn] fermentación *f*; **ferˈment·a·tive** [~tətiv] fermentativo.
fern [fə:rn] helecho *m*.
fe·ro·cious [fəˈrouʃəs] □ feroz; **fe·roc·i·ty** [fəˈrɔsiti] ferocidad *f*.
fer·ret [ˈferit] **1.** hurón *m* (*a. fig.*); **2.** cazar con hurones; ~ *about* buscar revolviéndolo todo; ~ *out* husmear; *secret* lograr saber.
fer·ric [ˈferik] férrico.
Fer·ris wheel [ˈferiswi:l] rueda *f* de feria, noria *f*.
fer·rous [ˈferəs] ferroso.
fer·rule [ˈferu:l] regatón *m*; ⊕ virola *f*.
fer·ry [ˈferi] **1.** pasaje *m*; balsadero *m*; (*boat*) balsa *f*, barca *f* (de pasaje); **2.** pasar ... a través del río *etc.*; ˈ**~·boat** balsa *f*, barca *f*; ˈ**fer·ry·man** balsero *m*.
fer·tile [ˈfə:rtl] fértil (*of*, *in* en; *a. fig.*), fecundo; **fer·til·i·ty** [fə:rˈtiliti] fertilidad *f*, fecundidad *f*; ˈ**fer·ti·lize** fertilizar, fecundar; 🌱 abonar; ˈ**fer·ti·liz·er** fertilizante *m*, abono *m*.
fer·ule [ˈferu:l] férula *f*.
fer·ven·cy [ˈfə:rvənsi] *fig.* fervor *m*; ˈ**fer·vent** □, **fer·vid** [ˈfə:rvid] □ fervoroso, ardiente.
fer·vor [ˈfə:rvər] fervor *m*, ardor *m*.
fes·tal [ˈfestl] □ festivo.
fes·ter [ˈfestər] ulcerarse, enconarse (*a. fig.*).
fes·ti·val [ˈfestəvl] **1.** fiesta *f*; ♪ festival *m*; **2.** festivo; **fes·tive** [ˈ~iv] □ festivo; regocijado; *the* ~ *season mst* Navidades *f*/*pl.*; **fesˈtiv·i·ty** fiesta *f*; festividad *f*; regocijo *m*.
fes·toon [fesˈtu:n] **1.** *sew.* festón *m*; **2.** *sew.* festonear; *fig.* engalanar, adornar.
fetch [fetʃ] *v*/*t.* traer; ir por, ir a buscar; hacer venir; *blow* dar; *price* venderse por (*or* a); *sigh* proferir; F atraer; ~ *up* vomitar; *v*/*i.* ~ *up at* llegar por fin a, ir a parar a; ~ *and carry* trajinar; ser un esclavo del trabajo; ˈ**fetch·ing** □ F atractivo.
fête [feit] **1.** fiesta *f*; **2.** festejar.
fet·id [ˈfetid] □ fétido.
fet·ish [ˈfetiʃ] fetiche *m*.
fet·lock [ˈfetlɔk] espolón *m*; (*hair*) cernejas *f*/*pl*.
fet·ter [ˈfetər] **1.** grillete *m*; ~*s pl.* grillos *m*/*pl.* (*a. fig.*); **2.** encadenar; trabar (*a. fig.*); *fig.* estorbar.
fet·tle [ˈfetl] estado *m*, condición *f*; *in fine* ~ de buen humor; en buenas condiciones.
fe·tus [ˈfi:təs] feto *m*.
feud [fju:d] enemistad *f* heredada (entre dos familias *etc.*); vendetta *f*, odio *m* de sangre; **feu·dal** [ˈ~dl] □ feudal; **feu·dal·ism** [ˈ~əlizm] feudalismo *m*; **feu·dal·i·ty** [~ˈdæliti] feudalidad *f*; (*holding*) feudo *m*; **feu·da·to·ry** [ˈ~dətɔ:ri] feudatorio *adj. a. su. m*.
fe·ver [ˈfi:vər] fiebre *f*; calentura *f*; **fe·vered** [ˈfi:vərd] *mst fig.* febril; ˈ**fe·ver·ish** □ febril (*a. fig.*), calenturiento.

few [fju:] pocos; (alg)unos; *a* ~ unos cuantos; *not a* ~ no pocos; F *a good* ~ un buen número (de); ~ *and far between* muy raros; *the* ~ la minoría.
fi·an·cé(**e** *f*) [fi:ɑ:nˈsei] *approx.* novio (a *f*) *m*, prometido (a *f*) *m*.
fi·as·co [fiˈæskou] fiasco *m*.
fi·at [ˈfaiæt] fiat *m*, autorización *f*; ~ *money* billetes *m/pl.* sin respaldo.
fib [fib] F **1.** mentirilla *f*, bola *f*; **2.** decir mentirillas; ˈ**fib·ber** F mentirosillo (a *f*) *m*.
fi·ber [ˈfaibər] fibra *f*; *fig.* carácter *m*; **fi·brin** [ˈ~brin] fibrina *f*; ˈ**fi·brous** □ fibroso.
fib·u·la [ˈfibjulə] *anat.* peroné *m*.
fick·le [ˈfikl] inconstante, mudable, veleidoso; ˈ**fick·le·ness** inconstancia *f*, veleidad *f*.
fic·tion [ˈfikʃn] ficción *f*; novelas *f/pl.*, género *m* novelístico; ˈ**fic·tion·al** □ novelesco.
fic·ti·tious [fikˈtiʃəs] □ ficticio.
fid·dle [ˈfidl] **1.** ♩ violín *m*; F trampa *f*; *be fit as a* ~ andar como un reloj; *play second* ~ desempeñar un papel secundario; **2.** ♩ tocar el violín; *sl.* agenciarse; ~ *away* desperdiciar; ~ *with* jugar con, manosear; **fid·dle-de·dee** [ˈ~diˈdi:] ¡tonterías!; ˈ**fid·dler** violinista *m/f*; ˈ**fid·dle·sticks** ¡qué disparate!; ˈ**fid·dling** trivial, insignificante; molesto.
fi·del·i·ty [fiˈdeliti] fidelidad *f*.
fidg·et [ˈfidʒit] F **1.** (*p.*) persona *f* inquieta; ~*s pl.* agitación *f* nerviosa; *have the* ~*s* no poder estar quieto; **2.** agitarse nerviosamente; ~ *with* manosear, jugar con; ˈ**fidg·et·y** F nervioso, azogado; *be* ~ tener azogue.
fi·du·ci·ar·y [fiˈdju:ʃiəri] fiduciario *adj. a. su. m.*
fief [fi:f] feudo *m*.
field [fi:ld] **1.** campo *m* (*a.* ⚔, ⚡, *sport*); prado *m*, pradera *f*; esfera *f of activities*; competidores *m/pl. in race*; *take the* ~ salir a palestra; **2.** *ball* parar, recoger; *team* presentar; ˈ~ **day** ⚔ día *m* de maniobras; *fig.* día *m* de gran éxito; ˈ**field·er** el que recoge la pelota; *baseball*: jardinero *m*.
field...: ˈ~ **fare** zorzal *m* real; ˈ~ **glass·es** *pl.* gemelos *m/pl.* (de campo); ˈ~ **gun** cañón *m* de campaña; ˈ~ ˈ**kit·chen** cocina *f* de campaña; ˈ~ ˈ**mar·shal** *approx.* mariscal *m* de campo; capitán *m* general del ejército; ˈ~ ˈ**of·fi·cer** jefe *m*; ˈ~ **sports** *pl.* caza *f*; ˈ~ **work** trabajo *m* en el propio campo.
fiend [fi:nd] demonio *m*, diablo *m*; desalmado *m*; fanático *m* (*for* de); ˈ**fiend·ish** □ diabólico.
fierce [firs] □ feroz, fiero; furioso; *heat* intenso; *supporter etc.* acérrimo; ˈ**fierce·ness** ferocidad *f*, violencia *f*; intensidad *f*.
fi·er·y [ˈfairi] □ ardiente; caliente; *fig.* vehemente; *horse* fogoso; *speech* apasionado.
fife [faif] pífano *m*.
fif·teen [ˈfifˈti:n] quince (*a. su. m*); ˈ**fifˈteenth** [~θ] décimoquinto;
fifth [fifθ] **1.** □ quinto; **2.** quinto *m*; quinta parte *f*; ♪ quinta *f*; ~ *column* quinta *f* columna; ~ *columnist* quintacolumnista *m/f*; **fif·ti·eth** [ˈ~tiiθ] quincuagésimo; ˈ**fif·ty** cincuenta; ˈ**fif·ty-ˈfif·ty**. *go* ~ ir a medias, pagar a escote.
fig [fig] (*green*) higo *m*; (*early*) breva *f*; ~ *leaf fig.* hoja *f* de parra; ~ *tree* higuera *f*; *I don't care a* ~ *for him* no se me da un higo.
fight [fait] **1.** pelea *f*, combate *m*; lucha *f* (*for* por); combatividad *f*, brío *m*; riña *f*; *put up a good* ~ dar buena cuenta de sí; *show* ~ enseñar los dientes; **2.** [*irr.*] *v/t.* combatir; batirse con; luchar con(tra); *battle* dar; *bull* lidiar; ~ *it out* decidirlo luchando; ~ *off* rechazar; *v/i.* batirse, pelear; luchar (*against* con, contra; *for* por); ~ *back* resistir; ~*ing chance* posibilidad *f* de éxito; ~*ing fit* en excelente salud; ˈ**fight·er** combatiente *m/f*; luchador (-a *f*) *m*; ✈ caza *m*; ~-*bomber* cazabombardero *m*; ˈ**fight·ing** combate *m*; lucha *f*; pendencia *f*; *attr.* guerrero; *cock* de pelea.
fig·ment [ˈfigmənt] ficción *f*, invención *f*.
fig·u·rant(**e** *f*) [ˈfigjurənt; (~ˈrænti)] figurante (a *f*) *m*.
fig·ur·a·tive [ˈfigərətiv] □ *sense* figurado; figurativo.
fig·ure [ˈfigər] **1.** figura *f*; tipo *m of body*; (*sketch etc.*) dibujo *m*, figura *f*; ♗ figura *f*; (*number*) cifra *f*; número *m*; ✝ precio *m*; (~ *of speech*) figura *f*, tropo *m*, figura retórica; *fig.* exageración *f*; *be good at* ~*s* ser fuerte en matemáticas; *cut a* ~ hacer papel; **2.**

v/t. figurar; representar; imaginar; calcular (*a.* ~ *up*); ~ *out* calcular; resolver; descifrar; *v/i.* figurar (*as* como, *among* entre); figurarse; ~ *on* contar con; incluir; proyectar; esperar; ~ *out at* venir a ser; '**~·head** ⚓ figurón *m* de proa, mascarón *m* (de proa); *fig.* figurante (a *f*) *m*, testaferro *m*; '**~ skat·ing** patinaje *m* de figura, patinaje artístico.

fig·u·rine [figju'ri:n] figurina *f*, figurilla *f*.

fil·a·ment ['filəmənt] *all senses*: filamento *m*.

fil·bert ['filbə:rt] avellana *f*.

filch [filtʃ] sisar, ratear.

file[1] [fail] **1.** carpeta *f*; fichero *m*; archivo *m*; legajo *m*; (*row*) fila *f*, hilera *f*; ~ *clerk* fichador *m*, archivero *m*; *the* ~*s pl.* los archivos; **2.** *v/t.* archivar (*a.* ~ *away*); clasificar; registrar; *v/i.* ~ *by*, ~ *past* desfilar; ~ *out* salir en fila; *filing cabinet* archivador *m*, clasificador *m*; *filing card* ficha *f*; *filing case* fichero *m*.

file[2] [~] ⊕ **1.** lima *f*; **2.** limar; *filings* limadura *f*, limalla *f*; '**~ cut·ter** picador *m* de limas.

fi·let [fi'lei] **1.** filete *m*; **2.** *v/t.* cortar en filetes.

fil·i·al ['filjəl] □ filial; **fil·i·a·tion** [fili'eiʃn] filiación *f*.

fil·i·bus·ter ['filibʌstər] **1.** filibustero *m*; *American Congress* (*p.*) obstruccionista *m*; (*act*) maniobra *f* obstruccionista; **2.** *American Congress* usar de maniobras obstruccionistas.

fil·i·gree ['filigri:] filigrana *f*.

fil·ings ['failiŋz] *pl.* limaduras *f/pl.*

fill [fil] **1.** llenar(se) (*with* de); rellenar(se); *post* ocupar; *vacancy* cubrir; *sails* hinchar(se); *space* llenar (*or* ocupar) completamente; *tooth* empastar; *tire* inflar; ~ *in form* llenar; *hole* terraplenar; llenar; *details* añadir; *outline etc.* completar; ~ *out form* llenar; (*p.*) engordar; *fig.* completar; ~ *up* llenar; colmar; **2.** hartazgo *m*; pipa *f of tobacco*; *eat one's* ~ hartarse; *have one's* ~ darse un hartazgo (*of* de).

fill·er ['filər] cargador *m of pen.*

fil·let ['filit] **1.** *all senses*: filete *m*; **2.** *fish* quitar la raspa de, cortar en filetes.

fill·ing ['filiŋ] relleno *m*; ⊕ empaquetadura *f*; empaste *m of tooth*; *mot.* ~ *station* estación *f* de servicio.

fil·lip ['filip] capirotazo *m with finger*; *fig.* estímulo *m*. [vivaz.]

fil·ly ['fili] potra *f*; *fig.* muchacha *f*

film [film] **1.** película *f*; capa *f of dust*; *fig.* velo *m*; *phot. a. thea.* película *f*, film *m*; ~ *library* cinemateca *f*; ~ *strip* tira *f* de película, tira proyectable; **2.** filmar; hacer una película de; rodar; ~ *over* empañarse, cubrirse con película; '**~ star** estrella *f* (*or* astro *m*) de cine, estrella de la pantalla; '**film·y** □ transparente, diáfano.

fil·ter ['filtər] **1.** filtro *m*; **2.** filtrar(se); ~ *in*, ~ *through* infiltrarse; *fig.* introducirse; '**~ pa·per** papel *m* de filtro; '**~ tip** embocadura *f* de filtro.

filth [filθ] inmundicia *f*; suciedad *f*, mugre *f*; '**filth·y** □ inmundo (*a. fig.*); sucio, mugriento.

fil·trate ['filtreit] filtrar(se); **fil'tra·tion** filtración *f*.

fin [fin] *all senses*: aleta *f*.

fi·nal ['fainl] **1.** □ final, último; decisivo, definitivo, terminante; ~*ly* finalmente, por último; **2.** *sport*: final *f*; *univ.* ~*s pl.* examen *m* final; **fi·nale** [fi'næli] ♪ final *m*; **fi·nal·ist** ['fainəlist] finalista *m/f*; **fi·nal·i·ty** [~'næliti] finalidad *f*; decisión *f*.

fi·nance [fi'næns] **1.** finanzas *f/pl.*; fondos *m/pl.*; asuntos *m/pl.* financieros; **2.** financiar; **fi'nan·cial** [~ʃl] □ financiero; bancario; monetario; **fi'nan·cier** [~sir] financiero *m*.

finch [fintʃ] *v. chaf*~ *etc.*

find [faind] **1.** [*irr.*] encontrar, hallar; dar con; descubrir; ⚖ declarar, fallar; (*supply*) proveer; lograr obtener, lograr reunir; ~ *o.s. fig.* descubrir su verdadera vocación; *all found* todo incluido; ~ *out* averiguar; (llegar a) saber; F conocer el juego de, calar; ~ *out about* informarse sobre; **2.** hallazgo *m*; '**find·er** el (la) que halla; *phot.* visor *m*; '**find·ing** descubrimiento *m*; ~*s pl.* ⚖ fallo *m*; recomendaciones *f/pl. of report.*

fine[1] [fain] **1.** □ fino; bello, hermoso; escogido, primoroso; refinado; *p.* admirable; magnífico; *iro.* bueno, lindo; *be* ~ (*weather*) hacer buen tiempo; *that's* ~! ¡estupendo!; *have a* ~ *time* divertirse mucho; F *you're a* ~ *one!* ¡qué tío!; ~ *arts pl.* bellas artes *f/pl.*; ~ *print* letra *f* menuda, tipo *m* menudo; ~*-spun* estirado en hilo finísimo; *fig.* alambicado; *~-toothed comb* lendrera *f*, peine *m* de púas finas; *go over with a ~-toothed comb* escudriñar minuciosamente; **2.** *adv.* F muy bien; *cut it ~* dejarse muy poco tiempo; *feel ~* estar de primera; **3.** *meteor.* buen tiempo *m*.

fine[2] [~] ⚖ **1.** multa *f*; *in ~* en resumen; **2.** multar.

fine-drawn ['fain'drɔːn] fino, sutil.

fine·ness ['fainnis] fineza *f etc.* (*v. fine*[1]); ley *f of metals*.

fin·er·y ['fainəri] galas *f/pl.*, adornos *m/pl.*

fi·nesse [fi'nes] discriminación *f* sutil; artificio *m*, sutileza *f*; tino *m*; *cards*: impase *m*.

fin·ger ['fiŋgər] **1.** dedo *m*; *~ dexterity* ♩ dedeo *m*; *little ~* dedo *m* meñique; *middle ~* dedo *m* del corazón; *ring ~* dedo *m* anular; *have a ~ in the pie* meter su cucharada; *put one's ~ on* señalar acertadamente; *slip through one's ~s* escaparse de entre los dedos de uno; *twist s.o. round one's little ~* hacer con uno lo que le da la gana; **2.** manosear; ♩ pulsar; ♩ teclear (*v/i*); '**~board** teclado *m*; ♩ teclado *m of piano*; diapasón *m of guitar*; '**~ bowl** lavadedos *m*, lavafrutas *m*; '**fin·gered** con ... dedos; '**fin·ger·ing** ♩ digitación *f*.

fin·ger...: '**~·nail** uña *f*; *~ polish* esmalte *m* para las uñas; '**~ post** poste *m* indicador; '**~·print 1.** huella *f* dactilar, huella digital; **2.** tomar las huellas dactilares a; '**~·stall** dedil *m*; '**~·tip** punta *f* del dedo; *~ control* mando *m* a punta de dedo; *have at one's ~s* saber al dedillo.

fin·i·cal ['finikl] □, '**fin·ick·ing,** '**fin·ick·y** melindroso, superferolítico.

fin·ish ['finiʃ] **1.** *v/t.* acabar (*a.* ⊕, *a. ~ up*); terminar; concluir; consumar; *~ off* completar; rematar; acabar con; F *p.* despachar; *~ed goods pl.* productos *m/pl.* acabados; *~ing touch* última mano *f*, aderezo *m* definitivo; *v/i.* acabar (*by* por; *ger.* de *inf.*); *~ up ger.* terminar *ger.*; *~ up at* ir a parar a; **2.** fin *m*, final *m*; conclusión *f*; remate *m*; *sport*: poste *m* de llegada; ⊕ acabado *m*; '**fin·ish·er** acabador *m*; ⊕ máquina *f* acabadora.

fi·nite ['fainait] □ finito (*a. gr.*).

Finn [fin] finlandés (-a *f*) *m*; **Finnish** ['~iʃ] finlandés *adj. a. su. m.*

fir [fəːr] abeto *m*; *Scotch ~* pino *m*; '**~ cone** piña *f* (de abeto).

fire ['faiər] **1.** fuego *m*; (*damaging*) incendio *m*; (*warming*) fuego *m*, lumbre *f*; *fig.* ardor *m*; viveza *f*; *be on ~* estar ardiendo; *catch ~* encenderse; *open ~* abrir fuego; *play with ~ fig.* jugar con fuego; *set on ~*, *set ~ to* pegar fuego a; *take ~* encenderse; **2.** *v/t.* encender, incendiar, quemar; *pottery etc.* cocer; *gun, shot* disparar; F *p.* despedir; *fig.* excitar, enardecer; *~ off* descargar; *v/i.* encenderse; ⚔ hacer fuego; *mot.* dar explosiones; *~ at*, *~ (up)on* hacer fuego sobre, tirar a; F *~ away!* ¡adelante!; *~ up* enfurecerse (*at* con); **3.** ¡fuego!; '**~ a·larm** alarma *f* de incendios; '**~·arm** arma *f* de fuego; '**~·ball** bola *f* de fuego; '**~·box** caja *f* de fuego; '**~·brand** *fig.* partidario *m* violento; '**~·brick** ladrillo *m* refractario; '**~ bri·gade** cuerpo *m* de bomberos; '**~·bug** F incendiario *m*; '**~ com·pa·ny** cuerpo *m* de bomberos; compañía *f* de seguros; '**~·crack·er** triquitraque *m*; '**~ cur·tain** *thea.* telón *m* a prueba de incendios; '**~·damp** ⚒ grisú *m*; '**~ de·part·ment** servicio *m* de bomberos; '**~·dog** morillo *m*; '**~ drill** ejercicio *m* para caso de incendio; '**~ en·gine** bomba *f* de incendios; '**~ es·cape** escalera *f* de incendios; '**~ ex·tin·guish·er** extintor *m*; '**~·fly** luciérnaga *f*; '**~·guard** alambrera *f*; guardafuego *m*; '**~·house** cuartel *m* de bomberos, estación *f* de incendios; '**~ hy·drant** boca *f* de incendio; '**~ in·sur·ance** seguro *m* de incendios; '**~ i·rons** *pl.* útiles *m/pl.* de chimenea; '**~·less** '**cook·er** cocinilla *f* sin fuego; '**~ light·er** *approx.* astillas *f/pl.* para encender el fuego, tea *f*; '**~·man** bombero *m*; 🚂 fogonero *m*; '**~·place** chimenea *f*; hogar *m*; '**~·plug** boca *f* de agua; '**~·proof** incombustible, a prueba de fuego, a prueba de incendio; '**~ sale** venta *f* de mercancías averiadas en un incendio; '**~ screen** pantalla *f* chimenea; '**~ ship** brulote *m*; '**~·side 1.** hogar *m*; **2.** familiar, hogareño, doméstico; '**~ sta·tion** parque *m* de bomberos; '**~·trap** edificio *m* sin medios adecuados de escape en caso de incendio; ˈ~ **wall** cortafuego *m*; ˈ~**·war·den** vigía *m* de incendios; ˈ~**·wa·ter** aguardiente *m*; ˈ~**·wood** leña *f*; ˈ~**·works** fuegos *m/pl.* artificiales; *fig.* explosión *f* de cólera *etc.*

fir·ing [ˈfairiŋ] (*fuel*) combustible *m*; (*act*) incendio *m*; cocción *f of pottery etc.*; *mot.* encendido *m*; ⚔ disparo *m*; tiroteo *m*; ~ *squad for executions*: pelotón *m* de ejecución, piquete *m* de ejecución; *for saluting at a burial*: piquete *m* de salvas.

fir·kin [ˈfəːrkin] *approx.* cuñete *m* (= *45,5 litros*).

firm [fəːrm] **1.** □ firme; **2.** firma *f*, casa *f* de comercio, empresa *f*.

fir·ma·ment [ˈfɔːrməmənt] firmamento *m*.

firm·ness [ˈfəːrmnis] firmeza *f*.

first [fəːrst] **1.** *adj.* primero; original, primitivo; **2.** *adv.* primero; en primer lugar; ~ *of all*, ~ *and foremost* ante todo; *at* ~ al principio; **3.** primero (a *f*) *m*; ✝ ~*s pl.* artículos *m/pl.* de primera calidad; ✝ ~ *of exchange* primera *f* de cambio; *from the* ~ desde el principio; *from* ~ *to last* desde el principio hasta el fin, de todo en todo; *be the* ~ *to inf.* ser el primero en *inf.*; *go* ~ entrar *etc.* el primero; 🚃 viajar en primera; ˈ~ ˈ**aid** primera curación *f*, primeros auxilios *m/pl.*, socorrismo *m*; ~ *kit* botiquín *m*; ~ *post* puesto *m* de socorro; ˈ~**-born** primogénito (a *f*) *m*; ˈ~ˈ**class** de primera (clase); ˈ~ ˈ**cous·in** primo *m* hermano, prima *f* hermana; ˈ~ eˈ**di·tion** edición *f* príncipe; ˈ~ **fruits** *pl.* primicias *f/pl.*; ˈ~ˈ**hand** de primera mano; ˈ~ **lieuˈten·ant** teniente *m*; ˈ**first·ly** en primer lugar; ˈ~ ˈ**mate** ⚓ piloto *m*; ˈ~ ˈ**name** nombre *m* de pila; **first night** estreno *m*; **first pa·pers** solicitud *f* preliminar de carta de naturaleza (*EE. UU.*); ˈ**first-rate** excelente, de primera.

firth [fəːrθ] ría *f*, estuario *m*.

fis·cal [ˈfiskl] fiscal; monetario; ~ *year* año *m* económico, ejercicio *m*.

fish [fiʃ] **1.** pez *m*; (*as food*) pescado *m*; F tipo *m*, tío *m*; *have other* ~ *to fry* tener cosas más importantes que hacer; **2.** *v/t.* pescar; *river* pescar en; F ~ *out* sacar; *v/i.* pescar; ~ *for* tratar de pescar; F *compliment etc.* andar a la pesca de; ˈ~**·bone** raspa *f*, espina *f* (de pez); ˈ~**·bowl** pecera *f*.

fish·er·man [ˈfiʃərmən] pescador *m*; ˈ**fish·er·y** pesquería *f*, pesquera *f*.

fish·hook [ˈfiʃhuk] anzuelo *m*.

fish·ing [ˈfiʃiŋ] pesca *f*; ˈ~ **boat** barca *f* pesquera; ˈ~ **grounds** *pl.* pesquera *f*; ˈ~ **reel** carrete *m*; ˈ~ **rod** caña *f* (de pescar); ˈ~ **tack·le** aparejo *m* de pescar.

fish...: ˈ~ **line** sedal *m*; ˈ~ **mar·ket** pescadería *f*; ˈ~**·plate** 🚃 eclisa *f*; ˈ~**·pond** piscina *f*; ˈ~ **sto·ry** F andaluzada *f*, patraña *f*; *tell fish stories* F mentir por la barba; ˈ~**·tail 1.** ✈ coleadura *f*; **2.** ✈ *v/i.* colear; ˈ~**·wife** pescadera *f*; (*foul-mouthed woman*) verdulera *f*; ˈ~**·worm** lombriz *f* de tierra (*cebo para pescar*); ˈ**fish·y** que huele o sabe a pescado; *eye* vidrioso; F dudoso, inverosímil; *it's* ~ me huele a camelo.

fis·sion [ˈfiʃn] *phys.* fisión *f*; *biol.* escisión *f*; ˈ**fis·sion·a·ble** fisionable; **fis·sure** [ˈfiʃər] **1.** grieta *f*, hendedura *f*; **2.** agrietar(se), hender(se).

fist [fist] puño *m*; F escritura *f*; ~ *fight* pelea *f* con los puños; *shake one's* ~ *at* amenazar con el puño; ~*ful* puñado *m*; **fist·i·cuffs** [ˈ~ikʌfs] *pl.* (pelea *f* a) puñetazos *m/pl.*

fis·tu·la [ˈfistjulə] fístula *f*.

fit[1] [fit] **1.** □ apto, a propósito; adecuado, conveniente, apropiado; listo (*for* para); hábil (*for a post* para); digno (*for a king* de); ⚕ sano, bien de salud; ~ *to eat* bueno de comer; *the wine is not* ~ *to drink* el vino no se puede beber; *see* ~ juzgar conveniente (*to inf.*); *survival of the* ~*test* supervivencia *f* de los mejor dotados; **2.** *v/t.* ajustar, acomodar (*to* a); encajar (*a.* ⊕); adaptar (*for* para); *clothes* probar (*a.* ~ *on*); *p.* (*clothes*) sentar a, venir bien a; *description* cuadrar con; *facts* estar de acuerdo con; ⊕ ~ *in*(*to*) encajar en; ~ *out*, ~ *up* equipar (*with* con); ⚓ armar; *v/i.* ajustarse; (*clothes*) entallar; encajar *in place*; (*facts*) estar de acuerdo; ~ *in* caber; ⊕ encajarse en; F *fig.* acomodarse; ~ *in with* cuadrar con, concordar con; (*p.*) llevarse bien con; *the dress fits well* el vestido le sienta bien, el vestido entalla bien; **3.** ajuste *m*, corte *m*; ⊕ encaje *m*; *it's a good* ~ le sienta bien.

fit[2] [~] acceso *m*, ataque *m*; arranque

m of anger; *by* ~*s and starts* a saltos, a rachas.

fit·ful [ˈfitful] □ espasmódico, caprichoso; ˈ**fit·ment** mueble *m*; ˈ**fit·ness** aptitud *f*; conveniencia *f*; ⚕ (buena) salud *f*; ˈ**fit·ter** ⊕ mecánico *m* ajustador; ˈ**fit·ting 1.** □ conveniente, apropiado; *it is not* ~ *that* no está bien que *subj.*; **2.** prueba *f of dress*; ajuste *m*; (*size*) medida *f*; ~*s pl.* guarniciones *f/pl.*; (*metal*) herrajes *m/pl.*; muebles *m/pl.*

five [faiv] cinco (*a. su. m*); ~*s sg.* juego *m* de pelota (*estilo inglés*); ~ *year plan* plan *m* quinquenal.

fix [fiks] **1.** fijar (*a. phot.*), asegurar; *attention* fijar (*on* en); *bayonet* calar; *blame* colgar (*on* a); *date* fijar, señalar (*a.* ~ *on*); *eyes* clavar (*on* en); *price* determinar, decidir; (*establish*) precisar; *sl.* pagar en la misma moneda; F = ~ *up* arreglar; componer; decidir, organizar; F ~ (*up*)*on* escoger, elegir; F ~ *up with* arreglarlo con; *p.* proveer de; **2.** F aprieto *m*; *get a* ~ *sl.* (*take drugs*) picarse, pincharse; **fix**ˈ**a·tion** fijación *f*; **fix·a·tive** [ˈ~ətiv] fijativo *adj. a. su. m*; **fixed** [ˈ~t] (*adv.* **fix·ed·ly** [ˈ~idli]) *all senses*: fijo; ˈ**fix·er** *phot.* fijador *m*; ˈ**fix·ing** fijación *f etc.*; F ~*s pl.* accesorios *m/pl.*, guarniciones *f/pl.*; ˈ**fix·i·ty** fijeza *f*; = **fix·ture** [ˈ~tʃər] cosa *f* fija; instalación *f* fija; *sport*: (fecha *f* de un) partido *m*; *fig.* (*p.*) ostra *f*; *lighting* ~*s pl.* guarniciones *f/pl.* de alumbrado.

fizz [fiz] **1.** sisear; **2.** siseo *m*; F gaseosa *f*; ˈ**fiz·zle 1.** sisear débilmente; F ~ *out* (*candle*) apagarse; *fig.* no dar resultado, fracasar; **2.** siseo *m* débil; F fracaso *m*; ˈ**fiz·zy** gaseoso.

flab·ber·gast [ˈflæbərgæst] pasmar, aturdir.

flab·by [ˈflæbi] □ flojo; blanducho; *fig.* débil.

flac·cid [ˈflæksid] □ fláccido.

flag[1] [flæg] **1.** bandera *f*, pabellón *m*; (*small*) banderín *m*; ~ *of truce*, *white* ~ bandera *f* de parlamento; **2.** hacer señales con bandera (a).

flag[2] [~] ⚠ **1.** losa *f*; **2.** enlosar.

flag[3] [~] ⚘ lirio *m*.

flag[4] [~] flaquear, decaer; (*conversation etc.*) languidecer; (*enthusiasm etc.*) aflojar, enfriarse.

Flag Day [ˈflægdei] fiesta *f* de la bandera (*14 junio, EE. UU.*).

flag·el·late [ˈflædʒeleit] flagelar; **flag·el**ˈ**la·tion** flagelación *f*.

flag·on [ˈflægən] *approx.* jarro *m*; ⚓ botella *f* de unos 2 litros.

fla·grant [ˈfleigrənt] □ notorio, escandaloso.

flag...: ˈ**~·pole**, ˈ**~·staff** asta *f* de bandera; ˈ**~·ship** capitana *f*; ˈ**~·stone** losa *f*.

flail [fleil] **1.** ✓ mayal *m*; **2.** *v/t. fig.* golpear, azotar; *v/i.*: ~ *about* debatirse.

flair [fler] instinto *m*, aptitud *f* especial (*for* para).

flake [fleik] **1.** escama *f*; hojuela *f*; copo *m of snow*; **2.** *v/t.* separar en escamas; *v/i.* desprenderse en escamas; ˈ**flak·y** escamoso; desmenuzable.

flam·beau [ˈflæmbou] antorcha *f*.

flam·boy·ant [flæmˈbɔiənt] □ extravagante; flameante (*a.* ⚠).

flame [fleim] **1.** llama *f*; fuego *m*; *co.* novio (a *f*) *m*; **2.** llamear; brillar; *fig.* estallar, encenderse (*a.* ~ *up*); ~ *up* inflamarse; ˈ**~·throw·er** lanzallamas *m*.

fla·min·go [fləˈmiŋgo] *zo.* flamenco *m*.

flange [flændʒ] pestaña *f*, reborde *m*.

flank [flæŋk] **1.** costado *m*; ijada *f of animal*; ⚔ flanco *m*; **2.** flanquear; *be* ~*ed by* tener a su lado; (*p.*) ir escoltado por.

flan·nel [ˈflænl] franela *f*; (*face*) paño *m*; ~*s pl.* pantalones *m/pl.* de franela; ropa *f* interior de lana.

flap [flæp] **1.** fald(ill)a *f on dress*; cartera *f of pocket*; hoja *f* plegadiza *of table*; solapa *f of envelope*; aletazo *m of wing*; *sl.* lío *m*; estado *m* nervioso; **2.** *v/t.* batir; sacudir; agitar; *v/i.* aletear; *sl.* ponerse nervioso.

flare [fler] **1.** *v/i.* resplandecer, llamear, destellar; ~ *up* encenderse; *fig.* (*p.*) encolerizarse; estallar; *v/t. skirt* nesgar; **2.** llamarada *f*, destello *m*; (*signal*) cohete *m* de señales; (*skirt*) nesga *f*; ˈ**~-up** llamarada *f*; *fig.* arranque *m of anger*; manifestación *f* súbita, estallido *m of trouble*.

flash [flæʃ] **1.** relámpago *m of lightning* (*a. fig.*); destello *m*, ráfaga *f of light*; fogonazo *m of gun*; rayo *m of hope etc.*; (*moment*) instante *m*; *phot.* = ~*light*; flash *m*, noticia *f* de última hora, mensaje *m* urgente; *in a* ~ en un instante; ~ *of wit* rasgo *m* de ingenio; ~ *in the pan* esfuerzo *m* abortado, éxito *m* único; **2.** *v/i.* relampaguear; destellar; ~ *past* pasar como un rayo; *v/t. light* despedir; *look* dirigir rápidamente; *message* transmitir rápidamente; F hacer ostentación de (*a.* ~ *about*); '**~·back** *film*: escena *f* retrospectiva; '**~ bulb** bombilla *f* fusible (*or* de flash), relámpago *m* fotogénico, bombilla *f* de destello; '**~·light** linterna *f* eléctrica, lámpara *f* eléctrica de bolsillo; (*of a lighthouse*) luz *f* intermitente, fanal *m* de destellos; *phot.* flash *m*, relámpago *m*; ~ *battery* pila *f* de linterna; ~ *bulb* bombilla *f* de linterna; '**~ point** punto *m* de inflamación; '**flash·y** □ llamativo; de relumbrón; *p.* charro, chulo.

flask [flæsk] frasco *m*; redoma *f*; ⚗ matraz *m*.

flat [flæt] **1.** □ llano; (*smooth*) liso; (*even*) igual; horizontal; (*stretched out*) tendido; *denial* terminante; *drink* muerto; *feeling* de abatimiento; *p.* alicaído; *taste* insípido; *tone* monótono; *tire* desinflado; *voice* desafinado; ♪ bemol; ✝ flojo; ~ *roof* azotea *f*; *sport*: *400 meters* ~ 400 metros lisos; *v. fall 2*; ~*top* ⚓ portaaviones *m*; ~*ware* vajilla *f* de plata; vajilla de porcelana; **2.** *adv.*: *sing* ~ desafinar; *turn down* ~ rechazar de plano; F *go* ~ *out* ir a máxima velocidad; **3.** *British* piso *m*; palma *f of hand*; plano *m of sword*; ♪ bemol *m*; ⚓ banco *m*; pantano *m*; *mot. sl.* pinchazo *m*; '**~·boat** chalana *f*; '**~·car** 🚃 vagón *m* de plataforma; '**~·foot** *sl.* polizonte *m*; '**~'foot·ed** que tiene los pies planos; F *fig.* pedestre, desmañado; indiscreto; F inflexible; '**~·i·ron** plancha *f*; '**flat·ness** llanura *f*; *fig.* insipidez *f*; '**flatten** allanar; aplanar(se); aplastar; ✈ ~ *out* enderezarse.

flat·ter ['flætər] adular, lisonjear; (*clothes*, *picture*) favorecer; '**flat·ter·er** adulador (-a *f*) *m*; '**flat·ter·ing** □ lisonjero; halagüeño; '**flat·ter·y** adulación *f*, lisonja *f*.

flat·u·lence, flat·u·len·cy ['flætjuləns(i)] flatulencia *f*; *fig.* hinchazón *f*; '**flat·u·lent** □ flatulento; *fig.* hinchado.

flaunt [flɔːnt] *v/t.* ostentar, lucir; *v/i.* pavonearse.

fla·vor ['fleivər] **1.** sabor *m*; gusto *m*; condimento *m* (*a.* ~*ing*); **2.** sazonar, condimentar; *fig.* dar un sabor característico a; '**fla·vored** con sabor a...; '**fla·vor·less** insípido, soso.

flaw [flɔː] tacha *f*; imperfección *f*; desperfecto *m*; defecto *m* (*a.* ⚖ *a.* ⊕); (*crack*) grieta *f*; '**flaw·less** □ intachable, perfecto.

flax [flæks] lino *m*; '**fla·xen** de lino; *hair* muy rubio.

flay [flei] desollar; *fig.* azotar; (*criticize*) flagelar.

flea [fliː] pulga *f*; ~ *market* mercado *m* de cosas viejas; El Rastro *en Madrid*; '**~·bite** picadura *f* de pulga; *fig.* pérdida *f* (*or* gasto *m*) insignificante.

fleck [flek] **1.** mancha *f*, punto *m*; **2.** puntear, salpicar (*with* de).

flec·tion ['flekʃn] flexión *f*.

fled [fled] *pret. a. p.p. of flee.*

fledge [fledʒ] emplumar; ~*d* plumado; *full-*~*d fig.* hecho y derecho; **fledg·ling** ['~liŋ] volantón *m*, pajarito *m*.

flee [fliː] [*irr.*] huir (*from* de).

fleece [fliːs] **1.** vellón *m*; lana *f*; *Golden* ♀ vellocino *m* de oro; **2.** esquilar; F pelar, mondar; '**fleec·y** lanudo; *cloud* aborregado.

fleet [fliːt] **1.** □ *poet.* veloz, ligero; **2.** flota *f*; armada *f*; escuadra *f of cars*; ♀ *Street* la prensa (*londinense*); '**fleet·ing** □ fugaz, efímero, pasajero.

Flem·ish ['flemiʃ] flamenco *adj. a. su. m.*

flesh [fleʃ] carne *f* (*a. fig.*); *in the* ~ en persona; *put on* ~ echar carnes; *of* ~ *and blood* de carne y hueso; ~*pot* olla *f*, marmita *f*; ~*pots* vida *f* regalona; suntuosos nidos *m/pl.* de vicios; '**flesh·ly** carnal, sensual; '**flesh wound** herida *f* superficial; '**flesh·y** (*fat*) gordo; ♀ *etc.* carnoso.

flew [fluː] *pret. of fly 2.*

flex [fleks] **1.** doblar(se); **2.** ⚡ hilo *m*, cordón *m* (de la luz); **flex·i·bil·i·ty** [~ə'biliti] flexibilidad *f* (*a. fig.*); '**flex·i·ble** □ flexible (*a. fig.*); **flex·ion** ['flekʃn] flexión *f* (*a. gr.*); **flex·or** ['~ksər] (músculo *m*) flexor *m*; **flex·ure** ['flekʃər] flexión *f*; corvadura *f*.

flick [flik] **1.** dar un capirotazo a; rozar levemente; *whip* chasquear; ~ *away* quitar *etc.* rápidamente; **2.** capirotazo *m of finger*; chasquido *m of whip*; golpe *m* rápido y ligero; *sl.* película *f*; *sl.* ~*s pl.* cine *m*.

flick·er ['flikər] **1.** (*light*) parpadear;

brillar con luz mortecina; (*flame*) vacilar; (*movement*) oscilar, vibrar; *fig.* fluctuar; **2.** parpadeo *m*; luz *f* mortecina; *without a ~ of* sin la menor señal de.

fli·er ['flaiər] = *flyer.*

flight [flait] ✈ vuelo *m*; (*distance*) recorrido *m*; (*unit*) escuadrilla *f*; ⚔ trayectoria *f of bullet etc.*; (*flock of birds*) bandada *f*; (*escape*) huida *f*, fuga *f*; escalera *f*, tramo *m of steps*; ~ *deck* ⚓ cubierta *f* de vuelo; ~ *of fancy* sueño *m*, ilusión *f*; *put to* ~ ahuyentar; *take* ~ alzar el vuelo; *take to* ~ ponerse en fuga; '**flight·y** □ coqueta, frívolo, veleidoso.

flim·flam ['flimflæm] **1.** F engaño *m*, trampa *f*; tontería *f*; **2.** F engañar, trampear.

flim·sy ['flimzi] **1.** □ débil, endeble; *fig.* baladí, frívolo; *cloth* muy delgado; **2.** papel *m* muy delgado.

flinch [flintʃ] acobardarse, retroceder (*from* ante); desistir de miedo (*from* de); *without* ~*ing* sin vacilar.

fling [fliŋ] **1.** baile *m* escocés; *have a* ~ *at* intentar; *have one's* ~ correrla; **2.** [*irr.*] *v/i.* arrojarse; ~ *out* salir muy enfadado; *v/t.* arrojar; tirar (*a.* ~ *away*); echar (*a.* ~ *out*); ~ *o.s.* arrojarse; ~ *down* echar al suelo; ~ *open* abrir de golpe.

flint [flint] pedernal *m*; piedra *f of lighter*; '**flint·y** *fig.* empedernido.

flip [flip] **1.** capirotazo *m*; ✈ *sl.* vuelo *m*; **2.** *coin etc.* echar de un capirotazo; mover de un tirón; ~ *side* contraportada *f* del disco.

flip·pan·cy ['flipənsi] ligereza *f*, frivolidad *f*; '**flip·pant** □ ligero, frívolo.

flip·per ['flipər] aleta *f* (*a. sl.*); ~*s pl.* (*frogfoot*) aletas *f/pl.*

flirt [flə:rt] **1.** coqueta *f*; mariposón *m*; **2.** coquetear (*with* con), flirtear, mariposear; *fig.* ~ *with idea* acariciar con poca seriedad; *death* jugar con; **flir'ta·tion** coqueteo *m*; flirteo *m.*

flit [flit] revolotear; volar con vuelo cortado; pasar rápidamente *before eyes etc.*; F mudarse a la chita callando.

flitch [flitʃ] hoja *f* de tocino.

fliv·ver ['flivər] F coche *m* barato.

float [flout] **1.** boya *f*, corcho *m*; balsa *f*; carroza *f in procession*; **2.** *v/t.* poner a flote; ☤ emitir; *company* lanzar; *v/i.* flotar; (*bather*) hacer la plancha; '**float·a·ble** flotable; **float'a·tion** flotación *f*; '**float·ing** *mst* flotante; *voter* indeciso.

flock[1] [flɔk] **1.** rebaño *m*; bandada *f of birds*; *eccl.* grey *f*; gentío *m of people*; **2.** congregarse, reunirse; *come* ~*ing* venir en masa.

flock[2] [~] (*wool*) borra *f.*

floe [flou] témpano *m* de hielo.

flog [flɔg] azotar; F ~ *a dead horse* machacar en hierro frío; '**flog·ging** paliza *f*, zurra *f.*

flood [flʌd] **1.** inundación *f*; diluvio *m*; avenida *in river*; *fig.* torrente *m*, plétora *f*; (*a.* ~ *tide*) pleamar *f*; *the* ♀ el Diluvio; *in* ~ crecido; **2.** *v/t.* inundar (*with* de; *a. fig.*), anegar; *v/i.* desbordar; ~ *in etc.* entrar a raudales; '~**·gate** compuerta *f*; esclusa *f*; '~**·light 1.** foco *m*; **2.** iluminar con foco(s).

floor [flɔ:r] **1.** suelo *m*; (*story*) piso *m*; fondo *m of sea*; *parl.* hemiciclo *m*; *first* ~ primer piso *m*, piso *m* principal; = *ground* ~ piso *m* bajo, planta *f* baja; *have the* ~, *hold the* ~ tener la palabra; *take the* ~ salir a bailar; *fig.* salir a palestra; ~ *show* espectáculo *m* de cabaret, atracciones *f/pl.* (en la pista de baile); **2.** solar, entarimar; *p.* derribar; *fig.* dejar sin réplica posible, confundir; '~ **cloth** bayeta *f*; '~**·ing** entarimado *m*, piso *m*, suelo *m*; '~ **lamp** lámpara *f* de pie; '~ **mat** *mot.* alfombrilla *f*; '~ **mop** fregasuelos *m*, estropajo *m*; '~ **plan** planta *f*; '**floor·walk·er** superintendente *m/f* de división; '~ **wax** cera *f* de pisos.

flop [flɔp] **1.** dejarse caer pesadamente; *sl.* fracasar; *thea.* venirse al foso; **2.** *thea.* caída *f*; *sl.* fracaso *m*; *sl.* ~*house* posada *f* de baja categoría; '**flop·py** flojo, colgante.

flo·ra ['flɔ:rə] flora *f.*

flo·ral ['flɔ:rəl] floral; de flores.

flo·res·cence [flɔ:'resns] florescencia *f.*

flor·id ['flɔrid] □ florido; *face* encarnado, subido de color.

flor·in ['flɔrin] florín *m* (*British* = 2 *chelines*).

flo·rist ['flɔrist] florista *m/f*; ~'s floristería *f.*

floss [flɔs] seda *f* floja (*a.* ~ *silk*); '**floss·y** *sl.* vistoso, cursi.

flo·ta·tion [flou'teiʃn] flotación *f*; ☤ lanzamiento *m.*

flo·til·la [flə'tilə] flotilla *f.*

flot·sam ['flɔtsəm] pecios *m/pl.*, restos *m/pl.* flotantes; ~ *and jetsam* pecios *m/pl.*, despojos *m/pl.*; (*trifles*) baratijas *f/pl.*; gente *f* trashumante, gente perdida.
flounce[1] [flauns] **1.** volante *m*; **2.** guarnecer con volantes.
flounce[2] [~]: ~ *out* salir airado, alejarse indignado.
floun·der[1] ['flaundər] *ichth.* platija *f*.
floun·der[2] [~] revolcarse, forcejear (*a.* ~ *about*).
flour ['flauər] harina *f*; ~ *mill* molino *m* de harina; ~*y* harinoso.
flour·ish ['flʌriʃ] **1.** rúbrica *f*, rasgo *m in writing*; ♪ floreo *m*; ♪ toque *m* de trompeta; ademán *m of hand*; *with a* ~ triunfalmente; **2.** *v/i.* florecer; prosperar; crecer rápidamente; *v/t. weapon* blandir; *stick* menear; *fig.* hacer alarde de, mostrar orgullosamente; '**flour·ish·ing** □ floreciente; (*healthy*) como un reloj.
flout [flaut] mofarse de, burlarse de.
flow [flou] **1.** corriente *f*; flujo *m*; (*amount*) caudal *m*; curso *m*; torrente *m of words etc.*; **2.** fluir; correr; (*tide*) subir; (*hair*) ondear; (*blood*) derramarse; *fig.* abundar (*with* en); ~ *away* deslizarse; ~ *from fig.* proceder de; ~ *into (river)* desembocar en.
flow·er ['flauər] **1.** flor *f*; *fig.* flor *f* (y nata); *in* ~ en flor; **2.** florecer; '~ **bed** cuadro *m*, macizo *m*; '~ **girl** florera *f*; (*at a wedding*) damita *f* de honor; '~ **pot** tiesto *m*, maceta *f*; '~ **shop** floristería *f*; '~ **show** exposición *f* de flores; '**flow·er·y** cubierto de flores; florido (*a. fig.*).
flown [floun] *p.p. of fly* 2.
flu [flu:] F = *influenza* gripe *f*.
fluc·tu·ate ['flʌktjueit] fluctuar; **fluc·tu'a·tion** fluctuación *f*.
flue [flu:] humero *m*, (cañón *m* de) chimenea *f*.
flu·en·cy ['fluənsi] fluidez *f*, facilidad *f*; dominio *m* (*in language* de); '**flu·ent** □ flúido, fácil; corriente; *be* ~ *in German, speak German* ~*ly* dominar el alemán.
fluff [flʌf] pelusa *f*, tamo *m*, lanilla *f*; F *bit of* ~ falda *f*, tia *f*; '**fluff·y** velloso; que tiene mucha pelusa.
flu·id ['flu:id] flúido *adj. a. su. m* (*a.* ⚡); líquido *m*; **flu'id·i·ty** fluidez *f*.
fluke [flu:k] *zo.* trematodo *m*; *ichth.* platija *f*; ⚓ uña *f*; F chiripa *f*.
flum·mox ['flʌməks] F confundir, desconcertar.
flung [flʌŋ] *pret. a. p.p. of fling* 2.
flunk [flʌŋk] F *v/t. p.* reprobar, dar calabazas a; *exam* perder; *v/i.* salir mal.
flunk·(e)y ['flʌŋki] lacayo *m* (*a. fig.*).
flu·o·res·cence [fluə'resns] fluorescencia *f*; **flu·o'res·cent** fluorescente.
fluor·i·date ['flɔ:rideit] fluorizar; **fluor·i'da·tion** fluorización *f*; '**fluor·ide** fluoruro *m*; '**fluor·o·scope** fluoroscopio *m*.
flur·ry ['flʌri] **1.** agitación *f*; conmoción *f*; nevisca *f*, ráfaga *f of snow*; **2.** agitar, hacer nervioso.
flush [flʌʃ] **1.** ⊕ nivelado; igual, parejo; F adinerado; ~ *outlet* ⚡ caja *f* de enchufe embutida; ~ *switch* ⚡ llave *f* embutida; **2.** rubor *m*, sonrojo *m*; abundancia *f*; *fig.* vigor *m*, plenitud *f*; *cards*: flux *m*; **3.** *v/t.* limpiar con chorro de agua (*a.* ~ *out*); *game* levantar; ~ *tank* depósito *m* de limpia; ~ *toilet* inodoro *m* con chorro de agua; *v/i.* ruborizarse, sonrojarse.
flus·ter ['flʌstər] **1.** confusión *f*, aturdimiento *m*; **2.** confundir, aturdir.
flute [flu:t] **1.** ♪ flauta *f*; ⚠ estría *f*; **2.** estriar, acanalar.
flut·ter ['flʌtər] **1.** revoloteo *m of wings*; palpitación *f of heart*; *fig.* agitación *f*; emoción *f*; *sl.* apuesta *f*; **2.** *v/t.* agitar, menear; *v/i.* (*bird etc.*) revolotear; (*heart*) palpitar; (*flag*) ondear; agitarse.
flux [flʌks] *fig.* flujo *m*; ⚗ fundente *m*; (*state*) continua mudanza *f*.
fly [flai] **1.** mosca *f*; (*trouser*) bragueta *f*; *thea. flies pl.* bambalinas *f/pl.*; *die like flies* morir como chinches; ~*catcher* moscareta *f*, papamoscas *m*; ~ *chaser* espantamoscas *m*; ~*-fish* pescar con moscas artificiales; ~ *in the ointment* mosca *f* muerta que malea el perfume; **2.** [*irr.*] *v/i.* volar; (*rush*) precipitarse; (*escape*) evadirse, huir; *I must* ~ tengo que darme prisa; *the flag is* ~*ing* la bandera está izada; *send* ~*ing* echar a rodar; *v. let*; ~ *at* lanzarse sobre; ~ *away* irse volando; ~ *ball baseball*: palomita *f*; ~*-by-night* indigno de confianza; ~ *in the face of* estar abiertamente opuesto a; desafiar; ~ *into a passion* montar en cólera; ~ *off* (*part*) desprenderse; (*bird*) alejarse volando; ~ *open* abrir-

se de repente; *v/t.* hacer volar; ✈ dirigir; transportar en avión; *ocean etc.* atravesar (en avión); *distance* recorrer (en avión); *flag* llevar, tener izado; *danger* huir (de); *country* abandonar; *let* ~ descargar, proferir (*at* contra); **3.** F despabilado, avispado.

fly·blown ['flaibloun] lleno de cresas; *fig.* contaminado.

fly·er ['flaiər] aviador *m*; tren *m etc.* rápido, *sl.* empresa *f* arriesgada; = *flier*.

fly·ing ['flaiiŋ] **1.** vuelo *m*; aviación *f*; **2.** *attr.* de vuelo; de aviación; *adj.* volante, volador; rápido, veloz; *visit* muy breve; ~ *boat* hidroavión *m*; ~ *bomb* bomba *f* volante; ~ *buttress* arbotante *m*; ~ *colors pl.* gran éxito *m*; ~ *field* campo *m* de aviación; ~ *fish* pez *m* volador; ~ *machine* avión *m*; ~ *saucer* platillo *m* volante; ~ *sickness* mal *m* de altura; ~ *time* horas *f/pl.* de vuelo; ~ *start* salida *f* lanzada; *get off to a* ~ *start* comenzar muy felizmente.

fly...: '~·**leaf** hoja *f* de guarda; '~ **net** *for a bed* mosquitero *m*; *for a horse* espantamoscas *m*; ~·**pa·per** papel *m* matamoscas; ~·**speck** mancha *f* de mosca; ~ **swat·ter** matamoscas *m*; ~·**trap** atrapamoscas *m*; '~·**weight** peso *m* mosca; '~·**wheel** volante *m* (*de motor*).

foal [foul] **1.** potro (a *f*) *m*; **2.** parir (*la yegua*).

foam [foum] **1.** espuma *f*; ~ *extinguisher* lanzaespumas *m*; ~ *rubber* espuma *f* de látex (*or* de caucho); **2.** espumar; echar espuma; ~ *at the mouth* espumajear; '**foam·y** espum(aj)oso.

fob[1] [fɔb] faltriquera *f* del reloj.

fob[2] [~]: ~ *off* apartar de un propósito con excusas; ~ *off with* persuadir a aceptar de modo fraudulento.

fo·cal ['foukl] focal; *phot.* ~ *distance* distancia *f* focal; *phot.* ~ *plane* plano *m* focal; ~ *point* punto *m* focal.

fo·cus ['foukəs] **1.** foco *m* (*a. fig.*); *in* ~ enfocado; *out of* ~ desenfocado; **2.** enfocar; *attention* fijar, concentrar (*on* en).

fod·der ['fɔdər] forraje *m*.

foe [fou] *lit.* enemigo *m*.

foe·tus ['fi:təs] = *fetus*.

fog [fɔg] **1.** niebla *f* (*a. fig.*); *fig.* confusión *f*; *phot.* velo *m*; **2.** *fig.* oscurecer; *issue* entenebrecer; *phot.* velar(se); '~-**bound** inmovilizado por la niebla.

fo·g(e)y ['fougi]: *old* ~ viejo *m* de ideas anticuadas.

fog·gy ['fɔgi] brumoso, nebuloso (*a. fig.*); *phot.* velado; *it is* ~ hay niebla; *I haven't the foggiest idea* no tengo la más remota idea; '**fog·horn** sirena *f* (de niebla).

foi·ble ['fɔibl] flaco *m*.

foil[1] [fɔil] hojuela *f* (de metal); *fig.* contraste *m*.

foil[2] [~] **1.** frustrar; *attempt* desbaratar; **2.** *fenc.* florete *m*.

foist [fɔist]: ~ *on* encajar a, lograr con engaño que ... acepte; imputar a.

fold[1] [fould] ✓ **1.** redil *m*, aprisco *m*; *eccl.* rebaño *m*; **2.** apriscar.

fold[2] [~] **1.** doblez *m*, pliegue *m* (*a. geol.*); arruga *f*; **2.** plegar(se), doblar(se); envolver (*in* en); *wings* recoger; ~ *one's arms* cruzar los brazos; ~ *in one's arms* abrazar tiernamente; ~ *down* doblar hacia abajo; ~ *up* doblar(se); F ⚕ quebrar; entrar en liquidación, liquidarse; '**fold·er** carpeta *f*; (*brochure*) folleto *m*.

fold·ing ['fouldiŋ] plegadizo; plegable; '~ **bed** catre *m* de tijera; '~ **chair** silla *f* de tijera, silla plegadiza; catrecillo *m of canvas*; '~ **cot** catre *m* de tijera; '~ **door** puerta *f* plegadiza; '~ **rule** metro *m* plegadizo.

fo·li·age ['fouliidʒ] follaje *m*; **fo·li'a·tion** foliación *f*.

fo·li·o ['fouliou] folio *m*, libro *m* en folio.

folk [fouk] *pl.* gente *f*; nación *f*; raza *f*; tribu *f*; F (*a.* ~*s pl.*) familia *f*; *the old* ~ los viejos; F *hello* ~! ¡hola, amigos!

folk·lore ['fouklɔ:r] folklore *m*; '**folk mu·sic** música *f* folklórica; '**folk song** canción *f* popular (*or* tradicional); **folk·sy** ['fouksi] F sociable, tratable; (*like common people*) F plebeyo; '**folk·way** costumbre *f* tradicional.

fol·low ['fɔlou] *v/t.* seguir; seguir la pista a; *news* interesarse en; *profession* ejercer; *p.* comprender; *argument* seguir el hilo de; ~ *through*, ~ *up* llevar hasta el fin; proseguir; *v. suit*; *v/i.* seguirse; resultar; *as* ~*s* como sigue; *it* ~*s that* síguese que; ~ *on from* ser la consecuencia lógica de; ˈ**fol·low·er** partidario (a *f*) *m*; secuaz *m*; imitador (-a *f*) *m*; discípulo *m*; ˈ**fol·low·ing 1.** partidarios *m/pl.*; secuaces *m/pl.*; séquito *m*; **2.** siguiente; *the* ~ lo siguiente; ~ *wind* viento *m* en popa; ˈ**fol·low-ˈup** *letter* recordativo; subsiguiente; de continuación.

fol·ly [ˈfɔli] locura *f*, desatino *m*.

fo·ment [fouˈment] fomentar (*a.* ⚕); provocar; nutrir; **fo·menˈta·tion** fomento *m* (*a.* ⚕); ⚕ fomentación *f*.

fond [fɔnd] □ cariñoso, afectuoso; *be* ~ *of* ser aficionado a, ser amigo de; *p.* tener mucho cariño a.

fon·dle [ˈfɔndl] acariciar.

fond·ness [ˈfɔndnis] cariño *m*; afición *f* (*for* a).

font [fɔnt] pila *f*.

food [fu:d] comida *f*; alimento *m*, alimentación *f*; provisiones *f/pl.*; (*dish*) manjar *m*; (*material*) comestible *m*; *fig.* alimento *m*, pábulo *m*; *give* ~ *for thought* dar materia en que pensar; ˈ~ **poi·son·ing** botulismo *m*; ˈ~**·stuffs** *pl.* comestibles *m/pl.*, artículos *m/pl.* alimenticios; ˈ~ **val·ue** valor *m* alimenticio.

fool [fu:l] **1.** tonto (a *f*) *m*, necio (a *f*) *m*; (*jester*) bufón *m*; *make a* ~ *of* poner en ridículo; *play the* ~ hacer el tonto; *all* ~*s' day* (*1 abril*) día *m* de inocentes (*28 diciembre*); ~*'s errand* empresa *f* descabellada; misión *f* inútil; ~*'s paradise* bienestar *m* ilusorio; **2.** F tonto; **3.** *v/t.* engañar, embaucar; confundir; F ~ *away* malgastar; *v/i.* chancear; tontear; (*a.* ~ *about*) juguetear (*with* con), divertirse (*with* con); F *no* ~*ing* en serio; F ~ *around* malgastar el tiempo neciamente; F ~ *with* manosear neciamente.

fool·er·y [ˈfu:ləri] bufonada *f*; tontería *f*; ˈ**fool·hard·y** □ temerario; ˈ**fool·ish** □ tonto, necio; *remark etc.* disparatado; indiscreto; ridículo; ˈ**fool·ish·ness** tontería *f*, necedad *f*; estupidez *f*; ridiculez *f*; ˈ**fool·proof** ⊕ a prueba de impericia; F infalible; ˈ**fools·cap** *approx.* papel *m* tamaño folio.

foot [fut] **1.** (*pl.* *feet*) pie *m*; pata *f of animal etc.*; ⚔ infantería *f*; ~*age* distancia *f* o largura *f* en pies; *on* ~ a pie; *fig.* en marcha; *fall on one's feet fig.* caer de pie; *have one* ~ *in the grave* estar con un pie en la sepultura; *keep one's feet* mantenerse en pie; *put one's* ~ *down* adoptar una actitud firme; F *mot.* acelerar; F *put one's* ~ *in it* meter la pata; *set on* ~ promover, iniciar; **2.**: ~ *the bill* pagar la cuenta; *fig.* pagar el pato; ~ *it* ir andando; ˈ~**-and-ˈmouth** (**dis·ease**) fiebre *f* aftosa; ˈ~**·ball** (*game*) fútbol *m*, balompié *m* (*estadunidense*); (*ball*) balón *m* (*estadunidense*); ~ *player* futbolista *m* (*estadunidense*); ~ *pool* quinielas *f/pl.*; ˈ~**·board** estribo *m*; ˈ~ **brake** pedal *m* del freno; freno *m* de pie; ˈ~**-bridge** puente *m* para peatones; ˈ**foot·ed** de ... pies; ˈ**foot·fall** pisada *f*, paso *m*; ˈ**foot·hills** *pl.* colinas *f/pl.* al pie de una sierra; estribaciones *f/pl.*; ˈ**foot·hold** (asidero *m* para el) pie *m*, pie *m* firme; *gain a* ~ ganar pie.

foot·ing [ˈfutiŋ] pie *m*; posición *f* estable(cida); condición *f*; *on an equal* ~ en un mismo pie de igualdad (*with* con); *on a war* ~ en pie de guerra; *gain a* ~ lograr establecerse.

foo·tle [ˈfu:tl] F hacer el tonto; ~ *away* disipar neciamente; ˈ**foot·ling** baladí, insignificante.

foot...: ˈ~**·lights** *pl.* candilejas *f/pl.*, batería *f*; *fig.* tablas *f/pl.*, escena *f*; ˈ~**·loose** libre; andariego; ˈ~**·man** lacayo *m*; ˈ~**·note** nota *f*; apostilla *f*; nota *f* al pie de la página; ˈ~**·pad** salteador *m* de caminos; ˈ~**·path** senda *f* para peatones, sendero *m*; ˈ~**·plate** plataforma *f* del maquinista; ˈ~**·print** huella *f*; ˈ~**·rest** apoyapié *m*; ˈ~ **rule** regla *f* de un pie; ˈ~ **sol·dier** soldado *m* de a pie; ˈ~**·sore** con los pies cansados; ˈ~**·step** paso *m*; *follow in the* ~*s of* seguir los pasos de; ˈ~**·stool** escabel *m*; ˈ~ **warm·er** calientapiés *m*; ˈ~**·wear** calzado *m*; ˈ~**·work** *sport*: juego *m* de piernas.

fop [fɔp] petimetre *m*, currutaco *m*; ˈ**fop·per·y** afectación *f*; ˈ**fop·pish** □ currutaco, afectado.

for [fɔ:r, fər] **1.** *prp.* para; por; a causa de; en honor de; en lugar de; ~ *all his wealth* a pesar de su riqueza; ~ *all that* con todo; ~ *3 days* (*past*) (durante) 3 días; (*present a. future*) por 3 días; *as* ~ en cuanto a; *as* ~ *me* por mi parte; *but* ~ a no ser por; F *I'm* ~ *London* yo voy a Londres; F *I'm all* ~ *it* lo apruebo sin reserva; *it is* ~ *you to decide* le toca a Vd. decidir; F *now we're* ~ *it* ahora nos va a tocar la gorda; *oh* ~ ...! ¡quién tuviera ...!; *time* ~ *dinner* hora *f* de comer; *there is nothing* ~ *it but to* no queda más remedio que *inf.*; *if it were not* ~ *him* si no fuera por él; *were it not* ~ *that* si no fuera por eso; **2.** *cj.* pues, ya que.

for·age ['fɔridʒ] **1.** forraje *m*; **2.** forrajear; dar forraje a; *fig.* buscar (*for acc.*).

for·ay ['fɔrei] correría *f*, incursión *f*.

for·bade [fər'beid] *pret. of forbid.*

for·bear [fɔːr'ber] [*irr.*] abstenerse (*from* de); contenerse; **for'bear·ance** paciencia *f*, dominio *m* sobre sí mismo.

for·bears ['fɔːrberz] *pl.* antepasados *m/pl.*

for·bid [fər'bid] [*irr.*] prohibir (*to inf.*; *a p. a th.* algo a alguien); *God* ~! ¡no lo permita Dios!; **for'bid·den** *p.p. of forbid*; **for'bid·ding** □ formidable; repugnante.

for·bore, for·borne [fɔːr'bɔːr(n)] *pret. u. p.p. of forbear.*

force [fɔːrs] **1.** fuerza *f*; personal *m*; ⚔ cuerpo *m*; ⚔ ~*s pl.* fuerzas *f/pl.* (armadas); F *the* ~ la policía; *by* ~ a la fuerza; *by* ~ *of* a fuerza de; *in* ~ en gran número; *in* ~ (*law*) vigente, en vigor; *be in* ~ (*price etc.*) regir, imperar; *v. join*; **2.** *mst* forzar (*to* a *inf.*; *upon a p.* a uno a aceptar); obligar; violentar; ↗ hacer madurar temprano; ~*d landing* aterrizaje *m* forzado, aterrizaje forzoso; ~*d march* marcha *f* forzada; *I am* ~*d to* me veo obligado a; ~ *back* hacer retroceder; ~ *down* (hacer) tragar por fuerza; ✈ obligar a aterrizar; ~ *in* introducir por fuerza; ~ *o.s. inf.* hacer un esfuerzo por *inf.*; ~ *open* forzar; ~ *a smile* sonreír forzadamente; **'forced** (*adv.* **forc·ed·ly** ['~idli]) *mst* forzado; *smile* que no le sale a uno; **force·ful** ['~ful] □ vigoroso, poderoso; **'force·meat** relleno *m* (de carne picada).

for·ceps ['fɔːrseps] fórceps *m*; tenacillas *f/pl.*; **force-pump** ['fɔːrspʌmp] bomba *f* impulsora.

for·cible ['fɔːrsəbl] □ vigoroso, poderoso, enérgico; concluyente; *entry* a viva fuerza.

forc·ing-house ['fɔːrsiŋhaus] invernadero *m*.

ford [fɔːrd] **1.** vado *m*; **2.** vadear; **'ford·a·ble** vadeable.

fore [fɔːr] **1.** *adv.*: *to the* ~ en la delantera; destacado; *come to the* ~ empezar a destacar; ⚓ ~ *and aft* de (*etc.*) popa a proa; **2.** *adj.* anterior, delantero; ⚓ de proa; **'~·arm** antebrazo *m*; **~'bode** presagiar, pronosticar; **~'bod·ing** presagio *m*, presentimiento *m*; **'~·cast 1.** pronóstico *m*; **2.** [*irr.* (*cast*)] pronosticar, prever; **'~·cas·tle** ['fouksl] castillo *m* de proa; **~'close** excluir; ⚖ extinguir el derecho de redimir; **'~·fa·thers** *pl.* antepasados *m/pl.*; **'~·fin·ger** dedo *m* índice; **'~·foot** pata *f* delantera; **'~·front** vanguardia *f*; sitio *m* de actividad más intensa; **~'go** [*irr.* (*go*)] = *forgo*; **~'go·ing** anterior, precedente; **'~'gone**: ~ *conclusion* conclusión *f* (*or* resultado *m*) inevitable; **'~·ground** primer plano *m* (*or* término *m*); **'~·hand** directo *m*; **~·head** ['fɔrid] frente *f*.

for·eign ['fɔrin] extranjero; *trade etc.* exterior; extraño, ajeno (*to* a); ~ *exchange* cambio *m* extranjero; (*currency*) divisa *f*, divisas *f/pl.*; ♀ *Office* Ministerio *m* de Asuntos Exteriores; ~ *trade* comercio *m* exterior; **'for·eign·er** extranjero (a *f*) *m*.

fore...: **'~'know·ledge** presciencia *f*; **'~·land** cabo *m*, promontorio *m*; **'~·leg** pata *f* delantera; **'~·lock** copete *m*; *take time by the* ~ tomar la ocasión por los cabellos; **'~·man** capataz *m*; maestro *m* de obras; ⚖ presidente *m* del jurado; **'~·mast** trinquete *m*; **'~·most** delantero; primero; principal; **'~·noon** mañana *f*.

fo·ren·sic [fə'rensik] forense.

fore...: **'~'run·ner** precursor (-a *f*) *m*; **~·sail** ['~seil, ⚓ '~sl] trinquete *m*; **~'see** [*irr.* (*see*)] prever; **~'see·a·ble** □ previsible; **~'shad·ow** prefigurar; prever, anunciar; **'~·shore** playa *f* (entre los límites de pleamar y bajamar); **~'short·en** escorzar; **'~·sight** previsión *f*; **'~·skin** prepucio *m*.

for·est ['fɔrist] bosque *m*; *attr.* forestal, del bosque; ~ *ranger* guarda *m* forestal.

fore·stall [fɔːr'stɔːl] *th.* prevenir; *p.* anticipar (e impedir).

for·est·er ['fɔristər] silvicultor *m*; ingeniero *m* forestal (*or* de montes); (*keeper*) guardabosques *m*; **'for·est·ry** silvicultura *f*.

fore...: **'~·taste** anticipo *m*; **~'tell** [*irr.* (*tell*)] predecir, pronosticar; presagiar; **'~·thought** providencia *f*, prevención *f*; *b.s.* premeditación *f*; '~**top** cofa *f* de trinquete; ~'**warn** prevenir; *be ~ed* precaverse; '~**word** prefacio *m*.

for·feit ['fɔːrfit] **1.** perdido; **2.** (*fine*) multa *f*; ⚖ pena *f*; prenda *f in game*; *~s pl.* juego *m* de prendas; **3.** perder (el derecho a); **for·fei·ture** ['~tʃər] pérdida *f*.

for·gath·er [fɔːr'gæðər] reunirse.

for·gave [fər'geiv] *pret. of forgive*.

forge[1] [fɔːrdʒ] **1.** (*fire*) fragua *f*; (*blacksmith's*) herrería *f*; (*factory*) fundición *f*; **2.** *metal* forjar, fraguar; *money etc.* falsificar, contrahacer; '**forg·er** falsificador *m*; '**for·ger·y** falsificación *f*.

forge[2] [~]: *~ ahead* avanzar constantemente; adelantarse muchísimo a todos.

for·get [fər'get] [*irr.*] *v/t.* olvidar(se de) (*to inf.*); *~ o.s.* propasarse; F *~ it!* ¡no se preocupe!; *v/i.* olvidarse; *I forgot freq.* se me olvidó; **for'get·ful** [~ful] □ olvidadizo; descuidado; **for'get·ful·ness** olvido *m*; descuido *m*; **for'get-me-not** nomeolvides *f*.

for·give [fər'giv] [*irr.*] perdonar (*acc. acc.*; *a p.* [*for*] *a th.* algo a alguien); **for'giv·en** *p.p. of forgive*; **for'give·ness** perdón *m*; misericordia *f*; **for'giv·ing** □ perdonador; magnánimo.

for·go [fɔːr'gou] [*irr.* (*go*)] renunciar, privarse de.

for·got [fər'gɔt], **for'got·ten** [~n] *pret. a. p.p. of forget*.

fork [fɔːrk] **1.** tenedor *m*; ✓ horca *f*; horquilla *f* (*a* ⊕); bifurcación *f in road*; horcajo *m in river*; horcadura *f in tree*; *anat.* horcajadura *f*, entrepierna *f*; *~lift truck* carretilla *f* elevadora de horquilla; **2.** *v/i.* (*road*) bifurcarse; *v/t.* cultivar (cavar, hacinar *etc.*) con horquilla; F *~ out* desembolsar de mala gana; F *~ over* entregar; '**forked** ahorquillado; *road* bifurcado; *lightning* en zigzag.

for·lorn [fər'lɔːrn] abandonado, desamparado; *appearance* triste, de abandono; *~ hope* empresa *f* desesperada; cosa *f* sumamente dudosa.

form [fɔːrm] **1.** forma *f*; figura *f*; (*condition*) estado *m*; (*formality*) formalidad *f*; (*seat*) banco *m*; *school*: clase *f*; (*document*) hoja *f*, formulario *m*; *be in* (*good*) *~ sport*: estar en forma; (*witty*) estar de vena; *be bad ~* ser de mal gusto; *for ~'s sake* por pura fórmula; **2.** formar(se); *habit* adquirir; ⚔ alinearse, formar (*a. ~ up*).

for·mal ['fɔːrml] □ formal; *manner etc.* ceremonioso; *visit* de cumplido; *dress etc.* de etiqueta; '**for·mal·ist** formalista *m/f*; **for·mal·i·ty** [fɔːr'mæliti] formalidad *f*; etiqueta *f*; *without formalities* prescindiendo de los trámites de costumbre; **for·mal·ize** ['fɔːrmәlaiz] formalizar.

for·mat ['fɔːrmæt] formato *m*.

for·ma·tion [fɔːr'meiʃn] *all senses*: formación *f*; **form·a·tive** ['fɔːrmәtiv] formativo.

for·mer ['fɔːrmәr] antiguo; anterior, primero, precedente; ex...; *the ~* ése *etc.*, aquél *etc.*; '**for·mer·ly** antes, antiguamente.

for·mic ['fɔːrmik]: *~ acid* ácido *m* fórmico.

for·mi·da·ble ['fɔːrmidәbl] □ formidable.

form·less ['fɔːrmlis] □ informe.

for·mu·la ['fɔːrmjulә], *pl. mst* **for·mu·lae** ['~liː] fórmula *f*; **for·mu·lar·y** ['~lәri] formulario *adj. a. su. m*; **for·mu·late** ['~leit] formular; **for·mu'la·tion** formulación *f*.

for·ni·cate ['fɔːrnikeit] fornicar; **for·ni·ca·tion** [~'keiʃn] fornicación *f*.

for·sake [fər'seik] [*irr.*] abandonar, dejar; desamparar; *opinion* renegar de; **for'sak·en** *p.p. of forsake*.

for·sook [fər'suk] *pret. of forsake*.

for·sooth [fər'suːθ] *iro.* en verdad.

for·swear [fɔːr'swer] [*irr.* (*swear*)] abjurar; *~ o.s.* perjurarse; **for'sworn** perjuro.

fort [fɔːrt] fuerte *m*, fortín *m*.

forte [~] *fig.* fuerte *m*.

forth [fɔːrθ] (a)delante, (a)fuera; *v. so*; *from this day ~* de hoy en adelante; ~'**com·ing** venidero, próximo; *book etc.* de próxima aparición; *p.* abierto, afable; *be ~ freq. th.* ser disponible; '~'**right** directo; franco; terminante; '~'**with** en el acto, sin dilación.

for·ti·eth ['fɔːrtiiθ] cuadragésimo.

for·ti·fi·ca·tion [fɔːrtifi'keiʃn] fortificación *f*; **for·ti·fy** ['~fai] ⚔ fortificar; *wine* encabezar; *opinion* corroborar; *p.* animar; *p.* confirmar (*in belief* en); **for·ti·tude** ['~tjuːd] fortaleza *f*, valor *m*, resistencia *f*.

fort·night ['fɔːrtnait] quince días *m/pl.*, quincena *f*; *this day ~* de hoy en

quince (días); ˈ**fort·night·ly** (que sale *etc.*) cada quince días; quincenal(mente).
for·tress [ˈfɔːrtris] fortaleza *f*, plaza *f* fuerte.
for·tu·i·tous [fɔːrˈtjuitəs] □ fortuito, casual; **forˈtu·i·ty** casualidad *f*.
for·tu·nate [ˈfɔːrtʃnit] □ afortunado; feliz; *~ly* afortunadamente.
for·tune [ˈfɔːrtʃn] fortuna *f*; suerte *f*; *cost a ~* valer un dineral; *tell one's ~* decirle a uno la buenaventura; ˈ**~ hunt·er** aventurero *m*; ˈ**~·tel·ler** adivina *f*.
for·ty [ˈfɔːrti] cuarenta.
fo·rum [ˈfɔːrəm] foro *m*; *fig.* tribunal *m*.
for·ward [ˈfɔːrwərd] **1.** *adj.* delantero; adelantado; precoz; ⚓ de proa; F descarado, impertinente; ⚓ *~ delivery* entrega *f* en fecha futura; *~ line* línea *f* delantera; **2.** *adv.* (hacia) adelante; ⚓ hacia la proa; *~ march!* de frente ¡mar!; **3.** *sport*: delantero *m*; **4.** *project* fomentar, promover, favorecer; ✉ hacer seguir; expedir; enviar; *~ing agent* agente *m* expedidor.
for·ward·ness [ˈfɔːrwərdnis] precocidad *f*; F descaro *m*, impertinencia *f*.
for·wards [ˈfɔːrwərdz] = *forward* 2.
for·went [fɔːrˈwent] *pret. of forgo.*
fosse [fɔs] ⚔ foso *m*; *anat.* fosa *f*.
fos·sil [ˈfɔsl] fósil *adj. a. su. m* (*a. fig.*); ˈ**fos·sil·ized** fosilizado.
fos·ter [ˈfɔstər] **1.** fomentar, favorecer; criar; **2.**: *~ brother* hermano *m* de leche; *~ home* hogar *m* de adopción; *~ mother* madre *f* adoptiva; (*nurse*) ama *f* de leche; *~ sister* hermana *f* de leche.
fought [fɔːt] *pret. a. p.p. of fight* 2.
foul [faul] **1.** □ sucio, puerco; asqueroso; *air* viciado; *blow, play* sucio, fco; *breath* fétido; *deed* vil; *weather* feo, muy malo; *fall ~ of* indisponerse con, ponerse a malas con; **2.** falta *f*, juego *m* sucio; **3.** ensuciar; chocar contra; enredarse en; obstruir; *sport*: cometer una falta contra; *~-* **mouthed** [ˈ~ˈmauðd] malhablado, deslenguado; ˈ**~-ˈsmell·ing** hediondo.
found[1] [faund] *pret. a. p.p. of find* 1.
found[2] [~] fundar, establecer; basar.
found[3] [~] ⊕ fundir.
foun·da·tion [faunˈdeiʃn] fundación *f*; *fig.* fundamento *m*, base *f*; *~s pl.* △ cimientos *m/pl.*; **faunˈda·tion school** escuela *f* dotada; **faunˈda·tion stone** primera piedra *f*.
found·er [ˈfaundər] **1.** fundador (-a *f*) *m*; **2.** ⊕ fundidor *m*; **3.** ⚓ irse a pique, hundirse (*a. fig.*).
found·ling [faundliŋ] niño *m* expósito.
found·ress [faundris] fundadora *f*.
found·ry [ˈfaundri] fundición *f*.
fount *poet.* [faunt] fuente *f*; *typ.* [fɔnt] fundición *f*.
foun·tain [ˈfauntin] fuente *f* (*a. fig.*); surtidor *m*; ˈ**~ˈhead** *fig.* fuente *f*, origen *m*; ˈ**~ ˈpen** (pluma *f*) estilográfica *f*, lapicero *m* fuente; pluma fuente *f S.Am.*
four [fɔːr] cuatro (*a. su. m*); *on all ~s* a gatas; *fig.* en completa armonía (*with* con); ˈ**~-ˈen·gined** cuatrimotor; ˈ**~ˈflush·er** *sl.* impostor *m*, embustero *m*; ˈ**~·fold** **1.** *adj.* cuádruple; **2.** *adv.* cuatro veces; ˈ**~-ˈfoot·ed** cuadrúpedo; ˈ**fourˈsquare** *fig.* firme; franco, sincero; ˈ**four-ˈstroke** de cuatro tiempos; **four·teen** [ˈ~ˈtiːn] catorce; **four·teenth** [ˈ~ˈtiːnθ] décimocuarto; **fourth** [fɔːrθ] **1.** cuarto; **2.** cuarto *m*; cuarta parte *f*; ♪ cuarta *f*; ˈ**fourth·ly** en cuarto lugar; ˈ**four-wheel ˈdrive** tracción *f* a las cuatro ruedas.
fowl [faul] ave *f* (de corral); gallina *f*; pollo *m*; *~ pest* peste *f* aviar; ˈ**fowl·er** cazador *m* de aves.
fowl·ing [ˈfauliŋ] caza *f* de aves; ˈ**~ piece** escopeta *f*.
fox [fɔks] **1.** zorra *f*; (*dog-*) zorro *m* (*a. fig.*); **2.** F engañar, confundir; **foxed** [ˈ~t] manchado.
fox...: ˈ**~·glove** dedalera *f*; ˈ**~·hole** zorrera *f*; ⚔ pozo *m* de lobo, hoyo *m* de protección; ˈ**~·hound** perro *m* raposero; ˈ**~ hunt** cacería *f* de zorras; ˈ**~·trot** fox *m*; ˈ**fox·y** *fig.* taimado, astuto.
foy·er [ˈfɔier] vestíbulo *m*, hall *m*; *in a theater* salón *m* de entrada, vestíbulo *m*.
fra·cas [ˈfrækəs] gresca *f*, riña *f*.
frac·tion [ˈfrækʃn] ⅍ fracción *f*, quebrado *m*; *fig.* parte *f* muy pequeña; ˈ**frac·tion·al** □ fraccionario.
frac·tious [ˈfrækʃəs] □ reacio, rebelón, arisco.
frac·ture [ˈfræktʃər] **1.** fractura *f*; **2.** fracturar(se), quebrar(se).
frag·ile [ˈfrædʒil] frágil; quebradizo; delicado; **fra·gil·i·ty** [frəˈdʒiliti] fragilidad *f*.

frag·ment [ˈfrægmənt] fragmento *m*; ˈ**frag·men·tar·y** □ fragmentario.
fra·grance [ˈfreigrəns] fragancia *f*; ˈ**fra·grant** □ fragante.
frail [freil] □ frágil; *fig*. débil, endeble; ˈ**frail·ty** *fig*. debilidad *f*, flaqueza *f*.
frame [freim] **1.** estructura *f*; esqueleto *m*; marco *m of picture*; *sew*., ⊕ bastidor *m*; armadura *f of spectacles*; ⊕ armazón *f*; *p.'s* forma *f*, figura *f*; ⚓ cuaderna *f*; ~ *house* casa *f* de madera; ~ *of mind* estado *m* de ánimo; **2.** formar; inventar; construir; *picture* poner un marco a; *fig*. servir de marco a; *question* formular, expresar; *sl*. incriminar por medio de una estratagema; arreglar bajo cuerda; ˈ**frame-up** F estratagema *f* para incriminar a alguien; complot *m*; ˈ**frame·work** ⊕ armazón *f*, esqueleto *m*, armadura *f*; *fig*. sistema *m*, organización *f*.
franc [fræŋk] franco *m*.
fran·chise [ˈfræntʃaiz] derecho *m* de votar, sufragio *m*.
Fran·cis·can [frænˈsiskən] franciscano *adj*. *a*. *su*. *m*.
Frank[1] [fræŋk] franco *m*.
frank[2] [~] □ franco.
frank[3] [~] 📯 franquear.
frank·furt·er [ˈfræŋkfəːrtər] salchicha *f* de carne de vaca y de cerdo.
frank·in·cense [ˈfræŋkinsens] incienso *m*.
frank·ness [ˈfræŋknis] franqueza *f*.
fran·tic [ˈfræntik] □ frenético, furioso; F desquiciado *with worry*.
fra·ter·nal [frəˈtəːrnl] □ fraternal, fraterno; **fraˈter·ni·ty** fraternidad *f*, hermandad *f*; *Am. univ*. club *m* de estudiantes; **frat·er·ni·za·tion** [frætərnaiˈzeiʃn] fraternización *f*; ˈ**frat·er·nize** fraternizar.
frat·ri·cide [ˈfreitrisaid] fratricidio *m*; (*p*.) fratricida *m*.
fraud [frɔːd] fraude *m*; (*p*.) impostor *m*, farsante *m*; **fraud·u·lence** [ˈ~julənsl] fraudulencia *f*; ˈ**fraud·u·lent** □ fraudulento.
fraught [frɔːt]: ~ *with* cargado de, lleno de.
fray[1] [frei] *v/i*. deshilacharse; ~*ed* raído; *v/t*. desgastar.
fray[2] [~] combate *m*; refriega *f*, riña *f*.
fraz·zle [ˈfræzl] F **1.**: *in a* ~ rendido de cansancio; *beat to a* ~ cascar; **2.** desgastar; rendir de cansancio.
freak [friːk] **1.** capricho *m of imagination*; (*p*.) fenómeno *m*; (*a*. ~ *of nature*) monstruo *m*, monstruosidad *f*; curiosidad *f*; **2.** = ˈ**freak·ish** □ caprichoso; inesperado, imprevisto.
freck·le [ˈfrekl] peca *f*; ˈ**freck·led** pecoso.
free [friː] **1.** □ *mst* libre (*from*, *of* de); franco; exento (*from* de); inmune (*from* contra); *p*. liberal; (*not fixed*) suelto; (*untied*) desatado; (*for nothing*) gratuito; *be* ~ *to inf*. poder libremente *inf*.; *be* ~ *with* dar abundantemente; no regatear; *be* ~ *with money* ser manirroto; *make* ~ *with* usar como si fuera cosa propia; *set* ~ libertar; ~ *and easy* despreocupado, poco ceremonioso; ~ *of charge* gratis; † ~ *on board* franco a bordo; ~ *of charge* gratis, de balde; ~ *fight*, F ~ *for all* sarracina *f*, riña *f* general; ~ *trade* libre cambio *m*; ~ *wheel* rueda *f* libre; **2.** librar (*from* de), libertar; eximir, exentar (*from*, *of* de); *place etc*. desembarazar, despejar; *knot etc*. soltar, desenredar; ˈ**~·boot·er** filibustero *m*; ˈ**free·dom** libertad *f*; exención *f*, inmunidad *f*; ~ *of assembly* libertad *f* de reunión; ~ *of a city* ciudadanía *f* de honor; ~ *of the press* libertad *f* de imprenta; ~ *of the seas* libertad *f* de los mares; ~ *of speech* libertad *f* de la palabra; ~ *of worship* libertad *f* de cultos.
free...: ˈ**~ en·ter·prise** libertad *f* de empresa; ˈ**~ hand** plena libertad *f*, carta *f* blanca; ˈ**~·hand** hecho a pulso; ~ *drawing* dibujo *m* a pulso; ~*ed* dadivoso, generoso; ˈ**~·hold** feudo *m* franco; ˈ**~·hold·er** poseedor *m* de feudo franco; ˈ**~-kick** golpe *m* franco; ˈ**~ ˈlance** (periodista *m etc*.) independiente; (*writer not on a regular salary*) destajista *m*/*f*; soldado *m* mercenario; ˈ**~ lunch** tapas *f*/*pl*., enjutos *m*/*pl*.; ˈ**~·man** hombre *m* libre; ciudadano *m* de honor *of city*; ˈ**♀·ma·son** francmasón *m*; ˈ**♀·ma·son·ry** francmasonería *f*; *fig*. compañerismo *m*; ˈ**~ port** puerto *m* franco; ˈ**~ˈride** llevada *f* gratuita; ˈ**~ˈser·vice** servicio *m* post-venta; ˈ**~-ˈspo·ken** franco, sin reserva; ˈ**~·stone** abridero *adj*. *a*. *su*. *m*; ˈ**~-ˈthink·er** librepensador (-a *f*) *m*; ˈ**~-ˈthink·ing** librepensamiento *m*; ˈ**~·way** *mot*. autopista *f*; ˈ**~ ˈwill**

(libre) albedrío *m*; *of one's own* ~ por voluntad propia.

freeze [fri:z] **1.** [*irr.*] helar(se); congelar(se) (*a. fig.*, ⚓ *etc.*); ~ *to death* morir de frío; ~-*dry* liofilizar; ~-*drying* liofilización *f*; F ~ *out competitor* deshacerse de (quitándole la clientela); **2.** helada *f*; congelación *f of wages etc.*; **'freez·er** heladora *f*, sorbetera *f*, congelador *m*; **'freez·ing** □ glacial (*a. fig.*), helado; F *it's* ~ *cold* hace terriblemente frío; ~ *mixture* mezcla *f* refrigerante; ~ *point* punto *m* de congelación.

freight [freit] **1.** flete *m*, carga *f*; *attr.* de mercancías; ~ *station* estación *f* de carga; ~ *train* mercancías *m/sg.*, tren *m* de mercancías; ~ *yard* patio *m* de carga; **2.** fletar, cargar; **'freight·age** flete *m*; **'freight car** vagón *m* de mercancías; **'freight·er** buque *m* de carga.

French [frentʃ] francés *adj. a. su. m*; ~ *bean* judía *f*; ~ *chalk* jaboncillo *m* de sastre; ~ *doors pl.* puertas *f/pl.* vidrieras dobles; ~ *dressing* salsa *f* francesa, vinagreta *f*; ~-*fried potatoes pl.* patatas *f/pl.* fritas en trocitos; ~ *horn* ♪ trompa *f* de armonía; ~ *horsepower* caballo *m* de fuerza, caballo de vapor; *take* ~ *leave* despedirse a la francesa; ~ *telephone* microteléfono *m*; ~ *toast* torrija *f*; ~ *window* puerta *f* ventana; **'~·man** francés *m*; **'~·wom·an** francesa *f*.

fren·zied ['frenzid] □ frenético; **'fren·zy** frenesí *m*, delirio *m*.

fre·quen·cy ['fri:kwənsi] frecuencia *f* (*a.* ⚡); **fre·quent 1.** ['~kwənt] □ frecuente; **2.** [~'kwent] frecuentar; **fre'quent·er** frecuentador (-a *f*) *m*.

fres·co ['freskou], *pl.* **fres·co(e)s** ['~z] fresco *m*.

fresh [freʃ] □ fresco; nuevo, reciente; *air* puro; *face* de buen color; *water* dulce; *wind* recio; *p.* nuevo, novicio; F fresco, descarado; *in the* ~ *air* al aire libre; **'fresh·en** refrescar(se); **'fresh·er** F = **'fresh·man** estudiante *m* de primer año; **'fresh·ness** frescura *f*; novedad *f*; **'fresh·wa·ter** de agua dulce; bisoño.

fret[1] [fret] ⊕ **1.** calado *m*; **2.** adornar con calados.

fret[2] [~] **1.** *v/t.* raer, rozar, corroer; *p.* irritar, molestar; *v/i.* inquietarse, apurarse, impacientarse (*at* por); **2.** estado *m* inquieto.

fret[3] [~] ♪ traste *m*.

fret·ful ['fretful] □ displicente, descontentadizo, impaciente.

fret·saw ['fretsɔ:] sierra *f* de calados.

fret·work ['fretwə:rk] calado *m*.

fri·a·ble ['fraiəbl] friable.

fri·ar ['fraiər] fraile *m*; fray *in titles*; **'fri·ar·y** convento *m* de frailes.

fric·as·see [frikə'si:] fricasé *m*.

fric·tion ['frikʃn] rozamiento *m* (*a. fig.*), fricción *f*; *fig.* desavenencia *f*; ~ *tape* cinta *f* aislante; *attr.* = **'fric·tion·al** de rozamiento, de fricción.

Fri·day ['fraidi] viernes *m*; *Good* ♀ Viernes *m* Santo.

fridge [fridʒ] F = *refrigerator* nevera *f*, refrigerador *m*.

friend [frend] amigo (a *f*) *m*; ♀ cuákero (a *f*) *m*; ~*!* ¡gente de paz!; *be* ~*s with* ser amigo de; *make* ~*s with* trabar amistad con; **'friend·less** sin amigos; **'friend·li·ness** cordialidad *f*, amigabilidad *f*; **'friend·ly** amistoso; cordial, amigable; *place etc.* acogedor; *v. society*; **'friend·ship** amistad *f*.

frieze [fri:z] friso *m*.

frig·ate ['frigit] fragata *f*.

fright [frait] susto *m*, sobresalto *m*; terror *m*; (*p.*) espantajo *m*; **'fright·en** asustar, espantar, sobresaltar; ~ *away*, ~ *off* ahuyentar, espantar; *be* ~*ed of* tener miedo a; **fright·ful** ['~ful] □ espantoso, horrible, horroroso (*a. fig.*); F tremendo; **'fright·ful·ness** horror *m*; ⚔ terrorismo *m*.

frig·id ['fridʒid] □ frío; frígido; **fri'gid·i·ty** frialdad *f*; frigidez *f*.

frill [fril] lechuga *f*, volante *m*; ~*s pl. fig.* afectación *f*, adornos *m/pl.*

fringe [frindʒ] **1.** franja *f*; borde *m*; orla *f*; flequillo *m of hair*; ~ *benefits* beneficios *m/pl.* accesorios; **2.** orlar (*with* de) (*a. fig.*).

frip·per·y ['fripəri] perifollos *m/pl.*; cursilería *f*.

frisk [frisk] *v/i.* retozar, cabriolar, juguetear; *v/t. sl.* palpar, registrar, cachear; **'frisk·y** □ retozón, juguetón; *horse* fogoso.

frit·ter ['fritər] **1.** fruta *f* de sartén, buñuelo *m*; **2.:** ~ *away* desperdiciar, disipar.

fri·vol·i·ty [fri'vɔliti] frivolidad *f*; **friv·o·lous** ['frivələs] □ frívolo; trivial.

frizz [friz] pelo *m* de rizos muy apretados; **friz·zle** [ˈ~l] freír, asar; ˈ**frizzled,** ˈ**friz·zly** muy ensortijado.

fro [frou]: *to and* ~ de un lado a otro, de aquí para allá.

frock [frɔk] vestido *m*; ˈ~ ˈ**coat** levita *f*.

frog [frɔg] rana *f*; ~ *in the throat* carraspera *f*; ˈ~·**man** hombre-rana *m*.

frol·ic [ˈfrɔlik] **1.** juego *m* alegre; travesura *f*; **2.** retozar, juguetear; **frol·ic·some** [ˈ~səm] □ retozón, juguetón; (*mischievous*) travieso.

from [frɔm, frəm] de; desde; *message* de parte de; *date* a partir de; *price* desde ... en adelante; ~ *above* desde encima; ~ *among* de entre; ~ *afar* desde lejos; ~ *memory* de memoria; ~ *what he says* según lo que dice; *judging* ~ juzgando por; *take s.t.* ~ *s.o.* quitar algo a alguien.

frond [frɔnd] fronda *f*.

front [frʌnt] **1.** frente *m* (*a.* ⚔, *meteor.*, *pol.*); parte *f* delantera (*or* anterior); fachada *f of house*; principio *m of book*; pechera *f of shirt*; *fig.* apariencia *f* falsa; *in* ~ delante (*of* de); *come to the* ~ empezar a destacar; *put on a bold* ~ hacer de tripas corazón; **2.** delantero; anterior; primero; ~ *door* puerta *f* principal; ⚔ ~ *line* primera línea *f*; ~ *matter* preliminares *m/pl. de un libro*; ~ *porch* soportal *m*; ~ *room* cuarto *m* que da a la calle; ~ *row* primera fila *f*; ~ *seat* asiento *m* delantero; ~ *steps pl.* escalones *m/pl.* de acceso a la puerta de entrada; ~ *view* vista *f* de frente; ~ *wheel drive* tracción *f* a las ruedas delanteras; **3.**: ~ *on* (*to*) dar a; ˈ**frontage** fachada *f*; terreno *m* delante de una casa; ˈ**fron·tal** frontal; ⚔ de frente; **fron·tier** [~ˈtir] **1.** frontera *f*; **2.** fronterizo; **fron·tis·piece** [ˈ~ispi:s] △ fachada *f*; △ frontispicio *m*; *typ.* portada *f*; ˈ**front-page** de primera página; *fig.* muy importante; ˈ**front** ˈ**page** primera plana *f*.

frost [frɔst] **1.** helada *f*; escarcha *f* (*a. hoar* ~, *white* ~); *sl.* fracaso *m*; **2.** cubrir de escarcha; *plant* quemar; ~*ed glass* vidrio *m* deslustrado; ˈ~·**bite** congelación *f*; ˈ**frost-bitten** congelado, helado; ˈ**frost·y** □ helado; escarchado; *fig.* glacial.

froth [frɔθ] **1.** espuma *f*; *fig.* bachillerías *f/pl.*; **2.** espumar; ~ *at the mouth* espumajear; ˈ**froth·y** □ espumoso; *fig.* frívolo.

frown [fraun] **1.** ceño *m*; entrecejo *m*; **2.** fruncir el entrecejo; ~ *at* mirar con ceño; ~ *on* desaprobar.

frow·sy, frow·zy [ˈfrauzi] desaliñado; maloliente.

froze [frouz] *pret. of freeze* 1; ˈ**froz·en** *p.p. of freeze* 1 *a. adj.*; ~ *foods* alimentos *m/pl.* congelados.

fruc·ti·fy [ˈfrʌktifai] *v/t.* fecundar; *v/i.* fructificar.

fru·gal [ˈfru:gəl] □ frugal; **fru·gal·i·ty** [fruˈgæliti] frugalidad *f*.

fruit [fru:t] **1.** fruto *m* (*a. fig.*); fruta *f*; ~ *cake* torta *f* de frutas; ~ *cup* compota *f* de frutas picadas; ~ *fly* mosca *f* del vinagre; mosca de las frutas; ~ *jar* tarro *m* para frutas; ~ *juice* jugo *m* de frutas; ~ *of the vine* zumo *m* de cepas o de parras; ~ *salad* ensalada *f* de frutas, macedonia *f* de frutas; ~ *salts* sal *f* de fruta; ~ *stand* puesto *m* de frutas; ~ *store* frutería *f*; ~ *tree* árbol *m* frutal; **2.** dar fruto, frutar; ˈ**fruiter·er** frutero *m*; ~'s frutería *f*; **fruitful** [ˈ~ful] □ fructífero; *fig.* fructuoso, provechoso; **fru·i·tion** [fruˈiʃn] cumplimiento *m*; fruición *f*; *come to* ~ verse logrado; ˈ**fruit·less** □ infructuoso; ˈ**fruit·y** con sabor de fruta; F verde.

frump [frʌmp] espantajo *m*, mujer *f* descuidada en el vestir; ˈ**frump·ish** desaliñado.

frus·trate [frʌsˈtreit] frustrar; *plot* desbaratar; **frusˈtra·tion** frustración *f*; desazón *f*.

fry [frai] **1.** fritada *f*; **2.** *ichth.* pececillos *m/pl.*; F *small* ~ gente *f* menuda; **3.** freír(se); *fried fish* pescado *m* frito; ˈ**fry·ing pan** sartén *f*.

fuch·sia [ˈfju:ʃə] fucsia *f*.

fud·dled [ˈfʌdld] borracho; aturdido.

fudge [fʌdʒ] **1.** hacer de modo chapucero; **2.** *dulce de leche, azúcar, etc.*

fu·el [ˈfjuəl] **1.** combustible *m*; carburante *m*; *fig.* pábulo *m*; ~ *cell* cámara *f* de combustible, célula *f* electrógena; ~ *oil* petróleo *m* combustible, aceite *m* combustible; ~ *tank* depósito *m* de combustible; **2.** aprovisionar(se) de combustible.

fug [fʌg] *mst British* aire *m* viciado (*or* confinado, cargado).

fu·gi·tive [ˈfju:dʒitiv] **1.** fugitivo; fugaz; de interés pasajero; **2.** fugitivo (a *f*) *m*, evadido *m*.

fugue [fju:g] fuga *f*.
ful·crum ['fʌlkrəm] fulcro *m*.
ful·fil [ful'fil] cumplir; realizar; *condition etc.* llenar; *orders* ejecutar; **ful·'fil·ment** cumplimiento *m*; realización *f*; ejecución *f*.
full[1] [ful] **1.** (*adv. fully*) *mst* lleno; *fig.* pleno; (*complete*) cabal, íntegro; *account* extenso; *bus* completo; *dress* (*formal*) de etiqueta; *meal* abundante; *member* de número; *session* plen(ari)o; *skirt* amplio; F ~ *up bus* completo; harto *with food*; *beat by a ~ minute* aventajar en un minuto largo; *a ~ hour* una hora entera; ~ *moon* luna *f* llena, plenilunio *m*; ~ *powers* plenos poderes *m/pl.*; *at ~ speed* a máxima velocidad, a toda máquina; ~ *stop* punto *m*; *fig.* parada *f* completa; *in ~ view* totalmente visible; **2.** *adv.* de lleno; ~ *well* muy bien, sobradamente; **3.**: *in ~* sin abreviar, por extenso; *pay in ~* pagar la deuda entera; *to the ~* completamente, al máximum.
full[2] [~] ⊕ abatanar.
full...: '**~-'blast** a máxima velocidad (*or* capacidad); en plena actividad; '**~-'blood·ed** vigoroso; de raza; '**~-'blown** hecho y derecho, desarrollado; ♀ abierto; '**~-'bod·ied** fuerte; *wine* generoso; '**~-'dress** de etiqueta, de gala.
full·er ['fulər] ⊕ batanero *m*; *~'s earth* tierra *f* de batán.
full...: '**~-'fash·ioned** de costura francesa; '**~-'fledged** *fig.* hecho y derecho; '**~-grown** crecido; '**~-'length** de cuerpo entero; ~ *film* (cinta *f* de) largo metraje *m*.
ful(l)·ness ['fulnis] plenitud *f*; *in the ~ of time* a su debido tiempo.
full time ['fultaim] jornada *f* completa, jornada de costumbre, jornada ordinaria; '**full-time** a tiempo completo, en plena dedicación.
ful·mi·nate ['fʌlmineit] **1.** *v/t.* fulminar; *fulminating powder* pólvora *f* fulminante; *v/i.* ~ *against* tronar contra; **2.** ⚗ fulminato *m*; **ful·mi'na·tion** fulminación *f*.
ful·some ['fulsəm] □ exagerado; repugnante; servil.
fum·ble ['fʌmbl] *v/t.* manosear, revolver *etc.* torpemente; *ball* dejar caer; ~ *one's way* ir a tientas; *v/i.* ~ *for* buscar con las manos; ~ *with* tocar (*or* manejar *etc.*) torpemente; tratar torpemente de abrir *etc.*
fume [fju:m] **1.**: *~s pl.* humo *m*, gas *m*, vapor *m*; **2.** humear; (*p.*) enfadarse; echar pestes (*at th.* contra, *p.* de).
fu·mi·gate ['fju:migeit] fumigar; **fu·mi'ga·tion** fumigación *f*.
fun [fʌn] diversión *f*; alegría *f*; *be* (*good, great*) ~ ser (muy) divertido; *for ~, in ~* en broma; *have ~* divertirse; *make ~ of* burlarse de, hacer chacota de.
func·tion ['fʌŋkʃn] **1.** función *f*; acto *m*, ceremonia *f*; cargo *m*; **2.** funcionar; '**func·tion·al** □ funcional; '**func·tion·ar·y** funcionario *m*.
fund [fʌnd] **1.** fondo *m* (*a. fig.*); *~s pl.* fondos *m/pl.*; *be in ~s* estar en fondos; **2.** *debt* consolidar.
fun·da·men·tal [fʌndə'mentl] □ fundamental; **fun·da'men·tals** [~z] *pl.* fundamentos *m/pl.*
fu·ner·al ['fju:nərəl] **1.** entierro *m*, funerales *m/pl.*; ~ *director* director *m* de funeraria; **2.** funeral, fúnebre; **fu·ne·re·al** [~'niriəl] □ fúnebre, funéreo.
fun·fair ['fʌnfer] *British* parque *m* de atracciones.
fun·gous ['fʌŋgəs] fungoso; **fun·gus** ['fʌŋgəs], *pl.* **fun·gi** ['~gai] hongo *m*.
fu·nic·u·lar [fju'nikjulər] (ferrocarril *m*) funicular.
funk [fʌŋk] F **1.** canguelo *m*, jindama *f*; (*p.*) gallina *m/f*, mandria *m/f*; *in a ~* aterrado; **2.** retraerse por miedo de; '**funk·y** F cobarde, miedoso.
fun·nel ['fʌnl] **1.** embudo *m*; ⚓, 🚂 chimenea *f*; (*tube for ventilation*) manguera *f*, ventilador *m* (*tubo de ventilación*); **2.** verter por medio de un embudo; *fig.* verter.
fun·ny ['fʌni] □ cómico, gracioso, divertido; chistoso; (*strange*) raro, curioso; *the ~ thing about it is* (*that*) lo gracioso del caso es (que); *find it ~ that, strike s.o. as ~ that* hacerle a uno mucha gracia que; '**~ bone** F hueso *m* de la alegría.
fur [fə:r] **1.** piel *f*; pelo *m*; saburra *f on tongue*; sarro *m in kettle etc.*; **2.** de piel(es); ~ *coat* abrigo *m* de pieles; **3.** guarnecer *etc.* con pieles; depositar sarro en.
fur·bish ['fə:rbiʃ] pulir; ~ *up* renovar, restaurar.

fu·ri·ous [ˈfjuriəs] □ furioso; frenético; violento.
furl [fəːrl] ⚓ aferrar; arrollar.
fur·long [ˈfəːrlɔŋ] estadio *m*.
fur·lough [ˈfəːrlou] **1.** licencia *f*; **2.** dar licencia a.
fur·nace [fəːrnis] horno *m*; lugar *m* de mucho calor.
fur·nish [ˈfəːrniʃ] suministrar, proporcionar (*with acc.*); equipar (*with* con); *proof* aducir; *room* amueblar (*with* de); ˈ**fur·nish·ings** *pl.*, **fur·ni·ture** [ˈfəːrnitʃər] muebles *m/pl.*, mueblaje *m*, mobiliario *m*; ~ *dealer* mueblista *m/f*; ~ *store* mueblería *f*; *piece of* ~ mueble *m*.
fur·ri·er [ˈfəːriər] peletero *m*.
fur·row [ˈfəːrou] **1.** surco *m*; **2.** surcar.
fur·ry [ˈfəːri] peludo.
fur·ther [ˈfəːrðər] **1.** *adj.* más lejano; nuevo, adicional; *till* ~ *orders* hasta nueva orden; **2.** *adv.* más lejos, más allá (*a.* ~ *on*); además; **3.** promover, fomentar; adelantar; ˈ**fur·ther·ance** promoción *f*, fomento *m*; adelantamiento *m*; ˈ**fur·ther**ˈ**more** además; ˈ**fur·ther·most** más lejano.
fur·thest [ˈfəːrðist] **1.** *adj.* más lejano; extremo; **2.** *adv.* (lo) más lejos.
fur·tive [ˈfəːrtiv] □ furtivo.
fu·ry [ˈfjuri] furor *m*, furia *f*; frenesí *m*; *like* ~ a toda furia.
furze [fəːrz] aulaga *f*, tojo *m*.
fuse [fjuːz] **1.** fundir(se) (*a.* ⚡); fusionar(se); *the lights* ~*d* se fundieron los plomos; **2.** ⚡ plomo *m*, fusible *m*, tapón *m*, cortacircuitos *m*; ⚔ espoleta *f*, mecha *f*; ~ *box* caja *f* de fusibles.
fu·se·lage [ˈfjuːzilɑːʒ] fuselaje *m*.
fu·si·ble [ˈfjuːzəbl] fusible, fundible.
fu·sil·ier [fjuːziˈlir] fusilero *m*.
fu·sil·lade [ˈfjuːzileid] descarga *f* cerrada; *fig.* torrente *m*.
fu·sion [ˈfjuːʒn] fusión *f* (*a. fig.*), fundición *f*.
fuss [fʌs] **1.** (*noisy*) bulla *f*, alharaca *f*; (*excessive display*) aspaviento *m*, hazañería *f*; (*trouble*) lío *m*; (*formalities*) ceremonia *f*; *kick up a* ~, *make a great* ~ dar cuatro voces, hacer una algarada; armar un lío; *make a* ~ *of* hacer mimos a; *there's no need to make such a* ~ no es para tanto; **2.** agitarse, inquietarse (por pequeñeces); ˈ**fuss·y** □ F exigente; remilgado.
fus·tian [ˈfʌstiən] fustán *m*, pana *f*.
fust·y [ˈfʌsti] □ mohoso, rancio; que huele a cerrado.
fu·tile [ˈfjuːtl] □ inútil, vano, infructuoso; frívolo; **fu·til·i·ty** [fjuˈtiliti] inutilidad *f*, lo inútil; frivolidad *f*.
fu·ture [ˈfjuːtʃər] **1.** futuro; **2.** porvenir *m*, futuro *m*; ✝ ~*s pl.* futuros *m/pl.*; *in* (*the*) ~ en el futuro, en lo sucesivo; *in the near* ~ en fecha próxima; ˈ**fu·tur·ism** futurismo *m*; **fu·tu·ri·ty** [fjuˈtjuriti] estado *m* futuro.
fuzz [fʌz] tamo *m*, pelusa *f*; *the* ~ *sl.* policía *m*, guardia *m* urbano; ˈ**fuzz·y** □ borroso; *hair* muy ensortijado.

G

gab [gæb] F locuacidad *f*; cháchara *f*; *have the gift of (the)* ~ tener mucha labia, ser un pico de oro.
gab·ar·dine ['gæbərdi:n] gabardina *f*.
gab·ble ['gæbl] **1.** algarabía *f*; cotorreo *m*; **2.** *v/t.* farfullar, decir atropelladamente; *v/i.* farfullar; cotorrear.
gab·er·dine ['gæbərdi:n] gabardina *f*.
ga·ble ['geibl] aguilón *m*; '~ **end** hastial *m*; '~ **roof** tejado *m* de dos aguas.
gad [gæd] (*mst* ~ *about*) andar de aquí para allá; corretear; viajar mucho; '**gad·a·bout** F corretero (a *f*) *m*, persona *f* andariega.
gad·fly ['gædflai] tábano *m*.
gadg·et ['gædʒit] F artilugio *m*, chisme *m*.
Gael·ic ['geilik] gaélico *adj. a. su. m.*
gaff [gæf] arpón *m*, garfio *m*; ⚓ cangrejo *m*; *sl.* teatrucho *m*; *sl. blow the* ~ descubrir el pastel, levantar la liebre.
gaffe [gæf] F plancha *f*.
gaf·fer ['gæfər] vejete *m*; tío *m*; (*foreman*) capataz *m*; (*boss*) jefe *m*.
gag [gæg] **1.** mordaza *f* (*a. fig.*); *thea.* morcilla *f*; *parl.* clausura *f*; F chiste *m*, morcilla *f*; *thea. use* ~*s* meter morcillas; *sl.* timo *m*; **2.** *v/t.* amordazar (*a. fig.*), dar bascas a; *v/i.* sentir bascas, arquear.
gai·e·ty ['geiəti] alegría *f*, regocijo *m*; diversión *f* alegre.
gai·ly ['geili] alegremente.
gain [gein] **1.** ganancia *f*; aumento *m*; provecho *m*; ⚡ amplificación *f*; **2.** *v/t.* ganar; conseguir; (*clock*) adelantarse; *v/i.* crecer, medrar; ganar terreno; ~ *on* ir alcanzando; '**gain·er**: *be the* ~ salir ganando; **gain·ful** ['~ful] □ ganancioso; ~ *employment* trabajo *m* remunerado; **gain·ings** ['~iŋz] *pl.* ganancias *f/pl.*
gain·say [gein'sei] *lit.* contradecir, negar.
gait [geit] paso *m*, andar *m*.
gai·ter ['geitər] polaina *f*.
gal [gæl] *sl.* chica *f*.
ga·la ['geilə] fiesta *f*; ~ *dress* vestido *m* de gala.
gal·ax·y ['gæləksi] *ast.* galaxia *f*; *fi* constelación *f*, pléyade *f*.
gale [geil] ventarrón *m*; (*esp. sout erly*) vendaval *m*; *poet.* brisa *f*.
gall[1] [gɔ:l] bilis *f*, hiel *f* (*a. fig.*); vejiga *f* de la bilis; *fig.* rencor *m*; *sl.* descaro *m*; ~ *bladder* vejiga *f* de la bilis, vesícula *f* biliar.
gall[2] [~] ♀ agalla *f*.
gall[3] [~] **1.** *vet.* matadura *f*; **2.** lastimar rozando; *fig.* irritar, mortificar.
gal·lant ['gælənt] **1.** □ (*brave*) gallardo, valiente; lucido; **2.** [*mst* gə'lænt] □ galante; **3.** [~] galán *m*; '**gal·lant·ry** gallardía *f*, valor *m*, bizarría *f*; galantería *f*, galanteo *m*.
gal·leon ['gæljən] galeón *m*.
gal·ler·y ['gæləri] galería *f* (*a.* ⚒, *thea.*); *art* ~ museo *m* de arte; *play to the* ~ actuar para la galería.
gal·ley ['gæli] ⚓ *a. typ.* galera *f*; ⚓ cocina *f*, fogón *m*; '~ **proof** galerada *f*; '~ **slave** galeote *m*.
Gal·lic ['gælik] galo; **Gal·li·can** ['~kən] galicano.
gal·li·vant ['gælivænt] F callejear; andar de visitas; viajar mucho; pindonguear.
gal·lon ['gælən] galón *m* (= *American 3,785 litros, British 4,546 litros*).
gal·lop ['gæləp] **1.** galope *m*; galopada *f*; *at full* ~ a galope tendido, a uña de caballo; **2.** galopar; '**gal·lop·ing** ⚕ galopante.
gal·lows ['gælouz] *sg.* horca *f*; '~ **bird** carne *f* de horca.
ga·lore [gə'lɔ:r] a porrilla, en abundancia.
ga·losh [gə'lɔʃ] chanclo *m*.
gal·van·ic [gæl'vænik] □ galvánico; **gal·va·nism** ['gælvənizm] galvanismo *m*; '**gal·va·nize** galvanizar; ~*d iron* hierro *m* galvanizado; **gal·va·no·plas·tic** [gælvənou'plæstik] galvanoplástico. [táctica *f*.]
gam·bit ['gæmbit] gambito *m*; *fig.*

gam·ble [ˈgæmbl] **1.** jugar; **2.** jugada *f*; empresa *f* arriesgada; ˈ**gam·bler** jugador (-a *f*) *m*, tahur *m*.
gam·bling [ˈgæmbliŋ] juego *m*; ˈ~ **den,** ˈ~ **house** garito *m*, casa *f* de juego.
gam·bol [ˈgæmbl] **1.** brinco *m*; retozo *m*; **2.** brincar, retozar, juguetear.
game [geim] **1.** juego *m* (*a.* F); partida *f*; (*match*) partido *m*; deporte *m*; *bridge*: manga *f*; *hunt.* caza *f*; *big* ~ caza *f* mayor; ~ *of chance* juego *m* de azar, juego de suerte; ~ *preserve* reserva *f* de caza; F *the* ~ *is up* ya se acabó; *play the* ~ *fig.* jugar limpio; **2.** F animoso, valiente; *leg* cojo; *be* ~ *for anything* atreverse a todo; **3.** jugar (por dinero); ˈ~ **bag** morral *m*; ˈ~ **cock** gallo *m* de pelea; ˈ~·**keep·er,** ˈ~ **war·den** guardabosques *m*; ˈ~ **li·cense** licencia *f* de caza; **game·ster** [ˈ~stər] jugador (-a *f*) *m*, tahur *m*; ˈ**gam·ing** juego *m*.
gam·ma [ˈgæmə] gama *f*; ˈ~ **rays** *pl.* rayos *m*/*pl.* gama.
gam·mer [ˈgæmər] abuelita *f*, vieja *f*.
gam·mon [ˈgæmən] **1.** a) jamón *m*; b) curar (jamón); **2.** a) lance *m* del juego del chaquete; engaño *m*; b) ganar doble partida al chaquete; engañar.
gamp [gæmp] F paraguas *m*.
gam·ut [ˈgæmət] gama *f*.
gam·y [ˈgeimi] manido, salvajino.
gan·der [ˈgændər] ganso *m* (macho).
gang [gæŋ] **1.** cuadrilla *f*; pandilla *f*; brigada *f of workers*; juego *m of tools*; **2.** *Scot.* ir; ~ *up* conspirar, obrar de concierto (*against, on* contra); **3.** ⊕ múltiple; **gang·er** [ˈgæŋər] capataz *m*; ˈ**gang·plank** ⚓ plancha *f*, pasarela *f*.
gan·gli·on [ˈgæŋgliən] ganglio *m*.
gan·grene [ˈgæŋgriːn] gangrena *f*.
gang·ster [ˈgæŋstər] pistolero *m*, atracador *m*, gángster *m*, pandillero *m*.
gang·way [ˈgæŋwei] paso *m*, pasadizo *m*, pasillo *m*; ⚓ plancha *f*, pasadera *f*; ⚓ (*opening*) portalón *m*; ⚓ pasamano *m*; ~! ¡abran paso!
gan·try [ˈgæntri] caballete *m*; ~ *crane* grúa *f* de caballete.
gaol [dʒeil] *British* = *jail*.
gap [gæp] portillo *m*, abertura *f*; brecha *f*, boquete *m*; quebrada *f in mountains*; vacío *m*, hueco *m*, claro *m*, laguna *f*.
gape [geip] **1.** bostezo *m*; abertura *f*, hendedura *f*; **2.** bostezar; embobarse, estar boquiabierto; ~ *at* mirar boquiabierto, embobarse de (*or* con, en).
ga·rage [gəˈrɑːʒ] **1.** garaje *m*; **2.** dejar en garaje.
garb [gɑːrb] **1.** traje *m*, vestido *m*; ropaje *m* (*a. fig.*); **2.** vestir.
gar·bage [ˈgɑːrbidʒ] basura *f*, bazofia *f*, desperdicios *m*/*pl.*; ~ *can* cubo *m* de basuras; ~ *collection* recogida *f* de basuras; ~ *disposal* evacuación *f* de basuras.
gar·ble [ˈgɑːrbl] mutilar; falsear (por selección).
gar·den [ˈgɑːrdn] **1.** jardín *m*; (*fruit a. vegetables*) huerto *m*; ~ *party* fiesta *f* que se da en un jardín o parque; **2.** cultivar un huerto (*or* jardín); trabajar en el huerto (*or* jardín); ˈ**gar·den·er** jardinero (a *f*) *m*; hortelano (a *f*) *m*; ˈ**gar·den·ing** jardinería *f*; horticultura *f*.
gar·gle [ˈgɑːrgl] **1.** gargarizar, hacer gárgaras; **2.** gargarismo *m*.
gar·goyle [ˈgɑːrgɔil] gárgola *f*.
gar·ish [ˈgeriʃ] □ chillón, llamativo.
gar·land [ˈgɑːrlənd] **1.** guirnalda *f*; **2.** enguirnaldar.
gar·lic [ˈgɑːrlik] ajo *m*.
gar·ment [ˈgɑːrmənt] prenda *f* (de vestir).
gar·ner [ˈgɑːrnər] almacenar.
gar·net [ˈgɑːrnit] granate *m*.
gar·nish [ˈgɑːrniʃ] adornar, guarnecer; aderezar (*a. cooking*); ˈ**gar·nish·ing** adorno *m*.
gar·ni·ture [ˈgɑːrnitʃər] adorno *m*, guarnición *f*.
gar·ret [ˈgærit] guardilla *f*, desván *m*.
gar·ri·son [ˈgærisn] **1.** guarnición *f*; **2.** guarnecer, guarnicionar; poner en guarnición.
gar·ru·li·ty [gæˈruːliti] garrulidad *f*;
gar·ru·lous [ˈgærulǝs] □ gárrulo.
gar·ter [ˈgɑːrtər] liga *f*; ~ *belt* portaligas *m*; *Order of the* ♀ orden *f* de la Jarretera.
gas [gæs] **1.** *pl.* **gas·es** [ˈ~iz] gas *m*; F parloteo *m*; = *gasoline*; ~ *heat* calefacción *f* por gas; ~*holder* gasómetro *m*; ~ *jet* mechero *m* de gas; llama *f* de gas; *mot.* *step on the* ~ acelerar la marcha; **2.** asfixiar con gas; F parlotear; ˈ~ **bag** ✈ cámara *f* de gas; F charlatán (-a *f*) *m*; ˈ~ **brack·et** brazo *m* de lámpara de gas; ˈ~ **burn·er**

mechero *m* de gas; ˈ~ ˈ**cook·er** cocina *f* de (*or* a) gas; ˈ~ **en·gine** motor *m* a gas; **gas·e·ous** [ˈgæsiəs] gaseoso; ˈ**gas fire** estufa *f* de gas; ˈ**gas fit·ter** gasista *m*; ˈ**gas fit·tings** *pl.* instalación *f* del gas; guarniciones *f/pl.* del gas; ˈ~ ˈ**gen·er·a·tor** gasógeno *m*.

gash [gæʃ] **1.** cuchillada *f*, chirlo *m*; raja *f*, hendedura *f*; **2.** acuchillar, herir.

gas·i·fy [ˈgæsifai] *v/t.* gasificar; *v/i.* gasificarse.

gas·ket [ˈgæskit] ⚓ tomador *m*; ⊕ empaquetadura *f*.

gas...: ˈ~ **light** luz *f* de gas, alumbrado *m* de gas; ˈ~ **main**(**s**) cañería *f* (maestra) de gas; ˈ~ **man·tle** manguito *m* incandescente; ˈ~ **mask** careta *f* antigás; ˈ~ **me·ter** contador *m* de gas; **gas·o·hol** [ˈgæsəhɔ:l] alconafta *f*; **gas·o·line** [ˈgæsəli:n] *mot.* gasolina *f*; ~ *pump* poste *m* distribuidor de gasolina, surtidor *m* de gasolina; **gas·o·m·e·ter** [gæˈsɔmitər] gasómetro *m*; ˈ**gas ov·en** cocina *f* de (*or* a) gas.

gasp [gæsp] **1.** (*esp. last* ~) boqueada *f*; grito *m* entrecortado; **2.** boquear; ~ *for breath* jadear; *fig.* ~ *for* anhelar.

gas pro·duc·er [ˈgæs prəˈdu:sər] gasógeno *m*; **gas-proof** [ˈgæsˈpru:f] a prueba de gas; ˈ**gas pump** surtidor *m* de gasolina, poste *m* distribuidor de gasolina; ˈ**gas range** cocina *f* de (*or* a) gas; ˈ**gas ring** hornillo *m* de gas; ˈ**gas sta·tion** estación *f* gasolinera, estación de gasolina; ˈ**gas stove** cocina *f* de (*or* a) gas; ˈ**gas·sy** gaseoso; *fig.* hinchado; ˈ**gas tank** gasómetro *m*; *mot.* depósito *m* de gasolina.

gas·tric [ˈgæstrik] gástrico; **gas·tri·tis** [gæsˈtraitis] gastritis *f*.

gas·tron·o·mist [gæsˈtrɔnəmist] gastrónomo (a *f*) *m*; **gas**ˈ**tron·o·my** gastronomía *f*.

gas works [ˈgæswə:rks] fábrica *f* de gas.

gat [gæt] *sl.* arma *f* de fuego, revólver *m*.

gate [geit] puerta *f*; verja *f of iron*; portal *m of town*; (*wicket*) portillo *m*; (*level crossing*) barrera *f*; *sport*: entrada *f*; ˈ~ **crash·er** *sl.* intruso (a *f*) *m*; ˈ~**-leg**(**·ged**) **ta·ble** mesa *f* de alas abatibles; ˈ~ **mon·ey** *sport*: ingresos *m/pl.* de entrada; ˈ~**·way** portal *m*; entrada *f*.

gath·er [ˈgæðər] **1.** *v/t.* recoger, reunir; acumular; *wood, flowers* coger; *crops* cosechar; *sew.* fruncir; *fig.* colegir, inferir, sacar la consecuencia (*that* que); *I* ~ *from A. that* ... según lo que me ha dicho A. ...; ~ *dust* empolvarse; ~ *speed* ir cada vez más rápidamente; ~ *strength* cobrar fuerzas; ~ *in* recoger; *money* recaudar; ~ *together* reunir, juntar; ~ *up* recoger; *v/i.* reunirse, juntarse, congregarse (*a.* ~ *together*); acumularse; condensarse; (*clouds*) amontonarse; ⚕ formar pus; **2.** (*mst* ~*s pl.*) frunce *m*; ˈ**gath·er·ing** reunión *f*, asamblea *f*; muchedumbre *f*; acumulación *f*; recolección *f*; ⚕ absceso *m*.

gaud·y [ˈgɔ:di] □ chillón, llamativo, vistoso.

gauge [geidʒ] **1.** (norma *f* de) medida *f*; calibre *m*; indicador *m*; manómetro *m*; ⊕ calibrador *m*; *carpentry*: gramil *m*; 🚂 entrevía *f*, ancho *m*; **2.** medir; calibrar; aforar; *fig.* estimar.

Gaul [gɔ:l] galo (a *f*) *m*.

gaunt [gɔ:nt] □ flaco, desvaído, macilento; sombrío.

gaunt·let [ˈgɔ:ntlit] guantelete *m*; guante *m*; *run the* ~ correr baquetas; *take up the* ~ recoger el guante; *throw down the* ~ arrojar el guante.

gauze [gɔ:z] gasa *f*; ˈ**gauz·y** diáfano.

gave [geiv] *pret. of* give.

gav·el [ˈgævl] martillo *m de los presidentes y subastadores*.

gawk [gɔ:k] F **1.** zote *m*, bobo *m*; **2.** papar moscas; ˈ**gawk·y** torpe, desgarbado.

gay [gei] **1.** *adj. a. su.* homosexual *m/f*; **2.** □ † alegre, festivo; (*brilliant*) vistoso; (*pleasure-loving*) amigo *m* de los placeres.

gaze [geiz] **1.** mirada *f* fija; contemplación *f*; **2.** *a.* ~ *at*, ~ *on* mirar con fijeza, contemplar.

ga·zelle [gəˈzel] gacela *f*.

ga·zette [gəˈzet] **1.** gaceta *f*; **2.** publicar en la gaceta oficial; **gaz·et·teer** [gæziˈtir] diccionario *m* geográfico.

gear [gir] **1.** aparejo *m*, pertrechos *m/pl.*, herramientas *f/pl.*; F cosas *f/pl.*, chismes *m/pl.*; (*attire*) atavío *m*; (*harness*) arreos *m/pl.*, arneses *m/pl.*; ⊕ aparato *m*, mecanismo *m*; ⊕ engranaje *m*, rueda *f* dentada; *mot.* marcha *f* (*low, bottom* primera, *second* segunda, *top* tercera *or* cuarta), velocidad *f*; *in* ~ en juego; *put into* ~ engranar; *throw out of* ~ desengranar; *fig.* desconcertar; **2.** aparejar; ⊕ engranar; ~ *up* multiplicar; ~ *down* desmultiplicar; ~ (*in*)*to* engranar con; ˈ~ **box,** ˈ~ **case** caja *f* de velocidades (*or* de engranajes); ˈ**gear·ing** engranaje *m*; ˈ**gear le·ver,** ˈ**gear·shift** (palanca *f* de) cambio *m* de marchas.

gee [dʒiː] ¡arre!; ¡caramba!

geese [giːs] *pl. of goose.*

gee·zer [ˈgiːzər] *sl.* vejancón *m*, tío *m*.

gel·a·tin(**e**) [ˈdʒelətin] gelatina *f*; **ge·lat·i·nize** [dʒiˈlætinaiz] gelatinizar(se); **geˈlat·i·nous** gelatinoso.

geld [geld] [*irr.*] castrar; ˈ**geld·ing** caballo *m* castrado.

gel·id [ˈdʒelid] gélido, helado.

gel·ig·nite [ˈdʒelignait] gelatina *f* explosiva.

gem [dʒem] gema *f*, piedra *f* preciosa; *fig.* joya *f*, preciosidad *f*.

gen·der [ˈdʒendər] género *m*.

gene [dʒiːn] *biol.* gen *m*.

gen·e·a·log·i·cal [dʒiːniəˈlɔdʒikl] □ genealógico; **gen·e·al·o·gy** [dʒiːniˈælədʒi] genealogía *f*.

gen·er·a [ˈdʒenərə] *v. genus.*

gen·er·al [ˈdʒenərəl] **1.** □ general; ~ *delivery* lista *f* de correos; ~ *practitioner* médico *m* general; *become* ~ generalizarse; *in* ~, *as a* ~ *rule* en general, por lo general, por regla general; ~ *election* elecciones *f*/*pl.* generales; **2.** ⚔ general *m*; F (= ~ *servant*) criada *f* para todo; **gen·er·alˈis·si·mo** generalísimo *m*; **gen·er·al·i·ty** [~ˈræliti] generalidad *f*; **gen·er·al·i·za·tion** [~rəlaiˈzeiʃn] generalización *f*; ˈ**gen·er·al·ize** generalizar; ˈ**gen·er·al·ly** generalmente, en general, por lo común; ˈ**gen·er·al·ship** generalato *m*; estrategia *f*; dirección *f*, don *m* de mando.

gen·er·ate [ˈdʒenəreit] engendrar (*a.* 🙰), generar (*a.* ⚡); *generating station* central *f* (generadora); **genˈer·a·tion** generación *f*; ˈ**gen·er·a·tive** generativo; ˈ**gen·er·a·tor** generador *m* (*a.* ⚡, ⊕).

ge·ner·ic [dʒiˈnerik] genérico.

gen·er·os·i·ty [dʒenəˈrɔsiti] generosidad *f*; ˈ**gen·er·ous** □ generoso; dadivoso; amplio, abundante.

gen·e·sis [ˈdʒenisis] génesis *f*; *Bible*: ♀ Génesis *m*.

ge·net·ic [dʒiˈnetik] □ genético, genésico; **geˈnet·ics** genética *f*.

gen·ial [ˈdʒiːnjəl] □ afable, complaciente, cordial; suave; **ge·ni·al·i·ty** [~niˈæliti] afabilidad *f*, cordialidad *f*.

gen·i·tal [ˈdʒenitl] genital; ~*s pl.* órganos *m*/*pl.* genitales.

gen·i·tive [ˈdʒenitiv] genitivo *m* (*a.* ~ *case*).

gen·ius [ˈdʒiːnjəs], *pl.* **gen·i·i** [ˈ~niai] (*deidad, espíritu tutelar*) genio *m*; *pl.* **gen·i·us·es** [ˈ~njəsiz] (*facultad, persona*) genio *m*.

gen·o·cide [ˈdʒenəsaid] (*act*) genocidio *m*; (*p.*) genocida *m*/*f*.

Gen·o·ese [dʒenouˈiːz] genovés *adj. a. su. m* (-a *f*).

gent [dʒent] F = *gentleman.*

gen·teel [dʒenˈtiːl] □ *mst iro.* fino, cortés, elegante, de buen tono; afectado, cursi; **genˈteel·ism** locución *f* afectada (*or* cursi).

gen·tian [ˈdʒenʃiən] genciana *f*.

gen·tile [ˈdʒentail] no judío *adj. a. su. m* (a *f*); (*pagan*) gentil *adj. a. su. m*/*f*.

gen·til·i·ty [dʒenˈtiliti] *mst iro.* fineza *f*, buen tono *m*; cursilería *f*; † nobleza *f*.

gen·tle [ˈdʒentl] □ suave, dulce; benigno; sosegado; *esp. animals* manso, dócil; moderado; ligero; lento, pausado; bien nacido; † caballeroso; ~ *sex* † bello sexo *m*, sexo débil; ˈ**~·folk** gente *f* bien nacida; ˈ**~·man** caballero *m*, señor *m*; (*at court*) gentilhombre *m*; *he is no* ~ es un mal caballero; ~*'s agreement* acuerdo *m* verbal; ˈ**~·man·ly** caballeroso; ˈ**gen·tle·ness** suavidad *f*, dulzura *f*; mansedumbre *f*; ˈ**gen·tle·wom·an** dama *f*, señora *f*; ˈ**gen·tly** suavemente; poco a poco, despacio; ~! ¡paso!

gen·try [ˈdʒentri] gente *f* bien nacida; alta burguesía *f*; pequeña aristocracia *f*; *contp.* gentuza *f*.

gen·u·flec·tion, gen·u·flex·ion [dʒenjuˈflekʃn] genuflexión *f*.

gen·u·ine [ˈdʒenjuin] □ auténtico, legítimo, genuino; sincero; ˈ**gen·u·ine·ness** autenticidad *f*, legitimidad *f*; sinceridad *f*.

ge·nus [ˈdʒiːnəs], *pl.* **gen·er·a** [ˈdʒenərə] género *m*.

ge·od·e·sy [dʒiˈɔdisi] geodesia *f*.

ge·og·ra·pher [dʒiˈɔgrəfər] geógrafo

m; **ge·o·graph·i·cal** [~ə'græfikl] □ geográfico; **ge·og·ra·phy** [~'ɔgrəfi] geografía *f*.

ge·o·log·ic, ge·o·log·i·cal [dʒiə'lɔdʒik(l)] □ geológico; **ge·ol·o·gist** [dʒi'ɔlədʒist] geólogo *m*.

ge·o·met·ric, ge·o·met·ri·cal [dʒiə'metrik(l)] □ geométrico; **ge·om·e·try** [~'ɔmitri] geometría *f*.

ge·o·phys·ics [dʒiou'fiziks] geofísica *f*.

ge·o·pol·i·tics [dʒiou'pɔlitiks] geopolítica *f*.

ge·ra·ni·um [dʒi'reinjəm] geranio *m*.

ger·i·a·trics [dʒeri'ætriks] geriatría *f*.

germ [dʒəːrm] *biol., fig. a.* ⚘ germen *m*; ⚘ microbio *m*; ~ *cell* célula *f* germen; ~ *warfare* guerra *f* bacteriológica, guerra bacteriana.

Ger·man[1] ['dʒəːrmən] **1.** alemán *adj. a. su. m* (-a *f*); ⚘ ~ *measles* rubéola *f*; ⊕ ~ *silver* plata *f* alemana; ~ *text typ.* letra *f* gótica; **2.** (*language*) alemán *m*.

ger·man[2] [~]: *brother etc.* ~ hermano *m etc.* carnal; **ger·mane** [dʒəːr'mein] relacionado (*to* con); pertinente (*to* a); oportuno.

Ger·man·ic [dʒəːr'mænik] germánico.

germ car·ri·er ['dʒəːrmkæriər] portador *m* de gérmenes.

ger·mi·cide ['dʒəːrmisaid] germicida *m*.

ger·mi·nal ['dʒəːrminl] germinal; **ger·mi·nate** ['~neit] (hacer) germinar; **ger·mi'na·tion** germinación *f*.

germ·proof ['dʒəːrmpruːf] a prueba de gérmenes.

ger·ry·man·der ['dʒerimændər] *pol. approx.* falsificar elecciones.

ger·und ['dʒerənd] gerundio *m*.

ges·ta·tion [dʒes'teiʃn] gestación *f*.

ges·tic·u·late [dʒes'tikjuleit] accionar, gesticular, manotear; **ges·tic·u'la·tion** gesticulación *f*, manoteo *m*.

ges·ture ['dʒestʃər] **1.** gesto *m*, ademán *m*; demostración *f*; (*small token*) muestra *f*, detalle *m*; *empty* ~ pura formalidad *f*; *noble* ~ rasgo *m*; **2.** hacer ademanes.

get [get] [*irr.*] **1.** *v/t.* obtener, adquirir; lograr, conseguir; coger; (*grasp*) asir, agarrar *S.Am.*; recibir; *wage etc.* cobrar; ganar; tomar, prender; (*hit*) dar en; captar; comprender; alcanzar; cazar; hallar; (*fetch*) buscar, traer; sacar; (dis)poner; procrear; *have got* tener; *have got to inf.* tener que *inf.*; ~ *it sl.* ser castigado; F (*do you*) ~ *it?* ¿comprendes?; F ~ *it bad* sufrir mucho; *I'll* ~ *him one day! sl.* ¡algún día me lo cargaré!; ~ *a p. to do s.t.* lograr que una p. haga algo; F ~ *religion* darse a la religión; ~ *s.t. done* hacer (*or* mandar) hacer una cosa; *that's what* ~*s me! sl.* ¡eso es lo que me irrita!; F ~ *across* hacer entender; ~ *away* quitar (de en medio); separar; conseguir que (una p.) se escape; ~ *back* recobrar; ~ *down* bajar; descolgar; tragar; apuntar; F (*state of mind*) abatir; ~ *in* hacer entrar; *harvest* recoger; *word* decir; *blow* dar; ~ *off clothes etc.* quitar(se); *stain* sacar; despachar; (*punishment*) librar; aprender; ~ *on clothes etc.* ponerse; ~ *out* sacar; publicar; *problem* resolver; ~ *over* hacer pasar por encima de; F hacer entender; terminar; *let's* ~ *it over with!* ¡vamos a concluir de una vez!; ~ *through* conseguir pasar (por); ~ *up* levantar; (hacer) subir; organizar; presentar; (*dress*) ataviar; (*disguise*) disfrazar; **2.** *v/i.* hacerse, llegar a ser, ponerse, volverse, quedar(se); ir; *sl.* largarse; venir; llegar; ~ *going* ponerse en marcha; empezar; ~ *going!* ¡menearse!; ~ *home* llegar a casa; *fig.* dar en el blanco; ~ *a. p.p. or adj. is often translated by passive, v/i. or v/r. corresponding to p.p. or adj.*: ~ *beaten* ser vencido; ~ *dark* oscurecer; ~ *old* envejecer(se); ~ *angry* enfadarse; ~ *married* casarse; ~ *about* ir a muchos sitios; (*after sickness etc.*) estar levantado y moverse; (*report*) divulgarse; ~ *abroad* salir (al extranjero); (*report*) divulgarse; ~ *across* lograr cruzar; F *thea.* surtir efecto, tener éxito; F indisponerse con; ~ *ahead* (*of*) adelantar(se a); ~ *along* seguir andando; (*depart*) marcharse; (*manage*) ir tirando; *how are you* ~*ting along?* ¿cómo te va?; ~ *along with* avenirse con; ~ *along with you!* ¡no digas bobadas!; ~ *along without* pasarse sin; ~ *around* viajar mucho; dar la vuelta a; *difficulty* soslayar; *p.* persuadir; (*report*) divulgarse; ~ *around to s.t.* llegar a una cosa (con el tiempo); ~ *at* alcanzar, llegar a; atacar; descubrir, averiguar; querer decir; F apuntar a; F sobornar; (*spoil*) estropear; ~ *away* escapar(se); conseguir marcharse; alejarse; ~ *away with fig.* hacer impunemente; ~ *back* volver; retroceder; ~ *behind* penetrar; quedarse atrás; ~ *by* lograr pasar; eludir; F arreglárselas; ~ *down* bajar; ~ *down to* emprender; *problem* abordar; ~ *down to work* ponerse a trabajar; ~ *in* (lograr) entrar (en); llegar, volver a casa; *pol.* ser elegido; ~ *in with* congraciarse con; hacerse amigo de; ~ *into* (lograr) entrar (en); *vehicle* subir a; *difficulties etc.* meterse en; *clothes* ponerse; ~ *off* apearse (de); bajar (de); marcharse; *punishment* librarse de; escaparse; ✈ despegar; ~ *off!* ¡suelta!; ¡fuera!; ~ *off with sl.* enamorar; ~ *on* subir a; ponerse encima de; (*make progress*) adelantar; (*continue*) seguir; (*prosper*) medrar, tener éxito; *it's* ~*ting on for 8* falta poco para las 8; ~ *on with a p.* congeniar con; llevarse (bien) con; ~ *out* salir; escaparse; (*news*) hacerse público; ~ *out of vehicle* bajar de; *responsibility etc.* librarse de; evadir; ~ *over* atravesar; *obstacle* vencer, superar; *illness etc.* reponerse de, salir de; *fright* sobreponerse a; ~ *through* (conseguir) pasar por; *time* pasar; *money* gastar; llegar al final de; terminar; penetrar; *exam* aprobar; ~ *through to* comunicar con; ~ *to* llegar a; empezar a; aprender a; ~ *together* reunirse; ~ *up* levantarse; ponerse de pie; subir; (*wind*) empezar a soplar recio; (*fire*) avivarse; **get·at·a·ble** [get'ætəbl] accesible; **get·a·way** ['getəwei] *sport*: salida *f*; escapatoria *f*; *make one's* ~ escaparse; '**get·up** (*dress*) atavío *m*; presentación *f*.

gew·gaw ['gju:gɔ:] fruslería *f*, chuchería *f*.

gey·ser ['gaizər] géiser *m*; ['gi:zər] *British* calentador *m*.

ghastly ['gæstli] horrible; pálido; cadavérico; F malo, desagradable, aburrido.

gher·kin ['gə:rkin] pepinillo *m*.

ghet·to ['getou] judería *f*.

ghost [goust] fantasma *m*, aparecido *m*, espectro *m*; alma *f*, espíritu *m*; sombra *f*; *Holy* ♀ Espíritu *m* Santo; ~ (*writer*) escritor *m* fantasma; ~ *story* cuento *m* de fantasmas; *give up the* ~ entregar el alma; perder la esperanza; *not the* ~ *of a chance* ni la más remota posibilidad; '**ghost·ly** espectral; espiritual; '**ghost·write** componer escritos por otra persona.

ghoul [gu:l] demonio *m* necrófago; persona *f* de gustos inhumanos; '**ghoul·ish** espantosamente cruel y malsano.

gi·ant ['dʒaiənt] **1.** gigante *m*; **2.** gigantesco; '**gi·ant·ess** giganta *f*.

gib·ber ['dʒibər] farfullar; hablar de una manera ininteligible; decir disparates; '**gib·ber·ish** galimatías *m*, guirigay *m*.

gib·bet ['dʒibit] **1.** horca *f*; **2.** ahorcar; *fig.* exponer a la vergüenza.

gibe [dʒaib] **1.** mofarse (*at* de); **2.** mofa *f*, escarnio *m*, pulla *f*.

gib·lets ['dʒiblits] *pl.* menudillos *m/pl.*

gid·di·ness ['gidinis] vértigo *m*; mareo *m*; atolondramiento *m*; frivolidad *f*; '**gid·dy** □ vertiginoso; mareado; atolondrado; ligero de cascos.

gift [gift] **1.** regalo *m*, dádiva *f*; (*esp. spiritual*) don *m*; (*personal quality*) dote *f*, talento *m*, prenda *f*; *eccl.* ofrenda *f*; ⚖ donación *f*; *sl.* ganga *f*; ~ *of gab* F facundia *f*, labia *f*; ~ *shop* tienda *f* de objetos de regalo; ~-*wrap* envolver en paquete regalo; *deed of* ~ escritura *f* de donación; *I wouldn't have it as a* ~ no lo quiero ni regalado; *don't look a* ~ *horse in the mouth* a caballo regalado no le mires el diente; **2.** dotar; '**gift·ed** talentoso.

gig [gig] calesín *m*; ⚓ canoa *f*.

gi·gan·tic [dʒai'gæntik] □ gigantesco.

gig·gle ['gigl] **1.** risita *f*, risa *f* ahogada, retozo *m* de la risa; **2.** *v/i.* reírse bobamente, reír con una risilla sofocada (*or* tonta).

gig·o·lo ['dʒigəlou] acompañante *m* profesional de mujeres; (*man supported by a woman*) mantenido *m*.

gild [gild] **1.** = *guild*; **2.** [*irr.*] (sobre)dorar; '**gild·er** dorador (-a *f*) *m*; '**gild·ing** doradura *f*.

gill¹ [dʒil] cuarta parte *f* de una pinta (*approx.* $^1/_8$ *litro*).

gill² [gil] *ichth.* agalla *f*; ♀ laminilla *f*; *fig.* papad(ill)a *f*.

gil·lie ['gili] ayudante *m* (*or* criado *m*) escocés.

gilt [gilt] **1.** *pret. a. p.p. of gild*; **2.** dorado *m*; *fig.* atractivo *m*; '~-**edged** con los cantos dorados; *fig.*

de toda confianza, de primer orden; ~ *security* papel *m* del Estado.

gim·crack [ˈdʒimkræk] **1.** fruslería *f*; **2.** de baratillo; mal hecho.

gim·let [ˈgimlit] barrena *f* de mano.

gim·mick [ˈgimik] *sl.* treta *f*, artilugio *m*; *thea.* truco *m* característico; ✝ truco *m* publicitario.

gin[1] [dʒin] (*drink*) ginebra *f*; ~ *fizz* ginebra *f* con gaseosa.

gin[2] [~] **1.** trampa *f*; ⊕ desmotadera *f* de algodón; **2.** coger con trampa; ⊕ desmotar.

gin·ger [ˈdʒindʒər] **1.** jengibre *m*; F brío *m*, viveza *f*; **2.** rojo; **3.** F (*mst* ~ *up*) animar, estimular; ˈ~ ˈ**ale,** ˈ~ ˈ**beer,** ˈ~ ˈ**pop** cerveza *f* de jengibre; gaseosa *f*; ˈ**~·bread** pan *m* de jengibre; ˈ**gin·ger·ly 1.** *adj.* cuidadoso, delicado; **2.** *adv.* con tiento, con pies de plomo; ˈ**gin·ger snap** galleta *f* de jengibre, galletita *f* de jengibre.

ging·ham [ˈgiŋgəm] guinga *f*.

gip·sy [ˈdʒipsi] = *gypsy*.

gi·raffe [dʒiˈræf] jirafa *f*.

gird [gə:rd] [*irr.*] ceñir; rodear; ~ *o.s. for the fray* aprestarse para la lucha.

gird·er [ˈgə:rdər] viga *f*.

gird·le [ˈgə:rdl] **1.** cinto *m*; (*belt a. fig.*) cinturón *m*; (*corset*) faja *f*; **2.** ceñir; cercar.

girl [gə:rl] (*mst young*) niña *f*; muchacha *f*, chica *f*; (*young woman*) joven *f*; (*servant*) criada *f*; ~ *scout* niña *f* exploradora; ˈ**~·friend** amiguita *f*; novia *f*; **girl·hood** [ˈ~hud] niñez *f*; mocedad *f*; ˈ**girl·ish** □ de niña; juvenil; afeminado; ˈ**girl·ish·ness** aire *m* (*or* modales *m*/*pl.*) de niña.

girt [gə:rt] *pret. a. p.p. of gird*.

girth [gə:rθ] **1.** (*horse's*) cincha *f*; cintura *f*; corpulencia *f*; circunferencia *f*; **2.** (*a.* ~ *up*) cinchar.

gist [dʒist] esencia *f*, quid *m*, meollo *m*.

give [giv] **1.** [*irr.*] *v*/*t.* dar; proporcionar; ofrecer; (*as present*) regalar; (*pass on*) transmitir; *disease* contagiar con; *punishment* imponer, condenar a, castigar con; *aid* prestar; (*produce*) dar por resultado, arrojar, producir; (*cause*) ocasionar; (*hand over*) entregar; (*grant*) otorgar, conceder; *time, energy* dedicar, consagrar; sacrificar; (*impart*) comunicar; *lecture* explicar; *thea.* representar; *speech* pronunciar; F ~ *it to a p.* regañar a una p.; pegar a una p.; ~ *us a song!* ¡cántanos algo!; ~ *away* regalar; (*get rid of*) deshacerse de; (*sell cheaply*) malvender; (*disclose*) revelar; (*betray*) traicionar; ~ *away the bride* ser padrino de boda; ~ *back* devolver; ~ *forth* publicar, divulgar; emitir, despedir; ~ *in* entregar; ~ *off* emitir, despedir, echar; ~ *out* distribuir, repartir; anunciar; divulgar; afirmar; emitir, despedir; ~ *over* entregar; transferir; F cesar (de); dejar (de); ~ *up* entregar; ceder; cesar (de), dejar (de); renunciar (a); ⚖ desahuciar; (*for lost*) dar por perdido; ~ *o.s. up to* entregarse a; dedicarse a; **2.** [*irr.*] *v*/*i.* dar; ceder; (*weaken*) flaquear; (*break*) romperse; (*cloth etc.*) dar de sí; ~ *in* ceder; consentir; darse por vencido; ~ *out* agotarse; fallar; F ~ *over* cesar; ~ *up* rendirse, darse por vencido; perder la esperanza; **3.** elasticidad *f*; **give-and-take** [ˈgivənˈteik] toma y daca *m*; concesiones *f*/*pl.* mutuas; **give·a·way** [ˈgivəˈwei] revelación *f* indiscreta; ~ *price* precio *m* obsequio; ˈ**giv·en** *p.p. of give*; ~ *name* nombre *m* de pila; ~ *that* dado que; ~ *to* dado a, adicto a; ˈ**giv·er** dador (-a *f*) *m*, donador (-a *f*) *m*.

giz·zard [ˈgizərd] molleja *f*; *it sticks in my* ~ no lo puedo tragar.

gla·ci·al [ˈgleiʃl] □ glacial; **gla·ci·a·tion** [gleiʃiˈeiʃn] glaciación *f*; **gla·cier** [ˈgleiʃər] ventisquero *m*, glaciar *m*; **gla·cis** [ˈglæsis] glacis *m*.

glad [glæd] □ contento, satisfecho; alegre, gozoso; ~ *hand* F acogida *f* efusiva; *be* ~ alegrarse (*of, to* de); tener mucho gusto (*to* en); ~*ly* con mucho gusto; alegremente; **glad·den** [ˈ~dn] alegrar, regocijar.

glade [gleid] claro *m* (en un bosque), calvero *m*.

glad·i·a·tor [ˈglædieitər] gladiador *m*.

glad·i·o·lus [glædiˈouləs], **glad·i·o·la,** *pl.* **glad·i·o·li** [~ˈoulai] estoque *m*, gladíolo *m*.

glad·ness [ˈglædnis] alegría *f*, gozo *m*; contento *m*; **glad·some** [ˈ~səm] *poet.* alegre.

glad·stone [ˈglædstən] (*a.* ~ *bag*) maletín *m*.

glam·or·ous [ˈglæmərəs] □ encantador, hechicero; **glam·our** [ˈ~mər] encanto *m*, hechizo *m*; ~ *girl* glamour *f*, chica *f* picante, belleza *f* exótica.

glance [glæns] **1.** (*look*) ojeada *f*, vistazo *m*; (*light*) destello *m*; golpe *m* oblicuo; resbalón *m*, rebote *m* *of projectile*; *at a* ~ de un vistazo; *at first* ~ a primera vista; **2.** destellar; (*a.* ~ *off*) rebotar de soslayo; ~ *at* ojear, echar un vistazo a; *book* (*a.* ~ *over*, ~ *through*) hojear; examinar de paso.

gland [glænd] *anat.*, ⚘ glándula *f*; ⊕ prensaestopas *m*; **glan·dered** [ˈ~ərd] amormado; **glan·ders** [ˈ~ərz] *sg.* muermo *m*; **glan·du·lar** [ˈ~julər] glandular.

glare [gler] **1.** luz *f* deslumbradora; deslumbramiento *m*; mirada *f* feroz; **2.** relumbrar, deslumbrar; mirar ferozmente, echar fuego por los ojos; **glar·ing** [ˈ~riŋ] □ deslumbrador; *color* chillón; de mirada feroz; *fig.* manifiesto, craso.

glass [glæs] **1.** vidrio *m*, cristal *m*; (*drinking*) vaso *m*; (*wine*) copa *f*; (*beer*) caña *f*; (*spyglass*) catalejo *m*; barómetro *m*; (*mirror*) espejo *m*; ~es *pl.* gafas *f/pl.*, anteojos *m/pl.*, lentes *m/pl.*; (*binoculars*) gemelos *m/pl.*; **2.** de vidrio, de cristal; ~ *case* escaparate *m*, vitrina *f*; ~ *door* puerta *f* vidriera (*or* de cristales); ˈ**~·blow·er** soplador *m* de vidrio; ˈ**~ cut·ter** cortavidrio *m*; **glass·ful** [ˈ~ful] vaso *m*; ˈ**glass-house** invernadero *m*; *sl.* ⚔ cárcel *f* militar; ˈ**glass·i·ness** lo espejado, vidriosidad *f*.

glass...: ˈ**~ pa·per** (papel *m* de) lija *f*; ˈ**~·ware** cristalería *f*; ˈ**~·works** *pl.* ⊕ vidriería *f*, cristalería *f*; ˈ**glass·y** □ vítreo; *water* espejado; *eyes* vidrioso.

glaze [gleiz] **1.** vidriado *m*, barniz *m*; **2.** vidriar; poner vidrios a; ~*d paper* papel *m* satinado; **gla·zier** [ˈgleiʒər] vidriero *m*; ˈ**glaz·ing** vidriado *m*; vidrios *m/pl.*

gleam [gli:m] **1.** rayo *m*, destello *m*; *a. fig.* vislumbre *f*; brillo *m*; **2.** brillar, destellar.

glean [gli:n] espigar (*a. fig.*); ˈ**glean-er** espigador (-a *f*) *m*; **glean·ings** [ˈ~iŋz] *pl.* moraga *f*; *fig.* fragmentos *m/pl.* recogidos.

glebe [gli:b] *eccl.* terreno *m* beneficial; *poet.* suelo *m*.

glee [gli:] regocijo *m*, júbilo *m*; ♪ canción *f* para voces solas; ~ *club* orfeón *m*; **glee·ful** [ˈ~ful] □ alegre, regocijado.

glen [glen] cañada *f*.

glen·gar·ry [glenˈgæri] gorra *f* escocesa.

glib [glib] □ de mucha labia; *explanation* fácil; ˈ**glib·ness** labia *f*; facilidad *f*.

glide [glaid] **1.** deslizamiento *m*; ✈ planeo *m*; **2.** deslizarse; ✈ planear, volar sin motor; ~ *away*, *off* escurrirse; ˈ**glid·er** planeador *m*; (*light*) velero *m*; ~ *pilot* piloto *m* de planeador; ˈ**glid·ing** vuelo *m* a vela.

glim·mer [ˈglimər] **1.** luz *f* trémula; *a. fig.* vislumbre *f*; **2.** brillar con luz tenue y vacilante.

glimpse [glimps] **1.** vistazo *m*, vislumbre *f*; *catch a* ~ *of* vislumbrar; **2.** vislumbrar, entrever; ver por un momento.

glint [glint] **1.** destello *m*, reflejo *m*, centelleo *m*; **2.** destellar, centellear.

glis·ten [ˈglisn] relucir, brillar, centellear.

glit·ter [ˈglitər] **1.** resplandecer, rutilar; *all that* ~*s is not gold* no es oro todo lo que reluce; **2.** resplandor *m*; brillo *m*; ˈ**glit·ter·ing** resplandeciente, brillante, reluciente.

gloam·ing [ˈgloumiŋ] crepúsculo *m*.

gloat [glout] (*mst* ~ *over*) deleitarse (en); relamerse.

glob·al [ˈgloubl] mundial, global;

globe [gloub] globo *m*; esfera *f*; *geog.* bola *f* del mundo; ˈ**globe-trot·ter** trotamundos *m*; **glo·bose** [ˈ~ous], **glob·u·lar** [ˈglɔbjulər] □ globoso; **glo·bos·i·ty** [glouˈbɔsiti] globosidad *f*; **glob·ule** [ˈglɔbju:l] glóbulo *m*.

gloom [glu:m], ˈ**gloom·i·ness** tenebrosidad *f*, lobreguez *f*, oscuridad *f*; melancolía *f*, abatimiento *m*, pesimismo *m*; ˈ**gloom·y** □ tenebroso, lóbrego; abatido, melancólico, pesimista.

glo·ri·fi·ca·tion [glɔ:rifiˈkeiʃn] glorificación *f*; **glo·ri·fy** [ˈ~fai] glorificar; ˈ**glo·ri·ous** □ glorioso; F magnífico, estupendo.

glo·ry [ˈglɔ:ri] **1.** gloria *f*; *be in one's* ~ estar en sus glorias; **2.** (*rejoice*) gloriarse (*in* en); (*boast*) gloriarse (*in* de).

gloss[1] [glɔs] **1.** glosa *f*; **2.** glosar.

gloss[2] [~] **1.** lustre *m*, brillo *m*; *put a* ~ *on* sacar brillo a; ~ *paint* pintura *f* esmalte; **2.** pulir, lustrar; ~ *over* paliar, colorear.

glos·sa·ry [ˈglɔsəri] glosario *m*.
gloss·i·ness [ˈglɔsinis] lustre *m*, brillantez *f*; ˈ**gloss·y** □ lustroso, pulido; *paper*, *cloth* satinado.
glot·tis [ˈglɔtis] glotis *f*.
glove [glʌv] guante *m*; ~ *compartment mot*. portaguantes *m*; ~ *stretcher* ensanchador *m*, juanas *f/pl*.; **gloved** [~d] enguantado; ˈ**glov·er** guantero (a *f*) *m*.
glow [glou] **1.** incandescencia *f*; brillo *m*; calor *m*; luz *f* (difusa); arrebol *m of sky*; color *m* vivo; sensación *f* de bienestar; ardor *m*; **2.** estar candente; brillar; estar encendido; arder.
glow·er [ˈglauər]: ~ *at* mirar con ceño.
glow·ing [ˈglouiŋ] candente; encendido; ardiente; *fig*. entusiasta.
glow·worm [ˈglouwəːrm] luciérnaga *f*, gusano *m* de luz.
glu·cose [ˈgluːkous] glucosa *f*.
glue [gluː] **1.** cola *f*; **2.** encolar, pegar; ˈ~ **pot** cazo *m* (de cola); ˈ**glue·y** pegajoso; encolado.
glum [glʌm] □ taciturno, sombrío, malhumorado.
glut [glʌt] **1.** hartazgo *m*; superabundancia *f*; *be a ~ on the market* abarrotar el mercado; abarrotarse *S.Am.*; **2.** hartar; *market* inundar.
glu·ti·nous [ˈgluːtinəs] □ glutinoso.
glut·ton [ˈglʌtn] glotón (-a *f*) *m*; *zo*. glotón *m*; *be a ~ for* ser insaciable de; ˈ**glut·ton·ous** □ glotón; ˈ**glut·ton·y** glotonería *f*.
glyc·er·in(e) [ˈglisərin] glicerina *f*.
G-man [ˈdʒiːmæn] F agente *m* secreto federal.
gnarled [nɑːrld] nudoso, rugoso; (*weather-beaten*) curtido.
gnash [næʃ] rechinar (los dientes).
gnat [næt] mosquito *m*; jején *m S.Am.*
gnaw [nɔː] roer; ˈ**gnaw·ing 1.** roedura *f*; **2.** roedor.
gnome [noum] gnomo *m*; **gnom·ic** [ˈnoumik] gnómico.
gnu [nuː] ñu *m*.
go [gou] **1.** [*irr*.] (*v. a. going, gone*) ir; viajar, caminar; (*no direction indicated*) andar; (*depart*) irse, marcharse; desaparecer; eliminarse; (*give way*) ceder, romperse, hundirse; ⊕ funcionar, trabajar, marchar; seguir; hacer (gestos *or* movimientos); (*be current*) correr; (*be habitually*) andar; (*turn out*) resultar, salir; (*become*) hacerse, ponerse, volverse; (*food*) pasarse; (*milk*) cortarse; (*be sold*) venderse; (*time*) pasar; (*reach*) alcanzar, llegar; (*fit*) ajustarse, caber; (*belong*) (deber) colocarse; *as far as it ~es* dentro de sus límites; *as they etc. ~* considerando lo que corre; F *here ~es!* ¡vamos a ver!; F *how ~es it?* ¿qué tal?; *the story ~es* se dice; *there ~es the bell* allí suena el timbre; *who ~es there?* ¿quién vive?; *~ and* (*or to*) *see* ir a ver; *v. bad*; *~ blind* quedarse ciego; *~ hungry* pasar hambre; *~ hunting* ir de caza; *sl*. *~ it* ir a toda velocidad; obrar enérgicamente; correrla; *sl*. *~ it alone* obrar sin ayuda; *~ one better* quedar por encima (*than* de); *~ about* andar (de un sitio para otro); circular; ocuparse en; emprender, hacer las gestiones para; ⚓ virar; *~ abroad* ir al extranjero; salir; *~ against* ir en contra de; oponerse a; chocar con; *~ ahead* ir adelante, continuar, avanzar; *~ ahead!* ¡adelante!; *~ along* ir por; marcharse; seguir andando; *~ at* lanzarse sobre; acometer; *~ away* irse, marcharse; desaparecer; *~ back* volver, regresar; retroceder; F *~ back on* desdecirse de; faltar a; *~ before* ir a la cabeza de; anteceder; comparecer ante; *~ behind* ir detrás de; *~ behind a p.'s back* obrar a espaldas de uno; *~ between* interponerse; mediar (entre); *~ beyond* ir más allá (de); exceder; *~ by* pasar (por); atenerse a; juzgar por; regirse por; *~ by the name of* conocerse por el nombre de; *~ down* bajar; (*sun*) ponerse; (*ship*) hundirse; sucumbir (*before* ante); F aceptarse, tragarse; pasar a la historia; *~ for* ir por; F atacar; F *that ~es for me too* yo contigo; *~ in* entrar (en); (*fit*) caber (en); *~ in for* dedicarse a; tomar parte en; *exam* tomar, presentarse para; comprar; *~ into* entrar en; caber en; investigar; *~ in with* asociarse con; *~ off* irse, marcharse; (*gun*) dispararse; (*explosion*) estallar; deteriorarse; *~ on* seguir (adelante); durar; pasar; F machacar; F echar pestes; *thea*. salir a escena; F *~ on!* ¡anda!; F *how are you ~ing on?* ¿qué tal?, ¿cómo te va?; F *~ on at*

reñir; ~ *on to inf.* pasar luego a *inf.*; ~ *on to say* decir a continuación; ~ *on with* continuar, proseguir; ~ *out* salir; (*light*) apagarse; F pasar de moda; ~ *over* recorrer, atravesar; examinar, repasar; (*to another party, etc.*) pasarse a; ~ *round* dar la vuelta a; circular; (*revolve*) girar; (*suffice*) alcanzar para todos; ~ *round to* hacer una visita a; ~ *through* pasar por; atravesar; penetrar; sufrir; experimentar; (*spend*) (mal)gastar; examinar; ~ *through with* llevar a cabo; ~ *to* (*bequest*) pasar a; servir para, ayudar a; destinarse a; ~ *under* (*ship*) hundirse; arruinarse; fracasar; *name* pasar por; ~ *up* subir (a); (*explode*) estallar; ~ *with* acompañar; (*agree*) estar de acuerdo con; hacer juego con; ir bien con; ~ *without* pasarse sin; **2.** F (*occurrence*) suceso *m*; (*fix*) lío *m*; energía *f*; turno *m*; F *be on the* ~ trajinar; F *have a* ~ probar suerte; tentar; *in one* ~ de una vez, de un tirón; F *is it a* ~? ¿hace?; F *it's a* ~! ¡trato hecho!; F *it's all the* ~ hace furor; *sl. it's no* ~ es inútil; no puede ser; F *it's your* ~ te toca a ti; *make a* ~ *of* tener éxito en.

goad [goud] **1.** aguijada *f*; (*a. fig.*) aguijón *m*; **2.** aguijonear; *fig.* irritar, incitar; ~ *into* provocar a; ~ *into fury* irritar hasta la furia.

go-a·head [ˈgouəhed] **1.** emprendedor; **2.** permiso *m* (*or* señal *f*) para seguir adelante.

goal [goul] meta *f*; *sport*: portería *f*, meta *f*; (*score*) gol *m*, tanto *m*; ˈ**~·keep·er** portero *m*, guardameta *m*; ˈ**~·post** poste *m* de la portería, larguero *m*.

goat [gout] cabra *f*, macho *m* cabrío; *sl. get a p.'s* ~ irritar a una p.; **goat**ˈ**ee** perilla *f*; **goat·herd** [ˈ~hə:d] cabrero *m*; ˈ**goat·ish** cabruno; lascivo.

gob [gɔb] salivazo *m*; *sl.* boca *f*; F marino *m*; **gob·bet** [ˈ~it] bocado *m*; pedazo *m*.

gob·ble [ˈgɔbl] **1.** engullir; (*turkey*) gluglutear; **2.** gluglú *m of turkey*; **gob·ble·dy·gook** [ˈgɔbldiguk] *sl.* jerga *f* burocrática.

go-be·tween [ˈgoubitwi:n] medianero (a *f*) *m*, tercero (a *f*) *m*; *b.s.* alcahuete (a *f*) *m*.

gob·let [ˈgɔblit] copa *f*.

gob·lin [ˈgɔblin] duende *m*, trasgo *m*.

go-by [ˈgoubai]: F *give the* ~ *to* desairar; pasar por alto de; evitar.

go-cart [ˈgouka:rt] cochecito *m* de niño; andaderas *f/pl*.

god [gɔd] dios *m*; 2 Dios *m*; ~*s thea.* F paraíso *m*, gallinero *m*; *please* 2 plegue a Dios; 2 *willing* Dios mediante; ˈ**god·child** ahijado (a *f*) *m*; ˈ**god·daugh·ter** ahijada *f*; ˈ**god·dess** diosa *f*; ˈ**god·fa·ther** padrino *m*; ˈ**god-fear·ing** timorato; ˈ**god-for·sak·en** dejado de la mano de Dios; abandonado; desierto; ˈ**god·head** divinidad *f*; ˈ**god·less** descreído; ˈ**god·like** (de aspecto) divino; ˈ**god·li·ness** piedad *f*, santidad *f*; ˈ**god·ly** piadoso; ˈ**god·moth·er** madrina *f*; *fairy* ~ hada madrina *f*; ˈ**god·par·ents** *pl.* padrinos *m/pl.*; ˈ**god·send** divina merced *f*; cosa *f* llovida del cielo; ˈ**god**ˈ**speed** bienandanza *f*; adiós *m*; *bid* (*or wish*) ~ desear un feliz viaje (*or* buena suerte).

go·er [ˈgouər] corredor (-a *f*) *m*.

go-get·ter [ˈgouˈgetər] *sl.* persona *f* emprendedora, buscavidas *m/f*.

gog·gle [ˈgɔgl] **1.** salirse a una p. los ojos de la cabeza; **2.** ~*s pl.* anteojos *m/pl.*; *sl.* gafas *f/pl.*; ~*-eyed* de ojos saltones.

go·ing [ˈgouiŋ] **1.** yendo, que va; en marcha, funcionando; F en venta; F disponible; F existente; *be* ~ *to inf.* ir a *inf.*; *it's* ~ *on for 5 o'clock* son casi las 5; *keep* ~ seguir; no cejar; *set* ~ poner en marcha; ~ *concern* empresa *f* en pleno funcionamiento (*or* que marcha bien); ~, ~, *gone!* ¡a la una, a las dos, a las tres!; **2.** ida *f*; partida *f*, salida *f*; marcha *f*, velocidad *f*; estado *m* del camino (*sport*: de la pista); *good* ~! ¡bien hecho!; ˈ**go·ings-**ˈ**on** *pl.* F actividades *f/pl.* (dudosas); jarana *f*.

goi·ter [ˈgɔitər] bocio *m*; **goi·trous** [ˈgɔitrəs] que tiene bocio.

gold [gould] **1.** oro *m*; **2.** de oro, áureo; *sl.* ~ *brick* estafa *f*; ~ *leaf* oro *m* batido; ~ *plate* vajilla *f* de oro; ~*-silver embroidery* cañutería *f*; ~ *standard* patrón *m* oro; ˈ**~ crest** reyezuelo *m* sencillo; ˈ**~ dig·ger** *sl.* aventurera *f*; ˈ**gold·en** áureo, de oro; dorado; *fig.*

excelente, próspero, feliz; ~ *age* edad *f* de oro, siglo *m* de oro; ~ *jubilee* quincuagésimo aniversario *m*; ~ *mean* justo medio *m*; ~*rod* ♣ vara *f* de oro, vara de San José; ~ *wedding* bodas *f/pl.* de oro; ˈ**gold·finch** jilguero *m*; ˈ**gold·fish** pez *m* de colores; ~ *bowl* pecera *f*; ˈ**gold mine** mina *f* de oro; *fig.* río *m* de oro, potosí *m*; ˈ**gold·smith** orfebre *m*.

golf [gɔlf] golf *m*; ~ *club* (*stick*) palo *m* de golf; club *m* de golf; ˈ**golf·er** jugador (-a *f*) *m* de golf; ˈ**golf links** terreno *m* (*or* campo *m*) de golf.

gol·li·wog(g) [ˈgɔliwɔg] negrito *m*.

go·losh [gəˈlɔʃ] chanclo *m*.

gon·do·la [ˈgɔndələ] ⚓ góndola *f*; ✈ barquilla *f*.

gone [gɔn] (*p.p. of go*) ido; pasado; desaparecido; arruinado; (*lost*) perdido; (*used up*) agotado; muerto; F chiflado; *be* ~!, *get you* ~! ¡vete!; F *far* ~ muy adelantado; cerca de la muerte; muy borracho; *sl.* ~ *on* loco por; enamorado de; ~ (*with child*) encinta; *it has* ~ *4 o'clock* ya dieron las 4; ˈ**gon·er** *sl.* persona *f* (dada por) muerta.

gong [gɔŋ] gong(o) *m*, batintín *m*.

good [gud] **1.** bueno; F ~ *and adj. or adv.* bien, muy; ~ *at* hábil en; *be* ~ *for* ser bueno para; servir para; F tener fuerzas para; F ser capaz de (hacer *or* pagar *or* dar); *that's a* ~ *one!* ¡ésa sí que es buena!; ~ *afternoon* buenas tardes *f/pl.*; ~ *appetite!* ¡buena pro!, ¡buen provecho!; ~ *day* buenos días *m/pl.*; ~ *evening* buenas noches *f/pl.*, buenas tardes *f/pl.*; ~ *fellow* F buen chico *m*, buen sujeto *m*; ~ *fellowship* compañerismo *m*; ♀ *Friday* Viernes *m* santo; ~ *graces pl.* favor *m*, estimación *f*; ~*-hearted* de buen corazón; ~*-humored* de buen humor; afable; ~ *looks pl.* hermosura *f*, guapeza *f*; ~ *morning* buenos días *m/pl.*; ♀ *Neighbor Policy* política *f* del buen vecino; ~ *night* buenas noches *f/pl.*; ~ *sense* buen sentido *m*, sensatez *f*; ~*-sized* bastante grande, de buen tamaño; ~ *speed* adiós *m* y buen suerte; ~*-tempered* de natural apacible; ~ *time* rato *m* agradable; *have a good* ~ divertirse; *make good* ~ ir a buen paso; llegar en poco tiempo; ~ *turn* favor *m*, servicio *m*; ~ *way* buen trecho *m*; **2.** bien *m*; provecho *m*, utilidad *f*; ~*s pl.* bienes *m/pl.*; ✝ géneros *m/pl.*, mercancías *f/pl.*; *do* ~ hacer bien; sentar bien; *for* ~ (*and all*) (de una vez) para siempre; *for the* ~ *of* en bien de, para el bien de; *it is no* ~ es inútil, no sirve (para nada); *he is up to no* ~ está urdiendo algo malo; *the* ~ lo bueno; los buenos; *what is the* ~ *of?* ¿para qué sirve?; *to the* ~ en el haber, de sobra; ~**-by,** ~**-bye 1.** [gudˈbai] adiós *m*; **2.** [ˈgudˈbai] ¡adiós!; ˈ~**-for-ˈnoth·ing 1.** inútil; **2.** haragán (-a *f*) *m*, ablandabrevas *m/f*; ˈ**good·li·ness** hermosura *f*; excelencia *f*; ˈ**good-look·ing** bien parecido, guapo; ˈ**good·ly** hermoso; considerable; ˈ**good-ˈna·tured** bondadoso; bonachón; ˈ**good·ness** bondad *f*; (*food*) sustancia *f*, lo mejor; ~! ¡válgame Dios!; *for* ~*' sake!* ¡por Dios!; ˈ**good ˈwill** buena voluntad *f* (*towards* hacia); buena gana *f*; ✝ clientela *f*, buen nombre *m*; ~ *mission* misión *f* de buena voluntad.

good·y[1] [ˈgudi] **1.** golosina *f*; **2.** *int.* ¡qué bien!, ¡qué alegría!

good·y[2] [~] (*a.* ~-~) beato *adj. a. su. m* (a *f*); santito *adj. a. su. m* (a *f*), santurrón *adj. a. su. m* (-a *f*).

goo·ey [ˈgu:i] *sl.* pegajoso, empalagoso, fangoso.

goof [gu:f] *sl.* bobo (a *f*) *m*; ˈ**goof·y** *sl.* bobo.

goon [gu:n] *sl.* zoquete *m*; gángster *m*, gorila *m*.

goose [gu:s], *pl.* **geese** [gi:s] ganso (a *f*) *m*, oca *f*, ánsar *m*; *fig.* tonto (a *f*) *m*; plancha *f* de sastre; *cook a p.'s* ~ pararle los pies a una p., acabar con una p.

goose·ber·ry [ˈgusbəri] uva espina *f*; F *play* ~ hacer de carabina; ~ *bush* grosella *f* silvestre.

goose...: ˈ~ **flesh,** ˈ~ **pim·ples** carne *f* de gallina; ˈ~ **step** paso *m* de ganso.

gore[1] [gɔ:r] sangre *f* (derramada).

gore[2] [~] **1.** *sew.* nesga *f*; **2.** cornear, acornar; *sew.* nesgar.

gorge [gɔ:rdʒ] **1.** garganta *f*, barranco *m*; (*meal*) atracón *m*; *my* ~ *rises at* me da asco; **2.** *v/t.* engullir; *v/i.* atracarse.

gor·geous [ˈgɔ:rdʒəs] □ magnífico, brillante, vistoso; F maravilloso, hermoso; ˈ**gor·geous·ness** magnificencia *f*, vistosidad *f*.

gor·mand·ize [ˈgɔ:rməndaiz] glotonear.

gorse [gɔ:rs] tojo *m*, aulaga *f*.

gor·y [ˈgɔːri] □ ensangrentado; sangriento.
gosh [gɔʃ] *sl.* ¡caray!
gos·hawk [ˈgɔshɔːk] azor *m.*
gos·ling [ˈgɔzliŋ] ansarino *m.*
gos·pel [ˈgɔspl] evangelio *m.*
gos·sa·mer [ˈgɔsəmər] (hilos *m/pl.* de) telaraña *f* (volantes); ⚘ gasa *f* sutil.
gos·sip [ˈgɔsip] **1.** hablador (-a *f*) *m*; *b.s.* chismoso (a *f*) *m*, murmurador (-a *f*) *m*; † comadre *f*; (*conversation*) charla *f*; comadreo *m*, murmuración *f*, chismes *m/pl.*, habladurías *f/pl.*; *piece of ~* chisme *m*, hablilla *f*; *~ column* gacetilla *f*, mentidero *m*; *~ columnist* gacetillero *m*, cronista *m/f* social; **2.** charlar; *b.s.* chismear; **ˈgos·sip·y** chismoso, hablador.
got [gɔt] *or* **got·ten** [ˈ~tn] *pret. a. p.p. of* get.
Goth [gɔθ] *hist.* godo (a *f*) *m*; *fig.* bárbaro (a *f*) *m*; **ˈGoth·ic** gótico (*a. su. m*); godo.
gouge [gaudʒ] **1.** ⊕ gubia *f*; **2.** (*mst ~ out*) excavar con gubia, acanalar; *sl.* estafar; *~ a p.'s eyes out* sacarle los ojos a una p.
gou·lash [ˈguːlæʃ] puchero *m* húngaro.
gourd [gɔːrd, gurd] calabaza *f.*
gour·mand [ˈgurmənd] glotón *m*, goloso *m*; gastrónomo *m.*
gour·met [ˈgurmei] gastrónomo *m* delicado.
gout [gaut] ⚕ gota *f*; **ˈgout·y** □ gotoso.
gov·ern [ˈgʌvərn] *v/t.* gobernar, regir (*a. fig.*, *gr.*); dominar; *v/i.* gobernar; *~ing body* junta *f* directiva; *~ing principle* principio *m* rector; **ˈgov·ern·a·ble** □ gobernable, dócil; **ˈgov·ern·ess** institutriz *f*; **ˈgov·ern·ment** gobierno *m*; (*a. gr.*) régimen *m*; *attr.* = **gov·ern·men·tal** [~ˈmentl] gubernativo, gubernamental, del gobierno; **ˈgov·er·nor** gobernador *m*; director *m*; alcaide *m of prison*; F jefe *m*; F (*father*) progenitor *m*, viejo *m S.Am.*; ⊕ regulador *m.*
gown [gaun] **1.** (*dress*) vestido *m*; ⚖, *univ.* toga *f*; traje *m* talar; **2.** vestir (con toga).
grab [græb] **1.** arrebatar; agarrar, coger; *fig.* apropiarse; *~ at* tratar de agarrar; **2.** arrebatiña *f*; agarro *m*; F robo *m*; ⊕ gancho *m* arrancador; ⊕ cubeta *f* draga, cuchara *f* de dos mandíbulas; **ˈgrab·ber** avaro (a *f*) *m*; ladrón (-a *f*) *m.*
grace [greis] **1.** (*favor, attractiveness, a. eccl.*) gracia *f*; elegancia *f*; armonía *f*, decoro *m*; (*at table*) bendición *f* de la mesa; (*deferment*) respiro *m*, demora *f*; 2s Gracias *f/pl.*; *~ note* nota *f* de adorno, apoyatura *f*; *act of ~* gracia *f*; *with* (*a*) *good* (*bad*) *~* de buen (mal) talante; *good ~s* favor *m*; *get into a p.'s good ~s* congraciarse con una p.; *period of ~* plazo *m*; *Your 2* Vuestra Ilustrísima; *eccl.* Monseñor, su Reverendísima; **2.** adornar, embellecer; favorecer; honrar; **grace·ful** [ˈ~ful] □ agraciado, gracioso; elegante; **ˈgrace·ful·ness** gracia *f*, graciosidad *f*; elegancia *f*; **ˈgrace·less** □ réprobo; desgraciado, sin gracia.
gra·cious [ˈgreiʃəs] □ clemente, benigno, graciable; gracioso; *good* (*ness*) *~!* ¡Dios mío!; **ˈgra·cious·ness** clemencia *f*; afabilidad *f.*
gra·da·tion [grəˈdeiʃn] graduación *f*; gradación *f*; paso *m* (gradual).
grade [greid] **1.** grado *m*; (*quality*) clase *f*, calidad *f*; (*mark*) nota *f*; (*slope*) pendiente *f*; *make the ~* vencer los obstáculos, tener éxito; 🚂 *~ crossing* paso *m* a nivel; *~ school* escuela *f* primaria; **2.** graduar, clasificar; *cattle* cruzar; 🚂 *etc.* nivelar, explanar.
gra·di·ent [ˈgreidiənt] declive *m*, pendiente *f.*
grad·u·al [ˈgrædjuəl] □ gradual; **grad·u·ate** **1.** [ˈ~eit] graduar(se); **2.** [ˈ~it] graduado *adj. a. su. m* (a *f*); **grad·u·a·tion** [~ˈeiʃn] graduación *f.*
graft[1] [græft] **1.** 🌱, ⚕ injerto *m*; **2.** 🌱, ⚕ injertar (*in, upon* en).
graft[2] [~] corrupción *f*, soborno *m*, chanchullos *m/pl.*; *sl. hard ~* trabajo *m* muy duro; **ˈgraft·er** F chanchullero *m.*
gra·ham [ˈgreiəm]: *~ bread* pan *m* integral; *~ flour* harina *f* de trigo sin cerner.
Grail [greil] grial *m.*
grain [grein] **1.** grano *m*; cereales *m/pl.*; fibra *f*, hebra *f of wood*; vena *f*, veta *f of stone*; flor *f of leather*; granilla *f of cloth*; (*particle*) pizca *f*; *~ elevator* elevador *m* de granos; (*tall building where grain is stored*) depósito *m* de cereales; *~field* sembrado *m*;

against the ~ *fig.* a contrapelo; *it goes against the* ~ *with me* se me hace cuesta arriba; *dyed in the* ~ teñido en rama; *with a* ~ *of salt* con un grano de sal; *saw with the* ~ aserrar a hebra; **2.** vetear; ˈ**grain·ing** veteado *m.*

gram [græm] gramo *m.*

gram·mar [ˈgræmər] gramática *f*; ~ *school* escuela *f* pública elemental; *British* instituto *m* (de segunda enseñanza), (*private*) colegio *m*; **gram·mar·i·an** [grəˈmeriən] gramático *m*; **gram·mat·i·cal** [grəˈmætikl] □ gramático, gramatical.

Gram·o·phone [ˈgræməfoun] gramófono *m*, gramola *f*; fonógrafo *m S.Am.*; ~ *pick-up* pick-up *m*; ~ *record* disco *m* (de gramófono).

gram·pus [ˈgræmpəs] orca *f.*

gran·a·ry [ˈgrænəri] granero *m.*

grand [grænd] **1.** □ magnífico, imponente, grandioso; espléndido; *p.* distinguido, soberbio; *style* elevado, sublime; noble; magno; gran(de); estupendo; ~*aunt* tía *f* abuela; ~ *duchess* gran duquesa *f*; ~ *duchy* gran ducado *m*; ~ *duke* gran duque *m*; ~ *jury* jurado *m* de acusación; ~ *larceny* hurto *m* mayor; ~ *lodge* gran oriente *m*; ~*nephew* resobrino *m*; ~*niece* resobrina *f*; ~*stand* gradería *f* cubierta, tribuna *f*; ~ *strategy* alta estrategia *f*; ~ *total* gran total *m*, suma *f* de totales; ~*uncle* tío *m* abuelo; ~ *vizier* gran visir *m*; **2.** ♪ (*a.* ~ *piano*) piano *m* de cola; *sl.* mil dólares *m/pl.*

gran·dad [ˈgrændæd] F abuelito *m*; **gran·dam(e)** [ˈ~dæm] abuela *f*; anciana *f*; ˈ**grand·child** nieto (a *f*) *m*; ˈ**grand·daugh·ter** nieta *f*; **grandee** [grænˈdiː] grande *m* (de España); **gran·deur** [ˈgrændʒər] magnificencia *f*, grandiosidad *f*; grandeza *f*; sublimidad *f*; ˈ**grand·father** abuelo *m*; ~(*'s*) *clock* reloj *m* de caja (*or* de pie).

gran·dil·o·quence [grænˈdiləkwəns] grandilocuencia *f*; **granˈdil·o·quent** □ grandílocuo.

gran·di·ose [ˈgrændious] □ grandioso; *b.s.* exagerado, hinchado.

grand·ma [grændmɑ] F abuelita *f.*

grand·moth·er [ˈgrændmʌðər] abuela *f*; ˈ**grand·ness** = *grandeur.*

grand·pa [ˈgrændpɑː] F abuelito *m.*

grand...: ˈ~**·par·ents** *pl.* abuelos *m/pl.*; ~**·sire** [ˈ~saiər] † abuelo *m*; antepasado *m*; ˈ~**·son** nieto *m.*

grange [greindʒ] granja *f*; casa *f* de campo; asociación *f* agrícola.

gran·ite [ˈgrænit] granito *m*; **gra·nit·ic** [græˈnitik] granítico.

gran·ny [ˈgræni] F nana *f*, abuelita *f*; viejecita *f.*

grant [grænt] **1.** concesión *f*; otorgamiento *m*; donación *f*; (*subsidy*) subvención *f*; (*for study*) beca *f*, pensión *f*; ⚖ cesión *f*; **2.** conceder; otorgar; ⚖ ceder; donar; asentir a; *take for* ~*ed* dar por supuesto, descontar; ~*ed that* dado que; ~*ing this* (*to*) *be so* dado que así sea; *God* ~*!* ¡ojalá!, ¡Dios lo quiera!; **granˈtee** ⚖ cesionario (a *f*) *m*; **grant-in-aid** [ˈgræntinˈeid] subvención *f*, pensión *f*; **grant·or** [~ˈtɔːr] ⚖ cesionista *m/f.*

gran·u·lar [ˈgrænjulər] granular; **gran·u·late** [ˈ~leit] granular(se); **gran·uˈla·tion** granulación *f*; **gran·ule** [ˈ~juːl] gránulo *m.*

grape [greip] uva *f*; *unfermented* ~ *juice* mosto *m*; *sour* ~*s!* ¡están verdes!; ˈ~ ˈ**ar·bor** parral *m*; ˈ~**·fruit** toronja *f*, pomelo *m*; ˈ~ ˈ**hy·a·cinth** sueldacostilla *f*; ˈ~ **juice** zumo *m* de uva, jugo *m* de uvas; ˈ~**·shot** metralla *f*; ˈ~ **sug·ar** glucosa *f*; ˈ~**·vine** vid *f*, parra *f*; *sl.* sistema *m* de comunicación clandestina, rumores *m/pl.*

graph [græf] gráfico *m*; ~ *paper* papel *m* cuadriculado; ˈ**graph·ic** □ gráfico; ~ *arts* artes *f/pl.* gráficas; **graph·ite** [ˈ~fait] grafito *m*; **graph·ol·o·gy** [~ˈfɔlədʒi] grafología *f.*

grap·nel [ˈgræpnəl] ⚓ rezón *m*, arpeo *m*; ✈ áncora *f.*

grap·ple [ˈgræpl] **1.** ⚓ arpeo *m*, rezón *m*; asimiento *m*; *wrestling*: presa *f*; ⊕ garfio *m*; **2.** *v/t.* ⚓ aferrar; agarrar, asir; *v/i.*: ~ *with* ⚓ aferrar con; luchar (a brazo partido) con; *fig.* esforzarse por resolver; ˈ**grappling iron** arpeo *m*, garfio *m.*

grasp [græsp] **1.** agarro *m*, asimiento *m*; (*handclasp*) apretón *m*; (*power*) poder *m*; (*range*) alcance *m*; comprensión *f*; *have a good* ~ *of* saber a fondo; *within the* ~ *of* al alcance de; **2.** *v/t.* agarrar, asir, empuñar; *hand* estrechar; apoderarse de; *fig.* comprender; *v/i.*: ~ *at* hacer por asir; ˈ**grasp·ing** □ codicioso, tacaño.

grass [græs] **1.** hierba *f*; (*sward*) césped *m*; (*grazing*) pasto *m*; *go to* ~ ir al pasto; *fig.* descansar; *put out to* ~ echar al pasto; **2.** cubrir de hierba;

apacentar; **'~·hop·per** saltamontes *m*; **'~·land** pradera *f*; **'~'plot** césped *m*; **'~-roots** básico; rústico, provinciano; popular; **'~ seed** semilla *f* de césped; **'~ 'wid·ow(·er)** F mujer *f* cuyo marido (hombre *m* cuya mujer) está ausente; **'grass·y** herboso; herbáceo.

grate[1] [greit] parrilla *f*; reja *f*; (*fireplace*) hogar *m*.

grate[2] [~] *v/t. food* rallar; *teeth* hacer rechinar; *v/i.* rechinar; ~ *(up)on fig.* irritar; ~ *on the ear* herir el oído.

grate·ful ['greitful] ☐ agradecido, reconocido; *th.* grato, agradable; *be* ~ *for* agradecer.

grat·er ['greitər] rallador *m*.

grat·i·fi·ca·tion [grætifi'keiʃn] satisfacción *f*; placer *m*; **grat·i·fy** ['~fai] satisfacer; complacer; **'grat·i·fy·ing** satisfactorio; grato.

grat·ing ['greitiŋ] **1.** ☐ rechinador, áspero; irritante; **2.** reja *f*, verja *f*; rechinamiento *m*.

gra·tis ['greitis] **1.** *adv.* gratis; **2.** *adj.* gratuito.

grat·i·tude ['grætitju:d] agradecimiento *m*, reconocimiento *m*, gratitud *f*.

gra·tu·i·tous [grə'tju:itəs] ☐ gratuito; **gra'tu·i·ty** gratificación *f*.

gra·va·men [grə'veimen] ⚖ querella *f*; lo más grave (de una acusación).

grave[1] [greiv] grave (*a. gr.*); solemne; serio.

grave[2] [~] **1.** fosa *f*, sepultura *f*; (*esp. monument*) tumba *f*, sepulcro *m*; **2.** [*irr.*] grabar, esculpir; **'~-dig·ger** sepulturero *m*, enterrador *m*.

grav·el ['grævl] **1.** grava *f*, recebo *m*; ⚕ litiasis *f*, arenillas *f/pl.*; **2.** engravar, recebar; desconcertar; **'grav·el·ly** arenisco, cascajoso.

grav·en ['greivən] *p.p. of grave*; ~ *image* ídolo *m*.

grave...: **'~·stone** lápida *f* sepulcral; **'~·yard** cementerio *m*, campo *m* santo.

grav·ing dock ['greiviŋ'dɔk] dique *m* de carena.

grav·i·tate ['græviteit] gravitar; *fig.* dejarse atraer [*to(wards)* por]; **grav·i'ta·tion** gravitación *f*; **grav·i'ta·tion·al** gravitatorio, gravitacional.

grav·i·ty ['græviti] gravedad *f*; seriedad *f*, solemnidad *f*; *center of* ~ centro *m* de gravedad; *specific* ~ peso *m* específico.

gra·vy ['greivi] salsa *f*; jugo *m* (de la carne); *sl.* ganga *f*; **'~ boat** salsera *f*.

gray [grei] **1.** ☐ gris (*a. fig.*); *horse* rucio; *weather* pardo; ~ *hairs* canas *f/pl.*; ~ *matter* substancia *f* gris; (*intelligence*) F materia *f* gris, seso *m*; **2.** *color* gris *m*; *horse* rucio *m*; **3.** volver(se) gris; *hair* encanecer; **'~-beard** anciano *m*, viejo *m*; **'~-haired, '~-headed** canoso, cano; **'~·hound** galgo *m*; **'~·ish** grisáceo; *hair* entrecano.

graze [greiz] **1.** *v/t. grass* pacer; *cattle etc.* apacentar, pastar; *v/i.* pacer; **2.** a) *v/t.* rozar; raspar; b) *su.* roce *m*, abrasión *f*, desolladura *f*.

grease [gri:s] **1.** engrasar; *v. palm*[2]; **2.** grasa *f*; (*dirt*) mugre *f*; **'~ box, '~ cup** vaso *m* de engrase, caja *f* de sebo; **'~ gun** *mot.* engrasador *m* de compresión, bomba *f* de engrase; **'~ lift** puente *m* de engrase; **'~ paint** maquillaje *m*; **'~-proof** impermeable a la grasa; *paper* apergaminado; **greas·er** ['gri:sər] engrasador *m*; **'greas·ing** *mot.*, ⊕ engrase *m*.

greas·y ['gri:zi] ☐ grasiento, pringoso; *surface* resbaladizo; *p.* adulón.

great [greit] **1.** gran(de); enorme, vasto; importante; *lit.* magno; principal; mucho; *time* largo; F excelente, estupendo; F ~ *at* fuerte en; F ~ *on* aficionado a; **2.** *the* ~ los grandes; **'~-aunt** tía abuela *f*; **'~·coat** sobretodo *m*; **'~-'grand·child** bisnieto (a *f*) *m*; **'~-'grand·fa·ther** bisabuelo *m*; **'~-'grand·moth·er** bisabuela *f*; **'~-'~-'grand·fa·ther** tatarabuelo *m*; **'~-'~-'grand·son** tataranieto *m*; **'~-'heart·ed** magnánimo, valiente; **'great·ly** grandemente, mucho, muy; **'great·ness** grandeza *f*.

grebe [gri:b] somormujo *m*, zampullín *m*.

Gre·cian ['gri:ʃn] griego.

greed [gri:d], **'greed·i·ness** codicia *f*, avaricia *f*; voracidad *f*, gula *f*; **'greed·y** ☐ codicioso, avaro; (*for food*) goloso, voraz.

Greek [gri:k] **1.** griego *adj. a. su. m* (*a f*); **2.** (*language*) griego *m*; *that is* ~ *to me* está en arábigo (*no entiendo palabra*).

green [gri:n] **1.** verde; fresco; *com-*

plexion pálido; (*raw*) crudo; F (*inexperienced*) novato; F (*credulous*) crédulo, bobo; *grow* ~, *look* ~ verdear; **2.** verde *m*; prado *m*; césped *m*; ~*s pl.* verduras *f/pl.*; *bright* ~ verdegay *adj. a. su. m*; *dark* ~ verdinegro; '**~·back** billete *m* de banco; '**green·er·y** verde *m*, verdura *f*.

green...: '**~·finch** verderón *m* común; '**~·fly** pulgón *m*; '**~'gage** claudia *f*; '**~·gro·cer** verdulero (a *f*) *m*; '**~·gro·cer·y** verdulería *f*; '**~horn** bisoño *m*; bobo *m*; '**~·house** invernáculo *m*; '**green·ish** verdoso.

Green·land·er ['gri:nləndər] groenlandés (-a *f*) *m*.

green light F señal *f* para seguir adelante, autorización *f*; '**green·ness** verdor *m*; F inexperiencia *f*, credulidad *f*; '**green·room** saloncillo *m*; chismería *f* de teatro.

green...: '**~·stuff** verduras *f/pl.*; '**~·sward** césped *m*.

greet [gri:t] saludar; recibir; *senses* presentarse a; (*welcome*) dar la bienvenida a; '**greet·ing** saludo *m*, salutación *f*; (*welcome*) bienvenida *f*; ~*s* (*in letters*) recuerdos *m/pl.*, expresiones *f/pl.*

gre·gar·i·ous [gre'geriəs] □ gregario; sociable.

grem·lin ['gremlin] *sl.* duendecillo *m*.

gre·nade [gri'neid] ⚔ granada *f*; **gren·a·dier** [grenə'dir] granadero *m*.

grew [gru:] *pret. of grow.*

grey [grei] = *gray.*

grid [grid] reja *f*; parrilla *f*; ⚡ red *f*; *radio*: rejilla *f*; *mot. sl.* armatoste *m*, rácano *m*; '**grid·i·ron** parrilla *f*; reja *f*; campo *m* de fútbol; 🚂 emparrillado *m*.

grief [gri:f] dolor *m*, pesar *m*, aflicción *f*; *come to* ~ malograrse; sobrevenirle *a una p.* una desgracia.

griev·ance ['gri:vəns] agravio *m*; motivo *m* de queja; **grieve** [gri:v] afligir(se), acongojar(se) (*at, over* de, por); ~ *for* llorar; '**griev·ous** □ doloroso, penoso; opresivo; lamentable, grave; '**griev·ous·ness** gravedad *f*, opresión *f*; dolor *m*.

grill [gril] **1.** parrilla *f*; (*meat*) asado *m* a la parrilla; **2.** asar a la parilla; *sl.* (*a un acusado*) someter a un interrogatorio muy apremiante, atormentar, interrogar; '**~·room** parrilla *f*.

grille [gril] rejilla *f*; (*window*) reja *f*; (*screen*) verja *f*.

grim [grim] □ severo; ceñudo; feroz; inflexible; horroroso; F muy aburrido, desagradable; ~ *facts* hechos *m/pl.* inexorables.

gri·mace ['grimis, gri'meis] **1.** mueca *f*, gesto *m*, visaje *m*; **2.** hacer muecas (*or* visajes).

gri·mal·kin [gri'mælkin] gato *m*; gata *f* vieja.

grime [graim] **1.** mugre *f*; tizne *mst m*; **2.** enmugrecer; '**grim·y** □ mugriento, sucio.

grin [grin] **1.** sonrisa *f* (abierta *or* burlona *or* feroz); (*grimace*) mueca *f*; **2.** sonreír (mostrando los dientes *or* irónicamente *or* ferozmente); ~ *and bear it* poner al mal tiempo buena cara.

grind [graind] **1.** [*irr.*] *v/t.* moler; pulverizar; (*sharpen*) amolar, afilar; *teeth etc.* hacer rechinar; *dentistry*: desgastar; (*oppress*) oprimir; ~ *down* desgastar; pulverizar; F oprimir, agobiar; ~ *out* (re)producir mecánicamente (*or* laboriosamente); *v/i.* moler(se); trabajar (*or* estudiar) laboriosamente; F quemarse las cejas; **2.** molienda *f*; F trabajo *m* de negros; F rutina *f*; '**grind·er** amolador *m*, afilador *m*; (*coffee etc.*) molin(ill)o *m*; (*stone, tooth*) muela *f*; '**grind·ing 1.** pulverización *f*; amoladura *f*; molienda *f*; (*teeth*) rechinamiento *m*; *dentistry*: desgaste *m*; **2.** opresivo, agobiante; '**grind·stone** muela *f*, piedra *f* de amolar; *keep one's nose to the* ~ batir el yunque.

grin·go ['griŋgou] *b.s.* gringo *m*.

grip [grip] **1.** asir, agarrar; (*squeeze*) apretar; *wheel* agarrarse (a); *fig.* absorber la atención (a); **2.** asimiento *m*, agarro *m*; (*handle*) agarradero *m*, empuñadura *f*; (*clutches*) garras *f/pl.*; (*handshake*) apretón *m*; *fig.* dominio *m*, comprensión *f*; (*bag*) maletin *m* (con cremallera); *come to* ~*s with* luchar (a brazo partido) con; F *lose one's* ~ estar desbordado.

gripe [graip] **1.** *esp.* ~*s pl.* retortijón *m* de tripas; **2.** dar cólico a; *sl.* quejarse.

grip·sack ['gripsæk] maletín *m*.

gris·ly ['grizli] horripilante, espantoso; F desagradable.

grist [grist] molienda *f*; ~ *mill* molino *m* harinero; *all is* ~ *that comes to his mill* saca partido de todo.

grist·le ['grisl] ternilla *f*, cartílago *m*; '**grist·ly** ternilloso, cartilaginoso.
grit [grit] **1.** arena *f*, cascajo *m*; *geol.* arenisca *f*; F valor *m*, firmeza *f*; ~s cereales *m/pl.* a medio moler; **2.** (hacer) rechinar; '**grit·ty** arenisco.
griz·zle ['grizl] F gimotear; '**griz·zled** = *grizzly* 1; '**griz·zly 1.** gris, grisáceo; canoso; **2.** oso *m* gris.
groan [groun] **1.** gemido *m*, quejido *m*; **2.** gemir, quejarse; (*with weight*) crujir.
groats [grouts] *pl.* avena *f* a medio moler.
gro·cer ['grousər] tendero (a *f*) *m* (de ultramarinos), abacero (a *f*) *m*; abarrotero (a *f*) *m S.Am.*; **gro·cer·ies** ['~riz] *pl.* comestibles *m/pl.*, ultramarinos *m/pl.*; abarrotes *m/pl. S.Am.*; '**gro·cer's (shop),** '**gro·cery store** tienda *f* de ultramarinos (*or* de comestibles), abacería *f*, colmado *m*; tienda *f* de abarrotes *S.Am.*
grog [grɔg] grog *m*; '**grog·gy** F vacilante, inseguro; turulato; débil; † calamocano; *boxing*: grogui.
groin [grɔin] *anat.* ingle *f*; ⚠ arista *f* de encuentro.
groom [grum] **1.** mozo *m* de caballos; *palace*: gentilhombre *m*; lacayo *m*; = *bridegroom*; **2.** *horse* almohazar, cuidar; *p.* acicalar; *fig.* preparar (para un puesto *or* para la vida pública); *well-~ed* acicalado; elegante; '**groom·ing** *p.* aseo *m*; '**grooms·man** padrino *m* de boda.
groove [gru:v] **1.** ranura *f*, estría *f*, acanaladura *f*; *phonograph record*: surco *m*; *fig.* rutina *f*; **2.** estriar, acanalar.
grope [group] andar a tientas; ~ *one's way* tentar el camino; ~ *for* buscar (a tientas).
gross [grous] **1.** □ *size*: grueso, espeso; enorme; total; † bruto; ~ *national product* renta *f* nacional; *character* grosero; *error etc.* craso; **2.** gruesa *f*; *by the* ~ en gruesas; *in* (*the*) ~ en grueso; al por mayor; '**gross·ness** gordura *f*; grosería *f*; enormidad *f*.
gro·tesque [grou'tesk] □ grotesco.
grot·to ['grɔtou] gruta *f*.
grouch [grautʃ] F **1.** mal humor *m*; **2.** estar de mal humor, refunfuñar; '**grouch·y** F malhumorado, refunfuñador.
ground[1] [graund] *pret. a. p.p. of grind*; ~ *glass* vidrio *m* deslustrado.
ground[2] [~] **1.** suelo *m*; (*earth a.* ⚡) tierra *f*; terreno *m* (*a. fig.*); (*wire*) ⚡ hilo *m* de masa *mot.*, alambre *m* de tierra *radio*; *sport*: campo *m*; ⚓ fondo *m*; (*reason*) causa *f*, motivo *m*; (*basis*) fundamento *m*; *paint.* primera capa *f*, fondo *m*; ~*s pl.* terreno *m*, jardines *m/pl.*; *fig.* fundamento *m*, motivo *m*; (*sediment*) poso *m*; F *down to the* ~ completamente, como un guante; *on the* ~ sobre el terreno; *on the* ~(s) *of* con motivo de, en virtud de; *on the* ~(s) *that* porque, por *inf.*; pretextando que; *fall to the* ~ venirse al suelo (*a. fig.*); *give* ~ ceder terreno; *hold* (*or stand*) *one's* ~ mantenerse firme; **2.** ⚓ (hacer) varar; poner en tierra; ⚡ conectar con (*or* a) tierra; establecer; basar; enseñar los rudimentos (*in* de); ✈ *be* ~*ed* no poder despegar; *well* ~*ed* bien fundado; versado (*in* en).
ground...: '~ '**floor** piso *m* bajo, planta *f* baja; '~**·ing** ⚡ puesta *f* a tierra; '~**·less** □ infundado; '~**·nut** cacahuete *m*; '~ '**plan** planta *f*; '~ '**rent** *approx.* canon *m*.
ground·sel ['graunsl] ⚘ hierba *f* cana.
ground...: '~ **staff** ✈ personal *m* de tierra; '~ '**swell** mar *m* de fondo; '~ **wire** ⚡ toma *f* de tierra; '~**·work** fundamento *m*, cimiento *m*.
group [gru:p] **1.** grupo *m*, agrupación *f*; (*team*) conjunto *m*; **2.** agrupar(se); **3.** colectivo.
grouse[1] [graus] *orn. black* ~ gallo *m* lira; *red* ~ lagópodo *m* escocés.
grouse[2] [~] F **1.** (motivo *m* de) queja *f*; **2.** quejarse, refunfuñar.
grove [grouv] soto *m*, arboleda *f*, boscaje *m*.
grov·el ['grɔvl] arrastrarse; envilecerse; '**grov·el·(l)er** persona *f* servil; '**grov·el·(l)ing 1.** rastrero, servil; **2.** servilismo *m*.
grow [grou] [*irr.*] *v/i.* crecer; cultivarse; (*become*) hacerse, ponerse, volverse; ~ *a. adj. is often translated by v/i. or v/r. corresponding to adj.*: ~ *angry* enfadarse; ~ *cold* enfriarse; ~ *dark* oscurecer(se); ~ *fat* engordar; ~ *old* envejecer(se); ~ *into* hacerse, llegar a ser; F ~ *on a p.* gustar cada vez más a una p.; (*habit*) arraigar en una p.; ~ *out of* resultar de; *clothes* hacérsele pequeña a una

p. la ropa; *habit* perder (con el tiempo); ~ *to inf.* llegar a *inf.*; ~ *up* hacerse hombre (*or* mujer); (*custom*) imponerse; ˈ**grow·er** cultivador (-a *f*) *m*.

growl [graul] **1.** gruñido *m*; rezongo *m*; **2.** gruñir, regañar; rezongar; decir rezongando.

growl·er [ˈgraulər] gruñón (-a *f*) *m*; *sl.* jarro *m* para cerveza.

grown [groun] **1.** *p.p. of grow*; **2.** *adj.* crecido, adulto, maduro; ~ *over with* cubierto de; ˈ**~-ˈup 1.** *adj.* adulto; **2.** *su.* persona *f* mayor; **growth** [grouθ] crecimiento *m*; desarrollo *m*; aumento *m*; cobertura *f*, vegetación *f*; ⚕ tumor *m*; *3 days' ~ on the chin* barba *f* de 3 días.

grub [grʌb] **1.** larva *f*, gusano *m*; *contp.* puerco (a *f*) *m*; *sl.* alimento *m*, comida *f*; **2.** *v/t.* desmalezar; (*a.* ~ *out*, ~ *up*) arrancar, desenterrar; *v/i.* cavar; afanarse (*a.* ~ *away*); emplearse en oficios bajos; ~ *for* buscar (cavando *or* laboriosamente); ˈ**grub·by** sucio, mugriento; ˈ**grub-stake** anticipo *m* (*dado a un explorador minero*) *a cambio de una participación en los beneficios*.

grudge [grʌdʒ] **1.** (motivo *m* de) rencor *m*, inquina *f*, resentimiento *m*; *bear* (*or have*) *a ~ against* guardar rencor a; **2.** escatimar, dar de mala gana; envidiar; ~ *no pains* no perdonar esfuerzos; **grudg·ing·ly** [ˈ~iŋli] de mala gana.

gru·el [ˈgruəl] *approx.* gachas *f/pl.*; ˈ**gru·el·ing 1.** castigo *m*; **2.** riguroso, penoso.

grue·some [ˈgru:səm] □ pavoroso, horripilante.

gruff [grʌf] □ *voice* (b)ronco; *manner* brusco, malhumorado.

grum·ble [ˈgrʌmbl] **1.** queja *f*, regaño *m*; ruido *m* sordo; **2.** quejarse (*at* de); murmurar; refunfuñar; (*thunder*) retumbar (a lo lejos); ˈ**grum·bler** murmurador (-a *f*) *m*, gruñón (-a *f*) *m*.

grump·y [ˈgrʌmpi] □ F malhumorado, gruñón.

grunt [grʌnt] **1.** gruñido *m*; **2.** gruñir.

guar·an·tee [gærənˈti:] **1.** garantía *f*; persona *f* de quien se sale fiador; garante *m/f*, fiador (-a *f*) *m*; **2.** garantizar; F asegurar; **guar·an·tor** [ˈ~tɔ:r] garante *m/f*; ˈ**guar·an·ty** garantía *f*.

guard [gɑ:rd] **1.** (*in general, p., act, a. of sword*) guarda *f*; (*fencing*, ⚔ *duty, regiment*) guardia *f*; (*soldier*) guardia *m*; (*sentry*) centinela *m*; (*safeguard*) resguardo *m*; 🚂 jefe *m* de tren; ~*'s van* furgón *m*; *off* (*one's*) ~ desprevenido; *on* ~ en guardia; ⚔ de guardia; alerta; *change* ~ relevar la guardia; *mount* ~ montar la guardia; **2.** *v/t.* guardar, proteger, defender (*against, from* de); vigilar; escoltar; *v/i.* ~ *against* guardarse de; ˈ**guard·ed** □ guardado; cauteloso, reservado, circunspecto; ˈ**guard·house** ⚔ cuartel *m* de la guardia; ⚔ prisión *f* militar; ˈ**guard·i·an** guardián (-a *f*) *m*; protector (-a *f*) *m*; ⚖ tutor (-a *f*) *m*; ~ *angel* ángel *m* custodio (*or* de la guarda); ˈ**guard·i·an·ship** ⚖ tutela *f*; protección *f*; **guards·man** [ˈgɑ:rdzmən] ⚔ guardia *m*.

Gua·te·ma·lan [gwɑ:tiˈmɑ:lən] guatemalteco *adj. a. su. m* (a *f*).

gua·va [ˈgwɑ:və] guayaba *f*.

gudg·eon [ˈgʌdʒən] *ichth.* gobio *m*; *fig.* bobo (a *f*) *m*; ⊕ gorrón *m*; ⊕ cuello *m* de eje; ˈ~ **pin** perno *m* de émbolo.

gue(r)·ril·la [gəˈrilə] guerrilla *f*; guerrillero (a *f*) *m*; ~ *war(fare)* guerra *f* de guerrillas.

guess [ges] **1.** adivinación *f*, conjetura *f*, suposición *f*; **2.** adivinar, conjeturar, suponer; *esp. Am.* creer; ~ *at* conjeturar, estimar aproximadamente; ˈ**guess·work** conjetura(s) *f* (*pl.*).

guest [gest] huésped (-a *f*) *m*; (*at meal*) convidado (a *f*) *m*; ~ *book* libro *m* de oro; ~ *room* cuarto *m* de reserva; ˈ**guest·house** casa *f* de huéspedes.

guf·faw [gʌˈfɔ:] **1.** risotada *f*; **2.** reírse a carcajadas.

guid·ance [ˈgaidəns] gobierno *m*, conducta *f*, dirección *f*; consejo *m*.

guide [gaid] **1.** (*p.*) guía *m/f*; *on a tour* (*p.*) jefe *m* del ruta; (*book*, ⊕, *fig. etc.*) guía *f*; *attr.* de guía; ~ *dog* perro-lazarillo *m*; ~*line* cuerda *f* de guía; (*rule, instruction*) norma *f*, pauta *f*, directorio *m*; *Girl* ♀ exploradora *f*; **2.** guiar; orientar; gobernar; ~*d missile* proyectil *m* (tele)dirigido; ˈ**~·board** señal *f* de carretera; ˈ**~·book** guía *f* (del viajero); ˈ**~·post** poste *m* indicador.

guild [gild] gremio *m*; cofradía *f*; ˈ**guildˈhall** casa *f* consistorial; ˈ**Guildˈhall** casa *f* de ayuntamiento (*esp. London*).
guile [gail] astucia *f*, maña *f*, malicia *f*, engaño *m*; **guile·ful** [ˈ~ful] □ astuto, mañoso; ˈ**guile·less** □ cándido, inocente, sincero.
guil·le·mot [ˈgilimɔt] arao *m* común.
guil·lo·tine [giləˈtiːn] **1.** guillotina *f* (*a.* ⊕); **2.** guillotinar.
guilt [gilt] culpa(bilidad) *f* (*a.* ˈ**guilt·i·ness**); ˈ**guilt·less** □ libre de culpa, inocente (*of* de); ˈ**guilt·y** □ culpable; *plead* ~ confesarse culpable.
guin·ea [ˈgini] guinea *f* (= *21 chelines*); ~ *hen* pintada *f*, gallina *f* de Guinea (*hembra*); ˈ~ **fowl** gallina *f* de Guinea; ˈ~ **pig** cobayo *m*, conejillo *m* de Indias; *fig.* cobayo *m*.
guise [gaiz] apariencia *f*; traje *m*; manera *f*; pretexto *m*; *in the* ~ *of* disfrazado de; *under the* ~ *of* so capa de.
gui·tar [giˈtɑːr] guitarra *f*; **guit·ar·ist** guitarrista *m*/*f*.
gulch [gʌltʃ] barranco *m*.
gulf [gʌlf] golfo *m*; abismo *m* (*a. fig.*); vorágine *f*.
gull[1] [gʌl] *orn.* gaviota *f*.
gull[2] [~] **1.** primo *m*, bobo *m*; **2.** engañar; inducir con engaños (*into* a).
gul·let [ˈgʌlit] esófago *m*; garganta *f*.
gul·li·bil·i·ty [gʌliˈbiliti] credulidad *f*, tragaderas *f*/*pl.*; **gul·li·ble** [ˈ~əbl] crédulo, simplón.
gul·ly [ˈgʌli] barranco *m*, hondonada *f*; canal *m*; (*a.* ˈ~ **hole**) (*gutter*) arroyo *m*, alcantarilla *f*.
gulp [gʌlp] **1.** trago *m*, sorbo *m*; **2.** *v*/*t*. (*a.* ~ *down*) tragar, engullir; *emotion* ahogar; *v*/*i*. ahogarse momentáneamente.
gum[1] [gʌm] *anat.* encía *f*.
gum[2] [~] **1.** goma *f*; (*chewing-*) chicle *m*; (*adhesive*) cola *f*; ~*s pl.* chanclos *m*/*pl.* de goma; **2.** engomar, pegar con goma; F (*esp.* ~ *up*) atascar; ˈ~**·drop** frutilla *f*; ˈ~ **tree** gomero *m*, eucalipto *m*; F *up a* ~ en un aprieto; ˈ**gum·my** gomoso.
gum·boil [ˈgʌmbɔil] flemón *m*.
gump [gʌmp] F majadero *m*.
gump·tion [ˈgʌmpʃn] F sentido *m* común; energía *f*.
gun [gʌn] **1.** arma *f* de fuego; cañón *m*; (*sporting*) escopeta *f*; (*rifle*) fusil *m*; F revólver *m*, pistola *f*; (*shot*) cañonazo *m*; F *big* (*or great*) ~ pájaro *m* gordo; *stick to one's* ~*s* seguir en sus trece; *a 21-*~ *salute* una salva de 21 cañonazos; **2.** F andar a caza (*for* de); ˈ~**·boat** cañonero *m*; ˈ~ **car·riage** cureña *f*; ˈ~ **cot·ton** algodón *m* pólvora; ˈ~**·fire** cañoneo *m*; ˈ~ **li·cense** licencia *f* de armas; ˈ~**·man** gángster *m*, pistolero *m*; ˈ~ **met·al** bronce *m* de cañón; ˈ**gun·ner** ⚔, ⚓, ✈ artillero *m*.
gun·ny [ˈgʌni]: ~ *sack* saco *m* de yute.
gun...: ˈ~**·pow·der** pólvora *f*; ˈ~ **run·ning** contrabando *m* de armas; ˈ~**·shot** cañonazo *m*, escopetazo *m*, tiro *m* de fusil; *within* ~ a tiro de fusil; ˈ~**·smith** escopetero *m*, armero *m*; ˈ~**·stock** caja *f* (de fusil); ˈ~ **tur·ret** torre(ta) *f*; **gun·wale** [ˈgʌnəl] borda *f*, regala *f*.
gur·gle [ˈgəːrgl] **1.** (*liquid*) gluglú *m*, gorgoteo *m*; (*baby*) gorjeo *m*; **2.** gorgotear, hacer gluglú; (*baby*) gorjear(se).
gush [gʌʃ] **1.** chorro *m*, borbotón *m*; *fig.* efusión *f*; **2.** chorrear, borbotar; manar a borbotones (*from* de); *fig.* hacer extremos; ˈ**gush·er** pozo *m* de petróleo; *fig.* persona *f* efusiva; ˈ**gush·ing** □ *fig.* efusivo.
gus·set [ˈgʌsit] escudete *m*.
gust [gʌst] ráfaga *f*, racha *f*; *fig.* acceso *m*, arrebato *m*, explosión *f*.
gus·to [ˈgʌstou] gusto *m*; entusiasmo *m*.
gus·ty [ˈgʌsti] borrascoso.
gut [gʌt] **1.** intestino *m*, tripa *f*; cuerda *f* de tripa; ⚓ estrecho *m*; *Am. sl.* descaro *m*; ~*s sl.* agallas *f*/*pl.*; F sustancia *f*; **2.** destripar; saquear (*or* destruir) lo interior de.
gut·ta-per·cha [ˈgʌtəˈpəːrtʃə] gutapercha *f*.
gut·ter [ˈgʌtər] **1.** *street*: arroyo *m*; *roadside*: cuneta *f*; *roof*: canal *m*, gotera *f*; *fig.* barrios *m*/*pl.* bajos; **2.** *v*/*t*. acanalar; *v*/*i*. gotear; (*candle*) correrse; ~ **press** prensa *f* sensacional(ista); ˈ~**·snipe** golfillo *m*.
gut·tur·al [ˈgʌtərəl] □ (sonido *m*) gutural.
guy[1] [gai] **1.** muñeco *m*, mamarracho *m*; espantajo *m*; F tío *m*, tipo *m*; **2.** ridiculizar.

guy² [~] (*a.* ~ *rope*) viento *m*; retenida *f*; ~ *wire* cable *m* de retén.

guz·zle ['gʌzl] tragar, engullir; beber con exceso.

gym [dʒim] = *gymnasium*.

gym·kha·na [dʒim'kɑːnə] fiesta *f* deportiva.

gym·na·si·um [dʒim'neizjəm] gimnasio *m*; **gym·nast** ['dʒimnæst] gimnasta *m/f*; **gym'nas·tic** 1. □ gimnástico; 2. ~*s pl*. gimnasia *f*.

gyn·e·col·o·gist [gaini'kɔlədʒist] ginecólogo *m*; **gyn·e'col·o·gy** ginecología *f*.

gyp [dʒip] 1. *sl*. estafa *f*, timo *m*; estafador *m*; 2. *sl*. estafar, timar.

gyp·se·ous ['dʒipsiəs] yesoso.

gyp·sum ['dʒipsəm] yeso *m*.

gyp·sy ['dʒipsi] gitano *adj*. *a*. *su*. *m* (a *f*); ~ *moth* lagarta *f*.

gy·rate [dʒai'reit] girar; **gy'ra·tion** giro *m*, vuelta *f*; **gy·ra·to·ry** ['dʒairətɔːri] giratorio.

gy·ro-com·pass ['dʒairə'kʌmpəs] brújula *f* giroscópica, girocompás *m*;

gy·ro·scope ['dʒairəskoup] giroscopio *m*; **gy·ro·scop·ic** [~'skɔpik] giroscópico.

gyve [dʒaiv] *poet*. 1. ~*s pl*. grillos *m/pl*.; 2. engrillar.

H

h [eitʃ]: *drop one's h's* hablar con poca corrección.
ha [hɑː] ¡ah!
ha·be·as cor·pus [ˈheibiæs ˈkɔːrpəs] hábeas corpus *m*.
hab·er·dash·er [ˈhæbərdæʃər] mercero (a *f*) *m*; camisero (a *f*) *m*; ~'s (*shop*) mercería *f*; camisería *f*; ˈ**hab·er·dash·er·y** mercería *f*.
hab·it [ˈhæbit] costumbre *f*; hábito *m* (*a. dress*); *v. riding-~*; *be in the ~ of ger.* acostumbrar *inf.*, soler *inf.*; ˈ**hab·it·a·ble** habitable, vividero; **hab·i·tat** [ˈ~tæt] habitat *m*, habitación *f*; **hab·i**ˈ**ta·tion** habitación *f*; ˈ**hab·it-**ˈ**form·ing** que conduce al hábito morboso.
ha·bit·u·al [həˈbitjuəl] □ habitual, acostumbrado; **ha**ˈ**bit·u·ate** [~eit] habituar, acostumbrar (*to* a); **ha**ˈ**bit·u·é** [~ei] habituado (a *f*) *m*, asiduo (a *f*) *m*.
hack[1] [hæk] **1.** ⊕ piqueta *f*; corte *m*, hachazo *m*; mella *f*; puntapié *m* (en la espinilla); **2.** cortar, acuchillar; picar; mellar; dar un puntapié (en la espinilla); *~ing cough* tos *f* seca.
hack[2] [~] **1.** caballo *m* de alquiler; rocín *m*; (*a. ~ writer*) escritorzuelo (a *f*) *m*, plumífero (a *f*) *m*; **2.** de alquiler; mercenario; *fig.* trillado, gastado, sin originalidad.
hack·le [ˈhækl] ⊕ rastrillo *m*; *orn.* plumas *f/pl.* del pescuezo.
hack·ney [ˈhækni] = *hack*[2] 1, 2; *~ carriage* coche *m* de alquiler; ˈ**hack·neyed** trillado, gastado.
hack·saw [ˈhæksɔː] sierra *f* de arco para metales, sierra *f* de armero.
had [hæd, həd] *pret. a. p.p. of have*.
had·dock [ˈhædək] eglefino *m*.
Had·es [ˈheidiːz] F infierno *m*.
haem·or·rh... = *hemorrh...*
haft [hæft] mango *m*, puño *m*.
hag [hæg] (*mst fig.*) bruja *f*; F callo *m*.
hag·gard [ˈhægərd] □ macilento; trasojado, trasnochado.
hag·gish [ˈhægiʃ] □ de bruja.
hag·gle [ˈhægl] (*a. ~ over*) regatear; ˈ**hag·gling 1.** regateo *m*; **2.** regatón.
hag-rid·den [ˈhægridn] atormentado (por una pesadilla); F dominado por una mujer.
hail[1] [heil] **1.** granizo *m*, pedrisco *m*; *fig.* granizada *f*; **2.** granizar (*a. fig.*).
hail[2] [~] **1.** *v/t.* llamar; saludar; aclamar; *v/i.*: *~ from* proceder de, ser natural de; **2.** llamada *f*, grito *m*; saludo *m*; *~!* ¡salud!, ¡salve!; ♀ *Mary* avemaría *f*; *within ~* al habla.
hail·stone [ˈheilstoun] piedra *f* de granizo; ˈ**hail·storm** granizada *f*.
hair [her] pelo *m*; cabello *m*; (*head of*) *~* cabellera *f*; (*down*) vello *m*; *~cloth* tela *f* de crin; *worn as a penance* cilicio *m*; *~ curler* rizador *m*, tenacillas *f/pl.*; *~ dye* tinte *m* para el pelo; *~ restorer* crecepelo *m*; *~ ribbon* cinta *f* para el cabello; *~ set* fijapeinados *m*; *~ shirt* cilicio *m*; *~ spray* laca *f*; *~spring* espiral *f*; *~ style* peinado *m*; *~ tonic* vigorizador *m* del cabello; F *let one's ~ down* echar una cana al aire; *tear one's ~* mesarse los cabellos; F *not to turn a ~* no inmutarse; *~'s breadth* (ancho *m* de un) pelo *m*; *escape by a ~'s breadth* escapar por un pelo; ˈ**~ brush** cepillo *m* para el cabello; ˈ**~·cut** corte *m* de pelo; *get a ~* hacerse cortar el pelo; ˈ**~·do** F peinado *m*; ˈ**~·dress·er** peluquero (a *f*) *m*; *~'s* (*shop*) peluquería *f*; ˈ**~ dry·er** secador *m* para el pelo.
hair...: ˈ**~·less** sin pelo; pelón, calvo; ˈ**~ net** redecilla *f*; ˈ**~·pin** horquilla *f*; *~ bend* viraje *m* en horquilla; ˈ**~-rais·ing** horripilante, espeluznante; ˈ**~-split·ting 1.** quisquilla *f*, argucia *f*; **2.** quisquilloso; ˈ**hair·y** peludo, velloso.
hake [heik] merluza *f*.
hal·cy·on [ˈhælsiən] **1.** alción *m*; **2.** apacible, feliz; *~ days pl.* días *m/pl.* tranquilos, época *f* de paz.
hale [heil] sano, robusto; *~ and hearty* sano y fuerte.
half [hæf] **1.** *su.* mitad *f*; *school*: trimestre *m*; ⚖ parte *f*; *~ and ~* mitad y mitad; mezcla *f* de leche y crema; F *better ~* cara mitad *f*; *by ~* con mucho;

~ *halves* a medias; *go halves with* ir a medias con; *in* ~ en dos mitades; **2.** *adj.* medio, semi...; ~*-blood* mestizo *m*; medio hermano *m*; ~ *boot* bota *f* de media caña; ~*-cocked* F con precipitación; *go off* ~*-cocked* obrar precipitadamente y antes del momento propicio; ~ *fare* medio billete *m*; ~ *hose* calcetines *m/pl.*; ~ *leather* encuadernación *f* a la holandesa, media pasta *f*; ~ *note* ♪ nota *f* blanca; ~ *pay* media paga *f*; medio sueldo *m*; ~ *pint* media pinta *f*; *little runt sl.* gorgojo *m*, mirmidón *m*; ~ *shell either half of a bivalve* concha *f*; *oysters on the* ~ *shell* en su concha; ~ *sole* media suela *f*; ~*-sole* poner media suela a; *at* ~ *staff* a media asta; ~*-timbered* entramado; ~ *title* anteportada *f*, falsa portada *f*, ~*-track* media oruga *f*, semitractor *m*; ~ *a crown*, ~*-crown* media corona *f*; *a pound and a* ~, *one and a* ~ *pounds* libra *f* y media; *two and a* ~ *hours*, *two hours and a* ~ dos horas *f/pl.* y media; **3.** *adv.* medio, a medias, mitad, semi...; casi; ~ *asleep* medio dormido, semidormido, dormido a medias; ~ *dressed* a medio vestir; F *not* ~ mucho; F *not* ~! ¡ya lo creo!; F *not* ~ *bad* bastante bueno; **~·back** [ˈ~ˈbæk] *sports*: medio *m*; **~-baked** [ˈ~ˈbeikt] *fig.* poco maduro, incompleto; poco juicioso, inexperto; **ˈ~ bind·ing** media pasta *f*, encuadernación *f* a la holandesa; **ˈ~-ˈbound** encuadernado en media pasta; **ˈ~-bred** mestizo; **ˈ~-breed** mestizo (a *f*) *m*; **ˈ~ ˈbroth·er** medio hermano *m*; **ˈ~-caste** mestizo *adj. a. su. m* (a *f*); **ˈ~ ˈfull** a medio llenar, mediado; **ˈ~-ˈheart·ed** □ sin ánimo, indiferente; *effort* débil; **ˈ~ ˈhol·i·day** medio día *m* festivo; **ˈ~-hour** media hora *f*; *on the* ~ a la media en punto; cada media hora; **ˈ~-ˈlength** de medio cuerpo; **ˈ~-ˈmast:** (*at*) ~ a media asta; **ˈ~ ˈmeas·ure** medida *f* poco eficaz; **ˈ~-ˈmoon** media luna *f*; **ˈ~ ˈmourn·ing** medio luto *m*; **~·pen·ny** [ˈheipni] **1.** medio penique *m*; **2.** de medio penique; **ˈ~ ˈprice** a mitad de precio; **~-seas-o·ver** [ˈhæfsi:zˈouvər] F calamocano; **ˈ~ sis·ter** media hermana *f*; **ˈ~ ˈtime** *sport*: descanso *m*; **ˈ~ tone** fotograbado *m* a media tinta; **ˈ~ ˈtruth** verdad *f* a medias; **ˈ~·ˈway 1.** *adv.* a medio camino; **2.** *adj.* intermedio; ~ *between* equidistante de; ~ *house* venta *f* situada a mitad del camino; *fig.* punto *m* intermedio, término *m* medio; ~ *through* a la mitad de; *meet* ~ partir el camino con; partir la diferencia con; hacer concesiones mutuas (*dos personas*); **ˈ~-ˈwit·ted** imbécil; **ˈ~-ˈyear·ly** semestral.

hal·i·but [ˈhælibət] halibut *m*.

hall [hɔ:l] vestíbulo *m*; sala *f*; recibimiento *m*; casa *f* señorial; = *guild*~, *music*-~, *town* ~; *univ.*: residencia *f*; comedor *m*; paraninfo *m*.

hal·le·lu·jah [hæliˈlu:jə] aleluya *f*.

hall·mark [ˈhɔ:lmɑ:rk] **1.** marca *f* del contraste; *fig.* sello *m*; **2.** contrastar; *fig.* sellar.

hal·lo [həˈlou] **1.** grito *m*; **2.** ¡hola!; *to incite dogs in hunting*: ¡sus!; **3.** *v/i.* gritar.

hal·loo [həˈlu:] **1.** ¡hola!; *hunt.* ¡sus!; **2.** grita *f*; llamada *f*; **3.** llamar; *hunt.* azuzar.

hal·low [ˈhælou] santificar; **Hal low·e'en** [ˈ~i:n] víspera de Todos los Santos.

hall-stand [ˈhɔ:lˈstænd] perchero *m*.

hal·lu·ci·na·tion [həlu:siˈneiʃn] alucinación *f*; **hal·lu·cin·o·gen·ic** [həlu:sənəˈdʒenik] alucinante.

ha·lo [ˈheilou] halo *m*; *fig.* aureola *f*.

halt [hɔ:lt] **1.** alto *m*, parada *f*; 🚃 apeadero *m*; interrupción *f*; *call a* ~ mandar hacer alto; *call a* ~ *to* atajar; *come to a* ~ pararse; interrumpirse; **2.** hacer alto; parar(se); (*hesitate*) vacilar; † (*be lame*) cojear; (*stammer*) tartamudear; **3.** cojo; **4.** ~! ¡alto!

hal·ter [ˈhɔ:ltər] cabestro *m*, ronzal *m*; (*noose*) dogal *m*.

halt·ing [ˈhɔ:ltiŋ] □ vacilante, titubeante.

halve [hæv] **1.** partir por mitad; **2.**

halves [~z] *pl. of half*.

hal·yard [ˈhæljərd] driza *f*.

ham [hæm] jamón *m*, pernil *m*; *sl.* ~ (*actor*) comicastro *m*, maleta *m*; *sl. radio*: radioaficionado *m*.

ham·burg·er [ˈhæmbə:rgər] hamburguesa *f*.

ham·let [ˈhæmlit] aldehuela *f*, caserío *m*.

ham·mer [ˈhæmər] **1.** martillo *m*; ♪ macillo *m*; percusor *m of firearm*; F ~ *and tongs* violentamente, a más no poder; *come under the* ~ subastarse; **2.** martillar; batir; (*a.* ~ *in*) clavar (con martillo); *stock exchange*: declarar insolvente; ~ (*away*) *at* trabajar asiduamente en; insistir con ahinco en; ~ *out* extender bajo el martillo; *fig.* elaborar (trabajosamente).

ham·mock [ˈhæmək] hamaca *f*; ⚓ coy *m*.

ham·per [ˈhæmpər] **1.** cesto *m*, canasta *f*, excusabaraja *f*; **2.** estorbar, embarazar, impedir.

ham·ster [ˈhæmstər] hámster *m*.

ham·string [ˈhæmstriŋ] **1.** tendón *m* de la corva; **2.** desjarretar; *fig.* incapacitar.

hand [hænd] **1.** mano *f*; (*worker*) operario (a *f*) *m*, obrero (a *f*) *m*, peón *m*; (*measure*) palmo *m*; manecilla *f of clock*; aguja *f of instrument*; (*writing*) escritura *f*; (*signature*) firma *f*; aplausos *m/pl.*; *fig.* habilidad *f*; *fig.* influencia *f*; *all* ~*s* ⚓ toda la tripulación; *fig.* todos *m/pl.*; *at* ~ a mano; *at first* ~ de primera mano, directamente; *at the* ~*s of* de manos de; *be an old* ~ ser perro viejo; *be a good* ~ *at* tener buena mano para; ~ *baggage* equipaje *m* de mano; ~*breadth* palmo *m* menor; ~*car* 🚂 carrito *m* de mano; ~*cart* carretilla *f* de mano; ~ *control* mando *m* a mano; ~ *glass* espejo *m* de mano; lupa *f*; ~ *in glove* uña y carne; ~ *grenade* granada *f* de mano; ~*-held calculator* calculador *m* de mano; ~ *organ* organillo *m*; ~*saw* serrucho *m*, sierra *f* de mano; ~*set* microteléfono *m*; ~*-to-*~ cuerpo a cuerpo; ~*-wrestle* pulsear; *bear a* ~ arrimar el hombro; *by* ~ a mano; *change* ~*s* cambiar de dueño; *live from* ~ *to mouth* vivir de la mano a la boca; *get one's* ~ *in* hacerse la mano; *have a* ~ *in* tomar parte en, tener mano en; *have a free* ~ tener carta blanca; *keep one's* ~ *in* conservar la práctica (*at* de, en); *in* ~ entre manos; *money* constante; dominado; *put in* ~ empezar; *take in* ~ hacerse cargo de; disciplinar; entrenar; *lay* ~*s on* echar mano a; conseguir; *eccl.* imponer las manos a; *lend a* ~ arrimar el hombro; ~*s off!* ¡fuera las manos!; *keep one's* ~*s off* no tocar; *on* ~ a la mano; entre manos; disponible; *on one's* ~*s* a su cargo; *on all* ~*s* por todas partes; *on the one* ~ por una parte; *on the other* ~ por otra parte; *out of* ~ en seguida; desmandado; ~ *over fist* rápidamente; *take a* ~ tomar parte, intervenir (*at*, *in* en); *to* (*one's*) ~ a mano; ~ *to* ~ cuerpo a cuerpo; *come to* ~ venir a mano; (*letter*) llegar a las manos; *put one's* ~ *to* emprender; firmar; *turn one's* ~ *to* dedicarse a; *he can turn his* ~ *to anything* vale tanto para un barrido como para un fregado; ~*s up!* ¡arriba las manos!; *v. high*; **2.** dar; entregar; alargar; ~ *down* bajar; *p.* ayudar a bajar; transmitir; ⚖ dictaminar; ~ *in* entregar; *p.* ayudar a entrar; ~ *out* distribuir; *p.* ayudar a salir; ~ *over* entregar; ~ *around* repartir; (hacer) pasar de uno a otro; ˈ**~·bag** bolso *m*, bolsa *f*; ˈ**~·ball** balonmano *m*; ˈ**~·bell** campanilla *f*; ˈ**~·bill** hoja *f* volante; ˈ**~·book** manual *m*; (*guide*) guía *f*; ˈ**~ brake** freno *m* de mano; ˈ**~·cuff 1.** ~*s pl.* esposas *f/pl.*, manillas *f/pl.* de hierro; **2.** poner las esposas a; ˈ**hand·ed** de ... mano(s); de mano(s) ...; para ... personas; **hand·ful** [ˈ~ful] puñado *m*, manojo *m*; F *be a* ~ tener el diablo en el cuerpo.

hand·i·cap [ˈhændikæp] **1.** desventaja *f*, obstáculo *m*; handicap *m* (*a. sport*); **2.** perjudicar, dificultar; handicapar.

hand·i·craft [ˈhændikræft] artesanía *f*; destreza *f* manual; ˈ**hand·i·ness** destreza *f*; conveniencia *f*; ˈ**hand·i·work** obra *f* (hecha a mano); hechura *f*.

hand·ker·chief [ˈhæŋkərtʃif] pañuelo *m*.

han·dle [ˈhændl] **1.** mango *m*, puño *m*; asidero *m*; (*lever*) palanca *f*; asa *f of basket*, *jug etc.*; tirador *m of door*, *drawer etc.*; (*winding*) manubrio *m*; *fig.* F título *m*; *fig.* pretexto *m*; *sl. fly off the* ~ salirse de sus casillas; **2.** tocar, manosear; manejar, manipular; gobernar; (*deal in*) comerciar en; ˈ**~·bar** manillar *m*; ˈ**han·dler** *sports*: entrenador *m*.

han·dling [ˈhændliŋ] manejo *m*; gobierno *m*; tratamiento *m*; manoseo *m*.

hand...: ˈ**~-ˈmade** hecho a mano; ~ *paper* papel *m* de tina; ˈ**~·maid(en)** † *or fig.* criada *f*, sirvienta *f*; ˈ**~-me-downs** F *pl.* ropa *f* hecha; traje *m* de segunda mano; ˈ**~·out** F limosna *f*; F distribución *f*; F nota *f* de prensa; ˈ**~-ˈpicked** escogido a mano; ˈ**~-rail** pasamano *m*, barandal *m*; ˈ**~·shake** apretón *m* de manos.

hand·some [ˈhænsəm] ☐ hermoso, guapo; buen mozo; *treatment etc.* generoso; *fortune etc.* considerable.

hand...: **ˈ~ˈspring** voltereta *f* sobre las manos; **ˈ~·work** trabajo *m* a mano; obra *f* hecha a mano; **ˈ~·writ·ing** escritura *f*, letra *f*; **ˈhand·y** □ a mano; conveniente, práctico, manuable; útil; *p.* diestro, hábil; *~ man* factótum *m*; *come in ~* venir bien.

hang [hæŋ] **1.** [*irr.*] *v/t.* colgar; suspender; *wallpaper* pegar; *head* inclinar; (*execute*) ahorcar; (*drape*) poner colgaduras en; *I'll be ~ed if I will* que me cuelguen si lo hago; *~ it (all)!* ¡por Dios!; *~ fire* estar en suspenso; *~ out* tender; *~ up* colgar; interrumpir; suspender; *v/i.* colgar, pender; estar suspendido; (*be executed*) ser ahorcado; (*garments*) caer; *~ in the balance* estar pendiente de un hilo; *~ about* frecuentar, rondar; (*idle*) haraganear; *~ back* resistirse a pasar adelante; vacilar; *~ on* colgar de; agarrarse (*to* a); persistir; depender de; estar pendiente de, F esperar; *~ out* asomarse (*of* por); *sl.* vivir; *~ over* cernerse sobre; *~ together* mantenerse unidos; ser consistente; **2.** caída *f of garment*; F modo *m* de manejar; F sentido *m*; *get the ~ of* (lograr) entender; *I don't care a ~* no me importa un ardite.

hang·ar [ˈhæŋər] hangar *m*.

hang·bird [ˈhæŋbɔːrd] pájaro *m* de nido colgante; (*Baltimore oriole*) cacique *m* veranero.

hang·dog [ˈhæŋdɔg] avergonzado; rastrero.

hang·er [ˈhæŋər] percha *f*, colgadero *m*; **~-on** [ˈ~rˈɔn] *contp. fig.* parásito *m*, pegote *m*.

hang·ing [ˈhæŋiŋ] **1.** colgante; digno de la horca; *~ committee paint.* junta *f* de una exposición; **2.** ahorcadura *f*; *~s pl.* colgaduras *f/pl*.

hang·man [ˈhæŋmən] verdugo *m*.

hang·nail [ˈhæŋneil] padrastro *m*, respigón *m*.

hang·out [ˈhæŋˈaut] *sl.* guarida *f*, nidal *m*.

hang·o·ver [ˈhæŋouvər] F resto *m*; *sl.* resaca *f after drinking*.

hank [hæŋk] madeja *f*.

han·ker [ˈhæŋkər]: *~ after* ambicionar, añorar; *~ for* anhelar; **ˈhan·ker·ing** anhelo *m*, ambición *f*; antojo *m*; añoranza *f*.

hank·y·pank·y [ˈhæŋkiˈpæŋki] F truco *m*, supercheria *f*.

han·som [ˈhænsəm] cab *m*.

hap [hæp] † casualidad *f*; suerte *f*; **ˈhapˈhaz·ard 1.** casualidad *f*; **2.** fortuito, casual; **ˈhapˈhaz·ard·ly** a troche y moche; **ˈhap·less** □ desgraciado.

hap·pen [ˈhæpən] pasar, suceder, ocurrir, acontecer, acaecer; *he ~ed to be at home* se hallaba en casa por casualidad; *as it ~s, it ~s that* da la casualidad que; *whatever ~s* suceda lo que suceda, venga lo que viniere; *Am.* F *~ in(to)* entrar por casualidad; *~ (up)on* tropezar con; acertar con; **ˈhap·pen·ing** suceso *m*, acontecimiento *m*.

hap·pi·ly [ˈhæpili] felizmente, afortunadamente.

hap·pi·ness [ˈhæpinis] felicidad *f*, dicha *f*.

hap·py [ˈhæpi] □ feliz, dichoso; *sl.* entre dos luces; *be ~ to* alegrarse de, tener gusto en; *be ~ about* estar contento de; *v. medium*; **ˈ~-go-luck·y** despreocupado, imprevisor.

ha·rangue [həˈræŋ] **1.** arenga *f*; **2.** arengar.

har·ass [ˈhærəs] acosar, hostigar; preocupar; agobiar; ⚔ picar.

har·bin·ger [ˈhɑːrbindʒər] **1.** precursor *m*, heraldo *m*; **2.** anunciar.

har·bor [ˈhɑːrbər] **1.** puerto *m*; **2.** abrigar (*a. fig.*); encubrir; **ˈ~ ˈdues** derechos *m/pl.* de puerto; **ˈ~ ˈmas·ter** capitán *m* de puerto.

hard [hɑːrd] **1.** *adj.* duro, endurecido; sólido, firme; difícil, arduo, penoso; fuerte, recio; severo, inflexible; *water* crudo; *climate* áspero; *blow* rudo; *it is ~ to know* es difícil saber; *he is ~ to beat* es malo de vencer, es difícil de vencer; *~ to deal with* intratable; *be ~ (up)on p.* estar muy duro con; *clothing etc.* gastar, echar a perder; *~ and fast* inflexible; *~ candy* caramelos *m/pl.*; *~ cash* dinero *m* contante; *~ cider* sidra *f* muy fermentada; *~ coal* antracita *f*; *~ court* pista *f* dura; *~ currency* moneda *f* dura; *~ drinker* bebedor (-a *f*) *m* empedernido (a); *~-earned* ganado a pulso; *~ facts* hechos *m/pl.* innegables; *~-fought* reñido; *~ labor* trabajos *m/pl.* forzados; *~ liquor* licor *m* espiritoso; *~ luck* mala suerte *f*; *~-luck story* F cuento *m* de penas; *tell a ~-luck story* F contar lástimas; *~-pressed* acosado; *for money* apurado, alcanzado; ~ *rubber* vulcanita *f*; ~ *sauce* mantequilla *f* azucarada; ~*tack* galleta *f*, sequete *m*; ~ *times pl.* período *m* de miseria, apuros *m/pl.*; ~ *up* apurado, alcanzado; ~ *of hearing* duro de oído; **2.** *adv.* duro, duramente; de firme; difícilmente; con ahinco; *look* fijamente; ~ *by* muy cerca; F ~ *up* apurado; *be* ~ *put to it* encontrar difícil; estar en un aprieto; *go* ~ *with a p.* irle mal a una p.; *ride* ~ cabalgar fuerte; **ˈ~-ˈbit·ten** terco; **ˈ~-ˈboiled** *egg* duro; F endurecido; **ˈhard·en** endurecer(se) (*a.* ⚘); solidificar(se); ~*ing* endurecimiento *m*.

hard...: **ˈ~-ˈhead·ed** astuto, práctico, poco sentimental; **ˈ~-ˈheart·ed** □ duro de corazón, sin entrañas; **har·di·hood** [ˈ~ihud] temeridad *f*; **ˈhar·di·ness** vigor *m*, robustez *f*; audacia *f*; **ˈhard·ly** duramente; difícilmente; mal; (*scarcely*) apenas, casi no; ~ *ever* casi nunca; **ˈhard·ness** dureza *f*; dificultad *f*; fuerza *f*; rigor *m*.

hard...: **ˈ~·pan** subsuelo *m* (arcilloso y) duro; *fig.* base *f* sólida; **ˈ~-shell** de caparazón duro; *fig.* intransigente; ~ *clam* almeja *f* redonda; ~ *crab* cangrejo *m* de cáscara; **ˈhard·ship** penas *f/pl.*, penalidad *f*; infortunio *m*; apuro *m*, privación *f*; **ˈhard·ware** ferretería *f*, quincalla *f*; ~*man* ferretero *m*, quincallero *m*; ~ *store* quincallería *f*, ferretería *f*; **ˈhard-ˈwear·ing** resistente, duradero; **ˈhard-ˈwon** ganado a pulso; **ˈhard·wood** madera *f* dura; árbol *m* de madera dura; ~ *floor* entarimado *m*; **ˈhard-ˈwork·ing** trabajador, hacendoso; **ˈhar·dy** □ robusto; audaz; ⚘ resistente.

hare [her] liebre *f*; **ˈ~·bell** campanilla *f* azul; **ˈ~·brained** ligero de cascos; **ˈ~ˈlip** *anat.* labio *m* leporino.

ha·rem [ˈherəm] harén *m*.

har·i·cot [ˈhærikou] (*a.* ~ *bean*) judía *f* blanca, alubia *f*; ~ *mutton* guisado *m* de carnero.

hark [hɑːrk] (*a.* ~ *at*, ~ *to*) escuchar; ~ *back hunt.* volver sobre la pista; *fig.* ~ *back to matter* volver a; *earlier occasion* recordar.

har·lot [ˈhɑːrlət] ramera *f*; **ˈhar·lot·ry** prostitución *f*.

harm [hɑːrm] **1.** daño *m*; mal *m*; perjuicio *m*; *out of* ~*'s way* a (*or* en) salvo; *there's no* ~ no hay ningún mal (*in* en); **2.** hacer mal (a), hacer daño (a); dañar; perjudicar; **harm·ful** [ˈ~ful] □ dañino, dañoso, perjudicial, nocivo; **ˈharm·less** □ inocuo, inofensivo.

har·mon·ic [hɑːrˈmɔnik] **1.** □ armónico; **2.** armónica *f*; **harˈmon·i·ca** [~ikə] armónica *f*; **har·mo·ni·ous** [hɑːrˈmounjəs] armonioso; **har·mo·ni·um** [hɑːrˈmounjəm] armonio *m*; **har·mo·nize** [ˈhɑːrmənaiz] armonizar; **ˈhar·mo·ny** armonía *f*.

har·ness [ˈhɑːrnis] **1.** guarniciones *f/pl.*, arreos *m/pl.*; † ⚔ arnés *m*; *die in* ~ morir con las botas puestas; *get back in* ~ volver a la rutina; **2.** enjaezar, poner guarniciones a; *fig.* hacer trabajar, utilizar; **ˈ~ mak·er** guarnicionero *m*.

harp [hɑːrp] **1.** arpa *f*; **2.** tañer el arpa; ~ *on* repetir constantemente; *stop* ~*ing on it!* ¡no machaques!; **ˈharp·ist** arpista *m/f*.

har·poon [hɑːrˈpuːn] **1.** arpón *m*; **2.** arpon(e)ar.

har·py [ˈhɑːrpi] arpía *f*.

har·ri·dan [ˈhæridən] bruja *f*.

har·ri·er [ˈhæriər] acosador *m*, asolador *m*; *sport*: corredor *m* a través del campo; *hunt.* perro *m* lebrel; *orn.* aguilucho *m*.

har·row [ˈhærou] **1.** ⚒ grada *f*; **2.** ⚒ gradar; *fig.* atormentar, horrorizar; **ˈhar·row·ing** horrendo, conmovedor.

har·ry [ˈhæri] acosar; asolar; atormentar, inquietar.

harsh [hɑːrʃ] □ áspero; *color* chillón; duro, severo, cruel; **ˈharsh·ness** aspereza *f*; rigor *m*; dureza *f*.

hart [hɑːrt] ciervo *m*.

har·um-scar·um [ˈherəmˈskerəm] F tarambana *adj. a. su. m/f*.

har·vest [ˈhɑːrvist] **1.** cosecha *f*, recolección *f*; (*reaping*) siega *f*; vendimia *f of grape*; ~ *festival*, ~ *thanksgiving* fiesta *f* de la cosecha; ~ *moon* luna *f* de la cosecha; **2.** cosechar (*a. fig.*); recoger; **ˈhar·vest·er** segador (-a *f*) *m*; (*machine*) cosechadora *f*.

has [hæz, həz] ha; tiene (*v. have*); **ˈ~-been** F persona *f* (*or* cosa *f*) que ya no sirve; vieja gloria *f*.

hash [hæʃ] picadillo *m*; guisote *m*; F embrollo *m*; lío *m*; ~ *house* F bodegón *m*; F *make a* ~ *of* estropear; F *settle a p.'s* ~ acabar con una p.

hash·ish [ˈhæʃiʃ] hachich *m*, hachís *m*.
hasp [hæsp] portacandado *m*, aldaba *f* de candado; manecilla *f*.
has·sock [ˈhæsək] *eccl.* cojín *m*.
hast [hæst] † has; tienes (*v. have*).
haste [heist] prisa *f*, apresuramiento *m*, precipitación *f*; *make* ~ darse prisa (*to* para, en), apresurarse (*to* a); *more* ~ *less speed, make* ~ *slowly* vísteme despacio que estoy de prisa; **has·ten** [ˈheisn] *v/t.* apresurar, abreviar, acelerar; *v/i.* apresurarse (*to* a), darse prisa (*to* para, en); **hast·i·ness** [ˈheistinis] apresuramiento *m*, precipitación *f*; impaciencia *f*; ˈ**hast·y** □ apresurado, precipitado; impaciente; inconsiderado.
hat [hæt] sombrero *m*; ~ *band* cintillo *m*; *worn to show mourning* gasa *f*; ~ *block* hormillón *m*; ~-*check girl* guardarropa *f*; *sl. my* ~! ¡vaya!; *keep it under your* ~ de esto no digas ni pío; *take off one's* ~ descubrirse; *take off one's* ~ *to fig.* quitarse el sombrero y hacer reverencia a; *talk through one's* ~ decir disparates; *throw one's* ~ *in the ring* F decidirse a bajar a la arena; ˈ~·**box** sombrerera *f*.
hatch¹ [hætʃ] **1.** *orn.* nidada *f*, pollada *f*; (*door*) media puerta *f*, postigo *m*; (*trap*) trampa *f*; compuerta *f*; ⚓ escotilla *f*; **2.** *v/t.* empollar, sacar del cascarón; *fig.* tramar, idear; *v/i.* salir del huevo; empollarse; *fig.* madurarse.
hatch² [~] plumear.
hatch·et [ˈhætʃit] destral *m*, machado *m*, hacha *f*; *bury the* ~ echar pelillos a la mar; ˈ~ **face** cara *f* de cuchillo.
hatch·way [ˈhætʃwei] ⚓ escotilla *f*.
hate [heit] **1.** odio *m* (*for* a), aborrecimiento *m* (*for* de); **2.** odiar, aborrecer; **hate·ful** [ˈ~ful] □ odioso, aborrecible; ˈ**hat·er** aborrecedor (-a *f*) *m*; **ha·tred** [ˈheitrid] = *hate* 1.
hat·ter [ˈhætər] sombrerero *m*; *mad as a* ~ más loco que una cabra.
haugh·ti·ness [ˈhɔːtinis] altanería *f*, altivez *f*; ˈ**haugh·ty** □ altanero, altivo.
haul [hɔːl] **1.** tirón *m*; (*journey*) recorrido *m*, trayecto *m*; redada *f of fish* (*a. fig.*); *fig.* botín *m*, ganancia *f*; **2.** tirar (de); arrastrar; acarrear, transportar; ⚓ (*a.* ~ *at*, ~ *on*) halar; ⚓ ~ *down* arriar; ⚓ ~ (*the wind*) virar para ceñir el viento; ˈ**haul·age** acarreo *m*, transporte *m*; arrastre *m*, gastos *m/pl.* de acarreo; tracción *f*; ~ *contractor* contratista *m* de transportes.
haunch [hɔːntʃ] anca *f*; (*meat*) [pierna *f*.]
haunt [hɔːnt] **1.** nidal *m*, querencia *f*, lugar *m* frecuentado (*of* por); (*animals'*) guarida *f*; **2.** frecuentar, rondar; *fig.* perseguir; (*ghosts*) aparecer en, andar por; ~*ed house* casa *f* de fantasmas; ˈ**haunt·ing** persistente, obsesionante.
Ha·van·a [həˈvænə] (*or* ~ *cigar*) habano *m*.
have [hæv, həv] **1.** [*irr.*] *v/t.* tener; poseer; gozar de; contener; obtener; *food, drink, lessons* tomar; (*cause*) hacer; sentir; pasar; decir; coger; vencer; dejar perplejo; engañar; tolerar, permitir; *child* tener, dar a luz; ~ *just p.p.* acabar de *inf.*; ~ *to do* tener que hacer; ~ *to do with* tener que ver con; *I* ~ *my hair cut* me hago cortar el pelo; *he had a suit made* mandó hacer un traje; *he had his leg broken* se (le) rompió una pierna; *I would* ~ *you know* sepa Vd.; *as Plato has it* según Platón; *he will* ~ *it that* sostiene que; *I had* (*just*) *as well* ... lo mismo da que yo ...; *I had better go* más vale que yo vaya; *I had rather go* preferiría ir; *it is not to be had* no se puede conseguir; no se vende; F *I* ~ *been had* me han engañado; *sl. he has had it* se acabó para él; ya perdió la oportunidad; *we can't* ~ *that* no se puede consentir (eso); *let a p.* ~ *it* facilitárselo a una p.; F dar una paliza a una p.; F decirle cuatro verdades a una p.; ~ *about one* llevar consigo; ~ *at him!* ¡dale!; F ~ *it in for* tener tirria a; ~ *on* F *p.* tomar el pelo a; *th.* llevar puesto; ~ *it out* resolverlo discutiendo (*or* peleando); F ~ *a p. up* llevar a una p. ante los tribunales; **2.** *v/aux.* haber; **3.** *mst the* ~*s* los ricos *m/pl.*
ha·ven [ˈheivn] puerto *m*; abrigo *m*, refugio *m*.
have-not [ˈhævnɔt]: *mst the* ~*s pl.* los desposeídos *m/pl.*
haven't [ˈhævnt] = *have not.*
hav·er·sack [ˈhævərsæk] morral *m*, mochila *f*.
hav·oc [ˈhævək] estrago *m*, destrucción *f*, ruina *f*; *make* ~ *of, play* ~

with (*or among*) hacer estragos en (*or* entre).

haw[1] [hɔː] ⚘ baya *f* del espino.

haw[2] [~] **1.** *mst hum and ~* vacilar (al hablar); **2.** tosecilla *f* (falsa).

hawk[1] [hɔːk] **1.** *orn.* halcón *m*; *v. sparrow*; **2.** cazar con halcones; ˈ**hawk·ing** halconería *f*, cetrería *f*.

hawk[2] [~] carraspear.

hawk[3] [~] vender por las calles; pregonar (*a. fig.*); **hawk·er** [ˈhɔːkər] vendedor (-a *f*) *m* ambulante.

haw·ser [ˈhɔːzər] guindaleza *f*, cable *m*, calabrote *m*.

haw·thorn [ˈhɔːθɔːrn] espino *m*.

hay [hei] **1.** heno *m*; *~fever* fiebre *f* del heno; *~field* henar *m*; *~fork* horca *f*; ⊕ elevador *m* de heno; *~maker boxing*: golpe *m* que pone fuera de combate; *~mow* henil *m*; acopio *m* de heno; *~rack* pesebre *m*; *~ ride* paseo *m* de placer en carro de heno; *sl. hit the ~* acostarse; *make ~ of* confundir, desbaratar; *make ~ while the sun shines* hacer su agosto; **2.** segar el heno; ˈ**~·cock** montón *m* de heno; ˈ**~·loft** henil *m*; ˈ**~·rick,** ˈ**~·stack** almiar *m*; ˈ**~·seed** simiente *f* de heno; *sl.* patán *m*; ˈ**~·wire** *sl.* en desorden; loco.

haz·ard [ˈhæzərd] **1.** azar *m*; riesgo *m*, peligro *m*; *run a ~* correr riesgo; **2.** arriesgar; *remark etc.* aventurar; ˈ**haz·ard·ous** □ peligroso, arriesgado.

haze[1] [heiz] calina *f*; *fig.* confusión *f*, vaguedad *f*.

haze[2] [~] vejar; *Am.* dar novatada a.

ha·zel [ˈheizl] **1.** avellano *m*; **2.** avellanado; ˈ**~·nut** avellana *f*.

ha·zy [ˈheizi] calinoso; *fig.* confuso, vago.

H-bomb [ˈeitʃbɔm] = *hydrogen bomb* bomba *f* de hidrógeno.

he [hiː] **1.** él; *~ who* el que, quien; **2.** macho *m*, varón *m*.

head [hed] **1.** cabeza *f*; *lit. or iro.* testa *f*; cabecera *f of bed*; espuma *f of beer*; punta *f of arrow*; altura *f* de caída *of water*; culata *f of cylinder*; ⚓ proa *f*; *geog.* punta *f*; ⚘ cabezuela *f*; (*p.*) jefe *m*, director (-a *f*) *m*; (*title*) encabezamiento *m*; sección *f*; *fig.* crisis *f*; *he is* (*or stands*) *~ and shoulders above the rest* sobresale de cabeza y hombros; *fig.* no le llegan a la suela del zapato; *crowned ~* testa *f* coronada; *~band* cinta *f* para la cabeza; cabezada *f of a book*; *~board* cabecera *f* de cama; *~cheese* queso *m* de cerdo; *~ first* de cabeza; *~ of hair* cabellera *f*; *~hunter* cazador *m* de cabezas; *~most* delantero, primero; *~ office* oficina *f* central; *~rest* apoyo *m* para la cabeza; *~set* auricular *m* de casco, receptor *m* de cabeza; *~s or tails* cara o cruz; *I can't make ~ or tail of it* no le veo ni pies ni cabeza; *~waiter* jefe *m* de camareros; encargado *m* de comedor; *~wear* prendas *f/pl.* de cabeza; *~work* trabajo *m* intelectual; *from ~ to foot* de pies a cabeza; *~ over heels* patas arriba; *fig.* completamente, perdidamente; *off one's ~* delirante, fuera de sí, loco; (*up*)*on one's* (*own*) *~* a su responsabilidad; *out of one's own ~* de su cosecha; *over one's ~* fuera de su alcance; por encima de uno; *bring to a ~* ✝ ultimar; provocar; *come to a ~* madurar, llegar a la crisis; ⚕ supurar; *get it into one's ~ that* metérsele a uno en la cabeza que; *give him his ~* darle rienda suelta; *it goes to his ~* se le sube a la cabeza; *keep one's ~* ser dueño de sí mismo; *lose one's ~* perder los estribos; *talk one's ~ off* hablar por los codos; *he took it into his ~ to* se le ocurrió *inf.*; **2.** principal, primero; delantero, de frente; ⚓ de proa; superior; **3.** *v/t.* encabezar, estar a la cabeza de; acaudillar; dirigir; poner cabeza a; *football* cabecear; *~ed for* con rumbo a; *~ off* interceptar; desviar; distraer; atajar; *v/i.* dirigirse (*for, towards* hacia); (*stream*) nacer; *~ing for* ⚓ con rumbo a; ˈ**head·ache** dolor *m* de cabeza; *fig.* quebradero *m* de cabeza; ˈ**head·dress** toca *f*, tocado *m*; ˈ**head·ed** con (*or* de) cabeza ...; ˈ**head·er** ⚠ tizón *m*; F caída *f* de cabeza, salto *m* de cabeza; *football*: cabezazo *m*; ˈ**head·gear** tocado *m*; sombrero *m*, gorro *m*; cabezada *f of horse*; ˈ**head·i·ness** impetuosidad *f*, fogosidad *f*; terquedad *f*; fuerza *f* embriagadora; ˈ**head·ing** encabezamiento *m*, título *m*; ˈ**head·land** promontorio *m*; ˈ**head·less** sin cabeza; descabezado; *fig.* sin jefe.

head...: ˈ**~·light** 🚗 farol *m*; *mot.* faro *m*; ˈ**~·line** titular *m*, cabecera *f*; F *he hits the ~s* se habla mucho de él en los periódicos; *~r sl.* atracción *f* principal; ˈ**~·long 1.** *adj.* de cabeza, precipitado; **2.** *adv.* de cabeza, precipitadamente; ˈ~·**man** jefe *m*, cacique *m*; (*foreman*) capataz *m*; ˈ~ˈ**mas·ter** director *m* (de colegio *etc.*); ˈ~ˈ**mis·tress** directora *f* (de colegio *etc.*); ˈ~ˈ**on** de frente; ~ *collision* choque *m* de frente; ˈ~·**phones** *pl.* auriculares *m/pl.*; ˈ~·**piece** casco *m*; F cabeza *f*; ⚡ auriculares *m/pl.*; *typ.* cabecera *f*; ˈ~ˈ**quar·ters** *pl.* ⚔ cuartel *m* general; sede *f*; jefatura *f*; oficina *f* central; ˈ**head·ship** dirección *f*, jefatura *f*; ˈ**heads·man** verdugo *m*.

head...: ˈ~·**stone** lápida *f* mortuoria; ˈ~·**strong** voluntarioso, impetuoso, cabezudo; ˈ~·**wat·ers** *pl.* cabecera *f* (de un río); ˈ~·**way**: *make* ~ adelantar, hacer progresos; ˈ~·**wind** viento *m* contrario; ˈ**head·y** □ impetuoso, fogoso; terco; *wine* cabezudo, embriagador.

heal [hiːl] curar, sanar (*of* de); *cut etc.* cicatrizar(se); *fig.* remediar; ~ *up* cicatrizarse; ˈ**heal·ing 1.** □ curativo, sanativo; cicatrizal; **2.** cura(ción) *f*; cicatrización *f*.

health [helθ] salud *f*; (*public*) sanidad *f*; ~ *insurance* seguro *m* de enfermedad; *be in good* (*bad*) ~ estar bien (mal) de salud; *drink* (*to*) *the* ~ *of* beber a la salud de; **health·ful** [ˈ~ful] □ sano; saludable, higiénico; ˈ**health·i·ness** buena salud *f*; salubridad *f*; ˈ**health re·sort** balneario *m*; ˈ**health·y** □ sano, saludable; *place etc.* salubre.

heap [hiːp] **1.** montón *m* (*a. fig.*); pila *f*, hacina *f*; F *we have* ~*s of time* nos sobra tiempo; F *struck all of a* ~ anonadado; **2.** amontonar, hacinar, apilar (*a.* ~ *up*); ~ *favors upon* colmar de favores; **3.** *adv.* F ~*s* mucho.

hear [hir] [*irr.*] oír, sentir; escuchar; ~ *about*, ~ *of* oír hablar de, enterarse de; *I won't* ~ *of it* no lo permito; ¡ni hablar!; ~ *from* recibir carta de, tener noticias de; ~ *that* oír decir que; ~! ~! ¡muy bien!; **heard** [həːrd] *pret. a. p.p. of hear*; **hear·er** [ˈhirər] oyente *m/f*; ˈ**hear·ing** (*sense*) oído *m*; audiencia *f*; ⚖ vista *f*; *in our* ~ en nuestra presencia; *within* ~ al alcance del oído; ~ *aid* aparato *m* del oído, aparato auditivo; **heark·en** [ˈhɑːrkən] *mst* ~ *to* escuchar; hacer caso de; **hear·say** [ˈhirsei] rumor *m*, voz *f* común; *by* ~ de oídas.

hearse [həːrs] coche *m* (*or* carro *m*) fúnebre.

heart [hɑːrt] corazón *m* (*a. fig.*); cogollo *m of lettuce*; (*soul*) alma *f*; prenda *f* (*a. dear* ~; *v. sweet*~); *cards*: ~*s pl.* corazones *m/pl.*, (*Spanish*) copas *f/pl.*; ~ *failure* debilidad *f* coronaria; *death* paro *m* del corazón; *faintness* desfallecimiento *m*, desmayo *m*; ~*ily* cordialmente; con buen apetito; de buena gana; bien, mucho; ~*seed* farolillo *m*; ~*sick* afligido, desconsolado; ~ *and soul* con toda el alma; ~*strings pl.* fibras *f/pl.* del corazón, entretelas *f/pl.*; ~-*to*-~ franco, sincero; *have* ~ *trouble* enfermar del corazón; *after my own* ~ de los que me gustan, enteramente a mi gusto; *at* ~ en el fondo; *be sick at* ~ tener la muerte en el alma; *have at* ~ tener presente; *by* ~ de memoria; *have one's* ~ *in one's mouth* tener el alma en un hilo; *from the* ~ de todo corazón; *have the* ~ *to* tener corazón para; *in good* ~ *p* lleno de confianza, ilusionado; *soil* en buen estado; *in his* ~ *of* ~*s* en lo más recóndito de su corazón; *lose* ~ descorazonarse; *set one's* ~ *on* tener la esperanza puesta en; poner el corazón en; *take* ~ cobrar ánimo; *take to* ~ tomar a pecho(s); *wear one's* ~ *on one's sleeve* llevar el corazón en la mano; *with all my* ~ con toda mi alma; ˈ~·**ache** angustia *f*, pesar *m*, ˈ~ **atˈtack** ataque *m* cardíaco; ˈ~·**beat** latido *m* del corazón; ˈ~·**break** congoja *f*, angustia *f*; ˈ~·**break·ing** □ angustioso, desgarrador; ˈ~·**bro·ken** con el corazón partido, acongojado, afligido; ˈ~·**burn** ⚕ acedía *f*; agriera *f S.Am.*; ˈ~·**burn·ing** descontento *m*, envidia *f*, rencor *m*; ˈ~ **dis·ease** enfermedad *f* del corazón, afección *f* cardíaca; ˈ**heart·ed** de corazón ...; ˈ**heart·en** alentar, animar; ˈ**heart·felt** cordial, sincero, hondo.

hearth [hɑːrθ] hogar *m* (*a. fig.*), chimenea *f*; ~*stone* solera *f* del hogar; (*home*) hogar *m*.

heart·i·ness [ˈhɑːrtinis] cordialidad *f*, sinceridad *f*; vigor *m*; campechanía *f*; ˈ**heart·less** □ despiadado, empedernido; ˈ**heart·rend·ing** angustioso, desgarrador, que parte el corazón.

heart...: ˈ~*s*·**ease** ⚘ trinitaria *f*; ˈ~·**strings** *pl. fig.* fibras *f/pl.* del corazón; ˈ**heart·y 1.** □ cordial, sincero; vigoroso, robusto; campechano; *be* *a ~ eater* tener buen diente; **2.** ⚓ compañero *m*; *univ.* deportista *m*.

heat [hiːt] **1.** calor *m* (*a. fig.*); ardor *m*; calefacción *f*; *zo.* celo *m*; *sport*: eliminatoria *f*; *dead ~* empate *m*; *in ~* en celo; **2.** calentar(se) (*a. ~ up*); acalorar(se) (*a. fig.*); ˈ**heat·ed** □ acalorado; ˈ**heat·er** calentador *m*.

heath [hiːθ] brezal *m*; ♀ brezo *m*; *native ~* patria *f* chica.

hea·then [hiːðən] gentil *adj. a. su. m/f*, pagano *adj. a. su. m* (a *f*); F bárbaro *adj. a. su. m* (a *f*); ˈ**hea·then·ish** □ pagano; bárbaro; ˈ**hea·then·ism** gentilidad *f*, paganismo *m*.

heath·er [ˈheðər] brezo *m*.

heat·ing [ˈhiːtiŋ] **1.** calefacción *f*, caldeo *m*; **2.** de calefacción, de caldeo; calentador.

heat...: ˈ**~-ˈproof** termorresistente, a prueba de calor; ˈ**~·stroke** ⚕ insolación *f*; ˈ**~ val·ue** poder *m* calorífico; ˈ**~ wave** ola *f* de calor.

heave [hiːv] **1.** esfuerzo *m* (para levantar); echada *f*; henchidura *f*; náusea *f*; jadeo *m*; **2.** *v/t.* levantar; cargar; lanzar; tirar; ⚓ jalar; *sigh* exhalar; *v/i.* levantarse con esfuerzo; subir y bajar; palpitar; ⚕ basquear; ⚓ (*at capstan*) virar; ⚓ *~ in*(*to*) *sight* aparecer; ⚓ *~ to* ponerse al pairo; *it makes me ~* me da asco.

heav·en [ˈhevn] (*a. ~s pl.*) cielo *m*; (*good*) *2s!* ¡Dios mío!; ˈ**heav·en·ly** celestial (*a. fig.*); *ast.* celeste; **heav·en·ward**(**s**) [ˈ~wərd(z)] hacia el cielo.

heav·i·ness [ˈhevinis] peso *m*; pesadez *f* (*a. fig.*); letargo *m*, modorra *f*; torpeza *f*; opresión *f*; abundancia *f*; fuerza *f*.

heav·y [ˈhevi] □ pesado; *atmosphere* opresivo; *burden fig.* oneroso; *cloth, line, sea* grueso; ⚡ *current*, ⚔ *fire* intenso; *emphasis, expense, meal, rain* fuerte; *feeling* aletargado; *heart* triste; *liquid* espeso; *loss* considerable; *movement* lento, torpe; *population, traffic* denso; *responsibility* grave; *sky* encapotado; *soil* arcilloso; *surface* difícil; *task* duro, penoso; *yield* abundante; *be a ~ drinker* (*eater, smoker*) beber (comer, fumar) mucho; ˈ**~·weight** *boxing*: peso *m* pesado; *fig.* persona *f* de peso.

He·bra·ic [hiˈbreiik] □ hebraico.

He·brew [ˈhiːbruː] hebreo *adj. a. su. m* (a *f*).

hec·a·tomb [ˈhekətoum] hecatombe *f*.

heck·le [ˈhekl] interrumpir (a un orador).

hec·tare [ˈhekter] hectárea *f*.

hec·tic [ˈhektik] □ F agitado, febril; ⚕ hé(c)tico.

hec·tor [ˈhektər] *v/t.* intimidar con bravatas; *v/i.* echar bravatas.

hedge [hedʒ] **1.** seto *m* (vivo); cerca *f*; **2.** *v/t.* cercar con seto; *~ about, ~ in* rodear, encerrar; poner obstáculos a; *~ off* separar (por un seto); *~ a bet* hacer apuestas compensatorias; *v/i.* eludir la respuesta, contestar con evasivas; vacilar; ˈ**~·hog** erizo *m*; puerco *m* espín; ˈ**~·hop** ✈ *sl.* volar a ras de tierra; ˈ**~·row** seto *m* vivo; ˈ**~ ˈspar·row** acentor *m* común.

he·don·ism [ˈhiːdənizm] hedonismo *m*.

heed [hiːd] **1.** atención *f*, cuidado *m*; *give ~ to* poner atención en; *take no ~ of* no hacer caso de; **2.** atender (a), hacer caso (de); **heed·ful** [ˈ~ful] □ atento (*of* a); cuidadoso; ˈ**heed·less** □ desatento, descuidado; distraído.

hee·haw [ˈhiːˈhɔː] **1.** rebuzno *m*; *fig.* risotada *f*; **2.** rebuznar; reírse a carcajadas.

heel[1] [hiːl] **1.** *anat.* calcañar *m*; *anat. a. fig.* talón *m*; tacón *m of shoe*; parte *f* inferior; parte *f* trasera; restos *m/pl.*; *sl.* sinvergüenza *m*; *be at* (*or on*) *a p.'s ~s* pisarle los talones a una p.; *cool one's ~s* hacer antesala; *down at ~* desaliñado, mal vestido; *take to one's ~s* poner pies en polvorosa; **2.** *shoe* poner tacón a; *football* talonar; ˈ**~ ˈclick·ing** taconazo *m*; ˈ**heeled** F provisto de dinero; ˈ**heel·er** *sl.* muñidor *m*.

heel[2] [~] ⚓ escorar; *~ over* zozobrar.

heel·tap [ˈhiːltæp] ⊕ tapa *f* (del tacón); escurridura *f*.

heft [heft] *v. haft*; **1.** F mayor parte *f*; **2.** F sopesar; ˈ**heft·y** F pesado; fuerte, fornido.

he·gem·o·ny [hiːˈgeməni] hegemonía *f*.

he-goat [ˈhiːgout] macho *m* cabrío.

heif·er [ˈhefər] novilla *f*, vaquilla *f*.

heigh [hei] ¡oye!, ¡eh!

heigh-ho [ˈheiˈhou] ¡ay!

height [hait] altura *f*; elevación *f*; altitud *f*; (*top*) cima *f*; *p.'s* estatura *f*; (*hill*) cerro *m*; crisis *f*; *the* ~ *of madness* el colmo de la locura; ˈ**height·en** elevar; hacer más alto; aumentar; (*enhance*) realzar; intensificar, avivar.

hei·nous [ˈheinəs] □ atroz, nefando.

heir [er] heredero *m*; *be* ~ *to* heredar; ~ *apparent*, ~ *at law* heredero *m* forzoso; ˈ**heir·dom** herencia *f*; ˈ**heir·ess** heredera *f*; F soltera *f* adinerada; ˈ**heir·less** sin heredero; **heir·loom** [ˈ~luːm] reliquia *f* de familia.

held [held] *pret. a. p.p. of hold* 2.

hel·i·cal [ˈhelikl] espiral.

hel·i·cop·ter [ˈhelikɔptər] helicóptero *m*.

he·li·o·graph [ˈhiːliougræf] heliógrafo *m*; **he·li·o·gra·vure** [ˈhiːliougrəˈvjur] heliograbado *m*; **he·li·o·trope** [ˈheljətroup] heliotropo *m*.

hel·i·port [ˈhelipɔːrt] helipuerto *m*.

he·li·um [ˈhiːliəm] helio *m*.

hell [hel] infierno *m*; (*a. gambling-*~) garito *m*; *sl. like* ~! ¡ni hablar!; F *oh* ~! ¡demonio!; *go to* ~! ¡vete al diablo!; F *what the* ~...? ¿qué demonios...?; F *a* ~ *of a noise* un ruido de todos los demonios; F *raise* ~ armar la de Dios es Cristo; *go* ~ *for leather* ir como el demonio, ir disparado.

hel·le·bore [ˈheliboːr] eléboro *m*.

Hel·lene [ˈheliːn] heleno (a *f*) *m*.

hell·ish [ˈheliʃ] □ infernal, diabólico.

hel·lo [ˈheˈlou; heˈlou] **1.** saludo *m*; **2.** ¡hola!, ¡qué tal!; *teleph.* ¡oiga!; (*answering teleph.*) ¡diga!, ¡dígame!

helm [helm] (caña *f or* rueda *f* del) timón *m*.

hel·met [ˈhelmit] casco *m*; † yelmo *m*.

helms·man [ˈhelmzmən] timonel *m*.

help [help] **1.** ayuda *f*, auxilio *m*; socorro *m*; remedio *m*; (*p.*) criada *f*; (*servants*) servidumbre *f*; ~! ¡socorro!; F *lady* ~ asistenta *f*; *mother's* ~ niñera *f*; criada *f*; *by the* ~ *of* con la ayuda de; *call for* ~ pedir socorro; *there's no* ~ *for it* no hay (más) remedio; **2.** *v/t.* ayudar (*to* a); auxiliar; socorrer; *pain* aliviar; remediar; facilitar; (*at table*) servir; ~ *a p. to a th.* servirle algo a una p.; ~ *o.s.* servirse; valerse por sí mismo; *I could not* ~ *laughing* no pude menos de reír; (*not*) *if I can* ~ *it* si puedo evitarlo; *it can't be* ~*ed* no hay (más) remedio; ~ *a p. on with* (*dress*) ayudar a una p. a ponerse; ~ *out* ayudar (a salir *or* a bajar); *v/i.* ayudar (*a.* ~ *out*); ˈ**help·er** ayudador (-a *f*) *m*; ayudante *m*; asistente (a *f*) *m*; colaborador (-a *f*) *m*; **help·ful** [ˈ~ful] □ útil, provechoso; *p.* servicial, comprensivo; ˈ**help·ing** ración *f*, porción *f*; plato *m*; ˈ**help·less** □ impotente; incapaz; desamparado; ˈ**help·less·ness** impotencia *f*; incapacidad *f*; desamparo *m*; ˈ**help-mate,** ˈ**help·meet** buen(a) compañero (a *f*) *m*; esposo (a *f*) *m*.

hel·ter-skel·ter [ˈheltərˈskeltər] atropelladamente.

helve [helv] mango *m*, astil *m*.

hem[1] [hem] **1.** dobladillo *m*, bastilla *f*; (*edge*) orilla *f*; **2.** dobladillar, bastillar; ~ *in* encerrar, cercar.

hem[2] [~] **1.** destoserse; **2.** ¡ejem!

he-man [ˈhiːmæn] *sl.* machote *m*.

hem·i·sphere [ˈhemisfir] hemisferio *m*.

hem·i·stich [ˈhemistik] hemistiquio [*m*.]

hem·lock [ˈhemlɔk] cicuta *f*.

hem·or·rhage [ˈhemɔridʒ] hemorragia *f*; **hem·or·rhoids** [ˈ~rɔidz] *pl.* hemorroides *f/pl.*

hemp [hemp] cáñamo *m*; ˈ**hemp·en** cañameño.

hem·stitch [ˈhemstitʃ] **1.** vainica *f*; **2.** hacer vainica (en).

hen [hen] gallina *f*; (*female bird*) hembra *f*; ~*'s egg* huevo *m* de gallina.

hen·bane [ˈhenbein] beleño *m*.

hence [hens] (*a. from* ~) (*place*) de aquí, desde aquí; fuera de aquí; (*time*) desde ahora; (*therefore*) por lo tanto, por eso; ~! ¡fuera (de aquí)!; *a year* ~ de aquí a un año; ˈ~ˈ**forth,** ˈ~-ˈ**for·ward** de aquí en adelante.

hench·man [ˈhentʃmən] secuaz *m*; munidor *m*; guardaespaldas *m*; † paje *m*.

hen·dec·a·syl·lab·ic [henˈdekəsiˈlæbik] endecasílabo.

hen·house [ˈhenhaus] gallinero *m*.

hen·na [ˈhenə] alheña *f*.

hen...: ˈ~ ˈ**par·ty** F tertulia *f* de mujeres; ˈ~**pecked** dominado por su mujer.

hep [hep] *sl.* enterado.

he·pat·ic [hiˈpætik] hepático.

hep·cat [ˈhepkæt] *sl.* conocedor (-a *f*) *m* del jazz.
hep·ta·gon [ˈheptəgən] heptágono *m*.
her [hə:r, hər] **1.** *possessive* su(s); **2.** *pron. acc.* la; *dat.* le; (*after prp.*) ella.
her·ald [ˈherəld] **1.** heraldo *m*; *fig.* anunciador *m*, precursor *m*; **2.** anunciar, proclamar; ser precursor de; **he·ral·dic** [heˈrældik] □ heráldico; **her·ald·ry** [ˈherəldri] heráldica *f*.
herb [(h)ə:rb] hierba *f*; **her·ba·ceous** [~ˈbeiʃəs] herbáceo; ˈ**herb·age** herbaje *m*; ⚖ derecho *m* de pastoreo; ˈ**herb·al** herbario *adj. a. su. m*; ˈ**her·bal·ist** herbolario (a *f*) *m*; **her·bar·i·um** [~ˈberiəm] herbario *m*; **her·biv·o·rous** [~ˈbivərəs] herbívoro.
Her·cu·le·an [hə:rkjuˈli:ən] hercúleo.
herd [hə:rd] **1.** manada *f*, hato *m*, rebaño *m*; piara *f of swine*; *fig.* muchedumbre *f*; *the common* ~ el vulgo; ~ *instinct* instinto *m* gregario; **2.** *v/t.* guardar; reunir (*or* llevar) en manada; *v/i.* (*a.* ~ *together*) reunirse en manada; ir juntos; ˈ**herds·man** manadero *m*, pastor *m*; vaquero *m*.
here [hir] aquí; acá; ~*!* ¡presente!; ~ *and there* aquí y allá; ~ *below* aquí abajo; ~*'s to...!* ¡vaya por...!; ¡a la salud de...!; ~ *it is* aquí lo tiene Vd.; *come* ~*!* ¡ven acá!; *that's neither* ~ *nor there* eso no viene al caso.
here·a·bout(s) [ˈhirəbaut(s)] por aquí (cerca); **here·aft·er** [hirˈæftər] **1.** de aquí en adelante; en lo futuro; en la vida futura; **2.** lo futuro; vida *f* futura; ˈ**here**ˈ**by** por este medio; por la presente.
her·e·dit·a·ment [heriˈditəmənt] bienes *m/pl.* heredables; **he·red·i·tar·y** [hiˈreditəri] hereditario; **he**ˈ**red·i·ty** herencia *f*.
here·in [ˈhirˈin] aquí dentro; en esto; **here·in**ˈ**aft·er** más abajo, más adelante; **here·in·be**ˈ**fore** en lo precedente; **here·of** [hirˈɔv] de esto.
her·e·sy [ˈherəsi] herejía *f*.
her·e·tic [ˈherətik] **1.** (*mst* **he·ret·i·cal** □ [hiˈretikl]) herético; **2.** hereje *m/f*.
here·to·fore [ˈhirtuˈfɔ:r] hasta ahora; antes; **here·up·on** [ˈhirəˈpɔn] en esto; en seguida; ˈ**here**ˈ**with** con esto; adjunto.
her·it·a·ble [ˈheritəbl] heredable; ˈ**her·it·age** herencia *f*.
her·maph·ro·dite [hə:rˈmæfrədait] hermafrodita *adj. a. su. m*.
her·met·ic [hə:rˈmetik] □ hermético.
her·mit [ˈhə:rmit] ermitaño *m*; ˈ**her·mit·age** ermita *f*.
her·ni·a [ˈhə:rnjə] hernia *f*; ˈ**her·ni·al** herniario.
he·ro [ˈhirou], *pl.* **he·roes** [ˈ~z] héroe *m*; **he·ro·ic** [hiˈrouik] □ heroico; **her·o·ine** [ˈherouin] heroína *f*; ˈ**her·o·ism** heroísmo *m*.
he·ro·in [ˈherouin] *pharm.* heroína *f*; ~ *addict* heroinómano *m*.
her·on [ˈherən] garza *f* real.
her·ring [ˈheriŋ] arenque *m*; ˈ**her·ring·bone** ⊕ espinapez *m*; ~ *pattern* muestra *f* espiga; ~ *stitch* punto *m* de escapulario.
hers [hə:rz] (el) suyo, (la) suya *etc.*
her·self [hə:rˈself] (*subject*) ella misma; *acc.*, *dat.* se; (*after prp.*) sí (misma).
hes·i·tance, hes·i·tan·cy [ˈhezitəns(i)] vacilación *f*; **hes·i·tant** [ˈ~tənt] □ vacilante, irresoluto; **hes·i·tate** [ˈ~teit] vacilar (*about, over, to* en); *speech*: titubear; **hes·i**ˈ**ta·tion** vacilación *f*, irresolución *f*; titubeo *m*.
hes·sian [ˈhesiən] tejido *m* basto de cáñamo y yute.
het [het]: F *get* ~ *up* aturrullarse, acalorarse (*about, over* por).
het·er·o·dox [ˈhetərədɔks] heterodoxo; ˈ**het·er·o·dox·y** heterodoxia *f*; **het·er·o·dyne** [ˈ~dain] heterodino *adj. a. su. m*; **het·er·o·ge·ne·i·ty** [~roudʒiˈni:iti] heterogeneidad *f*; **het·er·o·ge·ne·ous** [ˈ~rouˈdʒi:niəs] heterogéneo.
hew [hju:] [*irr.*] cortar, tajar; hachear; labrar; picar; ~ *down* talar; ~ *out* excavar; tallar; *fig.* hacerse; **hewn** [hju:n] *p.p. of hew*.
hex·a·gon [ˈheksəgən] hexágono *m*; **hex·ag·o·nal** [hekˈsægənl] □ hexagonal; **hex·am·e·ter** [hekˈsæmitər] hexámetro *m*.
hey [hei] ¡eh!, ¡oye!
hey·day [ˈheidei] auge *m*, apogeo *m*; buenos tiempos *m/pl.*; flor *f* de edad.
hi [hai] ¡oye!, ¡eh!, ¡hala!
hi·a·tus [haiˈeitəs] laguna *f*; interrupción *f*; *gr.*, 𝄞 hiato *m*.
hi·ber·nate [ˈhaibə:rneit] *biol.* hibernar; invernar; **hi·ber**ˈ**na·tion** hibernación *f*; invernada *f*.

hic·cup, *a.* **hic·cough** [ˈhikʌp] **1.** hipo *m*; **2.** *v/t.* decir con hipos; *v/i.* hipar.

hick [hik] *sl.* palurdo *m*; *attr.* de aldea.

hick·o·ry [ˈhikəri] nogal *m* americano.

hid [hid] *pret. a.* **hid·den** [ˈhidn] *p.p. of hide*².

hide¹ [haid] piel *f*, pellejo *m*; (*esp. tanned*) cuero *m*.

hide² [~] [*irr.*] **1.** *v/t.* esconder (*from* de), ocultar (*from* a, de); (en)cubrir; disimular; *v/i.* esconderse, ocultarse (*from* de); **2.** *hunt.* trepa *f*; ˈ**hide-and-ˈseek** escondite *m*; *play (at)* ~ jugar al escondite.

hide·bound [ˈhaidbaund] *fig.* rígido; conservador; aferrado a la tradición.

hid·e·ous [ˈhidiəs] □ horrible; feo; monstruoso.

hide·out [ˈhaidaut] F escondrijo *m*, guarida *f*.

hid·ing¹ [ˈhaidiŋ] F paliza *f*, tunda *f*.

hid·ing² [~] ocultación *f*; *in* ~ escondido; *go into* ~ ocultarse, refugiarse; ˈ~ **place** escondrijo *m*.

hie [hai] *poet.* (*ger. hying*) ir de prisa.

hi·er·arch·y [ˈhaiərɑːrki] jerarquía *f*.

hi·er·o·glyph [ˈhaiərəglif] jeroglífico *m*; **hi·er·oˈglyph·ic** □ jeroglífico *adj. a. su. m.*

hi-fi [ˈhaiˈfai] = *high fidelity* (de) alta fidelidad *f*.

hig·gle [ˈhigl] regatear.

hig·gle·dy-pig·gle·dy [ˈhigldiˈpigldi] F *contp.* **1.** *adj.* revuelto; **2.** *adv.* confusamente.

high [hai] **1.** *adj.* □ (*v. a.* ~*ly*) alto; *altar, mass, street* mayor; *color, price* subido; *game* manido; *manner* altanero; *meat* pasado; *number, speed* grande; *polish* brillante; *priest* sumo; *quality* superior; F (*intoxicated*) embriagado; *3 feet* ~ 3 pies de alto; ~ *and dry* en seco; F ~ *and mighty* encopetado; ~*est bid* mejor postura *f*; *with a* ~ *hand* arbitrariamente, despóticamente; ~ *altar* altar *m* mayor; ~ *antiquity* antigüedad *f* remota; ~ *blood pressure* hipertensión *f* arterial; ~*boy* cómoda *f* alta con patas altas; ~*chair* silla *f* alta; ♀ *Church* Alta Iglesia *f*; ⚔ ~ *command* alto mando *m*; ~ *cost of living* carestía *f* de la vida; ♀ *Court* tribunal *m* supremo; ~ *diving* saltos *m/pl.* de palanca; ~ *explosive* explosivo *m* rompedor; ~*falutin* F pomposo, presuntuoso; ~ *fidelity* alta fidelidad *f*; ⚡ ~ *frequency* alta frecuencia *f*; ~ *gear* marcha *f* directa, toma *f* directa; ~ *horse* ademán *m* arrogante; ~*jack* = *hijack*; ~ *jinks sl.* jarana *f*, payasada *f*; ~ *life* alta sociedad *f*; ~ *living* vida *f* regalada; *v. spirit, tea, tension, etc.*; ~ *noon* pleno mediodía *m*; ~*-pitched* agudo; tenso, impresionable; ~*-priced* de precio elevado; ~ *priest* sumo sacerdote *m*; ~ *rise* edificio *m* de muchos pisos; ~ *school* escuela *f* de segunda enseñanza; ~ *sea* mar *f* gruesa; ~ *seas pl.* alta mar *f*; ~ *society* alta sociedad *f*, gran mundo *m*; ~*-strung* tenso, impresionable; ~ *tide* pleamar *f*, marea *f* alta; *fig.* punto *m* culminante; ~ *time* hora *f* precisa; *it is* ~ *time for you to go* ya es hora de que Vd. se marche; ~ *treason* alta traición *f*; *v. water*; ~ *wind* ventarrón *m*; ~ *words* palabras *f/pl.* airadas; **2.** *meteor.* (zona *f* de) alta presión *f*; ♀ = *High Street*; ♀ = *High School*; *on* ~ en las alturas, en el cielo; **3.** *adv.* altamente; (en) alto; fuertemente; a gran precio; lujosamente; ~ *and low* por todas partes; *aim* ~ *fig.* picar muy alto; *fly* ~ ✈ volar por alto; *fig.* picar muy alto; ˈ~-ˈ**backed** de respaldo alto; ˈ~**·ball** highball *m*; ˈ~**·born** linajudo; ˈ~**·brow** F intelectual *adj. a. su. m/f*; ˈ~**-class** de marca, de clase superior; ˈ~-ˈ**col·ored** de colores vivos; *fig.* exagerado; ˈ~**-flown** hinchado, altisonante; ˈ~**-grade** de calidad superior; ˈ~-ˈ**hand·ed** arbitrario, despótico; ˈ~ ˈ**hat** *sl.* **1.** esnob *m/f*; **2.** encopetado; **3.** tratar con desdén; ˈ~-ˈ**heeled** *shoes* de tacones altos; ˈ~ **jump** salto *m* de altura; ˈ~**·land·er** montañés (-a *f*) *m* (de Escocia); ˈ~**·lands** tierras *f/pl.* altas, montañas *f/pl.*; ˈ~**·light** toque *m* de luz; *fig.* momento *m* culminante; ˈ**high·ly** altamente; mucho, muy; sumamente; muy favorablemente; *speak* ~ *of* decir mil bienes de; *think* ~ *of* tener en mucho; ~ *bred animals* de buena raza; ~ *paid* muy bien pagado; ~ *seasoned* picante; ~ *strung* muy excitable, neurasténico; ˈ**high-ˈmind·ed** magnánimo, de nobles pensamientos; ˈ**high·ness** altura *f*; ♀ Alteza *f*.

high...: ˈ~**-pow·ered** de gran potencia; ˈ~-ˈ**pres·sure** de alta presión; *fig.* enérgico, urgente; ˈ~ˈ**road** carretera *f*, camino *m* real (*a. fig.*); ˈ~-ˈ**sound·ing** altisonante; ˈ~-**speed** de alta velocidad; ˈ~-ˈ**spir·it·ed** animoso; *horse* fogoso ˈ~-**test fuel** supercarburante *m*; ˈ~ˈ**toned** F de alto copete; de buen tono; de tono elevado; ˈ~·**way** = ~*road*; ~ *code* código *m* de circulación; ˈ~·**way·man** salteador *m* de caminos.

hi·jack [ˈhaidʒæk] F robar *un avión o el licor (a un contrabandista)*; F robar *a un pasajero o a un contrabandista de licores*; ˈ~·**er** F atracador *m*, pirata *m* aéreo; ˈ~·**ing** piratería *f* aérea.

hike [haik] F **1.** caminata *f*, excursión *f* a pie; **2.** dar una caminata, ir de excursión; ˈ**hik·er** F excursionista *m/f*.

hi·lar·i·ous [hiˈleriəs] □ hilarante.

hi·lar·i·ty [hiˈlæriti] hilaridad *f*.

hill [hil] colina *f*, cerro *m*, otero *m*, collado *m*; (*slope*) cuesta *f*; ~·**bil·ly** [ˈ~bili] F rústico *m* montañés; ˈ~ **climb·ing** *mot.* subida *f* de cuestas; ~ (*con*)*test* prueba *f* de subida de cuestas; ˈ**hill·i·ness** montuosidad *f*; **hill·ock** [ˈ~ək] altillo *m*, montículo *m*, altozano *m*; ˈ**hill·side** ladera *f*; ˈ**hill·y** accidentado, montuoso; *road* de fuertes pendientes.

hilt [hilt] puño *m*, empuñadura *f*; *up to the* ~ hasta las cachas.

him [him] *acc.* lo, le; *dat.* le; (*after prp.*) él.

him·self [himˈself] (*subject*) él mismo; *acc., dat.* se; (*after prp.*) sí (mismo); *by* ~ solo, por sí (solo); *he said to* ~ dijo para sí.

hind[1] [haind] cierva *f*.

hind[2] [~] trasero, posterior; ~ *leg* pata *f* trasera; ~ *quarters* cuarto *m* trasero; **hin·der** [ˈhində] *v/t.* estorbar, dificultar; ~ *from* impedir *inf.* (*or* que *subj.*); **hind·most** [ˈhaindmoust] posterior, último.

hin·drance [ˈhindrəns] obstáculo *m*, estorbo *m*, impedimento *m* (*to* para).

Hin·du, *a.* **Hin·doo** [ˈhinˈdu:] hindú *adj. a. su. m/f*.

Hin·du·sta·ni [hinduˈstæni] **1.** indostánico; indostanés *adj. a. su. m* (-a *f*); **2.** (*language*) indostaní *m*, indostánico *m*.

hinge [hindʒ] **1.** gozne *m*, pernio *m*, bisagra *f*; *a. zo.* charnela *f*; *fig.* eje *m*; *off the* ~ desquiciado; **2.** *v/t.* engoznar, embisagrar; *v/i.*: ~ (*up*)*on* girar sobre; *fig.* depender de.

hin·ny [ˈhini] burdégano *m*.

hint [hint] **1.** indirecta *f*; indicación *f*; consejo *m*; *take the* ~ darse por aludido; darse cuenta de la indirecta; aprovechar la indicación; **2.** echar indirectas; (*a.* ~ *at*) insinuar.

hin·ter·land [ˈhintərlænd] traspaís *m*.

hip[1] [hip] *anat.* cadera *f*; ~ *and thigh* sin piedad.

hip[2] [~] ⚘ escaramujo *m*.

hip[3] [~]: *int.* ~! ~! *hurra*(*h*)! ¡hurra!, ¡viva!

hip-bath [ˈhipbæθ] baño *m* de asiento.

hip·bone [ˈhipboun] cía *f*.

hipped[1] [hipt] △ a cuatro aguas.

hipped[2] [~] melancólico; *sl.* obsesionado.

hip·po [ˈhipou] F = **hip·po·pot·a·mus** [hipəˈpɔtəməs], *pl. a.* **hip·po·ˈpot·a·mi** [~mai] hipopótamo *m*.

hire [ˈhaiər] **1.** alquiler *m*, arriendo *m*; salario *m*, jornal *m of p.*; *for* (*or on*) ~ de alquiler; **2.** alquilar, arrendar (*a.* ~ *out*); tomar en arriendo; *p.* contratar; **hire·ling** [ˈ~liŋ] *contp.* alquiladizo *adj. a. su. m* (a *f*), mercenario *adj. a. su. m* (a *f*).

hir·sute [ˈhə:rsju:t] hirsuto.

his [hiz] **1.** su(s); **2.** *pron.* (el) suyo, (la) suya *etc.*

His·pan·ic [hisˈpænik] hispánico *adj. a. su. m* (a *f*); **his·pan·ist** [ˈhispənist] hispanista *m/f*.

hiss [his] **1.** siseo *m*, silbido *m*; **2.** silbar, sisear (*a.* ~ *off*).

hist [s:t] ¡chitón!, ¡silencio!

his·tol·o·gy [hisˈtɔlədʒi] histología *f*.

his·to·ri·an [hisˈtɔ:riən] historiador (-a *f*) *m*; **his·tor·ic, his·tor·i·cal** [~ˈtɔrik(l)] □ histórico; **his·to·ri·og·ra·pher** [~tɔ:riˈɔgrəfər] historiógrafo *m*; **his·to·ry** [ˈ~təri] historia *f*.

his·tri·on·ic [histriˈɔnik] □ histriónico, teatral.

hit [hit] **1.** golpe *m* (bien dado); tiro *m* certero; acierto *m*; *fig., thea.*, ♪ éxito *m*, sensación *f*; ⚔ impacto *m*; sátira *f*; *make a* ~ *with* caer en gracia a; **2.** golpear, pegar; (*collide with*) chocar con(tra), dar con; *target* dar en, acertar; (*wound*) herir; (*damage*) hacer daño a; afectar; F llegar a; ~ *a p. a blow* asestarle un golpe a una p.; ~ *at* dirigir (un) golpe(s) a; *fig.* satirizar, apuntar a; ~ *off* remedar; *resemblance* coger; ~ *it off with* hacer buenas migas con; ~ *or miss* a la buena ventura; ~ *out* atacar; repartir golpes; ~ (*up*)*on* dar con; tropezar con; *I ~ on the idea* se me ocurrió la idea; ~ *and run* atacar y retirarse; *he ~ his head against a tree* dio con la cabeza contra un árbol; ~ *the nail on the head* dar en el clavo; *it ~s you in the eye* salta a la vista; **ˈ~-and-ˈrun driv·er** *mot.* conductor *m* que atropella y huye.

hitch [hitʃ] **1.** tirón *m*; ⚓ cote *m*, vuelta *f* de cabo; obstáculo *m*, dificultad *f*; *without a ~* a pedir de boca; **2.** mover de un tirón; amarrar; enganchar; atar; ~ *up trousers* alzar; **ˈ~·hike** hacer autostop.

hith·er [ˈhiðər] *mst lit.* acá, hacia acá; ~ *and thither* acá y acullá; **hith·er·to** [ˈ~ˈtu:] hasta ahora.

hive [haiv] **1.** *a. fig.* colmena *f*; ~s ⚕ urticaria *f*; **2.** enjambrar; acopiar (miel); *fig.* vivir aglomerados.

ho [hou] ¡eh!; ¡alto!, ¡hola!

hoar [hɔ:r] † cano; vetusto.

hoard [hɔ:rd] **1.** tesoro *m* (escondido); provisión *f*; acumulamiento *m*; **2.** (*a.* ~ *up*) atesorar; acumular (en secreto).

hoard·ing[1] [ˈhɔ:rdiŋ] atesoramiento *m*; acumulación *f*; acaparamiento *m*.

hoard·ing[2] [~] valla *f* de construcción; (*for posters*) cartelera *f*.

hoar·frost [ˈhɔ:rfrɔst] escarcha *f*.

hoar·i·ness [ˈhɔ:rinis] canicie *f*; vetustez *f*.

hoarse [hɔ:rs] □ ronco, enronquecido; **ˈhoarse·ness** ronquedad *f*; ⚕ ronquera *f*.

hoar·y [ˈhɔ:ri] cano; vetusto.

hoax [houks] **1.** mistificación *f*; burla *f*; engaño *m*; **2.** mistificar; burlar; engañar.

hob[1] [hɔb] repisa *f* interior de la chimenea.

hob[2] [~] = *hobgoblin*; F *play ~ with* trastornar.

hob·ble [ˈhɔbl] **1.** cojera *f*; maniota *f*; **2.** *v/i.* cojear; *v/t.* manear.

hob·ble·de·hoy [ˈhɔbldiˈhɔi] mozalbete *m* desgarbado.

hob·by [ˈhɔbi] pasatiempo *m*, afición *f*; tema *f*, manía *f*; *orn.* alcotán *m*; **ˈ~·horse** caballito *m* (de niños); caballo *m* mecedor; *fig.* tema *f*, caballo *m* de batalla.

hob·gob·lin [ˈhɔbgɔblin] duende *m*, trasgo *m*.

hob·nail [ˈhɔbneil] clavo *m* de botas.

hob·nob [ˈhɔbnɔb] F codearse (*with* con).

ho·bo [ˈhoubou] vagabundo *m*.

hock[1] [hɔk] **1.** *zo.* corvejón *m*; **2.** desjarretar.

hock[2] [~] vino *m* (blanco) del Rin.

hock[3] [~] *sl.* **1.** empeño *m*; **2.** empeñar; **ˈ~·shop** casa *f* de empeños.

hock·ey [ˈhɔki] hockey *m*.

ho·cus-po·cus [ˈhoukəsˈpoukəs] abracadabra *m*, mistificación *f*; engaño *m*; pasapasa *m*.

hod [hɔd] cuezo *m* (para llevar mortero y ladrillos).

hodge·podge [ˈhɔdʒpɔdʒ] olla *f* podrida; mezcolanza *f*, baturrillo *m*.

hoe [hou] **1.** azada *f*, azadón *m*; sacho *m*; **2.** azadonar; sachar.

hog [hɔg] **1.** cerdo *m*, puerco *m* (*a. fig.*); F *go the whole ~* llegar hasta el extremo; liarse la manta a la cabeza; **2.** *sl.* acaparar; tragarse lo mejor de; *credit etc.* atribuirse todo; **hog·gish** [ˈ~iʃ] □ puerco; glotón; **hogs·head** [ˈ~zhed] pipa *f*, bocoy *m*; *medida de capacidad* (= *52,5 o 54 galones ingleses*); **ˈhog·skin** piel *f* de cerdo; **ˈhog·wash** bazofia *f*.

hoist [hɔist] **1.** montacargas *m*; elevador *m S.Am.*; cabria *f*; alzamiento *m*; **2.** alzar; *flag* enarbolar; ⚓ izar.

hoi·ty-toi·ty [ˈhɔitiˈtɔiti] **1.** petulante, presuntuoso, picajoso; **2.** ¡cáspita!; ¡tate!.

ho·kum [ˈhoukəm] *sl.* efectismo *m*; cursilería *f*; tonterías *f/pl*.

hold [hould] **1.** agarro *m*; asimiento *m*; *wrestling*: presa *f*; *fig.* dominio *m*, influencia *f*; *fig.* arraigo *m*; (*place to grip*) asidero *m*, asa *f*; ⚓ bodega *f*; ♩ calderón *m*; *catch* (*or get, lay, take*) ~ *of* agarrar, coger; apoderarse de; *have a ~ on* (*or over*) dominar; *keep ~ of* seguir agarrado a; **2.** *v/t.* tener; retener, guardar; detener; (*in place*) sujetar; agarrar, coger; contener, tener cabida para; mantener; sostener (*a.* ♩); juzgar; *post* ocupar; *meeting* celebrar; *this box won't ~ them all* en esta caja no caben todos; ~ *back* retener; detener; refrenar; ~ *down* sujetar; oprimir; F ~ *down a job* mantenerse en un puesto; estar a la altura de un cargo; ~ *in* refrenar; ~ *off* mantener a distancia; ~ *on* sujetar; ~ *out* extender, ofrecer; ~ *over* aplazar, diferir; ~ *up* (*support*) apoyar, sostener; (*raise*) levantar; (*stop*) detener; parar; suspender; interrumpir; (*rob*) saltear; (*gangsters*) atracar; **3.** [*irr.*] *v/i.* mantenerse firme, resistir, aguantar; (de)tenerse; ser valedero; (*weather*) continuar; (*stick*) pegarse; ~ *back* refrenarse; vacilar; ~ *forth* perorar (*about, on* sobre); ~ *good* (*or true*) ser valedero; ~ *hard!* ¡tente!, ¡para!; ~ *off* mantenerse a distancia; esperar; ~ *on* agarrarse bien; aguantar; persisitir; ~ *on!* ¡espera!; ~ *out* resistir; durar; ~ *out for s.t.* no cejar hasta que se conceda algo; insistir en algo; ~ *to* atenerse a; afirmarse en; ~ *up* mantenerse en pie; (*weather*) seguir bueno; ~ *with* estar de acuerdo con; aprobar; '**hold-all** funda *f*, neceser *m*; '**hold·er** (*p.*) tenedor (-a *f*) *m*; (*tenant*) arrendatario (a *f*) *m*; (*office, title*) titular *m*/*f*; (*handle*) asidero *m*; receptáculo *m*; ⊕ soporte *m*; (*pad*) agarrador *m*; (*in compounds*) porta...; '**hold·fast** grapa *f*; '**hold·ing** posesión *f*; tenencia *f*; propiedad *f*; ⚕ ~*s* valores *m*/*pl.* en cartera; ⚕ ~ *company* sociedad *f* de control; compañía *f* tenedora; '**hold·o·ver** resto *m*, sobras *f*/*pl.*; consecuencias *f*/*pl.*; '**hold·up** F detención *f*; interrupción *f*; (*gangsters*) atraco *m*.

hole [houl] **1.** agujero *m*; cavidad *f*; (*a. golf*) hoyo *m*; bache *m in road*; rotura *f in clothes*; boquete *m in wall*; guarida *f of animals*; *fig.* cuchitril *m*; F *in a* ~ en un aprieto; F *pick* ~*s in* encontrar defectos en; **2.** agujerear; *ball* meter en el hoyo; '**hole-and-'cor·ner** furtivo.

hole·y ['houli] F agujereado.

hol·i·day ['hɔlədei] **1.** día *m* de fiesta, día *m* festivo; asueto *m*; ~(*s pl.*) vacaciones *f*/*pl.*; ~*s with pay* vacaciones *f*/*pl.* retribuidas; ~ *camp* colonia *f* veraniega; **2.** veranear; pasar las vacaciones.

ho·li·ness ['houlinis] santidad *f*.

hol·ler ['hɔlər] F gritar; llamar a gritos.

hol·low ['hɔlou] **1.** □ hueco, ahuecado; *eyes* hundido; *fig.* vacío, falso; *voice* sepulcral, cavernoso; **2.** F *adv.* *beat* (*all*) ~ cascar, vencer completamente; **3.** hueco *m*; (con)cavidad *f*; depresión *f*; hondón *m in terrain*; **4.** (*a.* ~ *out*) ahuecar, excavar, vaciar; '~ '**ground** vaciado; '**hol·low·ness** concavidad *f*; oquedad *f* (*a. fig.*); falsedad *f*.

hol·ly ['hɔli] acebo *m*.

hol·ly·hock ['hɔlihɔk] malva *f* loca, malvarrosa *f*.

holm-oak ['houm'ouk] encina *f*.

hol·o·caust ['hɔləkɔ:st] holocausto *m*; *fig.* destrucción *f* ocasionada por un incendio.

hol·ster ['houlstər] pistolera *f*.

ho·ly ['houli] santo; sagrado; ♀ *of Holies* sanctasanctórum *m*; ♀ *Thursday* jueves *m* santo; ~ *water* agua *f* bendita; ♀ *Week* semana *f* santa.

hom·age ['hɔmidʒ] homenaje *m*; *do* (*or pay, render*) ~ rendir homenaje (*to* a).

home [houm] **1.** hogar *m*; domicilio *m*, casa *f*; patria *f* (chica); (*institution*) asilo *m*; (*habitat*) habitación *f*; *sport*: meta *f*; *children's games*: la madre; *at* ~ en casa; *fig.* a gusto; **2.** *adj.* casero, doméstico; de casa; nativo; nacional; *a few* ~ *truths* cuatro verdades; ~*body* hogareño *m*; ~*bred* doméstico; sencillo, inculto, tosco; ~*coming* regreso *m* al hogar; ~ *country* suelo *m* natal; ~ *delivery* distribución *f* a domicilio; ~ *front* frente *m* doméstico; ~*land* tierra *f* natal, patria *f*; ~ *life* vida *f* de familia; ~*-loving* casero, hogareño; ~*maker* ama *f* de casa; ~ *office* domicilio *m* social, oficina *f* central; ♀ *Office* Ministerio *m* del Interior; (*Spain*) Ministerio *m* de la Gobernación; ~ *plate baseball*: puesto *m* meta; ~ *port* puerto *m* de origen; ~ *rule* autonomía *f*; ~ *run baseball*: jonrón *m*, cuadrangular *m*; ♀ *Secretary* Ministro *m* del Interior; (*Spain*) Ministro *m* de la Gobernación; ~ *straight racing*: recta *f* de la llegada; ~ *stretch* esfuerzo *m* final, último trecho *m*; ~ *team* equipo *m* de casa; ~ *town* ciudad *f* natal; ~*y* F íntimo, cómodo; **3.** *adv.* a casa; en casa; a fondo; *be* ~ estar de vuelta; *bring s.t.* ~ *to s.o.* hacer que alguien se dé cuenta de algo; *come* ~ volver a casa; *it came* ~ *to me* me llegó al alma; me di cuenta de ello; *hit* (*or strike*) ~ herir en lo vivo; dar en el blanco; ⊕ meter a fondo; **4.** volver a casa; buscar la querencia; ⚔ ~ *on the target* buscar al blanco; '~-'**baked** hecho en casa; '~-'**brewed** fermentado en casa; ~ **e·co'nom·ics** economía *f* doméstica; '~-'**grown** de cosecha propia; del país; '**home·less** sin casa ni hogar; '**home·li·ness** sencillez *f*; domesticidad *f*; comodidad *f*; fealdad *f*; '**home·ly** sencillo, llano; casero; familiar; feo; **home·made** ['houm'meid] casero, de fabricación casera, hecho en casa.

ho·me·o·path ['houmjəpæθ] homeópata *m*; **ho·me·o'path·ic** □ homeopático; **ho·me·op·a·thist** [~'ɔpəθist] homeópata *m*; **ho·me'op·a·thy** homeopatía *f*.

home...: '~**·sick** nostálgico; *be* ~ tener morriña; '~**·sick·ness** morriña *f*, nostalgia *f*; '~**·spun** 1. hilado (*or* tejido) en casa; casero; *fig.* llano; 2. tela *f* de fabricación casera; '~**·stead** hacienda *f*, granja *f*; heredad *f*; casa *f*, caserío *m*; '~**·ward(s)** hacia casa; hacia la patria; ⚓ ~ *bound* con rumbo al puerto de origen; '~**·work** deberes *m/pl*.

hom·i·cide ['hɔmisaid] homicidio *m*; (*p*.) homicida *m/f*.

hom·i·ly ['hɔmili] homilía *f*.

hom·ing ['houmiŋ] vuelta *f* (al palomar); ~ *pigeon* paloma *f* mensajera; ~ *rocket* cohete *m* autodirigido buscador del blanco.

ho·mo·ge·ne·i·ty [hɔmoudʒe'ni:iti] homogeneidad *f*; **ho·mo·ge·ne·ous** [~'dʒi:niəs] □ homogéneo; **ho·mol·o·gous** [hɔ'mɔləgəs] homólogo; **ho'mol·o·gy** [~dʒi] homología *f*; **hom·o·nym** ['hɔmənim] homónimo *m*; **ho·mo·sex·u·al** ['houmou'seksjuəl] homosexual.

hone [houn] 1. piedra *f* de afilar; 2. afilar.

hon·est ['ɔnist] □ honrado, recto, probo; (*chaste, decent, reasonable*) honesto; sincero, genuino; '**hon·es·ty** honradez *f*, rectitud *f etc.*

hon·ey ['hʌni] miel *f*; (*my*) ~! ¡vida mía!; '~**·bee** abeja *f* (obrera); '**hon·ey·comb** panal *m*; '**hon·ey·combed** apanalado; acribillado; **hon·eyed** ['hʌnid] meloso, melifluo; '**hon·ey·moon** 1. luna *f* de miel, viaje *m* de novios; 2. pasar la luna de miel; '**hon·ey·pot** mielera *f*; **hon·ey·suck·le** ['~sʌkl] madreselva *f*.

honk [hɔŋk] 1. graznido *m of goose*; bocinazo *m of horn*; 2. graznar; bocinar.

honk·y-tonk ['hɔŋkitɔŋk] *sl.* taberna *f* (*or* cabaret *m*) de mala fama.

hon·or ['ɔnər] 1. honor *m*; (*esp. good name*) honra *f*; condecoración *f*; ~*s pl.* honores *m/pl.*; *last* ~*s* honras *f/pl.* (fúnebres); ~ *system* acatamiento *m* voluntario del reglamento; *point of* ~ punto *m* de honor; *word of* ~ palabra *f* de honor; *Your* ♀ vuestra merced; ⚖ Su Señoría; *in* ~ *of* en honor de; (*up*)*on my* ~ a fe mía; *do the* ~*s of the house* hacer los honores de la casa; 2. honrar (*a.* ✝); *signature etc.* hacer honor a.

hon·or·a·ble ['ɔnərəbl] □ honorable; honrado; (*conferring honor*) honroso; *Right* ♀ Ilustrísimo; ~ *mention* mención *f* honorífica; '**hon·or·a·ble·ness** honorabilidad *f*, honradez *f*.

hon·o·rar·i·um [ɔnə'reriəm] honorario *m* (*mst pl.*); **hon·or·ar·y** ['ɔnərəri] honorario; no remunerado.

hooch [hu:tʃ] *sl.* licor *m*.

hood [hud] capucha *f*, capilla *f*; (*univ., penitent's, hawk's*) capirote *m*; *mot.* capota *f*; *mot.* capó *m*; *sl.* criminal *m*; '**hood·ed** encapuchado; encapirotado.

hood·lum ['hu:dləm] F matón *m*, gorila *m*.

hoo·doo ['hu:du:] aojo *m*; mala suerte *f*; *put the* ~ *on* aojar.

hood·wink ['hudwiŋk] vendar los ojos a; engañar.

hoo·ey ['hu:i] *sl.* tonterías *f/pl.*, música *f* celestial.

hoof [hu:f] 1. casco *m*, pezuña *f*; 2. F ~ *it* marcharse; ir a pie; **hoofed** [hu:ft] ungulado.

hook [huk] 1. gancho *m* (*a. boxing*); garfio *m*; (*fishing*) anzuelo *m*; (*door etc.*) aldabilla *f*; (*hanger*) colgadero *m*; ~*s and eyes* corchetes *m/pl.*; *by* ~ *or by crook* por fas o por nefas; ~, *line and sinker* totalmente; ~*nose* nariz *f* de pico de loro; 2. *v/t.* enganchar (*a. fishing*); pescar (*a. fig.*); encorvar; *sl.* hurtar; *sl.* ~ *it* largarse; ~ *up* enganchar; abrochar; *v/i.* engancharse; encorvarse; **hooked** [~t] ganchudo; '**hook·up** combinación *f*; conexión *f*; ⚡ acoplamiento *m*; *radio*: estaciones *f/pl.* conjugadas; '**hook·y:** *play* ~ hacer novillos, jubilarse, hacer corrales.

hoo·li·gan ['hu:ligən] gamberro *m*, rufián *m*, camorrista *m*; '**hoo·li·gan·ism** gamberrismo *m*.

hoop [hu:p] **1.** aro *m*; ~ *skirt* miriñaque *m*; **2.** enarcar; '**hoop·er** tonelero *m*.

hoo·poe ['hu:pu:] abubilla *f*.

hoot [hu:t] **1.** ululato *m of owl*; bocinazo *m of horn*; ⚓, ⊕ toque *m* de sirena; (*laugh*) risotada *f*; grito *m*; **2.** *v/i.* ulular; gritar; *mot.* tocar la bocina; ⚓, ⊕ tocar la sirena; *v/t.* manifestar a gritos; dar grita a; silbar, abuchear (*a.* ~ *at*, ~ *off*, ~ *out*); '**hoot·er** sirena *f*; *mot.* bocina *f*.

hop[1] [hɔp] ⚘ lúpulo *m* (*a.* ~*s pl.*).

hop[2] [~] **1.** salt(it)o *m*, brinco *m*; ✈ vuelo *m*, etapa *f*; F baile *m*; ~, *skip and jump* triple salto *m*; **2.** *v/i.* brincar, saltar; danzar; F ~ *off* marcharse; bajar de; F ~ *on* subir a; *v/t.* atravesar (de un salto); F ~ *it* escabullirse; largarse.

hope [houp] **1.** esperanza *f*; **2.** esperar (*for acc.*, *to inf.*); ~ *in* confiar en; ~ *against* ~ esperar desesperando; **hope·ful** ['~ful] □ esperanzado; optimista; esperanzador, que da esperanzas, prometedor; *be* ~ *that* esperar que; '**hope·less** □ desesperanzado; desesperado; imposible; ⚕ desahuciado.

hop·per ['hɔpər] ⊕ tolva *f*; 🚃 vagón tolva *m*; **hop·ping** ['hɔpiŋ]: F *he is* ~ *mad* está que bota.

hop·scotch ['hɔpskɔtʃ] infernáculo *m*.

horde [hɔ:rd] horda *f*.

ho·ri·zon [hə'raizn] horizonte *m*; **hor·i·zon·tal** [hɔri'zɔntl] □ horizontal.

hor·mone ['hɔ:rmoun] hormona *f*.

horn [hɔ:rn] **1.** cuerno *m*; asta *f of stag, bull*; ♪ trompa *f*; *mot.* bocina *f*, claxon *m*; ~ *of plenty* cuerno *m* de la abundancia; *on the* ~*s of a dilemma* entre la espada y la pared; **2.** *sl.* ~ *in* entrometerse; **horned** ['~id, *in compounds* hɔ:rnd] cornudo; de cuernos ...

hor·net ['hɔ:rnit] avispón *m*; *stir up a* ~*s' nest* armar cisco.

horn·less ['hɔ:rnlis] sin cuernos; mocho; '**horn·pipe** ♪ cornamusa *f*; baile *m* vivaz (de marineros); '**horn-rimmed** '**spec·ta·cles** anteojos *m/pl.* de concha; **horn·swog·gle** ['~swɔgl] *sl.* **1.** timo *m*; pamplinas *f/pl.*; **2.** timar; '**horn·y** □ córneo; *hands* calloso.

hor·o·scope ['hɔrəskoup] horóscopo *m*; *cast a* ~ sacar un horóscopo.

hor·ri·ble ['hɔrəbl] □ horrible, horroroso; **hor·rid** ['hɔrid] □ horroroso, horrible; F muy antipático; **hor·rif·ic** [hɔ'rifik] horrendo, horrífico; **hor·ri·fy** ['~fai] horrorizar; **hor·ror** ['hɔrər] horror *m* (*of* a); *the* ~*s* espasmo *m* de horror; espanto *m*; ~ *film*, ~ *movie* película *f* de terror.

hors d'œuvres [ɔ:r'də:rv] entremeses *m/pl.*

horse [hɔ:rs] **1.** *zo.*, *gymnastics*: caballo *m*; ⚔ caballería *f*; ⊕ caballete *m*; ~ *of a different color* harina *f* de otro costal; *eat like a* ~ comer como una vaca; *get on one's high* ~ darse aires de suficiencia; F *hold your* ~*s!* ¡para!, ¡despacito!; *take* ~ montar a caballo; ~ *artillery* artillería *f* montada; **2.** montar; proveer de caballos; '**~·back:** *on* ~ a caballo; '**~ blan·ket** manta *f* para caballo; '**~·box** vagón *m* para caballerías; '**~ break·er** domador *m* de caballos; '**~ 'chest·nut** castaña *f* de Indias; (*a.* ~ *tree*) castaño *m* de Indias; '**~ col·lar** collera *f*; '**~ deal·er** chalán *m*; '**~·fly** mosca *f* borriquera, tábano *m*; ♀ **Guards** *pl.* guardias *f/pl.* montadas; '**~·hair** crin *f*; '**~·laugh** F risotada *f*; '**~·man** jinete *m*, caballista *m*; '**~·man·ship** equitación *f*, manejo *m* (del caballo); ~ **op·er·a** *sl.* película *f* que se desarrolla en el oeste de EE.UU.; '**~ pis·tol** pistola *f* de arzón; '**~·play** payasadas *f/pl.*, travesuras *f/pl.*, pelea *f* amistosa; '**~·pow·er** caballo *m* (de fuerza); '**~ race** carrera *f* de caballos; '**~·rad·ish** rábano *m* picante; '**~ sense** sentido *m* común; '**~·shoe** herradura *f*; ~ *magnet* imán *m* de herradura; ~ *nail* clavo *m* de herrar; '**~ show** concurso *m* hípico; '**~ thief** abigeo *m*, cuatrero *m*; '**~-trade** chalanear; '**~ trad·er** chalán *m*; '**~ trad·ing** chalanería *f*; '**~-trad·ing** chalanesco; '**~ whip** látigo *m*; '**~·wom·an** amazona *f*.

hors·y ['hɔ:rsi] caballuno; aficionado a caballos; carrerista.

hor·ti·cul·tur·al [hɔ:rti'kʌltʃərəl] hortícola; '**hor·ti·cul·ture** horticultura *f*; **hor·ti'cul·tur·ist** horticultor (-a *f*) *m*.

hose [houz] **1.** † calzas *f/pl.*; ✝ medias *f/pl.*, calcetines *m/pl.*; (*a.* ˈ~ **pipe**) mang(uer)a *f*; **2.** regar (*or* limpiar) con manga.
ho·sier [ˈhouʒər] calcetero (a *f*) *m*; ˈ**ho·sier·y** calcetería *f*; géneros *m/pl.* de punto.
hos·pice [ˈhɔspis] hospicio *m*.
hos·pi·ta·ble [ˈhɔspitəbl] □ hospitalario.
hos·pi·tal [ˈhɔspitl] hospital *m*; **hos·pi·tal·i·ty** [~ˈtæliti] hospitalidad *f*; **hos·pi·tal·ize** [ˈ~təlaiz] hospitalizar; ˈ**hos·pi·tal** ˈ**ship** buque hospital *m*; ˈ**hos·pi·tal train** tren hospital *m*.
host[1] [houst] huésped *m* (*a. zo.*, ♀); anfitrión *m at meal*; hospedero *m of inn*.
host[2] [~] ⚔ hueste *f*, ejército *m*; muchedumbre *f*; sinnúmero *m*; *Lord of* ♀*s* Señor *m* de los ejércitos.
host[3] [~] *eccl.* hostia *f*.
hos·tage [ˈhɔstidʒ] rehén *m*.
hos·tel [ˈhɔstəl] albergue *m*; residencia *f* (de estudiantes).
host·ess [ˈhoustis] huéspeda *f* (*v. host*[1]); ✈ azafata *f*.
hos·tile [ˈhɔstail] hostil; **hos·til·i·ty** [hɔsˈtiliti] hostilidad *f*; *start hostilities* romper las hostilidades.
hos·tler [ˈɔslər] = *ostler*.
hot [hɔt] caliente; *climate* cálido; *day* caluroso, de calor; *sun* ardiente, abrasador; *taste* picante; ⊕ en caliente; *fig. dispute* acalorado; *supporter* vehemente, acérrimo; *p.* enérgico; apasionado; lujurioso; F *situation* difícil, de mucho peligro; *sl.* robado; *sl.* radiactivo; *be* ~ (*p.*) tener calor; (*weather*) hacer calor; (*th.*) estar caliente; F ~ *air* palabrería *f*; F ~ *dog* perro *m* caliente; *go like* ~ *cakes* venderse como pan bendito; *sl.* ~ *stuff* caliente; de rechupete; experto; ˈ**hot·bed** almajara *f*; *fig.* semillero *m*, foco *m*.
hotch·potch [ˈhɔtʃpɔtʃ] = *hodgepodge*.
ho·tel [houˈtel] hotel *m*.
hot...: ˈ~**·foot** a toda prisa; ˈ~**·head** persona *f* exaltada (*or* impetuosa), botafuego *m*; ˈ~**·house** invernáculo *m*; ˈ~ **plate** calientaplatos *m*; hornillo *m* eléctrico; ˈ~ **pot** estofado *m*; ˈ~ **press** prensar en caliente; ~ **rod** *sl.* bólido *m*; ˈ~-ˈ**wa·ter:** ~ *bottle*, ~ *bag* bolsa *f* de agua caliente; ~ *heater* calentador *m* de acumulación; ~ *heating* calefacción *f* por agua caliente; ~ *tank* depósito *m* de agua caliente.
hound [haund] **1.** perro *m* (de caza); podenco *m*; sabueso *m* de Artois; *fig.* canalla *m*; **2.** acosar, perseguir; ~ *on* incitar (*to* a).
hour [ˈauər] hora *f*; *fig.* momento *m*; *after* ~*s* fuera de horas; *by the* ~ por horas; *the small* ~*s* las altas horas; ˈ~**·glass** reloj *m* de arena; ˈ~ **hand** horario *m*; ˈ**hour·ly** (de) cada hora; por hora.
house 1. [haus], *pl.* **hous·es** [ˈhauziz] casa *f* (*a.* ✝); *thea.* sala *f*, público *m*, entrada *f*; edificio *m*; *parl.* cámara *f*; *univ.* colegio *m*; ~ *arrest* arresto *m* domiciliario; ~*broken* (*perro o gato*) enseñado *a hábitos de limpieza*; ~ *cleaning* limpieza *f* de la casa; ~ *current* sector *m* de distribución, canalización *f* de consumo; ~*ful* casa *f* llena; ~*furnishings pl.* menaje *m*, enseres *m/pl.* domésticos; *go* ~*-hunting* ir a buscar casa; ~ *meter* contador *m* de abonado; ~*mother* mujer *f* encargada de una residencia de estudiantes; ~ *of cards* castillo *m* de naipes; ~ *of ill fame* jupanar *m*, casa *f* de prostitución; ~*work* quehaceres *m/pl.* domésticos; ~ *and home* hogar *m*; F *it's on the* ~ está pagado (por el dueño); *keep* ~ llevar la casa; tener casa propia; *attr.* de (la) casa, domiciliario, doméstico; **2.** [hauz] *v/t.* alojar; domiciliar; almacenar; meter (en); ⊕ encajar; ⚓ estibar; *v/i.* vivir, alojarse; ~ **a·gent** [ˈhaus~] corredor *m* de casas; ˈ~**·boat** habitación *f* flotante; ˈ~**·break·er** ladrón *m* con escala; demoledor *m* de casas; ˈ~**·break·ing** escalo *m*, allanamiento *m* de morada; ˈ~**·coat** bata *f*; ˈ~**·fly** mosca *f* doméstica; ˈ~**·hold** casa *f*; familia *f*; menaje *m*; *attr.* casero, doméstico; *royal* ~ corte *f*; ~ *troops* guardia *f* real; *be a* ~ *word* andar en lenguas; ˈ~**·hold·er** cabeza *f* de familia; amo (a *f*) *m* de casa; inquilino (a *f*) *m*; ˈ~**·keep·er** ama *f* de casa (*or* de llaves); ˈ~**·keep·ing 1.** gobierno *m* de la casa; quehaceres *m/pl.* domésticos; **2.** doméstico; ˈ~**·maid** criada *f*; ˈ~ **paint·er** pintor *m* de brocha gorda; ˈ~ **phy**ˈ**si·cian** médico *m* residente; ˈ~ **room** alojamiento *m*; cabida *f* (de una casa); *give* ~ *to*

alojar, tener en casa; ˈ~-to-ˈ**house** de casa en casa; a domicilio; ˈ~•**top** tejado *m*; *shout from the* ~*s* pregonar a los cuatro vientos; ˈ~-**train•ed** bien enseñado, limpio; ˈ~-**warm•ing** (*a.* ~ *party*) fiesta *f* de estreno de una casa; ~•**wife** [ˈ~waif] ama *f* de casa; madre *f* de familia; mujer *f* casada; [ˈhʌzif] estuche *m* de costura; ~•**wife•ly** [ˈ~waifli] de ama de casa; hacendoso.

hous•ing [ˈhauziŋ] alojamiento *m*; (provisión *f* de) vivienda *f*; casas *f*/*pl.*; (*storage*) almacenaje *m*; ⊕ encaje *m*; ⊕ cárter *m*, caja *f*; ~ *estate* bloque *m* de casas protegidas; ~ *shortage* crisis *f* de vivienda.

hove [houv] *pret. a. p.p. of heave* 2.

hov•el [ˈhɔvl] casucha *f*, cuchitril *m*, tugurio *m*.

hov•er [ˈhɔvər] cernerse; revolotear; planear; estar suspendido; flotar (en el aire); rondar; vacilar; ✈ ~(*ing*) *plane* helicóptero *m*.

how [hau] cómo; *price*: a cómo; *before adj. or adv.* qué, cuán; ~ *large it is!* ¡qué grande es!, ¡cuán grande es!; ~ *large is it?* ¿cómo es de grande?, ¿de qué tamaño es?; *he does not know* ~ *large it is* no sabe lo grande que es, no sabe cuán grande es; ~ *are you?* ¿cómo está Vd.?; ¿qué tal? (F); ~ *about ...?* ¿qué tal si ...?; ¿qué te parece ...?; ¿qué tal anda ...?; *v. else, far*; ~ *long* cuánto tiempo; ~ *many* cuántos; ~ *much* cuánto; ~ *often* cuántas veces; ~ *old is he?* ¿cuántos años tiene?, ¿qué edad tiene?; ~-**d'ye-do** [ˈ~diˈdu:] F lío *m*, berenjenal *m*; ~ˈ**ev•er 1.** *adv.* comoquiera que; por más que; (*with adj. or adv.*) por (muy) ... que; ~ *clever he is* por (muy) hábil que sea; ~ *hot it is* por mucho calor que haga; ~ *much* por mucho que; **2.** *conj.* sin embargo, no obstante, con todo.

how•itz•er [ˈhauitsər] obús *m*.

howl [haul] **1.** aullido *m*; alarido *m*; chillido *m*; ⚡ silbido *m*; **2.** aullar; dar alaridos; F reír a carcajadas; ~ *down* abuchear; ˈ**howl•er** F plancha *f*, falta *f* garrafal; ˈ**howl•ing 1.** aullador; F formidable, clamoroso; **2.** aullido(s) *m*(*pl.*).

hoy[1] [hɔi] ¡eh!, ¡hola!

hoy[2] [~] ⚓ buque *m* costero; barcaza *f*.

hub [hʌb] cubo *m*; *fig.* eje *m*, centro *m*; ˈ~•**cap** tapacubos *m*, tapón *m* de cubo.

hub•bub [ˈhʌbʌb] baraúnda *f*, batahola *f*; alboroto *m*.

hub(•**by**) [ˈhʌb(i)] F marido *m*.

huck•ster [ˈhʌkstər] **1.** buhonero *m*; mercachifle *m*; **2.** (re)vender; regatear.

hud•dle [ˈhʌdl] **1.** pelotón *m*, montón *m*; grupo *m* apretado; *sl. go into a* ~ ir aparte para conferenciar; **2.** *v*/*t.* amontonar; confundir; hacer precipitadamente; *v*/*i.* amontonarse, apretarse (*a.* ~ *together, up*); acurrucarse (*a.* ~ *up*).

hue[1] [hju:] color *m*, tinte *m*; matiz *m*; tono *m*.

hue[2] [~]: ~ *and cry* alarma *f*; protesta *f* clamorosa.

huff [hʌf] mal humor *m*, pique *m*; rabieta *f*; *in a* ~ ofendido; ˈ**huff•y** □ malhumorado, ofendido; enojadizo.

hug [hʌg] **1.** abrazo *m*; **2.** abrazar; apretujar; *coast etc.* no apartarse de; *fig.* afirmarse en; *fig.* acariciar; ~ *o.s.* congratularse (*on* de, por).

huge [hju:dʒ] □ enorme, inmenso, descomunal; ˈ**huge•ness** inmensidad *f*.

hug•ger-mug•ger [ˈhʌgərmʌgər] F **1.** confusión *f*, desorden *m*; **2.** confuso, desordenado; **3.** *adv.* desordenadamente.

Hu•gue•not [ˈhju:gənɔt] hugonote *adj. a. su. m* (a *f*).

hulk [hʌlk] ⚓ casco *m* (arrumbado); pontón *m*, carraca *f*; *fig.* armatoste *m*; ˈ**hulk•ing** grande y pesado.

hull [hʌl] **1.** ⚓ casco *m*; ⚘ vaina *f*, cáscara *f*; **2.** mondar; desvainar; ⚓ dar en el casco de.

hul•la•ba•loo [hʌləbəˈlu:] baraúnda *f*, batahola *f*; vocería *f*.

hul•lo [ˈhʌˈlou] = *hello*.

hum [hʌm] **1.** zumbido *m*; tarareo *m*; murmullo *m*; **2.** zumbar; *tune* tararear; *v. haw*; F *make things* ~ avivarlo; desplegar gran actividad.

hu•man [ˈhju:mən] □ humano *adj. a. su. m*; **hu•mane** [hju:ˈmein] □ humano; compasivo; **hu•man•ism** [ˈhju:mənizm] humanismo *m*; ˈ**hu•man•ist** humanista *m*/*f*; **hu•man•i•tar•i•an** [hjumæniˈtɛəriən] humanitario *adj. a. su. m* (a *f*); **huˈman•i•ty** humanidad *f*; *humanities pl.* humanidades *f*/*pl.*; **hu•man•i•za•tion** [hju:mənaiˈzeiʃn] humanización *f*; ˈ**hu•man•ize** humanizar.

hum·ble [ˈhʌmbl] **1.** □ humilde; *my ~ self, your ~ servant* un servidor; *eat ~ pie* humillarse y pedir perdón; **2.** humillar.

hum·ble·ness [ˈhʌmblnis] humildad *f.*

hum·bug [ˈhʌmbʌg] **1.** bola *f,* farsa *f;* embaucamiento *m;* disparate *m;* (*p.*) farsante *m/f,* charlatán (-a *f*) *m,* embaucador (-a *f*) *m;* (*sweet*) caramelo *m* de menta; **2.** embaucar.

hum·ding·er [hʌmˈdiŋər] *sl.* (*p.*) machote *m;* cosa *f* estupenda.

hum·drum [ˈhʌmdrʌm] monótono; rutinario; aburrido.

hu·mid [ˈhjuːmid] húmedo; **huˈmid·i·ty** humedad *f.*

hu·mil·i·ate [hjuˈmilieit] humillar; **hu·mil·iˈa·tion** humillación *f.*

hu·mil·i·ty [hjuˈmiliti] humildad *f.*

hum·ming·bird [ˈhʌmiŋbəːrd] colibrí *m;* **hum·ming top** [ˈhʌmiŋtɔp] trompa *f.*

hum·mock [ˈhʌmək] morón *m,* montecillo *m.*

hu·mor [ˈhjuːmər] **1.** humor *m;* humorismo *m;* capricho *m;* (*situation*) comicidad *f; in a good* (*bad*) ~ de buen (mal) humor; *be in the ~ for* estar (de humor) para; *out of ~* de mal humor; **2.** seguir el humor a; complacer; mimar; **hu·mor·ist** [ˈhjuːmərist] humorista *m/f;* persona *f* chistosa; **ˈhu·mor·less** sin (sentido de) humor; **hu·mor·ous** [ˈhjuːmərəs] □ festivo, chistoso, humorístico.

hump [hʌmp] **1.** joroba *f,* corcova *f,* giba *f;* montecillo *m;* 🚂 lomo *m* para maniobras de gravedad; *fig.* mal humor *m,* abatimiento *m; give a p. the ~* jorobar; **2.** corcovar(se); *fig.* jorobar; F llevar al hombro; **ˈhump·back, ˈhump·backed** *v. hunchback.*

humph [mm] ¡bah!, ¡qué va!

hump·ty-dump·ty [ˈhʌmptiˈdʌmpti] F persona *f* rechoncha.

hump·y [ˈhʌmpi] desigual; giboso.

hu·mus [ˈhjuːməs] humus *m.*

hunch [hʌntʃ] **1.** *v. hump;* tajada *f,* pedazo *m* grande; F idea *f,* corazonada *f,* sospecha *f;* **2.** encorvar (*a. ~ up*); **ˈhunch·back** corcova *f,* joroba *f;* (*p.*) corcovado (a *f*) *m,* jorobado (a *f*) *m;* **ˈhunch·backed** corcovado, jorobado.

hun·dred [ˈhʌndrəd] **1.** cien(to); **2.** ciento *m;* centenar *m;* centena *f; in* (*by*) *~s* a centenares; **ˈhun·dred-fold 1.** *adj.* céntuplo; **2.** *adv.* cien veces; **hun·dredth** [ˈ~θ] centésimo (*a. su. m*); **ˈhun·dred·weight** (= *50,8 Kg.*) *approx.* quintal *m.*

hung [hʌŋ] *pret. a. p.p. of hang* 1.

Hun·gar·i·an [hʌŋˈgeriən] **1.** húngaro *adj. a. su. m* (a *f*); **2.** (*language*) húngaro *m.*

hun·ger [ˈhʌŋgər] **1.** hambre *f* (*a. fig.*) (*for* de); *~ strike* huelga *f* de hambre; **2.** hambrear; tener hambre (*after, for* de).

hun·gry [ˈhʌŋgri] □ hambriento; *land* pobre, estéril; *be ~* tener hambre, tener ganas (*for* de).

hunk [hʌŋk] F buen pedazo *m,* rebanada *f* gruesa.

hunk·y(**do·ry**) [ˈhʌŋki(ˈdɔːri)] *sl.* magnífico, de órdago.

hunt [hʌnt] **1.** (partida *f* de) caza *f,* cacería *f;* montería *f; on the ~ for* a caza de; **2.** *v/t.* cazar; perseguir; buscar; *hounds etc.* emplear en la caza; *country* recorrer de caza; *~ out, ~ up* rebuscar; *v/i.* cazar, buscar (*a. ~ for*); *go ~ing* ir de caza; **ˈhunt·er** cazador *m;* caballo *m* de caza; (*watch*) saboneta *f;* **ˈhunt·ing 1.** caza *f;* montería *f;* **2.** cazador; de caza; **ˈhunt·ing box** pabellón *m* de caza; **ˈhunt·ing ground** cazadero *m;* **ˈhunt·ress** cazadora *f;* **ˈhunts·man** montero *m,* cazador *m.*

hur·dle [ˈhəːrdl] valla *f* (*a. sport*); **ˈhur·dler** corredor (-a *f*) *m* en las carreras de vallas; **ˈhur·dle race** carrera *f* de vallas.

hur·dy-gur·dy [ˈhəːrdigəːrdi] organillo *m.*

hurl [həːrl] **1.** lanzamiento *m;* **2.** lanzar, arrojar.

hurl·y-burl·y [ˈhəːrlibəːrli] batahola *f,* tumulto *m.*

hur·ra(**h**) [huˈrɑː] ¡hurra!; *~ for ...!* ¡viva ...!

hur·ri·cane [ˈhʌrikən] huracán *m.*

hur·ried [ˈhʌrid] □ apresurado; hecho de (*or* a) prisa.

hur·ry [ˈhʌri] **1.** prisa *f; in a ~* de prisa; *be in a ~* (*to*) tener prisa (por); *is there any ~?* ¿corre prisa?; F *I won't come back here in a ~* aquí no pongo los pies nunca más; **2.** *v/t.* apresurar, dar prisa a, acelerar (*a. ~ on, ~ up*); *~ away, ~ off* hacer marchar de prisa; *v/i.* apresurarse (*to* a), darse prisa (*a. ~ up*) (*to* para, en); *~ away, ~ off* marcharse de prisa; ~ *over* pasar rápidamente por; concluir a prisa; hacer con precipitación; **'~-'scurry** 1. atropello *m*, precipitación *f*; 2. precipitadamente, atropelladamente.

hurt [hə:rt] 1. daño *m*, mal *m*; dolor *m*; herida *f*; 2. [*irr*.] *v/t*. lastimar, dañar; herir; perjudicar; hacer mal a; doler; ofender; *get* ~ lastimarse; *v/i*. doler; hacer mal; F sufrir daño; **hurt·ful** ['~ful] □ dañoso, perjudicial.

hur·tle ['hə:rtl] arrojarse con violencia; volar; caer con violencia.

hus·band ['hʌzbənd] 1. marido *m*, esposo *m*; 2. economizar; manejar con economía; **'hus·band·man** labrador *m*, granjero *m*, agricultor *m*; **'hus·band·ry** labranza *f*, agricultura *f*; granjería *f*; economía *f*; (buen) gobierno *m*.

hush [hʌʃ] 1. silencio *m*; quietud *f*; 2. *v/t*. acallar; apaciguar; ~ *up* echar tierra a; *v/i*. callar(se); 3. ¡chito!, ¡chitón!; '~-'~ F muy secreto; '~ **mon·ey** F precio *m* del silencio (de una p.).

husk [hʌsk] 1. cascabillo *m*; cáscara *f* (*a. fig*.); vaina *f*; 2. descascarar; desvainar; **'husk·i·ness** ronquedad *f*; **'husk·y**[1] □ ronco; ⚘ cascarudo; F fornido.

hus·ky[2] ['hʌski] esquimal *adj. a. su. m/f*; perro *m* esquimal, husky *m*.

hus·sar [hu'zɑ:r] húsar *m*.

hus·sy ['hʌsi] mujerzuela *f*; sinvergonzona *f*.

hus·tings ['hʌstiŋz] *pl*. elecciones *f/pl*.

hus·tle ['hʌsl] 1. prisa *f*; actividad *f* (febril); empuje *m*; ~ *and bustle* actividad *f* bulliciosa; 2. *v/t*. empujar; atropellar; apresurar, dar prisa a; *v/i*. apresurarse; F menearse; **'hus·tler** F persona *f* de empuje; trafagón *m*.

hut [hʌt] cabaña *f*; barraca *f* (*a*. ⚔); casucha *f*; casilla *f*; cobertizo *m*.

hutch [hʌtʃ] conejera *f for rabbit*; jaula *f*; arca *f*; cabaña *f*.

hut·ment ['hʌtmənt], **hut·ted camp** ['hʌtid kæmp] campamento *m* de barracas.

huz·za [hu'zɑ:] † ¡viva!, ¡vítor!

hy·a·cinth ['haiəsinθ] jacinto *m*.

hy·ae·na [hai'i:nə] hiena *f*.

hy·brid ['haibrid] híbrido *adj. a. su. m* (*a f*); **'hy·brid·ism** hibridismo *m*; **'hy·brid·ize** hibridar.

hy·dra ['haidrə] hidra *f*.

hy·dran·gea [hai'dreindʒə] hortensia *f*.

hy·drant ['haidrənt] boca *f* de riego.

hy·drate ['haidreit] 1. hidrato *m*; 2. hidratar(se).

hy·drau·lic [hai'drɔ:lik] 1. □ hidráulico; 2. ~s hidráulica *f*.

hy·dro... ['haidrou...] hidr(o)...; **'~'car·bon** hidrocarburo *m*; **'~'chlo·ric ac·id** ácido *m* clorhídrico; **'~·dy'nam·ics** hidrodinámica *f*; **'~·e'lec·tric** hidroeléctrico; ~ *generating station* central *f* hidroeléctrica; **hy·dro·gen** ['haidridʒən] hidrógeno *m*; ~ *bomb* bomba *f* de hidrógeno; **hy·dro·gen·at·ed** [hai'drɔdʒineitid], **hy'drog·e·nous** hidrogenado; **hy'drog·ra·phy** [~grəfi] hidrografía *f*; **hy·dro·path·ic** ['haidrou'pæθik] 1. hidropático; 2. (*a.* ~ *establishment*) establecimiento *m* hidropático; **hy·drop·a·thy** [hai'drɔpəθi] hidropatía *f*.

hy·dro...: '~'pho·bi·a hidrofobia *f*; **'~·plane** hidroplano *m*, hidroavión *m*; **'~'stat·ic** 1. hidrostático; 2. ~s hidrostática *f*.

hy·drox·ide [hai'drɔksaid] hidróxido *m*.

hy·e·na [hai'i:nə] hiena *f*.

hy·giene ['haidʒi:n] higiene *f*; **hy'gi·en·ic** 1. □ higiénico; 2. ~s higiene *f*.

hy·grom·e·ter [hai'grɔmitər] higrómetro *m*.

Hy·men ['haimen] himeneo *m*; ♀ *anat*. himen *m*; **hy·me·ne·al** [~'ni:əl] nupcial.

hymn [him] 1. himno *m*; 2. *v/t*. ensalzar con himnos; *v/i*. cantar himnos; **hym·nal** ['~nəl], **'hymn book** himnario *m*.

hy·per·bo·la [hai'pə:rbələ] ⩚ hipérbola *f*; **hy'per·bo·le** [~li] *rhet*. hipérbole *f*; **hy·per·bol·ic** [~'bɔlik], **hy·per'bol·i·cal** □ hiperbólico; **hy·per·crit·i·cal** ['~'kritikl] □ hipercrítico; **hy'per·tro·phy** [~trəfi] hipertrofia *f*.

hy·phen ['haifən] guión *m*; **hy·phen·ate** ['~eit] unir (*or* separar *or* escribir) con guión; ~*d American* norteamericano (a *f*) *m* de nacimiento extranjero.

hyp·no·sis [hip'nousis] hipnosis *f*.

hyp·not·ic [hip'nɔtik] □ hipnótico *adj. a. su. m* (a *f*); **hyp·no·tism** ['~nətizm] hipnotismo *m*; **'hyp·no·tist** hipnotista *m/f*; **hyp·no·tize** ['~taiz] hipnotizar.
hy·po ['haipou] hiposulfito *m* sódico.
hy·po·chon·dri·a [haipou'kɔndriə] hipocondría *f*; **hy·po'chon·dri·ac** [~driæk] hipocondríaco *adj. a. su. m* (a *f*); **hy·poc·ri·sy** [hi'pɔkrəsi] hipocresía *f*; **hyp·o·crite** ['hipəkrit] hipócrita *m/f*; **hyp·o'crit·i·cal** □ hipócrita; **hy·po·der·mic** [haipə'də:rmik] hipodérmico; **hy·pot·e·nuse** [hai'pɔtinju:z] hipotenusa *f*; **hy'poth·e·cate** [~θikeit] hipotecar; **hy'poth·e·sis** [~θisis], *pl.* **hy'poth·e·ses** [~θisi:z] hipótesis *f*; **hy·po·thet·ic, hy·po·thet·i·cal** [~pə'θetik(l)] □ hipotético.
hys·sop ['hisəp] ♀, *eccl.* hisopo *m.*
hys·te·ri·a [his'tiriə] ⚕ histerismo *m*; excitación *f* loca; **hys·ter·ic,** *mst* **hys·ter·i·cal** [his'terik(l)] □ histérico; **hys'ter·ics** paroxismo *m* histérico; *go into* ~ ponerse histérico.

I

I [ai] yo.

i·am·bic [aiˈæmbik] yámbico; **ˈi·amb, iˈam·bus** [~bəs] yambo *m.*

I·be·ri·an [aiˈbiriən] **1.** ibero (a *f*) *m*; **2.** ibérico.

i·bex [ˈaibeks] rebeco *m.*

ice [ais] **1.** hielo *m*; (*to eat*) helado *m*; *break the* ~ romper el hielo; F *cut no* ~ no pinchar ni cortar; **2.** *v/t.* helar; (*with sugar*) alcorzar, garapiñar; *v/i.* helarse (*a.* ~ *up*); **ˈ~·age** período *m* glacial; **ˈ~ axe** piolet *m*; **ˈ~ bag** bolsa *f* para hielo; **ice·berg** [ˈ~bəːrg] témpano *m*, iceberg *m.*

ice...: **ˈ~·bound** helado; preso entre los hielos; **ˈ~·box, ˈ~ chest** nevera *f*, fresquera *f*; **ˈ~·break·er** ⚓ rompehielos *m*; **ˈ~·cap** bolsa *f* para hielo; manto *m* de hielo; **ˈ~ cream** helado *m*, mantecado *m*; **ˈ~-cream** de helado; ~ *cone* cucurucho *m* de helado, barquillo *m* de helado; ~ *freezer* heladora *f*, garapiñera *f*; ~ *parlor* salón *m* de refrescos, tienda *f* de helados, heladería *f*; ~ *soda* agua *f* gaseosa con helado; **ˈ~ cube** cubito *m* de hielo; **ˈ~ floe** témpano *m*; **ˈ~ hockey** hockey *m* sobre hielo; **ˈ~·man** vendedor *m* de hielo, repartidor *m* de hielo; **ˈ~ pack** hielo *m* flotante; bolsa *f* de hielo; **ˈ~ pail** enfriadera *f*; **ˈ~ pick** picahielos *m*; **ˈ~ skate** patín *m* de cuchilla, patín de hielo; **ˈ~-skate** patinar sobre hielo; **ˈ~ skat·ing** patinaje *m* sobre hielo; **ˈ~ tray** bandejita *f* de hielo; **ˈ~ wa·ter** agua *f* helada.

Ice·land·er [ˈaisləndər] islandés (-a *f*) *m*; **Ice·land·ic** [aisˈlændik] islandés *adj. a. su. m.*

ich·thy·ol·o·gy [ikθiˈɔlədʒi] ictiología *f.*

i·ci·cle [ˈaisikl] carámbano *m.*

i·ci·ness [ˈaisinis] frialdad *f* (de hielo).

ic·ing [ˈaisiŋ] formación *f* de hielo; alcorza *f*, capa *f* de azúcar *on cake.*

i·con [ˈaikɔn] icono *m*; **i·con·o·clast** [aiˈkɔnəklæst] iconoclasta *m/f.*

i·cy [ˈaisi] □ helado; glacial (*a. fig.*); gélido (*mst lit.*).

i·de·a [aiˈdiə] idea *f*, concepto *m*; *bright* ~ ocurrencia *f*, idea *f* luminosa; *form* (*or get*) *an* ~ *of* hacerse una idea de; F *the very* ~! ¡ni hablar!; **iˈde·al 1.** □ ideal; perfecto; **2.** ideal *m*; **iˈde·al·ism** idealismo *m*; **iˈde·al·ist** idealista *m/f*; **i·de·alˈis·tic** □ idealista; **iˈde·al·ize** [~aiz] idealizar.

i·den·ti·cal [aiˈdentikl] □ idéntico; **iˈden·ti·cal·ness** identidad *f*; **i·den·ti·fiˈca·tion** identificación *f*; ~ *mark* señal *f* (*or* marca *f*) de identificación; ~ *card* (*abbr. I.D.*) carta *f* de identificación; carnet *m*; ~ *tag* disco *m* de identificación; *v. a. identity*; **iˈden·ti·fy** [~fai] identificar; **iˈden·ti·ty** identidad *f*; ~ *card* cédula *f* personal, carnet *m*; ~ *disk* placa *f* (*or* chapa *f*) de identidad.

id·e·o·log·i·cal [aidiəˈlɔdʒikl] □ ideológico; **id·e·ol·o·gy** [~ˈɔlədʒi] ideología *f.*

id·i·o·cy [ˈidiəsi] idiotez *f*, imbecilidad *f.*

id·i·om [ˈidiəm] modismo *m*, idiotismo *m*; lenguaje *m*; idioma *m*; estilo *m*; **id·i·o·mat·ic** [idiəˈmætik] □ idiomático.

id·i·o·syn·cra·sy [idiəˈsiŋkrəsi] idiosincrasia *f.*

id·i·ot [ˈidiət] idiota *m/f*, tonto (a *f*) *m*, imbécil *m/f*; **id·i·ot·ic** [idiˈɔtik] □ idiota, necio, imbécil.

i·dle [ˈaidl] **1.** □ ocioso; desocupado; ⊕ parado; inactivo; *p. contp.* holgazán, perezoso; vano, inútil; *talk* vacío, frívolo; ~ *hours* ratos *m/pl.* perdidos, horas *f/pl.* de ocio; ~ *question* pregunta *f* ociosa; ⊕ *run* ~ marchar en vacío; **2.** *v/t.* (*mst* ~ *away*) gastar ociosamente; perder; *v/i.* haraganear; vagar; ⊕ marchar en vacío; **ˈi·dle·ness** ociosidad *f*; desocupación *f*; holgazanería *f*; pereza *f*; frivolidad *f*; **ˈi·dler** ocioso (a *f*) *m*, haragán (-a *f*) *m*, zángano *m*, aplanacalles *m.*

i·dol [ˈaidl] ídolo *m*; **i·dol·a·ter** [aiˈdɔlətər] idólatra *m*; **iˈdol·a·tress**

idólatra *f*; **i'dol·a·trous** □ idólatra; idolátrico; **i'dol·a·try** idolatría *f*; **i·dol·ize** ['aidəlaiz] idolatrar.
i·dyll ['aidil] idilio *m*; **i'dyl·lic** □ idílico.
if [if] **1.** si; ~ *only* ...! ¡ojalá (que) ...!; ~ *so* si es así; **2.** hipótesis *f*; duda *f*; ~*s and buts* peros *m/pl.*, dudas *f/pl.*; **'if·fy** F dudoso.
ig·loo ['iglu] iglú *m*.
ig·ne·ous ['igniəs] ígneo.
ig·nite [ig'nait] encender(se); **ig·ni·tion** [~'niʃn] ignición *f*; *mot.* encendido *m*; ~ *key* llave *f* de contacto; ~ *switch* interruptor *m* de encendido.
ig·no·ble [ig'noubl] □ innoble.
ig·no·min·i·ous [ignə'miniəs] □ ignominioso; **'ig·no·min·y** ignominia *f*.
ig·no·ra·mus [ignə'reiməs] ignorante *m/f*; **ig·no·rance** ['ignərəns] ignorancia *f*; **'ig·no·rant** ignorante; F inculto; *be* ~ *of* ignorar, desconocer; **ig·nore** [ig'nɔːr] desatender, no hacer caso de (*a p.*).
i·lex ['aileks] encina *f*.
ilk [ilk] (mismo) nombre *m*; F especie *f*, jaez *m*.
ill [il] **1.** *su.* mal *m*; desgracia *f*; daño *m*; **2.** *adj.* malo; enfermo; *fall* (*or take*) ~ caer (*or* ponerse) enfermo; **3.** *adv.* mal; *v. ease*; *take it* ~ tomarlo a mal.
I'll [ail] = *I will, I shall*.
ill-ad·vised ['iləd'vaizd] malaconsejado.
il·la·tive [i'leitiv] ilativo.
ill...: '~-'**bred** malcriado; '~-**dis·'posed** malintencionado; maldispuesto (*to[wards]* a, hacia).
il·le·gal [i'liːgəl] □ ilegal; **il·le·gal·i·ty** [ili'gæliti] ilegalidad *f*.
il·leg·i·ble [i'ledʒəbl] □ ilegible.
il·le·git·i·ma·cy [ili'dʒitiməsi] ilegitimidad *f*; **il·le'git·i·mate** [~mit] □ ilegítimo.
ill...: '~-'**fat·ed** aciago; malhadado; malogrado; '~-'**fa·vored** feso, mal parecido; '~ '**feel·ing** hostilidad *f*, rencor *m*; '~-'**got·ten** mal adquirido; '~-'**hu·mored** malhumorado.
il·lib·er·al [i'libərəl] □ iliberal; **il·lib·er·al·i·ty** [ilibə'ræliti] iliberalidad *f*.
il·lic·it [i'lisit] □ ilícito.
il·lim·it·a·ble [i'limitəbl] ilimitable.
il·lit·er·a·cy [i'litərəsi] analfabetismo *m*; **il·lit·er·ate** ['~rit] □ analfabeto *adj. a. su. m* (a *f*); iletrado.
ill...: '~-'**judged** imprudente; '~-'**man·nered** grosero, mal educado; '~-'**na·tured** malicioso; malhumorado.
ill·ness ['ilnis] enfermedad *f*, mal *m*.
il·log·i·cal [i'lɔdʒikl] □ ilógico.
ill...: ~-**o·mened** ['il'oumend] de mal agüero; '~-'**starred** malhadado; '~-'**tem·pered** de mal genio; malhumorado; '~-'**timed** intempestivo; '~-'**treat** maltratar.
il·lu·mi·nant [i'ljuːminənt] (tipo *m* de) alumbrado *m*; **il'lu·mi·nate** [~neit] iluminar, alumbrar (*a. fig.*); ~*d sign* letrero *m* luminoso; **il'lu·mi·nat·ing** instructivo, aclaratorio; ⚡ de alumbrado; **il·lu·mi'na·tion** iluminación *f*; alumbrado *m*; **il'lu·mi·na·tive** [~neitiv] iluminativo; **il'lu·mi·na·tor** iluminador (-a *f*) *m*; **il'lu·mine** [~min] = *illuminate*.
ill-use ['il'juːz] maltratar.
il·lu·sion [i'luːʒn] ilusión *f*; **il'lu·sive** [~siv] □, **il'lu·so·ry** [~səri] □ ilusorio.
il·lus·trate ['iləstreit] ilustrar; **il·lus'tra·tion** ilustración *f*; **'il·lus·tra·tive** □ ilustrativo; *be* ~ *of* ejemplificar; **'il·lus·tra·tor** ilustrador (-a *f*) *m*.
il·lus·tri·ous [i'lʌstriəs] □ ilustre.
ill will ['il'wil] mala voluntad *f*; rencor *m*, odio *m*.
I'm [aim] = *I am*.
im·age ['imidʒ] **1.** imagen *f*; *be the very* (F *spitting*) ~ *of* ser el vivo retrato de; **2.** representar; retratar; imaginar; reflejar; **'im·age·ry** imaginería *f*.
im·ag·i·na·ble [i'mædʒinəbl] imaginable; **im'ag·i·nar·y** imaginario; **im·ag·i·na·tion** [~'neiʃn] imaginación *f*; **im'ag·i·na·tive** [~nətiv] □ imaginativo; **im'ag·i·na·tive·ness** imaginativa *f*; **im'ag·ine** [~dʒin] imaginar(se), figurarse; *just* ~! ¡imagínese!
im·be·cile ['imbisiːl] □ imbécil *adj. a. su. m/f*; **im·be·cil·i·ty** [~'siliti] imbecilidad *f*.
im·bibe [im'baib] (em)beber; *fig.* embeberse de (*or* en).
im·bro·glio [im'brouliou] embrollo *m*, lío *m*.
im·bue [im'bjuː] *fig.* imbuir (*with* de, en); empapar; teñir.
im·i·ta·ble ['imitəbl] imitable; **im·i·tate** ['~teit] imitar; *b.s.* remedar;

im·i'ta·tion imitación *f*; *b.s.* remedo *m*; *attr.* imitado, artificial; ~ *jewels* joyas *f/pl.* de imitación; **'im·i·ta·tive** □ imitativo; imitador; **'im·i·ta·tor** imitador (-a *f*) *m*.
im·mac·u·late [i'mækjulit] □ sin mancha, limpísimo; inmaculado; correcto; ♀ *Conception* Inmaculada (*or* Purísima) Concepción *f*.
im·ma·nent ['imənənt] inmanente.
im·ma·te·ri·al [imə'tiriəl] □ inmaterial; sin importancia; indiferente.
im·ma·ture [imə'tʃur] inmaturo; verde; **im·ma'tu·ri·ty** inmadurez *f*, inexperiencia *f*.
im·meas·ur·a·ble [i'meʒərəbl] □ inmensurable, inmenso.
im·me·di·ate [i'mi:djət] inmediato; **im'me·di·ate·ly 1.** *adv.* inmediatamente, luego, en seguida; **2.** *cj.* así que, luego que.
im·me·mo·ri·al [imi'mɔ:riəl] □ inmemorial, inmemorable.
im·mense [i'mens] □ inmenso, enorme, vasto; *sl.* estupendo; **im'men·si·ty** inmensidad *f*.
im·merse [i'mə:rs] sum(erg)ir; ~ *o.s. in fig.* sumergirse en; ~*d in fig.* absorto en; **im'mer·sion** [~ʒn] inmersión *f*, sumersión *f*; ~ *heater* calentador *m* de inmersión.
im·mi·grant ['imigrənt] inmigrante *adj. a. su. m/f*; **im·mi·grate** ['~greit] inmigrar; **im·mi'gra·tion** inmigración *f*.
im·mi·nence ['iminəns] inminencia *f*; **'im·mi·nent** □ inminente.
im·mo·bile [i'moubail] inmóvil, inmoble; **im·mo·bil·i·ty** [imou'biliti] inmovilidad *f*; **im·mo·bi·lize** [i'moubilaiz] inmovilizar.
im·mod·er·ate [i'mɔdərit] □ inmoderado; **im'mod·er·ate·ness** inmoderación *f*.
im·mod·est [i'mɔdist] □ inmodesto, impúdico; **im'mod·es·ty** inmodestia *f*, impudicia *f*.
im·mo·late ['imouleit] inmolar; **im·mo'la·tion** inmolación *f*.
im·mor·al [i'mɔrəl] □ inmoral; **im·mo·ral·i·ty** [imə'ræliti] inmoralidad *f*.
im·mor·tal [i'mɔ:rtl] □ inmortal *adj. a. su. m/f*; **im·mor·tal·i·ty** [~'tæliti] inmortalidad *f*; **im'mor·tal·ize** [~təlaiz] inmortalizar.
im·mov·a·ble [i'mu:vəbl] **1.** □ inmoble, inmóvil; inalterable; **2.** ~*s pl.* bienes *m/pl.* inmuebles.
im·mune [i'mju:n] inmune (*from, to* contra); exento (*from* de); **im'mu·ni·ty** inmunidad *f*; exención *f*; **'im·mu·nize** [~aiz] inmunizar.
im·mure [i'mjur] emparedar.
im·mu·ta·bil·i·ty [imju:tə'biliti] inmutabilidad *f*; **im'mu·ta·ble** □ inmutable.
imp [imp] trasgo *m*, duende *m*, diablillo *m* (*a. fig.*).
im·pact ['impækt] impacto *m* (*a. fig.*), choque *m*; *fig.* efecto *m*.
im·pair [im'per] perjudicar, menoscabar, deteriorar, debilitar.
im·pale [im'peil] empalar, espetar.
im·pal·pa·ble [im'pælpəbl] □ impalpable; *fig.* intangible.
im·pan·el [im'pænl] = *empanel*; inscribir en la lista de los jurados; elegir *un jurado*.
im·part [im'pɑ:rt] comunicar, hacer saber; impartir.
im·par·tial [im'pɑ:rʃl] □ imparcial; **im·par·ti·al·i·ty** ['~ʃi'æliti] imparcialidad *f*.
im·pass·a·ble [im'pæsəbl] □ intransitable, impracticable.
im·passe ['impæs] callejón *m* sin salida (*a. fig.*).
im·pas·sioned [im'pæʃnd] apasionado, ardiente.
im·pas·sive [im'pæsiv] □ impasible; **im'pas·sive·ness** impasibilidad *f*.
im·pa·tience [im'peiʃns] impaciencia *f*; **im'pa·tient** □ impaciente (*at, with* con, de, por); intolerante (*of* con, para); *be*(*come*) (*or get, grow*) ~ impacientarse (*at, with* ante, con; *to* por); *make* ~ impacientar.
im·peach [im'pi:tʃ] acusar (de alta traición); procesar; censurar; tachar; **im'peach·a·ble** censurable; susceptible de ser procesado; **im'peach·ment** procesamiento *m* (por alta traición); acusación *f*.
im·pec·ca·bil·i·ty [impekə'biliti] impecabilidad *f*; **im'pec·ca·ble** □ impecable, intachable.
im·pe·cu·ni·ous [impi'kju:niəs] inope, indigente.
im·pede [im'pi:d] dificultar, estorbar; impedir.
im·ped·i·ment [im'pedimənt] impedimento *m* (*a.* ⚖); estorbo *m* (*to* para); *speech*: defecto *m* del habla;

im·ped·i·men·ta [~ˈmentə] *pl.* equipaje *m*; ⚔ impedimenta *f*.
im·pel [imˈpel] impeler, impulsar (*to* a).
im·pend [imˈpend] pender; ser inminente; amenazar; **imˈpend·ing** inminente; pendiente.
im·pen·e·tra·bil·i·ty [impenitrəˈbiliti] impenetrabilidad *f*; **imˈpen·e·tra·ble** □ impenetrable (*by, to* a).
im·pen·i·tence [imˈpenitəns] impenitencia *f*; **imˈpen·i·tent** □ impenitente, incorregible.
im·per·a·tive [imˈperətiv] **1.** □ imperativo; imperioso; indispensable; *gr.* ~ *mood* = **2.** *gr.* (modo) imperativo *m*.
im·per·cep·ti·ble [impərˈseptəbl] □ imperceptible.
im·per·fect [imˈpəːrfikt] □ imperfecto (*a. gr.*); deficiente, defectuoso; **im·per·fec·tion** [~pərˈfekʃn] imperfección *f*; desperfecto *m*.
im·pe·ri·al [imˈpiriəl] **1.** □ imperial; imperatorio; **2.** (*beard*) perilla *f*; **imˈpe·ri·al·ism** imperialismo *m*; **imˈpe·ri·al·ist** imperialista *m/f*; **im·pe·ri·alˈis·tic** imperialista.
im·per·il [imˈperil] poner en peligro, arriesgar.
im·pe·ri·ous [imˈpiriəs] □ imperioso, arrogante; apremiante.
im·per·ish·a·ble [imˈperiʃəbl] imperecedero.
im·per·ma·nent [imˈpəːrmənənt] no permanente, fugaz.
im·per·me·a·ble [imˈpəːrmiəbl] impermeable.
im·per·son·al [imˈpəːrsnl] □ impersonal; **im·per·son·al·i·ty** [~səˈnæliti] impersonalidad *f*.
im·per·son·ate [imˈpəːrsɔneit] hacerse pasar por; hacer el papel de; *thea.* imitar; **im·per·sonˈa·tion** representación *f*; *thea.* imitación *f*; **imˈper·son·a·tor** representador (-a *f*) *m*; *thea.* imitador (-a *f*) *m*.
im·per·ti·nence [imˈpəːrtinəns] impertinencia *f*; insolencia *f*; **imˈper·ti·nent** □ impertinente; insolente.
im·per·turb·a·bil·i·ty [ˈimpərtəːrbəˈbiliti] imperturbabilidad *f*; **im·perˈturb·a·ble** □ imperturbable.
im·per·vi·ous [imˈpəːrviəs] □ impermeable, impenetrable (*to* a); *fig.* insensible (*to* a).
im·pet·u·os·i·ty [impetjuˈɔsiti] impetuosidad *f*; irreflexión *f*; **imˈpet·u·ous** □ impetuoso; irreflexivo;
im·pe·tus [ˈ~pitəs] ímpetu *m*; impulso *m* (*a. fig.*).
im·pi·e·ty [imˈpaiəti] impiedad *f*.
im·pinge [imˈpindʒ] incidir ([*up*]*on* en); chocar ([*up*]*on* con); tocar ([*up*]*on* en); **imˈpinge·ment** choque *m*; infracción *f*.
im·pi·ous [ˈimpiəs] □ impío.
imp·ish [ˈimpiʃ] □ endiablado; travieso; juguetón.
im·pla·ca·bil·i·ty [implækəˈbiliti] implacabilidad *f*; **imˈpla·ca·ble** □ implacable.
im·plant [imˈplænt] implantar; inculcar.
im·plau·si·ble [imˈplɔːzəbl] inverosímil.
im·ple·ment 1. [ˈimplimənt] utensilio *m*, herramienta *f*, instrumento *m*; ~*s pl.* ⚒ apero *m*; **2.** [ˈ~ment] poner por obra; llevar a cabo; cumplir; **im·ple·men·ta·tion** [~ˈteiʃn] cumplimiento *m*, ejecución *f*.
im·pli·cate [ˈimplikeit] implicar; comprometer; enredar; **im·pliˈca·tion** inferencia *f*; insinuación *f*; complicidad *f*; ~*s pl.* trascendencia *f*, consecuencias *f/pl*.
im·plic·it [imˈplisit] □ implícito; *faith etc.* absoluto, incondicional, ciego.
im·plied [imˈplaid] implícito; *be* ~ sobre(e)ntenderse.
im·plore [imˈplɔːr] implorar; **imˈplor·ing** [~riŋ] □ suplicante.
im·ply [imˈplai] implicar; (pre)suponer; dar a entender; insinuar.
im·po·lite [impəˈlait] □ descortés, mal educado.
im·pol·i·tic [imˈpɔlitik] □ impolítico.
im·pon·der·a·ble [imˈpɔndərəbl] **1.** imponderable; **2.** ~*s pl.* elementos *m/pl.* imponderables.
im·port 1. [ˈimpɔːrt] ⚕ importación *f*; mercancía *f* importada; importancia *f*; significado *m*; ~ *duty* derechos *m/pl.* de entrada; **2.** [imˈpɔːrt] importar (*a.* ⚕); significar; **imˈpor·tance** importancia *f*; **imˈpor·tant** □ importante; de categoría; **im·por·ta·tion** [~ˈteiʃn] importación *f*; **imˈport·er** importador (-a *f*) *m*.
im·por·tu·nate [imˈpɔːrtjunit] □ importuno, insistente; **im·por·tune** [~ˈpɔːrtjuːn] importunar; insistir en una pretensión; **im·porˈtu·ni·ty** importunidad *f*; insistencia *f*.

im·pose [im'pouz] imponer; cargar; hacer aceptar; ~ *upon* embaucar; abusar de; molestar; **im'pos·ing** □ imponente, impresionante, majestuoso; **im·po·si·tion** [~pə'ziʃn] imposición *f*; carga *f*; abuso *m*; *school*: ejercicio *m* de castigo.
im·pos·si·bil·i·ty [impɔsə'biliti] imposibilidad *f*; **im'pos·si·ble** □ imposible.
im·post ['impoust] impuesto *m*; **im·pos·tor** [im'pɔstər] impostor (-a *f*) *m*, embaucador (-a *f*) *m*; **im'pos·ture** [~tʃər] impostura *f*, fraude *m*.
im·po·tence ['impətəns] impotencia *f*; '**im·po·tent** impotente.
im·pound [im'paund] acorralar; encerrar; ⚖ embargar, confiscar.
im·pov·er·ish [im'pɔvəriʃ] empobrecer; **im'pov·er·ish·ment** empobrecimiento *m*.
im·prac·ti·ca·bil·i·ty [impræktikə'biliti] impracticabilidad *f*; **im'prac·ti·ca·ble** □ impracticable; intratable; **im'prac·ti·cal** *v. unpractical*.
im·pre·cate ['imprikeit] imprecar; **im·pre'ca·tion** imprecación *f*; **im·pre·ca·to·ry** ['~keitəri] imprecatorio.
im·preg·na·bil·i·ty [impregnə'biliti] inexpugnabilidad *f*; **im'preg·na·ble** □ inexpugnable; **im·preg·nate** ['~neit] impregnar; empreñar; *biol.* fecundar; imbuir; **im·preg'na·tion** impregnación *f*; fecundación *f*.
im·pre·sa·ri·o [imprə'sɑːrio] empresario *m*, empresario de teatro.
im·press 1. ['impres] impresión *f*; huella *f*; *fig.* sello *m*; **2.** [im'pres] imprimir; estampar; (*of emotions*) impresionar, imponer; grabar, inculcar (*s.t. on the mind* algo en el ánimo); *goods* confiscar, apoderarse de; ⚔ reclutar (a la fuerza); **im'press·i·ble** impresionable; **im'pres·sion** [~ʃn] impresión *f* (*a. fig.*); huella *f*; *fig.* efecto *m*; *make an* ~ hacer efecto; *make an* ~ *on* impresionar; *be under the* ~ *that* tener la impresión de que; **im'pres·sion·a·ble** impresionable; **im'pres·sion·ist** impresionista *m*/*f*; **im'pres·sive** □ impresionante, imponente.
im·print 1. [im'print] imprimir; estampar; *fig.* grabar; **2.** ['imprint] impresión *f*; huella *f*; *typ.* pie *m* de imprenta.
im·pris·on [im'prizn] encarcelar, aprisionar; **im'pris·on·ment** encarcelamiento *m*; prisión *f*.
im·prob·a·bil·i·ty [imprɔbə'biliti] improbabilidad *f*, inverosimilitud *f*; **im'prob·a·ble** □ improbable, inverosímil.
im·promp·tu [im'prɔmtuː] **1.** *su.* improvisación *f*; **2.** *adj.* improvisado; espontáneo; **3.** *adv.* de improviso.
im·prop·er [im'prɔpər] □ impropio; incorrecto; indecoroso; ~ *fraction* fracción *f* impropia; **im·pro·pri·e·ty** [imprə'praiəti] inconveniencia *f*; indecencia *f*; indecoro *m*; impropiedad *f of language*.
im·prov·a·ble [im'pruːvəbl] mejorable.
im·prove [im'pruːv] *v/t.* mejorar; perfeccionar; 🖌 abonar; enmendar; reformar; *opportunity* aprovechar; *yield etc.* aumentar; *v/i.* mejorar(se), medrar; perfeccionarse; aumentar(se); hacer progresos *in studies etc.*; ~ *upon* mejorar, perfeccionar; aventajar; **im'prove·ment** mejora *f*; ⚕ mejoría *f*; perfeccionamiento *m*; 🖌 abono *m*; enmienda *f*; reforma *f*; aprovechamiento *m*; aumento *m*; progreso *m*.
im·prov·i·dence [im'prɔvidəns] imprevisión *f*; **im'prov·i·dent** □ impróvido, desprevenido.
im·prov·ing [im'pruːviŋ] edificante, instructivo.
im·pro·vi·sa·tion [imprəvai'zeiʃn] improvisación *f*; **im·pro·vise** ['~vaiz] improvisar.
im·pru·dence [im'pruːdəns] imprudencia *f*; **im'pru·dent** □ imprudente, malaconsejado.
im·pu·dence ['impjudəns] impudencia *f*, descaro *m*, insolencia *f*, desvergüenza *f*; '**im·pu·dent** □ impudente, descarado, insolente, desvergonzado.
im·pugn [im'pjuːn] impugnar; poner en tela de juicio.
im·pulse ['impʌls] impulso *m*, impulsión *f*; ímpetu *m*; arranque *m*, arrebato *m*; **im'pul·sion** impulsión *f*; **im'pul·sive** □ impulsivo; irreflexivo; **im'pul·sive·ness** irreflexión *f*, carácter *m* impulsivo.
im·pu·ni·ty [im'pjuːniti] impunidad *f*; *with* ~ impunemente.

im·pure [im'pjur] □ impuro; adulterado; deshonesto; **im'pu·ri·ty** [~riti] impureza *f*.

im·put·a·ble [im'pju:təbl] imputable; **im·pu·ta·tion** [~'teiʃn] imputación *f*; **im·pute** [~'pju:t] imputar (*to* a).

in [in] **1.** *prp.* en; dentro de; ~ *Spain* en España; ~ *1990* en (el año) 1990; ~ *the box* en (*or* dentro de) la caja; ~ *a week* dentro de una semana, de aquí a 8 días; *the biggest* ~ *Spain* el más grande de España; *all the soldiers* ~ *the army* todos los soldados del ejército; ~ *this way* de esta manera; *dressed* ~ *white* vestido de blanco; *furnished* ~ *walnut* amueblado de nogal; *better* ~ *health* mejor de salud; ~ *the morning* por la mañana; *at 7* ~ *the morning* a las 7 de la mañana; ~ *the daytime* de día, durante el día; ~ *writing* por escrito; ~ *my opinion* a mi parecer; ~ (*good*) *time* (*early*) a tiempo, con tiempo; (*eventually*) andando el tiempo, con el tiempo; ~ *the Spanish fashion* a la (manera) española; ~ *the rear* a retaguardia; ~ *the reign of* bajo el reinado de; *one* ~ *four* uno sobre cuatro; *day* ~, *day out* día tras día; F *there's nothing* ~ *it* van muy iguales; no da ningún resultado; no tiene importancia; *it is not* ~ *him to* no es capaz de; *he has it* ~ *him to* tiene capacidad (*or* predisposición) para; ~ *that* en que, por cuanto; ~ *saying this* al decir esto; **2.** *adv.* (a)dentro; *be* ~ estar en casa (*or* en su oficina *etc.*); haber llegado; *parl.* estar en el poder; F estar en sazón; F estar de moda; *is John* ~*?* ¿está Juan?; F *be* ~ *for* estar expuesto a; *exam* presentarse a; *post* ser candidato a, solicitar; *competition* concurrir a; F *you're* ~ *for it now* la vas a pagar; F *you don't know what you're* ~ *for* no sabes lo que te pescas; F *be* ~ *on* (*it*) estar en el secreto, estar al tanto de; F *be* (*well*) ~ *with* estar muy metido con; estar asociado con; ~ *here* aquí dentro; ~ *there* allí dentro; **3.** *su.* ~*s and outs pl.* recovecos *m/pl.*; pormenores *m/pl*.

in·a·bil·i·ty [inə'biliti] incapacidad *f*; impotencia *f*; imposibilidad *f*.

in·ac·ces·si·bil·i·ty ['inæksesə'biliti] inaccesibilidad *f*; **in·ac'ces·si·ble** □ inaccesible; inasequible.

in·ac·cu·ra·cy [in'ækjurəsi] inexactitud *f*; incorrección *f*; **in'ac·cu·rate** [~rit] □ inexacto; incorrecto.

in·ac·tion [in'ækʃn] inacción *f*.

in·ac·tive [in'æktiv] □ inactivo; **in·ac'tiv·i·ty** inactividad *f*.

in·ad·e·qua·cy [in'ædikwəsi] insuficiencia *f*; **in'ad·e·quate** [~kwit] □ insuficiente, inadecuado.

in·ad·mis·si·bil·i·ty ['inədmisə'biliti] no admisibilidad *f*; **in·ad'mis·si·ble** □ inadmisible.

in·ad·vert·ence, in·ad·vert·en·cy [inəd'və:rtəns(i)] inadvertencia *f*; **in·ad'vert·ent** □ inadvertido; accidental; ~*ly a.* sin querer.

in·ad·vis·a·ble [inəd'vaizəbl] □ imprudente, no aconsejable.

in·al·ien·a·ble [in'eiliənəbl] □ inalienable.

in·am·o·ra·ta [inæmə'rɑ:tə] amada *f*.

in·ane [i'nein] □ necio, fatuo, inane.

in·an·i·mate [in'ænimit] □ inanimado.

in·a·ni·tion [inə'niʃn] inanición *f*.

in·an·i·ty [i'næniti] fatuidad *f*, sandez *f*; inanidad *f*.

in·ap·pli·ca·bil·i·ty ['inæplikə'biliti] no aplicabilidad *f*; **in'ap·pli·ca·ble** inaplicable.

in·ap·po·site [in'æpəzit] □ impertinente, inaplicable.

in·ap·pre·hen·si·ble [inæpri'hensəbl] □ inaprensible.

in·ap·pro·pri·ate [inə'proupriit] □ impropio, inoportuno, inadecuado.

in·ar·tic·u·late [inɑ:r'tikjulit] □ *p.* incapaz de expresarse; inarticulado; **in·ar'tic·u·late·ness** (*p.'s*) incapacidad *f* para expresarse; falta *f* de articulación.

in·ar·tis·tic [inɑ:r'tistik] □ antiestético; *p.* falto de talento artístico.

in·as·much [inəz'mʌtʃ]: ~ *as* ya que; en cuanto.

in·at·ten·tion [inə'tenʃn] desatención *f*; **in·at'ten·tive** □ desatento; distraído; descuidado.

in·au·di·ble [in'ɔ:dəbl] □ inaudible, imperceptible.

in·au·gu·ral [i'nɔ:gjurəl] inaugural; **in'au·gu·rate** [~reit] inaugurar; **in·au·gu'ra·tion** inauguración *f*; ♀ *day día de la instalación del presidente de EE.UU.*

in·aus·pi·cious [inɔ:s'piʃəs] □ poco propicio, desfavorable; ominoso.

in·board [ˈinbɔːrd] ⚓ **1.** *adj.* interior; **2.** *adv.* hacia dentro (del casco).
in·born [ˈinˈbɔːrn] innato.
in·bred [ˈinˈbred] innato; engendrado por endogamia.
in·breed·ing [ˈinbriːdiŋ] endogamia *f*.
in·cal·cul·a·ble [inˈkælkjuləbl] □ incalculable.
in·can·des·cence [inkænˈdesns] incandescencia *f*; **in·canˈdes·cent** incandescente.
in·can·ta·tion [inkænˈteiʃn] conjuro *m*; ensalmo *m*.
in·ca·pa·bil·i·ty [inkeipəˈbiliti] incapacidad *f*, inhabilidad *f*; **inˈca·pa·ble** □ incapaz; inhábil; imposibilitado; **in·ca·pac·i·tate** [inkəˈpæsiteit] incapacitar (*for*, *from* para); imposibilitar; **in·caˈpac·i·ty** incapacidad *f*; insuficiencia *f*.
in·car·cer·ate [inˈkɑːrsəreit] encarcelar; **in·car·cerˈa·tion** encarcelamiento *m*.
in·car·nate 1. [inˈkɑːrnit] encarnado; **2.** [ˈinkɑːrneit] encarnar; **in·carˈna·tion** encarnación *f*.
in·case [inˈkeis] *v.* *encase*.
in·cau·tious [inˈkɔːʃəs] □ incauto, imprudente.
in·cen·di·ar·y [inˈsendjəri] incendiario *adj. a. su. m* (a *f*); ~ *bomb* bomba *f* incendiaria.
in·cense¹ [ˈinsens] **1.** incienso *m* (*a. fig.*); **2.** incensar.
in·cense² [inˈsens] encolerizar, indignar.
in·cen·tive [inˈsentiv] incentivo *adj. a. su. m.*
in·cep·tion [inˈsepʃn] principio *m*, comienzo *m*; inauguración *f*; **inˈcep·tive** incipiente; *gr.* incoativo.
in·cer·ti·tude [inˈsəːrtitjuːd] incertidumbre *f*.
in·ces·sant [inˈsesnt] □ incesante.
in·cest [ˈinsest] incesto *m*; **inces·tu·ous** [inˈsestjuəs] □ incestuoso.
inch [intʃ] **1.** pulgada *f* (= *2,54 cm*); *fig.* pizca *f*; ~*es pl. a.* estatura *f*; ~ *by* ~, *by* ~*es* palmo a palmo; *every* ~ *a man* nada menos que todo un hombre; *within an* ~ *of* a dos dedos de; **2.**: ~ *forward etc.* avanzar *etc.* palmo a palmo.
in·cho·ate [inˈkoueit] incipiente, rudimentario; **in·cho·a·tive** [ˈinkoueitiv] incoativo.
in·ci·dence [ˈinsidəns] incidencia *f*; frecuencia *f*; extensión *f*; *angle of* ~ ángulo *m* de incidencia; **ˈin·ci·dent 1.** incidente *m*; episodio *m*; ocurrencia *f*; suceso *m*; **2.** incidente; propio (*to* de); **in·ci·den·tal** [~ˈdentl] **1.** cosa *f* accesoria (*or* sin importancia); **2.** □ incidental, incidente; accesorio; casual; ~*ly a.* a propósito.
in·cin·er·ate [inˈsinəreit] incinerar; **in·cin·erˈa·tion** incineración *f*; **inˈcin·er·a·tor** incinerador *m*.
in·cip·i·ent [inˈsipiənt] incipiente.
in·cise [inˈsaiz] cortar; grabar; tallar; **in·ci·sion** [~ˈsiʒn] incisión *f*; **in·ci·sive** [~ˈsaisiv] □ incisivo; *fig.* tajante; **inˈci·sor** [~zər] incisivo *m*.
in·cite [inˈsait] incitar, mover (*to* a); **inˈcite·ment** incitación *f*; incitamento *m*.
in·ci·vil·i·ty [insiˈviliti] descortesía *f*, incivilidad *f*.
in·clem·en·cy [inˈklemənsi] inclemencia *f*; intemperie *f of weather*; **inˈclem·ent** inclemente, riguroso; *weather* destemplado.
in·cli·na·tion [incliˈneiʃn] inclinación *f*; declive *m*; tendencia *f*; afición *f* (*for* a); gana(s) *f*(*pl.*) (*to*, *for* de); **in·cline** [~ˈklain] **1.** *v/t.* inclinar (*a. fig.*), ladear; ~*d plane* plano *m* inclinado; *fig. be* ~*d to* inclinarse a; *v/i.* inclinarse (*to* a); ladearse; estar inclinado, estar ladeado; **2.** *su.* [*mst* ˈ~klain] declive *m*, pendiente *f*.
in·close [inˈklouz] *v.* *enclose*.
in·clude [inˈkluːd] incluir; adjuntar; comprender; *be* ~*d in* figurar en; *everything* ~*d* todo comprendido; *including* incluso, inclusive; *not including* no comprendido.
in·clu·sion [inˈkluːʒn] inclusión *f*; **inˈclu·sive 1.** □ *adj.* inclusivo; completo; *be* ~ *of* incluir; ~ *terms* todo incluido; **2.** *adv.* inclusive; *Sunday to Saturday* ~ del domingo al sábado inclusive.
in·cog [inˈkɔg] F, **inˈcog·ni·to** [~nitou] **1.** incógnito *m*; **2.** de incógnito.
in·co·her·ence, in·co·her·en·cy [inkouˈhirəns(i)] incoherencia *f*; **in·coˈher·ent** □ incoherente; sin pies ni cabeza.
in·com·bus·ti·ble [inkəmˈbʌstəbl] □ incombustible.
in·come [ˈinkəm] ingreso(s) *m*(*pl.*); renta *f*; entrada *f*; *annual* ~ ingresos

m/*pl.* anuales; *family* ~ entradas *f*/*pl.* familiares; **in·com·er** [ˈinkʌmər] recién llegado (a *f*) *m*; forastero (a *f*) *m*; sucesor (-a *f*) *m*; ˈ**in·come tax** impuesto *m* sobre la renta.

in·com·ing [ˈinkʌmiŋ] **1.** entrada *f*; ~*s pl.* ingresos *m*/*pl.*; **2.** entrante; *tide* ascendente.

in·com·men·su·ra·ble [inkəˈmenʃərəbl] □ inconmensurable; **in·comˈmen·su·rate** [~rit] inconmensurable, desproporcionado.

in·com·mode [inkəˈmoud] incomodar, molestar; **in·comˈmo·di·ous** [~iəs] □ incómodo.

in·com·mu·ni·ca·bil·i·ty [ˈinkəmju:nikəˈbiliti] incomunicabilidad *f*; **in·comˈmu·ni·ca·ble** □ incomunicable; **in·com·mu·ni·ca·do** [inkəmjuniˈkɑ:dou] incomunicado.

in·com·pa·ra·ble [inˈkɔmpərəbl] □ incomparable.

in·com·pat·i·bil·i·ty [ˈinkəmpætəˈbiliti] incompatibilidad *f*; **in·comˈpat·i·ble** □ incompatible.

in·com·pe·tence, in·com·pe·ten·cy [inˈkɔmpitəns(i)] incompetencia *f*; incapacidad *f*; inhabilidad *f*; **inˈcom·pe·tent** □ incompetente; inhábil; incapaz.

in·com·plete [inkəmˈpli:t] □ incompleto; defectuoso; inconcluso.

in·com·pre·hen·si·bil·i·ty [inkɔmprihensəˈbiliti] incomprensibilidad *f*; **in·com·preˈhen·sible** □ incomprensible.

in·com·press·i·ble [inkəmˈpresəbl] incompresible.

in·con·ceiv·a·ble [inkənˈsi:vəbl] □ inconcebible.

in·con·clu·sive [inkənˈklu:siv] □ inconcluyente; poco convincente; indeterminado; **in·conˈclu·sive·ness** lo inconcluyente; indeterminación *f*.

in·con·gru·i·ty [inkɔŋˈgruiti] incongruencia *f*; **inˈcon·gru·ous** □ incongruo.

in·con·se·quence [inˈkɔnsikwəns] inconsecuencia *f*; **inˈcon·se·quent** □ inconsecuente; **in·con·se·quen·tial** [~ˈkwenʃl] □ inconsecuente; sin trascendencia.

in·con·sid·er·a·ble [inkənˈsidərəbl] □ insignificante; pequeño; **in·conˈsid·er·ate** [~rit] □ desconsiderado.

in·con·sist·en·cy [inkənˈsistənsi] inconsistencia *f*, inconsecuencia *f*; **in·conˈsist·ent** □ inconsistente, inconsecuente. [inconsolable.]

in·con·sol·a·ble [inkənˈsouləbl] □

in·con·spic·u·ous [inkənˈspikjuəs] □ que no llama la atención; poco aparente; modesto.

in·con·stan·cy [inˈkɔnstənsi] inconstancia *f*, veleidad *f*; **inˈcon·stant** □ inconstante, veleidoso.

in·con·test·a·ble [inkənˈtestəbl] incontestable.

in·con·ti·nence [inˈkɔntinəns] incontinencia *f* (*a.* ⚕); **inˈcon·ti·nent** □ incontinente; ~*ly a.* en seguida.

in·con·tro·vert·i·ble [ˈinkɔntrəˈvə:rtəbl] □ incontrovertible.

in·con·ven·ience [inkənˈvi:njəns] **1.** incomodidad *f*, inconveniencia *f*, molestia *f*; inoportunidad *f*; **2.** incomodar, molestar; **in·conˈven·ient** □ incómodo, inconveniente, molesto; inoportuno.

in·con·vert·i·bil·i·ty [ˈinkənvə:rtəˈbiliti] inconvertibilidad *f*; **in·conˈvert·i·ble** □ inconvertible.

in·cor·po·rate 1. [inˈkɔ:rpəreit] incorporar (*in*[*to*], *with* a, con, en); incluir; comprender; ⚖ constituir(se) en corporación (*or* sociedad anónima); **2.** [inˈkɔ:rpərit] incorpóreo; asociado, incorporado; **inˈcor·po·rat·ed** [~reitid] ✝ sociedad *f* anónima (*abbr.* S.A.); **in·cor·poˈra·tion** incorporación *f*; constitución *f* en sociedad anónima.

in·cor·po·re·al [inkɔ:rˈpɔ:riəl] incorpóreo, incorporal.

in·cor·rect [inkəˈrekt] □ incorrecto; inexacto; erróneo.

in·cor·ri·gi·bil·i·ty [inkɔridʒəˈbiliti] incorregibilidad *f*; **inˈcor·ri·gi·ble** □ incorregible, empecatado.

in·cor·rupt·i·ble [inkəˈrʌptəbl] □ incorruptible.

in·crease 1. [inˈkri:s] *v*/*t.* aumentar; acrecentar; multiplicar; *v*/*i.* aumentarse; crecer; multiplicarse; *increasing* creciente; *increasingly* cada vez más; **2.** [ˈinkri:s] aumento *m*, incremento *m*; crecimiento *m*; ganancia *f*; alza *f in price*; *be on the* ~ ir en aumento.

in·cred·i·bil·i·ty [inkrediˈbiliti] incredibilidad *f*; **inˈcred·i·ble** □ increíble.

in·cre·du·li·ty [inkriˈdju:liti] incredulidad *f*; **in·cred·u·lous** [inˈkredjuləs] □ incrédulo.

in·cre·ment ['inkrimənt] incremento *m*; añadidura *f*; (*a.* ~ *value*) plusvalía *f*.

in·crim·i·nate [in'krimineit] acriminar, incriminar; **in'crim·i·na·to·ry** [~əri] acriminador, incriminador.

in·crust [in'krʌst] incrustar(se); **in·crus'ta·tion** incrustación *f*; costra *f*.

in·cu·bate ['inkjubeit] empollar, incubar; **in·cu'ba·tion** incubación *f*; **'in·cu·ba·tor** incubadora *f*; **in·cu·bus** ['~bəs] íncubo *m*.

in·cul·cate ['inkʌlkeit] inculcar (*in* en); **in·cul'ca·tion** inculcación *f*.

in·cul·pate ['inkʌlpeit] inculpar; **in·cul'pa·tion** inculpación *f*; **in'cul·pa·to·ry** [~pətəri] inculpador.

in·cum·ben·cy [in'kʌmbənsi] *eccl.* (duración *f* de un) beneficio *m* eclesiástico; **in'cum·bent 1.** *eccl.* beneficiado *m*; **2.** incumbente, obligatorio; *be* ~ *upon* incumbir a.

in·cu·nab·u·la [inkju'næbjulə] *pl.* *typ.* incunables *m/pl.*

in·cur [in'kəːr] incurrir en; *debt* contraer.

in·cur·a·bil·i·ty [inkjurə'biliti] incurabilidad *f*; **in'cur·a·ble** □ incurable.

in·cu·ri·ous [in'kjuriəs] □ poco curioso.

in·cur·sion [in'kəːrʒn] incursión *f*, invasión *f*; *fig.* penetración *f*.

in·debt·ed [in'detid] adeudado; reconocido; obligado; *be* ~ *to* estar en deuda con; **in'debt·ed·ness** deuda *f*; obligación *f*.

in·de·cen·cy [in'diːsnsi] indecencia *f*; **in'de·cent** □ indecente; ~ *assault approx.* tentativa *f* de violación.

in·de·ci·pher·a·ble [indi'saifərəbl] indescifrable.

in·de·ci·sion [indi'siʒn] indecisión *f*; irresolución *f*; **in·de·ci·sive** [~'saisiv] □ indeciso; inconcluyente; dudoso.

in·de·clin·a·ble [indi'klainəbl] indeclinable.

in·dec·o·rous [in'dekərəs] □ indecoroso; **in'dec·o·rous·ness** = **in·de·co·rum** [indi'kɔːrəm] indecoro *m*.

in·deed [in'diːd] verdaderamente, de veras; por cierto; en efecto (*a. yes,* ~); ~? ¿de veras?; *yes,* ~! ¡sí, por cierto!

in·de·fat·i·ga·ble [indi'fætigəbl] □ infatigable, incansable.

in·de·fen·si·ble [indi'fensəbl] □ indefendible.

in·de·fin·a·ble [indi'fainəbl] indefinible.

in·def·i·nite [in'definit] □ indefinido; incierto; vago.

in·del·i·ble [in'delibl] □ indeleble; ~ *pencil* lápiz tinta *m*.

in·del·i·ca·cy [in'delikəsi] falta *f* de delicadeza; grosería *f*; **in'del·i·cate** [~kit] □ poco delicado, indecoroso, grosero.

in·dem·ni·fi·ca·tion [indemnifi'keiʃn] indemnización *f*, resarcimiento *m*; **in'dem·ni·fy** [~fai] indemnizar, resarcir (*a p. for, from, against* a una p. de); **in'dem·ni·ty** (*compensation*) indemnización *f*; indemnidad *f*.

in·dent 1. ['indent] mella *f*; muesca *f*; ✝ pedido *m*; ⚔ requisición *f*; = *indenture*; **2.** [in'dent] mellar; (en)dentar; *typ.* sangrar; ⚖ redactar (por duplicado) un contrato (de aprendizaje); ~ *upon a p. for s.t.* pedir algo a una p.; **in·den'ta·tion** mella *f*; muesca *f*; *typ.* sangría *f* = **in'den·tion; in'den·ture** [~tʃər] **1.** escritura *f*; contrato *m* (de aprendizaje); **2.** contratar (como aprendiz).

in·de·pend·ence [indi'pendəns] independencia *f*; **in·de'pend·ent** □ independiente *adj. a. su. m/f*; *of* ~ *means* acomodado.

in·de·scrib·a·ble [indis'kraibəbl] □ indescriptible; *b.s.* incalificable.

in·de·struct·i·ble [indis'trʌktəbl] □ indestructible.

in·de·ter·mi·na·ble [indi'təːrminəbl] □ indeterminable; **in·de'ter·mi·nate** [~nit] □ indeterminado; vago.

in·dex ['indeks] **1.** (*pl. a.* **in·di·ces** ['indisiːz]) (*finger, of book*) índice *m*; ⅍ exponente *m*; ~ *card* ficha *f* catalográfica; ~ *finger* dedo *m* índice; ~ *tab* pestaña *f*; ♀ *eccl.* índice *m* expurgatorio; **2.** *book* poner índice a; *entry* poner en un índice.

In·di·a ['indjə]: ~ *ink* tinta *f* china; ~ *paper* papel *m* de China, papel *m* biblia; ~ *rubber* goma *f* de borrar; caucho *m*.

In·di·an ['indjən] **1.** indio (a *f*) *m*; (*Red*) ~ piel roja *m/f*; **2.** indio; ~ *club* maza *f* (de gimnasia); ~ *corn* maíz *m*,

panizo *m*; ~ *file* fila *f* india; F ~ *giver* *b.s.* dador *m* interesado (*or* de toma y daca); ~ *summer* veranillo *m* de San Martín.
in·di·cate [ˈindikeit] indicar, señalar; **in·diˈca·tion** indicio *m*, señal *f*; indicación *f*; **in·dic·a·tive** [inˈdikətiv] indicativo *adj. a. su. m*; *be* ~ *of* indicar; **in·di·ca·tor** [ˈ~keitər] indicador *m* (*a.* ⊕, ⚗).
in·di·ces [ˈindisi:z] *pl. of index*.
in·dict [inˈdait] acusar (ante el juez) (*for, on a charge of* de); encausar; **inˈdict·a·ble** denunciable, procesable; **inˈdict·ment** acusación *f*; ⚖ sumaria *f*.
in·dif·fer·ence [inˈdifrəns] indiferencia *f*; desapego *m*; falta *f* de importancia; **inˈdif·fer·ent** □ indiferente; desinteresado; imparcial; *quality* mediano, ordinario.
in·di·gence [ˈindidʒəns] indigencia *f*.
in·dig·e·nous [inˈdidʒinəs] indígena (*to* de).
in·di·gent [ˈindidʒənt] indigente.
in·di·gest·i·ble [indiˈdʒestəbl] □ indigestible, indigesto; **in·diˈges·tion** indigestión *f*, empacho *m*.
in·dig·nant [inˈdignənt] □ indignado (*at a p.* con[tra]; *at a th.* de, por); **in·digˈna·tion** indignación *f*; ~ *meeting* mitin *m* de protesta; **inˈdig·ni·ty** [~niti] indignidad *f*, afrenta *f*.
in·di·go [ˈindigou] añil *adj. a. su. m*.
in·di·rect [indiˈrekt] □ indirecto; ~ *discourse* estilo *m* indirecto.
in·dis·cern·i·ble [indiˈsə:rnəbl] imperceptible.
in·dis·ci·pline [inˈdisiplin] indisciplina *f*.
in·dis·creet [indisˈkri:t] □ indiscreto; **in·dis·cre·tion** [~ˈkreʃn] indiscreción *f*.
in·dis·crim·i·nate [indisˈkriminit] □ promiscuo, sin distinción; falto de discernimiento; ˈ**in·dis·crim·i·ˈna·tion** falta *f* de discernimiento; indistinción *f*.
in·dis·pen·sa·ble [indisˈpensəbl] □ indispensable, imprescindible.
in·dis·pose [indisˈpouz] indisponer (*for* para); **in·disˈposed** ⚕ indispuesto; mal dispuesto; **in·dis·po·si·tion** [indispəˈziʃn] indisposición *f* (*to* para).
in·dis·pu·ta·ble [ˈindisˈpju:təbl] □ indisputable, incontestable.
in·dis·so·lu·bil·i·ty [ˈindisɔljuˈbiliti] indisolubilidad *f*; **in·dis·so·lu·ble** [~ˈsɔljubl] □ indisoluble.
in·dis·tinct [indisˈtiŋkt] □ indistinto; **in·disˈtinct·ness** indistinción *f*, vaguedad *f*; falta *f* de claridad.
in·dis·tin·guish·a·ble [indisˈtiŋgwiʃəbl] indistinguible.
in·dite [inˈdait] componer; redactar, poner por escrito.
in·di·vid·u·al [indiˈvidjuəl] **1.** individuo *m*; *mst contp.* sujeto *m*; **2.** □ individual; personal; particular; **in·diˈvid·u·al·ist** individualista *m/f*; **in·di·vid·u·al·i·ty** [~ˈæliti] individualidad *f*; **in·diˈvid·u·al·ize** [~əlaiz] individuar.
in·di·vis·i·bil·i·ty [ˈindiviziˈbiliti] indivisibilidad *f*; **in·diˈvis·i·ble** □ indivisible.
In·do... [ˈindou] indo..., ˈ~**-Eu·ro·ˈpe·an** indoeuropeo *adj. a. su. m*; **In·do·ne·sian** [indouˈni:ʒən] indonesio *adj. a. su. m* (a *f*).
in·doc·tri·nate [inˈdɔktrineit] adoctrinar (*with* en).
in·do·lence [ˈindələns] indolencia *f*; pereza *f*; ˈ**in·do·lent** □ indolente (*a.* ⚕); perezoso.
in·dom·i·ta·ble [inˈdɔmitəbl] □ indómito, indomable.
in·door [ˈindɔ:r] interior; de casa; de puertas adentro; *sport*: en sala; ~ *aerial* antena *f* de interior; ~ *games* diversiones *f/pl.* de salón; ~ *plant* planta *f* de salón; ~ *swimming pool* piscina *f* cubierta; **in·doors** [ˈinˈdɔ:rz] en casa; (a)dentro; bajo techado.
in·dorse *etc.* [inˈdɔ:rs] = *endorse etc.*
in·du·bi·ta·ble [inˈdju:bitəbl] □ indudable.
in·duce [inˈdju:s] inducir (*a.* ⚡) (*to* a); producir; ocasionar; *sleep* provocar; ~*d current* corriente *f* inducida; **inˈduce·ment** incentivo *m*; aliciente *m*; estímulo *m*.
in·duct [inˈdʌkt] *eccl.* instalar; **inˈduct·ance** inductancia *f*; **inˈduc·tion** *phls.*, ⚡ inducción *f*; *eccl.* instalación *f*; ~ *coil* carrete *m* de inducción; **inˈduc·tive** □ inductivo.
in·dulge [inˈdʌldʒ] *v/t. desires* gratificar, dar rienda suelta a; *p.* consentir, mimar; dar gusto a; *v/i.*: ~ *in*

darse a, entregarse a; darse el lujo de, permitirse; **inˈdul·gence** indulgencia *f* (*a. eccl.*); mimo *m*; gratificación *f*; abandono *m* (*in* a); desenfreno *m*; **inˈdul·gent** □ indulgente.

in·dus·tri·al [inˈdʌstriəl] industrial; ~ *court* tribunal *m* industrial; **inˈdus·tri·al·ism** industrialismo *m*; **inˈdus·tri·al·ist** industrial(ista) *m*; **inˈdus·tri·al·ize** [~aiz] industrializar; **inˈdus·tri·ous** □ industrioso, aplicado; **inˈdus·tri·ous·ness** industria *f*, aplicación *f*, laboriosidad *f*.

indus·try [ˈindəstri] industria *f*; laboriosidad *f*, diligencia *f*; *heavy* ~ industria *f* pesada.

in·e·bri·ate 1. [iˈni:brieit] embriagar, emborrachar; **2.** [iˈni:briit] borracho *adj. a. su. m* (a *f*); **in·e·briˈa·tion, in·e·bri·e·ty** [ini:ˈbraiəti] embriaguez *f*.

in·ed·i·ble [inˈedibl] incomible.

in·ed·it·ed [inˈeditid] inédito.

in·ef·fa·ble [inˈefəbl] □ inefable.

in·ef·face·a·ble [iniˈfeisəbl] □ imborrable.

in·ef·fec·tive [iniˈfektiv], **in·efˈfec·tu·al** [~tjuəl] □ ineficaz; vano; *p.* incapaz.

in·ef·fi·ca·cious [inefiˈkeiʃəs] □ ineficaz; **inˈef·fi·ca·cy** [~kəsi] ineficacia *f*.

in·ef·fi·cien·cy [iniˈfiʃənsi] ineficiencia *f*; **in·efˈfi·cient** □ ineficiente, ineficaz.

in·e·las·tic [iniˈlæstik] inelástico.

in·el·e·gance [inˈeligəns] inelegancia *f*; **inˈel·e·gant** □ inelegante.

in·el·i·gi·bil·i·ty [inelidʒəˈbiliti] no elegibilidad *f*; **inˈel·i·gi·ble** □ inelegible.

in·ept [iˈnept] □ inepto; **inˈept·i·tude** [~itju:d], **inˈept·ness** inepcia *f*, ineptitud *f*.

in·e·qual·i·ty [iniˈkwɔliti] desigualdad *f*.

in·eq·ui·ta·ble [inˈekwitəbl] injusto; **inˈeq·ui·ty** injusticia *f*.

in·e·rad·i·ca·ble [iniˈrædikəbl] □ no extirpable.

in·ert [iˈnə:rt] □ inerte; **in·er·tia** [iˈnə:rʃiə], **inˈert·ness** inercia *f*.

in·es·cap·a·ble [inisˈkeipəbl] ineludible.

in·es·sen·tial [ˈiniˈsenʃl] **1.** cosa *f* sin importancia; **2.** no esencial.

in·es·ti·ma·ble [inˈestiməbl] inestimable.

in·ev·i·ta·bil·i·ty [inˈevitəˈbiliti] inevitabilidad *f*, necesidad *f*; **inˈev·i·ta·ble** □ inevitable, ineludible; **inˈev·i·ta·ble·ness** = *inevitability*.

in·ex·act [inigˈzækt] inexacto; **in·exˈact·i·tude** [~itju:d], **in·exˈact·ness** inexactitud *f*.

in·ex·cus·a·ble [iniksˈkju:zəbl] □ inexcusable, imperdonable.

in·ex·haust·i·bil·i·ty [ˈinigzɔ:stəˈbiliti] lo inagotable; **in·exˈhaust·i·ble** □ inagotable, inexhausto.

in·ex·o·ra·bil·i·ty [ineksərəˈbiliti] inexorabilidad *f*; **inˈex·o·ra·ble** □ inexorable.

in·ex·pe·di·en·cy [iniksˈpi:diənsi] inoportunidad *f*, inconveniencia *f*, imprudencia *f*; **in·exˈpe·di·ent** □ inoportuno, inconveniente, imprudente.

in·ex·pen·sive [iniksˈpensiv] □ barato, económico.

in·ex·pe·ri·ence [iniksˈpiriəns] inexperiencia *f*, falta *f* de experiencia; **in·exˈpe·ri·enced** inexperto, novel.

in·ex·pert [ineksˈpə:rt] □ imperito, inexperto, inhábil.

in·ex·pli·ca·ble [inˈeksplikəbl] □ inexplicable.

in·ex·press·i·ble [iniksˈpresəbl] □ inexpresable, indecible.

in·ex·pres·sive [iniksˈpresiv] □ inexpresivo.

in·ex·tin·guish·a·ble [iniksˈtiŋgwiʃəbl] □ inextinguible.

in·ex·tri·ca·ble [inˈekstrikəbl] □ inextricable.

in·fal·li·bil·i·ty [infæləˈbiliti] infalibilidad *f*; **inˈfal·li·ble** □ infalible.

in·fa·mous [ˈinfəməs] □ infame; ⚖ infamante; **in·fa·my** [ˈ~mi] infamia *f*.

in·fan·cy [ˈinfənsi] infancia *f* (*a. fig.*); ⚖ menor edad *f*; *from* ~ desde niño; **in·fant** [ˈ~fənt] **1.** criatura *f*, infante *m*; niño (a *f*) *m*; ⚖ menor *m/f*; **2.** infantil.

in·fan·ta [inˈfæntə] infanta *f*; **in·fan·te** [~ti] infante *m*.

in·fan·ti·cide [inˈfæntisaid] infanticidio *m*; (*p.*) infanticida *m/f*; **in·fan·tile** [ˈinfəntail] infantil; pueril; aniñado; ~ *paralysis* parálisis *f* infantil.

in·fan·try [ˈinfəntri] infantería *f*; **ˈin·fan·try·man** infante *m*, soldado *m* de infantería.

in·fat·u·ate [inˈfætjueit] apasionar, amartelar; *be* ~*d with* apasionarse de (*or* por); F estar chiflado por; **in·fat·u'a·tion** apasionamiento *m*; F chifladura *f*.

in·fect [inˈfekt] infectar; inficionar (*a. fig.*); contagiar (*a. fig.*); *fig.* influenciar; **in'fec·tion** infección *f*; contagio *m* (*a. fig.*); **in'fec·tious** □ infeccioso; contagioso (*a. fig.*); **in'fec·tive** infectivo.

in·fe·lic·i·tous [infiˈlisitəs] □ infeliz; desacertado; *style* impropio; **in·fe'lic·i·ty** infelicidad *f*; desacierto *m*; impropiedad *f*.

in·fer [inˈfəːr] inferir; deducir, colegir; F conjeturar; **in'fer·a·ble** deducible, ilativo; **in·fer·ence** [ˈinfərəns] inferencia *f*; **in·fer·en·tial** [~ˈrenʃl] □ ilativo; **in·fer·en·tial·ly** [~ˈrenʃəli] por inferencia.

in·fe·ri·or [inˈfiriər] inferior *adj. a. su. m/f*; **in·fe·ri·or·i·ty** [~riˈɔriti] inferioridad *f*; ~ *complex* complejo *m* de inferioridad.

in·fer·nal [inˈfəːrnl] □ infernal; ~ *machine* máquina *f* infernal; **in·fer·no** [inˈfəːrnou] infierno *m*.

in·fer·tile [inˈfəːrtəl] infecundo, estéril, infértil; **in·fer·til·i·ty** [~ˈtiliti] infecundidad *f etc.*

in·fest [inˈfest] infestar; *be* ~*ed with* estar plagado de; **in·fes'ta·tion** infestación *f*.

in·fi·del [ˈinfidəl] infiel *adj. a. su. m/f*; pagano *adj. a. su. m* (a *f*); descreído *adj. a. su. m* (a *f*); **in·fi·del·i·ty** [~ˈdeliti] infidelidad *f* (*to* para [con]); perfidia *f*.

in·field [ˈinfiːld] *baseball*: cuadro *m* interior.

in·fight(**·ing**) [ˈinfait(iŋ)] *boxing*: cuerpo a cuerpo *m*.

in·fil·trate [ˈinfiltreit] infiltrar(se en); **in·fil'tra·tion** infiltración *f*.

in·fi·nite [ˈinfinit] □ infinito; **in·fin·i·tes·i·mal** [~ˈtesiml] infinitesimal (*a.* ♆); **in'fin·i·tive** infinitivo *m* (*a.* ~ *mood*); **in'fin·i·tude** [~tjuːd] infinitud *f*, infinidad *f*; **in'fin·i·ty** infinidad *f*; sinfín *m*; ♆ infinito *m*.

in·firm [inˈfəːrm] enfermizo, achacoso; débil; inestable; ~ *of purpose* irresoluto; **in'fir·ma·ry** enfermería *f*; hospital *m*; sala *f* de enfermos; **in'fir·mi·ty** achaque *m*; enfermedad *f*; debilidad *f*; (*moral*) flaqueza *f*; inestabilidad *f*.

in·fix [inˈfiks] encajar; clavar; fijar (en la mente).

in·flame [inˈfleim] inflamar (*a. fig. a.* ⚕); *be* ~*d with* inflamarse de (*or* en).

in·flam·ma·bil·i·ty [inflæməˈbiliti] inflamabilidad *f*; **in'flam·ma·ble** □ inflamable; **in·flam·ma·tion** [infləˈmeiʃn] inflamación *f* (*a.* ⚕); **in·flam·ma·to·ry** [inˈflæmətəri] ⚕ inflamatorio; inflamador; *speech* incendiario.

in·flate [inˈfleit] hinchar (*a. fig.*); inflar; **in'fla·tion** inflación *f* (*a.* ⚜); *of a tire*: inflado *m*; **in'fla·tion·ar·y** inflacionista; **in'flat·or** bomba *f* (para inflar).

in·flect [inˈflekt] torcer, encorvar; *voice* modular; *gr.* declinar, conjugar; ~*ed gr.* flexional; **in'flec·tion** inflexión *f*.

in·flex·i·bil·i·ty [infleksəˈbiliti] inflexibilidad *f*; **in'flex·i·ble** □ inflexible; **in'flex·ion** [~ʃn] *British* = *inflection*.

in·flict [inˈflikt] inferir, infligir (*on* a); *damage* causar; F ~ *o.s. on a p.* molestar a una p. acompañándole; **in'flic·tion** imposición *f*; castigo *m*; sufrimiento *m*.

in·flo·res·cence [infləˈresns] inflorescencia *f*. [2. afluir.]

in·flow [ˈinflou] 1. afluencia *f*;

in·flu·ence [ˈinfluəns] 1. influencia *f*, influjo *m* ([*up*]*on* sobre); valimiento *m* (*with* cerca de); ascendiente *m* (*over* sobre); F *have* ~ tener buenas aldabas; 2. influir en, influenciar; **in·flu·en·tial** [~ˈenʃl] □ influ(y)ente; *p.* prestigioso.

in·flu·en·za [influˈenzə] gripe *f*, trancazo *m*.

in·flux [ˈinflʌks] afluencia *f*.

in·form [inˈfɔːrm] *v/t.* informar (*of* de, *about* sobre); avisar, comunicar; enterar; (*well*) ~*ed* entendido; *be* (*well*) ~*ed about* estar enterado de, estar al corriente de; *keep a p.* ~*ed about* tener una p. al corriente de; *v/i.*: ~ *against* delatar; **in'for·mal** □ de confianza, sin ceremonia; familiar; sencillo; (*unofficial*) extraoficial; (*irregular*) informal; **in·for·mal·i·ty** [~ˈmæliti] falta *f* de ceremonia; familiaridad *f*; sencillez *f*; informalidad *f*; **in'form·ant** [~ənt] informante *m/f*; informador (-a *f*) *m*; = *informer*; **in·for·ma·tion** [infərˈmeiʃn] información *f* (*a. piece of* ~);

informe(s) *m(pl.)*; noticia(s) *f(pl.)*; dato(s) *m(pl.)*; conocimientos *m/pl.*; ⚖ denunciación *f*, delación *f*; ~ *bureau* oficina *f* de información; *gather* ~ tomar informes, informarse (*about* sobre); **in·form·a·tive** [inˈfɔːrmətiv] informativo; **inˈform·er** ⚖ denunciante *m/f*, delator (-a *f*) *m*; F soplón *m*.

in·frac·tion [inˈfrækʃn] infracción *f*.

in·fra·red [ˈinfrəˈred] infrarrojo.

in·fre·quen·cy [inˈfriːkwənsi] infrecuencia *f*; **inˈfre·quent** □ poco frecuente, infrecuente.

in·fringe [inˈfrindʒ] infringir, violar (*a.* ~ *upon*); **inˈfringe·ment** infracción *f*, transgresión *f*.

in·fu·ri·ate [inˈfjurieit] enfurecer, poner furioso.

in·fuse [inˈfjuːz] *all senses*: infundir (*into* a, en); **inˈfu·sion** [~ʒn] infusión *f*; **in·fu·so·ri·a** [infjuːˈsɔːriə] *pl.* infusorios *m/pl.*

in·gen·ious [inˈdʒiːnjəs] □ ingenioso, inventivo, hábil; listo; **in·ge·nu·i·ty** [indʒiˈnjuiti] ingenio *m*, ingeniosidad *f*; inventiva *f*; maña *f*; **in·gen·u·ous** [inˈdʒenjuəs] □ ingenuo; **inˈgen·u·ous·ness** ingenuidad *f*.

in·gest [inˈdʒest] ingerir; **inˈges·tion** ingestión *f*.

in·glo·ri·ous [inˈglɔːriəs] □ ignominioso; desconocido, sin fama.

in·go·ing [ˈingouiŋ] **1.** entrada *f* (*a.* ✝); **2.** entrante.

in·got [ˈiŋgət] lingote *m*; ~ *steel* acero *m* en lingotes.

in·grain [ˈinˈgrein] teñido en rama; *fig.* (*a.* ˈ**inˈgrained** [~d]) arraigado, inveterado; innato.

in·gra·ti·ate [inˈgreiʃieit]: ~ *o.s.* congraciarse, insinuarse (*with* con); **inˈgra·ti·a·ting** □ insinuante; congraciador; **in·grat·i·tude** [~ˈgrætitjuːd] ingratitud *f*, desagradecimiento *m*.

in·gre·di·ent [inˈgriːdiənt] ingrediente *m*, componente *m*.

in·gress [ˈingres] ingreso *m*; acceso *m*.

in·grow·ing [ˈingrouiŋ] que crece hacia dentro; ~ *nail* uñero *m*.

in·gui·nal [ˈiŋgwinl] inguinal.

in·hab·it [inˈhæbit] habitar; **inˈhab·it·a·ble** habitable; **inˈhab·it·an·cy** ⚖ habitación *f*; **inˈhab·it·ant** habitante *m/f*; íncola *m lit.*

in·hal·ant [inˈheilənt] inhalante *m*; **in·ha·la·tion** [inhəˈleiʃn] ⚕ inhalación *f*; **in·hale** [~ˈheil] inspirar; ⚕ inhalar; **inˈhal·er** ⚕ inhalador *m*.

in·har·mo·ni·ous [inhɑːrˈmounjəs] inarmónico; *fig.* discorde, poco armonioso.

in·here [inˈhir] ser inherente (*in* a); residir (*in* en); **inˈher·ence, inˈher·en·cy** [~rəns(i)] inherencia *f*; **inˈher·ent** □ inherente (*in* a).

in·her·it [inˈherit] heredar; **inˈher·it·a·ble** □ heredable; heredero; **inˈher·it·ance** herencia *f*; patrimonio *m*; **inˈher·i·tor** heredero *m*; **inˈher·i·tress, inˈher·i·trix** [~triks] heredera *f*.

in·hib·it [inˈhibit] inhibir; *eccl.* prohibir; impedir (*from inf.*); **in·hi·bi·tion** [~ˈbiʃn] inhibición *f*; **inˈhib·i·to·ry** [~təri] inhibitorio.

in·hos·pi·ta·ble [inˈhɔspitəbl] □ inhospitalario, inhóspito; **in·hos·pi·tal·i·ty** [ˈ~tæliti] inhospitalidad *f*.

in·hu·man [inˈhjuːmən] □ inhumano; **in·hu·man·i·ty** [~ˈmæniti] inhumanidad *f*.

in·hu·ma·tion [inhjuːˈmeiʃn] inhumación *f*.

in·hume [inˈhjuːm] inhumar.

in·im·i·cal [iˈnimikəl] enemigo (*to* de); contrario (*to* a).

in·im·i·ta·ble [iˈnimitəbl] □ inimitable.

in·iq·ui·tous [iˈnikwitəs] □ inicuo; **inˈiq·ui·ty** iniquidad *f*.

in·i·tial [iˈniʃl] **1.** □ inicial *adj. a. su. f*; **2.** marcar (*or* firmar) con iniciales; **in·i·ti·ate 1.** [iˈniʃiit] iniciado *adj. a. su. m* (a *f*); **2.** [iˈniʃieit] iniciar (*into* en); **in·i·tiˈa·tion** iniciación *f*; **inˈi·ti·a·tive** [~iətiv] **1.** iniciativa *f*; *on one's own* ~ por su propia iniciativa; *take the* ~ tomar la iniciativa; **2.** iniciativo; **inˈi·ti·a·tor** [~ieitər] iniciador (-a *f*) *m*; **inˈi·ti·a·to·ry** [~iətəri] iniciativo; de iniciación.

in·ject [inˈdʒekt] inyectar (*into* en); *fig.* introducir, injertar; **inˈjec·tion**, inyección *f*.

in·ju·di·cious [indʒuˈdiʃəs] □ imprudente, indiscreto.

in·junc·tion [inˈdʒʌŋkʃn] mandato *m*, precepto *m*; ⚖ entredicho *m*.

in·jure [ˈindʒər] *body* lastimar, herir, ⚕ lesionar, (*esp. permanently*) lisiar; (*damage*) dañar, perjudicar, averiar;

feelings, reputation injuriar, ofender; **in·ju·ri·ous** [in'dʒuriəs] □ dañoso, perjudicial; nocivo; injurioso; **in·ju·ry** ['indʒəri] herida *f*, lesión *f*; perjuicio *m*, daño *m*; injuria *f*.

in·jus·tice [in'dʒʌstis] injusticia *f*.

ink [iŋk] **1.** tinta *f*; **2.** entintar (*a.* ~ *in*); '~ **e·ras·er** goma *f* para tinta.

ink·ling ['iŋkliŋ] atisbo *m*; sospecha *f*; indicio *m*; idea *f*.

ink...: '~ **pad** almohadilla *f* (*or* tampón *m*) de entintar; '~ **pot** tintero *m*; '~ **stand** escribanía *f*; '~**·well** tintero *m*; '**ink·y** manchado de tinta; (negro) como la tinta.

in·laid ['inleid] *pret. a. p.p. of inlay*; ~ *floor* entarimado *m*; ~ *work* taracea *f*.

in·land ['inlənd] **1.** interior *m* (del país); **2.** (del) interior; **3.** [in'lænd] *adv.* tierra adentro; **in·land·er** ['inləndər] habitante *m/f* del interior.

in·lay ['in'lei] **1.** [*irr.* (*lay*)] taracear, embutir, incrustar; **2.** taracea *f*, embutido *m*.

in·let ['inlet] entrante *m*, ensenada *f*, cala *f*; ⊕ admisión *f*; ~ *valve* válvula *f* de admisión.

in·mate ['inmeit] (*in a hospital or home*) asilado *m* (a *f*), recluso *m* (a *f*), acogido *m* (a *f*); (*in a jail*) presidiario *m* (a *f*), preso *m* (a *f*).

in·most ['inmoust] (más) interior; más íntimo, más recóndito.

inn [in] posada *f*, mesón *m*; (*poor, wayside*) venta *f*; (*bigger*) fonda *f*.

in·nate ['i'neit] □ innato.

in·ner ['inər] interior, interno; secreto, oculto; ~*spring mattress* colchón *m* de muelles interiores; *mot. etc.* ~ *tube* cámara *f* (de neumático); '**in·ner·most** = *inmost*.

in·nings ['iniŋz] *sport:* turno *m*, entrada *f*; *fig.* oportunidad *f*.

inn·keep·er ['inki:pər] posadero (a *f*) *m*, mesonero (a *f*) *m*; ventero (a *f*) *m*; fondista *m/f*.

in·no·cence ['inəsns] inocencia *f*; **in·no·cent** ['~snt] □ inocente *adj. a. su. m/f* (*of* de).

in·noc·u·ous [i'nɔkjuəs] □ inocuo.

in·no·vate ['inouveit] innovar; **in·no'va·tion** innovación *f*; '**in·no·va·tor** [~tər] innovador (-a *f*) *m*.

in·nu·en·do [inju'endou] indirecta *f*, insinuación *f*, pulla *f*.

in·nu·mer·a·ble [i'nju:mərəbl] □ innumerable.

in·ob·serv·ance [inəb'zə:rvəns] inobservancia *f*.

in·oc·u·late [i'nɔkjuleit] inocular; **in·oc·u'la·tion** inoculación *f*.

in·o·dor·ous [in'oudərəs] inodoro.

in·of·fen·sive [inə'fensiv] □ inofensivo; **in·of'fen·sive·ness** inocuidad *f*.

in·op·er·a·tive [in'ɔpərətiv] inoperante.

in·op·por·tune [inɔpər'tju:n] □ inoportuno; ~*ly* a deshora.

in·or·di·nate [i'nɔ:rdinit] □ desmesurado, excesivo; inordenado.

in·or·gan·ic [inɔ:r'gænik] inorgánico.

in·pa·tient ['inpeiʃənt] paciente *m/f* interno (a).

in·put ['input] ⊕, ⚡ (potencia *f* de) entrada *f*; ✝ dinero *m* invertido (*or* gastado); *fig.* comentarios *m/pl.*, observaciones *f/pl.*, informes *m/pl.* confidenciales.

in·quest ['inkwest] diligencias *f/pl.* previas; encuesta *f*; *of coroner:* pesquisa *f* judicial, levantamiento *m* del cadáver, reconocimiento *m* médico.

in·quire [in'kwaiər] preguntar (*about, after, for* por; *of* a); pedir informes (*about* sobre); ~ *into* inquirir, averiguar, indagar; **in'quir·er** preguntador (-a *f*) *m*, interrogante *m/f*; investigador (-a *f*) *m*; inquiridor (-a *f*) *m*; **in'quir·ing** □ curioso, investigador; **in'quir·y** pregunta *f*; encuesta *f*; (*esp.* ⚖) pesquisa *f*; investigación *f*; petición *f* de informes; *make inquiries* pedir informes (*of* a; *about, on* sobre).

in·qui·si·tion [inkwi'ziʃn] inquisición *f*; 2 Inquisición *f*, Santo Oficio *m*; **in'quis·i·tive** □ *b.s.* curioso, preguntón; especulativo; **in'quis·i·tive·ness** curiosidad *f*; **in'quis·i·tor** inquisidor *m*; **in·quis·i·to·ri·al** [~'tɔ:riəl] □ inquisitorial.

in·road ['inroud] incursión *f*; *fig.* invasión *f*, usurpación *f* (*into, on* de).

in·rush ['inrʌʃ] afluencia *f*; irrupción *f*.

in·sa·lu·bri·ous [insə'lu:briəs] insalubre.

in·sane [in'sein] □ insano, loco, demente; (*senseless*) insensato; **in·san·i·tar·y** [~'sænitəri] □ insalubre, antihigiénico; **in'san·i·ty** insania *f*, locura *f*, demencia *f*.

in·sa·ti·a·bil·i·ty [inseiʃiə'biliti] insaciabilidad *f*; **in'sa·ti·a·ble, in'sa·ti·ate** [~ʃiət] insaciable.
in·scribe [in'skraib] inscribir (*a. fig.*, ⚘, ⚖); *book* dedicar.
in·scrip·tion [in'skripʃn] inscripción *f*; dedicatoria *f in book*.
in·scru·ta·bil·i·ty [inskru:tə'biliti] inescrutabilidad *f*; **in'scru·ta·ble** □ inescrutable, insondable.
in·sect ['insekt] insecto *m*; **in'sec·ti·cide** [~isaid] insecticida *adj. a. su. m*; **in·sec·tiv·o·rous** [~'tivərəs] insectívoro.
in·se·cure [insi'kjur] □ inseguro; **in·se'cu·ri·ty** [~riti] inseguridad *f*.
in·sem·i·na·tion [insemi'neiʃn] inseminación *f*, fecundación *f*; *artificial* ~ fecundación *f* artificial.
in·sen·sate [in'senseit] insensato; (*unfeeling*) insensible; **in·sen·si·bil·i·ty** [~sə'biliti] insensibilidad *f*; desmayo *m*; inconsciencia *f*; impasibilidad *f*; **in'sen·si·ble** □ insensible (*of*, *to* a); inconsciente (*of* de); impasible; imperceptible; **in'sen·si·tive** insensible (*to* a).
in·sep·a·ra·bil·i·ty [insepərə'biliti] inseparabilidad *f*; **in'sep·a·ra·ble** □ inseparable.
in·sert 1. [in'sə:rt] insertar, inserir; introducir; **2.** ['insə:rt] inserción *f*; hoja *f* insertada; **in'ser·tion** inserción *f*; *sew.* entredós *m*.
in·set ['inset] inserción *f*; intercalación *f*, encaje *m*; *typ.* medallón *m*, mapa *m* (*or* grabado *m*) en la esquina de la página.
in·shore ['in'ʃɔ:r] **1.** *adj.* cercano a la orilla; **2.** *adv.* cerca de la orilla; hacia la orilla.
in·side ['in'said] **1.** interior *m*; parte *f* de dentro; F entrañas *f/pl.*; *on the* ~ por dentro; ~ *out* al revés; *turn* ~ *out* volver(se) al revés; **2.** *adj.* interior; interno; F secreto, confidencial; ~ *information* informes *m/pl.* confidenciales; *sport*: ~ *left* interior *m* izquierdo; ~ *right* interior *m* derecho; **3.** *adv.* (a)dentro, hacia dentro; por dentro; **4.** *prp.* dentro de; **'in'sid·er** miembro *m*; iniciado (a *f*) *m*; persona *f* enterada (*or* privilegiada).
in·sid·i·ous [in'sidiəs] □ insidioso.
in·sight ['insait] penetración *f* (psicológica); perspicacia *f*; intuición *f*; *get an* ~ *into* formarse una idea de.
in·sig·ni·a [in'signiə] *pl.* insignias *f/pl.*
in·sig·nif·i·cance, *a.* **in·sig·nif·i·can·cy** [insig'nifikəns(i)] insignificancia *f*; **in·sig'nif·i·cant** □ insignificante.
in·sin·cere [insin'sir] □ poco sincero, falso; **in·sin'cer·i·ty** [~'seriti] falta *f* de sinceridad, falsedad *f*.
in·sin·u·ate [in'sinjueit] insinuar; ~ *o.s. into* insinuarse en; introducirse en; **in'sin·u·at·ing** □ insinuador; **in·sin·u'a·tion** insinuación *f*; indirecta *f*, pulla *f*.
in·sip·id [in'sipid] □ insípido, soso, insulso; **in·si'pid·i·ty** insipidez *f*, sosería *f*, insulsez *f*.
in·sist [in'sist] insistir ([*up*]*on* en, sobre; *on ger.* en *inf.*; *that* en que); empeñarse (en); porfiar; **in'sist·ence** insistencia *f*, empeño *m*, porfía *f*; **in'sist·ent** □ insistente, porfiado; urgente.
in·so·bri·e·ty [insou'braiəti] intemperancia *f*; embriaguez *f*.
in·so·la·tion [insou'leiʃn] ⚕ insolación *f*.
in·sole ['insoul] plantilla *f*.
in·so·lence ['insələns] insolencia *f*, descaro *m*; **'in·so·lent** □ insolente, descarado.
in·sol·u·bil·i·ty [insɔlju'biliti] insolubilidad *f*; **in'sol·u·ble** [~jubl] □ insoluble; *problem* indescifrable.
in·sol·ven·cy [in'sɔlvənsi] insolvencia *f*; **in'sol·vent** insolvente.
in·som·ni·a [in'sɔmniə] insomnio *m*.
in·so·much [insou'mʌtʃ]: ~ *as* ya que; ~ *that* hasta tal punto que.
in·spect [in'spekt] inspeccionar; examinar; registrar; ⚔ pasar revista a; **in'spec·tion** inspección *f*; examen *m*; registro *m*; ⚔ revista *f*; ~ *pit* foso *m* de reconocimiento; **in'spec·tor** inspector *m*; interventor *m*; 🚂 revisor *m*; **in'spec·tor·ate** [~tərit] inspectorado *m*.
in·spi·ra·tion [inspə'reiʃn] inspiración *f*; *find* ~ *in* inspirarse en; **in·spire** [~'spaiər] inspirar; mover (*to* a); ~ *s.t. in a p. or p. with s.t.* inspirar algo a (*or* en) una p.; **in·spir·it** [~'spirit] alentar, animar.
in·sta·bil·i·ty [instə'biliti] in(e)stabilidad *f*; inconstancia *f*, volubilidad *f*.
in·stall [in'stɔ:l] instalar; **in·stal·la·tion** [instə'leiʃn] instalación *f*.
in·stal(l)·ment [in'stɔ:lmənt] (*fitting*

out, *setting up*) instalación *f*; entrega *f*; ✝ plazo *m*; *payment by* (*or in*) ~*s* pago *m* a plazos; ~ *buying* compra *f* a plazos; ~ *plan* pago *m* a plazos, compra *f* a plazos; *buy on the* ~ *plan* comprar a plazos; *in* ~ por entregas; a plazos; *on the* ~ *plan* con facilidades de pago.

in·stance ['instəns] **1.** ejemplo *m*, caso *m*; vez *f*, ocasión *f*; petición *f*; (*urgent request a.* ⚖) instancia *f*; *at the* ~ *of* a instancia de; *for* ~ por ejemplo; *in the first* ~ en primer lugar; **2.** poner por caso, citar (como ejemplo).

in·stant ['instənt] **1.** instante *m*, momento *m*; *in an* ~, *on the* ~, *this* ~ al instante, en seguida; **2.** *cj.*: *the* ~ luego que, en cuanto; **3.** □ inmediato, urgente; corriente; † *the 10th* ~ (*mst inst.*) el 10 del (mes) corriente; **in·stan·ta·ne·ous** [~'teinjəs] □ instantáneo; **in·stan·ter** [in'stæntər], **in·stant·ly** ['instəntli] inmediatamente, al instante.

in·state [in'steit] instalar.

in·stead [in'sted] en cambio; en lugar de ello (*or* él, ella *etc.*); ~ *of* en lugar de, en vez de.

in·step ['instep] empeine *m*.

in·sti·gate ['instigeit] instigar; **in·sti'ga·tion** instigación *f*; *at the* ~ *of* a instigación de; **'in·sti·ga·tor** instigador (-a *f*) *m*.

in·stil(l) [in'stil] instilar; infundir, inculcar (*in*[*to*] en); **in·stil·la·tion** [insti'leiʃn] instilación *f*; inculcación *f*.

in·stinct 1. ['instiŋkt] instinto *m*; **2.** [in'stiŋkt]: ~ *with* animado de, lleno de; **in'stinc·tive** □ instintivo.

in·sti·tute ['institju:t] **1.** instituto *m*; asociación *f* (profesional); ⚖ ~*s pl.* instituta *f*; **2.** instituir; *proceedings etc.* iniciar, entablar; *p.* nombrar ([*in*]*to* para); instalar ([*in*]*to* en); **in·sti'tu·tion** institución *f*; fundación *f*, establecimiento *m*; iniciación *f*; instituto *m*; asilo *m*; costumbre *f*; F cosa *f* (*or* persona *f*) muy conocida; **in·sti'tu·tion·al·ize** [~əlaiz] reglamentar.

in·struct [in'strʌkt] instruir (*about*, *in* de, en, sobre); mandar (*to* a); **in'struc·tion** instrucción *f*; ~*s pl.* instrucciones *f*/*pl.*; indicaciones *f*/*pl.*; orden *f*; ~*s for use* modo *m* de empleo; *on the* ~*s of* por orden de; **in'struc·tion·al** educacional; **in'struc·tive** □ instructivo; **in'struc·tor** instructor *m*; *Am. univ.* profesor *m* auxiliar; **in'struc·tress** instructora *f*.

in·stru·ment ['instrumənt] *all senses*: instrumento *m*; ~*s pl.* ♪, 🎼 instrumental *m*; *mot.*, ✈ ~ *board*, ~ *panel* tablero *m* de instrumentos; *fly on* ~*s* volar por instrumentos; **in·stru·men·tal** [~'mentl] instrumental; *be* ~ *in* contribuir (materialmente) a, intervenir en, ayudar a; **in·stru'men·tal·ist** instrumentista *m*/*f*; **in·stru·men·tal·i·ty** [~'tæliti] intervención *f*, mediación *f*, agencia *f*; **in·stru·men'ta·tion** instrumentación *f*.

in·sub·or·di·nate [insə'bɔ:rdnit] insubordinado; **'in·sub·or·di'na·tion** insubordinación *f*.

in·suf·fer·a·ble [in'sʌfərəbl] □ insufrible, inaguantable.

in·suf·fi·cien·cy [insə'fiʃənsi] insuficiencia *f*; **in·suf'fi·cient** □ insuficiente.

in·su·lar ['insjulər] insular, isleño; *fig.* de miras estrechas; **in·su·lar·i·ty** [~'læriti] insularidad *f*; *fig.* estrechez *f* de miras; **in·su·late** ['~leit] aislar; **'in·su·lat·ing** aislador; ~ *tape* cinta *f* aisladora; **in·su'la·tion** aislamiento *m*; **'in·su·la·tor** aislador *m*, aislante *m*.

in·su·lin ['insjulin] insulina *f*.

in·sult 1. ['insʌlt] insulto *m*, ultraje *m*, injuria *f*; **2.** [in'sʌlt] insultar, ultrajar, injuriar; **in'sult·ing** □ insultante, injurioso.

in·su·per·a·bil·i·ty [insju:pərə'biliti] lo insuperable; **in'su·per·a·ble** □ insuperable.

in·sup·port·a·ble [insə'pɔ:rtəbl] □ insoportable.

in·sur·a·ble [in'ʃurəbl] asegurable; **in·sur·ance** [in'ʃurəns] aseguramiento *m*; ✝ seguro *m*; ~ *company* compañía *f* de seguros; ~ *policy* póliza *f*; ~ *premium* prima *f*, premio *m*; **in'sur·ant** asegurado (a *f*) *m*; **in·sure** [in'ʃur] asegurar; **in'sured** asegurado (a *f*) *m*; **in'sur·er** asegurador (-a *f*) *m*.

in·sur·gent [in'sə:rdʒənt] insurgente *adj. a. su. m*/*f*, insurrecto *adj. a. su. m* (a *f*).

in·sur·mount·a·ble [insər'mauntəbl] insuperable.

in·sur·rec·tion [insəˈrekʃn] insurrección *f*, levantamiento *m*; **in·surˈrec·tion·al, in·surˈrec·tion·ar·y** insurreccional; **in·surˈrec·tion·ist** [~ʃnist] insurrecto (a *f*) *m*, sedicioso (a *f*) *m*.

in·tact [inˈtækt] intacto, íntegro, ileso.

in·take [ˈinteik] ⊕ admisión *f*, toma *f*, entrada *f*; cantidad *f* admitida; número *m* admitido; ~ *manifold* múltiple *m* de admisión, colector *m* de admisión; ~ *valve* válvula *f* de admisión.

in·tan·gi·bil·i·ty [intændʒəˈbiliti] intangibilidad *f*; **inˈtan·gi·ble** [~dʒəbl] □ intangible.

in·te·ger [ˈintidʒər] (número *m*) entero *m*; **in·te·gral** [ˈ~grəl] **1.** □ (*whole*) íntegro; (*component*) integrante; ⅍ integral; **2.** ⅍ integral *f*; **in·te·grant** [ˈ~grənt] integrante; **in·te·grate** [ˈ~greit] integrar (*a.* ⅍); combinar en un todo (*with* con); **in·teˈgra·tion** integración *f*; **in·teg·ri·ty** [~ˈtegriti] integridad *f*, probidad *f*.

in·teg·u·ment [inˈtegjumənt] integumento *m*.

in·tel·lect [ˈintilekt] intelecto *m*, entendimiento *m*; **in·telˈlec·tu·al** [~tjuəl] □ intelectual *adj. a. su. m/f*; **in·tel·lec·tu·al·i·ty** [ˈ~ˈæliti] intelectualidad *f*.

in·tel·li·gence [inˈtelidʒəns] inteligencia *f*; información *f*, noticias *f/pl.*; ~ *quotient* cociente *m* intelectual; ~ *service* ⚔ servicio *m* de información; ~ *test* prueba *f* (*or* test *m*) de inteligencia; **inˈtel·li·genc·er** *mst* † noticiero *m*; espía *m*; gaceta *f*.

in·tel·li·gent [inˈtelidʒənt] □ inteligente; **in·tel·li·gent·si·a** [~ˈdʒentsiə] intelectualidad *f*; **in·tel·li·gi·bil·i·ty** [~dʒəˈbiliti] inteligibilidad *f*; **inˈtel·li·gi·ble** □ inteligible.

in·tem·per·ance [inˈtempərəns] intemperancia *f*; inmoderación *f*; exceso *m* en la bebida; **inˈtem·per·ate** [~rit] □ intemperante; inmoderado; descomedido; dado a la bebida.

in·tend [inˈtend] pensar, proponerse; (*mean*) querer decir (*by* con); destinar (*for* a, para); ~ *to do* pensar hacer; **inˈtend·ant** intendente *m*; **inˈtend·ed 1.** pensado; deseado; F prometido; *be* ~ *to* tener por fin; **2.** F prometido (a *f*) *m*, novio (a *f*) *m*.

in·tense [inˈtens] □ intenso; fuerte; extremado; *p.* apasionado; **inˈtense·ness** intensidad *f*; fuerza *f*; apasionamiento *m of p.*

in·ten·si·fi·ca·tion [intensifiˈkeiʃn] intensificación *f*; **inˈten·si·fy** [~fai] intens(ific)ar(se); reforzar (*a. phot.*); **inˈten·si·ty** = *intenseness*; **inˈten·sive** □ = *intense*; intensivo.

in·tent [inˈtent] **1.** □ absorto (*on* en); resuelto (*on* a); **2.** intento *m*, propósito *m*; *to all ~s and purposes* prácticamente, en realidad; *with ~ to* con el propósito de; **inˈten·tion** intención *f*; intento *m*, propósito *m*; significado *m*; **inˈten·tion·al** [~ʃnl] □ intencional; ~*ly* adrede, de propósito; **inˈten·tioned** intencionado; **inˈtent·ness** atención *f*; ahinco *m*.

in·ter [inˈtə:r] enterrar, sepultar.

in·ter... [ˈintər] inter...; entre.

in·ter·act [intərˈækt] obrar recíprocamente; **in·terˈac·tion** interacción *f*; efecto *m* recíproco.

in·ter·breed [ˈintərˈbri:d] [*irr.* (*breed*)] cruzar(se), entrecruzar(se).

in·ter·ca·late [inˈtə:rkəleit] intercalar; **in·ter·caˈla·tion** intercalación *f*.

in·ter·cede [intərˈsi:d] interceder, mediar (*with* con, *for* por).

in·ter·cept [intərˈsept] interceptar; detener; ⅍ cortar; **in·terˈcep·tion** interceptación *f*; **in·terˈcep·tor** interceptador *m* (*a.* ✈).

in·ter·ces·sion [intərˈseʃn] intercesión *f*.

in·ter·change 1. [intərˈtʃeindʒ] (inter)cambiar(se), trocar(se); alternar(se); **2.** [ˈ~ˈtʃeindʒ] intercambio *m*; canje *m of prisoners, publications*; (*on a highway*) correspondencia *f*; alternación *f*; **in·terˈchange·a·ble** intercambiable.

in·ter·col·le·giate [intərkəˈli:dʒit] interescolar; *v. interscholastic.*

in·ter·com [intərˈkɔm] F sistema *m* de intercomunicación, interfono *m*.

in·ter·com·mu·ni·cate [intərkəˈmju:nikeit] comunicarse; **ˈin·ter·com·mu·niˈca·tion** intercomunicación *f*; comercio *m*; **in·ter·comˈmun·ion** [~jən] intercomunión *f*.

in·ter·con·nect [ˈintərkəˈnekt] interconectar.

in·ter·con·ti·nen·tal [ˈintərkɔntiˈnentl] intercontinental.
in·ter·course [ˈintərkɔːrs] (*social*) trato *m*; comercio *m*; intercambio *m*; (*sexual*) coito *m*, trato *m* sexual; *have* ~ juntarse.
in·ter·de·nom·i·na·tion·al [intərdinɔmiˈneiʃnl] interconfesional.
in·ter·de·pend·ent [intərdiˈpendənt] interdependiente.
in·ter·dict **1.** [intərˈdikt] entredecir, interdecir; **2.** [ˈintərdikt] entredicho *m*, interdicto *m*; **in·terˈdic·tion** interdicción *f*.
in·ter·est [ˈint(ə)rist] **1.** interés *m* (*a.* ✝); ✝ rédito *m*; participación *f*; influencia *f* (*with* sobre); ~*s pl.* intereses *m/pl.*; personas *f/pl.* interesadas; *bear* ~ devengar intereses; *be of* ~ *to* interesar; *in the* ~ *of* en interés de; *put out at* ~ poner a interés; *repay with* ~ *fig.* devolver con creces; *take an* ~ interesarse (*in th.* en, *p.* por); **2.** interesar (*in* en); *be* ~*ed in*, ~ *o.s. in* interesarse por (*or* en); **ˈin·ter·est·ed** □ interesado; ~ *party* interesado (a *f*) *m*; **ˈin·ter·est·ing** □ interesante.
in·ter·fere [intərˈfir] (entro)meterse, mezclarse, intervenir (*in* en); ~ *with* estorbar; dificultar; meterse con; F tocar, manosear; *phys.* interferir; **in·terˈfer·ence** entrometimiento *m*; intervención *f*; estorbo *m*; *phys.*, ⚡ interferencia *f*; **in·terˈfer·ing** entrometido.
in·ter·fuse [intərˈfjuːz] mezclar(se).
in·ter·im [ˈintərim] **1.** intervalo *m*, intermedio *m*, ínterin *m*; *in the* ~ entretanto, en el ínterin, interinamente; **2.** interino, provisional.
in·te·ri·or [inˈtiriər] **1.** interior *m*; **2.** interior, interno; ~ *decoration* decoración *f* de interiores.
in·ter·ject [intərˈdʒekt] interponer; interrumpir (con); **in·terˈjec·tion** *gr.* interjección *f*; exclamación *f*.
in·ter·lace [intərˈleis] entrelazar(se), entretejer(se).
in·ter·lard [intərˈlɑːrd] *fig.* insertar, interpolar; ~ *with* salpicar de.
in·ter·leave [intərˈliːv] interfoliar.
in·ter·line [intərˈlain] interlinear; *sew.* entretelar; **in·ter·lin·e·ar** [intərˈliniər] interlineal; **in·ter·lin·e·a·tion** [ˈ~liniˈeiʃn] interlineación *f*; **in·ter·lin·ing** [ˈ~lainiŋ] *sew.* entretela *f*.
in·ter·link [intərˈliŋk] eslabonar.
in·ter·lock [intərˈlɔk] enclavar(se); engranar; en(tre)lazar(se); ~*ing device* sistema *m* de cierre (*or* de enclavamiento); ~*ing stitch* punto *m* indesmallable.
in·ter·lo·cu·tion [intərlouˈkjuːʃn] interlocución *f*; **in·ter·loc·u·tor** [~ˈlɔkjutər] interlocutor (-a *f*) *m*; **in·terˈloc·u·to·ry** ⚖ interlocutorio; dialogístico.
in·ter·lope [intərˈloup] ser intruso; entrometerse; ✝ traficar sin autorización; **ˈin·ter·lop·er** intruso (a *f*) *m*; ✝ intérlope *m*.
in·ter·lude [ˈintərluːd] ♪ interludio *m*; *thea.* intermedio *m*; intervalo *m*; descanso *m*.
in·ter·mar·riage [intərˈmæridʒ] casamiento *m* (*or* matrimonio *m*) entre parientes; matrimonio *m* entre personas de distintas razas, castas o religiones; **ˈin·terˈmar·ry** casarse (personas emparentadas *or* de distintas razas, castas o religiones).
in·ter·me·di·ar·y [intərˈmiːdiəri] intermediario *adj. a. su. m* (a *f*); **in·ter·me·di·ate** [~ˈmiːdiət] □ (inter)medio; intermediario; ~-*range rocket* cohete *m* de alcance medio; ~ *stop* escala *f*.
in·ter·ment [inˈtəːrmənt] entierro *m*.
in·ter·mez·zo [intərˈmedzou] ♪ intermezzo *m*; *thea.* intermedio *m*.
in·ter·mi·na·ble [inˈtəːrminəbl] □ interminable, inacabable.
in·ter·min·gle [intərˈmiŋgl] entremezclar(se), entreverar(se).
in·ter·mis·sion [intərˈmiʃn] interrupción *f*; intervalo *m*, pausa *f*; *thea.* entreacto *m*; 🕮 intermisión *f*.
in·ter·mit·tent [intərˈmitənt] □ intermitente (*a.* ⚕); ~*ly* a intervalos.
in·ter·mix [intərˈmiks] entremezclar(se).
in·tern [inˈtəːrn] recluir, internar.
in·tern(**e**) [ˈintəːrn] ⚕ practicante *m* de hospital.
in·ter·nal [inˈtəːrnl] □ interno, interior; *internal revenue* rentas *f/pl.* internas; ~-**comˈbus·tion en·gine** motor *m* de explosión, motor *m* de combustión interna.
in·ter·na·tion·al [intərˈnæʃnl] **1.** □ internacional; ~ *date line* línea *f* internacional de cambio de fecha; ~ *law* derecho *m* internacional (*or* de

gentes); **2.** ♀ *pol.* Internacional *f*; *sport*: partido *m* internacional; jugador (-a *f*) *m* internacional; **in·ter·ˈna·tion·al·ism** internacionalismo *m*; **in·terˈna·tion·al·ize** [~əlaiz] internacionalizar.

in·ter·ne·cine war [intərˈni:sinˈwɔ:r] guerra *f* de aniquilación mutua.

in·tern·ee [intərˈni:] internado (a *f*) *m*; **inˈtern·ment** internamiento *m*; ~ *camp* campo *m* de internamiento.

in·ter·pel·late [inˈtə:rpeleit] interpelar; **in·ter·pelˈla·tion** interpelación *f*.

in·ter·pen·e·trate [intərˈpenitreit] compenetrarse.

in·ter·plan·e·tar·y [intərˈplænitəri] interplanetario.

in·ter·play [ˈintərˈplei] interacción *f*.

in·ter·po·late [inˈtə:rpouleit] interpolar; **in·ter·poˈla·tion** interpolación *f*.

in·ter·pose [intərˈpouz] interponer(se); **in·ter·po·si·tion** [intərpəˈziʃn] interposición *f*.

in·ter·pret [inˈtə:rprit] interpretar; **in·ter·preˈta·tion** interpretación *f*; **inˈter·pre·ta·tive** interpretativo; **inˈter·pret·er** intérprete *m*/*f*.

in·ter·reg·num [ˈintəˈregnəm] interregno *m*.

in·ter·ro·gate [inˈterəgeit] interrogar, examinar; **in·ter·roˈga·tion** interrogación *f*, examen *m*; *note* (*or mark or point*) *of* ~ (punto *m* de) interrogación *f*; **in·ter·rog·a·tive** [~təˈrɔgətiv] □ interrogativo *adj.* *a.* *su.* *m*; **in·terˈrog·a·to·ry** [~təri] **1.** interrogatorio *m*; **2.** interrogativo.

in·ter·rupt [intəˈrʌpt] interrumpir; (entre)cortar; **in·terˈrupt·ed·ly** interrumpidamente; **in·terˈrupt·er** interruptor (-a *f*) *m*; **in·terˈrup·tion** interrupción *f*.

in·ter·scho·las·tic [intərskəˈlæstik] interescolar; *v.* *intercollegiate*.

in·ter·sect [intərˈsekt] *v*/*t.* cortar; *v*/*i.* intersecarse; **in·terˈsec·tion** intersección *f*; cruce *m*.

in·ter·space [ˈintərˈspeis] **1.** espacio *m* intermedio, intervalo *m*; **2.** espaciar.

in·ter·sperse [intərˈspə:rs] esparcir, entremezclar; salpicar (*with* de).

in·ter·state [ˈintərˈsteit] interestatal.

in·ter·stel·lar [ˈintərˈstelər] interestelar.

in·ter·stice [inˈtə:rstis] intersticio *m*; **in·ter·sti·tial** [intərˈstiʃl] □ intersticial.

in·ter·twine [intərˈtwain] entrelazar(se), entretejer(se); trenzar.

in·ter·val [ˈintərvəl] intervalo *m* (*a.* ♪); *thea.* entreacto *m*; descanso *m* (*a.* *sport*); pausa *f*; *at* ~*s* de vez en cuando, a intervalos.

in·ter·vene [intərˈvi:n] intervenir, interponerse, mediar; **in·ter·ven·tion** [~ˈvenʃn] intervención *f*.

in·ter·view [ˈintərvju:] **1.** entrevista *f*; (*press etc.*) interviú *f*; *have an* ~ *with* = **2.** entrevistarse con, interviuvar; **ˈin·ter·view·er** interviuvador (-a *f*) *m*; interrogador (-a *f*) *m*.

in·ter·weave [intərˈwi:v] [*irr.* (*weave*)] entretejer (*a.* *fig.*).

in·tes·ta·cy [inˈtestəsi] falta *f* de testamento; **inˈtes·tate** [~tit] intestado.

in·tes·ti·nal [inˈtestinl] intestinal; **inˈtes·tine** [~tin] intestino *adj.* *a.* *su.* *m*; *large* ~ intestino *m* grueso; *small* ~ intestino *m* delgado.

in·ti·ma·cy [ˈintiməsi] intimidad *f*; F trato *m* sexual; **in·ti·mate 1.** [ˈ~meit] intimar; dar a entender; **2.** [ˈ~mit] a) □ íntimo; estrecho; *knowledge* profundo, detallado; *become* ~ intimarse (*with* con); b) amigo (a *f*) *m* de confianza; **in·ti·ma·tion** [~ˈmeiʃn] intimación *f*; insinuación *f*, indirecta *f*; indicio *m*.

in·tim·i·date [inˈtimideit] intimidar, amedrentar, acobardar; **in·tim·iˈda·tion** intimidación *f*; **in·tim·iˈda·tor·y** [~ˈdeitəri] amenazador.

in·to [ˈintu, *before consonant* ˈintə] en; a; dentro de; hacia el interior de; ~ *the garden* al jardín; *fall* ~ *the sea* caer al (*or* en el) mar; *put it* ~ *the box* meterlo dentro de la caja.

in·tol·er·a·ble [inˈtɔlərəbl] □ intolerable, inaguantable; **inˈtol·er·ance** intolerancia *f*; **inˈtol·er·ant** □ intolerante (*of* con, para).

in·to·na·tion [intouˈneiʃn] entonación *f*; **in·to·nate** [ˈ~neit], **in·tone** [inˈtoun] entonar; *eccl.* salmodiar.

in·tox·i·cant [inˈtɔksikənt] **1.** embriagador; **2.** bebida *f* alcohólica; **inˈtox·i·cate** [~keit] embriagar (*a.* *fig.*); ⚕ intoxicar; **in·tox·iˈca·tion** embriaguez *f* (*a.* *fig.*); ⚕ intoxicación *f*.

in·trac·ta·bil·i·ty [intræktəˈbiliti]

intratabilidad *f*; **in'trac·ta·ble** □ *p.* intratable, insumiso; *materials* difícil de trabajar; *problem* insoluble.

in·tra·mu·ral ['intrə'mjurəl] interior, situado intramuros.

in·tran·si·gent [in'trænsidʒənt] intransigente.

in·tran·si·tive [in'trænsitiv] □ intransitivo *adj. a. su. m.*

in·tra·ve·nous ['intrə'vi:nəs] intravenoso.

in·trench [in'trentʃ] *v. entrench.*

in·trep·id [in'trepid] □ intrépido; **in·tre·pid·i·ty** [intri'piditi] intrepidez *f.*

in·tri·ca·cy ['intrikəsi] intrincación *f*; **in·tri·cate** ['~kit] □ intrincado.

in·trigue [in'tri:g] **1.** intriga *f*; amorío *m* secreto, lío *m*; *thea.* enredo *m*; **2.** intrigar; tener un lío; **in'tri·guer** intrigante *m/f.*

in·trin·sic [in'trinsik] □ intrínseco.

in·tro·duce [intrə'dju:s] introducir; meter, insertar; *p. to a p., parl. bill* presentar; dar a conocer; *book* prologar; *subject into conversation* sacar a colación; **in·tro·duc·tion** [~'dʌkʃn] introducción *f*; inserción *f*; presentación *f of p.*; prólogo *m to book*; *letter of* ~ carta *f* de recomendación; **in·tro'duc·to·ry** [~təri] introductor; preliminar; ~ *offer* ofrecimiento *m* de presentación, oferta *f* preliminar.

in·tro·it ['introit] introito *m.*

in·tro·spec·tion [introu'spekʃn] introspección *f*; **in·tro'spec·tive** □ introspectivo.

in·tro·ver·sion [introu'və:rʒn] introversión *f*; **in·tro·vert** ['~və:rt] introvertido *adj. a. su. m* (a *f*).

in·trude [in'tru:d] *v/t.* introducir (sin derecho), meter, encajar (*in* en); imponer (*upon* a); *v/i.* (entro)meterse, encajarse (*upon* en); pegarse; estorbar; **in'trud·er** intruso (a *f*) *m.*

in·tru·sion [in'tru:ʒn] intrusión *f*; **in·tru·sive** [in'tru:siv] □ intruso.

in·trust [in'trʌst] *v. entrust.*

in·tu·i·tion [intju'iʃn] intuición *f*; **in·tu·i·tive** [~'tjuitiv] □ intuitivo.

in·un·date ['inʌndeit] inundar; **in·un'da·tion** inundación *f.*

in·ure [i'njur] acostumbrar, endurecer (*to* a).

in·vade [in'veid] invadir (*a. fig.*); **in'vad·er** invasor (-a *f*) *m*; **in'vad·ing** invasor.

in·val·id 1. [in'vælid] inválido, nulo; **2.** ['invəlid] ⚔, ⚓ inválido *adj. a. su. m* (a *f*); enfermo *adj. a. su. m* (a *f*); ~ *carriage* cochecillo *m* de inválido; ~ *chair* sillón *m* para inválidos; **3.** [~] incapacitar; ⚔, ⚓ (*a.* ~ *out*) licenciar por invalidez; **in·val·i·date** [in'vælideit] invalidar; **in·val·i'da·tion** invalidación *f*; **in·va·lid·i·ty** [invə'liditi] invalidez *f.*

in·val·u·a·ble [in'væljuəbl] □ inestimable, inapreciable.

in·var·i·a·ble [in'veriəbl] □ invariable.

in·va·sion [in'veiʒn] invasión *f* (*a. fig.*, ⚕).

in·vec·tive [in'vektiv] invectiva *f*; improperio *m.*

in·veigh [in'vei]: ~ *against* vituperar, invectivar.

in·vei·gle [in'vi:gl] engatusar (*into* para que); inducir (engañosamente) (*into* a); **in'vei·gle·ment** engatusamiento *m*, persuasión *f.*

in·vent [in'vent] inventar; idear; fingir; **in'ven·tion** invención *f*, invento *m*; (*faculty*) inventiva *f*; ficción *f*; **in'ven·tive** □ inventivo; **in'ven·tive·ness** inventiva *f*; **in·ven·tor** inventor (-a *f*) *m*; **in·ven·to·ry** ['invəntɔri] **1.** inventario *m*; existencias *f/pl.*; **2.** inventariar.

in·verse ['in'və:rs] □ inverso; **in·ver·sion** [in've:rʒn] inversión *f.*

in·vert 1. [in'və:rt] invertir; trastrocar; volver al revés; ~*ed commas pl.* comillas *f/pl.*, ~*ed exclamation point* principio *m* de admiración; ~*ed question mark* principio *m* de interrogación; **2.** ['invərt] invertido (a *f*) *m.*

in·ver·te·brate [in'və:rtibrit] invertebrado *adj. a. su. m.*

in·vest [in'vest] *v/t.* ✝ invertir, colocar; ~ *with honor* investir de (*or* con); *garment, quality* revestir de (*or* con); ⚔ sitiar, cercar; *v/i.*: ~ *in* poner (*or* invertir) dinero en; F comprar.

in·ves·ti·gate [in'vestigeit] investigar; averiguar; examinar; **in·ves·ti'ga·tion** investigación *f*; averiguación *f*; pesquisa *f*; **in'ves·ti·ga·tor** [~geitər] investigador (-a *f*) *m.*

in·ves·ti·ture [in'vestitʃər] investidura *f*; **in'vest·ment** ✝ inversión *f*, colocación *f* (de fondos); ⚔ sitio *m*, cerco *m*; investidura *f*; ✝ ~*s pl.* valores *m/pl.* en cartera, fondos *m/pl.* invertidos; ~ *capital* capital *m* de

inversión; ~ *trust* compañía *f* inversionista; **in'vest·or** inversionista *m/f*; accionista *m/f*, inversor (-a *f*) *m*.
in·vet·er·a·cy [in'vetərəsi] lo inveterado; **in'vet·er·ate** [~rit] □ inveterado; *p.* habitual; *b.s.* empedernido.
in·vid·i·ous [in'vidiəs] □ aborrecible, odioso; parcial, injusto.
in·vig·i·late [in'vidʒileit] vigilar (durante los exámenes).
in·vig·or·ate [in'vigəreit] vigorizar, tonificar; **in'vig·or·a·ting** vigorizador; **in·vig·or'a·tion** tonificación *f*.
in·vin·ci·bil·i·ty [invinsi'biliti] invencibilidad *f*; **in'vin·ci·ble** □ invencible.
in·vi·o·la·bil·i·ty [invaiələ'biliti] inviolabilidad *f*; **in'vi·o·la·ble** □ inviolable; **in'vi·o·late** [~lit] inviolado.
in·vis·i·bil·i·ty [invizə'biliti] invisibilidad *f*; **in'vis·i·ble** □ invisible; ~ *ink* tinta *f* simpática.
in·vi·ta·tion [invi'teiʃn] invitación *f*, convite *m*; **in·vite** [in'vait] invitar (*to* a); (*esp. to food, drink*) convidar (*to* a); **in'vi·ting** □ atrayente; incitante; provocativo; *food* apetitoso.
in·vo·ca·tion [invou'keiʃn] invocación *f*; evocación *f of spirits*.
in·voice ['invɔis] **1.** factura *f*; **2.** facturar.
in·voke [in'vouk] invocar; *spirits* evocar.
in·vol·un·tar·y [in'vɔləntəri] □ involuntario.
in·vo·lute ['invəluːt] intrincado; vuelto hacia dentro; enrollado en espiral; **in·vo'lu·tion** intrincación *f*; *biol.*, ⚘ involución *f*; ⅍ elevación *f* a potencias.
in·volve [in'vɔlv] envolver; (*entangle*) enredar, enmarañar; complicar; (*entail*) traer consigo, acarrear; implicar; comprometer; *get ~d in* meterse en, embrollarse en; **in'volve·ment** envolvimiento *m*; enredo *m*; complicación *f*; compromiso *m*; apuro *m*, dificultad *f*.
in·vul·ner·a·bil·i·ty [invʌlnərə'biliti] invulnerabilidad *f*; **in'vul·ner·a·ble** □ invulnerable.
in·ward ['inwərd] **1.** *adj.* interior, interno; **2.** *adv.* (*mst* **in·wards** ['~z]) hacia dentro, para dentro, interiormente; **3.** *su.* F *~s* ['inərdz] *pl.* entrañas *f/pl.*; interiores *m/pl.*; **'in·ward·ly** interiormente; (hacia) dentro; para sí; **'in·ward·ness** esencia *f*; espiritualidad *f*.
in·wrought ['in'rɔːt] entretejido; incrustado, embutido (*with* con; *in*, *on* en).
i·od·ic [ai'ɔdik] yódico; **i·o·dide** ['aiədaid] yoduro *m*; **i·o·dine** ['~dain] yodo *m*.
i·o·do·form [ai'ɔdəfɔːrm] yodoformo *m*.
i·on ['aiən] ion *m*; ~ *trap* ⚡ trampa *f* de iones.
I·o·ni·an [ai'ounjən] jonio *adj. a. su. m* (a *f*), jónico *adj. a. su. m* (a *f*).
I·on·ic[1] [ai'ɔnik] jónico.
i·on·ic[2] [~] *phys.* iónico; **i·on·ize** ['aiənaiz] ionizar; **i·on·o·sphere** [ai'ɔnəsfir] ionosfera *f*.
i·o·ta [ai'outə] (*letter*) iota *f*; *fig.* jota *f*, ápice *m*, pizca *f*.
ip·e·cac·u·an·ha [ipikækju'ænə] ipecacuana *f*.
I·ra·ni·an [i'reinjən] iranio *adj. a. su. m* (a *f*), iranés *adj. a. su. m* (-a *f*).
I·ra·qi [i'ræki] irakí *adj. a. su. m/f*.
i·ras·ci·bil·i·ty [iræsi'biliti] irascibilidad *f*, iracundia *f*; **i'ras·ci·ble** [~sibl] □ irascible, iracundo.
i·rate [ai'reit] airado, colérico.
ire ['aiər] *poet.* ira *f*, cólera *f*.
ir·i·des·cence [iri'desns] iridescencia *f*, irisación *f*; **ir·i'des·cent** iridescente, irisado; tornasolado.
i·ris ['airis] *opt.* iris *m*; ⚘ lirio *m*; *phot.* ~ *diaphragm* diafragma *m* iris.
I·rish ['airiʃ] irlandés *adj. a. su. m*; *the ~ pl.* los irlandeses; **'I·rish·ism** idiotismo *m* irlandés; **'I·rish·man** irlandés *m*; **'I·rish·wom·an** irlandesa *f*.
irk [əːrk] fastidiar, molestar.
irk·some ['əːrksəm] □ fastidioso, molesto, cargante, pesado; **'irk·some·ness** fastidio *m*, molestia *f*, tedio *m*.
i·ron ['aiərn] **1.** hierro *m* (*a. fig., tool, weapon, golf*); (*a. flat-~*) plancha *f*; *~s pl.* hierros *m/pl.*, grillos *m/pl.*; *put in ~s* aherrojar; *strike while the ~ is hot* a hierro candente batir de repente; **2.** de hierro; férreo (*a. fig.*); ~ *curtain* telón *m* de acero; ~ *lung* pulmón *m* de hierro; ~ *ore* mineral *m* de hierro; ~ *ration* ración *f* de reserva; **3.** *clothes* planchar; aherrojar; herrar; ~ *out* allanar; '♀ **'Age** Edad *f* de Hierro; **'~·bound** zunchado con hierro; *fig.* férreo, inflexible; *coast* escabroso; **'~·clad** acorazado *adj. a. su. m*;

ˈi·ron found·ry fundición *f* de hierro; **ˈi·ron·hand·ed** severo; riguroso; de mano férrea.
i·ron·ic, i·ron·i·cal [aiˈrɔnik(l)] □ irónico.
i·ron·ing [ˈaiərniŋ] **1.** planchado *m*; **2.** de planchar; ˈ~ ˈ**board** tabla *f* de planchar.
i·ron...: ˈ**~·mas·ter** fabricante *m* de hierro; ˈ**~·mon·ger** ferretero *m*, quincallero *m*; *~'s* (*shop*) ferretería *f*, quincallería *f*; ˈ**~·mon·ger·y** quincalla *f*, ferretería *f*; ˈ**~·mo**(**u**)**ld** mancha *f* de orín; ˈ**~·stone** mineral *m* de hierro; ˈ**~-willed** de voluntad de hierro; ˈ**~·work** herraje *m*; obra *f* de hierro; ˈ**~·work·er** herrero *m* de grueso; ˈ**~·works** herrería *f*; fábrica *f* de hierro.
i·ro·ny [ˈairəni] ironía *f*.
ir·ra·di·ance, ir·ra·di·an·cy [iˈreidiəns(i)] luminosidad *f*; irradiación *f*; **irˈra·di·ant** luminoso, radiante.
ir·ra·di·ate [iˈreidieit] *v/t. phys.*, ⚕ irradiar; iluminar(se de); *fig.* derramar; *v/i.* brillar; **ir·ra·diˈa·tion** irradiación *f*.
ir·ra·tion·al [iˈræʃnl] □ irracional (*a.* ⅍); **ir·ra·tion·al·i·ty** [~ʃəˈnæliti] irracionalidad *f*.
ir·re·claim·a·ble [iriˈkleiməbl] □ irrecuperable; irredimible, incorregible; inservible.
ir·re·con·cil·a·ble [iˈrekənsailəbl] □ irreconciliable, intransigente.
ir·re·cov·er·a·ble [iriˈkʌvərəbl] irrecuperable; incobrable.
ir·re·deem·a·ble [iriˈdi:məbl] irredimible; ✝ perpetuo, no reembolsable, no amortizable.
ir·re·duc·i·ble [iriˈdju:səbl] irreducible.
ir·ref·u·ta·ble [iˈrefjutəbl] □ irrefutable.
ir·reg·u·lar [iˈregjulər] **1.** □ irregular; **2.** ⚔ guerillero *m*; **ir·reg·u·lar·i·ty** [~ˈlæriti] irregularidad *f*.
ir·rel·e·vance, ir·rel·e·van·cy [iˈrelivəns(i)] inconexión *f*; impertinencia *f*; inaplicabilidad *f*; **irˈrel·e·vant** □ fuera de propósito; impertinente; inaplicable; *be ~* no hacer al caso.
ir·re·li·gion [iriˈlidʒn] irreligión *f*; **ir·re·li·gious** [~dʒəs] □ irreligioso.
ir·re·me·di·a·ble [iriˈmi:diəbl] □ irremediable.
ir·re·mis·si·ble [iriˈmisəbl] □ irremisible.
ir·re·mov·a·ble [iriˈmu:vəbl] □ inamovible.
ir·rep·a·ra·ble [iˈrepərəbl] □ irreparable.
ir·re·place·a·ble [iriˈpleisəbl] insustituible, irreemplazable.
ir·re·press·i·ble [iriˈpresəbl] indomable; incorregible, incontrolable.
ir·re·proach·a·ble [iriˈproutʃəbl] □ irreprochable.
ir·re·sist·i·bil·i·ty [ˈirizistəˈbiliti] lo irresistible; invencibilidad *f*; **ir·reˈsist·i·ble** □ irresistible.
ir·res·o·lute [iˈrezəlu:t] □ irresoluto, irresuelto, indeciso; **irˈres·o·lute·ness, ir·res·oˈlu·tion** irresolución *f*, indecisión *f*.
ir·re·spec·tive [irisˈpektiv] □: *~ of* aparte de, prescindiendo de, sin consideración a.
ir·re·spon·si·bil·i·ty [ˈirispɔnsəˈbiliti] irresponsabilidad *f*; **ir·reˈspon·si·ble** □ irresponsable.
ir·re·triev·a·ble [iriˈtri:vəbl] irrecuperable, irreparable.
ir·rev·er·ence [iˈrevərəns] irreverencia *f*; **irˈrev·er·ent** □ irreverente.
ir·re·vers·i·ble [iriˈvə:rsəbl] irreversible; irrevocable.
ir·rev·o·ca·bil·i·ty [irevɔkəˈbiliti] irrevocabilidad *f*; **irˈrev·o·ca·ble** □ irrevocable.
ir·ri·gate [ˈirigeit] regar; irrigar (*a.* ⚕); **ir·riˈga·tion** riego *m*; irrigación *f*; *~ channel* acequia *f*, canal *m* de riego.
ir·ri·ta·bil·i·ty [iritəˈbiliti] irritabilidad *f*; ˈ**ir·ri·ta·ble** □ irritable; irascible; nervioso; ˈ**ir·ri·tant** irritante *adj. a. su. m*; **ir·ri·tate** [ˈ~teit] irritar; exasperar; azuzar; molestar; ˈ**ir·ri·tat·ing** □ irritador, irritante; enojoso; molesto; **ir·riˈta·tion** irritación *f*.
ir·rup·tion [iˈrʌpʃn] irrupción *f*.
is [iz] es; está (*v. be*).
i·sin·glass [ˈaiziŋglæs] colapez *f*; cola *f* de pescado.
Is·lam [ˈizlæm] islam *m*; **Is·lam·ic** [izˈlæmik] islámico.
is·land [ˈailənd] **1.** isla *f*; refugio *m in road*; **2.** isleño; ˈ**is·land·er** isleño (a *f*) *m*.
isle [ail] *mst poet.* isla *f*; **is·let** [ˈailit] isleta *f*; islote *m*.

ism [izm] F *mst contp.* ismo *m*; teoría *f*; sistema *m*.

isn't ['iznt] = *is not.*

i·so... ['aisou] iso...; '**~·bar** [~bɑːr] isobara *f*.

i·so·late ['aisəleit] aislar; apartar; **i·so·lat·ed** ['~id] aislado; insulado; alejado; **i·so'la·tion** aislamiento *m*, apartamiento *m*; ~ *hospital* hospital *m* de aislamiento (*or* de contagiosos); **i·so'la·tion·ism** aislacionismo *m*; **i·so'la·tion·ist** aislacionista *adj. a. su. m*, aislamentista *adj. a. su. m.*

i·so·met·ric [aisə'metrik] isométrico; ~s isométrica *f*.

i·so·sceles [ai'sɔsəliːz] isósceles.

i·so·therm ['aisouθəːrm] isoterma *f*.

i·so·tope ['aisoutoup] isótopo *m*.

Is·ra·el·i [iz'reili] israelí *adj. a. su. m/f.*

Is·ra·el·ite ['izriəlait] israelita *adj. a. su. m/f.*

is·sue ['iʃuː] **1.** salida *f*; distribución *f*; ⚕ emisión *f of coins, shares, stamps*; *publishing*: edición *f*, impresión *f*, tirada *f*; (*copy*) número *m*, entrega *f*; (*question*) cuestión *f*, problema *m*, punto *m* en disputa; (*outcome*) resultado *m*, consecuencia *f*, éxito *m*; (*offspring*) sucesión *f*, prole *f*; ⚕ flujo *m*; *at* ~ en disputa, en cuestión; *without* ~ sin sucesión; *side* ~ cuestión *f* secundaria; *evade the* ~ esquivar la pregunta; *face the* ~ afrontar la situación; *force the* ~ forzar una decisión; *join* (*or take*) ~ *with* oponer; llevar la contraria a; no estar de acuerdo con; disputar con; **2.** *v/t.* distribuir; expedir; ⚕ emitir; poner en circulación; publicar; *decree* promulgar; *v/i.* salir; brotar; provenir; emanar; fluir; ~ *in* dar por resultado; **3.** ⚔ reglamentario; '**is·sue·less** sin sucesión.

isth·mus ['isməs] istmo *m*.

it [it] **1.** (*subject, but gen. omitted*) él, ella, ello; *acc.* lo, la; *dat.* le; *after prp.* él, ella, ello; ~ *is I* (*or* ~*'s me*) soy yo; ~ *is raining* llueve; ~ *is said that* se dice que; ~ *is true that* es verdad que; ~ *is 2 o'clock* son las 2; F *how goes* (*or is*) ~? ¿qué tal?; *that's* ~ eso es; ya está; está bien; F *this is* ~ ya llegó la hora; **2.** F aquél *m*; atracción *f* sexual; lo necesario; (= *Italian*) vermut *m* italiano; **3.** F *pred.*: *you're* ~ *children's games*: tú te quedas; *he thinks he's* ~ se da mucho tono.

I·tal·ian [i'tæljən] **1.** italiano *adj. a. su. m* (a *f*); **2.** (*language*) italiano *m*.

i·tal·ic [i'tælik] **1.** (*a.* ♀) itálico; **2.** *typ. mst* ~s (letra *f*) bastardilla *f*; *in* ~s en bastardilla; en cursiva; **i·tal·i·cize** [i'tælisaiz] poner en (letra) bastardilla; subrayar.

itch [itʃ] **1.** ⚕ sarna *f*; picazón *f*; comezón *f*, prurito *m* (*a. fig. for* por, *to* de); **2.** picar; sentir comezón; *my arm* ~*es* me pica el brazo; ~ *to* sentir comezón (*or* prurito) de, rabiar por; '**itch·ing** prurito *m*, comezón *f* (*a. fig.*); *have an* ~ *palm* ser codicioso; '~ '**pow·der** polvos *m/pl.* de 'pica-pica'; '**itch·y** picante; sarnoso; *p.* nervioso; impaciente.

i·tem ['aitem] **1.** ítem *m*, artículo *m*; ⚕ partida *f*; número *m in program*; (*newspaper*) noticia *f*, suelto *m*; detalle *m*; **2.** *adv.* ítem; **i·tem·ize** ['aitəmaiz] detallar, especificar.

it·er·ate ['itəreit] iterar; **it·er'a·tion** iteración *f*; **it·er·a·tive** ['itərətiv] □ iterativo.

i·tin·er·ant [i'tinərənt] ambulante, errante; **i·tin·er·ar·y** [ai'tinərəri] **1.** itinerario *m*; ruta *f*; guía *f*; **2.** itinerario.

its [its] **1.** su(s); **2.** *pron.* (el) suyo, [(la) suya *etc.*]

it's [its] = *it is, it has.*

it·self [it'self] (*subject*) él mismo, ella misma, ello mismo; *acc.*, *dat.* se; (*after prp.*) sí (mismo [a]).

I've [aiv] = *I have.*

i·vied ['aiviːd] cubierto de hiedra.

i·vo·ry ['aivəri] **1.** marfil *m*; *sl. ivories pl.* teclas *f/pl.* de piano; bolas *f/pl.* de billar; dientes *m/pl.*; **2.** de marfil; *poet.* ebúrneo; ~ *tower* torre *f* de marfil; *fig.* inocencia *f*.

i·vy ['aivi] hiedra *f*.

J

jab [dʒæb] **1.** (*poke*) hurgonazo *m*; (*prick*) pinchazo *m*, piquete *m*; (*with elbow*) codazo *m*; *boxing*: golpe *m* rápido (dado sin extender el brazo); **2.** hurgonear; pinchar; clavar; dar un codazo a; golpear.
jab·ber [ˈdʒæbər] **1.** (*a.* ∼*ing*) jerigonza *f*; farfulla *f*, chapurreo *m*; **2.** farfullar, chapurrear; parlotear.
jack [dʒæk] **1.** ⊕, *mot.* gato *m*; ↯ enchufe *m* hembra; (*p.*) hombre *m*, mozo *m*; ⚓ marinero *m*; *cards*: sota *f*; *zo.* macho *m*; *ichth.* lucio *m* (joven); ⚓ bandera *f* de proa; torno *m* de asador; sacabotas *m* (*a.* boot ∼); **2.**: ∼ up alzar con el gato; price subir, aumentar.
jack·al [ˈdʒækɔːl] *zo.* chacal *m*; *fig.* paniaguado *m*.
jack·ass [ˈdʒækæs] burro *m* (*a. fig.*); ˈ**jack·boots** botas *f/pl.* fuertes; ˈ**jack·draw** grajilla *f*.
jack·et [ˈdʒækit] chaqueta *f*, americana *f*; saco *m S.Am.*; cubierta *f*; envoltura *f*; ⊕ camisa *f*, chaqueta *f*; (*book-*) sobrecubierta *f*, camisa *f*; potatoes in their ∼s patatas *f/pl.* enteras (*or* con su piel); strait ∼ camisa *f* de fuerza.
jack...: ˈ∼**-in-the-box** caja *f* sorpresa; ˈ∼**·knife** navaja *f*; ∼ dive salto *m* de la carpa; ˈ∼**-of-ˈall-trades** factótum *m*; hombre *m* de muchos oficios (and master of none y maestro de ninguno); ˈ∼**-of-ˈall-work** factótum *m*; ˈ∼**o'-lan·tern** fuego *m* fatuo; ˈ∼ **plane** garlopa *f*; ˈ∼**·pot** *cards*: bote *m*; premio *m* gordo; F hit the ∼ tener mucha suerte; ponerse las botas; ˈ∼ **rab·bit** liebre *m* grande.
Jac·o·be·an [dʒækəˈbiːən] de la época de Jacobo I; **Jac·o·bin** [ˈdʒækəbin] jacobino *adj. a. su. m* (a *f*); **Jac·o·bite** [ˈ∼bait] jacobita *adj. a. su. m/f*.
jade¹ [dʒeid] **1.** rocín *m*; *contp.* mujerzuela *f*, picarona *f*; mozuela *f*; **2.** cansar, rendir; saciar.
jade² [∼] *min.* jade *m*.
jag [dʒæg] **1.** diente *m*; púa *f*; mella *f*; (*tear*) siete *m*; *sl.* turca *f*, juerga *f*; **2.** dentar; mellar; rasgar; **jag·ged** [ˈ∼id] dentado, desigual, mellado; áspero; rasgado (en sietes).
ja·gu·ar [ˈdʒægjuər] jaguar *m*.
jail [dʒeil] **1.** cárcel *f*; **2.** encarcelar; ˈ∼**·bird** presidiario *m*; encarcelado *m*; ˈ∼**·break** escapatoria *f* de la cárcel.
jail·er [ˈdʒeilər] carcelero *m*.
ja·lop·y [dʒəˈlɔpi] F *mot.*, ✈ cacharro *m*, armatoste *m*; automóvil *m* ruin.
jam¹ [dʒæm] **1.** *approx.* mermela *f*, confitura *f*, compota *f*; F and on it y un jamón con chorrera; **2.** hacer mermelada de.
jam² [∼] **1.** apiñadura *f*; (*stoppage*) atasc(amient)o *m*; agolpamiento *m* of people; *sl.* aprieto *m*, lío *m*; traffic ∼ aglomeración *f* de tráfico, ensalada *f*; F ∼ session concierto *m* improvisado de jazz; **2.** apiñar(se); apretar(se); atascar(se); *radio*: interferir; ∼ on brakes echar (*or* poner) con violencia; hat encasquetar(se); ˈ∼**-packed** apiñado; apretujado.
Ja·mai·ca [dʒəˈmeikə] (*a.* ∼ rum) ron *m* de Jamaica; **Jaˈmai·can** [∼kən] jamaicano *adj. a. su. m* (a *f*).
jamb [dʒæm] jamba *f*.
jam·bo·ree [dʒæmbəˈriː] F francachela *f*, juerga *f*; congreso *m* de (niños) exploradores.
jam jar [ˈdʒæmdʒɑːr] pote *m* para mermelada.
jam·ming [ˈdʒæmiŋ] ↯ radioperturbación *f*; interferencia *f*.
jan·gle [ˈdʒæŋgl] **1.** sonido *m* discordante, cencerreo *m*; **2.** cencerrear, (hacer) sonar de manera discordante; ˈ**jan·gling** discordante, estridente, desapacible.
jan·i·tor [ˈdʒænitər] portero *m*, conserje *m*.
Jan·u·ar·y [ˈdʒænjuəri] enero *m*.
ja·pan [dʒəˈpæn] **1.** laca *f* negra; charol *m*; obra *f* laqueada japonesa; **2.** barnizar con laca japonesa; charolar.
Jap·a·nese [dʒæpəˈniːz] **1.** japonés

adj. a. su. m (-a *f*); *the* ~ *pl.* los japoneses; **2.** (*language*) japonés *m.*

jar¹ [dʒɑːr] tarro *m*; pote *m*; (*with handles*) jarra *f*; (*narrow-necked*) botija *f*; (*large*) tinaja *f*; Leyden ~ botella *f* de Leiden.

jar² [~] **1.** choque *m*, sacudida *f*; ruido *m* desapacible; sorpresa *f* desagradable; discordia *f*; **2.** chocar; sacudir; (hacer) vibrar; (*colors*) chillar; chirriar; ser discorde; ~ (*up*)*on* irritar, poner(le a una p.) los nervios en punta.

jar·gon [ˈdʒɑːrgən] jerigonza *f*; (*specialist*) jerga *f*; (*gibberish*) guirigay *m.*

jar·ring [ˈdʒɑːriŋ] discordante; desconcertante.

jas·min(**e**) [ˈdʒæsmin] jazmín *m.*

jas·per [ˈdʒæspər] jaspe *m.*

jaun·dice [ˈdʒɔːndis] ⚕ ictericia *f*; **ˈjaun·diced** ⚕ ictérico; cetrino; *fig.* avinagrado, envidioso.

jaunt [dʒɔːnt] **1.** caminata *f*, excursión *f*, paseo *m*; **2.** hacer una caminata, ir de excursión; **ˈjaun·ti·ness** viveza *f*, garbo *m*, soltura *f*; **ˈjaun·ty** □ garboso, airoso, ligero; vivaracho; de buen humor.

Jav·a·nese [dʒævəˈniːz] javanés *adj. a. su. m* (-a *f*).

jave·lin [ˈdʒævlin] jabalina *f*; *throwing the* ~ lanzamiento *m* de jabalina.

jaw [dʒɔː] **1.** quijada *f*, mandíbula *f*, maxilar *m*; *sl.* cháchara *f*, chismes *m/pl.*, charla *f*; ⊕ mordaza *f*, mandíbula *f*; ~*s pl.* boca *f*, garganta *f*; *fig.* garras *f/pl.*, fauces *f/pl.*; **2.** F *v/i.* chismear, charlar; *v/t.* regañar; **ˈ~·bone** maxilar *m*, quijada *f*, mandíbula *f*; **ˈ~·break·er** F trabalenguas *m*, palabra *f* kilométrica, terminacho *m* impronunciable.

jay [dʒei] *orn.* arrendajo *m*; F necio (a *f*) *m*; **ˈ~·walk** cruzar la calle temerariamente; **ˈ~·walk·er** peatón *m* imprudente.

jazz [dʒæz] **1.** jazz *m*; F (*and*) *all that* ~ (y) otras cosas por el estilo; **2.** de jazz; **3.** *v/t.* sincopar; *v/i.* tocar (*or* bailar) el jazz; **ˈ~ ˈband** orquesta *f* de jazz, jazz band *m*; **ˈjazz·y** F sincopado; de colores chillones.

jeal·ous [ˈdʒeləs] □ celoso, envidioso; cuidadoso, vigilante; *be* ~ *of a p.* tener celos de una p.; **ˈjeal·ous·y** celos *m/pl.*; envidia *f*; (*care*) celo *m.*

jeans [dʒiːnz] *pl.* F pantalones *m/pl.* de dril.

jeep [dʒiːp] jeep *m.*

jeer [dʒir] **1.** mofa *f*, befa *f*, escarnio *m*; (*shout*) grito *m* de sarcasmo (*or* protesta *etc.*); **2.** mofarse (*at* de), befar; **ˈjeer·er** mofador (-a *f*) *m*; **ˈjeer·ing** □ mofador.

je·june [dʒiˈdʒuːn] seco, árido; aburrido, insípido.

jell [dʒel] cuajarse; ponerse gelatinoso; **jel·ly** [ˈdʒeli] **1.** jalea *f*, gelatina *f*; **2.** convertir(se) en jalea; **ˈjel·ly-bean** frutilla *f*; **ˈjel·ly·fish** medusa *f.*

jeop·ard·ize [ˈdʒepərdaiz] arriesgar, comprometer; **ˈjeop·ard·y** riesgo *m*, peligro *m.*

jer·e·mi·ad [dʒeriˈmaiæd] jeremiada *f.*

jerk [dʒəːrk] **1.** tirón *m*, sacudida *f*, arranque *m*; espasmo *m* muscular; *by* (*or in*) ~*s* a sacudidas; *sl. put a* ~ *in it* menearse; F *physical* ~*s* ejercicios *m/pl.* físicos; **2.** *v/t.* sacudir; mover a tirones; arrojar; *meat* atasajar; *I* ~*ed it away from him* se lo quité de una sacudida; *v/i.* sacudirse; avanzar a tirones.

jer·kin [ˈdʒəːrkin] justillo *m.*

jerk·wa·ter [ˈdʒəːrkwɔːtər] F de poca monta.

jerk·y [ˈdʒəːrki] □ espasmódico, desigual; que se mueve a tirones.

Jer·ry [ˈdʒeri] F (soldado) alemán *m.*

jer·ry build·ing [ˈdʒeribildiŋ] construcción *f* (barata y) defectuosa; **ˈjer·ry-built** mal construido, de pacotilla.

jer·sey [ˈdʒəːzi] jersey *m.*

jes·sa·mine [ˈdʒesəmin] jazmín *m.*

jest [dʒest] **1.** chanza *f*, broma *f*; (*esp. verbal*) chiste *m*; cosa *f* de risa; *in* ~ de guasa, en broma; **2.** bromear, chancear(se); **ˈjest·er** bufón *m.*

Jes·u·it [ˈdʒezjuit] jesuita *adj. a. su. m*; **Jes·uˈit·ic, Jes·uˈit·i·cal** □ jesuítico.

jet¹ [dʒet] *min.* azabache *m.*

jet² [~] **1.** chorro *m*, surtidor *m*; (*burner*) mechero *m*; ⊕, ✈ *attr.* a reacción, a chorro; ~ *engine* reactor *m*, motor *m* a chorro; ~ *fighter* caza *f* de reacción; ~ *plane* avión *m* a reacción; ~ *propulsion* propulsión *f* por reacción (*or* a chorro); retropropulsión *f*; **2.** *v/t.* echar en chorro; *v/i.* chorrear.

jet-black [ˈdʒetˈblæk] azabachado.

jet...: **ˈ~-ˈpow·ered, ˈ~-proˈpelled** a reacción.

jet·sam [ˈdʒetsəm] ⚓ echazón *f*; *fig.* persona *f* rechazada o maltratada por la sociedad.

jet set [ˈdʒetset] F gente acomodada que viaja mucho por avión.

jet·ti·son [ˈdʒetisn] **1.** ⚓ echazón *f*; **2.** ⚓ echar al mar; *fig.* desechar, librarse de.

jet·ty [ˈdʒeti] malecón *m*; muelle *m*; embarcadero *m*.

Jew [dʒuː] judío (a *f*) *m*; ~'s *harp* birimbao *m*.

jew·el [ˈdʒuːəl] **1.** joya *f*; alhaja *f* (*a. fig.*); piedra *f* preciosa; rubí *m* of *watch*; **2.** enjoyar; **ˈ~ ˈcase** joyero *m*; **ˈjew·el·(l)ed** *watch* con rubíes; **ˈjew·el·er** joyero *m*; ~'s (*shop*) joyería *f*; **ˈjew·el·ry** joyas *f/pl.*; ✝ joyería *f*.

Jew·ess [ˈdʒuːis] judía *f*; **ˈJew·ish** judío; **Jew·ry** [ˈdʒuri] judería *f*, los judíos *m/pl*.

jib [dʒib] **1.** ⚓ foque *m*; ⊕ aguilón *m*; *fig. the cut of his* ~ su pergeño *m*; **2.** (*horse*) plantarse; resistirse, negarse (*at* a); **ˈjib ˈboom** botalón *m* de foque.

jibe [dʒaib] F concordar; compaginar; *v. gibe*.

jif·fy [ˈdʒifi] F instante *m*; *in a* ~ en un santiamén.

jig [dʒig] **1.** jiga *f*; ⊕ plantilla *f* (de guía); **2.** bailar (la jiga); mover(se) a saltitos.

jig·gered [ˈdʒigərd] F rendido; *I'm* ~ *if*... que me cuelguen si ...

jig·gle [ˈdʒigl] zangolotear; vibrar.

jig·saw [ˈdʒigsɔː] sierra *f* de vaivén; ~ *puzzle* rompecabezas *m*.

jilt [dʒilt] dar calabazas a, dejar plantado.

jim-jams [ˈdʒimdʒæmz] *sl.* delirium *m* tremens; *it gives me the* ~ me horripila.

jim·my [ˈdʒimi] palanqueta *f*.

jin·gle [ˈdʒiŋgl] **1.** (re)tintín *m*, cascabeleo *m*; rima *f* infantil; **2.** *v/t.* hacer sonar; *v/i.* cascabelear, tintinear.

jin·go [ˈdʒiŋgou] patriotero (a *f*) *m*, jingoísta *m/f*; F *by* ~! ¡caramba!; **ˈjin·go·ism** jingoísmo *m*, patriotería *f*.

jinks [dʒiŋks]: *high* ~ *pl.* jolgorio *m*; regocijo *m*.

jinx [~] *sl.* cenizo *m*, pájaro *m* de mal agüero, duendecillo *m*.

jit·ney [ˈdʒitni] coche *m* de pasaje.

jit·ter [ˈdʒitər] *sl.* **1.** temblar, estremecerse; bailar; **2.** ~*s pl.* inquietud *f*, nerviosidad *f*; **~·bug** [ˈ~bʌg] *sl.* (aficionado [a *f*] *m* a) bailar el jazz; **ˈjit·ter·y** *sl.* agitado, nervioso, inquieto.

jiu·jit·su [dʒuːˈdʒitsuː] jiu-jitsu *m*.

jive [dʒaiv] *sl.* (modo *m* de) bailar el jazz.

job [dʒɔb] **1.** tarea *f*, quehacer *m*; labor *m*; trabajo *m*; (*post*) empleo *m*, puesto *m*; (*piecework, contract*) destajo *m*; F asunto *m*; F cosa *f* difícil, faena *f*; *sl.* crimen *m*, robo *m*; *by the* ~ a destajo; *make a* (*good*) ~ *of it* hacerlo bien; *be on the* ~ estar trabajando; *sl.* estar al pie; *be out of a* ~ estar sin trabajo; *a bad* ~ mala situación *f*, caso *m* desahuciado; *odd* ~ tarea *f* suelta; *odd* ~ *man* hombre *m* que hace de todo; ~ *lot* ✝ lote *m* suelto de mercancías, saldo *m*, ~ *security* garantía *f* de empleo continuo; ~ *work typ.* remiendo *m*; **2.** alquilar; ceder por contrato; ✝ comprar y vender como corredor; ✝ especular; trabajar a destajo.

job·ber [ˈdʒɔbər] destajista *m/f*; ✝ agiotista *m*; ✝ corredor *m*; ✝ intermediario *m*; *b.s.* chanchullero *m*; **ˈjob·bing 1.** ✝ agiotaje *m*; ✝ comercio *m* de intermediario; trabajo *m* a destajo; **2.** que trabaja a destajo; **ˈjob·less** desempleado; desocupado; **ˈjob mar·ket** oportunidades *f/pl.* de empleo.

jock [dʒɔk] *sl.* atleta *m*; ~*strap* suspensorio *m* de atleta.

jock·ey [ˈdʒɔki] **1.** jockey *m*; **2.** *v/t.* embaucar (*into* para que); *v/i.* maniobrar (*for* para obtener).

jo·cose [dʒəˈkous] □, **joc·u·lar** [ˈdʒɔkjulər] □ jocoso.

joc·und [ˈdʒɔkənd] jocundo.

jodh·purs [ˈdʒɔdpʌrz] pantalones *m/pl.* de equitación.

jog [dʒɔg] **1.** empujoncito *m*, codazo *m*, sacudimiento *m* (ligero); trote *m* corto, paso *m* lento; *fig.* estímulo *m*; **2.** *v/t.* empujar (*or* sacudir) levemente; *fig.* estimular; *memory* refrescar; *v/i.* (*mst* ~ *along*, ~ *on*) andar a trote corto, avanzar despacio; **jog·ging** [ˈdʒɔgiŋ] trote *m* corto.

jog·gle [ˈdʒɔgl] **1.** traqueo *m*, sacudimiento *m*; ⊕ ensambladura *f* dentada; **2.** traquear, sacudir.

john [dʒɔn] F retrete *m*; inodoro *m*.
john·ny [ˈdʒɔni] F tipo *m*, chico *m*; currutaco *m*; ~ *cake* pan *m* de maíz.
join [dʒɔin] **1.** juntura *f*, costura *f*; **2.** *v/t.* unir, juntar; ⊕ ensamblar, acoplar; *lines* empalmar; reunirse con, unirse a; *society* ingresar en, hacerse socio de; ⚔ alistarse en; ~ *battle* trabar batalla; ~ *company* (*with*) reunirse (con); asociarse (con); F ~ *forces* juntar meriendas; ~ *hands* darse las manos; ~ *one's regiment* (*ship*) incorporarse a su regimiento (barco); ~ *a p. in* acompañar a una p. en; *v/i.* juntarse, unirse; (*lines*) empalmar; ~ *in* tomar parte (en), participar (en); ~ *up* alistarse; ~ (*up*) *with* asociarse con, acompañar.
join·er [ˈdʒɔinər] carpintero *m* (de blanco); ensamblador *m*; F persona *f* que se hace miembro de muchas asociaciones; ˈ**join·er·y** carpintería *f*.
joint [dʒɔint] **1.** junt(ur)a *f*; *anat.* articulación *f*, coyuntura *f*; ⚘ nudo *m*; ⚡ empalme *m*; ⊕ ensambladura *f*; (*hinge*) bisagra *f*; *sl.* garito *m*; *sl.* fonducho *m*; *out of* ~ descoyuntado; *fig.* fuera de quicio; *put out of* ~ descoyuntar; *put a p.'s nose out of* ~ suplantar a una p.; **2.** □ (en) común; mutuo; colectivo; conjunto; combinado; (*in compounds*) co...; ~ *account* cuenta *f* indistinta; ~ *communiqué* comunicado *m* conjunto; ~ *heir* coheredero (a *f*) *m*; ~ *responsibility* responsabilidad *f* solidaria; ~ *stock* fondo *m* social; **3.** juntar, unir; ⊕ ensamblar; articular; ˈ**joint·ed** articulado; ⚘ nudoso; ˈ**joint-stock** ˈ**com·pa·ny** sociedad *f* anónima; ˈ**joint·ure** ⚖ bienes *m/pl.* parafernales.
joist [dʒɔist] vig(uet)a *f*.
joke [dʒouk] **1.** broma *f*, chanza *f*; (*esp. verbal*) chiste *m*; (*laughing matter*) cosa *f* de reír; (*p.*) hazmerreír *m*; *play a* ~ (*on*) gastar una broma (a); *tell a* ~ contar un chiste; **2.** bromear, chancear(se); decir chistes; hablar en broma; F chunguear; ˈ**jok·er** bromista *m/f*; guasón (-a *f*) *m*; *cards*: comodín *m*; escapatoria *f*, cláusula *f* que permite evadir un contrato.
jol·li·fi·ca·tion [dʒɔlifiˈkeiʃn] regocijo *m*, alborozo *m*; festividades *f/pl.*; ˈ**jol·li·ty** alegría *f*, regocijo *m*; diversión *f*.
jol·ly [ˈdʒɔli] **1.** □ alegre, regocijado; jovial; divertido; F achispado; F agradable, estupendo; **2.** *adv.* F muy; **3.** F (*a.* ~ *along*) engatusar, seguir el humor a.
jol·ly boat [ˈdʒɔlibout] esquife *m*.
jolt [dʒoult] **1.** sacudida *f*; choque *m*; (*a.* ~*ing*) traque(te)o *m*; **2.** sacudir; traque(te)ar; ˈ**jolt·y** desigual; que traquetea.
jon·quil [ˈdʒɔŋkwil] junquillo *m*.
josh [dʒɔʃ] *sl.* **1.** broma *f*; **2.** burlarse de, tomar el pelo a; bromear.
jos·tle [ˈdʒɔsl] **1.** empujón *m*, empellón *m*, codazo *m*; **2.** empujar, dar empellones; codear.
jot [dʒɔt] **1.** jota *f*, pizca *f*; *I don't care a* ~ (*about*) no se me da un bledo (de); **2.**: ~ *down* apuntar; ˈ**jot·ter** taco *m* para notas; ˈ**jot·ting** apunte *m*.
jour·nal [ˈdʒəːrnl] (✝ libro *m*) diario *m* (⚓ de navegación); (*newspaper*) periódico *m*; (*review*) revista *f*; ⊕ gorrón *m*, mangueta *f*; ˈ~ ˈ**bear·ing**, ˈ~ ˈ**box** ⊕ cojinete *m*; 🚂 caja *f* de grasas; **jour·nal·ese** [ˈ~nəˈliːz] lenguaje *m* periodístico; ˈ**jour·nal·ism** periodismo *m*; ˈ**jour·nal·ist** periodista *m/f*; **jour·nalˈis·tic** □ periodístico.
jour·ney [ˈdʒəːrni] **1.** viaje *m*; **2.** viajar; ˈ~**man** oficial *m*.
joust [dʒaust] **1.** justa *f*, torneo *m*; **2.** justar.
jo·vi·al [ˈdʒouviəl] □ jovial; **jo·vi·al·i·ty** [~ˈæliti] jovialidad *f*.
jowl [dʒaul] quijada *f*; carrillo *m*; papada *f of cattle*; *cheek by* ~ lado a lado; ˈ~**y** mofletudo.
joy [dʒɔi] alegría *f*, júbilo *m*, regocijo *m*; deleite *m*; *a* ~ *to the eye* un gozo para la retina; **joy·ful** [ˈ~ful] □ alegre, regocijado; ˈ**joy·ful·ness** alegría *f*; ˈ**joy·less** □ sin alegría, triste; deprimente; ˈ**joy·ous** □ alegre; ˈ**joy·ride** F excursión *f* (desautorizada) en coche *etc.*; ˈ**joy·stick** ✈ *sl.* palanca *f* de gobierno.
ju·bi·lant [ˈdʒuːbilənt] □ jubiloso; triunfante; **ju·biˈla·tion** júbilo *m*; **ju·bi·lee** [ˈ~liː] *hist.*, *eccl.* jubileo *m*; quincuagésimo aniversario *m*; (*rejoicing*) júbilo *m*.
Ju·da·ism [ˈdʒuːdeiizm] judaísmo *m*; ˈ**Ju·da·ize** *v/i.* convertir al judaísmo; *v/t.* judaizar.
judge [dʒʌdʒ] **1.** juez *m*; *fig.* conocedor (-a *f*) *m*; *sport*: árbitro *m*; *be no* ~

of no entender de; **2.** juzgar; considerar; opinar; *judging by* a juzgar por; ~ *by appearances* juzgar sobre apariencias; ˈ~ ˈ**ad·vo·cate** ⚔ auditor *m* de guerra.

judge·ship [ˈdʒʌdʒʃip] judicatura *f*;

judg·ment [ˈ~mənt] juicio *m*; ⚖ sentencia *f*, fallo *m*; entendimiento *m*, discernimiento *m*; opinión *f*; *in my* ~ a mi parecer; *pronounce* ~ pronunciar sentencia (*on* en, sobre); *sit in* ~ *on* juzgar; *to the best of my* ~ según mi leal saber y entender; ♀ *Day* día *m* del juicio (final); ~ *seat* tribunal *m*.

ju·di·ca·ture [ˈdʒu:dikətʃər] judicatura *f*.

ju·di·cial [dʒuˈdiʃl] □ judicial; juicioso; ~ *murder* asesinato *m* legal.

ju·di·cious [dʒuˈdiʃəs] □ juicioso, sensato.

jug [dʒʌg] **1.** jarro *m*; pote *m*; *sl.* chirona *f*; **2.** *sl.* encarcelar.

Jug·ger·naut [ˈdʒʌgərnɔ:t] *fig.* monstruo *m* destructor de los hombres.

jug·gle [ˈdʒʌgl] **1.** juego *m* de manos; *b.s.* engaño *m*; **2.** *v/t.* escamotear; *b.s.* falsear; ejecutar (varias cosas) a la vez; *v/i.* hacer juegos malabares (*or* de manos); *b.s.* hacer trampas; ~ *with fig.* arreglar de otro modo; *b.s.* falsear; ˈ**jug·gler** malabarista *m/f*, jugador (-a *f*) *m* de manos; *b.s.* tramposo (a *f*) *m*; † juglar *m*; ˈ**jug·gler·y** juegos *m/pl.* malabares (*or* de manos); *b.s.* trampas *f/pl.*; fraude *m*.

Ju·go·slav [ˈju:gouˈslɑ:v] yugo(e)slavo *adj. a. su. m* (a *f*).

jug·u·lar [ˈdʒʌgjulər] yugular; ~ *vein* vena *f* yugular.

juice [dʒu:s] (*esp. fruit*) zumo *m*; jugo *m*; *mot. sl.* gasolina *f*; ⚡ *sl.* corriente *f*; **juic·i·ness** [ˈ~inis] jugosidad *f*; ˈ**juic·y** □ zumoso, jugoso; F picante, sabroso.

ju·jube [ˈdʒu:dʒu:b] ⚘ azufaifa *f*; pastilla *f*.

ju·jut·su [dʒu:ˈdʒutsu:] jiu-jitsu *m*.

juke·box [ˈdʒu:kbɔks] tocadiscos *m* (tragamonedas).

ju·lep [ˈdʒu:lep] julepe *m*.

Ju·ly [dʒuˈlai] julio *m*.

jum·ble [ˈdʒʌmbl] **1.** revoltijo *m*; confusión *f*; mezcolanza *f*; **2.** mezclar, emburujar; confundir.

jum·bly [ˈdʒʌmbli] revuelto, emburujado.

jum·bo [ˈdʒʌmbou] F elefante *m*; *attr.* enorme.

jump [dʒʌmp] **1.** salto *m*, brinco *m*; F *get* (*have*) *the* ~ *on* llevar la ventaja a; *give a* ~ dar un salto; **2.** *v/t.* saltar; *horse* hacer saltar; F ~ *the gun* madrugar; ~ *the rails* descarrilar; ~ *ship* desertar del buque; *v/i.* saltar; brincar; dar saltos; bailar; ✈ lanzarse; *fig.* ~ *at* lanzarse sobre, apresurarse a aprovechar; ~ *down* bajar de un salto; ~ *on* (*board*) saltar a; F regañar, poner verde; ~ *over* saltar (por); ~ *to conclusions* juzgar al (buen) tuntún; ˈ**jump·er** saltador (-a *f*) *m*; (*dress*) suéter *m*, jersey *m*; blusa *f*; ⚒ barrena *f* de percusión; ⚡ hilo *m* de cierre; ˈ**jump seat** *mot.* asiento *m* desmontable; traspuntín *m*; ˈ**jump suit** vestido *m* unitario (como de paracaidista); ˈ**jump·y** saltón; *fig.* asustadizo, nervioso.

junc·tion [ˈdʒʌŋkʃn] juntura *f*, unión *f*; conexión *f*; confluencia *f of rivers*; 🚂 (estación *f* de) empalme *m*; ⚡ ~ *box* caja *f* de empalmes; **junc·ture** [ˈ~tʃər] coyuntura *f*; (*critical*) trance *m*; ⚒ juntura *f*.

June [dʒu:n] junio *m*.

jun·gle [ˈdʒʌŋgl] jungla *f*; selva *f*; *fig.* maraña *f*.

jun·ior [ˈdʒu:njər] **1.** menor, más joven; más nuevo; subalterno; juvenil; *Paul Jones*, ~ Paul Jones, hijo; ~ *high school* escuela *f* de bachillerato elemental; ~ *partner* socio *m* menos antiguo; **2.** menor *m/f*; joven *m/f*; hijo *m*; alumno (a *f*) *m* de 8 a 11 años; *univ.* estudiante *m/f* de penúltimo año; *he is my* ~ *by 3 years, he is 3 years my* ~ es 3 años más joven que yo, le llevo 3 años.

ju·ni·per [ˈdʒu:nipər] enebro *m*.

junk[1] [dʒʌŋk] ⚓ junco *m*.

junk[2] [~] F trastos *m/pl.* viejos; (*iron*) chatarra *f*; (*cheap goods*) baratijas *f/pl.*; *fig.* disparates *m/pl.*; ⚓ (*salt meat*) carnaje *m*; *sl.* heroína *f* (*pharm.*); ~ *shop* tienda *f* de trastos viejos; ~ *yard* parque *m* de chatarra.

jun·ket [ˈdʒʌŋkit] **1.** dulce *m* de leche cuajada; (*a.* ~*ing*) francachela *f*, festividades *f/pl.*; jira *f*; **2.** festejar; banquetear; ir de jira.

junk·ie (*a.* **junk·y**) [ˈdʒʌŋki] *sl.* toxicómano *m*; narcotómano *m*.

jun·ta [ˈdʒʌntə] junta *f* militar; camarilla *f*; **jun·to** [ˈ~tou] camarilla *f*.

ju·rid·i·cal [dʒuˈridikl] □ jurídico.

ju·ris·dic·tion [dʒurisˈdikʃn] jurisdicción *f*; **ju·ris·pru·dence** [ˈ~pru:-dəns] jurisprudencia *f*.

ju·rist [ˈdʒurist] jurista *m*.

ju·ror [ˈdʒurər] (miembro *m* de un) jurado *m*.

ju·ry [ˈdʒuri] jurado *m*; ˈ**ju·ry box** tribuna *f* del jurado; ˈ**ju·ry·man** (miembro *m* de un) jurado *m*.

ju·ry-rig [ˈdʒuririg] ⚓ aparejar temporariamente.

just [dʒʌst] **1.** *adj.* □ justo; recto; exacto; **2.** *adv.* justamente, exactamente, ni más ni menos; precisamente; sólo, no más; apenas; recientemente, recién; en el (*or* este) mismo instante; F absolutamente, completamente; *I have (had) ~ finished it* acabo (acababa) de acabarlo; *~ appointed* recién nombrado; *~ received* acabado de recibir; *he was ~ going* estaba a punto de marchar; *~ imagine!* ¡imagínese!; *~ let me see!* ¡pues a ver!; *it's ~ perfect!* ¡es absolutamente perfecto!; *~ as* en el momento en que; (tal) como; *~ as you wish* como Vd. quiera; *~ by* muy cerca (de); *v. now*.

jus·tice [ˈdʒʌstis] justicia *f*; juez *m*; *~ of the peace approx.* juez *m* de paz; *chief ~* presidente *m* de la corte (suprema); *court of ~* tribunal *m* de justicia; *do ~ to p.* hacer justicia a, tratar debidamente; *meal* hacer los debidos honores a; *do oneself ~* quedar bien.

jus·ti·fi·a·ble [ˈdʒʌstifaiəbl] justificable; ˈ**jus·ti·fi·a·bly** con razón, con justicia.

jus·ti·fi·ca·tion [dʒʌstifiˈkeiʃn] justificación *f*; ˈ**jus·ti·fi·er** *typ.* justificador *m*.

jus·ti·fy [ˈdʒʌstifai] justificar (*a. typ.*); dar motivo para; *~ o.s.* sincerarse; acreditarse; *be justified in* tener motivo para.

just·ly [ˈdʒʌstli] justamente, con justicia; con derecho; debidamente; exactamente.

just·ness [ˈdʒʌstnis] justicia *f*; rectitud *f*; exactitud *f*.

jut [dʒʌt] **1.** saliente *m*, saledizo *m*; **2.** (*a. ~ out*) sobresalir, resaltar.

Jute[1] [dʒu:t] juto (a *f*) *m*.

jute[2] [~] yute *m*.

ju·ve·nile [ˈdʒu:vənail] **1.** joven *m/f*; niño (a *f*) *m*; **2.** juvenil; de (*or* para) niños (*or* menores); ≗ *Court* tribunal *m* juvenil; *~ delinquency* delincuencia *f* de menores; *~ delinquent* delincuente *m/f* juvenil; *~ lead thea.* galán *m* joven, galancete *m*.

jux·ta·pose [dʒʌkstəˈpouz] yuxtaponer; **jux·ta·po·si·tion** [~pəˈziʃn] yuxtaposición *f*.

K

Kaf·(f)ir ['kæfər] cafre *adj. a. su. m/f.*
kale [keil] col *f* (rizada); *sl.* guita *f.*
ka·lei·do·scope [kə'laidəskoup] ca-l(e)idoscopio *m*; *fig.* escena *f* animada y variadísima.
kan·ga·roo [kæŋgə'ru:] canguro *m.*
ka·o·lin ['keiəlin] caolín *m.*
ka·pok ['keipɔk] capoc *m*; lana *f* de ceiba.
ka·put [kə'put] *sl.* inútil; gastado; roto.
ka·ra·te [kə'rɔti] karate *m*; karaté *m.*
kay·ak ['kaiak] ⚓ kayak *m.*
kedge [kedʒ] anclote *m.*
keel [ki:l] **1.** ⚓, ✈., ⚘ quilla *f*, *on an even* ~ ⚓ en iguales calados; en equilibrio (*a. fig.*); *fig.* derecho, estable; **2.**: ~ *over* ⚓ dar de quilla; volcar(se); F caerse patas arriba; **'keeled** *zo.*, ⚘ carinado; **keel·haul** ['~hɔ:l] castigar pasando por debajo de la quilla.
keen [ki:n] □ agudo; *edge* afilado; *wind* penetrante; sutil; perspicaz; mordaz; *price* bajo; *emotion* vivo, ardiente, sentido; *appetite* bueno; *p.* entusiasta, celoso; ansioso; F *be* ~ *on th.* ser muy aficionado a; *p.* estar prendado de; *I'm not very* ~ *on him* no es santo de mi devoción; *be* ~ *to inf.* ansiar *inf.*, tener vivo deseo de *inf.*; **~-edged** ['~edʒd] cortante, afilado; **'keen·ness** agudeza *f*; perspicacia *f*; viveza *f*; entusiasmo *m*; afición *f*; ansia *f.*
keep [ki:p] **1.** mantenimiento *m*; subsistencia *f*; comida *f*; *hist.* torreón *m*, torre *f* del homenaje; F *for ~s* para siempre, para guardar; *earn one's* ~ estar (*or* trabajar) por la comida; producir (*or* trabajar) bastante; **2.** [*irr.*] *v/t.* guardar; tener guardado; (re)tener; reservar; (*not give back*) quedarse con; preservar; conservar; mantener; defender; cuidar, custodiar; (*delay a p.*) detener, entretener; *promise* cumplir; *house, accounts* llevar; *position* mantenerse (firme) en; *hotel, shop* dirigir; *law* observar; ~ *a p. waiting* hacer esperar a una p.; ~ *away* mantener a distancia; no dejar acercarse; ~ *back* retener; ocultar; no dejar avanzar; reprimir; ~ *down* no dejar subir; sujetar; oprimir; dominar; limitar; *price* mantener bajo; ~ *a p. from ger.* no dejar *inf.* a una p.; ~ *s.t. from a p.* ocultar algo a una p.; ~ *in p.* no dejar salir, tener encerrado; *feelings* contener; *fire* mantener encendido; ~ *off* tener a raya; cerrar el paso a; no dejar penetrar; ~ *on* no quitarse; tener puesto (*or* encendido *etc.*); ~ *out* excluir; no dejar entrar (*or* penetrar); ~ *s.t. to o.s.* guardar algo en secreto; ~ *together* mantener unido; ~ *under* sujetar; tener oprimido; ~ *up* mantener, conservar; sostener; *p.* hacer trasnochar; ~ *it up* no cejar; **3.** [*irr.*] *v/i.* quedar(se); permanecer; seguir, continuar; mantenerse; conservarse; estar(se); ~ *doing* seguir haciendo, continuar haciendo; ~ *still!* ¡estáte quieto!; ~ *well* conservarse bien; ~ *at* no cejar en; insistir en; F ~ *at it* machacar; ~ *away* mantenerse alejado (*from place* de); no dejarse ver; abstenerse (*from th.* de); no meterse (*from p.* con); ~ *back* hacerse a un lado; ~ *clear of* mantenerse libre de; no meterse con; ~ *from* guardarse de, abstenerse de; F ~ *in with* cultivar, mantener buenas relaciones con; ~ *off* mantenerse a distancia; *grass* no pisar; no tocar; *if the rain ~s off* si no llueve; ~ *on* continuar (*with* con); seguir (*doing* haciendo); ~ *out!* ¡prohibida la entrada!; ~ *out of place* no entrar en; *affair* no meterse en; *trouble* evitar; ~ *to direction* llevar; limitarse a; cumplir con; ~ *to one's bed* guardar (la) cama; ~ *together* mantenerse unidos; ~ *up* continuar; no rezagarse; ~ *up with* ir al paso de; emular; proseguir; ~ *with* seguir acompañando.
keep·er ['ki:pər] guarda *m*; custodio *m*; (*park etc.*) guardián (-a *f*) *m*; (*owner*) dueño (a *f*) *m*; (*a. game* ~) guardabosques *m*; archivero *m*; ⊕

cerradero *m*; culata *f*; ˈ**keep·ing** custodia *f*; guarda *f*; protección *f*; mantenimiento *m*; conservación *f*; observación *f*; celebración *f*; *in* ~ *with* de acuerdo con, en armonía con; *out of* ~ *with* en desacuerdo con; **keep-sake** [ˈ~seik] recuerdo *m*.

keg [keg] cuñete *m*, barrilete *m*.

ken [ken] **1.** alcance *m* de la vista; comprensión *f*, conocimiento *m*; **2.** † *or prov.* saber, (re)conocer.

ken·nel [ˈkenl] **1.** perrera *f*; jauría *f of hounds*; *fig.* cuchitril *m*; **2.** tener (*or* encerrar *or* estar) en perrera.

kept [kept] *pret. a. p.p. of keep* 2.

ker·chief [ˈkəːrtʃif] pañuelo *m*, pañoleta *f*.

ker·nel [ˈkəːrnl] almendra *f*, núcleo *m*; grano *m*; *fig.* meollo *m*.

ker·o·sene [ˈkerəsiːn] keroseno *m*.

kes·trel [ˈkestrəl] cernícalo *m* vulgar.

ketch [ketʃ] queche *m*.

ketch·up [ˈketʃəp] salsa *f* de tomate *etc.*; *v. catsup*.

ket·tle [ˈketl] *approx.* olla *f* en forma de cafetera, tetera *f*; pava *f S.Am.*; *here's a (pretty)* ~ *of fish!* ¡vaya un lío!; ˈ**~·drum** timbal *m*.

key [kiː] **1.** llave *f* (*a.* ⊕); tecla *f of piano, typewriter*; *tel.* manipulador *m*; ⊕ chaveta *f*; cuña *f*; *fig.*, △ clave *f*; ♪ tonalidad *f*, tono *m*; *in* ~ a tono, templado; *off* ~ desafinado, desafinadamente; ~ *industry* industria *f* clave; ~ *man* hombre *m* indispensable; **2.** ⊕ enchavetar, acuñar; ♪ afinar; ˈ**~·board** teclado *m*; ˈ**~·hole** ojo *m* (de la cerradura); ˈ~ *saw* sierra *f* de punta; ˈ~ **mon·ey** pago *m* ilícito al casero; ˈ**~·note** (nota *f*) tónica *f*; *fig.* idea *f* fundamental; ˈ**~·ring** llavero *m*; ˈ**~·stone** △ clave *f*; *fig.* piedra *f* angular.

khak·i [ˈkɑːki] (de) caqui *m*.

kib·itz·er [ˈkibitsər] F entrometido (a *f*) *m*; mirón (-a *f*) *m*.

ki·bosh [ˈkaibɔʃ] *sl.*: *put the* ~ *on* acabar con, desbaratar; imposibilitar.

kick [kik] **1.** puntapié *m*; patada *f*; coz *f of animal*; culatazo *m of firearm*; *fig.* (fuerza *f* de) reacción *f*; *sl.* fuerza *f of drink*; F queja *f*, protesta *f*; F *I get a* ~ *out of* me emociona, encuentro placer en; F *it's got a* ~ *to it* esto está que rabia; patea *S.Am.*; **2.** *v/t.* dar un puntapié a; dar de coces a; *goal* marcar; ~ *downstairs* echar escalera abajo; ~ *one's heels* esperar con impaciencia; ~ *out* echar (a puntapiés); F ~ *the bucket* morir; ~ *up the dust* levantar una polvareda; ~ *up a row* meter bulla; armar camorra; *v/i.* dar coces; cocear (*a. fig.*); patalear; *fig.* respingar, quejarse; (*gun*) dar culatazo(s); *football*: chutar; ~ *against the pricks* dar coces contra el aguijón; **~·back 1.** ⊕ contragolpe *m*; **2.** ✝ comisión *f* ilícita; propina *f* ilícita; ˈ**kick·er** caballo *m* coceador; F reparón (-a *f*) *m*, persona *f* quejumbrosa; ˈ**kick-ing** coces *f/pl.*, pataleo *m*; ˈ**kickˈoff** *football*: saque *m* inicial.

kid [kid] **1.** (*meat* carne *f* de) cabrito *m*, chivo *m*; (*leather*) cabritilla *f*; F crío *m*, niño (a *f*) *m*, chico (a *f*) *m*, chaval (-a *f*) *m*; *sl.* broma *f*; F *the* ~*s* la chiquillería *f*; ~ *gloves* guantes *m/pl.* de cabritilla; F trato *m* muy blando; **2.** *sl.* embromar, tomar el pelo a; *I was only* ~*ding* lo decía en broma; ˈ**kid·dy** F niño (a *f*) *m*.

kid·nap [ˈkidnæp] secuestrar; ˈ**kid-nap·(p)er** secuestrador (-a *f*) *m*, ladrón *m* de niños.

kid·ney [ˈkidni] riñón *m*; *fig.* especie *f*, índole *f*; ~ *bean* judía *f*, habichuela *f*.

kill [kil] **1.** matar (*a. fig.*); destruir, eliminar; *feeling* apagar; *parl. bill* ahogar; F hacer morir de risa; F hacer una impresión irresistible; ~ *off* exterminar; ~ *time* matar (*or* engañar) el tiempo; **2.** matanza *f*; golpe *m* (*or* ataque *m*) final; ˈ**kill·er** matador (-a *f*) *m*; asesino *m*; ˈ**kill·ing 1.** matanza *f*; F éxito *m* financiero; **2.** □ matador; destructivo; abrumador; F cómico; F irresistible; ˈ**kill·joy** aguafiestas *m/f*.

kiln [kiln, ⊕ kil] horno *m*; ˈ**~-dry** secar al horno.

kil·o·cy·cle [ˈkilousaikl] kilociclo *m*; **kil·o·gram** [ˈ~græm] kilo(gramo) *m*; **kil·o·me·ter** [ˈkiləmiːtər] kilómetro *m*; **kil·o·watt** [ˈkiləwɔt] kilovatio *m*; ˈ**kil·o·watt-ˈhours** kilovatios-hora *m/pl.*

kilt [kilt] **1.** tonelete *m* (*de los montañeses de Escocia*); **2.** plegar; arremangar.

kin [kin] familia *f*, parientes *m/pl.*, parentela *f*; *fig.* especie *f*; *next of* ~ pariente(s) *m(pl.)* más próximo(s); *kith and* ~ parientes *m/pl.*; deudos *m/pl.* y amigos *m/pl.*

kind [kaind] **1.** clase *f*, género *m*, especie *f*, suerte *f*; *a ~ of* uno a modo de; F *~ of* casi, más o menos, vagamente; *pay in ~* pagar en especie (*fig.* en la misma moneda); *of a ~* de una misma clase; *b.s.* inferior; *of all ~s* toda clase de..., ...de todas clases; *nothing of the ~!* ¡nada de eso!; **2.** □ bondadoso, bueno; benigno; amable; *v. regard*; *be ~ to* ser amable con, ser bueno para (con); *be so ~ as to* tener la bondad de.
kind·er·gar·ten ['kindərgɑːrtn] jardín *m* de (la) infancia; escuela *f* de párvulos.
kind-heart·ed ['kaind'hɑːrtid] de buen corazón, bondadoso.
kin·dle ['kindl] encender(se) (*a. fig.*); *fig.* incitar.
kind·li·ness ['kaindlinis] bondad *f*, benignidad *f*, benevolencia *f*.
kin·dling ['kindliŋ] (*act*) encendimiento *m*; (*wood*) encendajas *f/pl.*; leña *f* menuda.
kind·ly ['kaindli] **1.** *adj.* bondadoso, benévolo; *climate* benigno; **2.** *adv.* bondadosamente; benignamente; *~ wait a moment* haga el favor de esperar un momento; *take ~ to* aceptar de buen grado; sufrir; *he'd take it ~ if you...* le estaría agradecido si...
kind·ness ['kaindnis] bondad *f*; benevolencia *f*; amabilidad *f*; favor *m*.
kin·dred ['kindrid] **1.** (*kinship*) parentesco *m*; afinidad *f*; (*ps.*) parentela *f*, familia *f*, parientes *m/pl.*; **2.** allegado; afín.
kin·e·mat·o·graph [kaini'mætəgræf] cinematógrafo *m*.
kin·e·scope ['kinəskoup] cinescopio *m*.
ki·net·ic [kai'netik] cinético; **ki'net·ics** cinética *f*.
kin·folk ['kinfouk] F pariente(s) *m(pl.)*.
king [kiŋ] rey *m* (*a. fig.*, *chess*, *cards*); *checkers*: dama *f*; ♀'s *English* inglés *m* correcto; '**king·dom** reino *m*; '**king·fish·er** martín *m* pescador; '**king·ly** real, regio; digno de un rey; '**king·pin** perno *m* real, perno *m* pinzote; pivote *m*; *fig.* persona *f* principal, *b.s.* jefe *m* de criminales; '**king·post** pendolón *m*; '**king·ship** dignidad *f* real; monarquía *f*; '**king-size** F de tamaño extra.
kink [kiŋk] **1.** coca *f*, enroscadura *f*; *fig.* chifladura *f*, peculiaridad *f*; **2.** formar cocas; '**kink·y** enroscado, ensortijado; *sl.* perverso; raro.
kin...: '**~·ship** parentesco *m*, afinidad *f*; '**~s·man** pariente *m*; '**~·wom·an** parienta *f*.
ki·osk ['kiːɔsk] quiosco *m*; *teleph.* cabina *f*.
kip·per ['kipər] **1.** arenque *m* ahumado; *sl.* tío *m*; *sl.* mujerzuela *f*; **2.** curar al humo.
kirk [kəːrk] *Scot.* iglesia *f*.
kiss [kis] **1.** beso *m*; ósculo *m* (*lit.*); *fig.* roce *m*; **2.** besar(se).
kit [kit] avíos *m/pl.*; ⚔ equipo *m*; (*travel*) equipaje *m*; (*tools*) herramental *m*; (*first aid*) botequín *m*; cubo *m*; '**~·bag** ⚔ saco *m*; saco *m* de viaje.
kitch·en ['kitʃin] cocina *f*; *~ sink* fregadero *m*; *~ utensils* batería *f* de cocina; **kitch·en·ette** [~'net] cocina *f* pequeña.
kitch·en...: '**~ 'gar·den** huerto *m*; '**~ maid** fregona *f*; '**~ range** cocina *f* económica; '**~ sink** fregadero *m*; *everything but the ~* sin faltar apenas nada; completísimo.
kite [kait] *orn.* milano *m* real; cometa *f*; ⚕ giro *m* ficticio; *sl. fly a ~* sondar la opinión; intentar un timo; *~ balloon* globo *m* cometa.
kith [kiθ]: *~ and kin* parientes *m/pl.* (y amigos *m/pl.*).
kit·ten ['kitn] gatito (a *f*) *m*; '**kit·ten·ish** juguetón; coquetón.
kit·ty ['kiti] F gatito (a *f*) *m*; *cards etc.*: puesta *f*, bote *m*.
klax·on ['klæksn] claxon *m*.
klep·to·ma·ni·a [kleptou'meiniə] cleptomanía *f*; **klep·to'ma·ni·ac** [~niæk] cleptómano (a *f*) *m*.
knack [næk] tino *m*; maña *f*, destreza *f*; hábito *m*; truco *m*.
knack·er ['nækər] matarife *m* de caballos; contratista *m* de derribos.
knag [næg] nudo *m*.
knap·sack ['næpsæk] mochila *f*, barjuleta *f*.
knave [neiv] bellaco *m*, bribón *m*; *cards*: sota *f*; **knav·er·y** ['~əri] bellaquería *f*, bribonería *f*.
knav·ish ['neiviʃ] □ bellaco, bribón, ruin.
knead [niːd] amasar, sobar; '**knead·ing** amasijo *m*, soba *f*.

knee [niː] **1.** rodilla *f*; ⊕ ángulo *m*, cod(ill)o *m*; *on bended* ~, *on one's* ~*s* de rodillas; *fall on one's* ~*s* caer de rodillas; *go down on one's* ~*s to* implorar de rodillas; *bring a p. to his* ~*s* vencer a una p., humillar a una p.; **2.** dar un rodillazo a; *trousers* formar rodilleras en; ˈ~ **breech·es** calzón *m* corto; ˈ~**·cap** rótula *f*, choquezuela *f*; ˈ~-ˈ**deep** metido hasta las rodillas; ˈ~-**jerk** *sl. action* repentino y violento; reflexivo; ˈ~ **joint** articulación *f* de la rodilla; **kneel** [niːl] [*irr.*] (*a.* ~ *down*) arrodillarse, hincar la rodilla (*to* ante); estar de rodillas.

knell [nel] doble *m*, toque *m* de difuntos; *fig.* mal agüero *m*.

knelt [nelt] *pret. a. p.p. of kneel.*

knew [njuː] *pret. of know.*

knick·er·bock·ers [ˈnikərbɔkərz] *pl.* pantalones *m/pl.* cortos; ˈ**knick·ers** *pl.* F bragas *f/pl.*, pantalones *m/pl.* de señora; = *knickerbockers.*

knick·knack [ˈniknæk] chuchería *f*, baratija *f*; chisme *m*.

knife [naif] **1.** [*pl. knives*] cuchillo *m*; navaja *f*; ⊕ cuchilla *f*; *to the* ~ a muerte; *have one's* ~ *into* tener inquina a; **2.** acuchillar; apuñalar; ˈ~ **edge** filo *m* (de cuchillo); ˈ~ **grind·er** amolador *m*; ˈ~ **switch** interruptor *m* de cuchilla.

knight [nait] **1.** caballero *m*; *chess*: caballo *m*; **2.** armar caballero; **knight-er·rant** [ˈnaitˈerənt] caballero *m* andante; ˈ**knight-**ˈ**er·rant·ry** caballería *f* andante; **knight·hood** [ˈ~hud] caballería *f*; título *m* de caballero; ˈ**knight·li·ness** caballerosidad *f*; ˈ**knight·ly** caballeroso, caballeresco.

knit [nit] [*irr.*] **1.** *v/t.* hacer (a punto de aguja); *brows* fruncir; (*a.* ~ *together*) enlazar, unir; *v/i.* hacer calceta (*or* media *or* punto); (*bone*) soldarse; (*a.* ~ *together*) enlazarse, unirse; **2.** prenda *f* de punto; *a.* = *knitwear*; ˈ**knit·ting** labor *f* de punto; ˈ**knit·ting ma·chine** máquina *f* de hacer punto *etc.*; ˈ**knit·ting** ˈ**nee·dle** aguja *f* de hacer calceta; ˈ**knit·wear** géneros *m/pl.* de punto.

knives [naivz] *pl. of knife.*

knob [nɔb] protuberancia *f*, bulto *m*; botón *m*, perilla *f*; tirador *m of door, drawer*; puño *m of stick*; (*fragment*) terrón *m*; ˈ**knobbed,** ˈ**knob·bly,** ˈ**knob·by** nudoso.

knock [nɔk] **1.** golpe *m*; porrazo *m*; aldabonazo *m*, llamada *f on door*; ⊕ golp(et)eo *m*; pistoneo *m*; **2.** *v/t.* golpear; chocar contra; criticar, calumniar; hacer competencia (injusta) a; ~ *about* pegar; maltratar; ~ *down* derribar; echar por tierra; *price* rebajar; *auction*: adjudicar, rematar (*to* a, *for* en); ⊕ desmontar; *mot.* atropellar; ~ *in* hacer entrar a golpes; *nail* clavar; ~ *off* quitar (de un golpe); hacer caer; F *work* terminar, suspender; ⚕ rebajar; F ejecutar prontamente; *sl.* apropiarse, robar; matar; ~ *out mst boxing*: poner fuera de combate, noquear; eliminar; suprimir; ~ *over* volcar; ~ *together* construir (*or* armar) de prisa; ~ *up* despertar; F agotar, reventar; *building* construir a la ligera; *v/i.* **llamar a la puerta; ⊕ golpear, martillear;** F ~ *about* vagabundear, ver mucho mundo; *he's* ~*ing about* estará por ahí; ~ *against* chocar contra; ~ *into* topar con; F ~ *off* acabar (el trabajo), terminar; ~ *up tennis*: pelotear; ~ *up against* chocar contra; tropezar con; ~**·a·bout** [ˈ~əbaut] **1.** farsa *f* bulliciosa; **2.** bullicioso, turbulento; *clothes* para todos los días; ˈ~ˈ**down** que derriba; abrumador; ~ *price* precio *m* obsequio; ˈ**knock·er** aldaba *f*; *sl.* criticón (-a *f*) *m*; ˈ**knock-kneed** patizambo; *fig.* débil, irresoluto; ˈ**knock**ˈ**out** *boxing*: (*a.* ~ *blow*) knockout *m*, noqueada *f*; *sport*: eliminación *f* progresiva; *sl.* moza *f* (*or* cosa *f*) estupenda.

knoll [noul] otero *m*, montículo *m*.

knot [nɔt] **1.** nudo *m* (*a. fig.*, ⚓, ⚘); (*bow*) lazo *m*; corrillo *m of people*; *tied up in* ~*s* confuso, enmarañado; perplejo; ~*hole* agujero *m in wood*; **2.** *v/t.* anudar, atar; *v/i.* hacer nudos; enmarañarse; ˈ**knot·ty** nudoso; *fig.* difícil, complicado, espinoso.

know [nou] **1.** [*irr.*] saber; (*be acquainted with*) conocer; (*recognize*) **reconocer;** ~ *best* **saber lo que más conviene;** ~ *French* **saber francés;** ~ *how to inf.* saber *inf.*; ~ *of* saber de; tener conocimiento de; *come* (*or get*) *to* ~ *p.* llegar a conocer; *th.* enterarse de; **2.**: F *be in the* ~ estar enterado (*about* de); **know·a·ble** [ˈnouəbl] conocible; ˈ**know-how** F habilidad *f*, destreza *f*; experiencia *f*; ˈ**know·ing** □ inteligente; sabio; entendido;

b.s. astuto; malicioso; ~ *full well that* a sabiendas de que; ~*ly* a sabiendas; **'know-it-all** sabelotodo *m/f*.

knowl·edge ['nɔlidʒ] conocimiento(s) *m(pl.)*; saber *m*; *to my* ~ según mi leal saber y entender; que yo sepa; por lo que yo sé; *without my* ~ sin saberlo yo; **'knowl·edge·able** □ enterado, conocedor; **known** [noun] *p.p. of know*; *make* ~ publicar, comunicar.

knuck·le ['nʌkl] **1.** nudillo *m*; jarrete *m of meat*; *brass* ~*s weapon* bóxer *m*; llave inglesa *f*; **2.:** ~ *down to inf.* ponerse a *inf.* con ahinco; ~ *under* someterse; **'~ dust·er** puño *m* de hierro.

kook [kuːk] F tipo *m* raro; excéntrico *m*.

Ko·ran [kɔ'rɑːn] Alcorán *m*, Corán *m*.

ko·sher ['kouʃər] de ortodoxia judía; *sl.* genuino; auténtico.

kow·tow ['kau'tau] saludar humildemente; humillarse (*to* ante).

ku·dos ['kuːdɔs] renombre *m*, prestigio *m*.

L

lab [læb] F = *laboratory*.
la·bel ['leibl] **1.** rótulo *m*, marbete *m*, etiqueta *f*; tejuelo *m of book*; *fig.* calificación *f*, apodo *m*; **2.** rotular, poner etiqueta a; *fig.* calificar (*as* de); apodar.
la·bi·al ['leibiəl] labial *adj. a. su. f.*
la·bor ['leibər] **1.** trabajo *m*; labor *f*; faena *f*; esfuerzo *m*; pena *f*; (*a.* ~ *force*) mano *f* de obra; clase *f* obrera; (dolores *m/pl.* del) parto *m*; *hard* ~ trabajos *m/pl.* forzados; *be in* ~ estar de parto; **2.** *attr.* de trabajo; laboral; obrero; *pol.* ♀ laborista; ~ *camp* campamento *m* de trabajo; ~ *dispute* conflicto *m* laboral; ♀ (*Party*) Partido *m* Laborista; ~ *turnover* rotación *f* de la mano de obra; ~ *union* sindicato *m* (de trabajadores de la misma rama) industrial; **3.** *v/t.* desarrollar con nimiedad; insistir en; *v/i.* trabajar (*at* en); afanarse (*to* por); moverse penosamente; ~ *under* sufrir; ~ *under a delusion* estar equivocado.
lab·o·ra·to·ry ['læbrətɔri] **laboratorio** *m*; ~ *assistant* **ayudante** (**a** *f*) *m* (*or* **mozo** *m*) **de laboratorio.**
la·bor...: '**~ed** penoso, dificultoso; fatigoso; *style* premioso; '**~·er** trabajador *m*; obrero *m*; (*day*) jornalero *m*; (*unskilled*) peón *m*; bracero *m*; (*farm*) labriego *m*; **~i·ous** [lə'bɔːriəs] □ laborioso; '**~-sav·ing** que ahorra trabajo.
la·bur·num [lə'bəːrnəm] laburno *m*, codeso *m*.
lab·y·rinth ['læbərinθ] laberinto *m*; **lab·y·rin·thine** [~'rinθain] laberíntico.
lace [leis] **1.** cordón *m of shoes etc.*; encaje *m*; (*trimming*) puntilla *f*; **2.** atar; enlazar(se); *sew.* guarnecer con encajes; F (*a.* ~ *into*) dar una paliza a; *drink* echar licor a.
lac·er·ate ['læsəreit] lacerar; *feelings* herir; **lac·er'a·tion** laceración *f*.
lach·ry·mal ['lækriml] lagrimal; **lach·ry·ma·to·ry** ['~mətəri] lacrimatorio, lagrimal; ~ *gas* gas *m* lacrimógeno; **lach·ry·mose** ['~mous] lacrimoso.
lack [læk] **1.** carencia *f*; falta *f*; necesidad *f*; ausencia *f*; *for* (*or through*) ~ *of* por falta de; **2.** *v/t.* carecer de; necesitar; *he* ~*s money* le (hace) falta dinero; *v/i.*: *be* ~*ing* faltar; *he is* ~*ing in* le falta.
lack·a·dai·si·cal [lækə'deizikl] □ lánguido; indiferente; distraído.
lack·ey ['læki] lacayo *m*; *fig.* secuaz *m* servil.
lack·lus·ter ['læklʌstər] deslustrado, inexpresivo, apagado.
la·con·ic [lə'kɔnik] □ lacónico.
lac·quer ['lækər] **1.** (*a.* ~ *work*) laca *f*, maque *m*; **2.** laquear, maquear.
lac·ta·tion [læk'teiʃn] lactancia *f*.
lac·te·al ['læktiəl] lácteo; *anat.* quilífero.
lac·tic ['læktik] láctico.
lac·tose ['læktouz] lactosa *f*.
la·cu·na [lə'kjuːnə] laguna *f*; *fig.* omisión *f*.
lad [læd] muchacho *m*, chico *m*; zagal *m*, rapaz *m*.
lad·der ['lædər] escala *f* (*a.* ⚓); escalera *f* de mano; *fig.* escalón *m*; carrera *f in stocking*; *hook and* ~ carro *m* de escaleras de incendio.
lade [leid] [*irr.*] cargar; *v. ladle* 2; '**lad·en** cargado; **lad·ing** ['leidiŋ] cargamento *m*, flete *m*; *bill of* ~ conocimiento *m* de embarque.
la·dle ['leidl] **1.** cucharón *m*, cazo *m*; **2.** sacar (*or* servir) con cucharón (*a.* ~ *out*).
la·dy ['leidi] señora *f*; (*noble*) dama *f*; *young* ~ señorita *f*; *ladies and gentlemen!* ¡(señoras y) señores!; F ~ *doctor* médica *f*; ~ *of the house* señora *f* de la casa; ~*'s maid* doncella *f*; ~*'s* (*or ladies'*) *man* Perico *m* entre ellas; '**~·bird** mariquita *f*, vaca *f* de San Antón; '**~-in-'wait·ing** dama *f* (de honor); '**~·kill·er** F tenorio *m*; '**~·like** delicado; bien educado; elegante, distinguido; *contp.* afeminado; '**~·love** amada *f*, querida *f*; '**~·ship:** *her* ~, *Your* ♀ Su Señoría.
lag[1] [læg] **1.** retraso *m*, retardo *m*; **2.** (*a.* ~ *behind*) rezagarse; retrasarse.

lag[2] [~] ⊕ revestir, forrar; *boiler* calorifugar.
la·ger (beer) ['lɑːgər (bir)] cerveza *f* tipo Pilsen.
lag·gard ['lægərd] rezagado (a *f*) *m*; holgazán (-a *f*) *m*; persona *f* irresoluta.
la·goon [lə'guːn] laguna *f*.
la·i·cize ['leiəsaiz] laicizar.
laid [leid] *pret. a. p.p. of lay*[4] 2; *be ~ up* tener que guardar cama (*with* a causa de); *~ paper* papel *m* vergé (*or* vergueteado).
lain [lein] *p.p. of lie*[2].
lair [ler] cubil *m*, guarida *f*.
laird [lerd] *Scot.* señor *m*, propietario *m*.
la·i·ty ['leiiti] legos *m/pl.*, laicado *m*.
lake [leik] lago *m*.
lam [læm] *sl.* pegar, tundir (*a. ~ into*); huir; *on the ~* huido; escapado.
la·ma ['lɑːmə] lama *m*.
lamb [læm] 1. cordero (a *f*) *m* (*a. fig.*); (*older*) borrego (a *f*) *m*; (*meat*) carne *f* de cordero; 2. parir (*la oveja*).
lam·baste [læm'beist] F dar una paliza a; poner como un trapo.
lam·bent ['læmbənt] *flame* vacilante; centelleante.
lamb...: '~ '**chop** chuleta *f* de cordero; '**~·like** (manso) como un cordero; '**~·skin** corderina *f*, piel *f* de cordero; '**~s·wool** añinos *m/pl*.
lame [leim] 1. □ cojo; lisiado; *excuse* débil, poco convincente; *meter* defectuoso; *~ duck* persona *f* incapacitada (*or* ✝ insolvente); político *m* derrotado; *~ excuse* disculpa *f* de poco crédito; 2. lisiar, encojar; incapacitar; '**lame·ness** cojera *f*; incapacidad *f*; *fig.* debilidad *f*.
la·ment [lə'ment] 1. lamento *m*, queja *f*; *poet. etc.* elegía *f*; 2. lamentar(se de), llorar (*a. ~ for, over*); **lam·en·ta·ble** ['læməntəbl] □ lamentable, deplorable; lastimero; **lam·en'ta·tion** lamentación *f*.
lam·i·na ['læminə], *pl.* **lam·i·nae** ['~niː] lámina *f*; '**lam·i·nar** laminar; **lam·i·nate** ['~neit] laminar; dividir en láminas; *wood* contraplacar; **lam·i·nate** ['~nit], **lam·i·nat·ed** ['~neitid] laminado.
lamp [læmp] lámpara *f*; linterna *f*; (*street*) farol *m*, farola *f*; *mot.* faro *m*; (*bulb*) bombilla *f*; *fig.* antorcha *f*; '**~·black** negro *m* de humo; '**~ brack·et** brazo *m* (de lámpara); '**~ chim·ney**, '**~ glass** tubo *m* (de lámpara); '**~ hold·er** portalámpara(s) *m*; '**~·light** luz *f* de (la) lámpara; '**~·light·er** farolero *m*.
lam·poon [læm'puːn] 1. pasquín *m*; 2. pasquinar.
lamp·post ['læmppoust] poste *m* de farol.
lam·prey ['læmpri] lamprea *f*.
lamp·shade ['læmpʃeid] pantalla *f*.
lance [læns] 1. lanza *f*; 2. (a)lancear; ⚕ abrir con lanceta; '**~ 'cor·po·ral** soldado *m* (de) primera; **lanc·er** ['lænsər] lancero *m*; *~s* (*dance*) lanceros *m/pl*.
lan·cet ['lænsit] lanceta *f*; *~* **arch** ojiva *f* aguda; *~* **win·dow** ventana *f* ojival.
land [lænd] 1. *all senses*: tierra *f*; (*soil*) suelo *m*; (*nation*) país *m*; (*a. tract of ~*) terreno *m*; *by ~* por tierra; *dry ~* tierra *f* firme; *native ~* patria *f*; *promised ~* tierra *f* de promisión; *~ forces* fuerzas *f/pl.* terrestres; *~ reform* reforma *f* agraria; *see how the ~ lies* tantear (*or* reconocer) el terreno; 2. *v/t. passengers* desembarcar; *goods* descargar; ✈ poner en tierra; F conseguir, ganar; *blow* asestar; *boxing*: conectar; *v/i.* desembarcar; ✈ aterrizar; ✈ (*on sea*) amerizar, amarar; llegar; F caer; (*a. ~ up*) ir a parar; '**~ a·gent** corredor *m* de fincas rurales; administrador *m*; '**land·ed** hacendado; que consiste en tierras; *~ gentry* pequeña aristocracia *f* rural; *~ property* bienes *m/pl.* raíces.
land...: '**~·fall** ⚓ aterrada *f*; '**~·fill** tierra *f* y escombros *m/pl.*; '**~·hold·er** terrateniente *m/f*.
land·ing ['lændiŋ] aterraje *m*; desembarco *m of passengers*; desembarque *m of cargo*; ✈ aterrizaje *m*; (*stairs*) descanso *m*, rellano *m*; *~ craft* barcaza *f* de desembarco; *~ field* pista *f* de aterrizaje; *~ gear* tren *m* de aterrizaje; *~ ground* campo *m* de aterrizaje; *~ run* recorrido *m* de aterrizaje; '**~ stage** (des)embarcadero *m*.
land...: '**~·la·dy** dueña *f*; patrona *f*, huéspeda *f of boarding house*; '**~·locked** cercado de tierra; '**~·lord** propietario *m*, dueño *m of property*; patrón *m of boarding house*; posadero *m*, mesonero *m of inn*; '**~·lub·ber** ⚓ *contp.* marinero *m* de agua dulce;

hombre *m* de tierra; **'~·mark** ⚓ marca *f* (de reconocimiento); mojón *m*; punto *m* destacado; *fig.* monumento *m*, acontecimiento *m* que hace época; **'~ own·er** terrateniente *m/f*, propietario (a *f*) *m*; **~·scape** ['lændskeip] paisaje *m*; ~ *gardener* arquitecto *m* de jardines; ~ *painter* paisajista *m/f*; **'~·slide** corrimiento *m* de tierras (*a.* **'~·slip**); *pol.* victoria *f* electoral arrolladora; **~ tax** contribución *f* territorial; **~·ward** ['~wərd] hacia tierra.

lane [lein] (*country*) camino *m* (vecinal), vereda *f*; (*town*) callejón *m*; *sport:* calle *f*; *mot.* senda *f*; ⚓ ruta *f* de navegación.

lang·syne ['læŋ'sain] *Scot.* (tiempo *m* de) antaño.

lan·guage ['læŋgwidʒ] lenguaje *m* (*faculty of speech, particular mode of speech, style*); lengua *f*, idioma *m of nation*; *bad* ~ palabrotas *f/pl.*; *use bad* ~ ser mal hablado; *strong* ~ palabras *f/pl.* mayores; **'~ 'lab·o·ra·to·ry** laboratorio *m* de idiomas.

lan·guid ['læŋgwid] □ lánguido; **'lan·guid·ness** languidez *f*.

lan·guish ['læŋgwiʃ] languidecer; afectar languidez; mostrarse sentimental; consumirse (*for* por); pudrirse *in prison*; **'lan·guish·ing** □ lánguido; sentimental.

lan·guor ['læŋgər] languidez *f*; **'lan·guor·ous** □ lánguido; enervante.

lank [læŋk] □ alto y flaco; *hair* lacio; **'lank·y** □ larguirucho; zancudo.

lan·tern ['læntərn] linterna *f* (*a.* △); fanal *m of lighthouse*; ⚓ faro(l) *m*; *dark* ~ linterna *f* sorda; *magic* ~ linterna *f* mágica; ~ *lecture* conferencia *f* con proyecciones; **'~-jawed** chupado de cara.

lan·yard ['lænjərd] acollador *m*.

lap[1] [læp] **1.** regazo *m*; falda *f*; *fig.* seno *m*; *sport:* vuelta *f*; (*stage*) etapa *f*; ⊕ traslapo *m*; **2.** envolver (*in* en); traslapar(se) (*a.* ~ *over*); juntar a traslapo; *sport:* aventajar en una vuelta entera; ~ *about* (*with*) cercar (de).

lap[2] [~] **1.** lametada *f*; chapaleteo *m of waves*; **2.** lamer; (*waves*) chapalear; ~ *up* beber con la lengua; (*a. fig.*) tragar.

lap dog ['læpdɔg] perro *m* faldero.

la·pel [lə'pel] solapa *f*.

lap·i·dar·y ['læpidəri] lapidario *adj. a. su. m*; *fig.* sucinto.

Lap·land·er ['læplændər], **Lapp** [læp] lapón (-a *f*) *m*.

lapse [læps] **1.** (*moral, of time*) lapso *m*; desliz *m*; recaída *f* (*into* en); (*mistake*) equivocación *f*; ⚖ caducidad *f*, prescripción *f*; **2.** (*time*) transcurrir; pasar; caer (en la culpa *or* en el error); recaer (*into* en); ⚖ caducar, prescribir.

lap·wing ['læpwiŋ] avefría *f*.

lar·board ['lɑːrbərd] (de) babor *m*.

lar·ce·ny ['lɑːrsəni] latrocinio *m*; *petty* ~ robo *m* de menor cuantía; *grand* ~ hurto *m* mayor.

larch [lɑːrtʃ] alerce *m*.

lard [lɑːrd] **1.** manteca *f* (de cerdo), lardo *m*; **2.** lard(e)ar, mechar; *fig.* adornar (*with* con), salpicar (*with* de); **'lard·er** despensa *f*; **'lard·y** mantecoso.

large [lɑːrdʒ] grande; *as* ~ *as life* de tamaño natural; en persona; *at* ~ en libertad, suelto; en general; extensamente; por todas partes; *on the* ~ *side* algo grande; **'large·ly** grandemente; en gran parte; **'large·ness** grandeza *f*; gran tamaño *m*; vastedad *f*; **'large-'scale** en gran(de) escala; **'large-'sized** de gran tamaño.

lar·gess(e) ['lɑːrdʒes] largueza *f*; dádiva *f* espléndida.

lar·iat ['læriet] lazo *m*.

lark[1] [lɑːrk] *orn.* alondra *f* común.

lark[2] [~] **1.** juerga *f*; travesura *f*; broma *f*; **2.** (*a.* ~ *about*) hacer travesuras; andar de jarana.

lark·spur ['lɑːrkspəːr] espuela *f* de caballero.

lar·va ['lɑːrvə], *pl.* **lar·vae** ['~viː] larva *f*; **lar·val** ['~vl] larval.

lar·yng·i·tis [lærin'dʒaitis] laringitis *f*.

lar·ynx ['læriŋks] laringe *f*.

las·civ·i·ous [lə'siviəs] □ lascivo.

la·ser ['leizər] láser *m*.

lash [læʃ] **1.** tralla *f*; azote *m*; (*whip*) látigo *m*; (*stroke*) latigazo *m* (*a. fig.*); coletazo *m of tail*; *anat.* pestaña *f*; **2.** azotar, fustigar (*a. fig.*); provocar (*into* hasta); *tail* agitar; chocar con; (*bind*) atar, ⚓ trincar; ~ *out* tirar coces; dar golpes furiosos; estallar; **'lash·ing** azotamiento *m*; atadura *f*; ⚓ trinca *f*; ~*s sl.* montones *m/pl.*, derroche *m*.

lass [læs] chica *f*, muchacha *f*; za-

gala *f*; moza *f*; **las·sie** ['~i] muchachita *f*.
las·si·tude ['laesitju:d] lasitud *f*.
las·so ['læsou] **1.** lazo *m*; **2.** lazar.
last[1] [læst] **1.** *adj*. último; postrero; final; extremo; *week etc*. pasado; *the ~ to* el último en; *at the ~ moment* a última hora; *before ~* antepasado; *~ but one* penúltimo; **2.** último (a *f*) *m*; última cosa *f*; fin *m*; *my ~* mi última carta; *at ~* por fin; *at long ~* al fin y al cabo; *to the ~* hasta el fin; *breathe one's ~* exhalar el último suspiro; *see the ~ of* no volver a ver; *~-ditch* (*esfuerzo*) último; desesperante; **3.** *adv*. por último; por última vez; finalmente; *~ but not least* el último pero no el peor; *arrive ~* llegar el último.
last[2] [~] (per)durar; continuar; permanecer; resistir; subsistir, sostenerse, conservarse (*a. ~ out*).
last[3] [~] horma *f* (del calzado); *stick to your ~!* ¡zapatero, a tus zapatos!
last·ing ['læstiŋ] □ duradero, perdurable; constante; *color* sólido.
last·ly ['læstli] por último, finalmente.
latch [lætʃ] picaporte *m*; pestillo *m* de golpe; aldabilla *f*; *on the ~* cerrado con picaporte; '**~ key** llavín *m*.
late [leit] **1.** *adj*. tardío; *hour* avanzado; reciente, de ha poco; (*dead*) fallecido, difunto; (*former*) antiguo, ex...; *a ~ twelfth-century text* un texto de fines del siglo doce; *it is ~* es tarde; *he is ~* llega tarde; *I was ~ in ger*. tardé en *inf*.; *be 2 minutes ~* 🚂 *etc*. llegar con 2 minutos de retraso; *get* (*or grow*) *~* hacerse tarde; *keep ~ hours* acostarse a las altas horas de la noche; *of ~ years* en estos últimos años; **2.** *adv*. tarde; *~ in the afternoon* a última hora de la tarde; *~ in life* a una edad avanzada; *~ in the year* hacia fines del año; *as ~ as* todavía en; hasta; *at the ~st* a más tardar; *~r on* más tarde; *of ~* últimamente, recientemente; '**~-com·er** recién llegado (a *f*) *m*; rezagado (a *f*) *m*; '**late·ly** hace poco; últimamente, recientemente.
la·ten·cy ['leitənsi] estado *m* latente.
late·ness ['leitnis] retraso *m*; lo avanzado *of the hour*; lo tarde; lo reciente.
la·tent ['leitənt] □ latente.
lat·er·al ['lætərəl] □ lateral.
la·tex ['leiteks] ⚘ látex *m*.
lath [læθ] listón *m*.
lathe [leið] torno *m*.
lath·er ['læðər] **1.** jabonadura(s) *f*(*pl*.), espuma *f* (de jabón); *in a ~* F desconcertado; aturdido; **2.** *v/t*. (en)jabonar; *sl*. zurrar; *v/i*. hacer espuma.
Lat·in ['lætin] **1.** latino *adj*. *a*. *su*. *m* (a *f*); **2.** (*language*) latín *m*; '**~ A'mer·i·can** latinoamericano *adj*. *a*. *su*. *m* (a *f*); '**Lat·in·ism** latinismo *m*.
lat·i·tude ['lætitju:d] latitud *f*; *fig*. libertad *f*; **lat·i'tu·di·nal** latitudinal; **lat·i·tu·di·nar·i·an** ['~'neriən] latitudinario *adj*. *a*. *su*. *m* (a *f*).
la·trine [lə'tri:n] latrina *f*.
lat·ter ['lætər] más reciente; posterior; último; segundo *of 2*; *the ~* éste *etc*.; *~ end* muerte *f*; *the ~ end* (*or part*) *of* fines de; '**~-day** moderno, reciente; '**lat·ter·ly** recientemente, últimamente.
lat·tice ['lætis] **1.** enrejado *m* (*a*. '**~work**); celosía *f*; **2.** enrejar.
Lat·vi·an ['lætviən] letón *adj*. *a*. *su*. *m* (-a *f*).
laud [lɔ:d] *mst lit*. **1.** alabanza *f*; *~s eccl*. laudes *f*/*pl*.; **2.** alabar, loar, elogiar; **laud·a'bil·i·ty** laudabilidad *f*; '**laud·a·ble** □ laudable, loable; **laud·a·to·ry** ['~ətɔ:ri] □ laudatorio.
laugh [læf] **1.** risa *f*; (*loud*) carcajada *f*, risotada *f*; cosa *f* (*or* persona *f*) divertida; **2.** reír(se); *~ at* reírse de, burlarse de; *~ off* tomar a risa; *~ out* (*loud*) reírse a carcajadas; '**laugh·a·ble** □ risible, irrisorio; divertido; '**laugh·ing** **1.** risa *f*; **2.** risueño, reidor; *~ matter* cosa *f* de risa; '**laugh·ing·stock** hazmerreír *m*; '**laugh·ter** risa(s) *f*(*pl*.).
launch [lɔ:ntʃ] **1.** botadura *f*; (*boat*) lancha *f*; **2.** *v/t*. *ship* botar, echar al agua; (*throw*, *publicize*, *set up*) lanzar; dar principio a; poner en operación; ✝ emitir; *v/i*.: *~ forth*, *~ out* lanzarse, salir; *~* (*out*) *into* lanzarse a; engolfarse en; emprender; *speech* desatarse en; '**launch·ing** botadura *f*; lanzamiento *m*; iniciación *f*; ✝ emisión *f*; '**launch**(**·ing**) **pad** paraje *m* de lanzamiento; '**launch·ing site** rampa *f* de lanzamiento; '**launch·ing tower** torre *f* de lanzamiento.
laun·der ['lɔ:ndər] *v/t*. lavar (y planchar); *v/i*. resistir el lavado.
laun·dress ['lɔ:ndris] lavandera *f*;

ˈ**laun·dry** lavadero *m*; lavandería *f S.Am.*; (*clothes*) ropa *f* lavada (*or* por lavar).
lau·re·ate [ˈlɔːriit] (poeta *m*) laureado.
lau·rel [ˈlɔːrəl] laurel *m*; *win* ~*s* cargarse de laureles, laurearse.
la·va [ˈlɑːvə] lava *f*.
lav·a·to·ry [ˈlævətɔːri] wáter *m*, excusado *m*, inodoro *m*, retrete *m*; (*washplace*) lavabo *m*; *public* ~ evacuatorio *m* (público).
lav·en·der [ˈlævindər] espliego *m*, lavanda *f*.
lav·ish [ˈlæviʃ] **1.** □ pródigo (*of* de, *in* en); profuso; **2.** prodigar; ~ *s.t. upon a p.* colmar a una p. de algo; ˈ**lav·ish·ness** prodigalidad *f*; profusión *f*.
law [lɔː] ley *f*; (*study, body of*) derecho *m*; jurisprudencia *f*; *sport*: regla *f*; ~ *and order* orden *m* público; *by* ~ según la ley; *in* ~ según derecho; *...-in-*~ político; *go to* ~ poner pleito, recurrir a la ley; *have the* ~ *of* (*or on*) llevar a los tribunales; *lay down the* ~ **hablar autoritariamente**; *practice* ~ **ejercer** (la profesión) de abogado; *take the* ~ *into one's own hands* tomarse la justicia por su mano; ˈ**~-a·bid·ing** observante de la ley; morigerado; ˈ**~·break·er** infractor (-a *f*) *m* de la ley; ˈ**~ court** tribunal *m* de justicia; ˈ**law·ful** □ lícito, legítimo, legal; ˈ**law·less** □ ilegal; desaforado, desordenado; sin leyes; ˈ**law·mak·er** legislador (-a *f*) *m*.
lawn[1] [lɔːn] linón *m*.
lawn[2] [~] césped *m*; ˈ**~ mow·er** cortacésped *m*; ˈ~ ˈ**ten·nis** lawn tennis *m*, tenis *m*.
law·suit [ˈlɔːsuːt] pleito *m*, litigio *m*, proceso *m*; **law·yer** [ˈ~jər] abogado *m*; jurisconsulto *m*.
lax [læks] (*morally*) laxo; indisciplinado; negligente; vago; **lax·a·tive** [~ətiv] laxante *adj. a. su. m*; ˈ**lax·i·ty**, ˈ**lax·ness** laxitud *f*; relajamiento *m*; negligencia *f*.
lay[1] [lei] *pret. of lie*[2].
lay[2] [~] *lit.* trova *f*, romance *m*; caución *f*.
lay[3] [~] laico, lego, seglar; profano.
lay[4] [~] **1.** disposición *f*, situación *f*; *sl.* negocio *m*; **2.** [*irr.*] *v/t.* poner, colocar, dejar; (ex)tender; acostar; derribar; acabar con; ⚔ apuntar; *bet* hacer; *blame, foundations* echar; *claim* presentar; *dust* matar; *eggs, table* poner; *fears* aquietar; *fire* preparar; *money* apostar; *plans* formar; 🚂 *track* tender; ~ *aside*, ~ *away* echar a un lado, arrinconar; ahorrar; ~ *bare* poner al descubierto; ~ *before* **presentar a; exponer ante;** ~ *by* **poner a un lado; guardar; ahorrar;** ~ *down arms* deponer; *burden* posar; *life* dar; *principle* asentar; *ship* colocar la quilla de; guardar; afirmar (*that* que); ~ *in* (*stocks of*) proveerse de; almacenar; ~ *low* derribar; poner fuera de combate; ~ *off* poner a un lado; *workers* despedir (temporalmente); ~ *on* colocar sobre; aplicar; imponer; *blows* descargar; *water etc.* instalar; F ~ *it on* (*thick*) (*beat*) zurrar; (*exaggerate*) recargar las tintas; (*flatter*) adular; ~ *open* abrir; poner al descubierto; exponer (*a. fig.*); ~ *out* (ex)tender; F derribar, poner fuera de combate; disponer; trazar; ✝ invertir; gastar; ~ *o.s. out* hacer un gran esfuerzo (*to* por); molestarse (*for* por); ~ *up* almacenar, guardar, ahorrar; ⚕ obligar a guardar cama; ⚓ amarrar; *mot.* encerrar; *v/i.* (*hens*) poner; apostar (*a.* ~ *a wager*) (*that* a que); ~ *about one* dar palos de ciego; *sl.* ~ *into* atacar, dar una paliza a; ~ *off sl.* dejar en paz, quitarse de encima; *sl.* dejar; ⚓ virar de bordo; F ~ *on* descargar golpes.
lay·er [ˈleiər] **1.** capa *f*; lecho *m*; *geol.* estrato *m*; (gallina *f*) ponedora *f*; ⚘ acodo *m*; **2.** acodar.
lay·ette [leiˈet] canastilla *f*, ajuar *m* (de niño).
lay fig·ure [ˈleiˈfigər] maniquí *m*.
lay·ing [ˈleiiŋ] colocación *f*; tendido *m of cable*; postura *f of eggs*; ~ *on of hands* imposición *f* de manos.
lay·man [ˈleimən] seglar *m*, lego *m*; profano *m*.
lay...: ˈ**~·off** paro *m* involuntario; ˈ**~·out** trazado *m*; disposición *f*; equipo *m* ˈ**~·o·ver** parada *f* en un viaje.
laze [leiz] holgazanear; ˈ**laz·i·ness** pereza *f*, indolencia *f*, holgazanería *f*; ˈ**la·zy** □ perezoso, indolente, holgazán; ˈ**la·zy-bones** gandul (-a *f*) *m*.
lea [liː] *poet.* prado *m*.
lead[1] [led] **1.** plomo *m*; ⚓ sonda *f*, escandallo *m*; *typ.* regleta *f*; mina *f in pencil*; ~*s pl.* chapas *f/pl.* de plomo;

~*footed* indeciso; vacilante; ~ *pencil* lápiz *m*; ~ *poisoning* plumbismo *m*; **2.** emplomar; *typ.* regletear; ~*ed gasoline* gasolina *f* con plomo; ~*ed lights* cristales *m/pl.* emplomados.

lead² [li:d] **1.** delantera *f*, cabeza *f* (*a. sport*); iniciativa *f*; dirección *f*, mando *m*; ejemplo *m*; guía *f*; indicación *f*; *sport*: liderato *m*; *cards*: mano *f*; *thea.* papel *m* principal; traílla *f for dog*; ⚡ conductor *m*, avance *m*; *cards*: *it's my* ~ yo soy mano; *be in the* ~ ir en cabeza; *take the* ~ tomar la delantera (*or* la cabeza *or* el mando); **2.** *v/t.* conducir; guiar; encabezar; dirigir; mandar; *life* llevar; mover (*to inf.* a *inf.*); *card* salir con; ~ *astray* llevar por mal camino; ~ *on fig.* incitar (*to* a); seducir; *v/i.* llevar la delantera; tener el mando; conducir (*to* a); *cards*: ser mano; ~ *off* empezar; *sport*: abrir el juego; ~ *up to* conducir a; preparar (el terreno para).

lead·en ['ledn] plúmbeo, de plomo; *color* plomizo; *fig.* pesado; *fig.* triste.

lead·er ['li:dər] jefe (a *f*) *m*, líder *m*, caudillo *m*; guía *m/f*; conductor (-a *f*) *m*; cuadrillero *m of gang*; cabecilla *m of rebels*; director *m of band*; primer violín *m of orchestra*; artículo *m* de fondo *in newspaper*; '**lead·er·ship** jefatura *f*, liderato *m*; mando *m*, dirección *f*; iniciativa *f*; (*powers of*) ~ dotes *f/pl.* de mando; '**lead·er** '**wri·ter** editorialista *m*.

lead·ing ['li:diŋ] **1.** dirección *f*; **2.** principal, capital; director; primero; ~ *article* artículo *m* de fondo; ~ *lady* dama *f*, primera actriz *f*; ~ *man* primer galán *m*; ~ *question* ⚖ pregunta *f* capciosa.

leaf [li:f] **1.** (*pl. leaves*) hoja *f*; *shake like a* ~ temblar como un azogado; *take a* ~ *from a p.'s book* seguir el ejemplo de una p.; *turn over a new* ~ reformarse; **2.** ~ *through* hojear, trashojar; '~ **bud** yema *f*; '**leaf·less** deshojado, sin hojas; **leaf·let** ['~lit] hoja *f* volante, folleto *m*; '**leaf mold** abono *m* verde; '**leaf·y** frondoso.

league [li:g] **1.** (*measure*) legua *f*; *pol.*, *sport*: liga *f*; ♀ *of Nations* Sociedad *f* de las Naciones; *in* ~ coligado; F de manga; *in* ~ *with* de acicate con; **2.** (co)ligar(se).

leak [li:k] **1.** ⚓ vía *f* de agua; gotera *f in roof*; (*aperture*) agujero *m*, rendija *f*; salida *f*, escape *m*, fuga *f of gas, liquid*; filtración *f of data, news*; **2.** ⚓ hacer agua; salirse; gotear(se); ~ *out* rezumarse (*a. fig.*); *fig.* filtrarse; '**leak·age** escape *m*; derrame *m*; filtración *f*; *fig.* divulgación *f* no autorizada, noticia *f* oficiosa; '**leak·y** ⚓ que hace agua; *roof* llovedizo; que se rezuma; agujereado.

lean¹ [li:n] flaco; *meat* magro; *year etc.* de carestía.

lean² [~] **1.** [*irr.*] ladear(se), inclinar(se); ~ *against* arrimar(se) a; ~ *back* reclinarse, echar el cuerpo atrás; ~ *out of* asomarse a; ~ *to* inclinarse a (*or* hacia); ~ (*up*)*on* apoyarse en; **2.** (*a. fig.* **lean·ing**) inclinación *f*; tendencia *f*.

lean·ness ['li:nnis] flaqueza *f*; magrez *f*; *fig.* carestía *f*.

leant [lent] *pret. a. p.p. of lean²* 1.

lean-to ['li:n'tu:] colgadizo *m*.

leap [li:p] **1.** salto *m*, brinco *m*; *by* ~*s and bounds* a pasos agigantados; ~ *in the dark* salto *m* en el vacío; **2.** [*irr.*] saltar (*a.* ~ *over*); dar un salto (*a. fig.*); '~·**frog 1.** fil derecho *m*, pídola *f*; **2.** jugar a la pídola; saltar; **leapt** [lept] *pret. a. p.p. of leap* 2; '**leap year** año *m* bisiesto.

learn [lə:rn] [*irr.*] aprender (*to* a); instruirse (*about* en); enterarse de *a fact*; *I* ~*ed the news yesterday* supe la noticia ayer; *live and* ~ vivir para ver; **learned** [lə:rnd] = *learnt*; **learn·ed** ['~id] □ docto, sabio; erudito; *profession* liberal; '**learn·er** principiante *m/f*, aprendiz (-a *f*) *m*; estudioso (a *f*) *m*; '**learn·ing** el aprender; estudio *m*; erudición *f*, saber *m*; **learnt** [lə:rnt] *pret. a. p.p. of learn*.

lease [li:s] **1.** (contrato *m* de) arrendamiento *m*; *let out on* ~ dar en arriendo; *take on a new* ~ *of life* recobrar su vigor; renovarse; **2.** arrendar; dar (*or* tomar) en arriendo; ~·**hold** ['~hould] **1.** arrendamiento *m*; bienes raíces *m/pl.* arrendados; **2.** arrendado; '~·**hold·er** arrendatario (a *f*) *m*.

leash [li:ʃ] **1.** traílla *f*; **2.** atraillar; *fig.* poner límite a; reprimir.

least [li:st] **1.** *adj.* menor; más pequeño; mínimo; **2.** *adv.* menos; **3.** *su.* lo menos; menor *m/f*; *the* ~ *of the apostles* el menor de los apóstoles; *at* ~ a lo menos, al menos, por lo menos; *at the* (*very*) ~ lo menos; *not in the* ~ de ninguna manera; nada; *to say the* ~ para no decir más.

leath·er [ˈleðər] **1.** cuero *m*; piel *f*; F pellejo *m*; (*wash*) gamuza *f*; **2.** de cuero; **3.** F zurrar; **leath·er·ette** [~ˈret] cuero *m* artificial; **leath·ern** [ˈleðərn] de cuero; **ˈleath·er·neck** *sl.* soldado *m* de la infantería de marina de EE. UU.; **ˈleath·er·y** correoso; *skin* curtido.

leave [li:v] **1.** permiso *m*; ⚔ (*a.* ~ *of absence*) licencia *f*; (*a.* ~*-taking*) despedida *f*; *by your* ~ con permiso de Vd.; *on* ~ de licencia; *take* (*one's*) ~ despedirse (*of* de); **2.** [*irr.*] *v/t.* dejar; abandonar; salir de; marcharse de; legar *in will*; entregar; ceder; F ~ *it at that* dejar así las cosas; darse por satisfecho; ~ *it to me* yo me encargaré de eso; *it* ~*s much to be desired* deja mucho que desear; *3 from 5* ~*s* 2 de 5 a 3 van 2, 5 menos 3 son 2; ~ *alone p.* dejar en paz; no meterse con; *th.* no tocar, no manosear; ~ *it alone!* ¡déjalo!; ~ *behind* dejar atrás; olvidar; ~ *off clothes* no ponerse, quitarse; *habit* renunciar a; ~ *out* omitir; *v/i.* irse, marcharse; salir (*for* para); ~ *off ger.* cesar de *inf.*, dejar de *inf.*

leav·en [ˈlevn] **1.** levadura *f*; *fig.* influencia *f*, estímulo *m*, mezcla *f*; **2.** (a)leudar; *fig.* entremezclar; penetrar e influenciar.

leaves [li:vz] *pl. of leaf.*

leav·ings [ˈli:viŋz] *pl.* sobras *f/pl.*

Leb·a·nese [ˈlebəni:z] libanés *adj. a. su. m* (-a *f*).

lech·er·ous [ˈletʃərəs] □ lascivo; **ˈlech·er·y** lascivia *f*.

lec·tern [ˈlektərn] atril *m*.

lec·ture [ˈlektʃər] **1.** conferencia *f*; *univ. mst* lección *f*, clase *f*; *fig.* sermoneo *m*; *read a p. a* ~ sermonear a una p.; **2.** dar una conferencia, dar conferencias (*or* lecciones) (*on* sobre); *fig.* sermonear; **ˈlec·tur·er** conferenciante *m/f*; conferencista *m/f S.Am.*; *univ. approx.* profesor *m* adjunto; **ˈlec·ture room** sala *f* de conferencias; *univ.* aula *f*, sala *f* de clase; **ˈlec·ture·ship** *approx.* cargo *m* de profesor adjunto.

led [led] *pret. a. p.p. of lead*[2] 2.

ledge [ledʒ] repisa *f*, (re)borde *m*; (*shelf*) anaquel *m*; retallo *m along wall*; antepecho *m of window*.

ledg·er [ˈledʒər] ✝ libro *m* mayor; ⊕ travesaño *m* de andamio.

lee [li:] ⚓ (*attr.* de) sotavento *m*; (*shelter*) socaire *m*.

leech [li:tʃ] sanguijuela *f* (*a. fig.*); † médico *m*.

leek [li:k] puerro *m*.

leer [lir] **1.** mirada *f* (de reojo) con una sonrisa impúdica (*or* maligna); **2.** mirar (de reojo) con una sonrisa impúdica (*or* maligna) (*at acc.*).

leer·y [ˈliri] *sl.* suspicaz; cauteloso.

lees [li:z] *pl.* heces *f/pl.*, poso *m*.

lee·ward [ˈli:wərd] (*attr.* de, *adv.* a) sotavento *m*.

lee·way [ˈli:wei] ⚓ deriva *f*; *fig.* atraso *m*, pérdida *f* de tiempo; *Am.* F sobra *f* de tiempo, libertad *f*; ⚓ *make* ~ derivar, abatir; *fig. make up* ~ salir del atraso.

left[1] [left] *pret. a. p.p. of leave* 2; *be* ~ quedar(se); *be* ~ *over* sobrar.

left[2] [~] **1.** *su.* izquierda *f*; *pol.* izquierda(s) *f* (*pl.*); *on* (*or to*) *the* ~ a la izquierda; **2.** *adj.* izquierdo; *pol.* izquierdista; siniestro (*lit.*); **3.** *adv.* a (*or* hacia) la izquierda; **ˈ~-ˈhand**: ~ *drive mot.* conducción *f* a la izquierda; ~ *side* izquierda *f*; **ˈ~-ˈhand·ed** □ zurdo; *fig. p.* torpe, desmañado; *compliment* ambiguo, insincero; *marriage* de la mano izquierda; ⊕ a izquierdas; **ˈleft·ist** izquierdista *adj. a. su. m/f*.

left...: **ˈ~·o·vers** *pl.* sobras *f/pl.*; **ˈ~-ˈwing** *pol.* izquierdista.

leg [leg] pierna *f*; pata *f of animals, furniture*; (*support*) pie *m*; pernil *m of pork, trousers*; caña *f of stocking*; (*stage*) etapa *f*, recorrido *m*; F *give a p. a* ~ *up* ayudar a una p. a subir; F *be on one's last* ~*s* estar en las últimas; *pull a p.'s* ~ tomar el pelo a una p.; ~ *bail sl.* fuga *f*; evasión *f*; ~ *room* espacio *m* para las piernas *in a car etc.*

leg·a·cy [ˈlegəsi] legado *m*, herencia *f*.

le·gal [ˈli:gəl] □ legal; lícito; jurídico; *v. proceeding*; ~ *adviser* jurisconsulto *m*, abogado *m*; ~ *costs* litisexpensas *f/pl.*; ~ *entity* persona *f* jurídica; **le·gal·i·ty** [liˈgæliti] legalidad *f*; **le·gal·i·za·tion** [li:gəlaiˈzeiʃn] legalización *f*; **ˈle·gal·ize** legalizar.

leg·ate [ˈlegit] legado *m*.

leg·a·tee [legəˈti:] legatario (a *f*) *m*.

le·ga·tion [liˈgeiʃn] legación *f*.

leg·end [ˈledʒənd] leyenda *f*; **ˈleg·end·ar·y** legendario.

leg·er·de·main [ˈledʒərdəˈmein] juego *m* de manos; trapacería *f*.
leg·ged [ˈlegid], **legged** [legd] de ... piernas; **leg·gings** [ˈ~z] *pl.* polainas *f/pl.*; ˈ**leg·gy** zanquilargo.
leg·i·bil·i·ty [ledʒiˈbiliti] legibilidad *f*; **leg·i·ble** [ˈledʒəbl] □ legible.
le·gion [ˈliːdʒən] legión *f* (*a. fig.*); ˈ**le·gion·ar·y** legionario *adj. a. su. m.*
leg·is·late [ˈledʒisleit] legislar; **leg·isˈla·tion** legislación *f*; ˈ**leg·is·la·tive** □ legislativo; ˈ**leg·is·la·tor** legislador (-a *f*) *m*; **leg·is·la·ture** [ˈ~tʃər] legislatura *f*.
le·git·i·ma·cy [liˈdʒitiməsi] legitimidad *f*; **leˈgit·i·mate 1.** [~mit] □ legítimo; admisible; **2.** [~meit] legitimar (*a.* **leˈgit·i·mize**); **leˈgit·iˈma·tion** legitimación *f*.
leg·ume [ˈlegjuːm] legumbre *f*; **leˈgu·mi·nous** leguminoso.
lei·sure [ˈliːʒər, ˈleʒər] **1.** ocio *m*, tiempo *m* libre, desocupación *f*; *be at ~* estar desocupado; *at your ~* en sus ratos libres, cuando tenga tiempo; **2.** de ocio, desocupado, de pasatiempo; *~ activities* recreo(s) *m*(*pl.*); pasatiempos *m/pl.*; *~ time* horas *f/pl.* de ocio; *~ wear* ropa *f* de recreo; traje *m* informal; ˈ**lei·sured** desocupado; *class* acomodado; ˈ**lei·sure·ly 1.** *adj.* pausado, lento; **2.** *adv.* pausadamente, despacio, con calma.
lem·on [ˈlemən] **1.** limón *m*; (*a. ~ tree*) limonero *m*; *sl.* artículo *m* de fábrica defectuosa; **2.** *attr.* de limón; (*color*) limonado; **lem·on·ade** [~ˈneid] limonada *f*, gaseosa *f* de limón; ˈ**lem·on ˈsquash** limonada *f* (natural); zumo *m* de limón; ˈ**lem·on ˈsqueez·er** exprimelimones *m*.
lend [lend] [*irr.*] prestar; *fig.* dar, añadir; *~ o.s. to* prestarse a; *~ing library* biblioteca *f* circulante; ˈ**lend·er** prestador (-a *f*) *m*; prestamista *m/f*; ˈ**Lend-ˈLease Act** ley *f* de préstamos y arriendos.
length [leŋθ] largo(r) *m*, longitud *f*; ⚓ eslora *f*; *racing*: cuerpo *m*; duración *f of time*; corte *m of cloth*; tramo *m of track, road etc.*; *at ~* por fin; *at* (*great*) *~* detenidamente, por extenso; *v. full-~*; *go to any ~* no pararse en barras; hacer todo lo posible (*to* para); *go to great ~s in* extremarse en; *go to the ~ of* llegar al extremo de; ˈ**length·en** alargar(se), prolongar(se); ˈ**length·wise** longitudinal(mente); a lo largo; ˈ**length·y** largo; prolongado.
le·ni·ent [ˈliːniənt] □ indulgente, clemente, poco severo; **le·ni·ence, le·ni·en·cy** [ˈ~niəns(i)], **len·i·ty** [ˈleniti] lenidad *f*; ˈ**len·i·tive** lenitivo *adj. a. su. m.*
lens [lenz] *opt.*, *phot.* lente *f*; *anat.* cristalino *m*; *~ system* sistema *m* de lentes.
lent[1] [lent] *pret. a. p.p. of lend.*
Lent[2] [~] cuaresma *f*.
Lent·en [ˈlentən] cuaresmal.
len·til [ˈlentil] lenteja *f*.
le·o·nine [ˈliːənain] leonino.
leop·ard [ˈlepərd] leopardo *m*.
le·o·tard [ˈliːətɑːrd] traje *m* ajustado de ejercicio.
lep·er [ˈlepər] leproso (a *f*) *m*.
lep·ro·sy [ˈleprəsi] lepra *f*; ˈ**lep·rous** leproso.
Les·bi·an [ˈlezbiːən] lesbia *f*; lesbiana *f*; mujer *f* homosexual; ˈ**~·ism** lesbianismo *m*.
lese maj·es·ty [ˈliːzˈmædʒisti] lesa majestad *f*.
le·sion [ˈliːʒən] lesión *f*.
less [les] **1.** *adj.* (*size, degree*) menor, inferior; (*quantity*) menos; **2.** *adv.*, *prp.* menos; *~ and ~* cada vez menos; (*at*) *~ than* (en) menos que; *~ than 4* menos de 4; *~ than you say* menos de lo que dices; *grow ~* menguar, disminuir(se); *no ~* (*than*) nada menos (que); *no ~ a p. than* no otro que.
...less [lis] sin ...
les·see [leˈsiː] arrendatario (a *f*) *m*.
less·en [ˈlesn] *v/t.* disminuir, (a)minorar, reducir; *v/i.* disminuir(se), reducirse, menguar.
less·er [ˈlesər] menor, más pequeño; inferior.
les·son [ˈlesn] lección *f*; *fig.* escarmiento *m*; *~s pl.* clases *f/pl.*; *learn one's ~ fig.* escarmentar(se); *teach* (*or give*) *a ~* dar clase; dar una lección (*a. fig.*).
les·sor [leˈsɔːr] arrendador (-a *f*) *m*.
lest [lest] de miedo que, para que no, no sea que.
let[1] [let] [*irr.*] *v/t.* dejar, permitir (*he let me go* me dejó ir, me permitió ir); *property* alquilar, arrendar; *~ inf.* = *imperative*: *~ him come!* ¡que venga!; *~'s go!* ¡vamos!; *~ alone* no tocar; dejar en paz; sin mencionar, ni mucho menos; F *~ well alone* peor es meneallo; dejar las cosas como

están; F ~ *be* dejar en paz; ~ *by* dejar pasar; ~ *down* (dejar) bajar; *fig. p.* dejar plantado, faltar a, desilusionar; ~ *a p. down gently* castigar a una p. con poca severidad; ~ *o.s. down by* descolgarse con; ~ *fly* disparar (*at* contra); soltar (palabras duras) (*at* contra); ~ *go* soltar; *property* vender; (*miss, pass*) dejar pasar; F ~ *o.s. go* desfogarse; dejar de cuidarse *in appearance*; F ~ *a p. in for* meter a una p. en; ~ *in(to)* dejar entrar (en); *visitor* hacer pasar; ~ *a p. into a secret* revelar un secreto a una p.; ~ *a p. know* hacer saber a una p., avisar a una p.; ~ *loose* soltar; ~ *off p.* perdonar, dejar libre; ~ *out* dejar salir; poner en libertad; acompañar a la puerta; soltar; divulgar; (*for hire*) alquilar; *fire* dejar apagarse; *garment* ensanchar; ~ *through* dejar pasar (por); *v/i.* alquilarse (*at, for* en); F ~ *on* dejar saber; revelar el secreto; F ~ *up* moderarse (*on* en); trabajar menos, cesar.

let[2] [~]: *without ~ or hindrance* sin estorbo ni obstáculo.

let·down ['letdaun] desilusión *f*; chasco *m*.

le·thal ['li:θl] □ mortífero; *esp. poison* letal.

le·thar·gic, le·thar·gi·cal [le'θɑ:rdʒik(l)] □ letárgico; **leth·ar·gy** ['leθərdʒi] letargo *m* (*a. fig.*).

let·ter ['letər] **1.** carta *f*; letra *f of alphabet, typ. a. fig.*; ~*s pl.* (*learning etc.*) letras *f/pl.*; ~ *of credit* carta *f* de crédito; *by* ~ por escrito, por carta; *man of* ~*s* literato *m*; *small* ~ minúscula *f*; *to the* ~ a(l pie de) la letra; **2.** rotular; estampar con letras; '**let·ter car·rier** cartero *m*; '**let·tered** *p.* letrado; rotulado, marcado con letras; '**let·ter file** carpeta *f*, archivo *m*; '**let·ter·head** membrete *m*; pliego *m* con membrete; '**let·ter·ing** inscripción *f*, letras *f/pl.*

let·ter...: '~**·press** texto *m* impreso; '~ **press** prensa *f* de copiar cartas.

let·tuce ['letis] lechuga *f*.

let-up ['letʌp] cesación *f*; pausa *f*; F calma *f*, tregua *f*.

leu·ke·mia [lju'ki:miə] leucemia *f*.

Le·vant [lə'vænt] Levante *m*; **Le·vant·ine** ['levənti:n] levantino *adj. a. su. m* (a *f*).

lev·ee ['levi:] ribero *m*, dique *m*.

lev·el ['levl] **1.** (*flat place*) llano *m*; llanura *f*; (*instrument, altitude, degree*) nivel *m*; *dead* ~ superficie *f* completamente llana; *fig.* uniformidad *f*, monotonía *f*; *on a* ~ *with* al nivel de (*a. fig.*); a ras de, a flor de; *fig.* parangonable con; *sl. on the* ~ honrado; sin engaño, en serio; **2.** *v/t.* nivelar (*a. surv.*); igualar; allanar; derribar; *site* desmontar; *blow* asestar; *weapon* apuntar; *fig.* dirigir; ~ *with the ground* arrasar; ~ *down* rebajar (al mismo nivel); igualar; ~ *up* levantar (al mismo nivel); igualar; *v/i.*: ~ *at*, ~ *against* apuntar a; ~ *off* nivelarse; ✈ enderezarse; (*prices*) estabilizarse; **3.** raso, llano, plano; a nivel; nivelado; igual; *fig.* juicioso, ecuánime; *dead* ~ completamente a nivel; *my* ~ *best* todo lo que puedo; ~ *crossing* paso *m* a nivel; **4.** *adv.* a nivel; ras con ras; '~-'**head·ed** sensato, juicioso; '**lev·el(l)ing 1.** nivelación *f etc.*; **2.** nivelador.

le·ver ['li:vər, 'levər] **1.** palanca *f* (*a. fig.*); **2.** apalancar; '**le·ver·age** apalancamiento *m*; *fig.* influencia *f*, ventaja *f*.

le·vi·a·than [li'vaiəθən] leviatán *m*; *fig.* buque *m* enorme.

lev·i·tate ['leviteit] elevar(se) (por medios espiritistas).

Le·vite ['li:vait] levita *m*.

lev·i·ty ['leviti] frivolidad *f*, levedad *f*.

lev·y ['levi] **1.** exacción *f* (de tributos); impuesto *m*; ⚔ leva *f*, reclutamiento *m*; **2.** *tax* exigir, recaudar; ⚔ reclutar.

lewd [lu:d] □ lascivo, impúdico; '**lewd·ness** lascivia *f*, impudicia *f*.

lex·i·cal ['leksikl] □ léxico.

lex·i·cog·ra·pher [leksi'kɔgrəfər] lexicógrafo *m*; **lex·i·co·graph·i·cal** [~kou'græfikl] □ lexicográfico; **lex·i·cog·ra·phy** [~'kɔgrəfi] lexicografía *f*; **lex·i·con** ['leksikən] léxico *m*; lexicón *m*.

li·a·bil·i·ty [laiə'biliti] obligación *f*, compromiso *m*; responsabilidad *f*; riesgo *m*, exposición *f*; tendencia *f*; F desventaja *f*; ✝ *liabilities pl.* pasivo *m*, deudas *f/pl.*

li·a·ble ['laiəbl] responsable (*for* de); obligado; expuesto, sujeto, propenso (*to* a); ~ *to duty* sujeto a derechos.

li·ai·son [li'eizɔ:n] enlace *m* (*a.* ⚔); (*affair*) lío *m*, relaciones *f/pl.* amorosas; ~ *officer* (oficial *m* de) enlace *m*.

li·ar [ˈlaiər] embustero (a *f*) *m*, mentiroso (a *f*) *m*.

li·ba·tion [laiˈbeiʃn] libación *f*.

li·bel [ˈlaibl] **1.** (*written*) libelo *m* (*on* contra); difamación *f*, calumnia *f* (*on* de); **2.** difamar, calumniar; ˈ**li·bel·(l)ous** □ difamatorio, calumnioso.

lib·er·al [ˈlibərəl] **1.** □ liberal (*a. pol.*); generoso; tolerante; abundante; **2.** liberal *m/f*; ˈ**lib·er·al·ism** liberalismo *m*; **lib·er·al·i·ty** [~ˈræliti] liberalidad *f*.

lib·er·ate [ˈlibəreit] libertar, librar (*from* de); **lib·erˈa·tion** liberación *f*; ~ *theology* teología *f* liberacionista; ˈ**lib·er·a·tor** libertador (-a *f*) *m*.

lib·er·tar·ian [libərˈtæriən] libertarianista *m/f*.

lib·er·tin·age [ˈlibərtinidʒ] libertinaje *m*; **lib·er·tine** [ˈlibərtin] libertino; ˈ**lib·er·tin·ism** libertinaje *m*.

lib·er·ty [ˈlibərti] libertad *f*; ⚓ licencia *f*; *take liberties* permitirse (*or* tomar) libertades; *be at* ~ estar en libertad; *be at* ~ *to do* tener permiso para (*or* derecho de) hacer; *set at* ~ poner en libertad.

li·bid·i·nous [liˈbidinəs] □ libidinoso; **li·bi·do** [liˈbi:dou] libido *m*; libídine *f*.

li·brar·i·an [laiˈbreriən] bibliotecario (a *f*) *m*; **li·brar·y** [ˈlaibrəri] biblioteca *f*; (*esp. private*) librería *f*; ~ *science* bibliotecnia *f*; biblioteconomía *f*.

li·bret·tist [liˈbretist] libretista *m/f*.

li·bret·to [liˈbretou] libreto *m*.

Lib·y·an [ˈlibiən] **1.** libio (a *f*) *m*; **2.** *p.* libio; líbico.

lice [lais] *pl. of louse*.

li·cense [ˈlaisəns] **1.** licencia *f*; permiso *m*; autorización *f*; título *m*; cédula *f*; (*excess*) desenfreno *m*; **2.** licenciar; autorizar; dar licencia (*or* cédula *or* privilegio) a; **li·cen·see** [~ˈsi:] concesionario (a *f*) *m*; persona *f* que obtiene licencia; ˈ**li·cense plate** placa *f* de matrícula.

li·cen·ti·ate [laiˈsenʃiit] licenciado (a *f*) *m*.

li·cen·tious [laiˈsenʃəs] □ licencioso, disoluto.

li·chen [ˈlaiken] liquen *m*.

lick [lik] **1.** lamedura *f*; lamida *f S.Am.*; lengüetada *f*; F velocidad *f*; **2.** lamer; F vencer; F zurrar; ~ *the dust* morir, morder el polvo; F ~ *into shape* dar forma a; adiestrar; habilitar; ~ *one's lips* relamerse; **lick·e·ty-split** [ˈlikətiˈsplit] *sl. adv.* como un rayo; ˈ**lick·ing** lamedura *f*; F zurra *f*; ˈ**lick·spit·tle** lameculos *m*.

lic·o·rice [ˈlikəris] regaliz *m*.

lid [lid] tapa(dera) *f*; cobertera *f of pan etc.*; *anat.* párpado *m*; *sl.* (*hat*) techo *m*; F *blow one's* ~ enfurecerse; F *that's put the* ~ *on it* eso es el colmo; se acabó.

lie[1] [lai] **1.** mentira *f*; *give the* ~ *to* dar el mentís a; desmentir; *tell a* ~ = **2.** mentir.

lie[2] [~] [*irr.*] echarse, acostarse; estar echado, estar tumbado; descansar; estar (situado), hallarse; (*stretch*) extenderse; yacer, estar enterrado *in grave*; † dormir; ⚓ estar amarrado; ~ *about* estar esparcido(s); F holgazanear; ~ *back* recostarse; ~ *down* echarse, acostarse, tenderse; F ~ *down under it, take it lying down* tragarlo, soportarlo sin chistar; ~ *in* (*prp.*) consistir en; depender de; (*adv.*) estar de parto; ~ *in wait for* acechar; F ~ *low* agacharse, no chistar; ~ *over* aplazarse, quedar en suspenso; ⚓ ~ *to* estar (*or* ponerse) a la capa; ~ *under* estar bajo (el peso de); estar sometido (*or* expuesto) a; ~ *with* † dormir con; *fig.* corresponder a; *it* ~*s with you* la responsabilidad recae sobre Vd.

liege [li:dʒ] *hist.* **1.** feudatario; **2.** (*a.* ˈ~**·man** [ˈ~mæn]) vasallo *m*; (*a.* ~ *lord*) señor *m* feudal.

li·en [ˈli:ən] derecho *m* de retención; gravamen *m*.

lieu [lju:]: *in* ~ *of* en lugar de.

lieu·ten·an·cy [lu:ˈtenənsi] lugartenencia *f*; tenencia *f*; **lieu·ten·ant** [lu:ˈtenənt] lugarteniente *m*; ⚔ teniente *m*; ⚓ teniente *m* de navío; ⚔ *second* ~ alférez *m*; ⚓ *sub-*~ alférez *m* de navío; ˈ~ ˈ**colo·nel** teniente coronel *m*; ˈ~ **comˈmand·er** capitán *m* de corbeta; ˈ~ ˈ**gen·er·al** teniente general *m*; ˈ~ ˈ**gov·er·nor** vicegobernador *m*.

life [laif] (*pl. lives*) vida *f*; (modo *m* de) vivir *m*; ser *m*, existencia *f*; vivacidad *f*, animación *f*; (*period of validity*) vigencia *f*; *be the* ~ *and soul of the party* ser el alma de la fiesta; *for* ~ de por vida; *for one's* ~, *for dear* ~ para salvarse la vida; a más no poder; F *for the* ~ *of me* así me maten; *from* ~ del natural; *never in my* ~ en mi vida; F *not on your* ~! ¡ni hablar!; en absoluto; *see* ~ ver mundo; *take one's* ~ *in one's hands* jugarse la vida; *this is the* ~! ¡cómo la mamamos!, ¡esto es jauja!; *to the* ~ al vivo; ~ *sentence* condena *f* a perpetuidad; '~ **an·nu·i·ty** vitalicio *m*; '~ **as·sur·ance** = *life insurance*; '~ **belt** (cinturón *m*) salvavidas *m*; '~**·blood** sangre *f* vital; *fig.* alma *f*, nervio *m*, sustento *m*; '~**·boat** lancha *f* de socorro; (*ship's*) bote *m* salvavidas, bote *m* de salvamento; '~**·buoy** guindola *f*; '~ **ex'pect·an·cy** expectación *f* de vida; '~**·guard** ⚔ guardia *m* de corps; '~ **in·ter·est** usufructo *m* (vitalicio) (*in* de); '~ **in·sur·ance** seguro *m* sobre la vida; '~ **'jack·et** chaleco *m* salvavidas; '~**·less** □ sin vida, muerto; exánime; *fig.* desanimado; flojo; deslucido; '~**·less·ness** falta *f* de vida; inercia *f*; desánimo *m etc.*; '~**·like** natural; '~**·line** cuerda *f* salvavidas; '~**·long** de toda la vida; '~ **pre·serv·er** cachiporra *f*; '~ **raft** balsa *f* salvavidas; '~ **sav·ing** (de) salvamento *m*; '~-'**size** de tamaño natural; '~ **span** período *m* de vida; '~**·time** (transcurso *m* de la) vida *f*.

lift [lift] **1.** alzamiento *m*; esfuerzo *m* para levantar, empuje *m* para arriba; ayuda *f* (para levantar); *British* ascensor *m*, elevador *m S.Am.*; (*cargo*) montacargas *m*; F viaje *m* en coche ajeno; ✈ sustentación *f*; ⊕ altura *f* de elevación; ⊕ carrera *f of valve*; *fig.* estímulo *m*; *give a p. a* ~ ayudar a una p.; llevar a una p. gratis en coche; **2.** *v/t.* levantar, alzar, elevar (*a.* ~ *up*); transportar (en avión); *restrictions* suprimir; *hat* quitarse; *sl.* ratear, robar; F plagiar; *v/i.* levantarse; (*clouds etc.*) disiparse; '**lift·ing 1.** levantamiento *m*; **2.** ascensional, levantador; '**lift-off** despegue *m* (vertical) *of a rocket*; alzamiento *m*; '**lift truck** carretilla *f* montacargas.

lig·a·ment ['ligəmənt] ligamento *m*.

lig·a·ture ['ligətʃur] **1.** ligadura *f* (*a.* ♩, ⚕); *typ.* ligado *m*; **2.** ligar.

light[1] [lait] **1.** luz *f* (*a. fig. a. window*); lumbre *f*; fuego *m for cigarette etc.*; ⚓ faro *m*; *fig.* aspecto *m*, punto *m* de vista; ~*s pl.* luces *f/pl.*, conocimientos *m/pl.*; ~ *meter* exposímetro *m*; *according to his* ~*s* según Dios le da a entender; *against the* ~ al trasluz; *at first* ~ al rayar el día; *in the* ~ *of* a la luz de (*a. fig.*); *bring* (*come*) *to* ~ sacar (salir) a luz, descubrir(se); *cast* (*or shed or throw*) ~ *on* aclarar; F *give a* ~ *to* dar fuego a; *put a* ~ *to* encender; *see the* ~ ver la luz; caer en la cuenta; convertirse; ~ *bulb* bombilla *f*; ~ *wave* onda *f* luminosa; **2.** claro; *hair* rubio; *skin* blanco; **3.** [*irr.*] *v/t.* (*ignite*) encender; alumbrar, iluminar (*a.* ~ *up*); *v/i.* (*mst* ~ *up*) encenderse; alumbrarse, iluminarse; brillar; *sl.* ~ *into* atacar; *sl.* ~ *out* largarse.

light[2] [~] **1.** *adj.* □ *a. adv.* ligero (*a. fig.*); (*slight*) leve; (*bearable*) llevadero; (*unencumbered*) desembarazado; (*fickle, wanton*) liviano; (*cheerful*) alegre; *reading* ameno, de puro entretenimiento; ⚓ en lastre; 🚂 vacío; ~ *opera* opereta *f*, zarzuela *f*; *make* ~ *of* no dar importancia a; **2.:** ~ (*up*)*on* (*bird*) posarse en.

light·en[1] ['laitn] iluminar(se); clarear; relampaguear.

light·en[2] [~] *load etc.* aligerar(se); *heart* alegrar(se).

light·er[1] ['laitər] encendedor *m*; (*gasoline*) mechero *m*.

light·er[2] [~] ⚓ gabarra *f*, barcaza *f*.

light...: '~-'**fin·gered** largo de uñas; '~ **fix·ture** guarnición *f* (*or* artefacto *m*) del alumbrado; '~-'**head·ed** mareado; ligero de cascos; ⚕ delirante; '~-'**heart·ed** □ alegre (de corazón); poco serio; '~**·house** faro *m*; '~(**house**) **keep·er** torrero *m*.

light·ing ['laitiŋ] alumbrado *m*; iluminación *f*; encendido *m*; ~ *engineering* luminotecnia *f*; ⚡ ~ *point* tomacorriente *m* para lámpara.

light·ly ['laitli] *adv.* ligeramente; levemente; frívolamente; sin pensarlo bien; '**light-mind·ed** tonto; atolondrado; '**light·ness** ligereza *f*; levedad *f*; agilidad *f*; claridad *f*, luminosidad *f*.

light·ning ['laitniŋ] relámpago *m*, rayo *m* (*a.* ~ *flash*); relampagueo *m*; *attr.* relámpago, relampagueante; '~ **bug** luciérnaga *f*; '~ **con·duc·tor**, '~ **rod** pararrayos *m*.

lights [laits] F entendimiento *m*; inteligencia *f*.

light·ship ['laitʃip] buque *m* faro.

light·weight ['laitweit] persona *f* de poco peso (*a. fig.*); *boxing*: peso *m* ligero.

light-year ['lait'jir] año *m* luz.
lig·ne·ous ['ligniəs] leñoso; **lig·nite** ['lignait] lignito *m*; **lig·num vi·tae** ['lignəm 'vaiti:] palo *m* santo; (*tree*) guayacán *m*.
lik·a·ble ['laikəbl] simpático; **like** [laik] **1.** *adj*. parecido (a), semejante (a); igual; propio de, característico de; como; ~..., ~... tal..., tal...; ~ *father*, ~ *son* tal palo, tal astilla; *in* ~ *cases* en casos parecidos; *he has a house* ~ *mine* tiene una casa semejante a la mía; *eyes* ~ *stars* ojos como estrellas; *be* ~ parecerse a; *that's just* ~ *him* eso es muy de él; † *he is* ~ *to die* es probable que muera; *feel* ~ *ger*. tener ganas de *inf*.; *something* ~ algo así como; *that's more* ~ *it!* eso (sí que) se llama hablar; eso sí que es mejor; *what is he* ~? ¿cómo es?; **2.** *adv. or prp*. como; del mismo modo (que); igual (que); tal como; ~ *a hero* como un héroe; *nothing* ~ ni con mucho; **3.** *conj*. F como, del mismo modo que; F ~ *we used to (do)* como hacíamos; **4.** *su*. semejante *m/f*, semejanza *f*; ~*s pl*. simpatías *f/pl*., gustos *m/pl*.; *and the* ~, F *and such* ~ y otros por el estilo; F *the* ~*(s) of him* otro(s) como él; **5.** *vb*. gustar; querer; estar aficionado a; *I* ~ *bananas* me gustan los plátanos; *I don't* ~ *bullfighting* no estoy aficionado a los toros; *how do you* ~ *Madrid?* ¿qué te parece Madrid?; *as you* ~ como quieras, como gustes; *I would* ~ *time* desearía tiempo; *I would* ~ *to know* quisiera saber; *would you* ~ *to go to Madrid?* ¿te gustaría ir a Madrid?
'**like·able** = *likable*.
like·li·hood ['laiklihud] probabilidad *f*; '**like·ly 1.** *adj*. probable; verosímil; prometedor; *he is* ~ *to die* es probable que muera; *not* ~*!* ¡ni hablar!; **2.** *adv*. probablemente.
like...: '~-'**mind·ed** animado por los mismos sentimientos; '**lik·en** comparar (*to* con), asemejar (*to* a); '**like·ness** parecido *m*, semejanza *f*; imagen *f*; (*portrait*) retrato *m*; *family* ~ aire *m* de familia; '**like·wise** asimismo, igualmente; además; lo mismo.
lik·ing ['laikiŋ] gusto *m* (*for* por); afición *f* (*for* a); simpatía *f* (*for p*. hacia), cariño *m* (*for p*. a); *take a* ~ *to* tomar gusto a, cobrar afición a; *p*. tomar cariño a; *to one's* ~ del gusto de uno.
li·lac ['lailək] (de color de) lila *f*.
lilt [lilt] (canción *f* alegre con) ritmo *m* marcado.
lil·y ['lili] lirio *m*; azucena *f*; ~ *of the valley* muguete *m*, lirio *m* de los valles.
limb [lim] miembro *m of body*; rama *f of tree*; F *be out on a* ~ estar en un atolladero.
lim·ber ['limbər] **1.** ágil, flexible; **2.** hacer flexible; ~ *up* agilitarse.
lim·bo ['limbou] limbo *m*; *fig*. estado *m* neutro.
lime[1] [laim] **1.** cal *f*; (*a. bird* ~) liga *f*; **2.** encalar; untar con liga.
lime[2] [~] ⚘ (*a.* ~ *tree*) tilo *m*.
lime[3] [~] ⚘ lima *f*; (*tree*) limero *m*; '~ **juice** jugo *m* de lima.
lime...: '~ **kiln** horno *m* de cal; '~·**light** luz *f* de calcio; *thea*. luz *f* del proyector; *be in the* ~ estar a la vista del público; '~·**stone** (piedra *f*) caliza *f*.
lim·er·ick ['limərik] *especie de* quintilla *f* jocosa.
lim·it ['limit] **1.** límite *m*, confín *m*; *know no* ~*s* ser infinito; *p*. ser inmoderado; F *that's the* ~*!* ¡es el colmo!, ¡no faltaba más!; *to the* ~ hasta no más; **2.** limitar (*to* a), restringir; **lim·i'ta·tion** limitación *f*, restricción *f*; ⚖ prescripción *f*; '**lim·it·ed** limitado, restringido; ~ (*liability*) *company* sociedad *f* anónima, sociedad *f* (de responsabilidad) limitada; 🚂 ~ (*express train*) tren *m* de composición limitada; '**lim·it·less** □ ilimitado.
lim·ou·sine ['limuzi:n] limousine *f*, limusina *f*.
limp[1] [limp] **1.** cojera *f*; **2.** cojear.
limp[2] [~] □ flojo, lacio; flexible.
lim·pet ['limpit] lapa *f*; *fig*. persona *f* tenaz.
lim·pid ['limpid] □ límpido, cristalino, transparente; **lim'pid·i·ty**, '**lim·pid·ness** limpidez *f*, claridad *f*.
lim·y ['laimi] calizo; pegajoso.
linch·pin ['lintʃpin] pezonera *f*.
lin·den ['lindən] tilo *m* (*a.* ~ *tree*).
line[1] [lain] **1.** línea *f*; cuerda *f*; ⚓ cordel *m*; *fishing*: sedal *m*; ✝ ramo *m*, género *m*; 🚂 vía *f*; *typ*. renglón *m*; *poet*. verso *m*; (*row*) hilera *f*; (*wrinkle*) arruga *f*; F especialidad *f*; F profesión *f*; F plan *m*, norma *f*; ~*s pl*. principios *m/pl*., normas *f/pl*.;

plan *m*; *thea.* papel *m*; ⚔ líneas *f/pl.*; ⚓ formas *f/pl.*; ~ *of battle* línea *f* de batalla; *ship of the* ~ navío *m* de línea; F *hard* ~*s* mala suerte *f*; *draw the* ~ no pasar más allá (*at* de); *drop a* ~ poner unas letras (*to* a); *teleph. hold the* ~! ¡un moment(it)o!, ¡no cuelgue Vd.!; *in* ~ *with* conforme a, de acuerdo con; *that is not in my* ~ eso no es de mi especialidad; *fall into* ~ *with* conformarse con; *on the* ~*s of* conforme a, a tenor de; *sl. shoot a* ~ darse bombo; *take a ... line* adoptar una actitud ...; **2.** *v/t.* rayar; linear; *face etc.* arrugar; alinear (*a.* ~ *up*); ~ *the streets* ocupar las aceras; *v/i.*: ~ *up* alinearse; ponerse en fila; hacer cola; formar(se).

line² [~] *clothes* forrar; ⊕ revestir; *brakes* guarnecer; F ~ *one's pockets* ponerse las botas.

lin·e·age ['liniidʒ] linaje *m*; **lin·e·al** ['liniəl] □ lineal; en línea recta; **lin·e·a·ment** ['~iəmənt] lineamento *m*; **lin·e·ar** ['~iər] lineal; de longitud.

lin·en ['linin] **1.** lino *m*, hilo *m*; (*a piece of* un) lienzo *m*; (*sheets, underclothes etc.*) ropa *f* blanca; *dirty* ~ ropa *f* sucia; **2.** de lino; '~ **clos·et** armario *m* para ropa blanca.

lin·er ['lainər] ⚓ vapor *m* de línea, transatlántico *m*; **lines·man** ['lainzmən] (*a.* **line·man**) *sport*: juez *m* de línea; 🚂 guardavía *m*; ⚡ celador *m*; '**line'up** alineación *f*, formación *f*; rueda *f* de presos.

ling¹ [liŋ] *ichth. approx.* abadejo *m* largo.

ling² [~] ⚘ *approx.* brezo *m*.

lin·ger ['liŋgər] (*a.* ~ *on*) tardar (en marcharse [*or* morirse]); quedarse; persistir; ~ *over* hacer (*or* comer) despacio; dilatarse en; reflexionar; '**lin·ger·ing** □ prolongado, dilatado, lento, persistente.

lin·ge·rie ['lɑːnʒəriː] ropa *f* blanca (*or* interior) de mujer, lencería *f*.

lin·go ['liŋgou] F lengua *f*, jerga *f*, galimatías *m*.

lin·gua fran·ca ['liŋgwə 'fræŋkə] lengua *f* franca.

lin·guist ['liŋgwist] poligloto (a *f*) *m*; linguista *m/f*; **lin'guis·tic** □ lingüístico; **lin'guis·tics** lingüística *f*.

lin·i·ment ['linimənt] linimento *m*.

lin·ing ['lainiŋ] forro *m of clothes*; ⊕ revestimiento *m*; guarnición *f of brakes*.

link¹ [liŋk] **1.** eslabón *m*; *fig.* enlace *m*; ⊕ varilla *f*, corredera *f*; **2.** eslabonar(se), enlazarse (*a.* ~ *up*).

link² [~] *hist.* hacha *f* de viento.

link·age ['liŋkidʒ] enlace *m*, eslabonamiento *m*; ⊕ varillaje *m*.

links [liŋks] *pl.* campo *m* (*or* terreno *m*) de golf.

link·up ['liŋkʌp] conexión *f*; acoplamiento *m in space.*

lin·net ['linit] pardillo *m* común.

li·no·le·um [li'nouljəm] linóleo *m*.

lin·o·type ['lainoutaip] linotipia *f*.

lin·seed ['linsiːd] linaza *f*; ~ *oil* aceite *m* de linaza.

lint [lint] hilas *f/pl.*

lin·tel ['lintl] dintel *m*.

li·on ['laiən] león *m* (*a. astr. a. fig.*); *fig.* celebridad *f*; ~*'s share* parte *f* del león; *put one's head in the* ~*'s mouth* meterse en la boca del lobo; '**li·on·ess** leona *f*; '**li·on·ize** tratar como una celebridad.

lip [lip] labio *m* (*a. fig.*, ⚘); pico *m of jug*; borde *m of cup*; *sl.* insolencia *f*; *hang on a p.'s* ~*s* estar pendiente de las palabras de una p.; *keep a stiff upper* ~ no inmutarse; '~**read** leer en los labios; '~ **serv·ice** jarabe *m* de pico; '~**·stick** rojo *m* de labios, lápiz *m* labial.

liq·ue·fac·tion [likwi'fækʃn] licuefacción *f*; **liq·ue·fi·a·ble** ['~faiəbl] liquidable; **liq·ue·fy** ['~fai] liquidar(se).

li·queur [li'kəːr] licor *m*.

liq·uid ['likwid] **1.** líquido *m*; *gr.* líquida *f*; **2.** □ líquido; *fig.* límpido; ✝ realizable; ✝ ~ *assets* activo *m* líquido.

liq·ui·date ['likwideit] *all senses*: liquidar(se); **liq·ui'da·tion** liquidación *f*; '**liq·ui·da·tor** liquidador (-a *f*) *m*.

liq·uor ['likər] licor *m*; bebida *f* alcohólica; *in* ~ borracho.

liq·uo·rice ['likəris] regaliz *m*.

lisp [lisp] **1.** ceceo *m*; balbuceo *m as of child*; **2.** cecear; balbucear.

lis·som(e) ['lisəm] ágil, flexible.

list¹ [list] **1.** lista *f*, relación *f*; (*registration*) matrícula *f*; escalafón *m of officials*; orillo *m*, tira *f of cloth*; **2.** poner en una lista; hacer una lista de; inscribir; *it is not* ~*ed* no consta (en la lista).

list[2] [~] ⚓ **1.** escora *f*; **2.** escorar.
list[3] [~] † escuchar.
lis·ten [ˈlisn] escuchar, oír (*to acc.*); prestar atención, dar oídos, atender (*to* a); ~ *in* (*to*) *radio*: escuchar la radio; escuchar por radio; estar a la escucha (de); (*eavesdrop*) escuchar a hurtadillas; ˈ**lis·ten·er** oyente *m*/*f*; *radio*: (*a.* ˈ**lis·ten·er-ˈin**) radioescucha *m*/*f*, radioyente *m*/*f*.
lis·ten·ing [ˈlisniŋ] escucha *f*; *attr.* de escucha; ˈ~ **post** puesto *m* de escucha.
list·less [ˈlistlis] □ lánguido, apático, indiferente; ˈ~**·ness** apatía *f*; indiferencia *f*.
lists [lists] *pl. hist.* liza *f*.
lit [lit] *pret. a. p.p. of light*[1] 3; ~ *up sl.* achispado.
lit·a·ny [ˈlitəni] letanía *f*.
li·ter [ˈliːtər] litro *m*.
lit·er·a·cy [ˈlitərəsi] capacidad *f* de leer y escribir.
lit·er·al [ˈlitərəl] □ literal; ~**·ism** [ˈ~izm] literalismo *m*.
lit·er·ar·y [ˈlitərəri] □ literario; **lit·er·ate** [ˈlitərit] que sabe leer y escribir; **lit·e·ra·ti** [litəˈrɑːtiː] *pl.* literatos *m*/*pl.*; **lit·er·a·ture** [ˈlitəritʃər] literatura *f*; F impresos *m*/*pl.*, folletos *m*/*pl.*
lithe(**·some**) [ˈlaið(səm)] ágil, esbelto, flexible.
lith·o·graph [ˈliθəgræf] **1.** litografía *f*; **2.** litografiar; **li·thog·ra·pher** [liˈθɔgrəfər] litógrafo *m*; **lith·o·graph·ic** [liθəˈgræfik] litográfico; **li·thog·ra·phy** [liˈθɔgrəfi] litografía *f*.
Lith·u·a·ni·an [liθjuˈeinjən] lituano *adj. a. su. m* (a *f*).
lit·i·gant [ˈlitigənt] litigante *adj. a. su. m*/*f*; **lit·i·gate** [ˈ~geit] litigar; **lit·iˈga·tion** litigio *m*, litigación *f*; **li·ti·gious** [liˈtidʒəs] □ litigioso.
lit·mus (**pa·per**) [ˈlitməs (peipər)] (papel *m* de) tornasol *m*.
lit·ter [ˈlitər] **1.** litera *f*; ⚕ camilla *f*; lecho *m*, cama *f* de paja *for animals*; camada *f of young animals*; (cosas *f*/*pl.* esparcidas en) desorden *m*, revoltillo *m*; (*rubbish*) desperdicios *m*/*pl.*, basura *f*; **2.** poner en desorden; esparcir (cosas por); dar cama de paja; (*give birth*) parir; ˈ~ ˈ**bas·ket** basurero *m*; cubo *m* para desechos; ˈ~**·bug** caminante *m* desperdiciador.
lit·tle [ˈlitl] **1.** *adj.* pequeño; chico; menudo; poco; escaso; (*mean*) mezquino; ~ *money* poco dinero; *no* ~ *money* mucho dinero; *a* ~ *money* un poco de dinero; *a* ~ *house* una casa pequeña, una casita; *the* ~ *ones* los pequeños, los chiquillos, la gente menuda; *his* ~ *ways* sus cos(it)as; ~ *people* hadas *f*/*pl.*; **2.** *adv.* poco; *a* ~ *better* un poco mejor, algo mejor; ~ *does he know that* no tiene la menor idea de que; *not a* ~ *surprised* muy sorprendido; **3.** *su.* poco; *he knows* ~ sabe poco; ~ *he knows!* ¡maldito lo que él sabe!; *a* ~ un poco; ~ *by* ~ poco a poco; *for a* ~ (por *or* durante) un rato; *in* ~ en pequeño; *make* ~ *of* sacar poco en claro de; *not a* ~ mucho; ˈ**lit·tle·ness** pequeñez *f*; poquedad *f*; mezquindad *f*.
lit·to·ral [ˈlitərəl] litoral *adj. a. su. m.*
li·tur·gi·cal [liˈtəːrdʒikl] litúrgico.
lit·ur·gy [ˈlitərdʒi] liturgia *f*.
liv·a·ble [ˈlivəbl] *life* llevadero; F habitable.
live 1. [liv] *v*/*i.* vivir (*by, off, on* de); *long* ~! ¡viva(n)!; ~ *high* (*or well*) darse buena vida; ~ *in* vivir en, habitar; estar interno; ~ *on* seguir viviendo; ~ *together* convivir; ~ *to see* (vivir bastante para) ver; presenciar; ~ *up to promise* cumplir; *standard* vivir (*or* ser) en conformidad con; ~ *up to one's income* gastarse toda la renta; ~ *within one's means* vivir con arreglo a los ingresos; *v*/*t. life* llevar; *experience* vivir; ~ *down* lograr borrar; ~ *out* vivir hasta el fin de; *life* pasar el resto de; **2.** [laiv] vivo; ardiente, encendido; *issue etc.* de actualidad; ⚡ con corriente; ⚔ cargado; ~ *coal* ascua *f*; ~ *weight* peso *m* en vivo; *sl.* ~ *wire* polvorilla *m*/*f*; ˈ**live·a·ble** = *livable*; **live·li·hood** [ˈlaivlihud] vida *f*, sustento *m*; **live·li·ness** [ˈ~linis] viveza *f*, vivacidad *f*; animación *f*; **live·long** [ˈlivlɔŋ] *lit.* duradero; *all the* ~ *day* todo el santo día; **live·ly** [ˈlaivli] vivo, vivaz; animado, bullicioso; alegre.
liv·en [ˈlaivən] avivar; animar.
liv·er[1] [ˈlivər]: *fast* ~ calavera *m*; *good* ~ goloso *m*.
liv·er[2] [~] hígado *m*.
liv·er·y [ˈlivəri] librea *f*; *poet.* vestiduras *f*/*pl.*; pensión *f* (*or* alquiler *m*)

de caballos; ~ *company* gremio *m de la Ciudad de Londres*; ~ *stable* caballeriza *f* (*or* cochera *f*) de alquiler.

lives [laivz] *pl. of life*; ˈ**live·stock** ganado *m*, ganadería *f*.

liv·id [ˈlivid] lívido; F furioso.

liv·ing [ˈliviŋ] **1.** vivo, viviente; vital; ~ *conditions* condiciones *f/pl.* de vida; *in* ~ *memory* de que hay memoria; que se recuerde; ~ *wage* jornal *m* suficiente para vivir; **2.** vida *f*; sustento *m*; modo *m* de vivir; *eccl.* beneficio *m*; *the* ~ los vivientes; *earn* (*or make*) *a* ~ ganarse la vida; ˈ~ **room** sala *f* de estar, living *m*; ˈ~ **space** espacio *m* vital *of a nation.*

liz·ard [ˈlizərd] lagarto *m*.

lla·ma [ˈlɑːmə] llama *f*.

lo [lou] *mst* ~ *and behold!* ¡he aquí!, ¡mirad!

loach [loutʃ] locha *f*.

load [loud] **1.** carga *f* (*a. fig.*, ⊕, ⚡); peso *m*; F ~*s pl.* gran cantidad *f*, montones *m/pl.*; ~ *test* prueba *f* de (*or* en) carga; **2.** *v/t.* cargar (*with* con, de); (*oppress*) agobiar (*with* con, de); (*favor*) colmar (*with* de); ~*ed question* intencionado; *dice* cargados; *v/i.* (*a.* ~ *up*) cargar(se); tomar carga; ˈ**load·er** cargador *m*; ˈ**load·ing 1.** cargamento *m*, carga *f*; **2.** de carga; cargador; ~ *zone* zona *f* de carga; ˈ**load line** línea *f* de (flotación con) carga; ˈ**load·stone** piedra *f* imán.

loaf[1] [louf] (*pl. loaves*) pan *m*; (*large*) hogaza *f*; ~ *sugar* azúcar *m* de pilón.

loaf[2] [~] F haraganear, gandulear.

loaf·er [ˈloufər] haragán (-a *f*) *m*, gandul (-a *f*) *m*; (*street*) azotacalles *m/f*.

loam [loum] marga *f*; ˈ**loam·y** margoso.

loan [loun] **1.** préstamo *m*; (*public*) empréstito *m*; *on* ~ prestado; *ask for the* ~ *of* pedir prestado *acc.*; **2.** prestar.

loath [louθ] poco dispuesto (*to* a); *be* ~ *for a p. to* no querer que una p. *subj.*; *nothing* ~ de buena gana; **loathe** [louð] abominar, detestar, aborrecer; *I* ~ *cheese* me da asco el queso; **loath·ing** [ˈ~ðiŋ] asco *m*, detestación *f*, repugnancia *f*; **loath·some** [ˈ~ðsəm] asqueroso, repugnante, nauseabundo; ˈ~**·ness** repugnancia *f*.

loaves [louvz] *pl. of loaf*[1].

lob [lɔb] *tennis*: **1.** voleo *m* alto; **2.** volear por alto.

lob·by [ˈlɔbi] **1.** vestíbulo *m*; pasillo *m*; antecámara *f*; *government*: camarilla *f* de cabilderos; **2.** *government*: cabildear; ˈ**lob·by·ist** *government*: cabildero *m*.

lobe [loub] *anat.*, ⚘ lóbulo *m*.

lob·ster [ˈlɔbstər] langosta *f*; bogavante *m*.

lo·cal [ˈloukəl] **1.** □ local; vecinal; *he's a* ~ *man* es de aquí; *teleph.* ~ *call* llamada *f* local; ~ *color* color *m* local; ~ *government* administración *f* local; **2.** 🚂 (*a.* ~ *train*) tren *m* ómnibus (*or* suburbano); F *the* ~ la taberna *f*; F ~*s pl.* vecindario *m*; **lo·cale** [louˈkæl] lugar *m*; escenario *m* (de acontecimientos); **lo·cal·i·ty** [~ˈkæliti] localidad *f*; situación *f*; **lo·cal·ize** [ˈ~kəlaiz] localizar.

lo·cate [louˈkeit] situar; colocar; localizar, hallar; *be* ~*d* estar situado, hallarse; **loˈca·tion** localidad *f*; situación *f*; colocación *f*; ubicación *f*; localización *f*; *film*: rodaje *m* fuera del estudio.

loch [lɔx] *Scot.* lago *m*; ría *f*.

lock[1] [lɔk] **1.** cerradura *f*; traba *f*; retén *m*; (*wrestling a.* ⚔) llave *f*; esclusa *f on canal etc.*; F ~, *stock and barrel* por completo; *under* ~ *and key* bajo llave; **2.** *v/t.* cerrar con llave; encerrar; ⊕ trabar, enclavar; ~ *in* encerrar; ~ *out* cerrar la puerta a; ~ *up* encerrar; encarcelar; *capital* inmovilizar; *v/i.* cerrarse con llave; ⊕ trabarse; ~ *up* echar la llave.

lock[2] [~] mechón *m*; guedeja *f*; bucle *m*; ~*s pl.* cabellos *m/pl.*

lock·er [ˈlɔkər] armario *m* (particular); cajón *m* cerrado con llave; **lock·et** [ˈ~it] medallón *m*, guardapelo *m*.

lock...: ˈ~ ˈ**gate** puerta *f* de esclusa; ˈ~**·jaw** trismo *m*; ˈ~ **keep·er** esclusero *m*; ˈ~**·nut** contratuerca *f*; ˈ~ˈ**out** cierre *m*, paro *m* voluntario de patronos; ˈ~**·smith** cerrajero *m*; ˈ~**·stitch** punto *m* de cadeneta; ˈ~**·up 1.** cierre *m*; cárcel *f*; **2.** con cerradura.

lo·co [ˈloukou] *sl.* loco.

lo·co·mo·tion [loukəˈmouʃn] locomoción *f*; **lo·co·mo·tive** [ˈ~tiv] **1.** locomotora *f*; **2.** locomotor.

lo·cum (**te·nens**) ['loukəm ('tenənz)] interino (a *f*) *m*.
lo·cust ['loukəst] langosta *f* (*a. fig.*); ⚘ (*a.* ~ *tree*) acacia *f* falsa, algarrobo *m*.
lo·cu·tion [lou'kju:ʃn] locución *f*.
lode [loud] filón *m*; '**~·star** estrella *f* polar; *fig.* norte *m*; '**~·stone** piedra *f* imán.
lodge [lɔdʒ] **1.** casita *f*; casa *f* de campo; casa *f* de guarda; (*porter's*) portería *f*; (*masonic*) logia *f*; **2.** *v/t.* alojar, hospedar; colocar, depositar; introducir; *complaint* formular; *v/i.* alojarse; hospedarse; ir a parar; fijarse; '**lodg·er** huésped (-a *f*) *m*; '**lodg·ing** alojamiento *m*, hospedaje *m*; (*a.* ~*s pl.*) habitación *f*, aposento *m*; (*without board*) cobijo *m*; '**lodg·ing house** casa *f* de huéspedes; '**lodg·ment** alojamiento *m*; depósito *m*; ⚔ posición *f* ganada.
loft [lɔft] desván *m*; pajar *m for straw*; *eccl.* galería *f*; **loft·i·ness** ['~inis] altura *f*; eminencia *f*; nobleza *f*; altanería *f*; '**loft·y** □ alto, elevado; eminente; noble; sublime; altanero.
log [lɔg] **1.** leño *m*, tronco *m*, troza *f*; ⚓ corredera *f*; = ~*book*; *v. sleep*; **2.** cortar (y transportar) leños; apuntar, registrar.
log·a·rithm ['lɔgəriθm] logaritmo *m*.
log...: '**~·book** ⚓ cuaderno *m* de bitácora, diario *m* de navegación; ✈ libro *m* de vuelo(s); ⊕ cuaderno *m* de trabajo; '**~ cab·in** cabaña *f* de madera; **log·ger·head** ['lɔgərhed]: *be at* ~*s* estar de pique; '**log·ging** explotación *f* forestal; transporte *m* de leños.
log·ic ['lɔdʒik] lógica *f*; '**log·i·cal** □ lógico; **lo·gi·cian** [lɔ'dʒiʃən] lógico (a *f*) *m*; **lo·gis·tic** [lɔ'dʒistik] logístico; ~*s* logística *f*.
log·roll·ing ['lɔgrouliŋ] F toma y daca *m*; sistema *m* de bombos mutuos; *pol.* trueque *m* de favores políticos.
loin [lɔin] ijada *f*; lomo *m* (*a. of meat*); *gird up one's* ~*s fig.* apercibirse para la lucha; '**~·cloth** taparrabo *m*.
loi·ter ['lɔitər] holgazanear, perder el tiempo; rezagarse; vagar; '**loi·ter·er** holgazán (-a *f*) *m*; vago (a *f*) *m*; rezagado (a *f*) *m*.
loll [lɔl] repantigarse (*a.* ~ *about*); apoyarse con indolencia (*against*, *on* en); (*tongue*) colgar hacia fuera.
lol·li·pop ['lɔlipɔp] F gilda *f*.
lol·lop ['lɔləp] F correr (*or* moverse) torpemente, arrastrar los pies.
lol·ly ['lɔli] *sl.* parné *m*.
Lom·bard ['lɔmbərd] lombardo *adj. a. su. m* (a *f*).
Lon·don ['lʌndən] *adj.* londinense; '**Lon·don·er** londinense *m/f*.
lone [loun] solo, solitario; soltero; aislado; '**lone·li·ness** soledad *f*; '**lone·ly, lone·some** ['~səm] solitario, solo; aislado, remoto; '**lone 'wolf** *mst fig.* lobo *m* solitario.
long[1] [lɔŋ] **1.** *adj.* largo; extenso; prolongado; F alto; *it is 4 feet* ~ tiene 4 pies de largo; *be* ~ *in ger.* tardar en *inf.*; † *at* ~ *date* a largo plazo; *in the* ~ *run* a la larga; ~ *wave radio*: (de) onda *f* larga; *it is a* ~ *way* (*away*, *off*) está muy lejos, dista mucho; **2.** *su.* largo (*or* mucho) tiempo *m*; *the* ~ *and the short of it is* (*that*) en resumidas cuentas; *before* ~ en breve, dentro de poco; *for* ~ largo (*or* mucho) tiempo; *take* ~ *to inf.* tardar en *inf.*; **3.** *adv.* largo (*or* mucho) tiempo; largo rato; largamente; ~ *before* mucho antes; *as* ~ *as* mientras; con tal que *subj.*; *as* ~ *ago as 1950* ya en 1950; F *so* ~*!* ¡hasta luego!; *so* ~ *as* con tal que; ~*er* más tiempo; *how much* ~*er?* ¿cuánto tiempo más?; *no* ~*er* ya no; no más.
long[2] [~] anhelar (*for acc.*, *to inf.*), suspirar (*for*, *to* por).
long...: '**~·boat** lancha *f*; '**~·bow** arco *m*; '**~-'dat·ed** a largo plazo; '**~-'dis·tance** a (larga *or* gran) distancia; *sport*: de fondo; *teleph.* ~ *call* conferencia *f* interurbana; ~ *flight* vuelo *m* a distancia; **lon·gev·i·ty** [lɔn'dʒeviti] longevidad *f*; '**long·hair** *sl.* erudito; aficionado a la música clásica *adj. a. su.*; '**long·hand** escritura *f* normal (*or* sin abreviaturas).
long·ing ['lɔŋiŋ] **1.** anhelo *m*, añoranza *f*, ansia *f* (*for* de); **2.** □ anhelante.
long·ish ['lɔŋiʃ] algo (*or* bastante) largo.
lon·gi·tude ['lɔndʒitju:d] longitud *f*; **lon·gi'tu·di·nal** [~inl] □ longitudinal.
long...: '**~ johns** F ropa *f* interior que cubre brazos y piernas; '**~ 'jump** salto *m* de longitud; '**~-'leg·ged** zancudo; **~-lived** ['~'laivd, F '~-

ˈlivd] de larga vida, duradero; ˈ~-ˈ**play·ing** de larga duración; ˈ~-ˈ**range** ⚔ de gran alcance; ✈ de gran autonomía; ˈ**~·shore·man** estibador *m*, obrero *m* portuario; ˈ~-ˈ**sight·ed** présbita; *fig.* previsor, sagaz; ˈ~-ˈ**stand·ing** existente desde hace mucho tiempo; ˈ~-ˈ**suf·fer·ing** sufrido; ˈ~-ˈ**term** a largo plazo; ˈ**~·ways** longitudinalmente, a lo largo; ˈ~-ˈ**wind·ed** □ prolijo.

loo [luː] *sl.* retrete *m.*

look [luk] **1.** mirada *f*, vistazo *m*; (*a.* ~*s pl.*) aspecto *m*, apariencia *f*; aire *m*; *good* ~*s pl.* buen parecer *m*; *by the* ~ *of things* por lo visto; F *get* (*or have*) *a* ~ *in* poder participar; tener posibilidad de ganar; *have* (*or take*) *a* ~ *at* echar un vistazo a; *have a* ~ *for* buscar; *I like the* ~ *of him* me hace buena impresión; **2.** *v/i.* mirar; parecer; tener aire (de); buscar; considerar; ~ *before you leap* antes que te cases, mira lo que haces; ~ *here!* ¡oye!; ~ *like* parecerse a; *it* ~*s like rain* parece que va a llover; ~ *well* (*p.*) tener buena cara; *it* ~*s well on you* te sienta bien; ~ *about* mirar alrededor; ~ *about for* andar buscando; ~ *about one* mirar a su alrededor; *fig.* considerar las cosas con calma; ~ *after* ocuparse de, cuidar de; ~ *at* mirar; ~ *away* desviar los ojos; ~ *back* mirar hacia atrás; *fig.* volverse atrás; ~ *back on* recordar, evocar; ~ *down on* dominar; *fig.* mirar por encima del hombro, despreciar; ~ *for* buscar; esperar; ~ *forward to* anticipar con placer, esperar con ilusión; F ~ *in* hacer una visita breve (*on* a), pasar por la casa *etc.* (*on* de); mirar la televisión; ~ *into* investigar, examinar; ~ *on* mirar, estar de mirón; ~ *on to* caer a, dar a; ~ *out!* ¡cuidado!, ¡ojo!; ~ *out for* buscar; estar a la expectativa de; tener cuidado con; ~ *out of window* mirar por; ~ *out on* dar a, caer a; ~ *round* volver la cabeza; = ~ *about*; ~ *through window* mirar por; *book* hojear; (*search*) rebuscar entre, registrar; ~ *to* ocuparse de, mirar por; *p.* contar con, acudir a; tener puestas las esperanzas en; ~ *to a p. to inf.* esperar que una p. *subj.*; ~ *up* levantar los ojos; F mejorar; ~ (*up*)*on fig.* considerar, estimar; ~ *up to* respetar, admirar; **3.** *v/t. emotion* expresar con la mirada; *age* representar; ~ *a p. in the face* mirar a una p. cara a cara (*a. fig.*); ~ *out* buscar; escoger; ~ *over* examinar; recorrer; ~ *up* buscar, averiguar, consultar; F visitar; ~ *a p. up and down* mirar a una p. de arriba abajo; ˈ**~·a·like** doble; parecido *adj. a. su. m* (a *f*).

look·er-on [ˈlukərˈɔn] espectador (-a *f*) *m*, mirón (-a *f*) *m*; curioso *m.*

look·ing glass [ˈlukiŋglæs] espejo *m.*

look·out [ˈlukˈaut] (*p.*) vigía *m*, atalaya *m*; (*tower*) atalaya *f*; observación *f*, vigilancia *f*; perspectiva *f*; *be on the* ~ (*for*) estar a la mira (de); F *a poor* ~ *for* mala perspectiva para; F *that's his* ~ ¡eso a él!, ¡allá él!; ˈ**look-o·ver** *sl.* vistazo *m*; ojeada *f.*

loom[1] [luːm] telar *m.*

loom[2] [~] surgir, asomar(se), aparecer (*a.* ~ *up*); vislumbrarse; *fig.* amenazar; ~ *large* abultar; *fig.* ser (*or* parecer) de gran importancia.

loon [luːn] *Scot.* patán *m*; granuja *m*; tipo *m.*

loon·y [ˈluːni] *sl.* loco *adj. a. su. m* (a *f*); ˈ**~ bin** *sl.* manicomio *m.*

loop [luːp] **1.** gaza *f*, lazo *m*; (*fastening*) presilla *f*; (*bend*) curva *f*, vuelta *f*, recodo *m*; ⚡ circuito *m* cerrado; *radio*: ~ *aerial* antena *f* de cuadro; **2.** *v/t.* hacer gaza con; asegurar con gaza (*or* presilla); enlazar; ✈ ~ *the* ~ hacer (*or* rizar) el rizo; *v/i.* formar lazo(s); serpentear; ˈ**~·hole** ⚔ aspillera *f*, tronera *f*; *fig.* escapatoria *f*, evasiva *f*; ˈ**~ line** 🚂 vía *f* apartadero, vía *f* de circunvalación; ⚡ circuito *m* en bucle.

loose [luːs] **1.** □ (*free*; *separate*) suelto, desatado; (*not tight*) flojo, movedizo; (*unpacked*) sin envase; *dress* holgado; *wheel, pulley etc.* loco; *connexion* desconectado; poco exacto; aproximado; negligente; *thinking* ilógico, incoherente; *morals* relajado; *woman* fácil; ⚕ suelto de vientre; ~ *change* suelto *m*; ~ *end* cabo *m* suelto; *be at a* ~ *end* estar desocupado; *become* (*or get, work*) ~ aflojarse, desatarse; *break* ~ desatarse; escaparse; *fig.* desencadenarse; *cast* (*or let, set, turn*) ~ soltar; **2.** soltar; desatar; aflojar; (*a.* ~ *off*) disparar; ~ *one's hold on* soltar; **3.**: F *be on the* ~ estar en

libertad; estar de juerga; **ˈ~-leaf:** ~ *book* cuaderno *m* de hojas sueltas (*or* movibles); **loos·en** [ˈlu:sn] desatar(se), aflojar(se), soltar(se); ~ *up muscles* desentumecer; **ˈloose·ness** soltura *f*; flojedad *f*; holgura *f*; relajación *f*; ⚕ diarrea *f*.
loot [lu:t] **1.** botín *m*; F ganancias *f/pl.*; **2.** saquear, pillar; **ˈloot·er** saqueador (-a *f*) *m*.
lop [lɔp] *tree* (des)mochar; cercenar; ~ *away, off* cortar.
lope [loup] ir a medio galope, correr a paso largo.
lop...: **ˈ~-eared** de orejas caídas; **ˈ~ˈsid·ed** desproporcionado; ladeado; desequilibrado (*a. fig.*).
lo·qua·cious [louˈkweiʃəs] □ locuaz; **lo·quac·i·ty** [louˈkwæsiti] locuacidad *f*.
lo·ran [ˈlɔ:rən] ⚓ lorán *m*.
lord [lɔ:rd] **1.** señor *m*; (*title*) lord *m*; *the* ♀ el Señor; *my* ~ señor; Su Señoría; ♀*'s Prayer* padrenuestro *m*; ♀*'s Supper* (última) Cena *f*, *parl. the* (*House of*) ♀*s* (la Cámara de) los Lores; **2.:** ~ *it* hacer el señor; mandar despóticamente; ~ *it over* señorear, dominar; **ˈlord·li·ness** señorío *m*; altivez *f*; suntuosidad *f*; **ˈlord·ly** señoril; altivo; imperioso; espléndido; **ˈlord·ship** (*title*) señoría *f*; (*rule*) señorío *m*.
lore [lɔ:r] saber *m* (popular), ciencia *f*.
lor·gnette [lɔ:rnˈjet] impertinentes *m/pl*.
lose [lu:z] [*irr.*] *v/t.* perder; hacer perder; *that lost us the war* eso nos hizo perder la guerra; ~ *o.s.* perderse, errar el camino; *fig.* ensimismarse; *fig.* confundirse; *v/i.* perder; ser vencido; (*clock*) atrasar; **ˈlos·er** perdidoso (a *f*) *m*, perdedor (-a *f*) *m*; *sl.* persona *f* sin atractivo; F *come off the* ~ salir perdiendo; **ˈlos·ing** perdidoso; *team* vencido.
loss [lɔs] pérdida *f*; F *be a dead* ~ ser inútil; ser una nulidad; *be a total* ~ considerarse totalmente perdido; *at a* ~ ✝ con pérdida; *be at a* ~ estar perplejo, no saber qué hacer; *be at a* ~ *for* no encontrar; *be at a* ~ *to inf.* no saber cómo *inf.*; **ˈ~ lead·er** artículo *m* vendido a gran descuento.
lost [lɔst] *pret. a p.p. of lose*; ~ *in* abismado en, absorto en; *be* ~ *on a p.* no aprovechar a una p.; pasar inadvertido por una p.; ~ *to* insensible a; inaccesible a; **ˈ~-ˈprop·er·ty of·fice** oficina *f* de objetos perdidos.
lot [lɔt] ✝ lote *m*; porción *f*; (*fate*) suerte *f*; solar *m for building*; F gran cantidad *f*; F (*p.*) sujeto *m*, tipo *m*; F *a* ~ *of*, ~*s of* mucho, la mar de; F *a* ~ *of people* mucha gente; F *a bad* ~ un mal sujeto; *draw* ~*s* echar suertes; *fall to a p.'s* ~ caerle a una p. en suerte; incumbirle a una p.; F *the* ~ todo; *throw in one's* ~ *with* unirse a la suerte de.
lo·tion [ˈlouʃn] loción *f*.
lot·ter·y [ˈlɔtəri] lotería *f*.
lo·tus [ˈloutəs] loto *m*.
loud [laud] □ alto; fuerte, recio; ruidoso, estrepitoso; *color* chillón; (*in bad taste*) charro, cursi; **ˈloud-mouth** bocón *m* (-a *f*); **ˈloud·ness** (gran) ruido *m*; sonoridad *f*; fuerza *f*; *fig.* mal gusto *m*; **loudˈspeak·er** altavoz *m*, altoparlante *m*
lounge [laundʒ] **1.** salón *m*; sala *f* (de estar); sofá *m*; ~ *suit* traje *m* de calle; **2.** arrellanarse, repantigarse; pasearse perezosamente; haraganear; ~ *about* tirarse a la bartola; **ˈloung·er** haragán (-a *f*) *m*; azotacalles *m/f*.
lour [ˈlauər] *v. lower*².
louse [laus] (*pl. lice*) piojo *m*; **lous·y** [ˈlauzi] piojoso; *sl.* asqueroso, vil, malísimo.
lout [laut] patán *m*; gamberro *m*; **ˈlout·ish** grosero, zafio.
lov·a·ble [ˈlʌvəbl] □ amable.
love [lʌv] **1.** amor *m* (*of, for, towards* de, a); querer *m*; cariño *m*; (*p.*) amado (a *f*) *m*, querido (a *f*) *m*; afición *f*; F monada *f*, preciosidad *f*; *tennis*: cero *m*; *attr.* de amor, amoroso; *for* ~ por amor; F gratis; *for the* ~ *of* por el amor de; *give* (*or send*) *one's* ~ *to* (*in letters*) mandar cariñosos saludos a; *in* ~ *with* enamorado de; *fall in* ~ enamorarse (*with* de); *make* ~ *to* hacer el amor a; cortejar; F *not for* ~ *nor money* por nada del mundo; **2.** amar, querer, tener cariño a; ser muy aficionado a; *I would* ~ *to inf.* me gustaría mucho *inf.*; **ˈ~ af·fair** amores *m/pl.*; amorío(s) *m*(*pl.*) (F); **ˈ~·bird** periquito *m*; *fig.* palomito *m*; **ˈ~ child** hijo (a *f*) *m* del amor; **ˈ~ feast** ágape *m*; **ˈlove·less** sin amor; **ˈlove let·ter** carta *f* de amor; **ˈlove·li·ness** belleza *f*, hermosura *f*; encanto *m*; exquisitez *f*; **love·lorn** [ˈ~lɔ:rn] suspirando de amor, aban-

donado de su amante; ˈ**love·ly** bello, hermoso; encantador; exquisito; precioso; simpático; ˈ**love-making** galanteo *m*; trato *m* sexual; ˈ**love match** matrimonio *m* por amor; ˈ**lov·er** amante *m/f*; aficionado (a *f*) *m* (*of* a), amigo (a *f*) *m* (*of* de); *~s pl.* amantes *m/pl.*, novios *m/pl.*; ˈ**lovesick** enfermo de amor, amartelado.

lov·ing [ˈlʌviŋ] □ amoroso, amante; cariñoso.

low[1] [lou] **1.** bajo; *bow* profundo; *blow* sucio; *dress* escotado; *price* módico; *stocks* escaso; *diet* deficiente; ♪ grave; *spirits* abatido; *health* débil, gravemente enfermo; *rank* humilde; *manners* grosero; *character* vil, rastrero; *joke* verde; *opinion* malo; *~ comedy* farsa *f*; *~ trick* partida *f* serrana; F *be ~ on* estar escaso de; **2.** *meteor.* área *f* de baja presión; F punto *m* bajo; *mot.* primera marcha *f*; **3.** *adv.* bajo; bajamente; en voz baja.

low[2] [~] **1.** mugir; **2.** mugido *m*.

low...: ˈ**~born** de humilde cuna; ˈ**~brow** F (persona *f*) nada intelectual; ˈ**~-ˈcost** económico; ˈ**~-ˈdown** **1.** bajo, vil; **2.** [ˈ~] *sl.* verdad *f*, informes *m/pl.* confidenciales; pormenores *m/pl.*

low·er[1] [ˈlouər] **1.** más bajo *etc.* (*v. low*); inferior; bajo; *~ classes* clase *f* baja; **2.** bajar; disminuir; *price* rebajar; ⚓ arriar; ⚕ debilitar; abatir; humillar; *~ one's guard* aflojar la guardia.

low·er[2] [ˈlauər] fruncir el entrecejo, mirar con ceño; (*sky*) encapotarse; ˈ**low·er·ing** ceñudo; encapotado; amenazador.

low-key [ˈlouki:] modesto; moderado; retirado; **low·land** [ˈlouland] tierra *f* baja; **low life** gentuza *f*; ˈ**low·li·ness** humildad *f*; ˈ**low·ly** humilde; ˈ**low-ˈnecked** escotado; ˈ**low·ness** bajeza *f etc.*; ˈ**low-ˈpressure** de baja presión; ˈ**low-ˈtension** de baja tensión.

loy·al [ˈlɔiəl] □ leal, fiel; ˈ**loy·al·ist** legitimista *adj. a. su. m/f*, gubernamental *adj. a. su. m/f*; *Spain*: republicano *adj. a. su. m* (a *f*); ˈ**loy·al·ty** lealtad *f*, fidelidad *f*.

loz·enge [ˈlɔzindʒ] pastilla *f*; ⚜ *a. heraldry*: losange *m*.

lub·ber [ˈlʌbər] ⚓ marinero *m* de agua dulce; bobalicón *m*; ˈ**lub·ber·ly** torpe, tosco.

lu·bri·cant [ˈlu:brikənt] lubri(fi)cante *adj. a. su. m*; **lu·bri·cate** [ˈ~keit] lubri(fi)car, engrasar; **lu·briˈca·tion** lubri(fi)cación *f*, engrase *m*; ˈ**lu·bri·ca·tor** lubri(fi)cador *m*; **lu·bric·i·ty** [lu:ˈbrisiti] lubricidad *f*.

lu·cerne [luˈsə:rn] alfalfa *f*.

lu·cid [ˈlusid] □ lúcido; **luˈcid·i·ty** lucidez *f*.

luck [lʌk] suerte *f*, ventura *f*; fortuna *f*; azar *m*; *good ~* (buena) suerte *f*; *bad ~, hard ~, ill ~* mala suerte *f*; *be in ~* estar de suerte; F *be down on one's ~, be out of ~* estar de malas; *no such ~!* ¡ojalá!; *try one's ~* probar fortuna; *with any ~* a lo mejor; ˈ**luck·i·ly** afortunadamente, por fortuna; ˈ**luck·less** desafortunado, desdichado; ˈ**luck·y** □ afortunado; de buen agüero; *be ~* tener (buena) suerte; tener buena sombra; *~ hit, ~ break* racha *f* de suerte, chiripa *f*.

lu·cra·tive [ˈlu:krətiv] □ lucrativo, provechoso; **lu·cre** [ˈlu:kər] † lucro *m*; *filthy ~* el vil metal.

lu·cu·bra·tion [lu:kjuˈbreiʃn] lucubración *f*.

lu·di·crous [ˈlu:dikrəs] □ absurdo, ridículo.

luff [lʌf] **1.** orza *f*; **2.** orzar.

lug [lʌg] **1.** oreja *f*; ⊕ orejeta *f*; agarradera *f*; (*movement*) (es)tirón *m*; **2.** arrastrar; tirar de; F *~ about* llevar consigo (con dificultad) ; *fig. ~ in* traer a colación.

lug·gage [ˈlʌgidʒ] equipaje *m*; ˈ**~ boot** maleta *f*; ˈ**~ car·ri·er,** ˈ**~ grid** portaequipajes *m*; ˈ**~ rack** rejilla *f*; ˈ**~ van** furgón *m* de equipajes.

lug·ger [ˈlʌgər] lugre *m*.

lu·gu·bri·ous [lu:ˈgju:briəs] □ lúgubre.

luke·warm [ˈlu:kwɔ:rm] tibio (*a. fig.*), templado; *fig.* indiferente; ˈ**~ness** tibieza *f*.

lull [lʌl] recalmón *m*, intervalo *m* de calma; *fig.* tregua *f*, respiro *m*.

lull·a·by [ˈlʌləbai] nana *f*, canción *f* de cuna.

lum·ba·go [lʌmˈbeigou] lumbago *m*.

lum·ber [ˈlʌmbər] **1.** maderos *m/pl.*, maderas *f/pl.* (de sierra); trastos *m/pl.* viejos; **2.** moverse pesadamente (*or* con ruido sordo); cortar árboles; ˈ**lum·ber·ing** pesado; ˈ**lum·ber·jack,** ˈ**lum·ber·man** hachero

m, maderero *m*, leñador *m*; ˈ**lum·ber room** trastera *f*; ˈ**lum·ber·yard** corral *m* de madera.
lu·mi·nar·y [ˈlu:minəri] lumbrera *f*; *p.* celebridad *f*; ˈ**lu·mi·nous** □ luminoso.
lump [lʌmp] **1.** terrón *m* (*a. of sugar*); masa *f*; borujo *m*; (*swelling*) bulto *m*, hinchazón *f*; protuberancia *f*; (*pellet*) pella *f*; (*p.*) zoquete *m*; nudo *m in throat*; ~ *sugar* azúcar *m* en terrón; ~ *sum* suma *f* global; **2.** *v/t.* amontonar; aborujar; F aguantar, tragar; ~ *together* agrupar, mezclar; *v/i.* aborujarse; ˈ**lump·ing** F grueso, pesado; ˈ**lump·ish** torpe, pesado; ˈ**lump·y** □ aterronado; borujoso; *sea* agitado, picado.
lu·na·cy [ˈlu:nəsi] locura *f*.
lu·nar [ˈlu:nər] lunar; ~ ˈ**land·ing** alunizaje *m*; ~ ˈ**mod·ule** (*semi-independent spaceship*) módulo *m* lunar; ~ ˈ**walk** caminata *f* en la luna.
lu·na·tic [ˈlu:nətik] loco *adj. a. su. m* (*a f*), demente *adj. a. su. m/f*, ~ *asylum* manicomio *m*; F ~ *fringe* elementos *m/pl.* fanáticos (y estrafalarios).
lunch [lʌntʃ] **1.** almuerzo *m*, comida *f* (*a. more formally* ˈ**lunch·eon** [ˈ~ən]); lonche *m S.Am.*; (*snack*) bocadillo *m*, merienda *f*; **2.** almorzar, comer; tomar un bocadillo, merendar; ˈ**lunch hour** hora *f* del almuerzo.
lung [lʌŋ] pulmón *m*; ~ *cancer* cáncer *m* pulmonar.
lunge [lʌndʒ] **1.** *fenc.* estocada *f*; arremetida *f*; **2.** dar una estocada; arremeter (*at* contra).
lu·pin(**e**) [ˈlu:pin] altramuz *m*.
lurch¹ [lə:rtʃ] **1.** sacudida *f*, tumbo *m*, tambaleo *m* repentino; **2.** dar sacudidas, dar un tumbo, tambalearse.
lurch² [~]: *leave in the* ~ dejar plantado.
lure [lur] **1.** cebo *m*; señuelo *m* (*a. fig.*); aliciente *m*, seducción *f*; **2.** atraer (con señuelo); tentar; seducir.
lu·rid [ˈlurid] □ *color of skin etc.* lívido, cárdeno; *dress etc.* chillón; *account* sensacional; *detail* espeluznante.
lurk [lə:rk] ocultarse; estar en acecho; moverse furtivamente.
lus·cious [ˈlʌʃəs] □ delicioso, rico, exquisito, suculento; *b.s.* empalagoso.
lush [lʌʃ] jugoso, lozano.
lust [lʌst] **1.** lujuria *f*, lascivia *f*; (*greed*) codicia *f*; **2.** lujuriar; ~ *after* codiciar; ˈ**lust·ful** □ lujurioso, lascivo.
lus·ter [ˈlʌstər] lustre *m*, brillo *m*; ˈ**lus·ter·less** sin brillo, deslustrado; sin lustre.
lus·trous [ˈlʌstrəs] □ lustroso.
lust·y [ˈlʌsti] □ vigoroso, fornido, robusto; lozano.
lute [lu:t] ♪ laúd *m*.
Lu·ther·an [ˈlu:θərən] luterano *adj. a. su. m* (*a f*); ˈ**Lu·ther·an·ism** luteranismo *m*.
lux·u·ri·ance [lʌgˈʒuriəns] lozanía *f*, exuberancia *f*; **lux**ˈ**u·ri·ant** □ lozano, exuberante; **lux**ˈ**u·ri·ate** [~rieit] crecer con exuberancia; deleitarse (*in* con), entregarse al lujo (*in* de); **lux**ˈ**u·ri·ous** [~riəs] □ lujoso; **lux·u·ry** [ˈlʌkʃəri] lujo *m*; *attr.* de lujo.
ly·ce·um [laiˈsiəm] liceo *m*.
lye [lai] lejía *f*.
ly·ing [ˈlaiiŋ] **1.** *ger. of lie*¹ *a. lie*²; **2.** *adj.* mentiroso; ˈ~-ˈ**in** parto *m*; ~ *hospital* casa *f* de maternidad.
lymph [limf] linfa *f* (*a. poet.*); **lym·phat·ic** [~ˈfætik] □ (vaso *m*) linfático.
lynch [lintʃ] linchar; ˈ~ **law** ley *f* de Lynch; ley *f* de la soga.
lynx [liŋks] lince *m*; *be* ~*-eyed* tener ojos de lince.
lyre [ˈlaiər] lira *f*.
lyr·ic [ˈlirik] **1.** lírico; **2.** poesía *f* lírica; letra *f* (de una canción); ˈ**lyr·i·cal** □ lírico; F elocuente, entusiasmado.

M

ma [mɑː] F mamá *f*.
ma'am [mæm, F məm, m] = *madam*.
ma·ca·bre [məˈkɑːbr] macabro.
mac·ad·am [məˈkædəm] macadán *m*; **macˈad·am·ize** macadamizar.
mac·a·ro·ni [mækəˈrouni] macarrones *m/pl*.
mac·a·roon [mækəˈruːn] macarrón *m* (de almendras), mostachón *m*.
mace [meis] maza *f*; (*spice*) macis *f*; ˈ**~ bear·er** macero *m*.
mac·er·ate [ˈmæsəreit] macerar(se); **mac·erˈa·tion** maceración *f*.
mach·i·na·tion [mækiˈneiʃn] maquinación *f*; **mach·i·na·tor** [ˈ~tər] maquinador (-a *f*) *m*; **ma·chine** [məˈʃiːn] **1.** máquina *f* (*a. fig.*); aparato *m*; *mot.* coche *m*; (*cycle*) bicicleta *f*; ✈ avión *m*; *pol.* organización *f*, camarilla *f*; *attr.* mecánico, a máquina; ~ *fitter* montador *m*; **2.** elaborar (*or* acabar, coser) a máquina; **maˈchine gun 1.** ametralladora *f*; **2.** ametrallar; **maˈchine-made** hecho a máquina; **maˈchin·er·y** maquinaria *f*; mecanismo *m* (*a. fig.*); **maˈchine·shop** taller *m* de máquinas; **maˈchine tool** máquina herramienta *f*; **maˈchine trans·la·tion** traducción *f* automática; **maˈchine-wash·able** lavable en lavadora automática; **maˈchin·ist** maquinista *m/f*, operario (a *f*) *m* de máquina, mecánico *m*.
mack·er·el [ˈmækrəl] caballa *f*; escombro *m*; ˈ**~ˈsky** cielo *m* aborregado.
mack·in·tosh [ˈmækintɔʃ] impermeable *m*.
mac·ro... [ˈmækrou] macro...
mad [mæːd] □ loco, demente; F furioso; *dog* rabioso; *idea* insensato; F *be ~ about* (*on, for*) estar loco por, ser muy aficionado a; F *be ~ about* (*or at*) estar furioso con (*or* contra, por); *drive ~* enloquecer, volver loco; F *get ~* encolerizarse; *go ~* volverse loco, enloquecer; F *like ~* como un loco.
mad·am [ˈmædəm] señora *f*; F niña *f* precoz, niña *f* repipi.
mad·cap [ˈmædkæp] **1.** locuelo (a *f*) *m*, tarambana *m/f*; **2.** atolondrado;
mad·den [ˈmædn] enloquecer; enfurecer; *it's ~ing* es para volverse loco.
made [meid] *pret. a. p.p. of make* 1; ˈ**~-to-or·der** hecho a la medida.
made-up [ˈmeidˈʌp] hecho; compuesto; *story* ficticio; *face* pintado, maquillado; *dress* confeccionado.
mad·house [ˈmædhaus] manicomio *m*; casa *f* de locos (*a. fig.*); situación *f* caótica; ˈ**mad·man** loco *m*; lunático *m*; ˈ**mad·ness** locura *f*, demencia *f*; rabia *f*; furia *f*.
mad·ri·gal [ˈmædrigəl] madrigal *m*.
mael·strom [ˈmeilstroum] remolino *m*, vórtice *m*.
mag·a·zine [ˈmægəziːn, mægəˈziːn] revista *f*; ⚔ almacén *m*; ⚔ polvorín *m for powder*; ⚓ santabárbara *f*.
ma·gen·ta [məˈdʒentə] magenta *f*.
mag·got [ˈmægət] cresa *f*, gusano *m*; ˈ**mag·got·y** agusanado.
mag·ic [ˈmædʒik] **1.** magia *f*; *as if by ~* (como) por ensalmo; **2.** mágico; *v. lantern*; *~ wand* varilla *f* de virtudes; ˈ**mag·i·cal** □ mágico; **ma·gi·cian** [məˈdʒiʃn] mágico *m*, mago *m*; (*conjuror*) prestidigitador *m*.
mag·is·te·ri·al [mædʒisˈtiriəl] □ magistral; **mag·is·tra·cy** [ˈ~trəsi] magistratura *f*; **mag·is·trate** [ˈ~trit] magistrado *m*; juez *m* (municipal).
mag·na·nim·i·ty [mægnəˈnimiti] magnanimidad *f*; **mag·nan·i·mous** [~ˈnæniməs] magnánimo.
mag·nate [ˈmægneit] magnate *m*.
mag·ne·sia [mægˈniːʃə] magnesia *f*;
magˈne·sium [~ziəm] magnesio *m*.
mag·net [ˈmægnit] imán *m*; **mag·net·ic** [~ˈnetik] □ magnético; **mag·net·ism** [ˈ~nitizm] magnetismo *m*; **mag·net·i·za·tion** [~taiˈzeiʃn] magnetización *f*, iman(t)ación *f*; ˈ**mag·net·ize** magnetizar, iman(t)ar;
mag·ne·to [mægˈniːtou] magneto *f*.
mag·nif·i·ca·tion [mægnifiˈkeiʃn]

opt. (*high* gran, *low* pequeño) aumento *m*, (*high* alto, *low* bajo) enfoque *m*; *fig.* exageración *f*.

mag·nif·i·cence [mægˈnifisns] magnificencia *f*; **magˈnif·i·cent** magnífico; **mag·ni·fy** [ˈ~fai] *opt.* aumentar, magnificar; agrandar; *fig.* exagerar; *~ing glass* lupa *f*, lente *f* de aumento; **mag·ni·tude** [ˈ~tjuːd] magnitud *f*; *star of the first ~* estrella *f* de primera magnitud.

mag·no·li·a [mægˈnouljə] magnolia *f*.

mag·pie [ˈmægpai] urraca *f*, marica *f*.

ma·hog·a·ny [məˈhɔgəni] caoba *f*.

Ma·hom·et·an [məˈhɔmitən] mahometano *adj. a. su. m* (a *f*).

maid [meid] criada *f*, camarera *f*; *mst lit.* doncella *f*, virgen *f*; muchacha *f*; soltera *f*; *~ of honor* dama *f* de honor; *mst contp. old ~* solterona *f*.

maid·en [ˈmeidn] **1.** *mst lit.* doncella *f*, virgen *f*; muchacha *f*; soltera *f*; **2.** virginal, intacto; (de) soltera; *speech* primero; *voyage* inaugural; *~ name* apellido *m* de soltera; **ˈ~·hair** ⚘ culantrillo *m*, cabellos *m/pl.* de Venus; **ˈ~·head** doncellez *f*; himen *m*; **ˈ~·hood** doncellez *f*; **ˈmaid·en·ly** virginal; recatado, modesto.

maid-of-all-work [ˈmeidəvˈɔːlwɔːrk] criada *f* para todo; **ˈmaid-serv·ant** criada *f*, sirvienta *f*.

mail[1] [meil] ⚔ (cota *f* de) malla *f*.

mail[2] [~] **1.** ✉ correo *m*; correspondencia *f*; mala *f*; **2.** echar al correo, despachar; enviar (por correo).

mail...: **ˈ~bag** valija *f*, mala *f*; **ˈ~ boat** vapor *m* correo; **ˈ~·box** buzón *m*; **ˈ~ car·ri·er** cartero *m*; **ˈ~ coach** diligencia *f*, coche *m* correo; **ˈ~·man** cartero *m*; **ˈ~-or·der firm**, **ˈ~-order house** casa *f* de ventas por correo; **ˈ~ train** (tren *m*) correo *m*.

mail·ing list lista *f* de direcciones.

maim [meim] tullir; mutilar; estropear.

main [mein] **1.** principal; maestro; mayor; *by ~ force* por fuerza mayor; ✈ *~ plane* ala *f*; *the ~ thing* lo más importante, lo esencial; **2.** cañería *f* (maestra); *poet.* océano *m*; *~s pl.* ⚡ red *f* (eléctrica); *in the ~* en general, en su mayoría; **ˈ~·land** tierra *f* firme, continente *m*; **ˈmain·ly** principalmente, mayormente.

main...: **~·mast** [ˈ~mɑːst, ⚓ ˈ~məst] palo *m* mayor; **~·sail** [ˈ~seil, ⚓ ˈ~sl] vela *f* mayor; **~·spring** muelle *m* real; *fig.* causa *f* (*or* motivo *m*) principal, origen *m*; **ˈ~·stay** ⚓ estay *m* mayor; *fig.* sostén *m* principal; **ˈ~·stream** vía *f* principal; ♀-**Street** calle *f* mayor.

main·tain [meinˈtein] mantener, sostener; ⊕ entretener.

main·te·nance [ˈmeintinəns] mantenimiento *m*; sustento *m*; (gastos *m/pl.* de) conservación *f*; ⊕ entretenimiento *m*.

main·top [ˈmeintɔp] ⚓ cofa *f* mayor.

maize [meiz] maíz *m*.

ma·jes·tic [məˈdʒestik] □ majestuoso; **maj·es·ty** [ˈmædʒisti] majestad *f*; *His ♀* Su Majestad *f*; *Your ♀* (Vuestra) Majestad.

ma·jor [ˈmeidʒər] **1.** mayor (*a.* ♪); principal; importante; **2.** mayor *m/f* de edad; ⚔ comandante *m*; *phls.* mayor *f*; *Am. univ.* especialidad *f*; **3.** *Am. univ.* especializarse (*in* en); **~·do·mo** [ˈ~ˈdoumou] mayordomo *m*; **ˈ~ ˈgen·er·al** general *m* de división; **ma·jor·i·ty** [məˈdʒɔriti] mayoría *f*, mayor número *m*; ⚔ comandancia *f*; mayor edad *f*.

make [meik] **1.** [*irr.*] *v/t.* hacer; crear; formar; construir; practicar, ejecutar, efectuar; constituir; causar, ocasionar; componer; producir; terminar, acabar; creer; deducir, inferir; calcular; (*acquire*) ganar, obtener, granjear, adquirir; (*act as*) servir de, portarse como; (*agree on*) convenir en; (*compel*) forzar, obligar, compeler (*inf.* **a** *inf.*); (*equal*) ser (igual a); (*induce*) inclinar, inducir (*inf.* a *inf.*); (*manufacture*) fabricar, confeccionar, elaborar; (*prepare*) aderezar, preparar, disponer, arreglar; (*reach*) alcanzar, llegar a (*a.* ⚓); ⚡ *circuit* cerrar; *mistake* cometer; *speech* pronunciar; *~ a. adj. is often translated by v/t. corresponding to adj.*: *~ rich* enriquecer; F *~ a p.* hacerle la fortuna a una p., ser causa del éxito de una p.; *I made him write the letter* le hice escribir la carta; *that ~s 50* con éste van cincuenta; *I made one of the group* yo era (uno) del grupo; *~ believe* fingir(se); *~ good damage* reparar; *loss* compensar, indemnizar; completar, suplir; probar; *promise* cumplir;

accusation hacer bueno; F salir bien, tener éxito; F ~ *it* (*arrive*) llegar; (*succeed*) tener éxito; conseguir lo deseado; ~ *or break*, ~ *or mar* hacer la fortuna o ser la ruina de; ~ *into* convertir en, transformar en; ~ *of* sacar de, pensar de, inferir de; ~ *out document* extender; (*perceive*) distinguir, vislumbrar; *writing* descifrar; (*understand*) entender; justificar; dar la impresión de; sugerir; declarar; ~ *over* ceder, traspasar, transferir; ~ *up* hacer; preparar; fabricar; inventar; componer, formar; *collection* reunir; *total* completar; *typ.* compaginar; *clothes* confeccionar; *face* pintar, maquillar; *fire* echar carbón *etc.* a; *loss* subsanar; (re)compensar, indemnizar; *parcel* empaquetar; *time* recuperar; ~ *it up* hacer las paces; **2.** [*irr.*] *v/i.*: ~ *as if to*, ~ *as though to inf.* hacer como si quisiese *inf.*, fingir que va a *inf.*, aparentar *inf.*; ~ *after* (per)seguir; ~ *away with* llevarse, hurtar; suprimir; destruir; *p.* matar; ~ *away with o.s.* suicidarse; ~ *for place* dirigirse a, encaminarse a; *result* contribuir a, conducir a; (*attack*) abalanzarse sobre; ~ *off* largarse, escaparse; ~ *off with* alzarse con, llevarse; escaparse con; F ~ *out* arreglárselas, salir bien; *how did you ~ out?* ¿cómo te fue?; ~ *to inf.* ir a, hacer ademán de *inf.*; ~ *towards* dirigirse a; ~ *up* pintarse, maquillarse; *thea.* caracterizarse; ~ *up for* compensar; suplir; *lost time* recobrar; ~ *up to* (procurar) congraciarse con; halagar; adular; galantear; **3.** hechura *f*; confección *f*; corte *m of clothes*; manufactura *f*; fabricación *f*; (*brand*) marca *f*; modelo *m*; *sl. be on the* ~ echar el agua a su molino; *our own* ~ de fabricación propia; **'~-be·lieve 1.** ficción *f*, simulación *f*; **2.** simulado, falso, fingido; **'mak·er** hacedor (-a *f*) *m*, creador (-a *f*) *m*; fabricante *m*; artífice *m/f*; constructor (-a *f*) *m*; confeccionador (-a *f*) *m*; ♀ Hacedor *m*.

make...: '~·shift 1. improvisación *f*; expediente *m*; arreglo *m* provisional; **2.** improvisado, provisional; **'~-up** composición *f*; carácter *m*, modo *m* de ser; hechura *f*, confección *f of clothes*; maquillaje *m*, cosmético(s) *m(pl.) for face*; *thea.* caracterización *f*; *typ.* imposición *f*; ~ *man films*: maquillador *m*; **'~·weight** contrapeso *m*; *fig.* tapa(a)gujeros *m*.

mak·ing ['meikiŋ] creación *f*; formación *f*; fabricación *f*, confección *f*; hechura *f*; elementos *m/pl.* necesarios; *have the ~s of (p.)* tener talento para ser; *it was the ~ of him* fue la causa de su éxito.

mal·a·chite ['mæləkait] malaquita *f*.

mal·ad·just·ment ['mælə'dʒʌstmənt] mal ajuste *m*; inadaptación *f*.

mal·ad·min·is·tra·tion ['mælədminis'treiʃn] mala administración *f*.

mal·a·droit [mælə'drɔit] torpe.

mal·a·dy ['mælədi] mal *m*, enfermedad *f*.

mal·aise [mæ'leiz] malestar *m*.

mal·a·prop·ism ['mæləprɔpizm] despropósito *m*.

ma·lar·i·a [mə'leriə] paludismo *m*, malaria *f*; **ma'lar·i·al** palúdico.

ma·lar·key [mə'lɑːrki] *sl.* habla *f* necia; tontería(s) *f(pl.)*; mentira(s) *f(pl.)*.

Ma·lay [mə'lei] **1.** malayo (a *f*) *m*; (*language*) malayo *m*; **2.** malayo (*a.* **Ma'lay·an**).

mal·con·tent ['mælkəntent] malcontento *adj. a. su. m* (a *f*).

male [meil] **1.** macho; masculino; ~ *child* hijo *m* varón; ~ *nurse* enfermero *m*; ~ *screw* tornillo *m* (macho); **2.** macho *m*; varón *m*.

mal·e·dic·tion [mæli'dikʃn] maldición *f*.

mal·e·fac·tor ['mælifæktər] malhechor (-a *f*) *m*.

ma·lev·o·lence [mə'levələns] malevolencia *f*; **ma'lev·o·lent** □ malévolo.

mal·for·ma·tion ['mælfɔːr'meiʃn] malformación *f*, deformidad *f*.

mal·func·tion [mæl'fʌŋkʃn] **1.** malfuncionamiento *m*; **2.** ir de través; estropearse.

mal·ice ['mælis] malicia *f*, mala voluntad *f*; ⚖ intención *f* delictuosa; *bear* ~ guardar rencor.

ma·li·cious [mə'liʃəs] □ malicioso, maligno; rencoroso.

ma·lign [mə'lain] **1.** □ maligno; **2.** calumniar, difamar; **ma·lig·nan·cy** [mə'lignənsi] malignidad *f*; **ma'lignant** maligno; **ma'lig·ni·ty** malignidad *f*.

ma·lin·ger [mə'liŋgər] fingirse enfermo; hacer la zanguanga; **ma'lin-**

ger·er enfermo (a *f*) *m* fingido (a); zanguango *m*.
mal·lard ['mælərd] pato *m* real, ánade *m* real.
mal·le·a·bil·i·ty [mæliə'biliti] maleabilidad *f* (*a. fig.*); '**mal·le·a·ble** maleable (*a. fig.*).
mal·let ['mælit] mazo *m*, mallo *m*.
mal·low ['mælou] malva *f*.
mal·nu·tri·tion [mælnjuː'triʃn] desnutrición *f*.
mal·o·dor·ous [mæ'loudərəs] □ maloliente.
mal·prac·tice [mæl'præktis] procedimientos *m/pl.* ilegales; abuso *m* de autoridad.
malt [mɔːlt] **1.** malta *f*; ~ *liquor* cerveza *f*; **2.** preparar la malta; ~*ed milk* harina *f* lacteada.
Mal·tese ['mɔːl'tiːz] maltés *adj. a. su. m* (-a *f*); ~ *cross* cruz *f* de Malta.
mal·treat [mæl'triːt] maltratar; **mal'treat·ment** maltrat(amient)o *m*.
mal·ver·sa·tion [mælvəːr'seiʃn] malversación *f*.
ma·ma, mam·ma ['mɑːmə, mə'mɑː] mamá *f*.
mam·mal ['mæməl] mamífero *m*; **mam·ma·li·an** [mə'meiliən] mamífero *adj. a. su. m.*
mam·moth ['mæməθ] **1.** mamut *m*; **2.** gigantesco.
mam·my ['mæmi] F mamaíta *f*; madrecita *f*.
man [mæn, *in compounds* ... mən] **1.** (*pl. men*) hombre *m*; varón *m*; el género humano; (*servant*) criado *m*; (*workman*) obrero *m*; ⚔ soldado *m*; pieza *f in chess, etc.*; *a* ~ *needs friends* uno necesita amigos; ~ *about town* señorito *m*; F ~ *alive!* ¡hombre!; ~ *and boy* desde pequeño; ~ *and wife* marido *m* y mujer *f*; ~ *in the street* hombre *m* medio, hombre *m* de la calle; ~ *overboard!* ¡hombre a la mar!; ~ *of the world* hombre *m* de mundo; *no* ~ nadie; *to a* ~ por unanimidad, como un solo hombre; todos sin excepción; **2.** ⚓ tripular; ⚔ guarnecer; proveer de gente (armada); *guns* servir.
man·a·cle ['mænəkl] **1.** manilla *f*; ~*s pl.* esposas *f/pl.*; **2.** poner esposas a.
man·age ['mænidʒ] *v/t.* manejar; manipular; llevar; conseguir (hacer); guiar; regir; administrar; *business* dirigir; *house* gobernar; F comer; *can you* ~ *2 more?* ¿puedes llevar 2 más?; *can you* ~ *10 o'clock?* ¿puedes venir a las 10?; *v/i.* arreglárselas, componérselas; ir tirando; ~ *to inf.* lograr *inf.*, arreglárselas para *inf.*, ingeniarse para *inf.*; ~ *without* pasarse sin; '**man·age·a·ble** □ manejable; dócil; '**man·age·ment** dirección *f*, gerencia *f*; administración *f*; *thea.* empresa *f*; manejo *m*; gobierno *m*; conducta *f*; '**man·ag·er** director *m*, gerente *m*; administrador (-a *f*) *m*; jefe *m*; *thea.* empresario *m*; *she is a good* ~ es buena administradora, es muy económica; '**man·ag·er·ess** directora *f*; jefa *f*; administradora *f*; **man·a·ge·ri·al** [~ə'dʒiriəl] □ directivo; administrativo.
man·ag·ing ['mænidʒiŋ] directivo; *b.s.* mandón; ~ *director* director *m* gerente.
man-at-arms ['mænət'ɑːrmz] hombre *m* de armas.
man·da·rin ['mændərin] mandarín *m*; ⚘ (*a.* '**man·da·rine**) mandarina *f*.
man·da·tar·y ['mændətəri] mandatario *m*; **man·date** ['~deit] **1.** mandato *m*; **2.** asignar por mandato; ~*d territory* país *m* bajo mandato;
man·da·to·ry ['~dətəri] **1.** obligatorio; conferido por mandato; **2.** mandatario *m*.
man-day ['mæn'dei] día-hombre *m*.
man·di·ble ['mændibl] mandíbula *f*.
man·do·lin(e) ['mændəlin] mandolina *f*.
man·drake ['mændreik] mandrágora *f*.
man·drel ['mændril] ⊕ mandril *m*.
man·drill [~] *zo.* mandril *m*.
mane [mein] crin(es) *f* (*pl.*); melena *f of lion*.
man-eat·ing ['mæniːtiŋ] antropófago; caníbal.
ma·neu·ver [mə'nuːvər] **1.** maniobra *f*; **2.** *v/t.* hacer maniobrar, manipular; lograr con maniobras; *v/i.* maniobrar.
man·ful ['mænful] □ valiente, resuelto; '~**ness** virilidad *f*.
man·ga·nese [mæŋgə'niːz] manganeso *m*; ~ *steel* acero *m* al manganeso.
mange [meindʒ] *vet.* roña *f*, sarna *f*.
man·ger ['meindʒər] pesebre *m*; *dog in the* ~ perro *m* del hortelano.

man·gle[1] [ˈmæŋgl] **1.** exprimidor *m* de la ropa; rodillo *m*; **2.** pasar por el exprimidor.
man·gle[2] [~] lacerar, destrozar; mutilar (*a. fig.*); magullar; *fig.* estropear.
man·go [ˈmæŋgou] mango *m*.
man·gy [ˈmeindʒi] sarnoso, roñoso.
man...: ˈ**~·han·dle** ⊕ mover a brazo; (*roughly*) maltratar; ˈ**~·hole** registro *m*, pozo *m* de visita; agujero *m* de hombre *in boiler*; ˈ**~·hood** virilidad *f*; naturaleza *f* humana; hombres *m/pl.*; ˈ**~-ˈhour** hora-hombre *f*; ˈ**~·hunt** persecución *f* de un criminal.
ma·ni·a [ˈmeiniə] manía *f*; **ma·ni·ac** [ˈ~iæk] **1.** maníaco (a *f*) *m*; **2.** (*a.* **ma·ni·a·cal** [məˈnaiəkl] □) maníaco; ˈ**man·ic-deˈpress·ive** maníaco-depresivo.
man·i·cure [ˈmænikjur] **1.** manicura *f*; **2.** hacer manicura a; ˈ**~ case,** ˈ**~ set** estuche *m* de manicura.
man·i·cur·ist [ˈmænikjurist] manicuro (a *f*) *m*.
man·i·fest [ˈmænifest] **1.** □ manifiesto; *make* ~ poner de manifiesto; **2.** ⚓ manifiesto *m*; **3.** manifestar; hacer patente, revelar; **man·i·fesˈta·tion** manifestación *f*; **man·i·fes·to** [~ˈfestou] manifiesto *m*.
man·i·fold [ˈmænifould] **1.** □ múltiple; multiforme; numeroso; **2.** sacar muchas copias de; **3.**: *exhaust* ~ colector *m* de escape.
man·i·kin [ˈmænikin] maniquí *m*; enano *m*.
ma·nip·u·late [məˈnipjuleit] manipular, manejar; **ma·nip·uˈla·tion** manipulación *f*, manejo *m*; **maˈnip·u·la·tive** de manipulación; **maˈnip·u·la·tor** manipulador (-a *f*) *m*.
man·kind [ˈmænkaind, mænˈkaind] humanidad *f*, raza *f* humana; [ˈ~] sexo *m* masculino; ˈ**man·li·ness** virilidad *f*, masculinidad *f*; hombr(ad)ía *f*; ˈ**man·ly** varonil; masculino; valiente; ˈ**man-ˈmade** hecho por el hombre; manufacturado.
man·na [ˈmænə] maná *m*.
man·ne·quin [ˈmænikin] maniquí *m/f*, modelo *f*; ~ *parade* desfile *m* de modelos.
man·ner [ˈmænər] manera *f*, modo *m*; ademán *m*, aire *m of p.*; clase *f*; ~s *pl.* modales *m/pl.*, maneras *f/pl.*, crianza *f*, educación *f*; costumbres *f/pl.*; *he has no* ~*s* tiene malos modales, no tiene crianza, es un mal criado; *after* (*or in*) *the* ~ *of* a la manera de; *all* ~ *of* toda clase de; *by no* ~ *of means* de ningún modo; *in a* ~ (*of speaking*) en cierto modo; como si dijéramos; *in this* ~ de este modo, de esta forma; *to the* ~ *born* avezado desde la cuna; ˈ**man·nered** *style* amanerado; de modales...; ˈ**man·ner·ism** amaneramiento *m of style*; hábito *m*; idiosincrasia *f*; ˈ**man·ner·ly** cortés, bien criado.
man·nish [ˈmæniʃ] hombruno.
man·of·war [ˈmænəvˈwɔːr] buque *m* de guerra.
ma·nom·e·ter [məˈnɔmitər] manómetro *m*.
man·or [ˈmænər] solar *m*, finca *f* solariega, señorío *m*; (*a.* ˈ**~ house**) casa *f* señorial, casa *f* solariega; **ma·no·ri·al** [məˈnɔːriəl] señorial; solariego.
man·pow·er [ˈmænpauər] mano *f* de obra; potencial *m* humano.
man-serv·ant [ˈmænsəːrvənt] criado *m*.
man·sion [ˈmænʃn] palacio *m*, hotel *m*, casa *f* grande; casa *f* solariega.
man·slaugh·ter [ˈmænslɔːtər] homicidio *m* (sin premeditación).
man·tel [ˈmæntl] manto *m* (de chimenea); ˈ**~·piece** repisa *f* de chimenea.
man·til·la [mænˈtilə] mantilla *f*.
man·tle [ˈmæntl] **1.** manto *m* (*a. fig.*, *zo.*); (*incandescent* ~) manguito *m* incandescente; **2.** *v/t.* cubrir; ocultar; *v/i.* extenderse; (*cheeks*) ponerse encendido.
man·trap [ˈmæntræp] cepo *m*.
man·u·al [ˈmænjuəl] **1.** □ manual; **2.** manual *m*; ♪ teclado *m* de órgano.
man·u·fac·to·ry [mænjuˈfæktəri] fábrica *f*.
man·u·fac·ture [mænjuˈfæktʃər] **1.** fabricación *f*; (*product*) manufactura *f*; **2.** fabricar (*a. fig.*); manufacturar, elaborar; **man·uˈfac·tur·er** fabricante *m*, industrial *m*, manufacturero *m*; **man·uˈfac·tur·ing 1.** manufacturero, fabril; **2.** fabricación *f*.
ma·nure [məˈnjur] **1.** estiércol *m*, abono *m*; **2.** estercolar, abonar.
man·u·script [ˈmænjuskript] manuscrito *adj. a. su. m.*
Manx [mæŋks] **1.** de la Isla de Man; **2.** lengua *f* de la Isla de Man; *the* ~ los habitantes de la Isla de Man.

man·y [ˈmeni] **1.** muchos (*a. ~ a, ~ a one*); *~ a time* muchas veces; *~ people* mucha gente *f*; *as ~ as* tantos como; *as ~ as 50* hasta 50; *how ~* cuántos; *so ~* tantos; *too ~* demasiados; *one too ~* uno de más; **2.** gran número *m*; muchos (as *f/pl.*) *m/pl.*; *a good ~* un buen número (de); *a great ~* muchísimos; *the ~* la mayoría, las masas; **ˈ~-ˈcol·ored** multicolor; **ˈ~-ˈsid·ed** multilátero; *fig.* polifacético; complejo.

map [mæp] **1.** mapa *m*, carta *f* geográfica; plano *m*; F *off the ~* remoto, aislado; **2.** trazar el mapa (*or* plano) de; *fig.* planear, proyectar (*a. ~ out*).

ma·ple [ˈmeipl] arce *m*.

map·mak·ing [ˈmæpˈmeikiŋ], **map·ping** [ˈmæpiŋ] cartografía *f*.

mar [mɑːr] estropear; desfigurar; echar a perder; *enjoyment* aguar.

mar·a·schi·no [mɑːrəsˈkiːnou] (*liqueur*) marrasquino.

Mar·a·thon [ˈmærəθən] (*or ~ race*) carrera *f* de Maratón.

ma·raud [məˈrɔːd] merodear; **maˈraud·er** merodeador (-a *f*) *m*.

mar·ble [ˈmɑːrbl] **1.** mármol *m*; canica *f in game*; **2.** marmóreo (*a. fig.*); de mármol; **3.** crispir; jaspear.

March[1] [mɑːrtʃ] marzo *m*; *mad as a ~ hare* loco como una cabra.

march[2] [~] **1.** marcha *f* (*a.* ♪, *fig.*); *steal a ~ on a p.* ganarle por la mano a una p.; ⚔ *~ past* desfile *m*; **2.** *v/i.* marchar; caminar con resolución; ⚔ *forward ~!* de frente ¡mar!; *~ on* seguir marchando; *~ past* desfilar (ante); *v/t. p. etc.* hacer marchar; llevar; *distance* llevar andado, recorrer marchando.

march[3] [~] *hist.* marca *f*, frontera *f* (*mst ~es pl.*).

march·ing [ˈmɑːrtʃiŋ] de marcha, en marcha; *get one's ~ orders* F ser despedido.

mar·chion·ess [ˈmɑːrʃənis] marquesa *f*.

mare [mer] yegua *f*; *~'s nest* parto *m* de los montes, hallazgo *m* ilusorio.

mar·ga·rine [ˈmɑːrdʒərin] margarina *f*.

mar·gin [ˈmɑːrdʒin] margen *mst m* (*a. typ.*, ✝ *~ of profit*); reserva *f*; sobrante *m*; *~ of error* margen *m* de error; *~ of safety* margen *m* de seguridad; *in the ~* al margen; **ˈmar·gin·al** □ marginal; *~ note* acotación *f*.

Ma·ri·a [məˈraiə]: F *Black ~* coche *m* celular.

mar·i·gold [ˈmærigould] caléndula *f*, maravilla *f*.

mar·i·jua·na [mæriˈwɑːnə] mariguana *f*.

ma·ri·na [məˈriːnə] dársena *f*; **mar·i·nade** [ˈmærəneid] **1.** escabeche *m*; **2.** escabechar; marinar.

ma·rine [məˈriːn] **1.** marino, marítimo; **2.** marina *f*; soldado *m* de marina; *~s pl.* infantería *f* de marina; *tell that to the ~s!* ¡a otro perro con ese hueso!; **mar·i·ner** [ˈmærinər] marinero *m*, marino *m*.

mar·i·o·nette [mæriəˈnet] marioneta *f*, títere *m*.

mar·i·tal [ˈmæritl] □ marital; matrimonial; *~ status* estado *m* civil.

mar·i·time [ˈmæritaim] marítimo.

mar·jo·ram [ˈmɑːrdʒərəm] mejorana *f*; orégano *m*.

mark[1] [mɑːrk] (*coin*) marco *m*.

mark[2] [~] **1.** señal *f*; (*distinguishing, trade-*) marca *f*; impresión *f*; (*trace*) huella *f*; (*stain*) mancha *f*; (*sign*) indicio *m*; (*target*) blanco *m*; (*label*) marbete *m*; *exam*: calificación *f*, nota *f*; distinción *f*, categoría *f*; (*level*) nivel *m*; *sport*: raya *f*; *hit the ~* dar en el blanco, acertar; *make one's ~* firmar con una cruz; *fig.* señalarse, distinguirse; *of ~* célebre, distinguido; *up to the ~* satisfactorio; a la altura de las circunstancias; *wide of the ~* alejado de la verdad; errado; **2.** *v/t.* señalar; marcar; (*stain*) manchar; notar; apuntar; distinguir; *exam*: dar nota a, calificar; (*label*) rotular; indicar (el precio de); *~ down* ✝ rebajar (el precio de); apuntar; *fig.* señalar, escoger; *~ off* señalar; separar; definir; jalonar; *~ out* trazar; marcar; definir; jalonar; (*select*) escoger; *v. time*; **marked** [mɑːrkt] marcado; señalado; notable; *~ man* hombre *m* que ha llamado la atención; futura víctima *f*; **mark·ed·ly** [ˈmɑːrkidli] marcadamente; notablemente; **ˈmark·er** marcador *m* (*a. billiards*); ficha *f*; registro *m in book*.

mar·ket [ˈmɑːrkit] **1.** mercado *m*; (*a. ~ place*) plaza *f* (del mercado); ✝ bolsa *f*; *fig.* tráfico *m*; venta *f*; *be in the ~ for* estar dispuesto a comprar; *black ~* estraperlo *m*, mercado *m* negro; bolsa *f* negra *S.Am.*; *~ garden* huerto *m*; (*large*) huerta *f*; ~ *gardener* hortelano *m*; ~ *price* precio *m* corriente (*or* de mercado); ~ *research* investigación *f* mercológica; análisis *m* de mercados; *on the* ~ de venta; en la bolsa; *play the* ~ jugar a la bolsa; *ready* ~ fácil salida *f*; **2.** vender, poner a la venta; llevar al mercado; ˈ**mar·ket·a·ble** □ vendible, comerciable; **mar·ket·eer** [~ˈtir]: *black* ~ estraperlista *m/f*; ˈ**mar·ket·ing** venta *f*, comercialización *f*.

mark·ing [ˈmɑːrkiŋ] señal *f*, marca *f*; pinta *f on animals*; coloración *f*; ˈ~ **ink** tinta *f* de marcar.

marks·man [ˈmɑːrksmən] tirador (-a *f*) *m*; ˈ**marks·man·ship** buena puntería *f*.

marl [mɑːrl] marga *f*.

mar·ma·lade [ˈmɑːrməleid] mermelada *f* (de naranjas amargas).

mar·mo·re·al [mɑːrˈmɔːriəl] □ *poet.* marmóreo.

mar·mo·set [ˈmɑːrməzet] tití *m*.

mar·mot [ˈmɑːrmət] marmota *f*.

ma·roon[1] [məˈruːn] **1.** (*color*) marrón *m*; (*firework*) petardo *m*; **2.** marrón.

ma·roon[2] [~] abandonar (en una isla desierta).

mar·quee [mɑːrˈkiː] entoldado *m*; marquesina *f*.

mar·quess, *mst* **mar·quis** [ˈmɑːrkwis] marqués *m*.

mar·que·try [ˈmɑːrkitri] marquetería *f*.

mar·riage [ˈmæridʒ] matrimonio *m*; (*wedding*) boda(s) *f* (*pl.*), casamiento *m*; *fig.* unión *f*; *by* ~ político; *civil* ~ matrimonio *m* civil; ~ *license* licencia *f* para casarse; ~ *lines* partida *f* de matrimonio; ~ *portion* dote *f*; ~ *settlement* capitulaciones *f/pl.*; *related by* ~ emparentado; ˈ**mar·riage·a·ble** casadero, núbil.

mar·ried [ˈmærid] *p.* casado; *state etc.* conyugal; *get* ~ casarse (*to* con).

mar·row [ˈmærou] médula *f* (*or* medula *f*), tuétano *m*; meollo *m* (*a. fig.*); *to the* ~ hasta los tuétanos; ⚘ (*vegetable*) ~ calabacín *m*; ˈ~**·bone** hueso *m* con tuétano; ~*s pl. co.* rodillas *f/pl.*

mar·ry [ˈmæri] *v/t.* (*give or join in marriage*) casar (*to* con); (*take in marriage*) casar(se) con; *fig.* unir; *v/i.* casarse; ~ *again* casarse en segundas nupcias; ~ *into family* emparentar con.

marsh [mɑːrʃ] pantano *m*, marjal *m*; marisma *f*; ciénaga *f*; ~ *fever* paludismo *m*; ~ *gas* gas *m* de los pantanos.

mar·shal [ˈmɑːrʃəl] **1.** mariscal *m*; maestro *m* de ceremonias; oficial *m* de justicia; jefe *m* de policía; **2.** ordenar; conducir con ceremonia; dirigir; ˈ**mar·shal·(l)ing** ˈ**yard** 🚂 playa *f* de clasificación; ˈ**marsh·mal·low** ⚘ malvavisco *m*; bombón *m* de merengue blando; ˈ**marsh** ˈ**mar·i·gold** calta *f* (palustre); ˈ**marsh·y** pantanoso.

mar·su·pi·al [mɑːrˈsuːpiəl] marsupial *adj. a. su. m.*

mart [mɑːrt] emporio *m*; (*auction room*) martillo *m*; *poet.* plaza *f* del mercado.

mar·ten [ˈmɑːrtin] marta *f*; garduña *f*.

mar·tial [ˈmɑːrʃəl] □ marcial; castrense; ~ *law* ley *f* marcial; *under* ~ *law* en estado de sitio.

Mar·tian [ˈmɑːrʃən] marciano *adj. a. su. m* (a *f*).

mar·tin[1] [ˈmɑːrtin] *orn.* avión *m*.

Mar·tin[2] [~]: *St.* ~*'s summer* veranillo *m* de San Martín.

mar·ti·net [mɑːrtiˈnet] ordenancista *m/f*.

mar·ti·ni [mɑːrˈtiːniː] cóctel *m* confeccionado de ginebra con vermut.

Mar·tin·mas [ˈmɑːrtinməs] día *m* de San Martín (*11 noviembre*).

mar·tyr [ˈmɑːrtər] **1.** mártir *m/f*; **2.** martirizar; ˈ**mar·tyr·dom** martirio *m*; ˈ**mar·tyr·ize** martirizar.

mar·vel [ˈmɑːrvəl] **1.** maravilla *f*; prodigio *m*; **2.** maravillarse (*at* con, de).

mar·vel·(l)ous [ˈmɑːrviləs] □ maravilloso.

Marx·ian [ˈmɑːrksjən] marxista *adj. a. su. m/f*; **Marx·ism** [ˈ~izm] marxismo *m*; ˈ**Marx·ist** marxista *adj. a. su. m/f*.

mar·zi·pan [ˈmɑːrzipæn] mazapán *m*.

mas·ca·ra [mæsˈkærə] tinte *m* para las pestañas.

mas·cot [ˈmæskət] mascota *f*.

mas·cu·line [ˈmæskjulin] **1.** masculino; varonil; (*mst of woman*) hombruno; **2.** *gr.* masculino *m*.

mash [mæʃ] **1.** mezcla *f*; amasijo *m*; baturrillo *m*; *brewing*: malta *f* remojada; 🌱 afrecho *m* remojado; puré *m* (de patatas); **2.** majar, machacar;

mezclar; amasar; despachurrar; *~ed potatoes* puré *m* de patatas (papas *S.Am.*).

mask [mæsk] **1.** máscara *f* (*a. fig.*); careta *f*, antifaz *m*; (*p.*) máscara *m/f*; *v. masque*; (*death*) ~ mascarilla *f*; **2.** enmascarar; ocultar; *~ed ball* baile *m* de máscaras.

mas·och·ism [ˈmæzəkizm] masoquismo *m*; **mas·ochˈist·ic** masoquista *adj. a. su. m/f*.

ma·son [ˈmeisn] △ cantero *m*, albañil *m*; (*free-*) (franc)masón *m*; **ma·son·ic** [məˈsɔnik] masónico; **ˈma·son·ry** cantería *f*, albañilería *f*; sillería *f*; (franc)masonería *f*.

masque [mæsk] mascarada *f*; mojiganga *f*; **mas·quer·ade** [mæskəˈreid] **1.** mascarada *f*; (baile *m* de) máscaras *f/pl.*; *fig.* farsa *f*; **2.** enmascararse, ir disfrazado (*as* de); *fig.* hacer el papel (*as* de).

mass[1] [mæs] *eccl.* misa *f*; *High* ~ misa *f* mayor; *Low* ~ misa *f* rezada.

mass[2] [~] **1.** masa *f* (*a. phys.*); bulto *m* (informe); macizo *m of mountains*; montón *m*, gran cantidad *f*; muchedumbre *f*; *the ~es pl.* las masas; *the (great) ~ of* la mayoría de; *in the ~* en conjunto; *~ meeting* mitin *m* popular; *~ production* producción *f* en serie; *~ unemployment* desempleo *m* en masa; **2.** juntar(se) en masa, reunir(se); concentrar(se).

mas·sa·cre [ˈmæsəkər] **1.** matanza *f*; carnicería *f*; **2.** hacer una carnicería de, masacrar.

mas·sage [mæˈsɑːʒ] **1.** masaje *m*; **2.** dar masaje a.

mas·seur [mæˈsur] masajista *m*; **masˈseuse** [~uːz] masajista *f*.

mas·sive [ˈmæsiv] macizo, sólido; abultado; **ˈmas·sive·ness** macicez *f*, solidez *f*; gran bulto *m*.

mass me·dia [ˈmæsˈmiːdjə] medios *m/pl.* de comunicación en gran escala.

mast[1] [mæst] ⚓ mástil *m*, palo *m*, árbol *m*; *radio*: torre *f*.

mast[2] [~] *beech*: hayuco *m*; *oak*: bellota *f*.

mast·ed [ˈmæstid] ⚓ arbolado; de ... palos.

mas·ter [ˈmæstər] **1.** señor *m*; amo *m of house etc.*; (*owner*) dueño *m*; (*graduate, expert, teacher a. fig.*) maestro *m*; profesor *m in secondary school*; director *m of college*; ⚓ capitán *m*; patrón *m of small craft*; (*young*) señorito *m*; maestre *m of military order*; *v. art, ceremony*; *old ~* pintura *f* de uno de los grandes maestros; *be ~ of* dominar; poseer; *be ~ of the situation* ser dueño del baile; *I am the ~ here* aquí mando yo; *be one's own ~* ser independiente; trabajar por su propia cuenta; **2.** maestro; *fig.* magistral, superior, principal; **3.** dominar (*a. fig.*); llegar a ser maestro en; vencer; **ˈmas·ter ˈbuild·er** arquitecto *m*; maestro *m* de obras; constructor *m*; **mas·ter·ful** [ˈ~ful] □ imperioso, dominante; **ˈmas·ter-key** llave *f* maestra; **ˈmas·ter·ly** magistral; maestro; perfecto; **ˈmas·ter·mind** mente *f* directora; **ˈmas·ter·piece** obra *f* maestra; **ˈmas·ter·stroke** golpe *m* maestro; **ˈmas·ter·y** maestría *f*; dominio *m*; autoridad *f*.

mast·head [ˈmæsthed] ⚓ tope *m*; cabecera *f* editorial *of newspaper*.

mas·tic [ˈmæstik] mástique *m*; ⚘, *pharm*, almáciga *f*.

mas·ti·cate [ˈmæstikeit] mas(ti)car; **mas·tiˈca·tion** masticación *f*; **mas·ti·ca·to·ry** [ˈ~təri] masticatorio.

mas·tiff [ˈmæstif] mastín *m*; perro *m* alano.

mast·oid [ˈmæstɔid] mastoides *adj. a. su. f*.

mas·tur·bate [ˈmæstərbeit] masturbarse.

mat[1] [mæt] **1.** estera *f*; esterilla *f*; (*round*) ruedo *m*; felpudo *m at door*; salvamanteles *m for table*; (*lace etc.*) tapetito *m*; greña *f of hair*; **2.** esterar; enmarañar(se), entretejerse.

mat[2] [~] mate.

match[1] [mætʃ] cerilla *f*, fósforo *m*, mixto *m*; cerillo *m S.Am.*; (*fuse*) mecha *f*.

match[2] [~] **1.** igual *m/f*; compañero (a *f*) *m*; pareja *f*; matrimonio *m*; *sport*: partido *m*; concurso *m*; *be a ~ for* poder con; (*color etc.*) hacer juego con; *good ~* buena pareja *f*; buen partido *m in marriage*; *meet one's ~* hallar la horma de su zapato; **2.** *v/t.* (*pair*) emparejar; parear; igualar; competir con; *color etc.* hacer juego con; *~ a p. against another* hacer que una p. compita con otro; *v/i.* hacer juego, casar; *~ing, to ~* acompañado; a juego con; a tono (con).

match·box [ˈmætʃbɔks] cajita *f* de cerillas, fosforera *f*.
match·less [ˈmætʃlis] sin par, incomparable; ˈ**match·mak·er** casamentero (a *f*) *m*.
match·wood [ˈmætʃwud] madera *f* para fósforos; astillas *f/pl*.
mate[1] [meit] *chess*: **1.** mate *m*; **2.** dar jaque mate (a).
mate[2] [~] **1.** compañero *m*, camarada *m*; (*married*) cónyuge *m/f*, consorte *m/f*; ⚓ primer oficial *m*, segundo *m*, piloto *m*; (*assistant*) ayudante *m*, peón *m*; *zo*. macho *m*, hembra *f*; **2.** casar(se); *zo*. parear(se), acoplar(se); *mating season* época *f* de celo.
ma·te·ri·al [məˈtiriəl] **1.** □ material; importante, esencial; considerable; **2.** (*ingredient, equipment a. fig.*) material *m*; (*substance*) materia *f*; *fig*. datos *m/pl*.; (*cloth*) tejido *m*, tela *f*; ~s *pl*. material(es) *m*(*pl*.); *raw* ~s materias *f/pl*. primas; *writing* ~s efectos *m/pl*. de escritorio; **maˈte·ri·al·ism** materialismo *m*; **maˈte·ri·al·ist** materialista *adj. a. su. m/f*; **ma·te·ri·alˈis·tic** □ materialista; **ma·te·ri·al·i·za·tion** [~riəlaiˈzeiʃn] materialización *f*; realización *f*; **maˈte·ri·al·ize** materializar(se); realizarse.
ma·ter·nal [məˈtəːrnl] □ materno; *affection etc*. maternal; **maˈter·ni·ty** [~niti] maternidad *f*; ~ *benefit* subsidio *m* de natalidad; ~ *hospital* casa *f* de maternidad.
math [mæθ] F = *mathematics*; **math·e·mat·i·cal** [mæθiˈmætikl] □ matemático; **math·e·ma·ti·cian** [~məˈtiʃn] matemático *m*; **math·e·mat·ics** [~ˈmætiks] *mst sg*. matemática(s) *f*(*pl*.).
mat·i·née [ˈmætinei] función *f* de tarde.
mat·ins [ˈmætinz] *pl*. maitines *m/pl*.
ma·tri·arch [ˈmeitriɑːrk] matriarca *f*; **ma·tri·cide** [ˈ~said] matricidio *m*; (*p*.) matricida *m/f*.
ma·tric·u·late [məˈtrikjuleit] matricular(se); **ma·tric·uˈla·tion** matriculación *f*.
mat·ri·mo·ni·al [mætriˈmounjəl] □ matrimonial; conyugal; **mat·ri·mo·ny** [ˈmætrimouni] matrimonio *m*; vida *f* conyugal.
ma·trix [ˈmeitriks] matriz *f*.
ma·tron [ˈmeitrən] matrona *f*; *hospital*: enfermera *f* jefa; *school*: ama *f* de llaves; ~ *of honor* dama *f* de honor; ˈ**ma·tron·ly** matronal; respetable; maduro y algo corpulento.
mat·ter [ˈmætər] **1.** materia *f* (*a.* ⚕); material *m*; tema *m*; asunto *m*, cuestión *f*; motivo *m*; cosa *f*; *printed* ~ impresos *m/pl*.; *a* ~ *of* cosa de; obra de; *as a* ~ *of course* por rutina; *be a* ~ *of course* ser de cajón; ~ *of fact* hecho *m* positivo; *as a* ~ *of fact* en hecho de verdad; en realidad; el caso es que; ~ *of form* pura formalidad *f*; *in the* ~ *of* en materia de; ~ *in hand* asunto *m* de que se trata; *no* ~ no importa; *no* ~ *how* de cualquier modo; *no* ~ *who* quienquiera; *to make* ~*s worse* para colmo de desgracias; *for that* ~ en cuanto a eso; *what* ~? ¿qué importa?; *what's the* ~? ¿qué hay?; *what's the* ~ *with smoking?* ¿qué inconveniente hay en fumar?; *what's the* ~ *with you?* ¿qué te pasa?, ¿qué tienes?; **2.** importar; *it does not* ~ no importa, es igual; *what does it* ~? ¿qué importa?; ˈ**~-of-ˈfact** prosaico; práctico, positivista; flemático.
mat·ting [ˈmætiŋ] estera *f*.
mat·tock [ˈmætək] azadón *m*.
mat·tress [ˈmætris] colchón *m*.
ma·ture [məˈtjur] **1.** □ maduro (*a. fig*.); ⚜ vencido, pagadero; **2.** madurar; ⚜ vencer; **maˈtu·ri·ty** madurez *f*; ⚜ vencimiento *m*.
ma·tu·ti·nal [məˈt(j)uːtinəl] □ matutino.
maud·lin [ˈmɔːdlin] sensiblero; llorón.
maul [mɔːl] magullar; maltratar (*a. fig*.); F manosear.
maun·der [ˈmɔːndər] hablar (*or* errar) como atontado; chochear.
Maun·dy Thurs·day [ˈmɔːndiˈθəːrzdi] Jueves *m* Santo.
mau·so·le·um [mɔːsəˈliːəm] mausoleo *m*.
mauve [mouv] (de) color *m* de malva.
mav·er·ick [ˈmævərik] res *f* sin marcar; *pol*. disidente *m*.
maw [mɔː] estómago *m*; *ruminant*: cuajar *m*; *bird*: molleja *f*; F buche *m*; *fig*. abismo *m*.
mawk·ish [ˈmɔːkiʃ] □ insulso; empalagoso, dulzarrón; sensiblero; ˈ**mawk·ish·ness** sensiblería *f etc*.
max·il·lar·y [mækˈsiləri] maxilar.
max·im [ˈmæksim] máxima *f*; ˈ**max·i·mal** máximo; **max·i·mum** [ˈ~əm] **1.** máximo; **2.** máximo *m*, máximum *m*.

May[1] [mei] mayo *m*; ~ *Queen* maya *f*; ♀ ⚘ flor *f* del espino blanco.
may[2] [~] [*irr.*] poder; ser posible; tener permiso para; *I* ~ *come* puede (ser) que yo venga; *yes, I* ~ sí, es posible; *if I* ~ si me lo permites; ~ *I come in?* ¿se puede (pasar)?; *it* ~ *be that* puede ser que, tal vez, quizás; *it* ~ *snow* puede (ser) que nieve, es posible que nieve; ~ *you be lucky!* ¡que tengas suerte!
may·be ['meibi:] quizá(s), tal vez, acaso.
May Day ['meidei] (fiesta *f* del) primero *m* de mayo; **May·day!** ¡socorro! (*naves, aviones*).
may·on·naise [meiə'neiz] mayonesa *f*.
may·or ['meiər, mær] alcalde *m*; **'may·or·al** de alcalde; **'may·or·al·ty** alcaldía *f*; **'may·or·ess** alcaldesa *f*.
may·pole ['meipoul] mayo *m*.
maze [meiz] laberinto *m*; *fig.* enredo *m*, perplejidad *f*; **'ma·zy** □ laberíntico; perplejo.
me [mi:] me; (*after prp.*) mí; *with* ~ conmigo.
mead [mi:d] **1.** aguamiel *f*, hidrom(i)el *m*; **2.** *poet.* = *meadow*.
mead·ow ['medou] prado *m*; (*big*) pradera *f*; henar *m for hay*; **'~·sweet** reina *f* de los prados.
mea·ger ['mi:gər] □ escaso, exiguo, pobre; magro, flaco; **'mea·ger·ness** escasez *f etc.*
meal[1] [mi:l] comida *f*.
meal[2] [~] harina *f* (a medio moler).
meal·time ['mi:ltaim] hora *f* de comer.
meal·y ['mi:li] harinoso; pálido; **'~-mouthed** mojigato; excesivamente circunspecto.
mean[1] [mi:n] □ humilde, pobre; inferior; vil, bajo; sórdido; mezquino, tacaño; F malo, desconsiderado.
mean[2] [~] **1.** medio; *in the* ~ *time* = ~*time*; **2.** medio *m*; promedio *m*, término *m* medio; ℞ media *f*; ~*s sg. or pl.* medio(s) *m(pl.)*; manera *f*; ~*s pl.* recursos *m/pl.*, medios *m/pl.*, dinero *m*; *by all* ~*s* por todos los medios; F por cierto, con mucho gusto, no faltaba más; *by any* ~*s* de cualquier modo que sea; *not by any* ~*s* = *by no* ~*s* de ningún modo; *by fair* ~*s or foul* por las buenas o por las malas; *by* ~*s of* por medio de, mediante; *by this* ~*s* por este medio, de este modo; ~*s to an end* medio *m* para conseguir un fin.
mean[3] [~] [*irr.*] querer decir (*by* con); significar (*to* para); destinar (*for* para); decir en serio; ~ *to inf.* pensar *inf.*, proponerse *inf.*; *he didn't* ~ *to do it* lo hizo sin querer; ~ *well* (*ill*) tener buenas (malas) intenciones.
me·an·der [mi'ændər] **1.** meandro *m*, serpenteo *m*; **2.** serpentear; errar.
mean·ing ['mi:niŋ] **1.** □ significativo; **2.** significado *m*, sentido *m*; *what's the* ~ *of* ...? ¿qué significa ...?; **'mean·ing·less** sin sentido; insignificante; insensato.
mean·ness ['mi:nnis] humildad *f*; mezquindad *f*.
meant [ment] *pret. a. p.p. of mean*[3].
mean·time ['mi:ntaim], **mean·while** ['mi:nwail] entretanto, mientras tanto.
mea·sles ['mi:zlz] sarampión *m*; **'mea·sly** F pobre, despreciable.
meas·ur·a·ble ['meʒərəbl] □ mensurable; apreciable.
meas·ure ['meʒər] **1.** medida *f* (*a. fig.*); (*rule*) regla *f*; ♪ compás *m*; *parl.* (proyecto *m* de) ley *f*; *dry* ~ medida *f* para áridos; ~ *of capacity* medida *f* de capacidad; *beyond* ~ hasta no más; excesivamente; *for good* ~ por añadidura; *in a* ~, *in some* ~ hasta cierto punto; *in* (*a*) *great* ~ en gran manera; *made to* ~ hecho a medida; *take a p.'s* ~ *fig.* tomarle las medidas a una p.; **2.** medir (*a.* ~ *off*, ~ *out*); *p. for height* tallar; *p. for clothes* tomar las medidas a; ~ *one's length* medir el suelo; ~ *up to* estar a la altura de; ~*d* moderado; acompasado; deliberado; **'mea·sure·less** □ inmensurable, inmenso; **'meas·ure·ment** medida *f*; medición *f*.
meas·ur·ing ['meʒəriŋ] **1.** medición *f*; **2.** de medir.
meat [mi:t] carne *f*; † comida *f*; † alimento *m*; *fig.* meollo *m*, sustancia *f*; *cold* ~ fiambre *m*; ~ *ball* albóndiga *f*; ~ *fly* mosca *f* de la carne; ~ *head sl.* tonto *m*; bestia *m/f*; alcornoque *m*; ~ *pie* pastel *m* de carne, empanada *f*; **'~ chop·per** (*a.* **'~ grind·er**) picadora *f* de carne; **'~ safe** fresquera *f*; **'meat·y** carnoso; *fig.* sustancioso.
me·chan·ic [mi'kænik] mecánico *m*; **me'chan·i·cal** □ mecánico; ma-

quinal (*a. fig.*); ~ *engineering* ingeniería *f* mecánica; ~ *pencil* lapicero *m*; **me·chan·ics** [mi'kæniks] *mst sg.* mecánica *f*; mecanismo *m*, técnica *f*.

mech·a·nism ['mekənizm] mecanismo *m*; aparato *m*; *phls.* mecanicismo *m*; **mech·a·nize** ['~naiz] mecanizar.

med·al ['medl] medalla *f*; **me·dal·lion** [mi'dæljən] medallón *m*; **med·al·(l)ist** ['medlist] medallista *m*; persona *f* condecorada con una medalla.

med·dle ['medl] entrometerse (*in* en); meterse (*with* con); '**med·dler** entrometido (a *f*) *m*; **med·dle·some** ['~səm] □ entrometido; '**med·dle·some·ness** entrometimiento *m*.

me·di·a ['mi:diə] = *mass media*.

me·di'ae·val = *medieval*.

me·di·al ['mi:diəl] □ medial; '**me·di·an** mediano; ~ *strip* faja *f* divisora *of highway*.

me·di·ate 1. □ ['mi:diit] mediato; **2.** ['mi:dieit] mediar (*between* entre, *for* por, *in* en); **me·di'a·tion** mediación *f*; '**me·di·a·tor** mediador (-a *f*) *m*.

med·i·cal ['medikəl] médico; de medicina; medicinal; ~ *board* tribunal *m* médico; ~ *certificate* certificado *m* médico; ~ *corps* cuerpo *m* de sanidad; ~ *jurisprudence* medicina *f* legal; ~ *man* médico *m*; ~ *practitioner* médico (a *f*) *m*; ~ *officer* jefe *m* de sanidad municipal; ⚔ oficial *m* médico; ~ *student* estudiante *m/f* de medicina; **me'dic·a·ment** medicamento *m*; '**Me·di·care** seguros *m/pl.* de enfermedad para los viejos de EE.UU.

med·i·cate ['medikeit] medicar; impregnar; **med·i'ca·tion** medicación *f*.

me·dic·i·nal [me'disinl] □ medicinal; **med·i·cine** ['medsin] medicina *f*; medicamento *m*; ~ *chest* botiquín *m*; ~ *man* curandero *m*; hechizador *m*; *take one's* ~ pagar las consecuencias.

me·di·e·val [medi'i:vəl] □ medieval; **me·di'e·val·ism** medievalismo *m*; **me·di'e·val·ist** medievalista *m/f*.

me·di·o·cre [mi:di'oukər] mediano, mediocre; **me·di·oc·ri·ty** [~'ɔkriti] mediocridad *f*, medianía *f* (*a. p.*).

med·i·tate ['mediteit] meditar (*on acc.*); reflexionar (*on* en, sobre); **med·i'ta·tion** meditación *f*, reflexión *f*; '**med·i·ta·tive** □ meditabundo, meditador.

me·di·um ['mi:diəm] **1.** (*pl. a.* **me·dia** ['~diə]) medio *m*; (*p.*) médium *m*; *happy* ~ justo medio *m*; *through the* ~ *of* por medio de; **2.** mediano, intermedio, regular; '~-'**sized** de tamaño medi(an)o.

med·lar ['medlər] níspola *f*; (*a.* ~ *tree*) níspero *m*.

med·ley ['medli] mezcla *f*, mezcolanza *f*; miscelánea *f*; ♩ popurrí *m*.

me·dul·la [mi'dʌlə] médula *f*.

meed [mi:d] *poet.* galardón *m* (merecido).

meek [mi:k] □ manso, dócil, humilde; '**meek·ness** mansedumbre *f etc.*

meer·schaum ['mirʃəm] (pipa *f* de) espuma *f* de mar.

meet[1] [mi:t] *lit.*, † conveniente.

meet[2] [~] **1.** [*irr.*] *v/t.* encontrar(se con); (*come across*) tropezar con; (*on arrival*) ir a recibir, esperar; (*become acquainted with*) conocer; (*fight*) batirse con; *sport*: enfrentarse con; (*connect with* 🚂 *etc.*) empalmar con; (*suffer*) tener que aguantar; (*answer*) responder a; (*fall in with*) conformarse a; *request, need* satisfacer; *bill* pagar; *obligations* cumplir; *expense* hacer frente a; *go to* ~ ir al encuentro de; ~ *a p. half-way fig.* partir la diferencia, hacer concesiones a una p.; *v. please*; *v/i.* encontrarse; reunirse; conocerse; verse; (*fight*) batirse; (*join*) confluir; ~ *with* encontrarse con; reunirse con; *loss etc.* sufrir; *accident* tener; *till we* ~ *again* hasta más ver, hasta la vista; **2.** concurso *m* de cazadores (*or* deportistas).

meet·ing ['mi:tiŋ] reunión *f*; sesión *f*; (*public*) mitin *m*; encuentro *m*; (*by appointment*) cita *f*; confluencia *f of rivers*; *sport*: concurso *m*; '~ **house** iglesia *f* de disidentes; iglesia *f* cuáquera; '~-**place** lugar *m* de reunión (*or* de cita).

meg·a·bucks ['megəbʌks] *sl.* vastas cantidades de dinero; **meg·a·cy·cle** ['megəsaikl] megaciclo *m*; **meg·a·lo·ma·ni·a** ['~lou'meinjə] megalomanía *f*; **meg·a·phone** ['~foun] megáfono *m*; **meg·a·ton** ['~tʌn] megatón *m*.

mel·an·chol·ic [melən'kɔlik] melancólico; **mel·an·chol·y** ['~kɔli] **1.** melancolía *f*; **2.** melancólico.

mê·lee ['melei] pelea *f* confusa, refriega *f*.

mel·lif·lu·ent [me'lifluənt], *mst* **mel·lif·lu·ous** melifluo; dulcísono; (*trato*) suave, dulce.

mel·low ['melou] **1.** □ maduro, sazonado; *fig.* blando, suave, meloso; melodioso; *wine* añejo; *sl.* entre dos luces; **2.** madurar(se); suavizar(se); '**mel·low·ness** madurez *f etc.*

me·lo·di·ous [mi'loudjəs] □ melodioso; **me'lo·di·ous·ness** melodía *f*; '**mel·o·dra·ma** melodrama *m*; **mel·o·dra'mat·ic** melodramático; '**mel·o·dy** melodía *f*.

mel·on ['melən] melón *m*.

melt [melt] (*snow*) derretir(se); (*metal*) fundir(se); disolver(se); *fig.* ablandar(se); ~ *away* disolverse, desvanecerse; ~ *down* fundir; ~ *into tears* deshacerse en lágrimas; '~-**down** fusión *f*; *atomic reactor*: fusión *f* del combustible por fisión no controlada.

melt·ing ['meltiŋ] **1.** fusión *f*; derretimiento *m*; **2.** □ fundente; *fig.* tierno, dulce; '~ **point** punto *m* de fusión; '~ **pot** crisol *m* (*a. fig.*).

mem·ber ['membər] miembro *m* (*a. parl.*); socio (a *f*) *m*, individuo *m of society*; *parl.* diputado *m* (*Spanish*: a Cortes); '**mem·ber·ship** calidad *f* de miembro (*or* socio); asociación *f*; (número *m* de) miembros *m*/*pl. or* socios *m*/*pl.*; ~ *fee* cuota *f* (de socio).

mem·brane ['membrein] membrana *f*.

me·men·to [me'mentou] recuerdo *m*.

mem·oir ['memwɑ:r] memoria *f*; biografía *f*; ~*s pl.* memorias *f*/*pl*.

mem·o·ra·ble ['memərəbl] □ memorable.

mem·o·ran·dum [memə'rændəm] apunte *m*, memoria *f*; *pol.* memorándum *m*, memorando *m*.

me·mo·ri·al [mi'mɔ:riəl] **1.** conmemorativo; **2.** monumento *m* (conmemorativo); (*document*) memorial *m*; **me'mo·ri·al·ist** (*professional*) memorialista *m*/*f*, suplicante *m*/*f*; **me'mo·rial·ize** conmemorar; dirigir un memorial a.

mem·o·rize ['memәraiz] aprender de memoria.

mem·o·ry ['meməri] memoria *f*; recuerdo *m*; *computer*: memoria *f*; almacenaje *m* de datos; *from* ~ de memoria; *in* ~ *of* en memoria de.

men [men] *pl. of man*.

men·ace ['menəs] **1.** amenaza *f*; F sujeto *m* peligroso (*or* fastidioso); **2.** amenazar.

me·nag·er·ie [mi'nædʒəri] casa *f* (*or* colección *f*) de fieras.

mend [mend] **1.** *v*/*t.* remendar; componer, reparar; mejorar; reformar; (*darn*) zurcir; ~ *one's ways* enmendarse; *v*/*i.* mejorar(se); **2.** remiendo *m*; (*darn*) zurcido *m*; *be on the* ~ ir mejorando.

men·da·cious [men'deiʃəs] □ mendaz; **men·dac·i·ty** [~'dæsiti] mendacidad *f*.

men·di·can·cy ['mendikənsi] mendicidad *f*; '**men·di·cant** mendicante *adj. a. su. m*/*f*; **men'dic·i·ty** [~siti] mendicidad *f*.

mend·ing ['mendiŋ] compostura *f*; reparación *f*; (*darning*) zurcidura *f*; (*clothes*) ropa *f* de repaso.

men·folk ['menfouk] F hombres *m*/*pl*.

me·ni·al ['mi:niəl] *mst contp.* **1.** bajo; servil; doméstico; **2.** criado (a *f*) *m*; lacayo *m*.

men·in·gi·tis [menin'dʒaitis] meningitis *f*.

men·stru·al ['menstruəl] menstrual; **men·stru'a·tion** menstruación *f*.

men·su·ra·tion [mensju'reiʃn] mensura(ción) *f*.

men·tal ['mentl] □ mental; ~ *arithmetic* cálculo *m* mental; ~ *case* F paciente *m*/*f* mental; ~ *derangement* trastorno *m* mental; ~ *giant* F genio *m*; ~ *home*, ~ *hospital* manicomio *m*; ~ *hygiene* higiene *f* mental; ~ *reservation* reserva *f* mental; ~*ly ill* alienado;

men·tal·i·ty [~'tæliti] mentalidad *f*.

men·thol ['menθɔl] mentol *m*.

men·tion ['menʃən] **1.** mención *f*; alusión *f*; **2.** mencionar, mentar; (*in passing*) aludir a; *don't* ~ *it!* ¡no hay de qué!, ¡de nada!; *not to* ~ sin contar; además de.

men·tor ['mentɔ:r] mentor *m*.

men·u ['menju:] lista *f* (de platos), minuta *f*, menú *m*.

me·ow [mi'au] **1.** miau *m*; **2.** maullar.

mer·can·tile ['mə:rkəntail] mercantil, comercial; ~ *marine* marina *f* mercante.

mer·ce·nar·y [ˈmə:rsinəri] □ mercenario (⚔ a. su. m); interesado.
mer·cer [ˈmə:rsər] mercero m; sedero m; ˈ**mer·cer·y** mercería f; sedería f.
mer·cer·ize [ˈmə:rsəraiz] mercerizar.
mer·chan·dise [ˈmə:rtʃəndaiz] mercancía(s) f(pl.), géneros m/pl.
mer·chant [ˈmə:rtʃent] **1.** comerciante m/f, negociante m; F sujeto m; **2.** mercantil; ⚓ mercante; ~ *bank* banco m mercantil; ˈ**mer·chant·a·ble** comerciable; ˈ**mer·chant·man** buque m mercante; ˈ**mer·chant mar**ˈ**ine** marina f mercante.
mer·ci·ful [ˈmə:rsiful] □ misericordioso, piadoso; clemente.
mer·ci·less [ˈmə:rsilis] □ despiadado, inhumano; ~**·ness** inhumanidad f; crueldad f.
mer·cu·ri·al [mə:rˈkjuriəl] mercurial; (*lively*) vivo; (*changeable*) veleidoso; inconstante.
mer·cu·ry [ˈmə:rkjuri] mercurio m; ~ *relay* relé m de mercurio; ~ *switch* interruptor m de mercurio.
mer·cy [ˈmə:rsi] misericordia f, compasión f; clemencia f; favor m; merced f; *be at the ~ of* estar a la merced de; *it is a ~ that* gracias a Dios que; ~ *killing* eutanasia f.
mere[1] [mir] □ mero; simple; solo, no más que; ~*(st) nonsense* puro disparate m; *a ~ nothing* una friolera; ~ *words* palabras f/pl. al aire; ~*ly* meramente; sólo, nada más que.
mere[2] [~] lago m.
mer·e·tri·cious [meriˈtriʃəs] □ de oropel, postizo.
merge [mə:rdʒ] v/t. unir; mezclar; ✝ fusionar, enchufar; v/i. fundirse, ✝ fusionarse; ~ *into* ir convirtiéndose en; perderse en; ˈ**merg·er** fusión f.
me·rid·i·an [məˈridiən] **1.** *geog.*, *ast.* meridiano m; mediodía m; *Greenwich ~* meridiano m de Greenwich; **2.** meridiano; **meˈrid·i·o·nal** □ meridional.
me·ringue [məˈræŋ] merengue m.
mer·it [ˈmerit] **1.** mérito m, merecimiento m; ~*s* ⚖ méritos m/pl.; circunstancias f/pl. (de cada caso); **2.** merecer, ser digno de; **mer·i·to·ri·ous** [~ˈtɔ:riəs] □ meritorio.
mer·maid [ˈmə:rmeid] sirena f; **mer·man** [ˈ~mən] tritón m.
mer·ri·ment [ˈmerimənt] alegría f, regocijo m, alborozo m; hilaridad f.
mer·ry [ˈmeri] □ alegre, regocijado, alborozado; *sl.* calamocano; *make ~* divertirse, regocijarse; ~ *Christmas!* ¡felices pascuas!; ˈ**~-go-round** tiovivo m, caballitos m/pl.; ˈ**~·mak·ing** festividades f/pl.; alborozo m.
me·sa [ˈmeisə] *geog.* meseta f.
mes·en·ter·y [ˈmesəntəri] mesenterio m.
mesh [meʃ] **1.** malla f; ⊕ engran(aj)e m; *fig.* (*freq.* ~*es*) red f, trampa f; ⊕ *be in ~* estar engranado; **2.** v/t. *fig.* enredar; v/i. engranar (*with* con).
mes·mer·ism [ˈmezmərizm] mesmerismo m; ˈ**mes·mer·ize** hipnotizar.
mes·on [ˈmi:zɔn] *phys.* mesón m.
mess[1] [mes] **1.** revoltijo m, lío m, confusión f; asco m, suciedad f; *be in a ~* estar revuelto; (*p.*) estar en un aprieto; *make a ~ of* = **2.** v/t. (*a.* ~ *up*) echar a perder; desordenar; ensuciar; v/i.: F ~ *about* perder el tiempo (en tonterías); trabajar con desgana; ~ *about with* manosear; divertirse con; *stop ~ing about!* ¡déjate de tonterías!.
mess[2] [~] **1.** comida f; ⚔, ⚓ rancho m; ~ *kit* utensilios m/pl. de rancho; **2.** comer (juntos); arrancharse.
mes·sage [ˈmesidʒ] recado m, mensaje m; *mst tel.* parte m; *leave a ~* dejar un recado.
mes·sen·ger [ˈmesindʒər] mensajero (a f) m; mandadero (a f) m, recadero (a f) m; ~ *boy* botones m.
Mes·sieurs, *mst* **Messrs.** [ˈmesərz] s(eño)res m/pl.
mess·mate [ˈmesmeit] compañero m de rancho, comensal m; ˈ**mess·tin** ⚔ plato m de campaña.
mes·suage [ˈmeswidʒ] ⚖ finca f.
mes·sy [ˈmesi] desarreglado; sucio.
met [met] *pret. a. p.p. of meet*[2] 1.
met·a·bol·ic [metəˈbɔlik] metabólico; **meˈtab·o·lism** metabolismo m.
met·al [ˈmetl] **1.** metal m; *road:* grava f; *fig.* temple m; *fig.* ánimo m, brío m; ~*s pl.* 🚂 rieles m/pl.; ~ *polish* lustre m para metales; **2.** metálico; **3.** v/t. *road* engravar; **me·tal·lic** [miˈtælik] □ metálico; **met·al·lif·er·ous** [metəˈlifərəs] metalífero; **met·al·lur·gic, met·al·lur·gi·cal** [~ˈlə:rdʒik(l)] metalúr-

gico; ˈ**met·al·lur·gy** metalurgia *f*; ˈ**met·al·work** metalistería *f*.
met·a·mor·phose [metəˈmɔːrfouz] metamorfosear; **met·aˈmor·pho·sis** [~fəsis], *pl.* **met·aˈmor·pho·ses** [~fəsiːz] metamorfosis *f*.
met·a·phor [ˈmetəfər] metáfora *f*; **met·a·phor·ic,** *mst* **met·a·phor·i·cal** [~ˈfɔrik(l)] □ metafórico.
met·a·phys·i·cal [metəˈfizikl] □ metafísico; **met·aˈphys·ics** *mst sg.* metafísica *f*.
mete [miːt] (*mst* ~ *out*) repartir, distribuir; F *punishment* dar, imponer.
me·te·or [ˈmiːtiɔr] meteorito *m*; *fig.* meteoro *m*; **me·te·or·ic** [miːtiˈɔrik] meteórico; **me·te·or·ite** [ˈmiːtjɔrait] bólido *m*; **me·te·or·o·log·i·cal** [miːtjərəˈlɔdʒikl] □ meteorológico; **me·te·or·ol·o·gist** [~ˈrɔlədʒist] meteorologista *m/f*; **me·te·orˈol·o·gy** meteorología *f*.
me·ter [ˈmiːtər] **1.** contador *m*; medidor *m S.Am.*; (*measure*) metro *m*; **2.** medir (con contador).
meth·ane [ˈmeθein] metano *m*.
me·thinks [miˈθiŋks] (*pret.* *methought*) † *or co.* me parece.
meth·od [ˈmeθəd] método *m*, procedimiento *m*, sistema *m*; orden *m*; razón *f*; **me·thod·ic,** *mst* **me·thod·i·cal** [miˈθɔdik(l)] □ metódico; ordenado; **Meth·od·ism** [ˈmeθədizm] metodismo *m*; ˈ**Meth·od·ist** metodista *m/f*; ˈ**meth·od·ize** metodizar; **meth·od·ol·o·gy** [~ˈdɔlədʒi] metodología *f*.
meth·yl [ˈmeθil] metilo *m*; ~ *alcohol* alcohol *m* metílico; **meth·yl·at·ed spir·it** [ˈmeθileitid ˈspirit] alcohol *m* metilado (*or* desnaturalizado).
me·tic·u·lous [miˈtikjuləs] □ meticuloso; minucioso.
met·ric [ˈmetrik] métrico; ~ *system* sistema *m* métrico; ˈ**met·ri·cal** □ métrico; ˈ**met·rics** *pl. a. sg.* métrica *f*.
me·trop·o·lis [miˈtrɔpəlis] metrópoli *f*; **me·tro·pol·i·tan** [metrəˈpɔlitən] **1.** metropolitano; ♀ *Railway* metro(politano) *m*; **2.** *eccl.* metropolitano *m*.
met·tle [ˈmetl] ánimo *m*, brío *m*; temple *m*; *be on one's* ~ estar dispuesto a hacer grandes esfuerzos; *put a p. on his* ~ picar a una p. en el amor propio; **met·tle·some** [ˈ~səm] brioso, fogoso, animoso.
mewl [mjuːl] maullar; lloriquear.
mews [mjuːz] caballeriza *f*.
Mex·i·can [ˈmeksikən] mejicano (*in Mexico* mexicano) *adj. a. su. m* (a *f*).
mez·za·nine [ˈmezəniːn] entresuelo *m*.
mi·as·ma [maiˈæzmə], *pl. a.* **mi·as·ma·ta** [~tə] miasma *m*; **miˈas·mal** □ miasmático.
mi·ca [ˈmaikə] mica *f*.
mice [mais] *pl. of mouse*.
Mich·ael·mas [ˈmiklməs] fiesta *f* de San Miguel (*29 septiembre*).
mi·cro... [ˈmaikrou] micro...
mi·cro·bi·ol·o·gy [maikroubaiˈɔlədʒi] microbiología *f*; **mi·cro·bus** [ˈmaikroubʌs] microbus *m*; ˈ**mi·cro·card** (*a.* ˈ**~·fiche**) microficha *f*; **mi·cro·cosm** [ˈ~kɔzm] microcosmo *m*; ˈ**mi·cro·film** **1.** microfilm *m*; micropelícula *f*; **2.** microfilmar; ˈ**mi·cro·groove** microsurco.
mi·crom·e·ter [maiˈkrɔmitər] micrómetro *m*; **mi·cro·phone** [ˈmaikrəfoun] micrófono *m*; **mi·cro·scope** [ˈ~skoup] microscopio *m*; **mi·cro·scop·ic, mi·cro·scop·i·cal** [~sˈkɔpik(l)] □ microscópico; **mi·cro·wave** [ˈ~weiv] microonda *f*.
mid [mid] medio; *poet.* = *amid*; ~ˈ**air:** *in* ~ a medio del aire; ˈ~**course:** *in* ~ a media carrera; ˈ**~·day** **1.** mediodía *m*; **2.** de(l) mediodía.
mid·dle [ˈmidl] **1.** centro *m*, medio *m*, mitad *f*; (*waist*) cintura *f*; *in the* ~ *of* en medio de; en pleno; *in the* ~ *of the afternoon* a media tarde; *towards* (*or in*) *the* ~ *of June* a mediados de junio; **2.** medio, intermedio; de en medio; central; mediano; ~ *age* mediana edad *f*; ♀ *Ages* Edad *f* Media; ~ *class*(*es pl.*) clase *f* media; ~ *distance* segundo término *m*; ˈ**~-ˈaged** de mediana edad, de edad madura; ˈ~ ˈ**class** de la clase media; ˈ**~·man** intermediario *m*; corredor *m*; ˈ**~·most** más céntrico; ˈ**~-sized** de tamaño mediano; *p.* de estatura mediana; ˈ**~·weight** *boxing*: peso *m* medio.
mid·dling [ˈmidliŋ] **1.** *adj.* mediano, regular; mediocre; **2.** *adv.* así, así; medianamente.
mid·dy [ˈmidi] F = *midshipman*.
midge [midʒ] mosca *f* pequeña; enano (a *f*) *m*; **midg·et** [ˈ~it] **1.** enano (a *f*) *m*; **2.** (en) miniatura.

mid·land [ˈmidlənd] **1.** del interior, del centro (de un país); **2.** *the* ♀*s pl. región central de Inglaterra*; ˈ**mid·night** (de) medianoche *f*; *burn the* ~ *oil* quemarse las cejas; **mid·riff** [ˈ~rif] diafragma *m*; ˈ**mid·ship·man** guardia marina *m*; ˈ**mid·ships** en medio del navío; **midst** [midst] **1.** *in the* ~ *of* entre, en medio de; *in our* ~ entre nosotros; **2.** *prp. poet.* = *amidst*; ˈ**mid·stream:** *in* ~ en medio de la corriente; ˈ**mid·sum·mer** pleno verano *m*; solsticio *m* de verano; ♀ *Day* fiesta *f* de San Juan (*24 junio*); ˈ**mid·way 1.** (situado) a mitad del camino; **2.** mitad *f* del camino; avenida *f* central; ˈ**mid·wife** comadrona *f*, partera *f*; **mid·wife·ry** [ˈmidwaifri] partería *f*; ˈ**mid**ˈ**win·ter** pleno invierno *m*; solsticio *m* de invierno.

mien [mi:n] *lit.* semblante *m*; porte *m*, aire *m*.

might [mait] **1.** fuerza *f*, poder(ío) *m*; *with* ~ *and main* con todas sus *etc.* fuerzas, a más no poder; **2.** *pret. of may*[2]; podría *etc.*; ser posible; ojalá; *for many phrases, v. may*; *they* ~ *arrive today* es posible que lleguen hoy; **might·i·ness** [ˈ~inis] fuerza *f*; poder(ío) *m*; grandeza *f*; ˈ**might·y 1.** □ fuerte, potente; F enorme; **2.** *adv.* F muy.

mi·gnon·ette [minjəˈnət] reseda *f*.

mi·graine [ˈmai:grein] jaqueca *f*, migraña *f*.

mi·grant [ˈmaigrənt] **1.** migratorio; peregrino; nómada; ~ *worker* bracero *m* migratorio; **2.** (*bird*) ave *f* de paso.

mi·grate [maiˈgreit] emigrar; **mi**ˈ**gra·tion** migración *f*; **mi·gra·to·ry** [ˈ~grətəri] migratorio.

mike [maik] *sl.* micrófono *m*.

milch [miltʃ]: ~ *cow* vaca *f* lechera.

mild [maild] □ suave; manso; blando; apacible; dulce; *weather* templado; ⚕ benigno; (*slight*) ligero; *to put it* ~*ly* para no decir más.

mil·dew [ˈmildju:] **1.** moho *m*; añublo *m on wheat*; mildeu *m on vine*; **2.** enmohecer(se).

mild·ness [ˈmaildnis] suavidad *f etc.*

mile [mail] milla *f* (= *1609,34 m.*).

mile·age [ˈmailidʒ] número *m* de millas; distancia *f* en millas; *approx.* kilometraje *m*; ~ *ticket* billete *m* kilométrico.

mile·stone [ˈmailstoun] piedra *f* miliar(ia); mojón *m*; *fig. be a* ~ hacer época.

mi·lieu [milˈju:] medio *m*, ambiente *m*.

mil·i·tan·cy [ˈmilitənsi] belicosidad *f*; ˈ**mil·i·tant** □ militante; belicoso; agresivo; **mil·i·ta·rism** [ˈ~rizəm] militarismo *m*; ˈ**mil·i·tar·ize** militarizar; ˈ**mil·i·tar·y 1.** □ militar; de guerra; **2.** *the* ~ los militares; **mil·i·tate** [ˈ~teit] militar (*against* contra; *in favor of* a favor de); **mi·li·tia** [miˈliʃə] milicia *f*; **mi**ˈ**li·tia·man** [~mən] miliciano *m*.

milk [milk] **1.** leche *f*; ~ *diet* régimen *m* lácteo; ~ *of human kindness* compasión *f*; ~ *of magnesia* leche *f* de magnesia; ~ *tooth* diente *m* de leche; *powdered* (*whole*) ~ leche *f* en polvo (no desnatada); **2.** *v/t.* ordeñar; *fig.* chupar; *v/i.* dar leche; ˈ**milk-and-**ˈ**wa·ter** débil, flojo; ˈ**milk·er** ordeñador (-a *f*) *m*; vaca *f etc.* lechera; ˈ**milk·ing** ordeño *m*; ˈ**milk·ing ma**ˈ**chine** ordeñadora *f* (mecánica).

milk...: ˈ**~·maid** lechera *f*; ˈ**~·man** lechero *m*; ˈ~ ˈ**shake** batido *m* de leche; ˈ**~·sop** marica *m*; ˈ**milk·y** lechoso; ♀ *Way* Vía *f* Láctea.

mill[1] [mil] **1.** molino *m*; molinillo *m for coffee etc.*; (*factory*) fábrica *f*, taller *m*; *spinning*: hilandería *f*; *weaving*: tejeduría *f*; F pugilato *m*; ~ *end* retazo *m* de hilandería; F *go through the* ~ pasar por muchas cosas en la vida; aprender por experiencia; entrenarse rigurosamente; *put a p. through the* ~ pasar por la piedra; **2.** *v/t.* moler; ⊕ fresar; *coin* acordonar; *cloth* abatanar; *chocolate* batir; ~*ed edge* cordoncillo *m*; *v/i.*: ~ *around* circular en masa, moverse con impaciencia.

mill[2] [~] milésimo *m* de dólar.

mil·len·ni·al [miˈleniəl] milenario; **mil·le·nar·y** [ˈ~əri] milenario *adj. a. su. m*; **mil**ˈ**len·ni·um** [~iəm] milenario *m*, milenio *m*.

mil·le·pede [ˈmilipi:d] miriápodo *m*; miriópodo *m*; milípedo *m*.

mill·er [ˈmilər] molinero *m*.

mil·les·i·mal [miˈlesiməl] milésimo.

mil·let [ˈmilit] mijo *m*.

mill hand [ˈmilhænd] obrero (a *f*) *m*, operario (a *f*) *m*.

mil·li·ard [ˈmiljɑ:rd] mil millones *m/pl.*

mil·li·gram [ˈmiligræm] miligramo [*m.*}

mil·li·li·ter ['milili:tər] mililitro *m.*
mil·li·me·ter ['milimi:tər] milímetro *m.*
mil·li·ner ['milinər] sombrerera *f*, modista *f* (de sombreros); '**mil·li·ner·y** sombrerería *f*; sombreros *m/pl.* de señora.
mill·ing ['miliŋ] molienda *f*; cordoncillo *m of coin*; ⊕ ~ *cutter* fresa *f*; ~ *machine* fresadora *f.*
mil·lion ['miljən] millón *m*; *three* ~ *men* tres millones de hombres; **mil·lion·aire** [~'ner] millonario (a *f*) *m*; **mil·lionth** ['miljənθ] millonésimo *adj. a. su. m.*
mill...: '~ **pond** represa *f* de molino, cubo *m*; '~ **race** caz *m*; '~**·stone** piedra *f* de molino, muela *f.*
mil·om·e·ter [maɪ'lɔmɪtər] pedómetro *m*; *approx.* cuentakilómetros *m.*
milt[1] [milt] *ichth.* lecha *f.*
milt[2] [~] *anat.* bazo *m.*
mime [maim] **1.** mimo *m*; pantomima *f*, mímica *f*; **2.** *v/t.* remedar, hacer en pantomima; *v/i.* hacer de mimo.
mim·e·o·graph ['mimiəgræf] **1.** mimeógrafo *m*; **2.** mimeografiar.
mim·ic ['mimik] **1.** mímico; fingido; **2.** remedador (-a *f*) *m*; **3.** remedar; imitar; '**mim·ic·ry** mímica *f*, remedo *m*; *zo.* mimetismo *m.*
min·a·ret ['minəret] alminar *m.*
min·a·to·ry ['minətɔ:ri] amenazador.
mince [mins] **1.** *v/t.* picar; desmenuzar; *not to* ~ *matters, not to* ~ *one's words* no tener pelos en la lengua; *v/i.* andar con pasos menuditos; hablar remilgadamente; **2.** carne *f* picada (*a.* ~*d meat*); '~**·meat** (*carne picada con frutas*) cuajado *m*; *make* ~ *of* hacer pedazos; '~ '**pie** pastel *m* de cuajado; '**minc·er** molinillo *m*, máquina *f* de picar carne, picadora *f.*
minc·ing ['minsiŋ] remilgado, afectado; '~ **ma·chine** = *meat chopper.*
mind [maind] **1.** mente *f*; (*intellect*) inteligencia *f*, entendimiento *m*; (*not matter*) espíritu *m*; ánimo *m*; juicio *m*; (*opinion*) parecer *m*; inclinación *f*; gusto *m*; memoria *f*; ~*'s eye* imaginación *f*; *change one's* ~ cambiar de opinión, mudar de parecer; *give one's* ~ *to* aplicarse a; *give a p. a piece of one's* ~ decirle cuatro verdades a una p.; *I have* (*half*) *a* ~ *to go, I have a good* ~ *to go* estoy por ir; tengo ganas de ir; por poco me marcho; *know one's own* ~ saber lo que uno quiere; *bear* (*or keep*) *in* ~ tener presente, tener en cuenta; *have in* ~ pensar en; tener pensado; *put a p. in* ~ *of* recordarle a una p.; *be in one's right* ~ estar en sus cabales; *make up one's* ~ resolverse, decidirse (*to* a); determinar (*to inf.*); tomar partido; *of one* ~ unánimes; *have s.t. on one's* ~ estar preocupado; *out of* ~ olvidado; *out of one's* ~ fuera de juicio, (como) loco; *set one's* ~ *on* desear con vehemencia; estar resuelto a; *it slipped my* ~ se me escapó de la memoria; *speak one's* ~ decir su parecer, hablar con franqueza; *with one* ~ unánimemente; **2.** *v/t.* (*heed*) fijarse en, hacer caso de; (*bear in* ~) tener en cuenta; cuidar; (*beware of*) tener cuidado de; (*remember*) acordarse de; (*be put out by*) sentir molestia por; tener inconveniente en; *do you* ~ *the noise?* ¿le molesta el ruido?; *do you* ~ *lending it to me?* ¿no te importa prestármelo?; *would you* ~ *taking off your hat?* ¿quiere hacer el favor de quitarse el sombrero?; *v. business*; *v/i.* tener cuidado; sentir molestia; tener inconveniente; ~*!* ¡cuidado!; *never* ~*!* ¡no haga Vd. caso!; ¡no importa!; ¡no se preocupe!; ¿qué más da?; '~ **bend·ing** *sl.* alucinante; '~**-blow·ing** *sl.* alucinante en exceso; '~**-bog·gling** deslumbrante; abrumador; '**mind·ed** inclinado, dispuesto; de pensamientos...; '**mind·ful** □ atento (*of* a), cuidadoso (*of* de); '**mind·less** □ estúpido; absurdo; ridículo; negligente (*of* de).
mine[1] [main] (el) mío, (la) mía *etc.*
mine[2] [~] **1.** mina *f* (*a.* ⚓, ⚔, *fig.*); **2.** *v/t.* extraer; minar (*mst* ⚔); ⚔, ⚓ sembrar minas en; *v/i.* dedicarse a la minería; extraer minerales; ⚔ minar; '~**·field** campo *m* de minas; '~**·lay·er** buque *m* minador; '**min·er** minero *m.*
min·er·al ['minərəl] mineral *adj. a. su. m*; ~ *jelly* jalea *f* mineral; ~ *oil* aceite *m* mineral; ~ *water* agua *f* mineral; gaseosa *f* (*a.* F ~*s*); '**min·er·al·ize** mineralizar; **min·er·al·o·gist** [~'rælədʒist] mineralogista *m/f*; **min·er'al·o·gy** mineralogía *f.*
mine sweep·er ['mainswi:pər] barreminas *m*, dragaminas *m.*
min·gle ['miŋgl] mezclar(se), con-

fundir(se) (*in*, *with* con); asociarse, fraternizar (*with* con).
min·gy [ˈmindʒi] F cicatero, tacaño.
mi·ni... [ˈmini:] mini...
min·i·a·ture [ˈminjətʃər] **1.** miniatura *f*; modelo *m* pequeño; **2.** (en) miniatura; diminuto.
mi·ni·com·put·er [mini:kəmˈpju:tər] miniordenador *m*.
min·im [ˈminim] ♪ blanca *f*; *pharm.* mínima *f*; *eccl.* mínimo *m*; ˈ**min·i·mize** minimizar, reducir al mínimo; atenuar; empequeñecer; menospreciar; **min·i·mum** [ˈ~iməm] **1.** mínimo *m*, mínimum *m*; **2.** mínimo; ~ *wage* jornal *m* mínimo.
min·ing [ˈmainiŋ] **1.** minería *f*; extracción *f*; **2.** minero; ~ *engineer* ingeniero *m* de minas.
min·ion [ˈminjən] favorito (a *f*) *m*; paniaguado *m*; satélite *m*; *typ.* miñona *f*.
min·i·skirt [ˈmini:skərt] minifalda *f*.
min·i·ster [ˈministər] **1.** ministro *m*; **2.** ministrar; atender (*to* a); **min·is·te·ri·al** [~ˈtiriəl] □ *pol.* ministerial; de ministro.
min·is·trant [ˈministrənt] **1.** ministrador; **2.** *eccl.* oficiante *m*; **min·is·ˈtra·tion** ayuda *f*; servicio *m*; *eccl.* ministerio *m*; ˈ**min·is·try** ministerio *m*; *eccl.* sacerdocio *m*; *radio* ~ (*emisiones religiosas*) ministerio *m* radiofónico.
mink [miŋk] (piel *f* de) visón *m*.
min·now [ˈminou] pececillo *m* de agua dulce.
mi·nor [ˈmainər] **1.** menor (*a.* ♪); menor de edad; secundario; subalterno; *detail* sin importancia; ~ *key* tono *m* menor; ~ *third* tercera *f* menor; **2.** menor *m*/*f* de edad; *phls.* menor *f*; *Am. univ.* asignatura *f* secundaria; **mi·nor·i·ty** [maiˈnɔriti] minoría *f*; (*age*) minoridad *f*; ~ *government* gobierno *m* minoritario.
min·ster [ˈminstər] iglesia *f* de un monasterio; catedral *f*.
min·strel [ˈminstrəl] juglar *m*, trovador *m*; cantor *m*; cómico *m* (disfrazado de negro); **min·strel·sy** [ˈ~si] canto *m*; *hist.* arte *m* del trovador (*or* juglar); *hist.* gaya ciencia *f*.
mint[1] [mint] ⚘ hierbabuena *f*, menta *f*; (*sweet*) pastilla *f* de menta.
mint[2] [~] **1.** casa *f* de moneda; *a ~ of money* un dineral; **2.** sin usar; pristino; **3.** acuñar; *fig.* inventar; ˈ**mint·age** acuñación *f*; moneda *f* acuñada.
min·u·et [minjuˈet] minué *m*, minuete *m*.
mi·nus [ˈmainəs] **1.** *prp.* menos; F sin; **2.** *adj.* negativo; **3.** (signo) menos *m*.
mi·nute [maiˈnju:t] diminuto, menudo; minucioso; ˈ**~·ly** minuciosamente.
min·ute [ˈminit] **1.** minuto *m*; *fig.* instante *m*, momento *m*; (*note*) nota *f*, minuta *f*; **~s** *pl.* acta(s) *f*(*pl.*); procedimientos *m*/*pl.*; **2.** levantar acta de; minutar; ~ **book** libro *m* de actas; ˈ**min·ute hand** minutero *m*.
mi·nu·ti·a [miˈnju:ʃiə], *mst pl.* **miˈnu·ti·ae** [~ʃii:] detalle(s) *m*(*pl.*) minucioso(s).
minx [miŋks] picaruela *f*, moza *f* descarada.
mir·a·cle [ˈmirəkl] milagro *m*; **mi·rac·u·lous** [miˈrækjuləs] □ milagroso.
mi·rage [ˈmirɑ:ʒ] espejismo *m*.
mire [ˈmaiər] fango *m*, lodo *m*.
mirk [mə:rk] = *murk*.
mir·ror [ˈmirər] **1.** espejo *m* (*a. fig.*); *mot.* retrovisor *m*; **2.** reflejar.
mirth [mə:rθ] regocijo *m*, alegría *f*; hilaridad *f*, risa *f*; **mirth·ful** [ˈ~ful] □ alegre; reidor; ˈ**mirth·less** □ triste, sin alegría.
mir·y [ˈmairi] lodoso, fangoso; ~ *place* lodazal *m*.
mis... [mis] mal...
mis·ad·ven·ture [ˈmisədˈventʃər] desgracia *f*, accidente *m*.
mis·al·li·ance [misəˈlaiəns] casamiento *m* desigual.
mis·an·thrope [ˈmizənθroup] misántropo *m*; **mis·an·throp·ic, mis·an·throp·i·cal** [~ˈθrɔpik(l)] □ misantrópico; **mis·an·thro·pist** [miˈzænθrəpist] misántropo *m*; **misˈan·thro·py** misantropía *f*.
mis·ap·pli·ca·tion [ˈmisæpliˈkeiʃn] aplicación *f* errada; abuso *m*; **mis·ap·ply** [ˈ~əˈplai] aplicar mal; abusar de.
mis·ap·pre·hend [ˈmisæpriˈhend] entender mal; ˈ**mis·ap·preˈhen·sion** equivocación *f*; concepto *m* erróneo; *be under a ~* estar equivocado.
mis·ap·pro·pri·ate [ˈmisəˈproupri-eit] malversar; ˈ**mis·ap·pro·priˈa·tion** malversación *f*.

mis·be·got(·ten) [ˈmisbiˈgɔt(n)] bastardo, ilegítimo.
mis·be·have [ˈmisbiˈheiv] portarse mal; (*child*) ser malo; **ˈmis·beˈhav·ior** [~jər] mala conducta *f*, mal comportamiento *m*.
mis·be·lief [ˈmisbiˈliːf] error *m*; creencia *f* heterodoxa; **ˈmis·beˈliev·er** heterodoxo (a *f*) *m*.
mis·cal·cu·late [ˈmisˈkælkjuleit] calcular mal; **ˈmis·cal·cuˈla·tion** cálculo *m* errado; desacierto *m*.
mis·car·riage [misˈkæridʒ] malparto *m*, aborto *m*; malogro *m*, fracaso *m*; ✉ extravío *m*; ~ *of justice* error *m* judicial; **misˈcar·ry** malparir, abortar; salir mal, malograrse; ✉ extraviarse.
mis·ce·ge·na·tion [misidʒiˈneiʃn] entrecruzamiento *m* de razas.
mis·cel·la·ne·ous [misiˈleinjəs] misceláneo.
mis·cel·la·ny [miˈseləni] miscelánea *f*.
mis·chance [misˈtʃæns] mala suerte *f*; infortunio *m*; accidente *m*.
mis·chief [ˈmistʃif] daño *m*; mal *m*; malicia *f*; travesura *f*, diablura *f* *esp. of child*; picardía *f*; F (*p.*) diablillo *m*; **ˈ~·mak·er** enredador (-a *f*) *m*, chismoso (a *f*) *m*; alborotador (-a *f*) *m*.
mis·chie·vous [ˈmistʃivəs] dañoso, perjudicial; malo; malicioso; *child* travieso.
mis·con·ceive [ˈmiskənˈsiːv] entender mal, formar un concepto erróneo de; **mis·con·cep·tion** [ˈ~ˈsepʃn] concepto *m* erróneo, equivocación *f*.
mis·con·duct [ˈmisˈkɔndəkt] mala conducta *f*; adulterio *m*.
mis·con·struc·tion [ˈmiskənˈstrʌkʃn] mala interpretación *f*; **mis·con·strue** [ˈ~ˈstruː] interpretar mal.
mis·count [ˈmisˈkaunt] **1.** contar mal; **2.** cuenta *f* errónea.
mis·cre·ant [ˈmiskriənt] malandrín *adj. a. su. m* (-a *f*), bellaco *adj. a. su. m* (a *f*).
mis·date [misˈdeit] fechar erróneamente.
mis·deal [ˈmisˈdiːl] [*irr.* (*deal*)] dar mal (las cartas).
mis·deed [ˈmisˈdiːd] malhecho *m*, delito *m*.
mis·de·mean·or [ˈmisdiˈmiːnər] mala conducta *f*; ⚖ delito *m* de menor cuantía.
mis·di·rect [ˈmisdiˈrekt] dirigir mal; extraviar; **ˈmis·diˈrec·tion** mala dirección *f*; instrucciones *f/pl.* erradas.
mi·ser [ˈmaizər] avaro (a *f*) *m*.
mis·er·a·ble [ˈmizərəbl] □ triste; miserable; lastimoso; despreciable; F indispuesto.
mi·ser·ly [ˈmaizərli] avariento, tacaño.
mis·er·y [ˈmizəri] sufrimiento *m*; aflicción *f*; infelicidad *f*; miseria *f*.
mis·fire [ˈmisˈfaiər] **1.** falla *f* de tiro (*mot.* de encendido); **2.** fallar.
mis·fit [ˈmisfit] casa *f* mal ajustada; traje *m* que no cae bien; (*p.*) inadaptado (a *f*) *m*; *fig.* rebelde *m*.
mis·for·tune [misˈfɔːrtʃn] desgracia *f*, infortunio *m*, desventura *f*.
mis·giv·ing [misˈgiviŋ] recelo *m*, duda *f*; presentimiento *m*.
mis·gov·ern [ˈmisˈgʌvərn] gobernar mal, desgobernar; **ˈmisˈgov·ern·ment** desgobierno *m*; mala administración *f*.
mis·guide [ˈmisˈgaid] dirigir mal; aconsejar mal.
mis·han·dle [ˈmisˈhændl] manejar mal; maltratar.
mis·hap [ˈmishæp] contratiempo *m*, accidente *m*; desgracia *f*.
mish·mash [ˈmiʃˈmæʃ] baturrillo *m*; mezcolanza *f*.
mis·in·form [ˈmisinˈfɔːrm] informar mal, dar informes erróneos a; **ˈmis·in·forˈma·tion** informes *m/pl.* erróneos (*or* falsos).
mis·in·ter·pret [ˈmisinˈtəːrprit] interpretar mal; **ˈmis·in·ter·preˈta·tion** mala interpretación *f*.
mis·judge [ˈmisˈdʒʌdʒ] juzgar mal; **ˈmisˈjudg·ment** juicio *m* equivocado (*or* injusto).
mis·lay [misˈlei] [*irr.* (*lay*)] extraviar, perder.
mis·lead [misˈliːd] [*irr.* (*lead*)] extraviar; despistar; descarriar; engañar; **misˈlead·ing** engañoso.
mis·man·age [ˈmisˈmænidʒ] administrar mal, manejar mal; **ˈmisˈman·age·ment** mala administración *f*, desgobierno *m*; mal manejo *m*.
mis·no·mer [ˈmisˈnoumər] nombre *m* equivocado (*or* inapropiado).
mi·sog·a·mist [miˈsɔgəmist] misógamo (a *f*) *m*.
mi·sog·y·nist [maiˈsɔdʒinist] misógino *m*; **miˈsog·y·ny** misoginia *f*.

mis·place ['mis'pleis] colocar mal; poner fuera de su lugar; extraviar; *~d affection etc.* equivocado, inmerecido; '**mis'place·ment** colocación *f* fuera de lugar; extravío *m*.
mis·print ['mis'print] **1.** errata *f*, error *m* de imprenta; **2.** imprimir mal.
mis·pro·nounce ['misprə'nauns] pronunciar mal; **mis·pro·nun·ci·a·tion** ['~prənʌnsi'eiʃn] mala pronunciación *f*.
mis·quo·ta·tion ['miskwou'teiʃn] cita *f* falsa (*or* equivocada); '**mis'quote** citar mal.
mis·read ['mis'ri:d] [*irr.* (*read*)] leer mal; interpretar mal.
mis·rep·re·sent ['misrepri'zent] desfigurar, falsificar; describir engañosamente; '**mis·rep·re·sen'ta·tion** falsificación *f*, tergiversación *f*; descripción *f* falsa.
mis·rule ['mis'ru:l] **1.** desgobierno *m*; desorden *m*; **2.** desgobernar.
miss[1] [mis] señorita *f*; muchacha *f*; jovencita *f*; F niña *f* precoz.
miss[2] [~] **1.** tiro *m* errado; (*mistake*) falta *f*, desacierto *m*; (*failure*) malogro *m*, fracaso *m*; **2.** *v/t. aim, target, vocation* errar; *chance, train etc.* perder; *solution* no acertar; *th. sought* no encontrar; (*regret absence of*) echar de menos; *meaning* no entender; omitir (*a.* ~ *out*); (*overlook*) pasar por alto; ~ *one's footing* perder el pie; *the shot just ~ed me* por poco la bala me mató; *I ~ed your lecture* perdí su conferencia, no pude asistir a su conferencia; *I ~ed what you said* se me escapó lo que dijo Vd.; *v/i.* errar el blanco; fallar, salir mal; *mot.* ratear.
mis·sal [misl] misal *m*.
mis·shap·en ['mis'ʃeipən] deforme.
mis·sile [misl] misil *m*; proyectil *m*; arma *f* arrojadiza; cohete *m*; ~ *gap* desigualdad *f* de armas proyectiles poseídas por dos potencias; **mis·sile·ry** ['~ri] cohetería *f*; ciencia *f* de las armas proyectiles.
miss·ing ['misiŋ] ausente; perdido; ⚔ desaparecido; *be* ~ faltar.
mis·sion ['miʃn] misión *f*; '**mis·sion·ar·y** misionero *adj. a. su. m* (a *f*).
mis·sive ['misiv] misiva *f*.
mis·spell ['mis'spel] [*irr.* (*spell*)] deletrear (*or* escribir) mal; '**mis'spell·ing** error *m* de ortografía.
mis·spend ['mis'spend] [*irr.* (*spend*)] malgastar, desperdiciar, perder.
mis·state ['mis'steit] relatar mal; '**mis'state·ment** relación *f* inexacta (*or* falsa).
mis·sus ['misəz] F: *the* ~ la parienta.
miss·y ['misi] F señorita *f*, hija *f* mía.
mist [mist] **1.** niebla *f*; (*low*) neblina *f*; bruma *f at sea*; (*slight*) calina *f*; *Scotch* ~ llovizna *f*; **2.** an(i)eblar(se); empañar(se).
mis·tak·a·ble [mis'teikəbl] confundible, equívoco; sujeto a errores; **mis·take** [~'teik] **1.** [*irr.* (*take*)] *v/t.* entender mal; confundir, equivocar(se en); ~ *A for B* equivocar A con B; *be ~n* engañarse; equivocarse (*for* con); *v/i.* ⚒ equivocarse; **2.** equivocación *f*; error *m*; falta *f in exercise*; *by* ~ por equivocación; sin querer; *and no ~!* ¡sin duda alguna!, ¡ya lo creo!; *make a* ~ equivocarse; **mis'tak·en** □ equivocado; erróneo, incorrecto; ~ *identity* identificación *f* errónea.
mis·ter ['mistər] señor *m* (*abbr.* **Mr.**).
mis·time ['mis'taim] hacer (*or* decir) a deshora; cronometrar mal.
mist·i·ness ['mistinis] nebulosidad *f*.
mis·tle thrush [misl θrʌʃ] zorzal *m* charlo.
mis·tle·toe ['misltou] muérdago *m*.
mis·trans·late ['mistræns'leit] traducir mal; '**mis·trans'la·tion** mala traducción *f*.
mis·tress ['mistris] ama *f* de casa; dueña *f*; maestra *f* (de escuela), profesora *f*; amante *f*, querida *f*; señora *f* (*abbr.* **Mrs.** ['misiz]).
mis·tri·al [mis'traiəl] ⚖ pleito *m* (*or* juicio *m*) viciado de nulidad.
mis·trust ['mis'trʌst] **1.** desconfiar de; dudar de; **2.** desconfianza *f*, recelo *m*; '**mis'trust·ful** [~ful] □ desconfiado, receloso.
mist·y ['misti] □ nebuloso, brumoso; *fig.* vaporoso, vago; *glass* empañado.
mis·un·der·stand ['misʌndər'stænd] [*irr.* (*stand*)] entender mal, comprender mal; '**mis·un·der'stand·ing** equivocación *f*, concepto *m* erróneo; desavenencia *f*; malentendido *m*.
mis·use **1.** ['mis'ju:z] emplear mal; abusar de; maltratar; **2.** ['~'ju:s] mal uso *m*, abuso *m*; maltratamiento *m*.

mite[1] [mait] *zo.* ácaro *m* (doméstico).
mite[2] [~] (*coin*) ardite *m*; (*contribution*) óbolo *m*; pizca *f*; niño (a *f*) *m* muy pequeño (a).
mi·ter [ˈmaitər] **1.** mitra *f*; ⊕ inglete *m*; ~ *joint* ensambladura *f* de inglete; ~ *box* caja *f* de ingletes; **2.** ⊕ ingletear.
mit·i·gate [ˈmitigeit] mitigar; **mit·iˈga·tion** mitigación *f*.
mitt [mit] guante *m* forreado; *sl.* mano *f*; **mit·ten** [mitn] mitón *m*, guante *m* con solo el pulgar separado.
mix [miks] mezclar, mixturar; *flour, plaster etc.* amasar; *drinks* preparar; *salad* aderezar; combinar; confundir; ~*ed* mixto; mezclado; (*assorted*) variado, surtido; ~ *up* confundir; *be* (*or get*) ~*ed up in* (*or with*) mezclarse en, mojar en; *v/i.* mezclarse; (*p.*) asociarse; (*get on well*) llevarse bien; ~ *in* (*or with*) *high society* frecuentar la alta sociedad; ˈ**mix·er** mezclador *m* (*a. radio*); F persona *f* sociable; *be a good* ~ tener don de gentes; **mix·ture** [ˈ~tʃər] mezcla *f*, mixtura *f*; ˈ**mix-ˈup** confusión *f*; F lío *m*, enredo *m*.
miz·zen [ˈmizn] (palo *m* de) mesana *f*.
miz·zle [ˈmizl] F zafarse; F lloviznar.
mne·mon·ic [niˈmɔnik] **1.** (m)nemotécnico; **2. mneˈmon·ics** (m)nemotécnica *f*.
moan [moun] **1.** gemido *m*, quejido *m*; **2.** gemir; F quejarse.
moat [mout] **1.** foso *m*; **2.** fosar.
mob [mɔb] **1.** gentío *m*, muchedumbre *f*; *b.s.* chusma *f*, turba *f*, populacho *m*; *sl.* pandilla *f*; **2.** atropellar; atacar en masa; festejar tumultuosamente.
mob·cap [ˈmɔbkæp] cofia *f*; toca *f* de mujer.
mo·bile [ˈmoubil] móvil, movible; **mo·bil·i·ty** [mouˈbiliti] movilidad *f*; **mo·bi·li·za·tion** [moubilaiˈzeiʃn] movilización *f*; ˈ**mo·bi·lize** movilizar.
mob law [ˈmɔblɔː] ley *f* de Lynch.
mob·ster [ˈmɔbstər] *sl.* gángster *m*; panderillero *m*; ~**ism** [ˈ~izm] gangsterismo *m*; acción(es) *f*(*pl.*) de los gángsters.
moc·ca·sin [ˈmɔkəsin] mocasín *m*.
mock [mɔk] **1.** burla *f*; *make a* ~ *of* poner en ridículo; **2.** fingido, simulado; burlesco; **3.** *v/t.* burlarse de, mofarse de; (*mimic*) remedar; frustrar; decepcionar; *v/i.* mofarse (*at* de); ˈ**mock·er** mofador (-a *f*) *m*; burlador *m*; F = *mocking bird*; ˈ**mock·er·y** mofa *f*, burla *f*; hazmerreír *m*; parodia *f*, mal remedo *m*; *make a* ~ *of* hacer ridículo; ˈ**mock-heˈro·ic** heroicocómico; ˈ**mock·ing** **1.** burlas *f/pl.*; **2.** □ burlón; ˈ**mock·ing bird** sinsonte *m*; ˈ**mock-ˈor·ange** jeringuilla *f*; ˈ**mock·up** maqueta *f*, modelo *m* en escala natural.
mod·al [ˈmoudl] □ modal; **mo·dal·i·ty** [mouˈdæliti] modalidad *f*.
mode [moud] modo *m* (*a. phls.*, ♪); manera *f*; (*fashion*) moda *f*.
mod·el [ˈmɔdl] **1.** modelo *m* (*a. fig.*); ⚠ maqueta *f*; (*fashion*) ~ modelo *m/f*; *attr.* modelo; ~ *airplane* aeromodelo *m*; ~ *town* ciudad *f* modelo; **2.** *v/t.* modelar (*on* sobre); planear (*after, on* según); *v/i.* servir de modelo; **mod·el·er** [ˈmɔdlər] modelador (-a *f*) *m*; ˈ**mod·el·(l)ing** modelado *m*.
mod·er·ate **1.** [ˈmɔdərit] □ moderado (*pol. a. su. m*); regular, mediocre; *price* módico; **2.** [ˈ~reit] moderar(se), templar(se); (*wind*) amainar; ser interlocutor (*de debate, etc.*); **mod·er·a·tion** [~ˈreiʃn] moderación *f*; *in* ~ con moderación; ˈ**mod·er·a·tor** moderador (-a *f*) *m*; árbitro *m*; *eccl. presidente de la asamblea de la Iglesia Escocesa.*
mod·ern [ˈmɔdərn] **1.** moderno; **2.**: *the* ~*s pl.* los modernos; ˈ**mod·ern·ism** modernismo *m*; **mo·der·ni·ty** [mɔˈdəːrniti] modernidad *f*; ˈ**mod·ern·ize** modernizar(se).
mod·est [ˈmɔdist] □ modesto; moderado; púdico; ˈ**mod·es·ty** modestia *f*; moderación *f*; pudor *m*.
mod·i·cum [ˈmɔdikəm] cantidad *f* módica, poco *m*.
mod·i·fi·a·ble [ˈmɔdifaiəbl] modificable; **mod·i·fi·ca·tion** [~fiˈkeiʃn] modificación *f*; **mod·i·fy** [ˈ~fai] modificar(se).
mod·ish [ˈmoudiʃ] de moda, elegante.
mod·u·late [ˈmɔdjuleit] modular; **mod·uˈla·tion** modulación *f*; *radio*: *frequency* ~ modulación *f* de frecuencia; ˈ**mod·u·la·tor** modulador *m*.
Mo·gul [mouˈgʌl]: *the Great* ~ el Gran Mogol; ♀ magnate *m*.

mo·hair [ˈmouher] moer *m.*
Mo·ham·med·an [mouˈhæmidən] mahometano *adj. a. su. m* (a *f*).
moi·e·ty [ˈmɔiəti] mitad *f*; parte *f.*
moist [mɔist] húmedo; mojado; **mois·ten** [ˈmɔisn] humedecer(se); mojar(se); ˈ**moist·ness, mois·ture** [ˈ~tʃər] humedad *f.*
moke [mouk] *sl.* burro *m.*
mo·lar [ˈmoulər] molar *m*, muela *f.*
mo·las·ses [məˈlæsiz] melaza(s) *f*(*pl.*).
mold [mould] = *mo*(*u*)*ld.*
mole [moul] *zo.* topo *m*; (*spot*) lunar *m*; ⚓ malecón *m*, muelle *m*; ⚘ mola *f.*
mo·lec·u·lar [mouˈlekjulər] molecular; ~ *physics* física *f* molecular; ~ *weight* peso *m* molecular; **mol·e·cule** [ˈmɔlikjuːl] molécula *f.*
mole·hill [ˈmoulhil] topera *f*; *make a mountain out of a* ~ hacer de una pulga un elefante; ˈ**mole·skin** piel *f* de topo; molesquina *f.*
mo·lest [mouˈlest] importunar; faltar al respeto a; molestar; **mo·les·ta·tion** [moulesˈteiʃn] importunidad *f*; vejación *f*; molestia *f.*
moll [mɔl] *sl.* amiga *f*, ramera *f.*
mol·li·fy [ˈmɔlifai] apaciguar, mitigar.
mol·lusc, mol·lusk [ˈmɔləsk] molusco *m.*
mol·ly·cod·dle [ˈmɔlikɔdl] **1.** niño *m* mimado; alfeñique *m*, marica *m*; **2.** mimar; consentir.
mol·ten [ˈmoultən] fundido; derretido; *lava etc.* líquido.
mo·ment [ˈmoumənt] momento *m*; instante *m*; importancia *f*; *at any* ~ de un momento a otro; *at* (*or for*) *the* ~ de momento, por ahora; *at this* ~ en este momento; *in a* ~ en un momento; ˈ**mo·men·tar·y** □ momentáneo; **mo·men·tous** [~ˈmentəs] □ grave, trascendental, de suma importancia; **moˈmen·tum** [~təm] *phys.* momento *m*; ímpetu *m*; *gather* ~ cobrar velocidad.
mon·ad [ˈmɔnæd] mónada *f.*
mon·arch [ˈmɔnərk] monarca *m*; **mo·nar·chic, mo·nar·chi·cal** [mɔˈnɑːrkik(l)] □ monárquico; **mon·arch·ism** [ˈmɔnərkizm] monarquismo *m*; **mon·arch·y** [ˈ~ki] monarquía *f.*
mon·as·ter·y [ˈmɔnəsteri] monasterio *m*; **mo·nas·tic, mo·nas·ti·cal** [məˈnæstik(l)] □ monástico; **mon-ˈas·ti·cism** monacato *m*; monaquismo *m.*
Mon·day [ˈmʌndi] lunes *m.*
mon·e·tar·y [ˈmʌniteri] monetario; pecuniario; ~ *reform* reforma *f* monetaria.
mon·ey [ˈmʌni] dinero *m*; plata *f esp. S.Am.*; (*coin*) moneda *f*; *keep in* ~ proveer de dinero; *make* ~ ganar dinero; (*business*) dar dinero; *throw good* ~ *after bad* echar la soga tras el caldero; *v. paper*; *funny* ~ *sl.* dinero *m* contrahecho; *ready* ~ dinero *m* contante; ˈ~ **box** hucha *f*; ˈ~ **chang·er** cambista *m*/*f*; **mon·eyed** [ˈmʌnid] adinerado.
mon·ey...: ˈ~ **grub·ber** avaro (a *f*) *m*; ˈ~**·lend·er** prestamista *m*/*f*; ˈ~ ˈ**mar·ket** mercado *m* monetario; ~ *fund* fondo *m* de inversiones en el mercado monetario; ˈ~ ˈ**or·der** *approx.* giro *m* postal; ˈ~**'s worth:** *get one's* ~ *out of* sacar el valor de.
mon·ger [ˈmʌŋgər] traficante *m*/*f* en...; tratante *m* en...; *fig.* propalador (-a *f*) *m* de...; *war*~ atizador *m* de la guerra.
Mon·gol [ˈmɔŋgɔl], **Mon·go·lian** [~ˈgouljən] **1.** mogol *adj. a. su. m* (-a *f*); **2.** (*language*) mogol *m.*
mon·grel [ˈmʌŋgrəl] **1.** perro *m* mestizo, perro *m* callejero; mestizo (a *f*) *m*; **2.** mestizo.
mon·i·tor [ˈmɔnitər] **1.** *school*: monitor *m*; *radio*: radiorreceptor *m* de contrastación; *radio*: (*p.*) escucha *m*/*f*; **2.** vigilar; regular; contrastar; radiocaptar.
monk [mʌŋk] monje *m.*
mon·key [ˈmʌŋki] **1.** mono (a *f*) *m*, mico (a *f*) *m*; *fig.* diablillo *m*; ⊕ maza *f*; *sl.* 500 libras *f*/*pl.* esterlinas; F *get one's* ~ *up* hinchársele a uno las narices; F *make a* ~ *out of* tomar el pelo a; F ~ *business* trampería *f*, malas mañas *f*/*pl.*; F ~ *suit* frac *m*; F ~ *tricks* travesuras *f*/*pl.*, diabluras *f*/*pl.*; **2.** F hacer payasadas; ~ (*about*) *with* manosear; meterse con; ˈ~ **nut** cacahuete *m*; ˈ~ **puz·zle** araucaria *f*; ˈ~**·shine** *sl.* monada *f*; ˈ~ **wrench** ⊕ llave *f* inglesa.
monk·ish [ˈmʌŋkiʃ] *mst contp.* frailuno, de monje.
mo·no... [ˈmɔnou] mono...; **mon·o·chrome** [ˈmɔnəkroum] monocromo *adj. a. su. m*; **mon·o·cle** [ˈmɔnɔkl] monóculo *m*; **moˈnoc·u·lar** [~kju-

lər] monóculo; **moˈnog·a·my** [~gə-mi] monogamia *f*; **mon·o·gram** [ˈmɔnəgræm] monograma *m*; **mon-o·graph** [ˈ~græf] monografía *f*; **mon·o·lith** [ˈmɔnəliθ] monolito *m*; **mon·o·logue** [ˈmɔnəlɔg] monólogo *m*; **mon·o·ma·ni·a** [ˈmɔnouˈmei-niə] monomanía *f*; **mon·o·plane** [ˈmɔnəplein] monoplano *m*; **mo-nop·o·list** [məˈnɔpəlist] monopolista *m*/*f*; acaparador (-a *f*) *m*; **moˈnop·o·lize** [~laiz] monopolizar; acaparar (*a. fig.*); **moˈnop·o·ly** monopolio *m*; **mon·o·syl·lab·ic** [ˈmɔnəsiˈlæbik] □ *word* monosílabo; monosilábico; **mon·o·syl·la·ble** [ˈ~ləbl] monosílabo *m*; **mon·o·the-ism** [ˈmɔnouθiːizm] monoteísmo *m*; **mon·o·tone** [ˈmɔnətoun] monotonía *f*; **mo·not·o·nous** [məˈnɔtənəs] □ monótono; **moˈnot·o·ny** [~təni] monotonía *f*; **Mon·o·type** [ˈmɔnə-taip] monotipia *f*.

mon·soon [mɔnˈsuːn] monzón *m or f*.

mon·ster [ˈmɔnstər] monstruo *m*; *attr.* enorme, monstruoso.

mon·strance [ˈmɔnstrəns] custodia *f*.

mon·stros·i·ty [mɔnsˈtrɔsiti] monstruosidad *f*; **mon·strous** □ monstruoso.

mon·tage [mɔnˈtɑːʒ] montaje *m*.

month [mʌnθ] mes *m*; *100 pesetas a ~* 100 pesetas mensuales; F *in a ~ of Sundays* en mucho tiempo; ˈ**month-ly 1.** mensual(mente); **2.** revista *f* mensual.

mon·u·ment [ˈmɔnjumənt] monumento *m*; **mon·u·men·tal** [~ˈmentl] □ monumental; notable; *iro.* garrafal.

moo [muː] **1.** mugido *m*; **2.** mugir, hacer mu.

mooch [muːtʃ] F pedir de gorra; F *~ about* vagar, haraganear; *~ along* andar arrastrando los pies.

mood¹ [muːd] *gr.* modo *m*.

mood² [~] humor *m*; capricho *m*; *be in a good* (*bad*) *~* estar de buen (mal) humor; *be in the ~* estar de vena (*for* para).

mood·i·ness [ˈmuːdinis] mal humor *m*; melancolía *f*; carácter *m* caprichoso.

mood·y [ˈmuːdi] □ de mal humor; melancólico; caprichoso.

moon [muːn] **1.** luna *f*; *poet.* mes *m*; *v. full, new*; F *once in a blue ~* de Pascuas a Ramos; **2.** mirar a las musarañas, andar distraído (*mst ~ about*); ˈ**~·beam** rayo *m* de luna; ˈ**moon·light 1.** luz *f* de la luna; F *~ flit* mudanza *f* a la chita callando; **2.** tener empleo segundo; *moonlighting* pluriempleo *m*; ˈ**moon·lit** iluminado por la luna; *night* de luna.

moon...: ˈ**~·shine** F pamplinas *f*/*pl.*, música *f* celestial; F licor *m* destilado ilegalmente; ˈ**~·shin·er** F fabricante *m* de licor ilegal; ˈ**~·shot** lanzamiento *m* a la luna; ˈ**~·stone** adularia *f*; ˈ**~·struck** lunático; aturdido; ˈ**~-walk** = *lunar walk*.

Moor¹ [mur] moro (a *f*) *m*.

moor² [~] páramo *m*, brezal *m*.

moor³ [~] ⚓ *v*/*t*. amarrar; *v*/*i*. echar las amarras.

moor·hen [ˈmurhen] polla *f* de agua.

moor·ings [ˈmuriŋz] *pl.* ⚓ amarras *f*/*pl.*; (*place*) amarradero *m*.

Moor·ish [ˈmuriʃ] moro; ⚠ *etc.* árabe.

moor·land [ˈmurlənd] = *moor²*.

moose [muːs] alce *m* de América (*a.* ˈ**~ deer**).

moot [muːt] **1.** *hist.* asamblea *f* de ciudadanos; **2.**: *~ point*, *~ question* punto *m* discutible; **3.** proponer para la discusión.

mop [mɔp] **1.** fregasuelos *m*; mata *f*, greña *f of hair*; **2.** fregar; limpiar; secar; *~ up* secar; limpiar (*a.* ⚔ *fig.*); *sl.* beber(se); *sl.* acabar con, liquidar.

mope [moup] **1.** estar abatido (*or* aburrido); andar alicaído; **2.** melancólico (a *f*) *m*; *~s pl.* melancolía *f*.

mo·ped [ˈmouped] moto *f*.

mop·ing [ˈmoupiŋ] □, ˈ**mop·ish** □ abatido, melancólico.

mo·quette [məˈket] moqueta *f*.

mo·raine [mɔˈrein] *geol.* morena *f*.

mor·al [ˈmɔrəl] **1.** □ moral, ético; virtuoso; honesto; *~ victory* victoria *f* moral; **2.** moraleja *f*; *~s pl.* moral *f*; moralidad *f*; costumbres *f*/*pl.*; **mo-rale** [mɔˈræl] estado *m* de ánimo; **mo·ral·ist** [ˈmɔrəlist] moralista *m*/*f*; moralizador (-a *f*) *m*; **mo·ral·i·ty** [məˈræliti] moralidad *f etc.*; *~ play lit.* moralidad *f*; **mor·al·ize** [ˈmɔrəlaiz] moralizar.

mo·rass [məˈræs] cenagal *m*, pantano *m* (*a. fig.*).

mor·a·to·ri·um [mɔrəˈtɔːriəm] moratoria *f*.

mor·bid [ˈmɔːrbid] □ mórbido, morboso; *mind* malsano, enfermizo; **morˈbid·i·ty, ˈmor·bid·ness** morbosidad *f*; lo malsano.

mor·dant [ˈmɔːrdənt] **1.** mordaz; **2.** mordiente *m*.

more [mɔːr] *adj., adv., su.* más; ~ *and* ~ cada vez más; ~ *or less* (poco) más o menos; *v. than*; *no* (*or not any*) ~ ya no, no más; *once* ~ otra vez, una vez más; *so much* (*or all*) *the* ~ tanto más; *the* ~ *the merrier* cuanto(s) más, mejor; *the* ~ ... *the* ~ ... cuanto más ... (tanto) más ...

more·o·ver [mɔːrˈouvər] además (de eso), por otra parte.

mor·ga·nat·ic [mɔːrgəˈnætik] □ morganático.

morgue [mɔːrg] depósito *m* de cadáveres.

mor·i·bund [ˈmɔribʌnd] moribundo.

Mor·mon [ˈmɔːrmən] **1.** mormón (-a *f*) *m*; **2.** mormónico.

morn [mɔːrn] *poet.* mañana *f*, alborada *f*.

morn·ing [ˈmɔːrniŋ] **1.** mañana *f*; *good* ~! ¡buenos días!; *in the* ~ por la mañana; *at 6 o'clock in the* ~ a las 6 de la mañana; *tomorrow* ~ mañana por la mañana; **2.** matutino, matinal, de (la) mañana; ~ *coat* chaqué *m*; ~ *sickness* achaques *m/pl.* mañaneros; ~ *star* lucero *m* del alba.

Mo·roc·can [məˈrɔkən] marroquí *adj. a. su. m/f*, marrueco *adj. a. su. m* (a *f*).

mo·roc·co [məˈrɔkou] (*or* ~ *leather*) marroquí *m*, tafilete *m*.

mo·ron [ˈmɔːrɔn] imbécil *m/f*.

mo·rose [məˈrous] □ malhumorado, sombrío.

mor·phi·a [ˈmɔːrfjə], **mor·phine** [ˈmɔːrfiːn] morfina *f*.

mor·phol·o·gy [mɔːrˈfɔlədʒi] morfología *f*.

mor·row [ˈmɔrou] *mst poet.* día *m* siguiente; mañana *m*; *on the* ~ al día siguiente.

Morse [mɔːrs] (*a.* ~ *code*) (alfabeto) Morse *m*.

mor·sel [ˈmɔːrsəl] pedazo *m*; bocado *m*.

mor·tal [ˈmɔːrtl] □ mortal *adj. a. su. m/f*; **mor·tal·i·ty** [mɔːrˈtæliti] mortalidad *f*; (*muerte natural o prematura*) mortandad *f*.

mor·tar [ˈmɔːrtər] mortero *m* (*a.* ⚔).

mort·gage [ˈmɔːrgidʒ] **1.** hipoteca *f*; **2.** hipotecar; **mort·ga·gee** [~gəˈdʒiː] acreedor (-a *f*) *m* hipotecario (a); **mort·ga·gor** [~gəˈdʒɔːr] deudor (-a *f*) *m* hipotecario (a).

mor·tice [ˈmɔːrtis] = *mortise*.

mor·ti·cian [mɔːrˈtiʃn] director *m* de pompas fúnebres.

mor·ti·fi·ca·tion [mɔːrtifiˈkeiʃn] mortificación *f*; humillación *f*.

mor·ti·fy [ˈmɔːrtifai] *v/t.* mortificar; humillar; *v/i.* ⚕ gangrenarse.

mor·tise [ˈmɔːrtis] **1.** muesca *f*, mortaja *f*; **2.** hacer muescas en.

mor·tu·ar·y [ˈmɔːrtʃuəri] **1.** depósito *m* de cadáveres; **2.** mortuorio.

mo·sa·ic[1] [məˈzeiik] mosaico *m*.

Mo·sa·ic[2] [~] mosaico.

Mos·lem [ˈmɔzlem] musulmán *adj. a. su. m* (-a *f*) islámico (a), mahometano *adj. a. su. m* (a *f*).

mosque [mɔsk] mezquita *f*.

mos·qui·to [məsˈkiːtou], *pl.* **mosˈqui·toes** [~z] mosquito *m*; *mosquito net* mosquitero *m*.

moss [mɔs] musgo *m*; *geog.* pantano *m*; **ˈmoss·y** musgoso.

most [moust] **1.** *adj.* □ más; la mayor parte de; los más, la mayoría de; casi todos; ~ *people* la mayoría de la gente; *v. part*; **2.** *adv.* más; muy, sumamente; de lo más; ~ *of all* sobre todo; *a* ~ *interesting book* un libro interesantísimo, un libro de lo más interesante; **3.** *su.* la mayor parte; el mayor número, los más; *at* (*the*) ~ a lo más, a lo sumo, cuando más; *make the* ~ *of* sacar el mejor partido de; exagerar.

...most [moust, məst] *sup.* más...

most·ly [ˈmoustli] por la mayor parte; principalmente; en general.

mote [mout] mota *f*; átomo *m*.

mo·tel [mouˈtel] motel *m*.

mo·tet [mouˈtet] motete *m*.

moth [mɔθ] mariposa *f* (nocturna); polilla *f in clothes etc.*; **ˈ~·ball** bola *f* de naftalina; **ˈ~-eat·en** apolillado.

moth·er [ˈmʌðər] **1.** madre *f*; *attr.* madre, maternal, materno; ♀ *Church* la santa madre iglesia; iglesia *f* metropolitana; ~ *country* (madre) patria *f*; ~ *love* amor *m* maternal; ~ *tongue* lengua *f* materna, lengua *f* madre; ~ *wit* sentido *m* común; ingenio *m*; **2.** servir de madre a; mimar; *animal* ahijar; **moth·er·hood** [ˈ~hud] maternidad *f*; madres *f/pl.*;

ˈ**moth·er-in-law** suegra *f*; **moth·er·land** (madre) patria *f*; ˈ**moth·er·less** huérfano de madre, sin madre; ˈ**moth·er·ly** maternal.

moth·er...: ˈ**~-of-ˈpearl** 1. nácar *m*; 2. nacarado; ˈ**~ ship** buque *m* nodriza, buque *m* madre; ˈ**~ su·pe·ri·or** superiora *f*.

mo·tif [mouˈtiːf] ♪, *art*: motivo *m*; tema *m*; *sew.* adorno *m*.

mo·tion [ˈmouʃn] 1. movimiento *m*; ⊕ marcha *f*, operación *f*; ⊕ mecanismo *m*; *parl.* moción *f*; ademán *m*; señal *f*; ⚕ movimiento *m* del vientre, deyección *f*; *bring forward* (*or propose*) *a* ~ presentar una moción; *carry a* ~ (hacer) adoptar una moción; (*set*) *in* ~ (poner) en marcha; 2. *v/t.* indicar a *una p.* con la mano *etc.* (*to inf.* que *subj.*); *v/i.* hacer señas; ˈ**mo·tion·less** inmóvil; ˈ**mo·tion pic·ture** 1. película *f*; 2. cinematográfico; ~ *camera* cámara *f* cinematográfica.

mo·ti·vate [ˈmoutiveit] motivar; **mo·tiˈva·tion** motivación *f*.

mo·tive [ˈmoutiv] 1. motivo *m*; 2. motor, motivo; ~ *power* fuerza *f* motriz; ˈ**mo·tive·less** sin motivo.

mot·ley [ˈmɔtli] 1. abigarrado; vario; 2. botarga *f*.

mo·tor [ˈmoutər] 1. motor *m*; = ~*car*; 2. motor; ~ *ambulance* ambulancia *f*; ~ *mechanic* mecánico *m* (de automóviles), ~ *ship*, ~ *vessel* motonave *f*; 3. ir (*or* viajar) en automóvil; ˈ**~·bike** F moto *f*; ˈ**~·boat** gasolinera *f*; motora *f*, motorbote *m*; autobote *m*; ˈ**~ˈbus** autobús *m*; ˈ**~·cade** [ˈ~keid] caravana *f* de automóviles; ˈ**~·car** auto(móvil) *m*, coche *m*; carro *m S.Am.*; ˈ**~·coach** autocar *m*; ˈ**~ˈcy·cle** moto(cicleta) *f*; ˈ**~·cy·cling** motorismo *m*; ˈ**~·cy·clist** motociclista *m/f*, motorista *m/f*; **mo·tor·ing** [ˈmoutəriŋ] automovilismo *m*; ~ *school* escuela *f* automovilista; ˈ**mo·tor·ist** motorista *m/f*; automovilista *m/f*; **mo·tor·i·za·tion** [~raiˈzeiʃn] motorización *f*; ˈ**mo·tor·ize** motorizar; ˈ**mo·tor launch** lancha *f* (*or* canoa *f*) automóvil.

mo·tor...: ˈ**~·man** 🚋 conductor *m* (de locomotora eléctrica); ˈ**~ road** autopista *f*; ˈ**~ ˈscoot·er** vespa *f*; motoneta *f*; ˈ**~ truck** (auto)camión *m*.

mot·tled [ˈmɔtld] jaspeado, abigarrado.

mot·to [ˈmɔtou], *pl.* **mot·toes** [ˈ~z] lema *m*; *heraldry*: divisa *f*.

mo(u)ld[1] [mould] mantillo *m*; (*fungus*) moho *m*; (*iron* ~) mancha *f* de orín.

mo(u)ld[2] [~] 1. molde *m*; cosa *f* moldeada; *fig.* carácter *m*; 2. moldear; vaciar; amoldar (*a. fig.*) (*[up]on* a).

mo(u)ld·er[1] [ˈmouldər] moldeador (-a *f*) *m*.

mo(u)ld·er[2] [~] (*a.* ~ *away*) desmoronarse; convertirse en polvo; decaer.

mo(u)ld·i·ness [ˈmouldinis] moho *m*, enmohecimiento *m*.

mo(u)ld·ing [ˈmouldiŋ] amoldamiento *m*; vaciado *m*; ⚠ moldura *f*.

mo(u)ld·y [ˈmouldi] mohoso, enmohecido; *fig.* rancio, anticuado.

moult [moult] 1. muda *f*; 2. mudar (la pluma).

mound [maund] montón *m*; montículo *m*; terraplén *m*.

mount [maunt] 1. *poet. a. geog.* monte *m*; *horse etc.*: montura *f*, cabalgadura *f*; engaste *m of jewel*; base *f*; soporte *m*; fondo *m*; 2. *v/t.* montar (*a.* ⊕); (*climb*) subir; (*get on to*) subir a (*or* en); poner a caballo; proveer de caballos; *jewel* engastar; *v. guard*; *v/i.* subir a caballo; montar(se); aumentar (*a.* ~ *up*).

moun·tain [ˈmauntin] 1. montaña *f*; (*pile*) montón *m*; ~ *chain* cordillera *f*; ~ *range* sierra *f*; ~ *side* falda *f* (*or* ladera *f*) de una montaña; 2. montañés, de montaña; ~ *climbing* alpinismo *m*; montañismo *m*; **moun·tain·eer** [~iˈnir] 1. montañés (-a *f*) *m*; montañero (a *f*) *m*, alpinista *m/f*; 2. dedicarse al montañismo; **moun·tainˈeer·ing** 1. montañismo *m*; alpinismo *m*; 2. montañero; ˈ**moun·tain·ous** montañoso; *fig.* enorme.

moun·te·bank [ˈmauntibæŋk] saltabanco *m*, saltimbanqui *m*, charlatán *m*.

mount·ing [ˈmauntiŋ] montadura *f*; ⊕ montaje *m*; engaste *m of jewel*; soporte *m*; base *f*.

mourn [mɔːrn] *v/t.* llorar (la muerte de); lamentar; llevar luto por; *v/i.* lamentarse; estar de luto; ˈ**mourn·er** doliente *m/f*; (*hired*) plañidera *f*; **mourn·ful** [ˈ~ful] □ triste, dolori-

do, lúgubre, lastimero; ˈ**mourn·ful·ness** tristeza *f*, melancolía *f*.
mourn·ing [ˈmɔːrniŋ] **1.** luto *m*, duelo *m*; lamentación *f*; ~ *band* crespón *m* fúnebre; *be in* ~ estar de luto; *be in* ~ *for* llevar luto por; *deep* ~ luto *m* riguroso; *half* ~ medio luto *m*; **2.** de luto.
mouse 1. [maus] (*pl. mice*) ratón *m*; **2.** [mauz] cazar ratones; **mous·er** [ˈmauzər] gato *m* cazador de ratones; ˈ**mouse·trap** ratonera *f*.
mous·tache [məsˈtæʃ] bigote(s) *m*(*pl.*), mostacho *m*.
mous·y [ˈmausi] *p*. silencioso, tímido; *color* pardusco.
mouth [mauθ], *pl.* **mouths** [mauðz] **1.** boca *f* (*a. fig.*); (des)embocadura *f* *of river*; boquilla *f of wind instrument*; *down in the* ~ deprimido, alicaído; *keep one's* ~ *shut* tener la boca cerrada, guardar un secreto; *not to open one's* ~ no decir esta boca es mía; **2.** [mauð] *v/t.* pronunciar (con rimbombancia), proferir; *v/i.* hablar exagerando los movimientos de la boca; **mouthed** [mauðd] de boca ...; **mouth·ful** [ˈ~ful] bocado *m*.
mouth...: ˈ~ **or·gan** armónica *f* (de boca); ˈ~**·piece** boquilla *f*; ♪ estrangul *m*; *teleph.* micrófono *m*; *fig.* portavoz *m*; ˈ~**·wash** enjuague *m*; ˈ~-**wa·ter·ing** apetitoso.
mov(**e**)**·a·ble** [ˈmuːvəbl] **1.** movible; mueble; **2.** ~*s pl.* bienes *m*/*pl.* muebles.
move [muːv] **1.** *v/t.* mover; poner en marcha; trasladar *from one place to another*; *house* mudar de; (*disturb*) remover, sacudir; menear; *bowels* exonerar; *emotion*: conmover, enternecer; *parl.* proponer; ~ *a p. to inf.* mover (*or* impeler) a una p. a *inf.*; ~ *away* alejar; apartar; quitar; ~ *on* hacer circular; adelantar; ~ *up* ascender; subir; *v/i.* moverse; trasladarse; caminar; ponerse en marcha; menearse; mudar de casa; *games*: hacer una jugada; (*traffic*) circular; (*bowels*) exonerarse; ~ *about* ir y venir; moverse; ~ *away* apartarse; marcharse; ~ *forward* avanzar; ~ *in* instalarse (en); *society* frecuentar, alternar con; ~ *off* alejarse; ~ *on* avanzar; seguir (andando); circular; ~ *out* salir; abandonar la casa; ~ *up* ascender, subir; **2.** movimiento *m*; paso *m*; acción *f*; maniobra *f*; *game*: jugada *f*; mudanza *f of house*; *on the* ~ en movimiento; de viaje; F *get a* ~ *on* menearse, darse prisa; F *get a* ~ *on!* ¡anda, espabílate!; *have first* ~ *games*: salir; *make a* ~ dar un paso; hacer una jugada; ponerse en marcha; *whose* ~ *is it?* ¿a quién le toca (jugar)?; ˈ**move·ment** movimiento *m* (*a. fig.*); ⊕ mecanismo *m*; juego *m*; ♪ tiempo *m*; ⚕ defecación *f*; ✝ actividad *f*; circulación *f of traffic*; ˈ**mov·er** movedor (-a *f*) *m*; móvil *m*; (*proposer*) autor (-a *f*) *m*; *prime* ~ ⊕ máquina *f* motriz; *phls.* primer motor *m*; *fig.* promotor (-a *f*) *m*.
mov·ie [ˈmuːvi] F película *f*; ~*s pl.* cine *m*; ~ *star* cineasta *m*; ~-*goer* aficionado *m* al cine, cinéfilo *m*; ~*land* F cinelandia *f*; Hollywood.
mov·ing [ˈmuːviŋ] □ motor; movedor; movedizo; *fig.* conmovedor; ~ *picture* = *motion picture*; ~ *spirit* alma *f*.
mow [mou] [*irr.*] segar (*a.* ~ *down*); ˈ**mow·er** segador (-a *f*) *m*; = *mowing machine*; *power* ~ motosegadora *f*; ˈ**mow·ing 1.** siega *f*; **2.** segador; ˈ**mow·ing ma·chine** segadora *f* mecánica; cortacésped *m for lawn*; **mown** *p.p. of mow*.
Moz·ar·ab [mouzˈærəb] mozárabe *m*/*f*; **Moz**ˈ**ar·ab·ic** mozárabe.
much [mʌtʃ] *adj.* mucho; *adv.* mucho; (*before p.p.*) muy; (*almost*) casi, más o menos; (*by far*) con mucho; *su.* mucho; *as* ~, *so* ~ tanto; *as* ~ *again*, *as* ~ *more* otro tanto más; *as* ~ *as* tanto como; *how* ~ cuánto; *however* ~ por mucho que; *make* ~ *of* dar mucha importancia a; *p.* agasajar; ~ *as I should like* por más que yo quisiera; *not* ~ *of a* ... ... de poca cuantía; pobre, malo; *not so* ~ *as* ni siquiera; *think* ~ *of* estimar en mucho; *not to think* ~ *of* tener en poco; *I thought as* ~ ya me lo figuraba; *too* ~ demasiado.
mu·ci·lage [ˈmjuːsilidʒ] mucílago *m*; **mu·ci·lag·i·nous** [~ˈlædʒinəs] mucilaginoso.
muck [mʌk] **1.** ✓ estiércol *m*; suciedad *f*; F porquería *f* (*a. fig.*); **2.** estercolar; F ~ *about* perder el tiempo; F ~ *about with* manosear; F ~ *up* ensuciar; estropear; **muck·rake** [ˈ~reik] escarbar vidas ajenas;

ˈ**muck·rak·er** escarbador (-a *f*) *m* de vidas ajenas; ˈ**muck-up** F lío *m*, fracaso *m*; ˈ**muck·y** F puerco, sucio, asqueroso.

mu·cous [ˈmjuːkəs] mucoso; ~ *membrane* mucosa *f*.

mu·cus [~] moco *m*, mucosidad *f*.

mud [mʌd] lodo *m*, barro *m*; fango *m* (*a. fig.*); *sling* ~ *at* F vilipendiar; ~*slinger* menospreciador *m*; *stick in the* ~ F aguafiestas *m/f*; ˈ~ ˈ**bath** lodos *m/pl*.

mud·dle [ˈmʌdl] **1.** embrollo *m*, confusión *f*; F lío *m*; *get into a* ~ embrollarse; *make a* ~ causar confusión; armar un lío; **2.** *v/t*. embrollar, confundir (*a.* ~ *up*); *p*. aturdir; *v/i*. obrar confusamente (*or* sin ton ni son); ~ *through* salir del paso sin saber cómo; ˈ~**-head·ed** atontado, estúpido; confuso.

muddy [ˈmʌdi] **1.** □ lodoso, fangoso; *liquid* turbio; **2.** enlodar; enturbiar; manchar (*a. fig.*).

mud...: ˈ~ ˈ**flats** *pl*. marisma *f*; ˈ~**guard** guardafango *m*, guardabarros *m*; ˈ~**lark** F galopín *m*.

muff[1] [mʌf] *sport*: dejar escapar (la pelota); perder (la ocasión).

muff[2] [~] manguito *m*.

muf·fin [ˈmʌfin] *approx*. mollete *m*.

muf·fle [ˈmʌfl] **1.** ⊕ mufla *f*; **2.** embozar(se), tapar(se) (*a.* ~ *up*), envolver; amortiguar (el ruido de); *drum* enfundar; ˈ**muf·fler** bufanda *f*; ♪ sordina *f*; ⊕ silenciador *m*.

muf·ti [ˈmʌfti] traje *m* de paisano; *in* ~ vestido de paisano.

mug [mʌg] **1.** taza *f* (alta sin platillo); barro *m*, jarra *f of beer*; *sl*. (*face*) hocico *m*, jeta *f*; *sl*. (*p*.) bruto *m*; F gorila *m*; **2.** asaltar para robar; **mug·ger** [ˈmʌgər] ladrón *m* asaltador.

mug·gy [ˈmʌgi] húmedo y sofocante; bochornoso.

mug·wump [ˈmʌgwʌmp] votante *m* independiente.

mu·lat·to [mjuˈlætou] mulato *adj*. *a. su. m* (a *f*).

mul·ber·ry [ˈmʌlbəri] mora *f*; (*a.* ~ *tree*) morera *f*, moral *m*; *attr*. (*color*) morado.

mulch [mʌlʃ] ↗ (cubrir con) estiércol *m*, paja *f* y hojas *f/pl*.

mulct [mʌlkt] **1.** ⚒ multa *f*; **2.** multar (*a p.* [*in*] a una p. en); ~ *of* quitar.

mule [mjuːl] mulo (a *f*) *m*; (*slipper*) babucha *f*; *fig*. sujeto *m* terco; ⊕ máquina *f* de hilar intermitente, selfactina *f*; **mu·le·teer** [~iˈtir] mul(at)ero *m*, arriero *m*; ˈ**mule track** camino *m* de herradura.

mul·ish [ˈmjuːliʃ] □ terco, obstinado.

mull[1] [mʌl] calentar con especias.

mull[2] [~] chapucear, estropear; ~ *over* reflexionar sobre.

mul·let [ˈmʌlit] (*red*) salmonete *m*; (*grey*) mújol *m*.

mul·li·gan [ˈmʌligən] *sl*. puchero *m*; **mul·li·ga·taw·ny** [mʌligəˈtɔːni] sopa *f* muy condimentada.

mul·lion [ˈmʌljən] **1.** △ parteluz *m*; **2.** dividir con parteluz.

mul·ti·col·ored [ˈmʌltikʌlərd] multicolor; **mul·ti·far·i·ous** [~ˈferiəs] □ múltiple, vario; **mul·ti·form** [ˈ~fɔːrm] multiforme; **mul·ti·lat·er·al** [~ˈlætərəl] □ multilátero; **mul·ti·mil·lion·aire** [ˈ~miljəˈner] multimillonario (a *f*) *m*; **mul·ti·na·tion·al** [ˈ~ˈnæʃənl] multinacional; **mul·ti·ple** [ˈmʌltipl] **1.** múltiple; múltiplo; ~ *firm* casa *f* con muchas sucursales; ~ *stores* cadena *f* de almacenes; ~ *sclerosis* esclerosis *f* múltiple; **2.** múltiplo *m*; *lowest common* ~ mínimo común múltiplo *m*; ˈ**mul·ti·plex** múltiple; **mul·ti·pli·cand** [~ˈkænd] multiplicando *m*; **mul·ti·pliˈca·tion** multiplicación *f*; ~ *table* tabla *f* de multiplicar; **mul·ti·plic·i·ty** [~ˈplisiti] multiplicidad *f*; **mul·ti·pli·er** [ˈ~plaiər] multiplicador *m*; **mul·ti·ply** [ˈ~plai] multiplicar(se); **mul·ti·tude** [ˈ~tjuːd] multitud *f*, muchedumbre *f*; **mul·tiˈtu·di·nous** [~dinəs] □ multitudinario; muy numeroso.

mum[1] [mʌm] **1.** callado; *keep* ~ callarse; **2.** ~(*'s the word*)! ¡chito!, ¡chitón!; ¡ni una palabra!

mum[2] [~] F mamá *f*.

mum·ble [ˈmʌmbl] mascullar, musitar; hablar entre dientes.

mum·bo jum·bo [ˈmʌmbou ˈdʒʌmbou] F fetiche *m*; conjuro *m*; mistificación *f*; galimatías *m*.

mum·mer [ˈmʌmər] máscara *m/f*; histrión *m*; *contp*. comicastro *m*; ˈ**mum·mer·y** momería *f*, mojiganga *f*; *fig*. ceremonia *f* vana.

mum·mi·fi·ca·tion [mʌmifiˈkeiʃn] momificación *f*; **mum·mi·fy** [ˈ~fai] momificar(se).

mum·my¹ [ˈmʌmi] momia *f*.
mum·my² [~] F mamaíta *f*.
mumps [mʌmps] *sg*. papera *f*, parótidas *f*/*pl*.
munch [mʌntʃ] ronzar.
mun·dane [ˈmʌndein] □ mundano.
mu·nic·i·pal [mjuːˈnisipl] □ municipal; ~ *bond* bono *m* municipal (*or* estatal); **mu·nic·i·pal·i·ty** [~ˈpæliti] municipio *m*; **muˈnic·i·pal·ize** [~əlaiz] municipalizar.
mu·nif·i·cence [mjuːˈnifisns] munificencia *f*; **muˈnif·i·cent** □ munífico.
mu·ni·ments [ˈmjuːnimənts] documentos *m*/*pl*. (probatorios), archivos *m*/*pl*.
mu·ni·tions [ˈmjuːniʃnz] *pl*. municiones *f*/*pl*.
mu·ral [ˈmjurəl] **1.** mural; **2.** pintura *f* mural.
mur·der [ˈməːrdər] **1.** asesinato *m*; homicidio *m*; **2.** asesinar; *fig*. arruinar, estropear; *play* degollar; **ˈmur·der·er** asesino *m*; **ˈmur·der·ess** asesina *f*; **ˈmur·der·ous** □ asesino, homicida; sanguinario; intolerable.
murk [məːrk] oscuridad *f*, lobreguez *f*; **murk·y** [ˈməːrki] □ oscuro, lóbrego; tenebroso (*a. fig.*).
mur·mur [ˈməːrmər] **1.** murmullo *m*, murmurio *m* (*a. fig.*); **2.** murmurar (*a. fig.*) (*a.* ~ *against*, ~ *at*).
mur·rain [ˈmʌrin] morriña *f*.
mus·ca·dine [ˈmʌskədin], **mus·cat** [ˈ~kət], **mus·ca·tel** [~ˈtel] moscatel *adj. a. su. m*.
mus·cle [ˈmʌsl] **1.** músculo *m*; *fig*. fuerza *f* muscular; ~*bound* de musculatura desarrollada en exceso; **2.:** *sl*. ~ *in* entrar (*or* establecerse) por fuerza (en un negocio ilegal); **mus·cu·lar** [ˈmʌskjulər] (*of muscle*) muscular; (*having muscles*) musculoso; fornido.
Muse¹ [mjuːz] musa *f*.
muse² [~] meditar, reflexionar, rumiar; estar distraído; ~ (*up*)*on* contemplar.
mu·se·um [mjuˈziəm] museo *m*.
mush¹ [mʌʃ] gacha(s) *f*(*pl*.); *fig*. disparates *m*/*pl*.; *fig*. sensiblería *f*.
mush² [~] (hacer un) viaje *m* con trineo tirado por perros.
mush·room [ˈmʌʃrum] **1.** seta *f*, hongo *m*; champiñón *m*; *attr*. que aparece de la noche a la mañana; **2.** aparecer de la noche a la mañana; crecer rápidamente.
mush·y [ˈmʌʃi] pulposo, mollar; *fig*. sensiblero.
mu·sic [ˈmjuːzik] música *f*; F *face the* ~ pagar el pato; *set to* ~ poner música a, musicar; **ˈmu·si·cal 1.** □ músico, musical; *be very* ~ tener mucho talento para la música; ~ *box* caja *f* de música; ~ *instrument* instrumento *m* músico; **2.** comedia *f* musical; *approx*. opereta *f*, zarzuela *f*.
mu·sic hall [ˈmjuːzikhɔːl] teatro *m* de variedades; salón *m* de conciertos.
mu·si·cian [mjuˈziʃn] músico (a *f*) *m*; **ˈ~·ship** musicalidad *f*.
mu·sic...: **ˈ~ pa·per** papel *m* de música; **ˈ~ stand** atril *m*.
musk [mʌsk] (olor *m* de) almizcle *m*; ⚘ almizcleña *f*; **ˈ~ deer** almizclero *m*.
mus·ket [ˈmʌskit] mosquete *m*; **mus·ket·eer** [~ˈtir] mosquetero *m*; **ˈmus·ket·ry** mosquetes *m*/*pl*.; (*troops*) mosquetería *f*; fuego *m* de fusilería; tiro *m* de fusil.
musk·y [ˈmʌski] almizcleño, almizclado.
Mus·lim [ˈmʌzlim] = *Moslem*.
mus·lin [ˈmʌzlin] muselina *f*.
mus·quash [ˈmʌskwɔʃ] (piel *f* de) rata *f* almizclera.
muss [mʌs] F **1.** desaliño *m*, confusión *f*; **2.** desarreglar, poner en confusión.
mus·sel [ˈmʌsl] mejillón *m*.
Mus·sul·man [ˈmʌslmən] musulmán *adj. a. su. m* (-a *f*).
must¹ [mʌst, məst] deber; tener que; haber de; *probability*: deber (de); *I* ~ *do it now* tengo que hacerlo ahora; *I* ~ *keep my word* debo cumplir lo prometido; *he* ~ *be there by now* ya debe (de) estar allí, ya estará allí; *there* ~ *be an explanation* ha de haber una explicación; *it* ~ *be about* 2 serán las 2; *he* ~ *have gone* habrá ido.
must² [~] moho *m*.
must³ [~] mosto *m of wine*.
mus·tache [məsˈtæʃ] = *moustache*.
mus·tard [ˈmʌstərd] mostaza *f*; **ˈmus·tard gas** gas *m* mostaza; **ˈmus·tard pot** mostacera *f*.
mus·ter [ˈmʌstər] **1.** asamblea *f* (*a.* ⚔); ⚔ revista *f*; lista *f*, matrícula *f*; ⚓ rol *m*; *pass* ~ pasar revista; ser aceptable; **2.** *v*/*t*. llamar a asamblea; juntar para pasar revista; *fig*. (*a.* ~ *up*) cobrar, juntar; *v*/*i*. juntarse.

mus·ti·ness ['mʌstinis] moho *m*; ranciedad *f*; olor *m* a humedad; **'mus·ty** mohoso; rancio; que huele a humedad.

mu·ta·bil·i·ty [mju:tə'biliti] mutabilidad *f*; **'mu·ta·ble** □ mudable; **mu'ta·tion** mutación *f*.

mute [mju:t] **1.** □ mudo; silencioso; **2.** mudo (a *f*) *m*; ♪ sordina *f*; *gr.* (letra *f*) muda *f*; *deaf-~* sordomudo *m*; **3.** poner sordina a; apagar.

mu·ti·late ['mju:tileit] mutilar; **mu·ti'la·tion** mutilación *f*.

mu·ti·neer [mju:ti'nir] amotinado(r) *m*; **'mu·ti·nous** □ amotinado; turbulento, rebelde; **'mu·ti·ny** **1.** motín *m*, sublevación *f*; **2.** amotinarse, sublevarse.

mutt [mʌt] perro *m* cruzado; *sl.* bobo *m*.

mut·ter ['mʌtər] **1.** murmullo *m*, rumor *m*; **2.** *v/t.* murmurar, mascullar; *v/i.* murmurar; hablar entre dientes (*a.* *v/t.*).

mut·ton ['mʌtn] carne *f* de carnero; *leg of ~* pierna *f* de carnero; **'~'chop** chuleta *f* de carnero.

mu·tu·al ['mju:tʃuəl] □ mutuo; F común; *~ aid* socorros *m/pl.* mutuos; *~ consent* común acuerdo *m*; *~ fund* sociedad *f* inversionista mutualista; *~ insurance* seguro *m* mutuo; **mu·tu·al·i·ty** [~'æliti] mutualidad *f*.

muz·zle ['mʌzl] **1.** hocico *m*; bozal *m* *for dog*; boca *f* *of gun*; **2.** abozalar; (*gag*) amordazar; **'~·load·er** arma *f* que se carga por la boca.

muz·zy ['mʌzi] □ confuso, atontado.

my [mai] mi(s).

my·op·ic [mai'ɔpik] □ miope *adj.* *a.* *su.* *m/f*; **my·o·pi·a** [~'oupiə], **my·o·py** ['~oupi] miopia *f*.

myr·i·ad ['miriəd] **1.** miríada *f*; **2.** miríada de, sin cuento.

myr·mi·don ['mə:rmidən] *contp.* secuaz *m* fiel, satélite *m*; esbirro *m*.

myrrh [mə:r] mirra *f*.

myr·tle ['mə:rtl] arrayán *m*, mirto *m*.

my·self [mai'self] (*subject*) yo mismo, yo misma; *acc.*, *dat.* me; (*after prp.*) mí (mismo, misma).

mys·te·ri·ous [mis'tiriəs] □ misterioso.

mys·ter·y ['mistəri] misterio *m*; arcano *m*; *thea.* auto *m*, misterio *m*; † oficio *m*, mester *m*; (*a.* *~ novel*) novela *f* policíaca; *~ play* auto *m*, misterio *m*.

mys·tic ['mistik] **1.** (*a.* **'mys·ti·cal**) □ místico; **2.** místico (a *f*) *m*; **mys·ti·cism** ['~sizm] misticismo *m*, mística *f*; **mys·ti·fi·ca·tion** [~fi'keiʃn] mistificación *f*; *b.s.* superchería *f*; perplejidad *f*; misterio *m*; **mys·ti·fy** ['~fai] mistificar; dejar perplejo; ofuscar.

myth [miθ] mito *m*; **myth·ic, myth·i·cal** ['~ik(l)] □ mítico; fabuloso.

myth·o·log·ic, myth·o·log·i·cal [miθə'lɔdʒik(l)] □ mitológico; **my·thol·o·gy** [~'θɔlədʒi] mitología *f*.

myx·o·ma·to·sis [miksəmə'tousis] mixomatosis *f*.

N

nab [næb] coger, atrapar, prender.
na·bob [ˈneibɔb] nabab *m*.
na·celle [nəˈsel] ✈ barquilla *f*.
na·cre [ˈneikər] nácar *m*; **na·cre·ous** [ˈ~kriəs] nacarino, nacarado.
na·dir [ˈneidər] *ast*. nadir *m*; *fig*. punto *m* más bajo.
nag[1] [næg] jaca *f*; *contp*. rocín *m*.
nag[2] [~] regañar, importunar (*a*. ~ *at*); machacar; *fig*. hostigar, remorder.
Nai·ad [ˈnaiæd] náyade *f*.
nail [nail] **1.** *anat*. uña *f*; ⊕ clavo *m*; *on the* ~ en el acto; *pay on the* ~ pagar a toca teja; *bite one's* ~*s* comerse las uñas; **2.** clavar (*a*. *fig*.), enclavar; clavetear; F coger; ~ *down* sujetar con clavos; ~ *a p. down* comprometer a una p. (*to* a); poner a una p. entre la espada y la pared; ~ *up* cerrar con clavos; ~ (*to the counter*) demostrar la falsedad de, poner término a; ˈ~ **brush** cepillo *m* para las uñas; ˈ~ **clip·pers** cortaúñas *m*; ˈ~ **pol·ish** laca *f* de uñas; ˈ~ **scis·sors** *pl*. tijeras *f/pl*. para las uñas.
na·ïve [naiˈi:v], **na·ive** [neiv] □ ingenuo, cándido, sencillo; **na·ïve·té** [naiˈi:vtei], **na·ive·ty** [ˈneivti] ingenuidad *f etc*.
na·ked [ˈneikid] desnudo (*a*. *fig*.), en cueros; obvio; *fig*. desvergonzado; *with the* ~ *eye* a simple vista; ˈ**na·ked·ness** desnudez *f*.
nam·by·pam·by [ˈnæmbiˈpæmbi] **1.** soso, ñoño; melindroso; **2.** ñoño (a *f*) *m*, mirliflor *m/f*, melindroso (a *f*) *m*; insulseces *f/pl*.
name [neim] **1.** nombre *m* (*a*. *fig*.); (*surname*) apellido *m*; reputación *f*; *b.s.* apodo *m*; título *m of book etc.*; linaje *m*; *by* ~, *in* ~ de nombre; *by the* ~ *of* llamado, nombrado; bajo el nombre de; *call a p.* ~*s* poner motes a, injuriar; *in the* ~ *of* en nombre de, de parte de; *make a* ~ *for o.s.* darse a conocer; *my* ~ *is* me llamo; *what is your* ~? ¿cómo se llama?; **2.** nombrar; designar; (*mention*) mentar; *date, price etc.* fijar, señalar; bautizar *with Christian name*; apellidar *with surname*; ~*d p.* llamado; ˈ**name·less** □ anónimo, sin nombre; *vice* nefando; ˈ**name·ly** a saber (*abbr*. *viz*.); ˈ**name·plate** placa *f* rotulada, letrero *m* con nombre; ˈ**name·sake** tocayo (a *f*) *m*, homónimo (a *f*) *m*.
nan·ny [ˈnæni] F niñera *f*; ˈ~ **goat** F cabra *f*.
nap[1] [næp] *cloth*: lanilla *f*, flojel *m*.
nap[2] [~] **1.** sueño *m* ligero, duermevela *m*, dormirela *m*, (*afternoon*) siesta *f*; *take a* ~ descabezar el sueño; dormir la siesta; **2.** dormitar; *catch* ~*ping* coger desprevenido.
na·palm [ˈneipɑ:m] jalea *f* de gasolina.
nape [neip] cogote *m*, nuca *f* (*mst* ~ *of the neck*).
naph·tha [ˈnæfθə] nafta *f*; **naph·tha·lene** [ˈ~li:n] naftaleno *m*, naftalina *f*.
nap·kin [ˈnæpkin] servilleta *f* (*a*. *table*-~); pañal *m* (*a*. *baby's* ~); ˈ~ **ring** servilletero *m*.
narc [nɑ:rk] *sl*. agente *m* de policía antidroga.
nar·cis·sus [nɑ:rˈsisəs] narciso *m*.
nar·co·sis [nɑ:rˈkousis] narcosis *f*, narcotismo *m*; **nar·cot·ic** [~ˈkɔtik] narcótico *adj*. *a*. *su*. *m*; **nar·co·tize** [ˈnɑ:rkətaiz] narcotizar.
nard [nɑ:rd] nardo *m*.
nark [nɑ:rk] *sl*. soplón *m*.
nar·rate [næˈreit] narrar, referir, relatar; **narˈra·tion** narración *f*, relato *m*; **nar·ra·tive** [ˈ~rətiv] **1.** □ narrativo; **2.** narrativa *f*, narración *f*; **nar·ra·tor** [~ˈreitər] narrador (-a *f*) *m*.
nar·row [ˈnærou] **1.** □ estrecho (*a*. *fig*.); *passage etc*. angosto; reducido; *p*. de miras estrechas; *p*. tacaño; ~ *circumstances* estrechez *f*; **2.** ~*s pl*. ⚓ estrecho *m*; desfiladero *m*; **3.** estrechar(se), (en)angostar(se); reducir(se); encoger(se); ˈ~**-gauge** 🚂 de vía estrecha; ˈ~-ˈ**mind·ed** □ intolerante; de

miras estrechas; ˈ**nar·row·ness** estrechez *f*, angostura *f*; intolerancia *f*.

nar·whal [ˈnɑːrwəl] narval *m*.

na·sal [ˈneizl] □ nasal *adj. a. su. f*; *speak* ~*ly* ganguear; **na·sal·i·ty** [~ˈzæliti] nasalidad *f*; **na·sal·ize** [ˈ~zəlaiz] nasalizar.

nas·cent [ˈnæsnt] naciente.

nas·ti·ness [ˈnæstinis] suciedad *f etc.*

na·stur·tium [nəˈstəːrʃəm] capuchina *f*.

nas·ty [ˈnæsti] □ sucio, asqueroso; feo, repugnante; indecente; horrible; áspero; F peligroso; F difícil.

na·tal [ˈneitl] natal; **na·tal·i·ty** [nəˈtæliti] natalidad *f*.

na·tion [ˈneiʃn] nación *f*.

na·tion·al [ˈnæʃnl] □ nacional *adj. a. su. m/f*; ~ *debt* deuda *f* pública; ♀ *Socialism* nacionalsocialismo *m*; ˈ**na·tion·al·ism** nacionalismo *m*; ˈ**na·tion·al·ist** nacionalista *adj. a. su. m/f*; **na·tion·al·i·ty** [næʃəˈnæliti] nacionalidad *f*; **na·tion·al·ize** [ˈnæʃnəlaiz] nacionalizar.

na·tion-wide [ˈneiʃnwaid] por (*or* de) toda la nación.

na·tive [ˈneitiv] **1.** □ nativo (*a.* ⚒); natural; indígena, originario (*to* de); ~ *land* patria *f*; ~ *tongue* lengua *f* materna; F *go* ~ vivir como los indígenas; **2.** natural *m/f*; indígena *m/f*; nacional *m/f*; *I am a* ~ *of* soy natural de, nací en.

na·tiv·i·ty [nəˈtiviti] natividad *f*; (*Christmas*) Navidad *f*; *art*: nacimiento *m*; ~ *play* auto *m* del nacimiento.

nat·ty [ˈnæti] □ F fino, elegante; apuesto; majo.

na·tu·ral [ˈnætʃərəl] **1.** □ natural (*a.* ♪); nativo; innato; *p.* sencillo, llano; normal; *child* ilegítimo; ~ *history* historia *f* natural; ~ *sciences pl.* ciencias *f/pl.* naturales; **2.** (*p.*) idiota *m/f*; ♪ nota *f* natural; ♪ becuadro *m*; F cosa *f* de éxito certero; ˈ**nat·u·ral·ism** naturalismo *m*; ˈ**nat·u·ral·ist** naturalista *m/f*; ˈ**nat·u·ral·ist·ic** □ naturalista; **nat·u·ral·i·za·tion** [~laiˈzeiʃn] naturalización *f*; ~ *papers* carta *f* de naturaleza; ˈ**nat·u·ral·ize** naturalizar; **nat·u·ral·ly** naturalmente; F desde luego, claro; ˈ**nat·u·ral·ness** naturalidad *f*.

na·ture [ˈneitʃər] naturaleza *f*; *p.*'*s* natural *m*, temperamento *m*; (*kind*) género *m*, clase *f*; *from* ~ del natural; *in the* ~ *of* algo como; *good* ~ buen natural *m*; afabilidad *f*; ˈ**na·tured** de carácter…; de condición…

naught [nɔːt] nada; cero *m*; *bring to* ~ frustrar; destruir; *come to* ~ malograrse; reducirse a nada; *set at* ~ despreciar; contravenir; **naugh·ti·ness** [ˈ~tinis] travesura *f etc.*; ˈ**naugh·ty** travieso, pícaro; desobediente; *story* verde; *don't be* ~! (*to child*) ¡no seas malo!

nau·se·a [ˈnɔːsiə] náusea *f*, asco *m*; **nau·se·ate** [ˈ~sieit] dar asco (a); ˈ**nau·se·at·ing**, ˈ**nau·seous** □ nauseabundo; asqueroso.

nau·ti·cal [ˈnɔːtikl] □ náutico, marítimo; ~ *mile* milla *f* marina.

na·val [ˈneivəl] naval, de marina; ~ *base* base *f* naval; ~ (*dock*)*yard* arsenal *m*; ~ *officer* oficial *m* de marina; ~ *station* apostadero *m*.

nave [neiv] ⛪ nave *f* (principal).

na·vel [ˈneivəl] ombligo *m*; ˈ~ ˈ**or·ange** navel *m*; naranja *f* umbilicada.

nav·i·ga·ble [ˈnævigəbl] *river etc.* navegable; *ship etc.* gobernable, dirigible; **nav·i·gate** [ˈ~geit] navegar; *ship* marear; **nav·iˈga·tion** navegación *f*, náutica *f*; mareaje *m*; ˈ**nav·i·ga·tor** navegador *m*, navegante *m*.

na·vy [ˈneivi] marina *f* de guerra; armada *f*; ~ *blue* azul *m* marino (*or* de mar).

nay [nei] **1.** † *or prov.* no; *lit.* más aun, mejor dicho; **2.** negativa *f*.

Naz·a·rene [næzəˈriːn] nazareno *adj. a. su. m* (a *f*).

Na·zi [ˈnɑːtsi] nazi *adj. su. m/f*; **Na·zism** nazismo *m*.

N-bomb [ˈen bɔm] bomba *f* de neutrones.

neap [niːp] marea *f* muerta (*a.* ~ *tide*).

Ne·a·pol·i·tan [niəˈpɔlitən] napolitano *adj. a. su. m* (a *f*).

near [nir] **1.** *adj.* cercano, próximo; inmediato, vecino; *relationship* estrecho, íntimo; *translation etc.* aproximativo; *it was a* ~ *thing* escape *etc.* por un pelo; **2.** *adv.* cerca; ~ *at hand* a la mano, cerca; *come* (*or draw*) ~ acercarse (*to* a); **3.** *prp.* (*a.* ~ *to*) cerca de; próximo a, junto a; hacia; casi; **4.** acercarse a, aproximarse a; **near·by** [ˈ~bai] **1.** *adj.* próximo, cercano; **2.** *adv.* cerca; ˈ**near·ly** casi; de cerca; aproximadamente; *not* ~ ni con mucho; *I* ~ *lost it* por poco lo perdí;

we very ~ bought it en poco estuvo que lo comprásemos; **ˈnear·ness** proximidad *f*, cercanía *f*; intimidad *f*; **ˈnear·sight·ed** miope, corto de vista.

neat [ni:t] □ pulcro, esmerado, aseado; primoroso; (*shapely*) bien hecho, bien proporcionado; (*skillful*) diestro; *drink* puro, sin mezcla; **ˈneat·ness** aseo *m*; pulcritud *f etc.*

neb [neb] *Scot.* pico *m*; nariz *f*; punta *f*.

neb·u·la [ˈnebjulə] nebulosa *f*; **ˈneb·u·lar** *ast.* nebuloso; **ˈneb·u·lous** □ nebuloso.

nec·es·sar·y [ˈnesisəri] **1.** □ necesario, preciso, indispensable; **2.** cosa *f* necesaria, requisito *m* indispensable; lo necesario (*a. necessaries pl.*); **ne·ces·si·tate** [niˈsesiteit] necesitar, exigir; **neˈces·si·tous** necesitado, indigente; **neˈces·si·ty** necesidad *f*; requisito *m* indispensable; indigencia *f*; *of ~* de (*or* por) necesidad; *in case of ~* si fuese necesario; en caso de urgencia; *be under the ~ of ger.* verse obligado a *inf.*

neck [nek] **1.** cuello *m*; pescuezo *m of animal*; gollete *m of bottle*; mástil *m of violin etc.*; *geog.* istmo *m*; *sew.* escote *m* (*a.* **ˈ~·line**); *~ and ~* (a las) parejas; *~ and crop* enteramente; de cabeza; *sl. get it in the ~* recibir una peluca, pagarla(s), cargársela; **2.** *sl.* acariciarse, besuquearse; **neck·er·chief** [ˈnekətʃif] pañoleta *f*, pañuelo *m* de cuello; **neck·lace** [ˈ~lis], **neck·let** [ˈ~lit] collar *m*; **ˈneck·tie** corbata *f*.

ne·crol·o·gy [neˈkrɔlədʒi] necrología *f*; **nec·ro·man·cy** [ˈnekroumænsi] necromancía *f*, nigromancía *f*.

nec·tar [ˈnektər] néctar *m*.

née [nei] nacida; *Rosa Bell, ~ Martin* Rosa Martin de Bell.

need [ni:d] **1.** necesidad *f* (*for, of* de); requisito *m*; urgencia *f*; carencia *f*, falta *f* (*for, of* de); *bodily ~s pl.* menesteres *m/pl.*; *if ~ be* si fuera necesario; *in ~* necesitado; *be* (*or stand*) *in ~ of, have ~ of* necesitar; *in case of ~* en caso de necesidad (*or* urgencia); **2.** *v/t.* necesitar; requerir, exigir; carecer de; deber *inf.*; tener que *inf.*; *I ~ it* me hace falta, me falta, lo necesito; *I ~ to do it* tengo que hacerlo, debo hacerlo; *he ~s watching* hay que vigilarle; *a visa is ~ed* se exige visado; *it ~ not be done* no es preciso hacerlo; *v/i.* estar necesitado; **need·ful** [ˈ~ful] **1.** □ necesario; **2.** F lo necesario, conquibus *m*; **ˈneed·i·ness** necesidad *f*, estrechez *f*.

nee·dle [ˈni:dl] **1.** aguja *f*; **2.** F aguijar; fastidiar; *drink* añadir alcohol a; **ˈ~ case** alfiletero *m*.

need·less [ˈni:dlis] innecesario, superfluo, inútil; *~ to say* excusado es decir, huelga decir; claro está; **ˈ~·ly** inútilmente.

nee·dle...: **ˈ~·wom·an** costurera *f*; *be a good ~* coser bien; **ˈ~·work** costura *f*; labor *f* (de aguja); bordado *m*.

needs [ni:dz] necesariamente, forzosamente; **ˈneed·y** □ necesitado, indigente; *the ~* los pobres; los necesitados; los desamparados.

ne'er [ner] *poet.* nunca; **ˈ~·do·well** holgazán *m*, perdulario *m*.

ne·far·i·ous [niˈferiəs] □ nefario, malo, atroz.

ne·gate [niˈgeit] negar; anular, invalidar; **neˈga·tion** negación *f*, negativa *f*; anulación *f*; **neg·a·tive** [ˈnegətiv] **1.** □ negativo; **2.** negativa *f*; *phot.* negativo *m*; *gr.* negación *f*; ⚡ electricidad *f* negativa; ⚡ polo *m* negativo; **3.** negar; desaprobar; poner veto a; anular.

neg·lect [niˈglekt] **1.** negligencia *f*, descuido *m*; abandono *m*; inobservancia *f*; (*self-*) dejadez *f*; *fall into ~* caer en desuso; **2.** descuidar, desatender; abandonar; *duty etc.* faltar a; (*ignore*) no hacer caso de; *~ to inf.* dejar de *inf.*, olvidarse de *inf.*; **negˈlect·ful** [~ful] □ negligente, descuidado; *be ~ of* descuidar.

neg·li·gée [ˈnegli:ʒei] salto *m* de cama; bata *f*.

neg·li·gence [ˈneglidʒəns] negligencia *f*, descuido *m*; **ˈneg·li·gent** □ negligente, descuidado.

neg·li·gi·ble [ˈneglidʒəbl] insignificante; despreciable.

ne·go·ti·a·bil·i·ty [nigouʃiəˈbiliti] negociabilidad *f*; **neˈgo·ti·a·ble** □ negociable; *road etc.* transitable; **neˈgo·ti·ate** [~eit] *v/t.* negociar; gestionar, agenciar; pasar por; *obstacle* salvar; *bend* tomar; **ne·go·tiˈa·tion** negociación *f*; gestión *f*; *enter into ~ with* entrar en tratos con; **neˈgo·ti·a·tor** negociador (-a *f*) *m*.

Ne·gri·tude [ˈnegrətuːd] negrura *f*; calidad *f* de ser identificado con la raza negra; **Ne·gro** [ˈniːgrou] *mst contp.* negro *adj. a. su. m.*; **Ne·groid** [ˈniːgrɔid] negroide.

neigh [nei] **1.** relincho *m*; **2.** relinchar.

neigh·bor [ˈneibər] **1.** vecino (a *f*) *m*; prójimo (a *f*) *m*; **2.** (*a.* ~ *upon*) colindar con, estar contiguo a; ˈ**neigh·bor·hood** vecindad *f*, vecindario *m*; barrio *m*; alrededores *m*/*pl.*; *in the* ~ *of* cerca de; ˈ**neigh·bor·ing** vecino, colindante, cercano; de al lado; ˈ**neigh·bor·ly** (de) buen vecino; amistoso.

nei·ther [ˈniːðər, ˈnaiðər] **1.** ninguno (de los dos), ni (el) uno ni (el) otro; **2.** *adv.* ni; ~ ... *nor* ni ... ni; **3.** *conj.* ni; tampoco; ni ... tampoco.

nem·e·sis [ˈnemisis] *fig.* justicia *f*, justo castigo *m*.

ne·ol·o·gism [niˈɔlədʒizm] neologismo *m*.

ne·on [ˈniːən] neón *m*, neo *m*; ~ *light* lámpara *f* neón.

ne·o·phyte [ˈniːoufait] neófito (a *f*) *m*; novicio *m*; principiante *m*/*f*.

neph·ew [ˈnefjuː] sobrino *m*.

nep·o·tism [ˈnepətizm] nepotismo *m*.

nerd [nəːrd] *sl.* tipo *m* insípido; sujeto *m* estúpido.

Ne·re·id [ˈniriid] nereida *f*.

nerve [neːrv] **1.** nervio *m* (*a. fig.*); (*courage*) valor *m*, ánimo *m*; *sl.* descaro *m*, tupé *m*; F ~*s pl.* nerviosidad *f*; *get on a p.'s* ~*s* crisparle los nervios a una p.; ~ *center* centro *m* nervioso; *fig.* punto *m* neurálgico; **2.** esforzar, animar; ˈ~ ˈ**cell** neurona *f*; célula *f* nerviosa; ˈ**nerve-**ˈ**rack·ing** irritante; exasperante.

nerv·ous [ˈnəːrvəs] □ nerv(i)oso; tímido; ~ *breakdown* crisis *f* nerviosa; ~ *exhaustion* neurastenia *f*; ~ *system* sistema *m* nervioso; ˈ**nerv·ous·ness** nerviosidad *f*, nerviosismo *m*; timidez *f*.

nerv·y [ˈnəːrvi] F nervioso; *sl.* descarado; presumido.

nest [nest] **1.** nido *m* (*a. fig.*); nidada *f of eggs or young birds*; nidal *m of hen*; juego *m of drawers etc.*; **2.** anidar; buscar nidos; ˈ**nest egg** nidal *m*; *fig.* ahorros *m*/*pl.*, buena hucha *f*; **nes·tle** [ˈnesl] abrigar(se); anidar(se); arrimar(se) (*up to* a); apretar(se) (*up to* contra); **nest·ling** [ˈnesliŋ] pajarito *m* en el nido.

net[1] [net] **1.** red *f* (*a. fig.*); (*fabric*) tul *m*; redecilla *f for hair etc.*; **2.** coger (con red); enredar; cubrir con red.

net[2] [~] ✝ **1.** neto, líquido; ~ *income* renta *f* neta; ~ *price* precio *m* neto; ~ *weight* peso *m* neto; **2.** ganar (*or* producir) en neto.

neth·er [ˈneðər] inferior, más bajo; ~ *regions* infierno *m*; ˈ~**·most** (el *etc.*) más bajo.

net·ting [ˈnetiŋ] red(es) *f*(*pl.*); obra *f* de malla.

net·tle [ˈnetl] **1.** ortiga *f*; **2.** irritar, provocar; ˈ~**-rash** urticaria *f*.

net·work [ˈnetwəːrk] red *f* (*a. fig.*); malla *f*.

neu·ral·gia [njuˈrældʒə] neuralgia *f*; **neu·ras·the·ni·a** [njurəsˈθiːniə] neurastenia *f*; **neu·ras·then·ic** [~ˈθenik] neurasténico; **neu·ri·tis** [njuˈraitis] neuritis *f*; **neu·rol·o·gist** [~ˈrɔlədʒist] neurólogo *m*; **neu·rol·o·gy** [~ˈrɔlədʒi] neurología *f*; **neu·ron** [ˈ~rɔn] neurona *f*; **neu·ro·path** [~rouˈpæθ] neurópata *m*/*f*; **neu·ro·path·ic** [~rouˈpæθik] neuropático; **neu·ro·sis** [~ˈrousis] neurosis *f*; **neu·rot·ic** [~ˈrɔtik] □ neurótico *adj. a. su. m* (a *f*).

neu·ter [ˈnjuːtər] neutro.

neu·tral [ˈnjuːtrəl] **1.** □ neutral; ⚘, ⚡, ♏ *zo.* neutro; **2.** neutral *m*/*f*; *mot. in* ~ en punto muerto; **neu·tral·i·ty** [njuːˈtræliti] neutralidad *f*; **neu·tral·i·za·tion** [njuːtrəlaiˈzeiʃn] neutralización *f*; ˈ**neu·tral·ize** neutralizar.

neu·tri·no [nuːˈtriːnou] *phys.* neutrino *m*; **neu·tron** [ˈnjuːtrɔn] neutrón *m*; ~ *bomb* bomba *f* neutrónica.

nev·er [ˈnevər] nunca, jamás; de ningún modo; ni siquiera; ~ *again* nunca más; ~ *fear!* ¡no hay cuidado!; ~ *a word* ni una palabra; ˈ**never-**ˈ**more** nunca más; **never·the·less** [~ðəˈles] sin embargo, no obstante, con todo.

new [njuː] **1.** *adj.* nuevo; (*fresh*) fresco; *bread* tierno; *p.* inexperto; F *what's* ~*?* ¿qué hay de nuevo?; ~ *moon* novilunio *m*; ≈ *Testament* Nuevo Testamento *m*; ≈ *Year* Año *m* Nuevo; ~ *Year's Day* día *m* de Año Nuevo; ≈ *Yorker* neoyorquino (a *f*) *m*; ≈ *Zealander* neozelandés (-a *f*) *m*; **2.** *adv.* recién; ˈ**new**ˈ**born** recién nacido; ˈ**newˈcom·er** recién llegado (a *f*) *m*; **new·fan·gled** [ˈ~fæŋgld] *contp.* recién inventado, moderno; ˈ**new·ish** bastante nuevo; ˈ**new-laid** *egg* recién puesto, fresco; ˈ**new·ly** nuevamente, recién; ~ *wed* recién casado; ˈ**new·ness** novedad *f*; inexperiencia *f*.

news *mst sg.* noticia(s) *f* (*pl.*); nueva(s) *f* (*pl.*), novedad *f*; *radio*: noticiario *m*; *it was ~ to me* me cogió de nuevas; *what's the ~?* ¿qué hay de nuevo? *he is in the ~* se oye hablar mucho de él; ˈ~ **a·gen·cy** agencia *f* de información; ˈ~ **a·gent** vendedor (-a *f*) *m* de periódicos; ˈ~ ˈ**bul·le·tin** (boletín *m* de) noticias *f*/*pl.*, noticiario *m*; ˈ**~·cast** noticiario *m*; ˈ**~·cast·er** reportero *m* radiofónico; ˈ~ **con·fer·ence** conferencia *f* de prensa; ˈ**~·let·ter** circular *f* noticiera; ˈ**~·pa·per** periódico *m*, diario *m*; *attr.* periodístico; ˈ**~·pa·per·man** periodista *m*; ˈ**~-print** papel *m* prensa; ˈ**~·reel** noticiario *m*, actualidades *f*/*pl.*; ˈ**~·room** gabinete *m* de lectura; ˈ**~·stand** quiosco *m* de periódicos; **news·y** [ˈnjuːzi] F lleno de noticias; *p.* noticioso.

newt [njuːt] tritón *m*.

next [nekst] **1.** *adj.* próximo, siguiente; *year etc.* que viene; inmediato; *house etc.* de al lado, vecino; otro; *it's the ~ but one* es el segundo después de éste; *~ day* día *m* siguiente; *v. door*; *on the ~ page* a la vuelta, a la página siguiente; *~ time* la próxima vez; *~ week* la semana que viene; **2.** *adv.* luego, inmediatamente, después; la próxima vez; *~ best thing* lo mejor después de eso; *~ to* junto a, al lado de; primero después de; casi; *~ to nothing* casi nada; *v. what*.

nib [nib] pico *m*; plumilla *f*, plumín *m of fountain pen*.

nib·ble [ˈnibl] (*a. ~ at*) mordiscar; (*fish*) picar; *grass* rozar; *fig.* criticar; *fig.* tantear, considerar.

nibs [nibz]: *sl. his ~* su señoría.

nice [nais] □ ameno, agradable; bonito (*a. iro.*); bueno; *p.* simpático, amable; primoroso; fino, delicado; escrupuloso; exacto; meticuloso; F *~ and adj.* muy; bastante; *often rendered by diminutive* -ito; *~ and early* tempranito; *it's ~ and warm* hace un calor agradable; F *not ~* feo; *~ point* punto *m* delicado; ˈ**~-look·ing** F mono, guapo; ˈ**nice·ness** amenidad *f*; lo simpático, simpatía *f etc.*; **nice·ty** [ˈ~iti] exactitud *f*; sutileza *f*; refinamiento *m*; *niceties pl.* detalles *m*/*pl.*; *to a ~* con la mayor precisión.

niche [nitʃ] nicho *m*; *fig.* colocación *f* conveniente.

nick [nik] **1.** mella *f*; muesca *f*; *in the (very) ~ of time* de perilla, en el momento preciso (*or* crítico); **2.** mellar, hacer muescas en; *sl.* robar, ratear.

nick·el [ˈnikl] **1.** níquel *m* (*a. moneda de EE. UU. de 5 centavos*); **2.** niquelar (*a.* ˈ**~-plate**).

nick·name [ˈnikneim] **1.** apodo *m*, sobrenombre *m*, mote *m*; **2.** apodar, motejar.

nic·o·tine [ˈnikətiːn] nicotina *f*.

niece [niːs] sobrina *f*.

nif·ty [ˈnifti] □ *sl.* elegante, excelente, de primera; hábil.

nig·gard [ˈnigərd] tacaño *adj. a. su. m* (a *f*); ˈ**nig·gard·ly** tacaño, avariento, mezquino.

nig·gle [ˈnigl] inquietarse por pequeñeces; ˈ**nig·gling** nimio, minucioso; mezquino; insignificante.

nigh [nai] † *or prov.* cerca (de); casi.

night [nait] noche *f*; *attr.* nocturno; *at ~*, *by ~*, *in the ~* de noche, por la noche; *good ~!* ¡buenas noches!; *last ~* anoche; F *make a ~ of it* estar de juerga hasta muy entrada la noche; *the ~ before last* anteanoche; ˈ**~·cap** gorro *m*; F resopón *m*; ˈ**~club** cabaret *m*; ˈ**~·dress** camisón *m* (de noche); ˈ**~·fall** anochecer *m*; *at ~* al anochecer; ˈ~-ˈ**fight·er** ✈ caza *m* nocturno; ˈ**~·gown** camisa *f* de dormir; camisón *m*; **night·in·gale** [ˈ~iŋgeil] ruiseñor *m*; ˈ**night·light** mariposa *f*; ˈ**night·ly** de noche; (de) todas las noches.

night...: ˈ**~·mare** pesadilla *f* (*a. fig.*); ˈ~ **school** escuela *f* nocturna; ˈ**~-shade** dulcamara *f*, hierba *f* mora; *deadly ~* belladona *f*; ˈ**~·shift** turno *m* de noche; ˈ**~·spot** cabaret *m*; ˈ**~-time** noche *f*; horas *f* de noche; ˈ~ ˈ**watch·man** sereno *m*, vigilante *m* de noche; guardia *m* de noche.

ni·hil·ism [ˈnaiilizm] nihilismo *m*; ˈ**ni·hil·ist** nihilista *m*/*f*.

nil [nil] nada *f*, cero *m*.

nim·ble [ˈnimbl] □ ágil, activo, ligero; listo.

nim·bus [ˈnimbəs] nimbo *m.*
nin·com·poop [ˈninkəmpu:p] F bobo (a *f*) *m*, simplón (-a *f*) *m*, papirote *m.*
nine [nain] nueve (*a. su. m*); F *be dressed up to the* ~*s* estar hecho un brazo de mar; ˈ**~·pins** *pl.* (juego *m* de) bolos *m/pl.*; **nine·teen** [ˈ~ˈti:n] diecinueve; ˈ**~-**ˈ**one** (-ˈ**two** *etc.*) mil novecientos uno (dos *etc.*); ˈ**nine-**ˈ**teenth** [~θ] decimonoveno, decimonono; **nine·tieth** [ˈ~tiiθ] nonagésimo; ˈ**nine·ty** noventa.
nin·ny [ˈnini] F bobo (a *f*) *m*, mentecato (a *f*) *m.*
ninth [nainθ] noveno, nono.
nip[1] [nip] **1.** pellizco *m*, mordisco *m*; viento *m* frío; helada *f*; **2.** pellizcar, mordiscar; helar; (*wind*) picar; cortar, parar; ~ *in the bud* atajar en el principio.
nip[2] [~] trago *m*, sorb(it)o *m.*
nip[3] [~] F correr; ~ *in* colarse; ~ *off* pirarse.
nip·per [ˈnipər] *sl.* chiquillo *m.*
nip·ple [ˈnipl] pezón *m*; tetilla *f of male or bottle*; ⊕ boquilla *f* roscada, manguito *m* de unión; (*lubricating*) engrasador *m.*
nip·py [ˈnipi] ágil, listo; *temperature* helado.
nir·va·na [nirˈvɑ:nə] nirvana *m.*
nit [nit] liendre *f.*
ni·ter [ˈnaitər] nitro *m.*
ni·trate [ˈnaitreit] nitrato *m.*
ni·tric ac·id [ˈnaitrikˈæsid] ácido *m* nítrico.
ni·tro·gen [ˈnaitridʒən] nitrógeno *m*; **ni·trog·e·nous** [~ˈtrɔdʒinəs] nitrogenado; **ni·tro·glyc·er·in** [naitrouˈglisərin] nitroglicerina *f.*
ni·trous [ˈnaitrəs] nitroso.
nit·wit [ˈnitwit] *sl.* bobalicón *m*; ignorante *m.*
nix [niks] *sl.* nada; ~! ¡alto!, ¡cese Vd!, ¡no siga Vd!
no [nou] **1.** *adv.* no; **2.** *adj.* ninguno; ~ *man's land* tierra *f* de nadie; ~ *one* nadie, ninguno; *with* ~ sin; **3.** *su.* no *m*; voto *m* negativo.
nob[1] [nɔb] *sl.* cabeza *f.*
nob[2] [~] *sl.* pez *m* gordo; elegante *m*, majo *m.*
nob·ble [ˈnɔbl] *sl. p.* sobornar; *th.* birlar, ratear; *horse* narcotizar, estropear.
no·bil·i·ty [nouˈbiliti] nobleza *f*; hidalguía *f esp. of conduct.*
no·ble [ˈnoubl] **1.** □ noble; hidalgo, caballeroso; sublime; **2.** (*a.* ˈ**~·man**) noble *m*; hidalgo *m*; ˈ**no·ble·ness** nobleza *f*; hidalguía *f*; ˈ**no·ble-wom·an** dama *f* noble, hidalga *f.*
no·bod·y [ˈnoubədi] nadie, ninguno; *a* ~ un (don) nadie, un cualquiera.
noc·tur·nal [nɔkˈtə:rnl] nocturno.
nod [nɔd] **1.** menear la cabeza de arriba abajo; (*doze*) dar cabezadas, cabecear; indicar con la cabeza; decir que sí con la cabeza; ~*ding acquaintance* conocimiento *m* superficial; **2.** cabezada *f*; inclinación *f* de la cabeza; señal *f* hecha con la cabeza.
nod·dle [ˈnɔdl] F cabeza *f*, mollera *f.*
node [noud] protuberancia *f*; nudo *m*; ⚕, *ast.*, *phys.* nodo *m*; ⚘ nudo *m.*
nod·u·lar [ˈnɔdjulər] nodular.
nod·ule [ˈnɔdju:l] nódulo *m.*
nog·gin [ˈnɔgin] vaso *m* pequeño; *medida de licor* (= *1,42 decilitros*); *sl.* cabeza *f.*
no·how [ˈnouhau] F de ninguna manera.
noise [nɔiz] **1.** ruido *m*; clamor *m*; estrépito *m*; F *big* ~ pez *m* gordo; **2.**: ~ *about* divulgar, publicar.
noise·less [ˈ~lis] □ silencioso, sin ruido.
nois·i·ness [ˈnɔizinis] ruido *m*, estrépito *m*; lo ruidoso.
noi·some [ˈnɔisəm] apestoso; asqueroso; malsano, nocivo.
nois·y [ˈnɔizi] □ ruidoso, estrépitoso, clamoroso.
no·mad [ˈnɔməd] nómada *adj. a. su. m/f*; **no·mad·ic** [nouˈmædik] □ nómada.
nom de plume [ˈnɔmdəplum] seudónimo *m.*
no·men·cla·ture [nouˈmenklətʃər] nomenclatura *f.*
nom·i·nal [ˈnɔminl] □ nominal; ~ *value* valor *m* nominal; **nom·i·nate** [ˈ~neit] nombrar, proponer como candidato (*for* a); **nom·iˈna·tion** nombramiento *m*, nominación *f*; propuesta *f*; **nom·i·na·tive** [ˈ~nətiv] nominativo *adj. a. su. m*; **nom·i·nee** [~ˈni:] candidato *m* nombrado (*or* propuesto).
non [nɔn] *in compounds*: no, des..., in..., falta *f* de; **~·ac·cept·ance** [~ækˈseptəns] rechazo *m*; falta *f* de aceptación.
non·age [ˈnounidʒ] minoridad *f.*
non·a·ge·nar·i·an [nounədʒiˈneri-

ən] nonagenario (a *f*) *m*, noventón (-a *f*) *m*.

non·ag·gres·sion [ˈnɔnəˈgreʃn]: no agresión *f*; ~ *pact* pacto *m* de no agresión.

non·al·co·hol·ic [ˈnɔnælkəˈhɔlik] no alcohólico.

non·a·ligned [nɔnəˈlaind] *país* no comprometido *to a major power*.

non·ap·pear·ance [ˈnɔnəˈpirəns] ausencia *f*; ⚖ no comparecencia *f*.

non·at·tend·ance [ˈnɔnəˈtendəns] falta *f* de asistencia, ausencia *f*.

nonce [nɔns]: *for the* ~ por esta vez, por el momento.

non·cha·lance [ˈnɔnʃələns] indiferencia *f*; aplomo *m*; descuido *m*; **ˈnon·cha·lant** □ indiferente; descuidado.

non·com·bat·ant [ˈnɔnˈkɔmbətənt] no combatiente *adj. a. su. m/f*.

non·com·mis·sioned [ˈnɔnkəˈmiʃənd]: ~ *officer* ⚔ sargento *m or* cabo *m*; *marina* suboficial *m*.

non·com·mit·al [ˈnɔnkəˈmitl] que no compromete; ambiguo, evasivo.

non·com·pli·ance [ˈnɔnkəmˈplaiəns] falta *f* de cumplimiento, desobediencia *f* (*with* de).

non·con·duc·tor [ˈnɔnkənˈdʌktər] ⚡ aislador *m*.

non·con·form·ist [ˈnɔnkənˈfɔːrmist] disidente *adj. a. su. m/f*; *eccl.* no conformista *adj. a. su. m/f*; **ˈnon·conˈform·i·ty** disidencia *f*; no conformismo *m*.

non·de·script [ˈnɔndiskript] indefinido, inclasificable; *b.s.* mediocre.

none [nʌn] **1.** *pron.* (*p.*) nadie; (*p.*, *th.*) ninguno; (*th.*) nada; ~ *of that* nada de eso; ~ *of them* ninguno de ellos; **2.** *adv.* no; de ninguna manera, nada; ~*theless* sin embargo.

non·en·ti·ty [nɔˈnentiti] nulidad *f*, cero *m* a la izquierda.

non·es·sen·tial [ˈnɔniˈsenʃəl] no esencial.

non·ex·ist·ence [nɔnekˈzistəns] inexistencia *f*.

non·fer·rous [ˈnɔnˈferəs] no ferroso.

non·fic·tion [ˈnɔnˈfikʃn] literatura *f* no novelesca.

non·in·ter·ven·tion [ˈnɔnintərˈvenʃn] no intervención *f*.

non·pa·reil [nɔnpəˈrel] (persona *f or* cosa *f*) sin par; *typ.* nomparell *m*.

non·par·ti·san [ˈnɔnˈpɑːrtizn] imparcial; **non·par·ty** [ˈnɔnˈpɑːrti] *pol.* independiente.

non·plus [ˈnɔnˈplʌs] dejar perplejo, confundir.

non·prof·it [ˈnɔnˈprɔfit] sin fin *m* lucrativo; ~ *institution* institución *f* no lucrativa.

non·res·i·dent [ˈnɔnˈrezidənt] transeúnte *adj. a. su. m/f*; no residente *m/f*.

non·sense [ˈnɔnsəns] disparate *m*, desatino *m*, tontería *f*; ~! ¡tonterías!; **non·sen·si·cal** [~ˈsensikəl] □ disparatado, tonto, desatinado.

non·shrink [ˈnɔnˈʃriŋk] inencogible.

non·skid [ˈnɔnˈskid] antideslizante, antirresbaladizo.

non·smok·er [ˈnɔnˈsmoukər] no fumador *m*.

non·stop [ˈnɔnˈstɔp] **1.** *adj.* interminable; 🚂 directo; ✈ sin escalas; continuo; **2.** *adv.* sin parar.

non·un·ion [nɔnˈjuːnjən] no sindicalizado.

noo·dle [ˈnuːdl] tallarín *m*; fideo *m*; F cabeza *f*; ~ *soup* sopa *f* de pastas (*or* de fideos).

nook [nuk] rincón *m*, escondrijo *m*.

noon [nuːn] **1.** mediodía *m* (*a.* **ˈ~·day**, **ˈ~·tide**); *fig.* apogeo *m*; *at* ~ a(l) mediodía; **2.** de mediodía, meridional.

noose [nuːs] **1.** lazo *m* (corredizo); (*hangman's*) dogal *m*; **2.** coger con lazo.

nope [noup] F no.

nor [nɔːr] ni, no, tampoco; *neither* ... ~ ... ni ... ni ...; ~ *I* ni yo tampoco; ~ *was this all* y esto no fue todo.

Nor·dic [ˈnɔːrdik] nórdico.

norm [nɔːrm] norma *f*; modelo *m*; pauta *f*; **ˈnor·mal** □ **1.** normal (*a.* ⚕); regular, corriente; ~ *school* escuela *f* normal; **2.** estado *m* normal, nivel *m* normal; **ˈnor·mal·ize** normalizar.

Nor·man [ˈnɔːrmən] normando *adj. a. su. m* (a *f*).

north [nɔːrθ] **1.** norte *m*; **2.** *adj.* del norte, septentrional; **3.** *adv.* al norte, hacia el norte; **ˈ~ˈeast** noreste *adj.* (*a.* **ˈ~ˈeast·er·ly, ~ˈeast·ern**) *a. su. m*; **north·er·ly** [ˈ~ðərli] *direction* hacia el norte; *wind* del norte; **north·ern** [ˈ~ərn] (del) norte, norteño, septentrional; **ˈnorth·ern·er** habitante *m/f* del norte; **ˈnorth·ern·most** (el) más norte; **ˈnorth·ward(s)** hacia el norte.

north...: ˈ~ˈ**west** noroeste *adj.* (*a.* ˈ~ˈ**west·er·ly,** ˈ~ˈ**west·ern**) *a. su. m.*

Nor·we·gian [nɔːrˈwiːdʒən] **1.** noruego *adj. a. su. m* (a *f*); **2.** (*language*) noruego *m.*

nose [nouz] **1.** nariz *f*; narices *f/pl.* (F); hocico *m of animals*; (*sense of smell*) olfato *m*; ✈ morro *m*; ⚓ proa *f*; *blow one's* ~ sonarse (las narices); *follow one's* ~ ir todo seguido; dejarse llevar por el instinto; *have a good* ~ *for* tener buen olfato para; *look down one's* ~ *at* mirar por encima del hombro; *pay through the* ~ dejarse desollar; *turn up one's* ~ *at* desdeñar; *under the* (*very*) ~ *of* en las barbas de; **2.** *v/t.* husmear, olfatear (*a.* ~ *out*); restregar la nariz contra; ~ *one's way* avanzar con cautela; *v/i.*: ~ *about* curiosear; ˈ~ **bag** morral *m*, cebadera *f*; ˈ~**·bleed** hemorragia *f* nasal; ˈ~ **cone** cono *m* de proa *of a spacecraft*; **nosed** de nariz...

nose...: ˈ~ **dive** ✈ picado *m* vertical; (*involuntary*) caída *f* de bruces; ˈ~**·gay** ramillete *m.*

no-show [ˈnouʃou] F persona *f* que no se presenta cuando debe.

nos·tal·gi·a [nɔsˈtældʒiə] nostalgia *f*, añoranza *f*; **nosˈtal·gic** [~dʒik] □ nostálgico.

nos·tril [ˈnɔstril] (ventana *f* de la) nariz *f.*

nos·trum [ˈnɔstrəm] remedio *m* secreto, panacea *f.*

nos·y [ˈnouzi] F curioso; entremetido.

not [nɔt] no; ~ *I* yo no; ~ *to say* por no decir; ~ *thinking that* sin pensar que; *I think* ~ creo que no, no lo creo; *why* ~? ¿cómo no?

no·ta·bil·i·ty [noutəˈbiliti] notabilidad *f*; **no·ta·ble** [ˈnoutəbl] **1.** □ notable, señalado; **2.** notabilidad *f*; ~*s pl.* notables *m/pl.*

no·tar·i·al [nouˈtɛriəl] □ notarial; **no·ta·ry** [ˈnoutəri] notario *m* (*a.* ~ *public*).

no·ta·tion [nouˈteiʃn] notación *f.*

notch [nɔtʃ] **1.** muesca *f*, mella *f*; desfiladero *m*; **2.** mellar, cortar muescas en; *fig.* señalar.

note [nout] **1.** nota *f* (*a.* ♪); apunte *m*; marca *f*, señal *f*; (*letter*) esquela *f*, recado *m*; (*bank*) billete *m*; ⚕ vale *m*; *of* ~ notable; *make a* ~ *of* apuntar; *take* ~ *of* poner atención a; *take* ~*s* tomar notas, sacar apuntes; **2.** notar, observar, advertir; anotar, apuntar (*a.* ~ *down*); ˈ~**·book** cuaderno *m*, libro *m* de apuntes, libreta *f*; ˈ~**·case** cartera *f*; ˈ**not·ed** conocido, célebre (*for* por); ˈ**note pa·per** papel *m* para cartas; ˈ**note·wor·thy** notable, digno de notarse.

noth·ing [ˈnʌθiŋ] **1.** nada; ✗ cero *m*; friolera *f*, nadería *f* (*a. mere* ~); *sweet* ~*s pl.* ternezas *f/pl.*; ~ *else* nada más; ~ *much*, ~ *to speak of* poca cosa; *for* ~ (*free*) gratis, de balde; (*in vain*) en vano, en balde; *come to* ~ fracasar, reducirse a nada; *make* ~ *of* no sacar nada de, no entender; no aprovecharse de; no dar importancia a; *think* ~ *of* tener en poco; tener por fácil; no hacer caso de; **2.** *adv.* de ninguna manera, en nada; ~ *daunted* sin arredrarse; ~ *less* no menos; ni con mucho; ˈ**noth·ing·ness** nada *f*, inexistencia *f.*

no·tice [ˈnoutis] **1.** aviso *m*; (*poster etc.*) letrero *m*, anuncio *m*, cartel *m*; (*review*) reseña *f*, crítica *f*; (*reference*) nota *f*, mención *f*; observación *f*, atención *f*; *at short* ~ a corto plazo, con poco tiempo de aviso; *give* ~ *that* avisar que; *give a p. a week's* ~ despedir con una semana de plazo; avisar con una semana de anticipación; *take* ~ *of* observar, hacer caso de; *until further* ~ hasta nuevo aviso; **2.** notar, observar; hacer caso de; reparar, advertir, fijarse en; *book* reseñar; ˈ**no·tice·a·ble** □ evidente, perceptible; notable; ˈ**no·tice board** tablón *m* de anuncios.

no·ti·fi·a·ble [ˈnoutifaiəbl] de declaración obligatoria; **no·ti·fi·ca·tion** [~fiˈkeiʃn] notificación *f.*

no·ti·fy [ˈnoutifai] notificar, comunicar, intimar, avisar.

no·tion [ˈnouʃn] noción *f*, idea *f*; capricho *m*; inclinación *f*; ~*s pl.* mercería *f*; artículos *m/pl.* de fantasía; ˈ**no·tion·al** □ nocional; especulativo.

no·to·ri·e·ty [noutəˈraiəti] mala fama *f*; escándalo *m*; notoriedad *f*; **no·to·ri·ous** [nouˈtɔːriəs] □ de mala fama; notorio; célebre (*for* por).

not·with·stand·ing [nɔtwiθˈstændiŋ] **1.** *prp.* a pesar de; **2.** *adv.* no

obstante; **3.** *conj.* (*a.* ~ *that*) a pesar de que.
nou·gat [ˈnuːgət] *approx.* turrón *m.*
nought [nɔːt] ✠ cero *m*; nada.
noun [naun] nombre *m*, sustantivo *m.*
nour·ish [ˈnəːriʃ] nutrir, alimentar, sustentar; *fig.* fomentar, abrigar; ˈ**nour·ish·ing** nutritivo, alimenticio; ˈ**nour·ish·ment** nutrimento *m*, alimento *m*; nutrición *f.*
nov·el [ˈnɔvl] **1.** nuevo, original, insólito; **2.** novela *f*; **nov·el·ette** [nɔvəˈlet] novela *f* corta; ˈ**nov·el·ist** novelista *m*/*f*; **nov·el·ty** [ˈnɔvlti] novedad *f*; innovación *f*; ✝ baratija *f.*
No·vem·ber [nouˈvembər] noviembre *m.*
nov·ice [ˈnɔvis] novicio (a *f*) *m* (*a. eccl.*); principiante *m*/*f.*
no·vi·ti·ate [nouˈviʃiit] noviciado *m.*
now [nau] **1.** ahora; ya; *before* ~ antes, ya; *from* ~ *on*(*ward*) de aquí en adelante; *just* ~ ahora mismo; hace poco; ~ *and again*, ~ *and then* de vez en cuando, una que otra vez; ~ ... ~ ... ora ... ora ..., ya ... ya ..; **2.** *cj.* ahora bien, pues; ~ *that* ya que; **3.** actualidad *f.*
now·a·days [ˈnauədeiz] hoy en día, actualmente.
no·way(**s**) [ˈnouwei(z)], **no way** F de ninguna manera; ¡nunca!
no·where [ˈnouwer] en (*or* a) ninguna parte; ~ *else* en ninguna otra parte.
no·wise [ˈnouwaiz] de ninguna manera.
nox·ious [ˈnɔkʃəs] □ nocivo, dañoso; pestífero.
noz·zle [ˈnɔzl] ⊕ tobera *f*, inyector *m*; boquerel *m*, lanza *f of hose.*
nu·cle·ar [ˈnjuːkliər] nuclear; ~ *fission* fisión *f* nuclear, escisión *f* nuclear; ~ *physics* física *f* nuclear; ~-*powered* accionado por energía nuclear; **nu·cle·us** [ˈ~kliəs] núcleo *m.*
nude [njuːd] desnudo *adj. a. su. m.*
nudge [nʌdʒ] **1.** codazo *m* (ligero); **2.** dar un codazo a.
nud·ism [ˈnjuːdizm] (des)nudismo *m*; naturismo *m*; ˈ**nud·ist** desnudista *m*/*f*; ˈ**nu·di·ty** desnudez *f.*
nu·ga·to·ry [ˈnjuːgətəri] fútil, ineficaz, insignificante.
nug·get [ˈnʌgit] pepita *f* (de oro).
nui·sance [ˈnjuːsns] molestia *f*, fastidio *m*; plaga *f*; lata *f* (F); (*p.*) moscón *m*; *what a* ~! ¡qué lata!, ¡que fastidio!; *be a* ~, *make a* ~ *of o.s.* dar la lata.
nuke [nuːk] *sl.* **1.** arma *f* atómica; **2.** atacar con arma atómica; aniquilar.
null [nʌl] nulo, inválido (*a.* ~ *and void*); **nul·li·fy** [ˈ~ifai] anular, invalidar; ˈ**nul·li·ty** nulidad *f* (*a. p.*).
numb [nʌm] **1.** □ entumecido; insensible; **2.** entumecer; entorpecer.
num·ber [ˈnʌmbər] **1.** número *m*; (*figure*) cifra *f*; ~*s pl. poet.* versos *m*/*pl.*; *a* ~ *of* una porción de, varios; *v. back* ~; *sl. look after* ~ *one* cuidar de sí mismo; **2.** numerar; contar; poner número a; (*total*) ascender a; *be* ~*ed among* figurar entre, hallarse entre; *his days are* ~*ed* tiene los días contados; ˈ**num·ber·less** innumerable, sin número; ˈ**num·ber plate** *mot.* placa *f* de matrícula.
numb·ness [ˈnʌmnis] entumecimiento *m*; insensibilidad *f*; **numb·skull** [ˈnʌmskʌl] = *numskull.*
nu·mer·al [ˈnjuːmərəl] **1.** numeral; **2.** número *m*, cifra *f*, guarismo *m*; **nu·merˈa·tion** numeración *f*; ˈ**nu·mer·a·tor** numerador *m.*
nu·mer·i·cal [njuˈmerikl] □ numérico.
nu·mer·ous [ˈnjuːmərəs] □ numeroso; muchos.
nu·mis·mat·ic [njuːmizˈmætik] □ numismático; **nu·misˈmat·ics** *mst sg.* numismática *f*; **nu·mis·ma·tist** [njuˈmizmətist] numismático *m.*
num·skull [ˈnʌmskʌl] F zote *m*; mentecato *m*; imbécil *m.*
nun [nʌn] monja *f*, religiosa *f.*
nun·ci·o [ˈnʌnʃiou] nuncio *m* (apostólico).
nun·ner·y [ˈnʌnəri] convento *m* de monjas.
nup·tial [ˈnʌpʃəl] **1.** nupcial; **2.** ~*s* [ˈ~lz] *pl.* nupcias *f*/*pl.*
nurse [nəːrs] **1.** enfermera *f*; nodriza *f*, ama *f* de leche (*a. wet* ~); (*children's*) niñera *f*; **2.** *v*/*t. sick* cuidar; *child* criar, amamantar; mecer *in arms*; (*caress*) acariciar; *fig.* fomentar; ~ *a cold* tratar de curarse de un resfriado; *v*/*i.* ser enfermera; ˈ~**maid** niñera *f.*
nurs·er·y [ˈnəːrsəri] cuarto *m* de los niños; ✔ criadero *m*, semillero *m*; ✔, *fig.* plantel *m*; ~ *school* jardín *m* de la infancia; ˈ~**·man** horticultor *m*; encargado *m* de un semillero; ˈ~ **rhyme** canción *f* infantil; ˈ~ **school** escuela *f* materna; parvulario *m.*

nurs·ing [ˈnəːrsiŋ] lactancia *f*; crianza *f*; asistencia *f*; profesión *f* de enfermera; ~ *home* casa *f* de inválidos; residencia *f* de ancianos.
nur·ture [ˈnəːrtʃər] **1.** nutrición *f*; crianza *f*, educación *f*; **2.** nutrir, alimentar; criar, educar.
nut [nʌt] nuez *f*; ⊕ tuerca *f*; *sl.* cabeza *f*; loco *m*, estrafalario *m*, excéntrico *m*; *he is a jazz* ~ es un aficionado del jazz; *sl. be* ~*s about* estar loco por; *sl. drive* ~*s* volver loco; *a hard* ~ *to crack* hueso *m* duro de roer.
nu·ta·tion [njuːˈteiʃn] nutación *f*.
nut·cracker [ˈnʌtkrækər], *mst* (*a pair of* un) ~*s pl.* cascanueces *m*; **nut·meg** [ˈ~meg] nuez *f* moscada.
nu·tri·ent [ˈnjuːtriənt] **1.** nutritivo; **2.** nutrimento *m*; **ˈnu·triment** nutrimento *m*.
nu·tri·tion [njuːˈtriʃn] nutrición *f*, alimentación *f*; **nuˈtri·tion·al value** valor *m* nutritivo; **nuˈtri·tious, nu·tri·tive** [ˈ~tiv] □ nutritivo, alimenticio.
nuts [nʌts] *sl.* **1.** loco, estrafalario; **2.** ~*!* ¡no!; ¡de ninguna manera!; ¡niego!
nut·shell [ˈnʌtʃel] cáscara *f* de nuez; *in a* ~ en resumidas cuentas; **nut·ty** [ˈnʌti] de nuez; que sabe a nueces; *sl.* loco (*about* por).
nuz·zle [ˈnʌzl] *v/t.* hocicar; acariciar con el hocico; *v/i.* arrimarse cómodamente (*in to*, *up to* a).
ny·lon [ˈnailɔn] nailon *m*, nilón *m*; ~*s* medias *f/pl.* de nailon.
nymph [nimf] ninfa *f*.

O

o [ou] ¡oh!, ¡ah!, ¡ay!; ~ *that* ...! ¡ojalá (que) ...!
oaf [ouf] zoquete *m*, bobalicón *m*, patán *m*; ˈ**oaf·ish** lerdo, zafio.
oak [ouk] **1.** roble *m*; **2.** de roble; ˈ~ **ap·ple,** ˈ~ **gall** agalla *f* (de roble); ˈ**oak·en** ⚒ de roble.
oa·kum [ˈoukəm] estopa *f* (de calafatear).
oar [ɔːr] remo *m*; (*p.*) remero (a *f*) *m*; *fig. put one's* ~ *in* meter baza; *fig. rest on one's* ~*s* descansar; dormir en los laureles; **oars·man** [ˈɔːrzmən] remero *m*.
o·a·sis [ouˈeisis], *pl.* **oˈa·ses** [~siːz] oasis *m*.
oast [oust] secadero *m* para lúpulo.
oat [out] avena *f* (*mst* ~*s pl.*); *rolled* ~*s* copos *m*/*pl.* de avena; ˈ~**·cake** torta *f* de avena; ˈ**oat·en** de avena.
oath [ouθ], *pl.* **oaths** [ouðz] juramento *m*, jura *f*; *b.s.* blasfemia *f*, reniego *m*; *administer an* ~ *to* tomar juramento a; *under* ~, *on* ~ bajo juramento; *put a p. on* ~ hacer prestar juramento a una p.; *take an* (*or the*) ~ prestar juramento (*on* sobre).
oat·meal [ˈoutmiːl] harina *f* de avena.
ob·du·ra·cy [ˈɔbdjurəsi] obstinación *f*, terquedad *f*; **ob·du·rate** [ˈ~rit] □ obstinado, terco; empedernido.
o·be·di·ence [əˈbiːdjəns] obediencia *f*; *in* ~ *to* conforme a; **oˈbe·di·ent** □ obediente.
o·bei·sance [ouˈbeisns] reverencia *f*, acato *m*; homenaje *m*; *do* (*or make, pay*) ~ *to* acatar, tributar homenaje a.
ob·e·lisk [ˈɔbilisk] obelisco *m*.
o·bese [ouˈbiːs] obeso; **oˈbese·ness, oˈbes·i·ty** obesidad *f*.
o·bey [əˈbei] obedecer; *instructions* cumplir, observar; obrar de acuerdo con.
ob·fus·cate [ˈɔbfʌskeit] ofuscar.
o·bit·u·ar·y [əˈbitjuəri] **1.** necrología *f*; *eccl.* obituario *m*; **2.** necrológico; ~ *notice* necrología *f*.
ob·ject 1. [ˈɔbdʒikt] objeto *m*; (*thing*) cosa *f*, artículo *m*; *contp.* mamarracho *m*, facha *f*; *gr.* complemento *m*; *cost no* ~ no importa (el) precio; **2.** [əbˈdʒekt] *v*/*t.* objetar; *v*/*i.* poner reparos, hacer objeciones, oponerse (*to* a); sentir disgusto (*to* por); *if you don't* ~ si no tiene Vd. inconveniente; ˈ~ **glass** [ˈɔbdʒiktglæs] objetivo *m*.
ob·jec·tion [əbˈdʒekʃn] objeción *f*, reparo *m*; dificultad *f*, inconveniente *m*; *raise* ~*s to* poner reparos a; *there is no* ~ no hay inconveniente; **obˈjec·tion·a·ble** □ molesto, desagradable; ofensivo; censurable.
ob·jec·tive [ɔbˈdʒektiv] □ objetivo *adj. a. su. m*; **ob·jecˈtiv·i·ty** objetividad *f*.
ob·ject...: ˈ~ **lens** objetivo *m*; ˈ~ **lesson** lección *f* práctica, ejemplo *m*; **ob·jec·tor** [əbˈdʒektər] objetante *m*/*f*; *v. conscientious*.
ob·jur·gate [ˈɔbdʒəːrgeit] increpar, reprender.
ob·late [ˈɔbleit] □ *eccl.* oblato; ⚘ achatado por los polos.
ob·la·tion [ouˈbleiʃn] oblación *f*; (*gift*) oblata *f*.
ob·li·ga·tion [ɔbliˈgeiʃn] obligación *f*; deber *m*; compromiso *m*; *eccl. of* ~ de precepto; *be under* (*an*) ~ *to a p.* deber favores a una p.; *be under* ~ *to inf.* correr obligación a *inf.*; *without* ~ ✝ sin compromiso; **ob·lig·a·to·ry** [ˈ~gətəri] obligatorio.
o·blige [əˈblaidʒ] obligar, forzar (*to* a); complacer, hacer un favor a; *much* ~*d* muy agradecido (*for* por); *much* ~*d!* ¡se agradece!; *I should be much* ~*d if* ... agradecería que ...; ~ *with* hacer el favor de; **o·blig·ing** □ atento, servicial, complaciente.
ob·lique [əˈbliːk] □ oblicuo; indirecto, evasivo; **obˈlique·ness, obˈliq·ui·ty** [~kwiti] oblicuidad *f*; desviación *f*; aberración *f*.
ob·lit·er·ate [əˈblitəreit] borrar; destruir, aniquilar; ⚕ obliterar;

ob·lit·er'a·tion borradura *f*; destrucción *f*; aniquilación *f*; ⚕ obliteración *f*.

ob·liv·i·on [ə'bliviən] olvido *m*; **ob'liv·i·ous** □ olvidado, inconsciente (*of, to* de).

ob·long ['ɔblɔŋ] **1.** oblongo, rectangular, cuadrilongo; **2.** rectángulo *m*, cuadrilongo *m*.

ob·lo·quy ['ɔbləkwi] difamación *f*, calumnia *f*; deshonra *f*.

ob·nox·ious [əb'nɔkʃəs] □ detestable, ofensivo, odioso.

o·boe ['oubou] oboe *m*.

ob·scene [ɔb'si:n] □ obsceno, indecente; **ob'scen·i·ty** [~iti] obscenidad *f*.

ob·scu·ran·tism [ɔb'skjurӕntizm] oscurantismo *m*; **ob·scure** [əb'skjur] **1.** □ oscuro (*a. fig.*); **2.** oscurecer; eclipsar; esconder; **ob'scu·ri·ty** oscuridad *f* (*a. fig.*).

ob·se·quies ['ɔbsikwiz] *pl.* exequias *f/pl.*

ob·se·qui·ous [əb'si:kwiəs] □ servil; obsequioso; **ob'se·qui·ous·ness** servilismo *m*; obsequiosidad *f*.

ob·serv·a·ble [əb'zə:rvəbl] □ observable; **ob'serv·ance** observancia *f*; práctica *f*, costumbre *f*; **ob'serv·ant** □ observador; atento; perspicaz; vigilante; **ob·ser·va·tion** [ɔbzə:r'veiʃn] observación *f*; experiencia *f*; *under* ~ vigilado; 🚂 ~ *car* vagón-mirador *m*; **ob·serv·a·to·ry** [əb'zə:rvətɔ:ri] observatorio *m*; **ob'serve** observar; decir; *festival, silence* guardar; *p.* vigilar; **ob'serv·er** observador (-a *f*) *m*.

ob·sess [əb'ses] obsesionar, causar obsesión a; **ob·ses·sion** [əb'seʃn] obsesión *f*.

ob·so·les·cence [ɔbsə'lesns] caída *f* en desuso; **ob·so'les·cent** que cae en desuso.

ob·so·lete ['ɔbsəli:t] anticuado, desusado; *biol.* rudimentario.

ob·sta·cle ['ɔbstəkl] obstáculo *m*; impedimento *m*; inconveniente *m*; ~ *race* carrera *f* de obstáculos.

ob·ste·tri·cian [ɔbste'triʃn] obstétrico *m*; **ob'stet·rics** [~riks] obstetricia *f*.

ob·sti·na·cy ['ɔbstinəsi] obstinación *f etc.*; **ob·sti·nate** ['~nit] □ obstinado, terco, porfiado; pertinaz.

ob·strep·er·ous [əb'strepərəs] □ clamoroso; turbulento, desmandado.

ob·struct [əb'strʌkt] *v/t.* obstruir; *action* estorbar; *pipe etc.* atorar; *v/i.* estorbar; **ob'struc·tion** obstrucción *f* (*a. parl.*); estorbo *m*; **ob'struc·tion·ist** obstruccionista *m/f*; **ob'struc·tive** □ obstructivo; estorbador.

ob·tain [əb'tein] *v/t.* obtener; adquirir; lograr, conseguir; *v/i.* existir, prevalecer; **ob'tain·a·ble** asequible; *be* ~ ✝ estar de venta.

ob·trude [əb'tru:d] *v/t. opinions* imponer (*on* a), introducir a la fuerza; *v/i.* entrometerse; **ob'tru·sion** imposición *f*; entrometimiento *m*; **ob'tru·sive** [~siv] □ entrometido, intruso; importuno.

ob·tuse [əb'tju:s] □ obtuso (*a.* ⩓, *fig.*); *p.* estúpido, duro de mollera; **ob'tuse·ness** embotadura *f*; *fig.* estupidez *f*.

ob·verse ['ɔbvə:rs] (*adj.* del) anverso *m*.

ob·vi·ate ['ɔbvieit] obviar, evitar, eliminar.

ob·vi·ous ['ɔbviəs] □ evidente, obvio, patente; poco sutil, transparente; innegable.

oc·ca·sion [ə'keiʒən] **1.** ocasión *f*; vez *f*; coyuntura *f*, sazón *f*; motivo *m*; *on* ~ de vez en cuando; *on the* ~ *of* con motivo de; *rise to the* ~ estar a la altura de las circunstancias; **2.** ocasionar; **oc'ca·sion·al** □ poco frecuente; uno que otro; ~ *table* mesilla *f*; ~*ly* de vez en cuando.

oc·ci·dent ['ɔksidənt] *lit.* occidente *m*; **oc·ci·den·tal** [~'dentl] □ occidental.

oc·cult [ɔ'kʌlt] □ oculto, secreto; misterioso; sobrenatural; **oc·cul·ta·tion** [~'teiʃn] *ast.* ocultación *f*; **oc·cult·ism** ['ɔkəltizm] ocultismo *m*; **'oc·cult·ist** ocultista *m/f*.

oc·cu·pan·cy ['ɔkjupənsi] ocupancia *f*, tenencia *f*; **'oc·cu·pant** ocupante *m/f*; (*tenant*) inquilino (a *f*) *m*; **oc·cu'pa·tion** ocupación *f* (*a.* ⚔); tenencia *f*, inquilinato *m*; **oc·cu'pa·tion·al** de oficio, profesional; ~ *disease* enfermedad *f* profesional; ~ *hazard* riesgo *m* ocupacional; ~ *risks iro.* gajes *m/pl.* del oficio; ~ *therapy* terapia *f* vocacional; **oc·cu·pi·er** ['~paiər] inquilino (a *f*) *m*; **oc·cu·py** ['~pai] ocupar; *house* habitar; *time* emplear, pasar; ~ *o.s.* (*or be occupied*) *in or with* ocuparse de *or* en *or* con.

oc·cur [ə'kəːr] (*happen*) ocurrir, suceder, acontecer; (*be found*) encontrarse; *it ~red to me* (*to inf.*) se me ocurrió (*inf.*); **oc'cur·rence** [ə'kʌrəns] acontecimiento *m*, ocurrencia *f*; caso *m*, aparición *f*; *be of frequent ~* suceder a menudo.

o·cean ['ouʃn] océano *m*; *fig. ~s of* la mar de; **'~-go·ing** transoceánico; **o·ce·an·ic** [ouʃi'ænik] oceánico; **'o·cean·lin·er** buque *m* transoceánico.

o·cher ['oukər] ocre *m*.

o'clock [ə'klɔk] = *of the clock*; *it is 1 ~* es la una; *it is 5 ~* son las cinco; *at 2 ~* a las dos.

oc·ta·gon ['ɔktəgən] octágono *m*; **oc·tag·o·nal** [ɔk'tægənl] octagonal.

oc·tane ['ɔktein] octano *m*; *high ~ gasoline* gasolina *f* de alto octanaje.

oc·tave ['ɔktiv] octava *f*; **oc·ta·vo** [~'teivou] (libro *m*) en octavo.

Oc·to·ber [ɔk'toubər] octubre *m*.

oc·to·ge·nar·i·an ['ɔktoudʒi'neriən] octogenario *adj. a. su. m* (a *f*).

oc·to·pus ['ɔktəpəs] pulpo *m*.

oc·u·lar ['ɔkjulər] □ ocular *adj. a. su. m*; **'oc·u·list** oculista *m/f*.

odd [ɔd] *number* impar; desigual; (*isolated*) suelto, desparejado; (*extra*) sobrante; (*strange*) raro, extraño, estrambótico; (*occasional*) tal cual; *20 ~* veinte y pico, veinte y tantos; *~ moments* momentos *m/pl.* de ocio; *at ~ times* de vez en cuando; *be ~ man out* diferenciarse de los demás; estar excluido; ser de más; **'odd·ball** excéntrico; disidente *adj. a. su. m/f.*; **'odd·i·ty** rareza *f*, excentricidad *f*; ente *m* singular; cosa *f* rara; **'odd 'job(s)** empleo *m* al azar; tarea(s) *f* menor(es); **'odd·ment** retal *m*; artículo *m* suelto; sobra *f*; **odds** [ɔdz] *mst pl.* (*advantage*) ventaja *f*, superioridad *f*; (*chances*) probabilidades *f/pl.*; *betting*: puntos *m/pl.* de ventaja; *~ and ends* retazos *m/pl.*; chismes *m/pl.*; materiales *m/pl.* sobrantes; *the ~ are* lo más probable es que; *against ~* contra una fuerza superior; *be at ~* estar reñido, estar de punta (*with* con); *give ~* dar ventaja; F *it makes no ~* lo mismo da; *set at ~* enemistar; F *what's the ~?* ¿qué importa?

ode [oud] oda *f*; *fig.* elogio *m*.

o·di·ous ['oudjəs] □ odioso, detestable; infame; **o·di·um** ['oudiəm] oprobio *m*; odiosidad *f*; odio *m*.

o·don·to·lo·gy [ɔdɔn'tɔlədʒi] odontología *f*.

o·dor·if·er·ous [oudə'rifərəs] □ odorífero; **'o·dor·ous** oloroso, oliente.

o·dor ['oudər] olor *m*; fragancia *f*; *fig.* sospecha *f*; *fig.* estimación *f*; *be in bad ~* tener mala fama; *be in bad ~ with* llevarse mal con; **'o·dor·less** inodoro.

oec·u·men·i·cal [iːkjuː'menikl] = *ecumenical*.

oe·de·ma [iː'diːmə] = *edema*.

o'er [ouər] = *over*.

oe·soph·a·gus [iː'sɔfəgəs] = *esophagus*.

of [ɔv, *unstressed* əv, v] de; *I was robbed ~ my money* me robaron el dinero; *how kind ~ you to inf.* qué amable ha sido Vd. en *inf.*; *a friend ~ mine* un amigo mío; *it smells ~ roses* huele a rosas; *love ~ country* amor *m* a la patria; *~ a morning* † *or* F por la mañana; *I dream ~ you* sueño contigo; *I think ~ you* pienso en ti.

off [ɔːf] **1.** *adv.* lejos, a distancia; fuera; *mst in combination with vb.*: *be ~, go ~* marcharse *etc.*; *3 miles ~* a 3 millas (de distancia); *the exam is 3 days ~* faltan 3 días para el examen; *far ~,* (*a long*) *way ~* muy lejos; *~ and on* ya bien, ya mal; de vez en cuando, a intervalos; *hands ~!* ¡fuera las manos!; *have one's shoes ~* estar descalzo; *be badly ~* andar mal de dinero; *be well ~* estar acomodado; *there is nothing ~* ✝ no hay descuento; **2.** *prp.* lejos de; fuera de; separado de; de, desde; ⚓ a la altura de, frente a; al lado de; *work* libre de; *he has a button ~ his coat* a su chaqueta le falta un botón; *a street ~ the square* una calle que sale de la plaza; **3.** *adj.* separado; terminado; quitado; ⚡ desconectado; ⊕ parado; *water etc.* cortado; *brake* desapretado; *light* apagado; *tap* cerrado; *food* un poco pasado; *time* libre, sin trabajo; *side* derecho, de la derecha; F *~ day* día *m* malo, día *m* nulo; *day ~* día *m* libre; *~ season* estación *f* muerta; **4.** *su.* paro *m* (*a. ~ position*); **5.** *int.* ¡fuera (de aquí)! (*a. ~ with you!*).

of·fal ['ɔfəl] despojos *m/pl.*; asadura *f*, menudencias *f/pl.*

ˈ**offˈbeat** *sl.* insólito; original; ˈ**off-ˈcol·or** desteñido; F arriesgado; obsceno; de mal gusto.
off-du·ty hours [ˈɔːfdjuːti ˈauərz] horas *f/pl.* libres (de servicio).
of·fence [əˈfens] *British* = *offense.*
of·fend [əˈfend] ofender; *be* ~*ed* tomarlo a mal; ~ *against* pecar contra; violar; **ofˈfend·er** delincuente *m/f*; culpable *m/f*; ofensor (-a *f*) *m*; *first* ~ delincuente *m/f* sin antecedente penal.
of·fense [əˈfens] ofensa *f*; ⚖ violación *f* de la ley; delito *m*; *sport*, ⚔ ofensiva *f*; *give* ~ ofender; *no* ~ (*meant*) sin ofender a Vd.; *take* ~ ofenderse, resentirse (*at* de, por).
of·fen·sive [əˈfensiv] **1.** □ ofensivo, injurioso; repugnante; agresivo; **2.** ofensiva *f*; *take the* ~ tomar la ofensiva; **ofˈfen·sive·ness** repugnancia *f*; insolencia *f*.
of·fer [ˈɔfər] **1.** oferta *f* (*a.* ✝), ofrecimiento *m*; ✝ *on* ~ en oferta; **2.** ofrecer (*a.* ~ *up*); *prospect etc.* deparar, brindar; *resistance* oponer, intentar; ~ *to inf.* ofrecerse a *inf.*; ˈ**of·fer·ing** ofrecimiento *m*; *eccl.* ofrenda *f*; tributo *m*.
of·fer·to·ry [ˈɔfərtəri] ofertorio *m*; ofrenda *f*; ~ *box* cep(ill)o *m*.
off·hand [ˈɔːfˈhænd] **1.** *adj.* informal, brusco; despreocupado; improvisado; **2.** *adv.* de improviso, sin pensarlo.
of·fice [ˈɔfis] oficina *f*; (*room*) despacho *m*, escritorio *m*; (*lawyer's*) bufete *m*; (*function*) oficio *m* (*a. eccl.*); (*post*) cargo *m*; *good* ~*s* buenos oficios *m/pl.*; *be in* ~ estar en el poder, estar en funciones; ~ *boy* mandadero *m*; ~ *force* gente *f* de la oficina; cuerpo *m* de oficinistas; ~ *hours* horas *f* de oficina (de consulta, de negocio); ~ *seeker* aspirante *m*; ~ *worker* oficinista *m/f*.
of·fi·cer [ˈɔfisər] **1.** oficial *m* (*a.* ⚔); funcionario *m*; dignatario *m*; (agente *m* de) policía *m*; **2.** mandar; proveer de oficiales; *be well* ~*ed* tener buena oficialidad.
of·fi·cial [əˈfiʃl] **1.** □ oficial; formal; autorizado; ⚕ oficinal; **2.** oficial *m* (público), funcionario *m*; **ofˈfi·cial·dom** círculos *m/pl.* oficiales; *contp.* burocracia *f*.
of·fi·ci·ate [əˈfiʃieit] oficiar (*as* de).
of·fic·i·nal [ɔˈfisinl] oficinal.
of·fi·cious [əˈfiʃəs] oficioso, entrometido.
off·ing [ˈɔfiŋ] *mst in the* ~ cerca (⚓ de la costa), *fig.* en perspectiva.
off...: ˈ~-ˈ**peak** (*horas, estación, etc.*) de valle; de menor tránsito; ˈ~·**print** separata *f*, tirada *f* aparte; ˈ~·**set 1.** compensación *f*; ⚠ retallo *m*; *typ.* offset *m*; ⛏ acodo *m*; ⊕ recodo *m*; **2.** compensar; equilibrar; *typ.* imprimir por offset; ˈ~·**shoot** vástago *m*; *fig.* ramal *m*; ˈ~ˈ**side** *sport*: fuera de juego, offside; ˈ~ˈ**shore** costanero, costeño; ~ *fishing* pesca *f* de bajura; ˈ~·**spring** vástago *m*; prole *f*, descendencia *f*; *fig.* resultado *m*; ˈ~·**stage** (de) entre bastidores; ˈ~-**the-ˈre·cord** confidencial; no oficial.
of·ten [ˈɔfn, ˈɔftən], †, *poet. or in composition* **oft** [ɔft] a menudo, muchas veces, con frecuencia; *as* ~ *as* siempre que, tantas veces como; *how* ~ cuántas veces; *not* ~ pocas veces.
o·gi·val [ouˈdʒaivəl] ojival; **o·give** [ˈoudʒaiv] ojiva *f*.
o·gle [ˈougl] echar miradas amorosas (*or* incitantes) (a).
o·gre [ˈougər] ogro *m*.
oh [ou] ¡oh!, ¡ay!
ohm [oum] ohmio *m*; ohm *m*.
oil [ɔil] **1.** *mst* aceite *m*; *geol. etc.* petróleo *m*; *paint.*, *eccl.* óleo *m*; *paint in* ~*s* pintar al óleo; *strike* ~ *fig.* enriquecerse de súbito; ~ *lamp* velón *m*, quinqué *m*; candil *m*; **2.** lubri(fi)car, engrasar; aceitar; **3.** *adj.* de petróleo; petrolero; *sl. be well* ~*ed* ir a la vela; ˈ~·**can** aceitera *f*; ˈ~·**cloth** hule *m*; F linóleo *m*; ˈ~·**field** campo *m* petrolífero; yacimiento *m* de petróleo; ˈ~ **gauge** manómetro *m* de aceite; ˈ~ **glut** exceso *m* de petróleo; ˈ~ **paint·ing** pintura *f* al óleo; ˈ~ **short·age** carestía *f* (*or* escasez *f*) de petróleo; ˈ~·**skin** hule *m*; ~*s pl.* ⚓ chubasquero *m*; ˈ~ **stove** *cooking*: cocina *f* de petróleo; *heating*: estufa *f* de petróleo; ˈ~ **tank·er** ⚓ (buque) petrolero *m*; *S.Am.* tanquero *m*; ˈ~ **well** pozo *m* de petróleo; ˈ**oil·y** □ aceitoso, oleaginoso; *p.* zalamero, excesivamente obsequioso.
oint·ment [ˈɔintmənt] ungüento *m*.
O. K., o·kay [ˈouˈkei] **1.** ¡está bien!; ¡conforme!; ¡de acuerdo!; **2.** aprobar; **3.** aprobado; en buen orden;

satisfactorio; **4.** aprobación *f*; aprobado *m*.

old [ould] viejo; anciano (*p. only*); (*long-standing, former*) antiguo; *wine* añejo; *grow* ~ envejecer(se); *how* ~ *is he?* ¿cuántos años tiene?, ¿qué edad tiene?; *he is 6 years* ~ tiene 6 años (de edad); *of* ~ antiguamente, de antiguo; ~ *age* vejez *f*, senectud *f*; ~ *age pension* subsidio *m* de vejez; ~ *boy* antiguo alumno *m*; F viejo *m*; F amigo *m* mío; 2 *Glory bandera de los EE.UU.*; *my* ~ *man* F el pariente; 2 *Testament* Antiguo Testamento *m*; *my* ~ *woman* F la parienta; **'old·en** † *or poet.* antiguo; **'old-'fash·ioned** anticuado, pasado de moda; **'old·ish** que va para viejo, algo viejo; **'old-'maid·ish** de solterona; remilgado; **old·ster** ['~stər] F viejo *m*.

o·le·ag·i·nous [ouli'ædʒinəs] oleaginoso.

o·le·o·graph ['ouliougræf] oleografía *f*.

ol·fac·to·ry [ɔl'fæktəri] olfativo, olfatorio.

ol·i·garch·y ['ɔligɑːrki] oligarquía *f*.

ol·ive ['ɔliv] **1.** aceituna *f*, oliva *f*; (*a.* ~ *tree*) olivo *m*; ~ *oil* aceite *m* (de oliva); **2.** aceitunado; **'~ grove** olivar *m*.

O·lym·pi·ad [ou'limpiæd] olimpíada *f*.

O·lym·pi·an [ou'limpiən] olímpico; **O'lym·pic Games** *pl.* Juegos *m/pl.* Olímpicos.

om·e·let, om·e·lette ['ɔmlit] tortilla *f*.

o·men ['oumen] agüero *m*, presagio *m*.

om·i·nous ['ɔminəs] □ ominoso.

o·mis·sion [ou'miʃn] omisión *f*; *sin of* ~ pecado *m* por omisión.

o·mit [ou'mit] omitir; olvidar; suprimir; ~ *to inf.* dejar de *inf.*

om·ni·bus ['ɔmnibəs] **1.** autobús *m*; **2.** general, para todo.

om·nip·o·tence [ɔm'nipətəns] omnipotencia *f*; **om'nip·o·tent** □ omnipotente; todopoderoso.

om·ni·pres·ence ['ɔmni'prezəns] omnipresencia *f*; **'om·ni'pres·ent** □ omnipresente.

om·nis·cience [ɔm'niʃiəns] omnisciencia *f*; **om'nis·cient** □ omnisciente, omniscio.

om·niv·o·rous [ɔm'nivərəs] omnívoro.

on [ɔn] **1.** *prp.* en, sobre, encima de; (*concerning*) sobre, (acerca) de; ~ *arriving* al llegar; ~ *Sunday* el domingo; ~ *Sundays* los domingos; ~ *the third of May* el tres de mayo; ~ *and after* a partir de; ~ *his arrival* a su llegada; ~ *holiday* de vacaciones; ~ *my responsibility* bajo mi responsabilidad; ~ *the next page* a la página siguiente; ~ *this model* según este modelo; *get* ~ *a train* subir a un tren; F *do you have any change* ~ *you?* ¿tienes cambio encima?; F *this is* ~ *me* esto corre por mi cuenta; (*drinks*) invito yo; *march* ~ *London* marchar hacia Londres; *turn one's back* ~ *a p.* volver la espalda a una p.; **2.** *adv.* (hacia) adelante; encima; *vb.* ~ seguir *ger.*; *early* ~ temprano; *read* ~ seguir leyendo; *farther* ~ más allá, más adelante; *later* ~ más tarde; ~ *and* ~ sin cesar; *v.* so; *come* ~*!* ¡vamos!; **3.** *adj.* *clothes* puesto; *light* encendido; ⚡ conectado; ⊕ (puesto) en marcha; *brake* apretado; *tap* abierto; *side* izquierdo; ✝ *the deal is* ~ se ha cerrado el trato; *the race is* ~ ha comenzado la carrera; F *that's not* ~*!* ¡eso no se hace!; *what's* ~*? thea.* ¿qué representan?; **4.** *su.* marcha *f* (*a.* ~ *position*).

once [wʌns] **1.** *adv.* una vez; (*formerly*) antes, antiguamente; *at* ~ en seguida, inmediatamente; (*in one go*) de una vez; *all at* ~ (*suddenly*) de repente; (*in one go*) de una vez; (*all together*) todos juntos; (*just*) *for* ~ una vez siquiera; ~ (*and*) *for all* una vez para siempre; ~ *in a while* de tarde en tarde, de vez en cuando; ~ *more* otra vez; ~ *upon a time there was* érase que se era, había una vez; **2.** *su.* (una) vez *f*; *this* ~ esta vez; **3.** *cj.* una vez que.

once-o·ver ['wʌnsouvər] *sl.* vistazo *m*, examen *m* (rápido).

on·col·o·gy [ɔn'kɔlədʒi] oncología *f*; *approx.* cancerología *f*.

on·com·ing ['ɔnkʌmiŋ] inminente; pendiente.

one [wʌn] **1.** un(o); solo, único; un tal; igual; *his* ~ *care* su único cuidado; *it is all* ~ (*to me*) (me) es igual (*or* indiferente); ~ *day* un día; ~ *Jones* un tal Jones; ~ *or two* unos pocos; **2.** uno (a *f*) *m*; alguno (a *f*) *m*; (*hour*) la una; (*indefinite*) se, uno; *v. any, every, no*; *the black book and the gray* ~ el libro negro y el gris;

the little ~*s* los pequeños, los chiquillos, la gente menuda; ~ *and all* todos; ~ *another* se, uno(s) a otro(s); ~ *by* ~ uno a uno; ~ *does not know* no se sabe, uno no sabe; ~ *must work* hay que trabajar; ~'s su, el ... de uno; *the* ~ *that* (*or who*) el (la) que; *that* ~ ése (a *f*) *m*, aquél (-la *f*) *m*; *this* ~ éste (a *f*) *m*; '~-**eyed** tuerto; '~-'**hand·ed** manco; '~-'**horse** F insignificante, de poca monta; '**one·ness** unidad *f*; '**one-'piece** enterizo, de una pieza.

on·er·ous ['ɔnərəs] □ oneroso.

one...: ~'**self** (*subject*) uno mismo, una misma; (*acc., dat.*) se; (*after prp.*) sí (mismo), sí (misma); *by* ~ solo; por sí mismo; '~-'**sid·ed** □ unilateral; desequilibrado; parcial; *contest* desigual; '~**·time** antiguo; '~-**way:** ~ *street* calle *f* de dirección única; ~ *traffic* dirección *f* obligatoria.

on-go·ing ['ɔngouiŋ] F *adj*. continuo, en progreso.

on·ion ['ʌnjən] cebolla *f*.

on·look·er ['ɔnlukər] mirón (-a *f*) *m*, espectador (-a *f*) *m*.

on·ly ['ounli] **1.** *adj*. solo, único; **2.** *adv*. (tan) sólo, solamente; únicamente; no más que; nada más; *he* ~ *wanted*... quería... nada más; *if* ~...! ojalá...!; ~ *just* hace un momento; apenas; *the* ~ *thing* lo único; **3.** *cj*. ~ (*that*) sólo que, pero.

on·o·mat·o·poe·ia [ɔnəmætə'piːə] onomatopeya *f*; **on·o·mat·o'poe·ic** onomatopéyico.

on·rush ['ɔnrʌʃ] arremetida *f*; torrente *m*; ímpetu *m*.

on·set ['ɔnset] ataque *m*; acceso *m*, comienzo *m* (*a*. ⚕).

on·slaught ['ɔnslɔːt] embestida *f* furiosa.

o·nus ['ounəs] (*no pl.*) carga *f*, responsabilidad *f*.

on·ward ['ɔnwərd] **1.** *adj*. progresivo; hacia adelante; **2.** *adv*. (hacia) adelante (*a*. **on·wards** ['~z]).

on·yx ['ɔniks] ónice *m*.

oo·dles ['uːdlz] F: ~ *of* la mar de, montones de.

oomph [uːmf] *sl*. vigor *m*; atracción *f* sexual.

ooze [uːz] **1.** lama *f*, cieno *m*; **2.** rezumarse (*a*. ~ *out*), exudar.

o·pac·i·ty [ou'pæsiti] opacidad *f*.

o·pal ['oupəl] ópalo *m*; **o·pal·es·cent** [~'lesnt] opalescente.

o·paque [ou'peik] □ opaco.

o·pen ['oupən] **1.** □ abierto; (*uncovered*) descubierto, destapado; (*unfolded*) desplegado, extendido; *event etc*. público; libre; *p*. franco; *mind* receptivo, sin prejuicios; *race* muy igual; *sea* alta mar *f*; ~ *to* expuesto a; accesible a; ~ *to conviction* dispuesto a dejarse convencer; ~ *question* cuestión *f* pendiente (*or* sin resolver); ~ *secret* secreto *m* a voces; ~ *shop* taller *m* franco; *keep* ~ *house* ser muy hospitalario, invitar a casa todo el mundo; *leave* ~ *fig*. dejar sin resolver; **2.:** *in the* ~ al aire libre; en el campo; al descubierto; *bring into the* ~ hacer público; **3.** *v/t*. abrir; (*uncover*) descubrir, destapar; desplegar, extender (*a*. ~ *out*); *parcel* deshacer; *exhibition etc*. inaugurar; dar principio a; ~ *up* abrir; explorar; (*disencumber*) franquear; *v/i*. abrir(se) (*a*. ~ *out*); comenzar; extenderse; (*play*) estrenarse; ~ *into* comunicar con; (*street etc.*) desembocar en; ~ *on* (*to*) dar a, mirar a; ~ *up* franquearse, descubrir el pecho; ⚔ romper el fuego; '~'**cast** ⚒ a (*or* de) cielo abierto; '~-'**end·ed** sin límite; sin término fijo; '~-'**hand·ed** □ liberal, dadivoso; '**o·pen·ing 1.** abertura *f*; brecha *f in wall*; claro *m in woods*; *thea., school, chess:* apertura *f*; ⚕ salida *f*; oportunidad *f*; (*job*) vacante *f*; **2.** de apertura; inaugural; *remark etc*. primero; '**o·pen-'mind·ed** □ receptivo; imparcial; '**o·pen-'mouthed** boquiabierto; **o·pen·ness** ['oupnnis] espaciosidad *f*; abertura *f*; *fig*. franqueza *f*.

op·er·a ['ɔpərə] ópera *f*; '~ **glass**(**·es** *pl.*) gemelos *m/pl*. de teatro; '~ **hat** clac *m*; '~ **house** teatro *m* de la ópera; '~ '**sing·er** cantante *m/f* de la ópera, operista *m/f*.

op·er·ate ['ɔpəreit] *v/t*. hacer funcionar; actuar; impulsar; manejar, dirigir; *v/i*. funcionar; ⚕, ⚕, ⚔ operar; ~ *on* producir efecto en; ⚕ operar (*for* de); **op·er·at·ic** [~'rætik] operístico; **op·er·at·ing** ['ɔpəreitiŋ] operante; ~ *expenses pl*. gastos *m/pl*. de explotación; ~ *room* quirófano *m*; ~ *table* mesa *f* de operaciones; *v. theater*; **op·er'a·tion** operación *f* (*a*. ⚕, ⚕, ⚔); funcionamiento *m*; explotación *f*; manejo *m*; procedimiento *m*; *in* ~

⚖ en vigor; ⊕ en funcionamiento; *come into* ~ entrar en vigor; *put into* ~ poner por obra; **op·er'a·tion·al** ⚔ de operaciones; ⚔ en condiciones de servicio; ⊕ capaz de funcionar; **op·er·a·tive 1.** ['~reitiv] □ operativo; ⚖ en vigor; ⚕ operatorio; **2.** ['~rətiv] operario (a *f*) *m*; **op·er·a·tor** ['~reitər] ⊕ maquinista *m/f*; ⚕, *film*: operador (-a *f*) *m*; ⚜ agente *m*, corredor *m* de bolsa; *teleph.* telefonista *m/f*.

op·er·et·ta [ɔpə'retə] opereta *f*; *Spain*: zarzuela *f*.

oph·thal·mi·a [ɔf'θælmiə] oftalmía *f*; **oph'thal·mic** oftálmico; **oph·thal·mol·o·gist** [~'mɔlədʒist] oftalmólogo *m*.

o·pi·ate ['oupiit] **1.** opiata *f*, narcótico *m*; calmante *m*; **2.** opiato; calmante.

o·pine [ou'pain] opinar; **o·pin·ion** [ə'pinjən] opinión *f*, parecer *m*, juicio *m*, concepto *m*; *public* ~ opinión *f* pública; *be of (the)* ~ opinar, ser de la opinión (*that* que); *have a high* ~ *of o.s.* pagarse de sí mismo; *in my* ~ a mi parecer; **o'pin·ion·at·ed** [~eitid] porfiado, pertinaz; dogmático.

o·pi·um ['oupjəm] opio *m*; ~ *den* fumadero *m* de opio; ~ *poppy* ⚘ adormidera *f*.

o·pos·sum [ə'pɔsəm] zarigüeya *f*.

op·po·nent [ə'pounənt] adversario (a *f*) *m*, contrincante *m*, contrario (a *f*) *m*.

op·por·tune [ɔpər'tju:n] □ oportuno, tempestivo; **op·por'tun·ism** oportunismo *m*; **op·por'tun·ist** oportunista *m/f*; **op·por'tu·ni·ty** oportunidad *f*, ocasión *f* (*of ger.*, *to inf.* de *inf.*).

op·pose [ə'pouz] oponerse a; resistir, combatir; (*set against*) oponer; **op'posed** opuesto; *be* ~ *to* oponerse a; **op'pos·ing** opuesto, contrario; **op·po·site** ['ɔpəzit] **1.** □ opuesto, contrario; de enfrente; F ~ *number* persona *f* que ocupa un puesto correspondiente, colega *m*; *the house* ~ la casa de enfrente; **2.** *prp.* (*a.* ~ *to*) enfrente de, frente a; **3.** *adv.* enfrente; **4.** *su.* lo contrario, lo opuesto; **op·po'si·tion** oposición *f*; resistencia *f*; ⚜ competencia *f*.

op·press [ə'pres] oprimir; agobiar; **op·pres·sion** [ə'preʃn] opresión *f*; agobio *m*; **op'pres·sive** [~siv] □ opresivo; agobiador; *weather* sofocante; **op·pres·sor** [ə'presər] opresor (-a *f*) *m*.

op·pro·bri·ous [ə'proubriəs] □ oprobioso; **op'pro·bri·um** [~briəm] oprobio *m*.

opt [ɔpt] optar (*for* por).

op·tic ['ɔptik], **'op·ti·cal** □ óptico; **op·ti·cian** [ɔp'tiʃn] óptico *m*; **'op·tics** *sg.* óptica *f*.

op·ti·mism ['ɔptimizm] optimismo *m*; **'op·ti·mist** optimista *m/f*; **op·ti'mis·tic** □ optimista; **op·ti·mize** ['ɔptimaiz] mejorar en todo lo posible; **op·ti·mum** ['~məm] (lo) óptimo.

op·tion ['ɔpʃn] opción *f* (*on* a); **'op·tion·al** □ opcional, discrecional, facultativo.

op·u·lence ['ɔpjuləns] opulencia *f*; **'op·u·lent** □ opulento.

o·pus ['oupəs] ♪ obra *f*; opus *m*.

or [ɔ:r] o; (*before* o-, ho-) u; *after negative* ni; *either* ... ~ ... o ... o ...; ~ *else* o bien, si no.

or·a·cle ['ɔrəkl] oráculo *m*; F *work the* ~ dirigirlo todo entre bastidores; **o·rac·u·lar** [ɔ'rækjulər] de oráculo; *fig.* sentencioso; misterioso.

o·ral ['ɔ:rəl] oral; *anat.* bucal.

or·ange ['ɔrindʒ] **1.** naranja *f*; (*a.* ~ *tree*) naranjo *m*; ~ *blossom* azahar *m*; ~ *juice* zumo *m* de naranja; **2.** (a)naranjado; **or·ange·ade** ['~'eid] naranjada *f*.

o·rate [ɔ:'reit] *co.* perorar; **o'ra·tion** oración *f*, discurso *m*; **or·a·tor** ['ɔrətər] orador (-a *f*) *m*; **or·a·tor·i·cal** [ɔrə'tɔrikl] oratorio; **or·a·to·ri·o** [~'tɔ:riou] ♪ oratorio *m*; **or·a·to·ry** ['ɔrətɔ:ri] oratoria *f*; *eccl.* oratorio *m*.

orb [ɔ:rb] orbe *m*, globo *m*; **or·bit 1.** órbita *f* (*a. fig.*); *go into* ~ entrar en órbita; **2.** girar (alrededor de); **'or·bit·al** orbital; **'or·bit·er** (*astronavegación*) satélite *m* (artificial).

or·chard ['ɔ:rtʃərd] huerto *m*, huerta *f* (de árboles frutales); (*esp. apple* ~) pomar *m*.

or·ches·tra ['ɔ:rkistrə] orquesta *f*; *thea.* ~ *stall* butaca *f* de platea; **or·ches·tral** [ɔ:r'kestrl] orquestral; **or·ches·trate** ['ɔr:kistreit] orquestar; *fig.* ejecutar con cuidado.

or·chid ['ɔ:rkid], **or·chis** ['ɔ:rkis] orquídea *f*.

or·dain [ɔ:r'dein] ordenar (*a. eccl.*); decretar; disponer.

or•deal [ɔːrˈdiːl] prueba *f* rigurosa, experiencia *f* penosa; *hist.* ordalías *f/pl.*
or•der [ˈɔːrdər] **1.** (*method, class, disposition, peace*) orden *m*; (*command, society*) orden *f*; ⚕ pedido *m for goods*; ⚕ libranza *f for money*; ~ *blank* ⚕ hoja *f* de pedidos; ~ *of the day* ⚔ orden *f* del día; *fig.* moda *f*, lo que es de rigor; *in* ~ en regla, reglamentario; en orden; ⊕ en funcionamiento; *in* ~ *that* para que; *in* ~ *to* para; *of the* ~ *of* del orden de; *on the* ~*s of* por orden de; *out of* ~ desarreglado, descompuesto; ⊕ que no funciona; *parl.* fuera de orden; *till further* ~*s* hasta nueva orden; *to* ~ por encargo especial; ⚕ a la orden; *call to* ~ llamar al orden; *it is on* ~ está pedido; *keep* ~ mantener el orden; *put in* ~ poner en orden, arreglar; *take (holy)* ~*s* ordenarse; **2.** ordenar; mandar; (*arrange*) disponer; *goods* encargar, pedir; ~ *a suit* mandar hacer un traje; *I* ~*ed them to go* les mandé ir, mandé que fuesen; ~ *about*, ~ *around* mandar (para acá y para allá), ser muy mandón con; ~ *out* mandar salir; ˈ~ **book** ⚕ libro *m* de pedidos; ˈ**or•der•ly 1.** ordenado, metódico; regular; tranquilo; obediente; ⚔ ~ *officer* oficial *m* del día; ⚔ ~ *room* oficina *f*; **2.** ⚔ ordenanza *m*; ⚔ enfermero *m*.
or•di•nal [ˈɔːrdinl] ordinal *adj. a. su. m.*
or•di•nance [ˈɔːrdinəns] ordenanza *f*, decreto *m*.
or•di•nar•y [ˈɔːrdineri] **1.** □ común, corriente, normal; ordinario (*a. b.s.*); ~ *seaman* simple marin(er)o *m*; ~ *share* ⚕ acción *f* ordinaria; **2.**: *out of the* ~ fuera de lo común, extraordinario.
or•di•nate [ˈɔːrdnit] ordenada *f*.
or•di•na•tion [ɔːrdiˈneiʃn] ordenación *f*.
ord•nance [ˈɔrdnəns] artillería *f*; pertrechos *m/pl.* de guerra (*a.* ~ *stores*); ♀ *Corps* Cuerpo *m* de Armamento y Material; ♀ *Survey map approx.* mapa *m* del estado mayor.
or•dure [ˈɔːrdjur] excremento *m*, inmundicia *f*.
ore [ɔːr] mineral *m*, mena *f*.
or•gan [ˈɔːrgən] *all senses*: órgano *m*; ˈ~**grind•er** organillero (a *f*) *m*; **or•gan•ic** [ɔːrˈgænik] □ orgánico; **or•gan•ism** [ˈɔːrgənizm] organismo *m*; ˈ**or•gan•ist** organista *m/f*; **or•gan•i•za•tion** [~naiˈzeiʃn] organización *f*, organismo *m*; ˈ**or•gan•ize** organizar(se); *sl.* agenciar; ˈ**or•gan•iz•er** organizador (-a *f*) *m*; **or•gan loft** [ˈɔːrgən lɔft] tribuna *f* de órgano.
or•gasm [ˈɔːrgæzm] orgasmo *m*.
or•gias•tic [ɔːrˈdʒiæstik] orgiástico; **or•gy** [ˈɔːrdʒi] orgía *f*.
o•ri•el [ˈɔːriəl] mirador *m*.
o•ri•ent [ˈɔːriənt] **1.** ♀ Oriente *m*; oriente *m of pearl*; **2.** [ˈ~ent] orientar; guiar, dirigir; **o•ri•en•tal** [ˈ~entl] □ oriental *adj. a. su. m/f*; **o•ri•en•tate** [ˈɔrienteit] orientar(se); **o•ri•enˈta•tion** orientación *f*.
or•i•fice [ˈɔrifis] orificio *m*.
or•i•gin [ˈɔridʒin] origen *m*.
o•rig•i•nal [əˈridʒənl] **1.** □ original; primitivo, primordial; ~ *sin* pecado *m* original; **2.** original *m* (*a. p.*); prototipo *m*; **o•rig•i•nal•i•ty** [~ˈnæliti] originalidad *f*.
o•rig•i•nate [əˈridʒineit] originar(se); ~ *from*, ~ *in a th.* traer su origen de; ~ *with a p.* ser obra de; **oˈrig•i•na•tor** creador (-a *f*) *m*, inventor (-a *f*) *m*, autor (-a *f*) *m*.
o•ri•ole [ˈɔːrioul] oropéndola *f*.
or•mo•lu [ˈɔːrməluː] oro *m* molido; bronce *m* dorado.
or•na•ment 1. [ˈɔːrnəmənt] adorno *m*, ornato *m*; ornamento *m* (*a. fig.*); ~*s pl. eccl.* ornamentos *m/pl.*; **2.** [ˈ~ment] adornar, ornamentar; **or•naˈmen•tal** □ ornamental, decorativo.
or•nate [ɔːrˈneit] □ muy ornado; *language* florido.
or•ni•tho•log•i•cal [ɔːrniθəˈlɔdʒikl] □ ornitológico; **or•ni•thol•o•gist** [~ˈθɔlədʒist] ornitólogo *m*; **or•ni•thol•o•gy** ornitología *f*.
or•phan [ˈɔːrfən] huérfano *adj. a. su. m* (a *f*) (*adj. a.* ~*ed*); **or•phan•age** [~idʒ] orfanato *m*; (*condición*) orfandad *f*.
or•tho•dox [ˈɔːrθədɔks] ortodoxo; F correcto; auténtico; ˈ**or•tho•dox•y** ortodoxia *f*.
or•tho•graph•ic, or•tho•graph•i•cal [ɔːrθəˈgræfik(l)] □ ortográfico; **or•thog•ra•phy** [ɔːrˈθɔgrəfi] ortografía *f*.
or•tho•pe•dic [ɔːrθouˈpiːdik] ortopédico; **or•thoˈpe•dics** *sg.* ortopedia *f*; **or•thoˈpe•dist** (*a.* **or•tho•pod** [ˈ~pɔd]) ortopedista *m/f*.

os·cil·late [ˈɔsileit] oscilar; **os·cilˈla·tion** oscilación *f*; **ˈos·cil·la·tor** oscilador *m*; **os·cil·la·to·ry** [ˈ~tɔːri] oscilatorio; **os·cil·lo·graph** [ˈ~græf] ⚡ oscilógrafo *m*.
os·cu·late [ˈɔskjuleit] *mst co.* besar(se).
o·sier [ˈouʒər] mimbre *m or f*; (*bush*) mimbrera *f*.
os·prey [ˈɔspri] águila *f* pescadora.
os·se·ous [ˈɔsiəs] óseo; **os·si·fi·cation** [ɔsifiˈkeiʃn] osificación *f*; **os·si·fy** [ˈ~fai] osificar(se); F emborracharse totalmente; **os·su·ar·y** [ˈɔsjuəri] osario *m*.
os·ten·si·ble [ɔsˈtensəbl] □ supuesto, pretendido, aparente.
os·ten·ta·tion [ɔstenˈteiʃn] ostentación *f*; aparato *m*, boato *m*; **os·tenˈta·tious** □ ostentoso, aparatoso; *p.* ostentativo.
os·te·ol·o·gy [ɔstiˈɔlədʒi] osteología *f*; **os·te·o·path** [ˈɔstiəpæθ] osteópata *m*/*f*; **os·te·op·a·thy** [ɔstiˈɔpəθi] osteopatía *f*.
ost·ler [ˈɔslər] mozo *m* de cuadra.
os·tra·cism [ˈɔstrəsizm] ostracismo *m*; **os·tra·cize** [ˈ~saiz] condenar al ostracismo, excluir de la sociedad.
os·trich [ˈɔstritʃ] avestruz *m*.
oth·er [ˈʌðər] **1.** otro (*than* que); *the ~ day* el otro día; *some ~ day* otro día; *the ~ (one)* el otro; *this house and the ~ (one)* esta casa y la otra; *the ~s* los otros, los demás; *v. each*; *somebody or ~* alguien; **2.** *adv.*: *~ than* de otra manera que; otra cosa que; **ˈ~·wise** de otra manera, otramente; si no; (*in other respects*) por lo demás.
o·ti·ose [ˈouʃious] □ ocioso, superfluo.
ot·ter [ˈɔtər] nutria *f*.
Ot·to·man [ˈɔtəmən] otomano *adj. a. su. m* (a *f*); ♀ otomana *f*.
ought [ɔːt] **1.** = *aught* algo; **2.** *v/aux. mst* deber; *I ~ to do it* debo (debiera *or* debería) hacerlo; *I ~ to have done it* debiera haberlo hecho; *he ~ to have arrived* debe de haber llegado; *you ~ to have seen it* era de ver; *one ~ to drink water* conviene beber agua.
ounce [auns] onza *f* (= *28,35 gr.*) (*a. zo.*); *fig.* pizca *f*.
our [ˈauər] nuestro(s), nuestra(s); **ours** [ˈauərz] (el) nuestro, (la) nuestra *etc.*; **ourˈselves** (*subject*) nosotros mismos, nosotras mismas; (*acc., dat.*) nos; (*after prp.*) nosotros (mismos), nosotras (mismas).
oust [aust] desposeer; expulsar, desalojar; desahuciar.
out [aut] **1.** *adv.* afuera, fuera, hacia fuera; *a. in combination with vb.*: *come ~, go ~* salir; *run ~* salir corriendo; *be ~* haber salido; estar fuera (de casa); estar fuera de moda; (*book*) haberse publicado; (*bridge*) estar caído; derrumbado; (*fire*) estar apagado; (*secret*) haber salido a luz; (*striker*) estar en huelga; *sport*: estar fuera de juego; *Mr Jones is ~* no está el señor Jones; *be ~ for* buscar; ambicionar; *be ~ to inf.* esforzarse por *inf.*; proponerse *inf.*; *be ~ and about* estar levantado y salir; *have a day ~* tener un día libre; pasar el día fuera de casa; **2.** *prp.* *~ of* fuera de; de; entre; de entre; por; sin; *a chapter ~ of a novel* un capítulo de una novela; *read ~ of a novel* leer en una novela; *~ of gasoline* sin gasolina; *~ of spite* por despecho; *6 ~ of 7* de cada 7, 6; **3.** *int.* *~ with him!* ¡fuera con él!; F *~ with it!* ¡desembucha!; ¡habla sin rodeos!
out...: [~] **ˈ~-and-ˈ~** perfecto, rematado; *b.s.* redomado; **~ˈbid** [*irr.* (*bid*)] licitar más que; sobrepujar; **ˈ~·board** (*~ motor* motor *m*) fuera de borda; **ˈ~·break** erupción *f*; estallido *m*; rompimiento *m of war*; brote *m of disease*; **ˈ~·build·ing** dependencia *f*, edificio *m* accesorio; cobertizo *m*; **ˈ~·burst** explosión *f*, arranque *m*, acceso *m*; **ˈ~·cast** paria *m*/*f*, proscrito (a *f*) *m*; **~ˈclass** ser muy superior a, aventajar con mucho; **ˈ~·come** resultado *m*, consecuencia *f*; **ˈ~·crop** *geol.* afloramiento *m*; **ˈ~·cry** grito *m*, clamoreo *m*; protesta *f* (ruidosa); **~-ˈdat·ed** fuera de moda, anticuado; **~ˈdis·tance** dejar atrás; **~ˈdo** [*irr.* (*do*)] exceder, sobrepujar; *he was not to be outdone* no se quedó en menos; **ˈ~·door** *adj.* al aire libre; externo; **ˈ~ˈdoors** **1.** *adv.* fuera de casa, al aire libre; **2.** *su.* aire *m* libre, campo *m* raso.
out·er [ˈautər] exterior, externo; *~ cover* cubierta *f of tire*; *~ space* espacio *m* exterior; **ˈ~·most** (el) más exterior; extremo.
out...: **ˈ~·fall** desembocadura *f*; **ˈ~·field·er** (*baseball*) jardinero *m*; **ˈ~·fit** equipo *m*; (*suit*) traje *m*; (*tools*) juego *m* de herramientas; F⚔ cuerpo *m*; F organización *f*; **ˈ~·fit·ter** cami-

sero (a *f*) *m*; **~'flank** ⚔ flanquear; *fig.* burlar; **'~·flow** efusión *f*, derrame *m*, desagüe *m*; **'~·go·ing 1.** saliente; (*p.*) amigable; no reservado; **2.** (*mst* ~*s pl.*) gastos *m/pl.*; **~'grow** [*irr.* (*grow*)] crecer más que; hacerse demasiado grande (*or* viejo) para; *I have* ~*n my shoes* se me quedan chicos los zapatos; **'~·growth** excrecencia *f*; *fig.* consecuencia *f*; **'~·house** letrina *f* exterior.

out·ing ['autiŋ] excursión *f*, paseo *m*, jira *f*.

out...: **~'land·ish** estrafalario; **~'last** durar más que; sobrevivir a; **'~·law 1.** proscrito *m*, forajido *m*; **2.** proscribir; declarar fuera de la ley; **'~·law·ry** proscripción *f*; bandolerismo *m*; **'~·lay** desembolso *m*; **'~·let** salida *f* (*a. fig.*, ✝); ⚡ toma *f* de corriente; **'~·line 1.** contorno *m*, perfil *m*; trazado *m*; bosquejo *m* (*a. fig.*); *in* ~ *fig.* a grandes rasgos; **2.** perfilar, trazar; bosquejar (*a. fig.*); *policy* prefigurar; *be* ~*d against* destacarse contra; **~'live** sobrevivir a; durar más que; **'~·look** perspectiva(s) *f*(*pl.*) (*a. fig.*); punto *m* de vista; actitud *f*; **'~·ly·ing** remoto; exterior, de las afueras; **~ma'neu·ver** superar en la táctica; vencer por su mejor táctica; **~'mod·ed** anticuado, fuera de moda; **~'num·ber** exceder en número; **'~-of-'doors** = *outdoors*; **'~-of-the-way** apartado; poco concurrido; **~'pace** dejar atrás; **'~·pa·tient** paciente *m/f* externo (a) (del hospital); **'~·post** avanzada *f*, puesto *m* avanzado; **'~·pour·ing** chorro *m*; efusión *f* (*a. fig.*); **'~·put** producción *f*; ⊕ rendimiento *m*; ⚡ potencia *f* de salida; ~ *valve* válvula *f* de salida.

out·rage ['autreidʒ] **1.** atrocidad *f*; ultraje *m*, atropello *m*; violación *f* (*on* de); **2.** ultrajar; violentar; violar; **out'ra·geous** □ atroz; ultrajoso; violento; F monstruoso, inaudito.

out...: **'~·rid·er** escolta *m* a caballo; motociclista *m* de escolta; **'~·rig·ger** ⚓ botalón *m*; ⚓ (bote *m* con) portarremos *m* exterior; ⚓ balancín *m*; **~·right 1.** ['autrait] *adj.* completo, cabal, franco; **2.** [aut'rait] *adv.* de una vez, de un golpe; enteramente, de plano; sin rodeos; **~'ri·val** sobrepujar, exceder; **~'run** [*irr.* (*run*)] correr más que; *fig.* exceder; pasar los límites de; **'~·set** principio *m*, comienzo *m*; **~'shine** [*irr.* (*shine*)] brillar más que; *fig.* eclipsar, superar en brillantez; **'~'side 1.** exterior *m*; superficie *f*; apariencia *f*; *at the* ~ a lo sumo, cuando más; *on the* ~ por fuera; **2.** *adj.* exterior, externo; superficial; ajeno; extremo; *sport*: ~ *right* (*left*) extremo *m* derecho (izquierdo); **3.** *adv.* (a)fuera; ~ *of* = **4.** *prp.* fuera de; más allá de; **'~'sid·er** forastero (a *f*) *m*; intruso (a *f*) *m*; desplazado (a *f*) *m*; *racing*: caballo *m* que no figura entre los favoritos; **'~·size** de tamaño extraordinario; **'~·skirts** *pl.* afueras *f/pl.*, alrededores *m/pl.*, cercanías *f/pl.*; **~'smart** F ser más listo que; engañar; **~'spok·en** □ franco, abierto; *be* ~ no tener pelos en la lengua; **'~'spread** extendido, desplegado; **~'stand·ing** destacado, descollante; sobresaliente; ✝ pendiente, sin pagar; **~'stay** quedarse más tiempo que; **~'stretched** extendido; **~'strip** dejar atrás, aventajar; **~'vote** vencer en las elecciones; *proposal* rechazar por votación.

out·ward ['autwərd] **1.** □ exterior, externo; aparente; ~ *journey* (viaje *m* de) ida *f*; **2.** *adv.* (*mst* **out·wards** ['~z]) exteriormente, hacia fuera.

out...: **~'wear** [*irr.* (*wear*)] durar más que; gastar; **~'weigh** pesar más que; valer más que; **~'wit** ser más listo que; burlar; **'~·worn** gastado; anticuado.

o·val ['ouvl] **1.** oval(ado); **2.** óvalo *m*.

o·va·ry ['ouvəri] ovario *m*.

o·va·tion [ou'veiʃn] ovación *f*.

ov·en ['ʌvn] horno *m*, cocina *f*.

o·ver ['ouvər] **1.** *adv.* (por) encima; al otro lado; de un lado a otro; al revés; patas arriba; otra vez; de añadidura; *all* ~ por todas partes; *all* ~ *again* de nuevo; ~ *against* enfrente de; en contraste con; ~ *and* ~ *again* repetidas veces; ~ *here* acá; por aquí; ~ *there* allá; *10 times* ~ 10 veces (seguidas); **2.** *prp.* sobre, (por) encima de; al otro lado de; por, a través de; más allá de; *number* más de; (*concerning*) acerca de; por causa de; superior a; *all* ~ *Europe* por toda Europa; *be* ~ *30* tener más de 30 años; ~ *and above* además de, en exceso de; ~ *the way* enfrente, al otro lado; **3.** adicional, excesivo; acabado, concluido; *it's all* ~ se acabó.

o·ver...: ˈ~ˈ**act** exagerar (el papel); ˈ~·**all 1.** global; de conjunto; **2.** guardapolvo *m*; ~*s pl.* mono *m*; ~ˈ**awe** intimidar; ~ˈ**bal·ance** (hacer) perder el equilibrio; ~ˈ**bear·ing** □ despótico, dominante; ˈ~ˈ**blown** marchito, pasado; ˈ~·**board** ⚓ al mar, al agua; *man* ~*!* ¡hombre al agua!; *throw* ~ echar por la borda; F deshacerse de, abandonar; ~ˈ**bur·den** sobrecargar; oprimir, agobiar; ˈ~ˈ**cast** *sky* encapotado; ˈ~ˈ**charge** sobrecargar; ✝ cobrar un precio excesivo (a); ˈ~·**coat** abrigo *m*, sobretodo *m*, gabán *m*; ~ˈ**come** [*irr.* (*come*)] vencer; superar; (*sleep etc.*) rendir; ˈ~**con·fi·dent** □ demasiado confiado (*of* en); ˈ~·**conˈsump·tion** ✝ superconsumo *m*; ~ˈ**crowd** apiñar, atestar; congestionar; ~ˈ**crowd·ing** sobrepoblación *f*, congestionamiento *m*; ~ˈ**do** [*irr.* (*do*)] exagerar; llevar a exceso, excederse en; *food* recocer, requemar; ~ *it* F trabajar demasiado, fatigarse; ~·**done** [ouvərˈdʌn] exagerado; [ˈouvərˈdʌn] *food* muy hecho, requemado, pasado; ˈ~·**dose 1.** sobredosis *f*, dosis *f* excesiva; **2.** tomar una dosis excesiva; ˈ~·**draft** ✝ giro *m* en descubierto, saldo *m* deudor; ˈ~ˈ**draw** [*irr.* (*draw*)] ✝ girar en descubierto; ˈ~ˈ**dress** vestirse con exceso; ˈ~ˈ**drive** *mot.* superdirecta *f*; ˈ~ˈ**due** atrasado; ✝ vencido y no pagado; ˈ~ˈ**eat** [*irr.* (*eat*)] comer con exceso, atracarse; ˈ~·**emˈploy·ment** superempleo *m*; ˈ~ˈ**es·ti·mate** estimar en valor excesivo; tener un concepto exagerado de; ˈ~·**exˈpose** *phot.* sobreexponer; ˈ~·**exˈpo·sure** *phot.* sobreexposición *f*; ˈ~ˈ**feed** [*irr.* (*feed*)] sobrealimentar; ~·**flow 1.** [ouvərˈflou] [*irr.* (*flow*)] desbordar(se); rebosar (*a. fig.*) (*with* de); *the river* ~*ed its banks* se desbordó el río; **2.** [ˈouvərflou] desbordamiento *m*; derrame *m*; (*pipe*) rebosadero *m*, vertedor *m*, cañería *f* de desagüe; ˈ~ˈ**grown** entapizado, revestido, cubierto (*with* de); demasiado grande (para su edad); ~·**hang 1.** [ˈ~ˈhæŋ] [*irr.* (*hang*)] sobresalir (por encima de); estar pendiente (sobre); *fig.* amenazar; **2.** [ˈ~hæŋ] proyección *f*; alero *m of roof*; ~ˈ**haul 1.** revisar; rehabilitar, componer; (*catch up*) alcanzar; **2.** repaso *m*, revisión *f*; ~·**head 1.** [ouvərˈhed] *adv.* por lo alto, por encima de la cabeza; **2.** [ˈouvərhed] *adj.* de arriba; aéreo; ✝ general; ~ *cable* ⚡ línea *f* aérea; ~ *railway* ferrocarril *m* elevado; **3.** ✝ ~*s pl.* gastos *m/pl.* generales; ~ˈ**hear** [*irr.* (*hear*)] oír (por casualidad); acertar a oír; *conversation* sorprender; ˈ~ˈ**heat** recalentar; ˈ~·**inˈdulge** mimar demasiado; ~ *in* tomar con exceso; ~ˈ**joyed:** *be* ~ no caber de contento (*at* con); ˈ~·**kill 1.** exceso *m* de potencia (*or* eficacia); **2.** *fig.* exceder lo necesario; ˈ~·**land** por tierra, (por vía) terrestre; ~ˈ**lap 1.** traslapar(se); *fig.* coincidir en parte; **2.** solapo *m*, traslapo *m*; *fig.* coincidencia *f* (parcial); ~·**lay 1.** [ouvərˈlei] [*irr.* (*lay*)] cubrir (*with* con); dar una capa a; **2.** [ˈouvərlei] capa *f*; cubierta *f*; ˈ~ˈ**leaf** a la vuelta; ~·**load 1.** [ˈouvərˈloud] sobrecargar; **2.** [ˈouvərloud] sobrecarga *f*; ~ˈ**look** (*p.*) dominar con la vista; (*building*) dar a, caer a; vigilar; (*leave out*) pasar por alto, no hacer caso de; (*tolerate*) disimular; (*forgive*) perdonar; (*wink at*) hacer la vista gorda a; ˈ~·**lord** señor *m*; jefe *m* supremo; ˈ~ˈ**much** demasiado; ˈ~ˈ**night** de la noche a la mañana; *stay* ~ pernoctar (*at* en); ˈ~·**plus** sobrante *m*; ~ˈ**pow·er** vencer; subyugar; dominar; *senses* embargar; ˈ~·**proˈduc·tion** superproducción *f*; ˈ~ˈ**rate** exagerar el valor de; ~ˈ**reach:** *mst* ~ *o.s.* excederse; pasarse de listo; ~ˈ**ride** [*irr.* (*ride*)] no hacer caso de; anular; poner a un lado; ~ˈ**rid·ing** predominante, decisivo; ~ˈ**rule** anular; ⚖ denegar; ~ˈ**run** [*irr.* (*run*)] invadir; infestar; *time etc.* exceder; ˈ~ˈ**sea**(**s**) **1.** *adj.* de ultramar; **2.** *adv.* allende el mar, en ultramar; ˈ~ˈ**see** [*irr.* (*see*)] superentender, fiscalizar; ˈ~·**se·er** superintendente *m/f*; sobrestante *m*; (*foreman*) capataz *m*; ~ˈ**shad·ow** (en-) sombrear; *fig.* eclipsar; ˈ~·**shoe** chanclo *m*; ˈ~ˈ**shoot** [*irr.* (*shoot*)] tirar más allá de; ✈ sobrepasar; ~ *the mark* pasar de la raya, excederse; ˈ~·**sight** descuido *m*, inadvertencia *f*; equivocación *f*; (*supervision*) vigilancia *f*; ˈ~·**sim·pli·fiˈca·tion** supersimplificación *f*; ˈ~ˈ**sleep** [*irr.* (*sleep*)] dormir demasiado; *I overslept* durmiendo se me pasó la hora; ˈ~·**spill** desparramamiento *m* de población; ˈ~ˈ**state** exagerar; ˈ~ˈ**step** exceder; ~ *the mark* propasarse; ˈ~ˈ**stock:** *be ~ed with* tener surtido excesivo de; ˈ~ˈ**strain 1.** fatigar excesivamente; **2.** fatiga *f* excesiva, tensión *f* excesiva; ˈ~ˈ**strung** sobreexcitado, nervioso; *piano* cruzado; ˈ~**·sub**ˈ**scribe** contribuir más de lo pedido; ˈ~**·sup**ˈ**ply** proveer en exceso.

o·vert [ˈouvəːrt] □ abierto, manifiesto.

over...: ~ˈ**take** [*irr.* (*take*)] alcanzar; pasar, adelantar(se) a; *fig.* coger, sorprender; ˈ~ˈ**tax** oprimir con tributos; *fig.* agobiar; exigir demasiado a; ~ *o.s.* fatigarse demasiado; ~**·throw 1.** [ouvərˈθrou] [*irr.* (*throw*)] echar abajo; volcar; derrocar, derribar (*a. fig.*); **2.** [ˈouvərθrou] derrocamiento *m*, derribo *m*; ˈ~**·time** horas *f/pl.* extraordinarias; ˈ~**·tone** ♪ armónico *m*; *fig.* sugestión *f*, resonancia *f*; ˈ~ˈ**top** descollar sobre.

overture [ˈouvərtjur] ♪ obertura *f*; *fig.* proposición *f*; sondeo *m*.

o·ver...: ~**·turn** [ouvərˈtəːrn] *v/t.* volcar, trastornar; *v/i.* volcar; ⚓ zozobrar; ~ˈ**ween·ing** arrogante, presuntuoso; ˈ~ˈ**weight 1.** sobrepeso *m*, peso *m* de añadidura; **2.** excesivamente pesado; *be* ~ pesar demasiado; ~ˈ**whelm** abrumar; anonadar; inundar; ~ *with favors* colmar de favores; ~ˈ**whelm·ing** □ arrollador, aplastante, abrumador; ˈ~ˈ**work 1.** trabajo *m* excesivo; **2.** [*irr.* (*work*)] (hacer) trabajar demasiado; ˈ~ˈ**wrought** agotado por el trabajo; sobreexcitado.

o·vi·form [ˈouvifɔːrm] oviforme; **o·vip·a·rous** [ouˈvipərəs] ovíparo; **o·void** [ˈouvɔid] ovoide *adj. a. su. m.*

owe [ou] *v/t.* deber; estar agradecido por; ~ *a p. a grudge* guardar rencor a una p.; *v/i.* tener deudas; estar en deuda (*for* por).

ow·ing [ˈouiŋ] sin pagar; debido; ~ *to* debido a, por causa de; *be* ~ *to* deberse a.

owl [aul] (*barn*) lechuza *f* común; (*little*) mochuelo *m* común; (*long-eared*) búho *m* chico; (*tawny*) cárabo *m*; *night* ~ F trasnochador (-a *f*) *m*; **owl·et** [ˈaulit] lechuza *f etc.* pequeña; ˈ**owl·ish** □ de búho; parecido a un búho; estúpido.

own [oun] **1.** propio; particular; *my ~ self* yo (*after prp.* mí) mismo; yo por mi parte; **2.** *my* ~ (lo) mío; *come into one's* ~ entrar en posesión de lo suyo; tener el éxito merecido; *get one's* ~ *back* tomar su revancha; *hold one's* ~ no cejar, mantenerse firme; *on one's* ~ por su propia cuenta; a solas; *a house of one's* ~ una casa propia; **3.** poseer; ser dueño de; (*acknowledge*) reconocer; (*admit*) confesar (*a.* F ~ *up* [*to*]).

own·er [ˈounər] amo (a *f*) *m*, dueño (a *f*) *m*, poseedor (-a *f*) *m*, propietario (a *f*) *m*; ˈ**own·er·less** sin dueño; abandonado; ˈ**own·er·ship** posesión *f*, propiedad *f*.

ox [ɔks], *pl.* **ox·en** [ˈ~ən] buey *m*.

ox·al·ic ac·id [ɔkˈsælik ˈæsid] ácido *m* oxálico.

ox·ide [ˈɔksaid] óxido *m*; **ox·i·diz·a·tion** [ɔksidiˈzeiʃn] oxidación *f*; **ox·i·dize** [ˈɔksidaiz] oxidar(se).

Ox·o·ni·an [ɔkˈsounjən] oxoniense *adj. a. su. m/f.*

ox·y·a·cet·y·lene [ˈɔksiəˈsetiliːn]: ~ *burner* soplete *m* oxiacetilénico.

ox·y·gen [ˈɔksidʒən] oxígeno *m*; **ox·y·gen·ate** [ˈɔksidʒineit] oxigenar.

ox·y·hy·dro·gen [ˈɔksiˈhaidridʒən] gas *m* oxhídrico.

oys·ter [ˈɔistər] ostra *f*; ˈ~ **bed** ostral *m*; ˈ~ˈ**catch·er** *orn.* ostrero *m*.

o·zone [ˈouzoun] ozono *m*; ~ *layer* capa *f* de ozono.

P

P [pi:]: *mind one's Ps and Qs* cuidarse de no meter la pata, andar con cuidado con lo que dice uno.
pa [pɑ:] F papá *m.*
pace [peis] **1.** paso *m*; marcha *f*; velocidad *f*; *keep ~ with* llevar el mismo paso con; *fig.* correr parejas con; *put through one's ~s* poner a uno a prueba; demostrar las cualidades de uno; *set the ~* establecer el paso; **2.** *v/t. distance* medir a pasos (*a. ~ out*); *room* pasearse por; *competitor* marcar el paso para; *v/i.*: *~ up and down* pasearse de un lado a otro; ˈ**pace·mak·er** el que marca el paso, el que abre carrera; ⚕ marcapasos *m.*
pach·y·derm [ˈpækidə:rm] paquidermo *m.*
pa·cif·ic [pəˈsifik] □ pacífico; **pac·i·fi·ca·tion** [pæsifiˈkeiʃn] pacificación *f*; ˈ**pac·i·fism** pacifismo *m*; ˈ**pac·i·fist** pacifista *m/f*; **pac·i·fy** [ˈpæsifai] pacificar; apaciguar, calmar.
pack [pæk] **1.** (*bundle*) lío *m*, fardo *m*; (*animal's*) carga *f*; (*rucksack*) mochila *f* (*a.* ⚔); paquete *m*; cajetilla *f of cigarettes*; jauría *f of hounds*; manada *f of wolves*; baraja *f of cards*; montón *m of lies*; *~ animal* bestia *f* de carga; **2.** *v/t. case etc.* hacer; embaular *in trunk*, encajonar *in box*; (*a. ~ up*) empacar, empaquetar; (*wrap*) envasar; *place, container* atestar, llenar (*with* de); apretar *tightly*; meter apretadamente (*a. ~ in*); *court* llenar de partidarios; *the hall was ~ed* la sala estuvo de bote en bote; *be ~ed with* estar lleno de; *send ~ing* despedir con cajas destempladas; F *~ it in, ~ it up* dejarlo; *~ off* despachar; *v/i.* hacer las maletas; *~ up* hacer el equipaje; F terminar; liar el petate; ˈ**pack·age 1.** paquete *m*; bulto *m*; **2.** empaquetar; envasar; ˈ**pack·er** embalador (-a *f*) *m*; **pack·et** [ˈ~it] paquete *m*; cajetilla *f of cigarettes etc.*; (*a.* ˈ**~·boat**) paquebote *m*; ˈ**pack·horse** caballo *m* de carga; ˈ**pack·ing** (*act*) embalaje *m*, envase *m*; (*material, outer*) envase *m*; (*inner*) relleno *m*, empaquetadura *f*; *~ case* cajón *m* de embalaje; ˈ**pack·sad·dle** albarda *f.*
pact [pækt] **1.** pacto *m*; **2.** pactar.
pad[1] [pæd] (*a. ~ about etc.*) andar, pisar (sin hacer ruido *etc.*).
pad[2] [~] **1.** almohadilla *f*, cojinete *m*; (*ink-*) tampón *m*, almohadilla *f* para entintar; bloque *m*, bloc *m of paper*; *sl.* vivienda *f*; **2.** rellenar, forrear; *shoulders* bombear; *book etc.* hinchar con mucha paja (*a. ~ out*); ˈ**pad·ding** relleno *m*; paja *f in book etc.*
pad·dle [ˈpædl] **1.** canalete *m*, zagual *m*; **2.** *v/i.* remar con canalete; mojarse los pies, chapotear *in sea*; *v/t.* impulsar con canalete; apalear; ˈ**~ steam·er** vapor *m* de ruedas; ˈ**~·wheel** rueda *f* de paletas.
pad·dock [ˈpædək] *approx.* potrero *m*; *racing*: corral *m.*
pad·dy [ˈpædi] (*rice*) arroz *m* con cáscara; arrozal *m.*
pad·dy wag·on [ˈpædiwægən] *sl.* camión *m* de policía.
pad·lock [ˈpædlɔk] **1.** candado *m*; **2.** cerrar con candado.
pa·gan [ˈpeigən] pagano *adj. a. su. m* (a *f*); ˈ**pa·gan·ism** paganismo *m.*
page[1] [peidʒ] **1.** (*boy*) paje *m*; **2.** (*in hotel*) buscar llamando, hacer llamar por el botones *etc.*
page[2] [~] **1.** página *f*; *typ.* plana *f of newspaper etc.*; **2.** paginar.
pag·eant [ˈpædʒənt] espectáculo *m* brillante; desfile *m*; representación *f* de un episodio histórico *etc.* en una serie de cuadros; ˈ**pag·eant·ry** pompa *f*, boato *m*; lo espectacular.
pag·i·nate [ˈpædʒineit] paginar; **pag·iˈna·tion** paginación *f.*
pa·go·da [pəˈgoudə] pagoda *f.*
paid [peid] *pret. a. p.p. of pay 2*; asalariado; *put ~ to* acabar con; *~ up share* liberado.
pail [peil] cubo *m*, balde *m.*
pain [pein] **1.** dolor *m*; ⚕ *~s pl.* (*labor*) dolores *m/pl.* del parto; *~s fig.* trabajo *m*; *on ~ of* so pena de; *be in ~* estar con

dolor; get *for one's* ~s lograr después de tantos trabajos; *I have a* ~ *in my side* me duele el costado; *take* ~s esmerarse (*over* en); *take* ~s *to inf.* poner especial cuidado en *inf.*; **2.** doler; dar lástima; **pained** [peind] *expression* de disgusto; *voice* dolorido; **painful** ['~ful] □ doloroso; penoso; *decision* muy difícil; *duty* nada grato; **'pain·kil·ler** analgésico *m*; calmante *m* del dolor; **'pain·less** □ indoloro, sin dolor; **'pains·tak·ing** □ *p.*, *th.* esmerado; cuidadoso; laborioso.

paint [peint] **1.** pintura *f*; colorete *m for face*; *v. wet*; **2.** pintar (*red* de rojo); *face* pintarse; ~ *out* tachar con una mano de pintura; **'~ brush** (*small*) pincel *m*; (*large*) brocha *f*.

paint·er¹ ['peintər] pintor (-a *f*) *m*; retratista *m/f*; (*house*) pintor *m* de brocha gorda.

paint·er² ['peintər] ⚓ amarra *f*.

paint·ing ['peintiŋ] pintura *f*; cuadro *m*.

pair [per] **1.** par *m*; pareja *f of people*; *a* ~ *of scissors* unas tijeras; **2.** aparear(se) (*a. zo.*, *a.* ~ *off*).

pa·ja·mas [pə'dʒɑːməz] *pl.* pijama *m*.

pal [pæl] F **1.** compañero (a *f*) *m*; amigo (a *f*) *m*; **2.:** ~ *up* hacerse amigos; ~ *up with* hacerse amigo de.

pal·ace ['pælis] palacio *m*.

palaeo... *v. paleo...*

pal·at·a·ble ['pælətəbl] □ sabroso, apetitoso; F comible; *fig.* aceptable.

pal·a·tal ['pælətl] palatal *adj. a. su. f*; **'pal·a·tal·ize** palatalizar(se).

pal·ate ['pælit] paladar *m* (*a. fig.*).

pa·la·tial [pə'leiʃəl] □ suntuoso.

pal·a·tine ['pælətain] palatino.

pa·lav·er [pə'lævər] (*discussion*) conferencia *f*, parlamento *m*; F lío *m*; trámites *m/pl. etc.* largos y molestos; (*words*) palabrería *f*.

pale¹ [peil] **1.** □ pálido; *color* claro; *grow* ~ = **2.** palidecer; descolorarse; *fig.* dejar de tener importancia (*before* ante).

pale² [~] = *paling*; *beyond the* ~ excluido de la buena sociedad, indeseable.

pale·face ['peilfeis] F rostropálido *m*.

pale·ness ['peilnis] palidez *f*.

pa·le·o·gra·phy [peili'ɔgrəfi] paleografía *f*.

pa·le·on·tol·o·gy [pælion'tɔlədʒi] paleontología *f*.

Pal·es·tin·i·an [pæles'tiniən] palestino *adj. a. su. m* (a *f*).

pal·ette ['pælit] paleta *f*; ~ *knife* espátula *f*.

pal·frey ['pɔːlfri] palafrén *m*.

pal·ing ['peiliŋ] estaca *f*; (*fence*) estacada *f*.

pal·i·sade [pæli'seid] estacada *f*.

pall¹ [pɔːl] paño *m* mortuorio; *eccl.* palio *m*; capa *f of smoke*; ~*bearer* portaféretro *m*.

pall² [~] perder su sabor (*on* para), dejar de gustar (*on* a), empalagar (*on* a).

pal·let¹ ['pælit] (*bed*) jergón *m*.

pal·let² [~] ⊕ uña *f*.

pal·li·ate ['pælieit] paliar; **pal·li·a·tive** ['pæliətiv] paliativo *adj. a. su. m*.

pal·lid ['pælid] □ pálido; **'pal·lid·ness, pal·lor** ['pælər] palidez *f*.

palm¹ [pɑːm] ♆ palma *f* (*a. fig.*), palmera *f*; ♀ *Sunday* Domingo *m* de Ramos.

palm² [~] **1.** palma *f of hand*; *grease s.o.'s* ~ untar la mano a alguien; **2.** *card etc.* escamotear; ~ *off* encajar (*on* a); **palm·is·try** ['~istri] quiromancia *f*; **'palm oil** aceite *m* de palma; **'palm tree** palmera *f*; **'palm·y** próspero, floreciente.

pal·pa·ble ['pælpəbl] □ palpable (*a. fig.*).

pal·pi·tate ['pælpiteit] palpitar; **pal·pi'ta·tion** palpitación *f*.

pal·sy ['pɔːlzi] perlesía *f*.

pal·tri·ness ['pɔːltrinis] mezquindad *f*; insignificancia *f*; **pal·try** ['pɔːltri] □ insignificante, mezquino, baladí.

pam·pas ['pæmpəs] pampas *f/pl.*

pam·per ['pæmpər] mimar, consentir, regalar.

pam·phlet ['pæmflit] octavilla *f*; folleto *m*, panfleto *m*; **pam·phlet·eer** [~'tir] folletista *m/f*.

pan¹ [pæn] **1.** cazuela *f*; cacerola *f*; (*frying*) sartén *f*; perol *m*; **2.** *v/t. gold* separar en la gamella; F *play* criticar severamente; *cinematography*: panoramicar; *v/i.*: ~ *out* tener éxito; resultar (de modo satisfactorio *etc.*).

pan²... [~] pan...

pan·a·ce·a [pænə'siə] panacea *f*.

pan·ache [pən'æʃ] penacho *m*.

pan·cake ['pænkeik] hojuela *f*, tortita *f*; ~ *landing* aterrizaje *m* a vientre.

PQR

pan·da [ˈpændə] *zo.* panda *m/f.*
pan·de·mo·ni·um [pændiˈmounjəm] ruido *m* de todos los diablos, pandemonio *m.*
pan·der [ˈpændər] **1.** alcahuetear; ~ *to* ser indulgente a; desvivirse por complacer a; procurar sin escrúpulo satisfacer a; **2.** alcahuete *m.*
pane [pein] cristal *m*, (hoja *f* de) vidrio *m.*
pan·e·gyr·ic [pæniˈdʒirik] panegírico *m.*
pan·el [ˈpænl] panel *m*; (*door*) entrepaño *m*; (*ceiling*) artesón *m*; (*wall*) panel *m*; *sew.* paño *m*; *paint.* tabla *f*; tablero *m of instruments*; (*list*) lista *f*; tribunal *m of experts etc.*; ~ *discussion* coloquio *m* ante un auditorio; ˈ**pan·eled** artesonado; con paneles; de tableros; ˈ**pan·el·ing** entrepaños *m/pl. of door*; artesonado *m of ceiling*; paneles *m/pl. of wall.*
pang [pæŋ] punzada *f*, dolor *m* (agudo); ~ *of conscience* remordimiento *m.*
pan·han·dle [ˈpænhændl] F pedir limosna; ˈ**pan·han·dler** F mendigo *m*; pordiosero *m.*
pan·ic [ˈpænik] **1.** pánico; **2.** (terror *m*) pánico *m*; **3.** llenarse (sin motivo) de terror; aterrarse, ser preso de un terror pánico; ˈ~**-strick·en** lleno de terror, muerto de miedo; ˈ**pan·ick·y** F asustadizo.
pan·nier [ˈpæniər] cuévano *m*; serón *m*; ~ *bags pl.* (*motorcycle*) carteras *f/pl.*
pan·o·ply [ˈpænəpli] panoplia *f*; *fig.* esplendor *m.*
pan·o·ra·ma [pænəˈrɑːmə] panorama *m*; **pan·o·ram·ic** [~ˈræmik] □ panorámico.
pan·sy [ˈpænsi] ⚘ pensamiento *m*; F maricón *m.*
pant [pænt] jadear; resollar; ~ *after*, ~ *for* anhelar, suspirar por.
pan·tech·ni·con [pænˈteknikən] camión *m* de mudanzas.
pan·the·ism [ˈpænθiizm] panteísmo *m*; **pan·theˈis·tic** □ panteísta; **pan·the·on** [ˈpænθiən] panteón *m.*
pan·ther [ˈpænθər] pantera *f.*
pant·ies [ˈpæntiz] *pl.* F (*a pair of* unas) bragas *f/pl.*; pantaloncillas *f/pl.*
pan·to·mime [ˈpæntəmaim] pantomima *f.*
pan·try [ˈpæntri] despensa *f.*
pants [pænts] *pl.* F calzoncillos *m/pl.*; pantalones *m/pl.*
pap [pæp] papilla *f*, gachas *f/pl.*
pa·pa [pəˈpɑː] papá *m.*
pa·pa·cy [ˈpeipəsi] papado *m*, pontificado *m.*
pa·pal [ˈpeipəl] □ papal, pontifical.
pa·per [ˈpeipər] **1.** papel *m*; (*news-*) periódico *m*; (*learned*) comunicación *f*, ponencia *f*; (*written*) artículo *m*; ~*s pl.* (*identity etc.*) documentación *f*; *brown* ~ papel *m* de embalar, papel *m* de estraza; *on* ~ sobre el papel; **2.** *attr.* ... de papel; ~ *money* papel *m* moneda; **3.** *wall* empapelar; ˈ~**·back** libro *m* en rústica; ˈ~**·bag** saco *m* de papel; ˈ~ **clip** sujetapapeles *m*; clip *m*; ˈ~**-fast·en·er** grapa *f*; ˈ~**·hang·er** empapelador *m*; ˈ~ **knife** cortapapeles *m*; ˈ~ **mill** fábrica *f* de papel; ˈ~**·weight** pisapapeles *m*; ˈ~ **work** preparación *f* de escritos; papeleo *m*; *approx.* tramitación *f*; **pa·per·y** [ˈ~ri] parecido al papel; delgado como el papel.
pa·pier mâché [ˈpæpjeiˈmɑːʃei] (*attr.* de) cartón *m* piedra.
pa·pist [ˈpeipist] papista *m/f*; **pa·pis·try** [ˈpeipistri] papismo *m.*
pa·py·rus [pəˈpairəs] papiro *m.*
par [pɑːr] **1.** par *f*; *above* ~ a premio; *below* ~ ⚕ a descuento; ⚕ indispuesto; *fig.* inferior a la calidad normal; *golf*: *5 under* ~ 5 bajo par; *be on a* ~ correr parejas (*with* con); **2.** *value* nominal; *standard* normal.
par·a·ble [ˈpærəbl] parábola *f.*
pa·rab·o·la [pəˈræbələ] parábola *f*;
par·a·bol·ic, par·a·bol·i·cal [pærəˈbɔlik(l)] □ parabólico.
par·a·chute [ˈpærəʃuːt] **1.** paracaídas *m*; **2.** lanzar(se) en paracaídas; ˈ**par·a·chut·ing** *sport* paracaidismo *m*; ˈ**par·a·chut·ist** paracaidista *m.*
pa·rade [pəˈreid] **1.** ⚔ desfile *m*, parada *f*; (*road*) paseo *m*; *fig.* alarde *m*, ostentación *f*; *make a* ~ *of* hacer alarde de; ~ *ground* plaza *f* de armas; **2.** *v/t.* ⚔ formar; *streets* desfilar por; *th.* pasear (*through the streets* por las calles); (*show off*) hacer gala (*or* alarde) de, lucir; *v/i.* desfilar; formar en parada.
par·a·digm [ˈpærədaim] paradigma [*m.*]
par·a·dise [ˈpærədais] paraíso *m.*
par·a·dox [ˈpærədɔks] paradoja *f*; *fig.* persona *f etc.* enigmática; **par·aˈdox·i·cal** □ paradójico.

par·af·fin ['pærəfin] petróleo *m*, keroseno *m*; ~ *wax* parafina *f*.
par·a·gon ['pærəgən] dechado *m*.
par·a·graph ['pærəgræf] párrafo *m*; *typ*. suelto *m*; *new* ~ (punto y) aparte.
Pa·ra·guay·an [pærə'gwaijən] paraguayo *adj. a. su. m* (a *f*).
par·a·keet ['pærəki:t] perico *m*, periquito *m*.
par·al·lel ['pærəlel] **1.** paralelo; ⚡ en paralelo; *run* ~ *to* ir en línea paralela a; **2.** (línea *f*) paralela *f*; *geog*., *fig*. paralelo *m*; ~ *bars* paralelas *f/pl*.; ⚡ *in* ~ en paralelo; *without* ~ nunca visto; *have no* ~ no tener par; **3.:** *be* ~*led by* ir parejo con, correr parejas con; tener su paralelo en; '**par·al·lel·ism** paralelismo *m*; **par·al'lel·o·gram** [~əgræm] paralelogramo *m*.
pa·ral·y·sis [pə'rælisis] parálisis *f*; **par·a·lyt·ic** [pærə'litik] ☐ paralítico *adj. a. su. m* (a *f*); **par·a·lyze** ['pærəlaiz] paralizar (*a*. *fig*.).
pa·ram·e·ter [pə'ræmitər] parámetro *m*.
pa·ra·mil·i·ta·ry ['pærə'miləteri] seudomilitar; semimilitar.
par·a·mount ['pærəmaunt] supremo; *importance* capital.
par·a·mour ['pærəmur] *lit*. *or co*. querido (a *f*) *m*.
par·a·no·ia [pærə'nɔijə] paranoia *f*; **par·a·noid** ['~nɔid] paranoico *adj. a. su. m* (a *f*).
par·a·pet ['pærəpit] parapeto *m*.
par·a·pher·na·li·a [pærəfər'neiljə] trastos *m/pl*.; F avíos *m/pl*., chismes *m/pl*.; molestias *f/pl*., trámites *m/pl*. engorrosos.
par·a·phrase ['pærəfreiz] **1.** paráfrasis *f*; **2.** parafrasear.
pa·ra·ple·gia [pærə'pli:dʒə] paraplejía *f*.
par·a·site ['pærəsait] parásito *m* (*a*. *fig*.); *fig*. gorrista *m/f*; **par·a·sit·ic, par·a·sit·i·cal** [~'sitik(l)] ☐ parasítico, parasitario; parásito (*on* de).
par·a·sol [pærə'sɔl] sombrilla *f*, quitasol *m*.
par·a·troop·er ['pærətru:pər] paracaidista *m*.
par·a·ty·phoid ['pærə'taifɔid] (fiebre *f*) paratifoidea *f*.
par·boil ['pɑ:rbɔil] sancochar.
par·cel ['pɑ:rsl] **1.** paquete *m*; lío *m*; parcela *f of land*; **2.** (*a*. ~ *out*) *land* parcelar; repartir; ~ *up* empaquetar, embalar; **par·cel post** (servicio *m* de) paquetes *m/pl*. postales.
parch [pɑ:rtʃ] (re)secar, (re)quemar; *plants* agostar; *be* ~*ed* (*with thirst*) morirse de sed.
parch·ment ['pɑ:rtʃmənt] pergamino *m*.
par·don ['pɑ:rdn] **1.** perdón *m*; ⚖ indulto *m*; *I beg your* ~ le pido perdón, perdone; *I beg your* ~? ¿cómo?; **2.** perdonar, dispensar; F disculpar; ⚖ indultar; ~ *me* dispense Vd.; perdone Vd.; '**par·don·a·ble** ☐ perdonable.
pare [per] *stick etc*. adelgazar; *fruit etc*. mondar; *nails* cortar; *fig*. reducir, ir reduciendo (*a*. ~ *away*, ~ *down*).
par·ent ['perənt] **1.** padre *m*, madre *f*; ~*s pl*. padres *m/pl*.; **2.** madre; '**par·ent·age** nacimiento *m*; linaje *m*; **pa·ren·tal** [pə'rentl] de padre y madre, de los padres.
pa·ren·the·sis [pə'renθisis], *pl*. **pa'ren·the·ses** [~si:z] paréntesis *m*; **par·en·thet·ic, par·en·thet·i·cal** [pærən'θetik(l)] ☐ entre paréntesis; explicativo.
par·ent·hood ['perənthud] paternidad *f or* maternidad *f*; el ser padre(s), el tener hijos.
pa·ri·ah [pə'raiə, 'periə] paria *m/f*.
pa·ri·e·tal [pə'raiitl] parietal.
par·ish ['pæriʃ] **1.** parroquia *f* (*a*. ~ *church*); **2.** *attr*. parroquial; ~ *priest* párroco *m*; ~ *register* registro *m* parroquial; **pa·rish·ion·er** [pə'riʃənər] feligrés (-a *f*) *m*.
Pa·ri·sian [pə'rizjən] parisiense *adj. a. su. m/f*, parisino *adj. a. su. m* (a *f*).
par·i·ty ['pæriti] paridad *f*, igualdad *f*.
park [pɑ:rk] **1.** parque *m*; jardines *m/pl*.; *mot*. parque *m* de automóviles; **2.** *v/t*. estacionar; aparcar; F parquear; poner, dejar; *v/i*. estacionarse; aparcar; '**park·ing** estacionamiento *m*; aparcamiento *m*; *no* ~ prohibido estacionarse; ~ *attendant* celador *m*; ~ *fee* costa *f* de estacionamiento; ~ *lights pl*. luces *f/pl*. de estacionamiento; ~ *lot* parque *m* de estacionamiento; *sl*. parqueadero *m*; ~ *meter* reloj *m* de estacionamiento; parquímetro *m*.
par·lance ['pɑ:rləns] lenguaje *m*.
par·ley ['pɑ:rli] **1.** parlamento *m*; F charla *f* de negociación; **2.** parlamentar; F negociar.
par·lia·ment ['pɑ:rləmənt] parla-

mento *m*; (*Spanish*) Cortes *f/pl.*; *Houses of* ♀ Cámara *f* de los Lores y la de los Comunes; *member of* ~ diputado *m*, miembro *m* del parlamento; **par·lia·men·tar·i·an** [~menˈteriən] parlamentario *adj. a. su. m* (a *f*); **par·lia·men·ta·ry** [~ˈmentəri] parlamentario.

par·lor [ˈpɑːrlər] salón *m*, saloncito *m*; *eccl.* locutorio *m*; ~ *game* juego *m* de salón; ˈ~ **maid** camarera *f*.

par·lous [ˈpɑːrləs] peligroso; *state* lamentable.

pa·ro·chi·al [pəˈroukjəl] □ parroquial; *fig.* de miras estrechas, mezquino.

par·o·dist [ˈpærədist] parodista *m/f*; ˈ**par·o·dy 1.** parodia *f*; **2.** parodiar.

pa·role [pəˈroul] **1.** palabra *f* (de honor); libertad *f* bajo palabra; *on* ~ bajo palabra; *put on* ~ = **2.** dejar libre bajo palabra.

par·ox·ysm [ˈpærəksizm] paroxismo *m*.

par·quet [pɑːrˈkei] parquet *m*, entarimado *m* (de hojas quebradas); ˈ**par·quet·ry** (obra *f* de) entarimado *m*.

par·ri·cide [ˈpærisaid] parricidio *m*; (*p.*) parricida *m/f*.

par·rot [ˈpærət] **1.** loro *m*, papagayo *m*; ~ *fashion* mecánicamente; **2.** repetir servilmente; imitar servilmente.

par·ry [ˈpæri] *fenc.* parar, quitar; *fig.* esquivar, desviar (hábilmente).

parse [pɑːrz] *gr.* analizar.

Par·see [pɑːrˈsiː] parsi *m/f*.

par·si·mo·ni·ous [pɑːrsiˈmounjəs] □ parsimonioso; **par·si·mo·ny** [ˈpɑːrsimouni] parsimonia *f*.

pars·ley [ˈpɑːrsli] perejil *m*.

pars·nip [ˈpɑːrsnip] chirivía *f*.

par·son [ˈpɑːrsn] clérigo *m*, cura *m*; párroco *m*; ˈ**par·son·age** casa *f* del cura.

part [pɑːrt] **1.** parte *f*; porción *f*; ⊕ pieza *f*; *thea. a. fig.* papel *m*; ♪ parte *f*; (*hair*) raya *f*; crencha *f*; (*place*) lugar *m*, comarca *f*; (*duty*) deber *m*; ~*s pl.* † prendas *f/pl.*; (*region*) región *f*; *three* ~*s* tres cuartos; casi; *travel in foreign* ~*s* viajar por el extranjero; ~ *of speech* parte *f* de la oración; ~ *and parcel* parte *f* esencial; *man of* ~*s* hombre *m* de mucho talento; *for my (own)* ~ por mi parte; *for the most* ~ por la mayor parte; *in* ~ en parte; *in good* ~ en buena parte; *in these* ~*s* por aquí; en estos contornos; *on my* ~ por mi parte; *do one's* ~ cumplir con su obligación; *it is not my* ~ *to* no me toca a mí *inf.*; *look the* ~ vestir el cargo; *take* ~ *in* tomar parte en; **2.** *adv.* (en) parte; **3.** *adj.* parcial; co..., con; ~ *author* coautor (-a *f*) *m*; **4.** *v/t.* separar; dividir; partir; *v. company*; ~ *one's hair* hacerse la raya; *v/i.* separarse; (*come apart*) desprenderse; romperse; ~ *from* despedirse de; ~ *with* deshacerse de; ceder, entregar; *money* pagar, dar.

par·take [pɑːrˈteik] [*irr.* (*take*)]: ~ *of food etc.* comer *etc.*, aceptar; *quality* tener algo de.

par·terre [pɑːrˈter] *thea.* anfiteatro *m* debajo de la galería.

par·tial [ˈpɑːrʃl] □ parcial; predispuesto; ~ *to* aficionado a; **par·ti·al·i·ty** [pɑːrʃiˈæliti] (*bias*) parcialidad *f*; ~ *for*, ~ *to* afición *f* a.

par·tic·i·pant [pɑːrˈtisipənt] *mst* partícipe *m/f*; combatiente *m/f in fight*; **parˈtic·i·pate** [~peit] participar, tomar parte (*in* en); **par·tic·i·ˈpa·tion** participación *f*; **par·ti·ci·ple** [ˈpɑːrtsipl] participio *m*; *past* ~ participio *m* de pasado; *present* ~ participio *m* de presente.

par·ti·cle [ˈpɑːrtikl] partícula *f*; pizca *f*; ~ *physics* física *f* de las partículas.

par·tic·u·lar [pərˈtikjulər] **1.** □ particular; (*detailed*) detallado, minucioso; (*scrupulous*) escrupuloso; (*fastidious*) exigente, quisquilloso (*about*, [*as to*] *what* en cuanto a, en asuntos de); *be very* ~ *about* cuidar mucho de; *that* ~ *person* esa persona (y no otra); **2.** particularidad *f*; detalle *m*; ~*s pl.* detalles *m/pl.*; informe *m* pormenorizado; *in* ~ en particular; **par·tic·u·lar·i·ty** [~ˈlæriti] particularidad *f*; **parˈtic·u·lar·ize** *v/t.* particularizar; *v/i.* dar todos los detalles.

part·ing [ˈpɑːrtiŋ] **1.** separación *f*; despedida *f*; raya *f in hair*; ~ *of the ways fig.* momento *m* de separación; **2.** ... de despedida.

par·ti·san [pɑːrtiˈzæn] **1.** partidario (a *f*) *m*; ⚔ partisano *m*, guerrillero *m*; **2.** partidista; ~ *spirit* partidismo *m*; ˈ~**ship** parcialidad *f*; partidismo *m*.

par·ti·tion [pɑːrˈtiʃn] **1.** partición *f*, división *f*; ~ (*wall*) tabique *m*; **2.** (*share*) repartir; *country, room* divi-

dir; ~ *off* tabicar, separar con tabique.
par·ti·tive [ˈpɑːrtitiv] □ partitivo.
part·ly [ˈpɑːrtli] en parte; en cierto modo.
part·ner [ˈpɑːrtnər] **1.** ✝ socio (a *f*) *m*; compañero (a *f*) *m* (*a. cards*); pareja *f in dance, tennis etc.*; (*married*) cónyuge *m/f*; **2.** acompañar; *be ~ed by* ir acompañado de; ˈ**part·ner·ship** ✝ sociedad *f*; asociación *f*; vida *f etc.* en común; *enter into ~* asociarse (*with* con).
part...: ˈ**~ own·er** condueño (a *f*) *m*; ˈ**~ pay·ment** pago *m* en parte; *in ~* como parte del pago.
par·tridge [ˈpɑːrtridʒ] perdiz *f*.
part-time [ˈpɑːrtˈtaim] **1.** *adj.* en dedicación parcial, que trabaja por horas; **2.** *adv.*: *work ~* trabajar por horas.
par·ty [ˈpɑːrti] **1.** *pol.* partido *m*; grupo *m*; ⚔ pelotón *m*; *hunt. etc.* partida *f*; (*gathering*) reunión *f*; (*informal*) tertulia *f*; (*merry*) fiesta *f*, guateque *m*; ⚖ parte *f*; interesado (a *f*) *m*; F individuo *m*; *be ~ to* estar interesado en; ser cómplice en; *I will not be a ~ to* no quiero tener nada que ver con; *v. third*; **2.** *attr. pol.* de partido; *dress* de gala; *~-goer* tertuliano *m*, fiestero *m*; *approx.* juerguista *m/f*; *~ leader* jefe *m* de partido; *~ line teleph.* línea *f* de dos o más abonados; *pol.* línea *f* de partido; *~ politics b.s.* politiqueo *m*, partidismo *m*; *~ ticket* candidatura *f* apoyada por un partido; *~ wall* pared *f* medianera.
par·ve·nu [ˈpɑːrvənjuː] arribista *m/f*.
pas·chal [ˈpæskəl] pascual.
pa·sha [ˈpæʃə] pachá *m*, bajá *m*.
pass [pæs] **1.** *geog.* puerto *m*, paso *m*, desfiladero *m*; ⚔ *etc.* pase *m* (*a. fenc., sport*); salvoconducto *m*; *thea.* entrada *f* de favor; *univ. etc.* nota *f* de aprobado; *fig.* condición *f*; coyuntura *f*; *make a ~ at* requebrar de amores, echar un piropo a; **2.** *v/i.* pasar; *univ. etc.* aprobar, ser aprobado; *come to ~* suceder, acontecer; *let ~* dejar pasar, no hacer caso de; *~ away* fallecer; *~ by* (*adv.*) pasar de largo; (*prp.*) pasar delante de, pasar cerca de; *~ for* pasar por; *~ off* pasar; *~ on* fallecer; pasar; *~ out* salir; F desmayarse, caer redondo; *~ through* pasar por; *v/t.* pasar; pasar por delante de; (*overtake*) pasar, dejar atrás; *p.* cruzarse con *on street etc.*; *bill, candidate, exam, proposal* aprobar; *opinion* expresar; *sentence* pronunciar, dictar; *~ (me) the salt, please* ¿me hace el favor de pasar la sal?; *~ by* no hacer caso de, pasar por alto; *~ off coin etc.* pasar; *offence* disimular; *~ o.s. off as* hacerse pasar por; *~ on* pasar, transmitir; dar, decir; *~ over* pasar por alto; postergar *for promotion*; *~ around* pasar de uno a otro; F *~ up* renunciar a, rechazar; ˈ**pass·a·ble** □ (*tolerable*) pasadero, pasable; *pass etc.* pasadero, transitable.
pas·sage [ˈpæsidʒ] paso *m*; ⚓, ♪ pasaje *m*; ⚠ pasillo *m*, galería *f*; (*alley*) callejón *m*; (*underground*) pasadizo *m*; trozo *m of book*; *parl.* (*process*) trámites *m/pl.*, (*final*) aprobación *f of bill*; *bird of ~* ave *f* de paso (*a. fig.*); *~ of arms* combate *m*; *~ of time* paso *m* del tiempo; *in the ~ of time* andando el tiempo; ˈ**~ mon·ey** pasaje *m*; ˈ**~ way** = *passage* ⚠ *etc.*
pass·book [ˈpæsbuk] libreta *f* de banco.
pass·é [pæˈsei] pasado (de moda).
pas·sen·ger [ˈpæsindʒər] pasajero (a *f*) *m*, viajero (a *f*) *m*; *~ train* tren *m* de pasajeros.
passe-par·tout [ˈpæspɑːrˈtuː] paspartú *m*.
pass·er-by, *pl.* **pass·ers-by** [ˈpæsər(z)ˈbai] transeúnte *m/f*.
pass·ing [ˈpæsiŋ] **1.** paso *m*; (*death*) fallecimiento *m*; *in ~* de pasada, de paso; **2.** pasajero; corriente; casual; *~ fancy* capricho *m*; **3.** *adv.* † muy; ˈ**~ bell** toque *m* de difuntos.
pas·sion [ˈpæʃən] pasión *f*; (arranque *m* de) cólera *f*; *have a ~ for* tener pasión por; **pas·sion·ate** [ˈ~ʃenit] □ apasionado; (*angry*) colérico; *believer, desire* vehemente, ardiente; ˈ**pas·sion flow·er** pasionaria *f*; ˈ**pas·sion·less** sin compasión; frío; ˈ**pas·sion play** drama *m* de la Pasión.
pas·sive [ˈpæsiv] **1.** □ pasivo; inactivo, inerte; **2.** voz *f* pasiva; ˈ**pas·sive·ness, pas·siv·i·ty** [~ˈsiviti] pasividad *f*; inercia *f*.
pass·key [ˈpæskiː] llave *f* maestra.
Pass·o·ver [ˈpæsouvər] Pascua *f* de los hebreos.

pass·port [ˈpæspɔːrt] pasaporte *m*.
pass·word [ˈpæswəːrd] santo *m* y seña.
past [pæst] **1.** *adj*. pasado (*a. gr.*); *all that is now* ~ todo eso se acabó ya; *for some time* ~ de algún tiempo a esta parte; ~ *master fig*. maestro *m*, consumado (*adj*.) (*at, in* en); **2.** *adv*. por delante; *rush* ~ pasar precipitadamente; **3.** *prp*. *place* (*beyond*) más allá de; (*in front of*) por delante de; *number* más de; *time etc*. después de; *half* ~ *2* las 2 y media; *it's* ~ *12* dieron las 12 ya; F *I wouldn't put it* ~ *him* le creo capaz de eso; ~ *belief* increíble; ~ *comprehension* incomprensible; ~ *all doubt* fuera de toda duda; ~ *hope* sin esperanza; **4.** *su*. pasado *m* (*a. gr.*); antecedentes *m/pl*.; *woman with a* ~ mujer *f* que tiene historia.
paste [peist] **1.** pasta *f*; engrudo *m for sticking*; diamante *m* de imitación, bisutería *f*; **2.** engrudar; pegar (con engrudo); *sl*. pegar; *sport*: *sl*. cascar; ˈ~·**board** (*attr*. de) cartón *m*.
pas·tel [ˈpæstəl] pastel *m*; pintura *f* al pastel; ~ *shade* tono *m* pastel.
pas·tern [ˈpæstəːrn] cuartilla *f* (del caballo).
paste-up [ˈpeistʌp] montaje *m*; arreglo *m* compósito.
pas·teur·ize [ˈpæstʃəraiz] pasteurizar.
pas·tille [pæsˈtiːl] pastilla *f*.
pas·time [ˈpæstaim] pasatiempo *m*.
pas·tor [ˈpæstər] pastor *m*; ˈ**pas·to·ral** *lit*. pastoril; *economy etc*. pastoral; *eccl*. pastoral (*a. su. f*).
pas·try [ˈpeistri] (*dough*) pasta *f*; (*collectively*) pastas *f/pl*., pasteles *m/pl*.; (*art*) pastelería *f*; *flaky* (*or puff-*)~ hojaldre *m*; ˈ~ **cook** pastelero (a *f*) *m*; repostero (a *f*) *m*.
pas·tur·age [ˈpæstʃuridʒ] = *pasture* 1.
pas·ture [ˈpæstʃər] **1.** (*herbage, land*) pasto *m*, pastura *f*; (*land*) dehesa *f*; **2.** *v/t*. *animals* apacentar, pastorear; *herbage* comer; *v/i*. pastar, pacer.
past·y 1. [ˈpeisti] *material* pastoso; *color* pálido; **2.** [ˈpæsti] pastel *m* (de carne), empanada *f*.
pat [pæt] **1.** palmadita *f*; (*affectionate*) caricia *f*; palmada *f on shoulder*; pastelillo *m of butter*; **2.** dar una palmadita a; *shoulder* dar una palmada en; *dog etc*. acariciar (con la mano); pasar la mano por; ~ *on the back fig*. felicitar; **3.** *adj*. oportuno; perfecto; apto; **4.** *adv*.: *have* ~ saber al dedillo.
patch [pætʃ] **1.** remiendo *m in dress*; parche *m on tire, wound*; lunar *m* postizo *on face*; (*stain etc.*) mancha *f*; (*small area*) pequeña extensión *f*; ⸸ terreno *m*, cuadro *m*; **2.** remendar; ~ *up quarrel* componer; remendar (*or* componer) de modo provisional; ~·**work** [ˈpætʃwəːrk] labor *f* de retazos; ~ *quilt* centón *m*; ˈ**patch·y** desigual, poco uniforme.
pate [peit] mollera *f*.
pat·en [ˈpætən] patena *f*.
pat·ent [ˈpætnt] **1.** □ patente, palmario; ⚕ de patente, patente, patentado; *letters* ~ *pl*. patente *m* de privilegio; ~ *leather* charol *m*; ~ *medicine* específico *m*; medicamento *m* de patente; **2.** patente *f*, privilegio *m* de invención; ~ *agent* agente *m* de patentes; ~ *office* oficina *f* de patentes; **3.** patentar; **pat·ent·ee** [peitənˈtiː] poseedor *m* de patentes.
pa·ter·nal [pəˈtəːrnl] □ *quality* paternal; *relation* paterno; **paˈter·ni·ty** paternidad *f*.
path [pæθ], *pl*. **paths** [pæðz] senda *f*, sendero *m*; *fig*. camino *m*, trayectoria *f*; curso *m*; rastro *m*; marcha *f of storm*.
pa·thet·ic [pəˈθetik] □ patético, conmovedor.
path·less [ˈpæθlis] sin camino; desconocido.
path·o·log·i·cal [pæθəˈlɔdʒikl] □ patológico; **pa·thol·o·gist** [pəˈθɔlədʒist] patólogo *m*; **paˈthol·o·gy** patología *f*.
pa·thos [ˈpeiθɔs] patetismo *m*, lo patético.
path·way [ˈpæθwei] = *path*.
pa·tience [ˈpeiʃns] paciencia *f*; *cards*: solitario *m*; *be out of* ~ *with* no poder más sufrir, no tener simpatía alguna a; ˈ**pa·tient 1.** □ paciente, sufrido; **2.** paciente *m/f*, enfermo (a *f*) *m*.
pa·ti·o [ˈpætiou] patio *m*.
pa·tri·arch [ˈpeitriɑːrk] patriarca *m*; **pa·triˈar·chal** □ patriarcal.
pa·tri·cian [pəˈtriʃn] patricio *adj*. *a*. *su*. *m* (a *f*).
pat·ri·mo·ny [ˈpætrimouni] patrimonio *m*.
pa·tri·ot [ˈpeitriət] patriota *m/f*; **pa·tri·ot·ic** [~ˈɔtik] □ patriótico; **pa·tri·ot·ism** [ˈ~ətizm] patriotismo *m*.
pa·trol [pəˈtroul] **1.** ⚔ *etc*. patrulla *f*;

ronda *f*; ~ *car* coche *m* de policía; ~ *wagon* camión *m* de policía; **2.** patrullar (*v/t.* por); *fig.* rondar, pasearse (por); **~·man** [pəˈtroulmæn] guardia *m* municipal.

pa·tron [ˈpeitrən] ✝ parroquiano (a *f*) *m*; *lit.* mecenas *m*; protector *m*; *eccl.* patrono (a *f*) *m* (*a.* ~ *saint*); patrocinador (-a *f*) *m of enterprise*; **pa·tron·age** [ˈpeitrənidʒ] *lit.* mecenazgo *m*; *eccl.* patronato *m*; patrocinio *m of enterprise*; *under the* ~ *of* bajo los auspicios de; **pa·tron·ize** [ˈpeitrənaiz] *shop* ser parroquiano de; *enterprise* patrocinar; *b.s.* tratar con aire protector; **ˈpa·tron·iz·ing** □ *tone etc.* protector; condescendiente.

pat·ten [ˈpætn] zueco *m*, chanclo *m*.

pat·ter [ˈpætər] **1.** (*a.* ~ *about*) andar con pasos ligeros; (*rain*) tamborilear; **2.** pasos *m/pl.* ligeros *of feet*; tamborileo *m of rain etc.*; golpeteo *m*; ✝ jerga *f* (publicitaria *etc.*); (*rapid speech*) parloteo *m*.

pat·tern [ˈpætərn] **1.** (*design*) diseño *m*, dibujo *m*; modelo *m*; patrón *m for dress etc.*; **2.** modelar (*on* sobre); **ˈ~ mak·er** ⊕ carpintero *m* modelista.

pat·ty [ˈpæti] empanada *f*; *hamburger* ~ pastilla *f* de hamburguesa.

pau·ci·ty [ˈpɔːsiti] escasez *f*, insuficiencia *f*.

paunch [pɔːntʃ] panza *f*; **ˈpaunch·y** panzudo.

pau·per [ˈpɔːpər] pobre *m/f*, indigente *m/f*; **ˈpau·per·ism** pauperismo *m*; **ˈpau·per·ize** empobrecer.

pause [pɔːz] **1.** pausa *f*; *give* ~ *to* hacer vacilar, dar que pensar a; **2.** hacer una pausa, detenerse (brevemente); reflexionar.

pave [peiv] pavimentar, asfaltar; enlosar; ~ *the way* preparar el terreno (*for* a); **ˈpave·ment** acera *f*; pavimento *m*; asfaltado *m*.

pa·vil·ion [pəˈviljən] pabellón *m*; *sport*: caseta *f*, vestuario *m*.

pav·ing stone [ˈpeiviŋstoun] losa *f*.

paw [pɔː] **1.** pata *f*; (*cat's etc.*) garra *f*; (*lion's*) zarpa *f*; **2.** (*lion etc.*) dar zarpazos a; F manosear; *p.* sobar; ~ *the ground* piafar.

pawn[1] [pɔːn] *chess*: peón *m*; *fig.* instrumento *m*.

pawn[2] [~] **1.**: *in* ~ en prenda; **2.** empeñar, dejar en prenda; **ˈ~·bro·ker** prestamista *m*, prendero *m*; **ˈ~·bro·ker's**, **ˈ~·shop** casa *f* de empeños, prendería *f*; monte *m* de piedad; **ˈ~ tick·et** papeleta *f* de empeño.

pay [pei] **1.** paga *f*; sueldo *m*; *in the* ~ *of* asalariado de, al servicio de; *on half* ~ a medio sueldo; **2.** [*irr.*] *v/t.* pagar; *account* liquidar; (*be profitable*) ser provechoso a, rendir (bien, *etc.*); *attention* prestar; *respects* ofrecer; *visit* hacer; ~ *back* devolver; reembolsar; *fig.* pagar en la misma moneda; ~ *down* pagar al contado; pagar como desembolso inicial; ~ *off* pagar, liquidar; amortizar; *scores* ajustar; *workmen* pagar y despedir; ~ *out* desembolsar; *rope* ir dando; *p.* pagar en la misma moneda; ~ *up* pagar (de mala gana); *v/i.* pagar (*for acc.*); (*be profitable*) rendir, ser provechoso; *it doesn't* ~ *to* vale más no *inf.*; **ˈpay·a·ble** pagadero; **ˈpay·day** día *m* de paga; **pay dirt** grava *f* provechosa; **pay·ee** [~ˈiː] portador (-a *f*) *m*; tenedor (-a *f*) *m*; **ˈpay·er** pagador (-a *f*) *m*; **ˈpay·ing** provechoso; que rinde bien; ~ *guest* pensionista *m/f*; **ˈpay·load** carga *f* útil; **ˈpay·mas·ter** oficial *m* pagador; **ˈpay·ment** pago *m* (*a. fig.*); *in* ~ *for* en pago de; *on* ~ *of* pagando; *monthly* ~ mensualidad *f*.

pay...: **ˈ~-off** F colmo *m*; resultado *m*; momento *m* decisivo; **ˈ~ pack·et** sobre *m* de paga; **ˈ~·roll** nómina *f*; hoja *f* de paga; **ˈ~ sta·tion** teléfono *m* público.

pea [piː] guisante *m*; *be as like as 2* ~*s* parecerse como dos gotas de agua.

peace [piːs] paz *f*; *at* ~ en paz; *the* (*King's*) ~ orden *m* público; ~ *loving nation* nación *f* amante de la paz; *hold one's* ~ guardar silencio; *keep the* ~ mantener la paz; *make* ~ hacer las paces (*with* con); **ˈpeace·a·ble** □ pacífico, sosegado; **ˈPeace Corps** Cuerpo *m* de Paz; **peace·ful** [ˈ~ful] □ tranquilo; **ˈpeace·mak·er** pacificador (-a *f*) *m*; árbitro *m*.

peach [piːtʃ] ⚘ melocotón *m*; (*a.* ~ *tree*) melocotonero *m*; *sl.* monada *f*; *sl.* (*girl*) real moza *f*; chica *f* preciosa; **ˈpeach·y** *sl.* estupendo; magnífico.

pea·cock [ˈpiːkɔk] pavo *m* real, pavón *m*.

peak [piːk] pico *m*; cima *f*; cumbre *f* (*a. fig.*); visera *f of cap*; ~ *hours pl.* horas *f/pl.* punta; ~ *load* carga *f* máxima; ~ *season* época *f* más popular del año; ~ *traffic* movimiento *m* máximo; **peaked** [pi:kt] *cap* con visera; **peak·ed** ['pi:kid] pálido; enfermizo; fatigado; '**peak·y** pálido, enfermizo.

peal [pi:l] **1.** repique(teo) *m*; (*set*) juego *m* de campanas; ~ *of laughter* carcajada *f*; ~ *of thunder* trueno *m*; **2.** *v/i. a. v/t.* repicar, tocar a vuelo.

pea·nut ['pi:nʌt] cacahuete *m*; ~ *butter* manteca *f* de cacahuete; *work for* ~*s* F recibir poco sueldo.

pear [per] pera *f*; (*a.* ~ *tree*) peral *m*; ~ *shaped* de forma de pera.

pearl [pə:rl] perla *f* (*a. fig.*); ~ *barley* cebada *f* perlada; *attr.* = '**pearl·y** de perla(s); color de perla; perlino; nacarado.

peas·ant ['pezənt] campesino (a *f*) *m*, labrador (-a *f*) *m*; '**peas·ant·ry** campesinos *m/pl.*, gente *f* del campo.

pea shoot·er ['pi:ʃu:tər] cerbatana *f*.

pea soup ['pi:'su:p] puré *m* de guisantes; **pea-'soup·er** F niebla *f* muy densa, puré *m* de guisantes.

peat [pi:t] turba *f*; '~ **bog** turbera *f*; '**peat·y** turboso.

peb·ble ['pebl] guija *f*, guijarro *m*; '**peb·bly** guij(arr)oso.

pe·can ['pi:kæn; pi:'kæ:n] ⚘ pacana *f*.

pec·ca·dil·lo [pekə'dilou] falta *f* leve.

peck[1] [pek] *medida de áridos* (= *9,087 litros*); *a* ~ *of trouble* la mar de disgustos.

peck[2] [~] **1.** picotazo *m*; F beso *m* poco cariñoso; **2.** picotear; ~ *at food* comer melindrosamente; '**peck·er** picoteador *m*; rezongador *m*; *sl.* pene *m*.

pec·to·ral ['pektərəl] pectoral *adj. a. su. m.*

pec·u·la·tion [pekju'leiʃn] peculado *m*.

pe·cul·iar [pi'kju:ljər] □ peculiar; singular; ~ *to* propio de, privativo de; **pe·cu·li·ar·i·ty** [~li'æriti] peculiaridad *f*; singularidad *f*; rasgo *m* característico.

pe·cu·ni·ar·y [pi'kju:njəri] pecuniario.

ped·a·gog·ic, ped·a·gog·i·cal [pedə'gɔdʒik(l)] □ pedagógico; '**ped·a·gogue** [~gɔg] pedagogo *m* (*a. b.s.*); **ped·a·go·gy** ['~gi] pedagogía *f*.

ped·al ['pedl] **1.** pedal *m*; **2.** *v/i.* pedalear; F ir en bicicleta; *v/t.* impulsar pedaleando.

ped·ant ['pedənt] pedante *m*; **pe·dan·tic** [pi'dæntik] □ *p.* pedante; *manner* pedantesco; **ped·ant·ry** ['pedəntri] pedantería *f*.

ped·dle ['pedl] andar vendiendo (de puerta en puerta); '**ped·dler** vendedor *m* ambulante.

ped·er·as·ty ['pedəræsti] pederastia *f*.

ped·es·tal ['pedistl] pedestal *m*; **pe·des·tri·an** [pi'destriən] **1.** de (*or* para) peatones; pedestre (*a. fig.*); **2.** peatón *m*; paseante *m/f*.

pe·dia·tri·cian [pi:diə'triʃn] pediatra *m/f*; **pe·diat·rics** [pi:di'ætriks] pediatría *f*.

ped·i·cure ['pedikjur] quiropedia *f*.

ped·i·gree ['pedigri:] **1.** genealogía *f*, linaje *m*; árbol *m* genealógico; pedigrí *m*; **2.** de raza.

ped·i·ment ['pedimənt] frontón *m*.

pe·dom·e·ter [pi'dɔmitər] podómetro *m*.

pee [pi:] F **1.** orinar; mear; **2.** orina *f*.

peek [pi:k] **1.** mirada *f* furtiva; *take a* ~ (*at*) = **2.** mirar furtivamente.

peel [pi:l] **1.** piel *f*; (*removed*) pieles *f/pl.*, monda *f*, peladura(s) *f*(*pl.*); **2.** *v/t.* pelar, mondar; *paper etc.* quitar (una capa de); ~ *off dress* quitarse; *v/i.* ⚘ pelarse; ~ *off* desconcharse; F (*p.*) desnudarse; **peelings** *pl.* monda *f*, peladuras *f/pl.*

peep[1] [pi:p] **1.** pío *m*; **2.** piar.

peep[2] [~] **1.** mirada *f* (rápida, furtiva, por una rendija *etc.*); **2.** (*a.* ~ *at*) mirar (rápidamente, furtivamente, por una rendija *etc.*); atisbar; (*a.* ~ *out*) asomar; empezar a dejarse ver; '**peep·er** *sl.* ojo *m*; '**peep·hole** mirilla *f in door*, atisbadero *m*; **Peep·ing Tom** mirón *m*; '**peep·show** mundonuevo *m*; F vistas *f/pl.* sicalípticas.

peer[1] [pir] (*a.* ~ *at*) mirar de cerca; mirar con ojos de miope; ~ *into* mirar (de cerca) lo que hay dentro de.

peer[2] [~] (*noble*) par *m*; (*equal*) igual *m*; '**peer·age** nobleza *f*, paría *f*; '**peer·ess** paresa *f*; '**peer·less** sin par, incomparable.

peeved [pi:vd] F negro, irritado;

pee·vish ['pi:viʃ] □ malhumorado, displicente, cojijoso; '**pee·vish·ness** mal humor *m*, displicencia *f*.

pee·wit ['pi:wit] avefría *f*.

peg [peg] **1.** clavija *f*, claveta *f*; (*tent etc.*) estaca *f*; (*clothes*) pinza *f*; colgadero *m for coats*; *fig.* pretexto *m*; *take s.o. down a* ~ bajarle los humos a uno;

2. enclavijar; (*a.* ~ *down*) estaquillar; (*a.* ~ *out*) *area* señalar con estacas; *clothes* tender (con pinzas); *prices* fijar, estabilizar; F ~ *away* machacar; persistir, afanarse (*at* en); *sl.* ~ *out* estirar la pata; '~ **top** peonza *f*.
peign·oir ['peinwɑːr] bata *f*; peinador *m*.
pe·jo·ra·tive [pi'dʒɔːrətiv, 'piːdʒərətiv] □ peyorativo.
pel·i·can ['pelikən] pelícano *m*.
pel·let ['pelit] bolita *f*; bodoque *m*; ⚔ perdigón *m*.
pell·mell ['pel'mel] *adv.* en tropel, atropelladamente; precipitadamente.
pel·lu·cid [pe'ljuːsid] diáfano, cristalino.
pe·lo·ta [pe'loutə] pelota *f* (vasca).
pelt[1] [pelt] (*skin*) pellejo *m*.
pelt[2] [~] 1. *v/t.* tirar, arrojar; apedrear *with stones*; *they ~ed him with tomatoes* le tiraron tomates; *v/i.* llover a cántaros (*a.* ~ *with rain*); F ir a máxima velocidad; 2. F (*at*) *full* ~ a máxima velocidad, a todo correr.
pel·vis ['pelvis] pelvis *f*.
pen[1] [pen] 1. pluma *f*; (*fountain-*) estilográfica *f*; *ball* (*point*) ~ bolígrafo *m*; ~ *pal* amigo *m* por correspondencia; 2. escribir; redactar.
pen[2] [~] ↗ 1. corral *m*, redil *m*; 2. [*irr.*] encerrar, acorralar.
pe·nal ['piːnl] penal; ~ *code* código *m* penal; ~ *servitude* trabajos *m/pl.* forzados; **pe·nal·ize** ['~əlaiz] penar; (*accidentally*, *unfairly*) perjudicar; *sport*: castigar; **pen·al·ty** ['penlti] pena *f*; multa *f*; castigo *m*; *sport*: penálty *m*; ~ *area* área *f* de castigo; ~ *kick* golpe *m* de castigo, penálty *m*.
pen·ance ['penəns] penitencia *f*.
pence [pens] *pl. of penny*.
pen·chant ['pɑːŋʃɑːŋ] predilección *f* (*for* por), afición *f* (*for* a).
pen·cil ['pensl] 1. lápiz *m*; rayo *m of light*; 2. escribir con lápiz; '**pen·cil sharp·en·er** sacapuntas *m*.
pend·ant, pend·ent ['pendənt] 1. pendiente; 2. pendiente *m*, medallón *m*.
pend·ing ['pendiŋ] 1. *adj.* pendiente; 2. *prp.* durante; hasta.
pen·du·lous ['pendjuləs] colgante; **pen·du·lum** ['~ləm] péndulo *m*.
pen·e·trate ['penitreit] penetrar; '**pen·e·trat·ing** □ penetrante (*a. fig.*); **pen·e'tra·tion** penetración *f*; '**pen·e·tra·tive** □ penetrante.
pen·guin ['peŋgwin] pingüino *m*.
pen·hold·er ['penhouldər] portaplumas *m*.
pen·i·cil·lin [peni'silin] penicilina *f*.
pen·in·su·la [pi'ninsjulə] península *f*; **pen'in·su·lar** peninsular.
pe·nis ['piːnis] pene *m*.
pen·i·tence ['penitəns] penitencia *f*, arrepentimiento *m*; '**pen·i·tent** □ penitente *adj. a. su. m/f*; compungido, arrepentido; **pen·i·ten·tial** [~'tenʃl] penitencial; **pen·i·ten·tia·ry** [~'tenʃəri] cárcel *f*, presidio *m*.
pen·knife ['pennaif] navaja *f*, cortaplumas *m*.
pen·man·ship ['penmənʃip] caligrafía *f*.
pen name ['penneim] seudónimo *m*.
pen·nant ['penənt] ⚓ gallardete *m*; banderola *f*.
pen·ni·less ['penilis] sin dinero.
pen·non ['penən] pendón *m*.
pen·ny ['peni] penique *m*; centavo *m*; *cost a pretty* ~ costar un dineral; '**~-a-'lin·er** escritorzuelo *m*; '**~-'dread·ful** revista *f* juvenil de bajísima calidad; '**~·weight** *peso* (= *1,555 gr.*); **~·worth** ['~wəːrθ] valor *m* de un penique; *fig.* pizca *f*.
pen·sion ['penʃn] 1. pensión *f*; jubilación *f*; ⚔ retiro *m*; 2. pensionar; jubilar (*a.* ~ *off*); '**pen·sion·er** pensionado (a *f*) *m*, pensionista *m/f*; ⚔ inválido *m*.
pen·sive ['pensiv] □ pensativo; melancólico; preocupado.
pent [pent] *pret. a. p.p. of pen*[2]; ~ *up* reprimido.
pen·ta·gon ['pentəgən] pentágono *m*; **pen·tag·o·nal** [~'tægənl] pentagonal.
pen·tath·lon [pen'tæθlən] péntatlo *m*.
Pen·te·cost ['pentikɔst] Pentecostés *f*; **pen·te'cos·tal** de Pentecostés.
pent·house ['penthaus] colgadizo *m*; casa *f* de azotea.
pent-up ['pent'ʌp] contenido; reprimido.
pen·ul·ti·mate [pin'ʌltimit] penúltimo.
pe·num·bra [pi'nʌmbrə] penumbra *f*.
pe·nu·ri·ous [pi'njuriəs] □ miserable, pobrísimo; **pen·u·ry** ['penjuri] miseria *f*, pobreza *f*.
pe·o·ny ['piəni] peonía *f*.

peo·ple [ˈpi:pl] **1.** (*nation*) pueblo *m*, nación *f*; (*lower orders*) pueblo *m*, plebe *f*; (*in general*) gente *f*; personas *f/pl.*; *my etc.* ~ mi *etc.* familia; *the* ~ *of London* los londinenses, los habitantes de Londres; *English* ~ los ingleses; *the English* ~ el pueblo inglés; *old* ~ los viejos; *some* ~ algunos; *there are some* ~ *who say* hay quien dice que; ~ *say that* se dice que; *I like the* ~ *here* aquí la gente es muy simpática; **2.** poblar.
pep [pep] *sl.* **1.** ánimo *m*, vigor *m*; **2.**: ~ *up* animar, estimular; ~ *talk* palabras *f/pl.* alentadoras.
pep·per [ˈpepər] **1.** pimienta *f*; (*plant*) pimiento *m*; **2.** sazonar con pimienta; *fig.* salpicar; acribillar *with shot*; ˈ~ **box,** ˈ~ **pot** pimentero *m*; ˈ~**·corn** grano *m* de pimienta; ˈ~**·mint** (pastilla *f etc.* de) menta *f*; ˈ**pep·per·y** picante; *fig.* enojadizo, de malas pulgas.
pep·tic [ˈpeptik] péptico.
per [pə:r] por; ~ *annum* al año; ~ *cent* por ciento; *increase by 50* ~ *cent* aumentar en un 50 por ciento; ~ *capita*, ~ *person* por persona; cada uno; ~ se de por sí; *as* ~ según; F *as* ~ *usual* lo de siempre.
per·am·bu·late [pəˈræmbjuleit] *v/t.* recorrer (para inspeccionar); *v/i.* pasearse, deambular; **per·am·bu·ˈla·tion** visita *f* de inspección; paseo *m*; viaje *m*; **per·am·bu·la·tor** [ˈpræmbjuleitə] cochecito *m* de niño.
per·ceive [pərˈsi:v] percibir; ver; notar; comprender.
per·cent·age [pərˈsentidʒ] porcentaje *m*; proporción *f*; *sl.* tajada *f*; *attr.* porcentual.
per·cep·ti·ble [pərˈseptəbl] □ perceptible; **perˈcep·tion** percepción *f*; comprensión *f*; perspicacia *f*; **perˈcep·tive** □ perspicaz, penetrante.
perch[1] [pə:rtʃ] *ichth.* perca *f*.
perch[2] [~] **1.** *medida de longitud* (= *5,029 m.*); (*bird's*) percha *f*; posición *f* elevada; *fig.* posición *f* al parecer segura; **2.** *v/i.* posar(se); encaramarse; colocarse *etc.* en una posición elevada; *v/t.* colocar (en una posición elevada).
per·chance [pərˈtʃæns] quizá, por ventura.
per·cip·i·ent [pərˈsipiənt] perspicaz, penetrante.
per·co·late [ˈpə:rkəleit] filtrar(se), infiltrar(se); ˈ**per·co·la·tor** *approx.* cafetera *f* filtradora.
per·cus·sion [pə:rˈkʌʃn] (♪ *attr.* de) percusión *f*; ~ *cap* cápsula *f* fulminante.
per·di·tion [pə:rˈdiʃn] perdición *f*; infierno *m*.
per·e·gri·na·tion [perigriˈneiʃn] peregrinación *f*; ~*s pl. co.* vagabundeo *m*.
per·emp·to·ry [pəˈremtəri] □ perentorio; *p.* imperioso, autoritario.
per·en·ni·al [pəˈrenjəl] □ perenne *adj. a. su. m* (*a.* ⚘).
per·fect 1. [ˈpə:rfikt] □ perfecto (*a. gr.*); **2.** [~] (*a.* ~ *tense*) perfecto *m*; **3.** [pərˈfekt] perfeccionar; **per·fect·i·bil·i·ty** [~iˈbiliti] perfectibilidad *f*; **perˈfect·i·ble** [~təbl] perfectible; **perˈfec·tion** perfección *f*; *to* ~ a la perfección; **perˈfec·tion·ist** persona *f* que lo quiere todo perfecto; detallista *m/f*.
per·fid·i·ous [pərˈfidiəs] □ pérfido; **perˈfid·i·ous·ness, per·fi·dy** [ˈpə:rfidi] perfidia *f*.
per·fo·rate [ˈpə:rfəreit] perforar, horadar; ~*d stamp* dentado; **per·foˈra·tion** perforación *f*; trepado *m of stamp*; ˈ**per·fo·ra·tor** perforador (-a *f*) *m*.
per·force [pərˈfɔ:rs] forzosamente.
per·form [pərˈfɔ:rm] *v/t. task etc.* realizar, cumplir, hacer; *functions* desempeñar; ♪ *etc.* ejecutar; *play* representar, poner; *v/i.* ♪ tocar; *thea.* representar, actuar; tener un papel; ⊕ funcionar; **perˈform·ance** ejecución *f* (*a.* ♪); desempeño *m*; *thea.* representación *f*; función *f*; actuación *f* (brillante *etc.*); ⊕ funcionamiento *m*; rendimiento *m*; comportamiento *m*; performance *m in race etc.*; **perˈform·er** artista *m/f*; actor *m*, actriz *f*; ♪ ejecutante *m/f*; *etc.*; **perˈform·ing** *animal* amaestrado.
per·fume 1. [ˈpə:rfju:m] perfume *m*; **2.** [pərˈfju:m] perfumar; **perˈfum·er** perfumista *m/f*; **perˈfum·er·y** (*factory*) perfumería *f*; perfumes *m/pl.*
per·func·to·ry [pərˈfʌŋktəri] □ superficial, hecho *etc.* a la ligera.
per·haps [pərˈhæps] tal vez, quizá(s); puede que.
per·il [ˈperil] peligro *m*, riesgo *m*; ˈ**per·il·ous** □ peligroso, arriesgado; *come* ~*ly close to* acercarse de modo peligroso a; *fig.* rayar en.

per·i·me·ter [pe'rimitər] perímetro *m.*
pe·ri·od ['piriəd] período *m* (*a. gr.*), época *f*; término *m*; *typ.* punto *m*; *school*: clase *f*, hora *f*; ⚖ ~*s pl.* reglas *f pl.*; ~ *furniture* muebles *m/pl.* de época; **per·i·od·ic** [~'ɔdik] □ periódico; **pe·ri'od·i·cal 1.** □ periódico; **2.** periódico *m*, publicación *f* periódica.
per·i·pa·tet·ic [peripə'tetik] □ ambulante, sin residencia fija; *phls.* peripatético.
pe·riph·er·y [pe'rifəri] periferia *f.*
pe·riph·ra·sis [pə'rifrəsis], *pl.* **pe'riph·ra·ses** [~si:z] perífrasis *f*; **per·i·phras·tic** [peri'fræstik] □ perifrástico.
per·i·scope ['periskoup] periscopio *m.*
per·ish ['periʃ] *v/i.* perecer; (*material*) deteriorarse; ~ *the thought!* ¡ni por pensamiento!; *v/t.* deteriorar, echar a perder; F *be* ~*ed with cold* estar aterido; **'per·ish·a·ble 1.** perecedero; *food etc.* corruptible, que no se conserva bien; **2.** ~*s pl.* mercancías *f/pl.* corruptibles; **'per·ish·er** *sl.* tío *m*; (*little* ~) tunante *m*; **'per·ish·ing** *sl.*: *it's* ~ *cold* hace un frío helador.
per·i·style ['peristail] peristilo *m.*
per·i·to·ni·tis [peritə'naitis] peritonitis *f.*
per·i·win·kle ['periwiŋkl] ⚘ (vinca) pervinca *f*; *zo.* litorina *f.*
per·jure ['pə:rdʒər]: ~ *o.s.* perjurar(se); **'per·jured** *p.* perjuro; *evidence* falso; **'per·jur·er** perjuro *m*; **'per·ju·ry** perjurio *m*; *commit* ~ jurar en falso; dar falso testimonio.
perk [pə:rk] F: ~ *up* reanimarse, sentirse mejor; **'~·i·ness** viveza *f*; gallardía *f.*
perks [pə:rks] *pl.* F = *perquisites.*
perk·y ['pə:rki] F vivaracho; de excelente humor; despabilado.
perm [pə:rm] F **1.** ondulación *f* permanente; **2.**: *have one's hair* ~*ed* hacerse una permanente.
per·ma·nence ['pə:rmənəns], **'per·ma·nen·cy** permanencia *f*; **'per·ma·nent** □ permanente; fijo; duradero; ~ *wave* ondulación *f* permanente; ~ *press* planchado *m* permanente.
per·man·gan·ate [pə:r'mæŋgəneit] permanganato *m.*
per·me·a·bil·i·ty [pə:rmiə'biliti] permeabilidad *f*; **'per·me·a·ble** □ permeable; **per·me·ate** ['~mieit] penetrar; saturar; impregnar.
per·mis·si·ble [pər'misəbl] □ permisible; **per·mis·sion** [~'miʃn] permiso *m*; **per·mis·sive** [~'misiv] permisivo.
per·mit 1. [pər'mit] permitir (*to inf.*, que *subj.*); ~ *of* permitir, dar lugar a; *weather* ~*ting* si lo permite el tiempo; **2.** ['pə:rmit] permiso *m*; licencia *f*; ⚕ permiso *m* de importación *etc.*
per·mut·a·tion [pə:rmju:'teiʃn] permutación *f.*
per·ni·cious [pə:r'niʃəs] □ pernicioso, funesto.
per·nick·et·y [pər'nikiti] F quisquilloso, remirado.
per·o·ra·tion [perə'reiʃn] peroración *f.*
per·ox·ide [pə'rɔksaid] peróxido *m*; F ~ *blonde* rubia *f* de bote.
per·pen·dic·u·lar [pə:rpen'dikjulər] □ perpendicular *adj. a. su. f.*
per·pe·trate ['pə:rpitreit] perpetrar; **per·pe'tra·tion** perpetración *f*; **'per·pe·tra·tor** perpetrador (-a *f*) *m.*
per·pet·u·al [pər'petjuəl] □ perpetuo; ~ *motion* movimiento *m* perpetuo; **per'pet·u·ate** [~eit] perpetuar; **per·pet·u'a·tion** perpetuación *f*; **per·pe·tu·i·ty** [pə:rpi'tjuiti] perpetuidad *f*; *in* ~ para siempre.
per·plex [pər'pleks] confundir, dejar perplejo; **per'plexed** □ perplejo; **per'plex·ing** □ confuso, que causa perplejidad; **per'plex·i·ty** perplejidad *f.*
per·qui·site ['pə:rkwizit] obvención *f*; adehala *f*; gaje *m*; ~*s pl.* gajes *m/pl.*; *salary and* ~*s* un sueldo y lo que cae.
per·se·cute ['pə:rsikju:t] perseguir, acosar; **per·se'cu·tion** persecución *f*; ~ *mania* manía *f* persecutoria; **per·se·cu·tor** ['~tər] perseguidor *m.*
per·se·ver·ance [pə:rsi'virəns] perseverancia *f*; **per·se·vere** [~'vir] perseverar, persistir (*in* en); **per·se'ver·ing** □ perseverante.
Per·sian ['pə:rʒn] persa *adj. a. su. m/f.*
per·sist [pər'sist] persistir; porfiar, empeñarse (*in* en); **per·sist·ence, per·sist·en·cy** [pər'sistəns(i)] persistencia *f*; porfía *f*; pertinacia *f of disease etc.*; **per'sist·ent** □ persistente, porfiado; *disease etc.* pertinaz.
per·son ['pə:rsn] persona *f*; *in* ~ en

persona; *in the ~ of* en la persona de; ˈ**per·son·a·ble** bien parecido; ˈ**per·son·age** personaje *m*; ˈ**per·son·al** 1. □ personal; (*private*) privado; de uso personal; *cleanliness etc.* corporal; *interview etc.* en persona; ~ *property* bienes *m/pl.* muebles; *become* ~ (pasar a) hacer crítica personal; *make a ~ appearance* aparecer en persona; **2.** F nota *f* de sociedad; **per·son·al·i·ty** [~səˈnæliti] personalidad *f*; **per·son·al·ty** [ˈ~snlti] bienes *m/pl.* muebles; **per·son·ate** [ˈ~səneit] hacerse pasar por; *thea. etc.* hacer el papel de; **per·son·i·fi·ca·tion** [~sɔnifiˈkeiʃn] personificación *f*; **per·son·i·fy** [~ˈsɔnifai] personificar; **per·son·nel** [~səˈnel] personal *m*; ~ *management* relaciones *f/pl.* personales; ~ *manager* jefe *m* del personal.

per·spec·tive [pərˈspektiv] (*in* en) perspectiva *f*.

per·spi·ca·cious [pəːrspiˈkeiʃəs] □ perspicaz; **per·spi·cac·i·ty** [~ˈkæsiti] perspicacia *f*.

per·spi·ra·tion [pəːrspəˈreiʃn] transpiración *f*, sudor *m*; **per·spire** [pəːrˈspaiər] transpirar, sudar; **perˈspir·ing** sud(or)oso.

per·suade [pərˈsweid] persuadir, inducir (*to* a); convencer (*of* de, *that* de que).

per·sua·sion [pərˈsweiʒən] persuasiva *f*; (*act*) persuasión *f*; (*creed*) creencia *f*, secta *f*.

per·sua·sive [pərˈsweisiv] □ persuasivo.

pert [pəːrt] □ impertinente, respondón; fresco.

per·tain [pəːrˈtein]: ~ *to* (*concern*) referirse a, tener que ver con; (*belong to*) pertenecer con.

per·ti·na·cious [pəːrtiˈneiʃəs] □ pertinaz; **per·ti·nac·i·ty** [~ˈnæsiti] pertinacia *f*.

per·ti·nence, per·ti·nen·cy [ˈpəːrtinəns(i)] pertinencia *f*; ˈ**per·ti·nent** □ pertinente, oportuno.

pert·ness [ˈpəːrtnis] impertinencia *f*, frescura *f*.

per·turb [pərˈtəːrb] perturbar, inquietar; **per·tur·ba·tion** [pəːrtəːrˈbeiʃn] perturbación *f*.

pe·rus·al [pəˈruːzl] lectura *f* (cuidadosa); **pe·ruse** [pəˈruːz] leer (con atención), examinar.

Pe·ru·vi·an [pəˈruːviən] peruano *adj. a. su. m* (a *f*); ~ *bark* quina *f*.

per·vade [pəːrˈveid] extenderse por, difundirse por; impregnar, ocupar; **perˈva·sive** [~siv] penetrante; que lo impregna (*or* ocupa) todo.

per·verse [pərˈvəːrs] □ perverso; avieso; contumaz; **perˈverse·ness** = *perversity*; **perˈver·sion** perversión *f* (*a.* ⚕); **perˈver·si·ty** perversidad *f*; contumacia *f*.

per·vert 1. [pərˈvəːrt] pervertir; *taste etc.* estragar; *talent* emplear mal; **2.** [ˈpəːrvəːrt] ⚕ pervertido (a *f*) *m*; (*apostate*) apóstata *m/f*.

per·vi·ous [ˈpəːrviəs] permeable (*to* a).

pes·ky [ˈpeski] molesto.

pes·si·mism [ˈpesimizm] pesimismo *m*; ˈ**pes·si·mist** pesimista *m/f*; **pes·siˈmis·tic** □ pesimista.

pest [pest] *zo.* plaga *f*; insecto *m etc.* nocivo; *fig.* (*p.*) machaca *f*; (*th.*) molestia *f*; ~ *control* control *m* de los insectos; ˈ**pes·ter** molestar, acosar (con preguntas *etc.*), importunar.

pes·ti·cide [ˈpestisaid] insecticida *m*; **pes·tif·er·ous** [pesˈtifərəs] pestífero; **pes·ti·lence** [ˈpestiləns] pestilencia *f*; ˈ**pes·ti·lent** pestilente; *fig.* engorroso; **pes·ti·len·tial** [~ˈlenʃl] pestilencial.

pes·tle [ˈpesl] mano *f* de almirez.

pet[1] [pet]: *be in a ~* estar de mal humor, estar enojado.

pet[2] [~] **1.** animal *m* doméstico (*or* de casa); (*p.*) favorito (a *f*) *m*, persona *f* muy mimada; F *yes, my ~* sí, rico; F *he's rather a ~* es simpatiquísimo; **2.** *animal* doméstico, de casa, domesticado; (*favorite*) favorito; ~ *aversion* bestia *f* negra, pesadilla *f*; (*p.*) hincha *m/f*; ~ *name* nombre *m* cariñoso; diminutivo *m*; **3.** *v/t.* acariciar; (*spoil*) mimar; *v/i.* F besuquearse, sobarse.

pet·al [ˈpetl] pétalo *m*.

pe·ter [ˈpiːtər]: ~ *out* (*supply*) agotarse; ir disminuyendo; parar en nada; (*plan etc.*) no dar resultado.

pe·ti·tion [piˈtiʃn] **1.** petición *f*, memoria *f*, instancia *f*; **2.** suplicar, rogar (*for acc.*; *to inf.* que *subj.*); dirigir una instancia a; **peˈti·tion·er** suplicante *m/f*.

pet·rel [ˈpetrəl] petrel *m*, paiño *m*.

pet·ri·fac·tion [petriˈfækʃn] petrificación *f*.

pet·ri·fy [ˈpetrifai] petrificar(se) (*a. fig.*).

pe·tro·le·um [pi'troulijəm] petróleo *m*; ~ *jelly* vaselina *f*, jalea *f* de petróleo.
pe·trol·o·gy [pe'trɔlədʒi] petrología *f*.
pet·ti·coat ['petikout] enagua(s) *f*(*pl*.); (*slip*) combinación *f*; (*stiff*) falda *f* can-can; *attr*. ... de mujer(es).
pet·ti·fog·ger ['petifɔgər] picapleitos *m*; trapacista *m*/*f*; **pet·ti·fog·ging** ['petifɔgiŋ] insignificante; hecho *etc*. para entenebrecer (un asunto).
pet·ti·ness ['petinis] insignificancia *f* *etc*.
pet·tish ['petiʃ] □ malhumorado (de modo pueril).
pet·ty ['peti] □ insignificante, pequeño; despreciable; *p*. intolerante; que se para en menudencias; rencoroso; reparón; ~ *cash* gastos *m*/*pl*. menores; *v*. *larceny*; ~ *officer* suboficial *m* de marina; ~ *sessions pl*. *tribunal presidido por juez de paz*.
pet·u·lance ['petjuləns] mal humor *m*; **pet·u·lant** ['..lənt] □ malhumorado, enojadizo.
pew [pju:] **1.** banco *m* de iglesia; F asiento *m*; F *take a* ~! ¡siéntate!; **2.** *int*. ¡fo!
pew·ter ['pju:tər] (*attr*. de) peltre *m*; '~**·er** peltrero *m*.
pha·lanx ['fælæŋks] falange *f*.
phan·tasm ['fæntæzm] fantasma *m*; **phan·tas·ma·go·ri·a** [.~mə'gɔ:riə] fantasmagoría *f*.
phan·tom ['fæntəm] **1.** fantasma *m*; **2.** fantasmal.
phar·i·sa·ic, phar·i·sa·i·cal [færi'seiik(l)] □ farisaico.
Phar·i·see ['færisi:] fariseo *m*.
phar·ma·ceu·ti·cal [fɑ:rmə'su:tikl] farmacéutico; **phar·ma·ceu·tics** [fɑ:rmə'su:tiks] farmacéutica *f*; farmacia *f*; **phar·ma·cist** ['fɑ:rməsist] farmacéutico *m*; **phar·ma·col·o·gy** [~'kɔlədʒi] farmacología *f*; '**phar·ma·cy** farmacia *f*.
phar·ynx ['færiŋks] faringe *f*.
phase [feiz] fase *f*, etapa *f*.
pheas·ant ['feznt] faisán *m*.
phe·nom·e·nal [fi'nɔminl] □ fenomenal; **phe'nom·e·non** [~nən], *pl*. **phe'nom·e·na** [~nə] fenómeno *m*.
phew [fju:] ¡puf!; ¡caramba!
phi·al ['faiəl] frasco *m* (pequeño), redoma *f*.
phi·lan·der [fi'lændər] flirtear, mariposear; **phi'lan·der·er** tenorio *m*.
phil·an·throp·ic [filən'θrɔpik] □ filantrópico; **phi·lan·thro·pist** [fi'lænθrəpist] filántropo (a *f*) *m*; **phi'lan·thro·py** filantropía *f*.
phi·lat·e·list [fi'lætəlist] filatelista *m*/*f*; **phi'lat·e·ly** filatelia *f*.
phi·lip·pic [fi'lipik] filípica *f*.
Phi·lip·pine ['filipain] filipino *adj*. *a*. *su*. *m* (a *f*).
Phi·lis·tine ['filistain] filisteo (a *f*) *m*.
phil·o·log·i·cal [filə'lɔdʒikl] □ filológico; **phi·lol·o·gist** [fi'lɔlədʒist] filólogo *m*; **phi'lol·o·gy** filología *f*.
phi·los·o·pher [fi'lɔsəfər] filósofo *m*; ~'*s stone* piedra *f* filosofal; **phil·o·soph·ic, phil·o·soph·i·cal** [filə'sɔfik(l)] □ filosófico; **phi·los·o·phize** [fi'lɔsəfaiz] filosofar; **phi'los·o·phy** filosofía *f*; ~ *of life* filosofía *f* de la vida.
phil·ter, phil·tre ['filtər] filtro *m*.
phle·bi·tis [fli'baitis] flebitis *f*.
phlegm [flem] flema *f* (*a*. *fig*.); **phleg·mat·ic** [fleg'mætik] □ flemático.
Phoe·ni·cian [fi'niʃn] fenicio *adj*. *a*. *su*. *m* (a *f*).
phoe·nix ['fi:niks] fénix *m*.
phone [foun] F = *telephone*; ~ *call* llamada *f* telefónica.
pho·neme ['founi:m] fonema *m*.
pho·net·ic [fou'netik] □ fonético; **pho·ne·ti·cian** [founi'tiʃn] fonetista *m*/*f*; **pho·net·ics** [fou'netiks] fonética *f*; **phon·ics** ['founiks] fónica *f*.
pho·no·graph ['founəgræf] fonógrafo *m*.
pho·nol·o·gy [fou'nɔlədʒi] fonología *f*.
pho·n(e)**y** ['founi] *sl*. **1.** farsante *m*/*f*; persona *f* insincera; **2.** falso, postizo; sospechoso; insincero.
phos·phate ['fɔsfeit] fosfato *m*.
phos·pho·resce [fɔsfə'res] fosforecer; **phos·pho'res·cent** fosforescente; **phos·phor·ic** [~'fɔrik] fosfórico; **phos·pho·rous** ['~fərəs] fosforoso; **phos·pho·rus** ['~] fósforo *m*.
pho·to ['foutou] F foto *f*; '~**·cop·ier** fotocopiador *m*; fotóstato *m*; '~**·co·py** **1.** fotocopia *f*; **2.** fotocopiar; '~**·e'lec·tric 'cell** célula *f* fotoeléctrica; ~**·en·grav·ing** [~in'greiviŋ] fotograbado *m*; '~ **fin·ish** (resultado *m* comprobado por) fotocontrol *m*; *fig*. final *m* muy reñido; '~**·flash** flash *m*, magnesio *m*; **pho·to·gen·ic** [~'dʒenik] fotogénico (*a*. F).

pho·to·graph [ˈfoutəgræf] **1.** fotografía *f* (*foto*); **2.** fotografiar; **pho·tog·ra·pher** [fəˈtɔgrəfər] fotógrafo (a *f*) *m*; **pho·to·graph·ic** [foutəˈgræfik] □ fotográfico; **pho·tog·ra·phy** [fəˈtɔgrəfi] fotografía *f* (*arte*).

pho·to·gra·vure [foutəgrəˈvjur] fotograbado *m*, huecograbado *m*; **pho·tom·e·ter** [fouˈtɔmitər] fotómetro *m*; ˈ**pho·to·play** fotodrama *m*; **pho·to·stat** [ˈfoutoustæt] **1.** fotóstato *m*; **2.** fotostatar; **pho·toˈsyn·the·sis** fotosíntesis *f*; ˈ**pho·to·teˈleg·ra·phy** fototelegrafía *f*; **pho·to·type** [ˈ~taip] fototipo *m*; **pho·to·vol·ta·ic** [ˈ~vɔlˈteiik] fotovoltaico.

phrase [freiz] **1.** frase *f* (*a.* ♪); expresión *f*, locución *f*; **2.** expresar; **phra·se·ol·o·gy** [~iˈɔlədʒi] fraseología *f*.

phre·net·ic [friˈnetik] □ frenético.

phre·nol·o·gy [friˈnɔlədʒi] frenología *f*.

phthis·i·cal [ˈθaisikl] tísico; **phthi·sis** [ˈ~sis] tisis *f*.

phys·ic [ˈfizik] purgante *m*; † medicina *f*; ~*s sg*. física *f*; ˈ**phys·i·cal** □ físico; ~ *condition* estado *m* físico; ~ *culture* cultura *f* física; **phy·si·cian** [fiˈziʃn] médico *m*; **phys·i·cist** [ˈ~sist] físico *m*.

phys·i·og·no·my [fiziˈɔgnəmi] fisonomía *f*; **phys·i·og·ra·phy** [~ˈɔgrəfi] fisiografía *f*; **phys·i·ol·o·gy** [~ˈɔlədʒi] fisiología *f*.

phy·sique [fiˈziːk] físico *m*.

pi·an·ist [ˈpjænist, ˈpiənist] pianista *m/f*.

pi·a·no[1] [ˈpjænou] *adv*. piano, suavemente.

pi·an·o[2] [ˈpjænou, piˈɑːnou], *a*. **pi·an·o·for·te** [pjænouˈfɔːrti] piano(forte) *m*.

pi·az·za [piˈædʒə] plaza *f*; pórtico *m*, galería *f*.

pic·a·resque [pikəˈresk] picaresco.

pic·a·yune [pikəˈjuːn] **1.** persona *f* insignificante; bagatela *f*; **2.** de poca monta.

pick [pik] **1.** (~*axe*) (zapa)pico *m*, piqueta *f*; (*choice*) derecho *m* de elección; (*best*) lo más escogido, flor *f* y nata; F *it's your* ~ a ti te toca elegir; **2.** *v/t*. escoger (con cuidado); *bone* roer; *flower* coger; *fruit* recoger; *lock* forzar, abrir con ganzúa; *nose* hurgarse; *team* seleccionar; *teeth* mondarse; ~ *one's way* andar con mucho tiento; *v. bone*, *crow*, *pocket*; ~ *off paint etc.* separar, arrancar; (*shoot*) matar de un tiro; matar con tiros sucesivos; ~ *out* escoger; *color etc.* hacer resaltar; (*identify*) conocer, identificar; (*discern*) lograr ver; ~ *over* ir revolviendo y examinando; ~ *up* recoger *from floor etc.*; (*recover*) recobrar; (*casually*) saber (*or* encontrar *etc.*) por casualidad; (*learn*) lograr aprender; *radio*: captar; *v/i*. ~ *and choose* (hacer melindres al) escoger; F ~ *at*, F ~ *on* perseguir, criticar; ~ *up* ⚕ reponerse; ~**-a-back** [ˈ~əbæk] sobre los hombros; ˈ~**·axe** *v. pick* 1; **picked** [pikt] escogido; ˈ**pick·er** recogedor *m*.

pick·et [ˈpikit] **1.** estaca *f*; ⚔ piquete *m*; (guardia *f* de) vigilante(s) *m*(*pl*.) huelguista(s); **2.** *v/t*. *factory* cercar con un cordón de huelguistas; *v/i*. estar de guardia (los vigilantes huelguistas).

pick·ing [ˈpikiŋ] recolección *f of fruit etc.*; ~*s pl*. sobras *f/pl*.; (*profits*) ganancias *f/pl*.; lo robado *from theft*.

pick·le [ˈpikl] **1.** (*as condiment*) encurtido *m* (*a*. ~*s pl*.); (*fish, olives*) escabeche *m*; (*meat*) adobo *m*; (*salted*) salmuera *f*; F apuro *m*; lío *m*; F (*p*.) pillo *m*; **2.** escabechar; adobar; conservar; ~*d sl*. ajumado.

pick...: ˈ~**-me-up** F reconstituyente *m*; ⚕ tónico *m*; ˈ~**·pock·et** ratero *m*, carterista *m*; ˈ~**·up** pick-up *m*; ~ *arm* palanca *f*.

pic·nic [ˈpiknik] **1.** jira *f*, excursión *f* campestre, picnic *m*; *sl*. cosa *f* fácil; *go for a* ~ = **2.** ir de jira, merendar *etc.* en el campo.

pic·to·ri·al [pikˈtɔːriəl] □ pictórico; *magazine* gráfico, ilustrado.

pic·ture [ˈpiktʃər] **1.** cuadro *m*, pintura *f*; (*portrait*) retrato *m*; (*photo*) fotografía *f*; lámina *f in book*; *television*: cuadro *m*; (*spoken etc.*) descripción *f*; (*mental*) imagen *f*; visión *f* de conjunto; F *the* ~*s* el cine; *a* ~ *of health* la salud personificada; *the other side of the* ~ el reverso de la medalla; F *put a p. in the* ~ poner a una p. al corriente de una cosa; **2.** *attr*. *paper* ilustrado; *hat* de alas anchas; **3.** pintar; describir; ~ (*to o.s.*) imaginarse, representarse; ˈ~ **frame** marco *m*; ˈ~ **gal·ler·y** museo *m* de pintura; ˈ~**-go·er**

aficionado (a *f*) *m* al cine; '~ **post card** postal *f* ilustrada.
pic·tur·esque [piktʃə'resk] □ pintoresco.
pidg·in ['pidʒin] (*chino = business*): ~ *English lengua franca* (*inglés-chino*) *comercial del Lejano Oriente.*
pie [pai] (*sweet*) pastel *m*; (*meat etc.*) empanada *f*; *v. finger.*
pie·bald ['paibɔ:ld] pío, de varios colores; abigarrado.
piece [pi:s] **1.** (*fragment*) pedazo *m*, fragmento *m*; trozo *m*; ♪, *thea.*, ⚔, ⊕, *coin, chess etc.*: pieza *f*; *chess etc. a.* ficha *f*; F (*girl*) pizpireta *f*; *by the* ~ por pieza; *in* ~*s* hecho pedazos, roto; desmontado; *of a* ~ *with* de la misma clase que; conforme a; *two-shilling* ~ moneda *f* de 2 chelines; ~ *of advice* consejo *m*; ~ *of furniture* mueble *m*; ~ *of ground* terreno *m*; solar *m*; ~ *of news* noticia *f*; *break to* (*or in*) ~*s* hacer pedazos; *go to* ~*s fig.* sufrir un ataque de nervios; perder la salud; (*team*) desalentarse por completo; *take to* ~*s* desmontar; **2.** (*a.* ~ *together*) juntar (las piezas de); *fig.* atar cabos (e ir comprendiendo); '~**·meal** *adv.* a trozos; sin sistema fijo; '~**·work** trabajo *m* a destajo.
pied [paid] *animal* pío, de varios colores; *bird* manchado.
pier [pir] ⚠ estribo *m*, pila *f of bridge*; pilar *m*, columna *f*; ⚓ muelle *m*, malecón *m*, embarcadero *m*.
pierce [pirs] penetrar; taladrar, horadar, perforar; agujerear; pinchar; atravesar; **pierc·ing** ['pirsiŋ] □ penetrante, agudo.
pi·e·ty ['paiəti] piedad *f*, devoción *f*.
pif·fle ['pifl] F disparates *m/pl.*, tonterías *f/pl.*; **pif·fling** F de poca monta, insignificante.
pig [pig] cerdo *m*, puerco *m*, cochino *m*; F (*p.*) marrano *m*; *metall.* lingote *m*; *buy a* ~ *in a poke* cerrar un trato a ciegas; F *make a* ~ *of o.s.* comer demasiado; darse un atracón (*over* de).
pi·geon ['pidʒin] paloma *f*; '~**·hole 1.** casilla *f*; **2.** encasillar; clasificar; archivar (*fig.* en la memoria); (*shelve*) dar carpetazo a.
pig·ger·y ['pigəri] pocilga *f*.
pig-head·ed ['pig'hedid] □ terco, cabezudo.
pig i·ron ['pigaiərn] hierro *m* en lingotes.
pig·ment ['pigmənt] pigmento *m*.
pig·my ['pigmi] pigmeo *adj. a. su. m.*
pig...: '~**·skin** piel *f* de cerdo; *sl.* balón *m* de fútbol; ~**·sty** ['~stai] pocilga *f*, cochiquera *f* (*a. fig.*); '~**·tail** trenza *f*, coleta *f*.
pike [paik] ⚔ pica *f*; *ichth.* lucio *m*; '**pik·er** *sl.* cicatero *m*; cobarde *m*; '**pike staff:** *as plain as a* ~ claro como la luz del día.
pil·chard ['piltʃərd] sardina *f* arenque.
pile[1] [pail] **1.** montón *m*, pila *f*; mole *f of buildings*; F fortuna *f*; *phys.* (*atomic* ~) pila *f*; **2.** (*a.* ~ *up*) amontonar(se), apilar(se), acumular(se); F ~ *in*(*to*) entrar todos (en); ~ *on* ir aumentando; ~ *it on* exagerar.
pile[2] [~] ⚠ pilote *m*.
pile[3] [~] pelo *m of carpet*; pelillo *m of cloth.*
pile driv·er ['paildraivər] martinete *m*.
piles [pailz] *pl.* ⚕ almorranas *f/pl.*
pil·fer ['pilfər] ratear; '**pil·fer·ing** ratería *f*.
pil·grim ['pilgrim] peregrino (a *f*) *m*, romero (a *f*) *m*; '**pil·grim·age** peregrinación *f*, romería *f*; *make a* ~ ir en romería.
pill [pil] píldora *f*; *sl.* pelota *f*; *sl.* persona *f* molesta.
pil·lage ['pilidʒ] **1.** pillaje *m*; **2.** pillar.
pil·lar ['pilər] pilar *m*, columna *f*; *fig.* sostén *m*; *chase from* ~ *to post* no dejar a sol ni a sombra; '~ **box** buzón *m*.
pill·box ['pilbɔks] estuche *m* para píldoras; ⚔ fortín *m*.
pil·lion ['piljən]: ~ *seat* asiento *m* de atrás; *ride* ~ ir en el asiento de atrás.
pil·lo·ry ['piləri] **1.** picota *f*; **2.** *fig.* poner en ridículo, satirizar.
pil·low ['pilou] **1.** almohada *f*; **2.** apoyar sobre una almohada; servir de almohada a; '~ **case,** '~ **slip** funda *f* de almohada.
pi·lot ['pailət] **1.** ✈ piloto *m*; ⚓ práctico *m*; ~ *light mot.*, ✈ luz *f* de situación; mechero *m* encendedor *on stove*; ~ *plant* planta *f* piloto, fábrica *f* experimental; **2.** pilotar; *fig.* guiar; conducir.
pi·men·to [pi'mentou] pimienta *f*.
pimp [pimp] **1.** alcahuete *m*; **2.** alcahuetear.
pim·ple ['pimpl] grano *m*; '**pim·ply** granujoso.

pin [pin] **1.** alfiler *m*; ⊕ perno *m*; (*wooden*) clavija *f*; ~*ball* billar *m* romano; ~*s pl. sl.* piernas *f/pl.*; *like a new* ~ como una plata; *for 2* ~*s* por menos de nada; ~*s and needles* F hormiguillo *m*; **2.** prender con alfiler(es); sujetar (con perno *etc.*); ~ *down fig.* inmovilizar; *p.* obligar a que concrete; ~ *s.t. on s.o. fig.* acusar (falsamente) a uno de algo; ~ *up* fijar (con alfileres).
pin·a·fore [ˈpinəfɔːr] delantal *m* (de niña).
pin·cers [ˈpinsərz] *pl.* (*a pair of* ~ unas) tenazas *f/pl.*, pinzas *f/pl.*
pinch [pintʃ] **1.** pellizco *m with fingers*; *cooking*: pizca *f*; pulgarada *f of snuff*; *at a* ~ si es realmente necesario, en caso de apuro; *feel the* ~ pasar apuros; **2.** *v/t.* pellizcar *with fingers*; *finger* cogerse *in door etc.*; (*shoe*) apretar; *sl.* (*steal*) birlar, guindar; (*arrest*) prender; *v/i.* (*shoe*) apretar; *fig.* economizar; privarse de lo necesario; **pinched** [~t] aterido, chupado (*with cold* de).
pinch·beck [ˈpintʃbek] (*attr.* de) similor *m*.
pinch-hit [ˈpintʃhit] **1.** (*baseball*) batear de emergente; **2.** *sl.* servir de sustituto (*for* para).
pin cush·ion [ˈpinkuʃin] acerico *m*.
pine[1] [pain] ♀ pino *m*.
pine[2] [~] languidecer, consumirse (*a.* ~ *away*); ~ *for* penar por, anhelar.
pine...: ˈ**~·ap·ple** ananás *m*, piña *f*; ˈ**~ cone** piña *f*; ˈ**~ need·le** aguja *f* de pino; ˈ**~·wood** pinar *m*.
ping [piŋ] **1.** sonido *m* metálico; **2.** hacer un sonido metálico (como una bala); *mot.* picar (por autoencendido).
Ping-Pong [ˈpiŋpɔŋ] ping-pong *m*.
pin·ion [ˈpinjən] **1.** ⊕ piñón *m*; *poet.* ala *f*; **2.** *bird* cortar las alas a; *p.* atar los brazos de.
pink[1] [piŋk] **1.** ♀ clavel *m*, clavellina *f*; F *in the* ~ en perfecta salud; *in the* ~ *of* en perfecto estado de; **2.** rosado; color de rosa (*a. su. m*); *pol.* rojillo, procomunista.
pink[2] [~] *sew.* ondear, picar.
pin mon·ey [ˈpinmʌni] (dinero *m* para) alfileres *m/pl.*
pin·nace [ˈpinis] pinaza *f*.
pin·na·cle [ˈpinəkl] △ pináculo *m*, chapitel *m*; cumbre *f* (*a. fig.*).
pin...: ˈ**~·point** *fig.* indicar con toda precisión; ˈ**~·prick** alfilerazo *m*; *fig.* molestia *f* pequeña; ˈ**~·stripe** (pantalón *m*) a rayas.
pint [paint] pinta *f* (= *EE. UU.* 0,473, *British* 0,568 litros).
pin-up [ˈpinʌp] F foto *f* de muchacha guapa, pin-up *f*; *fig.* mujer *f* ideal.
pin·wheel [ˈpinwiːl] rueda *f* de fuego; *toy*: rehilandera *f*.
pi·o·neer [paiɔˈnir] **1.** explorador *m in country*; ⚔ zapador *m*; (*early settler*) colonizador *m*; iniciador *m*, promotor *m of scheme*; *be a* ~ *in the study of* ser de los primeros en estudiar *acc.*; **2.** *v/i.* explorar; *v/t. settlement etc.* preparar el terreno para; *scheme, study* iniciar, promover.
pi·ous [ˈpaiəs] □ piadoso, devoto.
pip[1] [pip] *vet.* pepita *f*.
pip[2] [~] ♀ pepita *f*; punto *m on card*; estrella *f on uniform*.
pip[3] [~] F (*defeat*) vencer; *exam* no aprobar; (*wound*) herir (con bala *etc.*).
pipe [paip] **1.** tubo *m*, caño *m*, cañería *f*; conducto *m*; cañón *m of organ*; ♪ caramillo *m*; pipa *f for tobacco*; ♪ ~*s pl.* gaita *f*; ~ *dream* esperanza *f* imposible; ~ *tobacco* tabaco *m* de pipa; **2.** *v/t.* conducir en cañerías *etc.*; decir en voz atiplada; *v/i.* tocar el caramillo; *sl.* ~ *down* callarse; F ~ *up* comenzar a hablar (inesperadamente); ˈ**~·clay** **1.** albero *m*; **2.** blanquear con albero; ˈ**~·line** (*oil*) oleoducto *m*; cañería *f*; ˈ**pip·er** flautista *m/f*; (*bag-*) gaitero *m*; *pay the* ~ cargar con los gastos.
pip·ing [ˈpaipiŋ] **1.** cañería(s) *f*(*pl.*); *sew.* ribete *m*; **2.:** ~ *hot* bien caliente.
pip·it [ˈpipit] bisbita *f*.
pip·pin [ˈpipin] camuesa *f*.
pip·squeak [ˈpipskwiːk] persona *f* sin importancia.
pi·quan·cy [ˈpiːkənsi] picante *m*; **pi·quant** [ˈpiːkənt] □ picante.
pique [piːk] **1.** pique *m*, resentimiento *m*; *be in a* ~ estar resentido; **2.** picar, herir; ~ *o.s. upon* enorgullecerse de.
pi·ra·cy [ˈpairəsi] piratería *f*; **pi·rate** [ˈ~rit] **1.** pirata *m*; ~ *radio* emisora *f* ilegal; **2.** pillar, robar; publicar fraudulentamente; ~(*d*) *edition* edición *f* furtiva (*or* pirateada); **pi·rat·i·cal** [paiˈrætikl] □ pirático.
pi·rou·ette [piruːˈet] **1.** pirueta *f*; **2.** piruetear.
piss [pis] *sl.* **1.** orina *f*; **2.** mear.

pis·til [ˈpistil] pistilo *m.*
pis·tol [ˈpistl] pistola *f*; revólver *m*; *sl.* persona *f* descarada.
pis·ton [ˈpistən] émbolo *m*, pistón *m*; ˈ~ **disˈplace·ment** cilindrada *f*; ˈ~ **ring** aro *m* (*or* segmento *m*) de pistón; ˈ~ **rod** vástago *m* de émbolo; ˈ~ **stroke** carrera *f* del émbolo.
pit [pit] **1.** hoyo *m*, hoya *f*, foso *m*; ⚒ mina *f* (de carbón); (*quarry*) cantera *f*; *thea.* parte *f* posterior del patio; boca *f of stomach*; *fig.* abismo *m*; (*danger*) escollo *m*; hueso *m of fruit*; **2.** marcar (con hoyas); (*match*) oponer (*against* a).
pit-(a-)pat [ˈpit(ə)ˈpæt]: *go* ~ latir rápidamente, hacer tictac.
pitch[1] [pitʃ] **1.** pez *f*, brea *f*; ~ *dark* negro como boca de lobo; **2.** embrear.
pitch[2] [~] **1.** (*throw*) lanzamiento *m*, echada *f*; ⚓ cabezada *f*; ♫ tono *m*; (*slope*) **grado** *m* **de inclinación; pendiente** *f of roof*; *sport*: **terreno** *m*, **campo** *m*; (*salesman's*) **puesto** *m*; *fig.* **punto** *m*, **grado** *m*, **extremo** *m*; **2.** *v/t.* **arrojar, echar; lanzar;** *tent* **armar;** ♪ **graduar el tono de;** *note* **entonar, dar;** F *tale* **contar;** ~*ed battle* **batalla** *f* **campal;** *v/i.* **caerse** (*into* **en**)**;** ⚓ **cabecear;** ~ *forward* **caer de cabeza;** F ~ *in* **ponerse a trabajar con afán; comenzar a comer;** F ~ *into* **arremeter contra, atacar vigorosamente;** F ~ *on* **elegir.**
pitch·er[1] [ˈpitʃər] cántaro *m*, jarro *m*.
pitch·er[2] [~] botador *m*, lanzador *m of baseball team.*
pitch·fork [ˈpitʃfɔːrk] **1.** horca *f*, tornadera *f*, bielda *f*; **2.**: *fig.* ~ *s.o. into s.t.* imponer inesperadamente a alguien una tarea.
pitch pine [ˈpitʃpain] pino *m* de tea.
pit·e·ous [ˈpitiəs] □ lastimero, lastimoso.
pit·fall [ˈpitfɔːl] *fig.* escollo *m*, trampa *f*.
pith [piθ] ⚘ médula *f* (*a. fig.*); *fig.* meollo *m*, jugo *m*; (*strength*) vigor *m*.
pit·head [ˈpithed] bocamina *f*.
pith·y [ˈpiθi] □ *fig.* sucinto, expresivo, lacónico.
pit·i·a·ble [ˈpitiəbl] □ enternecedor, digno de compasión.
pit·i·ful [ˈpitiful] □ lastimero, lastimoso; (*contemptible*) despreciable, lamentable.
pit·i·less [ˈpitilis] □ despiadado, implacable.
pit·tance [ˈpitəns] miseria *f*, renta *f* miserable; recursos *m/pl.* insuficientes.
pi·tu·i·tar·y [piˈtjuːitəri] **1.** pituitario; **2.** (*a.* ~ *gland*) glándula *f* pituitaria.
pit·y [ˈpiti] **1.** piedad *f*, compasión *f*; lástima *f*; *for* ~*'s sake!* ¡por piedad!; *it is a* ~ (*that*) es lástima (que *subj.*); *more's the* ~ desgraciadamente; *take* ~ *on* tener piedad de, apiadarse de; *what a* ~*!* ¡qué lástima!; **2.** tener piedad de, compadecer(se de).
piv·ot [ˈpivət] **1.** pivote *m*, gorrón *m*; *fig.* punto *m* central; **2.** *v/t.* montar sobre un pivote; *v/i.* girar (*on* sobre); *fig.* ~ *on* depender de; ˈ**piv·o·tal** central, fundamental.
pix·ie [ˈpiksi] duende *m*.
pix·i·lat·ed [ˈpiksəleitid] *sl.* chiflado; aturrulado.
pla·card [ˈplækɑːrd] **1.** cartel *m*, pancarta *f*; **2.** *wall* llenar de carteles.
pla·cate [pləˈkeit] aplacar.
place [pleis] **1.** sitio *m*, lugar *m*; (*enclosed*) local *m*; (*post*) puesto *m*, empleo *m*; (*rank*) lugar *m*, puesto *m*; (*seat*) plaza *f*; cubierto *m at table*; ~ *mat* estera *f* de cubierto; ♈ *to the third* ~ en milésimas; ~ *of worship* templo *m*, edificio *m* de culto; F *at my* ~ en mi casa; *in* ~ en su sitio; oportuno; *in his* ~ en su lugar; *in* ~ *of* en lugar de; *in the first* ~ en primer lugar; *out of* ~ fuera de (su) lugar; fuera de serie; fuera de propósito; *give* ~ *to* ceder el paso a; *it is not his* ~ *to* no le cumple a él *inf.*; *put s.o. in his* ~ bajarle los humos a uno; *know one's* ~ ser respetuoso; *take* ~ tener lugar; verificarse; **2.** colocar, poner; fijar; colocar *in post etc.*; (*recall*) acordarse bien de; (*identify*) identificar; *sport*: *be* ~*d* colocarse; ˈ~ **kick** puntapié *m* colocado; ˈ~ **name** topónimo *m*.
plac·id [ˈplæsid] □ plácido; **plaˈcid·i·ty** placidez *f*.
pla·gi·a·rism [ˈpleidʒiərizm] plagio *m*; ˈ**pla·gi·a·rist** plagiario (a *f*) *m*; ˈ**pla·gi·a·rize** plagiar.
plague [pleig] **1.** peste *f*, plaga *f*; **2.** plagar, infestar; *fig.* atormentar, molestar, acosar.
pla·guy [ˈpleigi] F engorroso.
plaice [pleis] platija *f*.
plaid [plæd] plaid *m*, manta *f* escocesa; *cloth* tartán *m*.

plain [plein] **1.** □ sencillo, llano; sin adornos; (*unmixed*) natural, puro; *face* sin atractivo, ordinario; *in ~ clothes* en traje de calle, de paisano; *in ~ English* hablando sin rodeos; *be ~ with* hablar claro a; *it is ~ that* es evidente que; *~ knitting* punto *m* de media; *~ truth* verdad *f* lisa y llana; **2.** *adv.* claro, claramente; **3.** llano *m*, llanura *f*; **'~·clothes man** agente *m* de policía que lleva traje de calle; **'plain·ness** llaneza *f*, franqueza *f*; falta *f* de atractivo *of face etc.*

plains·man ['pleinzmən] llanero *m*.

plain·song ['pleinsɔŋ] canto *m* llano.

plain·tiff ['pleintif] demandante *m/f*; **'plain·tive** □ dolorido, plañidero.

plait [plæt] **1.** trenza *f*; **2.** trenzar.

plan [plæn] **1.** proyecto *m*, plan *m*; ⚠ plano *m*; esquema *m*; programa *m*; *v.* five; **2.** *v/t.* planear, planificar; proyectar; idear; *~ned economy* economía *f* dirigida; *~ning board* comisión *f* planificadora; *v/i.* hacer proyectos (*for* para); *~ to* proponerse *inf.*, pensar *inf.*

plane[1] [plein] **1.** plano; **2.** ⩓ plano *m*; *fig.* nivel *m*, esfera *f*; ✈ avión *m*; ala *f*; ⊕ cepillo *m* (de carpintero); **3.** ⊕ acepillar; desbastar (*a. ~ down*).

plane[2] [~] ♀ plátano *m* (*a. ~ tree*).

plan·et ['plænit] planeta *m*.

plane-ta·ble ['pleinteibl] plancheta *f*.

plan·e·tar·i·um [plæni'teriəm] planetario *m*; **plan·e·tar·y** ['~təri] planetario.

pla·nim·e·try [plæ'nimitri] planimetría *f*.

plan·ish ['plæniʃ] aplanar.

plank [plæŋk] **1.** tablón *m*, tabla *f* (gruesa); *~s pl.* tablaje *m*; *mst Am. parl.* artículo *m* (de un programa político); **2.** entablar, entarimar; F *~ down* tirar, colocar firmemente; **'plank·ing** tablaje *m*; ⚓ maderamen *m* de cubierta.

plan·ning ['plæniŋ] planificación *f*.

plant [plænt] **1.** ♀ planta *f* (*a.* ⊕); ⊕ instalación *f*, maquinaria *f*; ⚡ grupo *m* electrógeno; (*factory*) fábrica *f*; *sl.* estratagema *f* para incriminar a una p.; **2.** plantar; (*sow*) sembrar; sentar, colocar; *blow* plantar; *sl. ~ a th. on a p.* ocultar algo para incriminar a una p.

plan·tain ['plæntin] llantén *m*.

plan·ta·tion [plæn'teiʃn] plantación *f of tea, sugar etc.*; vega *f S.Am. of tobacco*; arboleda *f of trees*; **plant·er** ['plæntər] plantador *m*; colono *m*.

plaque [plæk] placa *f*.

plas·ma ['plæzmə] plasma *m*.

plas·ter ['plæstər] **1.** yeso *m*; ⚠ argamasa *f*; (*layer*) enlucido *m*; ⚕ emplasto *m*; (*adhesive*) esparadrapo *m*; *~cast* vaciado *m*; ⚕ tablilla *f* de yeso; *~ of Paris* yeso *m* mate; **2.** enyesar, enlucir; ⚕ emplastar; *fig.* cubrir, llenar (*with* de); *posters* pegar; *sl. ~ed* ajumado; **'plas·ter·er** enlucidor *m*, yesero *m*.

plas·tic ['plæstik] **1.** plástico; *~ surgery* cirugía *f* estética (*or* plástica); **2.** plástico *m*; **plas·ti·cine** ['~tisi:n] plasticina *f*; **plas·tic·i·ty** [~'tisiti] plasticidad *f*.

plate [pleit] **1.** plato *m*; (*plaque*) placa *f*; ⊕ lámina *f*, chapa *f*, plancha *f*; (*silver*) vajilla *f* de plata; *typ.* lámina *f*; *phot.* placa *f*; (*a. dental ~*) (placa *f* de la) dentadura *f* postiza; *racing*: premio *m*; *~ glass* vidrio *m* cilindrado; F *hand s.o. s.t. on a ~* servirle algo a alguien en bandeja; F *have a lot on one's ~* estar muy ocupado; **2.** planchear, chapear; niquelar *etc.*

pla·teau [plæ'tou] meseta *f*.

plate·ful ['pleitful] plato *m*.

plate...: **'~ glass** vidrio *m* cilindrado; **'~ hold·er** *phot.* portaplacas *m*; **'~ lay·er** peón *m* (ferroviario).

plat·form ['plætfɔ:rm] plataforma *f*; tablado *m*; tribuna *f at meeting*; 🚂 andén *m*; *esp. Am. pol.* programa *m* electoral.

plat·ing ['pleitiŋ] enchapado *m*; capa *f* metálica.

plat·i·num ['plætinəm] platino *m*; *~ blonde* rubia *f* platino.

plat·i·tude ['plætitju:d] lugar *m* común, perogrullada *f*, platitud *f*; **plat·i'tu·di·nous** □ lleno de lugares comunes *etc.*

pla·toon [plə'tu:n] pelotón *m*.

plat·ter ['plætər] fuente *f*; *sl.* ♪ disco *m* (fonográfico).

plau·dits ['plɔ:dits] aplausos *m/pl.*

plau·si·ble ['plɔ:zəbl] □ especioso, aparente; *p.* bien hablado pero nada confiable.

play [plei] **1.** juego *m* (*a.* ⊕), recreo *m*; *thea.* obra *f* dramática, pieza *f*; *fair (foul)* ~ juego *m* limpio (sucio); ~ *on words* retruécano *m*, juego *m* de palabras; *sport*: *in* ~ en juego; *out of* ~ fuera de juego; *come into* ~ entrar en juego; *go to the* ~ ir al teatro; *make great* ~ *with* recalcar, insistir en; **2.** *v/i.* jugar (*at* a); divertirse; ♪ tocar; *thea.* representar; (*fountain*) correr; (*light*) reverberar; ~ *fast and loose with* portarse de modo irresponsable con; ~ *for time* tratar de ganar tiempo; ~ (*up*)*on* valerse de; ~ *up to* hacer la pelotilla a; *v/t. card* jugar; *game, cards etc.* jugar a; *opponent* jugar con(tra); *player* incluir *in team*; ♪ tocar; *thea. play* representar, poner; *part* hacer; *fig.* desempeñar; *character* hacer el papel de; *trick* hacer (*on* a); *fish* dejar que se canse; *hose* dirigir; ~ *back* repetir (lo grabado); *v. ball*; ~ *off A against B* oponer A a B, *be* ~*ed out* estar agotado (*a. fig.*); F ~ *up* burlarse de (la autoridad de); **'~·back** ⚡ lectura *f*; **'~·bill** cartel *m*; **'~·boy** señorito *m* amante de los placeres; **'play·er** jugador (-a *f*) *m*; *thea.* actor *m*, actriz *f*; ♪ músico (a *f*) *m*; ~ *piano* autopiano *m*; **'play fel·low** compañero *m* de juego; **play·ful** ['~ful] □ juguetón; *remark* dicho en broma.

play...: **'~·go·er** aficionado (a *f*) *m* al teatro; **'~·ground** patio *m* de recreo; **'~·house** teatro *m*; casita *f* de muñecas.

play·ing...: **'~ card** carta *f*; **'~ field** campo *m* de deportes.

play...: **'~·mate** compañero (a *f*) *m* de juego; **'~-off** (partido *m* de) desempate *m*; **'~·pen** parque *m* (de niño), corral *m*; **'~·thing** juguete *m* (*a. fig.*); **'~·time** hora *f* de recreo; **'~·wright** dramaturgo *m*.

plea [pli:] pretexto *m*, disculpa *f*; ⚖ (alegato *m* de) defensa *f*; contestación *f* a la demanda; (*request*) petición *f* (*for* a favor de); *put in a* ~ *for p.* hablar por; *th.* pedir.

plead [pli:d] *v/i.* suplicar (*with acc.*), rogar (*with s.o. for* a uno que conceda); ⚖ abogar; ~ *guilty* confesarse culpable; **'plead·er** ⚖ abogado *m*; **'plead·ing** (*a.* ~*s pl.*) súplicas *f/pl.*; ⚖ alegatos *m/pl.*

pleas·ant ['pleznt] □ agradable; *surprise etc.* grato; *manner, style* ameno; *p.* simpático; **'pleas·ant·ry** chiste *m*, dicho *m* gracioso.

please [pli:z] *v/i.* gustar; dar satisfacción; ~ *tell me* haga Vd. el favor de decirme, dígame por favor; *as you* ~ como Vd. quiera; *if you* ~! *iro.* ¡fíjese!; *v/t.* gustar, dar gusto a, caer en gracia a; ~ *o.s.* hacer únicamente lo que uno quiere; ~ *yourself!* como Vd. quiera; *be* ~*d* estar contento; *be* ~*d to* complacerse en; *we are* ~*d to inform you* nos es grato informarle; *I am* ~*d to meet you* tengo mucho gusto en conocerle; *be* ~*d with* estar satisfecho de; **'pleased** alegre; contento; **pleas·ing** ['pli:ziŋ] □ agradable, grato.

pleas·ur·a·ble ['pleʒərəbl] □ agradable, deleitoso.

pleas·ure ['pleʒər] placer *m*; gusto *m*; deleite *m*; (*will*) voluntad *f*; *it is a* ~ es un placer; *with (great)* ~ con (mucho) gusto; ~ *trip* viaje *m* de recreo; *take* ~ *in* deleitarse en *su.*, *inf.*; *b.s.* gozarse en *inf.*

pleat [pli:t] **1.** pliegue *m*; **2.** plegar, plisar.

ple·be·ian [pli'bi:ən] plebeyo *adj.* [*a. su. m* (a *f*).]

pleb·i·scite ['plebisit] plebiscito *m*.

plebs [plebz] plebe *f*.

pledge [pledʒ] **1.** (*security*) prenda *f* (*a. fig.*); (*promise*) promesa *f*; (*toast*) brindis *m*; *as a* ~ *of* en señal de; F *sign the* ~ jurar abstenerse del alcohol; **2.** (*pawn*) empeñar; (*promise*) prometer; (*toast*) brindar por.

ple·na·ry ['pli:nəri] plenario.

plen·i·po·ten·ti·ar·y [plenipə'tenʃəri] plenipotenciario *adj. a. su. m.*

plen·i·tude ['plenitju:d] plenitud *f*.

plen·te·ous ['plentiəs] □, **plen·ti·ful** ['plentiful] □ copioso, abundante.

plen·ty ['plenti] **1.** abundancia *f*; *horn of* ~ cuerno *m* de abundancia; cornucopia *f*; *in* ~ en abundancia; *we have* ~ *of* tenemos bastante..., tenemos una cantidad suficiente de; **2.** F: *know* ~ saber (lo) bastante; ~ *of people do* hay muchos que lo hacen; **3.** F completamente; mucho; muy.

ple·o·nasm ['pli:ənæzm] pleonasmo *m*.

pleth·o·ra ['pleθərə] plétora *f*; **ple·thor·ic** [ple'θɔrik] □ pletórico.

pleu·ri·sy ['plurisi] pleuresía *f*.

ple·xi·glass ['pleksiglæs] plexiglás *m*.

pli·a·ble [ˈplaiəbl] □, **pli·ant** [ˈplaiənt] □ flexible, plegable; *fig.* dócil, manejable.
pli·ers [ˈplaiərz] *pl.* (*a pair of* ~ unos) alicates *m/pl.*
plight[1] [plait] empañar.
plight[2] [~] apuro *m*, aprieto *m*; condición *f* (inquietante), situación *f* (difícil).
plinth [plinθ] plinto *m.*
plod [plɔd] (*a.* ~ *on*, ~ *one's way*) avanzar (*or* caminar) laboriosamente; trabajar laboriosamente (*away at* en); ˈ**plod·der** estudiante *m/f etc.* más aplicado que brillante; ˈ**plod·ding** □ perseverante, laborioso.
plop [plɔp] **1.** ¡paf!; **2.** caer dejando oír un paf.
plot[1] [plɔt] ✓ parcela *f*, terreno *m*; (*building*) solar *m*; cuadro *m* (de hortalizas *etc.*).
plot[2] [~] **1.** complot *m*, conspiración *f*; *thea. etc.* argumento *m*, trama *f*, intriga *f*; **2.** *v/t. course etc.* trazar; *downfall etc.* tramar, maquinar; *v/i.* conspirar, intrigar (*to* para); ˈ**plot·ter** conspirador (-a *f*) *m*, conjurado (a *f*) *m.*
plough [plau] = *plow.*
plov·er [ˈplʌvər] chorlito *m.*
plow [plau] **1.** arado *m*; **2.** *v/t.* arar; *fig.* surcar; *univ. sl.* dar calabazas a, escabechar; ⚜ ~ *back* reinvertir; ~ *up* arrancar con el arado; *v/i.* arar; *fig.* ~ *through snow etc.* abrirse con dificultad paso por; *book* leer con dificultad; ˈ**~·ing** arada *f*; ˈ**~·man** arador *m*; ˈ**~·share** reja *f* del arado.
ploy [plɔi] maniobra *f*; artimaña *f.*
pluck [plʌk] **1.** valor *m*, ánimo *m*; **2.** *v/t.* coger; arrancar; *bird* desplumar; *guitar* puntear; *v. courage*; *v/i.*: ~ *at* tirar de, dar un tirón a; **pluck·y** [ˈplʌki] □ valiente, animoso.
plug [plʌg] **1.** tapón *m*, taco *m*; tampón *m* (*a.* ⚕); *mot.* bujía *f*; ⚡ enchufe *m*; ⚡ (*wall*) toma *f*; (*fire*) boca *f* de agua; *sl.* anuncio *m* (*or* publicidad *f*) incidental; **2.** *v/t.* tapar, obturar; *tooth* empastar; *sl.* (*strike*) pegar; *sl.* (*shoot*) pegar un tiro a; *radio etc. sl.* dar publicidad incidental a; machacar en; ⚡ ~ *in* enchufar; *v/i. sl.* (*a.* ~ *away*) trabajar con ahinco (*at* en), seguir trabajando a pesar de todo; ˈ**~-in** enchufable.
plum [plʌm] ciruela *f*; (*a.* ~ *tree*) ciruelo *m*; F lo mejor; (*post*) pingüe destino *m.*
plum·age [ˈplu:midʒ] plumaje *m.*
plumb [plʌm] **1.** plomada *f*; **2.** *adj.* vertical, a plomo; **3.** *adv.* verticalmente, a plomo; F completamente; **4.** *fig.* sond(e)ar; **plum·ba·go** [~ˈbeigou] plombagina *f*; **plumb·er** [ˈ~mər] fontanero *m*; **plum·bic** [ˈ~mbik] plúmbico; **plumb·ing** [ˈ~miŋ] (*craft*) fontanería *f*; (*piping*) instalación *f* de cañerías; ˈ**plumb-line** cuerda *f* de plomada.
plume [plu:m] pluma *f*; penacho *m on helmet, of smoke.*
plum·met [ˈplʌmit] **1.** plomada *f*; **2.** caer a plomo.
plump[1] [plʌmp] **1.** rechoncho, rollizo; *fowl etc.* gordo; **2.** engordar (*v/i. a. v/t.*); hinchar(se).
plump[2] [~] **1.** dejar(se) caer pesadamente; ~ *for* optar por; **2.** *adv.* de lleno.
plump·ness [ˈplʌmpnis] gordura *f.*
plum pud·ding [ˈplʌmˈpudiŋ] pudín *m* inglés (*de Navidad*).
plun·der [ˈplʌndər] **1.** botín *m*, pillaje *m*; **2.** saquear, pillar; ˈ**plun·der·er** saqueador *m.*
plunge [plʌndʒ] **1.** zambullida *f*; salto *m*; **2.** zambullir(se); sumergir(se); *fig.* arrojar(se); precipitar(se); hundir(se) *into grief etc.*; *dagger* hundir; (*horse*) corcovear; ⚓ cabecear; **plung·er** [ˈplʌndʒər] émbolo *m.*
plu·per·fect [ˈplu:ˈpə:rfikt] pluscuamperfecto *m.*
plu·ral [ˈplurəl] plural *adj. a. su. m*; **plu·ral·i·ty** [~ˈræliti] pluralidad *f.*
plus [plʌs] **1.** *prp.* más, y; **2.** *adj.* ⚡ positivo; adicional; F y algo más, y pico; **~-fours** [ˈ~ˈfɔ:rz] *pl.* pantalones *m/pl.* holgados de media pierna.
plush [plʌʃ] **1.** felpa *f*; **2.** F lujoso, de buen tono.
plu·toc·ra·cy [plu:ˈtɔkrəsi] plutocracia *f*; **plu·to·crat** [ˈ~təkræt] plutócrata *m/f.*
plu·to·ni·um [plu:ˈtouniəm] plutonio *m.*
plu·vi·om·e·ter [plu:viˈɔmitər] pluviómetro *m.*
ply [plai] **1.**: *three* ~ de tres capas; *wool* de tres cordones; **2.** *v/t. tool* manejar, menear (vigorosamente); *trade* ejercer; *p.* acosar, importunar *with questions*; ofrecer repetidas veces; *v/i.*: ~ *between* hacer el servi-

cio entre; '~·**wood** madera *f* contrachapeada, panel *m*.
pneu·mat·ic [nju'mætik] □ neumático; ~ *drill* perforadora *f*, martillo *m* picador; ~ *tire* neumático *m*; llanta *f*.
pneu·mo·ni·a [nju'mounjə] pulmonía *f*.
poach[1] [poutʃ] *v/t. a. v/i.* cazar (*or* pescar) en vedado; *fig.* cazar en finca ajena.
poach[2] [~] *egg* escalfar.
poach·er ['poutʃər] cazador *m* furtivo; '**poach·ing** caza *f* furtiva.
pock·et ['pɔkit] **1.** bolsillo *m*; *fig.* bolsa *f* (*a.* ⚔, *geol.*), cavidad *f*; ✈ bolsa *f* de aire; *be in* ~ salir ganando; *be out of* ~ salir perdiendo; *pick s.o.'s* ~ robar la cartera *etc.* a alguien; **2.** embolsar; *b.s.* apropiarse; **3.** *attr.* ... de bolsillo; '~·**book** (*purse*) bolsa *f*; cartera *f*, portamonedas *m*; '~ '**cal·cu·la·tor** calculadora *f* de bolsillo; '~·**knife** cortaplumas *m*; '~·**mon·ey** dinero *m* para pequeños gastos personales; '~-**size** de bolsillo.
pock·marked ['pɔkmɑːrkt] picado de viruelas; *fig.* marcado de hoyos.
pod [pɔd] vaina *f*.
podg·y ['pɔdʒi] F gordinflón.
po·di·um ['poudiəm] ▲ podio *m*.
po·em ['pouim] poesía *f*, poema *m*.
po·et ['pouit] poeta *m*, poetisa *f*; **po·et·as·ter** [~'tæstər] poetastro *m*; '**po·et·ess** poetisa *f*; **po·et·ic, po·et·i·cal** [pou'etik(l)] □ poético; ~ *justice* justicia *f* poética; **po'et·ics** *pl.* poética *f*; '**po·et·ry** poesía *f*; *attr.* de poesía.
pog·rom ['pɔgrəm] pogrom(o) *m*, persecución *f* (antisemítica).
poign·an·cy ['pɔinənsi] patetismo *m*; intensidad *f*; '**poign·ant** □ conmovedor, patético; intenso, agudo.
point [pɔint] **1.** punto *m* (*a. sport, typ.*, ⚓; = *place, time*); (*sharp*) punta *f*; puntilla *f of pen*; *geog.* punta *f*, cabo *m*; cuarta *f of compass*; (*objective*) propósito *m*, finalidad *f*; gracia *f*, lo esencial *of joke*; rasgo *m of character*; ⚡ enchufe *m*, toma *f*; 🚂 ~*s pl.* agujas *f/pl.*; *the* ~ *is that* lo importante es que; *there is no* ~ *in ger.* no vale la pena *inf.*; ~ *of order* cuestión *f* de procedimiento; ~ *of view* punto *m* de vista; *in* ~ *of* en cuanto a; *in* ~ *of fact* en realidad; *off the* ~ fuera de propósito; *on* ~*s boxing*: por puntos; *up to a* ~ hasta cierto punto; *be beside the* ~ no venir al caso; *be on the* ~ *of* estar a punto de; *carry one's* ~ salirse con la suya; *come to the* ~ ir al grano, dejarse de historias; *keep to the* ~ no salir del tema; *make a* ~ *of ger.* insistir en *inf.*, no dejar de *inf.*; *make the* ~ *that* hacer ver que; *see the* ~ caer en la cuenta; *I do not see the* ~ *of ger.* no creo que sea necesario *inf.*; *speak to the* ~ hablar al caso; *stretch a* ~ hacer una excepción; **2.** *v/t.* (*sharpen*) afilar, aguzar; *pencil* sacar punta a; *gun etc.* apuntar (*at* a); ~ *a finger at* señalar con el dedo; ~ *out* indicar, señalar; advertir (*that* que); *v/i.*: *it* ~*s west* está orientado hacia el oeste; ~ *at* señalar (con el dedo); ~ *to* señalar; indicar (*a. fig.*); '~-'**blank** (*adj.* hecho *etc.*) a quemarropa (*a. fig.*); '**point·ed** □ puntiagudo; *remark* inequívoco; lleno de intención; '**point·er** indicador *m on gauge*; *fig.* indicación *f* (*to* de); (*dog*) perro *m* de muestra; '**point·less** □ inútil; '**point-to-'point** *carrera de caballos a través del campo*.
poise [pɔiz] **1.** equilibrio *m*; aplomo *m*; confianza *f* en sí mismo; **2.** *v/t.* equilibrar; balancear; *be* ~*d* estar suspendido; cernerse; *be* ~*d to inf.* estar ya en condiciones de *inf.*
poi·son ['pɔizn] **1.** veneno *m* (*a. fig.*); **2.** *attr.* venenoso; ~ *gas* gas *m* asfixiante; ~ *pen letter* carta *f* calumniosa; **3.** envenenar (*a. fig.*); '**poi·son·er** envenenador (-a *f*) *m*; '**poi·son·ing** envenenamiento *m*; '**poi·son·ous** □ venenoso; F pésimo.
poke [pouk] **1.** empuje *m*, empujón *m*; codazo *m*; hurgonazo *m of fire*; **2.** *v/t.* empujar; *hole* hacer a empujones; *fire* hurgar, atizar; introducir (*into* en); ~ *fun at* burlarse de; ~ *one's nose into* meterse en; *v/i.*: ~ *about*, ~ *around* andar buscando (vagamente).
pok·er[1] ['poukər] *approx.* atizador *m*, badila *f*.
po·ker[2] [~] *cards*: póker *m*, póquer *m*; ~ *face* cara *f* impasible.
pok·y ['pouki] lerdo; perezoso; *room* muy pequeño, mezquino.
po·lar ['poulər] polar; ~ *bear* oso *m* blanco; **po·lar·i·ty** [pou'læriti] polaridad *f*; **po·lar·i·za·tion** [poulərai'zeiʃn] polarización *f*; '**po·lar·ize** polarizar.
Pole[1] [poul] polaco (a *f*) *m*.

pole² [~] *geog.*, ⚡ *etc.* polo *m.*
pole³ [~] *medida de longitud* (= 5,029 *m.*); palo *m*, vara *f* larga; (*flag*) asta *f*; (*tent*) mástil *m*; (*telegraph*) poste *m*; (*vaulting etc.*) pértiga *f*; *sl. up the* ~ en un aprieto; chiflado; **ˈ~·ax(e)** desnucar; **ˈ~·cat** turón *m*; mofeta *f*.
po·lem·ic [pɔˈlemik] **1.** (*a.* **poˈlem·i·cal** □) polémico; **2.** (*a.* **po·lem·ics** *pl.*) polémica *f*.
pole·star [ˈpoulstɑːr] estrella *f* polar; *fig.* norte *m*.
pole vault [ˈpoulvɔːlt] salto *m* con pértiga.
po·lice [pəˈliːs] **1.** policía *f*; ~ *court* tribunal *m* de policía; ~ *force* (cuerpo *m* de) policía *f*; **2.** *frontier* vigilar, patrullar; *area* mantener servicio de policía en; **ˈ~·man** guardia *m*, policía *m*; agente *m* de policía; **ˈ~ re·cord** ficha *f*; **ˈ~ state** estado *m* policial; **ˈ~ sta·tion** comisaría *f*; **ˈ~·wom·an** policía *m* femenino.
pol·i·cy [ˈpɔlisi] política *f*; programa *m* político; normas *f*/*pl.* de conducta *of newspaper etc.*; (*insurance*) póliza *f*; ~ *holder* tenedor (-a *f*) *m* de póliza.
po·li·o(·my·e·li·tis) [ˈpouliou(maiəˈlaitis)] polio(mielitis) *f*.
Pol·ish [ˈpouliʃ] polaco *adj. a. su. m.*
pol·ish [ˈpɔliʃ] **1.** (*shine*) lustre *m*, brillo *m*, bruñido *m*; (*act*) pulimento *m*; (*shoe*) betún *m*; (*floor*) cera *f* de lustrar; *fig.* finura *f*; perfección *f*; **2.** *floor etc.* encerar, sacar brillo a; *pans etc.* abrillantar; *shoes* limpiar; *silver etc.* pulir; ⊕ pulimentar; *fig.* (*a.* ~ *up*) pulir, limar; F ~ *off* acabar con; **ˈpol·ished** *fig.* fino, elegante, acabado; **ˈpol·ish·er** (*p.*) pulidor (-a *f*) *m*; (*machine*) enceradora *f*; **ˈpol·ish·ing** **1.** el pulir *etc.*; **2.** *attr.* de lustrar *etc.*; ~ *machine* enceradora *f*.
po·lite [pəˈlait] □ cortés, atento, fino; *society* bueno, culto; **poˈlite·ness** cortesía *f etc.*
pol·i·tic [ˈpɔlitik] □ prudente, aconsejable; *body* ~ el estado; **po·lit·i·cal** [pəˈlitikl] □ político; **pol·i·ti·cian** [pɔliˈtiʃn] político *m*; *b.s.* politiquero *m*; **pol·i·tics** [ˈpɔlitiks] política *f*; *v. party*; **pol·i·ty** [ˈpɔliti] gobierno *m*; estado *m*.
pol·ka [ˈpɔlkə] polca *f*; diseño *m* de puntos.
poll [poul] **1.** (*election*) votación *f*, elección *f*; (*total votes*) votos *m*/*pl.*; (*public-opinion* ~) organismo *m* de sondaje; (*inquiry*) encuesta *f*, sondeo *m*; *go to the* ~(s) ir a votar; *take a* ~ hacer una encuesta; **2.** *v*/*t. votes* recibir; *cattle* descornar; *v*/*i.* recibir (muchos, *10.000 etc.*) votos.
pol·lard [ˈpɔlərd] **1.** árbol *m* desmochado; **2.** desmochar; **3.** desmochado.
pol·len [ˈpɔlin] polen *m*; **pol·lin·ate** [ˈpɔlineit] fecundar (con polen).
poll·ing [ˈpouliŋ] votación *f*; **ˈ~ booth** caseta *f* de votar; **ˈ~ day** día *m* de elecciones; **ˈ~ place, ˈ~ sta·tion** urnas *f*/*pl.* electorales.
poll tax [ˈpoultæks] capitación *f*.
pol·lu·tant [pəˈluːtənt] contaminante *m*; **pol·lute** [pəˈluːt] *water etc.* contaminar, ensuciar; *fig.* corromper; **polˈlu·tion** contaminación *f*; corrupción *f*.
po·lo [ˈpoulou] polo *m*.
pol·troon [pɔlˈtruːn] cobarde *m*/*f*.
po·lyg·a·mist [pəˈligəmist] polígamo (a *f*) *m*; **po·lyg·a·my** [pəˈligəmi] poligamia *f*; **pol·y·glot** [ˈpɔliglɔt] poligloto *adj. a. su. m* (a *f*); **pol·y·gon** [ˈ~gən] polígono *m*; **po·lyg·o·nal** [pɔˈligənl] poligonal; **pol·y·phon·ic** [~ˈfɔnik] □ polifónico; **pol·yp** [ˈ~ip], **pol·y·pus** [ˈ~pəs] pólipo *m*; **pol·y·syl·lab·ic** [ˈpɔlisiˈlæbik] □ polisílabo; **pol·y·syl·la·ble** [ˈ~siləbl] polisílabo *m*; **pol·y·tech·nic** [~ˈteknik] escuela *f* de formación profesional; **pol·y·the·ism** [ˈ~θiizm] politeísmo *m*; **po·ly·thene** [ˈ~θiːn] politene *m*.
po·made [pəˈmeid], **po·ma·tum** [pəˈmeitəm] pomada *f*.
pome·gran·ate [ˈpɔmigrænit] granada *f*.
pom·mel [ˈpʌml] **1.** pomo *m*; **2.** apuñear, dar de puñetazos.
pomp [pɔmp] pompa *f*; **pom·pos·i·ty** [pɔmˈpɔsiti] pomposidad *f etc.*; **ˈpomp·ous** □ pomposo; *language* hinchado, rimbombante.
pond [pɔnd] charca *f*; (*artificial*) estanque *m*; (*fish*) vivero *m*.
pon·der [ˈpɔndər] *v*/*t. a. v*/*i.* ponderar, considerar con especial cuidado; meditar (*on*, *over acc.*); **ˈpon·der·ous** □ pesado; laborioso.
pone [poun] pan *m* de maíz.
pon·iard [ˈpɔnjərd] *lit.* puñal *m*.
pon·tiff [ˈpɔntif] pontífice *m*; **ponˈtif·i·cal** □ pontificio, pontifi-

cal; **pon'tif·i·cate 1.** [~kit] pontificado *m*; **2.** [~keit] pontificar.
pon·toon [pɔn'tuːn] pontón *m*; *cards*: veintiuna *f*; ~ *bridge* puente *m* de pontones.
po·ny ['pouni] jaca *f*, caballito *m*, poney *m*; F chuleta *f*.
pooch [puːtʃ] *sl.* perro *m*.
poo·dle ['puːdl] perro *m* de lanas.
pooh [puː] ¡bah!, ¡qué va!
pooh-pooh [puː'puː] rechazar con desdén; negar importancia a.
pool [puːl] **1.** charca *f*; (*artificial*) estanque *m*; (*swimming*) piscina *f*; pozo *m*, remanso *m in river*; charco *m of spilt liquid*; *billiards*: trucos *m/pl.*; *cards etc.*: polla *f*; (*football*) quinielas *f/pl.*; *fig.* mancomunidad *f*, fusión *f* de intereses; ⚕ fondo *m* común; **2.** *resources* juntar, mancomunar; '**~·room** sala *f* de trucos; '**~·table** mesa *f* de trucos.
poop [puːp] popa *f*.
poor [pur] □ pobre; *quality* malo, bajo; *spirit* mezquino; *the* ~ los pobres; *be in* ~ *health* tener mala salud; '**~·box** cepo *m* para los pobres; '**~·house** asilo *m* de los pobres; '**~ law** *ley acerca de los menesterosos*; '**poor·ly 1.** *adj.* enfermo; **2.** *adv.* pobremente; mal.
pop[1] [pɔp] **1.** ligera detonación *f*; taponazo *m of cork*; ruido *m* seco *of fastener etc.*; F gaseosa *f*; **2.** *v/t.* F poner (rápidamente); *sl.* empeñar; ~ *corn* hacer palomitas de maíz; F ~ *the question* declararse; *v/i.* estallar (con ligera detonación); reventar; F ~ *in* entrar de sopetón, dar un vistazo; F ~ *out* salir un momento; F ~ *up* aparecer inesperadamente; **3.** ¡pum!
pop[2] [~] F (*abbr. of popular*): ~ *concert* concierto *m* popular.
pop[3] [~] F papá *m*.
pop·corn ['pɔpkɔːrn] rosetas *f/pl.*, palomitas *f/pl.*
pope [poup] papa *m*; **pop·er·y** ['~əri] papismo *m*.
pop-eyed ['pɔpaid] de ojos saltones.
pop·gun ['pɔpgʌn] taco *m*, fusil *m* de juguete.
pop·ish ['poupiʃ] papista, católico.
pop·lar ['pɔplər] (*white*) álamo *m*; (*black*) chopo *m*.
pop·lin ['pɔplin] popelín *m*, popelina *f*.
pop·py ['pɔpi] amapola *f*, adormidera *f*; '**~·cock** F ¡tonterías! (*a. su. f/pl.*).
pop·sy ['pɔpsi] *sl.* chica *f*.
pop·u·lace ['pɔpjuləs] pueblo *m*; *contp.* populacho *m*.
pop·u·lar ['pɔpjulər] □ popular; **pop·u·lar·i·ty** [~'læriti] popularidad *f*; **pop·u·lar·ize** ['~ləraiz] popularizar, vulgarizar.
pop·u·late ['pɔpjuleit] poblar; **pop·u'la·tion** población *f*; habitantes *m/pl.*
pop·u·lous ['pɔpjuləs] □ populoso.
por·ce·lain ['pɔːrslin] porcelana *f*.
porch [pɔːrtʃ] pórtico *m*; entrada *f*.
por·cu·pine ['pɔːrkjupain] puerco *m* espín.
pore[1] [pɔːr] poro *m*.
pore[2] [~]: ~ *over* estar absorto en el estudio de; estudiar larga y detenidamente.
pork [pɔːrk] carne *f* de cerdo (*or* puerco); ~ *chop* chuleta *f* de cerdo; '**pork·er** cerdo *m*, cochino *m*; '**pork·y** F gordo.
por·no·graph·ic [pɔːrnə'græfik] pornográfico; **por·no·gra·phy** [pɔːr'nɔgrəfi] pornografía *f*; **por·no queen** *sl.* actriz *f* de películas pornográficas.
po·ros·i·ty [pɔː'rɔsiti], **po·rous·ness** ['pɔːrəsnis] porosidad *f*; **po·rous** ['pɔːrəs] □ poroso.
por·phy·ry ['pɔːrfiri] pórfido *m*.
por·poise ['pɔːrpəs] marsopa *f*.
por·ridge ['pɔridʒ] *approx.* gachas *f/pl.* de avena.
port[1] [pɔːrt] ⚓ (*harbor*) puerto *m*.
port[2] [~] ⚓ (*~hole*) portilla *f*; † tronera *f*; ⊕ lumbrera *f*.
port[3] [~] ⚓ **1.** (*a.* ~ *side*) babor *m*; **2.** *helm* poner a babor.
port[4] [~] vino *m* de Oporto.
port·a·ble ['pɔːrtəbl] portátil.
por·tage ['pɔːrtidʒ] porteo *m*.
por·tal ['pɔːrtl] puerta *f* (grande e imponente).
port·cul·lis [pɔːrt'kʌlis] rastrillo *m*.
por·tend [pɔːr'tend] pronosticar; presagiar, augurar.
por·tent ['pɔːrtent] presagio *m*, augurio *m*; **por'ten·tous** □ portentoso.
por·ter ['pɔːrtər] portero *m*, conserje *m*; 🚂 mozo *m* (de estación); (*beer*) cerveza *f* negra; ~'s *lodge* conserjería *f*; **por·ter·age** ['~ridʒ] porte *m*; '**por·ter·house:** ~ *steak* biftec *m* de filete.
port·fo·li·o [pɔːrt'fouljou] cartera *f*

(*a. pol.*), carpeta *f*; *without* ~ sin cartera.
port·hole [ˈpɔːrthoul] portilla *f*.
por·ti·co [ˈpɔːrtikou] pórtico *m*.
por·tion [ˈpɔːrʃn] **1.** porción *f*, parte *f*; (*dowry*) dote *f*; (*helping*) ración *f*; **2.** (*a.* ~ *out*) repartir, dividir.
port·li·ness [ˈpɔːrtlinis] corpulencia *f*; **ˈport·ly** corpulento; grave.
port·man·teau [pɔːrtˈmæntou] baúl *m* de viaje; ~ *word* palabra *f* híbrida.
por·trait [ˈpɔːrtrit] retrato *m*; ~ *painter* = **ˈpor·trait·ist** retratista *m*/*f*; **por·trai·ture** [ˈ~tʃər] arte *m* de retratar; retrato *m*.
por·tray [pɔːrˈtrei] retratar; *fig.* describir; **porˈtray·al** *fig.* descripción *f* (gráfica), representación *f*.
Por·tu·guese [pɔːrtjuˈgiːz] **1.** portugués *adj. a. su. m* (-a *f*); **2.** (*language*) portugués *m*.
pose [pouz] **1.** postura *f of body*; *fig.* afectación *f*, pose *f*; **2.** *v/t. problem* plantear; *question* hacer, formular; *v/i.* (*model*) posar; darse tono (*affectedly*); ~ *as* hacerse pasar por, echárselas de; **ˈpos·er** pregunta *f* (*or* problema *m*) difícil.
posh [pɔʃ] F elegante, de lujo, lujoso; de mucho rumbo; cursi.
po·si·tion [pəˈziʃn] **1.** posición *f*, situación *f*; categoría *f*; (*post*) puesto *m*, colocación *f*; (*opinion*) opinión *f*; *be in a* ~ *to* estar en condiciones de *inf.*; **2.** colocar, disponer.
pos·i·tive [ˈpɔzətiv] **1.** □ positivo (*a.* ♆, ⚡, *phot.*); (*affirmative*) afirmativo; (*emphatic*) enfático, categórico; *be* ~ *that* estar seguro de que; F *it's a* ~ *nuisance* es realmente una molestia; ~*ly* realmente, absolutamente; **2.** *phot.* positiva *f*; **ˈpos·i·tiv·ism** positivismo *m*.
pos·se [ˈpɔsi] *fuerza civil armada bajo el mando del Sheriff etc.*; *fig.* grupo *m*, pelotón *m*.
pos·sess [pəˈzes] poseer (*a. be* ~*ed of*); ~ *o.s. of* tomar posesión de, apoderarse de; *be* ~*ed by idea* estar dominado por; *what can have* ~*ed you?* ¿cómo lo has podido hacer?; **posˈsessed** [~t] poseído, poseso; **pos·ses·sion** [pəˈzeʃn] posesión *f*; ~*s pl.* bienes *m*/*pl.*; *in the* ~ *of* en poder de; *take* ~ *of* tomar posesión de; **pos·ses·sive** [pəˈzesiv] **1.** □ *gr.* posesivo; *love etc.* dominante, tiránico; **2.** posesivo *m*; **posˈses·sor** poseedor (-a *f*) *m*.
pos·si·bil·i·ty [pɔsəˈbiliti] posibilidad *f*; **ˈpos·si·ble** □ posible; *as frequent(ly) as* ~ lo más frecuente(mente) posible; *as soon as* ~ cuanto antes; *do as much as* ~ *to* hacer lo posible para; *bring as much as* ~ traer todo lo que puede uno; **ˈpos·si·bly** posiblemente; tal vez; *if I* ~ *can* a serme posible; *he cannot* ~ *go* le es absolutamente imposible ir.
post¹ [poust] poste *m*.
post² [~] **1.** (*job*) puesto *m*; destino *m*; cargo *m*; ⚔ *etc.* puesto *m*; ✆ correo *m*; (casa *f* de) correos; (*collection*) recogida *f*; (*delivery*) entrega *f*; *by* ~ por correo; *by return of* ~ a vuelta de correo; *go to the* ~ ir a correos, ir al buzón; **2.** *poster etc.* fijar, pegar; ✆ echar al correo; mandar por correo, despachar; ⚔ *etc.* situar, apostar; mandar (*to* a); *keep a p.* ~*ed* tener a una p. al corriente.
post·age [ˈpoustidʒ] franqueo *m*, porte *m*; ~ *due* a pagar; ~ *stamp* sello *m* (de correo), estampilla *f S.Am.*
post·al [ˈpoustəl] □ postal, de correos; ~ *card* postal *f*; ~ *order approx.* giro *m* postal.
post...: **ˈ~ box** buzón *m*; **ˈ~ card** (tarjeta *f*) postal *f*; **ˈ~ˈdate** poner fecha adelantada a.
poste res·tante [ˈpoustˈrestɑːnt] lista *f* de correos.
post·er [ˈpoustər] cartel *m*.
pos·te·ri·or [pɔsˈtiriər] **1.** posterior; **2.** F *co.* asentaderas *f*/*pl*.
pos·ter·i·ty [pɔsˈteriti] posteridad *f*.
pos·tern [ˈpoustəːrn] postigo *m*.
post-free [ˈpoustˈfriː] porte pagado, franco de porte.
post·grad·u·ate [ˈpoustˈgrædjuit] postgraduado *adj. a. su. m* (a *f*); ~ *course* curso *m* para postgraduados.
post·haste [ˈpoustˈheist] a toda prisa, con toda urgencia.
post·hu·mous [ˈpɔstjuməs] □ póstumo.
pos·til·(l)ion [pəsˈtiljən] postillón *m*.
post...: **ˈ~·man** cartero *m*; **ˈ~·mark** **1.** matasellos *m*; **2.** matar (el sello de); **ˈ~·mas·ter** administrador *m* de correos; ♀ *General* director *m* general de correos.
post·me·rid·i·an [ˈpoustməˈridiən] postmeridiano; **post-mor·tem** [ˈ~ˈmɔːrtəm] autopsia *f*.
post...: **ˈ~ of·fice** (casa *f* de) correos;

general ~ administración *f* de correos; ~ *box* apartado *m* (de correos); ~ *savings bank* caja *f* postal de ahorros; '**~paid** porte pagado, franco de porte.

post·pone [poust'poun] aplazar; **post'pone·ment** aplazamiento *m*.

post·pran·di·al [poust'prændiəl] *co.* de sobremesa; *walk etc.* que se da después de comer.

post·script ['poustskript] posdata *f*.

pos·tu·lant ['pɔstjulənt] *eccl.* postulante (a *f*) *m*.

pos·tu·late **1.** ['pɔstjulit] postulado *m*; **2.** ['~leit] postular; **pos·tu'la·tion** postulación *f*.

pos·ture ['pɔstʃər] **1.** postura *f*, actitud *f*; **2.** adoptar una actitud (afectada).

post·war ['poust'wɔːr] de (la) pos(t)guerra.

po·sy ['pouzi] flor *f*; ramillete *m* de flores.

pot [pɔt] **1.** (*cooking*) olla *f*, puchero *m*, marmita *f*; (*preserving*) tarro *m*, pote *m*; (*flower*) tiesto *m*; (*chamber*) orinal *m*; F copa *f*; *sl.* mariguana *f*; F ~*s pl.* montones *m/pl.*; F *big* ~ pez *m* gordo; F *go to* ~ echarse a perder, arruinarse; **2.** *v/t. food* conservar (en botes *etc.*); *plant* poner en tiesto; ⚔ F matar (a tiros); *v/i.* F disparar (*at* contra).

pot·ash ['pɔtæʃ] potasa *f*.

po·tas·si·um [pə'tæsiəm] potasio *m*.

po·ta·tions [pou'teiʃnz] *pl.* libaciones *f/pl*.

po·ta·to [pə'teitou], *pl.* **po'ta·toes** [~z] patata *f*, papa *f S.Am.*; ~ *omelet* tortilla *f* española.

pot...: '**~bel·lied** barrigón; '**~-boil·er** obra *f* mediocre compuesta para ganar dinero; '**~ 'cheese** requesón *m*.

po·ten·cy ['poutənsi] potencia *f*; '**po·tent** □ potente; poderoso, eficaz; *drink etc.* fuerte; **po·ten·tate** ['~teit] potentado *m*; **po·ten·tial** [pə'tenʃl] potencial *adj. a. su. m*; **po·ten·ti·al·i·ty** [~ʃi'æliti] potencialidad *f*.

poth·er ['pɔðər] alharaca *f*, aspaviento *m*; lío *m*.

pot·hole ['pɔthoul] bache *m in road*; *geol.* marmita *f* de gigante; '**~hol·ing** espeleología *f*.

po·tion ['pouʃn] poción *f*, pócima *f*.

pot·luck ['pɔt'lʌk]: *take* ~ comer (*fig.* tomar) lo que haya.

pot shot ['pɔtʃɔt] tiro *m* a corta distancia; tiro *m* al azar.

pot·ter[1] ['pɔtər] ocuparse en fruslerías; ~ *round the house* hacer bagatelas en casa.

pot·ter[2] [~] alfarero *m*; ~'*s clay* arcilla *f* de alfarería; ~'*s field* hoyanca *f*; ~'*s wheel* torno *m* de alfarero; '**pot·ter·y** (*works, art*) alfarería *f*; (*pots*) cacharros *m/pl.*; (*archaeological etc.*) cerámicas *f/pl*.

pot·ty[1] ['pɔti] *sl.* (*small*) insignificante, miserable; (*mad*) chiflado.

pot·ty[2] [~] F orinal *m* de niño.

pouch [pautʃ] bolsa *f*; *hunt. etc.* morral *m*, zurrón *m*; (*tobacco*) petaca *f*; ⚔ cartuchera *f*.

poul·ter·er ['poultərər] pollero *m*.

poul·tice ['poultis] **1.** cataplasma *f*, emplasto *m*; **2.** poner una cataplasma a, emplastar.

poul·try ['poultri] aves *f/pl.* de corral; ~ *farm* granja *f* avícola; ~ *house* gallinero *m*; ~ *keeper* avicultor *m*.

pounce [pauns] **1.** salto *m*; ataque *m* súbito; **2.** atacar súbitamente; ~ *on* saltar sobre (*a. fig.*), precipitarse sobre, caer sobre.

pound[1] [paund] libra *f* (= *453,6 gr.*); ~ (*sterling*) libra *f* (esterlina) (*abbr.* £ = *20 shillings*); ~*cake* ponqué *m*.

pound[2] [~] corral *m* de concejo.

pound[3] [~] *v/t.* machacar, martillar, aporrear; dar de puñetazos *with fists*; (*grind*) moler; ⚔ bombardear; *v/i.* dar golpes (*at* en); *door etc.* aporrear (en); (*run*) correr *etc.* pesadamente.

pound·age ['paundidʒ] impuesto *m* exigido por cada libra.

pound·er ['paundər] de ... libras.

pour [pɔːr] *v/t.* (*a.* ~ *out*) echar, verter, derramar (*a. fig.*); *smoke* arrojar; ~ *away*, ~ *out* vaciar; *v/i.* correr, fluir (abundantemente); (*rain*) diluviar, llover a torrentes; ~ *in* (*out*) entrar (salir) a raudales, entrar (salir) a montones.

pout [paut] **1.** puchero *m*, mala cara *f*; **2.** *v/t.*: ~ *one's lips* = *v/i.* hacer pucheros, poner mala cara.

pov·er·ty ['pɔvərti] pobreza *f*, miseria *f*; escasez *f*; ~-*stricken* extremadamente pobre.

pow·der ['paudər] **1.** polvo *m*; (*face*) polvos *m/pl.*; (*gun-*) pólvora *f*; **2.**

(*reduce to* ~) pulverizar(se); (*dust with* ~) polvorear; *face, o.s.* empolvarse, ponerse polvos; ~*ed milk* leche *f* en polvo; ˈ~ **com·pact** polvera *f*; ˈ~ **puff** borla *f* para empolvarse; ˈ~ **room** cuarto *m* tocador; F retrete *m* de mujeres; ˈ**pow·der·y** *substance* en polvo; pulverizado; *surface* polvoriento; empolvado.

pow·er [ˈpauər] poder *m* (*a.* ⚖); poderío *m*; autoridad *f*; *pol.*, ⚔ potencia *f*; ⊕ potencia *f*, energía *f*; ⚡ fuerza *f*; (*gift*) facultad *f* (*of* de); (*drive*) empuje *m*, energía *f*; *the* ~*s that be* las autoridades (actuales); *be in* ~ estar en el poder; *do all in one's* ~ hacer lo posible (*to* por); ˈ~ **brake**(**s**) *mot.* servofreno *m*; ˈ~ **cut** corte *m* de corriente, apagón *m*; ˈ~ **drill** taladradora *f* de fuerza; ˈ~ **fail·ure** interrupción *f* de fuerza; **pow·er·ful** [ˈ~ful] □ poderoso; ⊕ potente; *engine, build* fuerte; *emotion etc.* intenso; *argument* convincente; ˈ**pow·er·house** central *f* eléctrica; ⊕ fábrica *f* de fuerza motriz; ˈ**pow·er·less** □ impotente; sin fuerzas (*to* para); sin autoridad (*to* para).

pow·er...: ˈ~ **line** ⚡ línea *f* de fuerza; ˈ~ **load·er** ⚒ rompedora-cargadora *f*; ˈ~ **plant** grupo *m* electrógeno; ˈ~ **saw** motosierra *f*; ˈ~ **sta·tion** central *f* eléctrica; ˈ~ **steer·ing** *mot.* servodirección *f*; ˈ~ **strug·gle** lucha *f* por control; ˈ~ **tool** herramienta *f* mecánica.

pow·wow [ˈpauˈwau] *fig.* conferencia *f*.

pox [pɔks] F sífilis *f*.

prac·ti·ca·ble [ˈpræktikəbl] □ practicable, hacedero; ˈ**prac·ti·cal** □ práctico; ~ *joke* trastada *f*, broma *f* pesada; **prac·ti·cal·i·ty** [~ˈkæliti] espíritu *m* práctico; **prac·ti·cal·ly** [ˈ~kli] prácticamente; casi, punto menos que.

prac·tice [ˈpræktis] **1.** práctica *f*; costumbre *f*; ejercicio *m*; ⚕ clientela *f*; *in* ~ (*not theory*) en la práctica; *be out of* ~ haber perdido la costumbre; *sport*: estar desentrenado; *make a* ~ *of ger.* acostumbrar *inf.*; *put into* ~ poner por obra; ~ *makes perfect* la práctica hace maestro; **2.** practicar; *profession etc.* ejercitar, ejercer; *piano etc.* hacer prácticas de; *sport*: hacer ejercicios de, entrenarse en; ~ *ger.* ensayarse a *inf.*; *v/i.* ensayarse, hacer ensayos (*on* en); (*professionally*) ejercer (*as* de); ⚕ practicar la medicina; ˈ**prac·ticed** *eye etc.* experto; ˈ**prac·tic·ing** practicante.

prac·ti·tion·er [prækˈtiʃənər] facultativo *m*, práctico *m*; *general* ~ médico *m* general.

prag·mat·ic [prægˈmætik] □ pragmático.

prai·rie [ˈpreri] pradera *f*, pampa *f S.Am.*

praise [preiz] **1.** alabanza(s) *f*(*pl.*), elogio(s) *m*(*pl.*); **2.** alabar, elogiar; ˈ~**·wor·thy** □ loable, digno de alabanza.

pram [præm] F cochecito *m* de niño.

prance [præns] cabriolar, encabritarse.

prank [præŋk] travesura *f*; broma *f*.

prate [preit] parlotear, charlar.

prat·tle [ˈprætl] **1.** parloteo *m*; (*child's*) balbuceo *m*; **2.** parlotear; (*child*) balbucear.

prawn [prɔːn] gamba *f*; (*large*) langostino *m*.

pray [prei] *v/i.* (*say one's prayers*) rezar; orar (*for* por, *to* a); *v/t.* rogar, pedir, suplicar (*for acc.*); ~ *tell me* haga el favor de decirme.

pray·er [ˈprer] oración *f*, rezo *m*; (*entreaty*) súplica *f*, ruego *m*; *Book of Common* ♀ *liturgia de la Iglesia Anglicana*; *say one's* ~*s* rezar; ˈ~ **book** devocionario *m*, misal *m*.

pre... [priː, pri] pre...; ante...

preach [priːtʃ] predicar (*a.* F, *b.s.*); *advantages etc.* celebrar; ˈ**preach·er** predicador *m*; ˈ**preach·ing** predicación *f*; *b.s.* sermoneo *m*; ˈ**preach·y** moralizador; moralizante.

pre·am·ble [priːˈæmbl] preámbulo *m*.

pre·ar·range [priːəˈreindʒ] arreglar (*or* fijar) de antemano.

preb·end [ˈprebənd] prebenda *f*; ˈ**pre·ben·dar·y** prebendado *m*.

pre·car·i·ous [priˈkeriəs] □ precario.

pre·cau·tion [priˈkɔːʃn] precaución *f*; **preˈcau·tion·ar·y** de precaución, preventivo.

pre·cede [priˈsiːd] preceder; **pre·ced·ence** [ˈpresidəns] precedencia *f*; *take* ~ *over* primar sobre; **prec·e·dent** [ˈpresidənt] precedente *m*; **preˈced·ing** precedente.

pre·cen·tor [priˈsentər] chantre *m*.

pre·cept [ˈpriːsept] precepto *m*; **pre·cep·tor** [priˈseptər] preceptor *m*.
pre·cinct [ˈpriːsiŋkt] recinto *m*; distrito *m* electoral; barrio *m*; ~s *pl*. contornos *m/pl.*; *within the* ~*s of* dentro de los límites de.
pre·ci·o·si·ty [presiˈɔsiti] preciosismo *m*.
pre·cious [ˈpreʃəs] **1.** □ precioso; *p*. amado, querido; *style* afectado, rebuscado; **2.** *adv*. F muy.
prec·i·pice [ˈpresipis] precipicio *m*, despeñadero *m*; **pre·cip·i·tance, pre·cip·i·tan·cy** [priˈsipitəns(i)] precipitación *f*; **preˈcip·i·tate 1.** [~teit] precipitar (*a*. ⚗); **2.** [~] ⚗ precipitado *m*; **3.** [~tit] precipitado; **pre·cip·i·ta·tion** [~ˈteiʃn] precipitación *f*; **preˈcip·i·tous** □ escarpado, cortado a pico.
pré·cis [ˈpreisiː] resumen *m*.
pre·cise [priˈsais] □ preciso, exacto; (*too* ~) afectado; *p*. escrupuloso, meticuloso; ~*ly!* perfectamente, eso es; **preˈcise·ness, pre·ci·sion** [priˈsiʒn] (*attr*. de) precisión *f*, exactitud *f*.
pre·clude [priˈkluːd] excluir, imposibilitar.
pre·co·cious [priˈkouʃəs] □ precoz; **preˈco·cious·ness, pre·coc·i·ty** [priˈkɔsiti] precocidad *f*.
pre·con·ceived [ˈpriːkənˈsiːvd] preconcebido.
pre·con·cep·tion [ˈpriːkənˈsepʃn] preconcepción *f*.
pre·cool [ˈpriːˈkuːl] preenfriar.
pre·cur·sor [priːˈkəːrsər] precursor (-a *f*) *m*.
pred·a·to·ry [ˈpredətɔːri] rapaz, de rapiña; depredador.
pre·de·cease [ˈpriːdiˈsiːs] morir antes que.
pred·e·ces·or [ˈpredisesər] predecesor (-a *f*) *m*, antecesor (-a *f*) *m*.
pre·des·ti·na·tion [pridestiˈneiʃn] predestinación *f*; **pre·des·tine** [priˈdestin] predestinar.
pre·de·ter·mine [ˈpriːdiˈtəːrmin] predeterminar.
pre·dic·a·ment [priˈdikəmənt] apuro *m*, situación *f* difícil; *phls*. predicamento *m*.
pred·i·cate [ˈpredikit] *gr*. predicado *m*.
pre·dict [priˈdikt] pronosticar, predecir; **pre·dic·tion** [~ˈdikʃn] pronóstico *m*, predicción *f*.
pre·di·lec·tion [priːdiˈlekʃn] predilección *f*.
pre·dis·pose [ˈpriːdisˈpouz] predisponer; **pre·dis·po·si·tion** [ˈ~dispəˈziʃn] predisposición *f*.
pre·dom·i·nance [priˈdɔminəns] predominio *m*; **preˈdom·i·nant** □ predominante; ~*ly* por la mayor parte, en su mayoría; **preˈdom·i·nate** [~neit] predominar.
pre·em·i·nence [priːˈeminəns] preeminencia *f*; **preˈem·i·nent** □ preeminente.
pre·emp·tion [priːˈempʃn] preempción *f*.
preen [priːn] *feathers* arreglarse (con el pico); *fig*. ~ *o.s.* pavonearse, atildarse.
pre·ex·ist [ˈpriːigˈzist] preexistir; **ˈpre·exˈist·ence** preexistencia *f*; **ˈpre·exˈist·ent** preexistente.
pre·fab [ˈpriːfæb] F casa *f* prefabricada; **ˈpreˈfab·ri·cate** [~rikeit] prefabricar; ~*d* prefabricado.
pref·ace [ˈprefis] **1.** prólogo *m*, prefacio *m*; **2.** *book etc.* prologar; *fig*. decir *etc*. a modo de prólogo a; introducir; *be* ~*d by* tener ... a modo de prólogo.
pref·a·to·ry [ˈprefətəri] preliminar, a modo de prólogo.
pre·fect [ˈpriːfekt] prefecto *m*; *school*: monitor *m*.
pre·fer [priˈfəːr] preferir (*to inf.*; *A to B* A a B); *p*. ascender, promover *to post*; *charge etc.* hacer, presentar; **pref·er·a·ble** [ˈprefərəbl] □ preferible; **ˈpref·er·a·bly** preferentemente, más bien; **ˈpref·er·ence** preferencia *f*; ~ *shares pl*. acciones *f/pl*. preferentes; **pref·er·en·tial** [~ˈrenʃl] □ preferente; **pre·fer·ment** [priˈfəːrmənt] promoción *f*, ascenso *m*.
pre·fix 1. [ˈpriːfiks] prefijo *m*; **2.** [~, priːˈfiks] prefijar.
preg·nan·cy [ˈpregnənsi] embarazo *m*; **ˈpreg·nant** □ embarazada, encinta, en estado; *fig*. preñado, lleno (*with* de).
pre·heat [ˈpriːˈhiːt] precalentar.
pre·hen·sile [priˈhensil] prensil.
pre·his·tor·ic [ˈpriːhisˈtɔrik] prehistórico.
pre·ig·ni·tion [ˈpriːigˈniʃn] preignición *f*.
pre·judge [ˈpriːˈdʒʌdʒ] prejuzgar.

prej·u·dice [ˈpredʒudis] **1.** prejuicio *m*; parcialidad *f*; *without* ~ *to* sin perjuicio de; **2.** *chances etc.* perjudicar; prevenir, predisponer (*against* contra); ~*d* parcial, interesado; lleno de prejuicios.
prej·u·di·cial [predʒuˈdiʃl] □ perjudicial.
prel·ate [ˈprelit] prelado *m*.
pre·lim [ˈpriːlim] F examen *m* preliminar; **pre·lim·i·nar·y** [priˈliminəri] preliminar *adj. a. su. m*; **preˈlim·i·na·ries** [~z] *pl.* preliminares *m/pl.*, preparativos *m/pl.*
prel·ude [ˈpreljuːd] **1.** preludio *m* (*a.* ♪); **2.** preludiar (*a.* ♪).
pre·mar·i·tal [priˈmæritl] premarital.
pre·ma·ture [priməˈtjur] prematuro; ~ *baldness* calvicie *f* precoz.
pre·med·i·tate [priˈmediteit] premeditar; **pre·med·iˈta·tion** premeditación *f*.
pre·mi·er [priˈmir, primˈjer] **1.** primero, principal; **2.** primer ministro *m*; **pre·mi·ère** [~] estreno *m*; **ˈpre·mi·er·ship** cargo *m* del primer ministro.
pre·mise [ˈpremis] premisa *f*; ~*s pl.* local *m*, casa *f*, tienda *f etc.*; *on the* ~*s* en el local, in situ.
pre·mi·um [ˈpriːmjəm] ✝ premio *m*; (*insurance*) prima *f*; *be at a* ~ ✝ estar sobre la par; *fig.* estar en gran demanda; *put a* ~ *on* estimular, fomentar; premiar (de modo injusto).
pre·mo·ni·tion [priːməˈniʃn] presentimiento *m*, premonición *f*; **pre·mon·i·to·ry** [priˈmɔnitəri] □ premonitorio.
pre·na·tal [ˈpriːˈneitl] prenatal.
pre·oc·cu·pa·tion [priːɔkjuˈpeiʃn] preocupación *f*; **pre·oc·cu·pied** [~ˈɔkjupaid] preocupado; **preˈoc·cu·py** [~pai] preocupar.
pre·or·dain [ˈpriːɔːrˈdein] predestinar.
prep [prep] **1.** F = *preparation*, *preparatory*; **2.** F prepare; make ready.
pre·pack·aged [priˈpækidʒd] precintado; **pre·paid** [priːˈpeid] pagado por adelantado.
prep·a·ra·tion [prepəˈreiʃn] preparación *f*; ~*s pl.* preparativos *m/pl.*; **preˈpar·a·to·ry** [~tɔːri] **1.** preparatorio, preliminar; **2.** *adv.*: ~ *to* con miras a, antes de.
pre·pare [priˈper] preparar(se), disponer(se), prevenir(se); ~ *to* disponerse a; *be* ~*d* estar listo; *be* ~*d to* estar dispuesto a; *be* ~*d for anything* estar dispuesto a aguantarlo todo; no dejarse sorprender; **preˈpar·ed·ness** preparación *f* (militar *etc.*).
pre·pay [ˈpriːˈpei] [*irr.* (*pay*)] pagar por adelantado; **ˈpreˈpay·ment** pago *m* adelantado.
pre·pon·der·ance [priˈpɔndərəns] preponderancia *f*; **preˈpon·der·ant** □ preponderante; **preˈpon·der·ate** [~reit] preponderar.
prep·o·si·tion [prepəˈziʃn] preposición *f*; **prep·oˈsi·tion·al** □ preposicional.
pre·pos·sess·ing [priːpəˈzesiŋ] □ agradable, atractivo.
pre·pos·ter·ous [priˈpɔstərəs] □ absurdo, ridículo.
pre·puce [ˈpriːpjuːs] prepucio *m*.
pre·re·cord [priːriˈkɔːrd] grabar de antemano.
pre·req·ui·site [ˈpriːˈrekwizit] requisito *m* previo.
pre·rog·a·tive [priˈrɔgətiv] prerrogativa *f*.
pres·age [ˈpresidʒ] **1.** presagio *m*; **2. pre·sage** [~, *a.* priˈseidʒ] presagiar.
pres·by·ter [ˈprezbitər] presbítero *m*; **Pres·by·te·ri·an** [~ˈtiriən] presbiteriano *adj. a. su. m* (a *f*); **pres·by·ter·y** [ˈ~təri] presbiterio *m*.
pre·sci·ence [ˈpreʃiəns] presciencia *f*; **ˈpre·sci·ent** presciente.
pre·scribe [prisˈkraib] prescribir, ordenar; ⚕ recetar.
pre·scrip·tion [prisˈkripʃn] prescripción *f*; ⚕ receta *f*; **preˈscrip·tive** □ legal; sancionado por la costumbre.
pre·seal·ed [priːˈsiːld] precintado.
pres·ence [ˈprezns] presencia *f*; asistencia *f* (*at* a); ~ *of mind* presencia *f* de ánimo; *in the* ~ *of* ante, en presencia de.
pres·ent[1] [ˈpreznt] **1.** □ presente, actual; ~! ¡presente!; *those* ~ los presentes; ~ *company excepted* mejorando lo presente, con perdón de los presentes; *be* ~ asistir (*at* a); **2.** presente *m*; actualidad *f*; *gr.* tiempo *m* presente; *at* ~ actualmente; al presente; *for the* ~ por ahora.
pre·sent[2] [priˈzent] presentar, ofrecer, dar; *case* exponer; ~ *o.s.* pre-

sentarse; ~ *arms!* ¡presenten armas!; ~ *with* obsequiar con; *occasion* deparar.
pres·ent[3] ['preznt] regalo *m*, presente *m*; *make a ~ of* regalar; *fig.* dar medio regalado.
pre·sent·a·ble [pri'zentəbl] presentable.
pres·en·ta·tion [prezən'teiʃn] presentación *f*; (*present*) obsequio *m*; ~ *copy* ejemplar *m* con dedicatoria del autor.
pres·ent-day ['prezntdei] actual.
pre·senti·ment [pri'zentimənt] presentimiento *m*, corazonada *f*; *have a ~ that* presentir que.
pres·ent·ly ['prezntli] luego, dentro de poco.
pres·er·va·tion [prezər'veiʃn] conservación *f*; preservación *f*; *in good ~* bien conservado; **pre·serv·a·tive** [pri'zə:rvətiv] preservativo *adj. a su. m.*
pre·serve [pri'zə:rv] **1.** conservar; preservar (*from* contra); guardar (*from* de); **2.** conserva *f*; confitura *f*, compota *f*; *hunt.* vedado *m*; **pre'served** *food* en conserva; **pre'serv·er** preservador *m*.
pre·side [pri'zaid] presidir (*at, over acc.*).
pres·i·den·cy ['prezidənsi] presidencia *f*; '**pres·i·dent** presidente *m*; ✝ director *m*; *Am. univ.* rector *m*; ~-*elect* presidente *m* electo (*todavía sin gobierno*); **pres·i·den·tial** [~'denʃl] presidencial.
press [pres] **1.** ⊕ *etc.* prensa *f*; imprenta *f*; (*pressure*) presión *f*; urgencia *f of affairs*; apiñamiento *m of people*; *be in ~* estar en prensa; *go to ~* entrar en prensa; *have a bad ~* tener mala prensa; **2.** *v/t.* ⊕ *etc.* prensar; apretar; *button etc.* pulsar, presionar, empujar; *clothes* planchar; *fig.* abrumar, acosar; apremiar; *claim* insistir en; ~ *s.t. (up)on s.o.* insistir en que uno acepte algo; ~ *s.o. to do s.t.* instar a uno a hacer algo; *be ~ed for time* tener poco tiempo; ~ *the point* insistir (*that* en que); ~ *into service* utilizar; *v/i.* urgir, apremiar; (*people*) apiñarse; *time ~es* el tiempo apremia; ~ *for* hacer propaganda a favor de; reclamar, pedir con urgencia; ~ *forward*, ~ *on* seguir adelante (a pesar de todo); **3.** *attr.* de prensa; de presión; '~ **a·gen·cy** agencia *f* de información; '~ **a·gent** agente *m* de publicidad; '~ **box** tribuna *f* de la prensa; '~ '**con·fer·ence** conferencia *f* de prensa; '**press·ing** ☐ urgente, apremiante, acuciante; '**press·man** periodista *m*; '**press mark** signatura *f*; '**press re·lease** comunicado *m* de prensa.
pres·sure ['preʃər] presión *f* (*a.* ⊕, *meteor.*); *fig.* urgencia *f*, apremio *m*; ⚕ tension *f* (nerviosa); impulso *m*, influencia *f*; '~ **cook·er** olla *f* a presión; '~ **gauge** manómetro *m*; '~ **group** grupo *m* de presión; '**pres·sur·ize** ✈ sobrecargar; '**pres·sur·ized** '**cab·in** cabina *f* a presión (*or* altimática).
pres·ti·dig·i·ta·tion ['prestididʒi'teiʃn] prestidigitación *f*.
pres·tige [pres'ti:ʒ] prestigio *m*.
pre·stressed con·crete ['pri:strest kən'kri:t] hormigón *m* pretensado.
pre·sum·a·bly [pri'zju:məbli] *adv.* según cabe presumir; ~ *it was he* supongo que era él; **pre'sume** presumir, suponer; ~ *to* atreverse a; ~ *(up)on* abusar de.
pre·sump·tion [pri'zʌmpʃn] presunción *f*; pretensión *f*; *the ~ is that* puede presumirse que; **pre'sump·tive** *heir* presunto; **pre'sump·tu·ous** [~tjuəs] ☐ presuntuoso, presumido.
pre·sup·pose [pri:sə'pouz] presuponer; **pre·sup·po·si·tion** [pri:sʌpə'ziʃn] presuposición *f*.
pre·tend [pri'tend] (*feign*) fingir, aparentar; (*claim*) pretender (*to acc.*); ~ *to quality* afirmar tener; ~ *to be asleep* fingir dormir, fingirse dormido; ~ *to be ill* fingirse enfermo; ~ *to be su.* fingirse *su.*, hacerse el (la) *su.*; **pre'tend·ed** ☐ pretendido; **pre'tend·er** pretendiente *m*/*f*; **pre·tense** [pri'tens] (*claim*) pretensión *f*; (*display*) ostentación *f*; (*pretext*) pretexto *m*; fingimiento *m*; *false ~s pl.* fraude *m*.
pre·ten·sion [pri'tenʃn] pretensión *f*; *have ~s to culture* tener pretensiones de cultura.
pre·ten·tious [pri'tenʃəs] ☐ pretencioso, presuntuoso; (*ostentatious*) aparatoso, ambicioso; cursi.
pret·er·it(e) ['pretərit] pretérito *m*.
pre·ter·nat·u·ral [pri:tər'nætʃərəl] ☐ preternatural.

pre·text [ˈpriːtekst] pretexto *m*; *under* ~ *of* so pretexto de.
pret·ti·fy [ˈpritifai] embellecer adornar (de modo ridículo).
pret·ti·ness [ˈpritinis] lindeza *f*.
pret·ty [ˈpriti] **1.** □ bonito, guapo, lindo; precioso, mono; *sum etc.* considerable; *iro.* bueno; **2.** *adv.* bastante, algo; ~ *difficult* bastante difícil; ~ *much the same* más o menos lo mismo; ~ *near ruined* casi arruinado; *be sitting* ~ estar en posición muy ventajosa.
pre·vail [priˈveil] prevalecer, imponerse; (*conditions*) reinar, imperar; ~ *upon* persuadir, inducir (*to* a); *be* ~*ed upon to* dejarse persuadir a *inf.*; **preˈvail·ing** reinante, imperante; predominante; general.
prev·a·lence [ˈprevələns] uso *m* corriente, costumbre *f*; frecuencia *f*; predominio *m*; **ˈprev·a·lent** □ corriente; extendido; frecuente; predominante.
pre·var·i·cate [priˈværikeit] buscar evasivas, tergiversar.
pre·vent [priˈvent] impedir ([*from*] *ger. inf.*), evitar, estorbar; **preˈvent·a·ble** evitable; **preˈvent·a·tive** [~tətiv] *v. preventive*; **preˈven·tion** prevención *f*; el impedir; **preˈven·tive 1.** □ preventivo, impeditivo; ~ *medicine* medicina *f* preventiva; **2.** preservativo *m*.
pre·view [ˈpriːvjuː] pre-estreno *m*; *fig.* vista *f* anticipada.
pre·vi·ous [ˈpriːviəs] □ previo, anterior; F prematuro; ~ *to* antes de; ~*ly* previamente, con anticipación; antes.
pre·war [ˈpriːˈwɔːr] de (la) preguerra.
prey [prei] **1.** presa *f*, víctima *f*; *bird of* ~ ave *f* de rapiña; *be a* ~ *to* ser víctima de; **2.:** ~ (*up*)*on* atacar, alimentarse de, pillar; *mind etc.* agobiar, remorder, preocupar.
price [prais] **1.** precio *m*; *at any* ~ a toda costa; *not at any* ~ de ningún modo; ~ *control* control *m* de precios; ~ *list* lista *f* de precios; **2.** tasar, fijar el precio de; **ˈprice·less** inapreciable; F divertidísimo, absurdo; **ˈprice war** guerra *f* de precios; **ˈprice·y** F caro.
prick [prik] **1.** pinchazo *m*, punzada *f*; alfilerazo *m with pin*; *sl.* pene *m*; **2.** *v/t.* pinchar, punzar; agujerear; marcar con agujerillos; *conscience* remorder; ~ *up one's ears* aguzar las orejas; *v/i.*: ~ *up* prestar atención; **prick·le** [ˈ~l] espina *f*, pincho *m*, púa *f*; **ˈprick·ly** espinoso; lleno de púas; *p.* malhumorado; ⚘ ~ *heat* salpullido *m* causado por exceso de calor; ~ *pear* chumbera *f*.
pride [praid] **1.** orgullo *m*; *b.s.* soberbia *f*, arrogancia *f*; *take* ~ *of place* venir primero, ocupar el primer puesto; *take* (*a*) ~ *in* = **2.:** ~ *o.s. on* enorgullecerse de, preciarse de.
priest [priːst] sacerdote *m*; cura *m*; **ˈpriest·ess** sacerdotisa *f*; **priest·hood** [ˈ~hud] (*function*) sacerdocio *m*; (*priests collectively*) clero *m*; **ˈpriest·ly** sacerdotal.
prig [prig] presumido (a *f*) *m*; pedante *m*/*f*; mojigato *m*; **ˈprig·gish** □ presumido; pedante; mojigato.
prim [prim] □ (*a.* ~ *and proper*) remilgado; etiquetero, estirado.
pri·ma·cy [ˈpraiməsi] primacía *f*;
pri·ma don·na [ˈpriːmə ˈdɔnə] primadonna *f*, diva *f*; **pri·ma·ri·ly** [praiˈmerili, ˈpraimərəli] ante todo; **ˈpri·ma·ry 1.** □ primario; **2.** *pol.* selección *f* preliminar; **pri·mate** [ˈ~mit] *eccl.* primado *m*; *zo.* primate *m*.
prime [praim] **1.** primero; principal; fundamental; *quality* selecto, de primera clase; ⅍ primo; ~ *minister* primer ministro *m*; ~ *number* número *m* primo; **2.** flor *f*, lo mejor; ~ *of life* la flor de la vida; **3.** *gun, pump* cebar; *surface etc.* preparar; *fig.* informar de antemano, instruir clandestinamente; (*with drink*) hacer beber, emborrachar.
prim·er 1. [ˈprimər] cartilla *f*; libro *m* de texto elemental; **2.** [ˈpraimər] (*for paint*) aprestado *m*; ⊕ cebedor *m*.
pri·me·val [praiˈmiːvəl] primitivo, prístino.
prim·ing [ˈpraimiŋ] preparación *f*; primera capa *f of paint*; *attr.* de cebar.
prim·i·tive [ˈprimitiv] □ primitivo; rudimentario, sencillo; F sucio, sórdido.
pri·mo·gen·i·ture [praimouˈdʒenitʃər] primogenitura *f*.
pri·mor·di·al [praiˈmɔːrdiəl] □ primordial.

prim·rose ['primrouz] primavera *f*; ~ *path* caminito *m* de rosas.
prince [prins] príncipe *m*; '**prince·ly** principesco, magnífico; **prin·cess** ['prinsis] princesa *f*.
prin·ci·pal ['prinsəpəl] 1. □ principal; *gr.* ~ *parts pl.* partes *f/pl.* principales; 2. principal *m* (*a.* ✝, ⚖); director (-a *f*) *m of a school*; **prin·ci·pal·i·ty** [prinsi'pæliti] principado *m*.
prin·ci·ple ['prinsəpl] principio *m*; *in* ~ en principio; *on* ~ por principio.
print [print] 1. (*mark*) marca *f*, impresión *f*; *typ.* tipo *m*; (*picture*) estampa *f*, grabado *m*; *phot.* impresión *f*, positiva *f*; (*cloth, dress*) estampado *m*; *in* ~ impreso; disponible; *in* (*cold*) ~ en letras de molde; *out of* ~ agotado; 2. *dress* estampado; 3. (hacer) imprimir (*a. phot.*); (*write*) escribir en caracteres de imprenta; '**print·ed** impreso; *dress etc.* estampado; *v. matter*; '**print·er** impresor *m*; ~*'s devil* aprendiz *m* de imprenta; ~*'s ink* tinta *f* de imprenta.
print·ing ['printiŋ] impresión *f*; tipografía *f*; (*quantity*) tirada *f*; *attr.* ... de imprenta; '~ **frame** prensa *f* de copiar; '~ **ink** tinta *f* de imprenta; '~ **of·fice** imprenta *f*; '~ **press** prensa *f* de imprenta; '**print·out** (*computer*) impreso *m* derivado.
pri·or ['praiər] 1. anterior; previo; 2. *adv.*: ~ *to* antes de; hasta; 3. *eccl.* prior *m*; '**pri·or·ess** priora *f*; **pri·or·i·ty** [~'ɔriti] prioridad *f*, precedencia *f*; **pri·o·ry** ['~əri] priorato *m*.
prism ['prizm] prisma *m*; ~ *binoculars* prismáticos *m/pl.*; **pris·mat·ic** [priz'mætik] □ prismático.
pris·on ['prizn] cárcel *f*, prisión *f*; *put in* ~ encarcelar; ~ *camp* campamento *m* para prisioneros; '**pris·on·er** ⚖ preso (a *f*) *m*; ⚔ prisionero *m*; *take* ~ hacer prisionero.
pris·sy ['prisi] F remilgado, melindroso.
pris·tine ['pristi:n, 'pristain] prístino.
pri·va·cy ['praivəsi] secreto *m*, reserva *f*, retiro *m*; aislamiento *m*; intimidad *f*.
pri·vate ['praivit] 1. □ privado; particular; secreto, reservado; *report etc.* confidencial; *conversation etc.* íntimo; *view* particular, personal; ~! prohibida la entrada; ~ *enterprise* iniciativa *f* privada; *in* ~ *life* en la intimidad; *parl.* ~ *member* miembro *m* (*que no lo es del gobierno*); ~ *secretary* secretario *m* particular; ~ *view* inauguración *f* privada; 2. ⚔ (*or* ~ *soldier*) soldado *m* raso; ~*s pl.*, ~ *parts pl.* partes *f/pl.* pudendas; *in* ~ en privado, en secreto.
pri·va·teer [praivi'tir] corsario *m*.
pri·va·tion [prai'veiʃn] estrechez *f*, miseria *f*; privación *f*.
pri·va·tive ['privətiv] privativo.
priv·et ['privit] ligustro *m*.
priv·i·lege ['privilidʒ] 1. privilegio *m*, prerrogativa *f*; 2. privilegiar; *be* ~*d to* tener el privilegio de; '**priv·i·leged** privilegiado.
priv·y ['privi] 1. □: *be* ~ *to* estar enterado secretamente de; ♀ *Council* consejo *m* privado; ~ *parts pl.* partes *f/pl.* pudendas; ~ *purse* gastos *m/pl.* personales del monarca; ♀ *Seal* sello *m* pequeño; 2. retrete *m*.
prize [praiz] 1. premio *m*; ⚓ *etc.* presa *f*; 2. premiado; digno de premio; de primera clase; ~ *money* premio *m*; ⚓ parte *f* de presa; 3. apreciar, estimar.
prize...: '~**fight·er** boxeador *m* profesional; '~ **giv·ing** distribución *f* de premios; '~ **mon·ey** bolsa *f*; '~ **win·ner** premiado (a *f*) *m*.
pro[1] [prou] en pro de; *v. con.*
pro[2] [~] F profesional *m/f*.
prob·a·bil·i·ty [prɔbə'biliti] probabilidad *f*; *in all* ~ según toda probabilidad; '**prob·a·ble** □ probable; '**prob·ab·ly** probablemente; *he* ~ *forgot* lo habrá olvidado.
pro·bate ['proubit] verificación *f* oficial de los testamentos.
pro·ba·tion [prə'beiʃn] probación *f*; ⚖ *approx.* libertad *f* condicional; *on* ~ a prueba; ⚖ bajo libertad condicional; ~ *officer oficial que vigila las personas que están en régimen de libertad condicional*; **pro'ba·tion·ar·y** de prueba; ⚖ ~ *period* período *m* de libertad condicional; **pro'ba·tion·er** ⚖ persona *f* en régimen de libertad condicional; *eccl.* novicio (a *f*) *m*; ⚕ aprendiza *f* de enfermera.
probe [proub] 1. ⚕ sonda *f*; (*rocket*) cohete *m*, proyectil *m*; *fig.* F investigación *f* (*into* de), encuesta *f*;

2. ⚕ sondar, tentar; *fig.* indagar, investigar.
prob·i·ty [ˈproubiti] probidad *f.*
prob·lem [ˈprɔbləm] problema *m*; *attr.* F difícil; **prob·lem·at·ic, prob·lem·at·i·cal** [~bliˈmætik(l)] problemático, dudoso. [F nariz *f.*]
pro·bos·cis [prəˈbɔsis] probóscide *f*;
pro·ce·dur·al [prəˈsi:dʒərəl] procesal; **proˈce·dure** [~dʒər] procedimiento *m*, proceder *m*; trámites *m/pl.*
pro·ceed [prəˈsi:d] proceder; (*continue*) seguir, continuar; obrar; ~ *against* proceder contra, procesar; ~ *from* proceder de, provenir de; salir de; ~ *on one's way* seguir su camino; ~ *to election* proceder a; *place* ir a, trasladarse a; ~ *to say etc.* decir *etc.* a continuación; (*unexpectedly*) ~ *to inf.* ponerse a *inf.*; ~ *with* proseguir; **proˈceed·ing** procedimiento *m*; ~*s pl.* actos *m/pl.*; transacciones *f/pl.*; (*published*) actas *f/pl.*; ⚖ proceso *m*, procedimiento *m*; *take* (*legal*) ~*s* entablar demanda, instruir causa; *take* ~*s against* proceder contra; **pro·ceeds** [ˈprousi:dz] *pl.* ganancia *f*, producto *m*; ingresos *m/pl.*
proc·ess [ˈprɔses] 1. procedimiento *m*, proceso *m*; *in* ~ *of construction* bajo construcción, en (vía de) construcción; *in the* ~ *of time* andando el tiempo; 2. *data* procesar; ⊕ preparar, tratar (*into* para hacer); **ˈproc·ess·ing** procesamiento *m*; tratamiento *m*; **pro·ces·sion** [prəˈseʃn] desfile *m*; *eccl.* procesión *f*; *funeral* ~ cortejo *m* fúnebre.
pro·claim [prəˈkleim] proclamar; ~ *o.s. king* proclamarse rey.
proc·la·ma·tion [prɔkləˈmeiʃn] proclamación *f.*
pro·cliv·i·ty [prəˈkliviti] propensión *f*, inclinación *f.*
procras·ti·nate [prəˈkræstineit] hablar *etc.* para aplazar una decisión, no decidirse; tardar; **pro·cras·tiˈna·tion** falta *f* de decisión, dilación *f*, discusión *f etc.* dilatoria.
pro·cre·ate [ˈproukrieit] procrear; **pro·creˈa·tion** procreación *f*; **ˈpro·cre·a·tive** procreador.
proc·tor [ˈprɔktər] ⚖ procurador *m*; *univ.* oficial que cuida de la disciplina.
pro·cur·a·ble [prəˈkjurəbl] asequible.
proc·u·ra·tor [ˈprɔkjureitər] procurador *m.*
pro·cure [prəˈkjur] *v/t.* obtener (*a p. a th.* algo para alguien), conseguir; lograr; gestionar; *girl* obtener para la prostitución; *v/i.* alcahuetear; **proˈcure·ment** obtención *f*; **proˈcur·er** alcahuete *m*; **proˈcur·ess** alcahueta *f.*
prod [prɔd] 1. empuje *m*; codazo *m with elbow*; estímulo *m*; 2. empujar; codear *with elbow*; estimular; *fig.* pinchar.
prod·i·gal [ˈprɔdigəl] □ pródigo (*of* de); *the* ~ *son* el hijo pródigo; **prod·i·gal·i·ty** [~ˈgæliti] prodigalidad *f.*
pro·di·gious [prəˈdidʒəs] □ prodigioso; enorme, ingente; **prod·i·gy** [ˈprɔdidʒi] prodigio *m*; (*a. child* ~, *infant* ~) niño *m* prodigio.
pro·duce 1. [ˈprɔdju:s] producto(s) *m*(*pl.*) (*esp.* agrícolas); 2. [prəˈdju:s] producir; *line* prolongar; (*show*) presentar, mostrar; sacar; (*cause*) causar, ocasionar, motivar; *thea.* (*stage*) presentar; *actors* dirigir; **proˈduc·er** productor (-a *f*) *m*; *thea.* director *m* de escena.
prod·uct [ˈprɔdəkt] producto *m*;
pro·duc·tion [prəˈdʌkʃn] producción *f*; producto *m*; *thea.* (re)presentación *f*; **proˈduc·tive** □ productivo; ~ *of* que produce...; abundante en, prolífico en; *error etc.* con tendencia a causar...; **pro·duc·tiv·i·ty** [prɔdʌkˈtiviti] productividad *f.*
prof [prɔf] F profesor *m.*
prof·a·na·tion [prɔfəˈneiʃn] profanación *f*; **pro·fane** [prəˈfein] 1. □ profano; impío; *language etc.* fuerte, indecente; 2. profanar; **pro·fan·i·ty** [prəˈfæniti] blasfemia *f*, impiedad *f*; F lenguaje *m* indecente, palabrotas *f/pl.*
pro·fess [prəˈfes] profesar; declarar, confesar; *regret etc.* manifestar; ~ *o.s. unable to inf.* declararse incapaz de *inf.*; ~ *to be su.* pretender ser *su.*; **proˈfessed** □ declarado; *b.s.* supuesto; *eccl.* profeso; **proˈfess·ed·ly** [~idli] declaradamente; *b.s.* supuestamente.
pro·fes·sion [prəˈfeʃn] profesión *f*; **proˈfes·sion·al** □ profesional (*a. su. m/f*), de profesión; **proˈfes·sion·al·ism** [~əlizm] *sport*: profesionalismo *m.*

pro·fes·sor [prəˈfesər] profesor (-a *f*) *m* (universitario [a]), catedrático (a *f*) *m*; **proˈfes·sor·ship** cátedra *f*.
prof·fer [ˈprɔfər] ofrecer.
pro·fi·cien·cy [prəˈfiʃənsi] pericia *f*, habilidad *f*; **proˈfi·cient** □ perito, hábil (*at*, *in* en).
pro·file [ˈproufail] **1.** perfil *m*; **2.** perfilar.
prof·it [ˈprɔfit] **1.** ganancia *f* (✝, *a*. ~*s pl*.); *fig*. provecho *m*, beneficio *m*; utilidad *f*; ~ *and loss* ganancias *f*/*pl*. y pérdidas; ~ *margin* excedente *m* de ganancia; **2.** *v*/*t*. servir a, aprovechar a; *v*/*i*.: ~ *by*, ~ *from* aprovechar, sacar partido de; *he does not seem to have* ~*ed* no parece haber sacado provecho de ello; **ˈprof·it·a·ble** □ provechoso; **prof·it·eer** [~ˈtir] **1.** acaparador *m*, el que hace ganancias excesivas; **2.** hacer ganancias excesivas; **prof·itˈeer·ing** (negocios *m*/*pl*. que dan) ganancias *f*/*pl*. excesivas; **ˈprof·it·less** □ inútil; **prof·it shar·ing** [ˈ~ʃeriŋ] participación *f* en los beneficios *by workers*, reparto *m* de los beneficios *by company*.
prof·li·ga·cy [ˈprɔfligəsi] libertinaje *m*; **prof·li·gate** [ˈ~git] □ libertino *adj*. *a*. *su*. *m*.
pro·found [prəˈfaund] □ profundo; **pro·fun·di·ty** [~ˈfʌnditi] profundidad *f*.
pro·fuse [prəˈfjuːs] □ profuso, abundante; pródigo; **proˈfuse·ness, pro·fu·sion** [~ˈfjuːʒn] profusión *f*.
pro·gen·i·tor [prouˈdʒenitər] progenitor *m*; **prog·e·ny** [ˈprɔdʒini] progenie *f*, prole *f*.
prog·no·sis [prɔgˈnousis], *pl*. **progˈno·ses** [~siːz] pronóstico *m*.
prog·nos·tic [prəgˈnɔstik] **1.** pronóstico *m*; **2.** pronosticador, pronóstico; **progˈnos·ti·cate** [~keit] pronosticar; **prog·nos·tiˈca·tion** pronosticación *f*, pronóstico *m*.
pro·gram [ˈprougræm] **1.** programa *m*; **2.** *computer* programar; **pro·gram·(m)er** [ˈprougræmər] programador (-a *f*) *m*; **pro·gram·(m)ing** [ˈprougræmiŋ] programación *f*; *computer* ~ programación *f* de ordenadores.
prog·ress 1. [ˈprɔgres, ˈprougres] progreso(s) *m*(*pl*.); marcha *f*; *in* ~ en vía de realizarse *etc*.; *make* ~ = **2. pro·gress** [prəˈgres] progresar, hacer progresos; **proˈgres·sion** [~ʃn] progresión *f* (*a*. ♈); **proˈgres·sive** □ progresivo; *pol*. progresista (*a*. *su*. *m*/*f*).
pro·hib·it [prəˈhibit] prohibir; **pro·hi·bi·tion** [prouiˈbiʃn] prohibición *f*; **pro·hiˈbi·tion·ist** prohibicionista *m*/*f*; **pro·hib·i·tive** [prəˈhibitiv] □ prohibitivo; *price* exorbitante.
proj·ect [ˈprɔdʒekt] proyecto *m*.
pro·ject [prəˈdʒekt] *v*/*t*. proyectar; *v*/*i*. (sobre)salir; resaltar; **pro·jec·tile** [prəˈdʒektil] proyectil *m*; misil *m*; misil *m*; **proˈject·ing** saliente; **proˈjec·tion** proyección *f*; (*overhang etc*.) saliente *m*, resalto *m*; **proˈjec·tor** *film*: proyector *m*.
pro·le·tar·i·an [prouleˈteriən] proletario *adj*. *a*. *su*. *m* (a *f*); **pro·leˈtar·i·at(e)** [~riət] proletariado *m*.
pro·lif·ic [prəˈlifik] □ prolífico (*of* en).
pro·lix [ˈprouliks] prolijo; **proˈlix·i·ty** prolijidad *f*.
pro·log(ue) [ˈproulɔg] prólogo *m* (*a*. *fig*.).
pro·long [prəˈlɔŋ] prolongar, alargar; **pro·lon·ga·tion** [proulɔŋˈgeiʃn] prolongación *f*.
prom·e·nade [prɔmiˈneid] **1.** paseo *m*; (*seaside*) paseo *m* marítimo; ~ *deck* cubierta *f* de paseo; **2.** pasear(se).
prom·i·nence [ˈprɔminəns] prominencia *f*; *fig*. eminencia *f*; **ˈprom·i·nent** □ saliente, prominente; *eyes* saltones; *fig*. eminente, conspicuo.
prom·is·cu·i·ty [prɔmisˈkjuːiti] promiscuidad *f*; **pro·mis·cu·ous** [prəˈmiskjuəs] □ promiscuo.
prom·ise [ˈprɔmis] **1.** promesa *f*; *have* ~, *be of* (*great*) ~ prometer (mucho); **2.** prometer (*to inf*.); asegurar; (*augur*) augurar, pronosticar; *I* ~ *you* se lo aseguro; *v*. *land*; **ˈprom·is·ing** □ prometedor, que promete; **ˈprom·is·so·ry note** pagaré *m*.
prom·on·to·ry [ˈprɔməntri] promontorio *m*.
pro·mote [prəˈmout] promover, fomentar; ascender *in rank*; *discussion etc*. estimular, facilitar; *parl*. *bill* presentar; *campaign* apoyar; ✝ *business* gestionar; *company* fundar, financiar; **proˈmot·er** promotor *m*; ✝ fundador *m*; *boxing*: empresario *m*, promotor *m*; **proˈmo·tion** promoción *f*, fomento *m*; ascenso *m in rank*.

prompt [prɔmpt] **1.** □ pronto, puntual; **2.** *adv.* puntualmente; *5 o'clock* ~ las 5 en punto; **3.** mover, incitar, estimular (*to* a); *thought etc.* inspirar, sugerir; *thea.* apuntar; **4.** ✝ plazo *m*; ˈ**prompt·er** apuntador *m*; *~'s box* concha *f*; **promp·ti·tude** [ˈ~itjuːd], ˈ**prompt·ness** prontitud *f*, puntualidad *f*.

pro·mul·gate [ˈprɔməlgeit] promulgar; **pro·mulˈga·tion** promulgación *f*.

prone [proun] postrado (boca abajo); *fig.* ~ *to* propenso a; ˈ**prone·ness** *fig.* propensión *f* (*to* a).

prong [prɔŋ] punta *f*, púa *f*; **pronged** [~d] de ... puntas.

pro·nom·i·nal [prəˈnɔminl] □ pronominal.

pro·noun [ˈprounaun] pronombre *m*.

pro·nounce [prəˈnauns] *v/t.* pronunciar (*a.* ⚖); (*with adj.*) declarar, juzgar; *v/i.*: ~ *on* expresar una opinión sobre, juzgar *acc.*; **proˈnounced** [~t] marcado, fuerte; decidido; **proˈnounce·ment** declaración *f*; decisión *f*; opinión *f*.

pron·to [ˈprɔntou] F pronto.

pro·nun·ci·a·tion [prənʌnsiˈeiʃn] pronunciación *f*.

proof [pruːf] **1.** prueba *f* (*a. typ.*); graduación *f* normal *of alcohol*; *in ~ of* en prueba de, en comprobación de; *be ~ against* ser (*or* estar) a prueba de; **2.** *drink* de graduación normal; *~ against* a prueba de; *bullet-~* a prueba de balas; **3.** impermeabilizar; **proof-read** [ˈpruːfriːd] corregir; ˈ**~·read·er** corrector *m* (de pruebas); ˈ**~-sheets** pruebas *f/pl.*; ˈ**~ spir·it** licor *m* de prueba.

prop [prɔp] **1.** ⚠ puntal *m*; sostén *m* (*a. fig.*); ⚒ entibo *m*; ⸙ rodrigón *m*; **2.** (*a. ~ up*) apuntalar; apoyar, sostener (*a. fig.*).

prop·a·gan·da [prɔpəˈgændə] propaganda *f*; **prop·aˈgan·dist** propagandista *m/f*; **prop·a·gate** [ˈprɔpəgeit] propagar; **prop·aˈga·tion** propagación *f*.

pro·pel [prəˈpel] ⊕ impeler, impulsar; empujar; **proˈpel·lant** propulsor *m*; (*rocket*) combustible *m*; **proˈpel·ler** hélice *f*; **proˈpel·ling pen·cil** lapicero *m*.

pro·pen·si·ty [prəˈpensiti] propensión *f* (*to* a).

prop·er [ˈprɔpər] □ propio (*to* de); conveniente, apropiado; (*decent*) decente, decoroso; (*prim and ~*) relamido, etiquetero; F (*fully formed*) hecho y derecho; consumado; *row etc.* de todos los diablos; *what is ~* lo que está bien; *architecture ~* la arquitectura propiamente dicha; *in the ~ sense of the word* en el sentido estricto de la palabra; *~ name* nombre *m* propio; ˈ**prop·er·ly:** *do s.t. ~* hacer algo bien (*or* como hace falta); (*correctly*) correctamente, debidamente; *behave ~* portarse correctamente, portarse decorosamente; *it puzzled him ~* le confundió completamente; ˈ**prop·er·ty** (*estate, quality*) propiedad *f*; hacienda *f*; bienes *m/pl.*; *man of ~* hacendado *m*; *thea. properties pl.* accesorios *m/pl.*; *~ owner* propietario *m* de bienes raíces; ˈ**prop·er·ty tax** impuesto *m* sobre la propiedad.

proph·e·cy [ˈprɔfisi] profecía *f*; **proph·e·sy** [ˈ~sai] profetizar; *fig.* augurar, prever.

proph·et [ˈprɔfit] profeta *m*; **pro·phet·ic, pro·phet·i·cal** [prəˈfetik(l)] □ profético.

pro·phy·lac·tic [prɔfiˈlæktik] □ profiláctico *adj. a. su. m.*

pro·pin·qui·ty [prəˈpiŋkwiti] propincuidad *f*; (*kinship*) consanguinidad *f*.

pro·pi·ti·ate [prəˈpiʃieit] propiciar; conciliar; **pro·pi·tiˈa·tion** propiciación *f*; **proˈpi·ti·a·to·ry** [~ʃiətəri] propiciatorio, conciliatorio.

pro·pi·tious [prəˈpiʃəs] □ propicio.

prop·jet [ˈprɔpˈdʒet] turbohélice *m*.

pro·po·nent [prəˈpounənt] defensor *m*; patrocinador *m*.

pro·por·tion [prəˈpɔːrʃn] **1.** proporción *f*; *in ~ as* a medida que; *in ~ to* en proporción con, a medida de; *out of ~* desproporcionado; *be out of ~* no guardar proporción (*to, with* con); **2.**: *well etc. ~ed* bien *etc.* proporcionado; **proˈpor·tion·al** □ proporcional; *~ representation* representación *f* proporcional; **proˈpor·tion·ate** [~it] □ proporcionado.

pro·pos·al [prəˈpouzəl] propuesta *f*, proposición *f*; oferta *f*; (*a. ~ of marriage*) oferta *f* de matrimonio, declaración *f*; **proˈpose** *v/t.* proponer; ofrecer; *v/i.* proponer; (*marriage*) pedir la mano, declararse (*to* a);

~ to *inf.* proponerse *inf.*, pensar *inf.*; **pro'pos·er** *parl. etc.* proponente *m*; **pro·po·si·tion** [prɔpə'ziʃn] proposición *f*; oferta *f*; F empresa *f*, cosa *f*, problema *m*.

pro·pound [prə'paund] proponer.

pro·pri·e·tar·y [prə'praiətəri] propietario; *article* patentado; **pro'pri·e·tor** propietario *m*; dueño *m*; **pro'pri·e·tress** propietaria *f*; dueña *f*; **pro'pri·e·ty** corrección *f*; conveniencia *f*; decoro *m*; *proprieties pl.* decoro *m*, convenciones *f/pl*.

pro·pul·sion [prə'pʌlʃn] propulsión *f*.

pro·rate [prou'reit] **1.** prorrata *f*; **2.** prorratear.

pro·ro·ga·tion [prourə'geiʃn] prórroga *f*, prorrogación *f*; **pro·rogue** [prə'roug] prorrogar.

pro·sa·ic [prou'zeiik] □ prosaico.

pro·scribe [prəs'kraib] proscribir.

pro·scrip·tion [prəs'kripʃn] proscripción *f*.

prose [prouz] **1.** prosa *f*; **2.** *attr.* de (*or* en) prosa.

pros·e·cute ['prɔsikju:t] ⚖ procesar, enjuiciar; proseguir, continuar; **pros·e'cu·tion** ⚖ (*case*) proceso *m*, causa *f*; ⚖ (*side*) parte *f* actora; prosecución *f*; **'pros·e·cu·tor** acusador *m*; (*a. public* ~) fiscal *m*.

pros·e·lyte ['prɔsilait] prosélito (a *f*) *m*; **pros·e·lyt·ism** ['~litizm] proselitismo *m*; **'pros·e·lyt·ize** *v/i.* ganar prosélitos.

pros·o·dy ['prɔsədi] métrica *f*, prosodia *f*.

pros·pect 1. ['prɔspekt] perspectiva *f*; (*view*) vista *f*; (*expectation*) expectativa *f*, esperanza *f*; (*chance*) probabilidad *f* (de éxito *etc.*); *have in* ~ esperar, anticipar; *hold out a* ~ *of* dar esperanzas de; **2.** [prɔs'pekt] *v/t.* explorar; *v/i.*: ~ *for* buscar; **pro'spect·ing** ⚒ prospección *f*; **pro'spec·tive** □ anticipado, esperado; futuro; **pros'pec·tor** ⚒ prospector *m*; **pro'spec·tus** [~təs] prospecto *m*.

pros·per ['prɔspər] *v/i.* prosperar, medrar; *v/t.* favorecer, fomentar; **pros·per·i·ty** [prɔs'periti] prosperidad *f*; **pros·per·ous** ['~pərəs] □ próspero.

pros·tate ['prɔsteit] **1.** próstata *f*; **2.** prostático; ~ *gland* glándula *f* prostática.

pros·ti·tute ['prɔstitju:t] **1.** prostituta *f*; **2.** prostituir; **pros·ti'tu·tion** prostitución *f*.

pros·trate 1. ['prɔstreit] postrado (*a. fig.*); *fig.* abatido (*with* por); **2.** postrar (*a. fig.*); *fig.* abatir; ~ *o.s.* postrarse; **pros'tra·tion** postración *f* (*a. fig.*); *fig.* abatimiento *m*.

pros·y ['prouzi] prosaico, aburrido.

pro·tag·o·nist [prou'tægənist] protagonista *m/f*.

pro·tect [prə'tekt] proteger (*from* de, contra); **pro'tec·tion** protección *f*; **pro'tec·tion·ist** proteccionista *adj. a. su. m/f*; **pro'tec·tive** □ protector; ~ *custody* custodia *f* preventiva; ~ *duty* impuesto *m* proteccionista; **pro'tec·tor** protector *m*; **pro'tec·tor·ate** [~tərit] protectorado *m*.

pro·té·gé(e) ['prɔteiʒei] protegido (a *f*) *m*, ahijado (a *f*) *m*.

pro·te·in ['prouti:n] proteína *f*.

pro·test 1. ['proutest] protesta *f*; queja *f*; *under* ~ haciendo objeciones; **2.** [prə'test] protestar (*against* de, *that* de que); quejarse; *innocence, loyalty etc.* declarar (enérgicamente).

Prot·es·tant ['prɔtistənt] protestante *adj. a. su. m/f*; **'Prot·es·tant·ism** protestantismo *m*.

prot·es·ta·tion [proutes'teiʃn] protesta *f*.

pro·to·col ['proutəkɔl] protocolo *m*.

pro·ton ['proutɔn] protón *m*.

pro·to·plasm ['proutɔplæzm] protoplasma *m*.

pro·to·type ['proutətaip] prototipo *m*.

pro·tract [prə'trækt] prolongar; **pro'trac·ted** □ largo, prolongado; **pro'trac·tion** prolongación *f*; **pro'trac·tor** transportador *m*.

pro·trude [prə'tru:d] *v/t.* sacar fuera; *v/i.* (sobre)salir, salir fuera; **pro'trud·ing** saliente; *eyes, teeth* saltones.

pro·tu·ber·ance [prə'tju:bərəns] protuberancia *f*, saliente *m*; **pro'tu·ber·ant** □ protuberante, saliente, prominente.

proud [praud] □ orgulloso; *b.s.* soberbio, engreído; (*imposing*) espléndido, imponente; *be* ~ *of* enorgullecerse de; ufanarse de; *be* ~ *to* tener el honor de; F *do o.s.* ~ darse buena vida; F *do a p.* ~ agasajar a una p., hacer fiestas a una p.

prove [pru:v] *v/t.* (com)probar; demostrar; *will* verificar; *v/i.* resultar (*that* que; *true* verdadero); ~ *otherwise* salir de otro modo; ~ *to be* resultar (ser), salir.

prov·e·nance [ˈprɔvinəns] (punto *m* de) origen *m.*

prov·en·der [ˈprɔvindər] forraje *m*; *co.* comida *f.*

prov·erb [ˈprɔvərb] refrán *m*, proverbio *m*; **pro·ver·bi·al** [prəˈvə:rbiəl] ☐ proverbial.

pro·vide [prəˈvaid] *v/t.* suminstrar, surtir; proporcionar; proveer, abastecer (*with* de); *v/i.*: ~ *against* precaverse de; ~ *for* prevenir; prever; *dependents* asegurar el porvenir de; ~ *that* disponer que, estipular que; **proˈvid·ed** (**that**) con tal que.

prov·i·dence [ˈprɔvidəns] providencia *f*; previsión *f*; ♀ (Divina) Providencia; ˈ**prov·i·dent** ☐ providente, previsor; ~ *society* sociedad *f* de socorro mutuo; **prov·i·den·tial** [~ˈdenʃl] ☐ providencial.

pro·vid·er [prəˈvaidər] proveedor (-a *f*) *m.*

prov·ince [ˈprɔvins] provincia *f*; *fig.* competencia *f*, jurisdicción *f.*

pro·vin·cial [prəˈvinʃl] **1.** provincial; de provincia; *contp.* provinciano; **2.** provinciano (a *f*) *m*; **proˈvin·cial·ism** provincialismo *m.*

prov·ing ground [ˈpru:viŋgraund] campo *m* de ensayos.

pro·vi·sion [prəˈviʒn] **1.** provisión *f*; (*condition*) disposición *f*, estipulación *f*; ~*s pl.* provisiones *f/pl.*, víveres *m/pl.*; *make* ~ *for* prevenir; *dependents* asegurar el porvenir de; **2.** aprovisionar, abastecer; **proˈvi·sion·al** ☐ provisional, interino.

pro·vi·so [prəˈvaizou] estipulación *f*; salvedad *f.*

prov·o·ca·tion [prɔvəˈkeiʃn] provocación *f*; **pro·voc·a·tive** [prəˈvɔkətiv] ☐ provocativo.

pro·voke [prəˈvouk] provocar (*to* a), incitar (*to* a); causar, motivar; (*anger*) irritar, indignar; **proˈvok·ing** ☐ provocativo; irritante, enojoso.

prov·ost [ˈprɔvəst] preboste *m*; *univ.* rector *m*; *Scot. approx.* alcalde *m*; *eccl.* prepósito *m*; ⚔ [ˈprouvou] ~ *marshal* capitán preboste *m.*

prow [prau] proa *f.*

prow·ess [ˈprauis] valor *m*; habilidad *f*, destreza *f.*

prowl [praul] **1.** ronda *f* en busca de presa *etc.*; *be on the* ~ = **2.** rondar (en busca de presa *etc.*); vagar (*v/t.* por); ~ **car** coche *m* de policía; ˈ**~er** rondador *m* sospechoso.

prox·im·i·ty [prɔkˈsimiti] proximidad *f*; inmediaciones *f/pl.*; **prox·i·mo** [ˈ~mou] ✝ del mes próximo.

prox·y [ˈprɔksi] (*power*) procuración *f*, poder *m*; (*p.*) apoderado (a *f*) *m*; *by* ~ por poder(es).

prude [pru:d] remilgada *f*, gazmoña *f.*

pru·dence [ˈpru:dəns] prudencia *f*; ˈ**pru·dent** ☐ prudente.

prud·er·y [ˈpru:dəri] remilgo *m*, gazmoñería *f*; ˈ**prud·ish** ☐ remilgado, gazmoño.

prune[1] [pru:n] ciruela *f* pasa.

prune[2] [~] podar; escamondar (*a. fig.*); ˈ**prun·ing** poda *f*; ~ *shears pl.* podadera *f.*

pru·ri·ence, pru·ri·en·cy [ˈpruriəns(i)] salacidad *f*, lascivia *f*; ˈ**pru·ri·ent** ☐ salaz, lascivo.

Prus·sian [ˈprʌʃn] prusiano *adj. a. su. m* (a *f*); ~ *blue* azul *m* de Prusia.

prus·sic ac·id [ˈprʌsikˈæsid] ácido *m* prúsico.

pry [prai] fisgar, fisgonear; curiosear; entrometerse (*into* en); *up, apart, etc.* apalancar; ˈ**pry·ing** ☐ fisgón, entrometido; curioso.

psalm [sɑ:m] salmo *m*; ˈ**psalm·ist** salmista *m*; **psal·mo·dy** [ˈsælmədi] salmodia *f.*

psal·ter [ˈsɔ:ltər] salterio *m.*

pseu·do... [ˈsu:dou] seudo...; falso, fingido; **pseu·do·nym** [ˈ~dənim] seudónimo *m*; **pseu·don·y·mous** [~ˈdɔniməs] ☐ seudónimo.

psych... psic..., psiqu...; *the Academy recommends the spelling* sic..., siqu...

psy·che [ˈsaiki] **1.** sique *f*; **2.** [saik]: *sl.* ganar ventaja a (s.o.) por psicología.

psy·chi·a·trist [saiˈkaiətrist] psiquiatra *m/f*; **psyˈchi·a·try** psiquiatría *f.*

psy·chic [ˈsaikik] ☐ psíquico.

psy·cho·a·nal·y·sis [saikouəˈnæləsis] psicoanálisis *m*; **psy·cho·an·a·lyst** [~ˈænəlist] psicoanalista *m/f.*

psy·cho·log·i·cal [saikəˈlɔdʒikl] ☐ psicológico; **psy·chol·o·gist** [saiˈkɔlədʒist] psicólogo *m*; **psyˈchol·o·gy** psicología *f.*

psy·cho·sis [saiˈkousis] psicosis *f.*

ptar·mi·gan [ˈtɑːrmigən] perdiz *f* blanca (*or* nival).
pto·maine [ˈtoumein] ptomaína *f*; ~ *poisoning* envenenamiento *m* ptomaínico.
pub [pʌb] F taberna *f*, tasca *f*; ˈ**~·crawl** *sl.* **1.** chateo *m* (de tasca en tasca); *go on a* ~ = **2.** ir de chateo, copear, alternar.
pu·ber·ty [ˈpjuːbərti] pubertad *f*.
pu·bes·cence [pjuˈbesns] pubescencia *f*; **puˈbes·cent** pubescente.
pub·lic [ˈpʌblik] **1.** □ público; ~ *address system* sistema *m* amplificador (de discursos públicos); ~ *enemy* enemigo *m* público; ~ *house* taberna *f*; posada *f*; ~ *library* biblioteca *f* pública; ~ *relations* relaciones *f*/*pl.* públicas; ~ *spirit* civismo *m*; *v. school*, *utility etc.*; **2.** público *m*; *in* ~ en público; **pub·li·can** [ˈ~kən] tabernero *m*; **pub·liˈca·tion** publicación *f*; **pub·li·cist** [ˈ~sist] publicista *m*; **pubˈlic·i·ty** [~siti] publicidad *f*; ~ *agent* agente *m* de publicidad; **pub·li·cize** [ˈ~saiz] publicar, dar publicidad a, anunciar; ˈ**pub·lic-ˈspir·it·ed** □ *action* de buen ciudadano; *p.* lleno de civismo.
pub·lish [ˈpʌbliʃ] publicar; ˈ**pub·lish·er** editor *m*; ˈ**pub·lish·ing** publicación *f* de libros; ~ *house* casa *f* editorial.
puce [pjuːs] (de) color purpúreo rojizo.
puck [pʌk] duende *m*.
puck·er [ˈpʌkər] **1.** *sew.* frunce *m*, fruncido *m*; (*accidental*) buche *m*; **2.** (*a.* ~ *up*) *v*/*t. sew.*, *brow* fruncir; *v*/*i.* arrugarse, formar buches.
pud·ding [ˈpudiŋ] pudín *m*.
pud·dle [ˈpʌdl] **1.** charco *m*; **2.** ⊕ pudelar; ˈ**pud·dler** ⊕ pudelador *m*; ˈ**pud·dling fur·nace** horno *m* de pudelar.
pudg·y [ˈpɔdʒi] F gordinflón; rechoncho.
pu·er·ile [ˈpjuəril] pueril; **pu·er·il·i·ty** [~ˈriliti] puerilidad *f*.
puff [pʌf] **1.** resoplido *m*, resuello *m*; soplo *m of air*, racha *f of wind*; bocanada *f*, humareda *f of smoke*; *cookery*: pastelillo *m* de crema; (*advert etc.*) bombo *m*; **2.** *v*/*t.* soplar; ~ *out smoke etc.* echar, arrojar; ~ *up* hinchar, inflar; *v*/*i.* soplar; (*a.* ~ *and blow*) jadear, acezar, resollar; ~ *at* chupar; ~ *out* (*train*) salir echando humo; **puffed** *eye* hinchado; *be* ~ (*out of breath*) estar sin aliento, acezar; *be* ~ *up with pride* engreírse; ˈ**puff·er** F locomotora *f*.
puf·fin [ˈpʌfin] frailecillo *m*.
puff pas·try [ˈpʌfˈpeistri] hojaldre *m*; **puf·fy** hinchado.
pug(**dog**) [ˈpʌg(dɔg)] doguillo *m*.
pu·gil·ism [ˈpjuːdʒilizm] pugilato *m*; ˈ**pu·gil·ist** púgil *m*; pugilista *m*; boxeador *m*.
pug·na·cious [pʌgˈneiʃəs] □ pugnaz; **pug·nac·i·ty** [~ˈnæsiti] pugnacidad *f*.
pug-nosed [ˈpʌgnouzd] chato, braco.
puke [pjuːk] vomitar.
puk·ka [ˈpʌkə] F genuino; elegante, lujoso.
pull [pul] **1.** tirón *m*; estirón *m*; chupada *f at pipe*; cuerda *f of bell*; *typ.* primeras pruebas *f*/*pl.*; F (*drink*) trago *m*; F (*influence*) buenas aldabas *f*/*pl.*; F *it's a long* ~ es mucho camino; **2.** *v*/*t.* tirar de; (*drag*) arrastrar; *muscle* torcerse, dislocarse; *face*(*s*) hacer; ~ *about* manosear, estropear; ~ *along* arrastrar; ~ *back* tirar hacia atrás; ~ *down house* derribar, demoler; *grade*, *price etc.* rebajar; ~ *in rope* cobrar; *suspect* detener; ~ *off* arrancar; quitar de un tirón; F ~ *it off* lograrlo, llevarlo a cabo, vencer (inesperadamente); ~ *out* sacar; arrancar; (*stretch*) estirar; F ~ *strings* usar enchufe; ~ *through* sacar de una enfermedad *etc.*; ~ *to pieces* deshacer, hacer pedazos; *fig. argument* deshacer; *p.* criticar severamente; ~ *o.s. together* sobreponerse, recobrar la calma; ~ *up root etc.* arrancar; *car* parar; *v*/*i.* tirar, dar un tirón; ~ *at pipe* chupar; *rope etc.* tirar de; ~ *in* 🚂 llegar al andén; *mot.* parar junto a la acera; ~ *on* tirar de; ~ *out* 🚂 salir de la estación; ⚔ retirarse; ~ *through* ⚕ recobrar la salud; salir de un apuro; ~ *up* pararse, detenerse; mejorar su posición.
pul·let [ˈpulit] poll(it)a *f*.
pul·ley [ˈpuli] polea *f*.
Pull·man car [ˈpulmənˈkɑːr] coche *m* Pullman.
pull·o·ver [ˈpulouvər] jersey *m*; pulóver *m*.
pul·mo·nar·y [ˈpʌlmənəri] pulmonar.
pulp [pʌlp] **1.** pulpa *f*; pasta *f* (*a. wood* ~); **2.** hacer pulpa.

pul·pit [ˈpulpit] púlpito *m.*
pulp·y [ˈpʌlpi] pulposo.
pul·sate [pʌlˈseit] pulsar, latir, vibrar; **pulˈsa·tion** pulsación *f*, latido *m.*
pulse [pʌls] **1.** pulso *m*; *feel one's* ~ tomar el pulso a; **2.** pulsar, latir.
pul·ver·i·za·tion [pʌlvəraiˈzeiʃn] pulverización *f*; ˈ**pul·ver·ize** pulverizar(se); F cascar.
pum·ice [ˈpʌmis] (*a.* ˈ~ **stone**) piedra *f* pómez.
pum·mel [ˈpʌml] *v. pommel.*
pump[1] [pʌmp] **1.** bomba *f*; **2.** sacar (*or* elevar *etc.*) con bomba; *arm* mover rápidamente de arriba para abajo; F *p.* sonsacar; ~ *dry* secar con bomba(s); ~ *up tire* inflar.
pump[2] [~] (*shoe*) zapatilla *f.*
pump·kin [ˈpʌmpkin] calabaza *f.*
pun [pʌn] **1.** juego *m* de palabras (*on* sobre); equívoco *m*; **2.** jugar del vocablo (*a.* ~ *on*).
punch[1] [pʌntʃ] **1.** ⊕ punzón *m*; **2.** punzar, taladrar; *ticket* picar.
punch[2] [~] **1.** (*blow*) puñetazo *m*; F empuje *m*, vigor *m*; *pull one's* ~*es* no emplear toda su fuerza; **2.** dar un puñetazo a, pegar con los puños; golpear; *cattle* guiar; acorralar; cuidar.
punch[3] [~] (*drink*) ponche *m.*
punch·ball [ˈpʌntʃbɔːl] saco *m* de arena, punching *m*; **punch-drunk** [ˈ~drʌŋk] *boxer* atontado.
punc·til·i·o [pʌŋkˈtiliou] puntillo *m*, etiqueta *f*; **punc·til·i·ous** [~ˈtiliəs] □ puntilloso, etiquetero.
punc·tu·al [ˈpʌŋktʃuəl] □ puntual; **punc·tu·al·i·ty** [~ˈæliti] puntualidad *f.*
punc·tu·ate [ˈpʌŋktʃueit] puntuar (*a. fig.*); **punc·tuˈa·tion** puntuación *f.*
punc·ture [ˈpʌŋktʃər] **1.** *mot. etc.* pinchazo *m*; puntura *f*, punzada *f of skin*; ⚕ punción *f*; *have a* ~ tener un neumático pinchado; **2.** pinchar; perforar, punzar.
pun·dit [ˈpʌndit] *contp.* erudito *m*; experto *m.*
pun·gen·cy [ˈpʌndʒənsi] picante *m*; lo acre; mordacidad *f*; ˈ**pun·gent** □ picante; *smell* acre; *remark etc.* mordaz, áspero.
pun·ish [ˈpʌniʃ] castigar; F maltratar; (*tax*) exigir esfuerzos sobrehumanos a; ˈ**pun·ish·a·ble** □ punible, castigable; ˈ**pun·ish·ment** castigo *m*; F tratamiento *m* severo.
pu·ni·tive [ˈpjuːnitiv] punitivo.
punk [pʌŋk] **1.** basura *f*, fruslerías *f/pl.*; *sl.* pillo *m*; **2.** *sl.* malo, baladí; **punk rock** [ˈpʌŋkrɔk] música *f* rock de efectos deliberadamente chocantes.
pun·ster [ˈpʌnstər] persona *f* aficionada a los juegos de palabras.
punt[1] [pʌnt] ⚓ **1.** batea *f*; **2.** *v/i.* ir en batea; *v/t.* impeler con botador.
punt[2] [~] jugar, hacer apuestas; ˈ**punt·er** jugador *m.*
pu·ny [ˈpjuːni] encanijado; insignificante; *effort etc.* débil.
pup [pʌp] **1.** cachorro (a *f*) *m*; **2.** parir (*la perra*).
pu·pil [ˈpjuːpl] alumno (a *f*) *m*; *anat.* pupila *f.*
pup·pet [ˈpʌpit] títere *m*; (*p.*) marioneta *f*; ~ *régime* régimen *m* marioneta; ˈ~ **show** (función *f* de) títeres *m/pl.*
pup·py [ˈpʌpi] cachorro (a *f*) *m*; perrito (a *f*) *m.*
pur·blind [ˈpəːrblaind] cegato; *fig.* falto de comprensión.
pur·chase [ˈpəːrtʃəs] **1.** compra *f*; *fig.* agarre *m* firme; ⊕ apalancamiento *m*; ~ *tax* impuesto *m* de venta; *get a* ~ *on rock etc.* tener donde agarrarse; *make* ~*s* hacer compras; **2.** comprar, adquirir; *purchasing power* poder *m* adquisitivo; ˈ**pur·chas·er** comprador (-a *f*) *m.*
pure [pjur] □ puro; casto; no mezclado; ˈ~**-bred** de pura sangre; ˈ**pure·ness** pureza *f.*
pur·ga·tion [pəːrˈgeiʃn] purgación *f*; **pur·ga·tive** [ˈ~getiv] purgativo; purgante (*a. su. m*); ˈ**pur·ga·to·ry** purgatorio *m.*
purge [pəːrdʒ] **1.** ⚕ purga *f*, purgante *m*; *pol.* purga *f*, depuración *f*; **2.** purgar; purificar, depurar; *pol. party* purgar, depurar; *member* liquidar.
pu·ri·fi·ca·tion [pjurifiˈkeiʃn] purificación *f*, depuración *f*; **pu·ri·fi·er** [ˈ~faiər] (*water*) depurador *m*; **pu·ri·fy** [ˈ~fai] purificar, depurar; *metall.* acrisolar; ˈ**pu·rist** purista *m/f*, casticista *m/f.*
pu·ri·tan [ˈpjuritən] puritano *adj. a. su. m* (a *f*); **pu·ri·tan·i·cal** [~ˈtænikl] □ puritano; **pu·ri·tan·ism** [ˈ~tənizm] puritanismo *m.*
pu·ri·ty [ˈpjuriti] pureza *f*; castidad *f.*

purl [pəːrl] **1.** punto *m* de media invertido; **2.** hacer un punto de media invertido.
pur·lieu [ˈpəːrljuː] *fig.* competencia *f*; ~*s pl.* alrededores *m/pl.*, immediaciones *f/pl.*
pur·loin [pəːrˈlɔin] hurtar, robar.
pur·ple [ˈpəːrpl] **1.** purpúreo, morado; ~ *patch* trozo *m* de estilo hinchado, pasaje *m* demasiado sentimental *etc.*; **2.** púrpura *f*; **3.** purpurar.
pur·port 1. [ˈpəːrpərt] significado *m*, tenor *m*; intención *f*; **2.** [pərˈpɔːrt] significar, dar a entender (*that* que); ~ *to inf.* pretender *inf.*
pur·pose [ˈpəːrpəs] **1.** propósito *m*, intención *f*; resolución *f*; *novel with a* ~ novela *f* de tesis; *strength of* ~ resolución *f*; *for the* ~ *of ger.* con el fin de *inf.*; *on* ~ adrede, de propósito; *to good* ~ con buenos resultados; *to no* ~ inútilmente, en vano; *serve one's* ~ servir para el caso; **2.** proponerse; proyectar; **pur·pose·ful** [ˈ~ful] □ determinado, resuelto; ˈ**purpose·less** □ sin propósito fijo, sin fin determinado; ˈ**pur·pose·ly** *adv.* adrede, de propósito.
purr [pəːr] **1.** (*cat, motor*) ronronear; *fig.* decir suavemente; **2.** ronroneo *m.*
purse [pəːrs] **1.** bolsa *f*; bolso *m*; (*prize*) premio *m*; **2.** *lips* fruncir; ˈ**purs·er** contador *m* de navío; ˈ**purse strings:** *hold the* ~ tener las llaves de la caja.
pur·su·ance [pərˈsjuːəns]: *in* ~ *of* con arreglo a, cumpliendo; **purˈsu·ant:** ~ *to* de acuerdo con.
pur·sue [pərˈsuː] (*hunt*) seguir (la pista de), cazar; (*a. fig.*) perseguir; acosar; *pleasures etc.* dedicarse a; *plan* proceder de acuerdo con; *profession* ejercer; *study, inquiry* proseguir; **purˈsu·er** perseguidor (-a *f*) *m*; **pur·suit** [~ˈsuːt] caza *f*, busca *f*; persecución *f*; (*occupation*) ocupación *f*; (*pastime*) pasatiempo *m*; *in* ~ *of* en pos de; ~ *plane* avión *m* de caza.
pu·ru·lent [ˈpjurulənt] □ purulento.
pur·vey [pəːrˈvei] suministrar, abastecer, proveer; **purˈvey·ance** suministro *m*, abastecimiento *m*; **purˈvey·or** abastecedor (-a *f*) *m*, proveedor (-a *f*) *m*.
pur·view [ˈpəːrvjuː] alcance *m*, esfera *f*.
pus [pʌs] pus *m*.
push [puʃ] **1.** empuje *m*, empujón *m*; ⚔ ofensiva *f*, avance *m*; agresividad *f*; *sl. give a p. the* ~ despedir a una p.; **2.** *v/t.* empujar; *enterprise* promover, fomentar; *claim* proseguir; F *product* hacer una campaña publicitaria a favor de; *p.* incitar, obligar (*to* a); F (*prod*) pinchar; ~ *one's way* abrirse paso empujando; F *be* ~*ed for* tener muy poco ... disponible; andar muy escaso de; ~ *away* apartar con la mano; empujar; ~ *back* echar atrás; ~ *in* introducir a la fuerza; ~ *off* ⚓ desatracar; ~ *out* empujar hacia fuera; expulsar; ~ *through measure* hacer aceptar a la fuerza; *v/i.* empujar, dar un empujón; hacer esfuerzos; ~ *off* ⚓ desatracarse, apartarse de la orilla; F largarse, marcharse; ~ *on* seguir adelante, continuar (a pesar de todo); avanzar; ˈ~**-but·ton** (*attr.* que tiene) pulsador *m*, botón *m* de llamada *etc.*; ~ *control* mando *m* por botón; ˈ~**-cart** carretilla *f* de mano; **push·ful** [ˈ~ful] □, ˈ**push·ing** □ emprendedor, vigoroso; *b.s.* agresivo; ˈ**push·ful·ness** empuje *m*; ˈ**push·o·ver** F cosa *f* muy fácil; persona *f* muy fácil de (con)vencer *etc.*; breva *f*; ˈ**push·y** F agresivo; presumido.
pu·sil·la·nim·i·ty [pjuːsiləˈnimiti] pusilanimidad *f*; **pu·sil·lan·i·mous** [~ˈlænimәs] □ pusilánime.
puss(·y) [ˈpus(i)] minimo *m*, micho *m*; F moza *f*; *sl.* cara *f*; ˈ**puss·y·foot** F moverse a paso de gato, andar a tientas; no declararse.
pus·tule [ˈpʌstjuːl] pústula *f*.
put [put] [*irr.*] **1.** *v/t.* poner; colocar; (*insert*) meter; *weight* lanzar, arrojar; *question* hacer; *motion* proponer, someter a votación; (*expound*) exponer, presentar; expresar, redactar *in words*; (*translate*) traducir (*into* a); (*estimate*) computar, estimar; tasar (*at* en); *for many phrases, see the corresponding su.*; ~ *it about that* dar a entender que; ~ *across meaning* comunicar, hacer entender; *idea, product* hacer aceptar; F ~ *it across* (*deceive*) engañar, embaucar; (*defeat*) cascar; ~ *aside* (*reject*) rechazar; (*save*) poner aparte, ahorrar; ~ *away* (*keep*) guardar; (*save*) ahorrar; volver a poner en su lugar; F *food* zampar; (*imprison*) encarcelar; *lunatic* meter en un manicomio;

~ *back th.* devolver a su lugar; *clock, process* retardar, atrasar; *function etc.* aplazar; ~ *by* poner aparte; *money* ahorrar; ~ *down revolt* suprimir; *burden* poner en el suelo; soltar; apuntar *in writing*; ⚕ sentar (*to* en la cuenta de); *I could not* ~ *the book down* me era imposible dejar el libro de la mano; ~ *down as* juzgar; ~ (*it*) *down to* atribuir(lo) a, achacar(lo) a; ~ *forth book etc.* publicar; *bud etc.* producir, echar; *effort* emplear; ~ *forward* presentar, proponer; *function, date* adelantar; ~ *o.s. forward* ofrecerse (con poca modestia), llamar sobre sí la atención; ~ *in* meter, insertar, introducir; *claim* presentar; *remark* interponer; *time* dedicar; ~ *off* (*postpone*) aplazar, dejar para después; *p.* quitar las ganas de, hacer perder el sabor de (*fig.* el deseo de); *scent* desviar de, apartar de; (*dissuade*) disuadir; (*evade*) dar largas a, apartar de su propósito (con evasivas); ~ *on clothes* ponerse; *shoes* calzarse; F ~ *it on* exagerar; emocionarse demasiado; darse tono; ⚕ engordar; ~ *out hand etc.* extender; *head etc.* asomar, sacar; *tongue* sacar; *shoot* echar; *bone* dislocar; *book* publicar; *fire, light* apagar; (*expel*) poner en la calle; (*inconvenience*) molestar, incomodar; (*disconcert*) desconcertar; ~ *over idea, product* hacer aceptar; *meaning* comunicar; ~ *o.s. over* impresionar con su personalidad; ~ *right watch* poner en hora; *difficulty* resolver, arreglar; *mistake* corregir; ~ *through task* llevar a cabo; *proposal* hacer aceptar; *teleph.* poner (*to* con); ~ *it to p.* decirlo a; sugerirlo a; proponerlo a; *be hard* ~ *to it to* tener mucha dificultad en *inf.*; ~ *together* añadir; juntar; ⊕ montar; ~ *up building* construir; *sword* envainar; *umbrella* abrir; *price* aumentar; *prize* ofrecer; *money* poner, contribuir; *game* levantar; *candidate* nombrar; apoyar; *guest* hospedar; *p.* ~ *up to* incitar a; **2.** *v/i.*: ~ *about* ⚓ cambiar de rumbo; ~ *in* ⚓ entrar a puerto; ~ *in at* ⚓ hacer escala en; ~ *in for post* presentarse a, solicitar; ~ *off*, ~ *out* ⚓ hacerse a la mar; ~ *up at* hospedarse en; ~ *up for* ser candidato a; ~ *up with* aguantar, resignarse a; ~ *upon* molestar, incomodar.

pu·ta·tive [ˈpjuːtətiv] putativo.

pu·tre·fac·tion [pjuːtriˈfækʃn] putrefacción *f*.

pu·tre·fy [ˈpjuːtrifai] pudrirse.

pu·tres·cence [pjuːˈtresns] pudrición *f*; **puˈtres·cent** putrescente.

pu·trid [ˈpjuːtrid] □ podrido, putrefacto; F malísimo, pésimo.

putt [pʌt] **1.** golpe *m* corto; **2.** golpear con poca fuerza.

put·ty [ˈpʌti] **1.** masilla *f*; **2.** enmasillar.

put-up job [ˈputʌpˈdʒɔb] *sl.* cosa *f* proyectada y preparada de antemano; asunto *m* fraudulento.

puz·zle [ˈpʌzl] **1.** problema *m*, enigma *m*; (*game*) rompecabezas *m*, acertijo *m*; **2.** *v/t.* intrigar, confundir, dejar perplejo; ~ *out* descifrar, resolver; *v/i.*: ~ *over* tratar de resolver, devanarse los sesos para descifrar; **ˈpuz·zled** intrigado; perplejo; **ˈpuz·zler** engima *m*, problema *m* difícil; **ˈpuz·zling** enigmático, misterioso.

pyg·my [ˈpigmi] pigmeo *adj. a. su. m.*

py·ja·mas [pəˈdʒɑːməz] *pl.* pijama *m.*

py·lon [ˈpailən] pilón *m*; ⚡ torre *f* de conducción eléctrica.

py·or·rh(o)e·a [paiəˈriə] piorrea *f*.

pyr·a·mid [ˈpirəmid] pirámide *f*; **py·ram·i·dal** [piˈræmidl] piramidal.

pyre [ˈpaiər] pira *f*; *fig.* hoguera *f*.

py·ret·ic [paiˈretik] pirético.

py·ri·tes [paiˈraitiːz] pirita *f*.

py·ro... [ˈpairou] piro...; **py·roˈtech·nics** *pl.* pirotecnia *f*.

py·thon [ˈpaiθən] pitón *m*.

pyx [piks] *eccl.* píxide *f*.

Q

quack[1] [kwæk] *approx.* **1.** graznido *m*; **2.** graznar.
quack[2] [~] **1.** charlatán *m*, curandero *m*; **2.** falso; fraudulento; *remedy* de curandero; **quack·er·y** ['~əri] charlatanismo *m*.
quad [kwɔd] = *quadrangle, quadrat, quadruplet(s)*.
quad·ran·gle ['kwɔdræŋgl] cuadrángulo *m*; ⚠ patio *m*.
quad·rant ['kwɔdrənt] cuadrante *m*.
quad·ra·phon·ic [kwɔdrə'fɔnik] cuadrafónico; **quad·rat** ['kwɔdræt] cuadrado *m*, cuadratín *m*; **quad·rat·ic** [kwɔ'drætik] de segundo grado; **quad·ra·ture** ['kwɔdrətʃər] cuadratura *f*.
quad·ri·lat·er·al [kwɔdri'lætərəl] cuadrilátero *adj. a. su. m.*
quad·ri·par·tite [kwɔdri'pɑːrtait] cuadripartido.
quad·ru·ped ['kwɔdruped] **1.** cuadrúpedo *m*; **2.** (*a.* **quad·ru·pe·dal** [kwɔ'druːpidl]) cuadrúpedo; **quad·ru·ple 1.** ['kwɔdrupl] cuádruple; **2.** [~] cuádruplo *m*; **3.** [~'rupl] cuadruplicar(se); **quad·ru·plets** [kwɔd'ruːplits] *pl.* cuatrillizos (as *f/pl.*) *m/pl.*; **quad·ru·pli·cate 1.** [kwɔ'druːplikit] (*in* por) cuadruplicado; **2.** [~keit] cuadruplicar.
quaff [kwæf] † beber; *~ off* beberse *acc.*, apurar.
quag·mire ['kwægmaiər] tremedal *m*, cenegal *m*.
quail[1] [kweil] *orn.* codorniz *f*.
quail[2] [~] acobardarse, descorazonarse.
quaint [kweint] □ curioso, original; pintoresco; típico; '**quaint·ness** singularidad *f*; lo pintoresco; tipismo *m*.
quake [kweik] **1.** temblor *m*; terremoto *m*; **2.** temblar, trepidar, estremecerse (*with, for* de).
Quak·er ['kweikər] cuáquero *m*; '**Quak·er·ism** cuaquerismo *m*.
qual·i·fi·ca·tion [kwɔlifi'keiʃn] calificación *f*; requisito *m*; modificación *f*, restricción *f*; *have the ~s* llenar los requisitos; *without ~* sin reserva; **qual·i·fied** ['~faid] *p.* c(u)alificado, habilitado, capacitado, competente; modificado, limitado; **qual·i·fy** ['~fai] *v/t.* calificar (*a. gr.*); habilitar; modificar, limitar; *drink* aguar; *v/i.* habilitarse, capacitarse; llenar los requisitos; *qualifying examination* examen *m* eliminatorio; **qual·i·ta·tive** ['~teitiv] □ cualitativo; '**qual·i·ty** (*type, character*) calidad *f*, categoría *f*, clase *f*; (*characteristic*) cualidad *f*, virtud *f*; *the ~* la aristocracia; *of low ~* de baja calidad; *he has many good qualities* tiene muchas buenas cualidades.
qualm [kwɔːm, kwɑːm] ⚕ bascas *f/pl.*, náusea *f*; duda *f*, escrúpulo *m of conscience*; inquietud *f*; '**qualm·ish** □ bascoso.
quan·da·ry ['kwɔndəri] incertidumbre *f*, perplejidad *f*, dilema *m*; *be in a ~* estar en un dilema.
quan·ti·ta·tive ['kwɔntiteitiv] □ cuantitativo; *~ analysis* análisis *m* cuantitativo; '**quan·ti·ty** cantidad *f*; *unknown ~* incógnita *f* (*a. fig.*); *~ surveyor* aparejador *m*.
quan·tum ['kwɔntəm] cantidad *f*; *phys.* cuanto *m*; *~ theory* teoría *f* cuántica (*or* de los cuanta).
quar·an·tine ['kwɔrəntiːn] **1.** cuarentena *f*; *place in ~* = **2.** poner en cuarentena.
quar·rel ['kwɔrəl] **1.** riña *f*, disputa *f*; (*violent*) reyerta *f*, pendencia *f*; *pick a ~* buscar camorra; **2.** reñir, disputar; pelear; **quar·rel·some** ['~səm] □ pendenciero.
quar·ry[1] ['kwɔri] **1.** cantera *f*; *fig.* mina *f*; **2.** sacar, extraer (*a. fig.*).
quar·ry[2] [~] *hunt.* presa *f*.
quar·ry·man ['kwɔrimən] cantero *m*.
quart [kwɔːrt] *cuarto de galón* (= *1,136 litros*).
quarte [kɑːrt] *fenc.* cuarta *f*.
quar·ter ['kwɔːrtər] **1.** cuarto *m*, cuarta parte *f*; *heraldry*: cuartel *m*; (*3*

months) trimestre *m*; cuarto *m of moon*; barrio *m of town*; *fig*. procedencia *f*; *moneda de 25 centavos*; (*weight*) (= *28 libras = 12,7 Kg*.) *approx*. arroba *f*; ~*s pl*. vivienda *f*; ⚔ cuartel *m*, alojamiento *m*; ~ *of an hour* cuarto *m* de hora; *from all* ~*s* de todas partes; *in this* ~ por aquí; *at close* ~*s* de cerca; ⚔ casi cuerpo a cuerpo; ⚔ *give no* ~ no dar cuartel; *have free* ~*s* tener alojamiento gratis; **2.** cuartear; *meat* descuartizar; *heraldry*: cuartelar; ⚔ acuartelar; *be* ~*ed* (*up*)*on* estar alojado en casa de; ˈ~ **day** día *m* en que se paga un trimestre; ˈ**~-deck** alcázar *m*; ˈ**quar·ter·ly 1.** trimestral; **2.** publicación *f* trimestral; **3.** cada tres meses, por trimestres; ˈ**quar·ter·mas·ter** *approx*. furriel *m*, comisario *m*; **quar·tern** [ˈ~ərn] cuarta *f*; (*a*. ~ *loaf*) pan *m* de 4 libras.

quar·tet(**te**) [kwɔːrˈtet] cuarteto *m*.

quar·to [ˈkwɔːrtou] en cuarto; (*paper*) tamaño holandesa.

quartz [kwɔːrts] cuarzo *m*.

qua·sar [ˈkweizɑːr] *ast*. fuente *f* cuasiestelar de radio.

quash [kwɔʃ] anular, invalidar.

qua·si [ˈkweisai] cuasi ...

qua·ter·na·ry [kwəˈtəːrnəri] cuaternario (*a. geol*.).

quat·rain [ˈkwɔtrein] estrofa *f* de 4 versos.

qua·ver [ˈkweivər] **1.** temblor *m*; ♪ trémolo *m*; (*note*) corchea *f*; **2.** temblar, vibrar; ♪ gorjear, trinar; ˈ**qua·ver·ing** □, ˈ**qua·ver·y** trémulo.

quay [kiː] muelle *m*, desembarcadero *m*.

quea·si·ness [ˈkwiːzinis] bascas *f/pl*.; propensión *f* a la náusea; ˈ**quea·sy** □ bascoso; delicado; *conscience* escrupuloso; *I feel* ~ me siento mal.

queen [kwiːn] **1.** reina *f* (*a. chess*); *cards*: dama *f*, (*Spanish*) caballo *m*; ~ *bee* abeja *f* reina; ~ *mother* reina *f* madre; **2.** *pawn* coronar; ~ *it* pavonearse; ˈ**queen·like**, ˈ**queen·ly** regio, de reina.

queer [kwir] □ raro, extraño; misterioso; excéntrico, extravagante; F ⚕ enfermo; F *contp*. maricón (*a. su. m*); F ⚕ *feel* ~ sentirse indispuesto.

quell [kwel] reprimir, domar; calmar.

quench [kwentʃ] *thirst etc*. apagar; extinguir, ahogar; ⊕ templar; ˈ**quench·er** F trago *m*; ˈ**quench·less** □ inapagable.

quern [kwəːrn] molinillo *m* de mano.

quer·u·lous [ˈkweruləs] □ quejumbroso, quejicoso.

que·ry [ˈkwiri] **1.** (*abbr*. **qu.**) pregunta *f*; duda *f*; punto *m* de interrogación [?]; **2.** preguntar; expresar dudas acerca de, dudar de; no estar conforme con.

quest [kwest] **1.** busca *f*, búsqueda *f*; pesquisa *f*; *in* ~ *of* en busca de; **2.** buscar (*for acc*.).

ques·tion [ˈkwestʃn] **1.** pregunta *f*; (*affair*) asunto *m*, cuestión *f*; problema *m*; ~ *mark* punto *m* de interrogación; *beyond all* ~ fuera de (toda) duda; *in* ~ en cuestión; *beg the* ~ ser una petición de principio; *call in* ~ poner en duda; *come into* ~ empezar a discutirse; *it is a* ~ *of* se trata de; *the* ~ *is* el caso es; *that is the* ~ ahí está el problema; *that is out of the* ~ es totalmente imposible; *there is no* ~ *of* no se trata de; **2.** interrogar, hacer preguntas a; examinar; (*doubt*) poner en duda; desconfiar de; ˈ**ques·tion·a·ble** □ cuestionable, dudoso; **ques·tion·naire** [kwestʃəˈner] cuestionario *m*; ˈ**ques·tion·er** interrogador (-a *f*) *m*.

queue [kjuː] **1.** cola *f*; **2.** hacer cola (*a*. ~ *up*).

quib·ble [ˈkwibl] **1.** evasión *f*, sofistería *f*; retruécano *m*; **2.** sutilizar; jugar del vocablo; buscar evasivas; ˈ**quib·bler** sofista *m/f*.

quick [kwik] **1.** rápido, veloz; pronto; vivo; ágil; *ear* fino; *eye, wit* agudo; **2.** carne *f* viva; *the* ~ los vivos; *cut to the* ~ herir en lo vivo; **3.** *v*. ~*ly*; ~ *march!* de frente ¡mar!; ˈ**~-change ac·tor** transformista *m*; ˈ**quick·en** acelerar(se), apresurar; vivificar; ˈ**quick-fir·ing** de tiro rápido; ˈ**quick-ˈfroz·en** de congelación rápida; **quick·ie** [ˈ~i] F pregunta *f* (*or* acción *f*) relámpago; ˈ**quick·lime** cal *f* viva; ˈ**quick·ly** pronto; de prisa, rápidamente; ˈ**quick·ness** presteza *f*, celeridad *f*; prontitud *f*; viveza *f*, penetración *f of mind*.

quick...: ˈ**~·sand** arena *f* movediza; ˈ**~·set** ⸙ plantón *m* (*esp*. espino *m*); seto *m* vivo (*a*. ~ *hedge*); ˈ**~-ˈsight·ed** de vista aguda; ˈ**~·sil·ver** azogue *m*, mercurio *m*; ˈ**~-ˈtem·pered** de genio vivo; ˈ**~-ˈwit·ted** agudo, perspicaz.

quid·di·ty ['kwiditi] *phls.* esencia *f*; sutileza *f*.
quid pro quo ['kwid prou 'kwou] compensación *f*; recompensa *f*.
qui·es·cence [kwai'esns] quietud *f*, tranquilidad *f*; **qui'es·cent** □ quieto, inactivo; latente.
qui·et ['kwaiət] **1.** □ (*silent*) silencioso, callado; (*motionless, not excited*) quieto, tranquilo; reposado; *color* no llamativo; *market* encalmado; *celebration etc.* sin ceremonias, más bien privado; *all* ~ sin novedad; *be* ~, *keep* ~ (*p.*) callarse; **2.** silencio *m*; tranquilidad *f*, reposo *m*; F *on the* ~ a la sordina; **3.** calmar(se), tranquilizar(se); F callarse (*a.* ~ *down*); **4.** ~! ¡silencio!; **'qui·et·ism** quietismo *m*; **'qui·et·ist** quietista *m*/*f*; **'qui·et·ness, qui·e·tude** ['~tjuːd] tranquilidad *f*, quietud *f*; silencio *m*.
qui·e·tus [kwai'iːtəs] golpe *m* de gracia; muerte *f*.
quill [kwil] **1.** pluma *f*; cañón *m* (de pluma); (*spine*) púa *f*; (*bobbin*) canilla *f*; **2.** plegar; **'quill pen** pluma *f* de ave (para escribir).
quilt [kwilt] **1.** colcha *f*; **2.** acolchar; estofar; pespunt(e)ar; **'quilt·ing** colchadura *f*; (*art*) piqué *m*.
quince [kwins] membrillo *m*.
qui·nine ['kwainain] quinina *f*.
quin·quen·ni·al [kwiŋ'kwenjəl] □ quinquenal.
quin·quen·ni·um [kwiŋ'kweniəm] quinquenio *m*.
quins [kwinz] F quintillizos (as *f*/*pl.*) *m*/*pl*.
quin·sy ['kwinzi] angina *f*.
quint·es·sence [kwin'tesns] quinta esencia *f*.
quin·tet(te) [kwin'tet] quinteto *m*.
quin·tu·ple ['kwintjupl] **1.** quíntuplo; **2.** quintuplicar(se); **quin·tu·plets** ['~plits] *pl.* quintillizos (as *f*/*pl.*) *m*/*pl*.
quip [kwip] **1.** agudeza *f*, pulla *f*, chiste *m*; **2.** echar pullas.
quire ['kwaiər] mano *f* de papel.
quirk [kwəːrk] (*oddity*) capricho *m*, idiosincrasia *f*, peculiaridad *f*; (*quip*) agudeza *f*; (*flourish*) rasgo *m*; ⚠ avivador *m*.
quit [kwit] **1.** *v*/*t*. dejar, abandonar; salir de; desocupar; ~ *ger.* dejar de *inf.*, desistir de *inf.*; *v*/*i*. retirarse, despedirse; rajarse; cejar; **2.** libre (*of* de); absuelto.
quite [kwait] totalmente, completamente; (*rather*) bastante; ~ *a hero* todo un héroe; ~ (*so*)! efectivamente, perfectamente; ~ *that!* ¡lo menos eso!, ¡ya lo creo!; F ~ *the go*, ~ *the thing* muy de moda.
quits [kwits]: *call it* ~ no seguir; descontinuar; *cry* ~ hacer las paces.
quit·ter ['kwitər] remolón *m*; F *approx.* faltón *m*, inconstante *m*; catacaldos *m*.
quiv·er[1] ['kwivər] **1.** temblar, estremecerse; **2.** temblor *m*.
quiv·er[2] [~] carcaj *m*, aljaba *f*.
quix·ot·ic [kwik'sɔtik] □ quijotesco.
quiz [kwiz] **1.** encuesta *f*; acertijo *m*; prueba *f*; ~ *show* torneo *m* radiofónico (*or* televisado); **2.** interrogar; mirar con curiosidad; **'quiz·zi·cal** □ burlón.
quod [kwɔd] *sl.* chirona *f*.
quoin [kɔin] ⚠ esquina *f*; piedra *f* angular; *typ.* cuña *f*.
quoit [kɔit] tejo *m*; ~*s pl.* juego *m* de tejos (*or* aros).
quon·dam ['kwɔndæm] antiguo.
quo·rum ['kwɔːrəm] quórum *m*.
quo·ta ['kwoutə] cuota *f*; contingente *m*, cupo *m*.
quo·ta·tion [kwou'teiʃn] cita *f*, citación *f*; ✝ cotización *f*; **quo'ta·tion marks** *pl.* comillas *f*/*pl*.
quote [kwout] **1.** citar; ✝ cotizar (*at* en); **2.** = *quotation*.
quoth [kwouθ]: † ~ *I* dije (yo).
quo·tient ['kwouʃənt] cociente *m*.

R

rab·bet ['ræbit] **1.** rebajo *m*; ensambladura *f*; ~ *plane* guillame *m*; **2.** embarbillar, ensamblar a rebajo.
rab·bi ['ræbai] rabino *m*; (*before name*) rabí *m*.
rab·bit ['ræbit] conejo *m*; *Welsh* ~ pan *m* con queso tostado; ~ *fever* tularemia *f*; ~ *punch* puñetazo *m* agudo en la nuca.
rab·ble ['ræbl] canalla *f*, chusma *f*; '~**rous·er** agitador *m*.
rab·id ['ræbid] □ rabioso (*a. fig.*); *fig.* fanático.
ra·bies ['reibi:z] rabia *f*.
race[1] [reis] raza *f* (*a. biol.*); estirpe *f*, casta *f*; *human* ~ género *m* humano.
race[2] [~] **1.** carrera *f*; regata *f on water*; (*current*) corriente *f* fuerte; (*mill-*) caz *m*, saetín *m*; *arms* ~ carrera *f* armamentista; ~*s pl.* carreras *f/pl.*; **2.** *v/i.* competir; ir a máxima velocidad; ⊕ girar a velocidad excesiva, embalarse; *v/t.* hacer correr; competir con; '~**course** hipódromo *m*, cancha *f S.Am.*
race ha·tred ['reis'heitrid] odio *m* racial.
race·horse ['reishɔ:rs] caballo *m* de carrera.
race meet·ing ['reis'mi:tiŋ] concurso *m* hípico, reunión *f*.
rac·er ['reisər] caballo *m* (*or* coche *m etc.*) de carrera.
race ri·ot ['reis 'raiət] disturbio *m* racista.
race track ['reistræk] pista *f*, cancha *f S.Am.*; *mot.* autódromo *m*.
ra·cial ['reiʃl] □ racial; **ra·cial·ism** ['~ʃəlism] racismo *m*.
rac·i·ness ['reisinis] sal *f*, vivacidad *f*, picante *m*.
rac·ing ['reisiŋ] carreras *f/pl.*; *attr.* de carrera(s); ~ *car* coche *m* de carreras; ~ *cyclist* corredor *m* ciclista; ~ *motorist* corredor *m* automovilista.
rac·ism ['reisizm] actitud *f* discriminatoria hacia razas específicas; racismo *m*; **rac·ist** ['reisist] practicante *m/f* o creyente *m/f* del racismo; racista *adj. a. su. m/f.*
rack[1] [ræk] **1.** estante *m*, anaquel *m*; (*torture*) potro *m*; ⊕ cremallera *f*; (*hat etc.*) percha *f*, cuelgacapas *m*; ~-*and-pinion steering mot.* dirección *f* de cremallera; **2.** atormentar; *v. brain.*
rack[2] [~]: *go to* ~ *and ruin* arruinarse.
rack[3] [~] *wine* trasegar, embotellar (*a.* ~ *off*).
rack·et[1] ['rækit], **racqu·et** [~] raqueta *f*; ~*s pl. especie de tenis jugado contra frontón.*
rack·et[2] [~] **1.** alboroto *m*, baraúnda *f*, jaleo *m*, estrépito *m*; F estafa *f*, chantaje *m*, trapacería *f*; **2.** jaranear; hacer ruido; **rack·et·eer** [~'tir] F estafador *m*, chantajista *m*, trapacista *m*; **rack·et'eer·ing** F chantaje *m* sistematizado.
rack·rent ['rækrent] alquiler *m* exorbitante.
ra(c)·coon [rə'ku:n] mapache *m*.
rac·y ['reisi] □ espiritoso; picante; castizo; *style* salado, vivaz.
ra·dar ['reidɑ:r] radar *m*; ~*scope* radarscopio *m*; ~ *scanner* explorado *m* de radar.
rad·dle ['rædl] **1.** almagre *m*; **2.** almagrar.
ra·di·al ['reidiəl] □ radial; ~ *engine* motor *m* radial.
ra·di·ance, ra·di·an·cy ['reidiəns(i)] brillantez *f*, resplandor *m*; '**ra·di·ant** □ radiante (*a. fig.*); brillante.
ra·di·ate 1. ['reidieit] (ir)radiar; *happiness etc.* difundir; **2.** ['~it] radiado; **ra·di'a·tion** (ir)radiación *f*; **ra·di·a·tor** ['~eitər] radiador *m*.
rad·i·cal ['rædikəl] □ *all senses*: radical *adj. a. su. m*; '**rad·i·cal·ism** radicalismo *m*.
ra·di·o ['reidiou] **1.** radio *f* (*a.* ~ set); radio(tele)fonía *f*; rayos *m/pl.* X (*or* Roentgen); *on* (*or over*) *the* ~ por radio; ~ *drama*, ~ *play* comedia *f* radiofónica; ~ *engineering* técnica *f* radiofónica; ~ *fan* radioexperimentador *m*; ~ *station* emisora *f*; ~ *studio* estudio *m* (de emisión); **2.** radiar, transmitir por radio; '~'**ac·tive**

radiactivo; ~ *waste* residuos *m/pl.* radiactivos; ˈ~·acˈtiv·i·ty radiactividad *f*; **ra·di·o·gram** [ˈ~græm] (*message*) radiograma *m*; (*set*) radiogramola *f*, radiofonógrafo *m S.Am.*; **ra·di·o·graph** [ˈ~græf] **1.** radiografía *f*; **2.** radiografiar; **ra·di·o·gra·phy** [reidiˈɔgrəfi] radiografía *f*; **ra·di·ol·o·gy** [reidiˈɔlədʒi] radiología *f*; **ra·di·os·co·py** [~ˈɔskəpi] radioscopia *f*; **ˈra·di·oˈtel·e·gram** radiograma *m*; **ra·di·oˈtel·e·scope** radiotelescopio *m*; **ˈra·di·oˈther·a·py** radioterapia *f*.

rad·ish [ˈrædiʃ] rábano *m*.

ra·di·um [ˈreidiəm] radio *m*.

ra·di·us [ˈreidiəs], *pl.* **ra·di·i** [ˈ~iai] *all senses*: radio *m*; *within a ~ of* en un radio de.

raff·ish [ˈræfiʃ] disipado, de vida airada.

raf·fle [ˈræfl] **1.** rifar, sortear; **2.** rifa *f*.

raft [ræft] **1.** balsa *f*, almadía *f*; **2.** transportar en balsa; **ˈraft·er** ⚠ cab(r)io *m*; traviesa *f*.

rag[1] [ræg] trapo *m*; andrajo *m*, harapo *m*; F (*newspaper*) periodicucho *m*; *in ~s* harapiento, andrajoso; *put on one's glad ~s* endomingarse; *sl. chew the ~* platicar.

rag[2] [~] *sl.* **1.** *v/t.* embromar, dar guerra a; *v/i.* guasearse, bromear, fisgar; **2.** guasa *f*, broma *f* pesada; broma *f* estudiantil; función *f* estudiantil benéfica.

rag·a·muf·fin [ˈrægəmʌfin] granuja *m*, galopín *m*.

rag bag [ˈrægbæg] talego *m* de recortes; *fig.* mezcolanza *f*, cajón *m* de sastre.

rage [reidʒ] **1.** rabia *f*, furor *m*; manía *f*, afán *m* (*for* de); *it's all the ~* es la moda, es la última; **2.** rabiar; (*storm etc.*) bramar.

rag·ged [ˈrægid] □ harapiento, andrajoso; *edge* desigual, mellado; ♪ poco suave.

rag·ing [ˈreidʒiŋ] rabioso, furibundo.

rag·man [ˈrægmən] trapero *m*.

ra·gout [ræˈguː] guisado *m*.

rag...: ˈ~·**tag** F chusma *f* (*freq.* ~ *and bobtail*); ˈ~·**time** ♪ tiempo *m* sincopado.

raid [reid] **1.** correría *f*, incursión *f*; ✈ ataque *m*, bombardeo *m*; **2.** invadir; atacar; ✈ bombardear.

rail[1] [reil] **1.** baranda *f*, barandilla *f*, pasamanos *m*; 🚃 riel *m*, carril *m*; *by ~* por ferrocarril; ⚕ *~s pl.* acciones *f/pl.* de sociedades ferroviarias; *get* (*or go or run*) *off the ~s* descarrilar; *fig.* extraviarse; **2.** (*a.* ~ *in*, ~ *off*) poner cerca (*or* barandilla) a; 🚃 transportar por ferrocarril.

rail[2] [~]: ~ *at*, ~ *against* protestar amargamente contra.

rail[3] [~] *orn.* rascón *m*.

rail·ing [ˈreiliŋ] (*a.* ~*s pl.*) verja *f*, barandilla *f*.

rail·lery [ˈreiləri] burla *f*, mofa *f*.

rail·road 1. [ˈreilroud] = **rail·way** [ˈreilwei] ferrocarril *m*; **2.** *attr.* ... ferroviario; **3.** F llevar a cabo muy precipitadamente; *sl.* encarcelar falsamente.

rail·way·man [ˈreilweimən] ferroviario *m*.

rai·ment [ˈreimənt] *lit.* vestimenta *f*.

rain [rein] **1.** lluvia *f* (*a. fig.*); **2.** llover (*a. fig.*); ~ *cats and dogs* llover a cántaros; ˈ~·**bow** arco iris *m*; ˈ~·**coat** impermeable *m*; ˈ~·**drop** gota *f* de agua; ˈ~·**fall** precipitación *f*; (cantidad *f* de) lluvia *f*; ~ **gauge** [ˈ~geidʒ] pluviómetro *m*; **ˈrain·i·ness** lo lluvioso; **ˈrain·proof** impermeable; **ˈrain·wa·ter** agua *f* llovediza; **ˈrain·y** □ lluvioso; ~ *day* día *m* de lluvia.

raise [reiz] levantar, alzar, elevar, subir, erguir; ⅌ elevar (a una potencia); ascender *in rank*; *sunken vessel* sacar a flote; *army* reclutar; *building* erigir; *claim* formular; *crop* cultivar; *dead* resucitar; *doubts, hopes* suscitar, excitar; *flag* izar, enarbolar; *livestock* criar; *money* reunir; *objection* poner, hacer; *question* plantear, suscitar; *siege, voice* levantar; *v. Cain*; ~ *a loan* reunir fondos; ~ *one's hat* descubrirse; **raised** en relieve.

rai·sin [ˈreizin] pasa *f*; uva *f* seca.

ra·ja(h) [ˈrɑːdʒə] rajá *m*.

rake[1] [reik] **1.** (*garden*) rastrillo *m*; (*farm*) rastro *m*; (*fire*) hurgón *m*; **2.** *v/t.* rastrillar; *fire* hurgar; ~ *together* (*off*) reunir (quitar) con el rastrillo; ~ *up the past etc.* remover; sacar a relucir; ⚔, ⚓ barrer; *v/i.* rastrear; ˈ~-**off** *sl.* tajada *f*.

rake[2] [~] ⚓ **1.** inclinación *f*; **2.** inclinar.

rake[3] [~] libertino *m*, calavera *m*. **rak·ish** [ˈreikiʃ] **1.** ⚓ de palos inclinados; veloz, ligero; gallardo (*a. fig.*); *at a ~ angle hat* echado al lado, a lo chulo; **2.** □ *p.* libertino.

ral·ly[1] [ˈræli] **1.** *mst pol.* reunión *f*, manifestación *f*; ⚕, ✝ recuperación *f*; ⚔ repliegue *m*; *mot.* rallye *m*; *tennis*: peloteo *m*; **2.** *v/i.* reunirse; ⚕, ✝ recuperarse; ⚔ replegarse, rehacerse; *v/t.* reanimar.

ral·ly[2] [~] ridiculizar, embromar, burlarse de.

ram [ræm] **1.** *zo.* carnero *m*; *ast.* Aries *m*; ⚔ ariete *m*; ⚓ espolón *m*; ⊕ pisón *m*; **2.** dar contra; ⚓ atacar con espolón; apisonar; (*fill*) rellenar (*with* de); *~ s.t. into* introducir algo por fuerza (*or* apretadamente) en.

ram·ble [ˈræmbl] **1.** paseo *m* por el campo, excursión *f* a pie; **2.** salir de (*or* hacer una) excursión a pie; divagar *in speech*; **ˈram·bler** vagabundo *m*; excursionista *m/f*; *~ rose* rosal *m* trepador; **ˈram·bling 1.** □ errante; ⚘ trepador; *speech* divagador; *house* laberíntico, construido sobre un plano poco lógico; **2.** excursionismo *m*.

ram·i·fi·ca·tion [ræmifiˈkeiʃn] ramificación *f*; **ram·i·fy** [ˈ~fai] ramificarse.

ram·jet (**en·gine**) [ˈræmdʒet (ˈendʒən)] motor *m* autorreactor; estatorreactor *m*.

ram·mer [ˈræmər] ⊕ pisón *m*.

ramp[1] [ræmp] *sl.* estafa *f*; usura *f*.

ramp[2] [~] rampa *f*; descendedero *m*; **ˈram·page** *co.* **1.** *v/i.* = **2.**: *be on the ~* desbocarse, desenfrenarse; **ˈramp·an·cy** exuberancia *f*; desenfreno *m*; **ˈramp·ant** □ prevaleciente; exuberante; desenfrenado; *heraldry*: rampante; *be ~* cundir.

ram·part [ˈræmpɑːrt] muralla *f*; terraplén *m*.

ram·rod [ˈræmrɔd] baqueta *f*, atacador *m*.

ram·shack·le [ˈræmʃækl] desvencijado, destartalado, ruinoso.

ran [ræn] *pret. of run* 1.

ranch [ræntʃ] hacienda *f*, rancho *m* *S.Am.*; **ˈranch·er** ganadero *m*.

ran·cid [ˈrænsid] □ rancio; **ran·cid·i·ty**, **ˈran·cid·ness** rancidez *f*, ranciedad *f*.

ran·cor [ˈræŋkər] rencor *m*; **ran·cor·ous** [ˈræŋkərəs] □ rencoroso.

ran·dom [ˈrændəm] **1.**: *at ~* al azar; **2.** fortuito, casual, impensado; aleatorio; *~ distribution* distribución *f* aleatoria; *~ sample* muestra *f* seleccionada al azar; *~ shot* tiro *m* sin puntería.

rang [ræŋ] *pret. of ring*[2] 2.

range [reindʒ] **1.** alcance *m*; extensión *f*; serie *f*; ⚡ gama *f* (de frecuencias); ✝ surtido *m*; gama *f of colors*; escala *f of prices, speeds*; amplitud *f of variation*; extensión *f of voice*; (*cattle*) dehesa *f*; (*mountain*) sierra *f*, cordillera *f*; (*stove*) fogón *m*; ⚔ alcance *m* (de tiro); ⚔ campo *m* de tiro; ⚓, ✈ autonomía *f*, radio *m* de acción; *take the ~* averiguar la distancia; *within ~* al alcance (*a. fig.*); **2.** *v/t.* ordenar; clasificar; colocar; *country* recorrer; *v/i.* extenderse; variar; alinearse; **ˈ~ find·er** telémetro *m*; **ˈrang·er** guardabosques *m*.

rank[1] [ræŋk] **1.** (*row*) fila *f* (*a.* ⚔), hilera *f*; (*status*) grado *m*, graduación *f*, rango *m*; dignidad *f*, categoría *f*; ⚔ *the ~s*, *the ~ and file* soldados *m/pl.* rasos; *fig.* masa *f*; *join the ~s* alistarse; *rise from the ~s* ascender desde soldado raso; **2.** *v/t.* clasificar, ordenar; *v/i.* clasificarse; figurar; *~ above* ser superior a; *~ among* estar al nivel de; *~ as* equivaler a; figurar como; *~ with* equipararse con.

rank[2] [~] □ *growth* lozano, exuberante; *smell etc.* maloliente, rancio; *fig. b.s.* redomado.

ran·kle [ˈræŋkl] *v/i.* roer, afligir (*with acc.*).

rank·ness [ˈræŋknis] exuberancia *f of growth*; fetidez *f of smell*.

ran·sack [ˈrænsæk] saquear; registrar (de arriba abajo).

ran·som [ˈrænsəm] **1.** rescate *m*; *eccl.* redención *f*; **2.** rescatar; redimir.

rant [rænt] **1.** lenguaje *m* campanudo (*or* declamatorio); **2.** despotricar, delirar, hablar con violencia; hablar en un estilo hinchado; **ˈrant·er** fanfarrón *m*; declamador *m*.

ra·nun·cu·lus [rəˈnʌŋkjuləs] ranúnculo *m*.

rap [ræp] **1.** golpecito *m*; *not to care a ~* no importarle un bledo a uno;

sl. take the ~ pagar la multa; **2.** golpear; ~ *a p.'s knuckles fig.* reprender severamente a una p.; ~ *out order* espetar.
ra·pa·cious [rə'peiʃəs] □ rapaz; **ra·paç·i·ty** [rə'pæsiti] rapacidad *f*.
rape¹ [reip] **1.** violación *f*, estupro *m*; **2.** violar, forzar, estuprar.
rape² [~] ⚘ colza *f*; '**~-oil** aceite *m* de colza; '**~·seed** nabina *f*.
rap·id ['ræpid] **1.** □ rápido, veloz; **2.** ~*s pl.* rápidos *m/pl.*, recial *m*, rabión *m*; **ra·pid·i·ty** [rə'piditi] rapidez *f*.
ra·pi·er ['reipiər] estoque *m*.
rap·ine ['ræpain] *lit.* rapiña *f*.
rap·ist ['reipist] violador *m*; estuprador *m*.
rap·proche·ment [ræ'prɔʃmɑ̃:ŋ] *pol.* acercamiento *m*.
rapt [ræpt] arrebatado, transportado; ~ *attention* atención *f* fija.
rap·ture ['ræptʃər] rapto *m*, éxtasis *m*, arrobamiento *m*; *in* ~*s* extasiado; *go into* ~*s* extasiarse; '**rap·tur·ous** □ extático.
rare [rer] □ raro, poco común; peregrino; *phys.* ralo; *meat* poco hecho; ~*ly* rara vez.
rare·bit ['rerbit]: *Welsh* ~ = *Welsh rabbit*.
rar·e·fac·tion [reri'fækʃn] rarefacción *f*; **rar·e·fy** ['~fai] enrarecer; '**rare·ness,** '**rar·i·ty** rareza *f*.
ras·cal ['ræskəl] pillo *m*, pícaro *m*; **ras·cal·i·ty** [~'kæliti] picardía *f*; **ras·cal·ly** ['~kəli] pícaro, truhanesco.
rash¹ [ræʃ] □ temerario; precipitado.
rash² [~] ⚕ erupción *f* (cutánea); salpullido *m*.
rash·er ['ræʃər] magra *f*, lonja *f*.
rash·ness ['ræʃnis] temeridad *f*; precipitación *f*.
rasp [ræsp] **1.** escofina *f*; **2.** escofinar, raspar; decir en voz áspera.
rasp·ber·ry ['ræzbəri] frambuesa *f*.
rasp·er ['ræspər] raspador *m*.
rasp·ing ['ræspiŋ] **1.** □ *voice* áspero; **2.** ~*s pl.* raspaduras *f/pl*.
rat [ræt] **1.** rata *f*; *sl.* canalla *m*; *pol.* desertor *m*; *sl.* ~*s!* ¡demonios!; *smell a* ~ oler el poste; ~ *race sl.* lucha *f* diaria por ganarse el pan; **2.** cazar ratas; *pol. a.* F desertar, ser esquirol; *sl.* ~ *on* chivatear contra, soplar contra.
rat·a·ble ['reitəbl] □ sujeto a contribución (municipal *etc.*); tasable.
ratch [rætʃ], **ratch·et** ['rætʃit] trinquete *m*; '**~ wheel** rueda *f* de trinquete.
rate¹ [reit] **1.** proporción *f*; relación *f*; tanto *m* (por ciento); (*speed*) velocidad *f*, paso *m*; (*price*) tasa *f*, precio *m*; (*hotel*) tarifa *f*; *mst* ~*s pl.* contribución *f* (municipal *etc.*); *at a cheap* ~ a un precio reducido; *at the* ~ *of* a razón de; *at any* ~ de todas formas; *at that* ~ de ese modo; ~ *of exchange* cambio *m*; ~ *of interest* tipo *m* de interés; ~ *of taxation* nivel *m* de impuestos; **2.** tasar (*at* en), valorar; clasificar; imponer contribución (municipal) a; ~ *s.o. highly* tener muy buen concepto de alguien.
rate² [~] regañar, reñir.
rate pay·er ['reitpeiər] contribuyente *m/f*
rath·er ['ræðər, 'rɑ:ðər] (*more*) mejor, primero, más bien; (*somewhat*) algo, bastante; F ~*!* ¡ya lo creo!; *or* ~ mejor dicho; *I had* (*or would*) ~ preferiría *inf.*; me gustaría más *inf.*; *I* ~ *expected it* ya lo preveía.
rat·i·fi·ca·tion [rætifi'keiʃn] ratificación *f*; **rat·i·fy** ['~fai] ratificar.
rat·ing ['reitiŋ] clasificación *f*; contribución *f*; ⚓ (*ship*) clase *f*; ⚓ marinero *m*; capacidad *f*; potencia *f*.
ra·tio ['reiʃiou] relación *f*, razón *f*, proporción *f*.
ra·tion ['ræʃn] **1.** ración *f*; ⚔ ~*s pl.* suministro *m*; ~ *book* (*or* ~ *card*) cartilla *f* de racionamiento; *off the* ~ no racionado; **2.** racionar.
ra·tion·al ['ræʃnl] □ racional, razonable; **ra·tion·al·ism** ['~nəlizm] racionalismo *m*; '**ra·tion·al·ist** racionalista *m/f*; **ra·tion·al·i·ty** [~'næliti] racionalidad *f*; **ra·tion·al·i·za·tion** ['~nəlai'zeiʃn] racionalización *f*; '**ra·tion·al·ize** hacer racional, organizar racionalmente; buscar pretexto racional a.
ra·tion·ing ['ræʃniŋ] racionamiento *m*.
rat·tle ['rætl] **1.** golpeteo *m*; traqueteo *m*; crujido *m*; sonsonete *m*; (*instrument*) matraca *f*, carraca *f*; (*child's*) sonajero *m*; *death* ~ estertor *m*; **2.** *v/i.* sonar, crujir, castañetear; F ~ *on* parlotear; *v/t.* agitar, sacudir; F desconcertar; ~ *off* enumerar rápida-

mente; ˈ~-**brained,** ˈ~-ˈ**pat·ed** ligero de cascos; ˈ**rat·tler** F = ˈ**rat·tle-snake** serpiente *f* de cascabel; ˈ**rat·tle·trap 1.** desvencijado; **2.** armatoste *m*; *mot.* cacharro *m*.

rat·tling [ˈrætliŋ] ruidoso; desconcertante; F *at a ~ pace* a gran velocidad; F *adv. ~ good* realmente estupendo.

rat·ty [ˈræti] *sl.* amostazado; *clothes* gastado; ruin.

rau·cous [ˈrɔːkəs] □ estridente, ronco.

rav·age [ˈrævidʒ] **1.** estrago *m*, destrozo *m*; **2.** destrozar, asolar; pillar.

rave [reiv] delirar, desvariar; F *~ about* pirrarse por, entusiasmarse por; *~ at* insultar frenéticamente de palabra.

rav·en [ˈreivn] cuervo *m*.

rav·en·ous [ˈrævnəs] □ famélico, voraz, hambriento; *be ~ly hungry* tener una hambre canina; ˈ**rav·en·ous·ness** voracidad *f*.

ra·vine [rəˈviːn] barranco *m*.

rav·ings [ˈreiviŋz] *pl.* delirio *m*, desvarío *m*.

rav·ish [ˈræviʃ] encantar, embelesar; *lit.* robar, violar; ˈ**rav·ish·er** raptor *m*; ˈ**rav·ish·ing** □ encantador, embelesador; ˈ**rav·ish·ment** éxtasis *m*; rapto *m*.

raw [rɔː] **1.** □ *food, weather* crudo; *spirit* puro; *substance* en bruto, sin refinar, crudo; (*inexperienced*) novato; F *~ deal* tratamiento *m* injusto; *v. material*; *~ recruit* soldado *m* bisoño; **2.** carne *f* viva; F *it gets me on the ~* me hiere en lo más vivo; ˈ~·**boned** huesudo; ˈ~·**hide** cuero *m* en verde; ˈ**raw·ness** crudeza *f*; inexperiencia *f*.

ray[1] [rei] **1.** rayo *m*; ⚘ bráctea *f*; ⚕ *~ treatment* tratamiento *m* con rayos; **2.** emitir rayos.

ray[2] [~] *ichth.* raya *f*.

ray·on [ˈreiɔn] rayón *m*.

raze [reiz] arrasar, asolar (*a. ~ to the ground*).

ra·zor [ˈreizər] (*open*) navaja *f*; (*safety*) maquinilla *f* de afeitar; ⚡ máquina *f* de afeitar, rasurador *m*; ˈ~-**blade** hoja *f* (*or* cuchilla *f*) de afeitar; ˈ~ **strop** suavizador *m*.

razz [ræz] *sl.* echar un rapapolvo a; ridiculizar.

raz·zle (**daz·zle**) [ˈræzl(dæzl)] *sl.* ostentación *f*; confusión *f*.

re [riː] respecto a, con referencia a.

re... [~] re...

reach [riːtʃ] **1.** alcance *m*; extensión *f*, distancia *f*; capacidad *f*; (*river*) extensión *f* entre dos recodos; *beyond ~, out of ~* fuera de alcance; *within* (*easy*) *~* al alcance; **2.** *v/i.* extenderse; *with hand* (*freq. ~ out*) alargar (*or* tender) la mano (*for* para tomar); *it won't ~* no llega; *v/t.* alcanzar; llegar a; lograr; *hand* alargar; *age* cumplir.

re·act [riˈækt] reaccionar (*against* contra; *to* a, ante; *upon* sobre).

re·ac·tion [riˈækʃn] reacción *f*; **re**ˈ**ac·tion·ar·y** *esp. pol.* reaccionario *adj. a. su. m* (a *f*).

re·ac·tive [riˈæktiv] reactivo *adj. a. su. m*; **re**ˈ**ac·tor** *phys.* reactor *m*.

read 1. [riːd] [*irr.*] *v/t.* leer; interpretar, descifrar; *typ.* corregir; *univ.* estudiar; cursar; *thermometer etc.* consultar; *~ lips* leer en los labios; *~ out* anunciar; *~ over* repasar; *v/i.* leer; (*notice etc.*) rezar, decir; (*thermometer etc.*) indicar, marcar; *~ aloud* leer en alta voz; *~ between the lines fig.* leer entre líneas; **2.** [red] *pret. a. p.p. of* 1; *adj. well ~* leído, instruido.

read·a·ble [ˈriːdəbl] □ legible; digno de leerse, entretenido.

read·er [ˈriːdər] lector (-a *f*) *m*; *typ.* corrector *m*; (*book*) libro *m* de lectura; *univ. profesor que ocupa el segundo rango, después del catedrático*; ˈ**read·er·ship** número *m* total de lectores (de un periódico); *univ. puesto del reader.*

read·i·ly [ˈredili] *adv.* de buena gana; fácilmente; ˈ**read·i·ness** prontitud *f*; alacridad *f*; buena disposición *f*; *in ~* preparado, listo; *~ of mind* (*or wit*) viveza *f*.

read·ing [ˈriːdiŋ] lectura *f* (*a. parl*); interpretación *f*; (*MS*) lección *f*; (*thermometer etc.*) indicación *f*, lectura *f*; *attr.* ... de lectura; *~ room* sala *f* de lectura.

re·ad·just [ˈriːəˈdʒʌst] reajustar; *pol. etc.* reorientar; ˈ**re·ad**ˈ**just·ment** reajuste *m*; reorientación *f*.

re·ad·mit [ˈriːədˈmit] readmitir.

read·y [ˈredi] **1.** □ listo, preparado (*for* para; *to* para *inf.*); pronto; (*inclined*) dispuesto (*to* a); ✝ contante, efectivo; *answer* fácil; *wit* agudo, vivo; *~ reckoner* libro *m* de cálculos hechos; *~ for action* dispuesto para el combate; *fig.* lanza en ristre; ~ *for use*, ~ *to use* listo para usar; ~ *to serve* preparado; get (*or make*) ~ preparar(se), disponer(se); **2.**: *at the* ~ ⚔ listo para tirar; apercibido; en ristre; ˈ**~-made**, ˈ**~-to-**ˈ**wear** ya hecho, confeccionado.

re·af·firm [riːəˈfəːrm] reafirmar, reiterar.

re·af·for·est·a·tion [ˈriːəfɔristˈeiʃn] repoblación *f* forestal.

re·a·gent [riˈeidʒənt] reactivo *m*.

re·al [riəl] □ **1.** real; verdadero; auténtico; genuino; legítimo; *v. estate*; **2.** F *adv.* verdaderamente; muy; ˈ**re·al·ism** realismo *m*; **re·al**ˈ**is·tic** □ realista; **re·al·i·ty** [riˈæliti] realidad *f*; **re·al·iz·a·ble** [ˈriəlaizəbl] □ realizable; **re·al·i**ˈ**za·tion** comprensión *f*; realización *f of plan*, *a*. ✝; verificación *f*; ˈ**re·al·ize** darse cuenta de; reconocer; ✝ realizar; *plan etc.* realizar, llevar a cabo; ˈ**re·al·ly** en realidad; verdaderamente, realmente; ~? ¿de veras?

realm [relm] reino *m*; *fig.* campo *m*.

Re·al·tor [ˈriəltər] corredor *m* de bienes raíces (*or* de fincas); ˈ**re·al·ty** ⚖ bienes *m/pl.* raíces.

ream[1] [riːm] (*paper*) resma *f*; F montón *m*.

ream[2] [~] ⊕ escariar; ˈ**ream·er** escariador *m*.

re·an·i·mate [riˈænimeit] reanimar.

reap [riːp] segar; cosechar (*a. fig.*); ˈ**reap·er** segador (-a *f*) *m*; (*machine*) segadora *f*; ˈ**reap·ing** siega *f*; ˈ**reap·ing hook** hoz *f*.

re·ap·pear [ˈriːəˈpir] reaparecer; ˈ**re·ap**ˈ**pear·ance** reaparición *f*.

re·ap·point [ˈriːəˈpɔint] volver a nombrar.

rear[1] [rir] *v/t.* criar; (*build*) erigir, alzar; *v/i.* encabritarse, ponerse de manos.

rear[2] [~] **1.** parte *f* posterior (*or* trasera); cola *f*; ⚔ última fila *f*; ⚔ retaguardia *f*; *bring up the* ~ cerrar la marcha; *at the* ~ *of*, *in* (*the*) ~ *of* detrás de; ⚔ *in the* ~ a retaguardia; **2.** trasero, posterior; de cola; ~ (*wheel*) *drive* tracción *f* trasera; ˈ**~** ˈ**ad·mi·ral** contraalmirante *m*; ˈ**~ end** *mot.* caja *f* de puente trasero; *sl.* culo *m*; ˈ**~·guard** retaguardia *f*; ˈ**~ lamp** luz *f* piloto (*or* trasera); ˈ**~ win·dow** *mot.* luneta *f*.

re·arm [ˈriːˈɑːrm] rearmar(se); ˈ**re**ˈ**ar·ma·ment** [~məmənt] rearme *m*.

rear·most [ˈrirmoust] trasero, último.

re·ar·range [ˈriːəˈreindʒ] ordenar de nuevo; ♪ volver a adaptar.

rear-view [ˈrirˈvjuː] retrovisor; de retrovisión.

rear·ward [ˈrirwərd] **1.** *adj.* trasero, de atrás; **2.** *adv.* (*a.* ˈ**rear·wards** [~z]) hacia atrás.

rea·son [ˈriːzn] **1.** razón *f*; motivo *m*, causa *f*; sensatez *f*, moderación *f*; *by* ~ *of* a causa de; en virtud de; *for this* ~ por esta razón; *within* ~ dentro de lo razonable; *listen to* ~ meterse en razón; *it stands to* ~ (*that*) es evidente (que), es lógico (que); **2.** *v/i.* razonar, discurrir; *v/t.* razonar; resolver pensando (*a.* ~ *out*); ~ *a p. into* (*out of*) *a th.* lograr con razones que una p. acepte (abandone) algo; ~*ed* razonado; ˈ**rea·son·a·ble** □ razonable; justo, equitativo; *p.* sensato; ˈ**rea·son·ing** razonamiento *m*; argumento *m*.

re·as·semble [ˈriːəˈsembl] volver a reunir(se); ⊕ montar de nuevo.

re·as·sert [ˈriːəˈsəːrt] reiterar, reafirmar.

re·as·sur·ance [ˈriːəˈʃurəns] noticia *f* (*or* promesa *f etc.*) tranquilizadora; **re·as·sure** [ˈ~ˈʃur] tranquilizar; alentar; **re·as**ˈ**sur·ing** □ tranquilizador.

re·bate[1] [ˈriːbeit] **1.** rebaja *f*, descuento *m*; **2.** rebajar, descontar.

re·bate[2] [~, ˈræbit] ⊕ *v. rabbet*.

re·bel **1.** [ˈrebl] rebelde *m/f*; **2.** [~] rebelde (*mst* **re·bel·lious** [riˈbeljəs]); **3.** [riˈbel] rebelarse, sublevarse; **re**ˈ**bel·lion** [~jən] rebelión *f*, sublevación *f*.

re·birth [ˈriːbəːrθ] renacimiento *m*.

re·bore [ˈriˈbɔːr] **1.** ⊕ rectificar; **2.** rectificado *m*.

re·bound [riˈbaund] **1.** rebotar; resaltar; **2.** rebote *m*; *on the* ~ de rebote, de rechazo.

re·buff [riˈbʌf] **1.** repulsa *f*, desaire *m*; **2.** rechazar, desairar.

re·build [ˈriːˈbild] [*irr.* (*build*)] reedificar, reconstruir; *mot.* componer completamente.

re·buke [riˈbjuːk] **1.** reprensión *f*, reprimenda *f*; **2.** reprender, censurar.

re·bus [ˈriːbəs] jeroglífico *m*.
re·but [riˈbʌt] rebatir, refutar; **reˈbut·tal** refutación *f*.
re·cal·ci·trant [riˈkælsitrənt] recalcitrante, refractorio.
re·call [riˈkɔːl] **1.** revocación *f*; retirada *f of ambassador, capital*; llamada *f* (para que vuelva una p.); *thea.* llamada *f* a escena; *beyond* ~, *past* ~ irrevocable; **2.** revocar; *ambassador, capital* retirar; llamar; hacer volver; recordar, traer a la memoria.
re·cant [riˈkænt] retractar(se); **re·can·ta·tion** [riːkænˈteiʃn] retractación *f*.
re·cap [riːˈkæp] *tires* recauchutar.
re·ca·pit·u·late [riːkəˈpitjuleit] recapitular; **ˈre·ca·pit·uˈla·tion** recapitulación *f*.
re·cap·ture [ˈriːˈkæptʃər] **1.** represa *f*, recobro *m*; **2.** represar, recobrar; volver a prender; *memory* hacer revivir.
re·cast [ˈriːkæst] [*irr.* (*cast*)] ⊕ refundir (*a. fig.*).
re·cede [riˈsiːd] retroceder, retirarse, alejarse; (*price*) bajar.
re·ceipt [riˈsiːt] **1.** recibo *m*; cobranza *f*; ✝ ~*s pl.* ingresos *m*/*pl.*; **2.** dar recibo (por).
re·ceiv·a·ble [riˈsiːvəbl] admisible; recibidero; ✝ por cobrar; **reˈceive** recibir, admitir; *guest etc.* acoger; *money* cobrar; *tennis etc.*: ser restador; **reˈceived** admitido, aprobado; **reˈceiv·er** recibidor (-a *f*) *m*; destinatario (a *f*) *m*; *radio*: receptor *m*; *teleph.* auricular *m*; *phys.*, ⚗ recipiente *m*; ⚖ (*official* ~) *approx.* síndico *m*; **reˈceiv·er·ship** ⚖ sindicatura *f*; **reˈceiv·ing** recepción *f* (*a. radio*); ~ set radiorreceptor *m*.
re·cen·sion [riˈsenʃn] recensión *f*.
re·cent [ˈriːsnt] □ reciente, nuevo.
re·cep·ta·cle [riˈseptəkl] receptáculo *m* (*a.* ⚘).
re·cep·tion [riˈsepʃn] recepción *f* (*a. radio*); recibimiento *m*; acogida *f*; (*royal*) besamanos *m*; **reˈcep·tion·ist** recibidor (-a *f*) *m*; **reˈcep·tion room** sala *f* de recibo.
re·cep·tive [riˈseptiv] □ receptivo; **re·cepˈtiv·i·ty** receptividad *f*.
re·cess [riˈses, ˈriːses] vacaciones *f*/*pl.*, intermisión *f*; *esp. parl.* suspensión *f*; intermedio *m between sittings*; ⊕ rebajo *m*; ⚠ hueco *m*, nicho *m*; ~es *pl. fig.* entrañas *f*/*pl.*; lo más recóndito.
re·ces·sion [riˈseʃn] retirada *f*, retroceso *m* (*a.* ✝); ✝ recesión *f*; **reˈces·sion·al** himno *m* (de fin de oficio).
re·cher·ché [rəˈʃerʃei] rebuscado.
re·ci·pe [ˈresipi] receta *f*.
re·cip·i·ent [riˈsipiənt] recibidor (-a *f*) *m*, recipiente *m*/*f*.
re·cip·ro·cal [riˈsiprəkəl] **1.** □ recíproco, mutuo; **2.** ⅍ recíproca *f*, inverso *m*; **reˈcip·ro·cate** [~keit] *v*/*i.* ⊕ oscilar, alternar; usar de reciprocidad, corresponder; *v*/*t.* intercambiar; corresponder a; devolver; **re·cip·roˈca·tion** reciprocación *f*; **rec·i·proc·i·ty** [resiˈprɔsiti] reciprocidad *f*.
re·cit·al [riˈsaitl] relación *f*, narración *f*; ♪ recital *m*; ⚖ parte *f* expositiva (de un documento); **rec·i·ta·tion** [resiˈteiʃn] recitación *f*; recitado *m*; **rec·i·ta·tive** [~təˈtiːv] ♪ recitativo *adj. a. su. m*; recitado *m*; **re·cite** [riˈsait] recitar; declamar; narrar, referir; **reˈcit·er** recitador (-a *f*) *m*.
reck·less [ˈreklis] □ temerario; imprudente; inconsiderado; **ˈreck·less·ness** temeridad *f*; imprudencia *f*.
reck·on [ˈrekn] *v*/*t.* contar, calcular; estimar; considerar (*as* como; *that* que); ~ *up* calcular, computar; *v*/*i.* calcular; F estimar, creer; ~ (*up*)*on* contar con; ~ *with* tener en cuenta; **ˈreck·on·er** calculador *m*; *v. ready* ~; **ˈreck·on·ing** cuenta *f*; cálculo *m*; *be out in one's* ~ equivocarse en el cálculo; *day of* ~ día *m* de ajuste de cuentas.
re·claim [riˈkleim] reclamar; amansar, reformar; *land* recuperar, hacer utilizable; (*from sea*) ganar; ⊕ utilizar, regenerar; **reˈclaim·a·ble** reclamable; utilizable.
rec·la·ma·tion [rekləˈmeiʃn] reclamación *f*; recuperación *f*, utilización *f*; *land* ~ rescate *m* de terrenos.
re·cline [riˈklain] reclinar(se), recostar(se); ~ *upon fig.* contar con, fiarse de; **reˈclin·ing chair** sillón *m* reclinable, poltrona *f*.
re·cluse [riˈkluːs] recluso, solitario *adj. a. su. m* (a *f*).
rec·og·ni·tion [rekəgˈniʃn] recono-

cimiento *m*; **rec·og·niz·a·ble** [ˈ~-naizəbl] □ reconocible; **rec·og·ni·zance** [riˈkɔgnizəns] ⚖ reconocimiento *m*; obligación *f* contraída; **rec·og·nize** [ˈrekəgnaiz] reconocer; admitir, confesar.
re·coil [riˈkɔil] **1.** recular, retroceder (de espanto); ⚔ retroceder, rebufar; *~ on* recaer sobre; **2.** reculada *f*, retroceso *m* (*a.* ⚔); ⚔ rebufo *m*.
rec·ol·lect [rekəˈlekt] recordar, acordarse de; **rec·ol·lec·tion** [rekəˈlekʃn] recuerdo *m*.
re·com·bin·ant [riˈkɔmbənənt] *biol.* recombinado.
re·com·mence [ˈriːkəˈmens] recomenzar.
rec·om·mend [rekəˈmend] recomendar, encarecer; **rec·omˈmend·a·ble** recomendable; **rec·om·menˈda·tion** recomendación *f*; **rec·omˈmend·a·to·ry** [~ətɔːri] recomendatorio.
re·com·mit [riːkəˈmit] volver a confiar; internar de nuevo.
rec·om·pense [ˈrekəmpens] **1.** recompensa *f*, compensación *f*; **2.** recompensar (*for acc.*).
re·com·pose [ˈriːkəmˈpouz] recomponer.
rec·on·cil·a·ble [ˈrekənsailəbl] reconciliable; **ˈrec·on·cile** (re)conciliar; *~ o.s. to* resignarse a, acomodarse con; **ˈrec·on·cil·er** reconciliador (-a *f*) *m*; **rec·on·cil·i·a·tion** [ˈ~siliˈeiʃn] reconciliación *f*.
rec·on·dite [riˈkɔndait] □ recóndito; elusivo; secreto.
re·con·di·tion [ˈriːkənˈdiʃn] reacondicionar.
re·con·nais·sance [riˈkɔnisəns] reconocimiento *m*.
rec·on·noi·ter, rec·on·noi·tre [rekəˈnɔitər] reconocer.
re·con·quer [ˈriːˈkɔŋkər] reconquistar; **ˈreˈcon·quest** [~kwest] reconquista *f*.
re·con·sid·er [ˈriːkənˈsidər] repensar, reconsiderar; **ˈre·con·sid·erˈa·tion** reconsideración *f*.
re·con·sti·tute [ˈriːˈkɔnstitjuːt] reconstituir; **ˈre·con·stiˈtu·tion** reconstitución *f*.
re·con·struct [ˈriːkənsˈtrʌkt] reconstruir; reedificar; **ˈre·conˈstruc·tion** reconstrucción *f*.
re·con·ver·sion [ˈriːkənˈvəːrʒn] reconversión *f*, reorganización *f*; **ˈre·conˈvert** reconvertir, reorganizar.
rec·ord 1. [ˈrekɔːrd] registro *m*; partida *f*; documento *m*; relación *f*; (*p.'s history*) historial *m*, curriculum vitae *m*, carrera *f*, antecedentes *m/pl.*; reputación *f*; ⚖ acta *f*; *sport*: record *m*, marca *f*; *~ breaker* plusmarquista *m/f*; ♪ disco *m*; *long-playing ~* disco *m* de larga duración; elepé *m*; *~ changer* tocadiscos *m* automático; *~s pl.* archivos *m/pl.*; *off the ~* no oficial, confidencial(mente); *place on ~* dejar constancia de; *it is on ~ that* consta que; *beat* (*or break*) *the ~* batir la marca; *set up* (*or establish*) *a ~* establecer un record; *~ card* ficha *f*; *~ library* discoteca *f*; ♀ *Office* Archivo *m* Nacional; **2.** [~] *attr.* sin precedentes, máximo; *~ time* tiempo *m* record; **re·cord** [riˈkɔːrd] registrar; hacer constar, consignar; inscribir; archivar; indicar; *voice etc* registrar, grabar; **reˈcord·er** registrador *m*, archivero *m*; ⚖ *approx.* juez *m* municipal; ♪ caramillo *m*; ⊕ indicador *m*; **reˈcord·ing** grabación *f*; grabado *m*; **ˈrec·ord ˈplay·er** tocadiscos *m*.
re·count[1] [riˈkaunt] (re)contar, referir.
re·count[2] [ˈriːˈkaunt] *parl.* segundo escrutinio *m*.
re·coup [riˈkuːp] recobrar; indemnizarse por.
re·course [riˈkɔːrs] recurso *m*; *have ~ to* recurrir a.
re·cov·er[1] [riˈkʌvər] *v/t.* recobrar, recuperar; *money* reembolsarse; recaudar; *v/i.* ⚕ restablecerse (*a.* ✝), reponerse; ⚖ ganar (*~ in a suit* un pleito).
re·cov·er[2] [ˈriːˈkʌvər] recubrir.
re·cov·er·a·ble [riˈkʌvərəbl] recuperable; **reˈcov·er·y** recobro *m*, recuperación *f*; ⚕ restablecimiento *m*, mejoría *f*; recaudación *f of money*.
rec·re·ate [ˈrekrieit] recrear(se), divertir(se); **rec·reˈa·tion** recreación *f*; *school*: recreo *m*; *~ ground* campo *m* de deportes; *~al vehicle* vehículo *m* de recreo; **ˈrec·re·a·tive** recreativo.
re·crim·i·nate [riˈkrimineit] recriminar; **re·crim·iˈna·tion** recriminación *f*.
re·cru·desce [riːkruːˈdes] recrudecer; **re·cruˈdes·cence** recrudescencia *f*.

re·cruit [ri'kru:t] **1.** recluta *m*; *fig.* novicio *m*; **2.** reclutar, alistar; ⚕ *etc.* restablecer(se), rehacer(se); **re'cruit·ing, re'cruit·ment** reclutamiento *m*.

rec·tan·gle ['rektæŋgl] rectángulo *m*; **rec'tan·gu·lar** [~gjulər] □ rectangular.

rec·ti·fi·a·ble ['rektifaiəbl] rectificable; corregible; **rec·ti·fi·ca·tion** [~fi'keiʃn] rectificación *f*; **rec·ti·fi·er** ['~faiər] *mst* rectificador *m*; ⊕ (*crankshafts etc.*) rectificadora *f*; **rec·ti·fy** ['~fai] *all senses*: rectificar; **rec·ti·lin·e·al** [rekti'linjəl], **rec·ti'lin·e·ar** [~njər] □ rectilíneo; **rec·ti·tude** ['~tju:d] rectitud *f*, probidad *f*.

rec·tor ['rektər] *Scot. univ.* rector *m*; *eccl.* párroco *m*; **rec·tor·ate** ['~rit], **'rec·tor·ship** rectorado *m*; **'rec·to·ry** rectoría *f*; casa *f* del cura.

rec·tum ['rektəm] recto *m*.

re·cum·bent [ri'kʌmbənt] □ reclinado, recostado; *statue* yacente.

re·cu·per·ate [ri'kju:pəreit] *v/t.* recuperar; *v/i.* ⚕ restablecerse; **re·cu·per'a·tion** recuperación *f*; ⚕ restablecimiento *m*; **re'cu·per·a·tive** [~rətiv] recuperativo.

re·cur [ri'kə:r] repetirse, producirse de nuevo, volver a ocurrir; (*idea*) volver a la mente; ~*ring decimal* decimal *f* (*or* fracción *f*) periódica pura; **re·cur·rence** [ri'kə:rəns] repetición *f*, reaparición *f*; **re'cur·rent** □ repetido; recurrente (*a. anat.*, ⚕); ⚡ periódico.

re·curve [ri:'kə:rv] recorvar(se).

rec·u·sant ['rekjuzənt] recusante *adj. a. su. m/f.*

red [red] **1.** rojo (*a. pol.*); colorado; encarnado; *wine* tinto; *face* encendido *with anger*, ruboroso *with shame*; *pol.* comunista; marxista; *sl. paint the town* ~ echar una cana al aire; ♀ *Cross* Cruz *f* Roja; ~ *currant* grosella *f* roja; ~ *deer* ciervo *m* común; ~ *heat* calor *m* rojo; ~ *herring fig.* pista *f* falsa, ardid *m* para apartar la atención del asunto principal; ~ *lead* minio *m*; ~ *tape* papeleo *m*, formalidades *f/pl.*, burocracia *f*; **2.** (color *m*) rojo *m*; (*pol.*) rojo *m*; comunista *m/f*; marxista *m/f*; *see* ~ sulfurarse, encolerizarse; F *be in the* ~ estar adeudado, estar en el libro de lo morosos.

re·dact [ri'dækt] redactar; **re'dac·tion** redacción *f*.

red·breast ['redbrest] (*freq. robin* ~) petirrojo *m*; **'red·cap** mozo *m* de estación; ⚔ *sl.* policía *m* militar; **red·den** ['redn] *v/t.* enrojecer, teñir de rojo; *v/i.* enrojecer(se) *with anger*; ponerse colorado, ruborizarse *with shame*; **'red·dish** rojizo; **red·dle** ['~l] almagre *m*, almazarrón *m*.

re·dec·o·rate ['ri:'dekəreit] *room* renovar; **'re·dec·o'ra·tion** renovación *f*.

re·deem [ri'di:m] redimir; *promise* cumplir; *pledge etc.* rescatar, desempeñar; ✝ amortizar; ~*ing virtue* virtud *f* compensadora; **re'deem·a·ble** redimible; ✝ amortizable; **Re'deem·er** Redentor *m*.

re·de·liv·er ['ri:di'livər] volver a entregar.

re·demp·tion [ri'dempʃn] redención *f*; rescate *m*; desempeño *m*; ✝ amortización *f*; *beyond* ~, *past* ~ sin esperanza, que no tiene remedio; **re'demp·tive** redentor.

re·de·ploy·ment ['ri:di'plɔiment] reorganización *f*.

red...: **'~-'haired, '~-'head·ed** pelirrojo; ~-**'hand·ed** con las manos en la masa, en flagrante; **'~-'hot** candente; *fig.* vehemente, acérrimo; *news* de última hora.

re·di·rect ['ri:di'rekt] *letter* reexpedir.

re·dis·cov·er ['ri:dis'kʌvər] volver a descubrir.

re·dis·trib·ute ['ri:dis'tribju:t] distribuir de nuevo.

red-let·ter day ['redletər'dei] día *m* festivo; *fig.* día *m* señalado.

red-light dis·trict ['redlait'distrikt] barrio *m* de los lupanares, barrio *m* chino.

red·ness ['rednis] rojez *f*, lo rojo; ⚕ inflamación *f*.

re·do ['ri:'du:] [*irr.* (*do*)] rehacer.

red·o·lence ['redələns] fragancia *f*, perfume *m*; **'red·o·lent** perfumado (*of* como); *fig. be* ~ *of* recordar, hacer pensar en.

re·dou·ble [ri'dʌbl] redoblar (*a. bridge*); intensificar.

re·doubt [ri'daut] reducto *m*; **re'doubt·a·ble** temible, formidable.

re·dound [ri'daund]: ~ *to* redundar en (*or* en beneficio de).

re·draft ['ri:dræft] **1.** nuevo borrador *m*; ✝ (letra *f* de) resaca *f*; **2.** *or*

re·draw [ˈriːˈdrɔː] [*irr.* (*draw*)] volver a dibujar (*or* redactar).
re·dress [riˈdres] **1.** reparación *f*, compensación *f*, resarcimiento *m*; derecho *m* a satisfacción; **2.** reparar, resarcir; enmendar; equilibrar.
red...: ˈ~·skin piel roja *m/f*; *contp.* indio *m* norteamericano; **ˈ~·start** colirrojo *m* real; **ˈ~ ˈtape** papeleo *m*; burocracia *f*.
re·duce [riˈdjuːs] *v/t.* reducir (*to* a, hasta; *a.* ⚗, ⚒); disminuir, abreviar; *price* rebajar; degradar *in rank*; *fort etc.* reducir, tomar; ~ *to writing* poner por escrito; *v/i.* ⚕ adelgazar; **reˈduc·i·ble** reducible; **re·duc·tion** [riˈdʌkʃn] reducción *f*; di(s)minución *f*; abreviación *f*; rebaja *f of price*; reducción *f*, toma *f of fort etc.*
re·dun·dance, re·dun·dan·cy [riˈdʌndəns(i)] redundancia *f*; **reˈdun·dant** □ redundante; *be* ~ estar de más.
re·du·pli·cate [riˈdjuːplikeit] reduplicar; **re·du·pliˈca·tion** reduplicación *f*.
red·wood [ˈredwud] ⚘ secoya *f*.
re·dye [ˈriːˈdai] reteñir.
re·ech·o [riːˈekou] repercutirse, resonar.
reed [riːd] ⚘ carrizo *m*, junco *m*, caña *f*; ♪ lengüeta *f*; ♪ (*pipe*) caramillo *m*.
re·ed·it [ˈriːˈedit] reeditar.
re·ed·u·ca·tion [ˈriːedjuˈkeiʃn] reeducación *f*.
reed·y [ˈriːdi] *place* cañoso; *voice* alto y delgado.
reef[1] [riːf] escollo *m*, arrecife *m*.
reef[2] [~] ⚓ **1.** rizo *m*; **2.** arrizar.
reef·er[1] [ˈriːfər] chaquetón *m*.
reef·er[2] [~] *sl.* pitillo *m* de mariguana.
reek [riːk] **1.** vaho *m*; hedor *m*; **2.** vahear, humear; heder, oler (*of* a).
reel [riːl] **1.** carrete *m*, tambor *m*; (*fishing*) carrete(l) *m*; *sew.* broca *f*, devanadera *f*; ♪ *baile escocés*; *phot.*, *film*: rollo *m*, cinta *f*, película *f*; F *off the* ~ seguido(s); **2.** *v/t.* devanar; ~ *off* enumerar rápidamente, ensartar; *v/i.* tambalear(se); (*enemy*) cejar.
re·e·lect [ˈriːiˈlekt] reelegir.
re·el·i·gi·ble [ˈriːˈelidʒəbl] reelegible.
re·en·act [ˈriːiˈnækt] ⚖ volver a promulgar; *thea.* volver a representar.
re·en·gage [ˈriːinˈgeidʒ] contratar de nuevo.
re·en·list [ˈriːinˈlist] reenganchar(se).
re·en·ter [ˈriːˈentər] reingresar en; reentrar en; **re·en·trant** [riːˈentrənt] entrante; **re·en·try** [riːˈentri] reingreso *m*; reentrada *f into earth's atmosphere*.
re·es·tab·lish [ˈriːisˈtæbliʃ] restablecer; **ˈre·esˈtab·lish·ment** restablecimiento *m*.
reeve [riːv] ⚓ *v/i.* laborear; *v/t.* pasar (por un ojal *etc.*).
re·ex·change [ˈriːiksˈtʃeindʒ] ✝ (letra *f* de) resaca *f*, recambio *m*.
re·fec·tion [riˈfekʃn] refacción *f*; **reˈfec·to·ry** [~təri] refectorio *m*.
ref·er [riˈfəːr] *v/t.* remitir (*a th. to a p.* algo a una p., *a p. to a th.* una p. a algo); *v/i.*: ~ *to* referirse a, hacer referencia (*or* alusión) a; **refˈer·a·ble:** ~ *to* referible a, asignable a; **ref·er·ee** [refəˈriː] **1.** *all senses*: árbitro *m*; **2.** arbitrar; **ref·er·ence** [ˈrefərəns] referencia *f*; alusión *f*; recomendación *f*; (*a.* ~ *mark*) llamada *f*; *with* (*or in*) ~ *to* en cuanto a, respecto a (*or* de); *make* ~ *to* referirse a, hacer alusión a; *terms of* ~ puntos *m/pl.* de consulta; *work of* ~, ~ *book* libro *m* de consulta; ~ *library* biblioteca *f* de consulta; ~ *number* número *m* de referencia; ~ *point* punto *m* de referencia.
ref·er·en·dum [refəˈrendəm] referéndum *m*.
re·fill [ˈriːˈfil] **1.** repuesto *m*, recambio *m*; mina *f for pencil*; **2.** rellenar.
re·fine [riˈfain] *v/t.* refinar (*a.* ⊕); purificar; ⊕ acrisolar, acendrar (*a. fig.*); *v/i.*: ~ (*up*)*on* sutilizar *acc.*; mejorar *acc.*; **reˈfined** fino, refinado; *p.* bien criado, culto; *b.s.* redicho; **reˈfine·ment** refinamiento *m*; esmero *m*, urbanidad *f*; ⊕ refinación *f*; **reˈfin·er** refinador *m*; **reˈfin·er·y** refinería *f*.
re·fit [ˈriːˈfit] **1.** reparar(se) (*a.* ⚓), componer(se); **2.** (*a.* **reˈfit·ment**) reparación *f*, compostura *f*.
re·flect [riˈflekt] *v/t.* reflejar; *v/i.* (*think*) reflexionar; *that* ~*s well* (*ill*) *upon him* eso le revela bajo una luz (poco) favorable; **reˈflec·tion** reflejo *m*, reflexión *f*; (*thinking*) reflexión *f*, consideración *f*, meditación *f*; (*censure*) reproche *m* (*on* a); *cast* ~*s on* reprochar *acc.*; **reˈflec·tive** □ reflexivo; **reˈflec·tor** reflector *m*; *mot. rear* ~ (placa *f* de) captafaros *m*.

re·flex [ˈri:fleks] reflejo *adj. a. su. m*; ~ *action physiol.* (acto *m*) reflejo *m*; *conditioned* ~ reflejo *m* acondicionado; **re·flex·ive** [riˈfleksiv] □ reflexivo.

re·float [ˈri:ˈflout] sacar a flote.

re·flux [ˈri:flʌks] reflujo *m*.

re·for·est·a·tion [ˈri:fɔrisˈteiʃn] repoblación *f* forestal.

re·form [riˈfɔ:rm] **1.** reforma(ción) *f*; **2.** reformar(se), enmendar(se); reconstituir; **ref·or·ma·tion** [refərˈmeiʃn] reformación *f*; *eccl.* ♀ Reforma *f*; **re·form·a·to·ry** [riˈfɔ:rmətɔ:ri] reformatorio *adj. a. su. m* (*mst* de jóvenes); **reˈformed** reformado; **reˈform·er** reformador (-a *f*) *m*.

re·found [ˈri:faund] refundir.

re·fract [riˈfrækt] refractar; ~*ing telescope* telescopio *m* de refracción; **reˈfrac·tion** refracción *f*; **reˈfrac·tive** refractivo; **reˈfrac·tor** refractor *m*; **reˈfrac·to·ri·ness** lo refractario (*a.* ⚗), obstinación *f*; **reˈfrac·to·ry** refractario (*a.* ⚗), obstinado.

re·frain[1] [riˈfrain] abstenerse (*from* de).

re·frain[2] [~] estribillo *m*.

re·fresh [riˈfreʃ] refrescar; **reˈfresh·er** F refresco *m*; ~ *course* curso *m* de repaso; **reˈfresh·ing** □ refrescante; **reˈfresh·ment** refresco *m*; ~*s pl.* refrescos *m/pl.*; ~ *room* cantina *f*.

re·frig·er·ant [riˈfridʒərənt] refrigerante *adj. a. su. m*; **reˈfrig·er·ate** [~reit] refrigerar; **reˈfrig·er·at·ing** refrigerativo; refrigerante; **re·frig·erˈa·tion** refrigeración *f*; **reˈfrig·er·a·tor** nevera *f*, refrigerador *m*; frigorífico *m*; ⚗ refrigerante *m*; ~ *truck* camión *m* frigorífico.

re·fu·el [ri:ˈfjuəl] reabastecer(se) de combustible, rellenar (de combustible).

ref·uge [ˈrefju:dʒ] refugio *m*, asilo *m*; *fig.* recurso *m*, amparo *m*; *mount.* albergue *m*; *take* ~ guarecerse; *take* ~ *in* acogerse a; **ref·u·gee** [~ˈdʒi:] refugiado (a *f*) *m*; ~ *camp* campo *m* de refugiados.

re·ful·gence [riˈfʌldʒəns] refulgencia *f*; **reˈful·gent** □ refulgente.

re·fund 1. [riˈfʌnd] devolver, reintegrar; **2.** [ˈri:fʌnd] devolución *f*.

re·fur·bish [ˈri:ˈfə:rbiʃ] restaurar, repulir.

re·fur·nish [ˈri:ˈfə:rniʃ] amueblar de nuevo.

re·fus·al [riˈfju:zl] negativa *f*; denegación *f*; rechazamiento *m*; ✝ opción *f* (exclusiva).

re·fuse 1. [riˈfju:z] *v/t.* rehusar, (de)negar, rechazar; no querer aceptar; ~ *o.s. s.t.* privarse de algo; *v/i.* (*horse*) rehusar, plantarse; ~ *to inf.* negarse a *inf.*, rehusar *inf.*; *he* ~*d* se negó a hacerlo; **2. ref·use** [ˈrefju:s] desechado; **3.** [~] basura *f*; desperdicios *m/pl.*; sobras *f/pl*; ~ *dump* terreno *m* echadizo.

ref·u·ta·ble [riˈfju:təbl, ˈrefjutəbl] □ refutable; **ref·uˈta·tion** refutación *f*; **re·fute** [riˈfju:t] refutar, rebatir.

re·gain [riˈgein] (re)cobrar.

re·gal [ˈri:gəl] □ regio; real.

re·gale [riˈgeil] regalar(se) (*on* con); agasajar, festejar.

re·ga·li·a [riˈgeiliə] *pl.* insignias *f/pl.* (reales).

re·gard [riˈgɑ:rd] **1.** consideración *f*, respeto *m*; estimación *f*; (*gaze*) mirada *f*; ~*s pl.* recuerdos *m/pl.*; *having* ~ *to* considerando; *in* (*or with*) ~ *to* con respecto a, en cuanto a; *out of* ~ *for* por respeto a; *with kind* ~*s* con muchos recuerdos; **2.** considerar (*as* como); observar; respetar; mirar; tocar a; *as* ~*s* por lo que se refiere a; **reˈgard·ful** □ atento (*of* a); **reˈgard·ing** en cuanto a; relativo a; **reˈgard·less 1.**: ~ *of* indiferente a; sin hacer caso de; sin miramientos de; **2.** *adv.* F pese a quien pese, a pesar de todo.

re·gat·ta [riˈgætə] regata *f*.

re·gen·cy [ˈri:dʒənsi] regencia *f*.

re·gen·er·ate 1. [riˈdʒenəreit] regenerar; **2.** [~rit] regenerado; **re·gen·erˈa·tion** regeneración *f*; **reˈgen·er·a·tive** [~rətiv] *radio*: regenerador.

re·gent [ˈri:dʒənt] regente *adj. a. su. m/f*; ˈ**~ship** regencia *f*.

reg·i·cide [ˈredʒisaid] regicidio *m*; (*p.*) regicida *m/f*.

ré·gime [reiˈʒi:m], **reg·i·men** [ˈredʒimen] régimen *m*.

reg·i·ment 1. [ˈredʒimənt] regimiento *m*; **2.** [ˈ~ment] *fig.* organizar muy estrictamente, reglamentar; **reg·iˈmen·tal** de(l) regimiento; **reg·iˈmen·tals** [~tlz] *pl.* ⚔ uniforme *m*; **reg·i·men'ta·tion** organización *f* estricta.

re·gion ['ri:dʒən] región *f*, comarca *f*; zona *f*; *in the* ~ *of fig.* alrededor de; '**re·gion·al** □ regional.

reg·is·ter ['redʒistər] **1.** registro *m* (*a.* ♪); lista *f*, padrón *m of members*; *univ.*, ⚓ matrícula *f*; ⊕ indicador *m*, registrador *m*; (*parish*) ~ registro *m* parroquial; ~ *office approx.* juzgado *m* (municipal); ⚓ ~ *ton* tonelada *f* de registro (= 2,832 m^3); **2.** *v/t.* registrar; inscribir, matricular; ⊕ indicar *emotion* manifestar; *letter* certificar; *luggage* facturar; *v/i.* inscribirse, matricular; *typ.* corresponder, estar en registro; *fig.* producir impresión; '**reg·is·tered** *letter* certificado; ~ *design* diseño *m* registrado; ~ *trade mark* marca *f* registrada.

reg·is·trar ['redʒistra:r, redʒis'tra:r] registrador *m*, archivero *m*; **reg·is·tra·tion** [~'treiʃn] registro *m*, inscripción *f*, matrícula *f*; ~ *fee* derechos *m/pl.* de matrícula; ~ *number mot.* matrícula *f*; '**reg·is·try** registro *m*, archivo *m*; ~ *office approx.* juzgado *m* (municipal), registro *m* civil; *servant's* ~ agencia *f* de colocaciones.

re·gress 1. ['ri:gres] retroceso *m*; **2.** [ri'gres] perder terreno; retroceder; **re·gres·sion** ['ri:greʃn] regresión *f*; **re·gres·sive** [ri'gresiv] □ regresivo.

re·gret [ri'gret] **1.** sentimiento *m*, pesar *m*; remordimiento *m*; *to my* ~ a mi pesar; ~*s pl.* excusas *f/pl.*; **2.** sentir, lamentar; arrepentirse de; **re'gret·ful** [~ful] □ pesaroso, arrepentido; ~*ly* con pesar, sentidamente; **re'gret·ta·ble** □ lamentable, deplorable.

re·group [ri:'gru:p] reagruparse.

reg·u·lar ['regjulər] **1.** □ regular (*a. eccl.*); normal; uniforme; ordenado; *attender etc.* asiduo; *reader* habitual; F cabal, verdadero; ⚔ regular, de línea; **2.** obrero *m* permanente; *eccl.* regular *m*; ⚔ soldado *m* de línea; F parroquiano *m*, asiduo *m*; **reg·u·lar·i·ty** [~'læriti] regularidad *f*; orden *m*; '**reg·u·lar·ize** regularizar.

reg·u·late ['regjuleit] regular (*a.* ⊕), arreglar, ajustar; '**reg·u·lat·ing** ⊕ regulador; **reg·u'la·tion 1.** regulación *f*; regla *f*, reglamento *m*; **2.** reglamentario; '**reg·u·la·tor** regulador *m* (*a.* ⊕).

re·gur·gi·tate [ri:'gə:rdʒiteit] *v/t.* vomitar (sin esfuerzo); *v/i.* regurgitar.

re·ha·bil·i·tate [ri:(h)ə'biliteit] rehabilitar; '**re·ha·bil·i'ta·tion** rehabilitación *f*.

re·hash ['ri:'hæʃ] *fig.* **1.** refundir, rehacer; **2.** refundición *f*; repetición *f* sin novedad.

re·hears·al [ri'hə:rsəl] enumeración *f*, repetición *f*; *thea.*, ♪ ensayo *m*; **re·hearse** [ri'hə:rs] enumerar, repetir; *thea.*, ♪ ensayar.

re·heat [ri:'hi:t] recalentar.

reign [rein] **1.** reinado *m*; *fig.* (pre)dominio *m*; **2.** reinar; *fig.* imperar, prevalecer; ~*ing* reinante.

re·im·burse ['ri:im'bə:rs] reembolsar; '**re·im'burse·ment** reembolso *m*.

rein [rein] **1.** rienda *f*; *give* ~ *to* dar rienda suelta a; **2.** *v/t.*: ~ *in*, ~ *back* refrenar; *v/i.*: ~ *in* detenerse.

rein·deer ['reindir] reno *m*.

re·in·force ['ri:in'fɔ:rs] reforzar (*a. fig.*); enfatizar; fortalecer; ~*d concrete* hormigón *m* armado; '**re·in'force·ments** *pl.* refuerzos *m/pl.*

re·in·state ['ri:in'steit] reinstalar; rehabilitar; '**re·in'state·ment** reinstalación *f*.

re·in·sur·ance ['ri:in'ʃurəns] reaseguro *m*; **re·in·sure** ['~'ʃur] reasegurar.

re·in·vest ['ri:in'vest] reinvertir.

re·is·sue ['ri:'iʃu:] **1.** *book* reimprimir; *patent etc.* reexpedir; *film* reestrenar; **2.** reimpresión *f etc.*

re·it·er·ate ['ri:'itəreit] reiterar; **re·it·er'a·tion** reiteración *f*.

re·ject [ri'dʒekt] *offer etc.* rechazar; *application* denegar; *plan etc.* desechar; *solution* descartar; **re'jec·tion** rechazamiento *m*; denegación *f*, desestimación *f*; **re'jec·tor circuit** *radio*: circuito *m* de repulsor.

re·joice [ri'dʒɔis] alegrar(se), regocijar(se) (*at*, *by* de); **re'joic·ing 1.** □ regocijado; **2.** (*freq.* ~*s pl.*) regocijo *m*, júbilo *m*, alegría *f*.

re·join 1. ['ri:'dʒɔin] reunirse con, volver a juntarse con; reincorporarse a; juntar de nuevo; **2.** [ri'dʒɔin] replicar; **re'join·der** réplica *f*.

re·ju·ve·nate [ri'dʒu:vineit] rejuvenecer; **re·ju·ve·na·tion** [ridʒu:vi'neiʃn] rejuvenecimiento *m*; **re·ju·ve·nes·cence** [~'nesns] rejuvenecimiento *m*.

re·kin·dle ['ri:'kindl] reencender.

re·lapse [ri'læps] **1.** ⚕ recaída *f*, recidiva *f*; reincidencia *f into crime etc.*; **2.** ⚕ recaer; reincidir *into crime etc.*; *eccl.* relapso *m into sin, heresy*.

re·late [ri'leit] *v/t.* relatar, contar; relacionar (*to, with* con); *v/i.*: ~ *to* relacionarse con; F ver con simpatía; **re'lat·ed** *subject* afín, conexo; *he is* ~ *to me* es pariente mío.

re·la·tion [ri'leiʃn] (*narration*) relato *m*, relación *f*; (~*ship*) conexión *f*, relación *f* (*to, with* con); (*kin*) pariente *m*/*f*; ~*s pl.* (*kin*) parientes *m*/*pl.*; (*good etc.*) relaciones *f*/*pl.*; *in* ~ *to* respecto de; *public* ~*s office* departamento *m* de relaciones públicas; **re'la·tion·ship** conexión *f*, afinidad *f* (*to, with* con); (*kinship*) parentesco *m*.

rel·a·tive ['relətiv] **1.** □ relativo (*to* a); **2.** *gr.* relativo *m*; (*kin*) pariente *m*/*f*; **rel·a'tiv·i·ty** relatividad *f*.

re·lax [ri'læks] *v/t.* relajar, aflojar; mitigar, suavizar; *v/i.* esparcirse, expansionarse, descansar; relajarse, mitigarse; F ~! ¡cálmate!; **re·lax'a·tion** esparcimiento *m*, recreo *m*, descanso *m*; relajación *f*, aflojamiento *m*.

re·lay[1] [ri'lei] **1.** parada *f*, posta *f of horses etc.*; tanda *f of workmen*; relevo *m*; ⚡ relé *m*, relai(s) *m*; ~ *race* (carrera *f* de) relevos *m*/*pl.*; **2.** *radio*: retransmitir.

re-lay[2] ['ri:'lei] volver a colocar.

re·lease [ri'li:s] **1.** liberación *f*; excarcelación *f from prison*; descargo *m from obligation*; *film*: estreno *m* general; ⚖ cesión *f*; ⊕, *phot.* disparador *m*; ⊕, *gases* escape *m*; **2.** soltar, libertar; descargar, absolver *from obligation*; *pressure etc.* aflojar; *brake* soltar; *film* estrenar; ⚖ ceder.

rel·e·gate ['religeit] relegar; **rel·e'ga·tion** relegación *f*.

re·lent [ri'lent] ablandarse, ceder; **re'lent·less** □ implacable, despiadado.

rel·e·vance, rel·e·van·cy ['relivəns(i)] pertinencia *f*; '**rel·e·vant** □ pertinente.

re·li·a·bil·ity [rilaiə'biliti] confiabilidad *f*; formalidad *f*; seguridad *f*; **re'li·a·ble** □ confiable; seguro; de fiar, de confianza; *p.* formal, de mucha formalidad; *news* fehaciente.

re·li·ance [ri'laiəns] confianza *f* (*on* en); dependencia *f* (*on* de).

re·li·ant [ri'laiənt] confiado; dependiente.

rel·ic ['relik] reliquia *f* (*a. eccl.*), vestigio *m*; antigüedad *f*; **rel·ict** ['relikt] viuda *f*.

re·lief [ri'li:f] alivio *m*; desahogo *m*; consuelo *m*; aligeramiento *m*; relevación *f*; (*a. poor* ~) socorro *m*, auxilio *m*; ⚔ (*troops*) relevo *m*; ⚔ descerco *m*, socorro *m of town*; ▲ relieve *m*; ⚖ satisfacción *f*, remedio *m*; *throw into* ~ hacer resaltar; F *that's a* ~! ¡menos mal!; ~ *map* mapa *m* en relieve; ~ *train* tren *m* suplementario; ~ *work* trabajos *m*/*pl.* de socorro; ~ *works* obras *f*/*pl.* públicas (para aliviar el desempleo).

re·lieve [ri'li:v] aliviar; (*reassure*) tranquilizar; *burden* aligerar; *poor* socorrer; *headache etc.* quitar, suprimir; ⚔ *men* relevar; ⚔ *town* socorrer, descercar; destituir (*of post* de); relevar, exonerar (*of duty* de); ~ *nature* hacer del cuerpo; ~ *one's feelings* desahogarse.

re·lie·vo [ri'li:vou] relieve *m*.

re·li·gion [ri'lidʒən] religión *f*.

re·li·gious [ri'lidʒəs] □ religioso; ~*ly fig.* puntualmente; **re'li·gious·ness** religiosidad *f*.

re·lin·quish [ri'liŋkwiʃ] abandonar, renunciar (a); **re'lin·quish·ment** abandono *m*, renuncia *f*.

rel·i·quar·y ['relikwəri] relicario *m*.

rel·ish ['reliʃ] **1.** sabor *m*, gusto *m*; apetito *m*, apetencia *f*; entremés *m*; (*sauce*) salsa *f*; **2.** saborear; gustar de; tener buen apetito para.

re·lo·cate [ri:'loukeit] mudar(se); cambiar de lugar.

re·luc·tance [ri'lʌktəns] desgana *f*, renuencia *f*, aversión *f*; *with* ~ a desgana; **re'luc·tant** □ maldispuesto; poco dispuesto (*to* a); ~*ly* a regañadientes, de mala gana.

re·ly [ri'lai]: ~ (*up*)*on* confiar en, fiarse de; contar con.

re·main [ri'mein] **1.** quedar(se), permanecer; (*be left over*) sobrar; ~ *the same*, ~ *unchanged* seguir siendo lo mismo; **2.** ~*s pl.* restos

m/pl.; sobras *f/pl.*; *mortal* ~ restos *m/pl.* mortales; **re'main·der 1.** resto *m*; ⅍ residuo *m*, resta *f*; (*books*) restos *m/pl.* de edición; **2.** *books* saldar.
re·make ['ri:'meik] rehacer.
re·mand [ri'mænd] **1.** reencarcelar; **2.:** *be on* ~ estar detenido.
re·mark [ri'mɑ:rk] **1.** observación *f*; **2.** *v/t.* observar, notar; *v/i.* hacer una observación ([*up*]*on* sobre); **re'mark·a·ble** ☐ notable; raro.
re·mar·ry ['ri:'mæri] volver a casarse.
re·me·di·a·ble [ri'mi:diəbl] ☐ remediable; **re·me·di·al** [ri'mi:diəl] ☐ remediador.
rem·e·dy ['remidi] **1.** remedio *m*; **2.** remediar.
re·mem·ber [ri'membər] acordarse de, recordar; (*mst in commands*) tener presente; ~ *me to him!* ¡déle Vd. recuerdos míos!; **re'mem·brance** recuerdo *m*, memoria *f*; recordación *f*; *in* ~ *of* que conmemora; ~*s pl.* recuerdos *m/pl.*
re·mind [ri'maind] recordar (*a p. of a th.* algo a una p.); ~ *o.s. that* recordarse que; **re'mind·er** recordatorio *m*, advertencia *f*.
rem·i·nisce [remi'nis] contar los recuerdos; **rem·i'nis·cence** [remi'nisns] reminiscencia *f*; **rem·i'nis·cent** ☐ evocador; recordativo; *be* ~ *of* recordar *acc.*
re·miss [ri'mis] ☐ negligente, descuidado; **re'mis·si·ble** [~əbl] remisible; **re·mis·sion** [~'miʃn] remisión *f*; perdón *m*; **re'miss·ness** negligencia *f*, descuido *m*.
re·mit [ri'mit] *all senses*: remitir; **re'mit·tance** remesa *f*; **re·mit'tee** consignatorio (a *f*) *m*; **re'mit·tent** (fiebre *f*) remitente; **re'mit·ter** remitente *m/f*.
rem·nant ['remnənt] resto *m*, residuo *m*; ✝ retazo *m of cloth.*
re·mod·el ['ri:'mɔdl] modelar de nuevo; refundir.
re·mon·strance [ri'mɔnstrəns] protesta *f*, reconvención *f*; **re'mon·strant** protestante *adj. a. su. m/f*; **re'mon·strate** [~streit] reconvenir (*with* a); protestar (*against* contra); poner reparos (*on* a).
re·morse [ri'mɔ:rs] remordimiento *m*; **re'morse·ful** [~ful] ☐ arrepentido; **re'morse·less** ☐ implacable, despiadado.
re·mote [ri'mout] ☐ remoto; *v. control*; **re'mote·ness** apartamiento *m*, alejamiento *m*.
re·mount [ri:'maunt] **1.** *v/t.* remontar (*a.* ⚔); *v/i.* volver a subir; **2.** remonta *f* (*a.* ⚔).
re·mov·a·ble [ri'mu:vəbl] separable; amovible; **re'mov·al** [~vəl] removimiento *m*, remoción *f*; mudanza *f of furniture*; destitución *f*, deposición *f from office*; ⊕ separación *f of part*; eliminación *f of obstacle, waste*; ⚕ extirpación *f*; **re·move** [~'mu:v] **1.** *v/t.* quitar, remover; trasladar (*to* a); *furniture* mudar; destituir *from office*; borrar *from list*; ⊕ *part* separar, retirar; *obstacle, waste* eliminar; ⚕ extirpar; *v/i.* mudarse, trasladarse; **2.** grado *m*; **re'mov·er** agente *m* de mudanzas; *spot* ~ quitamanchas *m*.
re·mu·ner·ate [ri'mju:nəreit] remunerar; **re·mu·ner'a·tion** remuneración *f*; **re'mu·ner·a·tive** [~rətiv] ☐ remunerador.
Ren·ais·sance [ri'neisəns] Renacimiento *m*.
re·nal ['ri:nl] renal.
re·name ['ri:'neim] dar nuevo nombre a.
re·nas·cence [ri'næsns] renacimiento *m*; **re'nas·cent** renaciente.
rend [rend] [*irr.*] *lit.* rasgar, hender.
ren·der ['rendər] hacer, volver; *service, honor, thanks* dar; *fat* derretir; (*translate*) traducir; ♪ interpretar, ejecutar; ✝ *account* pasar; ⊕ rendir, producir; **'ren·der·ing** interpretación *f*; traducción *f etc.*
ren·dez·vous ['rɔndivu:] (lugar *m* de una) cita *f*.
ren·di·tion [ren'diʃn] ♪ ejecución *f*.
ren·e·gade ['renigeid] renegado *adj. a. su. m* (a *f*).
re·new [ri'nju:] renovar; reanudar; **re'new·a·ble** renovable; **re'new·al** [~əl] renovación *f*; reanudación *f*.
ren·net ['renit] cuajo *m*.
re·nounce [ri'nauns] renunciar (*un derecho, a una cosa*).
ren·o·vate ['renouveit] renovar; **ren·o'va·tion** renovación *f*.
re·nown [ri'naun] *lit.* renombre *m*, nombradía *f*; **re'nowned** *lit.* renombrado, ínclito.
rent[1] [rent] **1.** *pret. a. p.p. of rend*; **2.** rasgón *m*; *fig.* cisma *m*.

rent² [~] **1.** alquiler *m*; arriendo *m*; **2.** alquilar; arrendar; ˈ**rent·a·ble** arrendable; ˈ**rent·al** alquiler *m*, arriendo *m*; ˈ**rent-**ˈ**free** exento de alquiler.

re·nun·ci·a·tion [rinʌnsiˈeiʃn] renuncia(ción) *f*.

re·o·pen [ˈriːˈoupn] reabrir(se); ˈ**re**ˈ**o·pen·ing** reapertura *f*.

re·or·ga·ni·za·tion [ˈriːɔːrgənaiˈzeiʃn] reorganización *f*; ˈ**re**ˈ**or·gan·ize** reorganizar.

rep [rep] ✝ reps *m*.

re·paint [ˈriːˈpeint] repintar.

re·pair¹ [riˈper] **1.** reparación *f*; compostura *f*; (*esp. shoes*) remiendo *m*; ~*s pl.* reparaciones *f/pl.*; *in* (*good*) ~ en buen estado; ~*man* reparador *m*; mecánico *m*; ~ *shop* taller *m* de reparaciones; **2.** reparar; componer; *shoes etc.* remendar.

re·pair² [~]: ~ *to* ir a, encaminarse a.

rep·a·ra·ble [ˈrepərəbl] reparable; **rep·a**ˈ**ra·tion** reparación *f*; satisfacción *f*; ~*s pol.* indemnizaciones *f/pl.*; *make* ~*s* dar satisfacción.

rep·ar·tee [repɑːrˈtiː] réplicas *f/pl.* agudas.

re·pass [ˈriːˈpæs] repasar.

re·past [riˈpæst] comida *f*.

re·pa·tri·ate **1.** [riːˈpætrieit] repatriar; **2.** [riːˈpætriit] repatriado *m*; ˈ**re·pa·tri**ˈ**a·tion** repatriación *f*.

re·pay [riːˈpei] [*irr.* (*pay*)] pagar, devolver; reembolsar; *p.* resarcir, compensar; **re**ˈ**pay·a·ble** reembolsable; **re**ˈ**pay·ment** reembolso *m*; devolución *f*.

re·peal [riˈpiːl] **1.** revocación *f*, abrogación *f*; **2.** revocar, abrogar.

re·peat [riˈpiːt] **1.** *v/t.* repetir; *thanks etc.* reiterar; (*aloud*) recitar; ✝ ~ *an order* (*for*) repetir el pedido (de); *v/i.* repetirse; (*rifle, clock, taste*) repetir; **2.** ♪ repetición *f*; *radio* (*a.* ~ *broadcast*): retransmisión *f*; ✝ (*freq.* ~ *order*) pedido *m* de repetición; **re**ˈ**peat·ed** □ repetido; **re**ˈ**peat·er** reloj *m* (rifle *m etc.*) de repetición.

re·pel [riˈpel] rechazar, repeler; *fig.* repugnar; **re**ˈ**pel·lent** repugnante.

re·pent [riˈpent] arrepentirse (*of* de).

re·pent·ance [riˈpentəns] arrepentimiento *m*; **re**ˈ**pent·ant** □ arrepentido.

re·peo·ple [ˈriːˈpiːpl] repoblar.

re·per·cus·sion [riːpəːrˈkʌʃn] repercusión *f* (*a. fig.*); *fig.* resonancia *f*.

rep·er·toire [ˈrepərtwɑːr], **rep·er·to·ry** [ˈrepərtɔːri] repertorio *m* (*a. fig.*).

rep·e·ti·tion [repiˈtiʃn] repetición *f*; ✝ ~ *order* pedido *m* de repetición; **re**ˈ**pet·i·tive** □ reiterativo.

re·pine [riˈpain] quejarse (*at* de), afligirse.

re·place [riːˈpleis] reemplazar, sustituir (*with, by* por); reponer, colocar nuevamente; **re**ˈ**place·ment** (*th.*) repuesto *m*; (*p.*) sustituto *m*; (*act*) reposición *f*; reemplazo *m*.

re·plant [ˈriːˈplænt] replantar.

re·plen·ish [riˈpleniʃ] rellenar, reaprovisionar; **re**ˈ**plen·ish·ment** rellenado *m*, reaprovisionamiento *m*.

re·plete [riˈpliːt] repleto (*with* de); **re**ˈ**ple·tion** repleción *f*; hartazgo *m of food*.

rep·li·ca [ˈreplikə] *paint. etc.* copia *f*, reproducción *f* (exacta); *fig.* segunda edición *f*.

re·ply [riˈplai] **1.** responder, contestar; ~ *to a letter* contestar (a) una carta; **2.** respuesta *f*, contestación *f*; ~ *post card* tarjeta *f* de porte pagado.

re·port [riˈpɔːrt] **1.** (*official*) informe *m*; parte *m*; relato *m*; (*newspaper*) información *f*, reportaje *m*, crónica *f*; *school*: papeleta *f*, nota *f*; estampido *m of gun*; ~ *card* certificado *m* escolar; *annual* ~ memoria *f* anual; **2.** *v/t.* relatar; *event etc.* informar acerca de; *crime* denunciar; ~ *that* comunicar que, informar que; *v/i.* hacer un informe (*on* acerca de); presentarse (*at* en); **re**ˈ**port·er** reportero *m*; repórter *m*; *approx.* periodista *m/f*.

re·pose [riˈpouz] **1.** reposo *m*; **2.** descansar, reposar; ~ *trust etc. in* poner confianza *etc.* en; **re·pos·i·to·ry** [riˈpɔzitɔːri] guardamuebles *m*; repositorio *m*; depósito *m*; (*p.*) depositario *m*.

re·pos·sess [ˈriːpəˈzes] recobrar.

rep·re·hend [repriˈhend] reprender; **rep·re**ˈ**hen·si·ble** □ reprensible; **rep·re**ˈ**hen·sion** reprensión *f*.

rep·re·sent [repriˈzent] representar; ⚖ ser apoderado de; ✝ ser agente (*or* representante) de; **rep·re·sen**ˈ**ta·tion** representación *f*; **rep·re**ˈ**sent·a·tive** [~tətiv] **1.** □ representativo; **2.** representante *m/f*; ⚖ apoderado

m; *House of* ℒ*s* Cámara *f* de Representantes (*EE.UU.*).
re·press [riˈpres] reprimir; **re·pression** [riˈpreʃn] represión *f*; **reˈpressive** □ represivo.
re·prieve [riˈpri:v] **1.** respiro *m*; ⚖ indulto *m*, suspensión *f* (*esp.* de la pena de muerte); **2.** indultar, suspender la pena de muerte de.
rep·ri·mand [ˈreprimænd] **1.** reprimenda *f*; **2.** reprender, reconvenir.
re·print [ˈri:ˈprint] **1.** reimprimir; **2.** reimpresión *f*.
re·pris·al [riˈpraizl] represalia *f*; *take* ~*s* tomar represalias.
re·proach [riˈproutʃ] **1.** reproche *m*; oprobio *m*; baldón *m*; **2.** reprochar (*s.o. for, with a th.* algo a alguien); **reˈproach·ful** [~ful] □ acusador, reprensor.
rep·ro·bate [ˈreproubeit] réprobo *adj. a. su. m* (a *f*); **rep·roˈba·tion** reprobación *f*.
re·pro·cess [ri:ˈprɔses] elaborar de nuevo; volver a confeccionar.
re·pro·duce [ri:prəˈdju:s] reproducir(se); **re·pro·duc·tion** [~ˈdʌkʃn] reproducción *f*; **re·proˈduc·tive** □ reproductor; *organ etc.* de la generación.
re·proof [riˈpru:f] reproche *m*, reprensión *f*.
re·prov·al [riˈpru:vl] reprobación *f*; **re·prove** [~ˈpru:v] reprobar, reprender (*s.o. for s.t.* algo a alguien).
rep·tile [ˈreptail] reptil *adj. a. su. m*.
re·pub·lic [riˈpʌblik] república *f*; **reˈpub·li·can** republicano *adj. a. su. m* (a *f*); **reˈpub·li·can·ism** republicanismo *m*.
re·pub·li·ca·tion [ˈri:pʌbliˈkeiʃn] reedición *f*.
re·pub·lish [ˈri:ˈpʌbliʃ] reeditar.
re·pu·di·ate [riˈpju:dieit] *charge etc.* desechar, negar, rechazar; *obligation etc.* desconocer, rechazar; *wife* repudiar; **repu·diˈa·tion** desconocimiento *m*; repudiación *f etc.*.
re·pug·nance [riˈpʌgnəns] repugnancia *f*; **reˈpug·nant** □ repugnante.
re·pulse [riˈpʌls] **1.** repulsión *f*, repulsa *f*, rechazo *m*; **2.** rechazar, repulsar; **reˈpul·sion** repulsión *f*, repugnancia *f*; **reˈpul·sive** □ repulsivo, repelente.
re·pur·chase [riˈpə:rtʃəs] readquirir.
rep·u·ta·ble [ˈrepjutəbl] □ *firm* acreditado; *p.* honroso, estimable; **rep·u·ta·tion** [~ˈteiʃn] reputación *f*, fama *f*; **re·pute** [riˈpju:t] **1.** reputación *f*; *by* ~ según la opinión común; *of* ~ acreditado; **2.** reputar; *be* ~*d to be or as* ser tenido por, tener fama de; **reˈput·ed** supuesto; **reˈput·ed·ly** según la opinión común.
re·quest [riˈkwest] **1.** petición *f*, instancia *f*, solicitud *f*; ✝ demanda *f*; *at the* ~ *of* a petición (*or* instancia) de; *by* ~ a petición; *on* ~ a solicitud; ~ *program* programa *m* a petición de radioyentes; ~ *stop* parada *f* discrecional; **2.** pedir; solicitar; suplicar.
re·qui·em [ˈrekwiem] réquiem *m*.
re·quire [riˈkwaiər] necesitar; exigir; requerir (*of* a; *a p. to do* que una p. haga); **reˈquired** requisito; obligatorio; **reˈquire·ment** requerimiento *m*; requisito *m*; necesidad *f*.
req·ui·site [ˈrekwizit] **1.** preciso, indispensable; **2.** requisito *m*; *toilet* ~*s pl.* artículos *m/pl.* de limpieza; **req·uiˈsi·tion 1.** requisición *f* (*a.* ⚔); pedido *m*; requerimiento *m*; **2.** ⚔ requisar; exigir.
re·quit·al [riˈkwaitl] compensación *f*; desquite *m*.
re·quite [riˈkwait] (re)compensar; desquitarse; corresponder a.
re·read [ˈri:ˈri:d] [*irr.* (*read*)] releer.
re·re·dos [ˈrirədɔs] retablo *m*.
re·run [ˈri:rʌn] exhibición *f* repetida *of film, play, etc.*; programa *m* repetido.
re·sale [ˈri:ˈseil] reventa *f*.
re·scind [riˈsind] rescindir.
re·scis·sion [riˈsiʒn] rescisión *f*.
re·script [ˈri:skript] rescri(p)to *m*.
res·cue [ˈreskju:] **1.** salvamento *m*; liberación *f*; rescate *m*; **2.** salvar; librar, libertar; rescatar; **ˈres·cu·er** salvador (-a *f*) *m*.
re·search [riˈsə:rtʃ] **1.** investigar; indagar; **2.** investigación *f* (*in, into* de); ~ *establishment* instituto *m* de investigaciones; ~ *worker* = **reˈsearch·er** investigador (-a *f*) *m*.
re·seat [ˈri:ˈsi:t] *valves* reasentar.
re·sell [ˈri:ˈsel] [*irr.* (*sell*)] revender.
re·sem·blance [riˈzembləns] semejanza *f*, parecido *m* (*to* a); **reˈsemble** [~bl] asemejarse a, parecerse a.

re·sent [riˈzent] resentirse de (*or* por); tomar a mal; **reˈsent·ful** [ˌful] □ resentido, ofendido (*at*, *of* por); **reˈsent·ment** resentimiento *m*.

res·er·va·tion [rezərˈveiʃn] (*act*) reserva *f*; reservación *f*; (*mental*) reserva *f*; salvedad *f*; (*in argument*) distingo *m*; plaza *f* reservada *on train etc.*; reserva *f* (de indios *etc.*).

re·serve [riˈzəːrv] **1.** reserva *f* (*a.* ⚔, ⚕); *sport*: suplente *m/f*; *in* ~ de reserva; ~ *price* precio *m* mínimo; **2.** reservar; ~ *one's strength* reservarse; **reˈserved** □ reservado, callado; sigiloso; ~ *seat* plaza *f* reservada.

re·serv·ist [riˈzəːrvist] reservista *m*.

res·er·voir [ˈrezərvwɑːr] embalse *m*, pantano *m of water*; depósito *m*; *fig.* fondo *m*.

re·set [ˈriːset] ⊕ reajustar; *jewel* reengastar; *typ.* recomponer.

re·set·tle [ˈriːˈsetl] *p.* restablecer; *land* colonizar; **ˈre·set·tle·ment** restablecimiento *m*; colonización *f*.

re·shuf·fle [ˈriːˈʃʌfl] **1.** *government* reconstruir; **2.** reconstrucción *f*.

re·side [riˈzaid] residir (*fig. in* en); **res·i·dence** [ˈrezidəns] residencia *f*; ~ *permit* visado *m* de permanencia; **ˈres·i·dent 1.** residente; **2.** residente *m/f*, vecino (a *f*) *m*; **res·i·den·tial** [ˌˈdenʃl] residencial.

re·sid·u·al [riˈzidjuəl] residual; **reˈsid·u·ar·y** restante; residual; ⚖ ~ *legatee* legatario (a *f*) *m* universal; **res·i·due** [ˈrezidjuː] residuo *m*; resto *m*; ⚕ *etc.* superávit *m*; **re·sid·u·um** [riˈzidjuəm] *esp.* ⚗, ⚗ residuo *m*.

re·sign [riˈzain] *v/t.* dimitir, renunciar, resignar; ~ *o.s.* resignarse (*to* a), conformarse (*to* con); *v/i.* dimitir (*from* de); **res·ig·na·tion** [rezigˈneiʃn] dimisión *f* (*from* de), renuncia *f*; resignación *f*; conformidad *f* (*to* con); **re·signed** [riˈzaind] □ resignado.

re·sil·i·ence [riˈziliəns] resistencia *f*; elasticidad *f*; *fig.* resistencia *f*, poder *m* de recuperación; **reˈsil·i·ent** elástico; resistente (*a. fig.*).

res·in [ˈrezin] **1.** resina *f*; **2.** tratar con resina; **ˈres·in·ous** resinoso.

re·sist [riˈzist] resistir (a); oponerse a; **reˈsist·ance** resistencia *f* (*a. phys.*, ⚡); **reˈsist·ant** resistente; **reˈsis·tor** ⚡ resistor *m*.

re·sole [ˈriːˈsoul] (sobre)solar.

res·o·lute [ˈrezəluːt] □ resuelto; **ˈres·o·lute·ness** resolución *f*.

res·o·lu·tion [rezəˈluːʃn] resolución *f*; *parl. etc.* acuerdo *m*; *pass a* ~ tomar un acuerdo; *good* ~*s* buenos propósitos *m/pl*.

re·solv·a·ble [riˈzɔlvəbl] soluble.

re·solve [riˈzɔlv] **1.** *v/t. all senses*: resolver (*into* en); *v/i.* resolverse (*into* en; *to* a); *parl. etc.* acordar (*to do* hacer); ~ (*up*)*on ger.* acordar *inf.*; **2.** resolución *f*; **reˈsolved** resuelto.

res·o·nance [ˈrezənəns] resonancia *f*; **ˈres·o·nant** □ resonante.

re·sorp·tion [riˈsɔːrpʃn] resorción *f*.

re·sort [riˈzɔːrt] **1.** recurso *m*; punto *m* de reunión; *health* ~ balneario *m*; *seaside* ~ punto *m* marítimo de veraneo, playa *f*; *summer* ~ punto *m* de veraneo; *in the last* ~, *as a last* ~ en último caso; **2.**: ~ *to* recurrir a, acudir a; *place* frecuentar.

re·sound [riˈzaund] resonar, retumbar; **reˈsound·ing** □ sonoro; *fig.* clamoroso, resonante.

re·source [riˈsɔːrs] recurso *m*, expediente *m*; inventiva *f*; ~*s pl.* recursos *m/pl.*; **reˈsource·ful** [ˌful] □ inventivo, ingenioso; **reˈsource·ful·ness** inventiva *f*, iniciativa *f*.

re·spect [risˈpekt] **1.** (*esteem*) respeto *m*, consideración *f* (*for* por); (*aspect*, *relation*) respecto *m*; ~*s pl.* recuerdos *m/pl.*, saludos *m/pl.*; *in* ~ *of* respecto a (*or* de); *in this* ~ por lo que se refiere a esto; *out of* ~ *for* por consideración a; *with* ~ *to* con respecto a; *pay one's* ~*s to* cumplimentar a; **2.** respetar; estimar; *law etc.* atenerse a; **re·spect·aˈbil·i·ty** respetabilidad *f*; **re·spect·a·ble** □ respetable; apreciable; **reˈspect·ful** [ˌful] □ respetuoso; *Yours* ~*ly* le saluda atentamente; **reˈspect·ful·ness** acatamiento *m*; **reˈspect·ing** con respecto a, en cuanto a; **reˈspec·tive** □ respectivo; **reˈspec·tive·ly** respectivamente.

res·pi·ra·tion [respəˈreiʃn] respiración *f*.

res·pi·ra·tor [ˈrespəreitər] máscara *f* (*or* careta *f*) antigás; **re·spir·a·to·ry** [ˈrəspərətɔri, risˈpairətəri] respiratorio.

re·spire [risˈpaiər] respirar.

res·pite [ˈrespit] **1.** respiro *m*, respiradero *m*; ⚖ prórroga *f*; *without* ~ sin tregua, sin respirar; **2.** aplazar, prorrogar; *p.* suspender la ejecución de.

re·splend·ence, re·splend·en·cy [ris'plendəns(i)] resplandor *m*; **re'splend·ent** □ resplandeciente.

re·spond [ris'pɔnd] responder; ~ *to treatment etc.* reaccionar a, ser sensible a; **re'spond·ent** ⚖ demandado *adj. a. su. m* (a *f*).

re·sponse [ris'pɔns] respuesta *f*; *fig.* reacción *f* (*to* a); *eccl.* responsorio *m*.

re·spon·si·bil·i·ty [rispɔnsə'biliti] responsabilidad *f* (*for* de); **re'spon·si·ble** responsable (*for* de); *post* de confianza; **re'spon·sive** □: ~ *to* sensible a.

rest[1] [rest] **1.** descanso *m*, reposo *m*; *fig.* paz *f*; (*support*) apoyo *m*; ♪ silencio *m*, pausa *f*; *at* ~ reposado; *fig.* en paz; *take a* ~ descansar un rato; **2.** *v/i.* **descansar; holgar; posar(se)** (*on* en); apoyarse (*on* en); (*matter*) quedar; *fig.* ~ (*up*)*on* descansar sobre; estribar en; *fig.* ~ *with* depender de; residir en; ~ *assured that* tener la seguridad de que; *v/t.* descansar; apoyar (*on* en).

rest[2] [~] resto *m*; ⚕ reserva *f*; *the* ~ lo demás, los demás *etc.*; *for the* ~ por lo demás.

re·state·ment ['ri:steitmənt] nueva exposición *f*.

res·tau·rant ['restərənt] restaurante *m*, restorán *m*; ~ *car* coche *m* restaurante, coche-comedor *m*.

rest cure ['restkjur] cura *f* de reposo.

rest·ful ['restful] □ descansado, sosegado; tranquilizador.

rest home ['resthoum] casa *f* de reposo.

res·ting place ['restiŋpleis] *fig.* última morada *f* (*a. last* ~).

res·ti·tu·tion [resti'tju:ʃn] restitución *f*; *make* ~ indemnizar.

res·tive ['restiv] □ intranquilo, inquieto; *horse etc.* rebelón; **'res·tive·ness** intranquilidad *f*.

rest·less ['restlis] □ inquieto; desasosegado; (*sleepless*) insomne; turbulento; **'rest·less·ness** inquietud *f*; desasosiego *m*; insomnio *m*; turbulencia *f*.

re·stock ['ri:'stɔk] reaprovisionar; repoblar.

res·to·ra·tion [restə'reiʃn] restauración *f*; devolución *f*; **re·stor·a·tive** [ris'tɔrətiv] reconstituyente *adj. a. su. m*.

re·store [ris'tɔ:r] restaurar; devolver; ~ *a p. to liberty* (*health*) devolver la libertad (la salud) a una p.; **re'stor·er** restaurador (-a *f*) *m*; *hair* ~ loción *f* capilar, restaurador *m* del cabello.

re·strain [ris'train] contener, refrenar, reprimir, tener a raya; ~ *s.o. from ger.* impedir que alguien *subj.*; **re'strained** templado, cohibido; refrenado; **re'straint** moderación *f*, comedimiento *m*; restricción *f*.

re·strict [ris'trikt] restringir, limitar; *be* ~*ed to* (*quality*) ser privativo de; **re'stric·tion** restricción *f*, limitación *f*; **re'stric·tive** □ restrictivo; ~ *practices pl.* normas *f/pl.* restrictivas.

rest room ['rest 'ru:m] sala *f* de descanso; *euph.* excusado *m*, retrete *m*.

re·sult [ri'zʌlt] **1.** resultado *m*; *as a* ~ por consiguiente; *as a* ~ *of* de resultas de; **2.** resultar (*from* de); ~ *in* terminar en, parar en; **re'sult·ant** resultante *adj. a. su. f* (⊕).

ré·su·mé ['rezu:mei] resumen *m*.

re·sume [ri'zju:m] reasumir; *journey etc.* reanudar; *seat* volver a tomar; **re·sump·tion** [ri'zʌmpʃn] reasunción *f*; reanudación *f*.

re·sur·gence [ri'sə:rdʒəns] resurgimiento *m*; **re'sur·gent** que está en trance de renacer.

res·ur·rect [rezə'rekt] resucitar; **res·ur'rec·tion** resurrección *f*.

re·sus·ci·tate [ri'sʌsiteit] resucitar (*v/t. a. v/i.*); **re·sus·ci'ta·tion** resucitación *f*.

re·tail **1.** ['ri:teil] venta *f* al por menor; *by* ~ al por menor; ~ *price* precio *m* al por menor (*or* al detalle); **2.** [~] *adj.*, *adv.* al (por) menor; ~ *bookseller* librero *m* al por menor; **3.** [ri:'teil] *v/t.* vender al (por) menor (*or* al detalle); *gossip* repetir; *v/i.* venderse al (por) menor (*at* a); **'re·tail·er** detallista *m/f*, comerciante *m/f* al por menor.

re·tain [ri'tein] retener; conservar; quedarse con; *lawyer* ajustar; *player* contratar; **re'tain·er** *hist.* adherente *m*, secuaz *m*; criado *m*; ⚖ (*a. retaining fee*) ajuste *m*, anticipo *m*.

re·take ['ri:'teik] [*irr.* (*take*)] volver a tomar.

re·tal·i·ate [riˈtælieit] desquitarse; tomar represalias; vengarse (*on* en); **re·tal·iˈa·tion** desquite *m*; represalias *f*/*pl*.; venganza *f*; **reˈtal·i·a·to·ry** [\~əri] vengativo.
re·tard [riˈtɑːrd] retardar, retrasar; **re·tard·a·tion** [\~ˈeiʃn] retardación *f*; **reˈtard·ed** subnormal, atrasado.
retch [retʃ] (esforzarse por) vomitar.
re·tell [ˈriːˈtel] [*irr*. (*tell*)] recontar.
re·ten·tion [riˈtenʃn] retención *f* (*a*. ⚕), conservación *f*; **reˈten·tive** □ retentivo.
re·think [ˈriːˈθiŋk] [*irr*. (*think*)] repensar.
ret·i·cence [ˈretisəns] reserva *f*; **ˈret·i·cent** □ reservado.
re·tic·u·late [riˈtikjulit], **reˈtic·u·lat·ed** [\~leitid] reticular; **ret·i·cule** [ˈretikjuːl] retículo *m*; (*a*. **re·ti·cle** [ˈretikl]) *opt*. retículo *m*.
ret·i·na [ˈretinə] retina *f*.
ret·i·nue [ˈretinjuː] séquito *m*, comitiva *f*.
re·tire [riˈtaiər] *v*/*i*. retirarse (*a*. ⚔); recogerse *to bed etc*.; jubilarse *from post*, retirarse *from army*; *v*/*t*. jubilar; **reˈtired** jubilado; ⚔ retirado; **reˈtire·ment** retiro *m*; ⚔ retirada *f*; jubilación *f from post*; \~ *pay* ⚔ retiro *m*; \~ *pension* jubilación *f*, pensión *f* de retiro; **reˈtir·ing** □ retraído, reservado; *member* saliente.
re·tort [riˈtɔːrt] **1.** réplica *f*; ⚗ retorta *f*; **2.** replicar (*a*. *v*/*i*.); *insult etc*. devolver; *argument* redargüir.
re·touch [ˈriːtʌtʃ] retocar (*a*. *phot*.).
re·trace [riˈtreis] volver a trazar; repasar; \~ *one's steps* desandar lo andado, volver sobre sus pasos.
re·tract [riˈtrækt] retractar(se); retraer(se); ⊕ replegar; **reˈtract·a·ble** retractable; ✈ replegable; **re·tracˈta·tion, reˈtrac·tion** retracción *f*, retractación *f*.
re·tread 1. [riˈtred] recauchutar; **2.** [ˈriːtred] llanta *f* recauchutada.
re·treat [riˈtriːt] **1.** retiro *m* (*a*. *eccl*.); retraimiento *m*; ⚔ retirada *f*; **2.** ⚔ retirarse, batirse en retirada (*a*. *beat a* \~); retroceder.
re·trench [riˈtrentʃ] *v*/*t*. cercenar; *v*/*i*. economizar; **reˈtrench·ment** cercenadura *f*; economías *f*/*pl*.
re·tri·al [riːˈtraiəl] revisión *f*.
ret·ri·bu·tion [retriˈbjuːʃn] justo castigo *m*; desquite *m*.
re·triev·a·ble [riˈtriːvəbl] reparable; recuperable; **reˈtriev·al** recobro *m*; cobra *f*.
re·trieve [riˈtriːv] (re)cobrar; *fortunes* reparar; *loss* resarcirse de; *hunt*. cobrar; **reˈtriev·er** perro *m* cobrador.
ret·ro... [ˈretrou] retro...; **re·troˈac·tive** □ retroactive; **ret·roˈcede** retroceder; **ret·roˈces·sion** retroceso *m*; **ret·ro·graˈda·tion** *ast*. retrogradación *f*; **ˈret·ro·grade 1.** retrógrado; **2.** *ast*. retrogradar.
ret·ro·gres·sion [retrouˈgreʃn] *ast*. retrogradación *f*; **ret·ro·roc·ket** [ˈ\~rɔkit] retrocohete *m*; **ret·ro·spect** [ˈ\~spekt] retrospección *f*; *in* \~ retrospectivamente; **ret·roˈspec·tion** retrospección *f*, consideración *f* de lo pasado; **ret·roˈspec·tive** □ retrospectivo; ⚖ retroactivo.
re·try [ˈriːˈtrai] ⚖ rever.
re·turn [riˈtəːrn] **1.** vuelta *f*, regreso *m*; devolución *f of book etc*.; ⚕ *etc*. reaparición *f*; (*reply*) respuesta *f*; recompensa *f for kindness*; (*report*) informe *m*, relación *f*; *parl*. elección *f*; resultado *m* (del escrutinio); △ marco *m*; vuelta *f*; † (*freq*. \~*s pl*.) ganancia *f*, rédito *m on capital etc*.; ingresos *m*/*pl*.; \~*s pl*. (*official*) estadística *f*; (*tax* \~) declaración *f* (de renta); *many happy* \~*s of the day!* ¡que los cumplas muy felices!; *in* \~ en cambio, en recompensa (*for* de); *by* \~ (*of post*) a vuelta de correo; \~ *match* (partido *m* de) desquite *m*, revancha *f*; \~ *ticket* (F \~) billete *m* de ida y vuelta; **2.** *v*/*i*. volver, regresar; (*reply*) responder; (*reappear*) reaparecer; ⚖ revertir; \~ *to theme, habit* volver a; *v*/*t*. devolver; † producir, rendir; *parl*. elegir; *ball* restar; *kindness etc*. corresponder a; *suit of cards* devolver; *thanks* dar; *verdict* dictar; *visit* pagar; **reˈturn·a·ble** restituible; ⚖ devolutivo; \~ *empties* envases *m*/*pl*. a devolver.
re·un·ion [ˈriːjuːnjən] reunión *f*; **re·u·nite** [ˈriːjuːˈnait] reunir(se); reconciliar(se).
rev [rev] *mot*. F **1.** revolución *f*; **2.** (*a*. \~ *up*) girar (el motor); acelerar.
re·val·or·i·za·tion [riːvælərəˈzeiʃn], **re·val·u·a·tion** [\~væljuˈeiʃn] revalor(iz)ación *f*; **reˈval·or·ize** [\~əraiz], **re·val·ue** [\~ˈvæljuː] revalorizar.
re·vamp [riːˈvæmp] renovar; remendar.

re·veal [ri'vi:l] revelar; **re'veal·ing** □ revelador.
re·veil·le ['revəli] (toque *m* de) diana *f*.
rev·el ['revl] **1.** (*freq.* ~*s pl.*) jarana *f*, juerga *f*, fiesta *f* bulliciosa; **2.** jaranear; ir de paranda; ~ *in* deleitarse en.
rev·e·la·tion [revi'leiʃn] revelación *f*.
rev·el·er ['revələr] jaranero *m*, juerguista *m*/*f*; '**rev·el·ry** jolgorio *m*, jarana *f*, diversión *f* tumultuosa.
re·venge [ri'vendʒ] **1.** venganza *f*; **2.** vengar(se); ~ *o.s.* (*or be* ~*d*) *on* vengarse en; **re'venge·ful** [~ful] □ vengativo; **re'venge·ful·ness** sed *f* de venganza; **re'veng·er** vengador (-a *f*) *m*.
rev·e·nue ['revinju:] rentas *f*/*pl*. públicas; (*a.* ~*s pl.*) ingresos *m*/*pl.*; rédito *m*, renta *f*; ~ *cutter* guardacostas *m*; ~ *officer* aduanero *m*; ~ *stamp* sello *m* fiscal.
re·ver·ber·ate [ri'və:rbəreit] retumbar; (*light*) reverberar; **re·ver·ber'a·tion** el retumbar; reverberación *f*; **re'ver·ber·a·tor** reverberador *m*; **re'ver·ber·a·to·ry furnace** horno *m* de reverbero.
re·vere [ri'vir] reverenciar, venerar; **rev·er·ence** ['revərəns] **1.** reverencia *f*; *Your* ♀ (su) Reverencia; **2.** reverenciar; '**rev·er·end 1.** reverendo; **2.** sacerdote *m*, pastor *m*.
rev·er·ent ['revərənt] □ reverente; **rev·er·en·tial** [~'renʃl] □ reverencial.
rev·er·ie ['revəri] ensueño *m*.
re·ver·sal [ri'və:rsəl] inversión *f*; cambio *m* completo *of policy etc.*; ⚖ revocación *f*; **re·verse** [~'və:rs] **1.** (*the* ~) lo contrario; *fig.* revés *m*, contratiempo *m*; reverso *m of coin*; revés *m of cloth*; ⊕ marcha *f* atrás; *quite the* ~ todo lo contrario; **2.** inverso, invertido; contrario; *mot.* ~ *gear* cambio *m* de marcha atrás; **3.** *v*/*t*. invertir; *opinion* cambiar completamente de; trastrocar; volver al revés; ⚖ revocar; ⊕ poner en marcha atrás; *v*/*i*. dar la marcha atrás; **re'vers·i·ble** *coat etc.* reversible; **re'vers·ing** ⊕ ... de marcha atrás.
re·ver·sion [ri'və:rʃn] reversión *f* (*a.* ⚖ *a. biol.*); *fortune in* ~ bienes *m*/*pl*. reversibles; **re'ver·sion·ar·y** reversible.
re·vert [ri'və:rt] volver(se) (*to* a); revertir (*a.* ⚖); *biol.* saltar atrás.
rev·er·y = *reverie*.
re·vet·ment [ri'vetmənt] ⊕ revestimiento *m*.
re·view [ri'vju:] **1.** revista *f* (⚓, ⚔, *magazine*); repaso *m*; ⚖ revisión *f*; reseña *f of book*; **2.** rever (*a.* ⚖); repasar; ⚓, ⚔ pasar revista a, revistar; *book* reseñar; **re'view·er** crítico *m*.
re·vile [ri'vail] ultrajar, injuriar.
re·vise [ri'vaiz] **1.** revisar; *lesson* repasar; *book* corregir, refundir; **2.** *typ.* segunda prueba *f*; **re'vis·er** revisor (-a *f*) *m*; *typ.* corrector *m*.
re·vi·sion [ri'viʒn] revisión *f*; repaso *m*; correción *f*, refundición *f of book*; *typ.* corrección *f*; '~**·ism** revisionismo *m*; '~**·ist** revisionista *adj. a. su. m*/*f*.
re·vis·it ['ri:'vizit] volver a visitar.
re·vi·so·ry [ri'vaizəri] revisor.
re·vi·tal·ize ['ri:'vaitəlaiz] revivificar.
re·viv·al [ri'vaivl] reanimación *f*; renacimiento *m*; *thea.* reposición *f*; *eccl.* despertamiento *m* religioso; '~**·ist** predicador *m* del renacimiento religioso; **re·vive** [~'vaiv] *v*/*t*. reanimar; restablecer; *fire* avivar; *hopes* despertar; *play* reponer; *v*/*i*. reanimarse; volver en sí; renacer; restablecerse; **re·viv·i·fy** [~'vivifai] revivificar.
rev·o·ca·ble ['revəkəbl] □ revocable; **rev·o·ca·tion** [~'keiʃn] revocación *f*.
re·voke [ri'vouk] *v*/*t*. revocar; *v*/*i*. *cards*: renunciar.
re·volt [ri'voult] **1.** rebelión *f*, sublevación *f*; **2.** *v*/*i*. rebelarse, sublevarse; *v*/*t*. *fig.* dar (*or* causar) asco a; repugnar; **re'volt·ing** □ asqueroso, repugnante.
rev·o·lu·tion [revə'lu:ʃn] revolución *f* (*a.* ⊕, *pol.*); vuelta *f*, rotación *f*; **rev·o'lu·tion·ary** revolucionario *adj. a. su. m* (a *f*); **rev·o'lu·tion·ize** revolucionar.
re·volve [ri'vɔlv] *v*/*i*. girar, dar vueltas; *ast.* revolverse; *fig.* depender (*round* de); *v*/*t*. (hacer) girar; *fig.* ponderar; **re'volv·er** revólver *m*; **re'volv·ing** giratorio; rotativo.
re·vue [ri'vju:] *thea.* revista *f*.
re·vul·sion [ri'vʌlʃn] ⚕ revulsión *f*; asco *m*; reacción *f*, cambio *m* re-

pentino; re'vul·sive □ ⚕ revulsivo.
re·ward [ri'wɔ:rd] **1.** recompensa *f*, premio *m*, galardón *m*; **2.** recompensar, premiar; **re'ward·ing** □ remunerador.
re·word ['ri:'wə:rd] formular en otras palabras.
re·write ['ri:'rait] [*irr.* (*write*)] refundir; escribir de nuevo.
rhap·so·dize ['ræpsədaiz] *fig.*: ~ *over* entusiasmarse por, extasiarse ante; **'rhap·so·dy** rapsodia *f*; *fig.* transporte *m* (de admiración *etc.*).
rhe·o·stat ['ri:oustæt] reóstato *m.*
rhet·o·ric ['retərik] retórica *f*; **rhe·tor·i·cal** [ri'tɔrikl] □ retórico; **rhet·o·ri·cian** [retə'riʃn] retórico *m.*
rheu·mat·ic [ru:'mætik] □ reumático; ~*s* F *pl.* = **rheu·ma·tism** ['ru:mətizm] reumatismo *m.*
rhi·no[1] ['rainou] *sl.* parné *m.*
rhi·no[2] [~] = **rhi·noc·er·os** [rai'nɔsərəs] rinoceronte *m.*
rhomb, rhom·bus ['rɔm(bəs)] rombo *m.*
rhu·barb ['ru:bɑ:rb] ruibarbo *m*; *sl.* lío *m*; pelea *f.*
rhyme [raim] **1.** rima *f*; poesía *f*; *without* ~ *or reason* sin ton ni son; **2.** rimar; **'rhym·er, rhyme·ster** ['~stər] rimador (-a *f*) *m.*
rhythm [riðm] ritmo *m*; **'rhyth·mic, 'rhyth·mi·cal** □ rítmico.
rib [rib] **1.** *anat.*, ⚓ costilla *f*; ⚘ nervio *m*; △ nervadura *f*; **2.** F tomar el pelo a.
rib·ald ['ribəld] obsceno; irreverente y regocijado; **'rib·ald·ry** obscenidad *f*; irreverencia *f* regocijada.
rib·and ['ribənd] = *ribbon.*
ribbed [ribd] nervudo; rayado.
rib·bon ['ribən] cinta *f* (*a. typewriter* ~); ⚔ galón *m*; ~*s pl. fig.* trizas *f/pl.*; F ~*s pl.* riendas *f/pl.*; ~ *development* desarrollo *m* en línea.
ri·bo·fla·vin [raibou'fleivin] ribofarina *f.*
rice [rais] arroz *m*; ~ *field* arrozal *m*; ~ *paper* papel *m* de paja de arroz.
rich [ritʃ] □ rico; (*lavish*) suntuoso; exquisito; *color* vivo; *food* rico, sabroso; *profits* pingüe; *soil* fértil; *style* opulento, copioso; *b.s.* empalagoso; *voice* sonoro; *wine* generoso; F muy divertido; *be* ~ *in* abundar de (*or* en); ~ *milk* leche *f* sin desnatar; **rich·es** ['~iz] *pl.* riqueza *f*; **'rich·ness** riqueza *f*; fertilidad *f of soil etc.*
rick[1] [rik] ✔ **1.** *approx.* montón *m* de paja (*or* heno *etc.*), almiar *m*; **2.** recoger en montones.
rick[2] [~] *v. wrick.*
rick·ets ['rikits] ⚕ raquitismo *m*, raquitis *f*; **'rick·et·y** ⚕ raquítico; *fig.* desvencijado, destartalado.
ri·co·chet ['rikəʃei] rebotar.
rid [rid] [*irr.*] librar, desembarazar (*of* de); *be* ~ *of* estar libre de; *get* ~ *of* deshacerse de; **'rid·dance** libramiento *m*; *good* ~! ¡enhoramala!, ¡vete con viento fresco!
rid·den ['ridn] *p.p. of ride* 2; ~ *by horse* montado por.
rid·dle[1] ['ridl] acertijo *m*, adivinanza *f*; (*p. etc.*) enigma *m.*
rid·dle[2] [~] **1.** criba *f* (gruesa); (*potato* ~) escogedor *m*; **2.** cribar; acribillar *with shot.*
ride [raid] **1.** cabalgata *f*; paseo *m*, viaje *m* (a caballo, en coche *etc.*); camino *m* de herradura; *sl. take s.o. for a* ~ decepcionar a alguien; *sl.* pasear a alguien; **2.** *v/i.* montar, cabalgar; ir, viajar, pasear(se) (en coche *etc.*); flotar; ~ *at anchor* estar fondeado; ~ *for a fall* presumir demasiado; *v/t. horse etc.* montar; *bicycle* ir en; *a distance* recorrer (a caballo *etc.*); *waves* hender, surcar; ~ *down* revolcar, atropellar; ~ *out storm* capear, hacer frente a; **'rid·er** jinete (a *f*) *m*, caballero *m*; (*cyclist*) ciclista *m/f*; (*clause*) aditamiento *m*; ⊕ pilón *m.*
ridge [ridʒ] cadena *f*, sierra *f of hills*; cresta *f of hill*; △ caballete *m* (*a.* ✔); ✔ caballón *m.*
rid·i·cule ['ridikju:l] **1.** irrisión *f*, burlas *f/pl.*; **2.** ridiculizar, poner en ridículo; **ri'dic·u·lous** [~julәs] □ ridículo.
rid·ing ['raidiŋ] **1.** equitación *f*; **2.** ... de montar; **'~ hab·it** traje *m* de montar; **'~ school** picadero *m*, escuela *f* de equitación.
rife [raif] corriente, frecuente; general; endémico; ~ *with* lleno de; *be* ~ cundir.
riff·raff ['rifræf] chusma *f*, bahorrina *f*; canalla *f.*
ri·fle[1] ['raifl] robar; saquear.
ri·fle[2] [~] **1.** rifle *m*, fusil *m*; ~*s pl.* rifleros *m/pl.*; **2.** ⊕ rayar; **'~·man**

riflero *m*; '~ **range** tiro *m* de rifle.
ri·fling ['raifliŋ] ⊕ rayado *m*.
rift [rift] hendedura *f*, rendija *f*; *fig*. grieta *f*, desavenencia *f*.
rig[1] [rig] *sl*. subvertir; manipular; *election* falsificar; ~ *the market* manipular la lonja.
rig[2] [~] **1.** ⚓ aparejo *m*; *mot*. tractocamión *m*; F atuendo *m*; **2.** ⚓ aparejar, enjarciar; F ~ *out* ataviar; F ~ *up* improvisar; '**rig·ger** ⚓ aparejador *m*; ✈ mecánico *m*; '**rig·ging** jarcia *f*; aparejo *m*; cordaje *m*.
right [rait] **1.** □ *side* derecho; (*correct*) correcto, exacto; (*true*) verdadero; (*just*) justo, equitativo; (*proper*) indicado, debido; (*in mind*) cuerdo; *conditions* favorable; *th. sought* que hace falta, que se busca; *be* ~ (*p*.) tener razón; *be* ~ *to inf*. hacer bien en *inf*.; *that's* ~ eso es; *put* (*or set*) ~ arreglar, ajustar; *all* ~! ¡bueno!; ¡conforme!, ¡está bien!, (*answering call*) ¡voy!; *be all* ~ estar bien (de salud); *it will be all* ~ todo se arreglará; *are we on the* ~ *road?* ¿vamos por buen camino?; **2.** *adv*. derechamente; directamente; bien; completamente; exactamente; correctamente; a la derecha; † muy; ~ *away* en seguida; ~ *here* aquí mismo; F ~ *now* ahorita; *sl*. ~ *on!* ¡olé!; ¡vaya!; ¡bravo!; **3.** derecho *m* (*to* a *su*., *inf*.); justicia *f*; título *m*; privilegio *m* (*of ger*. de *inf*.); (*side*) derecha *f* (*a. pol*.); *boxing*: derechazo *m*; ~*s pl*. propiedad *f of story etc*.; ~ *of way* derecho *m* de paso; *mot*. prioridad *f*; *by* ~(*s*) en justicia, según derecho; *by* ~ *of* por razón de; *in his own* ~ por derecho propio; *on* (*or to*) *the* ~ a la derecha; *be in the* ~ tener razón; *set* (*or put*) *to* ~*s* arreglar, ajustar; **4.** enderezar (*a*. ⚓); corregir, rectificar; ~ **an·gle** ['~'æŋgl] ⩓ ángulo *m* recto; '~-'**an·gled** rectangular; **right·eous** ['~ʃəs] □ justo, honrado, probo; '**right·eous·ness** honradez *f*, probidad *f*; **right·ful** ['~ful] □ justo; legítimo; '**right-hand:** ~ *drive mot*. conducción *f* a la derecha; ~ *man* mano *f* derecha; ~ *side* derecha *f*; '**right-'hand·ed** que usa (*or* ⊕ para) la mano derecha; '**right·ist** derechista *adj. a. su. m/f*; '**right-'mind·ed** honrado; '**right·ness** derechura *f*; justicia *f*; '**right-wing** *pol*. derechista.
rig·id ['ridʒid] □ rígido; **ri'gid·i·ty** rigidez *f*.
rig·ma·role ['rigməroul] galimatías *m*, relación *f* disparatada.
rig·or ['rigɔːr] rigor *m*, severidad *f*; ⚕ escalofríos *m/pl*.; ~ **mor·tis** ['mɔːrtis] rigidez *f* cadavérica; **rig·or·ous** ['rigərəs] □ riguroso.
rile [rail] F sulfurar, irritar, reventar.
rill [ril] *poet*. riachuelo *m*.
rim [rim] borde *m*, canto *m*; llanta *f of wheel*.
rime[1] [raim] *poet*. rima *f*.
rime[2] [~] (*frost*) escarcha *f*.
rind [raind] corteza *f*; cáscara *f*; piel *f*.
ring[1] [riŋ] **1.** (*finger*) anillo *m*; círculo *m*; (*iron*) argolla *f*; (*boxing*) cuadrilátero *m*; (*bull*) redondel *m*, plaza *f*; corro *m of people*; † confabulación *f*, pandilla *f*; (*on large scale*) cartel *m*; **2.** cercar, rodear (*by, with* de).
ring[2] [~] **1.** campanilleo *m*; toque *m* (de timbre); llamada *f at door*; *teleph*. telefonazo *m*; **2.** *v/i*. sonar; resonar (*with* con); (*bell*) repicar; campanillear; llamar *at door*; (*ears*) zumbar; ~ *off teleph*. colgar; *v/t*. *small bell* tocar; *large bell* tañer; (hacer) sonar; *teleph*. llamar (por teléfono) (*a*. ~ *up*); '~ '**bind·er** cuaderno *m* de hojas sueltas; '**ring·er** campanero *m*; '**ring·ing 1.** □ resonante; **2.** repique *m of bells*; zumbido *m in ears*; '**ring·lead·er** cabecilla *m*; **ring·let** ['~lit] rizo *m*; '**ring·worm** tiña *f*.
rink [riŋk] pista *f*.
rinse [rins] **1.** aclarar; enjugar (*a*. ~ *out*); **2.** = '**rins·ing** aclaración *f*; enjuague *m*; teñido *m* ligero *of the hair*.
ri·ot ['raiət] **1.** tumulto *m*, alboroto *m*, motín *m*; orgía *f* (*a. fig*.); *run* ~ desenfrenarse; F *it was a* ~ eso fue de miedo; **2.** amotinarse, alborotarse; '**ri·ot·er** manifestante *m/f*; amotinado(r) *m*; '**ri·ot·ous** □ alborotado; *life* desenfrenado; *party* bullicioso; F ~*ly funny* tremendamente divertido; '**ri·ot** '**squad** pelotón *m* de asalto.
rip[1] [rip] **1.** rasgón *m*, rasgadura *f*; **2.** rasgar(se); ~ *off* arrebatar; ~ *up* desgarrar, romper.
rip[2] [~] calavera *m*.
rip·cord ['ripkɔːrd] ✈ cabo *m* de desgarre.

ripe [raip] □ maduro; ˈ**rip·en** madurar; ˈ**ripe·ness** madurez *f*.
rip-off [ˈripɔf] *sl*. estafa *f*; timo *m*.
ri·poste [riˈpoust] *fenc*. estocada *f*; *fig*. respuesta *f* aguda, réplica *f*.
rip·ping [ˈripiŋ] □ *sl*. bárbaro, de aúpa.
rip·ple [ˈripl] **1.** rizo *m*; ondulación *f*; (*sound*) murmullo *m*; **2.** rizar(se), encrespar(se); (*sound*) murmurar.
rise [raiz] **1.** subida *f*, alza *f*, elevación *f of prices etc*.; ascenso *m in rank*; crecida *f of river*; nacimiento *m of spring*; (*hill*) cuesta *f*, elevación *f*; *fig*. origen *m*; *give* ~ *to* dar origen a, motivar, ocasionar; **2.** [*irr*.] subir; alzarse; levantarse; ponerse en pie; ascender *in rank*; (*sun*) salir; (*river*) nacer, brotar; (*swell*) hincharse; (*revolt*) sublevarse; (*cake*) leudarse; *parl*. suspenderse (la sesión); ~ *to* ser capaz de; *occasion* estar a la altura de, corresponder dignamente a; (*mountain*) elevarse a, alcanzar; **ris·en** [ˈrizn] *p.p. of rise*; ˈ**ris·er:** *early* ~ madrugador (-a *f*) *m*.
ris·i·bil·i·ty [riziˈbiliti] risibilidad *f*; ˈ**ris·i·ble** □ risible.
ris·ing [ˈraiziŋ] **1.** (*revolt*) sublevación *f*; levantamiento *m*; salida *f of sun*; *parl*. término *m* (de sesión); **2.** naciente, ascendiente; *sun* saliente; *ground* que sube; *generation* nuevo.
risk [risk] **1.** riesgo *m*; peligro *m*; *at the* ~ *of* con peligro de, arriesgando; *run a* (*or the*) ~ *of ger*. correr riesgo de *inf*.; **2.** arriesgar, exponer(se a); ~ *ger*. arriesgarse a *inf*.; ˈ**risk·y** □ arriesgado, aventurado.
ris·sole [ˈrisoul] *approx*. croqueta *f*, albóndiga *f*.
rite [rait] rito *m*; *last* (*or funeral*) ~*s pl*. exequias *f/pl*.; **rit·u·al** [ˈritjuəl] □ ritual *adj. a. su. m*.
ri·val [ˈraivl] **1.** rival *m/f*, competidor (-a *f*) *m*; **2.** rival, competidor (*a*. ✝); **3.** rivalizar con, competir con; ˈ**ri·val·ry** rivalidad *f*, competencia *f*.
riv·er [ˈrivər] río *m*; *down* ~ río abajo; *up* ~ río arriba; *attr*. fluvial; ˈ~ **ba·sin** cuenca *f* de río; ˈ~ **horse** caballo *m* marino; hipopótamo *m*; ˈ~**·side** ribera *f*, orilla *f*; *attr*. ribereño.
riv·et [ˈrivit] **1.** roblón *m*, remache *m*; **2.** ⊕ remachar; *fig*. clavar (*on*, *to* en).
riv·u·let [ˈrivjulit] riachuelo *m*.
roach [routʃ] cucaracha *f*; *ichth*. escarcho *m*.
road [roud] camino *m* (*to* de; *a*. *fig*.); carretera *f*; (*in town*) calle *f*; *by* ~ por carretera; ⚓ ~*s pl*. rada *f* (*a*. ˈ~**·stead**); *hold the* ~ agarrarse al camino; ˈ~ **hog** conductor *m* poco considerado, asesino *m* de carretera; ˈ~**·house** taberna *f*; posada *f*; ˈ~ **mend·er** peón *m* caminero; ˈ~**·race** carrera *f* sobre carretera; ˈ~**·side** borde *m* del camino; **road·ster** [ˈ~stər] coche *m* (*or* bicicleta *f etc*.) de turismo; ˈ**road·way** calzada *f*.
roam [roum] *v/i*. vagar; callejear *in town*; *v/t*. vagar por, recorrer; ˈ**roam·er** vag(abund)o *m*.
roan [roun] (caballo *m*) ruano; ⊕ badana *f*.
roar [rɔːr] **1.** rugir; bramar; (*with laughter*) reírse a carcajadas; **2.** rugido *m*; bramido *m*; **roar·ing** [ˈ~riŋ] **1.** *v*. *roar* 2; **2.** □ rugiente; bramante; ✝ *etc*. floreciente; F de aúpa.
roast [roust] **1.** asar; *coffee* tostar; **2.** asado; *coffee* tostado; ~ *beef* rosbif *m*; **3.** carne *f* asada, asado *m*; *rule the* ~ mandar.
rob [rɔb] robar (*s.o. of s.t*. algo a alguien); saltear *on highway*; ˈ**robber** ladrón *m*; salteador *m* (de caminos); ˈ**rob·ber·y** robo *m*.
robe [roub] **1.** túnica *f*, manto *m*; ⚖ toga *f*; vestido *m* talar; ~*s pl*. traje *m* de ceremonia; *gentlemen of the* ~ la curia; **2.** vestir(se).
rob·in [ˈrɔbin] petirrojo *m*.
ro·bot [ˈroubɔt] autómata *m*, robot *m*; **ro·bot·ics** [rouˈbɔtiks] ciencia o uso del robot; robótica *f*.
ro·bust [rəˈbʌst] □ robusto; recio; vigoroso; **roˈbust·ness** robustez *f*.
rock[1] [rɔk] roca *f*; peña *f*; ⚓ escollo *m*; *sl*. diamante *m*; *the* ♀ el Peñón (de Gibraltar); *get down to* ~ *bottom* llegar a lo más bajo; ~ *crystal* cristal *m* de roca; ~ *salt* sal *f* gema.
rock[2] [~] mecer(se), balancear(se); (*violently*) sacudir(se).
rock-bot·tom [ˈrɔkˈbɔtəm] F *price* más bajo, mínimo.
rock·er [ˈrɔkər] (eje *m* de) balancín *m*; F (*chair*) mecedora *f*; F músico *m* del rock.

rock·er·y ['rɔkəri] jardincito *m* rocoso, cuadro *m* alpino.
rock·et¹ ['rɔkit] **1.** cohete *m*; *sl.* peluca *f*; ~ *propulsion* propulsión *f* a cohete; **2.** subir como cohete; '**rock·et·ry** cohetería *f*.
rock·et² [~] ⚘ oruga *f*.
rock...: '~**·fall** deslizamiento *m* de montaña; '~ **gar·den** = *rockery*.
rock·ing... ['rɔkiŋ]: '~ **chair** mecedora *f*; '~ **horse** caballo *m* de balancín.
rock-'n'-roll (*a.* **rock**) ['rɔkən 'roul] rock *m* (*música popular de compás intenso, poca melodía y mucha percusión*).
rock·y ['rɔki] rocoso, peñascoso; *sl.* inestable; dificultoso.
ro·co·co [rə'koukou] rococó *adj. a. su. m.*
rod [rɔd] *medida de longitud* (= *5,029 m.*); var(ill)a *f*; barra *f*; vástago *m*; (*fishing*) caña *f*; *sl.* pistola *f*; quitapenas *m*.
rode [roud] *pret. of ride* 2.
ro·dent ['roudənt] roedor *m*.
ro·de·o ['roudiou, rou'deiou] rodeo *m*.
rod·o·mon·tade [rɔdə'mɔnteid] fanfarronada *f*.
roe¹ [rou] hueva *f* (*a. hard* ~); *soft* ~ lecha *f*.
roe² [~] *zo.* corzo (a *f*) *m*; '~**·buck** corzo *m*.
ro·ga·tion [rou'geiʃn] *eccl.* rogación *f*.
rogue [roug] pícaro *m*, pillo *m*; canalla *m*; ~*s' gallery* fichero *m* de delincuentes; '**ro·guer·y** picardía *f*; '**ro·guish** □ pícaro, picaruelo; travieso.
roist·er ['rɔistər] jaranear; '**roist·er·er** jaranero *m*.
role [roul] *thea.* papel *m* (*a. fig.*); *play* (*or take*) *a* ~ hacer un papel.
roll [roul] **1.** rollo *m*; ⊕ rodillo *m*; (*bread*) panecillo *m*; bollo *m*; (*list*) lista *f*; retumbo *m of thunder*; redoble *m of drum*; (*gait*) bamboleo *m*; ⚓ balance(o) *m*; fajo *m of notes*; **2.** *v/t.* hacer rodar; *soil* allanar; *cigarette* liar; *eyes* poner en blanco; *tongue* vibrar; ~ *up* arrollar, enrollar; *sleeves* arremangar; ~*ed gold* oro *m* laminado; *v/i.* rodar; revolcarse *on ground*; (*land*) ondular; (*thunder*) retumbar; (*gait*) bambolearse; ⚓ balancearse; F *be* ~*ing in* nadar en; ~ *up* (*car etc.*) llegar; F (*p.*) aparecer, presentarse; '~ **call** (acto *m* de pasar) lista *f*; '**roll·er** ✓, ⊕ rodillo *m*; ⚓ ola *f* larga; (*mst* ~ *bandage*) venda *f* enrollada; ~ *coaster* montaña *f* rusa; ~ *skates* patines *m/pl.* de ruedas; ~ *towel* toalla *f* de rodillo; '**roll film** película *f* en rollo.
rol·lick ['rɔlik] juguetear; '**rol·lick·ing** alegre, jovial.
roll·ing ['rouliŋ] **1.** rodante; rodadero; *ground* ondulado; **2.** rodadura *f*; ⚓ balanceo *m*; ~ *mill* tren *m* de laminación; ~ *pin* rodillo *m*; '~**·stock** material *m* rodante.
roll-top desk ['roultɔp'desk] buró *m*, escritorio *m* de tapa rodadera.
ro·ly-po·ly ['rouli'pouli] regordete.
Ro·man ['roumən] romano *adj. a. su. m* (a *f*); *typ.* (*mst* ♀) tipo *m* romano; ~ *candle* vela *f* romana.
ro·mance [rə'mæns] **1.** novela *f*; ficción *f*; lo pintoresco *of history etc.*; sentimentalismo *m*; F amoríos *m/pl.*, amores *m/pl.*; (*language*) romance *m*; **2.** soñar; exagerar; **3.** románico, romance; ~ *languages* lenguas *f/pl.* romances *or* románicas.
Ro·man·esque [roume'nesk], **Ro·man·ic** [rou'mænik] románico.
ro·man·tic [rə'mæntik] **1.** □ romántico; *affair* novelesco; *p.* sentimental; *place* pintoresco, encantado; **2.** romántico *m*; **ro'man·ti·cism** romanticismo *m*.
romp [rɔmp] **1.** retozo *m*, trisca *f*; **2.** retozar, juguetear, triscar; ~ *home* ganar fácilmente; '**romp·ers** traje *m* infantil de juego.
rood [ru:d] cruz *f*, crucifijo *m*.
roof [ru:f, ruf] **1.** tejado *m*, techo *m*; (*flat*) azotea *f*; ~ *of the mouth* paladar *m*; **2.** (*freq.* ~ *in, over*) techar; '**roof·ing 1.** techumbre *f*; **2.** ... para techos.
rook¹ [ruk] **1.** *orn.* graja *f*; **2.** trampear, estafar.
rook² [~] *chess*: torre *f*, roque *m*.
rook·er·y ['rukəri] nidada *f* de grajas.
rook·ie ['ruki] ⚔ *sl.* bisoño *m*.
room [ru:m, rum] cuarto *m*, habitación *f*; pieza *f*; (*large*) aposento *m*; (*space*) sitio *m*, espacio *m*; cabida *f*; ~*s pl.* alojamiento *m*; *make* ~ hacer lugar; *there is no* ~ *for* no cabe(n); ~ *and board* pensión *f* completa; **...roomed** [ru:md] de ... piezas; '**room·er** subinquilino (a *f*) *m*; huésped *m/f*; '**room·ing house** casa *f* donde se alquilan cuartos;

ˈ**room·mate** compañero (a *f*) *m* de cuarto; ˈ**room·y** □ espacioso, holgado.
roost [ruːst] **1.** percha *f*; gallinero *m*; *rule the* ~ mandar; **2.** (*bird*) descansar (en una percha); *fig.* pasar la noche; ˈ**roost·er** gallo *m*.
root [ruːt] **1.** *all senses*: raíz *f*; *take* (*or strike*) ~ echar raíces, arraigar; ~ *idea* idea *f* fundamental; ~ *and branch* del todo; **2.** *v/t.*: ~ *out*, ~ *up* arrancar, desarraigar, desenterrar, extirpar; F buscar; F hacer salir; *v/i.* ⚘ arraigar(se); (*pig*) hozar, hocicar; *sl.* ~ *for* hacer propaganda por; gritar por el éxito de; ˈ**root·er** *sl.* entusiasta *m*, partidario *m* (*for* de).
rope [roup] **1.** cuerda *f*; soga *f*; (*esp.* ⚓) maroma *f*, cable *m*; collar *m of pearls*; *mount. on the* ~ atado(s); *know the* ~*s* saber cuántas son cinco; **2.** atar, amarrar con cuerda(s) *etc.*; ~ *off* cercar con cuerdas; F ~ *a p. in* entruchar a una p., persuadir a una p. a que tome parte (*for s.t.* en algo); ˈ~ **lad·der** escala *f* de cuerda; ˈ~ **mak·er** cordelero *m*.
rop·y [ˈroupi] *liquid* viscoso.
ro·sa·ry [ˈrouzəri] *eccl.* rosario *m*; ⚘ jardín *m* de rosales.
rose¹ [rouz] ⚘ rosa *f*; (*color*) color *m* de rosa; roseta *f of can*; ⚠ rosetón *m* (*a.* ~ *window*).
rose² [~] *pret. of rise* 2.
ro·se·ate [ˈrouziit] róseo, rosado.
rose·bud [ˈrouzbʌd] capullo *m* de rosa; ˈ**rose bush** rosal *m*; ˈ**rose hip** ⚘ cinarrodón *m*; eterio *m*.
rose·mar·y [ˈrouzməri] romero *m*.
ro·sette [rouˈzet] escarapela *f*; ⚠ rosetón *m*.
ros·in [ˈrɔzin] **1.** colofonia *f*; **2.** frotar con colofonia.
ros·ter [ˈrɔstər] lista *f*.
ros·trum [ˈrɔstrəm] tribuna *f*; ♪ atril *m*.
ros·y [ˈrouzi] □ (son)rosado; *prospect* prometedor.
rot [rɔt] **1.** putrefacción *f*, podredumbre *f*; *sl.* tonterías *f/pl.*; ~*gut sl.* matarratas *m*, whisky *m* ruin; **2.** pudrir(se), corromper(se).
ro·ta [ˈroutə] lista *f* (de tandas *etc.*).
ro·ta·ry [ˈroutəri] rotativo, rotatorio; ~ *press* prensa *f* rotativa; **ro·tate** [rouˈteit] (hacer) girar; alternar(se); **ro·taˈtion** rotación *f* (*a.* ↗); alternación *f*; *in* ~ por turno; **ro·ta·to·ry** [~ˈtətɔːri] *v. rotary*.
rote [rout]: *by* ~ de coro, maquinalmente.
ro·tor [ˈroutər] rotor *m*.
rot·ten [ˈrɔtn] □ podrido, corrompido; *food* putrefacto; *wood* carcomido; *sl.* vil, ruin; *sl. feel* ~ estar muy malo; ˈ**rot·ten·ness** podredumbre *f*, putrefacción *f*.
rot·ter [ˈrɔtər] *sl.* canalla *m*, sinvergüenza *m*.
ro·tund [rouˈtʌnd] □ rotundo; *figure* corpulento; **roˈtun·da** [~də] ⚠ rotonda *f*; **roˈtun·di·ty** rotundidad *f*.
rouge [ruːʒ] **1.** colorete *m*, arrebol *m*; **2.** ponerse colorete, arrebolarse.
rough [rʌf] **1.** □ áspero; tosco; *estimate* aproximado; *ground* quebrado; *manners* grosero; *material* crudo, bruto; *play* duro; *sea* bravo; *treatment* brutal; *weather* tempestuoso; *work* chapucero; de preparación; ~ *and ready* tosco (pero eficaz); F *cut up* ~ sulfurarse; ~ *copy*, ~ *draft* borrador *m*; **2.** terreno *m* áspero, superficie *f* áspera; F matón *m*; *in the* ~ en bruto; *take the* ~ *with the smooth* aceptar la vida como es, tomarse las cosas filosóficamente; **3.** F ~ *it* pasar apuros, vivir sin comodidades; ~ *out* bosquejar, trazar de modo provisional; **rough·age** [ˈ~idʒ] alimento *m* poco digerible; ˈ**rough·cast** mezcla *f* gruesa; ˈ**rough·en** poner(se) áspero (*or* tosco).
rough...: ~**-hewn** [ˈ~ˈhjuːn] desbastado; ˈ~**·house** *sl.* trapatiesta *f*, trifulca *f*; ˈ~**·neck** *sl.* canalla *m*; matón *m*; ˈ**rough·ness** aspereza *f*, tosquedad *f etc.*; ˈ**rough rid·er** domador *m* de caballos; ˈ**rough·shod:** *ride* ~ *over* tratar sin miramientos, imponerse a.
rou·lette [ruːˈlet] ruleta *f*.
Rou·ma·nian *v. Rumanian*.
round [raund] **1.** □ redondo (*a. number*, *sum*); *denial etc.* rotundo, categórico; ~ *table* mesa *f* redonda; ~ *trip* viaje *m* de ida y vuelta; **2.** *adv.* alrededor; (*freq.* ~ *about*) a la redonda; *all* ~ por todos lados; *all the year* ~ durante todo el año; 2 feet ~ 2 pies en redondo; **3.** *prp.* alrededor de; cerca de, cosa de; ~ *about 5 o'clock* a eso de las 5; ~ *the corner* a la vuelta de esquina; ~ *the town* por

la ciudad; **4.** esfera *f*; círculo *m*; (*daily*) rutina *f*; (*tradesman's etc.*) recorrido *m*; (*slice*) rodaja *f*; (*drinks*; *meetings*) ronda *f*; *sport*: (*stage*) vuelta *f*; (*lap*) circuito *m*; *boxing*: asalto *m*; ⚔ salva *f*; ⚔ tiro *m*, cartucho *m*; **5.** redondear (*a.* ~ *off*, ~ *out*); *corner etc.* doblar; ~ *up* acorralar, rodear *S.Am.*

round·a·bout ['raundəbaut] **1.** indirecto; ambagioso; **2.** tiovivo *m*; (*traffic-*) glorieta *f*; **round·house** ['raundhaus] depósito *m* de locomotoras; '**round·ly** *adv.* rotundamente; '**round·ness** redondez *f*; '**round-'shoul·dered** cargado de espaldas; **rounds·man** ['~zmən] proveedor *m* casero; repartidor *m*; '**round-ta·ble con·fer·ence** reunión *f* de mesa redonda; '**round-'up** rodeo *m*.

rouse [rauz] despertar(se); *emotion* excitar; provocar *to fury etc.*; *game* levantar; '**rous·ing** conmovedor, emocionado.

roust·a·bout ['raustə'baut] peón *m* (*esp.* portuario).

rout [raut] **1.** cerrota *f* completa, fuga *f* desordenada; *put to* ~ = **2.** derrotar (completamente).

route [ru:t, ⚔ raut] ruta *f*, itinerario *m*, camino *m*; '~ **march** marcha *f* (de entrenamiento).

rou·tine [ru:'ti:n] **1.** rutina *f*; **2.** rutinario.

rove [rouv] vagar, errar (*the country* por el campo); '**rov·er** vagabundo (a *f*) *m*; '**rov·ing** errante; ambulante; *disposition* andariego.

row[1] [rou] fila *f* (*a. thea. etc.*), hilera *f*; *in a* ~ seguidos.

row[2] [~] ⚓ **1.** *v/i.* remar; *v/t.* conducir remando; **2.** paseo *m* en bote.

row[3] [rau] F **1.** (*noise*) ruido *m*, jaleo *m*, tremolina *f*, estrépito *m*; (*quarrel*) bronca *f*, pelea *f*, camorra *f*; lío *m*, escándalo *m*; follón *m*; **2.** pelearse (con); reñir.

row·an ['rauən, 'rouən] serbal *m*.

row·boat ['roubout] bote *m* (de remos).

row·dy ['raudi] gamberro *m*; quimerista *adj. a. su. m.*

row·er ['rouər] remero (a *f*) *m*; '**row·ing** remo *m*; ~ *boat* bote *m* (de remos).

row·lock ['rɔlək] escalamera *f*.

roy·al ['rɔiəl] □ real; regio; '**roy·al·ism** sentimiento *m* monárquico, monarquismo *m*; '**roy·al·ist** monárquico (a *f*) *m*; '**roy·al·ty** realeza *f*; personajes *m/pl.* reales; derechos *m/pl.* (de autor).

rub [rʌb] **1.** frotamiento *m*; roce *m*, rozadura *f*; *there's the* ~ ahí está el busilis; **2.** *v/t.* frotar; (*hard*) (r)estregar; limpiar frotando; ~ *down horse* almohazar; ~ *in* hacer penetrar frotando; ~ *it in* F reiterar (una cosa desagradable); ~ *off* quitar frotando; ~ *out* borrar; *sl.* asesinar; ~ *up* pulir; ~ *the wrong way* frotar a contrapelo; *v. shoulder*; *v/i.*: ~ *against*, ~ *on* rozar *acc.*; ~ *along* F ir tirando.

rub-a-dub ['rʌbədʌb] rataplán *m*.

rub·ber ['rʌbər] caucho *m*, goma *f*; (*eraser*) goma *f* de borrar; ⊕ paño *m etc.* de pulir; *bridge*: juego *m* (primero *etc.*); ~*s pl.* chanclos *m/pl.*; *attr.* de caucho, de goma; ~ *band* gom(it)a *f*; *sl.* ~ *check* cheque *m* no cobradero; ~ *solution* disolución *f* de goma; '~**neck** *sl.* **1.** mirón (-a *f*) *m*; **2.** curiosear; '~ **stamp** estampilla *f* (*or* sello *m*) de goma; '~**-stamp** F aprobar maquinalmente.

rub·bish ['rʌbiʃ] basura *f*; desperdicios *m/pl.*; desecho(s) *m(pl.)*; *fig.* disparates *m/pl.*, tonterías *f/pl.*; ~ *dump* vertedero *m*; '**rub·bish·y** de bajísima calidad.

rub·ble ['rʌbl] cascote *m*, escombros *m/pl.*; (*filling*) cascajo *m*.

rube [ru:b] *sl.* campesino *m*.

ru·bi·cund ['ru:bikənd] rubicundo.

ru·ble ['ru:bl] rublo *m*.

ru·bric ['ru:brik] rúbrica *f* (*a. eccl.*); **ru·bri·cate** ['~keit] rubricar.

ru·by ['ru:bi] **1.** rubí *m*; **2.** de color de rubí.

ruck(·le) ['rʌk(l)] (*mst* ~ *up*) arrugar(se).

ruck·sack ['ruksæk] mochila *f*.

ruc·tion ['rʌkʃn] F disturbio *m*, jaleo *m*; disgusto *m*.

rud·der ['rʌdər] timón *m* (*a.* ✈), gobernalle *m*.

rud·dle ['rʌdl] **1.** almagre *m*; **2.** marcar con almagre; '**rud·dy** rubicundo; rojizo; *sl.* condenado.

rude [ru:d] □ grosero, descortés; ofensivo; (*rough*) inculto, rudo, tosco; '**rude·ness** grosería *f*; rudeza *f*.

ru·di·ment ['ru:dimənt] *biol.* rudimento *m*; ~*s pl. fig.* rudimentos *m/pl.*; **ru·di·men·ta·ry** [~ˈmentəri] *biol.* rudimental; *fig.* rudimentario.

rue[1] [ruː] ⚘ ruda *f.*

rue[2] [~] arrepentirse de, lamentar.

rue·ful [ˈruːful] □ triste; arrepentido; lamentable; ˈ**rue·ful·ness** tristeza *f.*

ruff[1] [rʌf] gorguera *f.*

ruff[2] [~] *cards*: **1.** fallada *f*; **2.** fallar.

ruf·fi·an [ˈrʌfjən] rufián *m*; canalla *m*; pillo *m*; bribón *m*; ˈ**ruf·fi·an·ly** brutal.

ruf·fle [ˈrʌfl] **1.** *sew.* volante *m*; **2.** descomponer; perturbar; *water etc.* agitar, rizar; *sew.* fruncir.

rug [rʌg] alfombr(ill)a *f*; tapete *m*; manta *f* (de viaje).

rug·by [ˈrʌgbi] rugby *m.*

rug·ged [ˈrʌgid] □ *country* áspero, escabroso; *character* robusto; *b.s.* rudo, tosco; ˈ**rug·ged·ness** escabrosidad *f etc.*

ru·in [ˈruːin] **1.** ruina *f*; arruinamiento *m*; perdición *f*; ~*s pl.* ruinas *f/pl.*; *lay in* ~*s* asolar; **2.** arruinar; perder; estropear; estragar; **ru·in·ˈa·tion** F arruinamiento *m*; ˈ**ru·in·ous** □ ruinoso.

rule [ruːl] **1.** regla *f* (*a. eccl.*); reglamento *m*; norma *f*; mando *m*; dominio *m*; ⚖ fallo *m*, decisión *f*; (*a. standing* ~) estatuto *m*; ⊕ metro *m* (plegable *etc.*); *as a* ~ por regla general; ~ *of the road* reglamento *m* del tráfico; ✗ ~ *of three* regla *f* de tres; ~ *of thumb* regla *f* empírica; *be the* ~ ser de regla; *make it a* ~ *to* hacerse una regla de; **2.** *v/t.* mandar, gobernar (*a.* ~ *over*); regir; *line* trazar, tirar; *paper* rayar, reglar; ~ *that* decretar que; ~ *out* excluir; *be* ~*d by* guiarse por; *v/i.* gobernar; reinar; prevalecer; ✝ (*price*) regir; ˈ**rul·er** gobernante *m/f*; (*for lines*) regla *f*; ˈ**rul·ing** **1.** *esp.* ⚖ fallo *m*; **2.** ✝ *price* que rige; imperante.

rum [rʌm] ron *n*; aguardiente *m.*

Ru·ma·nian [ruːˈmeinjən] **1.** rumano *adj. a. su. m* (a *f*); **2.** (*language*) rumano *m.*

rum·ble [ˈrʌmbl] **1.** retumbo *m*; ruido *m* sordo; *sl.* pelea *f* callejera; ~ *seat* asiento *m* trasero (descubierto); **2.** retumbar; F (*stomach*) sonar.

ru·mi·nant [ˈruːminənt] rumiante *adj. a. su. m*; **ru·mi·nate** [ˈ~neit] rumiar (*a. fig.*); **ru·miˈna·tion** rumia(ción *f*) *f.*

rum·mage [ˈrʌmidʒ] **1.** buscar (*in* en) revolviéndolo todo; registrar; **2.** *attr.* ~ *sale* venta *f* de prendas usadas.

rum·my[1] [ˈrʌmi] *sl.* **1.** extraño, misterioso; **2.** *p.* alcohólico (a *f*) *m.*

rum·my[2] [~] *cards*: rummy *m.*

ru·mor [ˈruːmər] **1.** rumor *m*; **2.** rumorear; *it is* ~*ed* (*that*) se rumorea (que).

rump [rʌmp] *anat.* trasero *m*, ancas *f/pl.*; *cooking*: cuarto *m* trasero.

rum·ple [ˈrʌmpl] ajar, chafar.

rump·steak [ˈrʌmpˈsteik] biftec *m* del cuarto trasero.

rum·pus [ˈrʌmpəs] F tumulto *m*, batahola *f*, revuelo *m*; ~ **room** [ˈ~ruːm] cuarto *m* para recreo y fiestas.

rum run·ner [ˈrʌmrʌnər] contrabandista *m* de bebidas alcohólicas.

run [rʌn] **1.** [*irr.*] *v/i.* correr; apresurarse; (*continue*) seguir; (*reach*) extenderse; (*liquid*) correr, fluir; (*transport*) circular, ir; competir *in race*; (*melt*) derretirse; (*color*) desteñirse; *thea.* mantenerse en la cartelera; ⊕ funcionar, marchar, andar; ⚕ supurar; *parl.* ser candidato; ~ *across a p.* topar a una p.; ~ *away* huir; escaparse; (*horse*) dispararse; ~ *away with* arrebatar; fugarse con; *race* ganar fácilmente; ~ *down* (*watch*) acabarse la cuerda; ~ *dry* secarse; ~ *for parl.* ser candidato para; ~ *high* (*river*) estar crecido; (*feelings*) encenderse; ~ *in* entrar corriendo; ~ *in the family* venir de familia; ~ *into* extenderse a; (*meet*) topar a; (*crash*) chocar con; ~ *on* continuar; F parlotear; ~ *out* salir corriendo; (*stock*) agotarse, acabarse; (*term*) expirar; ~ *over* desbordar, rebosar; *v. short*; ~ *through money* derrochar, consumir; *book* hojear; ~ *to* extenderse a; F costear; ~ *up* acudir corriendo; ~ (*up*)*on* (*thoughts*) concentrarse en; ~ *up against* tropezar con, chocar con; ~ *with* abundar en; nadar en; ~ *with sweat* chorrear de sudor; **2.** [*irr.*] *v/t.* correr; *blockade* forzar, burlar; *business* dirigir, organizar; *candidate* proponer, apoyar; *city* gobernar; *contraband* pasar; *distance, race* correr; *errand* hacer; *line* trazar; *machine* manejar;

temperature tener; *vehicle* poseer; ~ *down* (*car*) atropellar; (*police*) acorralar, cazar; *reputation* desacreditar, desprestigiar, denigrar; ⚕ *be* ~ *down* estar debilitado; ~ *hard* acosar, hacer pasar apuros; ~ *in* ⊕, *mot.* rodar, ablandar; F *criminal* meter en la cárcel; ~ *into* hacer chocar con; ~ *off liquid* vaciar; *typ.* tirar, imprimir; ~ *over text* repasar; (*search*) registrar a la ligera; *p.* atropellar; ~ *one's eye over* examinar *acc.*; ~ *one's hand over* pasar la mano por, recorrer con la mano; ~ *a p. through* traspasar, espetar; ~ *up flag* izar; *debts* incurrir en; *house* construir (rápidamente); **3.** carrera *f* (*a. sport*); corrida *f*; *mot.* paseo *m* en coche; trayecto *m*, recorrido *m of vehicle*; ♪ glisado *m*, fermata *f*; ⚓ (*a. day's* ~) singladura *f*; *thea.* serie *f* de representaciones; ✓ terreno *m* de pasto; ✝ demanda *f* (*on* de); ✝ tendencia *f of market*; ✝ asedio *m* (*on a bank* de un banco); curso *m*, desarrollo *m of play etc.*; (*progress*) marcha *f*, progreso *m*; *the common* ~ el común (de las gentes); *dry* ~ ensayo *m*; recorrido *m* de prueba; *in the long* ~ a la larga; *on the* ~ en fuga desordenada; (*prisoner*) fugado; *have the* ~ *of* tener libre uso de.

run·a·bout [ˈrʌnəbaut] *mot.* coche *m* pequeño.

run·a·way [ˈrʌnəwei] **1.** fugitivo *m*; caballo *m* desbocado; **2.** *victory* fácil; *marriage* clandestino.

run-down [ˈrʌnˈdaun] desmantelado; inculto.

rune [ruːn] runa *f*.

rung[1] [rʌŋ] *p.p. of ring*[2] 2.

rung[2] [~] escalón *m* (*a. fig.*).

run·ic [ˈruːnik] rúnico.

run-in [ˈrʌnin] *typ.* palabra(s) *f* (*pl.*) insertada(s) en un párrafo; *sl.* riña *f*.

run·let [ˈrʌnlit], **run·nel** [ˈrʌnl] arroyuelo *m*.

run·ner [ˈrʌnər] corredor (-a *f*) *m*; caballo *m*; ⚔ ordenanza *m*, mensajero *m*; patín *m of sledge*; tapete *m of table*; (*carpet*) pasacaminos *m*; ⚘ serpa *f*; **~-up** [ˈ~ərˈʌp] subcampeón *m*.

run·ning [ˈrʌniŋ] **1.** *water* corriente; *knot* corredizo; *writing* cursivo; *commentary* continuo; ⚕ supurante; *two days* ~ dos días seguidos; ~ *mate* compañero *m* de candidatura; ~ *start* salida *f* lanzada; **2.** carrera *f*; ⊕ marcha *f*, funcionamiento *m of machine*; administración *f*, dirección *f of business*; *be in the* ~ tener posibilidades de ganar; ˈ**~ board** *mot.* estribo *m*; ˈ**~-ˈin** *mot.* (*adv.* en) rodaje *m*.

run-of-the-mill [ˈrʌnəvðəˈmil] F ordinario; mediocre.

runt [rʌnt] redrojo *m*, enano *m* (*a. fig.*); animal *m* achaparrado.

run·way [ˈrʌnwei] ✈ pista *f* de aterrizaje; *hunt.* pista *f*.

ru·pee [ruːˈpiː] rupia *f*.

rup·ture [ˈrʌptʃər] **1.** ⚕ hernia *f*, quebradura *f*; *fig.* ruptura *f*; **2.** ⚕ quebrarse (*a.* ~ *o.s.*).

ru·ral [ˈrurəl] □ rural.

rush[1] [rʌʃ] ⚘ junco *m*.

rush[2] [~] **1.** ímpetu *m*; ataque *m* (*a.* ⚔), acometida *f*; torrente *m of words etc.*; (*haste*) prisa *f*, precipitación *f*; agolpamiento *m of people*; (*disorderly*) desbandada *f* general; ✝ demanda *f* extraordinaria (*for, on* de); ✝ ~ *order* pedido *m* urgente; ~ *hours* horas *f/pl.* de máximo tránsito; **2.** *v/i.* precipitarse, lanzarse; venir *etc.* de prisa; ~ *at* arremeter contra; ~ *in* entrar precipitadamente; ~ *into print* publicar una obra sin reflexionar; *v/t. work* despachar (*or* ejecutar) de prisa; ⚔ asaltar; *sl.* hacer pagar; *parl.* ~ *through* aprobar de prisa.

rush·y [ˈrʌʃi] juncoso.

rusk [rʌsk] galleta *f* dura.

rus·set [ˈrʌsit] (color *m*) bermejo, rojizo.

Rus·sia leath·er [ˈrʌʃəˈleðər] piel *f* de Rusia; ˈ**Rus·sian** **1.** ruso *adj. a. su. m* (a *f*); **2.** (*language*) ruso *m*.

rust [rʌst] **1.** orín *m*, herrumbre *f*; ⚘ roya *f*; **2.** aherrumbrar(se), oxidar(se), tomarse de orín.

rus·tic [ˈrʌstik] **1.** □ rústico, palurdo; **2.** rústico *m*, palurdo *m*; **rus·ti·cate** [ˈ~keit] *v/t. univ.* suspender temporalmente; *v/i.* rusticar; **rus·tiˈca·tion** rusticación *f*; *univ.* suspensión *f* temporal; **rus·tic·i·ty** [~ˈtisiti] rusticidad *f*.

rus·tle [ˈrʌsl] **1.** (hacer) susurrar; (hacer) crujir; F hurtar (ganado); **2.** (*a.* ˈ**rus·tling**) crujido *m of paper*; susurro *m of wind*.

rust...: ˈ**~·less** inoxidable; ˈ**~ˈproof,** ˈ**~-re·sist·ant** a prueba de herrumbre; ˈ**rust·y** mohoso, enmohecido, herrumbroso, oxidado; *fig.* torpe; empolvado.

rut[1] [rʌt] *zo.* **1.** celo *m*; **2.** caer (*or* estar) en celo.

rut[2] [~] rodera *f*, rodada *f*, carril *m*; bache *m*; *fig.* rutina *f*; *be in a ~ fig.* ir encarrilado.

ruth·less [ˈru:θlis] □ despiadado; implacable; ˈ**ruth·less·ness** implacabilidad *f*.

rut·ted [ˈrʌtid] *road* lleno de baches.

rut·ting [ˈrʌtiŋ] *zo.* en celo; *~ season* época *f* de celo.

rut·ty [ˈrʌti] = *rutted*.

rye [rai] centeno *m*; whisky *m* de centeno.

S

sab·bath [ˈsæbəθ] (*Christian*) domingo *m*; (*Jewish*) sábado *m*.
sab·bat·ic, sab·bat·i·cal [səˈbætik(l)] □ sabático.
sa·ber [ˈseibər] 1. sable *m*; 2. herir } [a sablazos.
sa·ble [ˈseibl] 1. *zo.* cebellina *f*; *heraldry*: sable *m*; 2. negro.
sab·o·tage [ˈsæbətɑːʒ] 1. sabotaje *m*; 2. sabotear; **sab·o·teur** [sæbəˈtəːr] saboteador *m*.
sac·cha·rin [ˈsækərin] sacarina *f*; **sac·cha·rine** [ˈ~rain] sacarino; *fig.* azucarado; empalagoso.
sac·er·do·tal [sæsərˈdoutl] □ sacerdotal.
sack[1] [sæk] 1. saco *m*, costal *m*; (*a.* ~ *coat*) saco *m*, americana *f*; F *give the* ~ despedir; F *get the* ~ ser despedido; 2. ensacar; F despedir.
sack[2] [~] 1. saqueo *m*; *put to* ~ = 2. saquear.
sack·cloth [ˈsæckkləθ], ˈ**sack·ing** (h)arpillera *f*; **sack·ful** [ˈ~ful] saco *m* (lleno).
sac·ra·ment [ˈsækrəmənt] sacramento *m*; **sac·ra·men·tal** [~ˈmentl] sacramental.
sa·cred [ˈseikrid] □ sagrado; ˈ**sa·cred·ness** santidad *f*.
sac·ri·fice [ˈsækrifais] 1. sacrificio *m*; víctima *f*; ✝ *at a* ~ con pérdida; 2. sacrificar; ✝ malvender.
sac·ri·fi·cial [sækriˈfiʃl] de sacrificio.
sac·ri·lege [ˈsækrilidʒ] sacrilegio *m*; **sac·ri·le·gious** [~ˈlidʒəs] sacrílego.
sac·ris·tan [ˈsækristən] sacristán *m*.
sac·ris·ty [ˈsækristi] sacristía *f*.
sad [sæːd] □ triste; lamentable; *grow* ~ entristecerse.
sad·den [ˈsædn] entristecer.
sad·dle [ˈsædl] 1. silla *f*; (*cycle-*) sillín *m*; (*hill*) collado *m*; 2. ensillar (*a.* ~ *up*); *fig.* ~ *with* echar a cuestas a; ~ *o.s. with* cargar con; ˈ~**backed** ensillado; ˈ~**bag** alforja *f*; ˈ~**cloth** sudadero *m*; ˈ**sad·dler** talabartero *m*, guarnicionero *m*; ˈ**sad·dler·y** talabartería *f*.
sad·ism [ˈseidizm] sadismo *m*; **sadˈis·tic** □ sádico.
sad·ness [ˈsædnis] tristeza *f*.
sa·fa·ri [səˈfɑːri] safari *f*.
safe [seif] 1. □ seguro; intacto, ileso; *p.* digno de confianza; ~ *from* a salvo de, al abrigo de; ~ *and sound* sano y salvo; *to be on the* ~ *side* para mayor seguridad; 2. caja *f* de caudales; ~ *deposit box* caja *f* de seguridad; ~ *keeping* custodia *f*; lugar *m* seguro; *be in* ~ *keeping* (*p.*) estar en buenas manos; ˈ~**-blow·er** ladrón *m* de cajas de caudales; ~-ˈ**con·duct** salvoconducto *m*; ˈ~ **crack·er** ladrón *m* de cajas de caudales; ˈ~**guard** 1. salvaguardia *f*; protección *f*; 2. salvaguardar; ˈ**safe·ly** con toda seguridad; *arrive etc.* sin accidente, sin novedad; ˈ**safe·ness** seguridad *f*.
safe·ty [ˈseifti] 1. seguridad *f*; 2. *attr.* de seguridad; ˈ~ **belt** ✈ cinturón *m* de seguridad; ~ **cur·tain** *thea.* telón *m* de seguridad; ˈ~ **match** fósforo *m* de seguridad; ˈ~**-pin** imperdible *m*; ~ **ra·zor** maquinilla *f* de afeitar; ˈ~ **valve** válvula *f* de seguridad.
saf·fron [ˈsæfrən] 1. azafrán *m*; 2. azafranado.
sag [sæg] 1. combarse, hundirse; ✝ bajar; *fig.* aflojarse; 2. comba *f*.
sa·ga [ˈsɑːgə] saga *f*.
sa·ga·cious [səˈgeiʃəs] □ sagaz.
sa·gac·i·ty [səˈgæsiti] sagacidad *f*.
sage[1] [seidʒ] □ sabio *adj. a. su.* (a *f*).
sage[2] [~] ♀ salvia *f*.
sa·go [ˈseigou] sagú *m*.
said [sed] *pret. a. p.p. of say*; *esp.* ⚖ *the* ~ *articles* dichos artículos, los cuales artículos.
sail [seil] 1. vela *f*; paseo *m* en barco (de vela); aspa *f of mill*; *in full* ~ a todo trapo; set ~ hacerse a la vela; 2. *v/i.* navegar; darse a la vela; flotar; ~ *into sl.* atacar; *v/t. boat* gobernar; *sea* navegar; ˈ~**boat** barco *m* de vela; ˈ~**cloth** lona *f*; ˈ**sail·ing**: *be plain* ~ ser cosa de coser y cantar; ~

STU

orders pl. últimas instrucciones *f/pl.*; **'sail·ing ship** velero *m*; **'sail·or** marinero *m*, marino *m*; *be a bad* ~ marearse fácilmente; **'sail·plane** velero *m*, planeador *m*.

saint [seint] santo (a *f*) *m*; (*before most m names*) San ...; **'saint·ed** santo; que en santa gloria esté; **'saint·li·ness** santidad *f*; **'saint·ly** santo.

sake [seik]: *for the* ~ *of* por, por motivo de, en atención a; *for my* ~ por mí; *for God's* ~ por el amor de Dios.

sal [sæl]: ~ *ammoniac* sal *f* amoníaca; ~ *volatile* sal *f* volátil.

sa·la·cious [sə'leiʃəs] □ salaz.

sal·ad ['sæləd] ensalada *f*; ~ *bowl* ensaladera *f*; ~ *dressing* mayonesa *f*, aliño *m*.

sal·a·man·der ['sæləmændər] salamandra *f*.

sa·la·mi [sə'lɑːmi] salami *m*.

sal·a·ried ['sælərid] *p.* asalariado; *post* retribuido; ~ *employees* empleados *m/pl.* (de oficina); **'sal·a·ry** salario *m*, sueldo *m*; **'sal·a·ry earn·er** persona *f* que gana un sueldo.

sale [seil] venta *f*; (*clearance* ~) saldo *m*, liquidación *f*; (*a. public* ~) (pública) subasta *f*; *for* ~, *on* ~ de venta, en venta; se vende; **'sale·a·ble** vendible; **'sale room** sala *f* de subastas.

sales... [seilz]: **'~·man** dependiente *m*, vendedor *m*; viajante *m*; **'~·man·ship** arte *m* de vender; **'~·room** salón *m* de ventas; **'~·wom·an** dependienta *f*, vendedora *f*.

sa·li·ent ['seiliənt] □ (*fig.* sobre)-saliente *adj. a. su. m.*

sa·line 1. ['seilain] salino; **2.** [sə'lain] saladar *m*; **sa·lin·i·ty** [sə'liniti] salinidad *f*.

sa·li·va [sə'laivə] saliva *f*; **sal·i·var·y** ['sælivəri] salival; **sal·i'va·tion** salivación *f*.

sal·low[1] ['sælou] ⚘ sauce *m*.

sal·low[2] [~] cetrino, amarillento; **'sal·low·ness** amarillez *f*.

sal·ly ['sæli] **1.** ⚔ salida *f* (*a. fig.*); **2.** hacer una salida; ~ *forth* salir resueltamente.

salm·on ['sæmən] (color *m*) salmón *m*.

sa·loon [sə'luːn] salón *m*; ⚓ cámara *f*; bar *m*, taberna *f*; *mot.* limousine *f*, limusina *f*; **sa'loon car** 🚃 coche-salón *m*.

salt [sɔːlt] **1.** sal *f*; ~*s pl.* sales *f/pl.* medicinales; *old* ~ lobo *m* de mar; ~ *of the earth* sal *f* de la tierra; **2.** salado; salobre; **3.** salar; ~ *away* ocultar para uso futuro.

salt...: **'~·cel·lar** salero *m*; **'salt·ness** salinidad *f*; **salt·pe·ter** [~'piːtər] salitre *m*; **'salt shak·er** salero *m*; **'salt·works** salinas *f/pl.*; **'salt·y** salado.

sa·lu·bri·ous [sə'luːbriəs] □ salubre; **sa·lu·bri·ty** [sə'luːbriti], **sal·u·tar·i·ness** ['sæljutərinis] salubridad *f*; **sal·u·tar·y** ['sæljutəri] □ saludable.

sal·u·ta·tion [sælju'teiʃn] salutación *f*; **sa·lu·ta·to·ry** [səl'juːtətəri] de salutación; **sa·lute** [sə'luːt] **1.** saludo *m*; *co.* beso *m*; salva *f of guns*; **2.** saludar.

sal·vage ['sælvidʒ] **1.** salvamento *m*; objetos *m/pl.* salvados; **2.** salvar.

sal·va·tion [sæl'veiʃn] salvación *f*; ☉ *Army* Ejército *m* de Salvación; **sal'va·tion·ist** miembro *m* del Ejército de Salvación.

salve[1] [sælv] salvar.

salve[2] [sæv] **1.** *mst fig.* ungüento *m*; **2.** curar (con ungüento); *fig.* tranquilizar.

sal·ver ['sælvər] bandeja *f*.

sal·vo[1] ['sælvou] salvedad *f*, reserva *f*.

sal·vo[2] [~] ⚔ salva *f*.

Sa·mar·i·tan [sə'mæritn] samaritano *adj. a. su. m* (a *f*); *good* ~ buen samaritano *m*.

same [seim] mismo; igual, idéntico; *all the* ~ a pesar de todo; *it is all the* ~ *to me* me es igual, lo mismo me da; *the* ~ ... *as* el mismo ... que; *the* ~ *to you* igualmente; **'same·ness** igualdad *f*; identidad *f*; monotonía *f*.

samp [sæmp] maíz *m* molido grueso.

sam·ple ['sæmpl] **1.** *esp.* ✝ muestra *f*; **2.** probar; *wine etc.* catar; ⚒ muestrear; **'sam·pler** (*p.*) catador *m*; *sew.* dechado *m*; **'sam·pling** ⚒ muestreo *m*.

san·a·tive ['sænətiv], **san·a·to·ry** ['~təri] sanativo; **san·a·to·ri·um** [~'tɔːriəm] sanatorio *m*.

sanc·ti·fi·ca·tion [sæŋktifi'keiʃn] santificación *f*; **sanc·ti·fy** ['~fai] santificar; **sanc·ti·mo·ni·ous** [~'mounjəs] □ mojigato, santurrón; **sanc·tion** ['sæŋkʃn] **1.** sanción *f*; **2.** sancionar, autorizar; **sanc·ti·ty**

['~titi] santidad *f*; inviolabilidad *f*; ~ *of the mails* secreto *m* de correspondencia; **sanc·tu·ar·y** ['~tjuəri] santuario *m*; (*high altar*) sagrario *m*; *fig.* refugio *m*; *seek* ~ acogerse a sagrado; **sanc·tum** ['~təm] lugar *m* sagrado; *fig.* despacho *m* particular.
sand [sænd] **1.** arena *f*; ~*s pl.* arenal *m*, playa *f* (arenosa); **2.** enarenar; ⊕ lijar.
san·dal[1] ['sændl] sandalia *f*.
san·dal[2] [~], '**~·wood** sándalo *m*.
sand...: '**~·bag** saco *m* terrero; '**~·bank** banco *m* de arena; '**~·bar** barra *f* de arena; '**~·blast** ⊕ chorro *m* de arena; '**~·glass** reloj *m* de arena; '**~·pa·per 1.** papel *m* de lija; **2.** lijar; '**~·pit** arenal *m*; '**~·stone** piedra *f* arenisca.
sand·wich ['sændwitʃ] **1.** sándwich *m*; bocadillo *m*; **2.** poner (entre dos cosas *or* capas); apretujar; intercalar.
sand·y ['sændi] arenoso; *hair* rojo.
sane [sein] □ cuerdo, sensato.
San·for·ize ['sænfəraiz] sanforizar.
sang [sæŋ] *pret. of sing.*
san·gui·nary ['sæŋgwinəri] □ sanguinario; sangriento; **san·guine** ['~gwin] optimista; **san'guin·e·ous** [~niəs] sanguíneo.
san·i·tar·y ['~təri] □ sanitario; ~ *inspector* inspector *m* de sanidad; ~ *napkin* compresa *f* higiénica, paño *m* higiénico.
san·i·ta·tion [sæni'teiʃn] sanidad *f*; instalación *f* sanitaria, servicios *m/pl.*; saneamiento *m in house*; '**san·i·ty** cordura *f*, sensatez *f*.
sank [sæŋk] *pret. of sink* 1.
San·skrit ['sænskrit] sánscrito *adj. a. su. m.*
sap[1] [sæp] ♀ savia *f*; jugo *m*; *fig.* vitalidad *f*; *sl.* simplón *m*.
sap[2] [~] **1.** ⚔ zapa *f*; **2.** ⚔ zapar; socavar; *strength* minar.
sa·pi·ence ['seipiəns] *mst iro.* sapiencia *f*; '**sa·pi·ent** □ *mst iro.* sapiente.
sap·ling ['sæpliŋ] pimpollo *m*, árbol *m* nuevo; *fig.* jovenzuelo *m*.
sap·o·na·ceous [sæpou'neiʃəs] 🕮 *or co.* saponáceo.
sap·per ['sæpər] zapador *m*.
sap·phire ['sæfaiər] zafiro *m*.
sap·py ['sæpi] jugoso; *fig.* enérgico; *sl.* tonto.
Sar·a·cen ['særəsn] sarraceno *m*.
sar·casm ['sɑːrkæzm] sarcasmo *m*; **sar'cas·tic** □ sarcástico.
sar·coph·a·gus, *pl.* **sar'coph·a·gi** [sɑːr'kɔfəgəs, ~dʒai] sarcófago *m*.
sar·dine [sɑːr'diːn] sardina *f*.
Sar·din·i·an [sɑːr'dinjən] sardo *adj. a. su. m* (a *f*).
sar·don·ic [sɑːr'dɔnik] □ burlón, irónico; sardónico *S.Am.*
sar·to·ri·al [sɑːr'tɔːriəl] □ de sastrería; relativo al vestido.
sash[1] [sæʃ] marco *m* (corredizo) de ventana.
sash[2] [~] faja *f*; ⚔ fajín *m*.
sash win·dow ['sæʃ'windou] ventana *f* de guillotina.
sat [sæt] *pret. a. p.p. of sit.*
sa·tan·ic [sə'tænik] □ satánico; **sa·tan·ism** ['seitinizm] satanismo *m*.
satch·el ['sætʃl] cabás *m*; cartapacio *m*.
sate [seit] *v. satiate.*
sa·teen [sæ'tiːn] satén *m*.
sat·el·lite ['sætəlait] satélite *adj. a. su. m*; ~ *country* país *m* satélite; ~ *transmission* transmisión *f* por satélite.
sa·ti·ate ['seiʃieit] saciar, hartar; **sa·ti'a·tion, sa·ti·e·ty** [sə'taiəti] saciedad *f*, hartura *f*.
sat·in ['sætin] raso *m*.
sat·ire ['sætaiər] sátira *f*; **sa·tir·ic, sa·tir·i·cal** [sə'tirik(l)] □ satírico; **sat·i·rist** ['sætərist] escritor *m* satírico; '**sat·i·rize** satirizar.
sat·is·fac·tion [sætis'fækʃn] satisfacción *f*; **sat·is'fac·to·ry** [~təri] □ satisfactorio.
sat·is·fied ['sætisfaid] satisfecho; *be* ~ *that* estar convencido de que; **sat·is·fy** ['~fai] satisfacer.
sat·u·rate ['sætʃəreit] saturar; empapar; **sat·u'ra·tion** saturación *f*.
Sat·ur·day ['sætərdi] sábado *m*.
sat·ur·nine ['sætərnain] saturnino.
sat·yr ['sætər] sátiro *m*.
sauce [sɔːs] salsa *f*; (*sweet*) crema *f*; F impertinencia *f*, frescura *f*; '**~ boat** salsera *f*; '**~·pan** cacerola *f*, cazo *m*; '**sauc·er** platillo *m*.
sau·ci·ness ['sɔːsinis] F impertinencia *f*, descaro *m*, desfachatez *f*; **sau·cy** ['sɔːsi] F impertinente, descarado; fresco; coqueta.
saun·ter ['sɔːntər] **1.** paseo *m* lento y tranquilo; **2.** pasearse despacio y tranquilamente; deambular.
sau·ri·an ['sɔːriən] saurio *m*.

sau·sage ['sɔsidʒ] embutido *m*, salchicha *f*, chorizo *m*.
sav·age ['sævidʒ] **1.** □ salvaje; *attack* feroz; F rabioso; **2.** salvaje *m/f*; **3.** (*animal*) embestir; '**sav·age·ness**, '**sav·age·ry** salvajismo *m*; salvajería *f*; ferocidad *f*.
sa·van·na(h) [sə'vænə] sabana *f*.
save [seiv] **1.** *v/t.* salvar (*from* de); *time, money* ahorrar; *trouble* evitar; (*keep*) guardar; *v/i.* ahorrar, economizar; **2.** *lit. prp. a. cj.* salvo, excepto; ~ *for* excepto, si no fuera por; ~ *that* excepto que.
sav·e·loy ['sævilɔi] salchichón *m* seco y sazonado.
sav·ing ['seiviŋ] **1.**: ~ *clause* cláusula *f* que contiene una salvedad; ~ *grace* único mérito *m*; **2.** economía *f*; ~*s pl.* ahorros *m/pl.*; '~**s ac·count** cuenta *f* de ahorros; '~**s bank** caja *f* de ahorros.
sav·ior ['seivjər] salvador (-a *f*) *m*; ♀ Salvador *m*.
sa·voir faire ['sævwɑ:r'fer] desparpajo *m*, destreza *f*, aptitud *f* práctica.
sa·vor ['seivər] **1.** sabor *m*, gust(ill)o *m*; **2.** *v/i.* saber (*of* a), oler (*of* a) (*a. fig.*); *v/t.* saborear; **sa·vor·i·ness** ['~rinis] sabor *m*; '**sa·vor·less** insípido; '**sa·vor·y** **1.** sabroso; salado; **2.** ⚘ tomillo *m* salsero.
sa·voy [sə'vɔi] col *f* de Saboya.
sav·vy ['sævi] *sl.* **1.** comprender; **2.** comprensión *f*; conocimiento *m*.
saw[1] [sɔ:] *pret. of* see[1].
saw[2] [~] refrán *m*, dicho *m*.
saw[3] [~] ⊕ **1.** sierra *f*; **2.** (a)serrar; '~**·buck** cabrilla *f*; *sl.* billete *m* de diez dólares; '~**·dust** serrín *m*; '~**·fish** pez *m* sierra; '~**·horse** burro *m*; '~**·mill** aserradero *m*; **sawn** [sɔ:n] *p.p. of saw*[3] 2; **saw·yer** ['~jər] aserrador *m*.
Sax·on ['sæksn] sajón *adj. a su. m* (-a *f*).
sax·o·phone ['sæksəfoun] saxofón *m*.
say [sei] **1.** [*irr.*] decir; afirmar; (*text*) rezar; ~ *grace* bendecir la mesa; ~ *mass* decir misa; *that is to* ~ es decir; *to* ~ *nothing of* eso sin tomar en cuenta; *do you* ~ (*so*)? ¿de veras?; *you don't* ~ (*so*)! ¡parece mentira!; *I should* ~ *so!* ¡ya lo creo!; ~ *to o.s.* decir para sí; *it is said* se dice; *I* ~!, ~! ¡oiga!; ¡vaya!; **2.** voz *f*, (uso *m* de la) palabra *f*; *let him have his* ~ que hable él; *have a* (*or some*) ~ *in a th.* tener voz y voto; *have no* ~ *in a th.* no tener voz en capítulo; '**say·ing** dicho *m*, refrán *m*; *as the* ~ *goes* como dice el refrán; *it goes without* ~ eso cae de su peso.
scab [skæb] costra *f*; *vet.* roña *f*; F esquirol *m*.
scab·bard ['skæbərd] vaina *f*.
scab·by [skæbi] costroso.
sca·bi·es ['skeibii:z] sarna *f*.
sca·bi·ous ['skeibiəs] escabiosa *f*.
sca·brous ['skeibrəs] escabroso.
scaf·fold ['skæfəld] cadalso *m*; = '**scaf·fold·ing** andamiaje *m*, andamio *m*.
scald [skɔ:ld] **1.** escaldadura *f*; **2.** escaldar; (*mst* ~ *out*) limpiar con agua caliente; *milk* calentar.
scale[1] [skeil] **1.** (*fish*) escama *f*; **2.** *v/t.* escamar; descostrar; ⊕ raspar; *teeth* quitar el sarro a; *v/i.* descamarse (*freq.* ~ *off*).
scale[2] [~] **1.** platillo *m* de balanza; (*a pair of* una) ~*s pl.* balanza *f*; *ast.* Balanza *f*; *turn the* ~*s* decidir; **2.** pesar.
scale[3] [~] **1.** escala *f* (*a.* ♪); *to* ~ según escala; *on a large* ~ en gran(de) escala; **2.** *mountain* escalar, trepar a; ~ *down* reducir según escala; graduar.
scal·lop ['skɔləp] **1.** *zo.* venera *f*; *sew.* festón *m*; **2.** *sew.* festonear.
scalp [skælp] **1.** cuero *m* cabelludo; cabellera *f*; **2.** escalpar; *sl. billetes* revender a precio subido.
scal·pel ['skælpəl] escalpelo *m*.
scal·y ['skeili] escamoso.
scamp [skæmp] **1.** tunante *m/f*, bribón (-a *f*) *m*; (*child*) diablillo *m*; golfo *m*; **2.** chapucear, frangollar; '**scamp·er** **1.** (*a.* ~ *away*, ~ *off*) escabullirse, escaparse precipitadamente; **2.** huida *f etc.* precipitada.
scan [skæn] *v/t.* escudriñar, examinar; explorar (*a. television*); *verse* escandir; *v/i.* estar bien medido.
scan·dal ['skændl] escándalo *m*; ⚖ difamación *f*; *what a* ~!, *it's a* ~! ¡qué vergüenza!; '**scan·dal mon·ger** chismoso (a *f*) *m*; difamador (-a *f*) *m*; '**scan·dal·ous** □ escandaloso.
Scan·di·na·vi·an [skændi'neivjən] escandinavo *adj. a. su. m* (a *f*).
scan·ner ['skænər] (*radar*) antena *f* direccional giratoria; (*television*) dispositivo *m* explorador.
scan·sion ['skænʃn] escansión *f*.

scant [skænt] escaso; poco.
scant·i·ness [ˈskæntinis] escasez *f*, insuficiencia *f*.
scant·ling [ˈskæntliŋ] escantillón *m*; cuartón *m*; mínimo *m*.
scant·y [ˈskænti] □ escaso, corto; insuficiente.
scape·goat [ˈskeipgout] cabeza *f* de turco; víctima *f* propiciatoria.
scape·grace [ˈskeipgreis] bribón (-a *f*) *m*; pillo (a *f*) *m*.
scap·u·lar [ˈskæpjulər] **1.** *anat.* escapular; **2.** *eccl.* escapulario *m*.
scar [skɑːr] **1.** ⚕ cicatriz *f*, señal *f* (*a. fig.*); **2.** *v/t.* señalar; *v/i.* cicatrizarse.
scar·ab [ˈskærəb] escarabajo *m*.
scarce [skers] escaso; raro; F *make o.s.* ~ escabullirse, esfumarse; ˈ**scarce·ly** apenas; con dificultad; ~ *anybody* casi nadie; ~ *ever* casi nunca; ˈ**scar·ci·ty** escasez *f*; rareza *f*; carestía *f*.
scare [sker] **1.** espantar, asustar; ~ *away* ahuyentar; ~*d* sobresaltado; **2.** susto *m*, sobresalto *m*; ˈ**~·crow** espantapájaros *m*; *fig.* espantajo *m*; ˈ**~·head** titulares *m/pl.* grandes y sensacionales; ˈ**~·mon·ger** alarmista *m/f*.
scarf [skɑːrf] bufanda *f*; (*head*) pañuelo *m*; tapete *m*; ˈ**~·skin** epidermis *f*.
scar·i·fi·ca·tion [skerifiˈkeiʃn] ⚕ escarificación *f*; *fig.* crítica *f* mordaz; **scar·i·fy** [ˈ~fai] ⚕, ⚒ escarificar; *fig.* criticar severamente.
scar·la·ti·na [skɑːrləˈtiːnə] escarlatina *f*.
scar·let [ˈskɑːrlit] **1.** escarlata *f*, grana *f*; **2.** de color escarlata, de grana; ~ *fever* escarlatina *f*; ⚘ ~ *runner* judía *f* de España.
scarp [skɑːrp] escarpa *f*, declive *m*.
scarred [skɑːrd] señalado de cicatrices; *fig.* abusado; traumatizado.
scarves [skɑːrvz] *pl. of scarf*.
scar·y [ˈskeri] F asustadizo.
scath·ing [ˈskeiðiŋ] □ acerbo, mordaz.
scat·ter [ˈskætər] **1.** esparcir, desparramar(se); ⚔ dispersar(se); ~*ed* disperso; **2.** ⚛ dispersión *f*; ˈ**~·brain** F cabeza *m/f* de chorlito.
scav·enge [ˈskævindʒ] limpiar (las calles), recoger la basura; ˈ**scav·en·ger** basurero *m*; *zo.* animal *m etc.* que se alimenta de carroña.
sce·nar·i·o [siˈnæriou] guión *m*; escenario *m*; **sceˈnar·ist** guionista *m/f*.
scene [siːn] escena *f* (*a. thea.*); vista *f*, perspectiva *f*; paisaje *m*; teatro *m of events*; escenario *m of crime*; F escándalo *m*, jaleo *m*; *behind the* ~*s* entre bastidores; ˈ~ **paint·er** escenógrafo *m*; **scen·er·y** [ˈ~əri] paisaje *m*; *thea.* decoración(es) *f*(*pl.*); decorado *m*; ˈ**scene shift·er** tramoyista *m*.
sce·nic [ˈsiːnik] □ pintoresco; escénico; ~ *railway* montaña *f* rusa.
scent [sent] **1.** perfume *m*, olor *m*; (*sense*) olfato *m*; *hunt.* rastro *m*, pista *f*; **2.** perfumar; *danger etc.* sospechar, percibir; (*freq.* ~ *out*) olfatear, husmear; ˈ**scent·ed** perfumado; ˈ**scent·less** inodoro.
scep·tic [ˈskeptik] escéptico (a *f*) *m*; ˈ**scep·ti·cal** □ escéptico; **scep·ti·cism** [ˈ~sizm] escepticismo *m*.
scep·tre [ˈseptər] cetro *m*.
sched·ule [ˈskedjuːl] **1.** lista *f*; *esp.* ⚖ inventario *m*, apéndice *m*; programa *m*; cuestionario *m*; *esp. Am.* horario *m*; calendario *m* (de operaciones proyectadas); *on* ~ puntual; **2.** catalogar; fijar la hora de; proyectar; ~*d for demolition* se prevé su demolición.
scheme [skiːm] **1.** esquema *m*; plan *m*, proyecto *m*; (*plot*) ardid *m*, intriga *f*; **2.** *v/t.* proyectar; *b.s.* tramar; *v/i. b.s.* intrigar; ˈ**schem·er** intrigante *m/f*.
schism [ˈsizm] cisma *m*; **schis·mat·ic** [sizˈmætik] **1.** (*a.* **schisˈmat·i·cal** □) cismático; **2.** cismático *m*.
schist [ʃist] esquisto *m*.
schiz·o·phre·ni·a [skitsəˈfriːnjə] esquizofrenia *f*; **schiz·o·phre·nic** [~ˈfrenik] □ esquizofrénico.
schol·ar [ˈskɔlər] (*pupil*) colegial (-a *f*) *m*, escolar *m/f*; (*learned p.*) erudito (a *f*) *m*; *univ.* becario (a *f*) *m*; ˈ**schol·ar·ly** *adj.* erudito; ˈ**schol·ar·ship** erudición *f*; *univ.* beca *f*.
scho·las·tic [skəˈlæstik] □ escolástico *adj. a. su. m*.
school [skuːl] **1.** escuela *f* (*a.* ~ *of thought*); colegio *m*; *public* ~ *EE.UU. a. Scot.* escuela *f* pública; *England*: *approx.* internado *m* privado (con dote); *v. driving, grammar etc.*; *primary* ~ escuela *f* primaria; *high* ~, *secondary* ~ escuela *f* secundaria; **2.** instruir, enseñar; disciplinar; ˈ**~·boy** colegial *m*, escolar *m*; ˈ**~·girl** colegia-

la *f*, escolar *f*; ˈ**school·ing** instrucción *f*, enseñanza *f*; ˈ**~·man** escolástico *m*; ˈ**~·mas·ter** (*grammar school*) profesor *m* (de instituto); (*others*) maestro *m*; ˈ**~·mate** compañero (a *f*) *m* de clase; ˈ**~·mis·tress** (*grammar school*) profesora *f*; (*others*) maestra *f*; ˈ**~·room** (sala *f* de) clase *f*; ˈ**~·teach·er** maestro (a *f*) *m*.
schoon·er [ˈskuːnər] ⚓ goleta *f*.
sci·at·i·ca [saiˈætikə] ciática *f*.
sci·ence [ˈsaiəns] ciencia *f*; ~ *fiction* literatura *f* fictiva; novela *f* científica.
sci·en·tif·ic [saiənˈtifik] □ científico.
sci-fi [ˈsaiˈfai] *sl.* = *science fiction*.
scin·til·late [ˈsintileit] centellear, chispear; *fig.* brillar; ˈ**scin·til·lat·ing** □ *fig.* brillante.
sci·on [ˈsaiən] vástago *m* (*a. fig.*).
scis·sion [ˈsiʒn] escisión *f*; **scis·sors** [ˈsizərz] *pl.* (*a pair of* unas) tijeras *f/pl*.
scle·ro·sis [skliˈrousis] esclerosis *f*.
scoff [skɔf] **1.** mofa *f*, befa *f*; **2.** mofarse, burlarse (*at* de); *sl.* engullir; ˈ**scoff·er** mofador (-a *f*) *m*, burlón (-a *f*) *m*.
scold [skould] **1.** regañona *f*; **2.** regañar, reprender; ˈ**scold·ing** reprensión *f*, regaño *m*.
scol·lop [ˈskɔləp] *v.* *scallop*.
sconce[1] [skɔns] candelabro *m* de pared.
sconce[2] [~] ⚔ fortín *m*.
scon(**e**) [skɔn, skoun] *torta escocesa*.
scoop [skuːp] **1.** pal(et)a *f*; (*water-*) achicador *m*; cuchara *f* (de draga); ⚕ espátula *f*; *sl.* ganancia *f*; *sl.* primera publicación *f* de una noticia; **2.** (*mst* ~ *out*) sacar con pal(et)a; *water* achicar; *hole* excavar; *sl.* adelantarse a (un rival) publicando una noticia.
scoot·er [ˈskuːtər] (*child's*) patinete *f*; (*adult's*) vespa *f*; monopatín *m*.
scope [skoup] alcance *m*; extensión *f*; envergadura *f*; oportunidad *f*; esfera *f* de acción; *have free* ~ tener carta blanca; *there is* ~ *for* hay campo para.
scorch [skɔːrtʃ] *v/t.* chamuscar; (*sun, wind*) abrasar; ~*ed earth* tierra *f* quemada; *v/i.* F *mot.* ir volando; ˈ**scorch·er** F día *m* de mucho calor.
score [skɔːr] **1.** (*cut*) muesca *f*, entalladura *f*; (*line*) raya *f*; ♪ partitura *f*; (*20*) veintena *f*; *sport:* tanteo *m*; *four* ~ ochenta; *by the* ~ a granel; *on the* ~ *of* con motivo de; *on that* ~ a ese respecto; *pay off old* ~*s* ajustar cuentas viejas; *what's the* ~*?* ¿cómo estamos?; *keep* (*the*) ~ tantear; **2.** *v/t.* rayar; hacer cortes en; ♪ instrumentar; *sport*: *goal* marcar; *points* ganar; *total* apuntar (*a.* ~ *up*); F criticar severamente; *v/i.* marcar (un tanto), ganar (puntos); (*keep total*) tantear; F ~ *off a p.* triunfar a expensas de alguien; *that doesn't* ~ eso no puntúa; ˈ**score·board** tanteador *m*; ˈ**score card** anotador *m*; ˈ**scor·er** (*player*) marcador *m*; (*recorder*) tanteador *m*.
sco·ri·a, *pl.* **sco·ri·ae** [ˈskɔːriə, ˈ~riiː] escoria *f*.
scorn [skɔːrn] **1.** desprecio *m*, desdén *m*; **2.** despreciar, desdeñar; ~ *to* no dignarse *inf.*, desdeñarse de *inf.*;
scorn·ful [ˈ~ful] □ desdeñoso.
scor·pi·on [ˈskɔːrpjən] alacrán *m*.
Scot [skɔt] escocés (-a *f*) *m*.
Scotch[1] [skɔtʃ] **1.** escocés; *the* ~ los escoceses; **2.** F whisk(e)y *m* escocés.
scotch[2] [~] **1.** calce *m*, cuña *f*; **2.** *wheel* calzar, engalgar; *rumor* desmentir; *plan etc.* frustrar.
scot-free [ˈskɔtˈfriː] impune.
Scots [skɔts] escocés; ˈ**Scots·man** escocés *m*; ˈ**Scots·wom·an** escocesa *f*.
Scot·tish [ˈskɔtiʃ] escocés.
scoun·drel [ˈskaundrl] canalla *m*, bribón *m*.
scour[1] [ˈskauər] *dish* fregar; estregar; *channel* limpiar; ⚕ purgar.
scour[2] [~] *v/i.*: ~ *about* buscar por todas partes (*for acc.*); *v/t.* *country* recorrer, explorar (*for* buscando).
scourge [skəːrdʒ] *lit.* **1.** azote *m* (*a. fig.*); **2.** azotar, hostigar.
scout [skaut] **1.** explorador *m*, escucha *m*; F busca *f*, reconocimiento *m*; *univ.* fámulo *m*, criado *m*; *Boy* ♀ (niño *m*) explorador *m*; **2.** explorar; reconocer; F ~ *for* buscar.
scow [skau] gabarra *f*.
scowl [skaul] **1.** ceño *m*, sobrecejo *m*; **2.** fruncir el ceño; mirar con ceño (*a.* ~ *at*).
scrab·ble [ˈskræbl] garrapatear.
scrag [skræg] **1.** pescuezo *m*; **2.** torcer el pescuezo a; *sl.* aporrear; **scrag·gi·ness** [ˈ~inis] flaqueza *f*; ˈ**scrag·gy** □ enjuto, flaco.

scram [skræm] *esp. sl.* **1.** largarse, dar un zarpazo; **2.** *int.* ¡lárgate!

scram·ble ['skræmbl] **1.**: ~ *up* trepar a, subir gateando a; ~ *for* disputarse a gritos, andar a la rebatiña por; ~*d eggs* huevos *m/pl.* revueltos; **2.** subida *f* (*up* a); arrebatiña *f*, pelea *f* (*for* por).

scrap [skræp] **1.** pedazo *m*, fragmento *m*; *sl.* riña *f*, bronca *f*; ~*s pl.* sobras *f/pl.*; desperdicios *m/pl.*; *not a* ~ ni pizca; *contp.* ~ *of paper* papel *m* mojado; **2.** *v/t.* desechar; ⚓ reducir a chatarra; *v/i. sl.* reñir; '~**·book** álbum *m* de recortes; '~ **deal·er** chatarrero *m*.

scrape [skreip] **1.** raspadura *f*; F aprieto *m*, lío *m*; **2.** *v/t.* raspar, raer; ♪ *co.* rascar; (*a.* ~ *against*) rozar; ~ *off* quitar raspando; ~ *together*, ~ *up* arañar; ~ *acquaintance with* lograr conocer; *v/i.*: F ~ *along* ir tirando; F ~ *through exam* aprobar justo; '**scrap·er** (*tool*) raspador *m*, rascador *m*; limpiabarros *m for shoes*.

scrap heap ['skræp hi:p] montón *m* de desechos.

scrap·ings ['skreipi:ŋz] raspaduras *f/pl.*; *fig.* hez *f*.

scrap i·ron ['skræp 'aiərn] chatarra *f*; hierro *m* viejo.

scrap·py ['skræpi] fragmentario; inconexo; *sl.* pendencioso; combativo.

scratch [skrætʃ] **1.** rasguño *m*, arañazo *m*; raya *f on stone etc.*; *sport*: línea *f* de partida; *be* (*or come*) *up to* ~ estar en buena condición; (*p.*) estar al nivel de las circunstancias; *start from* ~ empezar sin nada, empezar desde el principio; **2.** *competitor* sin ventaja; *team etc.* improvisado, reunido de prisa; **3.** *v/t.* rasguñar; rascar; *stone* rayar; *earth* escarbar; *sport etc.*: borrar, retirar; ~ *out* borrar, raspar; *v/i.* rasguñar; rascarse; (*pen*) raspear; (*chicken*) escarbar; *sport*: retirarse; '**scratch·y** *pen* que raspea; *tone* áspero.

scrawl [skrɔ:l] **1.** garrapatear; **2.** garrapatos *m/pl.*

scraw·ny ['skrɔ:ni] F descarnado; huesudo, flaco.

scream [skri:m] **1.** chillido *m*, grito *m*; F *he's a* ~ es un chistoso; **2.** chillar, gritar (*a.* ~ *out*); *abuse etc.* vociferar.

scree [skri:] *ladera de montaña cubierta de piedras movedizas.*

screech [skri:tʃ] *v. scream*; '~**·owl** lechuza *f* común.

screed [skri:d] escrito *m* largo y aburrido.

screen [skri:n] **1.** (*cinema etc.*) pantalla *f*; (*folding*) biombo *m*; (*sieve*) tamiz *m*; ⚔ cortina *f*; *phot.* retícula *f*; *the* ~ la pantalla; ~ *advertising* publicidad *f* cinematográfica; *phot. focusing* ~ placa *f* esmerilada; ~ *play* cinedrama *m*; **2.** (*hide*) ocultar; (*protect*) proteger, abrigar; (*sift*) tamizar; *film* proyectar; *suspects* investigar.

screw [skru:] **1.** tornillo *m*; (*thread*) rosca *f*; ⚓, ✈ hélice *f*; *sl.* sueldo *m*; F *he has a* ~ *loose* le falta un tornillo; F *put the* ~(*s*) *on* apretar los tornillos a; **2.** atornillar; *sl.* traicionar; engañar; chingar; ~ *down* fijar con tornillos; ~ *up sl.* echar a perder, desordenar; *paper, face* arrugar; ~ *up one's courage* cobrar ánimo; '~**·ball** *sl.* estrafalario, excéntrico *adj. a. su. m*; '~**·driv·er** destornillador *m*; '~ **jack** gato *m* de tornillo; '~ **pro'pel·ler** hélice *f*; '**screw·y** *sl.* chiflado.

scrib·ble ['skribl] **1.** garrapatos *m/pl.*; **2.** garrapatear; ~ *over* emborronar; '**scrib·bler** autorzuelo *m*.

scribe [skraib] † *or co.* escriba *m*; amanuense *m/f*; *contp.* escritorzuelo *m*.

scrim·mage ['skrimidʒ] arrebatiña *f*, pelea *f*.

scrimp [skrimp] **1.** escatimar; **2.** (*a.* '**scrimp·y**) escatimoso.

scrip [skrip] vale *m*, abonaré *m*.

script [skript] escritura *f*, letra *f* (cursiva); manuscrito *m*; *film*: guión *m*; ~ *writer* guionista *m/f*.

Scrip·tur·al ['skriptʃərəl] escrituario; bíblico; **Scrip·ture** ['~tʃər] Sagrada Escritura *f*; (*lesson*) Historia *f* Sagrada.

scrof·u·la ['skrɔfjulə] escrófula *f*; '**scrof·u·lous** □ escrofuloso.

scroll [skroul] rollo *m* de pergamino *etc.*; ⚠ voluta *f*.

scro·tum ['skroutəm] escroto *m*.

scrounge [skraundʒ] *sl.* **1.** gorrón *m* (-a *f*); sujeto *m* vil; **2.** *v/i.* ir de gorra, gorronear, sablear; *v/t.* sacar por medio de gorronería.

scrub[1] [skrʌb] ⚘ maleza *f*, matas *f/pl.*, monte *m* bajo.

scrub[2] [~] **1.** fregar, (r)estregar; **2.** fregado *m* (*a.* '**scrub·bing**); jugador *m* no adiestrado.

scrub brush [ˈskrʌbrʌʃ] bruza *f*, estregadera *f*.
scrub·by [ˈskrʌbi] achaparrado, enano.
scrub wom·an [ˈskrʌb wumən] fregona *f*.
scruff of the neck [ˈskrʌfəvðəˈnek] pescuezo *m*; ˈ**scruf·fy** F sucio, desaliñado, piojoso.
scrump·tious [ˈskrʌmpʃəs] *sl.* magnífico; estupendo; de rechupete.
scrunch [skrʌntʃ] ronzar.
scrup·le [ˈskru:pl] **1.** escrúpulo *m* (*a. pharm.* = *20 granos* = *1,296 gramos*); *make no ~ to* no vacilar en; **2.** escrupulizar, vacilar (*to* en); **scru·pu·lous** [ˈ~julәs] □ escrupuloso (*about* en cuanto a); ˈ**scru·pu·lous·ness** escrupulosidad *f*.
scru·ti·nize [ˈskru:tinaiz] escudriñar; examinar; *votes* escrutar; ˈ**scru·ti·ny** escrutinio *m*; examen *m*.
scud [skʌd] correr (llevado por el viento), deslizarse rápidamente.
scuff [skʌf] **1.** rascadura *f*; **2.** rascar; desgastar.
scuf·fle [ˈskʌfl] **1.** refriega *f*, riña *f*; **2.** pelear(se).
scull [skʌl] **1.** remo *m* ligero; espadilla *f*; **2.** remar (con remo ligero); cinglar.
scul·ler·y [ˈskʌləri] trascocina *f*, fregadero *m*, office *m*; *~ maid* fregona *f*.
sculp·tor [ˈskʌlptər] escultor *m*.
sculp·tur·al [ˈskʌlptʃərəl] □ escultural; **sculp·ture** [ˈskʌlptʃər] **1.** escultura *f*; **2.** esculpir; ˈ**sculp·tur·ing** escultura *f*.
scum [skʌm] espuma *f*; *metall.* escoria *f*; verdín *m on pond*; *fig.* heces *f*/*pl.*; *fig.* canalla *f*; sujeto *m* ruin.
scup·per [ˈskʌpər] imbornal *m*.
scurf [skə:rf] caspa *f*; ˈ**scurf·y** casposo.
scur·ril·i·ty [skʌˈriliti] grosería *f*, procacidad *f*; ˈ**scur·ril·ous** □ grosero, procaz; difamatorio.
scur·ry [ˈskʌri] **1.** escabullirse; **2.** carrera *f* precipitada.
scur·vy[1] [ˈskə:rvi] ⚕ escorbuto *m*.
scur·vy[2] [~] □ vil, despreciable.
scut [skʌt] rabito *m*.
scutch·eon [ˈskʌtʃn] *v. escutcheon*.
scut·tle[1] [ˈskʌtl] (*coal*) cubo *m*.
scut·tle[2] [~] ⚓ **1.** escotilla *f*; **2.** barrenar, dar barreno a.
scut·tle[3] [~] **1.** fuga *f* (*or* retirada *f*) precipitada; **2.** escabullirse, echar a correr.
scythe [saið] **1.** guadaña *f*; **2.** guadañar.
sea [si:] mar *m or f*; océano *m*; (*waves*) marejada *f*; *at ~* en el mar; *fig.* (*all*) *at ~* despistado, perplejo; *by ~* por mar; *go to ~* hacerse marinero; *put to ~* hacerse a la mar; *sl. half ~s over* ajumado; ˈ**~·board** litoral *m*; ˈ**~·dog** lobo *m* de mar; (*seal*) foca *f*; ˈ**~·far·ing** marinero; **~ food** pescado *m*; (*a. ~s pl.*) mariscos *m*/*pl.*; ˈ**~·go·ing** de alta mar; ˈ**~ green** verdemar; ˈ**~·gull** gaviota *f*; ˈ**~ horse** caballito *m* de mar.
seal[1] [si:l] *zo.* foca *f*.
seal[2] [~] **1.** sello *m*; *great ~* sello *m* real; **2.** sellar; cerrar; lacrar *with wax*; *fig.* decidir; confirmar; *~ off* obturar; *~ up* cerrar; ⊕ precintar; *~* (*with lead*) emplomar.
sea legs [ˈsi:legz] pie *m* marino; *get one's ~* acostumbrarse a la vida de a bordo.
sea lev·el [ˈsi:levl] nivel *m* del mar.
seal·ing [ˈsi:liŋ] caza *f* de la foca.
seal·ing wax [ˈsi:liŋwæks] lacre *m*.
sea lion [ˈsi:laiən] león *m* marino.
seal·skin [ˈsi:lskin] piel *f* de foca.
seam [si:m] **1.** *sew* costura *f*; ⊕ juntura *f*; *geol.* filón *m*, veta *f*; *burst at the ~s* descoserse; **2.** coser.
sea·man [ˈsi:mən] marinero *m*; ˈ**sea·man·ship** marina *f*, náutica *f*.
seam·less [ˈsi:mlis] sin costura, inconsútil.
seam·stress [ˈsi:mstris] costurera *f*.
seam·y [ˈsi:mi] sórdido; vil; burdo; *~ side fig.* el revés de la medalla.
sé·ance [ˈseiɑ̃:ns] sesión *f* de espiritismo.
sea...: ˈ**~·plane** hidroavión *m*; ˈ**~·port** puerto *m* de mar; ˈ**~ po·wer** potencia *f* naval.
sear [sir] chamuscar; (*wind*) abrasar; *fig.* marchitar; ⚕ cauterizar; *~ing pain* dolor *m* punzante.
search [sə:rtʃ] **1.** busca *f*, buscada *f*, búsqueda *f* (*for* de); registro *m of house etc.*; ⚖ pesquisa *f*; *in ~ of* en busca de; **2.** buscar (*a. ~ for*); *place* explorar, registrar; *conscience* examinar; ⚕ tentar; *~ out* descubrir buscando; *~ into* investigar; F *~ me!* ¡qué sé yo!; ˈ**search·er** buscador (-a *f*) *m*; ˈ**search·ing** □ *look* penetrante; *question* agudo; ˈ**search·light** reflector *m*; ˈ**search war·rant** mandamiento *m* judicial.

sea...: **~·scape** ['si:skeip] marina *f*; '**~-'ser·pent** serpiente *f* de mar; '**~·shore** playa *f*; orilla *f* del mar; '**~·sick** mareado; *be ~* marearse; '**~·sick·ness** mareo *m*; '**~'side** playa *f* (*a. ~ place, ~ resort*); orilla *f* del mar; *go to the ~* ir a una playa (a veranear).

sea·son ['si:zn] **1.** estación *f of year*; (*indefinite*) época *f*; *social, sport*: temporada *f*; (*opportune time*) sazón *f*; *at this ~* en esta época (del año); *in (good or due) ~* a su tiempo; (*fruit*) en sazón; *out of ~* fuera de sazón; *at the height of the ~* en plena temporada; *with the compliments of the ~* deseándole felices Pascuas *etc.*; *close ~* veda *f*; **2.** sazonar, condimentar; *wood* curar; *fig.* templar; *fig.* acostumbrar (*to* a); '**sea·son·a·ble** □ propio de la estación; oportuno; **sea·son·al** ['si:znl] □ estacional; según la estación; '**sea·son·ing** condimento *m*; aderezo *m*; '**sea·son 'tick·et** abono *m* (de temporada); *~ holder* abonado *m*.

seat [si:t] **1.** asiento *m*, silla *f*; *thea.* localidad *f*; *parl.* escaño *m*; ✈ *etc.* plaza *f*; residencia *f*; sede *f of government*; fondillos *m/pl. of trousers*; *~ of war* teatro *m* de guerra; *v. country*; *take a back ~* dejar de figurar, quedar humillado; **2.** (a)sentar; establecer, fijar; *chair* poner asiento a; (*hall*) tener asientos para; *valve* ajustar; *~ o.s.* sentarse; *be ~ed* estar sentado; '**~ belt** cinturón *m* de asiento (*or* de seguridad); '**seat·er** *mot.*, ✈ de ... plaza(s); '**seat·ing ca'pac·i·ty** número *m* de asientos.

sea-ur·chin ['si:'ə:rtʃin] erizo *m* de mar; '**sea 'wall** dique *m* (marítimo); **sea·ward** ['~wərd] **1.** *adj.* del lado del mar; **2.** *adv.* (*a.* **sea·wards** ['~z]) hacia el mar.

sea...: '**~·weed** alga *f* (marina); '**~-wor·thy** marinero, en condiciones de hacerse a la mar.

se·cant ['si:kənt] secante *adj. a. su. f.*

sec·a·teurs [sekə'tə:rz] (*a pair of* una) podadera *f*.

se·cede [si'si:d] separarse; **se'ced·er** separatista *m*.

se·ces·sion [si'seʃn] secesión *f*; **se'ces·sion·ist** secesionista *m*.

se·clu·ded [si'klu:did] retirado, apartado; **se'clu·sion** [~ʒn] recogimiento *m*, retiro *m*.

sec·ond ['sekənd] **1.** □ segundo; *be ~ to none* no irle en zaga a nadie; *on ~ thoughts* después de pensarlo bien; *v. fiddle*; *~ sight* doble vista *f*; **2.** segundo *m*; *duel*: padrino *m*; *boxing*: segundante *m*; ♪ segunda *f*; ⚕ *~s pl.* artículos *m/pl.* de segunda calidad; **3.** apoyar, secundar; *p.* [si'kɔnd] trasladar temporalmente; '**sec·ond·ar·y** □ secundario (*a. school*); '**sec·ond-'best** **1.** expediente *m*, sustituto *m*; **2.** (el) mejor después del primero; F *come off ~* quedarse en segundo lugar; '**sec·ond·er** el (la) que secunda una moción; '**sec·ond-'hand** **1.** de segunda mano, de lance; *~ bookseller* librero *m* de viejo; *~ bookshop* librería *f* de viejo; **2.** segundero *m of watch*; '**sec·ond·ly** en segundo lugar; '**sec·ond-'rate** de segunda categoría; de calidad inferior.

se·cre·cy ['si:krisi] secreto *m*; discreción *f*; **se·cret** ['~krit] **1.** □ secreto; oculto; clandestino; **2.** secreto *m*; *in ~* en secreto; *be in the ~* estar en el secreto.

sec·re·tar·i·al [sekri'teriəl] de secretario; *~ course* curso *m* de secretaria;

sec·re·tar·i·at(**e**) ['~ət] secretaría *f*.

sec·re·tar·y ['sekrətəri] secretario (a *f*) *m*; ♀ *of State* Ministro *m*; Ministro *m* de Asuntos Exteriores; '**sec·re·tar·y·ship** secretaría *f*.

se·crete [si'kri:t] esconder; *physiol.* secretar; **se'cre·tion** *physiol.* secreción *f*; **se'cre·tive** □ callado, reservado; sigiloso; *be ~ about* hacer secreto de.

sect [sekt] secta *f*; **sec·tar·i·an** [~'teriən] sectario *adj. a. su. m* (a *f*).

sec·tion ['sekʃn] *mst* sección *f*; región *f of country*; barrio *m of city*; tramo *m of road etc.*; sector *m of opinion*; '**sec·tion·al** □ seccional; ⊕ fabricado en secciones; regional, local; '**sec·tion mark** párrafo *m*.

sec·tor ['sektər] sector *m*.

sec·u·lar ['sekjulər] □ secular; seglar; '**sec·u·lar·i'za·tion** secularización *f*; '**sec·u·lar·ize** secularizar.

se·cure [si'kjur] **1.** □ seguro; firme, fijo; a salvo; *~ against, ~ from* asegurado contra; **2.** asegurar (*against, from* contra); (*obtain*) conseguir, obtener.

se·cu·ri·ty [si'kjuriti] seguridad *f*; protección *f*; ✝ fianza *f on loan*, prenda *f*; (*p.*) fiador *m*; *stand* ~ *for* salir fiador de; *fig.* salir por; **se'cu·ri·ties** *pl.* acciones *f/pl.*; valores *m/pl.*, obligaciones *f/pl.*
se·dan [si'dæn] silla *f* de manos (*a.* ~ *chair*); *mot.* sedan *m.*
se·date [si'deit] **1.** □ sosegado, sentado, grave; **2.** ⚕ dar sedante *m*; **se'date·ness** compostura *f*, gravedad *f.*
sed·a·tive ['sedətiv] sedante *adj. a. su. m*; calmante *adj. a. su. m.*
sed·en·tar·y ['sedntəri] □ sedentario.
sedge [sedʒ] juncia *f.*
sed·i·ment ['sedimənt] sedimento *m* (*a. geol.*); poso *m*; **sed·i·men·ta·ry** [~'mentəri] sedimentario (*a. geol.*).
se·di·tion [si'diʃn] sedición *f.*
se·di·tious [si'diʃəs] □ sedicioso.
se·duce [si'dju:s] seducir; **se'duc·er** seductor *m*; **se·duc·tion** [~'dʌkʃn] seducción *f*; **se'duc·tive** □ seductor; seductivo.
sed·u·lous ['sedjuləs] □ diligente, asiduo.
see¹ [si:] [*irr.*] *v/i. a. v/t.* ver; observar; percibir; *fig.* comprender; (*visit*) visitar; (*receive*) recibir; (*vide*) véase; *I* ~ lo veo; ¡ya comprendo!; ~ *for yourself* véalo Vd.; *let's* ~ a ver; *let me* ~ vamos a ver; ~ *about a th.* atender a; encargarse de; ~ *off* despedir(se de); ~ *out* acompañar a la puerta; ~ *through a p.* calarle a uno; ~ *a p. through* ayudarle a uno hasta el fin; ~ *a th. through* llevar algo a cabo; ~ *to* atender a; ~ (*to it*) *that* hacer que, cuidar de que; ~ *home* acompañar a casa.
see² [~] sede *f*; *Holy* ♀ Santa Sede *f.*
seed [si:d] **1.** semilla *f*, simiente *f*; *fig.* germen *m*; ~ *potato* patata *f* de siembra; *go* (*or run*) *to* ~ granar, dar en grana; *fig.* echarse a perder; **2.** *v/t. land* sembrar; *sport*: seleccionar; *v/i.* dejar caer semillas; '~**bed** (*or* '~ **plot**) semillero *m*; **seed·i·ness** ['~inis] aspecto *m* raído; apariencia *f* decaído; '**seed·ling** planta *f* de semillero; **seeds·man** ['~zmən] vendedor *m* de semillas; '**seed·y** F ⚕ canijo, ojeroso; ⚕ achacoso; *appearance* raído; decaído; andrajoso; *place* asqueroso; decadente.
see·ing ['si:iŋ] **1.** vista *f*, visión *f*; *worth* ~ que vale la pena de verse; **2.** *cj.* ~ *that* visto que.
seek [si:k] [*irr.*] (*a.* ~ *after*, ~ *for*) buscar; *post* pretender, solicitar; *honor* ambicionar; (*search*) recorrer buscando; ~ *to* intentar, tratar de; '**seek·er** buscador (-a *f*) *m.*
seem [si:m] parecer; '**seem·ing 1.** □ aparente; **2.** apariencia *f*; '**seem·li·ness** decoro *m*; '**seem·ly** decoroso, decente, correcto.
seen [si:n] *p.p. of* see¹.
seep [si:p] rezumarse, filtrar(se); '**seep·age** filtración *f.*
seer ['si:ər] vidente *m/f*, profeta *m.*
see·saw ['si:'sɔ:] **1.** balancín *m*; columpio *m*; *fig.* vaivén *m*; **2.** columpiarse; *fig.* vacilar.
seethe [si:ð] hervir.
seg·ment ['segmənt] segmento *m.*
seg·re·gate ['segrigeit] segregar; **seg·re'ga·tion** segregación *f*; '~**·ist** segregacionista *adj. a. su. m/f.*
seine [sein] jábega *f.*
seis·mo·graph ['saizməgræf] sismógrafo *m.*
seize [si:z] *v/t.* agarrar, asir, coger; apoderarse de; ⚖ *p.* prender; *property* embargar; secuestrar; *opportunity* aprovechar; *v/i.* ⊕ (*a.* ~ *up*) (*valve, piston*) agarrotarse; (*motor*) calarse; ~ (*up*)*on fig.* fijarse en; **sei·zure** ['~ʒər] asimiento *m*; captura *f*; ⚖ prendimiento *m*; embargo *m*; ⚕ ataque *m.*
sel·dom ['seldəm] rara vez, raramente.
se·lect [si'lekt] **1.** escoger, elegir; *sport*: seleccionar; **2.** selecto, escogido; **se'lec·tion** selección *f* (*a.* ⚘, *zo.*); elección *f*; ♪ selecciones *f/pl.*; ✝ surtido *m*; **se'lec·tive** □ selectivo (*a. radio*); **se·lec·tiv·i·ty** [~'tiviti] *radio*: selectividad *f*; **se'lect·man** concejal *m*; **se'lec·tor** *radio*: selector *m*; *sport*: seleccionador *m.*
self [self] **1.** *pron.* se *etc.*; (*after prps.*) sí mismo *etc.*: ✝ *or* F = *myself etc.*; **2.** *adj. esp.* ⚘ unicolor; **3.** *su.* (*pl.* **selves** [selvz]) uno mismo; *the* ~ el yo; (*all*) *by one's* ~ (*unaided*) sin ayuda de nadie; (*alone*) completamente a solas; ~**-a'base·ment** rebajamiento *m* de sí mismo; ~**-'act·ing** automático; '~**-ad'ver·tise·ment** autobombo *m*; '~**-as'sur·ance** confianza *f* en sí mismo; '~**-'cen·tered** egocéntrico; '~**-'com-**

mand dominio *m* sobre sí mismo; ˈ~-conˈceit presunción *f*, arrogancia *f*; ˈ~-ˈcon·fi·dence confianza *f* en sí mismo; ˈ~-ˈcon·scious □ cohibido, tímido; ~-con·tained [ˈ~kənˈteind] independiente; reservado; *flat* completo en sí mismo; ˈ~-conˈtrol autodominio *m*, dominio *m* sobre sí mismo; ˈ~-deˈfense (*in* en) defensa *f* propia; ˈ~-deˈni·al abnegación *f*; ˈ~-de·ter·miˈna·tion autodeterminación *f*; ˈ~-ˈed·u·cat·ed autodidacto; ˈ~efˈfac·ing modesto, humilde; ˈ~-esˈteem amor *m* propio; ˈ~-ˈevi·dent patente, palmario; ˈ~-ˈgov·ern·ment autogobierno *m*, autonomía *f*; ˈ~-ˈfill·ing de relleno automático; ˈ~-ˈin·ter·est egoísmo *m*; ˈself·ish □ egoísta; ˈself·ish·ness egoísmo *m*.

self...: ˈ~-ˈmade man hijo *m* de sus propias obras; ˈ~-ˈpor·trait autorretrato *m*; ˈ~-posˈsessed sereno, dueño de sí mismo; ˈ~-pre·serˈva·tion propia conservación *f*; ˈ~-proˈpelled autopropulsado; automotriz (*f only*); ˈ~-reˈli·ance confianza *f* en sí mismo; ˈ~-reˈli·ant confiado en sí mismo; ˈ~-reˈspect amor *m* propio, dignidad *f*; ˈ~-ˈright·eous □ santurrón; ˈ~·same *lit.* mismísimo, mismo; ˈ~-ˈsat·is·fied pagado de sí mismo; ˈ~-seal·ing autopegado; ˈ~-ˈseek·ing egoísta; ˈ~-ˈserv·ice restau·rant autoservicio *m*; ˈ~-ˈstart·er *mot.* arranque *m* automático; ˈ~-ˈstyled supuesto, sediciente; ˈ~-sufˈfi·cien·cy independencia *f*; confianza *f* en sí mismo; ˈ~-ˈwilled terco, obstinado; ˈ~-wind·ing de cuerda automática.

sell [sel] **1.** [*irr.*] *v/t.* vender (*a. fig.*); F *idea* hacer aceptar; ✝ ~ *off* liquidar; ~ *out* saldar; *be sold out* estar agotado; *sl. be sold on* estar cautivado por; *v/i.* venderse, estar de venta; F ser aceptable; ~ *out*, ~ *up* venderlo todo, realizar; **2.** F decepción *f*, estafa *f*; ˈsell·er vendedor (-a *f*) *m*; ✝ *good* ~ artículo *m* que se vende bien; *best* ~ éxito *m* de librería; ˈsell·ing price precio *m* de venta.

selt·zer [ˈseltsər] (*or* ~ *water*) agua *f* (de) Seltz.

sel·vage, sel·vedge [ˈselvidʒ] borde *m*, orillo *m*.

se·man·tics [siˈmæntiks] semántica *f*.

sem·a·phore [ˈseməfɔːr] **1.** semáforo *m*; **2.** comunicar por semáforo.

sem·blance [ˈsembləns] apariencia *f*; simulacro *m*.

se·mes·ter [səˈmestər] semestre *m*.

sem·i... [ˈsemi] semi...; medio...; ˈ~·breve semibreve *f*; ˈ~·cir·cle semicírculo *m*; ˈ~ˈco·lon punto *m* y coma; ˈ~·deˈtached semiseparado; ˈ~ˈfi·nal semifinal *f*.

sem·i·nal [ˈseminl] seminal.

sem·i·nar [ˈseminɑːr], **sem·i·nar·y** [ˈ~əri] seminario *m*.

sem·i·of·fi·cial [ˈsemiəˈfiʃl] □ semioficial.

sem·i·qua·ver [ˈsemikweivər] semicorchea *f*.

Sem·ite [ˈsiːmait] semita *m/f*; **Se·mit·ic** [siˈmitik] semítico.

sem·i·tone [ˈsemitoun] semitono *m*.

sem·i·vow·el [ˈsemiˈvauəl] semivocal *f*; **sem·i·week·ly** [ˈ~ˈwiːkli] bisemanal.

sem·o·li·na [seməˈliːnə] sémola *f*.

sem·pi·ter·nal [sempiˈtəːrnl] □ *lit.* sempiterno.

semp·stress [ˈsempstris] costurera *f*.

sen·ate [ˈsenit] senado *m*; *univ. approx.* claustro *m*.

sen·a·tor [ˈsenətər] senador *m*; **sen·a·to·ri·al** [~ˈtɔːriəl] □ senatorial.

send [send] [*irr.*] enviar, mandar, despachar; remitir; expedir; *ball* lanzar; *radio* emitir; *telegram* poner; (*with adj.*) hacer, volver; *v. pack* 2, *word* 1; ~ *away* despedir; despachar; ~ *back* devolver; ~ *down univ.* expulsar; ~ *for* enviar por; ~ *in p.* hacer entrar; *name etc.* presentar; ~ *off p.* despedir; expedir; ~ *on* hacer seguir, dar curso a; ~ *out smoke etc.* arrojar, despedir; *signal* emitir; *invitations* mandar; distribuir; ˈsend·er remitente *m/f*; ⚡ transmisor *m*; ˈsend-ˈoff despedida *f*; principio *m*.

se·nile [ˈsiːnail] senil; caduco; **se·nil·i·ty** [siˈniliti] vejez *f*; ⚕ debilidad *f* senil.

sen·ior [ˈsiːnjər] **1.** mayor (de edad); más antiguo *in post* (to que); (*after names*) padre; ✝ ~ *partner* socio *m* más antiguo; **2.** mayor *m/f*; decano *m in group*; *univ.* alumno *m* del último año; *he is my* ~ *by a year* tiene un año más que yo; **sen·ior·i·ty** [siːniˈɔriti] antigüedad *f*; prioridad *f*.

sen·sa·tion [senˈseiʃn] sensación *f*; **senˈsa·tion·al** □ sensacional;

sen'sa·tion·al·ism sensacionalismo *m*.
sense [sens] **1.** sentido *m*; sensación *f*; juicio *m*; opinión *f of meeting*; ~ *of humor* sentido *m* de humor; *common* (*or good*) ~ sentido *m* común; *be out of one's* ~*s* haber perdido el juicio; *bring one to his* ~*s* hacerle volver en sí; *make* ~ tener sentido; *talk* ~ hablar con juicio; *in a* ~ en cierto sentido; *in the full* ~ *of the word* en toda la extensión de la palabra; **2.** sentir, percibir; intuir.
sense·less ['senslis] □ sin sentido; necio; (*mad*) insensato; **'sense·less·ness** insensatez *f*.
sen·si·bil·i·ty [sensi'biliti] sensibilidad *f* (*to* a).
sen·si·ble ['sensəbl] □ (*reasonable*) sensato, cuerdo; (*feeling*) sensible; *be* ~ *of* estar consciente de, darse cuenta de; **'sen·si·ble·ness** sensatez *f*.
sen·si·tive ['sensitiv] □ sensitivo; sensible (*to* a); impresionable; (*touchy*) susceptible; *phot.* sensibilizado; **'sen·si·tive·ness, sen·si·tiv·i·ty** [~'tiviti] sensibilidad *f* (*to* a); susceptibilidad *f*.
sen·si·tize ['sensitaiz] sensibilizar.
sen·so·ri·al [sen'sɔːriəl], **sen·so·ry** ['~səri] sensorio.
sen·su·al ['senʃuəl] □ sensual; **'sen·su·al·ism** sensualismo *m*; **'sen·su·al·ist** sensualista *m/f*; **sen·su·al·i·ty** [~'æliti] sensualidad *f*.
sen·su·ous ['senʃuəs] □ sensual.
sent [sent] *pret. a. p.p. of send*.
sen·tence ['sentəns] **1.** ⚖ sentencia *f*, condena *f*; fallo *m*; *gr.* frase *f*; oración *f*; *serve one's* ~ cumplir su condena; **2.** sentenciar, condenar (*to* a).
sen·ten·tious [sen'tenʃəs] □ sentencioso; **sen'ten·tious·ness** estilo *m* sentencioso.
sen·tient ['senʃnt] sensitivo, que siente.
sen·ti·ment ['sentimənt] sentimiento *m*; *v.* ~*ality*; **sen·ti·men·tal** [~'mentl] □ sentimental; *b.s.* sensiblero; ~ *value* valor *m* sentimental; **sen·ti·men·tal·i·ty** [~'tæliti] sentimentalismo *m*; sensiblería *f*.
sen·ti·nel ['sentinl], **sen·try** ['sentri] centinela *m*.
sen·try box ['sentribɔks] garita *f* de centinela.
se·pal ['siːpəl] sépalo *m*.
sep·a·ra·ble ['sepərəbl] □ separable; **sep·a·rate 1.** ['seprit] □ separado; distinto; suelto; **2.** ['~əreit] separar(se) (*from* de); desprender(se); apartar(se); **sep·a'ra·tion** separación *f*; **sep·a·ra·tist** ['~ərətist] separatista *m/f*; **sep·a·ra·tor** ['~reitər] *all senses*: separador *m*.
se·phar·dic [sə'fɑːrdik] sefardí *adj. a. su. m/f*; sefardita *adj. a. su. m/f*; *approx.* judáico-español.
se·pi·a ['siːpjə] *ichth.* jibia *f*; *paint.* sepia *f*.
se·poy ['siːpɔi] cipayo *m*.
sep·sis ['sepsis] sepsis *f*.
Sep·tem·ber [sep'tembər] se(p)tiembre *m*.
sep·tic ['septik] séptico; ~ *tank* depósito *m* para la desintegración de aguas cloacales.
sep·tu·a·ge·nar·i·an ['septjuedʒi'neriən] septuagenario *adj. a. su. m* (a *f*).
se·pul·chral [si'pʌlkrəl] sepulcral (*a. fig.*); **sep·ul·cher, sep·ul·chre** ['sepəlkər] *lit.* **1.** sepulcro *m*; **2.** sepultar en sepulcro; **sep·ul·ture** ['sepəltʃər] *lit.* sepultura *f*.
se·quel ['siːkwəl] secuela *f*; continuación *f of story*; resultado *m* (*to act* de); *in the* ~ como consecuencia.
se·quence ['siːkwəns] (orden *m* de) sucesión *f*; serie *f*; *film*: secuencia *f*; *gr.* ~ *of tenses* sucesión *f* de tiempos; **'se·quent** consecutivo.
se·ques·ter [si'kwestər] secuestrar; ~ *o.s.* apartarse (*from* de); ~*ed spot* aislado, retirado.
se·ques·trate [si'kwestreit] ⚖ secuestrar; **se·ques·tra·tion** [siːkwes'treiʃn] secuestro *m*; **'se·ques·tra·tor** secuestrador *m*.
se·quin ['siːkwin] lentejuela *f*.
se·quoi·a [si'kwɔiə] secoya *f*.
se·ragl·io [se'ræliou] serallo *m*.
ser·aph ['serəf], *pl. a.* **ser·a·phim** ['~fim] serafín *m*; **se·raph·ic** [se'ræfik] □ seráfico.
Serb, Ser·bi·an [səːrb, '~jən] servio *adj. a. su. m* (a *f*).
sere [sir] seco, marchito.
ser·e·nade [seri'neid] **1.** serenata *f*; **2.** dar serenata a.
se·rene [si'riːn] □ sereno; *Your* ♀ *Highness* Su Serenidad; **se·ren·i·ty** [si'reniti] serenidad *f*.
serf [səːrf] siervo (a *f*) *m* (de la gleba);

ˈserf·dom servidumbre *f* (de la gleba).
serge [səːrdʒ] estameña *f*.
ser·geant [ˈsɑːrdʒnt] sargento *m*; ˈ~ ˈ**ma·jor** *approx.* sargento *m* mayor, brigada *m*.
se·ri·al [ˈsiriəl] **1.** □ consecutivo; en serie; *number* de serie; *story* por entregas; **2.** serial *m*, novela *f* por entregas.
se·ries [ˈsiriːz] *sg. a. pl. all senses*: serie *f*; ⚡ *connect or join in* ~ conectar en serie; ˈ**~-wound** arrollado en serie.
se·ri·ous [ˈsiriəs] □ serio; *news, condition* grave; *be* ~ *(p.)* tomar las cosas en serio; ˈ**se·ri·ous·ness** seriedad *f*; gravedad *f*.
ser·mon [ˈsəːrmən] sermón *m* (*a. iro.*); ˈ**ser·mon·ize** sermonizar.
se·rol·o·gy [siˈrɔlədʒi] serología *f*.
ser·pent [ˈsəːrpənt] serpiente *f*, sierpe *f*; **ser·pen·tine** [ˈ~ain] **1.** serpentino; **2.** *min.* serpentina *f*.
ser·rate [ˈserit], **ser·rat·ed** [seˈreitid] serrado; **serˈra·tion** endentadura *f*.
ser·ried [ˈserid] apretado, apiñado.
se·rum [ˈsirəm] suero *m*.
serv·ant [ˈsəːrvənt] criado (a *f*) *m*; sirviente (a *f*) *m*; servidor (-a *f*) *m*; ~s *pl.* servidumbre *f*; ~s' *hall* comedor *m* de servicio; *v. civil*.
serve [səːrv] **1.** *v/t. p.* servir (a); estar al servicio de; *food* servir (*a.* ~ *out*, ~ *up*); abastecer; ser útil a; *tennis*: sacar; ⚖ *writ* entregar (*on a p.* a una p.); *it* ~*s him right* bien merecido lo tiene; *v. sentence*; *v/i.* servir (*a.* ⚔) (*as, for* de); ~ *at table* servir a la mesa; **2.** *tennis*: saque *m*; ˈ**serv·er** *tennis*: saque *m/f*; pala *f for fish etc.*; *eccl.* acólito *m*.
serv·ice [ˈsəːrvis] **1.** servicio *m*; vajilla *f*, juego *m*, servicio *m of crockery*; *tennis*: saque *m*; ⚓ forro *m* de cable; ⚖ entrega *f*; (*a. divine* ~) oficio *m* divino; misa *f*; *at your* ~ servidor de Vd.; *be at a p.'s* ~ estar a la disposición de alguien; *be of* ~ servir, ayudar; ⚔ *see* ~ prestar servicio; ⚔ *active* ~ servicio *m* activo; *be on active* ~ estar de activo; *after-sales* ~ servicio *m* de atención; ⚔ *the* ~*s pl.* las fuerzas armadas; *v. civil*; **2.** ⊕ atender, mantener, reparar; ˈ**serv·ice·a·ble** □ servible; útil; duradero.
serv·ice...: ˈ~ **line** *tennis*: línea *f* de saque; ˈ**~·man** militar *m*; mecánico *m*; ~ **sta·tion** estación *f* de servicio; taller *m* de reparaciones.
ser·vi·ette [seːrviˈet] servilleta *f*; ~ *ring* servilletero *m*.
ser·vile [ˈsəːrvil] □ servil; **ser·vil·i·ty** [~ˈviliti] servilismo *m*.
ser·vi·tude [ˈsəːrvitjuːd] servidumbre *f*; *v. penal*.
ses·a·me [ˈsesəmi] ⚘ *a. fig.* sésamo *m*; *open* ~! ¡sésamo ábrete!
ses·qui·pe·da·li·an [ˈseskwipiˈdeiljən] sesquipedal (*a. fig.*).
ses·sion [ˈseʃn] sesión *f*; *univ.* curso *m*; *v. petty*; F reunión *f*; F entrevista *f*; *be in* ~ sesionar; ˈ**ses·sion·al** de una sesión.
set [set] **1.** [*irr.*] *v/t.* poner, colocar; situar; establecer; arreglar, preparar; *alarm clock* regular; ⚕ *bone* reducir; *dog* azuzar (*at, on* a que embista a); *example* dar; *hair* fijar, marcar; *jewel* engastar, montar; *price* fijar; *problem* poner; *sail* desplegar; *saw* triscar; *task* imponer, asignar; *teeth* apretar; *time* fijar; *trap* armar; *watch* poner en hora; *v. fashion, fire, foot, heart, liberty, music, sail, store*; ~ *going* poner en marcha; ~ *a p. laughing* hacer reír a una p.; ~ *against* indisponer con; ~ *o.s. against* oponerse resueltamente a; ~ *apart* separar, segregar; ~ *aside* poner aparte; reservar; *petition* desatender; ⚖ anular; ~ *at ease, at rest* tranquilizar; ~ *back* detener; entorpecer; poner obstáculos a; ~ *down* poner por escrito; depositar; *passenger* dejar (apearse); ~ *forth* exponer; ~ *off* (*explode*) hacer estallar; (*contrast*) hacer resaltar, poner de relieve (*against* contra); ~ *out* exponer; sacar y disponer; ~ *up* fundar; *house, shop* poner; establecer, instalar; *p.* erigir (*as* en); *cry* levantar; ⊕ armar, montar; ~ *up* (*in type*) componer; *be well* ~ *up for* estar bien provisto de; ~ *upon* acometer; *be* ~ *upon* estar resuelto a; **2.** *v/i.* (*sun*) ponerse; (*jelly, mortar*) cuajarse; (*gum etc.*) endurecerse; *hunt.* estar de muestra (*dog*); ~ *about ger.* ponerse a *inf.*; ~ *about th.* emprender; *p.* F aporrear; atacar; ~ *forth* salir, partir; ponerse en camino; ~ *in* comenzar, declararse; (*night*) cerrar; ~ *off* partir; ~ *on* atacar; ~ *out* partir, ponerse

en camino; ~ *out to inf.* ponerse a *inf.*; tener la intención de *inf.*; ~ *to* aplicarse (con vigor), empezar; ~ *up as* erigirse en, constituirse en, dárselas de; **3.** *adj. purpose* resuelto, determinado; *readiness* listo; inflexible *in belief*; (*rigid*) rígido; (*usual*) reglamentario; *price etc.* fijo, firme; *barometer* estable; ~ (*up*)*on* empeñado en; ~ *with* adornado de; ~ *phrase* frase *f* hecha; *paint. etc.* ~ *piece* grupo *m*; ~ *speech* discurso *m* preparado de antemano; **4.** *su.* juego *m*; serie *f*; servicio *m* (de mesa); tendencia *f of mind*; pandilla *f*, clase *f of people*; caída *f of dress*; *thea.* decorado *m*, decoración *f*; (*radio-*) (aparato *m* de) radio *f*; ⊕ tren *m of gears*; *tennis*: set *m*; ↙ planta *f* de transplantar; *jet* ~, *smart* ~ mundo *m* elegante.

set·back [ˈsetbæk] contratiempo *m*, revés *m*; △ retraqueo *m*; ˈ**set-ˈoff** adorno *m*; contraste *m*; ✝ *etc.* compensación *f*.

set·tee [seˈtiː] canapé *m*, sofá *m*.

set·ter [ˈsetər] el que pone *etc.* (*v.* set 1); *hunt.* perro *m* de muestra.

set·ting [ˈsetiŋ] puesta *f of sun*; engaste *m*, montadura *f of jewels*; ⊕ ajuste *m*; alrededores *m/pl. of place*; *fig.* marco *m*; ♪ versión *f*, arreglo *m*; *thea.* escena *f*, escenario *m*; ˈ~ **lo·tion** *hair*: fijador *m*; ˈ~-**up** establecimiento *m*; ⊕ ajuste *m*; composición *f of type*.

set·tle [ˈsetl] **1.** banco *m* (largo); **2.** *v/t.* colocar; fijar; establecer; arreglar; calmar, sosegar; *account* ajustar, liquidar (*a.* ~ *up*); *fig.* saldar cuentas con (*a.* ~ *with*); *date* fijar; *deal* firmar; *income* asignar (*on* a); *land* colonizar, poblar; F *p.* vencer, confundir; *people* establecer; *quarrel* componer; *question* decidir, resolver; *v/i.* (*freq.* ~ *down*) asentarse (*liquid, building*); (*a.* ~ *o.s.*) sentarse, reposarse; (*bird etc.*) posar(se); (*p.*) instalarse, establecerse *in house, in town*; (*a.* ~ *down*) ⚓ hundirse lentamente; (*weather*) serenarse; *fig.* normalizarse; ~ *down to work* ponerse a trabajar; ~ *on* fijar; escoger; ~ *up* ajustar cuentas (*with* con).

set·tle·ment [ˈsetlmənt] establecimiento *m*; ✝ ajuste *m*, pago *m*, liquidación *f of account*; ⚖ asignación *f* (*on* a); (*agreement*) convenio *m*; colonización *f of land*; (*village*) colonia *f*, caserío *m*, núcleo *m* rural.

set·tler [ˈsetlər] colono (a *f*) *m*; colonizador *m*; poblador *m*.

set·tling [ˈsetliŋ] arreglo *m of dispute*; asentamiento *m*; ✝ ajuste *m*; *v.* settle 2.

set...: ˈ~-ˈ**to** F disputa *f*; pelea *f*; ˈ~-ˈ**up** F tinglado *m*, sistema *m*, organización *f*; *sl.* invitación *f* a beber.

sev·en [ˈsevn] siete (*a. su. m*); **sev·en·teen** [ˈ~ˈtiːn] diecisiete; **sev·enˈteenth** [~θ] decimoséptimo; **sev·enth** [ˈ~θ] □ séptimo (*a. su. m*); **sev·en·ti·eth** [ˈ~tiiθ] septuagésimo; ˈ**sev·en·ty** setenta.

sev·er [ˈsevər] separar, cortar; *relations* romper.

sev·er·al [ˈsevərəl] □ diversos, varios; respectivos; distintos; ⚖ *joint and* ~ solidario; ˈ**sev·er·al·ly** respectivamente; separadamente.

sev·er·ance [ˈsevərəns] separación *f*; ruptura *f of relations*.

se·vere [siˈvir] □ severo; *weather, winter, critic* riguroso; *storm* violento; *loss, wound* grave; *pain* intenso; *style* adusto; **se·ver·i·ty** [~ˈveriti] severidad *f*; rigor *m etc.*

Se·vil·lian [seˈviljən] sevillano *adj. a. su. m* (a *f*).

sew [sou] [*irr.*] coser; ~ *up* zurcir; F acabar, concluir.

sew·age [ˈsuːidʒ] aguas *f/pl.* residuales; ~ *farm* estación *f* depuradora.

sew·er [ˈsuːər] albañal *m*, alcantarilla *f*; ˈ**sew·er·age** alcantarillado *m*.

sew·ing [ˈsouiŋ] **1.** (labor *m* de) costura *f*; **2.** ... de coser; ˈ~ **ma·chine** máquina *f* de coser.

sewn [soun] *p.p. of sew*.

sex [seks] **1.** sexo *m*; *attr.* sexual; ~ *appeal* atracción *f* sexual, gancho *m*; **2.** *chicks etc.* sexar.

sex·a·ge·nar·i·an [seksədʒiˈneriən] sexagenario *adj. a. su. m* (a *f*); **sex·en·ni·al** [sekˈsenjəl] □ sexenal; **sex·tant** [ˈsekstənt] sextante *m*.

sex·ton [ˈsekstən] sacristán *m*; sepulturero *m*.

sex·tu·ple [ˈsekstjupl] séxtuplo.

sex·u·al [ˈsekʃuəl] □ sexual; ~ *desire* instinto *m* sexual; *v. intercourse*; **sex·u·al·i·ty** [~ˈæliti] sexualidad *f*; ˈ**sex·y** erótico; lozano; F provocativo.

sh [ʃ]: ~! ¡chitón!, ¡chis!

shab·bi·ness [ˈʃæbinis] lo raído *etc.*; ˈ**shab·by** □ *p.* pobremente vestido; *dress* raído, gastado; *place* en mal estado; *treatment* ruin, vil.
shack [ʃæk] casucha *f*; chabola *f*, choza *f*.
shack·le [ˈʃækl] **1.** grillete *m*, grillos *m/pl.* (*a. fig.*); *fig.* (*mst* ~*s pl.*) trabas *f/pl.*; ⊕, ⚓ eslabón *m*; **2.** encadenar; trabar; *fig.* poner trabas a.
shade [ʃeid] **1.** sombra *f*; matiz *m of color, meaning, opinion*; tonalidad *f of color*; (*fraction*) poquito *m*; (*lamp-*) pantalla *f*; (*eye-*) visera *f*; *in the* ~ *of* a la sombra de; F *put in the* ~ oscurecer; ~*s sl.* gafas *f/pl.* de sol; **2.** dar sombra a; (*protect*) resguardar; *paint.* sombrear; ~ *away*, ~ *off* cambiar poco a poco (*into* hasta hacerse), transformarse gradualmente (*into* en).
shad·i·ness [ˈʃeidinis] lo umbroso *etc.* (*v. shady*); ˈ**shad·ing** sombreado *m for eyes*; degradación *f of colors*.
shad·ow [ˈʃædou] **1.** *all senses*: sombra *f*; *the* ~*s* las tinieblas; ~ *boxing* boxeo *m* (*fig.* disputa *f*) con un adversario imaginario; **2.** sombrear; (*follow*) seguir y vigilar; (*mst* ~ *forth*) anunciar; indicar vagamente; ˈ**shad·ow·y** umbroso, sombroso; *fig.* vago, indefinido.
shad·y [ˈʃeidi] sombreado, umbroso; F turbio, sospechoso; F *on the* ~ *side of 40* más allá de 40 (años).
shaft [ʃæft] (*arrow*) flecha *f*, dardo *m*; (*handle*) mango *m*; vara *f of carriage*; agudeza *f of wit*; rayo *m of light*; ⊕ eje *m*; árbol *m*; ⚒ pozo *m*.
shag [ʃæg] † felpa *f*; tabaco *m* picado.
shag·gy [ˈʃægi] velludo, peludo; *sl.* ~ *dog story* chiste *m* goma.
sha·green [ʃəˈgriːn] chagrén *m*, zapa *f*.
Shah [ʃɑː] cha(h) *m*.
shake [ʃeik] **1.** [*irr.*] *v/t.* sacudir (*a.* ~ *off*); agitar; *head* mover, menear; *building* hacer retemblar; (*perturb*) perturbar; F sorprender; *hand* estrechar; ~ (*on it*)! ¡chócala!; ~ *hands* estrecharse la mano; ~ *down* bajar sacudiendo; *sl.* extorsionar; ~ *off fig.* zafarse de, dar esquinazo a; librarse de; ~ *up* remover, agitar; *fig.* descomponer; F reorganizar; *v/i.* agitarse; (*earth*) (re)temblar (*at, with* de); bambolear; ♪ trinar; ~ *with laughter* desternillarse de risa; **2.** sacudida *f*, sacudimiento *m*; meneo *m*, movimiento *m of head*; vibración *f of vehicle*; ♪ trino *m*; F instante *m*; F batido *m* (de leche *etc.*); F *no great* ~*s* poco extraordinario; *in a brace of* ~*s* en un periquete; ˈ~ˈ**down** *sl.* exacción *f* de dinero; ~ *cruise* ⚓ viaje *m* de pruebas; ˈ**shak·en** *p.p. of shake* 1; ˈ**shak·er** (*cocktail*) coctelera *f*.
shake-up [ˈʃeikˈʌp] F conmoción *f*; reorganización *f*.
shak·i·ness [ˈʃeikinis] falta *f* de solidez; ˈ**shak·y** □ tembloroso; *fig.* poco sólido; débil, debilitado.
shale [ʃeil] esquisto *m*; ~ *oil* aceite *m* esquistoso.
shall [ʃæl] [*irr.*] *v/aux.* que forma el [*futuro etc.*]
shal·lot [ʃəˈlɔt] chalote *m*.
shal·low [ˈʃælou] **1.** poco profundo; *fig.* somero, superficial; *p.* frívolo; **2.** ~*s pl.* bajío *m*; **3.** hacer(se) menos profundo; ˈ**shal·low·ness** poca profundidad *f*; *fig.* superficialidad *f*.
sham [ʃæm] **1.** falso, fingido, postizo; ~ *fight* simulacro *m* de combate; **2.** impostura *f*, engaño *m*; (*p.*) impostor *m*, farsante *m*; **3.** *v/i. a. v/t.* fingir(se), simular.
sham·bles [ˈʃæmblz] *pl. or sg.* lío *m*; desorden *m*; (lugar *m* de gran) matanza *f*; ruina *f*, escombrera *f*.
shame [ʃeim] **1.** vergüenza *f*; oprobio *m*, deshonra *f*; (*for*) ~!, ~ *on you!* ¡qué vergüenza!; *what a* ~! ¡qué lástima!; *put to* ~ avergonzar; *fig.* superar con mucho; **2.** avergonzar.
shame·faced [ˈʃeimfeist] □ vergonzoso, avergonzado; ˈ**shame·faced·ness** vergüenza *f*.
shame·ful [ˈʃeimful] □ vergonzoso; ignominioso; ˈ**shame·ful·ness** ignominia *f*.
shame·less [ˈʃeimlis] □ descarado, desvergonzado; ˈ**shame·less·ness** descaro *m*, desvergüenza *f*.
sham·my [ˈʃæmi] gamuza *f*.
sham·poo [ʃæmˈpuː] **1.** lavar la cabeza (*v/t.* a); **2.** champú *m*.
sham·rock [ˈʃæmrɔk] trébol *m* (*emblema nacional irlandés*).
shang·hai [ʃæŋˈhai] ⚓ *sl.* embarcar emborrachando.
shank [ʃæŋk] zanca *f of bird*; caña *f of leg*; ⚘ tallo *m*; ⊕ mango *m*; *ride* ♀'*s mare* ir en coche de San Fernando; andar a pie.

shan't [ʃænt, ʃɑːnt] = *shall not*.
shan·ty [ˈʃænti] choza *f*, cabaña *f*; ♪ saloma *f*.
shape [ʃeip] **1.** forma *f*; figura *f*; línea *f*; contorno *m*; configuración *f*; *take* ~ tomar forma; irse perfilando; *in bad* ~ ⚕ muy enfermo; arruinado; **2.** formar(se); modelar; tallar; *fig. course etc.* determinar; dirigir; **shaped** [~t] de ... forma; en forma de ...; ˈ**shape·less** □ informe; ˈ**shape·li·ness** buen talle *m*; elegancia *f*; ˈ**shape·ly** bien formado, bien tallado; (bien) proporcionado, elegante; de buen talle.
share [ʃer] **1.** parte *f*, porción *f*; participación *f*; interés *m*; cuota *f*, contribución *f*; ✝ acción *f*; *have a* ~ *in* participar en; *go* ~*s* ir a escote; ~ *and* ~ *alike* por partes iguales; **2.** *v/t.* (com)partir, dividir; *fig.* poseer en común; ~ *out* repartir; *v/i.*: ~ *in* tener parte en, participar en (*fig.* de); ˈ~**·crop·per** aparcero *m*; ˈ~**·hold·er** accionista *m/f*.
shark [ʃɑːrk] *ichth.* tiburón *m*; F estafador *m*; F caimán *m*; *sl.* perito *m*, as *m*.
sharp [ʃɑːrp] **1.** □ agudo; puntiagudo; *appearance* elegante; *bend* fuerte; *edge* afilado; *feature* bien marcado; *hearing* fino; *mind* listo, vivo; *outline* definido; *pace* rápido; *pain* agudo; *photo* nítido; *sight, wind* penetrante; *taste* acerbo, acre; *temper* áspero; *tongue* mordaz; *turn* (*tight*) cerrado, (*unexpected*) repentino; ♪ sostenido; F astuto, mañoso; avispado; **2.** *adv.* ♪ desafinadamente; F *4 o'clock* ~ las 4 en punto; *he turned* ~ *left* torció repentinamente a la izquierda; F *look* ~! ¡pronto!; *if you don't look* ~ si no te meneas; **3.** ♪ sostenido *m*; F estafador *m*; ˈ**sharp·en** afilar, aguzar (*a. fig.*); *pencil* sacar punta a; *feeling* agudizar; ˈ**sharp·en·er** afilador *m*, máquina *f* de afilar; ˈ**sharp·er** estafador *m*; *cards*: fullero *m*; ˈ**sharp·ness** agudeza *f etc.* (*v. sharp*).
sharp...: ˈ~**·shoot·er** tirador *m* certero; ˈ~-ˈ**sight·ed** de vista penetrante; ˈ~-ˈ**wit·ted** perspicaz.
shat·ter [ˈʃætər] romper(se), hacer(se) pedazos, estrellar(se); *health* quebrantar; *nerves* destrozar; *hopes* destruir; ˈ~**·proof** inastillable.
shave [ʃeiv] **1.** [*irr.*] afeitar(se); ⊕ (a)cepillar; (*skim*) pasar rozando; **2.** afeitada *f*, afeitado *m*; *have a* ~ afeitarse; *have a close* ~ escaparse por un pelo; *a close* ~, *a narrow* ~ cosa *f* de milagro; ˈ**shav·er**: F *young* ~ rapaz *m*.
Sha·vi·an [ˈʃeivijən] shaviano.
shav·ing [ˈʃeiviŋ] **1.** afeitada *f*; el afeitarse; ~*s pl.* virutas *f/pl.*, acepilladuras *f/pl.*; **2.** *attr.* de afeitar; ˈ~ **brush** brocha *f* (de afeitar).
shawl [ʃɔːl] chal *m*.
she [ʃiː] **1.** ella; **2.** hembra *f*.
she-... hembra *f of animals*.
sheaf [ʃiːf] (*pl. sheaves*) ✓ gavilla *f*; haz *m*; fajo *m of papers*.
shear [ʃir] **1.** [*irr.*] esquilar; trasquilar; ~ *off* cortar; ~ *through* hender, cortar; **2.** (*a pair of* unas) ~*s pl.* tijeras *f/pl.* (de jardín); ⊕ cizalla *f*; ˈ**shear·ing** esquileo *m*; ~*s pl.* lana *f* esquilada.
sheath [ʃiːθ] vaina *f* (*a.* ⚘); estuche *m*, funda *f*; cubierta *f*; **sheathe** [ʃiːð] envainar; enfundar; ⊕ revestir; ˈ**sheath·ing** ⊕ revestimiento *m*, forro *m*.
sheaves [ʃiːvz] *pl. of sheaf*.
she·bang [ʃəˈbæŋ] *sl.* taberna *f*; equipo *m*; *the whole* ~ todo el negocio.
shed[1] [ʃed] [*irr.*] *tears, light* verter; *blood* derramar; *skin etc.* mudar; *clothes, leaves* despojarse de; ~ *light on fig.* arrojar luz sobre.
shed[2] [~] cobertizo *m*; (*industrial*) nave *f*.
sheen [ʃiːn] lustre *m*, brillo *m*; ˈ**sheen·y** lustroso.
sheep [ʃiːp] oveja *f*; carnero *m*; *pl.* ganado *m* lanar; ˈ~**·cot** *v.* ~*fold*; ˈ~**·dog** perro *m* pastor; ˈ~**·fold** redil *m*, aprisco *m*; ˈ**sheep·ish** □ corrido; tímido; ˈ**sheep·ish·ness** timidez *f*.
sheep...: ˈ~**·man** dueño *m* de ganado lanar; ˈ~**·run** *v.* ~*walk*; ˈ~**·skin** zamarra *f*, badana *f*; F diploma *m* universitario; ˈ~**·walk** pasto *m* (*or* dehesa *f*) de ovejas.
sheer[1] [ʃir] **1.** *adj.* completo, cabal; puro; consumado; (*steep*) escarpado; *cloth* diáfano; fino; **2.** *adv.* directamente, completamente.
sheer[2] [~] **1.** ⚓ desviarse; ~ *off fig.* desviarse, largarse; **2.** ⚓ desviación *f*; ⚓ arrufadura *f*; *wind* ~ ✈ ráfaga *f* violenta.
sheet [ʃiːt] (*bed*) sábana *f*; hoja *f of paper, tin*; lámina *f of metal, glass*; (*news*) periódico *m*; extensión *f of*

water etc.; ⚓ escota *f*; ~ *copper etc.* cobre *m etc.* en láminas; ˈ~ **an·chor** ⚓ ancla *f* de la esperanza; *fig.* áncora *f* de salvación; ˈ**sheet·ing** tela *f* para sábanas; ˈ**sheet light·ning** relámpago *m* difuso.

sheik(h) [ʃeik] jeque *m.*

she·kel [ʃekl] siclo *m*; *sl.* ~*s pl.* parné *m.*

shelf [ʃelf] (*pl. shelves*) estante *m*, anaquel *m*; ⚓ banco *m* de arena, bajío *m*; *on the* ~ arrinconado, olvidado; (*girl*) *be on the* ~ quedarse para vestir santos.

shell [ʃel] **1.** cáscara *f of egg, nut, building*; concha *f*, caparazón *m*, carapacho *m of mollusc, tortoise etc.*; vaina *f of pea*; ⊕ armazón *f*; cubierta *f*; ⚔ granada *f*, proyectil *m*, bomba *f*; **2.** des(en)vainar, descascarar; ⚔ bombardear; *sl.* ~ *out money* desembolsar; (*v/i.*) desdinararse.

shel·lac [ʃeˈlæk] (goma *f*) laca *f.*

shelled [ʃeld] dotado de cáscara ...; (*without*) sin cáscara *etc.*

shell...: ˈ~ **fire** cañoneo *m*; ˈ~**·fish** mariscos *m/pl.*; *zo.* crustáceo *m*; ˈ~**·proof** a prueba de granadas; ˈ~ **shock** neurosis *f* de guerra.

shel·ter [ˈʃeltər] **1.** abrigo *m*, asilo *m*, refugio *m*; (*mountain*) albergue *m*; *fig.* resguardo *m*; *take* ~ = **2.** *v/i.* abrigarse, refugiarse, guarecerse; *v/t.* abrigar; guarecer; proteger.

shelve[1] [ʃelv] *fig.* arrinconar; dar carpetazo a; aplazar indefinidamente.

shelve[2] [~] *geog.* estar en declive.

shelves [ʃelvz] *pl. of shelf* estante *m etc.*; (*a.* **shelv·ing**) estantería *f.*

she·nan·i·gans [ʃiˈnænigənz] F travesuras *f/pl.*; embustes *m/pl.*

shep·herd [ˈʃepərd] **1.** pastor *m*; **2.** guiar; dirigir; ˈ**shep·herd·ess** pastora *f.*

sher·bet [ˈʃəːrbət] sorbete *m.*

sher·iff [ˈʃerif] sheriff *m*; alguacil *m* mayor.

sher·ry [ˈʃeri] jerez *m.*

shew [ʃou] ⚒ = *show* mostrar *etc.*

shib·bo·leth [ˈʃibəleθ] santo *m* y seña; *fig.* dogma *m* hoy desacreditado; convencionalismo *m.*

shield [ʃiːld] **1.** escudo *m* (*a. fig.*); ⊕ blindaje *m*; **2.** escudar (*a. fig.*), proteger, resguardar (*from* de); ˈ~ **bear·er** escudero *m.*

shift [ʃift] **1.** cambio *m*; movimiento *m*, cambio *m* de sitio; tanda *f*, turno *m at work*; astucia *f*; recurso *m*, expediente *m*; *make* ~ ingeniarse (*to* por), arreglárselas (*to* para); *make* ~ *with* ayudarse con; *make* ~ *without* pasarse sin; ~ *lever mot.* palanca *f* de cambios; **2.** *v/t.* cambiar (de sitio); mover; *v/i.* cambiar (de sitio, de puesto, de marcha); moverse; (*move house*) mudar; (*wind*) cambiar; F ir a gran velocidad; ~ *for o.s.* ayudarse (a sí mismo); ˈ**shift·ing** mudable; ~ *sands pl.* arenas *f/pl.* movedizas; ˈ**shift·less** □ agalbanado, indolente, inútil; ˈ**shift·y** □ taimado, furtivo; sospechoso.

shil·ling [ˈʃiliŋ] chelín *m.*

shil·ly-shal·ly [ˈʃiliʃæli] vacilar.

shim·mer [ˈʃimər] **1.** reflejo *m* (*or* resplandor *m*) trémulo; **2.** rielar.

shim·my[1] [ˈʃimi] *sl.* shimmy *m* (*baile*); *mot.* abaniqueo *m* (de ruedas); vibración *f.*

shim·my[2] [~] F camisa *f.*

shin [ʃin] **1.** (*or* ˈ~**·bone**) espinilla *f*; **2.**: ~ *up* trepar a.

shin·dig [ˈʃindig] *sl.* fiesta *f* ruidosa; juerga *f.*

shine [ʃain] **1.** lustre *m*, brillo *m*; buen tiempo *m*; F *take the* ~ *out of* eclipsar; *sl. take a* ~ *to* tomar simpatía por; **2.** [*irr.*] *v/i.* brillar (*a. fig.*), lucir (*a. fig.*); *v/t. shoes* limpiar; sacar brillo a.

shin·gle[1] [ˈʃiŋgl] **1.** ripia *f*; (*hair*) corte *m* a lo garçón; **2.** cubrir con ripias; *hair* cortar a lo garçón.

shin·gle[2] [~] guijo *m*; guijarral *m*; playa *f* guijarrosa.

shin·gles [ˈʃiŋglz] ⚕ *pl.* herpes *m or f/pl.*; zona *f.*

shin·gly [ˈʃiŋgli] guijarroso.

shin·ing [ˈʃainiŋ], **shin·y** [ˈʃaini] □ brillante, lustroso.

ship [ʃip] **1.** buque *m*, navío *m*, barco *m*; ~*'s company* tripulación *f*; *merchant* ~ mercante *m*; **2.** *v/t.* embarcar; ✝ transportar; enviar, expedir; *mast* izar; *oars* desarmar; *v/i.* embarcarse; ˈ~**·board:** *on* ~ a bordo; ˈ~**·build·er** constructor *m* de buques, ingeniero *m* naval; ˈ~**·build·ing** construcción *f* de buques; ˈ~ **ca·nal** canal *m* de navegación; ˈ~ ˈ**chan·dler** abastecedor *m* de buques; ˈ**ship·ment** embarque *m*; envío *m*, remesa *f*; ˈ**ship·own·er** naviero *m*; ˈ**ship·per** exportador *m*; remitente *m*; ˈ**shipping** buques *m/pl.*, flota *f*, marina *f*;

navegación *f*; embarque *m of goods*; ~ *agent* agente *m* marítimo; ~ *company* compañía *f* naviera.

ship...: **'~·shape** en buen orden; **'~·wreck 1.** naufragio *m*; **2.** naufragar (*a. be ~ed*); **'~·wrecked** náufrago; **'~·wright** carpintero *m* de navío; = *shipbuilder*; **'~·yard** astillero *m*, varadero *m*.

shire ['ʃaiər, *in compounds* ... ʃiər] condado *m*; ~ *horse* caballo *m* de tiro (inglés).

shirk [ʃəːrk] *v/t.* eludir, esquivar, desentenderse de; *v/i.* faltar al deber, gandulear; **'shirk·er** gandul *m*.

shirt [ʃəːrt] camisa *f*; *sl. keep one's ~ on* quedarse sereno; **'~·front** pechera *f*; **'shirt·ing** ✝ tela *f* para camisas; **'shirt·sleeve 1.**: *in ~s* en mangas de camisa; **2.** F sencillo, directo.

shit [ʃit] *sl.* **1.** mierda *f*; excremento *m*; **2.** evacuar el vientre; cagar.

shiv·er ['ʃivər] **1.** (*fear*) temblor *m*; (*cold*) tiritón *m*; F *the ~s pl.* dentera *f*, grima *f*; *it gives me the ~s* me da miedo; **2.** estremecerse; temblar *with fear*; tiritar *with cold*; **'shiv·er·y** estremecido; (*cold*) friolento.

shoal[1] [ʃoul] **1.** banco *m*, cardumen *m*; *fig.* muchedumbre *f*; **2.** reunirse en gran número.

shoal[2] [~] **1.** bajío *m*, banco *m* de arena; **2.** disminuir en profundidad.

shock[1] [ʃɔk] ✓ tresnal *m*.

shock[2] [~] **1.** choque *m* (*a.* ⚡); sacudida *f*; temblor *m* de tierra; sobresalto *m*; conmoción *f* desagradable; ⚕ shock *m*; *toxic ~ syndrome* síndrome *m* de choque tóxico; ⚔ ~ *troops pl.* tropas *f/pl.* de asalto; **2.** *fig.* chocar; sobresaltar; escandalizar; *be ~ed* asombrarse (*at* de).

shock[3] [~] greña *f of hair*.

shock ab·sorb·er ['ʃɔkəbsɔːrbər] *mot.* amortiguador *m*.

shock·er ['ʃɔkər] *sl.* novelucha *f*; película *f* horripilante.

shock·ing ['ʃɔkiŋ] □ chocante; escandaloso; *taste* pésimo.

shod [ʃɔd] *pret. a. p.p. of shoe* 2.

shod·dy ['ʃɔdi] de pacotilla, de pésima calidad; ~ *aristocracy* ricachos *m/pl.* ostentosos y vulgares.

shoe [ʃuː] **1.** zapato *m*; (*horse-*) herradura *f*; (*brake-*) zapata *f*; *I wouldn't be in his ~s* no quisiera estar en su pellejo; **2.** [*irr.*] calzar; *horse* herrar; **'~·black** limpiabotas *m*; **'~·blacking** betún *m*; **'~·horn** calzador *m*; **'~·lace** cordón *m*; **'~·mak·er** zapatero *m*; **'~ pol·ish** betún *m*; bola *f*; **'~·shine** brillo *m*; lustre *m*; **'~ boy** (*or shoeblack*) limpiabotas *m*; **'~·shop** zapatería *f*; **'~·string** cordón *m*; F *on a ~* con muy poco dinero.

shone [ʃɔn] *pret. a. p.p. of shine* 2.

shoo [ʃuː] **1.** *birds* oxear; ahuyentar; **2.** ¡zape!, ¡ox!

shook [ʃuk] *pret. of shake* 1.

shoot [ʃuːt] **1.** ⚘ renuevo *m*, vástago *m*; cacería *f*; tiro *m* (al blanco); conducto *m* inclinado; **2.** [*irr.*] *v/t.* disparar; tirar; herir (*or* matar) con arma de fuego; (*execute*) fusilar; *bolt* correr; *bridge* pasar debajo de; *film* rodar; *rapids* salvar; *sun* tomar la altura de; ~ *down* derribar; ~ *up sl.* destrozar a tiros; *v/i.* tirar (*at* a); *football*: chutar; ⚘ brotar; (*pain*) punzar; ~ *ahead* adelantarse mucho (*of* a); ~ *by*, ~ *past* pasar como un meteoro; ~ *forth* brotar; ~ *off*, ~ *out* salir disparado, precipitarse; ~ *up* crecer rápidamente, espigar; (*price*) elevarse rápidamente.

shoot·ing ['ʃuːtiŋ] **1.** tiros *m/pl.*; tiroteo *m*, cañoneo *m*; caza *f* con escopeta; rodaje *m of film*; *go ~* ir a la caza; **2.** *pain* punzante; **'~ box** pabellón *m* de caza; **'~ brake** rubia *f*; **'~ gal·ler·y** galería *f* de tiro (al blanco); **'~ match** certamen *m* de tiro al blanco; *sl.* conjunto *m*; negocio *m*; **'~ 'star** estrella *f* fugaz.

shoot·out ['ʃuːtaut] pelea *f* a tiros.

shop [ʃɔp] **1.** tienda *f*; (*large*) almacén *m*; ⊕ taller *m*; F *talk ~* hablar del propio trabajo; **2.** ir de compras (*mst go ~ping*); **'~ as'sist·ant** dependiente (*a f*) *m*; **'~·keep·er** tendero (*a f*) *m*; **'~·lift·er** mechera *f*; **'shop·per** comprador (*-a f*) *m*; **'shop·ping** compras *f/pl.*; ~ *center* centro *m* comercial; conjunto *m* de tiendas.

shop...: **'~-soiled** deteriorado; **'~ stew·ard** representante *m* de los obreros en la sección de una fábrica; **'~·walk·er** vigilante (*a f*) *m*; **'~ 'win·dow** escaparate *m*, vidriera *f S.Am.*; **'~·worn** desgastado antes de venderse.

shore[1] [ʃɔːr] playa *f*, orilla *f*, ribera *f*; *on ~* en tierra.

shore[2] [~] **1.** puntal *m*; **2.** apuntalar; *fig.* apoyar.

shorn [ʃɔːrn] *p.p. of shear* 1 esquilar *etc.*; ~ *of* despojado de.

short [ʃɔːrt] **1.** corto, breve; *p.* bajo; (*brusque*) brusco, seco; *memory* flaco; *pastry* quebrad(iz)o; ~ *wave radio*: onda *f* corta; *by a* ~ *head* por una cabeza escasa; *5* ~ 5 de menos, faltan 5; *for* ~ para abreviar; *in* ~ en breve; ~ *for* forma abreviada de; ~ *of* falto de, escaso de; *nothing* ~ *of* nada menos que; ~ *of lying* fuera de mentir; *cut* ~ acortar, abreviar; interrumpir; *fall* ~ *of* no alcanzar, no llegar a; no corresponder a; *run* ~ acabarse; *run* ~ *of* acabársele a uno; *stop* ~ parar de repente; *stop* ~ *of* detenerse antes de llegar a; *work* ~ *time* trabajar en jornadas reducidas; **2.** *film*: corto metraje *m*; ⚡ cortocircuito *m*; F ~*s pl.* pantalones *m*/*pl.* cortos; **3.** *v.* ~ *circuit*; ˈ**short·age** escasez *f*, falta *f*, carestía *f*; ✝ déficit *m*.

short...: ˈ**~·bread**, ˈ**~·cake** torta *f* seca y quebradiza; ˈ**~** ˈ**cir·cuit 1.** cortocircuito *m*; **2.** poner(se) en cortocircuito; **~**ˈ**com·ing** defecto *m*; **~·cut** atajo *m*; ˈ**short·en** acortar(se), reducir(se); ˈ**short·en·ing** acortamiento *m*; (*lard*) manteca *f*; grasa *f*.

short...: ˈ**~·fall** déficit *m*; ˈ**~·hand** taquigrafía *f*; ~ *writer* taquígrafo (a *f*) *m*; ~ *typist* taquimeca(nógrafa) *f*; ˈ**~**-ˈ**hand·ed** falto de mano de obra; **~-lived** [ˈ~ˈlaivd, F ˈ~ˈlivd] efímero; ˈ**short·ly** *adv.* en breve, dentro de poco; próximamente; ˈ**short·ness** pequeñez *f*.

short...: ˈ**~**-ˈ**sight·ed** miope, corto de vista; *fig.* falto de previsión; ˈ**~ sto·ry** cuento *m*; ˈ**~**-ˈ**tem·pered** enojadizo; ˈ**~-term** a plazo corto; ˈ**~-wave** *radio*: ... de onda corta; ˈ**~**-ˈ**wind·ed** corto de resuello.

shot[1] [ʃɔt] **1.** *pret. a. p.p. of shoot* 2; **2.** F (des)gastado; roto; inútil.

shot[2] [~] tiro *m*, disparo *m*; balazo *m*; (*a. small* ~) perdigones *m*/*pl.*; (*p.*) tirador (-a *f*) *m*; *sport*: tiro *m at goal*; (*stroke*) golpe *m*; (*weight*) pesa *f*; F tentativa *f*, conjetura *f*; *phot.* fotografía *f*; *film*: fotograma *m*; ⚕ inyección *f*; dosis *f*; *sl.* trago *m of rum etc.*; *have a* ~ probar suerte; *have a* ~ *at fig.* hacer una tentativa de; F *not by a long* ~ ni con mucho; F *like a* ~ acto seguido; como una bala; F *big* ~ pez *m* gordo; ˈ**~·gun** escopeta *f*; F ~ *marriage* casamiento *m* a la fuerza.

should [ʃud] **1.** *v*/*aux. que forma el condicional etc.*: *I* ~ *do it if I could* lo haría si pudiese; **2.** deber: *he* ~ *be here soon* debe llegar dentro de poco; *he* ~ *know that* debiera saberlo; *he* ~ *have gone last week* debiera haber ido la semana pasada.

shoul·der [ˈʃouldər] **1.** hombro *m*; espaldas *f*/*pl.*; lomo *m of hill etc.*; *give a p. the cold* ~ volver la espalda a una p.; *put one's* ~ *to the wheel* arrimar el hombro; *rub* ~*s with* codearse con; ~ *to* ~ hombro a hombro; **2.** llevar al hombro; *fig.* cargar con; empujar con el hombro; ⚔ ~ *arms!* ¡armas al hombro!; ˈ**~ blade** omóplato *m*; ˈ**~ knot** dragona *f*; ˈ**~ strap** tirante *m*, hombrera *f*.

shout [ʃaut] **1.** grito *m*; voz *f*; **2.** gritar; dar voces; ~ *down p.* protestar hasta hacer callar; *play* hundir a gritos; ˈ**~·ing match** riña *f* a gritos.

shove [ʃʌv] **1.** empujón *m*; **2.** *v*/*i.* dar empujones; ~ *off* ⚓ alejarse; *sl.* marcharse; *v*/*t.* empujar.

shov·el [ˈʃʌvl] **1.** pala *f*; cogedor *m*; **2.** traspalar.

show [ʃou] **1.** [*irr.*] *v*/*t.* mostrar, enseñar; (*prove*) probar, demostrar; señalar; manifestar; *film* poner, proyectar; *goods, pictures* exhibir; *loss* dejar; ~ *in* hacer pasar; ~ *off* hacer gala de; ~ *out* acompañar a la puerta; ~ *up* aparecer; presentarse; F desenmascarar; *v*/*i.* mostrarse, (a)parecer; (*film*) representarse; ~ *off* lucirse; fachendear; **2.** (*display*) exhibición *f*; exposición *f*; (*outward*) apariencia *f*; (*pomp*) boato *m*; manifestación *f*, demostración *f of feeling*; *thea.* función *f*, espectáculo *m*; ⛏ feria *f*; *sl.* cosa *f*, empresa *f*; ~ *of hands* votación *f* por manos levantadas; *dumb* ~ pantomima *f*; *on* ~ expuesto; F *give the* ~ *away* tirar de la manta; (*involuntary*) clarearse; *make a* ~ *of* hacer gala de; fingir; *sl. run the* ~ ser el todo; mandar; ˈ**~ bus·i·ness** comercio *m* (*or* vocación *f*) del entretenimiento público; ˈ**~·case** vitrina *f* (de exposición); ˈ**~·down** F momento *m* decisivo, revelación *f* decisiva; enfrentamiento *m* crítico.

show·er [ˈʃauər] **1.** chaparrón *m*, chubasco *m*; aguacero *m*; *fig.* rociada *f*, lluvia *f*; **2.** llover; derramar; *fig.* ~ *with* colmar de; ~ **bath** [ˈ~bæθ] ducha *f*; ˈ**show·er·y** lluvioso.

show·i·ness [ˈʃouinis] boato *m*; aparatosidad *f*; ˈ**show·ing** (*poor etc.*) actuación *f* (defectuosa *etc.*); ˈ**showman** empresario *m*; *fig.* hombre *m* ostentoso; ˈ**show·man·ship** teatralidad *f*; **shown** [ʃoun] *p.p. of show* 1; ˈ**show·room** salón *m* de demostraciones; ˈ**show win·dow** escaparate *m*; ˈ**show·y** □ vistoso, llamativo; aparatoso; *p.* ostentoso.

shrank [ʃræŋk] *pret. of shrink* 1.

shrap·nel [ˈʃræpnl] metralla *f*.

shred [ʃred] **1.** triza *f*, jirón *m*; fragmento *m*; *fig.* pizca *f*; **2.** [*irr.*] hacer trizas; desmenuzar.

shrew [ʃruː] *zo.* musaraña *f*; *fig.* arpía *f*, mujer *f* regañona, fierecilla *f*.

shrewd [ʃruːd] □ astuto, sagaz; ˈ**shrewd·ness** astucia *f*, sagacidad *f*.

shrew·ish [ˈʃruːiʃ] □ regañón.

shriek [ʃriːk] **1.** alarido *m*, chillido *m*; **2.** chillar (*a. fig.*).

shrill [ʃril] **1.** □ chillón (*a. fig.*), agudo y penetrante; **2.** chillar.

shrimp [ʃrimp] *zo.* camarón *m*; *fig.* enano *m*; individuo *m* sin importancia.

shrine [ʃrain] relicario *m*; capilla *f*, sepulcro *m* (de santo).

shrink [ʃriŋk] **1.** [*irr.*] *v/i.* encogerse, contraer(se); mermar; (*a.* ~ *back*) acobardarse, retirarse (*from*, *at* ante); ~ *from ger.* no atreverse a *inf.*; *v/t.* encoger, contraer; ⊕~ *on* montar en caliente; **2.** *sl.* psiquiatra *m/f*; ˈ**shrink·age** encogimiento *m*, contracción *f*.

shriv·el [ˈʃrivl] (*a.* ~ *up*) marchitar(se), arrugar(se); avellanarse.

shroud [ʃraud] **1.** sudario *m*, mortaja *f*; *fig.* velo *m*; **2.** amortajar; *fig.* velar.

shrouds [ʃraudz] ⚓ obenques *m/pl.*

Shrove·tide [ˈʃrouvtaid] carnestolendas *f/pl.*; **Shrove Tues·day** martes *m* de carnaval.

shrub [ʃrʌb] arbusto *m*; **shrub·ber·y** [ˈ~əri] plantío *m* de arbustos.

shrug [ʃrʌg] **1.** encogerse de hombros; **2.** encogimiento *m* (de hombros).

shrunk [ʃrʌŋk] *pret. a. p.p. of shrink* 1; ˈ**shrunk·en** *adj.* encogido; *fig.* mermado.

shud·der [ˈʃʌdər] **1.** estremecerse; **2.** estremecimiento *m*.

shuf·fle [ˈʃʌfl] **1.** *v/t.* mezclar, revolver; *cards* barajar; ~ *off* deshacerse de; **2.** *v/i.* arrastrar los pies; andar (bailar *etc.*) arrastrando los pies; **3.** *cards*: (*act*) barajadura *f*; (*turn*) turno *m* de barajar.

shun [ʃʌn] esquivar, evitar; retraerse de.

shunt [ʃʌnt] **1.** ⚡ derivación *f*, shunt *m*; *Am.* 🚂 aguja *f*, cambio *m* de vía; **2.** ⚡ poner en derivación; 🚂 maniobrar; apartar; ˈ**shunt·er** 🚂 guardagujas *m*, obrero *m* del servicio de maniobras; ˈ**shunt·ing** 🚂 maniobras *f/pl.*; ~ *engine* locomotora *f* de maniobras.

shut [ʃʌt] [*irr.*] *v/t.* cerrar; ~ *down factory* cerrar; *machine* parar; ~ *in* encerrar; cercar, rodear; ~ *off water etc.* cortar; aislar (*from* de); ~ *out* excluir; negar la entrada a; ~ *up* (en)cerrar; *opening* obturar; F *p.* hacer callar, reducir al silencio; *v/i.* cerrarse (*a.* ~ *down etc.*); F ~ *up* callarse; F ~ *up!* ¡cállate!; ˈ**~·down** cierre *m*; **~·out** *sport*: victoria *f* en que el contrario no gana un tanto; ˈ**shut·ter** contraventana *f*; *phot.* obturador *m*.

shut·tle [ˈʃʌtl] **1.** lanzadera *f*; ~ *service* tren *m etc.* que hace viajes cortos entre dos puntos; *space* ~ transbordador *m* (espacial); **2.** hacer viajes cortos entre dos puntos; ˈ**~·cock** volante *m*.

shy[1] [ʃai] **1.** □ tímido; recatado; huraño; vergonzoso; *sl. I'm $10* ~ me faltan 10 dólares; **2.** espantarse, respingar (*at* al ver).

shy[2] [~] F **1.** lanzar, arrojar; **2.** echada *f*; *have a* ~ probar; *have a* ~ *at* hacer una tentativa de.

shy·ness [ˈʃainis] timidez *f*; recato *m*; vergüenza *f*.

shy·ster [ˈʃaistər] *sl.* abogado *m* trampista.

Si·a·mese [saiəˈmiːz] siamés *adj. a. su. m* (-a *f*).

Si·be·ri·an [saiˈbiriən] siberiano *adj. a. su. m* (a *f*).

sib·i·lant [ˈsibilənt] □ sibilante *adj. a. su. f.*

sib·ling [ˈsibliŋ] hermano *m*; hermana *f*.

sib·yl [ˈsibil] sibila *f*.

sib·yl·line [siˈbilain] sibilino.

Si·cil·ian [siˈsiljən] siciliano *adj. a. su. m* (a *f*).

sick [sik] enfermo; mareado; *be* ~ estar enfermo; sentirse mareado; vomitar; *sl.* mórbido; perverso; *be* ~ *of* estar harto de; *get* ~ *of* coger asco a, hacérsele pesado; *fall* ~, *take* ~ caer enfermo; ausentarse debido a enfermedad; ˈ~ **bay** enfermería *f*; ˈ~**·bed** lecho *m* de enfermo; ˈ**sick·en** *v/i.* enfermar; ~ *at* sentir náuseas ante; ~ *for* añorar; ⚕ mostrar síntomas de; *v/t.* dar asco a; ˈ**sick·en·ing** □ asqueroso, nauseabundo.

sick·le [ˈsikl] hoz *f*.

sick leave [ˈsikli:v] permiso *m* de convalecencia; ˈ**sick·li·ness** achaque *m*; palidez *f*; ˈ**sick·ly** *p.* enfermizo, achacoso; pálido; *smell* nauseabundo; *smile* débil; *taste* empalagoso; ˈ**sick·ness** enfermedad *f*, mal *m*; náusea *f*; ˈ**sick pay** subsidio *m* de enfermedad.

side [said] **1.** lado *m*; costado *m of body, ship*; cara *f of solid, record*; falda *f*, ladera *f of hill*; orilla *f of lake*; (*party*) partido *m*; *sport*: equipo *m*; *fig.* aspecto *m*; F tono *m*, postín *m*; ~ *by* ~ lado a lado; *by the* ~ *of* al lado de; *on all* ~*s* por todas partes; *on the* ~ F incidentalmente, de paso; *sl.* bajo cuerda; *take* ~*s* tomar partido; **2.** lateral; secundario; indirecto; **3.:** ~ *with* declararse por; ˈ~ **arms** armas *f/pl.* de cinto; ˈ~**·board** aparador *m*; ˈ~**·car** sidecar *m*; ˈ**sid·ed** de ... lados.

side...: ˈ~**·kick** *sl.* compañero *m* regular; ˈ~**·light** luz *f* de costado; *fig.* detalle *m* (*or* información *f*) incidental; ˈ~**·line** 🚂 apartadero *m*; *sport*: línea *f* lateral; *fig.* empleo *m* (*or* negocio *m*) suplementario; ˈ~**·long** oblicuo; lateral; *glance* de soslayo.

si·de·re·al [saiˈdiriəl] sidéreo.

side...: ˈ~**-sad·dle 1.** silla *f* de mujer; **2.** *adv.* a mujeriegas, a la inglesa; ˈ~ **show** caseta *f* (de feria); ˈ~**-slip** ✈, *mot.* deslizamiento *m* lateral; ˈ~**-step 1.** esquivada *f* lateral; **2.** *fig.* evitar, esquivar; ˈ~**·stroke** natación *f* de costado; ˈ~**-track 1.** 🚂 apartadero *m*, vía *f* muerta; **2.** *fig.* desviar, apartar; ˈ~**·walk** acera *f*; *S.Am.* vereda *f*; **side·ward** [ˈ~wərd] *adj.* oblicuo; *adv.* (*a.* **side·wards** [ˈ~z], ˈ**side-ways,** ˈ**side·wise**) de lado, hacia un lado.

si·dle [ˈsaidl]: ~ *up to* acercarse cautelosamente (*or* servilmente) a.

siege [si:dʒ] cerco *m*, sitio *m*; *lay* ~ *to* asediar (*a. fig.*).

sieve [siv] **1.** cedazo *m*, tamiz *m*; (*kitchen*) coladera *f*; **2.** = *sift*.

sift [sift] tamizar, cerner; *fig.* examinar.

sigh [sai] **1.** suspiro *m*; **2.** suspirar (*after, for* por).

sight [sait] **1.** vista *f* (*a.* ⚓); visión *f*; escena *f*; espectáculo *m*; cosa *f* digna de verse; ⚔ puntería *f*; F espantajo *m*; ~*s pl.* cosas *f/pl.* de interés turístico; monumentos *m/pl.*; ⚔ miras *f/pl.*; *at* ~, *on* ~, *at first* ~ a primera vista; ⚓ a la vista; *by* ~ de vista; (*with*)*in* ~ *of* a la vista de; *out of* ~ invisible; *catch* ~ *of* alcanzar a ver; *lose* ~ *of* perder de vista (*a. fig.*); **2.** avistar, divisar; *gun* apuntar; ˈ~**·less** ciego; ˈ~**·see·ing** excursionismo *m*, turismo *m*; ˈ~**·se·er** excursionista *m/f*, turista *m/f*; ˈ~ **read·ing**, ˈ~ **sing·ing** ejecución *f* a la primera lectura.

sign [sain] **1.** señal *f*; indicio *m*; ⚕, ♪ *etc.* signo *m*; (*trace*) huella *f*, vestigio *m*; (*notice*) letrero *m*; (*shop-*) rótulo *m*; ~*s pl.* señas *f/pl.*; *in* ~ *of* en señal de; *show* ~*s of* dar muestras de; **2.** *v/t.* firmar; ~ *away* ceder; ~ *on*, ~ *up* contratar; ~*ed and sealed* firmado y lacrado; *v/i.* firmar; usar el alfabeto de los sordomudos; ~ *off* terminar; ~ *on* fichar (*for* por).

sig·nal [ˈsignl] **1.** señal *f*; *teleph. busy* ~ señal *f* de ocupado; ~*s pl.* ⚔ (cuerpo *m* de) transmisiones *f/pl.*; **2.** □ señalado, notable; **3.** señalar; hacer señales (*to* a); comunicar por señales (*that* que); ˈ~ **box** garita *f* de señales; **sig·nal·ize** [ˈ~nəlaiz] distinguir, marcar; ˈ**sig·nal·man** 🚂 guardavía *m*; ⚔ soldado *m* de transmisiones.

sig·na·to·ry [ˈsignətɔ:ri] firmante *adj. a. su. m* (a *f*), signatorio *adj. a. su. m* (a *f*); **sig·na·ture** [ˈsignitʃər] firma *f*; *typ.*, ♪ signatura *f*; ⚓ marca *f*; ~ *tune* sintonía *f*.

sign·board [ˈsainbɔ:rd] letrero *m*, muestra *f*; ˈ**sign·er** firmante *m/f*.

sig·net [ˈsignit] sello *m*; ˈ~ **ring** sortija *f* de sello.

sig·nif·i·cance, sig·nif·i·can·cy [sigˈnifikəns(i)] significación *f*, significado *m*; **sigˈnif·i·cant** □ significante, significativo; **sig·ni·fiˈca·tion** significación *f*; **sigˈnif·i·ca·tive** [~kətiv] significativo.

sig·ni·fy [ˈsignifai] significar; indicar; querer decir.
sign...: ˈ~ **paint·er** rotulista *m*; ˈ~·**post 1.** poste *m* indicador; señal *f*; **2.** señalizar.
si·lence [ˈsailəns] **1.** silencio *m*; ~! ¡silencio!; **2.** acallar (*a. fig.*), imponer silencio a; ˈ**si·lenc·er** *mot.* silenciador *m*.
si·lent [ˈsailənt] □ silencioso; callado; *be* ~, *remain* ~ callarse; ~ *film* película *f* muda; ✝ ~ *partner* socio *m* comanditario.
sil·hou·ette [siluːˈet] **1.** silueta *f*; **2.**: *be* ~*d against* destacarse sobre (*or* contra).
sil·i·ca [ˈsilikə] sílice *f*; **sil·i·cate** [ˈsilikit] silicato *m*; **si·li·ceous** [siˈliʃəs] silíceo.
silk [silk] **1.** seda *f*; **2.** *attr.* de seda; ~ *hat* sombrero *m* de copa; ˈ**silk·en** de seda; sedoso; ˈ**silk·i·ness** lo sedoso; ˈ**silk-**ˈ**stock·ing 1.** aristócrata *m/f*; **2.** aristocrático; ˈ**silk·worm** gusano *m* de seda; ˈ**silk·y** □ sedoso.
sill [sil] (*window*) alféizar *m*; antepecho *m*; (*door*) umbral *m*.
sil·li·ness [ˈsilinis] necedad *f*, tontería *f*; **sil·ly** [ˈsili] □ tonto, necio, bobo; ~ *season* época *f* de la serpiente de mar.
si·lo [ˈsailou] silo *m*, ensiladora *f*.
silt [silt] **1.** sedimento *m*, aluvión *m*; **2.** obstruirse con sedimentos (*mst* ~ *up*).
sil·ver [ˈsilvər] **1.** plata *f*; **2.** platear (*a.* ⊕ ˈ~-**plate**); *mirror* azogar; **3.** de plata; plateado; ~ *jubilee* vigésimo quinto aniversario *m*; ~ *paper* papel *m* de plata; ~ *wedding* bodas *f/pl.* de plata; ˈ~·**ware** vajilla *f* de plata; ˈ**sil·ver·y** plateado; *voice* argentino.
sim·i·lar [ˈsimilər] □ parecido, semejante; **sim·i·lar·i·ty** [~ˈlæriti] semejanza *f*.
sim·i·le [ˈsimili] símil *m*.
si·mil·i·tude [siˈmilitjuːd] similitud *f*.
sim·mer [ˈsimər] *v/i.* hervir (*v/t.* cocer) a fuego lento; *fig.* estar a punto de estallar.
si·mon·y [ˈsaiməni] simonía *f*.
sim·per [ˈsimpər] **1.** sonrisa *f* afectada (*or* boba); **2.** sonreír bobamente.
sim·ple [ˈsimpl] □ sencillo; simple; *style* llano; F bobo; ˈ~-ˈ**heart·ed** □ ingenuo, candoroso; ˈ~-ˈ**mind·ed** □ estúpido, idiota; candoroso; **sim·ple·ton** [ˈ~tən] inocentón *m*.
sim·plic·i·ty [simˈplisiti] sencillez *f*; llaneza *f of style*; F simpleza *f*; **sim·pli·fi·ca·tion** [~fiˈkeiʃn] simplificación *f*; **sim·pli·fy** [ˈ~fai] simplificar.
sim·ply [ˈsimpli] *adv.* sencillamente; simplemente.
sim·u·late [ˈsimjuleit] simular; **sim·u**ˈ**la·tion** simulación *f*.
si·mul·ta·ne·i·ty [simәltәˈniәti] simultaneidad *f*; **si·mul·ta·ne·ous** [~lˈteinjәs] □ simultáneo.
sin [sin] **1.** pecado *m*; **2.** pecar.
since [sins] **1.** *prp.* desde, a partir de, después de; **2.** *adv.* desde entonces, después; *long* ~ hace mucho (tiempo); *a short time* ~ hace poco; **3.** *cj.* desde que; puesto que, ya que; *it is an hour* ~ *he left* hace una hora que salió.
sin·cere [sinˈsir] □ sincero; *Yours* ~*ly* le saluda afectuosamente; **sin·cer·i·ty** [~ˈseriti] sinceridad *f*.
sine [sain] seno *m*.
si·ne·cure [ˈsainikjur] sinecura *f*.
sin·ew [ˈsinjuː] tendón *m*; *fig. mst* ~*s pl.* nervio *m*, fibra *f*; ˈ**sin·ew·y** nervudo, vigoroso.
sin·ful [ˈsinful] □ pecaminoso; *p.* pecador; ˈ**sin·ful·ness** maldad *f*.
sing [siŋ] [*irr.*] cantar; (*birds*) trinar; (*ears*) zumbar; F ~ *out* vocear; *sl.* confesar; ~ *small* achantarse; ~ *to sleep* arrullar, adormecer cantando; ~ *another song* (*or tune*) bajar el tono, verse obligado a cambiar de opinión.
singe [sindʒ] chamuscar; *hair* quemar las puntas de.
sing·er [ˈsiŋər] cantor (-a *f*) *m*; (*professional*) cantante *m/f*.
sing·ing [ˈsiŋiŋ] canto *m*; zumbido *m in ears*; ~ *bird* pájaro *m* cantor.
sin·gle [ˈsiŋgl] **1.** □ único, solo; simple; *room* individual; *ticket* sencillo; (*unmarried*) soltero; ~ *combat* combate *m* singular; ~ *file* fila *f* india; **2.** (*mst* ~ *out*) distinguir, singularizar; escoger; señalar; **3.** *tennis*: ~*s pl.* juego *m* de individuales (*or* de simples); ˈ~-ˈ**breast·ed** sin cruzar; ˈ~-ˈ**cham·ber** *pol.* unicameral; ˈ~-ˈ**en·gine**(**d**) ✈ monomotor; ˈ~-ˈ**hand·ed** sin ayuda (de nadie); ˈ~-ˈ**heart·ed** □, ˈ~-ˈ**mind·ed** □ resuelto, firme; sincero; ˈ**sin·gle·ness** resolución *f*, firmeza *f of purpose*; ˈ**sin·gles** F (los) no casados *a. adj.*; ˈ**sin·gle-seat·er** monoplaza *m*;

ˈ**sin·gle·stick** *fenc.* (esgrima *f* del) bastón *m*; **sin·glet** [ˈ~it] camiseta *f*; **sin·gle·ton** [ˈ~tən] semi-fallo *m*, carta *f* única de un palo; ˈ**sin·gle-**ˈ**track** de vía única.

sin·gly *adv.* individualmente; uno [a uno.

sing·song [ˈsiŋsɔŋ] **1.** (*tone*) salmodia *f*, sonsonete *m*; (*songs*) concierto *m* improvisado; **2.** *tone* monótono, cantarín.

sin·gu·lar [ˈsiŋgjulər] □ singular *adj. a. su. m*; **sin·gu·lar·i·ty** [~ˈlæriti] singularidad *f*.

Sin·ha·lese [sinhəˈliːz] cingalés *adj. a. su. m* (-a *f*).

sin·is·ter [ˈsinistər] □ siniestro.

sink [siŋk] **1.** [*irr.*] *v/i.* menguar, declinar; enviciarse; (*ship*) hundirse; (*sun*) ponerse; ⚕ debilitarse; dejarse caer *into chair*; *my heart sank* se me cayeron las alas del corazón; ~ *in* penetrar, calar; (*words*) tener efecto, hacer mella; *v/t.* sumergir; *ship* hundir; ⚒ *shaft* abrir, cavar; *well* perforar; *money* invertir; *teeth* hincar (*into* en); *differences* olvidar, suprimir; **2.** fregadero *m*, pila *f*; ⊕ sumidero *m*; *fig.* sentina *f*; ˈ**sink·er** ⚒ plomada *f*; (*fishing*) plomo *m*; ˈ**sink·ing** hundimiento *m*; ~ *fund* fondo *m* de amortización.

sin·ner [ˈsinər] pecador (-a *f*) *m*.

Sin·o... [ˈsinou] sino...; **si·nol·o·gy** [ˈsainɔlədʒi] sinología *f*; ˈ**si·nol·o·gist** sinólogo *m*.

sin·u·os·i·ty [sinjuˈɔsiti] sinuosidad *f*; ˈ**sin·u·ous** □ sinuoso.

si·nus [ˈsainəs] *anat.* seno *m*; **si·nus·i·tis** [~ˈsaitis] sinusitis *f*.

sip [sip] **1.** sorbo *m*; **2.** sorber.

si·phon [ˈsaifən] **1.** sifón *m*; **2.** sacar con sifón (*a.* ~ *off*).

sir [səːr] señor *m* (*in direct address*); sir *m* (*as title*); *Dear* ♀ muy señor mío.

sire [ˈsaiər] **1.** † *a. zo.* padre *m*; **2.** engendrar, ser el padre de.

si·ren [ˈsairin] *all senses*: sirena *f*.

sir·loin [ˈsəːrlɔin] solomillo *m*.

si·roc·co [siˈrɔkou] siroco *m*.

sis·sy [ˈsisi] marica *m*, mariquita *m*.

sis·ter [ˈsistər] hermana *f* (*a. eccl.*); *eccl.* (*as title*) Sor *f*; ~ *ship* (buque *m*) gemelo *m*; ~ *of charity* (*or mercy*) hermana *f* de la caridad; **sis·ter·hood** [ˈ~hud] hermandad *f*; cofradía *f* de mujeres; ˈ**sis·ter-in-law** cuñada *f*; ˈ**sis·ter·ly** de (*or* como) hermana.

sit [sit] *v/i.* sentarse (*a.* ~ *down*); estar sentado; (*assembly*) reunirse, celebrar junta; (*clothes*) sentar; (*hens*) empollar; posar *as model*; ~ *for portrait* hacerse; *painter* servir de modelo a; ~ *on committee* ser miembro de; F *p.* hacer callar; ser severo con; *objector* reprimir; ~ *up* incorporarse; velar *at night*; *make* (*a. p.*) ~ *up* sorprender; dar en qué pensar; *v/t.* sentar; *horse* montar; *exam* presentarse para; ~ *out dance* no bailar; *th.* aguantar hasta el fin; *p.* resistir durante más tiempo que;

sit·com [ˈsitkɔm] telecomedia *f* serial; ˈ**sit-down strike** huelga *f* de brazos caídos.

site [sait] **1.** sitio *m*; solar *m*, local *m*; **2.** situar.

sit-in [ˈsitin] manifestación *f* pacífica a modo de bloqueo.

sit·ter [ˈsitər] modelo *m* (de pintor); gallina *f* clueca; *sl.* cosa *f* fácil; *sport*: gol *m etc.* que se canta.

sit·ting [ˈsitiŋ] sesión *f*; nidada *f of eggs*; ˈ~ **room** sala *f* de estar.

sit·u·at·ed [ˈsitjueitid] situado; sito; **sit·u**ˈ**a·tion** situación *f*; (*post*) puesto *m*, colocación *f*.

six [siks] seis (*a. su. m*); *at* ~*es and sevens* en confusión; **six·teen** [ˈ~ˈtiːn] dieciséis; ˈ**six**ˈ**teenth** [~θ] decimosexto; **sixth** [~θ] sexto (*a. su. m*); **six·ti·eth** [ˈ~tiəθ] sexagésimo; ˈ**six·ty** sesenta.

siz·a·ble [ˈsaizəbl] □ considerable.

size[1] [saiz] **1.** tamaño *m*; talla *f*; dimensiones *f/pl.*; extensión *f*; número *m of shoes etc.*; **2.** clasificar según el tamaño; ~ *up* medir (*p.* con la vista); **-sized** de ... tamaño.

size[2] [~] **1.** cola *f*; apresto *m*; **2.** encolar; aprestar.

size·a·ble [ˈsaizəbl] □ = *sizable*.

siz·zle [ˈsizl] chisporrotear, churruscar, crepitar (al freírse).

skate [skeit] **1.** patín *m*; *v. roller*; *ichth.* raya *f*; **2.** patinar; ˈ**skat·er** patinador (-a *f*) *m*; ˈ**skat·ing rink** pista *f* de patinaje.

ske·dad·dle [skiˈdædl] F poner pies en polvorosa, largarse.

skein [skein] madeja *f*.

skel·e·ton [ˈskelitn] **1.** esqueleto *m*; *fig.* esquema *m*; ⊕ armazón *f*; **2.** reducido; esquemático; ~ *key* llave *f* maestra.

skep·tic [ˈskeptik] = *sceptic*.

sketch [sketʃ] **1.** croquis *m*; bosquejo *m*, boceto *m*; *thea.* pieza *f* corta; **2.** bosquejar, dibujar; ˈ**sketch·y** □ incompleto, superficial.
skew [skjuː] oblicuo, sesgado.
skew·er [ˈskuər] **1.** broqueta *f*, espetón *m*; **2.** espetar.
ski [skiː] **1.** esquí *m*; **2.** esquiar.
skid [skid] **1.** derrape *m*, patinazo *m*, deslizamiento *m*; ✈ patín *m*; **2.** derrapar, patinar, deslizarse.
skid·doo [skiˈduː] *sl.* largarse.
skid row [ˈskidˈrou] barrio *m* de mala vida.
ski·er [ˈskiːər] esquiador (-a *f*) *m*.
skiff [skif] esquife *m*.
ski·ing [ˈskiːiŋ] esquí *m*; ˈ**ski jump** salto *m* de esquí; ˈ**ski lift** telesquí *m*, telesilla *f*.
skil(l)·ful [ˈskilful] □ diestro, hábil; experto; ˈ**skil(l)·ful·ness, skill** [skil] destreza *f*, habilidad *f*; pericia *f*; **skilled** [skild] hábil, experto; *work, man* especializado; cualificado.
skil·let [ˈskilit] sartén *f*.
skim [skim] *v/t. milk* desnatar; espumar; (*graze*) rozar, rasar; *v/i.*: ~ *over* pasar rasando; ~ *through fig.* examinar ligeramente, hojear.
skimp [skimp] *v/t.* escatimar; *work* chapucear, frangollar; *v/i.* economizar; ˈ**skimp·y** □ escaso; tacaño.
skin [skin] **1.** piel *f*; cutis *m*; (*animal's*) pellejo *m*; (*hide*) cuero *m*; ⚘ corteza *f*; nata *f on milk*; (*wine-*) odre *m*; *by* (*or with*) *the* ~ *of one's teeth* por los pelos; **2.** *v/t.* despellejar (*a. sl.*); desollar; *fruit* pelar; *tree* descortezar; F ~ *alive* desollar vivo; *v/i.* ⚕ cicatrizarse (*a.* ~ *over*); ˈ~-ˈ**deep** superficial; ˈ~·**flint** cicatero *m*, tacaño *m*; ˈ~-**graft·ing** injerto *m* de piel; ˈ**skin·ner** peletero *m*; ˈ**skin·ny** flaco, magro; ˈ**skin**-ˈ**tight** ajustado al cuerpo.
skip [skip] **1.** brinco *m*, salto *m*; ⚒ jaula *f*; **2.** *v/i.* brincar, saltar (a la comba); *fig.* saltar *from one subject to another*; F escabullirse; *v/t.* (*a.* ~ *over*) omitir, saltar.
skip·per [ˈskipər] ⚓ patrón *m*; capitán *m* (*a. sport*).
skip·ping rope [ˈskipiŋroup] comba *f*.
skir·mish [ˈskəːrmiʃ] **1.** escaramuza *f*; **2.** escaramuzar; ˈ**skir·mish·er** escaramuzador *m*.
skirt [skəːrt] **1.** falda *f*; faldón *m of coat*; (*edge*) orilla *f*, borde *m*; **2.** orillar, ladear; ˈ**skirt·ing board** ⊕ rodapié *m*.
skit [skit] sátira *f*, pasquín *m* (*on* contra); *thea.* número *m* corto burlesco; ˈ**skit·tish** □ asustadizo (*esp. horse*); caprichoso, coqueta.
skit·tle [ˈskitl]: ~*s pl.* juego *m* de bolos; ˈ~ **al·ley** bolera *f*.
skiv·vy [ˈskivi] F *contp.* fregona *f*; esclava *f* del trabajo.
skul·dug·ger·y [skʌlˈdʌgəri] F trampa *f*, embuste *m*.
skulk [skʌlk] acechar; remolonear; ocultarse (en la sombra *etc.*).
skull [skʌl] cráneo *m*; calavera *f*.
skunk [skʌŋk] *zo.* mofeta *f*; F canalla *m*.
sky [skai] cielo *m*; ˈ~-ˈ**blue** azul celeste; ~·**div·ing** [ˈskaidaiviŋ] paracaidismo *m* con plomada suelta inicial; ˈ~-**high** por las nubes; ˈ~·**lark** **1.** alondra *f*; **2.** F jaranear; ˈ~·**light** tragaluz *m*; claraboya *f*; ˈ~·**line** (línea *f* del) horizonte *m*; silueta *f of building etc.*; ˈ~·**rock·et** **1.** cohete *m*; **2.** F subir (como un cohete); ˈ~-**scrap·er** rascacielos *m*; **sky·ward** (**-s**) [ˈ~wərd(z)] hacia el cielo; ˈ**sky-writ·ing** escritura *f* aérea.
slab [slæb] tabla *f* (*a.* ⊕), plancha *f of wood etc.*; losa *f of stone*; tajada *f* (gruesa) *of meat etc.*
slack [slæk] **1.** flojo (*a.* ⚓); (*lax*) descuidado, negligente; (*lazy*) perezoso; *student* desaplicado; ⚓ encalmado; *period etc.* de inactividad; ~ *water*, ~ *tide* repunte *m* de la marea; **2.** lo flojo; ⚓ estación *f* (*or* temporada *f*) de inactividad; ⚒ cisco *m*; ~*s pl.* pantalones *m/pl.* (flojos; *mst* de mujer); **3.** = ~*en*; = *slake*; F holgazanear; gandulear, racanear; ˈ**slack·en** *v/t.* aflojar (*a.* ~ *off*); disminuir; *v/i.* aflojarse; (*wind*) amainar; ~ *up* aflojar el paso; ˈ**slack·er** F gandul *m*, rácano *m*; haragán (-a *f*) *m*; ˈ**slack·ness** flojedad *f*; (*laxity*) descuido *m*; desaplicación *f*, inercia *f in studies*.
slag [slæg] escoria *f*; ˈ~·**heap** escorial *m*; escombrera *f*.
slain [slein] *p.p. of slay*.
slake [sleik] *all senses*: apagar.
sla·lom [ˈslɔːləm] eslálom *m*.
slam [slæm] **1.** golpe *m*; (*door*) portazo *m*; *cards*: bola *f*, capote *m*, slam

m; **2.** (*door*) cerrar(se) de golpe; colocar *etc.* con violencia; golpear.

slan·der [ˈslændər] **1.** calumnia *f*, difamación *f*; **2.** calumniar, difamar; decir mal de; ˈ**slan·der·er** calumniador (-a *f*) *m*; ˈ**slan·der·ous** □ calumnioso.

slang [slæŋ] **1.** argot *m*, jerga *f*; (*thieves'*) germanía *f*; vulgarismo *m*; **2.** poner como un trapo, llenar de insultos; ˈ**slang·y** □ *p.* que emplea (*or th.* lleno de) vulgarismos.

slant [slænt] **1.** inclinación *f*, sesgo *m*; F punto *m* de vista, parecer *m*; **2.** inclinar(se), sesgar(se); ˈ**slant·ing** □ inclinado, sesgado; ˈ**slant·wise** oblicuamente.

slap [slæp] **1.** palmada *f*, manotada *f*; ~ *in the face* bofetada *f*; *fig.* afrenta *f*; humillación *f*; golpe *m* (rudo); **2.** dar una palmada (*or* bofetada) a; pegar; **3.** ¡zas!; **4.** *adv.* (*full*) de lleno, directamente; (*suddenly*) de golpe; ˈ**~-dash** descuidado, de brocha gorda; ˈ**~·jack** torta *f* frita; ˈ**~·stick** payasadas *f/pl.*; ˈ**~-up** F de primera.

slash [slæʃ] **1.** cuchillada *f*; latigazo *m with whip*; *price* reducción *f*; **2.** *v/t.* acuchillar, rasgar; azotar *with whip*; F *price* machacar, cortar; reducir; criticar severamente; *v/i.* tirar tajos (*at* a); ˈ**slash·ing** □ *criticism* severo.

slat [slæt] tablilla *f*, hoja *f*.

slate [sleit] **1.** pizarra *f*; lista *f* de candidatos; **2.** cubrir de pizarra(s); *fig.* proyectar; catalogar; ˈ**~** ˈ**pen·cil** pizarrín *m*; ˈ**slat·er** pizarrero *m*.

slat·tern [ˈslætəːrn] **1.** mujer *f* desaseada; **2.** (*a.* ˈ**slat·tern·ly**) desaseado.

slaugh·ter [ˈslɔːtər] **1.** sacrificio *m*, matanza *f*; *fig.* carnicería *f*, mortandad *f*; **2.** sacrificar, matar; carnear *S.Am.*; ˈ**slaugh·ter·er** jifero *m*; ˈ**slaugh·ter·house** matadero *m*; ˈ**slaugh·ter·ous** mortífero.

Slav [slæv] eslavo *adj. a. su. m* (a *f*).

slave [sleiv] **1.** esclavo (a *f*) *m*; **2.** trabajar como un negro, sudar tinta; ˈ**slav·er**[1] ⚓ barco *m* negrero; (*p.*) (*a.* ˈ**slave**ˈ**driv·er**, ˈ**slave**ˈ**trad·er**) negrero *m* (*a. fig.*).

slav·er[2] [ˈslævər] **1.** baba *f*; **2.** babear.

slav·er·y [ˈsleivəri] esclavitud *f*.

Slav·ic [ˈslævik] eslavo *adj. a. su. m* (*a.* **Slav**ˈ**on·ic**).

slav·ish [ˈsleiviʃ] □ servil; ˈ**slav·ish·ness** servilismo *m*.

slaw [slɔː] ensalada *f* de col.

slay [slei] [*irr.*] matar; ˈ**slay·er** matador *m*; asesino *m*.

sled [sled], *mst* **sledge**[1] [sledʒ] **1.** trineo *m*; **2.** *v/i.* ir en trineo; *v/t.* llevar en trineo.

sledge[2] [~] acotillo *m*, macho *m* (*a.* ˈ**~ ham·mer**).

sleek [sliːk] **1.** □ liso y brillante; *p. etc.* pulcro, pulido; **2.** alisar, pulir; ˈ**sleek·ness** lisura *f etc.*

sleep [sliːp] **1.** [*irr.*] *v/i.* dormir; ~ *like a log* (*or top*) dormir como un lirón; ~ (*up*)*on s.t.* consultar algo con la almohada; *v/t.* pasar durmiendo (*a.* ~ *away*); ~ *off hangover etc.* dormir; ~ *it off* dormir la mona; **2.** sueño *m*; *go to* ~ dormirse (*a. of limb*); *put to* ~ *p.* dormir, adormecer; *pet* sacrificar; *send to* ~ dormir; ˈ**sleep·er** durmiente *m/f*; 🚂 traviesa *f*; (*coach*) coche-cama *m*; cama *f*; *be a light* (*heavy*) ~ tener el sueño ligero (profundo); ˈ**sleep·i·ness** somnolencia *f*; modorra *f*.

sleep·ing [ˈsliːpiŋ] adormecido; durmiente; *v. beauty*; ˈ**~ bag** saco *m* de dormir; ˈ**~ car** 🚂 coche-cama *m*; ˈ**~ pill**, ˈ**~** ˈ**tab·let** comprimido *m* para dormir, somnífero *m*; ˈ**~ sick·ness** enfermedad *f* del sueño.

sleep·less [ˈsliːplis] □ *p.* insomne; desvelado; *night* pasado en vela; ˈ**sleep·less·ness** insomnio *m*.

sleep·walk·er [ˈsliːpwɔːkər] sonámbulo (a *f*) *m*.

sleep·y [ˈsliːpi] *p.* soñoliento; *place* soporífero; *pear* fofo; *be* ~ tener sueño; ˈ**~·head** F dormilón (-a *f*) *m*.

sleet [sliːt] **1.** aguanieve *f*, nevisca *f*; **2.** caer aguanieve, neviscar.

sleeve [sliːv] manga *f*; ⊕ manguito *m*, enchufe *m*; *attr.* ... de enchufe; *have s.t. up one's* ~ tener algo en reserva; *laugh up one's* ~ reírse con disimulo; **sleeved** con mangas; ˈ**sleeve·less** sin mangas.

sleigh [slei] *v. sled.*

sleight [slait] (*mst* ~ *of hand*) escamoteo *m*, prestidigitación *f*.

slen·der [ˈslendər] □ delgado; *resources etc.* escaso, limitado; ˈ**slen·der·ness** delgadez *f*; escasez *f*.

slept [slept] *pret. a. p.p. of sleep* 1.

sleuth [sluːθ] (*a.* ˈ**~·hound**) sabueso *m*; *fig.* detective *m*.

slew [sluː] *pret. of slay.*

slice [slais] **1.** tajada *f*, lonja *f of meat*

etc.; raja *f of sausage*; rebanada *f*, trozo *m of bread*; (*round*) rodaja *f*; (*tool*) estrelladera *f*; **2.** cortar, tajar; *bread* rebanar; (*a.* ~ *off*) cercenar; ˈ**sli·cer** rebanador *m*.
slick [slik] F **1.** *adv.* directamente; **2.** *adj. p.* astuto, mañoso; listo; *movement* hábil.
slick·er [ˈslikər] F (*p.*) embaucador *m*; (*coat*) impermeable *m*.
slid [slid] *pret. a. p.p. of slide* 1.
slide [slaid] **1.** [*irr.*] *v/i.* resbalar; deslizarse (*along* por); *let* ~ no ocuparse de; *v/t.* correr, deslizar; **2.** resbaladero *m on ice*; ⊕ cursor *m*; corredera *f*; (*microscope*) portaobjeto *m*, platina *f*; (*lantern*) diapositiva *f*; ˈ**slide·rule** regla *f* de cálculo.
slid·ing [ˈslaidiŋ] **1.** deslizamiento *m*; **2.** corredizo; ~ *door* puerta *f* de corredera; *mot.* ~ *roof* techo *m* de corredera; ~ *scale* escala *f* móvil; ~ *seat* bancada *f* corrediza.
slight [slait] **1.** □ leve, ligero; insignificante; escaso, tenue; *stature* delgado, pequeño; *not in the* ~*est* ni en lo más mínimo; ~*ly* un poco; ligeramente; **2.** desaire *m*, desatención *f*; **3.** desairar, desatender; menospreciar; ˈ**slight·ing** □ menospreciativo; ˈ**slight·ness** insignificancia *f*; delgadez *f*.
slim [slim] **1.** □ delgado, esbelto; *resources, chance* escaso; **2.** adelgazar.
slime [slaim] limo *m*, légamo *m*; cieno *m*; baba *f of snail*; **slim·i·ness** [ˈslaiminis] lo limoso; viscosidad *f*.
slim·ness [ˈslimnis] delgadez *f*.
slim·y [ˈslaimi] □ limoso, legamoso; baboso; viscoso; *p.* puerco; vil; adulón.
sling [sliŋ] **1.** ⚔ honda *f*; ⚕ cabestrillo *m*; ⚓ eslinga *f*; braga *f*; **2.** [*irr.*] lanzar, tirar; colgar, suspender; ⚓ eslingar.
slink [sliŋk] [*irr.*] *v/i.* andar furtivamente; ~ *away* escabullirse; irse cabizbajo.
slip [slip] **1.** *v/i.* deslizarse; (*freq.* ~ *up*) resbalar; (*bone*) dislocarse; F declinar; ~ *away*, ~ *off* escabullirse; marcharse desapercibido; ~ *back* regresar con sigilo; ~ *by* pasar inadvertido; ~ *through* colarse; ~ *up* resbalar; *fig.* equivocarse; *let* ~ *chance* dejar pasar; *secret* decir inadvertidamente; *v/t.* deslizar; *bone* dislocarse; *guard* eludir; ~ *in remark* deslizar, insinuar; ~ *into* introducir en; ~ *off* (*on*) *coat etc.* quitarse (ponerse) de prisa; *it* ~*ped my mind* se me olvidó; F ~ *one over on* jugarle una mala pasada a; **2.** resbalón *m*; desliz *m* (*a. fig.*); *fig.* lapso *m*, equivocación *f*; ✎ esqueje *m*; (*dress*) combinación *f*; *geol.* dislocación *f*; ⚓ (*a.* ~*s pl.*) grada *f*; ~ *of paper* tira *f*, papeleta *f*; F ~ *of a girl* jovenzuela *f*; ~ *of the pen* lapsus *m* calami; ~ *of the tongue* lapsus *m* linguae; *give a p. the* ~ dar esquinazo a; ˈ~**·knot** lazo *m* corredizo; ˈ**slip·per** zapatilla *f*; babucha *f*; ˈ**slip·per·y** □ resbaladizo; *skin* viscoso; F *p.* astuto, zorro; **slip·shod** [ˈ~ʃɔd] descuidado; desaseado; ˈ**slip·stream** ✈ viento *m* de la hélice; ˈ**slip-up** F error *m*, desliz *m*; ˈ**slip·way** ⚓ gradas *f/pl.*
slit [slit] **1.** hendedura *f*, raja *f*; resquicio *m*; **2.** [*irr.*] hender, rajar, cortar.
slith·er [ˈsliðər] deslizarse, ir rodando; *p.*, *animal* culebrear.
sliv·er [ˈslivər] **1.** raja *f*; **2.** cortar en rajas.
slob [slɔb] persona *f* desaseada.
slob·ber [ˈslɔbər] **1.** baba *f*; **2.** babear; ~ *over* entusiasmarse de un modo ridículo por.
sloe [slou] (*fruit*) endrina *f*; (*tree*) endrino *m*.
slog [slɔg] F *v/i.* afanarse, sudar tinta; *v/t.* golpear (sin arte).
slo·gan [ˈslougən] slogan *m*, lema *m*; † grito *m* de combate.
sloop [slu:p] balandra *f*, corbeta *f*.
slop [slɔp] **1.**: ~*s pl.* agua *f* sucia, lavazas *f/pl.*; (*food*) gachas *f/pl.*; **2.** (*a.* ~ *over*) derramar(se), desbordarse.
slope [sloup] **1.** cuesta *f*, declive *m*; inclinación *f*; vertiente *f*, ladera *f of hill*; **2.** *v/t.* inclinar; sesgar; formar en declive; *v/i.* inclinarse; declinar; *sl.* ~ *off* largarse, escabullirse; ˈ**sloping** □ inclinado; en declive.
slop·py [ˈslɔpi] □ lleno de charcos; mojado; *fig. work* descuidado; *dress* desgalichado; F sentimental.
slosh [slɔʃ] F *v/i.* (*a.* ~ *about*) chapotear.
slot [slɔt] ⚔ muesca *f*, ranura *f*; *hunt.* rastro *m*.
sloth [slouθ] pereza *f*; *zo.* perezoso *m*; **sloth·ful** [ˈ~ful] □ perezoso.

slot ma·chine ['slɔtməʃiːn] tragamonedas *m*; tragaperras *m*.
slouch [slautʃ] **1.** *v/i.* estar sentado (*or* andar *etc.*) con un aire gacho; caminar arrastrando los pies; agacharse; *v/t. hat* agachar; **2.** postura *f* desgarbada; ~ *hat* sombrero *m* gacho; (*he is*) *no* ~ F (no es) nada incapaz.
slough [slʌf] **1.** *zo.* piel *f* (que muda la serpiente); ⚕ escara *f*; **2.** *v/i.* desprenderse; *v/t.* mudar, echar de sí (*a.* ~ *off*).
Slo·vak ['slouvæk] **1.** eslovaco (a *f*) *m*; **2.** = **Slo'va·ki·an** eslovaco.
slov·en ['slʌvn] persona *f* desaseada; **'slov·en·li·ness** desaseo *m*, dejadez *f*; **'slov·en·ly** desaseado, desaliñado, dejado; *work* descuidado.
slow [slou] **1.** □ lento; pausado; *clock* atrasado; (*dull*) torpe, lerdo; (*boring*) aburrido; *be* ~ *to* tardar en; *my watch is (10 minutes)* ~ mi reloj atrasa (10 minutos); ~ *lane* vía *f* de velocidad reducida; **2.** *adv.* (*a.* ~*ly*) despacio, lentamente; **3.** (*a.* ~ *down*, ~ *up*) *v/t.* retardar; ⊕ reducir la velocidad de, moderar la marcha de; *v/i.* ir más despacio; moderarse la marcha; **'~·down** reducción *f* de velocidad *or* ritmo; huelga *f* de brazos caídos; **'~-'mo·tion** *film* a cámara lenta; **'slow·ness** lentitud *f*; torpeza *f*; **'slow·worm** lución *m*.
sludge [slʌdʒ] lodo *m*, fango *m*; sedimento *m* fangoso.
slug[1] [slʌg] *zo.* babosa *f*.
slug[2] [~] **1.** ⚔ posta *f*; *typ.* lingote *m*; *sl.* porrazo *m*; puñetazo *m*; **2.** apuñear.
slug·gard ['slʌgərd] haragán (-a *f*) *m*; **'slug·gish** □ perezoso; tardo; inactivo.
sluice [sluːs] **1.** esclusa *f*; (*a.* **'~·way**) canal *m*; (*a.* **'~ gate**) compuerta *f*; **2.** regar, lavar (abriendo la compuerta).
slum [slʌm] barrio *m* bajo; (*house*) casucha *f*, tugurio *m*; ~*s pl.* barrios *m/pl.* bajos.
slum·ber ['slʌmbər] **1.** (*a.* ~*s pl.*) *lit.* sueño *m* (*mst* tranquilo); *fig.* inactividad *f*; **2.** dormir, dormitar; *fig.* permanecer inactivo.
slum·brous, slum·ber·ous ['slʌmbrəs, '~bərəs] □ soñoliento; inactivo.
'slum·lord ['slʌmlɔːrd] dueño *m* desinteresado de casas del barrio bajo.
slump [slʌmp] **1.** hundirse, bajar repentinamente; dejarse caer pesadamente *into chair*; **2.** ✝ baja *f* repentina *in price*; (*general*) declive *m* económico, retroceso *m*; bajón *m in morale*.
slung [slʌŋ] *pret. a. p.p. of sling* 2.
slunk [slʌŋk] *pret. a. p.p. of slink*.
slur [sləːr] **1.** reparo *m*; borrón *m* (en la reputación); ♪ ligado *m*; **2.** pasar por encima, ocultar (*a.* ~ *over*); *syllable* comerse; ♪ ligar.
slush [slʌʃ] nieve *f* a medio derretir; fango *m*; F sentimentalismo *m*, cursilería *f*; **'slush·y** fangoso; F sentimental, cursi.
slut [slʌt] marrana *f*, mujer *f* promiscua; **'slut·tish** sucio, desaliñado; promiscuo.
sly [slai] socarrón, taimado; astuto; furtivo; *on the* ~ a hurtadillas; **'sly·ness** socarronería *f*; astucia *f*.
smack[1] [smæk] **1.** sabor(cillo) *m*, dejo *m* (*of* a); **2.** saber (*of* a); ~ *of b.s.* tener resabios de.
smack[2] [~] **1.** (*slap*) manotada *f*; golpe *m*; **2.** dar una manotada a, pegar; golpear; *lips* relamerse; **3.** ¡zas!
smack[3] [~] ⚓ queche *m*.
smack·er ['smækər] *sl.* boca *f*; beso *m* sonado; dólar *m*.
smack·ing ['smækiŋ] F zurra *f*.
small [smɔːl] **1.** pequeño; chico; menudo; corto, exiguo; insignificante; *print* minúsculo; *voice* humilde; *p.* bajo (de estatura); *feel* ~ sentirse humillado; *v. beer, change, fry, hour, ware, etc.*; **2.**: ~ *of the back* parte *f* más estrecha (de la espalda); F ~*s pl.* paños *m/pl.* menores; **'~ arms** *pl.* armas *f/pl.* cortas; **'small-hold·ing** ⚘ parcela *f*; minifundio *m*; **'small·ish** más bien pequeño; **'small·ness** pequeñez *f*; **'small·pox** ⚕ viruela *f*; **'small talk** cháchara *f*; vulgaridades *f/pl.*; **'small-time** de poca importancia.
smalt [smɔːlt] esmalte *m*.
smarm·y ['smɑːrmi] F cobista.
smart [smɑːrt] **1.** □ listo, vivo; inteligente; *b.s.* ladino, astuto; *dress etc.* elegante; *appearance* pulcro; (*tidy*) aseado; *society* de buen tono; *pace* vivo; ~ *aleck* sabelotodo *m*; ~ *money fig.* inversionistas *m/pl.* astutos (*f/pl.*

as); gente *f* bien informada; **2.** escozor *m*; **3.** escocer; picar; ~ *under*, ~ *with fig.* resentirse de; *it makes my tongue* ~ escuece en la lengua; *you shall* ~ *for it* me lo pagará; ˈ**smart·en** hermosear (*mst* ~ *up*), arreglar; ˈ**smart·ness** elegancia *f*; vivacidad *f etc.*

smash [smæʃ] **1.** romper(se), hacer(se) pedazos; destrozar(se), aplastar(se) (*freq.* ~ *up*); ✝ quebrar; ~ *into* chocar con; **2.** 🚗 *etc.* choque *m* (violento), accidente *m*; ✝ quiebra *f*; *tennis*: golpe *m* violento; *go to* ~ hacerse pedazos; ~ *hit sl.* exitazo *m*; ˈ**smash·er** *sl.* (*girl*) bombón *m*, guayabo *m*; ˈ**smash·ing** *sl.* imponente, bárbaro; ˈ**smash-up** colisión *f* violenta.

smat·ter·ing [ˈsmætəriŋ] nociones *f/pl.*; barniz *m*; tintura *f*.

smear [smir] **1.** manchar(se) (*a. fig.*), embarrar(se), calumniar; **2.** mancha *f* (*a. fig.*), embarradura *f*.

smell [smel] **1.** olor *m* (*of* a); (*bad*) hedor *m*; (*sense of*) olfato *m*; **2.** [*irr.*] oler (*of* a); (*dog*) olfatear; ~ *out* husmear; ~*ing salts pl.* sales *f/pl.* (aromáticas).

smelt[1] [smelt] *pret. a. p.p. of smell* 2.

smelt[2] [~] *ichth.* eperlano *m*.

smelt[3] [~] fundir; ˈ**smelt·er** fundidor *m*; ˈ**smelt·ing** ˈ**fur·nace** horno *m* de fundición.

smile [smail] **1.** sonrisa *f*; **2.** sonreír(se) (*at* de); *fig.* ~ *on* favorecer; ˈ**smil·ing** □ risueño.

smirch [smə:rtʃ] *lit.* mancillar; desdorar.

smirk [smə:rk] **1.** sonreírse satisfecho; sonreírse afectadamente; **2.** sonrisa *f* satisfecha; sonrisa *f* afectada.

smite [smait] [*irr.*] † golpear (con fuerza); herir; castigar; afligir.

smith [smiθ] herrero *m*.

smith·er·eens [ˈsmiðəˈri:nz] *pl.* F añicos *m/pl.*; *smash to* ~ hacer añicos.

smith·y [ˈsmiði] herrería *f*.

smit·ten [ˈsmitn] **1.** *p.p. of smite*; **2.** *fig.* ~ *with* afligido por; F *idea* entusiasmado por; *p.* chalado por.

smock [smɔk] **1.** fruncir; **2.** blusa *f* (*a.* ˈ~ **frock**); bata *f*.

smog [smɔg] niebla *f* espesa con humo.

smoke [smouk] **1.** humo *m*; F pitillo *m*, tabaco *m*; F *have a* ~ echar un pitillo; **2.** *v/i.* fumar; (*chimney*) echar humo, humear; *v/t.* fumar; *bacon etc.* ahumar; ~ *out* ahuyentar con humo; ˈ~**-dried** ahumado; ˈ**smoke·less** □ sin humo; ˈ**smok·er** fumador (-a *f*) *m*; 🚃 coche *m* fumador; ˈ**smoke screen** cortina *f* de humo; ˈ**smoke·stack** chimenea *f*.

smok·ing [ˈsmoukiŋ] **1.** el fumar; *no* ~ prohibido fumar; **2.** ... de fumador(es); ˈ~ **com·part·ment** departamento *m* de fumadores; ˈ~ **room** salón *m* de fumar.

smok·y [ˈsmouki] □ *fire, chimney* humeante; *room* lleno de humo; *taste, surface etc.* ahumado.

smol·der [ˈsmouldər] = *smoulder*.

smooth [smu:ð] **1.** □ liso, terso; suave; llano, igual; *passage, water* tranquilo; *paste* liso, sin grumos; *manner* afable; *style* flúido; *p., b.s.* zalamero, meloso, astuto; *go* ~*ly* ir sobre ruedas; **2.** (*a.* ~ *out*, ~ *down*) alisar; suavizar; allanar; ⊕ desbastar; *p.* ablandar; (*a.* ~ *over*, ~ *away*) suprimir, allanar; ~*ing iron* plancha *f*; ˈ**smooth·ness** lisura *f*; suavidad *f etc.*

smote [smout] *pret. of smite*.

smoth·er [ˈsmʌðər] (*a.* ~ *up*) sofocar, ahogar; *fire* apagar; *yawn* contener; *doubts etc.* suprimir; *fig.* ~ (*a. p.*) *with* llenar de.

smoul·der [ˈsmouldər] arder sin llama; *fig.* estar latente.

smudge [smʌdʒ] **1.** manchar(se), tiznar(se); **2.** mancha *f*; ˈ**smudg·y** □ manchado; borroso.

smug [smʌg] □ pagado de sí mismo; presumido, vanidoso.

smug·gle [ˈsmʌgl] pasar de contrabando; ˈ**smug·gler** contrabandista *m/f*; ˈ**smug·gling** contrabando *m*.

smut [smʌt] **1.** tizne *m*; tiznón *m*; ⚘ tizón *m*; *fig.* obscenidad *f*; **2.** tiznar(se).

smut·ty [ˈsmʌti] □ tiznado; ⚘ atizonado; *fig.* obsceno, verde.

snack [snæk] bocadillo *m*, tentempié *m*; ˈ~ **bar** bar *m*; cafetería *f*; cantina *f*.

snag [snæg] nudo *m in wood*; tocón *m of tree*; raigón *m of tooth*; *fig.* tropiezo *m*; obstáculo *m*.

snail [sneil] caracol *m*; *at a* ~*'s pace* a paso de tortuga.

snake [sneik] culebra *f*, serpiente *f*; ~ *in the grass* sujeto *m* traidor; ˈ~**·weed** bistorta *f*.

snak·y [ˈsneiki] □ serpentino, tortuoso.
snap [snæp] 1. castañetazo *m of fingers*; chasquido *m of whip*; (*fastener*) corchete *m*, cierre *m*; F vigor *m*; *sl.* cosa *f* fácil; *phot.* foto *f*, instantánea *f*; *cold* ~ ola *f* de frío; 2. repentino, imprevisto; 3. *v/i.* (*break*) romperse; saltar; (*sound*) chasquear; ~ *at* querer morder; *fig.* contestar groseramente a; F ~ *into s.t.* emprender algo con vigor; F ~ *out of it* cambiarse repentinamente; ~ *out of it!* ¡menéate!, ¡ánimo!; *v/t.* romper; hacer saltar; *whip etc.* chasquear; *fingers* castañetear; *phot.* sacar una foto (*or* instantánea) de; ~ *one's fingers at* tratar con desprecio; ~ *shut* cerrar de golpe; F ~ *up* asir; comprar con avidez; 4. ¡crac!; ˈ**~·drag·on** cabeza *f* de dragón; ˈ**~ fas·ten·er** corchete *m* (de presión); ˈ**snap·pish** □ arisco; irritable; ˈ**snap·pish·ness** irritabilidad *f*; ˈ**snap·py** F enérgico; F *make it* ~! ¡pronto!; ˈ**snap·shot** 1. *phot.* instantánea *f*; 2. sacar una instantánea de.
snare [sner] 1. trampa *f*, lazo *m*; *fig.* engaño *m*; 2. coger con trampas; *fig.* hacer caer en el lazo.
snarl [snɑːrl] 1. gruñir; regañar; 2. gruñido *m*; regaño *m*; enredo *m*.
snatch [snætʃ] 1. arrebatamiento *m*; ♪ *etc.* trocito *m*; *by* ~*es* a ratos; 2. (~ *at* tratar de) arrebatar (*from* a); coger (al vuelo); ~ *up* asir.
sneak [sniːk] 1. *v/i.* ir (~ *in* entrar) a hurtadillas; ~ *away*, ~ *off* escabullirse; *v/t.* F hacer a hurtadillas; 2. soplón (-a *f*) *m*; ˈ**sneak·ers** *pl.* F zapatos *m/pl.* ligeros de goma; ˈ**sneak·ing** □ *manner* furtivo; *suspicion* inexplicable; secreto; ˈ**sneak thief** ratero *m*.
sneer [snir] 1. visaje *m* de burla y desprecio; 2. hacer un visaje de burla y desprecio; ~ *at* mofarse de, mirar al desgaire; ˈ**sneer·er** mofador (-a *f*) *m*; ˈ**sneer·ing** □ burlador y despreciativo.
sneeze [sniːz] 1. estornudar; 2. estornudo *m*.
snick [snik] tijeretear.
sniff [snif] 1. *v/i.* oler, ventear; ~ *at* husmear; F menospreciar; *v/t.* husmear, olfatear; sorber por las narices; 2. husmeo *m*; venteo *m*; sorbo *m* por las narices; ˈ**sniff·y** F estirado.
snig·ger [ˈsnigər] reírse con disimulo (*at* de).
snip [snip] 1. tijeretada *f*; recorte *m*; *sl.* ganga *f*; 2. tijeretear; recortar (*a.* ~ *off*).
snipe [snaip] 1. *orn.* agachadiza *f*; 2. ⚔ tirar desde un escondite; ~ *at* paquear; ˈ**snip·er** tirador *m* escondido.
snip·pets [ˈsnipits] *pl.* recortes *m/pl.*; *fig.* retazos *m/pl.*
snitch [snitʃ] *sl.* 1. (*nose*) naipas *f/pl.*; 2. soplar; escamotear; (*filch*) hurtar.
sniv·el [ˈsnivl] lloriquear; gimotear; ˈ**sniv·el·(l)ing** llorón.
snob [snɔb] (e)snob *m/f*; ˈ**snob·ber·y** (e)snobismo *m*; ˈ**snob·bish** □ (e)snob; (e)snobista.
snoop [snuːp] *sl.* 1. curiosear, fisgonear, ventear; 2. fisgón (-a *f*) *m*; ˈ**snoop·er** *sl.* investigador *m* furtivo.
snoot·y [ˈsnuːti] F fachendón.
snooze [snuːz] F 1. siestecita *f*, sueñecillo *m*; 2. dormitar; echar una siestecita.
snore [snɔːr] 1. ronquido *m* (*a.* ˈ**snor·ing**); 2. roncar.
snort [snɔːrt] 1. bufido *m*; *sl.* trago *m*; 2. *v/i.* bufar; *v/t.* decir con un bufido.
snot [snɔt] F mocarro *m*; ˈ**snot·ty** F mocoso; *sl.* insolente.
snout [snaut] hocico *m*, morro *m*.
snow [snou] 1. nieve *f*; *sl.* cocaína *f*; 2. nevar; *sl.* engañar; F *be* ~*ed under* estar inundado (*with*, *by* por); *be* ~*ed up* estar encerrado (*or* aislado) por la nieve; ˈ**~·ball** 1. bola *f* de nieve; 2. *v/t.* lanzar bolas de nieve a; *v/i. fig.* aumentar progresivamente; ˈ**~·bound** aprisionado por la nieve; ˈ**~·drift** ventisquero *m*; ˈ**~·drop** campanilla *f* blanca; ˈ**~·fall** nevada *f*; ˈ**~·flake** copo *m* de nieve; ˈ**~ job** *sl.* decepción *f*; engaño *m*; ˈ**~·man** figura *f* de nieve; ˈ**~·plow** (máquina *f*) quitanieves *m*; ˈ**~·shoe** raqueta *f* de nieve; ˈ**~·storm** nevasca *f*; ˈ**~ tire** llanta *f* de invierno; ˈ**~ˈwhite**, ˈ**snow·y** □ nevoso; *fig.* níveo.
snub [snʌb] 1. desairar; 2. desaire *m*; ˈ**snub-nosed** chato.
snuff [snʌf] 1. rapé *m*, tabaco *m* en polvo; 2. aspirar, sorber por la nariz (*a. take* ~); *candle* despabilar; *fig.* extinguir; ˈ**~·box** tabaquera *f*; ˈ**snuff·ers** *pl.* (*a pair of* ~ unas) despabiladeras *f/pl.*; **snuf·fle** [ˈ~l] 1. resollar; ganguear; 2. gangueo *m*.

snug [snʌg] □ cómodo; abrigado; *dress* ajustado; ⚓ bien aparejado; **ˈsnug·ger·y** cuarto *m* cómodo; **snug·gle** [ˈ~l] arrimarse (*up to* a); apretarse (para calentarse).

so [sou] así; por tanto, por consiguiente; (*and* ~) conque; ~ *good* tan bueno; ~ *much* tanto; ~ *many* tantos; *I think* ~ creo que sí; *or* ~ o así; más o menos; ~ *am I* yo también; *and* ~ *forth, and* ~ *on* y así sucesivamente; etcétera; *v. far*; ~ *much* ~ tan es así (*that* que); ~ *as to,* ~ *that* (*purpose*) para *inf.*, para que *subj.*; (*result*) de modo que.

soak [souk] **1.** remojar(se), empapar(se); F beber mucho; *sl.* desplumar, clavar un precio exorbitante a; *get* ~*ed to the skin* calarse hasta los huesos; *leave to* ~ dejar en remojo; ~ *in* penetrar; ~ *up* absorber, embeber; **2.** F borrachín *m*; **ˈsoak·ing** remojón *m*; ~ *wet* remojado; hecho una sopa.

so-and-so [ˈsouənsou] (*p.*) fulano (a *f*) *m*; F tío *m*; *Mr* ♀ Don Fulano (de Tal).

soap [soup] **1.** jabón *m*; *soft* ~ *sl.* coba *f*; **2.** (en)jabonar; **ˈ~·box** *fig.* caja *f* vacía empleada como tribuna (en la calle); ~ *orator* orador *m* de barricada; **ˈ~ dish** jabonera *f*; **ˈ~ op·er·a** *sl.* serial *m* radiofónico; telenovela *f*; serial *m* lacrimógeno; **ˈ~-suds** *pl.* jabonaduras *f/pl.*; **ˈsoap·y** □ jabonoso.

soar [sɔːr] encumbrarse (*a. fig.*); cernerse; volar a gran altura; *fig.* elevarse muchísimo.

sob [sɔb] **1.** sollozo *m*; **2.** sollozar; **3.** F sentimental.

so·ber [ˈsoubər] **1.** □ sobrio; serio; (*sensible*) cuerdo; moderado; *color* apagado; (*not drunk*) no embriagado; **2.** calmar(se) (*a.* ~ *down*); F ~ *up* desintoxicar(se), quitar(se) la sopa (a); **ˈso·ber·ness** sobriedad *f*; cordura *f*; **so·bri·e·ty** [souˈbraiəti] moderación *f*; sobriedad *f*.

sob-stuff [ˈsɔbstʌf] sentimentalismo *m*.

so-called [ˈsouˈkɔːld] llamado.

soc·cer [ˈsɔkər] F fútbol *m*.

so·cia·bil·i·ty [souʃəˈbiliti] sociabilidad *f*; **ˈso·cia·ble** □ sociable.

so·cial [ˈsouʃl] **1.** □ social; ~ *democrat* socialdemócrata *m/f*; ~ *insurance* (*or* ~ *security*) seguro *m* social; ~ *services pl.* servicios *m/pl.* sociales; **2.** reunión *f* (social), velada *f*; **ˈso·cial·ism** socialismo *m*; **ˈso·cial·ist** socialista *adj. a. su. m/f*; **so·cial·ite** [ˈsouʃəlait] F persona *f* conocidísima en la buena sociedad; **ˈso·cial·ize** socializar.

so·ci·e·ty [səˈsaiəti] sociedad *f*; asociación *f*; (*high* ~) buena sociedad *f*; *friendly* ~ montepío *m*, mutualidad *f*.

so·ci·o·log·i·cal [sousiəˈlɔdʒikl] □ sociológico; **so·ci·ol·o·gist** [~ˈɔlədʒist] sociólogo *m*; **so·ciˈol·o·gy** sociología *f*.

sock[1] [sɔk] calcetín *m*.

sock[2] [~] *sl.* **1.** tortazo *m*; puñetazo *m*; **2.** pegar; golpear.

sock·et [ˈsɔkit] cuenca *f of eye*; alvéolo *m of tooth*; ⚡, ⊕ enchufe *m*; cañón *m*; ~ *wrench* llave *f* de cubo (*or* de caja).

sod [sɔd] césped *m*, terrón *m*.

so·da [ˈsoudə] sosa *f*, soda *f* (*a. drink*); **ˈ~ foun·tain** sifón *m*; fuente *f* de sodas; **ˈ~ wa·ter** agua *f* de seltz; sifón *m*.

sod·den [ˈsɔdn] empapado, saturado; *p.* embrutecido por el alcohol.

so·di·um [ˈsoudjəm] sodio *m*.

so·ev·er [souˈevər] *in compounds*: ... de cualquier clase *etc.*

so·fa [ˈsoufə] sofá *m*.

soft [sɔft] **1.** □ blando; muelle; *sound, air, skin* suave; *water* blando; *metal* dúctil; *color* delicado; *hat* flexible; *character* débil, afeminado; F *heart* tierno; F *job* fácil; F (*foolish*) estúpido; F *drink* no alcohólico; **2.** (*a.* ~*ly*) suavemente, blandamente *etc.*;

soft·en [ˈsɔfn] ablandar(se); reblandecer; suavizar(se); templar(se);

soft·ness [ˈsɔftnis] blandura *f*; suavidad *f*; molicie *f*; ⊕ ductilidad *f*; **ˈsoft·ware** programas *m/pl.* (*or* operaciones *f/pl.*) de ordenador; **ˈsoft·y** mollejón (-a *f*) *m*.

sog·gy [ˈsɔgi] empapado; esponjoso.

soil[1] [sɔil] tierra *f* (*a. fig.*), suelo *m*.

soil[2] [~] ensuciar(se); manchar(se) (*a. fig.*).

soir·ée [ˈswɑːrei] sarao *m*, velada *f*.

so·journ [ˈsɔdʒəːrn] **1.** permanencia *f*, estancia *f*; **2.** permanecer, pasar una temporada.

sol·ace [ˈsɔləs] **1.** consuelo *m*; **2.** consolar.

so·lar [ˈsoulər] solar; ~ *plexus* plexo *m* solar; ~ *battery* fotopila *f*.

sold [sould] *pret. a. p.p. of sell* 1.

sol·der ['sɔldər] **1.** soldadura *f*; **2.** soldar; **sol·der·ing i·ron** ['~riŋ-aiərn] soldador *m*.

sol·dier ['souldʒər] **1.** soldado *m*; militar *m*; **2.** militar, ser soldado; **'sol·dier·like, 'sol·dier·ly** militar; **'sol·dier·y** soldadesca *f*.

sole[1] [soul] □ único, solo; exclusivo; *~ agent* agente *m* único; *~ right* exclusiva *f*.

sole[2] [~] **1.** suela *f*, piso *m of shoe*; *anat.* planta *f*; **2.** solar.

sole[3] [~] *ichth.* lenguado *m*.

sol·e·cism ['sɔlisizm] solecismo *m*.

sol·emn ['sɔləm] □ solemne; **so-lem·ni·ty** [sə'lemniti] solemnidad *f*; **sol·em·ni·za·tion** ['sɔləmnai-'zeiʃn] solemnización *f*; **'sol·em-nize** solemnizar.

sol·fa [sɔl'fɑː] **1.** solfa *f*; **2.** solfear.

so·lic·it [sə'lisit] solicitar (*a p. for a th. or a th. of a p.* algo a alguien); importunar; intentar seducir; **so-lic·i'ta·tion** solicitación *f*; **so'lic·i-tor** ⚖ *British approx.* abogado *m*; procurador *m*; (*oaths, wills etc.*) notario *m*; representante *m/f*; procurador *m* general del Estado; **so'lic·it·ous** □ solícito (*about, for* por); ansioso; **so'lic·i·tude** [~tjuːd] solicitud *f*, ansiedad *f*.

sol·id ['sɔlid] **1.** □ sólido (*a. fig.*, ⩓); *gold, tire etc.* macizo; *crowd* denso; *vote* unánime; *a ~ hour* una hora entera; ⩓ *~ geometry* geometría *f* del espacio; **2.** sólido *m*; **sol·i·dar·i·ty** [~'dæriti] solidaridad *f*; **so'lid·i·fy** [~fai] solidificar(se); **so'lid·i·ty** solidez *f*; **'sol·id-state** transistorizado.

so·lil·o·quize [sə'liləkwaiz] soliloquiar; **so'lil·o·quy** soliloquio *m*.

sol·i·taire [sɔli'ter] solitario *m* (*game, gem*); **sol·i·tar·y** ['~təri] □ solitario; retirado; único; *in ~ confinement* incomunicado; **sol·i·tude** ['~tjuːd] soledad *f*.

so·lo ['soulou] ♪, *cards*: solo *m*; ✈ *~ flight* vuelo *m* a solas; **'so·lo·ist** solista *m/f*.

sol·stice ['sɔlstis] solsticio *m*.

sol·u·bil·i·ty [sɔlju'biliti] solubilidad *f*; **sol·u·ble** ['sɔljubl] soluble.

so·lu·tion [sə'luːʃn] *all senses*: solución *f*.

solv·a·ble ['sɔlvəbl] soluble; **solve** [sɔlv] resolver; solucionar; *riddle* adivinar; **sol·ven·cy** ['~vənsi] solvencia *f*; **'sol·vent** solvente *adj*. (✝) *a. su. m* (⚗).

som·ber ['sɔmbər] □ sombrío.

some [sʌm, *unstressed* səm] **1.** *pron. a. adj.* un poco (de); alguno(s); unos; ciertos; *~ few* unos pocos; *~ 20 miles* unas 20 millas; *freq. not translated, e.g. do you want ~ bread?* ¿quiere pan?; *for ~ reason* (*or other*) por alguna que otra razón, por no sé qué razón; F *or Am. this is ~ house!* ¡esto es lo que se llama casa!; **2.** *adv.* algo; *Am.* F muy, mucho; **'~·bod·y, '~·one** alguien; F *be ~* ser un personaje; *~ else* otra persona; **'~·day** algún día; **'~·how** de algún modo; *~ or other* de un modo u otro; *~ or other I never liked him* por alguna que otra razón no me era simpático.

som·er·sault ['sʌmərsɔːlt] **1.** salto *m* mortal; (*car*) vuelco *m*; *turn ~s* = **2.** dar saltos mortales; (*car*) volcar.

some...: ~·thing ['sʌmθiŋ] algo; alguna cosa; *~ else* otra cosa; *that is ~* eso ya es algo; *~ of a* (*e.g. painter*) en cierto modo; **'~·time** **1.** algún día; alguna vez, en algún tiempo; **2.** antiguo; **~·times** [~z] algunas veces; a veces; **'~·what** algo, algún tanto; **'~·where** en (*motion* a) alguna parte; *~ else* en (*motion* a) otra parte.

som·nam·bu·lism [sɔm'næmbjulizm] somnambulismo *m*; **som-'nam·bu·list** somnámbulo (a *f*) *m*.

som·nif·er·ous [sɔm'nifərəs] □ somnífero.

som·no·lence ['sɔmnələns] somnolencia *f*; **'som·no·lent** □ soñoliento.

son [sʌn] hijo *m*.

so·na·ta [sə'nɑːtə] sonata *f*.

song [sɔŋ] canción *f*; canto *m*; cantar *m*; F *for a* (*mere*) *~* medio regalado; F *~ and dance* alharaca *f*; **'~·bird** pájaro *m* cantor; **'~ book** cancionero *m*; **'~ hit** canción *f* de moda; **'song·ster** pájaro *m* cantor.

son·ic bar·ri·er ['sɔnik 'bæriər] barrera *f* del sonido; **'son·ic 'boom** estampido *m* sónico.

son-in-law, *pl.* **sons-in-law** ['sʌn(z)inlɔː] yerno *m*, hijo *m* político.

son·net ['sɔnit] soneto *m*.

son·ny ['sʌni] F hijito *m*.

so·no·rous [sə'nɔːrəs] □ sonoro, resonante; so'**no·rous·ness** sonoridad *f*.

soon [suːn] pronto, temprano; ~ *after* poco después; *as* (*or so*) ~ *as* tan pronto como (*a. cj.*), luego que; *as* ~ *as possible* cuanto antes; '**sooner** más temprano; ~ *or later* tarde o temprano; ~ *than* antes que; *no* ~ ... *than* apenas; *I had* (*or would*) ~ ... preferiría ...; *I would just as* ~ *stay* igual me daría quedarme, estaría tan contento de quedarme.

soot [sut] hollín *m*.

sooth [suːθ]: *in* ~ en realidad.

soothe [suːð] calmar; aliviar; '**sooth·ing** □ calmante; tranquilizador.

sooth·say·er ['suːθseiər] adivino (a *f*) *m*.

soot·y ['suti] □ holliniento.

sop [sɔp] **1.** sopa *f*; *fig.* dádiva *f*; compensación *f*; *sl.* tonto *m*; **2.** empapar; ~ *up* absorber.

soph·ism ['sɔfizm] sofisma *m*.

soph·ist ['sɔfist] sofista *m*; **so·phis·tic, so·phis·ti·cal** [sə'fistik(l)] □ sofístico; so'**phis·ti·cat·ed** □ sofisticado; **soph·ist·ry** ['sɔfistri] sofistería *f*.

soph·o·more ['sɔfəmɔːr] *Am. univ.* estudiante *m*/*f* de segundo año.

so·po·rif·ic [soupə'rifik] □ soporífero *adj. a. su. m.*

sop·ping ['sɔpiŋ]: ~ *wet* hecho una sopa; '**sop·py** *sl.* tonto; sentimental.

so·pran·o [sə'prænou, sə'prɑːnou] soprano *f*, tiple *f*.

sor·cer·er ['sɔːrsərər] hechicero *m*, brujo *m*; '**sor·cer·ess** hechicera *f*, bruja *f*; '**sor·cer·y** hechicería *f*, brujería *f*.

sor·did ['sɔːrdid] □ asqueroso; vil, bajo; '**sor·did·ness** asquerosidad *f etc.*

sore [sɔːr] **1.** □ dolorido; doloroso; sensible; inflamado; *poet.* fuerte, grande; F irritable; F resentido; *be* ~ doler; **2.** llaga *f* (*a. fig.*), úlcera *f*; '**sore·head** F persona *f* resentida; '**sore·ly** *adv.* penosamente; con urgencia; muy; '**sore·ness** dolor *m*; inflamación *f*.

so·ror·i·ty [sə'rɔriti] *Am. univ.* hermandad *f* (de estudiantes).

sor·rel[1] ['sɔrəl] alazán *adj.* (*color*) *a. su. m* (*horse*).

sor·rel[2] [~] ♀ acedura *f*.

sor·row ['sɔrou] **1.** pesar *m*, dolor *m*, pena *f*; **2.** apenarse, afligirse (*at, for, over* de, por); **sor·row·ful** ['~ful] □ pesaroso, afligido.

sor·ry ['sɔri] □ pesaroso, apesadumbrado; apenado; arrepentido (*for th.* de); *condition, plight* desastrado, lastimoso; *excuse* poco convincente; *figure* ridículo; *sight* triste; *be* ~ sentirlo; *be* ~ *for p.* compadecer; *be* ~ *for o.s.* estar muy alicaído; *be* ~ *that* sentir que *subj.*; *be* ~ *to inf.* sentir *inf.*; (*I am*) (*so*) ~! lo siento (mucho); (*asking pardon*) ¡perdón!

sort [sɔːrt] **1.** clase *f*, especie *f*; *a* ~ *of* uno a modo de; *in some* ~, F ~ *of* algo; en cierta medida; *of all* ~*s* de toda clase; *something of the* ~, *that* ~ *of thing* algo por el estilo; *of* ~*s* de poco valor; *out of* ~*s* ⚕ indispuesto; de mal humor; *it takes all* ~*s* (*to make a world*) de todo hay en este mundo de Dios; F *he's a good* ~ es un buen chico; es buena persona; **2.** clasificar (*a.* ~ *out*); escoger; separar.

sor·tie ['sɔːrtiː] salida *f*.

so-so ['sousou] F regular; mediano.

sot [sɔt] borrachín *m*.

sot·tish ['sɔtiʃ] □ embrutecido (por el alcohol).

sought [sɔːt] *pret. a. p.p. of* **seek**; ['~-'**aft·er** solicitado.

soul [soul] alma *f* (*a. fig.*); *upon my* ~! ¡por vida mía!; '**soul·ful** □ sentimental; conmovedor; '**soul·less** □ desalmado.

sound[1] [saund] □ sano; firme, sólido; *p.* digno de confianza; *opinion* razonable, bien fundado, ortodoxo; *move* acertado, razonable, eficaz; *sleep* profundo; ⚚ solvente.

sound[2] [~] **1.** sonido *m*; son *m*; ruido *m*; *I don't like the* ~ *of it* no me gusta la idea; me inquieta la noticia; ~ *barrier* barrera *f* del sonido; ~ *effects pl.* efectos *m*/*pl.* sonoros; ~ *film* película *f* sonora; ~ *track film*: banda *f* sonora; ~ *wave* onda *f* sonora; **2.** *v*/*i.* (re)sonar; (*seem*) parecer; *v*/*t.* sonar; tocar; *alarm* dar la voz de; *praises* entonar; ⚔ ~ *the charge* tocar el zafarrancho de combate.

sound[3] [~] ⚓ estrecho *m*, brazo *m* de mar.

sound[4] [~] **1.** ⚕ sonda *f*; **2.** ⚓, ⚕ sondar; *chest* auscultar; *intentions, p.* sondear (*a.* ~ *out*).

sound·ing [ˈsaundiŋ] ⚓ sondeo *m.*
sound(·ing) board [ˈsaund(iŋ)-bɔːrd] ♪ secreto *m*; caja *f* de resonancia (*a. fig.*).
sound·less [ˈsaundlis] □ silencioso; ⊕ insonorizado.
sound·ness [ˈsaundnis] firmeza *f*, solidez *f etc.*
sound·proof [ˈsaundpruːf], **sound-tight** [ˈ~tait] insonorizado.
soup [suːp] (*thin*) caldo *m*, consomé *m*; (*thick*) puré *m*, sopa *f*; F *in the* ~ en apuros; ~ *tureen* sopera *f*.
sour [ˈsauər] **1.** □ agrio (*a. fig.*); acre (*a. fig.*); *milk* cortado; *land* maleado; *go* ~ (*milk*) cortarse; **2.** agriar(se); (*land*) malear(se); *fig.* amargar (*v/t.*).
source [sɔːrs] fuente *f*, nacimiento *m of river*; *fig.* fuente *f*; procedencia *f*.
sour·dough [ˈsauərdou] **1.** (pan *m* de) masa *f* fermentada; **2.** F explorador *m en Alaska*.
sour·ish [ˈsauəriʃ] agrete; ˈ**sour·ness** agrura *f* (*a. fig.*); acidez *f*;
sour·puss [ˈ~pus] *sl.* cascarrabias *m/f*.
souse [saus] **1.** escabechar; zambullir *into water*; mojar *with water*; *sl.* ~*d* ajumado; **2.** escabeche *m*.
south [sauθ] **1.** sur *m*, mediodía *m*; **2.** *adj.* del sur, meridional; **3.** *adv.* al sur, hacia el sur.
South A·mer·i·can [ˈsauθ əˈmerikən] sudamericano.
south...: ˈ~ˈ**east** sudeste *adj.* (*a.* ˈ~ˈ**east·er·ly,** ˈ~ˈ**east·ern**) *a. su. m.*
south·er·ly [ˈsʌðərli] *direction* hacia el sur; *wind* del sur; ˈ**south·ern** [~ərn] meridional; ˈ**south·ern·er** habitante *m/f* del sur (de los estados del sur *de EE.UU.*).
south·ern·most [ˈsʌðərnmoust] (el) más meridional.
south·paw [ˈsauθpɔː] jugador *m* zurdo; (*baseball*) lanzador *m* zurdo.
south·ward(s) [ˈsauθwərd(z)] hacia el sur.
south...: ˈ~ˈ**west** suroeste *adj.* (*a.* ˈ~ˈ**west·er·ly,** ˈ~ˈ**west·ern**) *a. su. m*; ˈ~ˈ**west·er** (*wind*) suroeste *m*; (*hat*) sueste *m*.
sou·ve·nir [ˈsuːvənir] recuerdo *m*.
sov·er·eign [ˈsɔvrin] soberano *adj. a. su. m* (a *f*); soberano *m* (*moneda de 1 libra*); ˈ**sov·er·eign·ty** soberanía *f*.
so·vi·et [ˈsouviət] **1.** soviet *m*; **2.** soviético.
sow[1] [sau] *zo.* cerda *f*; ⊕ galápago *m*.
sow[2] [sou] [*irr.*] sembrar (*a. fig.*); esparcir; plagar *with mines*; ˈ**sow·er** sembrador (-a *f*) *m*; ˈ**sow·ing** siembra *f*; ~ *time* sementera *f*; **sown** *p.p. of sow*[2].
so·ya [ˈsɔiə] soja *f*; ~ *bean* semilla *f* de soja.
spa [spɑː] balneario *m*.
space [speis] **1.** espacio *m* (*a. typ.*); ~ *helmet* casco *m* sideral; **2.** (*a.* ~ *out*) espaciar (*a. typ.*); **3.** espacial; ˈ~**ship** nave *f* espacial, astronave *f*; ˈ~ **shuttle** transbordador *m* (espacial); ˈ~ ˈ**sta·tion** apostadero *m* espacial; ˈ~**suit** escafandra *f* espacial.
spa·cious [ˈspeiʃəs] □ espacioso; *room* amplio; *living* holgado; **spa·cious·ness** amplitud *f*, extensión *f*.
spade [speid] laya *f*, pala *f*; *call a* ~ *a* ~ llamar al pan pan y al vino vino; *cards*: ~*s pl* picos *m/pl.*, pique *m*, (*Spanish*) espadas *f/pl*; ˈ~**work** trabajo *m* preliminar.
spag·hett·i [spəgˈeti] espagueti *m*; *approx.* fideos *m/pl*.
span[1] [spæn] **1.** palmo *m of hand*; ojo *m of bridge*; ✈ envergadura *f*; pareja *f* (de caballos); *fig.* extensión *f*, duración *f*; **2.** (*bridge*) extenderse sobre; (*builder*) tender (un puente) sobre; *time* abarcar.
span[2] [~] *pret. of spin* 1.
span·gle [ˈspæŋgl] **1.** lentejuela *f*; **2.** adornar con lentejuelas; *fig.* ~*d* estrellado.
Span·iard [ˈspænjərd] español (-a *f*) *m*.
span·iel [ˈspænjəl] perro *m* de aguas.
Span·ish [ˈspæniʃ] español *adj. a. su. m*; ˈ~-ˈ**speak·ing** hispanoparlante; hispanohablante; de habla española.
spank [spæŋk] F **1.** zurrar; manotear; ~ *along* ir volando; **2.** manotada *f*; ˈ**spank·er** ⚓ cangreja *f*; ˈ**spank·ing 1.** □ *pace* rápido; F fuerte, bárbaro; **2.** F zurra *f*.
span·ner [ˈspænər] llave *f* (inglesa).
spar[1] [spɑːr] ⚓ palo *m*, verga *f*.
spar[2] [~] *boxing*: hacer fintas; amagar (*at* a) (*a. fig.*); *fig.* disputarse (amistosamente); ~*ring partner* sparring *m*.
spare [sper] **1.** □ (*lean*) enjuto; (*left over*) sobrante; *room* disponible; para convidados; *time* libre, desocupado; *part* de repuesto, de recambio; ~ *time* ratos *m/pl.* libres, horas *f/pl.*

libres, ratos *m/pl.* de ocio; **2.** ⊕ (pieza *f* de) repuesto *m* (*or* recambio *m*); **3.** ahorrar, economizar; pasarse sin; dispensar de, excusar; *life* perdonar; (*and*) *to* ~ de sobra; *have … to* ~ disponer de; **spare·rib** [ˈ~rib] costilla *f* de cerdo con poca carne.

spar·ing [ˈsperiŋ] □ escaso; parco (*in, of* en), económico; ˈ**spar·ing·ness** parquedad *f*.

spark [spɑːrk] **1.** chispa *f*; *fig.* chispazo *m of wit*; átomo *m of life*; F ~*s sg.* telegrafista *m*; F *bright* ~ tipo *m* muy listo (*or* divertido); **2.** chispear; ~ *off* hacer estallar.

spar·kle [ˈspɑːrkl] **1.** centelleo *m*, destello *m*; *fig.* viveza *f*; **2.** centellear, chispear (*a. fig.*); relucir; *fig.* ser muy vivaz; ˈ**spar·kling** centelleante; *eyes, wit* chispeante; *wine* espumoso.

spark plug [ˈspɑːrkplʌg] bujía *f*.

spar·row [ˈspærou] gorrión *m*; ˈ~ **hawk** gavilán *m*.

sparse [spɑːrs] □ disperso; escaso; *hair* ralo.

spasm [ˈspæzm] ⚕ espasmo *m*; *fig.* arranque *m*; **spas·mod·ic, spas·mod·i·cal** [~ˈmɔdik(l)] □ espasmódico.

spat[1] [spæt] *zo.* freza *f*; masa *f* de ostras jóvenes.

spat[2] [~] disputa *f*; riña *f*; ~*s pl.* [botines *m/pl.*]

spat[3] [~] *pret. a. p.p. of spit*[2] 2.

spate [speit] avenida *f*; *fig.* torrente *m*; *in* ~ crecido.

spa·tial [ˈspeiʃl] □ espacial.

spat·ter [ˈspætər] salpicar, rociar (*with* de).

spat·u·la [ˈspætjulə] espátula *f*.

spav·in [ˈspævin] esparaván *m*.

spawn [spɔːn] **1.** freza *f*, huevas *f/pl.*; *fig.* prole *f*; **2.** *v/i.* desovar, frezar; *v/t. contp.* engendrar; ˈ**spawn·ing** freza *f*.

speak [spiːk] [*irr.*] hablar (*to* con, a); *truth* decir; *parl. etc.* hacer uso de la palabra; *teleph. Brown* ~*ing!* ¡Soy Brown!; *teleph. be* ~*ing* estar al habla; *so to* ~ por decirlo así; ~ *for* interceder por; representar; ~ *well for* demostrar el mérito de; ~ *out* hablar claro; osar hablar; ~ *up* hablar alto; ~ *up!* ¡más fuerte!; ˈ**~·eas·y** *sl.* taberna *f* clandestina; ˈ**speak·er** el (la) que habla; orador (-a *f*) *m*; hablante *m/f of language*; *parl.* presidente *m*; *radio*: (*loud*) altavoz *m*.

speak·ing [ˈspiːkiŋ] hablante; *likeness* perfecto; *we are not on* ~ *terms* no nos hablamos; ˈ~ **trum·pet** bocina *f*; ˈ~ **tube** tubo *m* acústico.

spear [spir] **1.** lanza *f*; (*fishing*) arpón *m*; **2.** alancear, herir con lanza; ˈ**~·head 1.** punta *f* de lanza (*a. fig.*); **2.** encabezar; dar impulso a.

spec [spek] F *sl.* (*on* como) especulación *f*; *sl. on* ~ por si acaso, a ver lo que sale; *sl.* ~*s* gafas *f/pl.*; anteojos *m/pl.*; especificaciones *f/pl.*

spe·cial [ˈspeʃl] **1.** □ especial, particular; **2.** *approx.* guardia *m* auxiliar (= ~ *constable*); número *m* extraordinario (= ~ *edition*); tren *m* especial (= ~ *train*); F oferta *f* extraordinaria; plato *m* del día; **spe·cial·ist** [ˈ~ʃəlist] especialista *m/f*; **spe·ci·al·i·ty** [speʃiˈæliti] especialidad *f*; **spe·cial·ize** [ˈspeʃəlaiz] especializarse (*in* en); **spe·cial·ty** [ˈ~ʃlti] especialidad *f*; (*talent*) fuerte *m*.

spe·cie [ˈspiːʃiː, ˈspiːsiː] metálico *m*, efectivo *m*.

spe·cies [ˈspiːʃiːz, ˈspiːsiːz] *sg. a. pl.* especie *f*.

spe·cif·ic [spiˈsifik] □ específico *adj.* (*all senses*) *a. su. m*; expreso.

spec·i·fi·ca·tion [spesifiˈkeiʃn] especificación *f*; plan *m* detallado; **spec·i·fy** [ˈ~fai] especificar; designar (en un plan).

spec·i·men [ˈspesimin] espécimen *m*, ejemplar *m*.

spe·cious [ˈspiːʃəs] □ especioso; ˈ**spe·cious·ness** lo especioso.

speck [spek] **1.** manchita *f*, mota *f*; grano *m of dust*; partícula *f*; *fig.* pizca *f*; **2.** *v. speckle* 2; **speck·le** [ˈ~kl] **1.** punto *m*, mota *f*; **2.** motear, salpicar de manchitas.

spec·ta·cle [ˈspektəkl] espectáculo *m*; (*a pair of* unas) ~*s pl.* gafas *f/pl.*, anteojos *m/pl*; ˈ**spec·ta·cled** con gafas.

spec·tac·u·lar [spekˈtækjulər] □ espectacular; aparatoso.

spec·ta·tor [spekˈteitər] espectador (-a *f*) *m*.

spec·tral [ˈspektrəl] □ espectral (*a. opt.*); **spec·ter** [ˈ~tər], **spec·trum** [ˈ~trəm] *opt.* espectro *m*.

spec·u·late [ˈspekjuleit] especular (*on* en; ⚚ *in* sobre); **spec·uˈla·tion** especulación *f*; **spec·u·la·tive** [ˈ~lətiv] □ especulativo; ˈ**spec·u·la·tor** especulador (-a *f*) *m*.

spec·u·lum [ˈspekjuləm] ⚕ espéculo *m*; *opt.* espejo *m* (metálico).
sped [sped] *pret. a. p.p. of speed* 2.
speech [spiːtʃ] (*faculty*) habla *f*; idioma *m* (*e. g., English* ~); (*style, manner*) lenguaje *m*; (*oration*) discurso *m, thea.*, ⚖ parlamento *m*; *make a* ~ pronunciar un discurso; ˈ~ **de·fect** defecto *m* del habla; ˈ**speech·less** □ mudo; estupefacto.
speed [spiːd] **1.** velocidad *f* (*a.* ⊕, *mot.*); prisa *f*, presteza *f*; *sl.* anfetaminas *f/pl.* tomadas como alucinantes; *at full* ~ a máxima velocidad, a toda máquina; *good* ~! ¡buen viaje!; **2.** *v/i.* apresurarse, darse prisa; *mot.* exceder la velocidad permitida; ~ *along* ir volando; ~ *past* pasar como un rayo; *v/t. guest* despedir; ~ *up* ⊕ acelerar; *p.* dar prisa a; *process* activar; ˈ~**·boat** lancha *f* rápida; ˈ**speed·i·ness** velocidad *f*, rapidez *f*; ˈ**speed lim·it** velocidad *f* máxima permitida; limite *m* de velocidad; **speed·om·e·ter** [spiˈdɔmitər] velocímetro *m*, cuentakilómetros *m*; ˈ**speed trap** trampa *f* para los cocheros que exceden el límite de velocidad permitida; ˈ**speed·way** carretera *f* para carreras; vía *f* de tráfico rápido; ˈ**speed·well** verónica *f*; ˈ**speed·y** □ veloz, rápido; *answer* pronto.
spe·le·ol·o·gy [spiːliˈɔlədʒi] espeleología *f*.
spell[1] [spel] **1.** tanda *f*, turno *m of work*; rato *m*, temporada *f*; *bad* ~ mala racha *f*; **2.** reemplazar; relevar.
spell[2] [~] **1.** encanto *m*, hechizo *m*; **2.** [*irr.*] *word* escribir; *fig. danger etc.* anunciar, significar; ~ *out* deletrear; ˈ~**·bind·er** orador *m* fascinante; ˈ~**·bound** *fig.* embelesado, hechizado; ˈ**spell·er** F abecedario *m*; *be a bad* ~ no saber escribir correctamente las palabras.
spell·ing [ˈspeliŋ] ortografía *f*; ˈ~ **bee** certamen *m* de ortografía; ˈ~ **book** abecedario *m*.
spelt[1] [spelt] *pret. a. p.p. of spell*[2] 2.
spelt[2] [~] ⚘ espelta *f*.
spel·ter [ˈspeltər] peltre *m*.
spend [spend] [*irr.*] *v/t. money, effort* gastar; *time* pasar; *anger* (*v/r.*) consumir(se); *v/i.* gastar dinero; ~*ing money* dinero *m* para gastos menudos; ˈ**spend·er** gastador (-a *f*) *m*.
spend·thrift [ˈspendθrift] derrochador (-a *f*) *m*, pródigo *m*.
spent [spent] **1.** *pret. a. p.p. of spend*; **2.** *adj.* agotado; gastado.
sperm [spəːrm] esperma *f*; **sper·ma·ce·ti** [~əˈseti] espermaceti *m*; **sper·ma·to·zo·on** [~ətouˈzouɔn], *pl.* **sper·ma·to·zo·a** [ˈ~zouə] espermatozoo *m*; **sperm whale** [ˈspəːrmˈweil] cachalote *m*.
spew [spjuː] vomitar.
sphere [sfir] esfera *f* (*a. fig.*); *ast.* esfera *f* celeste; **spher·i·cal** [ˈsferikl] □ esférico.
sphinc·ter [ˈsfiŋktər] esfínter *m*.
sphinx [sfiŋks] esfinge *f*.
spice [spais] **1.** especia *f*; *fig.* picante *m*; aliciente *m*; **2.** condimentar; *fig.* dar picante a.
spic·i·ness [ˈspaisinis] picante *m* (*a. fig.*); *fig.* F sicalipsis *f*.
spick-and-span [ˈspikənˈspæn] impecablemente limpio; *house etc.* como una tacita de plata; *p.* acicalado, pulcro.
spic·y [ˈspaisi] □ especiado; picante (*a. fig.*); *fig.* F sicalíptico.
spi·der [ˈspaidər] araña *f*; ~'*s web* telaraña *f*; ˈ**spi·der·y** muy delgado; *writing* de patas de araña.
spiel [spiːl] *sl.* arenga *f*; discurso *m* detallado.
spiff·y [ˈspifi] *sl.* guapo.
spig·ot [ˈspigət] espita *f of cask*; ⊕ espiga *f*.
spike [spaik] **1.** pincho *m*, púa *f*; escarpia *f*, espigón *m*; clavo *m on shoes*; ⚘ espiga *f*; **2.** sujetar con pincho *etc.*; *gun* clavar; *fig.* inutilizar; ~*d shoe* claveteado; **spike·nard** [ˈ~nɑːrd] nardo *m*; ˈ**spik·y** armado de púas.
spill [spil] **1.** [*irr.*] derramar(se); verter(se); *rider* desarzonar, hacer caer; *sl.* ~ *the beans* tirar de la manta; **2.** caída *f from horse*; vuelco *m*.
spill·way [ˈspilwei] bocacaz *m*; derramadero *m*.
spilt [spilt] *pret. a. p.p. of spill* 1.
spin [spin] **1.** [*irr.*] *thread* hilar; (*a.* ~ *round*) girar, hacer girar; *top* (hacer) bailar; ✈ entrar en barrena; ~ *along* correr rápidamente; ~ *out* alargar; **2.** vuelta *f*; ✈ barrena *f*; F paseo *m* en coche *etc.*
spin·ach [ˈspinidʒ] espinaca *f*.
spi·nal [ˈspainl] espinal; ~ *column* columna *f* vertebral; ~ *cord* médula *f* espinal.
spin·dle [spindl] (*spinning*) huso *m*;

⊕ eje *m*; ˈ**spin·dly** *leg* zanquivano; largo y delgado.

spin-dri·er [ˈspinˈdraiər] secador *m* centrífugo.

spin·drift [ˈspindrift] ⚓ rocío *m*.

spine [spain] *anat.* espinazo *m*; *zo.* púa *f*; ⚘ espina *f*; lomo *m of book*; ˈ**spine·less** □ *fig.* flojo, falto de voluntad; cobarde.

spin·ner [ˈspinər] hilandero (a *f*) *m*.

spin·ney [ˈspini] bosquecillo *m*.

spin·ning...: ~ **jen·ny** [ˈspiniŋˈdʒeni] máquina *f* de hilar de husos múltiples; ˈ~ **mill** hilandería *f*; ˈ~ **top** peonza *f*; ˈ~ **wheel** torno *m* de hilar.

spin...: ~ ˈ**off** ⊕, ✝ *byproduct, derivative* rendir; ˈ~-**off** ⊕, ✝ derivado *m*; subproducto *m*.

spin·ster [ˈspinstər] *mst contp.* soltera *f*; *contp.* solterona *f*.

spin·y [ˈspaini] espinoso (*a. fig.*).

spi·ra·cle [ˈspairəkl] espiráculo *m*.

spi·ral [ˈspairəl] **1.** □ (en) espiral; helicoidal; ~ *staircase* escalera *f* de caracol; **2.** espiral *f*, hélice *f*; **3.** dar vueltas en espiral.

spire [ˈspaiər] aguja *f*; chapitel *m*.

spir·it [ˈspirit] **1.** espíritu *m*; ánimo *m*, brío *m*; temple *m*, humor *m*; espectro *m*; ⚗ alcohol *m*; (*a. motor* ~) gasolina *f*; ~ *lamp* lámpara *f* de alcohol; ~ *level* nivel *m* de aire; ~*s pl.* ánimo *m*; humor *m*; ~ *of wine* espíritu *m* de vino; *keep up one's* ~*s* no desanimarse; *in (high)* ~*s* animado; *in low* ~*s* abatido; **2.**: ~ *away*, ~ *off* hacer desaparecer, llevarse misteriosamente.

spir·i·ted [ˈspiritid] □ animoso, brioso; *horse* fogoso.

spir·it·less [ˈspiritlis] □ apocado, sin ánimo; deprimido.

spir·it·u·al [ˈspiritjuəl] **1.** □ espiritual; **2.** tonada *f* espiritual; himno *m* religioso; ˈ**spir·it·u·al·ism** espiritismo *m*; **spir·it·u·al·i·ty** [~ˈæliti] espiritualidad *f*; **spir·it·u·al·ize** [ˈ~əlaiz] espiritualizar.

spir·it·u·ous [ˈspiritjuəs] espirit(u)oso.

spirt [spəːrt] **1.** salir a chorros, brotar a borbotones; **2.** chorretada *f*; *v. spurt*.

spit[1] [spit] **1.** espetón *m*, asador *m*; lengua *f of land*; **2.** espetar.

spit[2] [~] **1.** saliva *f*; F *be the* ~*ting image of* ser la segunda edición de; **2.** [*irr.*] *v/i.* escupir (*at* a, *on* en); (*cat*) bufar; ~ *with rain* chispear; *v/t.* (*mst* ~ *out*) escupir.

spit[3] [~] ⚒ azadada *f*.

spite [spait] **1.** rencor *m*, ojeriza *f*, despecho *m*; *in* ~ *of* a pesar de, a despecho de; **2.** mortificar, causar pena a.

spite·ful [ˈspaitful] □ rencoroso, malévolo; ˈ**spite·ful·ness** rencor *m*, malevolencia *f*.

spit·fire [ˈspitfaiər] fierabrás *m*.

spit·tle [ˈspitl] baba *f*, saliva *f*.

spit·toon [spiˈtuːn] escupidera *f*.

spiv [spiv] *sl. approx.* gandul *m*; sablista *m*, chanchullero *m*.

splash [splæʃ] **1.** salpicadura *f*, rociada *f*; (*noise*) chapoteo *m*; mancha *f of color*; F *make a* ~ impresionar; **2.** *v/t.* salpicar; *v/i.* chapotear (*a.* ~ *about*); F ~ *out* derrochar dinero; ˈ~·**down** *space capsule*: aterrizaje *m* en la mar; ˈ**splash·y** □ fangoso; llamativo.

splay [splei] **1.** bisel *m*; **2.** biselar; extender (sin gracia).

splay·foot [ˈspleifut] pie *m* aplastado y torcido; ~*ed* zancajoso.

spleen [spliːn] *anat.* bazo *m*; *fig.* esplín *m*, spleen *m*; rencor *m*.

splen·did [ˈsplendid] □, **splen·dif·er·ous** [~ˈdifərəs] F espléndido; **splen·dor** [ˈ~dər] esplendor *m*, brillantez *f*.

sple·net·ic [spliˈnetik] (*a.* **sple·net·i·cal** [~kl] □) *anat.* esplénico; *fig.* malhumorado, irritable.

splice [splais] **1.** empalme *m*; ⊕ (*wood*) junta *f*; **2.** empalmar; ⊕ juntar; *sl.* casar.

splint [splint] **1.** tablilla *f*; **2.** entablillar.

splin·ter [ˈsplintər] **1.** astilla *f*; ~ *group* grupo *m* disidente, facción *f*; **2.** astillar(se), hacer(se) astillas; ˈ~ **bone** peroné *m*; ˈ**splin·ter·less** inastillable.

split [split] **1.** hendedura *f*, raja *f*; *fig.* división *f*, cisma *m*; F *do the* ~*s* esparrancarse; **2.** partido, hendido; *fig.* dividido; **3.** partir(se); hender(se), rajarse; dividir(se); *sl.* irse; huir; ~ *hairs* ser quisquilloso; ~ *one's sides* desternillarse de risa; ~ *up* separar(se); ˈ**split·ting** *headache* enloquecedor.

splotch [splɔtʃ] borrón *m*, mancha *f*.

splurge [spləːrdʒ] **1.** F fachenda *f*; **2.** fachendear.

splut·ter [ˈsplʌtər] **1.** farfulla *f of*

speech; ⊕ chisporroteo *m*; **2.** (*p.*) farfullar; ⊕ chisporrotear.

spoil [spɔil] **1.** (*mst* ~*s pl.*) despojo *m*, botín *m*; *Am. pol.* ~*s system approx.* enchufismo *m*; **2.** [*irr.*] echar(se) a perder; estropear(se); dañar(se); malograr(se); deteriorar(se); *child* mimar; *be* ~*ing for* ansiar; ˈ**spoil·sport** aguafiestas *m/f*.

spoilt [spɔilt] **1.** *pret. a. p.p. of spoil* 2; **2.** *child* consentido, muy mimado.

spoke[1] [spouk] *pret. of speak*.

spoke[2] [~] (*wheel*) rayo *m*, radio *m*.

spo·ken [ˈspoukən] *p.p. of speak*.

spokes·man [ˈspouksmən] portavoz *m*; vocero *m*.

spo·li·a·tion [spouliˈeiʃn] despojo *m*; ⚖ expoliación *f*.

spon·dee [ˈspɔndiː] espondeo *m* (--).

sponge [spʌndʒ] **1.** esponja *f*; (*a.* ~ *cake*) bizcocho *m*; *boxing a. fig.*: *throw up the* ~ darse por vencido; **2.** lavar con esponja; F gorrear, vivir de gorra; F ~ *on* vivir a costa de; ~ *up* absorber; ˈ**spong·er** F gorrón *m*, sablista *m/f*.

spon·gi·ness [ˈspʌndʒinis] esponjosidad *f*; ˈ**spon·gy** esponjoso.

spon·sor [ˈspɔnsər] **1.** patrocinador *m*; ✝ fiador *m*; **2.** patrocinar; **spon·sor·ship** [ˈ~ʃip] patrocinio *m*.

spon·ta·ne·i·ty [spɔntəˈniːiti] espontaneidad *f*; **spon·ta·ne·ous** [~ˈteiniəs] ☐ *all senses*: espontáneo.

spoof [spuːf] *sl.* **1.** *v/t.* engañar; *v/i.* bromear; **2.** engaño *m*; broma *f*.

spook [spuːk] F espectro *m*; ˈ**~·y** F espeluznante; espectral.

spool [spuːl] **1.** carrete(l) *m*; canilla *f*; **2.** encanillar.

spoon [spuːn] **1.** cuchara *f*; **2.** cucharear (*a.* ~ *out*); *sl.* besuquearse; ˈ**~·drift** ⚓ rocío *m*; ˈ**spoon-fed** *fig.* muy mimado; **spoon·ful** [ˈ~ful] cucharad(it)a *f*; ˈ**spoon·y** F sobón; sentimental.

spo·rad·ic [spəˈrædik] ☐ esporádico.

spore [spɔːr] espora *f*.

sport [spɔːrt] **1.** deporte *m*; juego *m*, diversión *f*; juguete *m*; F (*a. good* ~) buen perdedor *m*; buen chico *m*; *biol.* mutación *f*; ~*s pl.* juegos *m/pl.* (atléticos); **2.** *v/i.* divertirse; juguetear; *v/t. clothes* lucir; ˈ**sport·ing** ☐ deportivo; (*fair*) ecuánime; *gun* de caza; *offer* arriesgado; ˈ**spor·tive** ☐ juguetón; **sports·man** [ˈ~smən] deportista *m*; persona *f* honrada; persona *f* temeraria; ˈ**sports·man·like** deportivo; leal y honrado; magnánimo; ˈ**sports·man·ship** deportividad *f*; magnanimidad *f*; ˈ**sports·wear** trajes *m/pl.* de deporte; ˈ**sports·wom·an** deportista *f*.

spot [spɔt] **1.** (*place*) sitio *m*, lugar *m*; (*mark*) punto *m*; (*stain*) mancha *f*; lunar *m*, grano *m on face*; F poquito *m*; *radio*: espacio *m* radiofónico (publicitario); F *ten* ~ billete *m* de 10 dólares; ~*s pl.* ✝ géneros *m/pl.* vendidos al contado; F *a* ~ *of* un poco de; *on the* ~ en el acto; al punto; *man* sobre el terreno; *sl.* (*put*) *on the* ~ (poner) en un aprieto; **2.** ✝ contante; disponible; **3.** manchar(se); salpicar; F notar, observar; descubrir; encontrar; F ~ *with rain* chispear; ˈ**spot·less** ☐ nítido; sin manchas, inmaculado; ˈ**spot·less·ness** nitidez *f*; ˈ**spot·light** arco *m*, proyector *m*; *mot.* faro *m* auxiliar orientable; *fig.* luz *f* concentrada; ˈ**spot·ted** manchado; moteado; ~ *fever* tifus *m* exantemático; ˈ**spot·ter** observador *m*; 🚂 *etc.* coleccionista *m* de números de locomotoras *etc.*; vigilante *m* secreto; ˈ**spot·ty** manchado (*face* de granos).

spouse [spauz] cónyuge *m/f*.

spout [spaut] **1.** pico *m*; pitón *m*; caño *m*; chorro *m of water*; ⚠ canalón *m*; *sl. up the* ~ en prenda; *fig.* arruinado; **2.** *v/t.* arrojar (en chorro); F declamar; *v/i.* chorrear.

sprain [sprein] **1.** torcedura *f*; **2.** torcer(se).

sprang [spræŋ] *pret. of spring* 2.

sprat [spræt] arenque *m* pequeño.

sprawl [sprɔːl] arrellanarse; tumbarse; (♀, *town*) extenderse.

spray[1] [sprei] ♀ ramita *f*.

spray[2] [~] **1.** rociada *f*; ⚓ espuma *f*; (*scent*) atomizador *m*; ⚘ riego *m* por aspersión; pulverización *f*; (*machine*) (*a.* ~*er*) pulverizador *m*; **2.** rociar; regar; pulverizar.

spread [spred] **1.** [*irr.*] extender(se); esparcir(se), desparramar(se); propagar(se), difundir(se); (*a.* ~ *out*) separar(se), abrir(se); *table* poner; *butter* untar; *wings* desplegar; ~ *o.s.* F ponerse a sus anchas; explayarse *in speech*; **2.** *pret. a. p.p. of* 1; **3.** extensión *f*; propagación *f*, difusión *f*; ✝ diferencia *f*; envergadura *f of wings*;

sl. comilona *f*, banquetazo *m*; **ˈ~ˈea·gled** con los miembros extendidos.

spree [spriː] F juerga *f*, parranda *f*; *go on a ~* ir de juerga.

sprig [sprig] ramita *f*; ⊕ puntilla *f*.

spright·li·ness [ˈspraitlinis] viveza *f*; **ˈspright·ly** vivo, animado.

spring [spriŋ] **1.** (*season*) primavera *f*; (*water*) fuente *f*, manantial *m*; (*jump*) salto *m*, brinco *m*; ⊕ muelle *m*, resorte *m*; elasticidad *f*; *fig.* móvil *m of action*; *hot ~* fuente *f* termal; **2.** *v/t. trap* hacer saltar; *mine* volar; ⚓ *~ a leak* abrirse una (vía de) agua; *~ a th. (up)on a p.* espetarle algo a alguien, decirle algo a alguien de buenas a primeras; *v/i.* saltar (*over acc.*); brincar; moverse rápidamente; brotar, nacer, proceder (*from* de); ⊕ torcerse, combarse; *~ at* abalanzarse sobre; *~ up* levantarse de un salto; ⚘, *fig.* brotar; (*breeze*) levantarse de pronto; *where have you sprung from?* ¿de dónde diablos ha salido Vd?; **3.** primaveral; ⊕ de muelle; *~ chicken* F joven *m/f*; *fig.* pollo *m* (a *f*); **ˈ~ ˈbal·ance** peso *m* de muelle; **ˈ~-board** trampolín *m*; **ˈ~·bolt** pestillo *m* de golpe; **ˈ~ ˈclean·ing** limpieza *f* en primavera.

springe [sprindʒ] lazo *m*.

spring gun [ˈspriŋgʌn] trampa *f* de alambre y escopeta; **ˈspring·i·ness** elasticidad *f*; **spring mat·tress** somier *m*; **ˈspring·tide** ⚓ marea *f* viva; *poet.* = **ˈspring·time** primavera *f*; **ˈspring·y** □ elástico; *turf* muelle, muy molido.

sprin·kle [ˈspriŋkl] *v/t.* salpicar, rociar (*with* de); sembrar (*with* de); asperjar *with holy water*; *v/i.* (*rain*) lloviznar; **ˈsprin·kler** regadera *f*; *eccl.* hisopo *m*; **ˈsprin·kling** rociada *f*; aspersión *f*; salpicadura *f*; *fig. a ~ of* unos cuantos.

sprint [sprint] **1.** sprint *m*; **2.** sprintar; **ˈsprint·er** esprínter *m*.

sprit [sprit] botavara *f*.

sprite [sprait] duende *m*, hada *f*.

sprock·et [ˈsprɔkit] rueda *f* de cadena.

sprout [spraut] **1.** *v/i.* brotar, germinar; crecer rápidamente; *v/t.* echar, hacerse; **2.** vástago *m*, retoño *m*; *~s pl.* col *f* de Bruselas.

spruce[1] [spruːs] □ apuesto, pulcro.

spruce[2] [~] ⚘ pícea *f* (*a. ~ fir*).

sprung [sprʌŋ] *pret.* (†) *a. p.p. of spring* 2.

spry [sprai] ágil, activo.

spud [spʌd] ⚒ escarda *f*; *sl.* patata *f*.

spume [spjuːm] *lit.* espuma *f*.

spun [spʌn] *pret. a. p.p. of spin* 1.

spunk [spʌŋk] coraje *m*, ánimo *m*; **ˈ~·y** animoso.

spur [spəːr] **1.** espuela *f* (*a. fig.*); *zo.* espolón *m*; *geog.* estribo *m*; *fig.* estímulo *m*, aguijón *m*; *on the ~ of the moment* impulsivamente, sin reflexión; *win one's ~s* distinguirse; *~ gear* rueda *f* dentada recta; *put (or set) ~s to* = **2.** espolear; *~ on* estimular, incitar (*to do* a que haga).

spurge [spəːrdʒ] euforbio *m*.

spu·ri·ous [ˈspjuriəs] □ espurio, falso; **ˈspu·ri·ous·ness** falsedad *f*.

spurn [spəːrn] desdeñar, rechazar.

spurt [spəːrt] **1.** chorretada *f*; arranque *m*; *sport etc.*: esfuerzo *m* supremo; **2.** salir a chorros; hacer un esfuerzo supremo; *v. spirt*.

sput·nik [ˈsputnik] sputnik *m*; satélite *m* artificial.

sput·ter [ˈspʌtər] *v. splutter*.

spy [spai] **1.** espía *m/f*; **2.** espiar (*on acc.*); columbrar, divisar; **ˈ~·glass** catalejo *m*; **ˈ~ hole** mirilla *f*.

squab·ble [ˈskwɔbl] **1.** riña *f*, disputa *f*; **2.** reñir, disputar; **ˈsquab·bler** pendenciero (a *f*) *m*.

squad [skwɔd] escuadra *f*, pelotón *m*;

squad·ron [ˈ~rən] ⚔ escuadrón *m*; ✈ escuadrilla *f*; ⚓ escuadra *f*.

squal·id [ˈskwɔlid] □ miserable, sucio; mezquino.

squall[1] [skwɔːl] **1.** chillido *m*, berrido *m*; **2.** chillar.

squall[2] [~] ⚓ ráfaga *f*, racha *f*, chubasco *m*; **ˈsquall·y** chubascoso.

squal·or [ˈskwɔlər] miseria *f*, suciedad *f*.

squan·der [ˈskwɔndər] malgastar, despilfarrar; disipar (*on* en).

square [skwer] **1.** □ cuadrado (*measure, mile,* & *root, etc.*); en ángulo recto (*to, with* con); *fig.* claro y directo; redondo; *deal* justo, equitativo; *p.* honrado; F inocente; *meal* abundante; *be all ~* estar en paz; (*sport*) ir iguales; *get ~ (with)* desquitarse (con); *~ dance* danza *f* de figuras; *~ sail* vela *f* de cruz; F *~ shooter* persona *f* honrada; *2 feet ~* 2 pies en cuadro; **2.** cuadrado *m* (*a.* &); cuadro *m* (*a.

⚔); ⚓, ⊕ escuadra *f*; plaza *f in town*; casilla *f of chessboard*; F *p.* inocente *m/f*; **3.** *v/t.* cuadrar (*a.* ♗); ⚓, ⊕ escuadrar; ajustar (*with* con; *a.* ⚕); *sl. p.* sobornar; persuadir; *~d paper* papel *m* cuadriculado; *v/i.* cuadrar, compaginar; conformarse (*with* con); **ˈ~·ly** *adv.* honradamente; directamente; **ˈ~-ˈrigged** de cruz.
squash [skwɔʃ] **1.** zumo *m* (de limón *etc.*); ⚘ calabaza *f*; frontón *m* con raqueta; F apiñamiento *m*, gentío *m*; **2.** aplastar; apretar, apiñar; F *argument* confutar; F *p.* apabullar.
squat [skwɔt] **1.** *p.* rechoncho; *building* desproporcionadamente bajo; **2.** agacharse, sentarse en cuclillas; *sl.* sentarse; establecerse (sin derecho) *on property*; **ˈsquat·ter** intruso *m*, colono *m* usurpador.
squaw [skwɔ:] india *f* norteamericana.
squawk [skwɔ:k] **1.** graznar, chillar; **2.** graznido *m*, chillido *m*.
squeak [skwi:k] **1.** chirriar, rechinar; **2.** chirrido *m*; *have a narrow ~* escaparse por un pelo; **ˈsqueak·y** □ chirriador.
squeal [skwi:l] **1.** chillido *m*, **2.** chillar; *sl.* cantar; delatar (*on* a).
squeam·ish [ˈskwi:miʃ] □ remilgado, escrupuloso, delicado, susceptible; **ˈsqueam·ish·ness** susceptibilidad *f*; repugnancia *f*.
squee·gee [ˈskwi:ˈdʒi:] enjugador *m* de goma (*a. phot.*).
squeeze [skwi:z] **1.** *v/t.* apretar, estrujar; oprimir; *~ out* exprimir; F *p.* excluir; *v/i.* introducirse, deslizarse (*in* en); **2.** estrujón *m*, estrujadura *f*; presión *f*; apretón *m of hand*; ⚕ restricción *f of credit*; F apiñamiento *m*; *tight ~* aprieto *m*; **ˈsqueez·er** exprimidor *m*.
squelch [skweltʃ] F *v/t.* despachurrar; *v/i.* andar chapoteando.
squib [skwib] buscapiés *m*; *fig.* pasquín *m*.
squid [skwid] calamar *m*.
squint [skwint] **1.** bizquear; torcer la vista; cerrar casi los ojos; **2.** estrabismo *m*; mirada *f* bizca; F vistazo *m*.
squire [ˈskwaiər] **1.** *approx.* propietario *m*, hacendado *m*; señor *m*; *hist.* escudero *m*; **2.** *lady* acompañar a.
squirm [skwə:rm] F retorcerse.
squir·rel [ˈskwirəl] ardilla *f*.
squirt [skwə:rt] **1.** chorro *m*; jeringazo *m*; F farolero *m*; *sl. little ~* enano *m*; chico *m*; **2.** *v/t.* jeringar; arrojar a chorros; *v/i.* salir a chorros.
stab [stæb] **1.** puñalada *f*; F tentativa *f*; **2.** apuñalar.
sta·bil·i·ty [stəˈbiliti] estabilidad *f*.
sta·bi·li·za·tion [steibilaiˈzeiʃn] estabilización *f*; **sta·bi·lize** [ˈsteibilaiz] estabilizar; **ˈsta·bi·liz·er** estabilizador *m*.
sta·ble¹ [ˈsteibl] □ estable.
sta·ble² [~] **1.** cuadra *f*; establo *m*; (*racing*) caballeriza *f*; **2.** poner (*or* guardar) en una cuadra.
stack [stæk] **1.** ✓ niara *f*, hacina *f*; montón *m* (*a.* F), rimero *m*, pila *f*; ⚔ pabellón *m* (de fusiles); canón *m of chimney*; **2.** ✓ hacinar; amontonar.
sta·di·um [steidiəm] estadio *m*.
staff [stæf] **1.** bastón *m*; palo *m*; *eccl. etc.* báculo *m*; *fig.* apoyo *m*; ♪ (*pl. staves* [steivz]) pentagrama *m*; ⚔ estado *m* mayor; profesorado *m of school*; personal *m of office*; (*servants*) servidumbre *f*; **2.** proveer de personal.
stag [stæg] *zo.* ciervo *m*, venado *m*; ⚕ especulador *m*; F soltero *m*.
stage [steidʒ] **1.** plataforma *f*, estrado *m*, tablado *m*; *thea.* escena *f*; *fig.* escenario *m*; *fig.* teatro *m*; (*stop*) parada *f*; posta *f*; fase *f*, etapa *f of progress*; *in ~s* por etapas; *in* (*or by*) *easy ~s* en cortas etapas; *go on the ~* hacerse actor; **2.** *play* representar; *recovery* efectuar, organizar; **ˈ~ ˈbox** palco *m* de proscenio; **ˈ~·coach** diligencia *f*; **ˈ~ di·rec·tion** acotación *f*; **ˈ~ door** entrada *f* de artistas; **ˈ~ fright** miedo *m* al público; **ˈ~·hand** tramoyista *m*; **ˈ~ man·ag·er** director *m* de escena; **ˈ~-struck** loco por el teatro; **ˈstag(e)·y** □ teatral.
stag·ger [ˈstægər] **1.** *v/i.* tambalear, titubear, hacer eses; *v/t.* asombrar, sorprender; *hours*, ⊕ escalonar; **2.** tambaleo *m*; *vet. ~s pl.* modorra *f*; **ˈstag·ger·ing** □ titubeante; *fig.* asombroso.
stag·nan·cy [ˈstægnənsi] estancamiento *m*; **ˈstag·nant** □ estancado (*a. fig.*); paralizado; ⚕ inactivo; **stag·nate** [ˈ~neit] estancarse; paralizarse; **stagˈna·tion** estancamiento *m* (*a. fig.*).
stag par·ty [ˈstægpɑ:rti] F tertulia *f* de solteros.
staid [steid] □ serio, formal; **ˈstaid·ness** seriedad *f*.

stain [stein] **1.** mancha *f* (*a. fig.*); tinte *m*, tintura *f* (*a.* ⊕); **2.** manchar(se) (*a. fig.*); teñir, colorar (*a.* ⊕); *~ed glass* vidrio *m* de color; **'stain·less** □ inmanchable; *fig.* inmaculado; ⊕ inoxidable.

stair [ster] peldaño *m*, escalón *m*; (*flight of* tramo *m* de) *~s pl.* escalera *f*; **'~·case,** *a.* **'~·way** escalera *f*; *moving ~* escalera *f* móvil.

stake [steik] **1.** estaca *f*, poste *m*; (*bet*) (a)puesta *f*, parada *f*; *fig.* interés *m*; *~s pl.* premio *m*; *at ~* en juego; en peligro; F *pull up ~s* mudar de casa; **2.** (*bet*) apostar (*on* a); ✝ aventurar, arriesgar; estacar *with wood* (*a. ~ off, ~ out*).

sta·lac·tite ['stæləktait] estalactita *f*.

stale [steil] *food* rancio, añejo, pasado; *bread* duro; *news* viejo; *air* viciado; *joke* mohoso; *p.* cansado.

stale·mate ['steil'meit] **1.** *chess*: tablas *f/pl.* por ahogo; *fig.* paralización *f*; *fig. reach a ~* llegar a un punto muerto; **2.** dar mate ahogado a; paralizar.

stalk[1] [stɔ:k] ⚘ tallo *m*; (*cabbage*) troncho *m*.

stalk[2] [~] *v/i.* andar con paso majestuoso; *v/t. hunt. etc.* cazar al acecho; acechar; **'stalk·ing horse** *fig.* pretexto *m*.

stall [stɔ:l] **1.** ✔ pesebre *m*; establo *m*; (*market*) puesto *m*, caseta *f*; *thea.* butaca *f*; *eccl.* sillería *f*; **2.** *v/t.* ⊕ parar, atascar; ✔ encerrar en establo; *v/i.* ⊕ pararse, atascarse; F buscar evasivas; **'~-fed** engordado en establo.

stal·lion ['stæljən] caballo *m* padre.

stal·wart ['stɔ:lwərt] **1.** □ (*sturdy*) fornido; *supporter etc.* leal; **2.** *pol.* partidario *m* leal.

sta·men ['steimen] estambre *m*.

stam·i·na ['stæminə] vigor *m*, resistencia *f*.

stam·mer ['stæmər] **1.** tartamudear, balbucir; **2.** tartamudeo *m*, balbuceo *m*; **'stam·mer·er** tartamudo (a *f*) *m*.

stamp [stæmp] **1.** (*postage*) sello *m*, estampilla *f S.Am.*; (*fiscal*) timbre *m*; marca *f*, impresión *f*; ⊕ cuño *m*; (*rubber*) estampilla *f*; patada *f of foot*; (*kind*) temple *m*, calaña *f*; **2.** *v/t. letter* sellar, franquear; estampillar; estampar; imprimir *on memory*; *fig.* marcar, señalar; *~ on* hollar, pisotear; *~ out fire* apagar pateando; *fig.* extirpar; *v/i.* patear; patalear *disapprovingly*; (*horse*) piafar; **'~ al·bum** álbum *m* (para sellos); **'~ col'lect·ing** filatelia *f*; **'~ du·ty** impuesto *m* del timbre.

stam·pede [stæm'pi:d] **1.** fuga *f* precipitada, estampida *f S.Am.*; movimiento *m* precipitado y unánime; **2.** (hacer) huir en desorden.

stamp pad ['stæmp pæd] tampón *m*.

stance [stæns] postura *f*.

stanch [stɔ:ntʃ, stæntʃ] **1.** restañar; **2.** = *staunch* 1.

stan·chion ['stænʃn] puntal *m*, montante *m*.

stand [stænd] **1.** [*irr.*] *v/i.* estar de pie; levantarse; (*be situated*) estar (situado); (*remain*) quedarse; (*remain in force*) mantenerse (en vigor); (*last*) (per)durar; (*stop*) pararse; (*measure*) medir; *how do we ~?* ¿cómo estamos?; *~ firm* resistir, mantenerse firme; *~ still* estarse quieto; *~ to win* tener probabilidad de ganar; *~ aside* apartarse; *~ back* retroceder; moverse hacia atrás; estar apartado; *~ by* estar alerta; estar cerca; estar a la expectativa; (*abide by*) atenerse a; (*support*) apoyar, sostener, no abandonar; *~ for* representar; significar; apoyar, apadrinar; *post, parl.* presentarse como candidato a; F aguantar; *~ in* ⚓ acercarse (*to* a); suplir (*for* a); *~ in with* declararse por; *~ off* apartarse (*a.* ⚓); *~ out* destacarse (*against sky etc.* contra); *esp. fig.* descollar, sobresalir; no ceder (*for* hasta obtener); *~ out against proposal etc.* oponerse a; *~ out for* insistir en; *~ out to sea* hacerse a la mar; *~ over* quedar en suspenso; *~ to* ⚔ estar sobre las armas; *v. reason*; *~ up* levantarse, ponerse de pie; *~ up for* defender; *~ up to* resistir resueltamente a; *test* salir muy bien de; **2.** [*irr.*] *v/t.* poner derecho; colocar; (*bear*) aguantar, soportar; *examination* resistir a; *test* salir muy bien de; F *drinks* pagar, invitar a; *I can't ~ him* no lo puedo ver; *v. chance, ground*; *sl. ~ a p. up* dar plantón a una p.; **3.** posición *f*, postura *f*; resistencia *f*; (*stall*) puesto *m*; quiosco *m*; *sport*: tribuna *f*; (*exhibition*) stand *m*; tarima *f*; (*band*) estrado *m*; ⊕ sostén *m*, pedestal *m*; estante *m*; (*taxi*) parada *f*, punto *m*; *make a* ~ resistir (*against* a).

stand·ard [ˈstændərd] **1.** patrón *m*, norma *f*, pauta *f*; nivel *m*; modelo *m*; ♂ árbol *m* de tronco derecho; (*flag*) estandarte *m*, bandera *f*; *gold* ~ patrón *m* oro; ~ *lamp* lámpara *f* de pie; ~ *of living* nivel *m* de vida; **2.** normal; corriente; standard, estándar; ~ *measure* medida *f* tipo; ~ *model* modelo *m* standard; ~ *work* obra *f* clásica; ˈ**~-bear·er** abanderado *m*; *fig.* jefe *m*; caudillo *m*; ~ **gauge** [ˈ~geidʒ] vía *f* normal; **stand·ard·i·za·tion** [ˈ~aiˈzeiʃn] normalización *f*, estandar(d)ización *f*; ˈ**stand·ard·ize** normalizar, regularizar, estandar(d)izar.

stand-by [ˈstændbai] **1.** recurso *m* seguro, persona *f* confiable, paño *m* de lágrimas; **2.** alternativo; de sustituto.

stand·ee [stænˈdiː] espectador *m* que asiste de pie.

stand-in [ˈstændin] doble *m*/*f*.

stand·ing [ˈstændiŋ] **1.** derecho, en (*or* de) pie; *army*, *committee* permanente; *grievance* constante; *order* vigente; *start* parado; *water* encharcado; ~ *order* reglamento *m*; **2.** posición *f*; reputación *f*; importancia *f*; (*of*) *long* ~ de mucho tiempo; ˈ~ **room** sitio *m* para estar de pie.

stand...: ˈ**~-off** reserva *f*; empate *m*; ˈ**~-ˈoff·ish** □ reservado; endiosado; poco amable; ~ˈ**pat·ter** *Am. pol.* F conservador *m*; ˈ**~·pipe** columna *f* de alimentación; ˈ**~·point** punto *m* de vista; ˈ**~·still** parada *f*, paro *m*; alto *m*; inactividad *f*; *be at a* ~ estar paralizado; *come to a* ~ pararse, paralizarse.

stank [stæŋk] *pret. of stink* 2.

stan·nic [ˈstænik] estánnico.

stan·za [ˈstænzə] estancia *f*, estrofa *f*.

sta·ple[1] [ˈsteipl] **1.** producto *m* principal; materia *f* prima; asunto *m* principal; fibra *f* (textil); **2.** principal; corriente.

sta·ple[2] [~] **1.** grapa *f*; **2.** sujetar con grapas; **sta·pler** [ˈsteiplər] grapadora *f*; cosepapeles *m*.

star [stɑːr] **1.** estrella *f* (*a. fig.*); *thea.* estrella *f*, vedette *f*, astro *m*; *typ.* asterisco *m*; ~*fish* estrella *f* de mar; *north* ~ estrella *f* del norte; *polar* ~ estrella *f* polar; ♀*s and Stripes* estrellas *f*/*pl.* y listas; **2.** *v*/*t.* adornar con estrellas; marcar con asterisco; (*film*) presentar como estrella; *v*/*i.* ser la estrella; **3.:** ~ *turn* atracción *f* especial (*or* estelar).

star·board [ˈstɑːrbərd] **1.** estribor *m*; **2.** *rudder* volver a estribor.

starch [stɑːrtʃ] **1.** almidón *m*; *biol.* fécula *f*; **2.** almidonar; ˈ**starch·y** □ feculento; *fig.* estirado, entonado.

star·dom [ˈstɑːrdəm] fama *f of an actor or performer*.

stare [ster] **1.** mirada *f* fija; **2.** mirar fijamente (*at acc.*); ~ *at* clavar la vista en; *it's staring you in the face* salta a la vista; **star·ing** [ˈ~riŋ] □ que mira fijamente; *eye* saltón.

stark [stɑːrk] (*stiff*) rígido (*sheer*) completo, puro; severo; (*unadorned*) escueto; ~ *mad* loco de atar; ~ *naked* en cueros.

star·ling [ˈstɑːrliŋ] estornino *m* pinto.

star·lit [ˈstɑːrlit] iluminado por las estrellas.

star·ring [ˈstɑːriŋ] que presenta como estrella...

star·ry [ˈstɑːri] estrellado; ˈ**~-ˈeyed** *fig.* inocentón, ingenuo; lleno de entusiasmo candoroso.

star-span·gled [ˈstɑːrspæŋgld]: ♀ *Banner* bandera *f* estrellada.

start [stɑːrt] **1.** comienzo *m*, principio *m*; (*departure*) salida *f* (*a. of race*); (*advantage*) ventaja *f*; (*surprise*) sobresalto *m*; respingo *m of horse*; *for a* ~ para empezar; *give a* ~ (*race*) dar una ventaja; (*surprise*) sobresaltar; **2.** *v*/*i.* empezar, comenzar, principiar (*to inf. or ger.* a *inf.*); iniciarse; (*depart*) ponerse en camino, salir (*a. in race*); sobresaltarse, sobrecogerse *with surprise* (*at* a); (*motor*) arrancar, ponerse en marcha; ~ *on* emprender; *v*/*t.* empezar, principiar; iniciar; *motor* arrancar; *vehicle etc.* poner en marcha; *game* levantar; *race* dar la señal de salida a.

start·er [ˈstɑːrtər] *sport*: stárter *m*, juez *m* de salida; *mot.* (motor *m* de, botón *m* de) arranque *m*.

start·ing [ˈstɑːrtiŋ]: ˈ~ **point** punto *m* de partida; ˈ~ **post** poste *m* de salida; ˈ~ **switch** botón *m* de arranque.

star·tle [ˈstɑːrtl] asustar, sobrecoger; ˈ**star·tling** □ alarmante; sorprendente.

star·va·tion [stɑːrˈveiʃn] inanición

f, hambre *f*; *attr.* .... de hambre; ~ *diet* régimen *m* de hambre; **starve** [stɑːrv] *v/i.* morir de hambre; padecer hambre; F tener mucha hambre; *v/t.* hacer morir de hambre; *fig.* privar (*of* de); ~ *out* hacer rendirse por hambre; ˈ**starv·ing** hambriento, famélico.

state [steit] **1.** estado *m* (*a. pol.*); condición *f*; pompa *f*, fausto *m*; *in* ~ con gran pompa; *lie in* ~ estar de cuerpo presente; F *be in a* ~ estar aturrullado; **2.** estatal; del estado; público; *occasion* de gala; *EE.UU.* ♀ *Department* Ministerio *m* de Asuntos Exteriores; ♀ *House* edificio *m* del Estado; **3.** declarar, manifestar, afirmar; exponer; *law* formular; *problem* plantear; ˈ**state·less** desnacionalizado; ˈ**state·li·ness** majestad *f*, majestuosidad *f etc.*; ˈ**state·ly** majestuoso, imponente; augusto; *carriage etc.* majestuoso, garboso; ~ *home* casa *f* solariega; ˈ**state·ment** declaración *f*; informe *m*; exposición *f*; relación *f*; ⚜ (*a.* ~ *of account*) estado *m* de cuenta(s); ˈ**state·room** camarote *m*; ˈ**state·side** F en (*or* a) los Estados Unidos.

states·man [ˈsteitsmən] estadista *m*, hombre *m* de estado; ˈ**states·man-like** digno de estadista; ˈ**states-man·ship** habilidad *f* de estadista; arte *m* de gobernar.

states' rights [ˈsteitsraits] derechos *m/pl.* de los Estados.

stat·ic [ˈstætik] □ *phys.* estático; *fig.* estancado, inactivo; ˈ**stat·ics** *pl. or sg. phys.* estática *f*; *pl. radio*: parásitos *m/pl.*

sta·tion [ˈsteiʃn] **1.** 🚂 *etc.* estación *f*; ⚓ apostadero *m* naval; puesto *m*; situación *f*; condición *f of life*; **2.** colocar, situar; ⚔ apostar, estacionar; ˈ**sta·tion·ar·y** □ estacionario; ~ *engine* máquina *f* fija; ˈ**sta·tion·er** papelero *m*; ~'s papelería *f*; ♀s' *Hall registro de libros publicados (en Londres)*; ˈ**sta·tion·er·y** papelería *f*, papel *m* de escribir; ˈ**sta·tion-mas·ter** jefe *m* de estación; **sta·tion wag·on** rubia *f*; furgoneta *f*.

sta·tis·ti·cal [stəˈtistikl] □ estadístico; **stat·is·ti·cian** [stætisˈtiʃn] estadístico *m*; **sta·tis·tics** [stəˈtistiks] *pl.* (*as science, sg.*) estadística *f*.

stat·u·ar·y [ˈstætjuəri] **1.** estatuario; **2.** (*p.*) estatuario *m*; (*art*) estatuaria *f*; (*collectively*) estatuas *f/pl.*; **stat·ue** [ˈ~tjuː] estatua *f*; **stat·u·esque** [~tjuˈesk] □ estatuario, escultural; **stat·u·ette** [~tjuˈet] figurina *f*.

stat·ure [ˈstætʃər] estatura *f*, talla *f*.

sta·tus [ˈsteitəs] estado *m*, condición *f*, rango *m*; ~ *seeker* ambicioso *m*; ~ *symbol* símbolo *m* de categoría social.

stat·ute [ˈstætjuːt] estatuto *m*; ~ *law* derecho *m* escrito; ˈ~ **book** código *m* de leyes.

stat·u·to·ry [ˈstætjutɔːri] □ estatutario; legal.

staunch [stɔːntʃ] **1.** □ leal, firme, constante; **2.** estancar; restañar.

stave [steiv] **1.** duela *f of barrel*; palo *m*; ♪ pentagrama *m*; **2.** [*irr.*] (*mst* ~ *in*) desfondar; romper; ~ *off* evitar, conjurar, diferir.

staves [steivz] *pl. of staff* 1 pentagrama *m*.

stay [stei] **1.** estancia *f*, permanencia *f*; visita *f*; ⚖ suspensión *f*, prórroga *f*; ⚓ estay *m*; ⊕ sostén *m*; ~s *pl.* corsé *m*; **2.** *v/t.* detener; poner freno a; *hunger* matar, engañar; ⚖ suspender; ⊕ sostener; ~ *one's hand* contenerse; *v/i.* quedar(se), permanecer; hospedarse (*at* en); esperar (*for* hasta); pararse; *they* ~*ed for tea* quedaron a merendar con nosotros; ~ *away* ausentarse; ~ *behind* quedarse; ~ *in* quedarse en casa; ~ *on* quedarse; ~ *out* quedarse fuera; *fig.* no tomar parte (*of* en); *fig.* ~ *put* mantenerse en su lugar; no cejar; ~ *up* velar, no acostarse; ~*ing power* resistencia *f*; ˈ**~-at-home** casero *m*, hogareño *m*; ˈ**stay·er** (*horse*) caballo *m* apto para carreras de distancia.

stead [sted]: *in his* ~ en su lugar; *stand a p. in good* ~ servirle a uno, serle útil a uno.

stead·fast [ˈstedfəst] □ constante, firme, resuelto; ˈ**stead·fast·ness** constancia *f*, resolución *f*.

stead·i·ness [ˈstedinis] constancia *f*; uniformidad *f etc.*

stead·y [ˈstedi] **1.** □ firme, fijo; estable; regular; constante; uniforme; sostenido, ininterrumpido; *p.* juicioso; ⚜ en calma; **2.** estabilizar; afirmar; *nerves* calmar; **3.** F novio (a *f*) *m* formal.

steak [steik] biftec *m*; tajada *f*.

steal [stiːl] **1.** [*irr.*] *v/t.* hurtar, robar; cautivar; *v/i.*: ~ *away* escabullirse;

marcharse sigilosamente; **2.** F ganga *f* extraordinaria.
stealth [stelθ] cautela *f*, sigilo *m*; *by* ~ a escondidas; **'~·ness** clandestinidad *f*; **'stealth·y** □ sigiloso; furtivo; clandestino.
steam [sti:m] **1.** vapor *m*; vaho *m*; *let off* ~ ⊕ descargar vapor; *fig.* desahogarse; **2.** de vapor; **3.** *v/i.* echar vapor; marchar (*or* funcionar) a vapor; navegar *etc.*; (*window*) empañarse; *v/t.* cocer al vapor; *window* empañar; **'steam en·gine** máquina *f* de vapor; **'steam·er** ⚓ (buque *m* de) vapor *m*; **'steam-roll·er 1.** apisonadora *f*; **2.** *fig.* aplastar, arrollar; **'steam·ship** = *steamer*; **'steam·y** □ lleno de vapor, vaporoso; *window* empañado.
ste·a·rin ['stirin, 'sti:ərin] estearina *f*.
steed [sti:d] *lit.* corcel *m*.
steel [sti:l] **1.** acero *m*; (*sharpener*) chaira *f*, eslabón *m*; **2.** de acero; acerado; **3.** ⊕ acerar; *fig.* ~ *o.s.* acorazarse; **'~-clad** revestido de acero; **'steel·y** *mst fig.* inflexible; **'steel·yard** romana *f*.
steep¹ [sti:p] □ empinado, escarpado, abrupto; F exorbitante, excesivo.
steep² [~] empapar (*a. fig.*); remojar.
stee·ple ['sti:pl] campanario *m*; aguja *f*; **'~·chase** carrera *f* de obstáculos; (*horses*) carrera *f* de vallas; **'~·jack** escalatorres *m*.
steep·ness ['sti:pnis] lo empinado *etc.*
steer¹ [stir] ✓ buey *m*; novillo *m*.
steer² [~] dirigir; *car* conducir; *ship* gobernar; ~ *for* dirigirse a; ~ *clear of* evitar.
steer·age ['stiridʒ] entrepuente *m*; **'~·way** empuje *m* del buque (necesario para gobernar).
steer·ing ['stiriŋ] dirección *f*; ⚓ gobierno *m*; *rack and pinion* ~ *mot.* dirección de cremallera; **'~ arm** *mot.* brazo *m* de dirección; **'~ col·umn** columna *f* de dirección; **'~ com·mit·tee** comité *m* planeador; **'~ wheel** volante *m*.
steers·man ['stirzmən] timonero *m*.
stel·lar ['stelər] estelar.
stem¹ [stem] **1.** ⚘ tallo *m*; ⊕ vástago *m*; *gr.* tema *m*; pie *m of glass*; cañón *m of pipe*; **2.**: ~ *from* provenir de, resultar de.
stem² [~] **1.** ⚓ roda *f*, tajamar *m*; *from* ~ *to stern* de proa a popa; **2.** *water* represar; *fig.* detener, contener.
stench [stentʃ] hedor *m*.
sten·cil ['stensl] **1.** ⊕ patrón *m* picado; estarcido *m*; (*typing*) cliché *m*; **2.** estarcir.
ste·nog·ra·pher [ste'nɔgrəfər] taquígrafo (a *f*) *m*; **ste·nog·ra·phy** [ste'nɔgrəfi] taquigrafía *f*.
step¹ [step] **1.** paso *m* (*a. fig.*); (*stair*) peldaño *m*, escalón *m*, grada *f*; estribo *m of car*; *fig.* medida *f*, gestión *f*; (*a. flight of*) ~*s pl.* escalera *f*, escalinata *f*; ~*s pl.* (*ladder*) escalera *f* de tijera; *at every* ~ a cada paso; *in* ~ llevando el paso; *fig.* de acuerdo (*with* con); *take* ~*s* tomar medidas (*to* para); *watch one's* ~ ir con tiento; **2.** *v/i.* dar un paso; andar, ir; pisar; ~ *aside* apartarse, hacerse a un lado; ~ *back* retroceder; dar un paso hacia atrás; ~ *down* bajar; *fig.* ceder su puesto; ~ *in* intervenir; ~ *in!* ¡adelante!; ~ *on* pisar; F ~ *on it!* ¡date prisa!; ~ *out* apretar el paso; ~ *this way* haga el favor de pasar por aquí; *v/t.* escalonar; *distance* medir a pasos (*a.* ~ *out*); ~ *up* aumentar, elevar.
step² [~]: **'~·fa·ther** padrastro *m*; **'~·son** hijastro *m*; *etc.*
steppe [step] estepa *f*.
step·ping stone ['stepiŋstoun] pasadera *f*; *fig.* escalón *m*.
ster·e·o... ['steriə]: **'~·phon·ic** □ estereofónico; **'~·scope** estereoscopio *m*; **'~·type 1.** clisé *m*, estereotipo *m*; F concepción *f* tradicional; **2.** clisar, estereotipar (*a. fig.*).
ster·ile ['steril] estéril; **ste·ril·i·ty** [~'riliti] esterilidad *f*; **ster·i·lize** ['~rilaiz] esterilizar.
ster·ling ['stə:rliŋ] **1.** genuino, de ley; *fig.* confiable; *pound* ~ libra *f* esterlina; **2.** libras *f/pl.* esterlinas.
stern¹ [stə:rn] □ severo, rígido; austero.
stern² [~] ⚓ popa *f*.
stern·ness ['stə:rnnis] severidad *f*, rigidez *f*.
ster·num ['stə:rnəm] esternón *m*.
steth·o·scope ['steθəskoup] estetoscopio *m*.
ste·ve·dore ['sti:vidɔ:r] estibador *m*.
stew [stju:] **1.** estofar; guisar; F contener el enojo; **2.** estofado *m*; guisado *m*; F apuro *m*.
stew·ard ['stjuərd] mayordomo *m*;

administrador *m*; ⚓, ✈ camarero *m*; ˈ**stew·ard·ess** ⚓ camarera *f*; ✈ azafata *f*, aeromoza *f*.

stew...: ˈ**~·pan,** ˈ**~·pot** cazuela *f*, cacerola *f*.

stick[1] [stik] **1.** palo *m*, vara *f*; porra *f*; (*walking*) bastón *m*; barra *f of soap etc.*; F *old* ~ tío *m*; ~*s pl.* leña *f*; **2.** ✓ apoyar con estacas.

stick[2] [~] [*irr.*] **1.** *v/i.* pegarse, adherirse (*to* a); atascarse *in mud etc.*; estar prendido; pararse, quedar parado; (*stay*) quedarse, permanecer; F ~ *around* esperar por ahí; ~ *at* persistir en; sentir escrúpulo por; ~ *at nothing* no tener ecrúpulos, no pararse en barras; ~ *fast* quedarse clavado; ~ *out* (sobre)salir; F ser evidente; ~ *out for* insistir en, no ceder hasta obtener; F ~ *to principle* aferrarse a; *p.* permanecer fiel a; (*follow*) *p.* pegarse a, seguir de cerca; ~ *together* quedarse unidos; ~ *up* asomarse por encima; (sobre)salir; (*hair etc.*) estar de punta; F ~ *up for* defender; **2.** *v/t.* (*gum etc.*) pegar, encolar (*a.* ~ *down*, ~ *together*); (*thrust*) clavar, hincar; (*pierce*) picar; F poner, meter; ~ *out* asomar, sacar; *sl.* ~ *it* (*out*) aguantar(lo) hasta el final; *sl.* ~ *up* atracar, encañonar; ˈ**stick·er** F persona *f* perseverante; etiqueta *f* engomada; ˈ**stick·i·ness** pegajosidad *f*; viscosidad *f*; ˈ**stick-in-the-mud** tardón *m*; aguafiestas *m*.

stick·le·back [ˈstiklbæk] espinoso *m*; ˈ**stick·ler** rigorista *m/f* (*for* en cuanto a).

stick-up [ˈstikʌp] *sl.* atraco *m*; asalto *m* con escopeta.

stick·y [ˈstiki] □ pegajoso; viscoso; F difícil; obstinado; *sl. end* triste.

stiff [stif] **1.** □ tieso, rígido; *collar* duro, almidonado; *door*, *joint* duro, tieso; *limb* entumecido; aterido *with cold*; *paste* espeso; *breeze* fuerte; *task*, *climb* difícil; *price* subido; *manner* estirado; F *bored* ~ aburrido como una ostra; F *scared* ~ muerto de miedo; **2.** *sl.* cadáver *m*; persona *f* cansada; ˈ**stiff·en** atiesar; endurecer(se); (*limb*) entumecerse; *morale etc.* fortalecer(se); ˈ**stiff·ness** entumecimiento *m of limb;* tiesura *f etc.*

sti·fle[1] [ˈstaifl] *vet.* babilla *f*.

sti·fle[2] [~] sofocar(se), ahogar(se); *fig.* suprimir; ˈ**sti·fling** sofocante, bochornoso.

stig·ma [ˈstigmə] *all senses*: estigma *m*; ˈ**stig·ma·tize** estigmatizar.

stile [stail] escalera *f* para pasar una cerca; ⚠ montante *m*.

sti·let·to [stiˈletou] estilete *m*.

still[1] [stil] **1.** *adj.* inmóvil; quieto, tranquilo; silencioso; *wine* no espumoso; **2.** *su. poet.* calma *f*, silencio *m*; *film*: vista *f* fija; **3.** *adv.* todavía, aún; **4.** *cj.* sin embargo, con todo; **5.** calmar, tranquilizar; acallar.

still[2] [~] alambique *m*.

still...: ˈ**~·born** nacido muerto; **~ life** bodegón *m*, naturaleza *f* muerta; ˈ**still·ness** inmovilidad *f*; quietud *f*; ˈ**still·y** *poet.* = *still*[1] 1.

stilt [stilt] zanco *m*; ˈ**stilt·ed** hinchado, afectado.

stim·u·lant [ˈstimjulənt] estimulante *adj. a. su. m*; **stim·u·late** [ˈ~leit] estimular (*to* a); **stim·uˈla·tion** estímulo *m*; excitación *f*; **stim·u·la·tive** [ˈ~lətiv] estimulador; **stim·u·lus** [ˈ~ləs] estímulo *m*.

sting [stiŋ] **1.** ⚘, *zo.* aguijón *m*; picadura *f*; escozor *m*, picazón *m*; *fig.* punzada *f*; **2.** [*irr.*] picar; punzar; escocer; *sl.* clavar.

stin·gi·ness [ˈstindʒinis] tacañería *f*.

sting(·ing) net·tle [ˈstiŋ(iŋ)netl] ortiga *f*.

stin·gy [ˈstindʒi] □ tacaño, cicatero.

stink [stiŋk] **1.** hedor *m*, mal olor *m*; **2.** [*irr.*] *v/i.* heder, oler mal (*of* a); *sl.* ser ricacho; *v/t.*: ~ *out* apestar; ˈ**~·er** *sl. p.* sinvergüenza *m/f*.

stint [stint] **1.** límite *m*, restricción *f*; destajo *m of work*; tarea *f*; **2.** limitar, restringir; ~ *o.s.* estrecharse.

sti·pend [ˈstaipend] estipendio *m*; **stiˈpen·di·ar·y** [~jəri] estipendario *adj. a. su. m.*

stip·ple [ˈstipl] puntear, granear.

stip·u·late [ˈstipjuleit] estipular (*for acc.*); **stip·uˈla·tion** estipulación *f*.

stir[1] [stəːr] **1.** agitación *f*; alboroto *m*; conmoción *f*, gran interés *m*; movimiento *m*; meneo *m*; hurgonada *f with poker*; *cause a* ~, *make a* ~ hacer ruido; **2.** *v/t.* (re)mover; agitar; *fire* hurgar; *liquid* revolver; *emotions* conmover; ~ *up passions* excitar; *rebellion* fomentar; *v/i.* moverse, menearse; *nobody is* ~*ring* están todavía en cama.

stir² [~] *sl.* chirona *f*; cárcel *f*.
stir·ring ['stə:riŋ] □ emocionante, conmovedor.
stir·rup ['stirəp] estribo *m*.
stitch [stitʃ] **1.** punto *m*, puntada *f*; ⚕ punzada *f*; *be in* ~*es* desternillarse de risa; **2.** coser (*a.* ⚕), hilvanar.
stoat [stout] armiño *m*.
stock [stɔk] **1.** (*family*) estirpe *f*, raza *f*; ⚘ tronco *m of tree*, cepa *f of vine*; ⚘ (*grafting*) patrón *m*; ⚘ (*flower*) alhelí *m*; (*handle*) mango *m*; ⚔ caja *f*; ⚚ surtido *m*, existencias *f/pl.*; ⚚ capital *m*; ⚒ (*a. live* ~) ganado *m*; (*a. dead* ~) aperos *m/pl.*; ⚚ ~*s pl.* acciones *f/pl.*, valores *m/pl.*; ⚓ ~*s pl.* astillero *m*; ~*s pl.* (*punishment*) cepo *m*; *in* ~ en almacén, en existencia; *on the* ~*s* ⚓ en vía de construcción; *fig.* en preparación; *take* ~ ⚚ hacer inventario (*of* de); *fig.* asesorarse (*of* de); *v. rolling* ~; **2.** consagrado; acostumbrado; *phrase* hecho; *thea.* de repertorio; **3.** proveer, abastecer; ⚚ tener existencias de; *pond etc.* poblar (*with* de); ~ *up* almacenar; acumular.
stock·ade [stɔ'keid] estacada *f*.
stock...: '~·**breed·er** ganadero *m*; '~·**brok·er** bolsista *m*, agente *m* de bolsa; '~ **ex·change** bolsa *f*; '~·**hold·er** accionista *m/f*.
stock·i·net ['stɔkinet] tela *f* de punto.
stock·ing ['stɔkiŋ] media *f*; (*knee-length*) calceta *f*.
stock·ist ['stɔkist] distribuidor *m*.
stock...: '~·**job·ber** agiotista *m*; '~·**job·bing** agiotaje *m*; '~·**pile** acumular; '~ **split** (*a.* '~ **div·i·dend**) reparto *m* de acciones gratis; '~-'**still** completamente inmóvil; '~·**tak·ing** inventario *m*, balance *m*; ~ *sale* venta *f* por balance; '**stock·y** rechoncho, achaparrado.
stodg·y ['stɔdʒi] □ indigesto, pesado.
sto·ic ['stouik] estoico *adj.* (*a.* '**sto·i·cal** □) *a. su. m*; '**sto·i·cism** estoicismo *m*.
stoke [stouk] cargar, cebar (*a. fig.*), echar carbón a; atizar; '**stok·er** fogonero *m*.
stole¹ [stoul] estola *f*.
stole² [~] *pret.*, '**sto·len** *p.p. of steal*.
stol·id ['stɔlid] □ impasible, imperturbable; **sto·lid·i·ty** [~'liditi] impasibilidad *f*.
stom·ach ['stʌmək] **1.** estómago *m*; *fig.* apetito *m*, deseo *m* (*for* de); ~ *ache* dolor *m* de estómago; ~ *pump* bomba *f* estomacal; **2.** *fig.* tragar, aguantar; '**stom·ach·er** peto *m*; **sto·mach·ic** [stə'mækik] □ estomacal *adj. a. su. m*.
stomp [stɔmp] pisar muy fuerte.
stone [stoun] **1.** piedra *f*; hueso *m of fruit*; (*commemorative*) lápida *f*; ⚕ cálculo *m*; (*weight*) catorce libras *f/pl.*; **2.** de piedra; ~*d sl.* borracho; narcotizado; **3.** lapidar, apedrear; *fruit* deshuesar; '~-'**blind** completamente ciego; '~-'**broke** arrancado; sin blanca; '~·**crop** pan *m* de cuco; '~-'**dead** más muerto que una piedra; '~-'**deaf** sordo como una tapia; '~·**ma·son** albañil *m*; cantero *m*; '~ **pit,** '~ **quar·ry** cantera *f*; '~'**wall·ing** *fig.* táctica *f* de cerrojo; '~·**ware** gres *m*.
ston·y ['stouni] *ground* pedregoso; *material* pétreo; *fig. silence, glance* glacial; *heart* empedernido; F ~ *broke* sin un cuarto.
stood [stud] *pret. a. p.p. of stand*.
stooge [stu:dʒ] paniaguado *m*, hombre *m* de paja.
stool [stu:l] taburete *m*, escabel *m*; ⚘ planta *f* madre; ⚕ evacuación *f*; (*folding*) silla *f* de tijera; *fall between two* ~*s* terminar siendo ni lo uno ni lo otro; fracasar por no saber a qué carta quedarse; '~ **pi·geon** soplón *m*, espía *m*.
stoop [stu:p] **1.** *v/i.* encorvarse, inclinarse; (*permanently*) ser cargado de espaldas; *fig.* rebajarse (*to* a); *v/t.* inclinar, bajar; **2.** cargazón *f* de espaldas; inclinación *f*; escalinata *f* de entrada.
stop [stɔp] **1.** *v/t.* detener, parar; *abuse, process etc.* poner fin a; *payment* suspender; *supply* cortar, interrumpir; *teeth* empastar; (*forbid*) prohibir, poner fin a; (*a.* ~ *up*) tapar, cegar; obstruir; ~ *s.o. talking* impedirle a uno hablar; ~ *s.o. going* prohibirle a uno ir; *v/i.* parar(se), detenerse; hacer alto; terminar(se), acabarse; cortarse; (*stay*) quedarse, hospedarse (*at* en); ~ *ger.* dejar de *inf.*; *I* ~*ped going* dejé de ir; *it has* ~*ped raining* ha dejado de llover; ~ *at nothing* no pararse en barras; ~ *dead* pararse en seco; ~ *in* no salir; F ~ *off* interrumpir el viaje (*at* en); ~ *over* quedar la noche; **2.** parada *f*; alto *m*; ⊕ tope *m*, retén *m*; ♪ registro *m of*

organ; ♪ llave *f*; *gr*. (*a. full* ~) punto *m*; *come to a* ~ venir a parar; *put a* ~ *to* poner fin a; ˈ**~·gap** recurso *m* provisional; (*p.*) tapa(a)gujeros *m*; ˈ**~·light** luz *f* de parada; ˈ**~-off,** ˈ**~·o·ver** parada *f* intermedia; ˈ**stop·page** cesación *f*; detención *f*; paro *m*, suspensión *f of work etc.*; interrupción *f*; ⊕ obstrucción *f*; ˈ**stop·per 1.** tapón *m*; ⊕ taco *m*; *radio*: ~ *circuit* circuito *m* anti-resonante; **2.** tap(o-n)ar; ˈ**stop·ping** empaste *m of tooth*; ˈ**stop-press news** "al cerrar la edición"; ˈ**stop·watch** cronómetro *m*.

stor·age [ˈstɔːridʒ] almacenaje *m*, depósito *m*; ~ *battery* acumulador *m*.

store [stɔːr] **1.** provisión *f*; (*reserve*) repuesto *m*; (~*house*) almacén *m*, depósito *m*; tienda *f*; ~*s pl.* provisiones *f/pl.*, víveres *m/pl.*; ⚔ ~*s pl.* pertrechos *m/pl.*; *in* ~ en almacén, en reserva; *be in* ~ *for a p.* esperarle a una p.; *set* (*or put*) *great* ~ *by* conceder mucha importancia a; **2.** almacenar; abastecer; ~ *away* tener en reserva, guardar, archivar; ~ *up* amontonar, acumular; ˈ**~·house** almacén *m*, depósito *m*; *fig.* mina *f*; ˈ**~·keep·er** almacenero *m*; tendero *m*; ˈ**~·room** despensa *f*; cuarto *m* de almacenar; ⚓ pañol *m*.

sto·rey [ˈstɔːri] *mst British* = *story*².

sto·ried [ˈstɔːrid] de ... pisos.

stork [stɔːrk] cigüeña *f*.

storm [stɔːrm] **1.** tormenta *f*, tempestad *f* (*a. fig.*), borrasca *f*; *take by* ~ tomar por asalto; ~ *cloud* nubarrón *m*; ~ *troops pl.* tropas *f/pl.* de asalto; **2.** *v/t.* ⚔ asaltar, tomar por asalto; *v/i.* rabiar, enfurecerse, tronar (*at* contra); ˈ**storm·y** □ tempestuoso, borrascoso (*a. fig.*).

sto·ry¹ [ˈstɔːri] cuento *m*, histori(et)a *f*; (*joke*) chiste *m*; anécdota *f*; argumento *m*, trama *f of novel etc.*; F mentira *f*, embuste *m*; *short* ~ cuento *m*; *that's* (*quite*) *another* ~ es harina de otro costal.

sto·ry² [~] piso *m*.

sto·ry·tell·er [ˈstɔːritelər] cuentista *m/f*; F embustero (a *f*) *m*.

stout [staut] **1.** □ robusto, sólido, macizo; *p.* gordo, corpulento; *fig.* animoso, valiente; **2.** stout *m* (*cerveza fuerte*); ˈ**~-ˈheart·ed** □ valiente; ˈ**stout·ness** gordura *f*, corpulencia *f*.

stove [stouv] **1.** estufa *f*; hornillo *m*; cocina *f* de gas *etc.*; **2.** *pret. a. p.p. of stave* 2; ˈ**~·pipe** tubo *m* de estufa; F (*top hat*) chistera *f*.

stow [stou] *v/t.* meter; esconder; ⚓ arrumar; *v/i.*: ~ *away* viajar de polizón; ˈ**stow·age** ⚓ arrumaje *m*; ⚓ (*place*) bodega *f*; ˈ**stow·a·way** polizón *m*.

strad·dle [ˈstrædl] esparrancarse encima de; *horse* montar a horcajadas; ⚔ *target* cubrir, caer a ambos lados de; favorecer a ambos lados en.

strafe [streif] bombardear.

strag·gle [ˈstrægl] rezagarse; extraviarse; vagar; ⚘ lozanear; ˈ**strag·gler** rezagado *m*; ⚔ extraviado *m*; ˈ**strag·gling** □ disperso; desordenado.

straight [streit] **1.** *adj.* derecho, recto; *back* erguido; *hair* lacio; (*honest*) honrado; *answer* franco, directo; *face* serio, impasible; *drink* sin mezcla; *pol. fight* sencillo, de dos candidatos; *Am. pol.* decidido, intransigente; *put* ~ arreglar; *sport*: *the* ~ la recta; **2.** *adv.* derecho; directamente; con franqueza; ~ *ahead*, ~ *on* todo seguido; ~ *away* en seguida; ~ *off* sin interrupción, de un tirón; F *go* ~ enmendarse; ˈ**straight·en** *v/t.* enderezar (*a.* ~ *out*); *fig.* arreglar (*a.* ~ *out*); *v/i.*: ~ *up* enderezarse; **straight-for·ward** [~ˈfɔːrwərd] □ honrado, franco; (*easy*) sencillo; ˈ**straight-ˈout** cabal; completo.

strain¹ [strein] **1.** tensión *f*, tirantez *f*; esfuerzo *m* grande; ⊕ deformación *f*; ⚕ torcedura *f of muscle*; ⚕ agotamiento *m* nervioso; ♪ ~*s pl.* aire *m*, melodía *f*, compases *m/pl.*; *put a great* ~ *on* someter a gran esfuerzo; **2.** *v/t.* estirar, tender con fuerza, poner tirante; ⊕ *machine* deformar; ⊕ (*filter*) colar, filtrar; *meaning* forzar; ⚕ *muscle* torcer; ⚕ *eyes* forzar, cansar; ~*ed relations* tirante; *v/i.* esforzarse (*after* por conseguir; *at* tirando de).

strain² [~] (*race*) linaje *m*, raza *f*; vena *f of madness*; (*style*) tono *m*, estilo *m*.

strain·er [ˈstreinər] colador *m*.

strait [streit] **1.** *geog.* estrecho *m* (*a.* ~*s pl.*); *fig.* ~*s pl.* estrecheces *f/pl.*, apuro *m*; *in dire* ~*s* en el mayor apuro; **2.**: ~ *jacket* camisa *f* de fuerza; ˈ**strait·en** estrechar; *in* ~*ed circumstances* apurado, en la necesidad; **strait-laced** ['~leist] gazmoño, remilgado, pudibundo.

strand[1] [strænd] **1.** *poet.* playa *f*, ribera *f*; **2.** ⚓ varar(se), encallar; *~ed fig.* desamparado; inmovilizado.

strand[2] [~] brizna *f*; ramal *m of rope*; hebra *f*.

strange [streindʒ] ☐ extraño, raro, peregrino; desconocido; nuevo, no acostumbrado; *it is ~ he has not come* es raro que no haya venido, me extraña que no haya venido; **'strange·ness** extrañeza *f*, rareza *f*; novedad *f*; **'stran·ger** desconocido (a *f*) *m*; forastero (a *f*) *m*; *be no ~ to* conocer bien.

stran·gle ['stræŋgl] estrangular; *fig.* ahogar; **'~·hold** *sport:* collar *m* de fuerza; *fig.* dominio *m* completo; *have a ~ on* tener asido por la garganta; *fig.* dominar completamente.

stran·gu·late ['stræŋgjuleit] ⚕ estrangular; **stran·gu'la·tion** estrangulación *f* (*a.* ⚕).

strap [stræp] **1.** correa *f*; tira *f*, banda *f*; *~hanger* pasajero *m* sin asiento; **2.** (*tie*) atar con correa; (*beat*) azotar con una correa; **'strap·ping** robusto, fornido.

strat·a·gem ['strætidʒəm] estratagema *f*.

stra·te·gic [strə'ti:dʒik] ☐ estratégico; **strat·e·gist** ['strætidʒist] estratega *m*; **'strat·e·gy** estrategia *f*.

strat·i·fy ['strætifai] estratificar(se).

stra·to·cruis·er ['streitoukru:zər] avión *m* estratosférico.

strat·o·sphere ['strætousfir] estratosfera *f*.

stra·tum, *pl.* **stra·ta** ['streitə(m)] estrato *m*; *fig.* capa *f*.

straw [strɔ:] **1.** paja *f*; (*drinking*) pajita *f*; (*mst ~ hat*) sombrero *m* de paja; *it's the last ~* no faltaba más; **2.** ... de paja; (*color*) pajizo; *~ vote Am. pol.* votación *f* de tanteo; **'~·ber·ry** fresón *m*; (*wild*) fresa *f*; *~ bed* fresal *m*; **'~ man** figura *f* de paja.

stray [strei] **1.** extraviarse; perderse; descarriarse; *~ from* apartarse de; **2.** (*a. ~ed*) extraviado; errante; aislado; *bullet* perdido; **3.** animal *m* extraviado.

streak [stri:k] **1.** raya *f*, lista *f*; vena *f of madness*; racha *f of luck*; *~ of lightning* rayo *m* (*a. fig.*); **2.** *v/t.* rayar, listar; *v/i.* pasar *etc.* como un rayo; **'streak·y** ☐ rayado, listado; *bacon* entreverado; *shot* afortunado.

stream [stri:m] **1.** arroyo *m*; corriente *f*; flujo *m*, chorro *m*; *fig.* oleada *f*, torrente *m*; *on ~* puesto en operación; en marcha; **2.** *v/i.* correr, fluir; ondear, flotar *in wind*; *~ forth*, *~ out* brotar, chorrear; (*people etc.*) salir a torrentes; *her eyes were ~ing* lloraba a mares; *her face was ~ing with tears* su cara estaba bañada de lágrimas; *v/t.* arrojar, derramar; *pupils* clasificar; **'stream·er** flámula *f*; (*paper*) serpentina *f*; ⚓ gallardete *m*.

stream·line ['stri:mlain] aerodinamizar; *fig.* coordinar, perfeccionar; *~d* perfilado, aerodinámico.

street [stri:t] calle *f*; *attr.* callejero; *on easy ~* con el bolsillo lastrado; **'~·car** tranvía *m*; **'~ floor** planta *f* baja; **'~·walk·er** prostituta *f* de calle; ramera *f*.

strength [streŋθ] fuerza *f*; intensidad *f*; resistencia *f*; ⚔ *etc.* número *m*; *on the ~ of* fundándose en; **'strength·en** fortalecer(se), reforzar(se), fortificar(se).

stren·u·ous ['strenjuəs] ☐ vigoroso, enérgico; arduo.

strep·to·my·cin [streptou'maisin] estreptomicina *f*.

stress [stres] **1.** esfuerzo *m*; presión *f*, compulsión *f*; ⚕ fatiga *f* (nerviosa); ⊕ tensión *f*, carga *f*; *rhet.* énfasis *m*; *gr.* acento *m*; *lay ~ (up)on* insistir en; **2.** ⊕ cargar; *rhet.* insistir en, recalcar; *gr.* acentuar.

stretch [stretʃ] **1.** extender(se); estirar(se); alargar(se); dilatar(se), ensanchar(se); *hand etc.* tender(se) (*mst ~ out*); *meaning etc.* forzar, violentar; desperezarse *after sleep*; *limb* desentorpecerse; *~ out on the ground* tenderse en el suelo; **2.** extensión *f*; (*act of stretching*) estirón *m*; ensanche *m*; esfuerzo *m of imagination*; (*distance*) trecho *m*; (*time*) período *m*; *at a ~* de un tirón; **'stretch·er** ⊕ ensanchador *m*; ⚕ camilla *f*; ⚠ soga *f*.

strew [stru:] [*irr.*] esparcir; derramar; *ground etc.* sembrar (*with* de); **strewn** [stru:n] *p.p. of strew*.

stri·ate ['straiit], **stri·at·ed** [strai'eitid] estriado.

strick·en ['strikən] afligido (*with* por).

strict [strikt] ☐ estricto; riguroso; severo; terminante; *~ly speaking* en rigor; **'strict·ness** rigor *m*; seve-

ridad *f*; **stric·ture** [ˈ~tʃər] censura *f*; ⚕ constricción *f*.
stride [straid] **1.** [*irr.*] *v/t. horse* montar a horcajadas; *v/i.* caminar a paso largo (*a.* ~ *along*), andar a trancos; **2.** zancada *f*, tranco *m*; *get into one's* ~ alcanzar el ritmo acostumbrado; *take it in one's* ~ sabérselo tomar bien.
stri·dent [ˈstraidnt] □ estridente.
strife [straif] *lit.* disensión *f*, contienda *f*.
strike [straik] **1.** huelga *f*; F descubrimiento *m* repentino *of oil etc.*; *baseball*: golpe *m*; *be on* ~ estar en huelga; *go on* ~ ponerse en huelga; *sit-down* ~ huelga *f* de asentados; **2.** [*irr.*] *v/t.* golpear; pegar; herir; *fig.* impresionar; *fig.* dar con; *attitude* tomar, adoptar, asumir; † *balance* hacer; † *bargain* cerrar; *blow* asestar; ⚓ *flag* arriar; (*clock*) *hour* dar; *match* frotar, encender; *medal* acuñar; ⚓ *mine* chocar con; *oil* descubrir; ⚘ *root* echar; *work* abandonar; ~ *down* derribar; ~ *off* borrar; cercenar; quitar de golpe; ~ *out* borrar, tachar; ~ *up* ♪ iniciar, empezar a tocar; *conversation* entablar; *friendship* trabar; *v/i.* golpear; chocar; ponerse (*or* estar) en huelga; (*clock*) dar (la una *etc.*); (*bell*) sonar; ⚘ echar raíces; ⚓ encallar *on reef*; ⚓ (*flag*) arriar la bandera; ~ *at* tratar de golpear; *fig.* acometer, amenazar; ~ *home* herir en lo vivo; dar en el blanco; ~ *into* penetrar en; ~ *out on one's own* campear por sus respetos; ~ *up* ♪ empezar a tocar; ˈ**~·break·er** rompehuelgas *m*; esquirol *m*; ˈ**~ pay** sueldo *m* de huelguista; ˈ**strik·er** huelguista *m/f*; ⊕ percutor *m*.
strik·ing [ˈstraikiŋ] □ impresionante; sorprendente; *color etc.* llamativo.
string [striŋ] **1.** cuerda *f* (*a.* ♪, *a. bow*); sarta *f of pearls, lies*; (*row*) hilera *f*, fila *f*; ristra *f of onions etc.*; retahila *f of curses*; ⚘ fibra *f*, nervio *m*; ~*s pl.* ♪ instrumentos *m/pl.* de cuerda; *have two* ~*s to one's bow* tener dos cuerdas en su arco; F *pull* ~*s* tocar resortes, mover palancas; **2.** *violin* encordar; *pearls etc.* ensartar; F ~ *along* traer al retortero; *sl.* hacer fisga a; ~ *out* extender; *sl.* ~ *up* ahorcar; ˈ**~ band,** ˈ**~ or·ches·tra** orquesta *f* de cuerdas; ˈ**~ bean** habichuela *f* verde; F persona *f* alta y flaca; **stringed** ♪ ... de cuerda(s).
strin·gen·cy [ˈstrindʒənsi] rigor *m*, severidad *f*; † tirantez *f*; ˈ**strin·gent** □ riguroso, estricto, severo; † tirante.
string·y [ˈstriŋi] fibroso.
strip [strip] **1.** *v/t.* despojar (*of* de); *p.* desnudar; *clothes* quitar, despojarse de (*a.* ~ *off*); *gears* estropear; ⊕ desmontar; *v/i.* desnudarse; **2.** tira *f*; faja *f*; *comic* ~ tira *f* cómica.
stripe [straip] **1.** raya *f*, lista *f*; banda *f*; ⚔ galón *m*; **2.** rayar, listar.
strip·ling [ˈstripliŋ] mozuelo *m*.
strip·tease [ˈstripti:z] espectáculo *m* de desnudamiento sensual.
strive [straiv] [*irr.*] esforzarse (*to* por); luchar (*against* contra); afanarse (*after*, *for* por conseguir);
striv·en [ˈstrivn] *p.p. of strive*.
strode [stroud] *pret. of stride* 1.
stroke [strouk] **1.** golpe *m* (*a. sport*); jugada *f*; estilo *m of swimming*; brazada *f of swimmer*; remada *f of oar*; (*oarsman*) primer remero *m*; (*caress*) caricia *f*; ⊕ carrera *f*; ⚕ ataque *m* fulminante, apoplejía *f*; campanada *f of bell*; pincelada *f of brush*; rasgo *m*, plumazo *m of pen* (*a. fig.*); ~ *of genius* rasgo *m* de ingenio; ~ *of lightning* rayo *m*; ~ *of luck* racha *f* de suerte; *at a* ~ de un golpe; *I haven't done a* ~ (*of work*) no he hecho absolutamente nada; **2.** acariciar; *chin* pasar la mano sobre.
stroll [stroul] **1.** pasearse, deambular, callejear; **2.** paseo *m*; *take a* ~ dar un paseo; ˈ**stroll·er** paseante *m/f*; cochecito *m*; ˈ**stroll·ing** *actor etc.* ambulante.
strong [strɔŋ] □ fuerte; recio, robusto; *accent* marcado; *conviction* profundo; *drink* potente, alcohólico; *emotion* intenso; *language* indecente; fuerte; *situation* dramático; *supporter* acérrimo; *tea* cargado; *terms* enfático; *verb* irregular, fuerte; *they were 100* ~ eran 100, ascendían a 100; *feel* ~*ly about* sentir profundamente *acc.*; F *going* ~ sin perder fuerza; lo bien de siempre; ˈ**~·box** caja *f* de caudales; ˈ**~·hold** fortaleza *f*, plaza *f* fuerte; *fig.* baluarte *m*; ˈ**~·point** fuerte *m*; ˈ**~-ˈwilled** obstinado.

strop [strɔp] **1.** suavizador *m*; **2.** suavizar.
stro·phe [ˈstroufi] estrofa *f*.
strove [strouv] *pret. of strive*.
struck [strʌk] *pret. a. p.p. of strike* 2.
struc·tur·al [ˈstrʌktʃərəl] ☐ estructural; **struc·ture** [ˈ~tʃər] estructura *f*; construcción *f*.
strug·gle [ˈstrʌgl] **1.** luchar (*to, for* por); esforzarse (*to* por); **2.** lucha *f* (*for* por); contienda *f*; esfuerzo *m*.
strum [strʌm] *v/t. guitar* rasguear (sin arte); *v/i.* cencerrear.
strum·pet [ˈstrʌmpit] ramera *f*.
strung [strʌŋ] *pret. a. p.p. of string* 2.
strut [strʌt] **1.** *v/i.* pavonearse, contonearse; *v/t.* ⊕ apuntalar; **2.** (*walk*) contoneo *m*; ⊕ puntal *m*, riostra *f*, tornapunta *f*.
strych·nine [ˈstrikni:n] estricnina *f*.
stub [stʌb] **1.** ✓ tocón *m*; colilla *f of cigarette*; cabo *m of pencil*; talón *m of check*; **2.**: ~ *out cigarette* apagar; ~ *one's toe* dar un tropezón.
stub·ble [ˈstʌbl] rastrojo *m*.
stub·bly [ˈstʌbli] *chin* cerdoso.
stub·born [ˈstʌbərn] ☐ tenaz, inflexible; *b.s.* terco, testarudo, porfiado; ˈ**stub·born·ness** tenacidad *f*; *b.s.* terquedad *f*, testarudez *f*.
stuc·co [ˈstʌkou] **1.** estuco *m*; **2.** estucar.
stuck [stʌk] *pret. a. p.p. of stick*²; *fig.* victimizado; arrinconado; F ~ *on* chalado por; ˈ~-ˈ**up** empingorotado, finchado, engreído.
stud¹ [stʌd] **1.** tachón *m*; (*boot*) taco *m*; botón *m* (de camisa); **2.** tachonar; *fig.* sembrar (*with* de).
stud² [~] caballeriza *f*; yeguada *f*; ˈ~ **book** registro *m* genealógico de caballos; ˈ~**·horse** caballo *m* padre.
stud·ding [ˈstʌdiŋ] ⚠ montantes *m/pl.* de tabique.
stu·dent [ˈstju:dənt] estudiante *m/f*; alumno (a *f*) *m*; investigador (-a *f*) *m*; ~ *body* estudiantado *m*.
stud·ied [ˈstʌdid] ☐ *insult* premeditado; *pose* afectado.
stu·di·o [ˈstju:diou] estudio *m* (*a. radio*); taller *m*; ~ *couch* sofá-cama *m*.
stu·di·ous [ˈstu:djəs] ☐ estudioso; asiduo, solícito; ˈ**stu·di·ous·ness** aplicación *f*.
stud·y [ˈstʌdi] **1.** estudio *m* (*a. paint.*, ♪, *room*); (*room*) despacho *m*, gabinete *m*; **2.** estudiar.
stuff [stʌf] **1.** materia *f*, material *m*; (*cloth*) tela *f*, paño *m*; *fig.* cosa *f*; *fig.* F chismes *m/pl.*; ~ *and nonsense!* ¡ni hablar!; **2.** *v/t.* llenar, hinchar, atestar, atiborrar (*with* de); meter sin orden (*into* en); atascar, tapar; *fowl* rellenar; *animal* disecar; ~ *away sl.* zampar; *sl.* ~*ed shirt* tragavirotes *m*; *v/i.* F atracarse, hartarse; ˈ**stuff·ing** borra *f*; *cooking*: relleno *m*; ˈ**stuff·y** ☐ *room* mal ventilado, sofocante; F relamido; F picajoso.
stul·ti·fi·ca·tion [stʌltifiˈkeiʃn] anulación *f*; situación *f* ridícula; **stul·ti·fy** [ˈ~fai] anular; hacer parecer ridículo; quitar importancia a.
stum·ble [ˈstʌmbl] **1.** tropezón *m*, traspié *m*; **2.** tropezar (*a. fig.*), dar un traspié; ~ *upon* tropezar con; ˈ**stum·bling block** *fig.* tropiezo *m*.
stump [stʌmp] **1.** tocón *m of tree*; muñón *m of leg etc.*; raigón *m of tooth*; cabo *m*; *cricket*: palo *m*; **2.** *v/t.* F confundir, dejar confuso; F *country* recorrer pronunciando discursos; F desafiar; *v/i.* cojear; pisar muy fuerte; *sl.* ~ *up* pagar (*for acc.*); ˈ~-ˈ**speak·er** orador *m* callejero; ˈ**stump·y** ☐ achaparrado.
stun [stʌn] aturdir, atolondrar (*a. fig.*).
stung [stʌŋ] *pret. a. p.p. of sting* 2.
stunk [stʌŋk] *p.p. of stink* 2.
stun·ner [ˈstʌnər] F persona *f* maravillosa; ˈ**stun·ning** ☐ F estupendo; bárbaro, imponente.
stunt¹ [stʌnt] F **1.** ✈ vuelo *m* acrobático; (*newspaper etc.*) treta *f* publicitaria; maniobra *f* sensacional; **2.** ✈ lucirse haciendo maniobras acrobáticas.
stunt² [~] atrofiar, impedir el crecimiento de; ˈ**stunt·ed** enano; raquítico.
stu·pe·fac·tion [stju:piˈfækʃn] estupefacción *f*.
stu·pe·fy [ˈstju:pifai] atolondrar; pasmar, causar estupor (a); dejar estupefacto.
stu·pen·dous [stju:ˈpendəs] ☐ estupendo.
stu·pid [ˈstju:pid] ☐ estúpido; **stu·pid·i·ty** [stju:ˈpiditi] estupidez *f*.
stu·por [ˈstju:pər] estupor *m* (*a. fig.*).
stur·di·ness [ˈstə:rdinis] robustez *f*, fuerza *f*; ˈ**stur·dy** ☐ robusto, fuerte; vigoroso; tenaz.

stur·geon ['stəːrdʒən] esturión *m.*
stut·ter ['stʌtər] **1.** *v/i.* tartamudear; *v/t.* balbucear; **2.** tartamudeo *m*; '~**er** tartamudo *adj. a. su.* (a *f*) *m.*
sty[1] [stai] pocilga *f*, zahurda *f*.
sty(e)[2] [~] orzuelo *m.*
style [stail] **1.** estilo *m* (*a.*); moda *f*; elegancia *f*; título *m*; (*of address*) tratamiento *m*; *do s.t. in* ~ hacer algo lo mejor posible; *live in* ~ darse buena vida; **2.** intitular, nombrar; *dress* cortar a la moda.
styl·ish ['stailiʃ] □ elegante; a la moda; '**styl·ish·ness** elegancia *f*.
styl·ist ['stailist] estilista *m/f*; **styl·ized** ['stailaizd] estilizado.
sty·lo·graph ['stailəgræf] estilógrafo *m.*
styp·tic ['stiptik] estíptico *adj. a. su. m*; ~ *pencil* lápiz *m* estíptico.
sua·sion ['sweiʒn] persuasión *f*.
suave [swaːv] □ afable, fino; *b.s.* zalamero; **suav·i·ty** ['swæviti] afabilidad *f*, finura *f*.
sub [sʌb] F *abbr.* = *submarine*; *subordinate* 2; *subscription*; *substitute* 2.
sub...: *mst* sub...
sub·ac·id ['sʌb'æsid] subácido.
sub·al·tern ['sʌbltərn] ⚔ alférez *m.*
sub·a·tom ['sʌb'ætəm] subátomo *m.*
sub·chas·er ['sʌb'tʃeisər] = *submarine chaser.*
sub·com·mit·tee ['sʌbkəmiti] subcomisión *f*.
sub·con·scious ['sʌb'kɔnʃəs] **1.** □ subconsciente; **2.** subcon(s)ciencia *f*.
sub·con·tract [sʌb'kɔntrækt] subcontrato *m.*
sub·cu·ta·ne·ous ['sʌbkjuː'teiniəs] □ subcutáneo.
sub·dean ['sʌb'diːn] subdecano *m.*
sub·di·vide ['sʌbdi'vaid] subdividir(se); **sub·di·vi·sion** ['~viʒn] subdivisión *f*.
sub·due [səb'djuː] sojuzgar, avasallar, dominar; suavizar, amansar; **sub'dued** *color* amortiguado; *emotion* templado; *light* tenue; *p.* deprimido, manso; *voice* bajo.
sub·head(·ing) ['sʌbhed(iŋ)] subtítulo *m.*
sub·ject ['sʌbdʒikt] **1.** sujeto; *people* subyugado, esclavizado; ~ *to* (*liable*) propenso a; ~ *to* (*exposed*) expuesto a; ~ *to the approval of* sujeto a la aprobación de; ~ *to change without notice* sujeto a cambio sin previo aviso; ~ *to correction* bajo corrección; ~ *to a fee* sujeto a derechos; **2.** *gr.* sujeto *m*; *pol.* súbdito (a *f*) *m*; (*matter*) tema *m*, materia *f*; materia *f*, asignatura *f in school*; asunto *m of talk etc.*; ♪, *paint.* tema *m*; *he is a nervous* ~ es un caso nervioso; **3.** [səb'dʒekt] someter *to test etc.*; (*conquer*) dominar, sojuzgar; ~ *o.s. to* sujetarse a; **sub'jec·tion** sujeción *f*; avasallamiento *m*; **sub·jec·tive** [sʌb'dʒektiv] □ subjetivo.
sub·join ['sʌb'dʒɔin] adjuntar.
sub·ju·gate ['sʌbdʒugeit] subyugar; **sub·ju'ga·tion** subyugación *f*.
sub·junc·tive [səb'dʒʌŋktiv] (*or* ~ *mood*) subjuntivo *m.*
sub·lease ['sʌb'liːs], **sub·let** ['~'let] [*irr.* (*let*)] realquilar, subarrendar.
sub·li·mate **1.** ['sʌblimit] ⚗ sublimado *m*; **2.** ['~eit] sublimar (*a.* ⚗); **sub·li'ma·tion** sublimación *f*; **sublime** [sə'blaim] **1.** □ (*the* lo) sublime; **2.** sublimar; **sub·li·min·al** [sʌb'liminəl] □ subliminal; **sublim·i·ty** [sə'blimiti] sublimidad *f*.
sub·ma·chine gun ['sʌbmə'ʃiːn-'gʌn] subfusil *m* ametrallador.
sub·ma·rine ['sʌbməriːn] submarino *adj. a. su. m*; '~ **chas·er** cazasubmarinos *m.*
sub·merge [səb'məːrdʒ] sumergir(se); **sub'mer·sion** sumersión *f*.
sub·mis·sion [səb'miʃn] sumisión *f*; **sub·mis·sive** [~'misiv] □ sumiso.
sub·mit [səb'mit] *v/t.* someter; *evidence* presentar; *esp. parl.* proponer; *I* ~ *that* me permito decir que; *v/i.* (*a.* ~ *o.s.*) someterse; *fig.* resignarse (*to* a).
sub·or·di·nate **1.** [sə'bɔːrdnit] □ subordinado (*a. gr.*), inferior; **2.** [~] subordinado (a *f*) *m*; **3.** [~'bɔːrdineit] subordinar; **sub·or·di'na·tion** subordinación *f*.
sub·orn [sʌ'bɔːrn] sobornar; **sub·or'na·tion** soborno *m.*
sub·poe·na [sə'piːnə] **1.** comparendo *m*; **2.** mandar comparecer.
sub·scribe [səb'skraib] su(b)scribir(se), abonarse (*to a paper* a un periódico); ✝ su(b)scribir (*for, to acc.*); ~ *to an opinion* su(b)scribir una opinión; **sub'scrib·er** su(b)scriptor (-a *f*) *m*; abonado (a *f*) *m.*
sub·scrip·tion [səb'skripʃn] su(b)-

scripción *f*; abono *m*; ~ *rate* tarifa *f* de su(b)scripción.
sub·se·quence [ˈsʌbsikwəns] subsecuencia *f*; ˈ**sub·se·quent** ☐ subsecuente, posterior (*to* a); ~*ly* con posterioridad, después.
sub·ser·vi·ence [səbˈsəːrviəns] subordinación *f*; servilismo *m*; **subˈser·vi·ent** ☐ subordinado; servil.
sub·side [səbˈsaid] (*water*) bajar; (*house*) hundirse; (*wind*) amainar; (*excitement*) calmarse; ~ *into chair etc.* dejarse caer en; **subˈsid·ence** hundimiento *m*, descenso *m of ground*; socavón *m in street*; bajada *f of water etc*; **sub·sid·i·ar·y** [~ˈsidjəri] **1.** ☐ subsidiario; auxiliar; ✝ afiliado, filial; **2.** filial *f*, sucursal *f*;
sub·si·dize [ˈsʌbsidaiz] subvencionar; ˈ**sub·si·dy** subvención *f*.
sub·sist [səbˈsist] subsistir; sustentarse (*on* con); **subˈsist·ence** subsistencia *f*; ~ *allowance* dietas *f/pl*.
sub·soil [ˈsʌbsɔil] subsuelo *m*.
sub·son·ic [sʌbˈsɔnik] subsónico.
sub·stance [ˈsʌbstəns] sustancia *f*; esencia *f*; *man of* ~ hombre *m* acaudalado.
sub·stand·ard [sʌbˈstændərd] inferior al nivel normal, deficiente.
sub·stan·tial [səbˈstænʃl] ☐ sustancial, sustancioso; *sum* considerable; *build* sólido; *p.* acomodado.
sub·stan·ti·ate [səbˈstænʃieit] establecer, verificar, justificar.
sub·stan·ti·val [sʌbstənˈtaivl] ☐ sustantivo; ˈ**sub·stan·tive** ☐ sustantivo *adj. a. su. m* (*a. gr.*).
sub·sta·tion [ˈsʌbˈsteiʃn] ⚡ subestación *f*; subcentral *m*.
sub·sti·tute [ˈsʌbstitjuːt] **1.** *v/t.* sustituir (*A for B* B por A); *v/i.* F suplir (*for* a); **2.** sustituto (a *f*) *m*; suplente *m/f*; reemplazo *m*; **3.** sucedáneo; de reemplazo; **sub·stiˈtu·tion** sustitución *f*; reemplazo *m*.
sub·stra·tum [ˈsʌbˈstreitəm] sustrato *m*.
sub·ten·ant [ˈsʌbˈtenənt] subarrendatario (a *f*) *m*.
sub·ter·fuge [ˈsʌbtərfjuːdʒ] subterfugio *m*.
sub·ter·ra·ne·an [sʌbtəˈreinjən] subterráneo.
sub·til·ize [ˈsʌtilaiz] sutilizar.
sub·ti·tle [ˈsʌbtaitl] subtítulo *m*.
sub·tle [ˈsʌtl] ☐ sutil; astuto; *b.s.* insidioso; ˈ**sub·tle·ty** sutileza *f*; astucia *f*.
sub·tract [səbˈtrækt] ⅍ sustraer, restar; **subˈtrac·tion** sustracción *f*, resta *f*.
sub·urb [ˈsʌbəːrb] suburbio *m*, arrabal *m*, barrio *m*; *the* ~*s pl.* los barrios (exteriores); **sub·ur·ban** [səˈbəːrbən] suburbano; 🚂 de cercanías; **sub·ur·bi·a** [sʌˈbəːrbiə] los suburbios *m/pl.*; las afueras *f/pl.*; vida *f* arrabalera.
sub·ven·tion [səbˈvenʃn] subvención *f*; ayuda *f* institucional; asistencia *f* financiera.
sub·ver·sion [sʌbˈvəːrʒn] subversión *f*; **subˈver·sive** ☐ subversivo.
sub·vert [sʌbˈvəːrt] trastornar, subvertir.
sub·way [ˈsʌbwei] paso *m* subterráneo; metro *m*; ferrocarril *m* subterráneo.
suc·ceed [səkˈsiːd] tener (buen) éxito, salir bien; ~ *in ger.* lograr *inf.*, conseguir *inf.*; ~ *to crown, post* suceder a; ~ *a p.* suceder a una p.; **sucˈceed·ing** subsiguiente.
suc·cess [səkˈses] (buen) éxito *m*; triunfo *m*; prosperidad *f*; *he was a (great)* ~ tuvo (mucho) éxito; *it was a (great)* ~ salió (muy) bien; *make a* ~ *of* tener éxito en; **sucˈcess·ful** [~ful] ☐ próspero, afortunado; feliz; *be* ~ tener (buen) éxito; *esp.* ✝ prosperar, medrar; **suc·ces·sion** [~ˈseʃn] sucesión *f* (*to* a); descendencia *f*; serie *f*; *in* ~ seguidos, uno tras otro; ~ *duty* derechos *m/pl.* de sucesión; **sucˈces·sive** ☐ sucesivo; **sucˈces·sor** sucesor (-a *f*) *m*.
suc·cinct [səkˈsiŋkt] ☐ sucinto.
suc·cor [ˈsʌkər] **1.** socorro *m*; **2.** socorrer.
suc·cu·lence [ˈsʌkjuləns] suculencia *f*; ˈ**suc·cu·lent** ☐ suculento.
suc·cumb [səˈkʌm] sucumbir (*to* a).
such [sʌtʃ] **1.** *adj.* tal, semejante; ~ *a man* tal hombre; *no* ~ *thing* no hay tal cosa; *and* ~ y tal; ~ *as* tal como; ~ *as to* de tal manera que, tal que; *as* ~ como tal; ~ *and* ~ tal o cual; ~ *is life* así es la vida; **2.** *adv.*: ~ *a big dog* perro tan grande; **3.** *pron.*: ~ *as* los que; ˈ**such·like 1.** *adj.* tal; **2.** *pron.* tales personas (*or* cosas).
suck [sʌk] **1.** chupar; mamar; ~ *in* sorber; *air* aspirar; ~ *up* absorber; **2.** chupada *f*; *give* ~ amamantar; ˈ**suck·er** ⊕ émbolo *m*; ⊕ caño *m* de bomba; ⚘ serpollo *m*, mamón *m*;

inocente *m/f*; bobo *m*; ˈ**suck·ing:** ~ *pig* lechoncillo *m*; **suck·le** [ˈ~l] *v/t*. amamantar; *fig*. criar; *v/i*. lactar; ˈ**suck·ling** mamón (-a *f*) *m*.
suc·tion [ˈsʌkʃn] **1.** succión *f*; **2.** ... de succión; aspirante; ~ *pump* bomba *f* aspirante.
sud·den [ˈsʌdn] □ repentino, súbito; imprevisto; *on a* ~, (*all*) *of a* ~ de repente; ˈ**sud·den·ly** de repente, de pronto; ˈ**sud·den·ness** precipitación *f*, rapidez *f*; lo imprevisto.
su·dor·if·ic [su:dəˈrifik] sudorífico *adj. a. su. m*.
suds [sʌdz] *pl*. jabonaduras *f/pl*.; *sl*. cerveza *f*.
sue [su:] *v/t*. procesar; demandar (*a p*. a una p.; *for* por); ~ *for peace* pedir la paz; ~ *out* rogar y obtener; *v/i*. poner pleito.
suede [sweid] suecia *f*.
su·et [ˈsu:it] sebo *m*; ˈ**su·et·y** seboso.
suf·fer [ˈsʌfər] sufrir; padecer (⚕ *from* de); aguantar; (*allow*) permitir; ~ *from fig*. adolecer de; ˈ**suf·fer·ance** sufrimiento *m*; (*on* por) tolerancia *f*; ˈ**suf·fer·er** víctima *f*; paciente *m/f*; ˈ**suf·fer·ing** dolor *m*.
suf·fice [səˈfais] *v/i*. bastar; *v/t*. satisfacer.
suf·fi·cien·cy [səˈfiʃənsi] cantidad *f* suficiente; suficiencia *f*; **sufˈfi·cient** □ suficiente.
suf·fix 1. [ˈsʌfiks, sʌˈfiks] añadir (como sufijo); **2.** [ˈsʌfiks] sufijo *m*.
suf·fo·cate [ˈsʌfəkeit] sofocar(se), asfixiar(se); ˈ**suf·fo·cat·ing** sofocante; **suf·foˈca·tion** sofocación *f*, asfixia *f*.
suf·fra·gan [ˈsʌfrəgən] (obispo *m*) sufragáneo; ˈ**suf·frage** sufragio *m*; aprobación *f*; **suf·fra·gette** [~əˈdʒet] sufragista *f*; **suf·fra·gist** [ˈ~dʒist] sufragista *m/f*.
suf·fuse [səˈfju:z] bañar (*with* de); difundirse por; **sufˈfu·sion** [~ʒn] difusión *f*.
sug·ar [ˈʃugər] **1.** azúcar *m a. f*; **2.** azucarar; ˈ~ **bowl** azucarero *m*; ˈ~ **cane** caña *f* de azúcar; ˈ~-ˈ**coat** azucarar; ˈ~·**loaf** pan *m* de azúcar; ˈ~·**plum** confite *m*; ˈ~ **tongs** *pl*. pinza *f* para azúcar; ˈ**sug·ar·y** azucarado; *fig*. almibarado.
sug·gest [səˈdʒest] sugerir; indicar; **sugˈges·tion** sugestión *f*; sugerencia *f*; indicación *f*; *fig*. sombra *f*, traza *f*.
sug·ges·tive [səˈdʒestiv] □ sugerente; sugestivo; *b.s*. sicalíptico; **sugˈges·tive·ness** *b.s*. sicalipsis *f*.
su·i·cid·al [sjuiˈsaidl] □ suicida; **su·i·cide** [ˈ~said] suicidio *m*; (*p*.) suicida *m/f*; *commit* ~ suicidarse.
suit [su:t] **1.** traje *m* (*a*. ~ *of clothes*); (*courtship*) galanteo *m*, cortejo *m*; ⚖ pleito *m*, petición *f*; *cards*: palo *m*; *follow* ~ servir del palo; *fig*. hacer lo mismo, seguir la corriente; **2.** *v/t*. adaptar, ajustar, acomodar (*to* a); convenir, satisfacer; (*clothes etc*.) sentar, caer bien a; *be* ~*ed* ir bien juntos; ~ *yourself* como Vd. quiera; *v/i*. convenir; **suit·aˈbil·i·ty** conveniencia *f*; idoneidad *f*; ˈ**suit·a·ble** □ conveniente, apropiado; idóneo, adecuado, indicado (*for* para); ˈ**suit·a·ble·ness** *v. suitability*; ˈ**suit·case** maleta *f*.
suite [swi:t] séquito *m*, comitiva *f*; mobiliario *m*, juego *m of furniture*; (*rooms*) habitaciones *f/pl*. (particulares); ♪ suite *f*.
suit·ing [ˈsu:tiŋ] ✝ tela *f* para trajes; ˈ**suit·or** pretendiente *m*, galán *m*; ⚖ demandante *m/f*.
sul·fur [ˈsʌlfər] = *sulphur*.
sulk [sʌlk] **1.** amohinarse; **2. sulks** *pl*. = **sulk·i·ness** [ˈ~inis] mohina *f*, murria *f*; ˈ**sulk·y** □ mohino, murrio; resentido.
sul·len [ˈsʌlən] □ hosco, malhumorado, resentido; *sky* plomizo; ˈ**sul·len·ness** hosquedad *f etc*.
sul·ly [ˈsʌli] *mst fig*. manchar.
sul·phate [ˈsʌlfeit] sulfato *m*; **sul·phide** [ˈ~faid] sulfuro *m*.
sul·phur [ˈsʌlfər] **1.** azufre *m*; **2.** azufrar; **sul·phu·re·ous** [sʌlˈfjuriəs] sulfúreo; **sul·phu·ric** [~ˈfjurik] sulfúrico; ~ *acid* ácido *m* sulfúrico; ˈ**sul·phu·rize** ⊕ azufrar.
sul·tan [ˈsʌltən] sultán *m*; **sul·tan·a** [sʌlˈtænə, sʌlˈtɑ:nə] sultana *f*.
sul·tri·ness [ˈsʌltrinis] bochorno *m*; **sul·try** [ˈsʌltri] □ bochornoso; sofocante; *fig*. seductor, provocativo.
sum [sʌm] **1.** suma *f*; total *m*; F problema *m* de aritmética; **2.** (*mst* ~ *up*) sumar; *fig*. resumir; F *p*., *situation* justipreciar; *to* ~ *up* en resumen.
sum·ma·rize [ˈsʌməraiz] resumir; ˈ**sum·ma·ry 1.** □ sumario (*a*. ⚖); **2.** resumen *m*, sumario *m*.
sum·mer[1] [ˈsʌmər] **1.** verano *m*,

estío *m*; *fig.* *of 20 ~s* de 20 abriles; **2.** de verano; veraniego; estival; *~ resort* lugar *m* de veraneo; **3.** veranear; **ˈ~·house** cenador *m*.
sum·mer² [~] ⚠ viga *f* maestra.
sum·mer·like [ˈsʌmərlaik], **sum·mer·y** [ˈ~ri] veraniego, estival.
sum·ming-up [ˈsʌmiŋʌp] recapitulación *f*.
sum·mit [ˈsʌmit] cima *f*, cumbre *f* (*a. fig.*); *~ conference* conferencia *f* en la cumbre.
sum·mon [ˈsʌmən] convocar; llamar; ⚖ citar, emplazar; *fig.* (*mst ~ up*) *memory* evocar; *courage* cobrar; **ˈsum·mon·er** ⚖ emplazador *m*; **sum·mons** [ˈ~z] **1.** ⚖ citación *f*; llamamiento *m*, requerimiento *m*; **2.** citar, emplazar.
sump [sʌmp] sumidero *m*, cárter *m*.
sump·tu·ar·y [ˈsʌmptjuəri] suntuario.
sump·tu·ous [ˈsʌmptjuəs] □ suntuoso; **ˈsump·tu·ous·ness** suntuosidad *f*.
sun [sʌn] **1.** sol *m*; **2.** ... solar; **3.** asolear; *~ o.s.* asolearse, tomar el sol (*a.* **ˈ~·bathe**); **ˈ~·baked** [~kt] asoleado; expuesto mucho al sol; **~·beam** [ˈsʌnbiːm] rayo *m* de sol; **ˈ~·blind** store *m*.
sun·burn [ˈsʌnbəːrn] solanera *f*; quemadura *f* del sol; **ˈsun·burnt** tostado (por el sol), bronceado.
sun·dae [ˈsʌnd(e)i] *helado con frutas, jarabes o nueces.*
Sun·day [ˈsʌndi] domingo *m*; *attr.* dominical; *~ best* trapos *m/pl.* de cristianar; *dress up in one's ~ best* endomingarse; *~ school escuela en que se da instrucción religiosa (los domingos).*
sun·der [ˈsʌndər] *poet.* romper; separar.
sun·di·al [ˈsʌndaiəl] reloj *m* de sol.
sun·down [ˈsʌndaun] puesta *f* del sol; *at ~* al anochecer.
sun·dry [ˈsʌndri] **1.** varios, diversos; *all and ~* todos y cada uno; **2. sun·dries** [ˈ~driz] *pl. esp.* ✝ géneros *m/pl.* diversos.
sun·flow·er [ˈsʌnflauər] girasol *m*.
sung [sʌŋ] *p.p. of sing.*
ˈsun·glass·es *pl.* (*a pair of ~* unas) gafas *f/pl.* de sol.
sunk [sʌŋk] *p.p. of sink* 1.
sunk·en [ˈsʌŋkən] **1.** *p.p. of sink* 1; **2.** *adj.* sumido, hundido (*a. fig.*).
sun·lamp [ˈsʌnlæmp] lámpara *f* de rayos ultravioletas.
sun·light [ˈsʌnlait] luz *f* solar, (luz *f* del) sol *m*.
sun·lit [ˈsʌnlit] iluminado por el sol; **ˈsun·ny** □ *place* (a)soleado; *day* de sol; *fig.* alegre, risueño; *be ~* hacer sol.
sun...: **ˈ~·rise** salida *f* del sol; **ˈ~·set** puesta *f* del sol; ocaso *m*; **ˈ~·shade** quitasol *m*; toldo *m*; **ˈ~·shine** sol *m*; *hours of ~* horas *f/pl.* de insolación; *mot. ~ roof* techo *m* corredizo; **ˈ~·spot** mancha *f* solar; **ˈ~·stroke** ⚕ insolación *f*; **ˈ~·up** salida *f* del sol.
sup [sʌp] *v/i.* cenar (*off, on acc.*); *v/t.* sorber.
su·per¹ [ˈsuːpər] (*abbr.*) **1.** *thea., film*: F figurante (a *f*) *m*, comparsa *m/f*; superintendente *m*; **2.** ✝ F superfino; *sl.* bárbaro; estupendo; magnífico.
su·per...:² [~] super...; sobre...; **~aˈbun·dant** □ sobreabundante; **~·an·nu·ate** [~ˈrænjueit] jubilar; **~d** jubilado; *fig.* anticuado; **~·an·nuˈa·tion** jubilación *f*.
su·perb [suˈpəːrb] □ soberbio; magnífico.
su·per...: **ˈ~·car·go** sobrecargo *m*; **ˈ~·charged** sobrealimentado; **ˈ~·charg·er** sobrealimentador *m*; **su·per·cil·i·ous** [~ˈsiliəs] □ desdeñoso, altanero, arrogante; **su·perˈcil·i·ous·ness** desdén *m*, arrogancia *f*; **su·per·er·o·ga·tion** [ˈ~rerəˈgeiʃn] supererogación *f*; **su·per·e·rog·a·to·ry** [ˈ~reˈrɔgətɔːri] supererogatorio; **su·per·fi·cial** [~ˈfiʃl] □ superficial; **su·per·fi·ci·al·i·ty** [~fiʃiˈæliti] superficialidad *f*; **su·per·fi·ci·es** [~ˈfiʃiːz] superficie *f*; **ˈsu·perˈfine** extrafino, superfino; **su·per·flu·i·ty** [~ˈfluiti] superfluidad *f*; **su·per·flu·ous** [suˈpəːrfluəs] □ superfluo; **su·perˈheat** sobrecalentar.
su·per...: **ˈ~ˈhu·man** □ sobrehumano; **~·imˈpose** sobreponer; **~·in·duce** [~ˈrinˈdjuːs] sobreañadir; **~·inˈtend** dirigir; vigilar; supervisar; **~·inˈtend·ence** superintendencia *f*; **~·inˈtend·ent** superintendente *m*; inspector *m*; supervisor *m*.
su·pe·ri·or [suˈpiriər] **1.** □ superior; *b.s.* orgulloso, arrogante; *~ officer* oficial *m* superior; **2.** superior *m*; (*eccl. a.*) superiora *f*; **su·pe·ri·or·i·ty** [~ˈɔriti] superioridad *f*.
su·per·la·tive [suˈpəːrlətiv] □ su-

perlativo *adj. a. su. m*; ˈ**su·per·man** superhombre *m*; ˈ**su·per·mar·ket** supermercado *m*; **su·perˈnat·u·ral** □ (*the* lo) sobrenatural; **su·per·nu·mer·ar·y** [~ˈnuːmərəri] supernumerario *adj. a. su. m* (a *f*); *thea.* figurante (a *f*) *m*, comparsa *m/f*; ˈ**su·per·poˈsi·tion** superposición *f*; ˈ**su·perˈscribe** sobrescribir; **su·perˈscrip·tion** sobrescrito *m*; **su·per·sede** [~ˈsiːd] reemplazar; sustituir; **su·per·son·ic** [~ˈsɔnik] □ supersónico; **su·per·sti·tion** [~ˈstiʃn] superstición *f*; **su·perˈsti·tious** [~ʃəs] □ supersticioso; **su·per·struc·ture** [ˈ~strʌktʃər] superestructura *f*; **su·per·tank·er** [ˈ~ˈtæŋkər] superpetrolero *m*; *S.Am.* supertanquero *m*; **su·per·tax** [ˈ~tæks] impuesto *m* adicional; **su·per·vene** [~ˈviːn] sobrevenir; **su·per·vise** [ˈ~vaiz] dirigir; vigilar; supervisar; **su·per·vi·sion** [~ˈviʒn] superintendencia *f*, vigilancia *f*; supervisión *f*; **su·per·vi·sor** [ˈ~vaizər] superintendente *m*; inspector *m*; supervisor *m*; ˈ**su·per·vi·so·ry** fiscalizador; de inspector.

su·pine [suːˈpain] **1.** *gr.* supino *m*; **2.** □ supino; *fig.* letárgico, flojo.

sup·per [ˈsʌpər] cena *f*.

sup·plant [səˈplænt] suplantar.

sup·ple [ˈsʌpl] □ flexible; *b.s.* dócil, servil.

sup·ple·ment 1. [ˈsʌplimənt] suplemento *m*; **2.** [ˈ~ment] suplir, complementar; **sup·pleˈmen·tal** □ suplemental; **sup·pleˈmen·ta·ry** suplementario.

sup·ple·ness [ˈsʌplnis] flexibilidad *f*.

sup·pli·ant [ˈsʌpliənt] □ suplicante *adj. a. su. m/f*.

sup·pli·cate [ˈsʌplikeit] suplicar; **sup·pliˈca·tion** súplica *f*; suplicación *f*.

sup·pli·er [səˈplaiər] suministrador (-a *f*) *m*; ✝ proveedor (-a *f*) *m*.

sup·ply [səˈplai] **1.** suministrar, facilitar; surtir; *city* aprovisionar; *want* suplir; ~ *with* abastecer de, proveer de; **2.** provisión *f*; suministro *m*; ✝ surtido *m*; *mst supplies pl.* provisiones *f/pl.*, víveres *m/pl.*; ⚔ pertrechos *m/pl.*; *be in short* ~ andar escaso; ✝ ~ *and demand* oferta y demanda.

sup·port [səˈpɔːrt] **1.** sostén *m*, apoyo *m* (⊕ *a. fig.*); ⚠ soporte *m*, pilar *m*; *in* ~ *of* en apoyo de; **2.** apoyar (⊕ *a. fig.*); sostener, mantener; *campaign* respaldar; ~ *o.s.* mantenerse; *film*: ~*ing program* películas *f/pl.* secundarias; *thea.* ~*ing role* papel *m* secundario; **supˈport·a·ble** □ soportable; **supˈport·er** partidario (a *f*) *m*; *sport*: seguidor (-a *f*) *m*; ⊕ soporte *m*, sostén *m*; ~*s' club* peña *f* deportiva.

sup·pose [səˈpouz] suponer; presumir; figurarse, imaginarse; F *he is* ~*d to go* debe ir; *let us* ~ pongamos por caso; ~ *or supposing (that)* ...? si...; F ~ *we try* y ¿si probamos?; *he is rich, I* ~ me imagino que es rico; *I* ~ *so* supongo que sí; (*resignedly*) no hay más remedio.

sup·posed [səˈpouzd] □ supuesto; pretendido; **supˈpos·ed·ly** [~idli] según lo que se supone.

sup·po·si·tion [sʌpəˈziʃn] suposición *f*; **sup·pos·i·ti·tious** [səpɔziˈtiʃəs] □ fingido, espurio; **supˈpos·i·to·ry** [~təri] supositorio *m*.

sup·press [səˈpres] suprimir; **sup·pres·sion** [səˈpreʃn] supresión *f*; **sup·pres·sor** *radio*: supresor *m*.

sup·pu·rate [ˈsʌpjureit] supurar; **sup·puˈra·tion** supuración *f*.

su·prem·a·cy [səˈpreməsi] supremacía *f*; **su·preme** [səˈpriːm] □ supremo.

sur·charge [ˈsəːrtʃɑːrdʒ] **1.** sobrecargar; **2.** sobrecarga *f*; sobretasa *f*.

surd [səːrd] (número *m*) sordo.

sure [ʃur] **1.** □ seguro; cierto; *aim etc.* certero; *manner, touch* firme; *to be* ~!, ~! ¡claro!; *to be* ~ sin duda; ~ *enough* efectivamente; ~ *fire* de éxito seguro; ~-*footed* de pie firme; *I am* ~ estoy seguro (*that* de que); *he is* ~ *to return* seguramente volverá; *make* ~ asegurar(se) (*that* de que); *make* ~ *of facts* verificar, cerciorarse de; ~ *thing* cosa *f* cierta; certeza *f*; **2.** *adv.*: *he* ~ *was mean* ése sí que era tacaño; ˈ**sure·ly** seguramente; ˈ**sure·ness** seguridad *f etc.*; ˈ**sure·ty** seguridad *f*, fianza *f*; (*p.*) fiador (-a *f*) *m*.

surf [səːrf] oleaje *m*; espuma *f*; rompientes *m/pl.*

sur·face [ˈsəːrfis] **1.** superficie *f*; firme *m of road*; ⚒ ~ *workers* personal *m* del exterior; **2.** *v/t.* ⊕ alisar; recubrir; *v/i.* (*submarine*) emerger.

surf·board [ˈsəːrfbɔːrd] patín *m* de mar.

sur·feit [ˈsəːrfit] **1.** hartura *f*; empa-

cho *m*; exceso *m*; **2.** hartar(se), saciar(se) (*on*, *with* de).
surf-rid·ing [ˈsəːrfraidiŋ] patinaje *m* sobre las olas.
surge [səːrdʒ] **1.** oleada *f*, oleaje *m*; **2.** agitarse, hervir.
sur·geon [ˈsəːrdʒən] cirujano *m*; **sur·ger·y** [ˈsəːrdʒəri] cirugía *f*; (*room*) consultorio *m*; clínica *f*; sala *f* de operaciones; ~ *hours* horas *f*/*pl.* de consulta; *v. plastic*; **sur·gi·cal** [ˈsəːrdʒikl] □ quirúrgico.
sur·li·ness [ˈsəːrlinis] aspereza *f*, malhumor *m*; ˈ**sur·ly** □ áspero, malhumorado, hosco.
sur·mise [səːrˈmaiz] **1.** conjetura *f*; suposición *f*; **2.** conjeturar; suponer.
sur·mount [səːrˈmaunt] superar, vencer; ~*ed by* (*or with*) coronado de; **surˈmount·a·ble** superable.
sur·name [ˈsəːrneim] **1.** apellido *m*; **2.** apellidar.
sur·pass [səːrˈpæs] *fig* aventajar, exceder, sobrepujar; **surˈpass·ing** □ sobresaliente, incomparable.
sur·plice [ˈsəːrpləs] sobrepelliz *f*.
sur·plus [ˈsəːrpləs] **1.** excedente *m*; sobrante *m*; ✝ superávit *m*; **2.** ... sobrante, de sobra.
sur·prise [sərˈpraiz] **1.** sorpresa *f*; asombro *m*; ⚔ (*a.* ~ *attack*) rebato *m*; *take by* ~ sobrecoger; *to my great* ~ con gran sorpresa mía; **2.** inesperado; **3.** sorprender; ⚔ coger por sorpresa; *be* ~*d at* sorprenderse de; **surˈpris·ing** □ sorprendente.
sur·re·al·ism [səˈriəlizm] surrealismo *m*; **surˈre·al·ist** surrealista *m*.
sur·ren·der [səˈrendər] **1.** rendición *f*; abandono *m*; entrega *f of documents*; renuncia *f of rights*; **2.** rendir(se); entregar(se); *rights* renunciar a.
sur·rep·ti·tious [sʌrəpˈtiʃəs] □ subrepticio *m*.
sur·ro·gate [ˈsʌrəgit] sustituto *m*; *eccl.* vicario *m*.
sur·round [səˈraund] cercar, circundar, rodear (*by* de); ⚔ copar; sitiar; **surˈround·ing** circundante; **surˈround·ings** *pl.* alrededores *m*/*pl.*, contornos *m*/*pl. of place*; *fig.* ambiente *m*.
sur·tax [ˈsəːrtæks] impuesto *m* adicional (sobre ingresos excesivos).
sur·veil·lance [səːrˈveiləns] vigilancia *f*.
sur·vey 1. [səːrˈvei] reconocer, registrar; inspeccionar, examinar; *surv.* medir; levantar el plano de; **2.** [ˈsəːrvei] reconocimiento *m*; inspección *f*, examen *m*; *surv.* medición *f*; *economic* ~ informe *m* económico; **surˈvey·ing** planimetría *f*; levantamiento *m* de planos; agrimensura *f*; **surˈvey·or** topógrafo *m*; agrimensor *m*.
sur·viv·al [sərˈvaivl] supervivencia *f*; **sur·vive** [~ˈvaiv] sobrevivir (*acc.* a *acc.*); perdurar; **surˈvi·vor** superviviente *m*/*f*.
sus·cep·ti·bil·i·ty [səseptəˈbiliti] susceptibilidad *f*; (*mst* ~*s pl.*) delicadeza *f*; **susˈcep·ti·ble** □ susceptible; sensible; (*easily moved*) impresionable; *be* ~ *of* admitir.
sus·pect 1. [səsˈpekt] sospechar, recelar; **2.** [ˈsʌspekt] sospechoso (a *f*) *m*; **3.** [~] sospechado, sospechoso.
sus·pend [səsˈpend] *all senses*: suspender; **susˈpend·ers** *pl.* ligas *f*/*pl.*; tirantes *m*/*pl.*
sus·pense [səsˈpens] incertidumbre *f*, duda *f*; ansiedad *f*; *thea. etc.* "suspense" *m*; *in* ~ en suspenso; **sus·pen·sion** [~ˈpenʃn] *all senses*: suspensión *f*; ~ *bridge* puente *m* colgante; **susˈpen·sive** □ suspensivo, interino; **sus·pen·so·ry** [~ˈpensəri] suspensorio *adj. a. su. m* (*a.* ~ *bandage*).
sus·pi·cion [səsˈpiʃn] sospecha *f*; recelo *m*; suspicacia *f*; *fig.* sombra *f*, traza *f* ligera; **sus·pi·cious** [~ˈpiʃəs] □ (*causing suspicion*) sospechoso; (*feeling suspicion*) receloso; suspicaz; **susˈpi·cious·ness** lo sospechoso; suspicacia *f*.
sus·tain [səsˈtein] sostener (*a.* ♪), apoyar; sustentar; *loss*, *injury* sufrir; **susˈtained** ininterrumpido, continuo.
sus·te·nance [ˈsʌstinəns] sustento *m*, subsistencia *f*.
su·ture [ˈsuːtʃər] **1.** *all senses*: sutura *f*; **2.** ⚕ suturar, coser.
su·ze·rain [ˈsuːzərein] soberano (a *f*) *m*; ˈ**su·ze·rain·ty** soberanía *f*.
svelte [svelt] esbelto.
swab [swɔb] **1.** estropajo *m*; ⚓ lampazo *m*; ⚕ algodón *m*; escob(ill)ón *m*; **2.** lampacear.
swad·dle [ˈswɔdl] **1.** empañar; *swaddling clothes pl.* pañales *m*/*pl.*; **2.** pañal *m*.
swag [swæg] *sl.* botín *m*, robo *m*.

swag·ger [ˈswægər] **1.** fanfarronear; pavonearse; **2.** F muy elegante; **3.** fanfarronada *f*; contoneo *m*; ˈ~ **cane** bastón *m* ligero de paseo.
swain [swein] zagal *m*; *co.* enamorado *m*.
swal·low[1] [ˈswɔlou] *orn.* golondrina *f*.
swal·low[2] [~] **1.** trago *m*; **2.** tragar (*a. fig.*, *a.* ~ *up*); deglutir; ~ *one's words* desdecirse; ~ *up savings etc.* consumir.
swam [swæm] *pret. of swim* 1.
swamp [swɔmp] **1.** pantano *m*; marisma *f*; **2.** sumergir; inundar; ⚓ hundir; *fig.* abrumar (*with work etc.* de); ˈ**swamp·y** pantanoso.
swan [swɔn] cisne *m*; ~ *dive* salto *m* de ángel.
swank [swæŋk] *sl.* **1.** ostentación *f*; fachenda *f*; (*p.*) currutaco *m*; cursi *m*/*f*; **2.** (*a.* ˈ**swank·y**) ostentoso, fachendoso.
swan·ner·y [ˈswɔnəri] colonia *f* de cisnes; ˈ**swan song** canto *m* del cisne.
swap [swɔp] F **1.** intercambio *m*, cambalache *m*, canje *m*; **2.** intercambiar, cambalachear, canjear.
swarm[1] [swɔːrm] **1.** enjambre *m* (*a. fig.*); *fig.* muchedumbre *f*, hormigueo *m*; **2.** enjambrar; (*people etc.*) hormiguear, pulular; (*place*) hervir (*with* de).
swarm[2] [~] trepar (*up* a).
swarth·i·ness [ˈswɔːrðinis] lo atezado; ˈ**swarth·y** □ atezado, moreno.
swash·buck·ler [ˈswɔʃbʌklər] espadachín *m*, matón *m*.
swas·ti·ka [ˈswɔstikə] svástica *f*.
swat [swɔt] *fly etc.* aplastar, aporrear.
swath [swɔθ, swɔːθ], *pl.* **swaths** [*a.* ~ðz] ✓ guadañada *f*; ringlera *f* de heno *etc.*
sway [swei] **1.** vaivén *m*, balanceo *m*; coletazo *m of train etc.* (*a.* ˈ**sway·ing**); *fig.* imperio *m*, dominio *m*; **2.** *v/t.* inclinar; hacer oscilar; *fig.* influir en; dominar; *v/i.* oscilar, mecerse; inclinarse, ladearse.
swear [swer] [*irr.*] *v/i.* jurar (*by* por); decir palabrotas; ~ *at* maldecir *acc.*, echar pestes de; ~ *by* tener entera confianza en; ~ *to* declarar bajo juramento; ~ *black and blue* echar sapos y culebras; *v/t.* jurar; juramentar; ~ *in* tomar juramento a; ~*word* palabrota *f*; voto *m*; F taco *m*.
sweat [swet] **1.** sudor *m* (*a. fig.* F); *by the* ~ *of one's brow* con el sudor de su frente, a pulso sudando; F *be in a* ~ estar en un apuro, encogérsele a uno el ombligo; ~*shirt* pulóver *m* de mangas largas; **2.** *v/i.* sudar; *v/t.* sudar; *workmen* explotar; *metall.* calentar hasta la fusión; ⊕ soldar; ˈ**sweat·er** suéter *m*; ˈ**sweat·ing** sud(or)oso; ˈ**sweat·shop** taller *m* de trabajo afanoso y de poco sueldo; ˈ**sweat·y** sud(or)oso.
Swede [swiːd] sueco (a *f*) *m*; ⚘♀ nabo *m* sueco.
Swed·ish [ˈswiːdiʃ] sueco *adj. a. su. m.*
sweep [swiːp] **1.** [*irr.*] *v/t.* barrer (*a.* ⚔); *chimney* deshollinar; ⚓ *mines* rastrear; *fig.* ~ *away* arrebatar, arrastrar; borrar, aniquilar; ~ *out*, ~ *up* barrer; ~ *the board* copar; *v/i.* barrer; (*mst with adv.*, ~ *by etc.*) pasar rápidamente, pasar majestuosamente; rozar; ir volando; descender precipitadamente; **2.** barredura *f*, escobada *f*; (*p.*) deshollinador *m*; redada *f by police*; *fig.* extensión *f*; recorrido *m*; *make a clean* ~ *of* cambiar completamente, hacer tabla rasa de; ˈ**sweep·er** barrendero (a *f*) *m*; (*machine*) barredera *f*; ˈ**sweep·ing** □ comprensivo (*or* extenso) pero infundado; (demasiado) comprensivo; ˈ**sweep·ings** *pl.* barreduras *f*/*pl.*; **sweep·stake** [ˈ~steik] lotería *f* de premio único.
sweet [swiːt] **1.** □ dulce; azucarado; suave; *smell* fragante; *land* fértil; (*not stale*) fresco; *face* lindo; *p.* amable, encantador; *th. admired* mono, majo; (*pleasing*) grato; *have a* ~ *tooth* ser goloso; ~ *pea* guisante *m* de olor; ~ *william* minutisa *f*; **2.** dulce *m*; caramelo *m*; (*course*) postre *m*; ~*s pl.* dulces *m*/*pl.*, bombones *m*/*pl.*, golosinas *f*/*pl.*; ˈ~**breads** *pl.* lechecillas *f*/*pl.*; ˈ**sweet·en** azucarar; endulzar (*a. fig.*); ˈ**sweet·heart** novio (a *f*) *m*; ˈ**sweet·ish** algo dulce; ˈ**sweet·meats** *pl.* confites *m*/*pl.*; dulces *m*/*pl.*; ˈ**sweet·ness** dulzura *f*, suavidad *f etc.*; ˈ**sweet poˈta·to** batata *f*; camote *m*; ˈ**sweet·shop** confitería *f*; ˈ**sweet-smell·ing** fragante.
swell [swel] **1.** [*irr.*] hinchar(se), inflar(se); crecer (*v/i.*); abultar(se); aumentar (*v/i. a. v/t.*); *numbers* engrosar (*v/t.*); ~ *with pride* envane-

cerse; F *have a ~ed head* subirle a uno humos a la cabeza; **2.** F muy elegante; *sl.* sobresaliente; estupendo; **3.** ♪ crescendo *m*; ⚓ marejada *f*, mar *m* de fondo, oleaje *m*; F guapo *m*, majo *m*; pez *m* gordo; **ˈswell·ing** hinchazón *f*; ⚕ chichón *m*, bulto *m*; protuberancia *f*.

swel·ter [ˈsweltər] sofocarse de calor, abrasarse; chorrear de sudor; **ˈswel·ter·ing** *heat* sofocante, abrasador.

swept [swept] *pret. a. p.p. of sweep* 1; ~ (*back*) *wings* en flecha.

swerve [swəːrv] **1.** *v/i.* desviarse (bruscamente); hurtar el cuerpo; torcer; *v/t.* desviar; *ball* cortar; **2.** desvío *m* (brusco); viraje *m*; esguince *m*, regate *m*.

swift [swift] **1.** □ rápido, veloz; repentino; pronto; **2.** *orn.* vencejo *m* común; **ˈswift·ness** rapidez *f etc.*

swig [swig] F **1.** tragantada *f*; **2.** beber a grandes tragos.

swill [swil] **1.** bazofia *f*; *contp.* aguachirle *f*; (*mst* ~ *out*) enjuagadura *f*; **2.** *v/t.* (*mst* ~ *out*) enjuagar; beber a grandes tragos; F emborracharse.

swim [swim] **1.** [*irr.*] *v/i.* nadar; (*head*) dar vueltas; *go ~ming* ir a bañarse; *v/t.* (*a.* ~ *across*) pasar a nado; **2.**: *go for a* ~ ir a nadar; *be in the* ~ estar al tanto.

swim·mer [ˈswimər] nadador (-a *f*) *m*.

swim·ming [ˈswimiŋ] natación *f*; **ˈswim·ming·ly** *adv.*: *go* ~ ir a las mil maravillas; **ˈswim·ming pool** piscina *f*; **ˈswim·suit** traje *m* de baño; bañador *m*.

swin·dle [ˈswindl] **1.** estafar, timar; ~ *out of* estafar *acc.*, quitar por estafa; **2.** estafa *f*, timo *m*; **ˈswin·dler** estafador *m*.

swine [swain] *zo. pl.* puercos *m/pl.*, cerdos *m/pl.*; F *sg.* canalla *m*; **ˈswine-herd** porquero *m*.

swing [swiŋ] **1.** [*irr.*] columpiar(se); balancear(se); (hacer) oscilar; *arm* menear; *door* girar; *pol. etc.* bascular; ~ *into action* ponerse en marcha; F *he'll* ~ *for it* le ahorcarán; **2.** columpio *m*; (*movement*) vaivén *m*, oscilación *f*; balance(o) *m*; ♪ swing *m*; ♪ ritmo *m* agradable; *pol. etc.* movimiento *m*, viraje *m*; *boxing*: golpe *m* lateral; *in full* ~ en plena actividad; **3.** giratorio; ~ **bridge** puente *m* giratorio; **ˈ~·ing ˈdoor** puerta *f* giratoria.

swipe [swaip] **1.** golpear fuertemente; *sl.* apandar, hurtar; **2.** golpe *m* fuerte.

swirl [swəːrl] **1.** arremolinarse; remolinar; **2.** remolino *m*; torbellino *m*.

swish [swiʃ] **1.** *v/t.* (*flog*) zurrar; *cane* agitar (produciendo un silbido); *v/i.* silbar; (*dress*) crujir; (*tail*) fustigar; **2.** silbido *m*; crujido *m of dress*; **3.** *sl.* guapo, majo.

Swiss [swis] suizo *adj. a. su. m* (a *f*); ~ *cheese* Gruyère *m*; queso *m* suizo.

switch [switʃ] **1.** (*stick*) varilla *f*; cambio *m of policy*; 🚂 agujas *f/pl.*, desviación *f*; ⚡ interruptor *m*; llave *f*; *sl.* cambio *m* engañoso; **2.** *v/t.* 🚂 desviar; *policy, positions* cambiar; ~ *on* ⚡ encender, poner, conectar; ~ *off* ⚡ apagar, cortar; *v/i.*: ~ *from A to B* (*or* ~ [*over*] *to B*) dejar A para tomar *etc.* B; **ˈ~·back** montaña *f* rusa; camino *m etc.* muy desigual; **ˈ~·board** cuadro *m* de distribución; *teleph.* cuadro *m* de conexión manual; centralita *f in office*.

swiv·el [ˈswivl] **1.** eslabón *m* giratorio; **2.** (hacer) girar.

swol·len [ˈswoulən] *p.p. of swell* 1.

swoon [swuːn] **1.** desmayo *m*; **2.** desmayar(se), desvanecerse.

swoop [swuːp] **1.** (*a.* ~ *down*) precipitarse (*on* sobre); (*bird*) calar; **2.** descenso *m* súbito.

sword [sɔːrd] espada *f*; *put to the* ~ pasar a cuchillo; **ˈ~·fish** pez *m* espada; **ˈ~ knot** borla *f* de espada; **ˈ~ rat·tling** fanfarronería *f*.

swords·man [ˈsɔːrdzmən] esgrimidor *m*; espadachín *m*; **ˈswords-man·ship** esgrima *f*.

swore [swɔːr] *pret. of swear*.

sworn [swɔːrn] *p.p. of swear*; *enemy* implacable.

swum [swʌm] *p.p. of swim* 1.

swung [swʌŋ] *pret. a. p.p. of swing* 1.

syb·a·rite [ˈsibərait] sibarita *m/f*.

syc·a·more [ˈsikəmɔːr] sicomoro *m*.

syc·o·phant [ˈsikəfənt] adulador *m*; **syc·o·phan·tic** [sikəˈfæntik] □ adulatorio.

syl·lab·ic [siˈlæbik] □ silábico; **syl·la·ble** [ˈsiləbl] sílaba *f*.

syl·la·bus [ˈsiləbəs] programa *m*.

syl·lo·gism [ˈsilədʒism] silogismo *m*.

sylph [silf] sílfide *f* (*a. fig.*); silfo *m*.

sylvan [ˈsilvən] selvático.

sym·bi·o·sis [simbiˈousis] simbiosis *f*; **sym·bi·o·tic** [~ˈɔtik] simbiótico.

sym·bol [ˈsimbəl] símbolo *m*; **sym·bol·ic, sym·bol·i·cal** [~ˈbɔlik(l)] □ simbólico; **sym·bol·ism** [ˈ~bəlizm] simbolismo *m*; ˈ**sym·bol·ize** simbolizar.

sym·met·ri·cal [siˈmetrikl] □ simétrico; **sym·me·try** [ˈsimitri] simetría *f*.

sym·pa·thet·ic [simpəˈθetik] □ compasivo; comprensivo; que simpatiza; simpático; **sym·pa·thize** [ˈ~θaiz] compadecerse; ~ *with* compadecer(se de); **sym·pa·thiz·er** [ˈ~θaizər] simpatizante *m/f* (*with* de); partidario (a *f*) *m*; **sym·pa·thy** [ˈ~θi] compasión *f*, conmiseración *f*; sentimiento *m*; simpatía *f*; ~ *strike* huelga *f* por solidaridad.

sym·phon·ic [simˈfɔnik] sinfónico; **sym·pho·ny** [ˈsimfəni] sinfonía *f*.

symp·tom [ˈsimptəm] síntoma *m*; **symp·to·mat·ic** [~ˈmætik] □ sintomático.

syn·a·gogue [ˈsinəgɔg] sinagoga *f*.

syn·chro·mesh gear [ˈsiŋkroumeʃˈgir] engranaje *m* sincronizado.

syn·chro·nic [siŋˈkrɔnik] síncrono, sincrónico; **syn·chro·nism** [ˈsiŋkrənizm] sincronismo *m*; ˈ**syn·chro·nize** *v/i.* ser sincrónico; *v/t.* sincronizar; ˈ**syn·chro·nous** □ síncrono, sincrónico.

syn·co·pate [ˈsiŋkəpeit] sincopar; **syn·coˈpa·tion, syn·co·pe** [ˈ~pi] síncopa *f*.

syn·dic [ˈsindik] síndico *m*; ˈ**syn·di·cal·ism** sindicalismo *m*; ˈ**syn·di·cal·ist** sindicalista *m*; **syn·di·cate** 1. [ˈ~kit] sindicato *m*; 2. [ˈ~keit] sindicar.

syn·drome [ˈsindroum] síndrome *m*; *toxic shock* ~ síndrome *m* del choque tóxico; *v. acquired immune-deficiency syndrome.*

syn·er·get·ic [sinərˈdʒetik] sinérgico; **syn·er·gism** [ˈsinərdʒizm] sinergia *f*.

syn·od [ˈsinəd] sínodo *m*; **syn·od·al** [ˈ~dl] sinodal; **syn·od·ic, syn·od·i·cal** [siˈnɔdik(l)] □ sinódico.

syn·o·nym [ˈsinənim] sinónimo *m*; **syn·on·y·mous** [siˈnɔniməs] □ sinónimo.

syn·op·sis [siˈnɔpsis], *pl.* **synˈop·ses** [~i:z] sinopsis *f*.

syn·op·tic, syn·op·ti·cal [siˈnɔptik(l)] □ sinóptico.

syn·tac·tic, syn·tac·ti·cal [sinˈtæktik(l)] □ sintáctico; **syn·tax** [ˈsintæks] sintaxis *f*.

syn·the·sis [ˈsinθisis], *pl.* **syn·the·ses** [ˈ~si:z] síntesis *f*; **syn·the·size** [ˈ~saiz] sintetizar; ˈ**syn·the·siz·er** sintetizador *m*.

syn·thet·ic, syn·thet·i·cal [sinˈθetik(l)] □ sintético.

syph·i·lis [ˈsifilis] sífilis *f*.

syph·i·lit·ic [sifiˈlitik] sifilítico.

sy·phon [ˈsaifən] *v. siphon.*

Syr·i·an [ˈsiriən] sirio *adj. a. su. m* (a *f*).

syr·inge [ˈsirindʒ] 1. jeringa *f*; 2. jeringar.

syr·up [ˈsirəp] jarabe *m*.

sys·tem [ˈsistim] sistema *m* (*a.* ⚕); ⚕ constitución *f*; ⊕ mecanismo *m*; ⚡ circuito *m*, instalación *f*; ~*s analysis* análisis *m* de sistemas; **sys·tem·at·ic** [~ˈmætik] □ sistemático.

T

T [ti:]: F *to a ~* exactamente.
tab [tæb] oreja *f*, lengüeta *f*; F *keep ~s on* vigilar, tener a la vista.
tab·ard [ˈtæbərd] tabardo *m*.
tab·by [ˈtæbi] **1.** (*mst ~ cat*) (*male*) gato *m* atigrado; (*female*) gata *f*; F solterona *f*; F chismosa *f*; **2.** atigrado.
tab·er·nac·le [ˈtæbərnækl] tabernáculo *m*.
ta·ble [ˈteibl] **1.** mesa *f*; ⚒ *etc.* tabla *f*; (*statistical*) cuadro *m*; ⚠ tablero *m*; *turn the ~s on* devolver la pelota a; *~ of contents* tabla *f* (*or* índice *m*) de materias; *~ d'hôte* mesa *f* redonda; **2.** *motion etc.* poner sobre la mesa, presentar; (*index*) catalogar; (*set out*) disponer en una tabla; *parl. bill* dar carpetazo a.
tab·leau [ˈtæblou] cuadro *m* vivo.
ta·ble...: ˈ**~·cloth** mantel *m*; ˈ**~·land** meseta *f*; ˈ**~ lin·en** mantelería *f*; ˈ**~ mat** apartador *m*, salvamanteles *m*; ˈ**~ nap·kin** servilleta *f*; ˈ**~·spoon** cuchara *f* grande, cuchara *f* para servir; *~ful* cucharada *f*.
tab·let [ˈtæblit] pastilla *f*; tableta *f*; tabla *f*; bloc *m* (de papel); (*inscribed*) lápida *f*; ⚕ comprimido *m*.
ta·ble...: ˈ**~ talk** conversación *f* de sobremesa; ˈ**~ ten·nis** tenis *m* de mesa.
tab·loid [ˈtæblɔid] *pharm.* (en forma de) tableta *f*; (*paper*) periódico *m* de formato reducido.
ta·boo [təˈbu:] **1.** tabú, prohibido; **2.** tabú *m*; prohibición *f*; **3.** declarar tabú, prohibir.
tab·u·lar [ˈtæbjulər] □ tabular; **tab·u·late** [ˈ~leit] exponer en forma de tabla, tabular.
tac·it [ˈtæsit] □ tácito; **tac·i·turn** [ˈ~tə:rn] □ taciturno; **tac·iˈtur·ni·ty** taciturnidad *f*.
tack [tæk] **1.** (*nail*) tachuela *f*; *sew.* hilván *m*; ⚓ virada *f*, bordada *f*; ⚓ amura *f of sail*; *fig.* rumbo *m*; línea *f* de conducta; *on the wrong ~* equivocado; **2.** *v/t.* clavar con tachuelas; *sew.* hilvanar; *fig.* añadir (*on, on to* a); *v/i.* ⚓ virar, cambiar de bordada.
tack·le [ˈtækl] **1.** ⚓, ⊕ aparejo *m*; ⚓ jarcia *f*; avíos *m/pl.*, aperos *m/pl.*; *sport*: atajo *m*; blocaje *m*; **2.** agarrar; *sport*: atajar; *problem* abordar; emprender.
tack·y [ˈtæki] pegajoso; F desaseado, cursi; vulgar.
tact [tækt] tacto *m*, discreción *f*; **tact·ful** [ˈ~ful] □ discreto; diplomático.
tac·ti·cal [ˈtæktikl] □ táctico; **tac·ti·cian** [~ˈtiʃn] táctico *m*; **tac·tics** [ˈ~iks] *pl.* táctica *f*.
tac·tile [ˈtæktil] táctil.
tact·less [ˈtæktlis] □ indiscreto.
tad·pole [ˈtædpoul] renacuajo *m*.
taf·fe·ta [ˈtæfitə] tafetán *m*.
tag [tæg] **1.** (*label*) etiqueta *f*, marbete *m*; herrete *m*; (*rag*) pingajo *m*; (*end*) rabito *m*; (*game*) tócame tú *m*; *fig.* dicho *m*; muletilla *f*; **2.** *v/t.* pegar una etiqueta a; F seguir los pasos de; (*baseball*) batear; *v/i.* F *~ along* seguir despacio su camino; F *~ on to* unirse a.
tail [teil] **1.** cola *f* (*a. fig.*), rabo *m*; trenza *f of hair*; cabellera *f of comet*; faldón *m*, faldillas *f/pl. of coat*; *~s* cruz *f of coin*; F *~s pl.* frac *m*; *turn ~* volver la espalda; **2.** *v/t.* (*follow*) seguir de cerca, vigilar; (*join*) añadir; *animal* descolar; *v/i.*: *~ away, ~ off* ir disminuyendo (*into* hasta [ser no más que]); ˈ**~·board** escalera *f*; ˈ**~ˈcoat** frac *m*; **tailed** con rabo; *long-~* rabilargo; ˈ**tail end** cola *f*; extremo *m*; *fig.* parte *f* que queda; porción *f* restante; ˈ**tail·gate** F *mot.* seguir demasiado de cerca; ˈ**tail·less** sin rabo; ˈ**tail·light** luz *f* piloto (*or* trasera).
tai·lor [ˈteilər] **1.** sastre *m*; **2.** *suit* confeccionar; *well ~ed suit* traje *m* que entalla bien; ˈ**tai·lor·ing** sastrería *f*; corte *m*; ˈ**tai·lor-made** hecho por sastre.
tail...: ˈ**~·piece** *typ.* florón *m*; *fig.* apéndice *m*; ˈ**~·pipe** *mot.* tubo *m* de

escape; ˈ~·**plane** (plano *m* de) cola *f*; ˈ~·**skid** ✈ patín *m* de cola; ˈ~ **u·nit** conjunto *m* de cola; ˈ~ˈ**wind** viento *m* de cola.

taint [teint] **1.** infección *f*; mancha *f*; *fig.* olor *m* (*of* a); **2.** manchar(se); corromper(se); viciar(se).

take [teik] **1.** [*irr.*] *v/t.* tomar; coger; *p.* llevar; (*by force*) asir; arrebatar; (*steal*) robar; (*accept*) aceptar; (*tolerate*) aguantar; (*catch*) coger; comer *at chess*; *city*, *decision*, *exercise*, *food*, *liberty*, *note* tomar; *advice* seguir; *fence* saltar; *illness* coger; *journal* abonarse a; *oath* prestar; *opportunity* aprovechar; *photo*, *ticket* sacar; *step*, *walk etc.* dar; *trip* hacer; *for many phrases, see under the corresponding substantive*; *I ~ it that* supongo que; *it ~s 2 hours* es cosa de 2 horas; tarda 2 horas (*to* en); *it ~s 2 men to lift it* se necesita 2 hombres para levantarlo; F *we can ~ it* lo aguantamos todo; *the devil ~ it!* ¡maldición!; *~ apart* desmontar, descomponer; *~ away* quitar; llevarse; △ restar; *~ back* recibir devuelto; volver a quitar (*from* a); (*return*) devolver; *p.* recibir otra vez; *words* retractar; *~ down* bajar; descolgar; ⊕ desmontar; *note* apuntar, poner por escrito; F *p.* quitar los humos a; *~ for* tomar por; *~ from* quitar a; privar de; △ restar de; *~ in* (*understand*) comprender; (*include*) abarcar; *clothes* achicar; *p.* acoger, recibir; *paper* abonarse a; *sail* desmontar; acortar, disminuir; *work* aceptar; F engañar; *~ off clothes* quitarse; *discount* descontar; F contrahacer, parodiar; *~ on* (*assume*) tomar; *duties* tomar sobre sí; F *p.* desafiar, luchar con; *work* emprender; aceptar; *workmen* contratar; *~ out* (*extract*) extraer, sacar; *children* llevar de paseo; *girl* escoltar, invitar; cortejar; *patent* obtener; *stain* quitar; F *~ it out of a p.* (*tire*) cansarle a uno; *b. s.* vengarse en una p.; *~ it out on a p.* desahogarse riñendo a una p.; vengarse en una p.; *~ over* tomar posesión de; encargarse de; *~ to pieces* desmontar; *~ up* subir; coger; absorber; *carpet* quitar; *passengers* tomar; *post* tomar posesión de; *residence* establecer, fijar; *room*, *time* ocupar, llenar; *story* empezar a contar; *study* dedicarse a; *~ a p. up on s.t.* censurar algo a alguien; (comenzar a) disputar con una p. sobre algo; *I ~ you up on that* no puedo aceptar eso; *~ upon o.s.* tomar sobre sí; encargarse de; *~ it upon o.s. to* atreverse a; **2.** [*irr.*] *v/i.* pegar; ser eficaz; resultar; ♀ arraigar (*a. fig.*); (*set*) cuajar; (*vaccination*) prender; F (*succeed*) tener éxito; *phot.* *he ~s well* saca buen retrato; *~ after* parecerse a; salir a; *~ off* salir; ✈ despegar; F *~ on* congojarse; quejarse; *don't ~ on so!* ¡no te apures!; *~ over* tomar posesión; *~ to p.* tomar cariño a; *th.* aficionarse a; *~ to ger.* aficionarse a *inf.*; ponerse a *inf.*; F *~ up with* relacionarse con, estrechar amistad con; **3.** toma *f*; *phot.* exposición *f*; *~-home pay* salario *m* neto.

tak·en [ˈteikn] *p.p. of take*; *be ~ with* estar cautivado por; *be ~ ill* enfermar; *be ~ up with* estar ocupado en; estar absorto en; F *be ~ in* tragar el anzuelo; *be ~ in by* dejarse engañar por; ˈ**takeˈoff** ✈ despegue *m*; ⊕ toma *f* de fuerza; F caricatura *f*, parodia *f* (*of*, *on* de); ˈ**tak·er** el (la) que acepta *a challenge etc.*

tak·ing [ˈteikiŋ] **1.** □ F atractivo, encantador; **2.** toma *f*; ˈ**tak·ings** *pl.* ingresos *m/pl.*

talc [tælk], **tal·cum pow·der** [ˈtælkəm ˈpaudər] talco *m.*

tale [teil] cuento *m* (*a. b.s.*); fábula *f*; relación *f*; historia *f*; *tell ~s* (*out of school*) soplar; chismear; ~·**bear·er** [ˈ~berər] soplón (-a *f*) *m*; chismoso (a *f*) *m.*

tal·ent [ˈtælənt] talento *m*; ˈ**tal·ent·ed** talentoso.

tal·is·man [ˈtælizmən] talismán *m.*

talk [tɔːk] **1.** conversación *f*; charla *f*; F palabras *f/pl.*; *there is ~ of ger.* se habla de *inf.*; *~ of the town* comidilla *f* de la ciudad; *~ show* F *television*: programa *m* de conversación e interviú; **2.** hablar (*to* con); charlar; *sense etc.* decir; *~ down* ✈ controlar el aterrizaje de (desde tierra); *~ into* persuadir a; convencer; *~ out of* disuadir de; *~ over* discutir; hablar de; *past events* pasar revista a; *~ over*, *~ round p.* convencer; **talk·a·tive** [ˈ~ətiv] □ locuaz, hablador; ˈ**talk·er** hablador (-a *f*) *m*; orador (-a *f*) *m*;

talk·ie [ˈ~i] F película *f* sonora; ˈ**talk·ing** parlante; *bird* parlero; **talk·ing-to** [ˈ~tu:] F rapapolvo *m*; amonestación *f*; sermón *m*.
tall [tɔ:l] alto; grande; *be 6 feet ~* tener 6 pies de alto; *sl. ~ order* cosa *f* muy difícil; *sl. ~ story, ~ tale* cuento *m* exagerado (*or* increíble); ˈ**tall·ness** altura *f*.
tal·low [ˈtælou] sebo *m*; ˈ**tal·low·y** seboso.
tal·ly [ˈtæli] **1.** (*stick*) tarja *f*; (*account*) cuenta *f*; número *m*; **2.** cuadrar, concordar, corresponder (*with* con).
tal·ly·ho [ˈtæliˈhou] *grito del cazador* (*de zorras*).
Tal·mud [ˈtælmu:d] Talmud *m*; **~·ic** [tælˈmu:dik] talmúdico.
tal·on [ˈtælən] garra *f*.
ta·lus [ˈteiləs] **1.** talud *m*; *geol.* talud *m* detrítico; **2.** *anat.* astrágalo *m*.
tam·a·ble [ˈteiməbl] domable.
ta·ma·le [təˈmæli *a.* təˈmɑ:li] tamal *m*.
tam·a·rind [ˈtæmərind] tamarindo *m*; **tam·a·risk** [ˈ~isk] tamarisco *m*.
tam·bour [ˈtæmbur] **1.** *sew.* tambor *m* (para bordar); ⚠ tambor *m*; **2.** bordar a tambor; **tam·bou·rine** [~bəˈri:n] pandereta *f*.
tame [teim] **1.** □ domesticado; manso; doméstico; amansado; *fig.* inocuo; F aburrido; **2.** domar, domesticar; amansar; ˈ**tame·ness** mansedumbre *f*; ˈ**tam·er** domador (-a *f*) *m*.
tam-o'-shan·ter [tæməˈʃæntər] boina *f* escocesa.
tamp [tæmp] apisonar; ⚒ atacar.
tam·per [ˈtæmpər]: *~ with* descomponer, estropear; tocar ajando; entrometerse en; *document* falsificar; *witness* sobornar.
tam·pon [ˈtæmpən] tapón *m*.
tan [tæn] **1.** bronceado *m*; (*bark*) casca *f*; **2.** *leather* curtir, adobar; (*sun*) tostar(se), broncear(se); F zurrar; **3.** leonado; *shoes* de color.
tan·dem [ˈtændəm] **1.** tándem *m*; **2.** *adj. a. adv.* ⚡ en tándem.
tang¹ [tæŋ] espiga *f of knife*; *fig.* gustillo *m*, dejo *m*; sabor *m* fuerte y picante.
tang² [~] **1.** retintín *m*; **2.** (hacer) retiñir.
tan·gent [ˈtændʒənt] tangente *adj. a. su. f*; *go* (*or fly*) *off at a ~* cambiar súbitamente de rumbo; **tan·gen·tial** [~ˈdʒenʃl] □ tangencial.
tan·ger·ine [tændʒəˈri:n] mandarina *f*.
tan·gi·bil·i·ty [tændʒiˈbiliti] tangibilidad *f*; **tan·gi·ble** [ˈtændʒəbl] □ tangible; *fig. a.* concreto.
tan·gle [ˈtæŋgl] **1.** enredo *m* (*a. fig.*), nudo *m*, maraña *f*; **2.** enredar(se), enmarañar(se); pelear, reñir (*with* con).
tan·go [ˈtæŋgou] tango *m*.
tank [tæŋk] tanque *m*; depósito *m*; ⚔ tanque *m*, carro *m* de combate; *~ car, ~ truck, ~ wagon* carro *m* cuba; 🚂 vagón *m* cisterna; *~ engine* locomotora *f* ténder; ˈ**tank·age** cabida *f* de un tanque.
tank·ard [ˈtæŋkərd] pichel *m*, bock *m*.
tank·er [ˈtæŋkər] petrolero *m*; tanquero *m S.Am.*
tan·ner [ˈtænər] curtidor *m*.
tan·ner·y [ˈtænəri] curtiduría *f*.
tan·nic [ˈtænik] tánico.
tan·nin [ˈtænin] tanino *m*.
tan·ning [ˈtæniŋ] curtido *m*; F paliza *f*.
tan·ta·lize [ˈtæntəlaiz] atormentar, tentar, dar dentera; ˈ**tan·ta·liz·ing** □ atormentador.
tan·ta·mount [ˈtæntəmaunt]: *~ to* equivalente a.
tan·trum [ˈtæntrəm] F rabieta *f*.
tap¹ [tæp] **1.** palmadita *f*, golpecito *m*; **2.** golpear ligeramente; dar golpecitos (*v/t.* a *or* en).
tap² [~] **1.** (*water*) grifo *m*; (*gas*) llave *f*; espita *f of barrel*; ⊕ macho *m* de terraja; *on ~* servido al grifo; *beer* sacado del barril; *fig.* a mano, disponible; **2.** *barrel* espitar; *tree* sangrar; *resources* explotar; ⚡ *wires* hacer una derivación en; *teleph. wire* intervenir, escuchar clandestinamente.
tap dance [ˈtæpdæns] zapateado *m*; **tap-dance** [~] zapatear.
tape [teip] **1.** cinta *f* (*a. sport*); cinta *f* adhesiva; (*ceremonial*) cinta *f* simbólica; cinta *f* magnetofónica *for recording*; *v. red ~*; **2.** F grabar sobre cinta; ˈ**~ meas·ure** cinta *f* métrica; ˈ**~-re·cord** grabar sobre cinta; ˈ**~ re·cord·er** magnetofón *m*; grabador *m* en cinta; ˈ**~ re·cord·ing** grabación *f* en cinta.
ta·per [ˈteipər] **1.** cerilla *f*; *eccl.* cirio *m*; **2.** ahusado; **3.** *v/i.* ahusarse; *~ away, ~ off* ir disminuyendo; *v/t.* afilar, ahusar; *~ing* = *~* 2.

tap·es·try ['tæpistri] tapiz *m*; tapicería *f*.
tape·worm ['teipwə:rm] tenia *f*, solitaria *f*.
ta·pi·o·ca [tæpi'oukə] tapioca *f*.
tap·per ['tæpər] ⚡ manipulador *m*.
tap·pet ['tæpit] ⊕ alzaválvulas *m*.
tap room ['tæpru:m] bodegón *m*.
tap root ['tæpru:t] raíz *f* central.
taps [tæps] toque *m* de silencio; *sl*. fin *m*; muerte *f*.
tap·ster ['tæpstər] mozo *m* de taberna.
tar [tɑ:r] **1.** alquitrán *m*; brea *f*; F marinero *m*; **2.** alquitranar; embrear; ~ *and feather* emplumar.
ta·ran·tu·la [tə'ræntjulə] tarántula *f*.
tar·di·ness ['tɑ:rdinis] tardanza *f*; lentitud *f*; '**tar·dy** □ (*late*) tardío; (*slow*) lento.
tare[1] [ter] ⚘ (*mst* ~*s pl*.) arveja *f*; (*Biblical*) cizaña *f*.
tare[2] [~] **1.** ✝ tara *f*; **2.** destarar.
tar·get ['tɑ:rgit] blanco *m* (*a. fig*.); ~ *practice* tiro *m* al blanco.
tar·iff ['tærif] tarifa *f*; arancel *m*; *attr*. arancelario.
tar·mac ['tɑ:rmæk] alquitranado *m*; asfaltado *m*.
tarn [tɑ:rn] lago *m* pequeño de montaña.
tar·nish ['tɑ:rniʃ] **1.** deslustrar(se) (*a. fig*.); **2.** deslustre *m*.
tar·pau·lin [tɑ:r'pɔ:lin] alquitranado *m*; lienzo *m* alquitranado (*or* encerado).
tar·ry[1] ['tæri] *lit*. tardar; detenerse; quedarse.
tar·ry[2] ['tɑ:ri] alquitranado; embreado.
tart [tɑ:rt] **1.** □ ácido, agrio; acre; *fig*. áspero; **2.** tarta *f*, torta *f*; *sl*. puta *f*, fulana *f*.
tar·tan ['tɑ:rtən] tartán *m*.
Tar·tar[1] ['tɑ:rtər] tártaro *m*; *fig*. arpía *f*, mujer *f* regañona; ~(e) *sauce* salsa *f* tártara.
tar·tar[2] [~] ⚗ tártaro *m*, sarro *m*.
task [tæsk] tarea *f*; faena *f*; *take to* ~ reprender (*for acc*.), llamar a capítulo; '**task force** agrupación *f* de fuerzas (para operación especial); '**task·mas·ter** capataz *m*; superintendente *m*; amo *m*.
tas·sel ['tæsl] borla *f*.
taste [teist] **1.** gusto *m*; sabor *m* (*of* a); (*sip*) sorbo *m*; (*sample*) muestra *f*; (*good*) ~ (buen) gusto *m*; *just a* ~ una pizca; *in bad* ~ de mal gusto; *to* ~ al gusto, a discreción; *acquire a* ~ *for* tomar gusto a; *be to one's* ~ gustarle a uno; *have a* ~ *for* gustar de, tener afición a; **2.** *v/t*. gustar; notar (un gusto de); (*try*) probar; *v/i*.: ~ *of* saber a; ~ *good* estar muy rico, estar sabroso, ser sabroso; **taste·ful** ['~ful] □ de buen gusto; elegante.
taste·less ['teistlis] □ insípido, soso; (*in bad taste*) de mal gusto; '**taste·less·ness** insipidez *f*; mal gusto *m*.
tas·ter ['teistər] catador *m*.
tast·y ['teisti] □ F sabroso.
tat[1] [tæt] *v*. *tit*[1].
tat[2] [~] *sew*. hacer frivolité.
tat·tered ['tætərd] andrajoso; en jirones; **tat·ters** ['tætərz] *pl*. andrajos *m/pl*.; jirones *m/pl*.; *in* ~ = *tattered*.
tat·tle ['tætl] **1.** parlotear; *b.s*. chismear; **2.** charla *f*; *b.s*. chismes *m/pl*., hablilla *f*; '**tat·tler** charlador (-a *f*) *m*; *b.s*. chismoso (a *f*) *m*.
tat·too[1] [tə'tu:] ⚔ (toque *m* de) retreta *f*; espectáculo *m* militar.
tat·too[2] [~] **1.** tatuar; **2.** tatuaje *m*.
taught [tɔ:t] *pret*. *a*. *p.p*. *of teach*.
taunt [tɔ:nt] **1.** mofa *f*; pulla *f*; dicterio *m*; **2.** reprochar con insultos (*for*, *with acc*.); mofar.
taut [tɔ:t] tieso, tenso, tirante; '**taut·en** *v/t*. te(n)sar; *v/i*. ponerse tieso.
tau·to·log·i·cal [tɔ:tə'lɔdʒikl] □ tautológico; **tau·to·lo·gy** [tɔ:'tɔlədʒi] tautología *f*.
tav·ern ['tævərn] taberna *f*; mesón *m*; bar *m*.
taw·dri·ness ['tɔ:drinis] lo charro *etc*.; '**taw·dry** □ charro; barato; deslucido; cursi; de oropel.
taw·ny ['tɔ:ni] leonado.
tax [tæks] **1.** impuesto *m* (*on* sobre), contribución *f*; *fig*. carga *f* (*on* sobre); esfuerzo *m* (*on* para); ~ *evasion* evasión *f* fiscal; **2.** *p*. imponer contribuciones a; *th*. imponer contribución sobre; ⚖ *costs* tasar; *fig*. *patience* agotar; *resources* someter a esfuerzo excesivo; *p*. acusar (*with* de); censurar (*with acc*.); '**tax·a·ble** imponible; sujeto a impuesto; **tax'a·tion** impuestos *m/pl*.; contribuciones *f/pl*.; sistema *m* tributario; '**tax col·lec·tor** recaudador *m* de contribuciones; '**tax de·duc·tion**

exclusión *f* de contribución; ˈ**tax-ˈfree** exento de contribuciones; ˈ**tax ha•ven** asilo *m* de los impuestos.
tax•i [ˈtæksi] **1.** = ˈ**~•cab** taxi *m*; **2.** ir en taxi; ✈ carretear; taxear.
tax•i•derm•ist [tæksiˈdəːrmist] taxidermista *m/f*.
tax•i...: ˈ**~ driv•er** taxista *m*; ˈ**~•meter** taxímetro *m*; ˈ**~ stand** parada *f* de taxis.
tax loss [ˈtækslɔs] pérdida *f* de reclamable; **tax•pay•er** [ˈtækspeiər] contribuyente *m/f*; ˈ**tax re•lief** aligeramiento *m* de impuestos; ˈ**tax re•turn** declaración *f* de renta.
tea [tiː] té *m*; (*meal*) merienda *f*; *high* ~ merienda-cena *f*; ˈ**~•bag** muñeca *f*.
teach [tiːtʃ] [*irr.*] enseñar (*to* a); *fig.* ~ *a lesson* escarmentar; ˈ**teach•a•ble** educable; ˈ**teach•er** profesor (-a *f*) *m*; maestro (a *f*) *m*; ˈ**teach•er ˈtrain•ing** formación *f* pedagógica; ˈ**teach•ing** enseñanza *f*; doctrina *f*; *attr.* docente.
tea...: ˈ**~ co•zy** cubretetera *f*; ˈ**~•cup** taza *f* para té; *tempest in a* ~ tormenta *f* en un vaso de agua; ˈ**~ dance** té *m* bailable.
teak [tiːk] (madera *f* de) teca *f*.
team [tiːm] **1.** *sport etc.*: equipo *m*; tiro *m of horses*; yunta *f of oxen*; **2.:** ~ *up* asociarse, formar un equipo; ˈ**~ ˈspir•it** compañerismo *m*, camaradería *f*; **team•ster** [ˈ~stər] tronquista *m*; camionista *m/f*; ˈ**team-work** cooperación *f*, colaboración *f*; solidaridad *f*.
tea•pot [ˈtiːpɔt] tetera *f*.
tear[1] [ter] **1.** [*irr.*] *v/t.* rasgar, desgarrar; romper; *flesh* lacerar; (*snatch*) arrancar; ~ *apart* despedazar; ~ *down building* derribar; *hangings, flag, poster etc.* arrancar, quitar (arrancando); ~ *off* arrancar; ~ *up paper etc.* romper; *plant* desarraigar; *v. hair*; *v/i.* rasgarse; F *with adv. or prp.* precipitarse, correr precipitadamente, ir con toda prisa; ~ *past* pasar como un rayo; **2.** rasgón *m*, desgarrón *m*; *v. wear*.
tear[2] [tir] lágrima *f*.
tear•ful [ˈtirful] □ lloroso, llorón; lacrimoso.
tear gas [ˈtirˈgæs] gas *m* lacrimógeno.
tea room [ˈtiːruːm] salón *m* de té.
tease [tiːz] **1.** *wool* cardar; *fig.* embromar, tomar el pelo a; jorobar; atormentar; **2.** embromador (-a *f*) *m*, guasón (-a *f*) *m*; **tea•sel** [ˈ~l] ⚘ cardencha *f*; ⊕ carda *f*; ˈ**teas•er** F rompecabezas *m*; incentivo *m*.
tea...: ˈ**~ set** servicio *m* de té; ˈ**~•spoon** cucharita *f*; ˈ**~ strain•er** colador *m* de té.
teat [tiːt] pezón *m*; teta *f*; chupador *m of bottle*.
tea•time [ˈtiːtaim] hora *f* del té.
tech•ni•cal [ˈteknikl] □ técnico; **tech•ni•cal•i•ty** [~ˈkæliti] tecnicidad *f*; cosa *f* técnica; (*word*) tecnicismo *m*; **tech•ni•cian** [tekˈniʃn] técnico *m*.
tech•ni•col•or [ˈteknikʌlər] (*attr.* en) tecnicolor *m*.
tech•nique [tekˈniːk] técnica *f*.
tech•no•log•i•cal [teknəˈlɔdʒikl] □ tecnológico; **tech•no•lo•gist** [tekˈnɔlədʒist] tecnólogo *m*; **techˈno•lo•gy** tecnología *f*.
ted•der [ˈtedər] heneador *m*.
ted•dy bear [ˈtediber] osito *m* de felpa; oso *m* de juguete.
te•di•ous [ˈtiːdiəs] □ aburrido, fastidioso; cansado; ˈ**te•di•ous•ness**, **te•di•um** [ˈtiːdiəm] tedio *m*; aburrimiento *m*.
tee [tiː] **1.** tee *m*; **2.:** ~ *off* golpear desde el tee.
teem [tiːm] hormiguear; abundar (*with* en), hervir (*with* de); ~ *with rain* diluviar, llover a cántaros.
teen-ag•er [ˈtiːneidʒər] joven *m/f* de 13 a 19 años.
teens [tiːnz] *pl.* edad *f* de 13 a 19 años; F juventud *f* de 13 a 19 años; *be in one's* ~ tener de 13 a 19 años.
tee•ny [ˈtiːni] F chiquito, chiquitín.
tee•ter [ˈtiːtər] F balancear, oscilar.
teeth [tiːθ] [*pl. of tooth*] dientes *m/pl.*
teethe [tiːð] endentecer, echar los (primeros) dientes; ˈ**teeth•ing** dentición *f*; ~ *ring* chupador *m*.
tee•to•tal [tiːˈtoutl] abstemio; **teeˈto•tal•er** abstemio (a *f*) *m*.
tel•e•gram [ˈteligræm] telegrama *m*.
tel•e•graph [ˈteligræf] **1.** telégrafo *m*; *attr.* telegráfico; ~ *pole* poste *m* telegráfico; **2.** telegrafiar; **tel•e•graph•ic** [~ˈgræfik] □ telegráfico; **te•leg•ra•phist** [tiˈlegrəfist] telegrafista *m/f*; **teˈleg•ra•phy** telegrafía *f*.
tel•e•path•ic [teliˈpæθik] □ telepático; **te•le•pa•thy** [tiˈlepəθi] telepatía *f*.
tel•e•phone [ˈtelifoun] **1.** teléfono *m*;

~ *booth* locutorio *m*, cabina *f* de teléfono; ~ *call* llamada *f*; ~ *directory* guía *f* telefónica; ~ *exchange* central *f* telefónica; ~ *operator* telefonista *m/f*; *be on the* ~ estar hablando por teléfono; **2.** llamar por teléfono, telefonear; **tel·e·phon·ic** [~ˈfɔnik] □ telefónico; **te·leph·o·nist** [tiˈlefənist] telefonista *m/f*; **teˈleph·o·ny** telefonía *f*.

tel·e·pho·to [ˈteliˈfoutou] **1.** telefotografía *f*; **2.** telefotográfico; ~ *lens* lente *f* telefotográfica.

tel·e·print·er [ˈteliprintər] teleimpresor *m*.

tel·e·scope [ˈteliskoup] **1.** telescopio *m*; catalejo *m*; **2.** telescopar(se); enchufar(se); **tel·e·scop·ic** [~ˈkɔpik] □ telescópico; de enchufe.

tel·e·type [ˈtelitaip] **1.** teletipo *m*; **2.** transmitir por teletipo; **ˈte·leˈtyp·er** teletipista *m/f*.

tel·e·vise [ˈtelivaiz] televisar; **tel·e·vi·sion** [ˈ~viʒn] (*attr.* de) televisión *f*; ~ *audience* telespectadores *m/pl.*; ~ *set* aparato *m* de televisión, televisor *m*; *cable* ~ televisión *f* por cable.

tel·ex [ˈteleks] servicio *m* comercial de teletipo.

tell [tel] [*irr.*] *v/t.* decir; *story* contar; conocer (*by* por); distinguir (*from* de); determinar; ~ *a p. to inf.* decirle a uno que *subj.*; *I have been told* (*that*) se me ha dicho (que); *you never can* ~ no se puede saber con certeza; F *you're* ~*ing me*! ¡a quién se lo cuentas!; ~ *off* mandar (*to inf.*); F reñir, regañar; *v/i.* hablar (*about, of* de); hacer mella, surtir efecto (*on* en); ~ *on health etc.* afectar, dejarse ver en; F ~ *on* soplar contra, chivatear contra; **ˈtell·er** narrador (-a *f*) *m*; *parl.* escrutador *m*; (*bank*) cajero *m*; **ˈtell·ing** □ eficaz; **tell·tale** [ˈ~teil] **1.** revelador; indicador; **2.** soplón (-a *f*) *m*; ⚓ axiómetro *m*; ~ *clock* reloj *m* registrador.

te·mer·i·ty [tiˈmeriti] temeridad *f*.

tem·per [ˈtempər] **1.** *all senses*: templar; *fig. a.* mitigar, moderar; **2.** humor *m*; disposición *f*; natural *m*; (*anger*) mal genio *m*; (*be in a* estar de) *good* ~ buen humor *m*; *keep one's* ~ contenerse; *lose one's* ~ perder la paciencia, enojarse; **tem·per·a·ment** [ˈ~rəmənt] temperamento *m*, disposición *f*; excitabilidad *f*; **tem·per·a·men·tal** [~ˈmentl] □ complexional; caprichoso, excitable; *be* ~ tener genio; **ˈtem·per·ance** templanza *f*; abstinencia *f* (del alcohol); ~ *hotel* hotel *m* donde no se sirven bebidas alcohólicas; **tem·per·ate** [ˈ~rit] □ templado; sobrio, abstemio; ~ *zone* zona *f* templada; **tem·per·a·ture** [ˈtempərətʃər] temperatura *f*; ⚕ calentura *f*; ⚕ ~ *chart* gráfico *m* de temperatura; **tem·pered** [ˈtempərd] templado.

tem·pest [ˈtempist] tempestad *f*; **tem·pes·tu·ous** [~ˈpestjuəs] □ tempestuoso.

Tem·plar [ˈtemplər] *hist* templario *m*.

tem·ple[1] [ˈtempl] templo *m*.

tem·ple[2] [~] *anat.* sien *f*.

tem·po·ral [ˈtempərəl] □ temporal; **tem·po·ral·i·ties** [~ˈrælitiz] *pl.* temporalidades *f/pl.*; **ˈtem·po·ra·ri·ly** temporalmente; **ˈtem·po·rar·y** □ temporáneo, provisional; transitorio; *official* interino; *worker* temporero; **ˈtem·po·rize** contemporizar.

tempt [tempt] tentar, provocar, inducir (*to* a); **tempˈta·tion** tentación *f*; **ˈtempt·er** tentador *m*; **ˈtempt·ing** □ tentador; *food* apetitoso; **ˈtempt·ress** tentadora *f*.

ten [ten] diez (*a. su. m*); decena *f*.

ten·a·ble [ˈtenəbl] defendible, sostenible.

te·na·cious [tiˈneiʃəs] □ tenaz; **te·nac·i·ty** [tiˈnæsiti] tenacidad *f*.

ten·an·cy [ˈtenənsi] inquilinato *m*, arriendo *m*.

ten·ant [ˈtenənt] **1.** arrendatario (a *f*) *m*, inquilino (a *f*) *m*; *fig.* habitante *m/f*; **2.** alquilar; *fig.* ocupar.

tend[1] [tend] tender (*to, towards* a).

tend[2] [~] *sick etc.* cuidar; vigilar; *machine* manejar, servir; *cattle* guardar.

tend·en·cy [ˈtendənsi] tendencia *f*; **ten·den·tious** [~ˈdenʃəs] □ tendencioso.

ten·der[1] [ˈtendər] □ tierno; *spot* delicado, sensible; ⚕ dolorido.

ten·der[2] [~] **1.** ✝ oferta *f*, proposición *f*; *legal* ~ moneda *f* de curso legal; **2.** *v/i.* ✝ ofertar; *v/t.* ofrecer; *thanks* dar; *resignation* presentar.

ten·der[3] [~] 🚂 ténder *m*; ⚓ gabarra *f*, embarcación *f* auxiliar.

ten·der·foot [ˈtendərfut] recién llegado *m*; novato *m*; **ten·der·loin**

['~lɔin] filete *m*; F barrio *m* de mala vida; '**ten·der·ness** ternura *f*; sensibilidad *f*.

ten·don ['tendən] tendón *m*.

ten·dril ['tendril] zarcillo *m*; (*vine-*) tijereta *f*.

ten·e·ment ['tenimənt] vivienda *f*; habitación *f*; ~ *house* casa *f* de vecindad.

ten·et ['tenit, 'ti:net] dogma *m*, credo *m*.

ten·fold ['tenfould] **1.** *adj*. décuplo; **2.** *adv*. diez veces.

ten·nis ['tenis] tenis *m*; '~ **court** pista *f* de tenis, cancha *f* de tenis *S.Am.*; '~ **play·er** tenista *m*/*f*.

ten·on ['tenən] espiga *f*, almilla *f*.

ten·or ['tenər] tenor *m* (*a*. ♪); curso *m*; tendencia *f*.

tense[1] [tens] *gr*. tiempo *m*.

tense[2] [~] **1.** □ tieso, tenso; *situation* crítico, lleno de emoción; **2.** te(n)sar; estirar; '**tense·ness** tirantez *f*; **tensile** ['tensil] tensor; de tensión; dúctil; ~ *strength* resistencia *f* a la tensión; **ten·sion** ['~ʃn] tensión *f*; tirantez *f* (*a*. *fig*.); *fig*. emoción *f*; ansia *f*; ⚡ *high* ~ (*attr*. de) alta tensión *f*.

tent [tent] tienda *f* (de campaña).

ten·ta·cle ['tentəkl] tentáculo *m*.

ten·ta·tive ['tentətiv] □ tentativo; provisional; de ensayo; ~*ly* provisionalmente, como tanteo.

ten·ter ['tentər] bastidor *m*; '~**·hook** escarpia *f*; *fig*. *be on* ~*s* estar en ascuas.

tenth [tenθ] décimo (*a*. *su*. *m*).

tent peg ['tentpeg] estaca *f* de tienda; '**tent pole** mástil *m* de tienda.

ten·u·i·ty [te'njuiti] tenuidad *f*; raridad *f* *of air*; **ten·u·ous** ['tenjuəs] □ tenue; sutil; *air* raro.

ten·ure ['tenjur] posesión *f*; tenencia *f*, ejercicio *m* *of office*.

tep·id ['tepid] □ tibio; **te'pid·i·ty**, '**tep·id·ness** tibieza *f*.

ter·cen·te·nar·y [tər'sentəneri], **ter·cen·ten·ni·al** [~'tenjəl] **1.** de trescientos años; **2.** tricentenario *m*.

term [tə:rm] **1.** término *m* (*end*, *word*, ℞, *phls*.); (*period*) plazo *m*, período *m*; condena *f* *of imprisonment*; mandato *m* *of president*; ⚖, *univ*., *school*: semestre *m*; trimestre *m*; ~*s pl*. condiciones *f*/*pl*.; ☤ precios *m*/*pl*.; (*relationship*) relaciones *f*/*pl*.; *in* ~*s of* en términos de; ☤ *on easy* ~*s* a plazos; *be on good* ~*s with* estar en buenos términos con; *come to* (*or make*) ~*s* llegar a un acuerdo; *fig*. *come to* ~*s with* conformarse con; **2.** nombrar, llamar; calificar (de).

ter·ma·gant ['tə:rməgənt] arpía *f*, fiera *f*.

ter·mi·na·ble ['tə:rminəbl] terminable; '**ter·mi·nal 1.** □ terminal (*a*. ⚘); último; **2.** ⚡ borne *m*; ⚡ polo *m*; (*port*) terminal *f*; 🚂 estación *f* de cabeza; **ter·mi·nate** ['~neit] *v*/*t*. *a*. *v*/*i*. terminar; despedir; **ter·mi'na·tion** terminación *f* (*a*. *gr*.); despido *m*.

ter·mi·nol·o·gy [tə:rmi'nɔlədʒi] terminología *f*.

ter·mi·nus ['tə:rminəs] término *m*; 🚂 estación *f* final (*or* de cabeza).

ter·mite ['tə:rmait] térmite *m*, comején *m*.

tern [tə:rn]: *common* ~ charrán *m* común.

ter·na·ry ['tə:rnəri] ternario.

ter·race ['terəs] **1.** terraza *f*, terraplén *m*; hilera *f* *of houses*; (*roof*) azotea *f*; **2.** terraplenar.

ter·rain ['terein] terreno *m*; *all-*~ todoterreno.

ter·res·tri·al [ti'restriəl] □ terrestre.

ter·ri·ble ['terəbl] □ terrible; F malísmo, pésimo.

ter·ri·er ['teriər] terrier *m*.

ter·rif·ic [tə'rifik] □ tremendo; F estupendo; imponente; **ter·ri·fy** ['terifai] aterrar, aterrorizar.

ter·ri·to·ri·al [teri'tɔ:riəl] **1.** □ territorial; ~ *waters pl*. aguas *f*/*pl*. territoriales (*or* jurisdiccionales); ♀ *Army* reserva *f* (del ejército); **2.** reservista *m*; **ter·ri·to·ry** ['~tɔ:ri] territorio *m*; *fig*. pertenencia *f*.

ter·ror ['terər] terror *m*, espanto *m*; '**ter·ror·ism** terrorismo *m*; '**ter·ror·ist** terrorista *m*; '**ter·ror·ize** aterrorizar.

ter·ry cloth ['teri'klɔθ] albornoz *m*.

terse [tə:rs] □ breve, conciso, lacónico; '**terse·ness** laconismo *m*.

ter·tian ['tə:rʃn] ⚕ terciana *f*; **ter·ti·ar·y** ['~ʃeri] terciario.

te·ry·lene ['terili:n] terylene *m*.

tes·sel·ate ['tesileit] formar con teselas; ~*d pavement* mosaico *m*.

test [test] **1.** prueba *f*, ensayo *m*; piedra *f* de toque; examen *m*; *psychological etc*.: test *m*; *acid* ~ *fig*. prueba *f*

de fuego; ~ *flight* vuelo *m* de ensayo; *put to the* ~ poner a prueba; *high-~ mot.* supercarburante; F súper; **2.** probar, ensayar; examinar; *sight* graduar.
tes·ta·ment [ˈtestəmənt] testamento *m*; **tes·ta·men·ta·ry** [~ˈmentəri] testamentario.
tes·ta·tor [tesˈteitər] testador *m*.
tes·ta·trix [tesˈteitriks] testadora *f*.
test ban [ˈtestˈbæn] prohibición *f* contra pruebas de armas nucleares.
test case [ˈtest keis] pleito *m* de ensayo (*para determinar la interpretación de una ley*).
tes·ter[1] [ˈtestər] (*bed*) baldaquín *m*.
test·er[2] [~] (*p.*) ensayador *m*.
tes·ti·cle [ˈtestikl] testículo *m*.
tes·ti·fy [ˈtestifai] testificar (*that* que); atestiguar (*to acc.*); atestar (*to acc.*) (*a. fig.*).
tes·ti·mo·ni·al [testiˈmounjəl] recomendación *f*; certificado *m*; **tes·ti·mo·ny** [ˈ~məni] testimonio *m*.
test·ing ground [ˈtestiŋ ˈgraund] zona *f* de pruebas.
test...: ~ **match** partido *m* internacional; ˈ~ **pa·per** *school*: papel *m* de examen; ⚗ papel *m* reactivo; ˈ~ **pi·lot** piloto *m* de pruebas; ˈ~ **print** *phot.* copia *f* de prueba; ˈ~ **tube** tubo *m* de ensayo; probeta *f*; ~ *baby* niño-probeta *m*.
tes·ty [ˈtesti] □, **tetch·y** [ˈtetʃi] □ enojadizo, picajoso.
te·ta·nus [ˈtetənəs] tétano *m*.
teth·er [ˈteðər] **1.** atadura *f*, traba *f*; *fig. be at the end of one's* ~ no poder más, estar para volverse loco; **2.** apersogar, atar.
Teu·ton [ˈtju:tən] teutón *m*; **Teu·ton·ic** [~ˈtɔnik] teutónico.
text [tekst] texto *m*; tema *m*; *typ.* ~ *hand* letra *f* cursiva grande; ˈ~**·book** libro *m* de texto.
tex·tile [ˈtekstail] **1.** textil; **2.** *mst* ~*s pl.* tejidos *m/pl.*
tex·tu·al [ˈtekstjuəl] □ textual.
tex·ture [ˈtekstʃər] textura *f* (*a. fig.*).
than [ðæn, *unstressed* ðən] que; *more* ~ *I* más que yo; *more* ~ *ten* más de diez; *not more* ~ *ten* no más que diez; *more money* ~ *we have* más dinero del que tenemos; *more books* ~ *we have* más libros de los que tenemos; *he is more stupid* ~ *we thought* es más estúpido de lo que creíamos.
thank [θæŋk] **1.** dar las gracias a; agradecer (*for acc.*); (*no*) ~ *you* (no) gracias; ~ *you!* (*stressed*) ¡a usted!; **2.** ~*s pl.* gracias *f/pl.*; agradecimiento *m*; ~*s to* gracias a; **thank·ful** [ˈ~ful] □ agradecido; *I was* ~ *to get out* me alegré de poder salir; ˈ**thank·less** □ *p.* ingrato; *task* ímprobo, sin recompensa; **thanks·giv·ing** [ˈ~sgiviŋ] acción *f* de gracias; ♀ (*Day*) Día *m* de acción de gracias.
that [ðæt, *unstressed* ðət] **1.** *pron.* (*pl. those*) *m*: ése, aquél (*more remote*); *f*: ésa, aquélla; *neuter*: eso, aquello; (*relative*) que, el cual *etc.*; *so* ~*'s* ~! se acabó; ~ *is* es decir; *at* ~ acto seguido, sin más; con todo; *like* ~ (*adv.*) de esa manera, de la misma manera; **2.** *adj.* (*pl. those*) *m*: ese, aquel (*more remote*); *f*: esa, aquella; **3.** *adv.* tan; ~ *far* tan lejos; ~ *much* tanto; **4.** *cj.* que; para que; *in* ~ en que, por cuanto; *so* ~ (*purpose*) para *inf.*, para que *subj.*; (*result*) de modo que.
thatch [θætʃ] **1.** (techo *m* de) paja *f*; **2.** poner un techo de paja a; badar.
thaw [θɔ:] **1.** deshielo *m*; **2.** deshelar(se), derretir(se); *fig.* ablandar(se).
the [ði:; *before vowel* ði, *before consonant* ðə] **1.** *article*: el, la; *pl.* los, las; (*stressed*) he's ~ *man for the job* es el único hombre para el puesto; *it's* ~ *thing, my dear* es lo último, querida; **2.** *adv.* ~ ... ~ cuanto más ... (tanto) más.
the·a·ter (*mst British a.* **the·a·tre**) [ˈθiətər] teatro *m* (*a. fig.*); *lecture* ~ aula *f*; *operating* ~ quirófano *m*, sala *f* de operaciones; **the·at·ri·cal** [θiˈætrikl] □ teatral; **theˈat·ri·cals** [~klz] *pl.* funciones *f/pl.* teatrales.
thee [ði:] † *or prov.* te; (*after prp.*) ti; *with* ~ contigo.
theft [θeft] hurto *m*, robo *m*.
their [ðer] su(s); **theirs** [~z] (el) suyo, (la) suya *etc.*
the·ism [ˈθi:izm] teísmo *m*.
them [ðem, ðəm] *acc.* los, las; *dat.* les; (*after prp.*) ellos, ellas.
theme [θi:m] tema *m*; ~ **song** motivo *m* principal; tema *m* central.
them·selves [ðəmˈselvz] (*subject*) ellos mismos, ellas mismas; *acc., dat.* se; (*after prp.*) sí (mismos, mismas).
then [ðen] **1.** *adv.* entonces; luego; después; *by* ~ para entonces; antes

de eso; *now* ~ ahora bien; *there and* ~ en el acto, acto seguido; **2.** *cj.* pues; conque; por tanto; **3.** *adj.* (de) entonces.
thence [ðens] *lit.* de(sde) allí; por eso.
thence·forth ['ðens'fɔːrθ] *lit.* de allí en adelante, desde entonces.
the·oc·ra·cy [θi'ɔkrəsi] teocracia *f*; **the·o·crat·ic** [θiə'krætik] □ teocrático.
the·o·do·lite [θiː'ɔdəlait] teodolito *m*.
the·o·lo·gi·an [θiə'loudʒiən] teólogo *m*; **the·o·log·i·cal** [~'lɔdʒikl] □ teológico; **the·ol·o·gy** [θi'ɔlədʒi] teología *f*.
the·o·rem ['θiərəm] teorema *m*; **the·o·ret·ic, the·o·ret·i·cal** [~'retik(l)] □ teórico; '**the·o·rist** teórico *m*, teorizante *m*; '**the·o·rize** teorizar; '**the·o·ry** teoría *f*; *in* ~ teóricamente.
the·os·o·phy [θi'ɔsəfi] teosofía *f*.
ther·a·peu·tic [θerə'pjuːtik] **1.** □ terapéutico; **2.** ~*s pl.* terapéutica *f*; **ther·a'peu·tist,** '**ther·a·pist** terapeuta *m*/*f*; '**ther·a·py** terapia *f*; terapéutica *f*; *occupational* ~ terapia *f* vocacional.
there [ðer] **1.** *adv.* allí, allá, ahí; F *all* ~ despierto, vivo; F *not all* ~ chiflado, tontiloco; ~ *is*, ~ *are* [ðə'riz, ðə'rɑːr] hay; **2.** *int.* ¡vaya!
there...: '~**·a·bout**(**s**) por ahí; ~'**after** después de eso; '~'**by** así, de ese modo; '~**·fore** por (lo) tanto, por consiguiente; ~'**in** en eso; en ese respecto; ~'**of** de eso; de lo mismo; '~**·up'on** por consiguiente; al momento, en seguida; ~'**with** con eso, con lo mismo.
ther·mal ['θəːrməl] □ termal; **thermic** ['~mik] □ térmico; **therm·i·on·ic** [~mi'ɔnik] *radio*: ~ *valve* lámpara *f* termiónica.
ther·mo·dy·nam·ics ['θəːrmoudai'næmiks] *sg.* termodinámica *f*.
ther·mo·e·lec·tric cou·ple ['θəːrmoui'lektrik'kʌpl] par *m* termoeléctrico; **ther·mom·e·ter** [θər'mɔmitər] termómetro *m*; **ther·mo·met·ric, ther·mo·met·ri·cal** [θəːrmə'metrik(l)] □ termométrico; **ther·mo·nu·cle·ar** ['~'nuːkliər] termonuclear; **ther·mo·pile** [~'moupail] termopila *f*; **Ther·mos** ['~mɔs] (*a.* ~ *bottle*) termos *m*; **ther·mo·stat** ['~moustæt] termóstato *m*.
these [ðiːz] (*pl. of this*) **1.** *pron. m*: éstos; *f*: éstas; **2.** *adj. m*: estos; *f*: estas.
the·sis ['θiːsis], *pl.* **the·ses** ['θiːsiːz] tesis *f*.
they [ðei] ellos, ellas; ~ *who* los que.
thick [θik] **1.** □ espeso; *smoke etc.* denso; *air* (*misty*) brumoso; (*foul*) viciado; *liquid* (*cloudy*) turbio; (*stiff*) viscoso; *voice* apagado, indistinto; F *p.* estúpido; F íntimo; 2 *inches* ~ 2 pulgadas de espesor; ~ *with place* atestado de; que abunda en; F *be* ~ (*as thieves*) intimar mucho, ser uña y carne; F *be* ~ *with* tener mucha intimidad con; *sl. it's a bit* ~! ¡es demasiado!; F *lay it on* ~ exagerar mucho; **2.**: *in the* ~ *of* en medio de; (*battle*) en lo más reñido de; *through* ~ *and thin* por las buenas y las malas; incondicionalmente; '**thick·en** espesar(se); (*plot*) complicarse; **thick·et** ['~it] matorral *m*, espesura *f*; '**thick-'head·ed** estúpido, torpe; '**thick·ness** espesura *f*; espesor *m*; grueso *m*; densidad *f*; consistencia *f*; '**thick-'skinned** *fig.* insensible.
thief [θiːf], *pl.* **thieves** [θiːvz] ladrón (-a *f*) *m*; **thieve** [θiːv] hurtar, robar; **thiev·er·y** ['~vəri], '**thiev·ing** robo *m*, latrocinio *m*.
thiev·ish ['θiːviʃ] □ ladrón; engatado.
thigh [θai] muslo *m*.
thim·ble ['θimbl] dedal *m*; ⚓ guardacabo *m*; **thim·ble·ful** ['~ful] dedal *m*; dedada *f*.
thin [θin] **1.** □ delgado; *p.* flaco; *covering* ligero; transparente; *air, scent, sound* tenue; *hair* ralo; *soup etc.* aguado; *crop, crowd* escaso (*a.* ~ *on the ground*); **2.** (*slim*) adelgazar(se); (*weaken*) enflaquecerse; (*a.* ~ *out*) entresacar; aclarar; (*crowd etc.*) reducir(se).
thine [ðain] (el) tuyo, (la) tuya *etc.*
thing [θiŋ] cosa *f*; asunto *m*; ~*s pl.* (*possessions*) efectos *m*/*pl.*; cosas *f*/*pl.*; F *the* ~ lo que está de moda; lo importante; F *the* ~ *is* el caso es que; *the best* ~ lo mejor; *the only* ~ lo único; *for one* ~ en primer lugar; *of all the* ~*s*! ¡qué sorpresa!; (*disgust*) ¡qué asco!; *as* ~*s stand* tal como están las cosas; ~*s are going better* las cosas van mejor; F *have a* ~ *about* estar obsesionado

por; F *it's not the (done)* ~ eso no se hace; F *know a ~ or two* saber cuántas son cinco; *not to know the first ~ about* no saber nada en absoluto de.

thing·um(·a)·bob ['θiŋəm(i)bɔb] F cosa *f*, chisme *m*.

think [θiŋk] [*irr.*] *v/i.* pensar (*about, of* en; *of* [*opinion*] de; *to inf., about, of ger.*: *all take inf.*); (*believe*) creer; reflexionar; meditar; *I ~ so* creo que sí; *I should ~ so!* ¡ya lo creo!; *v/t.* pensar; acordarse de; *not to know what to ~* no saber a qué carta quedarse; *~ better of it* mudar de parecer; *~ little of* tener en poco; *v. much, nothing*; *~ well of* tener buen concepto de; *~ out* resolver; *~ over* meditar *acc.*, pensar *acc.*; *~ up* idear; imaginar; '**think·a·ble** concebible; '**think·er** pensador *m*; '**think·ing 1.** intelectual, mental; *p.* razonable, considerado; **2.** pensamiento *m*; *way of ~* modo *m* de pensar.

thin·ness ['θinnis] delgadez *f*; tenuidad *f etc.*

third [θə:rd] **1.** tercero; F *~ degree* interrogatorio *m* brutal; *~ party* tercera persona *f*; **2.** tercio *m*; tercera parte *f*; ♪ tercera *f*; '**third·ly** en tercer lugar; '**third-rate** de tercer orden; *fig.* inferior; '**Third** '**World** Tercer(o) Mundo.

thirst [θə:rst] **1.** sed *f*; **2.** tener sed (*after, for* de); '**thirst·y** □ sediento; *land* árido; F *work* sudoroso; *be ~* tener sed.

thir·teen ['θə:r'ti:n] trece (*a. su. m*); '**thir'teenth** [~θ] decimotercio, decimotercero; **thir·ti·eth** ['~tiiθ] trigésimo; '**thir·ty** treinta.

this [ðis] (*pl. these*) **1.** *pron. m*: éste; *f*: ésta; *neuter*: esto; **2.** *adj. m*: este; *f*: esta; *~ morning* esta mañana.

this·tle ['θisl] cardo *m*.

thith·er ['ðiðər] *lit.* allá.

thong [θɔŋ] correa *f*.

tho·rax ['θɔ:ræks] tórax *m*.

thorn [θɔ:rn] espina *f*; '**thorn·y** espinoso (*a. fig.*).

thor·ough ['θə:rou] □ completo; cabal; concienzudo, minucioso; *~ly freq.* a fondo; '**~·bred** (de) pura sangre *m/f*; '**~·fare** vía *f* pública; carretera *f*; *no ~* se prohibe el paso; '**~·go·ing** cabal; totalista, de cuerpo entero; '**thor·ough·ness** minuciosidad *f*; lo concienzudo etc.

those [ðouz] (*pl. of that* 1, 2) **1.** *pron. m*: ésos, aquéllos (*more remote*); *f*: ésas, aquéllas (*more remote*); *~ who* los que, aquellos que *etc.*; **2.** *adj. m*: esos, aquellos; *f*: esas, aquellas (*v.* 1.).

thou [ðau] † *a. prov.* tú.

though [ðou] **1.** *cj.* aunque; si bien; *as ~* como si *subj.*; **2.** *adv.* sin embargo.

thought [θɔ:t] **1.** *pret. a. p.p. of think*; **2.** pensamiento *m*; reflexión *f*; solicitud *f*; *give ~ to* pensar, considerar *acc.*; **thought·ful** ['θɔ:tful] □ (*thinking*) pensativo; (*kind*) atento; considerado; (*farsighted*) previsor; '**thought·ful·ness** atención *f*; solicitud *f*; previsión *f*.

thought·less ['θɔ:tlis] □ irreflexivo; descuidado; inconsiderado; '**thought·less·ness** irreflexión *f*; descuido *m*.

thou·sand ['θauzənd] **1.** mil; *two ~ people* dos mil personas; **2.** mil *m*; millar *m*; **thou·sandth** ['~zənθ] milésimo (*a. su. m*).

thrall [θrɔ:l] *poet.* (*p.*) esclavo (a *f*) *m*; (*state*) esclavitud *f*.

thrash [θræʃ] *v/t.* golpear; azotar, zurrar; *~ out* resolver mediante larga discusión; *v/i.*: *~ about etc.* sacudirse, dar vueltas; *v. thresh*; '**thrash·ing** paliza *f*.

thread [θred] **1.** hilo *m* (*a. fig.*); hebra *f of silkworm*; filete *m*, rosca *f of screw*; *pick (or take) up the ~* coger el hilo; **2.** *needle* enhebrar; *beads* ensartar; ⊕ aterrajar; filetear; *~ one's way through* abrirse paso por; '**~·bare** raído, gastado.

threat [θret] amenaza *f*; '**threat·en** amenazar (*to* con); '**threat·en·ing** □ amenazante, amenazador.

three [θri:] tres (*a. su. m*); '**~-'col·or** de tres colores; '**~-'cor·nered** triangular; *~ hat* tricornio *m*; '**~-di'men·sion·al** tridimensional; '**~·fold 1.** *adj.* triple; **2.** *adv.* tres veces; **~-phase** ['θrifeiz] ⚡ trifásico; '**~-'ply** *wood* de 3 capas; *wool* triple; '**~-score** sesenta; '**~-way switch** conmutador *m* de tres terminales.

thresh [θreʃ] ✓ trillar; *v. thrash*.

thresh·ing ['θreʃiŋ] ✓ trilla *f*; '**~ floor** era *f*; '**~ ma·chine** trilladora *f*.

thresh·old ['θreʃhould] umbral *m*;

fig. on the ~ of en los umbrales de, al punto de.
threw [θru:] *pret. of throw* 1.
thrice [θrais] † tres veces.
thrift, thrift·i·ness [ˈθrift(inis)] economía *f*, frugalidad *f*; ˈ**thrift·less** □ malgastador, pródigo; ˈ**thrift·y** □ económico, frugal.
thrill [θril] **1.** emocionar(se), estremecer(se) (*with* de), conmover(se); *be ~ed with* estar cautivado por; **2.** emoción *f*; estremecimiento *m*; sensación *f*; ˈ**thrill·er** F novela *f* (película *f or* pieza *f*) escalofriante; novela *f* policíaca; ˈ**thrill·ing** □ emocionante; apasionante; cautivador.
thrive [θraiv] [*irr.*] medrar, florecer; **thriv·en** [ˈθrivn] *p.p. of thrive*; **thriv·ing** [ˈθraiviŋ] □ floreciente, próspero.
throat [θrout] garganta *f*; cuello *m*; *clear one's ~* aclarar la voz; ˈ**throat·y** □ gutural, ronco.
throb [θrɔb] **1.** latir, palpitar; (*engine*) vibrar; **2.** (*a.* ˈ**throb·bing**) latido *m*, pulsación *f*; vibración *f*.
throes [θrouz] *pl.* agonía *f*, dolores *m/pl.*; F *be in the ~ of* estar luchando con, sufrir todas las molestias de.
throm·bo·sis [θrɔmˈbousis] trombosis *f*.
throne [θroun] trono *m*.
throng [θrɔŋ] **1.** tropel *m*, muchedumbre *f*; **2.** *v/t.* atestar; *v/i.* apiñarse; acudir en tropeles.
throt·tle [ˈθrɔtl] **1.** ahogar, estrangular (*a.* ⊕); **2.** gaznate *m*; ⊕ (= ˈ**~ valve**) regulador *m*, válvula *f* reguladora; *mot.* acelerador *m*.
through [θru:] **1.** *prp.* por; a través de; por medio de, mediante, debido a; hasta (e incluso); **2.** *adv.* de parte a parte; (desde el principio) hasta el fin; *~ and ~* hasta los tuétanos; **3.** *adj. train* directo; F *be ~* haber terminado; haber acabado (*with* con); **~ˈout 1.** *prp.* (*time*) durante todo, en todo; (*place*) por todo; **2.** *adv.* (*time*) todo el tiempo, desde el principio hasta el fin; (*place*) en (*or* por) todas partes; en todo; ˈ**~·way** (*a.* ˈ**thru·way**) carretera *f* troncal.
throve [θrouv] *pret. of thrive*.
throw [θrou] **1.** [*irr.*] echar, lanzar, arrojar, tirar; *bridge* tender; *pot* hacer, dar forma a; *rider* desarzonar; *shadow* proyectar; ⊕ *silk* torcer; F *fight* perder con premeditación; *~ about* esparcir; *money* derrochar; *~ away* echar; malgastar; *chance* desperdiciar; *~ back enemy* arrollar; *offer* rechazar; *~ down ball etc.* echar a tierra; *building* derribar; *challenge* lanzar; *~ in* añadir; dar de más; *ball* sacar; *~ off clothes* quitarse; *burden* sacudirse; deshacerse de; *composition* hacer de prisa, improvisar; *~ out* echar; *p.* poner en la calle; *hint* proferir; *parl. bill* rechazar; *~ over* abandonar; *friend* despedir; *~ up defenses* levantar rápidamente; F vomitar; **2.** tirada *f*, tiro *m*, echada *f*; ˈ**~ˈback** *biol.* reversión *f*; ˈ**~-in** *sport*: saque *m*; **thrown** [θroun] *p.p. of throw*.
thru [θru:] = *through*.
thrum[1] [θrʌm] *weaving*: hilo *m* basto.
thrum[2] [~] ♪ *v/t. guitar* rasguear; *v/i.* teclear.
thrush[1] [θrʌʃ] *orn.* zorzal *m*.
thrush[2] [~] ⚕ ubrera *f*; *vet.* higo *m*.
thrust [θrʌst] **1.** estocada *f of sword*; ⚔ avance *m*; ataque *m*; ⊕ *a. fig.* empuje *m*; **2.** *v/t.* empujar (*forward etc.* hacia adelante *etc.*); *~ aside* rechazar bruscamente; *~ into* clavar en, hincar en; introducir en; *~ out* sacar; *hand* tender; *~ upon* imponer a; *v/i.*: *~ at* asestar un golpe a; *~ forward* seguir adelante; ⚔ avanzar; *~ through* abrirse paso por fuerza.
thud [θʌd] **1.** golpear con ruido sordo; **2.** ruido *m* sordo; (*fall*) baque *m*.
thug [θʌg] asesino *m*; ladrón *m* brutal; hombre *m* brutal, desalmado *m*.
thumb [θʌm] **1.** pulgar *m*; **2.** manosear; (*~ through*) hojear; F *~ a ride* hacer autostop; ˈ**~ in·dex** escalerilla *f*; índice *m* con pestañas; ˈ**~·print** impresión *f* del pulgar; ˈ**~·screw** *hist.* empulgueras *f/pl.*; ⊕ tornillo *m* de orejas; ˈ**~·tack** chinche *m*.
thump [θʌmp] **1.** golpazo *m*; porrazo *m*; **2.** *v/t.* golpear; aporrear; *v/i.* caer *etc.* con golpe pesado; (*heart*) latir con golpes pesados; ˈ**thump·ing** F enorme, grandote.
thun·der [ˈθʌndər] **1.** trueno *m*; *fig.* estruendo *m*; **2.** tronar; *threats etc.* fulminar; ˈ**~·bolt** rayo *m* (*a. fig.*); ˈ**~·clap** tronido *m*; ˈ**~·cloud** nubarrón *m*; ˈ**thun·der·ing** F enorme, imponente; ˈ**thun·der·ous** □ *applause* atronador; ˈ**thun·der-**

storm tronada *f*, tempestad *f* de truenos; **ˈthun·der·struck** *fig*. pasmado, estupefacto; **ˈthun·der·y** tormentoso.

Thurs·day [ˈθəːrzdi] jueves *m*.

thus [ðʌs] así; ~ *far* hasta aquí.

thwack [θwæk] *v. whack*.

thwart [θwɔːrt] **1.** frustrar, impedir, desbaratar; **2.** ⚓ bancada *f*.

thy [ðai] † tu(s).

thyme [taim] tomillo *m*.

thy·roid [ˈθairɔid] **1.** tiroideo; **2.** tiroides *m* (*a.* ~ *gland*).

thy·self [ðaiˈself] † (*subject*) tú mismo, tú misma; *acc.*, *dat.* te; (*after prp.*) ti (mismo, misma).

ti·a·ra [tiˈærə] diadema *f*; *papal* tiara *f*.

tib·i·a [ˈtibiə] tibia *f*.

tic [tik] ⚕ tic *m*.

tick[1] [~] *zo*. garrapata *f*.

tick[2] [~] (*mattress*) funda *f*.

tick[3] [~] **1.** tictac *m of clock*; (*mark*) señal *f*, marca *f*; F momento *m*; F *on* (*or to*) *the* ~ en punto, puntualmente; **2.** *v/i*. hacer tictac; ~ *over mot*. marchar en vacío; *v/t*. poner una señal contra (*a.* ~ *off*); *sl.* ~ *off* enojar a.

tic·ker [ˈtikər] teleimpresor *m*; *sl*. corazón *m*; **ˈtick·er tape** cinta *f* de cotizaciones.

tick·et [ˈtikit] **1.** billete *m*; *S.Am.* boleto *m*; *thea. etc.* entrada *f*, localidad *f*; (*counterfoil*) talón *m*; (*label*) etiqueta *f*, rótulo *m*; F multa *f* (*de conductor*); *parl*. candidatura *f*; F *that's the* ~ eso es lo que hacía falta; **2.** rotular, poner etiqueta a; **ˈ~ col·lec·tor** revisor *m*; **ˈ~ scal·per** revendedor *m* de billetes con mucha ganancia; **ˈ~ win·dow** ventanilla *f*; *thea.* taquilla *f*; 🚂 despacho *m* de billetes.

tick·le [ˈtikl] *v/i*. cosquillear, hacer cosquillas a; (*amuse*) divertir; *v/i.*: *my back* ~*s* siento cosquillas en la espalda; **ˈtick·ler** *radio*: (*or* ~ *coil*) bobina *f* de regeneración; **ˈtick·ling** cosquillas *f/pl.*; **ˈtick·lish** □ cosquilloso; *fig*. peliagudo; F difícil; delicado; *be* ~ tener cosquillas, ser cosquilloso.

tid·al [ˈtaidl] □ de marea; ~ *wave* ola *f* de marea.

tid·bit [ˈtidbit] golosina *f*; bocadito *m*.

tide [taid] **1.** marea *f*; *fig*. corriente *f*; marcha *f*; *low* ~ bajamar *f*; *fig*. punto *m* más bajo; *high* ~ pleamar *f*; *fig.* apogeo *m*; *turn of the* ~ cambio *m* de la marea; *fig*. momento *m* del cambio decisivo; **2.**: *fig*. ~ *over* sacar temporalmente de apuro; **ˈ~·wa·ter 1.** agua *f* de marea; **2.** *adj*. costanero.

ti·di·ness [ˈtaidinis] aseo *m*, buen orden *m*.

ti·dings [ˈtaidiŋz] *pl*. noticias *f/pl.*

ti·dy [ˈtaidi] **1.** □ aseado; ordenado; pulcro; F considerable; **2.** (*a.* ~ *up*) asear; arreglar; poner en orden.

tie [tai] **1.** corbata *f*; lazo *m*; ♪ ligado *m*; ⚠ tirante *m*; *fig*. (*hindrance*) estorbo *m*; (*bond*) vínculo *m*; *sport*, *voting*: empate *m*; (*match*) partido *m*; **2.** *v/t*. atar; liar; enlazar; ♪ *a. fig*. ligar; *tie* hacer; *fig*. (*a.* ~ *down*) limitar, confinar; (*hinder*) estorbar; ~ *up* atar; envolver; *traffic* obstruir; ⚓ atracar; F *business* despachar, arreglar; *v/i. sport etc.*: empatar; ⚓ atracar; **ˈ~·pin** alfiler *m* de corbata.

tier [tir] fila *f*, grada *f*, grado *m*.

tie-up [ˈtaiˈʌp] enlace *m*; paralización *f by strike*; bloqueo *m of traffic*.

tiff [tif] F riña *f* ligera; pique *m*.

ti·ger [ˈtaigər] tigre *m/f*; F persona *f* agresiva; **ˈti·ger·ish** □ *fig*. feroz.

tight [tait] □ apretado; estrecho; *clothes* ajustado; (*taut*) tirante; *box* bien cerrado; *curve* cerrado; *situation* difícil; ✝ *money* escaso; F (*mean*) agarrado; F (*drunk*) borracho; *hold* ~ agarrarse bien; F *sit* ~ estarse quieto; *be in a* ~ *corner* verse en un aprieto; estar en peligro; **ˈtight·en** (*a.* ~ *up*) apretar(se); atiesar(se); estrechar(se); **ˈtight-ˈfist·ed** agarrado; **ˈtight-ˈfit·ting** muy ajustado; **ˈtight-lipped** callado; que sabe guardar secretos; **ˈtight·ness** estrechez *f*; tirantez *f*; **ˈtight·rope walk·er** funámbulo *m*, equilibrista *m/f*; **tights** [~s] *pl*. traje *m* de malla; **ˈtight ˈsqueeze** aprieto *m*; **ˈtight·wad** *sl*. cicatero *m*.

ti·gress [ˈtaigris] tigresa *f*.

tile [tail] **1.** (*roof*) teja *f*; (*floor*) baldosa *f*; (*colored*) azulejo *m*; *sl*. sombrero *m*; *sl. on the* ~*s* de juerga; **2.** *roof* tejar; *floor* embaldosar.

till[1] [til] caja *f* registradora, cajón *m*.

till[2] [~] *prp*. hasta; *cj*. hasta que.

till[3] [~] 🌱 cultivar, labrar; **ˈtill·age** cultivo *m*, labranza *f*.

till·er [ˈtilər] ⚓ caña *f* del timón; 🌱 labrador *m*.

tilt [tilt] **1.** inclinación *f*; ⚔ torneo *m*;

(*at*) *full* ~ a toda velocidad; *on the* ~ inclinado; **2.** inclinar(se), ladear(se); ⚔ justar; ~ *at* arremeter contra.

tim·ber [ˈtimbər] **1.** madera *f* (de construcción); (*beam*) viga *f*; árboles *m/pl.* de monte; ⚓ cuaderna *f*; **2.** enmaderar; ~*ed* enmaderado; *land* arbolado; ˈ**tim·ber·ing** maderamen *m*; ˈ~ **line** límite *m* forestal.

time [taim] **1.** tiempo *m*; hora *f of day*; (*occasion*) vez *f*; época *f*; plazo *m*; horas *f/pl.* de trabajo; ♪ compás *m*; ~! ¡la hora!; ⅍ ~*s* por; ~ *to go* hora *f* de irse; *what is the* ~? ¿qué hora es?; *it is high* ~ *that* ya es hora de que; ~ *after* ~, ~ *and again* repetidas veces; *at a* ~, *at the same* ~ a la vez; *at any* ~ a cualquier hora; *at no* ~ nunca; *at one* ~ en cierta época; había momentos en que ...; *at* ~*s* a veces; *behind* ~ atrasado; *behind the* ~*s* anticuado; *between* ~*s* en los intervalos; *by that* ~ antes de eso; *every* ~! sin excepción; *for the* ~ *being* por ahora; *from* ~ *to* ~ de vez en cuando, con el tiempo; *in* (*good*) ~ (*early*) a tiempo, con tiempo; (*eventually*) andando el tiempo, con el tiempo; *in no* ~ en muy poco tiempo; *on* ~ puntual(mente); *beat* (*or keep*) ~ llevar el compás; F *do* ~ cumplir una condena; *have a bad* ~ pasarlo mal; *have a good* ~ divertirse (mucho); darse buena vida; *have no* ~ *for* no poder aguantar; *keep good* ~ (*clock*) andar bien; *mark* ~ ⚔ llevar el paso; *fig.* hacer tiempo; *take a long* ~ *to* tardar mucho en; *take one's* ~ no darse prisa; *v. mean*; **2.** *race* cronometrar; medir el tiempo de; *watch* regular; *action* hacer a tiempo oportuno; *the train is* ~*d for 5* el tren debe partir (llegar) a las 5; ˈ~ **bomb** bomba-reloj *f*; ˈ~ **ex·po·sure** *phot.* pose *f*; ˈ~-**hon·ored** tradicional, consagrado; ˈ~**·keep·er** reloj *m*; cronómetro *m*; (*p.*) cronometrador *m*; ˈ~**-lag** intervalo *m*; retraso *m*, retardo *m*; ˈ~**·less** eterno; sin limitación de tiempo; ˈ~ ˈ**lim·it** limitación *f* de tiempo; plazo *m*; fecha *f* tope; ˈ**time·ly** oportuno; ˈ**time** ˈ**pay·ment** pago *m* a plazos; ˈ**time·piece** reloj *m*; ˈ**tim·er** reloj *m* de arena; ⊕ reloj *m* automático; ⊕ distribuidor *m* de encendido *in engine*.

time...: ˈ~ ˈ**sig·nal** *radio*: señal *f* horaria; ˈ~**·ta·ble** horario *m*; programa *m*; ˈ~ ˈ**zone** huso *m* horario.

tim·id [ˈtimid] □ tímido; **ti·mid·i·ty** [tiˈmiditi] timidez *f*.

tim·ing [ˈtaimiŋ] medida *f* del tiempo; realización *f etc.* en momento oportuno *of action*; ⊕ cronometraje *m*; ~ *gear* engranaje *m* de distribución.

tim·or·ous [ˈtimərəs] □ temeroso, tímido.

tin [tin] **1.** estaño *m*; (*can*) lata *f*; ⊕ hoja *f* de lata, hojalata *f*; *sl.* parné *m*; **2.** de estaño, de hojalata; F inferior; ~ *hat* F casco *m* de acero; ~*horn sl.* vil y pretencioso; ~ *soldier* soldado *m* de plomo; **3.** ⊕ estañar; *food* conservar en latas; ~*ned meat* carne *f* en lata.

tinc·ture [ˈtiŋktʃər] **1.** tintura *f* (*a. fig.*); *pharm.* tintura *f*; **2.** tinturar, teñir.

tin·der [ˈtindər] yesca *f* (*a. fig.*); ~ *box* yescas *f/pl.*

tine [tain] púa *f*.

tin·foil [ˈtinˈfɔil] papel *m* de estaño.

tinge [tindʒ] **1.** tinte *m*; dejo *m*, matiz *m* (*a. fig.*); **2.** teñir (*with* de); matizar (*with* de) (*a. fig.*).

tin·gle [ˈtiŋgl] **1.** sentir comezón; *fig.* estremecerse (*with* de); **2.** (*a.* ˈ**tingling**) comezón *f*; estremecimiento *m*.

tink·er [ˈtiŋkər] **1.** calderero *m* remendón; **2.** *v/t.* remendar chapuceramente (*a.* ~ *up*); *v/i.*: ~ *with* tratar vanamente de reparar; jugar con; (*spoil*) estropear.

tin·kle [ˈtiŋkl] **1.** (hacer) retiñir; (hacer) campanillear; **2.** (*a.* ˈ**tinkling**) retintín *m*; campanilleo *m*.

tin·ny [ˈtini] ♪ cascado, que suena a lata; F desvencijado; ˈ**tin·plate** hojalata *f*.

tin·sel [ˈtinsl] **1.** oropel *m* (*a. fig.*); **2.** de oropel; **3.** oropelar.

tin·smith [ˈtinˈsmiθ] hojalatero *m*.

tint [tint] **1.** tinte *m*, matiz *m*; media tinta *f*; **2.** teñir, matizar.

tin·tin·nab·u·la·tion [ˈtintinæbjuˈleiʃn] 🕮 campanilleo *m*.

ti·ny [ˈtaini] menudo, diminuto, chiquitín.

tip [tip] **1.** punta *f*, extremidad *f*; casquillo *m of stick etc.*; embocadura *f of cigarette*; (*dump*) escombrera *f*; F (*gratuity*) propina *f*; F aviso *m*; soplo *m*; **2.** inclinar(se), ladear(se); *stick etc.* poner casquillo a; F dar propina (*v/t.* a); F *winner* recomendar; F ~ *off* advertir clandestinamente; ~ *over*, ~ *up* volcar(se); **ˈ~-off** F advertencia *f* clandestina.

tip·ple [ˈtipl] **1.** envasar, empinar el codo; **2.** bebida *f* (alcohólica); **ˈtip·pler** bebedor *m*.

tip·ster [ˈtipstər] pronosticador *m*.

tip·sy [ˈtipsi] □ achispado.

tip·toe [ˈtipˈtou]: *on* ~ de puntillas.

tip·top [ˈtipˈtɔp] F de primera, excelente.

tip-up [ˈtipʌp]: ~ *truck* basculante *m*; ~ *seat* asiento *m* abatible.

ti·rade [taiˈreid] diatriba *f*, invectiva *f*.

tire[1] [ˈtaiər] neumático *m*; llanta *f*; calce *m of metal*; ~ *chain* cadena *f* antirresbaladiza; ~ *pressure* presión *f* de inflado.

tire[2] [~] cansar(se) (*of* de); aburrir(se).

tired [ˈtaiərd] □ cansado (*fig. of* de); ~ *out* rendido; **ˈtired·ness** cansancio *m*.

tire·less [ˈtaiərlis] □ infatigable, incansable.

tire·some [ˈtaiərsəm] □ molesto, fastidioso; aburrido.

ti·ro [ˈtairou] novicio *m*, novato *m*.

tis·sue [ˈtiʃuː] tejido *m* (*a. anat.*); ✝ (*cloth*) tisú *m*; *fig.* sarta *f of lies etc.*; **ˈ~ ˈpa·per** papel *m* de seda.

tit[1] [tit]: ~ *for tat* donde las dan las toman.

tit[2] [~] = *teat*.

tit[3] [~] *orn. mst* herrerillo *m*.

Ti·tan [ˈtaitən] titán *m*; **ti·ta·nic** [~ˈtænik] □ titánico.

tithe [taið] *eccl.* diezmo *m*.

tit·il·late [ˈtitileit] estimular, excitar, titilar; **tit·ilˈla·tion** estimulación *f*, excitación *f*, titilación *f*.

tit·i·vate [ˈtitiveit] F emperejilar(se), ataviar(se).

ti·tle [ˈtaitl] **1.** título *m*; ⚖ título *m* de propiedad; *sport*: campeonato *m*; ~ *to* derecho *m* a; **2.** (in)titular; ~*d* titulado; **ˈ~ deed** título *m* de propiedad; **ˈ~·hold·er** *sport*: campeón *m*, titular *m*; **ˈ~·page** portada *f*; **ˈ~ ˈrole** papel *m* titular.

ti·trate [ˈtitreit] valorar; **tiˈtra·tion** valoración *f*.

tit·ter [ˈtitər] **1.** reírse a disimulo; **2.** risa *f* disimulada.

tit·tle [ˈtitl] *fig.* ápice *m*; partícula *f*.

tit·u·lar [ˈtitjulər] titular; nominal.

to [tuː; *in the sentence mst* tu, *before consonant* tə] **1.** *not translated before infinitive*: *to do* hacer; *I have letters* ~ *write* tengo cartas que escribir; *the book is still* ~ *be written* el libro está todavía por escribir; *I weep* ~ *think of it* lloro con sólo pensar en ello; **2.** *prp.* a; hacia; para; *I am going* ~ *Madrid* (*Spain*) voy a Madrid (España); *the road* ~ *Madrid* el camino de Madrid; *be kind* ~ *him* sé amable con él; ~ *my way of thinking* según mi modo de pensar; *a quarter* ~ *2* las 2 menos cuarto; *he gave it* ~ *me* me lo dio (a mí); *he gave it* ~ *his friend* se lo dio a su amigo; *secretary* ~ secretario de; *here's* ~ *you!* ¡por Vd.!; *from door* ~ *door* de puerta en puerta.

toad [toud] sapo *m*; **ˈ~·stool** hongo *m* (*freq.* venenoso).

toad·y [ˈtoudi] **1.** pelotillero *m*, adulador *m* servil; **2.** adular servilmente (*to* a); **ˈtoad·y·ing, ˈtoad·y·ism** adulación *f* servil.

toast [toust] **1.** pan *m* tostado; tostada *f*; brindis *m* (*to* por); F celebridad *f*; **2.** tostar; *p.* brindar por; **ˈtoast·er** (*electric*) tostadora *f*.

to·bac·co [təˈbækou] tabaco *m*; *smokeless* ~ tabaco *m* sin humo; ~ *pouch* petaca *f*; **toˈbac·co·nist** [~kənist] estanquero *m*, tabaquero *m*; ~*'s* (*shop*) estanco *m*, tabaquería *f*.

to·bog·gan [təˈbɔgən] **1.** tobogán *m*; **2.** deslizarse en tobogán.

toc·sin [ˈtɔksin] campana(da) *f* de alarma.

to·day [təˈdei] hoy; hoy día; *a week from* ~ de hoy en ocho días.

tod·dle [ˈtɔdl] hacer pinos, andar a tatas; F pasearse, irse (*a.* ~ *off*); **ˈtod·dler** pequeñito (a *f*) *m* (que aprende a andar).

tod·dy [ˈtɔdi] ponche *m*.

to-do [təˈduː] F lío *m*, alharaca *f*, alboroto *m*.

toe [tou] **1.** *anat.* dedo *m* del pie; punta *f* del pie; punta *f of sock*; puntera *f of shoe* (*a.* ~ *cap*); **2.** tocar con la punta del pie; ~ *the* (*party*) *line* conformarse; someterse.

tof·fee [ˈtɔfi] caramelo *m*.

to·ga [ˈtougə] toga *f*; ~ *party univ.* fiesta *f* bacanal; bacanal *f*.
to·geth·er [təˈgeðər] **1.** *adj.* juntos; *all* ~ todos juntos; *all* ~! *(pulling)* ¡bien, ahora!; **2.** *adv.* juntamente, junto; a la vez, a un tiempo; ~ *with* junto con.
tog·gle [ˈtɔgl] **1.** cazonete *m* de aparejo; **2.** asegurar con cazonete; ˈ~ ˈ**switch** interruptor *m* a palanca.
togs [tɔgz] *pl.* F ropa *f*.
toil [tɔil] **1.** fatiga *f*; afán *m*; **2.** fatigarse; afanarse.
toi·let [ˈtɔilit] atavío *m*, tocado *m*; lavabo *m*; inodoro *m*; retrete *m*; ˈ~ ˈ**bowl** inodoro *m*; ˈ~ **pa·per,** ˈ~ **roll** rollo *m* de papel higiénico; ˈ~ **set** juego *m* de tocador; ˈ~ **soap** jabón *m* de tocador; ˈ~ ˈ**wa·ter** agua *f* de tocador.
toils [tɔilz] *pl.* red *f*, lazo *m*.
to·ken [ˈtoukən] señal *f*; muestra *f*; prenda *f*; *(coin)* ficha *f*; tanto *m*; *attr.* simbólico; *in (or as a)* ~ *of* en señal de.
told [tould] *pret. a. p.p. of tell*; *all* ~ en total.
tol·er·a·ble [ˈtɔlərəbl] □ tolerable; *(fair)* mediano, regular; ˈ**tol·er·ance** tolerancia *f*; ˈ**tol·er·ant** □ tolerante; **tol·er·ate** [ˈ~reit] tolerar; aguantar; **tol·erˈa·tion** tolerancia *f*.
toll[1] [toul] peaje *m*; pontazgo *m*; *fig.* mortalidad *f*, número *m* de víctimas; *teleph.* ~ *call* conferencia *f* interurbana; *take* ~ *of* causar bajas en, tener su efecto en; ˈ~ **bridge** puente *m* de peaje; ˈ~**·gate** barrera *f* de peaje.
toll[2] [~] *v/i.* doblar (a muerto); *v/t.* tocar (a muerto), tañer, sonar.
tom [tɔm] macho *m* (*esp.* del gato); ˈ~**·cat** gato *m*.
tom·a·hawk [ˈtɔməhɔːk] tomahawk *m*.
to·ma·to [təˈmeitou], *pl.* **toˈma·toes** [~z] tomate *m*.
tomb [tuːm] tumba *f*, sepulcro *m*.
tom·boy [ˈtɔmbɔi] muchacha *f* traviesa; moza *f* retozona.
tomb·stone [ˈtuːmstoun] lápida *f* sepulcral.
tome [toum] tomo *m*; *co.* librote *m*.
tom·fool [ˈtɔmˈfuːl] necio *adj. a. su. m*; **tomˈfool·er·y** pataratas *f/pl.*, payasadas *f/pl.*
tom·my [ˈtɔmi] F soldado *m* inglés; ~ *gun* pistola *f* ametralladora; F ~ *rot* disparates *m/pl.*
to·mor·row [təˈmɔrou] mañana (*a. su. m*); *the day after* ~ pasado mañana.
tom·tom [ˈtɔmtɔm] tantán *m*.
ton [tʌn] tonelada *f*; F ~*s pl.* montones *m/pl.*
to·nal·i·ty [touˈnæliti] tonalidad *f*.
tone [toun] **1.** *all senses*: tono *m*; *radio*: ~ *control* control *m* de tonalidad; **2.** *v/t.* ♪, *paint.* entonar; *phot.* virar; ~ *down* suavizar (el tono de); ~ *up* tonificar, entonar; *fig.* embellecer; *v/i.* armonizar (*in with* con); ~ *down* moderarse.
tongs [tɔŋz] *pl.* (*a pair of* unas) (*sugar-*) tenacillas *f/pl.*; (*coal-*) tenazas *f/pl.*
tongue [tʌŋ] *mst* lengua *f*; ⊕ lengüeta *f* (*a. of scales*); *hold one's* ~ callar(se); *speak with one's* ~ *in one's cheek* hablar irónicamente; ˈ**tongue-tied** de lengua trabada; *fig.* premioso, tímido; ˈ**tongue twist·er** trabalenguas *m*.
ton·ic [ˈtɔnik] **1.** □ tónico; **2.** ♪ tónica *f*; ⚕ tónico *m* (*a. fig.*).
to·night [təˈnait] esta noche.
ton·nage [ˈtʌnidʒ] tonelaje *m*.
ton·ner [ˈtʌnər] de ... toneladas.
ton·sil [ˈtɔnsl] amígdala *f*; **ton·sil·li·tis** [~ˈlaitis] amigdalitis *f*.
ton·sure [ˈtɔnʃər] **1.** tonsura *f*; **2.** tonsurar.
ton·y [ˈtouni] *sl.* mundano; aristocrático, elegante.
too [tuː] demasiado; (*also*) también; ~ *much* demasiado; (*only*) ~ *well* de sobra.
took [tuk] *pret. of take*.
tool [tuːl] **1.** herramienta *f*; utensilio *m*; *fig.* instrumento *m*; (*set of*) ~*s pl.* útiles *m/pl.*, utillaje *m*; **2.** filetear *leather*; ˈ~ **bag,** ˈ~ **kit** herramental *m*, bolsa *f* de herramientas; ˈ~**·box** caja *f* de herramientas.
toot [tuːt] **1.** sonar (*v/i.* la bocina *etc.*); **2.** sonido *m* breve.
tooth [tuːθ] (*pl.* teeth) diente *m*; (*molar*) muela *f*; púa *f of comb*; *false teeth* dentadura *f* postiza; ~ *and nail* encarnizadamente; ˈ~**·ache** dolor *m* (*or* mal *m*) de muelas; ˈ~**·brush** cepillo *m* de dientes; **toothed** [~θt] dentado; con ... dientes; ˈ**tooth·ing** ⚠ adaraja *f*; ˈ**tooth·less** □ desdentado; ˈ**tooth·paste** pasta *f* dentífrica (*or* de dientes); ˈ**tooth·pick** palillo *m*; mondadientes *m*.
tooth·some [ˈtuːθsəm] □ sabroso.

top[1] [tɔp] **1.** cima *f*, cumbre *f*, ápice *m*; cabeza *f of page, list*; copa *f of tree*; remate *m of roof etc.*; coronilla *f of head*; imperial *f of bus*; (*lid*) tapa *f*; capuchón *m of pen*; *mot.* capota *f*; ⚓ cofa *f*; *sl. the* ~*s pl.* la flor de la canela; *at the* ~ *of* a la cabeza de; en la cumbre de; *at the* ~ *of one's voice* a voz en grito; *from* ~ *to bottom* de arriba abajo; de cabo a rabo; *from* ~ *to toe* de pies a cabeza; *on* ~ ganando; de arriba; *on* ~ *of* encima de; *fig.* además de; *fig. on* ~ *of that* por añadidura; **2.** (el) más alto; cimero; *floor* último; *price* tope; *speed* máximo; ~ *banana sl.* jefe *m*; persona *f* principal; ~ *people* la gente bien; **3.** coronar, rematar; *class* estar a la cabeza de; *fig.* superar, aventajar; ✓ descabezar, desmochar; F ~ *off* rematar.

top[2] [~] peonza *f*; peón *m*.

to·paz [ˈtoupæz] topacio *m*.

top·boots [ˈtɔpˈbuːts] botas *f/pl.* de campaña.

top·coat [ˈtɔpkout] sobretodo *m*.

top·er [ˈtoupər] borrachín *m*.

top...: ˈ**~·flight** F sobresaliente; **~-gal·lant** [ˈ~ˈgælənt, ⚓ təˈgælənt] (*or* ~ *sail*) juanete *m*; **~ hat** sombrero *m* de copa; chistera *f*; ˈ**~-ˈheav·y** demasiado pesado por arriba.

top·ic [ˈtɔpik] asunto *m*, tema *m*; ˈ**top·i·cal** □ (de interés) actual, corriente; ⚕ tópico.

top...: ˈ**~·knot** moño *m* (*a. orn.*); F cabeza *f*; ˈ**~·mast** mastelero *m*; ˈ**~·most** (el) más alto; ˈ**~·notch** F sobresaliente.

to·pog·ra·pher [təˈpɔgrefər] topógrafo *m*; **top·o·graph·ic, top·o·graph·i·cal** [tɔpəˈgræfik(l)] □ topográfico; **to·pog·ra·phy** [təˈpɔgrəfi] topografía *f*; **to·po·nym** [ˈtɔpənim] topónimo *m*.

top·per [ˈtɔpər] *sl.* chistera *f*; ˈ**top·ping** F estupendo; de primera; *cake* ~ garapiña *f*.

top·ple [ˈtɔpl] (*mst* ~ *down*, ~ *over*) *v/t.* derribar, volcar; *v/i.* volcar(se), venirse abajo.

top·sail [ˈtɔpsl] gavia *f*.

top-se·cret [ˈtɔpˈsiːkrit] ⚔ de máxima confidencia.

top·sy-tur·vy [ˈtɔpsiˈtəːrvi] trastornado; en desorden.

tor [tɔːr] colina *f* abrupta y rocosa.

torch [tɔːrtʃ] **1.** antorcha *f*; **2.** *sl.* pegar fuego a; ˈ**~·bear·er** portahachón *m*; ˈ**~·light** luz *f* de antorcha; ~ *procession* desfile *m* de portahachones; ˈ**~ song** canción *f* de murria; fado *m*.

tore [tɔːr] *pret. of tear*[1] 1.

tor·ment 1. [ˈtɔːrmənt] tormento *m*; **2.** [tɔːrˈment] atormentar; **torˈmen·tor** atormentador (-a *f*) *m*.

torn [tɔːrn] *p.p. of tear*[1] 1.

tor·na·do [tɔːrˈneidou], *pl.* **torˈna·does** [~z] huracán *m*, tornado *m*.

tor·pe·do [tɔːrˈpiːdou], *pl.* **torˈpe·does** [~z] **1.** *all senses*: torpedo *m*; **2.** torpedear (*a. fig.*); ˈ**~ boat** torpedero *m*; ˈ**~ tube** (tubo *m*) lanzatorpedos *m*.

tor·pid [ˈtɔːrpid] □ aletargado, inactivo; *fig.* torpe, entorpecido; **torˈpid·i·ty, ˈtor·pid·ness, tor·por** [ˈtɔːrpər] letargo *m*; *fig.* torpeza *f*, entorpecimiento *m*.

torque [tɔːrk] par *m* de torsión; ~ *converter mot.* convertidor *m* de par.

tor·rent [ˈtɔrənt] torrente *m* (*a. fig.*); **tor·ren·tial** [tɔˈrenʃl] □ torrencial.

tor·rid [ˈtɔrid] tórrido; ~ *zone* zona *f* tórrida.

tor·sion [ˈtɔːrʃn] torsión *f*; ˈ**tor·sion·al** torsional.

tor·so [ˈtɔːrsou] torso *m*.

tort [tɔːrt] agravio *m*.

tor·toise [ˈtɔːrtəs] tortuga *f*; ˈ**~·shell** carey *m*.

tor·tu·ous [ˈtɔːrtjuəs] □ tortuoso (*a. fig.*); *p.* torcido.

tor·ture [ˈtɔːrtʃər] **1.** tortura *f*; **2.** (a)tormentar; torturar; *fig.* torcer, violentar; ˈ**tor·tur·er** verdugo *m*.

To·ry [ˈtɔːri] tory *adj. a. su. m/f*, conservador *adj. a. su. m* (-a *f*).

toss [tɔs] **1.** meneo *m*, sacudida *f of head*; cogida *f by bull*; caída *f from horse*; echada *f of coin*; *argue the* ~ insistir con tesón; *it's a* ~ *up* puede ser lo uno tanto como lo otro; *win the* ~ ganar el sorteo; **2.** *v/t.* echar, tirar; lanzar al aire; agitar, menear; sacudir; *head* levantar airosamente; (*bull*) coger; mantear *in blanket*; *coin* echar a cara o cruz (*a.* ~ *up*); ~ *off drink* beber de un trago; *v/i.* agitarse; (~ *and turn*) revolverse *in bed*; ~ *up* jugar a cara o cruz (*for acc.*); *sport*: sortear (*for acc.*).

tot [tɔt] (*child*) nene (a *f*) *m*, párvulo *m*.

to·tal [ˈtoutl] **1.** □ total; **2.** total *m*; *sum* ~ (*of people*) colectividad *f*; **3.** *v/t.*

sumar; *v/i.* ascender a; **to·tal·i·tar·i·an** [ˈtoutæliˈteriən] totalitario; **ˈto·tal·iˈtar·i·an·ism** totalitarismo *m*; **toˈtal·i·ty** totalidad *f*; **To·tal·i·za·tor** [ˈ~təlәzeitәr] totalizador *m*; **to·tal·ize** [ˈ~təlaiz] totalizar; **to·tal wreck** [ˈ~ ˈrek] F automóvil *m* (*etc.*) hecho una ruina.

tote [tout] F llevar, acarrear; ~ *bag* bolsa *f* espaciosa.

tot·ter [ˈtɔtәr] tambalear(se); estar para desplomarse; **ˈtot·ter·ing** □, **ˈtot·ter·y** tambaleante; ruinoso.

touch [tʌtʃ] **1.** *v/t.* tocar; palpar; (*reach*) alcanzar; *food* tomar, probar; *emotions* conmover, enternecer; (*equal*) compararse con, igualar; *sl.* dar un sablazo a (*for* para sacar); ~ *off* hacer estallar (*a. fig.*); ~ *up* retocar (*a. phot.*); *v/i.* estar contiguo; tocarse; pasar rozando; ⚓ ~ *at* tocar en, hacer escala en; ~ *on* aludir brevemente a; **2.** tacto *m*; toque *m*; contacto *m*; ♪ pulsación *f*; *paint.* pincelada *f*; (*master's*) mano *f*; ⚕ ataque *m* leve; *fig.* rasgo *m*; *fig.* poquito *m*; *sport*: touche *f*; *in(to)* ~ fuera; *a* ~ *of the sun* una insolación; *be in* ~ (*with*) *th.* estar al tanto (de); *be in* ~ *with p.* estar en comunicación con; *get into* ~ *with* ponerse en contacto con; *keep in* ~ *with p.* mantener relaciones con; *th.* mantenerse al corriente de; **ˈ~-and-ˈgo 1.** difícil; dudoso; delicado; **2.:** *it's* ~ está en un vilo (*whether* si); **touched** conmovido; F chiflado; **ˈtouch·i·ness** susceptibilidad *f*; **ˈtouch·ing 1.** □ conmovedor; **2.** *prp.* tocante a; **ˈtouch·stone** piedra *f* de toque (*a. fig.*); **ˈtouch ˈtyp·ing** mecanografía *f* al tacto; **ˈtouch·y** □ quisquilloso, susceptible.

tough [tʌf] **1.** duro; resistente; tenaz; *meat* estropajoso; *task* difícil; *journey* arduo; F *luck* malo; F *p.* duro; malvado; criminal; **2.** F *esp.* machote *m*; gorila *m*; pendenciero *m*; criminal *m*; **ˈtough·en** endurecer; **ˈtough·ness** dureza *f*; tenacidad *f*; dificultad *f*.

tour [tur] **1.** viaje *m* (largo); excursión *f*; vuelta *f*; *sport etc.*: jira *f*, gira *f*; *on* ~ en jira; de viaje; **2.** *v/t.* viajar por, recorrer; *v/i.* viajar (de turista); **ˈtour·er** coche *m* de turismo; **ˈtour·ing 1.** turismo *m*; **2.** turístico; ~ *car* coche *m* de turismo; **ˈtour·ist** turista *m/f*; ~ *agency* agencia *f* de viajes; ~ *class* clase *f* turista, tarifa *f* turística.

tour·na·ment [ˈturnәmәnt], **tour·ney** [ˈturni] torneo *m*; concurso *m*.

tout [taut] **1.** (*agent*) gancho *m*; (*ticket*) revendedor *m*; *racing*: pronosticador *m*; **2.** solicitar (*v/i.* clientes; *for acc.*).

tow¹ [tou] **1.** (*on* a) remolque *m*; *take in* ~ dar remolque a; **2.** remolcar, llevar al remolque.

tow² [~] estopa *f*.

tow·age [ˈtouidʒ] (derechos *m/pl.* de) remolque *m*.

to·ward(s) [tɔːrd(z)] hacia; (*attitude*) para con; (*time*) cerca de.

tow·boat [ˈtoubout] remolcador *m*; **ˈtow·car** = *tow truck*.

tow·el [ˈtauәl] **1.** toalla *f*; **2.** sacar con toalla; **ˈ~ rack** toallero *m*.

tow·er [ˈtauәr] **1.** torre *f*; (*church*) campanario *m*; **2.** elevarse, encumbrarse; ~ *above*, ~ *over* dominar; *fig.* descollar entre; **ˈtow·er·ing** □ encumbrado; *rage* muy violento.

tow·line [ˈtoulain] sirga *f*.

town [taun] ciudad *f*; población *f*; pueblo *m*; ~ *clerk* secretario *m* particular del ayuntamiento; ~ *council* ayuntamiento *m*, concejo *m* municipal; ~ *councillor* concejal *m*; ~ *hall* ayuntamiento *m*, casa *f* consistorial; ~ *meeting* reunión *f* de los ciudadanos; *new* ~ poblado *m* de absorción; **ˈ~ ˈplan·ning** urbanismo *m*.

towns·folk [ˈtaunzfouk], **ˈtowns·peo·ple** ciudadanos *m/pl.*

town·ship [ˈtaunʃip] municipio *m*, término *m* municipal.

towns·man [ˈtaunzmәn] ciudadano *m*; vecino *m*.

tow·path [ˈtoupæθ] camino *m* de sirga.

tow·rope [ˈtouroup] sirga *f*; cable *m* de remolque; **ˈtow truck** camión-grúa *m*.

tox·ic [ˈtɔksik] □ tóxico; ~ *shock syndrome* síndrome *m* del choque tóxico; **tox·in** [ˈtɔksin] toxina *f*.

toy [tɔi] **1.** juguete *m*; chuchería *f*; **2.** *attr.* de jugar; muy pequeño; *dog* miniatura; **3.:** ~ *with* jugar con; *food* comer melindrosamente; *idea* acariciar; *affections* divertirse con; **ˈ~shop** juguetería *f*.

trace¹ [treis] **1.** huella *f*, rastro *m*; vestigio *m*; (*small amount*) pizca *f*; ~ *element* elemento *m* en rastro; **2.**

rastrear; (*find*) encontrar, averiguar el paradero de; *curve etc.* trazar; *drawing* calcar; ~ *back to* hacer remontar a; ~ *to* rastrear hasta llegar a.

trace[2] [~] tirante *m*; *kick over the* ~*s* rebelarse.

tra·cer [ˈtreisər] *phys. etc.* trazador; ~ *bullet* bala *f* trazadora; ˈ**trac·er·y** △ tracería *f*.

tra·che·a [ˈtreikiə] tráquea *f*.

trac·ing [ˈtreisiŋ] calco *m*; ˈ~ **pa·per** papel *m* transparente.

track [træk] **1.** huella *f*; *hunt.*, *sport*: pista *f*; (*path*) senda *f*, camino *m*; 🚂 vía *f*; ✈ *etc.* trayectoria *f*; (*wheel*) rodada *f*; ⊕ llanta *f* de oruga; ~ *events pl.* atletismo *m* en pista; *off the* ~ despistado; *be on s.o.'s* ~*s* andar a los alcances de alguien; *keep* ~ *of fig.* estar al tanto de; **2.** (*a.* ~ *down*) rastrear; averiguar el origen de; ˈ**track·er** rastreador *m*; ~ *dog* perro *m* rastrero; ˈ**track·ing** seguimiento *m of space vehicles*; ~ *station* estación *f* de seguimiento; ˈ**track·less** sin caminos; ˈ**track meet** concurso *m* de carreras y saltos.

tract[1] [trækt] región *f* (*a. anat.*); extensión *f*; *digestive* ~ canal *m* digestivo; *respiratory* ~ vías *f*/*pl.* respiratorias.

tract[2] [~] tratado *m*; folleto *m*.

trac·ta·ble [ˈtræktəbl] □ tratable, dócil; ⊕ dúctil, maleable.

trac·tion [ˈtrækʃn] tracción *f*; ~ *engine* locomóvil *m*; ˈ**trac·tive** tractivo; ˈ**trac·tor** tractor *m*; ~-*trailer* tractocamión *m*.

trade [treid] **1.** comercio *m*; industria *f*; negocio *m*; (*calling*) oficio *m*; *by* ~ de oficio; **2.** *v*/*i.* comerciar (*in* en, *with* con); F ~ *on* aprovecharse de, explotar; *v*/*t.* trocar, cambiar (*for* por); ~ *in* dar como parte del pago; ˈ~ **fair** feria *f* de muestras; ˈ~**-in** trueque *m*; canje *m*; ˈ~**·mark** marca *f* registrada; ˈ~ **name** razón *f* social; nombre *m* de fábrica; ˈ~ **price** precio *m* al por mayor; ˈ**trad·er** comerciante *m*, traficante *m*; ˈ**trade school** escuela *f* de artes y oficios; ˈ**trades·man** tendero *m*; artesano *m*; ~*'s entrance* puerta *f* de servicio; ˈ**trades·peo·ple** tenderos *m*/*pl.*; ˈ**trade un·ion** sindicato *m*; gremio *m*; *attr.* sindical, gremial; **trade** ˈ**un·ion·ism** sistema *m* de sindicatos, sindicalismo *m*; **trade** ˈ**un·ion·ist** miembro *m* de un sindicato, sindicalista *m*/*f*.

trade winds [ˈtreid windz] *pl.* vientos *m*/*pl.* alisios.

trad·ing [ˈtreidiŋ] comercial; mercantil; ~ *post* factoría *f*.

tra·di·tion [trəˈdiʃn] tradición *f*; **traˈdi·tion·al** □ tradicional.

traf·fic [ˈtræfik] **1.** (*trade, mot. etc.*) tráfico *m*; (*mot. etc.*) circulación *f*; (*trade*) comercio *m*; *b.s.* trata *f* (*in* de); *v. jam*; ~ *control* regulación *f* de tráfico; ~ *lights pl.* señales *f*/*pl.* luminosas, luces *f*/*pl.* de tráfico; **2.** traficar (*in* en); *b.s.* tratar (*in* en); ˈ**traf·fick·er** traficante *m*.

tra·ge·di·an [trəˈdʒiːdiən] trágico *m*; **trag·e·dy** [ˈtrædʒidi] tragedia *f*.

trag·ic [ˈtrædʒik] □ trágico.

trail [treil] **1.** rastro *m*, pista *f*; cola *f*; estela *f*; (*path*) sendero *m*; **2.** *v*/*t.* rastrear; seguir la pista de; (*drag*) arrastrar; *arms* bajar; *v*/*i.* arrastrar(se) (*a.* ⚘); (*be last*) rezagarse; ~ *away*, ~ *off* ir desapareciendo; ˈ**trail·er** *mot. etc.* remolque *m*; *film*: tráiler *m*; ⚘ planta *f* rastrera.

train [trein] **1.** 🚂 tren *m*; (*following*) séquito *m*; recua *f of mules*; cola *f of dress*; reguero *m of powder*; hilo *m of thought*; *by* ~ en tren, por ferrocarril; *in* ~ en preparación; **2.** adiestrar(se) (*a.* ⚔); preparar; *child etc.* enseñar; *voice etc.* educar; *sport*: entrenar(se); *gun* apuntar (*on* a); *plant* guiar; F 🚂 ir en tren; **trainˈee** *approx.* aprendiz *m* (*esp.* profesional); aspirante *m*; ˈ**train·er** *sport*: entrenador *m* (*a.* ✈); (*circus*) domador *m*.

train·ing [ˈtreiniŋ] educación *f*; preparación *f*; instrucción *f*; orientación *f*; *sport*: entrenamiento *m*; *physical* ~ gimnasia *f*; ˈ~ **col·lege** escuela *f* normal; ˈ~ **ship** buque-escuela *m*.

traipse [treips] andar sin cuidado o dirección.

trait [trei(t)] rasgo *m*.

trai·tor [ˈtreitər] traidor *m*; *be a* ~ *to* traicionar *acc.*; ˈ**trai·tor·ous** □ traidor; traicionero.

tra·jec·to·ry [trəˈdʒektəri] trayectoria *f*.

tram [træm] (*a.* ~*car*) tranvía *m*.

tram·mel [ˈtræml] **1.** ~*s pl. fig.* trabas *f*/*pl.*, impedimento *m*; **2.** poner trabas a, impedir.

tramp [træmp] **1.** marcha *f* pesada *of feet*; paseo *m* largo, excursión *f* a pie; (*p.*) vagabundo *m*; ⚓ (*a.* ~ *steamer*) vapor *m* volandero, mercante *m*; **2.** *v/i.* marchar pesadamente; viajar a pie; *v/t.* pisar con fuerza; recorrer a pie; **tram·ple** ['~l] *v/i.* patullar; *v/t.* (*a.* ~ *on*, ~ *underfoot*) pisar, hollar, pisotear.

tram·way ['træmwei] tranvía *m*.

trance [træns] éxtasis *m*; arrobamiento *m*; (*spiritualist's*) estado *m* hipnótico, trance *m*.

tran·quil ['træŋkwil] □ tranquilo; **'tran·quil·ize** tranquilizar; **'tran·quil·iz·er** calmante *m*; **tran'quil·li·ty** tranquilidad *f*.

trans·act [træn'zækt] llevar a cabo; tramitar; despachar; **trans'ac·tion** negocio *m*, transacción *f*; tramitación *f*; ~s *pl.* memorias *f/pl.*, actas *f/pl.* *of society*.

trans·at·lan·tic ['trænzət'læntik] transatlántico.

tran·scend [træn'send] exceder, superar; **tran'scend·ence, tran'scend·en·cy** [~dəns(i)] superioridad *f*; *phls.* tra(n)scendencia *f*; **tran'scend·ent** □ superior; sobresaliente; *a.* = **tran·scen·den·tal** [~'dentl] □ *phls.* tra(n)scendental.

tran·scribe [træns'kraib] transcribir.

tran·script ['trænskript] trasunto *m*; *univ.* certificado *m* de estudios; **tran'scrip·tion** transcripción *f*.

tran·sept ['trænsept] crucero *m*.

trans·fer 1. ['trænsfər, træns'fə:r] *v/t.* transferir (*a.* ⚖); trasladar; transbordar; *player* traspasar; *v/i.* trasladarse *to post*; cambiar (*de tren etc.*); **2.** ['trænsfər] transferencia *f* (*a.* ⚖), traspaso *m* (*a.* ✝, *sport*); transbordo *m*; traslado *m to post*; (*picture*) cromo *m*, calcomanía *f*; billete *m* de transferencia; **trans'fer·a·ble** □ transferible; *not* ~ inalienable; **trans·fer·ee** [~fə'ri:] ⚖ cesionario (a *f*) *m*; **trans·fer·ence** ['~fərəns] transferencia *f*; **trans'fer·or** ⚖ cesionista *m/f*.

trans·fig·u·ra·tion [trænsfigju'reiʃn] transfiguración *f*; **trans·fig·ure** [~'figər] transfigurar.

trans·fix [træns'fiks] traspasar, espetar; ~*ed fig.* atónito, pasmado (*with* de).

trans·form [træns'fɔ:rm] transformar; **trans·for·ma·tion** [~fər'meiʃn] transformación *f*; **trans·form·er** [~'fɔ:rmər] ⚡ transformador *m*.

trans·fuse [træns'fju:z] transfundir; *blood* hacer una transfusión de; *fig.* impregnar (*with* de); **trans'fu·sion** [~ʒn] (*esp.* ⚕) transfusión *f*.

trans·gress [træns'gres] *v/t.* violar, transgredir, traspasar; *v/i.* cometer transgresión; pecar; **trans·gres·sion** [~'greʃn] transgresión *f*; **trans·gres·sor** [~'gresər] transgresor (-a *f*) *m*.

tran·ship [træn'ʃip] transbordar; **tran'ship·ment** transbordo *m*.

tran·sience, tran·sien·cy ['trænʃəns(i)] lo pasajero; **tran·sient** ['trænziənt] **1.** pasajero, transitorio; **2.** transeúnte *m*.

tran·sis·tor [træn'sistər] ⚡ transistor *m*; **tran'sis·tor·ize** transistorizar.

trans·it ['trænsit] tránsito *m*; *in* ~ de (*or* en) tránsito.

tran·si·tion [træn'siʒn] transición *f*, paso *m*; **tran'si·tion·al** □ transicional, de transición.

tran·si·tive ['trænsitiv] □ transitivo.

tran·si·to·ry ['trænsitɔri] transitorio.

trans·late [træns'leit] traducir (*into* a); trasladar *to post*; **trans'la·tion** traducción *f*; **trans'la·tor** traductor (-a *f*) *m*.

trans·lu·cence, trans·lu·cen·cy [trænz'lu:sns(i)] translucidez *f*; **trans'lu·cent** □ translúcido.

trans·mi·grate ['trænzmaigreit] transmigrar; **trans·mi'gra·tion** transmigración *f*.

trans·mis·si·ble [trænz'misəbl] transmisible; **trans'mis·sion** *all senses*: transmisión *f*; *microwave* ~ emisión *f* en microonda.

trans·mit [trænz'mit] *all senses*: transmitir; **trans'mit·ter** transmisor *m*; *radio*: emisora *f*; **trans'mit·ting sta·tion** estación *f* transmisora.

trans·mog·ri·fy [trænz'mɔgrifai] F transformar (como por encanto).

trans·mut·a·ble [trænz'mju:təbl] □ transmutable; **trans·mu'ta·tion** transmutación *f*; *biol.* transformismo *m*; **trans·mute** [~'mju:t] transmutar.

tran·som ['trænsəm] travesaño *m*.

trans·par·en·cy [træns'perənsi] transparencia *f*; **trans'par·ent** □ transparente (*a. fig.*).

tran·spire [træns'paiər] transpirar; *fig.* revelarse, divulgarse; F tener lugar, acontecer; *it* ~*s that* se desprende que.

trans·plant [træns'plænt] **1.** trasplantar; **2.** trasplante *m.*
trans·port 1. [træns'pɔ:rt] transportar (*a. fig.*); **2.** ['trænspɔ:rt] *all senses*: transporte *m*; **trans'port·a·ble** transportable; **trans·por'ta·tion** transportación *f*; transporte(s) *m(pl.)*; ⚖ deportación *f.*
trans·pose [træns'pouz] transponer; ♪ transportar; **trans·po·si·tion** [~pə'ziʃn] transposición *f* (*a.* ♪).
trans·ship [træns'ʃip] transbordar.
tran·sub·stan·ti·ate [trænsəb'stænʃieit] transubstanciar; **'tran·sub·stan·ti'a·tion** transubstanciación *f.*
trans·ver·sal [trænz'və:rsl] □ (♣ línea *f*) transversal; **trans·verse** ['~və:rs] □ transverso, transversal.
trans·ves·tite [trænz'vestait] transvestido *adj. a. su. m/f*; **trans'ves·tism** transvestismo *m.*
trap [træp] **1.** trampa *f*; ⊕ bombillo *m*, sifón *m*; *sl.* boca *f*; ~*s pl.* equipaje *m*, cosas *f/pl.*; **2.** entrampar; atrapar; coger (en una trampa); hacer caer en el lazo; **'trap'door** trampa *f*; *thea.* escotillón *m.*
tra·peze [trə'pi:z] trapecio *m*; **trap·e·zoid** ['træpizɔid] trapezoide *m.*
trap·per ['træpər] cazador *m.*
trap·pings ['træpiŋz] *pl.* arreos *m/pl.*, jaeces *m/pl.*; *fig.* adornos *m/pl.*
trash [træʃ] pacotilla *f*, hojarasca *f*, cachivaches *m/pl.*; **'trash·y** □ cursi; baladí, despreciable.
trav·ail ['træveil] † *or lit.* **1.** dolores *m/pl.* del parto; afán *m*; *be in* ~ = **2.** estar de parto; afanarse.
trav·el ['trævl] **1.** *v/i.* viajar (*a.* ✈); ir *at a speed*; (*wine etc.*) poderse transportar; F ir a gran velocidad; ⊕ ~ *along etc.* correr por; *v/t.* recorrer; viajar por; **2.** viaje(s) *m(pl.)*; el viajar; ⊕ recorrido *m*; **'trav·el·er** viajero (a *f*) *m*; ✈ viajante *m*, agente *m* viajero *S.Am.*; ~*'s check* cheque *m* de viajeros; **'trav·el·ing** *salesman* ambulante; *rug etc.* de viaje; *crane* corredizo.
trav·e·log(ue) ['trævəlɔg] película *f* de (*or* conferencia *f* sobre) viajes.
trav·erse ['trævə:rs] **1.** *mount.* camino *m* oblicuo; ⊕ travesaño *m*; ⚔ través *m*; **2.** atravesar, cruzar; recorrer; ⚔ mover lateralmente.
trav·es·ty ['trævisti] **1.** parodia *f* (*a. fig.*); **2.** parodiar.
trawl [trɔ:l] **1.** red *f* barredera; **2.** rastrear, pescar a la rastra; **'trawl·er** barco *m* rastreador.
tray [trei] bandeja *f*; *phot. etc.* cubeta *f.*
treach·er·ous ['tretʃərəs] □ traidor, traicionero; *fig.* engañoso, incierto; *ground* movedizo; **'treach·er·y** traición *f.*
trea·cle ['tri:kl] melado *m*, melaza *f.*
tread [tred] **1.** [*irr.*] *v/i.* andar; poner el pie; ~ (*up*)*on* pisar; *v/t.* pisar, pisotear (*a.* ~ *down*); **2.** pisada *f*; paso *m*; huella *f of stair*; huella *f*, rodaje *m*, (banda *f* de) rodamiento *m of tire*; suela *f of shoe*; **trea·dle** ['~l] **1.** pedal *m*; **2.** pedalear; **tread·mill** ['~mil] rueda *f* de andar.
trea·son ['tri:zn] traición *f*; **'trea·son·a·ble** □ traidor.
treas·ure ['treʒər] **1.** tesoro *m*; ~ *trove* tesoro *m* hallado; **2.** atesorar (*a.* ~ *up*); apreciar mucho; guardar como un tesoro; **'treas·ur·er** tesorero *m.*
treas·ur·y ['treʒəri] tesoro *m*, tesorería *f*; ♀, ♀ *Department* Ministerio *m* de Hacienda; ~ *bill* vale *m* de la Hacienda; ~ *note* bono *m* del Ministerio de Hacienda.
treat [tri:t] **1.** *v/t.* tratar; (*invite*) convidar (*to* a); *v/i.*: ~ *of* tratar de, versar sobre; ~ *with* negociar con, tratar con; **2.** placer *m*, alegría *f*; recompensa *f* (especial); convite *m*, extraordinario *m*; F *it's my* ~ invito yo; **trea·tise** ['~iz] tratado *m*; **'treat·ment** tratamiento *m*; **'trea·ty** tratado *m.*
tre·ble ['trebl] **1.** □ triple; ♪ de tiple; ~ *clef* clave *f* de sol; **2.** ♪ tiple *m/f*; **3.** triplicar(se).
tree [tri:] **1.** árbol *m*; *v. family*; F *up a* ~ en un aprieto; **2.** ahuyentar por un árbol; **'tree·less** pelado, sin árboles.
tre·foil ['trefɔil] trébol *m* (*a.* ♣).
trek [trek] **1.** emigrar; viajar; F ir (a desgana); **2.** migración *f*; (*day's*) jornada *f*; F viaje *m* largo y aburrido.
trel·lis ['trelis] **1.** enrejado *m*, espaldar *m*; **2.** proveer de enrejado.
trem·ble ['trembl] **1.** temblar, estremecerse (*at* ante, *with* de); **2.** temblor *m*, estremecimiento *m.*
tre·men·dous [tri'mendəs] □ tremendo, formidable, imponente (*all a.* F).

trem·or ['tremər] temblor *m*; vibración *f*; *without a* ~ sin conmoverse.
trem·u·lous ['tremjuləs] □ trémulo; tímido.
trench [trentʃ] **1.** zanja *f*, foso *m*; ⚔ trinchera *f*; ~ *warfare* guerra *f* de trincheras; **2.** zanjar; hacer zanjas *etc.* en; ⚔ atrincherar; ⚒ excavar, remover; '**trench·ant** □ mordaz, incisivo, agudo; **trench coat** trinchera *f*.
trench·er ['trentʃər] tajadero *m*; '**trench·er·man:** *be a good* ~ tener siempre buen apetito.
trend [trend] **1.** tendencia *f*; dirección *f*; marcha *f*; **2.** tender; '**trend·y** de (última) moda.
trep·i·da·tion [trepi'deiʃn] turbación *f*, agitación *f*.
tres·pass ['trespəs] **1.** intrusión *f*, entrada *f* sin derecho; violación *f*; *eccl.* pecado *m*; **2.** entrar sin derecho (*on* en); penetrar en finca ajena; ~ *upon* violar; *fig.* abusar de; ~ *against* pecar contra; *no* ~*ing* prohibida la entrada; '**tres·pass·er** intruso (a *f*) *m*; ~*s will be prosecuted* se procederá contra los intrusos.
tress [tres] trenza *f*.
tres·tle ['tresl] caballete *m*; ~ *bridge* puente *m* de caballetes.
tri·ad ['traiəd] tríada *f*.
tri·al ['traiəl] prueba *f*, ensayo *m*; *fig.* aflicción *f*, adversidad *f*; ⚖ proceso *m*, juicio *m*, vista *f* de una causa; F molestia *f*; ~*s sport*, ⊕ *etc.*: pruebas *f/pl.*; *on* ~ a prueba; ⚖ en juicio; ~ *of strength* lucha *f*; ~ *and error* tanteo *m*; *give s.t. a* ~ ensayar, poner a prueba; *bring to* ~, *put on* ~ procesar, encausar; ~ **run**, ~ **trip** viaje *m* de ensayo.
tri·an·gle ['traiæŋgl] triángulo *m* (*a.* ♪); **tri·an·gu·lar** [~'æŋgjulər] □ triangular; **tri'an·gu·late** [~leit] triangular.
trib·al ['traibl] □ tribal; **tribe** [traib] tribu *f* (*a. zo.*); *contp.* tropel *m*; ralea *f*; **tribes·man** ['~zmən] miembro *m* de una tribu.
trib·u·la·tion [tribju'leiʃn] tribulación *f*.
tri·bu·nal [trai'bju:nl] tribunal *m* (*a. fig.*); **trib·une** ['tribju:n] tribuna *f*; (*p.*) tribuno *m*.
trib·u·tar·y ['tribjutəri] **1.** □ tributario; **2.** tributario *m*; (*river*) afluente *m*; **trib·ute** ['~bju:t] tributo *m*; *fig.* homenaje *m*; elogio *m*.
trice [trais]: *in a* ~ en un santiamén.
trick [trik] **1.** engaño *m*; truco *m*; burla *f*; trampa *f*; maña *f*; (*harmless*) travesura *f*; (*illusion*) ilusión *f*; (*conjuring*) juego *m* de manos; peculiaridad *f of style etc.*; *cards*: baza *f*; *dirty* ~ faena *f*, mala pasada *f*; ~ *photography* trucaje *m*; ~ *question* pregunta *f* de pega; **2.** engañar, trampear, burlar; ~ *into ger.* lograr con engaños que *subj.*; *be* ~*ed into ger.* dejarse persuadir por engaños a *inf.*; ~ *out of* estafar *acc.*; '**trick·er·y** astucia *f*; fraude *m*; malas artes *f/pl.*; **trick·ster** ['~stər] estafador *m*; burlador *m*.
trick·le ['trikl] **1.** gotear, escurrir; *fig.* salir *etc.* poco a poco; **2.** hilo *m*, chorro *m* delgado.
trick·y ['triki] □ *p.* tramposo; astuto, *situation etc.* delicado, difícil.
tri·col·or ['trikələr] bandera *f* tricolor.
tri·cy·cle ['traisikl] triciclo *m*.
tri·dent ['traidənt] tridente *m*.
tri·en·ni·al [trai'enjəl] □ trienal.
tri·fle ['traifl] **1.** friolera *f*, bagatela *f*, fruslería *f*; *fig.* pizca *f*; *cooking*: dulce *m* de bizcocho borracho *etc.*; **2.** *v/i.* chancear; jugar (*with* con); *v/t.*: ~ *away* malgastar; '**tri·fler** persona *f* frívola.
tri·fling ['traifliŋ] □ insignificante, fútil.
tri·fo·cal [trai'foukl] **1.** trifocal; **2.** lente *f* trifocal.
trig·ger ['trigər] **1.** gatillo *m*; ⊕ disparador *m*; **2.** iniciar; *fig.* provocar.
trig·o·no·met·ric, trig·o·no·met·ri·cal [trigənə'metrik(l)] □ trigonométrico; **trig·o·nom·e·try** [~'nɔmitri] trigonometría *f*.
tri·lin·gual ['trai'liŋgwəl] □ trilingüe.
trill [tril] **1.** trino *m* (*a.* ♪), gorjeo *m*; ♪ quiebro *m*; vibración *f of R*; **2.** trinar, gorjear; *R* pronunciar con vibración.
tril·lion ['triljən] trillón *m*; un millón de millones.
trim [trim] **1.** □ elegante; aseado; en buen estado; **2.** disposición *f*; (buena) condición *f*; recorte *m of hair etc.*; asiento *m of boat*; orientación *f of sails*; **3.** arreglar; ajustar;

componer; (re)cortar; ✓ podar; *boat* equilibrar; *sails* orientar; *dress* adornar, guarnecer (*with* de); *lamp* despabilar; *wood* alisar; ˈ**trim·ming** guarnición *f*, adorno *m*; orla *f*; ~*s pl.* recortes *m/pl.*; accesorios *m/pl.*; *contp.* arrequives *m/pl.*; ˈ**trim·ness** buen orden *m*; elegancia *f*.

Trin·i·ty [ˈtriniti] Trinidad *f*.

trin·ket [ˈtriŋkit] dije *m*; *contp.* ~*s pl.* baratijas *f/pl.*, chucherías *f/pl.*

tri·o [ˈtriːou] trío *m*.

trip [trip] **1.** excursión *f*; viaje *m*; tropiezo *m*, zancadilla *f with foot*; ⊕ trinquete *m*, disparo *m*; ego ~ *sl.* acción *f* vanidosa; **2.** *v/i.* tropezar (*on, over* en); ir (*or* correr *etc.*) con paso ligero; *v/i.* (*mst* ~ *up*) echar la zancadilla a; hacer tropezar; *fig.* coger en una falta.

tri·par·tite [ˈtraiˈpɑːrtait] tripartito.

tripe [traip] tripa *f* (*mst* ~*s pl.*); *cooking*: callos *m/pl.*; *sl.* tonterías *f/pl.*

tri·phase [ˈtraiˈfeiz] ⚡ trifásico.

trip·li·cate **1.** [ˈtriplikit] (*in* por) triplicado; **2.** [ˈ~keit] triplicar.

tri·pod [ˈtraipɔd] trípode *m*.

trip·per [ˈtripər] F excursionista *m/f* (de un día); ˈ**trip·ping** ☐ ligero, ágil.

trip·tych [ˈtriptik] tríptico *m*.

tri·sect [traiˈsekt] trisecar.

tris·yl·lab·ic [ˈtraisiˈlæbik] ☐ trisílabo; **tri·syl·la·ble** [ˈ~ˈsiləbl] trisílabo *m*.

trite [trait] ☐ trillado, trivial, vulgar; ˈ**trite·ness** trivialidad *f*, vulgaridad *f*.

tri·umph [ˈtraiəmf] **1.** triunfo *m*; **2.** triunfar (*over* de); **tri·um·phal** [~ˈʌmfəl] triunfal; ~ *arch* arco *m* triunfal; **triˈum·phant** ☐ triunfante.

triv·i·al [ˈtriviəl] ☐ trivial; frívolo; insignificante; **triv·i·al·i·ty** [~ˈæliti] trivialidad *f*.

tro·chee [ˈtroukiː] troqueo *m* (-◡).

trod [trɔd] *pret.*, **trod·den** [ˈ~n] *p.p. of tread.*

trog·lo·dyte [ˈtrɔglədait] troglodita *m*. [*su. m* (a *f*).}

Tro·jan [ˈtroudʒn] troyano *adj. a.*}

trol·ley [ˈtrɔli] carretilla *f*; (*a.* ˈ~ **car**) tranvía *m*; (*tea*) mes(it)a *f* de ruedas; ⚡ trole *m*; ⊕ corredera *f* elevada; ˈ~ **bus** trolebús *m*.

trol·lop [ˈtrɔləp] marrana *f*; ramera *f*.

trom·bone [trɔmˈboun] trombón *m*.

troop [truːp] **1.** tropa *f* (*a.* ⚔); ⚔ escuadrón *m of cavalry*; *thea.* compañía *f*; ~*s pl.* tropas *f/pl.*; **2.** reunirse; ~ *away*, ~ *off* marcharse en tropel; ˈ~ **car·ri·er** ⚓ transporte *m*; ⚔ camión *m* blindado; ˈ**troop·er** soldado *m* de caballería; policía *m* de a caballo; ˈ**troop·ship** transporte *m*.

tro·phy [ˈtroufi] trofeo *m*.

trop·ic [ˈtrɔpik] trópico *m*; ~*s pl.* trópicos *m/pl.*; ˈ**trop·ic**, ˈ**trop·i·cal** ☐ tropical.

trot [trɔt] **1.** trote *m*; *school sl.* chuleta *f*; F *be always on the* ~ estar siempre ocupado; F *on the* ~ seguidos; **2.** trotar; F ~ *out* sacar (para mostrar); *excuses etc.* ensartar.

troth [trouθ] † fe *f*; † *or co. plight one's* ~ desposarse, prometerse.

trot·ter [ˈtrɔtər] (caballo *m*) trotón *m*; *cooking*: pie *m* de cerdo *etc.*

trou·ble [ˈtrʌbl] **1.** aflicción *f*, congoja *f*; (*misfortune*) desgracia *f*, apuro *m*; dificultad *f*, disgusto *m*; (*unpleasantness*) sinsabor *m*; (*inconvenience*) molestia *f*; *pol.* trastorno *m*; ⚕ mal *m*; ⊕ falta *f*, fallo *m*; *be in* ~ verse en un apuro; *be worth the* ~ valer la pena; *go to great* ~ *to inf.* hacer un gran esfuerzo por *inf.*; *go to the* ~ *of ger.*, *take the* ~ *to inf.* tomarse la molestia de *inf.*; **2.** *v/t.* turbar; trastornar; afligir; molestar, fastidiar; incomodar; ~ *a p. for* pedirle a uno; *don't* ~ *yourself* no se moleste; no se preocupe; *v/i.* molestarse; ˈ**trou·bled** *p.* inquieto; apenado; ⚕ enajenado; *times* turbulento; *waters* revuelto, turbio; **trouble·some** [ˈ~səm] ☐ molesto; dificultoso; importuno.

trough [trɔf] (*drinking*) abrevadero *m*; (*feeding*) comedero *m*; (*kneading*) artesa *f*; canal *m*; seno *m of wave*; *meteor.* mínimo *m* de presión.

trounce [trauns] zurrar, pegar; *sport etc.*: cascar.

troupe [truːp] compañía *f*.

trou·sers [ˈtrauzərz] (*a pair of* un) pantalón *m*; pantalones *m/pl.*

trous·seau [ˈtruːsou] ajuar *m*.

trout [traut] trucha *f*.

trow·el [ˈtrauəl] ⚡ desplantador *m*; ⚠ paleta *f*, llana *f*.

troy (**weight**) [trɔi(weit)] peso *m* troy.

tru·an·cy ['tru:ənsi] ausencia *f* de clase sin permiso; evasión *f* de responsabilidad; '**tru·ant 1.** haragán; **2.** novillero *m*; *play* ~ hacer novillos (*or* toros).
truce [tru:s] tregua *f*.
truck[1] [trʌk] **1.** camión *m*; (*hand*) carretilla *f*; 🚂 vagón *m* (de mercancías); vagoneta *f*; **2.** transportar en camión.
truck[2] [~] cambio *m*, trueque *m*; (*mst* ~ *system*) pago *m* del salario en especie; *contp*. baratijas *f/pl*.; *have no* ~ *with* no tratar con.
truck·le ['trʌkl] someterse servilmente (*to* a).
truc·u·lence, truc·u·len·cy ['trʌkjuləns(i)] aspereza *f etc*.; '**truc·u·lent** □ áspero, hosco, arisco; agresivo.
trudge [trʌdʒ] caminar trabajosamente.
true [tru:] (*adv. truly*) verdadero; *account* verídico; *p*. leal; *copy* fiel, exacto; genuino; auténtico; *surface etc*. uniforme, a nivel; a plomo; *it is* ~ es verdad; ~ *to life* conforme con la realidad; *come* ~ realizarse; *too* ~*!* tiene Vd. razón; '~-'**blue** sumamente leal; '~·**bred** de casta legítima; '~·**love** fiel amante *m/f*, novio (a *f*) *m*.
truf·fle ['trʌfl] trufa *f*.
tru·ism ['tru:izm] truísmo *m*, perogrullada *f*.
tru·ly ['tru:li] verdaderamente; fielmente; efectivamente; *Yours* ~ su seguro servidor.
trump [trʌmp] **1.** triunfo *m*; **2.** fallar; ~ *up* forjar, falsificar; **trump·er·y** ['~əri] **1.** hojarasca *f*, oropel *m*; tontería *f*; **2.** frívolo; (*useless*) inútil; (*nonsensical*) tonto; (*trashy*) de relumbrón.
trum·pet ['trʌmpit] **1.** trompeta *f*; ~ *blast* trompetazo *m*; *v. ear* ~, *speaking* ~; **2.** trompetear; (*elephant*) barritar; *fig*. (*a*. ~ *forth*) pregonar (a son de trompeta); '**trum·pet·er** trompetero *m*, trompeta *m*.
trun·cate ['trʌŋkeit] truncar; **trun'ca·tion** truncamiento *m*.
trun·cheon ['trʌntʃn] (cachi)porra *f*.
trun·dle ['trʌndl] **1.** ruedecilla *f*; **2.** (hacer) rodar (*a*. ~ *along*); F transportarse.
trunk [trʌŋk] ⚘, *anat*. tronco *m*; (*case*) baúl *m*; (*elephant's*) trompa *f*; *mot*. portamaletas *m*; '~ **call** conferencia *f* interurbana; '~ **line** 🚂 línea *f* troncal; *teleph*. línea *f* principal; **trunks** *pl*. taparrabo *m*.
truss [trʌs] **1.** ⚒ haz *m*, lío *m*; ⚕ braguero *m*; ⚠ entramado *m*; **2.** atar, liar; *fowl* espetar; ⚠ apoyar con entramado.
trust [trʌst] **1.** confianza *f*; crédito *m*; obligación *f*, cargo *m*; ⚖ fideicomiso *m*; ☤ trust *m*; ~ *company* banco *m* fideicomisario; *breach of* ~ abuso *m* de confianza; *position of* ~ puesto *m* de confianza; *in* ~ en administración; *on* ~ a ojos cerrados; ☤ al fiado; **2.** *v/t*. confiar en, fiarse de; ~ *a p. with a th*. confiar algo a alguien; ~ *a p. to do* confiar en que uno haga; ~ *that* esperar que; ~ *him to do that!* no me extraña que lo haya hecho; *I wouldn't* ~ *him with your car* no le dejaría usar tu coche; *v/i*. confiar (*in, to* en).
trus·tee [trʌs'ti:] síndico *m*; depositario *m*; ⚖ fideicomisario *m*; administrador *m*; **trus'tee·ship** cargo *m* de fideicomisario *etc*.
trust·ful ['trʌstful] □, '**trust·ing** □ confiado.
trust·wor·thi·ness ['trʌstwə:rðinis] confiabilidad *f*; '**trust·wor·thy** *p*. confiable; *news etc*. fidedigno.
trust·y ['trʌsti] fiel, leal; seguro; *sl*. penitenciario *m* que goza de privilegios especiales.
truth [tru:θ, *pl*. ~ðz] verdad *f*.
truth·ful ['tru:θful] □ verídico; veraz; '**truth·ful·ness** veracidad *f*.
try [trai] **1.** *v/t*. intentar; (*test*) probar, ensayar (*a*. ~ *out*); ⚖ *p*. procesar (*for* por); *case* ver; *metall*. refinar; *eyes* cansar, irritar; (*sorely*) afligir; ~ *on clothes* probarse; F ~ *it on* fingirse (enfermo *etc*.); ~ *out* someter a prueba; *v/i*. probar; esforzarse; ~ *to*, F ~ *and inf*. tratar de *inf*., intentar *inf*.; ~ *for* tratar de obtener; **2.** F tentativa *f*; ensayo *m* (*a. rugby*), prueba *f*; '**try·ing** □ molesto; fatigoso; penoso; '**try'out** experimento *m*; prueba *f* (*a. sport*).
tryst [traist, trist] (lugar *m* de una cita *f*.)
Tsar [zɑ:r] zar *m*.
T-square ['ti:skwer] regla *f* T.
tub [tʌb] **1.** tina *f*; cubo *m*; cuba *f*; F (*bath*) baño *m*; F ⚓ carcamán *m*; **2.** entinar; F tomar un baño.

tu·ba [ˈtu:bə] tuba *f*.
tub·by [ˈtʌbi] rechoncho; bajo y gordo.
tube [tu:b] tubo *m* (*a. television*); *radio*: lámpara *f*; (*a. inner* ~) cámara *f*; 🚇 metro *m*; ˈ**~·less** *mot*. sin cámara; ⚡ sin tubo.
tu·ber [ˈtu:bər] tubérculo *m*; **tu·ber·cle** [ˈtu:bə:rkl] *all senses*: tubérculo *m*; **tu·ber·cu·lo·sis** [tubə:rkjuˈlousis] tuberculosis *f*; **tuˈber·cu·lous** tuberculoso.
tub·ing [ˈtu:biŋ] tubería *f*; trozo *m* de tubo.
tu·bu·lar [ˈtu:bjulər] tubular.
tuck [tʌk] **1.** alforza *f*; pliegue *m*; **2.** *v/t*. alforzar; plegar; ~ *away* encubrir, ocultar; *sl. food* zampar; ~ *up sleeves, skirt* arremangar; *bed* guarnecer; *p. in bed* arropar.
tuck·er [ˈtʌkər] F agotar, cansar.
Tues·day [ˈtju:zdi] martes *m*.
tuft [tʌft] copete *m*; penacho *m*; manojo *m of grass etc.*
tug [tʌg] **1.** tirón *m*; estirón *m*; ⚓ remolcador *m*; ~ *of war* lucha *f* de la cuerda; *fig*. lucha *f* (decisiva); **2.** tirar de; arrastrar; ⚓ remolcar; ˈ**~·boat** remolcador *m*.
tu·i·tion [tuˈiʃn] enseñanza *f*; cuota *f* de enseñanza.
tu·lip [ˈtu:lip] tulipán *m*.
tulle [tu:l] tul *m*.
tum·ble [ˈtʌmbl] **1.** *v/i*. caer; tropezar (*over* en); desplomarse, hundirse, venirse abajo (*a.* ~ *down*); ~ *out* salir en desorden; F caer en la cuenta (*to* de); *v/t*. derribar; derrocar; desarreglar; ~ *out* echar en desorden; **2.** caída *f*; voltereta *f*; *take a* ~ caerse; ˈ**~·down** destartalado, ruinoso; ˈ**tum·bler** (*glass*) vaso *m*; (*p.*) volteador (-a *f*) *m*; *orn*. pichón *m* volteador; seguro *m*, fiador *m of lock*.
tum·my [ˈtʌmi] F estómago *m*.
tu·mor [ˈtu:mər] tumor *m*.
tu·mult [ˈtu:mʌlt] tumulto *m*; **tu·mul·tu·ous** [tuˈmʌltjuəs] □ tumultuoso.
tun [tʌn] tonel *m*; † (*measure*) tonelada *f*.
tu·na [ˈtu:nə] atún *m*.
tune [tu:n] **1.** aire *m*, tonada *f*; armonía *f*; tono *m*; *in* ~ templado, afinado; *adv*. afinadamente; *fig. be in* ~ *with* concordar con; *out of* ~ destemplado, desafinado; *adv*. desafinadamente; *fig. be out of* ~ *with* desentonar con; *fig. change one's* ~ mudar de tono; F *to the* ~ *of* por la suma de; **2.** ♪ afinar, acordar, templar (*a.* ~ *up*); *radio*: ~ (*in*) sintonizar (*to acc.*); *mot*. ~ *up* poner a punto; **tune·ful** [ˈ~ful] □ melodioso, armonioso; ˈ**tune·less** □ disonante; ˈ**tun·er** afinador *m*; *radio*: sintonizador *m*.
tung·sten [ˈtʌŋstən] tungsteno *m*.
tu·nic [ˈtu:nik] túnica *f*.
tun·ing [ˈtu:niŋ] ♪ afinación *f*; *radio*: sintonización *f*; *fine* ~ sintonización *f* fina; ˈ**~ coil** bobina *f* sintonizadora; ˈ**~ fork** diapasón *m*.
tun·nel [ˈtʌnl] **1.** túnel *m*; ⚒ galería *f*; **2.** *v/t*. construir un túnel bajo (*or* a través de); *v/i*. construir un túnel; atravesar por túnel; ~ *vision* perspectiva *f* estrecha; prejuicio *m*.
tun·ny [ˈtʌni] atún *m*.
tur·ban [ˈtə:rbən] turbante *m*.
tur·bid [ˈtə:rbid] turbio.
tur·bine [ˈtə:rbin] turbina *f*.
tur·bo·fan [ˈtə:rboufæn] ✈ turboventilador *m*; **tur·bo·jet** [ˈtə:rbouˈdʒet] turborreactor (*a. su. m*); ˈ**tur·boˈprop** turbohélice (*a. su. m*); **tur·boˈsu·per·charg·er** turbosupercargador *m*.
tur·bot [ˈtə:rbət] rodaballo *m*.
tur·bu·lence [ˈtə:rbjuləns] turbulencia *f*; ˈ**tur·bu·lent** □ turbulento.
tu·reen [təˈri:n] sopera *f*.
turf [tə:rf] **1.** césped *m*; (*sod*) tepe *m*; (*peat*) turba *f*; *sport*: turf *m*; **2.** encespedar; *sl.* ~ *out* echar.
tur·gid [ˈtə:rdʒid] □ turgente; *fig*. hinchado; **turˈgid·i·ty** turgencia *f*.
Turk [tə:rk] turco (a *f*) *m*; *fig*. pícaro *m*.
tur·key [ˈtə:rki] pavo (a *f*) *m*; F *talk* ~ no tener pelos en la lengua.
Turk·ish [ˈtə:rkiʃ] turco *adj. a. su. m*; ~ *bath* baño *m* turco; ~ *towel* toalla *f* rusa.
tur·moil [ˈtə:rmɔil] desorden *m*; alboroto *m*, tumulto *m*; disturbio *m*.
turn [tə:rn] **1.** *v/t*. volver; ⊕ tornear; *ankle* torcer; *corner* doblar; *handle* girar, dar vueltas a; *key* dar vuelta a; *milk* agriar; *stomach* revolver; F ~ *color* cambiar de color; ~ *a p. against* predisponerle a uno en contra de; ~ *aside* desviar; ~ *away* apartar; despedir; ~ *back page* doblar; *p.* hacer retroceder; ~ *down page etc.* doblar;

gas etc. bajar; *offer* rehusar; *p.* no aceptar; ~ *in* doblar hacia adentro; *man* entregar, denunciar; ~ *into* convertir en, cambiar en; (*translate*) verter a; ~ *off light* apagar, *p.* desanimar; *tap* cerrar; *gas* cortar; ~ *on light* encender; *radio* poner; *tap* abrir; ~ *out light* apagar; *p.* echar, expulsar; *pocket* vaciar; *product* producir, fabricar; *be well* ~*ed out* ir bien vestido; ~ *over* volver; volcar; *pages* pasar; *motor* hacer girar; revolver *in mind*; entregar (*to* a); ✝ rendir; *v. leaf*; ~ *up* doblar hacia arriba; *earth* revolver; *gas* abrir (más); *reference* buscar, consultar; *radio* poner más fuerte; *sleeve* arremangar; **2.** *v/i.* volver(se); girar, dar vueltas; *mot.*, ✈ virar; torcer; (*become*) hacerse *su.*, ponerse, volverse *adj.*; (*milk*) agriarse, cortarse; (*tide*) repuntar; (*weather*) cambiar; ~ *about* dar una vuelta completa; ⚔ *about* ~! media vuelta ¡ar!; ~ *aside*, ~ *away* desviarse, alejarse; volver la espalda; ~ *back* volver (atrás), retroceder; ~ *from* apartarse de; ~ *in* doblarse hacia adentro; F acostarse; ~ *into* convertirse en; ~ *off* desviarse; ~ *on* depender de; *theme* versar sobre; *p.* volverse contra; ~ *out* salir de casa (*or* a la calle); resultar; F levantarse *from bed*; ~ *out to be* resultar; ~ *out well* salir bien; ~ *over* revolver(se); *mot.*, ✈ capotar; volcar; ~ *round* volverse; girar; ~ *to* (*for help*) recurrir a, acudir a; *stone etc.* convertirse en; ~ *to* (*adv.*) empezar (a trabajar); ~ *up* doblarse hacia arriba; aparecer; llegar, asistir, presentarse; ~ *upon v.* ~ *on*; **3.** vuelta *f*; giro *m*; revolución *f*; curva *f*, recodo *m in road etc.*; ⚓ *etc.* viraje *m*; *mot. etc.* giro *m*; (*change*) cambio *m*; repunte *m*, cambio *m of tide*; (*spell*) turno *m*; oportunidad *f*; propensión *f* (*for* a); sesgo *m*, disposición *f of mind*; F susto *m*; F ⚕ vahido *m*, desvanecimiento *m*; *thea.* número *m*; ~ *of phrase* giro *m*; *bad* ~ mala jugada *f*; *good* ~ favor *m*, servicio *m*; *it is my* ~ me toca a mí; *take a* ~ dar una vuelta; *take a* ~ *at* contribuir con su trabajo a; *take a* ~ *at the wheel* conducir por su turno; *take one's* ~ esperar su turno; *take* ~*s* turnar, alternar; *done to a* ~ en su punto; *at every* ~ a cada paso, a cada momento; *by* ~*s* por turnos; *in* ~ por turno; *in his* ~ a su vez; *out of* ~ fuera de orden; '~**·coat** renegado (a *f*) *m*; '~**·down 1.** doblado hacia abajo; **2.** negativa *f*; rechazamiento *m*; '**turn·er** tornero *m*.

turn·ing ['tə:rniŋ] vuelta *f*; ángulo *m*; '~ **lathe** torno *m* (de tornero); '~ **point** *fig.* punto *m* decisivo, coyuntura *f* crítica.

tur·nip ['tə:rnip] nabo *m*.

turn·key ['tə:rnki:] llavero *m* (de cárcel); '**turn·off** salida *f*; desviación *f of road*; F rechazamiento *m*; negativa *f*; '**turn·out** concurrencia *f*; entrada *f*; ✝ producción *f*; F atuendo *m*; '**turn·o·ver** ✝ (volumen *m* de) transacciones *f/pl.* (*or* operaciones *f/pl.*); movimiento *m* de mercancías (*or* de personal); *cooking*: pastel *m* con repulgo; '**turn·pike** barrera *f* de portazgo; autopista *f* de peaje; '**turn sig·nal** *mot.* señal *f* de dirección; '**turn·stile** torniquete *m*; '**turn·ta·ble** 🚂, *phonograph*: placa *f* giratoria; '**turn·up** vuelta *f of trousers*; F trifulca *f*; F racha *f* de buena suerte.

tur·pen·tine ['tə:rpəntain] trementina *f*.

tur·pi·tude ['tə:rpitju:d] *lit.* infamia *f*, vileza *f*.

tur·quoise ['tə:rkwɔiz] turquesa *f*.

tur·ret ['tʌrit] ⚠ torreón *m*; ⚔ torre *f*; ⚓ torreta *f* (acorazada); ✈ torreta *f* (de fuego); ⊕ cabrestante *m*; ⊕ ~ *lathe* torno *m* revolvedor.

tur·tle ['tə:rtl] tortuga *f* marina; *turn* ~ ⚓ zozobrar; (*car etc.*) volcar.

tur·tle dove ['tə:rtldʌv] tórtola *f*.

Tus·can ['tʌskən] toscano *adj. a. su. m* (a *f*).

tusk [tʌsk] colmillo *m*.

tus·sle ['tʌsl] **1.** lucha *f*; agarrada *f*, pelea *f*; **2.** luchar (*with* con); reñir (*over* a causa de).

tus·sock ['tʌsɔk] montecillo *m* de hierbas.

tut [tʌt] ¡bah!

tu·te·lage ['tju:tilidʒ] tutela *f*.

tu·tor ['tju:tər] **1.** preceptor *m*; ayo *m*; maestro *m* particular; ⚖ tutor *m*; **2.** enseñar, instruir; dar enseñanza particular a; **tu·to·ri·al** [tju'tɔ:riəl] **1.** preceptoral; ⚖ tutelar; **2.** *univ.* clase *f* particular; **tu·tor·ship** ['tju:tərʃip] ⚖ tutela *f*; *univ.* preceptorado *m*.

tux·e·do [tʌk'si:dou] smoking *m*.

twad·dle ['twɔdl] disparates *m/pl.*, tonterías *f/pl.*

twang [twæŋ] **1.** tañido *m*, punteado *m of guitar*; (*mst nasal* ~) gangueo *m*, timbre *m* nasal; **2.** *guitar* puntear.
tweak [twi:k] pellizcar retorciendo.
tweed [twi:d] cheviot *m*, mezcla *f* de lana; ~*s pl.* traje *m* de cheviot.
'tween [twi:n] = *between*.
tweez·ers [ˈtwi:zərz] *pl.* (*a pair of* ~ unas) bruselas *f*/*pl.*, pinzas *f*/*pl.*
twelfth [twelfθ] duodécimo (*a. su. m*); ˈ♀**-night** día *m* (*or* noche *f*) de Reyes.
twelve [twelv] doce (*a. su. m*).
twen·ti·eth [ˈtwentiiθ] vigésimo (*a. su. m*).
twen·ty [ˈtwenti] veinte; ~**·fold** [ˈ~-fould] *adv.* veinte veces (*adj.* mayor).
twerp [twə:rp] *sl.* tonto *m*; papanatas *m.*
twice [twais] dos veces; ~ *the sum* el doble; ~ *as much* dos veces tanto.
twid·dle [ˈtwidl] **1.** girar; jugar con, revolver ociosamente; **2.** vuelta *f* (ligera).
twig [twig] ramita *f*; ~*s pl.* leña *f* menuda.
twi·light [ˈtwailait] **1.** crepúsculo *m* (*a. fig.*); **2.** crepuscular; ~ *sleep* sueño *m* crepuscular.
twill [twil] **1.** tela *f* cruzada; **2.** cruzar.
twin [twin] gemelo *adj. a. su. m* (a *f*); ~**-en·gine**(**d**) [ˈ~ˈendʒin(d)] bimotor; ˈ~ ˈ**jet** birreactor *adj. a. su. m.*
twine [twain] **1.** guita *f*, bramante *m*; **2.** enroscar(se); (*mst with adv.*) retorcer(se); *fig.* ceñir (*with* de).
twinge [twindʒ] punzada *f.*
twin·ing [ˈtwainiŋ] ⚘ sarmentoso.
twin·kle [ˈtwiŋkl] **1.** centellear, titilar, parpadear; *fig.* moverse rápidamente; *in the twinkling of an eye* en un abrir y cerrar de ojos; **2.** centelleo *m*, parpadeo *m*; *in a* ~ en un instante.
twirl [twə:rl] **1.** vuelta *f* (rápida), giro *m*; rasgo *m of pen*; **2.** girar rápidamente; dar vueltas (*v*/*t.* a).
twist [twist] **1.** torcedura *f* (*a.* ⚕); torsión *f*; enroscadura *f*; torzal *m*; rollo *m of tobacco*; vuelta *f*, recodo *m in road*; sesgo *m*, peculiaridad *f of mind*; F baile *m* de rock 'n' roll; **2.** torcer(se) (*a. fig.*); retorcer(se); enroscar(se); trenzar, entrelazar(se); girar; (*road*) dar vueltas; F estafar; ˈ**twist·er** torcedor *m*; *meteor.* tromba *f*; tornado *m*; *baseball*: pelota *f* arrojada con efecto; F estafador *m*, tramposo *m.*
twit [twit] **1.** ~ *a p. with a th.* reprender (para divertirse) algo a alguien; **2.** F papanatas *m.*
twitch [twitʃ] **1.** *v*/*i.* crisparse; temblar; *v*/*t.* tirar ligeramente de; arrancar de un tirón; **2.** sacudida *f* repentina; ⚕ tic *m*, contracción *f* nerviosa; *vet.* acial *m.*
twit·ter [ˈtwitər] **1.** (*bird*) gorjear; *fig.* agitarse, temblar de inquietud; **2.** gorjeo *m*; *fig.* agitación *f*, inquietud *f*; F *be in a* ~ estar muy agitado.
two [tu:] dos (*a. su. m*); *in* ~ en dos; *in* ~*s*, ~ *by* ~ de dos en dos; *put* ~ *and* ~ *together* atar cabos; ˈ~**-bit** *sl.* inferior; cursi; ˈ~**-edged** de doble filo (*a. fig.*); ˈ~**-faced** *fig.* doble, falso; ˈ~**·fold 1.** *adj.* doble; **2.** *adv.* dos veces; ˈ~**-fist·ed** *fig.* fuerte; viril; ˈ~**-hand·ed** de (*or* para) dos manos; ˈ~**·pence,** ~**·pen·ny** [ˈtʌpni] *British* de dos peniques; *fig.* despreciable; ˈ~**-phase** ⚡ bifásico; ˈ~**-ply** de dos capas; ˈ~-ˈ**seat·er** *mot.* de dos plazas; ˈ~-ˈ**step** paso *m* doble; ˈ~-ˈ**sto·ry** de dos pisos; ˈ~-ˈ**stroke** de dos tiempos; ˈ~**-time** *sl.* engañar en amor; ˈ~-ˈ**tone** *mot.* bicolor; ˈ~**-way** ˈ**switch** ⚡ conmutador *m* de dos direcciones.
ty·coon [taiˈku:n] F magnate *m.*
tyke [taik] chiquillo *m*; F peque *m*/*f.*
tym·pa·num [ˈtimpənəm] *anat.*, ⚠ tímpano *m.*
type [taip] **1.** tipo *m*; *typ.* tipo *m*, carácter *m*; tipos *m*/*pl.*; **2.** escribir a máquina, mecanografiar; ˈ~**·script** (original *m*) mecanografiado; ˈ~**·set·ter** (*p.*) cajista *m*; (*machine*) máquina *f* de componer; ˈ~**·write** [*irr.* (*write*)] = *type* 2; ˈ~**·writ·er** máquina *f* de escribir; ~ *ribbon* cinta *f* para máquinas de escribir; ˈ~**-writ·ing** = *typing*; ˈ~**·writ·ten** escrito a máquina.
ty·phoid [ˈtaifɔid] fiebre *f* tifoidea.
ty·phoon [taiˈfu:n] tifón *m.*
ty·phus [ˈtaifəs] tifus *m.*
typ·i·cal [ˈtipikl] □ típico; **typ·i·fy** [ˈ~fai] simbolizar; representar; ser ejemplo de; **typ·ing** [ˈtaipiŋ] mecanografía *f*, dactilografía *f*; **typ·ist** [ˈtaipist] mecanógrafo (a *f*) *m*, dactilógrafo (a *f*) *m.*
ty·pog·ra·pher [taiˈpɔgrəfər] tipógrafo *m*; **ty·po·graph·ic, ty·po·graph·i·cal** [~pəˈgræfik(l)] □ tipo-

gráfico; **ty·pog·ra·phy** [~ˈpɔgrəfi] tipografía *f*.

ty·ran·nic, ty·ran·ni·cal [tiˈrænik(l)] □ tiránico; **tyr·an·ni·cide** [tiˈrænəsaid] tiranicidio *m*; **tyr·an·nize** [ˈtirənaiz] tiranizar (*over acc.*); **ˈtyr·an·ny** tiranía *f*.

ty·rant [ˈtairənt] tirano (a *f*) *m*.

ty·ro [ˈtairou] = *tiro*.

Tzar [zɑːr] zar *m*.

U

u·biq·ui·tous [juˈbikwitəs] □ ubicuo; **uˈbiq·ui·ty** ubicuidad *f*.
ud·der [ˈʌdər] ubre *f*.
ugh [ʌx, uh, əːh] ¡puf!
ug·li·fy [ˈʌglifai] F afear.
ug·li·ness [ˈʌglinis] fealdad *f*.
ug·ly [ˈʌgli] □ feo; *wound, situation* peligroso; *vice etc.* feo, asqueroso, repugnante; *sky etc.* amenazador; *rumor etc.* inquietante; F ~ *customer* sayón *m*; persona *f* de mal genio; *be in an ~ mood* (*p*.) estar de muy mal humor; (*mob*) amenazar violencia; *turn ~* (*situation*) ponerse peligroso; F (*p*.) mostrarse violento, ponerse negro.
U·krain·i·an [juːˈkreiniən] ucranio *adj. a. su. m* (a *f*).
u·ku·le·le [juːkəˈleili] guitarra *f* hawaiana.
ul·cer [ˈʌlsər] úlcera *f*; *fig.* llaga *f*; **ul·cer·ate** [ˈ~reit] ulcerar(se); **ul·ceˈra·tion** ulceración *f*; **ˈul·cer·ous** ulceroso.
ul·lage [ˈʌlidʒ] ⚓ merma *f* (de un tonel).
ul·na [ˈʌlnə], *pl.* **ul·nae** cúbito *m*.
ul·ster [ˈʌlstər] úlster *m*.
ul·te·ri·or [ʌlˈtiriər] ulterior; *motive* oculto.
ul·ti·mate [ˈʌltimit] □ último, final; fundamental; sumo; **ˈul·ti·mate·ly** últimamente; a la larga.
ul·ti·ma·tum [ʌltiˈmeitəm], *pl. a.* **ul·tiˈma·ta** [~tə] ultimátum *m*.
ul·ti·mo [ˈʌltimou] ⚓ del mes pasado.
ul·tra [ˈʌltrə] ultra...; **ˈ~ˈfash·ion·a·ble** muy de moda; **ˈ~ˈhigh** ⚡ ultraelevado; **~·maˈrine 1.** ultramarino; **2.** 🎨 *paint.* azul *m* de ultramar; **ˈ~ˈmod·ern** ultramoderno; **~·mon·tane** [~ˈmɔntein] ultramontano *adj. a. su. m*; **ˈ~ˈshort wave** (de) onda *f* extracorta; **ˈ~·sound** sonido *m* silencioso; **~ˈvi·o·let** ultravioleta.
ul·u·late [ˈjuːljuleit] ulular.
um·bel [ˈʌmbl] umbela *f*.
um·ber [ˈʌmbər] tierra *f* de sombra.
um·bil·i·cal [ʌmˈbilikl, ⚕ ~ˈlaikl] umbilical; ~ *cord* cordón *m* umbilical.
um·brage [ˈʌmbridʒ] *fig.* resentimiento *m*, pique *m*; *take ~* ofenderse (*at* por), resentirse (*at* de).
um·brel·la [ʌmˈbrelə] paraguas *m*; ⚔ cortina *f* de fuego (antiaéreo); **umˈbrel·la stand** paragüero *m*.
um·pire [ˈʌmpaiər] **1.** árbitro *m*; **2.** arbitrar.
ump·teen [ˈʌmtiːn] F muchísimos, tantísimos; **umpˈteenth** [~θ] F enésimo.
un... [ʌn...] in...; des...; no; poco.
un·a·bashed [ˈʌnəˈbæʃt] descarado, desvergonzado.
un·a·bat·ed [ˈʌnəˈbeitid] sin disminución.
un·a·ble [ˈʌnˈeibl] imposibilitado, incapaz (*to inf.* de *inf.*); *be ~ to inf.* no poder *inf.*
un·a·bridged [ˈʌnəˈbridʒd] íntegro.
un·ac·cent·ed [ˈʌnækˈsentid] inacentuado, átono.
un·ac·cept·a·ble [ˈʌnəkˈseptəbl] inaceptable.
un·ac·com·mo·dat·ing [ˈʌnəˈkɔmədeitiŋ] poco acogedor; intransigente.
un·ac·com·pan·ied [ˈʌnəˈkʌmpənid] sin acompañamiento.
un·ac·count·a·ble [ˈʌnəˈkauntəbl] □ inexplicable.
un·ac·cus·tomed [ˈʌnəˈkʌstəmd] insólito; no acostumbrado (*to* a).
un·ac·knowl·edged [ˈʌnəkˈnɔlidʒd] no reconocido.
un·ac·quaint·ed [ˈʌnəˈkweintid]: *be ~ with* desconocer, ignorar.
un·a·dorned [ˈʌnəˈdɔːrnd] sin adorno, sencillo; escueto.
un·a·dul·ter·at·ed [ˈʌnəˈdʌltəreitid] sin mezcla; puro.
un·ad·vis·a·ble [ˈʌnədˈvaizəbl] □ poco aconsejable.
un·af·fect·ed [ˈʌnəˈfektid] □ no afectado (*by* por); *fig.* sin afectación, natural.
un·a·fraid [ˈʌnəˈfreid] impertérrito.

un·aid·ed ['ʌn'eidid] sin ayuda.
un·al·loyed ['ʌnə'lɔid] puro, sin mezcla.
un·al·ter·a·ble [ʌn'ɔ:ltərəbl] □ inalterable.
un·am·big·u·ous ['ʌnæm'bigjuəs] □ inequívoco.
un·am·bi·tious ['ʌnæm'biʃəs] □ poco ambicioso.
un-A·mer·i·can ['ʌnə'merikən] antiamericano.
un·a·mi·a·ble [ʌn'eimjəbl] □ poco simpático.
u·na·nim·i·ty [ju:nə'nimiti] unanimidad *f*; **u·nan·i·mous** [ju:'næniməs] □ unánime.
un·an·swer·a·ble [ʌn'ænsərəbl] □ incontestable; irrebatible.
un·ap·peal·a·ble ['ʌnə'pi:ləbl] ⚖ inapelable.
un·ap·pe·tiz·ing ['ʌn'æpitaiziŋ] poco apetitoso.
un·ap·proach·a·ble ['ʌnə'proutʃəbl] □ inaccesible; *p.* intratable.
un·ap·pro·pri·at·ed ['ʌnə'prouprieitid] no asignado.
un·armed ['ʌn'ɑ:rmd] inerme, desarmado.
un·a·shamed ['ʌnə'ʃeimd; *adv.* ~midli] □ desvergonzado; sin remordimiento.
un·asked ['ʌn'æskt] no solicitado; sin ser convidado.
un·as·sail·a·ble [ʌnə'seiləbl] □ irrebatible.
un·as·sum·ing ['ʌnə'sju:miŋ] □ modesto, sin pretensiones.
un·at·tached ['ʌnə'tætʃt] suelto; *p.* no prometido; ⚔ de reemplazo; ⚖ no embargado.
un·at·tain·a·ble ['ʌnə'teinəbl] □ inasequible.
un·at·tend·ed ['ʌnə'tendid] desatendido; sin guardia.
un·at·trac·tive ['ʌnə'træktiv] □ poco atractivo.
un·au·thor·ized ['ʌn'ɔ:θəraizd] desautorizado.
un·a·vail·a·ble ['ʌnə'veiləbl] indisponible; '**un·a'vail·ing** □ infructuoso, inútil.
un·a·void·a·ble ['ʌnə'vɔidəbl] □ inevitable, ineludible.
un·a·ware ['ʌnə'wer]: *be* ~ ignorar (*of acc., that* que); '**un·a'wares** de improviso; inopinadamente; *catch a p.* ~ coger a una p. desprevenida.
un·backed ['ʌn'bækt] *fig.* sin respaldo; ✝ a descubierto.
un·bal·ance ['ʌn'bæləns] desequilibrio *m*; '**un'bal·anced** desequilibrado.
un·bap·tized ['ʌnbæp'taizd] sin bautizar.
un·bear·a·ble [ʌn'berəbl] □ inaguantable, insufrible.
un·beat·a·ble ['ʌn'bi:təbl] imbatible; *price* inmejorable.
un·beat·en [ʌn'bi:tn] *track* no trillado; *team* imbatido; *price* no mejorado.
un·be·com·ing ['ʌnbi'kʌmiŋ] □ indecoroso; impropio (*for, to* de); *dress* que sienta mal.
un·be·known ['ʌnbi'noun]: ~ *to me* sin saberlo yo.
un·be·lief ['ʌnbi'li:f] descreimiento *m*; '**un·be'liev·a·ble** □ increíble; '**un·be'liev·er** no creyente *m/f*, descreído (a *f*) *m*; '**un·be'liev·ing** □ incrédulo.
un·bend ['ʌnbend] [*irr.* (*bend*)] *v/t.* desencorvar, enderezar (*a.* ⊕); *v/i. fig.* relajarse, suavizarse; (*p.*) hacerse más expansivo; '**un'bend·ing** □ inflexible (*a. fig.*); *fig.* inconquistable, poco afable.
un·bi·ased ['ʌn'baiəst] imparcial.
un·bid, un·bid·den ['ʌn'bid(n)] sin ser convidado.
un·bind ['ʌn'baind] [*irr.* (*bind*)] desatar.
un·bleached ['ʌn'bli:tʃt] sin blanquear.
un·blem·ished [ʌn'blemiʃt] sin tacha.
un·blush·ing [ʌn'blʌʃiŋ] □ desvergonzado.
un·bolt ['ʌn'boult] desatrancar.
un·born ['ʌn'bɔ:rn] no nacido aún, nonato.
un·bos·om [ʌn'buzm]: ~ *o.s.* desahogarse, abrir su pecho (*to* a).
un·bound ['ʌn'baund] *book* sin encuadernar.
un·bound·ed [ʌn'baundid] ilimitado.
un·break·a·ble ['ʌnbreikəbl] irrompible.
un·bri·dled [ʌn'braidld] desenfrenado (*a. fig.*).
un·bro·ken ['ʌn'broukn] *seal* intacto; *time* no interrumpido; *horse* no domado.
un·buck·le ['ʌn'bʌkl] deshebillar.
un·bur·den ['ʌn'bə:rdn]: ~ *o.s.*, ~ *one's heart* desahogarse, aliviarse (*of* de).

un·bur·ied [ˈʌnˈberid] insepulto.
un·busi·ness·like [ˈʌnˈbiznislaik] poco práctico; informal.
un·but·ton [ˈʌnˈbʌtn] desabotonar.
un·called-for [ʌnˈkɔːldfɔːr] gratuito, inmerecido; impropio.
un·can·ny [ʌnˈkæni] □ misterioso; extraordinario.
un·cared-for [ˈʌnˈkerdˈfɔːr] *appearance* de abandono; *p. etc.* abandonado, desamparado.
un·ceas·ing [ʌnˈsiːsiŋ] □ incesante.
un·cer·e·mo·ni·ous [ˈʌnseriˈmounjəs] □ poco ceremonioso; *~ly* sin miramientos.
un·cer·tain [ʌnˈsəːrtn] □ incierto, dudoso; *be ~ of* no estar seguro de; **unˈcer·tain·ty** incertidumbre *f*, duda *f*.
un·chain [ˈʌnˈtʃein] desencadenar.
un·chal·lenge·a·ble [ˈʌnˈtʃælindʒəbl] incontestable; ˈ**unˈchal·lenged** incontestado.
un·change·a·ble [ʌnˈtʃeindʒəbl], **unˈchang·ing** □ incambiable, inalterable.
un·char·i·ta·ble [ʌnˈtʃæritəbl] □ poco caritativo; despiadado.
un·chaste [ˈʌnˈtʃeist] □ impúdico, incontinente.
un·checked [ˈʌnˈtʃekt] **1.** *adj.* desenfrenado; *fact etc.* no comprobado; **2.** *adv.* sin restricción; de una manera desenfrenada.
un·chris·tian [ˈʌnˈkristjən] indigno de un cristiano.
un·civ·il [ˈʌnˈsivl] □ incivil; ˈ**unˈciv·i·lized** [~vilaizd] incivilizado, inculto.
un·claimed [ˈʌnˈkleimd] sin reclamar.
un·clas·si·fied [ˈʌnˈklæsifaid] sin clasificar.
un·cle [ˈʌŋkl] tío *m*; *sl.* prestamista *m*, prendero *m*.
un·clean [ˈʌnˈkliːn] □ sucio; *fig.* impuro.
un·clench [ˈʌnˈklentʃ] desapretar.
un·clothed [ˈʌnˈklouðd] desnudo.
un·cloud·ed [ˈʌnˈklaudid] despejado.
un·coil [ˈʌnˈkɔil] desenrollar(se).
un·col·lect·ed [ˈʌnkəˈlektid] sin cobrar.
un·come·ly [ˈʌnˈkʌmli] desgarbado.
un·com·fort·a·ble [ʌnˈkʌmfərtəbl] □ incómodo.
un·com·mon [ʌnˈkɔmən] **1.** □ poco común, raro; **2.** *adv.* F extraordinariamente.
un·com·mu·ni·ca·tive [ˈʌnkəˈmjuːnikətiv] poco comunicativo.
un·com·plain·ing [ˈʌnkəmˈpleiniŋ] □ resignado, sumiso.
un·com·pli·men·ta·ry [ˈʌnˈkɔmpliˈmentəri] poco lisonjero; ofensivo.
un·com·pro·mis·ing [ˈʌnˈkɔmprəmaiziŋ] □ intransigente.
un·con·cern [ˈʌnkənˈsəːrn] despreocupación *f*; indiferencia *f*; ˈ**un·conˈcerned** [*adv.* ~idli] □ despreocupado; indiferente (*about* a).
un·con·di·tion·al [ˈʌnkənˈdiʃnl] □ incondicional.
un·con·fined [ˈʌnkənˈfaind] ilimitado, libre.
un·con·firmed [ˈʌnkənˈfəːrmd] no confirmado.
un·con·gen·ial [ˈʌnkənˈdʒiːnjəl] antipático; incompatible.
un·con·nect·ed [ˈʌnkəˈnektid] □ inconexo; no relacionado (*with* con).
un·con·quer·a·ble [ʌnˈkɔŋkərəbl] □ inconquistable, invencible.
un·con·sci·en·tious [ˈʌnkɔnʃiˈenʃəs] □ poco concienzudo.
un·con·scion·a·ble [ʌnˈkɔnʃənəbl] □ desmedido, desrazonable.
un·con·scious [ʌnˈkɔnʃəs] **1.** □ inconsciente (*of* de); no intencional; ⚕ sin sentido, desmayado; **2.** *the ~* lo inconsciente; **unˈcon·scious·ness** inconsciencia *f*; ⚕ insensibilidad *f*.
un·con·se·crat·ed [ˈʌnˈkɔnsikreitid] no consagrado.
un·con·sti·tu·tion·al [ˈʌnkɔnstiˈtjuːʃnl] □ inconstitucional.
un·con·strained [ˈʌnkənˈstreind] libre, no cohibido.
un·con·test·ed [ˈʌnkənˈtestid] incontestado.
un·con·trol·la·ble [ʌnkənˈtrouləbl] □ ingobernable.
un·con·ven·tion·al [ˈʌnkənˈvenʃnl] □ poco formalista, desenfadado, poco convencional; original.
un·con·vert·ed [ˈʌnkənˈvəːrtid] no convertido (*a.* ✝).
un·con·vinced [ˈʌnkənˈvinst] no convencido; ˈ**un·conˈvinc·ing** □ poco convincente.
un·cooked [ˈʌnˈkukd] sin cocer.
un·cork [ˈʌnˈkɔːrk] descorchar, destapar.
un·cor·rupt·ed [ˈʌnkəˈrʌptid] incorrupto.

un·count·a·ble [ˈʌnˈkauntəbl] incontable; ˈ**unˈcount·ed** sin cuenta.
un·cou·ple [ˈʌnˈkʌpl] desacoplar.
un·couth [ʌnˈku:θ] □ grosero; rústico; tosco.
un·cov·er [ʌnˈkʌvər] descubrir.
un·crit·i·cal [ˈʌnˈkritikl] □ falto de sentido crítico; poco juicioso.
un·crowned [ˈʌnˈkraund] sin corona.
unc·tion [ˈʌŋkʃn] unción *f* (*a. fig.*); *fig.* efusión *f* fingida, fervor *m* afectado; zalamería *f*; *eccl.* *extreme* ~ extremaunción *f*; **unc·tu·ous** [ˈʌŋktuəs] □ untuoso (*a. fig.*); *fig.* afectadamente fervoroso; zalamero.
un·cul·ti·vat·ed [ˈʌnˈkʌltiveitid] inculto (*a. fig.*).
un·cut [ˈʌnˈkʌt] sin cortar; *diamond* en bruto, sin tallar; *book* intonso.
un·dam·aged [ˈʌnˈdæmidʒd] ileso, indemne.
un·damped [ˈʌnˈdæmpt] *fig.* no disminuido.
un·dat·ed [ˈʌnˈdeitid] sin fecha.
un·daunt·ed [ʌnˈdɔ:ntid] □ impávido; intrépido.
un·de·ceive [ˈʌndiˈsi:v] desengañar.
un·de·ci·pher·a·ble [ˈʌndiˈsaifərəbl] indescifrable.
un·de·fend·ed [ˈʌndiˈfendid] indefenso; ⚖ ~ *suit* pleito *m* perdido por incomparecimiento.
un·de·feat·ed [ˈʌndiˈfi:tid] invicto.
un·de·filed [ˈʌndiˈfaild] inmaculado.
un·de·fined [ˈʌndiˈfaind] indefinido.
un·de·mon·stra·tive [ˈʌndiˈmɔnstrətiv] □ reservado.
un·de·ni·a·ble [ˈʌndiˈnaiəbl] □ innegable.
un·de·nom·i·na·tion·al [ˈʌndinɔmiˈneiʃnl] □ no sectario.
un·de·pend·a·ble [ˈʌndiˈpendəbl] poco confiable.
un·der [ˈʌndər] **1.** *adv.* debajo; abajo; **2.** *prp.* (*less precise*; *a. fig.*) bajo, (*more precise*) debajo de; *number* inferior a; *aged* ~ *21* que tiene menos de 21 años; **3.** *in compounds*: ... inferior; ... insuficiente(mente); (*clothes*) ... interior; ˈ**~ˈbid** [*irr.* (*bid*)] ofrecer precio más bajo que; ˈ**~·carriage,** F ˈ**~·cart** ✈ tren *m* de aterrizaje; ˈ**~·clothes,** ˈ**~·cloth·ing** ropa *f* interior; ˈ**~·coat** *paint.* primera capa *f*; ˈ**~·cur·rent** corriente *f* submarina, contracorriente *f*; *fig.* nota *f* callada; ˈ**~ˈcut** *competitor* competir con (rebajando los precios); ˈ**~·developed** subdesarrollado; ˈ**~·dog** desvalido *m*; ˈ**~ˈdone** poco hecho; medio asado; ˈ**~ˈes·ti·mate** subestimar; *p.* tener en menos de lo que merece; ˈ**~·exˈpose** *phot.* exponer insuficientemente; **~*d*** subexpuesto; ˈ**~ˈfed** subalimentado; ˈ**~ˈfeed·ing** subalimentación *f*; **~ˈfoot** debajo de los pies; **~ˈgo** [*irr.* (*go*)] sufrir, experimentar; **~ˈgrad·u·ate** estudiante *m*/*f* (no graduado); ˈ**~·ground 1.** *adj.* subterráneo; *fig.* clandestino; **2.** *adv.* bajo tierra; **3.** (= ~ *railway*) metro *m*; ⚔ resistencia *f*; ˈ**~·growth** maleza *f*; ˈ**~·hand** turbio, poco limpio; clandestino; ~ *service* saque *m* con la mano debajo del hombro; **~ˈlay** [*irr.* (*lay*)] reforzar; *typ.* calzar; **~ˈlie** [*irr.* (*lie*)] estar debajo de; servir de base a (*a. fig.*); **~ˈline** subrayar (*a. fig.*).
un·der·ling [ˈʌndərliŋ] subordinado *m*, inferior *m*; secuaz *m*; **un·derˈmanned** [ˈ~ˈmænd] sin la debida tripulación, sin el debido personal; **un·derˈmine** socavar; minar (*a. fig.*); ˈ**un·der·most** (el) más bajo; **un·der·neath** [~ˈni:θ] **1.** *pron.* debajo de, bajo; **2.** *adv.* debajo; **3.** *su.* superficie *f* inferior; ˈ**un·derˈnourished** desnutrido.
un·der...: ˈ**~·pants** *pl.* calzoncillos *m*/*pl.*; ˈ**~·pass** paso *m* inferior; ˈ**~ˈpay** [*irr.* (*pay*)] pagar insuficientemente; **~ˈpin** apuntalar; **~ˈpin·ning** apuntalamiento *m*; **~ˈpriv·i·leged** desvalido; **~ˈrate** menospreciar; subestimar; **~ˈscore** subrayar; ˈ**~ˈsec·re·tar·y** subsecretario *m*; ˈ**~ˈsell** [*irr.* (*sell*)] *p.* vender a menor precio que; *th.* malvender; ˈ**~ˈshirt** camiseta *f*; ˈ**~ˈside** superficie *f* inferior; revés *m*; ˈ**~·signed** infra(e)scrito (a *f*) *m*; abajo firmante *m*/*f*; ˈ**~ˈsized** de dimensión insuficiente; *p.* sietemesino; ˈ**~·skirt** enaguas *f*/*pl.*; **~ˈslung** *mot.* debajo del eje; **~ˈstaffed** sin el debido personal; **~ˈstand** [*irr.* (*stand*)] comprender, entender; sobre(e)ntender; *give to* ~ dar a entender; *make o.s. understood* hacerse entender; *it is understood that* se entiende que; *an understood thing* lo normal; **~ˈstand·a·ble** □ comprensible; **~ˈstand·ing 1.** entendimiento *m*; comprensión *f*; interpretación *f*; (*agreement*) acuerdo *m*; *on the* ~ *that* con tal que, bien entendido que; **2.** □ inteligente; razonable,

compasivo; comprensivo; **ˈ~ˈstate** exponer incompletamente; subestimar; **ˈ~ˈstate·ment** exposición *f* incompleta; subestimación *f*.

un·der...: ˈ~·stud·y *thea.* **1.** suplente *m/f*; **2.** aprender un papel para poder suplir a; **~ˈtake** [*irr.* (*take*)] *task etc.* emprender; *duty etc.* encargarse de; ~ *to inf.* comprometerse a *inf.*; prometer *inf.*; ~ *that* comprometerse a que, prometer que; **~ˈtak·er** empresario *m* de pompas fúnebres, director *m* de funeraria; *~'s* funeraria *f*; **ˈ~·tak·ing** (*business of funeral director*) funeraria *f*; ~ *establishment* funeraria *f*, empresa *f* de pompas fúnebres; **~ˈtak·ing** empresa *f*; (*pledge*) compromiso *m*, garantía *f*; promesa *f*; **ˈ~·tone** voz *f* baja; trasfondo *m of criticism etc.*; *in an* ~ en voz baja; **ˈ~ˈtow** resaca *f*; **ˈ~ˈval·ue** valor(iz)ar incompletamente; subestimar; menospreciar; **ˈ~ˈwa·ter** submarino; **ˈ~ˈwa·ter ˈfish·ing** pesca *f* submarina; **ˈ~·wear** ropa *f* interior, prendas *f/pl.* interiores; **ˈ~·weight** (*adj.* de) peso *m* insuficiente; **ˈ~·world** infierno *m*; (*criminal*) hampa *f*; **ˈ~·write** [*irr.* (*write*)] subscribir; (*to insure*) ☤ (re)asegurar; **ˈ~·writ·er** (re)asegurador *m*; compañía *f* aseguradora.

un·de·served [ʌndiˈzəːrvd] □ inmerecido; **ˈun·deˈserv·ing** indigno.

un·de·sir·a·ble [ˈʌndiˈzairəbl] □ indeseable.

un·de·terred [ˈʌndiˈtəːrd] sin dejarse intimidar.

un·de·vel·oped [ˈʌndiˈveləpt] sin desarrollar; *land* sin explotar; *phot.* sin revelar.

un·de·vi·at·ing [ʌnˈdiːvieitiŋ] □ constante.

un·dies [ˈʌndiz] F paños *m/pl.* menores.

un·di·gest·ed [ˈʌndiˈdʒestid] indigesto.

un·dig·ni·fied [ʌnˈdignifaid] indecoroso; poco digno.

un·di·min·ished [ˈʌndiˈminiʃt] no disminuido.

un·dis·cern·ing [ˈʌndiˈsəːrniŋ] sin discernimiento.

un·dis·ci·plined [ʌnˈdisiplind] indisciplinado.

un·dis·crim·i·nat·ing [ˈʌndisˈkrimineitiŋ] □ falto de sentido crítico.

un·dis·guised [ˈʌndisˈgaizd] □ franco, sin disfraz.

un·dis·mayed [ˈʌndisˈmeid] impávido; sin desanimarse.

un·dis·posed-of [ˈʌndisˈpouzdɔv] *mst* ☤ no vendido; no invertido.

un·dis·put·ed [ˈʌndisˈpjuːtid] □ incontestable.

un·dis·tin·guished [ˈʌndisˈtiŋgwiʃd] mediocre.

un·dis·turbed [ˈʌndisˈtəːrbd] sin tocar; *p.* imperturbado.

un·di·vid·ed [ˈʌndiˈvaidid] □ indiviso; entero.

un·do [ˈʌnˈduː] [*irr.* (*do*)] *work* deshacer; *knot* desatar; *clasp* desabrochar; **ˈunˈdo·ing** perdición *f*, ruina *f*; **undone** [ˈʌnˈdʌn]: *leave* ~ dejar sin hacer; *leave nothing* ~ no dejar nada por hacer; *he is* ~ está perdido; *come* ~ desatarse.

un·doubt·ed [ʌnˈdautid] □ indudable.

un·dreamt [ʌnˈdremt]: *~-of* no soñado.

un·dress [ˈʌnˈdres] **1.** desnudar(se); **2.** traje *m* de casa, des(h)abillé *m*; ⚔ traje *m* de cuartel.

un·drink·a·ble [ʌnˈdriŋkəbl] impotable.

un·due [ˈʌnˈdjuː] [*adv. unduly*] indebido; excesivo.

un·du·late [ˈʌndjuleit] ondular, ondear; **ˈun·du·lat·ing** ondeante, ondulante; *land* ondulado; **un·duˈlation** ondulación *f*; **ˈun·du·la·to·ry** ondulatorio.

un·dy·ing [ʌnˈdaiiŋ] imperecedero, inmarcesible.

un·earned [ˈʌnˈəːrnd] no ganado.

un·earth [ˈʌnˈəːrθ] desenterrar; descubrir (*a. fig.*); **unˈearth·ly** sobrenatural; espectral; F *hour* inverosímil.

un·eas·i·ness [ʌnˈiːzinis] inquietud *f*, desasosiego *m*; **unˈeas·y** □ inquieto (*about* por), desasosegado; *feel* ~ sentirse mal a gusto.

un·eat·a·ble [ˈʌnˈiːtəbl] incomible.

un·e·co·nom·ic, un·e·co·nom·i·cal [ˈʌnikəˈnɔmik(l)] □ antieconómico.

un·ed·i·fy·ing [ˈʌnˈedifaiiŋ] □ indecoroso.

un·ed·u·cat·ed [ˈʌnˈedjukeitid] ineducado.

un·e·mo·tion·al [ˈʌniˈmouʃnl] □ que no se deja emocionar; impasible; objetivo.

un·em·ployed [ˈʌnimˈplɔid] parado, sin empleo, desocupado; **ˈun·em·ploy·ment** paro *m* (forzoso), desempleo *m*, desocupación *f*; ~ *benefit* subsidio *m* de paro; ~ *insurance* seguro *m* de desempleo (*or* de desocupación), seguro contra el paro obrero.
un·end·ing [ˈʌnˈendiŋ] □ interminable, inacabable.
un·en·dur·a·ble [ˈʌninˈdjurəbl] □ inaguantable, insufrible.
un·en·gaged [ˈʌninˈgeidʒd] libre.
un·en·light·ened [ˈʌninˈlaitnd] poco instruido; *policy etc.* ignorante, estúpido.
un·en·ter·pris·ing [ˈʌnˈentərpraiziŋ] □ falto de iniciativa.
un·en·vi·a·ble [ˈʌnˈenviəbl] □ poco envidiable.
un·e·qual [ˈʌnˈiːkwəl] □ desigual; ~ *to* sin fuerzas para; **ˈunˈe·qualed** inigualado.
un·e·quiv·o·cal [ˈʌniˈkwivəkl] □ inequívoco.
un·err·ing [ˈʌnˈəːriŋ] □ infalible.
un·es·sen·tial [ˈʌniˈsenʃl] □ no esencial.
un·e·ven [ˈʌnˈiːvn] □ desigual; *road* ondulado; *number* impar; ~ *number* impar *m*; **unˈe·ven·ness** desigualdad *f*; lo ondulado.
un·e·vent·ful [ˈʌniˈventful] □ sin incidentes notables.
un·ex·am·pled [ˈʌnigˈzæmpld] sin igual.
un·ex·cep·tion·a·ble [ˈʌnikˈsepʃənəbl] □ intachable.
un·ex·pect·ed [ˈʌniksˈpektid] □ inesperado; inopinado.
un·ex·pired [ˈʌniksˈpaiərd] no expirado; *lease, ticket* no caducado; ✝ *bill* no vencido.
un·ex·plained [ˈʌniksˈpleind] inexplicado.
un·ex·plored [ˈʌniksˈplɔːrd] inexplorado.
un·ex·posed [ˈʌniksˈpouzd] *phot.* inexpuesto.
un·ex·pressed [ˈʌniksˈprest] no expresado.
un·ex·pur·gat·ed [ˈʌnˈekspəːrgeitid] sin expurgar, integro.
un·fad·ing [ʌnˈfeidiŋ] *m mst fig.* inmarcesible.
un·fail·ing [ʌnˈfeiliŋ] □ *zeal* infalible; *supply* inagotable.
un·fair [ˈʌnˈfer] □ *comment* injusto; *practice* sin equidad; *play* sucio; **ˈunˈfair·ness** injusticia *f etc.*
un·faith·ful [ˈʌnˈfeiθful] □ infiel; **ˈunˈfaith·ful·ness** infidelidad *f*.
un·fal·ter·ing [ʌnˈfɔːltəriŋ] □ resuelto.
un·fa·mil·iar [ˈʌnfəˈmiljər] desconocido (*to* a); *be* ~ *with* desconocer.
un·fash·ion·a·ble [ˈʌnˈfæʃnəbl] □ fuera de moda.
un·fas·ten [ˈʌnˈfæsn] desatar, soltar.
un·fath·om·a·ble [ʌnˈfæðəməbl] □ insondable.
un·fa·vor·a·ble [ˈʌnˈfeivərəbl] □ desfavorable.
un·feel·ing [ʌnˈfiːliŋ] □ insensible.
un·feigned [ʌnˈfeind, *adv.* ~nidli] □ no fingido.
un·fer·ment·ed [ˈʌnfəːrˈmentid] no fermentado.
un·fet·ter [ˈʌnˈfetər] destrabar; **unˈfet·tered** *fig.* sin trabas.
un·fin·ished [ˈʌnˈfiniʃt] inacabado, sin acabar; incompleto.
un·fit 1. [ˈʌnˈfit] incapaz (*for* de, *to* de); no apto (*for* para); *player* lesionado; **2.** [ʌnˈfit] inhabilitar; **ˈunˈfit·ness** incapacidad *f*; **unˈfit·ted** incapacitado (*for* para).
un·flag·ging [ʌnˈflægiŋ] □ incansable.
un·flat·ter·ing [ˈʌnˈflætəriŋ] □ poco lisonjero.
un·fledged [ˈʌnfledʒd] implume.
un·flinch·ing [ʌnˈflintʃiŋ] □ impávido.
un·fly·a·ble weath·er [ˈʌnˈflaiəbl ˈweðər] tiempo *m* que imposibilita la salida de aviones.
un·fold [ˈʌnˈfould] desplegar(se); desdoblar(se); desarrollar(se) (*a. fig.*); revelar; *idea* exponer.
un·fore·see·a·ble [ˈʌnfɔːrˈsiːəbl] □ imprevisible; **ˈun·foreˈseen** imprevisto.
un·for·get·ta·ble [ˈʌnfərˈgetəbl] □ inolvidable.
un·for·giv·a·ble [ˈʌnfərˈgivəbl] □ imperdonable; **ˈun·forˈgiv·ing** implacable.
un·for·ti·fied [ˈʌnˈfɔːrtifaid] no fortificado; *town* abierto.
un·for·tu·nate [ʌnˈfɔːrtʃənit] **1.** □ *p.* desgraciado, desafortunado; malogrado; *event* funesto; *p.'s manner* infeliz; *remark* que trae malas consecuencias; **2.** desgraciado (a *f*) *m*; **unˈfor·tu·nate·ly** por desgracia, desafortunadamente.
un·found·ed [ˈʌnˈfaundid] □ infundado.

un·fre·quent·ed [ˈʌnfriˈkwentid] poco frecuentado.
unˈfriend·ly [ˈʌnˈfrendli] poco amistoso, hostil.
un·fruit·ful [ˈʌnˈfru:tful] □ infructuoso.
un·ful·filled [ˈʌnfulˈfild] incumplido.
un·furl [ˈʌnˈfə:rl] desplegar.
un·fur·nished [ˈʌnˈfə:rniʃt] desamueblado, sin muebles.
un·gain·li·ness [ʌnˈgeinlinis] torpeza *f*; **unˈgain·ly** torpe, desgarbado.
un·gal·lant [ˈʌnˈgælənt] □ falto de cortesía.
un·gear [ˈʌnˈgir] ⊕ desembragar.
un·gen·er·ous [ˈʌnˈdʒenərəs] □ poco generoso.
un·gen·tle·man·ly [ʌnˈdʒentlmənli] poco caballeroso.
un·glazed [ˈʌnˈgleizd] no vidriado.
un·god·li·ness [ʌnˈgɔdlinis] impiedad *f*; **unˈgod·ly** impío, irreligioso; F atroz.
un·gov·ern·a·ble [ʌnˈgʌvərnəbl] □ ingobernable.
un·gra·cious [ˈʌnˈgreiʃəs] □ poco afable; descortés, grosero.
un·grate·ful [ʌnˈgreitful] □ desagradecido, ingrato.
un·grudg·ing [ˈʌnˈgrʌdʒiŋ] □ generoso.
un·gual [ˈʌŋgwəl] unguiculado.
un·guard·ed [ˈʌnˈgɑ:rdid] □ ⚔ indefenso; *words* imprudente; *moment* de descuido.
un·guent [ˈʌŋgwənt] ungüento *m*.
un·gu·late [ˈʌŋgjuleit] (*or* ~ *animal*) ungulado *m*.
un·ham·pered [ˈʌnˈhæmpərd] no estorbado; libre, sin estorbos.
un·hand [ʌnˈhænd] soltar; **unˈhand·y** □ *p*. desmañado; *th*. incómodo.
un·hap·pi·ness [ʌnˈhæpinis] infelicidad *f*, desdicha *f*; **unˈhap·py** □ *p*. infeliz, desdichado; desgraciado; *event* infausto.
un·harmed [ˈʌnˈhɑ:rmd] ileso, incólume.
un·har·mo·ni·ous [ˈʌnhɑ:rˈmounjəs] □ inarmónico.
un·har·ness [ˈʌnˈhɑ:rnis] desguarnecer.
un·health·y [ʌnˈhelθi] □ *p*. enfermizo; *place* malsano.
un·heard-of [ʌnˈhə:rdɔv] inaudito.
un·heed·ed [ʌnˈhi:did] desatendido.
un·hes·i·tat·ing [ʌnˈheziteitiŋ] □ resuelto; pronto, inmediato; ~*ly* sin vacilar.
un·hinge [ʌnˈhindʒ] desquiciar (*a. fig.*).
un·his·tor·ic, un·his·tor·i·cal [ˈʌnhisˈtɔrik(l)] □ antihistórico.
un·ho·ly [ʌnˈhouli] impío; F atroz.
un·hook [ˈʌnˈhuk] desenganchar; descolgar.
un·hoped-for [ʌnˈhouptfɔ:r] inesperado; **unˈhope·ful** [~ful] □ poco prometedor.
un·horse [ˈʌnˈhɔ:rs] desarzonar.
un·hurt [ˈʌnˈhə:rt] ileso, incólume.
u·ni·corn [ˈju:nikɔ:rn] unicornio *m*.
un·i·den·ti·fied [ˈʌnaiˈdentifaid] sin identificar; ~ *flying object* (*UFO*) objeto *m* volante no identificado (OVNI).
u·ni·fi·ca·tion [ju:nifiˈkeiʃn] unificación *f*.
u·ni·form [ˈju:nifɔ:rm] **1.** □ uniforme *adj. a. su. m*; **2.** uniformar; **u·niˈform·i·ty** uniformidad *f*.
u·ni·fy [ˈju:nifai] unificar.
u·ni·lat·er·al [ˈju:niˈlætərəl] □ unilateral.
un·im·ag·i·na·ble [ˈʌniˈmædʒinəbl] □ inimaginable; **ˈun·imˈag·i·na·tive** [~nətiv] □ poco imaginativo.
un·im·paired [ˈʌnimˈperd] no disminuido, no deteriorado; intacto.
un·im·peach·a·ble [ʌnimˈpi:tʃəbl] □ irrecusable.
un·im·ped·ed [ˈʌnimˈpi:did] □ sin estorbo.
un·im·por·tant [ˈʌnimˈpɔ:rtənt] □ insignificante; sin importancia.
un·in·formed [ˈʌninˈfɔ:rmd] poco instruido, ignorante.
un·in·hab·it·a·ble [ˈʌninˈhæbitəbl] inhabitable; **ˈun·inˈhab·it·ed** inhabitado.
un·in·jured [ˈʌnˈindʒərd] ileso.
un·in·sured [ˈʌninˈʃurd] no asegurado.
un·in·tel·li·gent [ˈʌninˈtelidʒənt] □ ininteligente; **ˈun·in·tel·li·giˈbil·i·ty** ininteligibilidad *f*; **ˈun·inˈtel·li·gi·ble** □ ininteligible.
un·in·tend·ed [ˈʌninˈtendid] □, **un·in·ten·tion·al** [ˈʌninˈtenʃnl] □ involuntario, no intencional; ~*ly* sin querer.
un·in·ter·est·ing [ˈʌnˈintristiŋ] □ falto de interés.
un·in·ter·rupt·ed [ˈʌnintəˈrʌptid] □ ininterrumpido.

un·in·vit·ed [ˈʌninˈvaitid] *guest* no convidado, (*adv.*) sin ser convidado; *comment* gratuito; ˈ**un·inˈvit·ing** □ poco atractivo.

un·ion [ˈjuːnjən] unión *f* (*a.* ⊕); (*marriage*) enlace *m*; *pol. etc.* sindicato *m*, gremio *m* (obrero); *attr.* gremial; ♀ *Jack bandera del Reino Unido*; ~ *shop* taller *m* de obreros agremiados; ~ *suit* traje *m* interior de una sola pieza; ˈ**un·ion·ism** *pol.* (*British*) conservatismo *m*; *v. trade*; ˈ**un·ion·ist** (*British*) conservador (-a *f*) *m*; *v. trade*; ˈ**un·ion·ize** agremiar(se).

u·nique [juːˈniːk] □ único.

u·ni·son [ˈjuːnizn] ♪ unisonancia *f*; armonía *f* (*a. fig.*); *in* ~ al unísono; **u·nis·o·nous** [juːˈnisənəs] ♪ unísono.

u·nit [ˈjuːnit] unidad *f* (*a.* ⚔, ⚕); ⚡ (*measurement*) unidad *f*; ⊕, ⚡ grupo *m*; **U·ni·tar·i·an** [juːniˈteriən] unitario *adj. a. su. m*; **u·ni·tar·y** [ˈ~təri] unitario; **u·nite** [juːˈnait] unir(se), juntar(se); (*marry*) casar, enlazar; **u·nit·ed** [juːˈnaitid] unido; ♀ *Nations* (*UN*) Organización *f* de las Naciones Unidas (ONU), Naciones *f*/*pl.* Unidas; **u·ni·ty** [ˈ~niti] unidad *f*; unión *f*.

u·ni·ver·sal [juːniˈvəːrsl] □ universal; ~ *heir* heredero *m* único; ⊕ ~ *joint* junta *f* cardán, junta *f* universal; ♀ *Postal Union* Unión *f* Postal Universal; ~ *product code* (*UPC*) código *m* universal de producto; ~ *suffrage* sufragio *m* universal; **u·ni·ver·sal·i·ty** [~ˈsæliti] universalidad *f*; **u·ni·verse** [ˈ~vəːrs] universo *m*; **u·niˈver·si·ty** universidad *f*; *attr.* universitario.

un·just [ˈʌnˈdʒʌst] □ injusto; **un·jus·ti·fi·a·ble** [ʌnˈdʒʌstifaiəbl] □ injustificable.

un·kempt [ˈʌnˈkempt] despeinado; *fig.* desaseado, descuidado.

un·kind [ʌnˈkaind] □ poco amable, poco compasivo; cruel, despiadado; *remark etc.* malintencionado.

un·known [ˈʌnˈnoun] **1.** desconocido; incógnito; *adv.* ~ *to me* sin saberlo yo; **2.** desconocido *m*; ⚕ *a. fig.* (*a.* ~ *quantity*) incógnita *f*; ~ *soldier* soldado *m* desconocido.

un·lace [ˈʌnˈleis] desenlazar.

un·lade [ˈʌnˈleid] [*irr.* (*lade*)] descargar.

un·la·dy·like [ˈʌnˈleidilaik] impropio de una señora.

un·la·ment·ed [ˈʌnləˈmentid] no lamentado.

un·latch [ˈʌnˈlætʃ] abrir (levantando el picaporte).

un·law·ful [ˈʌnˈlɔːful] □ ilegítimo, ilegal.

un·learn [ˈʌnˈləːrn] desaprender; ˈ**unˈlearn·ed** [~id] □ indocto, ignorante.

un·leash [ˈʌnˈliːʃ] destraillar; *fig.* desencadenar.

un·leav·ened [ˈʌnˈlevnd] ázimo, sin levadura.

un·less [ənˈles, ʌnˈles] a menos que, a no ser que.

un·let·tered [ˈʌnˈletərd] indocto.

un·li·censed [ˈʌnˈlaisənst] sin permiso, sin licencia.

un·like [ˈʌnˈlaik] **1.** desemejante; diferente (*a p.* de una p.); ⚡ de signo contrario; **2.** *prp.* a diferencia de; **unˈlike·li·hood** improbabilidad *f*; **unˈlike·ly** improbable; inverosímil.

un·lim·it·ed [ʌnˈlimitid] ilimitado.

un·lined [ˈʌnˈlaind] *coat* sin forro; *face* sin arrugas; *paper* sin rayar.

un·liq·ui·dat·ed [ˈʌnˈlikwideitid] ilíquido.

un·load [ˈʌnˈloud] descargar; ✝ deshacerse de.

un·lock [ˈʌnˈlɔk] abrir (con llave); *fig.* resolver.

un·looked-for [ʌnˈluktfɔːr] inesperado, inopinado.

un·loose, un·loos·en [ˈʌnˈluːs(n)] aflojar, desatar, soltar.

un·lov·a·ble [ˈʌnˈlʌvəbl] poco apetecible; *p.* antipático; ˈ**unˈlove·ly** desgarbado; ˈ**unˈlov·ing** □ desamorado; nada cariñoso.

un·luck·y [ʌnˈlʌki] □ desgraciado; desdichado; (*ill-starred*) nefasto, de mala suerte; *it's* ~ *to inf.* trae mala suerte *inf.*

un·make [ˈʌnˈmeik] [*irr.* (*make*)] deshacer.

un·man [ˈʌnˈmæn] acobardar.

un·man·age·a·ble [ʌnˈmænidʒəbl] □ inmanejable; *esp. p.* incontrolable.

un·man·ly [ˈʌnˈmænli] cobarde; afeminado.

un·man·ner·ly [ʌnˈmænərli] descortés, mal educado.

un·marked [ˈʌnˈmaːrkt] sin marca(r); intacto; (*unnoticed*) inadvertido; *sport*: desmarcado.

un·mar·ket·a·ble [ˈʌnˈmɑːrkitəbl] invendible.
un·mar·ried [ˈʌnˈmærid] soltero.
un·mask [ˈʌnˈmæsk] desenmascarar.
un·matched [ˈʌnˈmætʃt] incomparable.
un·men·tion·a·ble [ʌnˈmenʃnəbl] **1.** que no debe mencionarse; indecible; **2.** *co.* † ~*s pl.* pantalones *m/pl.* (de hombre).
un·mer·ci·ful [ʌnˈməːrsiful] □ despiadado.
un·mer·it·ed [ˈʌnˈmeritid] inmerecido.
un·me·thod·i·cal [ˈʌnmiˈθɔdikl] poco metódico.
un·mind·ful [ʌnˈmaindful] □ descuidado; *be* ~ *of* no pensar en.
un·mis·tak·a·ble [ˈʌnmisˈteikəbl] □ inconfundible; inequívoco.
un·mit·i·gat·ed [ʌnˈmitigeitid] no mitigado; *rogue* redomado.
un·mo·lest·ed [ˈʌnmouˈlestid] indemne.
un·mor·al [ʌnˈmɔrəl] amoral.
un·mort·gaged [ˈʌnˈmɔːrgidʒd] libre de hipoteca.
un·mount·ed [ˈʌnˈmauntid] *rider* desmontado; *stone* sin engastar; *phot.* sin pegar.
un·mourned [ˈʌnˈmɔːrnd] no llorado.
un·moved [ˈʌnˈmuːvd] *mst fig.* impasible, inmoble.
un·mu·si·cal [ˈʌnˈmjuːzikl] □ inarmónico; *p.* sin instinto musical.
un·named [ˈʌnˈneimd] sin nombre.
un·nat·u·ral [ʌnˈnætʃrl] □ innatural; desnaturalizado; afectado.
un·nav·i·ga·ble [ˈʌnˈnævigəbl] innavegable.
un·nec·es·sar·y [ʌnˈnesisəri] □ innecesario, superfluo.
un·neigh·bor·ly [ˈʌnˈneibərli] poco amistoso.
un·nerve [ˈʌnˈnəːrv] acobardar.
un·no·ticed [ˈʌnˈnoutist] inadvertido.
un·num·bered [ˈʌnˈnʌmbərd] *page etc.* sin numerar; *poet.* innumerable.
un·ob·jec·tion·a·ble [ˈʌnəbˈdʒekʃənəbl] □ intachable.
un·ob·serv·ant [ˈʌnəbˈzəːrvənt] □ inadvertido; distraído, que no se fija; ˈ**un·obˈserved** inadvertido.
un·ob·tain·a·ble [ˈʌnəbˈteinəbl] inasequible.
un·ob·tru·sive [ˈʌnəbˈtruːsiv] □ discreto; modesto.
un·oc·cu·pied [ˈʌnˈɔkjupaid] *house* deshabitado; *territory* sin colonizar; *seat* libre; *post* vacante; *p.* desocupado.
un·of·fi·cial [ˈʌnəˈfiʃl] □ extraoficial, no oficial.
un·o·pened [ˈʌnˈoupənd] sin abrir.
un·op·posed [ˈʌnəˈpouzd] sin oposición.
un·or·gan·ized [ˈʌnˈɔːrgənaizd] no organizado.
un·or·tho·dox [ˈʌnˈɔːrθədɔks] poco ortodoxo; *eccl.* heterodoxo.
un·os·ten·ta·tious [ˈʌnɔstənˈteiʃəs] □ sin ostentación.
un·pack [ˈʌnˈpæk] desembalar, desempaquetar; *case* deshacer.
un·paid [ˈʌnˈpeid] *bill* a pagar, por pagar; *work* no retribuido.
un·pal·at·a·ble [ʌnˈpælətəbl] desabrido (*a. fig.*), intragable (*a. fig.*).
un·par·al·leled [ʌnˈpærəleld] incomparable, sin par.
un·par·don·a·ble [ʌnˈpɑːrdnəbl] □ imperdonable.
un·par·lia·men·ta·ry [ˈʌnpɑːrliˈmentəri] □ antiparlamentario.
un·pat·ent·ed [ˈʌnˈpætəntid] sin patentar.
un·pa·tri·ot·ic [ˈʌnpætriˈɔtik] □ antipatriótico.
un·paved [ˈʌnˈpeivd] sin pavimentar.
un·per·ceived [ˈʌnpərˈsiːvd] inapercibido.
un·per·turbed [ˈʌnpərˈtəːrbd] impertérrito.
un·pick [ˈʌnˈpik] *seam* descoser.
un·pin [ˈʌnˈpin] desprender.
un·placed [ˈʌnˈpleist] *sport*: no colocado.
un·pleas·ant [ʌnˈpleznt] □ desagradable; *p.* antipático; **unˈpleas·ant·ness** lo desagradable; (*quarrel etc.*) desavenencia *f*, disgusto *m*.
un·plumbed [ˈʌnˈplʌmd] no sondado.
un·po·et·ic, un·po·et·i·cal [ˈʌnpouˈetik(l)] □ poco poético.
un·po·lished [ˈʌnˈpɔliʃt] sin pulir; *stone* en bruto; *fig.* grosero, tosco.
un·pol·lut·ed [ˈʌnpəˈluːtid] impoluto.
un·pop·u·lar [ˈʌnˈpɔpjulər] impopular; **un·pop·u·lar·i·ty** [ˈ~ˈlæriti] impopularidad *f*.

un·prac·ti·cal [ˈʌnˈpræktikl] □ *p.* desmañado; poco práctico; **ˈunˈprac·ticed, ˈunˈprac·tised** [~tist] inexperto.
un·prec·e·dent·ed [ʌnˈpresidəntid] □ inaudito, sin precedente.
un·pre·dict·a·ble [ˈʌnpriˈdiktəbl] □ impredictible, incierto; *p.* de (re)acciones imprevisibles.
un·prej·u·diced [ˈʌnˈpredʒudist] imparcial, sin prejuicios.
un·pre·med·i·tat·ed [ˈʌnpriˈmediteitid] □ impremeditado.
un·pre·pared [ˈʌnpriˈperd, *adv.* ~ridli] □ no preparado; *p.* desprevenido.
un·pre·pos·sess·ing [ˈʌnpri:pəˈzesiŋ] poco atractivo.
un·pre·sent·a·ble [ˈʌnpriˈzentəbl] mal apersonado.
un·pre·ten·tious [ˈʌnpriˈtenʃəs] □ modesto, sin pretensiones.
un·prin·ci·pled [ʌnˈprinsəpld] nada escrupuloso, sin conciencia.
un·print·a·ble [ˈʌnˈprintəbl] intranscribible.
un·pro·duc·tive [ˈʌnprəˈdʌktiv] □ improductivo.
un·pro·fes·sion·al [ˈʌnprəˈfeʃnl] □ *conduct* indigno de su profesión; (*unskilled*) inexperto.
un·prof·it·a·ble [ˈʌnˈprɔfitəbl] □ poco provechoso, nada lucrativo.
un·prom·is·ing [ˈʌnˈprɔmisiŋ] □ poco prometedor.
un·pro·nounce·a·ble [ˈʌnprəˈnaunsəbl] □ impronunciable.
un·pro·pi·tious [ˈʌnprəˈpiʃəs] □ impropicio.
un·pro·tect·ed [ˈʌnprəˈtektid] indefenso.
un·proved [ˈʌnˈpru:vd] no probado.
un·pro·vid·ed [ˈʌnprəˈvaidid] desprovisto (*with* de); **ˈun·proˈvid·ed-for** imprevisto; *child* desvalido.
un·pro·voked [ˈʌnprəˈvoukt] sin provocación.
un·pub·lished [ˈʌnˈpʌbliʃt] inédito.
un·punc·tu·al [ˈʌnˈpʌŋktʃuəl] □ impuntual; **un·punc·tu·al·i·ty** [ˈ~ˈæliti] impuntualidad *f.*
un·pun·ished [ˈʌnˈpʌniʃt] impune; *go* ~ escapar sin castigo.
un·qual·i·fied [ʌnˈkwɔlifaid] *p.* incompetente, inhábil; *teacher* sin título; *applicant* indocumentado; *success, assertion* incondicional; F *liar* redomado.
un·quench·a·ble [ʌnˈkwentʃəbl] □ inextinguible, insaciable (*a. fig.*).
un·ques·tion·a·ble [ʌnˈkwestʃənəbl] □ incuestionable; **unˈques·tioned** incontestable; **unˈques·tion·ing** □ incondicional.
un·qui·et [ˈʌnˈkwaiət] inquieto.
un·quote [ˈʌnˈkwout] terminar una cita; "~" (*in speech etc.*) fin *m* de la cita; **unˈquot·ed** † no cotizado.
un·rav·el [ʌnˈrævl] desenmarañar (*a. fig.*).
un·read [ˈʌnˈred] no leído; **un·read·a·ble** [ˈʌnˈri:dəbl] ilegible; *fig.* pesadísimo.
un·read·i·ness [ˈʌnˈredinis] desprevención *f*; **ˈunˈread·y** □ desapercibido, desprevenido.
un·re·al [ˈʌnˈriəl] irreal, ilusorio; **un·re·al·is·tic** [ˈʌnriəˈlistik] □ impracticable; fantástico; *p.* poco realista; **un·re·al·i·ty** [ˈ~ˈæliti] irrealidad *f*; **ˈunˈre·al·iz·a·ble** [~laizəbl] irrealizable.
un·rea·son [ˈʌnˈri:zn] insensatez *f*; **unˈrea·son·a·ble** □ irrazonable; *demand* excesivo; **unˈrea·son·ing** irracional.
un·re·claimed [ˈʌnriˈkleimd] *land* no utilizado.
un·rec·og·niz·a·ble [ˈʌnˈrekəgnaizəbl] □ irreconocible; **ˈunˈrec·og·nized** no reconocido.
un·re·cord·ed [ˈʌnriˈkɔ:rdid] no registrado.
un·re·deemed [ˈʌnriˈdi:md] *promise* sin cumplir; *pledge* no desempeñado; *fig.* no mitigado (*by* por).
un·re·dressed [ˈʌnriˈdrest] sin corregir.
un·re·fined [ˈʌnriˈfaind] no refinado; *fig.* inculto.
un·re·flect·ing [ˈʌnriˈflektiŋ] □ irreflexivo.
un·re·formed [ˈʌnriˈfɔ:rmd] no reformado.
un·re·gard·ed [ˈʌnriˈgɑ:rdid] desatendido.
un·re·gen·er·ate [ˈʌnriˈdʒenərit] empedernido.
un·reg·is·tered [ˈʌnˈredʒistərd] no registrado; *letter* no certificado.
un·re·gret·ted [ˈʌnriˈgretid] no lamentado.
un·re·lat·ed [ˈʌnriˈleitid] inconexo.
un·re·lent·ing [ˈʌnriˈlentiŋ] □ inexorable, implacable.

un·re·li·a·ble ['ʌnri'laiəbl] *p.* poco confiable; informal; *news* nada fidedigno.
un·re·lieved ['ʌnri'li:vd] □ no aliviado.
un·re·mit·ting ['ʌnri'mitiŋ] □ infatigable.
un·re·mu·ner·a·tive ['ʌnri'mju:nərətiv] □ poco lucrativo.
un·re·pealed ['ʌnri'pi:ld] no revocado.
un·re·peat·a·ble ['ʌnri'pi:təbl] que no puede repetirse.
un·re·pent·ant ['ʌnri'pentənt] □ impenitente.
un·re·quit·ed ['ʌnri'kwaitid] □ no correspondido; ~ *love* amor *m* no correspondido.
un·re·served ['ʌnri'zə:rvd, *adv.* ~vidli] □ no reservado, libre; ~*ly* sin reserva.
un·re·sist·ing ['ʌnri'zistiŋ] □ sumiso.
un·re·spon·sive ['ʌnris'pɔnsiv] insensible.
un·rest ['ʌn'rest] malestar *m*, zozobra *f*; *pol.* desorden *m*.
un·re·strained ['ʌnris'treind] □ desenfrenado.
un·re·strict·ed ['ʌnris'triktid] □ sin restricción *f*.
un·re·vealed ['ʌnri'vi:ld] no revelado.
un·re·ward·ed ['ʌnri'wɔ:rdid] sin recompensa; **un·re'ward·ing** sin provecho, infructuoso.
un·rig ['ʌn'rig] desaparejar.
un·right·eous [ʌn'raitʃəs] □ injusto; malvado.
un·ripe ['ʌn'raip] inmaturo, verde.
un·ri·valed [ʌn'raivəld] sin rival, incomparable.
un·roll ['ʌn'roul] desenrollar.
un·roof ['ʌn'ru:f] destechar.
un·rope ['ʌn'roup] *mount.* desatar(se).
un·ruf·fled ['ʌn'rʌfld] imperturbable.
un·ruled ['ʌn'ru:ld] *paper* sin rayar.
un·ru·ly [ʌn'ru:li] revoltoso, ingobernable.
un·sad·dle ['ʌn'sædl] *rider* desarzonar; *horse* desensillar.
un·safe ['ʌn'seif] □ inseguro.
un·said ['ʌn'sed] callado, no dicho.
un·sal(e)·a·ble ['ʌn'seiləbl] invendible.
un·sat·is·fac·to·ry ['ʌnsætis'fæktəri] □ insatisfactorio; **un'sat·is·fied** insatisfecho; **un'sat·is·fy·ing** □ insuficiente.
un·sa·vor·y ['ʌn'seivəri] desabrido; repugnante; *p.* indeseable.
un·say ['ʌn'sei] [*irr.* (*say*)] desdecirse de.
un·scathed ['ʌn'skeiðd] ileso.
un·sci·en·tif·ic ['ʌnsaiən'tifik] □ poco científico.
un·screw ['ʌn'skru:] destornillar.
un·scru·pu·lous [ʌn'skru:pjuləs] □ desaprensivo, poco escrupuloso.
un·seal ['ʌn'si:l] desellar.
un·sea·son·a·ble [ʌn'si:znəbl] □ intempestivo; '**un'sea·soned** sin sazonar; sin madurar; *wood* verde.
un·seat ['ʌn'si:t] *rider* desarzonar; destituir *from post*; *parl.* expulsar.
un·sea·wor·thy ['ʌn'si:wə:rði] innavegable.
un·seem·li·ness [ʌn'si:mlinis] lo indecoroso; **un'seem·ly** *adj.* indecoroso.
un·seen ['ʌn'si:n] **1.** invisible; inadvertido; **2.** (*a.* ~ *translation*) traducción *f* hecha a primera vista.
un·self·ish ['ʌn'selfiʃ] □ desinteresado, altruista.
un·serv·ice·a·ble ['ʌn'sə:rvisəbl] □ inservible.
un·set·tle ['ʌn'setl] desarreglar; *p.* inquietar; '**un'set·tled** *p.* inquieto; *weather* variable; *question* pendiente; *land* inhabitado, no colonizado; ✝ *market* in(e)stable; ✝ *account* por pagar.
un·shack·le ['ʌn'ʃækl] desencadenar.
un·shak·(e)a·ble ['ʌn'ʃeikəbl] □ inquebrantable; **un'shak·en** impertérrito.
un·shape·ly ['ʌn'ʃeipli] deforme.
un·shav·en ['ʌn'ʃeivn] sin afeitar.
un·sheathe ['ʌn'ʃi:ð] desenvainar.
un·ship ['ʌn'ʃip] desembarcar; *rudder* desmontar; F deshacerse de.
un·shod ['ʌn'ʃɔd] descalzo; *horse* desherrado.
un·shrink·a·ble ['ʌn'ʃriŋkəbl] inencogible; '**un'shrink·ing** □ impávido.
un·sight·ed ['ʌn'saitid] que tiene impedida la vista; **un'sight·ly** feo.
un·signed ['ʌn'saind] sin firmar.
un·skill·ful ['ʌn'skilful] □, '**un'skilled** inexperto, desmañado; *worker* no cualificado; ~ *laborer* bracero *m*, peón *m*.

un·skimmed ['ʌn'skimd] sin desnatar.
un·so·cia·ble [ʌn'souʃəbl] □ insociable.
un·sold ['ʌn'sould] sin vender.
un·sol·der [ʌn'sɑ:dər] desoldar; *fig.* desunir, separar.
un·sol·dier·ly ['ʌn'souldʒərli] indigno de un militar.
un·so·lic·it·ed ['ʌnsə'lisitid] no solicitado.
un·solv·a·ble ['ʌn'sɔlvəbl] irresoluble; '**un'solved** no resuelto.
un·so·phis·ti·cat·ed ['ʌnsə'fistikeitid] sencillo, cándido.
un·sought ['ʌn'sɔ:t] no solicitado.
un·sound ['ʌn'saund] □ defectuoso; *opinion* falso, erróneo; *fruit* podrido; *of* ~ *mind* insano, demente.
un·spar·ing ['ʌn'speriŋ] □ generoso, pródigo; *effort* incansable; (*cruel*) despiadado; *be* ~ *of* no escatimar *acc.*
un·speak·a·ble [ʌn'spi:kəbl] □ indecible; F horrible
un·spec·i·fied ['ʌn'spesifaid] no especificado.
un·spent ['ʌn'spent] no gastado.
un·spoiled ['ʌn'spɔild] sin menoscabo, intacto.
un·spo·ken ['ʌn'spoukn] tácito.
un·sport·ing ['ʌn'spɔ:rtiŋ] □, **unsports·man·like** ['ʌn'spɔ:rtsmənlaik] antideportivo; nada caballeroso.
un·spot·ted ['ʌn'spɔtid] inmaculado.
un·sta·ble ['ʌn'steibl] inestable.
un·stamped ['ʌn'stæmpt] ✉ sin franquear.
un·states·man·like ['ʌn'steitsmənlaik] indigno de un estadista.
un·stead·y ['ʌn'stedi] □ inestable, inseguro; inconstante; *p.* irresoluto.
un·stint·ed [ʌn'stintid] ilimitado, liberal.
un·stop ['ʌn'stɔp] destaponar.
un·stressed ['ʌn'strest] inacentuado, átono.
un·string ['ʌn'striŋ] [*irr.* (*string*)] ♪ desencordar; *nerves* trastornar; *pearls* desensartar.
un·stud·ied ['ʌn'stʌdid] natural, sin afectación.
un·sub·dued ['ʌnsəb'dju:d] indomado.
un·sub·mis·sive ['ʌnsəb'misiv] □ insumiso.
un·sub·stan·tial ['ʌnsəb'stænʃl] □ insustancial.
un·suc·cess·ful ['ʌnsək'sesful] □ *p.* fracasado; *effort etc.* infructuoso, ineficaz; *be* ~ malograrse; *be* ~ *in ger.* no lograr *inf.*
un·suit·a·ble ['ʌn'sju:təbl] □ inconveniente, inadecuado; impropio (*for a p.* de una p.); *p.* incompetente; '**un'suit·ed** inapto (*for, to* para); inadecuado.
un·sul·lied ['ʌn'sʌlid] inmaculado.
un·sure ['ʌn'ʃur] poco seguro.
un·sur·passed ['ʌnsə:r'pæst] insuperado.
un·sus·pect·ed ['ʌnsəs'pektid] insospechado; '**un·sus'pect·ing** □ confiado, nada suspicaz.
un·swerv·ing ['ʌn'swə:rviŋ] □ *resolve* inquebrantable; *course* sin vacilar.
un·sworn ['ʌn'swɔ:rn] no juramentado.
un·sym·pa·thet·ic ['ʌnsimpə'θetik] □ incompasivo, indiferente.
un·taint·ed ['ʌn'teintid] □ incorrupto; inmaculado.
un·tam(e)·a·ble ['ʌn'teiməbl] indomable; '**un'tamed** indomado.
un·tan·gle ['ʌn'tæŋgl] desenmarañar.
un·tanned ['ʌn'tænd] sin curtir.
un·tar·nished ['ʌn'tɑ:rniʃt] inmaculado.
un·tast·ed ['ʌn'teistid] sin probar.
un·taught ['ʌn'tɔ:t] no enseñado; espontáneo.
un·taxed ['ʌn'tækst] libre de impuesto.
un·teach·a·ble ['ʌn'ti:tʃəbl] indócil.
un·tem·pered ['ʌn'tempərd] ⊕ sin templar.
un·ten·a·ble ['ʌn'tenəbl] insostenible.
un·ten·ant·ed ['ʌn'tenəntid] desalquilado, desocupado.
un·think·a·ble [ʌn'θiŋkəbl] inconcebible; **un'think·ing** □ irreflexivo.
un·thread ['ʌn'θred] *cloth* deshebrar; *needle* desenhebrar; *pearls* desensartar.
un·thrift·y ['ʌn'θrifti] □ gastador.
un·ti·dy [ʌn'taidi] □ desaliñado, desaseado; *room* en desorden.
un·tie ['ʌn'tai] desatar; soltar.
un·til [ən'til, ʌn'til] **1.** *prp.* hasta; **2.** *cj.* hasta que.
un·tilled ['ʌn'tild] inculto.

un·time·ly [ʌnˈtaimli] intempestivo, prematuro.
un·tir·ing [ʌnˈtairiŋ] □ incansable.
un·to [ˈʌntu] † = *to* a *etc.*
un·told [ˈʌnˈtould] *story* nunca contado; *wealth* incalculable.
un·touch·a·ble [ˈʌnˈtʌtʃəbl] (*India*) intocable *adj.* *a.* *su.* *m/f*; **unˈtouched** intacto; incólume; *food* sin probar; *phot.* sin retocar; *fig.* insensible (*by* a).
un·to·ward [ʌnˈtɔ:rd] adverso; incómodo.
un·trained [ˈʌnˈtreind] no adiestrado, no entrenado.
un·trans·fer·a·ble [ˈʌntrænsˈfə:rəbl] intransferible.
un·trans·lat·a·ble [ˈʌntrænsˈleitəbl] intraducible.
un·trav·eled [ˈʌnˈtrævld] *place* inexplorado; *p.* que no ha viajado.
un·tried [ˈʌnˈtraid] no probado; ⚖ *p.* no procesado, *case* no visto.
un·trod, un·trod·den [ˈʌnˈtrɔd(n)] no trillado.
un·trou·bled [ˈʌnˈtrʌbld] tranquilo.
un·true [ˈʌnˈtru:] □ falso; inexacto; *p.* infiel.
un·trust·wor·thy [ˈʌnˈtrʌstwə:rði] □ indigno de confianza.
un·truth [ˈʌnˈtru:θ] mentira *f*; **unˈtruth·ful** □ mentiroso.
un·tu·tored [ˈʌnˈtju:tərd] no instruido, indocto.
un·twine [ˈʌnˈtwain], **un·twist** [ˈʌnˈtwist] destorcer; desenmarañar.
un·used [ˈʌnˈju:zd] inusitado; *stamp etc.* sin usar; no acostumbrado (*to* a); **un·u·su·al** [ʌnˈju:ʒuəl] □ insólito, extraordinario; nada usual, poco común.
un·ut·ter·a·ble [ʌnˈʌtərəbl] □ indecible.
un·var·nished [ˈʌnˈvɑ:rniʃt] sin barnizar; *fig.* puro.
un·var·y·ing [ʌnˈveriiŋ] □ invariable.
un·veil [ˈʌnˈveil] quitar el velo a; *statue etc.* descubrir.
un·versed [ˈʌnˈvə:rst] poco ducho (*in* en).
un·voiced [ˈʌnˈvɔist] *opinion* no expresado; *gr.* sordo.
un·vouched-for [ˈʌnˈvautʃdfɔ:r] no garantizado.
un·want·ed [ˈʌnˈwɔntid] superfluo; *child* no deseado.
un·war·i·ness [ʌnˈwerinis] imprudencia *f*, falta *f* de precaución.
un·war·like [ˈʌnwɔ:rlaik] pacífico.
un·war·rant·a·ble [ʌnˈwɔrəntəbl] □ injustificable; **ˈunˈwar·rant·ed** injustificado; desautorizado.
un·war·y [ˈʌnˈweri] □ imprudente, incauto.
un·wa·ver·ing [ʌnˈweivəriŋ] □ inquebrantable, resuelto.
un·wea·ry·ing [ʌnˈwiriiŋ] □ incansable.
un·wel·come [ʌnˈwelkəm] importuno, molesto.
un·well [ˈʌnˈwel] indispuesto.
un·whole·some [ˈʌnˈhoulsəm] insalubre; *p. etc.* indeseable.
un·wield·y [ʌnˈwi:ldi] pesado; abultado.
un·will·ing [ˈʌnˈwiliŋ] □ desinclinado; *be ~ to* estar poco dispuesto a; *~ly* de mala gana.
un·wind [ˈʌnˈwaind] [*irr.* (*wind*)] desenvolver.
un·wis·dom [ˈʌnˈwizdəm] imprudencia *f*; **un·wise** [ˈʌnˈwaiz] □ imprudente, malaconsejado.
un·wit·ting [ʌnˈwitiŋ] □ inconsciente; *~ly* sin saber.
un·wont·ed [ʌnˈwountid] □ insólito, inusitado.
un·work·a·ble [ˈʌnˈwə:rkəbl] impracticable.
un·world·ly [ˈʌnˈwə:rldli] no mundano, espiritual.
un·wor·thy [ʌnˈwə:rði] □ indigno.
un·wound·ed [ˈʌnˈwu:ndid] ileso.
un·wrap [ˈʌnˈræp] desenvolver, desempapelar; *parcel* deshacer.
un·writ·ten [ˈʌnˈritn] no escrito; *law* tradicional, tácito.
un·wrought [ˈʌnˈrɔ:t] no labrado.
un·yield·ing [ʌnˈji:ldiŋ] □ inflexible.
un·yoke [ˈʌnˈjouk] desuncir.
up [ʌp] **1.** *adv.* arriba; hacia arriba; en el aire, en (lo) alto; (*out of bed*) levantado; (*sun*) salido; (*standing*) de pie, en pie; (*time*) expirado; F *hard ~* apurado; F *it's all ~* todo se acabó; *it's all ~ with him* no hay remedio para él; F *~ against it* en apuros; *be ~ against p.* tener que habérselas con; F *what's ~?* ¿qué pasa?; *well ~ in* fuerte en; *~ to* hasta; *v. date, mark*; *be ~ to* ser capaz de; F *it's not ~ to much* no es para mucho; *it is ~ to me* me toca a mí; *what are you ~ to?* ¿qué haces allí?; **2.** *int.* ¡arriba!; **3.** *prp.* en lo

alto de; encima de; *~ a tree* en un árbol; *~ the street* calle arriba; **4.** *adj.*: *~ train* tren *m* ascendente; **5.** *su.*: F *on the ~ and ~* cada vez mejor; *the ~s and downs* vicisitudes *f/pl.*, altibajos *m/pl.*; **6.** *vb.*: F *to ~ and inf.* ponerse de repente a *inf.*

up-and-com·ing [ˈʌpənˈkʌmiŋ] F joven y prometedor.

up-and-down [ˈʌpənˈdaun] variable; accidentado.

up-and-up [ˈʌpənˈʌp]: *on the ~* F (*without fraud*) abiertamente, sin dolo; F (*improving*) mejorándose.

up·braid [ʌpˈbreid] reprochar, censurar (*a p. with a th.* algo a alguien).

up·bring·ing [ˈʌpbriŋiŋ] educación *f*, crianza *f*.

up·cast [ˈʌpkæst] ⚒ (*a. ~ shaft*) pozo *m* de ventilación.

up·coun·try [ˈʌpˈkʌntri] **1.** *adv.* tierra adentro; **2.** *adj.* del interior.

up·cur·rent [ˈʌpkʌrənt] ✈ viento *m* ascendente.

up·date [ʌpˈdeit, ˈʌpdeit] poner al día.

up·end [ˈʌpˈend] volver de arriba abajo.

up·grade [ˈʌpgreid] **1.** cuesta *f*, pendiente *f*; *on the ~ fig.* prosperando; ⚕ mejorando; **2.** mejorar.

up·heav·al [ʌpˈhiːvl] *geol.* solevantamiento *m*; *fig.* cataclismo *m*, sacudida *f*.

up·hill [ˈʌpˈhil] **1.** *adv.* cuesta arriba; **2.** *adj. task* arduo.

up·hold [ʌpˈhould] [*irr.* (*hold*)] sostener, defender; **upˈhold·er** *fig.* defensor (-a *f*) *m*.

up·hol·ster [ʌpˈhoulstər] (en)tapizar; **upˈhol·ster·er** tapicero *m*; **upˈhol·ster·y** tapicería *f*; tapizado *m*.

up·keep [ˈʌpkiːp] (gastos *m/pl.* de) conservación *f*, entretenimiento *m*.

up·land [ˈʌplənd] **1.** (*mst pl.*) tierras *f/pl.* altas; meseta *f*; **2.** de la meseta.

up·lift **1.** [ʌpˈlift] *fig.* inspirar, edificar; **2.** [ˈʌplift] *fig.* inspiración *f*, edificación *f*.

up·on [əˈpɔn] = *on* en, sobre *etc.*

up·per [ˈʌpər] **1.** superior; *~ berth* litera *f* alta, cama *f* alta; *~ case typ.* caja *f* alta; *~ class* clase *f* alta; *~ classes pl.* altas clases *f/pl.*; *~ deck* (*bus*) piso *m* de arriba; *the ~ hand* la ventaja; el dominio; *have the ~ hand* tener vara alta; *~ middle class* alta burguesía *f*; **2.** (*mst ~s pl.*) pala *f*; F *on one's ~s* sin un cuarto; **ˈ~-class** de la clase alta; **ˈ~·cut** *boxing*: golpe *m* de abajo arriba; **ˈ~·most** (el) más alto; predominante *in mind*.

up·pish [ˈʌpiʃ] □ F, **up·pi·ty** [ˈʌpiti] F engreído; atrevido.

up·raise [ʌpˈreiz] levantar.

up·right **1.** [ˈʌpˈrait] □ vertical; derecho (*a. adv.*); *fig.* honrado, probo; **2.** [ˈʌprait] montante *m*.

up·ris·ing [ʌpˈraiziŋ] alzamiento *m*, sublevación *f*.

up·roar [ˈʌprɔːr] *fig.* alboroto *m*, tumulto *m*; grita *f*; **upˈroar·i·ous** □ tumultuoso; clamoroso.

up·root [ʌpˈruːt] desarraigar (*a. fig.*), arrancar.

up·set [ʌpˈset] **1.** [*irr.* (*set*)] (*overturn*) volcar, trastornar; (*spill*) derramar; *fig. p. etc.* desconcertar, perturbar, trastornar; *plans* dar al traste con; *stomach* hacer daño a; F *~ o.s.* congojarse, apurarse; **2.** vuelco *m*; trastorno *m* (*a.* ⚕); contratiempo *m*; **3.** perturbado, preocupado; ⚕ indispuesto; *~ price* precio *m* mínimo *in auction*; **upˈset·ting** inquietante; desconcertante.

up·shot [ˈʌpʃɔt] resultado *m*; *in the ~* al fin y al cabo.

up·side [ˈʌpsaid]: *~ down* al revés; lo de arriba abajo; *fig.* en confusión; *turn ~ down* trastornar(se).

up·stage [ˈʌpˈsteidʒ] **1.** *adv.* (*be*) en el fondo de la escena; (*go*) hacia el fondo de la escena; **2.** *adj* F situado al fondo de la escena; F altanero, arrogante; **3.** [ʌpˈsteidʒ] *v/t.* F mirar por encima del hombro, desairar; *thea.* ir hacia el fondo de la escena a detrás de (*otro actor*); lograr captar la atención del público a costa de.

up·stairs [ˈʌpˈsterz] **1.** *adv.* arriba; **2.** *adj.* de arriba; **3.** piso *m* de arriba.

up·start [ˈʌpstɑːrt] arribista *adj. a. su. m*; advenedizo *adj. a. su. m*.

up·state [ˈʌpˈsteit] interior, septentrional (*esp. de Nueva York*).

up·stream [ˈʌpˈstriːm] río arriba, aguas arriba.

up·stroke [ˈʌpstrouk] plumada *f* (⊕ carrera *f*) ascendente.

up·surge [ˈʌpsəːrdʒ] acceso *m*, aumento *m* grande.

up·swing [ˈʌpˈswiŋ] *fig.* mejora *f*, prosperidad *f*.

up·take ['ʌpteik]: F *be quick* (*slow*) *on the* ~ ser muy listo (torpe).
up-to-date ['ʌptə'deit] corriente; reciente, moderno; de última hora, de última moda.
up-to-the-min·ute ['ʌptəθə'minit] al día, de actualidad.
up·town ['ʌp'taun] hacia (*adj.* de) la parte alta de la ciudad.
up·turn [ʌp'tə:rn] volver(se) hacia arriba; volcar.
up·ward ['ʌpwərd] **1.** *adj.* ascendente, ascensional; **2.** *adv.* = **up·wards** ['~z] hacia arriba; ~ *of* más de.
u·ra·ni·um [ju'reiniəm] uranio *m.*
ur·ban ['ə:rbən] urbano; **ur·bane** [ə:r'bein] □ urbano; **ur·ban·i·ty** [ə:r'bæniti] urbanidad *f*; **ur·ban·i·za·tion** [ə:rbənai'zeiʃn] urbanización *f*; '**ur·ban·ize** urbanizar.
ur·chin ['ə:rtʃin] galopín *m*, golf(ill)o *m.*
u·re·thra [ju:'ri:θrə] uretra *f.*
urge [ə:rdʒ] **1.** impeler, instar (*to* a *inf.*, a que *subj.*); incitar (*a p. to a th.*, *a th. on a p.* a una p. a algo); ~ *on* animar; **2.** impulso *m*; instinto *m*; **ur·gen·cy** ['~ənsi] urgencia *f*; '**ur·gent** □ urgente.
u·ric ['jurik] úrico.
u·ri·nal ['jurinl] urinario *m*; (*vessel*) orinal *m*; '**u·ri·nar·y** urinario; **u·ri·nate** ['~neit] orinar; **u·rine** ['~rin] orina *f*, orines *m/pl.*
urn [ə:rn] urna *f*; (*mst tea*) tetera *f.*
us [ʌs, əs] nos; (*after prp.*) nosotros, nosotras.
us·a·ble ['ju:zəbl] utilizable.
us·age ['ju:zidʒ] uso *m*; tratamiento *m.*
us·ance ['ju:zəns] ✝ plazo *m* a que se paga una letra de cambio; *bill at* ~ letra *f* de cambio pagadera a plazo.
use 1. [ju:s] uso *m*; utilidad *f*; manejo *m*, empleo *m*; *in* ~ en uso; *be of* ~ ayudar; *be of no* ~ no servir; *it is* (*of*) *no* ~ *ger.* (*or to inf.*) es inútil *inf.*; *have no* ~ *for* no necesitar; F tener en poco; *make* ~ *of* servirse de; *make good* ~ *of* aprovecharse de; *put to* ~ servirse de, sacar partido de; **2.** [ju:z] usar; emplear, manejar; utilizar; ~ *up* consumir, agotar; ~*d* usado; **used** ['ju:st]: *be* ~ *to* estar acostumbrado a; *get* ~ *to* acostumbrarse a; *I* ~ *to do* solía hacer, hacía; **use·ful** ['ju:sful] □ útil; ⊕ ~ *capacity*, ~ *efficiency* capacidad *f* útil; ~ *load* carga *f* útil; '**use·ful·ness** utilidad *f*; '**use·less** □ inútil; inservible; *p.* inepto; '**use·less·ness** inutilidad *f*; **us·er** ['ju:zər] usuario (a *f*) *m.*
ush·er ['ʌʃər] **1.** ujier *m*; portero *m*; *thea.* acomodador *m*; **2.** (*mst* ~ *in*) anunciar; introducir; hacer pasar; *thea.* acomodar.
ush·er·ette [ʌʃər'et] acomodadora *f.*
u·su·al ['ju:ʒuəl] □ usual, acostumbrado; corriente; *as* ~ como de costumbre.
u·su·fruct ['ju:sjufrʌkt] usufructo *m*; **u·su'fruc·tu·ar·y** [~tjueri] usufructuario (a *f*) *m.*
u·su·rer ['ju:ʒərər] usurero *m*; **u·su·ri·ous** [ju:'zjuriəs] □ usurario.
u·surp [ju:'zə:rp] usurpar; **u·sur'pa·tion** usurpación *f*; **u'surp·er** usurpador (-a *f*) *m*; **u'surp·ing** □ usurpador.
u·su·ry ['ju:ʒuri] usura *f.*
u·ten·sil [ju:'tensl] utensilio *m.*
u·ter·ine ['ju:tərin] uterino; **u·ter·us** ['~rəs] útero *m.*
u·til·i·tar·i·an [ju:tili'teriən] **1.** utilitarista *m/f*; **2.** utilitario; **u'til·i·ty 1.** utilidad *f*; *public* ~ empresa *f* de servicio público; **2.** *attr. clothing etc.* utilitario.
u·ti·li·za·tion [ju:tilai'zeiʃn] utilización *f*; '**u·ti·lize** utilizar.
ut·most ['ʌtmoust] extremo; último; supremo; *do one's* ~ hacer todo lo posible; *to the* ~ hasta más no poder.
u·to·pi·a [ju:'toupiə] utopía *f*; **u·to·pi·an** [ju:'toupjən] **1.** utópico; **2.** utopista *m/f.*
u·tri·cle ['ju:trikl] utrículo *m.*
ut·ter ['ʌtər] **1.** □ completo, absoluto, total; *fool etc.* de remate; **2.** pronunciar, proferir; *cry* dar; *money* poner en circulación; '**ut·ter·ance** declaración *f*; palabras *f/pl.*; *give* ~ *to* expresar; '**ut·ter·ly** totalmente, del todo; **ut·ter·most** ['~moust] más remoto; *v. utmost.*
u·vu·la ['ju:vjulə] úvula *f*; **u·vu·lar** [~r] uvular.

V

va·can·cy ['veikənsi] vacuidad *f*; vacío *m*; vaciedad *f of mind*; cuarto *m* vacante *in boarding house etc.*; (*office*) vacante *f*; *fill a* ~ proveer una vacante; **va·cant** ['~kənt] □ vacante; vacío; *seat* libre; desocupado; *p.* estólido; *look* vago, distraído.
va·cate ['veikeit] *house* desocupar; *post* dejar (vacante); **va'ca·tion 1.** vacación *f*, vacaciones *f/pl.*; **2.** tomar vacaciones; **va'ca·tion·ist** vacacionista *m/f*.
vac·ci·nate ['væksineit] vacunar; **vac·ci'na·tion** vacunación *f*; **vac·cine** ['~si:n] vacuna *f*.
vac·il·late ['væsileit] vacilar; **vac·il'la·tion** vacilación *f*.
va·cu·i·ty [væ'kjuiti] vacuidad *f* (*mst fig.*); **vac·u·ous** ['~kjuəs] □ *fig.* fatuo, necio; **vac·u·um** ['~əm] vacío *m*; ~ *brake* freno *m* de vacío; ~ *cleaner* aspirador *m*; ~ *bottle* termos *m*; ~ *tube* tubo *m* al vacío.
va·de me·cum ['veidi'mi:kəm] vademécum *m*.
vag·a·bond ['vægəbənd] vagabundo *adj. a. su. m* (a *f*); **vag·a·bond·age** ['~bɔndidʒ] vagabundeo *m*.
va·gar·y [və'geri] capricho *m*, extravagancia *f*.
va·gran·cy ['veigrənsi] vagancia *f*; **'va·grant 1.** vagabundo; vagante; *fig.* errante; **2.** vagabundo (a *f*) *m*.
vague [veig] □ vago; *p.* indeciso, distraído; **'vague·ness** vaguedad *f*.
vain [vein] □ vano; *p.* vanidoso; *in* ~ en vano; **~·glo·ri·ous** [~'glɔ:riəs] □ vanaglorioso; **~'glo·ry** vanagloria *f*.
val·ance ['væləns] *drapery*: cenefa *f*, doselera *f*; *across the top of a window*: guardamalleta *f*.
vale [veil] *poet. or in names*: valle *m*.
val·e·dic·tion [væli'dikʃn] despedida *f*; **val·e'dic·to·ry** [~təri] (discurso *m*) de despedida.
va·len·cy ['veilənsi] valencia *f*.
val·en·tine ['væləntain] tarjeta *f* del día de San Valentín (*14 febrero*); novio (a *f*) *m* (*escogido en tal día*).
va·le·ri·an [və'liriən] valeriana *f*.
val·et ['vælit] ayuda *m* de cámara.
val·e·tu·di·nar·i·an ['vælitju:di'neriən] valetudinario *adj. a. su. m* (a *f*).
val·iant ['væljənt] □ *lit.* esforzado, valiente.
val·id ['vælid] □ válido; valedero; ⚖ vigente; *be* ~ valer; **val·i·date** ['~deit] validar; **va·lid·i·ty** [və'liditi] validez *f*; ⚖ vigencia *f*.
val·ley ['væli] valle *m*.
val·or ['vælər] *lit.* valor *m*, coraje *m*.
val·or·i·za·tion [vælərai'zeiʃn] valorización *f*; **'val·or·ize** valorizar.
val·or·ous ['vælərəs] □ *lit.* valeroso.
val·our ['vælər] *mst British* = *valor*.
val·u·a·ble ['væljuəbl] **1.** □ valioso; precioso; estimable; **2.** ~*s pl.* objetos *m/pl.* de valor.
val·u·a·tion [vælju'eiʃn] valuación *f*; tasación *f*.
val·ue ['vælju:] **1.** valor *m*; **2.** valorar, tasar (*at* en); estimar, apreciar; tener en mucho; ~*-added tax* impuesto *m* sobre el valor añadido; impuesto al valor agregado; **'val·ue·less** sin valor; **'val·u·er** tasador *m*.
valve [vælv] *anat.*, ⊕ válvula *f*; ♀, *zo.* valva *f*; *radio*: lámpara *f*, válvula *f*, bulbo *m S.Am.*; llave *f of a trumpet*; ~ *cap* capuchón *m*; ~ *gears pl.* distribución *f*; ~*-in-head engine* motor *m* con válvulas en cabeza; ~ *lifter* levantaválvulas *m*; ~ *seat* asiento *m* de válvula; ~ *spring* muelle *m* de válvula; ~ *stem* vástago *m* de válvula; ~ *tester* comprobador *m* de lámparas.
va·moose [væ'mu:s] *sl.* largarse, poner pies en polvorosa.
vamp¹ [væmp] **1.** empella *f*; remiendo *m*; **2.** poner empella a; remendar; ♪ improvisar.
vamp² [~] F **1.** vampiresa *f*; **2.** coquetear con.
vam·pire ['væmpaiər] vampiro *m*; *fig.* vampiresa *f*.
van¹ [væn] camioneta *f*; furgoneta *f*; 🚃 furgón *m*.
van² [~] ⚔ *a. fig.* vanguardia *f*.
Van·dal ['vændl] **1.** vándalo *m*; **2.** vándalo, vandálico (*a.* **Van·dal·ic**

VWX

[~ˈdælik]); **van·dal·ism** [ˈ~dəlizm] vandalismo *m.*
vane [vein] (*weather*) veleta *f*; paleta *f of propeller*; aspa *f of mill.*
van·guard [ˈvængɑːrd] vanguardia *f.*
va·nil·la [vəˈnilə] vainilla *f.*
van·ish [ˈvæniʃ] desvanecerse, desaparecer.
van·ity [ˈvæniti] vanidad *f*; engreimiento *m*; ~ *case* neceser *m* de belleza, polvera *f* (de bolsillo).
van·quish [ˈvæŋkwiʃ] *lit.* vencer.
van·tage [ˈvæntidʒ] *tennis*: ventaja *f*; ˈ~ **ground** posición *f* ventajosa; ˈ~·**point** punto *m* panorámico *for views*; lugar *m* estratégico.
vap·id [ˈvæpid] □ insípido.
va·por [ˈveipər] **1.** vapor *m*; vaho *m*; exhalación *f*; ~ *bath* baño *m* de vapor; ~ *trail* ✈ estela *f* de vapor, rastro *m* de condensación; **2.** *fig.* fanfarronear.
va·por·ize [ˈveipəraiz] vaporizar(se); ˈ**va·por·iz·er** vaporizador *m.*
va·por·ous [ˈveipərəs] □ vaporoso (*a. fig.*); quimérico.
var·i·a·bil·i·ty [veriəˈbiliti] variabilidad *f*; ˈ**var·i·a·ble** □ variable *adj. a. su. f* (Å); ˈ**var·i·ance** desacuerdo *m*; desavenencia *f*; variación *f*; ⚖ discrepancia *f*; *at* ~ en desacuerdo (*with* con); ˈ**var·i·ant** variante *adj. a. su. f*; **var·iˈa·tion** variación *f* (*a.* ♪).
var·i·cose [ˈværikous] varicoso; ~ *veins* varices *f/pl.*
var·ied [ˈverid] □ variado; **var·i·e·gate** [ˈ~rigeit] abigarrar; jaspear; **var·i·eˈga·tion** abigarramiento *m*; **va·ri·e·ty** [vəˈraiəti] variedad *f* (*a. biol.*); diversidad *f*; *esp.* † surtido *m*; *thea.* ~ *artist* artista *m/f* de variedades; ~ *show* variedades *f/pl.*; ~ *theater* teatro *m* de variedades.
va·ri·o·la [vəˈraiələ] viruela *f.*
var·i·ous [ˈveriəs] □ vario, diverso.
var·mint [ˈvɑːrmint] F golfo *m*, bribón *m*; *hunt.* bicho *m.*
var·nish [ˈvɑːrniʃ] **1.** barniz *m* (*a. fig.*); *fig.* capa *f*, apariencia *f*; *nail* ~ laca *f*, esmalte *m* (para uñas); **2.** barnizar; *nails* laquear, esmaltar; *fig.* paliar, dar apariencia respetable a.
var·si·ty [ˈvɑːrsiti] **1.** *sports*: universitario; **2.** *sports*: equipo *m* principal de la universidad.
var·y [ˈveri] variar (*v/i. a. v/t.*); *decision* modificar.
vas·cu·lar [ˈvæskjulər] vascular.
vase [veiz] jarrón *m*; florero *m.*
Va·se·line [ˈvæsəliːn] vaselina *f.*
vas·sal [ˈvæsl] vasallo *m*; ˈ**vas·sal·age** vasallaje *m.*
vast [væst] □ vasto, inmenso; ~*ly* sumamente, en sumo grado; ˈ**vast·ness** inmensidad *f*, vastedad *f.*
vat [væt] **1.** tina *f*, tinaja *f*; **2.** poner en tina.
vau·de·ville [ˈvoudəvil] vaudeville *m.*
vault[1] [vɔːlt] **1.** △ bóveda *f*; (*wine-*) bodega *f*; (*tomb*) tumba *f*; **2.** abovedar.
vault[2] [~] **1.** saltar (*v/i. a. v/t.*); **2.** salto *m.*
vault·ing [ˈvɔːltiŋ] abovedado *m.*
vault·ing horse [ˈvɔːltiŋhɔːrs] potro *m* de madera.
vaunt [vɔːnt] *lit. v/i.* jactarse; *v/t.* jactarse de, hacer alarde de; ˈ**vaunt·ed** cacareado, alardeado; ˈ**vaunt·ing** □ jactancioso.
veal [viːl] carne *f* de ternera; ~ *chop* chuleta *f* de ternera.
ve·dette [viˈdet] centinela *f* de avanzada; buque *m* escucha.
veer [vir] virar (*a. fig., a.* ~ *round*); (*wind*) cambiar.
veg·e·ta·ble [ˈvedʒitəbl] **1.** vegetal; **2.** legumbre *f*; hortaliza *f*; (*in general*) vegetal *m*; ~*s pl. freq.* verduras *f/pl.*; ~ *garden* huerto *m* de hortalizas, huerto de verduras; ~ *soup* menestra *f*, sopa *f* de hortalizas; **veg·e·tar·i·an** [~ˈteriən] vegetariano *adj. a. su. m* (*a f*); **veg·e·tate** [ˈ~teit] vegetar (*a. fig.*); **veg·eˈta·tion** vegetación *f*; ˈ**veg·e·ta·tive** □ vegetativo.
ve·he·mence [ˈviːiməns] vehemencia *f*; ˈ**ve·he·ment** □ vehemente.
ve·hi·cle [ˈviːikl] *all senses*: vehículo *m*; **ve·hic·u·lar** [viˈhikjulər] de vehículos; ~ *traffic* circulación *f* rodada.
veil [veil] **1.** velo *m* (*a. fig. a. phot.*); **2.** velar (*a. fig.*); ˈ**veil·ing** † material *m* para velos; *phot.* velo *m.*
vein [vein] *all senses*: vena *f*; *be in the* ~ estar en vena (*for* para); **veined** venoso; veteado; ˈ**vein·ing** venas *f/pl.*
vel·lum [ˈveləm] vitela *f*; ~ *paper* papel *m* vitela.
ve·loc·i·ty [viˈlɔsiti] velocidad *f.*
vel·vet [ˈvelvit] **1.** terciopelo *m*; *hunt.* piel *f* velluda; *sl.* ganancia *f*

limpia; F *on* ~ en situación muy ventajosa; **2.** aterciopelado; de terciopelo; **vel·vet·een** [~'ti:n] pana *f*; '**vel·vet·y** aterciopelado.
ve·nal ['vi:nl] sobornable, venal; **ve·nal·i·ty** [vi'næliti] venalidad *f*.
vend [vend] *mst* ⚖ vender; vender como buhonero; '**vend·er**, '**vend·or** vendedor (-a *f*) *m*; buhonero *m*; '**vend·i·ble** vendible; '**vend·ing ma·chine** distribuidor *m* automático.
ve·neer [və'nir] **1.** chapa *f*, enchapado *m*; *fig.* apariencia *f*, barniz *m*; **2.** (en)chapar; *fig.* disfrazar.
ven·er·a·ble ['venərəbl] □ venerable; **ven·er·ate** ['~reit] venerar; **ven·er'a·tion** veneración *f*.
ve·ne·re·al [vi'niriəl]: ~ *disease* enfermedad *f* venérea.
Ve·ne·tian [vi'ni:ʃn] veneciano *adj. a. su. m* (a *f*); ~ *blind* persiana *f*.
Ve·ne·zuel·an [veni'zwi:lən] venezolano *adj. a. su. m* (a *f*).
venge·ance ['vendʒəns] venganza *f*; F *with a* ~ con creces, con extremo; **venge·ful** ['~ful] □ *lit.* vengativo.
ve·ni·al ['vi:niəl] □ venial.
ven·i·son ['venzn] carne *f* de venado.
ven·om ['venəm] veneno *m*; *fig.* virulencia *f*, malignidad *f*; '**ven·om·ous** □ venenoso; *fig.* virulento, maligno.
ve·nous ['vi:nəs] venal, venoso.
vent [vent] **1.** respiradero *m*; salida *f*; ⊕ válvula *f* de purga, orificio *m*, lumbrera *f*; *orn.* cloaca *f*; *give* ~ *to* desahogar, dar salida a; **2.** ⊕ purgar; *fig.* desahogar, descargar.
ven·ti·late ['ventileit] ventilar (*a. fig.*); **ven·ti'la·tion** ventilación *f* (*a. fig.*); '**ven·ti·la·tor** ventilador *m*.
ven·tral ['ventrəl] □ ventral.
ven·tri·cle ['ventrikl] ventrículo *m*.
ven·tril·o·quism [ven'triləkwizm] ventriloquia *f*; **ven·tril·o·quist** ventrílocuo (a *f*) *m*.
ven·ture ['ventʃər] **1.** empresa *f* (arriesgada); riesgo *m*; especulación *f*; *at a* ~ a la ventura; **2.** *v/t.* aventurar; *v/i.* aventurarse (*to* a), osar (*to inf.*); ~ (*up*)*on* arriesgarse en; **ven·ture·some** ['~səm] □ atrevido; emprendedor; azaroso.
ven·ue ['venju:] ⚖ lugar *m* donde se reúne el jurado; F lugar *m* de reunión.
ve·ra·cious [və'reiʃəs] □ veraz; **ve·rac·i·ty** [~'ræsiti] veracidad *f*.
ver·an·da [vər'ændə] veranda *f*.
verb [və:rb] verbo *m*; '**ver·bal** □ verbal; **ver·ba·tim** [~'beitim] palabra por palabra; **ver·bi·age** ['~biidʒ] palabrería *f*; **ver·bose** [~'bous] □ verboso; **ver·bos·i·ty** [~'bɔsiti] verbosidad *f*.
ver·dant ['və:rdənt] □ verde; F inocente.
ver·dict ['və:rdikt] ⚖ veredicto *m*; fallo *m*, juicio *m*; *fig.* opinión *f*, juicio *m* (*on* sobre); *bring in* (*or return*) *a* ~ dictar un veredicto.
ver·di·gris ['və:rdigris] verdete *m*, cardenillo *m*.
ver·dure ['və:rdʒər] verdura *f*.
verge[1] [və:rdʒ] vara *f of office*.
verge[2] [~] **1.** borde *m*, margen *m*; *fig. on the* ~ *of disaster* a dos dedos de, en el mismo borde de; *madness* al borde de; *discovery, triumph* en la antesala de; *fig. be on the* ~ *of ger.* estar a punto de *inf.*; **2.**: ~ *on* acercarse a, rayar en.
ver·ger ['və:rdʒər] sacristán *m*.
ver·i·fi·a·ble ['verifaiəbl] □ verificable; **ver·i·fi·ca·tion** [~fi'keiʃn] verificación *f*; **ver·i·fy** ['~fai] verificar; **ver·i·si·mil·i·tude** [~si'militju:d] verosimilitud *f*; '**ver·i·ta·ble** □ verdadero; '**ver·i·ty** † *or lit.* verdad *f*.
ver·mi·cel·li [və:rmi'seli] fideos *m/pl.*; **ver·mi·cide** ['~said] vermicida *m*; **ver·mic·u·lar** [~'mikjulər] vermicular; **ver·mi·form** ['~fɔ:rm] vermiforme; **ver·mi·fuge** ['~fju:dʒ] vermífugo *m*.
ver·mil·ion [vər'miljən] **1.** bermellón *m*; **2.** de color rojo vivo.
ver·min ['və:rmin] bichos *m/pl.*; sabandijas *f/pl.*; parásitos *m/pl.* (*a. fig.*); (*fox etc.*) alimañas *f/pl.*; '**ver·min·ous** verminoso; piojoso.
ver·mouth [vər'mu:θ] vermut *m*.
ver·nac·u·lar [vər'nækjulər] **1.** vernáculo; **2.** lengua *f* vernácula; F idioma *m* corriente.
ver·nal ['və:rnl] vernal.
ver·ni·er ['və:rniər] ⚒ vernier *m*.
ve·ron·i·ca [və'rɑ:nikə] ⚘ verónica *f*; *bullfighting*: verónica *f*; *representing the face of Christ*: lienzo *m* de la Verónica.
ver·sa·tile ['və:rsətil] □ versátil, flexible, adaptable, hábil para muchas cosas; **ver·sa·til·i·ty** [~'tiliti] versatilidad *f*, flexibilidad *f*.

verse [vəːrs] (*stanza*) estrofa *f*; (*poetry*) poesías *f/pl.*; (*line, genre*) verso *m*; versículo *m of Bible*; **versed** [vəːrst] versado (*in* en).

ver·si·fi·ca·tion [vəːrsifiˈkeiʃn] versificación *f*; **ver·si·fy** [ˈ~fai] versificar (*v/i. a. v/t.*).

ver·sion [ˈvəːrʒn] versión *f*.

ver·sus [ˈvəːrsəs] contra.

ver·te·bra [ˈvəːrtibrə], *pl.* **ver·te·brae** [ˈ~briː] vértebra *f*; **ver·te·bral** [ˈ~brəl] vertebral; **ver·te·brate** [ˈ~brit] vertebrado *adj. a. su. m.*

ver·tex [ˈvəːrteks], *pl. mst* **ver·ti·ces** [ˈ~tisiːz] vértice *m*; **ˈver·ti·cal** □ vertical; ~ *hold television* bloqueo *m* vertical; ~ *rudder* ✈ timón *m* de dirección.

ver·tig·i·nous [vəːrˈtidʒinəs] vertiginoso; **ver·ti·go** [ˈ~tigou] vértigo *m*.

verve [vəːrv] energía *f*, entusiasmo *m*, brío *m*.

ver·y [ˈveri] **1.** *adv.* muy; (*alone, in reply to question*) mucho; ~ *much* mucho, muchísimo; *the* ~ *best* el mejor (de todos); ~ *good mst* muy bueno, *but sometimes translated by absolute superlative of adj., e.g.* buenísimo, bonísimo, *and by prefix* re(quete)..., *e.g.* re(quete)bueno; **2.** *adj.* mismo; mismísimo; † verdadero; *it is* ~ *cold* hace mucho frío; *the* ~ *same* el idéntico; *to the* ~ *bone* hasta el mismo hueso; *it's the* ~ *thing* es exactamente lo que necesitábamos; *the* ~ *idea!* ¡ni hablar!; *the veriest rascal* el mayor bribón.

ves·i·cle [ˈvesikl] vesícula *f*.

ves·pers [ˈvespərz] vísperas *f/pl.*

ves·sel [ˈvesl] vasija *f*, recipiente *m*; *anat.*, ⚘ vaso *m*; ⚓ buque *m*, barco *m*, bajel *m* (*lit.*).

vest [vest] **1.** camiseta *f*; chaleco *m*; **2.** investir (*with* de); conferir (*in* a), conceder (*in* a); *~ed rights pl.* derechos *m/pl.* inalienables; *~ed interests pl.* intereses *m/pl.* creados.

ves·ta [ˈvestə] (*a. wax* ~) cerilla *f*.

ves·tal [ˈvestl] vestal *adj. a. su. f.*

ves·ti·bule [ˈvestibjuːl] vestíbulo *m*; zaguán *m*; 🚂 ~ *car* coche *m* de vestíbulo.

ves·tige [ˈvestidʒ] vestigio *m*; **vesˈtig·i·al** vestigial.

vest·ment [ˈvestmənt] vestidura *f*.

vest-pock·et [ˈvestˈpɔkit] *attr.* en miniatura, de bolsillo; diminuto.

ves·try [ˈvestri] sacristía *f*; **ˈ~·man** miembro *m* de la junta parroquial.

ves·ture [ˈvestʃər] *lit.* vestidura *f*.

vet [vet] F **1.** veterinario *m*; **2.** repasar, corregir; examinar, investigar; aprobar.

vetch [vetʃ] arveja *f*.

vet·er·an [ˈvetərən] veterano *adj. a. su. m.*

vet·er·i·nar·y [ˈvetərinəri] veterinario *adj. a. su. m* (*mst* ~ *surgeon*); ~ *medicine* veterinaria *f*, medicina *f* veterinaria.

ve·to [ˈviːtou] **1.** *pl.* **ve·toes** [ˈ~z] veto *m*; *put a* (*or one's*) ~ *on* = **2.** vedar, vetar.

vex [veks] vejar, fastidiar, enojar; **vexˈa·tion** vejación *f*, enojo *m*; **vexˈa·tious** □ vejatorio; fastidioso, engorroso; **ˈvexed** □ enojado, enfadado (*at a th.* de algo, *with a p.* con una p.); ~ *question* cuestión *f* batallona; **ˈvex·ing** □ fastidioso, molesto.

vi·a [ˈviːə, ˈvaiə] por (vía de).

vi·a·ble [ˈvaiəbl] viable.

vi·a·duct [ˈvaiədʌkt] viaducto *m*.

vi·al [ˈvaiəl] frasco *m* (pequeño).

vi·ands [ˈvaiəndz] *pl. lit.* manjares *m/pl.* (exquisitos).

vi·at·i·cum [vaiˈætikəm] viático *m*.

vi·brant [ˈvaibrənt] vibrante (*with* de).

vi·brate [vaiˈbreit] vibrar; **viˈbra·tion** vibración *f*; **vi·bra·to·ry** [ˈ~brətəri] vibratorio.

vic·ar [ˈvikər] vicario *m*; (*parish priest*) párroco *m*; ~ *general* vicario *m* general; **ˈvic·ar·age** casa *f* del párroco; **vi·car·i·ous** [vaiˈkeriəs] □ experimentado por otro; (*deputed*) vicario.

vice[1] [vais] vicio *m*.

vice[2] [~] ⊕ torno *m* (*or* tornillo *m*) de banco.

vice[3] **1.** [ˈvaisi] *prp.* en lugar de; que sustituye a; **2.** [vais] vice...; **ˈ~ˈad·mi·ral** vicealmirante *m*; **ˈ~ˈchair·man** vicepresidente *m*; **ˈ~ˈchan·cel·lor** vicecanciller *m*; *univ.* rector *m*; **ˈ~ con·sul** vicecónsul *m*; **ˈ~ˈpres·i·dent** vicepresidente *m*; **ˈ~ˈre·gal** virreinal; **ˈ~·roy** [ˈ~rɔi] virrey *m*.

vi·ce ver·sa [ˈvaisiˈvəːrsə] viceversa; a la inversa.

vi·cin·i·ty [viˈsiniti] vecindad *f*; proximidad *f* (*to* a); *in the* ~ cerca; *in the* ~ *of 25* alrededor de 25.

vi·cious ['viʃəs] □ vicioso; *criticism* virulento, rencoroso; *dog* bravo; *horse* arisco; *phls.* ~ *circle* círculo *m* vicioso.

vi·cis·si·tude [vi'sisitju:d]: *mst* ~*s pl.* vicisitud *f.*

vic·tim ['viktim] víctima *f*; '**vic·tim·ize** hacer víctima; escoger y castigar, tomar represalias contra.

vic·tor ['viktər] vencedor *m*; **Vic·to·ri·an** [vik'tɔ:riən] victoriano; **vic·'to·ri·ous** □ victorioso; **vic·to·ry** ['~təri] victoria *f.*

vict·ual ['vitl] **1.** abastecer(se), avituallar(se); F comer; **2.** ~*s pl.* vitualla(s) *f(pl.)*; víveres *m/pl.*; **vict·ual·er** ['vitlər] abastecedor (-a *f*) *m*; *licensed* ~ vendedor *m* de bebidas alcohólicas.

vi·de ['wi:də] vea, véase.

vi·de·li·cet [wi'deiliket] a saber.

vi·de·o ['vidiou] *radio*: ... de vídeo; ~ *recorder* magnetoscopia *f*; ~ *signal* señal *f* de vídeo; ~ *tape* cinta *f* grabada de televisión; ~*-tape recording* videograbación *f.*

vie [vai] rivalizar (con), competir (con); ~ *with s.o. for s.t.* disputar algo a alguien, disputarse algo.

view [vju:] **1.** vista *f*; perspectiva *f*; aspecto *m*; *paint.*, *phot.* panorama *m*; paisaje *m*; (*opinion*) opinión *f*, parecer *m*; *in* ~ visible; *in full* ~ totalmente visible; *in* ~ *of* en vista de; *in my* ~ en mi opinión; *have* (*or keep*) *in* ~ no perder de vista; *be on* ~ estar expuesto; *with a* ~ *to ger.* con miras a *inf.*, con el propósito de *inf.*; **2.** mirar; examinar; contemplar; considerar; '**view·er** espectador (-a *f*) *m*; telespectador (-a *f*) *m*; '**view·find·er** *phot.* visor *m*, mirilla *f*; '**view·point** mirador *m*, punto *m* panorámico; *fig.* punto *m* de vista.

vig·il ['vidʒil] vigilia *f*, vela *f*; '**vig·i·lance** vigilancia *f*; ~ *committee* comité *m* de vigilancia; '**vig·i·lant** □ vigilante; **vig·i·lan·te** [~'lænti] vigilante *m.*

vi·gnette [vi'njet] *typ.*, *phot.* viñeta *f.*

vig·or ['vigər] vigor *m*; **vig·or·ous** ['vigərəs] □ vigoroso.

vile [vail] □ vil; (*very bad*) horrible, pésimo, asqueroso; '**vile·ness** vileza *f.*

vil·i·fi·ca·tion [vilifi'keiʃn] vilipendio *m*; **vil·i·fy** ['~fai] vilipendiar.

vil·la ['vilə] *hist.* villa *f*; (*seaside etc.*) villa *f*, chalet *m*; (*country house*) quinta *f.*

vil·lage ['vilidʒ] aldea *f*, puebl(ecit)o *m*; lugar *m*; *attr.* aldeano; '**vil·lag·er** aldeano (a *f*) *m.*

vil·lain ['vilən] malvado *m*; *thea. etc.* malo *m*, traidor *m*; *hist.* villano *m*; *co.* tunante *m*; '**vil·lain·ous** □ vil, malvado; F pésimo, malísimo; '**vil·lain·y** maldad *f*, villanía *f.*

vil·lein ['vilin] villano (a *f*) *m.*

vim [vim] F fuerza *f*, energía *f.*

vin·di·cate ['vindikeit] vindicar; justificar; ~ *o.s.* justificarse; **vin·di·'ca·tion** vindicación *f.*

vin·dic·tive [vin'diktiv] □ vengativo, vindicativo.

vine [vain] vid *f*; (*climbing*) parra *f*; '~ **dress·er** viñador *m*; **vin·e·gar** ['vinigər] **1.** vinagre *m*; **2.** avinagrar (*a. fig.*); '**vin·e·gar·y** vinagroso; '**vine grow·er** viticultor *m*, viñador *m*; '**vine grow·ing** viticultura *f*; **vine·yard** ['vinjərd] viña *f*, viñedo *m.*

vi·nous ['vainəs] vinoso.

vin·tage ['vintidʒ] **1.** (*season*) vendimia *f*; *the 1987* ~ la cosecha de 1987; **2.**: ~ *wine* vino *m* añejo; vino de marca, vino de buena cosecha; ~ *year* año *m* de buen vino; F *car etc.* de época, clásico; '**vin·tag·er** vendimiador (-a *f*) *m*; **vint·ner** ['vintnər] vinatero *m.*

vi·o·la ♪ [vi'oulə] viola *f*; ⚘ ['vaiələ] viola *f.*

vi·o·late ['vaiəleit] *all senses*: violar; **vi·o'la·tion** violación *f*; '**vi·o·la·tor** violador *m.*

vi·o·lence ['vaiələns] violencia *f*; *do* ~ *to* agredir; *fig.* violentar; *offer* ~ mostrarse violento; '**vi·o·lent** □ violento.

vi·o·let ['vaiəlit] **1.** ⚘ violeta *f*; (*color*) violado *m*; **2.** violado.

vi·o·lin [vaiə'lin] violín *m*; '**vi·o·lin·ist** violinista *m/f.*

vi·o·lon'cel·lo [vaiələn'tʃelou] violoncelo *m.*

vi·per ['vaipər] víbora *f*; **vi·per·ine** ['~rain], **vi·per·ous** ['~rəs] □ *mst fig.* viperino.

vi·ra·go [vi'reigou] mujer *f* regañona.

vir·gin ['və:rdʒin] virgen *adj. a. su. f*; ~ *birth* parto *m* virginal de María Santísima; *zo.* partenogénesis *f*;

ˈ**vir·gin·al** □ virginal; **Vir·gin·ia** [vərˈdʒinjə]: ~ *creeper* ⚘ guau *m*; **Vir·gin·ian** [vərˈdʒinjən] (*or* ~ *tobacco*) tabaco *m* rubio; **vir·gin·i·ty** [vəːrˈdʒiniti] virginidad *f*.
vir·ile [ˈvirəl] viril; **vi·ril·i·ty** [viˈriliti] virilidad *f*.
vi·rol·o·gy [vaiˈrɑːlədʒi] virología *f*.
vir·tual [ˈvəːrtʃuəl] □ virtual; **vir·tue** [ˈ~tʃuː] virtud *f*; *in* (*or by*) ~ *of* en virtud de; **vir·tu·os·i·ty** [~tʃuˈɔsiti] virtuosismo *m*; **vir·tu·o·so** [~ˈouzou] *esp*. ♪ virtuoso *m*; ˈ**vir·tu·ous** □ virtuoso.
vir·u·lence [ˈvirjələns] virulencia *f* (*a. fig.*); ˈ**vir·u·lent** □ virulento (*a. fig.*).
vi·rus [ˈvairəs] virus *m*; ~ *disease* enfermedad *f* por virus.
vi·sa [ˈviːzə] **1.** visado *m*; **2.** visar.
vis·age [ˈvizidʒ] *lit*. semblante *m*.
vis-à-vis [ˈviːzəˈviː] respecto de.
vis·cer·a [ˈvisərə] 🕮 vísceras *f*/*pl*.
vis·cid [ˈvisid] □ viscoso.
vis·cose [ˈviskous] **1.** viscosa *f*; **2.** viscoso; **vis·cos·i·ty** [~ˈkɔsiti] viscosidad *f*.
vis·count [ˈvaikaunt] vizconde *m*; ˈ**vis·count·ess** vizcondesa *f*.
vis·cous [ˈviskəs] □ viscoso.
vi·sé [ˈviːzei] *v. visa*.
vis·i·bil·i·ty [viziˈbiliti] visibilidad *f*; **vis·i·ble** [ˈvizəbl] □ visible.
vi·sion [ˈviʒn] visión *f*; ˈ**vi·sion·ar·y** visionario *adj. a. su. m* (*a f*).
vis·it [ˈvizit] **1.** *v/t*. visitar; ~ *s.t. upon a p.* castigar una p. con algo; mandar algo a una p.; *v/i*. hacer visitas; F visitarse; **2.** visita *f*; *pay* (*return*) *a* ~ hacer (pagar) una visita; **vis·itˈa·tion** *eccl*. visitación *f*; F visita *f* larga y engorrosa; ˈ**vis·it·ing** ... visitante; ... de visita; ~ *card* tarjeta *f* (de visita); ~ *hours pl*. horas *f*/*pl*. de visita; ~ *nurse* enfermera *f* ambulante; ˈ**vis·i·tor** visitante *m*/*f*; visita *f to house*; turista *m*/*f*; forastero (*a f*) *m*; ~*s' book* libro *m* de visitas (*or* de honor).
vi·sor [ˈvaizər] visera *f*.
vis·ta [ˈvistə] perspectiva *f*, vista *f*, panorama *m*.
vis·u·al [ˈviʒuəl] □ visual; ˈ**vis·u·al·ize** representarse (en la mente); imaginarse; *situation* prever.
vit·al [ˈvaitl] □ vital; esencial; *p*. enérgico; ~*s pl*., ~ *parts pl*. partes *f*/*pl*. vitales; ~ *statistics pl*. estadística *f* vital; *co*. medidas *f*/*pl*. vitales; **vi·tal·i·ty** [~ˈtæliti] vitalidad *f*; **vi·tal·ize** [ˈ~təlaiz] vitalizar.
vi·ta·min [ˈvaitəmin] vitamina *f*; *attr*. vitamínico; **vi·ta·mi·nized** [ˈ~minaizd] reforzado con vitaminas.
vi·ti·ate [ˈviʃieit] viciar (*a*. ⚖).
vit·i·cul·ture [ˈvitikʌltʃər] viticultura *f*.
vit·re·ous [ˈvitriəs] □ vítreo.
vit·ri·fac·tion [vitriˈfækʃn] vitrificación *f*; **vit·ri·fy** [ˈ~fai] vitrificar(se).
vit·ri·ol [ˈvitriəl] vitriolo *m*; **vit·riˈol·ic** *fig*. mordaz, cáustico.
vi·tu·per·ate [viˈtjuːpəreit] vituperar, llenar de injurias; **vi·tu·perˈa·tion** vituperio *m*, injurias *f*/*pl*.; **viˈtu·per·a·tive** [~reitiv] □ vituperioso, injurioso.
Vi·tus [ˈvaitəs]: *St*. ~'(*s*) *dance* baile *m* de San Vito.
vi·va (**vo·ce**) [ˈvaivə(ˈvousi)] **1.** *adj*. oral; **2.** *adv*. de viva voz; **3.** examen *m* oral.
vi·va·cious [viˈveiʃəs] □ vivaz, animado; alegre; vivaracho; **vi·vac·i·ty** [~ˈvæsiti] vivacidad *f*; alegría *f*.
viv·id [ˈvivid] □ *impression, memory etc*. vivo; *color, light* intenso; *description* gráfico; ˈ**viv·id·ness** vivacidad *f*; intensidad *f etc*.
viv·i·fy [ˈvivifai] vivificar; **vi·vip·a·rous** [~ˈvipərəs] □ vivíparo; **viv·i·sec·tion** [~ˈsekʃn] vivisección *f*.
vix·en [ˈviksn] zorra *f*, raposa *f*; *fig*. mujer *f* regañona.
vo·cab·u·lar·y [vəˈkæbjuləri] vocabulario *m*.
vo·cal [ˈvoukl] □ vocal (*a*. ♪); *gr*. vocálico; *fig*. ruidoso, expresivo; ~ *cords pl*. cuerdas *f*/*pl*. vocales; ˈ**vo·cal·ist** cantante *m*/*f*; (*in cabaret etc*.) vocalista *m*/*f*; ˈ**vo·cal·ize** ♪ vocalizar; *gr*. vocalizar(se).
vo·ca·tion [vouˈkeiʃn] vocación *f*; **voˈca·tion·al** □ vocacional; ~ *guidance* guía *f* vocacional.
voc·a·tive [ˈvɔkətiv] vocativo *m* (*a*. ~ *case*).
vo·cif·er·ate [vouˈsifəreit] vociferar; **vo·cif·erˈa·tion** vociferación *f*; **voˈcif·er·ous** □ clamoroso; vocinglero.
vogue [voug] boga *f*, moda *f*; *in* ~ en boga.
voice [vɔis] **1.** voz *f* (*a. gr.*); *in* (*good*) ~ en voz; *with one* ~ a una voz, al

unísono; *give ~ to* expresar; *have no ~ in a matter* no tener voz en capítulo; **2.** expresar; hacerse eco de; *gr.* sonorizar(se); **voiced** *gr.* sonoro; ˈ**voice·less** □ *gr.* sordo.

void [vɔid] **1.** vacío; ⚖ nulo, inválido; *~ of* falto de, desprovisto de; **2.** vacío *m*; hueco *m*; *bridge*: fallo *m*; *the ~* la nada; **3.** evacuar, vaciar; ⚖ anular.

vol·a·tile [ˈvɔlətil] volátil (*a. fig.*); **vol·a·til·i·ty** [~ˈtiliti] volatilidad *f*; **vol·a·til·ize** [ˈvɔlətəlaiz] volatilizar(se).

vol·can·ic [vɔlˈkænik] □ volcánico; **vol·ca·no** [~ˈkeinou], *pl.* **volˈca·noes** [~z] volcán *m*.

vole [voul] campañol *m*.

vo·li·tion [vouˈliʃn] volición *f*; *of one's own ~* por voluntad propia.

vol·ley [ˈvɔli] **1.** ⚔ descarga *f*; lluvia *f of stones etc.*; salva *f of applause*; retahila *f of abuse*; *tennis*: volea *m*; **2.** *tennis*: volear; ⚔ lanzar una descarga; ˈ**vol·ley·ball** balón *m* volea, volibol *m*.

volt [voult] voltio *m*; ˈ**volt·age** voltaje *m*; **vol·ta·ic** [vɔlˈteiik] voltaico; **vol·ta·me·ter** [vɔlˈtæmitər] voltímetro *m*.

volte-face [vɔltˈfɑːs] viraje *m*, cambio *m* súbito (*or* total) de opinión.

vol·u·bil·i·ty [vɔljuˈbiliti] locuacidad *f*; **vol·u·ble** [ˈ~bl] □ locuaz.

vol·ume [ˈvɔljum] volumen *m*; tomo *m of book*; *fig.* masa *f*; *radio*: *~ of sound* volumen *m* sonoro; *~ control* control *m* del volumen sonoro; *speak ~s* ser de suma significación; *speak ~s for* evidenciar de modo inconfundible; **vo·lu·mi·nous** [vəˈljuːminəs] □ voluminoso.

vol·un·tar·y [ˈvɔləntəri] **1.** □ voluntario; *~ manslaughter* homicidio *m* intencional sin premeditación; **2.** solo *m* de órgano; **vol·un·teer** [~ˈtir] **1.** voluntario *m*; **2.** voluntario, de voluntarios; **3.** *v/i.* ofrecerse; ⚔ alistarse como voluntario; *v/t.* ofrecer; *remark* permitirse hacer.

vo·lup·tu·ar·y [vəˈlʌptjuəri] voluptuoso (a *f*) *m*.

vo·lup·tu·ous [vəˈlʌptjuəs] □ voluptuoso; **voˈlup·tu·ous·ness** voluptuosidad *f*.

vo·lute [vəˈljuːt] voluta *f*; **voˈlut·ed** en la forma de volutas.

vom·it [ˈvɔmit] **1.** vomitar; **2.** vómito *m*.

vo·ra·cious [vəˈreiʃəs] □ voraz; **voˈra·cious·ness, vo·rac·i·ty** [~ˈræsiti] voracidad *f*.

vor·tex [ˈvɔːrteks], *pl. mst* **vor·ti·ces** [ˈ~tisiːz] vórtice *m*.

vo·ta·ry [ˈvoutəri] devoto (a *f*) *m*; partidario (a *f*) *m*.

vote [vout] **1.** voto *m*; sufragio *m*; (*a. voting*) votación *f*; *by a majority ~* por la mayoría de los votos; *~ of confidence* voto *m* de confianza; *~ getter* acaparador *m* de votos; (*slogan*) consigna *f* que gana votos; *cast a ~* dar un voto; *put to the ~, take a ~ on* someter a votación; **2.** *v/t.* votar; *~ in* elegir; *v/i.* votar (*for* por); F proponer, sugerir (*that* que); *~ that* resolver (por voto) que; ˈ**vot·er** votante *m/f*; ˈ**vot·ing** votación *f*; *~ paper* papeleta *f*; *~ machine* máquina *f* registradora de votos; *~ power* potencia *f* electoral.

vo·tive [ˈvoutiv] votivo; *~ offering* exvoto *m*.

vouch [vautʃ] atestiguar; garantizar, confirmar; *~ for th.* responder de; *p.* responder por; ˈ**vouch·er** documento *m* justificativo; ☤ comprobante *m*; vale *m*; **vouchˈsafe** conceder, otorgar; dignarse hacer (*or* dar *etc.*).

vow [vau] **1.** voto *m*; promesa *f* solemne; **2.** hacer voto (*to* de); jurar; prometer solemnemente.

vow·el [ˈvauəl] vocal *f*.

voy·age [ˈvɔiidʒ] **1.** viaje *m* (por mar); travesía *f*; **2.** viajar (por mar); navegar; **voy·ag·er** [ˈvɔiidʒər] viajero (a *f*) *m*.

vul·can·ite [ˈvʌlkənait] vulcanita *f*, ebonita *f*; **vul·can·iˈza·tion** vulcanización *f*; ˈ**vul·can·ize** vulcanizar.

vul·gar [ˈvʌlgər] **1.** □ vulgar; *b.s.* grosero; (*in bad taste, showy*) cursi; *joke etc.* verde, indecente; *~ tongue* lengua *f* vulgar; **2.**: *the ~* el vulgo; ˈ**vul·gar·ism** vulgarismo *m*; **vul·gar·i·ty** [~ˈgæriti] vulgaridad *f*; grosería *f*; indecencia *f*; ˈ**vul·gar·ize** vulgarizar; ˈ**Vul·gar** ˈ**Lat·in** latín *m* vulgar, latín rústico; **Vul·gate** [ˈvʌlgit] Vulgata *f*.

vul·ner·a·bil·i·ty [vʌlnərəˈbiliti] vulnerabilidad *f*; ˈ**vul·ner·a·ble** □ vulnerable; ˈ**vul·ner·ar·y** vulnerario *adj. a. su. m.*

vul·pine [ˈvʌlpain] vulpino.

vul·ture [ˈvʌltʃər] buitre *m*.

vy·ing [ˈvaiiŋ] *ger. of vie*.

W

wack·y [ˈwæki] *sl.* chiflado.
wad [wɔd] **1.** taco *m*, tapón *m*; bolita *f* de algodón *etc.*; lío *m of papers*; F fajo *m of notes*; *sl.* pastel *m*; **2.** rellenar; acolchar; tapar; **ˈwad·ding** algodón *m* (en rama); taco *m*, relleno *m*; ⚕ algodón *m* absorbente (*or* hidrófilo).
wad·dle [ˈwɔdl] anadear.
wade [weid] *v/i.* caminar por el agua *etc.*; ~ *ashore* llegar a tierra vadeando; ~ *into* meterse en; F embestir con violencia; ~ *through book* leer a pesar de lo aburrido (*or* difícil *etc.*); *v/t.* vadear; **ˈwad·er** *orn.* ave *f* zancuda; ~*s pl.* botas *f/pl.* altas.
wa·fer [ˈweifər] galleta *f*; barquillo *m*; oblea *f for sealing*; *eccl.* hostia *f*.
waf·fle [ˈwɔfl] **1.** *approx.* churro *m*, buñuelo *m*; *sl.* palabrería *f*; **2.** *sl.* vacilar.
waft [wæft] **1.** traer, llevar (por el aire); **2.** soplo *m*.
wag[1] [wæg] **1.** menear(se); agitar(se); **2.** meneo *m*.
wag[2] [~] bromista *m*, zumbón *m*.
wage [weidʒ] **1.** *war* hacer; proseguir; **2.** (*a.* **wag·es** [ˈ~iz] *pl.*) salario *m*; (*mst day*) jornal *m*; **wage earn·er** [ˈ~əːrnər] asalariado (a *f*) *m*; obrero *m*; **ˈwage in·crease** aumento *m* de sueldo.
wa·ger [ˈweidʒər] *lit.* **1.** apuesta *f*; **2.** apostar (*on* a, *that* a que).
wag·ger·y [ˈwægəri] jocosidad *f*; chanzas *f/pl.*; **ˈwag·gish** □ zumbón, divertido.
wag·gle [ˈwægl] F *v. wag*[1].
wag·on [ˈwægən] carro *m*; 🚂 vagón *m*, furgón *m*; F *be on the* (*water*) ~ no beber.
wag·tail [ˈwægteil] aguzanieves *m*; lavandera *f*.
waif [weif] niño (a *f*) *m* abandonado (a); ~*s and strays pl.* niños *m/pl.* desamparados.
wail [weil] **1.** lamento *m*, gemido *m*; (*baby's*) vagido *m*; **2.** lamentarse, gemir; gimotear.
wain·scot [ˈweinskət] **1.** friso *m*; **2.** poner friso a.
waist [weist] cintura *f*; talle *m*; ⚓ combés *m*; **ˈ~·band** pretina *f*; **ˈ~·coat** chaleco *m*; **ˈ~-ˈdeep** hasta la cintura; **ˈ~·line** talle *m*.
wait [weit] **1.** *v/i.* esperar, aguardar (*for acc.*); (*a.* ~ *at table*) servir (*on acc.*); F ~ *about* estar esperando; ~ (*up*)*on p.* presentar sus respetos a; *decision* depender de; *keep s.o.* ~*ing* hacer que uno espere; ~ *and see!* espera y verás; *v/t.* esperar; F *meal* aplazar; **2.** espera *f*; ~*s pl.* murga *f* (de nochebuena); *have a long* ~ tener que esperar mucho tiempo; *be* (*or lie*) *in* ~ acechar (*for acc.*); **ˈwait·er** camarero *m*; mozo *m*.
wait·ing [ˈweitiŋ] espera *f*; servicio *m*; *in* ~ de honor; **ˈ~ list** lista *f* de espera; **ˈ~ room** sala *f* de espera.
wait·ress [ˈweitris] camarera *f*.
waive [weiv] *right* renunciar; *claim* desistir de; **ˈwaiv·er** renuncia *f*.
wake[1] [weik] ⚓ estela *f*; *fig. in the* ~ *of* siguiendo, como consecuencia de; tras.
wake[2] [~] **1.** [*irr.*] *v/i.* despertar(se) (*a.* ~ *up*); *v/t.* despertar; *corpse* velar; **2.** *hist.* verbena *f*; vela *f over corpse*; **wake·ful** [ˈ~ful] □ despierto; desvelado; **ˈwak·en** *v/i.* despertar(se); *v/t.* despertar.
walk [wɔːk] **1.** *v/i.* andar; caminar; (*stroll*) pasear(se); (*not ride*) ir a pie; ~ *about* pasearse; ~ *away with* llevarse; ~ *off with* llevarse; robar; ~ *out* (*strike*) declararse en huelga; retirarse (enfadado) *from conference*; salir repentinamente; F ~ *out on sweetheart* dejar plantado, plantar; dejar; *v/t. child etc.* pasear; *horse* llevar al paso; *distance* recorrer (a pie); (*tire*) cansar con tanto andar; ~ *off* deshacerse de ... andando; **2.** (*stroll*) paseo *m*; (*gait*) andar *m*, paso *m*; (*place*) paseo *m*, alameda *f*; *go for* (*or take*) *a* ~ dar un paseo; ~ *of life* profesión *f*, condición *f*; **ˈwalk·er**[1] paseante *m/f*, peatón *m*; *be a great* ~ ser gran andarín; **ˈwalk·er**[2] F figurante (a *f*) *m*.

walk·ie-talk·ie [ˈwɔːkiˈtɔːki] transmisor-receptor *m* portátil.
walk·ing [ˈwɔːkiŋ] **1.** excursionismo *m* a pie; el pasearse; **2.** ambulante; F ~ *papers pl.* despedida *f*; ~ *race* carrera *f* pedestre; ~ *tour* excursión *f* a pie; ˈ~ **stick** bastón *m*.
walk...: ˈ~**·out** huelga *f*; salida *f*; ˈ~**·over** *racing*: walkover *m*; *fig.* triunfo *m* fácil; ˈ~**-up** *house* sin ascensor.
wall [wɔːl] **1.** (*mst interior*) pared *f*; muro *m*; (*garden*) tapia *f*; (*city*) muralla *f*; *go to the* ~ ser desechado por inútil; quedar arrinconado; **2.** murar; *city* amurallar; ~ *up* emparedar; cerrar con muro.
wal·la·by [ˈwɔləbi] ualabi *m*.
wal·let [ˈwɔlit] cartera *f*.
wall...: ˈ~**·eyed** de ojos incolores; ˈ~**·flow·er** alhelí *m*; *fig. be a* ~ comer pavo; ˈ~ **fruit** fruta *f* de espalera; ˈ~ **map** mapa *m* mural.
wal·lop [ˈwɔləp] F **1.** golpear fuertemente; zurrar; **2.** golpazo *m*; zurra *f*; *sl.* fuerza *f of a drink*; ˈ**wal·lop·ing** F grandote.
wal·low [ˈwɔlou] revolcarse; *fig.* nadar (*in* en).
wall...: ˈ~**·pa·per** papel *m* pintado, papel *m* de empapelar; ˈ~ **sock·et** enchufe *m* de pared.
wal·nut [ˈwɔːlnʌt] nuez *f*; (*tree, wood*) nogal *m*.
wal·rus [ˈwɔːlrəs] morsa *f*..
waltz [wɔːls] **1.** vals *m*; **2.** valsar.
wan [wɔn] □ pálido, macilento.
wand [wɔnd] vara *f of office*; (*magic*) varita *f*.
wan·der [ˈwɔndər] errar, vagar; extraviarse; deambular (*a.* ~ *about*); *fig.* divagar *in mind*; salirse (*from theme etc.* de); ˈ**wan·der·er** vagabundo (a *f*) *m*; nómada *m*/*f*; ˈ**wan·der·ing 1.** □ errante; errabundo; *fig.* distraído; **2.** ⚕ delirio *m*; ~*s pl.* viajes *m*/*pl.*; errabundeo *m*; ˈ**wan·der·lust** [ˈ~lʌst] ansia *f* de viajar.
wane [wein] **1.** (*moon*) menguar; *fig.* disminuir; **2.** (*a.* ˈ**wan·ing**) menguante *f*; mengua *f*; *on the* ~ (*moon*) menguante; *fig.* menguando.
wan·gle [ˈwæŋgl] *sl.* **1.** chanchullo *m*, trampa *f*; **2.** mamarse, agenciarse; ˈ**wan·gler** chanchullero *m*.
wan·ness [ˈwɔnnis] palidez *f*.
want [wɔnt] **1.** (*lack*) falta *f*, carencia *f*; (*need*) necesidad *f*; (*poverty*) indigencia *f*; *for* ~ *of* por falta de; *be in* ~ estar necesitado; *fill a long-felt* ~ llenar un bien sentido vacío; F ~ *ad* anuncio *m* clasificado; **2.** *v/i.*: *be* ~*ing* faltar; *be* ~*ing in* estar falto de; ~ *for* necesitar, carecer de; *it* ~*s of* falta; *v/t.* querer, desear; (*need*) necesitar; (*lack*) carecer de; *he* ~*s energy* le falta energía; ~ *a p. to do* querer que una p. haga; F *you* ~ *to be careful* hay que tener ojo; ~*ed* (*in ads*) necesítase; (*police*) se busca; ˈ**want·ing** defectuoso; deficiente (*in* en), falto (*in* de).
wan·ton [ˈwɔntən] **1.** □ (*playful*) juguetón; (*rank*) lozano; caprichoso; *b.s.* lascivo; *destruction* sin propósito; **2.** libertino (a *f*) *m*; **3.** retozar; ˈ**wan·ton·ness** lascivia *f etc.*
war [wɔːr] **1.** guerra *f*; *attr.* ... de guerra, bélico; *at* ~ en guerra; *make* ~ hacer la guerra (*on* a); *cold* ~ guerra *f* fría; *hot* ~ guerra *f* a tiros; ~ *of nerves* guerra *f* de nervios; ~ *criminal* criminal *m* de guerra; ~ *dance* danza *f* guerrera; ~ *horse* corcel *m*; ~ *memorial* monumento *m* a los caídos; **2.** *lit.* guerrear.
war·ble [wɔːrbl] **1.** trinar, gorjear; **2.** trino *m*, gorjeo *m*; ˈ**war·bler** mosquitero *m*, curruca *f etc.*
ward [wɔːrd] **1.** (*p.*) pupilo (a *f*) *m*; (*wardship*) tutela *f*, custodia *f*; (*hospital*) sala *f*, crujía *f*; distrito *m* (electoral) *of city*; guarda *f of key*; *in* ~ bajo tutela; *casual* ~ asilo *m* para pobres; *Am. pol.* F ~ *heeler* muñidor *m*; F *walk the* ~*s* hacer práctica de clínica; **2.:** ~ *off* desviar, parar; *fig.* evitar, conjurar; ˈ**ward·en** carcelero *m*; guardián *m*; *univ. etc.* director *m*; (*in titles*) alcaide *m*; ˈ**ward·er** carcelero *m*, vigilante *m*; ˈ**ward·robe** guardarropa *m*; vestidos *m*/*pl.*; *thea.* vestuario *m*; ~ *dealer* ropavejero *m*; ~ *trunk* baúl *m* ropero; ˈ**ward·room** ⚓ cuarto *m* de los oficiales; ˈ**ward·ship** tutela *f*.
ware [wer] loza *f*; ~*s pl.* mercancías *f*/*pl.*; *small* ~*s pl.* mercería *f*.
ware·house 1. [ˈwerhaus] almacén *m*, depósito *m*; **2.** [ˈ~hauz] almacenar; ~**·man** [ˈ~hausmən] almacenista *m*.
war...: ˈ~**·fare** guerra *f*; ˈ~**·head** punta *f* de combate *of torpedo*; cabeza *f* de guerra *of rocket*.
war·i·ly [ˈwerili] cautelosamente;

war·i·ness [ˈ~inis] cautela *f*, precaución *f*.
war·like [ˈwɔːrlaik] guerrero, belicoso; castrense.
warm [wɔːrm] **1.** □ caliente; *day, greeting* caluroso; *climate* cálido; *heart* afectuoso; *argument* acalorado; *be* ~ (*p.*) tener calor; (*weather*) hacer calor; (*th.*) estar caliente; **2.** *v/t.* calentar; *heart* alegrar, regocijar; F zurrar; ~ *up food* recalentar; *v/i.* (*a.* ~ *up*) calentarse; (*argument*) acalorarse; *sport*: hacer ejercicios (para entrar en calor); ~ *to* (*heart*) ir cobrando afición a; ˈ**~-heart·ed** cariñoso; simpático; ˈ**warm·ing** F zurra *f*.
war·mon·ger [ˈwɔːrmʌŋgər] incendiario *m* de la guerra.
warmth [wɔːrmθ] calor *m*; *fig.* cordialidad *f*; entusiasmo *m*; ardor *m*.
warn [wɔːrn] avisar; advertir (*of acc.*); prevenir (*against* contra); amonestar (*to inf.*); ~ *off* expulsar *from racecourse etc.*; *he was* ~*ed off the subject* le advirtieron que no se metiese en el asunto; ˈ**warn·ing** aviso *m*; advertencia *f*; *be a* ~ servir de escarmiento (*to* a); *attr.* de aviso; de alarma; admonitorio.
warp [wɔːrp] **1.** (*weaving*) urdimbre *f*; alabeo *m of wood*; ⚓ espía *f*; *fig.* sesgo *m*; **2.** *v/i.* (*wood*) alabearse, torcerse; ⚓ espiarse; *v/t. wood* alabear, torcer; ⚓ mover con espía; *fig.* pervertir.
warp·ing [ˈwɔːrpiŋ] ✈ torsión *f*.
war·plane [ˈwɔːrplein] avión *m* militar.
war·rant [ˈwɔrənt] **1.** garantía *f*; autorización *f*, justificación *f*; ☤ cédula *f*, vale *m*; ⚖ mandato *m*; orden *f* (*of arrest* de prisión); **2.** *esp.* ☤ garantizar; autorizar, justificar; *I* ~ (*you*) se lo aseguro; ˈ**war·rant·a·ble** □ justificable; *stag* de edad para cazar; ˈ**war·rant·ed** ☤ garantizado; **war·ran·tee** [~ˈtiː] persona *f* afianzada; ˈ**war·rant of·fi·cer** ⚓ contramaestre *m*; ⚔ suboficial *m*; ˈ**war·ran·tor** [~tɔːr] garante *m*/*f*; ˈ**war·ran·ty** ☤ garantía *f*; *v. warrant*.
war·ren [ˈwɔrin] conejera *f*.
war·ri·or [ˈwɔriər] guerrero *m*.
war·ship [ˈwɔːrʃip] buque *m* de guerra.
wart [wɔːrt] verruga *f* (*a.* ♀); ˈ**wart·y** verrugoso.
war·y [ˈweri] □ cauto, cauteloso, prudente.
was [wɔz, wəz] *pret. of be.*
wash [wɔʃ] **1.** *v/t.* lavar (*a.* ~ *up*, ~ *out*); *dishes a.* fregar; bañar; ~ *away* quitar lavando; (*river*) llevarse; ~*ed out sl.* rendido; ~*ed up sl.* deslomado; *sl.* fracasado; ~ *one's hands of* desentenderse de; *v/i.* lavarse; lavar la ropa; (*water*) moverse; ~ *up* lavar (*or* fregar) los platos; **2.** lavado *m*; ropa *f* (para lavar); (*hung to dry*) tendido *m*; ⚓ estela *f*, remolinos *m*/*pl.*; movimiento *m of water*; ✈ disturbio *m* aerodinámico; (*hair*) champú *m*; *contp.* aguachirle *f*; ˈ**wash·a·ble** lavable; ˈ**wash-and-**ˈ**wear** *adj.* de lava y pon; ˈ**wash ba·sin** palangana *f*, lavabo *m*.
washed-up [ˈwɔʃtˈʌp] *sl.* fracasado.
wash·er [ˈwɔʃər] ⊕ arandela *f*; (*tap*) zapatilla *f*; ˈ**~·wom·an** lavandera *f*.
wash·ing [ˈwɔʃiŋ] **1.** ropa *f* (para lavar); lavado *m*; ~*s pl.* lavadura *f*; **2.**: ~ *machine* lavadora *f*; ~ *powder* jabón *m* en polvo; ~ *soda* sosa *f* de lavar; ˈ**~-**ˈ**up** platos *m*/*pl.* (para lavar); fregado *m*, lavado *m*.
wash...: ˈ**~ leath·er** gamuza *f*; ˈ**~**ˈ**out** *sl.* fracaso *m*; ˈ**~·rag** paño *m* de cocina; ˈ**~ stand** lavabo *m*, lavamanos *m*; ˈ**~·tub** tina *f* (de lavar); ˈ**wash·y** aguado, insípido; *fig.* flojo, insulso.
wasp [wɔsp] avispa *f*; ~*s' nest* avispero *m* (*a. fig.*); ˈ**wasp·ish** □ irascible; punzante.
wast·age [ˈweistidʒ] merma *f*, pérdida *f*; desgaste *m*.
waste [weist] **1.** (*rejected*) desechado; (*useless*) inútil; (*left over*) sobrante; *land* baldío, yermo; *lay* ~ asolar, devastar; ~ *paper* papel *m* viejo, papeles *m*/*pl.* usados; *biol.* ~ *products pl.* desperdicios *m*/*pl.*; ~ *steam* vapor *m* de escape; **2.** despilfarro *m*, derroche *m*; pérdida *f of time*; desgaste *m*; desperdicio(s) *m*(*pl.*); desecho *m*, basura *f*; (*land*) yermo *m*; *go* (*or run*) *to* ~ perderse; *radioactive* ~ residuos *m* radiactivos; **3.** *v/t.* malgastar; desperdiciar; derrochar; *time* perder; *v/i.* (des)gastarse; perderse; ~ *away* consumirse, mermar; **waste·ful** [ˈ~ful] □ pródigo; despilfarrado; antieconómico; ˈ**waste·ful·ness** despilfarro *m etc.*;

ˈ**waste·pa·per bas·ket** cesto *m* (para papeles); ˈ**waste pipe** tubo *m* de desagüe; ˈ**waste prod·uct** producto *m* de desecho; **wast·rel** [ˈweistrəl] derrochador *m*.

watch [wɔtʃ] **1.** reloj *m*; vigilia *f*; vigilancia *f*; ⚔, ⚓ guardia *f*, ⚓ vigía(s) *m(pl.)*; (*night*) ronda *f*; *be on the* ~ estar a la mira (*for* de); *keep* ~ estar de guardia; *keep* ~ *over p.* velar; *th.* vigilar por; **2.** *v/i.* velar; ~ *for* esperar; acechar; ~ *out* tener cuidado (*for* con); ~ *over* vigilar; *v/t.* mirar; observar; vigilar; guardar; ˈ~ **chain** cadena *f* de reloj; ˈ~·**dog** perro *m* guardián; ˈ**watch·er** observador *m*; **watch·ful** [ˈ~ful] □ vigilante; ˈ**watch·ful·ness** vigilancia *f*, desvelo *m*.

watch...: ˈ~·**mak·er** relojero *m*; ˈ~·**man** guardián *m*; (*night-*) sereno *m*; ˈ~·**tow·er** atalaya *f*; ˈ~·**word** ⚔ santo *m* y seña; *pol. etc.* lema *m*, consigna *f*.

wa·ter [ˈwɔːtər] **1.** agua *f*; *high* ~ pleamar *f*; *low* ~ bajamar *f*; *by* ~ por agua; por mar; *of the first* ~ de lo mejor; *drink* (*or take*) *the* ~*s* tomar las aguas; *get into deep* ~*s* meterse en honduras; F *get into hot* ~ cargársela (*for, over* en el asunto de); *hold* ~ retener el agua; *fig.* ser lógico; **2.** acuático; de agua, para agua; ~ *supply* abastecimiento *m* de agua; **3.** *v/t. land, plant* regar; *cattle* abrevar; *wine* aguar (*a.* ~ *down*); ~ *down fig.* suavizar, diluir; *v/i.* (*mouth*) hacerse agua; (*eyes*) llorar; ˈ~-**borne** llevado por barco *etc.*; ˈ~ **bot·tle** cantimplora *f*; ˈ~ **can·non** cañón *m* de agua; ˈ~ ˈ**car·ri·er** aguador *m*; ˈ~ **cart** cuba *f* de riego; ˈ~·**col·or** acuarela *f*; ˈ~-**cooled** refrigerado por agua; ˈ~ **cool·ing** refrigeración *f* por agua; ˈ~·**course** lecho *m*; arroyo *m*; ˈ~·**cress** berro *m*; ˈ~-**di**ˈ**vin·er** zahorí *m*; ˈ~·**fall** cascada *f*, salto *m* de agua; ˈ~·**fowl** *pl.* aves *f/pl.* acuáticas; ˈ~·**front** terreno *m* ribereño; ˈ**wa·ter·i·ness** acuosidad *f*.

wa·ter·ing [ˈwɔːtəriŋ] riego *m*; ˈ~ **can** regadera *f*; ˈ~ **place** (*spa*) balneario *m*; 🐄 abrevadero *m*.

water...: ˈ~ **jack·et** camisa *f* de agua; ˈ~ **lev·el** nivel *m* del agua; ⚓ línea *f* de agua; ˈ~ **lil·y** nenúfar *m*; ˈ~·**line** línea *f* de flotación; ˈ~·**logged** anegado; empapado; ˈ~ **main** cañería *f* maestra; ˈ~·**man** barquero *m*; ˈ~·**mark** filigrana *f*; ˈ~·**mel·on** sandía *f*; ˈ~·**mill** molino *m* de agua; ˈ~ **pipe** caño *m* de agua; ˈ~ **po·lo** polo *m* acuático; ˈ~ **pow·er** fuerza *f* hidráulica; ˈ~·**proof 1.** impermeable *adj. a. su. m*; **2.** impermeabilizar; ˈ~·**shed** línea *f* divisoria de las aguas; cuenca *f*; ˈ~·**side** orilla *f* del agua; ˈ~-ˈ**ski·ing** esquí *m* acuático; ˈ~·**spout** tromba *f* marina; ˈ~ **ta·ble** retallo *m* de derrame; ˈ~ **tank** cisterna *f*; ˈ~-**tight** estanco, hermético; *fig.* irrecusable; completamente lógico; ~ *compartment* compartimento *m* estanco; ˈ~·**wave 1.** ondulación *f* al agua; **2.** ondular al agua; ˈ~·**way** canal *m*, vía *f* fluvial; ˈ~·**wings** *pl.* nadaderas *f/pl.*; ˈ~·**works** *pl., a. sg.* central *f* depuradora; ˈ**wa·ter·y** acuoso; *eye* lagrimoso; *sky* que amenaza lluvia; *fig.* insípido; pálido.

watt [wɔt] vatio *m*; ˈ**watt·age** vatiaje *m*.

wat·tle [ˈwɔtl] zarzo *m*; *orn.* barba *f*.

wave [weiv] **1.** ola *f*; onda *f* (*a. phys., radio*); (*hair*) ondulación *f*; *fig.* oleada *f of strikes etc.*; señal *f*, ademán *m of hand*; *cold* ~ ola *f* de frío; **2.** *v/t.* agitar; *weapon etc.* blandir; *hair* ondular; ~ *aside* rechazar; ~ *a p. on* hacer señales a una p. para que avance; *v/i.* ondear; agitar el brazo; ~ *to a p.* hacer señales (con la mano) a una p.; ˈ~·**length** longitud *f* de onda; ˈ~ **me·ter** ondímetro *m*.

wa·ver [ˈweivər] vacilar, titubear.

wave...: ˈ~ **range** *radio*: gama *f* de ondas; ˈ~ **theo·ry** teoría *f* ondulatoria; ˈ~ **trap** *radio*: trampa *f* de ondas.

wav·y [ˈweivi] ondulado; ondeado.

wax[1] [wæks] **1.** cera *f*; **2.** encerar.

wax[2] [~] [*irr.*] (*moon*) crecer; (*with adj.*) ponerse.

wax·en [ˈwæksn] de cera; ceroso; ˈ**wax·work** figura *f* de cera; ~*s pl.* museo *m* de (figuras de) cera; ˈ**wax·y** □ ceroso; *sl.* enojadizo.

way [wei] camino *m* (*to* de); vía *f*; dirección *f*, sentido *m*; distancia *f*, trayecto *m*; viaje *m*; paso *m* (*a.* ~ *through*); costumbre *f*; respecto *m*; estado *m*; progreso *m*; (*means*) manera *f*, modo *m*; medio *m*; estilo *m of life*; ~ *in* entrada *f*; ~ *out* salida *f*; *a good* ~ un buen trecho; *this* ~ por aquí; de este modo; ~*s and means pl.* medios *m/pl.*; *across the*

~ enfrente; *by the* ~ de paso; a propósito; *by* ~ *of* por vía de; *fig.* a título de; *in a* ~ en cierto modo; *in every* ~ bajo todas los aspectos; *in no* ~ de ningún modo; *in a bad* ~ en mal estado; F *in a big* ~ en grande, en gran escala; *on the* ~ en el camino; *on the* ~ *to* camino de; *out of the* ~ arrinconado, aislado; insólito; *under* ~ en marcha; *be in the* ~ estorbar; *feel one's* ~ andar a tientas; *fig.* proceder con tiento; *get* (*or have*) *one's* ~ salirse con la suya; *get out of the* ~ quitar(se) de en medio; *give* ~ ceder (*to* el paso a); romperse; *mot.* ceder el paso; *go a long* ~ *towards ger.* contribuir mucho a *inf.*; *go one's own* ~ ir a la suya; *go out of one's* ~ desviarse del camino; *fig.* darse la molestia (*to inf.* de *inf.*); *have a* ~ *with* manejar bien; *have a* ~ *with people* tener don de gentes; *lead the* ~ ir primero; *lose one's* ~ extraviarse, errar el camino; *make one's* ~ abrirse camino (*through* por); dirigirse (*to* a); *make* ~ *for* hacer lugar para; *see one's* ~ *to ger. or inf.* ver la forma de *inf.*; ~ *station* estación *f* de paso; ˈ**~·bill** hoja *f* de ruta; ˈ**~·far·er** viajero (a *f*) *m*; caminante *m/f*; **~ˈlay** [*irr.* (*lay*)] asechar; detener; ˈ**~·side 1.** (*by the* al) borde *m* del camino; **2.** junto al camino.

way·ward [ˈweiwərd] voluntarioso; caprichoso; ˈ**way·ward·ness** voluntariedad *f*; lo caprichoso.

we [wiː, wi] nosotros, nosotras.

weak [wiːk] □ débil; flojo; *sound* tenue; ~ *point* flaco *m*; ˈ**weak·en** debilitar(se); atenuar(se); enflaquecer(se); ˈ**weak·ling** ⚕ canijo *m*; cobarde *m*; ˈ**weak·ly** enclenque, achacoso; ˈ**weak-ˈmind·ed** ⚕ imbécil; vacilante; ˈ**weak·ness** debilidad *f*; flaco *m*; *have a* ~ *for* ser muy aficionado a.

wealth [welθ] riqueza *f*; caudal *m*; *fig.* abundancia *f*; ˈ**wealth·y** □ rico, acaudalado.

wean [wiːn] destetar; *fig.* ~ *from*, ~ *of* apartar gradualmente de; ˈ**wean·ing** destete *m*, ablactación *f*.

weap·on [ˈwepən] arma *f*; ˈ**~·less** desarmado; inerme; ˈ**~·ry** armamento *m*.

wear [wer] **1.** [*irr.*] *v/t. clothes etc.* llevar; *shoes* calzar; *smile, look* tener; exhibir; ~ *away*, ~ *down*, ~ *out* (des)gastar; consumir; *patience* cansar; agotar; ~ *o.s. out* matarse; *v/i.* (*well*) durar; ~ *well* conservarse bien; ~ *away* desgastarse; ~ *off* pasar, desaparecer; ~ *on* (*time*) pasar (despacio); ~ *out* gastarse, usarse; **2.** desgaste *m*, deterioro *m*, uso *m* (*a.* ~ *and tear*); durabilidad *f*; (*clothes*) ropa *f*; moda *f*; *for everyday* ~ para todo trote; *for hard* ~ resistente, duradero; *the worse for* ~ deteriorado.

wea·ri·ness [ˈwirinis] cansancio *m*; aburrimiento *m*.

wea·ri·some [ˈwirisəm] □ fastidioso; aburrido.

wea·ry [ˈwiri] **1.** □ (*tired*) cansado (*of* de), fatigado; (*tiring*) fastidioso, aburrido; **2.** *v/t.* cansar; aburrir; *v/i.* cansarse (*of* de).

wea·sel [ˈwiːzl] comadreja *f*.

weath·er [ˈweðər] **1.** tiempo *m*; (*harsh*) intemperie *f*; *under the* ~ F ⚕ indispuesto; *sl.* borracho; **2.** *attr.* ⚓ de barlovento; meteorológico; **3.** *v/t.* ⚓ (*a.* ~ *out*) *storm* aguantar (*a. fig.*); *cape* doblar; *fig.* superar; *geol.* desgastar; *wood* curar al aire; *v/i.* curtirse a la intemperie; *geol.* desgastarse; **~-beat·en** [ˈ~biːtn] curtido por la intemperie; ˈ**~·bound** atrasado por el mal tiempo; ˈ**~ bu·reau** servicio *m* meteorológico; ˈ**~-chart** mapa *m* meteorológico; ˈ**~·cock** veleta *f*; ˈ**~ fore·cast** parte *m* (*or* boletín *m*) meteorológico; ˈ**~·proof** a prueba de la intemperie; ˈ**~ sta·tion** estación *f* meteorológica; ˈ**~-strip(·ping)** burlete *m*; ˈ**~ vane** veleta *f*.

weave [wiːv] **1.** [*irr.*] tejer; trenzar; *fig.* urdir, tramar; **2.** tejido *m*; ˈ**weav·er** tejedor *m*; ˈ**weav·ing** tejeduría *f*; *attr.* ... para tejer; de tejido(s).

web [web] tela *f*; tejido *m*; (*spider's*) telaraña *f*; *orn.* membrana *f*; ⊕ alma *f*; *printing*: rollo *m* de papel; **webbed** palmeado; ˈ**web·bing** cincha *f*; ˈ**web·foot·ed** palmípedo.

wed [wed] *v/t.* casarse con; *fig.* casar; *v/i.* casarse; ˈ**wed·ded** conyugal; *fig.* ~ *to* aferrado a; ˈ**wed·ding 1.** boda *f*, bodas *f/pl.*; casamiento *m*; **2.** *attr.*: ~ *breakfast* banquete *m* nupcial; ~ *cake* pastel *m* de boda; ~ *day* día *m* de boda; ~ *dress* traje *m* de novia; ~ *march* marcha *f* nupcial; ~ *ring* anillo *m* de boda.

wedge [wedʒ] **1.** cuña *f*; calce *m*; **2.** calzar, acuñar; ~ *in* introducir apretadamente, encajar.
wed·lock [ˈwedlɔk] matrimonio *m*.
Wed·nes·day [ˈwenzdi] miércoles *m*.
wee [wiː] F (*a. Scot.*) pequeñito, diminuto.
weed [wiːd] **1.** mala hierba *f*; F tabaco *m*; **2.** escardar; desherbar; ~ *out fig.* escardar, extirpar, eliminar; ˈ**~-kill·er** herbicida *m*.
weeds [wiːdz] *pl.* (*mst widow's* ~) ropa *f* de luto.
weed·y [ˈwiːdi] lleno de malas hierbas; F flaco, desmirriado.
week [wiːk] semana *f*; *this day* ~, *a* ~ *today* de hoy en ocho días; ~ *in*, ~ *out* semana tras semana; ˈ**~·day** día *m* laborable; ˈ~ˈ**end 1.** fin *m* de semana, weekend *m*; **2.** pasar el fin de semana; ˈ**week·ly 1.** semanal; **2.** semanalmente; **3.** (*a.* ~ *paper*) semanario *m*, hebdomadario *m*.
weep [wiːp] [*irr.*] llorar, lamentar (*for acc.*); *tears* derramar; ˈ**weep·ing 1.** lloroso; ~ *willow* sauce *m* llorón; **2.** llanto *m*, lágrimas *f/pl*.
wee·vil [ˈwiːvil] gorgojo *m*.
weft [weft] trama *f*.
weigh [wei] **1.** *v/t.* pesar (*a. fig.*, ~ *up*, *words etc.*); ~ *against* considerar en relación con; ~ *anchor* zarpar; ~ *down* sobrecargar; *fig.* agobiar (*with* de); *v/i.* pesar; *he* ~*s 80 kilogram* pesa 80 kilos; ~ *in with* intervenir afirmando; ~ *on* ser gravoso a; ~ *with* influir en; **2.**: ⚓ *under* ~ en marcha; ~*-in sports*: pesaje *m*; ˈ**weigh·ing ma·chine** báscula *f*.
weight [weit] **1.** peso *m* (*a. fig.*); pesa *f*; ~*s and measures pl.* pesos *m/pl.* y medidas; *carry great* ~ influir poderosamente (*with* en); *putting the* ~ lanzamiento *m* de pesos; ~ *lifting* halterofilia *f*; *throw* ~ *rocketry*: peso *m* de la carga a lanzarse; **2.** (sobre)cargar; sujetar con un peso; ponderar *statistically*; ˈ**weight·i·ness** peso *m*; *fig.* importancia *f*; ˈ**weight·less** ingrávido; ˈ**weight·less·ness** ingravidez *f*; gravedad *f* nula; ˈ**weight·y** □ pesado; *fig.* importante, de peso.
weir [wir] presa *f*, pesquera *f*.
weird [wird] □ fantástico, sobrenatural; F extraño, raro, curioso.
welch [welʃ] *sl.* dejar de pagar una apuesta (*on* a).
wel·come [ˈwelkəm] **1.** □ bienvenido; grato; *you are* ~ *to inf.* Vd. es muy dueño de *inf.*; *you are* ~ *to it* está a su disposición; F *you're* ~! no hay de qué; *iro.* ¡buen provecho le haga!; (*you are*) ~! ¡(sea Vd.) bienvenido!; **2.** bienvenida *f*; (buena) acogida *f*; **3.** dar la bienvenida a; acoger; recibir; ˈ**wel·com·ing** □ acogedor.
weld [weld] **1.** ⊕ soldar; *fig.* unir, unificar (*into* para formar); **2.** (*or* ~*ing seam*) soldadura *f*; ˈ**weld·er** soldador *m*; ˈ**weld·ing** ⊕ soldadura *f*; *attr.* ... soldador.
wel·fare [ˈwelfer] bienestar *m*; prosperidad *f*; asistencia *f* social; ~ *center* centro *m* de asistencia social; ~ *state* estado *m* benefactor; gobierno *m* socializante; ~ *worker* empleado (a *f*) *m* de asistencia social.
well[1] [wel] **1.** pozo *m*; *fig.* fuente *f*, manantial *m*; ⊕ pozo *m* (de petróleo); hueco *m of stairs*; **2.** (*a.* ~ *up*) brotar, manar.
well[2] [~] **1.** *adv.* bien; ~ *done!* ¡bien!; ~ *and good* enhorabuena; *he's* ~ *past 50* tiene mucho más de 50 años; *v. as*; **2.** *pred. adj.* bien (de salud); *it is just as* ~ *that* menos mal que; **3.** *int. etc.* ¡vaya!; bien; pues; ~ *then* pues bien; ˈ**~-adˈvised** bien aconsejado; ˈ**~-atˈtend·ed** muy concurrido; ˈ**~-beˈhaved** bien educado; ˈ~ˈ**be·ing** bienestar *m*; ˈ**~-ˈbred** bien criado; cortés; ˈ**~-disˈposed** bien dispuesto; benévolo (*to, towards* con); ˈ**~-ˈfa·vored** bien parecido; ˈ**~-heeled** F acomodado; ˈ**~-in·formed** (*in general*) instruido; bien enterado (*about matter* de).
Wel·ling·tons [ˈweliŋtənz] *pl.* botas *f/pl.* de goma.
well...: ˈ**~-inˈten·tioned** bienintencionado; ˈ**~-ˈjudged** bien calculado; ˈ**~-ˈknown** familiar, conocido; ˈ**~-ˈman·nered** cortés, urbano; ˈ**~-ˈmean·ing** bienintencionado; ˈ**~-nigh** casi; ˈ**~-ˈoff** F acomodado; ˈ**~-ˈread** muy leído; ˈ**~-ˈspo·ken** bienhablado; ˈ**~-ˈtimed** oportuno; ˈ**~-to-ˈdo** acomodado, pudiente; ˈ**~-ˈturned** *fig.* elegante; ˈ**~-ˈwish·er** amigo (a *f*) *m*; ˈ**~-ˈworn** *fig.* traído y llevado, trillado.
Welsh [welʃ] **1.** galés, de Gales; **2.** (*language*) galés *m*; ˈ**~·man** galés *m*.
welt [welt] **1.** vira *f of shoe*; (*weal*)

verdugón *m*; **2.** poner vira a; F zurrar.

wel·ter [ˈweltər] **1.** revolcarse; estar empapado (*in* de); **2.** confusión *f*; mar *m of blood etc.*; ˈ**~·weight** wélter *m*.

wen [wen] lobanillo *m*.

wench [wentʃ] moza *f*, mozuela *f*.

wend [wend]: ~ *one's way* dirigirse (*to* a).

went [went] *pret. of go* 1.

wept [wept] *pret. a. p.p. of weep.*

were [wəːr, wər] *pret. of be.*

west [west] **1.** oeste *m*, occidente *m*; **2.** *adj.* del oeste, occidental; **3.** *adv.* al oeste, hacia el oeste; *sl. go* ~ romperse; fracasar; (*die*) reventar.

west·er·ly [ˈwestərli] *direction* hacia el oeste; *wind* del oeste.

west·ern [ˈwestərn] **1.** occidental; **2.** ♀ película *f* que se desarrolla en el Oeste de EE. UU.; ˈ**west·ern·er** habitante *m/f* del oeste; ˈ**west·ern·most** (el) más occidental.

west·ward(**s**) [ˈwestwərd(z)] hacia el oeste.

wet [wet] **1.** mojado; *place* húmedo; *weather* lluvioso; *day* de lluvia; *paint* fresco; F antiprohibicionista; *v. blanket* 1; ~ *paint!* ¡ojo, se pinta!; ~ *steam* vapor *m* húmedo; ~ *through* mojado hasta los huesos; **2.** humedad *f*; (*rain*) lluvia *f*; **3.** mojar; F *bargain* cerrar con un brindis; ~ *one's whistle* remojar el gaznate.

wet·back [ˈwetbæk] *sl.* inmigrante *m/f* ilegal; ˈ**wet bar** bar *m* con agua corriente; ˈ**wet cell** ⚡ pila *f* húmeda.

weth·er [ˈweðər] carnero *m* castrado.

wet·ness [ˈwetnis] humedad *f*; (*raininess*) lo lluvioso.

wet nurse [ˈwetnəːrs] nodriza *f*.

whack [wæk] F **1.** golpear (ruidosamente); pegar; **2.** golpe *m* (ruidoso); *sl.* tentativa *f*; *sl.* parte *f*, porción *f*; *sl. have a ~ at* probar, tratar de hacer; ˈ**whack·ing** F **1.** zurra *f*; **2.** grandote, imponente.

whale [weil] ballena *f*; F *a ~ of ...* un enorme ...; F *have a ~ of a time* pasarlo en grande; ˈ**~·bone** ballena *f*; ˈ**whal·er** (*p.*) ballenero *m*; (*boat*) ballenera *f*; ˈ**whale oil** aceite *m* de ballena.

whal·ing [ˈweiliŋ] pesca *f* de ballenas; ~ *station* estación *f* ballenera.

whang [wæŋ] F **1.** golpe *m* resonante; **2.** golpear de modo resonante.

wharf [wɔːrf] (*pl. a.* **wharves** [wɔːrvz]) muelle *m*; **wharf·age** [ˈ~idʒ] muellaje *m*.

what [wɔt] **1.** *relative* lo que; *know ~'s ~* saber cuántas son cinco; ~ *money I had* el dinero que tenía; cuanto dinero tenía; ~ *with one thing and another* entre lo une y lo otro; *... and ~ not* y qué sé yo qué más; **2.** *interrogative* qué; cuál; *~?* (*surprise etc., asking for repetition*) ¿cómo?; *what book do you want?* ¿qué libro quieres?, ¿cuál de los libros quieres?; ~ *about...?* ¿qué te parece...?; ¿qué hay en cuanto a...?; ~ *about that book?* ¿y el libro aquel?; ~ *about me?* ¿y yo?; ~ *for?* ¿para qué?; ¿por qué?; ~ *of it?, so ~?* y eso ¿qué importa?; ~ *if...?* ¿y si...?; ~ *next?* ¿y luego?; ahora ¿qué?; F *~'s his name* Fulano; **3.**: ~ *luck!* ¡qué suerte!; ~ *a ...!* ¡qué...!; ˈ**what**(**·so**)ˈ**ev·er** **1.** cual(es)quiera que; todo lo que; **2.**: ~ *he says* diga lo que diga; *nothing ~* nada en absoluto.

wheal [wiːl] ⚕ verdugón *m*.

wheat [wiːt] trigo *m*; *attr.* triguero; ˈ**wheat·en** de trigo.

whee·dle [ˈwiːdl] engatusar (*into ger.* para que *subj.*); sonsacar (*a th. out of a p.* algo a alguien).

wheel [wiːl] **1.** rueda *f*; bicicleta *f*; (*steering*) volante *m*; ⚓ timón *m*; ⚔ conversión *f*; *big ~ sl.* persona *f* importante; **2.** *v/t.* hacer girar, hacer rodar; *bicycle* empujar; *child* pasear; *v/i.* girar, rodar; (*birds*) revolotear; ⚔ cambiar de frente; ~ *round* (*p.*) girar sobre los talones; ˈ**~·bar·row** carretilla *f*; ˈ**~ base** *mot.* distancia *f* entre ejes; batalla *f*; ˈ**~**ˈ**chair** silla *f* de ruedas; ˈ**wheeled** rodado; *4-~* de 4 ruedas; ~ *traffic* circulación *f* rodada; ˈ**wheel·er-**ˈ**deal·er** *contp.* explotador *m* tramoyista; empresario *m* pretendido; ˈ**wheel·wright** ruedero *m*; carretero *m*.

wheeze [wiːz] **1.** resollar (con ruido); **2.** resuello *m* (ruidoso), respiración *f* sibilante; *sl.* truco *m*, treta *f*, idea *f*; ˈ**wheez·y** □ que resuella (con ruido).

whelp [welp] *lit.* **1.** cachorro *m*; **2.** parir.

when [wen] **1.** ¿cuándo?; **2.** cuando.

whence [wens] *lit.* **1.** ¿de dónde?; **2.** por consiguiente.

when(·so)·ev·er [wen(sou)'evər] siempre que, cuandoquiera que; ~ *you like* cuando quieras.
where [wer] **1.** ¿(a)dónde?; **2.** donde; **~·a·bouts 1.** ['werə'bauts] *sl.* ¿dónde?; **2.** ['~] paradero *m*; **~'as** mientras (que); por cuanto; ⚖ considerando que; **~'at** con lo cual; **~'by** por lo cual, por donde; **'~·fore** por qué; por tanto; **~'in** en donde; **~'of** de que; **~'on** en que; **~·so'ev·er** dondequiera que; **~·up'on** acto seguido, después de lo cual; **wher'ev·er 1.** dondequiera que; **2.** F ¿dónde?; **where·with·al** [werwi'ðɔːl] F medios *m/pl.*, conquibus *m.*
whet [wet] *tool* afilar, amolar; *fig.* estimular, aguzar.
wheth·er ['weðər] si; ~ ... *or* sea ... sea; ~ *or no* en todo caso.
whet·stone ['wetstoun] muela *f*, piedra *f* de amolar.
whew [hwuː] ¡vaya!
whey [wei] suero *m.*
which [witʃ] **1.** ¿cuál(es)?; ¿qué?; ~ *book do you want?* ¿cuál de los libros quieres?, ¿qué libro quieres?; ~ *way?* ¿por dónde?; **2.** que; el (la, los, las) que; el (la) cual, los (las) cuales; lo cual (*e.g.*, *he came early, which was awkward* llegó temprano, lo cual creó dificultades); **~·ev·er** [~'evə] **1.** *pron.* cualquiera; el (la) que; **2.** *adj.* cualquier.
whiff [wif] soplo *m* (fugaz); vaharada *f*; fumada *f of smoke.*
whif·fle·tree ['wifltriː] volea *f.*
Whig [wig] † whig *m* (*liberal inglés*).
while [wail] **1.** rato *m*; *a good* ~ un buen rato; *for a* ~ durante un rato; F *worth* ~ que vale la pena; **2.**: ~ *away* entretener, pasar; **3.** (*a.* **whilst** [wailst]) mientras (que).
whim [wim] capricho *m*, antojo *m*; ⊕ malacate *m.*
whim·per ['wimpər] **1.** *v/i.* lloriquear, gimotear; *v/t.* decir lloriqueando; **2.** lloriqueo *m*, gimoteo *m.*
whim·si·cal ['wimzikl] □ caprichoso, fantástico; **whim·si·cal·i·ty** [~'kæliti] capricho *m*, fantasía *f.*
whim·s(e)y ['wimzi] fantasía *f* amena, extravagancia *f*; *v. whim.*
whine [wain] **1.** *v/i.* gimotear, quejarse; (*bullet*) silbar; *v/t.* decir gimoteando; **2.** gimoteo *m etc.*
whin·ny ['wini] **1.** relinchar; **2.** relincho *m.*
whip [wip] **1.** *v/t.* azotar; fustigar (*a. fig.*); *fig.* F derrotar; *cream* batir; ⚓ envolver con cuerda *etc.*; ~ *away* arrebatar (*from* a); *parl.* ~ *in* llamar (para que vote); ~ *off* (*on*) *clothes* quitarse (ponerse) de prisa; ~ *out* sacar de repente; ~ *up* confeccionar pronto; *v/i.* agitarse; ~ *round* volverse de repente; F hacer una colecta; **2.** látigo *m*; azote *m*; *parl.* llamada *f*; (*p.*) oficial *m* disciplinario de partido; F ~ *round* colecta *f*; **'~·cord** tralla *f*; **'whipped 'cream** crema *f* (*or* nata *f*) batida.
whip·per·snap·per ['wipərsnæpər] arrapiezo *m*; mequetrefe *m.*
whip·pet ['wipit] perro *m* lebrel.
whip·ping ['wipiŋ] flagelación *f*; vapuleo *m*; **'~ boy** cabeza *f* de turco; **'~ post** poste *m* de flagelación; **'~ top** peonza *f.*
whip·saw ['wipsɔː] sierra *f* cabrilla.
whirl [wəːl] **1.** *v/i.* arremolinarse; girar; (*head*) dar vueltas; *v/t.* hacer girar; agitar; llevar muy rápidamente; **2.** giro *m*, vuelta *f*; remolino *m*; serie *f* vertiginosa *of pleasures*; *in a* ~ (*head*) dando vueltas; **whirl·i·gig** ['~igig] tiovivo *m*; **'whirl·pool**, **'whirl·wind** torbellino *m*, remolino *m*; **'whir·ly·bird** F helicóptero *m.*
whir(r) [wəːr] **1.** zumbar, rechinar; **2.** zumbido *m*, rechino *m.*
whisk [wisk] **1.** (*brush*) escobilla *f*; (*fly*) mosqueador *m*; *cooking*: batidora *f*; **2.** *v/t. dust* quitar; *cooking*: batir; ~ *away* escamotear, arrebatar; llevar rápidamente; *v/i.* zamparse, desaparecer de repente; **'whisk·er** pelo *m* (de la barba); ~*s pl.* patillas *f/pl.*, bigotes *m/pl.* (*a. zo.*).
whis·k(e)y ['wiski] whisky *m.*
whis·per ['wispər] **1.** *v/i.* cuchichear; susurrar (*a. fig.*, *leaves*); *v/t.* decir al oído (*to* a); **2.** cuchicheo *m*; *fig.* susurro *m*; *fig.* rumor *m.*
whist [wist] whist *m.*
whis·tle ['wisl] **1.** silbar (*at acc.*); ~ *up* llamar con un silbido; **2.** ♪ silbato *m*, pito *m*; (*sound*) silbido *m*, silbo *m*; **'~ stop** población *f* pequeña.
whit [wit]: *not a* ~ ni pizca.
white [wait] **1.** blanco; *face* pálido; F honorable; *turn* ~ (*p.*) palidecer; ~ *coffee* café *m* con leche; ~ *heat* candencia *f*; ~ *horses* (*sea*) palomas *f/pl.*; ~ *lead* albayalde *m*;

~ *lie* mentirilla *f*; ~ *slave trade* trata *f* de blancas; **2.** blanco *m* (*a. of eye*); clara *f* del huevo; (*p.*) blanco (a *f*) *m*; ˈ**~·bait** salmonetes *m/pl.*; ˈ**~-col·lar** profesional; de oficina; *work* oficinesco; ~ *crime* crímenes *m/pl.* de oficinistas (*p. ej. contra la empresa*); ˈ**~-ˈhot** candente; *fig.* violento, ardiente; ˈ**whit·en** blanquear (*v/i. a. v/t.*); (*p.*) palidecer; ˈ**white·ness** blancura *f*; ˈ**whit·en·ing** tiza *f*; jalbegue *m*; ˈ**White Pa·per** *pol.* Libro *m* Blanco.

white...: ˈ**~ tie** (de) traje *m* de etiqueta; ˈ**~·wash 1.** jalbegue *m*; F encubrimiento *m* de faltas; **2.** enjalbegar, blanquear; F paliar (*p.* las faltas de).

whith·er [ˈwiðər] *lit.* ¿adónde?

whit·ing[1] [ˈwaitiŋ] blanco *m* de España.

whit·ing[2] [~] *ichth.* pescadilla *f*.

whit·ish [ˈwaitiʃ] blanquecino.

whit·low [ˈwitlou] panadizo *m*.

Whit·sun [ˈwitsn] **1.** ... de Pentecostés; **2.** Pentecostés *f*; **~·day** [ˈwitˈsʌndi] domingo *m* de Pentecostés; **~·tide** [ˈwitsntaid] Pentecostés *f*.

whit·tle [ˈwitl] *stick* cortar pedazos a; *fig.* ~ *away*, ~ *down* mermar (*or* reducir) poco a poco.

whiz(**z**) [wiz] **1.** silbar; (*arrow*) rehilar; F ~ *along* pasar como un rayo; **2.** silbido *m*, zumbido *m*; F *p.* experto *m*.

who [huː] **1.** que; quien(es); **2.** ¿quién(es)?; ~ *goes there?* ¿quién vive?; *Who's Who* Quién es Quién.

whoa [wou] ¡so!

who·dun·it [huːˈdʌnit] *sl.* novela *f* [policíaca.]

who·ev·er [huːˈevər] **1.** quienquiera que, cualquiera que; **2.** F ¿quién?

whole [houl] **1.** □ todo; entero; total; ⚕ sano; intacto; *the* ~ *world* el mundo entero; F *made out of* ~ *cloth* enteramente imaginario; ~ *milk* leche *f* sin desnatar; **2.** todo *m*; conjunto *m*; total *m*; totalidad *f*; *as a* ~ en su totalidad, en conjunto; *on the* ~ en general; ˈ**~ˈheart·ed** □ incondicional; cien por cien; ˈ**~·sale 1.** (*a.* ~ *trade*) venta *f* al (por) mayor; **2.** al (por) mayor; *fig.* en masa; general; ˈ**whole·sal·er** mayorista *m*; **whole·some** [ˈ~səm] □ saludable, sano; apetitoso; ˈ**whole wheat** trigo *m* entero.

whol·ly [ˈhouli] enteramente.

whom [huːm] *acc. of who.*

whoop [huːp] **1.** alarido *m*, grito *m*; **2.** gritar (fuertemente); *sl.* ~ *it up* armar una gritería; **whoop·ee** [ˈwuːpiː] F: *make* ~ divertirse una barbaridad; **whoop·ing cough** [ˈhuːpiŋkɔf] tos *f* ferina, coqueluche *f*.

whop [wɔp] *sl.* pegar; cascar; ˈ**whop·per** *sl.* enormidad *f*; (*lie*) mentirón *m*; ˈ**whop·ping** *sl.* enorme, grandísimo.

whore [hɔːr] puta *f*.

whorl [wəːrl] ⊕ espiral *f*; *zo.* espira *f*; ⚘ verticilo *m*.

whor·tle·ber·ry [ˈwəːrtlberi] arándano *m*.

whose [huːz] *genitive of who*: **1.** cuyo; de quien; **2.** ¿de quién?; **who·so·ev·er** [huːsouˈevər] quien(es)quiera que.

why [wai] **1.** ¿por qué?; ¿para qué?; **2.** vamos; pero; ¡hombre!; **3.** *su.* porqué *m*.

wick [wik] mecha *f*.

wick·ed [ˈwikid] □ malo, malvado; inicuo; *co.* F horroroso; ˈ**wick·ed·ness** maldad *f etc.*

wick·er [ˈwikər] (*attr.* de) mimbre *m or f*; ˈ**~·work 1.** rejilla *f*; cestería *f*; **2.** de mimbre.

wick·et [ˈwikit] postigo *m*, portillo *m*; *cricket*: (*stumps*) palos *m/pl.*; (*pitch*) terreno *m*.

wide [waid] **1.** □ ancho; extenso; amplio; *difference* considerable; *v. mark*; *be 3 feet* ~ ser ancho de 3 pies, tener 3 pies de ancho; **2.** *adv.* lejos; *v. awake*; ~ *open* abierto de par en par; *sl. city* que tiene mano abierta para el juego; *far and* ~ por todas partes; ˈ**~-an·gle** *phot.* de ángulo ancho; **wid·en** [ˈwaidn] ensanchar(se); ˈ**wide·ness** anchura *f*; ˈ**wide·spread** extenso, muy difundido.

wid·ow [ˈwidou] viuda *f*; ˈ**wid·owed** viudo; *be* ~ enviudar; ˈ**wid·ow·er** viudo *m*; **wid·ow·hood** [ˈ~hud] viudez *f*.

width [widθ] anchura *f*; extensión *f*; (*cloth*) ancho *m*; 2 *feet in* ~ ancho de 2 pies.

wield [wiːld] *lit.* manejar, empuñar; *power* ejercer; ~ *a pen* menear cálamo.

wife [waif] (*pl. wives*) mujer *f*, esposa *f*; ˈ**wife·ly** de esposa.

wig [wig] peluca *f*; *big* ~ F pájaro *m* de cuenta; **ˈwig·ging** F peluca *f*.

wig·gle [ˈwigl] menear(se) rápidamente.

wight [wait] *co.* criatura *f*.

wig·wam [ˈwigwæm] tienda *f* de indios norteamericanos.

wild [waild] **1.** □ salvaje; ♀ silvestre; feroz; violento; *weather* tormentoso; *child etc.* desmandado, desgobernado; (*rash, foolish*) insensato, temerario; (*frantic*) frenético; F (*angry*) negro; muy enfadado; ~ *beast* fiera *f*; *run* ~ vivir desenfrenadamente; ♀ crecer libre; F *be* ~ *about* andar loco por; **2.** ~*s pl. v. wilderness*; **ˈwild·cat 1.** *zo.* gato *m* montés; empresa *f* arriesgada; pozo *m* de petróleo de exploración; **2.** *fig.* quimérico; arriesgado; indisciplinado; (*strike*) sin autorización; **wil·der·ness** [ˈwildərnis] desierto *m*, yermo *m*; **wild·fire** [ˈwaildfaiər]: *spread like* ~ propagarse como la pólvora; **ˈwild-ˈgoose ˈchase** empresa *f* desatinada; **ˈwild·ness** ferocidad *f*; violencia *f etc.*

wiles [wailz] engaños *m/pl.*, ardides *m/pl.*, mañas *f/pl.*

wil·ful [ˈwilful] □ *p.* voluntarioso; *act* premeditado, intencionado.

wil·i·ness [ˈwailinis] astucia *f*

will [wil] **1.** voluntad *f*; placer *m*; ⚖ testamento *m*; *against one's* ~ a desgana; *at* ~ a voluntad; *with a* ~ resueltamente; *v. free* ~; **2.** [*irr.*] *v/aux. que forma el futuro etc.*: *he* ~ *come* vendrá; *I* ~ *do it* sí que lo haré; **3.** querer; lograr por fuerza de voluntad; ⚖ legar.

will·ing [ˈwiliŋ] □ complaciente; gustoso; *pred. be* ~ *to* estar dispuesto a; ~*ly* de buena gana; **ˈwill·ing·ness** buena voluntad *f*, complacencia *f*.

will-o'-the-wisp [ˈwiləðəwisp] fuego *m* fatuo; *fig.* quimera *f*.

wil·low [ˈwilou] sauce *m*; **ˈwil·low·y** *fig.* esbelto, cimbreño.

will pow·er [ˈwilpauər] fuerza *f* de voluntad.

wil·ly-nil·ly [ˈwiliˈnili] a la fuerza, quiera o no quiera.

wilt [wilt] marchitar(se); *fig.* acobardarse; languidecer.

wil·y [ˈwaili] □ astuto, mañoso.

wim·ple [ˈwimpl] griñón *m*.

win [win] **1.** [*irr.*] *v/t.* ganar; lograr; *sympathy* captar; *metal* arrancar; ⚔ *sl.* agenciarse; ~ *over*, ~ *round* conquistar; *v/i.* ganar; triunfar; ~ *through to* alcanzar; **2.** victoria *f*.

wince [wins] estremecerse, hacer una mueca de dolor.

winch [wintʃ] manubrio *m*, torno *m*.

wind[1] [wind] **1.** viento *m*; *fig.* (*breath*) aliento *m*; ⚕ flatulencia *f*; ♪ instrumento *m* de viento; *be in the* ~ estar pendiente; *get* ~ *of* husmear (*a. fig.*); *throw to the* ~*s* desechar; **2.** *hunt.* husmear; ⚕ dejar sin aliento.

wind[2] [waind] [*irr.*] *v/t.* enrollar, envolver (*a.* ~ *up*); *handle* dar vueltas a; *watch* dar cuerda a; *wool* devanar, ovillar; *horn* sonar; ~ *one's arms round* rodear de los brazos; ~ *up* concluir; ⚚ liquidar; *v/i.* serpentear; dar vueltas; ~ *round etc.* enroscarse; (re)torcerse.

wind... [wind]: **ˈ~·bag** charlatán *m*; **ˈ~·ed** sin aliento; **ˈ~·fall** fruta *f* caída; *fig.* golpe *m* de suerte inesperado; **ˈ~ gauge** anemómetro *m*; manga *f*.

wind·ing [ˈwaindiŋ] **1.** (*handle*) vuelta *f*; (*watch*) cuerda *f*; (*road etc.*) tortuosidad *f*; ⚡ bobinado *m*, devanado *m*; **2.** serpentino; sinuoso; tortuoso; ~ *staircase* escalera *f* de caracol; **ˈ~-ˈup** conclusión *f*; ⚚ liquidación *f*.

wind in·stru·ment [ˈwindinstrumənt] instrumento *m* de viento.

wind·jam·mer [ˈwinddʒæmər] buque *m* de vela (grande y veloz).

wind·lass [ˈwindləs] torno *m*.

wind·mill [ˈwindmil] molino *m* (de viento); (*toy*) molinete *m*.

win·dow [ˈwindou] ventana *f*; (*shop*) escaparate *m*; ventanilla *f of vehicle*; **ˈ~ dress·er** escaparatista *m/f*; **ˈ~ dress·ing** decoración *f* de escaparates; *fig.* camuflaje *m*.

win·dow...: ~ **en·ve·lope** sobre *m* de ventanilla; **ˈ~ frame** marco *m* (de ventana); **ˈ~ pane** cristal *m*; **ˈ~-shade** visillo *m*, transparente *m*; **ˈ~-shop** curiosear en las tiendas; **ˈ~ sill** alféizar *m*.

wind...: **ˈ~·pipe** tráquea *f*; **ˈ~·screen, ˈ~·shield** parabrisas *m*; ~ *washer* lavaparabrisas *m*; ~ *wiper* limpiaparabrisas *m*; **ˈ~ tun·nel** ✈ túnel *m* aerodinámico.

wind-up [ˈwaindʌp] final *m*; conclusión *f*; comienzo *m* del lanzamiento *of a baseball*.

wind·ward [ˈwindwərd] **1.** de barlovento; **2.** (*to* a) barlovento *m*.
win·dy [ˈwindi] □ ventoso; *day* de mucho viento; *place* expuesto al viento; *fig. speech* palabrero; *be* ~ hacer viento.
wine [wain] vino *m*; ˈ~ **cel·lar** bodega *f*; ˈ~**·glass** vaso *m* para vino; ˈ~**·grow·er** viñador *m*; ˈ~ **merchant** vinatero *m*; ˈ~ **press** lagar *m*; ˈ~**·skin** pellejo *m*, odre *m*.
wing [wiŋ] **1.** ala *f* (*a. pol.*, ⚔, ✈); F brazo *m*; *mot.* guardabarros *m*; *sport*: exterior *m*; *thea.* ~*s pl.* bastidores *m/pl.*; *be on the* ~ estar volando; *take* ~ irse volando; **2.** *v/t. bird* herir en el ala; *p.* herir en el brazo; ~ *one's way* volar; *v/i.* volar; ˈ~ **chair** sillón *m* de orejas; **winged** [~ŋd] alado; ˈ**wing nut** tuerca *f* mariposa; ˈ**wing·span,** ˈ**wing·spread** envergadura *f* (de alas).
wink [wiŋk] **1.** guiño *m*; pestañeo *m*; F *have* (*or take*) *40* ~*s* descabezar el sueño; F *not get a* ~ *of sleep* no pegar los ojos; *in a* ~ en un abrir y cerrar de los ojos; **2.** *v/t. eye* guiñar; *v/i.* guiñar el ojo; parpadear, pestañear, (*light*) titilar; ~ *at* guiñar el ojo a; *fig.* hacer la vista gorda a.
win·kle [ˈwiŋkl] **1.** bigarro *m*; **2.** F ~ *out* hacer salir; sacar con dificultad.
win·ner [ˈwinər] ganador (-a *f*) *m*, vencedor (-a *f*) *m*.
win·ning [ˈwiniŋ] **1.** □ vencedor, victorioso; *shot etc.* decisivo; *ways* encantador, persuasivo; **2.** ~*s pl.* ganancias *f/pl.*; ˈ~ **post** poste *m* de llegada.
win·now [ˈwinou] aventar; ~*ing machine* aventadora *f*.
win·ter [ˈwintər] **1.** invierno *m*; *attr.* invernal, de invierno; ~ *sports pl.* deportes *m/pl.* de invierno; **2.** invernar.
win·try [ˈwintri] invernal; *fig.* frío, glacial.
wipe [waip] **1.** enjugar; limpiar; ~ *off* quitar frotando; borrar; ~ *out* (*delete*) borrar, cancelar; (*destroy*) destruir, extirpar; aniquilar; *debt* liquidar; *sl.* ~ *the floor with* cascar; **2.** limpión *m*; limpiadura *f*; F golpe *m*.
wire [ˈwaiər] **1.** alambre *m*; F telegrama *m*; *attr.* ... de alambre; *sl. pull* ~*s* tocar resortes; tener un buen enchufe; **2.** *v/t. house* instalar el alambrado de; *fence* alambrar; F telegrafiar; *v/i.* F poner un telegrama; ˈ~ **cut·ters** *pl.* cizalla *f*; ˈ~ **gauge** calibre *m* para alambres; ˈ~**-haired** de pelo áspero; ˈ**wireless 1.** radio *f*, radiorreceptor *m* (*a.* ~ *set*); radiotelegrafía *f* (*a.* ~ *telegraphy*); radiograma *m* (*a.* ~ *message*); **2.** *attr.* radiofónico; ~ *operator* (radio)telegrafista *m*; ~ *station* estación *f* radiotelegráfica, emisora *f*; **3.** transmitir por radio(telegrafía); ˈ**wire ˈnet·ting** red *f* de alambre; ˈ**wire pull·er** *sl.* enchufista *m*; ˈ**wire pull·ing** *sl.* empleo *m* de resortes; ˈ**wire ser·vice** servicio *m* telegráfico y telefónico; ˈ**wire tapping** intercepcion *f* secreta de comunicaciones telefónicas.
wir·ing [ˈwairiŋ] instalación *f* de alambres; alambrado *m*; ⚡ alambres *m/pl.* tensores; ~ *diagram* esquema *m* del alambrado; ˈ**wir·y** □ delgado pero fuerte; nervudo.
wis·dom [ˈwizdəm] sabiduría *f*; prudencia *f*; ~ *tooth* muela *f* del juicio.
wise[1] [waiz] □ (*learned*) sabio; (*sensible etc.*) prudente; juicioso; acertado; *sl.* ~ *guy* sabelotodo *m*; tipo *m* atrevido; F *be* ~ *to* conocer el juego de; F *get* ~ caer en el chiste; F *put a p.* ~ ponerle a uno al tanto (*to, on* de).
wise[2] [~] † guisa *f*, modo *m*.
wise·a·cre [ˈwaizeikər] sabihondo *m*; ˈ**wise·crack 1.** cuchufleta *f*; **2.** cuchufletear.
wish [wiʃ] **1.** desear (*for acc.*; *to inf. inf.*); anhelar (*for acc.*); ~ *good morning* dar los buenos días (a); *I* ~ *I could inf.* ¡ojalá pudiera! *inf.*; ~ *a p. well* desearle a uno mucha suerte; **2.** deseo *m* (*for* de; *to inf.* de *inf.*); anhelo *m*; *best* ~*es* enhorabuena *f*; *with best* ~*es* (*in letter*) saludos *m/pl.*; **wish·ful** [ˈ~ful] □ deseoso (*to inf.* de *inf.*); ~ *thinking* espejismo *m*, ilusionismo *m*; ˈ**wish·bone** espoleta *f*.
wish·y-wash·y [ˈwiʃiwɔʃi] F soso, insípido.
wisp [wisp] manojito *m of grass*; mechón *m of hair*; jirón *m of cloud*.
wist·ful [ˈwistful] □ pensativo; anhelante; melancólico.
wit [wit] **1.** ingenio *m* (*a. p.*); agudeza *f*; sal *f*; (*p.*) chistoso *m*; ~*s pl.* juicio *m*; inteligencia *f*; *be at one's* ~*'s end* estar para volverse loco;

have (or keep) one's ~s about one tener ojo; *live by one's ~s* campar de golondro; *out of one's ~s* fuera de sí; **2.:** *to ~* a saber.

witch [witʃ] bruja *f*, hechicera *f*; *~ doctor* hechicero *m*; **ˈ~·craft** brujería *f*; **ˈ~ hunt** lucha *f* contra la subversión; *b.s.* persecución *f* (política).

with [wið] con; en compañía de; (*towards*) para con; de (*e.g., tremble with fear* temblar de miedo); *covered with* cubierto de; *the man with the grey suit* el del traje gris); a (*e. g., with all speed* a toda prisa); según (*e. g., it varies with the season* varía según la estación); sin (*e. g., with no trouble at all* sin dificultad alguna).

with·al [wiˈðɔːl] † además, también.

with·draw [wiðˈdrɔː] [*irr.* (*draw*)] *v/t.* retirar; sacar; retractar; *v/i.* retirarse (*from* de); recogerse; *sport:* abandonar; **withˈdraw·al** retirada *f* (*a.* ⚔, ⚕), retiro *m* (*a.* ⚕); *sport:* abandono *m*; *~ symptom* síntoma *m* de abstinencia.

with·er [ˈwiðər] (*a. ~ away*) *v/i.* marchitarse; *v/t.* marchitar; *fig.* aplastar, confundir; **ˈwith·er·ing** □ abrasador; *look* lleno de desprecio.

with·ers [ˈwiðərz] *pl.* cruz *f*.

with·hold [wiðˈhould] [*irr.* (*hold*)] retener; negar (*from* a); *payment* suspender; *reason etc.* no revelar (*from* a); *~ing tax* descuento *m* anticipado de los impuestos; **withˈin 1.** *adv. lit.* dentro; *from ~* desde dentro; **2.** *prp.* dentro de; al alcance de (*a. ~ reach of*); *~ call* al alcance de la voz; *~ doors* dentro de la casa; *~ an inch of fig.* a dos dedos de; *~ a mile of* a poco menos de una milla de; **withˈout 1.** *adv. lit.* (a)fuera; *from ~* desde fuera; **2.** *prp.* sin; *lit.* fuera de; *v. do;* **3.** *cj.* sin que; **withˈstand** [*irr.* (*stand*)] resistir a, aguantar.

wit·less [ˈwitlis] □ tonto, insensato.

wit·ness [ˈwitnis] **1.** (*p.*) testigo *m/f*; testimonio *m*; *in ~ of* en fe de; *bear ~* atestiguar (*to acc.*); **2.** presenciar; atestiguar (*to acc.*); *will etc.* firmar como testigo; **ˈ~-box, ˈ~ stand** barra *f* (*or* puesto *m*) de los testigos.

wit·ti·cism [ˈwitisizm] agudeza *f*, chiste *m*; **ˈwit·ti·ness** agudeza *f*, gracia *f*; **ˈwit·ting·ly** a sabiendas; **ˈwit·ty** □ ingenioso, chistoso, gracioso.

wives [waivz] *pl. of wife.*

wiz·ard [ˈwizərd] **1.** hechicero *m*, brujo *m*; F as *m*; **2.** *sl.* (*a.* **wiz** [wiz]) estupendo; mono; **ˈ~·ry** magia *f*.

wiz·ened [ˈwiznd] arrugado, apergaminado.

wo(**a**) [wou] ¡so!

wob·ble [ˈwɔbl] bambolear, tambalearse; ⊕ oscilar; *fig.* vacilar.

woe [wou] *lit. or co.* aflicción *f*, dolor *m*; *~ is me!* ¡ay de mí!; **ˈ~·be·gone** abatido, desconsolado; **ˈwoe·ful** □ triste, afligido; lamentable.

woke [wouk] *pret. a. p.p. of wake*[2].

wold [would] *approx.* páramo *m*, rasa *f* ondulada.

wolf [wulf] **1.** [*pl. wolves*] lobo (a *f*) *m*; *sl.* mujeriego *m*; *cry ~* gritar ¡el lobo!; **2.** F zampar, engullir; **ˈwolf·ish** □ lobuno.

wolf·ram [ˈwulfrəm] wolfram *m*, volframio *m*.

wolves [wulvz] *pl. of wolf* 1.

wom·an [ˈwumən] (*pl. women* [ˈwimin]) **1.** mujer *f*; F criada *f*; *young ~* joven *f*; **2.** femenino; de mujer; *~ doctor* médica *f*; **ˈwom·an-hat·er** misógino *m*; **wom·an·hood** [ˈ~hud] (*quality*) feminidad *f*; (*age*) edad *f* adulta; (*in general*) mujeres *f/pl.*, sexo *m* femenino; **ˈwom·an·ish** □ afeminado; mujeril; **ˈwom·an·kind** mujeres *f/pl.*, sexo *m* femenino; **ˈwom·an·like** mujeril; **ˈwom·an·ly** femenino, mujeril.

womb [wuːm] matriz *f*, útero *m*; *fig.* seno *m*.

wom·en [ˈwimin] *pl. of woman*; *~'s liberation* movimiento *m* feminista; *approx.* feminismo *m*; *~'s rights pl.* derechos *m/pl.* de la mujer; *~'s team* equipo *m* femenino; **wom·en·folk** [ˈ~fouk] las mujeres.

won [wʌn] *pret. a. p.p. of win* 1.

won·der [ˈwʌndər] **1.** (*object*) maravilla *f*, prodigio *m*; (*feeling*) admiración *f*; *it is no ~ that* no es mucho que; *work ~s* hacer milagros; **2.** admirarse, maravillarse (*at* de); preguntarse (*if, whether* si); *I ~ if she'll come* ¿si vendrá?; **won·der·ful** [ˈ~ful] □ maravilloso; **ˈwon·der·ment** asombro *m*, admiración *f*; **ˈwon·der-struck** pasmado.

won·drous [ˈwʌndrəs] □ *lit.* maravilloso.

won't [wount] = *will not.*
wont [wount] **1.** *pred.* acostumbrado; *be* ~ *to do* soler hacer; **2.** costumbre *f.*
woo [wu:] *lit.* cortejar, galantear; *fig.* tratar de conquistar.
wood [wud] (*trees*) bosque *m*; (*material*) madera *f*; (*fire*) leña *f*; *sport*: bola *f*; ♪ instrumento *m* de viento de madera; ~*s pl.* bosque *m*; ˈ~ **carv·ing** escultura *f* en madera; ˈ~**·cock** chocha *f* perdiz; ˈ~**·craft** destreza *f* en la montería; ˈ~**·cut** grabado *m* en madera; ˈ~**·cut·ter** leñador *m*; ˈ**wood·ed** arbolado, enselvado; ˈ**wood·en** □ de madera; *fig.* inexpresivo; rígido; ~ *shoe* zueco *m*; ˈ**wood en·grav·ing** grabado *m* en madera.
wood...: ˈ~**·land 1.** bosque *m*, arbolado *m*; monte *m*; **2.** selvático; ˈ~**·lark** totovía *f*; ˈ~**·louse** cochinilla *f*; ˈ~**·man** leñador *m*; ˈ~**·peck·er** *orn.* carpintero *m*; *green* ~ pito *m* real; ˈ~**·pi·geon** paloma *f* torcaz; ˈ~**·pile** montón *m* de leña; ˈ~ **pulp** pulpa *f* de madera; ˈ~ **shav·ings** *pl.* virutas *f*/*pl.*; ˈ~**·shed** leñera *f*; ˈ~**·wind** (*or* ~ *instruments*) *pl.* instrumentos *m*/*pl.* de viento de madera; ˈ~**·work** carpintería *f*, ebanistería *f*; ⚠ maderaje *m*; ˈ~**·worm** carcoma *f*; ˈ**wood·y** *tissue* leñoso; *country* arbolado.
woo·er [ˈwu:ər] pretendiente *m.*
woof [wu:f] trama *f.*
wool [wul] lana *f*; *attr.* de lana, lanar; *dyed in the* ~ *fig.* acérrimo, intransigente; ˈ~**·gath·er·ing 1.** absorción *f*; *go* ~ estar en Babia; **2.** absorto; ˈ**wool·en 1.** de lana; lanero; **2.** ~*s pl.* géneros *m*/*pl.* de lana; ˈ**wool·ly 1.** lanudo, lanoso; *paint.* borroso; *ideas* vago, confuso; **2.** F *woollies pl.* ropa *f* de lana.
wool...: ˈ~**·sack** saco *m* de lana; ˈ~ **sta·pler** lanero *m.*
word [wə:rd] **1.** palabra *f*; vocablo *m*; (*news*) noticia *f*; ⚔ santo *m* y seña; *the* ♀ el Verbo; ~*s pl. fig.* palabras *f*/*pl.* mayores; ♪ letra *f*; *by* ~ *of mouth* de palabra; ~ *for* ~ palabra por palabra; *in other* ~*s* en otros términos; *my* ~*!* ¡caramba!; *be as good as one's* ~ cumplir lo prometido; *not breathe a* ~ no decir palabra; *eat one's* ~*s* desdecirse; *give one's* ~ dar (*or* empeñar) su palabra; *have a* ~ *with* cambiar unas palabras con; *have* ~*s* reñir; *leave* ~ dejar dicho; *send* ~ mandar recado; *take a p. at his* ~ cogerle a uno la palabra; *take my* ~ *for it* se lo aseguro; **2.** redactar; expresar; ˈ~**·book** vocabulario *m*; glosario *m*; léxico *m*; ˈ**word·i·ness** verbosidad *f*; ˈ**word·ing** fraseología *f*, términos *m*/*pl.*; ˈ**word-ˈper·fect** *thea.* que sabe perfectamente su papel; ˈ**word proc·ess·ing** redacción *f* por medios electrónicos.
word·y [ˈwə:rdi] □ verboso.
wore [wɔ:r] *pret. of wear* 1.
work [wə:rk] **1.** trabajo *m*; labor *f*; (*lit. etc.*) obra *f*; ~*s pl.* ⊕ fábrica *f*; (*mechanism*) mecanismo *m*; (*lit. etc.*) obras *f*/*pl.*; *public* ~*s pl.* obras *f*/*pl.* públicas; *be in* ~ tener un empleo; *be out of* ~ estar desempleado; *make short* ~ *of* concluir con toda rapidez; F comerse rápidamente; *put* (*or throw*) *out of* ~ privar de trabajo; *set to* ~ poner(se) a trabajar; **2.** *v*/*i.* trabajar (*at* en; *hard* mucho); ⊕ funcionar, marchar; obrar; (*remedy*) surtir efecto, ser eficaz; ~ *loose* soltarse; ~ *out* resultar; resolverse; ~ *out at* (*cost*) llegar a; *v*/*t. p.* hacer trabajar; ⊕ manejar; hacer funcionar; *land* cultivar; *mine* explotar; *passage* pagar trabajando; *wonders etc.* hacer, efectuar; *wood* tallar; *sew.* bordar; F conseguir, agenciarse; ~ *in* introducir; ~ *off* deshacerse de ... trabajando; ~ *on* influir, trabajar; ~ *one's way* abrirse camino; ~ *out* calcular; *mine etc.* agotar; ~ *up business* desarrollar; *feeling* excitar (*into* hasta); *theme* elaborar; ~ *o.s. up* exaltarse.
work·a·ble [ˈwə:rkəbl] □ practicable; factible; práctico; ˈ**work·a·day** de cada día; *fig.* prosaico; **work-aˈhol·ic** individuo *m* con compulsión al trabajo; ˈ**work·bench** banco *m* de taller; ˈ**work·box** neceser *m* de costura; ˈ**work·day** día *m* laborable; ˈ**work·er** trabajador (-a *f*) *m*; obrero (a *f*) *m*; operario (a *f*) *m*; *zo.* abeja *f* obrera; ˈ**work force** personal *m* obrero; ˈ**work·house** asilo *m* de pobres; ˈ**work·ing 1.** funcionamiento *m*; explotación *f*; ⚒ ~*s pl.* labores *f*/*pl.*; **2.** obrero; de trabajo; *in* ~ *order* funcionando; ~ *capital* capital *m* de explotación; ~ *class* clase *f* obrera; ~ *day* (*weekday*) día *m* laborable; (*number of hours*) jornada *f*; ~ *expenses pl.* gastos *m*/*pl.* de explotación; ~ *hypothesis* hipótesis *f* de guía;

~ man obrero *m*; *~ party* comisión *f* de investigación.
work·man [ˈwəːrkmən] obrero *m*; trabajador *m*; operario *m*; ˈ**~·like** bien ejecutado, competente; ˈ**work·man·ship** hechura *f*; confección *f*; arte *m*, artificio *m*.
work...: **~·out** [ˈwəːrkaut] *sport*: entrenamiento *m*, ejercicio *m*; ˈ**~-room,** ˈ**~·shop** taller *m*; ˈ**~-ˈshy** perezoso.
world [wəːrld] mundo *m*; *attr*. mundial; *fig*. *a ~ of* la mar de; *~ class* sobresaliente; *for all the ~ like* (*or as*) (*if*) exactamente como (si); *in the ~ eccl*. en el siglo; *bring into the ~* echar al mundo; *come down in the ~* venir a menos; *feel on top of the ~* estar como un reloj; *see the ~* ver mundo; *think the ~ of* tener un altísimo concepto de; *~ champion* campeón *m* mundial; *~ power* potencia *f* mundial; ♀ *Series* Serie *f* Mundial; ˈ**world·li·ness** mundanería *f*.
world·ly [ˈwəːrldli] mundano; ˈ**~ˈwis·dom** mundología *f* (F), astucia *f*; ˈ**~-ˈwise** que tiene mucho mundo; astuto.
world-wide [ˈwəːrldˈwaid] mundial, universal.
worm [wəːrm] **1.** gusano *m*; (*earth*) lombriz *f*; *fig*. (*p*.) persona *f* vil; ⊕ filete *m*; ⊕ tornillo *m* sin fin; **2.** *fig*. insinuarse (*into* en); *~ o.s. through etc*. atravesar serpenteando; *~ a secret out of a p*. arrancar mañosamente (*or* sonsacar) un secreto a una p.; ˈ**~ drive** transmisión *f* por tornillo sin fin; ˈ**~-eat·en** *wood* carcomido; *cloth* apolillado; ˈ**~ gear** engranaje *m* de tornillo sin fin; = ˈ**~ wheel** rueda *f* de tornillo sin fin; ˈ**~·wood** ⚘ ajenjo *m*; *fig*. amargura *f*; ˈ**worm·y** gusanoso; carcomido.
worn [wɔːrn] *p.p. of wear* 1; ˈ**~-ˈout** gastado; inservible; anticuado; *be ~* (*p*.) estar rendido.
wor·ri·ment [ˈwəːrimənt] F inquietud *f*; ˈ**wor·ry 1.** inquietar(se), preocupar(se) (*about, over* por); molestar(se); (*dog*) pillar, morder sacudiendo; atacar; **2.** inquietud *f*, preocupación *f*; cuidado *m*; molestia *f*.
worse [wəːrs] **1.** peor (*a*. ⚕); *~ and ~* cada vez peor; *~ than ever* peor que nunca; *so much the ~* tanto peor; *the ~ for wear* deteriorado; *grow ~, make ~* empeorar; *~ luck!* ¡por desgracia!; *he is none the ~ for it* no se ha hecho daño; no se ha perjudicado; **2.** peor *m*; *from bad to ~* de mal en peor; ˈ**wors·en** empeorar.
wor·ship [ˈwəːrʃip] **1.** culto *m*; adoración *f*; oficio *m*; **2.** adorar; venerar; **wor·ship·ful** [ˈ~ful] *in titles*: excelente; ˈ**wor·ship·(p)er** adorador (-a *f*) *m*; devoto (a *f*) *m*.
worst [wəːrst] **1.** *adj. a. adv*. peor; **2.** lo peor; *at* (*the*) *~* en el peor de los casos; *do your ~!* ¡haz todo lo que quieras!, ¡haga cuanto daño quiera!; *get the ~ of it* llevar la peor parte; *if the ~ comes to the ~* si pasa lo peor; *the ~ of it is* (*that*) lo malo es que; **3.** vencer.
wor·sted [ˈwurstid] estambre *m*.
worth [wəːrθ] **1.** (*worthy of*) digno de; (*equal to*) equivalente a; *be ~* valer; merecer; *~ reading* que vale la pena de leerse; *~ seeing* digno de verse; *~ a million fig*. que vale un dineral; **2.** valor *m*; valía *f*; mérito *m*; **wor·thi·ness** [ˈ~ðinis] mérito *m*, merecimiento *m*; **worth·less** [ˈ~θlis] □ sin valor; indigno; inútil; despreciable; ˈ**worth-ˈwhile** valioso, digno de atención *etc*.; *be ~* valer la pena; **wor·thy** [ˈwəːrði] **1.** □ digno (*of* de); meritorio; benemérito; *be ~ of* merecer *acc*., ser digno de; **2.** dignidad *f*, notable *m*; *co*. personaje *m*.
would [wud] [*pret. of will*] *v/aux. que forma el condicional etc*.; *~ that ...!* ¡ojalá (que)...!
would-be [ˈwudbiː] supuesto; llamado; que presume de; aspirante a.
wouldn't [ˈwudnt] = *would not*.
wound[1] [wuːnd] **1.** herida *f*; **2.** herir; ˈ**wound·ing** □ *tone* hiriente.
wound[2] [waund] *pret. a. p.p. of wind*[2].
wove *pret*., **wo·ven** [ˈwouv(n)] *p.p. of weave* **1.**
wow [wau] **1.** *sl*. exitazo *m*; **2.** F (*int*.) ¡cielos!; **3.** F impresionar mucho a.
wrack[1] [ræk] ⚘ fuco *m*.
wrack[2] [~] = *rack*[2].
wraith [reiθ] fantasma *m*.
wran·gle [ˈræŋgl] **1.** reñir indecorosamente (*over* a causa de); **2.** riña *f* indecorosa; ˈ**wrang·ler** disputador *m*; F vaquero *m*.
wrap [ræp] **1.** *v/t*. envolver (*a*. *~ up*); *fig*. *be ~ped up in* estar absorto en; F *p*.

estar prendado de; *v/i.*: ~ *up* arroparse, arrebujarse; **2.** bata *f*, abrigo *m*; ˈ**wrap·per** envase *m*; (*postal*) faja *f*; ˈ**wrap·ping** envase *m*, envoltura *f*; ~ *paper* papel *m* de envolver (*or* embalar); ˈ**wrap up** concluir; acabar; ˈ**wrap-up** F conclusión *f*; resumen *m*.

wrath [ræθ] *lit. or co.* cólera *f*, ira *f*; **wrath·ful** [ˈ~ful] ☐ colérico, iracundo.

wreak [riːk] *lit. vengeance* tomar (*on* en); *wrath* descargar (*on* en); ~ *havoc* hacer estragos.

wreath [riːθ], *pl.* **wreaths** [~ðz] (*funeral*) corona *f*; guirnalda *f*; espiral *f*, penacho *m of smoke*; **wreathe** [riːð] [*irr.*] *v/t.* enguirnaldar; ceñir; tejer; ~*d in smiles* muy risueño; *v/i.* enroscarse, formar espirales.

wreck [rek] **1.** ⚓ (*act*) naufragio *m*; (*ship*) buque *m* naufragado; 🚂, *mot.* choque *m*; vehículo *m* (casa *f etc.*) destruido; *p.* quebrado; *fig.* ruina *f*, destrucción *f*; F *he's a* ~ está hecho polvo; **2.** ⚓ hacer naufragar; 🚂 hacer descarrilar; *fig.* arruinar, acabar con; ⚓ *be* ~*ed* naufragar; ˈ**wreck·age** ⚓ pecios *m/pl.*; restos *m/pl.*; escombros *m/pl. of house etc.*; (*act*) naufragio *m* (*a. fig.*), ruina *f*; ˈ**wreck·er** ⚓ raquero *m*; demoledor *m*; F camión-grua *m*; 🚂 descarrilador *m*; ˈ**wreck·ing**: ~ *service mot.* servicio *m* de auxilio.

wren [ren] chochón *m*.

wrench [rentʃ] **1.** arrancar; arrebatar (*from a p.* a una p.); torcer (*a.* ⚕); ~ *open* forzar; ~ *out* sacar violentamente; **2.** arranque *m*; ⚕ torcedura *f*; ⊕ llave *f* inglesa; *fig.* sacudida *f*, choque *m*; dolor *m*, momento *m* angustioso (de separación *etc.*).

wrest [rest] arrancar, arrebatar (*from* a); *fig.* sacar a duras penas.

wres·tle [ˈresl] **1.** *v/i.* luchar (*a. fig.*); *v/t.* luchar contra; **2.** = ˈ**wres·tling** lucha *f* (libre).

wretch [retʃ] desgraciado (a *f*) *m*; *poor* ~ pobrecito *m*; *co.* (*little* ~) pícaro *m*.

wretch·ed [ˈretʃid] ☐ miserable, desgraciado; *th.* pobre, mezquino; *taste etc.* pésimo; ˈ**wretch·ed·ness** miseria *f*; vileza *f etc.*

wrick [rik] **1.** torcer; **2.** torcedura *f*.

wrig·gle [ˈrigl] menearse; culebrear; ~ *out of* escaparse mañosamente de; *fig.* zafarse de.

wring [riŋ] [*irr.*] *clothes* escurrir, exprimir el agua de; *hands* retorcer; *neck* torcer; *heart* acongojar; *money, truth* sacar (*or* arrancar) por fuerza (*from, out of* a); ~*ing wet* muy mojado; ˈ**wring·er** secadora *f*, escurridor *m*.

wrin·kle[1] [ˈriŋkl] **1.** arruga *f*; **2.** arrugar(se); *brow* fruncir.

wrin·kle[2] [~] truco *m*; idea *f*; *new* ~ F novedad *f*; aspecto *m* nuevo.

wrist [rist] muñeca *f*; ~ *watch* reloj *m* de pulsera; ˈ~**·band** puño *m*; bocamanga *f*; **wrist·let** [ˈristlit] pulsera *f*, brazalete *m*.

writ [rit] *mst* ⚖ orden *f*, mandato *m*, auto *m*; *Holy* ♀ Sagrada Escritura *f*; ~ *for an election* autorización *f* para celebrar elecciones; ~ *of attachment* orden *f* de detención; ~ *of execution* auto *m* de ejecución.

write [rait] [*irr.*] *v/t.* escribir; redactar; ~ *down* poner por escrito; ♱ bajar el precio de; ♱ reducir el valor nominal de; ~ *off debt* cancelar; F dar por perdido; ~ *out* copiar; (*in full*) escribir sin abreviar; ~ *up ledger etc.* poner al día; *fig.* escribir una crónica de; describir exageradamente; *thea.* dar bombo a; *v/i.* escribir; ~ *back* contestar; ~ *for paper* colaborar a; ~ *off* escribir con prontitud (*for* pidiendo); F *nothing to* ~ *home about* nada de particular; ˈ~**-off** ♱ carga *f* por depreciación; F pérdida *f* total.

writ·er [ˈraitər] escritor (-a *f*) *m*, autor (-a *f*) *m*; *the* (*present*) ~ el que esto escribe; ~*'s cramp* calambre *m* de los escribientes.

write-up [ˈraitˈʌp] F (*report*) crónica *f*; *b.s.* bombo *m*, valoración *f* excesiva.

writhe [raið] retorcerse, contorcerse, debatirse.

writ·ing [ˈraitiŋ] (*in general*) el escribir; (*hand- etc.*) escritura *f*, letra *f*; (*thing written, work*) escrito *m*; profesión *f* de autor; *in* ~ por escrito; *attr.* ... de escribir; ˈ~ **case** recado *m* de escribir; ˈ~ **desk** escritorio *m*; ˈ~ **pad** taco *m* de papel, bloc *m*; ˈ~ **pa·per** papel *m* de escribir.

writ·ten [ˈritn] *p.p. of write*; *adj.* escrito.

wrong [rɔŋ] **1.** □ (*mistaken, false*) erróneo, incorrecto, equivocado; (*unfair*) injusto; (*wicked*) malo; inoportuno; impropio; *be* ~ (*p.*) no tener razón; equivocarse; *the* ~ *way* (*round*) al revés; *be the* ~ *side of 60* pasar ya de los 60; *there is something* ~ *with* algo le pasa a; *what's* ~ *with...?* ¿qué le pasa a...?; *what's* ~? ¿qué pasa?; ¿qué tiene Ud?; *it's* ~ no es justo; no es correcto; **2.** *adv.* mal; al revés; injustamente; *go* ~ funcionar mal; *fig.* extraviarse; **3.** mal *m*; injusticia *f*, entuerto *m*, agravio *m*; perjuicio *m*; *be in the* ~ no tener razón, equivocarse; *put a p. in the* ~ lograr que una p. parezca equivocada; echar la culpa a una p.; **4.** agraviar, ofender; ser injusto con; **ˈ~ˈdo·er** malhechor (-a *f*) *m*; **ˈ~ˈdo·ing** maldad *f*, perversidad *f*; **wrong·ful** [ˈ~ful] □ injusto; ilegal; **ˈwrong-ˈhead·ed** □ obstinado, perversamente equivocado; **ˈwrong·ness** injusticia *f*; error *m*; **ˈwrong ˈnumber** *teleph.* número *m* equivocado.

wrote [rout] *pret. of write.*

wroth [rouθ] † iracundo.

wrought [rɔːt] **1.** † *pret. a. p.p. of work* 2; *lit. he* ~ *great changes* llevó a cabo (*or* efectuó) grandes reformas; **2.** *adj.* forjado, labrado; ~ *iron* hierro *m* forjado (*or* batido).

wrung [rʌŋ] *pret. a. p.p. of wring.*

wry [rai] □ torcido, tuerto; *fig.* pervertido; ~ *face* mueca *f*.

X

X [eks] ✈ *a. fig.* **X.**

xer·o·graph·y [ziːˈrɔgræfi] xerografía *f* (*proceso de producir fotocopias instantáneas en seco*).

X-mas [ˈeksməs, ˈkrisməs] F Navidad *f*.

X-rat·ed [ˈeksˈreitid] F *film etc.* no recomendado; condenado; pornográfico.

X-ray [ˈeksˈrei] **1.** F radiografía *f*; ~**s** *pl.* rayos *m/pl.* X; **2.** radiográfico; **3.** radiografiar.

xy·log·ra·pher [zaiˈlɔgrəfər] xilógrafo *m*; **xy·lo·graph·ic, xy·lo·graph·i·cal** [~ləˈgræfik(l)] xilográfico; **xy·log·ra·phy** [~ˈlɔgrəfi] xilografía *f*.

xy·lo·phone [ˈzailəfoun] xilófono *m*.

Y

yacht [jɔt] **1.** (*mst large*) yate *m*, (*small*) balandro *m*; **2.** pasear en yate; ˈ**yacht club** club *m* náutico; ˈ**yacht·ing** paseo *m* en yate; regatas *f/pl.* de balandros; *attr.* de balandros; de balandristas; ˈ**yachts·man** deportista *m* náutico; balandrista *m*.

ya·hoo [jəˈhuː] patán *m*.

yam [jæm] batata *f*, ñame *m*.

yank[1] [jæŋk] F **1.** *mst* ~ *out* sacar de un tirón; **2.** tirón *m*.

Yank[2] [~] *v.* *Yankee.*

Yan·kee [ˈjæŋki] F yanqui *adj. a. su. m*; ~ *Doodle canción nacional norteamericana.*

yap [jæp] **1.** dar ladridos agudos; F charlar neciamente; F protestar (neciamente); **2.** ladrido *m* agudo.

yard[1] [jɑːrd] yarda *f* (= *91,44 cm.*); *approx.* vara *f*; ⚓ verga *f*.

yard[2] [~] corral *m*; patio *m*; *approx.* jardín *m*.

yard...: ˈ**~·arm** verga *f*; penol *m*; ˈ**~·stick** yarda *f*; *fig.* criterio *m*, norma *f*.

yarn [jɑːrn] **1.** hilo *m*, hilaza *f*; F cuento *m* (inverosímil); *spin a* ~ = **2.** F contar cosas inverosímiles.

yar·row [ˈjærou] milenrama *f*.

yaw [jɔː] **1.** ⚓ guiñada *f*; ✈ derrape *m*; **2.** ⚓ hacer una guiñada; ✈ derrapar.

yawl [jɔːl] yola *f*.

yawn [jɔːn] **1.** bostezar; *fig.* *~ing* muy abierto; **2.** bostezo *m*.

ye [jiː, ji] † vosotros, vosotras.

yea [jei] † sí (*a. su. m*); sin duda.

year [jir] año *m*; ~ *of grace* año *m* de gracia; ˈ**~·book** anuario *m*; ˈ**year·ling** primal *adj. a. su. m* (-a *f*); ˈ**year·ly** anual(mente *adv.*).

yearn [jəːrn] anhelar, añorar, ansiar (*after, for acc.*); suspirar (*for* por); ~ *to* anhelar *inf.*; ˈ**yearn·ing** anhelo *m*, añoranza *f*.

yeast [jiːst] levadura *f*; ˈ**yeast·y** □ espumoso; *fig.* frívolo.

yegg [jeg] *sl.* ladrón *m* (de cajas fuertes).

yell [jel] **1.** gritar; chillar; decir a gritos; **2.** grito *m*, alarido *m*; chillido *m*.

yel·low [ˈjelou] **1.** amarillo; F (*cowardly*) blanco; ~ *fever*, F ♀ *Jack* fiebre *f* amarilla; ~ *press* periódicos *m/pl.* sensacionales; **2.** amarillo *m*; **3.** *v/i.* amarillecer, amarillear; *v/t.* volver amarillo; ˈ**~·back** F novelucha *f*; ˈ**~·ham·mer** *orn.* picamaderos *m* norteamericano; ˈ**yel·low·ish** amarillento; ˈ**~·jac·ket** avispa *f*; avispón *m*.

yelp [jelp] **1.** gañido *m*; **2.** gañir.

yen [jen] *sl.* deseo *m* vivo.

yeo·man [ˈjoumən] *approx.* labrador *m* rico, pequeño terrateniente *m*; ~ *of the guard* alabardero *m* de la Casa Real; ˈ**yeo·man·ry** *approx.* clase *f* de los labradores ricos; ⚔ caballería *f* voluntaria.

yep [jep] F sí.

yes [jes] sí (*a. su. m*); ~ **man** [ˈ~mæn] [*sl.* pelotillero *m*.]

yes·ter·day [ˈjestərdi] ayer (*a. su. m*); ~ *afternoon* ayer por la tarde; *the day before* ~ anteayer; ˈ**yes·terˈyear** *poet.* antaño (*a. su. m*).

yet [jet] **1.** *adv.* todavía, aún; *as* ~ hasta ahora; *not* ~ todavía no; **2.** *cj.* sin embargo; con todo.

yew [juː] tejo *m*.

Yid·dish [ˈjidiʃ] lengua *f* de los judíos askenazis.

yield [jiːld] **1.** *v/t. crop, result* producir, dar (de sí); *profit* rendir; (*give up*) entregar; *v/i.* ↙ *etc.* producir, rendir; (*surrender*) rendirse, someterse; ceder; consentir (*to* en); **2.** ↙ cosecha *f*; producción *f*; ✝ rendimiento *m*, rédito *m on capital*; ˈ**yield·ing** □ flexible (*a. fig.*); *fig.* complaciente, dócil.

yo·del, yo·dle [ˈjoudl] **1.** canto *m* a la tirolesa; **2.** cantar a la tirolesa.

yo·ga [ˈjougə] yoga *f*; **yo·gi** [ˈjougiː] yogui *m*.

yo·gurt [ˈjougərt] yogurt *m*.

yoke [jouk] **1.** ↙ yunta *f*; *fig.* yugo *m*; ⊕ horquilla *f*; (*shoulder*) balancín *m*; *sew.* canesú *m*; **2.** ↙ uncir; acoplar; *fig.* unir.

yo·kel [ˈjoukl] F palurdo *m*, patán *m*.
yolk [jouk] yema *f* (de huevo).
yon [jɔn], **yon·der** [ˈjɔndər] † *or prov.* **1.** aquel; **2.** allá, a lo lejos.
yore [jɔːr] *lit.*: *of* ~ antaño, en otro tiempo.
you [juː] **1.** *familiar, with second p. verb*: (*nominative*) *sg.* tú, *pl.* vosotros, vosotras; (*acc., dat.*) *sg.* te, *pl.* os; (*after prp.*) *sg.* ti, *pl.* vosotros, vosotras; *with* ~ (*sg. reflexive*) contigo; **2.** *formal, with third p. verb*: (*nominative*) *sg.* usted, *pl.* ustedes; (*acc., dat.*) *sg.* le, la, *pl.* les; (*after prp.*) *sg.* usted, *pl.* ustedes; *with* ~ (*sg. a. pl. reflexive*) consigo; **3.** *when impersonal, often translated by reflexive*: ~ *can see it from here* se ve desde aquí; ~ *can't smoke here* no se puede fumar aquí; *also by* uno: ~ *never know whether...* uno nunca sabe si...
young [jʌŋ] **1.** joven; *brother etc.* menor; ~ *man* joven *m*; **2.** *zo.* cría *f*, hijuelos *m/pl.*; *the* ~ *pl.* los jóvenes, la juventud; *with* ~ encinta; **ˈyoung·ish** bastante joven; **ˈyoung·ster** joven *m/f*, jovencito (a *f*) *m*.
your [jur, jour, jɔːr, jər] tu(s); vuestro(s), vuestra(s); su(s); **yours** [~z] (el) tuyo, (la) tuya *etc.*; (el) vuestro, (la) vuestra *etc.*; (el) suyo, (la) suya *etc.*; (*ending letter*) cordialmente; **yourˈself**, *pl.* **your·selves** [~ˈselvz] (*subject*) tú mismo, vosotros mismos; usted(es) mismo(s); *acc., dat.* te, os, se; (*after prp.*) ti, vosotros, sí (mismo[s]); *f forms have* a(s).
youth [juːθ], *pl.* **youths** [juːðz] juventud *f*; (*p.*) joven *m*, mozo *m*; ~ *hostel* albergue *m* para jóvenes; **youth·ful** [ˈ~ful] □ juvenil; joven; **ˈyouth·ful·ness** juventud *f*; vigor *m*, espíritu *m* juvenil.
Yu·go·slav [ˈjuːgouslɑːv] yugo(e)slavo *adj. a. su. m* (a *f*).
Yule [juːl], **Yule·tide** [ˈjuːltaid] *lit.* Navidad *f*; ~ *log* leño *m* de Navidad.

Z

za·ny [ˈzeini] F tonto; loco.
zeal [ziːl] celo *m*, entusiasmo *m*; **zeal·ot** [ˈzelət] fanático *m*; **ˈzeal·ot·ry** fanatismo *m*; **ˈzeal·ous** □ celoso (*for* de); entusiasta (*for* de); apasionado (*for* por).
ze·bra [ˈziːbrə] cebra *f*.
ze·bu [ˈziːbuː] cebú *m*.
ze·nith [ˈziːniθ] cenit *m*; *fig.* apogeo *m*.
zeph·yr [ˈzefər] céfiro *m* (*a.* ✝ *cloth*).
ze·ro [ˈzirou] **1.** cero *m*; **2.** nulo; ~ *growth* sin aumento; estable; ~ *option* opción *f* zero (*or* nula); ~ **hour** ⚔ hora *f* de ataque.
zest [zest] gusto *m*, entusiasmo *m* (*for* por).
zig·zag [ˈzigzæg] **1.** zigzag *m*; **2.** (en) zigzag; **3.** zigzaguear, hacer eses.
zinc [ziŋk] **1.** cinc *m*; **2.** cubrir con cinc.
Zi·on·ism [ˈzaiənizm] sionismo *m*; **ˈZi·on·ist** sionista *adj. a. su. m*.
zip [zip] **1.** pasar volando; **2.** silbido *m*, zumbido *m*; F energía *f*; **ˈzip code** ✉ código *m* postal; **ˈzip·per** (cierre *m* de) cremallera *f*, cierre *m* relámpago; **ˈzip·py** F enérgico; rápido.
zith·er [ˈziθər] cítara *f*.
zo·di·ac [ˈzoudiæk] zodíaco *m*; **zo·di·a·cal** [zouˈdaiəkl] zodiacal.
zon·al [ˈzounl] □ zonal; **zone** [zoun] zona *f*.
zoo [zuː] F jardín *m* (*or* parque *m*) zoológico; casa *f* de fieras.
zo·o·log·i·cal [zouəˈlɔdʒikl] □ zoológico; ~ [zuˈlɔdʒikl] *gardens pl. v.* *zoo*; **zo·ol·o·gist** [zouˈɔlədʒist] zoólogo *m*; **zoˈol·o·gy** zoología *f*.
zoom [zuːm] F **1.** zumbar; ✈ empinarse; ~ *along*, ~ *by* ir con velocidad; **2.** zumbido *m*; ✈ empinadura *f*; ~ *lens phot.* lente *m* telefotográfico.
Zu·lu [ˈzuːluː] zulú *m*.
zy·mot·ic [zaiˈmɔtik] 🕮 cimótico.

Y Z

Appendices
Apéndices

American and British Abbreviations

Abreviaturas americanas y británicas

Each entry contains an expansion of the English abbreviation, and wherever possible the equivalent Spanish abbreviation with its expansion in parentheses.

A

AA *Automobile Association equivalente de* Real Automóvil Club *m* de España.
abbr. *abbreviated* abreviado; *abbreviation* abreviatura *f*.
ABC *American Broadcasting Company Compañía americana de radiotelevisión.*
A/C *account (current)* c.ta (c.te) (cuenta *f* [corriente]).
AC *alternating current* c.a. (corriente *f* alterna).
acc(t). *account* c.ta, cta (cuenta *f*).
AEC *Atomic Energy Commission* Comisión *f* de la Energía Atómica.
AFL-CIO *American Federation of Labor and Congress of Industrial Organizations Confederación general de los sindicatos de EE.UU.*
AFN *American Forces Network Red de radiodifusión de las Fuerzas Armadas de EE.UU.*
AIDS *acquired immune-deficiency syndrome* SIDA (síndrome *m* de inmunidad deficiente adquirida).
Ala *Alabama Estado de EE.UU.*
Alas *Alaska Estado de EE.UU.*
a.m. *ante meridiem (Latin = before noon)* de la mañana, antes del mediodía.
AP *Am. Associated Press Agencia de información.*
ARC *American Red Cross* Cruz *f* Roja Americana.
Ariz *Arizona Estado de EE.UU.*
Ark *Arkansas Estado de EE.UU.*
arr. *arrival* Ll. (llegada *f*).

B

BA 1. *Bachelor of Arts* Lic. en Fil. y Let. (Licenciado [a *f*] *m* en Filosofía y Letras); **3.** *British Airways Compañía británica de aviación.*
BBC *British Broadcasting Corporation* BBC *f* (*Radiotelevisión nacional de Gran Bretaña*).
BE *bill of exchange* letra *f* de cambio.
BFN *British Forces Network Red de radiodifusión de las Fuerzas Armadas de Gran Bretaña.*
BL 1. *bill of lading* conocimiento *m*; **2.** *Bachelor of Law* Licenciado (a *f*) *m* en Derecho.
BM 1. *British Museum* Museo *m* Británico; **2.** *Bachelor of Medicine* Licenciado (a *f*) *m* en Medicina.
BOT *Board of Trade* Ministerio *m* de Comercio (*británico*).
BR *British Rail Ferrocarriles británicos.*
Br(it). 1. *Britain* Gran Bretaña *f*; **2.** *British* británico.
Bros. *brothers* Hnos. (hermanos *m/pl.*).
BS *British Standard norma (industrial) británica.*
BS *Am.*, **B.Sc.** *Bachelor of Science* Licenciado (a *f*) *m* en Ciencias.
Bucks. *Buckinghamshire Condado inglés.*

C

c. 1. *cent(s)* céntimo(s) *m(pl.)* (*moneda americana*); **2.** *circa* h. (hacia); aproximadamente; **3.** *cubic* cúbico.
C. *Celsius, centigrade termómetro centígrado.*
C/A *current account* c/c (cuenta *f* corriente).
Cal(if) *California Estado de EE.UU.*
Cambs. *Cambridgeshire Condado inglés.*
Can. 1. *Canada* (el) Canadá; **2.** *Canadian* canadiense.

CC *continuous current* c.c. (corriente *f* continua).
cf. *confer* comp. (compárese).
Ches. *Cheshire Condado inglés.*
CIA *Central Intelligence Agency* CIA (Servicio *m* Secreto de Información *de EE.UU.*).
CID *Criminal Investigation Department Departamento de Investigación Criminal (británico), equivalente de* Brigada *f* Criminal.
c.i.f. *cost, insurance, freight* c.i.f., c.s.f. (costo, seguro, flete).
Co. 1. *Company* C., Cía. (compañía *f*); **2.** *county* condado *m* (*en EE.UU. e Irlanda*).
c/o. *care of* c/d (en casa de); a/c (al cuidado de).
COD *cash* (*Am. collect*) *on delivery* cóbrese a la entrega, contra re(e)mbolso.
Col *Colorado Estado de EE.UU.*
Conn *Connecticut Estado de EE.UU.*
cp. *compare* comp. (compárese).
c.w.o. *cash with order* pago *m* al contado.
cwt. hundredweight (= *50,8 kg.*) *approx.* quintal *m.*

D

DA 1. *deposit account approx.* cuenta *f* de ahorro; **2.** *Am. District Attorney* fiscal *m* de distrito.
DC 1. *direct current* c.c. (corriente *f* continua); **2.** *District of Columbia Washington, capital de EE.UU., y sus alrededores.*
Del *Delaware Estado de EE.UU.*
dep. *departure* S. (salida *f*).
Dept. *Department* dep. (departamento *m*).
Derby. *Derbyshire Condado inglés.*
disc(t). *discount* d.[to] (descuento *m*).
doz. *dozen* d.[na] (docena *f*).
Dur(h.) *Durham Condado inglés.*
dz. *dozen* d.[na] (docena *f*).

E

E. 1. *east(ern)* E (este [*m*]); **2.** *English* inglés.
EC *East Central Parte este del centro de Londres (distrito postal).*
ECE *Economic Commission for Europe* Comisión *f* Económica para Europa (*de las Naciones Unidas*).
ECOSOC *Economic and Social Council* Consejo *m* Económico y Social (*de las Naciones Unidas*).
Ed., ed. 1. *edition* ed. (edición *f*); **2.** *editor* director *m*, editor *m*, redactor *m*; **3.** *edited* editado.
EEC *European Economic Community* CEE (Comunidad *f* Económica Europea).
e.g. *exempli gratia* (*Latin* = *for example*) p.ej. (por ejemplo).
enc(l). *enclosure*(s) adjunto; anexo(s) *m*(*pl.*).
Esq. *Esquire* D. (Don); (*Esq., en el sobre después del apellido*).

F

f. 1. *fathom* (= *1,8288 m.*) braza *f*; **2.** *female, feminine* f. (femenino); **3.** *following* sgte. (siguiente).
F(ahr). *Fahrenheit termómetro Fahrenheit.*
FBI *Federal Bureau of Investigation Departamento de Investigación Criminal, equivalente de* Brigada *f* Criminal.
FC *Football Club* CF (Club *m* de Fútbol).
Fla *Florida Estado de EE.UU.*
fo(l). *folio* f.º, fol. (folio *m*).
f.o.b. *free on board* f.a.b. (franco a bordo).
for. *foreign* extranjero.
f.o.r. *free on rail* libre en la estación ferroviaria.
fr. *franc*(s) franco(s) *m*(*pl.*).
ft. *foot, pl. feet* (= *30,48 cm.*) pie(s) *m*(*pl.*).

G

g. *gram*(*me*[*s*]) gr(s). (gramo[s] *m*[*pl.*]).
Ga *Georgia Estado de EE.UU.*
gal. *gallon* (= *4,546 litros, Am. 3,785 litros*) galón *m.*
GB *Great Britain* Gran Bretaña *f.*
GI *Am. government issue* propiedad *f* del Estado; *por extensión, el soldado raso americano.*
Glos. *Gloucestershire Condado inglés.*
GMT *Greenwich Mean Time* T.M.G. (Tiempo *m* Medio de Greenwich).
GOP *Am. Grand Old Party* Partido *m* Republicano.
Govt. *Government* gob.[no] (gobierno *m*).

GPO *General Post Office* Oficina *f* Central de Correos.
gr. *gross* bruto.

H

h. *hour(s)* hora(s) *f(pl.)*.
Hants. *Hampshire Condado inglés.*
HBM *His (Her) Britannic Majesty* Su Majestad Británica.
HC *House of Commons* Cámara *f* de los Comunes.
Herts. *Hertfordshire Condado inglés.*
hf. *half medio.*
HI *Hawaii(an Islands)* (Islas *f/pl.*) Hawai.
HL *House of Lords* Cámara *f* de los Lores.
HM *His (Her) Majesty* S.M. (Su Majestad).
HMS 1. *His (Her) Majesty's Ship (Steamer)* buque *m* ([buque *m* de] vapor *m*) de Su Majestad; **2.** *His (Her) Majesty's Service* servicio *m* (de Su Majestad); ☏ oficial.
HO *Home Office* Ministerio *m* del Interior (*británico*).
Hon. *Honourable Título de la nobleza británica.*
h.p. *horse-power approx.* c.v. (caballo[s] *m[pl.]* de vapor).
HQ *Headquarters* Cuartel *m* General.
HR *Am. House of Representatives* Cámara *f* de Representantes (= *Diputados*).
HRH *His (Her) Royal Highness* S.A.R. (Su Alteza Real).
hrs. *hours* horas *f/pl.*

I

Ia *Iowa Estado de EE.UU.*
ID *Intelligence Department* Servicio *m* Secreto.
Id *Idaho Estado de EE.UU.*
i.e. *id est* (*Latin = that is*) es decir.
Ill *Illinois Estado de EE.UU.*
ILO *International Labour Organization* OIT (Organización *f* Internacional del Trabajo).
IMF *International Monetary Fund* FMI (Fondo *m* Monetario Internacional).
in. *inch(es)* (= *2,54 cm.*) pulgada(s) *f(pl.)*.
Inc. *Am. Incorporated* S.A. (Sociedad *f* Anónima).
Ind *Indiana Estado de EE.UU.*
inst. *instant* cte (corriente, de los corrientes).
IOC *International Olympic Committee* COI (Comité *m* Olimpico Internacional).
IQ *Intelligence Quotient* cociente *m* intelectual.
Ir. 1. *Ireland* Irlanda *f*; **2.** *Irish* irlandés.
IRA *Irish Republican Army* Ejército *m* Republicano Irlandés.
IRC *International Red Cross* Cruz *f* Roja Internacional.

J

JP *Justice of the Peace* juez *m* de paz.
Jr., Jun(r). *junior* hijo.

K

Kans *Kansas Estado de EE.UU.*
KO 1. *knock-out* k.o. (fuera *m* de combate); **2.** *knocked out* k.o. (fuera de combate).
Ky *Kentucky Estado de EE.UU.*

L

l. 1. *left* izquierdo; a la izquierda; **2.** *liter* l. (litro *m*).
La *Louisiana Estado de EE.UU.*
LA *Los Angeles* Los Ángeles.
Lancs. *Lancashire Condado inglés.*
lb. *pound* (= *453,6 gr.*) libra *f.*
LC *letter of credit* carta *f* de crédito.
Leics. *Leicestershire Condado inglés.*
Lincs. *Lincolnshire Condado inglés.*
LP 1. *long-playing* (de) larga duración *f*; **2.** *long-playing record* LP, elepé *m* (disco *m* de larga duración).
Ltd. *Limited* S. A. (Sociedad *f* Anónima).

M

m. 1. *male, masculine* m. (masculino); **2.** *meter* m. (metro *m*); **3.** *mile* (= *1609,34 m.*) milla *f*; **4.** *minute* m. (minuto *m*).
MA *Master of Arts* Maestro *m* en Artes.
Mass *Massachusetts Estado de EE.UU.*
MD *medicinae doctor* (*Latin = Doctor of Medicine*) Doctor *m* en Medicina.
Md *Maryland Estado de EE.UU.*
Me *Maine Estado de EE.UU.*

mi. *mile* (= *1609,34 m.*) milla *f.*
Mich *Michigan Estado de EE.UU.*
Middx. *Middlesex Condado inglés.*
Minn *Minnesota Estado de EE.UU.*
Miss *Mississippi Estado de EE.UU.*
Mo *Missouri Estado de EE.UU.*
MO *money order* giro *m* postal.
Mont *Montana Estado de EE.UU.*
MP 1. *Member of Parliament* miembro *m* del Parlamento; **2.** *Military Police* policía *f* militar.
m.p.h. *miles per hour* millas por hora.
Mr *Mister* Sr. (Señor *m*).
Mrs ['misiz] Sra. (Señora *f*).
MS 1. *manuscript* MS (manuscrito *m*); **2.** *motorship* motonave *f.*
Mt. *Mount* montaña *f*, monte *m.*

N

n. 1. *neuter* neutro; **2.** *noun* sustantivo *m*; **3.** *noon* mediodía *m.*
N. *North(ern)* N (norte [*m*]).
NASA *National Aeronautics and Space Administration* NASA (Administración *f* Nacional de Aeronáutica y del Espacio).
NATO *North Atlantic Treaty Organization* OTAN (Organización *f* del Tratado del Atlántico Norte).
NBC *National Broadcasting Company Compañía americana de radiotelevisión.*
NC *North Carolina Estado de EE.UU.*
ND(ak) *North Dakota Estado de EE.UU.*
NE *northeast(ern)* NE (noreste [*m*]).
Neb(r) *Nebraska Estado de EE.UU.*
Nev *Nevada Estado de EE.UU.*
NF *Newfoundland* Terranova *f.*
NH *New Hampshire Estado de EE.UU.*
NHS *National Health Service* Servicio *m* Nacional de Sanidad.
NJ *New Jersey Estado de EE.UU.*
NMex *New Mexico Estado de EE.UU.*
Norf. *Norfolk Condado inglés.*
Northants. *Northamptonshire Condado inglés.*
Northumb. *Northumberland Condado inglés.*
Notts. *Nottinghamshire Condado inglés.*
nt. *net* n.º (neto).
NW *northwest(ern)* NO (noroeste [*m*]).
NY *New York Estado de EE.UU.*
NYC *New York City* Ciudad *f* de Nueva York.

O

O *Ohio Estado de EE.UU.*
o/a *on account (of)* a/c. (de) (a cuenta [de]).
OAS *Organization of American States* OEA (Organización *f* de los Estados Americanos).
OECD *Organization for Economic Cooperation and Development* OCDE (Organización *f* para la Cooperación y el Desarrollo Económico).
OHMS *On His (Her) Majesty's Service* en el servicio de Su Majestad.
Okla *Oklahoma Estado de EE.UU.*
OPEC *Organization of Petroleum Exporting Countries* OPEP (Organización *f* de los Países Exportadores de Petróleo).
Ore(g) *Oregon Estado de EE.UU.*
Oxon. *Oxfordshire Condado inglés.*

P

Pa *Pennsylvania Estado de EE.UU.*
p.a. *per annum (Latin = yearly)* por año.
PanAm *PanAmerican Airways Compañía (Pan)americana de aviación.*
PAU *Panamerican Union* Unión *f* Panamericana.
PC *police constable* guardia *m.*
p.c. 1. *per cent* P%, %, p. c. (por cien[to]); **2.** *postcard* tarjeta *f* postal.
pd. *paid* pagado.
PEN Club *Poets, Playwrights, Editors, Essayists and Novelists* PEN (*Asociación internacional de escritores, etc.*).
Penn(a) *Pennsylvania Estado de EE.UU.*
per pro(c). *per procurationem (Latin = by proxy)* p.o. (por orden), p.p. (por poder).
Ph.D. *philosophiae doctor (Latin = Doctor of Philosophy)* Doctor *m* en Filosofía.
PLO *Palestine Liberation Organization* OLP (Organización *f* para la Liberación de Palestina).
p.m. *post meridiem (Latin = afternoon)* de la tarde.
PO 1. *Post Office* (Oficina *f* de) Correos *m/pl.*; **2.** *postal order* giro *m* postal.
POB *Post Office Box* apartado *m.*
p.o.d. *pay on delivery* (contra) re(e)mbolso.

p.p. **1.** *v. per pro(c)*; **2.** *past participle* participio *m* del pasado.
PS *postscript* PD (posdata *f*).
PTO *please turn over* véase al dorso.

Q

quot. *quotation* cotización *f*.

R

r. *right* derecho, a la derecha.
RAC *Royal Automobile Club equivalente de* Real Automóvil Club *m* de España.
RAF *Royal Air Force* Fuerzas *f/pl.* Aéreas Británicas.
Rd. *road* carretera *f*; c. (calle *f*).
ref. *(in) reference (to)* (con) referencia (a).
regd. *registered* certificado.
reg.tn. *register ton* tonelada *f* de arqueo.
resp. *respective(ly)* respectivamente.
ret. *retired* retirado.
Rev. *Reverend* R., Rdo (Reverendo).
RI *Rhode Island Estado de EE.UU.*
RN *Royal Navy* Marina *f* Real.
RP *reply paid* CP (contestación *f* pagada).
r.p.m. *revolutions per minute* r.p.m. (revoluciones *f/pl.* por minuto).
RR *Am. railroad* f.c. (ferrocarril *m*).
Ry. *railway* f.c. (ferrocarril *m*).

S

s. **1.** *second(s)* segundo(s) *m(pl.)*; **2.** *shilling(s)* chelín(es) *m(pl.)*.
S. *south(ern)* S (sur [*m*]).
SA **1.** *South Africa* Africa *f* del Sur; **2.** *South America* América *f* del Sur; **3.** *Salvation Army* Ejército *m* de Salvación.
SALT *Strategic Arms Limitation Talks* SALT (Conversaciones *f/pl.* para la limitación de las armas estratégicas).
SC **1.** *South Carolina Estado de EE.UU.*; **2.** *Security Council* Consejo *m* de Seguridad (*de las Naciones Unidas*).
SD(ak) *South Dakota Estado de EE.UU.*
SE **1.** *southeast(ern)* SE (sudeste [*m*]); **2.** *Stock Exchange* Bolsa *f*.
SEATO *South East Asia Treaty Organization* OTASE (Organización *f* del Tratado de Asia de Sudeste).
SHAPE *Supreme Headquarters Allied Powers Europe* Cuartel *m* General Supremo de los Aliados en Europa.
SJ *Society of Jesus* C. de J. (Compañía *f* de Jesús).
Soc. *Society* sociedad *f*.
Som. *Somerset Condado inglés.*
Sq. *square* plaza *f*.
sq. *square* cuadrado.
Sr. *senior* padre.
SS *steamship* vapor *m*.
St. **1.** *Saint* S. (San[ta]); **2.** *Street* calle *f*; **3.** *station* estación *f*.
Staffs. *Staffordshire Condado inglés.*
St. Ex. *Stock Exchange* Bolsa *f*.
stg. *sterling* moneda *f* esterlina.
Suff. *Suffolk Condado inglés.*
suppl. *supplement* suplemento *m*.
SW *southwest(ern)* SO (suroeste [*m*]).

T

t. *ton(s)* tonelada(s) *f(pl.)*.
Tenn *Tennessee Estado de EE.UU.*
Tex *Texas Estado de EE.UU.*
TO *Telegraph (Telephone) Office* Oficina *f* de Telégrafos (Teléfonos).
TU *Trade Union* sindicato *m*.
TUC *Trades Union Congress* Confederación *f* de Sindicatos.
TWA *Trans World Airlines Compañía americana de aviación.*

U

UFO *unidentified flying object* OVNI (objeto *m* volante no identificado).
UK *United Kingdom* RU (Reino *m* Unido: *Inglaterra, Escocia, Gales e Irlanda del Norte*).
UMW *Am. United Mine Workers* Sindicato *m* de Mineros.
UN *United Nations* NU, NN.UU. (Naciones *f/pl.* Unidas).
UNESCO *United Nations Educational, Scientific and Cultural Organization* UNESCO (Organización *f* de las Naciones Unidas para la Educación, la Ciencia y la Cultura).
UNICEF *United Nations (International) Children's (Emergency) Fund* UNICEF (Fondo *m* Internacional de Emergencia de las Naciones Unidas para la Infancia).
UNO *United Nations Organization* ONU (Organización *f* de las Naciones Unidas).

UPI *United Press International Agencia de información americana.*
US(A) *United States (of America)* EE.UU. (Estados *m/pl.* Unidos [de América]).
USAF(E) *United States Air Force (Europe)* Fuerzas *f/pl.* Aéreas de Estados Unidos (en Europa).
USN *United States Navy* Marina *f* Estadounidense.
USSR *Union of Soviet Socialist Republics* URSS (Unión *f* de las Repúblicas Socialistas Soviéticas).
UT *Utah Estado de EE.UU.*

V

v. 1. *verse* verso *m*; estrofa *f*; *(biblical)* vers.º (versículo *m*); **2.** *versus (Latin = against)* contra; **3.** *vide (Latin = see)* v. (véase), vid. (vide); **4.** *volt* v. (voltio *m*).
Va *Virginia Estado de EE.UU.*
VAT *value-added tax* IVA (impuesto *m* sobre el valor añadido).
VHF *very high frequency* MF (modulación *f* de frecuencia).
VIP *very important person* personaje *m* importante.
viz. *videlicet (Latin = namely)* v.gr. (verbigracia).
Vt *Vermont Estado de EE.UU.*
v.v. *vice versa (Latin = conversely)* viceversa.

W

W. *west(ern)* O (oeste [*m*]).
War. *Warwickshire Condado inglés.*
Wash *Washington Estado de EE.UU.*
WC 1. *West Central Parte oeste del centro de Londres (distrito postal)*; **2.** *water closet* WC (wáter *m*, inodoro *m*).
WHO *World Health Organization* OMS (Organización *f* Mundial de la Salud).
WI *West Indies* Antillas *f/pl.*
Wilts. *Wiltshire Condado inglés.*
Wis *Wisconsin Estado de EE.UU.*
wt. *weight* peso *m.*
WVa *West Virginia Estado de EE.UU.*
Wyo *Wyoming Estado de EE.UU.*

X

Xmas *Christmas* Navidad *f.*

Y

yd. *yard(s) (= 91,44 cm.)* yarda(s) *f(pl.).*
YMCA *Young Men's Christian Association* Asociación *f* Cristiana para los Jóvenes.
Yorks. *Yorkshire Condado inglés.*
yr(s). *year(s)* año(s) *m(pl.).*
YWCA *Young Women's Christian Association* Asociación *f* Cristiana para las Jóvenes.

English Proper Names

Nombres propios ingleses

A

Ab·er·deen [æbər'di:n] *Ciudad de Escocia.*
Ad·am ['ædəm] Adán.
Ad·e·laide ['ædəleid] **1.** *Ciudad de Australia*; **2.** Adelaida.
A·den ['eidn] Adén.
Ad·olf ['ædɔlf], **A·dol·phus** [ə'dɔlfəs] Adolfo.
Af·ghan·i·stan [æf'gænistæn] Afganistán *m.*
Af·ri·ca ['æfrikə] Africa *f.*
Ag·nes ['ægnis] Inés.
Al·a·bam·a [ælə'bæmə] *Estado de EE.UU.*
A·las·ka [ə'læskə] *Estado de EE.UU.*
Al·ba·ni·a [æl'beinjə] Albania *f.*
Al·bert ['ælbərt] Alberto.
Al·ber·ta [æl'bə:rtə] *Provincia de Canadá.*
Al·der·ney ['ɔ:ldərni] *Isla británica de las Islas Normandas.*
Al·ex·an·der [ælig'zændər] Alejandro.
Al·fred ['ælfrid] Alfredo.
Al·ge·ri·a [æl'dʒiriə] Argelia *f.*
Al·giers [æl'dʒiərz] Argel.
Al·ice ['ælis] Alicia.
Alps [ælps] *pl.* Alpes *m/pl.*
Am·a·zon ['æməzn] Amazonas *m.*
A·mer·i·ca [ə'merikə] América *f.*
An·des ['ændi:z] *pl.* Andes *m/pl.*
An·drew ['ændru:] Andrés.
Ann(e) [æn] Ana.
An·nap·o·lis [ə'næpəlis] *Capital del Estado de Maryland. Sede de la Academia de Marina.*
An·tho·ny ['æntəni] Antonio.
An·til·les [æn'tili:z] *pl.* Antillas *f/pl.*
Ap·pa·lach·i·ans [æpə'lei(t)ʃənz] *pl.* Apalaches *m/pl.*
A·ra·bia [ə'reibjə] Arabia *f.*
Ar·gen·ti·na [ɑ:rdʒən'ti:nə], *the* **Argen·tine** ['ɑ:rdʒəntin] (la) Argentina.
Ar·i·zo·na [ærə'zounə] *Estado de EE.UU.*
Ar·kan·sas ['ɑ:rkənsɔ:] *Estado, y* [ɑ:r'kænzəs] *Río de EE.UU.*
As·cot ['æskət] *Pueblo de Inglaterra con hipódromo de fama.*
A·sia ['eiʃə] Asia *f*; ~ *Minor* Asia *f* Menor.
Ath·ens ['æθənz] Atenas.
At·lan·tic (O·cean) [ət'læntik ('ouʃn)] (Océano *m*) Atlántico *m.*
Auck·land ['ɔ:klənd] *Puerto de Nueva Zelanda.*
Aus·tra·lia [ɔ:s'treiljə] Australia *f.*
Aus·tri·a ['ɔ:striə] Austria *f.*
A·von ['eivən, 'ævən] *Río de Inglaterra.*
A·zores [ə'zɔ:rz] *pl.* Azores *f/pl.*

B

Ba·ha·mas [bə'hɑ:məz] *pl.* Islas *f/pl.* Bahama, las Bahamas.
Ba·le·ar·ic Is·lands [bæli'ærik 'ailəndz] *pl.* Islas *f/pl.* Baleares.
Bal·kans ['bɔ:lkənz] Balcanes *m/pl.*
Bal·ti·more ['bɔ:ltəmɔ:r] *Puerto en la costa oriental de EE.UU.*
Be·a·trice ['biətris] Beatriz.
Bed·ford·shire ['bedfərdʃər] *Condado inglés.*
Bel·fast ['belfæst] *Capital de Irlanda del Norte.*
Bel·gium ['beldʒəm] Bélgica *f.*
Bel·grade [bel'greid] Belgrado.
Ben·ja·min ['bendʒəmin] Benjamín.
Ben Ne·vis [ben'nevis] *Pico más alto de Gran Bretaña (1343 m).*
Berk·shire ['berkʃər] *Condado inglés.*
Ber·lin [bə:r'lin] Berlín.
Ber·mu·das [bər'mju:dəz] Islas *f/pl.* Bermudas.
Bess(y) ['bes(i)] Isabelita.
Beth·le·hem ['beθlihem] Belén.
Bet·ty ['beti] Isabelita.
Bill, Bil·ly ['bil(i)] *nombre cariñoso de William.*
Bir·ming·ham ['bə:rmiŋhæm] *Ciudad industrial de Inglaterra; Ciudad de Alabama.*
Bis·cay ['bisk(e)i]: *Bay of* ~ Golfo *m* de Vizcaya.
Bob(·by) ['bɔb(i)] *nombre cariñoso de Robert.*

Bo·liv·i·a [bəˈlivjə] Bolivia *f.*
Bos·ton [ˈbɔstən] *Ciudad de EE.UU. con la Universidad de Harvard en el barrio de Cambridge.*
Bra·zil [brəˈzil] (el) Brasil.
Bridg·et [ˈbridʒit] Brígida.
Brigh·ton [ˈbraitn] *Ciudad en el sur de Inglaterra.*
Bris·tol [ˈbristl] *Puerto y ciudad industrial en el suroeste de Inglaterra.*
Bri·tain [ˈbritn] Gran Bretaña *f.*
Brook·lyn [ˈbruklin] *Barrio de Nueva York.*
Brus·sels [ˈbrʌslz] Bruselas.
Buck·ing·ham(·shire) [ˈbʌkiŋəm (-ʃər)] *Condado inglés.*
Bul·gar·i·a [bʌlˈgeriə] Bulgaria *f.*
Bur·ma [ˈbəːrmə] Birmania *f.*

C

Cal·i·for·nia [kæliˈfɔːrnjə] California *f* (*Estado de EE.UU.*).
Cam·bridge [ˈkeimbridʒ] *Ciudad universitaria inglesa*; *v.* Boston; **~shire** [ˈ~ʃər] *Condado inglés.*
Can·a·da [ˈkænədə] (el) Canadá.
Can·ar·y Is·lands [kəˈneri ˈailəndz] Islas *f/pl.* Canarias.
Can·ter·bur·y [ˈkæntərbəri] Cantórbery.
Cape Horn [keipˈhɔːrn] Cabo *m* de Hornos.
Car·diff [ˈkɑːrdif] *Capital de Gales.*
Ca·rib·be·an (Sea) [kæriˈbiːən (ˈsiː)] (Mar *m*) Caribe *m.*
Car·o·li·na [kærəˈlainə]: North ~ Carolina *f* del Norte; South ~ Carolina *f* del Sur (*Estados de EE.UU.*).
Cath·e·rine, Cath·a·rine [ˈkæθərin] Catalina.
Cec·i·ly [ˈsesəliː] Cecilia.
Cey·lon [siˈlɔn] Ceilán *m.*
Chan·nel Is·lands [ˈtʃænl ˈailəndz] *pl.* Islas *f/pl.* Normandas.
Charles [tʃɑːrlz] Carlos.
Char·lotte [ˈʃɑːrlət] Carlota.
Chesh·ire [ˈtʃeʃər] *Condado inglés.*
Chi·ca·go [ʃiˈkɑːgou] *Ciudad industrial de EE.UU.*
Chil·e, Chil·i [ˈtʃili] Chile *m.*
Chi·na [ˈtʃainə] China *f.*
Christ [kraist] Cristo.
Chris·to·pher [ˈkristəfər] Cristóbal.
Cin·cin·na·ti [sinsiˈnæti] *Ciudad de EE.UU.*
Cleve·land [ˈkliːvlənd] *Ciudad industrial y de comercio de EE.UU.*
Co·lom·bi·a [kəˈlʌmbiə] Colombia *f.*
Col·or·a·do [kɔləˈrædou] Colorado *m* (*Nombre de dos ríos y de un Estado de EE.UU.*).
Co·lum·bi·a [kəˈlʌmbiə] *Capital del Estado de Carolina del Sur.*
Co·lum·bus [kəˈlʌmbəs] Colón.
Con·nect·i·cut [kəˈnetikət] *Río y Estado de EE.UU.*
Co·pen·ha·gen [koupnˈheign] Copenhague.
Cor·do·va [ˈkɔːrdəvə] Córdoba.
Corn·wall [ˈkɔːrnwəl] Cornualles *m.*
Co·sta Ri·ca [ˈkɔstə ˈriːkə] Costa Rica *f.*
Cov·en·try [ˈkʌvəntri] *Ciudad industrial de Inglaterra.*
Crete [ˈkriːt] Creta *f.*
Cu·ba [ˈkjuːbə] Cuba *f.*
Cyp·rus [ˈsaiprəs] Chipre *f.*
Czech·o·slo·va·ki·a [ˈtʃekouslouˈvækiə] Checoslovaquia *f.*

D

Da·ko·ta [dəˈkoutə]: North ~ Dakota *f* del Norte; South ~ Dakota *f* del Sur (*Estados de EE.UU.*).
Da·niel [ˈdænjəl] Daniel.
Da·nube [ˈdænjuːb] Danubio *m.*
Da·vid [ˈdeivid] David.
Del·a·ware [ˈdeləwer] *Río y Estado de EE.UU.*
Den·mark [ˈdenmɑːrk] Dinamarca *f.*
Der·by(·shire) [ˈdəːrbi(ʃər)] *Condado inglés.*
De·troit [diˈtrɔit] *Ciudad industrial de EE.UU.*
Dev·on(·shire) [ˈdevn(ʃər)] *Condado inglés.*
Di·a·na [daiˈænə] Diana.
Dick [dik] *nombre cariñoso de* Richard.
Do·mi·ni·can Re·pub·lic [dəˈminikən riˈpʌblik] República *f* Dominicana.
Dor·set(·shire) [ˈdɔːrsit(ʃər)] *Condado inglés.*
Do·ver [ˈdouvər] *Puerto en el sur de Inglaterra.*
Down·ing Street [ˈdauniŋ ˈstriːt] *Calle de Londres con la sede del Primer Ministro.*
Dub·lin [ˈdʌblin] Dublín (*Capital de Irlanda*).
Dun·kirk [dʌnˈkəːrk] Dunquerque.
Dur·ham [ˈdʌrəm] *Condado inglés.*

E

Ed·in·burgh ['ed(i)nbərə] Edimburgo (*Capital de Escocia*).
E·gypt ['iːdʒipt] Egipto *m*.
Ei·re ['eərə] *Nombre irlandés de Irlanda*.
E·li·za·beth [i'lizəbəθ] Isabel.
El Sal·va·dor [el 'sælvədɔːr] El Salvador.
E·m(m)a·nu·el [i'mænjuəl] Manuel.
Eng·land ['iŋglənd] Inglaterra *f*.
Ep·som ['epsəm] *Pueblo inglés donde se verifican célebres carreras de caballos*.
Es·sex ['esiks] *Condado inglés*.
E·thi·o·pi·a [iːθi'oupiə] Etiopía *f*.
E·ton ['iːtn] *Pueblo inglés con colegio del mismo nombre*.
Eu·gene ['juːdʒiːn] Eugenio.
Eu·rope ['jurəp] Europa *f*.
Eve [iːv] Eva.

F

Falk·land Is·lands ['fɔːklənd 'ailəndz] (Islas *f/pl.*) Malvinas *f/pl*.
Fer·di·nand ['fəːrdinənd] Fernando.
Fin·land ['finlənd] Finlandia *f*.
Flor·i·da ['flɔridə] *Península y Estado de EE.UU*.
France [fræns] Francia *f*.
Fran·ces ['frænsis] Francisca.
Fran·cis ['frænsis] Francisco.
Frank [fræŋk] Paco.
Fred·e·rick ['fredrik] Federico.

G

Ge·ne·va [dʒi'niːvə] Ginebra.
Gen·o·a ['dʒenouə] Génova.
George [dʒɔːrdʒ] Jorge.
Geor·gia ['dʒɔːrdʒə] *Estado de EE.UU*.
Ger·ma·ny ['dʒərməni] Alemania *f*.
Get·tys·burg ['getizbərg] *Pueblo del Estado de Pensilvania* (*EE.UU.*).
Gib·ral·tar [dʒib'rɔltər] Gibraltar; *Rock of* ~ Peñón *m* de Gibraltar; *Straits of* ~ *pl*. Estrecho *m* de Gibraltar.
Giles [dʒailz] Gil.
Glas·gow ['glæsgou] *Puerto de Escocia*.
Glouces·ter ['glɔːstər] *Ciudad de Inglaterra*; **~·shire** ['~ʃər] *Condado inglés*.
Grand Can·yon [grænd 'kænjən] Gran Cañón *m del río Colorado* (*EE.UU.*).
Great Brit·ain ['greit 'britn] Gran Bretaña *f*.
Greece [griːs] Grecia *f*.
Green·land ['griːnlənd] Groenlandia *f*.
Green·wich ['grinidʒ] *Barrio de Londres*; ~ *Village* ['~'vilidʒ] *Barrio de los artistas de Nueva York*.
Gua·te·ma·la [gwɑːtə'mɑːlə] Guatemala *f*.
Guern·sey ['gəːrnzi] Guernesey *m*.
Gui·a·na [gai'ænə] Guayana *f*.
Guin·ea ['gini] Guinea *f*.
Guy [gai] Guido.

H

Hague [heig]: *The* ~ La Haya.
Hai·ti ['heiti] Haití *m*.
Hamp·shire ['hæmpʃər] *Condado inglés*.
Har·ry ['hæri] Enrique.
Har·vard U·ni·ver·si·ty ['hɑːrvərd juːni'vəːrsiti] *Universidad de fama de los EE.UU*.
Has·tings ['heistiŋz] *Ciudad en el sur de Inglaterra*.
Ha·van·a [hə'vænə] La Habana.
Ha·wai·i [hɑː'waiiː] (Islas *f/pl.*) Hawai.
Heb·ri·des ['hebridiːz] *pl*. Hébridas *f/pl*.
Hel·en ['helin] Elena.
Hen·ry ['henri] Enrique.
Her·e·ford(·shire) ['herifərd(ʃər)] *Condado inglés*.
Hert·ford(·shire) ['hɑːrfərd(ʃər)] *Condado inglés*.
Hol·ly·wood ['hɔliwud] *Ciudad de California y centro de la industria del cine de EE.UU*.
Hon·du·ras [hɔn'durəs] Honduras *f*.
Hud·son ['hʌdsn] *Río en el este de EE.UU*.
Hugh [hjuː] Hugo.
Hun·ga·ry ['hʌŋgəri] Hungría *f*.
Hu·ron ['hjurən]: *Lake* ~ el lago Hurón.
Hyde Park ['haid 'pɑːrk] *Parque público de Londres*.

I

Ice·land ['aislənd] Islandia *f*.

I·da·ho ['aidəhou] *Estado de EE.UU.*
Il·li·nois [ili'nɔi] *Río y Estado de EE.UU.*
In·dia ['indjə] (la) India.
In·di·an·a [indi'ænə] *Estado de EE.UU.*
In·dian O·cean ['indjən 'ouʃn] Océano *m* Indico.
In·dies ['indiz] Indias *f/pl*.
In·do·ne·sia [indou'niːʒə] Indonesia *f*.
I·o·wa ['aiouə, 'aiəwə] *Estado de EE.UU.*
I·raq [i'rɑːk, i'ræk] (el) Irak.
I·ran [i'rɑːn, i'ræn] (el) Irán.
Ire·land ['aiərlənd] Irlanda *f*.
Is·rael ['izriəl] Israel *m*.
It·a·ly ['it(ə)li] Italia *f*.
I·vo·ry Coast ['aivəri 'koust] Costa *f* de Marfil.

J

Jack [dʒæk] Juan(ito).
Ja·mai·ca [dʒə'meikə] Jamaica *f*.
James [dʒeimz] Diego; Jaime.
Jane [dʒein] Juana.
Ja·pan [dʒə'pæn] (el) Japón.
Jer·e·my ['dʒerəmi] Jeremías.
Jer·ome [dʒə'roum] Jerónimo.
Jer·sey ['dʒəːrzi] *Isla británica de las Islas Normandas*; ~ *City Ciudad a orillas del Hudson* (*EE.UU.*).
Je·ru·sa·lem [dʒə'ruːsələm] Jerusalén.
Je·sus ['dʒiːzəs] Jesús; *Jesus Christ* ['dʒiːzəs 'kraist] Jesucristo.
Jim(·my) ['dʒim(i)] *nombre cariñoso de James*.
Joan [dʒoun] Juana.
Joe [dʒou] Pepe.
John [dʒɔn] Juan.
Jor·dan ['dʒɔːrdn] (*river*) Jordán *m*; (*country*) Jordania *f*.
Jo·seph ['dʒouzif] José.
Jo·se·phine ['dʒouzifiːn] Josefina.
Ju·go·sla·vi·a [juːgou'slɑːvjə] Jugo(e)slavia *f*.
Ju·lian ['dʒuːljən] Juliano.

K

Kan·sas ['kænzəs] *Río y Estado de EE.UU.*
Kate [keit] *nombre cariñoso de Catherine*.
Kent [kent] *Condado inglés*.
Ken·tuck·y [ken'tʌki] *Río y Estado de EE.UU.*
Kit(·ty) ['kit(i)] *nombre cariñoso de Catherine*.
Ko·re·a [kə'riə] Corea *f*.

L

Lab·ra·dor ['læbrədɔːr] Labrador *m* (*Canadá*).
Lan·ca·shire ['læŋkəʃər] *Condado inglés*.
Lap·land ['læplənd] Laponia *f*.
Lat·in A·mer·i·ca ['lætn ə'merikə] América *f* Latina.
Leb·a·non ['lebənən] Líbano *m*.
Leeds [liːdz] *Ciudad industrial de Inglaterra*.
Leices·ter ['lestər] *Capital de Leicestershire*; **~·shire** ['~ʃər] *Condado inglés*.
Lew·is ['luːis] Luis.
Lib·y·a ['libiə] Libia *f*.
Lin·coln·shire ['liŋkənʃər] *Condado inglés*.
Lis·bon ['lizbən] Lisboa.
Liv·er·pool ['livərpuːl] *Puerto y ciudad industrial de Inglaterra*.
Lon·don ['lʌndən] Londres.
Los An·ge·les [lɔs 'ændʒələs] Los Angeles (*Ciudad de EE.UU.*).
Lou·i·si·an·a [luiːzi'ænə] Luisiana *f* (*Estado de EE.UU.*).
Luke [luːk] Lucas.
Lux·em·bourg ['lʌksəmbərg] Luxemburgo *m*.

M

Ma·dei·ra [mə'dirə] Madera *f*.
Mad·i·son ['mædisn] *Capital del Estado de Wisconsin* (*EE.UU.*).
Ma·gel·lan [mə'gelən] Magellanes; ~ *Straits pl*. Estrecho *m* de Magellanes.
Ma·hom·et [mə'hɔmət] Mahoma (*Fundador del Islam*).
Maine [mein] *Estado de EE.UU.*
Ma·jor·ca [mə'dʒɔːrkə] Mallorca *f*.
Man·ches·ter ['mæntʃestər] *Ciudad industrial de Inglaterra*.
Man·hat·tan [mæn'hætn] *Isla y centro de la ciudad de Nueva York*.
Man·i·to·ba [mæni'toubə] *Provincia de Canadá*.
Mar·ga·ret ['mɑːrgərit] Margarita.
Mark [mɑːrk] Marcos.

Mar·tin·ique [mɑːrtn'iːk] Martinica *f*.
Mar·y ['meri] María.
Mar·y·land ['merilənd] *Estado de EE.UU.*
Mas·sa·chu·setts [mæsə'tʃuːsəts] *Estado de EE.UU.*
Mat·thew ['mæθjuː] Mateo.
Mau·rice ['mɔːrəs] Mauricio.
Mau·ri·tius [mɔː'riʃəs] Mauricio *m (isla)*.
Med·i·ter·ra·ne·an (Sea) [meditə'reinjən (siː)] (Mar *m*) Mediterráneo *m*.
Mel·bourne ['melbərn] Melburne *(Australia)*.
Mex·i·co ['meksikou] Méjico *m*, México *m*.
Mi·am·i [mai'æmi] *Ciudad en el Estado de Florida (EE.UU.)*.
Mich·ael ['maikl] Miguel.
Mich·i·gan ['miʃigən] *Estado de EE.UU.*; Lake ~ el lago Michigan (*el tercero de los cinco Grandes Lagos de Norteamérica*).
Mid·dle·sex ['midlseks] *Condado inglés*.
Min·ne·ap·o·lis [mini'æpəlis] *Ciudad en el Estado de Minnesota (EE.UU.)*.
Min·ne·so·ta [mini'soutə] *Estado de EE.UU.*
Mi·nor·ca [mi'nɔːrkə] Menorca *f*.
Mis·sis·sip·pi [misi'sipi] Misisipi *m (Estado y río de EE.UU.)*.
Mis·sou·ri [mi'zuri] Misuri *m (Río y Estado de EE.UU.)*.
Mo·ham·med [mou'hæmed] Mahoma.
Mon·tan·a [mɔn'tænə] *Estado de EE.UU.*
Mont·re·al [mɔntri'ɔːl] *Ciudad de Canadá*.
Mo·roc·co [mɔ'rɔkou] Marruecos *m*.
Mos·cow ['mɔskou] Moscú.
Mo·ses ['mouziz] Moisés.

N

Ne·bras·ka [ni'bræskə] *Estado de EE.UU.*
Neth·er·lands ['neðərləndz] *pl.* (los) Países *m/pl.* Bajos.
Ne·vad·a [nə'vædə] *Estado de EE.UU.*
New Bruns·wick [n(j)uː 'brʌnzwik] *Provincia de Canadá*.
New·cas·tle ['n(j)uːkæsl] *Puerto en Gran Bretaña*.
New Eng·land [n(j)uː 'iŋglənd] Nueva Inglaterra *f*.
New·found·land ['n(j)uːfəndlənd] Terranova *f*.
New Guin·ea [n(j)uː 'gini] Nueva Guinea *f*.
New Hamp·shire [n(j)uː 'hæmpʃər] *Estado de EE.UU.*
New Jer·sey [n(j)uː 'dʒərzi] *Estado de EE.UU.*
New Mex·i·co [n(j)uː 'meksikou] *Estado de EE.UU.*
New Or·le·ans [n(j)uː 'ɔːrliːnz] Nueva Orleans *f*.
New South Wales ['n(j)uː'sauθ'weilz] Nueva Gales *f* del Sur (*Australia*).
New York [n(j)uː 'jɔːrk] Nueva York (*Ciudad y Estado de EE.UU.*).
New Zea·land [n(j)uː'ziːlənd] Nueva Zelanda *f*.
Ni·ag·a·ra [nai'ægərə] Niágara *m*.
Nic·a·ra·gua [nikə'rɑːgwə] Nicaragua *f*.
Nice [niːs] Niza.
Nich·o·las ['nikələs] Nicolás.
Ni·ge·ri·a [nai'dʒiːriə] Nigeria *f*.
Nile [nail] Nilo *m*.
No·ah ['nɔːə] Noé.
Nor·folk ['nɔːrfək] **1.** *Condado inglés*; **2.** *Puerto en Virginia (EE.UU.)*.
North·amp·ton·shire [nɔːr'θæmptənʃər] *Condado inglés*.
North·ern Ire·land ['nɔːrθərn 'aiərlənd] Irlanda *f* del Norte.
North Sea ['nɔːrθ'siː] Mar *m* del Norte.
North·um·ber·land [nɔːr'θʌmbərlənd] *Condado inglés*.
Nor·way ['nɔːrwei] Noruega *f*.
Not·ting·ham·shire ['nɔtiŋəmʃər] *Condado inglés*.
No·va Sco·tia ['nouvə'skouʃə] Nueva Escocia *f (Provincia de Canadá)*.

O

O·hi·o [ou'haiou] Ohío *m (Río y Estado de EE.UU.)*.
O·kla·ho·ma [ouklə'houmə] *Estado de EE.UU.*
On·tar·i·o [ɔn'teriou] *Provincia de Canadá*; Lake ~ el lago Ontario.
Or·e·gon ['ɔrigən] *Estado de EE.UU.*
Ork·ney Is·lands ['ɔːrkni 'ailəndz]

pl. (las) Orcadas *f/pl.* (*Archipiélago situado al norte de Escocia*).
Ot·ta·wa ['ɔtəwə] *Capital de Canadá.*
Ox·ford ['ɔksfərd] *Ciudad universitaria inglesa.*
Ox·ford·shire ['~ʃər] *Condado inglés.*

P

Pa·cif·ic (O·cean) [pə'sifik ('ouʃn)] (Océano *m*) Pacífico *m.*
Pa·ki·stan [pæki'stæn] Pakistán *m.*
Pal·es·tine ['pælistain] Palestina *f.*
Pall Mall ['pel'mel] *Nombre de una calle de Londres.*
Pan·a·ma [pænə'mɑː] Panamá *m.*
Par·a·guay ['pærəgwai] (el) Paraguay.
Par·is ['pæris] París.
Pat·rick ['pætrik] Patricio.
Paul [pɔːl] Pablo.
Pearl Har·bor ['pəːrl 'hɑːrbər] *Puerto cerca de Honolulú, Hawai.*
Pe·kin(g) [piː'kiŋ] Pekín.
Penn·syl·va·nia [pensil'veinjə] Pensilvania *f* (*Estado de EE.UU.*).
Pe·ru [pə'ruː] (el) Perú.
Pe·ter ['piːtər] Pedro.
Phil·a·del·phi·a [filə'delfjə] Filadelfia (*Gran ciudad de EE.UU.*).
Phil·ip ['filip] Felipe.
Phil·ip·pines ['filipiːnz] *pl.* Filipinas *f/pl.*
Phoe·nix ['fiːniks] *Capital de Arizona* (*EE.UU.*).
Pic·ca·dil·ly [pikə'dili] *Avenida principal en la parte occidental de Londres.*
Pitts·burgh ['pitsbərg] *Ciudad de EE.UU.*
Pi·us ['paiəs] Pío.
Plym·outh ['pliməθ] **1.** *Puerto de Inglaterra*; **2.** *Ciudad de EE.UU.*
Po·land ['poulənd] Polonia *f.*
Ports·mouth ['pɔːrtsməθ] *Puerto de Inglaterra.*
Por·tu·gal ['pɔːrtʃigəl] Portugal *m.*
Po·to·mac [pə'toumək] *Río de EE.UU.*
Prague [prɑːg] Praga.
Puer·to Ri·co ['pwertə 'riːkou] Puerto Rico *m.*
Pyr·e·nees [pirə'niːz] Pirineos *m/pl.*

Q

Que·bec [kwi'bek] *Provincia y ciudad de Canadá.*

R

Ra·phael ['ræfiəl] Rafael.
Rhine [rain] Rin *m.*
Rhode Is·land [roud'ailənd] *Estado de EE.UU.*
Rhone [roun] Ródano *m.*
Rich·ard ['ritʃərd] Ricardo.
Rich·mond ['ritʃmənd] **1.** *Capital de Virginia* (*EE.UU.*); **2.** *Barrio de Nueva York*; *barrio de Londres.*
Rob·ert ['rɔbərt], **Rob·in** ['rɔbən] Roberto.
Rock·y Moun·tains ['rɔki'mauntnz] *pl.* Montañas *f/pl.* Rocosas (*Sierra principal en el oeste de EE.UU.*).
Rome [roum] Roma.
Rose [rouz] Rosa.
Ru·ma·ni·a [ruː'meinjə] Rumania *f.*
Rus·sia ['rʌʃə] Rusia *f.*

S

Sa·har·a [sə'hɑːrə] Sáhara *m.*
Sam [sæm] *nombre cariñoso de Samuel.*
Sam·u·el ['sæmjəl] Samuel.
San Fran·cis·co [sænfrən'siskou] San Francisco (*EE.UU.*).
Sa·ra·gos·sa [særə'gɔsə] Zaragoza.
Sar·di·nia [sɑːr'dinjə] Cerdeña *f.*
Sas·katch·e·wan [səs'kætʃiwən] *Río y provincia de Canadá.*
Sau·di A·ra·bia ['sɔːdi ə'reibjə] Arabia *f* Saudita.
Scan·di·na·via [skændi'neivjə] Escandinavia *f.*
Scot·land ['skɔtlənd] Escocia *f*; *New* ~ *Yard Oficina central de la policía de Londres.*
Se·at·tle [si'ætl] *Puerto en el noroeste de EE.UU.*
Seine [sein] Sena *m.*
Se·ville ['səvil] Sevilla.
Shef·field ['ʃefiːld] *Ciudad industrial de Inglaterra.*
Si·be·ri·a [sai'biriə] Siberia *f.*
Sic·i·ly ['sisili] Sicilia *f.*
Si·er·ra Le·one [si'erə li'oun] Sierra *f* Leona.
Si·er·ra Ne·va·da [si'erə ni'vɑːdə] Sierra Nevada *en España y California.*
Si·mon ['saimən] Simón.
Sin·ga·pore [siŋgə'pɔːr] Singapur.
Snow·don ['snoudn] *Pico en Gales.*
Som·er·set·shire ['sʌmərsitʃər] *Condado inglés.*
Sou·dan [suː'dæn] Sudán *m.*

South Af·ri·ca: Re·pub·lik of ~ [ri'pʌblik əvsauθ'æfrikə] República *f* Sudafricana.
South A·mer·i·ca ['sauθ ə'merikə] América *f* del Sur.
South·amp·ton [sauθ'æmptən] *Puerto en Inglaterra.*
So·vi·et Un·ion ['souvjət 'ju:njən] Unión *f* Soviética.
Spain [spein] España *f*.
Sri Lan·ka [sri: 'lɑ:ŋkə] Sri Lanka *m*.
Staf·ford·shire ['stæfərdʃər] *Condado inglés.*
Ste·phen ['sti:vn] Esteban.
St. Lou·is [seint 'lu:əs] *Ciudad industrial de EE.UU.*
Stock·holm ['stɔkhɔlm] Estocolmo.
Stras·bourg ['stræzbərg] Estrasburgo.
Strat·ford ['strætfərd] *Nombre de varias poblaciones de Inglaterra y de EE.UU.*; ~-on-Avon *Lugar de nacimiento de Shakespeare.*
Stu·art ['st(j)u:ərt] Estuardo.
Su·dan [su:'dæn] Sudán *m*.
Su·ez Ca·nal ['su:ez kə'næl] Canal *m* de Suez.
Suf·folk ['sʌfək] *Condado inglés.*
Sur·rey ['sʌri] *Condado inglés.*
Su·san ['su:zn] Susana.
Sus·sex ['sʌsiks] *Condado inglés.*
Swe·den ['swi:dn] Suecia *f*.
Swit·zer·land ['switsərlənd] Suiza *f*.
Syd·ney ['sidni] *Puerto y ciudad industrial de Australia.*
Sy·ri·a ['siriə] Siria *f*.

T

Ta·gus ['teigəs] Tajo *m*.
Tan·gier [tæn'dʒiər] Tánger.
Ten·nes·see [tenə'si:] *Río y Estado de EE.U.U.*
Tex·as ['teksəs] Tejas *m* (*Estado de EE.UU.*).
Thames [temz] Támesis *m*.
Thom·as ['tɔməs] Tomás.
To·kyo ['toukjou] Tokio.
Tom(·my) ['tɔm(i)] *nombre cariñoso de Thomas.*
Ton·y ['touni] *nombre cariñoso de Anthony.*
To·ron·to [tə'rɔntou] *Ciudad de Canadá.*
Tra·fal·gar [trə'fælgər] *Promontorio cerca de Gibraltar.*
Tu·nis ['tu:nəs] Túnez.
Turk·ey ['tə:rki] Turquía *f*.

U

U·kraine [ju:'krein] Ucrania *f*.
Ul·ster ['ʌlstər] *Provincia de Irlanda.*
U·nit·ed King·dom [ju:'naitid 'kiŋdəm] (el) Reino Unido (*Gran Bretaña e Irlanda del Norte*).
U·nit·ed States (of A·mer·i·ca) [ju:'naitid 'steits (əvə'merikə)] *pl.* (los) Estados *m/pl.* Unidos (de América).
U·ru·guay ['urugwai] (el) Uruguay.
U·tah ['ju:tɑ:] *Estado de EE.UU.*

V

Van·cou·ver [væn'ku:vər] *Isla y ciudad en la costa occidental de Canadá.*
Vat·i·can ['vætikən] Vaticano *m*.
Ven·e·zue·la [vene'zweilə] Venezuela *f*.
Ven·ice ['venis] Venecia.
Ver·mont [vər'mɔnt] *Estado de EE.UU.*
Ver·sailles [ver'sai] Versalles.
Vi·en·na [vi'enə] Viena.
Vietnam ['vjet'næm] Vietnam *m*.
Vir·gin·ia [vər'dʒinjə] *Estado de EE.UU.*

W

Wales [weilz] Gales *f*.
Wall Street ['wɔ:lstri:t] *Calle de Nueva York y centro financiero de EE.UU.*
War·saw ['wɔ:rsɔ:] Varsovia.
War·wick(·shire) ['wɔrik(ʃər)] *Condado inglés.*
Wash·ing·ton ['wɔʃiŋtən] **1.** *Estado de EE.UU.*; **2.** *Capital federal y sede del gobierno de EE.UU.*
Wa·ter·loo [wɔ:tər'lu:] *Pueblo cerca de Bruselas* (*Bélgica*).
Wel·ling·ton ['weliŋtən] *Capital y puerto principal de Nueva Zelanda.*
West In·dies ['west 'indiz] *pl.* Antillas *f/pl.*
West·min·ster ['westminstər] *Barrio de Londres.*
West·mor·land ['westmərlənd] *Antiguo condado inglés.*
White·hall ['wait'hɔ:l] *Calle de Londres con edificios del gobierno inglés.*
White House ['wait 'haus]: the ~ la Casa Blanca (*sede oficial y residencia*

del presidente de EE.UU).
Wight: Isle of ~ [wait] *Isla en la costa meridional de Inglaterra.*
Will [wil], **Will·iam** ['wiljəm] Guillermo.
Wim·ble·don ['wimbldən] *Barrio de Londres (campeonatos de tenis).*
Wis·con·sin [wis'kɔnsn] *Estado de EE.UU.*
Worces·ter·shire ['wustərʃər] *Antiguo condado inglés.*
Wy·o·ming [wai'oumiŋ] *Estado de EE.UU.*

Y

Yale U·ni·ver·si·ty ['jeil juːni'vəːrsiti] Universidad de Yale (*en el Estado norteamericano de Connecticut*).
Yel·low·stone ['jeloustoun] *Río y parque nacional de EE.UU.*
York [jɔːrk] *Ciudad y sede arzobispal en Inglaterra.*
York·shire ['jɔːrkʃər] *Condado inglés.*
Yo·sem·i·te [jou'semiti] *Valle y parque nacional de EE.UU.*
Yu·go·sla·vi·a [juːgou'slɑːvjə] Yugo(e)slavia *f.*

Numerals – Numerales

Cardinal Numbers – Números cardinales

0 nought *cero*
1 one *uno, una*
2 two *dos*
3 three *tres*
4 four *cuatro*
5 five *cinco*
6 six *seis*
7 seven *siete*
8 eight *ocho*
9 nine *nueve*
10 ten *diez*
11 eleven *once*
12 twelve *doce*
13 thirteen *trece*
14 fourteen *catorce*
15 fifteen *quince*
16 sixteen *dieciséis*
17 seventeen *diecisiete*
18 eighteen *dieciocho*
19 nineteen *diecinueve*
20 twenty *veinte*
21 twenty-one *veintiuno*
22 twenty-two *veintidós*
30 thirty *treinta*
31 thirty-one *treinta y uno*
40 forty *cuarenta*
50 fifty *cincuenta*
60 sixty *sesenta*
70 seventy *setenta*
80 eighty *ochenta*
90 ninety *noventa*
100 a (*o* one) hundred *cien(to)*
101 a hundred and one *ciento uno*
110 a hundred and ten *ciento diez*
200 two hundred *doscientos -as*
300 three hundred *trescientos -as*
400 four hundred *cuatrocientos -as*
500 five hundred *quinientos -as*
600 six hundred *seiscientos -as*
700 seven hundred *setecientos -as*
800 eight hundred *ochocientos -as*
900 nine hundred *novecientos -as*
1000 a thousand *mil*
1959 nineteen hundred and fifty-nine *mil novecientos cincuenta y nueve*
2000 two thousand *dos mil*
1 000 000 a (*o* one) million *un millón (de)*
2 000 000 two million *dos millones (de)*

Ordinal Numbers – Números ordinales

1 first *primero*
2 second *segundo*
3 third *tercero*
4 fourth *cuarto*
5 fifth *quinto*
6 sixth *sexto*
7 seventh *séptimo*
8 eighth *octavo*
9 ninth *noveno, nono*
10 tenth *décimo*
11 eleventh *undécimo*
12 twelfth *duodécimo*
13 thirteenth *decimotercero, decimotercio*
14 fourteenth *decimocuarto*
15 fifteenth *decimoquinto*
16 sixteenth *decimosexto*
17 seventeenth *decimoséptimo*
18 eighteenth *decimoctavo*
19 nineteenth *decimono(ve)no*
20 twentieth *vigésimo*
21 twenty-first *vigésimo prim(er)o*
22 twenty-second *vigésimo segundo*
30 thirtieth *trigésimo*

31 thirty-first *trigésimo prim(er)o*
40 fortieth *cuadragésimo*
50 fiftieth *quincuagésimo*
60 sixtieth *sexagésimo*
70 seventieth *septuagésimo*
80 eightieth *octogésimo*
90 ninetieth *nonagésimo*
100 hundredth *centésimo*
101 hundred and first *centésimo primero*
110 hundred and tenth *centésimo décimo*
200 two hundredth *ducentésimo*
300 three hundredth *tricentésimo*
400 four hundredth *cuadringentésimo*
500 five hundredth *quingentésimo*
600 six hundredth *sexcentésimo*
700 seven hundredth *septingentésimo*
800 eight hundredth *octingentésimo*
900 nine hundredth *noningentésimo*
1000 thousandth *milésimo*
2000 two thousandth *dos milésimo*
1 000 000 millionth *millonésimo*
2 000 000 two millionth *dos millonésimo*

En inglés, los números ordinales suelen abreviarse **1**st., **2**nd., **3**rd., **4**th., **5**th., etc.

Fractions and other Numerals – Números quebrados y otros

½ one (*o* a) half *medio, media*; **1**½ one and a half *uno y medio*; **2**½ two and a half *dos y medio*; ½ h. half an hour *media hora*; **1**½ m. one and a half miles *milla y media*

⅓ one (*o* a) third *un tercio*; ⅔ two thirds *dos tercios*

¼ one (*o* a) quarter *un cuarto*; ¾ three quarters *tres cuartos*; ¼ h. (a) quarter of an hour *un cuarto de hora*; **1**¼ h. one and a quarter hours *hora y cuarto*

⅕ one (*o* a) fifth *un quinto*; **3**⅘ three and four fifths *tres y cuatro quintos*

1/11 one (*o* an) eleventh *un onzavo*

5/12 five twelfths *cinco dozavos*

75/100 seventy-five hundredths *setenta y cinco centésimos*

1/1000 one (*o* a) thousandth *un milésimo*

single *simple*
double *doble, duplo*
treble, triple, threefold *triple*
fourfold *cuádruplo*
fivefold *quíntuplo etc.*

once *una vez*
twice *dos veces*
three times *tres veces etc.*
seven times as big *siete veces más grande*; twice more *dos veces más*

firstly *en primer lugar*
secondly *en segundo lugar etc.*

7 + 8 = 15 seven and eight are fifteen *siete y ocho son quince*

10 − 3 = 7 three from ten leaves seven *diez menos tres igual siete, de tres a diez van siete*

2 × 3 = 6 two times three are six *dos por tres son seis*

20 ÷ 4 = 5 twenty divided by four is five *veinte dividido por cuatro es cinco.*

Notas sobre el verbo inglés

Notas sobre el verbo inglés

a) Conjugación

Modo indicativo.

1. **El tiempo presente** tiene la misma forma que el infinitivo en todas las personas menos la **3**a del singular; en ésta, se añade una -s al infinitivo, p.ej. *he brings*, o se añade -es si el infinitivo termina en sibilante (ch, sh, ss, zz), p. ej. *he passes*. Esta *s* tiene dos pronunciaciones distintas: tras consonante sorda se pronuncia sorda, p.ej. *he paints* [peints]; tras consonante sonora se pronuncia sonora, p.ej. *he sends* [sendz]; -es se pronuncia también sonora, sea la *e* parte de la desinencia o letra final del infinitivo, p.ej. *he washes* ['wɔʃiz], *he urges* ['əːrdʒiz]. Los verbos que terminan en *-y* la cambian en *-ies* en la tercera persona, p.ej. *he worries, he tries*, pero son regulares los verbos que en el infinitivo tienen una vocal delante de la *-y*, p.ej. *he plays*. El verbo *be* es irregular en todas las personas: *I am, you are, he is, we are, you are, they are*. Tres verbos más tienen forma especial para la tercera persona del singular: *do–he does, go–he goes, have–he has*.

   En los demás tiempos, todas las personas son iguales. **El pretérito** y **el participio del pasado** se forman añadiendo *-ed* al infinitivo, p.ej. *I passed, passed*, o añadiendo *-d* a los infinitivos que terminan en *e*, p.ej. *I faced, faced*. (Hay muchos verbos irregulares: *v.* abajo). Esta -(e)*d* se pronuncia generalmente como [t]: *passed* [pæst], *faced* [feist]; pero cuando se añade a un infinitivo que termina en consonante sonora o en sonido consonántico sonoro o en *r*, se pronuncia como [d]: *warmed* [wɔːrmd], *moved* [muːvd], *feared* [fird]. Si el infinitivo termina en *-d* o *-t*, la desinencia *-ed* se pronuncia [id]. Si el infinitivo termina en *-y*, ésta se cambia en *-ie* antes de añadirse la *-d*: *try–tried* [traid], *pity–pitied* ['pitid]. **Los tiempos compuestos del pasado** se forman con el verbo auxiliar *have* y el participio del pasado, como en español: **perfecto** *I have faced*, **pluscuamperfecto** *I had faced*. Con el verbo auxiliar *will* (*shall*) y el infinitivo se forma **el futuro,** p.ej. *I shall face*, y con el verbo auxiliar *would* (*should*) y el infinitivo se forma **el condicional,** p.ej. *I should face*.

   En cada tiempo existe además una forma continua que se forma con el verbo *be* (= estar) y el participio del presente (*v.* abajo): *I am going, I was writing, I had been staying, I shall be waiting*, etc.

2. **El subjuntivo** ha dejado casi de existir en inglés, salvo en algún caso especial (*if I were you, so be it, it is proposed that a vote be taken*, etc.). En el presente, tiene en todas las personas la misma forma que el infinitivo, *that I go, that he go*, etc.

3. **El participio del presente** y **el gerundio** tienen la misma forma en inglés, añadiéndose al infinitivo la desinencia *-ing*: *painting, sending*. Pero **1)** Los verbos cuyo infinitivo termina en -e muda la pierden al añadir *-ing*, p.ej. *love–loving, write–writing* (excepciones que conservan la -e: *dye–dyeing, singe–singeing, shoe–shoeing*); **2)** El participio del presente de los verbos *die, lie, vie*, etc. se escribe *dying, lying, vying*, etc.

4. Existe una clase de verbos ligeramente irregulares, que terminan en consonante simple precedida de vocal simple acentuada; en éstos, antes de añadir la desinencia *-ing* o *-ed*, se dobla la consonante:

to lob	lob*bed*	lob*bing*
to wed	wed*ded*	wed*ding*
to beg	beg*ged*	beg*ging*
to step	step*ped*	step*ping*
to quit	quit*ted*	quit*ting*
to compel	compel*led*	compel*ling*
to control	control*led*	control*ling*
to bar	bar*red*	bar*ring*
to stir	stir*red*	stir*ring*

Los verbos que terminan en *-l, -p,* aunque precedida de vocal átona, tienen doblada la consonante en los dos participios en el inglés escrito en Gran Bretaña, aunque no en el de Estados Unidos:

to travel	travel*led* *Am.* traveled	travel*ling* *Am.* traveling
to worship	worship*ped* *Am.* worshiped	worship*ping* *Am.* worshiping

Los verbos que terminan en *-c* la cambian en *-ck* al añadirse las desinencias *-ed, -ing*:

to traffic	traffic*ked*	traffic*king*

5. **La voz pasiva** se forma exactamente como en español, con el verbo *be* y el participio del pasado: *I am obliged, he was fined, they will be moved,* etc.

6. Cuando se dirige uno directamente a otra(s) persona(s) en inglés se emplea únicamente el pronombre *you,* con las formas correspondientes del verbo (2a persona del plural). *You* traduce por tanto el *tú, vosotros, usted y ustedes* del español. La segunda persona del singular en inglés (*thou*) no se emplea más que dialectalmente o en el rezo.

b) Los verbos irregulares ingleses

Se citan las tres partes principales de cada verbo: infinitivo, pretérito, participio del pasado.

abide - abode - abode
arise - arose - arisen
awake - awoke - awoke, awaked
be (am, is, are) - was (were) - been
bear - bore - borne (*llevado*), born (*nacido*)
beat - beat - beaten, beat
become - became - become
beget - begot, † begat - begotten
begin - began - begun
belay - belayed, belaid - belayed, belaid
bend - bent - bent
bereave - bereaved, bereft - bereaved, bereft
beseech - besought - besought
bestrew - bestrewed - bestrewed, bestrewn
bestride - bestrode - bestridden
bet - bet, betted - bet, betted
bid - bade, bid - bidden, bid
bind - bound - bound
bite - bit - bitten
bleed - bled - bled
blow - blew - blown
break - broke - broken
breed - bred - bred
bring - brought - brought
build - built - built
burn - burnt, burned - burnt, burned
burst - burst - burst
buy - bought - bought
can - could
cast - cast - cast
catch - caught - caught
chide - chid - chid, chidden
choose - chose - chosen

cleave - clove, cleft - cloven, cleft
cling - clung - clung
clothe - clothed, *lit.* clad - clothed, *lit.* clad
come - came - come
cost - cost - cost
creep - crept - crept
cut - cut - cut
dare - dared, † durst - dared
deal - dealt - dealt
dig - dug - dug
do - did - done
draw - drew - drawn
dream - dreamt, dreamed - dreamt, dreamed
drink - drank - drunk
drive - drove - driven
dwell - dwelt - dwelt
eat - ate - eaten
fall - fell - fallen
feed - fed - fed
feel - felt - felt
fight - fought - fought
find - found - found
flee - fled - fled
fling - flung - flung
fly - flew - flown
forbear - forbore - forborne
forbid - forbad(e) - forbidden
forget - forgot - forgotten
forgive - forgave - forgiven
forsake - forsook - forsaken
freeze - froze - frozen
geld - gelded, gelt - gelded, gelt
get - got - got, *Am.* gotten
gild - gilded, gilt - gilded, gilt
gird - girded, girt - girded, girt
give - gave - given
go - went - gone
grave - graved - graved, graven
grind - ground - ground
grow - grew - grown
hang - hung, ⚖ hanged - hung, ⚖ hanged
have - had - had
hear - heard - heard
heave - heaved, ⚓ hove - heaved, ⚓ hove
hew - hewed - hewed, hewn
hide - hid - hidden, hid
hit - hit - hit
hold - held - held
hurt - hurt - hurt
keep - kept - kept
kneel - knelt, kneeled - knelt, kneeled
knit - knitted, knit - knitted, knit
know - knew - known
lade - laded - laded, laden
lay - laid - laid
lead - led - led
lean - leaned, leant - leaned, leant
leap - leaped, leapt - leaped, leapt
learn - learned, learnt - learned, learnt
leave - left - left
lend - lent - lent
let - let - let
lie - lay - lain
light - lighted, lit - lighted, lit
lose - lost - lost
make - made - made
may - might
mean - meant - meant
meet - met - met
mow - mowed - mowed, mown
must - must
falta el presente - **ought**
pay - paid - paid
pen - penned, pent - penned, pent
put - put - put
read [ri:d] - read [red] - read [red]
rend - rent - rent
rid - rid - rid
ride - rode - ridden
ring - rang - rung
rise - rose - risen
rive - rived - riven
run - ran - run
saw - sawed - sawn, sawed
say - said - said
see - saw - seen
seek - sought - sought
sell - sold - sold
send - sent - sent
set - set - set
sew - sewed - sewed, sewn
shake - shook - shaken
shall - should
shave - shaved - shaved, (*mst adj.*) shaven
shear - sheared - shorn
shed - shed - shed
shine - shone - shone
shoe - shod - shod
shoot - shot - shot
show - showed - shown
shred - shredded - shredded, shred
shrink - shrank - shrunk
shut - shut - shut
sing - sang - sung
sink - sank - sunk
sit - sat - sat
slay - slew - slain
sleep - slept - slept

slide - slid - slid
sling - slung - slung
slink - slunk - slunk
slit - slit - slit
smell - smelt, smelled - smelt, smelled
smite - smote - smitten
sow - sowed - sown, sowed
speak - spoke - spoken
speed - sped, ⊕ speeded - sped, ⊕ speeded
spell - spelt, spelled - spelt, spelled
spend - spent - spent
spill - spilt, spilled - spilt, spilled
spin - spun, span - spun
spit - spat - spat
split - split - split
spoil - spoiled, spoilt - spoiled, spoilt
spread - spread - spread
spring - sprang - sprung
stand - stood - stood
stave - staved, stove - staved, stove
steal - stole - stolen
stick - stuck - stuck
sting - stung - stung
stink - stunk, stank - stunk
strew - strewed - (have) strewed, (be) strewn
stride - strode - stridden
strike - struck - struck
string - strung - strung
strive - strove - striven
swear - swore - sworn
sweep - swept - swept
swell - swelled - swollen
swim - swam - swum
swing - swung - swung
take - took - taken
teach - taught - taught
tear - tore - torn
tell - told - told
think - thought - thought
thrive - throve - thriven
throw - threw - thrown
thrust - thrust - thrust
tread - trod - trodden
wake - woke, waked - waked, woke(n)
wear - wore - worn
weave - wove - woven
weep - wept - wept
wet - wetted, wet - wetted, wet
will - would
win - won - won
wind - wound - wound
work - worked, ⊕ wrought - worked, ⊕ wrought
wring - wrung - wrung
write - wrote - written

Weights and Measures

Pesos y medidas

Weights and Measures

Pesos y medidas

1. Linear measures
Medidas de longitud

1 inch (in.)
= 2,54 cm.
1 foot (ft.)
= 12 inches = 30,48 cm.
1 yard (yd.)
= 3 feet = 91, 44 cm.

2. Distance and surveyors' measures
Medidas de distancia y de agrimensura

1 link (li., l.)
= 7.92 inches = 20,12 cm.
1 rod (rd.), pole *o* **perch (p.)**
= 25 links = 5,029 m.
1 chain (ch.)
= 4 rods = 20,12 m.
1 furlong (fur.)
= 10 chains = 201,17 m.
1 (statute) mile (mi.)
= 1,760 yards = 1609,34 m.

3. Nautical measures
Medidas náuticas

1 fathom (fm.)
= 6 feet = 1,83 m.
1 cable('s) length
= 100 fathoms = 183 m.
Am. 120 fathoms = 219 m.
1 nautical mile (n. m.)
= 10 cables' length = 1852 m.

4. Square measures
Medidas cuadradas

1 square inch (sq. in.)
= 6,45 cm².
1 square foot (sq. ft.)
= 144 square inches
= 929,03 cm².
1 square yard (sq. yd.)
= 9 square feet = 0,836 m².
1 square rod (sq. rd.)
= 30.25 square yards = 25,29 m².
1 rood (ro.)
= 40 square rods = 10,12 áreas.
1 acre (a.)
= 4 roods = 40,47 áreas.
1 square mile (sq. mi.)
= 640 acres = 2,59 km².

5. Cubic measures
Medidas de cubicación

1 cubic inch (cu. in.)
= 16,387 cm³.
1 cubic foot (cu. ft.)
= 1728 cubic inches
= 0,028 m³.
1 cubic yard (cu. yd.)
= 27 cubic feet = 0,765 m³.
1 register ton (reg. tn.)
= 100 cubic feet = 2,832 m³.

6. British measures of capacity
Medidas de capacidad (Gran Bretaña)

Dry and liquid measures

Medidas para áridos y líquidos

1 British *o* **Imperial gill (gi., gl.)**
= 0,142 l.
1 British *o* **Imperial pint (pt.)**
= 4 gills = 0,568 l.
1 British *o* **Imperial quart (qt.)**
= 2 Imp. pints = 1,136 l.
1 British *o* **Imp. gallon (Imp. gal.)**
= 4 Imp. quarts = 4,546 l.

Dry measures

Medidas para áridos

1 British *o* **Imperial peck (pk.)**
= 2 Imp. gallons = 9,087 l.
1 Brit. *o* **Imp. bushel (bu., bsh.)**
= 4 Imp. pecks = 36,36 l.

1 Brit. *o* **Imperial quarter (qr.)**
= 8 Imp. bushels = 290,94 l.

Medida para líquidos

Liquid measure

1 Brit. *o* **Imp. barrel (bbl., bl.)**
= 36 Imp. gallons = 1,636 Hl.

7. Medidas de capacidad (EE.UU.) Measures of capacity (U.S.A.)

Medidas para áridos

Dry measures

1 U.S. dry point
= 0,550 l.

1 U.S. dry quart
= 2 dry pints = 1,1 l.

1 U.S. peck
= 8 dry quarts = 8,81 l.

1 U.S. bushel *(granos)*
= 4 pecks = 35,24 l.

Medidas para líquidos

Liquid measures

1 U.S. liquid gill
= 0,118 l.

1 U.S. liquid pint
= 4 gills = 0,473 l.

1 U.S. liquid quart
= 2 liquid pints = 0,946 l.

1 U.S. gallon
= 4 liquid quarts = 3,785 l.

1 U.S. barrel
= $31^1/_2$ gallons = 119 l.

1 U.S. barrel petroleum
= 42 gallons = 158,97 l.

8. Medidas de boticario Apothecaries' fluid measures

1 minim (min., m.)
= 0,0006 dl.

1 fluid drachm, *Am.* **dram (dr. fl.)**
= 60 minims = 0,0355 dl.

1 fluid ounce (oz. fl.)
= 8 fluid dra(ch)ms = 0,284 dl.

1 pint (pt.)
= 20 fluid ounces = 0,568 l.
Am. 16 fluid ounces = 0,473 l.

9. Peso Avoirdupois Avoirdupois weight

1 grain (gr.)
= 0,0648 gr.

1 drachm, *Am.* **dram (dr. av.)**
= 27.34 grains = 1,77 gr.

1 ounce (oz. av.)
= 16 dra(ch)ms = 28,35 gr.

1 pound (lb. av.)
= 16 ounces = 0,453 kg.

1 stone (st.)
= 14 pounds = 6,35 kg.

1 quarter (qr.)
= 28 pounds = 12,7 kg.
Am. 25 pounds = 11,34 kg.

1 hundredweight (cwt.)
= 112 pounds = 50,8 kg
(*a.* long hundredweight: cwt. l.)
Am. 100 pounds = 45,36 kg.
(*a.* short hundredweight: cwt. sh.)

1 ton (tn., t.)
= 2240 pounds (= 20 cwt. l.) = 1016 kg. (*a.* long ton: tn. l.)
Am. = 2000 pounds (= 20 cwt. sh.) = 907,18 kg
(*a.* short ton: tn. sh.)

10. Peso Troy y de boticario Troy and apothecaries' weight

1 grain (gr.)
= 0,0648 gr.

1 scruple (s. ap.)
= 20 grains = 1,296 gr.

1 pennyweight (dwt.)
= 24 grains = 1,555 gr.

1 dra(ch)m (dr. t. *o* **dr. ap.)**
= 3 scruples = 3,888 gr.

1 ounce (oz. ap.)
= 8 dra(ch)ms = 31,104 gr.

1 pound (lb. t. *o* **lb. ap.)**
= 12 ounces = 0,373 kg.